Dictionary Catalog of the Arthur B. Spingarn Collection of Negro Authors

Howard University Library

Washington, D.C.

Volume 2

L – Z

*

Music Catalog

G. K. HALL & CO., 70 LINCOLN STREET, BOSTON, MASSACHUSETTS

1970

This publication is printed on permanent/durable acid-free paper.

TABLE of CONTENTS

Catalog

Là-bas, près de la Rivière.
M813.5 Wright, Richard, 1908-1960.
W93enl Les enfants de l'oncle Tom (Uncle Tom's children). Traduit de l'américain par Marcel Duhamel suivi de Là-bas, près de la Rivière traduit par Boris Vian. [Paris] Albin Michel [c1946]

241p. 17cm. (Le livre de poche)
Pocket book edition.

M323
C88t
Labor and laboring classes.
Crosswaith, Frank R
True freedom for Negro and white labor, by Frank R. Crosswaith and Alfred Baker Lewis; with introduction by Norman Thomas. New York, Negro Labor News Service, 1926.

59p. tables. 18cm.

Labor and laboring classes.
M06 Grimké, Archibald Henry, 1849-
Am3 ... Modern industrialism and the negroes of the United
no. 12 States, by Archibald H. Grimke ... Washington, D. C., The Academy, 1908.

18 p. 22cm. (Occasional papers, no. 12. The American negro academy)

1. Negroes—U. S. 2. Labor and laboring classes—U. S.

Library of Congress E184.N3A5 no. 12 9-35097
——— Copy 2. Library of Congress E184.N3G8

Trinidad
M822.91 Labistide, Neville
H55 One for the road.

Pp. 69-96.

In: Hill, Erroll G., ed. Caribbean plays, v.2. Mona, Jamaica, Mona, University of the West Indies, 1965.

M331 Labor and laboring classes.
D41 Denby, Charles
Workers battle automation. [Detroit, News and Letters, 1960]

62p. illus. 17cm.

1. Labor and laboring classes. 2. Automation. I. Title

Labor and laboring classes.
M304 Harris, Abram Lincoln
P19 The Negro worker, a problem of vital
v.4 concern of the entire labor movement.
no.4 New York, Conference for Progressive labor action, 1930.

17p. 16cm.

Labor, A B Merriman-
see
Merriman-Labor, A B

Labor and laboring classes
M306
At6 DuBois, William Edward Burghardt, 1868- ed.
No.7 The Negro artisan. Report of a social study made under the direction of Atlanta University, together with the proceedings of the seventh conference for the study of Negro problems, held at Atlanta University on May 27th, 1902. Edited by W.E.B. DuBois. Atlanta, Ga., Atlanta University Press, 1902.

viii, 192p. tables. 23cm.

M331
H334
Labor and laboring classes.
Haynes, Elizabeth Ross.
Negroes in domestic service in the United States, by Elizabeth Ross Haynes. Washington, D.C., Association for the study of Negro life and history, 1923.

384-442p. 25½cm.
Reprinted from the Journal of Negro History, vol. 8, no. 4, Oct. 1923.

Labor and laboring classes.
M331 Alston, Christopher C
A17h Henry Ford and the Negro people. Wash., D. C. National Negro Congress and the Michigan Negro Congress, 1940.

22p. 19cm.

Labor and laboring classes.
M304 Ford, James W 1893-
P19 The Negro people and the farmer-labor
v.1 party. New York, Harlem Division of the
no. 18 Communist Party, 1936.

11p. 16cm.

Labor and laboring classes.
M331.1 Hill, Herbert
H55 Labor unions and the Negro; the record of discrimination.

10p. 25½cm.
Reprint from Commentary, December, 1959.

1. Labor and laboring classes. 2. Labor Unions.

M331 Labor and laboring class.
B81s Brown, Earl Louis, 1900-
Summary of how management can integrate Negroes in war industries. n.p., n.d.

[3]p. 22cm.

Labor and laboring classes.
M331 Ginzberg, Eli, 1911- ed.
G43 The Negro challenge to the business community. New York, McGraw-Hill [1964]

vi, 111p. 22cm.

Labor and laboring classes.
M304 [James, Cyril Lionel Robert, 1901-
P19 Down with starvation wages in South-East
v.2, no.5 Missouri, 30 cents an hour—white and colored together. Published officially by Local 313, U. C. A. P. A. W. A.-C.I.O.
[10]p. 14cm.

Labor and laboring classes.
M973.6 Colored National Labor Convention, Washington,
C76w D. C.
1870 Proceedings of the Colored National labor convention held in Washington, D. C., on December 6th, 7th, 8th, 9th and 10th, 1869. Washington, D. C., Printed at the office of the New Era, 1870.
46p. 19cm.

Labor and laboring classes.
M331 Glazier, Harlan E.
G46 No Negro need apply; A brief glance at the employment situation in the District of Columbia as related to colored citizens, by Harlan E. Glazier, sponsored by the Inter-Racial Committee of the District of Columbia. Washington, The Committee, n.d.

8p. graphs. 23cm.

Labor and laboring classes.
Johnson, Charles Spurgeon, 1893-
M301 The Negro war worker in San Francisco, a local self-survey.
J63ne8 Technical staff: Charles S. Johnson, Herman H. Long [and] Grace Jones ... A project, financed by a San Francisco citizen, administered by the Y. W. C. A., and carried out in connection with the Race relations program of the American missionary association, Dr. Charles S. Johnson, director, and the Julius Rosenwald fund. [San Francisco] 1944.
2 p. l., 98 p. 28cm.
Reproduced from type-written copy.
1. Negroes—San Francisco. I. American missionary association. II. Julius Rosenwald fund. III. Title.

45-2580
Library of Congress F869.S3J57
[3] 331.98

M331 Labor and laboring classes.
C76c Congress of Industrial Organizations.
The C.I.O. and the Negro worker. Washington, Congress of Industrial Organizations, [193]

7p. 10x23cm.

M331 Labor and laboring classes
G76n Granger, Lester Blackwell, 1896-
The Negro worker in New York City, prepared by Lester B. Granger under direction of Committee on Negro Welfare. New York, Welfare Council of New York City, 1941.

32p. 19cm.

Labor and laboring classes.
M323 Johnson, James Weldon, 1871-1938.
J632c The changing status of Negro labor. Chicago, Ill., National Council of Social Work, 1918.

6p. 22cm.

Labor and laboring classes.
M331 L58
Lewis, Edward Erwin, 1900–
The mobility of the Negro; a study in the American labor supply, by Edward E. Lewis ... New York, Columbia university press; London, P. S. King & son, ltd., 1931.
144 p. illus. (maps) 23cm. (Half-title: Studies in history, economics and public law, ed. by the Faculty of political science of Columbia university, no. 342)
Published also as thesis (PH. D.) Columbia university.
"The third volume to appear as a result of studies in the field of Negro migration under grants by the Social science research council and the Columbia university Council for research in the social sciences."—Foreword.
"Selected bibliography": p. 134–135.
1. Negroes. 2. Negroes—Employment. 3. Southern states—Econ. condit.—1918– 4. Cotton growing and manufacture—Southern states. I. Social science research council. II. Columbia university. Council for research in the social sciences. III. Title.
Library of Congress H31.C7 no. 342 31—29612
——— Copy 2. E185.8.L47
[42q2] (306.2) 331.6

Labor and laboring classes.
M331 R27u
Reid, Ira De Augustine, 1901–
The urban Negro worker in the United States, 1925–1936; An analysis of the training types, and conditions of employment and the Negro workers. Volume I, statistics by regions, by Ira De A. Reid, Preston Valien, and Charles S. Johnson... Washington, D. C., Govt. Print. Off. 1938.
127p. tables. cm.

Labor and laboring classes-Dwellings.
M331.833 P92
President's conference on home building and home ownership, Washington, D. C., 1931.
Negro housing; report of the Committee on Negro housing, Nannie H. Burroughs, chairman; prepared for the committee by Charles S. Johnson; edited by John M. Gries and James Ford. Washington, D. C., The President's conference on home building and home ownership [1932]
xiv, 282 p. front., plates. 23½cm.
On cover: Physical aspects; social and economic factors; home ownership and financing.
(Continued on next card)
[43t2] 32—26008

Labor and laboring classes.
M304 P19 v.3, no.4
[Mc Dougald, Gertrude E.]
A new day for the colored woman worker. A study of the colored women in industry in New York City... Investigators Miss Jessie Clark and Mrs. Gertrude E. Mc Dougald. New York, Chas. P. Young, Co., 1919.
39p. illus. 22½cm.

Labor and laboring classes.
M323 R32n
Revolutionary Workers League.
The Negro under capitalism; Resolution adopted by the fourth plenum of the Central Committee of the Revolutionary Workers League of the United States, September 3–4, 1930. Detroit, Demos Press, 193 .
12p. 27cm.
Mimeographed.

Labor and laboring classes - Africa.
M910 H92d
Hunton, William Alphaeus, 1903–
Decision in Africa; sources of current conflict. With a foreword by W. E. B. Du Bois. New York, International Publishers [1957]
255 p. illus. 21 cm.
1. Africa—Econ. condit.—1945– 2. Labor and laboring classes—Africa. 3. Africa—Politics. I. Title.
HC502.H8 330.96 57—18398 ‡
Library of Congress [58f5]

Labor and laboring classes.
M304 P19 v.2,no.1
[National Negro Congress]
Negro workers after the war. New York, [National Negro congress, 1945]
23p. 15cm.
M331 N19n

Labor and laboring classes.
M331 R54f
Robeson, Paul, 1898–
Forge Negro-labor unity for peace and jobs. N.Y., Harlem Trade Union Council, 1950.
15p. 18½cm.

Labor and laboring classes - Africa, French West.
Cameroons, French M966.11 N62m
Minine, [Jules]
La main d'oeuvre indigène dans les colonies africaines ... Paris, Jouve and Cie, 1932.
241p. 25cm.
Thèse - Universite de Paris.
Bibliographie: p.[237]-238.

Labor and laboring classes.
Trinidad M330 P131
Padmore, George, 1903–
The life and struggles of Negro toilers, by George Padmore. London, Published by the R.I.L.U. Magazine for the International trade union committee of Negro workers, 1931.
126p. 22cm.

Labor and laboring classes.
M325 Un3n
U.S. Department of labor. Division of Negro economics.
Negro migration in 1916-17. Reports by R. H. Leavell, T. R. Snavely, T. J. Woofter,Jr., W. T. B. Williams and by J. H. Dillard. Washington, Government printing office, 1919.
158p. tables. 23cm.

Labor and laboring classes - Africa, South.
Africa M968 Na21r
National European-Bantu conference, Cape Town, 1929.
Report of the National European-Bantu conference. Cape Town, February 6-9, 1929. [Lovedale] Lovedale institution press [1929]
4 p. l., 227 p. 19cm.
1. Africa, South—Native races—Congresses. 2. Africa, South—Econ. condit.—1918– 3. Labor and laboring classes—Africa, South.
Library of Congress HC517.S7N25 1929 43-35525
[2]

Labor and laboring classes.
Trinidad M330 P13v
Padmore, George, 1903– ed.
The voice of coloured labour; Speeches and reports of colonial delegates to the world trade union conference, 1945. Manchester, Panaf Service [1945]
55p. 22cm.

Labor and laboring class
M331 W37ne
Weaver, Robert Clifton, 1907–
The Negro comes of age in industry. Washington, D.C., National CIO Committee to Abolish Racial Discrimination, 1943.
54-59p. 25½cm.
Reprinted from the Atlantic Monthly September 1943.

Labor and laboring classes - Cameroons, French.
Cameroons, French M966.11 N62m
Minine, [Jules]
La main d'oeuvre indigène dans les colonies africaines ... Paris, Jouve and Cie, 1932.
241p. 25cm.
Thèse - Universite de Paris.
Bibliographie: p.[237]-238.

Labor and laboring classes
M89 P25p
Parsons, Lucy Eldine (Gonzales)
Life of Albert R. Parsons, with brief history of the labor movement in America ... Chicago, L. E. Parsons, 1889.
xxviiip., 254p. 22½cm.

Labor and laboring classes
M331 W37n
Weaver, Robert Clifton, 1907–
Negro labor, a national problem [by] Robert C. Weaver. New York, Harcourt, Brace and company [1946]
xiv, 329 p. 21cm.
"First printing."
"Selected bibliography": p. 317-321.
1. Negroes—Employment. I. Title.
2. Labor and laboring classes.
Library of Congress E185.8.W38 46-25023
[5] 331.96

Labor and laboring classes-Europe.
M914.4 W272m
Washington, Booker Taliaferro, 1859?–1915.
The man farthest down; a record of observation and study in Europe, by Booker T. Washington, with the collaboration of Robert E. Park. Garden City, New York, Doubleday, Page & company, 1912.
4 p. l., 3-390 p., 1 l. fold. map. 20½cm.
1. Labor and laboring classes—Europe. 2. Poor—Europe. I. Park, Robert E., joint author. II. Title.
Library of Congress HD4851.W3 12—22002
——— Copy 2.
Copyright A 320538 [a39k1]

M301 R27t
Labor and laboring classes.
Reid, Ira DeAugustine, 1901–
Two hundred families of small wage earners- An analysis of their economic status as it relates to problems of housing, Newark, N.J. n.p., 1931.
4p. graphs. 27cm.
Mimeographed.

Labor and laboring classes-Biography.
M89 W199
Ward, Matthew
Indignant heart. New York, New Books, 1952.
184 p. 18 cm.
Pocketbook edition.

Labor and laboring classes - Haiti.
Haiti M972.94 Au4
Auguste, Gérard Bonaparte.
Les suicidés d'une classe. Port-au-Prince, Éditions ouvrières, 1957.
xv, 61 p. 21 cm.
1. Labor and laboring classes—Haiti. 2. Haiti—Soc. condit. I. Title.
A 59-3958
Florida. Univ. Library for Library of Congress [2]

Labor and laboring classes - Madagascar.

Cameroons, French
M966.11
N62m

Ninine, [Jules]
La main d'oeuvre indigène dans les colonies africaines ... Paris, Jouve and Cie, 1932.

241p. 25cm.
Thèse - Université de Paris.
Bibliographie: p.[237]-238.

Labor and laboring classes - West Indies, British.

St. Lucia
M330
L58L

Lewis, William Arthur, 1915-
Labour in the West Indies; the birth of a workers' movement, by W. Arthur Lewis; with a preface by A. Creech Jones, M. P. London, V. Gollancz ltd. and the Fabian society, 1939.

44p. 21½cm. (On cover: Fabian society. Research series, no. 44)

Labor Youth League.

M815.5
R54p

Robeson, Paul, 1898-
Paul Robeson speaks to youth. New York, Challenge, 1951.

[21]p. illus. 13cm.
Address delivered to the first national convention of the Labor Youth League, Nov. 24, 1950.

Labor and laboring classes- New York (City)

M331
F85

Franklin, Charles Lionel, 1910–
The Negro labor unionist of New York; problems and conditions among Negroes in the labor unions in Manhattan with special reference to the N. R. A. and post-N. R. A. situations, by Charles Lionel Franklin ... New York, 1936.

2 p. l., 7–417 p. 22½cm.
Thesis (PH. D.)—Columbia university, 1936.
Vita.
Published also as Studies in history, economics and public law, ed. by the Faculty of political science of Columbia university, no. 420.
Bibliography: p. 398–402.
1. Negroes—New York (City) 2. Negroes—Employment. 3. Trade-unions—New York (City) 4. Labor and laboring classes—New York (City) I. Title. II. Title: Negroes in the labor unions in Manhattan.

36—34118

Library of Congress E185.8.F732
Columbia Univ. Libr. [30d1] 331.88097471

Labor and laboring problems.

M304
P19
v.1
no. 2

Ford, James W
World problems of the Negro people. (a reputation of George Padmore) New York, issued by the Harlem section of the communist party [n.d.]

24p. 15cm. (Series on Negro problems)

Laboratories, Anatomical

See

Anatomical laboraties

Labor and laboring classes-New York (City)

M331
H33

Haynes, George Edmund, 1880–
The Negro at work in New York city; a study in economic progress, by George Edmund Haynes ... New York, 1912.

2 p. l., 7–159 p. incl. tables, diagrs. 25cm.
Thesis (PH. D.)—Columbia university, 1912.
Vita.
Published also as Studies in history, economics and public law, ed. by the Faculty of political science of Columbia university, vol. XLIX, no. 3, whole no. 124.
"Select bibliography": p. 154–156.

1. Negroes—New York (City) 2. Labor and laboring classes—New York (City) 3. Wages—New York (City) I. Title.

12—28454

Library of Congress E185.93.N56H41
Columbia Univ. Libr. 326.973
[45b1]

Labor costs - European Economic Community countries.

M380
P87

Powell, Adam Clayton, 1908-
Comparative wage costs and trade advantage: the European economic community, Great Britain, and the United States. Committee on Education and labor, House of Representatives, Eighty-eighth Congress, first session. Washington, U.S. Govt. Print. Off., 1963.

vi, 103p. 24cm.

Labour in the West Indies.

St. Lucia
M330
L58L

Lewis, William Arthur, 1915–
Labour in the West Indies; the birth of a workers' movement, by W. Arthur Lewis; with a preface by A. Creech Jones, M. P. London, V. Gollancz ltd. and the Fabian society, 1939.

44 p. 21½cm. (On cover: Fabian society. Research series, no. 44)

1. Labor and laboring classes—West Indies, British. 2. Trade-unions—West Indies, British. I. Title.

41-6878

Library of Congress HX11.N42 no. 44
[2] (335.1082) 331.8809729

Labor and laboring classes - New York (State).

M331
H25

Harris, Harry C
Apprentices, skilled craftsmen and the Negro; an analysis. New York, New York State Commission Against Discrimination [1960]

137p. 22½cm.
Includes bibliography.

1. Employees, Training of. 2. Discrimination in employment. 3. Apprentices. 4. Labor and laboring classes - New York (State). I. Title.

Labor costs - Gt. Brit.

M380
P87

Powell, Adam Clayton, 1908-
Comparative wage costs and trade advantage: the European economic community, Great Britain, and the United States. Committee on Education and labor, House of Representatives, Eighty-eighth Congress, first session. Washington, U. S.Govt. Print. Off., 1963.

vi, 103p. 24cm.

1. Competition, International. 2. Labor costs - European Economic Community countries. 3. Labor costs - Gt. Brit. 4. Labor costs - U.S. I. Title.

Labour unions

See

Trade unions

Labor and laboring classes—U.S.

M331
C31

Cayton, Horace R.
Black workers and the new unions, by Horace R. Cayton and George S. Mitchell. Chapel Hill, The University of North Carolina press, 1939.

xviii, 473 p. 23½cm.
"Three industries have been chosen for examination: iron and steel, meat packing, and railroad car shops."—Introd.
Bibliography: p. [458]–467.

1. Negroes—Employment. 2. Trade-unions—U. S. 3. Labor and laboring classes—U. S. I. Mitchell, George Sinclair, 1902– joint author. II. Title.

39-27580

Library of Congress E185.8.C39
[6] 331.6

Labor costs - U. S.

M380
P87

Powell, Adam Clayton, 1908-
Comparative wage costs and trade advantage: the European economic community, Great Britain, and the United States. Committee on Education and labor, House of Representatives, Eighty-eighth Congress, first session. Washington, U. S.Govt. Print. Off., 1963.

vi, 103p. 24cm.

1. Competition, International. 2. Labor costs - European Economic Community countries. 3. Labor costs - Gt. Brit. 4. Labor costs - U.S. I. Title.

Les laboureurs de la mer.

Haiti
M843.91
P191

Papailler, Hubert,
Les laboureurs de la mer. [Canada, n.p.] 1959.

143p. 18cm.

Labor and laboring classes- U.S.

M331
H24b

Harris, Abram Lincoln, 1899-
The black worker; the Negro and the labor movement, by Sterling D. Spero and Abram L. Harris. New York, Columbia university press, 1931.

x, 509 p., 1 l. 22½ cm.
Issued also as A. L. Harris's thesis (PH. D.) Columbia university. Mr. Harris wrote chapters 2-5, 10, 14-15, 17-19.
"Bibliography of works cited": p. 485–496.

1. Negroes—Employment. 2. Trade-unions—U. S. 3. Labor and laboring classes—U. S. 4. Negroes—Civil rights. 5. U. S.—Race question. I. Harris, Abram Lincoln, 1899– joint author. II. Title. III. Title: The Negro and the labor movement.

31—3610

Library of Congress E185.8.S74
[44p2] [325.26] 331.6

Labor relations.

see

Industrial relations.

Haiti
M841
C661

Les labours.
Colcou, Clément A 1894–
Les labours. Port-au-Prince [1948]
116 p. port. 22 cm. (Bibliothèque haïtienne)
Poems.

I. Title.

PQ3949.C58L3 A 50-821

New York. Public Libr. for Library of Congress [2]†

Labor and laboring classes-U. S. -Hist.

MB9
P25p

[Parsons, Lucy Eldine (Gonzalez)]
Life of Albert R. Parsons, with brief history of the labor movement in America ... Chicago, L. E. Parsons, 1889.

4 p. l., xxviii p., 2 l., 254 p. front., plates, ports., facsims., diagr. 22½cm.

1. Parsons, Albert Richard, 1848–1887. 2. Labor and laboring classes—U. S.—Hist. 3. Chicago. Haymarket square riot, 1886. I. Title.

15—1424

Library of Congress HX843.P3
[45r42d1]

Labor unions

See

Trade unions

MB9
B174

La Camara, Felix, comte de, 1897-
Mon sang dans tes veines, roman d'après une idée de Joséphine Baker [par] de La Camara et P. Abatino. Illustrations de G. De Pogedaieff. [Preface by Josephine Baker] Paris, Les Editions, Isis, 1931.

178p. illus., plates, port. 19cm.
White author.

1. Abatino, Petitos. II. Baker, Josephine, 1906- Preface. III. Title.

Uganda
M896.4
Oc3L

Lacan ma Kwo pe kinyero.
Ocitti, J P
Lacan ma Kwo pe kinyero [Every dog has his day] Ogoyo cal Vivienne Yates. Kampala, Eagle Press, 1960.

91p. illus. 21cm.
Written in Acoli.

Martinique
MB9
L11c

Lacenaire, Pierre-François, 1800-1836.
Cochinat, Victor ie. Jean Baptiste Thomas Victor 1823-1886.
Lacenaire, ses crimes, son procès et sa mort, suivis de ses poésies et chansons et de documents authentiques et inédits, recueillies par Victor Cochinat. Paris, Jules Laisné, 1857.

vii, 336p. 16½cm.

Uganda
M967.61
M46

Ladkin, R G
Medical Headquarters. Entebee, Uganda.
The laws that protect your health; a book of village hygiene with special reference to Uganda. Nairobi, East African Literature Bureau, 1956.

56p. illus. diagrs. 24½cm.

Réunion
M841
L11c

Lacaussade, Auguste
Cri de guerre; vae victoribus [poetry] Paris, Alphonse Lemerre, 1870.

16p. 18½cm.

I. Title.

Cuba
M972.91
L11

Lachatañeré, Rómulo.
... Manual de santería; el sistema de cultos "lucumís." La Habana, Cuba, Editorial Caribe, 1942.

88, [7] p. incl. illus. (facsim.) map, tables. 20½cm. (On cover: Estudios afro-cubanos)

At head of title: R. Lachatañeré.

1. Cuba—Religion. 2. ~~Negro race~~—Religion. 3. Negroes in Cuba. I. Title.

Library of Congress BL2530.C9L3 42—25316
[44c1] 299.64

MB9
Sp3

A lady of Boston.
Memoir of Mrs. Chloe Spear, a native of Africa, who was enslaved in childhood and died in Boston, Jan. 3, 1815 ... By a lady of Boston ... Boston, J. Loring, 1832.

1 p. l., iii, [9]-108 p. front. 15½cm.

1. Spear, Mrs. Chloe, 1750?-1815. I. A lady of Boston.

Library of Congress [31c1] 14-15962
E444.S74

Réunion
M841
L11pe

Lacaussade, Auguste, 1817-1897
Les épaves. Paris, Alphonse Lemerre, 1896.

306 p. 16 cm. (Petite bibliothèque littéraire)
At head of title: Poésies...

1. French poetry. I. Title.

M813.5
H87Lac2

Lachen, um nicht zu weinen.
Hughes, Langston, 1902-
Lachen, um nicht zu weinen: funf Erzahlungen. [Ubertragen von Paridam von dem Knesebeck. Weisbaden] Insel-Verlag, 1962.

79p. 18cm.
Translation of Laughing to keep from crying.

MB9
H721

Lady sings the blues.
Holiday, Billie, 1915-
Lady sings the blues [by] Billie Holiday with William Dufty. New York, Popular library (Paper back) 1958.
192p. 18cm.
Autobiography.

1. Musicians—Correspondence, reminiscences, etc. I. Title.

ML420.H58A3 927.8 56-5962
Library of Congress [15]

Réunion
M841
L11p
1897

Lacaussade, Auguste, 1817-1897.
Poèmes et payasages. Paris, Alphonse Lemerre, 1897.

360 p. 16 cm. (Petite bibliothèque littéraire)

At head of title: Poésies...

1. French poetry.

M813.5
H87Lac

Lachen um nict zu weinen.
Hughes, Langston, 1902-
Lachen um nicht zu weinen; erzahlungen. [Ubertragen von Paridam von dem Knesebeck. Wiesbaden] Im Insel-Verlag, 1958.

77p. 18cm.

Translation of Laughing to keep from crying.

I. Title.

MB9
H721

Lady sings the blues.
Holiday, Billie, 1915-
Lady sings the blues [by] Billie Holiday with William Dufty. [1st ed.] Garden City, N. Y., Doubleday, 1956.
250 p. illus. (on lining papers) 22 cm.
Autobiography.

1. Musicians—Correspondence, reminiscences, etc. I. Title.

ML420.H58A3 927.8 56—5962
Library of Congress [57q10]

Réunion
M841
L11p
1852

Lacaussade, Auguste, 1817-1897.
Poèmes et paysages. Paris, Marc Ducloux; Garnier Frères, 1852.

XXIII, 351p. 18cm.
Inscribed by author: A mon cher ami ... souvenir affectueuse. A Lacaussade.

1. French poetry

Ivory Coast
M966.68
Am6c

La côte, d'Ivoire dans la cité Africaine.
Amon D'aby, F J
La côte, d'Ivoire dans la cité Africaine. Paris, Éditions Larose, 1951.

206p. plates, maps. 25cm.

Cuba
M338.8
L13t

Lafargue, Paul, 1842-1911.
Les trusts américains; leur action—économique—sociale—politique; par Paul Lafargue ... Paris, V. Giard & E. Brière, 1903.
vi, [7]-146 p., 1 l. 19cm.

1. Trusts, Industrial. 2. Cuban author.

4-6974
Library of Congress

Réunion
M841
L11s

Lacaussade, Auguste, 1817-1897.
Le seige de Paris. Paris, Alphonse Lemerre, 1871.

31p. 18cm.
"A mon cher Prosper Guibert souvenir d'un ami. A Lacaussade."
MSS letter inserted dated November 19, 1871.

I. Title.

Guadeloupe
M843.91
L11s

Lacrosil, Michèle
Sapotille et le serin d'argile; roman. Paris, Gallimard [1960]

240p. 19cm.

1. Guadeloupe - Fiction. I. Title.

Haiti
M843.91
L13c

Lafontant, Delorme
Celie. Port-au-Prince, Haiti, 1939.

261p. port. 21cm.

1. Haitian fiction. I. Title.

M910
C77f

Lacaussade, Auguste, 1817-1897.
Cook, Mercer.
Five French Negro authors, by Mercer Cook ... Washington, D. C., The Associated publishers, inc. [1943]
xiv, 164 p. incl. front. ports. 19½ cm.
Bibliographical references included in "Notes" (p. 151-161)
CONTENTS.—Julien Raimond.—Charles Bissette.—Alexandre Dumas.—Auguste Lacaussade.—Rene Maran.

1. Raimond, Julien, 1743?-1802? 2. Bissette, Cyrille Charles Auguste, 1795-1858. 3. Dumas, Alexandre, 1802-1870. 4. Lacaussade, Auguste, 1817-1897. 5. Maran, René, 1887- 6. French literature—Hist. & crit. 7. Negro authors. I. Title.
[Full name: Will Mercer Cook]

Library of Congress PQ150.N4C6 43—13504
[44j5] 840.903

Nigeria
M896.2
L125

Ladipo, Duro
Three Yoruba plays: Oba Koso, Oba Moro [and] Oba Waja. English adaptations by Ulli Beier. Ibadan, Mbari Publications [1964]
75p. 21½cm.
Contents.- Oba Koso [The king does not hang.- Oba Moro [The ghost catcher.- Oba Waja [The king is dead]
1. African drama. I. Beier, Ulli, tr. II. Title. III. Mbari Plubications.

Haiti
M843.91
L13s

Lafontant, Delorme.
... Le soir; ou, Fleurs haïtiennes de sensibilité ... Port-au-Prince, Haïti [Imp. du Collège Vertières] 1942.
cover-title, 6 p. l., [11]-346 p. port. 21½cm.

I. Title. 1. Haitian fiction. [Full name: Jean Delorme Lafontant]

Library of Congress PQ3949.L28S 44-53543
[2] 843.91

La Fontaine, Jean de, 1621-1695.

M843.91
M32b

₍Marbot, François Achille₎ 1817-1866.
... Les Bambous; Fables de la Fontaine travesties en patois martiniquais Edition revue et augmentee d'une notice litteraire et d'une traduction Française par Louis Jaham-Desrivaux. Paris, J. Peyronnet & cie, 1931.

246p. 22cm.

La Fontaine, Jean de, 1621-1695. Fables

Haiti
M843.91
Sy5

Sylvain, Georges, 1866-
... Cric! Crac! Fables de La Fontaine, racontées par un montagnard haïtien, et transcrites en vers créoles par Georges Sylvain. 2. éd. Port-au-Prince (Haïti) En vente chez m^me Georges Sylvain, 1929.

2 p. l., 163, ₍1₎ p. front. (port.) illus. 17½cm. (Bibliothèque haïtienne)

Autographed presentation copy to Mr. and Mrs. Arthur Spingarn.

I. La Fontaine, Jean de, 1621-1695. Fables. II. Title.

Library of Congress PQ3949.S9C7 43-29668 ₍2₎

Kenya
M967.62
L18

La Fontaine, Sidney Hubert, 1887-
Thirikari ya handu o handũ Kenya; ₍Local government in Kenya₎ ihumo o na ũkũria wayo, rĩandĩkĩtwo nĩ S. H. La Fontaine magĩteithanagia wĩra wa rĩo na J. H. Mower. ₍Translated into Kikuyu by Mathayo Njeroge₎ Nairobi, Eagle Press, 1955.
63p. 21½cm.
Written in Kikuyu.
White author.
1. Local government - Kenya Colony and Protectorate. I. Title. II. Mower, J. H. III. Njerage, Mathayo, tr.

Haiti
M848
L13

Laforest, Clérie
Au clavier de la pensee. Haiti, Les Presses Libres, n.d.

49p. 22cm.

1. Haitian poetry
I. Title

Haiti
M941
L13c

Laforest, Edmond, 1876-1915
Cendres et flammes; poesies. Paris, Albert Messein, Editeur, 1912.
260p. 1 9cm.
Negro author.

1. Haitian literature. I. Title.

Haiti
M841
L13s

Laforest, Edmond, 1876-1915.
Sonnets-Médaillons du dix-neuvième siècle. Ornés de quatre-vingt-dix portraits authentiques et de douze fleurons originaux. Paris, Lib. Fischbacher, 1909.

LXVIII, 216p. ports. cm. (Collection des poetes Francias de l'etranger)

I. Title. 1. Haitian poetry.

Haiti
M843.91
L135t

Lagazy, Madeleine, 1911-
Terre d'enchantements, roman. Port-au-Prince, Haiti, Imprimerie de l'etat ₍1951₎
285 p. illus. 24 cm.

I. Title.

PQ2623.A27285T4 52-27982 ‡

Library of Congress ₍1₎

Jamacia
M966.9
C15f

Lagos - Description and travel.
Campbell, Robert
A few facts, relating to Lagos, Abbeokuta, and other sections of Central Africa. By Robert Campbell ... of the Niger Valley exploring party. Philadelphia, King & Baird Printers, 1860.

18p. 23cm.

Jamaica
M966.9
C15p

Lagos - Description and travel.
Campbell, Robert
A pilgrimage to my motherland. An account of a journey among the Egbas and Yorubas of Central Africa, in 1859-60. By Robert Campbell ... of the Niger Valley exploring party ... New-York, T. Hamilton; Philadelphia, The author, 1861.

145p. front. (port) double map. 19cm.

Jamaica
M966.9
C15p2

Lagos - Description and travel.
Campbell, Robert
A pilgrimage to my motherland; or, Reminiscenses of a sojourn among the Egbas and Yorubas of Central Africa, in 1859-60. By Robert Campbell. With an introduction by Sir Culling E. Eardley. London, William John Johnson, 1861.

116p. front. 19cm. illus.

Nigeria
M966.9
L89h

Lagos, Nigeria - History.
Losi, John B. Ogunjimi.
History of Lagos, by Prince John B. O. Losi... second edition. Lagos, C.M.S. Bookshop, 1921.

ii, 75p. plates. 22½cm.

Nigeria
M966.9
L89h

Lagos, Nigeria - History.
Losi, John B Ogunjimi.
Itan eko nipa Prince John B. O. Losi... third edition. Lagos, Church missionary society's press, 1921.

60p. plates. 22½cm.

M811.5
L13f

LaGrone, Oliver.
Footfalls; Poetry from America's becoming. Detroit, Darel press, 1949.

x, 37p. illus. 22cm.
Biographical sketch by Yale Soifer.

1. Poetry. I. Title.

M811.5
L13t

LaGrone, Oliver
They speak of dawns; a duo-poem; written for the Centennial year of the Emancipation Proclamation: 1863, in 1863. ₍Narrating: The Journeys of two modern contemporary travelers: the astronaut, the freedom rider₎ Brinkley Printers, 1963.
1 v. illus. 20½cm.
"Enscribed especially for Arthur B. Spingarn with respect, gratitude and Best wishes - Oliver LaGrone."
I. Title.

Puerto Rico
M863
L13c

Laguerre, Enrique A
La ceiba en el tiesto; novela. San Juan, Biblioteca de Autores Puertorriqueños, 1956.

146p. 22cm.

I. Title.

Puerto Rico
M863
L63d

Laguerre, Enrique A
Los dedos de la mano. ₍Novela₎ Mexico, Librería de M. Porrúa, 1951.
245 p. 21 cm.

I. Title.

PQ7439.L3D4 53-17263 ‡

Library of Congress ₍1₎

Puerto Rico
M863
L13L

LaGuerre, Enrique A
La Llamarada (novela). Edicion décimasegunda. Mexico, Editorial Orion, 1961.

295p. 19cm.

I. Title.

Puerto Rico
M863
L13i

Laguerre, Enrique A
...La llamarada novela 3rd ed. San Juan, Puerto Rico, Bibliotica de autores Puertorriquenos, 1945.

406p. 20½cm.

1. Puerto Rican fiction. I. Title.

Puerto Rico
M863
L63r

Laguerre, Enrique A
La resaca (bionovela). San Juan de Puerto Rico, Biblioteca de Autores Puertorriquenos, 1949.

452p. 18½cm.

I. Title.

Puerto Rico
M863
L13t

Laguerre, Enrique A
... El 30 de febrero (vida de un hombre interino) San Juan de Puerto Rico, Biblioteca de autores puertorriqueños, 1943.
383 p., 2 l. 20½cm.
A novel.

I. Title. 1. ~~Porto~~ Puerto Rican fiction. A 43-3168

Harvard univ. Library for Library of Congress PQ7439.L3T7 ₍3₎† 863.6

Puerto Rico
M863
L63s

Laguerre, Enrique A.
... Solar Montoya. ₍San Juan₎ Isla de Puerto Rico, América ₍Biblioteca de autores puertorriqueños, 1941₎
1 p. l., ₍5₎-351 p., 2 l. 22cm.
A novel.

I. Title. A 42-3487 Revised

Harvard univ. Library for Library of Congress PQ7439.L3S6 ₍r44c2₎† 863.6

South Africa
M896.3
L11an
La Guma, Alex, 1925-
And a threefold cord. Berlin, Seven Seas Publishers [1964]

173p. 19cm.

I. Title.

South Africa
M896
M88
La Guma, Alex, 1923-
Blankets

Pp. 268-273.

In: Mphahlele, Ezekiel, ed. African writing today. Baltimore, Penguin Books, 1967.

Africa
M808.83
B396
LaGuma, Alex, 1925-
A glass of wine.

Pp. 52-57.

In: Black Orpheus. Black Orpheus; an anthology of African and Afro-American prose. New York, McGraw-Hill, 1965.

South Africa
M896.3
L11s
La Guma, Alex, 1925-
The stone-country. Berlin, Seven Seas Publishers (1967).
160 p. 19 cm. (Seven seas books) DM 2.85
(GDB 68-A1-220)

I. Title. (Series)

PZ4.L178St 68-92086

Library of Congress [1]

Africa, South
M896.3
L11
La Guma, Alex, 1925-
A walk in the night. Ibadan, Nigeria, Mbari Publications [n.d.]

90p. 21½cm.

I. Title.

South Africa
M896.3
L11w
La Guma, Alex, 1925-
A walk in the night, and other stories. London, Heinemann, 1967.
[8], 136 p. 20½ cm. 18/-
(B 67-12815)

I. Title.

PZ4.L178Wal 4 67-112215

Library of Congress [2]

LaGuma, Alex, 1925-
Africa, South
M896.3
R52
Rive, Richard, 1931- ed.
Quartet; new voices from South Africa: Alex La Guma, James Matthews, Alf Wannenburgh, Richard Rive. New York, Crown Publishers [1963]

223p. 22cm.
Short stories.

Lagunes.
Guinea
M896.1
N34L
Nenekhaly-Camara, Condotto
Lagunes, [par] Nene Khaly. [n.p.] Editions de L'A.P.L.P. [n.d.]

22p. 19cm.
Autographed.

I. Title.

M813.5
L139b
LaHon, Vyola Therese
The big lie. New York, Vantage Press [1964]

68p. 20½cm.
Portrait of author on book jacket.

1. Southern states - Fiction.

M323
L14
Laidler, Harry Wellington, 1884- ed.
The role of the races in our future civilization; symposium, ed. by Harry W. Laidler. Participants: Pearl S. Buck, Walter White, Lester Granger, Hon. Adam Clayton Powell, Jr. and others ... New York, League for Industrial Democracy, 1942.

112p. 23cm. (On cover: L. I. D. Pamphlet series)
"All ... articles except those of Pearl S. Buck and Lester B. Granger were prepared for the L. I. D. Conference, May 8-9, 1942.

M323
L14
Laidler, Harry Wellington, 1884- ed.
The role of the races in our future civilization: (card 2)

Partial contents. -The Negro problem in America, by Walter White. -Abolish the color line, by Lester B. Granger.

1. Race problems. I. a.t. White, Walter II. a.t. Granger, Lester B.

M811.5
L14f
Laine, Henry Allen, 1870-
Footprints. [2d ed.] New York, Hobson Book Press, 1947.
xi, 144 p. group port. 22 cm.
Verse and prose.
Portrait of author in book.
Autographed.

I. Title.
PS3523.A355F6 1947 811.5 47-25285*
© Henry Allen Laine, Richmond, Ky., 22Apr47; A13993.

Library of Congress [2]

Gold Coast
M200
L14k
Laing, George E. F
A king for Africa. London and Redhill, United Society for Christian Literature, 1945.

63p. 18cm.

1. Religion.

Laity.
M260
R27
Reid, Gaines S 1890-
The church and the layman: man's duty to God; a plea for positive and dynamic support of the Christian church. Foreword by George W. Baber. [1st ed.] New York, Exposition Press [1959]
86 p. 21 cm.

1. Laity. I. Title.

BV4525.R43 241 59-3720 ‡

Library of Congress [2]

Laity.
M261.8
Sp31
Speers, Wallace Carter, 1896- ed.
Laymen speaking. New York, Association Press, 1947.
207 p. 19 cm.

1. Christian life. 2. Laity.

BV4495.S6 248 47-5820*

Library of Congress [60k1]

Lak tar miyo kinyero wi lobo.
Uganda
M896.3
P29L
p'Bitek Okot, J O 1931-
Lak tar miyo kinyero wi lobo [Are your teeth white? The laugh!] Kampala, The Eagle Press, 1953.

137p. illus. 18cm.
A novel depicting life in the towns and villages of East Africa, by an Acholi author.
Written in Lwo.

I. Title.

Lake Erie, Battle of.
M350
D29c
Davis, Harry E
Colored men in the battle of Lake Erie.
In: Annals of the Early Settlers Association of the Western Reserve. Proceedings of the year, 1938-1939... p. 22-26.

Nigeria
M398
L14p
Lakeru, J A ,comp.
Awọn owe ilẹ wa. Abeokuta, E.N.A. Press, 1916.

32p. 18½cm.
Translation: The proverbs of our land (Yoruba proverbs)

1. Yoruba - Proverbs. I. Title: The Proverbs of our land.

Nigeria
M398
L14p
Lakeru, J A , comp.
Awọn owe ilẹ wa. Abeokuta, E.N.A. Press, 1916.

32p. 18½cm.
Translation: The proverbs of our land (Yoruba proverbs)

1. Yoruba - Proverbs. I. Title: The Proverbs of our land.

Nigeria
M398
L14a
Lakeru, J A
Awon owe ile wa Ti a Kojo, Nipa Rev. J. A. Lakeru. Abeokuta, E.N.A. Press, [1916]

32 p. 18½ cm.

1. Nigeria-Folklore.

Lakor, Erica, tr.
Uganda
M649.1
D28
Davies, H F
Pit ki gwoko lotino [Infant welfare] Aye okobo Erica Lakor. [Revised by C. Moore and Labeka Auma] Kampala, Eagle Press, 1953.

20p. 18cm.
Written in Lwo. (Acoli)

1. Infants - Care and hygiene. I. Title. II. Lakor, Erica, tr.

Haiti
M848
L15

Laleau, Léon, 1892-
Apothéoses. Port-au-Prince, H. Deschamps [1952]
208 p. 20 cm. (Collection de la Bibliothèque nationale, 1)
CONTENTS.—Apothéoses.—De marbre et de bronze.—L'allée des tombeaux.—Textes parlés.

I. Title.
PQ3949.L3A8 848.91 53-16052
Library of Congress [1]

Lalela Zulu.

Africa, South
M780
T671e

Tracey, Hugh
Lalela Zulu; 100 Zulu lyrics. With illustrations by Eric Byrd. Foreword by A. W. Hoernle. Johannesburg, Published by African Music Society, 1948.

121p. illus. 25cm.

Lam, Wifredo.

Martinique
M841.91
G49t

Glissant, Édouard, 1928-
La terre inquiète. [poems] Frontispice de Wifredo Lam. Paris, Éditions du Dragon, 1955.

67p. 20cm.

Haiti
M841
L16

Lamarre, Joseph P V
L'aube rouge. Port-au-Prince, Imprimerie V. Valcin,

26p. 20½cm.

1. Haitian poetry. I. Title.

Haiti
M972.94
L16v

Lamaute, Emmanuel.
... Le vieux Port-au-Prince (une tranche de la vie haïtienne) suivi de quelques faits et dates ... Port-au-Prince, Haïti, Imprimerie de la Compagnie lithographique d'Haïti, 1939.
4 p. l., 7-256 p. front., plates (incl. music) ports. (part fold.) 22½cm.
"Errata": slip inserted.

Haiti
1. ~~Port-au-Prince, Haiti—Descr.~~ 2. Port-au-Prince, Haiti—Soc. life & cust. 3. Port-au-Prince, Haiti—Hist.—Chronology. I. Title.
Library of Congress F1929.P3L3 41-31912
[2] 917.294

M378Ho
L16

Lamb, Daniel Smith
Howard university, medical department, Washington, D.C. A historical, biographical and statistical souvenir, compiled and edited for and by authority of the medical faculty of Howard university. Washington, R. Beresford, 1900
301p. 27cm.
1. Howard university, Washington, D.C. Medical department.

Madagascar
M841.91
R11 1

Lamba, poème.
Rabemananjara, Jacques, 1913-
Lamba, poème. Paris, Présence africaine [1956]
78 p. 20 cm.

I. Title.
Illinois. Univ. Library for Library of Congress A 57-2128 [3]

Trinidad
M821.91
L17p

Lambert, Calvin Stollmeyer, 1913?-
Poems of a West-Indian. London, "Poetry of to-day", 1938.

35p. 20cm.
Inscribed: Calvin S. Lambert, With best wishes to Arthur Spingarn, C.S. Lambert, St. Bart's Hosp. London, E.C.I.

1. West Indian poetry. 1. Title.

Trinidad
M821.91
L17s

Lambert, Calvin Stollmeyer, 1913?-
Selected poems of a West-Indian, by Calvin S. Lambert. London, The Fortune press [1940]
57, [1] p. 19½cm.

1. West-Indian poetry

A 41-624
Harvard univ. Library for Library of Congress [2]

Haiti
M784
L17

Le Lambi; chansonnier scout Haitien, presente par Malfini des Hauteurs. Port-au-Prince, L'Etat, 1950.

31p. 23cm.

1. Haiti--Boy Scouts.

Nigeria
M610
L179

Lambo, T Adeoye
African traditional beliefs; concepts of health and medical practice; a lecture given before the Philosophical Society, University College, Ibadan, on 24 October, 1962. [Ibadan] Ibadan University Press, 1963.

11p. 21½cm.
Includes bibliography.

1. Medicine - Africa. 2. Africa - Health.
I. Title.

M811.5
H871

Lament for dark peoples and other poems.
Hughes, Langston, 1902-
Lament for dark peoples and other poems. London, 1944.

45 p. 22 cm.
No. 22 of a special edition of 50 copies printed on spiral paper.

West Indies
M820.8
C83

Lamming, George, 1927-
Birthday weather.

Pp. 88-94.

In: Coulthard, R. G. Caribbean literature. London, University of London Press, 1966.

Barbadoes
M823
L18em

Lamming, George, 1927-
The emigrants. New York, McGraw-Hill [1955, °1954]
282 p. illus. 21 cm.

I. Title.
PZ4.L232Em 2 55-7281 ‡
Library of Congress [7]

Barbados
M823
L18e

Lamming, George, 1927-
The emigrants. London, Michael Joseph, 1954.

271p. 21cm.
Illus. end papers.

I. title

Barbados
M823
L1811

Lamming, George, 1927-
Les iles fortunées [In the castle of my skin] Roman traduit de l'anglais par Colette Audry et Henriette Etienne. Paris, René Julliard, 1954.

338p. 19cm.

I. Title.

Barbados
M823
L1812

Lamming, George, 1927-
In the castle of my skin; with an introd. by Richard Wright. End papers and port. of the author by Denis Williams. New York, McGraw-Hill [1953]
313 p. illus. 22 cm.

I. Title. II. Wright, Richard.
PR6023.A518I 5 1953a 828.91 53-9014 ‡
Library of Congress [54k10]

Barbados
M823
L181

Lamming, George, 1927-
In the castle of my skin. London, Michael Joseph, 1953.

303p. 21cm.
Illus. end papers.

I. Title

M808.8
N42
v.4

Lamming, George, 1927-
In the castle of my skin.

(In: New world writing, 4. New York, New American Library, 1953. 18 cm.
p. 165-177)

I. Title.

Barbados
M823
L18o

Lamming, George, 1927-
Of age and innocence. London, Michael Joseph, [1958]

412p. 20cm.
Picture of the author on the book jacket.

I. Title.

Jamaica
M823.91
Sa3w

Lamming, George
Of Thornes and thistles.

Pp. 42-50.

In: Salkey, Andrew, ed. West Indian stories. London, Faber and Faber, 1960.

Barbados
M823
L18p
Lamming, George, 1927-
The pleasures of exile. London, M. Joseph [1960]
232 p. 23 cm.

1. Colonies. 2. West Indies, British. I. Title.
PR6023.A518P5 828.91 60-51766 ‡
Library of Congress [2]

M267.8
L19d
Lampton, Edward Wilkerson, 1857-1910
Digest of rulings and decisions of the bishops of the African Methodist Episcopal church from 1847 to 1907, by Edward W. Lampton, D. D. Washington, D. C., The Record publishing company, 1907.
334, xii p. incl. ports. 19½cm.

1. African Methodist Episcopal Church. Discipline
7-36266
Library of Congress (Copyright 1907 A 190489)

Jamaica
M823.91
H35L2
Land of the living.
Hearne, John, 1925-
Land of the living. [1st American ed.] New York, Harper & Row [1962]
280 p. 22 cm.

Portrait of author on book jacket.

I. Title.
Full name: John Edgar Caulwell Hearne.
PZ4.H435Lan 2 62-15725 ‡
Library of Congress [5]

Barbados
M823
L18s
Lamming, George, 1927-
Season of adventure. London, M. Joseph [1960]
366 p. 21 cm.
Portrait of author on book jacket.

I. Title.
PZ4.L232Se 60-52390 ‡
Library of Congress [3]

M813.5
W86
Lancaster triple thousand.
Woods, William B 1935-
Lancaster triple thousand; a novel of suspense. [1st ed.] New York, Exposition Press [1956]
77 p. 21 cm.
Portrait of author on jacket.

I. Title.
PZ4.W898Lan 56-7473 ‡
Library of Congress [3]

Jamaica
M823.91
H351
Land of the living.
Hearne, John, 1925-
Land of the living. London, Faber and Faber, 1961.
280p. 19½cm.

Jamaica
M823.91
Sa3w
Lamming, George
A wedding in spring.
Pp. 28-41.
In: Salkey, Andrew, ed. West Indian stories. London, Faber and Faber, 1960.

Land Grant Colleges, Conference of Presidents.
See
Conference of Presidents of Negro Land Grant Colleges.

M378Ho
M481
The land possessions of Howard university.
Melchor, Beulah H
The land possessions of Howard university, a study of the original ownership and extent of the holdings of Howard university in the District of Columbia [by] Beulah H. Melchor ... Washington, D. C., 1945.
85 p. illus. (plans) 28cm.
"This dissertation ... for a master's thesis [Howard university] ... covers the years 1651-1855."—Foreword.
Bibliography: p. 58-59.

1. Howard university, Washington, D. C.—Hist. 2. Land titles—District of Columbia. 3. Land titles—Maryland. I. Title.
45-16667
Library of Congress LC2851.H82M4
[3] 378.753

Haiti
M972.94
L191
Lamothe, Camille
Initiation à la coopération. Port-au-Prince, Editions Henri Deschamps, 196?
108p. 19½cm.

1. Haiti. I. Title.

M304
P19
v.3,no.12
...Land-grant colleges for Negroes.
Davis, John Warren, 1888-
... Land-grant colleges for Negroes, by President John W. Davis, West Virginia state college ... Institute, W. Va. [1934]
73 p. incl. tables, diagr. 23cm. (West Virginia state college. Dept. of education. Contribution no. 6)
At head of title: West Virginia state college bulletin ... April, 1934. Series 21, no. 5. Publications of West Virginia state college.
First published in abridged form in the Journal of Negro education. July, 1933. *cf.* foot-note, p. [8]
Bibliography: p. [69]-73.

1. Agricultural colleges—U. S. 2. Negroes—Education. 3. Universities and colleges—U. S. I. Title.
A 35-750
Title from Rochester Univ. LC2801.D26 1934
Printed by L. C.
[3]

S. Africa
M968
P69n
1916
Land tenure-Africa, South-Law.
Plaatje, Solomon Tshekisho, 1878-1936.
Native life in South Africa, before and since the European war and the Boer rebellion, by Sol. T. Plaatje ... London, P. S. King & son, ltd. [1916?]
xxxii, 352 p. 2 port. (incl. front.) 18½ cm.

Haiti
M843.91
L193
Lamothe, Leduc B
Sur la route de la vie; quelques pages de Dudel au coin des amateurs d'art. Préface de Me. J. B. Cinéas. Port-au-Prince, Editions Henri Deschamps, 1960.
112p. 21cm.
Portrait of author in book.
1. Short stories - Haiti. I. Title.

M812.5
Ed51
The land of cotton.
Edmonds, Randolph, 1900-
The land of cotton, and other plays by Randolph Edmonds ... Washington, D. C., The Associated publishers, inc. [°1942]
xii, 267 p. 21½cm.
CONTENTS.—The land of cotton.—Gangsters over Harlem.—Yellow death.—Silas Brown.—The High court of Historia.

I. Title. [*Full name:* Sheppard Randolph Edmonds]
43-5533
Library of Congress PS3509.D56L3
[4] 812.5

S. Africa
M968
P69n
Land tenure—Africa, South—Law.
Plaatje, Solomon Tshekisho. —1936.
Native life in South Africa, before and since the European war and the Boer rebellion, by Sol. T. Plaatje ... 2d ed. London, P. S. King & son, ltd. [1916?]
xxxii, 352 p. 2 port. (incl. front.) 18½cm.
"Report of the Lands commission, an analysis": p. iii-xxxii.

1. Africa, South—Native races. 2. Land tenure—Africa, South—Law. 3. Africa, South—Hist.—Rebellion, 1914-
17-13382
Library of Congress DT763.P7 1916

Haiti
M972.94
L19
[Lamour Jeune, Desilus]
Le moniteur haitien, devant la révolution de 1868. Etincelle politique, par un Jacmelien. D. L. J. Jacmel, Haiti, Librairie Dame Lamour & Cie, 1868.
111p. 18cm.
1. Haiti - History. I. Jacmelien, pseudonym.

Kenya
M967.65
G35
Land of sunshine.
Gicaru, Muga.
Land of sunshine; scenes of life in Kenya before Mau Mau. With foreword by Trevor Huddleston. London, Lawrence & Wishart, 1958.
175 p. illus. 23 cm.
Autobiographical.

1. Kenya Colony and Protectorate—Native races. I. Title.
DT434.E2G5 916.762 58-31946 ‡
Library of Congress [1]

Nigeria
M966.9
El4n
1962
Land tenure - Nigeria - Law.
Elias, Taslim Olawale.
Nigerian land law and custom. 3d ed. London, Routledge & K. Paul ~~[1951]~~ 1962
xxvii, ~~320~~ 386p. map. 23 cm.
Thesis—University of London.
Includes legislation.
Bibliography: p. 316-319.

1. Land tenure—Nigeria—Law. 2. Real property—Nigeria. I. Nigeria. Laws, statutes, etc. II. Title.
333.3 52—28040
Library of Congress [53e3]

Haiti
M972.94
B26
Lamour, Saladin, Supposed author
Refutation de faits controuvés et d'appreciations contradictoires que contient l'oeuvre intitulé: souvenirs historiques de Guy Joseph Bonnet. Port-au-Prince, Imprimerie de T. Bouchereau [1868]
113p. 23cm.
Supposed author - Saladin, Lamour

M973
F85L
Land of the free.
Franklin, John Hope, 1915- jt. auth.
Land of the free; a history of the United States, by John W. Caughey, John Hope Franklin [and] Ernest R. May. Educational advisers: Richard M. Clowes, [and] Alfred T. Clark, Jr. Pasadena, Calif., Designed and produced by the W. Ritchie Press for Franklin Publications, 1965.
xi, 658 p. illus. (part col.) maps, ports. 27 cm.
Includes bibliographical references.

1. U. S.—Hist. ~~I. Franklin, John Hope, 1915- joint author.~~ II. May, Ernest R., joint author. III. Title.
E178.1.C36 973 65-27033
Library of Congress [5]

Nigeria
M966.9
El4n
Land tenure - Nigeria - Law.
Elias, Taslim Olawale.
Nigerian land law and custom. London, Routledge & K. Paul [1951]
xxvii, 320 p. map. 23 cm.
Thesis—University of London.
Includes legislation.
Bibliography: p. 316-319.

1. Land tenure—Nigeria—Law. 2. Real property—Nigeria. I. Nigeria. Laws, statutes, etc. II. Title.
333.3 52—28040
Library of Congress [53e3]

Land tenure - Southern States.

M331 H335n Haywood, Harry, 1898-
Negro liberation. New York, International Publishers [1948]
245 p. map. 22 cm.
"Reference notes": p. [219]-230.

1. Negroes—Econ. condit. 2. Negroes—Moral and social conditions. 3. Land tenure—Southern States. I. Title.

E185.6.H43 325.260973 48-8881*
Library of Congress [15]

M976.1 L23 Landis, Benson Y
Cotton growing communities. Study no. 1, Case studies of 9 rural communities and 30 plantations in Alabama. New York, Federal council of churches of Christ in America 1934.
43p. 19cm.

M910 L241s Lane, James Franklin, 1874-
Some things we saw while abroad; a visit to Europe, the Holy Land and Egypt, by J. F. Lane ... and Mary Edna Lane ... Boston, The Christopher publishing house [c1941]
xv, 17-224 p. plates, ports. 19cm.

1. Europe—Descr. & trav. 2. Palestine—Descr. & trav. 3. Egypt—Descr. & trav. I. Lane, Mrs. Mary Edna (Johnson) 1872- joint author. II. Title.

Library of Congress D975.L24 42-2408
[4] 910.4

Land titles—Registration and transfer—Gt. Brit.

M347.2 C82a Cosey, Alfred Bonito.
American and English law on title of record, with practice and procedure supported by American and English decisions, by Alfred Bonito Cosey ... 1st ed. New York, Isaac Goldmann co., 1914.
415 p. 23½cm. $3.75

1. Land titles—Registration and transfer—U. S. 2. Land titles—Registration and transfer—Gt. Brit. [3. Recording and registry acts] I. Title.

Library of Congress 14-20229
——— Copy 2.
Copyright A 387454

M813.5 H914L The landlord.
Hunter, Kristin.
The landlord. New York, Scribner [1966]
338 p. 22 cm.

I. Title.

PZ4.H9457Lan 66-15075
Library of Congress [5]

M326.99B L24n Lane, Lunsford, 1803-
The narrative of Lunsford Lane, formerly of Raleigh, N. C., embracing an account of his early life, the redemption, by purchase of himself and family from slavery, and his banishment from the place of his birth for the crime of wearing a colored skin. Published by himself. 4th ed. Boston, Printed for the publisher, Hewes and Watson's print, 1848.
iv, [5]-54 p. 15½cm.

1. Slave narratives.

Library of Congress E444.L262 12-16469

Land titles—Registration and transfer—U. S.

M347.2 C82a Cosey, Alfred Bonito.
American and English law on title of record, with practice and procedure supported by American and English decisions, by Alfred Bonito Cosey ... 1st ed. New York, Isaac Goldmann co., 1914.
415 p. 23½cm. $3.75

1. Land titles—Registration and transfer—U. S. 2. Land titles—Registration and transfer—Gt. Brit. [3. Recording and registry acts] I. Title.

Library of Congress 14-20229
——— Copy 2.
Copyright A 387454

Nigeria M333 Ek34 Landlord and tenant - Nigeria.
Ekineh, Aliyi.
You and your landlord and you and the law of libel and slander. Lagos, Megida Printers and Publishers [1961]
50p. 22½cm. (Megida legal guide series, no.1)

M326.99B L24h Lane, Lunsford, 1803-
Hawkins, William George, 1823-1909.
Lunsford Lane; or, Another helper from North Carolina. By the Rev. William G. Hawkins ... Boston, Crosby & Nichols, 1863.
xii, 13-305 p. front. (port.) 19½cm.

1. Lane, Lunsford, 1803-

Library of Congress E444.L26 5-6449
——— Copy 2. [37e1]

Land titles-District of Columbia.

M378Ho M481 Melchor, Beulah H
The land possessions of Howard university, a study of the original ownership and extent of the holdings of Howard university in the District of Columbia [by] Beulah H. Melchor ... Washington, D. C., 1945.
85 p. illus. (plans) 23cm.
"This dissertation ... for a master's thesis [Howard university] ... covers the years 1651-1855."—Foreword.
Bibliography: p. 53-59.

1. Howard university, Washington, D. C.—Hist. 2. Land titles—District of Columbia. 3. Land titles—Maryland. I. Title.

45-16667
Library of Congress LC2851.H82M4
[3] 378.753

MB L23s Landrum, Bessie.
Stories of black folk for little folk, by Bessie Landrum. Atlanta, Ga., A. B. Caldwell publishing co., 1923.
103 p. illus. (ports.) 20½cm.

1. Negroes—Biog. I. Title.

Library of Congress E185.96.L25 24-2634
Copyright A 766907 [3]

Lane, Mrs. Mary Edna (Johnson) 1872- joint author.

M910 L241s Lane, James Franklin, 1874-
Some things we saw while abroad; a visit to Europe, the Holy Land and Egypt, by J. F. Lane ... and Mary Edna Lane ... Boston, The Christopher publishing house [c1941]
xv, 17-224 p. plates, ports. 19cm.

1. Europe—Descr. & trav. 2. Palestine—Descr. & trav. 3. Egypt—Descr. & trav. I. Lane, Mrs. Mary Edna (Johnson) 1872- joint author. II. Title.

Library of Congress D975.L24 42-2408
[4] 910.4

Land titles-Maryland.

M378Ho M481 Melchor, Beulah H
The land possessions of Howard university, a study of the original ownership and extent of the holdings of Howard university in the District of Columbia [by] Beulah H. Melchor ... Washington, D. C., 1945.
85 p. illus. (plans) 23cm.
"This dissertation ... for a master's thesis [Howard university] ... covers the years 1651-1855."—Foreword.
Bibliography: p. 53-59.

1. Howard university, Washington, D. C.—Hist. 2. Land titles—District of Columbia. 3. Land titles—Maryland. I. Title.

45-16667
Library of Congress LC2851.H82M4
[3] 378.753

M136 L24 Lane, Edward X.
I was a mental statistic; the true story of a man who came back. New York, Carlton Press [c1963]
92p. 21cm. (A Reflection book)
Portrait of author on book jacket.

1. Mental illness. I. Title.

Lang, Andrew, 1844-1912.

France M840 D89a2 Dumas, Alexandre, 1802-1870.
My memoirs, by Alexandre Dumas, tr. by E. M. Waller, with an introduction by Andrew Lang ... With a frontispiece. New York, The Macmillan company, 1907-09.
6 v. fronts. (v. 3-4, 6: ports.) 20cm.
Printed in Great Britain.
"The translator has, in the main, followed the edition published at Brussels in 1852-56, in the preface to which the publishers state that they have printed from 'le manuscrit autographe' of the author."

I. Waller, Emily Mary, tr. II. Lang, Andrew, 1844-1912.

Library of Congress PQ2230.A3W3 8-3121
[45h1]

Land without chimneys...

M910 C561 Coffin, Alfred Oscar
Land without chimneys; or the byways of Mexico, by Alfred Oscar Coffin...
Cincinnati, Ohio, The Editor Publishing Co., 1898.
352p. plates 20cm.

MB9 L24a Lane, Isaac, *bp.*, 1834-1937
Autobiography of Bishop Isaac Lane, LL. D.; with a short history of the C. M. E. church in America and of Methodism. Nashville, Tenn., Printed for the author, Publishing house of the M. E. church, South, 1916.
192 p. incl. plates, ports. front. 20cm. $1.00

Library of Congress 16-24333
Copyright A 445811

Langlois, Jean Thomas.

Guadeloupe M972.97 F84m Frasans, Hippolyte de.
Mémoire pour le chef de brigade Magloire Pélage et pour les habitans de la Guadeloupe, chargés, par cette colonie, de l'administration provisoire, après le départ du capitaine-général Lacrosse ... Paris, Desenne [etc.] an XI.—1803.
2 v. 20cm.
By H. de Frasans and Jean Thomas Langlois.

1. Guadeloupe—Hist. I. Langlois, Jean Thomas. II. Title.

Library of Congress F2066.F84 2-18833 rev.
[r37b2]

M784 L23 Landeck, Beatrice.
Echoes of Africa in folk songs of the Americas. Instrumental arrangements by Milton Kaye. English version of foreign lyrics by Margaret Marks. Drawings by Alexander Dobkin. New York, D. McKay Co. [1961]
viii, 184 p. illus. 29 cm.
Includes discussions of the origin of each folk song as well as technics of performance.
Instrumental arrangements consist of accompaniment of the songs by percussion instruments in varying combinations.
Bibliography: p. 182-183. Discography: p. 176-181.
White author.
1. Folk-songs, African—America. 2. Negro songs. 3. Jazz music. 4. Folk-songs, African—America—Discography. I. Kaye, Milton. II. Title.

M1680.L15E3 M 61—1013
Library of Congress [61x15]

MB9 L24s Lane, Isaac, Bp., 1834-1937.
Savage, Horace C
Life and times of Bishop Isaac Lane. Nashville, National Publication Co., 1958.
240 p. illus. 20 cm.

1. Lane, Isaac, Bp., 1834-1937.

BX8473.L3S3 922.773 58-30008 ‡
Library of Congress [1]

Langston, Charles H., p. 16-23.

MB9 B81tr A tribute of respect, commemorative of the worth and sacrifice of John Brown of Ossawatomie; it being a full report of the speeches made and the resolutions adopted by the citizens of Cleveland at a meeting held in the Melodeon on the evening of the day on which John Brown was sacrificed by the Commonwealth of Virginia: together with a sermon, commemorative of the sad event... Cleveland, Published for the benefit of widows and families of the Revolutionists of Harper's Ferry, 1859.
62p. 21½cm.

M323.4
L26e
Langston, John Mercer, 1829-1897.
"Equality before the law" Oration delivered by Prof. J.M. Langston, of Howard University, Washington, D.C., at the fifteenth amendment celebration, held in Oberlin Ohio, Thursday, May 14th, 1874. Oberlin, Ohio, Pratt & Battle, 1874.
8p. 23½cm.
1. Civil rights I. Title

Langston, John Mercer, 1829-1897
M973.6
N21c
1865
National equal rights league. Cleveland, Ohio.
Proceedings of the first annual meeting of the national equal rights league, held in Cleveland, Ohio, October 19, 20 and 21, 1865. Philadelphia, E. C. Markley & Son., 1865,
54p. 21cm.

Lanham, Peter, pseud.
See
Parker, Cecil John Lanham, 1899-

M815.4
L25e
Langston, John Mercer, 1829-1897.
The exodus, address by Hon. John M. Langston, delivered at Lincoln Hall, October 7, 1879, before the Emigrant Aid Society, District of Columbia. Washington, D.C., Rufus H. Darby, 1879.
25p. 23cm.
1. Emigration. I. Title.

Langston civic club of America.
MB9
At8c
Ruffin, George L.
Crispus Attucks, by George L. Ruffin. Phila⌊delphia⌋ Pa., The Langston civic club of America, °1942.
⌊16⌋ p. 14½cm.
1. Attucks, Crispus, d. 1770. I. Langston civic club of America.
Library of Congress E215.4.A8R8 42-12911
⌊2⌋ 973.3118

Nigeria
M896.3
L27
Laniyan, S Oladele
Asiri aiye. ⌊The secret of life⌋ ⌊London⌋ Longmans, Green and Co., 1961.
vi, 186p. 18½cm.
Written in Yoruba.
I. Title.

M815.4
L26
Langston, John Mercer, 1829-1897.
Freedom and citizenship. Selected lectures and addresses of Hon. John Mercer Langston ... With an introductory sketch by Rev. J. E. Rankin ... Washington, D. C., R. H. Darby, 1883.
286 p. front. (port.) 20cm.
1. Negroes. 2. U. S.—Pol. & govt.—1865-1898. I. Rankin, Jeremiah Eames, 1828-1904. II. Title. 3. Langston John Mercer, 1829-1897 (over)
Library of Congress E185.6.L28 15—10680
Copyright 1883: 19154 ⌊40b1⌋

The Langston Hughes reader.
M813.5
H871a
Hughes, Langston, 1902–
The Langston Hughes reader. ⌊1st ed.⌋ New York, G. Braziller, 1958.
501 p. 22 cm.
"Especially for Arthur - my latest and biggest to date - Sincerely, Langston, New York, March 29, 1958."
I. Title. *Full name: James Langston Hughes.*
PS3515.U274A6 1958 810.81 58—7871 ‡
Library of Congress ⌊59n10⌋

M811.08
L29c
1845
Lanusse, Armand, 1812-1867, comp.
Les Cenelles, choix de poesies indigenes ... Nouvelle Orleans, Imprime par H. Lauve et compagnie, 1845.
214p. 16½cm.
1. American poetry (French) - Louisiana.
2. French poetry - American authors.
3. Poetry.
I. Sejour, Victor. II. Valcour, B.
I. Title

MB9
L26
Langston, John Mercer, 1829-1897.
From the Virginia plantation to the national capitol; or, The first and only Negro representative in Congress from the Old Dominion. John Mercer Langston ... Hartford, Conn., American publishing company, 1894.
x, 11-534 p. front., plates, ports. 23cm.
I. Title.
Library of Congress E185.97.L27 12—3280
⌊a37b1⌋

Language and languages.
Nigeria
M401
Ok1
Okala, J B C Etuka
Bilingualism in Eastern region of Nigeria; a psychological and sociopsychological study. [Enugu, Eastern Nigeria Printing Corp., n.d.]
16p. 20½cm.
1. Bilingualism. 2. Language and languages.

Argentina
M982
L29
⌊Lanuza, José Luis⌋ *comp.*
Los morenos ... Buenos Aires, Emecé ⌊1942⌋
2 p. l., 7-95, ⌊1⌋ p. plates. 18cm. (Colección Buen aire. ⌊No. 10⌋)
"Selección de José Luis Lanuza."
1. Negroes in Argentine republic. I. Title.
A 43-1800
Harvard univ. Library for Library of Congress F3021.N3L3
⌊2⌋† 325.260982

M326
G87a
1854
Langston, John Mercer, 1829-1897.
The intellectual, moral, and spiritual condition of the slave.
(In: Griffiths, Julia ed. Autographs for freedom. Auburn, Alden, Beardsley, 1854. 19½cm. Pp. 147-150).

Africa
M496
L57
Language in Africa.
Leverhulme Conference on Universities and the Language Problems of Tropical Africa, *Ibadan, Nigeria, 1961-1962.*
Language in Africa; papers. Edited by John Spencer. Cambridge ⌊Eng.⌋ University Press, 1963.
vii, 167 p. 23 cm.
English or French.
Bibliographical footnotes.
1. Africa, Sub-Saharan—Languages. 2. Education—Africa, Sub-Saharan. I. Spencer, John Walter, ed. II. Title.
LA1503.7.L46 1961-1962 63-4814
Library of Congress ⌊5⌋

Guadeloupe
M972.97
L319c
Lara, H Adolphe.
Contributionde la Guadeloupe a la pensée francaise, 1635-1935. Preface de Léon Hennique. Paris, Editions Jean Crès, 1936.
301p. portraits. 22cm.
1. West Indian literature. 2. Guadeloupe-Biography. 3. French literature.

M973.8
L26o
Langston, John Mercer, 1829-1897.
The other phase of reconstruction. Speech of Hon. John Mercer Langston, delivered at Congregational tabernacle, Jersey City, New Jersey, April 17, 1877. Peaceful reconstruction possible ... Washington, D. C., Gibson brothers, printers, 1877.
16 p. 23½cm.
1. Reconstruction. I. Title
18-5993
Library of Congress E668.L28

Languages, African.
Senegal
M966.3
D62n
Diop, Cheikh Anta
Nations Nègres et culture. Paris, Éditions Africaines, 1955.
390p. illus. plates. 25cm.

Guadeloupe
M972.97
L32g
Lara, Oruno
La Guadeloupe, physique, economique, agricole, commerciale, financiere, politique, et sociale de la decouverte a nos jours (1492-1900). Paris, Nouvelle librairie universelle ⌊1922⌋
⌊16⌋ -340, 10p. illus., map. 26cm.
Portrait of author, p.9.
1. Guadeloupe.

Langston, John Mercer, 1829-1897.
M815
L26
Langston, John Mercer, 1829-1897.
Freedom and citizenship. Selected lectures and addresses of Hon. John Mercer Langston ... With an introductory sketch by Rev. J. E. Rankin ... Washington, D. C., R. H. Darby, 1883.
286 p. front. (port.) 20cm.
1. Negroes. 2. U. S.—Pol. & govt.—1865-1898. I. Rankin, Jeremiah Eames, 1828-1904. II. Title.
Library of Congress E185.6.L28 15—10680
Copyright 1883: 19154 ⌊40b1⌋

La langue du Rwanda et du Burundi expliquée aux autochtones.
Rwanda
M496
K11
Kagame, Alexis, 1912-
La langue du Rwanda et du Burundi expliquée aux autochtones. [Kabgayi, 1960]
252p. 20cm.

Guadeloupe
M972.97
L321
Lara, Oruno
La litterature Antillaise. Aux pays bleus. Notes de litterature et d'art etudes et critiques. La litterature Antillaise et le regionalisme chez les creoles ... Paris, Librairie "Le progres Vulgarisateur Fernand Drubay, 1913.
xiv. 206p. port. 18cm.
1. West Indian literature. 2. Creole literature dialects. 3. French literature.

Guadeloupe
M972.97
L32s
Lara, Oruno.
Sous le ciel bleu de la Guadeloupe...
Paris, Librairie Fischbacker, 1912.

174p. port. 18cm.

1. West Indian literature. 2. Guadeloupe - Life and customs. 3. French literature. 4. Creole dialects - literature.

M301
L326
Larkins, John Rodman.
Alcohol and the Negro: explosive issues, by John R. Larkins. Zebulon, N. C., Record Pub. Co., 1965.
xi, 251 p. illus. 24 cm.
Includes bibliographical references.

1. Alcohol and negroes. 2. Negroes—Moral and social conditions. I. Title.

E185.86.L36 309.173 65-28614
Library of Congress [5]

Nigeria
M496
L33
Lasebikan, Ebenezer Latunde
Ojúlówó Yoruba. Iwe kini: awon ilu nlá nlá ilẹ Yoruba. London, Oxford University Press [1961]

84p. illus. 18½cm.
"First published 1954."

1. Yoruba language - Grammar. I. Title.

Cuba
M29
M151
Lara Mena, María Julia de.
La familia Maceo. Cartas a Elena. Conversaciones patrióticas al calor del hogar, por la dra. María Julia de Lara Mena ... La Habana, Editorial selecta [1945]
141 p., 1 l. illus. (facsim.) 2 col. port. 20½cm.
On cover: 1845-centenario de Maceo-1945.
"'Los ancianitos.' Ejercicios" (music for physical exercises): p. 68.
"Bibliografía": p. [135]

1. Maceo family. I. González de Casaña, Elena. II. Title.

F1755.M3L3 929.2 A 46-5664
New York. Public library for Library of Congress [3]†

Trinidad
M821.91
L12
La Rose, Antony.
Foundations; a book of poems. London, New Beacon Publications [1966]

51p. 21cm.

I. Title.

M810.9
L33r
Lash, John S
Race consciousness of the American Negro author: Toward a reexamination of an orthodox critical concept.

(In: Social forces, 28:24-34, October 1949)
Detached copy.

Cuba
M613
L32s
Lara Mena, María Julia de.
Salud y belleza; divulgaciones científicas sobre anatomía, fisiología, patología, higiene y estética de la mujer, por la dra. María Julia de Lara ... Con un juicio crítico del profesor dr. W. H. Hoffmann ... Con 260 ilustraciones. La Habana, Cuba, Casa editora "La Propagandista," s. a., 1940.
xxxv, 663 p. illus. (incl. ports., facsim.) col. pl., tables, diagrs. 24cm.
"Bibliografía" at end of chapter 7.

1. Women—Health and hygiene. I. Title.
~~2. Cuban authors~~

A 41-189 rev
Harvard univ. Library for Library of Congress [r46c2]

M813.5
L32
Larsen, Nella.
Passing, by Nella Larsen. New York & London, A. A. Knopf, 1929.
6 p. l., 3-215, [1] p., 1 l. 19½cm.
"For Mr and Mrs Arthur Spingarn This serious examination of modern behaviour Nella Larson Imes. April 10, 1929 (Pub. date April 29, 1929)
ABS.

I. Title.

29-6090
Library of Congress PZ3.L33Pas
[44e1]

M728
L337
Lassiter, William Lawrence.
Shaker architecture; descriptions with photographs and drawings of Shaker buildings at Mount Lebanon, New York, Watervliet, New York [and] West Pittsfield, Massachusetts. Illustrated by Constantine Kermes. [1st ed.] New York, Vantage Press [1966]
127 p. illus., plans. 26 cm.
Bibliography: p. 127.
Portrait of author on book jacket.

1. Architecture, Shaker. 2. Architecture—New York (State) 3. Architecture—Designs and plans.

NA730.N4L3 728'.09747 66-23098
Library of Congress [5]

Haiti
M972.94
L32c
Laraque, Maurice.
... Constantin Mayard, étude par Maurice Laraque. Port-au-Prince, Haïti [Imp. Telhomme] 1944.
80 p. incl. port. 19cm. (Bibliothèque haïtienne)
"Cet petit 'essai' est extrait de mes 'Essais et portraits'."—Avant-propos.

1. Mayard, Constantin, 1882-1940.

F1926.M46L3 923.27294 47-21979
Library of Congress [1]

M813.5
L32q
Larsen, Nella.
Quicksand, by Nella Larsen. New York & London, A. A. Knopf, 1928.
4 p. l., 301, [1] p., 1 l. 19½cm.

Inscribed copy: For Mr. & Mrs. Spingarn, This tale of pride, prejuduce and passion, Nella Larsen

I. Title.

28-9740
Library of Congress PZ3.L33Qu
[43d1]

The last barbarian.

British Guiana
M823.91
C181
Carew, Jan Rynveld, 1923-
The last barbarian. London, Secker and Warburg, 1961.

286p. 20½cm.

Haiti
M844
L32
Large, Jacques
Choses & gens vus. Port-au-Prince, Haiti, n.d.

142p. 22½cm.

1. Description and Travel.

M323.3
L33
Larsson, Clotye Murdock, ed.
Marriage across the color line, edited by Clotye M. Larsson. Chicago, Johnson Pub. Co., 1965.
xi, 204 p. 22 cm.
Partial contents.- Miscegenation in America, by Lerone Bennett.- I don't want to marry your daughter, by Charles H. King.- Teaching children about race, by St. Clair Drake.- An African abdication, by Seretse Khama.- Five million white Negroes, by Roi Ottley.
Portrait of author on book jacket.

1. Miscegenation. 2. ~~U. S.~~—Race question. I. Title.
3. Marriage, Mixed.
HQ1031.L3 301.429 65-21549
Library of Congress [5]

Last call for peace.

M811.5
C831
Cox, Ollie
Last call for peace. New York, Arlain Printing Company, 1959.

87p. port. 21cm.

A larger manhood for the Negro.

M323
W281
Wassam, R Conkling
A larger manhood for the Negro ... by R. Conkling Wassam. Kansas City, Mo., Franklin Hudson publishing co., 1914.
80 [1] p. 17½cm.

Nigeria
M896.1
K621
Lasebikan, Ebenezer Latunde
Ijinlẹ ohun-ẹnu Yoruba; àkójọ kini.
Eni ti o ya àwòrán rẹ ni J. K. Oye.
[Ibadan] Ministry of Education, General Publications Division [1958]

51p. illus. 18½cm.
Written in Yoruba.
"Yoruba poetry book 1."

1. African poetry. I. Title.

The last enchantment.

Jamaica
M823.91
D321
Dawes, Neville
The last enchantment. London, MacGibbon & Kee, 1960.

288p. 19½cm.

M326.99B
D851
Larison, Cornelius Wilson, 1837-1910.
Silvia Dubois, (now 116 years old.) A biografy of the slav who whipt her mistres and gand her fredom. By C. W. Larison ... Ringos, N. J., C. W. Larison, 1883.
124 p. front. (port.) illus. 20cm.
Text in phonetic type.

1. Dubois, Silvia, b. 1768.

13-24983
Library of Congress PE1152.L48
Copyright 1883: 12148 [39f1]

Nigeria
M496.5
L331
Lasebikan, Ebenezer Latunde.
Learning Yoruba. London, Oxford University Press, 1958.
81 p. 19 cm.

1. Yoruba language—Grammar.

PL8821.L3 496.5 61-21789 ‡
Library of Congress [2]

Last of the conquerors.

M813.5
Sm651
Smith, William Gardner, 1926-
Last of the conquerors. New York, Farrar, Straus, 1948.

262p. 21cm.

M813.5
Sm681
1948

Last of the conquerors.
Smith, William Gardner, 1926-
Last of the conquerors. New York, The New American Library, 1948.

191p. 18cm. (A Signet Book)

M813.5
Sm681
1949

Last of the conquerors.
Smith, William Gardner, 1926-
New American Library, 1949.

191p. 18cm. (Signet books)
Pocket book edition.

M813.5
H83L

The last refuge of a scoundrel, and other stories.
Howard, Wendell.
The last refuge of a scoundrel, and other stories. New York, Exposition Press [1952]
85 p. 23 cm.

I. Title.

PZ4.H853Las 52-8701 ‡

Library of Congress

Jamaica
M823.91
Sa3L

The late emancipation of Jerry Stover.
Salkey, Andrew.
The late emancipation of Jerry Stover. London, Hutchinson, 1968.
[7], 246 p. 21 cm. 30/-
(SBN 09 085 530 2) (B 68-02620)

I. Title.

PZ4.S1687Lat 68-91611

Library of Congress

M621.326
L35

Latimer, Lewis Howard, 1848-1929.
Incandescent electric lighting. A practical description of the Edison system. By L. H. Latimer. To which is added the design and operation of incandescent stations. By C. J. Field. And a paper on the maximum efficiency of incandescent lamps. by John W. Howell. New York, D. Van Nostrand company, 1890.
71p. illus. diagrs. 15cm.

1. Electricity. I. Title.

Haiti
M972.94
B76et

Latin America.
Brierre, Paulette Fritz
Etau economique sur le monde; regards sur la situation Latino-Américaine programme de développment Haitien proposition universelle. Port-au-Prince, Imp. Les Presses Libres, 1961.

78p. 21cm.
Appendice: p. 66-75.

M973.8
F854

Latin America - Relations (general) with the U. S.
Hyman, Harold Melvin, 1924- , ed.
New frontiers of the American Reconstruction, edited by Harold M. Hyman. Urbana, University of Illinois Press, 1966.

x, 156p. 24cm.
Papers presented at a conference held at the University of Illinois in April 1965.
Includes bibliographical footnotes.
White editor.
Partial contents.- Reconstruction and the Negro, by John Hope Franklin.

W. Indies
M972.9
B41

Latin American economic institute.
... Economic problems of the Caribbean area; speeches, addresses and abstracts of papers, delivered at the public conference held in New York city jointly with the Women's international league for peace and freedom on May 1, 1943, by Dantes Bellegarde, Lawrence Berenson [and others] ... New York, 1943.
cover-title, 60 p. 23cm. (Its Pamphlet series, no. 7)

1. West Indies—Econ. condit. I. Women's international league for peace and freedom. II. Title. III. Williams, Eric. British possessions. IV. Bellegarde, Dantes - Haiti. V. Logan, Rayford - Agriculture & Industry. 44-47231.

Library of Congress HC161.L26 no. 7
[45d2] (330.82) 330.9729

W. Indies
M972.9
B41

Latin American economic institute.
...Economic problems of the Caribbean area.
(card 2)

Partial contents: -Haiti, by Dantes Bellegarde. British possessions, by Eric Williams. -Agriculture and industry, by Rayford Logan.

M812.5
R160

Latin drama.
Rankin, Wilfred.
Ovans L. aemilius paulus urbem ingreditur, a play in two acts. n.p. [193]

10p. 28cm.
Mimeographed.

Spain
M861.3
L34a

Latin literature - Mediaeval and modern.
Latino, Juan, fl.1573.
Ad Catholicum pariter et invictissimum Philippum dei gratia Hispaniarum regem, de foelicissima serenissimi Ferdinandi Principis nativitate, epigrammatum liber. Deque Sanctissimi PII Quinti Romanae Eclesiae Pontificis sumi, rebus et affectibus erga Philippum Regem Christianissimum Liber unus Austrias Carmen, De Ex Cellentissimi Domini. D. Ioannis ab Austria, Caroli Quinti filli,

(cont. on next card)

Spain
M861.3
L34a

Latin literature - Mediaeval and modern.
Latino, Juan, fl. 1573. Ad Catholicum pariter... (Card 2)

ac Philippi invictissimi fratris, re bene gesta, in victoria mirabili eiusdem Philippi adversus perfidos Turcas parta, Ad illustrissimum, pariter et Reverendissimum. D.D. Petrum a Deza Praesidem, ac pro Philippo Militiae prafectu. Per Magistrum Ioannem Latinum Garnatae studiosae ado Lescentiae

(cont. on next card)

Spain
M861.3
L34a

Latin literature - Mediaeval and modern.
Latino, Juan, fl.1573. Ad Catholicum pariter... (Card 3)

moderatorem. Libri duo. Cum Regiae Maiestatis Privilegio Garnatae. Ex officina Hugonis de Mena. Anno. 1573. Prastant in aedibus Ioannis Diaz Bibliopolae in vico santae Mariae.

44 [1], 35, [4] p. woodcuts. 20cm.
1. Austriad (poem). 2. Lepanto - Poems. 3. Latin literature - Mediaeval and modern. I. Title.

Spain
M861.3
L34a

Latino, Juan, fl. 1573.
Ad Catholicum pariter et invictissimum Philippum dei gratia Hispaniarum regem, de foelicissima serenissimi Ferdinandi Principis nativitate, epigrammatum liber. Deque Sanctissimi PII Quinti Romanae Eclesiae Pontificis sumi, rebus et affectibus erga Philippum Regem Christianissimum Liber unus Austrias Carmen, De Ex Cellentissimi Domini. D. Ioannis ab Austria, Caroli Quinti filli,

(cont. on next card)

Spain
M861.3
L34a

Latino, Juan, fl. 1573. Ad Catholicum pariter... (Card 2)

ac Philippi invictissimi fratris, re bene gesta, in victoria mirabili eiusdem Philippi adversus perfidos Turcas parta, Ad illustrissimum, pariter et Reverendissimum. D.D. Petrum a Deza Praesidem, ac pro Philippo Militiae prafectu. Per Magistrum Ioannem Latinum Garnatae studiosae ado Lescentiae

(cont. on next card)

Spain
M861.3
L34a

Latino, Juan, fl.1573. Ad Catholicum pariter... (Card 3)

moderatorem. Libri duo. Cum Regiae Maiestatis Privilegio Garnatae. Ex officina Hugonis de Mena. Anno. 1573. Prastant in aedibus Ioannis Diaz Bibliopolae in vico santae Mariae.

44 [1], 35, [4] p. woodcuts, 20cm.
1. Austriad (poem). 2. Lepanto - Poems. 3. Latin literature - Mediaeval and modern. I. Title.

MB9
L34m

Latino, Juan, fl. 1573.
Marín Ocete, Antonio
El Negro Juan Latino, ensayo, biográfico y critico. Granada, Libraria, Guevara, 1925.

94p. 27cm.

MB9
L34s

Latino, Juan, fl. 1573.
Spratlin, Valaurez Burwell.
Juan Latino, slave and humanist, by V. B. Spratlin ... New York, Spinner press, inc., 1938.
xiii, 216 p. 24cm.
Contents.—Introduction.—Juan Latino.—"The famous drama of Juan Latino", an adaptation in English from the Spanish of Diego Jiménez de Enciso.—Appendix: Diego Jiménez de Enciso.—Bibliography (p. 212-214)

1. Latino, Juan, 16th cent. I. Ximénez de Enciso, Diego. Comedia famosa de Juan Latino.

Library of Congress PA8540.L615Z8 38-31793
——— Copy 2.
Copyright A 122085 [40d1] 928.7

MB9
L35

Latta, Morgan London, 1853-
The history of my life and work. Autobiography by Rev. M. L. Latta ... Introduction by Rev. George Daniel, D. D., illustrations by the Tucker engraving company. Raleigh, Montreal [etc.] M. L. Latta [1903]
371 p. front., plates, ports. 21½ cm.

3—18966

Library of Congress E185.97.L35
[a48b1]

Guiana, British
M823.91
M691a

Latticed echoes.
Mittelholzer, Edgar, 1909-
Latticed echoes; a novel in the Leitmotiv Manner. London, Secker and Warburg, 1960.

254p. 19½cm.

MB9
B221a

Latrobe, John Hazlehurst Boneval, 1803-1891.
Memoir of Benjamin Banneker, read before the Maryland historical society ... by John H. B. Latrobe, esq. Published under direction of the society. Baltimore, Printed by J. D. Toy, 1845.
16 p. 23½cm.

1. Banneker, Benjamin, 1731-1806.

Library of Congress E185.97.B22 Rc-3345
——— Copy 2 [Maryland historical society. Publications. v. 2, no. 3] F176.M34 vol. 2
[33f1]

Laws and legislation.

M323.4 Jones, John.
J71b The black laws of Illinois, and a few reasons why they should be repealed. By John Jones ... Chicago, Tribune Book and Job Office, 1864.

16p. 22cm.

Law and legislation.

M815 Langston, John Mercer, 1829-1897.
L26 Freedom and citizenship. Selected lectures and addresses of Hon. John Mercer Langston... With an introductory sketch by Rev. J. E. Rankin... Washington, D. C., R. H. Darby, 1883.

286p. front. (port.) 20cm.

Laws and legislation.

M304 White, Walter Francis, 1893-
P19 The Negro and the supreme court, by
v.7 Walter White. Reprinted from Harper's
no.7 magazine, January, 1931 for the National association for the advancement of colored
M347.9 people, New York.
W58n 11p. 24½cm.

M323
W587ne3

Laws and legislation

M973. Woodson, Carter Godwin, 1875- ed.
W86fo Fifty years of Negro citizenship as qualified by the United States supreme court, by C.G. Woodson. Reprinted from the Journal of Negro history, 6; January 1921.
53P. 25cm.
Bound with: Free Negro owners of slaves in the United States, by C.G. Woodson.

Laws and legislation
M974.9
W93n Wright, Marion Thompson
New Jersey laws and the Negro. Washington, D.C., The Association for the Study of Negro Life and History, 1943.

45p. 24cm.
Reprinted from the Journal of Negro history, 28:no.2, April, 1943.
Inscribed by author.

Laws and legislations.
M304 Johnson, James Weldon
P19 Legal aspects of the Negro problem, by
V.7 James Weldon Johnson and Herbert J. Seligmann.
No.12 Reprinted from the Annals of the American Academy of Political and Social Science, November, 1928.

8p. 23½cm.

MB9
R321a Lawson, Elizabeth,
The gentleman from Mississippi; our first Negro congressman, Hiram R. Revels, by Elizabeth Lawson with an introduction by William L. Patterson. [New York, published by author, c 1960]

63p. ports. 19cm.
Reference notes: p. 54-63.
White author.

1. Revels, Hiram R ,1827-1901. I. Title. II. Patterson,William Lorenzo, 1891-

Lawson, Jesse, 1856- , ed.

M323. Washington conference on the race problem in the United
W279 States, *Washington, D. C.*, 1903.
How to solve the race problem. The proceedings of the Washington conference on the race problem in the United States under the auspices of the National sociological society, held at the Lincoln temple Congregational church; at the Nineteenth street Baptist church and at the Metropolitan A. M. E. church, Washington, D. C., November 9, 10, 11, and 12, 1903. Addresses, resolutions and debates by eminent men of both races and in every walk of life. Washington, D. C., Beresford, printer, 1904.
1 p. l., 286 p. front., illus. (port.) 23½cm.
Edited by Jesse Lawson. [45p1]
1. Negroes. 2. U. S.—Race question. I. Lawson, Jesse, ed. II. National sociological society.
Library of Congress E186.5.W32 4—14581

M811.4
D8991 Lawson, Victor.
Dunbar critically examined, by Victor Lawson ... Washington, The Associated publishers [°1941]
xvi, 151 p. 21½cm.
Thesis (M. A.)—Howard university.
Bibliography: p. 150-151.

1. Dunbar, Paul Laurence, 1872-1906. I. Title.
41—8322
Library of Congress PS1557.L3
[41e2] 811.49

Lawyers.

M342 Styles, Fitzhugh Lee, 1899-
St9 Negroes and the law in the race's battle for liberty, equality and justice under the Constitution of the United States; with causes celebres, by Fitzhugh Lee Styles ... Boston, The Christopher publishing house [°1937]
xi, [1], 13-320 p. front. (port.) 24cm.
The manuscript of the author's address before the National bar association at Baltimore, August 1934, on the battle of the Negro at the bar of justice, is the basis of this book. *cf.* Pref.
Bibliography: p. 320.
1. Negroes — Legal status, laws, etc. 2. Negroes—Biog. 3. Negro lawyers. 4. Law reports, digests, etc.—U. S. I. Title.
37—3583
Library of Congress E185.61.S92
——— Copy 2.
Copyright A 103799 [38g3] 325.260973

Lawyers.

M973 Woodson, Carter Godwin, 1875-
W86n The Negro professional man and the community, with special emphasis on the physician and the lawyer, by Carter Godwin Woodson. Washington, D. C., The Association for the study of Negro life and history, inc. [°1934]
1 p. l., v-xviii, 365 p. diagr. 23½cm.
"[This study forms] a part of the effort of the Association for the study of Negro life and history to portray the social and economic conditions obtaining among Negroes in the United States since the civil war."—Foreword.
1. Negroes—Employment. 2. Negroes—Moral and social conditions. 3. Negro physicians. 4. Negro lawyers. I. Association for the study of Negro life and history, inc. II. Title.
34—10066
Library of Congress E185.82.W88
[34f5] 325.260973

Lay my burden down...

M326.99B Federal writers' project.
F31 Lay my burden down; a folk history of slavery, edited by B. A. Botkin. Chicago, Ill., University of Chicago press [1945]
xxi, 285, [1] p. front., plates. 23½ cm.
Illustrated t.-p.
"A selection and integration of excerpts and complete narratives from the Slave narrative collection of the Federal writers' project."

1. Slavery in the U. S.—Condition of slaves. 2. Negroes—Biog. I. Botkin, Benjamin Albert, 1901- ed. II. Title.
A 45—5576
Chicago. Univ. Library for Library of Congress E444.F26
[47t²7] 326.973

The lay of the clay minstrel.

M811.5 Flanagan, Thomas Jefferon, 1890-
F61c The canyons at Providence (the lay of the clay minstrel) by Thomas Jefferson Flanagan.

21 3 p. illus. 23½cm.

Guinea
M896 Laye, Camara
L45 Camara Laye, écrivain Guinéen. [Textes commentés par Roger Mercier et M. et S. Battestini. Paris] Fernand Nathan [1964]
63p. 19½cm. (Classiques du monde. Littérature africaine, 2)
Portrait of author on book cover.
"Oeuvres": p. 6.

I. Mercier, Roger, ed. II. Series.

Fr. Guinea
MB9 Laye, Camara, 1924-
L45d The dark child. Translated from the French
1955 by James Kirkup with an introduction by William Plomer. London, Collins, 1955.

192p. 21cm.

1. Guinea, French - Soc. life and customs.
I. Title.

Laye, Camara, 1928-
French Guinea The dark child. With an introd. by Philippe Thoby-
MB9 Marcellin. Translated by James Kirkup, Ernest Jones [and]
L45d Elaine Gottlieb. New York, Noonday Press, 1954.
188 p. 21 cm.
Autobiographical story.

1. Guinea, French—Soc. life & cust. I. Title.
DT543.L313 916.652 54-11726 ‡
Library of Congress [20]

Guinea
M896.3 Laye, Camara, 1928-
L45dr Dramouss, roman. [Paris] Plon, 1966.
251 p. 20 cm. 12 F.
(F 66-10874)

I. Title.
PQ3989.L37D7 67-79125
Library of Congress [2]

French Guinea
MB9 Laye, Camara, 1928-
L45ef Einer aus kurussa (Lenfant noir). Zurich, Speer, 1954.

237p. 19cm.

French Guinea
MB9 Laye, Camara, 1928-
L45e L'enfant noir, roman. Paris, Plon [1953]
256 p. 19 cm.

I. Title.
A 54-2532
Illinois. Univ. Library for Library of Congress [2]

Africa
M808.83 Laye, Camara
B396 The eyes of the statue. Tr. by Una Maclean.

Pp. 118-130.

In: Black Orpheus. Black Orpheus; an anthology of African and Afro-American prose. New York, McGraw-Hill, 1965.

French Guinea
M966.52 Laye, Camara,1928-
L45ra The radiance of the king. Translated from the French by James Kirkup. London, Collins, 1956.

319p. 20½cm.

1. French Guinea-Fiction. I. Title.

French Guinea
M966.52
L45r

Laye, Camara, 1928–
Le regard du roi, roman. Paris, Plon [1954]

254 p. 19 cm.

I. Title.

Illinois. Univ. Library for Library of Congress [1]

A 55-3692

Laye, Camara, 1928–

Congo(Leopoldville)
M840.8
M971

Mushiete, Paul
La littérature française africaine; petite anthologie des écrivains noirs d'expression française. Leverville, Bibliothèque de l'Étoile, 1957.

40p. 17½cm.

Nigeria
M496
L45

Layeni, Olasiji
Yoruba course for secondary schools, Book I. Lagos, Pacific Printers [1962]

131p. 21cm.

1. Yoruba language - Grammar. I. Title.

Laymen speaking.

M261.8
Sp31

Speers, Wallace C , ed.
Laymen speaking, selected and edited by Wallace C. Speers. New York, Association Press, 1947.

207p. 19cm.

Lays in summer lands.

M811.4
M521

Menard, John Willis
Lays in summer lands. Poems, by J. Willis Menard. With the press notices of his speech and his appearance in Congress. Washington, Enterprise publishing company, 1879.
vii, 84p. 18cm.
1st edition.

Guadeloupe
M972.97
L49

Le Boucher, Léon
La Guadeloupe pittoresque, les volcans, les rivières du sud, les étangs. Paris, Societe d'Editions Geographiques, Maritimes et Coloniales, 1931.

256p. illus.

1. Guadeloupe - Descr. & trav.

Le Cap Français en 1792.

Haiti
M972.94
N349r

Nemours, Alfred, 1883–
... Les premiers citoyens et les premiers députés noirs et de couleur; la loi du 4 avril 1792, ses précédents, sa première application à Saint-Domingue, d'après des documents inédits de l'époque. Suivi de: Le Cap Français en 1792, à l'arrivée de Sonthonax, d'après des documents inédits de l'époque. Port-au-Prince, Haiti, Imprimerie de l'état, 1941.

2 p. l., 170 p. plates. 23cm.

At head of title: Général Nemours.
"Bibliographie": p. 167-168.

1. Haiti — Pol. & govt.—1791-1804. 2. France — Colonies — Santo Domingo. I. Title. II. Title: Le Cap Français en 1792.

Library of Congress F1923.N45 [2]

42-4318

972.94

Leadership.

M323
Ad1c

Adams, Julius J
The challenge, a study in Negro leadership. New York, W. Malliet, 1949.

154 p. 23 cm.

1. Negroes. 2. Leadership. I. Title.

E185.61.A233 325.26 50-4906

Library of Congress [2]

Leadership.

M378At
At62

Atlanta University
Leadership, the heart of the race problem. Atlanta, 1931.

44p. illus. 28cm.

At head of title: Atlanta University in affiliation with Morehouse College for men and Spelman College for women.

Kenya
M967.62
Oy3

Leadership

Oyende, J P
Chifu hodari wa kiafrika. The ideal African chief. Nairobi, Eagle Press, 1951.

14p. 18cm. (Mawazo ya wenzenu. Your friends are thinking series)
Written Swahili and English.

1. Leadership. 2. Africa - Native races. I. Title. II. Title: The ideal African chief. III. Series. IV. Series: Your friends are thinking series.

Leadership.

M323.1
T372

Thompson, Daniel Calbert.
The Negro leadership class. Englewood Cliffs, N. J., Prentice-Hall [1963]

174 p. 21 cm. (A Spectrum book)
Includes bibliography.

1. Negroes — New Orleans — Case studies. 2. Community leadership—Case studies. 3. Negroes—Civil rights. I. Title.

F379.N5T45 301.155 63-8286 ‡

Library of Congress [5]

Leaf, Earl. Isles of ryhthm.

M910
D92p

Dunham, Katharine
[Preface]

(In: Leaf, Earl. Isles of rhythm. New York, A. S. Barnes, [1948]. 24cm. p.vii-ix)

League of American Writers.

M813.5
H87a

League of American writers.
"We hold these truths..." Statements on anti-Semitism by 54 leading American writers, statesmen, educators, clergymen and trade-unionists. New York, N. Y., The League of American writers [°1939]

128 p. 20½cm.

"First printing March, 1939."
Errata slip inserted.
"A short bibliography relating to the Jewish question": p. 113-114.
"A partial list of anti-Semitic publishers, organizations and individuals in America": p. 115-123.

1. Jewish question. 2. Jews in the U. S. 3. National socialism. I. Title.

Library of Congress DS145.L47 [3]

39-32225

296

British
Guiana
M988.1
L49

League of Colored Peoples. British Guiana.
Seven amazing days in the life of Eze A. Ogueri II, compiled by the League of Colored Peoples, British Guiana. Boston, House of Edinboro, Publishers, 1954.

107p. port. illus. 20cm.

1. British Guiana. 2. Ogueri II, Eze A

League of nations.

Haiti
M972.94
N34c

Nemours, Alfred, 1883–
... Craignons d'être un jour l'Éthiopie de quelqu'un, conflit italo-éthiopien 1935. Port-au-Prince, Haiti, Imp. du Collège Vertières, 1945.

5 p. l., 9-82 p. 22½cm.

At head of title: Général Nemours.
"Références": p. 77-80.

1. Italo-Ethiopian war, 1935-1936. 2. League of nations. I. Title.

DT387.8.N33 A 47-2399

New York. Public library for Library of Congress [2]†

Africa
M304
P19
v.1, no.4

League of struggle for Negro rights.
Equality, land and freedom; a program for Negro liberation (draft submitted by the National council of the League of struggle for Negro rights) New York city, League of struggle for Negro rights, 1933.

46 p. 15 x 10½cm.

1. Negroes—Civil rights. I. Title.

45-46375

Library of Congress E185.61.L46 [2]

Learn Zulu.

S.Africa
M496.3
N981

Nyembezi, C L Sibusio
Learn Zulu. Pietermaritzburg, Shuter and Shooter, 1957.

151p. 18½cm.

The learning tree.

M813.5
P23Le

Parks, Gordon, 1912–
The learning tree. [1st ed.] New York, Harper & Row [1963]

303 p. 22 cm.

I. Title.

PZ4.P249Le 63-16528 ‡

Library of Congress [5]

H
M89
C461

Leconte, Vergniaud.
... Henri Christophe dans l'histoire d'Haïti ... Paris, Berger-Levrault, 1931.

vi, 461, [1] p. 17 pl. (incl. front., ports., plans, facsims., coat of arms) 25½cm.

1. Christophe, Henri, king of Haiti, 1767-1820. 2. Haiti—Hist.—Revolution, 1791-1804. 3. Haiti—Hist.—1804-1844.

32—1228

Library of Congress F1924.C48 [45c1]

923.17294

Haiti
M972.94
L49p

Lecorps, Louis Marceau, *ed.*
... La politique extérieure de Toussaint-Louverture; nos premières relations politiques avec les États-Unis, lettres de Toussaint-Louverture et d'Edward Stevens (1799-1800) Port-au-Prince, Cheraquit, 1935.

1 p. l., ii, [3]-107, vi p., 1 l. port. 22½cm.

At head of title: Ls. Marceau Lecorps.

1. Haiti—For. rel. 2. Haiti—For. rel.—U. S. 3. U. S.—For. rel.—Haiti. I. Toussaint Louverture, Pierre Dominique, 1746?-1803. II. Stevens, Edward.

A 41-3004

New York. Public library for Library of Congress [2]

A lecture.

M304
P19
v.6

Duvall, C H 1858-
A lecture; the building of a race, by C. H. Duvall ... Boston, Mass., The Everett print, ©1919.

1 p.l., 62, [1]p. front. (port.) 20cm.

Lecture on Haiti.

M815.4 D741 **Douglass, Frederick,** 1817-1895.
Lecture on Haiti. The Haitian pavilion dedication ceremonies delivered at the World's fair, in Jackson park, Chicago, Jan. 2d, 1893. By the Hon. Frederick Douglass ... Introductory by Prof. David Swing. Response of the Director-General Geo. R. Davis ... ₍Chicago, 1893₎
57 p. 22½cm.
1. Haiti—Descr. & trav. I. Title.
Library of Congress F1921.D73 2—12340 ₍a27c1₎

Lecuona, Pedro, tr.

M813.5 W93s **Wright, Richard,** 1908–
... Sangre negra ("Native son") Traducción de Pedro Lecuona. Buenos Aires, Editorial sudamericana ₍1941₎
4 p. l., 11-566, ₍1₎ p., 2 l. 18cm. (*On cover:* Colección Horisonte)
I. Lecuona, Pedro, tr. II. Title.
₍*Full name:* Richard Nathaniel Wright₎
Library of Congress PS3545.R815N258 42-18505 ₍2₎

M780 G47 Ledbetter, Huddie, 1885?- 1949.
The blues.
Pp. 15-16.
In: Gleason, Ralph J., ed. Jam session. New York, Putnam ₍1958₎.

M973.8 Am3 Lee, Benjamin Freanklin, 1841-1926
Negro organizations.
(In: American Academy of Political and Social Science. The Negro's progress in fifty years ... Philadelphia, 1913. 25cm. p. 129-137.)

M973 R72 Lee, Carlton L.
Religious roots of the Negro protest. Pp. 27-44.
In: Rose, Arnold Marshall, ed. Assuring freedom to the free. Detroit, Wayne State, 1964.

Lee, Charles.

M326.99B F31s **Fedric, Francis.**
Slave life in Virginia and Kentucky; or, Fifty years of slavery in the southern states of America. By Francis Fedric, an escaped slave. With preface, by the Rev. Charles Lee ... London, Wertheim, Macintosh, and Hunt, 1863.
viii, 115 p. 15½cm.
1. Slavery in the U. S.—Condition of slaves. I. Lee, Charles.
Library of Congress E444.F29 11—11611 ₍36b1₎

M813.5 L51 **Lee, George Washington,** 1894–
Beale street, where the blues began ₍by₎ George W. Lee; foreword by W. C. Handy. New York, R. O. Ballou ₍©1934₎
296 p. front., ports. 21cm.
1. Memphis—Streets—Beale avenue. 2. Negroes—Memphis. I. Title.
Library of Congress F444.M5L4 34-20400
——— Copy 2.
Copyright A 73530 ₍36f3₎ 917.68

M813.5 L51be Lee, George Washington, 1894-
Beale street sundown ₍by₎ George W. Lee. New York, House of Field Inc., 1942.
176p. 22cm.
I. Title. 1. Memphis—Fiction.

M813.5 L51r **Lee, George Washington,** 1894–
River George, by George W. Lee. New York, The Macaulay company ₍©1937₎
275 p. 19½cm.
I. Title.
Library of Congress PZ3.L5123Ri 37-8127
——— Copy 2.
Copyright A 105535 ₍3₎

M811.5 L51p **Lee, Harrison Edward.**
Poems for the day. New York, Comet Press Books ₍©1954₎
23 p. 23 cm.
I. Title.
PS3523.E334P6 811.5 54-9648 ‡
Library of Congress ₍3₎

M323.4 H36c Lee, J. Oscar, 1910- , jt. auth.
Height, Dorothy Irene, 1910–
The Christian citizen and civil rights; a guide to study and action, by Dorothy I. Height and J. Oscar Lee. New York, Woman's Press ₍1949₎
71 p. 21 cm. (Public affairs news service, v. 12, no. 4)
Includes bibliographies.
1. Civil rights—U. S. I. Lee, J. Oscar, 1910– joint author. II. Title. (Series)
H35.P83 vol. 12, no. 4 323.4 49-9198 rev*
Library of Congress ₍r52g5₎

M813.5 L513v **Lee, James F** 1928–
The victims. ₍1st ed.₎ New York, Vantage Press ₍1959₎
190 p. 21 cm.
Portrait of author on book jacket.
"For Long John - In appreciation for the many hours of entertainment your program has given me."
1. Juvenile delinquency. I. Title.
PZ4.L478Vi 59-65075 ‡
Library of Congress ₍2₎

MB9 L51r **Lee,** *Mrs.* **Jarena,** *b.* 1783.
Religious experience and journal of Mrs. Jarena Lee, giving an account of her call to preach the gospel. Rev. and cor. from the original manuscript, written by herself. Philadelphia, Pub. for the author, 1849.
97 p. front. (port.) 19cm.
Published Philadelphia, 1836, under title: The life and religious experience of Jarena Lee.
1. Narrative.
Library of Congress E185.97.L46 12—20711 ₍a41b1₎

M813.5 L513c **Lee, John M** 1907–
Counter-clockwise, by John M. Lee. New York, W. Malliet and company, 1940.
1 p. l., 5-103 p. 20cm.
"First edition."
I. Title.
Library of Congress PZ3.L5134Co 40-33588
——— Copy 2.
Copyright ₍4₎

Lee, Miriam, joint editor.

M811.08 Ai66 Ainsworth, Norma R ed.
The gift of Christmas; edited by Norma Ruedi Ainsworth and Miriam Lee. Illustrations by Ethel Gold. New York Scholastic Book Services ₍1965₎
94p. 19½cm.
White editor.
Partial contents.- Kid stuff, by Frank Horne.- Carol of the brown king, by Langston Hughes.
1. Christmas - Poetry. I. Lee, Miriam, jt. ed. II. Title.

MB9 L512 **Lee, Reba,** *pseud.*
I passed for white, by Reba Lee as told to Mary Hastings Bradley. ₍1st ed.₎ New York, Longmans, Green, 1955.
274 p. 21 cm.
I. Bradley, Mary (Hastings) II. Title.
E185.97.Z9L4 325.260973 55—11445 ‡
Library of Congress ₍56k10₎

MB9 L512w Lee, Reba
Ik wilde een blanke zijn; roman. Amsterdam, A. J. G. Strengholt U. M., n.d.
302p. 20cm.
Title: I passed for white.

Lee, Rossie.

MB9 L51s 1958 Sams, Jessie (Bennett)
White mother. ₍1st ed.₎ London, Michael Joseph, 1958.
224p. 21cm.
Autobiographical.
I. Lee, Rossie. I. Title.

Lee, Rossie.

MB9 L51s **Sams, Jessie (Bennett)**
White mother. ₍1st ed.₎ New York, McGraw-Hill ₍1957₎
241 p. 21 cm.
Autobiographical.
1. Lee, Rossie. I. Title.
CT275.L844S3 920.7 57-12911 ‡
Library of Congress ₍25₎

M329.6 R29p Lee, Samuel
Address.
(In: Republican Party. National Convention. 8th, Chicago, 1884. Proceedings... p. 174).

M960 Af8ac Lee, Ulysses Grant, 1913-1969
The ASNLH, the journal of Negro history, and American scholarly interest in Africa.
Pp. 401-418.
In: Africa seen by American Negroes. Paris, Présence Africaine, 1958.

M286
N52
Lee, William I
History of the church (Nineteenth Street Baptist Church, Wash. D.C.
(In: Nineteenth Street Baptist Church, Wash. D.C. One hundredth anniversary ... program. Wasington, D. C., 1939. 27cm. p. 1-11)

Legal aspects of the Negro problem.
M304
P19
V.7
No.12
Johnson, James Weldon
Legal aspects of the Negro problem, by James Weldon Johnson and Herbert J. Seligmann. Reprinted from the Annals of the American academy of political and social science, November, 1928.
8p. 23½cm.

Bahamas
M332
Sm61e
Legal tender.
Smith, James Carmichael, 1852-
Legal tender, correspondence with the editor of "The bankers' magazine." London. Kegan Paul, Trench, Trubner, 1909.
16p. graphs. 21½cm.

M286
N52
Lee, William I
A sketch of the life of Walter Henderson Brooks.
(In: Nineteenth Street Baptist Church, Wash. D.C. One hundredth anniversary ... program. Wasington, D.C., 1939. 27cm. p. 1-11)

Legal responsibility - Brazil.
Brazil
M869
B27m
Barreto de Menzes, Tobias, 1839-1889.
... Menores e Loucos e fundamento do direito de Punir. Sergipe Edição do Estado de Sergipe, 1926.
xx, 152p. 24cm. (Obras completas, v.V)

Bahamas
M332.
Sm61
Legal tender.
Smith, James Carmichael.
Legal tender; essays, by Jas. C. Smith ... London, K. Paul, Trench, Trübner & co., ltd., 1910.
3 p. l., v-xviii, 285 p. incl. tables. fold. diagr. 21½cm.
CONTENTS.—Economic definitions and illustrations.—Legal tender.—Taxation.—The money of India.—Money and currency.
1. Currency question—Gt. Brit. 2. Money. 3. Gt. Brit.—Econ. condit. I. Title.
13-8350
Library of Congress HG939.S7

Leeds, Eng. University.
Africa
M809
P912
Press, John, ed.
Commonwealth literature: unity and diversity in a common culture; extracts from the proceedings of a Conference held at Bodington Hall, Leeds, 9-12 September 1964, under the auspices of the University of Leeds. [London] Heinemann [1965]
223p. 22cm.
White editor.

M323.4
B93f
Legal status, laws, etc.
Friedman, Leon, *ed.*
Southern justice. With a foreword by Mark DeW. Howe. New York, Pantheon Books [1965]
ix, 306 p. 22 cm.
Bibliographical references included in "Notes" (p. [281]-306)
1. Justice, Administration of—Southern States. 2. Negroes—Legal status, laws, etc. 3. Civil rights—Southern States. I. Title.
323.4 65-14581
Library of Congress [5]

Le legende de m'pfoumou ma mazono.
Congo
(Brazzaville)
M967.26
M291
Malonga, Jean, 1907-
La legende de m'pfoumou ma mazono. Paris Editions Africaines, 1954.
153p. 18½cm.

M811.4
W58L
Leelah misled.
Whitman, Albery Allson, 1851-1901.
Leelah misled; a poem. By A. A. Whitman. Elizabeth-town [Ky.] . Richard Larue, printer, 1873.
39p. 14cm.

Legal status, laws, etc.
M323.4
G58
Goldwin, Robert A 1922- *ed.*
100 years of emancipation, essays by Harry V. Jaffa [and others] Edited by Robert A. Goldwin. Chicago, Rand McNally [1964]
217 p. 22 cm. (Rand McNally public affairs series)
Bibliographical footnotes.
1. Negroes—Civil rights. 2. Negroes—Legal status, laws, etc. 3. Emancipation proclamation. I. Jaffa, Harry V. II. Title.
E185.61.G62 1964a 323.4 64-14111
Library of Congress [10]

Haiti
M842
C397l
La légende des fleurs.
[Chauvet, Pierre]
La légende des fleurs, féerie en 1 acte, par Colibri [pseud] Port-au-Prince, Deschamps, [1947]
49p. 22cm.

M972.94
L522c
Lefèvre, Louis
Clergé, par Louis Lefèvre. Rennes, Paris, Typographie Oberthur, 1891.
101p. 22cm.
1. Haiti - Churches. 2. Haiti.
I. Title.

Legal status, laws, etc.
M06
Am3
no. 16
Grimke, Archibald Henry, 1849-
... The ballotless victim of one-party governments. An-nual address by Archibald H. Grimke ... Washington, D. C., The Academy, 1913.
18 p. 21½cm. (The American negro academy. Occasional papers, no. 16)
1. Negroes—Politics and suffrage. 2. Negroes—Legal status, laws, etc. I. Title.
13-18319
Library of Congress E185.5.A51 no. 16
——— Copy 2. JK1929.A2G8
——— Copy 3. JK1929.A2G8 copy 2

Légendes Africaines.
Dahomey
M966.8
Que 31
Quénum, Maximilien Possy Berry
Légendes Africaines; Côte d'Ivoire - Soudan-Dahomey. Illustrations de P. Tardy. Rochefort-Sur-Mer, Imprimerie A. Thoyon-Thèze, 1956.
101p. illus. 28cm.

M813.5
W147L
The legacy of a bet.
Walker, Claudius Roland.
The legacy of a bet. New York, Carlton Press, 1962.
149p. 20cm. (A Geneva book)

M342.73
M615
Legal statues, laws, etc.
Miller, Loren.
The petitioners; the story of the Supreme Court of the United States and the Negro. New York, Pantheon Books [1966]
xv, 461 p. 22 cm.
Bibliographical references included in "Notes" (p. [435]-455)
1. U. S. Supreme Court. 2. Negroes—Legal status, laws, etc. I. Title.
342.73 65-14583
Library of Congress [5]

... Légendes et traditions dans l'histoire.
M972.94
D251
Darondel, Louis.
... Légendes et traditions dans l'histoire de Saint-Domingue; essai de critique. Port-au-Prince, Impr. de la Compagnie lithographique d'Haïti [1939]
2 p. l., 3-60 p., 2 l. 21cm.
Bibliographical foot-notes.
1. Haiti—Hist.—To 1791. 2. Haiti—Hist.—Revolution, 1791-1804. I. Title.
41-9782
Library of Congress F1923.D3
[3] 972.94

M323
N21
Legal aid.
National Association for the Advancement of Colored People.
NAACP handbook; Outline of procedure for legal cases. N.Y., The Association [1944]
5-20p. 17cm.

Legal status, laws, etc.
M342
St9
Styles, Fitzhugh Lee, 1899-
Negroes and the law in the race's battle for liberty, equality and justice under the Constitution of the United States; with causes celebres, by Fitzhugh Lee Styles ... Boston, The Christopher publishing house [°1937]
xi, [1], 13-320 p. front. (port.) 24cm.
The manuscript of the author's address before the National bar association at Baltimore, August 1934, on the battle of the Negro at the bar of justice, is the basis of this book. *cf.* Pref.
Bibliography: p. 320.
1. Negroes — Legal status, laws, etc. 2. Negroes—Biog. 3. Negro lawyers. 4. Law reports, digests, etc.—U. S. I. Title.
37-8583
Library of Congress E185.61.S92
——— Copy 2.
Copyright A 103799 [38g3] 325.260973

Haiti
M843.91
L52c
Legendre, Franck.
... Contretemps, contes et fantaisies. Port-au-Prince, Haiti, Imprimerie Vertières [1941]
5 p. l., [9]-130, [1] p. 20cm.
I. Title. 1. Haitian fiction
42-48343 Revised
Library of Congress PQ3949.L4C6
[r44c2] 843.91

Legende - Brazzaville.
Congo (Brazzaville)
M967.26
M291
Malonga, Jean, 1907-
La legende de m'pfoumou ma mazono. Paris Editions Africaines, 1954.
153p. 18½cm.

Peru
M985
P18
Legends-Peru.
Palma, Ricardo, 1833-1919.
... La monja de la llave; prólogo de P. Matalonga ... México, D. F., Compañía general editora, s. a., 1940.
191, ⌊1⌋ p. 18½cm. (Colección Mirasol. ⌊4⌋)
"Forman este volumen dieciseis 'historias de amor,' extraídas de las 'Tradiciones peruanas'."—p. 11.
1. Legends—Peru. I. Matalonga, P., ed. II. Title.
⌊Full name: Manuel Ricardo Palma⌋
42-12809
Library of Congress F3409.P1733
⌊3⌋ 985

Peru
M985
P18t
Legends— Peru.
Palma, Ricardo, 1833-1919.
... Tradiciones peruanas escogidas (edición crítica) Prólogo, selección y notas de Luis Alberto Sánchez. Santiago de Chile, Ediciones Ercilla, 1940.
3 p. l., ⌊9⌋-215, ⌊3⌋ p. 18cm. (*Half-title:* Biblioteca Amauta (Serie América) ⌊V. 1⌋)
"Noticia bibliográfica": p. 14-16.
1. Legends—Peru. 2. Peru—Hist. I. Sánchez, Luis Alberto, 1900- ed. II. Title.
⌊Full name: Manuel Ricardo Palma⌋
41—9583
Library of Congress F3409.P1732
⌊44e1⌋ 985

Tobago
M972.98
Ot5L
Legends, true stories and old sayings from Trinidad and Tobago.
Ottley, Carlton Robert, 1914-
Legends, true stories and old sayings from Trinidad and Tobago, collected and told by C. R. Ottley. Port-of-Spain, College Press, 1962.
71p. 20cm.

Lauchmonen, pseud.
see
Kempadoo, Peter

M817
St45
Laughing on the outside.
Sterling, Philip, *ed.*
Laughing on the outside; the intelligent white reader's guide to Negro tales and humor. Introductory essay by Saunders Redding. Cartoons by Ollie Harrington. New York, Grosset & Dunlap ⌊1965⌋
254 p. illus. 22 cm.
Bibliography: p. ⌊251⌋-254.
1. Negro wit and humor. I. Title.
PN6231.N5S7 817.008 65-15349
Library of Congress ⌊5⌋

M813.5
H87Lac2
Laughing to keep from crying.
Hughes, Langston, 1902-
Lachen, um nicht zu weinen: funf Erzahlungen. ⌊Ubertragen con Paridam von dem Knesebeck. Weisbaden⌋ Insel-Verlag, 1962.
79p. 18cm.
Translation of Laughing to keep from crying.

M813.5
H87Lac
Laughing to keep from crying.
Hughes, Langston, 1902-
Lachen um nicht zu weinen; erzählungen. ⌊Ubertragen von Paridam von dem Knesebeck. Wiesbaden⌋ Im Insel-Verlag, 1958.
77p. 18cm.
Translation of Laughing to keep from crying.

M813.5
H87Lau
Laughing to keep from crying.
Hughes, Langston, 1902-
Laughing to keep from crying. ⌊1st ed.⌋ New York, Holt ⌊1952⌋
206 p. 21 cm.
Short stories.
I. Title. *Full name:* James Langston Hughes.
PZ3.H87313Lau 52-7952 ‡
Library of Congress ⌊30⌋

M323.2
L37p
Laura Spelman Rockefeller Memorial.
Proceedings of the inter-racial conference. Laura Spelman Rockefeller memorial. New Haven, Conn., Zeta Psi fraternity house, December 19-21, 1927.
11, 280p. 28cm.
Mimeographed.
1. Race relations I. Title: Inter-racial conference.

M973
W86fr
Laura Spelman Rockefeller Memorial, New York.
Woodson, Carter Godwin, 1875-
Free Negro heads of families in the United States in 1830, together with a brief treatment of the free Negro. Washington, D.C., The Association for the Study of Negro Life and History, Inc. c1925.
lviii, 296p. 25½cm.

M973
W86fo
Laura Spelman Rockefeller memorial, New York.
Woodson, Carter Godwin, 1875- *ed.*
Free Negro owners of slaves in the United States in 1830, together with Absentee ownership of slaves in the United States in 1830, compiled under the direction of, and edited by Carter G. Woodson ... Washington, D. C., The Association for the study of Negro life and history ⌊°1924⌋
viii, 78 p. 25cm.
This statistical report was made possible by an appropriation obtained from the Laura Spelman Rockefeller memorial. *cf.* Foreword.
1. Slavery in the U. S. 2. Negroes—Direct. I. Association for the study of Negro life and history, inc. II. Laura Spelman Rockefeller memorial, New York. III. Title. IV. Title: Absentee ownership of slaves in the United States in 1830.
25—28062
Library of Congress E185.W8873
⌊44n1⌋

Haiti
MB9
T641
Laurent, Gérard Mentor
Coup d'œil sur la politique de Toussaint-Louverture. ⌊Port-au-Prince, H. Deschamps, cover 1949⌋
xix, 350, ⌊4⌋ p. illus. 20 cm.
"Bibliographie": p. ⌊351⌋-⌊352⌋
1. Toussaint Louverture, Pierre Dominique, 1746?-1803. 2. Haiti—Hist.—Revolution, 1791-1804.
F1923.T858 923.27294 50-19137
Library of Congress ⌊1⌋

Haiti
M972.94
L37d
Laurent, Gérard Mentor
Documentation historique pour nos etudiants. Port-au-Prince, La Phalange, 1959.
299p. 19cm.
1. Haiti - History.

Haiti
M972.94
L37
Laurent, ~~Mentor,~~ Gérard Mentor
... Erreurs et vérités dans l'histoire d'Haïti, par Mentor Laurent ... Port-au-Prince, Haïti ⌊Imprimerie Telhomme⌋, 1945-
v. tables (1 fold.) 22cm. (Bibliothèque haïtienne)
"Bibliographie": v. 1, p. ⌊378⌋-381.
1. Haiti—Hist. I. Title.
A 46-2547
Harvard univ. Library for Library of Congress ⌊3⌋

Haiti
M972.94
L37p
Laurent, Gérard Mentor.
Pages d'histoire d'Haïti. Port-au-Prince, La Phalange, 1960.
271 p. 21 cm.
A selection from articles published in La Phalange. Cf. p. ⌊5⌋
Bibliography: p. ⌊269⌋-271.
1. Haiti—Hist.—Revolution, 1791-1804. 2. Haiti—Hist.—1804-1844. I. Title.
A 61-4316
Florida. Univ. Library for Library of Congress ⌊1⌋

M231
W62
Lavalais, Joseph George
Why I believe there is a God.
Pp. 66-72.
In: Why I believe there is a God. Chicago, Johnson Pub. Com., 1965.

France
M840
D89Lo
La Valliere, Louise Françoise de La Baume Le Blanc, duchesse de, 1644-1710 - Fiction.
Dumas, Alexandre, 1802-1870.
Louise de La Vallière; or, The love of Bragellone ⌊!⌋ A continuation of "The three musketeers", "Twenty years after", and "Bragelonne, the son of Athos". By Alex. Dumas. New rev. translation by H. Llewellyn Williams. New York, The F. M. Lupton publishing company ⌊°1892⌋
489 p. 19cm. (*On cover:* The elite series. no. 9)
Written in collaboration with Auguste Maquet.
A translation of the middle portion of the Vicomte de Bragelonne.
Sequel: The man in the iron mask.
1. La Vallière, Louise Françoise de La Baume Le Blanc, duchesse de, 1644-1710—Fiction. 2. France—Hist.—Louis XIV, 1643-1715—Fiction. 3. Man in the iron mask—Fiction. I. Maquet, Auguste, 1813-1888, joint author. II. Williams, Henry Llewellyn, jr., tr. III. Title.
6—43623
Library of Congress (⊛) (PZ3.D89Lo 2)
Copyright 1892: 3323 ⌊a37g1⌋

Martinique
M841.91
L39
Laviaux, Léon,
The ebon muse, and other poems, by Léon Laviaux; Englished by John Myers O'Hara. Portland, Me., Smith & Sale, 1914.
x p., 2 l., 3-51, ⌊1⌋ p., 1 l. 27½cm. $3.00
"Of this edition two hundred copies have been printed." No. 125.
I. O'Hara, John Myers, tr. II. Title. 1. Poetry.
14-12126
Library of Congress
——— Copy 2.
Copyright A 374599

M89
R871
Law, John
Franklin Delano Roosevelt, a friend to man. A tribute in verse by John Law. New York, William - Frederick press, 1946.
15p. 20cm.
1. Roosevelt, Franklin Delano, pres. of U. S., 1882-1945.

Brazil
M869
B27ed
Law.
Barreto de Menzes, Tobias, 1839-1889.
... Estudos de direito. ⌊Rio de Janeiro, Empreza graphica Editora, Paulo Pongetti & C., 1926⌋
2v. port. 24cm. (Edicao do estado de Sergipe)
Obras completas, v. 1,2.

Law—Study and teaching—Haiti.

Haiti
M972.94
D49a

Dévot, Justin.
Acta et verba ... par Justin Dévot ... Paris, F. Pichon, 1893.
xxii, 230 p., 1 l. 18cm.

1. Law—Haiti—Addresses, essays, lectures. 2. Law—Study and teaching—Haiti. I. Title.

46-38390

Library of Congress ⌊2⌋

Nigeria
M966.9
E114m

Law - Nigeria - Hist. & crit.

Elias, Taslim Olawale.
Makers of Nigerian law. ⌊London⌋ 1956.
55 p. 21 cm.
"Reprinted from West Africa, November 19, 1955–July 7, 1956."

1. Law—Nigeria—Hist. & crit. I. Title.

61-27123 ‡

Library of Congress ⌊8⌋

Nigeria
M966.9
E14n a

Law, Primitive - Africa.

Elias, Taslim Olawale.
The nature of African customary law. ⌊Manchester⌋ Manchester University Press ⌊1956⌋
318 p. 23 cm.
Includes bibliography.

1. Law, Primitive—Africa. I. Title.

349.6 57—1037 ‡

Library of Congress ⌊59e2⌋

M378Te
J63

Law - Study and teaching - Texas.

Johnson, Ozie Harold.
Price of freedom. ⌊Houston? Tex.⌋ °1954.
117 p. 24 cm.

1. Texas Southern University. School of Law. 2. Negroes—Texas. 3. Discrimination in education. 4. Law—Study and teaching—Texas. I. Title.

371.974 54-31912 ‡

Library of Congress ⌊1⌋

Nigeria
M966
E14

Law - Sierra Leone - History and criticism.

Elias, Taslim Olawale.
Ghana and Sierra Leone: the development of their laws and constitutions. London, Stevens, 1962.
xii, 334 p. 25 cm. (The British Commonwealth: the development of its laws and constitutions, v. 10)
Bibliography: p. 311-312.

1. Law—Ghana—Hist. & crit. 2. Law—Sierra Leone—Hist. & crit. 3. Ghana—Constitutional history. 4. Sierra Leone—Constitutional history. (Series)

63-2173

Library of Congress ⌊5⌋

M304
P19
v.7
no.17

Law and lawyers.

National bar association.
Addresses delivered before the fifth annual convention of the National bar association (incorporated) at Detroit, Mich. August 1st and 2nd, 1929.

51p. 23cm.

Nigeria
M966
E14

Law - Ghana - History and criticism.

Elias, Taslim Olawale.
Ghana and Sierra Leone: the development of their laws and constitutions. London, Stevens, 1962.
xii, 334 p. 25 cm. (The British Commonwealth: the development of its laws and constitutions, v. 10)
Bibliography: p. 311-312.

1. Law—Ghana—Hist. & crit. 2. Law—Sierra Leone—Hist. & crit. 3. Ghana—Constitutional history. 4. Sierra Leone—Constitutional history. (Series)

63-2173

Library of Congress ⌊5⌋

Gold Coast
M966.7
Sa7f

Law, Fanti.

Sarbah, John Mensah, 1864–1910.
Fanti customary laws. A brief introduction to the principles of the native laws and customs of the Fanti and Akan districts of the Gold coast, with a report of some cases thereon decided in the law courts. By John Mensah Sarbah ... London, W. Clowes and sons, limited, 1897.
xxiii, 295, ⌊1⌋ p. 22cm.

1. Law, Fanti.

5-32348

Library of Congress GN498.4.A9S3 ⌊a44c1⌋

M340
N21n

Law and lawyers.

National Bar Association.
National bar directory, compiled by Scovel Richardson. The Association, 1950.

13p. 23cm.
Inscribed: to Arthur B. Spingarn from Thurgood Marshall.

Nigeria
M325.342
E142

Law - Gt. Brit. - Colonies.

Elias, Taslim Olawale.
British colonial law; a comparative study of the interaction between English and local laws in British dependencies. London, Stevens, 1962.
323 p. 25 cm.

1. Law—Gt. Brit.—Colonies. I. Title.

325.342 62-6516 ‡

Library of Congress ⌊2⌋

Gold Coast
M966.7
Sa7fa

Law, Fanti.

Sarbah, John Mensah, 1864-1910.
Fanti law report of decided cases on Fanti customary laws. Second selection, by John Mensah Sarbah. Long, William Clowes and Sons, limited, 1904.

189p. 22cm.

M341.4
Sc81

The law of interstate rendition.

Scott, James Alexander, 1864–
The law of interstate rendition, erroneously referred to as interstate extradition; a treatise on the arrest and surrender of fugitives from the justice of one state to another; the removal of federal prisoners from one district to another; and the exemption of persons from service of civil process; and with an appendix of the statutes of the states and territories on fugitives from justice, by James A. Scott ... Chicago, Ill., S. Hight, 1917.
xiv, 584 p. 24cm.
1. Extradition—U. S. I. Title. II. Title: Interstate rendition.

Library of Congress 17—20646
——— Copy 2.
Copyright A 470090 ⌊a40b1⌋

Haiti
M972.94
D49a

Law—Haiti—Addresses, essays, lectures.

Dévot, Justin.
Acta et verba ... par Justin Dévot ... Paris, F. Pichon, 1893.
xxii, 230 p., 1 l. 18cm.

1. Law—Haiti—Addresses, essays, lectures. 2. Law—Study and teaching—Haiti. I. Title.

46-38390

Library of Congress ⌊2⌋

Gold Coast
M966.7
D23ca

Law, Primitive.

Danquah, Joseph Boakye, 1895– ed.
Cases in Akan law. Decisions delivered by The Honourable Nana Sir Ofori Atta. Edited with Introduction, Synopses, and notes by J.B. Danqua. London, Goerge Routledge, 1928.

xxxii, 28p. front. 22cm.

M323
N212

Law report, digest, etc.

National Association for the Advancement of Colored People. Legal Defense and Educational Fund.
Equal justice under law; ⌊Cases won before the United States Supreme Court⌋ New York, The Association, 1948.

16p. 22cm.

Nigeria
M966.9
E14gr

Law - Nigeria.

Elias, Taslim Olawale.
Groundwork of Nigerian law. London, Routledge & Paul ⌊1954⌋
xxx, 374 p. 23 cm.

1. Law—Nigeria. 2. Customary law—Nigeria. 3. Courts—Nigeria. I. Title.

54-36578

Library of Congress ⌊1⌋

Gold Coast
M966.7
D23g

Law, Primitive.

Danquah, Joseph Boakye, 1895–
Gold Coast: Akan laws and customs and the Akim Abuakwa constitution, by J. B. Danquah ... London, G. Routledge & sons, ltd., 1928.
x, 272 p. front. 22½cm.

1. Law, Primitive. 2. Ethnology—Gold Coast. 3. Customary law—Gold Coast. 4. Akim Abuakwa—Pol. & govt. I. Title. II. Title: Akan laws and customs.

29-12367

Library of Congress ⌊a44d1⌋

M323
N212

Law report, digest, etc.

National Association for the Advancement of Colored People. Legal Defense and Educational Fund.
Equal justice under law; ⌊Cases won before the United States Supreme Court⌋ New York, The Association, 1945.

16p. 22cm.

Nigeria
M966.9
E14ni

Law - Nigeria.

Elias, Taslim Olawale.
The Nigerian legal system. ⌊2d ed., rev.⌋ London, Routledge & Paul ⌊1963⌋
xxxvii, 386 p. 22 cm.
First ed. published in 1954 under title: Groundwork of Nigerian law.
"List of abbreviations" (bibliographical) p. xxxvii. Bibliographical footnotes.

1. Law—Nigeria. 2. Customary law—Nigeria. 3. Courts—Nigeria. I. Title.

63-24583

Library of Congress ⌊2⌋

Gold Coast
M966.7
Sa7fa

Law, Primitive.

Sarbah, John Mensah, 1864-1910.
Fanti law report of decided cases on Fanti customary laws. Second selection, by John Mensah Sarbah. Long, William Clowes and Sons, limited, 1904.

189p. 22cm.

M323
N212

Law report, digest, etc.

National Association for the Advancement of Colored People. Legal Defense and Educational Fund.
Equal justice under law; ⌊Cases won before the United States Supreme Court⌋ New York, The Association, 1944.

14p. 22cm.

Law report, digest, etc. - U. S.
M323. N212
National Association for the Advancement of Colored People. Louisville.
The history of Louisville segregation case and the decision of the Supreme Court. Louisville, The Association, Legal Committee, 1917?

Lawd Today.
M813.5 W93Law2
Wright, Richard, 1908-1960.
Lawd today. London, Anthony Blond 1965.
219p. cm.
I. Title.
PZ3.W9352Law 63—11769 ‡
Library of Congress 67f5

Haiti M972.94 L524h
Léger, Jacques Nicolas, 1859–
Haiti, her history and her detractors, by J. N. Léger ... New York and Washington, The Neale publishing company, 1907.
372 p. front., 14 pl. 22½cm.
1. Haiti—Hist.
7—25045
Library of Congress F1921.L485 40g1

M364 W67p
Law reports, digests, etc.
Williams, Thomas C
The people v. Diaz and DeJesus, brief v. To the honorable members of the legislature A series of miscarriages of justice... culminating in the railroading of two Puerto Rican youths to the chair. New York, 1946.
71p. 22cm.

Lawd today.
M813.5 W93Law
Wright, Richard, 1908-1960.
Lawd today. New York, Walker 1963
189 p. 22 cm.
I. Title.
Full name: Richard Nathaniel Wright.
PZ3.W9352Law 63-11769 ‡
Library of Congress 5

Haiti M972.94 L524h2
Leger, Jacques Nicolas, 1859-.
Haiti, son histoire et ses détracteurs, par J. N. Leger ... New York, The Neale publishing company, 1907.
411p. front., 14 pl. 22½cm.
1. Haiti-History.

Law reports, digests, etc.-Liberia.
Liberia M966.6 L610
Liberia. *Supreme court.*
Opinions delivered by the honourable the Supreme court of the republic of Liberia in cases decided during its November term A. D. 1933– New annual series no. 1– Monrovia, Liberia, Printed by authority at the Government printing office 1934?–
v. 25-26cm.
1. Law reports, digests, etc.—Liberia. I. Title.
38-19289
Library of Congress 2

Lawrence, Jacob, 1917– illus.
M811.5 H87o
Hughes, Langston, 1902–
One-way ticket poems illus. by Jacob Lawrence. 1st ed. New York, A. A. Knopf, 1949 °1948
xvii, 136 p. illus. 22 cm.
I. Lawrence, Jacob, 1917– illus. II. Title.
Full name: James Langston Hughes.
PS3515.U274O5 811.5 49-7018*
Library of Congress 20

Legislators-U.S.
MB M85s
Moseley, J H 1882–
Sixty years in Congress and twenty-eight out. 1st ed. New York, Vantage Press 1960
99 p. illus. 22 cm.
1. Legislators—U. S. 2. Negroes—Biog. I. Title.
JK1021.M75 923.273 60-3728 ‡
Library of Congress 2

Law reports, digests, etc.—U.S.
M342 St9
Styles, Fitzhugh Lee, 1899–
Negroes and the law in the race's battle for liberty, equality and justice under the Constitution of the United States; with causes celebres, by Fitzhugh Lee Styles ... Boston, The Christopher publishing house °1937
xi, 1, 13-320 p. front. (port.) 24cm.
The manuscript of the author's address before the National bar association at Baltimore, August 1934, on the battle of the Negro at the bar of justice, is the basis of this book. *cf.* Pref.
Bibliography: p. 320.
1. Negroes—Legal status, laws, etc. 2. Negroes—Biog. 3. Negro lawyers. 4. Law reports, digests, etc.—U. S. I. Title.
37—3563
Library of Congress E185.61.S92
——— Copy 2.
Copyright A 103799 38g3 325.260973

MB9 W69L
Lawrence, Versie Lee.
Deep south showman. New York, Carlton Press, 1962.
33p. 20½cm.
Portrait of author on book jacket.
1, Wilson, Eddie. I. Title.

Légitime, François Denis, 1833–
Haiti M972.94 H62g
Histoire du gouvernement du général Légitime, président de la République d'Haïti ... Paris, E. Leroux Angers, A. Burdin et cie. 1890.
4 p. l., xlvi, 422 p., 1 l. front. (port.) pl., fold. map. 24½cm.
Cover dated 1891.
1. Légitime, François Denis, 1833– 2. Haiti—Hist.—1844–
Library of Congress F1921.H63 37b2 2-12365 rev.

Law enforcement - Mississippi.
M352.2 M69
Mississippi black paper; fifty-seven Negro and white citizens' testimony of police brutality, the breakdown of law and order and the corruption of justice in Mississippi. Foreword by Reinhold Niebuhr. Introd. by Hodding Carter III. New York, Random House 1965
92 p. illus. 28 cm.
1. Police—Mississippi. 2. Law enforcement—Mississippi. 3. Negroes—Mississippi. I. Title: Fifty-seven Negro and white citizens' testimony of police brutality. II. Niebuhr, Reinhold, 1892–
HV8145.M7M5 323.11960762 65–18103
Library of Congress 8

M975 N31
Laws, J Bradford.
The Negroes of Cinclare Central Factory and Calumet Plantation, Louisiana. Bulletin of the Labor Dept. no.38, 1902, pp. 95-120.
In: The Negro in the black belt... Washington, D.C., Dept. of Labor, 189 - 19
1. Louisiana. 2. Plantation life. I. Title. II. T. - Negro in the black belt.

Africa M960 L527af
Legum, Colin, *ed.*
Africa; a handbook to the continent. Rev. and enl. ed. New York, Praeger 1966
xii, 558 p. illus., maps. 24 cm.
Includes bibliographies.
Partial contents.- Kenya, revised by John Nagenda.- The language of African literature, by Ezekiel Mphahlele.
1. Africa. I. Title.
DT30.L38 1966 916 66—12478
Library of Congress 66x5

U. S. M966.7 M96
Law in Africa. no. 1.
Murray, Pauli, 1910- jt. author.
The Constitution and Government of Ghana, by Leslie Rubin and Pauli Murray. London, Sweet & Maxwell, 1961.
xvi, 310p. 23cm. (Law in Africa, no. 1)

Laws against liberty.
M326. Sc71
Scarlett, George Chandler, 1880–
Laws against liberty, by George C. Scarlett ... New York, N. Y. Cosmos printing co., inc., °1937
135 p. 21cm.
1. Liberty. 2. Negroes. 3. U. S.—Race question. 4. Slavery in the U. S. I. Title.
A 39—1029
Yale law school. Library for Library of Congress 40c1

Africa M960 L527
Legum, Colin.
Pan-Africanism; a short political guide. London, Pall Mall Press 1962
296 p. map. 23 cm.
Bibliography: p. 279-285.
Appendices (p. 134-278) Documentary guide to Pan-Africanism.
White author.
1. Pan-Africanism. 2. Africa - Congresses.
DT30.L39 1962b 960 62-5026
Library of Congress 2

Nigeria M966.9 Od8
Law in Africa, no. 4.
Odumosu, Oluwole Idowu.
The Nigerian Constitution: history and development. London, Sweet & Maxwell, 1963.
xix, 407 p. 23 cm. (Law in Africa, no. 4)
"Originally ... submitted as a thesis for the award of the Ph. D. degree of the University of London."
"The Constitution of the Federation of Nigeria": p. 309-397.
Bibliographical footnotes.
1. Nigeria—Constitutional history. 2. Nigeria—Constitutional law. I. Nigeria. Constitution. (Series)
63-4741
Library of Congress 1

The laws and customs of the Yoruba people.
Nigeria M966.9 M782
Moore, E A Ajisafe
The laws and customs of the Yoruba people. Abeokuta, Nigeria, M. A. Ola Fola Bookshops n.d.
85p. 18cm.

Africa M960 L527a
Legum, Colin.
Pan-Africanism; a short political guide. New York, Praeger 1962
296 p. illus. 21 cm. (Books that matter)
Includes bibliography.
Appendices (p. 134-278) Documentary guide to Pan-Africanism.
White author.
1. Pan-Africanism. 2. Africa - Congresses.
DT30.L39 1962a 960 62-13489 ‡
Library of Congress 10

Leighton, George Ross, 1902- joint author.

M350 Brown, Earl Louis, 1900-
B798 ... The Negro and the war [by] Earl Brown and George R. Leighton ... [New York, Public affairs committee, inc.] 1942.
cover-title, 32 p. diagrs. 21cm. (Public affairs pamphlets, no. 71)
"First edition, August, 1942."
"For further reading": p. 32.

1. Negroes. 2. Negroes—Employment. 3. Negroes as soldiers. I. Leighton, George Ross, 1902- joint author. II. Title.
42-22892
Library of Congress E185.61.B877
[25] 325.260973

Martinique
M972.98 Lémery, Henri
L54d De la paix de Briand a la guerre de Hitler; préface de Albert Rivaud. Paris, Jean Vigneau, 1949.

243p. 19cm.

1. France-History-1914-1940. I. Title.

Leo, pseud.
see
Martin, Egbert, 1862-

Tobago
M821.91 Leighton-Mills, Horace E
L533 Anthology of poems and a 3-act play: Flora. [Trinidad, Busby's Printerie, 1966]

94p. 22cm.

I. Title. II. Title: Flora.

Martinique
M972.98 Lémery, Henry.
L54r La révolution française a'la Martinique. Paris, Chez Larose, 1936.

335p. plates. 20cm.

1. Martinique - History.

S.Africa
MB9 Leoatle, Edward Motsamai.
L55m Morena Moshoeshoe mor'a Mokhachane, Ka Edward Motsamai Leoatle Morija, Sesuto Book Depot, 1942.

iv, 84p. front. 18cm.
Story of Morena Moshoeshoe in Sotho.

1. Moshesh, 1790-1870.

Leisle, George.

M286 Adams, C C
Ad1n Negro Baptists and foreign missions; C. C. Adams and Marshall A. Talley, authors. Philadelphia, Pa., The Foreign mission board of the National Baptist convention, U. S. A., inc. [c1944]
84 p. 18½cm.

1. Baptists, Negro—Missions. 2. National Baptist convention of the United States of America—Missions. I. Talley, Marshall Alexander, 1877- joint author. II. National Baptist convention of the United States of America. Foreign mission board. III. Title.
45-15372
Library of Congress BV2521.A85
[3] 266.61

Haiti
M110 Lemoine, Raoul Fanini
L54 Principes de l'unite. [Port-au-Prince, Haiti, Imprimerie Théodore, n.d.]

31p. port. 21cm. (Serie des Santes-Ecritures)
Portrait of author in book.

1. Metaphysics. I. Title.

S.Africa
MB9 Leoatle, Edward Motsamai.
L55m Morena Moshoeshoe mor'a Mokhachane, Ka Edward Motsamai Leoatle Morija, Sesuto Book Depot, 1942.

iv, 84p. front. 18cm.
Story of Morena Moshoeshoe in Sotho.

1. Moshesh, 1790-1870.

Lekhethoa, Herbert H tr.

M334.4 Washington, Booker Taliaferro, 1859?-1915.
W27au5 Tokoloho bokhobeng: or Up from slavery phetolelo sesothong ke Herbert H. Lekhethoa. Morija, Basutoland, Morija Sesuto Book Depot, 1947.

146p. 18½cm.
Translated into Sesuto

M815.5 Lemon, Harriet Beecher Stowe Wright, comp.
L54r Radio speeches of Major R. R. Wright, Sr. compiled by his daughter, Harriet Beecher Stowe Lemon. Philadelphia, Pa., The Farmer Press, 1949.

189p. 18½cm.

I. Wright, Richard Robert, 1855-

Mexico
M860.4 León, Nicolás, 1859-
L55 El negrito poeta mexicano y sus populares versos. Contribucion para el folk-lore nacional, por el Dr. N. Leon ... Mexico, Imprenta del Museo nacional, 1912.
234 p. front. 16½cm.

1. Vasconcelos, José, 18th cent. 2. Mexican poetry.
13-17185
Library of Congress PQ7297.L4N8
——— Copy 2. [a28c1]

Haiti
M843.91 Lemaire, Emmeline Carriès
L54c Coeur de heros; coeur d'amant. Port-au-Prince, Le Matin, 1950.

154p. 23cm.
Inscribed by author.

1. Bolivar, Simon, 1783-1830 - Fiction.
I. Title. 1. Haitian fiction

Martinique Len Sly.
M843.91 Richer, Clément.
R392 Len Sly, roman. Paris, Plon [1949]
245 p. 19 cm.

I. Title.
A 50-3150
Illinois. Univ. Library
for Library of Congress [1]

Haiti Léon, Rulx.
M610 Les maladies en Haiti. Port-au-Prince.
L55 Imp. de l'Etat, [1954]

xxxiii, 345p. 18cm. (Collection du tricinquantenaire (1804-1954)

I. Title 1. Haiti - Medicine
2. Haiti - Diseases

Tanganyika
M967.82 Lemenye, Justin
L54m Maisha ya sameni ole kivasis yaani Justin Lemenye [The life of Justin Lemenye] Kampala, The Eagle Press, 1953.

71p. port. illus. 18½cm.
Written in Swahili.

1. Lemenye, Justin. 2. Tanganyika - history

Lena.

MB9 Horne, Lena.
H784 Lena, by Lena Horne and Richard Schickel. [1st ed.] Garden City, N. Y., Doubleday, 1965.
300 p. illus., ports. 22 cm.

1. Musicians—Correspondence, reminiscences, etc. I. Schickel, Richard, joint author. II. Title.
ML420.H65A35 792.7 (B) 65-16388/MN
Library of Congress [5]

Haiti
M610 Léon, Rulx
L55p Phytotherapie Haitienne nos simples. Port-au-Prince, Imprimerie de l'Etat, 1959.

79p. 21cm.

1. Haiti - Medicine.

Lemenye, Justin.

Tanganyika
M967.82 Lemenye, Justin
L54m Maisha ya sameni ole kivasis yaani Justin Lemenye [The life of Justin Lemenye] Kampala, The Eagle Press, 1953.

71p. port. illus. 18½cm.
Written in Swahili.

Lenga uzima.
Zanzibar
M636 Humphrey, Norman
H88y Ngombe zako hatarini! [Your cattle are in danger] Wanyama wana mahitaji sawasawa na wanadamu. [Tr. by D. E. Diva] Nairobi, Eagle Press, 1950.

13p. 21½cm. (Lenga uzima. Aim at healthy living series)
Written in Swahili.
White author.

1. Cattle. I. Title. II. Series.
III. Series: Aim at healthy living series.

Haiti
M972.34 Léon, Rulx.
L55p Propos d'histoire d'Haiti. Port-au-Prince, Imprimerie de l'etat, 1945.
xvi, 278p. 19½cm.

1. Haitian literature.

Guadeloupe
M841
A16
1770
Léonard, Nicolas Germain, 1744-1793.
A Mademoiselle C.
(In: Almanach des muses, 1770. Paris, Lelalain, 1770. 14 cm. p. 148)

Guadeloupe
M841
A16
1786
Léonard, Nicolas Germain, 1744-1793.
L'heure de Berger.
(In: Almanach des muses, 1786. Paris, Lelalain, 1786. 14 cm. p. 201-202)

Guadeloupe
M841
A16
1778
Léonard, Nicolas Germain, 1744-1793.
Les plaisers du rivage, idylle imitée de Moschus.
(In: Almanach des muses, 1778. Paris, Lelalain, 1778. 14 cm. p. 139-140)

Guadeloupe
M841
A16
1773
Léonard, Nicolas Germain, 1744-1793.
L'amour vengé, imitation de Montesquieu.
(In: Almanach des muses, 1773. Paris, Lelalain, 1773. 14 cm. p. 121-123)

Guadeloupe
M841
A16
1771
Léonard, Nicolas Germain, 1744-1793.
L'hiver, idylle imitée de M. Gesner.
(In: Almanach des muses, 1771. Pairs, Lelalain, 1771. 14 cm. p. 68-69)

Guadeloupe
M841
A16
1786
Léonard, Nicolas Germain, 1744-1793.
La prix de la défense.
(In: Almanach des muses, 1786. Paris, Lelalain, 1786. 14 cm. p. 33-34)

Guadeloupe
M841
A16
1767
Leonard, Nicolas Germain, 1744-1793.
Amytas; Idylle imitée de Gessner.
(In: Almanach des muses, 1767. Paris, Lelalain, 1767. 14 cm. p. 9-12)

Guadeloupe
M841
A16
1786
Léonard, Nicolas Germain, 1744-1793.
La caution.
(In: Almanach des muses, 1786. Paris, Lelalain, 1786. 14 cm. p. 6)

Guadeloupe
M841
A16
1778
Léonard, Nicolas Germain, 1744-1793.
La question indiscrette, idylle.
(In: Almanach des muses, 1778. Paris, Lelalain, 1778. 14 cm. p. 4)

Guadeloupe
M841
A16
1778
Léonard, Nicolas Germain, 1744-1793.
Les baisers rendus, idylle.
(In: Almanach des muses, 1778. Paris, Lelalain, 1778. 14 cm. p. 239-240)

Guadeloupe
M841
A16
1786
Léonard, Nicolas Germain, 1744-1793.
La consolateur.
(In: Alamach des muses, 1786. Paris, Lelalain, 1786. 14 cm p. 87-88)

Guadeloupe
M841
A16
1778
Léonard, Nicolas Germain, 1744-1793.
La récompense, idylle.
(In: Almanach des muses, 1778. Paris, Lelalain, 1778. 14 cm. p. 85)

Guadeloupe
M841
A16
1769
Léonard, Nicolas Germain, 1744-1793.
Le bonheur.
(In: Almanach des muses, 1769. Paris, Lelalain, 1769. 14 cm. p. 81-86)

Guadeloupe
M841
A16
1786
Léonard, Nicolas Germain, 1744-1793.
La conseil intéresse.
(In: Almanach des muses, 1786. Paris, Lelalain, 1786. 14 cm. p. 146)

Guadeloupe
M841
A16
1771
Léonard, Nicolas Germain, 1744-1793.
Romance, air note, n° 2.
(In: Almanach des muses, 1771. Paris, Lelalain, 1771. 14 cm. p. 136)

Guadeloupe
M841
A16
1770
Léonard, Nicolas Germain, 1744-1793.
Eglé et Milon, imitation d'une idylle de M. Gessner.
(In: Almanach des muses, 1770. Paris, Lelalain, 1770. 14 cm. p. 91-94)

Guadeloupe
M840
G15
Léonard, Nicloas Germain, 1744-1793.
Ouevres de Leónard, recueillies et publiées par Vincent Campenon. Paris, De l'Impreneries de Didot jeune, 1798.
3v. 19½cm.
I. Campenon François Nicolas Vincent, 1772-1843. ed.

Guadeloupe
M841
A16
1771
Léonard, Nicolas Germain, 1744-1793.
Le ruban, idylle; Lucette, Mirtil.
(In: Almanach des muses, 1771. Paris, Lelalain, 1771. 14 cm. p. 151-155)

Guadeloupe
M841
A16
1774
Léonard, Nicolas Germain, 1744-1793.
Epître à Lizette.
(In: Almanach des muses, 1774. Paris, Lelalain, 1774. 14 cm. p. 25-26)

Guadeloupe
M841
A16
1781
Léonard, Nicolas Germain, 1744-1793.
Le phénix.
(In: Almanach des muses, 1781. Paris, Lelalain, 1781. 14 cm. p. 188)

Guadeloupe
M841
A16
1774
Léonard, Nicolas Germain, 1744-1793.
Les souvenirs.
(In: Almanach des muses, 1774. Paris, Lelalain, 1774. 14 cm. p 171-174)

Guadeloupe
M841
A16
1781

Léonard, Nicolas Germain, 1744-1793.
Le village détruit, idylle.

(In: Almanach des muses, 1781. Paris, Lelalain, 1781. 14 cm. p. 223-228)

Guadeloupe
M841
A16
1769

Léonard, Nicolas Germain, 1744-1793.
Zila et Atis, idylle.

(In: Almanach des muses, 1769. Paris, Lelalain, 1769. 14 cm. p. 67-69)

Guadeloupe
M841
L55b

Léonard, Nicolas Germain, 1744-1793.
Barquissau, Raphaël.
Les poètes créoles du XVIIIe siècle (Parny, Bertin, Léonard) Paris, J. Vigneau, 1949.
249 p. ports. 24 cm.
Bibliography: p. [225]-233.
White author.

1. Parny, Évariste Désiré de Forges, vicomte de, 1753-1814. 2. Bertin, Antoine, chevalier de, 1752-1790. 3. Léonard, Nicolas Germain, 1744-1793. I. Title. II. Léonard, Nicolas Germain, 1744-1793

PQ427.B3 841.509 50-20934
Library of Congress [1]

Guadeloupe
M841
L55b

Léonard, Nicolas Germain, 1744-1793.
Barquissau, Raphaël.
Les poètes créoles du XVIIIe siècle (Parny, Bertin, Léonard) Paris, J. Vigneau, 1949.

249p. ports. 24cm.

Leonard, Nicolas Germain, 1744-1793.

Guadeloupe
M972.97
V46g

Vauchelet, Emile, 1830-1913.
La Guadeloupe ses enfants célèbres (Leonard, Lethière, Bernard, Poirie St. Auréle), par Vauchelet. Paris, Augustin Challamel, 1894.

130p. 18cm.

The leopard.

Jamaica
M823.91
R271

Reid, Victor Stafford, 1913-
The leopard. New York, Viking Press, 1958.
159 p. 21 cm.

I. Title.

PZ3.R2739Le 58-7064 ‡
Library of Congress [5]

The leopard.

Jamaica
M823.91
R271

Reid, Victor Stafford, 1913-
The leopard. London, Heinemann, 1958.

185p. 18½cm.

Sierra Leone
M896.3
N54t

The leopard hunt.

Nicol, Abioseh Davidson, 1929-
Two African tales: The leopard hunt, and The devil at Yolahun Bridge. Illustrated by Hassan Bangurah. Cambridge [Eng.] University Press, 1965.
76 p. illus. 21 cm.

I. Title. II. Title: The leopard hunt. III. Title: The devil at Yolahun Bridge.

PZ7.N559Tw 65-19166
Library of Congress [5]

Liberia
M398
L55

The leopard's daughter; a folk tale from Liberia. Translated from the Vai language by Princess Fatima Massaquoi. With illus. by Martha Burnham Humphrey. Boston, Bruce Humphries [1961]

14p. illus. 28cm.

1. Tales, Liberian. I. Massaquoi, Fatima, tr.

Martinique
M841.91
L55a

Léopold, Emmanuel Flavia.
Adieu foulards, adieu madras; chants pour la terre creole. Paris, Littre, [1948].

100 p. 19 cm.

I. Title.

Martinique
M841.91
L55a

Léopold, Emmanuel Flavia.
Adieu foulards, adieu madras; chants pour la terre créole. Paris, Littre, [1948].

100p. 19cm.

1. French poetry-Martinican authors.
I. Title.

Martinique
M841.91
L55c

Léopold, Emmanuel-Flavia
La clarté des jours, poèmes. Paris. Eugène Figuière, 1924.

93p. 16cm.

1. French poetry - Martinican authors.
I. title

Martinique
M841.91
L55p

Léopold, Emmanuel Flavia
Poèmes. Paris, Pierre Seghers [1949]

74p.

1. Martinique-poetry

Martinique
M841.91
L55so

Léopold, Emmanuel Flavia.
Soleils caraïbes. Poèmes. En ce temps de la terre. Toi qui n'étais que de lumière. Paris, Éditions Bellenand [1953]
158 p. 19 cm.
"A l'exception de Poèmes, publié en 1949 ... et des deux textes tirés de Adieu foulards, adieu madras, tous les poèmes de ce recueil sont inédits."

I. Title.

PQ2623.E555S6 A 55-2779
Illinois. Univ. Library for Library of Congress [1]†

Martinique
M841.91
L55su

Léopold, Emmanuel-Flavia
Suite pour un visage, poème suivi d'une ode. Paris, Éditions des Cahiers Libres, 1926.

23p. 19cm.
Inscribed by author.

I. title

Martinique
M841.91

Léopold, Emmanuel-Flavia
Le vagabond, poème. Carcassonne, Gabelle, 1931.

5p. 26cm.
Il a été tiré de ce poème: 10 exemplaires sur Japon numérotés de I à X, 10 exemplaires sur Holland numérotés de 11 à 20, et 500 exemplaires sur papier Bibliophile.
Inscribed by author.

(see other side)

Léopold Sédar Senghor.

Sénégal
M89
Se5g

Guibert, Armand
Léopold Sédar Senghor. Choix de testes, bibliographie, portraits, fac-similés. Paris, Editions Pierre Seghers, 1961.

215p. illus., ports. 16cm. (Poètes d'Aujour'd hui 82)
Portrait of biographee on front cover of book.

Leopoldville, Congo.

see

Congo (Democratic Republic)

Leo's local lyrics.

Brit. Guiana
M821
M361e

Martin, Egbert, 1862-1890.
Leo's local lyrics, illustrated by Charles Stephens. Demerara, Printed by Baldwin & Co., Georgetown, 1886.

viii, 75p. illus. 18cm.

Leo's poetical works.

Brit. Guiana
M821
M361

Martin, Egbert, 1862-1890.
Leo's poetical works. London, Printed for the author by W.H. and L. Collingridge, 1883.

224p. 16½cm.

Lepanto - Poems.

Spain
M861.3
L34a

Latino, Juan, fl. 1573.
Ad Catholicum pariter et invictissimum Philippum dei gratia Hispaniarum regem, de foelicissima serenissimi Ferdinandi Principis nativitate, epigrammatum liber. Deque Sanctissimi PII Quinti Romanae Eclesiae Pontificis sumi, robus et affectibus erga Philippum Regem Christianissimum Liber unus Austrias Carmen, De Ex Cellentissimi Domini. D. Ioannis ab Austria, Caroli Quinti filii,

(cont. on next card)

Spain
M861.3
L34a

Lepanto - Poems.

Latino, Juan, fl. 1573. Ad Catholicum pariter... (Card 2)

ac Philippi invictissimi fratris, re bene gesta, in victoria mirabili eiusdem Philippi adversus perfidos Turcas parta, Ad illustrissimum, pariter et Reverendissimum. D.D. Petrum a Deza Praesidem, ac pro Philippo Militiae prafectu. Per Magistrum Ioannem Latinum Garnatae studiosae ado lescentiae

(cont. on next card)

Haiti
M972.94
B64

Lescot, Elie, pres. Haiti, 1883-

Bonhomme, Colbert.

Les origines et les leçons d'une révolution profonde et pacifique, par Colbert Bonhomme ... préface de m. Samuel Devieux ... Port-au-Prince, Haïti, Imprimerie de l'état, 1946.

xvi, 74 p., 1 l. illus. (ports.) 22cm.

1. Haiti—Pol. & govt.—1844- 2. Haiti—Soc. condit. 3. Lescot, Elie, pres. Haiti, 1883- I. Title.

F1926.B7 972.94 47-24684

Library of Congress [1]

Africa
M398
L56

Leslau, Wolf, joint comp.

Leslau, Charlotte, comp.

African proverbs. Compiled by Charlotte and Wolf Leslau. With decorations by Jeff Hill. Mount Vernon, N. Y., Peter Pauper Press [1962]

61 p. col. illus. 19 cm.

White comp.

1. Proverbs, African. I. Leslau, Wolf, joint comp.

PN6519.A6L4 62-6237

Library of Congress [5]

Spain
M861.3
L34a

Lepanto - Poems.

Latino, Juan, fl 1573. Ad Catholicum pariter... (Card 3)

moderatorem. Libri duo. Cum Regiae Maiestatis Privilegio Garnatae. Ex officina Hugonis de Mena. Anno. 1573. Prastant in aedibus Ioannis Diaz Bibliopolae in vico santae Mariae.

44 [1], 35, [4] p. woodcuts. 20cm.

1. Austriad (poem). 2. Lepanto - Poems. 3. Latin literature - Mediaeval and modern. I. Title.

Haiti
M972.94
H36t

Lescot, Elie, pres. Haiti, 1883-

Hudicourt, Max Lelio

The triumph of fascism; or, the Haitian-American mutual responsibilities in the Haitian affaire. New York, Comite de Lutte pour une Haiti Democratique, [1945].

16p. port. 29cm.

Ethiopia
M896.3
Se48

Leslau, Wolf, tr.

Sellassie, Sahle, 1936-

Shinega's village; scenes of Ethiopian life. Translated from Chaha by Wolf Leslau. Illus. by Li Gelpke. Berkeley, University of California Press, 1964.

xi, 112 p. illus. 22 cm.

1. Ethiopia—Soc. life & cust. I. Leslau, Wolf, tr. II. Title.

PZ4.S4653Sh 64-12607

Library of Congress [5]

M972.94
L55

Lepelletier de Saint-Remy, R.

Saint-Domingue. Étude et solution nouvelle de la question haïtienne. Par m. R. Lepelletier de Saint-Remy ... Paris, A. Bertrand, 1846.

2 v. plan. 8°.

"Annexe bibliographique": v. 2, p. 537-548.

White author.

1. Haiti—Hist. 2. Finance—Haiti (Republic) 3. Finance—Dominican republic. I. Title.

2-12854

Library of Congress F1931.L59

[a27d1]

Haiti
M910
L56m

Lescouflair, Georges, 1882-

Mon vieux carnet; voyages--pensees--considerations--journal 1927. Montreal, Beauchemin, 1958.

178p. 16½cm.

1. Voyages and travels. I. Title.

The Leslie Uggams beauty book.

M646.7
Ug4

Uggams, Leslie.

The Leslie Uggams beauty book, by Leslie Uggams with Marie Fenton. Englewood Cliffs, N. J., Prentice-Hall [1966]

178 p. illus., ports. 26 cm.

1. Beauty, Personal. I. Fenton, Marie, joint author. II. Title.

RA778.U8 646.72 66-24987

Library of Congress [67d7]

Leprosy—Haiti.

Haiti
M972.94
V590

Vernet, E Louis.

... Les oubliés de chez nous, question hygiéno-sociale, par E. Louis Vernet ... [Port-au-Prince?] Imprimerie A. P. Barthélemy [1945?]

6 p. l., [12]-48 p., 1 l. 20½cm. (Bibliothèque haïtienne)

1. Leprosy—Haiti. I. Title.

RC154.55.H3V4 614.546 Med 47-1314 rev

Library of Congress [r47c2]

Haiti
M841
L56

Lescouflair, Georges

Visages familiers. Paris, Éditions d'Artrey, n.d.

103p. 19cm.

1. Haitian poetry
I. Title

Haiti
M841.91
L56c

Lespès, Anthony, 1907-

Les clefs de la lumière. Avec une illustration d'Elzire. [Port-au-Prince, Compagnie Lithographique d'Haiti, 1955]

23 leaves, illus. 20cm.

1. Haitian poetry.

Martinique
M843.9
L56

Lero, Yva,

Doucherie. Port-de-France, Horizons Caraibes [c 1958]

115p. illus. 21cm.

1. Martinique. I. Title.

Africa
M398
L56

Leslau, Charlotte, comp.

African proverbs. Compiled by Charlotte and Wolf Leslau. With decorations by Jeff Hill. Mount Vernon, N. Y., Peter Pauper Press [1962]

61 p. col. illus. 19 cm.

White comp.

1. Proverbs, African. I. Leslau, Wolf, joint comp.

PN6519.A6L4 62-6237

Library of Congress [5]

Haiti
M841.91
L56c

Lespès, Anthony, 1907-

Les clefs de la lumière. Avec une illustration d'Elzire. [Port-au-Prince. Compagnie Lithographique d'Haiti, 1955]

23 leaves, illus. 20cm.

1. Haitian poetry.

Haiti
M841
L56d

Leroy, Frantz

Du bec et des ongles. Port-au-Prince, 1962.

11p. port. 21cm.

Portrait of author in book.

I. Title.

Ethiopia
M896.8
L56f

Leslau, Wolf.

Falasha anthology, translated from Ethiopic sources with an introd. by Wolf Leslau. New Haven, Yale University Press, 1951.

xliii, 222 p. illus. 22 cm. (Yale Judaica series, v. 6)

Includes bibliographies.

1. Judaism—Collections. 2. Falashas. 3. Ethiopic literature—Translations into English. 4. English literature—Translations from Ethiopic. I. Title. (Series)

BM40.L37 296 51-7505

Library of Congress [52g3]

Haiti
M843.91
L56s

Lespes, Anthony, 1907-

Les semences de la colère. Port-au-Prince, Henri Deschamps, 1949.

215p. 19cm.

1. Haitian fiction. I. Title.

Martinique
M842.91
C33e

Et les chiens se taisaient, tragédie.

Césaire, Aimé.

Et les chiens se taisaient, tragédie. Arrangement théâtral. Paris, Présence africaine [1956]

121 p. 19 cm.

I. Title.

A 57-1537

Illinois. Univ. Library for Library of Congress [3]

Ethiopia
M963
C83

Leslau, Wolf, joint author.

Courlander, Harold, 1908-

The fire on the mountain, and other Ethiopian stories, by Harold Courlander and Wolf Leslau. Illustrated by Robert W. Kane. New York, Holt [1950]

141 p. illus., col. plates. 25 cm.

1. Tales, Ethiopic. I. Leslau, Wolf, joint author. II. Title.

GR360.E8C6 398.21 50-7265

Library of Congress [52k3]

Haiti
M972.94
L56g

Lespinasse, Pierre Eugène de.

... Gens d'autrefois. Vieux souvenirs ... Paris, La Revue mondiale, 1926-

v. ports. 19cm. (Collection haïtienne d'expression française)

Library has volume I.

1. Haiti—Hist.—1804- 2. Boyer, Jean Pierre, pres. Haiti, 1776-1850. 3. Pétion, Alexandre Sabès, pres. Haiti, 1770-1818. 4. Christophe, Henri, king of Haiti, 1767-1820. I. Title.

28-25703

Library of Congress F1924.L63

——— Copy 2. [3]

S. Africa
M896.3 L56s
Lestrade, G P
Some Kgatla animal stories; edited with English translation and notes. Cape Town, The Lovedale Press, 1948.
68p. 25cm
White author
1. Africa, South - Short stories. 2. Kgatla - Short stories. 3. Animals, Legends and stories of - Africa.

Let my people go.
Africa, South
M968 L971e2
Luthuli, Albert John, 1898-
Let my people go; an autobiography. Introd. by Charles Hooper. Johannesburg, Collins, 1962.
255 p. illus. 22 cm.
1. Africa, South—Race question. I. Title.
DT779.8.L8A3 1962a 323.168 62-51657 ‡
Library of Congress [1]

Let the righteous speak!
M323 Sa13
Sabourin, Clemonce.
Let the righteous speak! Travel memoirs. [1st ed.] New York, Pageant Press [1957]
80 p. 21 cm.
1. Negroes—Segregation. 2. Southern States—Descr. & trav. I. Title.
E185.61.S25 325.260975 57-8311 ‡
Library of Congress [2]

S. Africa
M896.3 L56
Lestrade, G P
Some Venda folk-tales; edited with English translations and notes. Cape Town, The Lovedale Press, 1949.
48p. 25cm.
White author
1. Venda - Folk-tales. 2. Africa, South - Folktales. I. Title.

Let my people go.
Africa, South
M968 L971e
Luthuli, Albert John, 1898-
Let my people go. New York, McGraw-Hill [1962]
255 p. illus. 22 cm.
Autobiography.
1. Africa, South—Race question. I. Title.
DT779.8.L8A3 323.168 62-13819 ‡
Library of Congress [63q5]

Let there be life.
MB9 G87b
Branson, Helen Kitchen, 1916-
Let there be life: the contemporary account of Edna L. Griffin, M. D. Pasadena, Calif., M. S. Sen [1947]
185 p. port. 24 cm.
1. Griffin, Edna La Flore, 1905- 2. U. S.—Race question. I. Title.
R154.G7678B7 926.1 48-2438*
Library of Congress [3]

Lessons of the hour.
M815.4 D74le
Douglass, Frederick, 1817-1895.
Address delivered in the Metropolitan A.M.E. church, Washington, D.C., Tuesday, January 9th, 1894, on the lessons for the hour. In which he discusses the various aspects of the so-called, but miscalled, Negro problem, Baltimore, Press of Thomas and Evans, 1894.
36p. 22cm.
Cover title: Lessons of the hour.

"Let my people go".
M813.5 W849
Wood, Lillian E.
"Let my people go". Philadelphia, Pa., A.M.E. book concern, n.d.
132p. 22cm.

M306 N213d
Let us build a National Negro Congress.
Davis, John Preston, 1905-
Let us build a National Negro Congress ... [Washington, National Sponsoring Committee, National Negro Congress, 1935]
31p. 18cm.

Lest we forget.
M811.5 B221
Banks, William Augustus.
"Lest we forget," by William Augustus Banks. Chattanooga, Tenn., Central High Press [1930]
11p. 20cm.

Let no man write my epitaph.
M813.5 M851
Motley, Willard, 1912-
Let no man write my epitaph. New York, Random House [1958]
467 p. 22 cm.
I. Title.
PZ3.M8573Le 58-7667 ‡
Library of Congress [58f5]

M323 N21
Let's be honest about democracy.
National Association for the Advancement of Colored People.
Let's be honest about democracy. New York, NAACP, 1939.
23p. illus. 22cm.

M813.5 At81
Let me breathe thunder.
Attaway, William.
... Let me breathe thunder. New York, Doubleday, Doran & company, inc., 1939.
4 p. l., 267 p. 19½cm.
"First edition."
I. Title.
M813.5 At8
Library of Congress PZ3.A882Le 39-17641
——— Copy 2.
Copyright A 130457 [5]

Let no man write my epitaph.
M813.5 K851
Motley, Willard, 1912-
Let no man write my epitaph. London, Longmans, 1958.
404p. 20½cm.
I. Title.

Let's face it; a guide to good grooming for Negro girls.
M646.7 Ar21
Archer, Elsie.
Let's face it; a guide to good grooming for Negro girls. With decorations by Harper Johnson. [1st ed.] Philadelphia, Lippincott [1959]
185 p. illus. 21 cm.
1. Beauty, Personal. I. Title. II. Title: Negro girls.
RA776.A62 646.7 59-6705 ‡
Library of Congress [50k10]

Let me live.
Temporary Card
MB9 H431
Herndon, Angelo, 1913-
[Russian edition of Let me live] Moscow, 1938.
306p. port. 17cm.
[To be transliterated]

Let noon be fair, a novel.
M813.5 M85Le
Motley, Willard, 1912-1965.
Let noon be fair, a novel. New York, Putnam [1966]
416 p. 22 cm.
I. Title.
PZ3.M8573Lg 65-20682
Library of Congress [8]

Let's go.
M910 R56
Robison, Lois
Let's go; teacher's book, junior. Greenwich, Connecticut, The Seabury Press, 1952.
48p. illus. 21cm.

Let me live.
MB9 H43
Herndon, Angelo, 1913-
Let me live [by] Angelo Herndon. New York, Random house [1937]
4 p. l., 3-409 p. front., ports. 21½cm.
"First printing."
I. Title.
37-5040
Library of Congress E185.97.H47
——— Copy 2. [5-5] 923.573

Let the ammunition roll.
M350 H24L
Harris, Elbert Leroy
Let the ammunition roll: The story of a Negro GI. N.Y. Exposition press, 1948.
30p. 22cm.

Let's make a play.
Kenya
M896.2 Mc4
MacPherson, Margaret
Let's make a play. With the acted version of Kintu; a play by E. C. N. Kironde. Kampala, Eagle Press, 1960.
vii, 44p. 21½cm.
White author.
1. Theater - Production and direction. I. Title. II. Kironde, E. C. N. Kintu. 2. Drama.

South Africa
M331.88 **Letsoaba, J**
L56 **The fight for trade union rights in South Africa. [London, Union of Democratic Control Publications, n.d.]**

13p. 21½cm.

1. Trade-unions - Africa, South. 2. Africa, South - Labor and laboring classes. I. Title.

Letter to Maurice Thorez.

Martinique
M843 Césaire, Aimé, 1913-
C331e Letter to Maurice Thorez. Paris, Presence Africaine [c1957]

16p. 18cm.

Letter writing, African.

Uganda
M808.6 **Ssekawma, J C**
Ss24 **Okuwandiika ebbaluwa [Letter writing] Nairobi, Eagle Press, 1960.**

108p. 21½cm. (East African Literature Bureau)
Written in Luganda.

1. Letter writing, African. I. Title.

Letterature dei negri d'America.

M810.9 **Piccioni, Leone.**
P581 Letteratura dei negri d'America. Milano, Gruppo editoriale "Academia" [1949]

344 p. 22 cm.
Includes bibliographical references.

1. American literature—Negro authors—Hist. & crit. 2. Negro literature (American)—Hist. & crit. 3. Negro poetry (American)—Translations into Italian. 4. Italian poetry—Translations from English. I. Title.

PS591.N4P5 50-24617
Library of Congress [1]

M808.8 **Letteratura Negra.** Prefazione di Pier Paolo
L718 Pasolini. [Roma, Editori Riuniti [1961]

2v. 22½cm.
Includes bibliography.

Contents.- [v.1] La paesia, a cura de Mario de Andrade.- [v.2] La Prosa, a cura di Leonard Sainville.

1. Literature. 2. African literature. 3. Poetry. 4. African poetry. I. Andrade, Mario de, 1893-1945. II. Sainville, Leonard.

Letters.

Brazil
M869.6 **Andrade, Mário de**
An2c **Cartas de Mário de Andrade a Manuel Bandeira. Prefácio e notas de Manuel Bandeira. Rio, Organização Simões Editôra, 1958.**

353p. 22½cm.

M815.2 Letters addressed to Dorothy Ripley, from
J711 several Africans and Indians, on subjects of
2d ed Christian experience, &c...Second edition... Bristol, printed by Philip Rose [n.d.]

38p. 18cm.
Bound with edition of 1807.

1. Jones, Absalom, 1746-1818. I. Allen, Richard, 1760-1831. II. Ripley, Dorothy.

M815.2 Letters addressed to Dorothy Ripley, from
J711 several Africans & Indians, on subjects of
1807 Christian experience, &c...Chester, printed by J. Hemingway, 1807.

58p. 16cm.

1. Jones, Absalom, 1746-1818. I. Allen, Richard, 1760-1831. II. Ripley, Dorothy.

Letters from a Jim Crow Army.

M323 Reddick, Lawrence Dunbar, 1910-
N78t Letters from a Jim Crow Army.

pp. 371-382.
In: Twice a year, ed. by Dorothy Norman. 1946.

Letters from my nephew slim.

M814.5 **Smith, Carl S**
Sm54 **Letters from my nephew slim. New York, Vantage Press [1965]**

120p. 20½cm.
Portrait of author on book cover.

Lettre d'un Africain.

Mali
M966.2 Ouane, Ibrahima Mamadou, 1908-
Ou1L Lettre d'un Africain. Monte-Carlo, Regain, 1958.

61p. port. 18½cm.

Cameroun Lettres de ma cambus.
M916.711 Ombede, Philippe-Louis.
Om1 Lettres de ma cambuse [par] R. Philombe [pseud.] Yaounde, Editions Abbia avec la collaboration de Cle, 1964.

62p. illus. 18cm.
Portrait of author on book cover.

1. Cameroun. I. Title.

Martinique **Lettres politiques sur les colonies.**
M972.98 **Bissette, Cyrille Charles Auguste, 1795-1858.**
B541 **Lettres politiques sur les colonies, sur l'esclavage et sur les questions qui s'y rettachent, par C. A. Bissette. Paris, Ebrard, Libraire, Passage des Panoramas, 1845.**

48p. 23cm.

Leurres et lueurs; poèmes.

Sénégal
M896.1 Diop, Birago, 1906-
D6221 Leurres et lueurs; poèmes. Paris, Présence Africaine, [1960].

86p. 19cm.

Levant - Description and travel.

M910 **Brooks, William Sampson, 1865-**
B791f Footprints of a black man; the Holy Land, by W. Sampson Brooks ... [St. Louis, Eden publishing house print, 1915]

317 p. front., illus. (incl. map) ports. 23½cm. $1.50

1. Levant—Descr. & trav. I. Title.

Library of Congress DS49.B7 16-4227
Copyright A 420741

Lève-toi amie viens.

Cameroun
M896.1 **Mveng, Engelbert**
M98L **Lève-toi amie viens, images et textes du Engelbert Mveng. Dakar, Librarie Clairafrique [1966]**

[53]p. illus. 24cm.

Levensgeschiedenis van den Amerikaanschen slaaf.

M810 **Brown, William Wells,** *b.* **1815.**
B779al Levensgeschiedenis van den Amerikaanschen slaaf, W.
1850 Wells Brown, Amerikaansch afgevaardigde bij het vredescongres te Parijs, 1849, door hem zelven beschreven. Naar den 5. Engelschen druk vertaald door M. Keijzer. Zwolle, W. E. J. Tjeenk Willink, 1850.

x, 119, [1] p. front. (port.) 23½cm.

Narrative of the author's experiences as a slave in St. Louis and elsewhere.

1. Slavery in the U. S.—Missouri. I. Keijzer, M., tr. II. Title.

Library of Congress E444.B885 1-6413

Africa
M496 **Leverhulme Conference on Universities and the Language**
L57 **Problems of Tropical Africa,** *Ibadan, Nigeria, 1961-1962.*
Language in Africa; papers. Edited by John Spencer. Cambridge [Eng.] University Press, 1963.

vii, 167 p. 23 cm.
English or French.
Bibliographical footnotes.

1. Africa, Sub-Saharan—Languages. 2. Education—Africa, Sub-Saharan. I. Spencer, John Walter, ed. II. Title.

LA1503.7.L46 1961-1962 63-4814
Library of Congress [5]

Levington, William, d. 1836.

M89 **Bragg, George Freeman, 1863-**
L57b The first negro priest on southern soil, by the Rev. George F. Bragg ... Baltimore, The Church advocate print, 1909.

72 p. front., illus. (incl. ports.) 20 cm.

1. Levington, William, d. 1836. I. Title.

Library of Congress BX5067.B8 9-30862
[a32b1]

Jamaica
M821.91 Levy, Ferdinand
L57f Flashes from the dark, by Ferdinand Levy, with sketch of the author by Louis Le Brocquy. Dublin, Sign of the three candles, 1941

45p. front. 20cm.

1. Jamaican poetry I.Title

M813.5 **Levy, Mimi Cooper.**
L57c Corrie and the Yankee. Illustrated by Ernest Crichlow. New York, Viking Press [1959]

189 p. illus. 22 cm.

White author.

I. Title. II. Crichlow, Ernest, illustrator.

PZ7.L5834Co 59-16931 ‡
Library of Congress [5]

Lewanika, king of Barotseland, d.1916.
Rhodesia, N.
M968.94
M18L
Mackintosh, Catharine Winkworth.
Lewanika, paramount chief of the Barotse and allied tribes, 1875-1916, by C.W. Mackintosh. London and Redhill, United society for Christian literature ⌈1942⌉

63, ⌈1⌉ p. 18½cm. (Half-title: Africa's own library ,no.4)

Lewanika, king of Barotseland, d. 1916.
Africa
MB9
L58m
Mackintosh, Catharine Winkworth.
Lewanika, paramount chief of the Barotse and allied tribes, 1875–1916, by C. W. Mackintosh. London and Redhill, United society for Christian literature ⌈1942⌉
63, ⌈1⌉ p. 18½cm. (*Half-title:* Africa's own library, no. 4)
"First published 1942."

1. Lewanika, king of Barotseland, d. 1916. 2. Missions—Barotseland. I. United society for Christian literature, London.
44-35506
Library of Congress DT964.B3M18
⌈2⌉ 968.961

M974.71
L58s
Lewin, Wilfred S.
A study of the Negro population of Mount Vernon, by Wilfrod S. Lewin. 1935.
52p. 28cm.
Typewritten

M026
L58
Lewinson, Paul, 1900–
A guide to documents in the National Archives: for Negro studies, compiled by Paul Lewinson for the Committee on Negro Studies of the American Council of Learned Societies. Washington, 1947.
x, 28 p. 24 cm. (American Council of Learned Societies Devoted to Humanistic Studies. Committee on Negro Studies. Publications, no. 1)

1. ~~Negroes~~—Bibl. I. U. S. National Archives. (Series)
A 50-2611
Columbia Univ. for Library of Congress Libraries ⌈3⌉

M817.5
L58
Lewis, Alethia (Lightner)
A true fairy tale; illustrated by Gloria Bultman. Boston, Christopher Pub. House ⌈1952⌉
107 p. illus. 21 cm.

1. Carver, George Washington, 1864?–1943—Fiction. I. Title.
PZ7.L5846Tr 52-8285 ‡
Library of Congress ⌈2⌉

M811.08
B98b
Lewis, Alexander.
⌈Poems⌉
(In: Byars, J. C. comp. Black and white. Washington, D. C. Crane Press, 1927. 24cm. p. 52-58).

M323.4
L58
Lewis, Anthony, 1927–
Portrait of a decade; the second American revolution ⌈by⌉ Anthony Lewis and the New York times. New York, Random House ⌈1964⌉
322 p. illus. 25 cm.
White author.
Partial contents.- A Negro assays to Negro mood, by James Baldwin.- Expalnation of the 'Black psyche', by John Oliver Killens.

1. ~~Negroes~~—Civil rights. I. New York times. II. Title. III. Title: The second American revolution.
E185.61.L52 1964 323.40973 64-14832
Library of Congress ⌈4-1⌉

M811.5
L58p
Lewis, Carrie Louise, 1932-
Polished pebbles; poems. New York, Exposition Press, 1960.
48p. 20½cm.
Portrait of author on book jacket.

1. Poetry-(American). I. Title.

MB9
P871
Lewis, Claude.
Adam Clayton Powell. Greenwich, Conn., Fawcett Publications ⌈1963⌉
127 p. 18 cm. (Gold medal books)
"K1361."

1. Powell, Adam Clayton, 1908–
E748.P86L4 64-708
Library of Congress ⌈5⌉

Lewis, Edmonia, 1845–
M304
P19
v.7
no.18
Our colored missions, vol. 17, no.11. New York City, The Catholic board for mission work among the colored people, November, 1931.
p. 164. 25½cm.

M331
L58
Lewis, Edward Erwin, 1900–
The mobility of the Negro; a study in the American labor supply, by Edward E. Lewis ... New York, Columbia university press; London, P. S. King & son, ltd., 1931.
144 p. illus. (maps) 23cm. (*Half-title:* Studies in history, economics and public law, ed. by the Faculty of political science of Columbia university, no. 342) White author.
Published also as thesis (PH. D.) Columbia university.
"The third volume to appear as a result of studies in the field of Negro migration under grants by the Social science research council and the Columbia university Council for research in the social sciences."—Foreword.
"Selected bibliography": p. 134–135.
~~1. Negroes.~~ 2. ~~Negroes~~ — Employment. 3. Southern states — Econ. condit.—1918– 4. Cotton growing and manufacture—Southern states. I. Social science research council. II. Columbia university. Council for research in the social sciences. III. Title.
Library of Congress H31.C7 no. 342 31—20612
——— Copy 2. E185.8.L47
⌈42q2⌉ (306.2) 331.6

M306
N21p
Lewis, Edward Shakespeare, 1901-
Progress in interracial relationships. New York, 1943.
In: National Conference of Social Work. Selected papers at seventieth annual meeting... 1943. New York, Columbia University for the Conference, 1943. 23cm. pp. 277-289.

1. Race relations.

Lewis, Ethel.
MB9
G19s
Suffrage league of Boston and vicinity. *Garrison centenary committee.*
The celebration of the one hundredth anniversary of the birth of William Lloyd Garrison, by the colored citizens of greater Boston under the auspices of the Suffrage league of Boston and vicinity, December tenth and eleventh, MCMV, with abridged accounts of celebrations held by certain churches of greater Boston, Sunday evening, December tenth, in response to appeal of the Suffrage league. Reported by Miss Ethel Lewis ... ed. by the secretary of the Suffrage league centenary committee. Boston, The Garrison centenary committee of the Suffrage league of Boston and vicinity, 1906.
3 p. l., 11–75, ⌈1⌉ p. front. (port.) illus. 24cm.
1. Garrison, William Lloyd, 1805–1879. I. Lewis, Ethel.
6—18976
Library of Congress E449.G257
Copyright A 137143 ⌈a27d1⌉

MB9
L58L
Lewis, Henry Harrison
Life of Rev. H. H. Lewis. Giving a history of his early life and services in the ministry. Written and compiled by himself. Philadelphia, S. L. Nichols, 1877.
54p. 16½cm.

M331
L58b
Lewis, Hylan.
Blackways of Kent. Chapel Hill, University of North Carolina Press, 1955.
xxiv, 337 p. diagrs., tables. 21 cm. (Field studies in the modern culture of the South)
Based on thesis, University of Chicago.

1. ~~Negroes~~—Southern States. I. Title. (Series)
E185.6.L4 55—62673
*301.451 325.260975
Library of Congress ⌈56k10⌉

M973
Am3
Lewis, Hylan
Racial situations and issues in Africa, by William O. Brown and Hylan Lewis. pp. 141-63.
In: American Assembly, The United States and Africa ... New York, 1958.

MB9
B681
Lewis, John W
The life, labors and travels of Elder Charles Bowles, of the Free Will Baptist denomination, by Eld. John W. Lewis. Together with an essay on the character and condition of the African race by the same. Also, an essay on the fugitive law of the U.S. congress of 1850, by Rev. Arthur Dearing Watertown, Ingalls and Stowell's steam press, 1852.
285 ⌈2⌉ p. 20cm.
1. Bowles, Charles, 1761-1843 2. Free Will Baptist.
3. Baptists.

M572.
L58
Lewis, Julian Herman, 1891-
The biology of the Negro, by Julian Herman Lewis ... Chicago, Ill., The University of Chicago press ⌈1942⌉
xvii, 433 p. incl. tables. 23½cm.
Bibliographical foot-notes.

1. ~~Negro race~~. I. Title.
42-14836
Library of Congress GN57.N4L4
⌈3⌉ 572.96

M304
P19
V.3,no.14
Lewis, Julian Herman, 1891-
Number and geographic location of Negro physicians in the United States. Reprinted from the Journal of the American Medical Association, 104:1272-73, April 6, 1935.

1. Physicians

Nigeria
M896.2
F13aL
Lewis, L J jt. auth.
Fagunwa, D O
Alàyé fun oluko nipa lilo iwe taiwo ati Kehinde, ⌈by⌉ D. O. Fagunwa and L. J. Lewis, London, Oxford univ. Press, 1954.
58p. 18cm.
Written in Yoruba.

M813.5
L58e
Lewis, Laura.
Enter in. Pictures by Ernest Crichlow. ⌈1st ed.⌉ New York, Pilot Pub. Corp. ⌈1959⌉
31 p. illus. 24 cm.
White author.

I. Title. II. Crichlow, Ernest, illus.
PZ8.3.L59En 59-12922 ‡
Library of Congress ⌈3⌉

M218
L58
1851
Lewis, Robert Benjamin
Light and truth; collected from the Bible and ancient and modern history, containing the universal history of the colored an the Indian race, from the creation of the world to the present time. By R. B. Lewis... Boston, published by Moses M. Taylor, 1851.

viii, 9-400p. 19cm.

1. History, Ancient. 2. Race. I. Title.

M218
L58
Lewis, Robert Benjamin.
Light and truth; collected from the Bible and ancient and modern history, containing the universal history of the colored and the Indian race, from the creation of the world to the present time. By R. B. Lewis ... Boston, Pub. by a committee of colored gentlemen, B. F. Roberts, printer, 1844.

viii, [9]-400 p. 18½ cm.

Originally issued in four monthly numbers, 1843? Copyright notice, 1836.

1. History, Ancient. 2. Negro race. 3. Indians—Origin. I. Title.
4. Haiti.

13—21188

Library of Congress D22.L5
[37b1-]

M811.5
L58
Lewis, Robert V
Selected poems. Detroit, Seminary Press, c1948.

22p. 22cm.
Autographed: "To Arthur B. Spingarn. With best wishes."

1. Poetry. I. Title.

Liberia
M966.6
B62c
1888
Lewis, Samuel, 1843-1903.

Blyden, Edward Wilmot, 1832-1912.
Christianity, Islam and the Negro race. By Edward W. Blyden... With an introduction by the Hon. Samuel Lewis... 2d ed. London, W.B. Whittingham & co., 1888.

3p. l., xv, 432p. front. (port.) 21½cm.

Liberia
M966.6
B62c
1887
Lewis, Samuel.

Blyden, Edward Wilmot, 1832-1912.
Christianity, Islam and the Negro race. By Edward W. Blyden... With an introduction by the Hon. Samuel Lewis. London, W.B. Whittingham & co., 1887.

vii, 423p.
Blyden's own copy containing his signature and corrections in his handwriting.

M973.9
F46
No.11
Lewis, Theophilus.
Fifty years of progress in the theatre. Pittsburgh, Pittsburgh Courier, 1950.

7p. illus. 24cm. (Fifty years of progress)

1. Theater. I. Series.

St. Lucia
M330
L58ec
Lewis, William Arthur, 1915-
Economic problems of to-day, by W. Arthur Lewis ... London, New York [etc.] Longmans, Green and co. [1940]

2 p. l., vii-xii, 175 p. diagr. 19cm.
"First published 1940."
"Suggestions for further reading" at end of each chapter.

1. Economic policy. 2. Gt. Brit.—Economic policy. I. Title.

A 40-3195

Harvard univ. Library for Library of Congress HD82.L4
[3] 330.904

St.Lucia
M330
L58d
Lewis, William Arthur, 1915-
Development planning; the essentials of economic policy [by] W. Arthur Lewis. [1st U. S. ed.] New York, Harper & Row [1966]

278 p. 22 cm.
Includes bibliographies.

1. Economic policy. I. Title.

HD82.L39 1966a 338.9 66-10655

Library of Congress [5]

St.Lucia
M330
L58e
Lewis, William Arthur, 1915-
Economic survey, 1919-1939. London, G. Allen and Unwin [~~1949~~] 1953.

221 p. diagrs., tables. 23 cm.
Bibliography: p. 214-218.

1. Economic conditions—1918-1945. I. Title.

HC57.L48 330.904 49—48124*

Library of Congress [58d1]

St. Lucia
M330
L58L
Lewis, William Arthur, 1915-
Labour in the West Indies; the birth of a workers' movement, by W. Arthur Lewis; with a preface by A. Creech Jones, M. P. London, V. Gollancz ltd. and the Fabian society, 1939.

44 p. 21½cm. (*On cover: Fabian society. Research series, no. 44*)

1. Labor and laboring classes—West Indies, British. 2. Trade-unions—West Indies, British. I. Title. 3. West Indies, British.

41-6878

Library of Congress HX11.N42 no. 44
[2] (355.1082) 331.8809729

St. Lucia
M330
L58o
Lewis, William Arthur, 1915-
Overhead costs; some essays in economic analysis. London, G. Allen & Unwin [~~1949~~] 1951

200 p. diagrs. 23 cm. (The Library of economics. Sect. 2: New works, 3)
Bibliographical footnotes.

1. Cost. 2. Price policy. 3. Monopolies. I. Title. (Series)

HB221.L54 338.52 49—6466*

Library of Congress [55c1]

Africa
M370
C83
Lewis, William Arthur, 1915-
Education and economic development.
Pp. 200-211.

In: Cowan, L. G., ed. Education and nation-building in Africa. New York, Praeger, 1965.

St. Lucia
M966
L589
Lewis, William Arthur, 1915-
Politics in West Africa [by] W. Arthur Lewis. Toronto, New York, Oxford University Press, 1965.

90 p. map. 19 cm. (The Whidden lectures, 1965)

1. Africa, West—Politics. 2. States, New. I. Title. (Series)

DT471.L57 320.966 65—8469

Library of Congress [68e2]

M909.82
C76
Lewis, W Arthur, 1915-
Economic problems of development.
Pp. 68-91.

In: Conference on Tensions in Development, Oxford University, 1961. Restless nations. New York, Dodd, Mead, 1962.

St. Lucia
M330
L58at
Lewis, William Arthur, 1915-
Attitude to Africa, by W. Arthur Lewis, Michael Scott, Martin Wight, and Colin Legum. With a map by Bip Pares. Middlesex, Penguin Books, 1951.

155p. 18cm.

1. Africa. I. Title.

St. Lucia
M330
L58p
Lewis, William Arthur, 1915-
The principles of economic planning; a study prepared for the Fabian Society. London, D. Dobson [1949]

128 p. 22 cm.
Imprint on label mounted on t. p.: London, Allen & Unwin.

1. Economic policy. I. Fabian Society, London.

HD82.L415 338.91 50—501

Library of Congress [53e1]

St.Lucia
M330
L58r
Lewis, William Arthur, 1915-
Report on industrialisation and the Gold Coast. Gold Coast, The Government Printing Department, 1953.

23p. 31½cm.

1. Gold Coast-Industry.

M909.82
C76a
Lewis, W Arthur, 1915-
Economic problems of development.
Pp. 68-91.

In: Conference on Tensions in Development. Restless nations. London, Allen and Unwin, 1962.

Africa
M960
Af83
Lewis, Sir William Arthur, 1915-
Aspects of economic development

Pp. 115-130.

In: African Conference on Progress through Cooperation. Africa. New York, Dodd, Mead, 1966.

M338.9
G92s
Lewis, William Arthur, 1915-
Science, men, and money.

Pp. 24-33.
In: Science and the new nations, edited by Ruth Griber. 1961.

I. Title.

St. Lucia
M330
L58t
Lewis, William Arthur, 1915-
The theory of economic growth. London, Allen & Unwin [1955]

453 p. 23 cm.

1. Industry. I. Title.

HD21.L43 330.1 55—43952 ‡

Library of Congress [61b2]

Ley municipal.
M972.95 P141
Pagán, Bolívar, 1899-
... Ley municipal, revisada, anotada y comentada, por Bolívar Pagán. (Contiene la Ley municipal y todas las demás leyes aplicables a los municipios, el acta orgánica, el reglamento de contabilidad municipal, y toda la jurisprudencia del Tribunal supremo sobre cuestiones municipales hasta el tomo 32, incl.) San Juan, Puerto Rico, La Correspondencia de Pto. Rico, inc., 1925.
xi, 13-256, [4] p. 22cm. (Biblioteca de divulgación legal, vol. I)
1. Municipal government—Puerto Rico. 2. Municipal corporations—Puerto Rico. I. Puerto Rico. Laws, statutes, etc. II. Title.
42-51912
Library of Congress JS2024.P3
[3]

Leyburn, James Graham. The Haitian people.
Haiti M972.94 M35
Mars, Jean Price, 1876-
Ebauches, 2eme série: De la prehistoire d'Haiti. Port-au-Prince, Impre. de l'État, 1962.
217p. tables 22cm.
Bibliographical footnotes.

Rhodesia M968.9 C43
Leys, Colin, *ed.*
A new deal in Central Africa, edited by Colin Leys and Cranford Pratt. New York, Praeger [1960]
226 p. illus. 22 cm. (Books that matter)
Includes bibliography.
Partial contents.- The meaning of good government in Central Africa, by Bernard Chidzero.- The essentials of a new deal, by Bernard Chidzero, Colin Leys and Cranford Pratt.
1. Rhodesia and Nyasaland. I. Pratt, Cranford, joint ed. II. Title.
DT856.L4 968.9 60-12201 ‡
Library of Congress [20]

La lézarde; roman.
Martinique M843.9 G49
Glissant, Èdouard, 1928-
La lézarde; roman. Paris, Editions du Seuil, 1958.
250p. 19cm.
"Autographed by author."

Haiti M841. L61c
Lhérisson, Justin, 1873- 1907.
... Les chants de l'aurore; primes rimes ... Port-au-Prince, Mprimerie [!] de la jeunesse A. Laforest, 1893.
72 p., 1 l. 20½cm.
Half-title: Primes rimes.
With this is bound the author's Passe-temps. (Tours) 1895.
I. Title. 1. Haitian poetry
25-20889
Library of Congress PQ3949.L5C5

Haiti M843.91 L61f
Lherisson, Justin, 1873-1907.
...Los fortunes de chez nous. La famille des pitite caille. 2e edit. Paris, Firmin Didot et Cie, 1929.
120p. front. 19cm.
1. Haitian fiction. I. Title.

Haiti M841 L61p
Lhérisson, Justin, 1873- 1907.
... Passe-temps, poésies ... [Tours, Imp. Deslis frères] 1895.
95, [1] p. front. (port.) 20½cm. [*With his* Les chants de l'aurore ... Port-au-Prince, 1893]
At head of title: Bibliothèque haïtienne ...
I. Title. 1. Haitian poetry.
25-20888
Library of Congress PQ3949.L5C5

Haiti M972.94 L61h
Lhérisson, Lélia Justin, 1873-1907.
Les héros de l'indépendance dans l'histoire d'Haïti. [Port-au-Prince, 1954?]
88 p. illus. 24 cm. (Collection du centcinquantenaire de l'indépendance d'Haïti)
Includes bibliography.
1. Haiti—Biog. 2. Haiti—Hist.—Revolution, 1791-1804.
F1914.L5 54-27072 ‡
Library of Congress [1]

Haiti M840.9 L61m
Lhérisson, Lélia Justin, 1873-1907.
... Manuel de littérature haitienne et textes expliqués. Littérature des Amériques. Port-au-Prince, Haiti, Imprimerie du Collège Vertières, 1945.
409 p. incl. illus. (incl. ports.) pl. 22cm.
At head of title: Lélia J. Lhérisson.
Correction slips inserted.
1. Haitian literature (~~French~~)—Hist. & crit. 2. French literature—Haitian authors. 3. Haitian literature (Selections: Extracts, etc.)
A 46-1904
New York. Public library for Library of Congress [3]

Haiti MB L61p
Lherisson, Justin, 1873-1907.
Portraitins; 1ere serie. Port-au-Prince, Imp., H. Amblard, 1894.
44p. 18cm.
Contents: Windsor Bellegatde. -Etienne Mathon. -Stenio Vincent. - Mirabeau Drice. -Louis Borno. - Massillon Coicou. -Amedee Brun. -Arsene Chevry. -Georges Sylvain. -Seymour Pradel.
1. Haiti - Biography. I. Title.

Haiti M972.94 L61n
Lherisson, Lelia Justin.
Notions de lecture. Cours preparatoire et cours elementaire ouvrage adopte par le department de l'instruction publique. Port-au-Prince [1931]
101p. 21cm.
1. Haiti--Education.

Haiti M972.94 L61p
Lhérisson, Lélia Justin
Premières notions de lectures. Cours préparatoire 1re. partie, par Lélia J. Lhérisson... Port-au-Prince, Haiti Imprimerie du College vertiers, 1929.
70 2p. illus. 22cm.
1. Haiti - Education. 2. Haitian textbooks.
I. Title.

Haiti M972.94 L614g
Liautaud, Andre
Geographie d'Haiti. 2ème livre. Cours elementaire et moyen, par Andre Liautaud avec la collaboration de Melle. Jeanne Sylvain. [Port-au-Prince] Editions Henri Deschamps [n.d.]
82p. 19cm.
1. Haiti. I.Title.

M973 L614n
Liberation Committee for Africa.
Nationalism, colonialism and the United States one minute to twelve; a forum. First anniversary celebration, June 2, 1961. [New York] Photo-Offset Process, 1961.
39p. 23cm.
1. Africa. 2. Cuba. 3. Colonialism. I. Title. II. Killens, John O. III. Worthy, William. IV. Baldwin, James, 1924- I. Title: Cuba: America's lost colony. VI.Make, Vsumsi.

Liberia M966.6 L61d
Liberia
Declaration of independence in convention, Town of Monrovia, June and July, 1847. Monrovia, Liberia, Dept. of State, 1937.
7p. 20cm.
Reprinted August 1937.
1. Liberia - Politics and Government.
I. Declaration of Independence, 1847.

Liberia M966.6 L610
Liberia. Supreme court.
Opinions delivered by the honourable the Supreme court of the republic of Liberia in cases decided during its November term A.D. 1933 and its April term A.D. 1934- New annual series no. 1- Monrovia, Liberia, Printed by authority at the Government printing office [1934?-
v. 25-25cm.
1. Law reports, digests, etc. - Liberia.
I. Title.

Liberia M966.6 L61t
Liberia. Supreme Court.
Two of the opinions and judgments of the Honourable the Supreme Court of Liberia. Delivered during the November term of Court, A.D. 1936, with a foreword by the Hon. Arthur Barclay. Monrovia, Methodist Mission Press, 1937.
31 p. 22 cm.
Cases: Wolo v. Wolo, Alimony; Prout v. Cooper, Objections to the probation of a deed of lease.
1. Liberia - laws and regulation..

Liberia M966.6 L61s
Liberia Republic. Grand Lodge, F.A. & A.M.
Souvenir programme for the observance of the semi-centennial anniversary of the grand lodge, F.A. & A.M. of the Republic of Liberia. A.D. 1867-1917, A.L. 5867-5917. At Monrovia, Liberia, W.A. Commencing Sunday, December 23rd to Saint John Evangelist's day, December 27th, A.D. 1917, A.L. 5917. Monrovia, Liberia, College of West Africa press, 1917.
11p. 19½cm.
1. Liberia
2. Freemasons.

Liberia.
Liberia M966.6 Af8p
Africa and the Africans. Proceedings on the occasion of a banquet, given at the Holborn restaurant, August 15th, 1903, to Edward W. Blyden...by West Africans in London. London, C.M. Phillips, 1903.
69p. 21cm.

Liberia.
M326.5 Am3r
American colonization society.
Memorial of the semi-centennial anniversary of the American colonization society, celebrated at Washington, January 15, 1867. With documents concerning Liberia. Washington, The Society, 1867.
viii, [9]-191, [1] p. 24cm.
1. Slavery in the U. S.—Societies. 2. Liberia. 3. Negroes—Colonization—Africa.
4—19676
Library of Congress E448.A53
[44c1]

M326 An8s
Liberia.
Anti-slavery conference, Paris, 1867.
Special report of the Anti-slavery conference, held in Paris in the Salle Herz, on the twenty-sixth and twenty-seventh August, 1867, hon. president. M. le duc de Broglie. President. Mons. Edouard Laboulaye ... London, Committee of the British and foreign anti-slavery society [1867]
1 p. l., ii, 166p. 24cm.
Partial contents: -On the Republic of Liberia; by the Hon. W.R.W. Johnson.

Liberia.

M326.5 ⌈Armistead, Wilson⌉ 1819?–1868.
Ar5
Calumny refuted by facts from Liberia; with extracts from the inaugural address of the coloured President Roberts; an eloquent speech of Hilary Teage, a coloured senator; and extracts from a discourse by H. H. Garnett, a fugitive slave, on the past and present condition, and destiny of the coloured race. Presented to the Boston Anti-slavery bazaar, U. S., by the author of "A tribute for the negro". London, C. Gilpin; New York, W. Harned, Anti-slavery office; ⌈etc., etc.⌉ 1848.

46 p. 18cm.

1. Liberia. 2. Negroes—Colonization—Africa. I. Roberts, Joseph Jenkins, pres. of Liberia, 1809–1876. II. Teage, Hilary. III. Garnett, H. H. IV. Title.

⌈33b1⌉ 24–3758

Library of Congress DT632.A5

Liberia.

M326.5 ⌈Armistead, Wilson⌉ 1819?–1868.
Ar5
Calumny refuted by facts from Liberia; with extracts from the inaugural address of the coloured President Roberts; an eloquent speech of Hilary Teage, a coloured senator; and extracts from a discourse by H. H. Garnett, a fugitive slave, on the past and present condition, and destiny of the coloured race. Presented to the Boston Anti-slavery bazaar, U. S., by the author of "A tribute for the negro". London, C. Gilpin; New York, W. Harned, Anti-slavery office; ⌈etc., etc.⌉ 1848.

46 p. 18cm.

1. Liberia. 2. Negroes—Colonization—Africa. I. Roberts, Joseph Jenkins, pres. of Liberia, 1809–1876. II. Teage, Hilary. III. Garnett, H. H. IV. Title.

⌈33b1⌉ 24–3758

Library of Congress DT632.A5

Liberia.

M326.5 Armistead, Wilson
Ar5
Calumny refuted, by facts from Liberia; with extracts from the inaugural address of the coloured president Roberts; an eloquent speech of Hilary Teage, a coloured senator; and extracts from a discourse by H. H. Garnett, a fugitive slave, on the past and present condition, and destiny of the coloured race. Presented to the Boston anti-slavery bazaar, by the author of "A tribute for the Negro." London, Charles Gilpin, 1848.

46, 1ip. 18½cm.

Liberia.

Nigeria
M966.9 Azikiwe, Nnamdi, 1904–
Az2L
Liberia in world politics, by Nnamdi Azikiwe ... London, A. H. Stockwell, ltd., 1934 ⌈*i. e.* 1935⌉

406 p. 19cm.

Includes bibliographies.

1. Liberia.

⌈*Full name:* Benjamin Nnamdi Azikiwe⌉

35–12624

Library of Congress DT632.A93

⌈3⌉ 966.6

Liberia.

Liberia
M966.6 ⌈Barclay, Arthur⌉ 1854–
B23m
Message of the president of Liberia communicated to the first session of the thirtieth legislature. Monrovia, R.A. Phillips, Government Printing Office, 1905.

20p. 21½cm.

M966.6 Liberia.
B44f
Benson, Stephen Allen, 1816–
...Fourth annual message of Stephen A. Benson, president of Liberia, delivered to the legislature, December 1858.

23 p. 21½ cm.
From the New York colonization journal, April 1859.

Liberia.

Liberia
M966.6 Blyden, Edward Wilmot, 1832-1912.
B62c
1888
Christianity, Islam and the Negro race. By Edward W. Blyden... With an introduction by the Hon. Samuel Lewis ... 2d ed. London, W.B. Whittingham & co., 1888.

3p. l., xv, 432p. front. (port.) 21½cm.

Liberia.

Liberia
M966.6 Blyden, Edward Wilmot, 1832-1912.
B62c
1887
Christianity, Islam and the Negro race. By Edward W. Blyden... With an introduction by the Hon. Samuel Lewis. London, W.B. Whittingham & co., 1887.

vii, 423p.
Blyden's own copy containing his signature and corrections in his handwriting.

Liberia.

Liberia
M966.6 Blyden, Edward Wilmot, 1832-1912.
B62r
A voice from bleeding Africa, on behalf of her exiled children, by Edward W. Blyden. Liberia, G. Killian, printer 1856.

33p. 20cm.

Liberia.

M810 Brawley, Benjamin Griffith, 1882–1939.
B73so
A social history of the American Negro, being a history of the Negro problem in the United States, including a history and study of the republic of Liberia, by Benjamin Brawley. New York, The Macmillan company, 1921.

xv, 420 p. 22½cm.

"Select bibliography": p. 390–408.

1. Negroes. 2. Slavery in the U. S. 3. U. S.—Race question. 4. Liberia. I. Title.

21—15578

Library of Congress E185.61.B82

⌈a48g1⌉

M326.5
B81 Liberia.
⌈Brown, Thomas C ⌉
Examination of Mr. Thomas C. Brown, a free colored citizen of S. Carolina, as to the actual state of things in Liberia in the years 1833 and 1834, at the Chatham Street Chapel, May 9th & 10th, 1834. New York, S. W. Benedict, 1834.

40p. 22cm.

Liberia Liberia.
M966.6 Cassell, Nathaniel H. B.
C27l
The baccalaureate, a discourse delivered by the Rev. Nathaniel H.B. Cassell... to the graduating class of 1914 in Trinity Memorial Church, Monrovia, Monvoria, Liberia, College of West Africa press, 1915.

29 p. illus. 21½ cm.
(Bound with: The Liberian scholar, by Nathaniel H. B. Cassell)

Liberia.

M283 Crummell, Alexander
C88e
The English language in Liberia. The annual address before the citizens of Maryland county, Cape Palmas, Liberia-July 26, 1860, being the day of national independence, by the Rev. Alex Crummell... New York, Bunce and co., 1861.

32p. 24cm.

Liberia.

M283 Crummell, Alexander, 1819–1898.
C88f
The future of Africa: being addresses, sermons, etc., etc., delivered in the republic of Liberia. By Rev. Alex. Crummell ... New York, C. Scribner, 1862.

354 p. 19½cm.

1. Africa. 2. Liberia. 3. Negro race. I. Title.

15—7448

Library of Congress DT632.C7

⌈42f1⌉

Trinidad Liberia.
M966.6 Durham, Frederick Alexander.
D93
The lone-star of Liberia; being the outcome of reflections on our own people. By Frederick Alexander Durham, an African ... With an introduction by Madame la comtesse C. Hugo. London, E. Stock, 1892.

xxi p., 1 l., 331 p. 20cm.

Contents.—The Africo-American.—Is the Ethiopian inferior to the Caucasian?—Immorality.—Superstition in the nineteenth century.—Under Caucasian rule.—Africa governed by Africans.—Repatriation and Liberia.

1. Negroes—Colonization—Africa. ~~2. Negro race.~~ 3. Liberia. I. Title.

5—15427

Library of Congress DT631.D96

Liberia
Ellis, George Washington, 1875-1919.
M910. Liberia in the political psychology of West
E15L Africa, by George W. Ellis... Reprinted from the Journal of The African Society, 1912.
52-70p. 22cm.

Liberia.

Africa, West
M966 Graves, Anna Melissa, ed.
G78g
Benvenuto Cellini had no prejudice against bronze; letters from West Africans, edited by Anna Melissa Graves. ⌈Baltimore, Waverly press, inc., 1943⌉

lxvi, 176p. front., plates, ports. 23½cm.

Liberia.

Liberia
M966.6 Grimes, L A
G88
1924
Report and opinions of L.A. Grimes. Third annual series with appendices 1, 2 and 3. Submitted to the 2nd session of the 25th legislature of the Republic of Liberia. Monrovia, 1924.

84p. 27cm.

Liberia.

Liberia
M966.6 Grimes, L A
G88
1923
Report and opinions of L.A. Gromes. ⌈for⌉ 1923. ⌈submitted to the 1st session of the 35th legislature of the Republic of Liberia. Monrovia, 1923⌉

68p. 27cm.

Liberia Liberia.
M966.6 Grimes, Louis Arthur, 1883-1948.
G38
1922
Report submitted to the 4th session of the 34th legislature of the Republic of Liberia and opinion filed by the Attorney General during the year 1922 with index. n.p. 1922.

98p. 27cm.

Liberia.

Liberia
M966.6 Hale, Sarah Josepha (Buell) 1788–1879.
H13L
Liberia; or, Mr. Peyton's experiments. Edited by Mrs. Sarah J. Hale ... New York, Harper & brothers, 1853.

iv, ⌈5⌉–304 p. 19½ cm.

Appendix, p. ⌈245⌉–304 contains documents for the most part written by colored persons from and about Liberia.

I. Title.

6–46208

Library of Congress PZ3.H135L

⌈a35d1⌉

Liberia
M966.6
L610

Liberia.

Liberia. *Supreme court.*

Opinions delivered by the honourable the Supreme court of the republic of Liberia in cases decided during its November term A. D. 1933– New annual series no. 1– Monrovia, Liberia, Printed by authority at the Government printing office [1934?–

v. 25–26cm.

1. Law reports, digests, etc.—Liberia. I. Title.

38-19289

Library of Congress [2]

Liberia
M966.6
R54a

Liberia.

Roberts, Joseph Jenkins, 1809-1876.

An address delivered at the fifty-second annual meeting of the American Colonization Society held in Washington, D. C., January 19, 1869. New York, American Colonization Society, [1869]

16 p. 23 cm.

M338.9
G92s

Liberia.

Weeks, Rocheforte L

Liberia.

Pp. 38-44.

In: Science and the new nations, edited by Ruth Gruber. 1961.

Liberia
M966.6
L61s

Liberia.

Liberia Republic. Grand Lodge, F.A. & A.M.

Souvenir programme for the observance of the semi-centennial anniversary of the grand lodge, F.A. &A.M. of the Republic of Liberia. A.D. 1867-1917, A.L. 5867-5917. At Monrovia, Liberia, W.A. Commencing Sunday, December 23rd to Saint John Evangelist's day, December 27th, A.D. 1917, A.L. 5917. Monrovia, Liberia, College of West Africa press, 1917.

11p. 19½cm.

MB9
K41s

Liberia.

Smith, C C

The life and work of Jacob Kenoly, by C. C. Smith. Cincinnati ... Methodist Book Company, c1912.

160p. 19cm.

M973
W67

Liberia.

Williams, George Washington, 1849-1891.

History of the Negro race in America from 1619 to 1880. Negroes as slaves, as soldiers, and as citizens; together with a preliminary consideration of the unity of the human family, an historical sketch of Africa, and an account of the Negro governments of Sierra Leone and Liberia. By George W. Williams ... Popular ed. ... New York & London, G. P. Putnam's sons [c1882]

2 v. in 1. front. (port.) 24cm.

Vol. 2 has half-title only.

1. Negroes. 2. Sierra Leone. 3. Liberia.

26—4240

Library of Congress E185.W69 [43d1]

Liberia
M966.6
L61s

Liberia.

Liberia Republic. Grand Lodge, F.A. & A.M.

Souvenir programme for the observance of the semi-centennial anniversary of the grand lodge, F.A. & A.M. of the Republic of Liberia. A.D. 1867-1917, A. L. 5867-5917. At Monrovia, Liberia, W.A. Commencing Sunday, December 23rd to Saint John Evangelist's day, December 27th, A.D. 1917, A.L. 5917. Monrovia, Liberia, College of West Africa press, 1917.

11p. 19½cm.

M910
St4

Liberia.

Stewart, Thomas McCants, 1853–

Liberia: the Americo-African republic. Being some impressions of the climate, resources, and people, resulting from personal observations and experiences in West Africa. By T. McCants Stewart ... With an introduction by Dr. G. W. Samson ... New York, E. O. Jenkins' sons, 1886.

107 p. illus. 20½cm.

1. Liberia. I. Title.

5-15270 Revised

Library of Congress DT625.S85 [r30c2]

Liberia
M966.6
Y15r

Liberia.

Yancey, Ernest Jerome.

The recent Liberian crisis and its causes; an address delivered at Buffalo, New York, August 12 and 14, 1934 under auspices of the Buffalo Liberian research society, by Ernest Jerome Yancy... [n.p., n.p., c1934]

12p. 23½cm.

1. Liberia.

Liberia
M966.6
T79p

Liberia.

Liberian Information Service.

The plot that failed; the story of the attempted assisination of President Tubman. Monrovia, Liberian Information Service [1959]

68p. ports. 21cm.

Autographed: "This was stolen from my house John B. Falconer by Arthur Spingarn."

Liberia
M966.6
T36

Liberia.

Thomas, W H

History of Liberia (revised and illustrated). Brewerville, Liberia, Lott Carey Mission press [1935] [ivy 61p. plates. 20½cm.

Liberia
M966.6
R391

Liberia.— Biographies.

Richardson, Nathaniel R

Liberia's past and present. London, The Diplomatic Press and Publishing Company, 1959.

348p. illus. ports. 28cm.

1. Liberia - History. 2. Liberia - Biographies.

Liberia
M966.6
L62

Liberia.

The Liberian year book. 1956–

London, Diplomatic Press and Pub. Co.

v. illus., ports., maps, diagrs. 22 cm.

Compiler: 1956– H. B. Cole.

1956

1. Liberia. I. Cole, Henry B., comp.

DT621.L53 916.66 56—45736

Library of Congress [57h5]

Liberia
M966.6
T79p

Liberia.

Tubman, William V S *Pres. Liberia*, 1895–

President Tubman of Liberia speaks; edited by E. Reginald Townsend. London, Consolidated Publications Co. [1959]

301 p. illus. 25 cm.

Portrait of author on book jacket.

1. Liberia.

DT624.T8 923.1666 60-34031 ‡

Library of Congress [1]

Liberia
M966.6
An2n

Liberia - Description and travel.

Anderson, Benjamin J K *b.* 1834.

Narrative of a journey to Musardu, the capital of the western Mandingoes. By Benjamin Anderson. New-York, S. W. Green, printer, 1870.

118 p. front. (fold. map) 2 pl. 18½cm.

—— Appendix to Benj. Anderson's Journey to Musadu. An exact fac-simile of a letter from the king of Musadu to the president of Liberia, written by a young Mandingo, at Musadu, in Arabic, in the latter part of 1868. Printed from photo-

(Continued on next card)

5-15274-5 Revised

[r42b2]

M910.
P54L

Liberia.

Phillips, Hilton Alonzo, 1905–

Liberia's place in Africa's sun, by Hilton Alonzo Phillips ... with a foreword by Hon. Hugh E. MacBeth ... New York, N. Y., The Hobson book press, 1946.

2 p. l., vii-xviii, 156 p. 21½cm.

Reproduced from type-written copy.

Bibliography: p. [153]–156.

1. Liberia. I. Title.

46-5061

Library of Congress DT632.P5 [5] 966.6

M910
W17r

Liberia.

Walton, Lester Agar, 1881–

Remarks of the Hon. Lester A. Walton... at cornerstone laying of the American Legation, Monrovia, Liberia, December 24, 1939. Monrovia, Liberia, The Lone Star Publishing co.

3 p. 15 cm.

Liberia
M966.6
An2n

Liberia.- Description and travel.

Anderson, Benjamin J K *b.* 1834. Narrative of a journey to Musardu ... 1870. (Card 2)

graphic relief plates. With a translation by the Rev. Edward W. Blyden ... New York, Lithographing, engraving & printing co., 1870.

14 p. 2 fold. facsim. 18½cm. [*With his* Narrative of a journey to Musardu. New-York, 1870]

1. Liberia—Descr. & trav. I. Blyden, Edward Wilmot, 1832–1912, tr.

5-15274-5 Revised

Library of Congress DT625.A54 [r42b2]

M326.5
P98r

Liberia.

Putnam, Lewis H

A review of the cause and the tendency of the issues between the two sections of the country, with a plan to consolidate the views of the people of the United States in favor of emigration to Liberia, as the initiative to the efforts to transform the present system of labor in the southern states into a free agricultural tenantry, by the respective legislatures with the support of Congress to make it a national measure. By Lewis H. Putnam...Albany,N.Y.,Weed Parsons & co., 1859.

29p. 24cm.

M338.9
G92s

Liberia.

Weeks, Rochsforte L

Liberia.

Pp. 38-44.

In: Science and the new nations, edited by Ruth Gruber. 1961.

M910
B64L

Liberia - Description and travel.

Boone, Clinton C

Liberia as I know it, by C. C. Boone ...
Richmond, Va. [n.d.] 1929.

xvi, 152p. illus. 21cm.

Liberia - Description and travel.

M910
D29t

Davis, Stanley A
This is Liberia; a brief history of this land of contradictions, with biographies of its founders and builders. New York, William-Frederick Press, 1953.
151 p. 23 cm.

1. Liberia—Descr. & trav. I. Title.
DT626.D3 966.6 52-12928 ‡
Library of Congress ₍3₎

Liberia - Description and travel.

M910
D37o

Delany, Martin Robison, 1812-1885
Official report of the Niger Valley exploring party. By M. R. Delany, chief commissioner to Africa. New York, T. Hamilton; ₍etc., etc.₎ 1861.
4 p. l., ₍5₎-75 p. 22½cm.

1. Liberia—Descr. & trav. 2. Yoruba—Descr. & trav. 3. Negroes—Colonization—Africa. I. Delany, Martin Robison, 1812-1885. II. Title.
5-15242
Library of Congress DT513.N68
——— Copy 2.

Liberia - Description and travel.

M301
D853v

Du Bois, William Burghardt, 1868-
A voyage to Liberia.

(In: Baker, Carlos Heard, ed. The American looks at the world. New York, Harcourt, Brace, 1944. 21cm. pp. 159-165).

Liberia - Description and travel.

M910.
H35b

Heard, William H 1850-
The bright side of African life, illustrated by Hon. William H. Heard ... Philadelphia, A. M. E. publishing house, ₍1898₎
2 p. l., 9-184 p. incl. illus., plates, ports. ports., fold. map. 22cm.
An account of Liberia.

1. Liberia—Descr. & trav. I. Title.
98-1026
Library of Congress DT626.H43
Copyright 1898: 49870 ₍37r28e1₎

Liberia - Description and travel.

Trinidad
M910
M69

Mitchell, Francis, 1910-
Grown up Liberia, by Francis Mitchell ... ₍Philadelphia, West Philadelphia multigraphing and printing company ₍1946₎ °1945.
144 p. plates. 22cm.

1. Liberia—Descr. & trav. I. Title.
46-21719
Library of Congress DT626.M55
₍47c1₎ 916.66

Liberia - Description & travel.

M910
M83

Morris, Wilson Major, 1884-
Africa, the great continent. New York, North River Press ₍1954₎
80 p. illus. 26 cm.

1. Africa, South—Descr. & trav. 2. Liberia—Descr. & trav. I. Title.
DT626.M62 916.66 54-4420 ‡
Library of Congress ₍5₎

Liberia - Economic conditions.

M910
B81

Brown, George William.
The economic history of Liberia, by George W. Brown ... Washington, D. C., The Associated publishers, inc. ₍°1941₎
2 p. l., iii-ix, 366 p. 23½cm.
Presented as the author's thesis (PH. D.) at the London school of economics and political science, 1938. *cf.* Acknowledgments.
"Selected bibliography": p. 310-323.

1. Liberia—Econ. condit. I. Title.
41-13981
Library of Congress HC591.L6B74
₍45i1₎ 330.9666

Liberia - Economic conditions.

Liberia
M966.6
In8e

International Commission of Inquiry.
Report ... Slavery and forced labor in the Republic of Liberia, Monrovia, Liberia, Sept. 8, 1930. Washington, D.C., Government Printing Office, 1931.

227p. 23cm.

Liberia-Education.

Liberia
M966.6
C271

Cassell, Nathaniel H. B.
The Liberian scholar, being the annual address delivered on the occasion of the commencement exercises of the College of West Africa, by the Rev. Nathaniel H. B. Cassell at the Hall of representatives, Monrovia, Liberia, Nov. 17th, 1915. Monrovia, Liberia, The government's printing press [1915.]

18p. 21½cm.

M 910
W17e

Liberia--Education.
Walton, Lester Agar, 1881-
Education; Commencement address delivered to the members of the graduating class of Liberia College, Monrovia, November 30, 1938. Monrovia, Liberia, Weekly Mirror, ₍1938₎.

8p. 22cm.

Liberia - History.

Liberia
M966.6
R391

Richardson, Nathaniel R
Liberia's past and present. London, The Diplomatic Press and Publishing Company, 1959.

348p. illus. ports. 28cm.

1. Liberia - History. 2. Liberia - Biographies.

Liberia - History.

Liberia
MB9
Si5me

Simpson, Clarence Lorenzo, 1896-
The memoirs of C. L. Simpson, former Liberian Ambassador to Washington and to the Court of St. James's; the symbol of Liberia. London, Diplomatic Press and Pub. Co. ₍1961₎
298 p. illus. 23 cm.

1. Liberia—Hist. I. Title.
DT636.S5A3 966.6 61-65890 ‡
Library of Congress ₍2₎

M910
T85u

Liberia - History.
Turner, Walter Lee
Under the skin in Africa; a complete outline of the history of the Republic of Liberia. Hot Springs, Arkansas, Connelly Printing Co., 1928.

152p. port. 18½cm.

Liberia - History.

M910
W15h

Walker, Thomas Hamilton Beb, 1873-
History of Liberia, by Thomas H. B. Walker ... Boston, The Cornhill publishing company ₍°1921₎
xx p., 1 l., 175 p. incl. front. plates, ports. 18½cm.

1. Liberia—Hist.
23-1388
Library of Congress DT631.W3
——— Copy 2.
Copyright A 654227 ₍41d1₎

Liberia—History.

Liberia
M966.6
Y15h

Yancy, Ernest Jerome.
Historical lights of Liberia's yesterday and today, by Ernest Jerome Yancy, A. B. ₍Xenia, O., The Aldine publishing company, °1934₎
xi, ₍1₎ p., 1 l., 15-323 p. incl. illus., port. 20cm.
"First edition."
Bibliography: p. xi.
Music: p. 293-302.

1. Liberia—Hist. 2. Liberia—Pol. & govt. I. Title.
35-608
Library of Congress DT631.Y3
——— Copy 2.
Copyright A 79022 ₍36d2₎ 966.6

M811.5
T58l

Liberia-History-Poetry.
Tolson, Melvin Beaunorus.
Libretto for the Republic of Liberia. New York, Twayne Publishers ₍1953₎
unpaged. 22 cm.

1. Liberia—Hist.—Poetry. I. Title.
PS3539.O334L5 811.5 53-13482 ‡
Library of Congress ₍7₎

M910
R56

Liberia - Juvenile literature.
Robison, Lois
Let's go; teacher's book, junior. Greenwich, Connecticut, The Seabury Press, 1952.

48p. illus. 21cm.

1.

Liberia
M966.6
L61t

Liberia - Laws and regulation.
Liberia. Supreme Court.
Two of the opinions and judgments of the Honourable the Supreme Court of Liberia. Delivered during the November term of Court, A.D. 1936, with a foreword by the Hon. Arthur Barclay. Monrovia, Methodist Mission Press, 1937.

31 p. 22 cm.
Cases: Wolo v. Wolo, Alimony; Prout v. Cooper, Objections to the probation of a deed of lease.

Liberia-Missions.

Liberia
M966.6
P93L

Price, Frederick A
Liberian odyssey "by hammock and surfboat"; the autobiography of F. A. Price. ₍1st ed.₎ New York, Pageant Press ₍1954₎
200 p. illus. 26 cm.

1. Missions—Liberia. I. Title.
BV3625.L6P7 922.7666 54-9267 ‡
Library of Congress ₍3₎

Liberia
M966.6
L61d

Liberia - Politics and Government.
Liberia
Declaration of independence in convention, Town of Monrovia, June and July, 1847. Monrovia, Liberia, Dept. of State, 1937.

7p. 20cm.
Reprinted August 1937.

Liberia - Politics and government.

Liberia
M966.6
Y15 h

Yancy, Ernest Jerome.
Historical lights of Liberia's yesterday and today, by Ernest Jerome Yancy, A. B. ₍Xenia, O., The Aldine publishing company, °1934₎
xi, ₍1₎ p., 1 l., 15-323 p. incl. illus., port. 20cm.
"First edition."
Bibliography: p. xi.
Music: p. 293-302.

1. Liberia—Hist. 2. Liberia—Pol. & govt. I. Title.
35-608
Library of Congress DT631.Y3
——— Copy 2.
Copyright A 79022 ₍36d2₎ 966.6

Liberia - Politics and government.

Liberia
M966.6
Y15re

Yancy, Ernest Jerome
The Republic of Liberia. London, George Allen & Unwin, 1959.

144p. port. illus. 18½cm.

Liberia-Postal service.

Liberia
M966.6
K14

Karnga, Abayomi.
Liberia official postal guide. Monrovia, The Montserrado Printing and publishing co., 1923.

28p. 20cm.

Liberia - Presidents.

M910
W15p

Walker, Thomas Hamilton Beb 1873-
The presidents of Liberia. A biographical sketch for students. Containing biographies of the presidents and some of the leaders in the making of the republic. With portraits, by Thos. H. B. Walker ... Jacksonville, Fla. [Mintz printing co.] 1915.

4 p. l., 11-96, [7] p. incl. plates, ports. 19½cm. $1.25

1. Liberia—Presidents. I. Title.

15-8010

Library of Congress DT636.A3W3
——— Copy 2.
Copyright A 398286

Liberia: the Americo-African republic.

M910
St4

Stewart, Thomas McCants, 1853-
Liberia: the Americo-African republic. Being some impressions of the climate, resources, and people, resulting from personal observations and experiences in West Africa. By T. McCants Stewart ... With an introduction by Dr. G. W. Samson ... New York, E. O. Jenkins' sons, 1886.

107 p. illus. 20½cm.

1. Liberia. I. Title.

Library of Congress DT625.S85 5-15270 Revised
[r30c2]

Liberia College.

Liberia
M966.6
B62ai

Blyden, Edward Wilmot, 1832-1912.
The aims and methods of a liberal education for Africans. Inaugural address, delivered by Edward Wilmot Blyden, January 5, 1881. Cambridge, John Wilson and Son, 1882.

30p. 23cm.

Liberian odyssey "by hammock and surfboat".

Liberia
M966.6
P93L

Price, Frederick A
Liberian odyssey "by hammock and surfboat"; the autobiography of F. A. Price. [1st ed.] New York, Pageant Press [1954]

269 p. illus. 26 cm.

1. Missions—Liberia. I. Title.

BV3625.L6P7 922.7666 54-9267 ‡

Library of Congress [8]

Liberia
M966.6
T79p

Liberian Information Service
The plot that failed; the story of the attempted assisination of President Tubman. Monrovia, Liberian Information Service [1959]

68p. ports. 21cm.
Autographed: "This was stolen from my house John B. Falconer by Arthur Spingarn."

1. Liberia. I. Title. II. Tubman, William V.S., Pres. of Liberia, 1895.

The Liberian scholar...

Liberia
M966.6
C271

Cassell, Nathaniel H. B.
The Liberian scholar, being the annual address delivered on the occasion of the commencement exercises of the College of West Africa, by the Rev. Nathaniel H. B. Cassell at the Hall of representatives, Monrovia, Liberia, Nov. 17th, 1915. Monrovia, Liberia, The government's printing press [1915]

18-. 21½cm.

Liberia
M966.6
L62

The Liberian year book. 1956-
London, Diplomatic Press and Pub. Co.

v. illus., ports., maps, diagrs. 22 cm.

Compiler: 1956- H. B. Cole.
1956

1. Liberia. I. Cole, Henry B., comp.

DT621.L53 916.66 56-45736

Library of Congress [57h5]

Liberia's place in Africa's sun.

M910
P54L

Phillips, Hilton Alonzo, 1905-
Liberia's place in Africa's sun, by Hilton Alonzo Phillips ... with a foreword by Hon. Hugh E. MacBeth ... New York, N. Y., The Hobson book press, 1946.

2 p. l., vii-xviii, 156 p. 21½cm.

Reproduced from type-written copy.
Bibliography: p. [153]-156.

1. Liberia. I. Title.

46-5061

Library of Congress DT632.P5
[5] 966.6

Liberté.

Senegal
M960
Se5

Senghor, Léopold Sédar, 1906-
Liberte. Paris, Éditions du Seuil, 1964-

v. 20½cm.
Contents.- v.1. Negritude et humanisme.

I. Liberté. II. Title: Negritude and humanisme.

Uganda
M323
B31

Liberty.
Lucas, Eric, ed.
What is freedom. London, Oxford University Press, 1963.

136p. 18cm.

M342
R15

Liberty.

Randolph, Asa Philip, 1889-
Chart and compass.

(In: Wise , James W. Our Bill of rights: what it means to me, ... New York, Bill of Rights Sesqui-centennial Committee, 1941. pp. 112-113.)

M326.
Sc71

Liberty.
Scarlett, George Chandler, 1880-
Laws against liberty, by George C. Scarlett ... New York, N. Y. [Cosmos printing co., inc., °1937]

185 p. 21cm.

1. Liberty. 2. Negroes. 3. U. S.—Race question. 4. Slavery in the U. S. I. Title.

A 39-1029

Yale law school. Library for Library of Congress [40c1]

Ghana
M89
D23

Liberty.
Danquah, Joseph Kwame Kyeretwie Boakye, 1895-1965.
Liberty; a page from the life of J. B. Accra, H. K. Akyeampong [1960]

34p. illus., ports. 22cm.

Liberty Baptist Church, Chicago

see

Chicago. Liberty Baptist Church

M326.
L61

The Liberty bell. By friends of freedom .. Boston, Massachusetts anti-slavery fair, 1839-46; National anti-slavery bazaar, 1847-58.

v. plates, ports. 17½-20cm.

"Edited and published annually in Boston, by Maria Weston Chapman, 1843 to 1858 (one or two years being omitted)"—Samuel May, Catalogue of anti-slavery publications in America.
No volumes issued for 1840, 1850, 1854-55, 1857. cf. Faxon, Literary annuals and gift books.

Library has: 1839, 1848.

1. Slavery in the U. S. 2. Gift-books (Annuals, etc.) I. Chapman, Maria (Weston) 1806-1885, ed. II. Massachusetts anti-slavery fair, III. National anti-slavery bazaar, Boston.

5-22887

Library of Congress E449.L69
[4311]

M784
C541

The liberty minstrel.
Clark, George W.
The liberty minstrel... by Geo. W. Clark. New York, Leavitt & Alden, etc., 1845.

184 [3]p. 18½cm.
Contains music-

Liberty of the press-Guadeloupe.

Guadeloupe
M972.97
B59c

Blanche, Lenis.
... Contribution à l'histoire de la presse à la Guadeloupe, par Lenis Blanche ... [Basse-Terre, Imprimerie catholique] 1935.

xiv, 85 p., 2 l. 28cm.

At head of title: Gouvernement de la Guadeloupe et dépendances.
"Publié à l'occasion du Tricentenaire des Antilles."

1. Press—Guadeloupe. 2. Liberty of the press—Guadeloupe. I. Guadeloupe.

37-7918

Library of Congress PN4969.G82B6
[3] 071.297

Haiti
M841.
L616b

Libose, Jean.
... Bouquet à la naïade, poème ... Port-au-Prince, Impr. du Collège Vertières, 1941.

3 p. l., v-xii, [12] p. 18½cm. (Bibliothèque haïtienne ... Collection capoise)

I. Title. 1. Haitian poetry.

44-53509

Library of Congress PQ3949.L53B6
[2] 841.91

Haiti
M841
L616p

Libose, Jean.
Une palme et des roses, poèmes. Port-au-Prince, Imprimerie du College Vertieres, 1941.

41p. 18cm.

1. Haitian poetry. I. Title.

Haiti M841 B94c
Libose, Jean
Burr-Reynaud, Frederic, 1884-
...La corbeille-poemes de Fred Burr-Reynaud, Luc Grimard, Dominique Hippolyte, Jean Libose, Edgar N. Numa. Port-au-Prince, Haiti, Imprimerie du College Vertieres, 1943.
34p. 19cm.

M026 H83a
Libraries - Special collections.
Howard University, Washington, D.C. Founders Library. Moorland Foundation.
The Arthur B. Spingarn collection of Negro authors. Washington, D.C. [1948]
[7]p. facisms. 21cm.

M261 L61s
Licorish, David Nathaniel, 1904-
Salute in Ghana - day of deliverance. New York, Abyssinian Baptist Church, 1957.
14p. 21cm.
1. Ghana.

M027 G47
Libraries.
Gleason, Eliza Valeria (Atkins) 1909-
The southern Negro and the public library; a study of the government and administration of public library service to Negroes in the South, by Eliza Atkins Gleason, with a foreword by Louis R. Wilson. Chicago, Ill., The University of Chicago press [1941]
xvi, 218 p. incl. tables, diagrs. 21 cm. (*Half-title:* The University of Chicago studies in library science)
Issued also in part as thesis (PH. D.) Chicago university, under title: The government and administration of public library service to Negroes in the South.
Bibliography: p. 199-202.
1. Libraries and Negroes. 2. Libraries—Southern states. I. Title.
Library of Congress Z711.9.G6 41—52062
[48r43x2] 027.636

M016.8 Oa4n 1937
Libraries - Special collections.
Oakland, California. Free Library.
The Negro literature collection; Books of Negro authorship to be found in the Oakland Free Library. Oakland, California, 1937.
11p. 22cm.
Mimeographed.

M261 L61t
Licorish, David Nathaniel, 1904-
Tomorrow's church in today's world; a study of the twentieth-century challenge to religion. [1st ed.] New York, Exposition Press [1956]
172 p. 21 cm.
1. Church and social problems. 2. Church. I. Title.
HN31.L55 *261.8 56-9408 ‡
Library of Congress [2]

M026 B63l
Libraries--Special collections.
Bolivar, William C
Library of William C. Bolivar, Philadelphia, Pennsylvania; Together with printed tracts, magazines, articles, reports, addresses and miscellaneous not enumerated; Americana, Negroana, manuscripts, autograph letters, Lincolniana, rare pamphlets, travels, Africana, etc... Philadelphia, 1914.
32p. 22cm.
Inscription on cover.

M026 P831
Libraries - Special collections
Porter, Dorothy Burnett, 1905-
A library on the Negro. The American scholar, 7:115-117, Winter 1938.
115-117p. 25cm.
Detached copy.

Congo Leopoldville M967.5 L97p
Lierde, Jean Van.
Lumumba, Patrice, 1925-1961
La pensée politique de Patrice Lumumba. Préface de Jean-Paul Sartre. Textes recueillis et présentes par Jean Van Lierde. Bruxelles, Le Livre Africaine, 1963.
401p. port. 21½cm.

M026 B64j
Libraries - Special Collections.
Bontemps, Arna Wendell, 1902-
The James Weldon Johnson Memorial Collection of Negro Arts and Letters. Yale University Library Gazette, 18:18-26, October 1943.
18-26p. port. 26cm.

M026 V26c
Libraries--Special collection.
Van Jackson, Wallace.
The Countee Cullen Memorial Collection at Atlanta University. Reprint from the Crisis, May 1947.
2p. 28cm.

M813.3 N312
The life and adventure of Zamba.
Neilson, Peter, 1795-1861.
The life and adventure of Zamba, an African negro king; and his experience of slavery in South Carolina. Written by himself. Corrected and arranged by Peter Neilson. London, Smith, Elder and co., 1847.
xx, 258 p. front. 20½ cm.
Written by Peter Neilson. *cf.* Dict. nat. biog.
1. Slavery in the U. S.—Fiction. 2. South Carolina—Soc. life & cust. I. Title.
Library of Congress PZ3.N318L 7—33168
[a28d1]

M026 B64s
Libraries - Special collections
Bontemps, Arna Wendell, 1902-
Special collections of Negroana. Reprinted from the Library quarterly, 14:187-206, June 1944.
187-206p. 24cm.

M026 P831
A library on the Negro.
Porter, Dorothy Burnett, 1905-
A library on the Negro. The American scholar, 7:115-117, Winter 1938.
115-117p. 25cm.
Detached copy.

Brit. Guiana M823.91 M691
The life and death of Sylvia.
Mittelhölzer, Edgar.
The life and death of Sylvia. London, Secker and Warburg, 1953.
287 p. 21 cm.
I. Title.
PZ3.M6977Li 53-31369 rev ‡
Library of Congress [r54b2]

M780 F54s
Libraries - Special collections
Fisk University. Nashville. Library.
Selected items from the George Gershwin Memorial collection of music and musical literature, founded by Carl Van Vechten. Nashville, 1947.
32p. 22cm.

M811.5 T58l
Libretto for the Republic of Liberia.
Tolson, Melvin Beaunorus.
Libretto for the Republic of Liberia. New York, Twayne Publishers [1953]
unpaged. 22 cm.
1. Liberia—Hist.—Poetry. I. Title.
PS3539.O334L5 811.5 53-13482 ‡
Library of Congress [7]

Brit. Guiana M823.91 M69l 1954
The life and death of Sylvia.
Mittelholzer, Edgar
The life and death of Sylvia, a novel. New York, John Day, 1954.
316p. 21cm.

M026 O95g
Libraries - Special collections.
Gumby, L S Alexander.
The Gumby scrapbook collection of Negroana. Columbia library world, v.5, no.1, January 1951.
8p. 22cm.

M261 L61
Licorish, David Nathaniel, 1904-
Adventures for today, by David Nathaniel Licorish. New York, Fortuny's [c1939]
111 [1] p. 19½cm.
1. Churches. I. Title.

Brit. Guiana M823.91 M69sy
The life and death of Sylvia, a novel.
Mittelhölzer, Edgar, 1909-
The life and death of Sylvia, a novel. [1st American ed.] New York, J. Day Co. [1953] [Dell Pub. Co.]
316 p. 21 cm.
I. Title.
PZ3.M6977Li 2 54-5014 ‡
Library of Congress [5]

The life and struggles of Negro toilers.
Trinidad
M330 Padmore, George, 1903-
P131 The life and struggles of Negro toilers, by George Padmore. London, Published by the R.I.L.U. Magazine for the International trade union committee of Negro workers, 1931.
126p. 22cm.

The life of Josiah Henson...
M326.99B Henson, Josiah, 1789-1881.
H39t The life of Josiah Henson, formerly a slave, now an inhabitant of Canada, as narrated by himself. London, Charles Gilpin, 1852.
iv, 76p. 17cm.

Light - Velocity.
M530 Alexis, Lucien Victor
A12s Simple formulae for measuring atoms, their speed, and the speed of light.
New Orleans, The Author, 1937.
[3]p. 21cm.

Life and health.
S. Africa
M968 Molema, Silas M
M73L Life and health, being health lectures delivered to Bechuanaland Bantu Societies... S. M. Molema... Lovedale, South Africa, Lovedale institution press 1924
69p. 18½cm.

Life on the Negro frontier.
M267.3 Arthur, George Robert, 1879-
Ar7 Life on the Negro frontier; a study of the objectives and the success of the activities promoted in the Young men's Christian associations operating in "Rosenwald" buildings [by] George R. Arthur. New York, Association press, 1934.
viii, 259 p. plates, maps. 19½cm.
1. Young men's Christian associations (Colored) 2. Rosenwald, Julius, 1862-1932. 3. Julius Rosenwald fund. 4. Negroes—Moral and social conditions. I. Title.
35-27187
Library of Congress BV1190.A7
——— Copy 2.
Copyright A 84475 [5-5] 267.3650973

Light ahead for the Negro.
M323 Johnson, Edward Augustus, 1860-
J631 Light ahead for the Negro, by E. A. Johnson ... New York, The Grafton press [1904]
vi p., 1 l., 132 p. 19½cm.
1. Negroes. I. Title.
4-27902
Library of Congress E185.6.J67
Copyright [a38b1]

Life can be meaningful.
M248 Harris, Marquis Lafayette, 1907-
H241 Life can be meaningful. Boston, Christopher [1951]
195 p. 21 cm.
1. Christian life. I. Title.
BV4501.H284 248 51-4686
Library of Congress [5]

The life story of Zik.
Nigeria
MB9 Mbah, A N
Az3m The life story of Zik. Onitsha, Nigeria, Appolos Brothers [1961]
32p. 18cm.

Light and shadows.
M811.5 Eastmond, Claude T.
Ea7 Light and shadows, by Claude T. Eastmond. Boston, The Christopher publishing house [1934]
1 p. l., [5]-66 p. 21cm.
Poems.
I. Title.
34-1959
Library of Congress PS3509.A754L5 1934
Copyright A 69220 [2] 811.5

Life line poems.
M811.5 Deas, Katherine.
D34L Life line poems. Chicago, Edward C. Deas.
32p. port. 18cm.

Life's red sea and other poems.
M811.5 Winston, Bessie Brent.
W731 Life's red sea and other poems. Washington, Review and Herald publishing association, 1950.
32p. 14cm.

Light and truth.
M318 Lewis, Robert Benjamin
L58 Light and truth; collected from the Bible
1851 and ancient and modern history, containing the universal history of the colored an the Indian race, from the creation of the world to the present time. By R.B. Lewis... Boston, Published by Moses H. Taylor, 1851.
viii, 9-400p. 19cm.

Life of Albert R. Parsons.
MB9 [Parsons, Lucy Eldine (Gonzalez)]
P25p Life of Albert R. Parsons, with brief history of the labor movement in America ... Chicago, L. E. Parsons, 1889.
4 p. l., xxviii p., 2 l., 254 p. front., plates, ports., facsims., diagr. 22½cm.
1. Parsons, Albert Richard, 1848-1887. 2. Labor and laboring classes—U. S.—Hist. 3. Chicago. Haymarket square riot, 1886. I. Title.
15—1424
Library of Congress HX843.P3
[45r42d1]

Lift every voice.
MB Quarles, Benjamin, jt. auth.
Qu26 ~~Sterling, Dorothy, 1913-~~
Lift every voice; the lives of Booker T. Washington, W. E. B. Du Bois, Mary Church Terrell, and James Weldon Johnson [by] Dorothy Sterling and Benjamin Quarles. Illustrated by Ernest Crichlow. [1st ed.] Garden City, N. Y., Doubleday, 1965.
116 p. illus., ports. 22 cm. (Zenith books)
1. Washington, Booker Taliaferro, 1859-1915—Juvenile literature. 2. Du Bois, William Edward Burghardt, 1868-1963—Juvenile literature. 3. Terrell, Mary (Church) 1863-1954—Juvenile literature. 4. Johnson, James Weldon, 1871-1938—Juvenile literature. I. Quarles, Benjamin, joint author. II. Title.
E185.96.S77 920.073 65-17237
Library of Congress [5]

Light and truth.
M318 Lewis, Robert Benjamin.
L58 Light and truth; collected from the Bible and ancient and modern history, containing the universal history of the colored and the Indian race, from the creation of the world to the present time. By R. B. Lewis ... Boston, Pub. by a committee of colored gentlemen, B. F. Roberts, printer, 1844.
viii, [9]-400 p. 18½ cm.
Originally issued in four monthly numbers, 1843? Copyright notice, 1836.
1. History, Ancient. 2. Negro race. 3. Indians—Origin. I. Title.
13—21188
Library of Congress D22.L5
[37b1-]

The life of Autumn Holliday.
Virgin Islands
M813.5 Pretto, Clarita C ,1934?-
P92 The life of Autumn Holliday; a novel. New York, Exposition Press, [1958]
95p. 20cm.

Lift every voice for victory.
M355.2 Jones, Claudia.
J73L Lift every voice for victory. New York, New Age, 1942.
14p. illus. 19cm.

The light and truth of slavery.
M326.99B Aaron's history. [Worcester, Mass., 184-?]
L62a 48p. illus. 23cm.
Caption title.
1. Slavery in the U.S. - Condition of slaves. 2. Aaron (slave)
3. Slave narratives

A life of Azikiwe.
Ghana
K39 Jones-Quartey, Kansen Asaasah Bremkong, 192?-
Az3j A life of Azikiwe. Baltimore, Penguin Books [1965]
272p. 18cm.
1. Azikiwe, Benjamin Nnamdi, 1904-
I. Title.

M323.2 Lifting the barriers at Sydenham Hospital.
L62 New York, Sydenham Institution,
18p. illus. 23cm.
1. Sydenham Hospital, New York.

Light from the Talmud.
M296 Russell, Charles L ed. and tr.
R91 Light from the Talmud ... by Charles L. Russell. New York, Bloch Publishing Co., 1942.
iv, 200p. incl. tab. 20cm.
Hebrew and English on opposite pages.

The light still shines.

M89 K251s
Keene, Royal D , 1895-
The light still shines. New York, Carlton Press, 1961.

40p. illus., ports. 20½cm.

M323 L73
Lightfoot, Claude.
Building a Negro and white alliance for Progress.
Pp. 22-45.

In: Winston, Henry M. Negro freedom. New York, New Current Publishers, 1964.

M335 L62
Lightfoot, Claude
The Negro question in the U.S.A.; resolution adopted by the 17th convention of the Communist party, U.S.A. together with the address to the convention by Claude Lightfoot. [New York, New Century Publishers, 1960]
23p. 20cm.

1. Race question. 2. Communism - U.S. I. Title.

M335.4 L62
Lightfoot, Claude
Turning point in freedom road; the fight to end jim crow now. New York, New Century Publishers, 1962.

32p. 18½cm.

1. Communism. 2. Race problems. I. Title.

Jamaica Lights and shadows of Jamaica history;
M972.92 H551
Hill, Richard, 1795-1872
Lights and shadows of Jamaica history; being three lectures delivered in aid of the mission schools of the colony, by Richard Hill...to which is added an appendix, with Ford and Gall's map of the island. Kingston, Ford and Gall, 1859.
164p. map. 19cm.

Haiti M396 L62
Ligue féminine d'action sociale (*Haiti*)
Femmes haïtiennes. [Port-au-Prince, H. Deschamps, 1953?]
263 p. 21 cm. (Collection du tricinquantenaire de l'indépendance d'Haïti)

1. Women in Haiti—Biog. I. Title. 2. Haiti-women.

F1914.L55 54-27866
Library of Congress [1]

Like one of the family...

M818.5 C431
Childress, Alice.
Like one of the family; conversations from a domestic's life. Brooklyn, Independence Publishers [1956]
226 p. illus. 21 cm.

I. Title.

PS3505.H76L5 818.5 56-9741 ‡
Library of Congress [2]

Li'l gal.

M811.4 D91Lig
Dunbar, Paul Laurence, 1872-1906.
Li'l' gal, by Paul Laurence Dunbar; illustrated with photographs by Leigh Richmond Miner ... decorations by Margaret Armstrong. New York, Dodd, Mead and co., 1904.
123, [1] p. incl. front., illus. 22½cm.
Ornamental borders.

I. Title.

4—30074
Library of Congress PS1556.L5 1904
[45f1]

Lillian Simmons.

M813.5 Sh1
Shackelford, Otis M 1871-
Lillian Simmons; or, The conflict of sections; a story by Otis M. Shackelford ... illustrated by William Hamilton. Kansas City, Mo., Burton publishing company [c1915]
2 p. l., 7-210 p. incl. plates. pl. 21cm. $1.50

1. U. S.—Race question—Fiction. I. Title.

15-16441
Library of Congress PZ3.S5228L
Copyright A 411052

M89 L631i
Lilly, William E.
Set my people free; a Negro's life of Lincoln, by William E. Lilly. New York, Farrar & Rinehart, incorporated [c1932]
viii, 269 p. front. (port.) 22½cm.

1. Lincoln, Abraham, pres. U. S., 1809-1865. I. Title.

32—1497
Library of Congress E457.L732
[43h1] 923.173

M89 L631i
Lilly, William E.
Set my people free; a Negro's life of Lincoln, by William E. Lilly. New York, Farrar & Rinehart, incorporated [c1932]
viii, 269 p. front. (port.) 22½cm.

1. Lincoln, Abraham, pres. U. S., 1809-1865. I. Title.

32—1497
Library of Congress E457.L732
[43h1] 923.173

Lily-skin lover.

M813.5 C911
Cunningham, George, 1927-
Lily-skin lover; his passion for light-complexioned women leads him to destruction. New York, Exposition Press, 1960.

54p. 21cm.
Portrait of author on book jacket.

Lima: coplas y guitarras.

Peru M860 D56
Diez Canseco, José
Lima: coplas y guitarras. Lima, 1949.

140p. illus. 22½cm. (His Obra Completas de, V. 1)

Brazil M869 L62a
Lima, Jorge de, 1893-1953.
... Anchieta. Rio de Janeiro, Civilização brasileira, s. a., 1934.
211 p., 2 l. 18½cm. (Bibliotheca brasileira de cultura, dirigida por Tristão de Athayde)
CONTENTS.—Anchieta.—Escola de Piratininga.—As reducções.—Iperoig.—Fundação do Rio de Janeiro.—Reritiba.—Bibliographia (p. [209]-211)

1. Anchieta, José de, 1534-1597. 2. Jesuits in Brazil. 3. Rio de Janeiro—Hist.

35—18715
Library of Congress F2528.A538
[a42c1] 922.281

Brazil M869 L62c
Lima, Jorge de
Calunga, romance. 2 ed. Rio de Janeiro, Alba Editora, 1943.
241p., 1 l. 19cm.

I. Title

Brazil M869.1 L621L
Lima, Jorge de, 1893-1953.
Les iles; poême. Traduit du Portugais par H. Usai. Rio de Janeiro, Artesanato Cristo Operário, 1952.

13 leaves. 24½cm.
Autographed.

I. Title.

Brazil M869. L62i
Lima, Jorge de, 1893-1953
Invenção de orfeu. Rio de Janeiro, Livros de Portugal, 1952.

xx, 431 p. 19cm.
[First edition]

I. Title 1. Brazilian poetry
II. Orpheus' invention.

Brazil M869 B27a
Lima, Hermes.
... Tobias Barreto (a época e o homem) (em apêndice o Discurso em mangas de camisa com as notas e adições) São Paulo [etc.] Companhia editora nacional, 1939.
4 p. l., 350 p., 1 l. IV pl. (incl. port., facsim.) on 2 l. 18½cm. (Biblioteca pedagogica brasileira. Ser. 5: Brasiliana. vol. 140)
White author.

1. Barreto de Menezes, Tobias, 1839-1889.

40-1548
Library of Congress PQ9697.B35Z7
[2] 928.6

Brazil M869 L62a2
Lima, Jorge de, 1893-1953
O anjo, romance. 2nd ed. Editora Getulio Costa,

132p. 20cm.

I. Title.

Brazil M869 L628
Lima, Jorge de, 1893-1953.
Obra completa. Organização de Afrânio Coutinho; introd. geral: Waltensir Dutra [e] Eurialo Canabrava. [1. ed.] Rio de Janeiro, J. Aguilar, 1958 [i. e. 1959]-
v. illus. 19 cm.
CONTENTS.—v. 1. Poesia e ensaios.

I. Coutinho, Afranio, ed.

PQ9697.L54 1959 60-17109 ‡
Library of Congress [3]

M869. L620
Lima, Jorge de. 1893-1953.
Obra poética. Edição completa, em um volume. Organizada por Otto Maria Carpeaux. Rio de Janeiro, Editora Getulio Costa, 1950.

657p. port. 20cm.

1. Brazilian poetry.

M808.8
N42
v.5
Lima, Jorge de 1893-1953
Poems: Calabar; Fear.
(In: New world writing, 5. New York, New American Library 1954. 18cm. pp. 73-74)

Latin America
M861.08
F56a
Lima, Jorge de, 1893-1953,
Pp. 74-93. In -
Fitts, Dudley, 1903- ed.
Anthology of contemporary Latin-American poetry, edited by Dudley Fitts. Norfolk, Conn., New directions [1942]
ix, [2], x-xxi, 667 p. 23½ cm.
Added t.-p.: Antología de la poesía americana contemporánea.
English and original text (Spanish, Portuguese or French) on opposite pages.
"Biographical and bibliographical notes, by H. R. Hays": p. 581-641.
1. Spanish-American poetry (Collections) 2. Spanish-American poetry—Translations into English. 3. English poetry—Translations from Spanish. 4. Spanish-American poetry—Bio-bibl. I. Hays, Hoffman Reynolds. II. Title.
PQ7084.F5 861.6082 43—485
Library of Congress [54r43k½7]

Brazil
M869.3
L62b
Lima Barreto, Afonso Henrique de, 1881-1922.
Bagatelas; romance. Prefácio de Astrojildo Pereira. São Paulo, Editôra Brasiliense, 1956.
821 p. ~~illus.~~ port. 21 cm. (*His* Obras, 9)
I. Title.
PQ9697.L544B3 58-42140 ‡
Library of Congress [8]

Brasil
M869.3
L62c
Lima Barreto, Afonso Henrique de, 1881-1922.
Clara dos Anjos. Rio de Janeiro, Editôra ~~Mérito [1948]~~ Brasiliense, 1956.
~~690 p.~~ 308p. 22 cm.
CONTENTS.—Clara dos Anjos (romance)—Contos: Um especialista. O filho da Gabriela. A nova Califórnia. O homem que sabia javanês. Um e outro. Miss Edith e seu tio. Como o "homem" chegou.
I. Title.
PQ9697.L544C5 50-26317
Library of Congress [4]

Brazil
M869.3
L62co
Lima Barreto, Afonso Henrique de, 1881-1922.
Coisas do reino do jambon; sátira e foeclore. São Paulo, Editôra Brasiliense, 1956.
320p. illus. 21cm.
I. Title.

Brazil
M869.3
L62d
Lima Barreto, Afonso Henrique de, 1881-1922.
Diário íntimo. São Paulo, Editôra Mérito [1953]
330 p. 21 cm.
I. Title.
PQ9697.L544Z54 55-41496 ‡
Library of Congress [3]

M869.3
L62f
Lima Barreto, Afonso Henrique de, 1881-1922.
Feiras e mafuás. ~~São Paulo, Editôra Mérito [1953]~~ Artigos e Crônicas. Brasiliense, 1956.
~~382 p.~~ 21 cm.
314p.
Essays.
I. Title.
PQ9697.L544F4 54-23465 rev ‡
Library of Congress [r57b3]

Brasil
M869.3
L62hi
Lima Barreto, Afonso Henrique de, 1881-1922.
Histórias e sonhos; contos. São Paulo, Editôra Brasiliense, 1956.
308p. illus. 21cm.
I. Title.

Brazil
M869.3
L62n
Lima Barreto, Afonso Henrique de, 1881-1922.
Numa e a ninfa (romance) ~~Rio [de Janeiro] Gráfica~~ Editôra Brasileira ~~[1950]~~ 1956. São Paulo,
~~306 p.~~ 21 cm. 285 illus.
~~L.C. copy imperfect.~~
~~"Aventuras do Dr. Bogoloff": p. [217]-306.~~
I. Title. ~~II. Title: Aventuras do Dr. Bogoloff.~~
PQ9697.L544N8 52-15661 ‡
Library of Congress [3]

Brazil
M869.3
L62br
Lima Barreto, Afonso Henrique de, 1881-1922.
Os bruzundangas; sátira. São Paulo, Editôra Brasiliense, 1956.
308p. illus. 21cm.
I. Title.

Brazil
M869.3
L62r
Lima Barreto, Afonso Henrique de, 1881-1922.
...Recordações do escrivão Caminha. Livraria, Classica Editoria de A.M. Teixeira & C. ia 1909.
316 p. 19 cm.
At head of title: Lima Barreto.

Brazil
M869.3
L62t
1915
Lima Barreto, Afonso Henrique de, 1881-1922
Triste fim de polycarpo quaresma. Rio de Faneiro, Revista dos Tribunaes, 1915.
352p. 19cm.
I. title

Brazil
M869.3
L62v
Lima Barreto, Afonso Henrique de, 1881-1922.
... Vida e morte de M. J. Gonzaga de Sá ... S. Paulo, ~~"Revista do Brasil," 1919.~~ Editora Brasiliense, 1956.
~~5 p. l., [13]-201 p., 1 l. 18cm.~~
At head of title: Lima Barreto.
Novel.
316p. port. 21cm.
I. Title.
Library of Congress PQ9697.L544V5 44-14444
[2]

Brit. Guiana
M827.91
W68
Limericks.
Wills, S E
50 local limericks, or 50 laughs by S. E. Wills. Georgetown, British Guiana, 1920.
12p. 21cm.

Nigeria
M096.1
Ok3L
Limits.
Okigbo, Christopher
Limits. [Ibadan] Mbari Publications [1964]
[23] p. 20cm.

M814.5
B791
Lincoln, Abraham, pres. U.S., 1809-1865.
Brooks, Walter Henderson, 1851-
Impressions at the tomb of Abraham Lincoln. n.p., n.d.
4p. 18cm.

Ghana
M966.7
D45
Lincoln, Abriaham, pres. U.S., 1809-1865.
Desewu, Paul M
Abraham Lincoln mutinya (second edition - rewritten). Published with the approval of the Education Department of the Gold Coast. London, Longmans, Green and Co., n.d.
106p. illus. 18½cm.

M815.4
D74s
Lincoln, Abraham, pres. U.S., 1809-1865.
Douglass, Frederick, 1817-1895.
Address at seventy-ninth anniversary of the birth of Abraham Lincoln.
(In: Republican National League. Services commemorative of the seventy-ninth anniversary of the birth of Abraham Lincoln...Washington, D.C. February 12th, 1888...Washington, Gibson Brass, 1888. 23cm. p. 14-18)

M815.4
D741
Lincoln, Abraham, pres. U. S. 1809-1865.
Douglass, Frederick, 1817-1895.
Inaugural ceremonies of the Freedmen's memorial monument to Abraham Lincoln. Washington City, April 14, 1876. Saint Louis, Levison & Blythe, 1876.
28p. front. 22½cm
Contains oration of Douglass, p. 16-26.

M304
P19
V.6,no.16
Lincoln, Abraham, pres. U.S. 1809-1865
Green, John Paterson, 1845-
The man Abraham Lincoln. An address, delivered before the Men's Club of the East Boulevard Presbyterian Church, by John P. Green, February 9, 1923. Cleveland, Ohio, Published by Riehl Printing Co. [1923]
[16] p. 23cm.

M59
L63hu
Lincoln, Abraham, pres. U. S., 1809-1865.
Hubert, James Henry, 1885-
The life of Abraham Lincoln, its significance to Negroes and Jews; an address delivered before Gad lodge, no. 11, Free sons of Israel, February 15, 1939, by James H. Hubert ... with an introduction by Dr. William Heard Kilpatrick ... and an extract from the presidential address on the test of American democracy delivered before the sixty-fifth annual session of the National conference of social work, by Dr. Solomon Lowenstein ... New York, N. Y., W. Malliet and company, 1939.
22 p. 23cm.
1. Lincoln, Abraham, pres. U. S., 1809-1865. 2. U. S.—Race question. 3. Negroes—Moral and social conditions. I. Lowenstein, Solomon, 1877-
40-34518 Revised
Library of Congress E457.2.H87
[r43e2] 923.173

Lincoln, Abraham, pres. U.S., 1809-1865.

M326.99B Keckley, Elizabeth (Hobbs) 1824-1907.
K23 Behind the scenes. By Elizabeth Keckley ... Or, Thirty years a slave, and four years in the White House. New York, G. W. Carleton & co., 1868.

2 p. l., [ix]-xvi, [17]-371 p. front. (port.) 19cm.

1. Lincoln, Abraham, pres. U. S., 1809-1865. 2. Lincoln, Mary (Todd) 1818-1882. I. Title.

Library of Congress E457.15.K26 5—4115
[45j1]

Lincoln, Abraham, pres. U.S., 1809-1865 - Addresses, sermons, etc.

M304 P19 v.5, no.5 Pickens, William, 1881-
Abraham Lincoln, man and statesman (abridged) by William Pickens. [New York, °1930.

cover-title, 15 p. 23cm.

1. Lincoln, Abraham, pres. U. S.—Addresses, sermons, etc.

Library of Congress E457.8.P596 30-6041
——— Copy 2.
Copyright AA 35230 [2]

M301 L63 Lincoln, Charles Eric, 1924-
My face is black, by C. Eric Lincoln. Boston, Beacon Press [1964]

137 p. 21 cm.
Bibliographical references included in "Notes" (p. [134]-137)

1. Negroes. 2. ~~U. S.~~—Race question. 3. Black Muslims. I. Title.

E185.61.L57 301.451 64—22695
Library of Congress [65f9]

Lincoln, Abraham, pres. U.S., 1809-1865.

MC9 L631i Lilly, William E.
Set my people free; a Negro's life of Lincoln, by William E. Lilly. New York, Farrar & Rinehart, incorporated [°1932]

viii, 269 p. front. (port.) 22½cm.

1. Lincoln, Abraham, pres. U. S., 1809-1865. I. Title.

32—4497
Library of Congress E457.L732
[43h1] 923.173

Lincoln, Abraham, pres. U.S., 1809-1865 - Poetry.

M811.5 J699s 1915 Jones, Edward Smyth, 1881-
The sylvan cabin, a centenary ode on the birth of Lincoln, by Edward Smyth Jones; with introduction taken from the N.Y. Times. San Francisco, published by the author, 1915.

9 unnumb. leaves port. (front.) 20½cm.
On cover: Panama-Pacific International Exposition Edition.

M973 L638 Lincoln, Charles Eric, 1924-
The Negro pilgrimage in America, by C. Eric Lincoln. New York, Bantam Books [1967]

184 p. illus., facsims., ports. 18 cm. (Bantam pathfinder editions)

1. Negroes—Hist. I. Title.

E185.L47 973'.0974'96 67-28881
Library of Congress [3]

Lincoln, Abraham, pres.U. S., 1809-1865.

MB9 L63na National Lincoln monument association.
Celebration by the Colored people's educational monument association in memory of Abraham Lincoln, on the Fourth of July, 1865, in the presidential grounds, Washington, D. C. ... Washington, D. C., McGill & Witherow, printers, 1865.

33, [1] p. 22½cm.

1. Lincoln, Abraham, pres. U. S., 1809-1865. I. Title.

Library of Congress E457.52.N22 12—30032
——— Copy 2. [a23d1]

Lincoln, Abraham, Pres. U.S., 1809-1865 - Relations with Negroes.

M973.7 Qu2 Quarles, Benjamin.
Lincoln and the Negro. New York, Oxford University Press, 1962.

275 p. illus. 21 cm.
Includes bibliography.

1. Lincoln, Abraham, Pres. U. S.—Relations with Negroes. 2. Lincoln, Abraham, Pres. U. S.—Views on slavery. I. Title.
Full name: Benjamin Arthur Quarles.

E457.2.Q3 923.173 62—9829 ‡
Library of Congress [63k5]

M323.4 L638 Lincoln, Charles Eric, 1924-
Sounds of the struggle; persons and perspectives in civil rights, by C. Eric Lincoln. New York, Morrow, 1967.

252 p. 22 cm.
Includes bibliographical references.
Portrait of author on book jacket.

1. Negroes—Civil rights—Addresses, essays, lectures. I. Title.

E185.615.L5 323.4'0973 67-29822
Library of Congress [5]

Lincoln, Abraham, pres. U. S., 1809-1865.

MB9 L63ri Rice, Allen Thorndike, 1851-1889, *ed.*
Reminiscences of Abraham Lincoln by distinguished men of his time, collected and edited by Allen Thorndike Rice ... New York, North American publishing company, 1886.

lxix, 2-18, 656 p. incl. facsims. front., plates, ports., fold. facsim. 23½cm.
Biographical sketches [of authors]: p. 609-649.

1. Lincoln, Abraham, pres. U. S., 1809-1865.
[*Full name:* Charles Allen Thorndike Rice]

Library of Congress E457.15.R49 1886 12-17395 rev
[r45b2]

Lincoln, Abraham, Pres. U.S., 1809-1865 - Views on slavery.

M973.7 Qu2 Quarles, Benjamin.
Lincoln and the Negro. New York, Oxford University Press, 1962.

275 p. illus. 21 cm.
Includes bibliography.

1. Lincoln, Abraham, Pres. U. S.—Relations with Negroes. 2. Lincoln, Abraham, Pres. U. S.—Views on slavery. I. Title.
Full name: Benjamin Arthur Quarles.

E457.2.Q3 923.173 62—9829 ‡
Library of Congress [63k5]

Lincoln, Charles Eric, 1924-
The sit-in comes to Atlanta.
pp. 259-265.

M323.4 W52 Westin, Alan F *ed.*
Freedom now! The civil-rights struggle in America. Edited by Alan F. Westin. New York, Basic Books [1964]

xv, 346 p. 22 cm.
Bibliography: p. [329]-341.

1. Negroes — Civil rights — Addresses, essays, lectures. 2. Civil rights—U. S.—Addresses, essays, lectures. I. Title.

E185.61.W54 301.451 64-17401
Library of Congress [5]

Lincoln, Abraham, pres. U. S., 1809-1865.

MB9 L63was Washington, John E.
They knew Lincoln, by John E. Washington, with an introduction by Carl Sandburg ... New York, E. P. Dutton & co., inc., 1942.

3 p. l., 11-244, [2] p. front., plates, ports., facsims. 22½cm.
"Personal narrative of a Negro boy and man who sought all that could be possibly known about Abraham Lincoln from Negroes having impressions on facts he considered worth record."—Introd.
"First edition."

1. Lincoln, Abraham, pres. U. S., 1809-1865. 2. Negroes—District of Columbia. I. Title.

Library of Congress E457.15.W32 42-8268
[30] 923.173

M973 R72 Lincoln, Charles Eric, 1924-
The Black Muslims as a protest movement.
Pp. 220-240.

In: Rose, Arnold Marshall, ed. Assuring freedom to the free. Detroit, Wayne State University, 1964.

Lincoln, Mary (Todd) 1818-1882.

M326.99B Keckley, Elizabeth (Hobbs) 1824-1907.
K23 Behind the scenes. By Elizabeth Keckley ... Or, Thirty years a slave, and four years in the White House. New York, G. W. Carleton & co., 1868.

2 p. l., [ix]-xvi, [17]-371 p. front. (port.) 19cm.

1. Lincoln, Abraham, pres. U. S., 1809-1865. 2. Lincoln, Mary (Todd) 1818-1882. I. Title.

Library of Congress E457.15.K26 5—4115
[45j1]

Lincoln, Abraham, pres. U.S., 1809-1865 - Addresses, sermons, etc.

M815.4 D74o Douglass, Frederick, 1817-1895.
Oration by Frederick Douglass, delivered on the occasion of the unveiling of the freedmen's monument in memory of Abraham Lincoln, in Lincoln park, Washington, D. C., April 14th, 1876. With an appendix. ~~Washington, D. C., Gibson brothers, printers, 1876.~~ N.Y. Fred. Douglass historical & cultural league, 1940.
cover-title, ~~24 p. 23cm.~~ 17cm.

1. Lincoln, Abraham, pres. U. S.—Addresses, sermons, etc. 2. Washington, D. C. Lincoln statue (Lincoln park)

Library of Congress E457.8.D73 12—6733
[28d1]

M363 L63b Lincoln, Charles Eric, 1924-
The Black Muslims in America. Foreword by Gordon Allport. Boston, Beacon Press [1961]

276 p. 21 cm.
"This book originated as a dissertation ... in the Graduate School of Boston University."
Includes bibliography.
Portrait of author on book jacket.

~~1. Negroes.~~ 2. U. S.—Race question. 3. Mohammedans in the U. S. I. Title.

E185.61.L56 363.973 61—5881 ‡
Library of Congress [62y5]

Lincoln and the Negro.

M973.7 Qu2 Quarles, Benjamin.
Lincoln and the Negro. New York, Oxford University Press, 1962.

275 p. illus. 21 cm.
Includes bibliography.

1. Lincoln, Abraham, Pres. U. S.—Relations with Negroes. 2. Lincoln, Abraham, Pres. U. S.—Views on slavery. I. Title.
Full name: Benjamin Arthur Quarles.

E457.2.Q3 923.173 62—9829 ‡
Library of Congress [63k5]

Lincoln, Abraham, pres. U.S., 1809-1865 - Addresses, sermons, etc.

M815.4 D74or Douglass, Frederick, 1817-1895.
Oration by Frederick Douglass, delivered on the occasion of the unveiling of the freedmen's monument in memory of Abraham Lincoln, in Lincoln park, Washington, D. C., April 14th, 1876. With an appendix. Washington, D. C., Gibson brothers, printers, 1876.

cover-title, 21 p. 23cm.

1. Lincoln, Abraham, pres. U. S.—Addresses, sermons, etc. 2. Washington, D. C. Lincoln statue (Lincoln park)

Library of Congress E457.8.D73 12—6733
[28d1]

M301 R11 Lincoln, Charles Eric, 1924-
The Black muslims in America.
Pp. 179-190.

(In: Raab, Earl. American race relations today. Garden City, N. Y., Doubleday, 1962)

M370. L63e Lincoln High School. Tallahassee, Florida.
The evolution of Susan Prim; a story developed by the Lincoln High and Elementary School faculties, in cooperation with the staff of the Secondary School study of the Association of Colleges and Secondary Schools for Negroes. Tallahassee, Florida, Lincoln High School, 1944.

59p. illus. 23cm.

1. Education, Secondary. I. Association of Colleges and Secondary Schools for Negroes, Secondary School study. 2. Florida - Education

Lincoln university, Jefferson City, Mo.—Hist.

M378L1
Sa9
Savage, William Sherman.
The history of Lincoln university ⌊by⌋ W. Sherman Savage ... Published under the direction of Lincoln university. Jefferson City, Mo. ⌊©1939⌋
xii, 302 p. illus. (incl. ports., maps, plan) diagrs. 23½cm.
Bibliography: p. 295–296.

1. Lincoln university, Jefferson City, Mo.—Hist.
40-6814
Library of Congress LC2851.L64288
⌊3⌋ 378.778

Lincoln University, Jefferson City, Mo. School of Journalism. Journalism series, no.2.
M016.07
B81c
Brown, Warren Henry, 1905–
Check list of Negro newspapers in the United States (1827–1946) Jefferson City, Mo., School of Journalism, Lincoln Univ., 1946.
cover-title, 37 p. 23 cm. (Lincoln University journalism series, no. 2)

1. Negro newspapers (American)—Bibl. I. Series: Lincoln University, Jefferson City, Mo. School of Journalism. Journalism series, no. 2.
Z6951.B88 016.071 48-326*
Library of Congress ⌊3⌋

Lincoln University poets.
M811.08
C91
Cuney, Waring, 1906– *ed.*
Lincoln University poets; centennial anthology ⌊1854–1954⌋ Edited by Waring Cuney, Langston Hughes, and Bruce McM. Wright. Foreword by Horace Mann Bond; introd. by J. Saunders Redding. ⌊1st ed.⌋ New York, Fine Editions Press ⌊1954⌋
72 p. 21 cm.
Inscribed by Langston Hughes.
Autographed by authors.

1. Negro poetry (American) I. Title.
PS591.N4C84 811.5082 54-2461 ‡
Library of Congress ⌊2⌋

Jamaica
M821.08
Ye3
Lindo, Archie. comp.
Year book of the Jamaica poetry league, 1939–
Kingston, Jamaica, The New Dawn Press, 1939–
v. 21cm.
Compiled by Archie Lindo.
See holdings card for issues in library.

Lindo, Cedric, jt. ed.
Jamaica
M820
H38
Hendriks, A L ed.
The independence anthology of Jamaican literature, selected by A. L. Hendriks and Cedric Lindo. With an introduction by Peter Abrahams. Kingston, The Ministry of Development and Welfare, 1962.
227p. 21½cm.

Lindsay, Arnett Grant.
M331
As7
Association for the study of Negro life and history, inc.
The Negro as a business man, by J. H. Harmon, jr., Arnett G. Lindsay, and Carter G. Woodson. Washington, D. C., The Association for the study of Negro life and history, inc. ⌊©1929⌋
v, 111 p. 25 cm.
CONTENTS.—The Negro as a local business man.—The Negro in banking.—Insurance business among Negroes.

1. Negroes—Employment. I. Harmon, John Henry, jr. II. Lindsay, Arnett Grant. III. Woodson, Carter Godwin, 1875– IV. Title.
30—21076
Library of Congress E185.8.A84
⌊48j1⌋ 325.26

Lines of life.
M811.5
B321
Batipps, Percy Oliver.
Lines of life, by Percy Oliver Batipps. Media, Penna., American publishing company, 1924.
118 p. 17½cm.
Verse.

I. Title.
24-31320
Library of Congress PS3503.A86L5 1924
Copyright A 814202 ⌊2⌋

Lingénu de Harlem.
M813.5
H87b5
Hughes, Langston, 1902–
Lingénu de Harlem, nouvelles traduites de l'Americain par F. J. Roy. Paris, Robert Laffont ⌊1967⌋
376p. 20cm. (Pavillons)
Translation of The best of simple.

I. Title.

The linguist.
Ghana
M966.7
W83p
Hayford, Casely, 1866–1930.
The linguist.
pp. 208–209.
In: Pageant of Ghana, by Freda Wolfson. 1958.

Links of friendship.
M811.5
C821
Cotter, Joseph Seamon, 1861– 1949.
Links of friendship, by Joseph S. Cotter ... Louisville, Ky., The Bradley & Gilbert company, 1898.
iv, ⌊5⌋–64 p. front. (port.) 18 cm.
Poems.
"Sketch of the author," signed Thomas G. Watkins: p. ⌊iii⌋–iv.

I. Title.
98—716
Library of Congress PS1449.C4L5
⌊40b1⌋

The lion and the archer.
M811.5
H32L
Hayden, Robert Earl
The lion and the archer: poems ⌊by Robert Hayden and Myron O'Higgins⌋ Nashville, Tenn., Mills Book Store, 1948.
28p. 24cm.

Nigeria
M896.2
So3f
The lion and the jewel.
Soyinka, Wole
Five plays: A dance of the forests, The lion and the jewel, The swamp dwellers, The trials of Brother Jero ⌊and⌋ The strong breed. London, Oxford University Press, 1964.
276p. 20cm. (A Three crowns book).

Nigeria
M896.2
So3L
The lion and the jewel.
Soyinka, Wole.
The lion and the jewel. London, Oxford University Press, 1963.
64p. 18cm.

The lion of Judah.
M813.5
J731
Dorsey, John T.
The lion of Judah, by John T. Dorsey ... illustrated by Clovis E. J. Fouché and W. E. Scott. Chicago, Fouché company, inc. ⌊©1924⌋
207 p. illus. 20cm.

I. Title.
Library of Congress PZ3.D7387Li 24-21151
Copyright A 800717 ⌊2⌋

M811.4
L65c
⌊Linton, William James⌋ 1812–1897.
Catoninetales; a domestic epic, by Hattie Brown ⌊*pseud.*⌋ a young lady of colour lately deceased at the age of 14. London, Laurence and Bullen, 1891.
5 p. l., ⌊3⌋–100 p. illus. 23cm.
Title vignette.
Half-title: Catoninetales: edited and illustrated by W. J. Linton.
"Only three hundred and thirty copies printed. no. 69."
Not Negro author.

I. Title.
6—25888
Library of Congress PR4889.L6C3
——— Copy 2. no. 57. ⌊a28c1⌋

Liphoofolo linonyana litaola, le lithoko tsa tsona.
Basutoland
M896.1
M3212
Mapetla, Joase
Liphoofolo linonyana litaola, le lithoko tsa tsona. ⌊Praise poems of animals, birds and divining bones⌋ Morija, Basutoland, Mroija Sesuto Book Depot, 1942.
30p. 16½cm.

Lipscomb, George Dewey, 1898– joint author.
M813.5
G76d
Graham, Shirley.
Dr. George Washington Carver, scientist, by Shirley Graham and George D. Lipscomb, illustrated by Elton C. Fax. New York, J. Messner, inc. ⌊1944⌋
viii, 248 p. incl. front. (port.) illus. 21½ cm.
Bibliography: p. 242–243.

1. Carver, George Washington, 1864?–1943. I. Lipscomb, George Dewey, 1898– joint author.
⌊*Full name:* Lola Shirley (Graham) McCanns⌋
44—40095
Library of Congress S417.C3G7
⌊46z²10⌋ 925

M813.5
L66
Lipscomb, Ken, 1921–
Duke Casanova; a novel. New York, Exposition Press, ⌊1958⌋
76p. 21cm.
Picture and biographical sketch of the author on the book jacket.

I. Title.

Lira Negra.
Latin America
M861.08
Sa
Sanz y Diaz, José
Lira Negra (Selecciones españolas y Afroamericanas.) Recopilacion prólogo y notas de José Sanz y Diaz. ⌊Madrid, M. Aguilar, 1945⌋
380p. 12½cm.

Lira negra.
M808.8
Sa59
Sanz y Díaz, José, 1907– *ed.*
Lira negra (selecciones españolas y afroamericanas) ⌊Madrid, M. Aguilar, 1945⌋
380 p. front. 12 cm. (Colección Crisol, núm. 21)
White editor.

1. Negro poetry. 2. Negro authors. 3. Negroes in literature. I. Title. (Series)
A 48-5448*
Yale Univ. Library for Library of Congress ⌊1⌋

M813.5
L68p
Liscomb, Harry F.
The Prince of Washington square; an up-to-the-minute story, by Harry F. Liscomb. New York, Frederick A. Stokes company, 1925.
ix p., 1 l., 180 p. 19cm.

I. Title.
25—6708
Library of Congress PZ3.L684Pr
⌊44d1⌋

M338.9 Lisette, Gabriel
G92s French Africa.

Pp. 44-48.
In: Science and the new nations, edited by Ruth Gruber. 1961.

1. Africa, French. I. Title.

Mauritius
M969.82 **Lislet-Geoffroy, Jean Baptiste,** 1755-1836.
G29m
Memoir and notice explanatory of a chart of Madagascar and the North-Eastern archipelago of Mauritius; drawn up according to the latest observations, under the auspices and government of His Excellency Robert Townsend Farquhar ... By Lislet Geoffroy ... Now first pub. in the original French, with an English translation, together with some observations on the coast of Africa, and a brief notice on the winds on the coast of Madagascar ₍by M. Barbarin₎ London, J. Murray, 1819.

v, 57 p. front. (fold. chart.) 28ᶜᵐ.
1. Pilot guides—Madagascar. 2. Pilot guides—Mauritius. I. Farquhar, Sir Robert Townsend, 1776-1830, ed. II. Barbarin, ———.
3. Madagascar. 4. Mauritius.

13—23158
Library of Congress VK891.G84
₍39b1₎

... Lisping leaves.
M811.5 **Rowland, Ida.**
R79
... Lisping leaves, by Ida Rowland. Philadelphia, Dorrance and company ₍ᶜ1939₎

55 p. 20ᶜᵐ. (Contemporary poets of Dorrance. (191))

I. Title.

40-1972
Library of Congress PS3535.O9658L5 1939
——— Copy 2.
Copyright A 135884 ₍2₎ 811.5

Liss, Howard, joint author.
M796 **Mays, Willie,** 1931-
M46m
My secrets of playing baseball, by Willie Mays with Howard Liss. Photos. by David Sutton. New York, Viking Press ₍1967₎

89 p. illus. (part col.) 27 cm.

1. Baseball—Juvenile literature. I. Liss, Howard, joint author. II. Title.

GV873.M35 796.3572 67-13502
Library of Congress ₍69-2₎

Liston, Sonny.
M89 **Young, Andrew Sturgeon Nash,** 1919-
L69y
Sonny Liston, the champ nobody wanted, by A. S. "Doc" Young. Chicago, Johnson Pub. Co. ₍1963₎

224 p. illus. 21 cm.

1. Liston, Sonny.

GV1132.L5Y6 927.9683 63-15652 ‡
Library of Congress ₍5₎

Dominican Republic
M860.9 Literary currents in Hispanic America.
H39L **Henríquez-Ureña, Pedro,** 1884-
Literary currents in Hispanic America, by Pedro Henríquez-Ureña. Cambridge, Mass., Harvard university press, 1945.

vi p., 2 l., ₍3₎-345 p. 21½ cm. (*Half-title:* The Charles Eliot Norton lectures, 1940-1941)
Bibliographical references included in "Notes" (p. ₍205₎-284) Bibliography: p. ₍285₎-295.

1. Spanish-American literature—Addresses, essays, lectures. 2. Spanish America—Civilization. I. Title.

A 45—2956
Harvard Univ. Library for Library of Congress ₍48c½₎

M810. Literature.
B73n6 Brawley, Benjamin Griffiths, 1822-1939.
1918
The Negro in literature and art, by Benjamin Brawley. New York, Duffield & company, 1918.

176p. portraits. 18cm.
List of books: p.160-74.

Literature.
M810. **Brawley, Benjamin Griffith,** 1882-1939.
B73n6
1910
The Negro in literature and art, by Benjamin Griffith Brawley ... ₍Atlanta? ᶜ1910₎

60 p. 17½ᶜᵐ.
List of books: p. ₍58₎-60.

1. Negroes—Biog. 2. Negro literature. I. Title.

10—12321
Library of Congress E185.82.B82
₍a41c1₎

Literature.
M810 **Butcher, Margaret (Just)** 1913-
B97n
The Negro in American culture; based on materials left by Alain Locke. ₍1st ed.₎ New York, Knopf, 1956.

294 p. 22 cm.

1. ~~Negroes in~~ literature. 2. ~~Negroes in~~ art. 3. ~~Negro literature~~ (American) 4. American literature—~~Negro~~ authors. 5. ~~Negro~~ art. 6. Music—~~Negroes.~~ 7. ~~Negroes~~ Dancing. I. Title.
II. Locke, Alain Leroy.
E185.82.B93 325.260973 56—5783 ‡
Library of Congress ₍57e30₎

Literature.
M810 Butcher, Margaret (Just), 1913-
B97no
Les noirs dans la civilisation Americaine.
The Negro in American culture, based on materials left by Alain Locke. Traduit de l'americain par Francoise Vernan et Jean Rosenthal. Paris, Buchet/Chastel, 1958.

320p. 16½cm.

Literature.
M810.8 **Calverton, Victor Francis,** 1900- *ed.*
C13
Anthology of American Negro literature, edited, with an introduction by V. F. Calverton. New York, The Modern library ₍ᶜ1929₎

xii, 535 p. 17ᶜᵐ. (*Half-title:* The modern library of the world's best books)

1. Negro literature. I. Title. II. Title: American Negro literature.

29—29948
Library of Congress PS591.N4C3
₍41n³3₎

Literature.
M814.5 **Ellison, Ralph.**
E159
Shadow and act. New York, Random House ₍1964₎

xxii, 317 p. 22 cm.

1. ~~Negroes in~~ literature. 2. ~~Negro authors.~~ I. Title.

PS153.N5E4 1964 809.8 64-18928
Library of Congress ₍4-1₎

Literature.
M813.09 **Gloster, Hugh Morris,** 1911-
G51n
Negro voices in American fiction. Chapel Hill, Univ. of North Carolina Press, 1948.

xiv, 295 p. 24 cm.
Bibliography: p. 273-288.

1. Negro fiction (American)—Hist. & crit. 2. Negroes in literature. 3. Negro fiction (American)—Bibl. I. Title.

PS374.N4G5 813.09 48—6740*
Library of Congress ₍50b²10₎

Literature.
M810.9 Hill, Herbert, ed.
H55a
Black voices; new writing by American Negroes, selected and edited, with an introduction and biographical notes, by Herbert Hill. London, Elek Books, ₍1964₎

617p. 21cm.
White editor.
American ed. (New York, Knopf) has title: Soon, one morning.

1. Literature. 2. American literature - Negro authors. I. Title.

Literature.
M810.9 **Hill, Herbert,** 1924- *ed.*
H55
Soon, one morning; new writing by American Negroes, 1940-1962. Selected and edited, with an introd. and biographical notes, by Herbert Hill. ₍1st ed.₎ New York, Knopf, 1963.

617 p. 22 cm.

1. Negro literature—U. S. 2. American literature—Negro authors. I. Title.

PS508.N3H5 810.89 62—15567 ‡
Library of Congress ₍63f5₎

Literature.
MSS Hill, Herbert, ed.
H55
Soon, one morning; new writing by American Negroes, 1940-62. Edited with an introduction by Herbert Hill. New York, Alfred A. Knopf, 1963.

2v. (leaves variously numbered) 30½cm.
"Uncorrected proof from Random House."
"Dear Mr. Spingarn - Here it is - at last - I hope this work pleases you, I should appreciate your comment, Herbert."
White editor.

1. Literature. 2. American literature - Authors. I. Title.

M973.9 Literature.
F46 Ivy, James Waldo.
No.8
Fifty years of progress in literature. Pittsburgh, Pittsburgh Courier, 1950.

7p. illus. 24cm. (Fifty years of progress)

Literature.
M810.8 **Johnson, Charles Spurgeon,** 1893- *ed.*
J63
Ebony and topaz, a collectanea, edited by Charles S. Johnson. New York, Opportunity, National urban league ₍ᶜ1927₎

6 p. l., 15-164 p. incl. illus., plates, ports., facsims. 30½ᶜᵐ.

1. Negro literature. 2. Negroes. I. Title.

28—2856
Library of Congress PS508.N3J6
——— Copy 2.
Copyright A 1018654 ₍39f1₎

Literature.
M808.8 Letteratura Negra. Prefazione di Pier Paolo
L718 Pasolini. ₍Roma₎ Editori Ruinti ₍1961₎

2v. 22½cm.

Literature.
M808 **Locke, Alain Le Roy,** 1886- *ed.*
L79n9
The new negro; an interpretation, edited by Alain Locke; book decoration and portraits by Winold Reiss. New York, A. and C. Boni, 1925.

xviii, 446 p. col. front., illus. (incl. music, facsims.) plates (part col.) col. ports. 24½ᶜᵐ.
Bibliography: p. 415-446.

1. Negroes. 2. Negro literature. I. Title.

25—25228
Library of Congress E185.82.L75
₍43b²2₎

Literature.
M812.08 **Locke, Alain Le Roy,** 1886- *ed.*
L79
Plays of Negro life; a source-book of native American drama, selected and edited by Alain Locke ... and Montgomery Gregory ... decorations and illustrations by Aaron Douglas. New York and London, Harper & brothers, 1927.

10 p. l., 3-430 p. front., plates. 22½ cm.
"Bibliography of Negro drama": p. 424-430.

1. Negroes in literature and art. 2. American drama (Collections) 3. Negro literature. I. Gregory, Montgomery, 1887- joint ed. II. Title. III. Title: Negro life, Plays of.

27—22553
Library of Congress PS627.N4L6
₍45x²1₎

Literature.

M792
M694
Mitchell, Loften.
Black drama; the story of the American Negro in the theatre. [1st ed.] New York, Hawthorn Books [1967]
248 p. illus., ports. 24 cm.

1. Negroes—in literature. 2. Theater—U. S.—H. 3. Negroes—Moral and social conditions. I. Title.

PS338.N4M5 792'.0973 66-22313

Library of Congress [5]

Literature - Bibliography

M01
H83
Howard university, Washington, D. C. Founders library. *Moorland foundation.*
A catalogue of books in the Moorland foundation, compiled by workers on projects 271 and 328 of the Works progress administration, Margaret R. Hunton and Ethel Williams, supervisors, Dorothy B. Porter, director. Washington, D. C., Howard university, 1939.
2 p. l., ii numb. l., 94, 166, 159, 23, 38, 19 p. 27½ x 21½cm.
Each part preceded by leaf with half-title not included in paging (6 leaves)
Mimeographed.
1. Negroes—Bibl. 2. Negro literature—Bibl. I. *Porter, Dorothy (Burnett) 1905- II. Hunton, Margaret R. III. Williams, Ethel. IV. U. S. Work projects administration.

39-14329 Revised

Library of Congress Z1361.N39H8 [r44f2] 016.325260973

Literature - Dictionaries.

M810.8
R26
The Reader's companion to world literature. Editor: Lillian Herlands Hornstein; co-editor: G. D. Percy [and others] General editor: Calvin S. Brown. [New York] New American Library [1956]
498 p. 18 cm. (A Mentor book, MD179)

1. Literature—Dictionaries. 2. Literature—Bio-bibl. 3. Literature—Hist. & crit. I. Hornstein, Lillian Herlands, 1909- ed.
I. Brown, Sterling, 1901-
PN41.R4 803 56—13345 ‡

Library of Congress [57e5]

Martinique Literature.

M608.8
Sa28
Sainville, Léonard.
Antholgie de la littérature Négro-Africaine. [Paris, Présence Africaine, 1963-]

v. 24cm.

Literature - Bibliography.

M016
J193
Jahn, Janheinz
Die Neoafrikanische Literatur Gesamtbibliographie von den Anfängen bis zur Gegenwart. Düsseldorf-Köln. Eugen Diederichs Verlag, 1965.

xxxv, 359p. map. 22cm.

1. Literature - Bibliography. I. Title.

Literature-Hist. & crit.

M810.
B73n2
Brawley, Benjamin Griffith, 1882-1939.
The Negro genius; a new appraisal of the achievement of the American Negro in literature and the fine arts, by Benjamin Brawley ... New York, Dodd, Mead & company, 1937.
xiii, 366 p. front., plates, ports. 20½ cm.
Bibliography: p. 331-350.

1. Negro authors. 2. Negro artists. 3. Negro musicians. 4. Negro literature—Hist. & crit. 5. Negroes in literature and art. I. Title.

37—4124

Library of Congress E185.82.B816 [47b²3] 325.260973

Literature.

M304
F19
v.5, no.18
Schomburg, Arthur Alfonso, 1874-1938.
Racial integrity; a plea for the establishment of a chair of Negro history in our schools and colleges, etc. Read before the teachers' summer class at Cheney Institute, July 1913. [n. p.] A. V. Bernier [1913?]
19 p. 23 cm. (Negro Society for Historical Research. Occasional paper no. 3)

1. Negroes—Hist. 2. Negro literature. I. Title. II. Series.

E185.5.N4 no. 3 48-32619*

Library of Congress [1]

Literature - Bibliography

M06
J61
no. 26
Locke, Alain Le Roy, 1886- *comp.*
A decade of negro self-expression, compiled by Alain Locke ... with a foreword by Howard W. Odum ... [Charlottesville, Va.] 1928.
20 p. 22½cm. (*On cover:* The Trustees of the John F. Slater fund. Occasional papers no. 26)
"This pamphlet is little more than an annotated list of books written by negroes since the outbreak of the world war."—p. [5]
Bibliography: p. [9]-20.

1. Negro literature—Bibl. I. Title.

30-31851

Library of Congress E185.5.J65 no. 26
———— Copy 2. PS153.N5L6
[35d2] (325.26) 016.81

Literature-Hist. & crit.

M260
M45ng
Mays, Benjamin Elijah, 1895-
The Negro's God as reflected in his literature [by] Benjamin E. Mays ... lithographs by James L. Wells. Boston, Chapman & Grimes, inc. [°1938]
viii p., 1 l., 269 p. 20cm.
Bibliography: p. 257-263.

1. Negro literature—Hist. & crit. 2. Negroes—Religion. 3. God. 4. Religion in literature. I. Title.

38—37550

Library of Congress PS153.N5M3
[43i1] [231] 810.9

Literature

M973
Un3s
U. S. *Library of Congress.*
75 years of freedom; commemoration of the 75th anniversary of the proclamation of the 13th amendment to the Constitution of the United States. The Library of Congress. [Washington, U. S. Govt. print. off., 1943]
cover-title, vi, 108 p. col. pl. 26cm.
"The contribution of the American Negro to American culture was the theme of a series of exhibits and concerts in the Library of Congress commencing on December 18th, the 75th anniversary of the proclamation of the Thirteenth amendment, which ended slavery in the United States."—p. v.
1. Negroes. 2. Negro songs. 3. Negro art. 4. Negro literature (American) I. Title.

43-52457

Library of Congress E185.6.U597 [15] 325.260973

Literature - Bibliography.

M016.8
Oa4n
1937
Oakland, California. Free Library.
The Negro literature collection; Books of Negro authorship to be found in the Oakland Free Library. Oakland, California, 1937.

11p. 22cm.
Mimeographed.

Literature - History & crit.

M810.8
R26
The Reader's companion to world literature. Editor: Lillian Herlands Hornstein; co-editor: G. D. Percy [and others] General editor: Calvin S. Brown. [New York] New American Library [1956]
498 p. 18 cm. (A Mentor book, MD179)

1. Literature—Dictionaries. 2. Literature—Bio-bibl. 3. Literature—Hist. & crit. I. Hornstein, Lillian Herlands, 1909- ed.
I. Brown, Sterling, 1901-
PN41.R4 803 56—13345 ‡

Library of Congress [57e5]

Literature.

M323
W587ne
White, Walter Francis, 1893-
The Negro's contribution to American culture, the sudden flowering of a genius-laden artistic movement, by Walter White. Girard Kansas, Haldeman - Julius publications c1928
64p. 13cm. (Little blue book no. 1306, edited by E. Haldeman - Julius)

Literature—Catholic authors.

M811.08
B73o
Braithwaite, William Stanley Beaumont, 1878- *ed.*
Our Lady's choir, a contemporary anthology of verse by Catholic sisters, edited by William Stanley Braithwaite; with a foreword by the Rev. Hugh Francis Blunt and an introduction by Ralph Adams Cram, LITT. D. Boston, B. Humphries, inc., 1931.
xxx, 213, [1] p. 21cm.
2575 copies printed. One of 2000 numbered copies on Hamilton's mellow book.

1. American literature—Catholic authors. 2. American poetry—20th cent. I. Title.

32—26225

Library of Congress PS591.C3B7
[44i1] 811.508

Literature-Hist. & crit.

M810.
R24to
Redding, Jay Saunders.
To make a poet black [by] J. Saunders Redding. Chapel Hill, The University of North Carolina press, 1939.
x p., 2 l., [3]-142 p. 22cm.
"Factual material and critical opinion on American Negro literature."—Pref.
Bibliography: p. [131]-136.

1. Negro literature—Hist. & crit. I. Title.

39—27275

Library of Congress PS153.N5R4
———— Copy 2.
Copyright A 127398 [41k8] 810.9

Literature.

M973
W93c
Writer's program. Illinois.
Cavalcade of the American Negro, compiled by the workers of the Writer's program of the work projects administration in the state of Illinois; frontispiece by Adrian Troy of the Illinois Art project. Chicago. Diamond jubilee exposition authority.

95p. incl. front. 23cm.

Literature - Collections.

M810.8
C76
Constelación Negra, antologia de la literatura Negro Americana. Traducción del inglés, selección y pórtico de Julio Gómez de la Serna. Barcelona, Ediciones Ayma, 1942.

142p. 19cm.

Literature - Study and teaching.

Africa
M809
P912
Press, John, ed.
Commonwealth literature: unity and diversity in a common culture; extracts from the proceedings of a Conference held at Bodington Hall, Leeds, 9-12 September 1964, under the auspices of the University of Leeds. [London] Heinemann [1965]
223p. 22cm.
White editor
Partial contents.- Some provisional

~~(Continued on next card)~~

Literature - Bibliography

M01
H18
Hampton, Va. Normal and agricultural institute. Collis P. Library.
A classified catalogue of the Negro collection in the Collis P. Huntington Library, Hampton Ins Institute. Compiled by workers of the Writers' program of the Works Projects Administration in the state of Virginia. Sponsored by Hampton Institute. [n.p.] 1940.

255p. 27½cm.
Reproduced from type-written copy.

Literature - Collections.

M810.8
D66
Dodd, Mead & Company, *publishers, New York.*
125th anniversary anthology, 1839-1964; a sampling of reading tastes from the lists of an American publisher with a brief historical commentary by the editors of Dodd, Mead. New York [1964]
xiii, 359 p. illus. 24 cm.

1. Literature—Collections. I. Title.

PN6014.D6 808.8 64-7501

Library of Congress [5]

Literature - Study and teaching.

M407
T48
Timmons, Eleanor Lewis
Teaching English. New York, Vantage Press, [1958]

96p. 20cm.

Lit[illegible] - Bio-Bibliography.

M810.8 R26

The Reader's companion to world literature. Editor: Lillian Herlands Hornstein; co-editor: G. D. Percy [and others] General editor: Calvin S. Brown. [New York] New American Library [1956]

498 p. 18 cm. (A Mentor book, MD179)

1. Literature—Dictionaries. 2. Literature—Bio-bibl. 3. Literature—Hist. & crit. ~~I. Hornstein, Lillian Herlands, 1909- ed.~~ I. Brown, Sterling, 1901-

PN41.R4 803 56—18345 ‡

Library of Congress [57o5]

Literature - Africa.

Cameroons M896 M49

Melone, Thomas

De la Négritude, dans la littérature - Négro-Africaine. Paris, Présence Africaine, 1962.

137p. 19cm. (Tribune des Jeunes, 2) Includes bibliography.

1. Negritude. 2. Literature - Africa. I. Title. II. Series.

Africa, South M960 M87

Literature - Africa.

Mphahlele, Ezekiel.

The African image. ~~New York, Praeger [1962]~~ London, Faber and Faber [1962]

240 p. 21 cm. ~~(Books that matter)~~

Includes bibliography.

1. Race. 2. Literature-Africa. ~~1. Negro race. 2. Negroes in literature.~~ I. Title. 3. Negritude. 4. Africa-Native races.

GN645.M7 1962a 809.93 62-19981 ‡

Library of Congress [5]

Literature - Africa.

South Africa M968 N65

Nkosi, Lewis, 1935-

Home and exile. [London] Longman's [1965]

136p. 20½cm.

1. South Africa. 2. Literature - Africa. 3. Race problems - Addresses, essays, lecture. I. Title.

Literature - Africa.

Africa M896.3 P741

Les plus beaux écrits de l'union française et du Maghreb, Présentés par Mohamed El Kholti, Leopold Sédar Senghor, [and others] Paris, Editions du Vieux, Colombier, 1947.

455p. 21cm.

Literature - Africa.

Africa M896 R93d2

Rutherfoord, Peggy, *ed.*

African voices; an anthology of native African writing. New York, Vanguard Press [1960, °1958]

208 p. 22 cm.

First published in 1958 under title: Darkness and light.

White editor.

1. Negro literature—Africa. 2. English literature—Translations from foreign literature. I. Title.

PN6014.R79 1960 808.89 60—9719 ‡

Library of Congress [60g15]

Africa M896 R93d

Literature - Africa.

Rutherfoord, Peggy, *ed.*

Darkness and light; an anthology of African writing. With a pref. by Trevor Huddleston. London, Faith Press [1958]

208 p. 23 cm.

1. Negro literature—Africa. 2. English literature—Translations from foreign literature. I. Title.

PN6014.R79 808.89 59-2791 ‡

Library of Congress [2]

Literature - Africa.

Ghana M896.8 V87v

Voices of Ghana; literary contributions to the Ghana broadcasting system 1955-57. Accra, Government Printer, 1958.

266p. 21½cm.

Africa M896 W58

Literature - Africa.

Whiteley, W H. comp.

A selection of African prose. Oxford, Clarendon Press, 1964.

2v. 22cm.

Contents.- v.1. Traditional oral texts.- v.2. Written prose.

Literature - Africa, Sub-Saharan.

U.S. M896.08 H87a2

Hughes, Langston, 1902- ed.

An African treasury; articles, essays, stories [and] poems by black Africans; selected by Langston Hughes. London, V. Gollancz, 1961.

xiv, 207p. 22cm.

"For Arthur - Sincerely, Langston. New York, July 13, 1965"

1. English literature - Africa, Sub-Saharan. 2. Literature - Africa, Sub-Saharan. I. Title.

Literature - Africa, Sub-Saharan.

U.S. M896.08 H87

Hughes, Langston, 1902- *ed.*

An African treasury: articles, essays, stories, poems, by black Africans. New York, Crown Publishers [1960]

207 p. 22 cm.

1. English literature—Africa, Sub-Saharan. 2. Negro literature—Africa, Sub-Saharan. I. Title.

Full name: James Langston Hughes.

PR9799.H8 808.89 60—8626 ‡

Library of Congress [61f30]

Literature - French African.

Congo (Leopoldville) M840.8 M971

Mushiete, Paul

La littérature française africaine; petite anthologie des écrivains noirs d'expression française. Leverville, Bibliothèque de l' Etoile, 1957.

40p. 17½cm.

Haiti M840.9 T75

Literature - Haiti.

Trouillot, Henock

Les origines sociales de la litterature Haitienne. Port-au-Prince, Imprimerie N. A. Theodore, 1962.

376p. 23½cm.

Special number, Revue de la societe Haitienne d'histoire de geographie et de geologie. January-July, 1962, v. 32, no. 109.

Literature-Haiti-History.

Haiti M840.9 P77m

Pompilus, Pradel

Manuel illustré d'histoire de la littérature Haitienne. Port-au-Prince, Editions Henri Deschamps, 1961.

613p. illus., ports. 19½cm.

Literature - Puerto Rico.

Puerto Rico M861 R71a

Rosa-Nieves, Cesáreo, 1904-

Aguinaldo lírico de la poesia Puertorriquenã. Prólogo, seleccion, ordenación y notas de Cesáreo Rosa-Nieves, Puerto Rico, Liberia Campos, 1957.

3v. 20cm.

Literature-Ruanda-Urundi-Hist. and Crit.

Rwanda M896.9 K11b

Kagame, Alexis, 1912-

Bref apercu sur la poésie dynastique du Rwanda. Bruxelles, Editions Universitaires, n.d.

30p.

[Extrait de la revue Zaire]

Literature - Southern states.

M813.08 H52s

Hibbard, Clarence Addison, 1887- *ed.*

Stories of the South, old and new, edited by Addison Hibbard, with an introduction, biographical notes, and bibliography by the editor. Chapel Hill, The University of North Carolina press; New York, W. W. Norton & company [°1931]

xvii, 520 p. 22cm.

1. Short stories, American. 2. American literature—Southern states. I. Title.

Library of Congress PZ1.H5228t 31—8688

[44j21]

Literature - U. S.

M810.8 R65

Rollins, Charlemae, *comp.*

Christmas gif'; an anthology of Christmas poems, songs, and stories, written by and about Negroes. Line drawings by Tom O'Sullivan. Book design by Stan Williamson. Chicago, Follett Pub. Co. [1963]

110 p. illus. 25 cm.

1. Christmas—Poetry. 2. Christmas stories. 3. American literature—Negro authors. 4. Negro literature—U. S. I. Title.

PS509.C56R6 810.89 63-17805

Library of Congress [5]

Literature (American)

M810. B73e

Brawley, Benjamin Griffith, 1882–1939, *ed.*

Early Negro American writers; selections with biographical and critical introductions, by Benjamin Brawley ... Chapel Hill, The University of North Carolina press, 1935.

ix, 305 p. 22cm.

1. Negro authors. 2. Negro literature (American) 3. American literature—Negro authors. I. Title.

35—7296

Library of Congress PS508.N3B7

[45g1] 810.822

Literature (American).

M810 B97n

Butcher, Margaret (Just) 1913-

The Negro in American culture; based on materials left by Alain Locke. [1st ed.] New York, Knopf, 1956.

294 p. 22 cm.

1. ~~Negroes in~~ literature. 2. ~~Negroes in~~ art. 3. ~~Negro~~ literature (American) 4. American literature—~~Negro~~ authors. 5. ~~Negro art.~~ 6. Music—~~Negroes.~~ 7. ~~Negroes—~~Dancing. I. Title. II. Locke, Alain Leroy.

E185.82.B89 325.260973 56—5783 ‡

Library of Congress [57e30]

Literature (American)

M813.08 C554

Clarke, John Henrik, 1915- *ed.*

American Negro short stories. [1st ed.] New York, Hill and Wang [1966]

xix, 355 p. 21 cm.

1. Short stories, American. 2. American literature—Negro authors. 3. Negro literature (American) I. Title.

PZ1.C563Am 66-23863

Library of Congress [3]

Literature (American)

M810.8 C88 Cromwell, Otelia ed.
Readings from negro authors, for schools and colleges, with a bibliography of negro literature, by Otelia Cromwell ... Lorenzo Dow Turner ... Eva B. Dykes ... New York, Harcourt, Brace and company [°1931]
xii, 388 p. 21cm.
"A bibliography of negro literature": p. 371-388; contains "Collateral reading."
1. Negro literature (American) 2. Negro literature (American)—Bibl. 3. American literature—Negro authors. I. Turner, Lorenzo Dow, joint ed. II. Dykes, Eva Beatrice, joint ed. III. Title.
31-31497
Library of Congress PS508.N3C7 [a45m1] 810.8

Literature, American

M813.5 Selc Seaver, Edwin, ed.
Cross section 1947; a collection of new American writing. New York, Simon and Schuster, 1947.
516p. 20cm.

Literature, Modern - 20th cent. - Hist.& crit.

M808.4 Sc8 Scott, Nathan A
Rehearsals of discomposure; alienation and reconciliation in modern literature: Franz Kafka, Ignazio Silone, D. H. Lawrence [and] T. S. Eliot. New York, King's Crown Press, 1952.
xv, 294 p. 21 cm.
Bibliography: p. [273]-288.
1. Religion and literature. 2. Literature, Modern—20th cent.—Hist. & crit. I. Title.
PN49.S33 809.04 52—13349
Library of Congress [53h7]

Literature (American)

M810.8 D81a Dreer, Herman, 1889–
American literature by Negro authors. New York, Macmillan, 1950.
xvii, 334 p. ports. 22 cm.
Bibliography: p. 327-332.
1. Negro literature (American) 2. American literature—Negro authors. 3. Negro authors. I. Title.
PS508.N3D7 810.82 50-9459
Library of Congress [30]

Literature (American) - Collections

M810.8 C22 The Carolina magazine; literary supplement to the Daily tar heel. Negro number, May 4, 1930. Chapel Hill, University of North Carolina.
8p. 38cm.

Literature, Primitive.

Africa M896.1 Sy25 Sydow, Eckart von, 1885-1942, ed.
Poesia dei popoli primitivi; lirica religiosa, magica e profana. Scelta, introd. e note di Eckart v. Sydow. [Traduzione di Roberto Bazlen. Modena, Guanda, 1951.
197 p. 24 cm. (Collezione Fenice; edizione fuori serie, 15)
1. Literature, Primitive. 2. Poetry—Collections. 3. Italian poetry—Translations from foreign literature. I. Title.
[PN1347.S] A 52-7577
Illinois. Univ. Library for Library of Congress [3]

Literature (American)

M810.9 H55an Hill, Herbert, 1924– ed.
Anger, and beyond: the Negro writer in the United States. [1st ed.] New York, Harper & Row [1966]
xxii, 227 p. 22 cm.
1. Negro authors. 2. Negro literature (American) 3. American literature—Negro authors. I. Title.
PS153.N5H5 810.9 65—14654
Library of Congress [66f4]

Literature, Modern - Translations into English.

West Indies M808.8 Howes, Barbara, ed.
From the green Antilles; writings of the Caribbean. New York, Macmillan [°1966]
xvi, 368 p. 21 cm.
1. Caribbean literature. 2. English literature—Translations from foreign literature. 3. Literature, Modern—Translations into English. I. Title.
PR9325.H6 808.890729 66-10593
Library of Congress [21-1]

Literature and art.

Latin America M861.08 B21a Ballagas, Emilio, ed.
... Antología de poesía negra hispano americana. Madrid, M. Aguilar, 1935.
8 p. l., [11]-182 p., 3 l. illus. 18½cm.
"Indice alfabético de autores y datos sobre los mismos": p. [175]-182.
1. Negroes in literature and art. 2. Spanish-American poetry (Collections) I. Title.
36—28887
Library of Congress PQ7084.B25 [48c1] 861.0822

Literature (American)

M810.8 W32 Watkins, Sylvestre C ed.
Anthology of American Negro literature, edited by Sylvestre C. Watkins, with an introduction by John T. Frederick. New York, The Modern library [1944]
xvii, 481 p. 18½ cm. (*Half-title: The modern library of the world's best books*)
"Bibliographical notes": p. [457]-481.
1. Negro literature (American) 2. American literature—Negro authors. I. Title.
44—6528
Library of Congress PS508.N3W3 [48b2] 810.82

West Indies Literature, Modern- Translations into English.

M808.8 H839 Howes, Barbara, ed.
From the green Antilles; writings of the Caribbean. New York, Macmillan [°1966]
xvi, 368 p. 21 cm.

Literature and art.

M812 B64 Bond, Frederick Weldon.
The Negro and the drama; the direct and indirect contribution which the American Negro has made to drama and the legitimate stage, with the underlying conditions responsible, by Frederick W. Bond. Washington, D. C., The Associated publishers, inc. [°1940]
x, 213 p. 20 cm.
Bibliography: p. 202-208.
1. Negro drama. 2. ~~Negroes in~~ literature and art. I. Title.
40-32025
Library of Congress PS338.N4B6 [3] 812.09

Literature (American)-Addresses, essays, lectures.

M808.08 C76a Conference of Negro Writers. *1st, New York, 1959.*
The American Negro writer and his roots; selected papers. New York, American Society of African Culture, 1960.
70 p. illus. 22 cm.
1. Negro literature (American)—Addresses, essays, lectures. 2. American literature—Negro authors—Addresses, essays, lectures. 3. Negro authors. I. Title.
PS153.N5C6 1959ac 809.8 60—10084 ‡
Library of Congress [60f5]

Literature, Modern-20th cent.

M808.8 N42 New world writing. 1st–
Apr. 1952–
[New York] New American Library.
v. 18 cm. (N. A. L. Mentor books)
1. Literature, Modern—20th cent. 2. American literature—20th cent.
PN6014.N427 808.8 52—1806
Library of Congress [54f5]

Literature and art.

M810. B73n 2 Brawley, Benjamin Griffith, 1882-1939.
The Negro genius; a new appraisal of the achievement of the American Negro in literature and the fine arts, by Benjamin Brawley ... New York, Dodd, Mead & company, 1937.
xiii, 366 p. front., plates, ports. 20½ cm.
Bibliography: p. 331-350.
1. Negro authors. 2. Negro artists. 3. Negro musicians. 4. Negro literature—Hist. & crit. 5. Negroes in literature and art. I. Title.
37—4124
Library of Congress E185.82.B816 [47b3] 325.260973

Literature (American)— Bibl.

M810.8 C88 Cromwell, Otelia ed.
Readings from negro authors, for schools and colleges, with a bibliography of negro literature, by Otelia Cromwell ... Lorenzo Dow Turner ... Eva B. Dykes ... New York, Harcourt, Brace and company [°1931]
xii, 388 p. 21cm.
"A bibliography of negro literature": p. 371-388; contains "Collateral reading."
1. Negro literature (American) 2. Negro literature (American)—Bibl. 3. American literature—Negro authors. I. Turner, Lorenzo Dow, joint ed. II. Dykes, Eva Beatrice, joint ed. III. Title.
31-31497
Library of Congress PS508.N3C7 [a45m1] 810.8

Literature, Modern - 20th century.

M808.8 N42 New World writing. 1st-
Apr. 1952-
[New York] New American Library.
v. 18cm. (N.A.L. Mentor books)

Literature and art.

M810.9 B81 Brown, Sterling Allen, 1901–
... The Negro in American fiction, by Sterling Brown ... Washington, D. C., The Association in Negro folk education, 1937.
3 p. l., 209 p. 21½cm. (Bronze booklet no. 6)
"Selected reading list": p. 207-209.
1. ~~Negro~~ fiction (American)—Hist. & crit. 2. ~~Negroes in~~ literature and art. I. Title.
38—20045
Library of Congress E185.5.B85 no. 6
——— Copy 2. PS374.N4B7
[45m1] (325.260973) 813.09

Literature, American.

M811.5 H87sp Hughes, Langston, 1902-
Selected works of Langston Hughes. Translated by Shojo Kojima. Japanese edition. Toyko, 1959.
300? p. port. 18½cm.

Literature, Modern-20th cent.-Hist.&crit.

M808.4 Sc8m Scott, Nathan A
Modern literature and the religious frontier. [1st ed.] New York, Harper [1958]
138 p. 22 cm.
Includes bibliography.
1. Religion and literature. 2. Literature, Modern—20th cent.—Hist. & crit. I. Title.
PN1077.S39 809.04 58-7476 ‡
Library of Congress [25]

Literature and art.

M810.9 B81n Brown, Sterling Allen, 1901–
... Negro poetry and drama, by Sterling A. Brown ... Washington, D. C., The Associates in Negro folk education, 1937.
3 p. l., 142 p. 21½cm. (Bronze booklet no. 7)
"Reading references" at end of each chapter.
1. ~~Negroes in~~ literature and art. 2. ~~Negro~~ poetry (American)—Hist. & crit. 3. Negro drama. I. Title.
38—20046
Library of Congress E185.5.B85 no. 7
——— Copy 2. PS153.N5B68
[42n2] (325.260973) 811.09

M910
C77n

Literature and art.
Cook, Mercer, ed.
Le noir; morceaux choisis de vingt-neuf Francais celebres, by Mercer Cook... New York, Cincinnati [etc.] American book company [c1934]

x, 173p. incl. front., ports. 19½cm.
On cover: W. Mercer Cook.
Selections for the use of French classes in colored schools.
Includes "Suggested readings."

Literature and art.
M757
C78
Cooper, William Arthur, 1895–
A portrayal of Negro life, by William Arthur Cooper. Published under the auspices of the Division of coöperation in education and race relations; coöperating organizations: State department of public instruction, Raleigh, N. C., University of North Carolina, Chapel Hill, N. C., Duke university, Durham, N. C. [Durham, N. C., The Seeman printery, inc.] 1936.
xi, 110 p. incl. plates, ports. 28½ cm.
"Portraits ... all of real people ... painted to portray some phase or mood of Negro life."—Pref.
1. Negroes in literature and art. I. Title.
36—10959
Library of Congress ND237.C68A4
[48f½] 757

Literature and art.
M808
D98
Dykes, Eva Beatrice.
The Negro in English romantic thought; or, A study of sympathy for the oppressed, by Eva Beatrice Dykes. Washington, D. C., The Associated publishers, inc., 1942.
5 p. l., 197 p. 23½cm.
Bibliography: p. 157-166.

1. Romanticism—England. 2. Negroes in literature and art. 3. English literature—18th cent.—Hist. & crit. 4. English literature—19th cent.—Hist. & crit. I. Title.
42—6447
Library of Congress PR447.D9
[45j2] 820.903

Literature and art.
M812.5
Ed5s
Edmonds, Randolph, 1900–
Six plays for a Negro theatre, by Randolph Edmonds ... foreword by Frederick H. Koch ... Boston, Walter H. Baker company [c1934]
3 p. l., 5-155 p. 19½cm.
CONTENTS.—Bad man.—Old man Pete.—Nat Turner.—Breeders.—Bleeding hearts.—The new window.

1. Negro drama. 2. Negroes in literature and art. I. Title: Plays for a Negro theatre.
[*Full name:* Sheppard Randolph Edmonds]
34—10819
Library of Congress PS3509.D56S6 1934
[44d1] 812.5

Literature and art.
M810.9
F75
Ford, Nick Aaron.
The contemporary Negro novel, study in race relations, by Nick Aaron Ford. Boston, Meador publishing company, 1936.
108 p. 21 cm.
Based on the author's thesis (M. A.) University of Iowa, presented in 1934 under title: A study of the race problem as it appears in contemporary novels written by Negroes.
Bibliography: p. 107-108.

1. Negro fiction (American)—Hist. & crit. 2. Negroes in literature and art. 3. Negroes. I. Title.
36—29260
Library of Congress PS374.N4F6
[a44e1] 813.509

Literature and art.
M323
J632b
Johnson, James Weldon, 1871–1938.
... Black Manhattan. New York, A. A. Knopf, 1930.
xvii p., 2 l., [3]–284, [xxi]–xxxiv p., 1 l. front., pl., ports., 2 maps on 1 pl., facsim. 19½cm.
Illustrated lining-papers.

1. Negroes—New York (City) 2. Harlem, New York (City) 3. Negroes in literature and art. I. Title.
30—18832
Library of Congress F128.9.N3J67
[43b²2] 325.26097471

Literature and art.
M806
L79n4
Locke, Alain LeRoy, 1886–
... Negro art: past and present, by Alain Locke ... Washington, D. C., Associates in Negro folk education, 1936.
3 p. l., 122 p. 20½cm. (Bronze booklet no. 3)
"Reading references" at end of each chapter.

1. Negro art. 2. Negroes in literature and art. I. Title.
37—7111
Library of Congress E185.5.B85 no. 3
——— Copy 2. E185.82.L74
[44h1] (325.260973) 709.73

Literature and art.
M323
J632r
Johnson, James Weldon, 1871-1938.
Race prejudice and the Negro artist, by James Weldon Johnson. Harpers monthly, November, 1928.

770-776p. 24½cm.

Uruguay
M864.6
P41m
Literature and art.
Pereda Valdés, Ildefonso, 1899–
... El negro rioplatense, y otros ensayos. Montevideo, C. García & cía, 1937.
187, [1] p., 1 l. plates. 17½cm.
CONTENTS.—Contribución al estudio del tema del negro en la literatura castellana hasta fines de la edad de oro.—Contribución al estudio de la música popular brasileña.—Supersticiones africanas del Río de la Plata.—Los pueblos negros del Uruguay y la influencia africana en el habla rioplatense.—Vocabulario de palabras de origen africano en el habla rioplatense.—El diablo mundo y Martín Fierro.—"La mojiganga de la muerte"; una pieza menor poco conocida de Calderón.—Los antiquijotes.—El "no" japonés y la tragedia griega.—Balzac, novelista de una época.—Las ideas ultraconservadoras de Chateaubriand.
1. Negroes in literature and art. 2. Negroes in South America. 3. Literature, Modern—Addresses, essays, lectures. I. Title.
39—16565
Library of Congress PQ8519.P26N4
[42c1] 864.6

Literature and art.
M812.08
R39n
Richardson, Willis, 1889– *ed.*
Negro history in thirteen plays, by Willis Richardson and May Miller. Washington, D. C., The Associated publishers, inc. [c1935]
vii, 333 p. 21½cm.

1. Negro drama. 2. Negroes in literature and art. I. Miller, May, joint ed. II. Title.
36—17
Library of Congress PS627.N4R47
[43u2] 812.50822

Literature and art.
M812.08
R39
Richardson, Willis, 1889– *comp.*
Plays and pageants from the life of the Negro [compiled by] Willis Richardson. Washington, D. C., The Associated publishers, inc. [c1930]
x, 373 p. incl. front., illus., plates. 22½cm.
CONTENTS.—Plays: Sacrifice, by Thelma M. Duncan. Antar of Araby, by Maud Cuney-Hare. Ti Yette, by John Matheus. Graven images, by May Miller. Riding the goat, by May Miller. The black horseman, by Willis Richardson. The king's dilemma, by Willis Richardson. The house of sham, by Willis Richardson.—Pageants: Two races, by Inez M. Burke. Out of the dark, by Dorothy C. Guinn. The light of the women, by Frances Gunner. Ethiopia at the bar of justice, by Edward J. McCoo.
1. Negro drama. 2. Negroes in literature and art. I. Title.
30—7094
Library of Congress PS627.N4R5
[43n1]

Literature and art.
M976.3
R76
Roussève, Charles Barthelemy.
The Negro in Louisiana; aspects of his history and his literature, by Charles Barthelemy Roussève, M. A. New Orleans, The Xavier university press, 1937.
xvii, 212 p. front., illus. (music) plates, diagrs. 20½cm.
"This work, prepared in 1935 in partial fulfillment of the requirements for the degree of master of arts, makes its appearance ... substantially as it was originally written, save for ... several minor alterations and the addition of a few details."—p. vii.
Bibliography: p. 193-201.
1. Negroes—Louisiana. 2. Negroes in literature and art. 3. Negro authors. I. Title.
38—525
Library of Congress E185.93.L6R6
[42h2] 325.2609763

Literature and art.
M813.5
W589
Whiting, Helen Adele (Johnson) 1885–
Negro art, music and rhyme, for young folks, by Helen Adele Whiting; illustrations by Lois Mailou Jones. Book II. Washington, D. C., The Associated publishers, inc. [c1938]
[38] p. illus. 23½cm.
Without music.
Book I published under title: Negro folk tales for pupils in the primary grades.

1. Negroes in literature and art. 2. Negro songs. I. Title.
38—17194
Library of Congress PE1119.W55
[45k1] 372.4

Guyana
M801
H249
Literature and society - Addresses, essays, lectures.
Harris, Theodore Wilson.
Tradition, the writer and society: critical essays; with an appendix by C. L. R. James. London, Port of Spain, New Beacon, 1967.
75 p. 18½ cm. 8/-
Appendix: Introduction to tradition and the West Indian novel, by C. L. R. James. (B 67-16502)

1. Literature and society—Addresses, essays, lectures. I. Title. II. James, Cyril Lionel Robert, 1901- Introduction to tradition and the West Indian novel.
PR6058.A692T7 801 67-101761
Library of Congress [3]

Congo (Leopoldville)
M840.8
M971
La littérature française africaine...
Mushiete, Paul
La littérature française africaine; petite anthologie des écrivains noirs d'expression française. Leverville, Bibliothèque de l'Étoile, 1957.

40p. 17½cm.

M781
R271
The literature of jazz, a selective bibliography.
Reisner, Robert George.
The literature of jazz, a selective bibliography. With an introd. by Marshall W. Stearns. [2d ed. rev. and enl.] New York, New York Public Library, 1959.
63 p. 26 cm.

1. Jazz music—Bibl. I. Title.
ML128.J3R4 1959 016.78157 59-9577
Library of Congress [5]

M810.8
F31
Lithographs, American.
Federal writers' project.
American stuff; an anthology of prose & verse by members of the Federal writers' project, with sixteen prints by the Federal art project. New York, The Viking press, 1937.
xvii, [1], 301 p. plates. 22cm.

1. American literature—20th cent. 2. Lithographs, American. 3. Drawings, American. I. Federal art project. II. Title.
37—28500
Library of Congress PS536.F4
[44u1] 810.822

Cameroun
M780
B36
Littérature et musique populaires en Afrique noire.
Belinga, M S Eno, 1935-
Littérature et musique populaires en Afrique noire. [Paris, Editions Cujas, 1965]

258p. illus. 18cm.
Includes bibliography.

Haiti
M840.9
V44L
... La littérature haitienne.
Vaval, Duraciné, 1879-
... La littérature haitienne; essais critiques ... Paris, Bibliotheque Internationale d'Edition, E. Sansot & Cie, 1911.

330p. front. 19½cm.

Haiti
M972.94
L71r
1791
Littey, Janvier.
Réponse de Janvier Littey. Homme de couleur de la Martinique, et député a la Covention nationale, A. P. J. Leborgne. [Paris; De l'Imprimerie de Cuffroy, [1791?]

10p. 22cm.

1. Santo Domingo - (French Colony).
2. Haiti - Pol. & govt., 1791-1804.

MB9
L72
Little, Malcolm, 1925–1965.
The autobiography of Malcolm X. With the assistance of Alex Haley. Introd. by M. S. Handler. Epilogue by Alex Haley. New York, Grove Press [1965]
xvi, 455 p. illus., ports. 24 cm.
Partial contents.- On Malcolm X, by Ossie Davis.

1. Black Muslims. I. Haley, Alex. II. Title.
E185.97.L5A3 301.451960730924 65—27331
Library of Congress [66w14]

M323.4 W52 Little, Malcolm, 1925-1965.
Black Muslims and Civil Rights.
pp. 52-58.
In: Westin, Alan F. Freedom now. New York, Basic Books, 1964.

M301 L726m Little, Malcolm, 1925-1965.
Malcolm X speaks; selected speeches and statements. ₑEdited with prefatory notes, by George Breitmanₐ New York, Merit Publishers, 1965
xiii, 242p. illus., ports. 22cm.
1. Race question. 2. Civil rights. 3. Black Muslims. I. Breitman, George, ed. II. Title.

M301 L726 Little, Malcolm, 1925-1965
Two speeches. ₍New York₎ Pioneer Publishers ₍1965₎
31p. 21cm.
"All of the material in this pamplhlet originally appeared in the Militant."
1. Civil rights.

Little, Malcolm, 1925-1965 - Poetry.
M811.08 R153 Randall, Dudley, 1914- comp.
For Malcolm; poems on the life and the death of Malcolm X. Edited by Dudley Randall and Margaret G. Burroughs. Pref. and eulogy by Ossie Davis. ₍1st ed.₎ Detroit, Broadside Press, 1967.
xxvi, 127 p. ports. 21 cm.
Bibliography: p. 113-120.
1. Little, Malcolm, 1925-1965—Poetry. I. Burroughs, Margaret G., 1917- joint comp. II. Title.
PS3568.A49F6 811'.008'03 66-28244
Library of Congress ₍3₎

Little brown baby.
M811.4 D91 11 Dunbar, Paul Laurence, 1872-1906.
Little brown baby ₍by₎ Paul Laurence Dunbar; poems for young people. Selections, with biographical sketch by Bertha Rodgers; illustrated by Erick Berry ₍*pseud.*₎ New York, Dodd, Mead & company, 1940.
xiv, 106 p. incl. plates. 21 cm.
1. Poetry.
I. Rodgers, Bertha, ed. II. Best, Allena (Champlin) 1892- illus. III. Title.
Library of Congress PZ8.3.D918Li 40—4721
₍45t1₎

A little dreaming.
M811.5 J6321 Johnson, Fenton.
A little dreaming, by Fenton Johnson. Chicago, The Peterson linotyping company, 1913.
80 p. front. (port.) pl. 20ᶜᵐ. $0.75
Poems.
I. Title.
Library of Congress PS3519.O245L5 1913 13-15814
Copyright A 347983

M615.4 P27l A little fun with the U.S.P.
Patrick, Thomas William, 1872-
A little fun with the U.S.P. (8th revision) before it leaves us. Boston, n.d.
₍5₎p. 18cm.

Little Rock, Arkansas.
MB9 B32 Bates, Daisy (Gatson)
The long shadow of Little Rock, a memoir. New York, David McKay Co. ₍1962₎
234 p. illus. 21 cm.
Portrait of author on book jacket.
1. Negroes—Little Rock, Ark. 2. Little Rock, Ark.—Public schools. I. Title.
F419.L7B3 920.7 62—20233 ‡
Library of Congress ₍62f2₎

Little Rock, Ark.
M976.7 W93 Writers' program. *Arkansas.*
Survey of Negroes in Little Rock and North Little Rock, compiled by the Writers' program of the Work projects administration in the state of Arkansas. Sponsored by the Urban league of greater Little Rock, Arkansas. ₍Little Rock, °1941₎
4 p. l., 101 p. incl. tables. 23ᶜᵐ.
Bibliography: p. 99-101.
1. Negroes—Little Rock, Ark. 2. Negroes—North Little Rock, Ark. I. Title.
Library of Congress F419.L7W85 41-4905
₍3₎ 323.2609767

Little Rock, Arkansas - Public schools.
MB9 B32 Bates, Daisy (Gatson)
The long shadow of Little Rock, a memoir. New York, David McKay Co. ₍1962₎
234 p. illus. 21 cm.
Portrait of author on book jacket.
1. Negroes—Little Rock, Ark. 2. Little Rock, Ark.—Public schools. I. Title.
F419.L7B3 920.7 62—20233 ‡
Library of Congress ₍62f2₎

A little souvenir...
M811.5 C59r Clem, Charles Douglass, 1875-
A little souvenir, by Chas. D. Clem. ₍n.p.n.p.₎ c1908.
₍8₎ p. port. 19½cm.

A little sunshine.
M811.5 T66b Todd, Walter E.
A little sunshine, by Walter E. Todd. ₍n.p., n.p., n.d.₎
61p. front. (port.) 15cm.
Poems.

Litwalton, Virginia.
M975 N31 Thom, William Taylor.
The Negroes of Litwalton, Virginia: A social study of the Oyster Negr. ₍Bulletin of the Labor Dept., no.37, 1901. pp. 1115-1170.
In: The Negro in the black belt... Washington, D.C., Dept. of Labor, ₍1897-1902₎

M616 W93t2 Liver.
Wright, Louis Tompkins, 1891-1952.
Traumatic rupture of the liver without penetrating wounds, a study of thirty-two cases. Chicago, American Medical Association, 1947.
20p. tables. 27cm.
Reprinted from the Archives of surgery, 54:613-632, June 1947.

The living and the dead, and other stories.
South Africa
M896.3 M87L Mphahlel, Ezekiel.
The living and the dead, and other stories. Illus. by Peter Clarke. Ibadan ₍Nigeria₎ Ministry of Education ₍196-?₎
66 p. illus. 21 cm.
I. Title.
PZ4.M94Li 62-50319 ‡
Library of Congress ₍1₎

The living dead.
M811.5 G78 Graves, Linwood D.
Poems of simplicity, and The living dead, a short true story, by Linwood D. Graves. ₍Kingsport, Tenn., Priv. print. ₍Kingsport press, inc.₎ 1938.
x, 116 p. incl. front. (port.) 20ᶜᵐ.
I. Title. II. Title: The living dead.
Library of Congress PS3601.G7P6 1938 40-3363
——— Copy 2.
Copyright ₍2₎ 811.5

The living is easy.
M813.5 W521 West, Dorothy.
The living is easy. Boston, Houghton, Mifflin Co., 1948.
347 p. 22 cm.
I. Title.
PZ3.W5174Li 48-6871*
Library of Congress ₍4₎

M810.4 H521 The living novel.
Hicks, Granville, 1901- ed.
The living novel, a symposium. New York, Macmillan, 1957.
xii, 230 p. 22 cm.
Ellison, Ralph. - Society, morality, and the novel. In: The living novel. pp. 58-91.
White author.
1. American fiction—Addresses, essays, lectures. I. Title.
PS379.H5 813.504 57—12221
Library of Congress ₍58f40₎

Living with others.
M370. Sc81 Scott, John Irving E.
Living with others; a foundation guidance program for junior high and upper elementary grades, by J. Irving E. Scott ... Boston, Meador publishing company, 1939.
110 p. incl. diagr., form. 21ᶜᵐ.
Includes bibliographies.
1. Education of children. I. Title.
39—10724
Library of Congress LB1027.S37
₍42d1₎ 370.15

Livingstone, David, 1813-1873.
Martinique
M843.9 M32L Maran, René, 1887-
... Livingstone et l'exploration de l'Afrique. Dix-huit reproductions et trois cartes. ₍Paris₎ Gallimard ₍1938₎
5 p. l., ₍13₎-276 p., 1 l. incl. plates, port., maps. 21ᶜᵐ. (La découverte du monde, collection dirigée par Raymond Burgard. ₍3₎)
1. Livingstone, David, 1813-1873. 2. Africa, Central—Disc. & explor. 3. Africa, South—Descr. & trav.
39-13318
Library of Congress DT731.L8M27
Copyright A—Foreign 39649
₍2₎ ₍922.842₎ 923.942

Livingston, David, 1813-1873.
MB9 L76r Rankin, Arthur Edward, 1879-
Livingstone returned; the story of a measureless labor of love. With an introd. by G. Lake Imes. ₍1st ed.₎ New York, Exposition Press ₍1955₎
131 p. 21 cm.
1. Livingstone, David, 1813-1873. I. Title.
DT731.L8R3 923.942 55-9409 ‡
Library of Congress ₍2₎

Livingstone College, Salisbury, N. C.

MB9
F73r
Fonvielle, W F
Reminiscences of college days, by W. F. Fonvielle ... Goldsboro, N. C., Printed for the author by Edwards & Broughton, 1904.
14.p. front. portraits. 20cm.

Lloyd, Lucy C., ed.

S. Africa
M398
B61b
Bleek, Wilhelm Heinrich Immanuel, 1827-1875, comp.
Specimens of Bushman folklore, collected by the late W. H. I. Bleek, PH. D., and L. C. Lloyd; ed. by the latter; with an introduction by George McCall Theal ... Translation into English; illustrations; and appendix. London, G. Allen & company, ltd., 1911.
xl, 468 p. plates (part col.) ports. (2 col., incl. front.) 22½cm.
"The original Bushman text ... is printed side by side with the English translation."
1. Folk-lore—Africa, South. 2. Bushmen. I. Lloyd, Lucy C., ed. II. Theal, George McCall, 1837-1919. III. Title: Bushmen folklore.
11—20041
Library of Congress GR360.B9B4 [43e1]

Uganda
M967.61
Ad45
Lobo Acoli.
Adimola, A B
Lobo Acoli [A geographical survey of Acoli district] Kampala, East African Literature Bureau, 1956.
37p. illus., maps. 21½cm.
Written in Acoli.

Livingstone returned.

MB9
L76r
Rankin, Arthur Edward, 1879–
Livingstone returned; the story of a measureless labor of love. With an introd. by G. Lake Imes. [1st ed.] New York, Exposition Press [1955]
131 p. 21 cm.
1. Livingstone, David, 1813-1873. I. Title.
DT731.L8R3 923.942 55-9409 ‡
Library of Congress [3]

Senegal
M966.3
T688
Lo, Mamadou, joint author.
Traoré, Bakary.
Forces politiques en Afrique noire, par Bakari Traoré, Mamadou Lô et Jean-Louis Alibert ... Paris, Presses universitaires de France, 1966.
viii, 312 p. 24 cm. (Travaux et recherches de la Faculté de droit et des sciences économiques de Paris. Série "Afrique," no 2) 20 F. (F 66-12565)
Includes bibliographies.
1. Political parties—Senegal. 2. Africa, Sub-Saharan—Politics. I. Title. (Series: Paris. Université. Faculté de droit et des sciences économiques. Série "Afrique," no 2) II. Lo, Mamadou. III. Alibert, Jean-Louis. IV. Series.
JQ3396.A979T7 329.9'663 67-74794
Library of Congress [5]

Ghana
M966.7
N67
Local government - Ghana.
Nsarkoh, J K
Local government in Ghana [by] J. K. Nsarkoh. Accra, Ghana Universities Press, 1964.
309 p. 23 cm.
"List of some local government books": p. [322]-323. Bibliographical footnotes.
1. Local government—Ghana. I. Title.
JS7649.G62N75 352.0667 64-6007
Library of Congress [1]

Martinique
M843.9
M321l
Le livre de la brousse, roman.
Maran, René, 1887–
... Le livre de la brousse, roman. Paris, A. Michel [1934]
287, [1] p. 19cm.
I. Title.
Library of Congress PQ2625.A74L5 1934 34-34731
Copyright A—Foreign 25210 [3] 843.91

Nigeria
M966.9
L78f
LoBagola, Bata Kindai Amgoza ibn.
The folk tales of a savage, by Lobagola; illustrated by Erick Berry. New York, A. A. Knopf, 1930.
7 p. l., 199, [1] p. front., illus. 20½cm.
Illustrated lining-papers.
1. Tales, African. I. Title.
30—21411
Library of Congress GR350.L6
——— Copy 2.
Copyright A 25961 [41j1] 398.21

Nigeria
M966.9
AK6e
Local government-Gt. Brit.-Colonies-Africa.
Akpan, Ntieyong U
Epitaph to indirect rule; a discourse on local government in Africa. London, Cassell [1956]
204 p. 19 cm.
1. Local government—Gt. Brit.—Colonies—Africa. 2. Local government—Nigeria. I. Title.
JS7525.A45 352.06 56-58715 ‡
Library of Congress [57c2]

Le livre d'or de l'effort colonial...

Madagascar
M325
B29l
Basquel, Victor, 1867–
... Le livre d'or de l'effort colonial français pendant la grande guerre, 1914-1918, publié ... par l'Institut colonial français ... Paris, Éditions de l'Institut colonial français, 1922-23.
2 v. 25½cm.
At head of title: Victor Basquel et Alcide Delmont.
Vol. 2 has imprint: Paris, Les Presses universitaires de France, 1923.
CONTENTS.—I. 1. Guadeloupe, Guyane, Inde française, Martinique, Océanie française, Réunion, Iles Saint-Pierre et Miquelon.—I. 2. Afrique occidentale et équatoriale françaises, Côte des Somalis.
No more published?
1. European war, 1914-1918—France. 2. France—Colonies. I. Delmont, Alcide, 1874– joint author. II. Institut colonial français, Paris. III. Title.
[Full name: Marie Sylvestre Victor Basquel]
24-918 Revised
Library of Congress D609.F82B3 [r41b2]

Nigeria
MB9
L781o
LoBagola, Bata Kindai Amgoza Ibn,
LoBagola; histoire d'un sauvage africain par lui-meme. Traduite de l'Anglais par G. M. Drucker. Paris, Albin Michel 1932.
312p. 19cm. (Collection des maitres de la litterature etrangere)
Autobiography.
1. Ethnology - Nigeria. 2. Nigeria. I. Title.

Kenya
M967.62
L18
Local government - Kenya Colony and Protectorate.
La Fontaine, Sidney Hubert, 1887–
Thirikari ya handu o handū Kenya; [Local government in Kenya] ihumo o na ūkūria wayo, rīandīkītwo nī S. H. La Fontaine magīteithanagia wīra wa rīo na J. H. Mower. [Translated into Kikuyu by Mathayo Njeroge] Nairobi, Eagle Press, 1955.
63p. 21½cm.
Written in Kikuyu.
1. Local government - Kenya Colony and Protectorate. I. Title. II. Mower, J. H. III. Njerage, Mathayo, tr.

Le livre du souvenir.

Martinique
M841.91
M321s
Maran, René, 1887–
Le livre du souvenir; poèmes (1909-1957). Paris, Présence Africaine, 1958.
142p. 19cm.

Nigeria
M966.9
L78 l
LoBagola, Bata Kindai Amgoza ibn.
LoBagola; an African savage's own story. New York, A. A. Knopf, 1930.
xxiii p., 1 l., 402 p., 1 l. 2 port. (incl. front.) facsims. 21cm.
1. Ethnology—Nigeria. 2. Nigeria.
30—12774
Library of Congress DT515.L6 [44n1] [572.9682] 920.9

Nigeria
M966.9
AK6e
Local government-Nigeria.
Akpan, Ntieyong U
Epitaph to indirect rule; a discourse on local government in Africa. London, Cassell [1956]
204 p. 19 cm.
1. Local government—Gt. Brit.—Colonies—Africa. 2. Local government—Nigeria. I. Title.
JS7525.A45 352.06 56-58715 ‡
Library of Congress [57c2]

Puerto Rico
M863
L13L
La Llamarada.
LaGuerre, Enrique A
La Llamarada (novela). Edicion décimasegunda. Mexico, Editorial Orion, 1961.
295p. 19cm.

Ivory Coast
M896.3
L78k
Loba, Aké.
Kocoumbo; L'étudian noir, roman. Paris, Flammarion, 1960.
267p.
I. Title.

Ghana
M966.7
N67
Local government in Ghana.
Nsarkoh, J K
Local government in Ghana [by] J. K. Nsarkoh. Accra, Ghana Universities Press, 1964.
309 p. 23 cm.
"List of some local government books": p. [322]-323. Bibliographical footnotes.
1. Local government—Ghana. I. Title.
JS7649.G62N75 352.0667 64-6007
Library of Congress [1]

La llamarada (novela)

M863.6
L131
Laguerre, Enrique A.
... La llamarada <novela> [Aguadilla, Puerto Rico, América [Tipografía Ruiz, 1935]
361 p., 2 l. 20½cm.
I. Title.
36-11864
Library of Congress PQ7439.L3L5
——— Copy 2.
Copyright A 90737 [2] 863.6

Rhodesia
M896.3
Sa46o
Lobengula, King of the Matabele, 1833 (ca.)-1893?- Fiction.
Samkange, Stanlake John Thompson, 1922–
On trial for my country [by] Stanlake Samkange. London, Heinemann, 1966.
viii, 160 p. 20½ cm. 18/- (B 66-17472)
Map on endpapers.
1. Lobengula, King of the Matabele, 1833 (ca.)-1893?—Fiction. 2. Rhodes, Cecil John, 1853-1902—Fiction. I. Title.
PZ4.S188On 67-70814
Library of Congress [3]

Haiti
M841.
L78c
Lochard, Paul, 1835-1919.
Les chants du soir; poesies, par P. Lochard. Paris, Imprimeries Typogrpahique Kugelmann, 1878.
210p. 18cm.
Negro author.
1. ~~Haitian poetry~~ 1. Haitian poetry.
I. Title.

Haiti M941 L78f
Lochard, Paul, 1835–1919.
... Les feuilles de chêne. Paris, Ateliers haïtiens, 1901.
2 p. l., [7]–190, [2] p. 22cm.
"Préface" (p. [7]–22) signed: A. Firmin.
I. Firmin, Anténor, 1850–1911. II. Title. 1. Haitian poetry.
25—20873
Library of Congress PQ3949.L6F4 [a40b1]

M808.8 N42 v.1
Locke, Alain Leroy, 1886-1954.
The Negro in American literature.
(In: New world writing, 1. New York, New American Library, 1952. 18 cm. p. 18-33)

M308 L79r
Locke, Alain Le Roy, 1886–1954
Le role du Nègre dans la culture des Amériques, conférences. Port-au-Prince, Haïti, Impr. de l'État, 1943.
141 p. 21 cm.
"La traduction française du texte anglais original est due à la précieuse collaboration du docteur et de madame Camille Lhérisson."
1. ~~Negroes~~ Race 2. ~~Negroes in America~~. 3. America—Civilization. I. Title.
E185.6.L78 325.26097 48-37282*‡
Library of Congress [1]

The Loci communes of Philip Melanchthon...
M230.41 M48
Melanchthon, Philipp, 1497–1560.
The Loci communes of Philip Melanchthon, with a critical introduction by the translator, Charles Leander Hill ... and a special introduction by Dean E. E. Flack ... Boston, Meador publishing company [°1944]
274 p. 20½cm.
Bibliographical foot-notes. "Bibliographia Melanchthoniana": p. 268–274.
1. Theology, Doctrinal. 2. Lutheran church—Doctrinal and controversial works. I. Hill, Charles Leander, tr. II. Title.
45—1360
Library of Congress BR336.L62 [46g2] 230.41

M808 L79n8
Locke, Alain Leroy, 1886-1954
The Negro in art, a pictorial record of the Negro artist and of the Negro theme in art. Edited and annotated by Alain Locke. Washington, D.C., Associates in Negro Folk Education, 1940.
223p. plates. 31cm.
1. Art.

M808 L79w
Locke, Alain Le Roy, 1886-1954 ed.
When peoples meet; a study in race and culture contacts, edited by Alain Locke ... and Bernhard J. Stern ... New York, Committee on workshops, Progressive education association [°1942]
xii, 756 p. 24½ cm. (*Half-title:* Progressive education association publications. Committee on workshops)
1. Acculturation. 2. Minorities. 3. Race problems. ~~I. Stern, Bernhard Joseph, 1894–~~ joint ed. II. Title.
42—326
Library of Congress CB5.L6 [45g5] 901

M06 J61 no.20
Locke, Alain Le Roy, 1886-1954 comp.
A decade of negro self-expression, compiled by Alain Locke ... with a foreword by Howard W. Odum ... [Charlottesville, Va.] 1928.
20 p. 22½cm. (*On cover:* The Trustees of the John F. Slater fund. Occasional papers no. 26)
"This pamphlet is little more than an annotated list of books written by negroes since the outbreak of the world war."—p. [5]
Bibliography: p. [9]–20.
1. Negro literature—Bibl. I. Title.
30-31351
Library of Congress E185.5.J65 no. 26
——— Copy 2. PS153.N5L6
[35d2] (325.26) 016.81

M306 N21p
Locke, Alain Leroy, 1886-1954
The Negro's contribution in art to American culture. Chicago, 1933.
In: National Conference of Social Work. Proceedings... of the fifty-ninth annual session. Chicago, Univ. of Chicago for the Conference, 1933. pp. 315-322.
1. Art. I. Title.

Locke, Alain Leroy, 1886-1954.
M810 B97n
Butcher, Margaret (Just) 1913-
The Negro in American culture; based on materials left by Alain Locke. [1st ed.] New York, Knopf, 1956.
294 p. 22 cm.
1. ~~Negroes in~~ literature. 2. ~~Negroes in~~ art. 3. ~~Negro~~ literature (American) 4. American literature—~~Negro~~ authors. 5. ~~Negro art~~. 6. Music—~~Negroes~~. 7. ~~Negroes~~—Dancing. I. Title. II. Locke, Alain Leroy.
E185.82.B89 325.260973 56—5783 ‡
Library of Congress [57e30]

M808 L78v
Locke, Alain 1886-1954.
Values and imperatives.
(In: Kallen, Horace M. ed. American philosophy today and tomorrow. New York, Lee Furman, 1935. cm. p. 313-333)
1. Philosophy.

M306 Am35
Locke, Alain LeRoy, 1886-1954
The Negro's contribution to American art and literature.
(In: American Academy of Political and Social Science, Philadelphia. The American Negro. Philadelphia. 1928. 24cm. pp.234-247.

Locke, Alain Leroy, 1886-1954.
M810 B97no
Butcher, Margaret (Just), 1913-
Les noirs dans la civilisation Américaine. The Negro in American culture, based on materials left by Alain Locke. Traduit de l'américain par Françoise Vernan et Jean Rosenthal. Paris, Bouchet/Chastel, 1958.
320p. 18½cm.

M808 L79n2
Locke, Alain LeRoy, 1886-1954
... The Negro and his music, by Alain Locke ... Washington, D. C., The Associates in Negro folk education, 1936.
3 p. l., 142 p. 20½ cm. (Bronze booklet no. 2)
"Reading references" at end of each chapter; "Recorded illustrations" at end of most of the chapters.
1. ~~Negro~~ musicians. 2. ~~Negro songs~~—Hist. & crit. 3. Music—U. S.—Hist. & crit. 4. Jazz music. 5. Phonograph records. I. Title.
37—10637
Library of Congress E185.5.B85 no. 2
———Copy 2. ML3556.L6N4
[42t2] (325.260973) 784.756

M808 L79n9
Locke, Alain Le Roy, 1886-1954 ed.
The new negro; an interpretation, edited by Alain Locke; book decoration and portraits by Winold Reiss. New York, A. and C. Boni, 1925.
xviii, 446 p. col. front., illus. (incl. music, facsims.) plates (part col.) col. ports. 24½cm.
Bibliography: p. 415-446.
1. ~~Negroes~~. 2. ~~Negro~~ literature. I. Title.
25—25228
Library of Congress E185.82.L75 [43b2]

Locke, Alain LeRoy, 1886-1954.
M974.7 C55
Holmes, Eugene C
The legacy of Alain Locke.
Pp. 43-55.
In: Clarke, John Henrik, ed. Harlem. a community in transition. New York, Citadel Press, 1965.

M808 L79n4
Locke, Alain LeRoy, 1886-1954
... Negro art; past and present, by Alain Locke ... Washington, D.C., Associates in Negro folk education, 1936.
3 p. l., 122 p. 20½cm. (Bronze booklet no. 3)
"Reading references" at end of each chapter.
1. ~~Negro~~ art. 2. ~~Negroes in~~ literature and art. I. Title.
37—7111
Library of Congress E185.5.B85 no. 3
——— Copy 2. E185.82.L74
[44h1] (325.260973) 709.73

M812.08 L79
Locke, Alain Le Roy, 1886-1954 ed.
Plays of Negro life; a source-book of native American drama, selected and edited by Alain Locke ... and Montgomery Gregory ... decorations and illustrations by Aaron Douglas. New York and London, Harper & brothers, 1927.
10 p. l., 3–430 p. front., plates. 22½ cm.
"Bibliography of Negro drama": p. 424–430.
1. ~~Negroes in literature and~~ Art. 2. American drama (Collections) 3. ~~Negro~~ literature. I. Gregory, Montgomery, 1887– joint ed. II. Title. III. Title: Negro life, Plays of.
27—22553
Library of Congress PS627.N4L6 [45x2]

Locke, Alain LeRoy, 1886-1954.
M973 H83n
Howard University, *Washington, D. C. Graduate School. Division of the Social Sciences.*
The new Negro thirty years afterward; papers contributed to the sixteenth annual spring conference ... April 20, 21 and 22, 1955. Edited by Rayford W. Logan, chairman, Eugene C. Holmes [and] G. Franklin Edwards. Washington, Howard University Press, 1955 [i. e. 1956]
iv, 96 p. 28 cm.
"Dedicated to the memory of Professor Alain Locke."
Includes bibliographies. "Bibliography of the writings of Alain Leroy Locke ... by Robert E. Martin": p. 89–96.
1. Locke, Alain Le Roy, 1886–1954. 2. Negroes—Addresses, essays, lectures. I. Title.
E185.5.H73 1955a 325.2604 56-7060
Library of Congress [2]

M808 L79n6
Locke, Alain Le Roy, 1886-1954
... The Negro in America, by Alain Locke. Chicago, American library association, 1933.
64 p. 18 cm. (Reading with a purpose, no. 68)
Title vignette; tail-piece.
"Books recommended in this course": p. 50.
1. ~~Negroes~~ History. 2. ~~Negroes~~—Bibl. I. American library association. II. Title.
33—15520
Library of Congress E185.6.L77 [48k2] 325.260973

M812.08 L79
Locke, Alain Le Roy, 1886-1954 ed.
Plays of Negro life; a source-book of native American drama, selected and edited by Alain Locke ... and Montgomery Gregory ... decorations and illustrations by Aaron Douglas. New York and London, Harper & brothers, 1927.
10 p. l., 3–430 p. front., plates. 22½ cm.
"Bibliography of Negro drama": p. 424–430.
1. Negroes in literature and art. 2. American drama (Collections) 3. Negro literature. I. Gregory, Montgomery, 1887– joint ed. II. Title. III. Title: Negro life, Plays of.
27—22553
Library of Congress PS627.N4L6 [45x2]

M813.5 H87negt
Locke, Alain LeRoy, 1886-1954
Hughes, Langston, 1902-
The Negro troops; The Negro in fiction and fact, by Langston Hughes, Lawrence Gellert, Melville J. Herskovits, Alain Locke.
(In: Stewart, D.O. ed. Fighting words. New York, Harcourt, Brace and company, 1940. 21cm. p. 58-73).

Locke, Pliny Ishmall, 1850-1892

MB9
C79r

Coppin, Fanny Jackson, 1837-1913
Reminiscences of school life, and hints on teaching, by Fanny Jackson Coppin. Introduction by William C. Bolivar. [Philadelphia, Pa., A.M.E. Book Concern, 1913]

191p. port. (front.) 20½cm.
Introduction by William C. Bolivar.

MB9
311

Lockwood, Lewis C
Mary S. Peake, the colored teacher at Fortress Monroe. By Rev. Lewis C. Lockwood... with an appendix. Boston, American tract society [n.d.]
64p. front. 15½cm.
1. Peake, Mary Smith Kelsey, 1823-

Locman,

See

Lukmān, called Al-Hakīm

Locomotive puffs from the back shop.

M811.5
H242

Harris, Leon R
Locomotive puffs from the back shop, by Leon R. Harris. Boston, B. Humphries, inc. [1946]
56 p. 19½cm.

1. Railroads—Poetry. I. Title.

Library of Congress PS3515.A755L6 46-18741
[3] 811.5

M331
L82

Loeb, Charles Harold, 1905-
The future is yours; the history of the Future Outlook League, 1935-1946. Cleveland, Future Outlook League [1947]
124 p. plates, ports. 22 cm.

1. Future Outlook League. 2. ~~Negroes~~—Cleveland. I. Title.

E185.5.L6 325.2609771 47-26371*
Library of Congress [48e2]

M975.6
L82

Logan, Frenise A
The Negro in North Carolina, 1876-1894. Chapel Hill, University of North Carolina Press [1964]
ix, 244 p. 24 cm.
Bibliography: p. [221]-233.

1. ~~Negroes~~—North Carolina. I. Title.

E185.93.N6L6 301.451 64-13554
Library of Congress [5]

W. Indies
M972.9
B41

Logan, Rayford Whittingham, 1897-
Agriculture and industry.

(In: Latin American Economic Institute. Economic problems of the Caribbean area; ... New York, 1943. 23cm. p. 39-47).

M973
L82at

Logan, Rayford Whittingham, 1897- ed.
The attitude of the southern white press toward Negro suffrage, 1932-1940; edited by Rayford W. Logan, PH. D., with a foreword by Charles H. Wesley, PH. D. Washington, D. C., The Foundation publishers, 1940.
cover-title, xii, 115 p. 23cm.

1. ~~Negroes~~—Politics and suffrage. 2. Press—Southern states. I. Title.

Library of Congress JK1929.A2L6 40-30270
[42f2] 324.15

M973
L82ne2

Logan, Rayford Whittingham, 1897-
The betrayal of the Negro, from Rutherford B. Hayes to Woodrow Wilson, by Rayford W. Logan. New enl. ed. New York, Collier Books [1965]
447 p. 19 cm.
"Originally published as The Negro in American life and thought: the nadir, 1877-1901."
Bibliographical references included in "Notes" (p. 397-430)

1. ~~Negroes~~—Civil rights. 2. ~~Negroes~~—Hist. I. Title.

E185.61.L64 1965 323.4 65-23835
Library of Congress [5]

M323
N21a

Logan, Rayford Whittingham, 1897-
The Charter of the United Nations and its provisions for human rights and the rights of minorities and decisions already taken under this charter.

(In: National Association for the Advancement of Colored People. An appeal to the world; ... New York, 1947. 21cm. p. 85-94).

Logan, Rayford Whittingham, 1897-
Comment on French Africa and the French union p.332-36

M960
H12a

Haines, Charles Grove, 1906- ed.
Africa today. Baltimore, Johns Hopkins Press [°1955]
xvi, 510 p. illus., maps. 24 cm.
Based on the proceedings of the conference on contemporary Africa which the Johns Hopkins University School of Advanced International Studies sponsored in Washington in August 1954.
Bibliographical footnotes.

1. Africa. I. Title.

DT5.H25 960 55-6220
Library of Congress [56x15]

M973
L82d

Logan, Rayford Whittingham, 1897-
The diplomatic relations of the United States with Haiti, 1776-1891, by Rayford W. Logan. Chapel Hill, The University of North Carolina press, 1941.
xi p., 2 l., 516 p. 24cm.
Bibliography: p. [459]-496. Bibliographical foot-notes.

1. U. S.—For. rel.—Haiti. 2. Haiti—For. rel.—U. S. I. Title.

Library of Congress E183.8.H2L6 41-6260
[42k4] 327.73097294

M973
L82e

Logan, Rayford Whittingham, 1897-
Education in Haiti. Reprinted from The Journal of Negro History, vol. XV, no. 4, Oct. 1930, 401-460.

1. Haiti. 2. Education - Haiti.
3. Haiti - Education.

M973
R72

Logan, Rayford Whittingham, 1897-
Educational changes affecting American Negroes.

Pp. 185-206.

In: Rose, Arnold Marshall, ed. Assuring freedom to the free. Detroit, Wayne State University, 1964.

M975.9
F46
No.12

Logan, Rayford Whittingham, 1897-
Fifty years of progress in Greek letter societies. Pittsburgh, Pittsburgh Courier, 1950.

7p. 24cm. (Fifty years of progress)

1. Greek letter societies. I. Series.

M323
N213a

Logan, Rayford Whittingham, 1897- Foreword
National Association for the Advancement of Colored People. Atlanta, Ga. Citizenship Training School.
A primer on citizenship, prepared and used by Citizenship Training School, conducted by Atlanta Branch, National Association for the Advancement of Colored People, Atlanta, Georgia, 1933.

13p. 21x10cm.
Foreword by Rayford W. Logan.

Africa
M960
Am3

Logan, Rayford Whittingham, 1897-
The historical aspects of Pan-Africanism, 1900-1945.

Pp. 37-52.

In: American Society of African Culture. Pan-Africanism reconsidered. Berkeley, University of California Press, 1962.

M815.5
H83n

Logan, Rayford Whittinham, 1897-
The historical setting of The New Negro.

(In: Howard University, Washington, D.C. Graduate School Div. of Social Sciences. The New Negro thirty years afterward .... Washington, Howard University, 1956. 23cm. pp. 18-25.)

M973
L82n

Logan, Rayford Whittingham, 1897-
The Negro and the post-war world, a primer, by Rayford Whittingham Logan ... Washington, D. C., The Minorities publishers, 1945.
viii p., 1 l., 95 p. 23cm.
Bibliography: p. 89-95.

1. ~~Negro race.~~ 2. ~~Negroes.~~ I. Title.

Library of Congress GN645.L55 46-376
[47q7] 325.26

M973
L82ne

Logan, Rayford Whittingham, 1897-
The Negro in American life and thought: the nadir, 1877-1901. New York, Dial Press, 1954.
x, 380 p. 21 cm.
Bibliographical references included in "Footnotes" (p. 341-365)

1. Negroes—Civil rights. 2. Negroes—Hist. I. Title.

E185.61.L64 *301.451 325.260973 54-6000
Library of Congress [54x20]

M973
L82n

Logan, Rayford Whittingham, 1897-
The Negro in the United States, a brief history. Princeton, N. J., D. Van Nostrand Co. [1957]
191 p. 19 cm. (An Anvil original, no. 19)
Includes bibliography.

History.
1. ~~Negroes~~. I. Title.

E185.L85 325.260973 56-12904 ‡
Library of Congress [58q7]

M973
L820
Logan, Rayford Whittingham, 1897-
The operation of the mandate system in Africa, 1919-1927, with an introduction on the problem of the mandates in the post-war world, by Rayford W. Logan. Washington, D. C., The Foundation publishers, inc., 1942.
xii, 50 p. 24½cm.
1. Mandates—Africa. I. Title.
42-51430
Library of Congress JQ3505.L6
[43d2] 321.027

Haiti
M972.94
An7
Loi promulguée le 9Aout 1926.
Annuaire Général d'haiti. C. Celestin, B. Danache, directeurs. Port-au-Prince, Haiti, 1926.
208, 107p. illus. 30cm.

M784
L83f
Lomax, Alan, 1915- ed.
The folk songs of North America, in the English language. Melodies and guitar chords transcribed by Peggy Seeger, with one hundred piano arrangements by Matyas Seiber and Don Banks. Illustrated by Michael Leonard. Editorial assistant, Shirley Collins. Garden City, N. Y., Doubleday [1960]
623 p. illus. 27 cm. White author.
Bibliography: p. 597-600.
Discography: p. 608-615.
1. Folk-songs, American. 2. Folk-songs, American—Discography. I. Title.
M1629.L83F6 1960a 784.497 M 60-1043
Library of Congress [61x40]

M973
L82s
Logan, Rayford Whittingham, 1897-
The Senate and the Versailles mandate system, by Rayford W. Logan ... Washington, D. C., The Minorities publishers, 1945.
vi p., 1 l., 112 p. 22½cm.
Bibliography: p. 105-108.
1. U. S. Senate. 2. Mandates. I. Title.
45-8821
Library of Congress JX4021.L6
[46g2] 321.027

Nigeria
M896.3
D37L
L'ojó ojó un.
Delano, Isaac O
L'ojó ojó un. [In the older days]
London, Thomas Nelson, 1963.
154p. 19cm.
Portrait of author in book.
Written in Yoruba.
I. Title.

M810
F31
Lomax, John A. Seven Negro convict songs.
Federal writers' project.
American stuff; an anthology of prose & verse by members of the Federal writers' project, with sixteen prints by the Federal art project. New York, The Viking press, 1937.
xvii, 1, 301 p. plates. 22cm.

M973
L82w
Logan, Rayford Whittingham, 1897- ed.
What the Negro wants, edited by Rayford W. Logan ... Chapel Hill, The University of North Carolina press [1944]
xxiii p., 1 l., 352 p. 23cm.
"Who's who": p. 345-352.
1. Negroes. I. Title.
44-47086
Library of Congress E185.61.L65
[46u²14] 325.260973

Lokman,
See
Lukmān; Called Al-Hakīm

M975
M834
Lomax, Louis Emanuel, 1922-
Georgia boy goes home.
Pp. 50-64.
In: Morris, Willie, ed. The South today. New York, Harper & Row [1965]

M323
L82n
Logan, Spencer, 1911-
A Negro's faith in America, by Spencer Logan. New York, The Macmillan company, 1946.
vi p., 1 l., 88 p. 21 cm.
"First printing."
1. Negroes. I. Title.
46-4456
Library of Congress E185.61.L66
[47j²7] 325.260973

Nigeria
M896.3
Ek87L
Lokotown and other stories.
Ekwensi, Cyprian Odiatu, 1921-
Lokotown and other stories. London, Ibadan [etc.] Heinemann, 1966.
[5], 152 p. 18½ cm. (African writers series, no. 19) 5/6
(B 66-8634)
I. Title.
PZ4.E349Lo 66-72751
Library of Congress [5]

M323.2
L83
Lomax, Louis Emanuel 1922-
The Negro revolt. [1st ed.] New York, Harper [1962]
271 p. 22 cm.
Includes bibliography.
Portrait of author on book jacket.
1. Negroes—Civil rights. 2. U. S.—Race question. I. Title.
E185.61.L668 301.451 62-7911 ‡
Library of Congress [10]

M370
W67p
Logan, Wenonah Bond.
Williams, Frances Harriet.
Pudge grows up; Series of meetings for high school girls, by Frances Williams and Wenonah Logan. New York, Womans press, 1936.
28p. 28cm.

South Africa
M896.4
W15
Lokwe, Victor Harold
Ukufana Kobu-Kristu Namasiko Olwendo Lwesintu.
Pp. 50-62.
Written in Xhosa.
In: Wallis, S. J., comp. and ed. Inkolo namasiko. London, Society for Promoting Christian Knowledge, 1930.

M323.2
L83a
Lomax, Louis Emanuel 1922-
The Negro revolt. [1st ed.] ~~New York, Harper, 1962~~
London, H. Hamilton 1963.
271 p. 22 cm.
Includes bibliography.
1. Negroes—Civil rights. 2. U. S.—Race question. I. Title.
E185.61.L668 301.451 62-7911 ‡
Library of Congress [10]

M808.83
L829
Loggem, Manuel von, 1916- comp.
Meesters der Neger vertelkunst, bijeengebracht en vertaald door Manuel von Loggem met medewerkung von Otto Sterman. [1. druk] Amsterdam, J. Meulenhoff [1966]
xv, 192p. 20cm. (Meesters der vertelkunst).
White compiler
1. Fiction - Collections. I. Title. (Series)

Congo(Leopoldville)
M896.3
L83n
Lomami-Tshibamba, Paul, 1914-
Ngando [le crocodile] Bruxelles, G. A. Deny [1949]
117 p. port. 23 cm.
"Prix littéraire de la Foire coloniale de Bruxelles, 1948."
I. Title. 1. Congo, Belgian-Folklore.
A 50-4465
Illinois. Univ. Library for Library of Congress [1]

M910
L83r
Lomax, Louis Emanuel, 1922-
The reluctant African. [1st ed.] New York, Harper [1960]
117 p. illus. 22 cm.
Portrait of author on book jacket.
1. Africa—Native races. 2. Africa—Politics. I. Title.
DT15.L65 323.1096 60-16472 ‡
Library of Congress [30]

M326.99B
L82
Loguen, Jermain Wesley, 1814-1872.
The Rev. J. W. Loguen, as a slave and as a freeman. A narrative of real life. Syracuse, N. Y., J. G. K. Truair & co., printers, 1859.
x, [11]-454 p. front. (port.) 18cm.
Written in the third person, but apparently the work of Loguen. Two letters at end of volume are dated 1860.
"Testimony of Rev. E. P. Rogers," including a poem "Loguen's position": p. 445-450.
3. Slave narratives.
1. Slavery in the U. S.—Fugitive slaves. 2. Slavery in the U. S.—Anti-slavery movements. 3. Underground railroad. I. Rogers, Ely. mas Payson, d. 1861.
14-15518
Library of Congress E444.L83
[48r42d1]

- Lomame-Tshibamba Paul, 1914-
Congo(Leopoldville)
M840.8
M971
Mushiete, Paul
La littérature française africaine; petite anthologie des écrivains noirs d'expression française. Leverville, Bibliothèque de l'Étoile, 1957.
40p. 17½cm.

U. S.
M959.3
L837
Lomax, Louis Emanuel, 1922-
Thailand; the war that is, the war that will be [by] Louis E. Lomax. New York, Random House [1967]
xiii, 175 p. map. 22 cm.
Portrait of author on book jacket.
1. Guerrillas—Thailand. 2. Communism—Thailand. I. Title.
DS586.L6 959.3'04 67-25075
Library of Congress [68n5]

M323.4 W52
Lomax, Louis Emanuel, 1922-
The unpredictable Negro.
pp. 22-25.
In: Westin, Alan F. Freedom now. New York, Basic Books, 1964.

M297 L83
Lomax, Louis Emanuel, 1922-
When the word is given; a report on Elijah Muhammad, Malcolm X, and the Black Muslim world. [1st ed.] Cleveland, World Pub. Co. [1963]
223 p. illus., ports. 21 cm.
"Suggested additional reading": p. 218-214.
1. Black Muslims. I. Title.
BP222.L6 290 63-21624
Library of Congress [64f3]

M301 Eb74
Lomax, Louis Emanuel, 1922-
The white liberal
Pp. 39-46
In: Ebony. The white problem in America. Chicago, Johnson Pub. Co., 1966.

London - Fiction.
M813.5 W688h
Wilson, Carl Thomas David.
The half caste, by Carl T. D. Wilson. Ilfracombe [Eng.] A.H. Stockwell [1964]
207p. 19cm.
Portrait of author on book jacket.

London - Social conditions.
West Indies M325.27 F21
Family Welfare Association, London.
The West Indian comes to England; a report prepared for the Trustees of the London Parochial Charities by the Family Welfare Association. Contributors: Douglas Manley, Ivo de Souza, Albert Hyndman, et al. Edited by S. K. Ruck. London, Routledge & K. Paul [1960]
187p. 23cm.

The lone-star of Liberia.
Trinidad M966.6 D93
Durham, Frederick Alexander.
The lone-star of Liberia; being the outcome of reflections on our own people. By Frederick Alexander Durham, an African ... With an introduction by Madame la comtesse C. Hugo. London, E. Stock, 1892.
xxi p., 1 l., 331 p. 20cm.
CONTENTS.—The Africo-American.—Is the Ethiopian inferior to the Caucasian?—Immorality.—Superstition in the nineteenth century.—Under Caucasian rule.—Africa governed by Africans.—Repatriation and Liberia.
1. Negroes—Colonization—Africa. 2. Negro race. 3. Liberia. I. Title.
5-15427
Library of Congress DT631.D96

Lonely crusade.
M813.5 H571
Himes, Chester B., 1909-
Lonely crusade. 1st ed. New York, A. A. Knopf, 1947.
[4] l., 3 398p. 22cm.

The lonely village.
Zambia M896.3 M38L
Massiye, A Sylvester
The lonely village. London, Thomas Nelson, 1951.
48p. map. 18½cm. (Eagle fiction library)

The lonely warrior: the life and times of Robert S. Abbott.
MB9 Ab2
Ottley, Roi, 1906-
The lonely warrior: the life and times of Robert S. Abbott. Chicago, H. Regnery Co., 1955.
381 p. illus. 22 cm.
Includes bibliographies.
1. Abbott, Robert Sengstacke, 1868-1940. 2. The Chicago defender. 3. Negroes. I. Title.
Full name: Roi Vincent Ottley.
PN4874.A23O7 920.5 55-8734 ‡
Library of Congress [55h7]

Lonesome boy.
M813.5 B641o
Bontemps, Arna Wendell, 1902-
Lonesome boy. Illustrated by Feliks Topolski. Boston, Houghton Mifflin, 1955.
28 p. illus. 22 cm.
I. Title.
PZ7.B6443Lo 54-9044 ‡
Library of Congress [55f5]

The lonesome road; the story of the Negro's part in America.
MB R24
Redding, Jay Saunders, 1906-
The lonesome road; the story of the Negro's part in America. [1st ed.] New York, Doubleday, 1958.
355 p. 24 cm. (Mainstream of America series)
Includes bibliography.
1. Negroes. 2. Negroes—Biog. 3. U. S.—Race question. I. Title.
E185.61.R298 58-6647 ‡
*301.451 325.260973
Library of Congress [58r30]

Jamaica M972.92 L85h
Long, Edward, 1734-1813.
The history of Jamaica: or, General survey of the antient and modern state of that island: with reflections on its situation, settlements, inhabitants, climate, products, commerce, laws, and government ... Illustrated with copper plates ... London, T. Lowndes, 1774.
3 v. fold. fronts. (v. 1-2) plates (1 fold.) fold. maps, plan. 28 x 22cm.
Vols. 2-3 paged continuously.
1. Jamaica. 2. Slavery in Jamaica. 3. Natural history—Jamaica. I. Title.
2-11578
Library of Congress F1863.L84
[40e1]

M331.833 L85p
Long, Herman Hodge.
People vs. property; race restrictive covenants in housing [by] Herman H. Long [and] Charles S. Johnson. Nashville, Fisk Univ. Press, 1947.
ix, 107 p. maps, diagrs. 21 cm.
Bibliographical footnotes.
1. Negroes—Housing. 2. Negroes—Segregation. 3. Real covenants—U. S. I. Johnson, Charles Spurgeon, 1893- joint author. II. Title.
E185.89.H6L7 325.260973 48-5205*
Library of Congress [48x10]

M323 L85c
Long, Herman Hodge
Race relations in the United States.
pp. 181-217. 25cm.
In: Coloured immigrants in Britain, by J. A. G. Griffith, et al. London, Oxford University Press, 1960.
1. Race relations. 2. Great Britain - Emigration and Immigration. I. Title.

M370 L85p
Long, Hollis Moody, 1900-
Public secondary education for Negroes in North Carolina, by Hollis Moody Long ... Published with the approval of Professor Grayson N. Kefauver, sponsor. New York city, Teachers college, Columbia university, 1932.
xi, 115 p. illus. (map) diagr. 23½ cm. (Teachers college, Columbia university. Contributions to education, no. 529)
Issued also as thesis (PH. D.) Columbia university.
Bibliography: p. 114-115.
1. Negroes—Education. 2. Negroes—North Carolina. 3. High schools—North Carolina. 4. Education, Secondary. 5. Education—North Carolina. I. Title.
Library of Congress LC2802.N8L6 1932a 32-23749
——— Copy 2. LB5.C8 no. 529
[42q1] 371.974

The long dream.
M813.5 W93L2
Wright, Richard, 1909-1960.
Den lange drøm [The long dream] på Dansk ved Kurt Kreutzfeld. [København] Gyldendal, 1959.
330p. 23cm.
Written in Danish.
1. Title. II. Title: The long dream.

The long dream.
M813.5 W931
Wright, Richard, 1909-
The long dream, a novel. [1st ed.] Garden City, N. Y., Doubleday, 1958.
384 p. 22 cm.
I. Title.
Full name: Richard Nathaniel Wright.
PZ3.W9352Lo 58-12059 ‡
Library of Congress [58f10]

The Long night.
M813.5 M451
Mayfield, Julian, 1928-
The Long night. London, Michael Joseph, 1960.
142p. 20½cm.
I. Title.

The long night.
M813.5 M451o
Mayfield, Julian, 1928-
The long night. London, Michael Joseph [1960]
142p. 21cm.

Long old road.
MB9 C31
Cayton, Horace Roscoe, 1903-
Long old road [by] Horace R. Cayton. New York, Trident Press, 1965 [c1964]
402 p. 22 cm.
Autobiography.
Portrait of author on book jacket.
I. Title.
E185.97.C35 1965 923.273 64-24280
Library of Congress [8]

The long search.
M813.5 B651
Bosworth, William, 1921-
The long search, a novel. [1st ed.] Great Barrington, Mass., Advance Pub. Co. [1957]
303 p. 23 cm.
I. Title.
PZ4.B7475Lo 56-12732 ‡
Library of Congress [2]

The long shadow of Little Rock.

MB9
B32
Bates, Daisy (Gatson)
The long shadow of Little Rock, a memoir. New York, David McKay Co. [1962]
234 p. illus. 21 cm.
Portrait of author on book jacket.

1. Negroes—Little Rock, Ark. 2. Little Rock, Ark.—Public schools. I. Title.

F419.L7B3 920.7 62—20233 ‡
Library of Congress [62f2]

Cuba
M861.08
L88
Lopez, Prieto, Antonio, 1847-1883,
Parnaso Cubano; coleccion de poesias selectas de autores Cubanos des de zequeira a nuestrosdias ... por D. Antonio Lopez Prieto ... Habana, Miguel de Villa [1881?]
[v]- 1 xxxi, 370p. 22½cm.

1. Cuban poetry.

St. Vincent
M233.5
L88g
Lord, Samuel Ebenezer Churchstone. 1874–
The God idea; a study in the development and perfection of man, by the Reverend Samuel Ebenezer Churchstone Lord ... [Philadelphia, A. M. E. book concern] 1922.
213 p. 19½ cm.

I. Title.

Library of Congress BT124.L6 25-15892
[2]

A long way from home.

Jamaica
MB9
M19
McKay, Claude, 1890–
A long way from home, by Claude McKay. New York, L. Furman, inc. [°1937]
6 p. l., 3-354 p. 21 cm.

I. Title.

37—8570
Library of Congress PS3525.A24785L6 1937
[45d1] 928.1

Peru
M863.6
L88c
López Albújar, Enrique, 1872-
Las caridades de la señora de Tordoya. Cuentos (Premio Nacional de 1950).
Lima, Juan Mejia Baca & P. L. Villanueva Editores, 1955.

212p. 22cm.
Inscribed.

I. Title.

Lord's Supper - Anglican Communion.

M265.3
W93
Wright, Nathan.
One bread, one body. Foreword by James A. Pike. Greenwich, Conn., Seabury Press, 1962.
148 p. 22 cm.
Includes bibliographies.

1. Lord's Supper—Anglican Communion. I. Title.

BX5949.C5W73 265.3 62-9618 ‡
Library of Congress [5]

Ghana
M966.7
L85
Longdon, J E
Ghana Adehyeman. Ghana Kasa ho dwumadzibea dze puee gua do. [Accra, Guinea Press] 1960.

60p. illus. ports. 20cm.

1. Ghana.

Peru
M863.6
L88m
López Albújar, Enrique, 1872-
Matalaché. Lima, Juan Mejia Baca & P. L. Villanueva, Editores, 19??

195p. 17½cm.
Inscribed.

I. Title.

Lord's supper - Art.

M740
C86a
Crite, Allan Rohan, 1910- illus.
All glory; brush drawing meditations on the Prayer of consecration. Cambridge, Mass., Society of Saint John the Evangelist, 1947.
[28] l. illus. 24 cm.

1. Lord's supper—Art. I. Protestant Episcopal Church in the U. S. A. Book of common prayer. Communion service. II. Title.

N8054.C7 741.6382 48-3019*
Library of Congress [2]

Ghana
M341.139
L85
Longdon, J E
Mr. Amoa learns about Uno, by J. E. Longdon and Ella Griffin. Cover design by R. Ohene Akyeampong. Accra, Bureau of Ghana Languages, 1959.

9p. 22cm.

1. United Nations. I. Griffin, Ella, jt. auth. II. Title.

Peru
M863.6
L88m
López Albújar, Enrique, 1872-
Matalaché. Segunda edicion. Lima, Juan Mejia Baca & P. L. Villanueva, Editores, 1955.

209p. 21½cm.
Inscribed.

I. Title.

Los Angeles.

M979
R24r
Reddick, Lawrence Dunbar, 1910- ed.
Race relations on the Pacific coast. New York, Journal of educational sociology. 1945.

129-208p. 23cm.
Special issue of The Journal of educational sociology, November 1945.
Partial contents: -The new race-relations frontiers, by L. D. Reddick. -Los Angeles, by Charles Bratt.

Longevity.

M612.68
P27
Patterson, John Andrew, 1875–
The breaking dawn; or, How long may we live in the body? By Rev. J. Andrew Patterson. Being a survey of the doctrines of renewed youth and the perpetuation of life in physical embodiment. Orange, N. J., The Chronicle publishing co., 1910.
ix, 121 p. front. (port.) 23 cm. $1.00

1. Hygiene. 2. Longevity.

10-13871
Library of Congress RA776.P3
© Apr. 14, 1910; 2c. June 2, 1910; A 265369; J. A. Patterson, Orange, N. J.

Peru
M863.6
L88n
López Albújar, Enrique, 1872–
... Nuevos cuentos andinos. Santiago de Chile, Ediciones Ercilla, 1937.
4 p. l., [11]-185 p., 1 l. 22 cm. (*Half-title: Biblioteca América*)
CONTENTS.—El brindis de los yayas.—Huayna-pishtanag.—El blanco.—Cómo se hiso pishtaco Calixto.—El trompiezo.—Juan Rabines no perdona.—Una posesión judicial.

I. Title. 1. Peruvian literature.

38—12446
Library of Congress PQ8497.L6N8
[45d1] 863.6

Los Angeles, California - History.

M979.493
B29f
Bass, Charlotta A
Forty years; memoirs from the pages of a newspaper. Los Angeles, The Author, 1960.

198p. illus., ports. 25½cm.

M324
N21L
Look at the filibuster.
National Association for the Advancement of Colored People.
Look at the filibuster. New York, 1949.

[8]p. illus. 21cm.

Lopoloko, Joseph Iyandza, 1927-

see

Iyandza-Lopoloko, Joseph, 1927-

Nigeria
M966.9
L89hi
Losi, John B Ogunjimi.
History of Abeokuta, by Prince J.B. Ogunjimi Losi. Lagos, Nigeria, Bosere Press, 1924.

176p. 21cm.

1. Nigeria - History. 2. Abeokuta - History.

The looming shadow.

Malawi
M896.3
K184L
Kayira, Legson.
The looming shadow. [1st ed.] Garden City, N. Y., Doubleday, 1967.
143 p. 22 cm.

I. Title.

PZ4.K234Lo 67-15367
Library of Congress [3]

M811.5
H87g
Lorca, Federico García Romancero Gitano.
Hughes, Langston, 1902- tr.
Gypsy ballads, by Federico García Lorca. Translated by Langston Hughes; illus. by John McNee; introduction by Robert H. Glauber. Beloit, Wisconsin, Beloit College, 1951.

40p. 22cm. (Chapbook no.1)
Special issue of the Beloit poetry journal, fall 1951.

Nigeria
M966.9
L89h
Losi, John B. Ogunjimi.
History of Lagos, by Prince John B. O. Losi...second edition. Lagos, C. M. S. Bookshop, 1921.

ii, 75p. plates. 22½cm.

1. Lagos, Nigeria-History
2. Nigeria-History

Nigeria
M966.9
L89hi

Losi, John B Ogunjimi.
Itan Abeokuta. Lati owo Prince John B. O. Losi. 2nd impression. Exeter, James Townsend & Co., 1920.

135p. 21½cm.
Bound with: John B.O. Losi's History of Abeokuta.

1. Abeokuta - History. 2. Nigeria - History.

Nigeria
M966.9
L89h

Losi, John B. .Ogunjimi.
Itan eko, nipa Prince John B. O. Losi... third edition. Lagos, Church missionary society's press, 1921.

60p. plates. 22½cm.
Bound with: John B. O. Losi's History of Lagos(1921)

1. Lagos, Nigeria— History. 2. Nigeria— History.

Nigeria
M966.92
L891

Losi, Prince John B Ogunjimi
Iwe itan ogun ati ote ilu-oke. Lagos, Church Missionary Society Bookshop, 1930.

32p. 18½cm.
A book of stories and political strifes of the Yoruba cities and towns North of Ibadan.

1. Nigeria - Cities and towns.

The lost zoo.

M811.5
C891

Cullen, Countee, 1903–
The lost zoo (a rhyme for the young, but not too young) by Christopher Cat and Countee Cullen, with illustrations by Charles Sebree. New York and London, Harper & brothers [°1940]

6 p. l., 72 p., 1 l. col. front., col. plates. 24ᶜᵐ.
Illustrated lining-papers in colors.
"First edition."

I. Sebree, Charles, illus. II. Title.

40—34870

Library of Congress PZ8.3.C889Lo
[45k1]

Lotteries.

M174.6
B45

Bernard, Ruth Thompson.
What's wrong with lottery? By Ruth Thompson Bernard. Boston, Meador publishing company [1943]

122 p. 20ᶜᵐ.

1. Gambling. 2. Lotteries. I. Title.

43—18105

Library of Congress HV6718.B47
[5] 174.6

MB9
L91r

Lotz, Philip Henry, 1889– *ed.*
... Rising above color, edited by Philip Henry Lotz ... New York, Association press; New York, Fleming H. Revell company, 1943.

viii, 112 p. 21 cm. (*His* Creative personalities. Vol. v)

"For further reading" at end of each chapter except one.

CONTENTS.—George Washington Carver, man with a magic wand, by F. G. Lankard.—Marian Anderson, singer, by H. B. Hunting.—W. E. B. DuBois, scoholar and fighter, by H. B. Hunting.—Robert Russa Moton, co-operator and educator, by H. B. Hunting.—Samuel Coleridge-Taylor, musician, by F. W. Clelland.—Richard Allen, first

(Continued on next card)
44—40017
[49w²5]

MB9
L91r

Lotz, Philip Henry, 1889– *ed.* ... Rising above color ... 1943. (Card 2)

CONTENTS—Continued.

Negro bishop, by Mary E. Moxcey.—Frederick Douglass, orator, by Mary E. Moxcey.—Daniel Hale Williams, surgeon, by Mary E. Moxcey.—Booker T. Washington, "Up from slavery," by F. G. Lankard.—Roland Hayes, world-renowned tenor, by F. G. Lankard. — Paul Laurence Dunbar, poet, by F. G. Lankard.—James Weldon Johnson, poet and diplomat, by Lucile Desjardins.—Walter White, crusader for justice, by Roy Wilkins.

1. ~~Negroes—Biog.~~ Biography I. Title.

44—40017

Library of Congress CT104.L68 vol. 5
[49w²5] (920.02) 920.073

Lotze, Hermann.

M100
J711

Jones, Gilbert Haven, 1881–
Lotze und Bowne. Eine Vergleichung ihrer philosophischen arbeit. Inaugural - Dissertation der philosophischen fakultät der universität Jena zur erlangung der doktorwürde. Weida i Th. Druck von Thomas & Hubert, 1909.

117p. 23½cm.

Haiti
M841
L93o

Louis, Janine Tavernier, 1935-
Ombre ensoleillée. Preface de Roland Morisseau. Illustration de Villard Denis. Port-au-Prince, Imprimerie Gervais Louis, 1961.

21p. 19½cm.
Portrait of author on back of book.

1. Haiti-Poetry. 2. Poetry, Haitian. I. Title.

1935-

Haiti
M841
L93s

Louis, Janine Tavernier, 1935-
Splendeur. Port-au-Prince, Imprimerie S. Bissainthe, [n.d.]

[16]p. 21cm.

1. Haitian portry. I. Title.

M796
L92h

Louis, Joe, 1914–
How to box, ed. by Edward J. Mallory. Philadelphia, D. McKay Co. [1948]

64 p. illus. 27 cm.

1. Boxing. I. Mallory, Edward J., ed. II. Title.

GV1137.L8 796.83 48—3663*

Library of Congress [50f²10]

MB9
L93m
1955

Louis, Joe, 1914–
The Joe Louis story. [Written with the editorial aid of Chester L. Washington and Haskell Cohen] New York, Grosset & Dunlap [~~1953~~] 1955

197 p. illus. 21 cm.
First ed. published in 1947 under title: My life story.

GV1132.L6A3 1953 927.9683 53-11991 ‡

Library of Congress [5]

MB9
L93m

Louis, Joe, 1914–
My life story, by Joe Louis ... New York, Duell, Sloan and Pearce [1947]

188, [2] p. plates, ports. 22ᶜᵐ.

"An Eagle book."
"Written with the editorial aid of Chester L. Washington and Haskell Cohen."
"First edition."
Contains Joe Louis' autograph.
I. Washington, Chester L. II. Cohen, Haskell.
GV1132.L6A3 927.9683 47-30240
© 19Mar47; author, New York; A11564.

Library of Congress [25]

Louis, Joe, 1914-

MB9
L93s

Scott, Neil.
Joe Louis, a picture story of his life. New York, Greenberg [1947]

[126] p. illus., ports. 21ᶜᵐ.

1. Louis, Joe, 1914–
GV1132.L6S35 927.9683 47-5025*
© Greenberg: Publisher; 25Jun47; A14096.

Library of Congress [15]

M616
W93

The Louis T. Wright Library of Harlem Hospital. Journal of the National Medical Association, 1952.

296-309p.
Reprinted from Journal of the National Medical Association, vo. 44, July 1952.
Speeches by: Walter White, W. Montague Cobb. Arthur B. Spingarn. Elmer Carter. Channing H. Tobias. William H. Hastie. Hon. Vincent R. Impellitteri. Eleanor Roosevelt. Louis T. Wright.

I. Wright, Lou is T

Louise de La Vallière.

France
M840
D89Lo

Dumas, Alexandre, 1802–1870.
Louise de La Vallière; or, The love of Bragellone [!] A continuation of "The three musketeers", "Twenty years after", and "Bragelonne, the son of Athos". By Alex. Dumas. New rev. translation by H. Llewellyn Williams. New York, The F. M. Lupton publishing company [°1892]
459 p. 19ᶜᵐ. (*On cover:* The elite series. no. 9)
Written in collaboration with Auguste Maquet.
A translation of the middle portion of the Vicomte de Bragelonne.
Sequel: The man in the iron mask.
1. La Vallière, Louise Françoise de La Baume Le Blanc, duchesse de, 1644–1710 — Fiction. 2. France — Hist. — Louis XIV, 1643–1715—Fiction. 3. Man in the iron mask—Fiction. I. Maquet, Auguste, 1813–1888, joint author. II. Williams, Henry Llewellyn, jr., tr. III. Title.

6—43623

Library of Congress (Ⓒ) (PZ3.D89Lo 2)
Copyright 1892: 5523 [a37g1]

Louisiana.

MB
D45

Desdunes, Rodolphe L
Nos hommes et notre histoire; notices biographiques accompagnées de reflexions et de souvenirs personnels, hommage à la population créole, en souvenir des grands hommes qu'elle a produits et des bonnes choses qu'elle a accomplies, par R.-L. Desdunes ... Montréal, Arbour & Dupont, 1911.

196 p. front., ports. 22½ᶜᵐ.

1. Negroes—Louisiana. 2. Creoles. 3. New Orleans—Biog. 4. American literature (French)—Louisiana. 5. French literature—American authors.

12-21176

Library of Congress E185.93.L6D4
[a44c1]

Louisiana.

M286
H52h

Hicks, William.
History of Louisiana Negro Baptists from 1804-1914. By Wm. Hicks... With a biographical introduction by Bishop W. B. Purvis. Nashville, Tenn., National Baptist publishing board [1914]

251p. illus., including ports. 20½cm.

Louisiana.

M810
H94mu
1936

Hurston, Zora Neale.
Mules and men, by Zora Neale Hurston; with an introduction by Frank Boas ... 10 illustrations by Miguel Covarrubias. Philadelphia, London, Kegan, Paul, Trench, Trubner, 1936.

342, [1] p. front., illus., plates. 22ᶜᵐ.

CONTENTS.—pt. I. Folk tales.—pt. II. Hoodoo.—Appendix. I. Negro songs with music (p. 309–[331]) II. Formulae of hoodoo doctors. III. Paraphernalia of conjure. IV. Prescriptions of root doctors.

1. Folk-lore, Negro. 2. Voodooism. 3. Negroes—Florida. 4. Negroes—Louisiana. 5. Negro songs. I. Title.

35—18525

Library of Congress GR103.H8
[45j²2] 398.09759

Louisiana.

M810
H94mu

Hurston, Zora Neale.
Mules and men, by Zora Neale Hurston; with an introduction by Frank Boas ... 10 illustrations by Miguel Covarrubias. Philadelphia, London, J. B. Lippincott company, 1935.

342, [1] p. front., illus., plates. 22ᶜᵐ.

CONTENTS.—pt. I. Folk tales.—pt. II. Hoodoo.—Appendix. I. Negro songs with music (p. 309–[331]) II. Formulae of hoodoo doctors. III. Paraphernalia of conjure. IV. Prescriptions of root doctors.

1. Folk-lore, Negro. 2. Voodooism. 3. Negroes—Florida. 4. Negroes—Louisiana. 5. Negro songs. I. Title.

35—18525

Library of Congress GR103.H8
[45j²2] 398.09759

Louisiana.

M975
N31

Laws, J Bradford.
The Negroes of Cinclare Central Factory and Calumet Plantation, Louisiana. [Bulletin of the Labor Dept. no.38, 1902] pp. 95-120.

In: The Negro in the black belt... Washington, D.C., Dept. of Labor, [189 - 190]

Louisiana.

M370. M11 **McAllister, Jane Ellen, 1899–**

The training of Negro teachers in Louisiana, by Jane Ellen McAllister ... New York city, Teachers college, Columbia university, 1929.

vi, 95 p. 23½ᶜᵐ. (Teachers college, Columbia university. Contributions to education; no. 364)

Published also as thesis (PH. D.) Columbia university.
Bibliography: p. 95.

1. Teachers, Training of—Louisiana. 2. Negroes—Education. 3. Negroes—Louisiana. I. Title. II. Title: Negro teachers in Louisiana, The training of.

30—11031

Library of Congress LC2802.L8M3 1929 a
——— Copy 2. LB5.C8 no. 364
Copyright A 21710 [41m1] 370.7

Louisiana.

M976.3 R76 **Roussève, Charles Barthelemy.**

The Negro in Louisiana; aspects of his history and his literature, by Charles Barthelemy Roussève, M. A. New Orleans, The Xavier university press, 1937.

xvii, 212 p. front., illus. (music) plates, diagrs. 20½ᶜᵐ.

"This work, prepared in 1935 in partial fulfillment of the requirements for the degree of master of arts, makes its appearance ... substantially as it was originally written, save for ... several minor alterations and the addition of a few details."—p. vii.
Bibliography: p. 193–201.

1. Negroes—Louisiana. 2. Negroes in literature and art. 3. Negro authors. I. Title.

38—525

Library of Congress E185.93.L6R6
[42h2] 325.2609763

Louisiana.

M976.3 Se6 The Sepia socialite.

... The Negro in Louisiana, seventy -eight years of progress. Fifth anniversary edition... New Orleans, Sepia socialite pub. co., 1942.

168p. illus. 38cm.
Dated on cover, July 1942; on t.-p. Apr, 1942.

Louisiana.

MB P41w **Who's who in colored Louisiana, 1930; A. E. Perkins ... editor.** Baton Rouge, La., Douglas loan co., inc. [1930]

153, [1] p. illus., plates (1 fold.) ports., facsim. 21ᶜᵐ.

1. Negroes—Louisiana. 2. Negroes—Biog. 3. Louisiana—Biog. I. Perkins, Archie Ebenezer, 1879– ed.

32-19208

Library of Congress E185.93.L6W5
[a44b1] 325.26

Louisiana - Civilization.

MB T49e **Tinker, Edward Larocque, 1881–**

Les écrits de langue française en Louisiane au XIXᵉ siècle; essais biographiques at bibliographiques par Edward Larocque Tinker ... Paris, H. Champion, 1932 [*i. e.* 1933]

2 p. l., 502 p. incl. plates, facsims. 25½ᶜᵐ. (*Added t.-p.:* Bibliothèque de la Revue de littérature comparée ... t. 85)

Authors, including Negroes, arranged alphabetically, with biographical and critical sketches written to show the characteristic French spirit which has left an impress in Louisiana, followed by the author's works including English titles of those writing in both languages. The location of a copy of the work is given, if known.

(Continued on next card)

33—21149

[45h1]

M976.3 A15s Louisiana--Economic conditions.

Allain, T T

Speech of Hon. T. T. Allain, of the delegate from the 14th senatorial district, delivered, May 24, 1879. Cosmopolitan Printing House, 1879.

[3] 7p. 23cm.

Louisiana - Education.

M370. B812a 1876 Brown, William G.

Annual report of the State Superintendent of Public Education, William G. Brwon, to the General Assembly of Louisiana, for the year 1875. Session of 1876. New Orlenas, Printed at the Republican Office, 1876.

392. xvixp. 22½cm.

Louisville, Ky.

M301 F86 **Frazier, Edward Franklin, 1894–**

Negro youth at the crossways, their personality development in the middle states, by E. Franklin Frazier; prepared for the American youth commission. Washington, D. C., American council on education, 1940.

xxiii, 301, [2] p. illus. (maps) diagr. 23½ cm.

"This volume .. describes the experiences of Negro boys and girls living in Washington, D. C., and Louisville, Kentucky; these communities were selected as examples of middle-area conditions."—Pref.

1. Negroes—Moral and social conditions. 2. Youth. 3. Personality. 4. Social psychology. 5. Negroes—District of Columbia. 6. Negroes—Louisville, Ky. I. American council on education. American youth commission. II. Title.

40—32764

Library of Congress E185.6.F74
[42z7] 325.2609753

Louisville, Ky.

M323. N213 National Association for the Advancement of Colored People. Louisville.

The history of Louisville segregation case and the decision of the Supreme Court. Louisville, The Association, Legal Committee, 1917?

Haiti M972.94 L93h Lourié, I

Haiti, the ally of democracies. Port-au-Prince, Imp. du College Veritères, 1942.

60p. 23cm.

1. Haiti

Louvain. Université catholique. Ecole des sciences politiques et socials. Collection no. 156.

Congo Leopoldville M325 M89i Mulenzi, Janvier

L'internationalisation du phénomène colonial. Bruxelles, Éditions du Treurenberg, 1958.

164p. 24cm. (Université de Louvain. Collection de l'École des sciences politiques et sociales, 156)
Bibliography: p. [154]-159.

1. Colonies - History. 2. International trusteeships. 3. Colonies (International Law) I. Title. II. Series: Louvain. Université catholique. École des sciences politiques et socials. Collection no. 156.

Louverture, Isaac. Supposed author.

M841.8 H12 L'Haitiade poéme epique en nuit chants, par un philanthrope Européen nouvelle edition, par Gragnon-Lacoste. Paris, A. Durand et Pedone-Lauriel, Editeurs, 1878.

xviii, 209p. 18cm.
Isaac Louverture, Suposed author.

Louverture family.

Haiti MB9 T46nh **Nemours, Alfred, 1883–**

... Histoire de la famille et de la descendance de Toussaint-Louverture. Avec des documents inédits et les portraits des descendants de Toussaint-Louverture jusqu'à nos jours. Port-au-Prince, Haiti, Imprimerie de l'État, 1941.

4 p. l., vii–viii, 308 p. front., pl., ports. 23ᶜᵐ.

At head of title: Général Nemours.
Bibliography: p. 290–302.

1. Toussaint Louverture, Pierre Dominique, 1746?–1803. 2. Louverture family. I. Title.

A 41—1743

Harvard univ. Library for Library of Congress F1923.T8907
[43c1] 923.27294

M286 L94 **Love, Emanuel King, 1850–1900.**

History of the First African Baptist church, from its organization, January 20th, 1788, to July 1st, 1888. Including the centennial celebration, addresses, sermons, etc. By Rev. E. K. Love ... Savannah, Ga., The Morning news print., 1888.

7 p. l., iii–v, 360 p. front., illus. 21ᶜᵐ.

1. Savannah. First African Baptist church. I. Title.

26—5886

Library of Congress BX6480.S45F5
Copyright 1888: 24385 [37b1]

M06 Am3 no.6 **Love, John L.**

The disfranchisement of the negro, by John L. Love ... Washington, D. C., The Academy, 1899.

27 p. 23ᶜᵐ. (American negro academy. Occasional papers, no. 6)

Disfranchisement

1. U. S.—Pol. & govt. ~~2. Negroes—U. S.~~

9—21947

Library of Congress E184.N3A5
——— Copy 2. JK1924.L89
[35b1]

M06 Am3 no. 11 Love, John L

The potentiality of the Negro vote.

(In: American Negro Academy. The Negro and the elective franchise. Washington, D.C., The Academy, 1905)

M811.5 L94w **Love, Melvin.**

War in heaven, and other poems. [1st ed.] New York, Exposition Press [1954]

64 p. 21 cm.

I. Title.

PS3523.O825W3 811.5 54-8269 ‡

Library of Congress [2]

M398 L94 **Love, Rose Leary, *ed.***

A collection of folklore for children in elementary school and at home. [1st ed.] New York, Vantage Press [1964]

83 p. illus. 21 cm.

Includes music.

"To Arthur - a charming little book by my cousin, Rose " Langston Hughes, 1964."

1. Folk-lore, American—Juvenile literature. I. Title. II. Title: Folklore for children.

GR105.L6 j 398 64-8852

Library of Congress [3]

M813.5 L94n **Love, Rose Leary.**

Nebraska and his granny, by Rose Leary Love; with illustrations by Preston Haygood. Tuskegee Institute, Ala., Tuskegee institute press, 1936.

5 p. l., 69 p. illus. 20ᶜᵐ.

I. Title.

37-2457

Library of Congress PZ7.L956Ne
——— Copy 2.
Copyright A 103569 [3]

Liberia M896.3 C78 Love in ebony.

Cooper, Charles Edward.

Love in ebony; a West African romance, by Varfelli Karlee [pseud]. With a foreword by Vernon Bartlett. London, John Murray [1932]

316 p. 19½ cm.

Love is a terrible thing.

M811.5 M951 Murphy, Beatrice M.

Love is a terrible thing, by Beatrice M. Murphy. New York, the Hobson Press, 1945.

ix, 65p. 21½cm.

M323.4
W52
Lomax, Louis Emanuel, 1922-
The unpredictable Negro.

pp. 22-25.

In: Westin, Alan F. Freedom now. New York, Basic Books, 1964.

The lonely village.
Zambia
M896.3
M38L
Massiye, A Sylvester
The lonely village. London, Thomas Nelson, 1951.

48p. map. 18½cm. (Eagle fiction library)

M370
L85p
Long, Hollis Moody, 1900-
Public secondary education for Negroes in North Carolina, by Hollis Moody Long ... Published with the approval of Professor Grayson N. Kefauver, sponsor. New York city, Teachers college, Columbia university, 1932.

xi, 115 p. illus. (map) diagr. 23½ cm. (Teachers college, Columbia university. Contributions to education, no. 529)

Issued also as thesis (PH. D.) Columbia university.
Bibliography: p. 114-115.

1. ~~Negroes~~ — Education. 2. ~~Negroes~~ — North Carolina. 3. High schools—North Carolina. 4. Education, Secondary. 5. Education — North Carolina. I. Title.

Library of Congress LC2802.N8L6 1932a 32—23749
——— Copy 2. LB5.C8 no. 529
[42q1] 371.974

M297
L83
Lomax, Louis Emanuel, 1922-
When the word is given; a report on Elijah Muhammad, Malcolm X, and the Black Muslim world. [1st ed.] Cleveland, World Pub. Co. [1963]

223 p. illus., ports. 21 cm.
"Suggested additional reading": p. 213-214.

1. Black Muslims. I. Title.

BP222.L6 290 63—21624
Library of Congress [64f3]

The lonely warrior: the life and times of Robert S. Abbott.
MB9
Ab2
Ottley, Roi, 1906-
The lonely warrior: the life and times of Robert S. Abbott. Chicago, H. Regnery Co., 1955.

381 p. illus. 22 cm.
Includes bibliographies.

1. Abbott, Robert Sengstacke, 1868-1940. 2. The Chicago defender. 3. Negroes. I. Title.
Full name: Roi Vincent Ottley.

PN4874.A23O7 920.5 55—8784 ‡
Library of Congress [55h7]

The long dream.
M813.5
W93L2
Wright, Richard, 1909-1960.
Den lange drøm [The long dream] pa Dansk ved Kurt Kreutzfeld. [København] Gyldendal, 1959.

330p. 23cm.

Written in Danish.

1. Title. II. Title: The long dream.

M301
Eb74
Lomax, Louis Emanuel, 1922-
The white liberal
Pp. 39-46

In: Ebony. The white problem in America. Chicago, Johnson Pub. Co., 1966.

Lonesome boy.
M813.5
B641o
Bontemps, Arna Wendell, 1902-
Lonesome boy. Illustrated by Feliks Topolski. Boston, Houghton Mifflin, 1955.

28 p. illus. 22 cm.

I. Title.

PZ7.B6443Lo 54—9044 ‡
Library of Congress [55d5]

The long dream.
M813.5
W931
Wright, Richard, ~~1908~~ 1909-
The long dream, a novel. [1st ed.] Garden City, N. Y., Doubleday, 1958.

384 p. 22 cm.

I. Title.
Full name: Richard Nathaniel Wright.

PZ3.W9352Lo 58—12059 ‡
Library of Congress [58f10]

London - Fiction.
M813.5
W688h
Wilson, Carl Thomas David.
The half caste, by Carl T. D. Wilson. Ilfracombe [Eng.] A.H. Stockwell [1964]

207p. 19cm.
Portrait of author on book jacket.

The lonesome road; the story of the Negro's part in America.
MB
R24
Redding, Jay Saunders, 1906-
The lonesome road; the story of the Negro's part in America. [1st ed.] New York, Doubleday, 1958.

355 p. 24 cm. (Mainstream of America series)
Includes bibliography.

1. Negroes. 2. Negroes—Biog. 3. U. S.—Race question. I. Title.

E185.61.R298 58—6647 ‡
*301.451 325.260973
Library of Congress [58f80]

The Long night.
M813.5
M451
Mayfield, Julian, 1928-
The Long night. London, Michael Joseph, 1960.

142p. 20½cm.

I. Title.

London - Social conditions.
West Indies
M325.27
F21
Family Welfare Association, London.
The West Indian comes to England; a report prepared for the Trustees of the London Parochial Charities by the Family Welfare Association. Contributors: Douglas Manley, Ivo de Souza, Albert Hyndman, et al. Edited by S. K. Ruck. London, Routledge & K. Paul [1960]

187p. 23cm.

Jamaica
M972.92
L85h
[Long, Edward] 1734-1813.
The history of Jamaica: or, General survey of the antient and modern state of that island: with reflections on its situation, settlements, inhabitants, climate, products, commerce, laws, and government ... Illustrated with copper plates ... London, T. Lowndes, 1774.

3 v. fold. fronts. (v. 1-2) plates (1 fold.) fold. maps, plan. 28 x 22cm.
Vols. 2-3 paged continuously.

1. Jamaica. 2. Slavery in Jamaica. 3. Natural history—Jamaica. I. Title.

Library of Congress F1868.L84 2—11573
[40c1]

The long night.
M813.5
M451o
Mayfield, Julian, 1928-
The long night. London, Michael Joseph [1960]

142p. 21cm.

The lone-star of Liberia.
Trinidad
M966.6
D93
Durham, Frederick Alexander.
The lone-star of Liberia; being the outcome of reflections on our own people. By Frederick Alexander Durham, an African ... With an introduction by Madame la comtesse C. Hugo. London, E. Stock, 1892.

xxi p., 1 l., 331 p. 20cm.

CONTENTS.—The Africo-American.—Is the Ethiopian inferior to the Caucasian?—Immorality.—Superstition in the nineteenth century.—Under Caucasian rule.—Africa governed by Africans.—Repatriation and Liberia.

1. ~~Negroes~~—Colonization—Africa. 2. ~~Negro race~~. 3. Liberia. I. Title.

5—15427
Library of Congress DT631.D96

M331.833
L85p
Long, Herman Hodge.
People vs. property; race restrictive covenants in housing [by] Herman H. Long [and] Charles S. Johnson. Nashville, Fisk Univ. Press, 1947.

ix, 107 p. maps, diagrs. 21 cm.
Bibliographical footnotes.

1. ~~Negroes~~ — Housing. 2. ~~Negroes~~ — Segregation. 3. Real covenants—U. S. I. Johnson, Charles Spurgeon, 1893- joint author. II. Title.

E185.89.H6L7 325.260973 48—5205*
Library of Congress [48x10]

Long old road.
MB9
C31
Cayton, Horace Roscoe, 1903-
Long old road [by] Horace R. Cayton. New York, Trident Press, 1965 [°1964]

402 p. 22 cm.
Autobiography.
Portrait of author on book jacket.

I. Title.

E185.97.C35 1965 923.273 64—24280
Library of Congress [8]

Lonely crusade.
M813.5
H571
Himes, Chester B., 1909-
Lonely crusade. 1st ed. New York, A. A. Knopf, 1947.

[4] l., 3 398p. 22cm.

M323
L85c
Long, Herman Hodge
Race relations in the United States.

pp. 181-217. 25cm.
In: Coloured immigrants in Britain, by J. A. G. Griffith, et al. London, Oxford University Press, 1960.

1. Race relations. 2. Great Britain - Emigration and Immigration. I. Title.

The long search.
M813.5
B651
Bosworth, William, 1921-
The long search, a novel. [1st ed.] Great Barrington, Mass., Advance Pub. Co. [1957]

303 p. 23 cm.

I. Title.

PZ4.B7475Lo 56—12732 ‡
Library of Congress [2]

The long shadow of Little Rock.

MB9
B32
Bates, Daisy (Gatson)
The long shadow of Little Rock, a memoir. New York, David McKay Co. [1962]
234 p. illus. 21 cm.
Portrait of author on book jacket.

1. Negroes—Little Rock, Ark. 2. Little Rock, Ark.—Public schools. I. Title.

F419.L7B3 920.7 62–20233 ‡
Library of Congress [62f2]

A long way from home.

Jamaica
MB9
M19
McKay, Claude, 1890–
A long way from home, by Claude McKay. New York, L. Furman, inc. [°1937]
6 p. l., 3-354 p. 21cm.

I. Title.

37–8570
Library of Congress PS3525.A24785L6 1937
[45d1] 928.1

Ghana
M966.7
L85
Longdon, J E
Ghana Adehyeman. Ghana Kasa ho dwumadzibea dze puee gua do. [Accra, Guinea Press] 1960.
60p. illus. ports. 20cm.

1. Ghana.

Ghana
M341.139
L85
Longdon, J E
Mr. Amoa learns about Uno, by J. E. Longdon and Ella Griffin. Cover design by R. Ohene Akyeampong. Accra, Bureau of Ghana Languages, 1959.
9p. 22cm.

1. United Nations. I. Griffin, Ella, jt. auth. II. Title.

Longevity.

M612.68
P27
Patterson, John Andrew, 1875–
The breaking dawn; or, How long may we live in the body? By Rev. J. Andrew Patterson. Being a survey of the doctrines of renewed youth and the perpetuation of life in physical embodiment. Orange, N. J., The Chronicle publishing co., 1910.
ix, 121 p. front. (port.) 23cm. $1.00

1. Hygiene. 2. Longevity.

10-13871
Library of Congress RA776.P3
© Apr. 14, 1910; 2c. June 2, 1910; A 265369; J. A. Patterson, Orange, N. J.

M324
N21l
Look at the filibuster.
National Association for the Advancement of Colored People.
Look at the filibuster. New York, 1949.
[8]p. illus. 21cm.

The looming shadow.

Malawi
M896.3
K184L
Kayira, Legson.
The looming shadow. [1st ed.] Garden City, N. Y., Doubleday, 1967.
143 p. 22 cm.

I. Title.

PZ4.K234Lo 67–15367
Library of Congress [3]

Cuba
M861.08
L88
Lopez, Prieto, Antonio, 1847-1883,
Parnaso Cubano; coleccion de poesias selectas de autores Cubanos des de zequeira a nuestrodias ... por D. Antonio Lopez Prieto ... Habana, Miguel de Villa [1881?]
[v]- 1 xxxi, 370p. 22½cm.

1. Cuban poetry.

Peru
M863.6
L88c
López Albújar, Enrique, 1872-
Las caridades de la señora de Tordoya. Cuentos (Premio Nacional de 1950). Lima, Juan Mejia Baca & P. L. Villanueva Editores, 1955.
212p. 22cm.
Inscribed.

I. Title.

Peru
M863.6
L88m
López Albújar, Enrique, 1872-
Matalaché. Lima, Juan Mejia Baca & P. L. Villanueva, Editores, 197?
195p. 17½cm.
Inscribed.

I. Title.

Peru
M863.6
L88m
López Albújar, Enrique, 1872-
Matalaché. Segunda edicion. Lima, Juan Mejia Baca & P. L. Villanueva, Editores, 1955.
209p. 21½cm.
Inscribed.

I. Title.

Peru
M863.6
L88n
López Albújar, Enrique, 1872–
... Nuevos cuentos andinos. Santiago de Chile, Ediciones Ercilla, 1937.
4 p. l., [11]–185 p., 1 l. 22cm. (*Half-title:* Biblioteca América)
CONTENTS.—El brindis de los yayas.—Huayna-pishtanag.—El blanco.—Cómo se hizo pishtaco Calixto.—El trompiezo.—Juan Rabines no perdona.—Una posesión judicial.

I. Title. 1. Peruvian literature.

38—12446
Library of Congress PQ8497.L8N8
[45d1] 863.6

Lopoloko, Joseph Iyandza, 1927-
see
Iyandza-Lopoloko, Joseph, 1927-

M811.5
H87g
Lorca, Federico García Romancero Gitano.
Hughes, Langston, 1902- , tr.
Gypsy ballads, by Federico García Lorca. Translated by Langston Hughes; illus. by John McNee; introduction by Robert H. Glauber. Beloit, Wisconsin, Beloit College, 1951.
40p. 22cm. (Chapbook no.1)
Special issue of the Beloit poetry journal, fall 1951.

St. Vincent
M233.5
L88g
Lord, Samuel Ebenezer Churchstone, 1874–
The God idea; a study in the development and perfection of man, by the Reverend Samuel Ebenezer Churchstone Lord ... [Philadelphia, A. M. E. book concern] ~~1925~~ 1922.
213 p. 19½cm.

I. Title.

25-15892
Library of Congress BT124.L6
[2]

Lord's Supper - Anglican Communion.

M265.3
W93
Wright, Nathan.
One bread, one body. Foreword by James A. Pike. Greenwich, Conn., Seabury Press, 1962.
148 p. 22 cm.
Includes bibliographies.

1. Lord's Supper—Anglican Communion. I. Title.

BX5949.C5W73 265.3 62–9618 ‡
Library of Congress [5]

Lord's supper - Art.

M740
C86a
Crite, Allan Rohan, 1910– *illus.*
All glory; brush drawing meditations on the Prayer of consecration. Cambridge, Mass., Society of Saint John the Evangelist, 1947.
[28] l. illus. 24 cm.

1. Lord's supper—Art. I. Protestant Episcopal Church in the U. S. A. Book of common prayer. Communion service. II. Title.

N8054.C7 741.6382 48-3019*
Library of Congress [2]

Los Angeles.

M979
B24r
Reddick, Lawrence Dunbar, 1910- ed.
Race relations on the Pacific coast. New York, Journal of educational sociology, 1945.
129-208p. 23cm.
Special issue of The Journal of educational sociology, November 1945.
Partial contents: -The new race-relations frontiers, by L. D. Reddick. -Los Angeles, by Charles Bratt.

Los Angeles, California - History.

M979.493
B29f
Bass, Charlotta A
Forty years; memoirs from the pages of a newspaper. Los Angeles, The Author, 1960.
198p. illus., ports. 25½cm.

Nigeria
M966.9
L89hi
Losi, John B Ogunjimi.
History of Abeokuta, by Prince J.B. Ogunjimi Losi. Lagos, Nigeria, Bosere Press, 1924.
176p. 21cm.

1. Nigeria - History. 2. Abeokuta - History.

Nigeria
M966.9
L89h
Losi, John B. Ogunjimi.
History of Lagos, by Prince John B. O. Losi,..second edition. Lagos, C. M. S. Bookshop, 1921.
ii, 75p. plates. 22½cm.

1. Lagos, Nigeria-History
2. Nigeria-History

Nigeria
M966.9
L89hi

Losi, John B Ogunjimi.
Itan Abeokuta. Lati owo Prince John B. O. Losi. 2nd impression. Exeter, James Townsend & Co., 1920.

135p. 21½cm.
Bound with: John B.O. Losi's History of Abeokuta.

1. Abeokuta - History. 2. Nigeria - History.

Nigeria
M966.9
L89h

Losi, John B. . .Ogunjimi.
Itan eko, nipa Prince John B. O. Losi... third edition. Lagos, Church missionary society's press, 1921.

60p. plates. 22½cm.
Bound with: John B. O. Losi's History of Lagos(...)

1. Lagos, Nigeria— History. 2. Nigeria— History.

Nigeria
M966.92
L891

Losi, Prince John B Ogunjimi
Iwe itan ogun ati ote ilu-oke. Lagos, Church Missionary Society Bookshop, 1930.

32p. 18½cm.
A book of stories and political strifes of the Yoruba cities and towns North of Ibadan.

1. Nigeria - Cities and towns.

The lost zoo.

M811.5
C891

Cullen, Countee, 1903–
The lost zoo (a rhyme for the young, but not too young) by Christopher Cat and Countee Cullen, with illustrations by Charles Sebree. New York and London, Harper & brothers [°1940]

6 p. l., 72 p., 1 l. col. front., col. plates. 24cm.
Illustrated lining-papers in colors.
"First edition."

I. Sebree, Charles, illus. II. Title.

40—34870

Library of Congress PZ8.3.C889Lo
[45k1]

Lotteries.

M174.6
B45

Bernard, Ruth Thompson.
What's wrong with lottery? By Ruth Thompson Bernard. Boston, Meador publishing company [1943]
122 p. 20cm.

1. Gambling. 2. Lotteries. I. Title.
43-13105

Library of Congress HV6713.B47
[5] 174.6

MB9
L91r

Lotz, Philip Henry, 1889– *ed.*
... Rising above color, edited by Philip Henry Lotz ... New York, Association press; New York, Fleming H. Revell company, 1943.

viii, 112 p. 21 cm. (*His* Creative personalities. Vol. v)
"For further reading" at end of each chapter except one.

Contents.—George Washington Carver, man with a magic wand, by F. G. Lankard.—Marian Anderson, singer, by H. B. Hunting.—W. E. B. DuBois, scholar and fighter, by H. B. Hunting.—Robert Russa Moton, co-operator and educator, by H. B. Hunting.—Samuel Coleridge-Taylor, musician, by F. W. Clelland.—Richard Allen, first

(Continued on next card)
44—40017
[49w²5]

MB9
L91r

Lotz, Philip Henry, 1889– *ed.* ... Rising above color ... 1943. (Card 2)

Contents—Continued.

Negro bishop, by Mary E. Moxcey.—Frederick Douglass, orator, by Mary E. Moxcey.—Daniel Hale Williams, surgeon, by Mary E. Moxcey.—Booker T. Washington, "Up from slavery," by F. G. Lankard.—Roland Hayes, world-renowned tenor, by F. G. Lankard.—Paul Laurence Dunbar, poet, by F. G. Lankard.—James Weldon Johnson, poet and diplomat, by Lucile Desjardins.—Walter White, crusader for justice, by Roy Wilkins.

1. ~~Negroes—Biog.~~ Biography I. Title.
44—40017

Library of Congress CT104.L68 vol. 5
[49w²5] (920.02) 920.073

Lotze, Hermann.

M100
J711

Jones, Gilbert Haven, 1861–
Lotze und Bowne. Eine Vergleichung ihrer philosophischen arbeit. Inaugural - Dissertation der philosophischen fakultät der universität Jena zur erlangung der doktorwürde. Weida i Th. Druck von Thomas & Hubert, 1909.

117p. 23½cm.

Haiti
M841
L93o

Louis, Janine Tavernier, 1935–
Ombre ensoleillée. Preface de Roland Morisseau. Illustration de Villard Denis. Port-au-Prince, Imprimerie Gervais Louis, 1961.

21p. 19½cm.
Portrait of author on back of book.

1. Haiti-Poetry. 2. Poetry, Haitian. I. Title.

1935

Haiti
M841
L93s

Louis, Janine Tavernier, 1935–
Splendeur. Port-au-Prince, Imprimerie S. Bissainthe, [n.d.]

[16]p. 21cm.

1. Haitian portry. I. Title.

M796
L92h

Louis, Joe, 1914–
How to box, ed. by Edward J. Mallory. Philadelphia, D. McKay Co. [1948]
64 p. illus. 27 cm.

1. Boxing. I. Mallory, Edward J., ed. II. Title.
GV1137.L8 796.83 48—3663*
Library of Congress [50f²10]

MB9
L93m
1955

Louis, Joe, 1914–
The Joe Louis story. [Written with the editorial aid of Chester L. Washington and Haskell Cohen] New York, Grosset & Dunlap [~~1953~~] 1955
197 p. illus. 21 cm.
First ed. published in 1947 under title: My life story.

GV1132.L6A3 1953 927.9683 53-11991 ‡

Library of Congress [5]

MB9
L93m

Louis, Joe. 1914–
My life story, by Joe Louis ... New York, Duell, Sloan and Pearce [1947]
188, [2] p. plates, ports. 22cm.
"An Eagle book."
"Written with the editorial aid of Chester L. Washington and Haskell Cohen."
"First edition."
Contains Joe Louis' autograph.
I. Washington, Chester L. II. Cohen, Haskell.
GV1132.L6A3 927.9683 47-30240
© 19Mar47; author, New York; A11564.

Library of Congress [25]

Louis, Joe, 1914–

MB9
L93s

Scott, Neil.
Joe Louis, a picture story of his life. New York, Greenberg [1947]
[126] p. illus., ports. 21cm.

1. Louis, Joe, 1914–
GV1132.L6S35 927.9683 47-5025*
© Greenberg: Publisher; 25Jun47; A14096.

Library of Congress [15]

M616
W93

The Louis T. Wright Library of Harlem Hospital.
Journal of the National Medical Association, 1952.

296-309p.
Reprinted from Journal of the National Medical Association, vo. 44, July 1952.
Speeches by: Walter White, W. Montague Cobb. Arthur B. Spingarn. Elmer Carter. Channing H. Tobias. William H. Hastie. Hon. Vincent R. Impellitteri. Eleanor Roosevelt. Louis T. Wright.

I. Wright, Lou is T

France
M840
D89Lo

Louise de La Vallière.
Dumas, Alexandre, 1802-1870.
Louise de La Vallière; or, The love of Bragellone [!] A continuation of "The three musketeers", "Twenty years after", and "Bragelonne, the son of Athos". By Alex. Dumas. New rev. translation by H. Llewellyn Williams. New York, The F. M. Lupton publishing company [°1892]
459 p. 19cm. (*On cover:* The elite series. no. 9)
Written in collaboration with Auguste Maquet.
A translation of the middle portion of the Vicomte de Bragelonne.
Sequel: The man in the iron mask.
1. La Vallière, Louise Françoise de La Baume Le Blanc, duchesse de, 1644-1710 — Fiction. 2. France — Hist. — Louis XIV, 1643-1715—Fiction. 3. Man in the iron mask—Fiction. I. Maquet, Auguste, 1813-1888, joint author. II. Williams, Henry Llewellyn, jr., tr. III. Title.
6—43023

Library of Congress (PZ3.D89Lo 2)
Copyright 1892: 5323 [a37g1]

Louisiana.

MB
D45

Desdunes, Rodolphe L
Nos hommes et notre histoire; notices biographiques accompagnées de reflexions et de souvenirs personnels, hommage à la population créole, en souvenir des grands hommes qu'elle a produits et des bonnes choses qu'elle a accomplies, par R.-L. Desdunes ... Montréal, Arbour & Dupont, 1911.
196 p. front., ports. 22½cm.

1. Negroes—Louisiana. 2. Creoles. 3. New Orleans—Biog. 4. American literature (French)—Louisiana. 5. French literature—American authors.
12-21176

Library of Congress E185.93.L6D4
[a44c1]

Louisiana.

M286
H52h

Hicks, William.
History of Louisiana Negro Baptists from 1804-1914. By Wm. Hicks... With a biographical introduction by Bishop W. B. Purvis. Nashville, Tenn., National Baptist publishing board [1914]

251p. illus., including ports. 20½cm.

Louisiana.

M810
H84mu
1936

Hurston, Zora Neale.
Mules and men, by Zora Neale Hurston; with an introduction by Frank Boas ... 10 illustrations by Miguel Covarrubias. Philadelphia, London, Kegan, Paul, Trench, Trubner, 1936.
342, [1] p. front., illus., plates. 22cm.
Contents.—pt. I. Folk tales.—pt. II. Hoodoo.—Appendix. I. Negro songs with music (p. 309-[331]) II. Formulae of hoodoo doctors. III. Paraphernalia of conjure. IV. Prescriptions of root doctors.

1. Folk-lore, Negro. 2. Voodooism. 3. Negroes—Florida. 4. Negroes—Louisiana. 5. Negro songs. I. Title.
35—18525

Library of Congress GR103.H8
[45j²2] 398.09759

Louisiana.

M810
H94mu

Hurston, Zora Neale.
Mules and men, by Zora Neale Hurston; with an introduction by Frank Boas ... 10 illustrations by Miguel Covarrubias. Philadelphia, London, J. B. Lippincott company, 1935.
342, [1] p. front., illus., plates. 22cm.
Contents.—pt. I. Folk tales.—pt. II. Hoodoo.—Appendix. I. Negro songs with music (p. 309-[331]) II. Formulae of hoodoo doctors. III. Paraphernalia of conjure. IV. Prescriptions of root doctors.

1. Folk-lore, Negro. 2. Voodooism. 3. Negroes—Florida. 4. Negroes—Louisiana. 5. Negro songs. I. Title.
35—18525

Library of Congress GR103.H8
[45j²2] 398.09759

Louisiana.

M975
N31

Laws, J Bradford.
The Negroes of Cinclare Central Factory and Calumet Plantation, Louisiana. [Bulletin of the Labor Dept. no.38, 1902] pp. 95-120.

In: The Negro in the black belt... Washington, D.C., Dept. of Labor, [189 - 190]

M370. M11

Louisiana.

McAllister, Jane Ellen, 1899–
The training of Negro teachers in Louisiana, by Jane Ellen McAllister ... New York city, Teachers college, Columbia university, 1929.
vi, 95 p. 23½cm. (Teachers college, Columbia university. Contributions to education; no. 364)
Published also as thesis (PH. D.) Columbia university.
Bibliography: p. 95.
1. Teachers, Training of—Louisiana. 2. Negroes—Education. 3. Negroes—Louisiana. I. Title. II. Title: Negro teachers in Louisiana, The training of.
Library of Congress LC2802.L8M3 1929 a 30—11031
——— Copy 2. LB5.C8 no. 364
Copyright A 21710 [41m1] 370.7

MJ01 F86?

Louisville, Ky.

Frazier, Edward Franklin, 1894–
Negro youth at the crossways, their personality development in the middle states, by E. Franklin Frazier; prepared for the American youth commission. Washington, D. C., American council on education, 1940.
xxiii, 301, [2] p. illus. (maps) diagr. 23½ cm.
"This volume ... describes the experiences of Negro boys and girls living in Washington, D. C., and Louisville, Kentucky; these communities were selected as examples of middle-area conditions."—Pref.
1. Negroes—Moral and social conditions. 2. Youth. 3. Personality. 4. Social psychology. 5. Negroes—District of Columbia. 6. Negroes—Louisville, Ky. I. American council on education. American youth commission. II. Title.
Library of Congress E185.6.F74 40—32764
[42z7] 325.2609753

M06 Am3 no.6

Love, John L.
The disfranchisement of the negro, by John L. Love ... Washington, D. C., The Academy, 1899.
27 p. 23cm. (American negro academy. Occasional papers, no. 6)
1. U. S.—Pol. & govt. ~~2. Negroes—U. S.~~
Library of Congress E184.N3A5 9—21947
——— Copy 2. JK1924.L89
[35b1]

M976.3 R76

Louisiana.

Roussève, Charles Barthelemy.
The Negro in Louisiana; aspects of his history and his literature, by Charles Barthelemy Roussève, M. A. New Orleans, The Xavier university press, 1937.
xvii, 212 p. front., illus. (music) plates, diagrs. 20½cm.
"This work, prepared in 1935 in partial fulfillment of the requirements for the degree of master of arts, makes its appearance ... substantially as it was originally written, save for ... several minor alterations and the addition of a few details."—p. vii.
Bibliography: p. 193–201.
1. Negroes—Louisiana. 2. Negroes in literature and art. 3. Negro authors. I. Title.
Library of Congress E185.93.L6R6 38—525
[42h2] 325.2609763

M323. N213l

Louisville, Ky.

National Association for the Advancement of Colored People. Louisville.
The history of Louisville segregation case and the decision of the Supreme Court. Louisville, The Association, Legal Committee, 1917?

M06 Am3 no. 11

Love, John L
The potentiality of the Negro vote.
(In: American Negro Academy. The Negro and the elective franchise. Washington, D.C., The Academy, 1905)

M976.3 Se6

Louisiana.

The Sepia socialite.
... The Negro in Louisiana, seventy -eight years of progress. Fifth anniversary edition... New Orleans, Sepia socialite pub. co., 1942.
168p. illus. 38cm.
Dated on cover, July 1942; on t.-p. Apr, 1942.

Haiti M972.94 L93h

Lourié, I
Haiti, the ally of democracies., Port-au-Prince, Imp. du College Veritères, 1942.
60p. 23cm.
1. Haiti

M811.5 L94w

Love, Melvin.
War in heaven, and other poems. [1st ed.] New York, Exposition Press [1954]
64 p. 21 cm.
I. Title.
PS3523.O825W3 811.5 54–8269 ‡
Library of Congress [2]

MB P41w

Louisiana.

Who's who in colored Louisiana, 1930; A. E. Perkins ... editor. Baton Rouge, La., Douglas loan co., inc. [1930]
153, [1] p. illus., plates (1 fold.) ports., facsim. 21cm.
1. Negroes—Louisiana. 2. Negroes—Biog. 3. Louisiana—Biog. I. Perkins, Archie Ebenezer, 1879– ed.
Library of Congress E185.93.L6W5 32—19208
[a44b1] 325.26

Congo Leopoldville M325 M89i

Louvain. Université catholique. Ecole des sciences politiques et socials. Collection no. 156.
Mulenzi, Janvier
L'internationalisation du phénomène colonial. Bruxelles, Éditions du Treurenberg, 1958.
164p. 24cm. (Université de Louvain. Collection de l'École des sciences politiques et sociales, 156)
Bibliography: p. [154]-159.
1. Colonies - History. 2. International trusteeships. 3. Colonies (International Law) I. Title. II. Series: Louvain. Université catholique. École des sciences politiques et socials. Collection no. 156.

M398 L94

Love, Rose Leary, ed.
A collection of folklore for children in elementary school and at home. [1st ed.] New York, Vantage Press [1964]
88 p. illus. 21 cm.
Includes music.
"To Arthur - a charming little book by my cousin, Rose " Langston Hughes, 1964."
1. Folk-lore, American—Juvenile literature. I. Title. II. Title: Folklore for children.
GR105.L6 j 398 64–2852
Library of Congress [3]

MB T49e

Louisiana - Civilization.

Tinker, Edward Larocque, 1881–
Les écrits de langue française en Louisiane au XIXe siècle; essais biographiques et bibliographiques par Edward Larocque Tinker ... Paris, H. Champion, 1932 [i. e. 1933]
2 p. l., 502 p. incl. plates, facsims. 25½cm. (Added t.-p.: Bibliothèque de la Revue de littérature comparée ... t. 85)
Authors, including Negroes, arranged alphabetically, with biographical and critical sketches written to show the characteristic French spirit which has left an impress in Louisiana, followed by the author's works including English titles of those writing in both languages. The location of a copy of the work is given, if known.
(Continued on next card)
33—21149
[45h1]

M841.8 H12

Louverture, Isaac. Supposed author.
L'Haïtiade poème épique en nuit chants, par un philanthrope Européen nouvelle edition, par Gragnon-Lacoste. Paris, A. Durand et Pedone-Lauriel, Editeurs, 1878.
xviii, 209p. 18cm.
Isaac Louverture. Supposed author.

M813.5 L94n

Love, Rose Leary.
Nebraska and his granny, by Rose Leary Love; with illustrations by Preston Haygood. Tuskegee Institute, Ala., Tuskegee institute press, 1936.
5 p. l., 69 p. illus. 20cm.
I. Title.
Library of Congress PZ7.L956Ne 37—2457
——— Copy 2.
Copyright A 103589 [3]

M976.3 Al5s

Louisiana--Economic conditions.
Allain, T T
Speech of Hon. T. T. Allain, of the delegate from the 14th senatorial district, delivered, May 24, 1879. Cosmopolitan Printing House, 1879.
[3] 7p. 23cm.

Haiti MB9 T46nh

Louverture family.

Nemours, Alfred, 1883–
... Histoire de la famille et de la descendance de Toussaint-Louverture. Avec des documents inédits et les portraits des descendants de Toussaint-Louverture jusqu'à nos jours. Port-au-Prince, Haiti, Imprimerie de l'État, 1941.
4 p. l., vii-viii, 308 p. front., pl., ports. 28cm.
At head of title: Général Nemours.
Bibliography: p. 290-302.
1. Toussaint Louverture, Pierre Dominique, 1746?-1803. 2. Louverture family. I. Title.
Harvard univ. Library for Library of Congress F1923.T8907 A 41—1743
[43c1] 923.27294

Liberia M896.3 C78l

Love in ebony.
Cooper, Charles Edward.
Love in ebony; a West African romance, by Varfelli Karlee [pseud.]. With a foreword by Vernon Bartlett. London, John Murray [1932]
316 p. 19½ cm.

M370. B812a 1876

Louisiana - Education.

Brown, William G.
Annual report of the State Superintendent of Public Education, William G. Brwon, to the General Assembly of Louisiana, for the year 1875. Session of 1876. New Orlenas, Printed at the Republican Office, 1876.
392, xvixp. 22½cm.

M286 L94

Love, Emanuel King, 1850–1900.
History of the First African Baptist church, from its organization, January 20th, 1788, to July 1st, 1888. Including the centennial celebration, addresses, sermons, etc. By Rev. E. K. Love ... Savannah, Ga., The Morning news print., 1888.
7 p. l., iii-v, 360 p. front., illus. 21cm.
1. Savannah. First African Baptist church. I. Title.
Library of Congress BX6480.S45F5 26—5886
Copyright 1888: 24385 [37b1]

M811.5 M951

Love is a terrible thing.

Murphy, Beatrice M.
Love is a terrible thing, by Beatrice M. Murphy. New York, the Hobson Press, 1945.
ix, 65p. 21½cm.

Love is a terrible thing.
M811.5 Murphy, Beatrice M
M951 Love is a terrible thing, by Beatrice M. Murphy. New York, The Hobson book, press, 1945.
ix, 65p. 21½cm.

Love knows no barriers.
M813.5 Thomas, Will, 1905-
T361 Love knows no barriers (God is for white folks). Rev. ed. New York, New American Library, 1950.
207p. 18cm. (Signet books)
At head of cover title: Original title: God is for white folks.
Pocket book edition.

Love leaps here.
Jamaica
M821.91 Figueroa, John
F469L Love leaps here. [Liverpool, printed by C. Tinling, 1962]
60p.
Poems

Love letters in rhyme.
M811.5 Brown, Samuel E
B811o Love letters in rhyme, by Samuel E. Brown. New York, Samuel E. Brown c 1930
29p. 19½cm.
Copy: no.3 First edition.
Autographed copy: Samuel E. Brown To Edward from your friend, Samuel. September 22nd, nineteen-thirty.

The love of Landry.
M813.4 **Dunbar, Paul Laurence, 1872-1906.**
D911 The love of Landry. By Paul Laurence Dunbar ... New York, Dodd, Mead and company [°1900]
3 p. l., 200 p. 18½ cm.
I. Title.
0—6621
Library of Congress PZ3.D911L
[42r27f1]

Love of this land; progress of the Negro...
M323 **Robinson, James Herman, ed.**
R561 Love of this land; progress of the Negro in the United States. Illustrated by Elton C. Fax. Philadelphia, Christian Education Press [1956]
76 p. illus. 23 cm.
1. ~~Negroes.—2. U. S.~~—Race question. I. Title.
E185.61.R68 325.260973 56-9433 ‡
Library of Congress [2]

Love shall never end.
Nigeria
M896.3 Uzoh, John E
Uz7L Love shall never end. Onitsha «Nigeria» Njoku and Sons Bookshop «n.d.»
48p. 21½cm.

Trinidad
M823.91 **Lovelace, Earl, 1935-**
L94w While gods are falling. Chicago, H. Regnery Co., 1966.
254 p. 21 cm.
Portrait of author on book jacket.
I. Title.
PZ4.L889Wh 66-17746
Library of Congress [3]

M812.08 **Lovell, John, 1907-**
L94d Digests of great American plays; complete summaries of more than 100 plays from the beginnings to the present. New York, Crowell [1961]
452 p. illus. 24 cm. (A Crowell reference book)
1. American drama—Stories, plots, etc. I. Title.
PS338.P5L6 812.0822 61—10482 ‡
Library of Congress [61f5]

M813.5 **Loveman, Amy, ed.**
H94v Varied harvest; a miscellany of writing by Barnard College women, edited by Amy Loveman, Frederica Barach, and Marjorie M. Mayer. New York, Putnam [1953]
304 p. 22 cm.
Partial contents.- Hurston, Zora Neale. The conscience of the court.
White editor.
1. American literature (Selections: Extracts, etc.) 2. Barnard College, New York—Alumnae. I. Title.
PS508.W7L6 810.82 53—12900 ‡
Library of Congress [15]

Lover man.
Panama
M813.5 Anderson, Alston, 1924-
An2101 Lover man. Garden City, N. Y., Doubleday, 1959.
1959 177 p. illus. 22 cm.
I. Title.
PZ4.A5446Lo2 59—10037 ‡
Library of Congress [60f7]

Lover man.
Panama
M813.5 Anderson, Alston, 1924-
An21 Lover man. London, Cassell, 1959.
1959
178p. illus. 21cm.
Portrait on jacket.
I. Title.

M811.5 Lovingood, Penman, 1895-
L95p Poems of a singer. Compton, Lovingood Company [1963]
68p. 16½cm.
I. Title.

M946 **Low, Mary.**
L95r Red Spanish notebook; the first six months of the revolution and civil war, by Mary Low and Juan Breá. London, M. Secker and Warburg, ltd., 1937.
x, 7-256 p. 19cm.
1. Spain—Hist.—Civil war, 1936- —Personal narratives. I. Breá, Juan. II. Title.
38-33711
Library of Congress DP269.L7
[3] 946.08

M796 Low, Nat
L95n The Negro in sports. San Francisco, The Daily People's World, 19 .
31p. illus. 19cm.
White author
1. Sports. I. Title.

M616 The low-down on tuberculosis.
B641 Bontemps, Arna Wendell, 1902-
The low-down on tuberculosis. National Tuberculosis Association, 1941.
7p. illus. 23cm.

Kenya
M630 Lowdermilk, Walter C
L95e Riathana ria ikumi na rimwe kana umenyeeri bwa muthetu [The eleventh commandment or Care of the land] [Tr. by Samson Mzee] [London, W. & J. Mackay, n.d.]
16p. 18cm.
Written in Meru.
White author.
1. Agriculture - Kenya. I. Title.

M811.08 **Lowenfels, Walter, 1897-** *ed.*
L95 Poets of today; a new American anthology. With a prologue poem by Langston Hughes. New York, International Publishers [1964]
143 p. 21 cm.
White editor.
Includes poems by 20 Negro authors.
1. American poetry—20th cent. I. Title.
PS614.L75 811.5082 64-8443
Library of Congress [5]

Lowenstein, A K joint author.
U. S.
M968 Marcum, John Arthur
Am3 Force: its thrust and prognosis, by J. A. Marcum and A. K. Lowenstein.
Pp. 249-277.
In: American Society of African Culture. Southern Africa in transition. New York, Praeger, 1966.

Lowenstein, Solomon, 1877-
M89 **Hubert, James Henry, 1885-**
L63hu The life of Abraham Lincoln, its significance to Negroes and Jews; an address delivered before Gad lodge, no. 11, Free sons of Israel, February 15, 1939, by James H. Hubert ... with an introduction by Dr. William Heard Kilpatrick ... and an extract from the presidential address on the test of American democracy delivered before the sixty-fifth annual session of the National conference of social work, by Dr. Solomon Lowenstein ... New York, N. Y., W. Malliet and company, 1939.
22 p. 23cm.
1. Lincoln, Abraham, pres. U. S., 1809-1865. 2. U. S.—Race question. 3. Negroes—Moral and social conditions. I. Lowenstein, Solomon, 1877-
40-34518 Revised
Library of Congress E457.2.H87
[r43e2]. 923.173

West Indies
M972.97 **Lowenthal, David.**
L95w The West Indies Federation; pespectives on a new nation. New York, Columbia University Press, 1961.
142 p. illus. 21 cm. (American Geographical Society. Research series, no. 23)
Includes bibliography.
1. West Indies (Federation)
F2131.L8 972.97 61—7176 ‡
Library of Congress [61k10]

Lowery, Irving E , 1850-
Pp. 217-24.
M973.5 L953 Jones, Katharine M 1900- ed.
The plantation South. [1st ed.] Indianapolis, Bobbs-Merrill [1957]
412 p. illus. 22 cm.
Includes bibliography.
White author.
1. Southern States—Descr. & trav. 2. Southern States—Soc. life & cust. 3. Plantation life.
F213.J6 917.5 57—9357 ‡
Library of Congress [a62y⁵8]

Haiti M89 D18L Lubin, Maurice A
Etape d'une visite culturelle [by] Malu [pseud.] Port-au-Prince, Imprimerie de l'Etat, 1964.
47p. illus. port. 23½cm.
Autographed.
1. Damas, Leon Gontran, 1912- I. Title.

Uganda M613.2 T75 Lubwama, Aloni, jt. tr.
Trowell, H C
Mmere ki gye tusaanira okulya? [What food should we eat?] kya H. C Trowell ne R. G. Ladin. Kyakyusibwa John W. S. Kasirye ne Aloni Lubwama. Nairobi, Eagle Press, 1951.
23p. illus. 18½cm. (Asika Obulamu Series)
Written in Luganda.
1. Nutrition. I. Title. II. Kasirye, John W. S., tr. III. Lubwama, Aloni, jt. tr. IV. Series.

M350 G192 1861 The loyalty and devotion of colored Americans in the Revolution and War of 1812.
Garrison, William Lloyd.
The loyalty and devotion of colored Americans in the Revolution and War of 1812. Boston, R. F. Wallcut, 1861.
24p. 18cm.

Haiti M972.94 L96e Lubin, Maurice A
De l'enseignement en Haiti, par Maurice A. Lubin. Collection: Servir. Port-au-Prince, Imprimerie du Commerce, 1946.
21p. 20cm.
1. Haiti--Education.

Uganda X367 P85 Lubwama, F. B., tr.
Potts, C W K
Social club mu Afrika [Social club in East Africa] Kyakyusibwa F. B. Lubwama. Nairobi, Eagle Press, 1953.
32p. 22½cm.
Written in Luganda.
White author.
1. Africa, East - Clubs. 2. Clubs. I. Title II. Lubwama, F. B., tr.

Uganda M967.61 L96e Lubambula, Y B
Ennyimba ezimu; Some Luganda songs. Nairobi, The Eagle Press, 1953.
17p. 18cm. (Eagle Improve Your Reading Series No. 2)
Written in Luganda.
1. Luganda songs.

Haiti M972.94 L96oe Lubin, Maurice A
Ou en sommes-nous avec l'elite intellectuelle d'Haiti.
Pp. 121-31 23cm.
Reprinted from Journal of Inter-American Studies, Vol. 3, No. 1, January 1961.
1. Haiti. 2. Elite. I. Title.

M813.5 L96a Lucas, Curtis, 1914-
Angel. New York, Lion Book, Inc., 1953.
160p. 16cm.
I. Title.

Haiti M844 L96f Lubin, J Dieudonné.
Les fauves c'est nous, petit thèse sociale. Port-au-Prince, L'Etat, 1950.
41p. port. 21cm.
1. Haitian essays. I. Title.

Haiti M841 L96p Lubin, Maurice A
Poesies Haitiennes. Rio de Janeiro, Livraria Editora da Casa, 1956.
147p. 22cm.
1. Poetry-Haitian.

M813.5 L96f Lucas, Curtis, 1914-
Flour is dusty, by Curtis Lucas. Philadelphia, Dorrance & company [1943]
166 p. 19½cm.
I. Title. 44-868
Library of Congress PZ3.L9614Fl [3]

Haiti M844 L96h Lubin, J Dieudonné
Heros et heroines de la liberté de la liberté d'Haiti et du monde. Port-au-Prince, Imp. de l'Etat.
89p. ports. 22cm. (Collection du tricinquantenaire)
1. Haitian poetry. I. Title.

Haiti M841 L96q Lubin, Maurice A
Quelques themes Haitiens de poesie. Presentation de Mr. Louis P. Baptiste. Port-au-Prince, 1959.
35p. 28cm.
Mimeographed.
1. Haitian Poetry.

M813.5 L96for Lucas, Curtis , 1914-
Forbidden fruit. [New York, Universal Publishing and Distributing Corporation] 1953.
190p. 18cm. (A Beacon Book)
I. Title.

Haiti M844 L96t Lubin, J Dieudonné.
Travaux de recherches et de documentation aux Etats-Unis et impressions de voyage. Port-au-Prince, L'Etat, 1951.
69p. port. 17cm.
1. U. S.--Description and travel.
2. Washington, Booker Taliaferro, 1859?-1915.

Lubin, Maurice A., ed.
Haiti M841.08 Sa2p Saint-Louis, Carlos, 1923- ed.
Panorama de la poésie haïtienne [par] Carlos St-Louis & Maurice A. Lubin. Port-au-Prince, H. Deschamps, 1950.
vi, 635 p. fold. col. map. 20 cm. (Collection Haitiana)
Includes bio-bibliographical sketches.
Bibliography: p. 634-635.
1. Haitian poetry (French) 2. French poetry—Haitian authors. I. Lubin, Maurice A., ed. (Series)
PQ3946.S3 52-18659
Library of Congress [1]

M813.5 L96fo Lucas, Curtis, 1914-
Forbidden fruit. New York, Universal. 1953.
135p. 18cm.
Bound with Taylor, Valerie. The lusty land. New York, 1953.
I. Title

Haiti M841 L96af Lubin, Maurice A
L'Afrique dans la poesie haitienne. Collection: etude individuelle des poètes Haitiens. Port-au-Prince, Editions Panorama, 1965.
99p. 22cm.
Autographed.
1. Haitian poetry. 2. Africa - Poetry. I. Title.

Lubwama, Aloni, tr.
Uganda M910 Sh61 Shillito, James
Ensi gye tulimu [The world in which we live] Kya kyucibwa Aloni Lubwama. Nairobi, Eagle Press, 1950.
39p. illus. 18½cm.
Written in Luganda.
White author.
1. Title. 1. Geography. II. Lubwama, Aloni, tr.

M813.5 L96s Lucas, Curtis, 1914-
So low, so lonely. New York, Lion Books, Inc. 1952.
158p. 16½cm.
I. Title.

M813.5
L96t
1952
Lucas, Curtis, 1914-
Third ward, Newark. New York, Lion Books, Inc., 1952.
160p. 16cm. (Lion books 80)
Pocket book edition.
I. Title

M813.5
L96t
Lucas, Curtis. 1914-
... Third ward, Newark. Chicago, New York, Ziff-Davis publishing company [1946]
3 p. l., 238 p. 21cm.
I. Title.
PZ3.L9614Th 46-8619
© 30Nov46; author, Newark, N. J.; A8896.
Library of Congress [4]

Uganda
M323
B31
Lucas, Eric, ed.
What is freedom. London, Oxford University Press, 1963.
136p. 18cm.
Partial contents.- On Political freedom, by B. K. Bataringaya.
1. Liberty. 2. Political rights. I. Title.

Nigeria
M966.9
L96
Lucas, J Olumide
The religion of the Yorubas; being an account of the religious beliefs and practices of the Yoruba peoples of Southern Nigeria, especially in relation to the religion of ancient Egypt. Lagos, C.M.S. Bookshop, 1948.
420p. illus. 21½cm.
1. Yorubas - Religion. 2. Nigeria - Religion.

Martinique
M972.98
L96h
Lucrèce, J
Histoire de la Martinique a l'usage des cours supérieur et complementaire des écoles primaires. Ouvrage illustre de 32 gravures, par J. Lucrèce. [Paris, Chez l'auteur, 1932]
173p. illus., ports. 17½cm.
1.Martinique--History. 2.Martinique--Description and travel. I. Achille, Louis.

Ludlow, Helen Wilhelmina, joint author.
M378H
Ar5h
Armstrong, Mary Frances (Morgan) *d.* 1903-
Hampton and its students. By two of its teachers, Mrs. M. F. Armstrong and Helen W. Ludlow. With fifty cabin and plantation songs, arranged by Thomas F. Fenner ... New York, G. P. Putnam's sons, 1874.
255, [1] p. fold, front., illus. 21½cm.
Songs (with music): p. [171]-255.
1. Hampton, Va. Normal and agricultural institute. 2. Negro songs. I. Ludlow, Helen Wilhelmina, joint author. II. Fenner, Thomas P.
Library of Congress LC2851.H32A7 7—42208
[45k1]

Congo
(Leopoldville)
M967.5
L96
Lufuluabo, François-Marie
La notion Luba-Bantoue de l'etre. Bakwanga, Imprimatur Jos. Nkongolo, 1164.
46p. 22½cm.
Portrait of author on back of book.
1. Bantus - Religion. I. Title.

Congo(Léopoldville)
M200
L96
Lufuluabo, François-Marie
Vers une théodicée bantoue. Mechliniae, Imprimi potest, 1961.
50p. 22½cm.
Portrait of author on back of book.
Includes bibliography.
1. Religion-Congo (Leopoldville) 2. Bantu - Relgion. I. Title.

Luganda language - Readers. speakers.
Uganda
M372.4
M46
Mdoe, Janet Naibirwa
Nze mmanyi okusoma [I know how to read] ebifaananyi byakubibwa Y. Kalanzi ne Alan Jarman. Nairobi, Eagle Press, 1960.
60p. illus. 18½cm.
Written in Luganda.
1. Luganda language - Readers. speakers. I. Title.

Luganda songs.
Uganda
M967.61
L96e
Lubambula, Y B
Ennyimba ezimu; Some Luganda songs. Nairobi, The Eagle Press, 1953.
17p. 18cm. (Eagle Improve Your Reading Series No. 2)
Written in Luganda.

Het luipaard.
Jamaica
M823.91
R271u
Reid, Victor Stafford, 1913-
Het luipaard; roman (The leopard). [Translated by Rosey E. Pool]. Amsterdam, Wereld-Bibliotheek, 1959.
133p. 20cm.

Luitpold, Josef, tr.
M811.08
N94
Nussbaum, Anna, *ed.*
Afrika singt, eine auslese neuer afro-amerikanischer lyrik, herausgegeben von Anna Nussbaum. Wien und Leipzig, F. G. Speidel [1929]
2 p. l., [7]-169, [5] p., 1 l. 22cm.
"Die nachdichtungen und übertragungen stammen von Hermann Kesser, Josef Luitpold, Anna Siemsen, Anna Nussbaum."
1. Negro poetry (American) I. Kesser, Hermann, 1880- tr. II. Luitpold, Josef, tr. III. Siemsen, Anna, 1882- tr.
Library of Congress PS591.N4SN8 29-21778
[2]

Kenya
M372.4
L92K
Bk.1
Lulagoli language - Readers and speakers.
Lwane, Benjamin G.
Kitabu chio kutanga chio kusoma mu Lulogooli. Kitabu 1 [Reader 1] chia Benjamin G. Lwane na Joseph G. Kisia. [illus. by Ruth Yudelowitz] Nairobi, Eagle Press, 1957.
30p. illus. 21-1/2cm.
Written in Lulagoli.
1. Lulagoli language - Readers and speakers. I. Kisia, Joseph G. jt. auth. II. Title.

Kenya
M372.4
L92K
Bk.2
Lulagoli language - Readers and speakers.
Lwane, Benjamin G.
Kitabu chio kaviri chio kusoma mu Lulogooli. Kitabu 2 [Reader 2] chla Benjamin G. Lwane na Joseph G. Kisia. [illus. by Ruth Yudelowitz] Nairobi, Eagle Press, 1957.
39p. illus. 21-1/2cm.
Written in Lulagoli.
1. Lulagoli language - Readers and speakers. I. Kisia, Joseph G., jt. author. II. Title.

Kenya
M372.4
L92
Lulagoli language - Readers and speakers.
Lwane, Benjamin G
Musomi wokutanga, chia Benjamin G. Lwane na Joseph G. Kisia. [Illustrated by Ruth Yudelowitz] Nairobi, Eagle Press, 1957.
24p. illus. 22cm.
Written in Lulagoli.

Uganda
M967.61
L97
Lule, Julia M.
Ssebato bazannya. London, Longmans, Green and Co., 1950.
44p. illus. 18½cm.
Written in Luganda

Lule, Vencent, tr.
Uganda
M967.61
G79
Gray, John Milner
Ebyafaayo ebitonotono ku Uganda [Short history of Uganda] Kyakyusibwa Vencent Lule. Kampala, East African Literature Bureau, 1956.
25p. 21½cm.
Written in Luganda.
White author.
1. Uganda - History. I. Lule, Vencent, tr. II. Title.

Congo,
Leopoldville
M967.5
L97
Lumanyisha, Dikonda wa
Face a face. [Vers quel destin le peuple Congolais est-il embraque? Préface de Jean Claude Tammaire] Bruxelles, Editions Remarques Congolaises, 1964.
109p. port. 19cm. (Collection Etudes Congolaises, no. 9)
Portrait of author in book.
1. Congo, Leopoldville. I. Title.

Lumbuti language.
Uganda
M496.3
K65f
Kivebulaya, Canon Apolo, trans.
First reading book. Lumbuti language (Pygmies of Central Africa). Translation by Rev. Canon Apolo Kivebulaya. London, The Religious Tract Society, n.d.
16p. 16½cm.

...Luminaires, poemes.
Haiti
M841
B411
Bélance, René.
... Luminaires, poèmes. Port-au-Prince, Haïti [Imp. Morissett] 1941.
2 p. l., 3-21, [1] p. 21 x 16cm.
I. Title.
Library of Congress PQ3949.B36L8 44-53608
[2] 841.91

The luminous darkness.
M301
T426
Thurman, Howard, 1899-
The luminous darkness; a personal interpretation of the anatomy of segregation and the ground of hope. [1st ed.] New York, Harper & Row [1965]
xi, 112 p. 20 cm.
1. Negroes—Segregation. 2. Church and race problems. I. Title.
E185.61.T47 301.45196073 65-20445
Library of Congress [5]

Uganda
M658
L97

Lumu, Nehemiah Bosa Eryan, 1912-
Oyinza okutunda edduka? [Can you run a shop?] Nairobi, Eagle Press, 1957.

59p. illus.
Written in Luganda.

1. Stores, Retail - Uganda. I. Title.

Congo
Léopoldville
M967.5
L97co

Lumumba, Patrice, 1925-1961.
Congo, my country. With a foreword by Colin Legum. New York, Praeger [1962]

195 p. illus. 23 cm. (Books that matter)
Translation of Le Congo, terre d'avenir, est-il menacé?

1. Congo (Leopoldville)—Pol. & govt. I. Title.
Full name: Patrice Emergy Lumumba.

DT657.L813 1962 967.5 62-18269 ‡
Library of Congress [3]

Congo
Leopoldville
M967.5
L97co2

Lumumba, Patrice, 1925-1961.
Congo, my country. With a foreword and notes by Colin Legum. Translated by Graham Heath. London, Pall Mall Press [°1962]

xxix, 195p. photos. 22cm.
Translation of Le Congo, terre d'avenir, est-il menacé?

1. Congo (Leopoldville)-Pol. & govt. I. Title.

Congo(Leopoldville)
M967.5
L97c

Lumumba, Patrice, 1925-1961
Le Congo terre d'avenir est-il menacé? Bruxelles, Office de Publicité, S. A., Éditeurs, 1961.

218p. 21.5cm.
Portrait of author on book jacket.

1. Congo. I. Title.

Congo
Leopoldville
M967.5
L97p

Lumumba, Patrice, 1925-1961
La pensée politique de Patrice Lumumba. Préface de Jean-Paul Sartre. Textes recueillis et Présentes par Jean Van Lierde. Bruxelles, Le Livre Africain, 1963.

401p. port. 21½cm.

1. Congo (Leopoldville)- Politics and government. I. Lierde, Jean Van. II. Sartre, Jean-Paul, 1905-Preface III. Title.

Lumumba, Patrice, 1925-1961.

Congo
Léopoldville
MB9
L97e

Europe; revue mensuelle.
Patrice Lumumba. [Paris] 1962.

173p. 21½cm.

Lumumba, Patrice, 1925-1961 - Drama.

Nigeria
M896.2
Oglp

Ogali, Ogali Agu, 1931-
Patrice Lumumba; a drama. Onitsha, Nigeria, Tabansi Printing Press, 1961.

40p. illus. 21½cm.
Portrait of author on book cover.

Lumumba, Patrice, 1925-1961.

Congo
(Léopoldville)
MB9
L97pt

Patrice Lumumba; la verite sur le crime odieux des colonialistes. Paris, Editions en Langues Etrangeres, 1961.

268p. 20cm.

Lumumba, Patrice, 1925-1961 - Drama.

Nigeria
M896.2
St43t

Stephen, Felix N
The trials and death of Lumumba. Onitsha [Nigeria] M.A. Ohaejesi [n.d.]

42p. ports. 20½cm.

Lumumba, Patrice, 1925-1961. Letters.

Congo
Léopoldville
MB9
L97e

Europe; revue mensuelle.
Patrice Lumumba. [Paris] 1962.

173p. 21½cm.

Lumumba, Patrice
The independence of the Congo, pp. 90-93.

Africa
M960.3
D87a

Duffy, James, 1923- ed.
Africa speaks. Edited by James Duffy and Robert A. Manners. Princeton, N.J., Van Nostrand [1961]

223p. 23cm.

MB
W58g

Lundy, Benjamin, 1789-1839.

pp. 13-18

In: Laureen White's Giants live in those days. 1959.

Kenya
M392
Om5

The Luo girl from infancy to marriage.
Ominde, Simeon H
The Luo girl from infancy to marriage. London, Macmillan, 1952.

69p. illus. 18½cm. (Custom and tradition in East Africa)

1. Girls. 2. Kenya - Social life and customs. 3. Family - Kenya. I. Title.

Lutheran church— Doctrinal and controversial works.

M230.41
M48

Melanchthon, Philipp, 1497-1560.
The Loci communes of Philip Melanchthon, with a critical introduction by the translator, Charles Leander Hill ... and a special introduction by Dean E. E. Flack ... Boston, Meador publishing company [°1944]

274 p. 20½cm.
Bibliographical foot-notes. "Bibliographia Melanchthoniana": p. 268-274.

1. Theology, Doctrinal. 2. Lutheran church—Doctrinal and controversial works. I. Hill, Charles Leander, tr. II. Title.

45—1360
Library of Congress BR336.L62 [46g2] 230.41

S. Africa
M960
Af78

Luthuli, Albert John Mvumbi, 1898-1967
Africa and freedom.

Pp. 9-23.

In: Africa's freedom. London, Unwin Books, 1964.

S. Africa
M968
Sp6s

Luthuli, Albert John Mvumbi, 1898-1967
The effect of minority rule on non-whites.

Pp. 109-118.

In: South Africa, the road ahead, comp. by Hildegarde Spottiswoode, 1960.

I. Title.

Luthuli, Albert John Mvumbi, 1898-1967. Foreword.

S. Africa
M968
R25

Reeves, Richard Ambrose, Bp., 1899-
Shooting at Sharpeville; the agony of South Africa. With a foreword by Chief Luthuli. [1st American edition] Boston, Houghton Mifflin, 1961 [°1960].

xvi, 141p. illus. map. 23cm.

S. Africa
M968
L97Le4

Luthuli, Albert John Mvumbi, 1898-1967
Giv mit folk fri. En biografi med forord af Per Wästberg. Denmark, Steen Hasselbalchs Forlag, 1963.

284p. 18½cm.

1. Africa, South - race question. I. Title.

S. Africa
M968
L971e

Luthuli, Albert John Mvumbi, 1898-1967
Let my people go. New York, McGraw-Hill Book Co., Inc., 1962.

255p. illus. 22cm.
Autobiography.

1. Africa, South - Race question. I. Title.
DT779.8.L8A3 323.168 62-13819

Africa, South
M968
L971e2

Luthuli, Albert John Mvumbi, 1898-1967
Let my people go; an autobiography. Introd. by Charles Hooper. Johannesburg, Collins, 1962.

255 p. illus. 22 cm.

1. Africa, South—Race question. I. Title.

DT779.8.L8A3 1962a 323.168 62-51657 ‡
Library of Congress [1]

Luthuli, Albert John Mvumbi, 1898-1967

S. Africa
M968
F914i

Friedmann, Marion Valerie, 1918- ed.
I will still be moved; reports from South Africa. Chicago, Quadrangle Books, 1963.

126p. illus. ports. 22cm.

Haiti
M972.94
M35?l

La lutte contre la folie.

Mars, Louis.
La lutte contre la folie. Port-Au-Prince, Haiti, 1947.
xi, 133 p., [1] l. 22 cm.

1. Insanity. [1. Mental disorders] 2. Psychiatry—Haiti. I. Title.

Med 48-1694

U. S. Army Medical Libr. for Library of Congress [WM100M368L 1947] [1]

Senegal
M796.81
Se5

La Lutte Sénégalaise.

Sène, Moustapha
La Lutte Sénégalaise [n.p., 1966]
18p. ports. 21cm.
"Comité de participation du Sénégal au premier festival mondial des arts Nègres."
Portrait of author on t.p.

1. Wrestling. I. Title.

Lutuli, Albert John Mvumbi.
see
Luthuli, Albert John Mvumbi, 1898-1967.

M366.1
F87d

Lux et veritas.
Freemason. Delaware.
Lux et veritas. Light and truth, or, the origin of ancient freemasonry among colored men in the state of Delaware. Published by a committee appointed December 17, A.D. 1855... by the Hiram Grand Lodge of A.Y.M. of the state of Delaware. Wilmington, Del., Henry Eckel and co., 1856.

53p. 18cm.

Kenya
M372.4
L92K

Lwane, Benjamin G
Kitabu chio kaviri chio kusoma mu Lulogooli. Kitabu 2 [Reader 2] chia Benjamin G. Lwane na Joseph G. Kisia. [illus. by Ruth Yudelowitz] Nairobi, Eagle Press, 1957.

39p. illus. 21-1/2cm.
Written in Lulagoli.

1. Lulagoli language - Readers and speakers. I. Kisia, Joseph G., jt. auth. II. Title.

Kenya
M372.4
L92K

Lwane, Benjamin G
Kitabu chio kutanga chio kusoma mu Lulogooli. Kitabu 1 [Reader 1] chia Benjamin G. Lwane na Joseph G. Kisia. [illus. by Ruth Yudelowitz] Nairobi, Eagle Press, 1957.

30p. illus. 21-1/2cm.
Written in Lulagoli.

1. Lulagoli language - Readers and speakers. I. Kisia, Joseph G., jt. auth. II. Title.

Kenya
M372.4
L92

Lwane, Benjamin G
Musomi Wokutanga, chia Benjamin G. Lwane na Joseph G. Kisia. [Illustrated by Ruth Yudelowitz] Nairobi, Eagle Press, 1957.

24p. illus. 22cm.
Written in Lulagoli.

1. Lulagoli language - Readers and speakers. I. Kisia, Joseph G., jt. auth. II. Title.

Sénégal
M966.3
L98c

Ly, Abdoulaye.
La Compagnie du Sénégal. [Paris] Présence africaine [1958]

310p. illus. 23cm. (Enquêtes et études)

1. Compagnie du Sénégal (Founded 1673) 2. France - Comm. - Africa, West. 3. Africa, West - Comm. - France. 4. Sénégal.

Sénégal
M966.3
L98e

Ly, Abdoulaye
L'etat et la production paysanne ou l'etat et la révolution au Sénégal 1957-1958. Paris, Présence Africaine, 1958.

79p. 19cm.

1. Sénégal. I. Title.

Sénégal
M966.3
L98ma

Ly, Abdoulaye
Les masses Africaines et l'actuelle condition humaine. Paris, Présence Africaine, 1956.

254p. 22½cm. (Enquêtes et Études)

1. Imperialism. 2. Africa. I. Title.

Sénégal
M966.3
L98m

Ly, Abdoulaye
Mercenaires noirs; notes sur une forme de l'exploitation des Africains. Paris, Présence Africaine, 1957.

67p. 19cm.

I. Title. 1. Sénégal. 2. Africa, French West.

France
M840
D891y

Lyderic.
Dumas, Alexander, 1802-1870.
Lyderic. Bruxelles, Societe Belge de Librairie, 1842.
231p. 16cm.

M378Al
L99c

Lyells, Ruby E Stutts
College spirit; The spirit of Alcorn A. and M. college by Ruby E. Stutts Lyells. Alcorn, Miss., Published at the request of members of the class of 1944 by M.J. and R.S. Lyells, 1944.

11p. 23cm.
1. Alcorn agriculture and mechanical college. I. Title

M616
W93a

Lymphogranuloma venereum.
Wright, Louis Tompkins, 1891-1952.
Anorectogenital lymphogranuloma venereum and granuloma inguinale treated with aureomycin, by Aaron Prigot, Louis T. Wright, Myra A. Logan and others. Reprinted from the New York State journal of medicine, 40:1911-1917, August 15, 1949.

M616.
W93a2

Lymphogranuloma venereum.
Wright, Louis Tompkins, 1891-1952.
Aureomycin, a new antibiotic with virucidal properties; A preliminary report on successful treatment in twenty-five cases of lymphogranuloma venereum, by Louis T. Wright, Murray Sanders, and Myra A. Logan. Chicago, American Medical Association, 1948.

12p. tables. 22cm.
Reprinted, with additions, from the Journal of the American Medical Association, 138:408-412, October 9, 1948.

M616
W631

Lymphogranuloma venereum.
Wright, Louis Tompkins, 1891-1952.
Incidence of asymptomatic lymphogranuloma venereum in a municipal hospital, by Louis T. Wright, Gerald A. Spencer, and Abraham Oppenheim. Reprinted from American journal of syphillis, gonorrhea, and venereal diseases, 31:282-288, May 1947.

M616
W93l

Lymphogranuloma venereum.
Wright, Louis Tompkins, 1891-1952.
Lymphogranulomatous strictures of the rectum; a resume of four hundred and seventy-six cases, by Louis T. Wright, W. Adrian Freeman and Joel V. Bolden. Reprinted from the Archives of Surgery, 53:499-544, November 1946.

Inscribed: To Arthur from Louis.

M616
W93os

Lymphogranuloma venereum.
Wright, Louis Tompkins, 1891-1952.
Osseous changes associated with lymphogranuloma venereum, by Louis T. Wright, and Myra Loga. Reprinted from the Archives of surgery, 39:108-121, July 1939.

M616
W93r6

Lymphogranuloma venereum.
Wright, Louis Tompkins, 1891-1952.
Rectal strictures due to lymphogranuloma venereum, with especial reference to Pauchet's excision operation, by Louis T. Wright, Benjamin N. Berg, Joel V. Bolden and W. Adrian Freeman. Reprinted from Surgery, Gynecology and Obstetrics, 82:449-462, April 1946.

Inscribed: To Arthur from Louis, May 10, 1946.

M616
W93t7

Lymphogranuloma venereum.
Wright, Louis Tompkins, 1891-1952.
The treatment of lymphogranuloma venereum and granuloma inguinale in humans with aureomycin, by L. T. Wright, M. Saunders, M. A. Logan, and others. Reprinted from the Annals of the New York Academy of Sciences, 51:318-330, November 30, 1948.

M329.6
R29p

Lynch, John Roy, 1847-1939
Address.

(In: Republican Party. National Convention, 8th, Chicago, 1884. Proceedings... p. 22, 86, 117).

Lynch, John Roy, 1847-1939
The facts of reconstruction, by John R. Lynch ... New York, The Neale publishing company, 1913.
325 p. front., ports. 19½cm.
"The state of Mississippi is made the pivotal one in the presentation of the facts and historical points touched upon in this work."—Pref.
1. Reconstruction. 2. Reconstruction—Mississippi. I. Title.
14—471
Library of Congress E668.L98
[a41c1]

Lynch law.
National Association for the Advancement of Colored People.
The fight against lynching; Anti-lynching work of the National Association for the Advancement of Colored People for the year nineteen eighteen. New York, NAACP, 1919.
20p. 23cm.

Lynching.

Douglass, Frederick, 1817-1895.
Lynching black people because they are black. In the Christian educator, vol. 5, April 1894.
95-108p. illus. 25cm.

Lynch, John Roy, 1847- 1939
Some historical errors of James Ford Rhodes, by Major John R. Lynch. Boston, New York, The Cornhill publishing company [c1922]
xx, 115 p. front., ports. 19cm.
1. Rhodes, James Ford, 1848- History of the United States from the compromise of 1850 ... 2. Negroes—Politics and suffrage. I. Title.
22—23557
Library of Congress E415.7.R479
——— Copy 2.
Copyright A 690397 [37d1]

Lynch law.

National association for the advancement of colored people.
Thirty years of lynching in the United States, 1889-1918. New York, The National association for the advancement of colored people, 1919.
105 p. incl. maps, tables, diagrs. 23cm.
1. Lynch law. I. Title.
20—13596
Library of Congress HV6457.N3
[37d1]

Lynching.

Spingarn, Joel Elias, 1875-1939.
[Statement at] Hearing before the Committee on the Judiciary, House of Representatives, sixty-fifth Congress, second session on H.R. 11279, to protect citizens against lynching. Washington, Govt. Print., Off., 1918.
14p. 23cm.
At head of title: To protect citizens against lynching.

Lynch law.

Haywood, Harry.
... Lynching, by H. Haywood and M. Howard. [New York] International pamphlets [1932]
cover-title, 15 p. 19cm. (International pamphlets. No. 25)
1. Mobs. 2. Negroes. 3. Lynch law. I. Howard, Milton, joint author. II. Title.
A 34—1451
Rochester univ. Libr. for Library of Congress HX81.I6 no. 25 [HX81.I6 no. 25]
[42c1]

Lynch law.

North, Joseph.
Behind the Florida bombings; who killed NAACP leader Harry T. Moore and his wife. New York, New Century, 1952.
23p. 19cm.

Lynching.

Weatherford, Willis Duke, 1875-
Lynching, removing its causes; Address delivered before the Southern Sociological Congress, New Orleans, La., April 14, 1916. Southern Sociological Congress, 1916.
18p. 16cm.

Lynch Law.

Johnson, James Weldon, 1871-1938.
Lynching, America's national disgrace, by James Weldon Johnson...New York City, National Association for the Advancement of Colored People, 1924.
6p. 24cm.
Reprinted by permission from Current History for January, 1924.

Lynch law.

U.S. Congress. House. Committee on the Judiciary.
Anti-lynching; Hearings before the Committee on the Judiciary, House of Representatives, sixty-sixth Congress, second session on H. R. 259, 4123, and 11873. Washington, Govt. Print. Off., 1920.

Lynching.

Wells, Ida Bernett.
Southern horrors. Lynch law in all its phases. New York, The New York Age Print, 1892.
24p. port. 23cm.

Lynch law.

National Association for the Advancement of Colored People.
An appeal to the conscience of the civilized world. New York, NAACP, 1920.
15p. illus. tables. 31cm.

Lynch law.

U. S. *Congress. Senate. Committee on the judiciary.*
Crime of lynching. Hearings before a subcommittee of the Committee on the judiciary, United States Senate, Seventy-sixth Congress, third session, on H. R. 801, an act to assure to persons within the jurisdiction of every state due process of law and equal protection of the laws, and to prevent the crime of lynching. February 6, 7, March 5, 12, and 13, 1940 ... Washington, U. S. Govt. print. off., 1940.
iii, 204 p. incl. tables. 23cm.
Printed for the use of the Committee on the judiciary. Frederick Van Nuys, chairman of subcommittee.
1. Lynch law. I. Title.
40—8628
Library of Congress HV6457.A5 1940
——— Copy 2. [41c2] 343.2

Lynching--Alabama.
Ransom, Leon Andrew, 1898-
Brief submitted to the United States Department of Justice in order to persuade the Federal government to take action against those guilty of the lynching of Dan Pippen and A. T. Harden at Tuscaloosa, Alabama, in August 1933, after the State authorities failed to do so, signed by Leon A. Ransom, Charles H. Houston, and Edward P. Lovett. New York, National Association for the Advancement of Colored People, 1933.
47p. 23cm.

Lynch law.

National Association for the Advancement of Colored People.
Burning at stake in the United States; A record of the public burning by mobs of five men, during the first five months of 1919, in the states of Arkansas, Florida, Georgia, Mississippi, and Texas, New York, NAACP, 1919.
19p. 23cm.

Lynch law.

White, Walter Francis, 1893-
Rope & faggot; a biography of Judge Lynch, by Walter White. New York & London, A. A. Knopf, 1929.
xiii p., 2 l., [3]-272, iv p., 1 l. incl. tables. front. 21½cm.
Bibliography: p. 269-272.
1. Lynch law. 2. Negroes. 3. U. S.—Race question. I. Title. II. Title: A biography of Judge Lynch.
29—10015
Library of Congress HV6457.W45
[44e1]

Lynching - Florida.

National Association for the Advancement of Colored People.
The lynching of Claude Neal. New York, 1934.
8p. illus. 28cm.

Lynch law.

National Association for the Advancement of Colored People.
Can the states stop lynching? New York, NAACP, [1937].
19p. illus. 18cm.

Lynching.

Commission on Interracial Cooperation.
The mob still rides; a review of the lynching record, 1931-1935. Atlanta, The Commission, n.d.
24p. 22cm.

Lynching - Georgia.

National association for the advancement of colored people.
The lynchings of May,1918 in Brooks and Lowndes counties, Georgia. An investigation made and published by the National association for the advancement of colored people. New York city, September, 1918.
6p. 24cm.

Lynching---Indiana.

[illegible] Pickens, William, 1881-1954.

P[illegible]af Aftermath of a lynching. New York, National Association for the Advancement of Colored People. 1931.

2p. 29cm.

Reprinted from the Nation April 15, 1931.

...Lynching.

M304 Haywood, Harry.

P19 ... Lynching, by H. Haywood and M. Howard. [New York,

v.1, no13 International pamphlets [1932]

cover-title, 15 p. 19cm. (International pamphlets. No. 25)

1. Mobs. 2. Negroes. 3. Lynch law. I. Howard, Milton, joint author. II. Title.

A 34—1451

Rochester univ. Libr. for Library of Congress HX81.I6 no. 25 [HX81.I6 no. 25] [42c1]

Lynching, America's National Disgrace.

M323 Johnson, James Weldon, 1871-1938.

J632c Lynching, America's national disgrace, by

no.4 James Weldon Johnson...New York City, National Association for the Advancement of Colored People, 1924.

6p. 24cm.

Reprinted by permission from Current History for January, 1924.

M343.3 Lynching in the Northern style.

M35p Marshall, Horace.

Police brutality; Lynching in the Northern style, with a special message from Councilman Benjamin J. Davis. New York, Office of Councilman Benjamin J. Davis, [c1947]

21p. illus. 21cm.

Lynching Negro children...

M304 North, Joseph.

P19 Lynching Negro children in Southern

v.1,no.13 courts (The Scottsboro case). New York, issued by International Labor Defense [n.d.]

15p. illus. 15cm.

Lynn, Eve, pseud.

See

Reynolds, Evelyn Crawford

M287.6 Lyon, Ernest, 1860-1938

L99n The negro's view of organic union, by Ernest Lyon ... introduction by George A. Owens. New York, Cincinnati, The Methodist book concern [1915]

64 p. 17½cm. $0.25

"The question of organic union of the Methodist Episcopal church and the Methodist Episcopal church, South."—Introd.

Inscribed copy: Compliments of the author.

I. Title.

16-7676

Library of Congress

Copyright A 427395

M304 Lyon, Ernest, 1860-1938.

P19 A protest against the title of James

v.4,no.6 Weldon Johnson's anomalous poem as a "Negro National Anthem" as subversive of patriotism [n.p. n.d.]

15p. 16cm.

1.Johnson, James Weldon.

2.Negro National Anthem.

Lyric and legend.

M811.5 Yeiser, Idabelle.

Y361 Lyric and legend. [Poems] Boston, Christopher Pub. House [1947]

77 p. 21 cm.

I. Title.

PS3547.E4L8 811.5 47-8097*

© Idabelle Yeiser, Philadelphia; 7Oct47; A17678.

Library of Congress [1]

Lyrics of life and love.

M811.5 Braithwaite, William Stanley Beaumont, 1878–

B73 Lyrics of life and love, by William Stanley Braithwaite. Boston, H. B. Turner & co., 1904.

80 p., 1 l. front. (port.) 20 x 12½cm.

I. Title.

4—27339

Library of Congress PS3503.R246L8 1904 [42d1]

British Guiana Lyrics of life and love.

M821 Gibson, Rufus

G35L Lyrics of life and love. New York, Carlton Press [1964]

96p. 20½cm. (A Lyceum book)

Lyrics of love.

M811.5 Dinkins, Charles Roundtree.

D611 Lyrics of love, by Charles R. Dinkins. Columbia, S. C., The State company [1904]

230 p. 2 port. (incl. front.) 19cm.

I. Title.

4—11500

Library of Congress PS3507.I 647L5 1904

Copyright [a39b1]

Lyrics of love and laughter.

M811.4 Dunbar, Paul Laurence, 1872–1906.

D911y Lyrics of love and laughter, by Paul Laurence Dunbar. New York, Dodd, Mead and company, 1903.

xi, 180 p. front. 17cm.

I. Title.

3—7777

Library of Congress PS1556.L55 1903 [44b1]

Lyrics of lowly life.

M811.4 Dunbar, Paul Laurence, 1872–1906.

D91 1yl Lyrics of lowly life, by Paul Laurence Dunbar, with an introduction by W. D. Howells. New York, Dodd, Mead and company, 1896.

xx, 208 p. front. (port.) 17cm.

I. Title. 1. Poetry.

4—18820

Library of Congress PS1556.L6 1896

——— Copy 2. 16cm. (p. 199–208 wanting) [42u2]

Lyrics of sunshine and shadow.

M811.4 Dunbar, Paul Laurence, 1872–1906.

D911yr Lyrics of sunshine and shadow, by Paul Laurence Dunbar. New York, Dodd, Mead & company, 1905.

x p., 1 l., 109 p. front. 17cm.

I. Title.

5—12695

Library of Congress PS1556.L65 1905

Copyright [36h1]

Lyrics of the hearthside.

M811.4 Dunbar, Paul Laurence, 1872–1906.

D911gh Lyrics of the hearthside, by Paul Laurence Dunbar. New York, Dodd, Mead and company, 1899.

x, 227 p. front. (port.) 16cm.

I. Title.

99—1025

Library of Congress PS1556.L7 1899 [43f1]

Lyrics of the Southland.

M811.5 Scott, Emory Elrage.

Sc81 Lyrics of the Southland, by Emory Elrage Scott. [Chicago, Printed by Wilton press, °1913]

3 p. l., 9-93 p. 18cm. $1.00

I. Title.

13-8600

Library of Congress PS3537.C88L8 1913

Copyright A 343964

Lyrics of the under world.

M811.5 Beadle, Samuel Alfred.

B351 Lyrics of the under world, by S. A. Beadle ... Jackson, Miss., W. A. Scott, 1912.

v, [2], 148, [3] p. incl. illus., plates. plates (1 col.) port. 22cm. $1.50

I. Title.

12-2948

Library of Congress PS3503.E15L8 1912

Copyright A 309190

Ma lutte, au Kasai, pour la verite au service de la justice.

Congo, Leopoldville

M967.5 Kalonji, Albert, 1929-

K127 Ma lutte, au Kasai, pour la verite au service de la justice; memorandum. [Barcelona, C. A. G. S. A., 1964]

52p. port. 21½cm.

1. Congo, Leopoldville. 2. Kalonji, Albert, 1929. I. Title.

Ma mystique liberatrice.

Haiti

M841 Augustin, Gérard.

Au5m Ma mystique liberatrice. Preface d'Hebel Ade. Saint-Marc, Haiti [n.p., n.d.]

42p. port. 20½cm.

Zambia

M392 Maango, David

M11 "Tell me, Josephine." [By David Maango, Barbara Hall and Kay Sifuniso] Edited by Barbara Hall. [Foreword by Kenneth D. Kaunda] New York, Simon and Schuster, 1964.

142p. 21cm.

Selections from the Tell me, Josephine column started in February, 1960, by the Central African mail, a weekly paper in Northern Rhodesia.

(Over)

South Africa
M496
M11
Mabille, Adolph, 1836-1894
Southern Sotho-English Dictionary, by A. Mabille and H. Dieterlen. Reclassified, revised and enlarged by R. A. Paroz. Morija, Basutoland, Morija Sesuto Book Depot, 1950.

xvi, 445p. 21½cm.
White authors.

1. Sotho language. I. Dieterlen, H. jt. auth. II. Title.

Nigeria
M966.9
B619
Mabogunje, Akin L
Land, people and tradition in Nigeria.

Pp. 11-36.

In: Blitz, L. Franklin, ed. The politics and administration of Nigerian government.

M266
M11h
McAfee, Sara Jane (Regulus) 1879–
History of the Woman's missionary society in the Colored Methodist Episcopal church, comprising its founders, organizations, pathfinders, subsequent developments and present status, by Mrs. L. D. McAfee ... ⌊Phenix City, Ala., Phenix City herald, 1945⌋

468, ⌊3⌋ p. illus. (ports.) fold. pl. 20ᶜᵐ.
"Corrections": slip inserted.
"Revised edition."

1. Colored Methodist Episcopal church. Woman's missionary society.

45-10781
Library of Congress BV2551.M3 1945
⌊2⌋ 266.79

M370.
M11
McAllister, Jane Ellen, 1899–
The training of Negro teachers in Louisiana, by Jane Ellen McAllister ... New York city, Teachers college, Columbia university, 1929.

vi, 95 p. 23½ᶜᵐ. (Teachers college, Columbia university. Contributions to education; no. 364)
Published also as thesis (PH. D.) Columbia university.
Bibliography: p. 95.

1. Teachers, Training of—Louisiana. 2. ~~Negroes~~—Education. 3. ~~Negroes~~—Louisiana. I. Title. II. Title: Negro teachers in Louisiana, The training of.

30—11031
Library of Congress LC2802.L8M3 1929 a
——— Copy 2. LB5.C8 no. 364
Copyright A 21710 ⌊41m1⌋ 370.7

M815.5
M12c
Macbeth, Hugh E
Colored America answers the challenge of Pearl S. Buck. Los Angeles, The author, 1942.

29p. 24cm. (Interracial reference series)
At head of title: Justice for all humanity.
Contents: -Pearl S. Buck's open letter to the colored people of America. -Pearl S. Buck's address to the colored leadership of the U.S.A. -Colored American leadership comes into action on behalf of the entire human race, by Hugh E. Macbeth.
1. Race problems.

M811.5
M12
McBrown, Gertrude Parthenia.
The picture-poetry book, by Gertrude Parthenia McBrown; illustrated by Lois Mailou Jones. Washington, D. C., The Associated publishers, inc., 1935.

x, 73 p. incl. front., illus. 22ᶜᵐ.
Verse for children.

I. Title. 1. Poetry. II. Jones, Lois Mailou illus.
36—4101
Library of Congress PZ8.3.M124Pi
⌊43d1⌋ 811.5

Trinidad
M700
H55
McBurnie, Beryl
West Indian dance.

Pp. 51-54.

In: Hill, Errol G., ed. The artists in West Indian society. Mona, Jamaica, University of the West Indies, 1963?.

McCarthy, Agnes

M973
R24w
Reddick, Lawrence Dunbar, 1910- jt. auth.
Worth fighting for; a history of the Negro in the United States during the Civil War and Reconstruction ⌊by⌋ Agnes McCarthy and Lawrence Reddick. Illustrated by Colleen Browning. ⌊1st ed.⌋ Garden City, N. Y., Doubleday, 1965.
118 p. col. illus., ports. 22 cm. (Zenith books)

1. Negroes—History, Juvenile. 2. U. S.—Hist.—Civil War—Negroes—Juvenile literature. I. ~~Reddick, Lawrence Dunbar, 1910- joint author.~~ II. Title.

E185.2.M23 973.715 65-10281
Library of Congress ⌊5⌋

M811.5
M128p
McClellan, George Marion, 1860-1934
The path of dreams, by George Marion McClellan. Louisville, Ky., J. P. Morton & company, incorporated ⌊©1916⌋

2 p. l., 76 p. 20½ᶜᵐ. $1.25
Poems.

I. Title. 1. Poetry.

16-9044
Library of Congress PS3525.A155P3 1916
Copyright A 428509

M811.5
M128po
McClellan, George Marion, 1860-1934.
Poems. Nashville, Tenn., Publishing House A.M.E. Church Sunday School Union, 1895.

145p. 19cm.

I. Title.

M811.5
M128s
McClellan, George Marion, 1860-1934.
Songs of a southerner, by George Marion McClellan. Boston, Press of Rockwell and Churchill, 1896.

16p. front. 22cm.

1. Poetry. I. Title.

Haiti
M447.9
M13y
McConnell, H Ormonde.
You can learn Creole; a simple introduction to Haitian Creole for English speaking people, by H. Ormonde McConnell ⌊and⌋ Eugene Swan. Port-au-Prince, Haïti, Impr. de l'État, 1945.

106 p. 24 cm.
Additional text on label mounted on p. ⌊89⌋

Haiti - Creole dialects
1. ~~Creole dialects—Haiti.~~ I. Swan, Eugene, joint author. II. Title.
2. Haiti - Language
PM7854.H3M3 447.9 47-27395*
Library of Congress ⌊1⌋

M812.5
M13e
McCoo, Edward J
Ethiopia at the bar of justice, by Rev. Edward J. Mc Coo. A pageant staged at the general conference of the African methodist episcopal church in Louisville, Ky., May, 1924; and at the sesqui-cen-tennial, Philadelphia, 1926... Newport, Ky., Edw. J. McCoo, c1924.
24p. 17cm.
1. Drama I. Title

M811.5
M13p.
McCorkle, George Washington
Poems of thought and cheer, by George Washington McCorkle. Petersburg, Va. n.d.

8p. 20½cm.
autographed by the author

1. Poetry

M811.5
M13po
McCorkle, George Washington
Poems of thought and cheer, ⌊by⌋ George Washington McCorkle. Washington, D.C., Published under the auspices of the National bureau of Negro writers and entertainers ⌊n.d.⌋
21p. 23½cm.
1. Poetry.
I. Title

M306
Sol
1913
McCulloch, James Edward, 1873- ed.
Southern sociological congress. *2d, Atlanta,* **1913.**
The human way. Addresses on race problems at the Southern sociological congress, Atlanta, 1913. Edited by James E. McCulloch. Nashville, Southern sociological congress, 1913.

146 p. 24ᶜᵐ.

Also included in "The South mobilizing for social service: addresses delivered at the Southern sociological congress", Nashville, 1913.
Bibliography: p. ⌊144⌋-146.

1. Negroes. 2. Sociology—Congresses. I. McCulloch, James Edward, 1873- ed. II. Title.
Agr 13-1850
U. S. Dept. of agr. Library for Library of Congress 280So8 E185.61.S72
⌊a33d1⌋

M306
Sol
1919
McCulloch, James Edward, 1873- ed.
Southern Sociological Congress. Knoxville. 1919
Distinguished service citizenship. Ed. by J. E. McCulloch. Washington, D.C., Southern Sociological Congress, 1919.

170 p. 23 cm.
Partial contents: Interracial co-operation and the south's new economic conditions, by Monroe Work.

McCulloch, James Edward, 1873- ed.

M306
Sol
1913
Southern Sociological Congress. 2d, Atlanta, 1913.
The South mobilizing for social service; addresses delivered at the Southern Sociological Congress, Atlanta, Gerogia, April 25-29, 1913. Ed. by James E. McCulloch. Nashville, 1913.

702p. 24cm.

M323
M13s
McCulloch, Margaret Callender, 1901–
Segregation, a challenge to democracy. Nashville, Race Relations Dept., American Missionary Association Division, Board of Home Missions, Congregational Christian Churches, Fisk University ⌊1950⌋

39 p. 23 cm.

1. ~~Negroes~~—Segregation. I. Title.

E185.61.M126 323.260973 50-2114
Library of Congress ⌊3⌋

M810.8
M139
McCullough, Esther Morgan, *ed.*
As I pass, O Manhattan; an anthology of life in New York. ⌊North Bennington, Vt.; Coley Taylor ⌊1956⌋

1236 p. illus. 25 cm.
Partial contents.- Miss Cynthie, by Rudolph Fisher.- Why, you reckon? By Langston Hughes.- Tableau ⌊poem⌋ by Countee Cullen.- ⌊Poems⌋ by Langston Hughes.
White editor.

1. American literature—New York (City) 2. New York City. I. Title.
PS549.N5M22 810.82 56-12429 ‡
Library of Congress ⌊3⌋

U.S.
M820.9
M139
McCullough, Norman Verrle, 1925-
The Negro in English literature; a critical introduction. Devon, Arthur H. Stockwell ⌊1962⌋

176p. 19cm.
Includes bibliography.

1. English literature - History and criticism. I. Title.

M811.5
M13o
McCullough, Norman Verrle, 1925–
The other side of hell; a tragedy in verse. New York, Exposition Press [1952]
62 p. 22 cm.

I. Title.

PS3525.A17964O7 811.5 51-13282 rev ‡
Library of Congress [r52b1]

M810.8
F31
McDaniel, Eluard Luchell
Bumming in California.

(In: Federal Writers' Project. American stuff; an anthology of prose & verse ... New York, The Viking press, 1937. pp. 112-118.)

M248
Mc14
McDaniels, Geraldine
God is the answer. [Rev. ed.] New York, Vantage Press [1965]

118 p. 21 cm.
Portrait of author on book jacket.

1. Christian life. I. Title.

M323
R38
McDonagh, Edward C jt. auth.
Richards, Eugene S
Ethnic relations in the United States [by] Edward C. McDonagh and Eugene S. Richards. New York, Appleton-Century-Crofts [1953]
xiv, 408 p. illus. 25 cm. (Appleton-Century-Crofts sociology series)
Includes bibliographies.

1. Minorities—U. S. 2. U. S.—Race question. I. ~~McDonagh,~~ ~~Edward C., joint author.~~ II. Title.
I. McDonagh, Edward C jt. auth.
E184.A1M137 325.73 52-13692
Library of Congress [20]

M350
M14w
MacDonald, Dwight.
The war's greatest scandal; The story of jim crow in uniform, by Dwight MacDonald, research by Nancy MacDonald. New York, March on Washington Movement, [1943]

15p. illus. 23cm.

1. World War, 1939-1945. 2. Jim Crow. I. Title.

MB9
M23
McDonald, Emanuel B 1884–
Sam McDonald's farm; Stanford reminiscences by Emanuel B. "Sam" McDonald. Stanford, Calif., Stanford University Press, 1954.
422 p. illus. 24 cm.

1. Stanford University—Hist. I. Title.
LD3027.M2 378.794 54-7166 ‡
Library of Congress [5]

Africa
M496
D141
MacDougald, Duncan.
... The languages and press of Africa, by Duncan MacDougald, jr. Philadelphia, University of Pennsylvania press, the University museum, 1944.
4 p. l., 86 p. map. 21½ᶜᵐ. (African handbooks, ed. by H. A. Wieschhoff. 4)
Bibliography: p. 83-86.
White author.

1. Africa—Languages. 2. Newspapers—Direct.
44—4429
Library of Congress PL8007.M3 [46k3] 496

M306
N21p
McDougald, Elise Johnson.
The School and its relation to the vocational life of the Negro.

(In: National Conference of Social Work. Proceedings, 1923. Chicago, University of Chicago, 1923. 22cm. p.415-418)

1. Vocational education.

M304
P19
v.3, no.4
[Mc Dougald, Gertrude E.]
A new day for the colored woman worker. A study of the colored women in industry in New York City... Investigators Miss Jessie Clark and Mrs. Gertrude E. Mc Dougald. New York, Chas. P. Young, Co. 1919.
39p. illus. 22½cm.
1. Labor and laboring classes
2. Women

MB9
E12e
[**McDougall, *Mrs.* Frances Harriet (Whipple) Greene,** 1805–1878.
Elleanor's second book ... Providence, B. T. Albro, printer, 1839.
128 p. front. (port.) 14ᶜᵐ.

1. Eldridge, Elleanor, b. 1785. I. Title.
8—25281
Library of Congress E185.97.E38
——— Copy 2. [a31d1]

MB9
E12m
[**McDougall, *Mrs.* Frances Harriet (Whipple) Greene,** 1805–1878.
Memoirs of Elleanor Eldridge ... Providence, B. T. Albro, printer, ~~1838.~~ 1846.
128 p. front. (port.) 14ᶜᵐ.

White author.

1. Eldridge, Elleanor, b. 1785. I. Title.
8—21103
Library of Congress E185.97.E37 [a28d1]

Cuba
M972.91
C57m
Maceo, Antonio, 1845-1896.
Clavijo Tisseur, Arturo, 1886–
Mis palabras en publico, panegiricos y conferencias. Santiago de Cuba, "Editorial Ros," 1941.
156 [3] p. 19½cm.

Cuba
M972.91
G59
Maceo, Antonio, 1845-1896.
Gómez Estévez, Rafael.
Reflexiones sobre José Martí y el Taboquero en la revolución Cubana, Habana, Impresos Economicos, 1929.

40p. port. 20cm.

Cuba
MB9
M15g
Maceo, Antonio, 1845-1896.
Griñán Peralta, Leonardo.
... Antonio Maceo, análisis caracterológico. (2. millar) La Habana, Editorial Trópico, 1936.
265 p., 1 l. front. (port.) 20½ᶜᵐ. (Biografías cubanas, 8)

1. Maceo, Antonio, 1845-1896.
40-24914
Library of Congress F1786.M15 [2] 923.57291

Cuba
MB9
M15g4
Maceo, Antonio, 1845-1956.
Griñán Peralta, Leonardo
La muerte de Antonio Maceo (Causas y consecuencias). La Habana, 1941.

79p. 20½cm.
Autographed.
Includes bibliography.

1. Maceo, Antonio, 1845-1956.
I. Title.

Maceo, Antonio, 1845-1896.
M973
H13s
Haley, James T. comp.
Sparkling gems of race knowledge worth reading. A compendium of valuable information and wise suggestions that will inspire noble effort at the hands of every race-loving man, woman, and child. Comp. and arranged by James T. Haley...Nashville, Tenn., J. T. Haley & company, 1897.

200p. incl. front., illus., ports. 20½cm.

Cuba
MB9
M151
Maceo family.
Lara Mena, María Julia de.
La familia Maceo. Cartas a Elena. Conversaciones patrióticas al calor del hogar, por la dra. María Julia de Lara Mena ... La Habana, Editorial selecta [1945]
141 p., 1 l. illus. (facsim.) 2 col. port. 20½ᶜᵐ.
On cover: 1845–centenario de Maceo–1945.
"'Los ancianitos.' Ejercicios" (music for physical exercises): p. 58.
"Bibliografía": p. [135]

1. Maceo family. I. González de Casaña, Elena. II. Title.
F1755.M3L3 929.2 A 46-5664
New York. Public library for Library of Congress [3]†

Jamaica
M821.91
M165a
McFarland, Harry Stanley, 1900–
Adopted son. n.p., n.d.

4 p. 15 cm.
Poetry.

I. Title.

Jamaica
M821.91
M165e
[**McFarland, Harry Stanley,** 1900–
Experiences of a heart, its joys; its sorrows, poems by Anonymous. Boston, Meador publishing company, 1931.
68 p. 20ᶜᵐ.

I. Title. II. Jamaican poetry
31-15665
Library of Congress PS3525.A2314E8 1931
Copyright A 37229 [2] 811.5

Jamaica
M821.91
M164g
McFarland, Harry Stanley, 1900–
Growing up; a book of verse. Boston, Meador Pub. Co. [1956]
88 p. 21 cm.

I. Title.
PS3525.A2314G7 811.5 56-14248 ‡
Library of Congress [2]

Jamaica
M821.91
M165m
McFarland, Harry Stanley, 1900–
Missing pages; poems. Boston, Forum Publishing Co., 1962.

72p. 18cm.

1. Poetry - Jamaica. I. Title.

Jamaica
M821.91
M165mo
McFarland, Harry Stanley, 1900-
More missing pages: a book of poems. New York, Carlton Press, 1966.

56p. 21cm.

I. Title.

Jamaica
M821.91
M167
McFarlane, John Ebenezer Clare, 1894-1962.
Selected shorter poems. Kingston, Pioneer Press [1954]

93p. 18cm.
Portrait of author on back cover of book.

1. Jamaican poetry. I. Title.

M378w
M17
McGinnis, Frederick Alphonso, 1887-
A history and an interpretation of Wilberforce university, by Frederick A. McGinnis ... Wilberforce, O. [Blanchester, O., Printed at the Brown publishing co.] 1941.
xii, 215 p. incl. tab. front., plates, ports. 23½cm.
Bibliography: p. 203-206.

1. Wilberforce university, Wilberforce, O.
2. Colleges and universities-History. 41-9156
Library of Congress LC2851.W62M2
[3] 378.771

Jamaica
M821.91
M165p
McFarland, Harry Stanley, 1900-
Passing thru; a collection of poems. [1st ed.] New York, W. Malliet, 1950.
120 p. 21 cm.

I. Title. 1. Jamaican poetry
PS3525.A2314P3 811.5 52-15269 ‡
Library of Congress [1]

Jamaica
M824
M16s
McFarlane, John Ebenezer Clare, 1894-1962.
Sex and Christianity; or The case against the system of monogamous marriage ... Kingston, Jamaica, Printed for the author by the Gleaner Co., 1932.

116p. 20cm.

1. Sex 2. Marriage 3. Jamaican literature

M811.4
M17
McGirt, James Ephraim.
Avenging the Maine, A drunken A. B., and other poems. By James Ephraim McGirt. ~~Raleigh, Edwards & Broughton, printers, 1899.~~ Philadelphia, George F. Lasher, Printer, 1901.
~~86 p.~~ 119p. front. (port.) 18cm.

I. Title. 1 Poetry.
Library of Congress PS3525.A235A8 1899 0-351
Copyright 1899: 68204 [a27f1]

Jamaica
M824
M16c
Mc Farlane, John Ebenezer Clare, 1894-1962.
The challenge of our time; A series of essays and addresses. Kingston, Jamaica, The New Dawn Press, 1945.

iii, 215p. 22½cm.

1. Jamaica I. title

Jamaica
M824
M16t
McFarlane, John Ebenezer Clare, 1894-1962.
A treasury of Jamaican poetry; selected and edited by J. E. Clare McFarlane. With and introduction by Hon. B.H. Easter. London, University of London Press, 1949.

159p. cm.

1. Jamaica.

M811.4
M17
McGirt, James Ephraim.
Avenging the Maine, A drunken A. B., and other poems. By James Ephraim McGirt. Raleigh, Edwards & Broughton, printers, 1899.
86 p. front. (port.) 18cm.

I. Title. 1. Poetry.
Library of Congress PS3525.A235A8 1899 0-351
Copyright 1899: 68204 [a27f1]

Jamaica
M824
M16d
McFarlane, John Ebenezer Clare, 1894-1962.-
Daphne, a tale of the hills of St. Clare Andrew, Jamaica. London, Fowler Wright, 1931.

93p. 19cm.

Poetry.

I. title 1. Jamaican poetry.

M910
M17b
McGee, Alice E.
Black America arboad[!] by Alice E. McGee. Boston, Meador publishing company, 1941.
289 p. front., plates, ports. 20cm.

1. Europe—Descr. & trav.—1919- 2. Germany—Descr. & trav.—1919- I. Title: Black America abroad.
41-24848
Library of Congress D921.M17
[a42f5] 914

M811.5
M17f
McGirt, James Ephraim.
For your sweet sake; poems, by James E. McGirt. Philadelphia, The John C. Winston co. ~~[c1906]~~ 1909.
2 p. l., 79 p. front. (port.) 20cm.
~~Ornamental borders.~~

I. Title. 1. Poetry
7-4788 Revised
Library of Congress PS3525.A235F6 1906
Copyright A 165080 [r30d2]

Jamaica
M824
M16e
McFarlane, John Ebenezer Clare, 1894-1962.
Essays and addresses. 1. The freedom of individual. Kingston, Jamaica, The New Dawn Press, 1940.

15p. 21cm. (The Challenge of our time)
Wilberforce centenary address delivered before the "Quill and Ink " Club, Port Maria, 28th July 1933.

1. Jamaican literature I. Freedom of the individual.

M343.3
R21s
McGee, Willie.
Raymond, Harry.
Save Willie McGee. New York, New Century, 1951.

14p. 19cm.

M811.4
M17s
McGirt, James Ephraim
Some simple songs and a few more ambitious attempts. By James E. McGirt...Philadelphia, George F. Lasher c1901
72p. front. plates. 18cm.

1. Poetry I. Title

Jamaica
M824
M16i
McFarlane, John Ebenezer Clare, 1894-1962
Introduction to Orange Valley and other poems.

(In: MacDermot, Thomas Henry. Orange valley and other poems. Kingston, Jamaica, Pioneer Press, 1951. 19cm. p. VII-XXVIII)

M811.5
Mc17t
McGehee, Maud
To get my name in the Kingdom book. Atlanta, Franklin Printing Co., 1962.

42p. 22½cm.

I. Title.

M811.4
M17t
McGirt, James Ephraim.
The triumphs of Ephraim by James E. McGirt. Philadelphia [The McGirt Publishing Co.] 1907.

131p. front. (port.) illus. 20cm.

I. Title.

Jamaica
M824
M16p
McFarlane, John Ebenezer Clare, 1894-1962.
Poems. Kingston, Jamaica, Printed by the Gleaner Co., 1924.

viii, 97p. 17½cm.
Autographed presentation copy.

1. Jamaican poetry.

M371.974
M17
McGinnis, Frederick Alphonso, 1887-
The education of Negroes in Ohio. Wilberforce, Ohio, 1962.
104 p. 21 cm.

1. Negroes—Education—Ohio. I. Title.
LC2802.O5M2 370.193 63-146 ‡
Library of Congress [3]

M323
W879
McGuinn, Henry J.
Woofter, Thomas Jackson, 1893- ed.
Negro problems in cities; a study made under the direction of T. J. Woofter, jr. Garden City, N. Y., Doubleday, Doran & company, inc., [c1928]
xiii p., 2 l., 17-284 p. illus. (maps) diagrs., form. 19½cm.
"The Institute of social and religious research ... is responsible for this publication."
CONTENTS.—pt. 1. Neighborhoods, by T. J. Woofter, jr.—pt. 2. Housing, by Madge Headley.—pt. 3. Schools, by W. A. Daniel.—pt. 4. Recreation, by H. J. McGuinn.

1. Negroes—Moral and social conditions. I. Headley, Madge. II. Daniel, William Andrew, 1895- III. McGuinn, Henry J. IV. Institute of social and religious research. V. Title.

Library of Congress E185.86.W91 28-8612
——— Copy 2.
Copyright A 1063386 [40x2]

Brazil
M89
M18v

Machado de Assis.

Vellinho, Moyses
Machado de Assis; histórias mal contadas e outros assuntos. Rio de Janeiro, Libraria São José, 1960.

106p. 19cm.

Brazil
M869.3
M18se

Machado de Assis, Joaquim Maria, 1839-1908
The attendant's confession. The fortune teller. Life. ⌊Selections from Varias historias⌋
(In: Goldberg, Isaac, ed. Brazilian tales. Boston, The Four Seas company, 1921. 19cm. pp. 43-104)
I. t.-Brazilian tales. II. Goldberg, Brazilian tales. III. t.-Varias historias. IV. Coelho Netto, Henrique. The pigeon.

Brazil
M869.3
M18co5

Machado de Assis, Joaquim Maria, 1839-1908.
Contos e crônicas; organização, prefácio e notes de R. Magalhães Júnior. Rio de Janeiro, Editôra Civilização Brasileira, 1958.

295p. 21½cm.

1. Brazil - Literature. 2. Magalhães, Raymundo, ed. I. Title.

Brazil
M869.3
M18co1

Machado de Assis, Joaquim Maria, 1839-1908.
Contos avulsos. Organização e prefácio de R. Magalhães Júnior. ⌊Rio de Janeiro⌋ Editora Civilização Brasileira especialmente para e Companhia Distribuidora de Livros ⌊1956⌋

264 p. 21 cm.

CONTENTS.—A anjo das donzelas.—O rei dos caiporas.—Diana.—Onda.—A vida eterna.—Possível e impossível.—Mariana.—Os óculos de Pedro Antão.—Uma por outra.—Um dia de entrudo.—O sainete.—D. Jucunda.—Tempo de crise.—Como se inventaram os almanaques.—A inglesinha Barcelos (fragmentos)

I. Title.

PQ9697.M18C56 — 57-15472 ‡

Library of Congress ⌊8⌋

Brazil
M869.3
M18co5

Machado de Assis, Joaquim Maria, 1839-1908.
Contos e crônicas; organização, prefácio e notes de R. Magalhães Júnior. Rio de Janeiro, Editôra Civilização Brasileira, 1958.

295p. 21½cm.

1. Brazil - Literature. 2. Magalhães, Raymundo, ed. I. Title.

Brazil
M869.3
M18co21

Machado de Assis, Joaquim Maria, 1839-1908.
Contos esparsos. Organização e prefácio de R. Magalhães Júnior. ⌊Rio de Janeiro⌋ Editora Civilização Brasileira especialmente para a Companhia Distribuidora de Livros ⌊1956⌋

282 p. 22 cm.

CONTENTS.—O anjo Rafael.—Não é o mel para a bôca do asno.—Antes que cases.—Quinhentos contos.—A menina dos olhos pardos.—Canseiras em vão.—Quem boa cama faz.—Uma visita de Alcibíades.—A felicidade.—Felicidade pelo casamento.—Habilidoso.—A idéia do Ezequiel Maia.—Um agregado.—Orai por êle!—Antes a rocha Tarpéia.

I. Title.

PQ9697.M18C57 — 57-15080 ‡

Library of Congress ⌊8⌋

Brazil
M869.3
M18co2

Machado de Assis, Joaquim Maria, 1839-1908.
Contos esquecidos. Organização e prefácio de R. Magalhães Júnior. ⌊Rio de Janeiro⌋ Editora Civilização Brasileira especialmente pará a Companhia Distribuidora de Livros ⌊1956⌋

271 p. 22 cm.

CONTENTS.—Decadência de dois grandes homens.—Muitos anos depois.—A melhor das noivas.—Um esqueleto.—Uma loureira.—Brincar com fogo.—A última receita.—O passado, passado.—D. Mônica.—Casa não casa.—Silvestre.—A pianista.—O machete.—Vidros quebrados.—Venus! divina Venus!

I. Title.

PQ9697.M18C58 — 56-45619 ‡

Library of Congress ⌊8⌋

Brazil
M869.3
M18co

Machado de Assis, Joaquim Maria, 1839-1908.
... Contos fluminenses. Nova ed. ... Rio de Janeiro, Paris, Garnier ⌊1924?⌋

2 p. l., 310, ⌊2⌋ p. 19cm. (*On cover:* Collecção dos autores celebres da litteratura brasileira)

At head of title: Machado de Assis.

CONTENTS.—Miss Dollar.—Luiz Soares.—A mulher de preto.—O segredo de Augusta.—Confissões de uma viuva moça.—Linha recta e linha curva.—Frei Simão.

I. Title. 1. Brasilian literature

30-718

Library of Congress PQ9697.M18C6 1924 ⌊2⌋

Brazil
M869.3
M18co3

Machado de Assis, Joaquim Maria, 1839-1908.
Contos recolhidos. Organização e prefácio de R. Magalhães Júnior. ⌊Rio de Janeiro⌋ Editora Civilização Brasileira especialmente para a Companhia Distribuidora de Livros ⌊1956⌋

277 p. 22 cm.

CONTENTS. — Francisca. — O oráculo. — O pai. — Fernando e Fernanda.—Rui de Leão.—Uma excursão milagrosa.—Astúcias de marido.—O capitão Mendonça.—Longe dos olhos.—O último dia de um poeta.—O que são as moças.—Cinco mulheres.

I. Title.

PQ9697.M18C65 — 56-45617 ‡

Library of Congress ⌊8⌋

Brazil
M869.3
M18co4

Machado de Assis, Joaquim Maria, 1839-1908.
Contos sem data. Organização e prefácio de R. Magalhães Júnior. ⌊Rio de Janeiro⌋ Editora Civilização Brasileira especialmente para a Companhia Distribuidora de Livros ⌊1956⌋

276 p. 22 cm.

CONTENTS.—O caso da viúva.—João Fernandes.—Duas juizas.—A mulher pálida.—Incorrigível.—O contrato.—Um bilhete.—A viúva Sobral.—História de uma lágrima.—Sales.—A chave.—Curiosidade.—Casa velha.—Um dístico.—O bote de rapé.—As fôrcas caudinas.

I. Magalhães, Raymundo, ed. II. Title.

PQ9697.M18C67 — 57-15483

Library of Congress ⌊8⌋

Brazil
M869.3
M18cor

Machado de Assis, Joaquim Maria, 1839-1908.
Correspondencia de Machado de Assis; com Joaquim Nabuco, José Verissimo, Lucio de Mendonça, Mario de Alencar e Outros, seguida das respostas dos destinatarios. Colegida e anotada por Fernando Nery. Rio de Janeiro, Officina Industrial Graphica, 1932.

266p. port. 18cm.

I. Title.

Brazil
M869.3
M18cr

Machado de Assis, Joaquim Maria, 1839-1908.
... Critica por Machado de Assis (coleção feita por Mario de Alencar) Rio de Janeiro, Paris, Livraria Garnier ⌊1924?⌋

2 p. l., 230 p., 1 l. 18 cm. (Collecção dos autores celebres da litteratura brasileira)

CONTENTS.—Literatura brazileira. Instinto de nacionalidade.—Guilherme Malta. — Castro Alves. — O Primo Bazilio. — Semana literaria.—Fagundes Varela.—A nova geração.—Antonio José.—Um livro (Cenas do Amazonas, de José Verissimo)—Secretario d'el-rei.—Horas sagradas e versos.—Pensées détachées et souvenirs, de Joaquim Nabuco.—Prefacios.

1. Brazilian literature—Addresses, essays, lectures. I. Alencar, Mario Cockrane de, 1872-1925, comp.

36—21928

Library of Congress PQ9551.M3 ⌊48b½⌋ 869.04

Brazil
M869.3
M18cr

Machado de Assis, Joaquim Maria, 1839-1908.
Crônicas de Lélia; organização, prefácio e notas de R. Magalhães, Júniôr. Rio de Janeiro, Editôra Civilização Brasileira, 1958.

328p. 21½cm.

1. Brazil - Literature. I. Magalhães, Raymundo, ed. II. Title.

Brazil
M869.3
M18di

Machado de Assis, Joaquim Maria, 1839-1908.
Diálogos e reflexões de um relojoeiro; escritos de 1886 ("A+B"), de 1888 e 1889 ("Bons dias"), recolhidos da "Gazeta de notícias." Organização, prefácio e notas de R. Magalhães Júnior. ⌊Rio de Janeiro⌋ Editora Civilização Brasileira, especialmente para a Companhia Distribuidora de Livros ⌊1956⌋

277 p. 21 cm.

I. Magalhães, Raymundo, ed. II. Title.

PQ9697.M18D5 — 57-25504 ‡

Library of Congress ⌊8⌋

Brazil
M869.3
M18d
1937

Machado de Assis, Joaquim Maria, 1839-1908.
... Dom Casmurro. Rio de Janeiro ⌊etc.⌋ W. M. Jackson inc., 1937.

426 p. 20cm.

At head of title: Machado de Assis.

I. Title. 1. Brasil - Fiction.

38—32239

Library of Congress PQ9697.M18D6 1937 ⌊43c1⌋ 869.3

Brazil
M869.3
M18d
1924

Machado de Assis, Joaquim Maria, 1839-1908.
... Dom Casmurro. Rio de Janeiro, Paris, Garnier ⌊1924?⌋

2 p. l., 404 p. 19cm. (Collecção dos autores celebres da litteratura brasileira)

At head of title: Machado de Assis.

I. Title. 1. Brasilian literature

29—25881

Library of Congress PQ9697.M18D6 ⌊42b1⌋

Brazil
M869.3
M18ep

Machado de Assis, Joaquim Maria, 1839-1908.
Epitaph of a small winner; translated from the Portuguese by William L. Grossman. Drawings by Shari Frisch. New York, Noonday Press, 1952.

223 p. illus. 21 cm.

Translation of Memorias posthumas de Braz Cubas.

I. Title.

PZ3.M1817Ep 869.3 52—36196 ‡

Library of Congress ⌊53d5⌋

Brasil
M869.3
M18es

Machado de Assis, Joaquim Maria, 1839-1908.
... Esaú e Jacob ⌊por⌋ Machado de Assis ... Rio de Janeiro, Paris, Garnier ⌊1920?⌋

3 p. l., 362 p. 18cm. (Collecção dos autores celebres da litteratura brasileira)

I. Title. 1. Brazilian literature.

29-2006

Library of Congress PQ9697.M18E7 ⌊2⌋

Brazil
M869.3
M18he

Machado de Assis, Joaquim Maria, 1839-1908.
... Helena. Rio de Janeiro, Paris, Garnier ⌊1929?⌋

3 p. l., 296, ⌊2⌋ p. 19cm. (Collecção dos autores celebres da litteratura brasileira)

At head of title: Machado de Assis.

I. Title. 1. Brazilian literature.

31-29254

Library of Congress PQ9697.M18H4 869.3

Brazil
M869.3
M18hel

Machado de Assis, Joaquim Maria, 1839-1908.
The heritage of Quincas Borba. A novel by Machado de Assis. Translated from the Portuguese by Clotilde Wilson. London, W. H. Allen, 19[illegible].

255p. 22cm.

I. Title.

Brazil
M869.3
M18hi

Machado de Assis, Joaquim Maria, 1839-1908.
... Historias da meia noite, por Machado de Assis ... Rio de Janeiro, Paris, Garnier ⌊1923⌋

242 p., 1 l. incl. front. (port.) 19cm. (Collecção dos autores celebres da litteratura brasileira)

CONTENTS.—A parasita azul.—As bodas de Luiz Duarte.—Ernesto de tal.—Aurora sem dia.—O relogio de ouro.—Ponto de vista.

I. Title. 1. Brazilian literature.

30-720

Library of Congress PQ9697.M18H5 ⌊2⌋

Brazil
M869.3
M18hi 2

Machado de Assis, Joaquim Maria, 1839–1908.
... Historias sem data ... Nova ed. rev. Rio de Janeiro, Paris, Garnier [1924?]
3 p. l., 224 p., 1 l. 19cm. (*On cover:* Collecção dos autores celebres da litteratura brasileira)
At head of title: Machado de Assis.

I. Title. 1. Brazilian literature
30-719
Library of Congress PQ9697.M18H52 1924
[2]

Brazil
M869.3
M18i

Machado de Assis, Joaquim Maria, 1839-1908.
Idéias e imagens de Machado de Assis; dicionário antológico, com mil verbêtes, abrangendo tôda a obra machadiana, desde a colaboração em "A Marmota" até o "Memorial de Aires," [ed. by Raymundo Magalhães, Junior] [Rio de Janeiro] Editora Civilização Brasileria, 1956.
220p. 21½cm.

1. Brazil-Literature. I. Magalhães, Raymundo, ed. II. Title.

Brazil
M869.3
M18ma

Machado de Assis, Joaquim Maria, 1839-1908.
A mão e a luva. Rio de Janeiro, W. M. Jackson, Inc. Editôres, 1957.
242p. 20½cm. (Obras completas de Machado de Assis.)

1. Brazilian literature. I. Title.

Brazil
M869.3
M18me

Machado de Assis, Joaquim Maria, 1839–1908.
... Memorial de Ayres. Rio de Janeiro, Paris, Garnier [1923]
5 p. l., [3]–273 p. 19cm. (Collecção dos autores celebres da litteratura brasileira)
At head of title: Machado de Assis.

I. Title. 1. Brazilian literature.
30-723
Library of Congress PQ9697.M18M47
[2]

Brazil
M869.3
M18me 3

Machado de Assis, Joaquim Maria, 1839–1908.
... Memorias posthumas de Braz Cubas, por Machado de Assis ... Rio de Janeiro, Paris, Garnier [1914]
x, 387 p. 18cm. (Collecção dos autores celebres da litteratura brasileira)
Continued in the author's Quincas Borba.

I. Title. 1. Brazilian literature.
20-20125
Library of Congress [35b1] PQ9697.M18M5

Brazil
M869.3
M18pag

Machado de Assis, Joaquim Maria, 1839-1908.
Páginas recolhidas. Rio de Janeiro, W. M. Jackson Inc. Editôres, 1957.
298p. 20½cm. (Obras completas de Machado de Assis)

1. Brazilian literature. I. Title.

Brazil
M869.3
M18pa

Machado de Assis, Joaquim Maria, 1839–1908.
... Papeis avulsos. Rio de Janeiro [etc.] Livraria Garnier, 1937.
318 p., 1 l. 20 cm. (Collecção dos autores celebres de la Litteratura Brasileira)
At head of title: Machado de Assis.
First published 1882.
CONTENTS.—O alienista.—Theoria do medalhão.—A chinella turca.—Na arca.—D. Benedicta.—O segredo do bonzo.—O annel de Polycrates.—O emprestimo.—A serenissima republica.—O espelho.—Uma visita de Alcibiades.—Verba testamentaria.

1. Brazilian literature.
38-32232
Library of Congress PQ9697.M18P35 1937
[2] 869.3

Brazil
M869.3
M18ph

Machado de Assis, Joaquim Maria, 1839–1908.
Philosopher or dog? (Quincas Borba) Translated from the Portuguese by Clotilde Wilson. New York, Noonday Press [°1954]
271 p. 21 cm.
Sequel to Epitaph of a small winner.

I. Title.
PZ3.M1817Ph 54-11195 ‡
Library of Congress [8]

Brazil
M869.3
M18po

Machado de Assis, Joaquim Maria, 1839–1908.
... Poesias completas: Chrysalidas, Phalenas, Americanas, Occidentaes. Rio de Janeiro, Paris, H. Garnier, 1901. 1902.
vi, 376 p. front. (port.) 18cm.
At head of title: Machado de Assis.

1. Brazilian literature.
41-35860
Library of Congress PQ9697.M18A17 1901
[2] 869.1

Brazil
M869.3
M18p

Machado de Assis, Joaquim Maria, 1839–1908.
The psychiatrist, and other stories. Translated by William L. Grossman & Helen Caldwell. Berkeley, University of California Press, 1963.
147 p. 22 cm.

I. Title. 1. Short stories, Brazilian.
PZ3.M1817Ps 63-9407 ‡
Library of Congress [5]

Brazil
M869.3
M18q

Machado de Assis, Joaquim Maria, 1839-1908.
... Quincas Borba. Rio de Janeiro, Paris, Garnier [1923]
3 p. l., 360p. 19cm. (Collecção dos autores celebres da litteratura brasileira)
At head of title: Machado de Assis.
A continuation of the author's Memorias posthumas de Braz Cubas.

I. Title 1. Brazilian literature.

Brazil
M869.3
M18r

Machado de Assis, Joaquim Maria, 1839-1908.
Ao redor de Machado de Assis (pesquisas e interpretações). (Edicão ilustrada, comemorativa do cinqüentenário da morte de Joaquim Maria Machado de Assis - 1839-1908). [ed. by Raymundo Magalhães, Junior] Rio de Janeiro, Editôra Civilizacão Brasileira, 1958.
285p. port. illus. 21½cm.

1. Brazil - literature. I. Magalhães, Raymundo, ed. II. Title.

Brazil
M869.3
M18re2
1957

Machado de Assis, Joaquim Maria, 1839-1908.
Relíquias de casa velha. Rio de Janeiro, W. M. Jackson Inc. Editôres, 1957.
2v. 20½cm. (Obras completas de Machado de Assis)

1. Brasilian literature. I. Title.

Brasil
M869.3
M18re2

Machado de Assis, Joaquim Maria, 1839–1908.
... Reliquias de casa velha, por Machado de Assis ... Rio de Janeiro, Paris, Garnier [1921?]
5 p. l., [3]–264 p., 1 l. 19cm. (Collecção dos autores celebres da litteratura brasileira)
CONTENTS.—A Carolina.—Pae contra mãe.—Maria Cora.—Marcha funebre.—Um capitão de voluntarios.—Suje-se gordo!—Umas ferias.—Evolução.—Pylades e Orestes.—Anecdota do cabriolet.—Paginas criticas e commemorativas.—Não consultes medico.—Licção de botanica.

I. Title. 1. Brasilian literature.
31-29718
Library of Congress PQ9697.M18R4 869.8

Brazil
M869.3
M18re7

Machado de Assis, Joaquim Maria, 1839–1908.
... Resurreição. Rio de Janeiro [etc.] W. M. Jackson inc., 1937.
235 p., 1 l. front. (port.) 20cm.
At head of title: Machado de Assis.
First published 1872.

I. Title. 1. Brazilian literature
38-32248
Library of Congress PQ9697.M18R45 1937
[2] 869.3

Brazil
M869.3
M18s

Machado de Assis, Joaquim Maria. 1839-1908
Seleção, prefacio e notas de Armando Correia Pacheco. Washington, União Pan-Americana, 1949.
78p. 20cm. (Escritores da América)

1. Brazil - Fiction

Brazil
M869.3
M18se

Machado de Assis, Joaquim Maria, 1839-1908.
A Semana. Rio de Janeiro, W. M. Jackson Inc. Editôres, 1957.
3v. 20½cm. (Obras completas de Machado de Assis).
Contents:-v. 1-1892-1893.-v.2-1894-1895.-v.3-1892-1900.

1. Brazilian literature. I. Title.

Brazil
M869.3
M18seu

Machado de Assis, Joaquim Maria, 1839-1908.
Seus 30 melhores contos. Precedidos de uma introdução geral. Rio de Janeiro, Editora Jose Aguilar, 1961.
478p. illus. 16cm.
Portrait of author.

I. Title.

Brazil
M869.3
M18t

Machado de Assis, Joaquim Maria, 1839-1908.
... Teatro. Colyido por Mario do Alencar. Rio de Janeiro, Paris Garnier. [n.d.]
369p. 1 l. 19cm.

1. Brazilian literature. I. Title

Brazil
M869.3
M18v

Machado de Assis, Joaquim Maria, 1839–1908.
... Varias historias ... Rio de Janeiro, Paris, Garnier [1924?]
2 p. l., [iii]–iv, 282 p., 1 l. 19cm. (Collecção dos autores celebres da litteratura brasileira)
At head of title: Machado de Assis.
CONTENTS.—A cartomante.—Entre santos.—Uns braços.—Um homem celebre.—A desejada das gentes.—A causa secreta.—Trio em lá menor.—Adão e Eva.—O enfermeiro.—O diplomatico.—Marianna.—Conto de escola.—Um apologo.—D. Paula.—Viver!—O conego; ou, Metaphysica do estylo.

1. Brazilian literature.
31-29717
Library of Congress PQ9697.M18V3 869.3

Brazil
M869.3
M18y

Machado de Assis, Joaquim Maria, 1839–1908.
... Yayá Garcia, por Machado de Assis. Nova ed. Rio de Janeiro, Paris, Garnier [1925?] 1919
2 p. l., 320 p. 19cm. (Collecção dos autores celebres da litteratura brasileira)

I. Title.
31-29263
Library of Congress PQ9697.M18Y3 1925 869.3

Machado de Assis, Joaquim Maria, 1839-1908.
Brazil
M869.3
M18ab
Bettencourt Machado, José.
Machado of Brazil, the life and times of Machado de Assis. New York, Bramerica, 1953.
246 p. illus. 22 cm.
Includes bibliography.
1. Machado de Assis, Joaquim Maria, 1839-1908. I. Title.
PQ9697.M18Z5678 928.69 53—4205 ‡
Library of Congress [54c2]

Machado de Assis, Joaquim Maria, 1839-1908.
Brazil
M869.3
M18am
Matos, Mário
Machado de Assis, o homem e a obra, os personagens explicam o autor. Rio de Janeiro, Companhia Editora Nacional, 1939.
454p. 19cm. (Brasiliana, Biblioteca pedagógica Brasileira. Serie 5 vol. 153)

Machado de Assis, Joaquim Maria, 1837-1908.
Brazil
M89
M18v
Vellinho, Moysés
Machado de Assis; historias mal contadas e outros assuntos. Rio de Janeiro, Libraria São José, 1960.
106p. 19cm.

Machado of Brazil.
Brazil
M869.3
M18ab
Bettencourt Machado, José.
Machado of Brazil, the life and times of Machado de Assis. New York, Bramerica, 1953.
246 p. illus. 22 cm.
Includes bibliography.
1. Machado de Assis, Joaquim Maria, 1839-1908. I. Title.
PQ9697.M18Z5678 928.69 53—4205 ‡
Library of Congress [54c2]

Machado y Gómez, Eduardo, 1836-1877.
Cuba
M861.5
V23g
García Garófalo y Mesa, Manuel, 1887-
... Plácido, poeta y mártir. México, Ediciones Botas, 1938.
295 p., 2 l. 19cm.
At head of title: M. García Garófalo Mesa.
"Plácido, poeta y mártir; Plácido, dichter und martyrer, por Durama de Ochoa [seudónimo de] Eduardo Machado Gómez. Hannover—1865. Traducido del francés": p. [279]-295.
1. Valdés, Gabriel de la Concepción, 1809-1844. I. Machado y Gómez, Eduardo, 1836-1877. Plácido, dichter und martyrer. II. Title.
39—8206
Library of Congress PQ7389.V3Z59
[44c1] 861.59

The machinery of justice in Nigeria.
Nigeria
M340
N97
Nwabueze, Benjamin Obi.
The machinery of justice in Nigeria. London, Butterworths, 1963.
xxi, 309 p. 23 cm. (Butterworth's African law series, no. 8)
Bibliographical references included in footnotes.
1. Justice, Administration of—Nigeria. I. Title.
2. Nigeria-Courts.
64-1951
Library of Congress [2]

Basutoland
M398
M18mp
Machobane, James J
Mphatlalatsane ea Sekhutlo. Morija, Basutoland, Sesuto Book Depot, 1947.
105p. 18cm.
Story of a bull.
1. Africa - folklore.

Basutoland
M398
M18ma
Machobane, James J.
Mahaheng a Matso. Morija, Basutoland, Sesuto Book Depot, 1946.
38p. 18cm.
"At the black caves."
1. Africa - Folklore.

Basutoland
M398
M18ma
Machobane, James J.
Mahaheng a Matso. Morija, Basutoland, Sesuto Book Depot, 1946.
38p. 18cm.
At the black caves.
1. Africa, South-Folklore.

Basutoland
M398
M18mp
Machobane, James J
Mphatlalatsane ea Sekhutlo. Morija, Sesuto Book Depot, 1947.
105p. 18cm.
Story of a bull
1. Africa, South - Folklore.

Uganda
M380
M18
Machyo, B Chango
Africa in world trade. [London] Africana Study Group, 1963.
16p. 22cm.
1. Commerce - Africa. I. Title.

Macina.
Mali
M966.2
Oule
Ouane, Ibrahima Mamadou, 1908-
L'énigme du Macina. Préface de Maurice Kaouza. Monte-Carlo, Regain, 1952.
187p. 19½cm.

MacIver, Robert Morrison, 1882- ed.
M323
In8u
Institute for religious and social studies, *Jewish theological seminary of America.*
... Unity and difference in American life, a series of addresses and discussions, edited by R. M. MacIver. New York and London, Pub. by Institute for religious & social studies, distributed by Harper & brothers [1947]
5 p. l., 3-168 p. 21 cm. (Religion and civilization series)
CONTENTS.—The common ground: Three paths to the common good, by Louis Finkelstein. The rise of an American culture, by Allan Nevins. What common ground has America won? By L. K. Frank.—The dividing issues: The racial issue, by E. F. Frazier. The ethnic issue, by Vilhjalmur Stefansson. The economic issue, by Eli Ginzberg.
(Continued on next card)
47—2731
[40k³7]

Jamaica
M823.91
M19ban
McKay, Claude, 1890—1948.
Banana bottom, traduit de l'Americain par F. W. Paparra. 8th ed. Paris, Les Editions Rieder, 1934.
ii, 333p. 19cm.
I. Title: Banana bottom (French translation)

Jamaica
M823.91
M19b
McKay, Claude, 1890-1948.
Banana Bottom [by] Claude McKay. New York, London, Harper & brothers, 1933.
4 p. l., 317 p. 20cm.
"First edition."
I. Title.
Library of Congress PZ3.M1926Bam 33-7952
——— Copy 2.
Copyright A 60896 [5]

Jamaica
M823.91
M19ba4
McKay, Claude, 1890-1948.
Banjo. Traduit de l'Americain par Ida Treat et Paul Vaillant-Couturier avec une préface de Georges Friedmann. Paris, Les Editions Rieder, 1931.
406p. 18½cm.
I. Title.

Jamaica
M823.91
M19ba
McKay, Claude, 1890-1948.
Banjo, a story without a plot, by Claude McKay ... New York and London, Harper & brothers, 1929.
5 p. l., 3-326 p., 1 l. 20cm.
First edition C-D
I. Title.
29-10436
Library of Congress PZ3.M1926Ban
——— Copy 2.
Copyright A 7868 [41c1]

Jamaica
M821.91
M19c
McKay, Claude, 1890-1948.
Constab ballads, by Claude McKay. London, Watts & co., 1912.
94p. 20cm.
1. Poetry. I. Title.

Jamaica
M398
Anl
McKay, Claude, 1890-1948
Dialect verse.
(In: Anancy stories and dialect verse.. 1st ed. Kingston, Jamaica, Pioneer Press, [1950]. 19cm. pp.91-93)

Jamaica
M823.91
M19g
McKay, Claude, 1890-1948.
Gingertown, by Claude McKay. New York and London, Harper & brothers, 1932.
vii p., 1 l., 274 p. 19½cm.
Short stories.
"First edition."
I. Title.
Library of Congress PZ3.M1926Gi 32-6427
——— Copy 2.
Copyright A 48892 [5]

Jamaica
M974.71
M19
McKay, Claude, 1890-1948.
Harlem: Negro metropolis, by Claude McKay; illustrated with photographs. New York, E. P. Dutton & company, inc. [c1940]
xi p., 1 l., 15-262 p. front., illus. (facsim.) plates, ports. 22½cm.
"First edition."
1. Harlem, New York (City) 2. Negroes—New York (City) I. Title: Negro metropolis.
40—32205
Library of Congress F128.68.H3M3
[47z2] 917.471

Jamaica
M821.91
M19h

McKay, Claude, 1890-1948.
Harlem shadows; the poems of Claude McKay, with an introduction by Max Eastman. New York, Harcourt, Brace and company [c1922]
xxi, 95 p. 19½cm.
Inscribed copy: Yours sincerely Claude McKay
Photograph of the author inlaid.

I. Title. 1. Poetry. 22—8610
Library of Congress PS3525.A24785H3 1922
——— Copy 2.
Copyright A 659695 [38g2]

Jamaica
M823.91
M19h2

McKay, Claude, 1890-1948.
Home to Harlem. New York, Avon Publishing Co., 1951.
157p. 16cm. (Avon pocket-size books, 376)
"Complete and unabridged."

I. Title

Jamaica
M823.91
M19h

McKay, Claude, 1890-1948.
Home to Harlem, by Claude McKay. New York and London, Harper & brothers, 1928.
5 p. l., 340 p. 19½cm.
First edition, A-C.

——— ——— 7th printing, C-C.

I. Title. 28—6523
Library of Congress PZ3.M1926Ho
[48d1]

Jamaica
M39
M19

McKay, Claude, 1890-1948.
A long way from home, by Claude McKay. New York, L. Furman, inc. [c1937]
6 p. l., 3-354 p. 21cm.

I. Title. 37—8570
Library of Congress PS3525.A24785L6 1937
[45d1] 928.1

M811.08
F825

McKay, Claude, 1890-1948.
[Poems]

(In: Four Negro poets: ... New York, Simon E. Schuster, n.d. 21½cm. p. 7-11).

Jamaica
M821.91
M19p

McKay, Claude, 1890-1948.
Poems. In: The Cambridge Magazine. Summer 1920, p. 55-59.

1. Poetry.

Jamaica
M823.91
M19h6

McKay, Claude, 1890-1948.
Quartier noir (Home to Harlem) traduit du Negre Americain par Louis Guilloux. Paris, Les Editions Rieder, 1932.
287p. 19cm.

I. Title. II. Guilloux, Louis.
III. Title: Home to Harlem.

M813.5
M19qu

McKay, Claude, 1890-1948.
Quasi blanca. Traducció de Josep Miracle. Barcelona, Edicions de la Rosa dels Vents, 1938.
45p. 18cm. (Biblioteca de la Rosa dels Vents, v. 62)

I. Title.

Jamaica
M821.91
M19s

McKay, Claude, 1890-1948.
Selected poems. With an introd. by John Dewey and a biographical note by Max Eastman. New York, Bookman Associates, 1953.
112 p. 23 cm.

PS3525.A24785A6 1953 811.5 53-6332 ‡
Library of Congress [5]

M810.8
F31

McKay, Claude, 1890-1948.
A song of the moon.
(In: Federal Writers' Project. American stuff: an anthology of prose & verse ... New York, The Viking press, 1937. p. 238.)

Jamaica
M821.91
M19son

McKay, Claude, 1890-1948.
Songs from Jamaica. London, Augener Ltd., 1912.
11p. 28½cm.
Words and music.
Six songs.

I. Title.

Jamaica
M821.91
M19so

McKay, Claude, 1890-1948.
Songs of Jamaica, by Claude McKay. With an introduction by Walter Jekyll... Kingston, Jamaica, Aston W. Gardner & Co., 1912.
140p. front. 18½cm.
Music.

1. Poetry. I. Title.

Jamaica
M821.91
M19sp

McKay, Claude, 1890-1948.
Spring in New Hampshire and other poems, by Claude McKay. London, Grant Richards, 1920.
40p. 20cm.

1. Poetry I. title

M813.08
C554

McKay, Claude, 1890-1948.
Truant
Pp. 41-54

In: Clarke, John Henrik, ed. American Negro short stories. New York, Hill and Wang, 1966.

McKay, Claude, 1890-1948.

Africa
M896
B36

Drayton, Arthur D
Claude McKay's human pity: a note on his protest poetry.
Pp. 76-88.

In: Beier, Ulli, comp. Introduction to African literature. London, Longmans, 1967.

M973.9
F46
No.13

McKenzie, Marjorie.
Fifty years of progress for Negro women. Pittsburgh, Pittsburgh Courier, 1950.
11p. illus. 24cm. (Fifty years of progress)

1. Women. I. Series.

M812.5
M19

McKetney, Edwin Charles.
Mr. Big. [A play in three acts. 1st ed.] New York, Pageant Press [1953]
74 p. 24 cm.

I. Title.
PS3525.A2576M5 812.5 53-10082 ‡
Library of Congress [5]

Mc Kinley, William.

M815.5
G88
V.1no.1

Grimke, Francis James, 1850-
Some lessons from the assassination of President William McKinley, by Rev. Francis J. Grimke,... delivered September, 1901.
15p. 23cm.

McKinley, William

M815.5
G88

Grimke, Francis James, 1850-
Some lessons from the assassination of President William McKinley, by Rev. Francis J. Grimke...delivered September 22, 1901.
15p. 23cm.

M378
M21r

McKinney, Richard Ishmael, 1906-
Religion in higher education among Negroes, by Richard I. McKinney ... New Haven, Yale university press; London, H. Milford, Oxford university press, 1945.
xvi, 165, [1] p. incl. tables. 23½cm. (*Half-title:* Yale studies in religious education, XVIII)
"The complete results of this study were presented as a dissertation ... for the degree of doctor of philosophy in Yale university [1942]."—p. xii.
Bibliography: p. [149]-161.

1. ~~Negroes~~— Education. 2. ~~Negroes~~— Religion. 3. Universities and colleges—Religion. I. Title.
A 45—4633
Yale univ. Library for Library of Congress BV1610.M33
[4617]†

M323.3
M21a

McKinney, Thomas Theodore, 1869-
All white America; a candid discussion of race mixture and race prejudice in the United States, by T. T. McKinney ... Boston, Meador publishing company, 1937.
214 p. 21 cm.
Bibliographical notes: p. 213-214.

1. U. S.—Race question. 2. Miscegenation. 3. Negroes. I. Title.
37-2557
Library of Congress E185.61.M156
[5] 325.260973

Africa
M960
M22a

MacLean, Joan Coyne, ed.
Africa: the racial issue. New York, Wilson, 1954.
198 p. map. 20 cm. (The Reference shelf, v. 26, no. 1)
Bibliography: p. [188]-198.

White editor.

1. Africa—Race question. I. Title. (Series)

DT15.M15 *301.451 325.6 54-7532
Library of Congress [60]

Mac Lean, Malcolm S.
M355.2
H18f
Hampton Institute. Hampton Va. Conference on the Participation of the Negro in National Defense.
Findings and principal addresses. Hampton, Va., 1940.

61p. 28cm.

M378
M22

McMillan, Lewis Kennedy., 1897-
Negro higher education in the State of South Carolina. [Orangeburg? S. C., 1953, °1952]
xii, 296 p. facsims. 24 cm.

1. ~~Negroes~~—Education—South Carolina. 2. Universities and colleges—South Carolina. I. Title.

LC2802.S6M25 378.757 53-2401
Library of Congress [54c2]

M811.5
M22s

McMorris, Thomas, 1897-
Striving to win. Boston, Christopher Pub. House [1949]
144 p. 20 cm.
Poems.

I. Title.

PS3525.A27755S7 811.5 49-3153*
Library of Congress [2]

Macon co., Ala.
M301
J63s

Johnson, Charles Spurgeon, 1893-
Shadow of the plantation, by Charles S. Johnson ... Chicago, Ill., The University of Chicago press [1934]
xxiv, 214, [1] p. front., plates, diagr. 22 cm.
Macon county, Alabama, was the area chosen for this survey. cf. Introd.

1. Plantation life. 2. Negroes—Macon co., Ala. I. Title.
34-19995

Library of Congress E185.93.A3J6
[44h1] 325.2609761

Kenya
M896.2
Mc4

MacPherson, Margaret
Let's make a play. With the acted version of Kintu; a play by E. C. N. Kironde. Kampala, Eagle Press, 1960.

vii, 44p. 21½cm.
White author.

1. Theater - Production and direction.
I. Title. II. Kironde, E. C. N. Kintu.
2. Drama.

Macunaíma.

Brazil
M869
An2ma

Andrade, Mário de, 1893-1945.
Macunaíma. São Paulo, Livraria Martins Editôra, 1944.

220p. 22cm. (Obras completas... Tomo IV)

The mad pagan and verse.
M811.5
Se8m
Seuell, Malchus M , 1911-
The mad pagan and verse. Downey, California, Elena Quinn, 1959.

72p. 22cm.

Madagascar.

Africa
M896.3
P741

Les plus beaux écrits de l'union française et du Maghreb, Présentés par Mohamed El Kholti, Léopold Sédar Senghor, [and others] Paris, Editions du Vieux, Colombier, 1947.

455p. 21cm.

Madagascar.
Madagascar
M969
An2t

Andriamanjato, Richard
Le tsiny et le tody dans la pensée Malgache. Paris, Presence Africaine, 1957.

100p. 25½cm.

Madagascar
M343.
B69s

Madagascar.
Boyer, Danika.
Sa majesté Ranavalo III, ma reine. Paris, Fasquelle Editeurs, 1946.

255 p. front (port.) 19 cm.

Madagascar.
Mauritius
M969.82
L29m

Lislet-Geoffroy, Jean Baptiste, 1755-1836.
Memoir and notice explanatory of a chart of Madagascar and the North-Eastern archipelago of Mauritius; drawn up according to the latest observations, under the auspices and government of His Excellency Robert Townsend Farquhar ... By Lislet Geoffroy ... Now first pub. in the original French, with an English translation, together with some observations on the coast of Africa, and a brief notice on the winds on the coast of Madagascar [by M. Barbarin] London, J. Murray, 1819.
v, 57 p. front. (fold. chart.) 28cm.
1. Pilot guides—Madagascar. 2. Pilot guides—Mauritius. I. Farquhar, Sir Robert Townsend, 1776-1830, ed. II. Barbarin, ———.
18-23158

Library of Congress VK891.G34
[39b1]

Madagascar - Drama.
Madagascar
M842.91
R11ag

Rabemananjara, Jacques, 1913-
Agapes des dieux; Tritriva; tragédie malgache. Paris, Présence Africaine [1962]

265p. 19cm.

Madagascar - Drama.

Madagascar
M842.91
R11b

Rabemananjara, Jacques, 1913-
Les boutriers de l'aurore; tragédie malgache en 3 actes, 6 tableaux. Paris, Présence Africaine, 1957.

231p. 19½cm.

Madagascar-History.
Madagascar
M969.1
T34m

Thierry, Solange
Madagascar. [Madagascar, 1967?]

189p. illus. 18cm.

Madagascar-Politics and government.
Madagascar
M969
R11n

Rabemananjara, Jacques, 1913-
Nationalisme et problèmes Malgaches. Paris, Presence Africaine, 1958.

219p. 22½cm.

1. Madagascar-Politics and government.
2. Poetry. I. Title.

Madagascar
M969
R11t

Madagascar - Politics and government.
Rabemananjara, Jacques, 1913-
Témoignage malgache et colonialisme. Paris, Présence africaine [1956]
46 p. 19 cm. (Collection "Le Colonialisme," 2)
First ed. published in 1946 under title: Un Malgache vous parle.

1. Madagascar—Pol. & govt. I. Title.

JQ3453 1956.R3 57-30796 ‡
Library of Congress [3]

Madagascar - Religion.
Madagascar
M969.1
R142

Ramandraivonona, Désiré.
Le Malgache; sa langue, sa religion. Paris, Présence africaine [1959]
241 p. 9 illus. 25 cm.
"Bibliographie": p. [239]-241.

1. Malagasy language. 2. Madagascar—Religion. I. Title.

PL5379.R3 A 59-8219
Chicago. Univ. Libr. for Library of Congress [a60b½]†

Madal, George, jt. author.
French Guiana
M840
J15d

Jadfard, Rene.
Deux hommes et l'adventure, par Rene Jadfard et George Madal. Toulouse, Editions S.T.A.E.L. 1945.

224p. 18cm.
French Guiana - author.

Madam President-elect; a novel.
M813.5
W24m

Warner, Samuel Jonathan, 1896-
Madam President-elect; a novel. [1st ed.] New York, Exposition Press [1956]
249 p. 21 cm.

I. Title.

PZ4.W284Mad 56-8723 ‡
Library of Congress [2]

Madden, Richard Robert, 1798-1886, tr.
Cuba
M861.6
M26

[Manzano, Juan Francisco] 1797-1854.
Poems by a slave in the island of Cuba, recently liberated; translated from the Spanish, by R. R. Madden, M. D., with the history of the early life of the negro poet, written by himself; to which are prefixed two pieces descriptive of Cuban slavery and the slave-traffic, by R. R. M. London, T. Ward & co., 1840.
4 p. l., v p., 1 l., [9]-188 p. 22½cm.

1. Slavery in Cuba. I. Madden, Richard Robert, 1798-1886, tr. II. Title.
1-13046 Revised

Library of Congress HT1076.M3
[r33b2]

M813.5
M26f
Madden, Will Anthony.
Five more short stories. New York, Exposition Press [1963]
64p. 21cm.
Portrait of author on book jacket.

1. Short stories. I. Title.

M813.5
M26tw
Madden, Will Anthony
Two and one; two short stories and a play. New York, Exposition Press, 1961.
50p. 21cm.
Portrait of author on back of book jacket.

1. Short stories. 2. Drama. I. Title.

The maddening scar, a mystery novel.

M813.5
C61m
Clinton, Dorothy Randle.
The maddening scar, a mystery novel. Boston, Christopher Pub. House [1962]
117 p. 21 cm.

I. Title.

PZ4.C6395Mad 62-17817 ‡
Library of Congress [5]

Senegal
M966.3
M26s
Maderba, Abd-el-kader
Au Sénégal et au Soudan Français. Paris, Librairie Larose, 1931.
116p. plates., maps. 25½cm.

1. Senegal. 2. France - Colonies.

M811.5
M26o
Madgett, Naomi Cornelia Long., 1923-
One and the many; [poems. 1st ed.] New York, Exposition Press [1956]
64 p. 21 cm.

I. Title.

PS3525.A318O5 811.5 56-12373 ‡
Library of Congress [2]

M811.5
M26s
Madgett, Naomi Cornelia Long, 1923-
Songs to a phantom nightingale, by Naomi Cornelia Long. New York, Fortuny's publishers, inc. [1941]
30 p. port. 19 cm.
Verse.
"First edition."

I. Title.

PS3525.A318S6 811.5 41-15740 rev
Library of Congress [r57c8]

M811.5
M26s
Madgett, Naomi Cornelia (Long), 1923-
Star by star; poems, by Naomi Long Madgett. [1st ed.] Detroit, Harlo Press, 1965.
64 p. 23 cm.
Portrait of author on book jacket.

I. Title.

PS3525.A318S7 811.52 65-27463
Library of Congress [3]

Madiana, roman poétique.

France
M841
A14m
Alie, Benoit.
Madiana, roman poétique. Paris, E. Edouard, c 1924.
92p. 19½cm.

... Madinina.

Martinique
M972.98
D87m
Dufougeré, William, 1878-
... Madinina, "Reine des Antilles", étude de mœurs martiniquaises; préface de M. le professeur A. Lacroix ... Avec 61 réproductions photographiques, couverture de Pierre Bodard ... frontispice en coleurs de Maurice Millière, bandeaux et culs-de-lampe d'après les dessins originaux de Colmet d'Aage. Paris, Berger-Levrault, 1929.
viii p., 1 l., 258 p., 1 l. col. front., illus., plates, fold. map. 24cm.
"Bibliographie": p. [241]-252.
1. Martinique—Descr. & trav. I. Title.
[Full name: William Marie Barbe Dufougeré]
30-14516
Library of Congress F2081.D86
Copyright A—Foreign 6543
[2]

M972.94
M26h
Madiou, Thomas, fils. 1814 - 1884.
Histoire d'Haiti, par Thomas Madiou, Annees 1843-1846 Prince, Impr. J. Verrollot, 1904
v. 26cm.

1. Haiti-History

Madison, James, pres. U. S., 1751-1836.

MB9
M26j
Jennings, Paul, b. 1799.
A colored man's reminiscences of James Madison. By Paul Jennings. Brooklyn, G. C. Beadle, 1865.
vi, [7]-21 p. front. (facsim.) 30cm. (Half-title: Bladensburg series. no. 2)
"Reprinted 1865. Seventy-five copies."
"Preface signed J. B. R."

1. Madison, James, pres. U. S., 1751-1836. I. J. B. R. II. R., J. B. III. Title.
12—20475
Library of Congress E342.J54
[a37b1]

La madone des roses.

M812.3
So4m
No.2
Séjour, Victor, 1816-1874.
La madone des roses, drame en cinq actes, en prose. Paris, Michel Lévy Frères, 1869.
149p. 19cm.

Maendeleo na jasho.

Tanganyika
M967.82
Om1ma
Omari, Dunstan Alfred, 1922- jt. auth.
Maendeleo na jasho. Progress & perspiration. [By C.W. W. Ryan and D. A. Omari] Dar es Salaam, Eagle Press, 1954.
19p. 18cm. (Mazungunmzo ya uraia. Talks on citizenship, no. 3)
Written in English and Swahili.

1. Tanganyika. I. Title. II. Title: Progress & perspiration. III. Series: Mazungunmzo ya uraia, no. 3. IV. Series: Talks on citizenship, no. 3. V. Ryan, C. W. W.

M323
M26k
Maffett, Robert Lee, 1920-
The kingdom within; a study of the American race problem and its solution. Foreword by Gaius Jackson Slosser. [1st ed.] New York, Exposition Press [1955]
182 p. 21 cm.

1. U. S.—Race question. 2. Negroes. I. Title.

E185.61.M2 325.260973 55-11124 ‡
Library of Congress [5]

Magalhães, Cruz.

Portugal
M869
C82v
Costa Alegre, Caetano da, 1864-1890.
Versos. Lisboa, Livraria Ferin, 1916.
167p. port. 19cm.
Collected and published by Cruz Magalhães.

Magalhães, Raymundo, ed.

Brazil
M869.3
M18co5
Machado de Assis, Joaquim Maria, 1839-1908.
Contos e crônicas; organização, prefácio e notes de R. Magalhães Júnior. Rio do Janeiro, Editôra Civilização Brasileira, 1958.
295p. 21½cm.

Brazil
M869.3
M18co4
Magalhães, Raymundo, ed.
Machado de Assis, Joaquim Maria, 1839-1908.
Contos sem data. Organização e prefácio de R. Magalhães Júnior. [Rio de Janeiro] Editora Civilização Brasileira especia[lmente para a Companhia Distribuidora de Livros [1956]
276 p. 22 cm.
CONTENTS.—O caso da vidva.—João Fernandes.—Duas juizas.—A mulher pálida.—Incorrigível.—O contrato.—Um bilhete.—A viúva Sobral.—História de uma lágrima.—Salea.—A chave.—Curiosidade.—Casa velha.—Um dístico.—O bote de rapé.—As fôrcas caudinas.

I. Magalhães, Raymundo, ed. II. Title.

PQ9697.M18C67 57-15483
Library of Congress [3]

Magalhaes, Raymundo

Brazil
M869.3
M18cr
Machado de Assis, Joaquim Maria, 1839-1908.
Crônicas de Lélio; organização, prefácio e notas de R. Magalhães, Júnior. Rio de Janeiro, Editôra Civilização Brasileira, 1958.
328p. 21½cm.

Brazil
M869.3
M18di
Magalhães, Raymundo, ed.
Machado de Assis, Joaquim Maria, 1839-1908.
Diálogos e reflexões de um relojoeiro; escritos de 1886 ("A+B"), de 1888 e 1889 ("Bons dias"), recolhidos da "Gazeta de notícias." Organização, prefácio e notas de R. Magalhães Júnior. [Rio de Janeiro] Editora Civilização Brasileira, especialmente para a Companhia Distribuidora de Livros [1956]
277 p. 21 cm.

I. Magalhães, Raymundo, ed. II. Title.

PQ9697.M18D5 57-25504 ‡
Library of Congress [3]

Magalhães, Raymundo, ed.

Brazil
M869.3
M18i
Machado de Assis, Joaquim Maria, 1839-1908.
Idéias e imagens de Machado de Assis; dicionário antológico, com mil verbêtes, abrangendo tôda a obra machadiana, desde a colaboração em "A Marmota" até o "Memorial de Aires," [ed. by Raymundo Magalhães, Junior] [Rio de Janeiro] Editora Civilização Brasileria, 1956.
220p. 21½cm.

Magalhaes, Raymundo, ed.

Brazil
M869.3
M18r
Machado de Assis, Joaquim Maria, 1839-1908.
Ao redor de Machado de Assis (pesquisas e interpretacões). (Edicão ilustrada, comemorativa do cinquentenário da morte de Joaquim Maria Machado de Assis - 1839-1908). [ed. by Raymundo Magalhães, Junior] Rio de Janeiro, Editôra Civilizacão Brasileira, 1958.
285p. port. illus. 21½cm.

Magazine verse.

M811.08 B73

Braithwaite, William Stanley Beaumont, 1878- ed.
Anthology of magazine verse for 1913-29 and yearbook of American poetry, edited by William Stanley Braithwaite. New York, G. Sully and company, inc. [1913]-29.
17 v. 22 cm.
1926: Sesqui-centennial edition.
Imprint varies: 1913-14, Cambridge, Mass., Issued by W. S. B.—1915, New York, Gomme & Marshall.—1916, New York, L. J. Gomme.—1917-22, Boston, Small, Maynard & company.—1923-27, Boston, B. J. Brimmer company.—1928, New York, H. Vinal, ltd.—1929, New York, G. Sulley and company, inc.
1. American poetry—20th cent. I. Title. II. Title: Magazine verse. III. Title: Yearbook of American poetry.
Library of Congress PS614.B7 15—26325 [47r36m1]

Magazine verse.

M811.08 B73

Braithwaite, William Stanley Beaumont, 1878- ed.
Anthology of magazine verse for 1913-29 and yearbook of American poetry, edited by William Stanley Braithwaite. New York, G. Sully and company, inc. [1913]-29.
17 v. 22 cm.
1926: Sesqui-centennial edition.
Imprint varies: 1913-14, Cambridge, Mass., Issued by W. S. B.—1915, New York, Gomme & Marshall.—1916, New York, L. J. Gomme.—1917-22, Boston, Small, Maynard & company.—1923-27, Boston, B. J. Brimmer company.—1928, New York, H. Vinal, ltd.—1929, New York, G. Sulley and company, inc.
1. American poetry—20th cent. I. Title. II. Title: Magazine verse. III. Title: Yearbook of American poetry.
Library of Congress PS614.B7 15—26325 [47r36m1]

M39 M27n

Magee, James H 1839-
The night of affliction and morning of recovery. An autobiography. By Rev. J. H. Magee ... Cincinnati, O., The author, 1873.
xi, [13]-173 p. front. (port.) 18½cm.
~~1. Biography~~. 2. Canada
Library of Congress F185.97.M19 12-21894
Copyright 1873: 4539

... Magia sexualis.

M176 R15

Randolph, Paschal Beverly, 1825-1874.
... Magia sexualis. Traduction français, par Maria de Naglowska. Edition originale, Paris, R. Télin, 1931.
218p. 1 l. illus. plates. (incl music port. col.) port. fold. tables. 23cm.
At head of title: P. B. Randolph.

Brazil M869.1 Iv7m

Magias.
Ivo, Lêdo.
Magias. [Poesia] Rio de Janeiro, AGIR, 1960.
83 p. 23 cm.
I. Title.
PQ9697.I 9M3 61-29628 ‡
Library of Congress [1]

Magic.

M133 B56

Black Herman's easy pocket tricks which you can do. All new tricks... [New York, Martin Publishing Co., n.d.]
160p. illus. 22½cm.

W. Indies M133 Ah5b

Magic.
Ahmed, Rollo.
The black art, by Rollo Ahmed; with an introduction by Dennis Wheatley, with 17 illustrations by C. A. Mills. London, J. Long, ltd. [1936]
292 p. incl. illus., plates. front. (port.) 22cm.
"First published 1936."
1. Magic. I. Title.
Library of Congress BF1589.A35 37-2818 [3] [159.9614] 133.4

Upper Volta Magic Africa.
M966.25 D59s

Dim Delobsom, A A.
... Les secrets des sorciers noirs. Avec une préface de Robert Randau [pseud.] ... Paris, Librairie Émile Nourry, 1934.
298 p., 1 l. illus., plates. 22½cm. (Collection science et magie. no 5)
At head of title: Dim Delobsom A. A.
"Cet ouvrage a obtenu le Grand prix de l'Afrique occidentale française (1934)"
1. Magic—Africa. I. Arnaud, Robert, 1873- II. Title.
A C 35-2867
Title from N. Y. Pub. Libr. Printed by L. C. [3]

South Africa
M916.8 M27

Magidi, Dora Thizwilondi, ~~pseud.~~ (1940-)
Black background; the childhood of a South African girl [by] John Blacking. New York, Abelard-Schuman [1964]
207 p. illus. 22 cm.
"Based on the autobiography of Dora Thizwilondi Magidi."
Bibliography: p. 203-207.
1. Negroes in South Africa. I. Blacking, John. II. Title.
DT761.M16 916.8 64-12734
Library of Congress [5]

Haiti M972.94 M27h

Magloire, Auguste.
Histoire d'Haiti d'apres un plan nouveau base sur l'observation des faits (1804-1909) Edition Speciale a l'usage des aduetes et des gens du monde... Port-au-Prince, Imprimerie-Lebrairie du "Matin", 1909-1911.
3v. 23½cm.
1. Haiti—History.

Haiti M844 M27r

Magloire, Jean.
... Remarques; préface de Léon Laleau. Port-au-Prince, Haïti, Impr. du Collège Vertières [1940?]
3 p. l., 5-103 p. 18cm.
1. Journalists—Correspondence, reminiscences, etc. I. Title.
44-38541
Library of Congress PQ3949.M15R4 [2] 848.91

Haiti M972.94 R72t

Magloire, Paul Eugene, pres. of Haiti, 1907-
Rosemond, Henri Chrysostome.
The truth about Haiti and the new deal government with Colonel Paul E. Magloire. N.Y., Haitian publishing co., 1950.
11p. 23cm.

Haiti M641 M27c

Magloire-Prophète, Herzulie.
Cuisine, selectionnée. Port-au-Prince [Impr. H. Deschamps, 1955]
xiv, 203 p. illus. 23 cm.
1. Cookery, Haitian.
A 57-4834
Florida. Univ. Library for Library of Congress [1]

Haiti M843.91 M26p

Magloire-Saint-Aude, Clément
Parias; documentaire. [Port-au-Prince, Imprimerie de l'Etat, 1949]
100p. 21cm.
I. Title.

West Indies M808.8 H839

Magloire-Saint-Aude, Clement
The wake. Translated by Frances Frenaye.
Pp. 202-204.
In: Howes, Barbara, ed. From the Green Antilles. New York, Macmillan, 1966.

Haiti M843.91 M27b

Magny, Elizabeth Arnoux
La belle de Montjoly; roman guyanais. Paris, Editions Denoël, 1941.
217p. 19cm.
I. Title.

Haiti M843.91 M27

Magny, Elizabeth Arnoux
Ces dames Catinat, roman. Port-au-Prince, Henri Deschamps, n.d.
144p. 21cm.
1. Haitian fiction
I. Title

Africa M266 St29t

Mahabane, Zaccheus Richard, 1881-
Problems of the African church.
Pp. 135-146.
In: Stauffer, Milton Theobald, ed. Thinking with Africa; chapters by a group of nationals interpreting the Christian movement. New York, Published for the Student Volunteer Movement for Foreign Missions by the Missionary Education Movement of the United States and Canada, 1927.

Mali M966.2 M31d

Mahmūd Kati ibn al-Ḥāj al-Mutawakkil Kāti 1468-1593.
Documents arabes relatifs à l'histoire du Soudan: Tarikh El-Fettach; où chronique du chercheur pour servir a l'histoire des Villes, des Armées et des principaux personages du Tekrour par Mahmoûd ben El 'Hâdj El-Mataouakkel Kâti. tr. Française par O. Houdas et M. Delafosse. Paris, Ernest Leroux, 1913.
2v. 28½cm.
Contents. V.1- Text Arabe. V.2.- Traduction par O. Houdas et M. Delafosse.
See next card

Card 2

Mali M966.2 M31d

Mahmūd Kati ibn al-Ḥāj al-Mutawakkil Kāti 1468-1593.
Documents arabes...Paris, Ernest Leroux, 1913.
Contents. V.1 - Text Arabe. V.2.- Traduction par O. Houdas et M. Delafosse.
1. Sudan, French-History. 2. Timbuktu-History. I. Houdas, Octave Victor, 1840-1916, tr. II. Delafosse, Maurice. III. Title: Tarikh El-Fettach.

Mahone, William.

M283 B73p No.8

Bragg, George Freeman, 1863-1940.
The hero of Jerusalem in honor of the one hundred anniversary of the birth of General William Mahone of Virginia, by the Rev. George F. Bragg.
[28] p. 20cm.

Mahone, William.

M283 Bragg, George Freeman, 1863-1940.
B73p The ehro of Jerusalem in honor of the One
no.8 hundreth anniversary of the birth of General
William Mahone of Virginia, by the Rev. George
F. Bragg.

[28]p. 20cm.

Jamaica
M823.91 Mais, Roger, 1905-1955.
M28f Face, and other short stories. Kingston,
Universal Printery, 1942.

109p.

1. Jamaican fiction 2. Jamaican poetry

Maitre Adam le Calabrais.

France
M840 Dumas, Alexandre, 1824-1895.
D891ma Maitre Adam le Calabrais. Bruxelles, Meline,
Cans et cie., 1839.

237p. 15cm.

Basutoland
M896 Mailo, Mallane L.
M28 Ngoanana ha a botsa telejane. Morija,
Sesuto Book Depot, 1947.

32 p. 18½ cm.
An unahppy young wife. Written in Sotho.

West Indies
M808.8 Mais, Roger, 1905-1955.
H839 Listen, the wind.

Pp. 87-92.

In: Howes, Barbara, ed. From the green
Antilles. New York, Macmillan, 1966.

Majors and minors;

M811.4 Dunbar, Paul Lawrence, 1872 - 1906
D91m Majors and minors; poems, by Paul Lawrence
Dunbar. [Toledo, Ohio, Hadley and Hadley,
printers, c1895]

Basutoland
M896 Mailo, Mallane L.
M28r Ramasoabi le potso. Morija, Sesuto
depot, 1947.

30 p. 18 cm.
"Father of weeping" written in Sotho.

Le maître d'école.

Guinea
M896.2 Fodeba, Keita, 1921-
F68m Le Maître d'école suivi de minuit.
Paris, Pierre Seghers [1932]

26p. 18cm.
Portrait of author on back cover.

I. Title: Le maîtee d'école. II. Title:
Minuit.

Africa,
South
M968 Makapan, Obed M , 1907-
Sp6s Apartheid as I see it.

pp. 119-122.
In: South Africa the road ahead, comp. by
Hildegarde Spottiswoode. 1960.

Maïmouna.

Sénégal
M896.3 Sadji, Abdoulaye, 1910-
Salm Maïmouna; roman. Paris, Présence Africaine,
1958.

251p. 18½cm.

S. Africa
M266 Majeke, Nosipho, pseud.
M28r The Rôle of the missionaries in conquest.
Johannesburg, Society of Young Africa, 195?

140p. 21½cm.

1. Africa, South - Missionaries. 2.
Missionaries - Africa, South. I. Title.

Make, Vsumsi.

M973 Liberation Committee for Africa.
L614n Nationalism, colonialism and the United
States one minute to twelve; a forum.
First anniversary celebration, June 2, 1961.
[New York] Photo-Offset Process, 1961.

39p. 23cm.

Zambia
M896.3 Mainza, M C
M28k Kabuca Uleta Tunji [Everyday brings some-
thing new] London, University of London
Press, 1956.

78p. 18cm.
Written in Tonga.

I. Title.

La Maison du bonheur.

Martinique
M843.9 Maran, René, 1887-
M32ma La maison du bonheur. Paris, Édition du
Beffroi, 1909.

163p. 19cm.

Make way for happiness.

M811.5 Butler, Alpheus.
B97 Make way for happiness, by Alpheus Butler. Boston, The
Christopher publishing house [1932]

x p., 1 l., [13]-133 p. 21cm.
Poems.

I. Title.

[Full name: James Alpheus Butler]
32-19489

Library of Congress PS3503.U84M3 1932
Copyright A 53240 [2] 811.5

Jamaica
M823.91 Mais, Roger, 1905-1955.
M28b Black lighnting. London, Jonathan Cape,
1955.

222p. 19½cm.
Portrait of author on jacket.

I. Title.

La Maison du Docteur.

France
M840 [Dumas, Alexandre] 1802-1870.
D89ri Richard Darlington, drame en trois actes
et en prose, précédé de La Maison de Docteur,
prologue par MM Dinaux, Paris, J. N. Barba,
Libraire, 1832.

132p. 20½cm.

Make way for happiness.

M811.5 Butler, Alpheus.
B97 Make way for happiness, by Alpheus Butler. Boston, The
Christopher publishing house [1932]

x p., 1 l., [13]-133 p. 21cm.
Poems.

I. Title.

[Full name: James Alpheus Butler]
32-19489

Library of Congress PS3503.U84M3 1932
Copyright A 53240 [2] 811.5

Jamaica
M823.91 Mais, Roger, 1905-1955.
Sa3w Blackout.

Pp. 182-185.

In: Salkey, Andrew, ed. West Indian
stories. London, Faber and Faber, 1960.

Maitre Adam le Calabrais.

France
M840 Dumas, Alexandre, 1824-1895
D891ma Maitre Adam le Calabrais. Bruxolles, Meline,
Cans et cie, 1839.

237p. 15cm.

South
Africa
M896.4 Makeba, Sol
W15 Ubugqira Kwa-Ntu.

Pp. 63-78.
Written in Xhosa.
In: Wallis, S. J., comp. and ed. Inkolo
namasiko. London, Society for Promoting
Christian Knowledge, 1930.

Makerere University College, Kampala
Africa
M960
Af83
African Conference on Progress Through Cooperation, Kampala, Uganda, 1965.
Africa; progress through cooperation. Edited by John Karefa-Smart. Introd. by S. O. Adebo. New York, Dodd, Mead, 1966.
xvi, 288 p. 22 cm.
"Organized by the Council on World Tensions in association with Makerere University College and held on the university campus in Kampala, Uganda, May 9-15, 1965."
1. Africa—Collections. I. Karefa-Smart, John, ed. II. Council on World Tensions. III. Kampala—Uganda. Makerere University College. IV. Title.
DT30.A382 1965aa 916.008 66-12609
Library of Congress

Malagasy language.
Madagascar
M969.1 Ramandraivonona, Désiré.
R142 Le Malgache; sa langue, sa religion. Paris, Présence africaine [1959]
241 p. 9 illus. 25 cm.
"Bibliographie": p. [239]-241.
1. Malagasy language. 2. Madagascar—Religion. I. Title.
PL5379.R3 A 59-8219
Chicago. Univ. Libr. for Library of Congress

Malawi
M968.97 Malekebu, Bennett E
M29 Unkhoswe waanyanja. [Dialogues on guardianship] Edited by Guy Atkins. Cape Town, London, Oxford University Press, 1952.
124p. 18½cm. (Annotated African Texts. Mananja, I)
Written in Nyanja.
1. Nyanja (African people) 2. Nyasaland. I. Title.

Nigeria Makers of Nigerian Law.
M966.9 Elias, Taslim Olawale.
EL4m Makers of Nigerian law. [London] 1956.
55 p. 21 cm.
"Reprinted from West Africa, November 19, 1955-July 7, 1956."
1. Law—Nigeria—Hist. & crit. I. Title.
61-27123 ‡
Library of Congress

Malagasy philosophy.
Madagascar
M969 Andriamanjato, Richard
An2t Le tsiny et le tody dans la pensée Malgache. Paris, Presence Africaine, 1957.
100p. 25½cm.

Congo, Leopolville
M896.3 Malembe, Timothée
M23 Le mystere de l'enfant disparu. Léopold-Bibliotheque de l'Etoile, [n.d.]
85p. illus. 20½cm. (Collection l'Afrique Reconte no. 1)
"Ouvrages consultes"; p. 85.
1. Africa, South-Fiction. I. Title.

Making your community Christian.
M261 Burroughs, Nannie Helen, 1879—
B94m Making your community Christian, by Nannie H. Burroughs. Washington, D. C., Woman's Convention [n.d.]
100 p. 19 cm.

Malagasy poetry.
Africa
M896.1 Wake, Clive, ed.
W137 An anthology of African and Malagasy poetry in French. London, Oxford University Press, 1965.
179p. 18½cm.
White editor.
1. African poetry. 2. Malagasy poetry. I. Title.

Le Malgache, sa langue, sa religion.
Madagascar
M969.1 Ramandraivonona, Désiré.
R142 Le Malgache; sa langue, sa religion. Paris, Présence africaine [1959]
241 p. 9 illus. 25 cm.
"Bibliographie": p. [239]-241.
1. Malagasy language. 2. Madagascar—Religion. I. Title.
PL5379.R3 A 59-8219
Chicago. Univ. Libr. for Library of Congress

Basutoland
M896
M29s Makoa, Jeremia.
Sefofu Bartimea. Morija, Sesuto Book Depot, 1939.
29 p. 17½ cm.
Bartimous, the blind man, a Bible story in Sotho.

Malawi - History.
Malawi
M968.97 Mwase, George Simeon, ca. 1880-1962.
M98 Strike a blow and die; a narrative of race relations in colonial Africa. Edited and introduced by Robert I. Rotberg. Cambridge, Mass., Harvard University Press, 1967.
xlii, 135 p. map, ports. 22 cm.
Bibliographical footnotes.
1. Chilembwe, John, d. 1915. 2. Malawi—Hist. I. Rotberg, Robert I., ed. II. Title.
DT862.M68 968.97'020924 (B) 66-21342
Library of Congress

Mali.
Sénégal
M966.3 Dia, Mamadou.
D54a The African nations and world solidarity. Translated from the French by Mercer Cook. New York, Praeger [1961]
145 p. 22 cm. (Books that matter)
1. Africa—Econ. condit.—1918- 2. Africa—Foreign economic relations. 3. Nationalism—Africa. 4. Mali. I. Title.
HC502.D417 960.3 61—17815 ‡
Library of Congress

Congo, Leopoldville
M396 Makonga, Bonaventure
M28 La mere Africaine. Bruxelles, Editions Remarques Congolaises, 1964.
113p. ports. 19cm. (Collection Etudes Congolaises, no. 11)
Portrait of author in book.
1. Women in the Congo. 2. Women, African. I. Title.

Malcolm X speaks.
M301 Little, Malcolm, 1925-1965.
L726m Malcolm X speaks; selected speeches and statements. [Edited with prefatory notes, by George Breitman] New York, Merit Publishers, 1965.
xiii, 242p. illus., ports. 22cm.
1. Race question. 2. Civil rights. 3. Black Muslims. I. Breitman, George, ed. II. Title.

Mali.
U.S.
M960 Skinner, Elliott Percival, 1924- ~~Chu, Daniel.~~
Sk34 A glorious age in Africa; the story of three great African empires [by] Daniel Chu and Elliott Skinner. Illustrated by Moneta Barnett. [1st ed.] Garden City, N. Y., Doubleday, 1965.
120 p. col. illus., col. maps. 22 cm. (Zenith books)
1. Africa—History, Juvenile. I. Chu, Daniel. ~~I. Skinner, Elliott Percival, 1924- joint author.~~ II. Title. 2. Mali. 3. Songhay.
DT23.C5 1965 j 960 65-10280
Library of Congress

La mala espalda.
Ecuador
M863.6 Ortiz, Adalberto, 1914-
Or8m La mala espalda, once relatos de aquí y de allá; ilustraciones de Enrique Tábara, Diógenes Paredes y de Albistur. la edición. Guayaquil, Ecuador, La Casa de la Cultura Ecuatoriana, 1952.
161p. 20cm.

A maldição de Canaan.
Brazil
M869.3 Crusoe, Romeu.
C88m A maldição de Canaan; romance. [Rio de Janeiro, Irmãos Di Giorgio, 1951.
231 p. 19 cm.
I. Title.
PQ9697.C753M3 52-22307 ‡
Library of Congress

Guinea Mali - History.
M966.24 Niane, Djibril Tamsir
N51r Recherches sur l'empire du Mali au Moyen Âge. Conakry, Institut National de Recherches et de Documentation, 1962.
70p. 24cm.
1. Mai - History. I. Title.

Les maladies en Haiti.
Haiti Léon, Rulx
M610 Les maladies en Haiti. Port-au-Prince, Imp. de l'Etat, [1954]
L55 xxxiii, 345p. 18cm. (Collection du tricinquantenaire (1804-1954)

M331 Male Negro skilled workers in the United States, 1930-1936.
W37 Weaver, Robert Clifton, 1907-
Male Negro skilled workers in the United States, 1930-1936, by Robert C. Weaver, Administrator of survey, Ira DeA. Reid ... Preston Valien ... Charles S. Johnson ... Sponsored by United States Department of the Interior .... Washington, D.C. Govt. Print. Off., 1939.
vi, 87p. tables graphs 29cm.

Mali - Politics and government - Addresses, essays, lectures.
Senegal
M335 Senghor, Léopold Sédar.
Se5 On African socialism. Translated and with an introd. by Mercer Cook. New York, Praeger [1964]
xv, 173 p. 21 cm.
Bibliographical references included in "Notes" (p. 167-173)
CONTENTS.—Nationhood: report on the doctrine and program of the Party of African Federation.—The African road to socialism.—The theory and practice of Senegalese socialism.
1. Senegal—Pol. & govt.—Addresses, essays, lectures. 2. Mali—Pol. & govt.—Addresses, essays, lectures. 3. Socialism in Africa—Addresses, essays, lectures. I. Title.
JQ3396.A91S4 1964 64—16419
Library of Congress

Mali Empire.
Guinea
M966.24
N51
Niane, Djibril Tamsir.
Soundjata; ou, L'épopée mandingue. Paris, Présence africaine [1960]
154 p. illus. 18 cm.

1. Mali Empire. I. Title. II. Title: L'épopée mandingue.

DT532.2.N5 61-48937 ‡
Library of Congress [1]

Kenya
M396
G19w
Malinda, T N tr.
Garriock, L H
Wia wa mũndũ mũka e mũsyĩ [The work of women in the home. Tr. by T. N. Malinda] Nairobi, Eagle Press, 1950.
16p. 18cm.
Written in Kamba.
Cover title.
White author.

Africa
M398
T69p
Malinké.
Travélé, Moussa.
Proverbs et contes Bambara accompagnés d'une traduction française et précédés d'un abrégé de droit coutumier Bambara et Malinke, par Moussa Travélé. Paris, Librairie Orientaliste Paul Geuthner, 1923.
240p. 22cm.

M326.99B
Al 1h
Mallalieu, Willard Francis, bp., 1828-
Albert, *Mrs.* Octavia Victoria (Rogers) 1853-1889?
The house of bondage; or, Charlotte Brooks and other slaves, original and life-like, as they appeared in their old plantation and city slave life; together with pen-pictures of the peculiar institution, with sights and insights into their new relations as freedmen, freemen, and citizens, by Mrs. Octavia V. Rogers Albert, with an introduction by Rev. Bishop Willard F. Mallalieu, D. D. New York, Hunt & Eaton; Cincinnati, Cranston & Stowe, 1890.
xiv p., 1 l., 161 p. incl. front. (port.) 19cm.
1. Slavery in the U. S.—Condition of slaves. 2. Negroes. I. Mallalieu, Willard Francis, bp., 1828-
Library of Congress E444.A33 10-33441
[30d1]

M89
P36m
Mallas, Aris A
Forty years in politics; the story of Ben Pelham, by Aris A. Mallas, Jr., Rea McCain [and] Margaret K. Hedden. Detroit, Wayne State University Press, 1957.
92 p. illus. 24 cm.

1. Pelham, Benjamin B., 1862-1948. 2. Finance, Public—Wayne Co., Mich. 3. Wayne Co., Mich.—Pol. & govt. I. Title.
4. Politics. II. The Plaindealer. 5. Detroit, Michigan.
F572.W4P4 923.573 57—10562 ‡
Library of Congress [59f5]

France
M840
D89ge
Mallefille, Jean Pierre Felicien, 1813-1868, supposed author.
Dumas, Alexandre, 1802-1870.
Dumas' Georges; an intermediate French reader; edited with introduction, notes, and vocabulary by W. Napoleon Rivers ... and John Frederic Matheus ... Washington, D. C., The Associated publishers [°1936]
2 p. l., vii-xi p., 1 l., 233 p. 17cm.
Attributed by Mirecourt to Mallefille. *cf.* A. F. Davidson, Alexandre Dumas, 1902, p. 397.
1. French language—Chrestomathies and readers. I. Rivers, William Napoleon, 1897- ed. II. Matheus, John Frederic, joint ed. III. Mallefille, Jean Pierre Félicien, 1813-1868, supposed author. IV. Title: Georges.
Library of Congress PQ2227.G4 1936 36-37277
——— Copy 2.
Copyright A 100966 [3] 843.76

M796
L92h
Mallory, Edward J., ed.
Louis, Joe, 1914-
How to box, ed. by Edward J. Mallory. Philadelphia, D. McKay Co. [1948]
64 p. illus. 27 cm.

1. Boxing. I. Mallory, Edward J., ed. II. Title.
GV1137.L8 796.83 48—3663*
Library of Congress [50f²10]

Kenya
M896.3
M29s
Malo, S
Sigend Luo ma duogo chuny [Merry stories] Ogor gi W. S. Agutu. Nairobi, Eagle Press, 1951.
42p. illus. 21½cm. (Treasury of East African stories)
Written in Luo.
1. Short stories - Kenya. I. Title. II. Agutu, W. S., illus. III. Series.

Kenya
M967.62
M29d
Malo, Shadrak
Dhoudi mag central Nyanza [Clans of central Nyanza] Kampala, The Eagle Press, 1953.
173p. map 21½cm. (A treasury of East African history)
Written in Luo
1. Kenya - history.

Trinidad
M323
M29af
Maloney, Arnold Hamilton, 1888-
After England—we; nationhood for Caribbea. Boston, Meador Pub. Co. [1949]
183 p. map. 21 cm.

1. West Indies—Pol. & govt. 2. West Indies—Econ. condit.—1918- 3. West Indies—Civilization. I. Title.
F1608.M28 972.9 49-5870*
Library of Congress [8]

Trinidad
M323
M29am
Maloney, Arnold Hamilton, 1888-
Amber gold; an adventure in autobiography, by A. H. Maloney ... Boston, Meador publishing company [1946]
448 p. 20½cm.

I. Title.
Library of Congress E185.97.M25A3 46-7137
[5] 920

Trinidad
M323
M29p
Maloney, Arnold Hamilton, 1888-
Pathways to democracy, by ... Arnold Hamilton Maloney ... Clarence McDonald Maloney ... [and] Arnold Hamilton Maloney, jr. ... Boston, Meador publishing company [1945]
589 p. 20½cm.

1. Democracy. 2. Minorities. ~~3. Negroes.~~ I. Maloney, Clarence McDonald, joint author. II. Maloney, Arnold Hamilton, 1916- joint author. III. Title.
Library of Congress * JC423.M32 45-1864
[8] 321.8

Trinidad
M323
M29s
Maloney, Arnold Hamilton. 1888-
Some essentials of race leadership, by Arnold Hamilton Maloney ... Xenia, O., The Aldine publishing house, 1924.
180, [4] p. 20cm.
Inscribed copy: For Mr. L. S. Alexander Gumby. With the compliments of the author, A. H. Maloney.

~~1. Negro race.~~ 2. U. S.—Race question. I. Title.
Library of Congress E185.61.M25 24-6120
——— Copy 2.
Copyright A 777566 [2]

Trinidad
M323
M29p
Maloney, Arnold Hamilton, 1916- joint author.
Maloney, Arnold Hamilton, 1888-
Pathways to democracy, by ... Arnold Hamilton Maloney ... Clarence McDonald Maloney ... [and] Arnold Hamilton Maloney, jr. ... Boston, Meador publishing company [1945]
589 p. 20½cm.

1. Democracy. 2. Minorities. 3. Negroes. I. Maloney, Clarence McDonald, joint author. II. Maloney, Arnold Hamilton, 1916- joint author. III. Title.
Library of Congress * JC423.M32 45-1864
[8] 321.8

Trinidad
M323
M29p
Maloney, Clarence McConald, joint author.
Maloney, Arnold Hamilton, 1888-
Pathways to democracy, by ... Arnold Hamilton Maloney ... Clarence McDonald Maloney ... [and] Arnold Hamilton Maloney, jr. ... Boston, Meador publishing company [1945]
589 p. 20½cm.

1. Democracy. 2. Minorities. 3. Negroes. I. Maloney, Clarence McDonald, joint author. II. Maloney, Arnold Hamilton, 1916- joint author. III. Title.
Library of Congress * JC423.M32 45-1864
[8] 321.8

Africa
M960
P92
no.16
Malonga, Jean, 1907-
Coeur D'Aryenne.
(In: Présence Africaine. Trois ecrivains noirs. Paris, Présence Africaine, 1954. 19cm. pp.161-285)

Congo
(Brazzaville)
M967.26
M291
Malonga, Jean, 1907-
La legende de m'pfoumou ma mazono. Paris Editions Africaines, 1954.
153p. 18½cm.

1. Legends-Brazzaville. I. Title.

Malu, pseud.
see
Lubin, Maurice

Congo, Leopoldville
M910
M29
Malula, Jos
Congo-Belgique. Bruxelles, Ultramare, 1953.
46p. illus. port. 21½cm.
Portrait of author in book.

1. Voyages and travels. I. Title.

Congo (Leopoldville)
M967.5
M29f
Malula, Joseph
Foyer heureux. Leverville, Bibliotheque de L'Etoile, 1951.
96p. 18½cm.

1. Marriage.

Congo
M896.3
K64c
Malulu, Paul.
Kitambala, Jérôme
Contes Africains, par Jerome Kitambala, Paul Malulu, Simon Mudiangu, and Robert Musungaie. Leverville (Congo Belge), Bibliotheque de l'Etoile, May 1955.
32p. illus. 18cm. (No. 97)

MB9
M29
Malvin, John, 1795-1880.
North into freedom; the autobiography of John Malvin, free Negro, 1795-1880. Edited and with an introd. by Allan Peskin. Cleveland, Press of Western Reserve University, 1966.
vii, 87 p. 23 cm.
"A book from Cleveland State University."
Bibliographical references included in "Notes to the introduction" (p. 22-24)
1. Negroes—Ohio. 2. Negroes—Civil rights. I. Peskin, Allan, ed. II. Title.
E185.97.M26A3 1966 66-28142
301.451960924 (B)
Library of Congress [8]

Mammy's cracklin' bread...
M811.5
Shlm
Shackelford, Theodore Henry.
Mammy's cracklin' bread, and other poems, by Theodore Henry Shackelford; cover illustration by the author ... [Philadelphia, Press of I. W. Klopp co., ©1916]
58 p., 1 l. front. (port.) 18cm. $0.50
I. Title.
Library of Congress PS3601.S5M3 1916 16-13167
Copyright A 433159

Man in the cane.
M813.5
C23m
Carrere, Mentis, 1891-
Man in the cane. [1st ed.] New York, Vantage Press [1956]
160 p. 21 cm.
I. Title.
PZ4.C315Man 56-5811 ‡
Library of Congress [2]

S. Africa
M896.1
M31a
Mama, G Soya
Amaqunube (imiHobe yesiXhosa), ngu G. Soya Mama no A. Z. T. Mbebe. London, Oxford University Press, 1950.
61p. 19cm.
1. Xhosa poetry. I. Title. II. Mbebe, A. Z. T.

Man.
M234.9
H58c
Hines, Samuel Theophilus.
Children of destiny, by Samuel Theophilus Hines. Los Angeles, Calif., DeVorss & co. [©1942]
3 p. l., 9-128 p. 21cm.
1. Fate and fatalism. 2. God. 3. Man. I. Title.
Library of Congress BL235.H5 42-8485
[2] 234.9

Man in the iron mask - Fiction.
France
M840
D89Lo
Dumas, Alexandre, 1802-1870.
Louise de La Vallière; or, The love of Bragelonne [!] A continuation of "The three musketeers", "Twenty years after", and "Bragelonne, the son of Athos". By Alex. Dumas. New rev. translation by H. Llewellyn Williams. New York, The F. M. Lupton publishing company [©1892]
459 p. 19cm. (On cover: The elite series. no. 9)
Written in collaboration with Auguste Maquet.
A translation of the middle portion of the Vicomte de Bragelonne.
Sequel: The man in the iron mask.
1. La Vallière, Louise Françoise de La Baume Le Blanc, duchesse de, 1644-1710—Fiction. 2. France—Hist.—Louis XIV, 1643-1715—Fiction. 3. Man in the iron mask—Fiction. I. Maquet, Auguste, 1813-1888, joint author. II. Williams, Henry Llewellyn, jr., tr. III. Title.
6—43423
Library of Congress (PZ3.D89Lo 2)
Copyright 1892: 5323 [a37g1]

Mamabolo, G G , jt. auth.
South Africa
M968
M36
Marwede, H T
Shall Lobolo live or die? Two opposing viewpoints on the passing of gift cattle in Bantu marriage, by H.T. Marwede and G.G. Mamabolo. Cape Town, The African Bookman, 1945.
30p. 18½cm.

Man.
Trinidad
M248
B394
Beguese, H Hugh
Man; evolutions unfinished product. New York, Vantage Press [1967]
119p. 21cm.
Portrait of author on book jacket.
I. Title.

Man know thyself.
M252
R13m
Raikes, John W 1850-
Man, know thyself. By John W. Raikes. 2d ed., rev. and enl. Wilmington, Del., H. A. Roop, printer, 1913.
92 p. 17½cm. $0.50
I. Title.
Library of Congress 13-8366
Copyright A 343851

Mamba na kima na hadithi nyingine.
Zanzibar
M896.3
D64ma
Diva, David Edward
Mamba na kima na hadithi nyingine [The crocodile and the monkey and other stories] London, University of London Press [1951]
32p. 18½cm.
Written in Swahili.
I. Title.

M323
W586am
A man called White.
White, Walter Francis, 1893-
A man called White, the autobiography of Walter White. New York, Viking Press, 1948.
viii, 382. 22cm.
Inscribed: For Arthur and Marian. Affectionately Walter White.
For other editions of this title, see entries under author's name.

The man next door.
M323
J13m
Jackson, Algernon Brashear, 1878-
The man next door, by Algernon Brashear Jackson ... Philadelphia, Neaula publishing company [©1919]
253 p. 19cm.
1. Negroes. 2. U. S.—Race question. I. Title.
Library of Congress E185.6.J12 20-3860
——— Copy 2.
Copyright A 565003 [4]

Haiti
M843.91
C27m
Mambo.
Casseus, Maurice A , 1909-
Mambo. Port-au-Prince, Seminaire Adventiste, 1949.
120p. illus. 22cm.
Edition du bi-centenaire de Port-au-Prince.

MB9
C53c
The man christened Josiah Clark.
Cade, John Brother, 1894-
The man christened Josiah Clark; who, as J. S. Clark, became president of a Louisiana State land grant college, by John B. Cade. 1st ed. New York, American Press, 1966.
202p. 21 cm.
Bibliography:p. 201-202.
Portrait of author on book cover.
1.Clark, Joseph Samuel, 1871-1944. 2.Southern University, Baton Rouge, La. I.Title.

Man of color.
MB9
So5m
1951
Somerville, John Alexander, 1882-
Man of color, an autobiography. With a Jamaica, Pioneer Press, 1951.
134p. 19cm.
Pocket book edition.

Mamie Mason ou un exercise de la bonne volonté.
M813.5
H57m
Himes, Chester B 1909-
Mamie Mason ou un exercise de la bonne volonté; roman. Traduit de l'Américain par Henri Collard. Paris, Plon, 1962.
229p. 25cm.

The man farthest down.
M314.4
W272m
Washington, Booker Taliaferro, 1859?-1915.
The man farthest down; a record of observation and study in Europe, by Booker T. Washington, with the collaboration of Robert E. Park. Garden City, New York, Doubleday, Page & company, 1912.
4 p. l., 3-390 p., 1 l. fold. map. 20½cm.
1. Labor and laboring classes—Europe. 2. Poor—Europe. I. Park, Robert E., joint author. II. Title.
12—22002
Library of Congress HD4851.W3
——— Copy 2.
Copyright A 320586 [a39k1]

Man of color.
MB9
So5m
Somerville, John Alexander, 1882-
Man of color, an autobiography. A factual report on the status of the American Negro today. [1st ed.] Los Angeles, L. L. Morrison, [1949.
170p. port. 24cm. (The Publisher's library. no.5)

"Mammy".
M813.5
B81m
Brown, Charlotte Hawkins.
"Mammy," an appeal to the heart of the South, by Charlotte Hawkins Brown ... [Boston, The Pilgrim press, ©1919]
viii, 18 p. front. (port.) 18½cm.
I. Title.
Library of Congress PS3503.R793M3 1919 20-12188
Copyright A 571301 [2]

Man has no rest in his life.
Nigeria
M896
O13m
Olisah, Sunday Okenwa, 1936-
Man has no rest in his life. [Onitsha, Nigeria, Okwumo Printing Press, n.d.]
40p. 21cm.

A man of the people.
Nigeria
M896.3
Ac4m
Achebe, Chinua, 1930-
A man of the people. London, Heinemann, [1966]
166p. 20½cm.
Portrait of author on book jacket.
I. Title.

Nigeria
M896.3
Ac4m2

A man of the people.
Achebe, Albert Chinua, 1930-
A man of the people. London, Heinemann, 1966.
[5], 167 p. 20½ cm. 18/-
(B 66-849)
A novel.
I. Title.
PZ4.A17Man 66-2335
Library of Congress [5]

Nigeria
M896.3
Ac4m3

A man of the people; a novel.
Achebe, Chinua
A man of the people; a novel. Introd. by K. W. J. Post. Garden City, N. Y., Doubleday, 1967.
141p. 18cm.
1. Title.

Nigeria
M896.3
Ol3ma

Man suffers.
Olisah, Sunday Okenwa, 1936-
Man suffers. [Makurdi, Nigeria, Progress Printing Works, 1960]
16p. 19½cm.

M191
M846

Man under stress.
Morton, Lena Beatrice.
Man under stress. New York, Philosophical Library [1960]
129 p. 22 cm.
Includes bibliography.
1. Philosophy. 2. Religion. I. Title.
B56.M65 101 60-13638 ‡
Library of Congress [5]

M813.5
S14m

Man walking on eggshells.
Simmons, Herbert.
Man walking on eggshells. Boston, Houghton Mifflin, 1962.
250 p. 21 cm.
I. Title.
Full name: Herbert Alfred Simmons.
PZ4.S593Man 62-7389 ‡
Library of Congress [5]

M811.5
D29m

The man with the pipe.
Davis, Walter Max.
The man with the pipe, by Walter Max Davis. Atlantic City, N.J., W. M. Davis, c 1945.
60p. 20½cm.

M813.5
W68m

The man who cried I am.
Williams, John Alfred, 1925-
The man who cried I am; a novel, by John A. Williams. [1st ed.] Boston, Little, Brown [1967]
403 p. 22 cm.
I. Title.
PZ4.W72624Man 67-18108
Library of Congress [68f5]

MB9
B798

Manchild in the promised land.
Brown, Claude, 1937-
Manchild in the promised land. New York, Macmillan [1965]
415 p. 22 cm.
Autobiographical.
1. Harlem, New York (City)—Soc. condit. I. Title.
E185.97.B86A3 309.17471 65-16938
Library of Congress [65f18]

Guadeloupe
M972.97
Al 1m

Le mandat colonial...
Alcandre, Jules
Le mandat colonial; analyse juridique et critique politique. Paris, Editions Europe-Colonies, 1935.
1?5p. 21cm.

M973
L82s

Mandates.
Logan, Rayford Whittingham, 1897-
The Senate and the Versailles mandate system, by Rayford W. Logan ... Washington, D. C., The Minorities publishers, 1945.
vi p., 1 l., 112 p. 22½cm.
Bibliography: p. 105-106.
1. U. S. Senate. 2. Mandates. I. Title.
45-8821
Library of Congress JX4021.L6 [46g2] 321.027

M973
L82o

Mandates - Africa.
Logan, Rayford Whittingham.
The operation of the mandate system in Africa, 1919-1927, with an introduction on the problem of the mandates in the post-war world, by Rayford W. Logan. Washington, D. C., The Foundation publishers, inc., 1942.
xii, 50 p. 24½cm.
1. Mandates—Africa. I. Title.
42-51490
Library of Congress JQ3505.L6 [43d2] 321.027

South Africa
M968
F9141

Mandela, Nelson Rolihlahla, 1918-
Friedmann, Marion Valerie, 1918- ed.
I will still be moved; reports from South Africa. Chicago, Quadrangle Books, 1963.
126p. illus., ports. 22cm.

South Africa
M968
F9141 2

Mandela, Nelson Rolihlahla, 1918-
Friedmann, Marion Valerie, 1918- ed.
I will still be moved; reports from South Africa. Chicago, Quadrangle Books, 1963.
126p. illus., ports. 22cm.

South Africa
M968
M313

Mandela, Nelson Rolihlahla, 1918-
No easy walk to freedom: articles, speeches, and trial addresses. Foreword by Ahmed Ben Bella. Introd. by Oliver Tambo. Edited by Ruth First. [London] Heinemann [1965]
xiv, 189p. ports. 22cm.
1. Segregation - Africa, South. 2. Africa, South - Race question. i. First, Ruth, ed. II. Title.

South Africa
M968
M313a

Mandela, Nelson Rolihlahla, 1918-
No easy walk to freedom: articles, speeches, and trial addresses. Foreword by Ahmed Ben Bella. Introd. by Oliver Tambo. Edited by Ruth First. New York, Basic Books [1965]
xiv, 189 p. ports. 22 cm.
1. Segregation—Africa, South. 2. Africa, South—Race question. I. First, Ruth, ed. II. Title.
DT779.7.M35 301.45196068 65-18219
Library of Congress [5]

M301
G623

Mandela, Nelson Rolihlahla, 1918-
Why I am ready to die.
Pp. 175-180
In: Goodman, Paul, 1911- ed. Seeds of liberation. New York, G. Braziller, 1965.

Fr. Guiana
M496
Eb71

Mandjia language - dictionary.
Éboué, Adolphe Felix Sylvestre, 1884-1944.
... Langues Sango, Banda, Baya, Mandjia. Notes grammatical s. Mots groupes d'après le sens. Phrases usuelles. Vocabulaire, par A. F. Éboué. Preface de M. Gaudefroy-Demombynes. Paris, Emile Larose, 1918.
iii, 109p. 19 x 11cm.

Haiti
M841
R81v

Les mandragores.
Roy, Herard C L.
... Les variations tropicales et Les mandragores. Port-au-Prince, Haiti, Imprimerie de l'état [193-?]
101 p. 19½cm.
Poems.
I. Title. II. Title: Les mandragores.
43-11373
Library of Congress PQ3949.R75V3 [2] 841.91

Kenya
M613.2
H88w

Mane midwaro?
Humphrey, Norman
Mane midwaro? Midenyo koso yieng'o? [Which do you want? Starvation or nutrition? Tr. by C. J. Amenya] Nairobi, Eagle Press, 1950
8p. illus. 21½cm. (Como ngima)
Written in Luo
I. Nutrition. I. Title. II. Series.
III. Amenya, C. J., tr.

Mauritius
M841
M44m

Les manèges de la mer.
Maunick, Edouard J
Les manèges de la mer. Paris, Présence Africaine [1964]
101p. 19½cm.
I. Title.

Basutoland
M896
M31h
1945

Mangoaela, Zekoa D.
Har'a libatana le linyamatsane. Morija, Sesuto Book Depot, 1945.
vi, 105 p. 16 cm.
Hunting stories. Written in Sesuto.

Basutoland
M896
M31h
1913

Mangoaola, Zokea D.
Har'a libatana le linyamatsane. Morija, Sesuto Book Depot, 1913.

205 p. 16 cm.
Written in Sesuto.

Basutoland
M896
M31l

Mangoaela, Zekea D.
Lithoko tsa Marena a Basotho, tse bokeletsoeng ke, Z. D. Mangoaela. Morija, Sesuto Book Depot, 1928.

246 p. 17½ cm.
"Praises of the Sotho Chiefs.

1. Poetry, African. 2. Basutoland.

Basutoland
M896
M31t

Mangoaela, Zakea D
Tsoelo-pele ea Lesotho. Morija, Sesuto Book Depot, 1928.

52 p. 18 cm.
The Progress of the Sotho People.

1. Africa, South-history.

Mangones, Edmond.

Haiti
M972.94
Ar7

L'art précolombien d'Haïti; catalogue de l'Exposition précolombienne organisée à l'occasion du IIIe Congrès des Caraibes sous le haut patronage de son excellence m^r^ Stenio Vincent, président de la République, présenté par mm. Edmond Mangones et le major Louis Maximilien. ₍Port-au-Prince, Imprimerie de l'état, 1941₎

29 p., 2 l. LXII pl. 28½^cm^.

"Il a été tiré de ce catalogue cinq cents exemplaires sur papier velvetone india paraphes."

1. Haiti—Antiq. 2. Indians of the West Indies—Haiti—Art. 3. Indians of the West Indies—Art. I. Congrès des Caraibes. 3d, Port-au-Prince, Haiti, 1941. II. Mangones, Edmond. III. Maximilien, Louis.

S 42-1 Revised

Smithsonian inst. Library for Library of Congress — F1909.A68 ₍r43c2₎† — 918.7294

M355.11
M31i

Manhattan Medical Society.
Identical care and treatment by the federal government; An open letter to the American Legion from The Manhattan Medical Society. New York, The Society, 1932.

M610
P19
V.1, no.11

3-10p. 23cm.

1. Veterans. 2. Hospitals, Military.
2. American Legion.

M610.6
M31p

Manhattan Medical Society. New York.
Past, present and future activities...; A brief review of major events and a forecast. ₍New York₎ the Society, 1935.

53p. 28cm. (Pamphlet no.3)
Mimeographed.

1. Medical societies.

M610
P19
v.1, no.10

Manhattan Medical Society, New York, N.Y.
Equal opportunity - no more - no less! Open letter to Mr. Edwin R. Embree, president of the Julius Rosenwald Fund, Chicago, Illinois from the Manhattan medical society. New York City, January 28, 1931.
8p. 20½cm.
1.Embree, Edwin R. 2.Hospitals. 3.Medicine. I.Title.

Nigeria
M966.9
M31z

Mani, Abdulmalik
Zuwan turawa nijeriya ta arewa. ₍Local history of Nigeria₎ Zaria, Norla; London, Longmans, Green and Co., 1957.

218p. 18½cm.
Written in Hausa.

1. Nigeria - History. I. Title.

Haiti
M972.94
M31r

Manigat, Leslie
La révolution de 1843; essai d'analyse historique d'une conjoncture de crise. ₍Port-au-Prince₎ le Normalien ₍1959₎

31p. 23cm.
Bibliography.

1. Haiti - History - Revolution. 2. Speeches. I. Title.

Haiti
M972.98
M31p

Manigat, Leslie F
La politique agraire du gouvernement d'Alexandre Petion (1807-1818). Port-au-Prince, Imp. La Phalange, 1962.

74p. 20½cm.

1. Haiti - History. 2. Pétion, Alexandre Sabès. I. Title.

Haiti
M972.94
M31p

Manigat, Leslie F
La politique agraire du gouvernement d'Alexandre Pétion (1807-1818). Port-au-Prince, Imp. La Phalange, 1962.

74p. 20½cm.

1. Haiti - History. 2. Pétion, Alexandre Sabès, Pres. Haiti, 1770-1818. Title.

Jamaica
M820
H38

Manley, Carmen
When fly bodder mauger mule.

Pp. 75-79.

In: Hendriks, A. L., ed. The independence anthology of Jamaican literature. Kingston, Arts Celebration Committee, Ministry of Development and Welfare, 1962.

Jamaica
M972.92
M31

Manley, Douglas
The West Indian in Britain, by Clarence Senior and Douglas Manley. Edited by Norman MacKenzie. London, Fabian Colonial Bureau, 1956.

29p. 21½cm.

1. West Indies-Emigration and Immigration.
2. Gt. Brit.-Emigration and Immigration.
I. Title.

Manley, Douglas.

West Indies
M325.27
F21

Family Welfare Association, *London.*
The West Indian comes to England; a report prepared for the Trustees of the London Parochial Charities by the Family Welfare Association. Contributors: Douglas Manley, Ivo de Souza, Albert Hyndman, et al. Edited by S. K. Ruck. London, Routledge & K. Paul ₍1960₎

187 p. 23 cm.

1. West Indians in Great Britain. I. Ruck, S. K., ed. II. Title.

DA125.W4F3 — 325.2729042 — 60-3053 ‡

Library of Congress ₍2₎

Jamaica
M820.8
M31b

Manley, Edna, *ed.*
Focus, Jamaica, 1943 ₍by₎ P. M. Sherlock, Cicely Howland, Roger Mais ... ₍and others₎ Edited by Edna Manley. ₍Kingston? City printery ltd., 1943?₎

cover-title, 180 (*i. e.* 181) p. plates. 23½^cm^.

"This collection of short stories, essays, plays and poems ... has been published by the co-operative effort of the contributors."—Foreword.

1. English literature (Selections, extracts) II. Title.

Jamaican lit.

A 46-602

New York. Public library for Library of Congress ₍2₎

Manners, Robert Alan, jt ed.

Africa
M960.3
D87a

Duffy, James, 1923- *ed.*
Africa speaks. Edited by James Duffy and Robert A. Manners. Princeton, N. J., Van Nostrand ₍1961₎

228 p. 23 cm.

1. Nationalism — Africa, Sub-Saharan. 2. Africa, South — Race question. I. Manners, Robert Alan, joint ed. II. Title.

Full name: James Edward Duffy.

DT30.D8 — 960.3 — 61-3312 ‡

Library of Congress ₍61q15₎

Man's relationship and duty to God.

M231
Sm63

Smith, Paul Dewey
Man's relationship and duty to God. New York, Carlton press ₍1964₎

546p. illus. 24cm. (A reflection book)

Haiti
M843.91
P41m

La mansarde.
Perez, Jeanne.
La mansarde. Port-au-Prince, Seminaire Adventiste, 1950.

175p. 19cm. (Collection La semeuse)

Mansart builds a school.

M301
D8530
V.2

Du Bois, William Edward Burghardt, 1868-
Mansart builds a school. New York, Mainstream Publishers, 1959.

367 p. 21 cm. (*His* The black flame, a trilogy, book 2)

I. Title.

PZ3.D8525Man — 59-65207 ‡

Library of Congress ₍2₎

Mantle, Robert Burns, 1873-1948, ed.

M812.5
B46

The Best plays. 1894/99-
New York ₍etc.₎ Dodd, Mead ₍etc.₎
v. illus. 21 cm.
Title varies: 1947/48-1949/50, The Burns Mantle best plays and the year book of the drama in America.—1950/51-1951/52, The Best plays and the year book of the drama in America.—1952/53, The Burns Mantle yearbook. The Best plays.
Other slight variations in title.
Added t. p., 1953/54- The Burns Mantle yearbook.
Editors: 1894/99, G. P. Sherwood, J. Chapman.—1899/1909-1946/47, B. Mantle (with G. P. Sherwood, 1899/1909-1909/19)—1947/48-1951/52, J. Chapman.—1952/53- L. Kronenberger.
INDEXES:
1899/1909-1949/50. 1 v.
1. Drama—20th cent. 2. Theater—U. S.—Yearbooks. 3. Drama—Bibl. I. Mantle, Robert Burns, 1873-1948, ed. II. Chapman, John Arthur, 1900- ed. III. Sherwood, Garrison P., ed. IV. Kronenberger, Louis, 1904- ed.
PN6112.B45 — 812.5082 — 20-21432*
Library of Congress ₍62r56t^56^15₎

The mantle of Dunbar and other poems.

M811.5
J624m

Johnson, Charles Bertram
The mantle of Dunbar and other poems. ₍by₎ Chas. Bertram Johnson. ₍Kirksville, Missouri₎ The author, 1917?₎
32p. 20cm.

... Manual de santería...

Cuba
M972.91 Lachatañeré, Rómulo.
L11

... Manual de santería; el sistema de cultos "lucumís." La Habana, Cuba, Editorial Caribe, 1942.

88, [7] p. incl. illus. (facsim.) map, tables. 20½cm. (On cover: Estudios afro-cubanos)

At head of title: R. Lachatañeré.

1. Cuba—Religion. 2. Negro race—Religion. 3. Negroes in Cuba. I. Title.

Library of Congress BL2530.C9L3 42—25316 [44c1] 299.64

Manuel d'histoire d'Haiti...1934.

M972.94 Brothers of Christian instruction of Ploërmel.
B79m

Manuel d'histoire d'Haïti, par le docteur J.-C. Dorsainvil, avec la collaboration des Frères de l'instruction chrétienne. Ouvrage approuvé par le Conseil de l'instruction publique d'Haïti, le 29 mars 1924. Port-au-Prince, Procure des Frères de l'instruction chrétienne, 1934.

3 p. l., 402 p. illus. (incl. ports., maps, facsims., coats of arms) 19½cm.

"Préface" signed: Frère Archange.

(Continued on next card)

A C 35—1591 [45r42e1]† 972.94

A manual on Action Group Party Organisation.

Nigeria
M966.9 Oredein, S T
Or27

A manual on Action Group Party Organisation. [Ibadan, Action Group Headquarter, n.d.]

57p. 21½cm.

A manual of research and thesis-writing...

M378 Ho Howard university, Washington, D. C.
H83m The Graduate School.

A manual of research and thesis-writing for graduate students. Washington, D. C., Howard university, The graduate school, 1941.

80p. 21cm.

Algeria
M965 Manuel de politique Musulmane.
Af8m

Paris, Brossard, 1925.

189p. 19cm.

1. Algeria. 2. Mohammedanism in Algeria. I. Title. II. Un Africain.

Manuel du conseiller général des colonies; les...

Guadeloupe
M972.97 Boisneuf, A René, 1873–
B63m

Manuel du conseiller général des colonies; les assemblées coloniales: conseils généraux, conseils coloniaux, par A. René-Boisneuf ... préface de M. Henry Simon ... Paris, E. Larose, 1922.

3 p. l., [v]–xiv p., 1 l., 482 p. 25½cm.

1. France—Colonies—Administration. 2. France—Colonies—Law. I. Title.

Library of Congress JV1862.B6 29-5055 [2]

Manuel illustré d'histoire de la littérature Haitienne.

Haiti
M840.9 Pompilus, Pradel
P77m

Manuel illustré d'histoire de la littérature Haitienne. Port-au-Prince, Editions Henri Deschamps, 1961.

613p. illus., ports. 19½cm.

M326.99B [illegible]
M24s

Strickland, S.

Negro slavery described by a Negro: being the narrative of Ashton Warner, a native of St. Vincent's. With an appendix containing the testimony of four Christian ministers recently returned from the colonies on the system of slavery as it now exists. By S. Strickland... London, Samuel Maunder, 1831.

144p. 15½cm.

Le manuscrit de mon ami.

Haiti
M843.9 Hibbert, Fernand.
H52m

... Le manuscrit de mon ami. Port-au-Prince, Imprimerie Chéraquit, 1923.

124 p., 1 l. 23cm. [With his Les simulacres ... Port-au-Prince, 1923]

I. Title.

Library of Congress PQ3949.H5S5 25-20878

Many a night's journey.

St. Kitts
M972.97 Thomas, Alexander, 1909–
T36m

Many a night's journey. New York, Comet Press Books, 1957.

143 p. 21 cm. (A Reflection book)

Autobiographical.

I. Title.

CT275.T536A3 818.5 57-8119 ‡

Library of Congress [3]

Many thousand gone.

M813.5 Fair, Ronald L
F15

Many thousand gone; an American fable, by Ronald L. Fair. [1st ed.] New York, Harcourt, Brace & World [°1965]

114 p. 21 cm.

Portrait of author on book cover.

I. Title.

PZ4.F1634Man 65-11987

Library of Congress [5]

Many thousand gone.

M326 Nichols, Charles Harold.
N515

Many thousand gone; the ex-slaves' account of their bondage and freedom, by Charles H. Nichols. Leiden, Brill, 1963.

xvi, 229 p. 25 cm. (Studies in American literature and history, 1)

Bibliography: p. [213]–224.

1. Negroes—Biog. 2. Slavery in the U. S.—Conditions of slaves. I. Title. (Series)

E444.N5 64-55501

Library of Congress [2]

S. Africa
M496 Manyase, ~~Lenchman Thozamile~~, 1915–
M31

Indlela yokubalwa kwamagama esi-Xhose ngolobalo olutsha. Lovedale, Lovedale Press, 1952.

20p. 18cm.

Collection of 27 exercises on the new Xhosa orthography.

Book review: South African Outlook, Dec. 1, 1952, p. 192.

1. Africa, South. 2. Xhosa grammar.

S. Africa
M896.1 Manyase, Lenchman Thozamile, 1915–
M31i

Izibongo Zabancinane. Johannesburg, The Lovedale Press, 1954.

38p. 18½cm.

1. Africa, South.

Uganda
M896.3 Manyindo, S T
M319h

Ha kyoto omu kairirizi [At the fireside in the evening. Ebisisani bikateerwa A.W.R. McCrae and Alan Jarman. Kampala, East African Literature Bureau, 1961.

44 p. illus. 21½ cm.

Written in Runyaro/Rutooro.

1. Title.

Manyolo, Betty, illus.

Uganda
M896.3 Mdoe, Janet Nsibirwa
M34e

Engero ennyimpi [Short stories] ebifaananyi byakubibwa Betty Manyolo. Nairobi, Eagle Press, 1960.

28p. illus. 24½cm.

Written in Luganda.

I. Title. II. Manyolo, Betty, illus.

Cuba
M861.6 [Manzano, Juan Francisco] 1797–1854.
M26

Poems by a slave in the island of Cuba, recently liberated; translated from the Spanish, by R. R. Madden, M. D., with the history of the early life of the negro poet, written by himself; to which are prefixed two pieces descriptive of Cuban slavery and the slave-traffic, by R. R. M. London, T. Ward & co., 1840.

4 p. l., v p., 1 l., [9]–188 p. 22½cm.

1. Slavery in Cuba. I. Madden, Richard Robert, 1798–1886, tr. II. Title. 2. Cuban poetry.

Library of Congress HT1076.M3 1-13046 Revised [r33b2]

Manzano, Juan Francisco, 1797–1854.

Cuba
MB Calcagno, Francisco, 1827–1903.
C12p
1887

Poetas de color, por Francisco Calcagno. Plácido, Manzano, Rodriguez, Echemendía, Silveira, Medina. Habana, Imp. militar de la v. de Soler y compañia, ~~1878~~. 1887

1 p. l., [5]–54 p. 23½cm.

1. Poets, Cuban. 2. Negro authors. I. Title.

[34b1] 22-9233

Library of Congress PQ7380.C3

Manzano, Juan Francisco, 1797–1854.

Cuba
MB Calcagno, Francisco, 1827–1903.
C12p

Poetas de color, por Francisco Calcagno. Plácido, Manzano, Rodriguez, Echemendía, Silveira, Medina. Habana, Imp. militar de la v. de Soler y compañia, 1878.

1 p. l., [5]–54 p. 23½cm.

1. Poets, Cuban. 2. Negro authors. I. Title.

[34b1] 22-9233

Library of Congress PQ7380.C3

A mão e a luve.

Brazil
M869.3 Machado de Assis, Joaquim Maria, 1839–1908.
M18ma

A mão e a luve. Rio de Janeiro, W. M. Jackson, Inc. Editôres, 1957.

242p. 20½cm. (Obras completas de Machado de Assis)

Basutoland Mapetla, Joase.
M896.1
M32L

Liphoofolo, Linonyana, Litaola le lithoko tsa tsona. Morija, Sesuto Book Depot, 1928.

32 p. 18½ cm.

In praise of animals, birds and divining bones with occasional comments.

Basutoland
M896.1 **Mapetla, Joase.**
M32L Liphoofolo, Linonyana, Litaola le lithoko tsa tsona. Morija, Sesuto Book Depot, 1928.

32p. 18½cm.
In praise of animals, birds and divining bones, with occasional comments.

1. Basutoland. Sotho language. Africa, South - literature.

Basutoland
M896.1 Mapetla, Joase
M32L2 Liphoofolo linonyana litaola, le lithoko tsa tsona. [Praise poems of animals, birds and divining bones] Morija, Basutoland, Mroija Sesuto Book Depot, 1942.

?0p. 16½cm.

I. Title.

Maps - Nigeria.
Nigeria
M912 **Oboli, Herbert Oguejiofo Nkemba**
Ob5 A sketch-map atlas of Nigeria, with notes and exercises. New ed. rev. London, George G. Harrap «1962»

46p. maps. 24½cm.

Maquet, Auguste, 1813-1888, joint author.
France
M840 Dumas, Alexandre, 1802-1870.
D89an Ange Pitou. Bruxelles, Meline, Cans and cie, 1851.

5 vols. 15½cm.

Maquet, Auguste, 1813-1888, joint author.
France
M840 Dumas, Alexandre, 1802-1870.
D89ch2 Le chevalier de Maison-Rouge. Bruxelles, Societe Belge de Librairie, 1845.

5 vols. in 2. 14½cm.

Maquet, Auguste, 1813-1888, jt. author.
France
M840 Dumas, Alexandre, 1802-1870.
D89co La collier de la reine, deuxième série des Mémoires d'un médecin. Bruxelles, Meline, Cans et compagnie, 1849.

6 vols. in 3. cm.

Maquet, Augusta, 1813-1888, joint author.
France
M840 Dumas, Alexandre, 1802-1870.
D89cou The Count of Monte-Cristo, Edmond Dantès. London Simpkin, Marshall & co., n.d.

339p. front., 19½cm.

Maquet, Auguste, 1813-1888, joint author.
France
M840 **Dumas, Alexandre, 1802-1870.**
D89Lo Louise de La Vallière; or, The love of Bragelione [!] A continuation of "The three musketeers", "Twenty years after", and "Bragelonne, the son of Athos". By Alex. Dumas. New rev. translation by H. Llewellyn Williams. New York, The F. M. Lupton publishing company [°1892]
459 p. 19 cm. (On cover: The elite series. no. 9)
Written in collaboration with Auguste Maquet.
A translation of the middle portion of the Vicomte de Bragelonne.
Sequel: The man in the iron mask.
1. La Vallière, Louise Françoise de La Baume Le Blanc, duchesse de, 1644-1710 — Fiction. 2. France — Hist. — Louis XIV, 1643-1715—Fiction. 3. Man in the iron mask—Fiction. I. Maquet, Auguste, 1813-1888, joint author. II. Williams, Henry Llewellyn, jr., tr. III. Title.
6—43623
Library of Congress (PZ3.D89Lo 2)
Copyright 1892: 5523 [a37g1]

Maquet, Auguste, 1813-1888, joint author.
France
M840 Dumas, Alexandre, 1802-1870.
D89me Mémoires d'un médecin, Joseph Balsamo. Bruxelles, Meline, Cans et Cie, 1846-1848.

10v. in 5. 16cm.
Written in collaboration with Auguste Maquet.
v. 3-4 missing.

Maquet, Auguste, 1813-1888, joint author.
France
M840 Dumas, Alexandre, 1802-1870.
D89sy Sylvandire. Bruxelles, Meline, Cans et cie., 1843.

2 vols.
Written in collaboration with Auguste Maquet.

El mar y la montana.
Cuba
M861.6 **Boti y Barreiro, Regine Eladio, 1878-**
B65m El mar y la montana (versiculos endennes) ...La Habana, Imprenta "El Siglo XX, 1921.

152p. 20½cm.

Brazil **...Mar morto, romance.**
M869.3 **Amado, Jorge.**
Amlm ... Mar morto, romance; 6th ed. Sao Paulo, Livraria Martins Editora, 1957.
251p. (His Os romances da Bahia. v)

I. Title.
87-16076
Library of Congress PQ9697.A647M3
[2] 869.3

Martinique
M843.9 Maran, René, 1887-
M32a Afrique équatoriale française, terres et races d'avenir. Texte de René Maran, illustré par Paul Jouve. Paris, Imprimerie de Vaugirard, 1937.

82p. plates, map 31½cm.

1. Africa, French Equatorial. I. Title.

Martinque
M843.9 **Maran, René, 1887-**
M32as Asepsie noire. Paris, Martinet, 1931.

45p. illus. 24cm.

1. Africa-Medicine. 2. Africa-Colonization. I. Title.

Martinique
M843.9 **Maran, René, 1887-**
M32b Bacouya, le cynocéphale, roman. Paris, A. Michel [1953]
241 p. 19 cm.

I. Title.
PQ2625.A74B24 53-32880 ‡
Library of Congress [1]

Martinique
M843.9 **Maran, René, 1887-**
M32ba ... Batouala; véritable roman nègre. Éd. définitive. Paris,
1938 A. Michel [1938]
3 p. l., [9]-250 p., 2 l. 19cm.
CONTENTS.—Batouala.—Youmba, la mangouste.

I. Title. II. Title: Youmba, la mangouste.
38-28241
Library of Congress PQ2625.A74B29 1938
Copyright A—Foreign 39301
[2]

Martinique
M843.9 **Maran, René, 1887-**
M32 ba Batouala, by René Maran. New York, T. Seltzer, 1922.
1922 4 p. l., 7-207 p. 19½cm.
N.Y. ed. Translated from the French by Adele Szold Seltzer.

I. Seltzer, Mrs. Adele Szold, 1876- tr. II. Title.
22—19479
Library of Congress PZ3.M33Ba
[45j1]

Martinique
M843.9 Maran, René, 1887-
M32ba Batouala, a Negro novel from the French of
1922 René Maran. London, Jonathan Cape, 1922.

192p. 22cm.
"Of this the first edition of Batouala, have been printed 1050 copies, of which 1000 only are for sale, copy no. 482."

I. Title.

Martinique
M843.9 Maran, René, 1887-
M32bat Batouala; ein echter Regerroman. Leipzig, Rhein, 1922.

211p. 18cm.

I. Title.

Martinique
M843.9 **Maran, René, 1887-**
M32ba ... Batouala; véritable roman nègre. Paris, A. Michel
1921 [°1921]
3 p. l., [9]-189 p., 1 l. 19cm.

I. Title.
21—21311
Library of Congress PQ2625.A74B29 1921
Copyright A—Foreign 18728
[39e1]

Martinique
M843.9 Maran, René,
B32ba Batoula, par René Maran, illustré de
1928 dessins par Iacovleff. Paris, Editions Mornay, 1928.

vii, 169p. illus. 25cm.

I. Title.

Martinique
M843.9
M32be
Maran, René, 1887-
...Les belles images; poèmes. Paris Editions Delmas, 1935.
86p. 19cm.
I. Title. 1. French poetry - Martinican authors.

Martinique
M89
M32f
Maran, René, 1887-
Félix Éboué, grand commis et loyal serviteur, 1885-1944. [Paris, Éditions parisiennes [°1957]
126 p. illus. 19 cm.
Includes bibliography.
1. Éboué, Adolphe Félix Sylvestre, 1884-1944.
DT546.E25M3 58-25839 ‡
Library of Congress [3]

Martinique
M843.9
M32ma
Maran, René, 1887-
La Maison du bonheur. Paris, Édition du Beffroi, 1909.
163p. 19cm.
I. Title.

Martinique
MB9
D87m
Maran, René, 1887-
Bertrand du Guesclin; l'épée du roi. Paris, Editions Albin Michel, 1960.
317p. maps. 20cm.
1. Du Guesclin, Bertrand. I. Title.

Martinique
M843.9
M32h
Maran, René, 1887-
Un homme pareil aux autres; roman. Paris, Editions arc-en-ciel, 1947.
248p. 18cm.
I. Title.

Martinique
M843.9
M32mb
Maran, René, 1887-
Mbala, l'éléphant. Illus. de André Collot. Paris, Éditions Arc-en-Ciel, 1943.
143 p. col. illus. 28 cm.
I. Title.
PQ2625.A74M3 843.91 49-33363*
Library of Congress [1]

Martinique
M843.9
M32bet
Maran, René, 1887-
... Bêtes de la brousse. Paris, A. Michel [1941]
3 p. l., [9]-258 p., 1 l. 18½cm.
I. Title. ~~1. French literature.~~
45-34153
Library of Congress PQ2625.A74B44
[2] 843.91

Martinique
M843.9
M32ho
Maran, René, 1887-
L'homme qui attend; roman inédit et complet, par René Maran.
(In: Les Oeuvres libres, v. 176. Paris, Fayard, 1936. 18cm. p.[37]-130)
I. Title.

Martinique
M843.9
M32pc
Maran, René, 1887-
... Le petit roi de Chimérie, conte; préface de Léon Bocquet. Paris, A. Michel [°1924]
237, [1] p. 19cm.
I. Bocquet, Léon, 1876- II. Title.
Library of Congress PQ2625.A74P4 1924 24-8818
Copyright A—Foreign 24205
[2]

Martinique
M843.9
M32br
Maran, René, 1887-
Brazza et la fondation de l'A.E.F. Cinquieme edition. Paris, Fallimard, 1941.
301p. illus. map. 21cm.
I. Title. 1. Congo, Belgian. 2. Brazzaville Congo, Belgian - Disc. & expl.

Martinique
M843.9
M32j
Maran, René, 1887-
Journal sans date.
(In: Les Oeuvres libres, v. 71. Paris, Fayard, 1927. 18cm. p. [105]-236)
I. Title.

Martinique
M843.9
M32pi
Maran, René, 1887-
... Les pionniers de l'empire ... Paris, A. Michel [1943-
2 v. port., maps (part double) 20cm.
"Bibliographie": v. 1, p. [335]-339.
CONTENTS.—1. Jean de Béthencourt. Anselme d'Isalguier. Binot le Paulmier de Gonneville. Jacques Cartier. Jean Parmentier. Nicolas Durand de Villegaignon. Jean Ribaut. —v.2 Samuel Champlain. Belain d'Esnambuc. Robert Cavelier de la Salle.
1. Explorers, French. 2. France—Colonies—Biog. I. Title.
46—13128
Library of Congress G255.M3
[47c1] 923.944

Martinique
M843.9
M32c
Maran, René, 1887-
... Le cœur serré, roman. Paris, A. Michel [°1931]
4 p. l., [11]-252 p. 19½cm.
I. Title.
Library of Congress PQ2625.A74C6 1931 31-20181
Copyright A—Foreign 12464
[2] 843.91

Martinique
M843.9
M32L
Maran, René, 1887-
... Livingstone et l'exploration de l'Afrique. Dix-huit reproductions et trois cartes. [Paris] Gallimard [1938]
5 p. l., [13]-276 p., 1 l. incl. plates, port., maps. 21cm. (La découverte du monde, collection dirigée par Raymond Burgard. [3])
1. Livingstone, David, 1813-1873. 2. Africa, Central—Disc. & explor. 3. Africa, South—Descr. & trav.
39-18318
Library of Congress DT731.L8M27
Copyright A—Foreign 30649
[2] [922.842] 923.942

Martinique
M843.9
M32s
Maran, René, 1887-
Savorgnan de Brazza. Éd. définitive. Paris, Éditions du Dauphin [1951]
246 p. illus. 21 cm.
1. Savorgnan de Brazza, Pierre Paul François Camille, comte, 1852-1905.
DC342.8.S27M37 52-29390 ‡
Library of Congress [3]

Martinique
M843.9
M32de
Maran, René, 1887-
Deux amis, nouvelle inédite.
(In: Les Oeuvres libres, v. 125. Paris, Fayard, 1931. 18cm. p. 85-128)
I. Title.

Martinique
M843.9
M32li
Maran, René, 1887-
... Le livre de la brousse, roman. Paris, A. Michel [1934]
287, [1] p. 19cm.
I. Title.
Library of Congress PQ2625.A74L5 1934 34-34731
Copyright A—Foreign 25210
[2] 843.91

Martinique
M843.9
M32t
Maran, René, 1887-
Le Tchad de sable et d'or, Documentation de Pierre Doloncle, couverture en couleurs de Charles Fouqueray. Paris, Librairie de la revue française [c1931]
159p. 21cm.
I. Title.

Martinique
M843.9
M32dj
Maran, René, 1887-
... Djouma, chien de brousse, roman. Paris, A. Michel [°1927]
3 p. l., [9]-253 p., 1 l. 19cm.
I. Title.
Library of Congress PQ2625.A74D5 1927 27-16567
Copyright A—Foreign 34923
[2]

Martinique
M841.91
M321s
Maran, René, 1887-
Le livre du souvenir; poèmes (1909-1957). Paris, Présence Africaine, 1958.
142p. 19cm.
I. Title.

Martinique
M843.9
M32v
Maran, René, 1887-
...La vie intérieure, poèmes, (1909-1912) Paris, Édition du Beffroi, 1912.
163p. 19cm.
I. Title. 1. French poetry - Martinican authors.

Martinique
M841.9 Maran, René.
M32vi

... Le visage calme, stances. ... Paris, Aux éditions du Monde nouveau, 1922.

3 p. l., [3]-86, [1] p., 1 l. 19½cm.

"L'edition originale."

"... quatre cent cinquante exemplaire sur papier Alfa satine, ... no. 219.

I. Title. 1. French poetry–Martinican authors ~~Poetry–French~~.

Library of Congress PQ2625.A74V5 1922 23-6702
Copyright A—Foreign 21496
[2]

Martinique
M843.9 Maran, René, 1887-
M32y

Yourba, la mangouste.

(In: Les Oeuvres libres, v. 159. Paris, Fayard, 1934. 19cm. p.[5]-48)

I. Title.

Maran, Rene, 1887-

M910 Cook, Mercer.
C77f

Five French Negro authors, by Mercer Cook ... Washington, D. C., The Associated publishers, inc. [1943]

xiv, 164 p. incl. front. ports. 19½ cm.

Bibliographical references included in "Notes" (p. 151-161)

CONTENTS.—Julien Raimond.—Charles Bissette.—Alexandre Dumas.—Auguste Lacaussade.—Rene Maran.

1. Raimond, Julien, 1743?-1802? 2. Bissette, Cyrille Charles Auguste, 1795-1858. 3. Dumas, Alexandre, 1802-1870. 4. Lacaussade, Auguste, 1817-1897. 5. Maran, René, 1887- 6. French literature—Hist. & crit. 7. Negro authors. I. Title.

[Full name: Will Mercer Cook]

Library of Congress PQ150.N4C6 43—13504
[44j5] 840.903

French Guiana
M841.08 Maran, René, 1887-
D18

Damas, Leon G ed., 1912-

Poètes d'expression française [d'Afrique Noire, Madagascar, Réunion, Guadeloupe, Martinique, Indochine, Guyane] 1900-1945. Paris, Éditions du Seuil [1947]

322p. (Lattitudes françaises, 1) Collection "Pierres vives."

Maran, Rene, 1887-

Guadeloupe
M843.91 Thomarel, André.
T36

Nuits tropicales. Avant-propos de René Marna. Paris, Les Editions du Scorpion, 1960.

159p. 19cm. (Collection Alternance).

Martinique
M398 [Marbot, Francois Achille, 1817-1866]
M32

Les bambous, fables de la Fontaine travesties en patois martiniquais. Edition revue et augmentée d'une notice littéraire et d'une traduction française par Louis Jaham-Desrivaux. Paris, J. Peyronnet, 1931.

246p. 23cm.
At head of title: Un vieux commandeur.

1. Fables, French. I. Jaham-Desrivaux, Louis, ed.

Haiti
M840.9 Marcelin, Emile, 1874-1936
M33m

Medaillons littéraires, poetes et prosateurs haitiens.. Port-au-Prince, Imp. de l'Abeille, 1906.

158p. 21½cm.

1. Hatian literature. I. Title.

Haiti
M972.94 Marcelin, Frédéric, 1848-1917.
M33a

Au gre du souvenir. Paris, Augustin Challamel, 1913.

198p. port. (front) 18½cm.

1. Haiti.

Haiti
M972.94 Marcelin, Frédéric, 1848-1917.
M33c

... Choses haïtiennes: politique et littérature ... Paris, P. Taillefer, 1896.

2 p. l., 163, [1] p. 18½cm.

1. Haiti.

Library of Congress F1921.M3 3-29006
[a44b1]

Haiti
M843.91 Marcelin, Frédéric, 1848-1917.
M33c

... La confession de Bazoutte. ~~2. éd.~~ Paris, ~~P. Ollendorff, 1909.~~ Societe D'Editions litteraires et artistiques, 1909.

3 p. l., 310 p., 1 l. 16cm.

CONTENTS.—Avis au lecteur.—La confession de Bazoutte.—Tristylya.—Pétionville.—Thalaza.—Sor Loute.—Pensées de pluie.—Manguiers et palmistes.—Souverain.—Toussaint-Louverture.—Alexander-Dumas.—Ensemble de méditations.—Pro patria.—Les deux voix.—En pleine nuit.—La presse, palladium des libertés publiques.—Entre voisins.—Au Champ de Mars.—Hier—aujour-d'hui—demain.—Le droit de la force.—L'apprenti.—Au bord d'un regard.—Marie-Madeleine.

1. Haitian fiction

I. Title.

Library of Congress PQ3949.M3C6 25-20473
[a44b1]

Haiti
M843.91 Marcelin, Frédéric, 1848-1917.
M33m

... Marilisse, roman haïtien. 3. éd. Paris, P. Ollendorff, 1903.

2 p. l., 349 p., 1 l. 16cm.

I. Title. 1. Haitian fiction

Library of Congress PQ3949.M3M3 1903 25-20469 Revised
[r44b2]

Haiti
M843.91 Marcelin, Frédéric, 1848-1917.
M33t

... Thémistocle-Épaminondas Labasterre; petit récit haïtien. Paris, P. Ollendorff, 1901.

3 p. l., 323 p. 16cm.

I. Title. 1. Haitian fiction.

Library of Congress PQ3949.M3T5 25-20468 Revised
[r44b2]

Haiti
M843.91 Marcelin, Frédéric, 1848-1917.
M33v

... La vengeance de Mama, roman haïtien. Paris, P. Ollendorff, 1902.

2 p. l., 276 p. 16cm.

I. Title. 1. Haitian fiction.

Library of Congress PQ3949.M3V4 25-20471
[a44b1]

Haiti
M972.94 Marcelin, L J 1861-
M33h

Haïti; ses guerres civiles—leurs causes, leurs conséquences présentes, leur conséquence future et finale. Moyens d'y mettre fin et de placer la nation dans la voie du progrès et de la civilisation. Études économiques, sociales et politiques, par L.-J. Marcelin ... Paris, A. Rousseau, 1892-93.

Haiti
M972.94
P19
V.2,no.10

3 v. 23-25 cm.

The designations "t. 1," and "t. 2" do not appear on the title-pages of the respective volumes, and the "Introduction," a separate part, is not uniform with the other volumes, being printed in larger type upon larger paper.

CONTENTS.—Introduction.—1. ptie. Situation actuelle: anarchie, décadence, mort.—2. ptie. Réorganisation, progrès, civilisation.

1. Haiti. Library has introduction.

Library of Congress F1921.M31 1—16604
[48d1]

Haiti
M133 Marcelin, Milo, 1910-
M33m

Mythologie vodou (rite rada) I: préface de F. Morisseau Leroy; illustration de Hector Hyppolite. Port-au-Prince, Les Éditions Haitiennes, 1949.

139p. illus. 23½cm.

1. Voodoism. 2. Folklore- Haiti.
I. Title. II. Hyppolite, Hedor, illus.

Marcelin, Philippe Thoby-

see

Thoby-Marcelin, Philippe

Haiti
M843.91 Marcelin, Pierre, 1908- joint author.
T35b

Thoby-Marcelin, Philippe, 1904–

The beast of the Haitian hills, by Philippe Thoby-Marcelin and Pierre Marcelin, translated from the French, La bête du Musseau, by Peter C. Rhodes. New York, Toronto, Rinehart & company, inc. [1946]

5 p. l., 3-210 p. 19½cm.

I. Marcelin, Pierre, 1908- joint author. II. Rhodes, Peter C., tr. III. Title.

[Full name: Émile Philippe Thoby-Marcelin]

PZ3.T35Be 843.91 46-8130
© 7Nov46; 2c 12Oct46; publisher, New York; A8804.

Library of Congress [5]

Haiti
M843.91 Marcelin, Pierre, 1908- joint author.
T35ca

Thoby-Marcelin, Philippe, 1904–

... Canapé-vert ... New York, N. Y., Éditions de la Maison française, inc., °1944.

2 p. l., [7]-255 p. 19cm.

At head of title: Philippe Thoby-Marcelin et Pierre Marcelin.
"Prix du roman haïtien, deuxième concours latino-américain."

I. *Marcelin, Pierre, 1908- joint author. II. Title.

[Full name: Émile Philippe Thoby-Marcelin]

Library of Congress PQ3949.T45C3 44-8279
[5] 843.91

Haiti
M843.91 Marcelin, Pierre, 1908-
T35c

Thoby-Marcelin, Philippe, 1904–

Canapé-Vert, by Philippe Thoby-Marcelin and Pierre Marcelin; translated by Edward Larocque Tinker. New York, Toronto, Farrar & Rinehart inc. [1944]

xxvii, 225 p. col. front. 21cm.

Illustrated lining-papers.
"Prize winning novel, second Latin American contest."

I. *Marcelin, Pierre, 1908- joint author. II. Tinker, Edward Larocque, 1881- tr. III. Title.

[Full name: Émile Philippe Thoby-Marcelin]

Library of Congress PZ3.T35Can 44—1710
[46f5]

Haiti
M843.91 Marcelin Pierre, 1908- joint author.
T35p2

Thoby-Marcelin, Phillippe, 1904-
~~Marcelin, Pierre, 1908-~~

Le crayon de Dieu, roman [par] Pierre Marcelin [et] Philippe Thoby-Marcelin. Paris, La Table ronde [1952]

254 p. 19 cm.

I. Marcelin, Pierre, 1908- ~~Thoby-Marcelin, Philippe, 1904-~~ joint author. II. Title.

Full name: Léonce Perceval Pierre Marcelin.

Illinois. Univ. Library for Library of Congress A 52-10337
[1]

Marcelin, Pierre, 1908- joint author.

Haiti
M843.91 Thoby-Marcelin, Philippe, 1904–
T35p2

The pencil of God, by Philippe Thoby-Marcelin and Pierre Marcelin; translated by Leonard Thomas, ~~with an introd. by Edmund Wilson. Boston, Houghton Mifflin, 1951.~~ London, Victor Gollancz, 1951.

xvii, 204 p. 22 cm.

I. Marcelin, Pierre, 1908- joint author. II. Title.

Full name: Émile Philippe Thoby-Marcelin.

PZ3.T35Pe 843.91 50-58334

Library of Congress [5]

Marcelin, Pierre, 1908- joint author.
Haiti
M843.91 Thoby-Marcelin, Philippe, 1904-
T35p The pencil of God, by Philippe Thoby-Marcelin and Pierre Marcelin; translated by Leonard Thomas, with an introd. by Edmund Wilson. Boston, Houghton Mifflin, 1951.
xvii, 204 p. 22 cm.

I. Marcelin, Pierre, 1908- joint author. II. Title.
Full name: Émile Philippe Thoby-Marcelin.
PZ3.T35Pe 843.91 50-58834
Library of Congress [5]

Marcos Antilla.
Cuba
M863.6 [Rodríguez, Luis Felipe] 1888-
R61m Marcos Antilla; relatos de cañaveral. La Habana, Editorial Hermes [1932]
4 p. l., iii-xxvi p., 1 l., 9-155 p. 20½cm.
Author's name on cover.
Contents.—Marcos Antilla contado por sí mismo.—Cama 1 y 2.—Fantasmas en el cañaveral. — El Pelirrojo. — La guardarraya. — Mister Lewis.—Los Almarales.—El ego de Nicolás.—Los subalternos.—El has de cañas.—La danza lucumí.

I. Title.
36-16055
Library of Congress PQ7389.R6M3 863.6

M811.5 Margetson, George Reginald, 1877-
M33s Songs of life, by George Reginald Margetson. Boston, Sherman, French & company, 1910.
3 p. l., 57 p. 19½cm. $1.00
Inscribed copy: "The gift of "Santa Claus" To Authur B. Spingarn Esq. From George Reginald Margetson, Cambridge Mass. Christmas, 1932. Original poem written on fly leaf "To the Critic"
1. Poetry. I. Title. 10-13842
Library of Congress
© June 7, 1910; 2c. June 10, 1910; A 265594; Sherman, French & co., Boston, Mass.

Jamaica
M820 March, Monica
H38 Lost in the shuffle.
Pp. 28-32.
In: Hendriks, A. L., ed. The independence anthology of Jamaican literature. Kingston, Arts Celebration Committee, Ministry of Development and Welfare, 1962.

U. S.
M968 Marcum, John Arthur
Am3 Force: its thrust and prognosis, by J. A. Marcum and A. K. Lowenstein.
Pp. 249-277.
In: American Society of African Culture. Southern Africa in transition. New York, Praeger, 1966.
I. Lowenstein, A K jt. auth.

Puerto Rico
M864 Marginalia.
F41 Ferrer, José.
... Marginalia. Margen del padre Rivera Viera. Puerto Rico [Imprenta Venezuela] 1939.
8 p. l., [9]-185 p., 2 l. 19cm.
Contents.—Carmelina Vizcarrondo, la infancia y Poemas para mi niño. — Vigil: El erial.—Los ídolos del foro, de Carlos Arturo Torres, ensayista colombiano. — Concha Meléndez: Signos de Iberoamérica. — Hostos, ciudadano de América.—Motivos de Carmen Alicia Cadilla.—Acentos y evocaciones: Juan Ramón Jiménez. Maestro. Claridad e iluminación. Cesáreo Rosa-Nieves. Tierra y estrella.
1. Spanish-American literature—Addresses, essays, lectures. I. Title.
40-17011
Library of Congress PQ7081.F4
——— Copy 2. [2] 860.4

The march of black men-Ethiopia leads.
Ethiopia
[illegible]
Bayen, Malaku E mmanuel, 1900-1940.
The march of black men-Ethiopia leads. Official report of the present state of affairs and prospectus. An authentic account of the determined fight of the Ethiopian people for their independence, edited by Malaku E. Bayen... New York, The Voice of Ethiopia press, 1939.
64p. illus. 23cm.

Africa
M960 Marcum, John Arthur.
Am3 Pan-Africanism: present and future.
Pp. 53-65.
In: American Society of African Culture. Pan-Africanism reconsidered. Berkeley, University of California Press, 1962.

Marguerite de Bourgogne, queen consort of Louis x, 1290-1315-Drama.
France Dumas, Alexandre, 1802-1870.
M840. La tour de Nesle, par Alexandre Dumas, père; edited with introduction, notes and vocabulary by T. A. Daley ... Williamsport, Pa., The Bayard press [°1935]
D89ta
v, 100 p. 21cm.
A drama originally written by Fréderic Gaillardet was rewritten by Dumas and first published in 1832 as the work of "MM. Gaillardet et * * *". In 1839 it was reprinted giving both authors' names.
1. Marguerite de Bourgogne, queen consort of Louis x, 1290-1315—Drama. I. *Gaillardet, Fréderic, 1808-1882, joint author. II. Daley, Tatham Ambersley, ed. III. Title.
36-13054
Library of Congress PQ2227.T6 1935
——— Copy 2.
Copyright A 90530 [3] 842.77

The march of progress.
M813.4 Chesnutt, Charles Waddell, 1858-1932.
C42u The March of Progress. From - Century Magazine. January 1901. p. 422-428.
Bound in his 6 Uncollected stories.

En marge de notre "Aperçu..."
Haiti
M972.94 Charlier, Etienne D
C376m En marge de notre "Aperçu..." (Response a Mr. Emmanuel C. Paul). Port-au-Prince, Les Presses Libres, 1955.
64p. 22cm.

Dominican Republic
M796.357 Marichal, Juan.
M337 A pitcher's story, by Juan Marichal with Charles Einstein. [1st ed.] Garden City, N. Y., Doubleday, 1967.
215 p. illus. 22 cm.
I. Einstein, Charles, joint author. II. Title.
GV865.M335A3 796.3572'2'0924 67-19069
Library of Congress [5]

March on Washington for Jobs and Freedom, 1963.
M323.4 Saunders, Doris E ed.
Sa87 The day they marched. With an introd. by Lerone Bennett, Jr. Designed by Herbert Temple. Chicago, Johnson Pub. Co. [°1963]
viii, 88 p. illus., ports. 28 cm.
1. March on Washington for Jobs and Freedom, 1963. I. Title.
F200.S2 323.41 63-23081
Library of Congress [5]

M811.5 Margetson, George Reginald, 1877-
M33e England in the West Indies; a neglected and degenerating empire, by George Reginald Margetson. Cambridge, Mass., The author c1906.
35p. 23½cm.
Inscribed copy: "The gift of "Santa Claus" to Arthur B. Spingarn, Esq., from George Reginald Margetson. Cambridge, Mass, Christmas 1932.
1. Poetry I. Title

Marie Antoinette-Fiction.
France
M840 Dumas, Alexandre, 1802-1870.
D89ch2 Le chevalier de Maison-Rouge. Bruxelles, Societe Belge de Librairie, 1845.
5 vols. in 2. 14½cm.

March on Washington movement.
M323 Myers, E Pauline
M99m The march on Washington movement mobilizes a gigantic crusade for freedom, by E. Pauline Myers. New York the March on Washington Movement n.d.
13p. 22cm.

M811.5 Margetson, George Reginald, 1877-
M33e Ethiopia's flight; the Negro question, or, the white man's fear, by George Reginald Margetson, Cambridge, Mass., George Reginald Margetson, c1907.
22p. 23cm.
1. Poetry
I. Title

Marie Antoinette - Fiction.
France
M840 Dumas, Alexandre, 1802-1870.
D89co La collier de la reine, deuxième série des Mémoires d'un médecin. Bruxelles, Moline, Cans et compagnie, 1849.
6 vols. in 3. cm.

Marching blacks.
M973 Powell, Adam Clayton, 1908-
P87 Marching blacks, an interpretive history of the rise of the black common man, by Adam Clayton Powell, jr. New York, Dial press, 1945.
4 p. l., 3-218 p. 21cm.
Bibliography: p. 215-218.
1. Negroes. 2. Negroes—Hist. I. Title.
46-1158
Library of Congress * E185.6.P6
[85] 325.260973

M811.5 Margetson, George Reginald, 1877-
M33f The fledgling bard and the poetry society, by George Reginald Margetson ... Boston, R. G. Badger; [etc., etc., °1916]
111 p. 19½ cm.
In verse.
Inscribed copy: To the Poet's Friend, poem written on fly leaf, by George Reginald Margetson. January, 1923.
I. Title. 1. Poetry.
16-10921
Library of Congress PS3525.A65F6 1916

Marie Antoinette - Fiction.
France
M840 Dumas, Alexandre, 1802-1870.
D89com La comtesse de Charny, par Alexandre Dumas... Bruxelles, Moline, Cans et cie 1852.
8 vols. in 4. 16cm.

Haiti
M843.91
V59

... Marie Villarceaux...

Verne, Marc.
... Marie Villarceaux, un roman d'amour ... ₍Port-au-Prince₎ Haïti, H. Deschamps ₍1945₎
xxii p., 1 l., 25-255 p. 20½cm. (On cover: Collection haïtienne)

I. Title.
PQ3949.V4M3 A 47-1717
New York. Public library for Library of Congress ₍3₎†

Haiti
M972.94
D15a

Marion, Ignace, 1777-1831
Expedition de Bolivar. Deuxieme edition conforme a l'originale et revue, par le Docteur Francois Dalencour.

(In: Dalencour, Francois. Alexandre Petion devant l'humanite... Port-au-Prince, Envente chez l'Auteur, n.d. pp. 71-100)

1. Bolivar, Simon

S. Africa
M968
Sp6s

Marolen, Daniel Paul Penry, 1916-
How I interpret Bantu education.

Pp. 123-126.

In: Spottiswoode, Hildegarde, comp. South Africa, the road ahead. London, Bailey Bros. and Swinfen, 1960.

1. Bantu - Education. 2. Education-Bantu. I. Title.

Haiti
M843.91
M33m

Marilisse.

Marcelin, Frédéric, 1848-1917.
... Marilisse, roman haïtien. 3. éd. Paris, P. Ollendorff, 1903.
2 p. l., 349 p., 1 l. 16cm.

I. Title.
Library of Congress PQ3949.M35M3 1903 25-20469 Revised ₍r44b2₎

M658.7
N31

Market surveys.

The Negro market, published in the interest of the Negro press. Atlanta, W. B. Ziff co., c 1932

39p. illus. 28cm.

M910.
D92

Maroons.

Dunham, Katherine.
Katherine Dunham's journey to Accompong; drawings by Ted Cook. New York, H. Holt and company ₍1946₎
ix p., 1 l., 162 p., 1 l. illus. 24cm.

1. Accompong, Jamaica. 2. Maroons. I. Cook, Proctor Fyffe, illus. II. Title: Journey to Accompong.
F1896.M3D8 917.292 47-30039
© 12Dec46; Henry Holt & co., inc.; A9175.
Library of Congress ₍47q10₎

MB9
L34m

Marín Ocete, Antonio
El Negro Juan Latino, ensayo biográfico y crítico. Granada, Librería, Guevara, 1925.

94p. 27cm.

1. Latino, Juan, fl. 1573. 2. Spanish literature.

M658.7
N31

Market surveys.
The Negro market, published in the interest of the Negro press. Atlanta, W.B. Ziff co. ₍c1932₎
39p. illus. 28cm.

M812.3
Se4m
no.1

Le marquis Caporal.

Séjour, Victor, 1816-1874.
Le marquis Caporal, drame en cinq actes, en sept tableaux. Paris, Michel Lévy Frères, 1865.

130p. 19cm.

1. French drama. I. Title.

Guadeloupe
M325
C16m

... La marine de la France.

Candace, Gratien, 1873-
... La marine de la France. Marine militaire.—Marine marchande. Paris, Payot, 1938.
2 p. l., ₍7₎-190 p., 1 l. incl. tables. 22½cm. (Bibliothèque politique et économique)

1. France—Navy. 2. Merchant marine—France. 3. Sea-power. I. Title.
New York. Public library for Library of Congress ₍3₎ A 39-675

M658.7
B21

Market surveys-Baltimore, Md.
Baltimore Afro-American.
Baltimore, America's 5th largest Negro market; a report on the characteristics of the Baltimore Negro market, its buying habits and brand preferences in 1945, from a survey by the Research company of America, N. Y., analyzed and projected by the Harry Hayden company, N. Y., compiled and published by the Baltimore Afro-American. ₍Baltimore, °1946.
1 p. l., 100 p. illus., diagrs. 28 x 22cm.

1. Market surveys—Baltimore. 2. Negroes—Baltimore. I. Research company of America, New York. II. Hayden (Harry) company, New York. III. Title.
HF3163.B2B3 658.8 47-16240
Library of Congress ₍3₎

MB9
M34j

Marrant, John, 1755-1791.
A journal of the Rev. John Marrant, from Aug. the 18th, 1785 to the 16th of March 1790. To which are added, Two sermons; one preached on Ragged Island on Sabbath day, the 27th day of Oct. 1787; the other at Boston, in New England, on Thursday, the 24th of June, 1787. London: Printed for the author: Sold by J. Taylor and Co. At the Royal Exchange; and Mr. Marrant, No. 2 Black Horse Court, in Aldergate-Street. 1790. Price 2s 6d.
106p. 20cm.

1. Sermons.

Trinidad
M972.98
M52m

The marine fishes of Trinidad.

Mendes, Alex. L.
The marine fishes of Trinidad ₍by₎ Alex. L. Mendes. Trinidad, B.W.I., Trinidad publishing co., Ltd., 1940.

28p. 21½cm.
Inscribed copy: To Captain A.A. Cepriani, with the compliments of the author, Alex. L. Mendes, 31 July 1940.

M658.7
B21

Market surveys—Baltimore, Md.

Baltimore Afro-American.
Baltimore, America's 5th largest Negro market; a report on the characteristics of the Baltimore Negro market, its buying habits and brand preferences in 1945, from a survey by the Research Company of America, N. Y. analyzed and projected by the Harry Hayden Company, N. Y. Compiled and published by the Baltimore Afro-American ₍Baltimore₎ c1946.

1p. 100p. illus. diagr. 28x22cm.

MB9
M34

Marrant, John, 1755-1791
A narrative of the life of John Marrant, of New York, in North America: giving an account of his conversion when only fourteen years of age: his leaving his mother's house from religious motives, wandering several days in the desert without food, and being at last taken by an Indian hunter among the Cherokees, where he was condemned to die. With an account of the conversion of the king of the Cherokees and his daughter, &c. &c. &c. The whole authenticated by the Reverend W. Aldridge. Leeds, Printed by Davies and co., 1810.
iv, ₍5₎-24 p. 21½cm.
Preface signed: W. Aldridge. London, July 19, 1786.
1. Indians of North America — Captivities. 2. Cherokee Indians. I. Aldridge, William, 1737-1797. 3. ~~Narratives.~~
Library of Congress E99.C5M35 2—8902

Cuba
M863.6
R61r

Marinello, Juan, 1899-
Americanismo y cubanismo literarios.

₍Rodríguez, Luis Felipe₎ 1888-
Relatos de Marcos Antilla, la tragedia del canaveral. La Habana, Impresora cubana, s.a. ₍1932?₎

3p. l., iii-xvii, 106p. 22½cm.
Author's name on cover.
First published 1928.

M658.7
W27

Market surveys—Washington, D. C.

Washington Afro-American.
The Washington Afro-American report on characteristics of the Washington Negro market... its product buying and brand preferences in 1945, compiled by the Washington Afro-American, from a survey conducted by the Research company of America. Washington, D. C. c1945.

92p. illus., diagrs. 28x22cm.

MB9
M34n

Marrant, John, 1755-1791.
A narrative of the life of John Marrant, of New York, in North America: giving an account of his conversion when only fourteen years of age; his leaving his mother's house from religious motives, wandering several days in the desert without food, and being at last taken by an Indian hunter among the Cherokees, where he was condemned to die. With an account of the conversion of the King of the Cherokees and his daughter, &c.&c.&c. The whole authenticated by the Rev. W. Aldridge.
Leeds: Printed by Davies and co. at the Stanhope press, Vicar-Lane, 1815.
1v, 5-24p. 21cm. 1. Biography.

Trinidad
M820
J23m

Mariners renegades and castaways.

James, Cyril Lionel Robert, 1901-
Mariners, renegades and castaways, the story of Herman Melville and the world we live in. New York, C.L.R. James, 1953.

203 p. 16cm.

Guyana
M364
M342

Marks, I Alexander
Thou shalt not kill. New York, Carolton Press ₍1967₎

125p. 21cm.
Portrait of author on book jacket.

1. Crime. I. Title.

MB9
M34

Marrant, John, 1755-1791
A narrative of the Lord's wonderful dealings with John Marrant, a black, (now going to preach the gospel in Nova-Scotia) born in New-York, in North-America. Taken down from his relation, arranged, corrected, and published by the Rev. Mr. Aldridge. The 4th ed. ... London, Printed by Gilbert and Plummer, ~~1785~~. 1802
v, 7-38 p. 22cm.
Preface signed: W. Aldridge, July 19th, 1785.
Also published under title: A narrative of the life of John Marrant ...

1. Cherokee Indians. 2. Indians of North America—Captivities. I. Aldridge, William, 1737-1797. 2. Narratives.
Library of Congress E99.C5M34 21-12609 ₍2₎

Marriage.
M323.3 Gardner, LeRoy.
G174 The truth about interracial marriage. [St. Paul? 1965]
ii, 148 p. 23 cm.

1. Miscegenation. 2. Negroes. I. Title.
HQ1031.G3 301.422 65-26932
Library of Congress [3]

Marriage - Nigeria.
Nigeria
M392 Ariwoola, Olagoke, 1940-
Ar46 The African wife. London, Kenion Press, 1965.
113p. 18½cm.
Portrait of author on book cover.

1. Marriage - Nigeria. 2. Family - Nigeria. 3. Nigeria - Social life and customs. I. Title.

Les marrons du syllabaire.
Haiti Fouchard, Jean
M370 Les marrons du syllabaire, quelques aspects
F82 du problème de l'instruction et de l'éducation des esclaves et affranchis de Saint-Domingue. Preface du Dr. Price-Mars. Port-au-Prince, Henri Deschamps, 1953.
167p. facsims. 21cm.

Marriage.
M173.1 Hudson, Elijah
H86h How to put sparkle and romance into marriage. New York, Carlton Press, 1962.
111p. 23½cm.
Portrait of author on book jacket.

Africa Marriage-Nigerian .
M966.9 Delano, Isaac O
D37a An African looks at marriage, by Isaac O. Delano ... London and Redhill, United society for Christian literature [1944]
47p. 18cm. (Africa' own library, no.5)

The marrow of tradition.
M813.4 Chesnutt, Charles Waddell, 1858-1932.
C42 The marrow of tradition, by Charles W. Chestnutt. Boston and New York, Houghton, Mifflin and company, 1901.
vi, 329, [1] p. 20cm.

I. Title.
1-25424
Library of Congress PZ3.C4253M
[45f1]

Zambia Marriage.
M392 Maango, David
X11 "Tell me, Josephine." [By David Maango, Barbara Hall and Kay Sifuniso] Edited by Barbara Hall. [Foreword by Kenneth D. Kaunda] New York, Simon and Schuster, 1964.
142p. 21cm.
Selections from the Tell me, Josephine column started in February, 1960, by the Central African mail, a weekly paper in Northern Rhodesia.
(Over)

Zanzibar Marriage - Zanzibar.
M392 Farsy, Muhammad Saleh, 1925-
F26 Ada za harusi, katika unguja [Marriage customs in Zanzibar] Dar es Salaam, East African Literature Bureau, 1956.
51p. illus. 18cm. (Desturi na masimulizi ya Afrika ya mashariki)
Written in Swahili.
1. Marriage - Zanzibar. 2. Zanzibar - Social life and customs. I. Title.

MB9 Marrs, Elijah P 1840-
M349m Life and history of the Rev. Elijah P. Marrs ... Louisville, Ky., The Bradley & Gilbert company, 1885.
146 p., 1 l. front. (port.) 19½cm.

1. Negroes—Kentucky. 2. U. S. artillery. 12th colored regt., 1863-1865. 3. U. S.—Hist.—Civil war—Personal narratives.
Library of Congress E185.97.M36M3 12-27743
Copyright 1885: 10739

Jamaica Marriage
M824 McFarlane, J E Clare, 1894-1962
M16s Sex and Christianity: or The case against the system of monogamous marriage ... Kingston, Jamaica, Printed for the author by the Gleaner Co., 1932.
116p. 20cm.
Autographed copy.

Marriage, Mixed.
M323.3 Larsson, Clotye Murdock, ed.
L33 Marriage across the color line, edited by Clotye M. Larsson. Chicago, Johnson Pub. Co., 1965.
xi, 204p. 22cm.

Nigeria
M641.5 Mars, J A ,compiler.
M35k Kudeti book of Yoruba cookery. Lagos, The Church Missionary Society's Bookshop, 1936.
39p. 20cm.

1. Yoruba cookery. 2. Africa, West - Cookery. 3. Nigeria. 4. Cookery.

Marriage.
Congo(Leopoldville)
M967.5 Malula, Joseph
M29f Foyer heureux. Leverville, Bibliotheque de L'Étoile, 1951.
96p. 18½cm.

Marriage across the color line.
M323.3 Larsson, Clotye Murdock, ed.
L33 Marriage across the color line, edited by Clotye M. Larsson. Chicago, Johnson Pub. Co., 1965.
xi, 204 p. 22 cm.

1. Miscegenation. 2. U. S.—Race question. I. Title.
HQ1031.L3 301.422 65-21549
Library of Congress [3]

M326.99B Mars, James, b. 1790.
M35 Life of James Mars, a slave; born and sold in Connecticut. 4th ed. Written by himself. Hartford, Press of Case, Lockwood & company, ~~1867.~~ 1868.
38 p. 19cm.

1. Slavery in the U. S.—Connecticut. 2. Slave narrative.
14-17088
Library of Congress E444.M36
[a37b1]

Ghana Marriage.
M392.6 Omari, T Peter.
Om12 Marriage guidance for young Ghanaians. With a foreword by Charles O. Easmon. London, New York, Nelson [1962]
148 p. illus. 20 cm.
Includes bibliography.

Portrait of author on back of book.

1. Marriage. 2. Family. I. Title.
HQ734.O63 63-4354 ‡
Library of Congress [2]

Ghana Marriage guidance for young Ghanaians.
M392.6 Omari, T Peter.
Om12 Marriage guidance for young Ghanaians. With a foreword by Charles O. Easmon. London, New York, Nelson [1962]
148 p. illus. 20 cm.
Includes bibliography.

Portrait of author on back of book.

1. Marriage. 2. Family. I. Title.
HQ734.O63 63-4354 ‡
Library of Congress [2]

M326.99B Mars, James, b. 1790.
M35 Life of James Mars, a slave born and sold in
1864 Connecticut. Written by himself. Hartford, Press, of Case Lockwood & Company, 1864.
32p. 17½cm.

1. Slavery in the U.S. - Connecticut.
2. Slave narrative.

Tanganyika Marriage.
M392 Saleh el-Busaidy, Hamed
Sa32 Ndoa na talaka [Marriage and divorce] Nairobi, Eagle Press, 1958.
45p. 21½cm.
Written in Swahili.

1. Marriage. 2. Divorce. I. Title.

Marriage law-U. S.
M323.3 Davenport, Charles Benedict, 1866-
D27s ... State laws limiting marriage selection examined in the light of eugenics, by Charles B. Davenport ... with two figures and four tables. Cold Spring Harbor [N. Y.] 1913.
66 p. tables (1 fold.) diagrs. (1 fold.) 23cm. (Eugenics record office. Bulletin no. 9)
Bibliography: p. 40.

1. Eugenics. 2. Marriage law—U. S. I. Title.
13-21086
Library of Congress HQ750.A1C5
[33f1]

Haiti Mars, Jean Price-, 1876- 1969
M398 ... Ainsi parla l'oncle...; essais d'ethnographie. [Port-
M35 au-Prince, Imprimerie de Compiègne, 1928.
3 p. l., iv, 243 p. illus. (incl. map, facsims., music) 25cm. (Bibliothèque haïtienne)
"Errata": 2 p. inserted.
"Bibliographie": p. [237]-239.

Haitian folk-lore
1. ~~Folk-lore—Haiti.~~ 2. ~~Ethnology—Haiti.~~ 3. Haiti—Soc. life & cust. 4. Voodooism. 5. ~~Ethnology—Africa.~~ I. Title.
Africa-Soc. life & cust.
33-13308
Library of Congress GR121.H3M3
[47d1] 398.097294

Haiti
M972.94
M35c
Mars, Jean Price, 1876-1969
Le cycle du Nègre essais de géographie humaine à propos de l'école d'anthropo-sociologie Brésilienne.

(In: Revue de la Société d Histoire et de Géographie d'Haiti. Port-au-Prince, Haiti, 1937. 24cm. v.8, Juin 1937. p.[1]-34)
Inscribed by author: Hommage particulier à M. Arthur B. Spingarn, Dr. Price-Mars, Juin 1937.

1. Brazil--African customs.

Haiti
MB9
C46m
Mars, Jean Price, 1876-1969
...Le sentiment de la valeur personnelle chez Henry Christophe en fonction de son role de chef psychologie d'un homme d'etat... Port-au-Prince, Haiti, V. Valcin, 1933.
21p. 24cm.
1. Christophe, Henri, King of Haiti, 1767-1820.
2. Haiti. I. Title

Haiti
M972.94
P281e
Mars, Jean Price, 1876-1969
Paultre, Emile
Essai sur M. Price-Mars (Prix de l'alliance Francaise.) Preface D'Etzer Vilaire. [Port-au-Prince] Imprimerie d'etat, 1933.

101p. 16cm.

Haiti
M972.94
M35s
Mars, Jean Price, 1876-1969
De Saint-Domingue a Haiti; essai sur la culture, les arts et la litterature. Paris, Presence Africaine, 1959.

170p. 18½cm.

1. Haitian art. 2. Haitian literature. 3. Saint-Domingue.

Haiti
M972.94
M35s
Mars, Jean Price, 1876-1969
Silhouettes de Nègres et de Négrophiles. Paris, Présence Africaine, 1959.

210p. illus., ports. 19cm.

1. Haiti - Biographies. 2. Biographies - Haiti. I. Title.

Mars, Jean Price, 1876-1969
Haiti
M972.94
T75p
Trouillot, Henock
La pensee de docteur Jean Price-Mars. Port-au-Prince, 1956.

101p. port. 23cm. (Numero special - Revue de la Societe Haitienne d'histoire de Geographie et de Geologie. Vol. 29, No. 102, Juillet-Octobre 1956)

Haiti
M972.94
M35d
Mars, Jean Price, 1876-1969
La diplomatie Haitienne et l'indépendance Dominicaine, 1858-1867; etude basée en partie sur des documents officiels et inédits dont nous devons la communication à la généreuse obligeance de M. M. Mentor Laurent et Edmond Mangonès.

(In: Revue de la Société d Histoire et de Géographie d'Haiti. Port-au-Prince, Haiti, 1939. v.10, Janvier 1939. p.1-72)
3. Dominican Republic - History
1. Haiti--History--1844- . 2. Haiti--Foreign relations--Dominican Republic. I.Title

---

Haiti
M972.94
M35u
Mars, Jean Price, 1876-1969
L'Unité politique de l'ile d'Haiti s'est-elle opérée en 1822 par la violence ou par le libre ralliement des Dominicains à la République d'Haiti?

(In: Revue de la Société d Histoire et de Géographie d'Haiti. Port-au-Prince, Haiti, 1937. 24cm. v.8, Octobre 1937. p.1-27)

1. Haiti--History--1804-1844. I. Title.

Mars, Jean Price, 1876-1969 Preface.
Haiti
M398
P612
Pierre-Louis, Ulysse
Sortilèges, Afro-Haitiens (contes et légendes). Préface du Dr. Jean Price-Mars. Port-au-Prince, Imprimeire de l'Etat, 1961.

120p. 18½cm.

Haiti
M972.94
M35
Mars, Jean Price, 1876-1969
Ebauches, 2eme série: De la prehistoire d'Haiti. Port-au-Prince, Impre. de lEtat, 1962.

217p. tables 22cm.
Bibliographical footnotes.

1. Haiti. I. Leyburn, James Graham. The Haitian people.

Haiti
M972.94
M35r
Mars, Jean Price, 1876-1969
La République d'Haïti et la République dominicaine; les aspects divers d'un problème d'histoire, de géographie et d'ethnologie. Depuis les origines du peuplement de l'île antiléenne en 1492, jusqu'à l'évolution des deux États qui en partagent la souveraineté en 1953. Port-au-Prince, 1953-

2 v. 23 cm. (Collection du tricinquantenaire de l'indépendance d'Haïti)

1. Haiti—For. rel.—Dominican Republic. 2. Dominican Republic—For. rel.—Haiti. 3. Haiti—Hist.

F1926.M363 54-27869 ‡

Library of Congress [1]

Haiti
M972.94
M352c
Mars, Louis
... La crise de possession dans le voudou, essais de psychiatrie comparee [by] Louis Mars... Port-au-Prince, Haiti, Imprimerie de l'Etat. 1946.

XV, 103p. 20cm. (Bibliotheque de l'Institut d'Ethnologie de Port-au-Prince)

1. Haiti-Psychiatry. 2. Psychiatry. 3. Voodooism. 4. Haiti - Voodooism. I. Title.

Son of Jean - [illegible]

Haiti
M972.94
M35
Mars, Jean Price, 1876-1969
Ebauches, 2eme série: De la prehistoire d'Haiti. Port-au-Prince, Impre. de l'Etat, 1962.

217p. tables 22cm.
Bibliographical footnotes.

1. Haiti. I. Leyburn, James Graham. The Haitian people.

Haiti
MB9
G94m
Mars, Jean Price, 1876-1969
... Vilbrun Guillaume-Sam ce Méconnu. Port-au-Prince, 1961.

175p. illus., port. 21½cm.

1. Guillaume-Sam, Vilbrun, 1860-
I. Title.

Haiti
M972.94
M352 l
Mars, Louis.
La lutte contre la folie. Port-Au-Prince, Haiti, 1947.
xi, 133 p., [1] l. 22 cm.

1. Insanity. [1. Mental disorders] 2. Psychiatry—Haiti. I. Title.

Med 48-1694

U. S. Army Medical Libr. for Library of Congress [WM100M363L 1947] [1]

Haiti
M972.94
M35f
Mars, Jean Price-, 1876-1969
... Formation ethnique, folk-lore et culture de peuple haïtien. Port-au-Prince, V. Valcin, imprimeur [1939]

iv p., 2 l., 151 p. 18cm.

"Voici un tout petit livre qui contient deux études ... La première est ma part de collaboration à une œuvre collective qui, sous la direction de m. Pattee devait paraître en langue anglaise ... La seconde, elle aussi, fait partie de l'enquête poursuivie par la Société haïtienne d'études scientifiques sur certains problèmes de notre communauté et doit paraître dans les Annales de la société."—Pref.
"Bibliographie générale": p. [149]-151.

1. Haiti—Nationality. 2. Haitian folklore 3. Haiti—Civilization. I. Title.

A 42-2340

New York. Public library for Library of Congress [2]

Haiti
M972.94
M35v
Mars, Jean Price, 1876-1969
...La vocation de l'élite, par Price-Mars. Port-au-Prince, Impr. E. Chenet, 1919.

2p. l., iv, 269p. 26cm. (Bibliothèque haitienne)

Errata slip inserted at end.

1. Haiti

Haiti
M972.94
M35e
Mars, Price.
... Une étape de l'évolution haïtienne. Port-au-Prince, Haïti, Impr. "La Presse" [1929?]
viii, [9]-208 p. 24½cm. (Bibliothèque haïtienne)

Contents.—L'intelligence haïtienne, études de socio-psychologie.—Les croyances, le sentiment et le phénomène religieux chez les nègres de St.-Domingue; conférence prononcée à la Société d'histoire et de géographie en 1926.—Magic island, par W. B. Seabrook ...—La Noël des humbles.—Les opinions à propos de "Black Haiti", une biographie de la fille aînée de l'Afrique, par Blair Niles.

1. Haiti—Soc. condit. 2. Haiti—Intellectual life. 3. National characteristics, Haitian. 4. Negroes in Haiti. I. Title.

30-15008

Library of Congress F1921.M36 [2]

Haiti
M972.94
M35j
Mars, Jean Price, 1876-1969
Jean-Pierre Boyer Bazelais et le drame de Miragoâne; à propos d'un lot d'autographes, 1883-1884. Port-au-Prince, Impr. de l'État, 1948.
135 p. ports., facsim. 21 cm. (Bibliothèque haïtienne)

1. Bazelais, Jean Pierre Boyer, 1833- 2. Haiti—Hist.—1844-

F1926.B35M35 972.94 49-26542*

Library of Congress [1]

Mars, Jean -Price, 1876-1969
Haiti
MB9
M35h
Haiti. Committee of friends of Haiti for the Promotion of the Candidacy of Dr. Jean Price-Mars to the Presidency of the Republic of Haiti.
A brief biography [of] Jean Price-Mars, presidential candidate in the Republic of Haiti. n.p. The Committee, n.d.

3p. port. 22½cm.

M784
M35
Marsh, J B T
The story of the Jubilee singers; with their songs. Ed. by J. B. T. [!] Marsh. 7th ed. London, Hodder and Stoughton, 1877.
vi, [2], 248 p. front. (mounted phot.) illus. 17½cm.

1. Jubilee singers. 2. Negro musicians. 3. Negro songs.

6-3204

Library of Congress M1607.F4 [45o1]

Marshall, Albert Prince, 1914- comp.

M016.05 M351
A Guide to Negro periodical literature. v. 1- Feb. 1941- Winston-Salem, N. C. [etc.], 1941-
v. 28cm. quarterly (irregular)
Reproduced from type-written copy.
Compiler: Feb. 1941- A. P. Marshall.

1. Negroes—Bibl.—Period. 2. Periodicals—Indexes. I. Marshall, Albert Prince, 1914- comp.

Library of Congress Z1361.N39G8 45-41371 [2] 016.32526

M813.5 M35b
Marshall, Paule, 1929-
Brown girl, brownstones. New York, Random House [1959]
310 p. 21 cm.

I. Title.

PZ4.M369Br 59-10804 ‡
Library of Congress [5]

M323 Su6
Marshall, Thurgood, 1908-
Speech.

Pp. 104-107.

In: Summit Meeting of National Negro Leaders, Washington, D. C. Report. Washington, National Newspaper Publishers Association, 1958.

M811.5 M35a
Marshall, Florence E.
Are you awake? by Florence E. Marshall. Lansing, Michigan, Sahw Publishing Co., c1936.
96p. 22½cm.

M813.08 C554
Marshall, Paule, 1929-
Reena
Pp. 264-282

In: Clarke, John Henrik, ed. American Negro short stories. New York, Hill and Wang, 1966.

M323.4 M35s
Marshall, Thurgood, 1908-
The supreme court as protector of civil rights; Equal protection of the laws. Reprinted from the Annals of the American Academy of Political and Social Science. Philadelphia, 1951.

101-110p. 24cm.

1. Civil rights. 2. Supreme Court.

Jamaica
M820 H38
Marshall, H V Ormsby
Poinsetta for Christmas.

Pp. 41-44.

In: Hendriks, A. L., ed. The independence anthology of Jamaican literature. Kingston, Arts Celebration Committee, Ministry of Development and Welfare, 1962.

M974.7 C55h
Marshall, Paule, 1929-
Some get wasted.

Pp. 316-327.

In: Clarke, J. H., ed. Harlem, U. S. A. Berlin Seven Seas Publishers, 1964.

Marshall, Thurgood, 1908, jt. author
M323. W587w
White, Walter Francis, 1893-
What caused the Detroit riot? An analysis by Walter White and Thurgood Marshall. New York, NAACP, 1943.

37p. 22½cm.

M910 M35
Marshall, *Mrs.* Harriet (Gibbs)
The story of Haiti, from the discovery of the island by Christopher Columbus to the present day, by Harriet Gibbs Marshall ... Boston, The Christopher publishing house [c1930]
177 p. front., plates, ports., fold. map. 20½cm.
"List of Haitian music": p. 139-141. "List of Haitian literature": p. 142-147.

1. Haiti—Hist. I. Title.

Library of Congress W1911.M36 30-18208 [42f1] 972.94

M813.5 M35s
Marshall, Paule, 1929-
Soul clap hands and sing. [1st ed.] New York, Atheneum, 1961.
177 p. 21 cm.
Four short novels.
Portrait of author on book jacket.

I. Title.

PZ4.M369So 61-16515 ‡
Library of Congress [5]

Marshall, Thurgood, 1908-
MB9 M358p
Poling, James.
Thurgood Marshall and the 14th Amendment. New York, Committee of 100, 1952.

29-[32]p. port. 31cm.
Reprinted from Colliers February 23, 1952.
white author.

MB9 A12m2
Marshall, Herbert, 1912-
Ira Aldridge, the Negro tragedian. By Herbert Marshall and Mildred Stock. London, Rockliff [c1958]

355p. ports. 22cm.
Bibliography: p. 337 - 342.
White authors.

1. Aldridge, Ira Frederick, d. 1867.
I. Stock, Mildred, Joint author.

Gold Coast
M966.7 M35p
Marshall, Percival G
The people's right in democracy. Accra, Lona Press Ltd., 1950.

36p. illus. 21cm.

1. Gold Coast - Pol and Govt. 2. Ansah-koi, 1904 -

Jamaica
M398 An1
Marson, Una M. 1905-
Dialect verse.

(In: Anancy stories and dialect verse... 1st ed. Kingston, Jamaica, Pioneer Press, [1950]. 19cm. pp. 97-98)

MB9 A12m
Marshall, Herbert, 1912-
Ira Aldridge, the Negro tragedian, by Herbert Marshall and Mildred Stock. ~~London, Rockliff~~ N.Y., Macmillan [1958]
355 p. illus. 23 cm.
Includes bibliographies.

White authors

1. Aldridge, Ira Frederick, d. 1867. I. Stock, Mildred, joint author.

PN2598.A52M3 927.92 59-22897 ‡
Library of Congress [59b15]

M323.4 M35m
Marshall, Thurgood, 1908-
Mr. Justice Murphy and civil rights. Reprinted from Michigan law review, 48:745-766, April 1950.

745-766p. 27cm.

1. Civil rights. 2. Murphy, Frank.
I. Title.

Jamaica
M821.91 M35m
Marson, Una M. 1905-
The moth and the star, by Una Marson. Kingston Jamaica, B.W.I. Published by the author, 1937.
xv, 103p. 21cm.
Autographed by the author

~~1. Poetry - Jamaica~~
2. Jamaican poetry
I. Title

M343.3 M35p
Marshall, Horace.
Police brutality; Lynching in the Northern style, with a special message from Councilman Benjamin J. Davis. New York, Office of Councilman Benjamin J. Davis, c1947]

21p. illus. 21cm.

1. New York - Police. 2. Police. I. Title. II. Davis, Benjamin Jefferson. III. Lynching in the Northern style.

M350 M35r
Marshall, Thurgood, 1908-
Report on Korea; The shameful story of the court martials of Negro GIs. New York, NAACP, 1951.

19p. 22cm.

1. Soldiers. 2. Korea - History - War and intervention, 1950-

---

Jamaica
M821.91 M35t
Marson, Una. M , 1905-
Towards the stars; poems by Una Marson, with a foreword by L. A. G. Strong. Bickley, Kent, University of London press ltd. [1945]
68 p. 16½cm.
"First printed February 1945."

I. Title.

Library of Congress PR6025.A695T6 45-6880 [3] 821.91

Jamaica
M820 H38
Marston, Beryl
The sound.
Pp. 65-68.
In: Hendriks, A. L., ed. The independence anthology of Jamaican literature. Kingston, Arts Celebration Committee, Ministry of Development and Welfare, 1962.

M331.833 M36
Martin, Isadore Maximilian
Housing problems of the Philadelphia nonwhite population. Philadelphia, Isadore Martin Realtor, 1953.
34p. tables. 28cm.
1. Housing I. Title

Martin, Rufus, joint author.
Virgin Is.
M972.97 J29vi
Jarvis, Jose Antonio, 1901-
Virgin Islands picture book, by J. Antonio Jarvis and Rufus Martin. Philadelphia, Dorrance [1948]
118 p. illus., ports., map (on lining-papers) 24 cm.
1. Virgin Islands—Descr. & trav. I. Martin, Rufus, joint author.
F2136.J39 917.297 48-5234*
Library of Congress [10]

Marti, José.
Cuba
M972.91 G59
Gómez Estévez, Rafael.
Reflexiones sobre José Marti y el Taboquero en la revolución Cubana. Habana, Impresos Economicos, 1929.
40p. port. 20cm.

M326 An8s
Martin, John Sella, 1832-
[Address]
(In: Anti-slavery Conference, Paris, 1867. Special report. London, Committee of the British and Foreign Anti-slavery Society 1867 Pp. 49-52).

Martin de Porres, Saint, 1579-1639.
MB9 M37t
Tarry, Ellen, 1906-
Martin de Porres, saint of the New World. Illustrated by James Fox. London, Burns and Oates; New York, Vision Books [1963]
173 p. illus. 22 cm. (Vision books, 57)
1. Martin de Porres, Saint, 1579-1639.
BX4700.M397T3 1963 [92] 63-9924 ‡
Library of Congress [5]

M191 M363
Martin, Clarence.
Universalism: faith in mankind. [1st ed.] New York, Vantage Press [1964]
58 p. illus. 21 cm.
Portrait of author on book jacket.
1. Humanism. I. Title.
B945.M383U5 191 64-22777
Library of Congress [5]

Cuba
M972.91 M35ec
Martin, Juan Luis
Ecué changó y Yemayá. Ensayos sobre la sub-religion de los Afro-Cubanos. Habana, Cultural, S. A., 1930.
164p. 20cm.
1. Cuba-Religion.

Martin Larwin.
Jamaica
M823.91 Sp3m
Spence, Tomas H
Martin Larwin [by] Tomas H. Spence [and] Eric Heath. [1st ed.] New York, Pageant Press [1954]
187 p. 21 cm.
I. Heath, Eric, joint author. II. Title.
PZ4.S744Mar 54-9825 ‡
Library of Congress [5]

Brit. Guiana
M821 M361e
Martin, Egbert, 1862-1890.
Leo's local lyrics, illustrated by Charles Stephens. Demerara, Printed by Baldwin & Co., George town, 1886.
viii, 75p. illus. 18cm.
1. British Guiana--Poetry. I. Title.

M371.974 C61n
Martin, Robert Earl
General education: its problems and promise in the education of Negroes.
Pp. 183-98.
In: Clift, Virgil A. Negro education in America. New York, Harper [1962]

Cuba
M861.09 M36m
Martin Llorente, Francisco, 1869-
La mujer vueltabajera en la poesia Cubana. La Habana, Molina y Compania, 1941.
28p. 22½cm.
At head of title: Armando Guera.
1. Cuban poetry-History and Criticism.

Brit. Guiana
M821 M361
Martin, Egbert, 1862-1890.
Leo's poetical works. London, Printed for the author by W. H. and L. Collingridge, 1883.
224p. 16½cm.
Clipping about Martin attached to cover of book.
1. British Guiana--Poetry. I. Title.

M975.5 M36n
Martin, Robert Earl
Negro disfranchisement in Virginia. Washington, D.C., Howard University, 1938.
49-188p. (Howard University studies in the social sciences. v.1, no.1)
Mimeographed.
Bound with Africa and the rise of capitalism by Wilson E. Williams.
1. Virginia. I. Title. II. Series.

Br. Honduras
M821.91 M36e
Martinez, J S
The Belize hurricane of September 10th, 1931, by J. S. Martinez. [n.p., The Trumpet press, 1931]
4 unnumb. p. 19cm.
Bound with Carribean jingles by J. S. Martinez.
1. ~~Poetry~~. 2. British Honduras ~~poet~~.
I. Title.

Brit. Guiana
M821 M36s
Martin, Egbert, 1862-1890.
Scriptology. A series of four short narratives by Leo. Demerara, Printed by Baldwin & Co., 1885.
58p. 18cm.
1. British Guiana--Poetry. I. Title.

M815.5 H83n
Martin, Robert Earl,
Professor Alain Locke-teacher.
(In: Howard University, Washington, D.C. Graduate School Div. of Social Sciences. The New Negro thirty years afterward ... Washington, Howard University, 1956. 23cm. pp. 8-11.)

Br. Honduras
M821.91 M36c
Martinez, J S
Carribean jingles. Dialect and other poems of British Honduras. By J. S. Martinez. [London, Waterlow & Sons, ltd., printers, 1925]
99p. front., plates. 19cm.
1. British Honduras ~~poet~~. 2. ~~Poetry~~.
I. Title.

MB M36
Martin, Fletcher, 1916- ,ed.
Our great Americans, the Negro contribution to American progress; compiled and edited by Fletcher Martin. Chicago, 1953.
96p. 28cm.
1. Biographies. I. Title

M811.5 M36e
Martin, Rose Hinton
Endearing endeavors. New York, Pageant Press, Inc., 1960.
56p. 20cm.
Portrait of author on book jacket.
1. Poetry-Biographical. I. Title.

Cuba
M972.91 M36
Martinez, Marcial
Cuba; la verdad de su tragedia. Colombia, Gráficos Galeza, 1958.
173p. 20cm.
1. Cuba - Race relations.

Puerto Rico
Martinez Nadal, Rafael, 1878-
M864 . Pagán, Bolívar, 1899-
P141 ... Ideales en marcha; discursos y artículos. San Juan, Puerto Rico, Biblioteca de autores puertorriqueños, 1939.

3 p. l., [9]-306 p., 3 l. 20cm.

"En homenaje a Bolívar Pagán [discurso pronunciado por Rafael Martínez Nadal, en junio 25, 1937]": p. [7]-19.
"Hablando con Bolívar Pagán [entrevista, de Angela Negrón Muñoz, abril 2, 1933]": p. [21]-38.

1. Puerto Rico—Pol. & govt.—1898- I. Martínez Nadal, Rafael, 1878- II. Negrón Muñoz, Angela. III. Title.

40—2968
Library of Congress F1975.P26
[42c1] 972.95

Martinican authors.
Guadeloupe
Satineau, Maurice, 1891-
M972.97 ... Histoire de la Guadeloupe sous l'ancien régime, 1635-1789.
Sa8h Paris, Payot, 1928.

3 p. l., 400 p. plates, map. 22½cm. (Bibliothèque historique)

On cover: Bibliothèque coloniale.
"Corrections supplémentaires de l'auteur après le tirage": 1 leaf inserted.
Bibliography: p. [386]-400.

1. Guadeloupe—Hist. 2. Guadeloupe—Econ. condit.

28-22435
Library of Congress F2066.S25
Copyright A—Foreign 39222
[2]

Martinican fiction.
Martinique
M843.9 Capécia, Mayotte.
C17j Je suis Martiniquaise. Paris, Editions Corrêa, 1948.

202p. 18½cm.
Received Grand Prix de Litérature des Antilles.

Martinican fiction.
Martinique
M843.9 Capécia, Mayotte
C17n La négresse blanche. Paris, Editions Corrêa 1950.

188p. 19cm.

Martinican fiction.
Martinique
M841.91 Romanette, Irmine
R66so ...Sonson de la Martinique, roman. Paris, Société Francaise d'Editions littéraires et Techniques, 1932.

248p. 18½cm.
At head of title: Bibliothèque du Hérisson.

Martinican fiction.
Martinique
M843.9 Tardon, Raphaël, 1911-
T17b Bleu des Iles, recits Martiniquais, Fasquelle Editeurs, 1946.

209p. 19cm.

Martinican fiction.
Martinique
M843.9 Tardon, Raphaël
T17c La Caldeira, roman. Paris, Fasquelle Editeurs, 1949.

264p. 23cm.

Martinican fiction.
Martinique
M843.9 Tardon, Raphaël, 1911-
T17c Christ au Poing, roman. Paris, Fasquelle [1950]

267p. 21cm.

Martinican fiction.
Martinique
M843.9 Tardon, Raphaël, 1911-
T17s Starkenfirst, roman. Paris, Fasquelle Editeurs, 1947.

201p. 22½cm.
Received Prix des Antilles

Martinican fiction.
Martinique
M843.9 Zobel, Joseph
Z71 Diab' - la; roman antillais. Préface de Georges Pillement. Paris, Nouvelles Editions Latines [1946]

174p. 18½cm.

Martinican literature.
Martinique
M972.98 Dufougeré, William 1878-
D87m ...Madinina, "Reine des Antilles", étude de moeurs martiniquaises; préface de M. le professeur A. Lacroix ... Avec 61 réproductions photographiques, couverture de Pierre Bodard ...frontispice en coleurs de Maurice Millière, bandeaux et culs-de-lampe d'après les dessins originaux de Colmet d'Aage, Paris, Berger-Levrault, 1929.

viii p., 1 l., 258p. 1 l. col. front., illus., plates, fold map. 24cm.

Martinican poetry.
Martinique
M841.91 Carbet, Claude
C17p ...Piment rouge, avec un portrait par Thérèse Ambourg. [by] Claude and Magdeleine carbet. Paris, Les Cahiers D'Art et D'Amitié, 1938.

35p. illus. 19cm. (La Poésie no. 15)

Martinican poetry.
Martinique
M841.91 Césaire, Aimé, 1913-
C33a ... Les armes miraculeuses. [Paris] Gallimard [1946]

2 p. l., 7-195, [1] p., 1 l. 19cm.

I. Title.
PQ4809.E69A8 842.91 47-15971
© 30 May46; Librairie Gallimard; AF2059.

Library of Congress [3]

Martinican poetry.
Martinique
M841.91 Césaire, Aimé
C33s Soleil cou-coupé. Paris, K, 1948.

123p. 23cm. (Collection Le Quadrangle)

Martinique
M841.91 Martinican poetry.
C81a Coridun, Victor.
A mes frères humains, sonnets & ballades. Fort-de-France, Imp. R. Illemay, 1934.

16 leaves. 21cm.
Martinican author.

Martinique
M841.91 Martinican poetry.
C81j Coridun, Victor.
"J'ai voulu venger mon frère;" sonnets & ballade. Ford-de-France, Imp. R. Illemay, 1936.

10 leaves. illus. 19cm.
Martinican author.
At head of title: Vers la revision du procès André Aliker.

Martinican poetry.
Martinique
M841.91 Coridun, Victor
C81p La promenade amoureuse "Vers le bonheur". sextour. Fort-de-France, Imp. R. Illemay, 1933.

121 22cm.
At head of title: Pour la propagande. Allons! ... Femme, en avant! ...

Martinican poetry.
Martinique
M841.91 Romanette, Irmine
R66s Sonate, poésies, Dessins de Georges Guiraud. Paris, Jouve, 1951, c1950.

190p. port. illus. 19cm.

Martinican poetry.
Martinique
M841.91 Thaly, Daniel Desiré Alin, 1879-
T32ch Chansons de mer et d'outre mer. Paris, Editions de la Phalange, 1911.

108p. 19½cm.

Martinican poetry.
Martinique
M841.91 Thaly, Daniel Desiré Alin, 1879-
T32c Chants de l'Atlantique suivis de sous le ciel des Antilles. Paris, La Muse Française, Garnier Editeur, 1928.

128p. port. 19½cm.

Martinican poetry.
Martinique
M841.91 Thaly, Daniel Desiré Alin, 1879-
T32cl La clarté du Sud; poèmes. Toulouse, Société Provinciale d'Edition, 1905.

107p. 18½cm.
Inscribed presentation copy.

Martinican poetry.
Martinique
M841.91 Thaly, Daniel Desiré Alin, 1879-
T32p Paysages invioles.

(In: Le Beffroi, 74:17-22, Janvier 1908)

Martinique Martinique.
M972.98 Thomarel, André
T36p Parfums et saveurs des Antilles. Préface de Daniel Thaly, illustré par Ardachés Baldjian. [Paris, Ch. Ebener, 1934]
42p. plates. 32cm.
This edition is printed on Japanese paper.

Martinique Martinique--Description and travel.
M972.98 Thomarel, André
T36c Contes & paysages de la Martinique. [Woodcuts by P.A. Bailly. Fort-de-France, Imprimerie Antillaise] 1930.
160p. illus. 24cm.

Martinique.
Martinique
M972.98 Daude, Théodore
D32m ...La Martinique. Paris, Société d'Editions, 1931.
29p. 28cm.
At head of title: Exposition Coloniale Internationale de Paris.

Martinique.
Martinique
M972.98 Thomarel, André
T36r ...Regrets et tendresses, Préface de Robert Chauvelot, 1936.
76p. 19cm.
At head of title: Sous le ciel des Antilles

Guadeloupe Martinique-Economic conditions.
M972.98 Banbuck, Cabuzel Andréa.
B22h ... Histoire politique, économique et sociale de la Martinique sous l'ancien régime (1635-1789) ... Paris, M. Rivière, 1935.
335 p., 2 l. col. front., fold. map. 25cm. (Bibliothèque d'histoire économique)
"Liste des principaux administrateurs de la Martinique, depuis 1637 jusqu'à 1789": p. [319]-321.
"Bibliographie": p. [13]-19.
1. Martinique—Hist. 2. Martinique—Econ. condit. 3. Martinique—Soc. condit.
36-1642
Library of Congress F2081.B35
[3] 972.98

Martinique.
Martinique
M843.9 Lero, Yva,
L56 Doucherie. Port-de-France, Horizons Caraibes [c 1958]
115p. illus. 21cm.

Martinique - Biography.
Martinique
MB Joyau, Auguste
J84 Dames de iles du temps jadis; récits historiques. Paris, Nouvelles Éditions Latines, 1948.
234p. 18½cm. (Bibliothèque l'Union Française)

Martinique - Fiction.
Martinique
M843.9 Capécia, Mayotte.
C17j Je suis Martiniquaise. Paris, Editions Corrêa, 1948.
202p. 18½cm.
Received Grand Prix de Litérature des Antilles.

Martinique Martinique.
M972.98 Miller, James Martin, 1859-1939.
M61m The Martinique horror and St. Vincent calamity, containing a full and complete account of the most appalling disaster of modern times ... by J. Martin Miller ... in collaboration with Hon. John Stevens Durham ... Philadelphia, National publishing co. [1902]
8, 17-560 p. 2 front., illus., plates, ports., maps. 23½cm.
Issued also under the title: True story of the Martinique and St. Vincent calamities ... by Prof. John Randolph Whitney.
1. La Soufrière, St. Vincent—Eruption, 1902. 2. Pelée, Mont—Eruption, 1902. 3. St. Vincent. 4. Volcanoes. I. Durham, John Stevens, 1861- joint author. II. Title.
2-17542
Library of Congress F2081.M64
[a44f1]

Martinique—Descr. & trav.
Martinique
M972.98 Dufougeré, William, 1878-
D87m ... Madinina, "Reine des Antilles", étude de mœurs martiniquaises; préface de M. le professeur A. Lacroix ... Avec 61 réproductions photographiques, couverture de Pierre Bodard ... frontispice en coleurs de Maurice Millière, bandeaux et culs-de-lampe d'après les dessins originaux de Colmet d'Aage. Paris, Berger-Levrault, 1929.
viii p., 1 l., 258 p., 1 l. col. front., illus., plates, fold. map. 24cm.
"Bibliographie": p. [241]-252.
1. Martinique—Descr. & trav. I. Title.
[Full name: William Marie Barbe Dufougeré]
30-14516
Library of Congress F2081.D86
Copyright A—Foreign 6543
[2]

Martinique - Fiction.
Martinique
M843.9 Capécia, Mayotte
C17n La négresse blanche. Paris, Editions Corrêa 1950.
18?p. 19cm.

Martinique.
Martinique
M972.98 Monplaisir, Emma
M75 La fille du caraïbe. Paris, Société d'Éditions Extérieures et Coloniales, 1960.
361p. 18½cm.

Martinique-Descr. & trav.
Martinique
M965. Fanon, Frantz, 1925-1962.
F21d Les damnés de la terre. Préface de Jean-Paul Sartre. Paris, François Maspero, 1961.
242p. 22cm.

Martinique Martinique-Fiction.
M972.98 Grandmaison, Daniel De
G76r Rendez-vous au Macouba; roman de moeurs Martiniquaises. Paris, Editions Littre, 1948.
201p. 19cm.

Martinique.
Martinique Philémon, Césaire.
M972.98 ... Galeries martiniquaises; population, mœurs, activités diverses et paysages de la Martinique; 3 cartes, 42 illustrations.
P53g 1. éd. Fort-de-France, Dans toutes les librairies et chez l'auteur; Paris, Chez l'auteur [1931]
480 p., 1 l. front., plates, ports., fold. maps. 23cm.
At foot of t.-p.: Exposition coloniale internationale, Paris, 1931.
1. Martinique. I. Paris. Exposition coloniale internationale, 1931. II. Title.
32-13871
Library of Congress F2081.P53
Copyright A—Foreign 14467
[3] 917.298

Martinique
Martinique--Description and travel.
M972.98 Lucrèce, J
L96h Histoire de la Martinique a l'usage des cours supérieur et complémentaire des écoles primaires. Ouvrage illustre de 32 gravures, par J. Lucrèce. [Paris, Chez l'auteur, 1932]
173p. illus., ports. 17½cm.

Martinique-Fiction.
Martinique
M841.91 Romanette, Irmine
R66so ...Sonson de la Martinique, roman. Paris, Société Francaise d'Editions littéraires et Techniques, 1932.
240p. 18½cm.
At head of title: Bibliothèque du Hérisson.

Martinique.
Martinique
M972.98 Pilotin, René A Th
P64f Face a l'univers (il faut réformer le conformisme). Paris, Jean D'Halluin, Editeur, 1959.
190p. 19cm. (Collection Alternance)

Martinique-Description and Travel.
Martinique
M972.98 Philémon, Césaire
P53s Souvenirs. Préface de F. Thizy. 2e ed. Paris, Exposition coloniale internationale, 1931.
176p. illus., ports. 22½cm.

Martinique-Fiction.
Martinique
M843.9 Tardon, Raphaël, 1911-
T17b Bleu des Iles, recits Martiniquais, Fasquelle Editeurs, 1946.
209p. 19cm.

Martinique - Fiction.
Martinique
M843.9 Tardon, Raphaël
T17c La Caldeira, roman. Paris, Fasquelle Editeurs, 1949.
264p. 23cm.

Martinique - History.
Martinique
M972.98 Lémery, Henry.
L54r La révolution francaise a'la Martinique. Paris, Chez Larose, 1936.
335p. plates. 20cm.

Nigeria Martyrdom, of Chief Obafemi Awolowo.
MB9 'Mosanya, Adio
Aw6m Martyrdom, of Chief Obafemi Awolowo. ₛn.p. n.d.₎
23p. 18½cm.

Martinique Martinique--Fiction.
M972.98 Thomarel, André
T35c Contes & paysages de la Martinique. ₍Woodcuts by P.A. Bailly₎ Fort-de-France, Imprimerie Antillaise, 1930.
160p. illus. 24cm.

Martinique
Martinique--History.
M972.98 Lucrèce, J
L96h Histoire de la Martinique a l'usage des cours supérieur et complémentaire des écoles primaires. Ouvrage illustre de 32 gravures, par J. Lucrèce. ₍Paris, Chez l'auteur, 1932₎
173p. illus., ports. 17½cm.

Le martyre du coeur.
M812.3 Séjour, Victor, 1816-1874.
Se4c Le martyre du coeur; drame en cinq actes, en prose, par Victor Séjour et Jules Brésil.
no.3 Paris, Michel Lévy Frères, 1858.
144p. 19cm.

Guadeloupe Martinique - Fiction.
M843.91 Thomarel, André.
T36 Nuits tropicales. Avant-propos de René Marna. Paris, Les Editions du Scorpion, 1960.
159p. 19cm. (Collection Alternance).

Martinique - Poetry.
France
M841 Alie, Benoit.
A14m Madiana, roman poétique. Paris, E. Edouard, c 1924.
92p. 19½cm.

The martyrs and the fugitive;
M813.3 Platt, S H
P69m The martyrs and the fugitive; or a narrative of the captivity, sufferings and death of an African family and the slavery and escape of their son. By Rev. S.H. Platt... New York, Printed by Daniel Fanshaw, 1859.
95p. 19½cm.

Martinique Martinique - Fiction.
M843.91 Zizine, Pierre
Z69t Théo le Paladin Martiniquais; récit. Paris, Les Editions du Scorpion ₍°1959₎
190p. 19cm. (Collection Alternance).

Martinique Martinique-poetry.
M841.91 Léopold, Emmanuel Flavia
L55p Poèmes. Paris, Pierre Seghers ₍1949₎
74p.
1. Martinique-poetry.

South Africa
M968 Marwede, H T
M36 Shall Lobolo live or die? Two opposing viewpoints on the passing of gift cattle in Bantu marriage, by H.T. Marwede and G.G. Mamabolo. Cape Town, The African Bookman, 1945.
30p. 18½cm.
1. Bantu-marriage laws & customs. II. Mamabolo, G G ,jt. auth.

Martinique - fiction.
Martinique
M843.9 Zobel, Joseph
Z71 Diab' - la; roman antillais. Préface de Georges Pillement. Paris, Nouvelles Editions Latines ₍1946₎
174p. 18½cm.

Guadaloupe. Martinique - Social conditions.
M972.98 Banbuck, Cabuzel Andréa.
B22h ... Histoire politique, économique et sociale de la Martinique sous l'ancien régime (1635–1789) ... Paris, M. Rivière, 1935.
335 p., 2 l. col. front., fold. map. 25ᶜᵐ. (Bibliothèque d'histoire économique)
"Liste des principaux administrateurs de la Martinique, depuis 1637 jusqu'à 1789": p. ₍319₎–321.
"Bibliographie": p. ₍13₎–19.
1. Martinique—Hist. 2. Martinique—Econ. condit. 3. Martinique—Soc. condit. 4. Guadaloupan author.
36-1642
Library of Congress F2081.B35
₍3₎ 972.98

Marxism and Negro liberation.
M335.4 Hall, Gus.
H14m Marxism and Negro liberation. New York, New Century, 1951.
24p. 19cm.

Guadeloupe Martinique-Hist.
M972.98 Banbuck, Cabuzel Andréa.
B22h ... Histoire politique, économique et sociale de la Martinique sous l'ancien régime (1635–1789) ... Paris, M. Rivière, 1935.
335 p., 2 l. col. front., fold. map. 25ᶜᵐ. (Bibliothèque d'histoire économique)
"Liste des principaux administrateurs de la Martinique, depuis 1637 jusqu'à 1789": p. ₍319₎–321.
"Bibliographie": p. ₍13₎–19.
1. Martinique—Hist. 2. Martinique—Econ. condit. 3. Martinique—Soc. condit.
36-1642
Library of Congress F2081.B35
₍3₎ 972.98

Martinique La Martinique et ses danses.
M793 Monplaisir, Emma
M75 La Martinique et ses danses. Conférence faite au Ciné-Théâtre le 1er Décembre 1961. Fort-de-France, Imp. Bezaudin, 1962.
32p. illus. 18cm

Ethiopia Mary, Virgin-Legends.
M963 Budge, *Sir* Ernest Alfred Thompson Wallis, 1857–1934, *ed.*
B85o One hundred and ten miracles of Our Lady Mary, translated from Ethiopic manuscripts for the most part in the British museum, with extracts from some ancient European versions, and illustrations from the paintings in manuscripts by Ethiopian artists, by Sir E. A. Wallis Budge ... London, Oxford university press, H. Milford, 1933.
lvii, ₍2₎, 355, ₍1₎ p. LXVI pl. (incl. front.) 19½ᶜᵐ.
A cheap edition of the one published by the Medici society in London, 1923. Contains all of the plates of the 1923 edition.
(Continued on next card)
A 34—1044
₍44e1₎

Martinique Martinique - History.
M972.98 Gratiant, Gilbert
G77f Ile fédérée Française de la Martinique. Paris, Editions Louis Soulanges, 1961.
110p. 18cm.

Martinique
The Martinique horror and St. Vincent calamity.
M972.98 Miller, James Martin, 1859–1939.
M61m The Martinique horror and St. Vincent calamity, containing a full and complete account of the most appalling disaster of modern times ... by J. Martin Miller ... in collaboration with Hon. John Stevens Durham ... Philadelphia, National publishing co. ₍1902₎
8, 17–560 p. 2 front., illus., plates, ports., maps. 23½ᶜᵐ.
Issued also under the title: True story of the Martinique and St. Vincent calamities ... by Prof. John Randolph Whitney.
1. La Soufrière, St. Vincent—Eruption, 1902. 2. Pelée, Mont—Eruption, 1902. 3. St. Vincent. 4. Volcanoes. I. Durham, John Stevens, 1861– joint author. II. Title.
2-17542
Library of Congress F2081.M64
₍a44f1₎

Mary Jane.
M813.5 Sterling, Dorothy, 1913–
St4m Mary Jane. Illustrated by Ernest Crichlow. ₍1st ed.₎ Garden City, N. Y., Doubleday, 1959.
214 p. illus. 22 cm.
I. Title.
PZ7.S8376Mar 59—7917 ‡
Library of Congress ₍60f7₎

M271.76
M360
[Mary Petra, *sister*] 1865–
Blossoms gathered from the lower branches; or, A little work of an Oblate sister of providence ... [St. Louis, Con. P. Curran printing co., °1914]
4 p. l., 7–69 p., 1 l. incl. pl., ports. 20cm.
1. Oblate sisters of providence. I. Title.
[*Secular name:* Mary Clopenia Boston]
Library of Congress BX4410.O2M3 15–4659 Revised
[r44b2]

Maryland.
M315.4
D772al
1893
Douglass, Frederick, 1817-1895.
Life and times of Frederick Douglass, written by himself. His early life as a slave, his escape from bondage, and his complete history to the present time, including his connection with the anti-slavery movement...With an introduction, by Mr. George L. Ruffin. New revised edition. Boston, DeWolfe, Fiske & Co., 1893.
752p. port. (front.) 19½cm.
"First edition of final revised edition with long autograph inscription by Frederick Douglass. (cont.)

Maryland.
M975
N31
Thom, William Taylor.
The Negroes of Sandy Spring, Maryland: A special study. Bulletin of the labor Dept., no.32, 1901. pp. 43-102.
In: The Negro in the black belt... Washington, D.C., Dept. of Labor, [1897-1902]

Maryland - Biographies
MB
B73m
1925
Bragg, George Freeman, 1863-
Men of Maryland. Baltimore, Md., Church Advocate Press, 1925.
160p. front. (3port.) port. 19½cm.
History and biographical sketches of Maryland Negroes.
On cover: Revised edition.

Maryland - Biographies
MB
B73m
Bragg, George Freeman, 1863-
Men of Maryland. Baltimore, Md., Church Advocate Press, 1914.
135p. incl. front. (group of ports.) 18½cm.
History and biographical sketches of Maryland Negroes.

Maryland-History.
MB
B73r
Bragg, George Freeman, 1863-1940.
A race with a history and a country [by] The Rev. George Freeman Bragg .... Baltimore, Md., C. M. Dorsey & sons [n.d.]
31 [5]p. 17½cm.

M500
M36n
Maryland. Morgan State College, *Baltimore.*
The Negro in science, by the Calloway Hall editorial committee: Julius H. Taylor, editor [and others. Baltimore] Morgan State College Press [1955]
viii, 192 p. illus. 26 cm.
Includes bibliographies.
1. Science—Addresses, essays, lectures. 2. Negro scientists. I. Taylor, Julius H., ed. II. Title.
Q171.M312 .504 55—63107
Library of Congress [56e2]

M975.26
M36
Maryland Commission on Interracial Problems and Relations.
An American city in transition; the Baltimore community self-survey of inter-group relations. Baltimore, Commission on Human Relations, 1955.
264p. illus. tables 23cm.
1. Baltimore, Maryland - History. 2. Inter-group problems. I. Title.

The Maryland Home for Friendless Colored Children.
M283
B73
no.9
Bragg, George F[reeman]
The twenty-fifty anniversary of the founding of the Maryland home for Friendless colored children, Baltimore County, Md. [Baltimore, Md., 1924]
38[p. 20cm.

Más allá canta el mar.
Cuba
M861.6
P34m
Pedroso, Regino, 1896–
Más allá canta el mar; poema de Regino Pedroso. Premio nacional de poesía, 1938. La Habana, En la Verónica, imprenta de Manuel Altolaguirre, 1939.
5 p. l., 13–66, [1] p., 2 l. 26½cm. (*On cover:* Ediciones "Heroe")
I. Title. A C 40-2435
Harvard univ. Library for Library of Congress [2]

MB9
M83m
Masa, Jorge O.
The angel in ebony; or, The life and message of Sammy Morris, by Jorge O. Masa; published by class of 1928 of Taylor university. Upland, Ind., Taylor university press [°1928]
131 p. front., plates, ports. 17½cm.
1. Morris, Samuel, 1873–1893. I. Title. 28–3768
Library of Congress E185.97.M86
——— Copy 2.
Copyright A 2861 [3]

Kenya Masai.
M572-967
J25
Janira, Simbo.
Kleiner grosser schwarzer Mann; Lebenserinnerungen eines Buschnegers. Während der Grabung nach dem afrikanischen Vormenschen aufgenommen von Ludwig Kohl-Larsen. Eisenach, E. Röth-Verlag [1956]
210 p. illus. 24 cm. (Das Gesicht der Völker)
1. Masai. I. Kohl-Larsen, Ludwig. II. Title.
DT429.J3 56-46187 ‡
Library of Congress [3]

Masai - Social life and customs.
Kenya
M967.62
M871i
Mpaayei, John Tompo Ole
Inkuti pukunot oo lmaasai. [Masai life and customs] Edited by A. N. Tucker. London, Oxford University Press, 1954.
74p. diagrs. 18½cm. (Annotated African Texts - III: Maasai)
Text in English and Masai.

Masai language - Readers and speakers.
Kenya
M372.4
M87
Mpaayei, John Tempo
Engolon eng'eno [Knowledge is power] Itung' ana kituaak too Imaasai, naitobirakasi J. T. Ole Mpaayei and Kariūki K. Njiiri. Eutaa Elizabeth Mooney. [Illus. by Ruth Yudelowitz] Nairobi, Eagle Press, 1960.
illus. 28cm.
Written in Masaai.
1. Masaai language - Readers and speakers. I. Title. II. Njiiri, Kariuki Karanja, 1928- jt. auth.

Uganda
M630
M37u
Masefield, G. B
Omulimi w'omu Uganda [The Uganda farmer] Kyakyusibwa E. Bulera. Nairobi, Eagle Press, 1951.
186p. illus. 18cm.
Written in Luganda.
White author.
1. Agriculture - Uganda. 2. Uganda - Agriculture. I. Title. II. Bulewa, E., tr.

M326.99B
M38
Mason, Isaac, 1822–
Life of Isaac Mason as a slave. Worcester, Mass., 1893.
74 p. incl. front. (port.) 26½cm.
Autobiography.
1. Slavery in the U. S.
2. Slave narratives. A 12–61
Title from Univ. of Chicago E444.M39 Printed by L. C.
[a32b1]

Masimulizi na desturi ya Afrika ya Mashariki.
Kenya
M967.62
N49
Ngala, Ronald Gideon, 1923-
Nchi na desturi za wagiriama [The land and customs of the Giriama] Nairobi, Eagle Press 1949.
41p. illus. 18cm. (Masimulizi na desturi ya Afrika ya Mashariki. Custom and tradition in East Africa series)
Written in Swahili.
1. Kenya - Native races. 2. Giryama tribe. I. Title. II. Series. III. Series: Custom and tradition in East Africa series.

Mawazo ya wenzenu.
Kenya
M967.6
K23
Kebaso, John K 1911-
Jinsi Afrika mashariki inavyowiwa deni kubwa na utawala wa dola ya kiingereza. East Africa owes much to British rule. Nairobi, Eagle Press, 1953.
[47]p. 18½cm. (Mawazo ya wenzenu. Your friends are thinking series)
Written in Swahili and English.
1. Africa, British East - Politics and government. I. Title. II. Title: East Africa owes much to British rule. III. Series. IV. Series: Your friends are thinking series.

U.S.
M960
C76a
Mason, Madison Charles Butler, 1859-1915
The Methodist Episcopal Church and the evangelization of Africa.
Pp. 143-148.
In: Congress on Africa, Atlanta, 1895. Africa and the American Negro. Atlanta, Gamma Theological Seminary, 1896.

M814.5
M38
Mason, Madison Charles Butler, 1859–1915.
Solving the problem; a series of lectures by the late Rev. M. C. B. Mason ... comp. by Mrs. M. C. B. Mason ... [Mt. Morris, Ill., Kable brothers company] 1917.
142 p. front. (port.) 20cm. $1.25
1. Mason, Mary E., "Mrs. M. C. B. Mason," comp. 2. Race problems
Library of Congress AC8.M384 17–30911
Copyright A 477487

Mason, Mary E., "Mrs. M. C. B. Mason." comp.
M814.5
M38
Mason, Madison Charles Butler, 1859–1915.
Solving the problem; a series of lectures by the late Rev. M. C. B. Mason ... comp. by Mrs. M. C. B. Mason ... [Mt. Morris, Ill., Kable brothers company] 1917.
142 p. front. (port.) 20cm. $1.25
1. Mason, Mary E., "Mrs. M. C. B. Mason," comp.
Library of Congress AC8.M384 17–30911
Copyright A 477487

M811.5
M38n
Mason, Mason Jordan
Notebook 1, 3-4, 23,
New Mexico, Motive Book Shop, n.d.,

v. illus. 21cm.

1. Poetry.

M304
P19
V.7
No.33
Masonic quarterly review, vol. 1, no.3
Brooklyn, N.Y., Prince Hall Masons, June 1920.

58 unnumb. p. 26½cm.

1. Freemasons. 2. Periodicals. I. Grimshaw, W. H. - Masonry is the one great association. II. Marrant, John - A sermon preached on the 24th day of June 1789.

Masques et visages.

Haiti
M843.91
H52ma
Hibbert, Fernand.
... Masques et visages. Port-au-Prince, Imprimerie-librairie du "Matin", 1910.

320 p. 20cm.

I. Title.

25-20876

Library of Congress PQ3949.H5M3

M811.5
M38n
Mason, Mason Jordan.
Notebook #23. New Mexico, Motive Book Shop, n.d.

13p. illus. 21cm.

1. Poetry. I. Title.

Masonry.

M815.5
B83
No.11
Bruce, John Edward, 1856-
The mission and the opportunity of the Negro mason. Notes on Solomon's Temple.

7p. 21cm.

Trinidad
M972.98
W67m
Massa day done.
Williams, Eric Eustace, 1911-
Massa day done; a masterpiece of political and sociological analysis. Address delivered on Wednesday, March 27, 1961. Port-of-Spain, PNM Pub. Co., 1961.

19p. 21cm.
Portrait of author on front cover.

M811.5
M38y
Mason, Mason Jordan
The yardarm of Murphey's kite. Ranches of Taos, New Mexico, Motive Press, 1956.

58p. illus. 24½cm.

1. Poetry. I. Title.

Masonry.

M815.5
B83
No.6
Bruce, John Edward, 1856-
Prince Hall, the Pioneer of Negro masonry. Proofs of the legitimacy of Prince Hall masonry, by John Edward Bruce. New York, 1921.

12p. 17cm.

Massachusetts.

M366.1
F87m4
Freemasons. Massachusetts. Prince Hall Grand Lodge.
Proceedings. 1st- [1791?]
17 -

v. 23cm. annual
Proceedings of special communications for 1908 and 1909 bound with 1909.
See holdings card for proceedings in library.

M356
M38
Mason, Monroe.
The American negro soldier with the Red Hand of France, by Monroe Mason and Arthur Furr ... Boston, The Cornhill company ~~1920~~ [1921]

180 p. front., plates, port., plan. 19cm.

1. European war, 1914-1918—Negroes. I. Furr, Arthur, joint author. II. Title.

21—14430

Library of Congress D639.N4M3
—— Copy 2.
Copyright A 622436 [a25c1]

Masonry.

M304
P19
V.6, no.7
Schomburg, Arthur Alfonso, 1874-
Masonic truths, a letter and a document. [lacks imprint]

43p. 20½cm.

Massachusetts anti-slavery fair.

M326.080
L61
The Liberty bell. By friends of freedom .. Boston, Massachusetts anti-slavery fair, 1839-46; National anti-slavery bazaar, 1847-58.

15 v. plates, ports. 17½-20cm.
"Edited and published annually in Boston, by Maria Weston Chapman, 1843 to 1858 (one or two years being omitted)"—Samuel May, Catalogue of anti-slavery publications in America.
No volumes issued for 1840, 1850, 1854-55, 1857. cf. Faxon, Literary annuals and gift books.
Volume for 1841 wanting in L. C. set.

1. Slavery in the U. S. 2. Gift-books (Annuals, etc.) I. Chapman, Maria (Weston) 1806-1885, ed. II. Massachusetts anti-slavery fair, III. National anti-slavery bazaar, Boston.

5—22887

Library of Congress E449.L69
[a31i1]

M304
P19
v.7
no.22
Mason, U G
An appeal to the white citizens for better Negro schools in the city of Birmingham, by U.G. Mason. [Reprint from Birmingham age-herald]
7p. 22cm.

1. Education - Birmingham.
2. Birmingham, Ala.

Masonry.

M304
P19
v.6,no.2
Williamson, Harry A.
Negroes and freemasonry. [lacks imprint, 1920]
24p. 18cm.

Les massacres de la syrie.

M812.3
Se4c
No.2
Séjour, Victor, 1816-1874.
Les massacres de la syrie; drame en huit tableaux, Paris, J. Barbré, n.d.

136p. 19cm.

M396
C26
Mason, Vivian C
Women in education.

Pp. 116-123.

In: Cassara, Beverly Benner, ed. American women. Boston, Beacon Press [1962]

Masonry among colored men in Massachusetts.

M366.1
H32m
[Hayden, Lewis]
Masonry among colored men in Massachusetts. To the Right Worshipful J. G. Findel, honorary grand master of the Prince Hall grand lodge, and general representative thereof to the lodges upon the continent of Europe. Boston, L. Hayden, 1871.
51 p. 23cm.
Signed: Lewis Hayden.
Appendix: no. 1. "Revolution and assumption." Remarks on G. M. Gardner's address before the G. L. of Massachusetts, March 7, 1870. By Bro. Jacob Norton. no. 2. The early history of masonry in Massachusetts. By Jacob Norton. no. 3. Extract from Report of Committee of G. L. of New Hampshire.
1. Freemasons, Negro. 2. Freemasons. Massachusetts. I. Findel, Gottfried Joseph Gabriel, 1828-1905. II. Norton, Jacob. III. Title.

17-15160

Library of Congress HS887.M4H4
—— Copy 2.

Massaquoi, Fatima, tr.

Liberia
M398
L55
The leopard's daughter; a folk tale from Liberia. Translated from the Vai language by Princess Fatima Massaquoi. With illus. by Martha Burnham Humphrey. Boston, Bruce Humphries [1961]

14p. illus. 28cm.

Masonic and other poems.

M811.5
G42m
Gilmore, F. Grant.
Masonic and other poems. n.p. n.p., 1908.

[21] p. port. (front) 18cm.

The masquerade.

Nigeria
M896.2
C54
Clark, John Pepper, 1935-
Three plays: Song of a goat; The masquerade; The raft. London, Oxford University Press, 1964.

134p. 18½cm.

M301
Eb74
Massaquoi, Hans J.
Would you want your daughter to marry one
Pp. 65-78

In: Ebony. The white problem in America. Chicago, Johnson Pub. Co., 1966.

Les masses Africianes et l'actuelle condition humaine.

Sénégal
M966.3
L98ma

Ly, Abdoulaye
Les masses Africaines et l'actuelle condition humaine. Paris, Présence Africaine, 1956.

254p. 22½cm. (Enquêtes et Études)

1. Imperialism. 2. Africa. I. Title.

M254
M38

Massey, James Earl
An introduction to the Negro churches in the Church of God Reformation Movement. With a foreword by Marcus H. Morgan. New York, Shining Light Survey Press, 1957.

70p. 21½cm.

1. Churches. 2. Church of God.

M248
M38wt

Massey, James Earl.
"When thou prayest"; an interpretation of Christian prayer according to the teachings of Jesus. Anderson, Ind., Warner Press [1960]

64 p. 19 cm.
Portrait of author on back of book.
"For Mr. Spingarn: with appreciation. James Earl Massey."

1. Prayer. I. Title.

BV215.M37 248.32 60-11403 ‡

Library of Congress [2]

M811.5
M39s

Massey, Joe C 1892-
Singing stars; verses. [1st ed.] New York, Greenwich Book Publishers [°1961]

57 p. 22 cm.
Portrait of author on book jacket.

I. Title.

PS3525.A827S5 811.54 61-14817 ‡

Library of Congress [3]

Zambia
M896.3
M38L

Massiye, A Sylvester
The lonely village. London, Thomas Nelson, 1951.

48p. map. 18½cm. (Eagle fiction library)

1. Rhodesia, Northern - Fiction.
2. Achewa - Fiction. I. Title

Master keys to anatomy.

M610
C63ma

Cobb, William Montague, 1904-
Master keys to anatomy, preliminary notes. Reprinted from the Journal of the National Medical Association, 35:75-86, May 1943.

75-86p. illus. 27cm.

Masterpieces of Negro eloquence.

M815
N33

Nelson, *Mrs.* Alice Ruth (Moore) Dunbar, 1875- *ed.*
Masterpieces of negro eloquence; the best speeches delivered by the negro from the days of slavery to the present time, ed. by Alice Moore Dunbar. New York, The Bookery publishing company [°1914]

512 p. front. (port.) 23cm.

1. American orations. I. Title. II. Title: Negro eloquence.

14-1930

Library of Congress PS663.N4N4
——— Copy 2.
Copyright A 362234 [33g1]

Haiti
M843.91
R76ma

Masters of the dew.
Roumain, Jacques, 1907-1945
Masters of the dew. Translated by Langston Hughes and Mercer Cook. New York, Reynal & Hitchcock, [1947]

180p. 19cm.

The Master's slave.

MB9
F53

Fisher, Miles Mark.
The Master's slave, Elijah John Fisher; a biography, by his son, Miles Mark Fisher ... with an introduction by the Rev. Lacey Kirk William, D. D., and an appreciation by the Hon. Martin B. Madden ... Philadelphia, Boston [etc.] The Judson press [1922]

12 p. l., 3-194 p. front., plates, ports. 20cm.

1. Fisher, Elijah John, 1858-1915. I. Title.

22-13782

Library of Congress BX6455.F5F5

[45c1]

M301
M39

Masuoka, Jitsuichi, 1903- ed.
Race relations: problems and theory; essays in honor of Robert E. Park. Edited by Jitsuichi Masuoka and Preston Valien. Chapel Hill, University of North Carolina Press [1961]

x 290p. 24cm.

Bibliographical footnotes.
White editor.
Partial contents.- Introduction: From race relations to human relations, by Charles S. Johnson.- Racial problems in world society, by

(Continued on next card)

M301
M39

Masuoka, Jitsuichi, 1903- ed.
Race relations: problems and theory. 1961.
(Card 2)

E. Franklin Frazier.- The Montgomery bus protest as a social movement, by Valion Preston.- Struggle for the vote at Tuskegee, by Lewis W. Jones.- Economic dimensions in race relations, by Vivian W. Henderson.

1. Race problems - Addresses, essays, lectures.
2. Race question - Addresses, essays lectures.
3. Park, Robert Emory, 1868-1942.
I. Valien, Preston, joint ed. II. Title.

Kenya
M896.3
M41b

Mataamu, Bwana
The beautiful Nyakiemo; the origin of the Kikuyu-Masai. Illustrated by Ruth Yudelowitz. London, Nelson [1951]

39p. illus. 18cm. (Eagle fiction library)

I. Title.

Matalaché.

Peru
M863.6
L88m

López Albújar, Enrique, 1872-
Matalaché. Lima, Juan Mejia Baca & P. L. Villanueva, Editores, 19??

195p. 17½cm.
Inscribed.

I. Title.

Matalaché.

Peru
M863.6
L88m

López Albújar, Enrique, 1872-
Matalaché. Segunda edicion. Lima, Juan Mejia Baca & P. L. Villanueva, Editores, 1955.

209p. 21½cm.
Inscribed.

I. Title.

Matalonga, P., ed.

Peru
M985
P18

Palma, Ricardo, 1833-1919.
... La monja de la llave; prólogo de P. Matalonga ... México, D. F., Compañía general editora, s. a., 1940.

191, [1] p. 18½cm. (Colección Mirasol. [4])

"Forman este volumen dieciseis 'historias de amor,' extraídas de las 'Tradiciones peruanas'."—p. 11.

1. Legends—Peru. I. Matalonga, P., ed. II. Title.

[Full name: Manuel Ricardo Palma]

42-12800

Library of Congress F3409.P1733

[3] 985

Ghana
M966.7
M41

Mate, C M O
A visual history of Ghana; illustrated by Ann and Donald Goring. London, Evans Brothers, 1959.

64p. illus. 24½cm.

1. Ghana-Hist. I. Title.

Maternal and infant welfare - Africa, West.

Nigeria
M966.9
On1

Onabamiro, Sanya Dojo.
Why our children die; the causes, and suggestions for prevention, of infant mortality in West Africa. With a foreword by Lancelot Hogben. London, Methuen [1949]

xi, 195 p. 20 cm.
"References": p. 187-190.

1. Infants—Mortality. 2. Maternal and infant welfare—Africa, West. 3. Obstetrics.

RG518.A3M3 618.2 50-15163

Library of Congress [3]

Mathematics.

M304
F19
v.3,no.10

Sherrod, Fletcher.
Geometry; the trisection of the angle and theorems and corollaries leading to it. Revised, 1933. Fletcher Sherrod, author and publisher. New Orleans, La., °1932-1933.

[14] p. diagrs. 21½cm.

1. Trisection of angle. I. Title.

CA 33-572 Unrev'd

Library of Congress QA468.S45 1933
Copyright AA 122420 513.9

Kenya
M173
W73

Mathenge, J. P., tr.
Windstedt, R O
Mũtũũrĩre na mwĩcĩrĩrĩe mwega [Right living and right thinking] Ritauritwo ni J. P. Mathenge na A. H. Kanyuru. Nairobi, Eagle Press, 1954.

89p. 18cm.
Written in Kikuyu.
White author.

1. Ethics. I. Title. II. Mathenge, J. P., tr. III. Kanyuru, A. H., jt. tr.

Mather, Frank Lincoln, ed.

MB
W62

Who's who of the colored race; a general biographical dictionary of men and women of African descent ... Chicago, 1915-

v. illus. 20cm.

Vol. 1 edited by Frank Lincoln Mather.
Vol. 1: Memento edition, half-century anniversary of Negro freedom in U. S.

1. Negroes—Biog. I. Mather, Frank Lincoln, ed.

15-25373

Library of Congress E185.96.W6

[a25g1]

Matheus, John Frederic, joint ed.

France
M840
D89ge

Dumas, Alexandre, 1802-1870.
Dumas' Georges; an intermediate French reader; edited with introduction, notes, and vocabulary by W. Napoleon Rivers ... and John Frederic Matheus ... Washington, D. C., The Associated publishers [°1936]

2 p. l., vii-xi p., 1 l., 233 p. 17cm.

Attributed by Mirecourt to Malleflle. *cf.* A. F. Davidson, Alexandre Dumas, 1902, p. 397.

1. French language—Chrestomathies and readers. I. Rivers, William Napoleon, 1897- ed. II. Matheus, John Frederic, joint ed. III. Mallefille, Jean Pierre Félicien, 1813-1868, supposed author. IV. Title: Georges.

36-37277

Library of Congress PQ2227.G4 1936
——— Copy 2.
Copyright A 100906 [3] 843.76

MP9
AL7m
Mathews Marcia M
Richard Allen. ₍1st ed.₎ Baltimore, Helicon ₍©1963₎
vi, 151 p. 23 cm.

1. Allen, Richard, Bp., 1760-1831.

BX8459.A4M3 922.773 63-19403

Library of Congress ₍5₎

Ruanda
M896.3
M42b
Mathieu, Jean
Le bien des etres; essai. Quatrieme edition. Bruxelles, Imprimerie des Sciences, 1952.

124p. 19cm.

I. Title.

Ruanda
M896.3
M42c
Mathieu, Jean
La consultation de midi; roman. Bruxelles, Imprimerie des Sciences, 1955.

166p. 19cm.

I. Title.

Ruanda
M896.3
M42h
Mathieu, Jean
Les hommes de l'aube; roman. Bruxelles, Imprimerie de Sciences, 1955.

110p. 20cm.

I. Title.

Haiti
M972.94
M42d
Mathon, Etienne *ed.*
Documents pour l'histoire d'Haïti; révolutions de 1888-1889; actes des trois départements du Nord, du Nord-ouest et de l'Artibonite, et du gouvernement provisoire du 27 novembre 1888, recueillis et annotés par M. E. Mathon ... Paris, H. Jouve, 1890.
2 p. l., 260 p. 23ᶜᵐ.

1. Haiti—Hist.—1844- —Sources. I. Title.

Library of Congress F1926.M48 1-27962
——— Copy 2. ₍a30d1₎

Haiti
M842
M42j
Mathon, Etienne.
...Judas: dreme Haitien en 4 actes en prose. Port-au-Prince, Imprimerie de l' Abeille, 1916.

63pl 20½cm.

1. Haitian drama. I. Title.

Cameroons, French
M896.3
M42b
Matip, Benjamin, 1932-
A la belle étoile; contes et nouvelles d'Afrique. Paris, Présence Africaine, 1962.

91p. 18cm.

I. Title.

Fr. Cameroons
M896.3
M42
Matip, Benjamin 1932.
Afrique, nous t'ignorons! Paris, Editions Renee Lacoste & Cie, 1956.

125p. 18½cm.
Portrait of author on cover.

I. Title.

Cameroons, French
M960
M43
Matip, Benjamin, 1932-
Heurts et malheurs des rapports Europe Afrique noire dans l'histoire moderne (du 15e au 19e siecle). ₍Paris₎ La Nef de Paris Editions ₍1958₎

124p. port., map. 18½cm.
Includes bibliography.

1. Europe - Relations (general) with Africa.
2. Africa - Relations (general) with Europe.
3. Africa - History. I. Title.

Brazil
M869.3
M18am
Matos, Mário
Machado de Assis, o homem e a obra, os personagens explicam o autor. Rio de Janeiro, Companhia Editora Nacional, 1939.

454p. 19cm. (Brasiliana, Biblioteca pedagógica Brasileira. Serie 5 vol. 153)

1. Machado de Assis, Joaquim Maria, 1839-1908

Congo (Leopoldville)
M967.5
M42
Matota, H
Influence des membres masculins de la famille sur l'enfant Mukongo; etude descriptive et interpretative. ₍Louvain, Institut de Psychologie Appliquee et de Pedagogie, 1958₎
261p. tables, map. 27cm.
Mimeographed.
At head of title: Université Catholique de Louvain. Institut de Psychologie Appliquée et de Pedagogie

(Continued on next card)

Congo (Leopoldville)
M967.5
M42
Matota, H Influence des membres masculins de la famille sur l'enfant Mukongo, 1958. (Card 2)

"Mémoire présenté par H. Matota, S. J., pour l'obtention du grade de licencié en psychologie appliquée."
"Références bibliographiques:" p. 252-256.
1. Congo, Belgian. 2. Family - Congo, Belgian. 3. Parent and child. 4. Children in the Congo. I. Title.

Africa, South
MB9
M43c
Matshikiza, Todd, 1920-1968
Chocolates for my wife. London, Hodder and Stoughton, 1961.

127p. 21cm.
Portrait of author and his wife on back of book jacket.

I. Title.

Matthews, James, 1929-
Africa, South
M896.3
R52
Rive, Richard, 1931- ed.
Quartet; new voices from South Africa: Alex La Guma, James Matthews, Alf Wannenburgh, Richard Rive. New York, Crown Publishers ₍1963₎

223p. 22cm.
Short stories.

M813.4
M42a
Matthews, ₍Victoria Earle₎, 1861-
Aunt Lindy; a story founded on real life, by Victoria Earle; illustrated by Mary L. Payne. New York ₍Press of J. J. Little & co.₎ 1893.
16 p. front., plates. 18½ᶜᵐ.

Library of Congress PZ3.E128A 6-36389†

Matthews, Victoria Earle, 1861-
M814.4
W272b
Washington, Booker Taliaferro, 1859?-1915.
Black-belt diamonds; gems from the speeches, addresses, and talks to students of Booker T. Washington ... selected and arranged by Victoria Earle Matthews; introduction by T. Thomas Fortune. New York, Fortune and Scott, 1898.
xii, 115 p. front. (port.) 15ᶜᵐ.

1. Negroes. I. Matthews, Victoria Earle.

Library of Congress E185.6.W3 98-552 Revised
Copyright 1898: 40043 ₍r32c2₎

M815.4
M43y
Matthews, William E.
'Young manhood: it's relations to a worthy future.' Address delivered before the literary societies of Wilberforce university, commencement week, June 15th, 1880, by William E. Matthews ... ₍Washington? D. C., 1880₎
cover-title, 1 p. l., 15 p. 20½ᶜᵐ.

1. Young men. 15-17286

Library of Congress BJ1671.M6

Africa, South
M968
Sp6s
Matthews, Zachariah Keodirelang, 1901- 1968
The education of the African.

pp. 169-192.
In: South Africa the road ahead, comp. by Hildegarde Spottiswoode. 1960.

1. Africa - Education. 2. Education - Africa. I. Title.

Mau Mau.
Kenya
M967.6
K14
Kariuki, Josiah Mwangi, 1929-
Mau Mau detainee; the account by a Kenya African of his experiences in detention camps, 1953-1960. Foreword by Margery Perham. London, Oxford University Press, 1963.
188 p. illus. 23 cm.

1. Mau Mau.
DT434.E27K3 1963 365.4 63-4983 ‡

Library of Congress ₍63c2₎

Maud Martha.
M811.5
B791m
Brooks, Gwendolyn, 1917-
Maud Martha, a novel. ₍1st ed.₎ New York, Harper ₍1953₎
180 p. 20 cm.

I. Title.
PZ4.B872Mau 53-7726 ‡
Library of Congress ₍54f5₎

Mauritius
M841
M44m
Maunick, Edouard J
Les manèges de la mer. Paris, Présence Africaine ₍1964₎

101p. 19½cm.

I. Title.

Mauritius. Archives Department.

Mauritius
M015.698
Ad72

Adolphe, H
Bibliography of Mauritius (1502-1954), covering the printed record, manuscripts, archivalia and carographic material, by A. Toussaint and H. Adolphe. Port Louis, Esclapon Ltd., 1956.

884p. 23cm.

Mauritius.

Mauritius
M969.82
G29m

Lislet-Geoffroy, Jean Baptiste, 1755-1836.
Memoir and notice explanatory of a chart of Madagascar and the North-Eastern archipelago of amuritius; drawn up according to the latest observations, under the auspices and government of His Excellency Robert Townsend Farquhar... By Lislet Geoffrey...London, J. Murray, 1819.

v, 57p. front (fold chart) 28cm.

Mauritius - Bibliographies.

Mauritius
M015.698
Ad72

Adolphe, H
Bibliography of Mauritius (1502-1954), coverning the printed record, manuscripts, archivalia and carographic material, by A. Toussaint and H. Adolphe. Port Louis, Esclapon Ltd., 1956.

884p. 23cm.

Kenya
M967.62
Oy3

Mawazo ya wenzenu.
Oyende, J P
Chifu hodari wa kiafrika. The ideal African chief. Nairobi, Eagle Press, 1951.

14p. 18cm. (Mawazo ya wenzenu. Your friends are thinking series)
Written Swahili and English.

1. Leadership. 2. Africa - Native races. I. Title. II. Title: The ideal African chief. III. Series. IV. Series: Your friends are thinking series.

Maxie Mongoose and other animal stories.

Jamaica
M398
B53

Bird, Laurice
Maxie Mongoose and other animal stories. With a foreword by C. Bernard Lewis ... Cover design and illustrations by D. G. Dunlop. Kingston, Jamaica, Pioneer Press, 1950.

93p. illus. 19cm.

Haiti
M972.94
M45

Maximilien, Louis.
... Le vodou Haitien; rite radas canzo; preface du Dr. Pierre Mabille. Port-au-Prince, Haiti, Imprimerie de l'etat 1945.
3 p. l., ix-xxviiii, 222 p., 2 l. port., illus., 21cm.

1. Haitian literature.

Maximilien, Louis.

Haiti
M972.94
r7

L'art précolombien d'Haïti; catalogue de l'Exposition précolombienne organisée à l'occasion du IIIe Congrès des Caraibes sous le haut patronage de son excellence mr. Stenio Vincent, président de la République, présenté par mm. Edmond Mangones et le major Louis Maximilien. [Port-au-Prince, Imprimerie de l'état, 1941]

29 p., 2 l. LXII pl. 28½cm.

"Il a été tiré de ce catalogue cinq cents exemplaires sur papier velvetone india paraphes."

1. Haiti—Antiq. 2. Indians of the West Indies—Haiti—Art. 3. Indians of the West Indies—Art. I. Congrès des Caraibes. 3d, Port-au-Prince, Haiti, 1941. II. Mangones, Edmond. III. Maximilien, Louis.

S 42-1 Revised

Smithsonian inst. Library for Library of Congress F1909.A68 [r43c2]† 918.7204

M81?.5
Sa4j

Maxims
Sampson, John Patterson
Jolly people. The author, n.d.

11, 5 p. 27cm.

Nigeria
M896.3
M45f

Maxwell, Highbred
Forget me not. [Onitsha, Nigeria, All Star Publishers, n.d.]

56p. 21cm.

I. Title.

Nigeria
M896.3
M45p

Maxwell, Highbred
Public opinion on lovers. Onitsha, Nigeria, Students' Own Bookshop [n.d.]

46p. 21cm.

I. Title.

Barbados
M942
M45

Maxwell, Neville George Anthony.
The power of Negro action, by Neville Maxwell. [London] N. G. A. Maxwell [1966]
1-59 p. 22 cm. 3/-
Bibliography: p. 57-58.

(B 66-5468)

1. West Indians in Great Britain. 2. Negroes in Great Britain. 3. Gt. Brit.—Race question. I. Title.

DA125.W4M3 301.45196042 66-70698

Library of Congress [5]

M796
M45t

Maxwell, Sherman Leander, 1906–
Thrills and spills in sports [by] Jocko Maxwell. New York, Fortuny's [1939]
101 p. 20cm.
"First edition."

1. Sports—Anecdotes, facetiae, satire, etc. I. Title.

40-35018

Library of Congress GV191.M3 [2] 796.0888

M973
F85L

May, Ernest R., joint author.
Franklin, John Hope, 1915– jt. auth.
Land of the free; a history of the United States, by John W. Caughey, John Hope Franklin [and] Ernest R. May. Educational advisers: Richard M. Clowes, [and] Alfred T. Clark, Jr. Pasadena, Calif., Designed and produced by the W. Ritchie Press for Franklin Publications, 1965.
xi, 658 p. illus. (part col.) maps, ports. 27 cm.
Includes bibliographical references.

1. U. S.—Hist. ~~I. Franklin, John Hope, 1915– joint author.~~ II. May, Ernest R., joint author. III. Title.

E178.1.C36 973 65-27033

Library of Congress [5]

M326.99B
P58k

May, Samuel J
Pickard, Kate E R.
The kidnapped and the ransomed. Being the personal recollections of Peter Still and his wife "Vina," after forty years of slavery. By Mrs. Kate E. R. Pickard. With an introduction, by Rev. Samuel J. May; and an appendix, by William H. Furness, D. D. Syracuse, W. T. Hamilton; New York [etc.] Miller, Orton and Mulligan, 1856.
xxiii (*i. e.* xxi), 25–409 p. 8 pl. (incl. front.) 19 cm.
Pages ix–x omitted in paging.
Added t.-p., engraved.
"Appendix. Seth Concklin [by William H. Furness]": p. 377–409.
1. Still, Peter. 2. Still, Lavinia. 3. Slavery in the U. S.—Kentucky. 4. Slavery in the U. S.—Alabama. 5. Concklin, Seth, 1802-1851. I. Furness, William Henry, 1802-1896. II. Title.

14—15958

Library of Congress E444.S85 [48g1]

Haiti
M972.94
L32c

Mayard, Constantin, 1883-1940.
Laraque, Maurice.
... Constantin Mayard, étude par Maurice Laraque. Port-au-Prince, Haïti [Imp. Telhomme] 1944.
80 p. incl. port. 19cm. (Bibliothèque haïtienne)
"Cet petit 'essai' est extrait de mes 'Essais et portraits'."—Avant-propos.

1. Mayard, Constantin, 1882-1940.

F1926.M46L3 923.27294 47-21979

Library of Congress [1]

M813.5
M45g

Mayfield, Julian, 1928–
The grand parade. New York, Vanguard Press [1961]
448 p. 22 cm.
Portrait of author on book jacket.

I. Title.

PZ4.M47Gr 61-5233 ‡

Library of Congress [2]

M813.5
M45g2

Mayfield, Julian, 1928–
The grand parade. ~~New York, Vanguard Press [1961]~~
London, Michael Joseph [1967]
448 p. 22 cm.

I. Title.

PZ4.M47Gr 61—5233 ‡

Library of Congress [62e2]

M974.7
C55h

Mayfield, Julian, 1928-
And then came Baldwin.

Pp. 158-173.

In: Clarke, J. H., ed. Harlem, U. S. A. Berlin Seven Seas Publishers, 1964

M813.5
M45c

Mayfield, Julian, 1928-
Un coup de chance (The Hit); roman. Traduit de l'Américan par Guy Le Clec'h. Paris, Editions Albin Michel, 1960.

219p. 18½cm.

I. Title.

M813.5
M45h2

Mayfield, Julian, 1928-
The hit. New York, Pocket Books [1959, ©1957]

154p. 18 cm.

I. Title.

M813.5
M45h

Mayfield, Julian, 1928–
The hit, a novel. New York, Vanguard Press [1957]
212 p. 21 cm.

I. Title.

PZ4.M47Hi 57-12251 ‡

Library of Congress [3]

M813.5 M451o Mayfield, Julian, 1928-
The long night. London, Michael Joseph [1960]

142p. 21cm.

I. Title.

M813.5 M451 Mayfield, Julian, 1928-
The Long night. London, Michael Joseph, 1960.

142p. 20½cm.

300498 I. Title.

M616 M45 Maynard, Aubre de L
Tetracycline hydrochloride studies on absorption, diffusion, excretion, and clinical trial by Aubre de L. Maynard, Joseph C. Andriola and Aaron Prigot. New York, Medical Encyclopedia, Inc., 1954.

102-107p. tables 25cm.
Reprinted from Antibiotics annual, 1953-54.

1. Antibiotics.

Nevis M242 M45 Maynard, Aurora
The inner guidance. New York, Vantage Press [1965]

116p. 20½cm.

1. Devotional literature. I. Title

M815.5 M44a Maynor, Dorothy, 1910-
Address on the occasion of the twenty-fifth anniversary celebration of Karamu House, December 17, 1944.

3p. cm.

1. Karamu House, Cleveland, Ohio.

M973.9 F46 No.14 Mays, Benjamin Elijah, 1895-
Fifty years of progress in the Negro church. Pittsburgh, Pittsburgh Courier, 1950.

7p. port. 24cm. (Fifty years of progress)

1. Church. I. Series.

M260 M45g Mays, Benjamin Elijah, 1895- comp.
A gospel for the social awakening; selections from the writings of Walter Rauschenbusch, compiled by Benjamin E. Mays, with an introd. by C. Howard Hopkins. New York, Association Press, 1950.

187 p. 20 cm. (A Haddam House book)
Bibliography: p. [6]

1. Sociology, Christian. I. Title.
II. Rauschenbusch, Walter, 1861-1918
BR115.S6R38 208.1 51-1462
Library of Congress [10]

Mays, Benjamin Elijah, 1895-
Living is a Christian calling.

pp. 155-57
(In: Young Men's Christian Associations. International Convention. Centennial. Report. New York, Association Press, 1951.)

M323 D22 Mays, Benjamin Elijah, 1895-
The moral aspects of segregation.

Pp. 170-176.

In: Bradford, Daniel, Ed. Black, white and gray. New York, Sheed and Ward, 1964.

M260 M45nc Mays, Benjamin Elijah, 1895-
The Negro's church, by Benjamin Elijah Mays and Joseph William Nicholson. New York, Institute of social and religious research [°1933]

xiii, 321 p. illus. (maps) 19½cm.

"The Institute of social and religious research ... is responsible for this publication."—p. [ii]

1. ~~Negroes—Religion.~~ 2. Churches—U. S. I. ~~Nicholson, Joseph William, joint author.~~ II. ~~Institute of social and religious research.~~ III. Title.

33—6349
Library of Congress BR563.N4M3
——— Copy 2.
Copyright A 59658 [a40q2] [261] 325.260073

M260 M45ng Mays, Benjamin Elijah, 1895-
The Negro's God as reflected in his literature [by] Benjamin E. Mays ... lithographs by James L. Wells. Boston, Chapman & Grimes, inc. [°1938]

viii p., 1 l., 269 p. 20cm.
Bibliography: p. 257-268.

1. Negro literature—Hist. & crit. 2. Negroes—Religion. 3. God. 4. Religion in literature. I. Title.

38—37550
Library of Congress PS153.N5M3
[43i1] [231] 810.9

M323 M45 Mays, Benjamin Elijah, 1895-
Race in America; the Negro perspective.

Pp. 65-72.

In: Smith, Huston, ed. The Search for America. Englewood Cliffs, N. J., Prentice-Hall, 1959.

M260 M45s Mays, Benjamin Elijah, 1895-
Seeking to be Christian in race relations. New York, Friendship Press, 1957.

84 p. 20 cm.

"Third printing" Revised with two new chapters added.

1. Race problems. 2. Church and social problems. I. Title.
BR115.R3M3 1957 °261.8 57—6580 ‡
Library of Congress [58k10]

M260 M45s Mays, Benjamin Elijah, 1895-
... Seeking to be Christian in Race Relations, by Benjamin E. Mays. New York, Friendship Press [1946]

48p. 18cm. (Study and action pamphlets on race relations)

M231 W62 Mays, Benjamin Elijah, 1895-
Why I believe there is a God.

Pp. 2-7.

In: Why I believe there is a God. Chicago, Johnson Pub. Co., 1965.

M231 W62 Mays, Benjamin Elijah, 1895-
Why I believe there is a God.

Pp. 2-7.

In: Why I believe there is a God. Chicago, Johnson Pub. Co., 1965.

M796 M45b Mays, Willie, 1931-
Born to play ball, by Willie Mays, as told to Charles Einstein. New York, Putnam [1955]

168 p. illus. 20 cm.

I. Einstein, Charles. II. Title.
GV865.M38A3 796.357 55—5779 ‡
Library of Congress [55q15]

M813.5 M454d Mays, Willie, 1931-
Danger in center field, by Willie Mays and Jeff Harris. Larchmont, N. Y., Argonaut Books [1963]

192 p. 21 cm. (Argonaut all-star baseball series)

I. Harris, Jeff, joint author. II. Title. 1. Baseball.- Fiction
PZ7.M4739Dan 63-11990 ‡
Library of Congress [5]

M796 M46m Mays, Willie, 1931-
My secrets of playing baseball, by Willie Mays with Howard Liss. Photos. by David Sutton. New York, Viking Press [1967]

89 p. illus. (part col.) 27 cm.

1. Baseball—Juvenile literature. I. Liss, Howard, joint author. II. Title.
GV873.M35 796.3572 67-13502
Library of Congress [60-2]

M796 M46 Mays, Willie, 1931-
Willie Mays: My life in and out of baseball, as told to Charles Einstein. [1st ed.] New York, Dutton, 1966.

320 p. illus., ports. 22 cm.

I. Einstein, Charles. II. Title. III. Title: My life in and out of baseball. 1. Baseball.
GV865.M38A32 796.3570924 (B) 66—11554
Library of Congress [66r67]

Haiti M972.94 V44r Mazeres, M
Vastey, Pompée Valentin, baron de, c. 1820?
Reflexions on the blacks and whites. Remarks upon a letter addressed by M. Mazeres, a French ex-colonist, to J. C. L. Sismonde de Sismondi, containing observations on the blacks and whites, the civilization of Africa, the kingdom of Haiti, & c. Translated from the French of the Baron DeVastey by W.H.M.B. London, Sold by J. Hatchard, 190 Piccadilly, and may be had of the Booksellers in general [1817]
83p. 17cm.

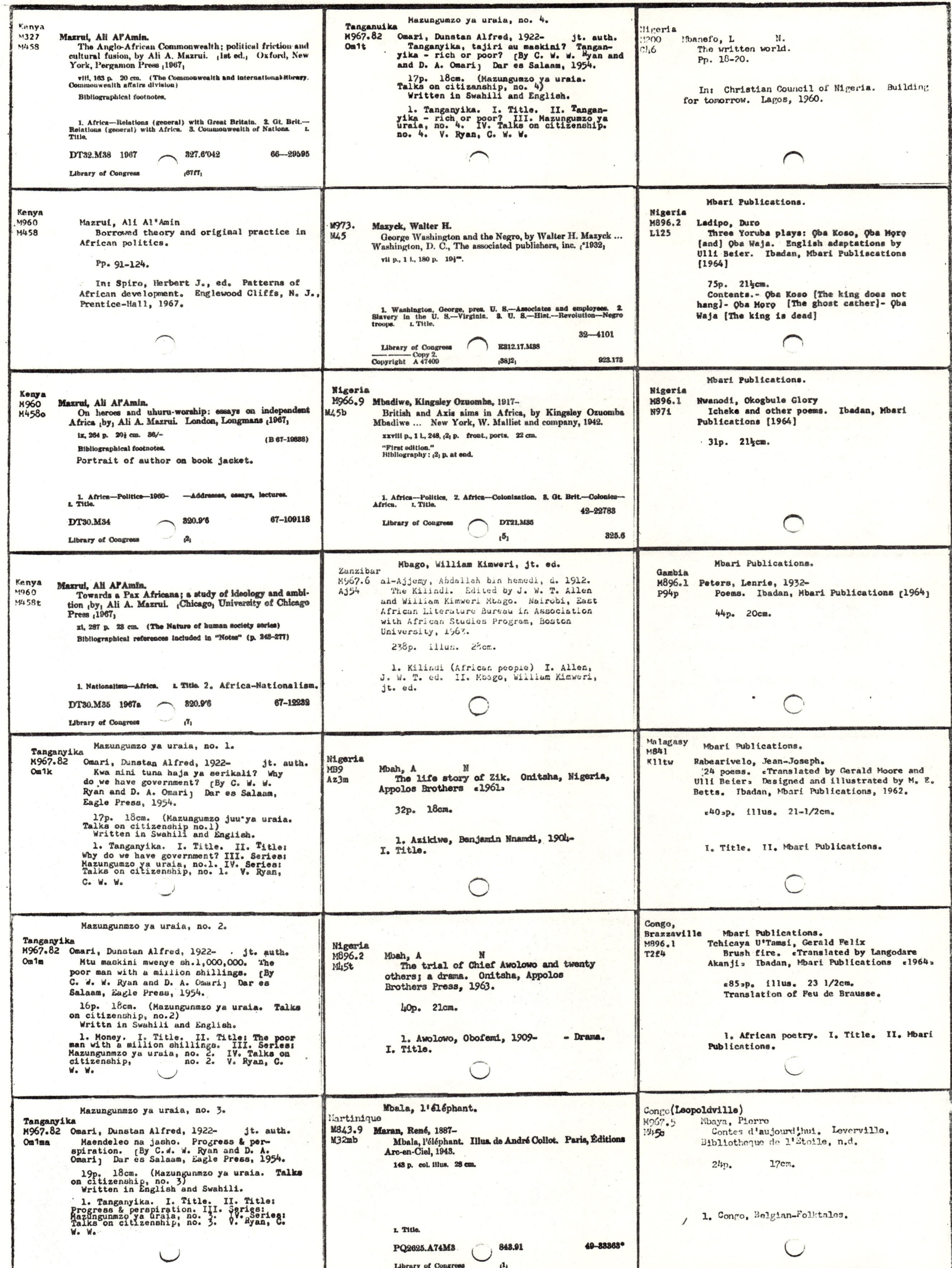

Kenya
M327
M458
Mazrui, Ali Al'Amin.
The Anglo-African Commonwealth; political friction and cultural fusion, by Ali A. Mazrui. [1st ed.] Oxford, New York, Pergamon Press [1967]
viii, 163 p. 20 cm. (The Commonwealth and international library. Commonwealth affairs division)
Bibliographical footnotes.
1. Africa—Relations (general) with Great Britain. 2. Gt. Brit.—Relations (general) with Africa. 3. Commonwealth of Nations. I. Title.
DT32.M38 1967 327.6'042 66—29595
Library of Congress [67f7]

Kenya
M960
M458
Mazrui, Ali Al'Amin
Borrowed theory and original practice in African politics.
Pp. 91-124.
In: Spiro, Herbert J., ed. Patterns of African development. Englewood Cliffs, N. J., Prentice-Hall, 1967.

Kenya
M960
M458o
Mazrui, Ali Al'Amin.
On heroes and uhuru-worship: essays on independent Africa [by] Ali A. Mazrui. London, Longmans [1967]
ix, 264 p. 20½ cm. 36/- (B 67-19888)
Bibliographical footnotes.
Portrait of author on book jacket.
1. Africa—Politics—1960- —Addresses, essays, lectures. I. Title.
DT30.M34 320.9'6 67-109118
Library of Congress [2]

Kenya
M960
M458t
Mazrui, Ali Al'Amin.
Towards a Pax Africana; a study of ideology and ambition [by] Ali A. Mazrui. [Chicago] University of Chicago Press [1967]
xi, 287 p. 23 cm. (The Nature of human society series)
Bibliographical references included in "Notes" (p. 242-277)
1. Nationalism—Africa. I. Title. 2. Africa-Nationalism.
DT30.M35 1967a 320.9'6 67-12232
Library of Congress [7]

Mazungumzo ya uraia, no. 1.
Tanganyika
M967.82
Om1k
Omari, Dunstan Alfred, 1922- jt. auth.
Kwa nini tuna haja ya serikali? Why do we have government? [By C. W. W. Ryan and D. A. Omari] Dar es Salaam, Eagle Press, 1954.
17p. 18cm. (Mazungumzo juu'ya uraia. Talks on citizenship no.1)
Written in Swahili and English.
1. Tanganyika. I. Title. II. Title: Why do we have government? III. Series: Mazungumzo ya uraia, no.1. IV. Series: Talks on citizenship, no. 1. V. Ryan, C. W. W.

Mazungunmzo ya uraia, no. 2.
Tanganyika
M967.82
Om1m
Omari, Dunstan Alfred, 1922- jt. auth.
Mtu maskini mwenye sh.1,000,000. The poor man with a million shillings. [By C. W. W. Ryan and D. A. Omari] Dar es Salaam, Eagle Press, 1954.
16p. 18cm. (Mazungunmzo ya uraia. Talks on citizenship, no.2)
Writtn in Swahili and English.
1. Money. I. Title. II. Title: The poor man with a million shillings. III. Series: Mazungunmzo ya uraia, no. 2. IV. Talks on citizenship, no. 2. V. Ryan, C. W. W.

Mazungunmzo ya uraia, no. 3.
Tanganyika
M967.82
Om1ma
Omari, Dunstan Alfred, 1922- jt. auth.
Maendeleo na jasho. Progress & perspiration. [By C.W. W. Ryan and D. A. Omari] Dar es Salaam, Eagle Press, 1954.
19p. 18cm. (Mazungunmzo ya uraia. Talks on citizenship, no. 3)
Written in English and Swahili.
1. Tanganyika. I. Title. II. Title: Progress & perspiration. III. Series: Mazungunmzo ya Uraia, no. 3. IV. Series: Talks on citizenship, no. 3. V. Ryan, C. W. W.

Mazungumzo ya uraia, no. 4.
Tanganuika
M967.82
Om1t
Omari, Dunstan Alfred, 1922- jt. auth.
Tanganyika, tajiri au maskini? Tanganyika - rich or poor? [By C. W. W. Ryan and and D. A. Omari] Dar es Salaam, 1954.
17p. 18cm. (Mazungumzo ya uraia. Talks on citizenship, no. 4)
Written in Swahili and English.
1. Tanganyika. I. Title. II. Tanganyika - rich or poor? III. Mazungumzo ya uraia, no. 4. IV. Talks on citizenship. no. 4. V. Ryan, C. W. W.

M973.
M45
Mazyck, Walter H.
George Washington and the Negro, by Walter H. Mazyck ... Washington, D. C., The associated publishers, inc. [°1932]
vii p., 1 l., 180 p. 19½cm.
1. Washington, George, pres. U. S.—Associates and employees. 2. Slavery in the U. S.—Virginia. 3. U. S.—Hist.—Revolution—Negro troops. I. Title.
32—4101
Library of Congress E312.17.M38
——— ——— Copy 2.
Copyright A 47409 [38j2] 923.173

Nigeria
M966.9
M45b
Mbadiwe, Kingsley Ozuomba, 1917–
British and Axis aims in Africa, by Kingsley Ozuomba Mbadiwe ... New York, W. Malliet and company, 1942.
xxviii p., 1 l., 248, [2] p. front., ports. 22 cm.
"First edition."
Bibliography: [2] p. at end.
1. Africa—Politics. 2. Africa—Colonization. 3. Gt. Brit.—Colonies—Africa. I. Title.
42-22783
Library of Congress DT21.M35
[5] 325.6

Mbago, William Kimweri, jt. ed.
Zanzibar
M967.6
Aj54
al-Ajjemy, Abdallah bin hemedi, d. 1912.
The Kilindi. Edited by J. W. T. Allen and William Kimweri Mbago. Nairobi, East African Literature Bureau in Association with African Studies Program, Boston University, 1963.
238p. illus. 23cm.
1. Kilindi (African people) I. Allen, J. W. T. ed. II. Mbago, William Kimweri, jt. ed.

Nigeria
MB9
Az3m
Mbah, A N
The life story of Zik. Onitsha, Nigeria, Appolos Brothers [1961]
32p. 18cm.
1. Azikiwe, Benjamin Nnamdi, 1904- I. Title.

Nigeria
M896.2
M45t
Mbah, A N
The trial of Chief Awolowo and twenty others; a drama. Onitsha, Appolos Brothers Press, 1963.
40p. 21cm.
1. Awolowo, Obofemi, 1909- - Drama. I. Title.

Mbala, l'éléphant.
Martinique
M843.9
M32mb
Maran, René, 1887–
Mbala, l'éléphant. Illus. de André Collot. Paris, Éditions Arc-en-Ciel, 1943.
143 p. col. illus. 28 cm.
I. Title.
PQ2625.A74M3 843.91 49-33363*
Library of Congress [1]

Nigeria
M200
C46
Mbanefo, L N.
The written world.
Pp. 18-20.
In: Christian Council of Nigeria. Building for tomorrow. Lagos, 1960.

Mbari Publications.
Nigeria
M896.2
L125
Ladipo, Duro
Three Yoruba plays: Ọba Koso, Ọba Mọrọ [and] Ọba Waja. English adaptations by Ulli Beier. Ibadan, Mbari Publiscations [1964]
75p. 21½cm.
Contents.- Ọba Koso [The king does not hang]- Ọba Mọrọ [The ghost cather]- Ọba Waja [The king is dead]

Mbari Publications.
Nigeria
M896.1
N971
Nwanodi, Okogbule Glory
Icheke and other poems. Ibadan, Mbari Publications [1964]
31p. 21½cm.

Mbari Publications.
Gambia
M896.1
P94p
Peters, Lenrie, 1932-
Poems. Ibadan, Mbari Publications [1964]
44p. 20cm.

Malagasy
M841
K11tw
Mbari Publications.
Rabearivelo, Jean-Joseph.
24 poems. [Translated by Gerald Moore and Ulli Beier] Designed and illustrated by M. E. Betts. Ibadan, Mbari Publications, 1962.
[40]p. illus. 21-1/2cm.
I. Title. II. Mbari Publications.

Congo, Brazzaville
M896.1
T2f4
Mbari Publications.
Tchicaya U'Tamsi, Gerald Felix
Brush fire. [Translated by Langodare Akanji] Ibadan, Mbari Publications [1964]
[85]p. illus. 23 1/2cm.
Translation of Feu de Brausse.
1. African poetry. I. Title. II. Mbari Publications.

Congo(Leopoldville)
M967.5
M45c
Mbaya, Pierre
Contes d'aujourd'hui. Leverville, Bibliotheque de l'Etoile, n.d.
24p. 17cm.
1. Congo, Belgian-Folktales.

Senegal
M896.1
M45k
Mbaye, Annette
Kaddu; poèmes. [Dakar, Imprimerie A. Diop, n.d.]
29p. illus. 21cm.
I. Title.

Rhodesia, N.
M968.94
M45
Mbikusita, Godwin.
A visit to England. London, United Society for Christian Literature, 1946.
64p. 18½cm.

Kenya
M960
M45
Mboya, Thomas Joseph, 1930-1969.
Conflict & nationhood; the essentials of freedom in Africa. [London, Africa Bureau, 1963]
12p. 21½cm.
"This anniversary address was delivered to the annual general meeting of the Africa Bureau in London on 30th September 1963."
1. Africa. 2. Nationalism-Africa. I. Title.

Senegal
M896.1
M45p
M'baye, Annette
Poèmes Africains. [Paris] Centre d'Art National Français [1965]
[10]p. 19cm. (Collection Art et Poesie)
I. Title.

Kenya
M398
M45
Mbiti, John Samuel, 1931- , ed. and tr.
Akamba stories; [translated and edited by] the Reverend John S. Mbiti. Oxford, Clarendon P., 1966.
x, 240 p. 22½ cm. (Oxford library of African literature) 45/-
(B 67-1173)
Bibliography: p. 41.
1. Tales, Kamba. 2. Kamba tribe. 3. Folklore - Kenya. 4. Tales, Kenyan. I. Title.
PL8351.M2 67—72464
Library of Congress [67c2]

Kenya
M967.6
M45ke
Mboya, Thomas Joseph, 1930-1969.
Kenya faces the future. New York, American Committee on Africa, 1959.
32p. 21cm. (Africa Today pamphlets: 3)
1. Kenya - Politics and government. I. Title.

Mbebe, A Z T
S. Africa
M896.1
M31a
Mama, G Soya
Amaqunube (imiHobe yesiXhosa), ngu G. Soya Mama no A. Z. T. Mbebe. London, Oxford University Press, 1950.
61p. 19cm.

Kenya
M496.3
M11e
Mbiti, John Samuel, 1931-
English-Kamba vocabulary. Nairobi, The Eagle Press, 1959.
52p. 15½cm.
1. Kenya - Dictionaries. 2. Kamba language - Dictionaries. I. Title.

Mboya, Thomas Joseph, 1930-1969,
Vision of Africa, pp. 13-27.
Africa
M960.3
D87a
Duffy, James, 1923- ed.
Africa speaks. Edited by James Duffy and Robert A. Manners. Princeton, N.J., Van Nostrand [1961]
223p. 23cm.

S. Africa
M968
M451
Mbeki, Govan Archibald Mvunyelwa, 1910-
Let's do it together. What cooperative societies are and do. Cape Town, South Africa, The African Bookman, 1944.
12p. 18cm. (Six penny library, #12)
1. Africa - cooperatives.

Kenya
M896.3
M11m
Mbiti, John Samuel, 1931-
Mutunga na ngewa yake. Illustrated by Ruth Yudelowitz. London, Thomas Nelson and Sons, Ltd., 1954.
60p. illus. 18½cm.
1. Kenya-Fiction. I. Title.

Africa
M960
F76
Mboya, Thomas Joseph, 1930-1969.
The party system and democracy in Africa.
Pp. 327-338.
Kenya author.
In: Foreign Affairs (New York). Africa. New York, Praeger, 1964.

South Africa
M968
M45s
Mbeki, Govan Archibald Mvunyelwa, 1910-
South Africa: the peasants' revolt [by] Govan Mbeki. Baltimore, Penguin Books [1964]
156, [3] p. map, port. 18 cm. (Penguin African library, AP9)
Portrait of author on book cover.
1. Africa, South—Native races. 2. Kaffraria—Pol. & govt. 3. Negroes in Africa, South—Segregation. I. Title.
DT846.K2M3 323.1 64-57150
Library of Congress [2]

Kenya
M823
St48t
Mbiti, John Samuel, 1931- tr.
Stevenson, Robert Louis
Kithamani kya uthwii [Treasure Island. Retold by Haydn Perry] Kitungitwe J. S. Mbiti. Nairobi, Eagle Press, 1955.
45p. 18½cm.
Written in Kamba.
I. Title. II. Mbiti, John Samuel, 1931- tr.

Africa
M960
Af83
Mboya, Thomas Joseph, 1930-1969.
The need for cooperation in Africa.
Pp. 31-38.
In: African Conference on Progress through Cooperation. Africa. New York, Dodd, Mead, 1966.

S. Africa
M496
B85k
Mbelle, Isaiah Budlwana, 1870-1847
Kafir scholar's companion, by I. Bud-M'belle. Lovedale, South Africa, Lovedale Missionary Press, 1903.
xxiii, 181p. 22cm.
"Kafir literature": p. 1 -11.
"Publications in which references are made to native races south of the Zambesi, with notes": p. 140 -173.
1. Kafir language (Bantu)
Library of congress PL8321.B8

Kenya
M967.6
M45u3
Mbotela, James Juma
The freeing of the slaves in East Africa. London, Evans Bros. [1965]
87p. 19cm.
Translation of Uhuru wa Watumwa.
1. Africa, British East - History. 2. Slavery in Africa. I. Title.

Africa
M960
Af83
Mboya, Thomas Joseph, 1930-1969.
Planning in an African economy, with particular reference to Kenya.
Pp. 131-137.
In: African Conference on Progress through Cooperation. Africa. New York, 1966.

S.Africa
M896.1
M45z
Mbidlana, Mafuya
Zangen' iinkomo. Indlalo-Isiyoliso; Ngemihla kaPhalo, Phefeya kweNciba, Elalini ENgoko ngaloo Mihla. Johannesburg, The Lovedale Press, 1954.
75p. 18½cm.
1. Africa, South - Poetry.

Kenya
M967.6
M45u
Mbotela, James Juma
Uhuru wa watumwa [The slaves who were brought to Freetown] Nairobi, Eagle Press, 1951.
102p. illus. 18cm.
Written in Swahili.
English ed. has title: The freeing of the slaves in East Africa.
1. Africa, British East - History. 2. Slavery in Africa. I. Title.

Kenya
M967.62
M45f3
Mboya, Thomas Joseph, 1930-1969.
Afrika frit - og hvad sa? [n.p.] Fremads Fokusbøger, 1964.
235p. illus., ports. 18½cm.
Translation of Freedom and after.
Autobiographical
Written in Danish
1. Kenya Colony and Protectorate. 2. Africa - Politics. 3. Pan-Africanism. I. Title.

Kenya
M967.62 **Mboya, Thomas Joseph, 1930-1969.**
M45f
Freedom and after. [1st ed.] Boston, Little, Brown [1963]
x, 288 p. illus., ports., map (on lining papers) 22 cm.
Autobiographical.

1. Kenya Colony and Protectorate—2. Africa—Politics—1960- 3. Pan-Africanism. I. Title.
DT434.E27M35 967.62 63-20102
Library of Congress [5]

Kenya
M967.62 **Mboya, Thomas Joseph, 1930-1969.**
M45f2
Freedom and after. ~~1st ed., Boston, Little, Brown 1963,~~ [London] A. Deutsch [1963]
~~x, 288 p.~~ illus., ports., map (on lining papers) 22 cm. 271p.
Autobiographical.

1. Kenya Colony and Protectorate—2. Africa—Politics—1960- 3. Pan-Africanism. I. Title.
DT434.E27M35 967.62 63-20102
Library of Congress [5]

Kenya
M967.6 **Mboya, Thomas Josephy, 1930-1969.**
M45K
The Kenya question: an African answer. Foreword by Margery Perham. London, Fabian Colonial Bureau, 1956.
48p. 21½cm. (Fabian tract 302)
"With my very best wishes, T. Mboya 9/10/56"

1. Kenya.

Africa
1960 **Mboya, Thomas Joseph, 1930-1969.**
Af78
African socialism.
Pp. 78-87.

In: Africa's freedom. London, Unwin Books, 1964.

Africa
1960 **Mboya, Thomas Joseph, 1930-1969.**
Af78
Tensions in African development.
Pp. 55-66.

In: Africa's freedom. London, Unwin Books, 1964.

M909.82 **Mboya, Thomas Joseph, 1930-1969.**
C76a
Tensions in African development.
Pp. 40-52.

In: Conference on Tensions in Development. Restless nations. London, Allen and Unwin, 1962.

M909.82 **Mboya, Thomas Joseph, 1930-1969.**
C.6
Tensions in African development.
Pp. 40-52.

In: Conference on Tensions in Development, Oxford University, 1961. Restless nations. New York, Dodd, Mead, 1962.

Kenya
M967.6 **Mboya, Paul**
M451u
Utawala na Maendeleo ya local government South Nyanza 1926-1957. (The work and progress of local government in South Nyanza, Kenya; 1926-1957.) Nairobi, The Eagle Press, 1959.
32p. illus. 18½cm.
Text in: Swahili.

1. Kenya - Politics and government. 2. South Nyanza, Kenya - Politics and government.

Mc

Names beginning with Mc are filed as if spelled Mac

Uganda
M896.3 **Mdoe, Janet Nsibirwa**
M45aw
Awo olwatuuka [Once upon a time] Ebifaananyi Byakubibwa Betty Manyolo. Nairobi, Eagle Press, 1960.
51p. illus. 24½cm.
Written in Luganda.

I. Title.

Uganda
M896.3 **Mdoe, Janet Nsibirwa**
M34e
Engero ennyimpi [Short stories] ebifaananyi byakubibwa Betty Manyolo. Nairobi, Eagle Press, 1960.
28p. illus. 24½cm.
Written in Luganda.

I. Title. II. Manyolo, Betty, illus.

Uganda
M372.4 **Mdoe, Janet Nsibirwa**
M46
Nze mmanyi okusoma [I know how to read] ebifaananyi byakubibwa Y. Kalanzi ne Alan Jarman. Nairobi, Eagle Press, 1960.
60p. illus. 18½cm.
Written in Luganda.

1. Luganda language - Readers. speakers. I. Title.

Me.

M818 **Samuels, Calvin Henry McNeal.**
Sa49
Me. New York, Comet Press Books [©1954]
41 p. 22 cm.
Anecdotes, essays, and poetry.

I. Title.
PS3537.A58M4 818.5 55-578 ‡
Library of Congress [2]

Brazil Mealheiro de Agripa.
M869 **Campos, Humberto de, 1886-1934.**
C157
... Mealheiro de Agripa. 2.a edição. Rio de Janeiro, W. M. Jackson, 1945.
269p. 20cm.
"Crônicas."

The meaning of Black Power.

M301 Jackson, James E
J135
The meaning of Black Power. Introduction by Henry Winston. New York, New Outlook Publishers, 1966.
15p. 22cm.
Reprinted from Political affairs, September 1966.

1. Black Power. I. Title.

The meaning of the sit-ins.

M323 **Wilkins, Roy, 1901-**
W65m
The meaning of the sit-ins. New York, [National Association for the Advancement of Colored People, 1960]
11p. 23cm.

M811.5 **Means, St. Elmo.**
M46p
Rev. St. Elmo Means' poems, essays, musings and quotations, ed. by Rev. St. Elmo Means. [Columbia, S. C., University press, ©1920]
3 p. l., 5-97 p. front. (port.) 15½cm. Inscribed copy: To Alex. Bumby, From H. S. Johnson

1. Poetry.
Library of Congress PS3601.M4A16 1920 20-15164
Copyright A 571832 [3]

M811.5 Means, Sterling M
M46b
The black devils and other poems, by Sterling M. Means. Louisville, Ky., Pentecostae publishing co., 1919.
56p. 19cm.
1. Poetry

M811.5 **Means, Sterling M.**
M46d
The deserted cabin, and other poems, by Rev. Sterling M. Means. Atlanta, Ga., A. B. Caldwell, 1915.
2 p. l., 13-96 p. 20½cm. $0.50
Autographed copy: Robert Kerlin, Lexington, Va.

I. Title. 1. Poetry.
Library of Congress PS2377.M8D4 1915 15-9551
Copyright A 398657

Meat - preservation.
M630.7 Carver, George Washington, 1864-1943.
C25pi
The pickling and curing of meat in hot weather. Second edition. Tuskegee Institute, Alabama, Tuskegee Institute press, 1925.
23p. 23cm. (Bulletin no. 23 June 1925)

The meat man.

M813.5 **Jordan, Moses.**
J76m
The meat man; a romance of life, of love, of labor, by Moses Jordan; illustrated with scenes from Wm. S. Scott studio. Chicago, Judy publishing company [©1923]
96 p. front., illus. 18½cm.

I. Title.
Library of Congress PZ3.J768Me 24-1180
Copyright A 765621 [2]

Medaillon civique.

Haiti M B [illegible]
Nazon, Emmanuel.
Médaillon civique, par me Emmanuel Nazon ... Port-au-Prince, Haïti, Imp. N. Telhomme, 1938.
2 p. l., 110 p., 1 l. port. 19cm.
"Hommage au docteur Alonzo P. B. Holly."
CONTENTS.—L'homme.—"God and the Negro."—Appendice: Lettre (de) Decatur McGill. Fête jubilaire. Félicitations. Extrait de "Miami times." Appréciations.

1. Holly, Alonzo Potter Burgess, 1865- I. Title.
45-47668
Library of Congress E185.97.H72
(2) 926.1

Medical education
See
Medicine--Study and teaching

M616 W93au4
Medical research.
Wright, Louis Tompkins, 1891-1952.
Aureomycin in the treatment of cervical tuberculous lymphadenopathy, report of twenty-five cases, by John W. V. Cordice, Lyndon M. Hill and Louis T. Wright. Reprinted from the Harlem hospital bulletin, 3:162-176, March 1951.

Medaillons litteraires.

Haiti M840.9 M33m
Marcelin, Emile.
Medaillons littéraires, poetes et prosateurs haitiens... Port-au-Prince, Imp. de l'Abeille, 1906.
158p. 21½cm.

Medical geography—Africa, West.

Sierra Leone M966.4 H78p
Horton, James Africanus Beale.
Physical and medical climate and meteorology of the west coast of Africa with valuable hints to Europeans for the preservation of health in the tropics. By James Africanus B. Horton ... London, J. Churchill & sons, 1867.
xix, 321 p. 23½cm.

1. Africa, West—Climate. 2. Medical geography—Africa, West. 3. Tropics—Diseases and hygiene.
7—39467
Library of Congress RA943.H82
(a27d1)

M616 W93c
Medical research.
Wright, Louis Tompkins, 1891-1952.
Congenital arteriovenous aneurysm of right upper extremity, by Louis T. Wright, and Arthur C. Logan. Reprinted from the American journal of surgery, new series, 48:658-663, June 1940.

The Medea and some poems.

M811.5 C89m
Cullen, Countee, 1903–
The Medea and some poems, by Countee Cullen. New York and London, Harper & brothers, 1935.
vi p., 2 l., 3-97 p., 1 l. 21cm.
"The Medea of Euripides, a new version by Countee Cullen": p. 1-64.
"First edition."

I. Euripides. Medea. II. Title.
35—13206
Library of Congress PS3505.U287M4 1935
(43i1) 811.5

Uganda M367.61 M46
Medical Headquarters. Entebee, Uganda.
The laws that protect your health; a book of village hygiene with special reference to Uganda. Nairobi, East African Literature Bureau, 1956.
56p. illus. diagrs. 24½cm.

1. Uganda - Hygiene. I. Ladkin, R G

M616 W93d
Medical research.
Wright, Louis Tompkins, 1891-1952.
Deaths from dicumarol, by Louis T. Wright and Milton Rothman. Chicago, American Medical Association, 1951.
6p. graphs. 26cm.
Reprinted with additions from the A.M.A. Archives of surgery, 62:23-28, January 1951.

... La médecine en Haiti.

M972.94 P92m
Pressoir, Catts.
... La médecine en Haiti. Port-au-Prince (Haiti) Imprimerie modèle, 1927.
3 p. l., (v)-xii, 254 p., 1 l. 22cm.
At head of title: Dr C. Pressoir.

1. Medicine—Haiti. I. Title.
28-16277
Library of Congress R475.H2P7

M616 W93a
Medical research.
Wright, Louis Tompkins, 1891-1952.
Anorectogenital lymphogranuloma venereum and granuloma inguinale treated with aureomycin, by Aaron Prigot, Louis T. Wright, Myra A. Logan and others. Reprinted from the New York State journal of medicine, 40:1911-1917, August 15, 1949.

M616 W93e2
Medical research.
Wright, Louis Tompkins, 1891-1952.
The effect of sulfathalidine on the bleeding and clotting time of the blood and prolongation reduction by the administration of vitamin K, by Louis T. Wright, Frank R. Cole, and Lyndon M. Hill. Reprinted from Surgery, gynecology and obstetrics, 88:201-208, February 1949.

M610 C63me8
Medical associations
Cobb, William Montague, 1904-
Medico-Chi: Whence and whither? Reprinted from the Journal of the National Medical Association, 37:75-80, May 1945.
75-80p. 27cm.

M616 W93a2
Medical research.
Wright, Louis Tompkins, 1891-1952.
Aureomycin, a new antibiotic with virucidal properties; A preliminary report on successful treatment in twenty-five cases of lymphogranuloma venereum, by Louis T. Wright, Murray Sanders, and Myra A. Logan. Chicago, American Medical Association, 1948.
12p. tables. 22cm.
Reprinted, with additions, from the Journal of the American Medical Association, 138:408-412, October 9, 1948.

M616 W93e5
Medical research.
Wright, Louis Tompkins, 1891-1952.
An evaluation of teropterin therapy in metastatic neoplasms, by Solomon Weintraub, Isidore Arons, Louis T. Wright, and others. Reprinted from New York State journal of medicine, 51:2159-2162, September 15, 1951.

Medical care and the plight of the Negro.

M610 C63me2
Cobb, William Montague, 1904-
Medical care and the plight of the Negro. New York, National Assn. for the Advancement of Colored People, 1947.
38p. illus. 22cm.

M616 W93a4
Medical research.
Wright, Louis Tompkins, 1891-1952.
Aureomycin as an adjunct in the treatment of major burns, by Louis T. Wright, Joseph A. Tamerin, William I. Metzer, and Arthur L. Garnes, Reprinted from Surgery, 29:763-771, May 1951.
11p. illus. 26cm.

M616 W93g
Medical research.
Wright, Louis Tompkins, 1891-1952.
Gunshot wounds of the abdomen, by Robert S. Wilkinson, Lyndon M. Hill and Louis T. Wright. Reprinted from Surgery, 19:415-429, March 1946.
15p. tables. 26cm.
Inscribed: To Arthur from Louis.

M610 C63d6
Medical colleges.
Cobb, William Montague, 1904-
Discussion of paper, Medical manpower, by Thomas Parran. Reprinted from Journal of Association of American Medical Colleges, v.27, 1948.
27-28p. 27cm.
Mimeographed.

M616 W93au3
Medical research.
Wright, Louis Tompkins, 1891-1952.
Aureomycin hydrochloride in actinomycosis, Louis T. Wright, and Harry J. Lowen. Chicago, American Medical Association, 1950.
5p. illus. 22cm.
Reprinted from the Journal of the American Medical Association, 144:21-22, September 2, 1950.

M616 W93h
Medical research.
Wright, Louis Tompkins, 1891-
Head injuries, by Louis T. Wright.
(In: Scudder, Charles L. Treatment of fractures. Philadelphia, W.B. Saunders, 1938. 25½cm. pp. 417-459).
Reprint of chapter xxii.

M616
W63i

Medical research.
Wright, Louis Tompkins, 1891-1952.
Incidence of asymptomatic lymphogranuloma venereum in a municipal hospital, by Louis T. Wright, Gerald A. Spencer, and Abraham Oppenheim. Reprinted from American journal of syphillis, gonorrhea, and venereal diseases, 31:282-288, May 1947.

M616
W93l

Medical research.
Wright, Louis Tompkins, 1891-1952.
Lymphogranulomatous strictures of the rectum; a resume of four hundred and seventy-six cases, by Louis T. Wright, W. Adrian Freeman and Joel V. Bolden. Reprinted from the Archives of Surgery, 53:499-544, November 1946.

Inscribed: To Arthur from Louis.

M616
W93ob

Medical research.
Wright, Louis Tompkins, 1891-1952.
Oblique subcervical (reverse intertrochanteric) fractures of the femur. American Orthopaedic Association, 1947.

4p. illus. 26cm.
Reprinted from the Journal of bone and joint surgery 29:707-710, July 1947.

M616
W93op

Medical research.
Wright, Louis Tompkins, 1891-1952.
Operative reduction and fixation by means of a specially devised blade plate for the treatment of supracondylar and T. fractures of the lower end of the femur and T fractures of the upper end of the tibia, preliminary report. Reprinted from the Harlem Hospital bulletin, 1:17-24, June 1948.

M616
W93os

Medical research.
Wright, Louis Tompkins, 1891-1952.
Osseous changes associated with lymphogranuloma venereum, by Louis T. Wright, and Myra Logan. Reprinted from the Archives of surgery, 39:108-121, July 1939.

M616
W93pr

Medical research.
Wright, Louis Tompkins, 1891-1952.
Prevention of postoperative adhesions in rabbits with streptococcal metabolites, Louis T. Wright, David H. Smith, Milton Rothman and others. Society for Experimental Biology and Medicine, 1950.

[3]p. illus. 25cm.
Reprinted from Proceedings of the Society.

M616
W93py

Medical research.
Wright, Louis Tompkins, 1891-1952.
Pyoderma gangrenosum in chronic non-specific ulcerative colitis treated with aureomycin, by Louis T. Wright, and Selig Strax. Reprinted from the Harlem Hospital bulletin, 1:99-112, December 1948.

M616
W93r4

Medical research.
Wright, Louis Tompkins, 1891-1952.
Recent advances in antibiotic therapy, by Selig Strax and Louis T. Wright. Reprinted New York State journal of medicine, 49:1797-1801, August 1, 1949.

M616
W93r6

Medical research.
Wright, Louis Tompkins, 1891-1952.
Rectal strictures due to lymphogranuloma venereum, with especial reference to Pauchet's excision operation, by Louis T. Wright, Benjamin N. Berg, Joel V. Bolden and W. Adrian Freeman. Reprinted from Surgery, Gynecology and Obstetrics, 82:449-462, April 1946.

Inscribed: To Arthur from Louis, May 10, 1946.

M616
W93s

Medical research.
Wright, Louis Tompkins, 1891-1952.
Sulfathalidine in low postoperative fistulas of the ileum, by Louis T. Wright, and Frank R. Cole. Reprinted from the American journal of surgery. 75:852-853, June 1948.

M616
W93t3

Medical research.
Wright, Louis Tompkins, 1891-1952.
Traumatic rupture of the intestines without penetrating wounds, by Louis T. Wright, Aaron Prigot, and Frances E. Stein. Reprinted from the Harlem Hospital bulletin, 1:116-139, December 1948.

M616
W93t2

Medical research.
Wright, Louis Tompkins, 1891-1952.
Traumatic rupture of the liver without penetrating wounds, a study of thirty-two cases. Chicago, American Medical Association, 1947.

20p. tables. 27cm.
Reprinted from the Archives of surgery, 54:613-632, June 1947.

M616
W93t5

Medical research.
Wright, Louis Tompkins, 1891-1952.
Treatment of acute peritonitis with aureomycin, by Louis T. Wright, William I. Metzger, and Edward B. Shapero. Reprinted from the American journal of surgery, 78:15-22, July 1949.

M616
W93t7

Medical research.
Wright, Louis Tompkins, 1891-1952.
The treatment of lymphogranuloma venereum and granuloma inguinale in humans with aureomycin, by L. T. Wright, M. Sanders, M. A. Logan, and others. Reprinted from the Annals of the New York Academy of Sciences, 51:318-330, November 30, 1948.

M616
W93t8

Medical research.
Wright, Louis Tompkins, 1891-1952.
Treatment of non-specific ulcerative colitis with aureomycin, by Louis T. Wright, Selig Strax, and Jerome A. Marks. Reprinted from the Annals of western medicine and surgery, November 1950.

M616
W93u3

Medical research.
Wright, Louis Tompkins, 1891-1952.
The use of alkyl-dimethyl-benzyl-ammonium chloride in injury, by Louis T. Wright, and Robert S. Wilkinson. Reprinted from the American journal of surgery, 44:626-630, June 1939.

Inscribed: To my friend Arthur from Louis.

M616
W93u

Medical research.
Wright, Louis Tompkins, 1891-1952.
Use of teropterin in neoplastic disease; a preliminary clinical report, by S. P. Lehv, L. T. Wright, S. Weintraub, and I. Arons. Reprinted from the Transaction of the New York Academy of Sciences, 10:75-81, January 1948.

75-81p. tables, graphs, illus. 25cm.
Inscribed: To Arthur from Louis.

Medical schools.

M362
C21a

Carnegie, Amos H
Address by the founder - Rev. Amos H. Carnegie of the organization of the national board of trustees of the Negro national hospital fund on March 23rd, 1934 held in the Methodist book concern chapel, New York City
14p. 23cm.

M378M
M47s

Medical schools.
Meharry Medical College. Nashville.
Souvenir [pictorial] of the dedication of Meharry's new educational and hospital buildings. Nashville, The College, [19]

25p. illus. tables. 29cm.

M378M
R66

Medical schools.
Roman, Charles Victor, 1864-1934.
Meharry medical college, a history, by Charles Victor Roman ... Nashville. Sunday School publishing board of the National Baptist convention, inc., 1934.

xi, 41, 224p. plates. 23½cm.

Medical societies.

M610.6
M31p

Manhattan Medical Society. New York.
Pa t, present and future activities...; A brief review of major events and a forecast. [New York] the Society, 1935.

53p. 28cm. (Pamphlet no.3)
Mimeographed.

Medical societies

M610.6
M46o
Medico-Chirurgical Society of the District of Columbia.
Officers, committees, members, schedule of meetings, officers of women's auxiliary 1945. Washington, D.C., the Society. 1945.

[4]p. 14cm.

M610
M96n
Medicine.
Murray, Peter Marshall, 1888-
N.M.A. president's address. n.p. 1952.

15p. 28cm.
Delivered at Washington, August 16, 1952.
Mimeo.

Medicine - Integration.

M610
C63me3
Cobb, William Montague, 1904-
Medicine. Reprint from the Integration of the Negro into American society, n.d.

77-85p. tables 23cm.

1. Medicine - Integration

Medical symphony.

St. Lucia
M610
Sp3m
Spencer, Gerald Arthur, 1902-
Medical symphony, a study of the contributions of the Negro to medical progress in New York. [New York, °1947]

120 p. ports. 21 cm.
"References": p. 9.

1. Medicine—New York (City) 2. Negro physicians. I. Title.

R292.N7S63 610.97471 48-3224*

Library of Congress [3]

M610
P93c
Medicine.
Pringle, Henry F
The color line in medicine, by Henry F. and Katharine Pringle. New York, Committee of 100, 1948.

12p. graphs. 23cm.
Reprinted from Saturday Evening Post, Jan. 24, 1948.

Medicine - Periodicals.
Bulletin of the Medico-Chirurgical Society of the District of Columbia, 1-
1941, 1945-

v. illus. tables. 29cm. irregular.
See holdings card for issues in library.
Editor: W. Montague Cobb.

Medicine.
M304
P19
v.3, no.15
Bousfield, Midian O
Presidential address. [Read at the Nashville meeting of the N.M.A., Aug. 14, 1934] Reprinted from Journal of the National Medical Association, Nov. 1934.
p. 1 - 8.

M614
R66c
Medicine.
Roman, Charles Victor, 1864-1934.
The cultural background of modern medicine. Reprinted from the Journal of the National Medical Association, July-September, 1924.

4p. 26cm.

M610.
C63fe
Medicine--Study and teaching.
Cobb, William Montague, 1904-
Federal aid to medical education. Reprinted from Journal of the National Medical Association, 42:87-94, March 1950.

Medicine.
M610
C63me2
Cobb, William Montague, 1904-
Medical care and the plight of the Negro. New York, National Assn. for the Advancement of Colored People, 1947.

38p. illus. 22cm.
"Literature cited": p. 37-38.

M614
R66m
Medicine.
Roman, Charles Victor, 1864-1934.
The medical phase of the South's ethnic problem. Reprinted from the Journal of the National Medical Association. 8:150-152. [1916]

Medicine - Study and teaching.
M610.
C63ni
Cobb, William Montague, 1904-
The 1939 scientific exhibit of the Howard University School of Medicine. Reprinted from the Journal of the National Medical Association, 32:216-218, September 1940.

Medicine.
M610
C63p7
Cobb, William Montague, 1904-
Progresses and portents for the Negro in medicine. New York, National Assn. for the Advancement of Colored People, 1948.

53p. illus. ports. map. 22cm.
"Literature cited": p. 46-47.

Medicine.
M610
P19
v.1
no.1
Steward, S Maria, 1845-
Women in medicine; a paper read before the National association of Colored Women's clubs at Wilberforce, Ohio, August 6, 1914. by S. Maria Steward... Wilberforce, Ohio [The author] 1914.

24p. ports. 19½cm.

Medicine - Study and teaching.
M610.
C63sc
Cobb, William Montague, 1904-
The scientific exhibit of the Howard University School of Medicine at the 1939 convention of the National Medical Association, n.p., 1939.

51 28cm.
Mimeographed.

Medicine.

MB
K39n
Kenney, John A 1874-
The Negro in medicine, by John A. Kenney ... [Tuskegee Institute, Ala., Printed by the Tuskegee institute press, °1912]
60 p. front., plates (part fold.) ports. 24½cm.

1. ~~Negro physicians~~ Physicians 2. ~~Negroes~~—Education. I. Title.
3. Biography 4. Medicine.
12—25563

Library of Congress E185.82.K36
Copyright A 327638 [a37b1]

Medicine.
M610
P19
v.1
no.12
Wright, Louis Tompkins, 1891-
Diagnosis and treatment of fractured skulls by Louis T. Wright, Jesse J. Greene and David H. Smith.... Reprinted from the Archives of surgery, vol. 27, November 1933.

19p. 25½cm.

M614
R66sk
Medicine--Study and teaching.
Roman, Charles Victor, 1864-1934.
Skeletology. Reprinted from the Journal of the National Medical Association, Oct.-Dec. 1922.

2p. 27cm.

Medicine.
M610
P19
v.1, no. 10
Manhattan medical society.
Equal opportunity - no more - no less! Open letter to Mr. Edwin R. Embree, president of the Julius Rosenwald Fund, Chicago, Illinois from the Manhattan medical society. New York City, January 23, 1931.
8p. 20½cm.

M614
R66fo
Medicine - Formulae.
Roman, Charles Victor, 1864-1934. comp.
... Formulae supplemental to those in U.S. pharmacopoeia and national formulary, with explanatory notes and appendix, compiled by the chief of the clinic. [Nashville, 1909]
57p. 13cm.
Cover title: Eye, ear, nose and throat formulary of remedies used in Dr. Roman's Clinic, Meharry Medical College.
Contains: The Deontological orientation of its membership the chief function of a medical society, by C.V. Roman.

Medicine - Africa.
Guadeloupe
M610
B14d
Baghio'oh, Jean Louis
Dictionnaire de médicine Africaine ou l'art de guérir avec les plantes toutes les maladies, même dites incurables, telles que l'Asthme, le Cancer, le Paludisme, les Rhumatismes, la Tuberculose, etc. 6th éd. Première partie. Guise, l'Imprimerie l'Espoir, 1955.

55p. port. 21½cm. (Le livre de la Santé)

Nigeria
M610
L172

Medicine - Africa.
Lambo, T Adeoye
African traditional beliefs; concepts of health and medical practice; a lecture given before the Philosophical Society, University College, Ibadan, on 24 October, 1962. Ibadan, Ibadan University Press, 1963.

11p. 21½cm.
Includes bibliography.

Senegal
M610
T68

Medicine - Africa.
Traore, Dominique
Comment le noir se soigne-t-il? Ou médecine et magie Africaines. Paris, Présence Africaine, [1965]

643p. 21½cm.

1. Medicine - Africa. 2. Africa - Social life and customs. I. Title.

St. Lucia
M610
Sp3m

Medicine - New York (City)
Spencer, Gerald Arthur, 1902-
Medical symphony, a study of the contributions of the Negro to medical progress in New York. [New York, °1947]
120 p. ports. 21 cm.
"References": p. 9.

1. Medicine—New York (City) 2. Negro physicians. I. Title.
R292.N7S63 610.97471 48-3224*
Library of Congress [8]

Senegal
M610
Sa58

Medicine - Senegal.
Sankalé, Marc
Médecine sociale au Sénégal, par Marc Sankalé et Pierre Pène. Dakar, Afrique documents, 1960.

104p. illus., map. 24cm. (Cahiers documents, no. 1, March 1960)
Includes bibliography.

Senegal
M610
Sa58

Médecine social au Sénégal.
Sankalé, Marc
Médecine sociale au Sénégal, par Marc Sankalé et Pierre Pène. Dakar, Afrique documents, 1960.

104p. illus., map. 24cm. (Cahiers documents, no. 1, March 1960)
Includes bibliography.

M610.
C63me8

Medico-Chi: Whence and whither?
Cobb, William Montague, 1904-
Medico-Chi: Whence and whither? Reprinted from the Journal of the National Medical Association, 37: 75-80, May 1945.

75-80p. 27cm.

Medico-Chirurgical Society of the District of Columbia.
Bulletin of the Medico-Chirurgical Society of the District of Columbia, 1- 1941, 1945-

v. illus. tables. 29cm. irregular.
See holdings card for issues in library.
Editor: W. Montague Cobb.

M610.6
M46o

Medico-Chirurgical Society of the District of Columbia.
Officers, committees, members, schedule of meetings, officers of women's auxiliary 1945. Washington, D.C., the Society, 1945.

[7]p. 14cm.

1. Medical societies

M610.
C63f1

Medico-chirurgical society of the District of Columbia.
Cobb, William Montague, 1904-
The first Negro medical society; a history of the Medico-chirurgical society of the District of Columbia, 1884-1939, by W. Montague Cobb ... Washington, D. C., The Associated publishers, 1939.
x, 159 p. 19½ᶜᵐ.
"Publications by society and members": p. 104-119; Bibliography: p. 135.

1. Medico-chirurgical society of the District of Columbia. I. Title.
39-19710
Library of Congress R15.M573C6
[45f1] 610.62753

M610.
C63me7

Medico-Chirurgical Society of the District of Columbia
Cobb, William Montague, 1904-
Medico-Chi: 1945-1947; Address of the retiring president, Medico-Chirurgical Society of the District of Columbia, January 22, 1948, Howard Medical School. Rev. for publication. Washington, The Society, 1948.

3-15p. illus. 21cm.

M610.
C63me8

Medico-Chirurgical Society of the District of Columbia
Cobb, William Montague, 1904-
Medico-Chi: Whence and whither? Reprinted from the Journal of the National Medical Association, 37:75-80, May 1945.

75-80p. 27cm.

M610.
C63me5

Medico-Chirurgical Society of the District of Columbia.
Cobb, William Montague, 1904-
Medico-Chi and the national selective service. Reprinted from the Journal of the National Medical Association 37:192-197, November, 1945.

MB
C12p

Medina, Antonio.
Calcagno, Francisco, 1827-1903.
Poetas de color, por Francisco Calcagno. Placido, Manzano, Rodriguez, Echemendia, Silveira, Medina. Habana, Imp. militar de la v. de Soler y compania, 1878.
1 p. l., [5]-54 p. 23½cm.

MB
C12p

Medina, Antonio.
Calcagno, Francisco, 1827-1903.
Poetas de color, por Francisco Calcagno. Placido, Manzano, Rodriguez, Echemendia, Silveira, Medina. Habana, Imp. militar de la v. de Soler y compania, 1878.
1 p. l., [5]-54 p. 23½cm.

M200
T42d

Meditations for apostles of sensitiveness.
Thurman, Howard, 1899-
Deep is the hunger; meditations for apostles of sensitiveness. [1st ed.] New York, Harper [1951]
x, 212 p. 22 cm.
An expansion of the author's Meditations for apostles of sensitiveness, published in 1948.

1. Devotional literature. I. Title. II. Title: Meditations for apostles of sensitiveness.
BV4832.T558 242 51-9391
Library of Congress [51b7]

M811.5
C85m

Meditations of solitude.
Crawford, Isaac
Meditations of solitude. Hixson, Tennessee, 1916.

63p. 20cm.

M200
T42m

Meditations of the heart.
Thurman, Howard, 1899-
Meditations of the heart. [1st ed.] New York, Harper [1953]
216 p. 22 cm.

1. Devotional literature. I. Title.
BV4832.T57 242 53-10980 ‡
Library of Congress [10]

Tanganyika
M398.6
M47

Meena, E K
Vitendawili [Riddles] Kutoka makabila mbalilbali ya Tanganyika, kimetungwa na E. K. Meena, G. V. Mmari na H. H. Sangiwa. London, Oxford University Press, 1960.
27p. illus. 18½cm.
Written in Swahili.

1. Riddles, African. I. Mmari, G. V., jt. auth. II. Sangiwa, H. H., jt. auth. III. Title.

M808.83
L829

Meesters der Neger vertelkunst.
Loggem, Manuel von, 1916- comp.
Meesters der Neger vertelkunst, bijeengebracht en vertaald door Manuel von Loggem met medewerkung von Otto Sterman. [1. druk] Amsterdam, J. Meulenhoff [1966]
xv, 192p. 20cm. (Meesters der vertelkunst)
White compiler

1. Fiction - Collections. I. Title. (Series)

M810.8
Sm5m

Meet an American.
Smith, Elmer Reid, 1904- ed.
Meet an American! Edited by Elmer R. Smith ... New York, Chicago, Harcourt, Brace and company [1944]
xiv, 480 p. incl. front., illus. 20½ᶜᵐ.

1. American literature (Selections: Extracts, etc.) 2. National characteristics, American. 3. U. S.—Civilization. I. Title.
44-4431
Library of Congress PS500.H5S5
[25] 810.82

MB
D75

Meet the Negro.
Downs, Karl E
Meet the Negro [by] Karl E. Downs. Los Angeles, Calif., The Methodist youth fellowship, Southern California-Arizona annual conference [1943]
5 p. l., xiii-xvi p., 2 l., 21-179 p. illus. (ports.) 20ᶜᵐ.
"First edition."
Includes bibliographies.

1. Negroes—Biog. I. Methodist youth fellowship. II. Methodist church (United States) Conferences. Southern California-Arizona. III. Title.
44-3249
Library of Congress E185.96.D68
[45l5] 825.260073

The meeting point.
Barbados
M823.91 Clarke, Austin Chesterfield, 1932–
C55m The meeting point [by] Austin C. Clarke. Toronto, Macmillan of Canada [1967]
249 p. 23 cm. $5.95 Can. (C 67-2753)
I. Title.
PZ4.C5973Me 67-93890
Library of Congress [3]

Meier, August, 1923– joint editor.
M973 Broderick, Francis L ed.
B78 Negro protest thought in the twentieth century. Edited by Francis L. Broderick and August Meier. Indianapolis, Bobbs-Merrill Co. [1966, °1965]
xliii, 444 p. 21 cm. (The American heritage series)
Excerpts and extracts by Negro authors.
White editor.
1. Negroes—Hist.—Sources. 2. Negroes—Civil rights—Addresses, essays, lectures. I. Meier, August, 1923– joint ed. II. Title.
E185.B87 301.45196073 65–23012
Library of Congress [67o3]

M301 Melady, Thomas Patrick.
Ah5n African independence and the Negro peoples.
(In: Ahmann, Mathew H ed. The new Negro. Notre Dame, Ind., Fides Publishers [1961] 21cm. pp. 89-106)

Meeting Street Baptist Church, Providence, R.I.
MB9 Asher, Jeremiah, 1812–
As3a An autobiography with details of a visit to England, and some account of the history of the Meeting Street Baptist Church, Providence, R.I., and of the Shiloh Baptist Chruch, Philadelphia, Pa., by Rev. Jeremiah Asher, with an introduction by Rev. J. Wheaton Smith... Philadelphia, the author, 1862.
x, 227p. front. 17½cm.

Les meilleurs poètes et romanciers Haitiens.
Haiti
M840 Gouraige, Ghislain
G74m Les meilleurs poètes et romanciers Haitiens (pages choisies). Paris, Imp. La Phalange, 1963.
414p. 20½cm.

Melady, Thomas Patrick, ed.
Zambia
M968.94 Kaunda, Kenneth David, Pres. Zambia, 1924–
K16k Kenneth Kaunda of Zambia; selections from his writings, edited by Thomas Patrick Melady. New York, Issued for the Africa Service Institute of New York by Praeger [1964]
254p. 22cm.

Nigeria Megida legal guide series, no. 1.
B33 Ekineh, Aliyi.
E34 You and your landlord and you and the law of libel and slander. Lagos, Megida Printers and Publishers [1961]
50p 22½cm. (Megida legal guide series, no. 1)

M811.08 Meine dunklen hände, moderne Negerlyrik in
M47 original und nachdichtung. München, Nymphenburger Verlagshandlung, 1953.
90p. 20cm.
Partial contents: Arna Bontemps. Gwendolyn Brooks, Leslie M. Collins. Joseph Cotter, jr. Countee Cullen. Waring Cuney. Frank Marshall Davis. Richard V. Durham. Robert E. Hayden. Langston Hughes. Fenton Johnson. James Weldon Johnson. Melvin B. Tolson. Jean Toomer.
(continued)

M230.41 Melanchthon, Philipp, 1497–1560.
M48 The Loci communes of Philip Melanchthon, with a critical introduction by the translator, Charles Leander Hill ... and a special introduction by Dean E. E. Flack ... Boston, Meador publishing company [°1944]
274 p. 20½cm.
Bibliographical foot-notes. "Bibliographia Melanchthoniana": p. 268–274.
1. Theology, Doctrinal. 2. Lutheran church—Doctrinal and controversial works. I. Hill, Charles Leander, tr. II. Title.
45–1360
Library of Congress BR336.L62
[46g2] 230.41

M378M Meharry Medical College. Nashville.
M47s Souvenir [pictorial] of the dedication of Meharry's new educational and hospital buildings. Nashville, The College, [19]
25p. illus. tables. 29cm.
1.Medical schools.

M811.08 Meine dunklen hände, moderne Negerlyrik in
M47 original und nachdichtung. München, Nymphenburger Verlagshandlung, 1953.
(card 2)
90p. 20cm.
Inscribed by Langston Hughes: "For Arthur Spingarn with all my best --Sincerely, Langston" New York, October 10, 1953.
1. Poetry - Collections.

M811.5 Melancon, Norman
M481 I'll just be me, poems for young and old. New York, Exposition Press [1967]
32p. 21cm.
I. Title.

M614
R66fo Meharry Medical College, Nashville, Dr. Roman's Clinic.
Roman, Charles Victor, 1864–1934. comp.
... Formulae supplemental to those in U.S. pharmacopoeia and national formulary, with explanatory notes and appendix, compiled by the chief of the clinic. [Nashville, 1909]
57p. 13cm.
Cover title: Eye, ear, nose and throat formulary of remedies used in Dr. Roman's Clinic, Meharry Medical College.
Contains: The Deontological orientation of its membership the chief function of a medical society, by C.V. Roman.

M808.81 Los Mejores versos de la poesía negra. [Buenos Aires, 1943]
M479 40 p. illus. 22 x 10 cm. (Cuadernillos de poesía, 23)
Cover title.
"For Arthur - Sincerely, Langston, con amistad. Harlem, January, 1967, p. 10-11.
1. Negro poetry.
PN6109.7.M4 57–32512
Library of Congress [1]

MB9
M48 Melbourn, Julius, b. 1790.
1851 Life and opinions of Julius Melbourn; with sketches of the lives and characters of Thomas Jefferson, John Quincy Adams, John Randolph, and several other eminent American statesmen. Ed. by a late member of Congress. Syracuse, Hall, 1851.
xii, 258p. (port.) 20cm.

M378M Meharry medical college. Nashville.
R66 Roman, Charles Victor, 1864–1934.
Meharry medical college, a history, by Charles Victor Roman ... Nashville, Sunday School publishing board of the National Baptist convention, inc., 1934.
xi, 41, 224p. plates. 23½cm.

M811.3 Menken, Adah Isaacs, 1835–1868.
M52i Infelicia, by Adah Isaacs Menken. Philadelphia, J. B. Lippincott & co., 1868.
124 p. 15cm.
Poems.
Photograph of author mounted on verso of half-title.
I. Title.
33–566
Library of Congress PS2389.M24 1868 a
[42b1] 811.39

MB9
M48 Melbourn, Julius, b. 1790.
1851 Life and opinions of Julius Melbourn.
(card 2)
1. Slavery in the U.S. - North Carolina. 2. U.S. - Descrip. & trav. 3. U.S.-Pol. & govt. - 1815-1861. I. Hammond, Jabez Delano, 1778-1885, ed.

M378M Meharry Medical College, Nashville.
R66 Roman, Charles Victor, 1864–1934.
Meharry medical college, a history, by Charles Victor Roman ... Nashville, Sunday School publishing board of the National Baptist convention, inc., 1934.
xi, 41, 224p. plates. 23½cm.

M811.3 Menken, Adah Isaacs, 1835–1868.
M521 Infelicia, by Adah Isaacs Menken. ~~Philadelphia, J. B. Lippincott & co.~~ London, Paris, New York, 1868.
~~124 p. 15cm.~~ 4, 141p., illus., 15cm.
Poems.
Photograph of author mounted on verso of half-title.
I. Title.
33–566
Library of Congress PS2389.M24 1868 a
[42b1] 811.39

MB9 Melbourn, Julius, b. 1790.
M48 Life and opinions of Julius Melbourn; with sketches of the lives and characters of Thomas Jefferson, John Quincy Adams, John Randolph, and several other eminent American statesmen. Ed. by a late member of Congress. Syracuse, Hall & Dickson; [etc., etc.] 1847.
239 p. front. (port.) 20cm.
1. Slavery in the U. S.—North Carolina. 2. U. S.—Descr. & trav. 3. U. S.—Pol. & govt.—1815–1861. I. Hammond, Jabez Delano, 1778–1855, ed.
12–30047
Library of Congress E338.M51
[45c1]

M378Ho
M481
Melchor, Beulah H
The land possessions of Howard university, a study of the original ownership and extent of the holdings of Howard university in the District of Columbia ₍by₎ Beulah H. Melchor ... Washington, D. C., 1945.
85 p. illus. (plans) 28ᶜᵐ.
"This dissertation ... for a master's thesis ₍Howard university₎ ... covers the years 1651-1855."—Foreword.
Bibliography: p. 53-59.
1. Howard university, Washington, D. C.—Hist. 2. Land titles—District of Columbia. 3. Land titles—Maryland. I. Title.
45-16667
Library of Congress LC2851.H82M4
₍3₎ 378.753

Meltzer, Milton, 1915- joint author.
M813.5
H87pi
Hughes, Langston, 1902–
A pictorial history of the Negro in America, by Langston Hughes & Milton Meltzer. New York, Crown ₍1956₎
316 p. illus., ports., maps, facsims. 29 cm.
Bibliography: p. 313.
1. Negroes—Hist.—Pictorial works. I. Meltzer, Milton, 1915– joint author. II. Title.
Full name: James Langston Hughes.
E185.H83 325.260973 56—7192
Library of Congress ₍57f20₎

Memoirs of a Monticello slave.
MB9
J35
Jefferson, Isaac, b. 1775.
Memoirs of a Monticello slave, as dictated to Charles Campbell in the 1840's by Isaac, one of Thomas Jefferson's slaves. Edited by Rayford W. Logan. Charlottesville, Published by the University of Virginia Press for the Tracy W. McGregor Library, 1951.
45 p. port. 24 cm.
"Appeared simultaneously in the autumn 1951 William and Mary quarterly."
"Bibliographical note": p. 37-38.
1. Jefferson, Thomas, Pres. U. S., 1743-1826. 2. Monticello, Va. I. Campbell, Charles, 1807-1876. II. Virginia. University. Library. Tracy W. McGregor Library. III. Title.
E444.J4 923.173 51—13833
Library of Congress ₍52m5₎

Mellow musings.
M811.5
W51
Whitney, Salem Tutt
Mellow musings, by Salem Tutt Whitney, with an introduction by Thomas L. G. Oxley ... Boston, Mass., The Colored poetic league of the world, 1926.
XXV, 126p. plates. 19cm.

Melville, Herman.
Trinidad
M820
J23m
James, Cyril Lionel Robert, 1901-
Mariners, renegades and castaways, the story of Herman Melville and the world we live in. New York, C.L.R. James, 1953.
203 p. 16cm.

Memoirs of a Monticello slave.
MB9
J35
1951
Jefferson, Isaac, b. 1775.
Memoirs of a Monticello slave, as dictated to Charles Campbell in the 1840's by Isaac, one of Thomas Jefferson's slaves. Charlottesville, Published by the University of Virginia Press for the Tracy W. McGregor Library, 1951.
86p. port. 24cm.

Mellows; a chronicle of unknown singers.
M784
K38
Kennedy, Robert Emmet, 1877-
Mellows; a chronicle of unknown singers. Decorations by Simmons Persons. New York, Albert and Charles Boni, 1925.
183p. illus. 30cm.

MB9
A119
Memoir and theatrical career of Ira Aldridge the African Roscuis ... London, Published by Onwhyn, Catharine Street, Strand, n.d.
28p. 21cm.
Presentation copy inscribed by Ira Aldridge "July 12, 1852."
1. Aldridge, Ira, 1804 (?) - 1867.

The memoirs of C. L. Simpson.
Liberia
MB9
Si5me
Simpson, Clarence Lorenzo, 1896–
The memoirs of C. L. Simpson, former Liberian Ambassador to Washington and to the Court of St. James's; the symbol of Liberia. London, Diplomatic Press and Pub. Co. ₍1961₎
298 p. illus. 23 cm.
1. Liberia—Hist. I. Title.
DT636.S5A3 966.6 61-65820 ‡
Library of Congress ₍2₎

Cameroons
M896
M45
Melone, Thomas
De la Négritude, dans la littérature - Négro-Africaine. Paris, Présence Africaine, 1962.
137p. 19cm. (Tribune des Jeunes, 2)
Includes bibliography.
1. Negritude. 2. Literature - Africa. I. Title. II. Series.

MB9
C89m
Memoir of Captain Paul Cuffee, a man of color; to which is subjoined The epistle of the Society of Sierra Leone, in Africa, &c. ... York, W. Alexander, 1812.
32 p. 16½ x 10ᶜᵐ.
Publisher's book list (paged ₍31₎-32) follows p. 32.
1. Cuffee, Paul, 1759?-1817.
15—839
Library of Congress E185.97.C96M5
₍28c1₎

Memoirs of Elleanor Eldridge...
MB9
El2m
₍McDougall, Mrs. Frances Harriet (Whipple) Greene₎ 1805–1878.
Memoirs of Elleanor Eldridge ... Providence, B. T. Albro, printer, 1838.
128 p. front. (port.) 14ᶜᵐ.
1. Eldridge, Elleanor, b. 1785. I. Title.
8—21168
Library of Congress E185 97.E57
₍a28d1₎

M973
M496
Meltzer, Milton.
In their own words; a history of the American Negro. New York, Crowell ₍1964-67₎
3v. illus., facsims., ports. 23cm.
Includes bibliographies.
Contents.- ₍1.₎ 1619-1865.- ₍2.₎ 1865-1916.- ₍3.₎ 1916-1966.
Contains extracts from letters, diaries, autobiographies, speeches and etc. by the Negro.
White author.
1. History - Sources. I. Title.

MB9
Sp3
Memoir of Mrs. Chloe Spear, a native of Africa, who was enslaved in childhood and died in Boston, Jan. 3, 1815 ... By a lady of Boston ... Boston, J. Loring, 1832.
1 p. l., iii, ₍9₎-108 p. front. 15½ᶜᵐ.
1. Spear, Mrs. Chloe, 1750?-1815. I. A lady of Boston.
~~2. Narrative.~~ 14-15962
₍31c1₎
Library of Congress E444.S74

Memoranda of a soldier.
M350
W38m
Webb, Percy R , 1917-
Memoranda of a soldier. New York, Vantage Press, 1961.
61p. 20cm.
Portrait of author on back of book jacket.

Meltzer, Milton, 1915- joint author.
M790
H87
Hughes, Langston, 1902-1967.
Black magic; a pictorial history of the Negro in American entertainment ₍by₎ Langston Hughes ₍and₎ Milton Meltzer. Englewood Cliffs, N. J., Prentice-Hall ₍1967₎
375 p. illus., ports. 29 cm.
1. Negro actors. 2. Entertainers — U. S. I. Meltzer, Milton, 1915- joint author. II. Title.
PN2286.H75 790.2'09174'96 67—22993
Library of Congress ₍68k7₎

Memoire pour le chef de brigade Magloire Pelage.
Guadeloupe
M972.97
F84m
Frasans, Hippolyte de.
Mémoire pour le chef de brigade Magloire Pélage et pour les habitans de la Guadeloupe, chargés, par cette colonie, de l'administration provisoire, après le départ du capitaine-général Lacrosse ... Paris, Desenne ₍etc.₎ an XI.—1803.
2 v. 20ᶜᵐ.
By H. de Frasans and Jean Thomas Langlois.
1. Guadeloupe—Hist. I. Langlois, Jean Thomas. II. Title.
2-13833 rev.
Library of Congress F2066.F84
₍r37b2₎

M06
J61
no. 17
... Memorial addresses in honor of Dr. Booker T. Washington. Lynchburg, Va., J. P. Bell company, inc., printers, 1916.
cover-title, 31 p. 23ᶜᵐ. (The trustees of the John F. Slater fund. Occasional papers no. 17)
"A memorial meeting in honor of Dr. Booker T. Washington was held in Carnegie hall, New York city ... February 11, 1916. The meeting was held under the auspices of Hampton institute, Tuskegee institute, and the National league on urban conditions."—Note, p. ₍2₎
1. Washington, Booker Taliaferro, 1859?-1915.
16—17488
Library of Congress E185.5.J65 no. 17
——— Copy 2. E185.97.W25
₍a39b1₎

Meltzer, Milton, 1915- jt auth.
M813.5
H87pi2
Hughes, Langston, 1902–
A pictorial history of the Negro in America, by Langston Hughes & Milton Meltzer. New rev. ed. New York, Crown Publishers ₍1963₎
337, ₍10₎ p. illus., ports., maps, facsims. 29 cm.
Bibliography: p. ₍341₎
1. Negroes—Hist.—Pictorial works. I. Meltzer, Milton, 1915– joint author. II. Title.
E185.H83 1963 325.2670973 63-12074
Library of Congress ₍5₎

Mémoires d'un médecin.
France
M840
D89me
Dumas, Alexandre, 1802-1870.
Mémoires d'un médecin, Joseph Balsamo. Bruxelles, Meline, Cans et Cie, 1846-1848.
10v. in 5. 16cm.
Written in collaboration with Auguste Maquet.
v. 3-4 missing.

Memorial de Ayres.
Brazil
M869.3
M18me
Machado de Assis, Joaquim Maria, 1839-1908.
... Memorial de Ayres. Rio de Janeiro, Paris, Garnier ₍1923₎
5 p. l., ₍3₎-273 p. 19ᶜᵐ. (Collecção dos autores celebres da litteratura brasileira)
At head of title: Machado de Assis.
I. Title.
30-723
Library of Congress PQ9697.M18M47
₍2₎

M326.5
L51 Memorial of Leonard Dugged, George A. Bailey, and 240 other free colored persons of California, praying for Congress to provide means for their colonization to some country in which their color will not be a badge of degradation. [Wash., D.C., G.P.O., 1862].

[6]p. 23cm. U.S. House. Mis Doc., no.31
At head title: Colonization of free blacks.

1. Colonization ... 2. Dugged, Leonard.

Men and matters in Nigerian politics (1934-58).
Nigeria
MB
An9m Anyiam, Frederick Uzoma, 1914-
Men and matters in Nigerian politics (1934-58). Yaba, Printed by John Okwesa & Co., 1958.

90p. ports., illus. 23cm.

Mende language—Grammar.
Sierra Leone
M496
Su6hm **Sumner, A T**
A hand-book of the Mende language, by the Rev. A. T. Sumner ... Freetown, Government printing office, 1917.

2 p. l., [vii]-xiv, 191 p. 21½cm.

1. Mende language—Grammar.

Library of Congress PL8511.S8 44-17472
[2] 496.4

Memorias posthumas de Braz Cubas.
Brasil
M869.3
M18m e3 **Machado de Assis, Joaquim Maria, 1839-1908.**
... Memorias posthumas de Braz Cubas, por Machado de Assis ... Rio de Janeiro, Paris, Garnier [1914]

x, 387 p. 18cm. (Collecção dos autores celebres da litteratura brasileira)
Continued in the author's Quincas Borba.

1. Title.

20-20125

Library of Congress [33b1] PQ9697.M18M5

M815.4
D74m **Douglass, Frederick, 1817-1895.**
Men of color, to arms! A call by Frederick Douglass.
Rochester, March 2, 1863.
1p. 21½cm.

The Mende language.
Sierra Leone
M496
M48 **Migeod, Frederick William Hugh.**
The Mende language, containing useful phrases, elementary grammar, short vocabularies, reading materials, by F. W. H. Migeod ... London, K. Paul, Trench, Trübner & co., ltd., 1908.

xv p., 1 l., [17]-271, [1] p. 19½cm.

9-403 Revised

Library of Congress [r28d2]

Memories of a retired Pullman porter.
MB9
T857 **Turner, Robert Emanuel, 1875-**
Memories of a retired Pullman porter. [1st ed.] New York, Exposition Press [1954]

191 p. illus. 21 cm.

1. Porters—Correspondence, reminiscences, etc. I. Title.
Full name: Robert Emmanuel Hammond Turner.

HD8039.R37T8 923.873 54-10978 ‡

Library of Congress [2]

Men of Maryland.
MB
B73m
1925 **Bragg, George Freeman, 1863-**
Men of Maryland, by the Reverend George F. Bragg, jr. ... Baltimore, Md., Church advocate press, 1925.

160 p. front. (3 port.) port. 19½cm.
History and biographical sketches of Maryland negroes.
On cover: Revised edition.

1. Negroes—Biog. 2. Negroes—Maryland. I. Title.

Library of Congress E185.93.M2B8 1925 25-12623
——— Copy 2.
Copyright A 861085 [36c1]

Trinidad
M972.98
M52m Mendes, Alex. L.
The marine fishes of Trinidad [by] Alex. L. Mendes. Trinidad, B.W.I., Trinidad publishing co., Ltd., 1940.

28p. 21½cm.
Inscribed copy: To Captain A. A. Cepriani, with the compliments of the author, Alex. L. Mendes, 31 July 1940.

1. Trinidad. 2. Fishes. I. Title.

Memories of east South America.
M910
H47m **Hershaw, Fay McKeene.**
Memories of east South America; an appreciation in story and pictures, by Fay McKeene Hershaw ... Boston, Meador publishing company, 1940.

144 p. incl. front. (map) plates. 20cm.

1. South America—Descr. & trav. I. Title. II. Title: East South America, Memories of.

Library of Congress F2223.H42 40-5440
——— Copy 2.
Copyright A 139001 [2] 918

Men of Maryland.
MB
B73m **Bragg, George Freeman, 1863-**
Men of Maryland, by the Rev. George F. Bragg ... Baltimore, Md., Church advocate press, 1914.

135 p. incl. front. (group of ports.) 18½cm.
History and biographical sketches of Maryland Negroes.

1. Negroes—Biog. 2. Negroes—Maryland. I. Title. 14—18558

Library of Congress E185.93.M2B8
Copyright A 379795 [a40g1]

Mendoza, Carlos Antonio, 1856-
Panama
MB9
M52w Westerman, George W
Carlos Antonio Mendoza father of Panama's Independence Act in commemoration of the Centennial of his birth, October 31, 1856. Panama, Published by the Bellas Artes Department and also Publications from the Educational Department Panama, 19??

83p. illus., port. 21½cm.
Bound with: Carlos Antonio Mendoza padre del acta de independencia de Panama. 83p.

MB9
B81m Memories of John Brown of Osawatomie. [New York, Frederick Douglass Chapter of the John Brown Memorial Association, 1928.]

18p. port. 13cm.
A reprint from a June number of Current history.

1. Brown, John, 1800-1859.

Men with backbone and other pleas for progress...
Jamaica
M972.92
W69m Wilson, C A
Men with backbone and other pleas for progress, by Rev. C.A. Wilson. Second edition. Kingston, Jamaica, The Educational supply company, 1913.
98 3 p. plates. 19cm.

M811.3
M52i Menken, Adah Isaacs, 1835-1868.
Infelicia. London, Chatto & Windus, Piccadilly, 1888.

126p. illus. 21cm.

Memphis—Fiction.
M813.5
L51be Lee, George Washington, 1894-
Beale street sundown [by] George W. Lee. New York, House of Field, inc., 1942.

176p. 22cm.

M811.4
M521 Menard, John Willis, 1838-1893
Lays in summer lands. Poems, by J. Willis Menard. With the press notices of his speech and his appearnace in Congress. Washington, Enterprise publishing company, 1879.
vii, 84p. 18cm.
1st edition.
Inscribed copy: Presented to Col. John Hay with the Author's compliments. Dec. 6, 1879.

1. Poetry. I. Title.

Menores e Loucos e fundamento do direito de Punir.
Brazil
M869
B27m Barreto de Menzes, Tobias, 1839-1889.
... Menores e Loucos e fundamento do direito de Punir. Sergipe Edição do Estado de Sergipe. 1926.
xx, 152p. 24cm. (Obras completas. v.V)

Memphis—Streets—Beale avenue.
M813.5
L51 **Lee, George Washington, 1894-**
Beale street, where the blues began [by] George W. Lee; foreword by W. C. Handy. New York, R. O. Ballou [°1934]

296 p. front., ports. 21cm.

1. Memphis—Streets—Beale avenue. 2. Negroes—Memphis. I. Title.

Library of Congress F444.M5L4 34-20400
——— Copy 2.
Copyright A 73530 [36f3] 917.68

Mende language - Grammar.
Sierra Leone
M496
M48 **Migeod, Frederick William Hugh.**
The Mende language, containing useful phrases, elementary grammar, short vocabularies, reading materials, by F. W. H. Migeod ... London, K. Paul, Trench, Trübner & co., ltd., 1908.

xv p., 1 l., [17]-271, [1] p. 19½cm.

9-403 Revised

Library of Congress [r28d2]

Haiti
M972.94
M52a Menos, Solon, d. 1918.
L'Affaire Luders.... Port-au-Prince, Imprimerie J. Verrollot, 1898.
1 p. l., iii, 393p., 1 l. 25cm.

1. Haitian literature.

Haiti
M840.9
Au8

Menos, Solon.
Auteurs Haitiens, morceaux choisis, précédes de notices biographiques, par Solon Menos, Dantes Bellegarde, A. Duval, Georges Sylvain; prose. Port-au-Prince, Imp. de F. Smith, 1904.

351p. 19cm. (Oeuvre des écrivains Haitiens)

Haiti
M841
M52m

Ménos, Solon, 1859-1918.
Les mnemoniennes. Premiere serie La Licence es-Joies (1876-1879). Paris, A. Cotillon & cie, 1882.
vii, 170 [1]p. 19cm.

1. Haitian poetry. I. Title.

Mensah, Albert Kayper.
The perfect understander, p. 228.

M808.8
N42
v.15

New world writing. 1st–
Apr. 1952–
[New York] New American Library.
v. 18 cm. (N. A. L. Mentor books)

1. Literature, Modern—20th cent. 2. American literature—20th cent.

PN6014.N457 808.8 52—1806
Library of Congress [60p5]

... The mental abilities of twenty-nine deaf and partially deaf Negro children.

M370
G61

Goodlett, Carlton Benjamin.
... The mental abilities of twenty-nine deaf and partially deaf Negro children, by Carlton B. Goodlett and Vivian R. Greene (with a foreword by Harry W. Greene) ... [Charleston, W. Va., Jarrett printing company, 1940]
23 p. incl. illus., tables, diagr. 23cm. (West Virginia state college bulletin ... Ser. no. 4. June, 1940)
"Contribution no. 1 of the Departments of psychology and education, West Virginia state college, in cooperation with the West Virginia school for the colored deaf and blind, Institute, West Virginia."
"Publications of West Virginia state college."
Bibliographical foot-notes.
1. Mental tests. 2. Negroes—Education. 3. Deaf—Education and institutions. [3. Deaf and dumb—West Virginia] I. Greene, Vivian R., joint author. II. West Virginia. School for the colored deaf and blind, Institute. III. Title.
U. S. Off. of educ. Library for Library of Congress BF432.N5G6 [a44c1]† E 40-493 371.912

Mental ability.

M378
C161

Canady, Herman G
The intelligence of Negro college students and parental occupation by Herman G. Canady. Reprinted... from The American journal of sociology, vol. 42, no.3, November 1936
388 - 399p. table 24cm.

M370
B47s

Mental defectives.
Bice, Harry V.
A study of Negro and white pupils in Piedmont North Carolina, by Harry V. Bice. [Raleigh, N.C., State board of charities and public welfare, 1938.]

28p. 23cm. (North Carolina State board of public welfare. Special bulletin no. 16)

Mental disorders

Haiti
M972.94
M352 R

Mars, Louis.
La lutte contre la folie. Port-Au-Prince, Haiti, 1947.
xi, 133 p., [1] l. 22 cm.

1. Insanity. [1. Mental disorders] 2. Psychiatry—Haiti. I. Title.

Med 48-1694
U. S. Army Medical Libr. for Library of Congress [WM100M363L 1947] [1]

Mental illness.

MB9
H83

Howell, Jinxy Red, 1930-
All the hairs on my head hurt. New York, Exposition Press, 1964.

197p. 20½cm.
Portrait of author on book jacket.

1. Mental illness. I. Title.

M136
L24

Mental illness.
Lane, Edward X.
I was a mental statistic; the true story of a man who came back. New York, Carlton Press [1963]

92p. 21cm. (A Reflection book)
Portrait of author on book jacket.

Mental tests.

M378
C16

Canady, Herman George.
... Individual differences among freshmen at West Virginia state college and their educational bearings, by Herman G. Canady ... Institute, W. Va., West Virginia state college 1936]
42 p. tables, diagrs. 23½cm. (West Virginia state college bulletin, series 23, no. 2. April 1936. Contribution no. 8 of the Department of psychology and philosophy)
Bibliography: p. [40]–42.

1. Mental tests. 2. Personnel service in education. I. Title.

E 39-40
U. S. Off. of educ. Library for Library of Congress LB1131.C28 [2]

Mental tests.

M370
G61

Goodlett, Carlton Benjamin.
... The mental abilities of twenty-nine deaf and partially deaf Negro children, by Carlton B. Goodlett and Vivian R. Greene (with a foreword by Harry W. Greene) ... [Charleston, W. Va., Jarrett printing company, 1940]
23 p. incl. illus., tables, diagr. 23cm. (West Virginia state college bulletin ... Ser. no. 4. June, 1940)
"Contribution no. 1 of the Departments of psychology and education, West Virginia state college, in cooperation with the West Virginia school for the colored deaf and blind, Institute, West Virginia."
"Publications of West Virginia state college."
Bibliographical foot-notes.
1. Mental tests. 2. Negroes—Education. 3. Deaf—Education and institutions. [3. Deaf and dumb—West Virginia] I. Greene, Vivian R., joint author. II. West Virginia. School for the colored deaf and blind, Institute. III. Title.
U. S. Off. of educ. Library for Library of Congress BF432.N5G6 [a44c1]† E 40-493 371.912

Menus of love.

M811.5
W152me

Walker, James Robert.
Menus of love. New York, Carlton Press, 1963.

130p. 20cm. (A Lyceum book)

Mercenaires noirs; notes sur une forme de l'exploitation des Africains.

Sénégal
M966.3
L98m

Ly, Abdoulaye
Mercenaires noirs; notes sur une forme de l'exploitation des Africains. Paris, Présence Africaine, 1957.

67p. 19cm.

Merchant marine-France.

Guadeloupe
M325
C16m

Candace, Gratien, 1873–
... La marine de la France. Marine militaire.—Marine marchande. Paris, Payot, 1938.
2 p. l., [7]–190 p., 1 l. incl. tables. 22½cm. (Bibliothèque politique et économique)

1. France—Navy. 2. Merchant marine—France. 3. Sea-power. I. Title.

A 39-675
New York. Public library for Library of Congress [3]

Merchant marine-France.

Guadeloupe
M325
C16ma

Candace, Gratien, 1873–
... La marine marchande française et son importance dans la vie nationale; préface de M. Aristide Briand ... Paris, Payot, 1930.
2 p. l., [7]–589 p. 23cm. (Bibliothèque politique et économique)
"Bibliographie": p. [585]–586.

1. Merchant marine—France. 2. France—Comm.

30-29002
Library of Congress HE833.C35
Copyright A—Foreign 8650
[3] 387.50944

Merchant marine-Germany.

Guadeloupe
M325
G32m

Gerville-Réache, Maxime.
La marine marchande en France et en Allemagne; subventions et primes, par Maxime Gerville-Réache ... Paris, A. Pedone, 1909.
114 p., 1 l. 25cm.
"Bibliographie": p. [5]–6.

1. Merchant marine—France. 2. Merchant marine—Germany. 3. Shipping bounties and subsidies.

10-24538
Library of Congress. HE743.F8G5

Merchant marine - U. S.

MB9
M92

Mulzac, Hugh, 1886–
A star to steer by; by Hugh Mulzac, as told to Louis Burnham and Norval Welch. New York, International Publishers [1963]
251 p. illus. 21 cm.

1. Merchant marine—U. S.—Negroes. 2. Merchant marine—U. S.—Officers—Correspondence, reminiscences, etc. I. Burnham, Louis E., 1915 or 16–1960. II. Welch, Norval. III. Title.

E185.63.M8 923.573 63–14260 ‡
Library of Congress [5]

Merchant marine - U. S. - Officers - Correspondence, reminiscences, etc.

MB9
M92

Mulzac, Hugh, 1886–
A star to steer by; by Hugh Mulzac, as told to Louis Burnham and Norval Welch. New York, International Publishers [1963]
251 p. illus. 21 cm.

1. Merchant marine—U. S.—Negroes. 2. Merchant marine—U. S.—Officers—Correspondence, reminiscences, etc. I. Burnham, Louis E., 1915 or 16–1960. II. Welch, Norval. III. Title.

E185.63.M8 923.573 63–14260 ‡
Library of Congress [5]

Merchant seamen - U.S.

MB9
W67k

Williams, James H 1864–1927.
Blow the man down! A Yankee seaman's adventures under sail; an autobiographical narrative based upon the writings of James H. Williams as arranged and edited by Warren F. Kuehl. [1st ed.] New York, Dutton, 1959.
255 p. illus. 22 cm.

1. Merchant seamen—U. S. I. Kuehl, Warren F., 1924– ed. II. Title.

HD8039.S42U74 923.873 59–5821 ‡
Library of Congress [15]

Haiti
M972.94
M53c

Mercier, Louis
Contribution de l'île d'Haïti à l'histoire de la civilisation. Haiti, Cap-Haïtien, Imprimerie "Les Presses Capoises." c1947
83p. 19cm.

1. Haiti—History.

Mercier, Roger, ed.

Dahomey
M896.3
B46

Bhely-Quenum, Olympe
Olympe Bhêly-Quénum, écrivian Dahomeen. [Textes commentés par Roger Mercier et M. et S. Battestini. Paris; Fernand Nathan [1964]
63p. 19½cm. (Classiques du monde. Litterature africaine, 5)
"Oeuvres": p. 5.
Portrait of author on book cover.

Mercier, Roger, ed.
Cameroons
M896.3 Biyidi, Alexandre, 1932-
B55m Mongo Beti, écrivian Camerounais. [Textes commentés par Roger Mercier et M. Et S. Battestini. Paris[Fernand Nathan [1964]
63p. 19½cm. (Classiques du monde. Littérature africaine, 6)
"Bibliographie": p. 5.
Portrait of author on book cover.

Ivory Coast Mercier, Roger, ed.
M896 Dadié, Bernard
D12 Bernard Dadié, écrivian Ivoirien. [Textes commentés par Roger Mercier et M. et S. Battestini. Paris] Fernand Nathan [1964]
63p. 19½cm. (Classiques du monde. Littérature africaine, 7)
"Oeuvres": p. 4.
Portrait of author on book cover.

Mercier, Roger, ed.
Senegal
M896.3 Diop, Birago
D59b Birago Diop, écrivain Sénégalais. [Textes commentés par Roger Mercier et M. et S. Battestini. Paris] Fernand Nathan [1964]
63p. 19½cm. (Classiques dummonde. Littérature africaine, 6)
"Bibliographie": p.8.
Portrait of author on book cover.

Mercier, Roger, ed.
Senegal
M896.3 Kane, Cheikh Hamidou, 1928-
K13 Cheikh Hamidou Kane, écrivain Sénégalais. [Textes commentés par Roger Mercier et M. et S. Battestini. Paris] Fernand Nathan [1964]
63p. 19½cm. (Classiques du monde. Littérature africaine, 1)
Portrait of author on book cover.
"Oeuvres": p.6.
I. Mercier, Roger, ed. II. Series.

Guinea Mercier, Roger, ed.
M896 Laye, Camara
L45 Camara Laye, écrivain Guinéen. [Textes commentés par Roger Mercier et M. et S. Battestini. Paris] Fernand Nathan [1964]
63p. 19½cm. (Classiques du monde. Littérature africaine, 2)
Portrait of autho on book cover.
"Oeuvres": p. 6.
I. Mercier, Roger, ed. II. Series.

Cameroons Mercier, Roger ed.
M896.3 Oyono, Ferdinand, 1929-
Oy4 Ferdinand Oyono; écrivain camerounais. [Textes commentés par Roger Mercier et M. et S. Battestini. Paris] Fernand Nathan [1964]
62p. 19½cm. (Classiques du monde. Littérature africaine, 8)
"Oeuvres": p.5.
Portrait of author on book cover.

Mercier, Roger, ed.
Senegal
M896.1 Senghor, Leopold Sédar, 1906-
Se5 L. S. Senghor, poète Sénégalais. [Textes commentés par Roger Mercier et M. et S. Battestini. Paris] Fernand Nathan [1964]
63p. 19½cm. (Classiques du monde. Littérature africaine, 3)
Bibliographie: p. 6-7.
Portrait of author on book cover.
I. Mercier, Roger, ed. II. Series.

Merciria ma arata anyu.
Kenya
M170 Gakwa, Silvanus Njendu
G12 Haría tūrī rīu. Where we are now. Nairobi, Eagle Press, 1949.
[25p. 18½cm. (Merciria ma arata anyu. Your friends are thinking series)
Written in English and Kikuyu.
1. Ethics. I. Title. II. Series. III. Series: Your friends are thinking series. IV. Title: Where we are now.

Congo, La mere Africaine.
Leopoldville
M396 Makonga, Bonaventure
M28 La mere Africaine. Bruxelles, Editions Remarques Congolaises, 1964.
113p. ports. 19cm. (Collection Etudes Congolaises, no. 11)
Portrait of author in book.
1. Women in the Congo. 2. Women, African. I. Title.

France Mère et jeune fille.
M841 Ségálas, Anaïs (Ménard) 1814-1895.
Se3m Mère et jeune fille. [a poem] Extract from Journal des Demouelles, 1840.
[2] p. 20 cm.

M378 **Meredith, James Howard, 1933-**
M541 **Three years in Mississippi [by] James Meredith. Bloomington, Indiana University Press [1966]**
328 p. 24 cm.
Autobiographical.
1. Mississippi. University—Hist. I. Title.
LD3412.9.M4A3 378.762 66-12731
Library of Congress [5]

Merrick, John, 1859-1919.
MB9 **Andrews, Robert McCants.**
M55a John Merrick, a biographical sketch, by R. McCants Andrews. [Durham, N. C., Press of the Seeman printery, °1920]
5 p. l., 9-229 p. front., plates, ports., facsim. 20½cm.
1. Merrick, John, 1859-1919. 2. North Carolina mutual and provident association.
20-22635
Library of Congress E185.97.M56
[48d1]

Sierra Leone
M966.4 Merriman-Labor, A B C
M55 Britons through Negro spectacles, or a Negro on Britons, with a description of London (illustrated) by A. B. C. Merriman-Labor London, The Imperial and Foreign company [1900]
238p. plates. 21½cm.
1. Great Britain. I. Title.

M811.5 **Merritt, Alice Haden, 1905-**
M55d ... Dream themes, and other poems, by Alice Haden Merritt. Philadelphia, Dorrance and company [°1940]
57 p. 20cm. (Contemporary poets of Dorrance (204))
I. Title. 1. Poetry.
40-6064
Library of Congress PS3525.E677D7 1940
——— Copy 2.
Copyright A 139154 [2] 811.5

M811.5 Merritt, Alice Haden, 1905-
M55p Psalms and Proverbs, a poetical version, by Alice Haden Merritt. Philadelphia, Dorrance & Co., 1941.
64p. 19cm.
1. Bible. O.T. Proverbs. Paraphrases.
2. Bible. N.T. Psalms. Paraphrases.
3. Bible. Paraphrases.

M811.5 **Merritt, Alice Haden, 1905-**
M55w Whence waters flow; poems for all ages from Old Virginia. Richmond, Dietz Press [1948]
69 p. illus. 26 cm.
I. Title.
PS3525.E677W5 811.5 49-16964*
Library of Congress [1]

MB9 **Merritt, Raleigh Howard.**
C25me From captivity to fame; or, The life of George Washington Carver, by Raleigh H. Merritt. Boston, Mass., Meador publishing company [°1929]
196 p. front., plates, ports. 20½cm.
"The supplementary section of this book is composed of bulletins on food and food subjects, etc., issued by Dr. Carver."—Pref.
1. Carver, George Washington, 1864- 2. Agriculture. 3. Cookery, American. I. Title.
30-7
Library of Congress S417.C3M4
[41n2]

M811.5 **Merriweather, Claybron W.**
M553g Goober peas, by Claybron W. Merriweather ... Boston, The Christopher publishing house [°1932]
xii, 13-174 p. 21cm.
Poems.
I. Title. 1 Poetry
32-19484
Library of Congress PS3525.E687G6 1932
Copyright A 53239 [2] 811.5

M811.5 **Merriweather, Claybron W.**
M553 The pleasures of life, lyrics of the lowly, essays, and other poems, by Claybron W. Merriweather ... [Hopkinsville, Ky., The New era printing company, 1931]
156 p. 20cm.
Autographed copy.
I. Title.
31-17719
Library of Congress PS3525.E687P6 1931
Copyright A 39248 [2] 810.81

...Mes années d'esclavage et de liberte.
M815.4 Douglass, Frederick, 1817-1895.
D739am ...Mes années d'esclavage et de liberte par Frédérik Douglass. Paris, E. Plon et Cie, 1883.
IV, 322p. 17½cm.
At head of title: Traducteur de la grande armee des miserables.

Mes combats.
MB9 Johnson, Jack, 1878-
J63 Mes combats. Paris, Pierre Lafitte, [c 1914]
93p. ports. 16cm. (Les petits bouquins)

Martinique
M841.91 A mes frères humains, sonnets & ballades.
C81a Coridun, Victor.
A mes frères humains, sonnets & ballades. Fort-de-France, Imp. R. Illemay, 1954.

16 leaves. 21cm.
Martinican author.

Mes transes a trente ans.
Rwanda
M89
N14m Naigiziki, Joseph Saverio, 1915-
Mes transes a trente ans. 2. De pis en mieux. Histoire vécue, mêlée de roman. Astrida, Groupe Scolaire, 1955.

487p. 23cm.

Haiti
M847.91 Messac, Achille
M56v Vie d'exil. Roman. Haiti, Port-au-Prince, 1955.

245p. 16cm.

1. Haiti-Fiction. I.Title.

M297 Message to the blackman in America.
P782 Poole, Elijah.
Message to the blackman in America, by Elijah Muhammad. Chicago, Muhammad Mosque of Islam No. 2 [1965]
xxvii, 355 p. 22 cm.

1. Black Muslims—Doctrinal and controversial works. 2. Negroes. I. Title.

BP222.P6 297.87 65-9666
Library of Congress [3]

Haiti Messages...
M841.1
In6m Innocent, Luc B
Messages ... [Poèmes] Port-au-Prince, Impr. Renelle, 1955.
59 p. port. 20 cm.

I. Title.

Florida. Univ. Library for Library of Congress [1] A 58-2092

The messenger.
M813.5 Wright, Charles Stevenson, 1932-
W92m The messenger. New York, Farrar, Straus [1963]
217 p. 22 cm.

I. Title.

PZ4.W9477Me 63-11709 ‡
Library of Congress [5]

Haiti Metaphysics.
M110 Lemoine, Raoul Fanini
L54 Principes de l'unite. [Port-au-Prince, Haiti, Imprimerie Théodore, n.d.]

31p. port. 21cm. (Serie des Saintes-Ecritures)
Portrait of author in book.

Metaphysics.
M113 Wilhite, William Hugh.
W64 The universe of universes, by William Hugh Wilhite. St. Louis, Mo., Keymer Printing company, 1923.

117 [10]p. 19½cm.

Methodism.
M287.8 Baxter, Daniel Minort, 1872-
B33 Back to Methodism, by Daniel Minort Baxter ... Philadelphia, A. M. E. book concern [°1926]
205 p. port. 20cm.

1. Methodism. I. Title.

Library of Congress BX8331.B35 26-8622
Copyright A 890256 [2]

Methodism.
M252 Turner, Henry McNeal, 1834-1915.
T85g The genius and theory of Methodist policy, or the machinery of Methodism. Practically illustrated through a series of questions and answers, by Bishop H. M. Turner...Philadelphia, A.M.E. Church [1885]

xii, 342p.

Methodist church-Sermons.
M252 Carter, Randall Albert, bp., 1867-
C24g Gathered fragments, by Bishop Randall Albert Carter ... Nashville, Tenn., The Parthenon press [°1939]
278 p. 21cm.

1. Methodist church—Sermons. 2. Sermons, American. I. Title.

Library of Congress BX8333.C35G3 39-32500
——— Copy 2.
Copyright A 134070 [2] 252.076

Methodist Church - Sermons.
M252 Wynn, Daniel Webster, 1919-
W98 Timeless issues [by] Daniel W. Wynn. New York, Philosophical Library [1967]
x, 144 p. 22 cm.

1. Methodist Church—Sermons. 2. Sermons, American. I. Title.

BX8472.W9 252.07 66-20219
Library of Congress [3]

M614 Methodist Church (Canada).
R66fr Roman, Charles Victor, 1864-1934.
Fraternal message from the African Methodist Episcopal Church to the Methodist Church of Canada, together with comments by reporters and editors. Nashville, Hemphill press, 1920.

36p. port. 19cm.

Methodist Church (United States) Conferences. Southern California-Arizona.
MB
D75 Downs, Karl E
Meet the Negro. Los Angeles, Calif., The Methodist Youth Fellowship, Southern California-Arizona Annual Conference, [1943].

xiii-xvi, 21-179p. 20cm.
First edition
Includes bibliographies.

Methodist Episcopal church.
M287.6 Hagood, Lewis Marshall, 1853-1936.
H12 The colored man in the Methodist Episcopal church. By the Rev. L. M. Hagood ... Cincinnati, Cranston & Stowe; New York, Hunt & Eaton, 1890.
327 p. front., plates, port. 19½cm.

1. Methodists, Negro. 2. Methodist Episcopal church. I. Title.

Library of Congress BX8435.H3 42-1798
[2]

Methodist Episcopal church-Government.
M323 Reed, John Hamilton.
R25 Racial adjustments in the Methodist Episcopal church, by John H. Reed ... with an introduction by Adna B. Leonard ... New York, The Neale publishing company, 1914.
193 p. 19cm.

1. Methodist Episcopal church—Government. 2. Methodists, Negro. I. Title.

Library of Congress BX8435.R4 14-17108 Revised
Copyright A 380509 [r40b2]

Methodist youth fellowship.
MB Downs, Karl E
D75 Meet the Negro [by] Karl E. Downs. Los Angeles, Calif., The Methodist youth fellowship, Southern California-Arizona annual conference [1943]
5 p. l., xiii-xvi p., 2 l., 21-179 p. illus. (ports.) 20cm.
"First edition."
Includes bibliographies.

1. Negroes—Biog. I. Methodist youth fellowship. II. Methodist church (United States) Conferences. Southern California-Arizona. III. Title.

Library of Congress E185.96.D68 44-3249
[4515] 325.260973

Methodists.
M287.8 Arnett, Benjamin W , editor.
Ar6b The budget of 1904 containing a complete organization of the church, facts, figures, historical data of the colored Methodist Church in particular and universal Methodism in general political and general information pertaining to the colored race, also portraits of each bishop and his wife; the portrait of many prominent men of the race and church, church edifices and institutions. Edited by Benjamin W. Arnett... Philadelphia, Pa.
373p. illus. tables. 22cm.

Methodists.
M287.6 Hagood, Lewis Marshall, 1853-1936.
H12 The colored man in the Methodist Episcopal church. By the Rev. L. M. Hagood ... Cincinnati, Cranston & Stowe; New York, Hunt & Eaton, 1890.
327 p. front., plates, port. 19½cm.

1. Methodists, Negro. 2. Methodist Episcopal church. I. Title.

Library of Congress BX8435.H3 42-1798
[2]

Methodists.
M287.1 Johnson, Charlest R.H. comp.
J62h A history of the Wesleyan Methodist Church of America. The story of one hundred years, 1842-1942 of the First Wesleyan Methodist church at Dayton, Ohio. Compiled and edited by Charlest R.H. Johnson.

74p. illus. 24cm.

Methodists, ~~Negro~~.
M323 Reed, John Hamilton.
R25 Racial adjustments in the Methodist Episcopal church, by John H. Reed ... with an introduction by Adna B. Leonard ... New York, The Neale publishing company, 1914.
193 p. 19cm.

1. Methodist Episcopal church—Government. 2. Methodists, Negro. I. Title.

Library of Congress BX8435.R4 14-17108 Revised
Copyright A 380509 [r40b2]

Metropolitan areas.
301.36 Weaver, Robert Clifton, 1907-
W37 The urban complex; human values in urban life [by] Robert C. Weaver. [1st ed.] Garden City, N. Y., Doubleday, 1964.
xii, 297 p. 22 cm.
Bibliographical footnotes.
1. Urbanization—U. S. 2. Urban renewal—U. S. 3. Metropolitan areas—U. S. 4. Cities and towns—Growth. I. Title.
HT123.W38 301.360973 64-15800
Library of Congress [5]

M813.5 Micheaux, Oscar, 1884-1951
M58c The case of Mrs. Wingate, by Oscar Micheaux ... New York, Book supply company, 1944. 1945.
518 p., 1 l. col. front. 21½cm.
Picture of author on jacket.
I. Title.
46-2765
Library of Congress PZ3.M5809Cas [2]

Haiti
M972.94 Michel, Antoine.
M58d ... La XIVe. législature ... Port-au-Prince, Haiti, Imprimerie "La Presse", 1932-
3 v. 23½cm.
At head of title, v. 1- : Au service de la jeunesse haïtienne.
1. Haiti (Republic) Assemblée nationale, 1873-1874. 2. Haiti—Pol. & govt.—1844- I. Title.
33-12850
Library of Congress F1926.M63 [2] 972.94

M89 Metropolitan Baptist church, N.Y.
B816p Phillips, Porter William, 1896-
W.W. Brown, host, by Porter W. Phillips... New York [etc.] Fleming H. Revell company [c1941]
102p. pl., ports. 19cm.

M813.5 [Micheaux, Oscar] 1884-1951
M579 The conquest; the story of a negro pioneer, by the pioneer. Lincoln, Nebr., The Woodruff press, 1913.
311 p. front. (port.) plates. 20cm.
I. Title.
13-10925
Library of Congress E185.97.M62M6

Haiti
M841 Michel, Jacques P
M58am Amour immorte'elie; poèmes. [Port-au-Prince, Imprime au Centre Audio Visuel, n.d.]
41p. leaves illus., port. 20½cm.
Cover title.
Portrait of author in book.
1. Poetry, Haitian. I. Title.

Mexico Mexican poetry.
M860.4 León, Nicolás, 1859-
L55 El negrito poeta mexicano y sus populares versos. Contribucion para el folk-lore nacional, por el Dr. N. Leon ... Mexico, Imprenta del Museo nacional, 1912.
234 p. front. 16½cm.
1. Vasconcelos, José, 18th cent.
13-17185
Library of Congress PQ7297.L4N3
——— Copy 2. [a28c1]

M813.5 Micheaux, Oscar, 1884-1951
M58f The forged note; a romance of the darker races, by Oscar Micheaux ... illustrated by C. W. Heller. Lincoln, Neb., Western book supply company, 1915.
9 p. l., 15-521 p. incl. front., illus. 20cm. $1.50
Ilus. t.-p. and lining-papers.
Picture of author on jacket pasted in book.
I. Title.
15-26847
Library of Congress PZ3.M5809F
Copyright A 414909

Michel-ange.
France
M840 Dumas, Alexandre, 1824-1895.
D891mi Michel-ange suivi de Titien Vecelli. Bruxelles et Leipzig, Meline, Cans et cie., 1844.
278p. 15cm.

S. Africa Mhudi.
M968 Plaatje, Solomon Tshekisho, 1878-1936.
P69mh Mhudi; an epic of South African native life a hundred years ago. Lovedale, Lovedale Press [1930]
225 p. 19 cm.

M813.5 Micheaux, Oscar, 1884-1951.
M58m The masquerade, an historical novel, by Oscar Micheaux. New York, Book Supply Co., c 1947.
401p. 21½cm.
I. Title.

Michel-ange suivi de Titien Vecelli.
France
M840 Dumas, Alexandre, 1824-1895
D89mic Michel-ange suivi de Titien Vecelli. Bruxelles et Leipzig, Meline, Cans, et compagnie, 1844.
278p. 15½cm.

Mi vida de Negro.
M813.5 Wright, Richard, 1909-
W93a2 Mi vida de Negro, de la niñez y la juventud, tr. de Clara Diament. Buenos Aires, Editorial Sudamericana. [1946].
391p. 19cm.
Spanish translation of Black boy.

M813.5 Micheaux, Oscar, 1884-1951
M58s The story of Dorothy Stanfield, based on a great insurance swindle, and a woman! A novel by Oscar Micheaux ... New York, Book supply company, 1946.
416 p. col. front. 22½cm.
I. Title.
46-2507
Library of Congress PZ3.M5809St [3]

Michelet, Jules, 1798-1874.
M89 Johnson, Mary Elisabeth.
M58j Michelet et le Christianisme. Paris, Librairie Nizet [1955]
262 p. 20 cm.
Bibliographie: p. [247]-255.
1. Michelet, Jules, 1798-1874.
BR139.M5J6 56-35674
Library of Congress [3]

Bahamas
M821 Michael, Julia Warner
C89 [Poems].
(In: Culmer, Jack, comp. A book of Bahamian verse. 2d ed. London, J. Culmer, 1948. 23cm. pp. 33-39.)

M813.5 Micheaux, Oscar, 1884-1951.
M58w The wind from nowhere... By Oscar Micheaux. New York, Book Supply Co., 1944.
385p. illus. 21½cm.
I. Title.

Africa Michelet, Raymond.
M960 African empires and civilisation. [Tr. from the French by Sir Edward Cunard, bt.; Foreword by Nancy Cunard.
M58a [Manchester, Eng.] Panaf Service [1945?]
v, 39 p. 19 cm. (International African Service Bureau. Publications, 4)
Cover title.
White author.
Reprinted from Negro anthology, made by Nancy Cunard, 1931-1933, pub. 1934.
Padmore, George-editorial note.
1. Africa—Hist. 2. ~~Negroes in Africa.~~ I. Title. II. ~~Cunard, Sir Edward, bart., 1898-~~ ~~(Series)~~
DT22.M5 960 A 48-7661*
Harvard Univ. Library for Library of Congress [2]†

M251 Michaux, Lightfoot Solomon, 1884-1968
M58 Sparks from the anvil of Elder Michaux, compiled and edited by Pauline Lark. Washington, Happy News Pub. Co., 1950.
ix, 139 p. port. 24 cm.
1. Homiletical illustrations. I. Title.
BV4225.M5 251 50-2492
Library of Congress [2]

Haiti
M972.94 Michel, Antoine.
M58em ... L'emprunt de trois millions de piastres ... Port-au-Prince, Haïti, Imprimerie "La Presse", 1934.
xix, 251 p. 23cm. (Au service de la jeunesse haïtienne)
Haiti-Finance
1. ~~Finance—Haiti.~~ 2. Haiti—Pol. & govt.—1844- 3. ~~Debts, Public—Haiti.~~ I. Title.
35-10792
Library of Congress HJ858.M5 [44c1] 336.7294

Kenya
M967.62 Michuki, D N
M58 Būrūri wa Embu [The story of the people of Embu. Nairobi, East African Literature Bureau, 1962.
119p. 18½cm.
Written in Kikuyu.
1. Embu tribe. 2. Kenya - Native races. I. Title.

Middle classes - U.S.

M301
F86b
1962

Frazier, Edward Franklin, 1894–1962.
Black bourgeoisie. With a new pref. by the author. New York, Collier Books [1962]

222 p. illus. 18 cm. (Collier books, AS347)

1. Negroes. 2. U. S.—Race question. 3. Middle classes—U. S. I. Title.

E185.61.F833 1962 325.2670973 A 62-8728 ‡

Library of Congress [5]

Migration.

M815
L26

Langston, John Mercer, 1829-1897.
Freedom and citizenship. Selected lectures and addresses of Hon. John Mercer Langston... With an introductory sketch by Rev. J. E. Rankin ... Washington, D. C., R. H. Darby, 1883.
286 p. front. (port.) 20cm.

Migration during the war, Negro.

M325
Sco84m

Scott, Emmett Jay, 1873–
... Negro migration during the war, by Emmett J. Scott ... New York [etc.] Oxford university press, 1920.

v p., 2 l., 3-189 p. 25cm. (Preliminary economic studies of the war, ed. by David Kinley ... no. 16)

At head of title: Carnegie endowment for international peace. Division of economics and history.
Bibliography: p. 175–183.

1. Negroes. 2. European war, 1914-1918—Economic aspects—U. S. I. Title. II. Title: Migration during the war, Negro.

20—9134

Library of Congress HC56.P7 no. 16 [41v2]

Middle classes.

M301
F86b1

Frazier, Edward Franklin, 1894–
Black bourgeoisie. Glencoe, Ill., Free Press [1957]

264 p. 22 cm.
Includes bibliographies.

1. Negroes. 2. U. S.—Race question. 3. Middle classes—U. S. I. Title.

E185.61.F833 325.260973 56—11964 ‡

Library of Congress [57o20]

Migration.

M331
L58

Lewis, Edward Erwin, 1900–
The mobility of the Negro; a study in the American labor supply, by Edward E. Lewis ... New York, Columbia university press; London, P. S. King & son, ltd., 1931.
144 p. illus. (maps) 23cm. (*Half-title:* Studies in history, economics and public law, ed. by the Faculty of political science of Columbia university, no. 342)
Published also as thesis (PH. D.) Columbia university.
"The third volume to appear as a result of studies in the field of Negro migration under grants by the Social science research council and the Columbia university Council for research in the social sciences."—Foreword.
"Selected bibliography": p. 184–185.
1. Negroes. 2. Negroes — Employment. 3. Southern states — Econ. condit.—1918– 4. Cotton growing and manufacture—Southern states. I. Social science research council. II. Columbia university. Council for research in the social sciences. III. Title.
Library of Congress H31.C7 no. 342 31—20612
—— —— Copy 2. E185.8.L47
[42q2] (306.2) 331.6

Mijn Harlem.

MB9
B798a4

Brown, Claude
Mijn Harlem «Manchild in the promise land» Rotterdam, Lemniscaat «1966»

411 p.
Written in Dutch.

I. Title.

Middle classes - U.S.

M301
F86b

Frazier, Edward Franklin, 1894–
Bourgeoisie noire. Paris, Librairie Plon [1955]

233 p. illus. 20 cm. (Recherches en sciences humaines, 7)

1. Negroes. 2. U. S.—Race question. 3. Middle classes—U. S. I. Title.

E185.61.F83 56-27366 ‡

Library of Congress [3]

Migration.

M323.
Su7n

Survey midmonthly.
... The Negro in the cities of the North ... New York, The Charity organization society, °1905.

2 p. l., 96 p. illus., plates. 26cm.

At head of title: Charities publication committee.
Reprint of Charities, October 7, 1905.

1. Negroes. I. Survey associates, inc., New York. II. Title.

6-2281 Revised

Library of Congress E185.9.S96 [r45c2]

M740
D74

Miles, Hamish tr.
Douglas, Aaron, illus.
Black magic, by Paul Morand. Translated from the French by Hamish Miles. Illus. by Aaron Douglas. New York, Viking Press, 1929.

vi, 218 p. 22 cm.
A group of stories on the modern Negro.
Walter White assisted the author.

M811.5
M58d

Middleton, Henry Davis.
Dreams of an idle hour, by Henry Davis Middleton ... [Chicago, Advocate publishing co., °1908]

70 p., 1 l. 21½cm.

1. Poetry. I. Title.

9-5468

Library of Congress (Copyright 1908 A 224562)

Migration.

M326
Un3n

U.S. Department of labor. Division of Negro economics.
Negro migration in 1916-1917. Reports by R. H. Leavell, T. R. Snavely, T. J. Woofter, Jr. W. T. B. Williams and Francis D. Tyson, with an introduction by J. H. Dillard. Washington, Government printing office, 1919.

158p. tables. 23cm.

Haiti
M972.94
M59

[Milescent, Claude Michel Louis]
Essai sur l'amolioration du sort des esclaves. [Paris, 1791].

[1], 26-39 p. 23 cm.
Signed: Milescent, creole.
"Claude Michel Louis Milscent, the author of this pamphlet was a white man & the father of Jules S. Milscent, the Haytian poet."

1. Slavery-Condition of slaves.

Sierra Leone
M496
M48

Migeod, Frederick William Hugh.
The Mende language, containing useful phrases, elementary grammar, short vocabularies, reading materials, by F. W. H. Migeod ... London, K. Paul, Trench, Trübner & co., ltd., 1908.

xv p., 1 l., [17]-271, [1] p. 19½cm.

1. Mende language - Grammar.

9-405 Revised

Library of Congress [r28d2]

Migration.

M304
P19
V.5, no.15

Waldron, Eric D.
The Negro exodus from the South. In: Three articles on the Negro problem. (Published in current history magazine, Sept. 1923) p. 23-29.

Nigeria
M966.9
Aj11

Milestones in Nigerian history.
Ajayi, J F Ade.
Milestones in Nigerian history. Ibadan, Nigeria, University College [1962]

47 p. illus., ports., map. 22 cm.
"For further reading": p. 47.

1. Nigeria—Hist. I. Title.

DT515.5.A64 63-6467

Library of Congress [1]

Migration.

M323
C43

Chicago. Mayor. Conference on Race Relations. February, 1944.
Proceedings... Chicago, The Committee, 1944.

64p. 28cm.

Migration, Internal - U.S.

M973
B64t2

Bontemps, Arna Wendell, 1902–
Anyplace but here [by] Arna Bontemps and Jack Conroy. New York, Hill and Wang [1966]

viii, 372 p. 21 cm.

"A revised and expanded version of They seek a city."—Dust jacket.
Bibliography: p. 349-360.

1. Negroes—Hist. 2. Negroes—Biog. 3. Migration, Internal—U. S. I. Conroy, Jack, 1899– joint author. II. Title.

E185.6.B75 1966 301.32973 66–15898

Library of Congress [15]

Milestones in the history of the Gold Coast.

Ghana
MB9
N58

Nii Kwabena Bonne III, 1888–
Milestones in the history of the Gold Coast; autobiography of Nii Kwabena Bonne III, Osu Alata Mantse, also Nana Owusu Aktenten III, Oyokohene of Techiman, Ashanti. [London] Diplomatist Publications [1953]

92 p. illus. 19 cm.

1. Gold Coast—Hist. I. Title.

DT511.N5 966.7 54–1186 ‡

Library of Congress [2]

Migration.

M815.4
D74f

Douglass. Frederick, 1817-1895.
Frederick Douglass, on the exodus. Resolutions submitted by Mr. Douglass, preliminary to his debate with Prof. R.T. Greener on the impolicy of the exodus of colored people from the South to Kansas and oth r nor h rn states, n.p., n.p., n.d.
7p. 23½cm.

Migration, Internal- U.S.

M973
B64t

Bontemps, Arna Wendell, 1902–
... They seek a city. Garden City, New York, Doubleday, Doran and company, inc., 1945.

xvii p., 1 l., 266 p. 21½cm.

At head of title: Arna Bontemps and Jack Conroy.
"First edition."
"A selected list of references and sources": p. 253–258.

1. Negroes—Hist. 2. Negroes—Biog. 3. Migration, Internal—U. S. I. Conroy, Jack, 1899– joint author. II. Title.

45—35114

Library of Congress E185.6.B75 [47g5] 325.260973

Les milices du Rwanda précolonial.

Rwanda
M967.57
K11m

Kagame, Alexis, 1912–
Les milices du Rwanda précolonial. [Bruxelles, 1963]

196 p. 25 cm. (Académie royale des sciences d'outre-mer. Classe des sciences morales et politiques. Mémoires in 8°. Nouv. sér., t. 28, fasc. 3)

1. Ruanda-Urundi—Soc. life & cust. 2. Ruanda-Urundi—History, Military. I. Title. (Series)

[DT641.A27 n. s., t. 28, fasc. 3] A 63-770

Yale Univ. Library for Library of Congress [1]

M973 F85m
The militant South, 1800-1861.
Franklin, John Hope, 1915–
The militant South, 1800–1861. Cambridge, Belknap Press of Harvard University Press, 1956.
317 p. 22 cm.
Includes bibliography.
1. Southern States—Hist.—1775–1865. 2. Militarism. I. Title.
F213.F75 975 56—10160 ‡
Library of Congress [57x20]

M973 F85m
Militarism.
Franklin, John Hope, 1915–
The militant South, 1800–1861. Cambridge, Belknap Press of Harvard University Press, 1956.
317 p. 22 cm.
Includes bibliography.
1. Southern States—Hist.—1775–1865. 2. Militarism. I. Title.
F213.F75 975 56—10160 ‡
Library of Congress [57x20]

M350 Yo8m
Military morale of nations and races.
Young, Charles, 1864–1922.
Military morale of nations and races, by Charles Young ... Kansas City, Mo., Franklin Hudson publishing co., 1912.
273 p. 22½cm.
Bibliography: p. [7]
1. National characteristics. 2. Ethnopsychology. 3. Soldiers. 4. Morale. I. Title.
14—8826
Library of Congress U21.Y6
[a41b1]

M973.9 F46 No.9
Military service.
Johnson, Campbell Carrington.
Fifty years of progress in the armed forces. Pittsburgh, Pittsburgh Courier, 1950.
11p. 24cm. (Fifty years of progress)

Uganda MB9 K11m
Millar, Ernest editor
Mukasa, Ham
Uganda's Katikiro in England, being the official account of his visit to the coronation of his majesty King Edward VII. By his secretary Ham Mukasa; translated and edited by the Rev. Ernest Millar... with an introduction by Sir H.H. Johnston. London, Hutchinson & Co., 1904.
xxiv, 278p. 21½cm.

MB9 B32m
Millar, Gerard.
Life, travels and works of Miss Flora Batson, deceased queen of song, by Gerard Millar. [n.p.] T. M. R. M. Company [n.d.]
[7]-92p. 17½cm.
1. Batson, Flora.

France M840. D89mi
Les mille et un fantomes.
Dumas, Alexandre, 1802–1870.
Les mille et un fantômes, par Alexandre Dumas. Bruxelles, Meline, Cans et compagnie; [etc., etc.] 1849.
3 v. 16 cm.
Written in collaboration with Paul Bocage.
I. Bocage, Paul Tousez, called, 1824–1887, joint author. II. Title.
12—12590
Library of Congress PQ2227.M6 1849
[48b1]

France M840 D89te
Les mille et un fantomes.
Dumas, Alexandre, 1802-1870.
Le testament de M. de Chauvelin, par Alexandre Dumas. Lo Mayro, Chez les Meri Tioro Doorman, 1850.
212p. 15cm.
At head of title: Les mille et un fantomes.

M811.5 M591
Miller, Clifford Leonard,
Imperishable the temple; a collection of verse. Mexico City, 1962.
[69]p. 21cm.
Portrait of author.
"In appreciation of your services to my race, my country, and humanity.- Clifford L. Miller."
1. Poetry. I. Title.

M812.5 M61
Miller, Clifford Leonard
Wings over dark waters, a poetic drama. [1st ed.] New York, Great Concord Publishers [1954]
270 p. illus. 21 cm.
I. Title.
PS3525.I 5223W5 812.5 54-8457 ‡
Library of Congress [2]

M286.7 M61a
Miller, George Frazier, 1864–
Adventism answered (the Sabbath question) Part first: Passing of the law and the introduction of grace. Part second: Some phases of the gospel liberty. By George Frazier Miller ... Brooklyn, N. Y., Guide printing and publishing company, 1905.
214 p. 20½cm.
Inscribed copy: Mr. Arthur B. Spingarn with the compliment of George Frazier Miller. Jan. 10, 1935.
1. Seventh-day Adventists. I. Title.
6–5699 Revised
Library of Congress BX6124.M46
[r41b2] 286.7

M304 P19 v.6, no.15
Miller, George Frazier, 1864–
A discussion. Is religion reasonable? Mr. Clarence Darrow says no and to the Black man it is self-stultification. Bishop Jones says yes it is the Universal Ground of Hope. A challenge by Dr. Du Bois, Editor of The Crisis. The objection and the challenge met, by George Frazier Miller. [Brooklyn, The Henne Press, n.d.]
[8] p. 22cm.

M304 P19 v.6, no.13
Miller, George Frazier, 1864–
A reply to the political plea of Bishop Cleland K Nelson and Bishop Thomas F. Gailor at the Cathedral of St. John the Divine in the city of New York, Sunday evening, October 19, 1913. A sermon by Reverend George Frazier Miller...October 26, 1913. Brooklyn, The interboro Press, 1913.
[18 p.] 22cm.

M304 P19 v.5, no. 14
Miller, George Frazier, 1864–
The sacredness of humanity, annual sermon of the conference of church workers (Episcopal) among colored people at St. Philip's church, New York, October 6-9, 1914. Brooklyn, Frank R. Chisholm, printer, 1914.
12p. 23p.
1.Religion. 2.Sermons.

MB9 D37m
Miller, Henry
The amazing and invariable Beauford Delaney, by Henry Miller. [New York] Alicat Book Shop, 287 S. Broadway, Yonkees 5, 1945]
24p. 21½cm. ("Outcast" series of chapbooks, no.2.)
1. Art
2. Delaney, Beauford.

M323 M59b
Miller, Henry Jefferson, 1877–
Blasted barriers; views of a reporter in story and song. Boston, Christopher Pub. House [1950]
140 p. 21 cm.
I. Title. 1. Race problems
PS3525.I 5455B5 325.260973 50–34016
Library of Congress [1]

Martinique M972.98 M61m
Miller, James Martin, 1859–1939.
The Martinique horror and St. Vincent calamity, containing a full and complete account of the most appalling disaster of modern times ... by J. Martin Miller ... in collaboration with Hon. John Stevens Durham ... Philadelphia, National publishing co. [1902]
8, 17–560 p. 2 front., illus., plates, ports., maps. 23½cm.
Issued also under the title: True story of the Martinique and St. Vincent calamities ... by Prof. John Randolph Whitney.
1. La Soufrière, St. Vincent—Eruption, 1902. 2. Pelée, Mont—Eruption, 1902. 3. St. Vincent. 4. Volcanoes. I. Durham, John Stevens, 1861– joint author. II. Title.
White author. Negro.
5. Martinique.
2–17542
Library of Congress F2081.M64
[a44f1]

M973 H55f
Miller, Jesse W., 1920– joint author.
Hill, Arthur C 1918–
From yesterday thru tomorrow, by Arthur C. Hill and J. W. Miller. New York, Vantage Press [1951]
142 p. 23 cm.
1. Negroes. 2. Slavery in the U. S. I. Miller, Jesse W., 1920– joint author. II. Title.
E185.6.H5 325.260973 51–2475
Library of Congress [10]

M323. M6la
Miller, Kelly, 1863–1939.
An appeal to conscience; America's code of caste a disgrace to democracy, by Kelly Miller ... with an introduction by Albert Bushnell Hart. New York, The Macmillan company, 1918.
108 p. 17cm.
1. Negroes. 2. U. S.—Race question. I. Title.
18—12463
Library of Congress E185.61.M63
[a44b1]

M304 P19 v.7 no. 16
M304 P19 V.5, no.7
Miller, Kelly, 1863–1939
As to The leopard's spots; an open letter to Thomas Dixon, jr., by Kelly Miller ... Washington, D. C., K. Miller [°1905]
21 p. 23cm.
1. Dixon, Thomas, 1864– 2. ~~Negroes.~~ 3. ~~U. S.~~—Race question. I. Title. 3. Race relations
5—33680
Library of Congress E185.61.M643
Copyright [36b1]

M323 M61d
Miller, Kelly, 1863–1939
The disgrace of democracy; open letter to President Woodrow Wilson, by Kelly Miller ... [Washington, 1917]
cover-title, 3–18 p. 21cm.
1. Negroes. 2. U. S.—Race question. I. Title.
17–28905
Library of Congress E185.61.M644

M323
M61e
Miller, Kelly, 1863-1939.
The everlasting stain, by Kelly Miller ... Washington, D. C., The Associated publishers [°1924]
xiii p., 1 l., 352 p. 19½cm.
"The essays in this collection center about the issues growing out of the world war and the Negro's relation to them."—Pref.
1. Negroes. 2. U. S.—Race question. I. Title. 25—2654
Library of Congress E185.61.M6442 [a41e1]

M329
M61p
Miller. Kelly, 1863-1939
...The political plight of the Negro, by Kelly Miller. Washington, D.C., Murray bros. printing co., inc., 1913.
21 3 p. 22cm. (Kelly Miller's mongraphic magazine, vol. 1, May1913)
1. Politics. I. Title

M342.73
M615
Miller, Loren B , 1903-
The petitioners; the story of the Supreme Court of the United States and the Negro. New York, Pantheon Books [1966]
xv, 461 p. 22 cm.
Bibliographical references included in "Notes" (p. [435]-455)
1. U. S. Supreme Court. 2. Negroes—Legal status, laws, etc. I. Title.
342.73 65-14583
Library of Congress [5]

M06
Am35
Miller, Kelly, 1863-1939.
Government and the Negro.
(In: American Academy of Political and Social Science, Philadelphia. The American Negro. Philadelphia, 1928. 24cm. p. 98-104.

M973.8
Am3
Miller, Kelly, 1863-1939
Professional and skilled occupations.
(In: American Academy of Political and Social Science. The Negro's progress in fifty years ... Philadelphia, 1913. 25cm. p. 10-18).

M811.5
M61i
Miller, May
Into the clearing. Washington, The Charioteer Press, 1959.
24p. 19cm.
Author's full name: May Miller Sullivan.
1. Poetry. I. Title.

M378
F92
Miller, Kelly, 1863-1939.
Howard University.
(In: From servitude to service ... Boston, American Unitarian Association, 1905. 20cm. pp. 1-47).

M973
M61p
Miller, Kelly, 1863-1939.
Progress and achievements of the colored people ... Kelly Miller and Joseph R. Gay ... Washington, D. C., Austin Jenkins co. [c1917]
490 p, plates. 21½cm.
1. History. I. Gay, Joseph R II. Title.

Miller, May
Door - Stops.
M810.8
C22
The Carolina magazine; literary supplement to the Daily tar heel. Negro number. May 4, 1930. Chapel Hill, University of North Carolina.
8p. 38cm.

M350
M61
Miller, Kelly, 1863-1939
Kelly Miller's history of the world war for human rights, being an intensely human and brilliant account of the world war and why and for what purpose America and the allies are fighting and the important part taken by the Negro including the horrors and wonders of modern warfare, the new and strange devices, etc... by Kelly Miller ... illustrated with 128 genuine pictures from recent official photographs also outline map ...
(cont'd)

M323
M61r
Miller, Kelly, 1863-1939.
Race adjustment; essays on the Negro in America, by Kelly Miller. New York and Washington, The Neale publishing company, 1908.
306 p. 21cm.
CONTENTS.—Radicals and conservatives.—As to The leopard's spots.—An appeal to reason on the race problem.—The Negro's part in the Negro problem.—Social equality.—The city Negro.—Religion as a solvent of the race problem.—Plea of the oppressed.—The land of Goshen.—Surplus Negro women.—Rise of the professional class.—Eminent Negroes.—What Walt Whitman means to the Negro.—Frederick Douglass.—Jefferson and the Negro.—The artistic gifts of the Negro.—The early struggle for education.—A brief for the higher education of the Negro.—Roosevelt and the Negro.
1. Negroes. I. Title. 8—24845
Library of Congress E185.5.M64 [a42g1]

Miller, May, joint ed.
M812.08
R39n
Richardson, Willis, 1889- ed.
Negro history in thirteen plays, by Willis Richardson and May Miller. Washington, D. C., The Associated publishers, inc. [°1935]
vii, 333 p. 21cm.
1. Negro drama. 2. Negroes in literature and art. I. Miller, May, joint ed. II. Title.
36—17
Library of Congress PS627.N4R47 [43u2] 812.50822

M350
M61
drawings made especially for this volume. Washington, D.C., Austin Jenkins co. [1919]
xiii, 495p. front. maps. plates. 21½cm.

M323.4
M615
Miller, Loren B 1903-
[Equality]
Pp. 3-39.
In: Equality. New York, Pantheon Books, 1965.

Miller, Queen Elizabeth (Taylor).
MB9
M61b
Blackford, Audrey.
The royal Queen Elizabeth Miller; the inspiring true story of a woman who built a kingdom for children whom the world had cast away. [1st ed.] New York, Greenwich Book Publishers [°1961]
52 p. 21 cm.
1. Miller, Queen Elizabeth (Taylor)
HV28.M48B55 60-53447 ‡
Library of Congress [3]

M06
Am3
no. 11
Miller, Kelly, 1863-1939
Migration and distribution of the Negro population.
(In: American Negro Academy. The Negro and the elective franchise. Washington, D.C., The Academy, 1905.)

Miller, Loren B , 1903-
Freedom now - but what then?
pp. 41-47.
M323.4
W52
Westin, Alan F ed.
Freedom now! The civil-rights struggle in America. Edited by Alan F. Westin. New York, Basic Books [1964]
xv, 346 p. 22 cm.
Bibliography: p. [329]-341.
1. Negroes—Civil rights—Addresses, essays, lectures. 2. Civil rights—U. S.—Addresses, essays, lectures. I. Title.
E185.61.W54 301.451 64-17401
Library of Congress [5]

M326
M61s
Miller, Richard Roscoe.
Slavery and Catholicism. Durham, N. C., North State Publishers [1957]
259 p. illus. 22 cm.
1. Slavery and the church—Catholic Church. 2. Slavery in the U. S. I. Title. 3. Catholicism.
E441.M65 326.973 57—8157 ‡
Library of Congress [57f5]

M323.X
M610
Miller, Kelly, 1863-1939.
Out of the house of bondage, by Kelly Miller ... New York, The Neale publishing company, 1914.
242 p. 19½cm.
Reprinted from various periodicals.
CONTENTS.—Oath of Afro-American youth.—A moral axiom.—Out of the house of bondage.—The physical destiny of the American negro.—Education for manhood.—Crime among negroes.—The American negro as a political factor.—Fifty years of negro education.—Negroes in professional pursuits.—"The negro in the New world" and "The conflict of color."—The ministry.—The ultimate race problem.—I see and am satisfied.
1. Negroes. 2. U. S.—Race question. I. Title.
(over) 14—9858
Library of Congress E185.6.M633 [a43f1]

M323.4
W52
Miller, Loren B , 1903-
Negroes and the police in Los Angeles.
pp. 224-228.
In: Westin, Alan F. Freedom now. New York, Basic Books, 1964.

Mills, Victoria. Cooperation of pastor and people, p. 7-16.
M287.8
Af8p
African methodist episcopal church. Mite missionary society.
In the Philadelphia conference branch mite missionary society's pamphlet. Philadelphia, A.M.E. publishing house, 1905, p. 7-16.
28p. 16½cm.

M343.3 Milton, William.
Sh6k
Shields, Art.
The killing of William Milton; Introduction by Simon W. Gerson. New York, Daily Worker, 1948.

14p. 18cm.

... Mimola...
Haiti
M843.91 Innocent, Antoine.
In6
... Mimola, ou L'histoire d'une cassette. Petit tableau de mœurs locales. Port-au-Prince, Imprimerie E. Malval, 1906.

2 p. l., [vii]-xiv, 175 p. 20cm.

I. Title. II. Title: L'histoire d'une cassette.

25-20874

Library of Congress PQ3949.I 5M5

M343.3 Mims, Florida.
N81b
North, Joseph.
Behind the Florida bombings; Who killed NAACP leader Harry T. Moore and his wife. New York, New Century, 1952.

23p. 19cm.

The mind of Africa.

Ghana
M960 Abraham, Willie E 1934-
Ab81
The mind of Africa. London, Weidenfeld and Nicholson [1962]

206p. 23cm. (The Nature of human society)
Portrait of author on book jacket.

The mind of Africa.

Ghana
M960 Abraham, Willie E
Ab81a
The mind of Africa. [Chicago] University of Chicago Press [1962]

206 p. 23 cm. (The Nature of human society)

1. Africa—Civilization. 2. Africa—Econ. condit. 3. Pan-Africanism. I. Title.

DT30.A2 916 63—9733 ‡

Library of Congress [63f5]

The mind of the Negro.

M301 Thorpe, Earl E
T39m
The mind of the Negro; an intellectual history of Afro-Americans. Baton Rouge, La., Printed by Ortlieb Press [1961]

562 p. 24 cm.
Includes bibliography.

1. Negroes—Intellectual life. 2. Negroes—Psychology. I. Title.

E185.82.T5 325.2670973 61—16125 ‡

Library of Congress [62k5]

Mind of the Negro.
M973. Woodson, Carter Godwin, 1875- ed.
W86m
The mind of the Negro as reflected in letters written during the crisis, 1800-1860, edited by Carter G. Woodson ... Washington, D. C., The Association for the study of Negro life and history, inc. [°1926]

5 p. l., v-xxxii, 672 p. 24cm.

1. Negroes. 2. Negroes—Moral and social conditions. 3. Slavery in the U. S.—Emancipation. I. Association for the study of Negro life and history, inc. II. Title.

26—14304

Library of Congress E185.W8877

[45m1]

Mine boy.
S. Africa
M896.3 Abrahams, Peter, 1919-
Ab8m
Mine boy. [1st American ed.] New York, Knopf, 1955.

252 p. 19 cm.

I. Title.

Full name: Peter Henry Abrahams.

PZ3.A1576Mi 3 55-8788 ‡

Library of Congress [5]

M323
N21a
Ming, William Robert , 1911-
The present legal and social status of the American Negro.

(In: National Association for the Advancement of Colored People. An appeal to the world; ... New York, 1947. 21cm. p. 47-61).

M331.833 Ming, William Robert , 1911-
M66r
Racial restrictions and the fourteenth amendment: The restrictive covenant cases. Reprinted from the University of Chicago law review, 16:203-238, Winter 1949.

203-238p. 24cm.

1. U.S. Constitution, 14th, Amendment.
2. Covenants.

Brazil Miniaturas.
M869.1 Gonçalves Crespo, Antonio Candido, 1846-1883.
G579m
Miniaturas, por Antonio Candido Gonçalves Crespo ... Coimbra, Impr. da Universidade, 1871.

3 p. l., 5-148 p. 21cm.
Poems.

I. Title.

32-14070

Library of Congress PQ9261.G65M5 869.1

The minister...
M250 Fisher, Charles Lewis.
F53m
The minister, a brief handbook on pastoral theology with helpful suggestions for young ministers, by the Rev. C.L. Fisher... covering over a quarter of a century of ministerial services and kingdom work, with an introduction by Rev. J.T.Brown...M. p., n.p., n.d.
56p. 19½cm.

Ministers.

M06 Moorland, Jesse Edward, 1863-1940.
Am3
no. 13
... The demand and the supply of increased efficiency in the negro ministry. By Jesse E. Moorland ... Washington, D. C., The Academy, 1909.

14 p. 22cm. (Occasional papers, no. 13. American negro academy)

1. Negroes—Education. 2. Religious education.

10—2009

Library of Congress E185.5.A51 no. 13
——— Copy 2. E185.82.M82

[a42d1]

The minister's wife.
Ross, Mrs. Solomon D.
MB
R73m
The minister's wife, by Mrs. S.D.Ross. [Detroit, Arbora publishing co., c1946]
78p.

Minneapolis.

M311.833 Tillman, James A.
T466
Not by prayer alone; a report on the Greater Minneapolis Interfaith Fair Housing Program [by] James A. Tillman, Jr. Philadelphia, United Church Press [1964]

223p. 23cm.

Minnesota. University. General extension division.
M323 Mudgett, Helen (Parker) 1900-
M88d
Democracy for all, a study program by Helen Parker Mudgett ... Minneapolis, Minn., General extension division, University of Minnesota [1945]

87, [1] p. diagrs. 23 cm.
Includes bibliographies.

1. Citizenship—Study and teaching. 2. Democracy. I. Minnesota. University. General extension division. II. Title.

45—37084

Library of Congress JA88.U6M8

[49e2] 323.607

Minorities.

M370 Caliver, Ambrose, 1894-
C12e
Education of teachers for improving majority-minority relationships. Course offerings for teachers to learn about racial and national minority groups. By Ambrose Caliver ... Federal security agency. Paul V. McNutt, administrator. U. S. Office of education, John W. Studebaker, commissioner. Washington, U. S. Govt. print. off., 1944.

iv, 64 p. incl. illus., tables. 23cm. (U. S. Office of education. Bulletin 1944, no. 2)
"Selected references and sources of information": p. 60-64.
1. U. S.—Race question. 2. Minorities. 3. Teachers, Training of—U. S. 4. Universities and colleges—Curricula. I. Title.

E 45—7

U. S. Off. of educ. Library for Library of Congress L111.A6 1944, no. 2
——— Copy 2. E184.A1C3
[46k3]† (370.6173) 325.73

Minorities.
M323 Gittler, Joseph Bertram, 1912- ed.
G44u
Understanding minority groups. Contributors: John Collier [and others] New York, Wiley [1956]

xii, 139 p. illus. 24 cm.
Includes bibliographical references.

1. Minorities—U. S. I. Collier, John, 1884- II. Title.

E184.A1G5 325.73 56—11777

Library of Congress [57f15]

Minorities.

Granger, Lester Blackwell, 1896-
M331
G76t
Toward job adjustment, with specific reference to the vocational problems of racial, religious and cultural minority groups, by Lester B. Granger ... Louis H. Sobel ... [and] William H. H. Wilkinson ... Prepared under the direction of Committee on minority groups, Section on employment and vocational guidance, Welfare council of New York city. [New York] Welfare council of New York city [°1941]

78 p., 1 l. illus. 21½cm.
Bibliography: 76-78.
1. Interviewing. 2. Employment agencies. 3. Minorities. I. Sobel, Louis Harry, joint author. II. Wilkinson, William H. H. III. Welfare council of New York city. Section on employment and vocational guidance. IV. Title.

41-16628

Library of Congress HD5861.G65

[10] 331.11511

Minorities.
M323 Imbert, Dennis I
Im1
The stranger within our gates; a South American's impression of America's social problems, byD.I. Imbert. First edition... New Orleans, La., Watson bros. press, 1945.
102p. plate. 15cm.

Minorities.

M323 Institute for religious and social studies, *Jewish theological seminary of America.*
In5a
... Unity and difference in American life, a series of addresses and discussions, edited by R. M. MacIver. New York and London, Pub. by Institute for religious & social studies, distributed by Harper & brothers [1947]

5 p. l., 3-168 p. 21 cm. (Religion and civilization series)

CONTENTS.—The common ground: Three paths to the common good, by Louis Finkelstein. The rise of an American culture, by Allan Nevins. What common ground has America won? By L. K. Frank.—The dividing issues: The racial issue, by E. F. Frazier. The ethnic issue, by Vilhjalmur Stefansson. The economic issue, by Eli Ginzberg.

(Continued on next card)

47—2731

[49k7]

Minorities.

M...
L79 w

Locke, Alain Le Roy, 1886– *ed.*
When peoples meet; a study in race and culture contacts, edited by Alain Locke ... and Bernhard J. Stern ... New York, Committee on workshops, Progressive education association, [°1942]
xii, 756 p. 24½ cm. (*Half-title:* Progressive education association publications. Committee on workshops)

1. Acculturation. 2. Minorities. 3. Race problems. I. Stern, Bernhard Joseph, 1894– joint ed. II. Title.
42—326
Library of Congress CB5.L6
[45g²5] 901

Minorities.

Trinidad
M323
M29p

Maloney, Arnold Hamilton, 1888–
Pathways to democracy, by ... Arnold Hamilton Maloney ... Clarence McDonald Maloney ... [and] Arnold Hamilton Maloney, jr. ... Boston, Meador publishing company [1945]
589 p. 20½ cm.

1. Democracy. 2. Minorities. 3. Negroes. I. Maloney, Clarence McDonald, joint author. II. Maloney, Arnold Hamilton, 1916– joint author. III. Title.
45-1864
Library of Congress ° JC423.M32
[8] 321.8

Minorities.

M301
R11

Raab, Earl, *ed.*
American race relations today. [1st ed.] Garden City, N. Y., Doubleday, 1962.
195 p. 18 cm. (Anchor books, A318)
Partial contents.-Changing social role in the new south, by Joseph S. Himes.-The sit-ins and the new Negro student, by Charles U. Smith (abridged).-The Black muslims in America by C. Eric Lincoln.
White editor.
1. ~~U. S.~~—Race question. 2. Minorities—~~U. S.~~ I. Title.
E184.A1R19 301.451 62-15926 ‡
Library of Congress [8]

M323
R38

Minorities

Richards, Eugene S
Ethnic relations in the United States [by] Edward C. McDonagh and Eugene S. Richards. New York, Appleton-Century-Crofts [1953]
xiv, 408 p. illus. 25 cm. (Appleton-Century-Crofts sociology series)
Includes bibliographies.

1. Minorities—U. S. 2. U. S.—Race question. I. ~~[struck out]~~ II. Title.
I. McDonagh, Edward C jt. auth.
E184.A1M137 325.73 52-13692
Library of Congress [20]

Minorities.

...4.5
...7u

Writers' congress, *University of California at Los Angeles,* 1943.
Writers' congress; the proceedings of the conference held in October 1943 under the sponsorship of the Hollywood writers' mobilization and the University of California. Published in coöperation with the Writers' congress continuations committee of the Hollywood writers' mobilization. Berkeley and Los Angeles, University of California press, 1944.
xx, 663 p. incl. front. (facsim.) 23 cm.

1. Authors. 2. World war, 1939– —Addresses, sermons, etc. I. Hollywood writers' mobilization. II. California. University. University at Los Angeles.
A 44-8485
California. Univ. Libr. for Library of Congress [12]

Minorities - Bibliography

M01
W36

Waxman, Julia.
Race relations, a selected list of readings on racial and cultural minorities in the United States, with special emphasis on Negroes, by Julia Waxman. Chicago, Ill., Julius Rosenwald fund, 1945.
47 p. 22½ cm.
Classified and annotated.

1. Negroes—Bibl. 2. U. S.—Race question—Bibl. 3. Minorities—U. S.—Bibl. I. Julius Rosenwald fund. II. Title.
45-7918
Library of Congress ° Z1361.N39W3
[20] 016.3231

Jamaica
M972.92
C69

Minorities - Great Britain.

Collins, Sydney.
Coloured minorities in Britain; studies in British race relations based on African, West Indian, and Asiatic immigrants. London, Lutterworth Press [1957]
258 p. 23 cm.

1. Minorities—Gt. Brit. I. Title.
DA120.C6 *301.451 325.42 58-1658 ‡
Library of Congress [2]

Panama
M986.2
W52m

A minority group in Panama.
Westerman, George W
A minority group in Panama; Some aspects of West Indian life. 3rd ed. Panama, National Civic League, 1950.

32 p. 21 cm.
English and Spanish text, separately paged; added t.p. in Spanish.
Inscribed by author: Sincere regards, G. W. Westerman.

M306
N21m

Minority groups;Segregation and integration.
National Conference of Social Work.
Minority groups: segregation and integration. Papers presented at the 82d annual forum of the National Conference of Social Work. [Editorial Committee: Irving Weissman, chairman, Lois Clarke and others. Editorial work: Dorothy Swart] New York, Published for the National Conference of Social Work by Columbia University Press, 1955.
vi, 110 p. 24 cm.

1. Segregation—U. S. 2. Social case work. I. Title.
HV95.N35 1955 *301.45 325.73 56—5879
Library of Congress [56f15]

... Minority peoples in a nation at war.

M323
Am3m

American academy of political and social science, *Philadelphia.*
... Minority peoples in a nation at war, edited by J. P. Shalloo ... and Donald Young ... Philadelphia, 1942.
viii, 276 p. 23½ cm. (*Its* Annals, v. 223, September 1942)
Contents.—The need for national solidarity.—The Negro and the war.—Minorities of alien origin.—The treatment of minorities in a democracy.

1. U. S.—Foreign population. 2. Negroes. 3. World war, 1939– —U. S. I. Shalloo, Jeremiah Patrick, 1898– ed. II. Young, Donald Ramsey, 1898– joint ed. III. Title.
42-36334
Library of Congress H1.A4 vol. 223
———— Copy 2. E184.A1A53
[45] (306.273) 323.173

Minstrels.

M792
F63

Fletcher, Tom, 1873–1954.
100 years of the Negro in show business; the Tom Fletcher story. 1st ed. New York, Burdge [1954]
337 p. illus. 23 cm.

1. Negro minstrels. 2. Theater—U. S.—Hist. I. Title.
ML3561.N4F5 927.8 55-1843 ‡
Library of Congress [2]

M331
M66

Minton, Henry M.
Early history of Negroes in business in Philadelphia. Read before the American Historical Society, March 1913, by Henry M. Minton. [Nashveille, Tenn., A.N.E.S.S. Union, 1913 ?]
20p. 22½cm.

1. Business 1. Philadelphia

Trinidad
M820
J23mi

Minty alley.
James, Cyril Lionel Robert, 1901–
Minty alley; a novel by C. L. R. James. London, M. Secker & Warburg, ltd., 1936.
320 p. 19 cm.

I. Title.
36-34613
Library of Congress PZ3.J2314Mi
Copyright A ad int. 22085 [3]

Guinea
M896.2
F68m

Minuit.
Fodeba, Keita, 1921-
Le Maître d'école suivi de Minuit.
Paris, Pierre Seghers [1952]

26p. 18cm.
Portrait of author on back cover.

I. Title: Le maître d'école. II. Title: Minuit.

Haiti
M841
M66m

Minuty, Julien V
Le miracle negre. Port-au-Prince, 1959.

198p. illus. 21cm.
Bibliography: p. 198.

1. Haitian poetry. I. Title.

Haiti
M841
M66

Minuty, Julien V
, Orchidees, poèmes. Port-au-Prince, Imp. de l'État, 1953.

9-49p. (port) 18cm. (Collection du sesquicentenaire de l'indépendance d'Haiti)

1. Haitian poetry I. Title.

Kenya
M896.1
H119

Miqdad & Mayasa, the story of.
Hadithi ya Mikidadi na Mayasa.
The story of Miqdad & Mayasa, from the Swahili-Abrabic text of Alice Werner.
Medstead, Hampshire, Azania Press, 1932.
90p. illus. 19cm.
Written in Swahili and English.

1. Swahili language - Texts. I. Werner, Alice, 1859-1935, tr. II. Title. III. Title: Miqdad & Mayasa, The story of.

Haiti
M841
M66m

Le miracle negre.

Minuty, Julien V
Le miracle negre. Port-au-Prince, 1959.

198p. illus. 21cm.
Bibliography: p. 198.

Senegal
M896.3
D62m

Mirages de Paris.
Diop, Ousmane Socé, 1911-
Mirages de Paris, roman suivi des rythmes du Khalam (poemes) [par] Ousmane Soce [pseud.] Paris, Nouvelles Editions Latines, 1955.
285p. 19cm.
Autographed.

I. Title.

Senegal
M896.3
D62m2

Mirages de Paris.
Diop, Ousmane Socé, 1911-
Mirages de Paris. Paris, Nouvelles Editions Latines [1964]
187p. 18½cm.

I. Title.

U.S.
M839
Iv3m

Miriam.
Sommerfelt, Aimee, 1892-
Miriam. Translated by Pat Shaw Iversen. London, New York, Abelard-Schuman °1965.

160p. 22cm.

Miriamy; a West Indian play in three acts.

Guiana, British M822.91 P64m

Pilgrim, Frank
Miriamy; a West Indian play in three acts. [Georgetown, British Guiana, B. G. Lithographic Co., 1963]

67p. 20½cm.

I. Title.

A mirror for magistrates.

M813.5 G35m

Gibson, Richard, 1931-
A mirror for magistrates; a novel. London, Anthony Blond, 1958.

172p. 19cm.

Haiti M972.94 M67

Mirville, Solon
L'ecole primaire & la lutte contre l'analphabetisme en Haiti. Port-au-Prince, La Phalange, 1959.

58p. 20½cm. (Etude Statistique)

1. Haiti - Education. 2. Education - Haiti.

The mis-education of the Negro.

M973 W86m

Woodson, Carter Godwin, 1875-
The mis-education of the Negro, by Carter Godwin Woodson. Washington, D. C., The Associated publishers, inc. [°1933]
xiv p., 1 l., 207 p. 19 cm.

1. Negroes—Education. 2. Negroes—Moral and social conditions. 3. Negroes—Employment. I. Title.

Library of Congress E185.82.W86 [45i1] 33—3606 371.974

Mis experiencias a través de 70 años.

Puerto Rico M972.95 C27m

Castrillo, Valentin
Mis experiencias a través de 70 años. Cagnuas, Puerto Rico, 1960.

Unpaged port. 20½cm.

Puerto Rico M972.95 C27

Mis experiencias a traves de cincuenta años.

Castrillo, Valenrin
Mis experiencias a traves de cincuenta años. Caguas, Puerto Rico, La Primavera, Inc., 1952.

213p. port. 23cm.

Jamaica M821.91 B43

Mis' Lulu sez.
Bennett, Louise.
Jamaican dialect poems. Kingston, Jamaica, The Gleaner co., n.d.

185 p. 21 cm.
Cover title: Mis' Lulu sez...
"Cover designed by Eric Coverley."

Miscegenation.

M323 A15a

Allen, William G.
The American prejudice against color. An authentic narrative, showing how easily the nation got into an uproar. By W. G. Allen, a refugee from American despotism. London, W. and F. G. Cash; [etc., etc.] 1853.
2 p. l., 107, [1] p. 16½cm.
The author, a quadroon, married a white girl of Fulton, N. Y. An attempt was made to mob him at Phillipsville, N. Y., on January 30, 1853.

1. Miscegenation. I. Title.

Library of Congress E185.62.A43 1—26231
———— Copy 2. [Tracts [Cambridge, etc., 1840?]-59. [no. 4]]
[37r23e1]

Miscegenation.

M323. D11

Dabney, Wendell Phillips, 1865 -
The wolf and the lamb, by Wendell P. Dabney. Cincinnati, O., The author, c 1913.

Cover-title. 15p. illus. 23cm.

M304 P19 V.5,no.6

Miscegenation.

M323.3 D27s

Davenport, Charles Benedict, 1866-
... State laws limiting marriage selection examined in the light of eugenics, by Charles B. Davenport ... with two figures and four tables. Cold Spring Harbor [N. Y.] 1913.
66 p. tables (1 fold.) diagrs. (1 fold.) 23cm. (Eugenics record office. Bulletin no. 9)
Bibliography: p. 40.

1. Eugenics. 2. Marriage law—U. S. I. Title.

Library of Congress HQ750.A1C5 [33f1] 13—21086

Miscegenation.

M323 G12w

Gaines, Gartrell J
Where do we stand? The Negro in the South today. [1st ed.] New York, Vantage Press [1957]
76 p. illus. 21 cm.

1. Southern States—Race question. 2. Negroes. 3. Miscegenation. I. Title.

E185.61.G15 *301.451 325.260975 57—7789 ‡

Library of Congress [20]

Miscegenation.

M323.3 G174

Gardner, LeRoy.
The truth about interracial marriage. [St. Paul? 1965]
ii, 143 p. 23 cm.

1. Miscegenation. 2. ~~Negroes.~~ I. Title.

HQ1031.G3 301.422 65—26932

Library of Congress [3]

Miscegenation.

M301 H43

Hernton, Calvin C
Sex and racism in America [by] Calvin C. Hernton. [1st ed.] Garden City, N.Y., Doubleday, 1965.
180 p. 22 cm.
Bibliographical footnotes.

1. ~~U. S.~~—Race question. 2. Sex (Psychology) 3. Miscegenation. I. Title.

E185.62.H4 301.451 64—20676

Library of Congress [5]

Miscegenation.

M220 H91

Hunter, W L
Jesus Christ had Negro blood in his veins. The wonder of the twentieth century. By W.L. Hunter. 1st edition Brooklyn, New York, Nolan bro's print., 1901.

45p. 22cm.

Miscegenation.

M323.3 L33

Larsson, Clotye Murdock, ed.
Marriage across the color line, edited by Clotye M. Larsson. Chicago, Johnson Pub. Co., 1965.
xi, 204 p. 23 cm.

1. Miscegenation. 2. ~~U. S.~~—Race question. I. Title.

HQ1031.L3 301.422 65—21549

Library of Congress [3]

Miscegenation.

M323.3 M21a

McKinney, Thomas Theodore, 1869-
All white America; a candid discussion of race mixture and race prejudice in the United States, by T. T. McKinney ... Boston, Meador publishing company, 1937.
214 p. 21 cm.
Bibliographical notes: p. 213-214.

1. U. S.—Race question. 2. Miscegenation. 3. Negroes. I. Title.

37—2557

Library of Congress E185.61.M156 [5] 325.260973

Miscegenation

M973 R63a

Rogers, Joel Augustus, 1880-
As nature leads; an informal discussion of the reason why Negro and Caucasian are mixing in spite of opposition. By J. A. Rogers ... [Chicago, Printed by M. A. Donohue & co., °1919]
2 p. l., [7]-207 p. 20 cm.
Errata slip attached to fly-leaf.

1. U. S.—Race question. 2. Negroes. 3. Miscegenation. I. Title.

19—9528

Library of Congress E185.62.R72 [48d½]

Miscegenation.

M973 R63s

Rogers, Joel Augustus, 1880-
Sex and race; Negro-Caucasian mixing in all ages and all lands, by J. A. Rogers ... New York city, J. A. Rogers publications [1940-44]
3 v. fronts. (v. 1-2) illus. (incl. ports., map, facsims.) 23½cm.
Vol. 2 has subtitle: A history of white, Negro and Indian miscegenation in the two Americas.
Includes bibliographies.
CONTENTS.—v. 1. The old world.—v. 2. The new world.—v. 3. Why white and black mix in spite of opposition.

1. Race problems. 2. Negroes. 3. Miscegenation. I. Title.

41—20

Library of Congress GN237.R6 1940 [45r45e2] 572

Miscegenation.

M575 Sa4

[Sampson, John Patterson, 1839-
Mixed races: their environment, temperament, heredity and phrenology. Hampton, Va., Normal school steam press, 1881.

ix, [12] - 159p. front. 22½cm.

Miscegenation.

M304 P19 v.5, no. 15

Winston, Robert Watson.
Should the color line go. In: Three articles on the Negro Problem (Published in Current History Magazine, Sept. 1923) p. 1-10.

White author.

La misère au sein des richesses.

Haiti M972.94 D38mi

Delorme, Démesvar, 1833-
La misère au sein des richesses. Réflexions diverses sur Haiti. Par D. Delorme ... Paris, E. Dentu, 1873.
2 p. l., 138 p. 22½cm.

1. Haiti—Hist. I. Title.

Library of Congress F1926.D35 26—21820

Nigeria
M896.2
Ar6m
Miss Appolo's pride.
Ariríguzo, Cyril Nwakunwa
Miss Appolo's pride lead her to be unmarried. "Pride goeth before a fall." Onitsha, Nigeria, Ariríguzo & Sons [n.d.]
22p. 18½cm.

Cameroons
M896.3
M55mis
Mission terminee.
Biyidi, Alexandre, 1932-
Mission terminee; roman by Mongo Beti [pseud.] Paris, Correa [1957]
254p. 19cm.

Missionaries - Africa, South.
S. Africa
M266
M28r
Majeke, Nosipho
The Rôle of the missionaries in conquest. Johannesburg, Society of Young Africa, 195?
140p. 21½cm.

Nigeria
M896.2
Ar6mi
Miss Comfort's heart cries for Tonny's love.
Aririguzo, Cyril Nwakuna
Miss Comfort's heart cries for Tonny's love. Onitsha, Nigeria [Eastern Niger Printing Press, 1960]
23p. 18½cm.

Nigeria
M327.667
B215
Mission to Ghana.
Balogun, Kolawole, 1922-
Mission to Ghana; memoir of a diplomat. [1st ed.]
73p. 21cm.

Missionary story sketches...
M910
C15m
Camphor, Alexander Priestley.
Missionary story sketches, folk-lore from Africa, by Alexander Priestley Camphor ... with an introduction by the Rev. M. C. B. Mason ... Cincinnati, Jennings and Graham; New York, Eaton and Mains [°1909]
346 p. front., 8 pl. 20cm.
Library of Congress 9-15872
Copr. May 5, '09; A 258487; 2c. June 3, '09; Jennings & Graham, Cincinnati.

Nigeria
M896.3
N971m
Miss Cordelia in the romance of destiny.
Nwosu, Cletus Gibson
Miss Cordelia in the romance of destiny; that most sensational love intricacy that has ever happened in West Africa. Port Harcourt, [Nigeria] Vincent C. Okeanu [n.d.]
43p. 19cm.

Cameroons
M896.3
B65mi
Mission to Kala...
Biyidi, Alexandre, 1932-
Mission to Kala; a novel by Mongo Beti [pseud.] Translated from the French by Peter Green. London, Frederick Muller, Ltd., [1958]
206p. 20½cm.
Picture and biographical sketch of author on book jacket.

M266
B23
Missions.
Barber, Jesse Belmont.
Climbing Jacob's ladder; story of the work of the Presbyterian Church U. S. A. among the Negroes. New York, Board of National Missions, Presbyterian Church in the U. S. A. [1952]
103 p. 23 cm.
"Originally prepared and published as a master's thesis in the Department of Church History of Auburn Theological Seminary ... revised and brought down to date."
Includes bibliography.
1. Negroes—Missions. 2. Presbyterians, Negro. 3. Presbyterian Church—Missions. I. Title.
BX8946.N4B3 [266.5] 277.3 52-11209 ‡
Library of Congress [2]

Nigeria
M641.5
W67m
Miss Williams' cookery book.
Johnston, Rhoda Omonsunloda (Williams)
Miss Williams' cookery book. London, Longmans, Green and Co., 1957.
260p. illus. 19½cm.
Portrait of author on book jacket.

MB9
J63t
Missionaries
Johnson, Thomas L
Twenty - eight years a slave; or the story of my life in three continents, by Thomas L. Johnson ... Bourne mouth, W. Mate and Sons, limited, 1909.
xvi, 266p. front. plates. 19cm.

M266
B43w
Missions.
Bennett, Ambrose
Woman's missionary society guide, arranged and edited by Ambrose Bennett. Nashville, Tenn., National Baptist convention [n.d.]
99p. 19½cm.

Jamaica
M821.91
M165m
Missing pages.
McFarland, Harry Stanley, 1900-
Missing pages; poems. Boston, Forum Publishing Co., 1962.
72p. 18cm.

MB9
St4m
Missionaries.
[Mitchell, Joseph]
The missionary pioneer or a brief memoir of the life, labour, and death of John Stewart (man of colour) founder, under God of the mission among the Wyandotts at Upper Sandusky, Ohio. Published by Joseph Mitchell, New York, Printed by J. C. Totten, 1827.
viii, 96p. 15cm.

Basutoland
M968.6
D18p
Missions.
Damane, Mosebi
Peace, the mother of nations. The "Saga" of the origin of the Protestant church in [Basutoland. Basutoland, Morija Printing works of the Paris Evangelical Missionary Society] 1947.
54p. 24cm.

M350
W65
Missing pages in American history.
Wilkes, Laura Eliza, 1871-
Missing pages in American history, revealing the services of negroes in the early wars in the United States of America, 1641-1815, by Laura E. Wilkes ... [Washington, D. C., Press of R. L. Pendleton, °1919]
91 p. 22cm.
On cover: Armistice edition.
Bibliography: p. 85-87.
1. Negroes as soldiers. 2. U. S.—History, Military. I. Title.
19-10083
Library of Congress E185.63.W68
Copyright A 515580 [3]

MB9
St4m
Missionaries.
[Mitchell, Joseph]
The missionary pioneer, or a brief memoir of the life, labours, and death of John Stewart, (man of coulour) founder, under God of the mission among the Wyandotts at Upper Sandusky, Ohio. Published by Joseph Mitchell. New York, Printed by J.C. Totten, 1827.
viii, 96p. 15cm.

MB
D91p
Missions
Duncan, Sara J
Progressive missions in the south and addresses with illustrations and sketches of missionary workers and ministers and bishops' wives. Atlanta Ga., The Franklin Printing and Publishing Co., 1906.
[8]-299p. 20½cm.

Cameroons
M896.3
B65ms
Mission accomplished.
Biyidi, Alexandre, 1932-
Mission accomplished. [By Mongo Beti, pseud.] Translated from the French by Peter Green. New York, Macmillan, 1958.
200p. 22cm.
A novel.
I. Title.

Gold Coast
M966.7
T45r
Missionaries.
Tidsley, Alfred.
The remarkable work achieved by Rev. Dr. Mark C. Rayford, in promotion of the spiritual and material welfare of the natives of West Africa, and proposed developments; with a foreword by Rev. Thos. Nightingale and appreciations from the President of the United States of America, the King of England, the President of France. London, Morgan & Scott, 1926.
36,[2]p. port. illus facsms. 22cm.

M266
J63
Missions.
Johnson, James H A, 1835-
The pine tree mission. By James H.A. Johnson... Baltimore, J. Lanahan, 1893.
114p. port. plates. 18cm.

Missions - Congresses.

Ghana M266 In8

International Missionary Council. *Assembly, Accra, 1957-1958.*
The Ghana assembly of the International Missionary Council, 28th December, 1957 to 8th January, 1958; selected papers, with an essay on the rôle of the I. M. C. Edited by Ronald K. Orchard. London, Published for the International Missionary Council by Edinburgh House Press, 1958.
240 p. 23 cm.

1. Missions—Congresses. I. Orchard, Ronald Kenneth, ed. II. Title.

A 59-3551 rev

Union Theol. Sem. Libr. for Library of Congress ⌈r59f4⌉

Missions—Africa, South.

M910 W93b

Wright, Charlotte (Crogman)
Beneath the Southern Cross; the story of an American bishop's wife in South Africa. ⌈1st ed.⌉ New York, Exposition Press ⌈1955⌉
184 p. 21 cm.

1. Missions—Africa, South. 2. African Methodist Episcopal Church—Missions. I. Title.

BV3555.W7 [266.78] 276.8 55-11138 ‡

Library of Congress ⌈2⌉

Missions. - Kongo, Belgian

M285 Sh4p

Sheppard, William Henry, 1865-1927.
Presbyterian pioneers in Congo, by William H. Sheppard. Introduction by Rev. S.H. Chester, d.d. Richmond, Va., Presbyterian committee of publication ⌈1917⌉
157p. incl. front., illus. (incl. map) ports. 19½cm.

Missions - Africa.

U.S. M960 C76a

Congress on Africa, *Atlanta,* **1895.**
Africa and the American Negro. Addresses and proceedings of the Congress on Africa, held under the auspices of the Stewart missionary foundation for Africa of Gammon theological seminary, in connection with the Cotton states and international exposition, December 13-15, 1895. Edited by Prof. J. W. E. Bowen ... secretary of the congress. Atlanta, Gammon theological seminary, 1896.
59, ⌈2⌉, 61-242 p. front., plates, ports. 23cm.

~~1. Missions—Africa. 2. Missions—Congresses. 3. Negroes—Congresses. I. Gammon theological seminary, Atlanta, Ga. Stewart missionary foundation for Africa. II. Bowen, John Wesley Edward, 1855- III. Title.~~

15-9181

Library of Congress BV3500.C7 ⌈42c1⌉

Africa M966 Sm5

Missions-Africa, West.

Smith, Charles Spencer, *bp.,* **1852-**
Glimpses of Africa, West and Southwest coast, containing the author's impressions and observations during a voyage of six thousand miles from Sierra Leone to St. Paul de Loanda and return, including the Rio del Ray and Cameroons rivers, and the Congo River, from its mouth to Matadi, by C. S. Smith, introduction by Bishop H. M. Turner ... Nashville, Tenn., Publishing house A. M. E. Church Sunday school union, 1895.
288 p. incl. plates, ports., maps. 20cm.

1. Africa, West—Descr. & trav. 2. Missions—Africa, West. I. Title.

Library of Congress DT471.S6 14-17784

Nigeria M200 C46

Missions - Nigeria.

Christian Council of Nigeria.
Building for tomorrow; a pictorial history of the protestant church in Nigeria. Lagos, Christian council of Nigeria, 1960.
35p. illus., ports. 28cm.

Missions - Congresses.

U.S. M960 C76a

Congress on Africa, *Atlanta,* **1895.**
Africa and the American Negro. Addresses and proceedings of the Congress on Africa, held under the auspices of the Stewart missionary foundation for Africa of Gammon theological seminary, in connection with the Cotton states and international exposition, December 13-15, 1895. Edited by Prof. J. W. E. Bowen ... secretary of the congress. Atlanta, Gammon theological seminary, 1896.
59, ⌈2⌉, 61-242 p. front., plates, ports. 23cm.

~~1. Missions—Africa. 2. Missions—Congresses. 3. Negroes—Congresses. I. Gammon theological seminary, Atlanta, Ga. Stewart missionary foundation for Africa. II. Bowen, John Wesley Edward, 1855- III. Title.~~

15-9181

Library of Congress BV3500.C7 ⌈42c1⌉

Missions - Angola.

M266.58 C67p

Coles, Samuel B *d.* **1957.**
Preacher with a plow. Boston, Houghton Mifflin ⌈1957⌉
241 p. illus. 21 cm.

1. Missions—Angola. I. Title.

BV3625.A6C57 [266.58] 276.73 57-8223 ‡

Library of Congress ⌈15⌉

Africa MB9 R17

Missions-Nigeria.

Delano, Isaac O
The singing minister of Nigeria; the life of the Rev. Canon J. J. Ransome-Kuti, by Isaac O. Delano ... London, United society for Christian literature ⌈1942⌉
63, ⌈1⌉ p. 18½cm. (*Half-title: Africa's own library, no. 2*)

1. Ransome-Kuti, Josaiah Jesse, 1855-1930. 2. Missions—Nigeria. I. United society for Christian literature, London. II. Title.

44-35318

Library of Congress BV3625.N6R3 ⌈2⌉ 922

Liberia M966.6 B62a

Missions-Africa.

Blyden, Edward Wilmot, 1832-1912.
African life and customs; reprinted from "The Sierra Leone weekly news." By Edward Wilmot Blyden ... London, C. M. Phillips, 1908.
91 p. 22cm.

1. Missions—Africa. 2. Africa—Soc. condit. I. Title.

9-20227

Library of Congress D14.B5

Missions-Catholic.

M304 P19 v.7 no.18

Our colored missions, vol. 17, no.11. New York City, The Catholic board for mission, work among the colored people, November, 1931.
162-176p.
25½cm.

Malawi MB9 M1

Missions - Nyasaland.

Fraser, Donald, 1870-1933.
The autobiography of an African. Retold in biographical form and in wild African setting of the life of Daniel Mtusu. London, Seeley, Service and Co., 1925.
209p. ports. 20cm.

Missions-Africa.

Sierra Leone M276 K14h

Karefa-Smart, John.
The halting kingdom; Christianity and the African revolution, by John and Rena Karefa-Smart. New York, Friendship Press ⌈1959⌉
86 p. 19 cm.
Includes bibliography.

1. Africa—Church history. 2. Missions—Africa. 3. Africa—Civilization. I. Karefa-Smart, Rena, joint author. II. Title.

BR1360.K3 276 59-6044 ‡

Library of Congress ⌈60d5⌉

Missions-Gold coast.

Gold Coast M966.7 A15g

Alleyne, Cameron Chesterfield, *bp.*
Gold coast at a glance, by Cameron Chesterfield Alleyne ... with an introduction by Bishop Paris Arthur Wallace. New York, The Hunt printing company ⌈1931⌉
6 p. l., 11-143 p. 18cm.
"Specially adapted to missions study classes."—1st prelim. leaf.

1. Gold coast. 2. Gold coast—Soc. life & cust. 3. Missions—Gold coast. 4. African Methodist Episcopal Zion church—Missions.

31-20518

Library of Congress DT511.A6
——— Copy 2.
Copyright A 40549 ⌈3⌉ [266.7] 276.67

Mississippi.

M323.4 H742

Holt, Len, 1928-
The summer that didn't end. New York, Morrow, 1965.
351 p. map. 22 cm.

1. Civil rights—Mississippi. 2. ~~Negroes—Civil rights.~~ I. Title.

E185.61.H75 323.4 65-18521

Library of Congress ⌈5⌉

U. S. M960 Sch89

Missions - Africa.

Schuyler, Philippa.
Jungle saints; Africa's heroic Catholic missionaries. ⌈Rome⌉ Herder ⌈1963⌉
223p. photos. 21cm.

Africa M967.5 B64c

Missions-Kongo.

Boone, Clinton C.
Congo as I saw it, by C. C. Boone ... who represented in Congo the Lott Carey Baptist foreign missionary convention of the U. S. A. and the American Baptist foreign missionary society of Boston, Mass., from 1901 to 1906. ⌈New York, Printed by J. J. Little and Ives company, °1927⌉
viii, 96 p. front. (port.) 19½cm.

1. Missions—Kongo. 2. Kongo—Descr. & trav. I. Title.

27-12519

Library of Congress BV3625.K6B6
Copyright A 990279 ⌈28c2⌉

Mississippi.

M323 J71b

Jones, Laurence Clifton, 1884-
The bottom rail; addresses and papers on the Negro in the lowlands of Mississippi and on inter-racial relations in the South during twenty-five years, by Laurence C. Jones ... with an introduction by Francis S. Harmon ... New York ⌈etc.⌉ Fleming H. Revell company ⌈°1935⌉
96 p. front. (port.) 19½cm. Inscribed: To A. B. Spingarn fsm.—To Miss Mary White Ovington, in appreciation of her efforts to strengthen the Bottom Rail, Laurence C. Jones, Piney Woods, Miss. 1935.

1. Negroes—Mississippi. 2. U. S.—Race question. 3. Piney Woods country life school, Braxton, Miss. I. Title.

35-4380

Library of Congress E185.93.M6J6 ⌈45f1⌉ 325.2609762

Africa M266 St29t

Missions—Africa.

Stauffer, Milton Theobald, 1885- *ed.*
... Thinking with Africa; chapters by a group of nationals interpreting the Christian movement, assembled and edited by Milton Stauffer ... New York, Pub. for the Student volunteer movement for foreign missions by the Missionary education movement of the United States and Canada ⌈°1927⌉
xviii p., 1 l., 184 p. 19½cm. (Christian voices around the world)

1. Missions—Africa. 2. Africa—Religion. 3. Africa—Civilization. I. Title.

28-8082

Library of Congress BV3500.S65 ⌈40i1⌉

Missions - Kongo, Belgian.

M285 Sh4e

Sheppard, William Henry, 1865-1927.
Experiences of a pioneer missionary on the Congo.

(In: Student Volunteer Movement for Foreign Missions. International Convention. 5th, Nashville, 1906. Students and the modern missionary crusade; addresses... New York, Student Volunteer Movement for Foreign Missions, 1906. 24cm. p. 291-296)

Mississippi.

M352.2 M69

Mississippi black paper; fifty-seven Negro and white citizens' testimony of police brutality, the breakdown of law and order and the corruption of justice in Mississippi. Foreword by Reinhold Niebuhr. Introd. by Hodding Carter III. New York, Random House ⌈1965⌉
92 p. illus. 28 cm.

1. Police—Mississippi. 2. Law enforcement—Mississippi. 3. Negroes—Mississippi. I. Title: Fifty-seven Negro and white citizens' testimony of police brutality. II. Niebuhr, Reinhold, 1892-

HV8145.M7M5 323.11960762 65-18103

Library of Congress ⌈3⌉

M343.5 Mississippi.
R21s Raymond, Harry.
Save Willie McGee. New York, New Century, 1951.

14p. 19cm.

Mississippi.

M370 Wilson, Charles H 1905–
W69e Education for Negroes in Mississippi since 1910, by Charles H. Wilson, sr. ... Boston, Meador publishing company ₍1947₎

641 p. illus. (incl. ports.) $20\frac{1}{2}$ᶜᵐ.

Bibliography: p. 595–607.

1. Negroes—Mississippi. 2. Negroes—Education. 3. Education—Mississippi. I. Title.

LC2802.M7W5 371.974 47–3639

© 16Apr47; Edward K. Meador, Boston; A12739.

Library of Congress ₍5₎

M370. Mississippi. Superintendent of public
M68 education.
Annual report of the state superintendent of public education, for the scholastic year, 1874. Jackson, Miss., Pilot publishing company, 1875.

100p. 27cm.
Library has: 1875

1. Education - Mississippi. I. Cardozo, T W

Mississippi. University - Hist.
M378 Meredith, James Howard.
M541 Three years in Mississippi ₍by₎ James Meredith. Bloomington, Indiana University Press ₍1966₎

328 p. 24 cm.
Autobiographical.

1. Mississippi. University—Hist. I. Title.

LD3412.9.M4A3 378.762 66–12731

Library of Congress ₍3₎

M352.2 Mississippi black paper; fifty-seven Negro and white citi-
M69 zens' testimony of police brutality, the breakdown of law and order and the corruption of justice in Mississippi. Foreword by Reinhold Niebuhr. Introd. by Hodding Carter III. New York, Random House ₍1965₎

92 p. illus. 28 cm.

1. Police—Mississippi. 2. Law enforcement—Mississippi. 3. Negroes—Mississippi. I. Title: Fifty-seven Negro and white citizens' testimony of police brutality. II. Niebuhr, Reinhold, 1892–

HV8145.M7M5 323.11960762 65–18103

Library of Congress ₍8₎

Mississippi minister.

M287.8 Morant, John J
M79 Mississippi minister. ₍1st ed.₎ New York, Vantage Press ₍1958₎

80 p. illus. 21 cm.

1. African Methodist Episcopal Church—Hist. I. Title.

BX8443.M6 922.773 57–11254 ‡

Library of Congress ₍2₎

M973.9 Missouri. *Dept. of education.*
M69s A suggestive outline for the study of the Negro in history. Missouri state Department of education. Special bulletin, 1941 ... ₍Jefferson City, Mid-state printing co., 1941₎

100 p. incl. tables. 23ᶜᵐ.
Bibliography at end of each unit.

~~1. Negroes 2. Negro race.~~ 1. History-Outline.

42–37368

Library of Congress E185.6.M7
₍48c2₎ 325.260975

Missouri.

M366.1 Freemasons. Missouri. Grand Lodge.
F87m8 Proceedings. 1st- 1867-
St. Louis. 1867-

v. 22cm. annual
See holdings card for proceedings in library.
Special communication held Dec. 20, 1866 in St. Louis. bound with the 1867 proceedings.

Mr. Amo learns about Uno.

Ghana
M341.139 Longdon, J E
L85 Mr. Amoa learns about Uno, by J. E. Longdon and Ella Griffin. Cover design by R. Ohene Akyeampong. Accra, Bureau of Ghana Languages, 1959.

9p. 22cm.

Mr. Big.

M812.5 McKetney, Edwin Charles.
M19 Mr. Big. ₍A play in three acts. 1st ed.₎ New York, Pageant Press ₍1953₎

74 p. 24 cm.

I. Title.

PS3525.A2576M5 812.5 53–10082 ‡

Library of Congress ₍5₎

M823 Mr. Charlie, let's you and I talk.
H33m Hayward, Ernest, 1927-
Mr. Charlie, let's you and I talk. New York, Vantage Press [1966]
173p. 21cm.

M323.4 Mr. Justice Murphy and civil rights.
M35m Marshall, Thurgood, 1908-
Mr. Justice Murphy and civil rights. Reprinted from Michigan law review, 48:745-766, April 1950.

745-766p. 27cm.

M304 Mr. President: Free the Scottsboro
P19 ₍International Labor Defense₎
v.1, no.16 Mr. President: Free the Scottsboro boys! ₍New York, International Labor Defense, 1934.₎

3-30p. 19cm.

M9 Mitchell, Arthur W., 1883-
M69 The Negro, a factor in the history of the world. Remarks of Hon. Arthur W. Mitchell of Illinois in the house of Representatives, Wednesday, February 7, 1940. Washington, Government Printing Office, 1940.

8p. 23cm.

M323 Mitchell, Arthur W , 1883-
M690 Overcoming difficulties under adverse conditions, address... in the House of Representatives, Thursday, April 6, 1939. Washington, Govt. Print. Off. 1939.

15p. 23cm.
Founder's Day address delivered at Tuskegee Institute, Alabama, April 2, 1939.

1. Washington, Booker Taliaferro, 1859?- 2. Race problems. I. Title.

M973 Mitchell, Arthur W , 1883-
W86n ₍Woodson, Carter Goodwin, 1875-1950₎
The Negro a factor in the history of the world; Remarks of Hon. Arthur W. Mitchell of Illinois in the House of Representatives. Washington, Govt. Print. Off., 1940.

3-8p. 23cm.
Letter from Dr. Woodson read by Representative Mitchell.

M323
So8 Mitchell, Clarence M , 1911-
Democrats versus Dixiecrats.
The Southern Negro, 1952; Warning to Ike and the Dixiecrats, a special issue. New York, The Nation, 1952.

243-284p. illus. 29cm.
Special issue of The Nation, September 27, 1952.

M89 Mitchell, Clarence M , 1911-
C12m ₍Statement at the₎ Hearing before a subcommittee of the Committee on Armed Services, United States Senate, Eighty-second congress, first session on nomination of Millard Frank Caldwell, jr. to be Federal Civil Defense Administrator. Washington, D.C., Govt. Print. Off, 1951.

1-10p. 23cm.
At head of title: Nomination of Millard Frank Caldwell to be federal civil defense administrator.
1. Caldwell, Millard Frank.

Trinidad
M910 Mitchell, Francis, 1910–
M69 Grown up Liberia, by Francis Mitchell ... ₍Philadelphia, West Philadelphia multigraphing and printing company ₍1946₎ ᶜ1945.

144 p. plates. 22ᶜᵐ.

1. Liberia—Descr. & trav. I. Title.

46—21719

Library of Congress DT626.M55
₍47c1₎ 916.66

Mitchell, George S , 1911-
The extension of citizenship, pp.50-55.
M371.974 Tuskegee Institute.
T87n The new south and higher education: what are the implications for higher education of the changing socio-economic conditions of the south? A symposium and ceremonies held in connection with the inauguration of Luther Hilton Foster, fourth president of Tuskegee Institute ₍October 31 and November 1, 1953. Tuskegee, Ala.₎ Dept. of Records and Research, Tuskegee Institute, 1954.

x, 145p. map. 24cm.

Mitchell, George Sinclair, 1902- joint author.

M331 Cayton, Horace R.
C31 Black workers and the new unions, by Horace R. Cayton and George S. Mitchell. Chapel Hill, The University of North Carolina press, 1939.

xviii, 473 p. $23\frac{1}{2}$ᶜᵐ.

"Three industries have been chosen for examination: iron and steel, meat packing, and railroad car shops."—Introd.
Bibliography: p. ₍458₎–467.

1. Negroes—Employment. 2. Trade-unions—U. S. 3. Labor and laboring classes—U. S. I. Mitchell, George Sinclair, 1902– joint author. II. Title.

39–27580

Library of Congress E185.8.C39
₍6₎ 331.6

M323
S08
Mitchell, George Sinclair, 1902-
How far has southern labor advanced?
The Southern Negro, 1952: Warning to Ike and the Dixiecrats, a special issue. New York, The Nation, 1952.

243-284p. illus. 29cm.
Special issue of The Nation, September 27, 1952.

M973
M69q
Mitchell, George Washington, 1865-
The question before Congress, a consideration of the debates and final action by Congress upon various phases of the race question in the United States, by Geo. W. Mitchell. Philadelphia, Pa., The A. M. E. book concern [°1918]

247 p. 23½cm.

1. Slavery in the U. S. 2. ~~Negroes~~ U. S. Congress. 3. U. S.—Race question. I. Title.

Library of Congress E441.M68 18—21546 [43g1]

M301
M69
Mitchell, Glenford E ed.
The angry black South. Edited by Glenford E. Mitchell and William H. Peace, III. New York, Corinth Books, 1962.

159p. 21cm.
Portrait of authors on back of book.

Contents.- The long struggle, by C. B. Robson. - Beginnings of a new age, by E. N. French. - School desegregation, by F. H. Moore.-

Continued on next card.

M301
M69
Mitchell, Glenford E ed.
The angry black south. Edited by Glenford E. Mitchell and William H. Peace, III. New York, Corinth Books, 1962. (Card 2)

Contents - Continued
College students take over, by G.E. Mitchell. - The South reacts, by W.H. Peace.- Nonviolence, by R.B. Gore.- The continuing struggle, by G.E. Mitchell and W.H. Peace.

1. Southern States. 2. Race question. 3. Sit-in demonstrations. I. Peace, William H., jt. ed. II. Title.

M301
M69
Mitchell, Glenford E
College students take over.

Pp. 73-95.
In: Mitchell, Glenford E., ed. The angry black south. New York, Corinth Books, 1962.

M301
M69
Mitchell, Glenford E
The continuing struggle, by Glenford E. Mitchell and William H. Peace.

Pp. 152-159.
In: Mitchell, Glenford E., ed. The angry black south. New York, Corinth Books, 1962.

I. Peace, William H., jt. auth.

M368
M69c
Mitchell, James B
The collapse of the National Benefit Life Insurance Company; A study in high finance among Negroes. Washington, D.C. Howard University, Graduate School for the Division of Social Sciences, 1939.

150p. tables. 24cm. (Howard University. Studies in the social sciences, v.2, no.1)

1. Insurance. I. National Benefit Life Insurance Company.

MB9
St4m
[Mitchell, Joseph]
The missionary pioneer, or a brief memoir of the life, labours and death of John Stewart (man of colour) founder, under God of the mission among the Wyandott's at Upper Sandusky, Ohio. Published by Joseph Mitchell. New York, Printed by J. C. Totten, 1827.

viii, 96p. 15cm.
1. Wyandott Mission. 2. Stewart, John 1786-1823. 3. Missionaries.

MB9
St4m
[Mitchell, Joseph]
The missionary pioneer, or a brief memoir of the life, labours and death of John Stewart, (man of colour) founder, under God of the missing among the Wyandotts at Upper Sandusky, Ohio. Published by Joseph Mitchell. New York, Printed by J. C. Totten, 1827.

viii, 96p. 15cm.
Reprinted by Joint Centenary Committee, 1918.
1. Wyandott,Mission. 2. Stewart, John, 1786-1823. 3. Missionaries.

M792
M694
Mitchell, Loften.
Black drama; the story of the American Negro in the theatre. [1st ed.] New York, Hawthorn Books [1967]

248 p. illus., ports. 24 cm.
Portrait of author on book jacket.

1. ~~Negroes in~~ literature. 2. Theater—~~U. S.~~ 3. ~~Negroes~~—Moral and social conditions. I. Title.

PS338.N4M5 792'.0973 66-22313

Library of Congress [5]

M974.7
C55
Mitchell, Loften
The Negro Theatre and the Harlem community.

Pp. 146-156.

In: Clarke, John Henrik, ed. Harlem, a community in transition, New York, Citadel Press, 1965.

1. Theatre - New York (City)

M974.7
C55h
Mitchell, Loften
The Negro theatre and the Harlem community.

Pp. 108-120.

In: Clarke, J. H., ed. Harlem, U. S. A. Berlin Seven Seas Publishers, 1964.

M326.
M69
1860
Mitchell, William M.
The underground railroad from slavery to freedom. By the Rev. W. M. Mitchell ... 2d ed. London, W. Tweedie; [etc., etc.] 1860.

~~xx, 10, 191 p.~~ front. (port.) ~~18½cm.~~
xv, 172, xi p. 19cm.

1. Underground railroad. 2. Slavery in the U. S.—Fugitive slaves. 3. ~~Negroes~~—Ontario.

10—34480

Library of Congress E450.M68 [a35b1]

...Os mitos africanos no Brasil.

Brazil
M398
S08
Souza Carneiro, A J de.
... Os mitos africanos no Brasil, ciencia do folk-lore; ilustrado com 30 gravuras e as fontes etimologicas de mais de 500 termos afro-brasileiros, ilustrações de Cicero Valladares. São Paulo [etc.] Companhia editora nacional, 1937.

506 p., 1 l. illus. 18½cm. (Biblioteca pedagogica brasileira. Ser. 5.ª: Brasiliana. v. 103)

At head of title: Souza Carneiro.

1. Folk-lore, Negro. 2. Negroes in Brazil. I. Title.

38—4942

Library of Congress GR133.B6S6 [45d1] 398.0981

Brit. Guiana
M823.91
M69a
Mittelhölzer, Edgar, 1909-1965.
The adding machine; a fable for capitalists and commercialists. Kingston, Jamaica, Pioneer Press [1954]

102 p. illus. 20 cm.

I. Title. *Full name:* Edgar Austin Mittelhölzer.

PZ3.M6977Ad 55-18824 ‡

Library of Congress [1]

Brit. Guiana
M823.91
M69c
Mittelhölzer, Edgar, 1909-1965.
Children of Kaywana. London, P. Nevill [1952]

515 p. 21 cm.

I. Title.

PZ3.M6977Ch 52-35370 ‡

Library of Congress [1]

Brit. Guiana
M823.91
M69v
Mittelholzer, Edgar, 1909-1965.
De vrouw Kaywana. Geautoriseerde vertaling van Hans de Vries. Den Haag, Zuid-Hollandsche Uitgevers Maatschappij [n.d.]

400p. map. 23cm.
Title: Children of Kaywana.
Dutch edition

I. Title.

Guiana, British
M823.91
M69el
Mittelholzer, Edgar, 1909-1965.
Eltonsbrody; a novel. London, Secker and Warburg, 1960.

191p. 18½cm.
Portrait of author on book jacket.

I. Title.

Brit. Guiana
M823.91
M69wel
Mittelholzer, Edgar, 1909-1965.
En welke is onze zonde; roman. Amsterdam, EM. Querido's Uigeversmij, 1953.

295p. 21cm.
Title: Shadows move among them.
Dutch edition.

I. Title.

British Guiana
M823.91
M69en
Mittelholzer, Edgar, 1909-1965.
Les enfants de Kaywana. (Children of Kaywana). Traduit de l'anglais par Clement Leclerc. Paris, La Table Ronde [1954]

618p. 23cm.
Biographical note concerning author on jacket.

I. Title.

Brit. Guiana
M823.91
M69h
Mittelhölzer, Edgar, 1909-1965.
The harrowing of Hubertus. London, Secker & Warburg, 1954.

308 p. 21 cm.

I. Title. *Full name:* Edgar Austin Mittelhölzer.

PZ3.M6977Har 54-25253 ‡

Library of Congress [1]

Brit. Guiana
M823.91 Mittelhölzer, Edgar, 1909-1965.
M69hu Hubertus, a novel. [1st American ed.] New York, J. Day Co. [1955, °1954]
308 p. 22 cm.
First published in London in 1954 under title: The harrowing of Hubertus.
I. Title.
Full name: Edgar Austin Mittelhölzer.
PZ3.M6977Hu 54-10461 ‡
Library of Congress [5]

Jamaica
M823.91 Mittelholzer, Edgar, 1909-1965.
Sa3a Miss Clark is dying.
Pp. 211-217.
In: Salkey, Andrew, comp. Stories from the Caribbean. London, Elek Books, 1965.

British Guiana
M823.91 Mittelhölzer, Edgar, 1909-1965.
M69p The piling of clouds. London, Putnam [1961]
262 p. 21 cm.
I. Title.
Full name: Edgar Austin Mittelhölzer.
PZ3.M6977Pi 62-4087 ‡
Library of Congress [8]

British Guiana
M823.91 Mittelhölzer, Edgar, 1909-1965.
M69j The Jilkington drama. London, New York, Abelard-Schuman [1965]
190 p. 23 cm.
I. Title.
PZ3.M6977Ji 66-10125
Library of Congress [5]

Jamaica
M823.91 Mittelholzer, Edgar, 1909-1965.
Sa3w A morning at the office.
pp. 13-19
In Andrew Salkey's West Indian Stories. 1960.

British Guiana
M823.91 Mittelholzer, Edgar, 1909-1965.
M69sa Savage destiny. Original title: Children of Kayana. Abridged. New York, Dell Printers, 1960.
384p. 16½cm.
I. Title.

British Guiana
M823.91 Mittelhölzer, Edgar, 1909-1965.
M69k Kaywana blood. London, Secker & Warburg, 1958.
523 p. illus. 21 cm.
"Sequel to Children of Kaywana."
I. Title.
Full name: Edgar Austin Mittelhölzer.
PZ3.M6977Kay 58-22204 ‡
Library of Congress [8]

Brit. Guiana
M823.91 Mittelhölzer, Edgar, 1909-1965.
M69m3 A morning in Trinidad. [1st ed.] Garden City, N. Y., Doubleday, 1950.
250 p. 21 cm.
A novel.
I. Title.
PZ3.M6977Mo 50-7594
Library of Congress [5]

Brit. Guiana
M823.91 Mittelholzer, Edgar, 1909-1965.
M69s Shadows move among them. London, Peter Nevill, 1951.
334p. 18cm.
I. Title.

Guiana, British
M823.91 Mittelholzer, Edgar, 1909-1965.
M691a Latticed echoes; a novel in the Leitmotiv Manner. London, Secker and Warburg, 1960.
254p. 19½cm.
I. Title.

Brit. Guiana
M823.91 Mittelhölzer, Edgar, 1909-1965.
M69m2 A morning at the office, a novel. London, Hogarth Press, 1950.
246 p. 19 cm.
Author is from British Guiana.
I. Title.
PZ3.M6977Mn 50-26028
Library of Congress [4]

British Guiana
M89 Mittelhölzer, Edgar, 1909- 1965.
M69 A swarthy boy. London, Putnam [1963]
157p. port. 21½cm.
"A childhood in British Guiana." Autobiographical.
I. Title.

Brit. Guiana Mittelholzer, Edgar, 1909-1965.
M823.91 The life and death of Sylvia, a novel.
M69l New York, John Day, 1954.
1954 316p. 21cm.
I. title

Brit. Guiana
M823.91 Mittelholzer, Edgar, 1909-1965.
L69mi My bones and my flute. London, Secker & Warburg, 1955.
222p. 19cm.
I. Title.

Brit. Guiana
M823.91 Mittelholser, Edgar, 1909-1965.
M69t A tale of three places. London, Secker and Warburg, 1957.
347p. 20cm.

Brit. Guiana
M823.91 Mittelhölzer, Edgar, 1909-1965.
M69sy The life and death of Sylvia, a novel. [1st American ed.] New York, J. Day Co. [1953] [Dell Pub. Co.]
316 p. 21 cm.
I. Title.
PZ3.M6977Li 2 54-5014 ‡
Library of Congress [5]

Brit. Guiana
M823.91 Mittelhölzer, Edgar, 1909-1965.
M69o Of trees and the sea. With decorations by the author. London, Secker & Warburg, 1956.
256 p. illus. 19 cm.
I. Title.
Full name: Edgar Austin Mittelhölzer.
PZ3.M6977Of 57-20080 ‡
Library of Congress [8]

British Guiana
M823.91 Mittelholzer, Edgar, 1909-1965.
M69th Thunder returning; a novel in the Leitmotiv manner. London, Secker and Warburg, 1961.
240p. 20½cm.
I. Title.

Brit. Guiana
M823.91 Mittelhölzer, Edgar, 1909-1965.
B691 The life and death of Sylvia. London, Secker and Warburg, 1953.
287 p. 21 cm.
I. Title.
PZ3.M6977Li 53-31369 rev ‡
Library of Congress [r54b2]

Brit. Guiana
M823.91 Mittelhölzer, Edgar, 1909-1965.
M69ol The old blood. [1st ed.] Garden City, N. Y., Doubleday, 1958.
576 p. illus. 22 cm.
I. Title.
Full name: Edgar Austin Mittelhölzer.
PZ3.M6977Ol 58-8104 ‡
Library of Congress [5]

British Guiana
M823.91 Mittelholzer, Edgar, 1909-1965.
M69ti A tinkling in the twilight; a novel. London, Secker & Warburg, 1959.
269p. 19½cm.
I. Title.

British Guiana
M823.91 Mittelhölzer, Edgar, 1909-1965.
M69u Uncle Paul. London, McDonald [1963]

222p. 20cm.

I. Title.

British Guiana
M823.91 Mittelholzer, Edgar, 1909-1965.
M69wo The wounded and the worried. London, Putnam, c1962.

223p. 21cm.

I. Title.

Haiti Les mnemoniennes.
M841. Menos, Solon, 1859-1918.
M52m Les mnemoniennes. Premiere serie La Licence es-Joies (1876-1879). Paris, A. Cotillon & cie, 1882.

vii, 170 1 p. 19cm.

Brit. Guiana
M823.91 Mittelholzer, Edgar, 1909-1965.
M69v Vie et mort de Sylvia (The life and death of Sylvia); roman, traduit de l'anglais par Jacques et Jean Tournier. Paris, Librairie Plon, [1956]

339p. 20cm. (Feux Croises, ames et terres etrangeres)

I. Title.

M89 Mix, Mrs. Edward, 1832-1884.
M691 In memory of departed worth. The life of Mrs. Edward Mix, written by herself in 1880. With appendix. Torrington, Conn., Press of register printing co., 1884.
24p. front. 17cm.
~~1. Biography~~

Tanganyika
M967.82 Mnyampala, Mathias E
M71h Historia, milia, na desturi za Wagogo wa Tanganyika [History and customs of the Wagogo of Tanganyika] Kampala, The Eagle Press, 1954.

116p. 15cm. (Custom and tradition in East Africa series)

Written in Swahili.

1. Tanganyika.

Jamaica
M823.91 Mittelholzer, Edgar, 1909-1965.
Sa3w We know not whom to mourn.

pp. 20-27

In Andrew Salkey's West Indian Stories. 1960.

Mixed races.

M575 [Sampson, John Patterson, 1839-
Sa4 Mixed races: their environment, temperament, heredity and phrenology. Hampton, Va., Normal school steam press, 1881.

ix, [13] - 159p. front. 22½cm.

Tanganyika
M896.3 Mnyampala, Mathias E
M71k Kisa cha mrina asali na wenzake wawili [The adventures of a honey-gatherer and his two friends] Dar es Salaam, Eagle Press, 1961.

77p. illus. 18cm. (Hadith za Tanganyika. Kitabu cha pili)
Written in Swahili.

I. Title.

W. Indies
M823 Mittelhölzer, Edgar, 1909-1965.
C23 We know not whom to mourn.

(In: Caribbean anthology of short stories,... Kingston, Jamaica, Pioneer Press 1953. 19cm. pp.35-42.)

South Africa
M968 Mlotyna, Stephen V
M71n Nozipo [Story of native life. [Lovedale, South Africa] Lovedale Institution Press [1923]

41p. 18½cm.
Written in Xhosa.

1. Africa, South. I. Title.

S. Africa
M968 Mnyanda, B J
M71i In search of truth; a commentary on certain aspects of Southern Rhodesia's Native Policy. Bombay, Hind Kitabs Ltd., 1954.

173p. port. map. 21cm.

1. Southern Rhodesia

Brit. Guiana
M823.91 Mittelholzer, Edgar, 1909-1965.
M69we The Weather family; a novel. London, Secker & Warburg, 1958.

339p. 23cm.

I. Title.

Tanganyika Mmari, G V., jt. auth.
M398.6 Meena, E K
M47 Vitendawili [Riddles] Kutoka makabila mbalimbali ya Tanganyika, kimetungwa na E. K. Meena, G. V. Mmari na H. H. Sangiwa. London, Oxford University Press, 1960.

27p. illus. 18½cm.
Written in Swahili.

1. Riddles, African. I. Mmari, G. V., jt. auth. II. Sangiwa, H. H., jt. auth. III. Title.

The mob still rides.

M323.2 Commission on Interracial Cooperation.
C73m The mob still rides; A review of the lynching record, 1931-1935. Atlanta, The Commission, n.d.

24p. 22cm.

Brit. Guiana

M823.91 Mittelhölzer, Edgar, 1909- 1965.
M69w The weather in Middenshot, a novel. [1st American ed.] New York, J. Day Co. [1953, °1952]

280 p. 20 cm.

The author is from British Guiana.

1. Title.

PZ3.M6977We 2 53-1289 ‡

Library of Congress [5]

Uganda Mmere ki gye tusaanira okulya?
M613.2 Trowell, H C
T75 Mmere ki gye tusaanira okulya? [What food should we eat?] kya H. C Trowell ne R. G. Ladin. Kyakyusibwa John W. S. Kasirye ne Aloni Lubwama. Nairobi, Eagle Press, 1951.
23p. illus. 18½cm. (Asika Obulamu Series)
Written in Luganda.

1. Nutrition. I. Title. II. Kasirye, John W. S., tr. III. Lubwama, Aloni, jt. tr. IV. Series.

Mob violence

See

Lynch law

Brit. Guiana
M823.91 Mittelhölzer, Edgar., 1909-1965.
M69wi With a Carib eye. London, Secker & Warburg, 1958.
192 p. illus. 21 cm.

1. Caribbean area—Descr. & trav. I. Title.
Full name: Edgar Austin Mittelhölzer.

F2171.M55 917.29 58-44418 ‡

Library of Congress [1]

Ghana Mmɔdenbɔ.
M896.3 Adaye, J J
Ad19 Mmɔdenbɔ by mmusu abasa so, [Perseverance conquers evil] short stories in Twi. Collected and edited by C. A. Akrofi. London, Thomas Nelson and Sons, 1948.

76p. 18cm.

I. Title.

Congo(Leopoldville)
M896.3 Mobiala, Louis
M71 Une nuit tragique. Leverville (Congo Belge) Bibliotheque de l'Etoile, 1954.

52p. illus.

I. Title.

M034
P19
V.5,no.9
Mobile Emancipation Association, Mobile, Ala.
Programme fifty-sixth anniversary, January 1, 1919; together with the names of all officers of the association, the members of the executive committee, also a complete report of the retiring general chairman, Dr. H. Roger Williams. Lacks imprint.

12p. 23cm.

1. Emancipation Day Celebrations. 2. Alabama. I. Williams, H. Roger, ed.

Basutoland
M896
M71t2
Mocoancoeng, Jacob G
Tseleng ea Bophelo, le lithothokiso tse ncha [The path of life, a drama and new poems. 2d ed.] Johannesburg, Witwatersrand University Press, 1955.

52p. 19cm. (The Bantu treasury x, ed. by C. M. Doke)
Written in Sotho.

I. Title.

Modern literature and the religious frontier.
M808.4
Sc8m
Scott, Nathan A
Modern literature and the religious frontier. [1st ed.] New York, Harper [1958]
138 p. 22 cm.
Includes bibliography.

1. Religion and literature. 2. Literature, Modern—20th cent.—Hist. & crit. I. Title.
PN1077.S39 809.04 58-7476 ‡
Library of Congress [25]

The mobility of the Negro.
M331
L58
Lewis, Edward Erwin, 1900–
The mobility of the Negro; a study in the American labor supply, by Edward E. Lewis ... New York, Columbia university press; London, P. S. King & son, ltd., 1931.
144 p. illus. (maps) 23cm. (Half-title: Studies in history, economics and public law, ed. by the Faculty of political science of Columbia university, no. 342)
Published also as thesis (PH. D.) Columbia university.
"The third volume to appear as a result of studies in the field of Negro migration under grants by the Social science research council and the Columbia university Council for research in the social sciences."—Foreword.
"Selected bibliography": p. 134–135.
1. Negroes. 2. Negroes — Employment. 3. Southern states — Econ. condit.—1918– 4. Cotton growing and manufacture—Southern states. I. Social science research council. II. Columbia university. Council for research in the social sciences. III. Title.
Library of Congress H31.C7 no. 342 31—29612
——— Copy 2. E185.8.L47
[42q2] (306.2) 331.6

Basutoland
M896
M71t
Mocoancoeng, Jacob G
Tseleng ea Bophelo. Le lithokhokiso tse ncha. Johannesburg, Witwatersrand University press, 1947.

52p. 18cm. (The Bantu Treasury)
"The Path of Life" a drama, and "New Poems" in S. Sotho.

1. Africa, South - Poetry. 2. Africa, South - Drama

Modern Negro art.
M709
P83m
Porter, James Amos, 1905–
Modern Negro art, by James A. Porter ... With eighty-five halftone plates. New York, The Dryden press, 1943.
viii, 272 p. incl. plates. 21cm.
Bibliography: p. 183–192.

1. Negro art. 2. Negro artists. I. Title.
43-16044 Revised
Library of Congress N6538.N5P6
[r45f2l0] 709.9

Mobs

See also

Lynch law

Mod en anden himmel [Another country]
M813.5
B19an4
Baldwin, James
Mod en anden himmel [Another country] [Copenhagen] Steen Hasselbalchs Forlag, 1963.

447p. 22cm.
Portrait of author on book cover.
"Overstat fra engelskaf Michael Tejn"

I. Title. II. Tejn, Michael, tr.

The modern waiter.
M642
H71m
Holland, Edwin Clifford
The modern waiter, a formula for correct and perfect dining room service. The waiter's criterion, by E.C. Holland... Columbus, Ohio, Lutheran book concern, 1920.
89p. front, illus. 19½cm.

Mobs.
M343.3
Ed5c
Edmonds, Henry M
The cost of the mob, sermon. Atlanta, Commission on Interracial Cooperation, 1933.

[6] 23cm.
Reprinted from the Birmingham age-herald, October 8, 1933.

Model questions & answers on English.
Nigeria
M428
On9
Onukwu, G C
Model questions & answers on English language for R.S.A. School & R.S.A. Inter Stage II certificate from (1958-1962). Forworded by M.C. Oji. Onitsha, [Etudo, 1963]

63p. tables 21cm.

The moderns.
M810.8
J72
Jones, LeRoi, ed.
The moderns; an anthology of new writing in America. New York, Corinth Books, 1963.
xvi, 351 p. 22 cm.
Bibliographical references included in "Acknowledgments" (p. [vii–viii])

1. American literature—20th cent. I. Title.
PS536.J6 813.54082 63-11408
Library of Congress [4-1]

Mobs.
M304
P19
v.1,no.12
Haywood, Harry.
... Lynching, by H. Haywood and M. Howard. [New York] International pamphlets [1932]
cover-title, 15 p. 19cm. (International pamphlets. No. 25)

1. Mobs. 2. Negroes. 3. Lynch law. I. Howard, Milton, joint author. II. Title.
A 34—1451
Rochester univ. Libr. for Library of Congress HX81.I 6 no. 25 [HX81.I 6 no. 25]
[42c1]

The modern African.
Nigeria
M960
Ob82
Obukar, Charles.
The modern African, by Charles Obukar and John Williams. London, Macdonald & Evans, 1965.
x, 149 p. illus., ports. 23 cm.

1. Africa, Sub-Saharan—Soc. condit. ~~I. Fosphong, Fritz-Karl, 1914– joint author.~~ II. Title.
HN797.O2 66-34222
Library of Congress [1]

South Africa
MB9
M72a
Modisane, Bloke, 1923-
Blame me on history. London, Thames and Hudson [1963]

311p. 22cm.
Autobiography.

I. Title. 1. Africa, South.

Tanganyika
M896.3
M715h
Mochiwa, Anthony
Habari za wazigua [Stories about Wazigua] London, Macmillan, 1954.

54p. 18½cm. (Desturi na masimulizi ya Afrika ya mashariki)
Written in Swahili.

I. Title.

Modern African stories.
Africa
M896.3
K83
Komey, Ellis Ayitey, ed.
Modern African stories, edited by Ellis Ayitey Komey and Ezekiel Mphahlele. London, Faber and Faber, 1964.

227p. 20cm.
Ghanaian and South African editors.

1. Short stories, African. I. Mphahlele, Ezekiel, jt. ed. II. Title.

South Africa
MB9
M72
Modisane, Bloke, 1923–
Blame me on history. [1st ed.] New York, Dutton, 1963.
311 p. 22 cm.
Autobiography.

I. Title. 1. Africa, South.
CT1929.M6A3 920 63-20846
Library of Congress [8]

Kenya
M967.65
M71a
Mockerie, Parmenas Githendu.
An African speaks for his people [by] Parmenas Githendu Mockerie; with a foreword by Professor Julian Huxley. London, L. and Virginia Woolf at the Hogarth press, 1934.
95 p. front. (port.) 19cm.

1. Kenya colony and protectorate. 2. Kikuyu tribe. 3. Gt. Brit.—Colonies—Kenya colony and protectorate. I. Title.
35-13386
Library of Congress DT434.E2M57
[3] 916.76

...Modern industrialism and the negroes of the United States...
M06
Am3
no. 12
Grimké, Archibald Henry, 1849–
... Modern industrialism and the negroes of the United States, by Archibald H. Grimke ... Washington, D. C., The Academy, 1908.
18 p. 22cm. (Occasional papers, no. 12. The American negro academy)

1. Negroes—U. S. 2. Labor and laboring classes—U. S.
9-35097
Library of Congress E184.N3A3 no. 12
——— Copy 2. Library of Congress E184.N3C8

Africa
M808.83
B396
Modisane, Bloke, 1923-
The situation.

Pp. 58-70.

In: Black Orpheus. Black Orpheus; an anthology of African and Afro-American prose. New York, McGraw-Hill, 1965.

Modou Fatim.
Senegal
M896.3 Sadji, Abdoulaye, 1910-
Sa15m Modou Fatim. ‹Dakar, Imprimerie A. Diop, n.d.›

54p. 16cm. (Collection "Mer-Gaddou")

Basutoland
M896.2 Mofokeng, Sophonia Machabe
M72s Senkatana. Johannesburg, Witwatersrand University Press, 1952.

71p. 17cm (The Bantu treasury, XII, ed. by C. M. Doke)
Written in Sotho.

I. Title.

Basutoland
M896.3 Mofolo, Thomas, 1873-1948.
M72t The traveller of the East, by Thomas Mofolo. London, Society for Promoting Christian knowledge, n.d.

125p. 18cm.

I. Title.

French Guinea
M966.1 Modupe, Prince, 1901-
M72i I was a savage. Foreword by Elspeth Huxley.
1958 Illustrations and sketch map by Rosemary Grimble. London, Museum Press, 1958.

168p. illus. 21½cm.

1. Africa, French West - Social life and customs. I. Title.

Basutoland
M896.2 Mofokeng, Twentyman M.
M72 Sek'ona sa joala; papali oa tsa motse, Morija, Sesuto Book Depot, 1929.

45p. 17½cm.
A village play.
In Sotho.

1. Africa, South-Drama.

Cameroun
M896 Mohamadou, Eldridge, comp.
M72 Contes et poèmes Foulbé de la Bénoué - Nord-Cameroun, présentés par Eldridge Mohamadou et Henriette Mayssal. Yaounde, Editions Abbia avec la collaboration de CLE, 1965.

84p. illus. 24cm.

1. African poetry. 2. African short stories.

French Guinea
M966.1 Modupe, *Prince*, 1901-
M72i I was a savage. [1st ed.] New York, Harcourt, Brace
1957 [1958, ©1957]

185 p. 21 cm.

1. Africa, French West—Soc. life & cust. I. Title.

DT530.M58 916.6 57-10058 ‡

Library of Congress [30]

Basutoland
M896.3 Mofolo, Thomas, 1873-1948.
M72c3 Chaka der Zulu; roman. Zurich. Manesse verlag, ‹1953›

268p. 15½cm.

Cameroun
M967.11 Mohamadou, Eldridge
M725 L'histoire de Tibati, chefferie Foulbe du Cameroun. Yaounde, Editions Abbia avec la collaboration de CLE, 1965.

72p. 18cm. illus., maps.

Portrait of author on book cover.

1. Fulahs. 2. Tibati, Cameroun. I. Title.

U.S.
M839 Moe, Jørgen Engebretsen, 1813-1882, joint comp.
Iv3n Asbjørnsen, Peter Christen, 1812-1885, *comp.*
Norwegian folk tales, from the collection of Peter Christen Asbjørnsen [and] Jørgen Moe. Illustrated by Erik Werenskiold [and] Theodor Kittelsen. Translated by Pat Shaw Iversen [and] Carl Norman. New York, Viking Press [1960]

188 p. illus. 28 cm.

1. Fairy tales. I. Moe, Jørgen Engebretsen, 1813-1882, joint comp. II. Title.

PZ8.A89Nq 61-16057 ‡

Library of Congress [15]

Basutoland
M896.3 Mofolo, Thomas, 1873-1948.
M72c 2 Chaka, an historical romance, by Thomas Mofolo, with an introduction by Sir Henry Newbolt ... translated from the original Sesuto by F. H. Dutton ... London, Pub. for the International institute of African languages & cultures by Oxford university press, H. Milford, 1931.

xv, 198 p., 1 l. 19½cm.

1. Chaka, Zulu chief, 1786 (ca.)-1828. I. Dutton, Frederick Hugh, tr. II. International institute of African languages and cultures. III. Title.

32-12705

Library of Congress DT878.Z9M6
[a38f2] 896.2

Liberia
M966.6 Mohammedanism.
B62w Blyden, Edward Wilmot, 1832-
West Africa before Europe, and other addresses, delivered in England in 1901 and 1903, by Edward Wilmot Blyden ... With an introduction by Casely Hayford ... London, C. M. Phillips, 1905.

4 p. l., iv, 158 p. front. (port.) 19cm.

Includes the author's article, "Islam in the Western Soudan," reprinted from Journal of African society, October, 1902.

1. Africa, West. 2. Negroes—Africa. 3. Mohammedanism.

Library of Congress DT471.B5 6-27329

Moeti oa bochabela
Basutoland
M896.3 Mofolo, Thomas, 1873-1948
M72tm Moeti oa bochabela. ‹Morija, Sesuto book depot, 1938›

156p. 15cm.

"A visitor to the East."

Basutoland
M896.3 Mofolo, Thomas, 1873-1948.
M72c Chaka. Morija, Sesuto Book Depot, 1925.

288p. front. 15½cm.

Mohammedanism - Readers and speakers.
M372.4 Johnson, Christine.
J63 Muhammads children; a first grade reader. ‹Chicago, University of Islam, 1963›

130p. 23cm.

M783
M72 Moffatt, Nona (Stein)
How to organize a music department for a church; a handbook by a successful choir director. [1st ed.] New York, Exposition Press [1963]

75 p. 21 cm. (An Exposition-banner book)
Includes bibliography.

1. Choirs (Music) 2. Conducting, Choral. 3. Choral music—Bibl. I. Title.

MT88.M78 783.8 63-2545 ‡/MN

Library of Congress [5]

Basutoland
M896.3 Mofolo, Thomas, 1873-1948
M72tm Moeti oa bochabela. ‹Morija, Sesuto book depot, 1938›

156p. 15cm.

"A visitor to the East."

I. Title.

Mohammedanism in Algeria.
Algeria
M965 Manuel de politique Musulmane.
Af8m Paris, Brossard, 1925.

189p. 19cm.

Basutoland
M896.2 Mofokeng, Sophonia Machabe
M72s2 Senkatana. [Reprinted in new orthography] Johannesburg, Witwatersrand University Press, 1962.

71p. 17cm. (The Bantu treasury, ed. by D. T. Cole)
Written in Sotho.

I. Title.

Basutoland
M896.3 Mofolo, Thomas, 1873-1948.
M72p Pitseng ‹by› Thomas Mofolo. Morija, Sesuto book depot, 1930.

433p. 16cm.
Love story.

I. Title.

Mohammedans.
Liberia
M966.6 Blyden, Edward Wilmot, 1832-1912.
B62c Christianity, Islam and the Negro race. By
1887 Edward W. Blyden,.. With an introduction by the Hon. Samuel Lewis. London, W.B. Whittingham & co., 1887.

vii, 423p.
Blyden's own copy containing his signature and corrections in his handwriting.

Mohammedans in the U. S.

M323
B19f
Baldwin, James, 1924–
The fire next time. New York, Dial Press, 1963.
120 p. 21 cm.

1. Negroes. 2. U. S.—Race question. 3. Mohammedans in the U. S. I. Title.

E185.61.B195 301.451 63—11713 ‡
Library of Congress [63g10]

Mohammedans in the U. S.

M323
B19f2
Baldwin, James, 1924–
~~The fire next time. New York, Dial Press, 1963.~~ London, M. Joseph [1963]
~~120 p.~~ 21 cm. 112p.

1. Negroes. 2. U. S.—Race question. 3. Mohammedans in the U. S. I. Title.

E185.61.B195 301.451 63—11713 ‡
Library of Congress [63g10]

Mohammedans in the U. S.

Nigeria
M297
Es77
Essien-Udom, Essien Udosen.
Black nationalism; a search for an identity in America. [Chicago] University of Chicago Press [1962]
xiii, 367 p. illus., ports. 25 cm.
Bibliography: p. 331-360.

1. Mohammedans in the U. S. 2. Negroes. 3. U. S.—Race question. I. Title.

E185.61.E75 297.0973 62—12632
Library of Congress [62x5]

Mohammedans in the U.S.

M363
L63b
Lincoln, Charles Eric.
The Black Muslims in America. Foreword by Gordon Allport. Boston, Beacon Press [1961]
276 p. 21 cm.
"This book originated as a dissertation ... in the Graduate School of Boston University."
Includes bibliography.
Portrait of author on book jacket.

1. Negroes. 2. U. S.—Race question. 3. Mohammedans in the U. S. I. Title.

E185.61.L56 363.973 61—5881 ‡
Library of Congress [62y²5]

Basutoland
M968.6
M72a
Mohapeloa, J M
Africans and their chiefs; should Africans be ruled by their chiefs or by elected leaders. Cape Town, The African Bookman, 1945.
26p. 18½cm.

1. Basutoland. 2. Chieftianship.

S.Africa
M784
M72
1947
Mohapeloa, J P
Meloli le lithallere tsa Africa. Morija, Basutoland, Morija Sesuto Book Depot, 1947.
68p. 18cm.
Sotho Songs.

1. Songs, African.

S. Africa
M784
M72
1945.
Mohapeloa, J P
Meloli le lithallere tsa Afrika. Morija, Sesuto Book Depot, 1945.
79 p. 18 cm.
Sotho songs.

S. Africa
M398
M72L
Moikangoa, Cornelius Rakhosi, 1877-1957
Litšomo tsa Ma-Afrika (African folk-tales). Maseru, Basutoland, Mazenod Institute, n.d.
78p. ports. 18cm.

1. Africa, South - folklore.

Brazil
M869.1
C88po
Moiséx, Massaud.
Cruz e Souza, João da, 1861-1898.
Poemas escholhidos. Seleção e introducã o de Massaud Moises. São Paulo, Editôra Cultrix [1961]
158p. 19½cm.

M813.5
P53m
Mojo hand.
Phillips, Jane, 1944–
Mojo hand. New York, Trident Press [1966]
180 p. 22 cm.

I. Title.

PZ4.P558Mo 66-24884
Library of Congress [3]

S.Africa
M89
M42
Molahlehi.
Matlosa, Sebolai.
Molahlehi. Morija, Basutoland, Morija Sesuto Book Depot, 1946.
66p. 18½cm.

Haiti
M972.94
J98q
Môle Saint-Nicolas.
Justin, Joseph
La question du Môle Saint-Nicolas, par Joseph Justin. Paris, A. Giard, Librarie-Editeur, 1891.
32p. 22½cm.

S. Africa
M896.3
B43
Molefe, George Benjamin, 1901- , ed.
Bennie, William Govan, 1868-1942, ed.
Izincwadi zesiZulu zabafundi, elandela eyokuqala. Edited by W. G. Bennie, in collaboration with G. B. Molefe. Lovedale, South Africa, The Lovedale Press, 1945.
63p. illus. 18½cm.

S. Africa
M968
M73b
Molema, Silas Modiri, 1892-1965
The Bantu past and present; an ethnographical and historical study of the native races of South Africa, by S. M. Molema. Edinburgh, W. Green and Son, Ltd., 1920.
xix, 398p. maps. 22½cm.
Bibliography: p. ix-xii.

1. Bantus. DT764.B2M6 21-5104

S. Africa
M968
M73l
Molema, Silas Modiri, 1892-1965
Life and health, being health lectures delivered to Bechuanaland Bantu Societies. Lovedale, South Africa, Lovedale institution press, 1924.
69p. 18½cm.

1. Bechuanaland Bantu Society. I. Title.
2. Health.

South
Africa
M968.1
M732
Molema, Silas Modiri, 1892-1965
Montshiwa, 1815-1896, Barolong chief and patriot [by] S. M. Molema. Cape Town, C. Struik, 1966.
233 p. illus., ports. 22 cm.

1. Montshiwa, Barolong chief, 1815-1896. 2. Bechuanaland—Hist.

DT795.M6M6 968'.1'040924 67-73802
Library of Congress [3]

Africa,
South
M968
Sp6s
Molteno, Donald B , 1908-
The South African constitution.
pp. 193-204.
In: South Africa the road ahead, comp. by Hildegarde Spottiswoode. 1960.
White South African

1. Africa, South - Politics and govt.
I. Title.

Moment musical.

M780.4
C54m
Clark, Edgar Rogie.
Moment musical; ten selected newspaper articles by Edgar Rogie Clark. Fort Valley, Ga., Department of music, Fort Valley state college, 1940.
24 p. 1 illus. 21½ᶜᵐ.

1. Music—Addresses, essays, lectures. 2. Music—Negroes. I. Title.

Library of Congress ML60.C537M6 40-31976
——— Copy 2.
Copyright AA 338881 [2] 780.4

Moment of time, poems.

Trinidad
M821.91
AL52
Allen, Oswald, 1927-
Moment of time, poems. 2nd ed. Port-of-Spain, Trinidad & Tobago Printing Works, 1964.
39p. ports. 21cm.
Portrait of author in book.

Mon ame Negre!

Haiti
M841
B447
Bernard, Gerard C
Mon ame Negre! Port-au-Prince, Imp. de l'Etat, 1953.
52 p. port. 24cm.

Mon amour pour toi est éternel.

Cameroun
M896.1
M98m
Mveng, Engelbert
Mon amour pour toi est éternel. [Paris] Mame [1963]
21p. illus. 12cm.

I. Title.

Mon pays a travers les légendes...

Martinique
M398.2
C27
Cassius de Linval, Paule
Mon pays a travers les légendes; contes Martiniquais. Paris, Editions de la Revue Moderne, 1960.

163p. 18½cm.

Haiti
M398
M74c
Mondesir, Luxembourg.
Cauzemen paysan, souveni, conte, provbbe ak gnou roman dramatik. Port-au-Prince, Imp. du Commerce, 1948.

142p. 18½cm.
At head of title: Creol haitien.

1. Creole dialects--Folklore. 2. Haitian folklore. 3. Haiti--Creole dialects. I. Title.

[illegible]
M332
Sm61e
Money.
Smith, James Carmichael, 1852-
Legal tender, correspondence with the editor of "The bankers' magazine." London, Kegan Paul, Trench, Trubner, 1909.

16p. graphs. 21½cm.

Mon sang dans tes veines.

MB9
B174
LaCamara, Felix, comte de, 1897-
Mon sang dans tes veines, roman d'après une idée de Joséphine Baker [par] de La Camara et P. Abatino. Illustrations de G. De Pogedaieff. [Preface by Josephine Baker] Paris, Les Editions, Isis, 1931.

178p. illus., plates, port. 19cm.
White author.

1. Abatino, Petitos. II. Baker, Josephine, 1906- Preface. III. Title.

Sudan
M962.4
Y16
Mondini, A G ed.
Yangu, Alexis Mbali
The Nile turns red; Azanians chose freedom against Arab bondage. Edited by A. G. Mondini. [1st ed. New York] Pageant Press [©1966]

xviii, 184p. map. 21cm.
Bibliography: p. 182-184
Portrait of author on book jacket.

Bahamas
M332
Sm6m
Money.
Smith, James Carmichael, 1852-
Money and profit-sharing; or, The double standard money system, by Jas. C. Smith ... London, K. Paul, Trench, Trübner & co., 1st, 1908.

xix, 232 p. incl. tables. fold. tab., fold. diagr. 22cm.

1. Money. 2. Profit-sharing. 3. Currency question—Gt. Brit. 4. Value. I. Title. II. Title: Double standard money system.

9—3071

Library of Congress HG221.S62

Mon vieux carnet.

Haiti
M910
L56m
Lescouflair, Georges, 1882-
Mon vieux carnet; voyages--pensees--considerations--journal 1927. Montreal, Beauchemin, 1958.

178p. 16½cm.

U. S.
M968
Am3
Mondlane, Eduardo C
The struggle for independence in Mozambique.

Pp. 197-209.

In: American Society of African Culture. Southern Africa in transition. New York, Praeger, 1966.

Bahamas
M332
Sm6e
Money - Gt. Brit.
Smith, James Carmichael, 1852-
Economic reconstruction; a paper read at the Royal colonial institute, on 15th June, 1916, by Jas. C. Smith ... London, P. S. King & son, ltd., 1918.

23, [1] p. 21½cm.
Preface signed: A. H. Mackmurdo.

1. European war, 1914- —Economic aspects—Gt. Brit. 2. Money—Gt. Brit. I. Title.

18-20511

Library of Congress HC256.2.S6

Mona, Jamaica. University of the West Indies. Dept of Extra-Mural Studies.

Trinidad
M700
H55
Hill, Errol G., ed.
The artist in West Indian society; a symposium. [Mona, Jamaica, University of the West Indies, Dept. of Extra-Mural Studies [1963?]]

79 p. 21 cm.
"The contributions ... were first delivered in a seminar organised by the University of the West Indies' Department of Extra-Mural Studies during May and June, 1963, in Port-of-Spain, Trinidad."

1. Art — West Indies, British. 2. Performing arts — West Indies, British. 3. Art and society. I. Mona, Jamaica. University of the West Indies. Dept. of Extra-Mural Studies. II. Title.

N6591.H5 65-3616

Library of Congress [1]

Money.

Tanganyika
M967.82
Om1m
Omari, Dunstan Alfred, 1922- jt. auth.
Mtu maskini mwenye sh.1,000,000. The poor man with a million shillings. [By C. W. W. Ryan and D. A. Omari] Dar es Salaam, Eagle Press, 1954.

16p. 18cm. (Mazungunmzo ya uraia. Talks on citizenship, no.2)
Writtn in Swahili and English.

1. Money. I. Title. II. Title: The poor man with a million shillings. III. Series: Mazungunmzo ya uraia, no. 2. IV. Talks on citizenship, no. 2. V. Ryan, C. W. W.

Bahamas
M332
Sm6m
Money and profit-sharing.
Smith, James Carmichael, 1852-
Money and profit-sharing; or, The double standard money system, by Jas. C. Smith ... London, K. Paul, Trench, Trübner & co., 1st, 1908.

xix, 232 p. incl. tables. fold. tab., fold. diagr. 22cm.

1. Money. 2. Profit-sharing. 3. Currency question—Gt. Brit. 4. Value. I. Title. II. Title: Double standard money system.

9—3071

Library of Congress HG221.S62

Cuba
M39
M74g
Moncada, Guillermo, 1838-
Boti y Barreiro, Regino Eladio,
Guillermon, notas biográficas del general Guillermo Moncada. Guantánamo, Librería y Papelería, La Imperial, [1911]

127p. Port. on cover. 15cm.

Bahamas
M332
Sm6d
Money
Smith, James Carmichael, 1852-
The distribution of the produce, by James C. Smith. London, Kegan Paul, Trench, Trübner & Co., 1892.

77p. 19cm.

Nigeria
M896.3
OL3m
Money hard to get but easy to spend.
Olisah, Sunday Okenwa, 1936-
Money hard to get but easy to spend. Onitsha, Nigeria, General Printing Press [1960]

32p. port. 19½cm.
Portrait of author in book.

Le monde Africain noir.

Upper Volta
M960
K65
Ki-Zerbo, Joseph
Le monde Africain noir; Histoire et civilisation. Paris, Hatier, 1963.

94p. illus. maps. 20½cm.

1. Africa - History. 2. Africa - Civilization. I. Title.

Bahamas
M332.
Sm61
Money.
Smith, James Carmichael, 1852-
Inter-temporary values; or, The distribution of the produce in time. By James C. Smith ... London, K. Paul, Trench, Trübner, & co., ltd., 1906.

2 p. l., 136 p. incl. tables. charts (1 fold.) 22cm.
Appendixes: A. Coinage act, 1870.—B. [Miscellaneous charts]—C. Wholesale and retail prices.—D. The double monetary unit.—E. Inter-temporary value.

1. Money. 2. Value.

A 10-1897

Title from National Monetary Commission. Printed by L. C.

Nigeria
M896.3
M74w
Moneyhard, C N Onuoha
Why harlots hate married men and love bachelors. Port Harcourt, Fenu Press [n.d.]

32p. illus., ports. 20½cm.
Portrait of author in book.
Cover title.

I. Title.

Africa
M960
M74
Le Monde noir, dirigé par Théodore Monod. [Paris], Seuil, 1950.

443p. illus. 23cm.

(Special number of Presence africaine, no. 8-9.)

1. Africa.

Bahamas
M332
Sm61
Money.
Smith, James Carmichael.
Legal tender; essays, by Jas. C. Smith ... London, K. Paul, Trench, Trübner & co., ltd., 1910.

3p. l., v-xviii, 285 p. incl. tables. fold. diagr. 21½cm.

Congo
Leopoldville
M896.2
M74n
Mongita, A
Ngombe. [Bruxelles, 1957]

19 leaves 28cm.

Mimeographed.

1. African drama. I. Title.

La monja de la llave.

Peru
M985
P18

Palma, Ricardo, 1833–1919.
... La monja de la llave; prólogo de P. Matalonga ... México, D. F., Compañía general editora, s. a., 1940.
191, [1] p. 18½cm. (Colección Mirasol. [4])
"Forman este volumen dieciseis 'historias de amor,' extraídas de las 'Tradiciones peruanas'."—p. 11.

1. Legends—Peru. I. Matalonga, P., ed. II. Title.
[Full name: Manuel Ricardo Palma]
42-12800
Library of Congress F3400.P1738
[3] 985

Martinique
M972.98
M75

Monplaisir, Emma
La fille du caraïbe. Paris, Société d'Éditions Extérieures et Coloniales, 1960.

361p. 18½cm.

1. Martinique. I. Title.

La montagne Pelée et l'effroyable...

Martinique
M972.98
P53m

Philémon, Césaire.
... La montagne Pelée et l'effroyable destruction de Saint-Pierre (Martinique) le 8 mai 1902; le brusque réveil du volcan en 1929. Éd. originale. Fort-de-France, Chez l'auteur; Paris, Impressions Printory et G. Courville [°1930]
4 p. l., [11]-211 p., 1 l. plates, fold. maps. 22½cm.
"Il a été tiré de cet ouvrage cinquante exemplaires sur papier pur fil Lafuma, numérotés de 1 à 50, qui constituent l'édition originale."

1. Pelee peak—Eruption, 1902. 2. Saint-Pierre, Martinique. I. Title.
31-13052
Library of Congress F2081.P54
Copyright A—Foreign 10883
[2] [917.298] 551.21097298

Monod, Theodore, ed.

Africa
M960
P92
no.8-9

Présence Africaine.
Le monde noir. Paris, Présence Africaine, 1950.

443p. illus. plates. 21½cm.

Martinique
M793
M75

Monplaisir, Emma
La Martinique et ses danses. Conférence faite au Ciné-Théâtre le 1er Décembre 1961. Fort-de - France, Imp. Bezaudin, 1962.
32p. illus. 18cm.

1. Dancing - Martinique. I. Title.

M813.5
M76o

Montague, W Reginald, 1903–
Ole Man Mose; a novel of the Tennessee Valley. [1st ed.] New York, Exposition Press [1957]
121 p. 21 cm.

I. Title.

PZ4.M76O1 57-10665 ‡
Library of Congress [2]

Monogenism and polygenism.

M573.5
D37

Delany, Martin Robison, 1812–1885.
Principia of ethnology: the origin of races and color, with an archeological compendium of Ethiopian and Egyptian civilization, from years of careful examination and enquiry, by Martin R. Delany ... Philadelphia, Harper & brother, ~~1879~~. 1880. 2d. ed.
viii, [9]-~~95~~ p. incl. illus., pl., map. 2 pl. 20½cm.

1. Monogenism and polygenism. 2. Color of man. 3. Egypt—Civilization. 4. Negro race.
5-29787
Library of Congress GN370.D33
[a33b1]

Monroe, N. C.

M323.1
W67

Williams, Robert Franklin, 1925–
Negroes with guns. Edited by Marc Schleifer. New York, Marzani & Munsell [°1962].
128 p. illus. 21 cm.

1. Negroes—Monroe, N. C. 2. Civil rights—Monroe, N. C. I. Title.

F264.M75W5 323.1 63-1716 ‡
Library of Congress [1]

Haiti
M383
M76

Montès, Léon
La timbrologie Haitienne, 1881-1954. Port-au-Prince, Henri Deschamps, 1954.

iv, 205p. illus. 21cm.

I. Title 1. Postage stamps - Haiti

Monogenism and polygenism.

Haiti
M972.94
P93r

Price, Hannibal, d. 1893.
De la réhabilitation de la race noire par la république d'Haïti, par Hannibal Price ... Port-au-Prince, J. Verrollot, 1900.
1 p. l., xvii, 736 p. 24½cm.

1. Haiti—Hist. 2. Negroes in Haiti. 3. Monogenism and polygenism.
3-32007
Library of Congress F1921.P94
[44d1]

Monselet, Charles, 1825-1888, ed.

Guadeloupe
M848
P13pa
1885

Privat d'Anglemont, Alexandre, d.ca. 1815-1859.
...Paris anecdote, avec une préface et des notes par Charles Monselet. Éd. illustrée de cinquante dessins à la plume par J. Belon, et d'un portrait de Privat d'Anglemont gravé à l'eauforte par R. de Los Rios. Paris, P. Rouquette, 1885.
2p. l., 278p., 1 l. front. (port.) illus. 25cm.

M370
M76p

Montgomery, Bishop Marteinne.
Parent-teacher cooperation, by Bishop Marteinne Montgomery ... Birmingham, Ala., Progressive publishing co., 1942, °1946.
xvi, 158 p. diagrs. 20½cm.
Imprint date, 1942, blotted out; "copyright 1946" stamped on t.-p.
Includes bibliographies.

1. Parents' and teachers' associations. 2. ~~Negroes~~—Education. I. Title.
46-7021
Library of Congress LC225.M6
[47c2] 371.103

Monographs on Negro education.

M370
C13m
No.1-5

Caliver, Ambrose, 1894–
Monographs on Negro education, by Ambrose Caliver.

p. 24cm.
Cover title.
no. 7, no. 8, no. 10, no. 17, no. 19

Monsieur Toussaint.

Martinique
M842.91
G49m

Glissant, Édouard, 1928–
Monsieur Toussaint; théâtre. Paris, Éditions du Seuil, 1961.

237p. 18½cm.

M210
M76a

Montgomery, Leroy Jeremiah
An analysis of two distinct religions: organized christianity and the religion of Jesus Christ. New York, New Voices Publishing Co., 1956.

32p. 21½cm.

1. Religion. 2. Christianity.

Basutoland Monono ke moholi ke mouoane.
M396
Se7m2

Segoete, Everitt Lechesa
Monono ke moholi ke mouoane. [Riches, their worthlessness] Morija, Basutoland, Morija Book Depot, 1948.

107p. 17½cm.
Written in Sotho.

Montage of a dream deferred.

M811.5
H87mo

Hughes, Langston, 1902–
Montage of a dream deferred [1st ed.] New York, Holt [c1951]

75p. 22cm.
In verse.

M323
M76n

Montgomery, Leroy Jeremiah
The Negro problem; its significance, strength and solution. New York, Island Press [1950]
87 p. 22 cm.

Race question
1. ~~Negroes.~~ I. Title.

E185.61.M7 325.260973 50-10696
Library of Congress [3]

Monopolies.

St. Lucia
M330
L58o

Lewis, William Arthur, 1915–
Overhead costs; some essays in economic analysis. London, G. Allen & Unwin [~~1949~~] 1951
200 p. diagrs. 23 cm. (The Library of economics. Sect. 2: New works, 3)
Bibliographical footnotes.

1. Cost. 2. Price policy. 3. Monopolies. I. Title. (Series)

HB221.L54 338.52 49-6466*
Library of Congress [55c½]

La montagne ensorcelée.

Haiti
M843.91
R76m

Roumain, Jacques, 1907-1945.
La montagne ensorcelée. Preface du Dr. Price, Mars. [Port-au-Prince, Haiti] Collection Indigene, 1931.

113p. 18cm.

M210
M76t

Montgomery, Leroy Jeremiah
Two distinct religions, Christanity and the religion of Jesus Christ, by Leroy Jeremiah Montgomery... Houston, Texas, Informer publishing company [n.d.]
69p. 17½cm.

1. Religion I. Title.

Montgomery, Ala.

M976.14
F46
Fields, Uriah J 1930–
The Montgomery story; the unhappy effects of the Montgomery bus boycott. [1st ed.] New York, Exposition Press [1959]
87 p. 21 cm.

1. Segregation in transportation—Montgomery, Ala. 2. Negroes—Montgomery, Ala. 3. Montgomery, Ala.—Race question. I. Title.

E185.89.T8F5 301.451 59–4227 ‡
Library of Congress [5]

Montgomery, Ala.

M323
K58s
King, Martin Luther.
Stride toward freedom; the Montgomery story. [1st ed.] New York, Harper [1958]
230 p. illus. 21 cm.

1. Segregation in transportation—Montgomery, Ala. 2. Negroes—Montgomery, Ala. 3. Montgomery, Ala.—Race question. I. Title.

E185.89.T8K5 *301.451 325.2609761 58–7099 ‡
Library of Congress [59d⁴30]

Montgomery, Ala.-Race question.

M976.14
F46
Fields, Uriah J 1930–
The Montgomery story; the unhappy effects of the Montgomery bus boycott. [1st ed.] New York, Exposition Press [1959]
87 p. 21 cm.

1. Segregation in transportation—Montgomery, Ala. 2. Negroes—Montgomery, Ala. 3. Montgomery, Ala.—Race question. I. Title.

E185.89.T8F5 301.451 59–4227 ‡
Library of Congress [5]

Montgomery, Ala. - Race question.

M323
K58s
King, Martin Luther.
Stride toward freedom; the Montgomery story. [1st ed.] New York, Harper [1958]
230 p. illus. 21 cm.

1. Segregation in transportation—Montgomery, Ala. 2. Negroes—Montgomery, Ala. 3. Montgomery, Ala.—Race question. I. Title.

E185.89.T8K5 *301.451 325.2609761 58–7099 ‡
Library of Congress [59d⁴30]

Montgomery, Ala. - Race question - Poetry.

M811.5
M83m
Morris, Joseph C
Montgomery on the march; a symbol, the bus boycott in Montgomery, Ala. and its meaning, 1955-1956. [New York] Joseph C. Morris, 1956.

9p. 13cm.

1. Poetry - Segration in transportation - Montgomery, Ala. 2. Montgomery, Ala. - Race question - Poetry. I. Title.

Montgomery on the march.

M811.5
M83m
Morris, Joseph C
Montgomery on the march; a symbol, the bus boycott in Montgomery, Ala. and its meaning, 1955-1956. [New York] Joseph C. Morris, 1956.

9p. 13cm.

1. Poetry - Segration in transportation- Montgomery, Ala. 2. Montgomery, Ala. - Race question - Poetry. I. Title.

The Montgomery story...

M976.14
F46
Fields, Uriah J 1930–
The Montgomery story; the unhappy effects of the Montgomery bus boycott. [1st ed.] New York, Exposition Press [1959]
87 p. 21 cm.

1. Segregation in transportation—Montgomery, Ala. 2. Negroes—Montgomery, Ala. 3. Montgomery, Ala.—Race question. I. Title.

E185.89.T8F5 301.451 59–4227 ‡
Library of Congress [5]

Monticello, Va.

MB9
J35
Jefferson, Isaac, b. 1775.
Memoirs of a Monticello slave, as dictated to Charles Campbell in the 1840's by Isaac, one of Thomas Jefferson's slaves. Edited by Rayford W. Logan. Charlottesville, Published by the University of Virginia Press for the Tracy W. McGregor Library, 1951.
45 p. port. 24 cm.
"Appeared simultaneously in the autumn 1951 William and Mary quarterly."
"Bibliographical note": p. 37–38.
1. Jefferson, Thomas, Pres. U. S., 1743–1826. 2. Monticello, Va. I. Campbell, Charles, 1807–1876. II. Virginia. University. Library. Tracy W. McGregor Library. III. Title.

E444.J4 923.173 51–13833
Library of Congress [52m5]

Monticello, Va.

MB9
J35
1951
Jefferson, Isaac, b. 1775.
Memoirs of a Monticello slave, as dictated to Charles Campbell in the 1840's by Isaac, one of Thomas Jefferson's slaves. Charlottesville, Published by the University of Virginia Press for the Tracy W. McGregor Library, 1951.

86p. port. 24cm.

Guinea

M896.3
M76n
Montrat, Maurice
N'Na ou la maman noire. [Versailles, Imprimerie Ch. Barbier] 1957.

56p. 18½cm.

I. Title.

South Africa
M968.1
M732
Montshiwa, Barolong chief, 1815-1896.
Molema, S M
Montshiwa, 1815–1896, Barolong chief and patriot [by] S. M. Molema. Cape Town, C. Struik, 1966.
233 p. illus., ports. 22 cm.

1. Montshiwa, Barolong chief, 1815–1896. 2. Bechuanaland—Hist.

DT795.M6M6 968'.1'040924 67-78802
Library of Congress [3]

M200
M77
Moon, Bertha Louise Hardwick
The bird on the limb. New York, Comet Press, 1959.

40p. 21cm.
Portrait of author on book jacket.

1. Religion. I. Title.

M810.8
M77p
Moon, Bucklin, 1911– ed.
Primer for white folks, edited by Bucklin Moon. Garden City, New York, Doubleday, Doran and co., inc., 1945.
xiv p., 1 l., 491 p. 21½ cm.
"First edition."

~~1. Negroes.~~ I. Title.

Library of Congress E185.5.M72 45–7185
[47q⁴5] 325.260973

M810.8
M77p
Moon, Bucklin, 1911– ed.
Primer for white folks. (card 2)

Partial contents: African culture, by W.E.B. DuBois. -The revolt of the evil fairies, by Ted Poston.- Slave on the block, by Langston Hughes. The ethics of living Jim Crow, by Richard Wright. Report from England, by Roi Ottley. Count us in, by Sterling A. Brown. -The truth about the Detroit riot, by Earl Brown. -The Negro comes of age in industry, by Robert C. Weaver. What shall we do about the south? by Langston Hughes. -Democracy is for the unafraid, by Chester B. Himes.

M324
M77b
Moon, Henry Lee, 1901–
Balance of power: the Negro vote. [1st ed.] Garden City, N. Y., Doubleday, 1948.
256 p. 22 cm.
Bibliographical footnotes. 192254

1. Negroes—Politics and suffrage. 2. Elections—U. S. I. Title.

JK2275.N4M6 324.15 48–6926*
Library of Congress [50d⁴15]

M323
So8
Moon, Henry Lee, 1901–
The Negro vote in the South, 1952.
The Southern Negro, 1952: Warning to Ike and the Dixiecrats, a special issue. New York, The Nation, 1952.

243-284p. illus. 29cm.
Special issue of The Nation, September 27, 1952.

Nigeria
M896.1
G25m
The moon cannot fight.
Gbadamosi, Bakare, jt. comp.
The moon cannot fight; Yoruba children's poems. Collected and translated by Ulli Beier and Bakare Gbadamosi. Illustrated by Georgina Betts. [Ibadan] Mbari Publications, [n.d.]

[44]p. illus. 20½cm.

Moon on a rainbow shawl.

Trinidad
M823
J61
John, Errol.
Moon on a rainbow shawl, a play in three acts. London, Faber and Faber [1958]
71 p. 22 cm.

I. Title.

A 59–6662
Rochester. Univ. Libr. for Library of Congress PR6019 [1]

MB9
M78a
Moore, Archie, 1916–
The Archie Moore story. [1st ed.] New York, McGraw-Hill [1960]
240 p. illus. 21 cm.
Portrait of author on book jacket.

I. Title.

Full name: Archie Lee Moore.

GV1132.M75A3 927.9683 60–12825 ‡
Library of Congress [20]

MB9
M78
Moore, Archie, 1916–
The Archie Moore story. ~~[1st ed.] New York, McGraw-Hill [1960]~~ London, Nicholas Kaye [1960]
240 p. illus. 21 cm.

I. Title.

GV1132.M75A3 927.9683 60–12825 ‡
Library of Congress [a64x2]

Liberia
M896.1
M78e
Moore, Bai Tamia, 1916–
Ebony dust. [n.p., 1963]

111p. 20½cm.

I. Title.

Nigeria
M966.9 Moore, E A Ajisafe
M782 The laws and customs of the Yoruba people. Abeokuta, Nigeria, M. A. Ola Fola Bookshops [n.d.]

85p. 18cm.

1. Nigeria - Native races. 2. Yorubas. I. Title.

Barbados
M301 Moore, Richard B
M78n The name "Negro," its origin and evil use. [1st ed.] New York, Afroamerican Publishers, 1960.

82 p. illus. 23 cm.
Portrait of author on book jacket.

1. Negroes—Names. I. Title.

E185.89.N3M6 301.451 60-50723 ‡

Library of Congress [2]

Basutoland
M896.3 Mopeli-Paulus, Attwell Sidwell, 1913-
M79b Blanket boy, by Peter Lanham [pseud.] Based on an original story by A. S. Mopeli-Paulus. New York, Crowell [1953.]

309p. 21cm.

I. Parker, Cecil John Lanham, 1899- II. Title.

M506 Moore, E W
N212 Address.

(In: National Negro Conference. Proceedings. New York, [1909] p.217-219)

M814.5 Moore, S Benjamin editor.
M78p ..."Poor Ben's choice pebbles, edited by S. Benj. Moore...Durham, N.C., The Moore Print, 1908.

28p. port. 20½cm.

1. Poetry. 2. Orations. I. Title.

Basutoland
M896.3 Mopeli-Paulus, Attwell Sidwell, 1913-
M79bL Blanket boy's moon, by Peter Lanham pseud. Based on an original story by A.S. Mopeli-Paulus. London, Collins, 1953.

320p. 21cm.

I. Parker, Cecil John Lanham, 1899- II. Title.

M301 Moore, Fred Henderson
M69 School desegregation.

Pp. 52-72.
In: Mitchell, Glenford E., ed. The angry black south. New York, Corinth Books, 1962.

M811.5 Moorer, Lizelia Augusta Jenkins.
M78 Prejudice unveiled, and other poems, by Lizelia Augusta Jenkins Moorer. Boston, Roxburgh publishing company, 1907.

170 p. front. (port.) 19cm.

I. Title. 1. Poetry.

Library of Congress PS3525.O582P7 1907 7—28034

Copyright A 178092 [a36b1]

Basutoland
M896.3 Mopeli-Paulus, Attwell Sidwell, 1913-
M79blu Blut hat hur eine farbe, roman (Blanket boy's moon), [by] Peter Lanham, nach einem Tatsachenbericht von A.S. Mopeli-Paulus. Munchen, R. Piper, 1953.

398p. 19cm.

I. Parker, Cecil John Lanham, 1899- II. Title.

M343.3 Moore, Harry T
N81b North, Joseph.
Behind the Florida bombings; Who killed NAACP leader Harry T. Moore and his wife. New York, New Century, 1952.

23p. 19cm.

MB9 Moorfield Storey. Memorial Exercises in Park St
St7 Street church, Boston, March 19, 1930. Boston, National Association for the Advancement of Colored People [1930]

vi, 37p. port. (front) 23cm.

Basutoland
M896.3 Mopeli-Paulus, Attwell Sidwell, 1913-
M79d Dekenjongen. Door Peter Lanham en A.S.Mopeli-Paulus, Stamhoofd van Basoetoland, Zuid-Afrika. Amsterdam, Uitgeverij Nieuwe Wieken [1952]

269p. 23cm.
Title: Blanket boy's moon.

I. Title. II. Parker, Cecil John Lanham, 1899-

M323 Moore, Harry T. p.267.
So8 The Southern Negro, 1952; Warning to Ike and the Dixiecrats, a special issue. New York, The Nation, 1952.

243-284p. illus. 29cm.
Special issue of The Nation, September 27, 1952.
Partial contents: -The Negro vote in the South, 1952, by Henry Lee Moon. -How far has southern labor advanced? by George S. Mitchell. -Democrats versus Dixiecrats, by Clarence Mitchell.

Moorish Science Temple, the Divine and National Movement of North America, Inc.
M290 Scott-Bey, R
Sc8 The door to God-Allah's kingdom is open, who will enter? Brooklyn, N.Y. Moorish Science Temple, the Divine and National Movement of North America, Inc., n.d.

6p. 22cm.

Basutoland
M896.1 Mopeli-Paulus, Attwell Sidwell, 1913-
M79 Ho Tsamaea ke ho bona. Lithothokiso. Morija, Basutoland, Sesuto Book Depot, 1945.

47p. 18cm.

1. Africa, South.

M974.8 Moore, Martha Edith (Bannister) 1910-
M78 Unmasked; the story of my life on both sides of the race barrier, by Martha B. Moore. [1st ed.] New York, Exposition Press [1964]

106 p. 21 cm.
Portrait of author on bookjacket.

1. Discrimination—Pittsburgh. 2. Pittsburgh. I. Title.

E185.97.M8A3 301.451 64-4395

Library of Congress [5]

M06 Moorland, Jesse Edward, 1863-1940.
Am3 ... The demand and the supply of increased efficiency in the negro ministry. By Jesse E. Moorland ... Washington, D. C., The Academy, 1909.
no. 13

14 p. 22cm. (Occasional papers, no. 13. American negro academy)

1. Negroes—Education. 2. Religious education. 3. Ministers.

10—2009

Library of Congress E185.5.A51 no. 13
——— Copy 2. E185.82.M82
[a42d1]

Basutoland
M896.3 Mopeli-Paulus, Attwell Sidwell, 1913-
M79t Turn to the dark, by A. S. Mopeli-Paulus & Miriam Basner. London, Cape [1956]

287 p. 21 cm.

I. Basner, Miriam, 1920- joint author. II. Title.

PZ4.M828Tu 57-27405 ‡

Library of Congress [8]

Moore, Peter Weddick.
MB Newbold, Nathan Carter, 1871- ed.
N42 Five North Carolina Negro educators; prepared under the direction of N.C. Newbold. Chapel Hill, The University of North Carolina press, 1939.

Xii, 142p. ports. 22cm.

Moorland, Jesse Edward, 1863-1940
M370. Hampton negro conference.
H18a Annual report, Hampton negro conference. no. 2-16; July 1898-1912. [Hampton, Va., Press of the Hampton normal and agricultural institute, 1898-1912]

15 v. in 5. illus. 22cm.

The report of the first conference, July 1897, is contained in v. 26, no. 9 (Sept. 1897) of the Southern workman.
Title varies: 1898-1901 (no. 2-5) Hampton negro conference.
1902-04 (no. 6-8) Proceedings of the Hampton negro conference.
1905-1912 (no. 9-16) ... Annual report, Hampton negro conference.
Imprint varies.
On cover of no. 9-16, The Hampton bulletin ...
No more published.
1. Negroes—Congresses.

Library of Congress E185.5.H23 4-19200 Revised
——— 2d set. [r35b2]

Congo(Leopoldville)
M967.5 Mopila, Francisco José, 1915-
M79 Memorias de un congolés; ensayo de auto-biografía. Madrid, Consejo Superior de Investigaciones Científicas, Instituto de Estudios Africanos, 1949-

v. illus., port. 24 cm.

1. Congo, Belgian—Soc. life & cust.

DT663.M6A3 52-22604

Library of Congress [8]

Haiti
M972.94
M79e

Moral, Paul
L'economie Haitienne; publié sous les auspices de la cour supérieure des comptes. Port-au-Prince, Imprimerie de l'Etat, 1959.

190p. 23½cm.

1. Haiti - Economic conditions.

Moral and social conditions.

M267.3
Ar7

Arthur, George Robert, 1879–
Life on the Negro frontier; a study of the objectives and the success of the activities promoted in the Young men's Christian associations operating in "Rosenwald" buildings [by] George R. Arthur. New York, Association press, 1934.

viii, 259 p. plates, maps. 19½cm.

1. Young men's Christian associations (Colored) 2. Rosenwald, Julius, 1862–1932. 3. Julius Rosenwald fund. 4. Negroes—Moral and social conditions. I. Title.

35–27187

Library of Congress BV1190.A7
——— Copy 2.
Copyright A 84475 [5-5] 267.3650973

M306
At6
no.2

Moral and social conditions.
Atlanta University. Conference for the Study of Problems Concerning Negro City Life.
Social and physical condition of Negroes in cities; Report of an investigation under the direction of Atlanta University: and Proceedings of the second Conference for the Study of Problems Concerning Negro City Life, held at Atlanta University, May 25-26, 1897. Atlanta, Atlanta University Press, 1897.

72, 14p. incl. tables. 22½cm.

Moral and social conditions.

M370
B64e

Bond, Horace Mann, 1904–
The education of the Negro in the American social order, by Horace Mann Bond ... New York, Prentice-Hall, inc., 1934.

xx, 501 p. illus. (maps) diagrs. 21cm.
Bibliography: p. [465]–481.

1. Negroes—Education. 2. Negroes—Moral and social conditions. I. Title.

34–33611

Library of Congress LC2801.B65
[45v2] 371.9740973

M378
B81s

Moral and social conditions.
Brown, Ina Corinne, 1896–
Socio-economic approach to educational problems, by Ina Corinne Brown, with an introduction by Fred J. Kelly. Washington, U.S. Govt. Print. Off., 1942.

xii, 166p. maps, tables, diagrs.
(U.S. Office of Education. Misc ellaneous no.6)
At head of title: National survey of the higher education of Negroes, v.1.

M370
C12m
no.2

Moral and social conditions.
Caliver, Ambrose, 1894–
... A background study of Negro college students, by Ambrose Caliver, senior specialist in the education of Negroes, Office of education ... Washington, U.S. Govt. print. off., 1933.
vii, 132 p. incl. tables, diagrs. 23cm. (U. S. Office of education. Bulletin, 1933, no. 8)
At head of title: United States Department of the interior. Harold L. Ickes, secretary. Office of education. William John Cooper, commissioner.
Bibliography: p. 116–117.
1. Negroes—Education. 2. Personnel service in education. 3. Negroes—Moral and social conditions. I. Title. II. Title: Negro college students.

E 33–1322

U. S. Off. of educ. Library L111.A6 1933 no. 8
——— Copy 2. LC2801.C32
for Library of Congress L111.A6 1933 no. 8
——— Copy 2. LC2801.C23
[a38t1] (370.6173) 371.9740973

M323
C38o

Moral and social conditions.
Charles, Charles V
Optimism and frustration in the American Negro. Reprinted from the Psychoanalytic review, 29:270-299, July, 1942.

270-299p. 24cm. (Psychogenetic studies in race psychology, no.6)

Moral and social conditions.

M370
C89

Cuthbert, Marion Vera, 1896–
Education and marginality; a study of the Negro woman college graduate, by Marion Vera Cuthbert ... New York city, 1942.

xviii, 167 p. incl. tables. 24cm.
Thesis (PH. D.)—Columbia university, 1942.
Vita.
Bibliography: p. 161–166.

1. Women, Negro. 2. Education of women—U. S. 3. Negroes—Education. 4. Negroes—Moral and social conditions. I. Title.

A 42–5388

Columbia univ. Libraries for Library of Congress LC2781.C8
[44e2]† 376.873

Moral and social conditions.

M323
D29c

Davis, Allison, 1902–
Children of bondage; the personality development of Negro youth in the urban South, by Allison Davis and John Dollard, prepared for the American youth commission. Washington, D. C., American council on education, 1940.

xxviii, 299, [1] p., 1 l. diagrs. 23½cm.
Illustration mounted on cover.

1. Negroes—Moral and social conditions. 2. Personality. 3. Social psychology. I. *Dollard, John, 1900– joint author. II. American council on education. American youth commission. III. Title.

[Full name: William Allison Davis]

40–13685

Library of Congress E185.86.D38
[a45r41j³10] 325.260975

M323
D291a

Moral and social conditions.
Davis, Robert E
The American Negro's dilemma; the Negro's self-imposed predicament. New York, Philosophical Library [1954]

147 p. 22 cm.

1. Negroes—Econ. condit. 2. Negroes—Moral and social conditions. I. Title.

E185.6.D35 54–13471 ‡
*301.451 325.260973

Library of Congress [10]

Moral and social conditions.

M323
D77

Doyle, Bertram Wilbur, 1897–
The etiquette of race relations in the South; a study in social control, by Bertram Wilbur Doyle ... Chicago, Ill., The University of Chicago press [°1937]

xxv, 249 p. 22 cm.
Bibliography: p. 173–190.

1. Negroes. 2. U. S.—Race question. 3. Negroes—Moral and social conditions. 4. Slavery in the U. S. I. Title. II. Title: Race relations in the South.

37–20152

Library of Congress E185.61.D764
[39u4] 325.260975

M306
At6
no.14

Moral and social conditions.
Du Bois, William Edward Burghardt, 1868– ed.
Efforts for Social betterment among Negro Americans; Report of a social study made by Atlanta University under the patronage of the trustees of the John F. Slater Fund; together with the Proceedings of the 14th annual Conference for the Study of the Negro Problems, held at Atlanta University on Tuesday, May the 24th, 1909. Ed. by W.E. Burghardt Du Bois. Atlanta, Atlanta University Press, 1909.

136p. 22cm. (Atlanta University publications no. 14)

M301
D85.3r7

Moral and social conditions.
Du Bois, William Edward Burghardt, 1868–
The revelation of Saint Orgne the damned, by W. E. Burghardt Du Bois. Commencement, 1938, Fisk university. [Nashville, Hemphill press [°1939]

16 p. 23cm.
Copy number: 64
Autographed: W.E.B DuBois

1. Negroes—Education. 2. Negroes—Moral and social conditions. I. Title.

39–8222

Library of Congress E185.6.D795
——— Copy 2.
Copyright A 126710 [2] 325.26

Moral and social conditions.

M370
Ev2c

Everett, Faye Philip, *ed.*
The colored situation; a book of vocational and civic guidance for the Negro youth, by Faye Philip Everett ... Boston, Meador publishing company, 1936.

312 p. illus. (ports.) 20½cm.
On cover: The colored situation [by] Faye P. Everett & others.
"Articles and books written by Dr. A. B. Jackson": p. 242–243.

1. Negroes—Employment. 2. Profession, Choice of. 3. Negroes—Moral and social conditions. I. Title. II. Title: Vocational and civic guidance for the Negro youth.

36–9272

Library of Congress E185.8.E94
[4212] [371.425] 325.260973

M301
F86f

Moral and social conditions.
Frazier, Edward Franklin, 1894–
The free Negro family; a study of family origins before the civil war, by E. Franklin Frazier ... Nashville, Tenn., Fisk university press, 1932.

5 p. l., 75 p. illus. (maps) 24 cm. (*Half-title:* Fisk university social science series)
"Selected bibliography": p. 73–75.

1. Negroes. 2. Freedmen. 3. Mulattoes. 4. Negroes—Moral and social conditions. 5. Slavery in the U. S.—Emancipation. I. Title.

32–14425

Library of Congress E185.F88
[41f1] 325.26

M301
F86nf3

Moral and social conditions.
Frazier, Edward Franklin, 1894–
The Negro family in Chicago, by E. Franklin Frazier ... Chicago, Ill., The University of Chicago press [°1932]

xxv, 294 p. incl. maps, diagrs. 20cm. (*Half-title:* The University of Chicago sociological series)
"Selected bibliography": p. 277–286.

1. Negroes—Chicago. 2. Negroes—Moral and social conditions. I. Title.

32–2328

Library of Congress F548.9.N3F8
[45q1] 325.26097731

M301
F86nf5
1951

Moral and social conditions.
Frazier, Edward Franklin, 1894–
The Negro family in the United States. Rev. and abridged ed. New York, Dryden Press, ~~1948~~ 1951.
~~xxxi, 372~~ 372p. 22 cm. (The Dryden Press sociology publications)
Bibliographical footnotes.
Reprint of the 1948 rev. & abr. ed.

1. Negroes—Moral and social conditions. 2. Family. I. Title.

E185.86.F74 1948 325.260973 48–7000*

Library of Congress [54b²1]

M301
F86nf5

Moral and social conditions.
Frazier, Edward Franklin, 1894–
The Negro family in the United States, by E. Franklin Frazier ... Chicago, Ill., The University of Chicago press [1939]

xxxii, 686 p. incl. illus., tables, diagrs. 20 cm. (*Half-title:* The University of Chicago sociological series)
"A classified bibliography": p. 641–669.

1. Negroes—Moral and social conditions. 2. Family. I. Title.

39–20651

Library of Congress E185.86.F74
[47k²2] 325.260973

M301
F86ni

Moral and social conditions.
Frazier, Edward Franklin, 1894–
The Negro in the United States. New York, Macmillan Co., 1949.

xxxi, 767p. illus. maps. 22cm.
"A clasified bibliography" :p.707-750.

M301
F86ny

Moral and social conditions.
Frazier, Edward Franklin, 1894–
Negro youth at the crossways, their personality development in the middle states, by E. Franklin Frazier; prepared for the American youth commission. Washington, D. C., American council on education, 1940.

xxiii, 301, [2] p. illus. (maps) diagr. 23½ cm.
"This volume ... describes the experiences of Negro boys and girls living in Washington, D. C., and Louisville, Kentucky; these communities were selected as examples of middle-area conditions."—Pref.

1. Negroes—Moral and social conditions. 2. Youth. 3. Personality. 4. Social psychology. 5. Negroes—District of Columbia. 6. Negroes—Louisville, Ky. I. American council on education. American youth commission. II. Title.

40–32764

Library of Congress E185.6.F74
[42z²7] 325.2609753

M973
F95

Moral and social conditions.
Fuller, Thomas Oscar, 1867–
Pictorial history of the American Negro, by Thomas O. Fuller; a story of progress and development along social, political, economic, educational and spiritual lines. Memphis, Tenn., Pictorial history, inc., 1933.

xxiii, 375 p. col. front., illus. (incl. ports., maps) 28½cm.
Bibliography: p. 361–363.

1. Negroes 2. Negroes — Education. 3. Negroes — Moral and social conditions. 4. Negroes—Biog. I. Title.

33–17135

Library of Congress E185.F97
[43o1] 325.260973

Moral and social conditions.

M331 G82n

Greene, Lorenzo Johnston, 1899–
The Negro wage earner, by Lorenzo J. Greene and Carter G. Woodson. Washington, D. C., The Association for the study of Negro life and history, inc. [°1930]
xiii p., 1 l., 388 p. incl. tables, diagrs. 22½ᶜᵐ.
Bibliography: p. [369]–380.

1. Negroes—Employment. 2. Negroes—Moral and social conditions. I. Woodson, Carter Godwin, 1875– II. Association for the study of Negro life and history, inc. III. Title.

31—493

Library of Congress E185.8.G79 [44r37z1] 325.26

Moral and social conditions.

M301 J63ne2

Johnson, Charles Spurgeon, 1893–
The Negro college graduate, by Charles S. Johnson ... Chapel Hill, The University of North Carolina press, 1938.
xvii, 399 p. incl. tables, diagrs. maps (part fold.) 23½ᶜᵐ.
Bibliography: p. 378–384.

1. Negroes—Education. 2. Negroes—Moral and social conditions. 3. Universities and colleges—U. S. I. Title.

38—9887

Library of Congress LC2781.J6
———— Copy 2.
Copyright A 116318 [40w5] 371.9740973

Moral and social conditions.

M331.833 P92

President's conference on home building and home ownership, *Washington, D. C.,* 1931.
Negro housing; report of the Committee on Negro housing, Nannie H. Burroughs, chairman; prepared for the committee by Charles S. Johnson; edited by John M. Gries and James Ford. Washington, D. C., The President's conference on home building and home ownership [°1932]
xiv, 282 p. front., plates. 23½ᶜᵐ.
On cover: Physical aspects; social and economic factors; home ownership and financing.

(Continued on next card)

32—26908

[48t2]

Moral and social conditions.

M331 H14

Hall, Egerton E 1886–
The Negro wage earner of New Jersey; a study of occupational trends in New Jersey, of the effect of unequal racial distribution in the occupations and of the implications for education and guidance. By Egerton E. Hall, ED. D. New Brunswick, Rutgers university, School of education [°1935]
115 p. 2 maps (incl. front.) diagrs. 23½ᶜᵐ.
Bibliography: p. 114–115.

1. Negroes—New Jersey. 2. Negroes—Employment. 3. Negroes—Education. 4. Negroes—Moral and social conditions. I. Title.

35—2951

Library of Congress E185.93.N54H3
———— Copy 2.
Copyright A 79060 [a41f1] 325.2600749

Moral and social conditions.

M323 J632n

Johnson, James Weldon, 1871–1938.
Negro Americans, what now? By James Weldon Johnson. New York, The Viking press, 1934.
viii, 103 p. 19½ᶜᵐ.

1. Negroes. 2. U. S.—Race question. 3. Negroes—Civil rights. 4. Negroes—Moral and social conditions. I. Title.

34—35660

Library of Congress E185.61.J69 [44g²2] 325.260973

Moral and social conditions.

M301 R271

Reid, Ira DeAugustine, 1901–
In a minor key; Negro youth in story and fact, by Ira DeA. Reid; prepared for the American youth commission. Washington, D. C., American council on education, 1940.
8 p. l., 3–134 p., 1 l. diagrs. 26ᶜᵐ.
"Authorities for the facts": p. [121]–134.

1. Negroes—Moral and social conditions. 2. Negroes—Education. I. American council on education. American youth commission. II. Title. III. Title: Negro youth in story and fact.

40—10435

Library of Congress E185.6.R45 [10] 325.260973

Moral and social conditions.

M06 J61 no.19

Hammond, *Mrs.* Lily (Hardy) 1859–
Southern women and racial adjustment, by L. H. Hammond. [Lynchburg, Va., J. P. Bell company, inc., printers] 1917.
32 p. 23½ᶜᵐ. (*On cover:* The trustees of the John F. Slater fund. Occasional papers, no. 19)

1. Negroes—Moral and social conditions. I. Title.

17—27879

Library of Congress E185.5.J65 no. 19 [40b1]

Moral and social conditions.

M331.833 J71

Jones, William Henry, 1896–
The housing of negroes in Washington, D. C.; a study in human ecology, by William Henry Jones ... Washington, D. C., Howard university press, 1929.
191 p. incl. front. (port.) plates, maps, diagrs., form. 22ᶜᵐ.
"An investigation made under the auspices of the Interracial committee of the Washington federation of churches."
Bibliography: p. [157]–158.

1. Negroes—District of Columbia. 2. Negroes—Moral and social conditions. 3. Housing—Washington, D. C. I. Washington federation of churches. Interracial committee. II. Title.

29—22528

Library of Congress E185.93.D6J6 [41i1]

Moral and social conditions.

M362.7 Sa5

Sanders, Wiley Britton, 1898– *ed.*
Negro child welfare in North Carolina, a Rosenwald study, directed by Wiley Britton Sanders ... under the joint auspices of the North Carolina State board of charities and public welfare and the School of public welfare, the University of North Carolina. Chapel Hill, Pub. for the North Carolina State board of charities and public welfare by the University of North Carolina press, 1933.
xiv p., 2 l., [3]–326 p. 24ᶜᵐ.
1. Negroes—North Carolina. 2. Negroes—Moral and social conditions. 3. Charities—North Carolina. 4. Children—Charities, protection, etc.—North Carolina. 5. Juvenile delinquency—North Carolina. 6. Social surveys I. North Carolina. State board of charities and public welfare. II. North Carolina. University. School of public welfare. III. Title.

33—18906

Library of Congress E185.93.S27 [45t1] 325.2609756

Moral and social conditions.

M331 H335n

Haywood, Harry, 1898–
Negro liberation. New York, International Publishers [1948]
245 p. map. 22 cm.
"Reference notes": p. [219]–230.

1. Negroes—Econ. condit. 2. Negroes—Moral and social conditions. 3. Land tenure—Southern States. I. Title.

E185.6.H43 325.260973 48–8881*

Library of Congress [15]

Moral and social conditions.

M975.3 J71

Jones, William Henry, 1896–
Recreation and amusement among Negroes in Washington, D. C.; a sociological analysis of the Negro in an urban environment, by William H. Jones ... Washington, D. C., Howard university press, 1927.
4 p. l., xi–xv, 17–216 p. plates (1 fold.) map, diagr. 21½ cm. (*Half-title:* Howard university studies in urban sociology)
Bibliography: p. 203–207.

1. Negroes—District of Columbia. 2. Washington, D. C.—Amusements. 3. Negroes—Moral and social conditions. I. Title.

27—24235

Library of Congress E185.93.D6J7 [3]

Moral and social conditions.

M323 St4

Stemons, James Samuel.
As victim to victims; an American Negro laments with Jews, by James Samuel Stemons. New York, Fortuny's [°1941]
268 p. 22½ᶜᵐ.
"First edition."

1. Negroes—Moral and social conditions. 2. Jewish question. 3. Race problems. I. Title. II. Title: An American Negro laments with Jews.

41—9105

Library of Congress E185.61.S8 [42d2] 325.260973

Moral and social conditions.

MB9 H358

Hedgeman, Anna (Arnold)
The trumpet sounds; a memoir of Negro leadership. [1st ed.] New York, Holt, Rinehart and Winston [1964]
202 p. 22 cm.
Portrait of author on book jacket.

1. Negroes—Civil rights. 2. Negroes—Moral and social conditions. I. Title.

E185.97.H44 323.4 64–21938

Library of Congress [7–1]

Moral and social conditions.

M301 L326

Larkins, John Rodman.
Alcohol and the Negro: explosive issues, by John R. Larkins. Zebulon, N. C., Record Pub. Co., 1965.
xi, 251 p. illus. 24 cm.
Includes bibliographical references.

1. Alcohol and negroes. 2. Negroes—Moral and social conditions. I. Title.

E185.86.L36 309.173 65–28614

Library of Congress [5]

Moral and social conditions.

M378 Un3na

U. S. *Office of education.*
National survey of the higher education of Negroes ... Federal security agency, Paul V. McNutt, administrator. U. S. Office of education, John W. Studebaker, commissioner. Washington, U. S. Govt. print. off., 1942–43.
4 v. maps, tables, diagrs. 29 x 23 cm. (*Its* Miscellaneous, no. 6)
CONTENTS.—[I] Socio-economic approach to educational problems, by Ina C. Brown, with an introduction by F. J. Kelly.—[II] General studies of colleges for Negroes.—[III] Intensive study of selected colleges for Negroes, by L. E. Blauch and M. D. Jenkins. IV. A summary, by Ambrose Caliver.

(Continued on next card)

E 42–362 rev

[r45v²7]†

Moral and social conditions.

MB9 L63hu

Hubert, James Henry, 1885–
The life of Abraham Lincoln, its significance to Negroes and Jews; an address delivered before Gad lodge, no. 11, Free sons of Israel, February 15, 1939, by James H. Hubert ... with an introduction by Dr. William Heard Kilpatrick ... and an extract from the presidential address on the test of American democracy delivered before the sixty-fifth annual session of the National conference of social work, by Dr. Solomon Lowenstein ... New York, N. Y., W. Malliet and company, 1939.
22 p. 23ᶜᵐ.
1. Lincoln, Abraham, pres. U. S., 1809–1865. 2. U. S.—Race question. 3. Negroes—Moral and social conditions. I. Lowenstein, Solomon, 1877–

40–34518 Revised

Library of Congress E457.2.H87 [r43e2] 923.173

Moral and social conditions.

M792 M694

Mitchell, Loften.
Black drama; the story of the American Negro in the theatre. [1st ed.] New York, Hawthorn Books [1967]
248 p. illus., ports. 24 cm.

1. Negroes in literature. 2. Theater—U. S. 3. Negroes—Moral and social conditions. I. Title.

PS338.N4M5 792'.0973 66–22313

Library of Congress [5]

Moral and social conditions.

M323 W37

Weatherford, Willis Duke, 1875–
Race relations; adjustment of whites and Negroes in the United States, by Willis D. Weatherford ... and Charles S. Johnson ... Boston, New York [etc.] D. C. Heath and company [°1934]
x, 590 p. 22½ cm. (*On cover:* Social relations series)
Bibliography: p. 556–576.

1. Negroes. 2. U. S.—Race question. 3. Negroes—Moral and social conditions. 4. Slavery in the U. S. I. Johnson, Charles Spurgeon, 1893– joint author. II. Title.

34—36788

Library of Congress E185.W42 [40h²3] 325.260973

Moral and social conditions.

M323.1 J35o

Jefferson, Thomas Le Roy, 1867–
The old Negro and the new Negro, by T. Le Roy Jefferson, M. D. Boston, Meador publishing company, 1937.
118 p. 20½ᶜᵐ.

1. Negroes—Moral and social conditions. I. Title.

37—38290

Library of Congress E185.86.J45 [42f1] 325.260973

Moral and social conditions.

M973.8 P38u

Penn, Irvine Garland, 1867– *ed.*
The united negro: his problems and his progress, containing the addresses and proceedings the Negro young people's Christian and educational congress, held August 6–11, 1902; introduction by Bishop W. J. Gaines ... edited by Prof. I. Garland Penn ... Prof. J. W. E. Bowen ... Atlanta, Ga., D. E. Luther publishing co., 1902.
xxx, 600 p. illus., plates, ports. 21ᶜᵐ.

1. Negroes—Moral and social conditions. 2. Negroes—Religion. I. Bowen, John Wesley Edward, 1855– joint ed. II. Title.

3—1805

Library of Congress E185.5.P41 [a45e1]

Moral and social conditions.

M370. W58c

Whiting, Helen Adele (Johnson) 1885–
Climbing the economic ladder. [Atlanta, 1948]
100 p. illus. 23 cm.
Cover title.
"Selected references for understanding and improving Southern life": p. 90–100.

1. Negroes—Econ. condit. 2. Negroes—Moral and social conditions. 3. Negroes—Education. I. Title.

E185.8.W48 325.260975 49–601*

Library of Congress [7]

Moral and social conditions.

M323 W67 **Williams, Frances Harriet.**
The business girl looks at the Negro world, a study course, by Frances Harriet Williams ... New York, The Womans press, 1937.
3 p. l., 55 p. illus. (maps) 21½cm.

1. Negroes—Moral and social conditions. 2. Negroes—Stat. 3. U. S.—Race question. I. Title.
37—4315
Library of Congress E185.61.W73
[42d1] 325.260973

Moral and social conditions.

M323.4 Y87 **Young, Whitney M**
To be equal [by] Whitney M. Young, Jr. [1st ed.] New York, McGraw-Hill [1964]
254 p. 22 cm.

1. Negroes—Civil rights. 2. Negroes—Moral and social conditions. I. Title.
E185.61.Y73 323.41 64-23179
Library of Congress [7-1]

Morale.

M350 Y08m **Young, Charles, 1864–1922.**
Military morale of nations and races, by Charles Young ... Kansas City, Mo., Franklin Hudson publishing co., 1912.
273 p. 22½cm.
Bibliography: p. [7]

1. National characteristics. 2. Ethnopsychology. 3. Soldiers. 4. Morale. I. Title.
14—8826
Library of Congress U21.Y6
[a41b1]

Moral and social conditions.

M973 W86m **Woodson, Carter Godwin, 1875– ed.**
The mind of the Negro as reflected in letters written during the crisis, 1800–1860, edited by Carter G. Woodson ... Washington, D. C., The Association for the study of Negro life and history, inc. [°1926]
5 p. l., v–xxxii, 672 p. 24cm.

1. Negroes. 2. Negroes—Moral and social conditions. 3. Slavery in the U. S.—Emancipation. I. Association for the study of Negro life and history, inc. II. Title.
26—14304
Library of Congress E185.W8877
[45m1]

Moral and social conditions - Pictorial works.

M301 R676 **Williamson, Stanford Winfield.**
With grief acquainted. Photographs: James Stricklin, Don Sparks [and] Jerry Cogbill. Chicago, Follett Pub. Co. [1964]
127 p. illus., port. 29 cm.
Portrait of author in book.

1. ~~Negroes~~—Moral and social conditions—Pictorial works. I. Stricklin, James, illus. II. Title.
E185.86.W5 301.451 64-21580
Library of Congress [5]

Cuba
M365 R618 Morales Rodríquez, René, 1923-
Dos cruces (Two crosses). La Habana, 1958.
xx, iii, 332p. 22cm.
Autographed.

1. Prisoners - Personal narratives - Cuba. I. Title.

Moral and social conditions.

M973 W86m **Woodson, Carter Godwin, 1875–**
The mis-education of the Negro, by Carter Godwin Woodson. Washington, D. C., The Associated publishers, inc. [°1933]
xiv p., 1 l., 207 p. 19 cm.

1. Negroes—Education. 2. Negroes—Moral and social conditions. 3. Negroes—Employment. I. Title.
33—3606
Library of Congress E185.82.W86
[45i1] 371.974

Moral behavior and the Christian ideal.

M171.1 W98 **Wynn, Daniel Webster, 1919–**
Moral behavior and the Christian ideal; an explanation of Christian ethics for the layman in our time. [1st ed.] New York, American Press [°1961]
123 p. 22 cm.

1. Christian ethics. I. Title.
BJ1261.W9 171.1 61-9470 ‡
Library of Congress [5]

West Indies
M808.8 H839 Morand, Florette
The umbrella lady. Translated by Merloyd Lawrence.
Pp. 179-183.
In: Howes, Barbara, ed. From the green Antilles. New York, Macmillan, 1966.

Moral and social conditions.

M973 W86np **Woodson, Carter Godwin, 1875–**
The Negro professional man and the community, with special emphasis on the physician and the lawyer, by Carter Godwin Woodson. Washington, D. C., The Association for the study of Negro life and history, inc. [°1934]
1 p. l., v–xviii, 365 p. diagr. 23½cm.
"[This study forms] a part of the effort of the Association for the study of Negro life and history to portray the social and economic conditions obtaining among Negroes in the United States since the civil war."—Foreword.
1. Negroes—Employment. 2. Negroes—Moral and social conditions. 3. Negro physicians. 4. Negro lawyers. I. Association for the study of Negro life and history, inc. II. Title.
34—10066
Library of Congress E185.82.W88
[34f5] 325.260973

Moral conditions.

M309 P949 **Provost, C Antonio, 1910–**
The birth of the modern renaissance (and the rise of the U. S. A.) by C. Antonio Provost. Illus. [by] Art Henkel. [1st ed.] New York, Pageant Press [1965–
v. illus. 21 cm.
Bibliographical footnotes.

1. U. S.—Moral conditions. 2. U. S.—Soc. condit. I. Title.
HN65.P7 309.173 65-29725
Library of Congress [2]

M740 D74 **Morand, Paul, 1888–**
... Black magic; translated from the French by Hamish Miles; illustrated by Aaron Douglas. New York, The Viking press, 1929.
vi p., 3 l., 3–218 p. plates. 21½cm.
A group of stories on the modern Negro.
Walter White assisted the author.

1. ~~Negro race.~~ I. ~~Miles, Hamish, 1894–~~ White, Walter tr. II. Douglas, Aaron, 1898– illus. III. Title.
29—10406
Library of Congress GN645.M68
[42e1]

Moral and social conditions.

M973 W86r **Woodson, Carter Godwin, 1875–**
The rural Negro, by Carter Godwin Woodson. Washington, D. C., The Association for the study of Negro life and history, inc. [°1930]
xvi p., 1 l., 265 p. illus. (incl. map) 22cm.
"Another by-product of the three-year survey of the social and economic conditions of the Negroes of the United States since the civil war ... undertaken by the Association for the study of Negro life and history in 1926."—Introd.
1. Negroes—Moral and social conditions. 2. Negroes—Employment. 3. Sociology, Rural. 4. Country life—U. S. I. Association for the study of Negro life and history, inc. II. Title.
30—21077
Library of Congress E185.86.W896
[43u²2] 325.26

Moral education.

M362.7 G158 **Gantt, Christopher H 1899–**
Juvenile delinquency and its primary cause, by Christopher H. Gantt. [1st ed.] New York, American Press [1964]
24 p. 21 cm.

1. Juvenile delinquency. 2. Moral education. I. Title.
HV9069.G3 64-16191
Library of Congress [5]

M287.8 M79 **Morant, John J , 1882–**
Mississippi minister. [1st ed.] New York, Vantage Press [1958]
80 p. illus. 21 cm.

1. African Methodist Episcopal Church—Hist. I. Title.
2. Biography.
BX8443.M6 922.773 57-11254 ‡
Library of Congress [2]

Moral and social conditions.

M323 W879 **Woofter, Thomas Jackson, 1893– ed.**
Negro problems in cities; a study made under the direction of T. J. Woofter, jr. Garden City, N. Y., Doubleday, Doran & company, inc. [°1928]
xiii p., 2 l., 17–284 p. illus. (maps) diagrs., form. 19½cm.
"The Institute of social and religious research ... is responsible for this publication."
CONTENTS.—pt. 1. Neighborhoods, by T. J. Woofter, jr.—pt. 2. Housing, by Madge Headley.—pt. 3. Schools, by W. A. Daniel.—pt. 4. Recreation, by H. J. McGuinn.
1. Negroes—Moral and social conditions. I. Headley, Madge. II. Daniel, William Andrew, 1895– III. McGuinn, Henry J. IV. Institute of social and religious research. V. Title.
28—8612
Library of Congress E185.86.W91
——— Copy 2.
Copyright A 1069386 [40x2]

M323 F63c Moral Reform League of the United States American Citizens.
Fletcher, Otis Gaus.
Colored Americans ask for a good name, and for an investigation of dictionaries and encyclopedias published and circulated in the United States of America with a view to delete evil designed names. Lexington, Kentucky, The author, 1946.
32p. port. 19cm.
Autographed.

Haiti
M841 M79a Moravia, Charles, 1875-1938, tr.
Autres poèmes de Henri Heine mis en vers français d'après la traduction de Gérard de Nerval; précédés d'un supplément à l'intermezzo. New York, The Haytian library [1918].
xvi, 92, 76p. 18½cm. (Bibliothèque Haitienne Charles Moravia)
Bound with: Heine, Heinrich, L'intermezzo ... d'apres la traduction de Gerard de Nerval. 1917.
(Tracings - over)

Moral and social conditions.

M813.5 W93t **Wright, Richard, 1909–**
12 million black voices; a folk history of the Negro in the United States; text by Richard Wright, photo-direction by Edwin Rosskam. New York, The Viking press, 1941.
152 p. illus. 26cm.
"First published in October 1941."

1. Negroes—Moral and social conditions. I. *Rosskam, Edwin, 1903– II. Title.
[Full name: Richard Nathaniel Wright]
41—25589
Library of Congress E185.6.W9
[45n2] 325.260973

The moral significance of the XVth amendment.

M287.8 P29m Payne, Daniel Alexander, 1811-1893.
The moral significance of the XVth amendment. Xenia, Ohio, Printed by the Xenia Gazette company, 1870.
8p. 21½cm.

Haiti
M841 M79c **Moravia, Charles, 1876–1938.**
... La Crête-à-Pierrot, poème dramatique en trois tableaux et en vers, représenté pour la première fois sur le théâtre du Petit séminaire-collège St-Martial de Port-au-Prince, le samedi, 13 avril 1907. Port-au-Prince, Imprimerie J. Verrollot, 1908.
xi p., 1 l., 80 p. 24cm.
At head of title: Bibliothèque haïtienne ...

I. Title. 1. Haitian poetry.
25-20869
Library of Congress PQ3949.M6C7

Haiti
M842
M79f

Moravia, Charles, 1876-1928.
...Le fils du tapissier (episode de la vie de Moliére) Poéme dramatique en un acte et en vers, représenté pour la première fois sur la scène de variétés la 7 mars 1922.
viii, 37p. 19cm.

1. Haitian drama. I. Title.

Haiti
M841
M79r

Moravia, Charles, 1876-1938.
... Roses et camélias, poésies par Charles Moravia. Port-au-Prince, Impr. Madame F. Smith, 1903.
3 p. l., 127, [1] p. 16cm.
At head of title: Bibliothèque haitienne.

I. Title. 1. Haitian poetry
Library of Congress PQ3949.M6R6 1903 26-3538
——— Copy 2.
With this are bound: Heine, H. L'intermezzo. 1917. Copy 2, and Heine, H. Autres poèmes. 1918. Copy 4.

More cuties in arms.
M741
C15c
Campbell, Elmer Simms, 1906-
More cuties in arms, by E. Simms Campbell. Philadelphia, David McKay company [c1943]
94 unnumb. p. illus. 19cm.

More Liberian tales.
Liberia
M398
F87
Freeman, Edwin O K
More Liberian tales. London, Sheldon Press, 1941.
69p. 18cm.

1. Tales, African. I. Title.

More missing pages: a book of poems.
Jamaica
M821.91
M165mo
McFarland, Harry Stanley, 1900-
More missing pages: a book of poems. New York, Carlton Press, 1966.
56p. 21cm.

I. Title.

More powerful than the a-bomb.
M815.5
B88m
Bunche, Ralph Johnson, 1904-
More powerful than the a-bomb. American Association for the United Nations [195]
[4]p. 28cm.
Reprinted from the Progressive, but originally adapted from a speech presented at the World Affairs Institute at the University of Denver.

More stories of life.
Kenya
M896.3
In7m
Inoti, F M
More stories of life. London, Sheldon Press, 1949.
15p. illus. 17cm. (African home library)

I. Title.

More than once.
Nigeria
M896.3
Ag95m
Agunwa, Clement, 1933-
More than once: a novel. London, Longmans, 1967.
[7], 211 p. 20½ cm. 21/-
(B 67-9223)

I. Title.
PZ4.A28Mo 67-88831
Library of Congress [3]

Moreau de St. Méry, Médéric Louis Elie, 1750-1819.
Haiti
M972.94
R13re
1791
Raimond, Julien, 1743?-1802?
Reponse aux considerations de M. Moreau, dit Saint-Méry, député à l'assemblée nationale, sur les colonies; par M. Raymond, citoyen de couleur de Saint-Domingue ... A Paris, De l'Imprimerie de Patriote François, 1791.
68p. 20½cm.

Morehouse college, Atlanta.
M378M
B73
Brawley, Benjamin Griffith, 1882-
History of Morehouse college, written on the authority of the Board of trustees, by Benjamin Brawley ... Atlanta, Ga., Morehouse college, 1917.
218 p. incl. front. plates, ports. 19cm.

1. Morehouse college, Atlanta. 17-6218
Library of Congress LC2851.M72B7
——— Copy 2.
Copyright A 457114

Morehouse College, Atlanta Ga.
M378At
At6
The Atlanta University system; Atlanta University, Morehouse College, Spelman College, The Atlanta University School of Social Work. n.p., 1939.
1 fold. l, 7 columns.
Originally published in the City builder, August 1934.

Los morenos.
Argentina
M982
L29
[Lanuza, José Luis] comp.
Los morenos ... Buenos Aires, Emecé [1942]
2 p. l., 7-95, [1] p. plates. 18cm. (Colección Buen aire. [No. 10])
"Selección de José Luis Lanuza."

1. Negroes in Argentine republic. I. Title.
A 43-1800
Harvard univ. Library for Library of Congress F3021.N3L3
[2] † 325.260982

M616
M82
Morgan, E Gates
Studies of the obsorption, distribution and excretion of magnamycin. New York, Harlem Hospital Bulletin, 1953.
84-88p. tables 23cm.
Reprinted from the Harlem Hospital Bulletin, September 1953.

1. Antibiotics.

M811.5
M82p.
Morgan, James H , 1916-
Poems by candelight and the flare of a match. New York, Vantage Press, 1967.
152p. 22cm.
Portrait of author on book jacket.

I. Title.

Morgan's daughter.
Jamaica
M823.91
D37m
De Lisser, Herbert George, 1878-1944.
Morgan's daughter. London, Ernest Benn [1961]
255p. 17½cm.

I. Title.

Morgue guide; a manual of embalming.
M393
P61
Pierce, Samuel Henry, 1913-
Morgue guide; a manual of embalming. [Atlanta?] °1954.
94 p. illus. 23 cm.

1. Embalming. I. Title.
RA623.P5 55-15209 ‡
Library of Congress [2]

Haiti
M841
M82f
Morisseau, Roland
5 poèmes de reconnaissance. Port-au-Prince, Imprimerie Theodore, 1961.
29p. 18½cm.
Portrait of author on back of book.

1. Poetry, Haitian. 2. Haiti-Poetry. I. Title.

Haiti
M841
M82c
Morisseau, Roland
Clef du soleil. [Port-au-Prince] Editions Les Araignees du Soir, 1963.
Folder([5]p.) 19½cm. (Collection Haiti literataire)
Printed on verso of Philoctete, Rene Promesse. [Port-au-Prince] 1963.
Poem.

I. Title. 1. Haitian poetry.

Haiti
M841
M82g
Morisseau, Roland
Germination d'espoir. Illustration de Ti-Ga. Port-au-Prince, Imprimerie N.A. Theodore, 1962.
42p. 18½cm. (Collection Haiti Litteraire)

1. Haitian poetry. I. Title.

Haiti
M842
M81
Morisseau-Leroy, Felix, 1912-
Antigone en creole. Pétion-Ville, Haiti. Culture, 1953.
74 p. 21cm.

1. Title - Antigone.

Haiti
M972.9
M819d
Morisseau-Leroy, Felix, 1912-
...Le destin des Caraïbes. El destin del Caribe. Port-au-Prince, Haiti [Imprimerie Telhomme] 1941.
1p. l., [1], 6-107, [1]p. 21cm.
French and Spanish on opposite pages, numbered in duplicate.
"Traduction espagnole de Miguel Sangenis."
"La première ... [de ce] travail ... a été
over

Haiti
M841
M83d
Morisseau-Leroy, Felix, 1912-
Diacoute. [Port-au-Prince, Henri Deschamps, 19]
30p. 21cm.
1. Haitian poetry
I. Title

Moron, Alonzo G
Salutation to the new president for Hampton Institute, p. 115.
M371.974
T87n
Tuskegee Institute.
The new south and higher education: what are the implications for higher education of the changing socio-economic conditions of the south? A symposium and ceremonies held in connection with the inauguration of Luther Hilton Foster, fourth president of Tuskegee Institute [October 31 and November 1, 1953. Tuskegee, Ala.] Dept. of Records and Research, Tuskegee Institute, 1954.
x, 145p. map. 24cm.

Haiti
M844
M82
Morpeau, Marie, -1949.
[Letters]
Morpeau, Hélène M
Pages de Marie et d'Helene. Port-au-Prince, Les Presses Libres, 1954.
XIV, 219p. illus. 22cm. (Collection du tricinquantenaire.)

Haiti
M841
M83n
Morisseau-Leroy, Felix, 1912-
Natif-natal, un conte en vers. Port-au-Prince, Editions Haitiennes [1948]
61p. 22cm.
1. Haitian poetry. I. Title.

Haiti
M972.94
M82c
Morpeau, Emmanuel
Contre la revision de la constitution, par Emmanuel Morpeau. Cayes, Haiti, Imprimerie Bonnefil, 1914.
46p. 21cm.
1. Haitian constitution. I. La "Dessalinienne" [poem] bound in.

Haiti
M972.94
M821
no.2
Morpeau, M[oravia]
Discours prononcé par M. M. Morpeau, avocat senateur de la republique a la séance de constitution du senat, en date du 21 avril 1914. Port-au-Prince, Imprimerie Edmond Chenet, 1914.
8p. 24½cm.
1. Haiti - History.

Haiti
M843.91
M83r
Morisseau-Leroy, Felix, 1912-
Recolte, Port-au-Prince, Les Editions Haitiennes, 1946.
146p. 20cm.
1. Haitian fiction. I. Title.

Haiti
M972.94
M82h
Morpeau, Emmanuel
Haiti au point de vue critique. Port-au-Prince, Haiti, Imprimerie Aug. A. Heraux, 1915.
42p. 23cm.
1. Haiti.

Haiti
M972.94
M821i
Morpeau[Moravia]
Instruction pour tous. Conference sur Toussaint Louverture, prononcée en 1921 au théatre cinématographique aux Gonaives et a Parisiana au Port-au-Prince, Imp. V. Pierre-Noël[1922]
42p. 25cm.
1. Toussaint Louverture, Pierre Dominque, 1746-1803

A morning at the office.
Brit. Guiana
M823.91
M69m2
Mittelhölzer, Edgar.
A morning at the office, a novel. London, Hogarth Press, 1950.
246 p. 19 cm.
I. Title.
PZ3.M6977Mn 50-26028
Library of Congress

Haiti
M844
M82
Morpeau, Hélène M
Pages de Marie et d'Helene. Port-au-Prince, Les Presses Libres, 1954.
XIV, 219p. illus. 22cm. (Collection du tricinquantenaire)
I. Morpeau, Marie, -1949. II. Title.
[Letters]
1. Women - Haitian. 2. Haiti.

Haiti
M972.94
M82d
[Morpeau, Moravia] ed.
Documents inedits pour l'histoire. Correspondance concernant l'emprisonnement et la mort de Toussaint Louverture. Procesverbal de l'autopsie de son cadavre au Fort de Jouv (Jura) France et rapport des médecin et chirurg en memoire du commissaire Julien Raymond sur la colonie de Saint-Domingue au premier consul Bonaparte publiés par M. Morpeau. Port-au-Prince, Imprimerie et Librairie dor Sacre Coeur, 1920.
16p. 23cm.
1.Haiti. 2.Toussaint Louverture, Pierre Dominique, 1746-1803. 3.Raymond, Julien.

Morning glories.
M811.4
H35m
Heard, Josephine D. (Henderson), 1861-
Morning glories, by Josephine D. (Henderson) Heard, Philadelphia, Penna. March 17, 1890.
108p. port. 18cm.

Haiti
M841.08
M82a
Morpeau, Louis, 1895- *comp.*
... Anthologie d'un siècle de poésie haïtienne, 1817-1925, avec une étude sur la muse haïtienne d'expression française et une étude sur la muse haïtienne d'expression créole. Les morceaux choisis de chaque auteur sont précédés de notices bibliographiques, critiques et biographiques. Preface de M. Fortunat Strowski ... Paris, Bossard, 1925.
xvi, 273 p., 1 l. 19ᶜᵐ.
"Bibliographie": p. [31]-32.
1. Haitian poetry ~~(French)~~ 2. ~~French poetry—Haitian authors~~ I. Title.
Library of Congress PQ3946.M6 26-23023
[a44c1]

Haiti
M972.94
M821e
Morpeau[Moravia]
L'exposition nationale et l'avenir d'Haiti, par M. Morpeau...Port-au-Prince, Imprimerie Vve J. Chenet, 1897.
16p. 21½cm.
1. Haiti-Exposition.

A morning in Trinidad.
Brit. Guiana
M823.91
M69m3
Mittelhölzer, Edgar.
A morning in Trinidad. [1st ed.] Garden City, N. Y., Doubleday, 1950.
250 p. 21 cm.
A novel.
I. Title.
PZ3.M6977Mo 50-7594
Library of Congress

Haiti
M840.9
M82a
Morpeau, Louis
Anthologie haitienne des poètes contemporains (1904-1920) comprenant les poetes qui ont continué ou commencé d'écrire après 1904... Port-au-Prince, Haiti, Imprimerie Aug. A. Heraux, 1920.
iii, 237p. 20cm.
Autographed copy.
1. Haitian literature.

Haiti
M972.94
M821p
Morpeau [Moravia]
Pro Patria, par M. Morpeau...2d ed. Port-au-Prince, Imprimerie H. Amblard, 1908.
59p. 22½cm.
1. Haiti

Morning songs.
M811.5
T37 1h
Thompson, Aaron Belford.
Morning songs. By Aaron Belford Thompson. Rossmoyne, O., The author, 1899.
82 p., 1 l. port. 18ᶜᵐ.
I. Title.
0-77 Revised
Library of Congress PS3539.H63M6 1899
Copyright 1899: 70950

Haiti
M972.94
M821p
Morpeau, Louis.
Pages de jeunesse et de foi. Port-au-Prince, Imprimerie du Sacré Coeur, 1919.
106p. 20cm.
1. Haiti-Education.

Haiti
M972.94
M821r
no.1
Morpeau, M[oravia]
...La résolution-Morpeau... 2nd ed. Port-au-Prince, Imp. V. Pierre - Noel, 1923.
12p. 23cm.
1. Haiti - History

Haiti
M972.94 Morpeau, M[oravia]
M821 Simples considérations patriotiques par
no.3 Me M. Morpeau avocat, suivies du discours
de l'auteur au centenaire de J.J. Dessalines.
Premier fascicule. Cayes, Imprimerie Bonnefil,
1908.

10p. 21cm.

1. Haiti-History

Morpeau, Moravia, ed.
Haiti
M972.94 **Haiti** (*Republic*) *Laws, statutes, etc.*
H12c ... Code de procédure civile annoté avec commentaires, jurisprudence et formules, par M. Morpeau ... Port-au-Prince,
1909 Imprimerie de l'Abeille, 1909–
v. 21cm. (Les codes haitiens)
Cover of v. 1 dated 1910.

1. Civil procedure — Haiti. 2. Forms (Law) — Haiti. [2. Forms — Haiti] I. Morpeau, Moravia, ed. II. Title.

31-14026

Library of Congress [3]

Haiti Morpeau, Moravia.
M520 Tippenhauer, Louis Gentil, 1867-
T49pr La préconnaissance du futur; interview
relative a la decouv rte de la loi du temps.
Port-au-Prince, Fondation Internationale de
Meterologie de Prt-au-Prince, 1950.

32p. illus. 23cm.
Interview de Pierre Moraviah Morpeau avec
... Docteur Louis Geatil Tippenhauer.

M304 Morris, Charles S.
P19 The nation and the Negro. [lacks imprint]
v.4, no.14 24p. 21cm.

1. Politics.
I. Douglass, Frederick. Letter to C.S.
Morris from Port-au-Prince, Jan. 30, 1891

Morris, Colin, 1930-
Northern Rhodesia
M968.94
K16 Kaunda, Kenneth, 1924-
Black government; a discussion between Colin
Morris and Kenneth Kaunda. Lusaka, Northern
Rhodesia, United Society for Christian
Literature, 1960.

116p. ports. 22cm.
Biographies included.

Zambia Morris, Colin M., 1930
M960 **Kaunda, Kenneth David,** *Pres., Zambia, 1924–*
F16 A humanist in Africa: letters to Colin M. Morris from Kenneth D. Kaunda. London, Longmans, 1966.
3–136 p. 20½ cm. 16/-

(B 66-10714)

1. Nationalism — Africa — Addresses, essays, lectures. 2. Pan-Africanism—Addresses, essays, lectures. I. Morris, Colin M. II. Title.

DT963.6.K3A45 320.15808 66-76308

Library of Congress [3]

M813.5 **Morris, Earl J**
M83 The cop, a novel. New York, Exposition Press [1951]
126 p. 22 cm.

I. Title.

PZ4.M877Co 51-2763

Library of Congress [2]

Uganda
M896.1 **Morris, Henry F** *ed.*
M83 The heroic recitations of the Bahima of Ankole, by H. F. Morris. With a foreword by A. T. Hatto. Oxford, Clarendon Press, 1964.
xii, 142, [1] p. illus., geneal. table, maps. 23 cm. (Oxford library of African literature)
Based on thesis, University of London in 1957, under the title: The heroic recitations of the Banyankore.
In part, English or Runyankore.
Bibliography: p. [143]

1. Epic poetry, Nyankole. 2. Bahima (African people) 3. Nyankole language. I. Title.

PL8594.N3M6 896.3 64-5119

Library of Congress [3]

M811.5 **Morris, James Cliftonne.**
M83c Cleopatra, and other poems. [1st ed.] New York, Exposition Press [1955]
64 p. 21 cm.

I. Title.

PS3525.O7455C6 811.5 55-12131 ‡

Library of Congress [2]

M818 **Morris, James Cliftonne.**
M832 From a tin-mouth god to his brass-eared subjects: "A is for aphorism," by James C. Morris. New York, Greenwich Book Publishers [1966]
141 p. 21 cm.
Portrait of author on book jacket.

I. Title.

PS3525.O7455F7 66-20518

Library of Congress [3]

M811.5 Morris, Joseph C
M83m Montgomery on the march; a symbol, the
bus boycott in Montgomery, Ala. and its
meaning, 1955-1956. [New York] Joseph C.
Morris, 1956.

9p. 13cm.

1. Poetry - Segration in transportation-
Montgomery, Ala. 2. Montgomery, Ala. - Race
question - Poetry. I. Title.

Africa
M323 Morris, Mervyn
T139 Feeling, affection, respect.

Pp. 5-26.

In: Tajeil, Henri, ed. Disappointed
guests. London, Oxford University Press,
1965.

Morris, Mildred, ed.
M09 **Harrison, Juanita.**
H24m My great, wide, beautiful world, by Juanita Harrison; arranged and prefaced by Mildred Morris. New York, The Macmillan company, 1936.
xii p., 1 l., 318 p. 20½cm.
"Condensed version first appeared in the 1935 autumn numbers of the Atlantic monthly."—Pref.

1. Voyages and travels. I. Morris, Mildred, ed. II. Title.

Library of Congress G463.H33 36—27252
[43i2] 910.4

Morris, Samuel, 1873-1893.
M89 **Masa, Jorge O.**
M83m The angel in ebony; or, The life and message of Sammy Morris, by Jorge O. Masa; published by class of 1928 of Taylor university. Upland, Ind., Taylor university press [1928]
131 p. front., plates, ports. 17½cm.

1. Morris, Samuel, 1873-1893. I. Title.

29-3768

Library of Congress E185.97.M86
——— Copy 2.
Copyright A 2861 [2]

M808.81 Morris, Tina, ed.
M83 Victims of our fear. [Blackburn, Eng.]
Screeches Publication, n.d.

[36]p. 25½cm.
Mimeographed.
White editor.

1. Poetry. I. Title.

M975 **Morris, Willie,** *ed.*
M834 The South today, 100 years after Appomattox. [1st ed.] New York, Harper & Row [1965]
ix, 149 p. 22 cm.
Most of these essays, now rev. and extended, originally appeared in a supplement to the April 1965 issue of Harper's magazine.
Partial contents.- Georgia boy goes home,
by Louis E. Lomax.- A vanishing era, by Whitney
M. Young.- Why I returned, by Arna Bontemps.

1. Southern States — Race question. 2. Southern States — Soc. condit. I. Harper's magazine. Supplement. II. Title.

E185.61.M95 301.45196075 65-21004

Library of Congress [8]

M910 **Morris, Wilson Major,** 1884-
M83 Africa, the great continent. New York, North River Press [1954]
80 p. illus. 26 cm.

1. Africa, South—Descr. & trav. 2. Liberia—Descr. & trav. I. Title.

DT626.M62 916.86 54-4420 ‡

Library of Congress [5]

M220.95 **Morrisey, Richard Alburtus,** 1865–
M83 Colored people in Bible history, by Rev. R. A. Morrisey ... Hammond, Ind., Printed for the author by W. B. Conkey company, 1925.
133 p. front. (port.) plates. 19½cm.
Earlier editions published under title: Bible history of the negro.

1. Negro-race. I. Title.

26-2304

Library of Congress HT1589.M75
——— Copy 2.
Copyright A 875992 [2]

M301 Morrison, Allan
Eb74 The White power structure
Pp. 129-140

In: Ebony. The white problem in America.
Chicago, Johnson Pub. Co., 1966.

M815.5 Morrison, Elizabeth (Jenkins)
M82t There is something within; a series of
talks given before religious, educational
and parents' groups, by E. J. Morrison,
assisted by Mr. and Mrs. H. Holliday.
Detroit, Harlo Press, 1964.

126p. 20½cm.
Picture of author on book jacket.

I. Title.

W. Indies
M823 Morrison, Hugh Panton
C23 Home is the hunter.

(In: Caribbean anthology of short stories...
Kingston, Jamaica, Pioneer Press 1953.)
19cm. pp. 134-146.)

M811.5
M83d
Morrison, William Lorenzo.
Dark rhapsody; poems by William Lorenzo Morrison. New York, H. Harrison [1945]
62 p. 20½cm.
I. Title. 1. Poetry.
46-796
Library of Congress PS3525.O7504D3
[3] 811.5

M973.92
M83
Morrow, Everett Frederic, 1909–
Black man in the White House; a diary of the Eisenhower years by the administrative officer for special projects, the White House, 1955–1961. New York, Coward-McCann [1963]
306 p. 22 cm.
1. U. S.—Pol. & govt.—1953–1961. 2. Negroes—Civil rights. 3. Presidents—U. S.—Staff. 4. Eisenhower, Dwight David, Pres. U. S., 1890– I. Title.
E835.M58 323.40973 63—13310 ‡
Library of Congress [64f14]

M815.5
M83d
Morse, Leonard F
The dawn of tomorrow, by Rev. Leonard F. Morse... Delivered at Emancipation Celebration, Yorktown Baptist church, Plateau, Alabama, Monday evening, January 1, 1923
27p. plate. 16½cm.
1. Orations. I. Title

La mort de Chaka.
Mali
96.2
B14m
Badian, Seydou
La mort de Chaka; piéce en cinq tableaux. Paris, Présence Africaine, 1961.
59p. 22½cm.

Mortality.
M306
At6
no.1
Atlanta University. Conference for the Investigations of City Problems.
Mortality among Negroes in cities; Proceedings of the Conference for the Investigations of City Problems, held at Atlanta University, May 26-27, 1896. Ed. by Thomas N. Chase. Atlanta, Atlanta University Press, 1903.
51p. 22½cm. (Atlanta University publications, no.1)

Mortality.
M304
P19
v.3,no.5
Nathan, Winfred Bertram.
... Health conditions in North Harlem, 1923–1927, by Winfred B. Nathan ... an abstract, by Mary V. Dempsey. New York, National tuberculosis association [°1932]
68 p. incl. maps. 23cm. ([National tuberculosis association] Social research series. no. 2)
The death rates were revised on the basis of the 1930 census population figures. *cf.* Foreword.
"This study is ... largely a study of negro health."—Introd.
1. Harlem, New York (City)—Sanit. affairs. 2. Negroes—New York (City) 3. Negroes—Mortality. 4. Negroes—Statistics, Vital. 5. New York (City)—Statistics, Vital. 6. Health surveys. I. Dempsey, Mary V., ed. II. Title.
32—21088
Library of Congress RA448.H3N3
[42d1] 614.097471

Mortality among Negroes in cities.
M306
At6
no.1
Atlanta University. Conference for the Investigations of City Problems.
Mortality among Negroes in cities; Proceedings of the Conference for the Investigations of City Problems, held at Atlanta University, May 26-27, 1896. Ed. by Thomas N. Chase. Atlanta, Atlanta University Press, 1903.
51p. 22½cm. (Atlanta University publications, no.1)

M780
G47
Morton, Ferdinand Joseph, 1885-1941.
A discourse on jazz.
Pp. 30-33.
In: Gleason, Ralph J., ed. Jam session. New York, Putnam [1958]

M780
G47
Morton, Ferdinand Joseph, 1885-1941.
A New Orleans funeral.
Pp. 27-29.
In: Gleason, Ralph J., ed. Jam session. New York, Putnam [1958]

M370
M83f
Morton, Lena Beatrice
Farewell to the public schools, I'm glad we met. Boston, Meador Publishing Company, 1952.
223 p. 21cm.
1. Public schools. I. Title

M191
M846
Morton, Lena Beatrice.
Man under stress. New York, Philosophical Library [1960]
129 p. 22 cm.
Includes bibliography.
1. Philosophy. 2. Religion. I. Title.
B56.M65 101 60-13638 ‡
Library of Congress [5]

MB9
M846
Morton, Lena Beatrice.
My first sixty years: passion for wisdom. New York, Philosophical Library [1965]
175 p. port. 22 cm.
1. Negro teachers—Correspondence, reminiscences, etc. I. Title.
LC2731.M6 923.773 65-11951
Library of Congress [3]

M811.09
M84
Morton, Lena Beatrice.
Negro poetry in America, by Lena Beatrice Morton. Boston, Mass., The Stratford company, 1925.
4 p. l., 71 p. illus. (music) 16cm.
"The tragedy": p. 37–71.
Bibliography: p. 36; "References used": p. 71.
1. Negro poetry (American)—Hist. & crit. 2. Tragedy. I. Title.
25—15782
Library of Congress PS310.N4M6
——— Copy 2.
Copyright A 861050 [41g1]

Morua Delgado, Martin, -1910.
M972.91
C16a
Canales Carozo, Juan
Amarguras y realidades recopilación de datos relativos à la labor del ilustre Cubano desaparecido Martin Morua Delgado como literato, como constituyente, en la asamblea, como legislador en el senador y como politica. Habana, Imp. O'Reilly num. 11, 1910.
291p. port. 21½cm.
1. Cuba--Politics. 2. Morua Delgado, Martin, -1910.

Mosaic templars.
M366.7
B96h
Bush, A E
History of the mosaic templars of America - its founders and officials, edited by A. E. Bush and P. L. Dorman. Little Rock, Central printing company, 1924.
291p. front. plates. 19½cm.

British Guiana
M823.91
C18g2
Moscow is not my mecca.
Carew, Jan Rynveld, 1923-
Moscow is not my mecca. London, Secker & Warburg [1964]
192p. 20cm.
American ed. (New York, Stein and Day) has title: Green winter.
I. Title.

MB
M85s
Moseley, J H 1882–
Sixty years in Congress and twenty-eight out. [1st ed.] New York, Vantage Press [1960]
99 p. illus. 22 cm.
1. Legislators—U. S. 2. Negroes—Biog. I. Title.
JK1021.M75 923.273 60-3728 ‡
Library of Congress [2]

Moseley, J H p. 93-97.
M378A1
D29p
Davis, Walker Milan, 1908-
Pushing forward; a history of Alcorn A. & M. college and portraits of some of its successful graduates, by W. Milan Davis... Okolona, Miss., The Okolona industrial school, 1938.
x, 124 p. illus. (incl. ports.) 23½cm.

M331.833
P92r
Moses, Earl R
Study of economic and social factors in housing conditions among Negroes in Chicago with special reference to juvenile delinquency. Prepared for President's Conference on Home Building and Home Ownership.
(In: President's Conference on Home Building and Home Ownership. Report, part II. Washington, D. C. Comm. on Negro Housing, 1931. 27cm. 71p.)
1. Housing--Chicago.

M252
M85f
Moses, William Henry, 1872-
Five commandments of Jesus, Matthew 5: 21-48... Study daily each in the light of all by W.H. Moses.
162p. 16cm.
1. Sermons.
I. Title.

M270
M85w
Moses, William Henry, 1872-
The white peril, by W. H. Moses... [Philadelphia, Pa., Lisle - Carey press, 1919]
xxxii, 260p. 19cm.
1. Baptists. 2. Religion - History.
I Title

Moses—Fiction.

M810
H94mo

Hurston, Zora Neale.
Moses, man of the mountain, by Zora Neale Hurston. Philadelphia, New York [etc.] J. B. Lippincott company [°1939]
351 p. 22cm.
"First edition."

1. Moses—Fiction. I. Title.

39-30582

Library of Congress PZ3.H945Mo
——— Copy 2.
Copyright A 134029 [15]

Moses: a story of the Nile.

M811.4
H23m

Harper, Frances Ellen Watkins, b. 1825.
Moses: a story of the Nile, by Mrs. F.E.W. Harper. Second edition. Philadelphia, Merrihew and son, 1869.
47p. 15cm.

Moses, man of the mountain,

M810
H94mo

Hurston, Zora Neale.
Moses, man of the mountain, by Zora Neale Hurston. Philadelphia, New York [etc.] J. B. Lippincott company [°1939]
351 p. 22cm.
"First edition."

1. Moses—Fiction. I. Title.

39-30582

Library of Congress PZ3.H945Mo
——— Copy 2.
Copyright A 134029 [15]

Basutoland
M896.1
B45L

Moshesh, 1790-1870.
Bereng, David Cranmer Theko.
Lithothokiso tsa Moshoeshoe le tse ling [by] David Cranmer Theko Bereng. Morija, Sesuto Book Depot, 1931.
114 p. 19 cm.

Moshesh, 1790-1870.

Basutoland
M896.2
K52m

Khaketla, B Makalo
Moshoeshoe le baruti. E ngotsoe ke B. Makalo Khaketla... Morija, Basutoland, Morija Sesuto Book depot, 1947.
xi, 95p. 18½cm.

Moshesh, 1790-1870.

S.Africa
M39
L55m

Leoatle, Edward Motsamai.
Morena Moshoeshoe mor'a Mokhachande, Ka Edward Motsamai Leoatle Morija, Sesuto Book Depot, 1942.
iv, 84p. front. 18cm.

Moshoeshoe.

Africa
M896.1
D24a

Darlow, D J
African heroes - Ntsikana, Tshaka, Khama, Moshoeshoe. Poems, by D.J. Darlow. [Lovedale S.A.] Lovedale press [n.d.]
75p. illus. 21½cm.

Moss, Frank, 1860- comp.

M974.7
C49

Citizens' protective league, *New York*.
Story of the riot, pub. by the Citizens' protective league. [New York, 1900]
cover-title, 79 p., 1 l. 22½cm.
"Persecution of negroes by roughs and policemen, in the city of New York, August, 1900. Statement and proofs written and compiled by Frank Moss and issued by the Citizens' protective league."

1. New York (City)—Riot, August, 1900. 2. Negroes—New York (City) I. Moss, Frank, 1860- comp. II. Title.

5-42437

Library of Congress F128.9.N3C6
[a39b1]

Haiti
MB9
T64m

Mossell, Charles W
Toussaint L'Ouverture, the hero of Saint Domingo, soldier statesman, martyr; or, Hayti's struggle, triumph, independence, and achievements. By Rev. C. W. Mossell ... Lockport, N. Y., Ward & Cobb, 1896.
2 p. l., [vii]-xxx, [31]-485, x p. front., illus., plates, ports., fold. map. 23 cm.
The work includes (p. [31]-319) without acknowledgment, a translation of Thomas Prosper Gragnon-Lacoste's Toussaint Louverture. Paris, 1877.

1. Toussaint Louverture, Pierre Dominique, 1746-1803. 2. Haiti—Hist.—Revolution, 1791-1804. 3. Haiti—Hist.—1804- I. Gragnon-Lacoste, Thomas Prosper, b. 1820.

1-6703

Library of Congress F1923.T80
[33e1]

MB
M85

Mossell, Gertrude E H Bustill, 1855-
The work of the Afro-American woman, by Mrs. N.F. Mossell. Philadelphia, Geo. S. Ferguson company, 1894.
178p. front. 17½cm.
1. Biography. I. Title

Mossi (African people)

Upper Volta
M966.25
D59e

Dim Delobsom, A A.
... L'empire du mogho-naba; coutumes des Mossi de la Haute-Volta. Préface de Robert Randau. Paris, Les éditions Domat-Montchrestien, 1932.
3 p. l., vii, 303 p. front., plates, ports., map. 25½cm. (Institut de droit comparé. Études de sociologie et d'ethnologie juridiques ... xi)
Cover dated 1933.

1. Mossi (African people) 2. Customary law—Upper Volta. 3. Ethnology—Upper Volta. I. Title.

33-19717

Library of Congress [3]

U. S.
M966.1
Sk34

Mossi (African people).
Skinner, Elliott Percival, 1927-
The Mossi of the Upper Volta; the political development of a Sudanese people. Stanford, Calif., Stanford University Press, 1964.
ix, 236 p. illus., map. 24 cm.
Bibliography: p. [225]-227.

1. Mossi (African people) I. Title.

GN655.M6S55 916.61 64—12074

Library of Congress [a64c2]

U. S.
M966.1
Sk34

The Mossi of the Upper Volta.
Skinner, Elliott Percival, 1927-
The Mossi of the Upper Volta; the political development of a Sudanese people. Stanford, Calif., Stanford University Press, 1964.
ix, 236 p. illus., map. 24 cm.
Bibliography: p. [225]-227.

1. Mossi (African people) I. Title.

GN655.M6S55 916.61 64—12074

Library of Congress [a64c2]

M811.5
M87n

Most, Marty
New Orleans blues. Photography by the author. [n.p., 1964]
88p. illus., ports. 21cm.

I. Title.

Bechuanaland
M896.2
R119m

Mot 5 wasele II.
Raditladi, L D
Mot 5 wasele II. [2d ed.] Johannesburg, Witwatersrand University Press, 1954.
65p. 17cm. (The Bantu treasury, ed. by D. T. Cole)
Written in Tswana.

Jamaica
M821.91
M35m

The moth and the star.
Marson, Una M 1905-
The moth and the star. Kingston Jamaica, B.W.I., Published by the author, 1937.
xv, 103p. 21cm.
Autographed by the author

"Mother"...

M811.5
G78m

Graves, Linwood D.
"Mother", also "the hidden flower... by Linwood D. Graves. Big Stone Gap, Va., The author, n.d.
4 unnumb. p. 21½cm.

A motif for living and other sermons.

M252
Se89

Sewell, George A.
A motif for living and other sermons. New York, Vantage Press [1963.
66p. 21cm.

Motion pictures.

M814.5
W93u

Writers' congress, *University of California at Los Angeles*, 1943.
Writers' congress; the proceedings of the conference held in October 1943 under the sponsorship of the Hollywood writers' mobilization and the University of California. Published in coöperation with the Writers' congress continuations committee of the Hollywood writers' mobilization. Berkeley and Los Angeles, University of California press, 1944.
xx, 663 p. incl. front. (facsim.) 23cm.

1. Authors. 2. World war, 1939- —Addresses, sermons, etc. I. Hollywood writers' mobilization. II. California. University. University at Los Angeles.

A 44-8435

California. Univ. Libr. for Library of Congress [12]

Basutoland
M896
M85

Motlamello, Paulus.
Ngaka ea Mosotho [Lacks imprint] 1937.
160 p. 15 cm.
Concerning Sotho doctor.

M813.5
M851

Motley, Willard, 1912-1965
Let no man write my epitaph. New York, Random House [1958]
467 p. 22 cm.

I. Title.

PZ3.M8573Le 58—7667 ‡

Library of Congress [58f5]

M813.5
M851
Motley, Willard, 1912- 1965
Let no man write my epitaph. London, Longmans, 1958.
404p. 20½cm.
I. Title.

M813.5
M85Le
Motley, Willard, 1912-1965.
Let noon be fair, a novel. New York, Putnam [1966]
416 p. 22 cm.
I. Title.
PZ3.M8578Lg 65-20682
Library of Congress

M813.5
M85kl
Motley, Willard, 1912-1965
Klop maar op'n deur. Geautoriseerde vertaling van Hans De Vries. Den Haag, Ad. M. C. Stok, n.d.
581p. 19cm.
Title: Knock on any door.
I. Title.

M813.5
M85k
1950
Motley, Willard, 1912- 1965
Knock on any door. New York, The American Library, 1950.
512p. 18cm. (A Signet Book)
I. Title.

M813.5
M85k
1948
Motley, Williard, 1912-1965
...Knock on any door. London, Collins, 1948]
479p. 18cm. (Fontana books)
Pocket book edition.
I. Title.

M813.5
M85k
1947
Motley, Willard, 1912-1965
Knock on any door. New York, The New American Library, 1947.
607p. 18cm. (A Signet Book)
Portrait of author on book cover on back.
I. Title.

M813.5
M85w
Motley, Williard, 1912- 1965
We fished all night. New York, New American Library, 1953.
598p. 18cm. (Signet books)
Pocket book edition.
I. Title.

M813.5
M85w
Motley, Willard, 1912-1965
We fished all night. New York, Appleton-Century-Crofts [1951]
560 p. 22 cm.
I. Title.
PZ3.M8578We 51-14180
Library of Congress

MB9
M85m
Moton, Robert Russa, 1867-1940.
Finding a way out; an autobiography, by Robert Russa Moton. Garden City, New York, Doubleday, Page & company, 1920.
ix, 295, [1] p. 21cm.
I. Title.
Library of Congress E185.97.M9 20—10075
[a42j1]

MB9
J71j
Moton, Robert Russa, 1867-1940.
My faith.
Johnson, Charles Spurgeon
Eugene Kinckle Jones (A Negro leader's contribution to racial adjustment).
(In: Northern Baptist Convention. Board of Education. The road to brotherhood. New York, Baptist Board of Education, 1924. 19½cm. p. 57-67).

M306
Am35
Moton, Robert Russa, 1867-1940.
Organized Negro effort for racial progress.
(In: American Academy of Political and Social Science, Philadelphia. The American Negro. Philadelphia, 1928. 24cm. p. 257-263.

M323.1
M85s
Moton, Robert Russa, 1867-1940.
Some elements necessary to race development [an address delivered at the Tuskegee Commencement, May 1912] Hampton, Press of the Hampton Normal and Agricultural Institute, 1913.
22p. 13cm.
"Reprinted from the Southern workman for July, 1912."
1. Race question. I. Title.

M323.1
M85
Moton, Robert Russa, 1867-1940.
What the Negro thinks, by Robert Russa Moton. Garden City, N. Y., Doubleday, Doran and company, inc., 1929.
vii p., 2 l., 267 p. 21½cm.
"First edition."
1. Negroes. 2. U. S.—Race question. I. Title.
29—9727
Library of Congress E185.61.M934
[45y1]

MB9
M85h
Moton, Robert Russa, 1867-1940.
Hughes, William Hardin, 1881- ed.
Robert Russa Moton of Hampton and Tuskegee, edited by William Hardin Hughes [and] Frederick D. Patterson. Chapel Hill, University of North Carolina Press [1956]
238 p. illus. 24 cm.
"Volume of tributes to the life of Dr. Robert Russa Moton."
1. Moton, Robert Russa, 1867-1940. 2. Tuskegee Institute. 3. Hampton Institute, Hampton, Va. I. Patterson, Frederick Douglas, 1901- joint ed.
E185.97.M92H8 923.773 56—14299
Library of Congress [5717]

Haiti
M972.94
Un3r
Moton, Robert Russa, 1867-1940.
U.S. Commission on education in Haiti.
...Report of the United States Commission on education in Haiti. October 1, 1930. Washington, U.S. Govt. print. off., 1931.
vii, 74, [2] p. incl. map, tables 24½cm. ([Publication, no. 166] Latin American series, no. 5)
R.R. Moton, chairman.

Basutoland
M896.3
M85m
Motsamai, Edward.
Mehla ea malimo. Morija, Sesuto Book Depot, 1912.
143p. 16cm.
Times of the Cannibals.
1. Africa, South - literature. 2. Sotho language.

Basutoland
M896.3
M858
Motsatse, Ratsebe L , 1911-
Khopotso ea bongoana. Morija, Sesuto Book Depot, 1938.
112 p. 18 cm.
A reminder of one's childhood days.
1. Africa, South-Fiction.

S. Africa
M896.2
R11m
Motswaĕle II.
Raditladi, L D
Motswaĕle II, ke L. D. Raditladi. Johannesburg, University of Witwatersrand Press, 1945.
65 p. 18 cm. (Bantu Treasury series no. IX)
Historical drama in Tswana.

MB9
M85c
Mott, Lucretia (Coffin) 1793-1880.
Cromwell, Otelia.
Lucretia Mott. Cambridge, Harvard University Press, 1958.
241 p. illus. 24 cm.
Includes bibliography.
1. Mott, Lucretia (Coffin) 1793-1880.
E449.M964C7 923.673 58—10399
Library of Congress [50k15]

Congo(Leopoldville)
M967.5
M85am
Motuli, Pierre
Amour-marriage. Leopoldville, Centre d'Etudes Pastorales, 1961.
90p. 18½cm.
Portrait of author on front of book.
1. Congo (Léopoldville)-Social life and customs. 2. Congo (Léopoldville)-Marriage. I. Title.

Cameroons
M967.11
M86
Moukouri, Jacques Kuoh
Doigts noirs; je fus ecrivan au Cameroun. Montreal, Canada, Les Editions à la Page [1963]
203p. 18½cm.
Portrait of author on book cover.
"Avec les hommages respectueux de l'auteur, ce "Doigts Noirs" a Madame Dorothy B. Porter, cette 'Africaine de coeur' par pratigues son française 18, Juilliet 1963".
1. Cameroons. I. Title.

M370.
M86m
Moultrie High and Elementary school. Moultrie, Georgia.
Miss Parker, the new teacher; An account of how a school took its first cooperative steps in establishing and maintaining working relationships, developed by the faculty of the Moultrie High and Elementary School in cooperation with the Secondary school study of the Association of Colleges and Secondary Schools for Negroes. Albany, Georgia, Albany State College, 1946.
73p. illus. 23cm.
(over)

Cameroons
M966.11
M86c
Moumé- Etia, Isaac.
Conversation grammar, English and Duala, by Isaac Mume-Etia. 1st ed. ⌈Paris, Imprimerie des Orphelius d'Auteuil, 1928⌉
59p. 21cm.
1. Douala language - Grammar. 2. Cameroons. 3. Doualà - English language - Grammar.

Cameroons
M966.11
M86c
Moumé-Etia, Isaac.
Dictionnaire du langage Franco-Douala contenant tous les mots usuels par Isaac Moumé Etia. 1st. ed. Clermont-Ferrand, Imprimerie Générale, 1928.
198p. 23cm.
Bound with author's - Conversation Grammar.
1. Douala - french language - dictionary. 2. Cameroons.

Cameroons
M398
M86
Moumé-Etia, Isaac.
Les fables de Douala (Cameroun) En deux langues: Français-Douala, par Isaac Moumé-Etia. Bergerac, Imprimerie Générale du Sud-Quest, 1930.
98. port. 20cm.
1. Douala - Fables. 2. Cameroons-Folktales. 3. Folktales - Cameroons.

Cameroons
M398
M86
Moumé-Etia, Isaac.
Les fables de Douala (Cameroun) En deux langues: Françaés-Douala, par Isaac Moumé-Etia. Bergerac, Imprimerie Générale du Sud-Quest, 1930.
98p. port. 20cm.

Cameroons
M496
M86g
Moumé Etia, Isaac.
Grammaire abrégée de la langue douala (Cameroun); a l'usage de tous ceux qui veulent apprendre le douala rapidement, par Isaac Moumé Etia. ⌈n.p. Imprimerie "Je Sers" Clamart, n.d.⌉
54p. 18cm.

Cameroons
M966.11
M86c
Moumé-Etia, Isaac.
La Langue de Douala (Cameroun) par vous-même (grammaire, Exercises, Conversations, par Moumé-Etia, Isaac. Clermont-Ferrand, Imprimerie Générale, 1929.
109p. 21cm.
1. Douala language - grammar. 2. Douala - French language - grammar. 3. Cameroons.

Cameroons
M966.11
M86f
Moumé-Etia, Isaac.
Quelques renseignements sur la coutume locale chez les Doualas (Camerous) par Isaac Moumé Etia. Brest, Imprimerie de l' "Union Republicaine du Finistère", 1928.
15p. 21½cm.
1. Cameroons - Social life and customs. 2. Douala.

Cameroons
M966.11
M86
Moumé-Etia, Isaac.
Quelques renseignements sur la coutume locale chez les Doualas (Cameroun) par Isaac Moumé Etia. Troisieme partie. Lodève, Imprimerie-Papeterie-Libraire Julian.
25p. 21cm.

Cameroons
M966.11
M86f
Moumé-Etia, Isaac.
Quelques renseignements sur la coutume locale chez les Doualas (Cameroun) par Isaac Moumé Etia. Troisieme partie. Lodève, Imprimerie-Papeterie-Librairie Julian.
25p. 21cm.
1. Cameroons - Social life and customs. 2. Douala.

Cameroons
M966.11
M86f
Moumé-Etia, Isaac.
Quelques renseignements sur la coutume locale chez les Doualas (Cameroun) par Issac Moumé Etia. Quatrième partie. Brest, Imprimerie de l'Union Republicaine du Finistère, 1928.
20p. 21cm.
1. Douala - Social life and customs. 2. Cameroons - Social life and customs.

Cameroons
M966.11
M86f
Moumé-Etia, Isaac.
Quelques renseignements sur la coutume locale chez les Doualas (Cameroun) par Isaac Moumé-Etia. Primiere edition. ⌈1927⌉
16p. 21cm.
Typewritten copy.
1. Cameroons-Social life and customs. 2. Douala.

Guinea
M370
M86
Moumouni, Abdou
L'éducation en Afrique. Paris, Francois Maspero, 1964.
399p. tables. 21½cm (Les textes à l'appui)
Includes bibliography.
1. Education - Africa, Sub-Saharan. I. Title.

Mount Ascutney.
MB9
W27m
Washington, Vivian Edwards, 1914-
Mount Ascutney. New York, Comet Press Books, 1958.
66p. 20½cm.
Picture and biographical sketch of the author on the book jacket.

Mount Olivet Baptist Church - Drama.
M812.5
W15
Wallace, Richetta G (Randolph)
Mount Olivet yesterday and today, a panorama in five acts. n.p. 1953.
28p. 25cm.
"Presented May 1953 ... in celebration of Mount Olivet's Seventy-fifth Anniversary."
Inscribed by author.
1. Mount Olivet Baptist Church - Dram.

Mount Vernon, N.Y.
M974.71
L58s
Lewin, Wilfred S.
A study of the Negro population of Mount Vernon, by Wilfred S. Lewin. 1935.
52p. 28cm.
Typewritten

Senegal
MB9
B219t
Mouridisme.
Thiam, Medoune Diarra
Cheickh Ahmadou Bamba; fondateur du Mouridisme (1850-1927). ⌈Conakry, Imprimerie Nationale, 1964⌈
32p. illus., ports. 27cm.
Portrait of author in book.

Guinea
M896.1
Yo83
Moussa, enfant de Guinée.
Youla, Nabi
Moussa, enfant de Guinée; Aux enfants de Guinée et a leurs petits amis de tous les pays. Regensburg, Josef Habbel [1964]
[68pp. illus. 30cm.
Text in French and Dutch.

West Indies
M823.91
D65m
A mouthful of life.
Dobson, Hastin.
A mouthful of life. New York, Dragon Press, 1964.
289 p. 23 cm.
I. Title.
PZ4.D636Mo 64-20358
Library of Congress ⌈5⌉

The Movable school goes to the Negro farmer.
M379.173
C15
Campbell, Thomas Monroe, 1883-
The Movable school goes to the Negro farmer, by Thomas Monroe Campbell ... Tuskegee Institute, Ala., Tuskegee institute press ⌈°1936.
xiv, 170 p. front., plates, ports. 23½cm.
CONTENTS.—pt. I. Semi-autobiography.—pt. II. The school on wheels.
1. Agricultural education—Alabama. 2. Negroes—Education. 3. Negroes—Alabama. 4. Tuskegee normal and industrial institute. 5. U. S. Extension service. I. Title.
36—7891
Library of Congress LC2802.A2C3
⌈44m1⌉ 371.97409761

The movement.
M323.4
H198
Hansberry, Lorraine, 1930- 1965.
The movement; documentary of a struggle for equality. New York, Simon and Schuster, 1964.
127 p. (chiefly illus., ports.) 28 cm.
1. Negroes—Civil rights—Pictorial works. I. Title.
E185.61.H24 301.451 64-24334
Library of Congress ⌈5⌉

Movin' on up.
M89 J136
Jackson, Mahalia, 1911-
Movin' on up. With Evan McLeod Wylie. [1st ed.] New York, Hawthorn Books [1966]
212, [7] p. illus., ports. 24 cm.
Discography: p. [215], [218]-[219]
1. Musicians—Correspondence, reminiscences, etc. I. Wylie, Evan McLeod, 1916- II. Title.
ML420.J17A3 784.0924 66-22315/MN
Library of Congress [5]

Mpala, awaragan naka esapat loka Afrika.
Uganda
M896.3 H44m
Hertslet, Jessie
Mpala, awaragan naka esapat loka Afrika [Mpala, the story of an African boy] [Nuejuli K. Y. S. Oumo] Nairobi, Eagle Press, 1951.
81p. 18cm.
Written in Ateso
White author.
I. Title. II. Oumo, K. Y. S., tr.

South Africa
M896 M88
Mphahlele, Ezekiel L 1919- ed.
African writing today, 1967. (Card 3)
(Partial contents.- Continued)
Jean-Baptiste Mutabaruka.- The wages of good, by Birago Diop.- To the mystery-mongers, by Birago Diop.- Flowers! Lively flowers!, by Joseph Zobel.- Death of the princess, by Leopold Sedar Senghor.- Negro mask, by Leopold Sedar Senghor.- Autobiography, by Mbella Sonne Dipoko.- Love, by Mbella Sonne Dipoko.- Burial,
(Continued on next card)

Moving-picture plays - Collections.
Trinidad
M822.91 J63
John, Errol.
Force majeure, The dispossessed, Hasta Luego: three screenplays. London, Faber, 1967.
194 p. 21 cm. 25/-
(B 67-14340)
1. Moving-picture plays—Collections. I. Title. II. Title: The dispossessed. III. Title: Hasta luego.
PN1997.J47 67-97528
Library of Congress [3]

Uganda
M896.3 M87s
Mpalanyi, Solomon E K
Ssanyu teribeerera [You can't always be happy] Ebifaananyi byakubibwo. M. E. Gregg. Kampala, Eagle Press, 1961.
32p. 18½cm.
Written in Luganda.
I. Title.

South Africa
M896 M88
Mphahlele, Ezekiel L 1919- ed.
African writing today, 1967. (Card 4)
(Partial contents.- Continued)
by Paulin Joachim.- The fetish tree, by Jean Pliya.- After they put down their overalls, by Lenrie Peters.- Remarks on Negritude, by Ezekiel Mphahlele.- Extract from an African autobiography, by Ezekiel Mphahlele.- Dagga-smoker's dream, by Richard Rive.- Blankets, by Alex La Guma.- The urchin, by Can Themba.-
(Continued on next card)

Moving pictures.
M05 R29
Ellison, Ralph
The shadow and the act; A critic comments on four films about Negroes ...
(In: The Reporter, 1:17-19, December 6, 1949)

S. Africa
M896 M871
Mpanza, James Sofasonke, 1889-
Izimpa Zondlela yomkrestu. Lovedale. Lovedale press, [1936]
55 p. 18 cm.
Battles in the life of a christian.

South Africa
M896 M88
Mphahlele, Ezekiel L 1919- ed.
African writing today, 1967. (Card 5)
(Partial contents.- Continued)
Let not this plunder be misconstrued!, by Dennis Brutus.- Universal live, by Mazisi Kunene.- The prisoner, by Lewis Nkosi.- Friend Mussunda, by Agostinho Neto.- Dina, by Luis Bernardo Honwana.- Dream of the black mother, by Kalungano.- Poem of the conscripted warrior, by Rui Nogra.
(Over)

Mower, J. H.
Kenya
M967.62 L18
La Fontaine, Sidney Hubert, 1887-
Thirikari ya handu o handũ Kenya; [Local government in Kenya] ihumo o na ũkũria wayo, rĩandĩkĩtwo nĩ S. H. La Fontaine magĩteithanagia wĩra wa rĩo na J. H. Mower. [Translated into Kikuyu by Mathayo Njeroge] Nairobi, Eagle Press, 1955.
63p. 21½cm.
Written in Kikuyu.
1. Local government - Kenya Colony and Protectorate. I. Title. II. Mower, J. H. III. Njerage, Mathayo, tr.

Africa
M960 J88
Mphahlele, Ezekiel L 1919-
African culture trends.
Pp. 109-139.
In: Judd, Peter, ed. African independence. New York, Dell Pub. Co., 1963.

South Africa
MB9 M87
Mphahlele, Ezekiel L 1919-
Down Second Avenue. London, Faber and Faber, 1959.
222p. 22cm.
I. Title.

Kenya
M372.4 M87
Mpaayei, John Tempo Ole.
Engolon eng'eno [Knowledge is power] Itung' ana kituaak too Imaasai, naitobirakasi J. T. Ole Mpaayei and Kariũki K. Njiiri. Eutaa Elizabeth Mooney. [Illus. by Ruth Yudelowitz] Nairobi, Eagle Press, 1960.
illus. 28cm.
Written in Masaai.
1. Masaai language - Readers and speakers. I. Title. II. Njiiri, Kariuki Karanja, 1928- jt. auth.

Africa, South
M960 M87
Mphahlele, Ezekiel L 1919-
The African image. London, Faber and Faber [1962]
240p. 21cm.
Includes bibliography.
1. Race. 2. Literature - Africa. 3. Negritude. 4. Africa-Native races.

Africa
M808.83 B396
Mphahlele, Ezekiel L 1919-
He and the cat.
Pp. 46-51.
In: Black Orpheus. Black Orpheus; an anthology of African and Afro-American prose. New York, McGraw-Hill, 1965.

Kenya
M967.62 M871i
Mpaayei, John Tompo Ole
Inkuti pukunot oo lmaasai. (Masai life and customs) Edited by A. N. Tucker. London, Oxford University Press, 1954.
74p. diagrs. 18½cm. (Annotated African Texts - III: Maasai)
Text in English and Masai.
1. Masai - Social Life and customs.

South Africa
M896 M88
Mphahlele, Ezekiel L 1919- ed.
African writing today. Harmondsworth, Penguin, 1967.
347 p. 20 cm. 7/6
(B 67-3152)
Includes African Portuguese literature.
Partial contents.- Night of freedom, by Cyprian Ekwensi.- Life is sweet at Kumansenu, by Abioseh Nicol.- Bindeh's gift, by Sarif Easom.- The harvest, by Kwesi Brew.-
~~1. African literature—Translations into English. 2. English literature—Translations from African. I. Title.~~
(Continued on next card)
PL8013.E5M64 896 67-76486
Library of Congress [3]

Africa
M896 B36
Mphahlele, Ezekiel L 1919-
Langston Hughes.
Pp. 69-75.
In: Beier, Ulli, comp. Introduction to African literature. London, Longmans, 1967.
1. Hughes, Langston, 1902-

Mpaayei, John Tompo Ole, joint author.
M496(Masai) T79
Tucker, Archibald Norman.
A Maasai grammar, with vocabulary, by A. N. Tucker and J. Tompo Ole Mpaayei. London, New York, Longmans, Green [1955]
xvii, 317 p. 2 maps (1 fold.) 22 cm. (Publications of the African Institute, Leyden, no. 2)
Includes bibliographical references.
1. Masai language—Grammar. I. Mpaayei, John Tompo Ole, joint author. II. Title. (Series: Afrika-Instituut (Netherlands) Publications, no. 2)
PL8501.T8 1955 64-3463
Library of Congress [1]

South Africa
M896 M88
Mphahlele, Ezekiel L 1919- ed.
African writing today, 1967. (Card 2)
(Partial contents.- Continued)
The message, by Christina Ama Ata Aidoo.- Rediscovery, by George Awoonor-Williams.- Bad blood, by Kuldip Sondhi.- New life, by Joseph E. Kariuki.- Tekayo, by Grace Ogot.- Presence, by Felix Tchikaya U'Tam'si.- The dark room, by Sylvain Bemba.- A fistful of news, by Antoine-Roger Bolamba.- Song of the drum, by
(Continued on next card)

South Africa
M960 L527af
Mphahlele, Ezekiel L 1919-
The language of African literature.
Pp. 394-406.
In: Legum, Colin, ed. Africa. New York, Praeger, 1966.

South Africa
M896.3 **Mphahlel, Ezekiel. L** 1919-
M87L The living and the dead, and other stories. Illus. by Peter Clarke. Ibadan [Nigeria] Ministry of Education [196-?]

66 p. illus. 21 cm.

I. Title.

PZ4.M94Li 62-50812 ‡
Library of Congress [3]

South Africa
M896.3 Mphahlele, Ezekiel L 1919-
M87m Man must live and other stories. Cape Town, South Africa, African Bookman, 1946.

46p. illus. 20cm.

1. Africa - Fiction.

Africa Mphahlele, Ezekiel L . 1919- jt. ed.
M896.3 Komey, Ellis Ayitey, ed.
K83 Modern African stories, edited by Ellis Ayitey Komey and Ezekiel Mphahlele. London, Faber and Faber, 1964.

227p. 20cm.
Ghanaian and South African editors.

1. Short stories, African. I. Mphahlele, Ezekiel, jt. ed. II. Title.

Mphahlele, Ezekiel L 1919- Preface.
Ghana
M896 Ademola, Frances, ed.
Ad34 Reflections; Nigerian prose and verse. [Preface by Ezekiel Mphahlele] Lagos [Nigeria] African Universities Press [1962]

123p. 18½cm.
Ghanaian editor.

South Africa
M896 Mphahlele, Ezekiel L 1919-
M88 Remarks on Negritude.

Pp. 247-253.

In: Mphahlele, Ezekiel, ed. African writing today. Baltimore, Benguin Books, 1967.

S. Africa
M896 Mqhayi, Samuel Edward Krune, 1875- 1945
M87i ...Imihobe nemibongo, yokufundwa ezikolweni. Yenziwe. London, The Sheldon press [1927]

viii, 116 p. 16½ cm.
At head of title: xosa poetry for schools.

1. Africa, South-Poetry. 2. Xhosa poetry.

S. Africa
M896 Mqhayi, Samuel Edward Krune, 1875- 1945
M87in I-nzuzo... [by] S.E.K. Mqhayi [with an introduction by] Rev. R. Godfrey. Johannesburg. The University of Witwatersrand press, 1942.

viii, 96 p. port. 17 cm.

1. Africa, South-Poetry. 2. Xhosa poetry.

South Africa
M896 **Mqhayi, Samuel Edward Krune, 1875- 1945**
M87in2 Inzuzo [Reward] Amazwi okugabula izigcawu enziwe ngu Rev. R. Godfrey. [Reprinted in new orthography] Johannesburg, Witwatersrand University Press, 1957.

96p. 18cm. (Bantu treasury, edited by D. T. Cole, VII)
Written in Xhosa..

1. Poetry - Xhosa. 2. Xhosa Poetry.
I. Title.

S. Africa
M896 Mqhayi, Samuel Edward Krune, 1875-1945
M87it Ityala lama-wele. Ngama swembe-zwembe
1914 akwa Gxuluwe. [Lovedale] Ushicilelo Lwesi-tandatu [1914]

viii, 136 p. ports. 19 cm.
The story of a Lawsuit.
Written in Xhosa.

1. Africa, South-Fiction.

S. Africa
M896 Mqhayi, Samuel Edward Krune, 1875- 1945
M87it Ityala lama-wele. Ngamawembe-zwembe
1931 akwagxuluwe. Lovedale, The Lovedale press [1931]

167 p. ports. 19 cm.
The story of a Lawsuit.
Written in Xhosa.

1. Africa, South-Fiction.

S. Africa
M896 Mqhayi, Samuel Edward Krune, 1875- 1945
M87u U-Bom bom-Fundsi u John Knox Bokwe. Lovedale, Lovedale Institution Press 1925.

92 p. front. portraits. 22½ cm.

1. Bokwe, John Knox, 1855-

S. Africa
M896 Mqhayi, Samuel Edward Krune, 1875- 1945
M87it U-Don Jadu: "Ukuhamba yi Mfundo." Imbali yokukutaza u manyano ne nqubela Pambili. Lovedale, Lovedale Press, 1929.

77 p. port. 18 cm.
Bound with: Mqhayi, Samuel E. K. Itayala... (1914).
Don Juda: Travel is education.

1. Africa, South.

S. Africa
M896 Mqhayi, Samuel Edward Krune, 1875- 1945
M87in U-Don Jadu: "UkuHamba yimFundo." Imbali
1944 yokukhuthaza uManyano nenKqubela-Phambili. Lovedale, Lovedale Press, 1944.

68 p. port. 18 cm.

1. Africa, South.

S. Africa
M896 Mqhayi, Samuel Edward Krune, 1875- 1945
M87um U-Mqhayi wase-Ntab'ozuko. Lovedale, Lovedale Press, 1939.

87 p. 18½ cm.

1. Mqhayi, Samuel Edward Krune, 1875-

Mqhayi, Samuel Edward Krune, 1875- 1945
S. Africa
M896 Mqhayi, Samuel Edward Krune, 1875- 1945
M87um U-Mqhayi wase-Ntab'ozuko. Lovedale, Lovedale Press, 1939.

87 p. 18½ cm.

South Africa
M968.4 Mseleku, William J 1911-ca.1962.
M87z Zulu solfa music. Mariannhill, South Africa, Mariannhill mission press, 1936.

31p. port. 24½cm.

1. Zulu music.

Congo
M335 Msemakweh, R J
M87 Communisme neo-colonialisme. Leopoldville, Éditions C.E.P. [1961]

258p. 19cm.
"Ouvrages consultés" : p. 256-258.

1. Communism. 2. Communism - Anti-communistic literature. 3. Communism - Congo, Belgian. 4. Congo, Belgian - Communism. I. Title.

Zanzibar
M896.1 Msham, Mwana Kupona (Binti) 1810-1860?
M87 The advice of Mwana Kupona upon the wifely duty, from the Swahili texts by Alice Werner and William Hichens. Medstead, Hampshire, The Azania press [1934]

95p. illus. 19½cm.

1. African poetry. 2. Swahili literature. I. Werner, Alice, 1395-1935. II. Hichens, William.

Msyamboza, Chewa headman, 1830 (ca.)-1926.
Malawi
M968.97 **Ntara, Samuel Yosia,** 1904 *or* 5-
M87h Headman's enterprise; an unexpected page in central African history, tr. and ed. with a pref. by Cullen Young from the Cewa original. London, Lutterworth Press [1949]

213 p. illus., map. 19 cm.

1. Msyamboza, Chewa headman, 1830 (ca.)-1926. I. Title.

DT864.N78 923.1678 50-12132
Library of Congress [2]

South Africa
M968.91 **Mishali, Benedict Vulindlela**
M879 Rhodesia: background to conflict [by] B. Vulindlela Mishali. New York, Hawthorn Books [1967]

235 p. 24 cm. (Revolution of color)

Bibliographical references included in "Notes": p. 208-211. "The politics of southern Africa, 1960-1966, a selective bibliography": p. 215-244.

Portrait of author on book jacket.

1. Rhodesia—Pol. & govt. I. Title. (Series: Revolution of color series)

DT948.M7 968.9'1 67-15557
Library of Congress [5]

Mtu maskini mwenye sh.1,000,000.
Tanganyika
M967.82 Omari, Dunstan Alfred, 1922- . jt. auth.
Om1m Mtu maskini mwenye sh.1,000,000. The poor man with a million shillings. [By C. W. W. Ryan and D. A. Omari] Dar es Salaam, Eagle Press, 1954.

16p. 18cm. (Mazungumzo ya uraia. Talks on citizenship, no.2)
Writtn in Swahili and English.

1. Money. I. Title. II. Title: The poor man with a million shillings. III. Series: Mazungunmzo ya uraia, no. 2. IV. Talks on citizenship, no. 2. V. Ryan, C. W. W.

Mtusu, Daniel, d. 1917.

Malawi
MB9
M1

Fraser, Donald, 1870-1933.
The autobiography of an African. Retold in biographical form and in wild African setting of the life of Daniel Mtusu. London, Seeley, Service and Co., 1925.

209p. ports. 20cm.

Arabia
M892.8
M88s

Mu'allakāt. *English.*
The seven odes; the first chapter in Arabic literature ₍by₎ A. J. Arberry. London, G. Allen & Unwin; New York, Macmillan ₍1957₎

258 p. 22 cm.

1. Arberry, Arthur John, 1905- tr. II. Title.

PJ7642.E5A7 892.71 57-13808 ‡

Library of Congress ₍10₎

Uganda
M967.61
M88e

Mubiru, Wilson
Ebyafa e Ssaayi ₍ The story of Ssaayi ₎ Nairobi, The Eagle Press, 1952.

9p. illus. 18cm.

Written in Luganda.

1. Uganda.

Uganda
M967.61
M88p

Mubiru, Wilson
Paspalum ₍The value of Paspalum grass₎ Nairobi, The Eagle Press, n.d.

18p. illus. 20½cm.

Written in Luganda.

1. Uganda.

Kenya
M610
M89

Muceera na mukundu akundukaga o taguo.
Ngurungu, Sospeter Kunuhe, tr.
Muceera na mukundu akundukaga o taguo ₍V.D. and drunkenness₎ ₍Tr. with a new preface by Sospeter Kunuhue Ngurungu₎ Nairobi, Eagle Press, 1950.

16p. 22cm. (Taanya Ũgima-inĩ. Aim at healthy living series)
Written in Kikuyu.

1. Venereal diseases. 2. Alcoholism. I. Title. II. Series. III. Aim at healthy living series.

Haiti
M841
M88

Mucius, Marguerite
Au-delà de l'ether, poèmes. Port-au-Prince, Imp. du Commerce, n.d.

7-129p. 21cm.

1. Haitian poetry. I. Title

M323
M88d

Mudgett, Helen (Parker) 1900-
Democracy for all, a study program by Helen Parker Mudgett ... Minneapolis, Minn., General extension division, University of Minnesota ₍1945₎

87, ₍1₎ p. diagrs. 23 cm.
Includes bibliographies.

1. Citizenship—Study and teaching. 2. Democracy. I. Minnesota. University. General extension division. II. Title.

45-37084

Library of Congress JA88.U6M8 ₍49e2₎ 323.607

Mudiangu, Simon

Congo(Leopoldville)
M896.3
K64c

Kitambala, Jérôme
Contes Africains, par Jerome Kitambala, Paul Malulu, Simon Mudiangu, and Robert Musungaie. Leverville (Congo Belge), Bibliotheque de l'Etoile, May 1955.

32p. illus. 18cm. (No. 97)

La muerte de Antonio Maceo.

Cuba
MB9
M15g4

Griñán Peralta, Leonardo
La muerte de Antonio Maceo (Causas y consecuencias). La Habana, 1941.

79p. 20½cm.
Autographed.
Includes bibliography.

1. Maceo, Antonio, 1845-1896.
I. Title.

Mugwanya, Stanislaus.

Uganda
M967.61
K15s

Kasirye, Joseph S
Stanislaus Mugwanya. Nairobi, The Eagle Press, 1953.

22p. 18cm.
Written in Luganda.

Muhammads children.

M372.4
J63

Johnson, Christine.
Muhammads children; a first grade reader. Chicago, University of Islam, 1963.

130p. 23cm.

La mujer.

Cuba
M972.91
G98m

Gutiérrez, José Margarito, 1855-
La mujer, defensa de sus derechos e ilustración; ensayo literario por José Margarito Gutiérrez. 2. ed. Habana, Imprenta de Rambla, Bouza y ca., 1929.

2 p. l., ₍3₎-66 p. 23cm.

1. Woman—Social and moral questions. 2. Woman—Legal status, laws, etc. I. Title.

30-29572

Library of Congress HQ1227.G9 1929 ₍2₎ 396.2

Mukalazi, Jechoada K S , jt.auth.

Uganda
M896.3
Se3s

Segganyi, Edward A K
Ssebato bafuma. (Short stories and folklore). ₍By₎ Edward A. K. Segganyi, Erasmus K. Kizito ne Jechoada K. S. Mukalazi. ... Nairobi, The Eagle Press, 1959.

164p. illus. 18½cm.
Text in: Luganda.

Mukamba wa wo,

Kenya
M967.62
K57

Kimilũ, David N
Mũkamba wa wo ₍A typical Mkamba₎ Literature Bureau, 1962.

139p. 21½cm.
Written in Kamba.

1. Kamba tribe. 2. Kenya - Native races.
I. Title.

U.S.
M967.5
Ed55

Mukanda muibidi wa Agalonomie.
Edmiston, Alonzo Lemore, 1904-
Guide pratique d'agriculture. Luebo, American₎ P₍resbyterian₎ C₍ongo₎ M₍ission₎. 1931.

203p. illus. 22cm.
Added t.p., in Luba.
Written in Luba.

1. Agriculture - Congo, Belgian. 2. Congo, Belgian. I. Title. II. Title: Mukanda muibidi wa Agalonomie. III. American Presbyterian Congo Mission.

Uganda
MB9
K11m

Mukasa, Ham
Uganda's Katikiro in England, being the official account of his visit to the coronation of his majesty King Edward VII. By his secretary Ham Mukasa; translated and edited by the Rev. Ernest Millar... with an introduction by Sir H.H. Johnston. London, Hutchinson & Co., 1904.

xxiv, 278p. 21½cm.

1. Katikiro of Uganda. Apolo Kagwa.
2. Kagwa, Apolo, 1863?-1927. 3. Africa
I. Millar, Ernest, editor.

Uganda
MB9
K11m

Mukasa, Ham
Uganda's Katikiro in England, being the official account of his visit to the coronation of his majesty King Edward VII. By his secretary Ham Mukasa; translated and edited by the Rev. Ernest Millar... with an introduction by Sir H.H. Johnston. London, Hutchinson &. Co., 1904.

xxiv, 278p. 21½cm.

1. Katikiro of Ugandu, Apolo Kagwa.
2. Kagwa, Apolo, 1863?-1927. 3. Africa
I. Miliar, Ernest, editor

S. Africa
M398
M89

Mukhombo, Aron S
A nkutsulani wa matimu ya batswa; a timhaka ta kale ti khedzelwe. Cleveland, Central Mission Press, 1931.

127p. port. 20½cm.
Tswa legends.

1. Tswa language. 2. South African legends.

Uganda
M967.61
M89L

Mukwaya, A B
Land tenure in Buganda; present day tendencies. Nairobi, The Eagle Press, 1953.

79p. tables graphs 21cm.
(East African Studies, No.I)

1. Buganda Province . Uganda.

Africa.
M960
As6a

Mulago, Vincent
Dialectique existentielle des Bantu, et sacramentalisme.

Pp. 146-171.
In: Aspects de la culture noire. 1958.

1. Bantu. I. Title.

Mulambwa santulu u amuhela bo mwene.

Zambia
M968.94
M93

Mupatu, Y W
Mulambwa Santulu u amuhela bo mwene. ₍Mulambwa Santulu welcomes the Mbunda chiefs₎ London, Macmillan, 1958.

37p. 18cm. (Bantu heritage series)
Written in Lozi.

1. Rhodesia, Northern - Native races.
I. Title.

Mulatto.

M812.5 H87m
Hughes, Langston, 1902-
Mulatto, dramma in due atti e tre scene. Italy, Arnoldo Mondadori, 1949.

158p. 18cm. (Biblioteca moderna mondadori, 58)
Inscribed by author: To Arthur Spingarn, Sincerely, Langston. New York, March 13, 1952.

Mulattoes.

M301 F86f
Frazier, Edward Franklin, 1894-
The free Negro family; a study of family origins before the civil war, by E. Franklin Frazier ... Nashville, Tenn., Fisk university press, 1932.

5 p. l., 75 p. illus. (maps) 24 cm. (*Half-title: Fisk university social science series*)

"Selected bibliography": p. 73-75.

1. Negroes. 2. Freedmen. 3. Mulattoes. 4. Negroes—Moral and social conditions. 5. Slavery in the U. S.—Emancipation. I. Title.

32—14425

Library of Congress E185.F83
[41f1] 325.26

Mulattoes

M813.5 J63 1948
Johnson, James Weldon, 1871-1938
The autobiography of an ex-coloured man, with an introduction by Charles S. Johnson. New York, New American Library, 1948.

142p. 18cm.
Pocketbook edition.

Mulattoes.

M813.5 J63 1927
Johnson, James Weldon, 1871-1938.
...The autobiography of an ex-coloured man by James Weldon Johnson. Garden City, N. Y., Garden City publishing co., inc., [c1927]

211p. cm. (A Star Book)

Mulattoes.

M813.5 J63 1927
[Johnson, James Weldon] 1871-1938.
The autobiography of an ex-colored man. Boston, Sherman, French & company, 1912.

3 p. l., 207 p. 21cm.

1. Mulattoes. 2. Negroes. I. Title.

12—15155

Library of Congress PZ3.J633Au
[47d1]

Mulattoes.

M813.5 J63
[Johnson, James Weldon] 1871-1938.
The autobiography of an ex-colored man. Boston, Sherman, French & company, 1912.

3 p. l., 207 p. 21cm.

1. Mulattoes. 2. Negroes. I. Title.

12—15155

Library of Congress PZ3.J633Au
[47d1]

Congo Leopoldville
M325 M891
Mulenzi, Janvier
L'internationalisation du phénomène colonial. Bruxelles, Éditions du Treurenberg, 1958.

164p. 24cm. (Université de Louvain. Collection de l'École des sciences politiques et sociales, 156)
Bibliography: p. [154]-159.

1. Colonies - History. 2. International trusteeships. 3. Colonies (International Law) I. Title. II. Series: Louvain. Université catholique. École des sciences politiques et socials. Collection no. 156.

Congo Leopoldville
M325 M89
Mulenzi, Janvier.
La tutelle internationale et le problème des unions administratives. Préf. de Guy Malengreau. Louvain, Nauwelaerts, 1955.

228 p. 21 cm.
Includes bibliography.

1. International trusteeships. I. Title.

JX4021.M9 57-26550 ‡

Library of Congress [3]

Mules and men.

M810 H94mu 1936
Hurston, Zora Neale.
Mules and men, by Zora Neale Hurston; with an introduction by Frank Boas ... 10 illustrations by Miguel Covarrubias. Philadelphia, London, Kegan, Paul, Trench, Trubner, 1936.

342, [1] p. front., illus., plates. 22cm.

CONTENTS.—pt. I. Folk tales.—pt. II. Hoodoo.—Appendix. I. Negro songs with music (p. 309-[331]) II. Formulae of hoodoo doctors. III. Paraphernalia of conjure. IV. Prescriptions of root doctors.

1. Folk-lore, Negro. 2. Voodooism. 3. Negroes—Florida. 4. Negroes—Louisiana. 5. Negro songs. I. Title.

35—18525

Library of Congress GR103.H8
[45j²2] 398.09759

Mules and men.

M810 H94mu
Hurston, Zora Neale.
Mules and men, by Zora Neale Hurston; with an introduction by Frank Boas ... 10 illustrations by Miguel Covarrubias. Philadelphia, London, J. B. Lippincott company, 1935.

342, [1] p. front., illus., plates. 22cm.

CONTENTS.—pt. I. Folk tales.—pt. II. Hoodoo.—Appendix. I. Negro songs with music (p. 309-[331]) II. Formulae of hoodoo doctors. III. Paraphernalia of conjure. IV. Prescriptions of root doctors.

1. Folk-lore, Negro. 2. Voodooism. 3. Negroes—Florida. 4. Negroes—Louisiana. 5. Negro songs. I. Title.

35—18525

Library of Congress GR103.H8
[45j²2] 398.09759

Mulwinda, S. K., tr.

Uganda M636 H88an
Humphrey, Norman
Ensolo zirina ebyetaago bimu nga ffe [Animals have the same needs as we do] Translated by S. K. Mulindwa. Kampala, East African Literature Bureau, 1950.
10p. 22cm. (Aim at healthy living series) Written in Luganda.
1. Animals, Treatment of. I. Title. II. Mulwinda, S. K., tr.

Uganda M967.61 M890 Pt. I.
Mulira, Enoch Emmanuel K
Olugero lwa Kintu [Story of the first king of Buganda] Part. I. Nairobi, The Eagle Press 1951.

31p. illus. 20cm.

Written in Luganda.

1. Kintu, King of Buganda. 2. Uganda.

Uganda M967.61 M890 Pt.II
Mulira, Enoch Emmanuel K
Olugero lwa Kintu [Story of Kintu the first king of Buganda: Pt. II] Nairobi, The Eagle Press, 1951.

30p. illus. 20cm.

Written in Luganda.

1. Uganda.

Uganda M967.61 M91t
Mulira, Enoch Emmanuel K
Troubled Uganda. London, Fabian Publications and Victor Gollancz [1950]

44p. 18cm. (Colonial controversy series, no.6)

1. Uganda.

Uganda M967.61 M91v
Mulira, Enoch Emmanuel K
The vernacular in African education. London, Longmans, Green and Co., [1951]

55p. 18½cm.

1. Uganda - Education. I. Title.

Uganda M372.4 M89
Mulira, Enoch Emmanuel K
Bagishu bosi basoma. [Ligusi adult literacy primer] Bifaani bya L. N. Sekaboga. Kampala, Eagle Press, 1951.

29p. illus. 24½cm.
Written in Lugisu.

I. Title.

S. Africa M280 M91i
Müller, Edward Mnganga, 1877-1946
Isigunqulo sama Protestanti saciteka kanjani namazwe amaningi. Mariannhill Mission press, 1929.

94p. front. (port.) 18cm.

1. Africa, South. 2. Church - History.

S. Africa M280 M91u
Müller, Edward Mngnanga, 1877-1946
Umlando weBandhla. Mariannhill, Mission press, 1929.

57p. front. (port.) 18½cm.
History of the Roman Catholic Church in Zulu.

1. Africa, South. 2. Roman Catholic Church. 3. Church - History.

MB9 M92
Mulzac, Hugh, 1886-
A star to steer by; by Hugh Mulzac, as told to Louis Burnham and Norval Welch. New York, International Publishers [1963]

251 p. illus. 21 cm.

1. Merchant marine—U. S.—Negroes. 2. Merchant marine—U. S.—Officers—Correspondence, reminiscences, etc. I. Burnham, Louis E., 1915 or 16-1960. II. Welch, Norval. III. Title.

E185.63.M8 923.573 63-14260 ‡

Library of Congress [5]

Mume-Etia, Isaac

See

Moumé-Etia, Isaac.

Puerto Rico M864 P141
Municipal corporations-Puerto Rico.
Pagán, Bolívar, 1899-
... Ley municipal, revisada, anotada y comentada, por Bolívar Pagán. (Contiene la Ley municipal y todas las demás leyes aplicables a los municipios, el acta orgánica, el reglamento de contabilidad municipal, y toda la jurisprudencia del Tribunal supremo sobre cuestiones municipales hasta el tomo 32, incl.) San Juan, Puerto Rico, La Correspondencia de Pto. Rico, inc., 1925.

xi, 13-256, [4] p. 22cm. (Biblioteca de divulgación legal, vol. I)

1. Municipal government—Puerto Rico. 2. Municipal corporations—Puerto Rico. I. Puerto Rico. Laws, statutes, etc. II. Title.

42-51912

Library of Congress JS2024.P3
[3]

Puerto Rico M864 P141

Municipal government—Puerto Rico.
Pagán, Bolívar, 1899–
... Ley municipal, revisada, anotada y comentada, por Bolívar Pagán. (Contiene la Ley municipal y todas las demás leyes aplicables a los municipios, el acta orgánica, el reglamento de contabilidad municipal, y toda la jurisprudencia del Tribunal supremo sobre cuestiones municipales hasta el tomo 32, incl.) San Juan, Puerto Rico, La Correspondencia de Pto. Rico, inc., 1925.
xi, 13–256, [4] p. 22ᶜᵐ. (Biblioteca de divulgación legal, vol. I)
1. Municipal government—Puerto Rico. 2. Municipal corporations—Puerto Rico. I. Puerto Rico. Laws, statutes, etc. II. Title.
42-51912
Library of Congress JS2024.P3 [3]

Nigeria M896.3 M726o **Munonye, John, 1929–**
The only son. London, Heinemann, 1966.
[5], 202 p. 20½ cm. 18/-
(B 66-7524)
Portrait of author on book jacket.
I. Title.
PR6063.U48O5 66-74105
Library of Congress [5]

Zambia M968.94 M93 Mupatu, Y W
Mulambwa Santulu u amuhela bo mwene. [Mulambwa Santulu welcomes the Mbunda chiefs] London, Macmillan, 1958.
37p. 18cm. (Bantu heritage series)
Written in Lozi.
1. Rhodesia, Northern - Native races.
I. Title.

M231 W62 Murchison, Elisha P , 1907–
Why I believe there is a God.
Pp. 34–40.
In: Why I believe there is a God. Chicago, Johnson Pub. Co., 1965.

M331 M93s Murchison, John Prescott
[Statement at] Hearings before the Committee on Labor, House of Representatives, seventy-second Congress, first session on Relief of distress due to unemployment. Wash., D.C., Govt. Print. Off., 1932.
45–51p. 23cm.
At head of title: Relief of distress due to unemployment. Detached copy.
1. Unemployment.

M029.6 M95c Murphy, Beatrice M Clay, 1908–
Catching the editor's eye; a manual for writers. Rev. Washington, D.C., Author 1962.
10p. 21½cm.
1. Writing. I. Title.

M811.08 M951 **Murphy, Beatrice M Clay, 1908– , ed.**
Ebony rhythm, an anthology of contemporary Negro verse. New York, Exposition Press [1948]
162 p. 23 cm.
1. Negro poetry (American) I. Title.
PS591.N4M76 811.5082 48-1162 rev*
Library of Congress [r48f3]

M811.5 M951 Murphy, Beatrice M Clay, 1908–
Love is a terrible thing, by Beatrice M. Murphy. New York, The Hobson book press, 1945.
ix, 66p. 21½cm.
1. Poetry. I. Title.

M811.08 M95 **Murphy, Beatrice M Clay, 1908– , ed.**
... Negro voices, edited by Beatrice M. Murphy; illustrations by Clifton Thompson Hill. New York, H. Harrison [°1938]
173, [3] p. illus. 21½ᶜᵐ.
At head of title: An anthology of contemporary verse.
1. Negro poetry (American) I. Title.
39-2667
Library of Congress PS591.N4M8 [43d1] 811.50822

Murphy, Beatrice M. Clay, 1908– , p. 57.
M810.8 P24 The Parnassian; prose and poetry by sixteen members of the younger generation, with an introduction by Alpheus Butler. Chicago, Washington [etc.] Laurel publishers, 1930.
64p. 21cm.
"Limited edition."
"First printing September 1930."

M323.4 M35m Murphy, Frank.
Marshall, Thurgood, 1908–
Mr. Justice Murphy and civil rights. Reprinted from Michigan law review, 48:745–766, April 1950.
745–766p. 27cm.

M323 N21 Murphy, George
National association for the advancement of colored people.
Resources in Negro youth. New York city, National association for the advancement of colored people, 1940.
18p. 20cm.

M89 M95 Murphy, John Henry, 1896–1922.
Sergeant Murphy, Story of a Civil War veteran. Afro-American Newspapers, [1942].
23p. illus. ports. 16cm.
1. Afro-American Newspapers.

M808.8 N42 v. 4 Murray, Albert, 1916–
The Luzana Cholly kick.
(In: New world writing, 4. New York, New American Library, 1953. 18 cm. p. 228–243)

M810.9 H55an Murray, Albert, 1916–
Something different, something more.
Pp. 112–137.
In: Hill, Herbert, ed. Anger and beyond. New York, Harper & Row, 1966.

M813.08 C594 Murray, Albert, 1916– .
Train whistle guitar
Pp. 209–226
In: Clarke, John Henrik, ed. American Negro short stories. New York, Hill and Wang, 1966.

M89 B22a Murray, Daniel Alexander Payne, 1852–1925, jt. author.
Allen, Will W.
Banneker, the Afro-American astronomer, from data collected by Will W. Allen assisted by Daniel Murray ... Washington, D. C., 1921.
80 p. incl. front. (port.) 17½ᶜᵐ.
1. Banneker, Benjamin, 1731–1806. I. Murray, Daniel, 1852– joint author.
21-17456
Library of Congress QB36.B22A4
——— Copy 2.
Copyright A 627219 [2]

M304 P19 v.7 no.24 Murray, Daniel Alexander Payne, 1852–1925
Murray's historical and biographical encyclopedia of the colored race throughout the world... Daniel Murray, editor in chief.. Chicago, World's cyclopedia company [n.d.]
15 unnumb p. 26cm.
Prospectus of proposed encyclopedia.
1. History
2. Biography.

M304 P19 v.3, no.2 **Murray, Daniel Alexander Payne, 1852–1925, *comp.***
Preliminary list of books and pamphlets by negro authors, for Paris exposition and Library of Congress. Comp. by Daniel Murray ... [Washington, D. C., U. S. commission to the Paris exposition, 1900]
8 p. 23½ᶜᵐ.
1. Negro authors.
1-6011
Library of Congress Z1361.N39M9 [a27e1]

Murray, Florence, ed.
M310 M96 The Negro handbook ... 1942–
New York, N. Y., W. Malliet and company, 1942–
v. tables. 24 cm.
Editor: 1942– Florence Murray.
"Books and periodicals, a list of books by and about Negroes": 1942, p. 194–200.
1. Negroes—Year-books. I. Murray, Florence, ed.
42-22818
Library of Congress E185.5.N382 [45k⁷] 325.260973

M730 M96e **Murray, Freeman Henry Morris.**
... Emancipation and the freed in American sculpture; a study in interpretation, by Freeman Henry Morris Murray, introduction by John Wesley Cromwell ... Washington, D. C., The author, 1916.
xxviii p., 2 l., 239, [1] p. plates. 19 cm. (Black folk in art series)
"This monograph is chiefly the expansion of papers which were read as lectures ... at the Summer school and Chautauqua of the National religious training school at Durham, N. C., in 1913. Some of the matter has also appeared in the A. M. E. church review."—Pref.
1. Negroes—Iconography. 2. Sculpture, American. I. Title.
19-2859
Library of Congress E185.89.I 2M9 [36d1]

M324
M96s
Murray, George Washington, 1853-1926.
Speech of Hon. G.W. Murray of South Carolina, on The Repeal of the Federal election laws, in the House of Representatives, October 5, 1893. [Lacks imprint]
14p. 24cm.
1. Politics 2. Elections
I. Repeal of the Federal Election laws.

M811.5
M96
Murray, Henry Clifford
The sight of dawn-poems. New York, Exposition Press, 1959.
61p. 21cm.
Portrait of author on book jacket.
I. Title.

M910
M96e
Murray, James A
Ethiopia, Italy and the Roman Church; a study of Bible prophecies, their past, present and future fulfillment. Stanberry, Missouri, The Church of God Publishing House, n.d.
54p. illus. 21½cm.
1. Ethiopia. 2. Bible.

U. S.
M966.7
M96
Murray, Pauli, 1910- jt. author.
The Constitution and Government of Ghana, by Leslie Rubin and Pauli Murray. London, Sweet & Maxwell, 1961.
xvi, 310p. 23cm. (Law in Africa, no. 1)
"The Constitution of the Republic of Ghana": p. 250-266.
Bibliography: p. 285-287.
1. Ghana-Constitutional law.
II. Ghana. Constitution. (Series)
III. Rubin. Leslie.

M89
M96p
Murray, Pauli, 1910-
Proud shoes; the story of an American family. [1st ed.] New York, Harper [1956]
276 p. 22 cm.
I. Title.
E185.97.M95 920 56-10698 ‡
Library of Congress [15]

M323
M78t
Murray, Pauli, 1910-
The right to equal opportunity in employment.
pp. 383-407.
In: Twice a year, ed. by Dorothy Norman. 1946.
1. Employment. I. Title.

M323.4
M96s
Murray, Pauli, 1910- ed.
States' laws on race and color, and appendices containing international documents, federal laws and regulations, local ordinances and charts. [Cincinnati, Woman's Division of Christian Service, Board of Missions and Church Extension, Methodist Church] 1950 [i. e. 1951]
x, 746 p. forms. 24 cm.
1. ~~Negroes~~—Legal status, laws, etc. 2. Race discrimination—~~Unit.~~ I. Title.
325.260973 51-2354
Library of Congress [51u10]

M610
F19
V.1
No.8
Murray, Peter Marshall.
Harlem's health. Reprinted from Hospital Social Service, 22, 1930.
309-315p. 20cm.
1. Harlem - Health. 2. Health.

M610
F19
V.1
No.7
Murray, Peter Marshall.
Hospital provision for the Negro race, by Peter Marshall Murray... Reprinted from the Bulletin of the American hospital association for July, 1930.
37-46p. 20cm.
1. Hospitals. I. Title.

M610
M96n
Murray, Peter Marshall, 1888-
N.M.A. president's address. n.p. 1932.
15p. 28cm.
Delivered at Washington, August 16, 1932.
Mimeo.
1. Medicine. I. National Medical Association.

Jamaica
M784
M95
Murray, Tom, ed. and arr.
Folk songs of Jamaica. London, Oxford University Press [1951]
9p. 25½cm
1. Songs - Jamaica. 2. Folk songs - Jamaica. I. Title.

M170
T34
Murrow, Edward R
This I believe: 2; The personal philosophies of one hundred thoughtful men and women in all walks of life - twenty of whom are immortals in the history of ideas, eighty of whom are our contemporaries of today. Written for Edward R. Murrow. Edited by Raymond Swing. New York, Simon and Schuster, 1954.
233p. 20cm.

M792
M97w
Muse, Clarence
Way down south, by Clarence Muse and David Arlen. Wood cuts by Blanding Sloan. Hollywood, Calif., David Graham Fischer Publisher, 1932.
145p. illus. 26½cm.
"For Walter White: From a friend of the Negro to a friend of the Negro-this romance of colored show business. We trust you will approve it. David Arlen."
(continued on next card)

M792
M97w
Muse, Clarence
Way down south, by Clarence Muse and David Arlen. Wood cuts by Blanding Sloan. Hollywood, Calif., David Graham Fischer Publisher, 1932.
(Card 2)
"Inscribed for Arthur B. Spingarn-to vouch for his having come by this volume through proper means-Walter White."
I. Title. II. Arlen, David, jt. au.

Congo (Leopoldville)
M840.8
M971
Mushiete, Paul
La littérature française africaine; petite anthologie des écrivains noirs d'expression française. Leverville, Bibliothèque de l'Etoile, 1957.
40p. 17½cm.
I. Title. 1. Literature-French African. 2. Rabemananjara, Jacques, 1913- 3. Césaire, Aimé, 1913- 4. Dadie, Bernard B , 1916- 5. Senghor, Léopold Sédar, 1906- 6. Laye, Camara, 1928- 7. Lomami-Tshibamba Paul, 1914- 8. Kagame, Alexis, 1912-

Congo, Leopoldville
M840.8
M97n
Mushiete, Paul
Notes sur la littérature congolaise.
pp. 608-620 24cm.
In: La Revue Nouvelle, Tome XXV, No. 6, Juin 15, 1957)
1. Congo, Belgian - Literature. 2. African literature.

Music.
M810
B97n
Butcher, Margaret (Just) 1913-
The Negro in American culture; based on materials left by Alain Locke. [1st ed.] New York, Knopf, 1956.
294 p. 22 cm.
1. ~~Negroes in~~ literature. 2. ~~Negroes in~~ art. 3. ~~Negro~~ literature (American) 4. American literature—~~Negro~~ authors. 5. ~~Negro art.~~ 6. Music—~~Negroes.~~ 7. ~~Negroes~~—Dancing. I. Title.
II. Locke, Alain Leroy.
E185.82.B88 325.260973 56-5783 ‡
Library of Congress [57e*30]

Music.
M810
B97no
Butcher, Margaret (Just), 1913-
Les noirs dans la civilisation Américaine. The Negro in American culture, based on materials left by Alain Locke. Traduit de l'américain par Françoise Vernan et Jean Rodenthal. Paris, Bouchet/Chastel, 1958.
320p. 18½cm.

Music.
M784
C53
Clark, Edgar Rogie, 1914- , comp.
Negro art songs; album by contemporary composers for voice and piano. New York, Edward B. Marks Music Corp., 1956.
72p. illus. 33cm.

Music.
M780
C54b
Clark, F A
The black music master, by F.A. Clark...
Philadelphia, Pa., F.A., c 1923.
32p. 19cm.

M784
C541
Music.
Clark, George W.
The liberty minstrel... by Geo. W. Clark. New York, Leavitt & Alden, etc., 1845.
184 [3] p. 18½cm.
Contains music.

Music.
M784 C83
Courlander, Harold, 1908–
Negro folk music, U. S. A. New York, Columbia University Press, 1963.
x, 324 p. illus., music. 24 cm.
"The music" (melodies with words): p. [221]–287.
Bibliography: p. [299]–301; Discography: p. [302]–308.
1. Music—Negroes. 2. Negro songs—Hist. & crit. 3. Negro songs—Discography. 4. Negro songs. I. Title.
ML3556.C7 784.756 63—18019/MN
Library of Congress [a63d3]

Music.
M780 J72
Jones, LeRoi.
Blues people; Negro music in white America. New York, W. Morrow, 1963.
xii, 244 p. 22 cm.
Bibliographical footnotes.
1. Music—Negroes. 2. Jazz music. 3. Negroes. I. Title.
ML3556.J73 781.773 63—17688/MN
Library of Congress [64k5]

Music-Addresses, essays, lectures.
M780.4 C54m
Clark, Edgar Rogie.
Moment musical; ten selected newspaper articles by Edgar Rogie Clark. Fort Valley, Ga., Department of music, Fort Valley state college, 1940.
24 p. 1 illus. 21½cm.
1. Music—Addresses, essays, lectures. 2. Music—Negroes. I. Title.
40-31976
Library of Congress ML60.C537M6
——— Copy 2.
Copyright AA 338881 [2] 780.4

Music.
M780.9 C83
Cowell, Henry, 1897– ed.
American composers on American music; a symposium edited by Henry Cowell. [Stanford University, Calif.] Stanford university press, 1933.
xii, 226 p. illus. (music) diagrs. 22 cm.
Composers reviewed include Carl Ruggles, Adolph Weiss, Colin McPhee, Edgar Varèse, Aaron Copland, Henry Cowell, Roy Harris, Wallingford Riegger, Roger Sessions, J. J. Becker, Henry Brant, Howard Hanson, Carlos Salzedo, Carlos Chávez, Nicolas Slonimsky, Ruth Crawford, Charles Seeger, Walter Piston and C. E. Ives.
"Biographical notes on composers ... together with lists of their principal works": p. 201–218.
White editor.
1. Music—~~U. S.~~—Hist. & crit. 2. Musicians, ~~American~~. 3. Music, ~~American~~. I. Title.
ML200.5.C87A5 780.97 33—13037
Library of Congress [50h1]

M784 N42o
Music.
New Orleans University Singers.
The only original New Orleans university singers. A colored double quartette. Voices unrivalled. Pronounced the best troupe now before the public. Philadelphia. Wm. Syckelmoore. 1881.
22p. 14cm.
Hymns and songs.

Music, Africa.
Nigeria M784 P54
Phillips, Ekundayo
Yoruba music (African); fusion of speech and music. Johannesburg, African Music Society, 1953.
58p. diagrs. 24½cm.

Music.
M89 H11d
Davenport, M Marguerite.
Azalia : the life of Madame E. Azalia Hackley. Boston, Chapman & Grimes, inc. [c 1947]
196p. ports. 19½cm.

Music.
M781 R14br
Ramsey, Frederic, 1915–
Been here and gone. New Brunswick, N. J., Rutgers University Press [1960]
177 p. illus. 24 cm.
1. Music—Negroes. 2. Negroes—Southern States. 3. Southern States—Soc. life & cust.—1865— —Illustrations. I. Title.
Full name: Charles Frederic Ramsey.
ML3556.R3 781.775 59—7514
Library of Congress [61o²20]

Music - Catalogs.
M784 H192
Handy Bros. Music Co., Inc.
Catalog of music from the House of Handy. New York, Handy Bros. Music Co. [1948]
160p. 20cm.
Music
1. Music - Catalogs. I. Title. II. Handy, William Christopher, 1873-1958.

Music.
M780 D42
Dennison, Tim.
The American Negro and his amazing music. [1st ed.] New York, Vantage Press [1963]
76 p. 21 cm.
1. Music—Negroes. I. Title.
ML3556.D45 781.773 63—24847/MN
Library of Congress [5]

Music.
Ghana M784 R54
Roberts, J T
A hymn of thanksgiving and other songs. Accra, Accra High School, 1953.
10p. port. 25cm.

Music - Biography.
M780 P19
Panassié, Hugues.
Guide to jazz, by Hugues Panassié and Madeleine Gautier. Translated by Desmond Flower; edited by A. A. Gurwitch. Introd. by Louis Armstrong. Boston, Houghton Mifflin, 1956.
vii, 312 p. illus., ports. 22 cm.
"First published in Paris, May 1954, under the title Dictionnaire du jazz. In its present form the book has been brought up to date and expanded for American publication."
1. Music—Bio-bibl. 2. Jazz music—Dictionaries. I. Gautier, Madeleine, 1905– joint author. II. Title.
ML102.J3P33 *785.42 781.5 56—10291
Library of Congress [57l²10]

Music.
M780.9 F31e
Feather, Leonard, comp.
The encylopedia of jazz. New ed., completely rev. and brought up to date. New York, Bonanza Books, 1962.
527p. 26cm.
Partial contents.- The encyclopedia of jazz, by Duke Ellington.

Music.
M973.9 F46 No.19
Still, William Grant, 1895-
Fifty years of progress in music. Pittsburgh, Pittsburgh Courier, 1950.
7p. illus. port. 24cm. (Fifty years of progress)

Music - Theory, Elementary.
M781 Sm64
Smith, Ruby R
The rudiments of music, step by step, by Ruby R. Smith. [1st ed.] New York, Vantage Press [1965]
71 p. illus., music. 21 cm.
1. Music—Theory, Elementary. I. Title.
MT7.S673R8 781.2 64-24743/MN
Library of Congress [5]

Music.
M784 H19b
Handy, William Christopher, 1873-1958, ed.
Blues, an anthology. With an introduction by Abbe Niles. Illustrations by Miguel Convarrubias. New York, Albert & Charles Boni, 1926.
180p. illus. 29cm.
1. Music. I. Title.

Music.
M780 T21t
Taylor, J Hillary
Taylor's music questionnaire. 250 questions and answers upon many phases of the art for the music lover, student amateur and musician, by J. Hillary Taylor. Washington, D.C., The author c1936
29p. 21cm.

Music-Africa.
Haiti M780 C39m
Chauvet, Stéphen, 1885–1950.
Musique nègre, par Stéphen-Chauvet ... Paris, Société d'éditions géographiques, maritimes et coloniales, 1929.
3 p. l., 242 p., 1 l. incl. illus., plates. 31 cm.
Error in paging: p. 230 numbered 228.
"Recueil de 118 airs de musique nègre": p. [127]–165.
"Bibliographie": p. [229]–228 [i. e. 230]
1. Folk-songs, African. 2. Music—Africa. 3. Music, Primitive. 4. Musical instruments, Primitive. I. Title.
ML3760.C4 780.96 31—22284
Library of Congress [57e½]

Music.
M780 J72b
Jones, LeRoi, 1934–
Black music. New York, W. Morrow, 1967.
221 p. illus. 22 cm.
1. Music—~~Negroes~~. 2. Jazz music. 3. ~~Negro~~ musicians. 4. ~~Negroes~~. I. Title.
ML3556.J728 781.7'296 67—29644/MN
Library of Congress [68h5]

Music - Addresses, essays, lectures.
Brazil M781 An2
Andrade, Mario de, 1893–1945.
Musica, doce musica. São Paulo, Martins [1963]
420 p. 22 cm. (*His* Obras completas, v. 7)
"A expressão musical dos Estados Unidos": p. [393]–417.
1. Music—Addresses, essays, lectures. 2. Music—Brazil. I. Title. II. Title: A expressão musical dos Estados Unidos.
ML60.A55O6 1963 64-3352/MN
Library of Congress [1]

Music-Africa.
M780.9 H22
Hare, Maud (Cuney) 1874–1936.
Negro musicians and their music, by Maud Cuney-Hare. Washington, D. C., The Associated publishers, inc. [°1936]
xii, 439 p. plates, ports., facsim. 21 cm.
Includes music.
Bibliography: p. 419–428.
1. Negro musicians. 2. Negro songs—Hist. & crit. 3. Music—U. S.—Hist. & crit. 4. Folk-songs, African. 5. Music—Africa.
36—11223
Library of Congress ML3556.H3N4
[37u5] 780.96

Music - America.

M789 **Howard, Joseph H**
H834 Drums in the Americas, by Joseph H. Howard. New York, Oak Publications [1967]

xv, 319 p. illus., maps, music, 74 photos. 24 cm.

Bibliography: p. 294-311.

1. Drum. 2. Music—America. I. Title.

ML1035.H69 789'.01 67-15826/MN

Library of Congress [3]

Music - Brazil.

Brazil
M781 **Andrade, Mario de, 1893-1945.**
An2 Musica, doce musica. São Paulo, Martins [1963]

420 p. 22 cm. (*His* Obras completas, v. 7)

"A expressão musical dos Estados Unidos": p. [395]-417.

1. Music—Addresses, essays, lectures. 2. Music—Brazil. I. Title. II. Title: A expressão musical dos Estados Unidos.

ML60.A55O6 1963 64-3352/MN

Library of Congress [1]

Music - Brazil.

Brazil
M869 **Andrade, Mario de, 1893–1945.**
An2m Música del Brasil. Traducción de Delia Bernabó. Buenos Aires, Editorial Schapire [1944]

128 p. illus. 19 cm. (Colección Alba. [17])

CONTENTS.—Evolución social de la música brasileña (1930)—Danzas dramáticas ibero-brasileñas (1939)

1. Music—Brazil. 2. Dancing—Brazil. I. Bernabó, Delia, tr. II. Series.

ML232.A725 780.981 47—28413*

Library of Congress [48b1]

Music - Brazil - History and criticism.

Brazil
M780 **Andrade, Mario de, 1893–1945.**
An24 Ensaio sôbre a música brasileira. São Paulo, Martins [1962]

188 p. music. 21 cm. (*His* Obras completas, 6)

Part 2, "Exposição de melodias populares," contains a collection of folk-songs (melodies with words)

1. Music—Brazil—Hist. & crit. 2. Folk-songs, Brazilian.

ML232.A7E6 1962 63—25845/MN

Library of Congress [63b1]

Music - Brazil - History and criticism.

Brazil
M780 **Andrade, Mario de, 1893–1945.**
An24m Música de feitiçaria no Brasil. Organização, introd. e notas de Oneyda Alvarenga. São Paulo, Livraria Martins Editôra [1963]

205 p. 22 cm. (*His* Obras completas, v. 13)

Includes unacc. melodies.
Bibliography: p. [282]-295.

1. Folk-songs, Brazilian—Hist. & crit. 2. Folk-songs, Brazilian.
3. Music - Brazil - Hist. & crit. I. Title.

ML3575.B7A5 64-55465/MN

Library of Congress [1]

Music - Haiti.

Haiti
M792.94 **Fouchard, Jean, 1912–**
F82a Artistes et répertoire des scènes de Saint-Domingue. Port-au-Prince, Impr. de l'État, 1955.

271 p. 21 cm.

Includes bibliographical references.

1. Theater—Haiti. 2. Music—Haiti. I. Title.

PN2416.F58 56-58737

Library of Congress [2]

Music--Madagascar.

Madagascar
M841 Rajaona, Henri
R13c Chants des écoliers Malgaches, paroles de H. Rajaona, musique de J. Landeroin. Paris, Librairie Armand Colin, 1904.

41p. 16½cm.

Music - U. S. - History & criticism.

M780.9 **Cowell, Henry, 1897–** *ed.*
C83 American composers on American music; a symposium edited by Henry Cowell. [Stanford University, Calif.] Stanford university press, 1933.

xii, 226 p. illus. (music) diagrs. 22 cm.

Composers reviewed include Carl Ruggles, Adolph Weiss, Colin McPhee, Edgar Varèse, Aaron Copland, Henry Cowell, Roy Harris, Wallingford Riegger, Roger Sessions, J. J. Becker, Henry Brant, Howard Hanson, Carlos Salzedo, Carlos Chávez, Nicolas Slonimsky, Ruth Crawford, Charles Seeger, Walter Piston and C. E. Ives.

"Biographical notes on composers ... together with lists of their principal works": p. 201-218.

White editor.

1. Music—~~U. S.~~—Hist. & crit. 2. Musicians, ~~American~~. 3. Music, ~~American~~. I. Title.

ML200.5.C87A5 780.97 33—13037

Library of Congress [59h½]

Music-U. S.-Hist. & crit.

M780.9 **Hare, Maud (Cuney) 1874–1936.**
H22 Negro musicians and their music, by Maud Cuney-Hare. Washington, D. C., The Associated publishers, inc. [°1936]

xii, 439 p. plates, ports., facsim. 21 cm.

Includes music.
Bibliography: p. 419-423.

1. Negro musicians. 2. Negro songs—Hist. & crit. 3. Music—U. S.—Hist. & crit. 4. Folk-songs, African. 5. Music—Africa.

36—11923

Library of Congress ML3556.H3N4
[37u5] 780.9

Music— U.S.—Hist. & crit.

M808. **Locke, Alain LeRoy, 1886–**
L79n2 ... The Negro and his music, by Alain Locke ... Washington, D. C., The Associates in Negro folk education, 1936.

3 p. l., 142 p. 20½ cm. (Bronze booklet no. 2)

"Reading references" at end of each chapter; "Recorded illustrations" at end of most of the chapters.

1. Negro musicians. 2. Negro songs—Hist. & crit. 3. Music—U. S.—Hist. & crit. 4. Jazz music. 5. Phonograph records. I. Title.

37—10637

Library of Congress E185.5.B85 no. 2
———Copy 2. ML3556.L6N4
[42i2] (325.260973) 784.756

Music-Zulu.

Africa, South
M780
T671e Tracey, Hugh
Lalela Zulu; 100 Zulu lyrics. With illustrations by Eric Byrd. Foreword by A. W. Hoernle. Johnnesburg, Published by African Music Society, 1948.

121p. illus. 25cm.

Music, African.

Cameroun
M780 Belinga, M S Eno, 1935-
B*6 Littérature et musique populaires en Afrique noire. [Paris, Éditions Cujas, 1965]

258p. illus. 18cm.
Includes bibliography.

1. Music, African. 2. Africa - Music.
I. Title.

Music, African.

Africa
M780.9 Brandel, Rose
B73mu The music of Central Africa; an ethnomusical study. The Hague, Martinus Nijhoff, 1961.

272p. illus. 27cm.
Includes bibliography.

Rhodesia
M780 Music, African.
J71 **Jones, A M**
Studies in African music. London, New York, Oxford University Press, 1959.

2 v. xvili plates (photos.) charts, music. 22, 23 x 32 cm.

Vol. 2 contains music dealt with in text of vol. 1 in full score; principally dance music for voices and percussion.

1. Music, African — Hist. & crit. 2. Music, Primitive. 3. Music, African. I. Title.

ML3760.J63 59—1858

Library of Congress [60j10]

Nigeria Music, African.
M784 **King, Anthony.**
K58 Yoruba sacred music from Ekiti. [Nigeria] Ibadan University Press, 1961.

ix, 45, xlix p. illus., music. 22 cm.

Music: xlix p. at end.

1. Music, African. 2. Music, Primitive. 3. Yorubas—Music. 4. Percussion music—Hist. & crit. I. Title.

ML3760.K47 62-752

Library of Congress [1]

Ghana Music, African.
M789.1 Nketia, J H Kwabena.
N65 Drumming in Akan communities of Ghana. [London] Published on behalf of the University of Ghana by Nelson [1963]
212p. 23½cm. illus.
"Recordings of Akan music and poetry"; p. 201-203.

Rhodesia, N.
M780 Music, African - Hist. & crit.
J71 **Jones, A M**
Studies in African music. London, New York, Oxford University Press, 1959.

2 v. xviii plates (photos.) charts, music. 22, 23 x 32 cm.

Vol. 2 contains music dealt with in text of vol. 1 in full score; principally dance music for voices and percussion.

1. Music, African — Hist. & crit. 2. Music, Primitive. 3. Music, African. I. Title.

ML3760.J63 59—1858

Library of Congress [60j10]

Music, Brazilian - History.

Brazil
M869 Andrade, Mário de, 1893-1945.
An2pe Pequena história de musica. 5ª edicão. São Paulo, Livraria Martins Editôra, 1958.

232p. illus., port. 21½cm.
(Obras Completas de Mário de Andrade)

Music, Popular (Songs, etc) - Trinidad.

M784 **Attaway, William.**
At8c Calypso song book. Edited and compiled by Lyle Kenyon Engel. Illus. by William Charmatz. [1st ed.] New York, McGraw-Hill [°1957]

64 p. col. illus. 26 cm.

"What is calypso?": p. 6-13.

1. Music, Popular (Songs, etc.)—Trinidad. I. Title.

M1681.T7A8 M 57—1008

Library of Congress [58b15]

Music, Popular (Songs, etc) - U. S.

M784 **Charters, Ann,** *ed.*
C38 The ragtime songbook; songs of the ragtime era by Scott Joplin ... and others. Compiled and edited, with historical notes concerning the songs and the times, by Ann Charters. New York, Oak Publications [1965]

112 p. illus. 26 cm.

Principally unacc., with chord symbols.
"Introduction": p. 8-34.

1. Music, Popular (Songs, etc.)—U. S. 2. Music, Popular (Songs, etc.)—U. S.—Hist. & crit. I. Title.

M1630.18.C515R3 784.7 65-22694/M

Library of Congress [2]

Music, Popular (Songs, etc.)-U.S.

M784 **Handy, William Christopher, 1873–** *ed.*
H19tr A treasury of the blues; complete words and music of 67 great songs from Memphis blues to the present day. With an historical and critical text by Abbe Niles. With pictures by Miguel Covarrubias. [New York] C. Boni; distributed by Simon and Schuster [1949]

258 p. illus. 29 cm.

First ed. published in 1926 under title: Blues, an anthology.
"A selective bibliography": p. 254-255.

1. Music, Popular (Songs, etc.)—U. S. I. Niles, Abbe, 1894– II. Title.

M1630.18.H26B5 1949 784 49—50282*

Library of Congress [56f2]

Music, Popular (Songs, etc.) - U. S.

M780 **Shirley, Kay,** *ed.*
Sh66 The book of the blues. Annotated by Frank Driggs. Record research by Joy Graeme. Music research by Bob Hartsell. New York, Leeds Music Corp. ⌊1963⌋

301 p. 32 cm.

Unacc., with guitar chords.
Background notes, list of recordings, and chord diagrams for guitar and tenor banjo, precede each song.

1. Music, Popular (Songs, etc.)—U. S. 2. Folk-songs, American. 3. Negro songs. I. Title.

M1629.S557B6 63-18895/M

Library of Congress ⌊3⌋

Music, Popular (Songs, etc.) - U. S. - History and criticism.

M784 **Charters, Ann,** *ed.*
C38 The ragtime songbook; songs of the ragtime era by Scott Joplin ... and others. Compiled and edited, with historical notes concerning the songs and the times, by Ann Charters. New York, Oak Publications ⌊1965⌋

112 p. illus. 26 cm.

Principally unacc., with chord symbols.
"Introduction": p. 8-34.

1. Music, Popular (Songs, etc.)—U. S. 2. Music, Popular (Songs, etc.)—U. S.—Hist. & crit. I. Title.

M1630.18.C515R3 784.7 65-22694/M

Library of Congress ⌊2⌋

Music, Popular (Songs, etc.) - West Indies.

M784 **Belafonte, Harold, 1927-** *comp.*
B41 Songs Belafonte sings. Illustrated by Charles White. ⌊1st ed.⌋ New York, Duell, Sloan and Pearce ⌊1962⌋

x, 196 p. illus. 29 cm.

Commentary on each song by Belafonte.
Music editor: Bob Bollard; piano arrangements: Joseph Mazzu.

CONTENTS.—Around the world.—The American Negro.—The West Indies.

1. Folk-songs. 2. Negro songs. 3. Negro spirituals. 4. Music, Popular (Songs, etc.)—West Indies. I. Title.

Full name: Harold George Belafonte.

M1627.B36S6 M62-1000

Library of Congress ⌊5⌋

Music, Primitive.

Haiti
M780 **Chauvet, Stéphen, 1885–1950.**
C39m Musique nègre, par Stéphen-Chauvet ... Paris, Société d'éditions géographiques, maritimes et coloniales, 1929.

3 p. l., 242 p., 1 l. incl. illus., plates. 31 cm.

Error in paging: p. 230 numbered 228.
"Recueil de 118 airs de musique nègre": p. ⌊127⌋-165.
"Bibliographie": p. ⌊229⌋-228 ⌊*i. e.* 230⌋

1. Folk-songs, African. 2. Music—Africa. 3. Music, Primitive. 4. Musical instruments, Primitive. I. Title.

ML3760.C4 780.96 31—22284

Library of Congress ⌊57e½⌋

Rhodesia, N.
M780 Music, Primitive.
J71 **Jones, A M**
Studies in African music. London, New York, Oxford University Press, 1959.

2 v. xviii plates (photos.) charts, music. 22, 23 x 32 cm.

Vol. 2 contains music dealt with in text of vol. 1 in full score; principally dance music for voices and percussion.

1. Music, African — Hist. & crit. 2. Music, Primitive. 3. Music, African. I. Title.

ML3760.J63 59—1858

Library of Congress ⌊60j10⌋

Nigeria Music, Primitive.
M784 **King, Anthony.**
K58 Yoruba sacred music from Ekiti. ⌊Nigeria⌋ Ibadan University Press, 1961.

ix, 45, xlix p. illus., music. 22 cm.

Music: xlix p. at end.

1. Music, African. 2. Music, Primitive. 3. Yorubas—Music. 4. Percussion music—Hist. & crit. I. Title.

ML3760.K47 62-752

Library of Congress ⌊1⌋

Music, Primitive.

Uganda
M967.61 **Kyagambiddwa, Joseph.**
K98 African music from the source of the Nile. With introductions by J. LaFarge and Josephine Shine. New York, Praeger ⌊1955⌋

xii, 255 p. illus., ports., map. 29 cm. (Books that matter)

Includes music.

1. Folk music—Africa. 2. Folk-songs, African. 3. Music, Primitive.

ML3760.K9 781.76 55-9485

Library of Congress ⌊10⌋

Music and musicians.

MB9 Handy, William Christopher, 1873-
H19b Father of the blues; an autobiography.
1957 Edited by Arna Bontemps. With a foreword by Abbe Niles. London, Sidgwick and Jackson, 1957.

317p. port., illus.

Music and musicians.

M784 **Oliver, Paul.**
O13 **Blues fell this morning - the meaning of the blues. With a foreword by Richard Wright. New York, Horizon Press, 1960.**

355p. 21½cm.

Music and musicians.

M784 **Pittman, Evelyn LaRue**
P68r **Rich heritage; songs about American Negro heroes. Oklahoma City, Oklahoma, Harlow Publishing Corporation, 1944.**

48p. illus. ports. 30cm.

The music of Central Africa.

Africa
M780.9 Brandel, Rose
B73mu The music of Central Africa; an ethno-musical study. The Hague, Martinus Nijhoff, 1961.

272p. illus. 27cm.
Includes bibliography.

Music on my mind.

M780 **Smith, Willie, 1897-**
Sm68 Music on my mind; the memoirs of an American pianist, by Willie the Lion Smith with George Hoefer. Foreword by Duke Ellington. ⌊1st ed.⌋ Garden City, N. Y., Doubleday, 1964.

xvi, 318 p. 22 cm.

Includes bibliographies, list of Willie Smith's compositions, and discography.

1. Musicians—Correspondence, reminiscences, etc. 2. Jazz music. I. Hoefer, George. II. Title.

ML417.S675A3 781.57 64-13840/MN

Library of Congress ⌊5⌋

Brazil **Musica, doce musica.**
M781 **Andrade, Mario de, 1893–1945.**
An2 Musica, doce musica. São Paulo, Martins ⌊1963⌋

420 p. 22 cm. (*His* Obras completas, v. 7)

"A expressão musical dos Estados Unidos": p. ⌊398⌋-417.

1. Music—Addresses, essays, lectures. 2. Music—Brazil. I. Title. II. Title: A expressão musical dos Estados Unidos.

ML60.A55O6 1963 64-3352/MN

Library of Congress ⌊1⌋

Musica de feiticaria no Brasil.

Brazil
M780 Andrade, Mario de, 1893-1945.
An24m Musica de feiticaria no Brasil. Organizacao, introd. e notas de Oneyda Alvarenga. Sao Paulo, Livraria Martins Editora, 1963

295p. 22cm. (His Obras completas, v.13)

Includes unacc. melodies.
Bibliography:p. 282-295.

1. Folk-songs, Brazilian - Hist. & crit. 2. Folk-songs, Brazilian. 3. Music - Brazil - Hist. & crit. I. Title.

The musical bride.

British Guiana
M823.91 Talbot, Dave
T14m The musical bride. New York, Vantage Press, 1962.

249p. 23cm.
Portrait of author on book jacket.

Musical instruments.

M789 **Howard, Joseph H**
H834 Drums in the Americas, by Joseph H. Howard. New York, Oak Publications ⌊1967⌋

xv, 319 p. illus., maps, music, 74 photos. 24 cm.

Bibliography: p. 294-311.
Portrait of author on book jacket.

1. Drum. 2. Music—America. I. Title.
3. Musical instruments.

ML1035.H69 789'.01 67-15326/MN

Library of Congress ⌊3⌋

Musical instruments - Juvenile literature.

M785 **Goward, Gladys McFadden.**
G74 See how they play; a pictorial tour through the orchestra. New York, Exposition Press ⌊1953⌋

50 p. illus. 21 cm.

1. Musical instruments—Juvenile literature. I. Title.

ML3930.A2G7 785 53-10540 ‡

Library of Congress ⌊2⌋

Musical instruments, Primitive.

Haiti
M780 **Chauvet, Stéphen, 1885–1950.**
C39m Musique nègre, par Stéphen-Chauvet ... Paris, Société d'éditions géographiques, maritimes et coloniales, 1929.

3 p. l., 242 p., 1 l. incl. illus., plates. 31 cm.

Error in paging: p. 230 numbered 228.
"Recueil de 118 airs de musique nègre": p. ⌊127⌋-165.
"Bibliographie": p. ⌊229⌋-228 ⌊*i. e.* 230⌋

1. Folk-songs, African. 2. Music—Africa. 3. Music, Primitive. 4. Musical instruments, Primitive. I. Title.

ML3760.C4 780.96 31—22284

Library of Congress ⌊57e½⌋

Musicians.

MB9 Bethune, Thomas Greene, 1849-1908.
B46b The marvelous musical prodigy, Blind Tom, the Negro boy pianist whose performances at the great St. James and Egyptian halls, London, and Salle Hertz, Paris, have created such a profound sensation. Anecdotes, songs, sketches of the life, testimonials of musicians, and savans and opinions of the American and English press of "Blind Tom." New York, French and Wheat ⌊n.d.⌋

30p. 23cm.

Musicians.

M810. **Brawley, Benjamin Griffith, 1882-1939.**
B73n2 The Negro genius; a new appraisal of the achievement of the American Negro in literature and the fine arts, by Benjamin Brawley ... New York, Dodd, Mead & company, 1937.

xiii, 366 p. front., plates, ports. 20½ cm.

Bibliography: p. 331-350.

1. Negro authors. 2. Negro artists. 3. Negro musicians. 4. Negro literature—Hist. & crit. 5. Negroes in literature and art. I. Title.

37—4124

Library of Congress E185.82.B816 ⌊47b³3⌋ 325.260973

Musicians.

M780.9 **Cowell, Henry, 1897-** *ed.*
C83 American composers on American music; a symposium edited by Henry Cowell. ⌊Stanford University, Calif.⌋ Stanford university press, 1933.

xii, 226 p. illus. (music) diagrs. 22 cm.

Composers reviewed include Carl Ruggles, Adolph Weiss, Colin McPhee, Edgar Varèse, Aaron Copland, Henry Cowell, Roy Harris, Wallingford Riegger, Roger Sessions, J. J. Becker, Henry Brant, Howard Hanson, Carlos Salzedo, Carlos Chávez, Nicolas Slonimsky, Ruth Crawford, Charles Seeger, Walter Piston and C. E. Ives.
"Biographical notes on composers ... together with lists of their principal works": p. 201-218.
White editor.

1. Music—~~U. S.~~—Hist. & crit. 2. Musicians, ~~American~~. 3. Music, ~~American~~. I. Title.

ML200.5.C87A5 780.97 33—13037

Library of Congress ⌊59h½⌋

M780.9 Musicians.
F31e Feather, Leonard, comp.
The encylopedia of jazz. New ed., completely rev. and brought up to date. New York, Bonanza Books, 1962.
527p. 26cm.
Partial contents.- The encyclopedia of jazz, by Duke Ellington.

M813.5 Musicians.
H87fam Hughes, Langston, 1902-
Famous Negro music makers; illustrated with photos. New York, Dodd, Mead, 1955.
179 p. illus. 22 cm. (Famous biographies for young people)
1. Negro musicians. I. Title.
Full name: James Langston Hughes.
ML3556.H9 927.8 55—9419 ‡
Library of Congress ₍56x15₎

M784 Musicians.
T75 Trotter, James M.
Music and some highly musical people: containing brief chapters on I. A description of music. II. The music of nature. III. A glance at the history of music. IV. The power, beauty, and uses of music. Following which are given sketches of the lives of remarkable musicians of the colored race. With portraits, and an appendix containing copies of music composed by colored men. By James M. Trotter ... Boston, Lee and Shepard; New York, C. T. Dillingham, 1878.
353 p., 1 l., 152 p. incl. pl. front., ports. 19½cm.
Music: Appendix, p. 4-152.
1. Negro musicians.
Library of Congress ML60.T85 5—38530
₍41c1₎

M780.9 Musicians.
F31 Feather, Leonard
The encyclopedia of jazz. Foreword by Duke Ellington. New York, Horizon Press, 1955.
359p. ports. 25½cm.
Includes bibliography.
White author.

M780 Musicians.
J72b Jones, LeRoi, 1934-
Black music. New York, W. Morrow, 1967.
221 p. illus. 22 cm.
1. Music—Negroes. 2. Jazz music. 3. Negro musicians. 4. Negroes. I. Title.
ML3556.J728 781.7'296 67—29844/MN
Library of Congress ₍68b5₎

MB9 Musicians
W29h Waters, Ethel, 1900-
His eye is on the sparrow; an autobiography by Ethel Waters with Charles Samuels. ₍1st ed.₎ Garden City, N.Y., Doubleday, 1951.
278p. 22cm.

M780 Musicians.
G47 Gleason, Ralph J ed.
Jam session; an anthology of jazz. New York, Putnam ₍1958₎
319 p. illus. 22 cm.
1. Jazz music—Addresses, essays, lectures. I. Title.
ML3561.J3G56 *785.42 780.973 57—6725 ‡
Library of Congress ₍58q10₎

M308 Musicians.
L79n 2 Locke, Alain LeRoy, 1886-
... The Negro and his music, by Alain Locke ... Washington, D. C., The Associates in Negro folk education, 1936.
3 p. l., 142 p. 20½ cm. (Bronze booklet no. 2)
"Reading references" at end of each chapter; "Recorded illustrations" at end of most of the chapters.
1. Negro musicians. 2. Negro songs—Hist. & crit. 3. Music—U. S.—Hist. & crit. 4. Jazz music. 5. Phonograph records. I. Title.
Library of Congress E185.5.B85 no. 2 37—10637
———— Copy 2. ML3556.L6N4
₍42i2₎ (325.260973) 784.756

M784 Musicians.
W33 Watson, Deek.
The story of the "Ink Spots," by Deek Watson with Lee Stephenson. ₍1st ed.₎ New York, Vantage Press ₍1967₎
72 p. 21 cm.
1. Ink Spots. I. Stephenson, Lee, joint author. II. Title.
3. Musicians.
ML400.W23 784'.0922 67-5817/MN
Library of Congress ₍3₎

MB9 Musicians
G83b Greenfield, Elizabeth T
A brief memoir of the "black swan," Miss E.T. Greenfield, the American vocalist. London ₍n.p.₎ 1853.
16p. 22cm.
Portrait on cover.

M784 Musicians.
M35 Marsh, J B T
The story of the Jubilee singers; with their songs. Ed. by J. B. T. ₍!₎ Marsh. 7th ed. London, Hodder and Stoughton, 1877.
vi, ₍2₎, 248 p. front. (mounted phot.) illus. 17½cm.
1. Jubilee singers. 2. Negro musicians. 3. Negro songs.
6—3204
Library of Congress M1607.F4
₍45o1₎

MB9 Musicians-Correspondence, reminiscences, etc.
An24o Anderson, Marian, 1902-
My Lord, what a morning. London, The Cresset Press, 1957.
240p. illus. 22cm.

M780.9 Musicians.
H19n Handy, William Christopher, 1873-
Negro authors and composers of the United States, by W. C. Handy. New York, N. Y., Handy brothers music co., inc. ₍1938?₎
cover-title, 24 p. illus. (port.) 23cm.
Bibliography: p. 24.
1. Negro musicians. I. Title.
38—19429
Library of Congress ML3556.H23N3
₍41c2₎ 780.973

M784 Musicians.
P63 Pike, Gustavus D
The Jubilee singers, and their campaign for twenty thousand dollars. By G. D. Pike ... Boston, Lee and Shepard; New York, Lee, Shepard and Dillingham, 1873.
219 p., 1 l. incl. front. ports. 20½ cm.
Includes a brief account of Fisk university, Nashville.
"Jubilee songs": p. ₍161₎-219.
1. Jubilee singers. 2. Negro musicians. 3. Fisk university, Nashville. 4. Negro songs. I. Title.
6—3203
Library of Congress ML400.P63
₍45o1₎

MB9 Musicians-Correspondence, reminiscences, etc.
An24 Anderson, Marian, 1902-
My Lord, what a morning; an autobiography. New York, Viking Press, 1956.
312 p. illus. 22 cm.
"A condensed version ... appeared in serial form in the Woman's home companion."
1. Musicians—Correspondence, reminiscences, etc. I. Title.
ML420.A6A3 927.8 56—10402 ‡
Library of Congress ₍57m²20₎

M780.9 Musicians.
H22 Hare, Maud (Cuney) 1874-1936.
Negro musicians and their music, by Maud Cuney-Hare. Washington, D. C., The Associated publishers, inc. ₍°1936₎
xii, 439 p. plates, ports., facsim. 21 cm.
Includes music.
Bibliography: p. 419-423.
1. Negro musicians. 2. Negro songs—Hist. & crit. 3. Music—U. S.—Hist. & crit. 4. Folk-songs, African. 5. Music—Africa.
36—11223
Library of Congress ML3556.H3N4
₍37u5₎ 780.96

M781 Musicians.
R14j Ramsey, Frederic, 1915- ed.
Jazzmen, edited by Frederic Ramsey, jr., and Charles Edward Smith. With 32 pages of illustrations. New York, Harcourt, Brace and company ₍1939₎
xv, 360 p. plates, ports. 22 cm.
Contributors (in addition to the editors): William Russell, S. W. Smith, E. Simms Campbell, E. J. Nichols, Wilder Hobson, Otis Ferguson and R. P. Dodge.
"First edition."
White author.
1. Jazz music. 2. Negro musicians. 3. Musicians, American. I. Smith, Charles Edward, joint ed. II. Title.
Full name: Charles Frederic Ramsey.
ML3561.R24J2 780.973 39—31807
Library of Congress ₍59f2₎

M780 Musicians-Correspondence, reminiscences, etc.
Ar5 Armstrong, Louis, 1900-
Satchmo; my life in New Orleans. New York, Prentice-Hall ₍1954₎
240 p. illus. 21 cm.
1. Musicians—Correspondence, reminiscences, etc. 2. Jazz music. I. Title.
ML419.A75A3 927.8 54—9628 ‡
Library of Congress ₍54d²30₎

MB9 Musicians.
H7841 Horne, Lena.
In person, Lena Horne; as told to Helen Arstein and Carlton Moss. ₍New York₎ Greenberg ₍1950₎
249p. illus. 21cm.

M780 Musicians.
Sp32 Spellman, A B 1935-
Four lives in the bebop business, by A. B. Spellman. New York, Pantheon Books ₍1966₎
xiv, 241 p. 22 cm.
Portrait of author on book jacket.
1. Jazz musicians. 2. Negro musicians. I. Title.
ML394.S74 780.922 66-10410/MN
Library of Congress ₍3₎

M780 Musicians-Correspondence, reminiscences, etc.
Ar5s Armstrong, Louis, 1900-
Satchmo; my life in New Orleans. London, The Harborough Publishing Co., Ltd., 1954.
157p. 18cm.
Paper back edition.

Musicians - Correspondence, reminiscences, etc.
MB9 H72 1
Holiday, Billie, 1915-
Lady sings the blues [by] Billie Holiday with William Dufty. [1st ed.] New York, Popular Library (paper back) 1958.
192p. illus. (on lining papers) 18cm.
Autobiography.
1. Musicians—Correspondence, reminiscences, etc. I. Title.
ML420.H58A3 927.8 56-5962
Library of Congress [15]

Musings of a minister.
M811.5 G34m
Gholson, Edward.
Musings of a minister, by Rev. Edward Gholson. Boston, The Christopher publishing house [1943]
viii, 9-101 p. 19cm.
Poems.
I. Title.
43-11475
Library of Congress PS3513.H6M8
[3] 811.5

Uganda
MB9 Ag38m
Musson, M
Aggrey loka Achimota [Aggrey of Achimota] Loejuli E. Y. A. Otim. Nairobi, Eagle Press, 1951.
42p. 21cm.
Written in Ateso
White author.
1. Aggrey, James Emman Kwegyir, 1875-1927. I. Otim, E. Y. A., tr. II. Title.

Musicians - Correspondence, reminiscences, etc.
MB9 H784
Horne, Lena.
Lena, by Lena Horne and Richard Schickel. [1st ed.] Garden City, N. Y., Doubleday, 1965.
300 p. illus., ports. 22 cm.
1. Musicians—Correspondence, reminiscences, etc. I. Schickel, Richard, joint author. II. Title.
ML420.H65A35 792.7 (B) 65-18388/MN
Library of Congress [5]

Musique Nègre.
Haiti M780 C39m
Chauvet, Stéphen, 1885-1950.
Musique nègre, par Stéphen-Chauvet ... Paris, Société d'éditions géographiques, maritimes et coloniales, 1929.
3 p. l., 242 p., 1 l. incl. illus., plates. 31 cm.
Error in paging: p. 230 numbered 228.
"Recueil de 118 airs de musique nègre": p. [127]-165.
"Bibliographie": p. [229]-228 [i. e. 230]
1. Folk-songs, African. 2. Music—Africa. 3. Music, Primitive. 4. Musical instruments, Primitive. I. Title.
ML3760.C4 780.96 31--22284
Library of Congress [57e1]

Gold Coast
MB9 Ag8m Gold Coast
Musson, M
Aggrey of Achimota, by M. Musson...London and Redhill, United society for Christian literature, 1944.
56p. 18½cm. (Africa's own library, no.7)
1. Aggrey, James Emman Kwegyir, 1875-1925.
2. Gold Coast.

Musicians - Correspondence, reminiscences, etc.
MB9 K65
Kitt, Eartha.
Thursday's child. [1st ed.] New York, Duell, Sloan and Pearce [1956]
250 p. illus. 21 cm.
Autobiographical.
1. Musicians—Correspondence, reminiscences, etc. I. Title.
ML420.K5A3 927.8 56-9590 ‡
Library of Congress [15]

M976.6 M97n
Muskogee, Oklahoma.
Negro city directory, including the town of Taft, 1941-1942. Muskogee, 1942.
127p. 22cm.
1. Directories.

Must Negro-Americans wait another hundred years for freedom?
M323.4 D29
Davis, Benjamin J.
Must Negro-Americans wait another hundred years for freedom? Against tokenism and gradualism. New York, New Century Publishers, 1963.
15p. 19½cm.

Musicians - Correspondence, reminiscences, etc.
MB9 J136
Jackson, Mahalia, 1911-
Movin' on up. With Evan McLeod Wylie. [1st ed.] New York, Hawthorn Books [1966]
212, [7] p. illus., ports. 24 cm.
Discography: p. [215], [218]-[219]
1. Musicians—Correspondence, reminiscences, etc. I. Wylie, Evan McLeod, 1916- II. Title.
ML420.J17A3 784.0924 66-22315/MN
Library of Congress [5]

Kenya M372.4 L92
Musomi Wokitanga.
Lwane, Benjamin G
Musomi Wokutanga, chia Benjamin G. Lwane na Joseph G. Kisia. [Illustrated by Ruth Yudelowitz] Nairobi, Eagle Press, 1957.
24p. illus. 22cm.
Written in Lulagoli.

Musungaie, Robert
Congo(Leopoldville)
M896.3 K64c
Kitambala, Jérôme
Contes Africains, par Jerome Kitambala, Paul Malulu, Simon Mudiangu, and Robert Musungaie. Leverville (Congo Belge), Bibliotheque de l'Etoile, May 1955.
32p. illus. 18cm. (No. 97)

Musicians - Correspondence, reminiscences, etc
M780 Sm68
Smith, Willie, 1897-
Music on my mind; the memoirs of an American pianist, by Willie the Lion Smith with George Hoefer. Foreword by Duke Ellington. [1st ed.] Garden City, N. Y., Doubleday, 1964.
xvi, 318 p. 22 cm.
Includes bibliographies, list of Willie Smith's compositions, and discography.
1. Musicians—Correspondence, reminiscences, etc. 2. Jazz music. I. Hoefer, George. II. Title.
ML417.S675A3 781.57 64-13840/MN
Library of Congress [5]

Jamaica M821.91 M97m
Musson, Flora Elaine.
A magazine of verse. n.p., n.d.
21p. Portrait. 22cm.
Inscribed by author: Compliments of the author, Flora E. Roberts.
~~1. Poetry.~~ 1. Jamaican poetry

South Africa M896 M88
Mutabaruka, Jean-Baptiste, 1937-
Song of the drum.
Pp. 145-148.
In: Mphahlele, Ezekiel, ed. African writing today. Baltimore, Penguin Books, 1967.

Nigeria M780 D28
Musicians, African.
Davies, Hezekiah Olufela, 1943-
The Victor Olaiya story; a biography of Nigeria's evil genius of highly life, Victor Abimbola Olaiya. [Ikeja, Nigeria, Sankey Printing Works, n.d.]
52p. illus. 18cm.
Cover title.

Jamaica M821.91 M97p
Musson, Elora Elaine.
Poems. n.p., n.d.
[5]p. 21cm.
Inscribed by author: Compliments of the author, Flora E. Roberts.
~~1. Poetry.~~ 1. Jamaican poetry

Uganda M967.61 M98
Mutesa II, King of Buganda. (1924-1969)
Desecration of my kingdom [by] the Kabaka of Buganda. London, Constable, 1967.
194p. illus., ports. 23cm.
Bibliographical footnotes.
1. Buganda - History. I. Title.

Musings of childhood.
M811.5 W152m
Walker, James Robert.
Musings of childhood. New York, Comet Press Books, 1960.
115p. 21cm.
Portrait of author on book jacket.

M821.91 M97v
Musson, Flora Elaine.
Voices of spring. Port-of-Spain, B.W.I., Guardian Commercial Printery, 1943.
39p. port. 23cm.
~~xxxxxxxxxxx~~ I. Title.
1. Jamaican poetry

Zambia M896.3 C44m
Mutolalibona.
Chimuka, Simasiku S
Mutolalibona. London, Evans Brothers in assocation with the Northern Rhodesia and Nyasaland Publications Bureau [1962]
64p. 19cm.
Written in Lozi.
I. Title.

Congo(Leopoldville)
M967.5 Mutombo, Dieudonne
M98h Hygiene de l'alimentation. Leverville, Bibliotheque de l'etoile, 1954.

39p. illus. 17½cm.

1. Congo, Belgian - health.

Congo(Leopoldville)
M967.5 Mutombo, Dieudonné
M98v Victoire de l'amour. Leverville, Bibliotheque de l'etoile, 1953.

127p. illus. 18½cm.

1. Fiction - Belgian Congo.

The Mutual baseball almanac.

M796 Kahn, Roger, ed.
K12 The Mutual baseball almanac, edited by Roger Kahn and Al Helfer in co-operation with the Mutual sports staff. Garden City, N.Y., Doubleday, 1954.

254p. illus. 22cm.

Mutunga na ngewa yake.

Kenya
M896.3 Mbiti, John Samuel, 1931-
M11m Mutunga na ngewa yake. Illustrated by Ruth Yudelowitz. London, Thomas Nelson and Sons, Ltd., 1954.

60p. illus. 18½cm.

Kenya
M173 Mũtũũrĩre na mwicirirĩe mwega.
W73 Windstedt, R O
Mũtũũrĩre na mwicirirĩe mwega [Right living and right thinking] Ritauritwo ni J. P. Mathenge na A. H. Kanyuru. Nairobi, Eagle Press, 1954.

89p. 18cm.
Written in Kikuyu.
White author.

1. Ethics. I. Title. II. Mathenge, J. P., tr. III. Kanyuru, A. H., jt. tr.

South Africa
M968 Mutwa, Vusamazulu Credo, 1921-
M98 Indaba, my children. Johannesburg, Blue Crane Books [1965]

562p. illus., ports. 25cm.

1. Zulus. 2. Zululand - Social life and customs. 3. Africa, South - Native races. I. Title.

Kenya
M896.1 Muyaka bin Haji al-Ghassaniy, 1776-1840.
M98d Diwani ya Muyaka bin Haji al-Ghassaniy «Swahili poems of Muyaka» Pamoja na khabari za maisha yake ambazo zimehadithiwa ni W. Hichens. Johannesburg, University of Witwatersrand Press, 1940.

115p. 18cm. (Bantu treasury, no. 4)

I. Title.

Cameroun
M960 Mveng, Engelbert
M98 Dossier culturel Pan-Africain. Paris Présence Africaine [1965]

236p. maps. 18cm.

1. Africa. I. Title.

Cameroons
M967.11 Mveng, Engelbert
M98 Histoire du Cameroun. Paris, Présence Africaine, 1963.

533p. illus., maps. 21cm.
Bibliography: p. 503-526.

1. Cameroons - History. I. Title.

Cameroun
M896.1 Mveng, Engelbert
M98L Lève-toi amie viens, images et textes du Engelbert Mveng. Dakar, Librarie Clairafrique [1966]

[53]p. illus. 24cm.

I. Title.

Cameroun
M896.1 Mveng, Engelbert
M98m Mon amour pour toi est éternel. [Paris] Mame [1963]

21p. illus. 12cm.

I. Title.

Cameroun
M896.1 Mveng, Engelbert
M98s Si quelqu'un ... chemin de croix. [Paris] Mame [1962]

[29]p. illus. 19cm.

1. Jesus Christ - Poetry. I. Title.

Cameroun
M896.1 Mveng, Engelbert
M98t Take up your cross. Meditations on the way of the cross. Translated by Douglas Lord. London, Geoffrey Chapman [1963]

[30]p. illus. 20cm.
Translation of Si quelqu'un... chemin de croix.

1. Jesus Christ - Poetry. I. Title.

Mvulana na nguruwe na hadithi nyingine

Zanzibar
M896.3 Diva, David Edward
D64m Mvulana na nguruwe na hadithi nyingine [The boy and the pig and other stories] London, University of London Press, 1951.

31p. 18½cm.
Written in Swahili.

I. Title.

Kenya
M896.3 Mwandia, David
M98k Kĩlovoo. Illustrated by Ruth Yudelowitz. London, Thomas Nelson [1952]

44p. illus. 18cm. (Eagle fiction library)
Written in Kamba.

I. Title.

Malawi
M968.97 Mwase, George Simeon, *ca.* 1880-1962.
M98 Strike a blow and die; a narrative of race relations in colonial Africa. Edited and introduced by Robert I. Rotberg. Cambridge, Mass., Harvard University Press, 1967.

xiii, 135 p. map, ports. 22 cm.

Bibliographical footnotes.

1. Chilembwe, John, d. 1915. 2. Malawi—Hist. I. Rotberg, Robert I., ed. II. Title.

DT862.M68 66-21342

968.97'020924 (B)

Library of Congress [5]

Tanganyika
M896.3 Mwonge, Elias G L
M99u Usia wa baba na hadithi nyingine [Father's last will and other Heke stories] Dar es Salaam, East African Literature Bureau, 1962.

14p. illus. 18cm. (Hadith za Tanganyika, Kitabu cha Tano)
Written in Swahili.

I. Title. II. Series.

My Africa.

Nigeria
M966.9 Ojike, Mbonu.
Oj3m ... My Africa ... New York, The John Day company [1946]

xiii, [1], 350 p. illus. (incl. map, plan) plates, ports. 22cm.

"Annotated book list": p. 342-345.

1. Africa—Soc. life & cust. I. Title.

46-25033

Library of Congress * DT14.O4

[20] 916

My bondage and my freedom.

M815.4 Douglass, Frederick, 1817-1895.
D739ab My bondage and my freedom ... By Frederick Douglass. With an introduction. By Dr. James M'Cune Smith. New York, Miller, Orton & Mulligan, 1855.

xxxi, [33]-464 p. front. (port.) 2 pl. 18½cm.

Enlarged and published under title: Life and times of Frederick Douglass. Hartford, 1881.

1. Slavery in the U. S.—Anti-slavery movements. 2. Slavery in the U. S.—Maryland. I. Title.

14—4878

Library of Congress E449.D738

[42n1]

My bones and my flute.

Brit. Guiana
M823.91 Mittelholzer, Edgar.
L69mi My bones and my flute. London, Secker & Warburg, 1955.

222p. 19cm.

My country and I.

MB9 Christian, Malcolm Henry, 1904-
C46 My country and I; the interracial experiences of an American Negro. With essays on interracial understanding. [1st ed.] New York, Exposition Press [1963]

96 p. 22 cm.

1. Negroes. I. Title.

E185.97.C5A3 920 63-496 ‡

Library of Congress [5]

My country, and other poems.

M811.5 Sh1

Shackelford, Theodore Henry.
My country, and other poems, by Theodore Henry Shackelford, illustrated by the author, introduction by Charles Hastings Dodd ... [Philadelphia, Press of I. W. Klopp co., °1918]
216 p. front. (port.) plates. 19½cm.
"Contains all the poems included in ... 'Mammy's cracklin' bread'."
Music: p. [158]-[161]
I. Title. 1.Poetry.
18—12942
Library of Congress PS3601.S5M8 1918 [43b1]

My first sixty years: passion for wisdom.

MB9 M846

Morton, Lena Beatrice.
My first sixty years: passion for wisdom. New York, Philosophical Library [1965]
175 p. port. 22 cm.
1. Negro teachers—Correspondence, reminiscences, etc. I. Title.
LC2731.M6 923.773 65-11951
Library of Congress [5]

My life in the Bush of Ghosts.

Nigeria M896.3 T88m Amer. ed

Tutuola, Amos.
My life in the Bush of Ghosts. With a foreword by Geoffrey Parrinder. New York, Grove Press [1954]
174 p. 21 cm.
I. Title.
[PZ4] 54-12101 ‡
Printed for U. S. Q. B. R. by Library of Congress [2]

M811.5 H19m

My deeply solemn thoughts.
Handy, Olive Lewis.
My deeply solemn thoughts. n.p. 1939.
35p. 19cm.
Autographed.

My great wide, beautiful world.

M910.4 H24

Harrison, Juanita.
My great, wide, beautiful world, by Juanita Harrison; arranged and prefaced by Mildred Morris. New York, The Macmillan company, 1936.
xii p., 1 l., 318 p. 20½cm.
"Condensed version first appeared in the 1935 autumn numbers of the Atlantic monthly."—Pref.
1. Voyages and travels. I. Morris, Mildred, ed. II. Title.
36—27252
Library of Congress G463.H33 [43i²2] 910.4

My life in the South.

MB9 St8

Stroyer, Jacob, 1849–
My life in the South. By Jacob Stroyer. New and enl. ed. Salem, Salem observer book and job print, 1889.
83 p. 19½ cm.
On verso of t.-p.: Third edition.
"The autobiography of an emancipated slave, born and raised on an extensive plantation in central South Carolina."—Introd.
1. Slavery in the U. S.—South Carolina. I. Title.
14—6299
Library of Congress E444.S92 [48c1]

My dog Rinty.

M813.5 T17m2

Tarry, Ellen, 1906–
My dog Rinty, by Ellen Tarry and Marie Hall Ets, illustrated by Alexander and Alexandra Alland. New York, The Viking press, ~~1946~~. [1964]
[48] p. incl. front., illus. 24½ x 19½ cm.
"First published May 1946."
1. Dogs—Legends and stories. I. Ets, Marie Hall, 1895– joint author. II. Title.
PZ10.3.T1386My 46—4736
Library of Congress [59b1]

M814.4 W27 am

My larger education.
Washington, Booker Taliaferro, 1859?–1915.
My larger education; being chapters from my experience, by Booker T. Washington ... illustrated from photographs. Garden City, New York, Doubleday, Page & company, 1911.
viii, 313 p. front., plates, ports. 20½cm.
1. Negroes. I. Title.
11—29623
Library of Congress E185.97.W28 [36j1]

MB9 C88

My life is an open book.
Crumes, Cole
My life is an open book. New York, Carlton Press [1965]
80p. ports. 21cm.
Portrait of author on book jacket.

My dog Rinty.

M813.5 T17m

Tarry, Ellen, 1906–
My dog Rinty, by Ellen Tarry and Marie Hall Ets, illustrated by Alexander and Alexandra Alland. New York, The Viking press, 1946.
[48] p. incl. front., illus. 24½ x 19½cm.
"First published May 1946."
1. Dogs—Legends and stories. I. Ets, Marie Hall, joint author. II. Title.
46—4736
Library of Congress PZ10.3.T1386My [47m5]

My life.

Nigeria MB9 B41m

Bellos, Sir Ahmadu, 1909-
My life. Cambridge [Eng.] University Press, 1962.
245p. illus. 23cm.

My lives and how I lost them.

M813.5 C89m

Cullen, Countee, 1903–
My lives and how I lost them, by Christopher Cat in collaboration with Countee Cullen, with drawings by Robert Reid Macguire. New York and London, Harper & brothers [°1942]
xiv p., 1 l., 160 p. illus. 24½cm.
"First edition."
1. Cats—Legends and stories. I. Title.
42—11447
Library of Congress PZ3.C8976lMy [44f2]

My dream world of poetry.

M813.5 W32m

Watkins, Violette Peaches.
My dream world of poetry; poems of imagination, reality, and dreams. [1st ed.] New York, Exposition Press [1955]
128 p. 21 cm.
I. Title.
PS3545.A8284M9 811.5 55-11196 ‡
Library of Congress [2]

Dominican Republic M796.357 AL73

My life and baseball.
Alou, Felipe, 1935–
Felipe Alou: my life and baseball, by Felipe Alou with Herm Weiskopf. Waco, Tex., Word Books [1967]
154 p. illus., ports. 23 cm.
I. Weiskopf, Herm, joint author. II. Title: My life and baseball.
GV865.A38A3 796.3576'4'0924 67-18977
Library of Congress [5]

My Lord, what a morning.

MB9 An24

Anderson, Marian, 1902–
My Lord, what a morning; an autobiography. New York, Viking Press, 1956.
312 p. illus. 22 cm.
"A condensed version ... appeared in serial form in the Woman's home companion."
1. Musicians—Correspondence, reminiscences, etc. I. Title.
ML420.A6A3 927.8 56—10402 ‡
Library of Congress [57m²20]

My dreams of a greater Nigeria.

Nigeria M966.9 N98m

Nwigwe, Henry Emezuem
My dreams of a greater Nigeria. [Yaba, West African Pilot, n.d.]
48p. port. 20½cm.
Portrait of author in book.

My life in and out of baseball.

M796 M46

Mays, Willie, 1931–
Willie Mays: My life in and out of baseball, as told to Charles Einstein. [1st ed.] New York, Dutton, 1966.
320 p. illus., ports. 22 cm.
I. Einstein, Charles. II. Title. III. Title: My life in and out of baseball.
GV865.M38A32 796.3570924 (B) 66—11554
Library of Congress [66r67]

My Lord, what a morning.

MB9 An24o

Anderson, Marian, 1902-
My Lord, what a morning. London, The Cresset Press, 1957.
240p. illus. 22cm.

My face is black.

M301 L63

Lincoln, Charles Eric.
My face is black, by C. Eric Lincoln. Boston, Beacon Press [1964]
137 p. 21 cm.
Bibliographical references included in "Notes" (p. [134]-137)
1. Negroes. 2. ~~U. S.~~—Race question. 3. Black Muslims. I. Title.
E185.61.L57 301.451 64—22695
Library of Congress [65f9]

My life in the bush of ghosts.

Nigeria M896.3 T88m

Tutuola, Amos.
My life in the Bush of Ghosts; with a foreword by Geoffrey Parrinder. London, Faber and Faber [1954]
174 p. 21 cm.
I. Title.
PZ4.T968My 54-21029 ‡
Library of Congress [1]

My Lord, What a Morning.

MB9 An24u

Anderson, Marian, 1902-
Un radiante spiritual. [Traducción de Luisa Rivaud] Buenos Aires, Compania General Fabril Editora, 1958.
309p. 19½cm.
Title: My Lord, What a Morning.
Portrait of author on book jacket.

My Lord, what a morning; an autobiography.

MB9
An241
Anderson, Marion, 1902-
My Lord, what a morning; an autobiography. New York, Avon Publications, Inc., 1956.

253p. 16½cm.

My master and I.

M811.5
B77m
Britt, Nellie.
My master and I; poems that will encourage, inspire and strengthen. New York, Carlton Press [1964]
48p. 20½cm. (A Lyceum book)
Portrait of author on book jacket.

My memories of the century club, 1919-1958.

MB9
D22
Daniel, William.
My memories of the century club, 1919-1958. [n.p.] Privately printed for the members of the Century Association [1959]

158p. 21cm.

My memory gems.

M811.5
T72m
Trent, Hattie Covington
My memory gems. North Carolina, Livingstone College, 1948.

87p. ports. 22cm.
Autographed.

My mother who fathered me.

Jamaica
M392.3
C55
Clarke, Edith, 1896–
My mother who fathered me; a study of the family in three selected communities in Jamaica. With a pref. by Hugh Foot. London, G. Allen & Unwin [1957]
215 p. illus. 23 cm.

1. Family—Jamaica. 2. Jamaica—Soc. condit. I. Title.

HQ584.C6 *301.42 392.3 58–22516 ‡
Library of Congress [60e2]

Mozambique
M796.334
F414
My name is Eusébio.
Ferreira, Eusébio da Silva, 1942–
My name is Eusébio, by Eusébio da Silva Ferreira assisted by Fernando F. Garcia, translated by Derrik Low. London, Routledge & K. Paul, 1967.
[8], 166 p. 32 plates. 19 cm. 18/-
(B 67-7585)
Translation of Meu nome é Eusébio.

I. Garcia, Fernando F. II. Title.

GV939.F4A33 796.334'0924 67-83079
Library of Congress [3]

My neighbor's island.

M813.5
J62m
Johnson, Evelyn Allen
My neighbor's island. New York, Exposition Press [1965]

55p. 21cm.

1. Race relations - Fiction. 2. Discrimination in housing - Fiction. I. Title.

My recollections of African M. E. ministers.

M287.8
W36
Wayman, Alexander Walker, *bp.*, 1821–1895.
My recollections of African M. E. ministers, or, Forty years' experience in the African Methodist Episcopal church. By Rev. A. W. Wayman ... With an introduction by Rev. B. T. Tanner, D. D. Philadelphia, A. M. E. book rooms, 1881.
xxi, 250 p. front. (port.) 20ᶜᵐ.

1. Title. II. Title: Forty years' experience in the African Methodist Episcopal church.

37-12169
Library of Congress BX8473.W35A4
Copyright 1881: 761 [2] 922.773

My secrets of playing baseball.

M796
M46m
Mays, Willie, 1931–
My secrets of playing baseball, by Willie Mays with Howard Liss. Photos. by David Sutton. New York, Viking Press [1967]
89 p. illus. (part col.) 27 cm.

1. Baseball—Juvenile literature. I. Liss, Howard, joint author. II. Title.

GV873.M35 796.3572 67-13502
Library of Congress [69-2]

My songs.

M784
H32
Hayes, Roland, 1887–
My songs; Aframerican religious folk songs arr. and interpreted by Roland Hayes. [1st ed.] Boston, Little, Brown, 1948.
x, 128 p. 29 cm.
"An Atlantic Monthly Press book."

1. Negro spirituals. I. Title.

M1670.H4M9 48–8965*
Library of Congress [58o1]

My southern home.

M810.
B81m
Brown, William Wells, *b.* 1814.
My southern home: or, The South and its people. By Wm. Wells Brown ... ~~3d ed.~~ Boston, A. G. Brown & co., ~~1882.~~ 1880
vii, 253 p. illus. 19½ᶜᵐ.
Portrait.

1. Negroes. 2. Slavery in the U. S. 3. Southern states—Soc. life & cust. I. Title.

Library of Congress E185.B88 2—7207
[37b1]

My story in black and white.

MB9
T36
Thomas, Jesse O 1885–
My story in black and white; the autobiography of Jesse O. Thomas. Foreword by Whitney M. Young, Jr. [1st ed.] New York, Exposition Press [1967]
300 p. 21 cm. (An Exposition-banner book)

I. Title.

E185.97.T49A3 973.9'0924 (B) 67-24271
Library of Congress [5]

My thirty years backstairs at the White House.

MB9
P23m
Parks, Lillian (Rogers)
My thirty years backstairs at the White House [by] Lillian Rogers Parks in collaboration with Frances Spatz Leighton. New York, Fleet Pub. Corp. [1961]
346 p. 21 cm.
Portrait of author on book jacket.

1. Presidents—U. S.—Biog. 2. Presidents—U. S.—Wives. 3. Washington, D. C. White House. I. Title.

E176.1.P37 923.173 61—7626 ‡
Library of Congress [61t30]

M323
B81m
My tour through Dixie.
Browning, Matthew.
My tour through Dixie. Minneapolis, Martin Brown, 1947.

[9]p. 20cm.

My trip through Egypt and the Holy Land.

M910
B14m
Bagley, *Mrs.* Caroline.
My trip through Egypt and the Holy Land, by Caroline Bagley. New York, The Grafton press [°1928]
223 p. front. (map) plates, ports. 21ᶜᵐ.

1. Egypt—Descr. & trav. 2. Palestine—Descr. & trav. I. Title.

Library of Congress DT55.B25 28-16113
——— Copy 2.
Copyright A 1077917 [3]

My 21 years in the White House.

MB9
F46m
Fields, Alonzo.
My 21 years in the White House. New York, Coward-McCann [1961]
223 p. 22 cm.

1. Washington, D. C. White House. 2. Washington, D. C.—Soc. life & cust. 3. Presidents—U. S.—Biog. 4. Presidents—U. S.—Wives. 5. Visits of state—U. S. I. Title.

F204.W5F5 923.173 61—15068 ‡
Library of Congress [62b5]

M812.5
V94m
My unfinished portrait.
Voteur, Ferdinand.
My unfinished portrait; drama in three acts and seven scenes. Boston, Bruce Humphries [°1951]
78 p. 24 cm.

I. Title.

PS3543.O98M9 812.5 52-14695 ‡
Library of Congress [3]

M370
N213m
My vocation.
National Urban League. Dept. of Industrial Relations.
My vocation, with special reference to the problems faced by Negro youth. New York, n.d.

16p. 19cm.

My wonderful year.

M910
T85m
Turner, Zatella R.
My wonderful year, by Zatella R. Turner. Boston, The Christopher publishing house [°1939]
xi, 13–117 p. front. 19½ᶜᵐ.

1. England—Descr. & trav. 2. Europe—Descr. & trav.—1919– I. Title.

39-31530
Library of Congress D921.T87
——— Copy 2.
Copyright A 134074 [2] 914

My work and public sentiment.

MB9
W67m
Williams, Maria P
My work and public sentiment, by Maria P. Williams ... Kansas City, Mo., Burton publishing co. [c1916]

1. Women. I. Title.

Myers, C. S.

Jamaica
M398
J38
Jekyll, Walter, *comp. and ed.*
Jamaican song and story: Annancy stories, digging sings, ring tunes, and dancing tunes, collected and edited by Walter Jekyll: with an introduction by Alice Werner, and appendices on traces of African melody in Jamaica by C. S. Myers, and on English airs and motifs in Jamaica, by Lucy E. Broadwood ... London, Pub. for the Folk-lore society by D. Nutt, 1907.
xxxviii p., 1 l., 288 p. illus. (music) 22½ᶜᵐ. (*Added t.-p.:* ... Publications of the Folk-lore society, LV)

I. Werner, Alice, 1859–1935. II. Myers, C. S. III. Broadwood, Lucy Etheldred, d. 1929.

7—23639
Library of Congress GR121.J2J4
[44h1]

M323
M99m
Myers, Evelyn Pauline
The march on Washington movement mobilizes a gigantic crusade for freedom, by E. Pauline Myers. New York the March on Washington Movement n.d.
13p. 22cm.

1. March on Washington movement.

Africa
M398
Ar66
Mythology, African.
Arnott, Kathleen.
African myths and legends, retold by Kathleen Arnott. Illustrated by Joan Kiddell-Monroe. [1st American ed.] New York, H. Z. Walck, 1963 [°1962]
211 p. illus. 23 cm. (Oxford myths and legends)

1. Tales, African. 2. Mythology, African. I. Title.
PZ8.1.A73Af2 398.096 63-7590 ‡
Library of Congress [5]

Tanganyika
M967.82 Mzirai, Robert R K
M99
Maandishi ya barua zetu. Kimetungwa na. Kampala, The Eagle Press, 1957.
107p. 18½cm.
Written in Swahili.
English translation: The writing of letters.

1. Tanganyika.

Myrdal, Gunnar, 1898-
An American dilemma.
M973
Ap8n
Aptheker, Herbert, 1915–
The Negro people in America [by] Herbert Aptheker. A critique of Gunnar Myrdal's "An American dilemma." Introduction by Doxey A. Wilkerson. New York, International publishers [1946]
80 p. 20½cm.
"Reference notes": p. 68-80.
1. *Myrdal, Gunnar, 1898– An American dilemma. 2. Negroes. I. Title.
E185.6.M9517 325.260973 46-8650
© 13Nov46; International publishers co., inc.; A8978.
Library of Congress [5]

U.S.
M839
Iv3o
Mythology, Norse.
Iiveberg, Harald, 1900-
Of Gods and giants, Norse mythology. Translated by Pat Shaw Iversen. Illustrated by Kai Ovre. Oslo, Johan Grundt Tanum Forlag [1962]
72p. illus. 21cm. (Tanums tokens of Norway)
Translation of Norrøn mytologi.

N.A.A.C.P.
M396
C59
The Clennon King story; the shocking story of another incident in which a Negro, who dared to speak out against the NAACP, was intimidated and threatened with death. [A compilation of newspaper clippings] Jackson, Miss., Mississippi State Times, 1957
1. N.A.A.C.P. I. King, Clennon.

Myrdal, Gunnar, 1898-
An American dilemma.
M323
St4n
Stewart, Maxwell Slutz, 1900–
... The Negro in America, by Maxwell S. Stewart. [New York, Public affairs committee, inc., 1944]
cover-title, 32 p. 1 illus., diagrs. 21cm. (Public affairs pamphlet, no. 95)
"First edition, August 1944."
"Summary of An American dilemma ... by Gunnar Myrdal."—p. [1]
"For further reading": p. 32.

1. Negroes. I. *Myrdal, Gunnar, 1898– An American dilemma. II. Title.
Library of Congress E185.6.M952 44-9455
[35] 325.260973

S.Africa
M220
M991
Mzamo, W F Daniel.
Intshumayezo ye Ngelosi. Iguqulwe kwinteto ya mangesi, ngu Daniel Mzamo. 2d.ed. Lovedale, Ishicilelwe nge sishicilelo saba fundisi, 1905.
34p. 18cm.
In Zulu
1. Africa - Bible stories.

NAACP - School segregation in education.
M323
Un30
U. S. Supreme Court. Brief for appellants in Nos. 1, 2 and 4 and for respondents in No.10... October Term, 1953.
235p. 23½cm.

Congo,
Leopoldville
M896.3
M23
Le mystere de l'enfant disparu.
Malembe, Timothée
Le mystere de l'enfant disparu. Léopoldville, Bibliotheque de l'Etoile, [n.d.]
85p. illus. 20½cm. (Collection l'Afrique Reconte no. 1)

M114
B812
1919
The mystery of space.
Browne, Robert T.
The mystery of space; a study of the hyperspace movement in the light of the evolution of new psychic faculties and an inquiry into the genesis and essential nature of space, by Robert T. Browne. New York, E. P. Dutton & company [°1919]
xvi p., 1 l., 395 p. diagrs. 21cm.
Bibliography: p. 359-365.

1. Hyperspace. I. Title.
19-18843
Library of Congress QA691.B8
[44f1]

The NAACP versus Negro revolutionary protest.
M323
W98n
Wynn, Daniel Webster, 1919–
The NAACP versus Negro revolutionary protest; a comparative study of the effectiveness of each movement. [1st ed.] New York, Exposition Press [1955]
115 p. 21 cm. (Exposition—University book)
Bibliography: p. [108]-110.

1. Negroes—Civil rights. 2. National Association for the Advancement of Colored People. 3. Communism—U. S.—1917– I. Title.
E185.61.W98 325.260973 54-13180
Library of Congress [56b5]

Les mystères du temple.
M812.3
Se4q
No.3
Séjour, Victor, 1816-1874.
Les mystères du temple, drame en cinq actes et nuit tablaux. Paris, Michel Lévy Frères [1862]
24p. 31cm.

South
Africa
MB9
M99
Mzimba, Livingstone Ntibane.
Ibali lobomi nomsebenzi womfi umfundisi Pambani Jeremiah Mzimba. Libalwe ngunyana wake U-Livingstone Ntibane Mzimba. Lovedale, Lovedale Insitution Press, 1923.
93p. port. illus. 21cm.
Work of Rev. P. J. Mzimba.

1. Mzimba, Pambani Jeremiah, 1850-1911
2. Xhosa Language. 3. Africa, South

M331.88
N21n
The N.M.U. fights jim crow.
National Maritime Union.
The N.M.U. fights jim crow. New York, 1943.
13p. illus. 23cm.

The myth that threatens America.
M323.
W93m
The Writers' Board.
The myth that threatens America. New York, The Board.
3-35p. 21cm.

South
Africa
MB9
M99
Mzimba, Pambani Jeremiah, 1850-1911
Mzimba, Livingstone Ntibane. ca. 1888-
Ibali lobomi nomsebenzi womfi umfundisi Pambani Jeremiah Mzimba. Libalwe ngunya wake U-Livingstone Ntibane Mzimba. Lovedale, Lovedale Institution Press, 1923.
93p. port. illus. 21cm.
Work of Rev. P. J. Mzimba.

Naeste gang [The fire next time]
M323
B19f4
Baldwin, James
Naeste gang [The fire next time. Oversat fra Engelsk af Gudrun Vergmann. København] Steen Hasselbalchs Forlag, 1963.
117p. 21cm.
Written in Danish.

Haiti
M133
M33m
Mythologie vodou (rite rada)
Marcelin, Milo.
Mythologie vodou (rite rada) I; preface de F. Morisseay Leroy; illustration de Hector Hyppolite. Port-au-Prince, Les Éditions Haitiennes, 1949.
139p. illus. 23½cm.

Zanzibar
M896.3
Ab
Mzimu wa watu wa kale.
Abdulla, Muhammed Said
Mzimu wa watu wa kale. [Stories of the older generation] Dar es Salaam, Eagle Press 1960.
86p. 19½cm.
Written in Swahili.

I. Title.

Uganda
M960
L527af
Nagenda, John, 1939-
Kenya.
Pp. 109-116.
In: Legum, Colin, ed. Africa. New York, Praeger, 1966.

Naglooskaea, tr.
M176 Randolph, Paschal Beverly, 1825-1874.
R15 ... Magia sexualis. Traduction française, par Maria de Naglowska. Edition originale. Paris, R. Télin, 1931.
218p., 1 l. illus. plates. (incl. music port. col.) port. fold. tables. 23cm.
At head of title: P. B. Randolph.

Nigeria Na'ibi, Mallam Shuaibu, jt. auth.
M966.9 Hassan, Sarkin Ruwa Abuja
H27a A chronicle of Abuja; translated and arranged from the Hausa of Alhaji Hassan and Mallam Shuaibu Na'ibi by Frank Heath. ₑRev. and enl. ed.ₒ Lagos, African Universities Press, 1962.
91p. illus. 25cm.

Rwanda
M39 Naigisiki, Joseph Saverio, 1915-
N14e ...Escapade Ruandaise. Journal d'un clerc en sa trentième année. Preface de M.J.M. Jadot. Bruxelles, G. A. Deny, Librairie Editeur ₍1950₎
208 p. 22 cm.
Congo Belgian author.
1. French literature - Belgian Congo. I. Title. 2. Congo, Belgian.

Naigiziki, J. Saverio,
See
Naigisiki, Joseph Saverio.

Rwanda
M896.2 Naigiziki, Joseph Saverio, 1915-
N14o L'Optimiste; pièces en trois actes. Preface de Madame Emma Maquet. Astrida, Frères de la Charité, 1954.
58p. 21cm.
1. Drama, African. 2. Congo, Belgian - Drama. I. Title.

Rwanda
M39 Naigiziki, Joseph Saverio, 1915-
N14m Mes transes a trente ans. 2. Dé pis en mieux.Histoire vécue, mêlée de roman. Astrida, Groupe Scolaire, 1955.
487p. 23cm.
I. Title. 1. Congo, Belgian.

Trinidad The naked fear.
M823.91 Offord, Carl Ruthven, 1910-
Of4n The naked fear. New York, Ace Books, Inc., 1954.
160p. 19cm. (Ace books S-54)
Pocket book edition.

The Naked Frame.
M811.5 **Oden, Gloria.**
Od2 The naked frame, a love poem and sonnets. ₍1st ed.₎ New York, Exposition Press ₍1952₎
unpaged. 21 cm.
I. Title.
PS3529.D44N3 811.5 52-10288 ‡
Library of Congress ₍3₎

The naked truth.
M813.5 Farrell, John T
F24n The naked truth. New York, Vantage Press ₍1961₎
196p. 21cm.

Nakupenda, lakini...
Kenya
M896.2 **Kuria, Henry**
K96n Nakupenda, lakini ... ₍I love you, but ...₎ Nairobi, Eagle Press, 1957.
42p. 22cm. (Watu wa Africa ya mashariki)
Written in Swahili.
I. Title. II. Series

The name "Negro," its origin and evil use.
Barbados
M301 **Moore, Richard B**
M78n The name "Negro," its origin and evil use. ₍1st ed.₎ New York, Afroamerican Publishers, 1960.
82 p. illus. 23 cm.
1. Negroes—Names. I. Title.
E185.89.N3M6 301.451 60-50723 ‡
Library of Congress ₍2₎

Names.
Barbados
M301 **Moore, Richard B**
M78n The name "Negro," its origin and evil use. ₍1st ed.₎ New York, Afroamerican Publishers, 1960.
82 p. illus. 23 cm.
1. Negroes—Names. I. Title.
E185.89.N3M6 301.451 60-50723 ‡
Library of Congress ₍2₎

Nigeria Names, African.
M929.4 Coker, Increase
C66 Grammar of African names; a guide to the appreciation of the cosmic significance of Nigerian and Ghanian names. ₑLagos, Times Press, n.d.ₒ
40p. illus., ports. 24½cm.
Portrait of author in front of book.
Includes bibliography.
"A daily times publication."

Nigeria Names, Personal - Africa.
M929.4 Coker, Increase
C66 Grammar of African names; a guide to the appreciation of the cosmic significance of Nigerian and Ghanian names. ₑLagos, Times Press, n.d.ₒ
40p. illus., ports. 24½cm.
Portrait of author in front of book.
Includes bibliography.
"A daily times publication."

The Namon Wise story.
M248 Wise, Namon.
W75 The Namon Wise story. New York, Carlton Press ₑ1964ₒ
38p. 21cm.

Nigeria Nancy in blooming beauty.
M896.3 Okeanu, Vincent C.
Ok2n Nancy in blooming beauty. 2d. ed. Port Harcourt ₍Nigeria₎ Eastern City Press, 1961.
37p. illus., port. 19cm. (Pens series)
I. Title.

M815.4 Napier, James Carroll, 1848-1940
N16d Discussion of national questions, by Hon. J.C. Napier... Decide views on financial matters and operation of Dingley law. The Spanish-American war and its results... Nashville, Tenn. National Baptist publishing board, 1898.
21p. port. 22cm.
1. Orations

Napoléon I, emperor of the French, 1769-1821.
France
M840 Dumas, Alexandre, 1802-1870.
D89n Napoléon. Bruxelles, Meline, Cans et cie., 1840.
355p. 16cm.
1. Napoléon I, emperor of the French, 1769-1821.

Narrative of James Williams...
M326.99B Williams, James, b. 1805-
W67n Narrative of James Williams, an American slave. In anti-slavery examiner no.6 1838
8p. 30cm.

Narrative of James Williams.
M326.99B **Williams, James, b. 1805.**
W67n Narrative of James Williams. An American slave; who was
1838 for several years a driver on a cotton plantation in Alabama ... New-York, The American anti-slavery society, 1838.
xxiii, ₍25₎-108 p. front. (port.) 15cm.
Written by J. G. Whittier from the verbal narrative of Williams. *cf.* G. R. Carpenter, John Greenleaf Whittier, 1903, p. 165.
1. Slavery in the U. S.—Alabama. I. Whittier, John Greenleaf, 1807-1892. II. American anti-slavery society, New York. III. Title.
17—5248
Library of Congress E444.W743 ₍39c1₎

Narrative of Sojourner Truth.
M326.99B ₍Gilbert, Olive₎
T77g Narrative of Sojourner Truth; a bonds-woman of olden
1875 time, emancipated by the New York Legislature in the early part of the present century; with a history of her labors and correspondence drawn from her "Book of life." ~~XXXXXXXX~~ Boston, ~~XXXX~~., For the author, ~~XXXX~~ 1875.
xi, 13-324p. ~~xii, 13-320 p.~~ front. (port.) illus. 20cm.
Narrative of Sojourner Truth, by Olive Gilbert. Book of life, by Frances W. Titus.
1. Truth, Sojourner, d. 1883. I. Titus, Frances W. II. Title.
29—25244
Library of Congress E185.97.T875 ₍a35b1₎

Narrative of Sojourner Truth...

M326.99B
T77g
1850

[Gilbert, Olive]
Narrative of Sojourner Truth, a northern slave, emancipated from bodily servitude by the state of New York, in 1828. With a portrait ... Boston, Printed for the author, 1850.
xi, [1], [13]-144 p. incl. front. (port.) 18½cm.

1. Truth, Sojourner, d. 1883. I. Title.
11—27426
Library of Congress E185.97.T87
[a37d1]

A narrative of the life and adventure of Venture.

M326.99B
Sm6n
1897

Smith, Venture, 1729–1805.
A narrative of the life and adventures of Venture, a native of Africa, but resident above sixty years in the United States of America. Related by himself, New London: Printed in 1798. Reprinted A. D. 1835, and published by a descendant of Venture. Rev. and republished with traditions by H. M. Selden, Haddam, Conn., 1896. Middletown, Conn., J. S. Stewart, printer, 1897.
iv, [5]-41 p. 23½cm.

1. Slavery in the U. S.—Connecticut. I. Selden, Henry M. II. Title.
4—17888
Library of Congress E444.S66
[a29c1]

Narrative of the life and adventures of Paul Cuffe.

MB9
C89n

[Cuffee, Paul] b. 1796?
Narrative of the life and adventures of Paul Cuffe, a Pequot Indian: during thirty years spent at sea, and in travelling in foreign lands. Vernon, Printed by H. N. Bill, 1839.
21 p. 21½cm.
Signed: Paul Cuffe, Stockbridge, N. Y. March 18, 1839.

I. Title.
38-11820
Library of Congress E99.C95C8
[2]
970.2

A narrative of the life and adventures of Venture.

M326.99B
Sm6n
1835

Smith, Venture, 1729-1805.
A narrative of the life and adventures of Venture, a native of Africa, but resident above sixty years in the United States of America. Related by himself, New London: Printed in 1798. Reprinted A.D. 1835, and published by a descendant of Venture.
24p. 20cm.

A narrative of the proceedings of the black people.

M974.811
J71n

[Jones, Absalom]
A narrative of the proceedings of the black people, during the late awful calamity in Philadelphia, in the year 1793: and a refutation of some censures, thrown upon them in some late publications. By A. J. and R. A. Philadelphia: Printed for the authors, by William W. Woodward, at Franklin's head, no. 41, Chesnut-street. 1794.
28 p. 18½cm.
"To Matthew Clarkson, esq. mayor of the city of Philadelphia [with reply]": p. 21-23. "An address to those who keep slaves, and approve the practice": p. 23-26. "To the people of colour": p. 26-27. "A short address to the friends of him who hath no helper" [signed Absalom Jones, Richard Allen, followed by five stanzas of verse]: p. 27-28.

(Continued on next card)
2-13737
[a38b1]

The narrow path.

Ghana
M896.3
Se49n

Selormey, Francis, 1927-
The narrow path. [London] Heinemann [1966]
183p. 20cm.
Portrait of author on book jacket.

The narrows.

M813.5
P44n2

Petry, Ann
The narrows. London, Victor Gollanz, Ltd. 1954.
428p. 19½cm.

The narrows.

M813.5
P44n

Petry, Ann (Lane) 1911-
The Narrows. Boston, Houghton Mifflin, 1953.
428 p. 22 cm.
First edition.

I. Title.
PZ3.P44904No 53-5729 ‡
Library of Congress [7]

Africa
MB9
St7

Narwimba.
Stories of old times, being the autobiographies of two women of East Afric. Translated and abridged from The German of Frau Elise Kootz-Kretschmer, and published by kind permission of the Verlag der. Missionsbuchhadnlung, Herrnhut, and of Dietrich Rumer, Berlin. London, The Sheldon press, 1932.
32p. 18½ (Little books for Africa)

Brazil
M869.2
N17d

Nascimento Abdias do, 1914- ed.
Dramas para Negroes e prólogo para brancos; antologia de teatro Negro-brasileiro. Rio de Janeiro, Teatro Experimental do Negro, 1961.
419p. illus., ports. 22cm.
Contents.- O filho prodigo, por I. Cardoso.- O castigo de oxalá, por Romeu Crusoé.- Auto da noiva, por Rosario Fusco.-
(Continued on next card)

Brazil
M869.2
N17d

Nascimento Abdias do, 1914- ed.
Dramas para Negroes e prólogo para brancos, 1961. (Card 2)
(Contents.- Continued)
Sortilegio, por Abdias do Nascimento.- Além do rio, por Agostinh Olavo.- Filhos de Santo, por José Pinho.- Aruanda, por Joaquim Ribeiro.- Anjo Negro, por Nélson Rodrigues.- Oemparedado, por Tasso da Silveira.
Autographed. (over)

Brazil
M869.2
N17d

Nascimento, Abdias do, 1914-
Sortilégio.
Pp. 159-197.
In: Nascimento, Abdias do, ed. Dramas para Negroes e prologo para brancos. Rio de Janeiro, Teatro Experimental do Negro, 1961.
I. Title.

Brazil
M869.2
N17

Nascimento, Abdias do, 1914-
Sortilegio (Misterio Negro). Rio, [Teatro Experimental do Negro] 1959.
81p. 22½cm.
"Para National Association for the Advancement of the Colored People, comas homenagens, do autor, Abdias Nascimento, Rio-Setembro - 1959."
Copy 183.
1. Brazilian drama. 2. Drama - Brazil. I. Title.

Brazil
M869.3
N172

Nascimento, Edson Arantes do, 1940-
Eu sou Pelé; narrativa. [Apresentação de Benedito Ruy Barbosa. Capa e ilus. de Cyro del Nero. Estudo especial de Thomaz Massoni. São Paulo, 1961]
191p. illus. 24cm. (Contrastes e confrontes, 3)
I. Title. II. Series.

Nash, Diane
Inside the sit-ins and freedom rides: testimony of a southern student, pp. 43-60.

M301
Ah5n

Ahmann, Mathew H ed.
The new Negro. Contributors: Stephen J. Wright [and others] In the symposium: James Baldwin [and others] Notre Dame, Ind., Fides Publishers [1961]
xii, 145p. 21cm.
Includes papers presented at the 1st convention of the National Catholic Conference for Interracial Justice, held in Detroit in 1961.

M813.4
N17l

Nash, T[heodore] E[dward] D[elafayette] 1881-
Love and vengeance; or, Little Viola's victory; a story of love and romance in the South; also society and its effects. By T. E. D. Nash. [Portsmouth, Va., T. E. D. Nash, °1903]
1 p. l., 171, [1] p. front. (port.) 23cm.

Library of Congress Copyright 4-35722

Nashville, Tenn.

M323
J132

Jackson, James Edward
3 brave men tell how freedom comes to an old South City, Nashville, Tenn. [New York, Publisher's New Press, 1963]
27p. 22½cm
1. Race relations. 2. Nashville, Tenn. I. Title.

Natchez, Miss. - Soc. life & customs.

MB9
J639

Johnson, William, 1809-1851.
William Johnson's Natchez; the ante-bellum diary of a free Negro. Edited by William Ransom Hogan and Edwin Adams Davis. [Baton Rouge] Louisiana State University Press [1951]
ix, 812 p. illus., facsims. 24 cm. (Source studies in Southern history, no. 1)

1. Natchez, Miss.—Soc. life & cust. I. Title. (Series)
E185.97.J697A3 325.2609762 51—3489
Library of Congress [52k5]

M304
P19
v.3,no.5

Nathan, Winfred Bertram.
... Health conditions in North Harlem, 1923-1927, by Winfred B. Nathan ... an abstract, by Mary V. Dempsey. New York, National tuberculosis association [°1932]
68 p. incl. maps. 23cm. ([National tuberculosis association] Social research series. no. 2)
The death rates were revised on the basis of the 1930 census population figures. cf. Foreword.
"This study is ... largely a study of negro health."—Introd.
1. Harlem, New York (City)—Sanit. affairs. 2. ~~Negroes~~—New York (City) 3. ~~Negroes~~—Mortality. 4. ~~Negroes~~—Statistics, Vital. 5. New York (City)—Statistics, Vital. 6. Health surveys. I. Dempsey, Mary V., ed. II. Title.
32—21038
Library of Congress RA448.H3N3
[42d1] 614.097471

Natif-natal, un conte en vers.

Haiti
M841
M83n

Morisseau-Leroy, Felix, 1912-
Natif-natal, un conte en vers. Port-au-Prince, Editions Haitiennes [1948]
61p. 22cm.

Nation et voie Africaine du socialisme.

Sénégal
M966.3
Se5nt

Senghor, Léopold Sédar, 1906-
Nation et voie Africaine du socialisme. Paris, Présence Africaine, 1961.
138p. 21½cm.

M323
J632a

The Nation, New York.

Johnson, James Weldon, 1871–

L'autonomie d'Haïti, par James Weldon Johnson. Qurtre [!] articles reproduits de la revue "The Nation", comprenant le compte-rendu d'une enquête effectuée pour le compte de l'Association nationale pour l'avancement des gens de couleur, et traduits en français par les soins de l'Union patriotique haïtienne. New York, Association nationale pour l'avancement des gens de couleur; Port-au-Prince, Comité central de l'Union patriotique, 1921.

35 p. 21½cm.

1. Haiti—For. rel.—U. S. 2. U. S.—For. rel.—Haiti. 3. Haiti—Pol. & govt.—1844– I. The Nation, New York. II. National association for the advancement of colored people. III. Union patriotique haïtienne. IV. Title. *Translation of* Self-determining Haiti.

32-24487

Library of Congress F1926.J83

[2] [327.7294] 972.94

The Nation, New York.

M323
J632s

Johnson, James Weldon, 1871–1938.

Self-determining Haiti, by James Weldon Johnson. Four articles reprinted from the Nation embodying a report of an investigation made for the National association for the advancement of colored people, together with official documents ... [New York, The Nation, °1920]

M323
J632a
no.3

48 p. 28cm.

1. Haiti—For. rel.—U. S. 2. U. S.—For. rel.—Haiti. 3. Haiti—Pol. & govt. I. The Nation, New York. II. National association for the advancement of colored people. III. Title.

A 21—1238

Stanford univ. Library for Library of Congress [a41d1]

La Nation haitienne.

Haiti
M972.94
B41

Bellegarde, Dantès, 1877–

... La nation haïtienne. Paris, J. de Gigord, 1938.

2 p. l., [vii]–x, 361, [1] p. illus. (incl. ports., maps (1 double)) 25cm.

"Bibliographie": p. [354]–359.

1. Haiti. 2. Haiti—Hist. I. Title.

[*Full name:* Louis Dantès Bellegarde]

38-37781

Library of Congress F1921.B47

[3] 972.94

The Nation transformed.

M973
D541

Diamond, Sigmund, *ed.*

The Nation transformed; the creation of an industrial society. Selected and edited, with introd. and notes by Sigmund Diamond. New York, G. Braziller, 1963.

xiv, 528 p. 24 cm.

Bibliography: p. 524–528.

1. ~~U. S.~~—Soc. condit.—Addresses, essays, lectures. 2. ~~U. S.~~—Civilization—Addresses, essays, lectures. I. Title.

HN57.D53 309.173 63—17876

Library of Congress [67n4]

M704
P19
v.6, no.2

National Afro-American council.

The National Afro-American council, organized 1898. A history of the organization, its objects, synopses of proceedings, constitution and by-laws, plan of organization, annual topics, etc. Comp. by Cyrus Field Adams, secretary ... Washington, D. C., C. F. Adams, 1902.

29, [2] p. 23cm.

1. Negroes—Societies. I. Adams, Cyrus Field, comp.

12—2898

Library of Congress E185.5.N27

[41b1]

National anti-slavery bazaar, Boston.

M326.080
L61

The Liberty bell. By friends of freedom .. Boston, Massachusetts anti-slavery fair, 1839–46; National anti-slavery bazaar, 1847–58.

15 v. plates, ports. 17½–20cm.

"Edited and published annually in Boston, by Maria Weston Chapman, 1843 to 1858 (one or two years being omitted)"—Samuel May, Catalogue of anti-slavery publications in America.

No volumes issued for 1840, 1850, 1854–55, 1857. *cf.* Faxon, Literary annuals and gift books.

Volume for 1841 wanting in L. C. set.

1. Slavery in the U. S. 2. Gift-books (Annuals, etc.) I. Chapman, Maria (Weston) 1806–1885, ed. II. Massachusetts anti-slavery fair. III. National anti-slavery bazaar, Boston.

5—22887

Library of Congress E449.L69

[43l1]

National anti-slavery bazaar, Boston.

M326.080
L61

The Liberty bell. By friends of freedom .. Boston, Massachusetts anti-slavery fair, 1839–46; National anti-slavery bazaar, 1847–58.

15 v. plates, ports. 17½–20cm.

"Edited and published annually in Boston, by Maria Weston Chapman, 1843 to 1858 (one or two years being omitted)"—Samuel May, Catalogue of anti-slavery publications in America.

No volumes issued for 1840, 1850, 1854–55, 1857. *cf.* Faxon, Literary annuals and gift books.

Volume for 1841 wanting in L. C. set.

1. Slavery in the U. S. 2. Gift-books (Annuals, etc.) I. Chapman, Maria (Weston) 1806–1885, ed. II. Massachusetts anti-slavery fair. III. National anti-slavery bazaar, Boston.

5—22887

Library of Congress E449.L69

[43l1]

M323
N21

National Association for the Advancement of Colored People.

An appeal to the conscience of the civilized world. New York, NAACP, 1920.

15p. illus. tables. 31cm.

1. Lynch law.

M323
N21

National Association for the Advancement of Colored People.

An appeal to the world; A statement on the denial of human rights to minorities in the case of citizens of Negro descent in the United States of America and An appeal to the United Nations for redress. Prepared for the National Association for the Advancement of Colored People, under the editorial supervision of W.E. Burghardt DuBois. New York, 1947.

94p. tables. 21cm.

M323
N21

National Association for the Advancement of Colored People. (card 2)

An appeal to the world ...

Contents: Introduction, by W.E.B. Du Bois. The denial of legal rights of American Negroes, 1787–1914, by E.B. Dickerson. The present legal and social status of the American Negro, by W.R. Ming. -Patterns of discrimination in fundamental human rights, by Leslie S. Perry. -The legal status of Americans of Negro descent since World War I, by M.R. Konvitz. The Charter of the United Nations and its provisions for human rights, by Rayford Logan.

M323
N21

National Association for the Advancement of Colored People. (card 3)

An appeal to the world ...

I. Du Bois, William Edward Burghardt, 1868– ed
II. a.t. Dickerson, E.B. III. a.t. Ming, W.R.
IV. a.t. Perry, Leslie S. V. a.t. Logan, Rayford W.
VI. a.t. DuBois Introduction
1. Civil rights. 2. Discrimination
3. Social equality.

M323
N21

[National association for the advancement of colored people]

Anti-Negro propaganda in school textbooks. [New York, The National association for the advancement of colored people, 1939]

18 p. 21cm.

1. Negroes. 2. Text-books—U. S. I. Title.
II. White, Walter, 1893–

42-30658

Library of Congress E185.61.N23

[2] 325.260973

MB
N198

National Association for the Advancement of Colored People.

Black heroes of the American revolution, 1775–1783. New York [1965?]

31p. 28cm.

1. Biography. I. Title.

M323
N21

National Association for the Advancement of Colored People.

Burning at stake in the United States; A record of the public burning by mobs of five men, during the first five months of 1919, in the states of Arkansas, Florida, Georgia, Mississippi, and Texas. New York, The Association, 1919.

19p. 23cm.

1. Lynch law. I. Title.

M323
N21

National Association for the Advancement of Colored People.

Can the states stop lynching? New York, NAACP, [1937].

19p. illus. 18cm.

1. Lynch law. I. Title.

M323
N21

National Association for the Advancement of Colored People.

Civil rights handbook. New York, 1953.

44, vii p. 23 cm.

Sources of information: p.vi-vii.

1. Civil rights. I. Title.

M323
N21

National Association for the Advancement of Colored People.

Civil rights in the United States; A balance sheet of group relations, 194-

New York, American Jewish Congress and the National Association for the Advancement of Colored People, 194-

v. 23 cm. annual.

See holdings card for issues in library.

1. Civil rights. 2. Race relations.

M323
N21

N.A.A.C.P.

Civil rights in the U.S.

Volume	Year	Month	Volume	Year	Month
	1948				
	1949				
	1950				
	1952				

M323
N21

National Association for the Advancement of Colored People.

Civil rights in the United States, a balance sheet of group relations, 194 -

New York; Published jointly by American Jewish Congress and the National Association for the Advancement of Colored People, 194 -

v. 22cm. annual.

See holdings card for issues in collection.

S.L.

M323
N21

National Association for the Advancement of Colored People.

Civil rights in the United States; A balance sheet of group relations, 194-

New York, American Jewish Congress and the National Association for the Advancement of Colored People, 194-

v. 23 cm. annual.

See holdings card for issues in library.

1. Civil rights. 2. Race relations.

M323
N21

National Association for the Advancement of Colored People.

The day they changed their minds. [New York, 1960]

unp. illus. 21½cm.

1. Civil rights. I. Title.

M321
N21 National Association for the Advancement of Colored People.
Defending your civil rights; Handbook on what to do. New York, n.d.

[11]p. 21cm.

1. Civil rights.

M323
N21 National Association for the Advancement of Colored People.
Georgia justice; The Ingram case... New York, n.d.

8p. illus. 22cm.

1. Ingram, Rosa Lee. 2. Georgia. 3. Civil rights, Denial of. I. Title.

M323
N 21 National Association for the Advancement of Colored People.
Look at the filibuster. New York, 1949.

[8]p. illus. 21cm.

1. ----Politics and government. 2. Filibuster. I. Title.

M323
N21 National Association for the Advancement of Colored People.
Emancipation's unfinished business. 54th annual convention souvenir program book. Morrison Hotel, Chicago, Ill., July 1st-6th, 1963.

1 v. illus., port.

I. Title.

M323
N21 National Association for the Advancement of Colored People.
Groveland U.S.A. New York, 1949.

[6]p. 20cm.

1. Groveland, Florida. 2. Riots--Florida.

M323
N21 National Association for the Advancement of Colored People.
The lynching of Claude Neal. New York, 1934.

8p. illus. 28cm.

1. Lynching - Florida. 2. Greenwood, Florida. 3. Neal, Claude.

M323
N21 National Association for the Advancement of Colored People.
The fight against lynching; Anti-lynching work of the National Association for the Advancement of Colored People for the year nineteen eighteen. New York, NAACP, 1919.

20p. 23cm.

1. Lynch law.

M323
N21 National Association for the Advancement of Colored People.
How about a decent school for me? New York.

20p. illus. 20cm.

M323
N21 National association for the advancement of colored people.
The lynchings of May, 1918 in Brooks and Lowndes counties, Georgia. An investigation made and published by the National association for the advancement of colored people. New York city, Spetember, 1918.

6p. 24cm.

1. Lynching - Georgia. I. White, Walter Francis.

M323
N21 National Association for the Advancement of Colored People.
The first line of defense; A summary of 20 years civil rights struggle for American Negroes. New York, NAACP, n.d.

[7]p. 21cm.

1. Civil rights.

M323
N21 National Association for the Advancement of Colored People.
How they stand on civil rights, the voting record of your senators and representatives in the 82nd Congress; 1951-52. New York, n.d.

11p. 28cm.

I. Title. 1. Civil rights.

M323
N21 National Association for the Advancement of Colored People.
The Massacre of East St. Louis, compiled from facts and pictures collected by Martha Gruening and W. E. Burghardt Du Bois. Reprinted from The Crisis.

M704
P19
V.7, no.23 20p. illus. 25cm.

1. Riots--East St. Louis.
2. East St. Louis, Ill.

M323
N21 National Association for the Advancement of Colored People.
The first 1000. New York, National Association for the Advancement of Colored People [1958]

[14]p. 21cm.

1. National Association for the Advancement of Colored People - Membership.

M323
N21 National Association for the Advancement of Colored People.
How your congressman voted on major issues affecting civil rights; The NAACP legislative scoreboard, 81st Congress, second session. Reprinted from the Crisis magazine, October 1950.

19p. tables. 20cm.

1. Civil rights.

M323
N21 National Association for the Advancement of Colored People.
NAACP handbook; Outline of procedure for legal cases. N.Y., The Association [1944]

5-20p. 17cm.

1. Legal aid.

M323
N21 National Association for the Advancement of Colored People.
Food costs more in Harlem; A comparative survey of retail food prices. New York, NAACP.

21p. 22cm.

1. Cost and standard of living.

M323
N21 National Association for the Advancement of Colored People.
In freedom's vanguard, NAACP report for 1963. New York [1964]

127p. illus., ports. 21½cm.

I. Title.

M323
N21 National Association for the Advancement of Colored People.
The Negro and the labor union with especial reference to the action of the American Federation of Labor in conference at Atlantic City, June, 1919. New York, 1919.

[3] p. 24cm.

1. American Federation of Labor. 2. Trade Unions.

M323
N21 National Association for the Advancement of Colored People.
The forgotten people. New York, New York State conference of NAACP Branches.

22p. illus. 22cm.

M323
N21 National Association for the Advancement of Colored People.
Let's be honest about democracy. New York, NAACP, 1939.

23p. illus. 22cm.

1. Race problems. I. Title.

M323
N213 National Association for the Advancement of Colored People.
Negro heroes of emancipation. New York, 1964.

unp. illus. 21cm.

1. Biography. I. Title.

M331.1
N213n
National Association for the Advancement of Colored People.
The Negro wage-earner and apprenticeship training programs; a critical analysis with recommendations. New York, NAACP, 1960.

60p. 27½cm.

1. Employment. I. Title.

M323
N21
National Association for the Advancement of Colored People.
A new birth of freedom; NAACP report for 1964. New York [1965]

110p. illus.

I. Title.

M323
N21
National Association for the Advancement of Colored People.
Now is the time for civil rights. New York, 1949.

[4]p. 28cm.

1. Civil rights.

M323
N21
National Association for the Advancement of Colored People.
Our democratic navy... New York, 1941.

[4]p. 22cm.

1. U. S. Navy.

M323
N21
National association for the advancement of colored people.
Racial inequalities in education. New York, The national association for the advancement of colored people, 1938.

cover-title, 24 p. tables. 22½cm.
Illustrations on cover.
Foreword signed: Walter White.

1. ~~Negroes~~—Education. 2. ~~Negroes~~—Race question. I. Title.

A 40-2768

Duke univ. Library for Library of Congress [2]

M323
N21
National Association for the Advancement of Colored People.
Report.
New York, 19-

v. illus. (map) ports. 16-23 cm. annual.
Each report has a special title.
See holdings card for reports in library.

1. Race relations. 2. Civil rights.

M232 323
N21
Country ~~NAACP~~ NAACP ~~XXXXXX~~ Dept.
Title Report Frequency Annual

LIBRARY HAS THOSE THAT ARE CHECKED

1901	1911	1921	1931 X	1941 X	1951 X	1961	1971
1902	1912	1922	1932	1942 X	1952 X	1962	1972
1903	1913 X	1923	1933	1943 X	1953	1963	1973
1904	1914	1924	1934 X	1944	1954	1964	1974
1905	1915	1925	1935	1945	1955 X	1965	1975
1906	1916	1926	1936 X	1946	1956	1966	1976
1907	1917	1927 X	1937 X	1947 X	1957	1967	1977
1908	1918	1928	1938 X	1948 X	1958	1968	1978
1909	1919	1929	1939 X	1949 X	1959	1969	1979
1910	1920	1930	1940 X	1950 X	1960	1970	1980

Place Pub. Source
Gift; Purchase
Library Bureau Cat. no. 1163.1 Document record (by year) KP 14694

M323
N21
National association for the advancement of colored people.
Resources in Negro youth. New York city, National association for the advancement of colored people, 1940.
18p. 20cm.
1. Youth I. Title
II. Robinson, James H
III. Murphy, George

M323
N21
National Association for the Advancement of Colored People.
Segregation and the schools, with the co-operation fo the National Association for the Advancement of Colored People. New York, Public Affairs Committee, 1954.

28p. 18cm. (Public affairs pamphlet no. 209)
1. Education - Integration. I. Title.
II. Series.

M323
N21
National Association for the Advancement of Colored People.
Target for 1963, goals of the fight for freedom. New York, 1954.

15 p. cm.

1. Integration. 2. Civil rights. I. Title.

M323
N21
National association for the advancement of colored people.
Teachers' salaries in black and white, a pamphlet for teachers and their friends, prepared by the National association for the advancement of colored people ... New York, N. Y. [1942]

15 p. illus. (ports.) 23cm.
"Reprinted February, 1942."

1. Teachers—U. S.—Salaries, pensions, etc. 2. ~~Negroes~~—Education. I. Title.

Library of Congress LB2843.N4N35 43-8228
[3] 371.161

M323
N21
National association for the advancement of colored people.
Thirty years of lynching in the United States, 1889-1918. New York, The National association for the advancement of colored people, 1919.

105 p. incl. maps, tables, diagrs. 23cm.

1. Lynch law. I. Title.

Library of Congress HV6457.N3 20-13596
[37d1]

M323
N21
[National Association for the Advancement of Colored People]
Veterans' handbook. New York, NAACP, n.d.

24p. 18cm.

1. Veterans.

M976.8
D29r
National Association for the Advancement of Colored People.
Davis, John P
Report of the chief social and economic problems of Negroes in the TVA: A survey prepared for the National Association for the Advancement of Colored People. New York, 1935.

41p. tables. 28cm.
Mimeographed.

National Association for the Advancement of Colored People
M323
J632a
Johnson, James Weldon, 1871-
L'autonomie d'Haiti. Qutre [4] articles reproduits de la revue "The Nation", comprenant le compte-rendu d'une enquête effectuée pour l'anvancement des gens de couleur, et traduits en français par les soins de l'Union patriotique haïtienne. New York, NAACP; Port-au-Prince, Comité central del'Union patriotique, 1921.

35p. 21½cm.

National association for the advancement of colored people,
M350
H270
Hastie, William Henry, 1904–
On clipped wings; the story of Jim Crow in the Army air corps, by William H. Hastie. [New York, National association for the advancement of colored people, 1943]

27 p. illus. (incl. ports.) 21½cm.

1. U. S. Army—Negro troops. 2. Negroes as soldiers. 3. U. S. Army air forces. I. National association for the advancement of colored people. II. Title.

A 44-3618

Harvard univ. Library for Library of Congress [3]

National association for the advancement of colored people.
M323
J632s
Johnson, James Weldon, 1871–1938.
Self-determining Haiti, by James Weldon Johnson. Four articles reprinted from the Nation embodying a report of an investigation made for the National association for the advancement of colored people, together with official documents ... [New York, The Nation, °1920]

M323
J632s
no.3
48 p. 23cm.

1. Haiti—For. rel.—U. S. 2. U. S.—For. rel.—Haiti. 3. Haiti—Pol. & govt. I. The Nation, New York. II. National association for the advancement of colored people. III. Title.

A 21—1238

Stanford univ. Library for Library of Congress [a41d1]

National association for the advancement of colored people.
M812.5
R38p
Richardson, Thomas.
Place: America (a theatre piece) by Thomas Richardson, based on the history of the National association for the advancement of colored people, foreword by Sterling A. Brown. New York, National association for the advancement of colored people [°1939]

51 p. 20cm.

I. National association for the advancement of colored people. II. Title.

Library of Congress PN6120.N4R45 40-8718
———— Copy 2.
Copyright D pub. 66008 [2] 812.5

National Association for the Advancement of Colored People.
M306
W67a
Willkie Memorial Building. Seven Organizations.
Annual report at the birthday anniversary dinner in memory of Wendell L. Willkie. New York, Willkie Memorial of Freedom, 1947.

20p. 23cm.

M343.3
B63c
National Association for the Advancement of Colored People.
Boardman, Helen.
The Crawford case; A reply to the N.A.A.C.P., by Helen Boardman and Martha Gruening. New York, the authors, 1935.

30p. 21cm.
Cover title: Who is the N.A.A.C.P.?
White author.

National Association for the Advancement of Colored People.
MSS
B73
Branch, William Blackwell
"Fifty steps toward freedom." A dramatic presentation in observance of the fiftieth anniversary of the National Association for the Advancement of Colored People, 1909-1959.

48p.
"Corrected Proof."
"For Arthur Spingarn."

M323.4
H87f

National Association for the Advancement of Colored People.
Hughes, Langston, 1902–
Fight for freedom; the story of the NAACP. New York, ~~Norton, 1962,~~ Berkley Pub. Corp. [1962]
224 p. illus. 22 cm.
Includes bibliography.
Portrait of author on book jacket.
1. National Association for the Advancement of Colored People. I. Title.
Full name: James Langston Hughes.
E185.5.N276H8 325.2670973 62—14352 ‡
Library of Congress [63k1]

M323.4
H87f2

National Association for the Advancement of Colored People.
Hughes, Langston, 1902–
Fight for freedom; the story of the NAACP, New York, Berkely Pub. Corp, c1962.
224p. illus. 22cm. (Berkley medalion, F590)

M323
N214j

National association for the advancement of colored people.
Jack, Robert L.
History of the National association for the advancement of colored people, by Robert L. Jack ... Boston, Meador publishing company, 1943.
xiv p., 1 l., 110 p. port. 20½cm.
Bibliography: p. 102–106.
1. National association for the advancement of colored people.
43—8386
Library of Congress E185.5.N276J3 [43f3] 325.260973

M301
D852g

National Association for the Advancement of Colored People.
Graham, Shirley, 1904–
Why was Du Bois fired?
(In: Masses & mainstream, 1:15–27, November 1948)

M323
N214o

National Association for the Advancement of Colored People.
Ovington, Mary White.
How the National Association for the Advancement of Colored People began. New York, NAACP, 1945.
5p. 23cm.

M323
Sa2

National Association for the Advancement of Colored People.
St. James, Warren D 1921–
The National Association for the Advancement of Colored People: a case study in pressure groups. Foreword by Ulysses S. Donaldson. [1st ed.] New York, Exposition Press [1958]
252 p. 21 cm. (An Exposition-university book)
Bibliography: p. [248]–252.
1. National Association for the Advancement of Colored People. 2. Pressure groups.
E185.5.N276S3 *301.451 325.260973 57—10668
Library of Congress [59b7]

M323.4
Un3n

National Association for the Advancement of Colored People.
U.S. Supreme Court.
Petition for writ of certiorari to the Supreme Court of Alabama. National Association for the Advancement of Colored People, a corporation, petitioner, v. State of Alabama, ex rel. John Petterson, Attorney General. In the Supreme Court of the United States, October Term, 1956.
22p. 23cm.

M347.9
Un34

National Association for the Advancement of Colored People.
U. S. District Court. Virginia (Eastern District) Richmond Division.
National Association for the Advancement of Colored People, a corporation, N.A.A.C.P. Legal Defense and Educational Fund, Incorporated, a corporation, plaintiffs, against Kenneth C. Patty...defendants. Civil actions nos. 2435 and 2436. [n.p.] NAACP Legal Defense and Educational Fund [n.d.]
64p. 27cm.
"A reprint of the decision."
1. National Association for the Advancement of Colored People.

M323
N214w

National Association for the Advancement of Colored People
Wilkins, Roy, 1901–
40 years of the NAACP, keynote address at 40th annual conference, National Association for the Advancement of Colored People, Los Angeles, California, July 12, 1949. New York, NAACP, 1949.
16p. 21x10cm.

M323
W98n

National Association for the Advancement of Colored People.
Wynn, Daniel Webster, 1919–
The NAACP versus Negro revolutionary protest; a comparative study of the effectiveness of each movement. [1st ed.] New York, Exposition Press [1955]
115 p. 21 cm. (Exposition—University book)
Bibliography: p. [108]–110.
1. Negroes—Civil rights. 2. National Association for the Advancement of Colored People. 3. Communism—U. S.—1917– I. Title.
E185.61.W98 325.260973 54—13180
Library of Congress [56h5]

M323
N213a

National Association for the Advancement of Colored People. Atlanta, Ga. Citizenship Training School.
A primer on citizenship, prepared and used by Citizenship Training School, conducted by Atlanta Branch, National Association for the Advancement of Colored People, Atlanta, Georgia, 1933.
13p. 21x10cm.
Foreword by Rayford W. Logan.
1. Citizenship. I. Logan, Rayford Whittingham

M323
N212

National Association for the Advancement of Colored People. Legal Defense and Educational Fund.
Assault at 75 feet. New York, NAACP, Legal Defense and Educational Fund, 1951.
6p. illus. 22cm.
1. Ingram, Mack. 2. North Carolina. 3. Civil rights, Denial of. I. Title.

M323
N212

National Association for the Advancement of Colored People. Legal Defense and Educational Fund.
Equal justice under law; [Cases won before the United States Supreme Court]. New York, The Association, 1948.
16p. 22cm.
1. Civil rights. 2. Law - Reports, digest, etc. I. Title.

M323
N212

National Association for the Advancement of Colored People. Legal Defense and Educational Fund.
Equal justice under law; [Cases won before the United States Supreme Court]. New York, The Association, 1945.
16p. 22cm.
1. Civil rights. 2. Law - Reports, digest, etc. I. Title.

M323
N212

National Association for the Advancement of Colored People. Legal Defense and Educational Fund.
Equal justice under law; [Cases won before the United States Supreme Court]. New York, The Association, 1944.
14p. 22cm.
1. Civil rights. 2. Law - Reports, digest, etc. I. Title.

M323
N212

National Association for the Advancement of Colored People. Legal Defense and Educational Fund.
The fantastic case of the Trenton six. New York, 1951.
5p. 22cm.
1. Trenton, New Jersey. 2. Trenton six. 3. Civil rights, Denial of. I. Title.

M323
N212

National Association for the Advancement of Colored People. Legal Defense and Educational Fund.
Mutiny? The real story of how the Navy branded 50 fear-shocked sailors as mutineers. New York, 1945.
16p. 21cm.

M323
N212

National Association for the Advancement of Colored People. Legal Defense and Educational Fund.
Segregation in public schools; brief for reargument in the Supreme Court of the United States, October term, 1953.
xxxii, 235 p. 24 cm.
1. Education - integration. I. U.S. Supreme Court.

MB9
B88e

National Association for the Advancement of Colored People. Legal Defense and Educational Fund.
Equal justice under law, [souvenir program]; on the occasion of the dinner in honor of Ralph J. Bunche, 1950 Nobel Peace laureate, launching the 1951 appeal of the N.A.A.C.P., Legal Defense and Educational Fund. New York, N.A.A.C.P., 1951.
[22p.] 31cm.

M323
N213l

National Association for the Advancement of Colored People. Louisville.
The history of Louisville segregation case and the decision of the Supreme Court. Louisville, The Association, Legal Committee, 1917?
32p. 14cm.
1. Louisville, Ky. 2. Law - Reports, digests, etc. - U.S.

M362.11
C63s

National Association for the Advancement of Colored People, National Medical Committee.
Cobb, William Montague, 1904–
Statement of W. Montague Cobb, representing the National Medical Committee of the National Association for the Advancement of Colored People, in opposition to S. 1414; A bill to provide for the establishment of a veterans hospital for Negro veterans at the birthplace of Booker T. Washington in Franklin County, Va., 1948.
5p. 28cm.
Mimeographed.

National Association for the Advancement of Colored People - Drama.
M812.5 B73f Branch, William Blackwell
"Fifty steps toward freedom." A dramatic presentation in observance of the fiftieth anniversary of the National Association for the Advancement of Colored People 1909-1959. Premier performance, July 14, 1959, during NAACP Golden Anniversary Convention at New York Coliseum, New York, N. Y. Produced and directed by Dick Campbell. Music by the Edna Gay Chorus. Balladeer, Johnny Barracuda. Narration by Ossie Davis. [New York, N.A.A.C.P. 1959]

26p. 21½cm.

National Association for the Advancement of Colored People - Membership.
M323 N21 National Association for the Advancement of Colored People.
The first 1000. New York, National Association for the Advancement of Colored People [1958]

[14]p. 21cm.

1. National Association for the Advancement of Colored People - Membership.

M610.73 N21s National Association of Colored Graduate Nurses.
A salute to democracy at mid-century. New York, 1951.

[48]p. 21cm.
Testimonial dinner honoring organizations and individuals who have helped further democracy in nursing.
Where service is needed, by Langston Hughes.

1. Nurses and nursing. I. Hughes, Langston Where service is needed.

M371.974 W65 National Association of Intergroup Relations Officials. Commission on School Integration.
Public school segregation and integration in the North; analysis and proposals of the [NAIRO] Commission on School Integration [prepared by Doxey A. Wilkerson] Washington, 1963.

vi, 104p. tables. 22cm.
Special issue of the Journal of Intergroup Relations.
Bibliography: p. 87-104.
(Continued on next card)

M371.974 W65 National Association of Intergroup Relations Officials. Commission on School Integration. Public school. 1963. (Card 2)

1. Segregation in education. I. Wilkerson, Doxey Alphonso, 1905- II. Journal of intergroup relations. III. Title.

M304 P19 v.7 no.19 National association of teachers in colored schools.
The National notebook, vol. 1, no.1, Augusta, Ga., National association of teachers in colored schools, Ja 1919.

15p. 25½cm.
Editor: Silas X. Floyd.

National Baptist convention.
M818.5 F95f Fuller, Thomas Oscar, 1867-1942
Flashes and gems of thought and eloquence heard from the platform of the National Baptist convention 1900-1920. By Rev. T.C. Fuller. Memphis, Tenn., n.p. c1920
49p. 17½cm.

M220 Su7c National Baptist Convention, U.S.A.
Sunday School Publishing Board. Commentary on the international and improved uniform lessons for 1937. Nashville, The Board, 19

321p. illus. map. 24cm.
Editor: J. T. Brown.

1. Baptists. 2. Sunday-school literature.

National Baptist convention of the United States of America. Foreign mission board.
M286 Ad1n Adams, C C
Negro Baptists and foreign missions; C. C. Adams and Marshall A. Talley, authors. Philadelphia, Pa., The Foreign mission board of the National Baptist convention, U. S. A., inc. [°1944]
84 p. 18½cm.

1. Baptists, Negro—Missions. 2. National Baptist convention of the United States of America—Missions. I. Talley, Marshall Alexander, 1877- joint author. II. National Baptist convention of the United States of America. Foreign mission board. III. Title.

45-15372
Library of Congress BV2521.A85
[3] 266.61

National Baptist Convention of the U.S. of America - History.
M286 P36s Pelt, Owen D
The story of the National Baptists, by Owen D. Pelt and Ralph Lee Smith. [1st ed.] New York, Vantage Press [1960]
272 p. illus. 22 cm.
Includes bibliography.

1. National Baptist Convention of the United States of America—Hist. I. Smith, Ralph Lee, joint author.

BX6443.P4 286.173 60-15470 ‡
Library of Congress [5]

National Baptist convention of the United States of America-Missions.
M286 Ad1n Adams, C C
Negro Baptists and foreign missions; C. C. Adams and Marshall A. Talley, authors. Philadelphia, Pa., The Foreign mission board of the National Baptist convention, U. S. A., inc. [°1944]
84 p. 18½cm.

1. Baptists, Negro—Missions. 2. National Baptist convention of the United States of America—Missions. I. Talley, Marshall Alexander, 1877- joint author. II. National Baptist convention of the United States of America. Foreign mission board. III. Title.

45-15372
Library of Congress BV2521.A85
[3] 266.61

National Baptist jubilee melodies.
M245 N21 National jubilee melodies ... [16th ed.] Nashville, Tenn., National Baptist publishing board [n. d.]
156, [3] p. 22cm.
Running title: National Baptist jubilee melodies.

I. National Baptist publishing board. II. Title: National Baptist jubilee melodies. III. Title: Jubilee melodies.

27-7076
Library of Congress M1670.N316

National Baptist publishing board.
M245 N21 National jubilee melodies ... [16th ed.] Nashville, Tenn., National Baptist publishing board [n. d.]
156, [3] p. 22cm.
Running title: National Baptist jubilee melodies.

I. National Baptist publishing board. II. Title: National Baptist jubilee melodies. III. Title: Jubilee melodies.

27-7076
Library of Congress M1670.N316

M304 P19 v.7 no.17 National bar association.
Addresses delivered before the fifth annual convention of the National bar association (incorporated) at Detroit, Mich. August 1st and 2nd, 1929.
51p. 23cm.

1. Law and lawyers.

M340 N21n National Bar Association.
National bar directory, compiled by Scovel Richardson. The Association, 1950.

13p. 23cm.
Inscribed: to Arthur B. Spingarn from Thurgood Marshall.

1. Law and lawyers. I. Title.

National bar directory.
M340 N21n National Bar Association.
National bar directory, compiled by Scovel Richardson. The Association, 1950.

13p. 23cm.
Inscribed: to Arthur B. Spingarn from Thurgood Marshall.

M368 M69c National Benefit Life Insurance Company.
Mitchell, James B
The collapse of the National Benefit Life Insurance Company; A study in high finance among Negroes. Washington, D.C. Howard University, Graduate School for the Division of Social Sciences, 1939.

150p. tables. 24cm. (Howard University. Studies in the social sciences, v.2, no.1)

M016 N213 National Book League.
Imaginative literature from the Commonwealth. London, National Book League, 1965.
41p. 22cm.

1. Bibliography. 2. Gt. Brit. - Colonies - Literature - Bibliography. I. Title.

National capital code of etiquette.
M395 G82 Green, Edward S.
National capital code of etiquette, by Edward S. Green. Washington, D. C., Austin Jenkins company [°1920]
138, [2] p. incl. front., illus. 20½cm.
With this is bound: Silas X. Floyd's Short stories for colored people both old and young. Washington, D. C., °1920.

I. Title.
Library of Congress 20-8875
——— Copy 2.
Copyright A 565923 [2]

National Catholic Conference for Interracial Justice. 1st convention, Det., 1961.
M301 Ah5n Ahmann, Mathew H ed.
The new Negro. Contributors: Stephen J. Wright [and others] In the symposium: James Baldwin [and others] Notre Dame, Ind., Fides Publishers [1961]
xii, 145 p. 21 cm.
Includes papers presented at the 1st convention of the National Catholic Conference for Interracial Justice, held in Detroit in 1961.

1. Negroes—Addresses, essays, lectures. I. Wright, Stephen J. II. National Catholic Conference for Interracial Justice. 1st convention, Detroit, 1961. III. Title.

E185.6.A26 301.451 61—17712
Library of Congress [62f5]

National characteristics.
M350 Yo8m Young, Charles, 1864-1922.
Military morale of nations and races, by Charles Young ... Kansas City, Mo., Franklin Hudson publishing co., 1912.
278 p. 22½cm.
Bibliography: p. [7]

1. National characteristics. 2. Ethnopsychology. 3. Soldiers. 4. Morale. I. Title.

14—8826
Library of Congress U21.Y6
[a41b1]

M973
R543a
National characteristics, American.
Robeson, Eslanda (Goode), 1896- jt. auth.
American argument, Pearl S. Buck with Eslanda Goode Robeson. New York, J. Day Co. [1949]
xii, 206p. 21cm.

National characteristics, American.
M301
Se4s
Sellers, Charles Grier, ed.
The southerner as American. [By] John Hope Franklin [and others] Chapel Hill, University of North Carolina Press [1960]
216 p. 24 cm.
Includes bibliography.
1. National characteristics, American. 2. Southern States—Civilization. 3. Southern States — Hist. — Historiography. 4. Southern States—Race question. I. Title.
F209.S44 917.5 60—4104 ‡
Library of Congress [61r*30]

National characteristics, Haitian.
Haiti
M972.94
M35e
Mars, Price.
... Une étape de l'évolution haïtienne. Port-au-Prince, Haïti, Impr. "La Presse" [1929?]
viii, [9]–208 p. 24½cm. (Bibliothèque haïtienne)
CONTENTS. — L'intelligence haïtienne, études de socio-psychologie. — Les croyances, le sentiment et le phénomène religieux chez les nègres de St.-Domingue; conférence prononcée à la Société d'histoire et de géographie en 1926.—Magic island, par W. B. Seabrook ...—La Noël des humbles.—Les opinions à propos de "Black Haiti", une biographie de la fille aînée de l'Afrique, par Blair Niles.
1. Haiti—Soc. condit. 2. Haiti—Intellectual life. 3. National characteristics, Haitian. 4. Negroes in Haiti. I. Title.
30-15008
Library of Congress F1921.M36 [2]

National characteristics, West African.
M910
F28w2
Fax, Elton C
West Africa vignettes. [Translations by Jacques Leger. 2d ed. New York] American Society of African Culture [1963]
92 p. illus., ports., map. 26 cm.
French and English.
1. National characteristics, West African. 2. Africa, West—Biog.—Portraits. I. Title.
DT494.F3 1963 916.6 63–11211
Library of Congress [3]

National characteristics, West African.
M910
F28w
Fax, Elton C
West Africa vignettes. [New York] American Society of African Culture [1960]
62 p. illus. 26 cm.
1. National characteristics, West African. 2. Africa, West—Biog.—Portraits. I. Title.
DT494.F3 916.6 60-11410 ‡
Library of Congress [5]

S. Africa
M968
N21f
National coloured-European conference. *1st, Cape Town, 1933.*
First National coloured-European conference. Report of proceedings. Cape Town, June 26, 27, 28, 1933. Cape Town, Atlas printing works (Pty.) Ltd. [1933]
116 p. 25 cm.
Africa Africa,South Africa,S.
1. ~~Negroes~~—Congresses. 2. ~~Negroes in Africa~~. 3. ~~Negroes~~—Education. 4. ~~Negroes~~—Economic conditions. 5. Race problems.
Africa,S Africa,S.
A 37—536
Teachers College Libr., for Library of Congress Columbia Univ. [a54c1]

S. Africa.
M968
N21f
National coloured-European conference. *1st, Cape Town, 1933.*
First National coloured-European conference. Report of proceedings. Cape Town, June 26, 27, 28, 1933. Cape Town, Atlas printing works (Pty.) Ltd. [1933]
116 p. 25 cm.
1. Negroes—Congresses. 2. Negroes in Africa. 3. Negroes—Education. 4. Negroes—Economic conditions. 5. Race problems.
A 37—536
Teachers College Libr., for Library of Congress Columbia Univ. [a54c1]

M331.1
N21f
National Community Relations Advisory Council.
FEPC reference manual prepared by the Committee on Employment Discrimination of the National Community Relations Advisory Council. 1948 ed. New York [1948]
70 p. 22 cm.
Bibliography: p. 69–70.
1. Discrimination in employment—~~U.S.~~ 2. U. S. Committee on Fair Employment Practice (1943–1946) I. Title.
3. Fair employment practice legislation
HD4903.N25 331.11 48–4697*
Library of Congress [2]

National Conference of Charities and Correction (name changed in 1916)
see
National Conference of Social Work

M973.6
N21t
1879
National Conference of Colored Men. Nashville.
Proceedings of the National Conference of Colored Men of the United States, held in the State Capitol at Nashville, Tennessee, May 6, 7, 8, and 9, 1879.
107p. 19cm.
1. Congresses and conventions. I. Pinchback, Pickney Benton Stewart, 1837-1923.
II. Augusta, Alexander T.
Sanitary conditions of the people of the United States. p. 42-50.

National Conference of Colored Men. Nashville. (card 2)
VI. Cromwell, John Wesley, 1846-
The necessity of industrial and technical education, p. 79-83.
VII. Barnett, Ferinand L , 1859-
Race unity -- its importance and necessity, p. 83-86.
VIII. Green, Theo H
Elements of prosperity, p. 86-94.

M306
N21m
National Conference of Social Work.
Minority groups: segregation and integration. Papers presented at the 82d annual forum of the National Conference of Social Work. [Editorial Committee: Irving Weissman, chairman, Lois Clarke and others. Editorial work: Dorothy Swart] New York, Published for the National Conference of Social Work by Columbia University Press, 1955.
vi, 110 p. 24 cm.
1. Segregation—U. S. 2. Social case work. I. Title.
HV95.N35 1955 *301.45 325.73 56—5879
Library of Congress [56f*15]

M306
N21p
National conference of social work.
Proceedings ... Selected papers [of the] ... annual meeting. 1st-
1874- **See holdings card for issues in library.**
New York [etc.] 1874–19
v. ports., tables (part fold.) diagrs. 22–24 cm.
Issued under earlier names of the conference as follows: 1874, Conference of boards of public charities; 1875–79, Conference of charities; 1880–81, Conference of charities and corrections; 1882–1916, National conference of charities and correction (varies slightly)
Title varies slightly.
Vol. for 1874 (originally published in the Journal of social science, no. 6) was issued without title by the American social science association; reprinted in 1885 under title Proceedings of the first Conference of charities and correction.
See S.L. for annalytics made. (Continued on next card)
8–35377 rev 2
[r46p*20]

M306
N21p
National conference of social work. Proceedings ...
1874–19 (Card 2)
Vols. for 1875–81 are regarded as extra numbers of the Journal of social science, though only the issue for 1875 was so designated on the title-page.
~~1934.~~ ~~Library has: 1919, 1924,~~ HV88.A3 ~~1926, 1928,~~ 1929
——— A guide to the study of charities and correction by means of the Proceedings of the ... conference ... using thirty-four volumes, 1874–1907. Compiled by Alexander Johnson ... [Indianapolis?] 1908.
xi, 353 p. 23 cm.
(Continued on next card)
8–35377 rev 2
[r46p*20]

M306
N21p
National conference of social work. Proceedings ...
1874–19 (Card 3)
INDEXES:
Vols. 1–33, 1874–1906. 1 v. (Issued in 4 pts. as appendices to its National bulletin (later called Conference bulletin)
Vols. 1–60, 1874–1933. 1 v.
Library ~~has: 1919, 1924, 1926, 1928,~~ 1929, ~~1934.~~
~~1. Public welfare—Congresses. 2. Charities—Congresses.~~ 3. Public welfare—~~U. S.~~ 4. Charities—~~U. S.~~ I. Johnson, Alexander, 1847–1941. II. American social science association. III. National conference of social work. Conference bulletin. Supplement.
8–35377 rev 2
Library of Congress HV88.A813
[r46p*20]

National conference of social work.
Conference bulletin. Supplement.
M306
N21p
National conference of social work.
Proceedings ... Selected papers [of the] ... annual meeting. 1st-
1874- Library has: 1919, 1924
New York [etc.] 1874–19
v. ports., tables (part fold.) diagrs. 22–24 cm.
Issued under earlier names of the conference as follows: 1874, Conference of boards of public charities; 1875–79, Conference of charities; 1880–81, Conference of charities and corrections; 1882–1916, National conference of charities and correction (varies slightly)
Title varies slightly.
Vol. for 1874 (originally published in the Journal of social science, no. 6) was issued without title by the American social science association; reprinted in 1885 under title Proceedings of the first Conference of charities and correction.
(Continued on next card)
8–35377 rev 2
[r46p*20]

National conference on human relations education: proceedings of the national conference...
M370
An8c
Anti-defamation League.
Current problems and issues in human relations education; proceedings of the national conference on human relations education, Commodore Hotel, New York City, April 29–30, 1955. Editor: Gertrude Noar, national director of education. [New York, 1955]
ix, 70 p. 26 cm.
Includes bibliographical references.
1. Intercultural education. I. Noar, Gertrude, ed. II. Title. III. Title: National conference on human relations education.
CB199.A54 370.19 56–58171
Library of Congress [2]

National Conference on Small Business.
M658
F57
Fitzhugh, H Naylor, ed.
Problems and opportunities confronting Negroes in the field of business; report on the National Conference on Small Business. Washington, D. C., U. S. Dept. of Commerece, 1962.
103p. 23½cm.

M323
N217
National Conference on the Problems of the Negro and Negro Youth.
Report. Washington, D.C. 1937.
48p. 27cm.
Mimeographed.
1. Race problems.

M973.6
N21w
National convention of colored men, Washington, D. C.
Proceedings of the national convention of the colored men of America, held in Washington, D. C., on January 13, 14, 15 and 16, 1869. Washington, D. C., Great Republic book and newspaper printing establishment, 1869.
42, xv p. 21cm.
1. Congresses and conventions. 2. Washington, D. C.

National Convention of Colored Men. Louisville.
MB15.4
D74a2
Douglass, Frederick, 1817-1895.
Address delivered at the National Convention of Colored Men at Louisville, Ky., September 24, 1883. Louisville, Courier-Journal Job Printing Company, 1883.
9p. 19cm.

M973.6
N21
1847

National Convention of Colored People. Troy, New York.
Proceedings of the National Convention of Colored People and their friends, held in Troy, N.Y., on the 6th, 7th, 8th and 9th, 1847. Troy, N.Y., Steam Press of J. C. Kneeland and Co., 1847.

32p. 19cm.

1. Congresses and conventions 2. New York(State)

M973.6
N21c
1865
176217

National equal rights league. Cleveland, Ohio.
Proceedings of the first annual meeting of the national equal rights league, held in Cleveland, Ohio, October 19, 20 and 21, 1865. Philadelphia, E. C. Markley & Son, 1865.
54p. 21cm.

1. Congresses and conventions. 2. Langston, John Mercer. 3. Ohio. I. Forten, William D. Address and resolutions. p. 37-44. II. Nesbitt, William. Address to the colored people of the United States, p.48-54.

Sp

MB9
L63na

National Lincoln monument association.
Celebration by the Colored people's educational monument association in memory of Abraham Lincoln, on the Fourth of July, 1865, in the presidential grounds, Washington, D. C. ... Washington, D. C., McGill & Witherow, printers, 1865.
33, [1] p. 22½cm.

1. Lincoln, Abraham, pres. U. S., 1809-1865. I. Title.

Library of Congress E457.52.N22 12—30032
——— Copy 2. [a23d1]

M331.1
N213a

National Council for a Permanent FEPC.
Answer the critics of F.E.P.C. Washington, D.C., National Council for a Permanent FEPC.

15p. 23cm.

1. Fair employment practice legislation.

M968
Na21r

National European-Bantu conference, *Cape Town*, 1929.
Report of the National European-Bantu conference. Cape Town, February 6-9, 1929. [Lovedale, Lovedale institution press [1929]
4 p. l., 227 p. 19cm.

1. Africa, South—Native races—Congresses. 2. Africa, South—Econ. condit.—1918- 3. Labor and laboring classes—Africa, South.

Library of Congress HC517.S7N25 1929 43-35525
[2]

M331.88
N21n

National Maritime Union.
The N.M.U. fights jim crow. New York, 1943.

13p. illus. 23cm.

1. Trade unions. I. Title.

M355.4
F75a

National council of Jewish Communists.
Ford, James W 1893-
... Anti-Semitism and the struggle for democracy ... New York city, The National council of Jewish Communists [1939?]
19 p. 19½cm.
"Based on the report to a special meeting of the Harlem division of the Communist party, by Theodore R. Bassett (December 22, 1938), and the speech of James W. Ford at the national conference of the Jewish Communists, December 24, 25, and 26, 1938."

1. Jewish question. 2. Jews in the U. S. 3. Negroes. I. Bassett, Theodore R. II. National council of Jewish Communists. III. Title.

Library of Congress DS145.F65 44-34986
[3]

M331
H76b

National industrial recovery act, 1933.
Hoover, Isaac James.
Banishing the ghost of unemployment, by Isaac James Hoover. Boston, Meador publishing company, 1934.
2 p. l., 7-105 p. 19½cm.
"The fallacies of the 'new deal' exposed."—Publisher's announcement.

1. Unemployed—U. S. 2. U. S.—Economic policy. 3. National industrial recovery act, 1933. I. Title.

Library of Congress HD5724.H6 34-39702
——— Copy 2.
Copyright A 78288 [5] 331.137973

M610.
C63sci

National Medical Association.
Cobb, William Montague, 1904-
The 1939 scientific exhibit of the Howard University School of Medicine. Reprinted from the Journal of the National Medical Association, 32:216-218, September 1940.

M641.5
N21

National Council of Negro Women.
The historical cookbook of the American Negro. Published under the auspices of the Council's Archives and Museum Dept. Compiled and edited by Sue Bailey Thurman, chairman. [Washington] Corporate Press, °1958.
144 p. illus. 22 cm.

1. Cookery, Negro. 2. Cookery, American. I. Thurman, Sue Bailey, ed. II. Title.
TX715.N326 59-24514 ‡
Library of Congress [1]

M301
J63ne6

National interracial conference, Washington, 1928.
Johnson, Charles Spurgeon, 1893-
The Negro in American civilization; a study of Negro life and race relations in the light of social research, by Charles S. Johnson... London, Constable and co., 1931.
xiv, 538p. diagrs. 22½cm.
Results of social research for the National interracial conference and problems discussed at its meeting in Washington, D.C., December 16-19, 1928.
Bibliography: p485-509 (over)

M610.
C63sc

National Medical Association.
Cobb, William Montague, 1904-
The scientific exhibit of the Howard University School of Medicine at the 1939 convention of the National Medical Association, n.p., 1939.

51 28cm.
Mimeographed.

MB
R39

The National cyclopedia of the colored race; editor-in-chief, Clement Richardson ...
Montgomery, Ala., National publishing company, inc., 1919-
v. illus., ports. 31cm.

1. Negroes. 2. ~~Negroes—Biog.~~ Biography I. Richardson, Clement, 1878- ed.

Library of Congress E185.N27 19—15870
[a41f1]

M245
N21

National jubilee melodies ... [16th ed.] Nashville, Tenn., National Baptist publishing board [n. d.]
156, [3] p. 22cm.
Running title: National Baptist jubilee melodies.

I. National Baptist publishing board. II. Title: National Baptist jubilee melodies. III. Title: Jubilee melodies.
1. Hymns.

Library of Congress M1670.N316 27-7076

M610
M96n

National Medical Association.
Murray, Peter Marshall, 1888-
N.M.A. president's address. n.p. 1932.

15p. 28cm.
Delivered at Washington, August 16, 1932.
Mimeo.

M973.6
N21cl
1854

National emigration convention, Cleveland, Ohio.
Arguments, pro and con, on the call for a national emigration convention, to be held in Cleveland, Ohio, August, 1854, by Frederick Douglass, W. J. Watkins, & J. M. Whitfield. With a short appendix of the statistics of Canada West, West Indies, Central and South America. Published by M. T. Newsome. Detroit, George E. Pomeroy & co., 1854.
34p. 19cm.

1. Congresses and conventions. 2. Ohio. 3. Colonization. 4. Emigration. I. Newsome, M T

(over)

M973.6
C76w
1870

National labor union.

Colored National Labor Convention, Washington, D. C.
Proceedings of the Colored National labor convention held in Washington, D. C., on December 6th, 7th, 8th, 9th and 10th, 1869. Washington, D. C., Printed at the office of the New Era, 1870.
46p. 19cm.

MB9
P42f

National Medical Association.
Perry, John Edward, 1870-
Forty cords of wood; memoirs of a medical doctor ... Jefferson City, Mo., Lincoln university [1947]
xvi, 459 p. illus., ports. 23½cm.

1. [Negro physicians] I. Title.
R154.P43A3 926.1 Med 47-944
© 6Mar47; publisher; A11697.

U. S. Army medical library for Library of Congress [W1045P462f 1947]
[4]†

M973.6
P83pe
1866

National Equal Rights' League.
Pennsylvania State Equal Rights' League.
Preamble and constitution of the Pennsylvania State Equal Rights' League, acting under the jurisdiction of the National Equal Rights' League of the United States of America and Constitution for Subordinate Leagues... Philadelphia, J. Mc C. Crummill, 1866.

30p. 14cm.

National League for Protection of Colored Women.

See

National Urban League

M614
R66pe

National Medical Association.
Roman, Charles Victor, 1864-1934.
Personality in progress. Reprinted from the Journal of the National Medical Association, April-June, 1922.

broadside 32cm.

M286
R17c

National ministers' institute, Virginia. Union university, Richmond.
Ransome, William Lee, 1879–
Christian stewardship and Negro Baptists, by W. L. Ransome ... Richmond, Virginia, National ministers' institute, Virginia union university. Richmond, Va., Brown print shop, inc., 1934.
193 p. 20cm.
"A short bibliography": p. 190.

1. Stewardship, Christian. 2. Baptists, Negro. 3. Baptists—Missions. I. National ministers' institute, Virginia. Union university, Richmond. II. Title.
36-30056
Library of Congress BV772.R25
——— Copy 2. [3] 254

M306
N21pe

[National Negro Congress]
A petition... to the United Nations on behalf of 13 million oppressed Negro citizens of the United States of America. New York, 1946.
15p. 23cm.
Contains also: The oppression on the American Negro: the facts, by Herbert Aptheker: p. 8.14.

I. Title. 1. Race problems.

M368.3
N21

National Negro insurance association.
Proceedings..., annual session. Richmond, Va., Quality printing co., 19
v. charts
Library has: 1937

1. Insurance

M304
P19
v.7
no.4

National Negro business league.
Annual report of the secretary's office, National Negro business league for the fiscal year ending August 15th, 1930.
16p. 23cm.

1. Business

M306
N213p

National Negro Congress
Proceedings.
Washington, 1936–
v. 20cm.
See holdings card for proceedings in library.

1. Congresses and conventions. 2. Race relations.

National Newspaper Publishers Association.

M323
Su6

Summit Meeting of National Negro Leaders, Washington, D. C., 1958.
Report of proceeding [of] Summit Meeting of Negro Leaders, Washington, D.C., May 12, 13, 1958. Sponsored by National Newspaper Publishers Association. [Washington, National Newspaper Publishers Association] 1958.
137p. illus. 33cm.
Contents.- Speech, by William O. Walker.- Speech, by A. Philip Randolph.- Speech, by Paul H. Cooke.- Address, by Roy Wilkins.-
(Continued on next card)

M334
N21

National negro business league.
Proceedings of the ... annual meeting of the National negro business league ...
1st–
1900–
[Nashville, Tenn., °1901–
v. fronts., ports. 21–23cm.
Title varies: 1st– Proceedings ...
Report of the ... annual convention.
... Annual report of the sixteenth session and the fifteenth anniversary convention.
... Report of the annual session.
Proceedings of the ... annual meeting.
1. Negroes—Employment. FOR LIBRARY HOLDINGS SEE NEXT CARD
1-31348 Revised
Library of Congress E185.8.N27
[r24e2]

M306
N214r

National Negro Congress.
Proceedings.

Volume	Year	Month	Volume	Year	Month
	1936				
	1937				

National Newspaper Publishers Association.

M323
Su6

Summit Meeting of National Negro Leaders, Washington, D. C., 1958. Report of proceedings. 1958. (Card 2)

Contents - Continued.
Speech by Thurgood Marshall.- How shall we travel the road of freedom together, by F. L. Shuttleworth.
At head of title: Lighting the way to freedom.
Mimeographed.
1. Race relations. 2. Civil rights. 3. Freedom. I. Title. II. National Newspaper Publishers Association.

M334
N21

National Negro Business League.
Proceedings.

Volume	Year	Month	Volume	Year	Month
1	1900		22	1921	
4	1903		25	1924	
6	1905				
7	1906				
9	1908				
11	1910				
13	1912				
14	1913				
15	1914				
18&19	1917-18				
20	1919				

M306
N213r

National Negro Congress
Resolutions of the National Negro Congress. Held in Chicago, Ill., February 14, 15, 16, 1936. [Washington, D.C., 1936?]
4-44p. 20cm.

M304
P19
v.7
no.19

The National notebook, vol. 1, no.1, Augusta, Ga., National association of teachers in colored schools, Ja 1919.
16p. 25½cm.
Editor: Silas X. Floyd.
1. Education
2. Teachers
I. National association of teachers in colored schools.
3. Periodicals.

M306
N212

National Negro Conference. New York, 1909.
Proceedings. New York, [1909].
229p. 19cm.
Contents: -Politics and industry, by W.E.B. DuBois. -Race prejudice as viewed from an economic standpoint, by William L. Bulkley. The Race problem, by Rev. Jenkins Lloyd Jones. -Evolution of the race problem, by W.E.B. Du Bois. -The problem's solution, by Rev. J. M. Waldron. -Civil and political status of the Negro, by A. Walters. -Lynching our national
(continued on card 2)

National Negro congress.

M815.4
D739k

Kingston, Steve.
Frederick Douglass, abolitionist, liberator, statesman, by Steve Kingston ... [Brooklyn and New York, National Negro congress, Brooklyn and Manhattan councils, 1941?]
45 p. 18½cm.

1. Douglass, Frederick, 1817–1895. I. National Negro congress.
42-50808
Library of Congress E449.D7675
[2] 923.673

M304
P19
v.7, no.19

The National notebook. Augusta Ga.

Volume	Year	Month	Volume	Year	Month
	1919				

M306
N212

National Negro Conference. New York, 1919. (Card 2)
crime, by Ida Wells-Barnett. -The Negro and the nation, by William S. Sinclair. -Address, by Charles E. Russell. -XXXXXXXXXXXXXXXXXXXXXX XXXXXXXXXXXXXX -Lynching our national crime, by Ida Wells-Barnett.
~~I. a.t. Woolley.~~ II. a.t. Du Bois. III. a.t. Jones. IV. a.t. Du Bois. V. a.t. Waldron. VI. a.t. Walters. VII. a.t. Sinclair. VIII. a.t. Moore. IX. a.t.

M306
N213d

National Negro Congress.
Davis, John Preston, 1905–
Let us build a National Negro Congress ... [Washington, National Sponsoring Committee, National Negro Congress, 1935?]
31p. 18cm.

M311.1
N21s

National Planning Association. *Committee of the South.*
Selected studies of Negro employment in the South, prepared for the NPA Committee of the South. Washington, National Planning Association [1953–54]
5 v. (x, 483, a-l p.) illus. 23 cm. (*Its* Reports, no. 6)
Bibliographical footnotes.
CONTENTS.—1. Negro employment in 3 southern plants of International Harvester Company, by J. Hope, II.—2. 4 studies of Negro employment in the Upper South, by D. Dewey.—3. Negro employment in the Birmingham metropolitan area, by L. T. Hawley.—4. 2 plants: Little Rock, by E. W. Eckard and B. U. Ratchford. 3 companies: New Orleans area, by H. W. Wissner.—5. Negro employment practices in the Chattanooga area, by W. H. Wesson, jr.
——— Copy 2. E185.8.N29
(Continued on next card)
53-12662 rev
[r56x9]

M304
P19
v.2,no.1
M331
N19n

[National Negro Congress]
Negro workers after the war. New York, [National Negro congress, 1945]
23p. 15cm.

1. Labor and laboring classes.

M304
P19
v.2, no. 8

National Negro Congress.
Yergan, Max, 1894–
Democracy and the Negro people today. Washington, D.C., National Negro Congress, [1940].
3-14p. port. (cover) 15cm.

M311.1
N21s

National Planning Association. *Committee of the South.*
Selected studies of Negro employment in the South ... [1953–54] (Card 2)
——— Another issue. [1955]
x, 483, a-l p. illus. 24 cm. (*Its* Report no. 6)
HN79.A2N35 no. 6 1955

1. ~~Negroes~~—Employment. 2. ~~Negroes~~—Southern States. I. Title. II. Title: Negro employment in the South. (Series)
HN79.A2N35 no. 6 1953 53-12662 rev
*331.63 331.98
Library of Congress [r56x9]

M332
Sm6n

The National providence.
Smith, James C.
The National providence; essays, by Jas. C. Smith... London, Kegan Paul, Trench, Trubner & Co., 1910.

vi, 1 *l*. 103p. 21½cm.

National socialism.

M323.2
L47w

League of American writers.
"We hold these truths..." Statements on anti-Semitism by 54 leading American writers, statesmen, educators, clergymen and trade-unionists. New York, N. Y., The League of American writers [°1939]

128 p. 20½cm.

"First printing March, 1939."
Errata slip inserted.
"A short bibliography relating to the Jewish question": p. 113-114.
"A partial list of anti-Semitic publishers, organizations and individuals in America": p. 115-123.

1. Jewish question. 2. Jews in the U. S. 3. National socialism. I. Title.

Library of Congress DS145.L47 39-32225
[3] 296

National sociological society.

M323.
W279

Washington conference on the race problem in the United States, *Washington, D. C.*, 1903.
How to solve the race problem. The proceedings of the Washington conference on the race problem in the United States under the auspices of the National sociological society, held at the Lincoln temple Congregational church; at the Nineteenth street Baptist church and at the Metropolitan A. M. E. church, Washington, D. C., November 9, 10, 11, and 12, 1903. Addresses, resolutions and debates by eminent men of both races and in every walk of life. Washington, D. C., Beresford, printer, 1904.

1 p. l., 286 p. front., illus. (port.) 23½cm.
Edited by Jesse Lawson. [45p1]
1. Negroes. 2. U. S.—Race question. I. Lawson, Jesse, ed. II. National sociological society.
Library of Congress E185.5.W32 4—14581

M370
C12n

National survey of the higher education of Negroes.
Caliver, Ambrose, 1894-
National survey of the higher education of Negroes, a summary. Washington, U.S. Govt. Print. Off., 1943.

50p. 29cm. (U.S. Office of Education. Miscellaneous, no.6)
At head of title: National survey of the higher education of Negroes, v.4).

National survey of vocational education and guidance of Negroes.

M371.425
C12

Caliver, Ambrose, 1894-
... Vocational education and guidance of Negroes; report of a survey conducted by the Office of education, by Ambrose Caliver, senior specialist in the education of Negroes ... United States Department of the interior. Harold L. Ickes, secretary. Office of education, J. W. Studebaker, commissioner. Washington, U. S. Govt. print. off., 1938.

x, 187 p. incl. tables, diagrs. 23cm. (U. S. Office of education. Bulletin, 1937, no. 38)

At head of title: Project in vocational education and guidance of Negroes.
On p. [2] of cover: National survey of vocational education and guidance of Negroes.

(Continued on next card)

E 39-3 †
[a46d²3]†

M304
P19
v.7
no.25

National urban league
After the depression - What?
Statement of the pruposes and plans of the third vocational opportunity campaign to improve the status of Negro workers. New York City, National urban league [1932]
4p. 28cm.
1. Vocational guidance.

M306
N21a

National Urban League.
... And the pursuit of happiness. 40th anniversary year book. New York, National Urban League, 1950.

128p. ports. illus. 28½cm.

1. National Urban League - Yearbooks.
2. Yearbooks - National Urban League.

M304
P19
v.7
no.27

National urban league
Bibliography... The exonomic life of the Negro in America New York [National urban league, 1932]
2p. 28cm.
Mimeographed.

1. Bibliography - Economic conditions.
2. Economic conditions - Bibliography.

M306
N214f

National Urban League ~~(for Social Service among Negroes)~~
40th anniversary year book, 1950. [New York, 1951]
128 p. illus. 29 cm.

1. ~~Negroes.~~ Social service

E185.5.N33F67 325.260973 52-69 ‡
Library of Congress [12]

M331
N21

National urban league ~~(for social service among Negroes)~~
Negro membership in American labor unions, by the Department of research and investigations of the National urban league, Ira De A. Reid, director. New York, N. Y. [The Alexander press, 1930]

175 p. 23½cm.

1. ~~Negroes~~—Employment. 2. Trade-unions—U. S. I. Title.
30—29407
Library of Congress E185.8.N31
[44r39t1] [331.8806] 325.26

M306
N214n

National Urban League.
No man... is an island. New York, the League, [1946]

8p. 22cm.

1. National Urban League. I. Title.

M331.833
N214r

National urban league.
Racial problems in housing. [New York] National urba n league [1944]
30p. illus. 27½cm. (Interacial planning for community organization. Bulletin no.2)

1. Housing
I. Title.

M306
N214r

National Urban League.
Report. 1-
New York, 1911-

v. tables. 23cm. annual.
Three organizations combined in 1911 to form the League: Committee on Urban Conditions among Negroes, National League for Protection of Colored Women, Committee for Improving the Industrial Condition of Negroes in New York.
First reports published in The Bulletin of the League.
See holdings card for reports in library.

M306
N214r

National Urban League.
Report, 1911-

Volume	Year	Month	Volume	Year	Month
22	1932		32	1942	
23	1933				
24			34	1944	
			35	1945	
26	1936		36	1946	
27	1937				
28	1938		38	1948	
29	1939				
30	1940		40	1950	
31	1941				
			42	1952	

2

M304
P19
v.7
no.5

National urban league
The right vocation; program helps for high schools and colleges participating in the vocational opportunity campaign, April 17-24, 1932. ...New York, National urban league, 1932.
4p. 24½cm.

MB
N21t

National urban league.
They crashed the color line! ...New York City, Department of industrial relations, National urban league [c1937]

31p. illus. 23cm. (On cover: The color line series, no. 5.)

1. Biography. I. Title.

M304
P19
v.7
no.32

National urban league
Unemployment status of Negroes; a compilation of facts and figures respecting unemployment among Negroes in one hundred and six cities. New York, National urban league, 1931.
56p. 26cm.

1. Unemployment. 2. Economic conditions.

M304
P19
v.7
no.28

National urban league
Vocational guidance: bibliography. New York, National urban league, 1932.
9p. 28cm.
Mimeographed.

1. Bibliography - Vocational guidance.
2. Vocational guidance - Bibliography.

M304
P19
v.7, no.26

National urban league
Vocational mindedness, a statement of the purpose and plans of the vocational opportunity campaign to improve the status of Negro workers. New York, National urban league [1931]
4p. 28cm.

1. Vocational guidance.

M301
R27so

National Urban League.
Reid, Ira DeAugustine, 1901-
Social conditions of the Negro in the hill district of Pittsburgh; survey conducted under the direction of Ira DeA. Reid. [Pittsburgh] General Committee on the Hill Survey, 1930.

117p. diagrs. 24½cm.
Bibliography: p. 116-117.

M370
N213m

National Urban League. Dept. of Industrial Relations.
My vocation, with special reference to the problems faced by Negro youth. New York, n.d.

16p. 19cm.

1. Vocational guidance. I. Title.

M975.8 N21n
National Youth Administration. Georgia.
Negro youth in Georgia study their problems; Based on the first state Negro youth conference ... by William H. Shell and Gabriel S. Alexander. ⌊Atlanta, 1940⌋
85p. 28cm. (Bulletin, no.3)
Mimeographed.
1. Georgia. 2. Youth.

Nationalism - Africa.
Kenya M960 M458t
Mazrui, Ali Al'Amin.
Towards a Pax Africana; a study of ideology and ambition ₍by₎ Ali A. Mazrui. ₍Chicago₎ University of Chicago Press ₍1967₎
xi, 287 p. 23 cm. (The Nature of human society series)
Bibliographical references included in "Notes" (p. 243-277)
1. Nationalism—Africa. I. Title. 2. Africa-Nationalism.
DT30.M35 1967a 320.9'6 67-12232
Library of Congress ₍7₎

Nationalism - Africa, Sub-Saharan.
Africa M960 F76
Foreign affairs (New York)
Africa; a Foreign affairs reader, edited by Philip W. Quigg. Foreword by Hamilton Fish Armstrong. ₍1st ed.₎ New York, Published for the Council on Foreign Relations by Praeger ₍1964₎
xii, 346 p. 25 cm.
1. Africa, Sub-Saharan—Politics—Addresses, essays, lectures. 2. Nationalism—Africa, Sub-Saharan. 3. Africa, South—Native races—Addresses, essays, lectures. I. Quigg, Philip W., ed. II. Title.
DT352.F6 1964 960.3082 64-12589
Library of Congress ₍5₎

National Urban League.
M06 N214n
National Urban League.
No man... is an island. New York, the League, ⌊1946⌋
8p. 22cm.

Kenya M960 M45
Nationalism - Africa.
Mboya, Thomas, 1930-
Conflict & nationhood; the essentials of freedom in Africa. ⌊London, Africa Bureau, 1963⌋
12p. 21½cm.

Nationalism - Congo, Belgian.
Congo (Democratic Republic) M967.5 K13t
Kanza, Thomas R
Tôt ou tard ... (Ata ndele ...) Bruxelles, Le Livre africain ₍1959?₎
87 p. 19 cm.
1. Nationalism—Congo, Belgian. 2. Congo, Belgian—Native races. I. Title.
DT644.K3 60-31883 ‡
Library of Congress ₍8₎

M06 N214r
National Urban League.
Riis, Roger William.
The answer to the Negro problem. Reprinted from Coronet, April 1949.
4p. 19cm.

Nationalism - Africa.
Rhodesia M968.91 S18a
Sithole, Ndabaningi, 1920-
African nationalism. With a foreword by R. S. Garfield Todd. Cape Town, New York, Oxford University Press, 1959.
174 p. 19 cm.
1. Nationalism—Africa. I. Title.
DT31.S55 960.3 59-16995 ‡
Library of Congress ₍60f5₎

Guinea M966.52 T64ac
Nationalism - Guinea, French.
Touré, Sékou, Pres. Guinea, 1922-
L'action politique du Parti démocratique de Guinée pour l'émancipation africaine. ₍Conakry, Impr. nationale₎ 1959-
v. illus. 24 cm.
1. Nationalism—Guinea, French. 2. Parti démocratique de Guinée. I. Title.
DT543.T6 60-22321 rev ‡
Library of Congress ₍r62b1₎

National Urban League - Yearbooks.
M306 N21a
National Urban League.
... And the pursuit of happiness. 40th anniversary year book. New York, National Urban League, 1950.
128p. ports. illus. 28½cm.

Dahomey M966.8 T29
Nationalism-Africa.
Tevoedjre, Albert, 1929-
L'Afrique révoltée. Préf. d'Alioune Diop. Paris, Présence africaine ₍1958₎
157 p. illus., ports. 20 cm. (Tribune de la jeunesse, 1)
Errata leaf inserted.
Portrait of author.
1. Nationalism—Africa. 2. France—Colonies—Africa. I. Title.
DT33.T4 59-30412
Library of Congress ₍8₎

Nationalism, colonialism and the United States one minute to twelve.
M973 L614n
Liberation Committee for Africa.
Nationalism, colonialism and the United States one minute to twelve; a forum. First anniversary celebration, June 2, 1961. ⌊New York⌋ Photo-Offset Process, 1961.
39p. 23cm.

Nationalism-Africa.
Sénégal M966.3 D54a
Dia, Mamadou.
The African nations and world solidarity. Translated from the French by Mercer Cook. New York, Praeger ₍1961₎
145 p. 22 cm. (Books that matter)
1. Africa—Econ. condit.—1918- 2. Africa—Foreign economic relations. 3. Nationalism—Africa. 4. Mali. I. Title.
HC502.D417 960.3 61-17815 ‡
Library of Congress ₍62q5₎

Nationalism - Africa - Addresses, essays, lectures.
Africa M370 C83
Cowan, Laing Gray, ed.
Education and nation-building in Africa. Edited by L. Gray Cowan, James O'Connell ₍and₎ David G. Scanlon. New York, F. A. Praeger ₍1965₎
x, 403 p. 21 cm.
Bibliography: p. 397-403.
1. Education—Africa—Addresses, essays, lectures. 2. Nationalism—Africa—Addresses, essays, lectures. I. O'Connell, James, 1925- joint ed. II. Scanlon, David G., joint ed. III. Title.
LA1501.C6 1965 370.96 65-12193
Library of Congress ₍8₎

Nationalism and religion - Africa.
Northern Rhodesia M968.94 K16
Kaunda, Kenneth, 1924-
Black government; a discussion between Colin Morris and Kenneth Kaunda. Lusaka, Northern Rhodesia, United Society for Christian Literature, 1960.
116p. ports. 22cm.
Biographies included.

Senegal M966.3 D54a2
Nationalism - Africa.
Dia, Mamadou.
Nations Africaines et solidarite mondiale. ⌊2d. ed.⌋ Paris, Presses Universitaires de France, 1963.
174p. 22cm.
1. Africa - Econ. condit. - 1945 - 2. Africa - Foreign economic relations. 3. Nationalism - Africa. I. Title.

Nationalism - Africa - Addresses, essays, lectures.
Zambia M960 K16
Kaunda, Kenneth David, Pres., Zambia, 1924-
A humanist in Africa: letters to Colin M. Morris from Kenneth D. Kaunda. London, Longmans, 1966.
3-136 p. 20½ cm. 16/-
(B 66-10714)
1. Nationalism — Africa — Addresses, essays, lectures. 2. Pan-Africanism—Addresses, essays, lectures. I. Morris, Colin M. II. Title.
DT963.6.K3A45 320.15808 66-76308
Library of Congress ₍3₎

Nationalisme et problèmes Malgaches.
Madagascar M969 R11n
Rabemananjara, Jacques, 1913-
Nationalisme et problèmes Malgaches. Paris, Presence Africaine, 1958.
219p. 22½cm.
1. Madagascar-Politics and government. 2. Poetry. I. Title.

Nationalism - Africa.
Nigeria M960 F215
Fani-Kayode, Remi, 1921-
Blackism. Lagos, London ⌊V. Cooper⌋ 1965
99p. 20½cm.
Portrait of author on book cover.
1. Nationalism - Africa. 2. Africa. I. Title.

Nationalism - Africa, Sub-Saharan.
Africa M960.3 D87a
Duffy, James, 1923- ed.
Africa speaks. Edited by James Duffy and Robert A. Manners. Princeton, N. J., Van Nostrand ₍1961₎
223 p. 23 cm.
1. Nationalism — Africa, Sub-Saharan. 2. Africa, South — Race question. I. Manners, Robert Alan, joint ed. II. Title.
Full name: James Edward Duffy.
DT30.D8 960.3 61-3312 ‡
Library of Congress ₍61q15₎

Nationalisme et problemes Malgaches.
Madagascar M969 R11n
Rabemananjara, Jacques, 1913-
Nationalisme et problemes Malgaches. Paris, Presence Africaine, 1958.
219p. 22½cm.
1. Madgascar - Politics and government. 2. Poetry. I. Title.

Senegal
M966.3
Se5nt2

Nationhood and the African road to socialism.
Senghor, Léopold Sédar, 1906-
Nationhood and the African road to socialism. Translated by Mercer Cook. Paris, Presence Africaine [1962]

130p. 21½cm.
Includes bibliography.

1. Africa. 2. Socialism. I. Title. II. Cook, Mercer, tr.

M813.5
W93n5

Native son.
Wright, Richard
Native son. New York, Grosset & Dunlap, 1940.

359p. 21cm.

Jamaica
M972.92
G69n

Natural history—Jamaica.
Gosse, Philip Henry, 1810-1888.
A naturalist's sojourn in Jamaica. By Philip Henry Gosse ... assisted by Richard Hill ... London, Longmans, Brown, Green and Longmans, 1851.

1 p. l., [v]-xxiv, 508 p. front., VII col. pl. 19 cm.

1. Natural history—Jamaica. I. Hill, Richard, 1795-1872. II. Title.

6—5293

Library of Congress QH109.J5G6 [37d1-]

Senegal
M966.3
D54a2

Nations Africaines et solidarite mondiale.
Dia, Mamadou.
Nations Africaines et solidarite mondiale. [2d. ed.] Paris, Presses Universitaires de France, 1963.

174p. 22cm.

1. Africa - Econ. condit. - 1945 - 2. Africa - Foreign economic relations. 3. Nationalism - Africa. I. Title.

Native son.
M813.5
W93n4

Wright, Richard.
Native son, by Richard Wright ... New York and London, Harper & brothers, 1940.

xi, 359 p. 21 cm.
"First edition."

I. Title.

40—4862

Library of Congress PZ3.W9352Nat [45o1]

Natural history—Jamaica.
Jamaica
M972.92
L85h

[Long, Edward] 1734-1813.
The history of Jamaica: or, General survey of the antient and modern state of that island: with reflections on its situation, settlements, inhabitants, climate, products, commerce, laws, and government ... Illustrated with copper plates ... London, T. Lowndes, 1774.

3 v. fold. fronts. (v. 1-2) plates (1 fold.) fold. maps, plan. 28 x 22cm.
Vols. 2-3 paged continuously.

1. Jamaica. 2. Slavery in Jamaica. 3. Natural history—Jamaica. I. Title.

3—11578

Library of Congress F1868.L84 [40e1]

Native African races and culture...
M323
J632e
no. 6

Johnson, James Weldon, 1871-1938.
Native African races and culture, by James Weldon Johnson ... [Charlottesville, Va.] 1927.

26 p. 23cm. (On cover: The Trustees of the John F. Slater fund. Occasional papers. no. 25)
"Works cited": p. 26.

1. Ethnology—Africa. 2. Africa—Civilization. I. Title.

29—8772

Library of Congress E185.5.J65 no. 25
——— Copy 2. GN645.J55 [a39f1]

M813.5
W93n3

Native son.
Wright, Richard
Native son. London, Victor Gollancz, 1940.

459p. 20cm.

Jamaica
M972.92
G69n

A naturalist's sojourn in Jamaica.
Gosse, Philip Henry, 1810-1888.
A naturalist's sojourn in Jamaica. By Philip Henry Gosse ... assisted by Richard Hill ... London, Longmans, Brown, Green and Longmans, 1851.

1 p. l., [v]-xxiv, 508 p. front., VII col. pl. 19 cm.

1. Natural history—Jamaica. I. Hill, Richard, 1795-1872. II. Title.

6—5293

Library of Congress QH109.J5G6 [37d1-]

"Native disabilities" in South Africa...
S. Africa
M968
J11n

Jabavu, Davidson Don Tengo, 1885-
"Native disabilities" in South Africa, by D. D. T. Jabavu. [Lovedale, Cape province, South Africa] The Lovedale press [1932]

26 p. 21½cm.
Bibliography: p. 25-26.

1. Africa, South—Native races. 2. Africa, South—Race question. I. Title.

45-28700

Library of Congress DT763.J3 [2] 323.168

Native son.
M813.5
W93n2

Wright, Richard, 1909-
Native son. New York, Harper, 1939.

134 (i.e. 268)p. 30cm.
Inscriptions: Kind wishes. Paul Robeson.
Galley proof.

La nature du droit coutumier Africain.
Nigeria
M966.9
E14nt

Elias, Taslim Olawale
La nature du droit coutumier Africain. Traduit de l'anglais par Decouflé et Dessau. Paris, Présence Africaine, 1961.

327p. 22½cm.

Native races.
Haiti
M325
Sy5

Sylvain, Benito.
Du sort des indigènes dans les colonies d'exploitation; par Benito Sylvain ... Paris, L. Boyer, 1901.

528 p., 1 l. incl. port. 22½cm.

1. Native races. 2. Slavery. 3. Colonies.
4. Haitian author

3-3141

Library of Congress JV305.S9

Native son, a play.
M813.5
W93n7

Wright, Richard, 1909-
Native son (the biography of a young American) a play in ten scenes by Paul Green and Richard Wright, from the novel by Richard Wright. A Mercury production by Orson Welles, presented by Orson Welles and John Houseman. New York and London, Harper & brothers [°1941]

ix p., 1 l., 148 p. front. 21cm.
Includes songs with music.
"First edition."

I. *Green, Paul, 1894- joint author. II. Title.
[Full name: Richard Nathaniel Wright]

41-6481

Library of Congress PS3545.R815N25 [12] 812.5

The nature of African customary law.
Nigeria
M966.9
E14na

Elias, Taslim Olawale.
The nature of African customary law. [Manchester] Manchester University Press [1956]

318 p. 23 cm.
Includes bibliography.

1. Law, Primitive—Africa. I. Title.

349.6 57—1037 ‡

Library of Congress [59e2]

Native son.
M813.5
W93n9

Wright, Richard, 1909-
Native son. New York, Grossett & Dunlap Publishers, 1940.

359p. 19½cm.

Native son.
M813.5
W93s

Wright, Richard, 1909-1960.
Sangre Negra (Native son). Traducción de Pedro Lecuona. Buenos Aires, Editorial Sudamericana, 1959.

567p. 18½cm.

Nature's garden for victory and peace.
M630.7
C25n

Carver, George Washington, 1864-1943.
Nature's garden for victory and peace. Revised and reprinted. Tuskegee Institute, Alabama, Agricultural research and experiment station, 1942.

23p. illus. 22cm. (Bulletin no.43, October 1942)

M813.5
W93n6

Native son.
Wright, Richard, 1909-
Native son. New York, New American Library, 1950.

413p. 18cm. (Signet books)
Pocket book edition.

Natural history.
Kenya
4574
K119

Kago, Fred K
Ciũmbe cia ngai [God's creatures] London, Macmillan, 1959.

48p. illus. 18cm.
"Published in association with the East African Literature Bureau."
Written in Kikuyu.

1. Natural history. 2. Zoology. I. Title.

Haiti
M972.94
N22h

Nau, Émile, baron, 1812-1860.
Histoire des caciques d'Haïti; par le baron Émile Nau. 2. éd. publiée avec l'autorisation des héritiers de l'auteur par Ducis Viard. Paris, G. Guérin et cie, 1894.

viii, 365 p. incl. port. plates, port., fold. map. 23cm.
"Notice biographique, Émile Nau": p. [vii]-viii.
Appendice: Géographie primitive d'Haïti; De la langue et de la littérature des aborigènes d'Haïti.—Flore indienne d'Haïti par Eugène Nau.

Haiti - Botany

1. Haiti—Hist.—To 1791. 2. [struck out] 3. Indians of the West Indies—Haiti. I. Viard, Ducis, ed. II. Nau, Eugène. III. Title.

2—12605

Library of Congress F1911.N28 [37e1-]

Nau, Eugène.

Haiti
M972.94 Nau, Émile, baron, 1812-1860.
N22h Histoire des caciques d'Haïti; par le baron Émile Nau. 2. éd. publiée avec l'autorisation des héritiers de l'auteur par Ducis Viard. Paris, G. Guérin et cie, 1894.

viii, 365 p. incl. port. plates, port., fold. map. 23cm.

"Notice biographique, Émile Nau": p. vii-viii.
Appendice: Géographie primitive d'Haïti; De la langue et de la littérature des aborigènes d'Haïti.—Flore indienne d'Haïti par Eugène Nau.

1. Haiti—Hist.—To 1791. 2. Botany—Haiti. 3. Indians of the West Indies—Haiti. I. Viard, Ducis, ed. II. Nau, Eugène. III. Title.

2—12695

Library of Congress F1911.N28 [37e1]

S. Africa
M968 Ncwana, K K
N24a Amanqakwana Ngcemeinombo yezizwe zaso-mbo. Lovedale press, 1953.

64p. 18½cm.
History of the abaMbo clans
Review in South African Outlook, July, 1954, p. 112.

Africa, South
M896.3 Ndawo, Henry Masila, 1883-1949
N24in Uhambo Luka Gqoboka. Lovedale, Lovedale Institution Press, 193?

93p. 18½cm
Gqoboka's travels.
Bound with the author's InXenye YenTsomi Zase Zweni. [Natal, 1920]

1. Africa, South - Literature. 2. Xhosa language. I. Title. II. Title: Gqoboka's travels.

Navy.

M359 Nelson, Dennis Denmark, 1907-
N331 The integration of the Negro into the U.S. Navy. New York, Farrar, Straus and Young [c1951]

xv, 238p. illus., ports. 22cm.
Bibliography: p. 235-238.

Ndabi, D. Wahome, tr.

Kenya
M613.2 Culwick, G M
C89w Tũrĩrĩa kĩ? [What shall we eat?]Tr. by D. Wahone Ndabi] Nairobi, Eagle Press, 1950.

24p. illus. 21½cm. (Taanya Ũgima-ini. Aim at healthy living series)
Written in Kikuyu.
White author.

1. Nutrition. I. Title. II. Ndabi, D. Wahome, tr.

S. Africa
M896.3 Ndawo, Henry Masila, 1883-1949
N241 Uhambo luka-Gqoboka. Lovedale, South Africa, The Lovedale Press, 1952.

92p. 18½cm.

1. Gqoboka's Travels.

Navy.

M359 Nelson, Dennis Denmark, 1907-
N331 The integration of the Negro into the United States Navy,
1948 1776-1947, with a brief historical introduction. [Washington, 1948.

1 v. (various pagings) illus., ports. 27 cm.
Cover title.
"A monograph from the thesis by the same title submitted to the Department of Sociology, Howard University, in partial fulfillment of the requirements for the degree of master of arts."
Seal of Navy Department, United States of America, on cover.
"Navexos-P-526."
Bibliography: p. 209-212.

1. U. S. Navy—Negroes. 2. Negroes as seamen. I. U. S. Navy Dept. II. Title.

E185.63.N4 1948 325.260973 48—46195*

Library of Congress [48c2]

S.Africa
M968 Ndamase, Victor Poto, 1897-
N23a Ama-Mpondo. Ibali ne- Ntalo, ngu Victor Poto Ndamase. Lovedale, Ishicilelwe e-Lovedale 1925?

xiv, 158p. illus. ports. 19½cm.
Pondo history.

1. Africa, South - history. 2. Pondo - history.

Africa, South
M896.3 Ndawo, Henry Masila, 1883-1949
N24in U-Nolishwa. Lovedale, The Lovedale Press, 1939.

126p. port. 18½cm.
Story of Noliswa.
Bound with the author's InXenye YenTsomi Zase Zweni. [Natal, 1920]

1. Africa, South - Literature. 2. Xhosa language. I. Title. II. Title: Story of Noliswa.

Haiti
M972.94 Nazaire, D
N14s Sentinelle perdue, ouvrage apologetique des dogmes de la doctrine du Roi de l'humanité par D. Nazaire. Port-au-Prince, Imprimerie du Commerce [1947].

133p. 22½cm.

I. Title
II Haiti

Africa
M370 Ndamukong, L M
C83 Education at the crossroads.
Pp. 388-395.

In: Cowan, L. G., ed. Education and nation-building in Africa. New York, Praeger, 1965.

S. Africa
M572 Ndawo, Henry Masila, 1883-1949
N24u UNomathamsanqa noSigebenga-i Gazi liyintSikelelo noXolelaniso-imbali engokuwa kuka-Ntu nokusindiswa kwakhe. Lovedale, Lovedale press, 1943.

48p. 18½cm.

Cuba ... Los Nazi-fascistas del Parque o el Espiá
M862.6
C57n Clavijo Tisseur, Arturo, 1886-
... Los Nazi-fascistas del Parque o el Espiá no. 2. Melodrame en un acto y diez cuadros. Musica: Anglel Alvarez Acosta. La Habana, Tipografia la universal, 1944.

[25] p. 19cm.

Africa, South
M896.3 Ndawo, Henry Masila, 1883-1949.
N24in InXenye YenTsomi Zase Zweni. Natal, Mariannhill Mission Press, 1920.

73p. illus. 18½cm.
Common folktales - Xhosa, Zulu.

Bound with the author's Izibongo zenkosi zama-Hlubi nezema-Bâca. [Natal, 1928] U-Nolishwa. [Lovedale, 1939] and Uhambo Luka Gqoboka. [Lovedale, n.d.]

1. Africa, South - Literature. 2. Xhosa language. I. Title.

South Africa
M896.2 Ndebele, Nimrod Njabulo T , 1913-
N24u2 Ugubudele Namazimuzimu [Gubudele and the Cannibals] (umdlalo osenzo-sinye esinemiboniso emihlanu). [Reprinted in the new orthography] Johannesburg, Witwatersrand University Press, 1959.

62p. 18cm. (Bantu treasury, edited by D. T. Cole, VI)

1. Drama - Zulu. 2. Zulu - Drama. I. Title. II. Title: Gubudele and the Cannibals. III. Series

---

Haiti
M39 Nazon, Emmanuel.
H72m Médaillon civique, par me Emmanuel Nazon ... Port-au-Prince, Häiti, Imp. N. Telhomme, 1938.

2 p. l., 110 p., 1 l. port. 19cm.
"Hommage au docteur Alonso P. B. Holly."
Contents.—L'homme.—"God and the Negro."—Appendice: Lettre de Decatur McGill. Fête jubilaire. Félicitations. Extrait de "Miami times." Appréciations.

1. Holly, Alonzo Potter Burgess, 1865- I. Title.

45-47668

Library of Congress E185.97.H72 [2] 926.1

Africa, South
M896.3 Ndawo, Henry Masila, 1883-1949
N24in Izibongo zenkosi zama-Hlubi nezama-Baca. Natal, The Mariannhill Mission Press, 1928.

39p. 18½cm.
Common folktales - Xhosa, Zulu.
Bound with the author's InXenye YenTsomi Zase Zweni. [Natal, 1920]

1. Africa, South - Folklore. 2. Xhosa language. 3. Tales, African. I. Title.

S. Africa
M896.2 Ndebele, Nimrod Njabulo T , 1913-
N24u UGubudele namaZimuzimu. (Umdlalo osenzosinye esinemiboniso emihlanu.) Johannesburg, South Africa, University of the Witwatersrand Press, 1941.

75p. 17½cm.

A Zulu play - Gubudele and the Cannibals.

Nchi na desturi za wagiriama.

Kenya
M967.62 Ngala, Ronald Gideon, 1923-
N49 Nchi na desturi za wagiriama [The land and customs of the Giriama] Nairobi, Eagle Press 1949.

41p. illus. 18cm. (Masimulizi na desturi ya Afrika ya Mashariki. Custom and tradition in East Africa series)
Written in Swahili.

1. Kenya - Native races. 2. Giryama tribe. I. Title. II. Series. III. Series: Custom and tradition in East Africa series.

S. Africa
M572 Ndawo, Henry Masila, 1883-1949
N241 Iziduko zama-Hlubi. Lovedale, Lovedale Press, 1939.

39p. 18½cm.
Damily names of the Hlubi tribe in Xhosa

1. Ethnology. 2. Xhosa language.

Nigeria
M966.9 Ndem, Eyo B E
N29 Ibos in contemporary Nigerian politics; a study in group conflict. Onitsha, Nigeria, Etudo Limited, 1961.

44p. 21½cm.

1. Ibo tribe. 2. Nigeria - Politics. I. Title.

Senegal
M966.3 N22
Ndiaye, H jt. auth.
Sénégal; récits historiques, cours élémentaire [par] M. Guilhem [et] H. Ndiaye. Paris, Ligel [1964]
107p. illus., maps. 22cm.
1. Senegal - History. I. Guilhem, M

Cameroons, French
M896.3 N23
N'djok, Kindengve.
Kel'lam, fils d'Afrique; récit. Jaquette de Ch. Lemmel. Illus. intérieures de P. Joubert. Paris, Éditions Alsatia [1958]
263 p. illus. 20 cm. (Rubans noirs)
1. Cameroons, French - Civilization -Fiction.
1. ~~Cameroons, French—Civilization~~ I. Title.
PQ3989.N4K4 62-28686 ‡
Library of Congress

Un Nègre a Paris.
Ivory Coast
M896.3 D12n
Dadie, Bernard B ,1916-
Un Nègre a Paris. Paris, Présence Africaine, 1956.
217p. 18cm.

Senegal
M370 N23
N'Diaye, Jean Pierre.
Enquête sur les étudiants noirs en France. Paris, Éditions "Réalités africaines" [1962]
315 p. illus. 25 cm.
Portrait of author on cover.
1. Negroes in France—Education. I. Title. 2. France.
LC2806.F8N4 63-36674 ‡
Library of Congress

Neal, Claude.
M323 N21
National Association for the Advancement of Colored People.
The lynching of Claude Neal. New York, 1934.
8p. illus. 28cm.

Le nègre masqué.
Haiti
M843.91 A12n
Alexis, Stephen.
Le nègre masqué, roman tranche de vie haitienne. Port-au-Prince, Haiti [Imp. de l'etat] 1933.
171p. 21cm.

Senegal
M973 N23
N'Diaye, Jean Pierre.
Les noirs aux États-Unis pour les africains, par J. P. N'Diaye, J. Bassene, B. Poyas. [Paris, 1964]
184 p. illus. 21 cm. (Réalités africaines, no 7)
Includes bibliographical references.
1. ~~Negroes~~—Hist. 2. Black Muslims. I. Bassene, J., joint author. II. Poyas, B., joint author. III. Title. (Series)
E185.R38 no. 7 65-44441
Library of Congress

Nebraska.
M978.2 W93n
Writers' program. *Nebraska.*
The Negroes of Nebraska, written and compiled by workers of the Writers' program, Work projects administration in the state of Nebraska. Sponsored by the Omaha urban league community center. Drawings by Paul Gibson. Lincoln, Neb., Woodruff printing company, 1940.
48 p. illus. 21½cm.
1. Negroes—Nebraska. I. Title.
40—13925
Library of Congress E185.93.N5W7
[42d1] 325.2609782

Le Nègre qui chante.
M784 J68
Jolas, Eugene, 1894- tr.
Le Nègre qui chante; chansons traduites et introduction par Eugène Jolas. Paris, Éditions de cahiers libres [1928]
85p. cm.

Senegal
M960 N23
N'Diaye, Massata Abdou
Afrique unie et renovation mondiale. [Doullens, France, Imprimerie Dessaint, n.d.]
172p. 19cm.
1. Africa - Politics. 2. Africa - Civilization. I. Title.

Nebraska and his granny.
M813.5 L94n
Love, Rose Leary.
Nebraska and his granny, by Rose Leary Love; with illustrations by Preston Haygood. Tuskegee Institute, Ala., Tuskegee institute press, 1936.
5 p. l., 69 p. illus. 20cm.
I. Title. 37-2457
Library of Congress PZ7.L956Ne
——— Copy 2.
Copyright A 103569 [3]

La négresse blanche.
Martinique
M843.9 C17n
Capécia, Mayotte
La négresse blanche. Paris, Editions Corrêa 1950.
188p. 19cm.

Senegal
M960 N23
N'diaye, Massata Abdou
Le Sénégal a l'heure de indépendence. [Doullens, France, Imprimerie Dessaint, n.d.]
Pp. 69-168. 19cm.
Bound with the author's Afrique unie et rénovation mondiale. Doullens, France, n.d.
1. Senegal. I. Title.

The negative forces vs. the positive qualities.
M323 Z65
Zilton, A W
The negative forces vs. the positive qualities. [n.p., n.p., 1942]
40p. illus. (ports) 23cm.
Cover title.

Negrito.
M811.5 B75
Brewer, John Mason, 1896-
Negrito, Negro dialect poems of the Southwest, by J. Mason Brewer; illustrations by Tom Smith. San Antonio, Tex., Naylor printing company, 1933.
3 p. l., 9-97 p., 1 l. illus. 20 cm.
I. Title. 33-28762
Library of Congress PS3503.R496N4 1933
[2] 811.5

Senegal
M966.3 N23
N'Diaye, Massata Abdou
Le Sénégal a l'heure de l'independance. [Doullens, France, Imprimerie Dessaint, n.d.]
104p. port. 19cm.
1. Senegal. I. Title.

De Neger zingt.
M811.08 Eel
Eekhout, Jan H., comp.
De Neger zingt; Amerikaansche Negerlyriek. Amsterdam, Derde Druk Uitgeversmaatschappuholland, n.d.
67p. 19cm.
White compiler.

El Negrito.
M813.5 W93ne
Wright, Richard, 1909-
El Negrito. (The Black boy). Madrid, Afrodisio Aguado, S. A., 195?
345p. 19cm.
Portrait of author on book jacket.

Cameroon
M896.1 N239f
N'Dintsouna, Francesco.
Fleurs de latérite. Monte-Carlo, Regáin [1954]
29p. 19cm. (Poètes de notre temps, no. 83)
I. Title.

M973 W51n
Neglected history.
Wesley, Charles Harris, 1891-
Neglected history; essays in Negro history by a college president: Charles H. Wesley. Wilberforce, Ohio, Central State College Press, 1965.
200 p. 28 cm.
Bibliographical references included in "Historical notes" p. 184-187)
1. Negroes—Hist.—Addresses, essays, lectures. I. Title.
E185.W46 973.0917496 65-5958
Library of Congress [2]

Negritude.
M960 Am3
American Society of African Culture.
Pan-Africanism reconsidered. Berkeley, University of California Press, 1962.
xix, 376 p. tables. 25 cm.
"Speeches, papers, and comments given at the Third Annual Conference of the American Society of African Culture, which was held in Philadelphia at the University of Pennsylvania from June 22 to June 26, 1960."
Bibliographical footnotes.
1. Pan-Africanism—Addresses, essays, lectures. 2. Africa—Civilization—Addresses, essays, lectures. 3. ~~Negro race.~~ I. Title.
3. Negritude. 4. Africa-Social thought.
DT30.A53 301.451 62-11491
Library of Congress

Negritude.

Cameroons
M896
M49

Melone, Thomas
De la Négritude, dans la littérature - Négro-Africaine. Paris, Présence Africaine, 1962.

137p. 19cm. (Tribune des Jeunes, 2)
Includes bibliography.

1. Negritude. 2. Literature - Africa.
I. Title. II. Series.

Africa, South Negritude.
M960
M87

Mphahlele, Ezekiel.
The African image. London, Faber and Faber c1962.
240 p. 21 cm.
Includes bibliography.

1. Race. 2. Literature-Africa. I. Title.
3. Negritude. 4. Africa-Native races.
GN645.M7 1962a 809.93 62-19981 ‡
Library of Congress [5]

Négritude.

Haiti
M972.94
P662n

Piquion, René
Négritude. Port-au-Prince, Imprimerie de l'Etat, 1961.

501p. 21½cm.
"À M. Arthur Spingarn hommage de l'auteur. René Piquion."

Negritude and humanisme.

Senegal
M960
Se5

Senghor, Léopold Sédar, 1906-
Liberte. Paris, Éditions du Seuil, 1964-

v. 20½cm.
Contents.- v.1. Negritude et humanisme.

I. Liberté. II. Title: Negritude and humanisme.

El Negro.

Cuba
M972.91
B46n

Betancourt, Juan René
El Negro: ciudadano del futuro. La Habana, Impreso en los Talleres Tipograficos de Cardenas y Cia, 1959.

248p. illus. 23½cm.

The Negro.

M301.
D853ne2

Du Bois, William Edward Burghardt, 1868-
The Negro, by W. E. Burghardt Du Bois ... New York, H. Holt and company; [etc., etc., °1915]
254 p. illus. (maps) 17cm. (Home university library of modern knowledge. no. 91)
"Suggestions for further reading": p. 244-252.

15-12642
Library of Congress HT1581.D8 [42q2]

The Negro

M01
H75

Homer, Dorothy R , comp.
The Negro, a selected bibliography. Compiled by Dorothy R. Homer and Evelyn R. Robinson. 7th ed. rev. New York, New York Public Library, 1955.

23p. 25cm.
Reprinted from the New York Public Library Bulletin, March 1955.

1. Bibliographies. I. Title.
II. Robinson, Evelyn R., jt. auth.

The Negro.

M01
N42no

New York (City) Public Library. 135th Street Branch.
The Negro, a selected bibliography. New York, The Library, 1940.

19p. 25cm.

The Negro.

M973
R246

Redding, Jay Saunders, 1906-
The Negro, by Saunders Redding. Washington, Potomac Books, 1967.
xii, 101 p. illus. 22 cm. (The U. S. A. survey series)
Bibliography: p. 91-94.

1. Negroes—Hist. I. Title.
E185.R42 301.451'96'073 66-19024 rev
Library of Congress [r68f5]

The Negro;

Mo1
T25

Tennessee. ***Dept. of education. Division of school libraries.***
The Negro; a selected list for school libraries of books by or about the Negro in Africa and America, compiled by the Division of school libraries. Revised and reprinted through courtesy of the Julius Rosenwald fund. Nashville, Tenn., State department of education, 1941.
48 p. illus. 23cm.
Classified and annotated, with author and title index.
"A list of bibliographies consulted": p. 10-11.

1. Negroes—Bibl. I. Title.
41-9406
Library of Congress Z1361.N39T3 1941 [44f2] 016.325260973

"Negro", Definition of term.

M572
B99n

[Byer, Dabron P]
The name "Negro", a compendium of some pertinent facts by Aldebaran. [Los Angeles, California, The National Publishing Board, [n.d.]

[48] 15cm.

M304
P19
v.4, no.20

The Negro, a monthly publication devoted to critical discussions of race problems involved in the mental moral, social, and material condition of the Negroes in the United States. Boston, the Negro , 1886.
v.1, nǹo.1 July 1885.
I. Periodicals make holdings record card.

M304
P19
v.4, no.20

The Negro, a monthly publication.

Volume	Year	Month	Volume	Year	Month
v.1, nol	1886	July			

The Negro, too, in American history.

M973
Ep7n

Eppse, Merl Raymond, 1893-
The Negro, too, in American history. Nashville, National Publication Co., 1949.
xxii, 644 p. illus., ports., maps. 22 cm.
Bibliographical references included in introduction. "Reading material": p. 551-572.

1. Negroes—Hist. 2. Slavery in the U. S.—Hist. I. Title.
E185.E696 1949 325.260973 49-1908 rev*
Library of Congress [r50h3]

The Negro after the war.

M323
Im1n

Imbert, Dennis I
The Negro after the war, by D. I. Imbert ... 1st ed. New Orleans, La., Williams printing service, 1943.
3 p. l., 74 p., 2 l. 21½cm.

1. Negroes. I. Title.
44-27088
Library of Congress E185.61.I 5 [3] 325.260973

The Negro after the war.

M323.2
Im1

Imbert, Dennis I
The Negro after the war, by D. I. Imbert ... 1st ed. New Orleans, La., Williams printing service, 1943.
3 p. l., 74 p., 2 l. 21½cm.

1. Negroes. I. Title.
44-27088
Library of Congress E185.61.I 5 [3] 325.260973

The Negro American.

M301
D122

Dædalus.
The Negro American. Edited and with introductions by Talcott Parsons and Kenneth B. Clark, and with a foreword by Lyndon B. Johnson. Illustrated with a 32 page portfolio of photos. by Bruce Davidson, selected and introduced by Arthur D. Trottenberg. Boston, Houghton Mifflin, 1966.
xxix, 781 p. illus. 24 cm. (The Daedalus library [v. 7])
Most of the essays, some in slightly different form, appeared originally in the Fall 1965 and Winter 1966 issues of Daedalus.
Includes bibliographical references.
1. Negroes—Addresses, essays, lectures. 2. Negroes—Civil rights—Addresses, essays, lectures. I. Parsons, Talcott, 1902- ed. II. Clark, Kenneth Bancroft, 1914- ed. III. Title.

E185.6.D24 301.45196073 66—17174
Library of Congress [67f14]

The Negro American.

M973
Qu25ne

Quarles, Benjamin, jt. auth.
The Negro American; a documentary history [by] Leslie H. Fishel, Jr. [and] Benjamin Quarles. Glenview, Ill., Scott, Foresman [1967]
536 p. illus., facsims., maps, ports. 24 cm.
Bibliographical footnotes.

1. Negroes—Hist.—Sources. I. Quarles, Benjamin, joint author. II. Title.
E185.F5 973 67—26184
Library of Congress [68f5]

Negro Americans, what now?

M323
J632n

Johnson, James Weldon, 1871-1938.
Negro Americans, what now? By James Weldon Johnson. New York, The Viking press, 1934.
viii, 103 p. 19½cm.

1. Negroes. 2. U. S.—Race question. 3. Negroes—Civil rights. 4. Negroes—Moral and social conditions. I. Title.
34—35660
Library of Congress E185.61.J69 [44g2] 325.260973

The Negro and Christianity in the U. S.

M277
W27

Washington, Joseph R
Black religion; the Negro and Christianity in the United States [by] Joseph R. Washington, Jr. Boston, Beacon Press [1964]

ix, 308p. 22cm.
Bibliographical references included in "Notes" (p. 298-303)

The Negro and defense.

M323.
C83n

Council for Democracy.
The Negro and defense: A test of democracy. New York, the council, 1941.

40p. illus. 20cm. (Democracy in action, no.3)

The Negro and economic restruction.

M331
H55

Hill, Timothy Arnold, 1888–

... The Negro and economic reconstruction, by T. Arnold Hill ... Washington, D. C., The Associates in Negro folk education, 1937.

2 p. l., 78 p. II tab. (1 fold.) 21cm. (Bronze booklet no. 5)

"Selected readings" at end of each chapter.

1. Negroes—Econ. condit. 2. Negroes—Employment. I. Title.

A 41—963

New York univ. Wash sq. for Library of Congress Library E185.5.B85 no. 5

[43r42t2]†

The Negro and fusion politics in North Carolina, 1894–1901.

M324
Ed57n

Edmonds, Helen G

The Negro and fusion politics in North Carolina, 1894–1901. Chapel Hill, University of North Carolina Press [1951]

viii, 260 p. illus., maps. 25 cm.

Bibliography: p. 239–247.

1. Negroes—North Carolina. 2. North Carolina—Pol. & govt.—1865– 3. Negroes—Politics and suffrage. I. Title.

E185.93.N6E4 325.2609756 51—4106

Library of Congress [53q5]

... The Negro and his music.

M780
L79n2

Locke, Alain LeRoy, 1886–

... The Negro and his music, by Alain Locke ... Washington, D. C., The Associates in Negro folk education, 1936.

3 p. l., 142 p. 20½ cm. (Bronze booklet no. 2)

"Reading references" at end of each chapter; "Recorded illustrations" at end of most of the chapters.

1. Negro musicians. 2. Negro songs—Hist. & crit. 3. Music—U. S.—Hist. & crit. 4. Jazz music. 5. Phonograph records. I. Title.

37—10637

Library of Congress E185.5.B85 no. 2
——— Copy 2. ML3556.L6N4

[42t2] (325.260973) 784.756

The Negro and his songs...

M784
Od8

Odum, Howard Washington, 1884–

The Negro and his songs; a study of typical Negro songs in the south, by Howard W. Odum and Guy B. Johnson. Chapel Hill, University of North Carolina Press; London, Humphrey Milford, Oxford University Press, 1925.

306p. 23cm.

1. Songs. 2. Songs-Hist. & crit. I. Johnson, Guy Benton, 1901– jt. auth. II. Title.

M89
B799n

The Negro and justice.

Yergan, Max, 1894–

The Negro and justice; A plea for Earl Browder, by Max Yergan and Paul Robeson. New York, Citizens' Committee to Free Earl Browder, 1941.

11p. illus. 19cm.

...The Negro and the Atlanta exposition...

M06
J61
no. 7

Bacon, Alice Mabel, 1858–1918.

... The negro and the Atlanta exposition, by Miss Alice M. Bacon ... Baltimore, The Trustees, 1896.

28 p. 24½cm. (The trustees of the John F. Slater fund. Occasional papers, no. 7)

Address by Booker T. Washington, at opening of Atlanta exposition, September 18, 1895, p. 12–16.

1. Negroes. 2. Atlanta. Cotton states and international exposition, 1895. I. Washington, Booker Taliaferro, 1859?–1915. II. Title.

8—13186

Library of Congress E185.5.J65 no. 7
——— Copy 2. [35c1]

The Negro and the democratic front.

M329
F75

Ford, James W., 1893–

The Negro and the democratic front, by James W. Ford; introduction by A. W. Berry. New York, International publishers [°1938]

viii, 9–222 p. front. (port.) 22cm.

1. Negroes. 2. Communism—U. S.—1917– I. Title.

38—30079

Library of Congress E185.6.F67

[a45h2] 325.260973

The Negro and the drama.

M812
B64

Bond, Frederick Weldon.

The Negro and the drama; the direct and indirect contribution which the American Negro has made to drama and the legitimate stage, with the underlying conditions responsible, by Frederick W. Bond. Washington, D. C., The Associated publishers, inc. [°1940]

x, 213 p. 20 cm.

Bibliography: p. 202–208.

1. Negro drama. 2. Negroes in literature and art. I. Title.

40—32025

Library of Congress PS338.N4B6

[3] 812.09

The Negro and the labor movement.

M331
H24b

Harris, Abram Lincoln, 1899–

The black worker; the Negro and the labor movement, by Sterling D. Spero and Abram L. Harris. New York, Columbia university press, 1931.

x, 509 p., 1 l. 22½ cm.

Issued also as A. L. Harris's thesis (PH. D.) Columbia university. Mr. Harris wrote chapters 2–5, 10, 14–15, 17–19.

"Bibliography of works cited": p. 485–496.

1. Negroes—Employment. 2. Trade-unions—U. S. 3. Labor and laboring classes—U. S. 4. Negroes—Civil rights. 5. U. S.—Race question. I. Harris, Abram Lincoln, 1899– joint author. II. Title. III. Title: The Negro and the labor movement.

31—3610

Library of Congress E185.8.S74

[44p²2] [325.26] 331.6

The Negro and the nation.

M323
H24n

Harrison, Hubert H.

The Negro and the nation, by Hubert H. Harrison. New York, Cosmo-advocate publishing co. [pref. 1917]

64 p. 16½cm.

1. Negroes. 2. U. S.—Race question. I. Title.

22—16697

Library of Congress E185.61.H28

[41b1]

The Negro and the post-war world.

M973
L82n

Logan, Rayford Whittingham, 1897–

The Negro and the post-war world, a primer, by Rayford Whittingham Logan ... Washington, D. C., The Minorities publishers, 1945.

viii p., 1 l., 95 p. 23cm.

Bibliography: p. 89–95.

1. Negro race. 2. Negroes. I. Title.

46—376

Library of Congress GN645.L65

[47q7] 325.26

... The Negro and the war.

M350.
B798

Brown, Earl Louis, 1900–

... The Negro and the war [by] Earl Brown and George R. Leighton ... [New York, Public affairs committee, inc.] 1942.

cover-title, 32 p. diagrs. 21cm. (Public affairs pamphlets, no. 71)

"First edition, August, 1942."

"For further reading": p. 32.

1. Negroes. 2. Negroes—Employment. 3. Negroes as soldiers. I. Leighton, George Ross, 1902– joint author. II. Title.

42—22292

Library of Congress E185.61.B877

[25] 325.260973

Negro anthology.

M810.8
C91

Cunard, Nancy, 1896– *comp.*

Negro anthology, made by Nancy Cunard, 1931–1933. London, Published by Nancy Cunard at Wishart & co., 1934.

viii, 854, [2] p. illus. (incl. ports., facsims.) maps (1 fold.) 32cm.

Contains music.

CONTENTS.—America.—Negro stars.—Music. — Poetry. — West Indies and South America.—Europe.—Africa.

1. Negroes. I. Title.

[*Full name:* Nancy Clara Cunard]

34—13895

Library of Congress HT1581.C8

[3] 325.26

The Negro around the world.

M973
P93

Price, Willard.

The negro around the world, by Willard Price ... pictorial maps by George Annand. New York, George H. Doran company [°1925]

75 p. incl. front., maps. 19½cm.

1. Negro race. I. Title.

25—9188

Library of Congress HT1581.P7

[a25d3]

... Negro art: past and present.

M700
L79n4

Locke, Alain LeRoy, 1886–

... Negro art: past and present, by Alain Locke ... Washington, D. C., Associates in Negro folk education, 1936.

3 p. l., 122 p. 20½cm. (Bronze booklet no. 3)

"Reading references" at end of each chapter.

1. Negro art. 2. Negroes in literature and art. I. Title.

37—7111

Library of Congress E185.5.B85 no. 3
——— Copy 2. E185.82.L74

[44h1] (325.260973) 709.73

Negro art, music and rhyme, for young folks.

M813.5
W589

Whiting, Helen Adele (Johnson) 1885–

Negro art, music and rhyme, for young folks, by Helen Adele Whiting; illustrations by Lois Mailou Jones. Book II. Washington, D. C., The Associated publishers, inc. [°1938]

[38] p. illus. 23½cm.

Without music.

Book I published under title: Negro folk tales for pupils in the primary grades.

1. Negroes in literature and art. 2. Negro songs. I. Title.

38—17194

Library of Congress PZ1119.W55

[45k1] 372.4

Negro art songs.

M784
C53

Clark, Edgar Rogie, 1914– , comp.

Negro art songs; album by contemporary composers for voice and piano. New York, Edward B. Marks Music Corp., 1956.

72p. illus. 33cm.

The Negro as a biological element in the American population.

M610
C63ne3

Cobb, William Montague, 1904–

The Negro as a biological element in the American population. Reprinted from the Journal of Negro education. 8:336-348, July 1939.

336-348p. 25cm.

The Negro as a business man.

M331
As7

Association for the study of Negro life and history, inc.

The Negro as a business man, by J. H. Harmon, jr., Arnett G. Lindsay, and Carter G. Woodson. Washington, D. C., The Association for the study of Negro life and history, inc. [°1929]

v, 111 p. 25 cm.

CONTENTS.—The Negro as a local business man.—The Negro in banking.—Insurance business among Negroes.

1. Negroes—Employment. I. Harmon, John Henry, jr. II. Lindsay, Arnett Grant. III. Woodson, Carter Godwin, 1875– IV. Title.

30—21076

Library of Congress E185.8.A84

[48j1] 325.26

The Negro as a soldier.

M350
F62

Fleetwood, Christian A.

The Negro as a soldier; written by Christian A. Fleetwood, late sergeant-major 4th U. S. colored troops, for the Negro congress, at the Cotton states and international exposition, Atlanta, Ga., November 11 to November 23, 1895. Published by Prof. Geo. Wm. Cook. Washington, D. C., Howard university print, 1895.

1 p. l., 19 p. 23cm.

1. Negroes. 2. U. S.—History—Civil war—Negro troops. I. Cook, George William, pub. II. Atlanta. Cotton states and international exposition, 1895. III. Title.

A 12—751 x¹

Stanford univ. Library for Library of Congress E185.63.F59

[a40b1]

The Negro as capitalist;

M331
H24

Harris, Abram Lincoln, 1899–

The Negro as capitalist; a study of banking and business among American Negroes, by Abram L. Harris ... Philadelphia, The American academy of political and social science, 1936.

xii, 205 p. diagrs. 23½cm. [Monographs of the American academy of political and social science ... no. 2]

1. Negroes—Econ. condit. 2. Banks and banking—U. S.—Hist. I. Title. II. Title: Banking and business among American Negroes.

36—18585

Library of Congress E185.8.H26
——— Copy 2.
Copyright A 97182 [41n2] [332.10973] 325.260973

The Negro at work in New York city.

M3.23.2
H33n

Haynes, George Edmund, 1880–
The Negro at work in New York city; a study in economic progress, by George Edmund Haynes ... New York, 1912.
2 p. l., 7–159 p. incl. tables, diagrs. 25cm.
Thesis (PH. D.)—Columbia university, 1912.
Vita.
Published also as Studies in history, economics and public law, ed. by the Faculty of political science of Columbia university, vol. XLIX, no. 3, whole no. 124.
"Select bibliography": p. 154–156.
1. Negroes—New York (City) 2. Labor and laboring classes—New York (City) 3. Wages—New York (City) I. Title.
12—28454
Library of Congress E185.93.N56H41
Columbia Univ. Libr. 326.973
[45b1]

Negro authors and composers of the United States.

M780.9
H19n

Handy, William Christopher, 1873–
Negro authors and composers of the United States, by W. C. Handy. New York, N. Y., Handy brothers music co., inc. [1938?]
cover-title, 24 p. illus. (port.) 23cm.
Bibliography: p. 24.
1. Negro musicians. I. Title.
38—19429
Library of Congress ML3556.H23N3
[41e2] 780.973

M814.5
J15n

Negro authors must eat.
Jacobs, George W
(In: Copy, 1930 stories, plays, poems, and essays selected ... from the published work of students in the special courses in writing, University extension, Columbia University. New York, London, D. Appleton and co., 1930. 19½cm. p.173-176)
Reprinted from The Nation.

M286
J76

Negro Baptist history, U. S. A., 1750, 1930.
Jordan, Lewis Garnett, 1854?–
... Negro Baptist history, U. S. A., 1750, 1930, by Rev. Lewis G. Jordan ... Nashville, Tenn., The Sunday school publishing board, N. B. C. [1930]
394 p. plates (1 fold.) ports. 22½cm.
"Minutes of the Baptist foreign mission convention of the United States of America held in Montgomery, Ala., November 24, 25, 26, 1880" (p. [153]–170) and "Minutes of the fourth annual session of the Baptist foreign mission convention of the United States of America, held with the First Baptist church, Manchester, Virginia, September 19–22, 1883" (p. [217]–236) have special title-pages.
Bibliography: p. 392–394.
1. Baptists, Negro—Hist. I. Title.
31—8788
Library of Congress BX6443.J6
——— Copy 2.
Copyright A 32956 [a40d1] 286.173

Negro Baptists and foreign missions.

M286
Adln

Adams, C C
Negro Baptists and foreign missions; C. C. Adams and Marshall A. Talley, authors. Philadelphia, Pa., The Foreign mission board of the National Baptist convention, U. S. A., inc. [©1944]
84 p. 18½cm.
1. Baptists, Negro—Missions. 2. National Baptist convention of the United States of America—Missions. I. Talley, Marshall Alexander, 1877– joint author. II. National Baptist convention of the United States of America. Foreign mission board. III. Title.
45-15372
Library of Congress BV2521.A85
[3] 266.61

Negro Baptists of Tennessee.

M286
F95

Fuller, Thomas Oscar, 1867–
History of the Negro Baptists of Tennessee, by T. O. Fuller ... [Memphis, Tenn., Haskins print, ©1936]
346 p. front., plates, ports. 18½cm.
1. Baptists, Negro—Tennessee. 2. Negroes—Tennessee. I. Title: Negro Baptists of Tennessee.
36—16373
Library of Congress BX6444.T4F8
[44c1] 286.1768

M976.4
Y41n

The Negro blue - book of Washington county.
Yancy, J W.
The Negro blue - book of Washington county, Texas, by J. W. Yancy... Brenham, Texas, Brenham banner press, 1936
viii, 138p. illus. 23cm.

Negro builders and heroes.

MB
B739n

Brawley, Benjamin Griffith, 1882–
Negro builders and heroes, by Benjamin Brawley ... Chapel Hill, The University of North Carolina press, 1937.
xi p., 1 l., 315 p. front., ports. 22cm.
"Bibliographical notes": p. 298–304.
1. Negroes—Biog. I. Title.
37—19626
Library of Congress E185.96.B797
[45i3] [325.260973] 920.073

M811.5
J24n

The Negro business league.
Jamison, Roscoe C
The Negro business league of St. Joseph, Mo.
2p. 19cm.
Bound with: Roscoe C. Jamison's Negro soldiers.

The Negro challenge to the business community.

M331
G43

Ginzberg, Eli, 1911– ed.
The Negro challenge to the business community. New York, McGraw-Hill [1964]
vi, 111 p. 22 cm.
"Highlights of a conference held at Arden House on January 15 to 17, 1964 under the auspices of the executive program of the Graduate School of Business, Columbia University."
1. Negroes—Econ. condit. 2. Negroes—Employment. I. Columbia University. Graduate School of Business. II. Title.
E185.8.G57 331.63 64-7743
Library of Congress [7-1]

Negro child welfare in North Carolina.

M362.7
Sa5

Sanders, Wiley Britton, 1898– ed.
Negro child welfare in North Carolina, a Rosenwald study, directed by Wiley Britton Sanders ... under the joint auspices of the North Carolina State board of charities and public welfare and the School of public welfare, the University of North Carolina. Chapel Hill, Pub. for the North Carolina State board of charities and public welfare by the University of North Carolina press, 1933.
xiv p., 2 l., [3]–326 p. 24cm.
1. Negroes—North Carolina. 2. Negroes—Moral and social conditions. 3. Charities—North Carolina. 4. Children—Charities, protection, etc.—North Carolina. 5. Juvenile delinquency—North Carolina. 6. Social surveys I. North Carolina. State board of charities and public welfare. II. North Carolina. University. School of public welfare. III. Title.
33—18006
Library of Congress E185.86.S27
[45t1] 325.2600756

M323
H73n

The Negro chooses democracy.
Holmes, Dwight Oliver Wendell, 1877-
The Negro chooses democracy. Reprinted from the Journal of Negro education. [8:620-633]. October, 1939.
Dedicatory address, The Savery Library, Talladega College, April 16, 1939.

M323
T69

Negro Christian student conference. *Atlanta*, 1914.
The new voice in race adjustments; addresses and reports presented at the Negro Christian student conference, Atlanta, Georgia, May 14–18, 1914. A. M. Trawick, editor ... Pub. by order of the executive committee of the conference. New York city, Student volunteer movement [1914]
1 p. l., [v]–vi p., 1 l., 230 p. 23½cm.
"Best books on the Negro in America and Africa": p. 221–224.
1. Negroes—Congresses. 2. Negroes—Race question. I. Trawick, Arcadius McSwain, 1869– ed. II. Title.
Springfield. Public library for Library of Congress E185.5.N38 A 15–837
[a35f1]

M277
F86

The Negro church in America.
Frazier, Edward Franklin, 1894-1962.
The Negro church in America. New York, Schocken Books [1964, ©1963]
xii, 92p. 23cm. (Studies in sociology)
Bibliographical footnotes.

Negro church, The history of the.

M973
W86 h

Woodson, Carter Godwin, 1875–
The history of the Negro church, by Carter G. Woodson ... Washington, D. C., The Associated publishers [©1921]
x, 330 p. front., plates, ports. 20½cm.
1. Negroes—Religion. I. Title. II. Title: Negro church, The history of the.
22—985
Library of Congress BR563.N4W6
[44q1]

Negro churches, Year book of.

M280
Y33

Year book of Negro churches, with statistics and records of achievements of Negroes in the United States ... 1935/36–
Wilberforce, O., Printed at Wilberforce university [19
v. 22½cm.
Editor: 1935/36– Reverdy C. Ransom.
"Published by authority of the bishops of the A. M. E. church."
1. Negroes. 2. Negroes—Religion. 3. Churches—U. S. 4. Negroes—Stat. I. Ransom, Reverdy Cassius, bp., 1861– ed. II. African Methodist Episcopal church. III. Title: Negro churches, Year book of.
37—22490
Library of Congress E185.7.Y43
[44e1] 325.260073

M05
R29

The Negro citizen. New York, The Reporter, 1949.
2-19, 35-37p. 29cm.
Special feature of the Reporter, December 6, 1949.
1. Race Problems. I.a.t. Brown - Ralph Bunche. II. a.t. Poston - Negro press. III. a.t. Ellison - Shadow.

The Negro citizen of West Virginia...

M975.4
P84n

Posey, Thomas Edward, 1901–
The Negro citizen of West Virginia, by Thomas E. Posey ... Institute, W. Va., Press of West Virginia state college [1934]
1 p. l., [5]–119 p. plates, ports., diagrs. 24cm.
Bibliography: p. [116]–112.
1. Negroes—West Virginia. I. Title.
37-27796
Library of Congress E185.93.W5P6
[2] 325.2609754

Negro clergymen, sixteen essays by.

M231
W62

Why I believe there is a God; sixteen essays by Negro clergymen. With an introd. by Howard Thurman. Chicago, Johnson Pub. Co., 1965.
xiii, 120 p. 22 cm.
1. God—Proof—Addresses, essays, lectures. I. Title: Negro clergymen, sixteen essays by.
BT102.W5 231.082 65–17082
Library of Congress [5]

The Negro college.

M378
H73

Holmes, Dwight Oliver Wendell, 1877–
The evolution of the Negro college, by Dwight Oliver Wendell Holmes ... New York city, Teachers college, Columbia university, 1934.
xi, 221 p. 23½cm. (Teachers college, Columbia university. Contributions to education, no. 609)
Issued also as thesis (PH. D.) Columbia university.
Bibliography: p. 211–221.
1. Negroes—Education. 2. Universities and colleges—U. S. I. Title. II. Title: The Negro college.
34—33600
Library of Congress LC2801.H57 1934 a
——— Copy 2. LB5.C8 no. 609
Copyright A 75062 [40o2] [378.73] 371.9740973

The Negro college graduate.

M301
J63ne2

Johnson, Charles Spurgeon, 1893–
The Negro college graduate, by Charles S. Johnson ... Chapel Hill, The University of North Carolina press, 1938.
xvii, 399 p. incl. tables, diagrs. maps (part fold.) 23½cm.
Bibliography: p. 378–384.
1. Negroes—Education. 2. Negroes—Moral and social conditions. 3. Universities and colleges—U. S. I. Title.
38—6887
Library of Congress LC2781.J6
——— Copy 2.
Copyright A 116318 [40w5] 371.9740973

Negro college life.

M378 W51 Wesley, Charles Harris, 1891-
The history of Alpha phi alpha; a development in Negro college life, by Charles H. Wesley ... Washington, D. C., The Foundation publishers, Howard university [1935]
xix, 21-352 p. illus. (incl. ports.) fold. pl. 22½cm.
"Second edition, revised and enlarged."
"National Alpha phi alpha hymn" (words and music): p. [311]-[313]
1. Alpha phi alpha. 2. Negroes. I. Title: Negro college life.
36-3087
Library of Congress LJ121.A55W4 1935
——— Copy 2.
Copyright A 90328 [3] 371.855

Negro colleges.

M378 W15c Wallace, William James Lord, 1908-
... Chemistry in Negro colleges, by William J. L. Wallace ... [Institute, W. Va., 1940]
34 p. tables. 22½cm. (West Virginia state college bulletin ... Ser. no. 2, Apr. 1940)
Contribution no. 3 of the Research council, West Virginia state college.
Publications of West Virginia state college.
1. Chemistry — [Study and teaching—[Universities and colleges] 2. Universities and colleges — U. S. — Curricula. 3. Negroes — Education. I. Title. II. Title: Negro colleges.
E 40-858 Revised
U. S. Off. of educ. Library for Library of Congress QD40.W26
[r44c2]† 540.71173

The Negro comes of age in industry.

M331 W37ne Weaver, Robert Clifton, 1907-
The Negro comes of age in industry. Washington, D.C., National CIO Committee to Abolish Racial Discrimination, 1943.
54-59p. 25½cm.
Reprinted from the Atlantic Monthly, September 1943.

The Negro committee to aid Spain.

MB9 K24n The Negro committee to aid Spain.
A Negro nurse in republican Spain. New York, issued by the Negro committee to aid Spain... n.d.
14p. port. 18cm.
1. Kee, Salaria. 2. Spain

The Negro community within American Protestantism, 1619-1844.

M261 H33 Haynes, Leonard L 1923-
The Negro community within American Protestantism, 1619-1844. Boston, Christopher Pub. House [1953]
264 p. 21 cm.
1. Negroes—Religion. 2. Protestant churches—U. S. I. Title.
BR563.N4H38 *261.8 53—4230 ‡
Library of Congress [54d2]

Negro culture in West Africa.

M910 E15 Ellis, George Washington, 1875-1919.
Negro culture in West Africa; a social study of the Negro group of Vai-speaking people, with its own invented alphabet and written language shown in two charts and six engravings of Vai script, twenty-six illustrations of their arts and life, fifty folklore stories, one hundred and fourteen proverbs, and one map, by George W. Ellis ... Introduction by Frederick Starr ... New York, The Neale publishing company, 1914.
290 p. front., plates, map. 20½cm.
1. Vei (Negro tribe) 2. Folk-lore, Vei. 3. Vei language. I. Title.
15—1680
Library of Congress DT630.5.V2E6
[42l1]

Negro directory of Indiana.

M310 N31d Negro directory of Indiana.
Indianapolis [The Johnson Advertising Agency, 1939]
30p. illus. 23cm.
Library has: 1939-40.
1. Indiana—Directory.

Negro disfranchisement in Virginia.

M975.5 M36n Martin, Robert E
Negro disfranchisement in Virginia. Washington, D.C., Howard University, 1938.
49-188p. (Howard University studies in the social sciences, v.1, no.1)
Mimeographed.
Bound with Africa and the rise of capitalism by Wilson E. Williams.

Negro doctor.

MB9 P46q Peyton, Thomas Roy, 1897-
Quest for dignity, an autobiography of a Negro doctor. Los Angeles, W. F. Lewis [1950]
vii, 156 p. 24 cm.
I. Title. II. Title: Negro doctor.
R154.P49A3 926.1 50-13642
Library of Congress [a50e2]

Negro education in Alabama.

M370 B64n Bond, Horace Mann, 1904-
Negro education in Alabama; a study in cotton and steel ... by Horace Mann Bond, PH. D. Washington, D. C., The Associated publishers, inc., 1939.
6 p. l., 358 p. illus. (maps, facsim.) diagrs. 23½ cm.
"The Susan Colver Rosenberger prize essay, 1937, the University of Chicago."
Issued also as thesis (PH. D.) University of Chicago, under title: Social and economic influences on the public education of Negroes in Alabama, 1865-1930.
Bibliography: p. 296-304.
1. Negroes—Education. 2. Negroes—Alabama. 3. Education—Alabama. 4. Alabama—Econ. condit. I. Title.
39—18307
Library of Congress LC2802.A2B6 1939
[45n2] 371.97409761

Negro education in America.

M371.974 C61n Clift, Virgil A ed.
Negro education in America; its adequacy, problems, and needs. Edited by Virgil A. Clift, Archibald W. Anderson [and] H. Gordon Hullfish. [1st ed.] New York, Harper [1962]
xxiii, 315 p. 22 cm. (Yearbook of the John Dewey Society, 16th)
Bibliographical footnotes.
1. Negroes—Education. I. Title. (Series: John Dewey Society. Yearbook, 16th)
L101.U6J6 16th, 1962 371.974 62-9485
Library of Congress [15]

Negro education in east Texas.

M370 D29 Davis, William Riley, 1886-
The development and present status of Negro education in east Texas, by William R. Davis ... New York city, Teachers college, Columbia university, 1934.
viii, 150 p. illus. (maps) diagrs. 23½cm. (Teachers college, Columbia university. Contributions to education, no. 626)
Issued also as thesis (PH. D.) Columbia university.
Bibliography: p. 139-150.
1. Negroes—Education. 2. Negroes—Texas. I. Title: Negro education in east Texas.
35-8311
Library of Congress LC2802.T4D3 1934 a
——— Copy 2. LB5.C8 no. 626
Copyright A 77765 [12] 371.97409764

Negro eloquence.

M815 N33 Nelson, Mrs. Alice Ruth (Moore) Dunbar, 1875- ed.
Masterpieces of negro eloquence; the best speeches delivered by the negro from the days of slavery to the present time, ed. by Alice Moore Dunbar. New York, The Bookery publishing company [°1914]
512 p. front. (port.) 23cm.
1. American orations. I. Title. II. Title: Negro eloquence.
14—1930
Library of Congress PS663.N4N4
——— Copy 2.
Copyright A 362234 [33g1]

... El Negro en Cuba.

Cuba M972.91 Ar6n Arredondo, Alberto.
... El negro en Cuba, ensayo. La Habana, Editorial "Alfa", 1939.
174 p., 1 l. 20½cm.
"Fe de erratas": slip laid in.
1. Negroes in Cuba. 2. Cuba—Race question. I. Title.
41—9675
Library of Congress F1789.N3A7
[43c1] 325.26097291

Negro-English dialects.

Jamaica M398 B38 Beckwith, Martha Warren, 1871-
Jamaica Anansi stories, by Martha Warren Beckwith; with music recorded in the field by Helen Roberts. New York, American folk-lore society, 1924.
xiii, 295 p. 25cm. (Half-title: Memoirs of the American folk-lore society, vol. XVII)
1. Folk-lore—Jamaica. 2. Negro-English dialects. I. Roberts, Helen Heffron, 1888- II. Title. III. Title: Anansi stories.
26—10868
Library of Congress GR1.A5 vol. XVII
[42e1]

Negro-English dialects.

M811.5 H38 Henderson, Elliott Blaine.
Plantation echoes; a collection of original Negro dialect poems, by Elliott Blaine Henderson. Columbus, O., Press of F. J. Heer, 1904.
95 p. 19½cm.
1. Negro-English dialects. I. Title.
5—20529
Library of Congress PS3515.E434P6 1904
[a37b1]

Negro-English dialects - Texts.

Jamaica M398 An1 Anancy stories and dialect verse; by Louise Bennett [and others] With an introd. by P. M. Sherlock. [1st ed.] Cover design after a drawing by Stella Shaw. Kingston, Jamaica, Pioneer Press [1950]
101 p. 19 cm.
Partial contents: Louise Bennett. Dorothy Clarke. Una Wilson. Claude McKay. Una Marson.
1. Tales, Jamaican. 2. Negro-English dialects—Texts. I. Bennett, Louise.
PZ8.1.A5 51-17383
Library of Congress [1]

The Negro entrepreneur.

M07 Oa1 Oak, Vishnu Vitthal, 1900-
The Negro entrepreneur. Yellow Springs, Ohio, Print. by the Antioch Press, 1948-
v. illus. 21 cm.
Bibliography: v. 1, p. 138-150.
CONTENTS.—v. 1. The Negro newspaper.
1. Negro newspapers (American) 2. Negro newspapers (American)—Direct. I. Title. II. Title: The Negro newspaper.
E185.8.O2 071 48—6779*
Library of Congress [50q7]

A Negro explorer at the North pole.

MB9 H39h Henson, Matthew Alexander, 1866-
A negro explorer at the North pole, by Matthew A. Henson; with a foreword by Robert E. Peary ... and an introduction by Booker T. Washington; with illustrations from photographs. New York, Frederick A. Stokes company [1912]
xx p., 1 l., 200 p. front., plates, ports. 19½ cm.
1. Arctic regions. 2. North pole. 3. Peary, Robert Edwin, 1856-1920. I. Title.
12—4225
Library of Congress G670 1909.H5
[42m1]

The Negro family in Chicago.

M301 F86 nf3 Frazier, Edward Franklin, 1894-
The Negro family in Chicago, by E. Franklin Frazier ... Chicago, Ill., The University of Chicago press [°1932]
xxv, 294 p. incl. maps, diagrs. 20cm. (Half-title: The University of Chicago sociological series)
"Selected bibliography": p. 277-286.
1. Negroes—Chicago. 2. Negroes—Moral and social conditions. I. Title.
32—2328
Library of Congress F548.9.N3F8
[45q1] 325.26097731

The Negro family in the United States.

M301 F86nf5 1951 Frazier, Edward Franklin, 1894-
The Negro family in the United States. Rev. and abridged ed. New York, Dryden Press, ~~1948~~ 1951.
~~xxxxxxxxx~~ 372p. 22 cm. (The Dryden Press sociology publications)
Bibliographical footnotes.
Reprint of the 1948 rev. & abr. ed.
1. Negroes—Moral and social conditions. 2. Family. I. Title.
E185.86.F74 1948 325.260973 48—7000*
Library of Congress [54b2]

The Negro family in the United States.

M301 F86n25
Frazier, Edward Franklin, 1894–
The Negro family in the United States, by E. Franklin Frazier ... Chicago, Ill., The University of Chicago press [1939]
xxxii, 686 p. incl. illus., tables, diagrs. 20 cm. (*Half-title:* The University of Chicago sociological series)
"A classified bibliography": p. 641–669.
1. Negroes—Moral and social conditions. 2. Family. I. Title.
39—20651
Library of Congress E185.86.F74 [47k2] 325.260973

... The Negro federal government worker...

M331 H32
Hayes, Laurence John Wesley, 1908–
... The Negro federal government worker; a study of his classification status in the District of Columbia, 1883–1938, by Laurence J. W. Haynes, M. A. Washington, D. C., The Graduate school, Howard university, 1941.
156 p. incl. tables, diagr. 23½ᶜᵐ. (The Howard university studies in the social sciences, vol. III, no. 1)
Thesis (M. A.)—Howard university, 1941.
Bibliographical foot-notes.
1. Negroes—Employment. 2. Civil service—U. S. 3. Negroes—District of Columbia. I. Title.
42—10174
Library of Congress H31.H66 vol. 3, no. 1 [a43j3] 325.2609753

Negro firsts in sports.

M796 Y84n
Young, Andrew Sturgeon Nash, 1919–
Negro firsts in sports, by A. S. "Doc" Young. With illus. by Herbert Temple. Chicago, Johnson Pub. Co. [1963]
301 p. illus. 22 cm.
1. Negro athletes. I. Title.
GV697.A1Y6 927.96 62—21535 ‡
Library of Congress [63f10]

Negro folk music, U. S. A.

M784 C83
Courlander, Harold, 1908–
Negro folk music, U. S. A. New York, Columbia University Press, 1963.
x, 324 p. illus., music. 24 cm.
"The music" (melodies with words): p. [221]–287.
Bibliography: p. [299]–301; Discography: p. [302]–308.
1. Music—Negroes. 2. Negro songs—Hist. & crit. 3. Negro songs—Discography. 4. Negro songs. I. Title.
ML3556.C7 784.756 63—18019/MN
Library of Congress [a63d3]

Negro folk rhymes.

M811.08 T14
Talley, Thomas Washington, *comp.*
Negro folk rhymes, wise and otherwise, with a study by Thomas W. Talley ... New York, The Macmillan company, 1922.
xii p., 1 l., 347 p. illus. (incl. music) 19½ᶜᵐ.
1. Negro songs. I. Title.
22—1477
Library of Congress PS595.N3T3 [41t1]

Negro folk tales.

M813.5 W589n
Whiting, Helen Adele (Johnson) 1885–
Negro folk tales, for pupils in the primary grades, by Helen Adele Whiting; illustrations by Lois Mailou Jones. Book I. Washington, D. C., The Associated publishers, inc. [°1938]
[28] p. illus. 23½ cm.
Book II published under title: Negro art, music and rhyme, for young folks.
1. Folk-lore, Negro. I. Title.
38—17132
Library of Congress PE1119.W54 [a45d1] 372.4

Negro folktales in Michigan.

M398 D73
Dorson, Richard Mercer, 1916– ed.
Negro folktales in Michigan. Cambridge, Harvard University Press, 1956.
245 p. illus. 22 cm.
1. Negro tales. 2. Folk-lore, Negro. 3. Negroes. I. Title.
GR103.D6 398.21 56—6516 ‡
Library of Congress [15]

The Negro freedman.

M326 D71
Donald, Henderson Hamilton.
The Negro freedman; life conditions of the American Negro in the early years after emancipation. New York, H. Schuman, 1952.
270 p. 24 cm.
Bibliography: p. [255]–258.
1. Freedmen. I. Title.
E185.2.D65 326.8 52—7163
Library of Congress [52u10]

Negro freedom.

M323 W73n
Winston, Henry M.
Negro freedom, a goal for all Americans, by Henry M. Winston and others. New York, New Currents Publishers, 1964.
56p. 18cm.

The Negro from 1863 to 1963.

M973 W56
Wheadon, Augusta Austin.
The Negro from 1863 to 1963. [1st ed.] New York, Vantage Press [1964, °1963]
91 p. 21 cm.
Bibliography: p. 91.
Portrait of author on book jacket.
1. Negroes. 2. Negroes—Biog. I. Title.
E185.6.W55 325.2670973 64—3283
Library of Congress [5]

Negro frontiersman.

MB9 F64a4
Flipper, Henry O . 1856-1940.
Negro frontiersman; the western memoirs of Henry O. Flipper, first Negro graduate of West Point, edited with an introduction by Theorode D. Harris. El Paso, Texas Western College Press, 1963.
54p. 23cm.

The Negro genius.

M810. B73n2
Brawley, Benjamin Griffith, 1882-1939.
The Negro genius; a new appraisal of the achievement of the American Negro in literature and the fine arts, by Benjamin Brawley ... New York, Dodd, Mead & company, 1937.
xiii, 366 p. front., plates, ports. 20½ cm.
Bibliography: p. 331–350.
1. Negro authors. 2. Negro artists. 3. Negro musicians. 4. Negro literature—Hist. & crit. 5. Negroes in literature and art. I. Title.
37—4124
Library of Congress E185.82.B816 [47b3] 325.260973

The Negro ghetto.

M331.833 W37n
Weaver, Robert Clifton, 1907-
The Negro ghetto. New York, Harcourt, Brace & co., 1948.
xviii, 404p. 21cm.

The Negro handbook.

M310 Eb7
Ebony.
The Negro handbook, compiled by the editors of Ebony. Chicago, Johnson Pub. Co., 1966.
535 p. 24 cm.
Includes bibliographies.
1. Negroes—Handbooks, manuals, etc. I. Title.
E185.E2 973.9'02'02 66—27479
Library of Congress [67d9]

M310 M96
The Negro handbook ... 1942–
New York, N. Y., W. Malliet and company, 1942–
v. tables. 24 cm.
Editor: 1942– Florence Murray.
"Books and periodicals, a list of books by and about Negroes": 1942, p. 194–200.
See holdings card for issues in library.
1. Negroes—Year-books. I. Murray, Florence, ed.
42—22818
Library of Congress E185.5.N382 [45k7] 325.260973

M310 M96
The Negro handbook, 1942-

Volume	Year	Month	Volume	Year	Month
	1942				
	1946				
	1949				

Negro heroes of emancipation.

M323 N213
National Association for the Advancement of Colored People.
Negro heroes of emancipation. New York, 1964.
unp. illus. 21cm.

Negro higher education in the State of South Carolina.

M378 M22
McMillan, Lewis Kennedy.
Negro higher education in the State of South Carolina. [Orangeburg? S. C., 1953, °1952]
xii, 296 p. facsims. 24 cm.
1. Negroes—Education—South Carolina. 2. Universities and colleges—South Carolina. I. Title.
LC2802.S6M25 378.757 53—2401
Library of Congress [54c2]

Negro historians in the United States.

M301 T39n
Thorpe, Earle E
Negro historians in the United States.
Baton Rouge, La., Fraternal Press [1958]
188p. 22cm.
Includes bibliography.

Negro history in thirteen plays.

M812.08 R39n
Richardson, Willis, 1889– ed.
Negro history in thirteen plays, by Willis Richardson and May Miller. Washington, D. C., The Associated publishers, inc. [°1935]
vii, 333 p. 21ᶜᵐ.
1. Negro drama. 2. Negroes in literature and art. I. Miller, May, joint ed. II. Title.
36—17
Library of Congress PS627.N4R47 [43u2] 812.50822

Negro housing.

M331.833 P92
President's conference on home building and home ownership, *Washington, D. C.*, 1931.
Negro housing; report of the Committee on Negro housing, Nannie H. Burroughs, chairman; prepared for the committee by Charles S. Johnson; edited by John M. Gries and James Ford. Washington, D. C., The President's conference on home building and home ownership [°1932]
xiv, 282 p. front., plates. 23½ᶜᵐ.
On cover: Physical aspects; social and economic factors; home ownership and financing.
(Continued on next card)
32—26008
[43t2]

The Negro immigrant.

M301 R27n4 **Reid, Ira De Augustine, 1901–**

The Negro immigrant, his background, characteristics and social adjustment, 1899–1937, by Ira De A. Reid ... New York, Columbia university press; London, P. S. King & son, ltd., 1939.

261 p. incl. tables. 23cm. (*Half-title:* Studies in history, economics and public law, ed. by the Faculty of political science of Columbia university. no. 449)

Issued also as thesis (PH. D.) Columbia university.
Bibliography: p. 253–258.

1. Negroes. 2. U. S.—Race question. 3. U. S.—Emig. & immig. I. Title.

Library of Congress H31.C7 no. 449 39—19099
——— Copy 2. JV6895.N44R4 1939 a
Copyright A 126486 [40k5] (308.2) 325.260973

M331.833 W37n3 The Negro in a program of public housing.
Weaver, Robert Clifton, 1907-
The Negro in a program of public housing.
Reprinted from Opportunity, July 1938.

6p. illus. 28cm.

The Negro in Africa and America, a bibliography of.

M01 W89 **Work, Monroe Nathan, 1866–** comp.

A bibliography of the Negro in Africa and America, compiled by Monroe N. Work ... New York, The H. W. Wilson company, 1928.

xxi, [1] p., 1 l., 698 p. 26½cm.

Classified, with author index.
"List of periodicals from which references for the bibliography were taken": p. [661]–674.
"A bibliography of bibliographies on Africa": pt. I, p. [242]–247.
"A bibliography of bibliographies on the Negro in the United States": pt. II, p. [630]–636.

(Continued on next card)
28—17150
[42w2]

The Negro in America...

M302 L79n6 **Locke, Alain Le Roy, 1886–**

... The Negro in America, by Alain Locke. Chicago, American library association, 1933.

64 p. 18 cm. (Reading with a purpose, no. 68)

Title vignette; tail-piece.
"Books recommended in this course": p. 59.

1. Negroes. 2. Negroes—Bibl. I. American library association. II. Title.

Library of Congress E185.6.L77 33—15520
[48k2] 325.260973

... The Negro in America.

M323 St4n **Stewart, Maxwell Slutz, 1900–**

... The Negro in America, by Maxwell S. Stewart. [New York, Public affairs committee, inc., 1944]

cover-title, 32 p. 1 illus., diagrs. 21cm. (Public affairs pamphlet, no. 95)

"First edition, August 1944."
"Summary of An American dilemma ... by Gunnar Myrdal."—p. [1]
"For further reading": p. 32.

1. Negroes. I. *Myrdal, Gunnar, 1898– An American dilemma. II. Title.

Library of Congress E185.6.M962 44-9455
[35] 325.260973

The Negro in American business.

M658 K62 Kinzer, Robert H
The Negro in American business; the conflict between separatism and integration, by Robert H. Kinzer & Edward Sagarin. [1st ed.] New York, Greenberg [c1950]

vi, 220p. 21cm.

M301 J63ne6 The Negro in American civilization.
Johnson, Charles Spurgeon, 1893-
The Negro in American civilization; a study of Negro life and race relations in the light of social research, by Charles S. Johnson ... London, Constable and co., 1931.

xiv, 538 p. diagrs. 22½cm.
Results of social research for the National interracial conference and problems discussed at its meeting in Washington, D.C., December 16-19, 1928.
Bibl: p. 485-509.

The Negro in American civilization.

M323 J63 **Johnson, Charles Spurgeon, 1893–**

The Negro in American civilization; a study of Negro life and race relations in the light of social research, by Charles S. Johnson ... New York, H. Holt and company [°1930]

xiv, 538 p. diagrs. 22½cm. (*Half-title:* American social science series; general editor, H. W. Odum)

Results of social research for the National interracial conference and problems discussed at its meeting in Washington, D. C., December 16–19, 1928.
Bibliography: p. 485–509.

1. Negroes. 2. U. S.—Race question. I. National interracial conference, Washington, 1928. II. Title.

Library of Congress E185.6.J665 30—15942
[a48k3] 325.260973

The Negro in American culture...

M810 B97n **Butcher, Margaret (Just) 1913–**

The Negro in American culture; based on materials left by Alain Locke. [1st ed.] New York, Knopf, 1956.

294 p. 22 cm.

1. ~~Negroes in~~ literature. 2. ~~Negroes in~~ art. 3. ~~Negro~~ literature (American) 4. American literature—~~Negro~~ authors. 5. ~~Negro art.~~ 6. Music—~~Negroes.~~ 7. ~~Negroes~~—Dancing. I. Title.
II. Locke, Alain Leroy.

E185.82.B89 325.260973 56—5783 ‡

Library of Congress [57e20]

The Negro in American fiction.

M810.9 B81 **Brown, Sterling Allen, 1901–**

... The Negro in American fiction, by Sterling Brown ... Washington, D. C., The Association in Negro folk education, 1937.

3 p. l., 209 p. 21½cm. (Bronze booklet no. 6)

"Selected reading list": p. 207–209.

1. ~~Negro~~ fiction (American)—Hist. & crit. 2. ~~Negroes in~~ literature and art. I. Title.

Library of Congress E185.5.B85 no. 6 38—20045
——— Copy 2. PS374.N4B7
[45m1] (325.260973) 813.09

The Negro in American history.

M973 C88 **Cromwell, John Wesley, 1846–**

The Negro in American history; men and women eminent in the evolution of the American of African descent, by John W. Cromwell ... Washington, The American Negro academy, 1914.

xiii, 284 p. front., plates, ports. 23½cm.

Bibliography: p. 257–262.

1. Negroes. 2. Negroes—Biog. 3. Slavery in the U. S. I. Title.

Library of Congress E185.C92 14—7742
——— Copy 2.
Copyright A 369777 [46o1]

M973 L82ne The Negro in American life and thought.
Logan, Rayford Whittingham, 1897–

The Negro in American life and thought: the nadir, 1877–1901. New York, Dial Press, 1954.

x, 380 p. 21 cm.

Bibliographical references included in "Footnotes" (p. 341–365)

1. Negroes—Civil rights. 2. Negroes—Hist. I. Title.

E185.61.L64 *301.451 325.260973 54—6000

Library of Congress [54x20]

The Negro in American national politics.

M324 N86 **Nowlin, William Felbert, 1897–**

The Negro in American national politics, by William F. Nowlin, A. M. Boston, Mass., The Stratford company [°1931]

4 p. l., 148 p. 19½ cm.

Bibliography: p. 145–148.

1. Negroes—Politics and suffrage. I. Title.

Library of Congress JK2275.N4N6 32—5242
[49e½] 325.26

M813.4 C42u The Negro in art; how shall he be portrayed.
Chesnutt, Charles Waddell, 1858-1932.
The Negro in art; how shall he be portrayed.
From The Crisis, No., 1926. p.28-29.

Bound in his - Uncollected stories.

The Negro in business.

M331.4 W272n **Washington, Booker Taliaferro, 1859?–1915.**

The Negro in business, by Booker T. Washington ... Boston, Chicago, Hertel, Jenkins & co. [°1907]

1 p. l., 379 p. 18 pl. (incl. front., ports.) 20½ cm.

Plates printed on both sides.

1. Negroes—Employment. I. Title.

Library of Congress E185.8.W31 7—37616
[41g1]

M326. G83n The Negro in colonial New England, 1620-1776.
Greene, Lorenzo Johnston, 1899–

The Negro in colonial New England, 1620–1776, by Lorenzo Johnston Greene ... New York, Columbia university press; London, P. S. King & Staples, ltd., 1942.

404 p. 23 cm. (*Half-title:* Studies in history, economics and public law, ed. by the Faculty of political science of Columbia university. No. 494)

Issued also as thesis (PH. D.) Columbia university.
Bibliography: p. 361–384.

1. Slavery in the U. S.—New England. 2. Negroes—New England. 3. New England—Hist.—Colonial period. I. Title.

Library of Congress H31.C7 no. 494 43—2384
——— Copy 2. E444.N5G7 1942a
[48x2] (308.2) 326.974

The Negro in English literature.

U.S. M820.9 M139 McCullough, Norman Verrle
The Negro in English literature; a critical introduction. Devon, Arthur H. Stockwell [1962]

176p. 19cm.
Includes bibliography

The Negro in English romantic thought.

M808 D98 **Dykes, Eva Beatrice.**

The Negro in English romantic thought; or, A study of sympathy for the oppressed, by Eva Beatrice Dykes. Washington, D. C., The Associated publishers, inc., 1942.

5 p. l., 197 p. 23½cm.

Bibliography: p. 157–166.

1. Romanticism—England. 2. Negroes in literature and art. 3. English literature— 18th cent. — Hist. & crit. 4. English literature — 19th cent.—Hist. & crit. I. Title.

Library of Congress PR447.D9 42—6447
[45j2] 820.903

The Negro in etiquette.

M395 W86 Woods, E M.

The negro in etiquette: a novelty. St. Louis, Buxton & Skinner, 1899.

1 p. l., 163 p. port. 12°.

Mar. 1, 1900-190

Library of Congress, no. Copyright.

The Negro in literature and art.

M810. B73n6 1910 **Brawley, Benjamin Griffith, 1882–1939.**

The Negro in literature and art, by Benjamin Griffith Brawley ... [Atlanta? °1910]

60 p. 17½cm.

List of books: p. [58]–60.

1. Negroes—Biog. 2. Negro literature. I. Title.

Library of Congress E185.82.B82 10—12321
[a41c1]

The Negro in Louisiana.

M976.3 R76 **Roussève, Charles Barthelemy.**

The Negro in Louisiana; aspects of his history and his literature, by Charles Barthelemy Roussève, M. A. New Orleans, The Xavier university press, 1937.

xvii, 212 p. front., illus. (music) plates, diagrs. 20½cm.

"This work, prepared in 1935 in partial fulfillment of the requirements for the degree of master of arts, makes its appearance ... substantially as it was originally written, save for ... several minor alterations and the addition of a few details."—p. vii.
Bibliography: p. 193–201.

1. Negroes—Louisiana. 2. Negroes in literature and art. 3. Negro authors. I. Title.

Library of Congress E185.93.L6R6 38—525
[42h2] 325.260763

The Negro in masonic literature.
M366.1 W67n Williamson, Harry A.
The Negro in Masonic literature, compiled by Harry A. Williamson... ₍New York, Prince Hall Masonic publishing co., c1922₎
30p. 21½cm.

The Negro in our history.
M973 W86 Woodson, Carter Godwin, 1875–
The Negro in our history, by Carter G. Woodson ... Washington, D. C., The Associated publishers, inc. ₍°1922₎
xv, 898 p. incl. front., illus. 20ᶜᵐ.
1. Negroes. 2. Slavery in the U. S. I. Title.
22—14504
Library of Congress E185.W89 ₍a35p2₎

The Negro in the American rebellion.
M210 B81n Brown, William Wells, b. 1815.
The negro in the American rebellion, his heroism and his fidelity, by William Wells Brown ... Boston, Lee & Shepard, 1867.
xvi, 380 p. 19ᶜᵐ.
1. U. S.—Hist.—Civil war—Negro troops. I. Title.
2—5868
Library of Congress E540.N3B8 ₍37g1₎

The Negro in medicine.
MB K39n Kenney, John A 1874–
The Negro in medicine. Tuskegee Institute Ala., Printed by the Tuskegee Institute Press, c1912.
60p. front. plates (part fold.) ports. 24½cm.

The Negro in science.
M500 M36n Maryland. Morgan State College, *Baltimore.*
The Negro in science, by the Calloway Hall editorial committee: Julius H. Taylor, editor ₍and others. Baltimore₎ Morgan State College Press ₍1955₎
viii, 192 p. illus. 26 cm.
Includes bibliographies.
1. Science—Addresses, essays, lectures. 2. Negro scientists. I. Taylor, Julius H., ed. II. Title.
Q171.M312 504 55—63107
Library of Congress ₍56e2₎

The Negro in the American Revolution.
M973 Qu2n Quarles, Benjamin.
The Negro in the American Revolution. Chapel Hill, Published for the Institute of Early American History and Culture, Williamsburg, Va., by University of North Carolina Press ₍1961₎
xiii, 231 p. front. 24 cm.
Bibliography: p. ₍201₎–223.
1. U. S.—Hist.—Revolution—Negroes. I. Institute of Early American History and Culture, Williamsburg, Va. II. Title.
Full name: Benjamin Arthur Quarles.
E269.N3Q3 973.315967 61—66795
Library of Congress ₍62k10₎

The Negro in modern American history textbooks.
M371.32 S1.52 Sloan, Irving
The Negro in modern American history textbooks: a study of the Negro in selected junior and senior high history textbooks as of September, 1966. ₌Chicago₌ American Federation of Teachers ₌1966₌
47p. 20cm.
White author?

The Negro in sports.
M796 H38 1949 Henderson, Edwin Bancroft, 1883–
The Negro in sports. Rev. ed. Washington, Associated Publishers, 1949.
xvi, 507 p. illus., ports. 21 cm.
1. Negro athletes. 2. Sports—U. S. 3. Negroes—Biog. I. Title.
GV161.H4 1949 796.0973 50—6466
Library of Congress ₍15₎

The Negro in the Americas.
M323.1 W51 Wesley, Charles Harris, 1891– *ed.*
... The Negro in the Americas, edited by Charles H. Wesley ... Washington, D. C., The Graduate school, Howard university ₍1940₎
3 p. l., 86 p. 23½ᶜᵐ. (Public lectures of the Division of the social sciences of the Graduate school, Howard university. vol. 1)
CONTENTS.—The Negro in the British West Indies, by Eric Williams.—Notes on the Negro in the French West Indies, by L. T. Achille.—The Negro in Spanish America, by R. W. Logan.—The Negro in Brazil, by Richard Pattee.—The Haitian nation, by Dantes Bellegarde.—Race, migration and citizenship, by Ira De A. Reid.—The Negro in the United States and Canada, by C. H. Wesley.
1. Negroes in America. I. Title.
40—34259
Library of Congress H31.H65 vol. 1
——— Copy 2. E29.N3W5
₍44f1₎ (308.2) 325.26097

The Negro in New York.
M974.7 A153 Allen, James Egert, 1896–
The Negro in New York. Foreword by Hon. Arthur Levitt. New York, Exposition Press ₌1964₌
94p. 21cm.

The Negro in sports.
M796 H38 Henderson, Edwin Bancroft, 1883–
The Negro in sports, by Edwin Bancroft Henderson ... Washington, D. C., The Associated publishers, inc. ₍°1939₎
5 p. l., 371 p. illus. (incl. ports.) 21 cm.
1. Negro athletics. 2. Sports—U. S. 3. Negroes—Biog. I. Title.
39—29452
Library of Congress E185.86.H45 ₍40k5₎ 796.0973

M975 N31 The Negro in the black belt; Some social sketches and other economic and social studies published by the Department of Labor. Washington, D.C. ₍1897-1902₎.
1v. (various paging) tables, maps. 23cm.
Eight separately issued Labor Dept. Bulletins.
1. South.

The Negro in North Carolina, 1876-1894.
M975.6 L82 Logan, Frenise A
The Negro in North Carolina, 1876–1894. Chapel Hill, University of North Carolina Press ₍1964₎
ix, 244 p. 24 cm.
Bibliography: p. ₍221₎–233.
1. Negroes—North Carolina. I. Title.
E185.93.N6L6 301.451 64—13554
Library of Congress ₍5₎

The Negro in sports.
M796 L95n Low, Nat
The Negro in sports. San Francisco, The Daily People's World, 19 .
31p. illus. 19cm.

The Negro in the black belt...
M975 N31 Condition of the Negro in various cities. ₍Bulletin of the Labor Dept., no.10, 1897₎ Pp. 257-369.
In: The Negro in the black belt... Washington, D.C., Dept. of Labor, ₍1897-1902₎

The Negro in North Carolina prior to 1861...
M975.6 B69 Boykin, James H
The Negro in North Carolina prior to 1861; an historical monograph. ₍1st ed.₎ New York, Pageant Press ₍1958₎
84 p. 21 cm.
Includes bibliography.
1. Negroes—North Carolina. I. Title.
E185.93.N6B6 325.2609756 58—1347 ‡
Library of Congress ₍58c5₎

The Negro in Tennessee.
M973.8 T21ne Taylor, Alrutheus Ambush.
The Negro in Tennessee, 1865–1880, by Alrutheus Ambush Taylor ... Washington, D. C., The Associated publishers, inc., 1941.
5 p. l., 306 p. 23½ᶜᵐ.
Bibliography: p. 267–273. Bibliographical notes: p. 275–300.
1. Negroes—Tennessee. I. Title.
41—5247
Library of Congress E185.93.T3T3 ₍43h1₎ 325.2609768

The Negro in the black belt.
M975 N31 Du Bois, William Edward Burghardt, 1868–
The Negro in the black belt; Some social sketches. ₍Bulletin of the Labor Dept., no.22, 1899₎ Pp. 401-417.
In: The Negro in the black belt. Washington, D.C., Dept. of Labor. ₍1897-1902.₎

The Negro in our history.
M973 W86 1928 Woodson, Carter Godwin, 1875–
The Negro in our history, by Carter G. Woodson... fifth edition (further revised and enlarged). Washington, D.C., The Associated publishers, inc. ₍c1928₎
xxx, 628p. front. illus. 21½cm.

Negro in Texas politics.
M324 B76n Brewer, John Mason, 1896–
Negro legislators of Texas and their descendants; a history of the Negro in Texas politics from reconstruction to disfranchisement, by J. Mason Brewer ... with an introduction by Herbert P. Gambrell ... Dallas, Tex., Mathis publishing co. ₍°1935₎
x, 134 p. ports. (1 fold.) map. 20ᶜᵐ.
1. Negroes—Texas. 2. Negroes—Politics and suffrage. 3. Texas—Pol. & govt.—1865– 4. Negroes—Biog. I. Title. II. Title: Negro in Texas politics.
35-17051
Library of Congress E185.93.T4B7
——— Copy 2.
Copyright A 86409 ₍36d3₎ 325.2609764

Negro in the black belt.
M975 N31 Du Bois, William Edward Burghardt, 1898–
The Negro landholder of Georgia. ₍Bulletin of the Labor Dept., no.35., 1901₎ pp. 647-777.
In: The Negro in the black belt... Washington, D.C., Dept. of Labor, ₍1897-1902₎

Negro in the black belt.

M975 N31 Du Bois, William Edward Burghardt, 1898-
The Negroes of Farmville, Virginia: A social study. ⌊Bulletin of the Labor Dept., no.14, 1898⌋ pp. 1-38.

In: The Negro in the black belt... Washington, D.C., Dept. of Labor ⌊1897-1902⌋

Negro in the black belt.

M975 N31 Laws, J Bradford.
The Negroes of Cinclare Central Factory and Calumet Plantation, Louisiana. ⌊Bulletin of the Labor Dept. no.38, 1902⌋ pp. 95-120.

In: The Negro in the black belt... Washington, D.C., Dept. of Labor, ⌊189 - 190 ⌋

Negro in the black belt.

M975 N31 Thom, William Taylor.
The Negroes of Litwalton, Virginia: A social study of the Oyster Negro. ⌊Bulletin of the Labor Dept., no.37, 1901. pp. 1115-1170.

In: The Negro in the black belt... Washington, D.C., Dept. of Labor, ⌊1897-1902⌋

Negro in the black belt.

M975 N31 Thom, William Taylor.
The Negroes of Sandy Spring, Maryland: A social study. Bulletin of the Labor Dept., no.32. pp. 43-102.
In: The Negro in the black belt... Washington, D.C., Dept. of Labor, ⌊1897-1902⌋

Negro in the black belt.

M975 N31 Wright, Richard Robert, Jr., 1878-
The Negroes of Xenia, Ohio: A social study. ⌊Bulletin of the Labor Dept., no.48. 1903⌋ pp. 1007-1044.
In: The Negro in the black belt... Washington, D.C., Dept. of Labor ⌊1897-1902⌋

The Negro in the building of America.

M973 R24n Reddick, Lawrence Dunbar. 1910-
The Negro in the building of America.
New York. National Committee for the Participation of Negroes in the American Common World's Fair of 1920 in New York. 1940.

447p. 23cm.
In: Souvenir program of Negro week on the American Common. World's Fair of 1940 in New York.

... The Negro in the Caribbean.

Trinidad M700 W67n Williams, Eric, 1911-
... The Negro in the Caribbean, by Eric Williams ... Washington, D. C., The Associates in Negro folk education, 1942.
4 p. l., 119 p. incl. tab. 22cm. (Bronze booklet no. 8)
"Reference notes": p. 110-114. "Select bibliography": p. 115-117.

1. Negroes in the West Indies. I. Title.
42—16832
Library of Congress E185.5.B85 no. 8
——— Copy 2. F1623.W48
⌊45j2⌋ (325.260973) 325.2609729

The Negro in the Christian pulpit.

M287.8 H76n Hood, James Walker, bp., 1831-
The Negro in the Christian pulpit; or the two characters and two destines, as delineated in twenty-one practical sermons. By J. W. Hood ... with an appendix containing specimen sermons by other bishops of the same church. Introduction by Rev. A. G. Haygood... Raleigh, Edwards Broughton & co., 1884.

363p. plates. 19cm.

...The Negro in the cities of the North.

M323.22 Su7n Survey midmonthly.
... The Negro in the cities of the North ... New York, The Charity organization society, °1905.
2 p. l., 96 p. illus., plates. 26cm.
At head of title: Charities publication committee.
Reprint of Charities, October 7, 1905.

1. Negroes. I. Survey associates, inc., New York. II. Title.
6-2281 Revised
Library of Congress E185.9.S96
⌊r45c2⌋

The Negro in the Civil War.

M973 Q25 Quarles, Benjamin.
The Negro in the Civil War. ⌊1st ed.⌋ Boston, Little, Brown ⌊1953⌋
xvi, 379 p. illus. 21 cm.
Bibliography: p. ⌊349⌋-360.

1. U. S.—Hist.—Civil War—Negroes. I. Title.
E540.N3Q3 973.715 53—7309
Library of Congress ⌊54z10⌋

The Negro in the making of America.

M973 Q25n Quarles, Benjamin.
The Negro in the making of America. ⌊1st ed.⌋ New York, Collier Books ⌊1964⌋
288 p. 18 cm. (A Collier books original)
"AS 534."
Bibliography: p. 267-271.

1. Negroes—Hist. I. Title.
E185.Q2 301.451 64-21838
Library of Congress ⌊4-1⌋

The Negro in the organization of abolition.

M326. W51n Wesley, Charles Harris, 1891-
The Negro in the organization of abolition. Reprinted from Phylon. 2:223-235. Third quarter 1941.

223-235p. 25cm.
Paper read at the meeting of the American Historical Association, 1940.

The Negro in the Philadelphia press...

M07 S15 Simpson, George Eaton, 1904-
The Negro in the Philadelphia press ... ⌊by⌋ George Eaton Simpson. Philadelphia, 1936.
xv, 158 p. incl. illus. (map) tables, diagrs. 28cm.
Thesis (PH. D.)—University of Pennsylvania, 1934.
"Planoprinting."
An analysis of Negro material published in the Philadelphia record, Public ledger, Evening bulletin and Philadelphia inquirer during 1908-1932.
Bibliography: p. ⌊153⌋-156.

1. Negroes. 2. Negroes—Stat. 3. American newspapers—Philadelphia. I. Title.
37—1807
Library of Congress PN4899.P4885 1934
Univ. of Pennsylvania Libr.
——— Copy 2. ⌊38g5⌋ 071.4811

The Negro in the political classics.

M324 Sm5n Smith, Arthur J.
The Negro in the political classics of the American government, by Arthur J. Smith. Washington, D. C. ⌊°1937⌋
cover-title, 25 l. 12 x 18½cm.
"A short biography of each Negro United States senator and representative, elected and seated ... since 1870."

1. Negroes—Biog. 2. Negroes—Politics and suffrage. I. Title.
39-33068
Library of Congress E185.96.S65
——— Copy 2.
Copyright AA 232559 ⌊2⌋ 923.273

The Negro in the reconstruction of Virginia.

M973.8 T21n Taylor, Alrutheus Ambush.
The Negro in the reconstruction of Virginia, by Alrutheus Ambush Taylor ... Washington, D. C., The Association for the study of Negro life and history ⌊°1926⌋
iv, 300 p. 24½cm.
Bibliography: p. 287-292.

1. Negroes—Virginia. 2. Reconstruction—Virginia. I. Association for the study of Negro life and history, inc. II. Title.
27—5705
Library of Congress E185.93.V8T3
⌊43g1⌋

The Negro in the St. Louis Economy, 1954.

M330 H24 Harris, Harry C
The Negro in the St. Louis Economy, 1954, by Irwin Sobel, Werner Z. Hirsch and Harry C. Harris. St. Louis, Urban League of St. Louis, Inc., 1954.

95p. tables 23cm.

The Negro in the South.

M814.4 W272n2 Washington, Booker Taliaferro, 1859?-1915.
The Negro in the South, his economic progress in relation to his moral and religious development; being the William Levi Bull lectures for the year 1907, by Booker T. Washington ... and W. E. Burghardt Du Bois ... Philadelphia, G. W. Jacobs & company ⌊1907⌋
222 p. 19½cm.
CONTENTS.—I. The economic development of the Negro race in slavery, by B. T. Washington.—II. The economic development of the Negro race since its emancipation, by B. T. Washington.—III. The economic revolution in the South, by W. E. B. Du Bois.—IV. Religion in the South, by W. E. B. Du Bois.—Notes to chapters III and IV (Bibliography: p. 220-222)

1. ~~Negroes.~~ I. Du Bois, William Edward Burghardt, 1868- II. Title.
7—21310
Library of Congress E185.6.W316
⌊4511⌋

The Negro in the United States.

M301 F86n1 Frazier, Edward Franklin, 1894-
The Negro in the United States. New York, Macmillan Co., 1949.

xxxi, 767p. illus. maps. 22cm.
"A classified bibliography": p. 707-750.

The Negro in the United States, a brief history.

M973 L82n Logan, Rayford Whittingham, 1897-
The Negro in the United States, a brief history. Princeton, N. J., D. Van Nostrand Co. ⌊1957⌋
191 p. 19 cm. (An Anvil original, no. 19)
Includes bibliography.

1. ~~Negroes.~~ History. I. Title.
E185.L85 325.260973 56—12904 ‡
Library of Congress ⌊58q7⌋

The Negro in the United States.

M01 N42ne 1965 New York, Public Library.
The Negro in the United States; a list of significant books. 9th rev. ed. New York, New York Public Library, 1965.

24p. 25½cm.

The Negro in the viceroyalty of the Rio de la Plata.

M910 D56n Diggs, Irene.
The Negro in the viceroyalty of the Rio de la Plata. Reprinted from the Journal of Negro History, 36:281-301, July 1951.

281-301p. 25cm.

The Negro in Virginia.

M975.5 N93

Writers' program. *Virginia.*

The Negro in Virginia, compiled by workers of the Writers' program of the Work projects administration in the state of Virginia ... Sponsored by the Hampton institute. New York, Hastings house, 1940.

xii, 380 p. plates, ports. 21cm.

Map on lining-papers.
Bibliography: p. 353-367.

1. Negroes—Virginia. I. Title.

40-12192

Library of Congress E185.93.V8W7
———— Copy 2.
Copyright [4] 325.2609755

The Negro in World War II.

M358 S13n

Silvera, John D

The Negro in World War II, by John D. Silvera. Baton Rouge, La. Military press of Louisiana, 1946.

140 unnumbered p. illus. 27cm.

Negro institutions.

M378 C16p

Canady, Herman George, 1901–

... Psychology in Negro institutions, by Herman G. Canady ... Institute, W. Va., West Virginia state college [1939]

24 p. tables. 23cm. (West Virginia state college bulletin. Series 26, no. 3. June, 1939)

"Contribution no. 1 of the Research council at West Virginia state college—curricula studies."

1. Psychology—[Study and] teaching. 2. Universities and colleges—U. S.—Curricula. 3. Negroes—Education. I. Title. II. Title: Negro institutions.

E 39-308

U. S. Off. of educ. Library for Library of Congress LC2801.C4 [4]

Negro journalism.

M07 G66n

Gore, George William, *jr.*

Negro journalism; an essay on the history and present conditions of the negro press, by George W. Gore, jr. ... Greencastle, Ind., 1922.

35 p. illus. 23cm.

Advertising matter: p. 33-35.

1. Journalism I. Title.

Library of Congress PN4888.N4G6 23-9635
———— Copy 2.
Copyright A 696986 [32c1]

Negro labor, a national problem.

M331 W37n

Weaver, Robert Clifton, 1907–

Negro labor, a national problem [by] Robert C. Weaver. New York, Harcourt, Brace and company [1946]

xiv, 329 p. 21cm.

"First printing."
"Selected bibliography": p. 317-321.

1. Negroes—Employment. I. Title.

46-25023

Library of Congress * E185.8.W38 [35] 331.98

Negro labor in the United States, 1850-1925...

M331 W51

Wesley, Charles Harris, 1891–

Negro labor in the United States, 1850-1925; a study in American economic history, by Charles H. Wesley ... New York, Vanguard press, 1927.

xiii, 343 p. illus. (map) 18½cm.

Bibliography: p. 321-330.

1. Negroes—Employment. I. Title.

27—7288

Library of Congress HD6305.C7W4 [44h1]

The Negro labor unionist of New York.

M331 F85

Franklin, Charles Lionel, 1910–

The Negro labor unionist of New York; problems and conditions among Negroes in the labor unions in Manhattan with special reference to the N. R. A. and post-N. R. A. situations, by Charles Lionel Franklin ... New York, 1936.

2 p. l., 7-417 p. 22½cm.

Thesis (PH. D.)—Columbia university, 1936.
Vita.
Published also as Studies in history, economics and public law, ed. by the Faculty of political science of Columbia university, no. 420.
Bibliography: p. 398-402.

1. Negroes—New York (City) 2. Negroes—Employment. 3. Trade-unions—New York (City) 4. Labor and laboring classes—New York (City) I. Title. II. Title: Negroes in the labor unions in Manhattan.

36—34118

Library of Congress E185.8.F732
Columbia Univ. Libr. [39d1] 331.88097471

The Negro landholder of Georgia.

M975 N31

Du Bois, William Edward Burghardt, 1898–

The Negro landholder of Georgia. [Bulletin of the Labor Dept., no.35, 1901] pp. 647-77.

In: The Negro in the black belt... Washington, D.C., Dept. of Labor, 1897-1902]

... Negro leaders.

M378 G83n

Greene, Harry Washington, 1896–

... Negro leaders; a study of educational and social background factors of prominent Negroes whose life sketches are carried in national directories, by Harry W. Greene ... Institute, W. Va., West Virginia state college [1936]

30 p. tables. 28cm. (West Virginia state college. Bulletin. Series 23, no. 6. November 1936. Contribution no. 7 of the Department of education)

Bibliography: p. 27.

1. Negroes—[U. S.] 2. Negroes—[U. S.]—Education. I. Title.

E 37—404

U. S. Off. of educ. Library for Library of Congress E185.82G7 [42c1]

The Negro leadership class.

M323.1 T372

Thompson, Daniel Calbert.

The Negro leadership class. Englewood Cliffs, N. J., Prentice-Hall [1963]

174p. 21cm. (A Spectrum book)

Includes bibliography.

Negro legislators of Texas.

M324 B75n

Brewer, John Mason, 1896–

Negro legislators of Texas and their descendants; a history of the Negro in Texas politics from reconstruction to disfranchisement, by J. Mason Brewer ... with an introduction by Herbert P. Gambrell ... Dallas, Tex., Mathis publishing co. [c1935]

x, 134 p. ports. (1 fold.) map. 20cm.

1. Negroes—Texas. 2. Negroes—Politics and suffrage. 3. Texas—Pol. & govt.—1865– 4. Negroes—Biog. I. Title. II. Title: Negro in Texas politics.

35-17051

Library of Congress E185.93.T4B7
———— Copy 2.
Copyright A 86409 [36d3] 325.2609764

Negro liberation.

M331 H335n

Haywood, Harry, 1898–

Negro liberation. New York, International Publishers [1948]

245 p. map. 22 cm.

"Reference notes": p. [219]-230.

1. Negroes—Econ. condit. 2. Negroes—Moral and social conditions. 3. Land tenure—Southern States. I. Title.

E185.6.H43 325.260973 48-8881*

Library of Congress [15]

The Negro Library Association.

M026 Sch64

Schomburg, Arthur A , comp.

Exhibition catalogue, first annual exhibition of books, manuscripts, paintings, engravings, sculptures, et cetera, by The Negro Library Association at the Carlton Avenue Young Men's Christian Association, Brooklyn, August 7 to 16, 1918 ... Compiled by Arthur A. Schomburg ... [New York, The Pool Press Association Printers, 1918]

23p. 23cm.

Negro life, Plays of.

M812.08 L79

Locke, Alain Le Roy, 1886– ***ed.***

Plays of Negro life; a source-book of native American drama, selected and edited by Alain Locke ... and Montgomery Gregory ... decorations and illustrations by Aaron Douglas. New York and London, Harper & brothers, 1927.

10 p. l., 3-430 p. front., plates. 22½ cm.

"Bibliography of Negro drama": p. 424-430.

1. Negroes in literature and art. 2. American drama (Collections) 3. Negro literature. I. Gregory, Montgomery, 1887– joint ed. II. Title. III. Title: Negro life, Plays of.

27—22553

Library of Congress PS627.N4L6 [45x2 1]

Negro life in rural Virginia.

M975.5 EL59

Ellison, John Malcus, 1889– jt. auth.

Negro life in rural Virginia, 1865-1934, by William Edward Garnett and John Malcus Ellison. [Blacksburg, Va., Virginia Polytechnic Institute, 1934]

35p. illus., maps. 23cm. (Virginia Polytechnic Institute Bulletin 295)

1. Virginia - Rural conditions. 2. Rural conditions. I. Garnett, William Edward. II. Title.

A Negro looks at war.

M350 W67n

Williams, John Henry.

A Negro looks at war, by John Henry Williams ... [New York, Workers library publishers, inc., 1940]

31 p. 19cm.

1. Negroes. 2. Negroes as soldiers. I. Title.

44-35049

Library of Congress E185.61.W735 [2] 325.260973

The Negro looks into the South.

M323 G34n

Gholson, Edward.

The Negro looks into the South. Boston, Chapman & Grimes [1947]

115 p. 21 cm.

1. Negroes. I. Title.

E185.6.G5 325.260975 47-6394*

Library of Congress
Copyright [3]

Negro makers of history.

M973 W86ne

Woodson, Carter Godwin, 1875–

Negro makers of history, by Carter G. Woodson ... Washington, D. C., The Associated publishers, inc. [c1928]

2 p. l., iii-vi, 362 p. illus. (incl. ports., facsims.) double map. 20 cm.

"An adaptation of [the author's] The Negro in our history to the capacity of children in the elementary schools."—Pref.

1. Negroes. 2. Slavery in the U. S. I. Title.

29—458

Library of Congress E185.W895 [43j1]

The Negro market.

M658.7 N31

The Negro market, published in the interest of the Negro press. Atlanta, W. B. Ziff co., c 1932.

39p. illus. 28cm.

M658.7 N31

The Negro market, published in the interest of the Negro press. Atlanta, W. B. Ziff co., c1932

39p. illus. 28cm.

1. Market surveys. ~~I. Title.~~

Negro membership in American labor unions.

M331 N21

National urban league (for social service among Negroes)

Negro membership in American labor unions, by the Department of research and investigations of the National urban league, Ira De A. Reid, director. New York, N. Y. [The Alexander press, 1930]

175 p. 23½cm.

1. Negroes—Employment. 2. Trade-unions—U. S. I. Title.

30—29407

Library of Congress E185.8.N31 [44r30i1] [331.8808] 325.26

Jamaica M974.71 M19
Negro metropolis.
McKay, Claude, 1890–
Harlem: Negro metropolis, by Claude McKay; illustrated with photographs. New York, E. P. Dutton & company, inc. [°1940]
xi p., 1 l., 15–262 p. front., illus. (facsim.) plates, ports. 22½cm.
"First edition."
1. Harlem, New York (City) 2. Negroes—New York (City) I. Title: Negro metropolis.
Library of Congress F128.68.H3M3 40—32905
[47z2] 917.471

M811.5 H87negm
The Negro mother and other dramatic recitations.
Hughes, Langston, 1902–
The Negro mother and other dramatic recitations by Langston Hughes. With decorations by Prentiss Taylor. New York The Golden Stair press 1931
20p. illus. 24cm.
"One of 17 signed copies bound in Robin's paper for presentations only.

M304 P19 v.2,no10
...The Negro people and the Communists.
Wilkerson, Doxey Alphonso, 1905–
... The Negro people and the Communists. [New York] Workers library publishers, inc., 1944]
23 p. 18cm.
At head of title: Doxey A. Wilkerson.
Portrait on title-page.
M335.4 W65n
1. Negroes. 2. Communism—U. S. I. Title.
Harvard univ. Library for Library of Congress E185.61.W67 A 44—2215
[45c1]†

M973 W86c
Negro migration.
Woodson, Carter Godwin, 1875–
A century of Negro migration, by Carter G. Woodson ... Washington, D. C., The Association for the study of Negro life and history, 1918.
vii, 221 p. maps, diagrs. 20½cm.
Bibliography: p. 193–211.
1. Negroes. I. Title. II. Title: Negro migration.
Library of Congress E185.9.M89 18—17856
[47q1]

M304 P19 v.4, no.6
Negro National Anthem.
Lyon, Ernest, 1860-1938.
" protest against the title of James Weldon Johnson's anomalous poem as a "Negro National Anthem" as subversive of patriotism [n.p. n.d.]
15p. 16cm.

M304 p19 v.2 no.3
The Negro people and the new world situation.
Ford, James W 1893–
The Negro people and the new world situation, by James W. Ford. [New York, Workers library publishers, inc., 1941]
15 p. 19cm.
"James W. Ford [biographical sketch]": p. [2]
M335.2 F75n2
1. World war, 1939– —Negroes. I. Title.
Library of Congress D810.N4F7 42-15016
[2] 940.5403

M325 Sco84m
... Negro migration during the war.
Scott, Emmett Jay, 1873–
... Negro migration during the war, by Emmett J. Scott ... New York [etc.] Oxford university press, 1920.
v p., 2 l., 3–189 p. 25cm. (Preliminary economic studies of the war, ed. by David Kinley ... no. 16)
At head of title: Carnegie endowment for international peace. Division of economics and history.
Bibliography: p. 175–183.
1. Negroes. 2. European war, 1914–1918—Economic aspects—U. S. I. Title. II. Title: Migration during the war, Negro.
Library of Congress HC56.P7 no. 16 20—9134
[41v2]

M07 Oal
The Negro newspaper.
Oak, Vishnu Vitthal, 1900–
The Negro entrepreneur. Yellow Springs, Ohio, Print. by the Antioch Press, 1948–
v. illus. 21 cm.
Bibliography: v. 1, p. 138–150.
Contents.—v. 1. The Negro newspaper.
1. Negro newspapers (American) 2. Negro newspapers (American)—Direct. I. Title. II. Title: The Negro newspaper.
E185.8.O2 071 48—6779*
Library of Congress [50q7]

M973 Ap8n
The Negro people in America.
Aptheker, Herbert, 1915–
The Negro people in America [by] Herbert Aptheker. A critique of Gunnar Myrdal's "An American dilemma." Introduction by Doxey A. Wilkerson. New York, International publishers [1946]
80 p. 20½cm.
"Reference notes": p. 63–80.
1. *Myrdal, Gunnar, 1898– An American dilemma. 2. Negroes. I. Title.
E185.6.M9517 325.260973 46–8650
© 13Nov46; International publishers co., inc.; A8978.
Library of Congress [3]

M325 Un3n
Negro migration in 1916-17.
U.S. Department of labor. Division of Negro economics.
Negro migration in 1916-17. Reports by R. H. Leavell, T. R. Snavely, T. J. Woofter, Jr., W. T. B. Williams and Francis D. Tyson, with an introduction by J. H. Dillard. Washington, Government printing office, 1919.
158p. tables. 23cm.

Brasil M981 C76 1937
O negro no Brasil.
Congresso afro-brasileiro. 2d, Bahia, 1937.
... O negro no Brasil; trabalhos apresentados ao 2.° Congresso afro-brasileiro (Bahia) ... Rio de Janeiro, Civilização brasileira s/a, 1940.
367 p. illus., fold. tab. 18½cm. (Bibliotheca de divulgação scientifica, dirigida pelo prof. dr. Arthur Ramos, vol. xx)
At head of title: Varios autores.
Includes bibliographies.
1. Negroes in Brazil. 2. Brazil—Race question. I. Title.
Library of Congress F2659.N4C65 42-3122
[2] 325.260981

M355.4 D29n
The Negro people in the struggle for peace and freedom.
Davis, Benjamin Jefferson, 1903–
The Negro people in the struggle for peace and freedom. New York, New Century, 1951.
23p. 19cm.
Report to the 15th convention, Communist party.

M207 D22
Negro ministers, The education of.
Daniel, William Andrew, 1895–
The education of Negro ministers, by W. A. Daniel; based upon a survey of theological schools for Negroes in the United States made by Robert L. Kelly and W. A. Daniel. New York, George H. Doran company [°1925]
vii p., 2 l., 13–187 p. 19½cm.
"The Institute of social and religious research ... is responsible for this publication."
1. Theological seminaries. 2. Theology—Study and teaching. 3. Negroes—Education. I. Institute of social and religious research. II. Title. III. Title: Negro ministers, The education of.
Library of Congress BV4080.D3 25—15962
[39p2]

M810.9 H87n
The Negro novelist.
Hughes, John Milton Charles, 1923–
The Negro novelist; a discussion of the writings of American Negro novelists, 1940–1950, by Carl Milton Hughes [pseud.] New York, Citadel Press [1953]
288 p. 22 cm.
Bibliography: p. [279]–285.
1. Negro fiction (American)—Hist. & crit. I. Title.
PS374.N4H8 813.509 53—11130
Library of Congress [54n10]

M335.4 D29ne
The Negro people on the march.
Davis, Benjamin Jefferson, 1903–
The Negro people on the march. New York, New Century Publishers, 1956.
48p. 18cm.
1. Communism. I. Title.

M301 B439
The Negro mood, and other essays.
Bennett, Lerone, 1928–
The Negro mood, and other essays. Chicago, Johnson Pub. Co., 1964.
ix, 104 p. 22 cm.
1. U.S.—Race question. 2. Negroes. I. Title.
E185.61.B43 301.451 64-8370
Library of Congress [5]

M973 W86ne
Negro orators and their orations.
Woodson, Carter Godwin, 1875– ed.
Negro orators and their orations, by Carter G. Woodson ... Washington, D. C., The Associated publishers, inc. [°1925]
xi p., 1 l., 711 p. 22½cm.
1. Orations. I. Title.
Library of Congress PS663.N4W6 25—20484
[45h1]

M973 L638
The Negro pilgrimage in America.
Lincoln, Charles Eric.
The Negro pilgrimage in America, by C. Eric Lincoln. New York, Bantam Books [1967]
184 p. illus., facsims., ports. 18 cm. (Bantam pathfinder editions)
1. Negroes—Hist. I. Title.
E185.L47 973'.0974'96 67-28881
Library of Congress [5]

M811.5 H87negm 1931
The Negro mother...
Hughes, Langston, 1902–
The Negro mother and other dramatic recitations, by Langston Hughes. With decorations by Prentiss Taylor. New York The Golden Stair Press c1931
20p. 24cm.

M606 T36
Negro participation in the Texas centennial...
Thomas, Jesse O 1883–
Negro participation in the Texas centennial exposition, by Jesse O. Thomas. Boston, The Christopher publishing house [°1938]
154 p. front. (port. group) plates. 20cm.
1. Negroes—Texas. 2. Dallas. Texas centennial central exposition, 1936. I. Title.
Library of Congress E185.93.T4T5 38—30208
[42d1] 325.260973

M372.4 C35b
Negro pioneers.
Chambers, Lucille Arcola
Booker T. Washington, educator. Art by John Neal. New York, C & S Ventures, 1965.
[23]p. illus. 31cm. (Negro pioneers)
"Compliments of Lucille Arcola Chambers, '67."
I. Title. II. Series.

Negro pioneers.
M372.4 C35p Chambers, Lucille Arcola
Phillis Wheatley, poetess. Art by John Neal. New York, C. & S Ventures, 1965.
[23]p. illus. 31cm. (Negro pioneers)
"Compliments of Lucille Arcola Chambers, '67."
I. Title. II. Series.

Negro population 1790-1915.
M312 Un3cr U. S. *Bureau of the census.*
... Negro population 1790-1915. Washington, Govt. print. off., 1918.
844 p. incl. maps, tables, diagrs. 30cm.
At head of title: Department of commerce. Bureau of the census. Sam. L. Rogers, director.
"Prepared by Dr. John Cummings in the Division of revision and results, under the general supervision of Dr. Joseph A. Hill."—"Letter of transmittal," p. 13.
1. Negroes. I. Cummings, John, 1868-1936. II. Hill, Joseph Adna, 1860- III. Title.
18—26864
Library of Congress HA205.A33 [42t2]

The Negro professional man and the community.
M973 W86np Woodson, Carter Godwin, 1875–
The Negro professional man and the community, with special emphasis on the physician and the lawyer, by Carter Godwin Woodson. Washington, D. C., The Association for the study of Negro life and history, inc. [c1934]
1 p. l., v–xviii, 365 p. diagr. 23½cm.
"This study forms a part of the effort of the Association for the study of Negro life and history to portray the social and economic conditions obtaining among Negroes in the United States since the civil war."—Foreword.
1. Negroes—Employment. 2. Negroes—Moral and social conditions. 3. Negro physicians. 4. Negro lawyers. I. Association for the study of Negro life and history, inc. II. Title.
34—10066
Library of Congress E185.82.W88 [34f5] 325.260973

Negro pioneers.
M372.4 C35 Chambers, Lucille Arcola
The story of George Washington Carver, scientist. Art by John Neal. New York, C & S Ventures, 1965.
[21]p. illus. 31cm. (Negro pioneers)
"Compliments, of Lucille Arcola Chambers, '67."
I. Title. II. Series.

The Negro press hits back.
M07 W65 Wilkins, Roy.
The Negro press hits back. Toronto, Reprinted from the Magazine digest, April 1943.
3-7p. 19cm.

The Negro protest.
M323.4 C54 Clark, Kenneth Bancroft, 1914–
The Negro protest: James Baldwin, Malcolm X, Martin Luther King talk with Kenneth B. Clark. Boston, Beacon Press [1963]
56 p. 21 cm.
1. Negroes. 2. U. S.—Race question. I. Title.
E185.61.C62 323.40973 63—21975
Library of Congress [64f20]

Negro poems melodies, plantation pieces, camp meeting songs, etc.
M811.5 B56n Blades, William C.
Negro poems, melodies, plantation pieces, camp meeting songs, etc., by William C. Blades. Boston, R. G. Badger [c1921]
1 p. l., 5-168 p. 20½cm.
I. Title.
22—2065
Library of Congress PS3503.L3N4 1921
——— Copy 2.
Copyright A 654342 [36c1]

The Negro press re-examined.
M07 B79n Brooks, Maxwell R
The Negro press re-examined; political content of leading Negro newspapers. Boston, Christopher Pub. House [1959]
125 p. 21 cm.
Includes bibliographies.
1. Negro press. I. Title.
PN4888.N4B7 071.3 59—8809 ‡
Library of Congress [60d5]

Negro protest thought in the twentieth century.
M973 B78 Broderick, Francis L ed.
Negro protest thought in the twentieth century. Edited by Francis L. Broderick and August Meier. Indianapolis, Bobbs-Merrill Co. [1966, c1965]
xliii, 444 p. 21 cm. (The American heritage series)
Excerpts and extracts by Negro authors.
White editor.
1. Negroes—Hist.—Sources. 2. Negroes—Civil rights—Addresses, essays, lectures. I. Meier, August, 1923– joint ed. II. Title.
E185.B87 301.45196073 65—23019
Library of Congress [67o3]

... Negro poetry and drama.
M810.9 B81n Brown, Sterling Allen, 1901–
... Negro poetry and drama, by Sterling A. Brown ... Washington, D. C., The Associates in Negro folk education, 1937.
3 p. l., 142 p. 21½cm. (Bronze booklet no. 7)
"Reading references" at end of each chapter.
1. Negroes in literature and art. 2. Negro poetry (American)—Hist. & crit. 3. Negro drama. I. Title.
38—20946
Library of Congress E185.5.B85 no. 7
——— Copy 2. PS153.N5B68
[42n2] (825.260973) 811.09

M323 N31 The Negro problem; a series of articles by representative American Negroes of today; contributions by Booker T. Washington ... W. E. Burghardt Du Bois, Paul Laurence Dunbar, Charles W. Chesnutt, and others. New York, J. Pott & company, 1903.
234 p. front., ports. 19cm.
CONTENTS.—Washington, B. T. Industrial education for the Negro.—Du Bois, W. E. B. The talented tenth.—Chesnutt, C. W. The disfranchisement of the Negro.—Smith, W. H. The Negro and the law.—Kealing, H. T. The characteristics of the Negro people.—Dunbar, P. L. Representative American Negroes.—Fortune, T. T. The Negro's place in American life at the present day.
1. Negroes. I. Washington, Booker Taliaferro, 1859?-1915, ed.
Industrial education for Negro p. 7-30 (over)
3—23404
Library of Congress E185.5.N39 [41j1]

Negro public school teachers in Tennessee.
M370. G66 Gore, George William, 1901–
In-service professional improvement of Negro public school teachers in Tennessee, by George W. Gore, jr. ... New York, Teachers college, Columbia university, 1940.
xi p., 1 l., 142 p. incl. illus., tables. 23½cm. (Teachers college, Columbia university. Contributions to education, no. 786)
Issued also as thesis (PH. D.) Columbia university.
Bibliography: p. 123-130.
1. Negroes—Education. 2. Teachers, Training of—Tennessee. 3. Education—Tennessee. 4. Teachers—Tennessee. I. Title. II. Title: Negro public school teachers in Tennessee.
40—30014
Library of Congress LC2802.T2G6 1940 a
——— Copy 2. LB5.C8 no. 786
Copyright A 139131 [41k10] 371.97409768

Negro poetry in America.
M811.09 M84 Morton, Lena Beatrice.
Negro poetry in America, by Lena Beatrice Morton. Boston, Mass., The Stratford company, 1925.
4 p. l., 71 p. illus. (music) 16cm.
"The tragedy": p. 37-71.
Bibliography: p. 36; "References used": p. 71.
1. Negro poetry (American)—Hist. & crit. 2. Tragedy. I. Title.
25—15782
Library of Congress PS310.N4M6
——— Copy 2.
Copyright A 861050 [41g1]

The Negro Problem.
M323 W93n Wright, Richard Robert, 1878–
The negro problem; being extracts from two lectures on "The sociological point of view in the study of race problems," and "The negro problem; what it is not and what it is," by R. R. Wright, jr. [Philadelphia, Printed by the A. M. E. book concern, c1911]
47 p. 18cm. $0.25
1. Negroes. 2. U. S.—Race question. I. Title.
12-1050
Library of Congress E185.61.W95
Copyright A 305268

Negro publication society of America.
M326.99B P58k 1941 Pickard, Kate E R
The kidnapped and the ransomed, by Kate E. R. Pickard ... [New York] Negro publication society of America, inc., 1941.
315, [1] p. 22cm. ([Negro publication society of America. Publications] Series I, History. No. 1)
"The first edition ... appeared in 1856."—Editor's note.
"Appendix. Seth Conklin [by W. H. Furness]": p. 293-315.
1. Still, Peter. 2. Still, Lavinia. 3. Slavery in the U. S.—Kentucky. 4. Slavery in the U. S.—Alabama. 5. Concklin, Seth, 1802-1851. I. Furness, William Henry, 1802-1896. II. Negro publication society of America. III. Title.
43—17335
Library of Congress E444.8855 [45e1] 326.92

Negro poets and their poems.
M811.08 K45 Kerlin, Robert Thomas, 1866–
Negro poets and their poems, by Robert T. Kerlin ... Washington, D. C., Associated publishers, inc. [c1923]
xv, 285 p. front., illus. (incl. ports.) 19½cm.
1. Negro authors. 2. Negro poetry (American) I. Title.
24—1295
Library of Congress PS591.N4K4 [44e1]

The Negro problem; its significance...
M323 M76n Montgomery, Leroy J
The Negro problem; its significance, strength and solution. New York, Island Press [1950]
87 p. 22 cm.
1. Negroes. I. Title.
E185.61.M7 325.260973 50-10696
Library of Congress [8]

The Negro question.
M323 St7n Storey, Moorfield.
The Negro question; An address delivered before the Wisconsin Bar Association, June 27, 1918. New York, NAACP [1918]
30p. 23cm.

The Negro politician, his success and failure.
M324 C579 Clayton, Edward Taylor, 1921–
The Negro politician, his success and failure [by] Edward T. Clayton. With an introd. by Martin Luther King, Jr. Chicago, Johnson Pub. Co., 1964.
xiv, 213 p. 22 cm.
1. Negroes—Politics and suffrage. I. Title.
E185.6.C637 62—21536
Library of Congress [65d4]

Negro problems in cities.
M323 W879 Woofter, Thomas Jackson, 1893– ed.
Negro problems in cities; a study made under the direction of T. J. Woofter, jr. Garden City, N. Y., Doubleday, Doran & company, inc., [c1928]
xiii p., 2 l., 17-284 p. illus. (maps) diagrs., form. 19½cm.
"The Institute of social and religious research ... is responsible for this publication."
CONTENTS.—pt. 1. Neighborhoods, by T. J. Woofter, jr.—pt. 2. Housing, by Madge Headley.—pt. 3. Schools, by W. A. Daniel.—pt. 4. Recreation, by H. J. McGuinn.
1. Negroes—Moral and social conditions. I. Headley, Madge. II. Daniel, William Andrew, 1895– III. McGuinn, Henry J. IV. Institute of social and religious research. V. Title.
28—8612
Library of Congress E185.86.W91
——— Copy 2.
Copyright A 1069386 [40x2]

The Negro question in the U.S.A.
M335 L62 Lightfoot, Claude
The Negro question in the U.S.A.; resolution adopted by the 17th convention of the Communist party, U.S.A. together with the address to the convention by Claude Lightfoot. [New York, New Century Publishers, 1960]
23p. 20cm.
1. Race question. 2. Communism - U.S. I. Title.

Gold Coast Negro race.
M966.7
D36a
1955
De Graft-Johnson, John Coleman, 1919–
African glory; the story of vanished Negro civilizations. New York, Praeger [1955, °1954]
209 p. illus. 23 cm. (Books that matter)
First edition published in England in 1954.
1. Africa—Hist. 2. Negro race. I. Title.
DT22.D4 1955 960 55—8000 ‡
Library of Congress [55h7]

Negro race.
M910
H81
Houston, Drusilla Dunjee.
Wonderful Ethiopians of the ancient Cushite empire, by Drusilla Dunjee Houston ... Oklahoma City, Okla., The Universal publishing company, 1926–
v. illus. 20½ cm.
1. Cushites. 2. Negro race. 3. Civilization, Ancient. I. Title. II. Title: Cushite empire.
Library of Congress GN545.H6 27—5026
——— Copy 2.
Copyright A 967452 [39d1]

Negro race.
M813.5
W93w
Wright, Richard, 1908–
White man, listen! [1st ed.] Garden City, N. Y., Doubleday, 1957.
190 p. 22 cm.
1. Negro race. I. Title.
Full name: Richard Nathaniel Wright.
HT1581.W7 *301.451 325.26 57—9702 ‡
Library of Congress [58x15]

Negro read, write and color book.
M372.45
K82
Koger, Earl
Negro read, write and color book; educational enterataining, inspiring [Illus. by Robert Louis Cooper. Baltimore]
24p. illus. 28cm.

M335.4
P42n
Negro representation - a step towards Negro freedom.
Perry, Pettis
Negro representation - a step towards Negro freedom. Introduction by Betty Gannett. New York, New Century Publishers, 1952.
24 p. 19 cm.

The Negro revolt.
M323.2
L83a
Lomax, Louis E 1922–
The Negro revolt. [1st ed.] ~~New York, Harper [1962]~~
London, H. Hamilton c1963.
271 p. 22 cm.
Includes bibliography.
1. Negroes—Civil rights. 2. ~~U. S.~~—Race question. I. Title.
E185.61.L668 301.451 62—7911 ‡
Library of Congress [10]

The Negro revolt.
M323.2
L83
Lomax, Louis E 1922–
The Negro revolt. [1st ed.] New York, Harper [1962]
271 p. 22 cm.
Includes bibliography.
1. Negroes—Civil rights. 2. U. S.—Race question. I. Title.
E185.61.L668 301.451 62—7911 ‡
Library of Congress [10]

El negro rioplatense, y otros ensayos.
M864.6
P41m
Pereda Valdés, Ildefonso, 1899–
... El negro rioplatense, y otros ensayos. Montevideo, C. García & cía, 1937.
187, [1] p., 1 l. plates. 17½ cm.
CONTENTS.—Contribución al estudio del tema del negro en la literatura castellana hasta fines de la edad de oro.—Contribución al estudio de la música popular brasileña.—Supersticiones africanas del Río de la Plata.—Los pueblos negros del Uruguay y la influencia africana en el habla rioplatense.—Vocabulario de palabras de origen africano en el habla rioplatense.—El diablo mundo y Martín Fierro.—"La mojiganga de la muerte"; una pieza menor poco conocida de Calderón.—Los antiquijotes.—El "no" japonés y la tragedia griega.—Balzac, novelista de una época.—Las ideas ultraconservadoras de Chateaubriand.
1. Negroes in literature and art. 2. Negroes in South America. 3. Literature, Modern—Addresses, essays, lectures. I. Title.
Library of Congress PQ8519.P26N4 39—10565
[42c1] 864.6

Negro Rural School Fund, Inc.
see
Rural School Fund Inc.

Negro sermons in verse.
M811.5
J63g
Johnson, James Weldon, 1871–1938.
God's trombones; seven Negro sermons in verse, by James Weldon Johnson, drawings by Aaron Douglas, lettering by C. B. Falls. New York, The Viking press, 1927.
4 p. l., 56 p. plates. 23 cm.
I. Title. II. Title: Negro sermons in verse.
Library of Congress PS3519.O2625G6 1927 27—12269
[a41j2]

The Negro since emancipation.
M973
W75
Wish, Harvey, 1909– ed.
The Negro since emancipation. Englewood Cliffs, N. J., Prentice-Hall [1964]
vi, 184 p. 21 cm. (A Spectrum book)
Bibliography: p. 183–184.
White editor.
An anthology of excerpts from the writings of 15 Negro leaders.
1. Negroes—Hist.—Addresses, essays, lectures. 2. ~~U.S.~~—Race question—Addresses, essays, lectures. I. Title.
E185.61.W79 301.451 64—23550
Library of Congress [5]

Negro slave songs in the United States.
M784
F53
Fisher, Miles Mark, 1899–
Negro slave songs in the United States. With a foreword by Ray Allen Billington. Ithaca, Cornell University Press for the American Historical Association [1953]
xv, 223 p. 24 cm.
Includes texts of the songs, without the music.
Bibliography: p. 193–213.
1. Negro songs. I. Title.
M1670.F35N4 53—13501
Library of Congress [54w15]

Negro society for historical research.
Occasional paper no. 2.
M396
F95p
[Fulton, David Bryant] 1863–
... A plea for social justice for the negro woman... Issued by the Negro society for historical research, Yonkers, N. Y. [New York] Lincoln press ass'n., 1912.
cover-title, 11p. 17½cm. (Negro society for historical research. Occasional paper no. ")
Signed: Jack Thorne [pseud.]

Negro Society for Historical Research.
Occasional paper no.3.
M304
P19
v.5, no.18
Schomburg, Arthur Alfonso, 1874–1938.
Racial integrity; a plea for the establishment of a chair of Negro history in our schools and colleges, etc. Read before the teachers' summer class at Cheney Institute, July 1913. [n. p.] A. V. Bernier [1913?]
19 p. 23 cm. (Negro Society for Historical Research. Occasional paper no. 3)
1. Negroes—Hist. 2. Negro literature. I. Title. II. Series.
E185.5.N4 no. 3 48—32619*
Library of Congress [1]

Negro soldiers.
M811.5
J24n
Jamison, Roscoe, C
Negro soldiers ("these truly are the brave") and other poems, by Roscoe C. Jamison. Second edition. St. Joseph, Mo., William F. Neil, 1918.
12 unnumb. p. port. 21½cm.

The Negro south and north.
M973
D85n
DuBois, William Edward Burghardt, 1868–
The Negro south and north, by Professor W. E. Burghardt DuBois. [Reprinted from the Bibliotheca sacra, July 1905]
500-513p. 22cm.

The Negro south and north.
M301
D853ne5
Du Bois, William Edward Burghardt, 1868–
The Negro south and north, by Professor W.E. Burghardt Du Bois. [Reprinted from the Bibliotheca sacra, July 1905]
500-513p. 22cm.

A Negro speaks of life.
M811.5
C65a
Coffey, John
A Negro speaks of life. Karlsruhe, Germany, Printed by Engelhardt and Bauer, 1961.
31p. 18cm.

The Negro spiritual speaks of life and death.
M200
T42n
Thurman, Howard, 1899–
The Negro spiritual speaks of life and death. New York, Harper [1947]
55 p. 18 cm. (The Ingersoll lecture, Harvard University, 1947)
1. Negro spirituals—Hist. & crit. I. Title. (Series)
ML3556.T56 784.756 47—12396*
Library of Congress [49n5]

Negro stars in all ages of the world.
MB
Q4n
Quick, William Harvey, 1856–
Negro stars in all ages of the world, by W. H. Quick ... ~~Henderson, N. C., D. E. Aycock, printer, 1890.~~
Richmond, Va., S.B. Adkins & Co., 1898.
272 p. 22 cm.
1. Negroes—Biog. I. Title.
Library of Congress E185.96.Q6 13-18465
Copyright 1888: 30864

Negro students & their colleges
M378
Sc8n
Scott, John Irving E
Negro students & their colleges. Boston, Meador Pub. Co. [1949]
179 p. 21 cm.
1. Negroes—Education. 2. Universities and colleges—U. S.—Direct. I. Title.
L901.S48 378.73 49—6113*
Library of Congress [15]

M974.8 P38m
... Negro survey of Pennsylvania.
Pennsylvania. *Dept. of welfare.*
... Negro survey of Pennsylvania. Harrisburg [1928]
97 p. incl. tables, diagrs. 23cm.
At head of title: Commonwealth of Pennsylvania. Department of welfare.
1. Negroes—Pennsylvania. I. Title.
28-27371 Revised
Library of Congress E185.93.P41P32
[r31d2]

Negro verse.
M808.81 H728
Hollo, Anselm, comp.
Negro verse. London, Vista Books, 1964.
48p. 18½cm.
White compiler.

M301. J63ne8
The Negro war worker in San Francisco,
Johnson, Charles Spurgeon, 1893–
The Negro war worker in San Francisco, a local self-survey. Technical staff: Charles S. Johnson, Herman H. Long [and] Grace Jones ... A project, financed by a San Francisco citizen, administered by the Y. W. C. A., and carried out in connection with the Race relations program of the American missionary association, Dr. Charles S. Johnson, director, and the Julius Rosenwald fund. [San Francisco?] 1944.
2 p. l., 98 p. 28cm.
Reproduced from type-written copy.
1. Negroes—San Francisco. I. American missionary association. II. Julius Rosenwald fund. III. Title.
45-2580
Library of Congress F869.S3J57
[8] 331.98

M304 P19 v.3,no.6
...Negro survey of Pennsylvania.
Pennsylvania. *Dept. of welfare.*
... Negro survey of Pennsylvania. Harrisburg [1928]
97 p. incl. tables, diagrs. 23cm.
At head of title: Commonwealth of Pennsylvania. Department of welfare.
1. Negroes—Pennsylvania. I. Title.
28-27371 Revised
Library of Congress E185.93.P41P32
[r31d2]

... Negro voices.
M811.08 M95
Murphy, Beatrice M *ed.*
... Negro voices, edited by Beatrice M. Murphy; illustrations by Clifton Thompson Hill. New York, H. Harrison [c1938]
173, [3] p. illus. 21½cm.
At head of title: An anthology of contemporary verse.
1. Negro poetry (American) I. Title.
39-2667
Library of Congress PS591.N4M8
[43d1] 811.50822

M335.4 W73n
Negro-white unity.
Winston, Henry.
Negro-white unity. New York, New Outlook Publishers, 1967.
31p. 20cm.
1. Race relations. 2. Communism. I. Title.

M610. C63ne5
Negro survival.
Cobb, William Montague, 1904–
Negro survival. Reprinted from the Journal of Negro education. 7:564-566, October 1938.
[564-566]p 25cm.

Negro voices in American fiction.
M811.09 G51n
Gloster, Hugh Morris, 1911–
Negro voices in American fiction. Chapel Hill, Univ. of North Carolina Press, 1948.
xiv, 295 p. 24 cm.
Bibliography: p. 273-288.
1. Negro fiction (American)—Hist. & crit. 2. Negroes in literature. 3. Negro fiction (American)—Bibl. I. Title.
PS374.N4G5 813.09 48-6740*
Library of Congress [50b²10]

M396.5 B81n
...The Negro woman worker.
Brown, *Mrs.* Jean (Collier)
... The Negro woman worker, by Jean Collier Brown ... Washington, U. S. Govt. print. off., 1938.
v, 17 p. pl. 23cm. (Bulletin of the [U. S.] Women's bureau, no. 165)
At head of title: United States Department of labor. Frances Perkins, secretary. Women's bureau. Mary Anderson, director.
"Selected references on Negro women workers": p. 16-17.
1. Women, Negro. 2. Woman—Employment—U. S. I. Title.
L 39-7
U. S. Dept. of labor Libr. for Library of Congress HD6008.A3 no. 165 HD6093.A35 no. 165
——— Copy 2. [a40f3] (331.406173)

M813.5 C82
Negro tales.
Cotter, Joseph Seamon, 1861–
Negro tales, by Joseph S. Cotter. New York, The Cosmopolitan press, 1912.
148 p. front. (port.) 19cm. $1.00
I. Title.
Library of Congress PZ3.C8274N 13-384
Copyright A 332036

M331 G82n
The Negro wage earner.
Greene, Lorenzo Johnston, 1899–
The Negro wage earner, by Lorenzo J. Greene and Carter G. Woodson. Washington, D. C., The Association for the study of Negro life and history, inc. [c1930]
xiii p., 1 l., 388 p. incl. tables, diagrs. 22½cm.
Bibliography: p. [360]-380.
1. Negroes—Employment. 2. Negroes—Moral and social conditions. I. Woodson, Carter Godwin, 1875– II. Association for the study of Negro life and history, inc. III. Title.
31-493
Library of Congress E185.8.G79
[44r37z1] 325.26

M378 N66n
The Negro woman's college education.
Noble, Jeanne L.
The Negro woman's college education. New York, Teachers College, Columbia University, 1956.
x, 163 p. form, 39 tables. 22 cm. (TC studies in education)
Bibliography: p. 145-150.
1. Women, Negro. 2. Education of women—U. S. I. Title. (Series: Teachers College studies in education)
LC1605.N6 378.73 56-8941
Library of Congress [10]

M370. M11
Negro teachers in Louisiana, The training of.
McAllister, Jane Ellen, 1899–
The training of Negro teachers in Louisiana, by Jane Ellen McAllister ... New York city, Teachers college, Columbia university, 1929.
vi, 95 p. 23½cm. (Teachers college, Columbia university. Contributions to education; no. 364)
Published also as thesis (PH. D.) Columbia university.
Bibliography: p. 95.
1. Teachers, Training of—Louisiana. 2. Negroes—Education. 3. Negroes—Louisiana. I. Title. II. Title: Negro teachers in Louisiana, The training of.
30-11081
Library of Congress LC2802.L8M3 1929 a
——— Copy 2. LB5.C8 no. 364
Copyright A 21710 [41m1] 370.7

M331.1 N213n
The Negro wage-earner and apprenticeship training programs.
National Association for the Advancement of Colored People.
The Negro wage-earner and apprenticeship training programs; a critical analysis with recommendations. New York, NAACP, 1960.
60p. 27½cm.

M331.4 Un3
...Negro women in industry.
U. S. *Women's bureau.*
... Negro women in industry. Washington, Govt. print. off., 1922.
v, 65, [1] p. front. 23cm. (Bulletin no. 20)
At head of title: U. S. Department of labor. James J. Davis, secretary. Women's bureau. Mary Anderson, director.
"This investigation was made by Miss Emma L. Shields ... in conjunction with the Division of Negro economics in the Department of labor."—Letter of transmittal.
1. Negroes—Employment. 2. Woman—Employment—U. S. 3. Women, Negro. I. U. S. Dept. of labor. Division of Negro economics. II. Shields, Emma L. III. Title.
L 22-164
U. S. Dept. of labor. Libr. for Library of Congress HD6093.A35 no. 20
[a41n1]

M979.4 B38
The Negro trail blazers of California...
Beasley, Delilah Leontium, 1871–
The negro trail blazers of California; a compilation of records from the California archives in the Bancroft library at the University of California, in Berkeley; and from the diaries, old papers and conversations of old pioneers in the state of California. It is a true record of facts, as they pertain to the history of the pioneer and present day negroes of California, by Delilah L. Beasley. Los Angeles, Cal. [Times mirror printing and binding house] 1919.
6 p. l., [17]-317 (*i. e.* 323) p. incl. ports. front. (port.) 25cm.
"Authorities consulted": 5th prelim. leaf.
1. Negroes—California. 2. California—Hist. I. Title.
19-8159
Library of Congress F870.N3B3
——— Copy 2.
Copyright A 525348 [33f1]

M331 H14
The Negro wage earner of New Jersey;
Hall, Egerton E 1886–
The Negro wage earner of New Jersey; a study of occupational trends in New Jersey, of the effect of unequal racial distribution in the occupations and of the implications for education and guidance. By Egerton E. Hall, ED. D. New Brunswick, Rutgers university, School of education [c1935]
115 p. 2 maps (incl. front.) diagrs. 23½cm.
Bibliography: p. 114-115.
1. Negroes—New Jersey. 2. Negroes—Employment. 3. Negroes—Education. 4. Negroes—Moral and social conditions. I. Title.
35-2951
Library of Congress E185.93.N54H3
——— Copy 2.
Copyright A 79660 [a41f1] 325.2609749

M304 P19 v.1, no.3
Negro women workers in the U.S.A.
Gordon, Eugene, 1890–
The position of Negro women, by Eugene Gordon and Cyril Briggs ... [New York, Workers library publishers, 1935]
15, [1] p. 15½cm.
Caption title: Negro women workers in the U. S. A.
Illustration on t.-p.
1. Women, Negro. 2. Woman—Employment. I. Briggs, Cyril V., 1888– joint author. II. Title. III. Title: Negro women workers in the U. S. A.
45-48360
Library of Congress E185.8.G67
[2]

M323 R32n
The Negro under capitalism.
Revolutionary Workers League.
The Negro under capitalism; Resolution adopted by the fourth plenum of the Central Committee of the Revolutionary Workers League. of the United States, September 3-4, 1930. Detroit, Demos Press, 193 .
12p. 27cm.
Mimeographed.

M323 W65n
The Negro wants full equality.
Wilkins, Roy, 1901-
The Negro wants full equality. New York, Committee on 100 [c1945]
14p. 23cm.
Reprinted from What the Negro wants, ed. by Rayford Logan 1944.

M784 Od8n
Negro workaday songs.
Odum, Howard Washington, 1884–
Negro workaday songs, by Howard W. Odum ... and Guy B. Johnson ... Chapel Hill, The University of North Carolina press; London, H. Milford, Oxford university press, 1926.
3 p. l., [ix]-xii, 2 l., 278 p. illus. (music) diagrs. 23½ cm. (*Half-title:* The University of North Carolina. Social study series)
"Selected bibliography": p. [265]-270.
1. Negro songs. 2. Negro songs—Hist. & crit. I. Johnson, Guy Benton, 1901– joint author. II. Title.
ML3556.O32 26-14118
Library of Congress [54g1]

M331
G76n

The Negro worker in New York City.

Granger, Lester Blackwell, 1896-

The Negro worker in New York City, prepared by Lester B. Granger under direction of Committee on Negro Welfare. New York, Welfare Council of New York City, 1941.

32p. 19cm.

M310
N31

Negro year book, an annual encyclopedia of the Negro ... 1912-

Tuskegee Institute, Ala., Negro year book publishing co., °1912-

v. illus. (incl. maps) diagrs. 19½-24cm.

No editions were published for 1920/21, 1923/24, 1927/28-1929/30.
Editor: 1912: M. N. Work.
Publishers: 1913, Negro year book co.—1914/15- Negro year book publishing co.
Title varies slightly.

See holdings card for issues in library.

1. Negroes—Year-books. I. Work, Monroe Nathan, 1866- ed.

12—14974

Library of Congress E185.5.N41

[43t2]

M310
N31

Negro year book, 1912-

Volume	Year	Month	Volume	Year	Month
	1912 1913		1952		
	1918-19 1921-22				
	1925-26 1931-32 1937-38				
	1947				

M301
F86ry

Negro youth at the crossways.

Frazier, Edward Franklin, 1894-

Negro youth at the crossways, their personality development in the middle states, by E. Franklin Frazier; prepared for the American youth commission. Washington, D. C., American council on education, 1940.

xxiii, 301, [2] p. illus. (maps) diagr. 23½ cm.

"This volume ... describes the experiences of Negro boys and girls living in Washington, D. C., and Louisville, Kentucky; these communities were selected as examples of middle-area conditions."—Pref.

1. Negroes—Moral and social conditions. 2. Youth. 3. Personality. 4. Social psychology. 5. Negroes—District of Columbia. 6. Negroes—Louisville, Ky. I. American council on education. American youth commission. II. Title.

40—32764

Library of Congress E185.6.F74

[42z7] 325.2609753

Negro youth in story and fact.

M301
R271

Reid, Ira DeAugustine, 1901-

In a minor key; Negro youth in story and fact, by Ira DeA. Reid; prepared for the American youth commission. Washington, D. C., American council on education, 1940.

8 p. l., 3-134 p., 1 l. diagrs. 20cm.

"Authorities for the facts": p. [121]-134.

1. Negroes—Moral and social conditions. 2. Negroes—Education. I. American council on education. American youth commission. II. Title. III. Title: Negro youth in story and fact.

40-10435

Library of Congress E185.6.R45

[10] 325.260973

M366.1
Am3

Negroes and freemasonry.

Williamson, Harry A.

Negroes and freemasonry [path 1] The American freemason. 7:104-111, January 1916.

M366.1
Am3

Negroes and freemasonry.

Williamson, Harry A.

Negroes and freemasonry [part 2] The American freemason. 7:153-196 February 1916.

Negroes and the law in the race's battle for liberty.

M342
St9

Styles, Fitzhugh Lee, 1899-

Negroes and the law in the race's battle for liberty, equality and justice under the Constitution of the United States; with causes celebres, by Fitzhugh Lee Styles ... Boston, The Christopher publishing house [°1937]

xi, [1], 13-320 p. front. (port.) 24cm.

The manuscript of the author's address before the National bar association at Baltimore, August 1934, on the battle of the Negro at the bar of justice, is the basis of this book. *cf.* Pref.
Bibliography: p. 320.

1. Negroes — Legal status, laws, etc. 2. Negroes—Biog. 3. Negro lawyers. 4. Law reports, digests, etc.—U. S. I. Title.

37—8583

Library of Congress E185.61.892
———— Copy 2.
Copyright A 103799 [38g3] 325.260973

Negroes and the national war front.

M815.4
D74n

Douglass, Frederick, 1817-1895.

Negroes and the national war front. An address by Frederick Douglass, with a foreword, by James W. Ford. New York, Workers library, 1942.

15p. 13 cm.

M350
Ow2n

Negroes and the war.

Owen, Chandler.

Negroes and the war. Washington, D. C., Office of War Information, 194 .

6p. illus. 34cm.

...The Negroes in a soviet America.

M304
F19
v.1, no.4

Ford, James W 1893-

... The Negroes in a soviet America. [New York, Workers library publishers, 1935]

48, [1] p. 19cm.

At head of title: By James W. Ford and James S. Allen.

M335.4
F75n

1. Negroes. 2. Communism—U. S. I. Allen, James Stewart, 1906- joint author. II. Title.

E185.61.F7 325.260973 47-38478

Library of Congress [1]

Africa
M960
N717

Negroes in Africa.

Nolen, Barbara, 1902- ed.

Africa is people; firsthand accounts from contemporary Africa. With an introd. by Mercer Cook. [1st ed.] New York, Dutton [1967]

xviii, 270p. illus., ports. 24cm.
Bibliography: p. [263]-264.
Includes extracts from books by African authors.
White editor.

1. Africa, Sub-Saharan - Civilization. 2. Negroes in Africa. I. Title. II. Cook, Mercer, 1903- Introduction.

Barbados
M942
M45

Negroes in Great Britain.

Maxwell, Neville George Anthony.

The power of Negro action, by Neville Maxwell. [London, N. G. A. Maxwell [1966]

1-69 p. 22 cm. 3/-

(B 66-5466)

Bibliography: p. 57-58.

1. West Indians in Great Britain. 2. Negroes in Great Britain. 3. Gt. Brit.—Race question. I. Title.

DA125.W4M3 301.45196042 66-70698

Library of Congress [5]

Senegal
M370
N23

Negroes in France - Education.

N'Diaye, Jean Pierre.

Enquête sur les étudiants noirs en France. Paris, Éditions "Réalités africaines" [1962]

315 p. illus. 25 cm.

1. Negroes in France—Education. I. Title.

LC2806.F8N4 63-36674 ‡

Library of Congress [61]

Negroes in literature.

M808.8
Sa59

Sanz y Díaz, José, 1907- ed.

Lira negra (selecciones españolas y afroamericanas) [Madrid, M. Aguilar, 1945]

380p. front. 12cm. (Colección Crisol, núm. 21)

White editor.

Negroes in rural communities, Availability of education to.

M379.173
C12

Caliver, Ambrose, 1894-

... Availability of education to Negroes in rural communities, by Ambrose Caliver, senior specialist in the education of Negroes, Office of education ... Washington, U. S. Govt. print. off., 1936.

iv, 86 p. tables. 23cm. (U. S. Office of education. Bulletin, 1935, no. 12)

At head of title: United States Department of the interior, Harold L. Ickes, secretary. Office of education, J. W. Studebaker, commissioner.

1. Negroes—Education. I. Title. II. Title: Negroes in rural communities, Availability of education to.

E 36—2

U. S. Off. of educ. Library L111.A6 1935 no. 12
———— Copy 2. LC2801.C346
for Library of Congress L111.A6 1935, no. 12
———— Copy 2. LC2801.C21

[a41n2]

M370
C12a

Negroes in rural communities, Availability of education to.

Caliver, Ambrose, 1894-

...Availability of education to Negroes in rural communities, by Ambrose Caliver, senior specialist in the education of Negroes. Office of education ... Washington, U.S. Govt. print. off., 1936.

iv, 86p. tables. 23cm. (U.S. Office of Education. Bulletin, 1935. no.12)

At head of title: United States Department of the interior, Harold L. Ickes, secretary.

(over)

Negroes in South Africa.

South Africa
M916.8
M27

Magidi, Dora Thizwilondi, *pseud.*

Black background; the childhood of a South African girl [by] John Blacking. New York, Abelard-Schuman [1964]

207 p. illus. 22 cm.

"Based on the autobiography of Dora Thizwilondi Magidi."
Bibliography: p. 203-207.

1. Negroes in South Africa. I. Blacking, John. II. Title.

DT761.M16 916.8 64-12734

Library of Congress [5]

Negroes in the labor unions in Manhattan.

M331
F85

Franklin, Charles Lionel, 1910-

The Negro labor unionist of New York; problems and conditions among Negroes in the labor unions in Manhattan with special reference to the N. R. A. and post-N. R. A. situations, by Charles Lionel Franklin ... New York, 1936.

2 p. l., 7-417 p. 22½cm.
Thesis (PH. D.)—Columbia university, 1936.
Vita.
Published also as Studies in history, economics and public law, ed. by the Faculty of political science of Columbia university, no. 420.
Bibliography: p. 398-402.
1. Negroes—New York (City) 2. Negroes—Employment. 3. Trade-unions—New York (City) 4. Labor and laboring classes—New York (City) I. Title. II. Title: Negroes in the labor unions in Manhattan.

36—34118

Library of Congress E185.8.F732
Columbia Univ. Libr. [39d1] 331.88097471

Negroes in the making of America.

M301
D853g

Du Bois, William Edward Burghardt, 1868-

The gift of black folk; the Negroes in the making of America, by W. E. Burghardt Du Bois ... introduction by Edward F. McSweeney ... Boston, Mass., The Stratford co., 1924.

2 p. l., iv, 349 p. 19½cm. (*On cover:* Knights of Columbus racial contribution series)

1. Negroes. 2. U. S.—Race question. I. Title. II. Title: Negroes in the making of America.

24—17975

Library of Congress E185.D83

[45v1]

The Negroes of Cinclare Central Factory and Calumet Plantation.

M975
N31

Laws, J Bradford

The Negroes of Cinclare Central Factory and Calumet Plantation, Louisiana. [Bulletin of the Labor Dept. no.38, 1902] pp. 95-120.

In: The Negro in the black belt... Washington, D.C., Dept. of Labor, [189 - 190]

The Negroes of Farmville, Virginia.

M975
N31

Du Bois, Willia, Edward Burghardt, 1898-
The Negroes of Farmville, Virginia: A social study. [Bulletin of the Labor Dept., no.14, 1898] pp. 1-38.

In: The Negro in the black belt... Washington, D.C., Dept. of Labor, [1897-1902]

The Negroes of Litwalton,

M975
N31

Thom, William Taylor.
The Negroes of Litwalton, Virginia: A social study of the Oyster Negro. [Bulletin of the Labor Dept., no.37, 1901. pp. 1115-1170.

In: The Negro in the black belt... Washington, D.C., Dept. of Labor [1897-1902]

The Negroes of Nebraska.

M978.2
W93n

Writers' program. *Nebraska.*
The Negroes of Nebraska, written and compiled by workers of the Writers' program, Work projects administration in the state of Nebraska. Sponsored by the Omaha urban league community center. Drawings by Paul Gibson. Lincoln, Neb., Woodruff printing company, 1940.

48 p. illus. 21½cm.

1. Negroes—Nebraska. I. Title.

40—13925

Library of Congress E185.93.N5W7
[42d1] 325.2609782

M973.8
W51n

The Negroes of New York in the emancipation movement.
Wesley, Charles Harris, 1891-
The Negroes of New York in the emancipation movement. Reprinted from the Journal of Negro history, 24:65-103, January 1939.

65-103p. 24½cm.

The Negroes of Sandy Spring, Maryland.

M975
N31

Thom, William Taylor.
The Negroes of Sandy Spring, Maryland: A social study. Bulletin of the Labor Dept., no.32. 1901. pp. 43-102.
In: The Negro in the black belt... Washington, D.C., Dept. of Labor, [1897-1902]

The Negroes of Xenia, Ohio.

M975
N31

Wright, Richard Robert, Jr., 1878-
The Negroes of Xenia, Ohio: A social study. [Bulletin of the Labor Dept., no.48. 1903] pp. 1007-1044.
In: The Negro in the black belt... Washington, D.C., Dept. of Labor [1897-1902]

Negroes with guns.

M323.1
W67

Williams, Robert Franklin, 1925-
Negroes with guns. Edited by Marc Schleifer. New York, Marzani & Munsell [©1962]

128p. illus. 21cm.

Puerto Rico
M864.
P141

Negron Munoz, Angela.
Pagán, Bolívar, 1899-
... Ideales en marcha; discursos y artículos. San Juan, Puerto Rico, Biblioteca de autôres puertorriqueños, 1939.

3 p. l., [9]-306 p., 3 l. 20cm.

"En homenaje a Bolívar Pagán [discurso pronunciado por Rafael Martínez Nadal, en junio 25, 1937]": p. [7]-19.
"Hablando con Bolívar Pagán [entrevista, de Angela Negrón Muños, abril 2, 1933]": p. [21]-38.

1. Puerto Rico—Pol. & govt.—1898- I. Martínez Nadal, Rafael, 1878- II. Negrón Muñoz, Angela. III. Title.

40—2988

Library of Congress F1975.P26
[42c1] 972.95

The Negro's adventure in general business.

M07
Oal

Oak, Vishnu Vitthal, 1900-
The Negro entrepreneur. Yellow Springs, Ohio, Print. by the Antioch Press, 1948-

v. illus. 21 cm.

Bibliography: v. 1, p. 133-150.

CONTENTS.—v. 1. The Negro newspaper.

1. ~~Negro~~ newspapers (American) 2. ~~Negro~~ newspapers (American)—Direct. I. Title. II. Title: The Negro newspaper.

E185.8.O2 071 48—6779*

Library of Congress [50q7]

Brasil
M869
C21n

Negros bantus.
Carneiro de Souza, Edison, 1912-
...Negros bantus; notas de ethnographia religiosa e de folklore. Rio de Janeiro, Civilização brasileira, s. a., 1937.

187, [2]p. plates, ports., map. 18½cm. (Biblioteca de divulgação scientifica, sob a direcção de Arthur Ramos. vol. xiv)

The Negro's church.

M260
M45nc

Mays, Benjamin Elijah, 1895-
The Negro's church, by Benjamin Elijah Mays and Joseph William Nicholson. New York, Institute of social and religious research [©1933]

xiii, 321 p. illus. (maps) 19½cm.

"The Institute of social and religious research ... is responsible for this publication."—p. [ii]

1. Negroes—Religion. 2. Churches—U. S. I. Nicholson, Joseph William, joint author. II. Institute of social and religious research. III. Title.

33—6340

Library of Congress BR563.N4M3
——— Copy 2.
Copyright A 59658 [a40q2] [261] 325.260073

The Negro's contribution in art to American culture.

M306
N21p

Locke, Alain Leroy, 1886-
The Negro's contribution in art to American culture. Chicago, 1933.

In: National Conference of Social Work. Proceedings... of the fifty-ninth annual session. Chicago, Univ. of Chicago for the Conference, 1933. pp. 315-322.

The Negro's contribution to American culture.

M810.9
W58n

White, Walter Francis, 1893-
The Negro's contribution to American culture, the sudden flowering of a genius-laden artistic movement, by Walter White. Girard Kansas, Haldeman - Julius publications c1928
64p. 12½cm. (Little blue book no. 1306, edited by E. Haldeman - Juilus)

A Negro's faith in America.

M323
L82n

Logan, Spencer, 1911-
A Negro's faith in America, by Spencer Logan. New York, The Macmillan company, 1946.

vi p., 1 l., 88 p. 21 cm.

"First printing."

1. Negroes. I. Title.

46—4456

Library of Congress E185.61.L66
[47j7] 325.260973

The Negro's God as reflected in his literature.

M260
M45ng

Mays, Benjamin Elijah, 1895-
The Negro's God as reflected in his literature [by] Benjamin E. Mays ... lithographs by James L. Wells. Boston, Chapman & Grimes, inc. [©1938]

viii p., 1 l., 269 p. 20cm.

Bibliography: p. 257-263.

1. Negro literature—Hist. & crit. 2. Negroes—Religion. 3. God. 4. Religion in literature. I. Title.

38—37550

Library of Congress PS153.N5M3
[43i1] [231] 810.9

Ghana
M966.7
C89n

The Negro's memorial, or abolitionist's catechism; by an abolitionist. London, Printed for the author and sold by Hatchard and Co., 1825.

127p. 21½cm.
Includes: Ottobah Cugoana's narrative.

1. Abolitionist.

The Negro's progress in fifty years.

M973.8
Am3

American academy of political and social science, *Philadelphia.*
The Negro's progress in fifty years ... Philadelphia, American academy of political and social science [©1913]

vi p., 1 l., 266 p. 25cm. (*Its* Annals. vol. XLIX, whole no. 138)

"The papers in this publication were collected and edited by J. P. Lichtenberger."

CONTENTS.—pt. I. Statistical: Negro population in the United States, by T. J. Jones.—pt. II. Business activities and labor conditions: Professional and skilled occupations, by K. Miller. The Negro in unskilled labor, by R. R. Wright, jr. Development in the tidewater counties of Virginia, by T. C. Walker. The Negro and the immigrant in the two Americas, by J. B. Clarke. The tenant system and some changes since

(Continued on next card)

13—22311

[42n2]

The Negro's view of organic union.

M287.6
L99n

Lyon, Ernest, 1860-
The negro's view of organic union, by Ernest Lyon ... introduction by George A. Owens. New York, Cincinnati, The Methodist book concern [©1915]

64 p. 17½cm. $0.25

"The question of organic union of the Methodist Episcopal church and the Methodist Episcopal church, South."—Introd.

I. Title.

Library of Congress 16-7676
Copyright A 427395

Negros famosos da América do norte.

M813.5
H87negf

Hughes, Langston, 1902-
Negros famosos da América do norte. (Famous American Negroes). Tradução de Helena R. Gandelman e Maris Helená Muus. São Paulo, Editôra Clássico-Cientifica, 1957.

114p. 21½cm.
"For Arthur Spingarn - Sincerely - Langston Hughes, New York, October, 1958."

M813.3
N312

Neilson, Peter, 1795-1861.
The life and adventure of Zamba, an African negro king; and his experience of slavery in South Carolina. Written by himself. Corrected and arranged by Peter Neilson. London, Smith, Elder and co., ~~1847.~~ 1850.

xx, 258 p. front. 20½ cm.

Written by Peter Neilson. *cf.* Dict. nat. biog.

1. Slavery in the U. S.—Fiction. 2. South Carolina—Soc. life & cust. I. Title. II Zamba, an African negro king

Library of Congress PZ3.N318L 7—33168
[a28d1]

Jamaica
M820
N38

Neita, Hartley
The mermaid's comb.

Pp. 61-64.

In: Hendriks, A. L., ed. The independence anthology of Jamaican literature. Kingston, Arts Celebration Committee, Ministry of Development and Welfare, 1962.

M89 H87a6
Nel mare della vita.
Hughes, Langston, 1902-
Nel mare della vita. Einaudi, 1948.
439 p. 19 cm.

M350 N32c
Nell, William Cooper, 1816-1874.
The colored patriots of the American revolution, with sketches of several distinguished colored persons: to which is added a brief survey of the condition and prospects of colored Americans. By William C. Nell. With an introduction by Harriet Beecher Stowe. Boston, R. F. Wallcut, 1855.
396 p. 2 pl. (incl. front.) fold. facsim. 19½cm.
1. U. S.—Hist.—Revolution—Negro troops. 2. Negroes. I. Stowe, Mrs. Harriet Elizabeth (Beecher) 1811-1896. II. Title.
4—5729
Library of Congress E269.N3N4 [42g1]

M350 N32 1851
Nell, William Cooper, 1816-1874
Services of colored Americans, in the wars of 1776 and 1812. By William C. Nell. Boston, Printed by Prentiss & Sawyer, 1851.
24 p. 23½cm.
1. U. S.—Hist.—Revolution—Negro troops. 2. U. S.—Hist.—War of 1812—Negro troops. 3. Soldiers.
5-23354
Library of Congress E269.N3N43

M350 N32 1852
Nell, William Cooper, 1816-1874
Services of colored americans, in the wars of 1776 and 1812. By William C. Nell. 2nd ed. Boston, Robert F. Wallcut, 1852.
40p. 30cm.
1. U. S.—Hist.—Revolution
2. U. S.—Hist.—War of 1812
3. Soldiers

M815 N33d
Nelson, Alice Ruth (Moore) Dunbar, 1875-1935 ed.
The Dunbar speaker and entertainer, containing the best prose and poetic selections by and about the Negro race, with programs arranged for special entertainments ed. by Alice Moore Dunbar-Nelson, with an introduction by Leslie Pinckney Hill ... Naperville, Ill., J. L. Nichols & co. [c1920]
288 p. front., illus., plates, ports. 21½ cm.
1. Readers and speakers—1870-
20—21507
Library of Congress PN4305.N5N4 [41f1]

M813.4 D911g
Nelson, Mrs. Alice Ruth (Moore) Dunbar, 1875-1935 ed.
The goodness of St. Rocque, and other stories, by Alice Dunbar. New York, Dodd, Mead and company, 1899.
5 p. l., [3]-224 p. 17½cm.
CONTENTS.—The goodness of Saint Rocque.—Tony's wife.—The fisherman of Pass Christian.—M'sieu Fortier's violin.—By the bayou St. John.—When the bayou overflows.—Mr. Baptiste.—A carnival jangle.—Little Miss Sophie.—Sister Josepha.—The praline woman.—Odalie.—La Juanita.—Titee.
I. Title.
99—5827
Library of Congress PZ3.N328Go [a42r21f1]

M815 N33
Nelson, Mrs. Alice Ruth (Moore) Dunbar, 1875-1935 ed.
Masterpieces of negro eloquence; the best speeches delivered by the negro from the days of slavery to the present time, ed. by Alice Moore Dunbar. New York, The Bookery publishing company [c1914]
512 p. front. (port.) 23cm.
(over)
1. American orations. I. Title. II. Title: Negro eloquence.
14—1960
Library of Congress PS663.N4N4
——— Copy 2.
Copyright A 362234 [33g1]

M813.5 N33a
Nelson, Annie (Greene)
... After the storm, a novel. Columbia, S. C., Hampton publishing company, 1942.
131 p. 23½cm.
I. Title.
42-14035
Library of Congress PZ3.N329Af [2]

M813.5 N33d
Nelson, Annie (Greene)
... The dawn appears, a novel. Columbia, S. C., Hampton publishing company, 1944.
4 p. l., 135 p. 20cm.
I. Title.
44-4354
Library of Congress PZ3.N329Daw [3]

M323.4 N33
Nelson, Bernard Hamilton, 1911-
The fourteenth amendment and the Negro since 1920; a dissertation... by Bernard H. Nelson. Washington, The Catholic university of American press, 1946.
viii, 185p. 22½cm.
1. Fourteenth amendment.

M304 P19 v.6, no.13
Nelson, Cleland K
Miller, George Frazier
A reply to the political plea of Bishop Cleland K Nelson and Bishop Thomas F. Gailor at the Cathedral of St. John the Divine in the city of New York, Sunday evening, October 19, 1913. A sermon by Reverend George Frazier Miller... October 26, 1913. Brooklyn, The interboro Press, 1913.
[8]p. 22cm.

M359 N331
Nelson, Dennis Denmark, 1907-
The integration of the Negro into the U. S. Navy. New York, Farrar, Straus and Young [1951]
xv, 238 p. illus., ports. 22 cm.
Bibliography: p. 235-238.
1. U. S. Navy—Negroes. 2. Negroes as seamen. I. Title. ViHaI
E185.63.N4 1951 325.260973 51-12820
Library of Congress [20]

M359 N331 1948
Nelson, Dennis Denmark, 1907-
The integration of the Negro into the United States Navy, 1776-1947, with a brief historical introduction. [Washington] 1948.
1 v. (various pagings) illus., ports. 27 cm.
Cover title.
"A monograph from the thesis by the same title submitted to the Department of Sociology, Howard University, in partial fulfillment of the requirements for the degree of master of arts."
Seal of Navy Department, United States of America, on cover.
"Navexos-P-526."
Bibliography: p. 209-212.
1. U. S. Navy—Negroes. 2. Negroes as seamen. I. U. S. Navy Dept. II. Title.
E185.63.N4 1948 325.260973 48—46195*
Library of Congress [48c2]

M261 N33c
Nelson, William Stuart, 1895- ed.
The Christian way in race relations. [1st ed.] New York, Harper [1948]
ix, 256 p. 21 cm.
"The result of a co-operative enterprise on the part of the members of the Institute of Religion."
1. U. S.—Race question. 2. Church and social problems—U. S. I. Institute of Religion, Howard University, Washington, D. C. II. Title.
BR115.R3N4 261 48—5726*
Library of Congress [49d10]

M973 N33
Nelson, William Stuart. 1895-
... La race noire dans la démocratie américaine. Paris, Groupe d'études en vue du rapprochement international [L'émancipatrice imprimerie] 1922.
x, 84, [2] p. illus. 18cm.
1. Negroes. I. Title.
24—195
Library of Congress E185.N43 [41b1]

Haiti M972.94 N34
Nemours, Alfred, 1883-
... La charte des Nations unies; étude comparative de la charte avec: les propositions de Dumbarton Oaks, le covenant de la Société des nations, les conventions de la Haye, les propositions et doctrines inter américaines. Port-au-Prince, Haïti, H. Deschamps, 1945.
xv, 17-188 p., 1 l. 20½cm.
At head of title: Général Nemours.
"Liste des ouvrages du général Nemours": p. viii-x.
1. United nations. Charter.
JX1976.N36 341.1 46-22436
Library of Congress [2]

Haiti M972.94 N34c
Nemours, Alfred, 1883-
... Craignons d'être un jour l'Éthiopie de quelqu'un, conflit italo-éthiopien 1935. Port-au-Prince, Haïti, Imp. du Collège Vertières, 1945.
5 p. l., 9-82 p. 22½cm.
At head of title: Général Nemours.
"Références": p. 77-80.
1. Italo-Ethiopian war, 1935-1936. 2. League of nations. I. Title.
DT387.8.N33 A 47-2399
New York. Public library for Library of Congress [2]†

Haiti M972.94 N34ha
Nemours, Alfred. 1883-
Haiti et la Guerre de l'Indépendance Américaine. Port-au-Prince, Henri Deschamps, 1952.
xi, 121 p. 19cm.
1. U.S. - Hist. - Revolution.
I. Title. 2. Haiti - History - To 1791.

Haiti M972.94 M34hie
Nemours, Alfred, 1883-
Histoire de la captivité et de la mort de Toussaint Louverture. Notre pèlerinage au Fort de Joux, avec les documents inedits. Paris, Editions Berger-Levrault, 1929.
315[2]p. 22cm.
At head of title: Général Nemours.
1. Toussaint Louverture, Pierre Dominique, 1746?-1803. 2. Haiti.

Haiti M89 T64nh
Nemours, Alfred, 1883-
... Histoire de la famille et de la descendance de Toussaint-Louverture. Avec des documents inédits et les portraits des descendants de Toussaint-Louverture jusqu'à nos jours. Port-au-Prince, Haïti, Imprimerie de l'État, 1941.
4 p. l., vii-viii, 303 p. front., pl., ports. 23cm.
At head of title: Général Nemours.
Bibliography: p. 290-302.
1. Toussaint Louverture, Pierre Dominique, 1746?-1803. 2. Louverture family. I. Title.
A 41—1743
Harvard univ. Library for Library of Congress F1923.T8007 [43c1] 923.27294

Haiti M972.94 N34hi
Nemours, Alfred, 1883-
... Histoire des relations internationales de Toussaint Louverture. Avec des documents inédits. Port-au-Prince, Haïti, Impr. du Collège Vertières, 1945.
208 p. incl. port. 22½ cm.
At head of title: Général Nemours.
"Liste des ouvrages du général Nemours": p. [7]-[0] "Bibliographie": p. 202-206.
1. Toussaint Louverture, Pierre Dominique, 1746?-1803. 2. Haiti—For. rel. I. Title.
A 45—4110
Harvard Univ. Library for Library of Congress [48c1]

Haiti
M972.94
N34h
Nemours, Alfred, 1883-
... Histoire militaire de la guerre d'indépendance de Saint-Domingue ...
Paris, Berger-Levrault, 1925- 1928
2v. fold. map. 22½cm.

1. Haiti—Hist.—Revolution, 1791-1804. I. Title.
Library of Congress F1923.N44 27-8243 [2]

Haiti
M841
N35g
Neptune, Louis. 1920-
Couttes de fiel. Collection de la vie violente. Port-au-Prince, Haiti, Imp. Henri Deschamps [1946].
19p. port. 21½cm.
1. Haitian poetry.
I. Title

A new birth of freedom.
M323
N21
National Association for the Advancement of Colored People.
A new birth of freedom; NAACP report for 1964. New York [1965]
110p. illus.

Haiti
M972.94
N34Pr
Nemours, Alfred, 1883-
... Les premiers citoyens et les premiers députés noirs et de couleur; la loi du 4 avril 1792, ses précédents, sa première application à Saint-Domingue, d'après des documents inédits de l'époque. Suivi de: Le Cap Français en 1792, à l'arrivée de Sonthonax, d'après des documents inédits de l'époque. Port-au-Prince, Haiti, Imprimerie de l'état, 1941.
2 p. l., 170 p. plates. 23cm.
At head of title: Général Nemours.
"Bibliographie": p. 167-168.
1. Haiti — Pol. & govt.—1791-1804. 2. France — Colonies — Santo Domingo. I. Title. II. Title: Le Cap Français en 1792.
Library of Congress F1923.N45 42-4318 [2] 972.94

Nesbitt, C. R., ed.
M811.4
B69v
Boyd, John.
The vision, and other poems, in blank verse, by John Boyd, a man of colour. Pub. for the author's benefit, and prefaced by some preliminary observations, by C. R. Nesbitt ... Exeter, Printed by R. J. Trewman; London, Longman and co., 1834.
xix, 23, [1] p. 18½cm.
I. Nesbitt, C. R., ed. II. Title.
Library of Congress PR4161.B46V5 1834 18-14708

New Caravan.
M810.8
Am29
1936
The American caravan, a yearbook of American literature...New York, The Macaulay company, 1936.
ix, 663p. 22cm.
Title varies: The New caravan.
Partial contents: Big boy leaves home, by Richard Wright. -Blue meridian, [poem], by Jean Toomer.

Haiti
M972.94
N34p
Nemours, Alfred, 1883-
Princesses creoles. Lettre-preface de M. Claude Farrere. Paris, Berger-Levrouet, editeurs, 1927.
69 1 p. 15cm.
1. Creole dialects. I. Title.
2. Haiti - Creole dialects.

Nesbitt, William
Address to the colored people of the United States
M973.6
N21c
1865
National Equal Rights League. Cleveland, Ohio
Proceedings of the first annual meeting of the National Equal Rights League, held in Cleveland, Ohio, October 19, 20 and 21, 1865. Philadelphia, E. C. Markley & Son, 1865.
54p. 21cm.

A new deal in Central Africa.
Rhodesia
M968.9
C43
Leys, Colin, ed.
A new deal in Central Africa, edited by Colin Leys and Cranford Pratt. New York, Praeger [1960]
226 p. illus. 22 cm. (Books that matter)
Includes bibliography.
1. Rhodesia and Nyasaland. I. Pratt, Cranford, joint ed. II. Title.
DT856.L4 968.9 60-12201 ‡
Library of Congress [20]

H
M 844.8
N34p
Nemours, Alfred, 1883-
Princesses creoles. Lettre-preface de M. Claude Farrere. Paris, Berger-Levrouet, editeurs, 1927.
69 1 p. 19cm.
1. Haitian literature. I. Title.

Netherlands-Hist.-1648-1714-Fiction.
France
M840
D89tu
Dumas, Alexandre, 1802-1870.
La tulipe noire. Bruxelles, Meline, Cans et cie., 1850.
2 vols in one. 15cm.

New England.
M326.
G83n
Greene, Lorenzo Johnston, 1899-
The Negro in colonial New England, 1620-1776, by Lorenzo Johnston Greene ... New York, Columbia university press; London, P. S. King & Staples, ltd., 1942.
404 p. 23 cm. (*Half-title:* Studies in history, economics and public law, ed. by the Faculty of political science of Columbia university. No. 494)
Issued also as thesis (PH. D.) Columbia university.
Bibliography: p. 361-384.
1. Slavery in the U. S.—New England. 2. Negroes—New England. 3. New England—Hist.—Colonial period. I. Title.
Library of Congress H31.C7 no. 494 43-2384
——— Copy 2. E444.N5G7 1942a
[48x2] (308.2) 326.974

Haiti
M89
T64nt
Nemours, Alfred, 1883-
... Toussaint Louverture fonde à Saint-Domingue la liberté et l'égalite, avec des documents inédits. Port-au-Prince, Haïti, Imp. du Collège Vertières, 1945.
104 p. group port. 23cm.
At head of title: Général Nemours.
"Bibliographie": p. 97-102.
1. Toussaint Louverture, Pierre Dominique, 1746?-1803. 2. Haiti—Hist.—Revolution, 1791-1804.
F1923.T89072 923.27294 A 46-6000
New York. Public library for Library of Congress [2]†

S.Africa
M896
M88
Neto, Antonio Agostinho, 1922-
Friend Mussunda
Pp. 311-312
In: Mphahlele, Ezekiel, ed. African writing today. Baltimore, Pengrin Books, 1967.

New England-Hist.-Colonial period.
M326.
G83n
Greene, Lorenzo Johnston, 1899-
The Negro in colonial New England, 1620-1776, by Lorenzo Johnston Greene ... New York, Columbia university press; London, P. S. King & Staples, ltd., 1942.
404 p. 23 cm. (*Half-title:* Studies in history, economics and public law, ed. by the Faculty of political science of Columbia university. No. 494)
Issued also as thesis (PH. D.) Columbia university.
Bibliography: p. 361-384.
1. Slavery in the U. S.—New England. 2. Negroes—New England. 3. New England—Hist.—Colonial period. I. Title.
Library of Congress H31.C7 no. 494 43-2384
——— Copy 2. E444.N5G7 1942a
[48x2] (308.2) 326.974

Guinea
M896.1
N34L
Nenekhaly-Camara, Condotto
Lagunes. [par] Nene Khaly. [n.p.] Editions de L'A.P.L.P. [n.d.]
22p. 19cm.
Autographed.
I. Title.

Africa
M896
N297
Neves, João Alves das, ed.
Poetas e contistas Africanos de expressão Portuguesa: Cabo verde, Guiné, São Tomé e príncipe, Angola, Moçambique. [São Paulo] Editôra Braziliense [1963]
211p. 20½cm.
White editor
1. Portuguese literature - Africa.
2. African literature. I. Title.

New frontiers of the American Reconstruction.
M973.8
F854
Hyman, Harold Melvin, 1924- , ed.
New frontiers of the American Reconstruction, edited by Harold M. Hyman. Urbana, University of Illinois Press, 1966.
x, 156p. 24cm.
Papers presented at a conference held at the University of Illinois in April 1965.
Includes bibliographical footnotes.
White editor.
Partial contents.- Reconstruction and the Negro, by John Hope Franklin.

Ghana
M960
N65n
Neo-colonialism; the last stage of imperialism.
Nkrumah, Kwame, *Pres. Ghana*, 1909-
Neo-colonialism; the last stage of imperialism. New York, International Publishers [1966, °1965]
xx, 280 p. col. map (on lining papers) 24 cm.
Bibliography: p. 260-262.
1. Investments, Foreign—Africa. 2. Africa—Foreign economic relations. 3. Africa—Indus. I. Title.
HC502.N5 1966 338.96 66—18026
Library of Congress [66f5]

New American caravan.
M810.8
Am29
1929
The American caravan, a yearbook of American literature...New York, The Macaulay company, 1929.
viii, 465p. 21cm.
Title varies: The New American caravan.
Partial contents: York Beach by Jean Toomer.

The new grand army.
M811.5
P182n
Palmer, Vernon Urquhart, 1930-
The new grand army; poems. New York, Vantage Press [1965]
64p. 21cm.
I. Title.

M378
C68c
New Haven, Connecticut.
College for colored youth: An account of the New-Haven city meeting and resolutions, with recommendations of the college, and strictures upon the doings of New-Haven. New York. Published by the Committee ⌊for superintending the application for funds for the College of Colored Youth⌋ 1831.

24p. 20½cm.

New Jersey.
M973.6
C83
1849
Coloured Citizens of New Jersey.
Proceedings and address of the coloured citizens of N.J. convened at Trenton, August 21st and 22nd, 1849, for the purpose of taking the initiatory measure for obtaining the right of suffrage, in this our native state.
⌊Lacks imprint, 1849⌋
9p. 14½cm.

New Jersey.
M331
H14
Hall, Egerton E 1886–
The Negro wage earner of New Jersey; a study of occupational trends in New Jersey, of the effect of unequal racial distribution in the occupations and of the implications for education and guidance. By Egerton E. Hall, ED. D. New Brunswick, Rutgers university, School of education ⌊°1935⌋

115 p. 2 maps (incl. front.) diagrs. 23½cm.

Bibliography: p. 114–115.

1. Negroes—New Jersey. 2. Negroes—Employment. 3. Negroes—Education. 4. Negroes—Moral and social conditions. I. Title.

Library of Congress E185.93.N54H3 35—2951
——— Copy 2.
Copyright A 79660 ⌊a41f1⌋ 325.2600749

M304
P19
V.7,no.3
New Jersey.
New Jersey Conference of Social Work.
Interracial Committee.
New Jersey's twentieth citizen; The Negro. Newark, Interacial Committee of the New Jersey Conference of Social Work, 1932.

18p. illus. 23cm.

M301
R27n5
New Jersey.
Reid, Ira DeAugustine, 1901–
The Negro in New Jersey; report of a survey by the Interracial committee of the New Jersey Conference of Social Work in cooperation with the state Department of Institutions and Agencies. ⌊Ira DeA. Reid, director⌋
⌊Newark⌋ 1932.

116p. incl. front. (map) diagrs. 28cm.

M370
W92
New Jersey.
Wright, *Mrs.* Marion Manola (Thompson) 1904–
The education of Negroes in New Jersey ⌊by⌋ Marion M. Thompson Wright ... New York, Teachers college, Columbia university, 1941.

ix p., 1 l., 227 p. 23½cm. (Teachers college, Columbia university. Contributions to education, no. 815)

Issued also as thesis (PH. D.) Columbia university.
Bibliography: p. 212–227.

1. Negroes—Education. 2. Negroes—New Jersey. I. Title.

41–19595 Revised
Library of Congress LC2802.N5W7 1941
⌊r42i3⌋ 371.97409749

New Jersey
M974.9
W93n
Wright, Marion Thompson
New Jersey laws and the Negro. Washington, D.C., The Association for the Study of Negro Life and History, 1943.

45p. 24cm.
Reprinted from the Journal of Negro History, 28, no.2, April, 1943.

M323.4
N45c
New Jersey. *Committee on Civil Liberties.*
Civil liberties in New Jersey; a report submitted to Alfred E. Driscoll, Governor of New Jersey. ⌊Trenton⌋ 1948.

viii, 24 p. 23 cm.

1. Civil rights—New Jersey.

JC599.U52N4 1948 323.4 48–45368*
Library of Congress ⌊2⌋

M301
R27n5
New Jersey, Dept. of Institutions and Agencies.
Reid, Ira DeAugustine, 1901–
The Negro in New Jersey; report of a survey by the Interracial committee of the New Jersey Conference of Social Work in cooperation with the state Department of Institutions and Agencies. ⌊Ira DeA.Reid, director⌋
⌊Newark⌋ 1932.

116p. incl. front. (map) diagrs. 28cm.

M304
P19
V.7,no.3
New Jersey Conference of Social Work.
Interracial Committee.
New Jersey's twentieth citizen; The Negro. Newark, Interacial Committee of the New Jersey Conference of Social Work, 1932.

M304
P19
V.7,no.31
18p. illus. 23cm.

1. Race Relations - New Jersey. 2. New Jersey.

M301
R27n5
New Jersey Conference of Social Work.
Interracial Committee.
Reid, Ira DeAugustine, 1901–
The Negro in New Jersey; report of a survey by the Interracial committee of the New Jersey Conference of Social Work in cooperation with the state Department of Institutions and Agencies. ⌊Ira DeA. Reid, director⌋
⌊Newark⌋ 1932.

New Jersey laws and the Negro
M974.9
W93n
Wright, Marion Thompson
New Jersey laws and the Negro. Washington, D.C., The Association for the Study of Negro Life and History, 1943.

45p. 24cm.
Reprinted from the Journal of Negro history, 28, no.2, April 1943.
Inscribed by author.

New Orleans.
M813.5
Im1c
Imbert, Dennis I.
The colored gentleman, a product of modern civilization, by D. I. Imbert. 1st ed. New Orleans, La., Williams printing service, 1931.

2 p. l., 86 p., 3 l. front., ports. 21½cm.

"Supplement: Prominent leaders of the colored race in New Orleans who have achieved success" (3 l. and 12 port. at end)

1. U. S.—Race question. 2. Negroes—New Orleans. I. Title.

31–13090
Library of Congress PZ3.I 313Co
——— Copy 2.
Copyright A 38301 ⌊3⌋

New Orleans—Biog.
MB
D45
Desdunes, Rodolphe L
Nos hommes et notre histoire; notices biographiques accompagnées de reflexions et de souvenirs personnels, hommage à la population créole, en souvenir des grands hommes qu'elle a produits et des bonnes choses qu'elle a accomplies, par R.-L. Desdunes ... Montréal, Arbour & Dupont, 1911.

196 p. front., ports. 22½cm.

1. Negroes—Louisiana. 2. Creoles. 3. New Orleans—Biog. 4. American literature (French)—Louisiana. 5. French literature—American authors.

12–21176
Library of Congress E185.93.L6D4
⌊a44c1⌋

New Orleans - Case studies.
M323.1
T372
Thompson, Daniel Calbert.
The Negro leadership class. Englewood Cliffs, N. J., Prentice-Hall ⌊1963⌋

174 p. 21 cm. (A Spectrum book)
Includes bibliography.

1. Negroes — New Orleans — Case studies. 2. Community leadership—Case studies. 3. Negroes—Civil rights. I. Title.

F379.N5T45 301.155 63–8286 ‡
Library of Congress ⌊8⌋

New Orleans, Battle of, 1815.
M326.99B
R54n
Roberts, James, *b.* 1753.
The narrative of James Roberts, soldier in the revolutionary war and at the battle of New Orleans. Chicago: printed for the author, 1858. Hattiesburg, Miss., The Book farm, 1945.

cover-title, viii, ⌊9⌋–32 p. 21½cm. ⌊Heartman's historical series, no. 71⌋

"Photo-lithoprint reproduction."
"One hundred and thirty-six copies reprinted from the apparently unique copy in the Charles E. Heartman collection of material relating to Negro culture."

1. Slavery in the U. S.—Condition of slaves. 2. New Orleans, Battle of, 1815.

45–9855
Library of Congress E444.R7
⌊4⌋ 326.92

New Orleans blues.
M811.5
M87n
Most, Marty
New Orleans blues. Photography by the author. ⌊n.p. 1964⌋

88p. illus., ports. 21cm.

I. Title.

M784
N42o
New Orleans University Singers.
The only original New Orleans university singers. A colored double quartette. Voices unrivalled. Pronounced the best troupe now before the public. Philadelphia. Wm. Syckelmoore, 1881.

22p. 14cm.
Hymns and songs.

1. Music. 2. Hymns.

Trinidad
M220
C86n
The new birth; a handbook of Scriptural doc...
Crichlow, Cyril A 1889–
The new birth; a handbook of Scriptu⌊r⌋al documentation. ⌊1st ed.⌋ New York, Pageant Press ⌊1956⌋

143 p. 21 cm.

1. Regeneration (Theology) I. Title.

BT790.C7 234.4 56–11348 ‡
Library of Congress ⌊2⌋

Jamaica
M823.91
R27n
1950
New day.
Reid, Victor Stafford, 1913–
New day. London, William Heinemann, 1950.

344p. 19cm.

Jamaica
M823.91
R27n
New day.
Reid, Victor Stafford, 1913–
New day. 1st ed. New York, A. A. Knopf, 1949.

viii, 374p. 20cm.

The new Ghana; the birth of a nation.

Ghana
M966.7
Aml

Amamoo, J Godson.
The new Ghana; the birth of a nation. London, Pan Books [1958]
145 p. illus. 18 cm. (A Pan original, G120)
Includes bibliography.

1. Ghana—Hist. I. Title.

DT510.A75 966.7 58-42940 ‡

Library of Congress [3]

New homes for today.

M728.6
W67n

Williams, Paul R 1894–
New homes for today, by Paul R. Williams, A. I. A. Hollywood [Calif.] Murray & Gee, incorporated, 1946.
95 p. illus. (incl. plans) 27½ x 21½ cm.
On cover: Remodeling interiors; duplexes, ranch houses.

1. Architecture, Domestic—Designs and plans. 2. House decoration. I. Title.

46-3841

Library of Congress NA7127.W612 [47z7] 728.6084

The new man.

MB9
M83

Bruce, Henry Clay, 1836–1902.
The new man. Twenty-nine years a slave. Twenty-nine years a free man. Recollections of H. C. Bruce. York, Pa., P. Anstadt & sons, 1895.
x, [11]–176 p. front. (port.) 23½ cm.
Narrative of slave life, mainly in Missouri.

1. Slavery in the U. S.—Missouri. I. Title.

14-7617

Library of Congress E444.B9
Copyright 1895: 15098 [40f1]

The New Negro.

M301
Ah5n

Ahmann, Mathew H ed.
The new Negro. Contributors: Stephen J. Wright [and others] In the symposium: James Baldwin [and others] Notre Dame, Ind., Fides Publishers [1961]
xii, 145 p. 21 cm.
Includes papers presented at the 1st convention of the National Catholic Conference for Interracial Justice, held in Detroit in 1961.

1. Negroes—Addresses, essays, lectures. I. Wright, Stephen J. II. National Catholic Conference for Interracial Justice. 1st convention, Detroit, 1961. III. Title.

E185.6.A26 301.451 61-17712

Library of Congress [62f5]

The new Negro.

M323
P58n

Pickens, William, 1881–1954.
The new negro, his political, civil and mental status, and related essays, by William Pickens ... New York city, The Neale publishing company, 1916.
239 p. 19 cm. $1.50

1. Negroes. I. Title.

17-2640

Library of Congress E185.6.P59
——— Copy 2.
Copyright A 455221 [s19d3]

The new Negro; an interpretation.

M808
L79n9

Locke, Alain Le Roy, 1886– ed.
The new negro; an interpretation, edited by Alain Locke; book decoration and portraits by Winold Reiss. New York, A. and C. Boni, 1925.
xviii, 446 p. col. front., illus. (incl. music, facsims.) plates (part col.) col. ports. 24½ cm.
Bibliography: p. 415–446.

1. Negroes. 2. Negro literature. I. Title.

25-25228

Library of Congress E185.82.L75 [43b2]

M304
F19
v.4, no.19

New Negro Art Theatre.
First Negro dance recital in America. The new Negro art theatre presents Edna Guy, Hemsley Winfield, assisted by a dance group... at the Theatre in the Clouds... April 29, 1931.

Folio.

1. Dancers and dancing.

M973
N42

A new Negro for a new century; an accurate and up-to-date record of the upward struggles of the Negro race. The Spanish-American war, causes of it; vivid descriptions of fierce battles; superb heroism and daring deeds of the Negro soldier ... Education, industrial schools, colleges, universities and their relationship to the race problem, by Prof. Booker T. Washington. Reconstruction and industrial advancement by N. B. Wood ... The colored woman and her part in race regeneration ... by ... Fannie Barrier Williams ... Chicago, Ill., American publishing house [1900]
428 p. front., illus. (ports) 20 cm.

(Continued on next card)

0-5252

[44g1]

M973
N42

A new Negro for a new century ... [1900] (Card 2)
Folded plate inserted.

~~1. Negroes.~~ 2. Slavery in the U. S. 3. U. S.—Hist.—War of 1898—Negro troops. ~~I. MacBrady, John E., ed.~~ II. Washington, Booker Taliaferro, 1859?–1915. III. Williams, Fannie Barrier. ~~IV. Wood, Norman Barton, 1857–~~

0-5252

Library of Congress E185.N53 [a44g1]

M323.4
C246

The new Negro of the South.
Carter, Wilmoth Annette, 1916–
The new Negro of the South; a portrait of movements and leadership, by Wilmoth A. Carter. [1st ed.] New York, Exposition Press [1967]
58 p. 21 cm. (An Exposition-university book)
Bibliography: p. [57]–58.

1. Negroes—Civil rights—Hist. I. Title.

E185.61.C285 301.451'96'073 67-24259

Library of Congress [5]

New Negro poets U. S. A.

M811.08
H87

Hughes, Langston, 1902– ed.
New Negro poets U. S. A. Foreword by Gwendolyn Brooks. Bloomington, Indiana University Press [1964]
127 p. 21 cm.

1. American poetry—Negro authors. I. Title. 2. Poetry.

PS591.N4H8 811.54082 64-10836

Library of Congress [5]

The new Negro thirty years afterward...

M973
H83n

Howard University, Washington, D. C. *Graduate School. Division of the Social Sciences.*
The new Negro thirty years afterward; papers contributed to the sixteenth annual spring conference ... April 20, 21 and 22, 1955. Edited by Rayford W. Logan, chairman, Eugene C. Holmes [and] G. Franklin Edwards. Washington, Howard University Press, 1955 [i. e. 1956]
iv, 96 p. 28 cm.
"Dedicated to the memory of Professor Alain Locke."
Includes bibliographies. "Bibliography of the writings of Alain Leroy Locke ... by Robert E. Martin": p. 89–96.

1. Locke, Alain Le Roy, 1886–1954. 2. Negroes—Addresses, essays, lectures. I. Title.

E185.5.H73 1955a 325.2604 56-7060

Library of Congress [2]

The new Nigerian elite.

M910
Sm9n

Smythe, Hugh H
The new Nigerian elite [by] Hugh H. Smythe and Mabel M. Smythe. Stanford, Calif., Stanford University Press, 1960.
ix, 196 p. map. 24 cm.
Bibliographical references included in "Notes" (p. [175]–191)

1. Upper classes—Nigeria. 2. Nigeria—Soc. condit. I. Smythe, Mabel M., joint author. II. Title.

HN800.N5S56 301.4409669 60-13870

Library of Congress [61f10]

M811.5
N42n

New poems by American poets. no. [1]–
New York, Ballantine Books, 1953–
v. 18–21 cm.
Editor: no. 1– R. Humphries.

1. American poetry—20th cent. I. Humphries, Rolfe, ed.

PS614.N35 811.5082 57-4075 ‡

Printed for A. B. P. by Library of Congress [59r58k10]

The new South and higher education.

M371.974
T87n

Tuskegee Institute.
The new South and higher education: what are the implications for higher education of the changing socio-economic conditions of the South? A symposium and ceremonies held in connection with the inauguration of Luther Hilton Foster, fourth president of Tuskegee Institute [October 31 and November 1, 1953. Tuskegee, Ala.] Dept. of Records and Research, Tuskegee Institute, 1954.
x, 145 p. map. 24 cm.

~~(Continued on next card)~~

54-12394

[5615]

The new South investigated.

M973.8
St8

Straker, David Augustus, d. 1908.
The new South investigated. By D. Augustus Straker ... Detroit, Mich., Ferguson printing company, 1888.
viii p., 1 l., 11–230 p. front. (port.) 20 cm.

1. Southern states. 2. Negroes. I. Title.

1-21239

Library of Congress F215.S89
Copyright 1888: 23618 [a30c1]

A new survey of English literature.

M810
B73n8

Brawley, Benjamin Griffith, 1882–
A new survey of English literature; a text book for colleges, by Benjamin Brawley. New York, A. A. Knopf, 1925.
xv, 388 p. 21½ cm.
"Brief bibliography": p. 359–368.

1. English literature—Hist. & crit. I. Title.

26-4014

Library of Congress PR85.B68 [45g1]

New thought.

M131
An2u

Anderson, Garland.
Uncommon sense; the law of life in action, by Garland Anderson ... ~~London, L. N. Fowler & co.~~ [1933] [New York, The author]
220 p. 19 cm.

1. New thought. 2. Faith-cure. 3. Success. I. Title.

34-488

Library of Congress BF639.A68 1933
——— Copy 2.
Copyright A ad int. 18321 [3] [159.91324] 131.324

The new voice in race adjustments;

M323
T69

Negro Christian student conference. *Atlanta,* 1914.
The new voice in race adjustments; addresses and reports presented at the Negro Christian student conference, Atlanta, Georgia, May 14–18, 1914. A. M. Trawick, editor ... Pub. by order of the executive committee of the conference. New York city, Student volunteer movement [1914]
1 p. l., [v]–vi p., 1 l., 230 p. 23½ cm.
"Best books on the Negro in America and Africa": p. 221–224.

1. Negroes—Congresses. 2. U. S.—Race question. I. Trawick, Arcadius McSwain, 1869– ed. II. Title.

A 15-837

Springfield. Public library for Library of Congress E185.5.N38 [a35f1]

New voices from South Africa.

Africa, South
M896.3
R52

Rive, Richard, 1931– ed.
Quartet; new voices from South Africa: Alex La Guma, James Matthews, Alf Wannenburgh, Richard Rive. New York, Crown Publishers [1963]
223 p. 22 cm.
Short stories.

1. Short stories, South African. I. Title. II. Title: New voices from South Africa. 2. Africa, South - Short stories.

PZ1.R44Qar 63-21108

Library of Congress [5]

The new West Africa.

W.Africa
M966
Ad3

Ademola, Adenekan .
The new West Africa; problems of independence, by F. Le Gros Clark [and others] Edited by Basil Davidson and Adenekan Ademola. Introd. by Ritchie Calder. London, Allen & Unwin [1953]
184p. map. 22cm.
Includes bibliographies.

M. Africa 1966 Ad3
The new West Africa.
Ademola, Adenekan, ed.
The new West Africa; problems of independence, by F. Le Gros Clark [and others] Edited by Basil Davidson and Adenekan Ademola. Introd. by Ritchie Calder. London, Allen & Unwin [1953]
184 p. map. 22 cm.
Includes bibliographies.
1. Africa, West. I. Davidson, Basil, 1914- II. Clark, Frederick Le Gros, 1892- III. Title.
DT503.D3 966.7 54—19854
Library of Congress [54b5]

M974.71 Ot8
'New world a-coming'.
Ottley, Roi.
'New world a-coming'; inside black America, by Roi Ottley ... Boston, Houghton Mifflin company, 1943.
vi, [2], 364 p. incl. front., illus. 21½ cm. (Life-in-America prize book[s])
Illustrated lining-papers in colors.
Bibliography: p. [349]-354.
1. Negroes—New York (City) 2. Harlem, New York (City) I. Title.
Library of Congress F128.9.N3O75 43-11506
[20] 325.2609747

M808.8 N42
New world writing. 1st-
Apr. 1952-
[New York] New American Library.
v. 18 cm. (N. A. L. Mentor books)
1: The Negro in American literature, by Alain Locke. The seed among thorns, by Giuseppe Berto; tr. by Ben Johnson. -2: Roy's wound, by James Baldwin. The village washer, by Samuel Selvon. The House of the customs men [poem], tr. by Ben Johnson. -4: In the castle of my skin,
1. Literature, Modern—20th cent. 2. American literature—20th cent.
PN6014.N457 808.8 52—1806
Library of Congress [54j5]

M808.8 N42
New world writing. 1st- (card 2)
by George Lamming. The Luzana Cholly kick, by Albert Murray. Drawings by Wilson Bigaud and Dieudonné Cédor. -5: Poems, by Jorge de Lima. Did you ever dream lucky? by Ralph Ellison. Storyville days and nights, by Louis Armstrong.

M815.2 J71t
New Year's anthem...
Fortune, Michael
New Year's anthem, sung in the African episcopal church of St. Thomas, Jan.1, 1808.
[2] - 24p.
Bound in Absalom Jones, a thanksgiving sermon, preached January 1, 1808 in St. Thomas's or the African episcopal church, Philadelphia.

M814.4 W272bi
New York. People's Institute.
Washington, Booker Taliaferro, 1859?-1915
[Bishop Potter and the Negro, address]
(In: New York. People's Institute. Memorial to Henry Codman Potter by the People's Institute, Cooper Union,... December twentieth, MCMVIII. New York, [Cheltenham Press] 1909. 21cm. pp. 60-67)

M252 J63p
New York. St. Martin's Church.
Johnson, John Howard, 1897-
A place of adventure; essays and sermons. Foreword by Hughell E. W. Fosbroke. [Rev. ed.] Greenwich, Conn., Seabury Press, 1955.
130 p. 19 cm.
1. New York. St. Martin's Church. 2. Protestant Episcopal Church in the U. S. A.—Sermons. 3. Sermons, American. I. Title.
BX5980.N5M34 1955 283.747 55-13760 ‡
Library of Congress [3]

M362.7 C43o
New York (City)
The Children's Aid Society. New York.
Off Harlem's streets. New York, The Society, 1940.
[24]p. illus. diagrs. tables. 28cm.

M323.2 C49
New York (City)
Citizens Emergency Conference for Interracial Unity, Hunter College, 1943.
Report of the Citizens Emergency Conference for Interracial unity held at Hunter College... September 25, 1943, New York, The Conference, [1943]
30p. 22½cm.

M974.7 C49
New York (City).
Citizens' protective league, *New York.*
Story of the riot, pub. by the Citizens' protective league. [New York, 1900]
cover-title, 79 p., 1 l. 22½ cm.
"Persecution of negroes by roughs and policemen, in the city of New York, August, 1900. Statement and proofs written and compiled by Frank Moss and issued by the Citizens' protective league."
1. New York (City)—Riot, August, 1900. 2. Negroes—New York (City) I. Moss, Frank, 1860- comp. II. Title.
Library of Congress F128.9.N3C6 5-42437
[a39b1]

M974.7 C54
New York (City)
Clark, Kenneth Bancroft, 1914-
Dark ghetto; dilemmas of social power, by Kenneth B. Clark. Foreword by Gunnar Myrdal. [1st ed.] New York, Harper & Row [1965]
xxix, 251 p. illus. 22 cm.
1. ~~Negroes~~—New York (City) 2. ~~Negroes~~—Segregation. 3. Harlem, New York (City)—Soc. condit. I. Title.
F128.9.N3C65 301.451 64—7834
Library of Congress [65a14]

M974.7 C55
New York (City)
Clarke, John Henrik, 1915- *ed.*
Harlem, a community in transition. [1st ed.] New York, Citadel Press [°1964]
223 p. illus., ports. 21 cm.
"Much of the material in this book is from the Summer 1963 (Volume III, no. 3) issue of Freedomways."
Bibliographical footnotes.
1. Harlem, New York (City) 2. ~~Negroes~~—New York (City)
F128.68.H3C55 917.471 64-21891
Library of Congress [5]

M974.7 C55h
New York (City)
Clarke, John Henrik, 1915- ed.
Harlem, U.S.A.; the story of a city within a city, told by James Baldwin [and others] Edited, and with an introd. by John Henrik Clarke. Berlin, Seven Seas Publishers [1964]
361p. 18½cm.
"The contents of this book, in part, have been taken from various issues of Freedomways."
(Continued on next card)

M974.7 C55h
New York (City)
Clarke, John Henrik, 1915- ed. Harlem, U.S.A.; the story of a city within a city. [1964] (Card 2)
Partial contents.- The legacy of Alain Locke, by Eugene C. Holmes.- My early days in Harlem, by Langston Hughes.- The Nationalist movements of Harlem, by E. U. Essien-Udom.- How Bootsie was born, by Ollie Harrington.- The Negro theatre and the Harlem community, by Loften Mitchell.- A challenge to artists, by Lorraine Hansberry.- Purlie told me, by
(Continued on next card)

M974.7 C55h
New York (City)
Clarke, John Henrik, 1915- ed. Harlem, U.S.A.; the story of a city within a city. [1964] (Card 3)
Partial contents - Continued.
Ossie Davis.- And then came Baldwin, by Julian Mayfield.- A talk to Harlem teachers, by James Baldwin.- Birmingham's Harlem, by L. W. Holt.- HARYOU: An experiment, by Kenneth Clark.- A house is not always a home, by G. F. Brown.- The alienation of James Baldwin, by J. H. Clarke.- Revolt of
(Continued on next card)

M974.7 C55h
New York (City)
Clarke, John Henrik, 1915- ed. Harlem, U.S.A. the story of a city within a city. [1964] (Card 4)
Partial contents - Continued.
the angels, by J. H. Clarke.- The Harlem rat, by J. H. Jones.- Winds if change, by Loyle Hairston.- The health card, by Alice Childress.- I go to a funeral, by Alice Childress.- Who is simple, by Langston Hughes.- Banquet in honor, by Langston Hughes.- Dear Dr. Butts, by Langston Hughes.- Some get wasted, by
(Continued on next card)

M974.7 C55h
New York (City)
Clarke, John Henrik, 1915- ed. Harlem, U.S.A.; the story of a city within a city. [1964] (Card 5)
Partial contents - Continued.
Paule Marshall.
1. Harlem, New York (City). 2. New York (City).

M301 D853so6
New York (city)—Statistics.
Du Bois, William Edward Burghardt, 1868-
Some notes on the Negroes in New York city, compiled from the reports of the United States census and other sources, by W.E. Burghardt Du Bois, Atlanta, Ga., Atlanta University press, 1903.
5p. 22½cm. (Atlanta University Conference, special report, January 1903)

M304 P19 v.1, no.7
New York (City).
Ford, James W 1893-
Hunger and terror in Harlem, by James W. Ford ... [New York, Harlem section, Communist party, 1935]
23, 14, [1] p. 17½ cm.
Caption title: The causes and the remedies for the March 19th outbreak in Harlem. Testimony of James W. Ford, secretary of the Harlem section of the Communist party. Prepared for the Mayor's commission on conditions in Harlem. April, 1935.
1. Negroes—New York (City) 2. Harlem, New York (City) I. Communist party of the United States of America. Harlem section. II. Title.
Library of Congress F128.9.N3F6 45-46484
[2]

M331 F85
New York. (City)
Franklin, Charles Lionel, 1910-
The Negro labor unionist of New York; problems and conditions among Negroes in the labor unions in Manhattan with special reference to the N. R. A. and post-N. R. A. situations, by Charles Lionel Franklin ... New York, 1936.
2 p. l., 7-417 p. 22½ cm.
Thesis (PH. D.)—Columbia university, 1936.
Vita.
Published also as Studies in history, economics and public law, ed. by the Faculty of political science of Columbia university, no. 420.
Bibliography: p. 398-402.
1. Negroes—New York (City) 2. Negroes—Employment. 3. Trade-unions—New York (City) 4. Labor and laboring classes—New York (City) I. Title. II. Title: Negroes in the labor unions in Manhattan.
Library of Congress E185.8.F732 36-34118
Columbia Univ. Libr. [39d1] 331.88097471

M331 G76n
New York (City)
Granger, Lester Blackwell, 1896-
The Negro worker in New York City, prepared by Lester B. Granger under direction of Committee on Negro Welfare. New York, Welfare Council of New York City, 1941.
32p. 19cm.

M362.7 H226
New York (City).
Harlem Youth Opportunities Unlimited, New York.
Youth in the ghetto; a study of the consequences of powerlessness and a blueprint for change. [1st ed.] New York, 1964.
xxi, 614p. illus., maps, tables. 28cm.
Bibliographical footnotes.

M323.2 H33n
New York (City)
Haynes, George Edmund, 1880–
The Negro at work in New York city; a study in economic progress, by George Edmund Haynes ... New York, 1912.
2 p. l., 7–159 p. incl. tables, diagrs. 25cm.
Thesis (PH. D.)—Columbia university, 1912.
Vita.
Published also as Studies in history, economics and public law, ed. by the Faculty of political science of Columbia university, vol. XLIX, no. 3, whole no. 124.
"Select bibliography": p. 154–156.
1. Negroes—New York (City) 2. Labor and laboring classes—New York (City) 3. Wages—New York (City) I. Title.
12—28454
Library of Congress E185.93.N56H41
Columbia Univ. Libr. 326.973
[45b1]

M813.5 H875w
New York (City).
Hughes, Langston, 1902- joint author.
The sweet flypaper of life [by] Roy De Carava and Langston Hughes. [New York, Simon and Schuster, 1955]
98 p. illus. 19 cm.
1. Negroes—New York (City) 2. Harlem, New York (City)—Descr.—Views. I. Hughes, Langston, 1902– joint author. II. Title.
F128.9.N3D4 325.2609747 55—10048 ‡
Library of Congress [56k10]

M323. J632b
New York (City)
Johnson, James Weldon, 1871–1938.
... Black Manhattan. New York, A. A. Knopf, 1930.
xvii p., 2 l., [3]–284, [xxi]–xxxiv p., 1 l. front., pl., ports., 2 maps on 1 pl., facsim. 19½cm.
Illustrated lining-papers.
Inscribed copy: For my friend, Arthur B. Spingarn Sincerely, James Weldon Johnson.
1. ~~Negroes~~—New York (City) 2. Harlem, New York (City) 3. ~~Negro~~ literature and art. I. Title.
30—18832
Library of Congress F128.9.N3J67
[43b²2] 325.26097471

M810.8 M139
New York (City)
McCullough, Esther Morgan, ed.
As I pass, O Manhattan; an anthology of life in New York. [North Bennington, Vt.] Coley Taylor [1956]
1236 p. illus. 25 cm.
1. American literature—New York (City) 2. New York City. I. Title.
PS549.N5M22 810.82 56-12422 ‡
Library of Congress [3]

Jamaica M974.71 M19
New York (City).
McKay, Claude, 1890–
Harlem: Negro metropolis, by Claude McKay; illustrated with photographs. New York, E. P. Dutton & company, inc. [c1940]
xi p., 1 l., 15–262 p. front., illus. (facsim.) plates, ports. 22½cm.
"First edition."
1. Harlem, New York (City) 2. Negroes—New York (City) I. Title: Negro metropolis.
40—32205
Library of Congress F128.68.H3M3
[47z2] 917.471

M304 P19 v.3,no.5
New York (City)
Nathan, Winfred Bertram.
... Health conditions in North Harlem, 1923–1927, by Winfred B. Nathan ... an abstract, by Mary V. Dempsey. New York, National tuberculosis association [c1932]
68 p. incl. maps. 23cm. ([National tuberculosis association] Social research series. no. 2)
The death rates were revised on the basis of the 1930 census population figures. cf. Foreword.
"This study is ... largely a study of negro health."—Introd.
1. Harlem, New York (City)—Sanit. affairs. 2. Negroes—New York (City) 3. Negroes—Mortality. 4. Negroes—Statistics, Vital. 5. New York (City)—Statistics, Vital. 6. Health surveys. I. Dempsey, Mary V., ed. II. Title.
32—21088
Library of Congress RA448.H3N3
[42d1] 614.097471

M326 N48
New York (City)
New York committee of vigilance.
... Report of the New York committee of vigilance, with interesting facts relative to their proceedings. [N.Y.] Published by direction of the committee, O. Vale, jun. printer, 1842.
38p. 21cm.
See holdings card.
1842 report signed by W. Johnston.

M323.2 N419
New York (City)
New York (State) Temporary commission on the condition of the urban colored population.
... Second report of the New York state Temporary commission on the condition of the colored urban population to the Legislature of the state of New York, February, 1939. Created by chapter 858, Laws of 1937, continued by Chapter 677, Laws of 1938. Albany, J. B. Lyon company, printers, 1939.
190 p. 23cm.
At head of title: Legislative document (1939) no. 69. State of New York.
1. Negroes—New York (State) 2. Negroes—New York (City) 3. Negroes—Employment. 4. Negroes—Health and hygiene. 5. Housing—New York (State) I. Title.
40—30459
Library of Congress E185.93.N56N472
[42c1] 325.2600747

M974.71 Ot8
New York (City)
Ottley, Roi.
'New world a-coming'; inside black America, by Roi Ottley ... Boston, Houghton Mifflin company, 1943.
vi, [2], 364 p. incl. front., illus. 21½cm. (Life-in-America prize book[s])
Illustrated lining-papers in colors.
Bibliography: p. [349]–354.
1. Negroes—New York (City) 2. Harlem, New York (City) I. Title.
43-11506
Library of Congress F128.9.N3O75
[20] 325.2609747

M977 R24n
New York (City)
Reddick, Lawrence Dunbar, 1910– ed.
The Negro in the north during wartime. New York, Journal of educational sociology. 1944.
257-320p. 23cm.
Special issue of The Journal of educational sociology, January 1944.
Partial contents: -Chicago, by J. G. St. Clair Drake. -New York, by W. M. Banner.

M280 H66e
New York(City)-Churches.
Hodges, George W
Early Negro Church life in New York, by George W. Hodges. [New York] The author, c 1945.
25p. 21cm.

M280 H66e2
New York (City)-Churches.
Hodges, George W
Early Negro church life in New York. New York, The author, 1945
5-25p. 21cm. (Layman series, no.1)
Inscribed by author: To the Crisis Bookshop, George W. Hodges.

M323 N78t
New York (City) - Juvenile delinquency.
Wright, Richard, 1909-1960.
Urban misery in an American City; juvenile delinquency in Harlem.
pp. 339-346.
In: Twice a year, ed. by Dorothy Norman. 1946.

M811.5 T58h
New York (City) - Poetry.
Tolson, Melvin Beaunorus.
Harlem gallery, by M. B. Tolson. With an introd. by Karl Shapiro. New York, Twayne [1965–
v. 21 cm.
Poetry.
CONTENTS.—book 1. The curator.
1. Negroes—New York (City)—Poetry. 2. Harlem, New York (City)—Descr.—Poetry. 3. Poetry of places—Harlem, New York (City) I. Title.
PS3539.O334H3 811.52 64-25063
Library of Congress [5]

M974.7 C49
New York (City) - Riot, August, 1900.
Citizens' protective league, New York.
Story of the riot, pub. by the Citizens' protective league. [New York, 1900]
cover-title, 79 p., 1 l. 22½cm.
"Persecution of negroes by roughs and policemen, in the city of New York, August, 1900. Statement and proofs written and compiled by Frank Moss and issued by the Citizens' protective league."
1. New York (City)—Riot, August, 1900. 2. Negroes—New York (City) I. Moss, Frank, 1860– comp. II. Title.
5—42437
Library of Congress F128.9.N3C6
[a39b1]

M304 P19 v.3,no.5
New York (City)- Statistics, Vital.
Nathan, Winfred Bertram.
... Health conditions in North Harlem, 1923–1927, by Winfred B. Nathan ... an abstract, by Mary V. Dempsey. New York, National tuberculosis association [c1932]
68 p. incl. maps. 23cm. ([National tuberculosis association] Social research series. no. 2)
The death rates were revised on the basis of the 1930 census population figures. cf. Foreword.
"This study is ... largely a study of negro health."—Introd.
1. Harlem, New York (City)—Sanit. affairs. 2. Negroes—New York (City) 3. Negroes—Mortality. 4. Negroes—Statistics, Vital. 5. New York (City)—Statistics, Vital. 6. Health surveys. I. Dempsey, Mary V., ed. II. Title.
32—21088
Library of Congress RA448.H3N3
[42d1] 614.097471

M331.833 N42h
New York (City). Citizens Housing Council. Committee on Inter-racial Problems in Housing.
Harlem housing, prepared by Franklin O. Nichols in cooperation with the Committee on Inter-racial problems in Housing, Citizens' Housing Council of New York. New York, The Council, 1939.
32p. tables, diagrs. 28cm.
Mimeographed.
1. Housing. 2. Harlem, New York (City)—Housing. I. Title.

M815.4 D74e
New York (City) Colored citizens.
Douglass, Frederick, 1817-1895.
Eulogy of the late Hon. Wm. Jay, by Frederick Douglass, delivered on the invitation of the colored citizens of New York city in Shiloh Presbyterian church, New York, May 12, 1859. Rochester, Press of A. Strong & co., 1859.
32 p. 23cm.
1. Jay, William, 1789–1858. I. New York (City) Colored citizens. II. New York (City) Shiloh Presbyterian church.
A 17-1157
Title from Harvard Univ. Printed by L. C.

New York (City). Harlem Hospital.
See
Harlem Hospital. New York (City)

M974.71 N42s
New York (City) Mayor's Commission to Inquire into Conditions in Harlem following the March, 1935, Rioting.
Social and economic study of Harlem. New York, Amsterdam News, 193 .
58p. 28cm.
Mimeographed.
1. Harlem, New York (City). 2. Riots- New York (City).

M796
N42r
New York (City) Mayor's Committee on Baseball
Report... to Mayor F. H. La Guardia.
n.p., 1945.
11p. 23cm.
1. Baseball.

New York (State)
M973.6
N21
1853
Colored National Convention. ~~Rochester, New York~~
Proceedings of the Colored National Convention, held in Rochester, July 6th, 7th and 8th, 1853. Rochester, Printed at the Office of Frederick Douglass' paper, 1853.
57p. 21½cm.

New York (State)
M323.2
M419
New York (*State*) *Temporary commission on the condition of the urban colored population.*
... Second report of the New York state Temporary commission on the condition of the colored urban population to the Legislature of the state of New York, February, 1939. Created by chapter 858, Laws of 1937, continued by Chapter 677, Laws of 1938. Albany, J. B. Lyon company, printers, 1939.
100 p. 23cm.
At head of title: Legislative document (1939) no. 69. State of New York.
1. Negroes—New York (State) 2. Negroes—New York (City) 3. Negroes—Employment. 4. Negroes—Health and hygiene. 5. Housing—New York (State) I. Title.
Library of Congress E185.93.N56N472 40—30459
[42c1] 325.2600747

M378.
N42r
New York (City) Mayor's Committee on Unity.
Report on inequality of opportunity in higher education. New York, 1946.
19p. 26cm.
1. Education - New York. I. Tobias, Channing.

New York (State)
M331.
D29
Davis, John A
How management can integrate Negroes in war industries, prepared by John A. Davis. [Albany?] New York State war council, Committee on discrimination in employment, 1942.
1 p. l., v-viii, 43, [1] p. 23cm.
Bibliography: p. 42-43.
1. Negroes—Employment. 2. Negroes—New York (State) I. New York (State) State war council. Committee on discrimination in employment. II. Title.
42—52790
Library of Congress E185.8.D3
[44d2] 331.98

New York. (State).
M323.
R21
Raymond, Harry.
Dixie comes to New York; Story of the Freeport GI slayings. Introduction by Benjamin J. Davis, Jr. New York, Daily Worker, 1946.
14p. illus. 19cm.

M01
N42ne
1965
New York (City). Public Library.
The Negro in the United States; a list of significant books. 9th rev. ed.
New York, New York Public Library, 1965.
24p. 25½cm.
I. Title.

New York (State)
M366.1
F87n7
Freemasons. New York (State) United Grand Lodge.
Constitution and Statutes. rev. New York, Tobitt & Bunce, printers, 1876.
43p. 18cm.

New York (State)
M974.7
W93a
Wright, Theodore Sedgewick.
An address to the three thousand colored citizens of New York who are the owners of one hundred and twenty thousand acres of land in the state of New York, given to them by Gerrit Smith... September 1, 1846. New York n.p. 1846.
20p. 23cm.

M01
N42ne
New York (City) Public Library. 135th Street Branch.
The Negro, a selected bibliography. New York, The Library, 1940.
19p. 25cm.
1. Bibliography. I. Title.

New York (State).
M366.1
F87n7
Freemasons. New York (State) Grand Lodge.
Proceedings. 1st- 1845-
New York, 18 -
v. 24, 20 22cm. annual
See holdings card for proceedings in library

M370
N42a
New York (State) Dept. of Investigation.
Administration of human relations program in New York City schools, report to Honorable F. H. La Guardia. New York, 1945.
102p. 25cm.
1. Education--N.Y. 2. Intercultural education.

New York (City) Shiloh Presbyterian church.
M815.4
D74e
Douglass, Frederick, 1817-1895.
Eulogy of the late Hon. Wm. Jay, by Frederick Douglass, delivered on the invitation of the colored citizens of New York city in Shiloh Presbyterian church, New York, May 12, 1859. Rochester, Press of A. Strong & co., 1859.
32 p. 23cm.
1. Jay, William, 1789-1858. I. New York (City) Colored citizens. II. New York (City) Shiloh Presbyterian church.
A 17-1157
Title from Harvard Univ. Printed by L. C.

New York (State).
M974.71
L58s
Lewin, Wilfred S.
A study of the Negro population of Mount Vernon, by Wilfred S. Lewin. 1935.
52p. 28cm.
Typewritten

M331.1
N42n
New York (State) State Commission against Discrimination.
A new technique for an old problem. New York, State Commission against Discrimination, [1947].
837-862p. 26cm.
Reprint from the Yale law journal, May 1947.
1. Civil rights.
2. Fair employment practice legislation.
3. Discrimination in employment - New York (State).

M331
G76n
New York (City) Welfare Council. Committee on Negro Welfare.
Granger, Lester Blackwell, 1896
The Negro worker in New York City, prepared by Lester B. Granger under direction of Committee on Negro Welfare. New York, Welfare Council of New York City, 1941.
32p. 19cm.

New York (State)
M973.6
N21
1847
National Convention of Colored People. Troy New York
Proceedings of the National Convention of Colored People and their friends, held in Troy, N.Y., on the 6th, 7th, 8th, and 9th, 1847. Troy, N.Y., Steam Press of J. C. Kneeland and Co., 1847.
32p. 19cm.

M331.1
N42r2
New York (*State*) *State Commission Against Discrimination.*
Report. 1946-
[New York]
v. 28 cm. annual.
See holdings card for issues in library.
1. Discrimination in employment—New York (State)
HD4903.N67 331.11 A 47-3440 rev*
New York. State Libr. for Library of Congress [r50c1]†

M974.7
N153
New York (State).
Allen, James Egert, 1896-
The Negro in New York. Foreword by Hon. Arthur Levitt. New York, Exposition Press c1964.
94p. 21cm.

New York (State)
M323.2
N42
New York (State) State Temporary Commission Against Discrimination.
Report of the New York state Temporary Commission Against Discrimination. Albany, Williams press, 1945.
88p. 23cm.
At head of title: Legislative document (1945) no.6 New York State.

M331.1
N42a
New York (State) State Temporary Commission Against Discrimination.
Report.
Albany, Williams press, 1945.
88p. 23cm.
At head of title: Legislative document (1945) no.6. New York state.
1. Discrimination in employment - New York (State).

M331.1 N42r
New York (State) State Commission Against Discrimination.
Review of first year's operation of the New York State law against discrimination, July 1945–July 1946. [New York, 1946]
15 p. 23 cm.
1. Discrimination in employment—New York (State)
HD4903.N72 1946 331.11 A 47-5155 rev*
New York. State Libr. for Library of Congress [r50c2]†

M331.1 C24n
New York (State) Commission Against Discrimination.
Carter, Elmer Anderson, 1890-
The New York Commission succeeds. New York, New York State Commission against Discrimination, [1947].
2p. port. 24cm.
Reprinted from Interracial review, November 1947.

New York (State) State war council. Committee on discrimination in employment.
M331. D29
Davis, John A
How management can integrate Negroes in war industries, prepared by John A. Davis. [Albany?] New York State war council, Committee on discrimination in employment, 1942.
1 p. l., v-viii, 43, [1] p. 23ᶜᵐ.
Bibliography: p. 42-43.
1. Negroes—Employment. 2. Negroes—New York (State) I. New York (State) State war council. Committee on discrimination in employment. II. Title.
Library of Congress E185.8.D3 43—52790
[44d2] 331.98

New York City.
M331.833 B22
Banner, Warren M, 1910-
The housing of Negro families in greater New York.
4p.
A reprint of an abstract of a doctor's dissertation, University of Pittsburgh Bulletin, v. 36, no.4, Jan. 15, 1940.

M326 N48
New York committee of vigilance.
... Report of the New York committee of vigilance, with interesting facts relative to their proceedings. [N.Y.] Published by direction of the committee, G. Vale, jun. printer, 1842.
38p. 21cm.
See holdings card.
1842 report signed by W. Johnston.
1. New York City. 2. Slavery in the U.S.-Fugitive slaves. I. Johnston, William.

M323.4 N42
New York Herald Tribune Forum on Current Problems
The struggle for justice as a world force; Report of the 1946 annual New York Herald Tribune Forum on Current Problems. New York, 1946.
296p. ports. 24cm.
Partial contents: Colonial Africa's frontiers, by Robert Kweku Atta Gardiner. -Frontiers still left in America: The Negro's part, by Oliver Harrington.
1. Civil rights. I. a.t. Gardiner. II. a.t. Harrington.

New York times.
M323.4 L58
Lewis, Anthony, 1927-
Portrait of a decade; the second American revolution [by] Anthony Lewis and the New York times. New York, Random House [1964]
322 p. illus. 25 cm.
White author.
Partial contents.- A Negro assays the Negro mood, by James Baldwin.- Explanation of the 'Black psyche', by John Oliver Killens.
1. ~~Negroes~~—Civil rights. I. New York times. II. Title. III. Title: The second American revolution.
E185.61.L52 1964 323.40973 64-14832
Library of Congress [4-1]

M301 R27t
Newark, N. J.
Reid, Ira DeAugustine, 1901-
Two hundred families of small wage earners- An analysis of their economic status as it relates to problems of housing. Newark, N.J. n.p., 1931.
4p. graphs. 27cm.
Mimeographed.

Newark, N. J.
M309.1 W934
Wright, Nathan.
Ready to riot. [1st ed.] New York, Holt, Rinehart and Winston [1968]
148 p. illus., maps. 22 cm.
Bibliographical footnotes.
1. Newark, N. J.—Soc. condit. 2. Negroes—Newark, N. J. I. Title.
HN80.N685W74 309.1'749'32 68-12218
Library of Congress [15-2]

Newark, N. J. - Social conditions.
M309.1 W934
Wright, Nathan.
Ready to riot. [1st ed.] New York, Holt, Rinehart and Winston [1968]
148 p. illus., maps. 22 cm.
Bibliographical footnotes.
1. Newark, N. J.—Soc. condit. 2. Negroes—Newark, N. J. I. Title.
HN80.N685W74 309.1'749'32 68-12218
Library of Congress [15-2]

MB N42
Newbold, Nathan Carter, 1871- ed.
Five North Carolina Negro educators; prepared under the direction of N. C. Newbold. Chapel Hill, The University of North Carolina press, 1939.
xii, 142 p. ports. 22ᶜᵐ.
Biographical sketches composed by committees organized in nine North Carolina colleges, each committee consisting of one faculty adviser and one or more students. cf. Introd.
"Published under the auspices of the Division of cooperation in education and race relations; cooperating organizations: State department of public instruction, University of North Carolina [and] Duke university."
CONTENTS.—Simon Green Atkins.—James Benson Dudley.—Annie Wealthy Holland.—Peter Weddick Moore.—Ezekiel Ezra Smith.
1. ~~Negroes—Education~~. 2. ~~Negroes—Biog.~~ I. Title.
Education - North Ca. Biography
Library of Congress LC2802.N8N4 39-24948
[42c3] 923.773

Newbold, Nathan Carter, 1871-
M370 N81r
North Carolina. Governor's commission for the study of problems in the education of Negroes in North Carolina.
... Report of the Governor's commission for the study of problems in the education of Negroes in North Carolina. Issued by the state superintendent of public instruction, Raleigh, N. C. [Raleigh, 1935]
96 p. incl. tables, diagrs. 23½ᶜᵐ. ([North Carolina. Dept. of public instruction] Publication no. 183)
N. C. Newbold, chairman of the commission.
1. Negroes—Education. 2. Negroes—North Carolina. [1, 2. Negroes—North Carolina—Education] I. Newbold, Nathan Carter, 1871- II. Title.
E 36-191
U. S. Off. of educ. Library for Library of Congress LC2802.N8A4 [L184.B22 no. 183] [37c2]

News & letters.
M323 H18
Hamilton, Mary
Freedom riders speak for themselves [by] Mary Hamilton, Louise Inghram, and others. [Detroit, News & letters, 1961]
62p. illus. 18½cm.
"A News & letters pamphlet."

M811.5 N47
Newsome, Effie Lee.
Gladiola garden; poems of outdoors and indoors for second grade readers, by Effie Lee Newsome; illustrations by Lois Mailou Jones. Washington, D. C., The Associated publishers, 1940.
xv, [1], 167 p. incl. front., illus. 23½ᶜᵐ.
Illustrated lining-papers in color.
I. Title. 1. Poetry. II. Jones, Lois Mailou
[Full name: Mary Effie (Lee) Newsome]
41-3681 illus.
Library of Congress PZ8.3.N467Gl
[a45d1]

Newsome, M T
M973.6 N21cl 1854
National emigration convention, Cleveland, Ohio.
Arguments, pro and con, on the call for a national emigration convention, to be held in Cleveland, Ohio, August, 1854, by Frederick Douglass, W. J. Watkins, & J. M. Whitfield. With a short appendix of the statistics of Canada, West Indies, Central and South America. Published by M. T. Newsome, Detroit, George E. Pomeroy & co., 1854.
34p. 19cm.

Newspapers.
M05 R29
Poston, Theodore Roosevelt, 1906-
The Negro press. (The Reporter, 1:14-17, December 6, 1949.)
(In: The Reporter, 1:14-17, December 6, 1949.)

Newspapers.
M071 V87
Voice of the fugitive, v.1-2, Jan. 1851- Dec. 1852.
Sandwich, Canada West, 1851-52.
2v. 49cm. semi-weekly.
H. Bibb, editor.
52 no. in 2 v. lacks: V.2, no.6,7,8.

Newspapers.
M07 W65
Wilkins, Roy.
The Negro press hits back. Toronto, Reprinted from the Magazine digest, April 1943.
3-7p. 19cm.

Newspapers - Bibliography
M016.07 B81c
Brown, Warren Henry, 1905-
Check list of Negro newspapers in the United States (1827-1946) Jefferson City, Mo., School of Journalism, Lincoln Univ., 1946.
cover-title, 37 p. 23 cm. (Lincoln University journalism series, no. 2)
1. ~~Negro~~ newspapers (American)—Bibl. I. Series: Lincoln University, Jefferson City, Mo. School of Journalism. Journalism series, no. 2.
Z6951.B88 016.071 48-326*
Library of Congress [3]

Newspapers - Direct.
Africa M496 D141
MacDougald, Duncan.
... The languages and press of Africa, by Duncan MacDougald, jr. Philadelphia, University of Pennsylvania press, the University museum, 1944.
4 p. l., 86 p. map. 21½ᶜᵐ. (African handbooks, ed. by H. A. Wieschhoff. 4)
Bibliography: p. 83-86.
1. Africa—Languages. 2. Newspapers—Direct.
Library of Congress PL8007.M3 44-4429
[46k3] 496

Newspapers
See also
Press

M39
N48o
Newton, Alexander Herritage, 1837–
Out of the briars; an autobiography and sketch of the Twenty-ninth regiment, Connecticut volunteers, by A. H. Newton ... with introduction by Rev. J. P. Sampson ... [Philadelphia, The A. M. E. book concern, °1910]
xv p., 1 l., 19–269 p. front., plates, ports. 21cm.
10–25801
Library of Congress

S. Africa
M896.1
N49i
Ngani, Alfred Z , ca.1912–1950
Intlaba-mkhosi (izibongo zesiXhosa). Lovedale, The Lovedale Press, 1952.
60p. 18½cm.
1. Xhosa Poetry.

Congo, Leopoldville
M967.5
N49
Ngoma, Ferdinand
L'initiation Ba-Kongo et sa signification. [Paris] Sorbonne, 1963.
196p. 24½cm.
Theses (Ph.D) Université de Paris.
1. Bakongo (African tribe) 2. Congo, Leopoldville – Native races. I. Title.

M248
N48
Newton, Percy John.
The road to happiness, and other essays. Boston, Chapman & Grimes [1955]
153 p. illus. 22 cm.
1. Christian life. I. Title.
BV4501.N46 248 54–7551 ‡
Library of Congress [2]

S. Africa
M968
N51u
Ngani, Alfred Z , ca.1912–1950
Ubom buka-Kama [The life of Kama]. Lovedale, The Lovedale press, 1952.
55p. 18½cm.
1. Africa, South–History. 2. Kama.

Ngombe.
Congo Leopoldville
M896.2
M74n
Mongita, A
Ngombe. [Bruxelles, 1957]
19 leaves 28cm.
Mimeographed.

The next emancipation.
M323
O88
Oneal, James, 1875–
The next emancipation. With introd. by Frank R. Crosswaith. [4th ed.] New York, Negro Labor News Service [°1929]
30 p. 19 cm.
Cover title.
1. Negroes. I. Title.
E185.61.O56 1929 49–41115*
Library of Congress [1]

Uganda
M967.61
N51a
Nganwa, Kesi K.
Abakozire eby'okutangaza. Omuri. Ankole. Nairobi, Published for the Ankole literature committee by The Eagle Press, 1949.
36p. illus. 21cm.
1. Uganda literature. 2. Ankole.literature.

Zanzibar
M636
H88y
Ngómbe zako hatarini!
Humphrey, Norman
Ngómbe zako hatarini! [Your cattle are in danger] Wanyama wana mahitaji sawasawa na wanadamu. [Tr. by D. E. Diva] Nairobi, Eagle Press, 1950.
13p. 21½cm. (Lenga uzima. Aim at healthy living series)
Written in Swahili.
White author.
1. Cattle. I. Title. II. Series. III. Series: Aim at healthy living series.

M378F
N49
Neyland, Leedell W
The history of Florida Agricultural and Mechanical University [by] Leedell W. Neyland [and] John W. Riley. Gainesville, University of Florida Press, 1963.
xi, 303 p. illus., ports. 24 cm.
Bibliography: p. 281–282.
1. Florida. Agricultural and Mechanical University, Tallahassee. I. Riley, John W., joint author. 2. Universities and colleges.
LC2851.F63N4 630.711 63–17301
Library of Congress [5]

Uganda
M967.61
N51e
Nganwa, Kesi K
Emi twarize ya wakami [Traditional stories of the Ankole people of Uganda] Nairobi, The Eagle Press, 1951.
35p. 21cm.
Written in Runyankore
1. Uganda–Folktales. 2. Ankole People.

Kenya
M896.3
N51ki
Ngotho, Thomas M
Kimena kya nzou na mbũi [The enmity between the elephant and the goat] Nairobi, East African Literature Bureau, 1962.
35p. 18cm.
Written in Kamba.
1. African fiction. I. Title.

Kenya
M967.62
N49
Ngala, Ronald Gideon, 1923–
Nchi na desturi za wagiriama [The land and customs of the Giriama] Nairobi, Eagle Press 1949.
41p. illus. 18cm. (Masimulizi na desturi ya Afrika ya Mashariki. Custom and tradition in East Africa series)
Written in Swahili.
1. Kenya – Native races. 2. Giryama tribe. I. Title. II. Series. III. Series: Custom and tradition in East Africa series.

S. Africa
M968
C135
Ngcobo, Selby Bangani, 1908–
The Bantu peoples.
(In: Calpin, George Harold, The South African way of life. New York, Columbia University Press, 1953. 23cm. pp. 48–69).
1. Africa, South.

Kenya
M896.3
N51k
Ngotho, Thomas M
Kũtheea kuma yayayani [From the sky] African Literature Bureau, 1963.
35p. 18cm.
Written in Kambia.
1. African fiction. I. Title.

Congo (Leopoldville)
M896.3
L83n
Ngando [le crocodile]
Lomami-Tshibamba, Paul, 1914–
Ngando [le crocodile] Bruxelles, G. A. Deny [1949]
117p. port. 23cm.
"Prix littéraire de la Foire coloniale de Bruxelles, 1948."

Kenya
M896.3
N51n
Ngewa nyanya; na moelyo.
Ngotho, Thomas M
Ngewa nyanya; na moelyo [Eight stories and exercises] Nairobi, East African Literature Bureau, 1963.
24p. 18cm.
Written in Kamba.
I. Title.

Kenya
M896.3
N51n
Ngotho, Thomas M
Ngewa nyanya; na moelyo [Eight stories and exercises] Nairobi, East African Literature Bureau, 1963.
24p. 18cm.
Written in Kamba.
I. Title.

S. Africa
M968
N511
Ngani, Alfred Z ca.1912–1950
Ibali lamagqunukwebe. Lovedale, Lovedale press [1937]
vii, 38p. 18½cm.
History of the Gqunukwebe tribe.
1. Africa, South–History.

Nigeria
M896.3
N49f
Ngoh, John Emmanuel Akwo
Florence in the river of temptations. Onitsha [Nigeria] Century Printing Press, 1960.
40p. 18cm.
I. Title.

S. Africa
M968
N51af
Ngubane, Jordan Kush, 1917–
An African explains apartheid. New York, Praeger [1963]
243 p. illus. 22 cm. (Books that matter)
1. Africa, South—Hist. 2. Segregation—Africa, South. 3. Communism—Africa, South. I. Title. 4. Apartheid.
DT763.N45 968.06 63–7569 ‡
Library of Congress [5]

S. Africa
M968
N51af2 Ngubane, Jordan Kush, 1917-
An African explains apartheid. ~~New York, Praeger [1963]~~ London, Pall Mall [1963]
243 p. illus. 22 cm. ~~(Books that matter)~~

1. Africa, South—Hist. 2. Segregation—Africa, South. 3. Communism—Africa, South. I. Title. 4. Apartheid.

DT763.N45 968.06 63-7569 ‡
Library of Congress [5]

South Africa
M968
N51s Ngubane, Jordan Kush, 1917-
Should the natives representative council be abolished? Cape Town, The African Bookman, 1946.

28p. 18½cm. (Pro and Con Pamphlets)

1. Africa, South - Native Law. 2. Africa, South - Politics and government.

Kenya
M896.3 Ngugi, James, 1938-
N49g A grain of wheat. London, Heinemann, 1967.
vii, 280 p. 19½ cm. 25/-

Portrait of author on book jacket. (B 67-7107)

I. Title.

PZ4.N5688Gr 67-02814
Library of Congress [3]

South Africa
M896.3 Ngugi, James, 1938-
R52m The martyr.

Pp. 204-214.

In: Rive, Richard, ed. Modern African prose. London, Heinemann Educational Books, 1964.

Kenya
M896.3 Ngugi, James, 1938-
N49r The river between. London, Heinemann [1965]

174p. 18½cm.

1. Kenya - Fiction. I. Title.

Kenya
M896.3 Ngugi, James, 1938-
N49w Weep not, child. London, Heinemann, 1964.
153p. 18½cm.

1. Kenya - Fiction. I. Title.

Kenya
M610 Ngurungu, Sospeter Munuhe, tr.
N49 Muceera na mukundu akundukaga o taguo [V.D. and drunkenness] [Tr. with a new preface by Sospeter Munuhue Ngurungu] Nairobi, Eagle Press, 1950.

16p. 22cm. (Taanya ũgima-inĩ. Aim at healthy living series)
Written in Kikuyu.

1. Venereal diseases. 2. Alcoholism. I. Title. II. Series. III. Aim at healthy living series.

Congo (Leopoldville)
M967.5 Ngwete, Martin
N51m Les maladies vénériennes. Congo Belge, Bibliothèque de L'Etoile, 1951.

71p. 18½cm.

1. Congo, Belgian-Health.

S. Africa
M496 Nhlapo, Jacob Mfaniselwa, 1904-1957
N51b Bantu babel. Will the Bantu languages live? Cape Town, The African Bookman, 1944.

15p. 18cm. (The Sixpenny library, #4)

1. Africa, South - Bantu languages.
2. Bantu languages.

S. Africa
M496 Nhlapo, Jacob Mfaniselwa, 1904-1957
N51n Nguni and Sotho. A practical plan for the unification of the South African Bantu languages. Cape Town, The African Bookman, 1945.

22p. 18½cm.

1. Africa, South - Bantu languages.
2. Bantu languages.

Guinea
M966 Niane, Djibril Tamsir
N51 Histoire de l'Afrique Occidentale, par Djibril Tamsir Niane et J. Suret-Canale. [Paris] Présence Africaine [1961]

223p. maps. 24cm.

1. Africa, West - History. I. Suret-Canale, Jean, jt. auth. II. Title.

Guinea
M966.24 Niane, Djibril Tamsir
N51r Recherches sur l'empire du Mali au Moyen Âge. Conakry, Institut National de Recherches et de Documentation, 1962.

70p. 24cm.

1. Mali - History. I. Title.

Guinea
M966.24 Niane, Djibril Tamsir.
N51 Soundjata; ou, L'épopée mandingue. Paris, Présence africaine [1960]
154 p. illus. 18 cm.

1. Mali Empire. I. Title. II. Title: L'épopée mandingue.

DT532.2.N5 61-48937 ‡
Library of Congress [3]

Guinea
M398.2 Niane, Djibrie Tamsir
N51 Sundiata; an epic of old Mali. Translated by G. D. Pickett. [London] Longmans [1965]

96p. map. 20½cm.

1. Tales, African. I. Title.

Nicaraguan poetry.
Nicaragua
M861.6 Darío, Rubén, 1867-1916.
D24a ... Antología poética; selección y prólogo de Raúl Silva Castro. [Santiago de Chile, Edición Zig-zag [1936]
283 p., 2 l. 19½cm. [Antologías poéticas, 1]

I. Silva Castro, Raúl, comp. 38-12190
Library of Congress PQ7519.D3A6 1936
[3] 861.6

Nicaraguan poetry.
Nicaragua
M861.6 Darío, Rubén, 1867-1916.
D248 Prosas profanas and other poems, by Ruben Dario; tr. from the Spanish by Charles B. McMichael. New York, Nicholas L. Brown, 1922.
4 p. l., 11-60 p. 19½cm.

I. McMichael, Charles Barnsley, 1850- tr. II. Title.
22-3798
Library of Congress PQ7519.D3P73
[42c1]

Nicholas, James Lawrence, 1890-
[Gibson, John William] 1841- ed.
M973.8 Progress of a race; or, The remarkable advancement of the
G35 American Negro, from the bondage of slavery, ignorance, and poverty to the freedom of citizenship, intelligence, affluence, honor and trust. Rev. and enl. by J. L. Nichols ... and William H. Crogman ... With special articles by well known authorities, Mrs. Booker T. Washington, Charles M. Melden ... M. W. Dogan ... Albon L. Holsey ... and an introduction by Robert R. Moton ... Naperville, Ill., J. L. Nichols & company [c1920]
480 p. front., illus., ports. 21½cm. (Continued on next card)
20-22088
[44l1]

Nicholas, James Lawrence, 1890-
[Gibson, John William] 1841- ed. Progress of a race
M973.8 ... [c1920] (Card 2)
G35 "Who's who in the Negro race": p. 329-460.
Published in 1912 by John William Gibson and William H. Crogman.
First edition published under title: The colored American.

1. Negroes. I. Nicholas, James Lawrence, 1890- II. Crogman, William Henry, 1841- III. Title.
20-22088
Library of Congress E185.G452
[44l1]

M326 Nichols, Charles Harold.
N515 Many thousand gone; the ex-slaves' account of their bondage and freedom, by Charles H. Nichols. Leiden, Brill, 1963.
xvi, 229 p. 25 cm. (Studies in American literature and history, 1)
Bibliography: p. [218]-224.
"To Arthur Spingarn, with high esteem, Charles H. Nichols."
1. Negroes—Biog. 2. Slavery in the U. S.—Conditions of slaves. I. Title. (Series)

E444.N5 64-55501
Library of Congress [3]

M06 Nichols, Franklin O
Am35 Health measures as they relate to the Negro race.

(In: American Academy of Political and Social Science, Philadelphia. The American Negro. Philadelphia, 1928. 24cm. p. 294-298.

M306 Nichols, Franklin O.
N21p Public health education in the Negro group.
In: National Conference of Social Work. Pp. 186-188, 1928.

M810 Nichols, Franklin O
F19 Some public health problems of the Negro.
v.1, no.9 Reprinted from the Journal of social hygiene, vol.8, July 1922.
281-285p. 26cm.

1.Health. I.Title.

M811.5 Nichols, James Emanuel
N51v Verse fragments. New York, Vantage Press, 1958.

77p. 21cm.
Portrait of author on book jacket.

1. Poetry, American. I. Title.

M973 **Nichols, James Lawrence,** *d.* 1895.
N51s Safe citizenship; or, Issues of the day ... and a complete dictionary of civil government. By J. L. Nichols ... 2d ed. Naperville, Ill., Toronto, Ont., J. L. Nichols & co., 1896.
1 p. l., 7-591 p. incl. illus., port. front. 18cm.

1. U. S.—Pol. & govt.—Handbooks, manuals, etc.
8-4876 Revised
Library of Congress JK246.N5 1896
Copyright 1896: 38454 [r30d2]

MB9 **Nicholson, Alfred William,** 1861–
B46m Brief sketch of the life and labors of Rev. Alexander Bettis; also an account of the founding and development of the Bettis academy, by Alfred W. Nicholson. Trenton, S. C., The author, 1913.
92 p. plates, 2 port. (incl. front.) 23cm. $1.00

1. Bettis, Alexander, 1836-1895. 2. Bettis academy, Aiken Co., S. C.
13-22301
Library of Congress E185.97.N62
Copyright A 357145

A nickel and a prayer.
MB9 **Hunter, Jane Edna (Harris)** 1882–
H91n A nickel and a prayer, by Jane Edna Hunter. [Nashville, The Parthenon press, ©1940]
198 p. 2 pl. (incl. port.) on 1 l. 19½cm.

1. Negroes—Charities. I. Phillis Wheatley association. II. Title.
41—7251
Library of Congress HV3181.H8
[a43f2] 923.673

South Africa
M896.3 Nicol, Abioseh Davidson, 1929-
R52m As the night the day.

Pp.36-52.

In: Rive, Richard, ed. Modern African prose. London, Heinemann Educational Books, 1964.

South Africa
M896 Nicol, Abioseh, Davidson, 1929-
M88 Life is sweet at Kumansenu.

Pp. 61-68.

In: Mphahlele, Ezekiel, ed. African writing today. Baltimore, Penguin Books, 1967.

Sierra Leone
M896.3 Nicol, Abioseh Davidson, 1929-
N54t The truly married woman and other stories. Illustrated by J. H. Vandi. London, Oxford University Press, 1965.

120p. 18½cm.

I. Title.

Sierra Leone
M896.3 **Nicol, Abioseh** Davidson, 1929-
N54tw Two African tales: The leopard hunt, and The devil at Yolahun Bridge. Illustrated by Hassan Bangurah. Cambridge [Eng.] University Press, 1965.
76 p. illus. 21 cm.

I. Title. II. Title: The leopard hunt. III. Title: The devil at Yolahun Bridge.
PZ7.N559Tw 65-19166
Library of Congress [8]

Sierra Leone
M960 Nicol, Davidson Sylvester Hector Willoughby
N541 Africa - a subjective review. [London] Longmans [in association with] Ghana Universities Press [1964]
88p. 21cm. (The Aggrey, Fraser, Guggisburg memorial lectures, 1963)
"References": p. 81-88.
Portrait of author on book jacket.

1. Africa. 2. Africa - Politics.
I. Title. II. Series.

Africa
M370 Nicol, Davidson Sylvester Hector Willoughby
C83 Politics, nationalism and universities in Africa.

Pp. 281-290.

In: Cowan, L. G., ed. Education and nation-building in Africa. New York, Praeger, 1965.

Haiti
M972.94 Nicolas, Hogar
N54o L'occupation Americaine d'Haiti; la revanche de l'histoire. Preface Pradel Pompilus. Madrid, Industrias Graficas Espana, 1956.

305p. 21cm.

1. Haiti I. Title.

Haiti
M972.94 Nicolas, Schiller
N54b Bases essentielles d'un redressement economique, par Schiller Nicolas. Port-au-Prince, Haiti, Imprimerie de l'etat [n.d.]

32p. 21cm.

1. Haiti-Economic conditions. I. Title.

Guyana
M823.91 **Nicole, Christopher,** 1930-
N54r Ratoon. New York, St. Martin's Press [1962]
256 p. 22 cm.

I. Title.
PZ4.N6425Rat 62-11111 ‡
Library of Congress [8]

British Guiana
M796 Nicole, Christopher, 1930-
N54 West Indian cricket; the story of cricket in the West Indies with complete records. London, Phoenix Sports Books [1957]

256p. ports. 22cm.

1. Cricket. I. Title.

Niebuhr, Reinhold, 1892-
M352.2 **Mississippi** black paper; fifty-seven Negro and white citi-
M69 zens' testimony of police brutality, the breakdown of law and order and the corruption of justice in Mississippi. Foreword by Reinhold Niebuhr. Introd. by Hodding Carter III. New York, Random House [1965]
92 p. illus. 28 cm.

1. Police — Mississippi. 2. Law enforcement — Mississippi. 3. Negroes—Mississippi. I. Title: Fifty-seven Negro and white citizens' testimony of police brutality. II. Niebuhr, Reinhold, 1892-
HV8145.M7M5 323.11960762 65-18103
Library of Congress [8]

Niger expedition.
Nigeria
M966.9 Crowther, Samuel Adjai, 1806-1891.
C88g The gospel on the banks of the Niger. Journals and notices of the native missionaries accompanying the Niger expedition of 1857-1859. By the Rev. Samuel Crowther and the Rev. John Christopher Taylor. London, Church Missionary House, 1859.

x, 451p. map. 20cm.

Niger River.
Nigeria
M966.9 Crowther, Samuel Adjai, 1806-1894.
C88jo Journals of the Rev. James Frederick Schon and Mr. Samuel Crowther, who, with the sanction of her majesty's government, accompanied the expedition up the Niger in 1841 in behalf of the church missionary society. With appendices and map. London, Hatchard and son, 1842.

xxii, 393p. map. 20½cm.

Nigeria Niger River.
M966.21 Issa, Ibrahim
Is7g Grandes eaux noires. Paris, Les Editions du Scorpion, 1959.

122p. 19cm. (Collection Alternance).

Niger Valley Exploring Party.
Delany, Martin Robison, 1812-1855
M910 Official report of the Niger Valley exploring party.
D37o By M. R. Delany, chief commissioner to Africa. New York, T. Hamilton; [etc., etc.] 1861.
4 p. l., [5]-75 p. 22½cm.

1. Liberia—Descr. & trav. 2. Yoruba—Descr. & trav. 3. Negroes—Colonization—Africa. I. Delany, Martin Robison, 1812-1885. II. Title.
5-15242
Library of Congress DT513.N68
—— —— Copy 2.

Nigeria
M966.9 Nigeria. Commerce and Industry.
N56hd Handbook,

Lagos, Federal Department of Commerce and Industries, 1952,

v. illus., maps. 24cm.

1. Nigeria-Industries. 2. Nigeria-Commerce.

Nigeria. Constitution.
Nigeria
M966.9
Id8
Odumosu, Oluwole Idowu.
The Nigerian Constitution: history and development. London, Sweet & Maxwell, 1963.
xix, 407 p. 23 cm. (Law in Africa, no. 4)
"Originally ... submitted as a thesis for the award of the Ph. D. degree of the University of London."
"The Constitution of the Federation of Nigeria": p. 309-397.
Bibliographical footnotes.
1. Nigeria—Constitutional history. 2. Nigeria—Constitutional law. I. Nigeria. Constitution. (Series)
63-4741
Library of Congress [1]

Nigeria
M966.9
Az2zi
Nigeria.
Azikiwe, Benjamin Nnamdi, 1904-
Zik on African unity; opening address to the heads of African and Malagasy States Conference in Lagos, 25th Jan. 1962 & Respect for human dignity; inaugural address delivered on 16th November 1960. Lagos, Udo-Na-Meche Stores, 1962.
21p. 22½cm.
Cover title.

Nigeria.
Nigeria
M966.9
C66o
Coker, Increase
Our oil palm industry. Lagos, Public Relations Department, n.d.
16p. illus. 20½cm. (Crownbird Series No. 20)

Nigeria
M966.9
N98
Nigeria. Constitution.
Nwabueze, B O
Reflections on the review of the Nigerian constitution. [Lagos, Times Press, 1963]
32p. 24cm.

Nigeria.
Nigeria
M966.9
Az2z
Azikiwe, Nnamdi, 1904-
Zik; a selection from the speeches of Nnamdi Azikiwe. Cambridge, University Press, 1961.
344p. port. 22cm.
Portrait of author on book jacket.

Nigeria
M966.9
C88g
Nigeria.
Crowther, Samuel Adjai, 1806-1891.
The gospel on the banks of the Niger. Journals and notices of the native missionaries accompanying the Niger expedition of 1857-1859. By the Rev. Samuel Crowther and the Rev. John Christopher Taylor. London, Church Missionary House, 1859.
x,451p. map. 20cm.

Nigeria
M966.9
N56ng
Nigeria. Federal Ministry of Commerce and Industry.
The Nigeria exhibition, 1st - 22nd October, 1960, Victoria Island, Lagos. Organized by the Federal Ministry of Commerce and Industry. Lagos [Federal Government Printing Department] 1960.
192 + 8p. ports. 25cm.
I. Title.

Nigeria
Nigeria
M966.9
Az2re
Azikiwe, Nnamdi, 1904-
Respect for human dignity; an inaugural address delivered by His Excellency Dr. Nnamdi Azikiwe, Governor General and Commander-in-Chief [of the] Federation of Government Printer] 1960.
25p. ports. 25cm.
Biographical data: pp. 19-25.

Nigeria
M966.9
C88j
1854
Nigeria.
Crowther, Samuel Adjai, 1806-1891.
Journal of an expedition up the Niger and Tshadda rivers, undertaken by McGregor Laird Esq. in connection with the British government in 1854. By the Rev. Samuel Crowther. With map and appendix. London, Church Missionary house, 1855.
xxxi, 233p. maps. 20½cm.

Nigeria. Laws, statutes, etc.
Nigeria
M966.9
El4n
1962
Elias, Taslim Olawale. 3d ed.
Nigerian land law and custom. London, Routledge & K. Paul [1951] 1962
xxvii, 336 p. map. 23 cm. 386p.
Thesis—University of London.
Includes legislation.
Bibliography: p. 316-319.
1. Land tenure—Nigeria—Law. 2. Real property—Nigeria. I. Nigeria. Laws, statutes, etc. II. Title.
333.3 52-28040
Library of Congress [58e8]

Nigeria
M966.9
B11o
Nigeria.
Babamuboni, I E
Ojo Oluwa (Sunday) lati owo Mr. I.E. Babamuboni. Lagos, Tanimola printing and bookbinding works, 1927.
12p. 18½cm.
In Yoruba.

Nigeria.
Nigeria
M966.9
C88o
[Crowther, Samuel Ajayi] bp., 1806-1891.
Omode ẹru-kunrin ti o di bisọpu, tabi itan Samuel Ajayi Crowther. 5th ed. Lagos, C.M.S. bookshop, 1931.
31p. port. illus. 21½cm.
The young slave who became a bishop.
In Yoruba.

Nigeria
M966.9
Ak5k
Nigeria.
Akinsuroju, Olurundayomi, 1925-
Knowing Nigeria, questions and answers on Nigeria's history. [Apapa, Nigeria, Times Press, n.d.]
15p. 21½cm.
"A daily times publication."

Nigeria.
Nigeria
M966.9
C15f
Campbell, Robert.
A few facts, relating to Lagos, Abbeokuta, and other sections of Central Africa. By Robert Campbell ... of the Niger Valley exploring party. Philadelphia, King & Baird, printers, 1860.
cover-title, [3]-18 p. 23cm.
1. Abeokuta, Africa—Descr. 2. Lagos—Descr. & trav.
5-14431†
Library of Congress DT513.C18
———— Copy 2.

Nigeria
M966.9
C88s
Nigeria.
Crowther, Samuel Adjai, 1806-1891.
Slave trade-African squadron. Letters from the Rev. Samuel Crowther...and the Rev. Henry Townsend ...London, John Mortimer, 1850.
15p. 22cm.
"Extracted from the Colonial magazine for December, 1850"

Nigeria.
Nigeria
M966.9
Ar42
Arikpo, Okoi, 1916-
The development of modern Nigeria. Harmondsworth, Penguin, 1967.
176 p. map. 18 cm. (Penguin African library) 4/6
(B 67-6778)
Bibliography: p. 170-[172]
1. Nigeria. I. Title.
DT515.A77 320.9'669 67-88269
Library of Congress [3]

Nigeria.
Nigeria
M966.9
The Catholic Church in an independent Nigeria.
A joint pastoral letter of the Nigerian Hierarchy. [Ibadan, Claverianum Press] 1960.
40p. 20cm.

Nigeria.
Nigeria
MB9
R17
Delano, Isaac O
The singing minister of Nigeria; the life of the Rev. Canon J. J. Ransome-Kuti, by Isaac O. Delano ... London, United society for Christian literature [1942]
63, [1] p. 18½cm. (Half-title: Africa's own library, no. 2)
1. Ransome-Kuti, Josaiah Jesse, 1855-1930. 2. Missions—Nigeria. I. United society for Christian literature, London. II. Title.
44-35818
Library of Congress BV3625.N6R3
[2] 922

Nigeria
M966.9
Az2r
Nigeria.
Azikiwe, Benjamin Nnamdi, 1904-
Renascent Africa, by Nnamdi Azikiwe...Accra, Gold Coast, West Africa, The author [1937]
313p. port. 22cm.

Nigeria.
Nigeria
M966.9
C34o
Chadwick, E R
Our community effort in the east. Lagos, Public Relations Department, n.d.
32p. illus. 20½cm. (Crownbird Series No. 30 Special)

Nigeria
M966.9
D37s
Nigeria.
Delano, Isaac O
The soul of Nigeria, by Isaac O. Delano. London, T. Werner Laurie [1937]
251 [1]p. front. (port) plates. 22cm.

Nigeria
M966.9
D54
Nigeria.
Diamond, Stanley
Nigeria; model of a colonial failure. New York, American Committee on Africa, 1967.

88p. map. 22cm. (Occassional paper, 6)
White author.

Partial contents.- The tragedy of Professor Diamond, by Simon Obi Anekive.- Does Stanley Diamond exist? By F. U. Anyiam.- Diamond

(Continued on next card)

Nigeria
M966.9
D54
Nigeria.
Diamond, Stanley. Nigeria, 1967. (Card 2)

(Partial contents.- Continued) was prophetic, by Akintunde Emiola.

1. Nigeria. I. American Committee on Africa. II. Title.

Nigeria
M966.9
Ed4b
Nigeria.
Edegbe, Joshua E
Benin-English grammar, by J. E. Edegbe. Lagos, C.M.S. Bookshop, 1936.

62p. 18½cm.

Nigeria
M966.9
Ed4e
Nigeria.
Edegbe, Joshua E.
Emwe Ebo kevbe edo, (colloquial English) vbobo Jeshua E. Edegbe. Lagos, Church Missionary Bookshop, 1935.

28p. 18cm.
In Benin.

Nigeria
M966.9
E14f
Nigeria.
Elias, Taslim Olawa le
Federation vs. confederation and the Nigerian federation. "Whitehall" Port-of-Spain, Office of the Premier of Trinidad and Tobago, 1960.

50p. 24½cm.

Nigeria
M966.9
Ep2o
Nigeria.
Epelle, Kiea, 1928-
Our land and people Part I - The East. Lagos, Public Relations Department, n.d.

16p. illus. 20½cm. (Crownbird Series no.31.)

Nigeria
M896.3
F13a
Nigeria.
Fagunwa, D O
Adìítú Olódùmarè. ... London, Thomas Nelson and Sons, Ltd., 1960.

148p. illus. 18½cm.
Text in dialect.

Nigeria
M966.9
G15o
Nigeria.
Gana, Mallam Abba
Our land and people; Part II - The north. Lagos, Public Relations Department, n.d.

16p illus. 20½cm.

Nigeria
M966.9
G35h
Nigeria.
Gibson, Thomas Ogbe.
A handbook on West African native laws and customs (with particular reference to Southern Nigeria), by Thomas Ogbe Gibson [n.p., n.p., n.d.]

26p. front. (port.) 13cm.

Nigeria
M966.9
G72
Nigeria.
Goubadia, B A A
Our olympic adventure. Lagos, Public Relations Department, n.d.

12p. illus. 20½cm. (Crownbird Series No. 17)

Nigeria
M966.9
H27
Nigeria.
Hassan, Sarkin Ruwa, Abuja.
A chronicle of Abuja. Translated and arranged from the Hausa of Malam Hassan and Malam Shuaibu. Ibadan, The University Press, 1952.

92p. illus. 22½cm.

Nigeria
M966.9
Il18
Nigeria.
Ilogu, Edmund
Social philosophy for the new Nigeria nation. Onitsha, Etudo Limited [1962]

42p. 21½cm.

M338.9
G92s
Nigeria.
Imoke, S E
Nigeria.

Pp. 33-34.
In: Science and the new nations, edited by Ruth Gruber. 1961.

M338.9
G92s
Nigeria.
Ita, Eyo, 1904-
Nigeria.

Pp. 35-38.
In: Science and the new nations, edited by Ruth Gruber. 1961.

Nigeria
M966.9
J71i
Nigeria.
Jones, Melville, bp.
Isin Kristi ati Isin Momodu, [Christianity and Mohammedanism] lati owo Bisopu Melville Jones. Lagos, printed and published by the C.M.S. Press, 1920.

62p. 19cm.
In Yoruba.

Nigeria
M966.9
L621
Nigeria.
Lijadu, E M
Ifa: imole rè ti ise ipilè isin ni ile Yoruba, [Sayings of the Yoruba] nipa E.M. Lijadu. Exeter, printed by James Townsend & Sons, 1923.

72p. front. (port.) 21½cm.
In Yoruba.

Nigeria
M966.9
L781
Nigeria.
LoBagola, Bata Kindai Amgoza ibn.
LoBagola; an African savage's own story. New York, A. A. Knopf, 1930.

xxiii p., 1 l., 402 p., 1 l. 2 port. (incl. front.) facsims. 21cm.

1. Ethnology—Nigeria.

Library of Congress DT515.L6 30—12774
[44n1] [572.9662] 920.9

Nigeria
M89
L781o
Nigeria.
LoBagola, Bata Kindai Amgoza Ibn.
LoBagola; histoire d'un sauvage africain par lui-meme. Traduite de l'Anglais par G. M. Drucker. Paris, Albin Michel 1932.

312p. 19cm. (Collection des maitres de la litterature etrangere)
Autobiography.

Nigeria
M641.5
M35k
Nigeria.
Mars, J A , compiler.
Kudeti book of Yoruba cookery. Lagos, The Church Missionary Society's Bookshop, 1936.

39p. 20cm.

Nigeria
M966.9
N98m
Nigeria.
Nwigwe, Henry Emezuem
My dreams of a greater Nigeria. [Yaba, West African Pilot, n.d.]

48p. port. 20½cm.
Portrait of author in book.

Nigeria
M966.9
Og1
Nigeria.
Ogbalu, F. Chidozie.
Dr. Zik of Africa; biography and speeches. [2d ed. Nigeria. African Literature Bureau [1961]

272p. ports. 20cm.

Nigeria M966.9 Og9s
Nigeria.
Ogumefu, M I
The staff of Oranyan and other Yoruba tales, by M. I. Ogumefu. London, The Sheldon Press, [1930]
iv, 5-32p. illus. 18½cm.

Nigeria M966.9 T32o
Nigeria.
Thanni, Ade.
Our coronation visitors. Lagos, Public Relations Department, n.d.
32p. illus. 20½cm. (Crownbird Series No. 35 (Special)

Nigeria M200 C46
Nigeria - Churches - Protestant.
Christian Council of Nigeria.
Building for tomorrow; a pictorial history of the protestant church in Nigeria. Lagos, Christian Council of Nigeria, 1960.
35p. illus., ports. 28cm.

Nigeria M966.9 Og9t
Nigeria.
Ogumefu, M I
Tales of tortoise, Yoruba tales, by M. I. Ogumefu. London, The Sheldon Press [n.d.]
v, 7-32p. illus. 18½cm.

Nigeria M896.4 Ok5r
Nigeria - Addresses, essays, lectures.
Okoye, Mokwugo, 1926-
The rebel line; memoirs of revolutionary struggle and a penetrating study of life and literature with moving panegyrics on love and liberty. [Onitsha, Nigeria, Etudo Limited, 1962]
111p. 21cm.

Nigeria M966.92 L891
Nigeria - Cities and towns.
Losi, Prince John B Ogunjimi
Iwe itan ogun ati ote ilu-oke. Lagos, Church Missionary Society Bookshop, 1930.
32p. 18½cm.
A book of stories and political strives of the Yoruba cities and towns North of Ibadan.

Nigeria M966.9 Og9y
Nigeria.
Ogumefu, M I
Yoruba legends. London, The Sheldon Press [1929]
87p. 17½cm.

Nigeria M966.9 St6o
Nigeria - Art.
Stocker, John
Our festival of the arts. Lagos, Public Relations Department, n.d.
19p. illus. 20½cm. (Crwonbird Series No. 5)

Nigeria M966.9 N56hd
Nigeria-Commerce.
Nigeria. Commerce and Industry.
Handbook,
Lagos, Federal Department of Commerce and Industries, 1952,
v. illus., maps. 24cm.

Nigeria M966.9 Og9a
Nigeria.
Ogunbiye, Thomas A J
Awon Serafu [by] Thos. A. J. Ogunbiye. Lagos, C.M.S. press, 1926.
14p. 18½cm.
In Yoruba.

Nigeria M966.9 At8a
Nigeria - Bible, Personalities in.
Atundaolu, H
Awon enia inu Bibeli. Lagos, [n.p.] 1906.
208p. 21½cm.
Translation: Personalities in the Bible.

Nigeria M966.9 Ez3c
Nigeria - Constitutional history.
Ezera, Kalu.
Constitutional developments in Nigeria; an analytical study of Nigeria's constitution-making developments and the historical and political factors that affected constitutional change. Cambridge, University Press, 1960.
xv, 274 p. maps (1 fold.) 23 cm.
Bibliography: p. 262-270.
1. Nigeria—Constitutional history. I. Title.
JQ3082.E95 342.66909 60—50924
Library of Congress [61f5]

Nigeria M966.9 Oj3p
Nigeria.
Ojike, Mbonu.
Portrait of a boy in Africa [by] Mbonu Ojike. New York, East and West association [c1945]
36p. illus. 23cm.

Nigeria MB An91
Nigeria - Biography.
Anyiam, Frederick Uzoma, 1914-
Among Nigerian celebrities. Lagos, Yaba, 1960.
71p. ports. 21cm.

Nigeria M966.9 Id8
Nigeria - Constitutional history.
Odumosu, Oluwole Idown.
The Nigerian Constitution: history and development. London, Sweet & Maxwell, 1963.
xix, 407p. 23cm. (Law in Africa, no. 4)

Nigeria M966.9 P96o
Nigeria.
Public Relations Department
Our delegates in London. Lagos, Public Relations Department, n.d.
14p. illus. 20½cm. (Crownbird Series No.34)
1. Nigeria.

Nigeria M966.9 Ik7o
Nigeria - Biography.
Ikoli, Ernest
Our Council of ministers. Lagos, Public Relations Department, n.d.
22p. illus. 20½cm. (Crownbird Series No.11)

Nigeria M966.9 Ek34
Nigeria - Constitutional law.
Ekineh, Aliyi
Democratic rights during a period of emergency. A study of the 1962 Nigerian Emergency. [Yaba, Nigeria, The Pacific Printers, n.d.]
68p. 20½cm.

Nigeria. M966.9 So5o
Nigeria.
Sowunmi, Akintunde
Our land and People. Part III - the west. Lagos, Public Relations Department, n.d.
16p. illus. map. 20½cm. (Crownbird Series No. 33)

Nigeria MB9 N56e
Nigeria - Biog.
Nigerian Broadcasting Corporation.
Eminent Nigerians of the nineteenth century, a series of studies originally broadcast by the Nigerian Broadcasting Corporation. Cambridge, University Press, 1960.
97 p. 19 cm.
1. Nigeria—Biog. 2. Nigeria—Hist. I. Title.
DT515.N49 920.0669 60—3478 ‡
Library of Congress [61c5]

Nigeria M966.9 N98
Nigeria - Constitutional law.
Nwabueze, B O
Reflections on the review of the Nigerian constitution. [Lagos, Times Press, 1963]
32p. 24cm.

Nigeria M966.9 Od8

Nigeria - Constitutional law.
Odumosu, Oluwole Idowu.
The Nigerian Constitution: history and development. London, Sweet & Maxwell, 1963.

xix, 407p. 23cm. (Law in Africa, no. 4)

Nigeria M966.9 C47a

Nigeria - Economic conditions.
Chukwuemeka, Nwankwo.
African dependencies, a challenge to western democracy; a study of the resources, commerce and industries of Nigeria and suggestions for the economic development of the dependency. New York, William-Frederick Press, 1950.

207 p. map. 24 cm.
Bibliography: p. 198-200.

1. Nigeria—Econ. condit. I. Title.

HC517.N48C5 330.9669 50-2945

Library of Congress [8]

Nigeria M896.3 AJ74y

Nigeria - Fiction.
Ajose, Audrey
Yomi's adventure. With drawings by Mick Pilcher. Cambridge, University Press, 1964.

90p. illus. 18½cm.

Nigeria M340 N97

Nigeria - Courts.
Nwabueze, Benjamin Obi.
The machinery of justice in Nigeria. London, Butterworths, 1963.

xxi, 309p. 23cm. (Butterworth's African law series, no. 8)

Nigeria M966 D56t

Nigeria - Econ condit.
Dike, K Onwuka.
Trade and politics in the Niger Delta, 1830-1885; an introduction to the economic and political history of Nigeria. Oxford, Clarendon Press, 1956.

vi, 250 p. fold. map, tables. 22 cm. (Oxford studies in African affairs)

"Grew out of [the author's] ... thesis for the degree of doctor of philosophy (history) in the University of London."
Bibliographical references included in "Note on the sources" (p. [224]-230)

1. Nigeria—Econ. condit. 2. Nigeria—Pol. & govt. (Series)

HC517.N48D5 56-13763

Library of Congress [8]

Nigeria M896.3 AL81on

Nigeria - Fiction.
Aluko, Timothy Mofolorunso, 1918-
One man, one matchet. London, Heinemann, 1964.

196p. 18½cm.
Portrait of author on book jacket.

Nigeria M966.9 AJ51a

Nigeria - Customary law.
Ajisafẹ, Ajayi Kọlawọle.
Laws and customs of the Benin People, by A.K. Ajisafẹ. Lagos, Kash & Klare Bookshop, 1945.

101p. front. 18½cm.

Nigeria M966.9 It2r

Nigeria - Economic conditions.
Ita, Eyo, 1904-
Reconstructing towards wider integration; A theory of social symbiosis. Calabar, W.A.P.I. press.

9p. 18cm.

Nigeria M896.3 At47i

Nigeria - Fiction
Atilade, Emmanuel Adekunle, 1911-
Irin ajo Ọpáläbä si ilu ọba ajántálá; apa I. Lagos, Ife-Olu Printing Works, n.d.

73p. illus. 21½cm.
Written in Yoruba.

Nigeria M966.9 AJ51

Nigeria-Customary laws.
Ajisafẹ, Ajayi Kọlawọle.
The laws and customs of the Yoruba people, by A.K. Ajisafẹ. London, George Routledge & Sons, Ltd., 1924.

97p. front. 17½cm.

Nigeria M338 On9

Nigeria - Economic policy.
Onyemelukwe, Clement Chukwukadibia.
Problems of industrial planning and management in Nigeria [by] C. C. Onyemelukwe. London, Longmans, 1966.

vii, 330 p. tables, diagrs. 22½ cm. 42/-

Bibliography: p. 319-322.

(B 66-14302)

1. Nigeria—Economic policy. 2. Nigeria—Indus. I. Title.

HC517.N48O55 338.9669 66-74020

Library of Congress [3]

Nigeria M896.3 At47i Bk.2

Nigeria - Fiction.
Atilade, Emmanuel Adekunle, 1911-
Irin ajo Ọpalaba si ilu ọba ajantala; apa II. Lagos, New Nigeria Press, 1963.

93p. 21cm.
Written in Yoruba.
Translated title: Journey of Opalaba to the country of King Ajantala, Part II.

Nigeria M966.9 El4nt

Nigeria-Customs.
Elias, Taslim Olawale
La nature du droit coutumier Africain. Traduit de l'anglais par Decouflé et Dessau. Paris, Présence Africaine, 1961.

327p. 22½cm.

Nigeria M378 Ad31

Nigeria - Education.
Adetoro, J E ,ed.
The handbook of education, Nigeria, 1960; an independence souvenir. [Oshogbo] Schools and General Publication Services.

280p. 21cm.

Nigeria M896.3 Ek87b

Nigeria - Fiction.
Ekwensi, Cyprian
Burning grass; a story of the Fulani of Northern Nigeria. Illustrations by A. Folarin. Cover drawings by Dennis Duerden. London, Heinemann [1962]

150p. illus. 18½cm. (African writers series, 2)

Jamaica M966.9 C15f

Nigeria - Description and travel.
Campbell, Robert
A few facts, relating to Lagos, Abbeokuta, and other sections of Central Africa. By Robert Campbell ... of the Niger Valley exploring party. Philadelphia, King & Baird Printers, 1860.

18p. 23cm.

Nigeria M370 Ik3

Nigeria - Education.
Ikejiani, Okechukwu, ed.
Nigeria education. Edited and introduced by Okechukwu Ikejiani with a foreword by Nnamdi Azikiwe. Ikeja, Nigeria, Longmans of Nigeria, 1964.

Nigeria M966.3 F13ig

Nigeria - Fiction.
Fagunwa, D O
Igbo olodumare; apa keji ogboju ọdẹ ninu igbo irunmalẹ. Edinburgh, Thomas Nelson and Sons, Ltd., 1949.

165p. illus. 19cm.

1. Nigeria - fiction. I. Title.

Nigeria M966.9 D37n

Nigeria - Descr. and trav.
Delano, Isaac O
Notes and comments from Nigeria, by Isaac O. Delano...London, The United Society for Christian Literature [1944]

64p. 18½cm (Africa's own library no.8)

Nigeria M370 So42

Nigeria - Education.
Solarin, Tai,
Towards Nigeria's moral self-government. Ikenne, Tai Solarin, 1959.

95p. 21cm.

Nigeria M966.3 F13ir

Nigeria - Fiction.
Fagunwa, D O
Irèkè-onibùdo. Edinburgh, Thomas Nelson and Sons, Ltd., 1949.

141p. illus. 19cm.

1. Nigeria - fiction. I. Title.

Nigeria - Fiction.
Nigeria
M966.3
F131
Fagunwa, D O
Irinkerindo ninu igbo elégbêje; apa keta ogboju ọdẹ ninu igbo irunmalẹ. Edinburgh, Thomas Nelson and Sons, Ltd., 1954.
117p. illus. 19cm.
1. Nigeria - fiction. I. Title.

Nigeria - Folklore.
Nigeria
M398
Ep20
Pt.2
Epelle, Kiea.
Our folk lore and fables. Part II Lagos, Public Relations Department, n.d.
16p. illus. 20½cm. (Crownbird Series, no. 37)

Nigeria - History.
Nigeria
M966.9
Ak52
Akinyede, Gilbert Benjamin Akinyemi
The political and constitutional problems of Nigeria. ₛLagos, Nigerian Print. and Pub. Co., 1957ₛ
88p. port. 21½cm.
Portrait of author in book.
References: p. ₛ2ₛ

Nigeria
M896.3
N97d
Nigeria - Fiction.
Nwankwo, Nkem
Danda. ₛLondonₛ A. Deutsch ₛ1964ₛ
205p. 20cm.
Portrait of author on book jacket.

Nigeria - Folklore.
Nigeria
M398
F95o
Fuja, S A
Our folklore and fables by J. A. Danford and S. A. Fuja. Lagos, Public Relations Department, n.d.
14p. illus. 20½cm. (Crownbird Series No.14)
1. Nigeria - folklore.

Nigeria-History.
Nigeria
M966.9
A11a
Alagoa, E J
The Akassa raid, 1895-[Ibadan], [printed at the Ibadan University Press], [1960].
20p. 22cm.

Nigeria - Fiction.
Nigeria
M896.3
N98b
Nzekwu, Onuora, 1928-
Blade among the boys. London, Hutchinson [1962]
191p. 20cm.

Nigeria
M398
L14a
Nigeria-Folklore.
Lakeru, J A
Awon owe ile wa Ti a Kojo, Nipa Rev. J. A. Lakeru. Abeokuta, E.N.A. Press, [1916]
32 p. 18½ cm.

Nigeria - History.
Nigeria
M966.9
An34
Anene, Joseph C
Southern Nigeria in transition, 1885-1906; theory and practice in a colonial protectorate. Cambridge, Cambridge U. P., 1966.
xii, 360 p. illus., 9 plates (incl. map, ports.) tables. 22½ cm. 45/-
(B 66-5470)
Bibliography: p. 340-346.
1. Nigeria—Hist. I. Title.
DT515.7.A48 966.903 66-70318 rev
Library of Congress [r66f5]

Nigeria
M896.3
Ok1v
Nigeria - Fiction.
Okara, Gabriel
The voice, a novel. ₛLondonₛ A. Deutsch ₛ1964ₛ
157p. 19cm.
Portrait of author on book jacket.

Nigeria - History.
Nigeria
M966.9
Ad34
Ademoyega, 'Wale.
The Federation of Nigeria, from earliest times to independence. Illustrated by Ben Enwonwu. London, Harrap [1962]
208 p. illus. 20 cm.
Includes bibliography.
1. Nigeria—Hist.
DT515.5.A3 63-33532 ‡
Library of Congress [3]

Nigeria
M966.9
F178
Nigeria - History.
Fajana, A
Nigeria and her neighbours. Lagos, African Universities Press, 1964.
92p. illus., photos., maps. 18cm.

Nigeria - Fiction.
Nigeria
M896.3
T88f
Tutuola, Amos
Feather woman of the jungle. London, Faber and Faber, 1962.
132p. 21cm.

Nigeria
M966.9
Aj11
Nigeria - Hist.
Ajayi, J F Ade.
Milestones in Nigerian history. Ibadan, Nigeria, University College [1962]
47 p. illus., ports., map. 22 cm.
"For further reading": p. 47.
1. Nigeria—Hist. I. Title.
DT515.5.A64 63-6467
Library of Congress [1]

Nigeria - History.
Nigeria
M89
Ik7
Ikoli, Ernest.
Our northern warriors. Lagos, Public Relations Department, n.d.
12p. illus. 20½cm. (Crownbird Series No.15)

Nigeria - Fiction.
Nigeria
M896.3
T88p
Tutuola, Amos.
The palm-wine drinkard and his dead palm-wine tapster in the Deads' Town. London, Faber and Faber [1952]
125 p. 21 cm.
I. Title.
PZ4.T968Pal 52-43382 ‡
Library of Congress [58b1]

Nigeria
M966.9
Aj1ly
Nigeria - History.
Ajayi, J F Ade.
Yoruba warfare in the nineteenth century, by J. F. Ade Ajayi and Robert Smith. Cambridge [Eng.] University Press, 1964.
x, 160 p. maps, plans, plate. 23 cm.
Bibliography: p. 148-151. Bibliographical footnotes.
1. Yorubas. 2. Nigeria—Hist. I. Smith, Robert Sydney. II. Title.
DT513.A48 966.9 64-21522
Library of Congress [5]

Nigeria
M966.9
L89hi
Nigeria - History.
Losi, John B Ogunjimi.
History of Abeokuta, by Prince J.B. Ogunjimi Losi. Lagos, Nigeria, Bosere Press, 1924.
176p. 21cm.

Nigeria - Fiction.
Nigeria
M896.3
T88s
Tutuola, Amos.
Simbi and the satyr of the dark jungle. London Faber and Faber, 1955.
136p. 20½cm.

Nigeria
M966.9
Aj5h
Nigeria - History.
Ajisafe, Ajayi Kolawole.
History of Abeokuta, by Ajayi Kolawole Ajisafe. Bungay, Suffolk, Printed for the Author by Richard Clay & sons, Ltd., 1924.
225p. plates, 18cm.

Nigeria
M966.9
L89h
Nigeria - History.
Losi, John B. Ogunjimi.
History of Lagos, by Prince John B. O. Losi... second edition. Lagos, C.M.S. Bookshop, 1921.
ii, 75p. plates 22½cm.

Nigeria - History.
Nigeria
M966.9
L89hi
Losi, John B Ogunjimi.
Itan Abeokuta. Lati owo Prince John B.O. Losi. 2nd impression. Exeter James Townsend & Co., 1920.
135p. 21½cm.
Bound with: John B.O. Losi's History of Abeokuta.

Nigeria - History.
Nigeria
M966.9
L89h
Losi, John B Ogunjimi.
Itan eko, nipa Prince John B. O. Losi... third edition. Lagos, Church missionary society's press, 1921.
60p. plates. 22½cm.

Nigeria - History.
Nigeria
M966.9
M31z
Mani, Abdulmalik
Zuwan turawa nijeriya ta arewa. ‹Local history of Nigeria› Zaria, Norla; London, Longmans, Green and Co., 1957.
218p. 18½cm.
Written in Hausa.

Nigeria - History.
Nigeria
M89
N56e
Nigerian Broadcasting Corporation.
Eminent Nigerians of the nineteenth century, a series of studies originally broadcast by the Nigerian Broadcasting Corporation. Cambridge, University Press, 1960.
97 p. 19 cm.
1. Nigeria—Biog. 2. Nigeria—Hist. I. Title.
DT515.N49 920.0669 60—3478 ‡
Library of Congress ₍61c5₎

Nigeria - History.
Nigeria
M966.9
Ok52
Okonkwo, D Onuzulike
History of Nigeria in a new setting. ₍Aba, International Press, 1962.₎
378p. illus. 19cm.
Includes bibliography.

Nigeria - History.
Nigeria
M966.9
P96
Public Relations Department.
100 facts about Nigeria. Lagos, Public Relations Department, n.d.
8p. map 20½cm.

Nigeria - History.
Nigeria
M900
Sa58
Sangowawa, Bennett Adetola Oluwole (1915-)
Scholars' handbook of history, Part II. Rev. and enl. ed., Ijebu-Ode, Nigeria, Benson House of Commerce ‹1958›
121p. 18cm.

Nigeria-Industries.
Nigeria
M966.9
N56hd
Nigeria. Commerce and Industry.
Handbook,
Lagos, Federal Department of Commerce and Industries, 1952,
v. illus., maps. 24cm.

Nigeria - Industries.
Nigeria
M338
On9
Onyemelukwe, Clement Chukwukadibia.
Problems of industrial planning and management in Nigeria ₍by₎ C. C. Onyemelukwe. London, Longmans, 1966.
vii, 330 p. tables, diagrs. 22½ cm. 42/-
(B 66-14802)
Bibliography: p. 319-322.
1. Nigeria—Economic policy. 2. Nigeria—Indus. I. Title.
HC517.N48O55 338.9669 66-74020
Library of Congress ₍3₎

Nigeria - Juvenile literature.
Nigeria
M372.8
B813
Brown, Godfrey M
Stories from the south of Nigeria. Illustrated by M. A. Ajayi. London, Allen ₍1966₎
79p. illus. 18cm. (African social studies for the primary school)
1. Nigeria - Juvenile literature. I. Title.

Nigeria - Land tenure.
Nigeria
M966.9
Ak5o
Akinyele, I B
The outlines of Ibadan history, by Chief I.B. Akinyele. Lagos, Alebiosu printing press, 1946.
135p. front. (port.) 18½cm.

Nigeria-Laws.
Nigeria
M966.9
El4nt
Elias, Taslim Olawale
La nature du droit coutumier Africain. Traduit de l'anglais par Decouflé et Dessau. Paris, Présence Africaine, 1961.
327p. 22½cm.

Nigeria - Laws, statutes, etc.
Nigeria
M966.9
El4n
Elias, Taslim Olawale.
Nigerian land law and custom. London, Routledge & K. Paul ₍1951₎
xxvii, 326p. map. 23cm.
Thesis-University of London.
Includes legislation.
Bibliography: p. 316-319.

Nigeria - Laws, statutes, etc.
Nigeria
M966.9
N56c
Nigeria's constitutional story (1862-1954)
Lagos, A Federal Information Service Publications, 1954.
24p. illus. 21cm.

Nigeria-Music.
A
M784
Aw6
₍Ransome-Kuti, Josiah Jessie, 1855-1930₎
Awọn orin mimọ ni ede ati ohùn ile wa. Yoruba sacred songs. Lagos, C.M.S. Bookshop, 1925.
556-617p. 18½cm.

Nigeria - Nationalist movement.
Nigeria
M966.9
Og9a
Ogumbiyi, Thomas A J
Awon serafu. (The seraphum). Lagos, Church Missionary Society Press, 1926.
14p. 19cm.

Nigeria - Native races.
Nigeria
M966.9
H27a
Hassan, Sarkin Ruwa Abuja
A chronicle of Abuja; translated and arranged from the Hausa of Alhaji Hassan and Mallam Shuaibu Na'ibi by Frank Heath. ‹Rev. and enl. ed.› Lagos, African Universities Press, 1962.
91p. illus. 25cm.

Nigeria - Native races.
Nigeria
M966.9
M782
Moore, E A Ajisafe
The laws and customs of the Yoruba people. Abeokuta, Nigeria, M. A. Ola Fola Bookshops ₍n.d.₎
85p. 18cm.
1. Nigeria - Native races. 2. Yorubas. I. Title.

Nigeria - Poetry.
Nigeria
M896.1
Aj5g
Ajiṣafẹ, Ayaji Kolawole.
Ọrúnmìla, (a ko gbọdọ dà a ko laigbaẹ). Suffolk, Richard Clay & Sons, Ltd., 1923.
16p. 18cm.
Boundwith: Gbadebo Alake, by Ajayi Kolawole Ajisafe. 1922. 26p.

Nigeria - Poetry.
Nigeria
M896.1
Aj5g
Ajiṣafẹ, Ajayi Kọlawọle.
Gbadebọ Alake (lati Ogosti 8, 1898 titi de May 28, 1920). ₍A bibliography of Gbadebo Alake from August 8, 1898 to May 28, 1920₎, Bungay, Suffolk, Printed for the author by Richard Clay & Sons, Ltd., 1922.
26p. port. 18cm.

Nigeria - Police.
Nigeria
M966.9
Ou7p
Our police force. Lagos, Public Relations Department, nd. Crownbird series, No. 10 (Special).
28p. illus. 20½cm.
1. Nigeria-police.

Africa
M896.1
B29a

Nigeria - Poetry.
Bassir, Olumbe, 1920- , comp.
An anthology of West African verse. Ibadan, Ibadan University Press, 1957.
68p. 20½cm.
Nigerian compiler.

Nigeria
M966.9
Uw1

Nigeria - Politics.
Uwanaka, Charles U.
Awolowo and Akintola in political storm. Yaba, Published by the author and printed by John Okwesa and Company. ⌊1964⌋
119p. port., 20½cm.

Nigeria
MB9
B41m

Nigeria - politics and government.
Bello, *Sir* Ahmadu, 1909-
My life. Cambridge ⌊Eng.⌋ University Press, 1962.
245 p. illus. 23 cm.
1. Nigeria—Pol. & govt.
DT515.6.B4A3 966.9 63-6 ‡
Library of Congress ⌊2⌋

Nigeria
M896.1
Ob1i

Nigeria-Poetry.
Obasa, Denrele Adetimkan.
Iwe kinni ti awon Akewi (Yoruba philosophy) nipa Denrele Adetimkan Obasa. Published by Egbe Agba-'O-Tan. Ibaden, The Ilard, ⌊1927⌋
61 p. 19 cm.

Nigeria
M966.9
Ak5n

Nigeria-politics and government.
Akinsuroju, O
Nigeria political theatre (1923-53). Lagos, published by the City Publishing Association, ⌊1953⌋.
28p. port. 19cm.

Nigeria
M966.9
B52e

Nigeria - Politics and government.
Biobaku, Saburi Oladeni.
The Egba and their neighbours, 1842-1872. Oxford, Clarendon Press, 1957.
vi, 128 p. maps, tables. 22 cm. (Oxford studies in African affairs)
"Based on a Ph. D. thesis submitted to the University of London in May 1951."
Bibliography: p. ⌊106⌋-118.
1. Egba (African tribe) 2. Nigeria—Pol. & govt. (Series)
DT515.B5 966.92 57-59620
Library of Congress ⌊5⌋

Nigeria
M896.1
So9a

Nigeria - Poetry.
Sowande, J S
Awọn àrofo-orin ti Sọbọ A-ró-bi-odu li ọdun 1930. Ake Abeokuta, 1931.
47p. 20½cm.
Written in Yoruba.
Translation: A series of poems.
"Alias Sobo a-ró-bi-odu"

Nigeria
M966.9
Ak52

Nigeria - Politics and government.
Akinyede, Gilbert Benjamin Akinyemi
The political and constitutional problems of Nigeria. ⌊Lagos, Nigerian Print. and Pub. Co., 1957⌋
88p. port. 21½cm.
Portrait of author in book.
References: p. ⌊2⌋

Nigeria
M966.9
B619

Nigeria - Politics and government.
Blitz, L Franklin, ed.
The politics and administration of Nigerian government, edited by Franklin Blitz. Contributors: M. J. Campbell ⌊and others⌋ New York, Praeger, 1965.
xiv, 281p. illus. 22cm.
Partial contents.- Land, people and tradition in Nigeria, by Akin L. Mabogunje.- Constitutional development, by Oluwole Idowu Odumosu.
Bibliography: p. 265-271.
White editor.

Nigeria
M966.9
Ac85

Nigeria - Politics.
Action Group of Nigeria.
1956 summer school lectures. Ibadan, The Action Group Bureau of Information, ⌊1957⌋
38p. 24cm.

Nigeria
M966.9
A18p

Nigeria - Politics and government.
Aluko, S A
The problems of self-government for Nigeria; a critical analysis. Ilfracombe, Devon, Arthur H. Stockwell ⌊1956⌋
62p. 18½cm.

Nigeria
M966.9
D28n

Nigeria-Pol. & govt.
Davies, Hezekiah Oladipo.
Nigeria: the prospects for democracy. London, Weidenfeld and Nicolson ⌊1961⌋
185 p. 22 cm.
1. Nigeria—Pol. & govt.
DT515.8.D3 62-2967 ‡
Library of Congress ⌊3⌋

Nigeria
M966.9
B195

Nigeria - Politics.
Balewa, Alhaji Sir Abubakar Tafawa, 1912-
Nigeria speaks; speeches made between 1957 and 1964. Selected and introduced by Sam Epelle. Foreword by T.O.S. Benson. ⌊Ikeja, Nigeria⌋ Longmans of Nigeria ⌊1964⌋
178p. illus. ports. 22cm.

Nigeria
MB
An9m

Nigeria - Politics and government.
Anyiam, Frederick Uzoma, 1914-
Men and matters in Nigerian politics (1934-58). Yaba, Printed by John Okwesa & Co., 1958.
90p. ports., illus. 23cm.

Nigeria
M966.9
D56t

Nigeria - Pol. & govt.
Dike, K Onwuka.
Trade and politics in the Niger Delta, 1830-1885; an introduction to the economic and political history of Nigeria. Oxford, Clarendon Press, 1956.
vi, 250 p. fold. map, tables. 22 cm. (Oxford studies in African affairs)
"Grew out of ⌊the author's⌋ ... thesis for the degree of doctor of philosophy (history) in the University of London."
Bibliographical references included in "Note on the sources" (p. ⌊224⌋-230)
1. Nigeria—Econ. condit. 2. Nigeria—Pol. & govt. (Series)
HC517.N48D5 56-13763
Library of Congress ⌊3⌋

Nigeria
M966.9
N29

Nigeria - Politics.
Ndem, Eyo B E
Ibos in contemporary Nigerian politics; a study in group conflict. Onitsha, Nigeria, Etudo Limited, 1961.
44p. 21½cm.

Nigeria
M966.9
Aw6p

Nigeria - Pol. & govt.
Awolowo, Obafemi, 1909-
Path to Nigerian freedom; with a foreword by Margery Perham. London, Faber and Faber ⌊1947⌋
137 p. 23 cm.
1. Nigeria—Pol. & govt. I. Title.
JQ3082.A85 342.66909 47—24937*
Library of Congress ⌊a56c½⌋

Nigeria
MB9
En11

Nigeria - Pol. & govt.
Enahoro, Anthony Eronsele Oseghale, 1923-
Fugitive offender; the story of a political prisoner ⌊by⌋ Anthony Enahoro. London, Cassell ⌊1965⌋
xi, 436 p. illus., map, plan, ports. 22 cm.
Autobiographical.
1. Nigeria—Pol. & govt. I. Title.
DT515.8.E5 966.9050924 66-2006
Library of Congress ⌊2⌋

Nigeria
M966.9
Or27

Nigeria - Politics.
Oredein, S T
A manual on Action Group Party Organisation. ⌊Ibadan, Action Group Headquarter, n.d.⌋
57p. 21½cm.

Nigeria
M966.9
Aw6t

Nigeria - Politics and government.
Awolowo, Obafemi, 1909-
Thoughts on Nigerian constitution. Ibadan, London, Oxford U. P., 1966.
xii, 196 p. front. (map), tables. 21½ cm. 19/6
(B 67-10848)
1. Nigeria—Pol. & govt. I. Title.
JQ3083 1966.A9 342.669'03 67-90818
Library of Congress ⌊3⌋

Nigeria
M966.9
Ep2p

Nigeria-Politics and govt.
Epelle, Sam, 1930-
The promise of Nigeria. London, Pan Books Ltd., 1960.
252p. 17½cm.
Portrait of author on book cover.

Nigeria
M966.9
It2a

Nigeria - Pol. & Govt.
Ita, Eyo, 1904-
The assurance of freedom. Calabar, W.A.P.I. press, 1949.

62p. 18cm.

Nigeria
M290
Eg39

Nigeria - Religion.
Egharevba, Jacob Uwadiae, 1893-
Some tribal gods of Southern Nigeria. ‹Benin City, The Author› 1951.

59p. 18cm.
Portrait of author.

Nigeria
M39.
Ar46

Nigeria - Social life and customs.
Ariwoola, Olagoke, 1940-
The African wife. London, Kenion Pre , 196.

113p. 18½cm.
Portrait of author on book cover.

1. Marriage - Nigeria. 2. Family - Nigeria. 3. Nigeria - Social life and customs. I. Title.

Nigeria
M966.9
J21

Nigeria - Politics & government.
Jakande, L K
The trial of Obafemi Awolowo, by L. K. Jakande. London, Secker & Warburg; Lagos, John West Publications, 1966.

xiv, 354 p. front. (port.) 7 plates (incl. facsims., ports.) 22½ cm. 42/- (B 66-24229)

1. Awolowo, Obafemi, 1909- 2. Nigeria—Pol. & govt. I. Title.

343.31 67-71061

Library of Congress [3]

Nigeria
M966.9
L96

Nigeria - Religion.
Lucas, J Olumide
The religion of the Yorubas; being an account of the religious beliefs and practices of the Yoruba peoples of Southern Nigeria, especially in relation to the religion of ancient Egypt. Lagos, C.M.S. Bookshop, 1948.

420p. illus. 21½cm.

Nigeria
MB9
Ok1

Nigeria - Social life and customs.
Okafor-Omali, Dilim
A Nigerian villager in two worlds. London, Faber and Faber [1965]

159p. 19cm.

1. Nigeria - Social life and customs. I. Title.

Nigeria
MB9
Aw6m

Nigeria - Politics and government.
'Mosanya, Adio
Martyrdom, of Chief Obafemi Awolowo. ‹n.p., n.d.›

23p. 18½cm.

Nigeria
M173.1
At47

Nigeria - Social conditions.
Atilade, Emmanuel Adekunle, 1911-
Iwe asaro lori awọn nkan ti nmu; ikọsilẹ wa lẹjin igbeyawo. Mushin, New Nigeria Press ‹1964›

83p. 20cm.
Written in Yoruba.

Nigeria
M966.9
Ok5i

Nigeria-Social life and customs.
Okojie, Christopher Gbelokoto, 1920-
Ishan native laws and customs. Yaba, John Okwesa & Co., 1960.

338p. illus., ports. 24cm.

Nigeria
M966.9
Or3

Nigeria- Pol. & Govt.
Oresanya, A O Compiler.
An outline of the system of administration in Nigeria; being excerpts from the Nigeria handbook and other publications, compiled by A. O. Oresanya. 6th ed. Lagos, The Ife-Olu Printing Works, 1942.

45p. 18½cm.

Nigeria
M966.9
Or1w

Nigeria--Social conditions.
Orizu, Akweke Abyssinia Nwafor, 1920-
Without bitterness; western nations in post-war Africa, by A. A. Nwafor Orizu. New York, N. Y., Creative age press, inc. [1944]

xiv, 395 p. 21cm.

1. Africa—Civilization. 2. Africa—Native races. 3. Nigeria—Soc. condit. 4. Reconstruction (1939-)—Africa. I. Title.

44—7985

Library of Congress DT14.O7 [46q7] 960

Nigeria
M784
R17a

Nigeria - Songs.
Ransome-Kuti, Josaiah Jesse, 1855-1930.
Awọn orin mimọ ni ede ati Ohùn Ilẹ Wa. Yoruba sacred songs. Lagos, C.M.S. Bookshop, 1925.

Pp. 556-617 18½cm.

Translation: A series of sacred songs in the language and the tone of our land.

Nigeria
M966.9
P96ou

Nigeria - Politics and government.
Public Relations Department
Our ministers speak. Lagos, Public Relations Department, n.d.

20p. illus. 20½cm. (Crownbird Series No.24)

1. Nigeria - Politics and government.

M910
Sm9n

Nigeria - Social conditions.
Smythe, Hugh H
The new Nigerian elite [by] Hugh H. Smythe and Mabel M. Smythe. Stanford, Calif., Stanford University Press, 1960.

ix, 196 p. map. 24 cm.
Bibliographical references included in "Notes" (p. [175]-191)

1. Upper classes—Nigeria. 2. Nigeria—Soc. condit. I. Smythe, Mabel M., joint author. II. Title.

HN800.N5S56 301.4409669 60—13870

Library of Congress [61f10]

Nigeria
M336.2
Or14

Nigeria - Taxation.
Orewa, G Oka.
Taxation in Western Nigeria; the problems of an emergent state. [London] Published for the Nigerian Institute of Social and Economic Research [by] Oxford University Press, 1962.

xvii, 169 p. fold. map, tables. 19 cm. (Nigerian social and economic studies, no. 4)
Bibliography: p. [165]-166.

1. Taxation—Western Nigeria. (Series) 2. Nigeria-Taxation. 3. Income tax - Nigeria.
HJ3069.W4O7 336.209669 62-6142

Library of Congress [5] (over)

Nigeria
M966.9
Uz7n

Nigeria-Politics and government.
Uzo, T M
The Nigerian political evolution, by T. M. Uzo... Lagos, C.M.S. Bookshops, [1950].

80 p. map. 22 cm.

Nigeria
M966.9
Aj51

Nigeria-Social life & Customs.
Ajisafẹ, Ajayi Kọlawọle.
The laws and customs of the Yoruba people, by A.K. Ajisafẹ. London, George Routledge & Sons, Ltd., 1924.

97p. front. 17½cm.

Nigeria
M370
So42

Nigeria - Teachers.
Solaru, T T
Teacher training in Nigeria, by T. T. Solaru. Edited, and with a final chapter by Ian Espie. Ibadan, Ibadan University Press, 1964.

109p. maps. 21½cm.
Includes bibliography.

Nigeria
M333
Ek34

Nigeria - Real property.
Ekineh, Aliyi.
You and your landlord and you and the law of libel and slander. Lagos, Megida Printers and Publishers ‹1961›

50p. 22½cm. (Megida legal guide series, no.1)

Nigeria
M966.9
Ak6r

Nigeria - Social life and customs.
Akpan, Ntieyong U , 1924-
The reservoir. Abridged and adapted by G. Plummer. Illustrated by E.F. Gibbons. London, Longmans, Green and Co., 1959.

86p. 18cm. (New English Supplementary Reader. Stage 5)

Nigeria
M966.9
D54

Nigeria; model of a colonial failure.
Diamond, Stanley
Nigeria; model of a colonial failure. New York, American Committee on Africa, 1967.

88p. map. 22cm. (Occasional paper, 6)
White author.
Partial contents.- The tragedy of Professor Diamond, by Simon Obi Anekive.- Does Stanley Diamond exist? By F. U. Anyiam.- Diamond (Continued on next card)

Nigeria; model of a colonial failure.
Nigeria M966.9 D54
Diamond, Stanley. Nigeria, 1967. (Card 2)
(Partial contents.- Continued). was prophetic, by Akintunde Emiola.
1. Nigeria. I. American Committee on Africa. II. Title.

Nigeria Missions - History.
Nigeria M966.9 D56o
Dike, Kenneth Onwuka, 1917-
Origins of the Niger Mission, 1841-1891; a paper read at the centenary of the Mission at Christ Church, Onitsha, on 13 November 1957. Ibadan, Ibadan University Press, 1957.
21p. 22cm.
Bibliography: p. 21

Nigerian land law and custom.
Nigeria M966.9 El4n
Elias, Taslim Olawale.
Nigerian land law and custom. London, Routledge & K. Paul [1951]
xxvii, 326 p. map. 23 cm.
Thesis—University of London.
Includes legislation.
Bibliography: p. 316-319.
1. Land tenure—Nigeria—Law. 2. Real property—Nigeria. I. Nigeria. Laws, statutes, etc. II. Title.
333.3 52—28040
Library of Congress [53e8]

Nigeria, History.
Nigeria M966.9 Ak5o
Akinyele, I B
The outlines of Ibadan history, by Chief I.B. Akinyele. Lagos, Alebiosu printing press, 1946.
135p. front. (port.) 18½cm.

Nigeria political theatre (1923-53).
Nigeria M966.9 Ak5n
Akinsuroju, O
Nigeria political theatre (1923-53). Lagos, published by the City Publishing Association, [1953].
28p. port. 19cm.

The Nigerian legal system.
Nigeria M966.9 El4ni
Elias, Taslim Olawale.
The Nigerian legal system. [2d ed., rev.] London, Routledge & Paul [1963]
xxxvii, 386 p. 22 cm.
First ed. published in 1954 under title: Groundwork of Nigerian law.
"List of abbreviations" (bibliographical) p. xxxvii. Bibliographical footnotes.
1. Law—Nigeria. 2. Customary law—Nigeria. 3. Courts—Nigeria. I. Title.
63-24583
Library of Congress [2]

Nigeria, Marriage in.
Nigeria M966.9 D37a
Delano, Isaac O
An African looks at marriage, by Isaac O. Delano... London and Redhill, United society for Christian literature [1944]
47p. 18cm. (African's own library no.5)

Nigeria speaks.
Nigeria M966.9 B195
Balewa, Alhaji Sir Abubakar Tafawa, 1912-
Nigeria speaks; speeches made between 1957 and 1964. Selected and introduced by Sam Epelle. Foreword by T.O.S. Benson. [Ikeja, Nigeria] Longmans of Nigeria [1964]
178p. illus. ports. 22cm.

Nigerian literature.
Ghana M896 Ad34
Ademola, Frances, ed.
Reflections; Nigerian prose and verse. [Preface by Ezekiel Mphahlele] Lagos [Nigeria] African Universities Press [1962]
123p. 18½cm.
Ghanaian editor.

Nigeria and her neighbours.
Nigeria M966.9 F178
Fajana, A
Nigeria and her neighbours. Lagos, African Universities Press, 1964.
92p. illus., photos., maps. 18cm.

Nigeria M378.66N Az2
Nigeria University, Nsukka.
First graduation convocation, 15th June, 1963. [Aba, Nigeria, International Press, 1963]
87p. illus. port. 24½cm.
Partial contents: Origins of the University of Nigeria, and address delivered by Dr. Nnamdi Azikiwe.

Nigerian public finance.
Nigeria M336 Ok3
Okigbo, Pius Nwabufo C 1924-
Nigerian public finance [by] P. N. C. Okigbo. Evanston [Ill.] Northwestern University Press, 1965.
xiii, 245 p. 21 cm. (Northwestern University [Evanston, Ill.] African studies, no. 15)
Bibliographical footnotes.
1. Finance, Public—Nigeria. I. Title. (Series)
HJ1609.N5O5 336.669 65-15473
Library of Congress [3]

Nigeria army.
Nigeria M966.9 Ou7r
Our regiment. Lagos, Public Relations Department, n.d. Crownbird Series, No. 29, Special.
32p. illus. 20½cm.

Nigerian Broadcasting Corporation.
Nigeria MB9 N56e
Eminent Nigerians of the nineteenth century, a series of studies originally broadcast by the Nigerian Broadcasting Corporation. Cambridge, University Press, 1960.
97 p. 19 cm.
1. Nigeria—Biog. 2. Nigeria—Hist. I. Title.
DT515.N49 920.0669 60—3478 ‡
Library of Congress [61c5]

Nigerian social and economic studies, no. 4.
Nigeria M336.2 Or14
Orewa, O Oka.
Taxation in Western Nigeria; the problems of an emergent state. [London] Published for the Nigerian Institute of Social and Economic Research [by] Oxford University Press, 1962.
xvii, 169p. fold, map, tables, 19cm. (Nigerian social and economic studies, no. 4)
Bibliography: p. [165]-166.
1. Taxation -Western Nigeria. (Sieries) 2. Nigeria-Taxation. 3. Income tax-Nigeria. (over)

Nigeria education.
Nigeria M370 Ik3
Ikejiani, Okechukwu, ed.
Nigeria education. Edited and introduced by Okechukwu Ikejiani with a foreword by Nnamdi Azikiwe. Ikeja, Nigeria, Longmans of Nigeria, 1964.
xix, 234p. 22cm.

The Nigerian Constitution.
Nigeria M966.9 Od8
Odumosu, Oluwole Idowu.
The Nigerian Constitution: history and development. London, Sweet & Maxwell, 1963.
xix, 407 p. 23 cm. (Law in Africa, no. 4)
"Originally ... submitted as a thesis for the award of the Ph. D. degree of the University of London."
"The Constitution of the Federation of Nigeria": p. 309-397.
Bibliographical footnotes.
1. Nigeria—Constitutional history. 2. Nigeria—Constitutional law. I. Nigeria. Constitution. (Series)
63-4741
Library of Congress [1]

Nigerian student verse.
Nigeria M896.1 B22
Banham, Martin, ed.
Nigerian student verse, 1959. [Ibadan] Ibadan University Press, 1960.
33p. 21½cm.

The Nigeria exhibition, 1st-22nd October, 1960.
Nigeria M966.9 N56ng
Nigeria. Federal Ministry of Commerce and Industry.
The Nigeria exhibition, 1st-22nd October, 1960. Victoria Island, Lagos. Organized by the Federal Ministry of Commerce and Industry. Lagos [Federal Government Printing Department] 1960.
192+8p. ports. 25cm.

Nigerian land law and custom.
Nigeria M966.9 El4n 1962
Elias, Taslim Olawale.
Nigerian land law and custom. 3d ed. London, Routledge & K. Paul [1951] 1962
xxvii, ~~326~~ 386 p. map. 23 cm.
Thesis—University of London.
Includes legislation.
Bibliography: p. 316-319.
1. Land tenure—Nigeria—Law. 2. Real property—Nigeria. I. Nigeria. Laws, statutes, etc. II. Title.
333.3 52—28040
Library of Congress [53e8]

A Nigerian villager in two worlds.
Nigeria MB9 Ok1
Okafor-Omali, Dilim
A Nigerian villager in two worlds. London, Faber and Faber [1965]
159p. 19cm.
1. Nigeria - Social life and customs. I. Title.

Nigeria
M327.667
B215

Nigerians in Ghana.
Balogun, Kolawole, 1922-
Mission to Ghana; memoir of a diplomat. «1st ed.» New York, Vantage Press «1963»
73p. 21cm.

MB9
G862

Nigger.
Gregory, Dick.
Nigger; an autobiography, by Dick Gregory with Robert Lipsyte. [1st ed.] New York, Dutton, 1964.
224 p. illus., ports. 21 cm.
Portraits of author in book.
1. Negroes—Civil rights. I. Title.
PN2287.G68A3 927.92 64—11067
Library of Congress [64f7]

M813.5
V37

Nigger heaven.
Van Vechten, Carl, 1880-
Nigger heaven, by Carl Van Vechten. New York, London, A. A. Knopf, 1926.
5 p. l., 3-286 p., 1 l. 19½cm.
I. Title.
Library of Congress PZ3.V368Ni 26-15403
[5]

South Africa
M896.3
Ab8n

A night of their own.
Abrahams, Peter, 1919-
A night of their own. [1st American ed.] New York, Knopf, 1965.
ix, 286 p. 22 cm.
I. Title.
PZ3.A1576Ni 65-12051
Library of Congress [4-1]

South Africa
M896
Ab8n2

A night of their own.
Abrahams, Peter, 1919-
A night of their own. London, Faber and Faber, 1965.
ix, 269p. 22cm.

M813.5
W672n

Night song.
Williams, John Alfred, 1925-
Night song. New York, Farrar, Straus and Cudahy [1961]
219 p. 21 cm.
Portrait of author on book jacket.
I. Title.
PZ4.W72624Ni 61-16740 ‡
Library of Congress [5]

Ghana
MB9
N58

Nii Kwabena Bonne III, 1888-
Milestones in the history of the Gold Coast; autobiography of Nii Kwabena Bonne III, Osu Alata Mantse, also Nana Owusu Aktenten III, Oyokohene of Techiman, Ashanti. [London] Diplomatist Publications [1953]
92 p. illus. 19 cm.
1. Gold Coast—Hist. I. Title.
DT511.N5 966.7 54-1186 ‡
Library of Congress [2]

Sudan
M962.4
Y16

The Nile turns red.
Yangu, Alexis Mbali.
The Nile turns red; Azanians chose freedom against Arab bondage. Edited by A. G. Mondini. [1st ed. New York] Pageant Press [°1966]
xviii, 184 p. map. 21 cm.
Bibliography: p. 182-184.
1. Sudan—Hist. 2. Sudan—Race question. I. Title.
DT108.7.Y3 962.9'04 66-29146
Library of Congress [5]

M784
H19tr

Niles, Abbe, 1894-
Handy, William Christopher, 1873- ed.
A treasury of the blues; complete words and music of 67 great songs from Memphis blues to the present day. With an historical and critical text by Abbe Niles. With pictures by Miguel Covarrubias. [New York] C. Boni; distributed by Simon and Schuster [1949]
258 p. illus. 29 cm.
First ed. published in 1926 under title: Blues, an anthology.
"A selective bibliography": p. 254-255.
1. Music, Popular (Songs, etc.)—U. S. I. Niles, Abbe, 1894- II. Title.
M1630.18.H26B5 1949 784 49—50282*
Library of Congress [58f2]

M204
B41

Ninako, S. Gyasi - The Catechist and his books.
Belshaw, Harry
The catechist and his work. London and Redhill United Society for Christian Literature, 1947.
186p. 18½cm.

M204
B41

Ninako, S. Gyasi - The "Amoguo way" of preaching.
Belshaw, Harry.
The catechist and his work. London and Redhill United Society for Christian Literature. 1947.
186p. 18½cm.

Nigeria
M966.9
Ac85

1956 summer school lectures.
Action Group of Nigeria.
1956 summer school lectures. Ibadan, The Action Group Bureau of Information, «1957»
38p. 24cm.

Nigeria
M966.9
Ek34

1962 Nigerian emergency.
Ekineh, Aliyi
Democratic rights during a period of emergency. A study of the 1962 Nigerian Emergency. «Yaba, Nigeria, The Pacific Printers, n.d.»
68p. 20½cm.

M610.
C63s

The 1939 scientific exhibit of the Howard University School of Medicine.
Cobb, William Montague, 1904-
The 1939 scientific exhibit of the Howard University School of Medicine. Reprinted from the Journal of the National Medical Association, 32:216-218, September 1940.

M286
N62

Nineteenth Street Baptist Church, Wash. D.C.
One hundredth annniversary of the Nineteenth Street Baptist Church, 1839-1939; fifty-seventh anniversary, Rev. Walter H. Brooks, 1882-1939, program. Washington, D.C. 1939.
23p. illus. 27cm.
Partial contents: History of the church, and A Sketch of the life of Walter Henderson Brooks, by William I. Lee, Sr.
(see other side)

M206
H36

Nineteenth Street Baptist Church, Wash., D.C. Helping Hand Club.
The history of the Helping Hand Club of the Nineteenth Street Baptist Church. Washington, D.C. The Associated Publishers, 1948.
86p. port. 19½cm.
1. Nineteenth Street Baptist Church, Washington, D.C. 2. Washington, D.C.-Churches. 3. Cabaniss, Mary Emma.

Niniche, See, Gaillard, Viard

Cameroons, French
M966.11
N62m

Ninine, [Jules]
La main d'oeuvre indigeñe dans les colonies africaines ... Paris, Jouve and Cie, 1932.
241p. 25cm.
These - Universite de Paris.
Bibliographie: p.[237] - 238.
(contined on next card)

Cameroons, French
M966.11
N62m

Ninine, [Jules]
La main d'oeuvre indigeñe dans les colonies africaines ... Paris, Jouve and Cie, 1932. (Card 2)
1. Labor and laboring classes - Cameroons, French. 2. Labor and laboring classes - Africa, French West. 3. Labor and laboring classes - Madagascar.

Guadeloupe
M972.97
N63

Nithila, Georges, 1912-
Essai de géographie médicale de la Gaudeloupe These présentée et publiquement soutenue devant la faculté de Médecine de Montpellier le 2 Juin 1943. Montpellier, Imprimerie de la Presse, 1943.
73p. 25cm.
Autographed.
I. Title.

Kenya
M967.62
L18

Njerage, Mathayo, tr.
La Fontaine, Sidney Hubert, 1887-
Thirikari ya nandu o nandũ Kenya; [Local government in Kenya] ihumo o na ũkũria wayo, rĩandĩkĩtwo nĩ S. H. La Fontaine magĩteithanagia wĩra wa rĩo na J. H. Mower. [Translated into Kikuyu by Mathayo Njeroge] Nairobi, Eagle Press, 1955.
63p. 21½cm.
Written in Kikuyu.
1. Local government - Kenya Colony and Protectorate. I. Title. II. Mower, J. H. III. Njerage, Mathayo, tr.

Kenya
M613
N65
Njiiri, Kariũki K
Karanja mũndũ mũugĩ; ibuku ria mbere;
Njĩra Njega cia Ũtheru [Karanja, the wise man. Illustrated by William Agutu] Nairobi, Eagle Press, 1960.
32p. illus.
Written in Kikuyu.
1. Hygiene, Public. I. Title.

Njiiri, Kariuki Karanja, 1928- jt. auth.
Kenya
M372.4
M87
Mpaayei, John Tempo
Engolon eng'eno [Knowledge is power]
Itung' ana kituaak too Imaasai, naitobirakasi J. T. Ole Mpaayei and Kariũki K. Njiiri. Eutaa Elizabeth Mooney. [Illus. by Ruth Yudelowitz] Nairobi, Eagle Press, 1960.
illus. 28cm.
Written in Masaai.
1. Masaai language - Readers and speakers. I. Title. II. Njiiri, Kariuki Karanja, 1928- jt. auth.

Nigeria
M392.5
N65
Njoku, N O
Why boys nowadays don't marry in time.
Onitsha, Nigeria, Njoku and Sons Bookshop, [n.d.]
44p. 21cm.

Kenya
M398
N65
Njururi, Ngumbu, 1930- *comp.*
Agikuyu folk tales. London, Oxford U. P., 1966.
ix, 100 p. 22½ cm. 13/6
(B 66-11838)
1. Tales, Kikuyu. I. Title.
GR360.K5N55 398.2096762 66-72313
Library of Congress [5]

Africa
M261
D45
Nketia, J H.
The contribution of African culture of christian worship.
Pp. 109-123.
In: Desai, Ram, ed. Christianity in Africa as seen by Africans. Denver, A. Swallow [1962]

Gold Coast
M966.7
N65f
Nketia, J H
Funeral dirges of the Akan people.
Achimota, University College of the Gold Coast, 1955.
296p. 18½cm.
1. Gold Coast.

Ghana
M789.1
N65
Nketia, J H Kwabena.
Drumming in Akan communities of Ghana.
London, Published on behalf of the University of Ghana by Nelson [1963]
212p. 23½cm. illus.
"Recordings of Akan music and peotry": p. 201-203.
Includes bibliography.
1. Drum. 2. Music, African. I. Title.

Ghana
M784
N63
Nketia, J H Kwabena, *ed.*
Folk songs of Ghana. Legon, University of Ghana, 1963.
205 p. 26 cm.
For solo voice and chorus; words in Akan language.
1. Folk-songs, Ghana. I. Title.
M1838.G5N6 63-24154/M
Library of Congress [1]

Ghana
M784
N63
Nketia, J H Kwabena, ed.
Folk songs of Ghana. Legon, University of Ghana, 1963.
205p. 26cm.
For solo voice and chorus; words in Akan language.
1. Folk-songs, Ghana. I. Title. 2. Akan language - Music.

Nketia, J H Kwabena.
Introductory note, p. 189.
M808.8
N42
v.15
New world writing. 1st-
Apr. 1952-
[New York] New American Library.
v. 18 cm. (N. A. L. Mentor books)
1. Literature, Modern—20th cent. 2. American literature—20th cent.
PN6014.N457 808.8 52—1806
Library of Congress [54j5]

Nketia, J H Kwabena.
The poetry of drums, pp. 190-197.
M808.8
N42
v.15
New world writing. 1st-
Apr. 1952-
[New York] New American Library.
v. 18 cm. (N. A. L. Mentor books)
1. Literature, Modern—20th cent. 2. American literature—20th cent.
PN6014.N457 808.8 52—1806
Library of Congress [54j5]

Africa
M896
B36
Nketia, Kwabena
Akan poetry.
Pp. 23-33
In: Beier, Ulli, comp., Introduction to African literature. London, Longmans, 1967.
1. Akan poetry.

Nketta mu bizinga.
Uganda
M896.3
K17n
Kawere, Edward K N
Nketta mu bizinga [I spy on the islands, a detective story. Cover design by M. E. Gregg] Nairobi, Eagle Press, 1960.
148p. 21½cm. (East African Literature Bureau)
Written in Luganda.

Malawi
M896.3
N65u
Nkomba, Lester L
Ukawamba. Edited by Guy Atkins. Cape Town; London, Oxford University Press, 1953.
134p. 18½cm. (Annotated African Texts - II: Cewa)
1. Nyasaland - Fiction. 2. Cewa - Fiction. I. Title.

Nkomo, Joshua
Southern Rhodesia: apartheid country, pp. 130-143.
Africa
M960.3
D87a
Duffy, James, 1923- ed.
Africa speaks. Edited by James Duffy and Robert A. Manners. Princeton, N.J., Van Nostrand [1961]
223p. 23cm.

Nkomo, Joshua Mqabuko-, jt. auth.
Malawi
M968.9
C44
Chiume, Kanyama, 1929-
The Federation of Rhodesia and Nyasaland: the future of the dilemma [by] Channing Richardson, Kanyama Chiume, Joshua Nkomo [and others. New York] American Committee on Africa ©1959]
38p. 22cm. (Africa today pamphlets, 4)

South Africa
M378.3
N65
Nkomo, Simbini Mamba
Facts brought out by the survey as to the influence of returned students in the homelands.
Pp. 93-96.
In: Commission on Survey of Foreign Students in the United States of America. The foreign student in America. New York, Association Press, 1925.

Ruanda-Urundi
M398.9
N65
Nkongori, Laurent
Proverbes du Rwanda, par Laurent Nkongori. Avec la collaboration de Thomas Kamanzi. Tervuren, Annales du Musée Royal du Congo Belge, 1957.
79p. 27cm.
1. Ruanda-Urundi - Proverbs. I. Kamanzi, Thomas, jt. auth.

Africa
M960
K617
Nkosi, Lewis, 1935-
English - speaking West Africa: synthesizing past and present.
Pp. 285-295.
In: Kitchen, Helen, ed. A handbook of African Affairs. New York, Praeger, 1964.

Africa, South
M968
F914i
Nkosi, Lewis, 1935-
Farm jails.
Pp. 61-71.
In: Friedmann, M. V. I will still be moved. Chicago, Quadrangle Books, 1963.

Africa
M896
B36
Nkosi, Lewis
Fiction by black South Africans: Richard Rive; Bloke Modisane; Ezekiel Mphahlele; Alex la Guma.
Pp. 211-217.
In: Beier, Ulli, comp. Introduction to African literature. London, Longmans, 1967.
1. African fiction - History and criticism.

South Africa
M968 Nkosi, Lewis, 1935-
N65 Home and exile. [London] Longman's [1965]

136p. 20½cm.

1. African, South. 2. Literature - Africa. 3. Race problems - Addresses, essays, lecture. I. Title.

G
M960 Nkrumah, Kwame, Pres. Ghana, 1909-
N65al All-African People's Conference. Speeches by the Prime Minister of Ghana at the opening and closing sessions on December 8th and 13th, 1958. [at the] Community Centre, Accra. [Accra, Govt. Printer, 1958].
12p. 21½cm.
Cover title.

1. Africa - Politics. I. Title.

Ghana
M89 Nkrumah, Kwame, 1909-
N93n Funeral oration ... on the occasion of the interment of the ashes of the late George Padmore at Christiansborg Castle, Osu, Accra, Sunday 4th October 1959. Accra, Government Printers, 1959.

2p. 25cm.

1. Nurse, Malcolm, 1903-1959. 2. Padmore, George, 1903-1959, pseud.

South Africa
M896 Nkosi, Lewis, 1935-
N88 The Prisoner.

Pp. 294-307

In: Mphahlele, Ezekiel, ed. African writing today. Baltimore, Penguin Books, 1967.

Ghana
M966.7 Nkrumah, Kwame, 1909-
N65G The autobiography of Kwame Nkrumah. Edinburgh, Thomas Nelson and Sons, [1957]

310p. illus. port. 24cm.

1. Gold Coast-Politics and government. I. Title.

Ghana
M966.7 **Nkrumah, Kwame, 1909-**
N65G Ghana; the autobiography of Kwame Nkrumah. New York, Nelson [1957]
302 p. illus. 24 cm.

1. Gold Coast—Pol. & govt. I. Title.

DT511.N55 ~~967.8~~ 57—8425 ‡

Library of Congress [57x20]

U. S.
M968 Nkosi, Lewis, 1935-
Am3 Propaganda in the South African struggle.

Pp. 229-239.

In: American Society of African Culture. Southern Africa in transition. New York, Praeger, 1966.

Ghana
M966.7 **Nkrumah, Kwame,** *Pres. Ghana,* 1909-
N65ax Axioms of Kwame Nkrumah. London, Nelson, 1967.
[7], 85 p. 19 cm. 10/6 (B 67-1758)

I. Title.

DT510.6.N5A25 1967 354.667'035 67-81818

Library of Congress [3]

Ghana
M966.7 Nkrumah, Kwame, 1909-
N65h Hands off Africa. Some famous speeches by Dr. The Rt. Hon. Kwame Nkrumah, P.C., M.P. (First President of the Republic of Ghana); with a tribute to George Padmore written by Tawia Adamafio, General Secretary of C.P.P. Accra, Kwabena Owusu-Akyem [1960]

62p. ports. 21cm.

1. Ghana. 2. Speeches. I. Title. II. Padmore, George, 1913-1959. III. Adamafio, Tawia.

Africa, South
M896.2 Nkosi, Lewis, 1935-
N65 The rhythm of violence. London, Oxford University Press, 1964.

69p. 18½cm.
"A three crowns book"

1. Johannesburg, South Africa - Drama. I. Title.

Ghana
M966.7 Nkrumah, Kwame, Pres. Ghana, 1909-
N65b Blueprint for the future: sessional address delivered at the State Opening of the First Session of the Second Parliament of the Republic of Ghana on August 24th, 1965. [Accra, Information Division of the Ghana High Commission] 1965.
10p. 29½cm.
"Supplement with Ghana today of Aug. 25, 1965."
1. Ghana. I. Title.

Ghana
M966.7 **Nkrumah, Kwame,** *Pres. Ghana,* 1909-
N65i I speak of freedom; a statement of African ideology. New York, Praeger [1961]
291 p. illus. 21 cm. (Books that matter)

1. Ghana—Hist. 2. Africa—Politics. I. Title.

DT512.N55 1961 966.7 61-14200 ‡

Library of Congress [15]

Africa
M960 Nkosi, Lewis, 1935-
K617 South Africa: literature of protest.

Pp. 275-284.

In: Kitchen, Helen, ed. A handbook of African Affairs. New York, Praeger, 1964.

Ghana
M967.5 **Nkrumah, Kwame,** *Pres. Ghana,* 1909-
N65 Challenge of the Congo. ~~New York, International Publishers [1967]~~ [London] Nelson [1967]
xvi, 304 p. facsim., map. 24 cm.
Bibliography: p. [295]-296.

1. Congo (Democratic Republic)—Hist.—1960- I. Title.

DT658.N43 1967a 967.503 67—670

Library of Congress [67f5]

Ghana
M960 **Nkrumah, Kwame,** *Pres. Ghana,* 1909-
N65n Neo-colonialism; the last stage of imperialism. New York, International Publishers [1966, °1965]
xx, 280 p. col. map (on lining papers) 24 cm.
Bibliography: p. 260-262.

1. Investments, Foreign—Africa. 2. Africa—Foreign economic relations. 3. Africa—Indus. I. Title.

HC502.N5 1966 338.96 66—18026

Library of Congress [66f5]

Ghana
M966.7 Nkrumah, Kwame, 1909-
N65a Address by the Prime Minister of Ghana, The Honorable Dr. Kwame Nkrumah...to the International Missionary Assembly at Accra. 28th December, 1957. [Accra, Government Printer, 1957]

3p. 21½cm.

1. Ghana.

Ghana
M966.7 Nkrumah, Kwame, 1909-
N65ch Christmas eve broadcast. 24th December, 1957. Accra, Government Printer, 1957.

4p. 21cm.

I. Title.

Gold Coast
M966.7 Nkrumah, Kwame, 1909-
N65n The new stage (C.P.P. versus imperialism, by Kwame Nkrumah. Accra, Nyaniba Press and Publishing Co., Ltd., 1951.

10p. port. on cover, 18cm.

1. Gold Coast - Politics.

Africa
M960 Nkrumah, Kwame, Pres. Ghana, 1909-
F76 African prospect.

Pp. 272-282.

In: Foreign Affairs (New York). Africa. New York, Praeger, 1964.

Ghana
M335 Nkrumah, Kwame, Pres. Ghana, 1909-
N65 Consciencism; philosophy and ideology for decolonization and development with particular reference to the African revolution. New York, Monthly Review Press [1965, °1964]

vi, 122p. 23cm.

1. Socialism in Africa. 2. Philosophy, African. 3. Africa-Socialism. I. Title.

Ghana
M966.7 Nkrumah, Kwame, 1909-
W83p Nkrumah speaks.

pp. 255-256.
In: Pageant of Ghana, by Freda Wolfson. 1958.

I. Title.

Ghana
M966.7
N65p
Nkrumah, Kwame, Pres. Rep. of Ghana, 1909-
Peace! The world from African eyes. Address by the President of the Republic of Ghana, Osagyefo Dr. Kwame Nkrumah, to the 15th session of the United Nation's General Assembly September 28, 1960. [Chicago, Afro-American Heritage Ass'n, 1960]
27p. 21cm.
Portrait on cover.
I. Ghana. I. DuBois, W.E.B. II. Title.

Ghana
M966.7
N65s
Nkrumah, Kwame, 1909-
Statement on industrial promotion. In the National Assembly on 3rd September, 1958. Accra, Government Printer, 1958.
3p. 22cm.
1. Ghana - Industries.

Nkrumah, Kwame, 1909-
Sierra Leone
M39
N65t
Timothy, Bankole
Kwame Nkrumah, his rise to power. London, George Allen & Unwin, Ltd. 1955.
198p. portraits. 21cm.

Nkrumah, Kwame, 1909-
Positive action in Africa, pp.48-57.
Africa
M960.3
D87a
Duffy, James, 1923- ed.
Africa speaks. Edited by James Duffy and Robert A. Manners. Princeton, N.J., Van Nostrand [1961]
223p. 23cm.

Nkrumah, Kwame, 1909-
Africa
M960
C76sp
Conference of Independent African States.
Speeches delivered at the close of the conference, 22nd April, 1958. Second edition. Accra, Government Printer, 1958.
30p. 21½cm.

Nkrumah, Kwame, 1909-
Gold Coast
M966.7
Ye3a
Yen, Kwesi.
The Achievements of Dr. Kwame Nkrumah. Accra, The Heal Press, 1954.
19p. port. 18cm.

Africa
M370
C8x
Nkrumah, Kwame, 1909-
The role of the university.
Pp. 314-316.
In: Cowan, L. G., ed. Education and nation-building in Africa. New York, Praeger, 1965.

Nkrumah, Kwame, 1909-
Africa
M960
C76t
Conference of Independent African States.
Tour of Ghana Prime Minister; broadcast and communiques. Accra, Government Printer, 1958.
12p. 21½cm.

Nkrumah speaks.
Ghana
M966.7
W83p
Nkrumah, Kwame, 1909-
Nkrumah speaks.
pp. 255-256.
In: Pageant of Ghana, by Freda Wolfson. 1958.

Ghana
M89
N65s
Nkrumah, Kwame, 1909-
Schwarze fanfare. München, Paul List Verlag, 1958.
268p. 18½cm.
1. Ghana. I. Title.

Nkrumah, Kwane, 1909-
Gold Coast
M966.7
C76f
Convention People's Party.
Forward to freedom with the common people. Manifesto for the general election, 1954. Vote C.P.P. and we shall finish the job. 104-freedom. Accra, Convention People's Party. 1954.
20p. 21½cm.

Africa
M960
Af83
N'Liba-N'Guímbous, Français A
Progress through cooperation.
Pp. 138-147.
In: African Conference on Progress through Cooperation. Africa. New York, Dodd, Mead, 1966.

Ghana
M266
In8
Nkrumah, Kwame, 1909-
Speech.
Pp. 148-150.
In: International Missionary Council. Assembly, Accra, 1957-1958. The Ghana assembly. London, Edinburgh House Press, 1958.

Nkrumah, Kwame, 1909-
Gold Coast
M966.7
Ed8h
Edu, John E
How Dr. Kwame Nkrumah conquered Colonialism. Accra, The Heal Press, n.d.
44p. (port.) illus. 21½cm.

N'Na ou la maman noire.
Guinea
M896.3
M76n
Montrat, Maurice
N'Na ou la maman noire. [Versailes, Imprimerie Ch. Barbier] 1957.
56p. 18½cm.
I. Title.

Ghana
M966.7
N65sta
Nkrumah, Kwame, Pres. Ghana, 1909-
State opening of Parliament, 4th July, 1961. [Accra, Ministry of Information] 1961.
22p. 25cm.
1. Ghana - Politics and government.

Nkrumah, Kwame, Pres. Ghana, 1909-
Ghana
M966.7
Sp26
The Spark.
Some essential features of Nkrumaism, by the editors of the Spark. New York, International Publishers [1965, °1964]
127 p. 18 cm. (Little new world paperbacks, LNW-8)
1. Nkrumah, Kwame, Pres. Ghana, 1909- I. Title.
DT510.6.N5S65 1965 320.531 65-24380
Library of Congress [8]

...No alabaster box and other poems.
M811.5
R33m
Ryenolds, Evelyn Crawford.
...No alabaster box and other poems, by Eve Lynn, [pseud.] introduction by Gene Rhodes. Philadelphia, Alpress, 1936.
37p. 24cm.
Limited edition of 350 copies. This copy is number 264.

Ghana
M966.7
N65st
Nkrumah, Kwame, 1909-
Statement on foreign policy. In the National Assembly on 3rd September, 1958. Accra, Government Printer, 1958.
6p. 21½cm.
1. Ghana - Politics and government. 2. Ghana - Foreign Affairs. I. Title.

Nkrumah, Kwame, 1909-
Ghana
M896.1
St4a
Stewart, MacNeill
Appeal to reason -- to the political leaders of the country this poem is respectfully dedicated --. Accra, 1951.
4p. ports. 18cm.

No boot straps.
M248
B912
Burgess, Lois F
No boot straps. n.p., n.p., 1965.
36p. 18cm.

No day of triumph.

M810
R24n

Redding, Jay Saunders.
No day of triumph, by J. Saunders Redding, with an introduction by Richard Wright ... New York and London, Harper & brothers [1942]
6 p. l., 3-342 p. 22½cm.
"First edition."

1. Negroes. I. Title.

Library of Congress E185.6.R42 42—22760
[44x5] 325.260973

Nigeria
M896.3
Ac4n

No longer at ease.

Achebe, Chinua.
No longer at ease. New York, I Obolensky [1961, ©1960]
170 p. 21 cm.
Portrait of author on book jacket.

I. Title.

Full name: Albert Chinua Achebe.

PZ4.A17No 2 61—7356 ‡
Library of Congress [61e2]

M811.5
N66g

Noad, Emma M.
Golden sunshine and other poems, by Emma M. Noad. London, Arthur H. Stockwell, n.d.
24p. 19cm.

1. Poetry. I. Title.

No easy task.

Malawi
M896.3
K113n

Kachingwe, Aubrey, 1926-
No easy task. [London] Heinemann [1966]
233p. 20½cm.
Portrait of author on book jacket.

I. Title.

Nigeria
M896.3
Ac4n2

No longer at ease.

Achebe, Chinua. London, Heneman, 1960.
No longer at ease. ~~New York, I. Obolensky [1961, ©1960]~~
170 p. 21 cm.

I. Title.

Full name: Albert Chinua Achebe.

PZ4.A17No 2 61—7356 ‡
Library of Congress [2]

M370
An8c

Noar, Gertrude, ed.

Anti-defamation League.
Current problems and issues in human relations education; proceedings of the national conference on human relations education, Commodore Hotel, New York City, April 29-30, 1955. Editor: Gertrude Noar, national director of education. [New York, 1955]
ix, 70 p. 26 cm.
Includes bibliographical references.

1. Intercultural education. I. Noar, Gertrude, ed. II. Title. III. Title: National conference on human relations education.

CB199.A54 370.19 56-58171
Library of Congress [2]

South Africa
M968
M313

No easy walk to freedom.

Mandela, Nelson Rolihlahla, 1918-
No easy walk to freedom: articles, speeches, and trial addresses. Foreword by Ahmed Ben Bella. Introd. by Oliver Tambo. Edited by Ruth First. [London] Heinemann [1965]
xiv, 189p. ports. 22cm.

1. Segregation - Africa, South. 2. Africa, South - Race question. I. First, Ruth, ed. II. Title.

M06
N214n

No man... is an island.

National Urban League.
No man... is an island. New York, the League, [1946]
8p. 22cm.

M948.5
Ar5p

Nobel Laureation Festival, 1947.

Armattoe, Raphael Ernest Grail.
Personal recollections of the Nobel Laureation festival of 1947, by R. E. G. Armattoe. Londerry, England, David Irvine, Ltd.
62p. front. (port.) illus. 24½cm.

No easy walk to freedom.

South Africa
M968
M313a

Mandela, Nelson Rolihlahla, 1918-
No easy walk to freedom: articles, speeches, and trial addresses. Foreword by Ahmed Ben Bella. Introd. by Oliver Tambo. Edited by Ruth First. New York, Basic Books [1965]
xiv, 189 p. ports. 22 cm.

1. Segregation—Africa, South. 2. Africa, South—Race question. I. First, Ruth, ed. II. Title.

DT779.7.M35 301.45196068 65-18219
Library of Congress [5]

M811.5
Sm6

No middle ground.

Smith, Lucy.
No middle ground, a collection of poems by Philadelphia, The Phila. Council Arts, Sciences and Professions, 1952.
29 p. 22 cm.

M948.5
Ar5p

Nobel prizes.

Armattoe, Raphael Ernest Grail.
Personal recollections of the Nobel Laureation festival of 1947, by R. E. G. Armattoe. Londonerry, England, David Irvine, Ltd.
62p. front. (port.) illus. 24½cm.

No flesh shall glory.

M200
Ol3n

Oliver, C Herbert, 1925-
No flesh shall glory. [Nutley, N. J., Presbyterian and Reformed Pub. Co., 1959.
96 p. 21 cm.

1. Race. 2. Segregation—Religious aspects. 3. Sociology, Biblical. I. Title.

BT734.O4 261.83 59-14513 ‡
Library of Congress [2]

Barbados
M610
St2n

No time for prejudice.

Staupers, Mabel Keaton, 1890-
No time for prejudice; a story of the integration of Negroes in nursing in the United States. New York, Macmillan [1961]
206 p. illus. 22 cm.

1. Negro nurses. I. Title.

RT83.5.S75 610.7306273 61—7432 ‡
Library of Congress [61k10]

M378
N66n

Noble, Jeanne L. , 1926-
The Negro woman's college education. New York, Teachers College, Columbia University, 1956.
x, 163 p. form, 39 tables. 22 cm. (TC studies in education)
Bibliography: p. 145-150.

1. Women, Negro. 2. Education of women—U. S. I. Title. (Series: Teachers College studies in education)

LC1605.N6 378.73 56-8941
Library of Congress [10]

M323
Ot5n2

No green pastures.

Ottley, Roi, 1906-
No green pastures. ~~New York, Scribner, 1951.~~ London, J. Murray [1952]
ix, 234 p. 22 cm.
Bibliography: p. 221-229.

1. Negroes in Europe. I. Title.

Full name: Roi Vincent Ottley.

HT1581.O8 323.1 51-7318
Library of Congress [15]

MB9
P264

No time for tears.

Patterson, Katheryn
No time for tears. Chicago, Johnson Pub. Co., 1965.
109p. 21cm.

1. Patterson, Katheryn. 2. Handicapped children. I. Title.

M323
B19n2

Nobody knows my name...

Baldwin, James, 1924-
Nobody knows my name; more notes of a native son. ~~New York, Dial Press, 1961.~~ London, Michael Joseph [1964]
~~241 p. 22 cm.~~
196p. 22cm.

~~1. Negroes.~~ 2. ~~U. S.~~—Race question. I. Title.

E185.61.B197 301.451 61—11596 ‡
Library of Congress [63c5]

No green pastures.

M323.
Ot5n

Ottley, Roi, 1906-
No green pastures. New York, Scribner, 1951.
ix, 234 p. 22 cm.
Bibliography: p. 221-229.

1. Negroes in Europe. I. Title.

Full name: Roi Vincent Ottley.

HT1581.O8 323.1 51—7318
Library of Congress [a52q15]

M813.5
An18n

No use cryin'.

Anderson, Henry L
No use cryin'; [a novel] London, Los Angeles, Western Publisher, 1961.
208 p. 23 cm.

I. Title.

PZ4.A54725No 61-16299 ‡
Library of Congress [3]

M323
B19n

Nobody knows my name.

Baldwin, James, 1924-
Nobody knows my name; more notes of a native son. New York, Dial Press, 1961.
241 p. 22 cm.

1. Negroes. 2. ~~U. S.~~—Race question. I. Title.

E185.61.B197 301.451 61—11596 ‡
Library of Congress [61o20]

Nocturnes; poèmes.
Sénégal
M896.1 Senghor, Léopold Sédar, 1906-
Se5n Nocturnes; poèmes. Paris, Éditions de Seuil, [1961].

94p. 18½cm.
"A Monsieur Spingarn en hommage".

Les noirs dans la civilisation Américaine.
M810 Butcher, Margaret (Just), 1913-
B97no Les noirs dans la civilisation Américaine. The Negro in American culture, based on materials left by Alain Locke. Traduit de l'américain par François Vernan et Jean Rosenthal. Paris, Bouchet/Chastel, 1958.

320p. 18½cm.

Noma nini.
S.Africa
M896 Vilakazi, Benedict Wallet, d. 1947.
V71n Noma nini. Mariannhill, Natal, Yacindezelwa Emshinini Was'emhlathuzane [pref. 1935]

184p. illus. 19cm.

Tanganyika Nodoa na talaka.
M392 Saleh el-Busaidy, Hamed
Sa32 Ndoa na talaka [Marriage and divorce] Nairobi, Eagle Press, 1958.

45p. 21½cm.
Written in Swahili.

1. Marriage. 2. Divorce. I. Title.

Noirs et blancs.
Martinique
M323 Tardon, Raphaël, 1911-
T17n Noirs et blancs; une solution: l'apartheid? Paris, Denoël, 1961.

171p. 18½cm.

S. Africa Nomalizo.
M896.3 Guma, Enoch S
G95n Nomalizo or "The Things of this life are sheer vanity," by Enoch S. Guma, translated into English by the Rev. S. J. Wallis. London, The Sheldon press, 1928.

vii, 9-64 p. 18½ cm.
Story of a little girl named Nomalizo- which means "mother of gifts."

South Africa
M896 Nogar, Rui
N88 Poem of the Conscripted Warrior.

Pp. 337-338.

In: Mphahlele, Ezekiel, ed. African writing today. Baltimore, Penguin Books, 1967.

Les noirs et la coulture.
Mali
M301 Sissoko, Fily-Dabo, d. 1964
Si8 Les noirs et la culture (introduction au probleme de l'evolution culturelle des peuples Africains). New York, 1950.

71p. 20cm.

1. Africa - Social life and customs. 2. Culture - Africa. I. Title.

Noms de lieux d'époque coloniale.en Haiti.
Haiti
M972.94 Romain, J B
R66n Noms de lieux d'époque coloniale en Haiti; essai sur la toponymie du nord a l'usage des etudiants. Port-au-Prince, Imprimerie de l'Etat, 1960.

205p. illus. 23½cm. (Revue de la Faculte d'Ethnologie No. 3).

Brazil
M869.1 Nogueira da Silva, M
G58a ... Bibliografia de Gonçalves Dias, por M. Nogueira da Silva. Rio de Janeiro, Imprensa nacional, 1942.

4 p. l., [11]-203 p. 37 pl. (incl. ports., facsims.) 24½cm. (Ministério da educação e saude. Instituto nacional do livro. Coleção B 1. Bibliografia II)

White author

1. Gonçalves Dias, Antonio, 1823-1864—Bibl.

A 43-3594

Harvard univ. Library for Library of Congress Z8354.2.N78 [3] 012

Ivory Coast Nokan, Charles, 1936-
M896.2 Le soleil noir point. Préface de Pierre
N69s Stibbe. Paris, Présence Africaine [1962]

70p. 21cm.
Portrait of author on back cover.

I. Title.

Non-self-governing territories.
Panama
M986.2 Westerman, George W
W52n Non-self-governing territories and the United Nations. Panama, 1958.

33p. 22½cm.
Spanish text: 36p.

M910
C77n Le noir.
Cook, Mercer, ed.
Le noir; morceaux choisis de vingt-neuf Français célèbres, by Mercer Cook... New York, Cincinnati [etc] American book company [c1934]

x, 173p. incl. front., ports. 19½cm.
On cover: W. Mercer Cook.
Selections for the use of French classes in colored schools.
Includes "Suggested readings."

Nokwe, Philemon Pearce Duma, 1927-
S. Africa
M968 Friedmann, Marion Valerie, 1918- , tr.
F914i I will still be moved; reports from South Africa. Chicago, Quadrangle Books, 1963.

126p. illus. ports. 23cm.

Non-self-governing territories and the United Nations.
Panama
M986.2 Westerman, George W
W52n Non-self-governing territories and the United Nations. Panama, 1958.

33p. 22½cm.
Spanish text: 36p.

Le Noir Americain et les elections.
M324 Butcher, Margaret Just, 1913-
B97noi Le Noir Americain et les elections. [Maroc, le Service Americain d'Information, 1960?]

8p.; 8p. 21cm.
In French and Arabic.
Autographed.

Dominican Republic
M861.6 Nolasco, Flérida de.
N71p ... La poesía folklórica en Santo Domingo. Santiago, República dominicana, Editorial El Diario [1946]

4 p. l., [11]-367, [1] p. 23cm.

Contents.—Conferencia.—Provincia de Azua.—Provincia de Barahona.—Cabral.—Enriquillo.—Provincia Bahoruco.—Provincia Benefactor.—Las Matas de Farfán.—Provincia Trujillo Valdez.—Distrito de Santo Domingo.—Provincia del Seibo.—Higuey.

1. Dominican poetry (Collections) 2. Folk-lore, Dominican. 3. Dominican poetry—Hist. & crit. I. Title.

PQ7406.N6 47-844

Library of Congress [4]

None good but God.
M252 Horace, J Gentry.
H78 None good but God; a general introduction to scientific christianity in the form of a spiritual key to Matthew 19:16-22. New York, Exposition Press [1962]

105p. 21cm.
"An Exposition-testament book."
Portrait of author on book jacket.

Senegal Les noirs aux États-Unis pour les africains.
M973 N'Diaye, Jean Pierre.
N23 Les noirs aux États-Unis pour les africains, par J. P. N'Diaye, J. Bassene, B. Poyas. [Paris, 1964]

184 p. illus. 21 cm. (Réalités africaines, no 7)
Includes bibliographical references.

1. Negroes—Hist. 2. Black Muslims. I. Bassene, J., joint author. II. Poyas, B., joint author. III. Title. (Series)

E185.R38 no. 7 65-44441

Library of Congress [1]

Africa
M960 Nolen, Barbara, 1902- ed.
N717 Africa is people; firsthand accounts from contemporary Africa. With an introd. by Mercer Cook. [1st ed.] New York, Dutton [1967]

xviii, 270p. illus., ports. 24cm.
Bibliography: p. [263]-264.
Includes extracts from books by African authors.
White editor.
1. Africa, Sub-Saharan - Civilization. 2. Negroes in Africa. I. Title. II. Cook, Mercer, 1903- Introduction.

Jamaica
M821.91 Nonsense verses.
Sa3 Salmon, Lisa
Frankie frog, nonsense rhymes and sketches. Kingston, Jamaica, The Pioneer Press, 1952.

30p. illus. 24cm.

Haiti
Le Nord-Ouest dominicain...

M972.94
F46n

Fignolé, Daniel.
Le Nord-Ouest dominicain... Port-au-Prince, Imp. Barthelemy, 1948.

16p. 19½cm. (Mouvement ouvrier-paysan) Publication du Bureau de Propagande et d'Education du Parti.

M01
N76n

Norfolk, Va. Journal and Guide.
News index of the Journal and guide, 1936 ... Prepared by the staff of the library of Fisk University under the supervision of Carl M. White, librarian as a reliable source of information on contemporary Negro life and activities. Norfolk, Va. Guide publishing co., 1936.

53p. 22cm.

I. Fisk University. Nashville. Library.

Normal schools - Southern states.

M06
J61
no.23

Favrot, Leo Mortimer, 1874–
A study of county training schools for Negroes in the South, by Leo Mortimer Favrot ... Charlottesville, Va., 1923.

85 p. tables (2 fold.) diagrs. 23cm. (*On cover: The Trustees of the John F. Slater fund. Occasional papers, no. 23*)

1. Negroes—Education. 2. Normal schools—Southern states.
I. Title: County training school for Negroes in the South.

24—1381

Library of Congress E185.5.J65 no. 23
[44f1]

M323
N78t

Norman, Dorothy, ed.
Twice a year. A Book of literature, the arts and civil liberties. New York, Twice A Year Press, 1946.

513p. 23cm.
Double Number - Fourteen - Fifteen
Fall - Winter - 1946-1947.
Richard Wright, Association editor.

1. Race relations. I. Title.

M814.5
N78t

Norman, Henry, 1845-1933
Thoughts I met on the highway. By Henry Norman. ~~Lynn, Mass., R. Y. Russell, printer, 1891.~~ Boston, Mass., The Everett Press, 1905
105 p. 17½cm. front (port.)

Library of Congress 7-22651†

M910
N79e

Norris, John William.
The Ethiopian's place in history, and his contribution to the world's civilization; the negro—the Hamite, the stock, the stems and the branches of the Hamitic people. By Rev. John William Norris ... Baltimore, The Afro-American co., 1916.

5 p. l., 60 p. 23½cm. $0.75

1. Negro race. I. Title. 1. Ethiopa.

16-6281

Library of Congress HT1589.N57
———— Copy 2.
Copyright A 427196

M945.3
N81b

North, Joseph.
Behind the Florida bombings; Who killed NAACP leader Harry T. Moore and his wife. New York, New Century, 1952.

23p. 19cm.

1. Moore, Harry T. 2. Mims, Florida.
3. Mob violence. I. Title.

M304
F19
V.1, no.13

North, Joseph
Lynching Negro children in southern courts (The Scottsboro case). New York, Issued by International Labor Defense, n.d.

15p. illus. 15cm.

1. Scottsboro case
I. title

North, Sterling, 1906–

M910.4
D34

Dean, Harry, 1864–
The Pedro Gorino; the adventures of a Negro sea-captain in Africa and on the seven seas in his attempts to found an Ethiopian empire; an autobiographical narrative by Captain Harry Dean, with the assistance of Sterling North. Boston and New York, Houghton Mifflin company, 1929.

xvi, 262 p. illus. 22½cm.

1. Seafaring life. 2. Voyages and travels. 3. Africa, South.
I. North, Sterling, 1906– II. Title.

29—6322

Library of Congress G530.D4
[a44u1]

Haiti
M970

North America - History.
Balin, Marc
Les Africains en Amerique, avant et aprés Christophe Colomb. [n.p., n.d.]

85 leaves. illus. 28cm.
Mimeographed.

North American Negro poets...

M01
P83n

Porter, Dorothy (Burnett) 1905–
North American Negro poets, a bibliographical checklist of their writings, 1760–1944, by Dorothy B. Porter. Hattiesburg, Miss., The Book farm, 1945.

90 p. 23½ cm. (Heartman's historical series no. 70)

"An expansion of the Schomburg checklist."—Pref.

1. Negro poetry (American)—Bibl. I. Schomburg, Arthur Alfonso, 1874–1938. A bibliographical checklist of American Negro poetry. II. Title.

Full name: Dorothy Louise (Burnett) Porter.

Z1361.N39P6 016.811 45—4014

Library of Congress [a58n½]

M370
N81r

North Carolina. *Governor's commission for the study of problems in the education of Negroes in North Carolina.*
... Report of the Governor's commission for the study of problems in the education of Negroes in North Carolina. Issued by the state superintendent of public instruction, Raleigh, N. C. [Raleigh, 1935]

96 p. incl. tables, diagrs. 23½cm. ([North Carolina. Dept. of public instruction] Publication no. 183)

N. C. Newbold, chairman of the commission.

1. Negroes—Education. 2. Negroes—North Carolina. [1, 2. Negroes—North Carolina—Education] I. Newbold, Nathan Carter, 1871–
II. Title.

E 36-191

U. S. Off. of educ. Library for Library of Congress LC2802.N8A4 [L184.B22 no. 183]
[37c2]

North Carolina.

M975.6
B69

Boykin, James H
The Negro in North Carolina prior to 1861; an historical monograph. [1st ed.] New York, Pageant Press [1958]

84 p. 21 cm.
Includes bibliography.

1. Negroes—North Carolina. I. Title.

E185.93.N6B6 325.260975G 58—1347 ‡

Library of Congress [58c5]

North Carolina.

M324
Ed57n

Edmonds, Helen G
The Negro and fusion politics in North Carolina, 1894–1901. Chapel Hill, University of North Carolina Press [1951]

viii, 260 p. illus., maps. 25 cm.
Bibliography: p. 239–247.

1. Negroes—North Carolina. 2. North Carolina—Pol. & govt.—1865– 3. Negroes—Politics and suffrage. I. Title.

E185.93.N6E4 325.2609756 51—4106

Library of Congress [53q5]

North Carolina.

M975.6
F85

Franklin, John Hope.
The free Negro in North Carolina, 1790–1860, by John Hope Franklin ... Chapel Hill, The University of North Carolina press, 1943.

x, 271 p. illus. (maps) tables. 23½cm.
Bibliography: p. [247]–258.

1. Freedmen in North Carolina. I. Title.

43-5088

Library of Congress E185.93.N6F7
[15] 326.8

North Carolina.

M975.6
L82

Logan, Frenise A
The Negro in North Carolina, 1876–1894. Chapel Hill, University of North Carolina Press [1964]

ix, 244 p. 24 cm.
Bibliography: p. [221]–233.

1. ~~Negroes~~—North Carolina. I. Title.

E185.93.N6L6 301.451 64–13554

Library of Congress [5]

M323.
N212

North Carolina.
National Association for the Advancement of Colored People. Legal Defense and Educational Fund.
Assault at 75 feet. New York, NAACP, Legal Defense and Educational Fund, 1951.

6p. illus. 22cm.

North Carolina.

M362.7
Sa5

Sanders, Wiley Britton, 1898– *ed.*
Negro child welfare in North Carolina, a Rosenwald study, directed by Wiley Britton Sanders ... under the joint auspices of the North Carolina State board of charities and public welfare and the School of public welfare, the University of North Carolina. Chapel Hill, Pub. for the North Carolina State board of charities and public welfare by the University of North Carolina press, 1933.

xiv p., 2 l., [3]–326 p. 24cm.

1. Negroes—North Carolina. 2. Negroes—Moral and social conditions. 3. Charities—North Carolina. 4. Children—Charities, protection, etc.—North Carolina. 5. Juvenile delinquency—North Carolina. 6. Social surveys I. North Carolina. State board of charities and public welfare. II. North Carolina. University. School of public welfare. III. Title.

33—18006

Library of Congress E185.93.N6S27
[45t1] 325.2600756

North Carolina.

M370
N81r

North Carolina. *Governor's commission for the study of problems in the education of Negroes in North Carolina.*
... Report of the Governor's commission for the study of problems in the education of Negroes in North Carolina. Issued by the state superintendent of public instruction, Raleigh, N. C. [Raleigh, 1935]

96 p. incl. tables, diagrs. 23½cm. ([North Carolina. Dept. of public instruction] Publication no. 183)

N. C. Newbold, chairman of the commission.

1. Negroes—Education. 2. Negroes—North Carolina. [1, 2. Negroes—North Carolina—Education] I. Newbold, Nathan Carter, 1871–
II. Title.

E36-191

U. S. Off. of educ. Library for Library of Congress LC2802.N8A4 [L184.B22 no. 183]
[37c2]

North Carolina.

M334
P68c

Pitts, Nathan Alvin, 1913–
The cooperative movement in Negro communities of North Carolina. Washington, Catholic University of America Press, 1950.

xii, 201 p. maps. 23cm. (The Catholic University of America. Studies in sociology, v.33)

Thesis - Catholic University of America.
Bibliography: p. [193]–196

North Carolina.

M815.5
Sh4r

Shepard, James Edward, 1875–
Racial and inter-racial relations in North Carolina and the south; Speech delivered by, on the twentieth anniversary of the Michigan avenue Y.M.C.A., Buffalo, New York, October 22, 1943.

20 leaves. 28cm.
Mimeographed.

North Carolina - Crimes.

M975.6
N81c

North Carolina state board of charities and public welfare.
Capital punishment in North Carolina. Raleigh, N.C., N. C. state board of charities and public welfare, 1929.
173p. illus. 23cm. (Special bulletin number 10)
"Lawrence A. Oxley... is due chief credit for the collection of the material."

North Carolina—Education.

M370
N81r

North Carolina. ***Governor's commission for the study of problems in the education of Negroes in North Carolina.***
... Report of the Governor's commission for the study of problems in the education of Negroes in North Carolina. Issued by the state superintendent of public instruction, Raleigh, N. C. ⌊Raleigh, 1935⌋
96 p. incl. tables, diagrs. 23½ᶜᵐ. (⌊North Carolina. Dept. of public instruction⌋ Publication no. 183)
N. C. Newbold, chairman of the commission.
1. Negroes—Education. 2. Negroes—North Carolina. ⌊1, 2. Negroes—North Carolina—Education⌋ I. Newbold, Nathan Carter, 1871– II. Title.
E 36-191
U. S. Off. of educ. Library for Library of Congress LC2802.N8A4 [L184.B22 no. 183] ⌊37c2⌋

North Carolina - Pol. & govt. - 1775-1865.

M975.6
B69n

Boykin, James H
North Carolina in 1861. New York, Bookman Associates ⌊1961⌋
237 p. 21 cm.
Includes bibliography.
1. North Carolina—Soc. condit. 2. Secession. 3. North Carolina—Pol. & govt.—1775-1865.
F258.B6 975.603 61-15678 ‡
Library of Congress ⌊2⌋

North Carolina-Politics-govt.-1865-

M324
Ed57n

Edmonds, Helen G
The Negro and fusion politics in North Carolina, 1894–1901. Chapel Hill, University of North Carolina Press ⌊1951⌋
viii, 260 p. illus., maps. 25 cm.
Bibliography: p. 239-247.
1. Negroes—North Carolina. 2. North Carolina—Pol. & govt.—1865– 3. Negroes—Politics and suffrage. I. Title.
E185.93.N6E4 325.2609756 51—4106
Library of Congress ⌊53q5⌋

North Carolina-Pol. & govt.-1865-

MB9
F95t

Fuller, Thomas Oscar, 1867–
Twenty years in public life, 1890–1910, North Carolina-Tennessee, by Thomas O. Fuller. Nashville, Tenn., National Baptist publishing board, 1910.
279, ⌊1⌋ p. illus., ports. 20 cm.
1. Negroes—North Carolina. 2. North Carolina—Pol. & govt.—1865– 3. Negroes—Tennessee. I. Title.
E185.97.F9 10-18964 rev
Library of Congress ⌊r47b1⌋

North Carolina - Social conditions.

M975.6
B69n

Boykin, James H
North Carolina in 1861. New York, Bookman Associates ⌊1961⌋
237 p. 21 cm.
Includes bibliography.
1. North Carolina—Soc. condit. 2. Secession. 3. North Carolina—Pol. & govt.—1775-1865.
F258.B6 975.603 61-15678 ‡
Library of Congress ⌊2⌋

North Carolina, College, Durham

M378N
H78

Heningburg, Alphonse
North Carolina College for Negroes.
n.p. n.d.
⌊6⌋ p. 22cm.

North Carolina mutual and provident association.

MB9
M55a

Andrews, Robert McCants.
John Merrick, a biographical sketch, by R. McCants Andrews. ⌊Durham, N. C., Press of the Seeman printery, ᶜ1920⌋
5 p. l., 9–229 p. front., plates, ports., facsim. 20½ᶜᵐ.
1. Merrick, John, 1859–1919. 2. North Carolina mutual and provident association.
20—22635
Library of Congress E185.97.M56 ⌊43d1⌋

M975.6
N81c

North Carolina state board of charities and public welfare.
Capital punishment in North Carolina. Raleigh, N.C., N.C. state board of charities and public welfare, 1929.
173p. illus. 23cm. (Special bulletin number 10)
"Lawrence A. Oxley... is due chief credit for the collection of the material."
1. North Carolina - Crimes.
I. Title

North into freedom.

MB9
M29

Malvin, John, 1795–1880.
North into freedom; the autobiography of John Malvin, free Negro, 1795–1880. Edited and with an introd. by Allan Peskin. Cleveland, Press of Western Reserve University, 1966.
vii, 87 p. 23 cm.
"A book from Cleveland State University."
Bibliographical references included in "Notes to the introduction" (p. 22-24)
1. Negroes—Ohio. 2. Negroes—Civil rights. I. Peskin, Allan, ed. II. Title.
E185.97.M26A3 1966 66-28142
301.451960924 (B)
Library of Congress ⌊8⌋

North Little Rock, Ark.

M976.7
W93

Writers' program. ***Arkansas.***
Survey of Negroes in Little Rock and North Little Rock, compiled by the Writers' program of the Work projects administration in the state of Arkansas. Sponsored by the Urban league of greater Little Rock, Arkansas. ⌊Little Rock, ᶜ1941⌋
4 p. l., 101 p. incl. tables. 23ᶜᵐ.
Bibliography: p. 99–101.
1. Negroes—Little Rock, Ark. 2. Negroes—North Little Rock, Ark. I. Title.
41–4905
Library of Congress F419.L7W85 ⌊3⌋ 325.2609767

North pole.

MB9
H39h

Henson, Matthew Alexander, 1866–
A negro explorer at the North pole, by Matthew A. Henson; with a foreword by Robert E. Peary ... and an introduction by Booker T. Washington; with illustrations from photographs. New York, Frederick A. Stokes company ⌊1912⌋
xx p., 1 l., 200 p. front., plates, ports. 19½ cm.
1. Arctic regions. 2. North pole. 3. Peary, Robert Edwin, 1856–1920. I. Title.
12—4225
Library of Congress G670 1909.H5 ⌊42m1⌋

MB9
N81
1853

Northup, Solomon, *b.* 1808.
... Twelve years a slave. Narrative of Solomon Northup, a citizen of New-York, kidnapped in Washington city in 1841, and rescued in 1853, from a cotton plantation near the Red river, in Louisiana. Auburn, Derby and Miller; Buffalo, Derby, Orton and Mulligan; ⌊etc., etc.⌋ 1853.
xvi, ⌊17⌋–336 p. front., pl. 19½ cm.
At head of title: Tenth thousand.
Preface signed: David Wilson.
3. Slave narratives.
1. Plantation life. 2. Slavery in the U. S.—Louisiana. I. Wilson, David, 1818–1887, ed.
10—34503
Library of Congress E444.N87 ⌊30h1⌋

Northwest, Pacific.

M979
C44

Chittick, Victor Lovitt Oakes, 1882– ***ed.***
Northwest harvest, a regional stocktaking. Contributions by Peter H. Odegard ⌊and others⌋ New York, Macmillan Co., 1948.
xvi, 226 p. 22 cm.
"The printed record of the Writers' Conference on the Northwest, held in Portland, Oregon, October 31, November 1 and 2, 1946, under the joint sponsorship of the Library Association of Portland and Reed College."
1. Northwest, Pacific. 2. Alaska. I. Odegard, Peter H., 1901– II. Writers' Conference on the Northwest, Portland, Or., 1946. III. Title.
F852.C57 979.50082 48—5145*
Library of Congress ⌊40u10⌋

Northwest harvest, a regional stocktaking.

M979
C44

Chittick, Victor Lovitt Oakes, 1882– ***ed.***
Northwest harvest, a regional stocktaking. Contributions by Peter H. Odegard ⌊and others⌋ New York, Macmillan Co., 1948.
xvi, 226 p. 22 cm.
"The printed record of the Writers' Conference on the Northwest, held in Portland, Oregon, October 31, November 1 and 2, 1946, under the joint sponsorship of the Library Association of Portland and Reed College."
1. Northwest, Pacific. 2. Alaska. I. Odegard, Peter H., 1901– II. Writers' Conference on the Northwest, Portland, Or., 1946. III. Title.
F852.C57 979.50082 48—5145*
Library of Congress ⌊40u10⌋

Norton, Jacob.

M366.1
H32m

⌊Hayden, Lewis⌋
Masonry among colored men in Massachusetts. To the Right Worshipful J. G. Findel, honorary grand master of the Prince Hall grand lodge, and general representative thereof to the lodges upon the continent of Europe. Boston, L. Hayden, 1871.
51 p. 23ᶜᵐ.
Signed: Lewis Hayden.
Appendix: no. 1. "Revolution and assumption." Remarks on G. M. Gardner's address before the G. L. of Massachusetts, March 7, 1870. By Bro. Jacob Norton. no. 2. The early history of masonry in Massachusetts. By Jacob Norton. no. 3. Extract from Report of Committee of G. L. of New Hampshire.
1. Freemasons, Negro. 2. Freemasons. Massachusetts. I. Findel, Gottfried Joseph Gabriel, 1828–1905. II. Norton, Jacob. III. Title.
17–15160
Library of Congress HS887.M4H4
——— Copy 2.

U.S.
MB39
Iv3n

Norwegian folk tales.
Asbjørnsen, Peter Christen, 1812–1885, *comp.*
Norwegian folk tales, from the collection of Peter Christen Asbjørnsen ⌊and⌋ Jørgen Moe. Illustrated by Erik Werenskiold ⌊and⌋ Theodor Kittelsen. Translated by Pat Shaw Iversen ⌊and⌋ Carl Norman. New York, Viking Press ⌊1960⌋
188 p. illus. 28 cm.
1. Fairy tales. I. Moe, Jørgen Engebretsen, 1813–1882, joint comp. II. Title.
PZ8.A89Nq 61-16057 ‡
Library of Congress ⌊15⌋

Norwich, Conn.

M326.99B
Sm6

Smith, James Lindsay
Autobiography of James L. Smith, including, also, reminiscences of slave life, recollections of the war, education of freedmen, causes of the exodus, etc. Norwich Conn. Press of the Bulletin company, 1881.
xiii p., 1 l., 150 p. front. (port.) 2 pl. 20cm.

Nós, os cabindas.

Angola
M967.3
F85n

Franque, Domingos José
Nós, os cabindas. Lisboa, Editora ARGO, 1940.
230p. port. 19cm.

Nose.

M610
C63w

Cobb, William Montague, 1904–
"Wolf snout" and other anomalies in monovular twins: a case report. Reprinted from the Freedmen's hospital bulletin, 1:27-32, September 1934.
6p. illus. 28cm.

Nose.

M610
C63y

Cobb, William Montague, 1904–
Your nose won't tell. Reprinted from the Crisis, 45:332, 336, October 1938.
one leaf, 3 columns. 30cm.

... Nosotros, poemas.
Cuba
M861.6 Pedroso, Regino, 1898–
P34n ... Nosotros, poemas. La Habana, 1933.
2 p. l., 9–70 p. 21cm.

I. Title.

38-22228
Library of Congress PQ7389.P28N6
[2] 861.6

Martinique Nostalgies françaises (1908-1913).
M841.91 Thaly, Daniel Desire Alin, 1879-
T32n Nostalgies françaises (1908-1913). Paris, Editions de lá Phalange, 1913.

134p. 19cm.
"Hommage de l'auteur a Monsieur le Prince de Bauffremont. Daniel Thaly, Roseau 14 Mon 1916.

Not a man, and yet a man.
M811.4 Whitman, Albery Allson, 1851–1901.
W59n Not a man, and yet a man: by A. A. Whitman. Springfield, O., Republic printing company, 1877.
254 p. front. (port.) $19\frac{1}{2}$cm.
Poems.

1. Slavery in the U. S.—Poetry. I. Title.

31-28854 Revised
Library of Congress PS3187.W2N6
[r42b2]

Not by prayer alone.
M331.833
T466 Tillman, James A
Not by prayer alone; a report on the Greater Minneapolis Interfaith Fair Housing Program [by] James A. Tillman, Jr. Philadelphia, United Church Press [1964]
223 p. 28 cm.

1. Greater Minneapolis Interfaith Fair Housing Program. 2. Discrimination in housing—Minneapolis. 3. Negroes—Housing. 4. Church and race problems. I. Title.

E185.89.H6T5 301.451 64-19721
Library of Congress [5]

Not only war.
M813.5 Daly, Victor.
D33 Not only war, a story of two great conflicts, by Victor Daly. Boston, The Christopher publishing house [°1932]
106 p. 21cm.

1. European war, 1914–1918—Fiction. I. Title.

[Full name: Victor Reginald Daly]
32-1646
Library of Congress PZ3.D179No
——— Copy 2.
Copyright A 46912 [3]

Not without dust.
M813.5 Chantrelle, Seginald.
C36 Not without dust, a novel. [1st ed.] New York, Exposition Press [1954]
123 p. 21 cm.

I. Title.

PZ4.C459No 54-12467 ‡
Library of Congress [3]

Not without laughter.
M813.5 Hughes, Langston
H87ni Niet zonder lachen. Uit het Amerikaans Vertaald door Em. Van Loggem. Amsterdam, F. G. Kroonder, 1941.

255p. 20cm.
"To Arthur Spingarn - yours, Langston Hughes. New York, August 9, 1960."
Title: Not without laughter.

I. Title.

Not without laughter.
M813.5 Hughes, Langston, 1902–
H87no Not without laughter, by Langston Hughes. New York, London, A. A. Knopf, 1930.
viii, 324 p., 1 l. $19\frac{1}{2}$cm.

I. Title.

[Full name: James Langston Hughes]
30-19627
Library of Congress PZ3.H87318No
[a45m1]

Not without laughter.
M813.5 Hughes, Langston, 1902-
H87p Piccola America Negra, romanzo. Milano, Italy, Longanesi, 1948.

372 p. 18 cm. (La Gaja scienza, v. 27)
Translation of Not without laughter.

Not without laughter.
M813.5 Hughes, Langston, 1902-
H87s ... Sandy; Not without laughter, traduit de l'Americain par Garbiel Beauroy. Paris, Les Editions Rieder, 1934.

[9] 304 p. 19 cm.

Not without tears.
M89 Day, Helen Caldwell, 1926–
D285n Not without tears. New York, Sheed and Ward, 1954.
270 p. 22 cm.

1. Blessed Martin House of Hospitality, Memphis. I. Title.

BX4705.D284A3 922.273 54-11149 ‡
Library of Congress [10]

Not yet Uhuru: the autobiography of Oginga Odinga.
Kenya
M967.62 Odinga, Ajuma Oginga, 1911-
Od3 Not yet Uhuru: the autobiography of Oginga Odinga; with a foreword by Kwame Nkrumah. London, Heinemann, 1967.

xv, 323p. plates (incl. facsims., ports.), map. 20½cm.
Map on endpapers.
African author.

1. Kenya - Politics and government.
I. Title.

Notebook 23.
M811.5 Mason, Jordan Mason.
M38n Notebook # 23. New Mexico, Motive Book Shop, n.d.

13p. illus. 21cm.

Notes for a glossary of words and phrases of Barbadian dialect.
Barbados
M427.972 Collymore, Frank A , 1893-
C58 Notes for a glossary of words and phrases of Barbadian dialect. 2d ed. Advocate Company, 1957.

94p. 20cm.

Notes of a native son.
M813.5 Baldwin, James, 1924–
B19n2 Notes of a native son. ~~New York, Dial Press, 1963 [°1955]~~ London, M. Joseph [1964]
~~158 p. 21 cm.~~ 165p. 21½cm.
Essays.

1. Negroes. 2. U. S.—Race question. I. Title.

E185.61.B2 1963 64-115
Library of Congress [5]

Notes of a native son.
M813.5 Baldwin, James, 1924–
B19n Notes of a native son. Boston, Beacon Press [1955]
175 p. 22 cm.
Essays.

1. Negroes. 2. U. S.—Race question. I. Title.

E185.61.B2 55-11825 ‡
*301.451 325.260973
Library of Congress [12]

...Notes on the sounds and vocabulary.
M427. Turner, Lorenzo Dow
T85m ...Notes on the sounds and vocabulary of Gullah. Reprinted... from Publication of the American Dialect Society, no.3, May 1945.
13-28p. 22½cm.
Inscribed copy: To Dr. Arthur B. Spingarn, with the cordial regards of Lorenzo D. Turner, December 9, 1945.

Notes sur la democratie en pays Toucouleur.
Senegal
M966.3 Ba, Oumar
B12 Notes sur la democratie en pays Toucouleur. [Dakar, Imprimerie A. Diop, n.d.]

52p. 22cm.

1. Toucouleurs. 2. Senegal - Native races. I. Title.

Nothing personal.
M301 Baldwin, James, 1924-
B19 Nothing personal. Photos. by Richard Avedon and text by James Baldwin. [New York, Atheneum, 1964]
1 v. (chiefly illus., ports.) 37 cm.

1. Photography—Portraits. I. Baldwin, James, 1924–
II. Title.

TR680.A89 301.2 64-23632
Library of Congress [4-1]

Notice sur notre legislature.
Congo(Leopoldville)
M967.5 Batibuka, Jean
B32 Notice sur notre legislature (observations de deux ans). Bukavu, La Presse Congolaise, 1962.

143p. 21cm.
Portrait of author.

La notion Luba-Bantoue de l'etre.
Congo
(Leopoldville)
M967.5 Lufuluabo, François-Marie
L96 La notion Luba-Bantoue de l'etre. Bakwanga, Imprimatur Jos. Nkongolo, 1164.

46p. 22½cm.
Portrait of author on back of book.

1. Bantus - Religion. I. Title.

Haiti
M133
H72n

Notions méthaphysiques.

Holly, Théodose A
... Notions méthaphysiques [!] et autres, révélées ou confirmées par la radiesthésie ... Port-au-Prince, Haïti, Imp. V. Valcin [194-?]
v. 23cm.
CONTENTS.—1. Dieu et l'univers (mécanisme du monde)

1. Radiesthesia. I. Title.

44-30292

Library of Congress BF1142.H6 [2] 133

Nova-Scotia- Folklore.

M398
F27f

Fauset, Arthur Huff, ed.
Folklore from Nova Scotia, collected by Arthur Huff Fauset. New York, The American folk-lore society, G. E. Stechert and co., agents, 1931.
xxii, 204 p. 24½cm. (Half-title: Memoirs of the American folklore society. vol. xxiv)

1. Folk-lore—Nova Scotia.

32-8895

Library of Congress GR1.A5 vol. 24 [3] (398) 398.09716

Uganda
M967.61
N87m

Nsimbi, Michael B
Muddu awulira. ("The obedient servant...") Michael B. Wamala. Nairobi, The Eagle Press, 1959.

82p. 21½cm.
Text in: Luganda.

1. Uganda.

Haiti
M972.94
F46no

Notre Neybe ou leur Bahoruco?

Fignolé, Daniel.
Notre Neybe ou leur Bahoruco? Port-au-Prince, Imp. Valcin, 1948.

25p. 19½cm. (Mouvement ouvrier-paysan) Publication du Bureau d'Education du Parti.

"How I am civilized."

M813.5
H87n

Huffman, Eugene Henry.
"Now I am civilized" [by] Eugene Henry Huffman; illustrated by Herbert Rasche. Los Angeles, Calif., Wetzel publishing co., inc., 1930.
6 p. l., 11-208 p. illus. 20½cm.

I. Title.

30-24532

Library of Congress PN6161.H837
———— Copy 2.
Copyright A 27390 [2] 818.5

Uganda
M967.61
N87s

Nsimbi, Michael B
Siwa muto lugero. London, Longmans, Green and Co., 1957.

80p. 18½cm.

I. Title.

Haiti
M841
B76d

...Nous garderons le dieu.

Brierre, Jean Fernand, 1909-
...Nous garderons le dieu. En hommage au grand leader haïtien de gauche: Jacques Roumain. Port-au-Prince, Imprimerie H. Deschamps, 1945.

1p. l., 27p. 20 x 15cm.
At head of title: Jean F. Brierre.
Poems.

M324
N86

Nowlin, William Felbert, 1897-
The Negro in American national politics, by William F. Nowlin, A. M. Boston, Mass., The Stratford company [°1931]
4 p. l., 148 p. 19½ cm.
Bibliography: p. 145-148.

1. Negroes—Politics and suffrage. I. Title.

32—5242

Library of Congress JK2275.N4N6 [49e½] 325.26

Uganda
M967.61
N87w

Nsimbi, Michael B
Waggumbulizi. Eyawandiika; Omugaso gw' Okugunjulwa, Siwa Muto Lugero, Olulimi Oluganda, Muddu Awulira. Kampala, Uganda Bookshop, 1952.

111p. illus. 18½cm.

I. Title. 1. Uganda

Sénégal
M896.3
D59n

Les nouveaux contes d'Amadou Koumba.
Diop, Birago, 1906-
Les nouveaux contes d'Amadou Koumba. Préface de Léopold Sédar. Paris, Présence Africaine, 1958.

173p. 18½cm.

Nozipo

South Africa
M968
M71n

Mlotyna, Stephen V
Nozipo [Story of native life] [Lovedale, South Africa] Lovedale Institution Press [1923]

41p. 18½cm.
Written in Xhosa.

1. Africa, South. I. Title.

Malawi
M968.97
N87h

Ntara, Samuel Yosia, 1904 or 5-
Headman's enterprise; an unexpected page in central African history, tr. and ed. with a pref. by Cullen Young from the Cewa original. London, Lutterworth Press [1949]
213 p. illus., map. 19 cm.

1. Mayambosa, Chewa headman, 1830 (ca.)-1926. I. Title.
2. Nyasaland.
DT864.N78 923.1678 50-12132

Library of Congress [2]

Haiti
M841
P21n

Nouvelle floraison.

Paret, Timothee, Louis Joseph, 1887-1942.
Nouvelle floraison, poémes. Paris, Editions de la revue mondiale, 1927.
194 [cxcvii-ccvi]p. 18cm.

Ghana
M966.7
N67

Nsarkoh, J K
Local government in Ghana [by] J. K. Nsarkoh. Accra, Ghana Universities Press, 1964.
309 p. 23 cm.
"List of some local government books": p. [232]-233. Bibliographical footnotes.

1. Local government—Ghana. I. Title.

JS7649.G62N75 352.0667 64-6007

Library of Congress [1]

Malawi
M968.97
N87m

Ntara, Samuel Yosia, 1904 or 5-
Man of Africa, by Samuel Yosia Ntara; translated and arranged from the original Nyanja by T. Cullen Young. Foreword by Professor Julian Huxley ... London, The Religious tract society [1934]
180, [1] p. front., plates. 19cm.
"Prize-winning biography under authority of the International institute of African languages and cultures ... 1933."—p. [3]

1. Ethnology—Nyasaland. I. Young, T. Cullen, tr. II. Religious tract society, London. III. International institute of African languages and cultures.

35-6977

Library of Congress DT864.N8 [5] 572.96897

Haiti
M917.94
F77n

Nouvelle geographie de l'ile d'Haiti.

Fortunat, Dantès, 1851-
Nouvelle géographie de l'île d'Haïti: contenant des notions historiques et topographiques sur les autres Antilles, par Dantès Fortunat ... Port-au-Prince, Chez l'auteur; Paris, H. Noirot, 1888.
1 p. l., xxvi, 537 p. front. (port.) illus. (incl. plates, ports., maps, tables) fold. map. 18cm.

1. Haiti—Descr. & trav. I. Title.

4—2407

Library of Congress F1901.F73 [42d1]

Uganda
M967.61
N87o

Nsimbi, M B
Olulimi Oluganda [Correct Luganda] Nairobi, The Eagle Press, 1955.

52p. 21½cm.

1. Uganda.

Tanganyika
M967.82
N88d

Ntiro, S J
Desturi za Wachagga [Customs and traditions of the Chagga people of Tanganyika] Nairobi, The Eagle Press, 1953.

50p. illus. 22½cm.
Written in Swahili.

1. Tanganyika - History. 2. Chaggas.

Haiti
M972.94
O1n

Les nouvelles tendances du droit public de la républic d'Haïti.
O'Callachan, Georges.
Les nouvelles tendances du droit public de la république d'Haiti. Port-au-Prince, Imprimerie du Collège Vertières, 1940.

21p. 21½cm.

Uganda
M967.61
N87a

Nsimbi, Michael B
Amannya amaganda n'ennono zaago. Kampala, East African Literature Bureau, 1956.

323p. illus., maps. 21½cm.

1. Uganda. I. Title.

Basutoland
M896
N88ma

Ntsane, K E
Masoabi. Ngoan'a Mosotho 'a Kajeno. Morija, Basutoland, Sesuto Book Depot, 1947.

139 p. 18 cm.

1. Africa South-Folktales.

Basutoland
M896
N88mu
Ntsane, K E
'Musa-pelo. Morija, Basutoland, Sesuto Book Depot, 1946.
76 p. 18½ cm.
The heart restorer. Written in Sotho.

Uganda
M967.61
N88r
Ntungwerisho, Yemima K tr.
Ruhondeza mwene busasi [Rip Van Winkle] Nairobi, The Eagle Press, 1950.
22p. 18cm.
Written in Runyankore.
I. Rip Van Winkle.

Haiti
M841.
B94c
Numa, Edgar N., 1881-
Burr-Reynaud, Frederic, 1884-
...La corbeille-poemes de Fred Burr-Reynaud, Luc Grimard, Dominique Hippolyte, Jean Libose, Edgar N. Numa. Port-au-Prince, Haiti, Imprimerie du College Vertieres, 1943.
34p. 19cm.

S Africa
M89
N879b
Ntsikana, [Ibali Lika]
Bokwe, John Knox, 1855-1922.
Ntsikana: the story of an African convert, with an appendix "Ibali lika Ntsikana" in the native language. By John Knox Bokwe... second edition. [Lovedale, South Africa, printed at the mission press, 1914.]
67p. port. plates. 21½cm.

Nude to the meaning of tomorrow.
M813.5
W85n
Wooby, Philip
Nude to the meaning of tomorrow. New York, Exposition Press, 1959.
285p. 21cm.

Nigeria
M966.9
N916
Numa, Frederick Yamu, 1916-
The pride of Urhobo nation. Lagos, Ribway Press [1950]
56p. illus., port. 18cm.
Portrait of author in book.
1. Sobo (African people). I. Title.

S. Africa
M968
J11im
Ntsikana celebrations.
Jabavu, Davidson Don Tengo, 1885-
Imbumba yamaNyama. Lovedale, Lovedale Press, 1952.
v, 105 p. 19 cm.

Peru
M863.6
L88n
Nuevos cuentos andinos.
López Albújar, Enrique, 1872-
... Nuevos cuentos andinos. Santiago de Chile, Ediciones Ercilla, 1937.
4 p. l., [11]-185 p., 1 l. 22cm. (Half-title: Biblioteca América)
CONTENTS.—El brindis de los yayas.—Huayna-pishtanag.—El blanco.—Cómo se hizo pishtaco Calixto.—El trompiezo.—Juan Rabines no perdona.—Una posesión judicial.
I. Title.
38—12446
Library of Congress PQ8497.L8N8
[45d1] 863.6

Brazil
M869.3
L62n
Numa e a ninfa.
Lima Barreto, Afonso Henrique de, 1881-1922.
Numa e a ninfa (romance) Rio [de Janeiro] Gráfica Editôra Brasileira [1950]
~~308 p.~~ 21 cm. 285 illus.
~~L.C. copy imperfect.~~
~~"Aventuras do Dr. Bogoloff": p. [217]-308.~~
I. Title. ~~II. Title: Aventuras do Dr. Bogoloff.~~
PQ9697.L544N8 52-15661 ‡
Library of Congress [1]

South Africa
M896.4
W15
Ntsonkota, Elda Blanche
Ukukubekisa Kobu-Gqwira Entla-Lweni Yobu-Kristu.
Pp. 85-92.
Written in Xhosa
In: Wallis, S. J., comp. and ed. Inkolo namasiko. London, Society for Promoting Christian Knowledge, 1930.

Cameroun
M896.1
N98
La nuit de ma vie.
Nyunai, Jean-Paul
La nuit de ma vie. Paris, Debresse-Poesie, 1961.
47p. 19cm.
I. Title.

South Africa
M335.4
N916
Numade, N
Three essays on the African revolution. With a foreword by Benjamin J. Davis. New York, New Century Publishers, 1963.
48p. 19cm.
Contents: Marxism and African revolutions.- The choice before new Africa.- The working class and the African revolution.
1. Communism - Africa. 2. Africa - Communism. I. Davis, Benjamin F. Introduction.

South Africa
M896.3
N87
Ntuli, F L tr.
Umbuso ka Shaka. [Translated] from Nada the lily [R. Haggard] Mariannhill, Natal, Mariannhill Mission Press [1933]
350p. 18½cm.
Written in Zulu.
1. Zululand - History - Fiction. I. Haggard, Sir Henry Rider, 1856-1925. Nada the lily. II. Title.

Congo(Leopoldville)
M896.3
M71
Une nuit tragique.
Mobiala, Louis
Une nuit tragique. Leverville (Congo Belge) Bibliotheque de l'Etoile, 1954.
52p. illus.
I. Title.

Dominican Republic
M860.9
H39i
Nunez de Caceres, Jose, 1772?-1846—Fiction.
Henríquez Ureña, Max, 1885-
... La independencia efímera. Paris, F. Sorlot, 1938.
2 p. l., 7-213 p., 1 l. 18½cm.
At head of title: Episodios dominicanos.
"Erratas más notables": slip mounted on first blank leaf.
"Principales obras históricas consultadas": p. 195-197.
"Trabajos relativos a Núñez de Cáceres y a la revolución de 1821": p. 197-200.
"Escritos de Núñez de Cáceres y de sus hijos": p. 200-208.
1. Dominican republic—Hist.—Fiction. 2. Núñez de Cáceres, José, 1772?-1846—Fiction. I. Title. II. Title: Episodios dominicanos.
41—717
Library of Congress F1931.H514
[45c1] 972.93

Uganda
M967.61
N88ek
Ntungwerisho, Yemima K
Ekirooto ky'omufuzi era ekimuli sekisumuluzo [The ruler's dream and the key flower] Nairobi, The Eagle Press, 1949. African home library No. 37.
14p. 18cm.
Written in Luganda.
1. Uganda.

Dahomey
M896.1
Og6n
Nuits.
Ogoundele-Tessi, Jean
Nuits; extrait 1 - poèmes. Porto-Novo [Dahomey] Imprimerie Rapidex [n.d.]
15p. 21cm.
I. Title.

M811.08
N92
Nuovissima poesia Americana e Negra con testo a fronte, 1949-1953. Introduzione versione e note c cura di Carlo Izzo. Parma, Ugo Guanda Editore, 1953.
XXVII, 419p. 24cm.
Partial contents: Frances E.W. Harper. W.E.B. DuBois. James Weldon Johnson. Paul Lawrence Dunbar. Grimke. Fenton Johnson, Frank Horne. Sterling A. Brown. Arna Bontemps. Langston Hughes. Countee Cullen. Waring Cuney. Richard Wright. Frederick Douglass. Margaret Walker. Gwendolyn Brooks, Spirituals.
1. Poetry - Collections.

Uganda
M967.61
N88e
Ntungwerisho, Yemima K
Ensulo era n'ekitole ky'ebbumba [The source and a handful of clay] Nairobi, The Eagle Press, 1949.
10p. 18½cm.
(African home library, No. 63)
Written in Luganda.
1. Uganda.

Guadeloupe
M843.91
T36
Nuits tropicales.
Thomarel, André.
Nuits tropicales. Avant-propos de René Marna. Paris, Les Editions du Scorpion, 1960.
159p. 19cm. (Collection Alternance.

Nurse, Malcolm, See
Padmore, George, 1903-1959, pseud.

Nurses and nursing.

M610.73 N21s National Association of Colored Graduate Nurses.
A salute to democracy at mid-century. New York, 1951.

[48]p. 21cm.
Testimonial dinner honoring organizations and individuals who have helped further democracy in nursing.
Where service is neede, by Langston Hughes.

Nutrition.

Kenya M613.2 H88w Humphrey, Norman
Mane midwaro? Midenyo koso yieng'o? [Which do you want? Starvation or nutrition? Tr. by C. J. Amenya] Nairobi, Eagle Press, 1950
8p. illus. 21½cm. (Como ngima)
Written in Luo
I. Nutrition. I. Title. II. Series. III. Amenya, C. J., tr.

Nigeria M896.3 N97d Nwankemo, Nkem
Danda. [London] A. Deutsch [1964]
205p. 20cm.
Portrait of author on book jacket.
1. Nigeria - Fiction. I. Title.

Nurses and nursing.

Jamaica M89 Se2s Seacole, Mary.
Wonderful adventures of Mrs. Seacole in many lands. Edited by W. J. S. With an introductory preface by W. H. Russell ... London, J. Blackwood, 1857.
xii, 200 p. double front. 17cm.
Largely devoted to an account of the author's experiences as a sutler during the Crimean war.

1. Crimean war, 1853-1856—Personal narratives. I. S., W. J., ed. II. Title.

H. E. Huntington library for Library of Congress A 25-224

Nutrition.

Kenya M613.2 H55f Humphrey, Norman
Pong'o ic ok e gago ringruok [Feeding the body is more than filling the stomach. [Tr. by C. J. Amenya] Nairobi, Eagle Press, 1950.
14p. 21½cm. (Como ngima. Aim at healthy living series)
Written in Luo.
1. Nutrition. I. Title. II. Series. III. Aim at healthy living series. IV. Amenya, C. J., tr.

Nigeria M896.3 N97t Nwankwo, Nkem
Tales out of school. Illustrated by Adebayo Ajayi. Lagos, African Universities Press [1963]
90p. illus. 20cm. (African Reader's Library, no. 2)
I. Title. II: Series: African reader's library, 2.

Nurses and nursing.

Barbados M610 St2n Staupers, Mabel Keaton, 1890-
No time for prejudice; a story of the integration of Negroes in nursing in the United States. New York, Macmillan [1961]
206 p. illus. 22 cm.

1. Negro nurses. I. Title.

RT83.5.S75 610.7306273 61—7432 ‡
Library of Congress [61k10]

Nutrition.

Virgin Islands M641 J726 Jones, Trandailer
Impressions of nutrition habits in the Virgin Islands. [Saint Thomas, V. I.] Nutrition Division, Virgin Islands Department of Health [1952]
54p. illus. 23cm.
1. Nutrition. 2. Virgin Islands. I. Title.

Nigeria M896.1 N97i Nwanodi, Okogbule Glory
Icheke and other poems. Ibadan, Mbari Publications [1964]
31p. 21½cm.
1. African poetry. I. Title. II. Mbari Publications.

Nurses and nursing.

MB T38p Thoms, Adah B.
Pathfinders, a history of the progress of colored graduate nurses, compiled by Adah B. Thoms ... with biographies of many prominent nurses ... [New York, Printed at Kay printing house, inc., °1929]
xvi, 240 p. front., 1 illus., plates, ports. 23½cm.

1. Nurses and nursing. 2. Negroes—Biog. 3. Women, Negro. 4. Nurses and nursing—Study and teaching. I. Title.
[Full name: Adah B. Glassell Thoms]

Library of Congress RT71.T45 29—19412
[41g1]

Nutrition.

Uganda M613.2 T75 Trowell, H C
Mmere ki gye tusaanira okulya? [What food should we eat?] kya H. C Trowell ne R. G. Ladin. Kyakyusibwa John W. S. Kasirye ne Aloni Lubwama. Nairobi, Eagle Press, 1951.
23p. illus. 18½cm. (Asika Obulamu Series)
Written in Luganda.
1. Nutrition. I. Title. II. Kasirye, John W. S., tr. III. Lubwama, Aloni, jt. tr. IV. Series.

Nigeria M896.3 N973e Nwapa, Flora, 1931-
Efuru. [London] Heinemann [1966]
281p. 20½cm.
Portrait of author on book jacket.
I. Title.

M811.08 N94 Nussbaum, Anna, *ed.*
Afrika singt, eine auslese neuer afro-amerikanischer lyrik, herausgegeben von Anna Nussbaum. Wien und Leipzig, F. G. Speidel [1929]
2 p. l., [7]-169, [5] p., 1 l. 22cm.
"Die nachdichtungen und übertragungen stammen von Hermann Kesser, Josef Luitpold, Anna Siemsen, Anna Nussbaum."

1. ~~Negro~~ poetry (~~American~~)— I. Kesser, Hermann, 1880- tr. II. Luitpold, Josef, tr. III. Siemsen, Anna, 1882- tr.

29-21778
Library of Congress PS591.N43N8
[2]

Nutt, Howard, 1909- Special laughter.

M813.5 W931 Wright, Richard, 1909-
Introduction.
(In: Nutt, Howard, Special laughter, poems. Prairie City, Illinois, Press of James A Decker, 1940. pp. ix-xii)

Africa M323 T139 Nwariaku, Chickwenda
The paternal posture.
Pp. 75-86.
In: Tajeil, Henri, ed. Disappointed guests. London, Oxford University Press, 1965.

Nutrition.

Kenya M613.2 C89w Culwick, G M
Tũrĩrĩa kĩ? [What shall we eat?]Tr. by D. Wahone Ndabi] Nairobi, Eagle Press, 1950.
24p. illus. 21½cm. (Taanya Ũgima-ini. Aim at healthy living series)
Written in Kikuyu.
White author.
1. Nutrition. I. Title. II. Ndabi, D. Wahome, tr.

Nigeria M340 N97 Nwabueze, Benjamin Obi.
The machinery of justice in Nigeria. London, Butterworths, 1963.
xxi, 309 p. 23 cm. (Butterworth's African law series, no. 8)
Bibliographical references included in footnotes.

1. Justice, Administration of—Nigeria. I. Title
2. Nigeria-Courts.
64-1951
Library of Congress [3]

Nigeria M966.9 N98m Nwigwe, Henry Emezuem
My dreams of a greater Nigeria. [Yaba, West African Pilot, n.d.]
48p. port. 20½cm.
Portrait of author in book.
1. Nigeria. I. Title.

Nutrition.

Kenya M613.2 H88f3 Humphrey, Norman
Kũiyũria nda tikou gũthodeka mwĩrĩ [Feeding the body is more than filling the stomach. Tr. by J. M. Ruthuku] Nairobi, Eagle Press, 1950.
16p. 22cm. (Taanya Ũgima-ini. Aim at healthy living series)
Written in Kikuyu.
White author.
1. Nutrition. I. Title. II. Series. III. Aim at healthy living series. IV. Ruthuku, J. M., tr.

Nigeria M966.9 N98 Nwabueze, Benjamin Obi
Reflections on the review of the Nigerian constitution. [Lagos, Times Press, 1963]
32p. 24cm.
1. Nigeria. Constitution. 2. Nigeria - Constitutional law. I. Title.

Nwoko, Demas, illus.

Nigeria M896.1 Ok3h Okigbo, Christopher
Heavensgate. Drawings by Demas Nwoko. Ibadan, Mbari Publications, 1962.
39p. illus. 20cm.
1. African poetry. I. Title. II. Nwoko, Demas, illus.

Nigeria
M896.3
N974m

Nwosu, Cletus Gibson
Miss Cordelia in the romance of destiny; that most sensational love intricacy that has ever happened in West Africa. Port Harcourt, ‹Nigeria› Vincent C. Okeanu ‹n.d.›

43p. 19cm.

I. Title.

Africa
M261
D45

Nyabongo, Akiki K 1905-
African life and ideals.
Pp. 37-48.

In: Desai, Ram, ed. Christianity in Africa as seen by Africans. Denver, A. Swallow ‹1962.

Uganda
M967.61
N93a

Nyabongo, Akiki K 1905-
Africa answers back, by H. H. Prince Akiki K. Nyabongo; with an introduction by Dr. William Lyon Phelps; illustrated by Eleanor Maroney. London, G. Routledge & sons, ltd., 1936.

x, 278 p. incl. plates. front. (port.) 19cm.

Erratum slip inserted.
American edition (New York, C. Scribner's sons, 1935) has title: The story of an African chief.

1. Africa, Central—Soc. life & cust. I. Title.

36-35185
Library of Congress DT351.N9 1936 Provisional
[3] 916.7

Uganda
M967.61
N98b

Nyabongo, Akiki K 1905-
The "Bisoro" stories, by Akiki K. Nyabongo. Oxford, Basil Blackwell [1927]

ix, 111p. illus. 21½cm.

1. Folklore - Africa. 2. African Folklore. I. Title.

Uganda
M967.61
N98

Nyabongo, Akiki K 1905-
Oruhenda; obukama bwa toro [Dialect of the palace. Kampala, The Author, n.d.]

75p. illus., ports. 31cm.
Written in Luganda.

I. Title.

Uganda
M967.61
N98s

Nyabongo, Akiki K 1905-
The story of an African chief, by Akiki K. Nyabongo; illustrations by Eleanor Maroney; with an introduction by William Lyon Phelps. New York, C. Scribner's sons, 1935.

x p., 2 l., 3-312 p. incl. front., plates. 22cm.

1. Africa, Central—Soc. life & cust. I. Title.

35-7987
Library of Congress DT351.N9 Provisional
——— Copy 2.
Copyright A 83492 [5-5] 916.7

Uganda
M967.61
N98w

Nyabongo, Akiki K 1905-
Winds and lights; African fairy tales, by H. H. Prince Akiki K. Nyabongo; with illustrations by B. Hewitt. New York, N. Y., The Voice of Ethiopia [°1939]

[45] p. illus., port. 24cm.
"Errata" slip mounted on lining-paper.

1. Tales, African. I. Title.

39-17420
Library of Congress PZ8.1.N86W1
——— Copy 2.
Copyright A 131104 [3]

Uganda
M967.61
N98w

Nyabongo, Akiki K 1905-
Winds and lights; African fairy tales, by H. H. Prince Akiki K. Nyabongo; with illustrations by B. Hewitt. New York, N. Y., The Voice of Ethiopia [°1939]

[45] p. illus., port. 24cm.
"Errata" slip mounted on lining-paper.

1. Tales, African. I. Title.

39-17420
Library of Congress PZ8.1.N86W1
——— Copy 2.
Copyright A 131104 [3]

M811.5
N98p

Nyabongo, Virginia Lee (Simmons) 1913-
Les palmiers. La Habana, 1951.
60 p. port. 25 cm.
Poems.

I. Title.

PQ3989.N9P3 51-27375
Library of Congress [1]

M811.5
N98w

Nyabongo, Virginia Lee (Simmons), 1913-
Whitecaps [by] Virginia Simmons. [Yellow Springs, O., The Antioch press, 1942]

79p. illus. 21cm.

1. Poetry. I. Title.

Uganda
M896.3
N98

Nyakatuura, John William, 1895-
Enganikyo zaitu [Our stories] Kampala, East African Literature Bureau, 1961.

49p. illus. 18½cm.
Written in Ngoro-Tooroo.

I. Title.

Kenya
M641.5
N98

Nyakiyo.
Kūrīa wega [Good eating] Nairobi, Eagle Press, 1960.

48p. 18cm.
Written in Kikuyu.

1. Cookery, Kenyan. I. Title.

Nyanja (African people)

Malawi
M968.97
M29

Malekebu, Bennett E
Unkhoswe waanyanja. [Dialogues on guardianship] Edited by Guy Atkins. Cape Town: London. Oxford University Press, 1952.

124p. 18½cm. (Annotated African Texts. Mananja, I)
Written in Nyanja.

1. Nyanja (African people) 2. Nyasaland. I. Title.

Nyankole languages.

Uganda
M896.1
M83

Morris, Henry F ed.
The heroic recitations of the Bahima of Ankole, by H. F. Morris. With a foreword by A. T. Hatto. Oxford, Clarendon Press, 1964.

xii, 142, [1] p. illus., geneal. table, maps. 23 cm. (Oxford library of African literature)

Based on thesis, University of London in 1957, under the title: The heroic recitations of the Banyankore.
In part, English or Runyankore.
Bibliography: p. [143]

1. Epic poetry, Nyankole. 2. Bahima (African people) 3. Nyankole language. I. Title.

PL8594.N3M6 896.3 64-5119
Library of Congress [3]

Nyankonsem (Fables of the celestial.)

Ghana
M896.2
D23

Danquah, Joseph Kwame Keyeretwi Boakeye, 1895-
Nyankonsem (Fables of the celestial.) Agoru bi A wɔakye my Abiesa. A play in three acts. Done entirely in Twi language by J. B. Danquah. [New ed. Accra, Scottish Mission Book Depot [1954]

56p. 19cm.
"The version used in this play is based on R. S. Rattray's rendition in Akan-Ashanti folk tales."
Written in Twi.

Nyasaland.

Nyasaland
M968.97
C43m2

Chibambo, Yesaya Mlonyeni,
My Ngoni of Nyasaland. Translated by Rev. Charles Stuart. London, United Society for Christian Literature, n.d.

63p. 19cm. (Africa's own library, no.3)
Footnotes.

Nyasaland.

Malawi
M968.97
N87h

Ntara, Samuel Yosia, 1904 or 5
Headman's enterprise; an unexpected page in in central African history, tr. and ed. with a preface by Cullen Young from the Cewa original. London, Lutterworth Press 1949.
213p. illus., map. 19cm.

Nyasaland - Fiction.

Malawi
M896.3
N65u

Nkomba, Lester L
Ukawamba. Edited by Guy Atkins. Cape Town; London, Oxford University Press, 1953.

134p. 18½cm. (Annotated African Texts - II: Cewa)

Nydia y Fidel.

Cuba
M863.6
P86n

Poveda Ferrer, Simeon.
Nydia y Fidel; novela cubana por Simeon Poveda Ferrer. Habana, Imprenta "La Prueba", 1920.

274p. port. 19½cm.

S. Africa
M496.3
N98l

Nyembezi, Cyril Lincoln Sibusiso, 1919-
Learn Zulu. Pietermaritzburg, South Africa, Shuter and Shooter, 1957.

151p. 18½cm.

1. Zulu - Grammar. I. Title.

South Africa
M896.
N98r

Nyembezi, Cyril Lincoln Sibusiso, 1919-
A review of Zulu literature. University lecture delivered in the University of Natal, Pietermaritzburg, 7th June, 1961. Pietermaritzburg, University of Natal Press, 1961.

10p. 21½cm.

1. Zulu literature - History and criticism. I. Title.

S. Africa
M398.9
N98
Nyembezi, Cyril Lincoln Sibusiso, 1919-
Zulu proverbs. Johannesburg, South Africa, Witwatersrand University Press, 1954.

238p. 22½cm.

1. Zulu proverbs.

Africa
M960
Af78
Nyerere, Julius Kambarage, Pres. Tanzania, 1922-
'Ujamaa': the basis of African socialism.
Pp. 67-77.

In: Africa's freedom. London, Unwin Books, 1964.

Nigeria
M896.3
N98b
Nzekwu, Onuora, 1928-
Blade among the boys. London, Hutchinson [1962]
191 p. 20 cm.

I. Title. 1. Nigeria - Fiction.

PZ4.N998Bl 62-50521 ‡

Library of Congress [3]

Africa
M370
C83
Nyerere, Julius Kambarage, 1921-
An address at the inauguration of the University of East Africa.
Pp. 309-313.

In: Cowan, L. G., ed. Education and nation-building in Africa. New York, Praeger, 1965.

Africa
M960
Af78
Nyerere, Julius Kambarage, 1921-
A United States of Africa.
Pp. 88-94.

In: Africa's freedom. London, Unwin Books, 1964.

Nigeria
M896.3
N98e
Nzekwu, Onuora, 1928-
Eze goes to school, by Onuora Nzekwu and Michael Crowder. Illustrated by Adebayo Ajayi. Lagos, African Universities Press [1963]

89p. illus. 20cm. (African Reader's Library, no. 4)

I. Title. II. Series. III. Crowder, Michael, jt. auth.

Nyerere, Julius Kambarage.
The African and democracy, pp. 28-34.

Africa
M960.3
D87a
Duffy, James, 1923- ed.
Africa speaks. Edited by James Duffy and Robert A. Manners. Princeton, N.J., Van Nostrand [1961]

223p. 23cm.

Nyithindo e dala kendo e skul.

Kenya
M372.1
H44c
Hertslet, Jessie
Nyithindo e dala kendo e skul [Children at home and at school] [Translated by Mary O. Oloo] Nairobi, Eagle Press, 1950.

70p. 21½cm.
Written in Luo.
Translated from the English.
White author.

1. Children - Care and hygiene. I. Title. II. Oloo, Mary O., tr.

Nigeria
M896.3
N98h
Nzekwu, Onuora, 1928-
Highlife for lizards. London, Hutchinson [1965]

192p. 20½cm.
Portrait of author on book jacket.

I. Title.

Nyerere, Julius Kambarage.
Africa's place in the world, pp. 148-63.

Africa
M960.3
Sy6s
Symposium on Africa, Wellesley College, 1960.
Symposium on Africa. Wellesley, Mass., Wellesley College, 1960.

163p. 23cm.

South Africa
M896.4
W15
Nyoka, A D
Ukucinga Kwabantsundu Ngentlalo Yompefumlo Emva Kokufa.

Pp. 29-37.
Written in Xhosa.

In: Wallis, S. J., comp. and ed. Inkolo namasiko. London, Society for Promoting Christian Knowledge, 1930.

Nigeria
M896.3
N98w
Nzekwu, Onuora, 1928-
Wand of noble wood. London, Hutchinson, 1961.

208p. 19cm.

I. Title.

M301
G623
Nyerere, Julius Kambarage, Pres. Tanzania, 1922-
Communitarian socialism.

Pp. 184-191.

In: Goodman, Paul, 1911- ed. Seed of liberation. New York, G. Braziller, 1965.

Cameroun
M896.1
N98
Nyunai, Jean-Paul
La nuit de ma vie. Paris, Debresse-Poesie, 1961.
47p. 19cm.

I. Title.

Cameroun
M896.3
N98s
Nzouankeu, Jacques Mariel, 1938-
Le souffle des ancêtres. Yaounde, Editions Abbia, avec la collaboration de CLE, 1965.

107p. 18cm.
Portrait of author on book cover.
Contents.- Le souffle des ancêtres.- Les dieux de Bangoulap.- Le parole de Mouan Koum.- La dame d'eau.

I. Title.

Tanganyika
M967.8
N59
Nyerere, Julius Kambarage. Forword.
Stahl, Kathleen Mary, 1918-
Tanganyika: sail in the wilderness. [Forword by Julius Nyerere] 'S-Gravenhage, Mounton, 1961.

100p. plates. maps. 22cm.
White author.

1. Tanganyika-Description and travel. I. Nyerere, Julius Kambarge, Forword. II. Title.

Central African Republic
M896.1
D18
Nzakara (African people) - Poetry.
Dampierre, Eric de, ed.
Poetes nzakara. Paris, Julliard, 1962-

v. 24cm. (Classiques africains, I)
White editor.

M307
Oa1
Oak, Vishnu Vitthal, 1900-
The Negro entrepreneur. Yellow Springs, Ohio, Print. by the Antioch Press, 1948-
2 v. illus. 21 cm.
Bibliography: v. 1, p. 138-150.
CONTENTS.—v. 1. The Negro newspaper. v. 2. The Negro's adventure in general business.

Business
1. ~~Negro newspapers (American)~~ 2. ~~Negro~~ newspapers (~~American~~)—Direct. I. Title. II. Title: The Negro newspaper. III. T. The negro's adventure in general business.
E185.8.O2 071 48—6779*

Library of Congress [50q7]

Tanganyika
M960
N98
Nyerere, Julius Kambarage, *Pres. Tanzania*, 1922-
Freedom and unity: Uhuru na umoja; a selection from writings and speeches, 1952-65 [by] Julius K. Nyerere. London, Nairobi [etc.] Oxford U. P., 1967.
xiii, 366 p. front., 8 plates (incl. ports.) 22½ cm. 45/-
(B 67-3232)

1. Africa—Politics—Addresses, essays, lectures. I. Title. II. Title: Uhuru na umoja.

DT446.N9A5 320.9'6 67-77497

Library of Congress [3]

Nze mmanyi okusoma.

Uganda
M372.4
M46
Mdoe, Janet Naibirwa
Nze mmanyi okusoma [I know how to read] ebifaananyi byakubibwa Y. Kalanzi ne Alan Jarman. Nairobi, Eagle Press, 1960.
60p. illus. 18½cm.
Written in Luganda.

1. Luganda language - Readers. speakers. I. Title.

Oak and ivy.

M811.4
D91o
Dunbar, Paul Lawrence, 1872-1906.
Oak and ivy, by Paul Dunbar. Dayton, Ohio, Press of United brethen publishing house, 1893.
[5]-62p. 19½cm.

M016.8 Oa4n 1937
Oakland, California. Free Library.
The Negro literature collection; Books of Negro authorship to be found in the Oakland Free Library. Oakland, California, 1937.
11p. 22cm.
Mimeographed.
1. Literature - Bibliography. 2. Libraries - Special collections.

Colombia MB9 Ob2c
Obeso, Candelario, 1849-1884.
Caraballo, Vicente.
El negro Obeso (apuntes biográficos) y Escritos varios, por Vicente Caraballo ... Bogotá, Editorial ABC, 1943.
2 p. l., 7-202 p. port. 18cm.
"Fuentes de información": p. 88.
1. Obeso, Candelario, 1849-1884.
Library of Congress PQ8179.O198N4 44-42726
[2] 928.6

Nigeria M912 Ob5
Oboli, Herbert Oguejiofo Nkemba
A sketch-map atlas of Nigeria, with notes and exercises. New ed. rev. London, George G. Harrap [1962]
46p. maps. 21½cm.
1. Maps - Nigeria. I. Title.

M016.8 Oa4n 1930
Oakland, California. Free Library.
Dewitt, Josephine, , comp.
The black man's point of view; A list of references to material in the Oakland Free Library, compiled with an emphasis on the creative work of the black race. All the books and magazine article listed are by Negro authors, except some collections of songs and few references to art... compiled by Josephine DeWitt... Oakland, California, Acorn Club of Oakland, California and the Oakland Free Library, 1930.
30p. 37cm.
Mimeographed.

Colombia MB9 Ob2u
Obeso, Candelario, 1849-1884.
Uribe, Juan De D.
Candelario Obeso, por Juan de D. Uribe y Antonio J. Restrepo. Bogota, Imprenta de Vapor de Zalemea Hermanes, 1886.
28p. 17cm.

Africa M960 Af83
Obote, Milton Apollo, 1925-
Problems of progress through cooperation.
Pp. 11-17.
In: African Conference on Progress through Cooperation. Africa. New York, Dodd, Mead, 1966.

Oaks of Eden.
M813.5 T85o
Turner, Allen Pelzer.
Oaks of Eden, a novel. New York, Exposition Press [1951]
185 p. 23 cm.
I. Title.
PZ4.T745Oak 51-11875
Library of Congress [2]

Nigeria M309.22 Ob3
Obi, Enuenwemba.
Peace-corpsism. [1st ed.] New York, Pageant Press [1962]
78 p. 20 cm.
Portrait ofauthor on book jacket.
1. U. S. Peace Corps. I. Title.
HC60.5.O2 309.2206173 62-20947 ‡
Library of Congress [5]

Uganda M967.61 Ob5
Oboth-Ofumbi, Arphaxed Charles K, 1932-
Padhola [History and customs of the Jo Pahdola] Nairobi, Eagle Press, 1960.
84p. 21½cm.
Written in Luo (Ludoma)
1. Jopadhola. 2. Uganda - Native races. I. Title.

Obadzeng goes to town.
Ghana M896.2 Ac75o
Acquaye, Saka
Obadzeng goes to town. London, Evans Bros, 1965.
30p. 18½cm.
At head of title: Plays for African schools.
I. Title.

Nigeria M340 Ob3
Obi, Samuel Nwanko Chiawuba.
The Ibo law of property. London, Butterworths, 1963.
239 p. illus. 23 cm. (Butterworth's African law series, no. 6)
Includes bibliography.
1. Property (Ibo law) I. Title. 2. Customary law - Nigeria. 3. Africa - Law.
347.309669 64-3242 ‡
Library of Congress [3]

O'Brien, Edward Joseph Harrington, 1890-1941, ed.
M813.08 B46a
The Best American short stories ... and the Yearbook of the American short story ... 1915-
Boston, Houghton Mifflin company [1916]
v. 19½-21 cm.
Title varies: 1915-41, The Best short stories.
1942- The Best American short stories.
Editors: 1915-41, E. J. O'Brien.—1942- Martha Foley.
Imprint varies: 1915-25, Boston, Small, Maynard & company.—1926-32, New York, Dodd, Mead and company.—1933- Boston, Houghton Mifflin company.
1. Short stories, American. 2. Short stories—Bibl. I. O'Brien, Edward Joseph Harrington, 1890-1941, ed. II. Foley, Martha, ed. III. Yearbook of the American short story.
Library of Congress PZ1.B446235 16—11387
[49r43u²30] 813.0822

Kenya M630 Ob1
Obama, Barack H
Otieno Jarieko. kitabu mar ariyo - yore mabeyo mag puro puothe; ma eni en kitabu maluwo kitabu mokuongo e somoni - Yore Mabeyo Mag Rito Ngima. [Otieno, the wise man: a series of readers to follow the Luo Adult Literacy Primer. Book 2. Wise ways of farming] [Illus. by William Agutu] Nairobi, Eagle Press, 1959.
40p. illus. 24cm.
Written in Luo.
1. Agriculture - Kenya. I. Title. II. Agutu, William, illus.

Nigeria M650 Ob6
Obioha, Louis Nwakile
Guide to local businessmen. [Port Harcourt, C. M. S. Press, 1967.
24p. illus., port. 18cm.
1. Businessmen - Nigeria. I. Title.

O'Brien, Edward Joseph Harrington, 1890-1941, ed.
M813.5 B19t
The Best American short stories ... and the Yearbook of the American short story ... 1915-
Boston, Houghton Mifflin company [1916]-
v. 19½-21 cm.
Title varies: 1915-41, The Best short stories.
1942- The Best American short stories.
Editors: 1915-41, E. J. O'Brien.—1942- Martha Foley.
Imprint varies: 1915-25, Boston, Small, Maynard & company.—1926-32, New York, Dodd, Mead and company.—1933- Boston, Houghton Mifflin company.
1. Short stories, American. 2. Short stories—Bibl. I. O'Brien, Edward Joseph Harrington, 1890-1941, ed. II. Foley, Martha, ed. III. Yearbook of the American short story.
PZ1.B446235 813.0822 16—11387
Library of Congress [61r43c²30]

Nigeria M896.1 Ob1i
Obasa, Denrele Adetimkan.
Iwe kinni ti awon Akewi (Yoruba philosophy) nipa Denrele Adetimkan Obasa. Published by Egbe Agba-'O-Tan. Ibaden, The Ilard, [1927]
61 p. 19 cm.
1. Nigeria-Poetry.

Nigeria M896.3 Ob3b
Obioha, Raphael I M
Beauty is a trouble. Five men scrambling for Adamma. [Onitsha, Nigeria, Highbred Maxwell, 1962]
49p. illus. 20cm.
I. Title.

Obstetrics.
Nigeria M96?.9 Onl w
Onabamiro, Sanya Dojo.
Why our children die; the causes, and suggestions for prevention, of infant mortality in West Africa. With a foreword by Lancelot Hogben. London, Methuen [1949]
xi, 195 p. 20 cm.
"References": p. 187-190.
1. Infants—Mortality. 2. Maternal and infant welfare—Africa, West. 3. Obstetrics.
RG518.A3M3 618.2 50-15163
Library of Congress [1]

Ghana MB9 Ag3ok
Oben-Addae, H E
Okunini Aggrey. London, Thomas Nelson and Sons, Ltd., 1947.
66p. illus., map. 18½cm.
African author.
Portrait of biographee on front of book.
1. Aggrey, James Emman Kwegyir, 1875-1925. I. Title.

Oblate sisters of providence.
[Mary Petra, sister], 1865-
M271.76 M36o
Blossoms gathered from the lower branches; or, A little work of an Oblate sister of providence ... [St. Louis, Con. P. Curran printing co., °1914]
4 p. l., 7-69 p., 1 l. incl. pl., ports. 20cm.
1. Oblate sisters of providence. I. Title.
[Secular name: Mary Clopenia Boston]
15-4659 Revised
Library of Congress BX4410.O2M3
[r44b2]

Nigeria M960 Ob82
Obukar, Charles.
The modern African, by Charles Obukar and John Williams. London, Macdonald & Evans, 1965.
x, 149 p. illus., ports. 23 cm.
1. Africa, Sub-Saharan—Soc. condit. ~~I. ... joint author.~~ II. Title. I. Williams, John, jt. author.
HN797.O2 66-34229
Library of Congress [1]

Haiti
M972.94 O'Callaghan, Georges.
Oln
... Les nouvelles tendances du droit public de la république d'Haïti. Port-au-Prince, Haïti, Imprimerie du Collège Vertières, 1940.

21 p. 22cm. (Bibliothèque juridique haïtienne)

1. Haiti—Constitutional law. I. Title.

Library of Congress JL1083.1940.O3 42-45293 [3]

Ghana
M966.7 Ocansey, John E , -1889.
W83p
An African trader.

pp. 169-171.
In: Pageant of Ghana, by Freda Wolfson.

I. Title.

Occasional publications of the Illinois State Historical Society. Publication no.50.

MB9 Ayers, James T 1805-1865.
Ay2f
The diary of James T. Ayers, Civil War recruiter; ed., with an introd., by John Franklin. Springfield, Printed by authority of the State of Illinois, 1947.

xxv, 138p. illus., port., facsims. 24cm.

Haiti ...L'occupation américaine d'Haïti.
M972.94 Bellegarde, Dantès, 1877-
B41e
...L'occupation américaine d'Haïti, ses conséquences morales et économiques. Port-au-Prince, Chéraquit, 1929.

3p. l, 44p. 24cm.

Haiti L'occupation Americaine d'Haiti...
M972.94 Nicolas, Hogar
N54o
L'occupation Americaine d'Haiti; la revanche de l'histoire. Preface Pradel Pompilus. Madrid, Industrias Graficas Espana, 1956.

305p. 21cm.

Occupations.

M373 Canady, Herman G
C161
The intelligence of Negro college students and parental occupation by Herman G. Canady. Reprinted... from The American journal of sociology, vol. 42, no.3, November 1936
388 - 399p. table 24cm.

Occupations.

M06 Gannett, Henry, 1846-1914.
J61
no.6
... Occupations of the Negroes, by Henry Gannett ... Baltimore, The Trustees, 1895.

16 p. map, diagrs. 24½cm. (The trustees of the John F. Slater fund. Occasional papers, no. 6)

1. Negroes. I. Title.

Library of Congress E185.5.J65 no. 6
———— Copy 2. E185.8.G19
6-42728 [43r33d1]

Occupations.

M396 Iota Phi Lambda Sorority.
Io8s
Survey on white collar occupations of Negro women... [1947] the Sorority, 1948.

11p. graphs. 23cm.

...Occupations of the Negroes,..

M06 Gannett, Henry, 1846-1914.
J61
no.6
... Occupations of the Negroes, by Henry Gannett ... Baltimore, The Trustees, 1895.

16 p. map, diagrs. 24½cm. (The trustees of the John F. Slater fund. Occasional papers, no. 6)

1. Negroes. I. Title.

Library of Congress E185.5.J65 no. 6
———— Copy 2. E185.8.G19
6-42728 [43r33d1]

Occupied Haiti.

M972.94 Balch, Emily Greene, 1867- *ed.*
B18
Occupied Haiti; being the report of a committee of six disinterested Americans representing organizations exclusively American, who, having personally studied conditions in Haiti in 1926, favor the restoration of the independence of the Negro republic, edited by Emily Greene Balch. New York, The Writers publishing company, inc., 1927.

viii p., 1 l., 186 p. 19½cm.

1. Haiti—Pol. & govt.—1844- 2. Haiti—For. rel.—U. S. 3. U. S.—For. rel.—Haiti. I. Title.

Library of Congress F1926.B17 27-16258 [47q1]

Occult sciences.

M176 Randolph, Paschal Beverly, 1825-1874.
R15
... Magia sexualis. Traduction française, par Maria de Naglowska. Edition originale. Paris, R. Télin, 1931.

218p. 1 l. illus. plates. (incl. music, port. col.) port. fold. tables. 23cm.
At head of title: P. B. Randolph.

An ocean to ourselves.

Trinidad
M910.45 La Borde, Harold, 1933-
L11
An ocean to ourselves. New York, J. de Graff [1962]

189 p. illus. 22 cm.

1. Humming Bird (Ketch) 2. Atlantic Ocean. I. Title.

G530.L29 910.45 63-1332 ‡

Library of Congress [5]

Ocee McRae, Texas.

West Indies
M823.91 Ferguson, Ira Lunan
F38o
Ocee McRae, Texas; a novel of passion, petroleum and politics in the Pecos River Valley. New York, Exposition Press [1962]

182p. cm.

The ochre people.

Africa, South
M968 Jabavu, Noni.
J11$
The ochre people; scenes from a South African life. [London] J. Murray [1963]

261p. 22cm.

Uganda
M896.4 Ocitti, J P
Oc3L
Lacan ma Kwo pe kinyero [Every dog has his day] Ogoyo cal Vivienne Yates. Kampala, Eagle Press, 1960.

91p. illus. 21cm.
Written in Acoli.

I. Title.

O'Connell, Daniel, 1775.

M815 Langston, John Mercer, 1829-1897.
L26
Freedom and citizenship. Selected lectures and addresses of Hon. John Mercer Langston... With an introductory sketch by Rev. J. E. Rankin... Washington, D. C., R. H. Darby, 1883.
286 p. front. (port.) 20cm.

Africa O'Connell, James, 1925- joint ed.
M370 Cowan, Laing Gray, *ed.*
C83
Education and nation-building in Africa. Edited by L. Gray Cowan, James O'Connell [and] David G. Scanlon. New York, F. A. Praeger [1965]

x, 403 p. 21 cm.

Bibliography: p. 397-403.

1. Education—Africa—Addresses, essays, lectures. 2. Nationalism—Africa—Addresses, essays, lectures. I. O'Connell, James, 1925- joint ed. II. Scanlon, David G., joint ed. III. Title.

LA1501.C6 1965 370.96 65-12193

Library of Congress [5]

S. Africa
M398 O'Connell, Ruby M Agar-
Oc51
Iintsomi; Bantu folk stories. Illustrations by G.M. Pemba and others; Xhosa translations by B. A. Bangeni. Lovedale press, [1938?]

47p. illus. 29cm.
English and Xhosa in parallel columns.
White author.

1. Africa, South-folktales. I. Title. II. Bantu folk stories. III. Bangani, B.A. tr. IV. Pemba, G.M. -illus.

Brazil Octaviano de Almeida Rosa, Francisco, 1825-1889.
M869.4 Pinheiro, Xavier.
P65f
... Francisco Octaviano, Carioca illustre nos letros, no jornalismo, napolitica, na tribuna e na diplomacia. Rio de Janeiro, Edicao da Revista de Lingua Portugues a. [n.d.]

477 p. 25 cm.
White author.

Oda oak oracle.

Ethiopia
M896.2 Gabre-Medhin, Tsegaye, 1935-
G114o
Oda oak oracle; a legend of black peoples, told of gods and God, of hope and love, and of fears and sacrifices. London, Oxford University Press, 1965.

54p. 18½cm.

I. Title.

Africa
M960 Odaka, Samuel N 1933-
Af83
Cooperation in Africa and in the United Nations.

Pp. 197-202.

In: African Conference on Progress through Cooperation. Africa. New York, Dodd, Mead, 1966.

Odd-fellows, Grand united order of, in America.

M366.3
B79
1902

Brooks, Charles H.
The official history and manual of the grand united order of odd fellows in America. A chronological treatise of the origin, growth... Prepared by most venerable patriarch Chas. H. Brooks... Philadelphia, Odd fellows journal print, 1902.

274 ₍2₎ p. front., plates. 21½cm.

M813.5
Y46od

An odor of sanctity.
Yerby, Frank, 1916-
An odor of sanctity; a novel of medieval Moorish Spain. New York, Dial Press ₍1965₎
vi, 563 p. 24 cm.

I. Title.

PZ3.Y415Od 65-23964

Library of Congress ₍3₎

Nigeria
M372.4
Od83iw
Bk. 2

Odunjo, J Folahan
Iwe-keji Alawiye, fun awọn ọmọde; ati awọn agbà ti o nkọ iwe Yoruba ni kikà. London, Longmans, Green and Co., 1949.

64p. illus. 18½cm.
Translated title: Yoruba Alawiye readers, 2.
Written in Yoruba.

1. Yoruba language - Readers and speakers.
I. Title.

Odell, Margaretta Matilda.

M811.1
W56m
1835

Wheatley, Phillis, afterwards Phillis Peters, 1753?-1784.
Memoir and poems of Phillis Wheatley, a native African and a slave. Dedicated to the friends of the Africans. Second edition. Boston, Light & Horton, 1835.

viii, ₍9₎ 110p. front. (port.) 17½cm.
Memoir (p. ₍9₎-29) by Margaretta Matilda Odell.

Nigeria
M372.4
Od8
Bk. 2

Odujinrin, J S A
ABD asiko; apa kejo. ₍Ebute-Metta, Nigeria Service Printers₎ 1963.

55p. illus. 18cm.
Written in Yoruba.
Translated title: Timely ABD, Part 2.
1. Yoruba language - Readers and speakers. 2. Yoruba language - Grammar.
I. Title.

Nigeria
M372.4
Od83iw
Bk. 3

Ọdunjọ, J Folahan
Iwe-kẹta alawiye. ₍2nd ed. London₎ Longmans ₍1960₎

97p. illus. 18½cm.
Translated title: Yoruba Alawiye reader, 3.
Written in Yoruba.

1. Yoruba language - Readers and speakers.
I. Title.

Odell, Margaretta Matilda.

M811.1
W56m

Wheatley, Phillis, *afterwards* Phillis Peters, 1753?-1784.
Memoir and poems of Phillis Wheatley, a native African and a slave. Dedicated to the friends of the Africans. ~~Boston, G. W. Light, 1834.~~ ₍2nd ed.₎ Boston, Light & Horton ₍1835.
viii, ₍9₎-108 p. front. (port.) 17½cm.
Memoir (p. ₍9₎-29) by Margaretta Matilda Odell.

I. Odell, Margaretta Matilda. 30-20914

Library of Congress PS866.W5 1834 ₍42b1₎

Nigeria
M372.4
Od8
Bk. 1

Odujinrin, J S A
ABD asiko; apa kin-ni. Lagos, Olufunmiso Printing Works, 1963?

56p. illus. 18cm.
Translated title: Timely ABD, part 1.
1. Yoruba language - Readers and speakers. 2. Primers, African. I. Title.

Nigeria
M372.4
Od83i

Odunjo, J Folahan
Iwe-kini Alawiye; fun alakọ̀bẹ̀rẹ̀ ẹ̀kọ́ Yoruba l'omode ati l'agbà. Eni ti o ya àwòran rè ni Tayo Aiyegbusi. Ikeja ₍Nigeria₎ Longmans of Nigeria, 1963.

62p. illus. 18½cm.
Translated title: Alawiye primer and reader.
Written in Yoruba.

1. Primers, African. 2. Yoruba language - Readers and speakers. I. Title.

Odell, Margaretta Matilda.

M811.1
W56m

Wheatley, Phillis, *afterwards* Phillis Peters, 1753?-1784.
Memoir and poems of Phillis Wheatley, a native African and a slave. Dedicated to the friends of the Africans ... Boston, G. W. Light, 1834.
viii, ₍9₎-108 p. front. (port.) 17½cm.
Memoir (p. ₍9₎-29) by Margaretta Matilda Odell.

I. Odell, Margaretta Matilda. 30-20914

Library of Congress PS866.W5 1834 ₍42b1₎

Nigeria
M896.2
Od8ag

Odunjo, J Folahan.
Agbàlọwọ̀meri bàlẹ jòntolo; itàn eré aláḍun. Enti ti o ya àwòran rẹ̀ ni J. K. Oye. London, Longmans, Green and Co., 1958.

76p. illus.
Written in Yoruba.
Translated title: An extortioner, the chief of Jolonto.
1. Yoruba language - Drama. I. Title.

M784
Od8

Odum, Howard Washington, 1884-
The Negro and his songs; a study of typical Negro songs in the south, by Howard W. Odum and Guy B. Johnson. Chapel Hill, University of North Carolina Press; London, Humphrey Milford, Oxford University Press, 1925.

306p. 23cm.

1. Songs. 2. Songs-Hist. & crit. I. Johnson, Guy Benton, 1901- jt. auth. II. Title.

M811.5
Od2

Oden, Gloria.
The naked frame, a love poem and sonnets. ₍1st ed.₎ New York, Exposition Press ₍1952₎
unpaged. 21 cm.

I. Title.

PS3529.D44N3 811.5 52-10288 ‡

Library of Congress ₍3₎

A
M496.4
Od81

Odunjo, J Folahan.
Iwe-Kini A B D Alawiye, fun awon omode ati awon agbalagba... Revised edition. ₍Lagos, The Ife-Olu printing works₎ 1946.

32p. 18½cm.

1. Nigeria—Language. I. Title.

M784
Od8n

Odum, Howard Washington, 1884-
Negro workaday songs, by Howard W. Odum ... and Guy B. Johnson ... Chapel Hill, The University of North Carolina press; London, H. Milford, Oxford university press, 1926.
8 p. l., ₍ix₎-xii, 2 l., 278 p. illus. (music) diagrs. 23½ cm. (*Half-title:* The University of North Carolina. Social study series)
"Selected bibliography": p. ₍265₎-270.
with author
1. Negro songs. 2. Negro songs—Hist. & crit. I. Johnson, Guy Benton, 1901- joint author. II. Title.

ML3556.O32 26-14118

Library of Congress ₍54g1₎

M811.5
Od9t

Oden, Thomas Hildred.
Two Gun Bill ₍by₎ Benny Burleigh ₍pseud.₎ New York, Comet Press Books ₍1957₎
44 p. 21 cm.
Poems.

I. Title.

PS3529.D45T85 811.5 57-7019 ‡

Library of Congress ₍2₎

Nigeria
M896.3
Od8

Ọdunjọ, J Folahan.
Kuye (Itan ọmọ odi ti ẹdá rọ̀pin). Àwòrán yiyà láti ọwọ́ Adebayọ Ajayi. Lagos, African Universities Press, 1964.

123p. illus. 18cm.
Written in Yoruba.

I. Title.

Nigeria
M966.9
B619

Odumosu, Oluwole Idowu.
Constitutional development.

Pp. 37-55.

In: Blitz, L. Franklin, ed. The politics and administration of Nigerian government.

Kenya
M967.62
Od3

Odinga, Ajuma Oginga, 1911-
Not yet Uhuru: the autobiography of Oginga Odinga; with a foreword by Kwame Nkrumah. London, Heinemann, 1967.

xv, 323p. plates (incl. facsims., ports.), map. 20½cm.
Map on endpapers.
African author.

1. Kenya - Politics and government.
I. Title.

Nigeria
M372.4
Od83iw
Bk.6

Ọdunjọ, J Folahan
Iwe-kẹfà alawiye. Ẹni ti o ya àwòrán rẹ̀ ni Cyril Deakins. London, Longmans, 1961.

128p. illus. 18½cm.
Translated title: Yoruba Alawiye readers, 6.
Written in Yoruba.

1. Yoruba language - Readers and speakers.
I. Title.

Nigeria
M966.9
Od8

Odumosu, Oluwole Idowu.
The Nigerian Constitution: history and development. London, Sweet & Maxwell, 1963.
xix, 407 p. 23 cm. (Law in Africa, no. 4)
"Originally ... submitted as a thesis for the award of the Ph. D. degree of the University of London."
"The Constitution of the Federation of Nigeria": p. 309-397.
Bibliographical footnotes.

1. Nigeria—Constitutional history. 2. Nigeria—Constitutional law. I. Nigeria. Constitution. (Series)

63-4741

Library of Congress ₍1₎

The odyssey of Homer...

Ghana
M966.7
Of6

Ofosu-Appiah, L H
The odyssey of Homer; a Twi translation of book 8, line 461, to the end of book 12. London, Longmans Green and Co., 1957.

75p. 18½cm.
Written in Twi.

Brit. Guiana Of trees and the sea.
M823.91
M69o

Mittelhölzer, Edgar.
Of trees and the sea. With decorations by the author. London, Secker & Warburg, 1956.

256 p. illus. 19 cm.

I. Title.

Full name: Edgar Austin Mittelhölzer.

PZ3.M6977Of 57-20080 ‡

Library of Congress [3]

Trinidad
M823.91
Of4n

Offord, Carl Ruthven, 1910-
The naked fear. New York, Ace Books, Inc., 1954.

160p. 19cm. (Ace books S-54)
Pocket book edition.

I. Title

...Oeuvres créoles; poésies, fables...

Guadeloupe
M848
B32o

Baudot, Paul, 1801-1870.
...Oeuvres créoles; poésies, fables, théatre, contes. Basse-Terre, Guadeloupe, Imprimerie du governement, 1923.

vii, 165p. 19cm.

Off my chest.

M796
B813

Brown, James Nathaniel, 1936-
Off my chest, by Jimmy Brown with Myron Cope. [1st ed.] Garden City, N.Y., Doubleday, 1964.

x, 230p. illus., ports. 22cm.

1. Football. I. Cope, Myron. II. Title.

M813.08
C554

Offord, Carl Ruthven, 1910-
So peaceful in the country
Pp. 123-130

In: Clarke, John Henrik,, ed. American Negro short stories. New York, Hill and Wang, 1966.

Of age and innocence.

Barbados
M823
L18o

Lamming, George, 1927-
Of age and innocence. London, Michael Joseph, [1958]

412p. 20cm.
Picture of the author on the book jacket.

Martinique Offenses against the person.
M965
F21d4

Fanon, Frantz, 1925-1961.
The wretched of the earth. Pref. by Jean-Paul Sartre. Translated from the French by Constance Farrington. [Harmondsworth, Eng.] Penguin Books [1967]

255p. 18cm.
Translation of Les deamnés de la terre.

1. France—Colonies—Africa. 2. Algeria—Hist.—1945- 3. Offenses against the person. I. Title.

DT33.F313 301.24 65—14196

Library of Congress [67f3]

Trinidad
M823.91
Of4w

Offord, Carl Ruthven, 1910-
... The white face. New York, R. M. McBride & company [1943]

317 p. 21cm.
"First edition."

I. Title.

43-8249

Library of Congress PZ3.O825Wh [4]

U.S.
M839
Iv3o

Of Gods and giants, Norse mythology.
Hveberg, Harald, 1900-
Of Gods and giants, Norse mythology. Translated by Pat Shaw Iversen. Illustrated by Kai Ovre. Oslo, Johan Grundt Tanum Forlag [1962]

72p. illus. 21cm. (Tanums tokens of Norway)
Translation of Norrøn mytologi.

Martinique Offenses against the person.
M965
F21d3

Fanon, Frantz, 1925-1961.
The wretched of the earth. Pref. by Jean-Paul Sartre. Translated from the French by Constance Farrington. New York, Grove Press [1965, °1963]

255 p. 21 cm.
Translation of Les damnes de la terre.

1. France—Colonies—Africa. 2. Algeria—Hist.—1945- 3. Offenses against the person. I. Title.

DT33.F313 301.24 65-14196

Library of Congress [5]

Ghana
M343
Of6

Ofori, David
Why kibi ritual murder? An inside story of a sensational so-called "ritual murder" case. [Accra, Heal Press, 1954]

36p. illus., port. 21cm.
Portrait of author on t.p.

1. Rites and ceremonies - Ghana. 2. Ritual murder. I. Title.

Of love and dust.

M813.5
G128o

Gaines, Ernest J., 1933-
Of love and dust, by Ernest J. Gaines. New York, Dial Press, 1967.

281 p. 22 cm.

I. Title.

PZ4.G1422Of 67-25308

Library of Congress [20-3]

M230
Of4g

[Offley, Greensbury W.] 1808-
God's immutable declaration of his own moral and assumed natural image, and likeness in man, declared (Genesis 1:26-27.) and revealed to the Prophet Daniel, 7-9, and to St. John, Rev. 1:13-14; or, The Nations weighed in the balance. New Bedford, Mercury Stean Printing House, 1875.

30p. illus. 22½cm.

1. Religion.

Ghana
M966.7
Of6

Ofosu-Appiah, L H
The odyssey of Homer; a Twi translation of book 8, line 461, to the end of book 12. London, Longmans, Green and Co., 1957.

75p. 18½cm.
Written in Twi.

I. Title.

Of men and trees.

M811.5
W971

Wright, Ethel Williams.
Of men and trees; poems. [1st ed.] New York, Exposition Press [1954]

64 p. 21 cm.

I. Title.

PS3545.R34O5 811.5 54-9542 ‡

Library of Congress [3]

M326.99B
Of3

Offley, Greensbury W , 1808-
A narrative of the life and labors of the Rev. G. W. Offley, a colored man, and local preacher, who lived twenty-seven years at the South and twenty-four at the north... Hartford, Conn., 1860.

52p. 17cm.

1. Slave narrative.

Nigeria
M896.3
Ogle

Ogali, Ogali Agu, 1931-
Eddy the coal-city boy; a novel. [Enugu, Zik Enterprises, n.d.]

27p. port. 19½cm.
Portrait of author in book.

I. Title.

Of sight and sound.

M910
G76

Granger, Lester Blackwell, 1896-
Of sight and sound; letters from an American abroad. New York, National Urban League, Inc., 1959.

60p. 23cm.
"These letters were originally addressed to Theodore W. Kheel, President of the National Urban League."

1. Asia - Descr. & Travel. 2. Africa.- Descr. & Travel. I. Title.

Trinidad
M810.8
C884
1944

Offord, Carl Ruthven, 1910-
Low sky, [prose]

(In: Cross Section ... A collection of new American writing, 1944. New York, L. B. Fischer, 1944. p. 304-313).

Nigeria
M896.3
Oglo

Ogali, Ogali Agu, 1931-
Okeke the magician, a novel. Onitsha, Nigeria, Appolos Brothers [n.d.]

39p. port. 21cm.
Portrait of author in book.

Nigeria
M896.2
Oglp

Ogali, Ogali Agu, 1931-
Patrice Lumumba; a drama. Onitsha, Nigeria, Tabansi Printing Press, 1961.

40p. illus. 21½cm.
Portrait of author on book cover.

1. African drama. 2. Lumumba, Patrice, 1925-1961 - Drama. I. Title.

Nigeria
M896.2
Oglv

Ogali, Ogali Agu, 1931-
Veronica my daughter; a drama. Aba ⌊Nigeria⌋ Okeudo and Sons Press ⌊n.d.⌋

40p. port. 20½cm.
Portrait of author in book.

1. African drama. I. Title.

Nigeria
M966.9
Ogl

Ogbalu, F. Chidozie.
Dr. Zik of Africa; biography and speeches. ⌊2d ed. Nigeria⌋ African Literature Bureau ⌊1961⌋

272p. ports. 20cm.

1. Azikiwe, Benjamin Nnamdi, 1904-. 2. Nigeria. I. Azikiwe, Benjamin Nnamdi, 1904- II. Title.

Ogboju ode ninu igbo irunmale.

Nigeria
M896.3
F13o

Fagunwa, D O
Ogboju ode ninu igbo irunmale. Illustrated by Onasanya. London, Thomas Nelson and Sons, Ltd., 1950.

102p. illus. 18cm

I. Title.

M378
F92

Ogden, Robert Curtis, 1836-1913.
From servitude to service; being the Old South lectures on the history and work of southern institutions for the education of the Negro. Boston, American Unitarian association, 1905.

3 p. l., ⌊v⌋-x, 232 p. 20cm.

CONTENTS.—Introduction, by R. C. Ogden.—I. Howard university, by K. Miller.—II. Berea college, by W. G. Frost.—III. Tuskegee institute, by R. C. Bruce.—IV. Hampton institute, by H. B. Frissell.—V. Atlanta university, by W. E. B. Du Bois.—VI. Fisk university, by J. G. Merrill.

1. Negroes—Education. I. Ogden, Robert Curtis, 1836-1913. II. Miller, Kelly, 1863- III. Frost, William Goodell, 1854- IV. Bruce, Roscoe Conkling. V. Frissell, Hollis Burke, 1851- VI. Du Bois, William Edward Burghardt, 1868- VII. Merrill, James Griswold, 1840-

5—36403

Library of Congress LC2741.F7

Copyright A 128426 ⌊30j2-⌋

Ogé, Jacques Vincent, 1791.

M972.93
As7ada

Assemblée des Citoyens de Couleur, des Isles et Colonies Françoises. Paris.
Adresse a l'assemblée-nationale, pour les Citoyens-libres de Couleur, des Isles & Colonies Francoises, 18 Octobre 1789 ⌊Lacks imprint⌋

9p. 19cm.
Signed by De Joly; Raimond; Oge, etc.

Ogé, Jacques Vincent, 1791.

M972.93
As7ac
1790

Assemblée des Citoyens de couleur des Isles & colonies Françoises. Paris.
Adresse des Citoyens deCouleur des Isles, & Colonies Françoises; a l'assemblée Génerale des représentans de la commune de Paris; prononcée, le premier Février 1790, par M. de Joly... Paris, 1790.

15p. 21½cm.
Signed by De Joly, Raimond, Oge, etc.

Ogé, Jacques Vincent, 1791.

M972.93
As71
1789

Assemblée des Citoyens de Couleur, des Isles et Colonies Françoises. Paris.
Lettre des Citoyens de Couleur, des isles & colonies, françoises, a MM. les membres du Comite de Verification de l'Assemblée Nationale, du 23 Novembre 1789. Paris, De L'Imprimerie de Lottin l'aine & Lottin de S. Germain, Imprimeurs-Libraires Ordinaires de la Ville, 1789.

24p. 20½cm.
Signed by: Dr. Joly Raimond; Oge, etc.

Ogé, Jacques Vincent, 1791.

M972.93
As7rec

Assemblée des Citoyens de Couleur, des Isles et Colonies Françoises. Paris.
Réclamation des Citoyens de Couleur; des Isles & colonies Françoises; sur le Decret du 8 Mars 1790.

23p. 20cm.
Signed by De Joly; Raimond; Oge, etc.

Ogé, Jacques Vincent, 1791.

M972.93
As7s

Assemblée des Citoyens de Couleur des Isles et Colonies Françoises. Paris.
Supplique et petition des citoyens de couleur des Isles & colonies Françoises, Tendante à obtenir un jugement. 30 janvier 1790.

4p. 19½cm.
Signed by De Joly; Raimond; Oge, etc.

Ogé, Jacques Vincent, 1791.

M972.93
As7s

Assemblée desCitoyens de Couleur des Isles et Colonies Françoises. Paris.
Supplique et petition des citoyens de Couleur des Isles & colonies Françoises sur le motion faite le 27 Novembre 1789, par M. de Curt, député de la Guadeloupe, au nom des colonies reunies... 1789. Paris, 1789.

21p. 19½cm.
Signed: by De Joly; Raimond; Oge, etc.

Jamaica
M823.91
Og4

Ogilvie, William George.
Cactus Village. Kingston, Jamaica, Pioneer Press ⌊1953⌋

171 p. illus. 19 cm.

I. Title.

Full name: William George Graham Ogilvie.

PZ4.O342Cac 54-17746 ‡

Library of Congress ⌊1⌋

Jamaica
M823.91
Og4g

Ogilvie, William George Graham
The Ghost Bank. Kingston, Jamaica, Pioneer Press ⌊1953⌋

124 p. illus. 19 cm.
Portrait of author on book cover.

I. Title.

Full name: William George Graham Ogilvie.

PZ4.O342Gh 55-26933 ‡

Library of Congress ⌊1⌋

Jamaica
M823
F82

Ogilvie, William George Graham
The great kranjie.

Pp. 31-35.

In: 14 Jamaican short stories. Jamaica, Pioneer Press, 1950.

Jamaica
M823
F82

Ogilvie, William George Graham
Half a fork.

Pp. 83-95.

In: 14 Jamaican short stories. Jamaica, Pioneer Press, 1950.

W. Indies
M823
C23

Ogle, C W
Unguarded moment.

(In: Caribbean anthology of short stories.... Kingston, Jamaica, Pioneer Press 1953. 19cm. pp. 43-46.)

South Africa
M896
M88

Ogot, Grace, 1930-
Tekayo.

Pp. 109-120.

In: Mphahlele, Ezekiel, ed. African writing today. Baltimore, Penguin Books, 1967.

Dahomey
M896.1
Og6n

Ogoundele-Tessi, Jean
Nuits; extrait 1 - poèmes. Porto-Novo ⌊Dahomey⌋ Imprimerie Rapidex ⌊n.d.⌋

15p. 21cm.

I. Title.

Nigeria
M896.2
Og9r

Ogu, H O
Rose only loved my money. Aba ⌊Nigeria⌋ Treasure Press ⌊n.d.⌋

32p. 18cm. (Treasure series, no. 1)

1. African drama. I. Title.

British Guiana
M988.1
L49

Ogueri II, Eze A
League of Colored Peoples. British Guiana.
Seven amazing days in the life of Eze A. Ogueri II, compiled by the League of Colored Peoples, British Guiana. Boston, House of Edinboro, Publishers, 1954.

187p. port. illus. 20cm.

Nigeria
M820.7
Og9

Oguine, O D M
Questions and answers on twelfth night, with summaries. Onitsha ⌊Nigeria, Etudo, 1962⌋

58p. 21cm.

1. Shakespeare, William - Study. I. Title.

Nigeria
M966.9
Og9a
Ogumbiyi, Thomas A J
Awon serafu. (The seraphum). Lagos, Church Missionary Society Press, 1926.

14p. 19cm.

1. Nigeria - Nationalist movement.

Nigeria
M372.6
Og9
Bk.1
Ogunlesi, Josiah Soyemi, 1904- jt. auth.
English for Africans, 1, by Ronald Ridout and J. S. Ogunlesi. Illustrated by J. D. Akeredolu. ‹London, Ginn, 1960›

32p. illus. 26cm.

1. English - Study and teaching - Africa. I. Ridout, Ronald. II. Title.

Ohio.
M973.6
C77oh
1852
Convention of the Colored freemen of Ohio.
Proceedings of the convention of the Colored freemen of Ohio, held in Cincinnati, January 14, 15, 16, 17 and 19. Cincinnati, Printed by Dumas & Lawyer, 1852.
28p. 19cm.

Nigeria
M784
Og9y
Ogumefu, Ebun.
Yoruba melodies, adapted by Ebun Ogumefu. London, Society for promoting Christian knowledge ‹1929›

16 p. 18½ cm.

1. Yoruba-Music.

Nigeria
M372.6
Og9
Bk.2
Ogunlesi, Josiah Soyemi, 1904- jt. auth.
English for Africans, 2, by Ronald Ridout and J. S. Ogunlesi. Illustrated by A. Adenuga. ‹London, Ginn, 1955›

32p. illus. 26cm.

1. English - Study and teaching - Africa. I. Ridout, Ronald. II. Title.

Ohio
M366.1
F87o3
Freemasons. Ohio. Grand Lodge.
Proceedings. 1st- 1850-
Cleveland, 18 -

v. 22cm. annual
Place of publication varies.
See holdings card for proceedings in library

Nigeria
M966.9
Og9s
Ogumefu, M I
The staff of Oranyan and other Yoruba tales, by M. I. Ogumefu. London, The Sheldon Press, ‹1930›

iv, 5-32p. illus. 18½cm.

1. Folklore - Yoruba. 2. Nigeria.
3. Yorubas - Folklore.

Nigeria
M372.6
Og9
Bk3
Ogunlesi, Josiah Soyemi, 1904- . jt. auth.
English for Africans, 3, by Ronald Ridout and J. S. Ogunlesi. Illustrated by A. Adenuga. ‹London, Ginn, 1959›

32p. illus. 26cm.

1. English - Study and teaching - Africa. I. Ridout, Ronald. II. Title.

Ohio.
M366.1
F88o
Freemasons. Ohio. Knights Templars. Grand Commandery.
Proceedings. 1st- 1871?-
Chillicothe, etc. 18 -

v. 23cm. annual
Place of publication varies.
Constitution, statutes, regulations and by-laws included in the 1875 proceedings.

Nigeria
M966.9
Og9t
Ogumefu, M I
Tales of tortoise, Yoruba tales, by M. I. Ogumefu. London, The Sheldon Press ‹n.d.›

v. 7-32p. illus. 18½cm.

1. Folklore - Yoruba. 2. Nigeria.
3. Yorubas - Folklore.

Nigeria
M630
Og9
Ogunlesi, Josiah Soyemi, 1904-
Kokó tabi agbado? Cocoa or corn?
‹Ibadan, Abiodun Printing Works, 1961›

31p. 20cm.
In Yoruba and English.

1. Agriculture - Nigeria. I. Title.
II. Title: Cocoa or corn?

Ohio.
M366.1
F89o
Freemasons. Ohio. Royal Arch Masons.
Transactions. 1st- 1871-
Cleveland, etc. 1872-

v. 22cm. anual.
Place of publication varies.
Constitution and by-laws included in 1870 transactions.
See holdings card for proceedings.

Nigeria
M966.9
Og9y
Ogumefu, M I
Yoruba legends. London, The Sheldon Press ‹1929›

87p. 17½cm.

1. Yorubas-Folklore. 2. Nigeria

Africa
M960
P26
Ogunsheye, Ayo.
Problems of Federation in Africa.
Pp. 89-98.

In: Passin, Herbert, ed. Africa; the dynamics of change. Ibadan, Ibadan University Press, 1963.

Ohio
M977.1
J66h
Joiner, William A
A half century of freedom of the Negro in Ohio, compiled and arranged by W.A. Joiner... Xenia, O, Press of Smith Adv. co. 1915?
134p. illus. 23½cm.

Nigeria
M966.9
Og9a
Ogunbiye, Thomas A J
Awon Serafu ‹by› Thos. A.J. Ogunbiye. Lagos, C.M.S. press, 1926.

14p. 18½cm.
In Yoruba.

1. African Sermons. 2. Nigeria.
3. Yorubas - Religion. I. Title.

O'Hara, John Myers, . -1944
Martinique
M841.91
L39
Laviaux, Léon.
The ebon muse, and other poems, by Léon Laviaux; Englished by John Myers O'Hara. Portland, Me., Smith & Sale, 1914.
x p., 2 l., 3-51, ‹1› p., 1 l. 27½cm. $3.00
"Of this edition two hundred copies have been printed."

I. O'Hara, John Myers, tr. II. Title.
Library of Congress 14-12126
——— Copy 2.
Copyright A 374599

Ohio.
MB9
M29
Malvin, John, 1795-1880.
North into freedom; the autobiography of John Malvin, free Negro, 1795-1880. Edited and with an introd. by Allan Peskin. Cleveland, Press of Western Reserve University, 1966.
vii, 87 p. 23 cm.
"A book from Cleveland State University."
Bibliographical references included in "Notes to the introduction" (p. 22-24)
1. Negroes—Ohio. 2. Negroes—Civil rights. I. Peskin, Allan, ed. II. Title.
E185.97.M26A3 1966 66-28142
301.451960994 (B)
Library of Congress ‹8›

Gold Coast
M896
Og9
Ogundele, Joseph Ogunsina
Ibú- Olókun. London, University of London, 1956.

128p. illus. 18½cm.

I. Title.

M811.5
H32L
O'Higgins, Myron, jt. auth.
Hayden, Robert Earl
The lion and the archer: poems ‹by Robert Hayden and Myron O'Higgins› Nashville, Tenn., Mills Book Store, 1948.

28p. 24cm.

Ohio.
M973.6
N21cl
1854
National emigration convention, Cleveland, Ohio.
Arguments, pro and con, on the cal. for a national emigration convention, to be held in Cleveland, Ohio. August, 1854, By Frederick Douglass, W. J. Watkins, & J. M. Whitfield. With a short appendix of the statistics of Canada, West Indies, Central and South America. Published by M. T. Newsome. Detroit, George E. Pomeroy & co., 1854.
34p. 19cm.

Ohio.
M973.6 National equal rights league. Cleveland, Ohio.
N21c Proceedings of the first annual meeting of the
1865 national equal rights league, held in Cleveland, Ohio, October 19, 20 and 21, 1865. Philadelphia, E. C. Markley& Son, 1865.
54p. 21cm.

Ohio.
M973.6 Ohio state convention of colored men, Columbus,
Oh3c Ohio.
1871 Proceedings of the Ohio state convention of colored men [held in the city of Columbus, Ohio, on Wednesday, January 15, 1871] In: The Convention reporter, v.2, no.4, Feb. 15, 1871. [no imprint] p. 79-92.

Ohio.
M973.6 State convention of the colored citizens of
St2c Ohio. Columbus, Ohio.
1849 Minutes and address of the State Convention of colored citizens of Ohio, convened at Columbus, January 10th, 11th, 12th and 13th, 1849. Oberlin, From J. M. Fitch's Power Press, 1849.
28p. 19cm.

Ohio.
M973.6 State convention of the colored citizens of
St2c Ohio, Columbus, Ohio.
1850 Minutes of the state convention of the colored citizens of Ohio, convened at Columbus, January 9th, 10th, 11th and 12th, 1850. Columbus, Printed at the Ohio Standard Office, by Gale & Cleveland, 1850.
22p. 19cm.

Ohio.
M973.7 Wesley, Charles Harris, 1891-
W516 Ohio Negroes in the Civil War. [Columbus, Ohio State University Press for the Ohio Historical Society [1962]
46 p. 24 cm. (Publications of the Ohio Civil War Centennial Commission, no. 6)
Includes bibliography.

1. U. S.—Hist.—Civil War—Negro troops. 2. Negroes—Ohio. I. Title.

E525.O337 no. 6 62-63753 ‡

Library of Congress [5]

Ohio
M975 Wright, Richard Robert, Jr., 1878-
N31 The Negroes of Xenia, Ohio: A social study. [Bulletin of the Labor Dept., no.48. 1903] pp. 1007-1044.
In: The Negro in the black belt... Washington, D.C., Dept. of Labor, [1897-1902]

Ohio-Hist.-Civil war.
M350 Clark, Peter H.
C55b The black brigade of Cincinnati; being a report of its labors and a muster-roll of its members; together with various orders, speeches, etc., relating to it. By Peter H. Clark. Cincinnati, Printed by J. B. Boyd, 1864.
30 p. 22½cm.

1. U. S.—Hist.—Civil war—Campaigns and battles. 2. Kentucky—Hist.—Civil war. 3. Cincinnati. Black brigade. 4. Ohio—Hist.—Civil war. I. Title.

2—17175

Library of Congress E474.3.C59 [30d1]

Ohio Negroes in the Civil War.
M973.7 Wesley, Charles Harris, 1891-
W516 Ohio Negroes in the Civil War. [Columbus, Ohio State University Press for the Ohio Historical Society [1962]
46 p. 24 cm. (Publications of the Ohio Civil War Centennial Commission, no. 6)
Includes bibliography.

1. U. S.—Hist.—Civil War—Negro troops. 2. Negroes—Ohio. I. Title.

E525.O337 no. 6 62-63753 ‡

Library of Congress [5]

M973.6 Ohio state convention of colored men, Columbus,
Oh3c Ohio.
1871 Proceedings of the Ohio state convention of colored men [held in the city of Columbus, Ohio, on Wednesday, January 18, 1871] In: The Convention reporter, v.2, no.4, Feb. 15, 1871. [no imprint] p. 79-92.

1. Congresses and conventions. 2. Ohio.

Ohio state university, Columbus. College of education.
M378. Greene, Harry Washington, 1896-
G83a ... An adventure in experimental co-operative teaching; a general account of recent work in progressive education conducted jointly by members of the Department of education of the Ohio state university and the West Virginia state college, by Harry W. Greene ... Institute, W. Va., 1938.
vi, [7]-36 p. 22½cm. (West Virginia state college bulletin ... November, 1938. ser. 25, no. 6 ... Contribution no. 9 of the Dept. of education)
Bibliography: p. 32-36.
1. Teachers, Training of. 2. Education—Experimental methods. I. Ohio state university, Columbus. College of education. II. West Virginia state college, Institute. III. Title.

A 40-1473

Teachers college library, for Library of Congress Columbia univ. [2]

Oil - Texas.
M976.4 Williams, Jerome Aredell
W67 The tin box; a story of Texas cattle and oil. New York, Vantage Press, 1958.
275p. 21cm.

Africa
M261 Ojike, Mbonu.
D45 Christianity in Africa.
Pp. 60-66.
In: Desai, Ram, ed. Christianity in Africa as seen by Africans. Denver, A. Swallow [1962]

Nigeria
M966.9 Ojike, Mbonu.
Oj3m ... My Africa ... New York, The John Day company [1946]
xiii, [1], 350 p. illus. (incl. map, plan) plates, ports. 22cm.
"Annotated book list": p. 342-346.

1. Africa—Soc. life & cust. I. Title.

46-25033

Library of Congress DT14.O4 [20] 916

Nigeria
M966.9 Ojike, Mbonu.
Oj3p Portrait of a boy in Africa [by] Mbonu Ojike. New York, East and West association [c1945]
36p. illus. 23cm.

1. Africa, West. 2. Nigeria.

Africa
M261 Ojike, Mbonu.
D45 Religious life in Africa.
Pp. 49-59.
In: Desai, Ram, ed. Christianity in Africa as seen by Africans. Denver, A. Swallow [1962]

Nigeria
M966.9 Ojo, G J Afolabi.
Oj5 Yoruba culture: a geographical analysis [by] G. J. Afolabi Ojo; foreword by S. O. Biobaku. Ife, University; London, University of London P. [1967]
308 p. front., 20 plates, maps, plans, tables. 22½ cm. 30/-
(B 67-1219)
Revision of author's thesis, National University of Ireland. Bibliography: p. [279]-290.

1. Yorubas. I. Title. II. Biobaku, S O

DT513.O36 1967 916.69 67-78331

Library of Congress [5]

Nigeria
M728 Ojo, G J Afolabi.
Oj5 Yoruba palaces: a study of Afins of Yorubaland [by] G. J. Afolabi Ojo. London, University of London P. [1967]
~~142~~ p. plates, maps, plans, tables. 21 cm. 12/6 110p.
(B 67-2079)
Bibliography: p. 106.

1. Palaces—Yoruba. I. Title.

NA1597.Y6O38 728.8'2 67-75209

Library of Congress [2]

Nigeria Oju mi ri ni India.
M954 Ariyo, J O
Ar42 Oju mi ri ni India. [A Soldier's experiences in India. [Ibadan] Ministry of Education General Publications Section [1957]
96p. illus. 18½cm.
Written in Yoruba.

Ojúlówó Yoruba.
Nigeria
M496 Lasebikan, Ebenezer Latunde
L33 Ojúlówó Yoruba. Iwe kini: awon ilu nlá nlá ilẹ Yoruba. London, Oxford University Press [1961]
84p. illus. 18½cm.
"First published 1954."

Gold Coast
M966.7 Okae, J D
Ok1t Twi action songs and singing games. London, etc., Thomas Nelson and Sons, Ltd.; Accra, Scottish Mission Book Depot, 1953.
25p. illus. 24½cm.

1. Gold Coast - Songs. 2. Gold Coast - Games.

Gold Coast
M966.7 Okae, J D
Ok1w Why so stories; Twi stories. London, The Sheldon Press, ND.
16p. illus. 16cm.

1. Gold Coast - Folktales

Nigeria
M89
Okl

Okafor-Omali, Dilim
A Nigerian villager in two worlds. London, Faber and Faber [1965]

159p. 19cm.

1. Nigeria - Social life and customs.
I. Title.

Nigeria
M401
Ok1

Okala, J B C Etuka
Bilingualism in Eastern region of Nigeria; a psychological and sociopsychological study. [Enugu, Eastern Nigeria Printing Corp., n.d.]

16p. 20½cm.

1. Bilingualism. 2. Language and languages.

Africa
M808.83
B396

Okara, Gabriel
Okole.

Pp. 109-117.

In: Black Orpheus. Black Orpheus; an anthology of African and Afro-American prose. New York, McGraw-Hill, 1965.

Nigeria
M896.3
Ok1v

Okara, Gabriel
The voice, a novel. [London] A. Deutsch [1964]

157p. 19cm.
Portrait of author on book jacket.

1. Nigeria - Fiction. I. Title.

Nigeria
M896.3
Ok2n

Okeanu, Vincent C
Nancy in blooming beauty. 2d. ed. Port Harcourt [Nigeria] Eastern City Press, 1961.

37p. illus., port. 19cm. (Pens series)

I. Title.

Uganda
M967.61
Ok2t

Okech, Lacito
Tekwaro ki ker lobo acholi [History and chieftainship records of the land of the Acholi people of Uganda] Nairobi, The Eagle Press, 1953.

90p. 21cm.
Written in Lwo

1. Uganda - History. 2. Acholi people.

Nigeria
M370
Ik3

Okeke, P Uduaroh
Background to the problems of Nigerian education.

Pp. 1-18.

(In: Ikejiani, Okechukwu, ed. Nigerian education. Ikeja, Nigeria, Longmans, 1964)

Nigeria
M370
Ik3

Okeke, P Uduaroh
Education for efficiency: knowledge for use.

Pp. 93-114.

(In; Ikejiani, Okechukwu, ed. Nigerian education. Ikeja, Nigeria, Longmans, 1964)

Nigeria
M741
Ok2

Okeke, Uche, 1933–
Drawings. [Ibadan, Nigeria, Mbari Publications, 1961]
[24] p. illus. 28 cm. (New African artists, no. 1)

1. Drawings. 2. Art, African. 3. Art - Nigeria.

(Series)

NC1260.O4 63-2068

Library of Congress [1]

Nigeria
M741
Ok3

Okeke, Uche, 1933-
Drawings, Ibadan, Mbari Publications, 1961.

24p. illus. 28cm. (New African Artists, No. 1)

1. Art, African. 2. Africa - Art.
I. Title.

Nigeria
M896.3
Og1o

Okeke the magician, a novel.

Ogali, Ogali Agu, 1931-
Okeke the magician, a novel. Onitsha, Nigeria, Appolos Brothers [n.d.]

39p. port. 21cm.
Portrait of author in book.

Nigeria
M896.1
Ok3h

Okigbo, Christopher
Heavensgate. Drawings by Demas Nwoko. Ibadan, Mbari Publications, 1962.

39 p. illus. 20 cm.

1. African poetry. I. Title.
II. Nwoko, Demas, illus.

Nigeria
M896.1
Ok3L

Okigbo, Christopher
Limits. [Ibadan] Mbari Publications [1964]

[23]p. 20cm.

1. African poetry. I. Title.

Nigeria
M330
Ok3

Okigbo, Pius Nwabufo C 1924–
Africa and the Common Market [by] P. N. C. Okigbo. London, Longmans, 1967.
xv, 183 p. tables. 22½ cm. 27/6 (B 67-21004)
Bibliographical footnotes.

1. European Economic Community—Africa. 2. Africa—Economic integration. I. Title.

HC241.25.A3O45 1967b 382'.9142 67—112037

Library of Congress [68c1]

Nigeria
M336
Ok3

Okigbo, Pius Nwabufo C 1924–
Nigerian public finance [by] P. N. C. Okigbo. Evanston [Ill.] Northwestern University Press, 1965.
xiii, 245 p. 21 cm. (Northwestern University [Evanston, Ill.] African studies, no. 15)
Bibliographical footnotes.

1. Finance, Public—Nigeria. I. Title. (Series)

HJ1609.N5O5 336.669 65-15473

Library of Congress [3]

M304
P19
v.4, no. 16

Oklahoma.
Johnson, N.J.
Caesar F. Simmons, his life and accomplishments. Oklahoma's foremost member of the Negro race - 1923.
32p. portraits, 21cm.

Nigeria
M896.1
Ok5s

Okogie, M O
Songs of Africa. Ilfracombe, Arthur H. Stockwell [1961]

47p. port. 18½cm.
Portrait of author in book.

1. African poetry. I. Title.

Nigeria
M966.9
Ok5i

Okojie, Christopher Gbelokoto, 1920-
Ishan native laws and customs. Yaba, John Okwesa & Co., 1960.

338p. illus., ports. 24cm.

1. Nigeria-Social life and customs.
2. Ishan (African tribe). I. Title.

Gold Coast
M896.2
D36o

Okomfo Anokye's golden stool.

Dei-Anang, Michael F , 1909-
Okomfo Anokye's golden stool (a play in three acts). Ilfracombe, Devonshire, Arthur H. Stockwell Ltd., n.d.

54p. 18½cm.

Nigeria
M966.9
Ok52

Okonkwo, D Onuzulike
History of Nigeria in a new setting. [Aba, International Press, 1962.]

378p. illus. 19cm.
Includes bibliography.

1. Nigeria - History. I. Title.

Nigeria
M896.2
Ok5g

Okonkwo, R
The game of love; a classical drama from West Africa. Onitsha, Nigeria, J. C. Brothers Book-shop [n.d.]

48p. 21cm.

1. African drama. I. Title.

Nigeria
M960 Okoye, Mokwugo, 1926-
Ok5 African responses. Ilfracombe [Eng.] A. H. Stockwell [1964]
420 p. 22 cm.
Bibliography: p. 407-411.

1. Africa—Hist. 2. Africa—Civilization. I. Title.

DT20.O35 64-55286
Library of Congress [3]

Uganda
M896.3 Okwi, Erusa
Ok8ak Akonye-auni [Three eyes] Ekenomunan aputosia Margaret E. Gregg. Kampala, East African Literature Bureau, 1962.
20p. illus. 21½cm
Written in Atese.

I. Title.

The old blood.
Brit. Guiana
M823.91 Mittelhölzer, Edgar, 1909-
M69ol The old blood. [1st ed.] Garden City, N. Y., Doubleday, 1958.
576 p. illus. 22 cm.

I. Title. *Full name:* Edgar Austin Mittelhölzer.

PZ3.M6977Ol 58-8104 ‡
Library of Congress [5]

Nigeria
M896.4 Okoye, Mokwugo, 1926-
Ok5r The rebel line; memoirs of revolutionary struggle and a penetrating study of life and literature with moving panegyrics on love and liberty. [Onitsha, Nigeria, Etudo Limited, 1962]
111p. 21cm.

1. Nigeria - Addresses, essays, lectures. I. Title.

Nigeria
M896.2 Olagoke, D Olu
OL1in The incorruptible judge. London, Evans Bros., 1962.
48p. 18½cm.
At head of title: Plays for African schools.

I. Title.

Old fashioned black fo'ks.
M811.5 Henderson, Elliott Blaine.
H38o Old fashioned black fo'ks; poems, by Elliott Blaine Henderson. Columbus, Ohio, Published by the author, 1913.
54p. 18½cm.

Gold Coast Okraku, John Atua Simeon.
M496 Dagomba grammar, with exercises and vocabularies, by John Atua Simeon Okraku. Cambridge, Printed at the University Press, 1917.
Ok6
152p. 18½cm.

1. Dagomba language - grammar. 2. Gold Coast. I. Title.

Nigeria
M896.2 Olagoke, D Olu
OL1i The Iroko-man and the wood-carver. London, Evans Brothers [1963]
44p. 18cm. (Plays for African Schools)

1. African drama. I. Title.

The old gods laugh.
M813.5 Yerby, Frank, 1916-
Y46o The old gods laugh, a modern romance. New York, Dial Press, 1964.
408p. 22cm.

Kenya
M967.5 Okumu, Washington A Jalango.
Ok7 Lumumba's Congo: roots of conflict. Foreword by Rupert Emerson. New York, I. Obolensky [1963]
250 p. 22 cm.
Includes bibliography.

1. Congo (Leopoldville)—Hist.

DT657.O35 967.5 62-18793 ‡
Library of Congress [5]

Nigeria Olaiya, Victor Abimbola, 1931-
M780 Davies, Hezekiah Olufela, 1943-
D28 The Victor Olaiya story; a biography of Nigeria's evil genius of highly life, Victor Abimbola Olaiya. [Ikeja, Nigeria, Sankey Printing Works, n.d.]
52p. illus. 18cm.
Cover title.

The old Negro and the new Negro.
M323.1 Jefferson, Thomas Le Roy, 1867-
J35o The old Negro and the new Negro, by T. Le Roy Jefferson, M. D. Boston, Meador publishing company, 1937.
118 p. 20½cm.

1. Negroes—Moral and social conditions. I. Title. 37-38290
Library of Congress E185.86.J45
[42f1] 325.260973

Okunini Aggrey.
Ghana
M89 Oben-Addae, H E
Ag30k Okunini Aggrey. London, Thomas Nelson and Sons, Ltd., 1947.
66p. illus., map. 18½cm.
African author.
Portrait of biographee on front of book.

Brazil
M869.2 Olavo, Agostinho.
N17d Além do rio.
Pp. 200-231.
In: Nascimento, Abdias do, ed. Dramas para Negroes e prologo para brancos. Rio de Janeiro, Teatro Experimental do Negro, 1961.

I. Title.

Old songs hymnal.
M784 Bolton, Dorothy G ed.
B63 Old songs hymnal; words and melodies from the state of Georgia, collected by Dorothy G. Bolton; music arranged by Harry T. Burleigh. New York, London, The Century co. [c1929]
x p., 1 l., [208] p. 20½cm.
Spirituals.

I. Burleigh, Harry Thacker, 1866- II. Title. 29-22095
Library of Congress M1670.B68
[42c1]

Nigeria
M200 Okunsanya, I O S.
Ok6 The place of women in the new Nigeria. Pp. 21-22.
In: Christian Council of Nigeria. Building for tomorrow. Lagos, 1960.

1. Women in Nigeria.

M610 Old age homes-Pennsylvania-Direct.
P19 Pennsylvania. *Dept. of welfare.*
v.1 ... Directory of Pennsylvania institutions caring for the sick
no.14 and the aged. Prepared by the Bureau of assistance. [Harrisburg] 1930.
58 p. 23cm. (*Its* Bulletin no. 51)

1. Old age homes — Pennsylvania — Direct. 2. Hospitals — Pennsylvania—Direct.
46-36707
Library of Congress HV1468.P4A5 1930
[2]

An old story for this new day...
M252 Ransome, William Lee
R17o An old story for this new day and other sermons and addresses. Richmond, Central Publishing co., 1954.
207p. 20cm.

Okuwandiika ebbaluwa.
Uganda
M808.6 Seekamwa, J C
Se24 Okuwandiika ebbaluwa [Letter writing] Nairobi, Eagle Press, 1960.
108p. 21½cm. (East African Literature Bureau)
Written in Luganda.

1. Letter writing, African. I. Title.

Sierra Leone Old and new in Sierra Leone.
M966.4 Gorvie, Max.
G68o Old and new in Sierra Leone, by Max Gorvie ... London and Redhill, United society for Christian literature [1945]
79, [1] p. 18cm. (*Half-title:* Africa's own library, no. 9)
"First published 1945."

1. Ethnology—Sierra Leone. 2. Sierra Leone—Soc. life & cust. I. Title.
S D 46-18 Revised
U. S. Dept. of state. Libr. for Library of Congress DT516.G6
[r46d2]

Old Thom's harvest.
Guyana
M823.91 Kempadoo, Peter
K32o Old Thom's harvest, by Lauchmonen [pseud.] Spottiseoode [1965]
195p. 19½cm.

Old-time Negro preaching.

M251 Pipes, William Harrison, 1912-
P66s Say amen, brother! Old-time Negro preaching: a study in American frustration. New York, William-Frederick Press, 1951.

1, 210 p. 24cm.
Bibliography: p. 201-205.

M398 Old-time Negro proverbs.
B75o Brewer, John Mason, 1896-
Old-time Negro proverbs.

(In: Dobie, James Frank. ed. Spur-of-the-cock ... Austin, Texas, Texas Folk-lore Society, 1933. 22½cm. pp. 101-105).

Ole Man Mose; a novel of the Tenn. Valley.

M813.5 Montague, W Reginald, 1903-
M76o Ole Man Mose; a novel of the Tennessee Valley. ₍1st ed.₎ New York, Exposition Press ₍1957₎

121 p. 21 cm.

I. Title.

PZ4.M76Ol 57-10665 ‡

Library of Congress ₍2₎

Oleander.

M634 Pleasants, Clarence
P72 Galveston, the Oleander City; an appreciation. New York, Exposition Press ₍1966₎

31 p. 21 cm.

1. Oleander. 2. Galveston, Tex. - Description.

Nigeria
M896.2 Oleyede, S P
OL2 The trial of Hitler; a play. Aba ₍Nigeria₎ International Press, n.d.

12p. 15cm.

1. African drama. I. Title.

Uganda
M967.61 Olinga, Enoch
O12k Kidar Aijarakon ₍Look after you life.₎ Kampala, The Eagle Press ₍1952₎

48p. 18cm.
Written in Ateso

1. Uganda - health.

Uganda
M967.61 Olinga, Enoch O
O12ki Kimonyia oni akwap. (The Country is crying out for us; a discussion of economic, social and health problems) Nairobi, The Eagle Press, 1959.

28p. illus. 21½cm.
Text in: Teso.

1. Uganda - Social conditions. 2. Uganda - Economic conditions. 3. Uganda-Health.

Nigeria
M896.2 Olisah, Sunday Okenwa, 1936-
OL3ab About husband and wife who hate themselves; a drama. Onitsha, Nigeria, Highbred Maxwell, n.d.

48p. 20½cm.
At head of title: My wife.

1. African drama. I. Title.

Nigeria
M896.3 Olisah, Sunday Okenwa, 1936-
OL3d Dangerous man; vagabond versus princess, ₍Onitsha, New Era Printing Press, n.d.₎

16p. illus. 18½cm.

I. Title.

Nigeria
M896.2 Olisah, Sunday Okenwa, 1936-
OL3h How Lumumba suffered in life and died in Katanga. ₍Onitsha, Nigeria, Central Printing Press, n.d.₎

53p. illus. 20cm.

1. African drama. I. Title.

Nigeria
M896 Olisah, Sunday Okenwa, 1936-
OL3m Man has no rest in his life. ₍Onitsha, Nigeria, Okwumo Printing Press, n.d.₎

40p. 21cm.

I. Title.

Nigeria
M896.3 Olisah, Sunday Okenwa, 1936-
OL3ma Man suffers. ₍Makurdi, Nigeria, Progress Printing Works, 1960₎

16p. 19½cm.

I. Title.

Nigeria
M896.3 Olisah, Sunday Okenwa, 1936-
OL3m Money hard to get but easy to spend. Onitsha, Nigeria, General Printing Press ₍1960₎

32p. port. 19½cm.
Portrait of author in book.

I. Title.

Nigeria
M896.3 Olisah, Sunday Okenwa, 1936-
OL3w This world is hard. Onitsha, Nigeria, The Author ₍n.d.₎

20p. 18cm.

I. Title.

M200 Oliver, C Herbert, 1925-
O13n No flesh shall glory. ₍Nutley, N. J., Presbyterian and Reformed Pub. Co., 1959.

96 p. 21 cm.
Portrait of author on book jacket.

1. Race. 2. Segregation—Religious aspects. 3. Sociology, Biblical. I. Title.

BT734.O4 261.83 59-14513 ‡

Library of Congress ₍2₎

M814.5 Oliver, Clinton
O14h Henry James as a social critic. Reprinted from Antioch review, Summer 1947.

243-258p. 24cm.
Inscribed by author: For Mr. Arthur Spingarn, Sincerely yours, Clinton Oliver.

1. James, Henry, 1843-1916. I. Title.

M784 Oliver, Paul.
O13 Blues fell this morning - the meaning of the blues. With a foreword by Richard Wright. New York, Horizon Press, 1960.

355p. 21½cm.
White author.

1. Music and musicians. 2. Blues. I. Title.

M784 Oliver, Paul.
O13b Blues fell this morning; the meaning of the blues. With a foreword by Richard Wright. London, Cassell and Co., Ltd., 1960.

355p. 21½cm.
White author.

1. Blues. 2. Music and musicians. I.Title.

Jamaica
MB9 Olivier, Sydney Haldane Olivier, *baron*, 1859-1943.
O14 Letters and selected writings, edited with a memoir by Margaret Olivier. With some impressions by Bernard Shaw. ~~New York, Macmillan ₍1948₎~~ London, Allen & Unwin 1948

252 p. plates, ports. 22 cm.

1. West Indies - History.

[DA566.9.O43A] 923.242 A 50-4870

New York Univ. Wash. Sq. Library for Library of Congress ₍3₎

Ollennu,

Ghana
M896.1 Stewart, MacNeill
St4a Appeal to reason -- to the political leaders of the country this poem is respectfully dedicated --. Accra, 1951.

4p. ports. 18cm.

Jamaica
M972.92 Olley, Philip Peter, *ed.*
O14g Guide to Jamaica, compiled and edited by Philip P. Olley ... for the Tourist trade development board, Kingston, Jamaica, B. W. I. ₍Glasgow, Printed by R. Maclehose and co., ltd., The University press₎ 1937.

347 p. incl. front., illus., plates. maps (part fold.) 17½cm.
"First published 1937."

1. Jamaica—Descr. & trav.—Guide-books. I. Tourist trade development board of Jamaica, Kingston, Jamaica.

38—7270

Library of Congress F1869.O55 ₍38d3₎ 917.292

Ollie Miss.

M813.5
H88
Henderson, George Wylie.
Ollie Miss, a novel by George Wylie Henderson; blocks by Lowell Leroy Balcolm. New York, Frederick A. Stokes company, 1935.
4 p. l., 276 p. incl. illus., plates. front. 21½cm.

I. Title.

Library of Congress PZ3.H38450l 35—2970
[4241]

Olympic athletes.

Nigeria
M966.9
G72
Goubadia, B A A
Our olympic adventure. Lagos, Public Relations Department, n.d.

12p. illus. 20½cm. (Crownbird Series No. 17)

Tanganyika
M967.82
Om1ma
Omari, Dunstan Alfred, 1922- jt. auth.
Maendeleo na jasho. Progress & perspiration. [By C.W. W. Ryan and D. A. Omari] Dar es Salaam, Eagle Press, 1954.
19p. 18cm. (Mazungunmzo ya uraia. Talks on citizenship, no. 3)
Written in English and Swahili.
1. Tanganyika. I. Title. II. Title: Progress & perspiration. III. Series: Mazungunmzo ya uraia, no. 3. IV. Series: Talks on citizenship, no. 3. V. Ryan, C. W. W.

Olódùmarè.

Nigeria
M290
Id5
Idowu, E Bolaji.
Olódùmarè; God in Yoruba belief. [London] Longmans [1962]
222 p. illus. 23 cm.

1. Yorubas—Religion. I. Title. II. Title: God in Yoruba belief.

BL2480.Y6I3 62-52364 ‡

Library of Congress [2]

Olympio, Sylvanus
Reflections on Togolese and African problems, pp. 72-79.

Africa
M960.3
D87a
Duffy, James, 1923- ed.
Africa speaks. Edited by James Duffy and Robert A. Manners. Princeton, N.J., Van Nostrand [1961]

223p. 23cm.

Tanganyika
M967.82
Om1m
Omari, Dunstan Alfred, 1922- jt. auth.
Mtu maskini mwenye sh.1,000,000. The poor man with a million shillings. [By C. W. W. Ryan and D. A. Omari] Dar es Salaam, Eagle Press, 1954.
16p. 18cm. (Mazungunmzo ya uraia. Talks on citizenship, no.2)
Writtn in Swahili and English.
1. Money. I. Title. II. Title: The poor man with a million shillings. III. Series: Mazungunmzo ya uraia, no. 2. IV. Talks on citizenship, no. 2. V. Ryan, C. W. W.

Nigeria
M896.3
OL7
Ologbosere, N A.
Elophosa; an original novel of African life written by an African. [London, African Tribune Publication Dept.] 1961.

116p. 18cm.

1. African fiction. I. Title.

Africa
M960
F76
Olympio, Sylvanus E , 1902-1963.
African problems and the Cold War.

Pp. 292-301.

In: Foreign Affairs (New York). Africa. New York, Praeger, 1964.

Tanganuika
M967.82
Om1t
Omari, Dunstan Alfred, 1922- jt. auth.
Tanganyika, tajiri au maskini? Tanganyika - rich or poor? [By C. W. W. Ryan and D. A. Omari] Dar es Salaam, 1954.
17p. 18cm. (Mazungumzo ya uraia. Talks on citizanship, no. 4)
Written in Swahili and English.
1. Tanganyika. I. Title. II. Tanganyika - rich or poor? III. Mazungumzo ya uraia, no. 4. IV. Talks on citizenship. no. 4. V. Ryan, C. W. W.

Oloo, Mary O., tr.

Kenya
M372.1
H44c
Hertslet, Jessie
Nyithindo e dala kendo e skul [Children at home and at school] [Translated by Mary O. Oloo] Nairobi, Eagle Press, 1950.

70p. 21½cm.
Written in Luo.
Translated from the English.
White author.

1. Children - Care and hygiene. I. Title. II. Oloo, Mary O., tr.

Zanzibar
M896.3
Om1h
Omar, C A Shariff
Hadithi ya hazina binti Sultani. [The tale of Hazina, the Sultan's daughter] Nairobi, Eagle Press, 1951.
33p. illus. 21½cm. (A Treasury of East African Literature)
Written in Swahili.

I. Title. II. Series.

Ghana
M392.6
Om12
Omari, T Peter.
Marriage guidance for young Ghanaians. With a foreword by Charles O. Easmon. London, New York, Nelson [1962]
148 p. illus. 20 cm.
Includes bibliography.

Portrait of author on back of book.

1. Marriage. 2. Family. I. Title.

HQ734.O63 63-4354 ‡

Library of Congress [2]

Nigeria
M378
O19e
Olubummo, Adegoke.
The emergent university, with special reference to Nigeria [by] Adegoke Olubummo and John Ferguson. [London] Longmans [1960]
122 p. 20 cm.
Includes bibliographies.

1. Education, Higher. 2. Ibadan, Nigeria. University College. I. Ferguson, John, 1921- joint author. II. Title.

LB2321.O48 378.669 61-2482

Library of Congress [5]

Zanzibar
M896.3
Om1k
Omar, C A Shariff
Kisa cha hasan-Li-Basir. [The adventures of Hasan-Li-Basir] Nairobi, Eagle Press, 1951.

30p. illus. 21cm. (Treasury of East African literature)
Written in Swahili.

I. Title. II. Series.

Ombrages; pièce en trois actes.

Dahomey
M896.2
F11
Fabo, Paul
Ombrages; pièce en trois actes. Preface de René Lyr. Bruxelles, Les Editions F. Wellens-Pay, 1948.

91p. 19cm.

Nigeria
M378.3
OL9
Olugboji, Dayo
The problem of Nigerian students overseas. [Lagos, C. M. S. Press, 1959]

28p. 21½cm.

1. African students. I. Title.

Zanzibar
M967.8
Om1
Omar, C A Shariff
Kisiwa cha Pemba; historia na masimulizi [History and traditions of the Island of Pemba] Nairobi, Eagle Press, 1951.
21p. illus., port., maps. 21cm.
Written in Swahili.

1. Pemba. - History. 2. Pemba. - Social life and customs. 3. Zanzibar. I. Title.

Ombre ensoleillée.

Haiti
M841
L93o
Louis, Janine Tavernier
Ombre ensoleillée. Preface de Roland Morisseau. Illustration de Villard Denis. Port-au-Prince, Imprimerie Gervais Louis, 1961.

21p. 19½cm.
Portrait of author on back of book.

Nigeria
M966.9
O19
Olugboji, Dayo
The United States of West Africa and realpolitik. Lagos, Nigeria Press, 1959.

44p. 22cm.

1. West Africa - Politics and government. I. Title.

Tanganyika
M967.82
Om1k
Omari, Dunstan Alfred, 1922- jt. auth.
Kwa nini tuna haja ya serikali? Why do we have government? [By C. W. W. Ryan and D. A. Omari] Dar es Salaam, Eagle Press, 1954.
17p. 18cm. (Mazungumzo juu ya uraia. Talks on citizenship no.1)
Written in Swahili and English.
1. Tanganyika. I. Title. II. Title: Why do we have government? III. Series: Mazungumzo ya uraia, no.1. IV. Series: Talks on citizenship, no. 1. V. Ryan, C. W. W.

Cameroun
M916.711
Oml
Ombede, Philippe-Louis.
Lettres de ma cambuse [par] R. Philombe [pseud.] Yaounde, Editions Abbia avec la collaboration de Cle, 1964.
62p. illus. 18cm.
Portrait of author on book cover.

1. Cameroun. I. Title.

Omega Psi Phi.

M378 Cobb, William Montague, 1904-
C63o The delinquent laureate. Reprinted from The Oracle, June 1941.

[3]p. 27cm.

Omega Psi Phi.

M378 Cobb, William Montague, 1904-
C63o Omega academic awards. Reprinted from the Oracle.

28cm.

Omega psi phi.

M378. Dreer, Herman, 1889-
D81 The history of the Omega psi phi fraternity, a brotherhood of Negro college men, 1911 to 1939, by Herman Dreer. [Washington, D. C., The Fraternity [°1940]

2 p. l., a-d p., 2 l., iv, 331, [1] p. incl. illus., facsims. plates (1 fold.) 23½cm.

Includes songs with music.

1. Omega psi phi. I. Title.

41-814

Library of Congress LJ75.O55D7

——— Copy 2.

Copyright [2] 371.855

Kenya
M392 Ominde, Simeon H
Om5 The Luo girl from infancy to marriage. London, Macmillan, 1952.

69p. illus. 18½cm. (Custom and tradition in East Africa)

1. Girls. 2. Kenya - Social life and customs. 3. Family - Kenya. I. Title.

Nigeria
M896.3 Omoyajowo, J Akin
Om6i Itan adegbedan. Pelu awon aworan lati owo Cyril Deakins. «London» Longmans «1961»

72p. illus. 18½cm.
Translated title: Story of Adegbesan.
Written in Yoruba.

I. Title.

Omulini gw'omukazi my maka.

Uganda
M396 Garriock, L H
G19w Omulini gw'omukazi my maka [The work of women in the home] Kyakyusibwa Emmanuel B. Ongoye. [Kampala, East African Literature Bureau, n.d.]

16p. 18½cm. (Weemanyiizenga okusoma)
Written in Luganda.

1. Home labor. I. Title. II. Ongoye, Emanuel B., tr.

Omulimi w'omu Uganda.

Uganda
M630 Masefield, G. B
M37u Omulimi w'omu Uganda [The Uganda farmer] Kyakyusibwa E. Bulera. Nairobi, Eagle Press, 1951.

186p. illus. 18cm.
Written in Luganda.

1. Agriculture - Uganda. 2. Uganda - Agriculture. I. Title. II. Bulewa, E., tr.

Omuseveni eyagenda okusevena.

Uganda
M916 Serunkuma, J N B
Se6 Omuseveni eyagenda okusevena [One of the seventh (K. A. R.) goes 'a-severing'] Kampala, Eagle Press, 1959.

68p. 21½cm.
Written in Luganda.

1. Africa - Description and travel. I. Title.

Senegal On African socialism.
M335 Senghor, Léopold Sédar.
Se5 On African socialism. Translated and with an introd. by Mercer Cook. New York, Praeger [1964]

xv, 173 p. 21 cm.

Bibliographical references included in "Notes" (p. 167-173)

CONTENTS.—Nationhood: report on the doctrine and program of the Party of African Federation.—The African road to socialism.—The theory and practice of Senegalese socialism.

1. Senegal—Pol. & govt.—Addresses, essays, lectures. 2. Mali—Pol. & govt.—Addresses, essays, lectures. 3. Socialism in Africa—Addresses, essays, lectures. I. Title.

JQ3396.A91S4 1964 64—16419

Library of Congress [64f4]

M310 On being a Negro in America.
R24o Redding, Jay Saunders, 1906-
On being Negro in America. [1st ed.] Indianapolis, Bobbs-Merrill [1951]

156 p. 21 cm.

1. Negroes. I. Title.

E185.61.R3 325.260973 51—13473 ‡

Library of Congress [52x7]

France On board the Emma.
M940 Dumas, Alexandre, 1802-1870.
D89o On board the Emma, adventures with Garibaldi's "Thousand" in Sicily, by Alexandre Dumas, translated and with an introduction by R. S. Garnett. New York, D. Appleton and company, 1929.

xvi p., 2 l., 568 p. front., pl., ports., map, facsim. 22½cm.

"Facsimile pages from ms. of book" on end-papers.

1. Garibaldi, Giuseppe, 1807-1882. 2. Italy — Hist. — War of 1860-1861. I. Garnett, Robert Singleton, 1866-1932, tr. II. Title.

29—23710

Library of Congress DG554.D8 [44a1]

On clipped wings.

M350 Hastie, William Henry, 1904-
H27o On clipped wings; the story of Jim Crow in the Army air corps, by William H. Hastie. [New York, National association for the advancement of colored people, 1943]

27 p. illus. (incl. ports.) 21½cm.

1. U. S. Army—Negro troops. 2. Negroes as soldiers. 3. U. S. Army air forces. I. National association for the advancement of colored people. II. Title.

A 44-3616

Harvard univ. Library for Library of Congress [3]

On heroes and uhuru-worship.

Kenya
M960 Mazrui, Ali Al'Amin.
M458o On heroes and uhuru-worship: essays on independent Africa [by] Ali A. Mazrui. London, Longmans [1967]

ix, 264 p. 20½ cm. 36/- (B 67-19838)

Bibliographical footnotes.

1. Africa—Politics—1960- —Addresses, essays, lectures. I. Title.

DT30.M34 320.9'6 67-109118

Library of Congress [2]

MB On our way; Young pages from American
On2 autobiography, selected by Robert Patterson, Mildred Mebel, Lawrence Hill. Illus. by Robert Patterson. New York, Holiday House, 1952.

372p. 22cm.
Partial contents:-Frederick Douglass, Covey the Negro breaker. -Langston Hughes, Haunted ship. -Walter White, The Cry of the mob. -William C. Handy, Devil's plaything.

(Tracings - over).

On the air.

Ghana
M896.8 Blay, J Benibengor, 1915-
B61o On the air (B.B.C. talks). Aboso, published by the Author, 1952.

36p. 18cm.

On the exodus.

M815.4 Douglass, Frederick, 1817-1895.
D74f Frederick Douglass, on the exodus. Resolutions submitted by Mr. Douglass
pr preliminary to his debate with Prof. R.T. Greener on the impolicy of the exodus of colored people from the South to Kansas and other northern states, n.p. n.p., n.d.

7p. 23½cm.

On the tiger's back.

Nigeria
M335.4 Ajao, Aderogba, 1930-
Aj1o On the tiger's back. London, Allen & Unwin [1962]

149 p. illus. 23 cm.

1. Communism. I. Title.

HX450.N5A7 1962a 62-52690 ‡

Library of Congress [3]

On the trail of Negro folk-songs.

M784 Scarborough, Dorothy, 1878-1935.
Sc7 On the trail of Negro folk-songs, by Dorothy Scarborough, assisted by Ola Lee Gulledge. Cambridge, Harvard university press, 1925.

5 p. l., [3]-289 p. illus. (music) 24½ cm.

1. Negro songs. I. Gulledge, Ola Lee. II. Title.

M1670.S3 25—19922

Library of Congress [50s1]

On these I stand.

M811.5 Cullen, Countee, 1903-1946.
C89p On these I stand; an anthology of the best poems of Countee Cullen. Selected by himself and including six new poems never before published. New York and London, Harper & brothers [1947]

x, 197, [1] p. 21cm.

"First edition."

I. Title.

PS3505.U287A6 1947 811.5 47-30109

© 22Jan47; publisher, New York; A10416.

Library of Congress [20]

On trial for my country.

Rhodesia
M896.3 Samkange, Stanlake John Thompson, 1922-
Sa46o On trial for my country [by] Stanlake Samkange. London, Heinemann, 1966.

viii, 160 p. 20½ cm. 18/- (B 66-17472)

Map on endpapers.

1. Lobengula, King of the Matabele, 1833 (ca.)-1893?—Fiction. 2. Rhodes, Cecil John, 1853-1902—Fiction. I. Title.

PZ4.S188On 67-70814

Library of Congress [3]

Nigeria
M966.9 Onabamiro, Sanya Dojo.
On1w Why our children die; the causes, and suggestions for prevention, of infant mortality in West Africa. With a foreword by Lancelot Hogben. London, Methuen [1949]

xi, 195 p. 20 cm.

"References": p. 187-190.

1. Infants—Mortality. 2. Maternal and infant welfare—Africa, West. 3. Obstetrics.

RG518.A3M3 618.2 50-15163

Library of Congress [1]

Nigeria
M966.9
On1

Onabamiro, Sanya Dojo.
Why our children die; the causes, and suggestions for prevention, of infant mortality in West Africa. With a foreword by Lancelot Hogben. London, Methuen [1949]

xi, 195 p. 20 cm.

"References": p. 187–190.

1. Infants—Mortality. 2. Maternal and infant welfare—Africa, West. 3. Obstetrics.

RG518.A3M3 618.2 50–15163

Library of Congress [1]

Nigeria
M896.3 Onadipe, Kola.
On1 The adventures of Souza, the village lad. Illustrated by Adebayo Ajayi. Lagos, African Universities Press [1963]

92p. 20cm. (African readers library, 5)

1. Africa, West-Fiction. I. Titles.

Once upon a school day.

M793 Kelly, Dolores Evangeline
K29 Once upon a school day, little stories of fun at school. Illustrated by Alan Moyer. New York, Exposition Press [1962]

48p. 21cm.
Portrait of author on book jacket.

M812.5 One act play magazine, v.1 New York,
H87s Contemporary play publications, 19
v 25cm.
Library has: July 1937.

M812.5 One act play magazine, v 1.
H87d New York, Contemporary play publications, 19

v. 25cm.
Library has: October 1938

One Act Play Magazine. New York, N.Y.

Volume	Year	Month	Volume	Year	Month
1	1938	Oct.			

Nigeria The one and the many.
M370 Brooks, John Nixon, 1920-
D56 The one and the many: the individual in the modern world. By John Brooks, with essays by Charles Habib Malik [and others]. 1st ed.

xvi, 331p. 24cm.

One and the many; [poems. 1st ed.]

M811.5 **Madgett, Naomi Cornelia Long.**
M26o One and the many; [poems. 1st ed.] New York, Exposition Press [1956]

64 p. 21 cm.

I. Title.

PS3525.A318O5 811.5 56–12373 ‡

Library of Congress [2]

One bread, one body.

M265.3 **Wright, Nathan.**
W93 One bread, one body. Foreword by James A. Pike. Greenwich, Conn., Seabury Press, 1962.

148 p. 22 cm.
Includes bibliographies.

1. Lord's Supper—Anglican Communion. I. Title.

BX5949.C5W73 265.3 62–9618 ‡

Library of Congress [5]

One continual cry.

M326 **Aptheker, Herbert, 1915–**
W15 One continual cry; David Walker's Appeal to the colored
1965 citizens of the world, 1829–1830, its setting & its meaning, together with the full text of the third, and last, edition of the Appeal. New York, Published for A. I. M. S. by Humanities Press [1965]

150 p. 22 cm.
Bibliography: p. 149–150.

1. Slavery in the U. S.—Controversial literature—1830. I. Walker, David, 1785–1830. Walker's appeal, in four articles; together with a preamble, to the coloured citizens of the world. II. Title.

E446.W2A6 301.4522 65–16703

Library of Congress [6]

Ethiopia One hundred and ten miracles.
M963 **Budge, *Sir* Ernest Alfred Thompson Wallis, 1857–1934, *ed.***
B85o One hundred and ten miracles of Our Lady Mary, translated from Ethiopic manuscripts for the most part in the British museum, with extracts from some ancient European versions, and illustrations from the paintings in manuscripts by Ethiopian artists, by Sir E. A. Wallis Budge ... London, Oxford university press, H. Milford, 1933.

lvii, [2], 355, [1] p. LXVI pl. (incl. front.) 19½ cm.

A cheap edition of the one published by the Medici society in London, 1923. Contains all of the plates of the 1923 edition.

(Continued on next card)

A 34—1044

[44e1]

M940.3 128 genuine pictures from recent official
M61 photographs, also outline map drawings made especially for this volume. Washington, D.C., Austin Jenkins, co. 1919

viii, 495p. front. maps plates. 21½cm.

M810.8 125th anniversary anthology, 1839-1964.
D66 **Dodd, Mead & Company, *publishers, New York.***
125th anniversary anthology, 1839–1964; a sampling of reading tastes from the lists of an American publisher with a brief historical commentary by the editors of Dodd, Mead. New York [1964]

xiii, 359 p. illus. 24 cm.

1. Literature—Collections. I. Title.

PN6014.D6 808.8 64–7501

Library of Congress [5]

---

100 years of emancipation.

M323.4 **Goldwin, Robert A 1922– *ed.***
G58 100 years of emancipation, essays by Harry V. Jaffa [and others] Edited by Robert A. Goldwin. Chicago, Rand McNally [1964]

217 p. 22 cm. (Rand McNally public affairs series)
Bibliographical footnotes.

1. Negroes—Civil rights. 2. Negroes—Legal status, laws, etc. 3. Emancipation proclamation. I. Jaffa, Harry V. II. Title.

E185.61.G62 1964a 323.4 64–14111

Library of Congress [10]

---

100 years of Negro freedom.

MB **Bontemps, Arna Wendell, 1902–**
B64o 100 years of Negro freedom. New York, Dodd, Mead, 1961.

276 p. illus. 22 cm.
Includes bibliography.
Portrait of author on book jacket.

1. Negroes. 2. Negroes—Biog. I. Title.

E185.6.B74 325.2670973 61—11716 ‡

Library of Congress [62o25]

---

100 years of the Negro in show business.

M792 **Fletcher, Tom, 1873–1954.**
F63 100 years of the Negro in show business; the Tom Fletcher story. 1st ed. New York, Burdge [1954]

337 p. illus. 23 cm.

1. Negro minstrels. 2. Theater—U. S.—Hist. I. Title.

ML3561.N4F5 927.8 55–1843 ‡

Library of Congress [2]

One man, one matchet.

Nigeria
M896.3 Aluko, Timothy Mofolorunso, 1918-
AL81on One man, one matchet. London, Heinemann, 1964.

196p. 18½cm.
Portrait of author on book jacket.

One man, one wife.

Nigeria
M896.3 Aluko, T M ,1920-
A18o One man, one wife. Lagos, Nigerian Printing and Publishing Co., Ltd., 1959.

200p. 19cm.
Portrait of author on book jacket.

One more tomorrow.

M813.5 Puckett, G Henderson
P96 One more tomorrow. New York, Vantage Press, 1959.

288p. 21cm.

One tenth of a nation.

MB **Taylor, Harold William, 1903–**
T21o One tenth of a nation, by Harold W. Taylor. Corona, L. I., N. Y., Progressive book shop, °1946.

31 p. 15 x 11½ cm.

Contributions made by the Negro people in building a democratic America. cf. Foreword.
Bibliography: p. 31. "Books to read": p. 31.

1. Negroes. 2. Negroes—Biog. I. Title.

E185.6.T3 325.260973 47–15548

Library of Congress [3]

1,000 Kikuyu proverbs.

Kenya
M398 Barra, G
B27 1,000 Kikuyu proverbs with translations and English equivalents. [2d ed.] London, Macmillan and Co., Ltd., 1960.

123p. 18½cm.

One-way ticket.

M811.5 H87o Hughes, Langston, 1902-
One-way ticket [poems] illus. by Jacob Lawrence. [1st ed.] New York, A. A. Knopf, 1949 [°1948]
xvii, 136 p. illus. 22 cm.

I. Lawrence, Jacob, 1917- illus. II. Title.
Full name: James Langston Hughes.

PS3515.U274O5 811.5 49-7018*
Library of Congress [20]

Nigeria M960 On4af Bk. 1
Onibon-Oje, G O
Africa in the ancient world. [Rev. ed.] [Ibadan, Onibon-Oje Press, n.d.]

135p. illus., maps. 18cm. (History for secondary modern schools, Book I)

1. Africa - History. I. Title.

Nigeria M428 On9
Onukwu, G C
Model questions & answers on English language for R.S.A. School & R.S.A. Inter Stage II certificate from (1958-1962). Foreworded by M.C. Oji. Onitsha, [Etudo, 1963]

63p. tables 21cm.

1. English language - Study and teaching - Africa. I. Title.

One way to heaven.

M813.5 C89o Cullen, Countee, 1903-
One way to heaven, by Countee Cullen. New York and London, Harper & brothers, 1932.
4 p. l., [3]-280 p. 20cm.
"First edition."

I. Title. 32-4559
Library of Congress PZ3.C897610n
[41g1]

Nigeria M960 On4af Bk. 3
Onibon-Oje, G O
Africa in the modern world (the last 100 years). [Ibadan, United Printing Press, n.d.]

174p. illus., ports., maps. 18cm. (History for secondary modern schools with the optional extras and Teacher Training Colleges, Book 3)

1. Africa - History. I. Title.

Nigeria M335 On9
Onuoha, Bede
The elements of African socialism. [London] Andre Deutsch [1965]

139p. 22½cm.
Includes bibliography.

1. Socialism - Africa. 2. Africa - Socialism. I. Title.

Ongoye, Emanuel B., tr.

Uganda M396 G19w
Garriock, L H
Omulini gw'omukazi my maka [The work of women in the home] Kyakyusibwa Emmanuel B. Ongoye. [Kampala, East African Literature Bureau, n.d.]

16p. 18½cm. (Weemanyiizenga okusoma)
Written in Luganda.

1. Home labor. I. Title. II. Ongoye, Emanuel B., tr.

Onion to orchid.

M811.5 H83 Howard, Alice Henrietta.
Onion to orchid; poems by Alice Henrietta Howard. New York, The William-Frederick press, 1945.
32 p. 19½cm. (*On cover:* The William-Frederick poets. (No. 18))

I. Title. 46-1804
Library of Congress PS3515.O81505
[3] 811.5

Trinidad M972.98 R39
Onward Trinidad.
Richardson, E C
Onward Trinidad; the solution to our economic and social problems. [Port-of-Spain, Enterprise Electric Printery, n.d.]

25p. 22½cm.

1. Trinidad - Economic condition.
2 Trinidad - Social conditions. I. Title.

M323 C88 Oneal, James, 1875-
The next emancipation. With introd. by Frank R. Crosswaith. [4th ed.] New York, Negro Labor News Service [°1929]
30 p. 19 cm.
Cover title.

~~1. Negroes.~~ I. Title. II. Crosswaith, Frank Rudolph, 1892- Foreword.
E185.61.O56 1929 49-41115*
Library of Congress [1]

Onkel Toms børn [Uncle Tom's children]

M813.5 W93u4 Wright, Richard, 1908-1960
Onkel Toms børn [Uncle Tom's children] Pa dansk ved Kurt Kreutzfeld. [København] Gyldendal, 1957

245p. 21cm.
Written in Danish.

Onward Trinidad; the solution to our economic and social problems.

Trinidad M972.98 R39
Richardson, E C
Onward Trinidad; the solution to our economic and social problems. [Port-of-Spain, Enterprise Electric Printery, n.d.]

25p. 22½cm.

1. Trinidad - Economic condition.
2 Trinidad - Social conditions. I. Title.

M89 On21 O'Neal, William.
Life and history of William O'Neal; or, The man who sold his wife. St. Louis, Mo., A. R. Fleming & Co., 1896.

55 p. front. 20cm.

Nigeria M896.3 M726o
The only son.
Munonye, John, 1929-
The only son. London, Heinemann, 1966.
[5], 202 p. 20½ cm. 18/- (B 66-7524)

I. Title.
PR6063.U48O5 66-74105
Library of Congress [5]

Nigeria M896.3 On9
Onwuamaegbu, Moses Obumnene, 1924- , comp.
Akụkọ ife nke ndi Igbo. [Selection of stories in Igbo] Collection and edited by M. O. Onwuamaegbu and M. M. Green. London, Oxford University Press, 1962.

16p. 22cm.
Written in Ibo.

(Continued on next card)

M810.8 Am295 O'Neill, Eugene Gladstone, 1888-
All God's chillun got wings.

(In: The American mercury. The American mercury reader, ... Garden City, New York, Blue Ribbon Books, c1944. 19½cm. pp. 159-175).

Ontario.

M366.1 F87o5 Freemasons. Ontario. Grand Lodge.
Proceedings. 1st- 1874-
Windsor, 1874-

v. 21cm. annual
See holdings card for proceedings in library.

Nigeria M896.3 On9
Onwuamaegbu, Moses Obumnene, 1924- , comp.
Akụkọ ife nke ndi Igbo, 1962. (Card 2)

Contents.- Mbe na Enyi, by M. O. Onwuamaegbu.- Okwa na Ọgụrụ, by G. E. Igwe.- Manụụba, J. O. Iroaganachi.- Ilu, by A. O. Onyekwere.- Agu na mbe, J. O. Ioaganachi.- Nkịta Atọ, by J. A. Dureke.- Ibgo script and spelling, by J. O. Iroaganachi.

I. Title.

Uganda M398 On2a
Onen, S F
Agda yil ku wade; lem'abola ku titi. (Alur proverbs and riddles.) Nairobi, The Eagle Press, 1959.

26p. 18cm.
Text in: Lwo (Alur)

1. Uganda - Proverbs. 2. Uganda - Riddles.

Ontario.

M326. M69 1860
Mitchell, William M.
The underground railroad from slavery to freedom. By the Rev. W. M. Mitchell ... 2d ed. London, W. Tweedie; [etc., etc.] 1860.
ix, [10]-191 p. front. (port.) 16½cm.

1. Underground railroad. 2. Slavery in the U. S.—Fugitive slaves. 3. Negroes—Ontario.
10-34489
Library of Congress E450.M68
[a35b1]

Nigeria M896.3 On9
Onwuamaegbu, Moses Obumnene, 1924-
Mbe na Enyi.

pp. 3-4.

In: Onwuamaegbu. M. O., comp. Akụkọ ife nke ndi Igbo. London, Oxford University Press, 1962

Nigeria
M896.3 On9
Onyekwere, A O
Ilu.

pp. 10.

In: Onwuamaegbu, M. O., comp. Akụkọ ife ake ndi Igbo. London, Oxford University Press, 1962.

Nigeria
M338 On9
Onyemelukwe, Clement Chukwukadibia.
Problems of industrial planning and management in Nigeria ₍by₎ C. C. Onyemelukwe. London, Longmans, 1966.
vii, 330 p. tables, diagrs. 22½ cm. 42/-
(B 66-14302)
Bibliography: p. 319-322.

1. Nigeria—Economic policy. 2. Nigeria—Indus. I. Title.

HC517.N48O55 338.9669 66-74020

Library of Congress ₍3₎

Op de klank der Tamboerijnen.
M813.5 H87op
Hughes, Langston, 1902-
Op de klank der Tamboerijnen: roman. (Tambourines to glory). Uitgever, F. G. Kroonder, 1961?

188p. 20cm.

M973 D541
An open letter to President McKinley by the colored people of Massachusetts.

p. 401

In: Diamond, Sigmund, ed. The nation transformed, New York, G. Braziller, 1963.

Opera.
M784 J63c
Johnson, James Weldon, 1871-1938. tr.
Goyescas, or The rival lovers; opera in three tableaux. The book by Fernando Periquet, the music by Enrique Granados, English version by James Weldon Johnson. New York, G. Schirmer ₍c1915₎

42p. 24½cm. (G. Schirmer's collection of opera-librettos)
Inscribed copy: To Captain A. B. Spingarn, Yours sincerely, James Weldon Johnson.
White author.

Opera.
M784 J63go
Johnson, James Weldon, 1871-1938. tr.
Goyescas; an opera in three tableaux. The book by Fernando Periquet. The music by Enrique Granados. English version by James Weldon Johnson. New York, G. Schirmer, 1915.

165p. 29½cm.

Operas - Librettos.
M811.5 H87t
Hughes, Langston, 1902-
Troubled island; An opera in three acts. Libretto. Music by William Grant Still. Libretto by Langston Hughes. Hollywood, Leeds Music Corporation, 1949.

38p. 22cm.

1. Operas - Librettos. I. Title.
II. Still, William Grant, 1895-

The operation of the mandate system in Africa.
M973 L820
Logan, Rayford Whittingham.
The operation of the mandate system in Africa, 1919-1927, with an introduction on the problem of the mandates in the post-war world, by Rayford W. Logan. Washington, D. C., The Foundation publishers, inc., 1942.
xii, 50 p. 24½cm.

1. Mandates—Africa. I. Title.

42-51480

Library of Congress JQ3505.L6
₍43d2₎ 321.027

Opinions... Supreme cont... Liberia.
M966.6 L610
Liberia. *Supreme court.*
Opinions delivered by the honourable the Supreme court of the republic of Liberia in cases decided during its November term A. D. 1933– New annual series no. 1–
Monrovia, Liberia, Printed by authority at the Government printing office ₍1934?–
v. 25-26cm.

1. Law reports, digests, etc.—Liberia. I. Title.

35-19289

Library of Congress ₍2₎

Opoku, Andrew Amankwa.
Afram, pp. 205-211.
M808.8 N42 v.15
New world writing. 1st–
Apr. 1952–
₍New York₎ New American Library.
v. 18 cm. (N. A. L. Mentor books)

1. Literature, Modern—20th cent. 2. American literature—20th cent.

PN6014.N457 808.8 52—1806

Library of Congress ₍60p8₎

M323 C38o
Optimism and frustration in the American Negro.
Charles, Charles V
Optimism and frustration in the American Negro. Reprinted from the Psychoanalytic review, 29:270-299, July, 1942.

270-299p. 24cm. (Psychogenetic studies in race psychology, no.6)

The optimist.
M811.5 H39o
Henry, Thomas Millard.
The optimist, by Thomas Millard Henry. ₍New York, Hebbons press, ©1928₎
1 p. l., v-xii, 49 p. incl. port. 16½cm.
Poems.

I. Title.

28-14449

Library of Congress PS3515.E579O7 1928
———— Copy 2.
Copyright A 1077617 ₍2₎

L'Optimiste; pièces en trois actes.
Rwanda
M896.2 N14o
Naigiziki, Joseph Saverio, 1915-
L'Optimiste; pièces en trois actes. Preface de Madame Emma Maquet. Astrida, Frères de la Charité, 1954.

58p. 21cm.

Uganda
M967.61 Op9
Opwa, Antonio
An East African Chief in England. Nairobi, The Eagle Press, 1952.

38p. illus. 21½cm.

Or uranium, cuivre, radium.
Haiti
M841 B760
Bierre, Jean Fernand, 1909-
Or uranium, cuivre, radium; poèmes. ₍Port-au-Prince₎ N. A. Théodore, 1961.

26p. 19cm. (Collection librairie indigène)

L'oracle; poème dramatique haitien.
Haiti
M841 C66o
Coicou, Massillon, 1867-
L'oracle; poème dramatique haitien. Paris, Ateliers Haitiens, 1901.

50p. 17cm.

Martinique
M972.98 P53a
An oration, pronounced on the 29th of July, 1829, after the funeral dirge of Doctor John Baptista Philip, who died on the 16th of June, 1829, in Trinidad. London, printed by C. Lawler, n.d.

30p. 20cm.
Bound with: Philip, John Baptist - An address to the Right Hon. Earl Bathurst.

1. Philip, John Baptist, d. 1829.

Oration on Charles Sumner.
MB9 Su6e
Evangeline, *pseud.*
Oration on Charles Sumner, addressed to colored people ... By Evangeline. Albany, Weed, Parsons & co., printers, 1874.
53 p. 23cm.
Illustrated cover.
Cover-title: Sumner, the friend of humanity. Oration delivered at Washington by Evangeline.
Blank verse.

1. Sumner, Charles, 1811-1874. I. Title.

19-12977

₍33b1₎

Library of Congress E415.9.S9E9

Orations.
MB9 B79a
Brooks, Walter Henderson, 1851-
Address by Rev. Walter H. Brooks delivered at a luncheon given in his honor by Dr. Henry Goddard, research editor of the Forum, at the Hotel Ambassador, New York, April 23, 1935.
9 unnumb. p. photos. 23cm.

Orations.
M815.4 D74an
Douglass, Frederick, 1817-1895.
The anti-slavery movement. A lecture by Frederick Douglass, before the Rochester ladies' anti-slavery society. Rochester ₍N. Y.₎ Press of Lee, Mann & co., 1855.
44 p. 21½cm.

1. Slavery in the U. S.—Anti-slavery movements.

11-7348

Library of Congress E449.D731

Orations
M815.4 D74co
Douglass, Frederick, 1817-1895.
The Constitution of the United States: is it pro-slavery or anti-slavery? By Frederick Douglass. A speech delivered in Glasgow, March 26, 1860, in reply to an attack made upon his view by Mr. George Thompson. ₍Halifax, T. and W. Birtwhistle, printers, 1860?₎
16 p. 18½cm.
Caption title.
From the Glasgow daily mail.

1. U. S. Constitution. 2. Slavery in the U. S. 3. Thompson, George, 1804-1878.

A 17-1156

Title from Harvard Univ. Printed by L. C.

Orations.

M815.4
D74e

Douglass, Frederick, 1817-1895.
Eulogy of the late Hon. Wm. Jay, by Frederick Douglass, delivered on the invitation of the colored citizens of New York city in Shiloh Presbyterian church, New York, May 12, 1859. Rochester, Press of A. Strong & co., 1859.
32 p. 23cm.

1. Jay, William, 1789-1858. I. New York (City) Colored citizens. II. New York (City) Shiloh Presbyterian church.

A 17-1157

Title from Harvard Univ. Printed by L. C.

Orations.

MB9
B813d

Douglass, Frederick, 1817-1895.
John Brown. An address by Frederick Douglass, at the fourteenth anniversary of Storer college, Harper's Ferry, West Virginia, May 30, 1881. Dover, N. H., Morning star job printing house, 1881.
28 p. 20½cm.
Presented by the author to Storer college, the proceeds to go to the endowment of a John Brown professorship.

1. Brown, John, 1800-1859.

7-12896

Library of Congress E451.D18
——— Copy 2. [a41b1]

Orations.

M815.4
D74o

Douglass, Frederick, 1817-1895.
Oration, delivered in Corinthian hall, Rochester, by Frederick Douglass, July 5th, 1852 ... Rochester, Printed by Lee, Mann & co., 1852.
39 p. 22½cm.

1. Slavery in the U. S.—Controversial literature—1852. 2. Fourth of July orations.

16-25947

Library of Congress E449.D7526

Orations.

M815.4
D74a

Douglass, Frederick, 1817-1895.
Proceedings of the civil rights mass meeting held at Lincoln hall, October 22, 1883. Speeches held at Lincoln hall, October 22, 1883. Speeches of Hon. Frederick Douglass and Robert G. Ingersoll. Washington, D.C., C.P. Farrell, 1883.
53p. 23cm.

Orations.

M815.4
D74r

Douglass, Frederick, 1817-1895.
Report of the proceedings of the great anti-slavery meeting held in the Rev. Mr. Cairns's church on Wednesday, 23d September, 1846, including the speeches of Wm. Lloyd Garrison and Frederick Douglass. Taken in short hand by Cincinnatus. n.p., Alex. Gardner, printer, 1846
16p. 17½cm.

Orations.

M815.4
D47tw

Douglass, Frederick, 1817-1895.
Two speeches by Frederick Douglass; one on West India emancipation, delivered at Canandaigua, Aug. 4th, and the other on the Dred Scott decision, delivered in New York, on the occasion of the anniversary of the American abolition society, May 1857. Rochester, N. Y., C. P. Dewey, printer [1857]
46 p. 22cm.
The speeches are paged continuously.
The second speech has a half-title which reads: "The Dred Scott decision; speech delivered in part, at the anniversary of the American abolition society, held in New York, May 14th, 1857."

1. Slavery in the U. S.—Emancipation. 2. Scott, Dred. I. American abolition society.

A 17-1159

Title from Harvard Univ. Printed by L. C.

Orations.

M815.2
J71t

Jones, Absalom, 1746-1818.
A Thanksgiving sermon, preached January 1, 1808, in St. Thomas's or the African Episcopal Church, Philadelphia; an account of the abolition of the African slave trade on that day by the congress of the United States... Philadelphia, Printed for the use of the congregation, Fry and Kammerer, printers, 1808.
22 [2]p. 21½cm.

Orations.

M814.5
M78p

Moore, S Benjamin editor.
..."Poor Ben's choice pebbles, edited by S. Benj. Moore...Durham, N.C., The Moore Print, 1908.
28p. port. 20½cm.

Orations.

M815.5
M83d

Morse, Leonard F
The dawn of tomorrow, by Rev. Leonard F. Morse... Delivered at Emancipation Celebration, Yorktown Baptist church, Plateau, Alabama, Monday evening, January 1, 1923
27p. plate. 16½cm.

Orations.

M815.4
N16d

Napier, James C
Discussion of national questions, by Hon, J.C. Napier... Decide views on financial matters and operation of Dingley law. The Spanish-American war and its results... Nashville, Tenn. National Baptist publishing board, 1898.
21p. port. 22cm.

Orations.

M815.4
P55s

Pinchback, Pinckney Benton Stewart, 1837-1923.
Remarks of Hon. P.B.S. Pinchback of Louisiana in the House of representatives, Monday June 8th, 1874 on his right to a seat as representative at large from the state of Louisiana, as against the claim of Hon. George E. Sheridan.
15p. 21½cm.
Bound with: Speech... on the election bill.

Orations.

M815.4
P65s

Pinchback, Pinckney Benton Stewart, 1837-1923.
Speech of Hon. P.B.S. Pinchback on the election bill delivered in the Louisiana state senate, Friday, January 21st, 1870. New Orleans, New Orleans standard print, 1870.
8p. 22cm.

Orations.

M815.5
R17s

Ransome, Reverdy Cassius, 1861-
The spirit of freedom and justice; orations and speeches, by Reverdy C. Ransom. Nashville, Tenn., A.M.E. Sunday School Union, 1926.
175p. portraits, 23cm.

Orations.

M815.5
W154c

Walker, William.
Walker's complete book of welcome address and response for all occasion... Chicago, Ill., The author, c 1944.
31p. port. 21cm.

Orations.

MB9
W52

Wilson, John R.
Life and speeches of Ransom W. Westberry, by Prof. John R, Wilson... Atlanta, Ga., A.B. Caldwell publishing company, 1921.
130p. illus. 23cm.

Orations.

M973
W86 ne

Woodson, Carter Godwin, 1875- *ed.*
Negro orators and their orations, by Carter G. Woodson ... Washington, D. C., The Associated publishers, inc. [°1925]
xi p., 1 l., 711 p. 22½cm.

1. Orations. I. Title.

25-20484

Library of Congress PS663.N4W6
[45h1]

Oratory.

M808.5
B64s

Bond, Frederick Weldon.
Speech construction, by Frederick W. Bond ... Boston, The Christopher publishing house [°1936]
2 p. l., 7-146 p. 20½cm.
Bibliography: p. 141-146.

1. Speech. 2. Elocution. 3. Oratory. I. Title.

36-10026

Library of Congress PN4121.B53
[37c1] 808.5

Orchidees.

Haiti
M841
M66

Minuty, Julien V
Orchidees, poèmes. Port-au-Prince, Imp. de l'État, 1953.
9-49p. (port) 18cm. (Collection du sesquicentenaire de l'indépendance d'Haiti)

M326.5
Orla

Orcutt, John, 1807-1879.
African colonization. [New York city, American colonization society, 1868]
3 unnumb. p. 20½cm.
White author?

1. American colonization society. I. Title.

The ordeal of Mansart.

M301
D853o

Du Bois, William Edward Burghardt, 1868-
The ordeal of Mansart. New York, Mainstream Publishers, 1957.
316 p. 22 cm. (*His* The black flame, a trilogy, book 1)

I. Title.

PZ3.D8525Or 57-13796 ‡

Library of Congress [8]

Order of the eastern star (Colored)

M366
B81h

Brown, Sue M (Wilson) *"Mrs. S. Joe Brown,"* **1877-**
The history of the Order of the eastern star among colored people, by Mrs. S. Joe Brown ... Des Moines, Ia. [The Bystander press] 1925.
3 p. l., [13]-88 p., 1 l. front., plates, ports. 18½cm.

1. Order of the eastern star (Colored) 2. Negroes—Societies.

25-10755

Library of Congress HS895.E33 1925
Copyright A 830384 [2]

Nigeria
M966.9
Or27
Oredein, S T
A manual on Action Group Party Organisation. Ibadan, Action Group Headquarter, n.d.
57p. 21½cm.
1. Action Group of Nigeria. 2. Nigeria - Politics. I. Title.

The Origin of Christianity.
M230
V44
Vassall, William F
The origin of Christianity; a brief study of the world's early beliefs and their influence on the early Christian church, including an examination of the lost books of the Bible. [1st ed.] New York, Exposition Press [1952]
183 p. 21 cm.
1. Religions—Hist. 2. Christianity—Origin. 3. Bible. N. T. Apocryphal books—Criticism, interpretation, etc. I. Title.
BL80.V27 290 52-10685 ‡
Library of Congress [3]

Nigeria
M966.9
D56o
Origins of the Niger Mission, 1841-1891.
Dike, Kenneth Onwuka, 1917-
Origins of the Niger Mission, 1841-1891; a paper read at the centenary of the Mission at Christ Church, Onitsha, on 13 November 1957. Ibadan, Ibadan University Press, 1957.
21p. 22cm.
Bibliography: p. 21

Nigeria
M966.9
Or3
Oresanya, A O Compiler.
An outline of the system of administration in Nigeria; being excerpts from the Nigeria handbook and other publications, compiled by A. O. Oresanya. 6th ed. Lagos, The Ife-Olu Printing Works, 1942.
45p. 18½cm.
1. Nigeria-Pol. & Govt. 2. Africa, West

Africa
M398
B396
The origin of life and death.
Beier, Ulli, *ed.*
The origin of life and death: African creation myths. London, Ibadan [etc.] Heinemann, 1966.
x, 65 p. 18½ cm. (African writers series, 23) 5/-
(B 66-17612)
1. Creation. 2. Tales, African. I. Title.
GR355.B4 398.36 66-77882
Library of Congress [3]

Haiti
M398
Or1
Oriol, Jacques
Le mouvement folklorique en Haiti; intro. de MM. Lorimer Denis et Francois Duvalier. Port-au-Prince, Imp. de l'Etat, 1952.
115p. 19 cm.
1. Haiti - Folklore.

Nigeria
M336.2
Or14
Orewa, G Oka.
Taxation in Western Nigeria; the problems of an emergent state. [London] Published for the Nigerian Institute of Social and Economic Research [by] Oxford University Press, 1962.
xvii, 169 p. fold. map, tables. 19 cm. (Nigerian social and economic studies, no. 4)
Bibliography: p. [165]-166.
1. Taxation—Western Nigeria. (Series) 2. Nigeria - Taxation. 3. Income tax - Nigeria. 4. Finance, Public - Nigeria.
HJ3069.W4O7 336.209669 62-6142
Library of Congress [5]

The origin of the black man.
M973.2
T97
Tyndall, John William, 1877-
The origin of the black man, by John W. Tyndall ... St. Louis, Mich., Metropolitan correspondence Bible college [°1927]
3 p. l., 114, [1] p. 19cm.
1. Negro race. I. Title.
27-15666
Library of Congress HT1589.T8
[2]

Africa
M960
M22a
Orizu, A A Nwafor.
History of the Union of South Africa.
(In: MacLean, Joan Coyne, ed. Africa: the racial issue. New York, Wilson, 1954. 20cm. pp. 91-98.)

Organizations.
M367
D27t
Davis, Elizabeth Lindsey
The story of the Illinois Federation of Colored Women's Clubs, 1900-1922.
137p. ports. 22cm.

Original handbook of Harlem jive.
M427.9
B92o
Burley, Dan.
Dan Burley's Original handbook of Harlem jive; illustrations by Melvin Tapley. New York, N. Y., °1944.
158 p., 1 l. illus. 19½cm.
1. English language—Slang. 2. Americanisms. I. Title: Original handbook of Harlem jive. II. Title: Harlem jive.
45-15088
Library of Congress PE3711.B8
[3] 427.9

Nigeria
M966.9
Or1w
Orizu, Akweke Abyssinia Nwafor, 1920-
Without bitterness; western nations in post-war Africa, by A. A. Nwafor Orizu. New York, N. Y., Creative age press, inc. [1944]
xiv, 395 p. 21cm.
1. Africa—Civilization. 2. Africa—Native races. 3. Nigeria—Soc. condit. 4. Reconstruction (1939-)—Africa. I. Title.
44-7985
Library of Congress DT14.O7
[46q7] 960

M806
P83o
The organized educ. activities of lit. soc.
Porter, Dorothy Burnett, 1905-
The organized educational activities of Negro literary societies, 1828-1846.
Reprinted from the Journal of Negro education, October, 1936.
555-576p. 25cm.

M813.5
R46o
Original sin.
Rimanelli, Giose, 1926-
Original sin. Translated from the Italian by Ben Johnson. New York, Random House [1957]
179 p. 21 cm.
A novel.
I. Title.
PZ3.R4568Or 57-5376 ‡
Library of Congress [5]

Brazil
M869.
L621
Orpheus' invention.
Lima, Jorge de, 1893-1953
Invenção de orfeu. Rio de Janeiro, Livros de Portugal, 1952.
xx, 431 p. 19cm.
[First edition]

Guadeloupe
M325
Is20
L'Orientation de la politique coloniale...
Isaac, Al
L'Orientation de la politique coloniale et le ministere des colonies. Paris, Revue politique et parlementaire, Octobre 1894.
32p. 25cm.

Haiti
M972.94
B64
Les origines et les lecons d'une revolution...
Bonhomme, Colbert.
Les origines et les leçons d'une révolution profonde et pacifique, par Colbert Bonhomme ... préface de m. Samuel Devieux ... Port-au-Prince, Haïti, Imprimerie de l'état, 1946.
xvi, 74 p., 1 l. illus. (ports.) 22cm.
1. Haiti—Pol. & govt.—1844- 2. Haiti—Soc. condit. 3. Lescot, Élie, pres. Haiti, 1883- I. Title.
F1926.B7 972.94 47-24684
Library of Congress [1]

Ecuador
M863.6
Or8c
Ortiz, Adalberto, 1914-
Los contrabandistas, viñotos del autor. Mexico, Coleccion "Lunes", 1945.
35p. illus. 21cm.
I. Title.

Africa
M896
C771
Origin East Africa; a Makerere anthology.
Cook, David, *ed.*
Origin East Africa; a Makerere anthology. London, Heinemann Educational Books [1965]
xii, 188 p. 19 cm. (African writers series, 15)
1. African literature—Translations into English. 2. English literature—Translations from African. I. Title.
PL8013.E5C6 896 66-83082
Library of Congress [2]

Haiti
M840.9
T75
Les origines sociales de la litterature Haitienne.
Trouillot, Henock
Les origines sociales de la litterature Haitienne. Port-au-Prince, Imprimerie N. A. Theodore, 1962.
376p. 23½cm.
Special number, Revue de la societe Haitienne d'histoire de geographie et de geologie. January-July, 1962, v. 32, no. 109.

Ecuador
M863.6
Or8j
Ortiz, Adalberto.
... Juyungo, historia de un negro, una isla y otros negros ... Buenos Aires, Editorial Americalee [1943]
3 p. l., 9-268 p., 1 l. 21cm.
"Primer premio del Concurso nacional ecuatoriano de novelas de 1942."
I. Title. 1. Ecuadorian literature.
45-12333
Library of Congress PQ8219.O7J8
[2] 863.6

Ecuador
M863.6 Ortiz, Adalberto, 1914-
Or8m La mala espalda, once relatos de aquí y de allí; ilustraciones de Enrique Tábara, Diógenes Paredes y de Albistur. la edición. Guayaquil, Ecuador, La Casa de la Cultura Ecuatoriana, 1952.

161p. 20cm.

I. Title.

Ghana
M960 Osei, Gabriel K.
Os2af The African: his antecedents, his genuis, and his destiny. London, African Publication Society, 1967.

210p. port. 22cm.

1. Africa. I. Title.

Othello's countrymen.

Sierra Leone
M822.09 Jones, Eldred.
J714 Othello's countrymen; the African in English Renaissance drama. London, Published on behalf of Fourah Bay College, the University College of Sierra Leone [by] Oxford University Press, 1965.

ix, 158 p. illus., facsims., map. 23 cm.

Bibliography: p. [150]-152.
Portrait of author on book jacket.

1. English drama—Early modern and Elizabethan—Hist. & crit. 2. Africa in literature. I. Freetown, Sierra Leone. Fourah Bay College. II. Title.

PR658.A4J6 822.09003 65-5002

Library of Congress [3]

Ecuador
M863.6 Ortiz, Adalberto.
Or8t ... Tierra, son y tambor; cantares negros y mulatos. Prólogo de Joaquín Gallegos Lara y 28 grabados originales de Galo Galecio. México, D. F., Ediciones La Cigarra, 1945.

2 p. l., [7]-81 p., 2 l. illus. 23cm.

Without music.

1. Negroes—Poetry. 2. Negro songs. I. Title. 3. Ecuadorian literature.

46-18308

Library of Congress PQ8219.O7T5

[2] 861.6

Ghana
M960 Osei, Gabriel K
Os2 Fifty unknown facts about the African; with complete proof. London, The Author, 1962.

12p. 21cm.

1. Africa - History. I. Title.

Other leopards.

British Guiana
M823.91 Williams, Denis, 1923-
W67o Other leopards. [London, New Authors Limited, 1963]

221p. 21½ cm.

Portrait of author on book jacket.

1. Title.

Orton, Joseph.

M326.99B Strickland, S
St8n Negro slavery described by a Negro: being the narrative of Ashton Warner, a native of St. Vincent's. With an appendix containing... recently returned from the colonies on the system of slavery as it now exists. By S. Strickland... London, Samuel Maunder, 1831.

W24s

144p. 15½cm.

Ghana
MB Osei, Gabriel K
Os22 The forgotten great Africans, 3000 B.C. to 1959 A.D. London, G. K. Osei, 1965.

80p. port. 20cm.
Portrait of author on book cover.

1. Biography. I. Title.

The other phase of reconstruction.

M973.8 Langston, John Mercer, 1829-1897.
L26o The other phase of reconstruction. Speech of Hon. John Mercer Langston, delivered at Congregational tabernacle, Jersey City, New Jersey, April 17, 1877. Peaceful reconstruction possible ... Washington, D. C., Gibson brothers, printers, 1877.

16 p. 23½cm.

1. Reconstruction.

18-5993

Library of Congress E668.L28

M326.99B Orton, Joseph.
W24s Strickland, S.
Negro slavery described by a Negro: being the narrative of Ashton Warner, a native of St. Vincent's. With an appendix containing the testimony of four Christian ministers recently returned from the colonies on the system of slavery as it now exists. By S. Strickland... London, Samuel Maunder, 1831.

144p. 15½cm.

Ghana
M960 Osei, Gabriel K
Os2j A journey into the African past. London, The Author, 1964.

16p. 21cm.

1. Africa - History. I. Title.

The other side of hell.

M811.5 McCullough, Norman Verrle, 1925-
M13o The other side of hell; a tragedy in verse. New York, Exposition Press [1952]

62 p. 22 cm.

I. Title.

PS3525.A17964O7 811.5 51-13282 rev

Library of Congress [r52b1]

Oruhenda; obukama bwa toro.

Uganda
M967.61 Nyabongo, Akiki K 1905-
N98 Oruhenda; obukama bwa toro [Dialect of the palace] [Kampala, The Author, n.d.]

75p. illus., ports. 31cm.
Written in Luganda.

I. Title.

Ghana
M966.7 Osei, Gabriel K
Os22 The spirit and structure of Nkrumah's Convention People's Party. [London, G. K. Osei, 1962]

48p. 21½cm.

1. Ghana. 2. Convention People's Party. I. Title.

The other side of the wall.

M812.5 Amis, Lola (James)
Am57 3 plays: The other side of the wall, The place of wrath, Helen. New York, Exposition Press [1965]

88p. 21cm.

I. Title: The other side of the wall. II. Title: The place of wrath. III. Title: Helen.

Os brunzundangas; sátira.

Brazil
M869.3 Lima Barreto, Afonso Henrique de, 1881-1922.
L62br Os brunzundangas; sátira. São Paulo, Editôra Brasiliense, 1956.

308p. illus. 21cm.

I. Title.

Kenya
M967.62 Osogo, John.
Os5 A history of the Baluyia. Nairobi, New York, Oxford University Press, 1966.

162 p. maps, group port. 22 cm.
Bibliography: p. 145.

1. Kavirondo (African people) I. Title. 2. Baluyia. 3. Kenya. 4. Africa, East.

DT429.O83 572.8'963 67-1231

Library of Congress [3]

Kenya
M967.62 Otiende, Joseph Daniel, 1917-
Ot2 Habari za Abaluyia [The Abaluyia of Nyanza Province, Kenya] Nairobi, Eagle Press, 1949.

51p. illus. 18½cm. (Desturi na masimulizi ya Afrika ya Mashariki. Custom and tradition in East Africa series)
Written in Swahili.

1. Kenya - Native races. I. Title. II. II. Series. III. Series: Custom and tradition in East Africa series)

Nigeria
M896.1 Osadebay, Dennis Chukude, 1911-1964
Os1 Africa sings, by Dennis Chukude Osadebay. Ilfracombe, Arthur H. Stockwell, 1952.

104 p. 19 cm.

1. African poetry. I. Title.

Othello.

M815.5 Bruce, John Edward, 1856-
B83 Was Othello a Negro? By John E. Bruce.
No.3 New York, 1920.

15p. 15cm.

Otieno Jarieko, kitabu mar ariyo.

Kenya
M630 Obama, Barack H
Ob1 Otieno Jarieko, kitabu mar ariyo - yore mabeyo mag puro puothe; ma eni en kitabu maluwo kitabu mokuongo e somoni - Yore Mabeyo Mag Rito Ngima. [Otieno, the wise man: a series of readers to follow the Luo Adult Literacy Primer. Book 2. Wise ways of farming] [Illus. by William Agutu] Nairobi, Eagle Press, 1959.

40p. illus. 24cm.
Written in Luo.

1. Agriculture - Kenya. I. Title. II. Agutu William, illus.

Uganda
MB9
Ag38m
Otim, E. Y. A., tr.
Musson, M
Aggrey loka Achimota [Aggrey of Achimota] Loejuli E. Y. A. Otim. Nairobi, Eagle Press, 1951.
42p. 21cm.
Written in Ateso
White author.
1. Aggrey, James Emman Kwegyir, 1875-1927. I. Otim, E. Y. A., tr. II. Title.

Uganda
M630
St1
Otim, Lakana, tr.
Staples, E G
Pwonye me pur [Lectures in elementary agriculture. Translated by Lakana Otim and T. L. Lawrence. Rev. by Tomasi Otim and others] Nairobi, Eagle Press, 1949.
25p. 18½cm.
Written in Acoli.
White author.
1. Agriculture. I. Title. II. Otim, Lakana, tr.

M808.8
N42
v.15
Otoo, Samuel Kofi.
Fisherman's day, pp. 198-204.
New world writing. 1st- Apr. 1952- [New York] New American Library.
v. 18 cm. (N. A. L. Mentor books)
1. Literature, Modern—20th cent. 2. American literature—20th cent.
PN6014.N457 808.8 52—1806
Library of Congress [54j5]

Tobago
M972.98
Ot5a
Ottley, Carlton Robert, 1914-
An account of the life in Spanish Trinidad (from 1498-1797) with a chronological table of events and sundry appendices. Trinidad, Printed by the college press, 1955.
135p. illus. 21cm.
1. Trinidad.

Tobago
M352.2
Ot5
Ottley, Carlton Robert
A historical account of the Trinidad and Tobago police force from the earliest times. Trinidad, The Author, 1964.
152p. illus., port. 18½cm.
1. Police - Trinidad and Tobago. 2. Trinidad and Tobago. I. Title.

Tobago
M972.98
Ot5L
Ottley, Carlton Robert, 1914-
Legends, true stories and old sayings from Trinidad and Tobago, collected and told by C. R. Ottley. Port-of-Spain, College Press, 1962.
71p. 20cm.
1. Trinidad and Tobago. 2. Folklore - Trinidad. 3. Folklore - West Indies. 4. Tales, West Indies. I. Title.

Tobago
M972.98
Ot5to
Ottley, Carlton Robert, 1914-
Tobago legends and West Indian lore. [Trinidad, 1950]
137p. illus. 19cm.
1. Tobago, Island of. 2. West Indies-Folklore.

Tobago
M972.98
Ot5tr
Ottley, Carlton Robert, 1914-
Trinidad; land of the calypso, steelband, humming bird, pitch lake, and the Caadura. Tobago, Robinson Crusoe's Isle. Port-of-Spain, Trinidad, 1954.
36p. illus. 21½cm.
1. Trinidad. 2. Tobago, Island of.

M973
Ot8
1949
Ottley, Roi, 1906-1960
Black odyssey, the story of the Negro in America. London, John Murray, 1949.
viii, 340p. 22cm.
I. Title

M973
Ot8
Ottley, Roi, 1906-1960
Black odyssey, the story of the Negro in America. New York, C. Scribner's Sons, 1948.
viii, 340 p. 22 cm.
Bibliography: p. 315-322.
1. Negroes—History. I. Title. *Full name:* Roi Vincent Ottley.
E185.O85 325.260973 48-9099*
Library of Congress [40]

M973
Ot81
Ottley, Roi, 1906-1960
Die schwarze odyssee. (Black Odyssey). Die geschichte der Neger in Amerika. Hamburg, Europäische Verlagsanstalt Gmbh., 1949.
308p. 19½cm.
Portrait of author on book jacket.
I. Title.

M323.3
L33
Ottley, Roi, 1906-1960
Five million white Negroes.
Pp. 189-194.
In: Larsson, Cloyte, ed. Marriage across the Color line. Chicago, Johnson Pub. Co., 1965.

M973
Ot81
Ottley, Roi, 1906-1960
Inside black America. London, Eyre & Spottiswoode, [1948].
280p. 22cm.
I. Title

MB9
Ab2
Ottley, Roi, 1906-1960
The lonely warrior: the life and times of Robert S. Abbott. Chicago, H. Regnery Co., 1955.
381 p. illus. 22 cm.
Includes bibliographies.
1. Abbott, Robert Sengstacke, 1868-1940. 2. The Chicago defender. 3. Negroes. I. Title. *Full name:* Roi Vincent Ottley.
PN4874.A23O7 920.5 55—8734 ‡
Library of Congress [55h7]

M812.08
B26r
Ottley, Roi, 1906-1960
The Negro domestic.
(In: Barnouw, Erik, ed. Radio drama in action;... N.Y., Farrar & Rinehart, 1945. 21cm. p. 353-368.)

M792
B26r
Ottley, Roi, 1906-1960
The Negro domestic (radio script)
(In: Barnouw, Erik. Radio drama in action... New York, Farrar & Rinehart, Inc. [1945] 21cm. pp.354-68)

M792
B26r
Ottley, Roi, 1906-1960
The Negro domestic. (radio script)
(In: Barnouw, Erik. Radio drama in action... New York, Farrar & Rinehart, Inc. [1945] 21cm. pp.354-68)

M974.71
Ot8
Ottley, Roi, 1906-1960
'New world a-coming'; inside black America, by Roi Ottley ... Boston, Houghton Mifflin company, 1943.
vi, [2], 364 p. incl. front., illus. 21½cm. (Life-in-America prize book[s])
Illustrated lining-papers in colors.
Bibliography: p. [349]-354.
1. Negroes—New York (City) 2. Harlem, New York (City) I. Title.
Library of Congress F128.9.N3O75 43-11506
[20] 325.2609747

M323
Ot5n2
Ottley, Roi, 1906-1960
No green pastures. ~~New York, Scribner, 1951.~~ London, J. Murray [1952]
ix, 234 p. 22 cm.
Bibliography: p. 221-229.
1. Negroes in Europe. I. Title.
Full name: Roi Vincent Ottley.
HT1581.O8 323.1 51-7318
Library of Congress [15]

M323.
Ot5n
Ottley, Roi, 1906-1960
No green pastures. New York, Scribner, 1951.
ix, 234 p. 22 cm.
Bibliography: p. 221-229.
1. Negroes in Europe. I. Title. *Full name:* Roi Vincent Ottley.
HT1581.O8 323.1 51—7318
Library of Congress [a52q15]

M810.8
M77p
Ottley, Roi, 1906-1960
Report from England.
(In: Moon, Bucklin, ed. Primer for white folks. Garden City, N. Y. Doubleday, Doran, 1945. 21½cm. pp. 395-403).

M813.5
Ot8
Ottley, Rol, 1906-1960
White marble lady. New York, Farrar, Straus and Giroux [1965]
278 p. 22 cm.
I. Title.
PZ4.O804Wh 65-13727
Library of Congress [8]

Mali
M966.2
Ouli
Ouane, Ibrahima Mamadou, 1908-
L'Islam et la civilisation Française. Préface de Marguerite et Gabriel Schoell-Langlois. Paris, Les Presses Universelles, 1957.
44p. port. 19cm.
I. Title.

S. Africa
M896.2
Ou5i
Ouless, E U
Iziganeko zom-Kristu-uhambo lo mbambizenziwe undlalo, ngu E. U. Ouless. Lovedale, Lovedale Institution Press, 1928.
35p. 18½cm.
A play founded on Bunyon's Pilgrim's Progress.
1. Africa, South-literature. 2. Xhosa language. 3. Africa, South - Drama.

Ou en sommes-nous avec l'elite intellectuelle d'Haiti.
Haiti
M972.94
L96oe
Lubin, Maurice A
Ou en sommes-nous avec l'elite intellectuelle d'Haiti.
Pp. 121-31 23cm.
Reprinted from Journal of Inter-American Studies, Vol. 3, No. 1, January 1961.

Mali
M966.2
OuiL
Ouane, Ibrahima Mamadou, 1908-
Lettre d'un Africain. Monte-Carlo, Regain, 1958.
61p. port. 18½cm.
1. Title.

M896.2
Ou5i
Ouless, E U.
Iziganeko zom-Kristu-uhambo lo mbambizenziwe undlalo, ngu E. U. Ouless. Lovedale, Lovedale Institution press, 1928.
35p. 18½cm.
A play founded on Bunyan's Pilgrim's Progress
1. Africa, South - literature. 2. Xhosa language. 3. Africa, South - Drama.

Ouagadougou, Ivory Coast.
Upper Volta
M966.68
T44
Tiendrebéogo, Yamba, 1907-
Histoire et coutumes royales des Mossi de Ouagadougou; rédaction et annotations de Robert Pageard. Ouagadougou, Chez le Larhallé Naba, 1964.
208p. ports. 20cm.
1. Ivory Coast - Social life and customs. 2. Ivory Coast - History. 3. Ouagadougou, Ivory Coast. I. Title.

Mali
M966.2
Oulp
Ouane, Ibrahima Mamadou, 1908-
La pratique du droit Musulman. Loire, Société d'exploitation imprimerie moderne a Andrezieux, 1958.
43p. port. 18cm.
1. Title.

Oumo, K. Y. S., tr.
Uganda
M896.3
H44m
Hertslet, Jessie
Mpala, awaragan naka esapat loka Afrika [Mpala, the story of an African boy] [Nuejuli K. Y. S. Oumo] Nairobi, Eagle Press, 1951.
81p. 18cm.
Written in Ateso
White author.
I. Title. II. Oumo, K. Y. S., tr.

Mali
M966.2
Oulc
Ouane, Ibrahima Mamadou, 1908-
Le collier de coquillages. Loire, Société d'exploitation imprimerie moderne a Andrézieux, 1958.
70p. port. 18½cm.
I. Title.

Mali
M966.2
Oul
Ouane, Ibrahima Mamadou, 1908-
Le principe du droit Musulman. Paris, Les Presses Universelles, 1957.
91p. port. 19cm.
1. Title.

Our Baptist ministers and schools.
MB
P34o
Pegues, Albert Witherspoon.
Our Baptist ministers and schools. By A. W. Pegues... with an introduction by C. L. Purce... illustrated. [Springfield, Mass., Springfield printing and binding co., 1892.
622, 18p. plates. 20½cm.

Mali
M966.2
Oule
Ouane, Ibrahima Mamadou, 1908-
L'énigme du Macina. Préface de Maurice Kaouza. Monte-Carlo, Regain, 1952.
187p. 19½cm.
1. Africa, French West - History. 2. Sudan, French. 3. Macina. I. Title.

Oubangui - Chari languages - dictionary.
M496
Eb71
Éboué, Adolphe Felix Sylvestre, 1884-1944.
... Langues Sango, Banda, Baya, Mandjia. Notes grammaticales. Mots groupés d'après le sens. Phrases usuelles. Vocabulaire, par A. F. Éboué. Preface de M. Gaudefroy-Demombynes. Paris, Emile Larose, 1918.
iii, 109p. 19 x 11cm.

Our Bill of rights.
M342
R15
Randolph, Asa Philip, 1889-
Chart and compass.
(In: Wise, James W. Our Bill of rights; what it means to me, ... New York, Bill of Rights Sesqui-centennial Committee, 1941. pp. 112-113.)

Mali
M966.2
Oulf
Ouane, Ibrahima Mamadou, 1908-
Fädimätä; la princesse du désert; suivi du drame de Déguerbéré. Paris, Les Presses Universelles, 1955.
107p. port. 18½cm.
I. Title.

Les oubliés de chez nous.
Haiti
M972.94
V59o
Vernet, E Louis.
... Les oubliés de chez nous, question hygiéno-sociale, par E. Louis Vernet ... [Port-au-Prince!] Imprimerie A. P. Barthélemy [1945!]
6 p. l., [12]-48 p., 1 l. 20½cm. (Bibliothèque haitienne)
1. Leprosy—Haiti. I. Title.
RC154.55.H3V4 614.546 Med 47-1314 rev
Library of Congress [r47c2]

M304
P19
v.7
no.18
Our colored missions, vol. 17, no.11. New York City, The Catholic board for mission work among the colored people, November, 1931.
162-176p. 25½cm.
1. Missions-Catholic
2. Lewis, Edmonia, 1845-
I. DuBois, W.E.B. [Statement by p. 163-64.]

Mali
M960
Ou1
Ouane, Ibrahima Mamadou, 1908-
Les filles de la reine Cléopatre. Paris, Les Paragraphies Littéraires de Paris [1961]
188p. 19cm.
1. Colonies - Africa. 2. Africa - History. I. Title.

Oui ...c'est moi...pardon! ...
Guadeloupe
M843.91
G65o
Goram, Abel
Oui...c'est moi... pardon! ...
Paris, Jean D'Halluin, Éditeur, 1961.
157p. 19cm. (Collection Alternance)

Our fourth anniversary.
Trinidad
M329
W67o
Williams, Eric Eustace, 1911-
Our fourth anniversary, the last lap; political leader's address on September 24, 1960, at the University of Woodford Square, marking the fourth year of P.N.M.'s first term of office. [Port-of-Spain, P.N.M. Publishing Co., 1960]
15p. 21cm.
Portrait on cover.
1. People's National Movement. 2. Trinidad - Political parties. 3. Political parties - Trinidad. I. Title.

Our great Americans.
MB Martin, Fletcher , ed.
M39o Our great Americans, the Negro contribution to American progress; compiled and edited by Fletcher Martin. Chicago, 1953.

96p. 28cm.

Nigeria Our regiment. Lagos, Public Relations
M966.9 Department, n.d. Crownbird Series, No. 29,
Ou7r Special.

32p. illus. 20½cm.

1. Nigeria army.

Sénégal
M896.3 Ousmane, Sembene, 1923-
Ou8p Ô pays, mon beau peuple; roman. Paris, Le Livre contemporain [1957]

234 p. 19 cm.

I. Title.

Illinois. Univ. Library for Library of Congress [8] A 58-6146

Our homeland.
Togoland
M966.81 Chapman, D A
C35o Our homeland; a regional geography. With 22 maps. Achimota, Achimota Press, 1943.

124p. maps. 20cm.
Book I-South-East Gold Coast.

M910 Ourika.
C77m Cook, Mercer, 1903- ed.
Madame de Duras' Ourika, followed by Delphine Gay's poem Ourika. Edited with a foreword, notes and vocabulary by Mercer Cook and Guichard Parris. Atlanta, Atlanta University, 1936.

49 p. 28 cm. (Atlanta University french series).

Senegal
M896.3 Ousane, Sembene.
Ou8v Voltaique; nouvelles. [Paris] Présence Africaine [1962]

204p. 20cm.

I. Title.

Our inheritance.
M323. Withers, Zachary.
W77 Our inheritance, by Z. Withers ... Oakland, Cal., Tribune publishing co. print, 1909.

104 p. front. (port.) 18½cm.

"This essay ... argues for the rights of my [the negro] people before an unbiased and just American public."

1. Negroes. I. Title.

Library of Congress E185.6.W82 9-17565
Copyright A 242779 [34b1]

Un ours pour le F. B. I.
M813.5 Van Peebles, Melvin
V34o Un ours pour le F. B. I. Traduit de l'americain par Paule Truffert. Paris, Buchet/Chastel [1964]

190p. 19½cm.

I. Title.

Ousmane, Sembène, 1923-
Congo
Léopoldville
MB9 Europe; revue mensuelle.
L97e Patrice Lumumba. [Paris] 1962.

173p. 21½cm.

Our Lady's choir.
M811.08 Braithwaite, William Stanley Beaumont, 1878- ed.
B73o Our Lady's choir, a contemporary anthology of verse by Catholic sisters, edited by William Stanley Braithwaite; with a foreword by the Rev. Hugh Francis Blunt and an introduction by Ralph Adams Cram, LITT. D. Boston, B. Humphries, inc., 1931.

xxx, 213, [1] p. 21cm.

2575 copies printed. One of 2000 numbered copies on Hamilton's mellow book.

1. American literature—Catholic authors. 2. American poetry—20th cent. I. Title.

Library of Congress PS591.C3B7 32—26225
[44i1] 811.508

Sénégal
M896.3 Ousmane, Sembene, 1923-
Ou8b Les bouts de bois de Dieu; Banty Mam Yall. Marseille, Le Livre Contemporain, 1960.

380p. 21cm.
Portrait of author on front of book jacket.

1. Sénégal-Fiction. I. Title.

Ousmane Socé, Diop
see
Diop, Ousmane Socé, 1911-

Our Nig.
MB9 Wilson, H E
W69 Our Nig; or, sketches from the life of a free black in a two story white house, north. Showing that slavery's shadows fall even there ... By "Our Nig." Boston, Geo. C. Rand, 1859.

140p. 21cm.

Sénégal
M896.3 Ousmane, Sembène, 1923-
Ou8d Le docker noir [roman] Paris, Nouvelles Editions Debresse, 1956.

221p. [port. on cover] 19½cm.

I. Title.

Out of Bondage.
Puerto Rico
M364 Schomburg, Arthur Alfonso, 1874-
Sch6f Foreword.

(In: Robinson, Rowland Evans. Out of bondage and other stories; foreword by Arthur Schomburg,... Rutland, Vt., C.E. Tuttle company [c1936] 24cm. pp. [5]-9.)

Sierra Our people of the Sierra Leone protectrate.
Leone Gorvie, Max.
M966.4 Our people of the Sierra Leone protectorate, by Max Gorvie.
G68 London and Redhill, United society for Christian literature [1944]

64, [1] p. 18½cm. (Half-title: Africa's own library, no. 6)
"First published 1944."

1. Ethnology—Sierra Leone. I. United society for Christian literature, London. II. Title.

New York. Public library for Library of Congress [3] A 46-333

Senegal
M896.3 Ousmane, Sembene.
Ou8b2 God's bits of wood. Translated by Francis Price. [1st ed.] Garden City, N. Y., Doubleday, 1962.

333 p. 22 cm.

I. Title.

PZ4.O935Go 62-11298 ‡
Library of Congress [5]

Out of my dreams, and other verses.
M811.5 Eaton, Estelle Atley.
Ea8o Out of my dreams, and other verses. Boston, Christopher Pub. House [1959]

105 p. 21 cm.

I. Title.

PS3509.A825O8 811.54 59-8803 ‡
Library of Congress [2]

Nigeria
M966.9 Our police force. Lagos, Public Relations
Ou7p Department, nd. Crownbird series, No. 10 (Special).

28p. illus. 20½cm.

1. Nigeria-police.

Senegal
M896.3 Ousmane, Sembene, 1923-
Ou8h L'hartmattan. Paris, Présence Africaine [1964]

299p. 18½cm. (Référendum I.)

1. Senegal - Fiction. I. Title.

Out of my heart.
M811.5 Hamilton, Sarah B Edmonds
H18ot Out of my heart; poems. New York, Exposition Press, 1961.

96p. 20½cm.
Portrait of author on back of book jacket.

Out of the dark.

M812.5 Guinn, Dorothy C
G940 Out of the dark, a pageant of the Negro by Dorothy C. Guinn. New York, the Woman's press [c1924]

36p. 18½cm.

Out of the darkness.

M813.5 Grant, John Wesley, 1850–
G766o Out of the darkness; or, Diabolism and destiny. By J. W. Grant ... Nashville, Tenn., National Baptist publishing board, 1909.

1 p. l., 5–316 p. 20½cm.

I. Title.

9—15098

Library of Congress PZ3.G7658O

Copyright A 238469 [a38b1]

Out of the depths.

M811.5 Bradley, Henry T.
B720 Out of the depths, by Henry T. Bradley. New York, The Avondale press incorporated [°1928]

113, [1] p. 20cm.

Poems.

I. Title.

29-596

Library of Congress PS3503.R221O8 1928

——— Copy 2

Copyright A 3405 [2]

Out of the house of bondage.

M323.2 Miller, Kelly, 1863–1939.
M610 Out of the house of bondage, by Kelly Miller ... New York, The Neale publishing company, 1914.

242 p. 19½cm.

Reprinted from various periodicals.

CONTENTS.—Oath of Afro-American youth.—A moral axiom.—Out of the house of bondage.—The physical destiny of the American negro.—Education for manhood.—Crime among negroes.—The American negro as a political factor.—Fifty years of negro education.—Negroes in professional pursuits.—"The negro in the New world" and "The conflict of color."—The ministry.—The ultimate race problem.—I see and am satisfied.

1. Negroes. 2. U. S.—Race question. I. Title.

14—9858

Library of Congress E185.6.M633 [a43f1]

Out of wedlock.

M813.5 Henry, William S.
H39o Out of wedlock, by William S. Henry. Boston, R. G. Badger [°1931]

7, 5–220 p. 20cm.

I. Title.

32-3903

Library of Congress PZ3.H3972Ou

——— Copy 2.

Copyright A 47586 [3]

The Outsider.

M813.5 Wright, Richard, 1909–
W93rx El extraño. (The outsider). Traducción de León Mirlas. Buenos Aires, Editorial Sudamericana, 1954.

615p. 18½cm.

I. Title. II. Title: The Outsider.

The outsider.

M813.5 Wright, Richard, 1909–
W93o The outsider. New York, New American
1954 Library, 1954.

384p. 18cm. (Signet giant, S1114)
Pocket book edition.
"Complete and unabridged."

M813.5 The outsider.
W93o Wright, Richard, 1909–
The outsider. [1st ed.] New York, Harper [1953]

405 p. 22 cm.

I. Title. *Full name:* Richard Nathaniel Wright.

PZ3.W9352Ou 53-5383 ‡

Library of Congress [10]

The outsider.

M813.5 Wright, Richard, 1908–1960.
W93ou The outsider. [New York] New American Library [c1953]

384p. 18cm. (Signet Books)
Pocket book edition
"Complete and unabridged."

M323 Overcoming difficulties under adverse conditions.
M690 Mitchell, Arthur W , 1883–
Overcoming difficulties under adverse conditions, address...in the House of Representatives, Thursday, April 6, 1939. Washington, Govt. Print. Off. 1939.

15p. 23cm.
Founder's Day address delivered at Tuskegee Institute, Alabama, April 2, 1939.

Overhead costs; some essays in economic analysis

St.Lucia
M330 Lewis, William Arthur, 1915–
L58o Overhead costs; some essays in economic analysis. London, G. Allen & Unwin [1949] 1951

200 p. diagrs. 23 cm. (The Library of economics. Sect. 2: New works, 3)

Bibliographical footnotes.

1. Cost. 2. Price policy. 3. Monopolies. I. Title. (Series)

HB221.L54 338.52 49—6466*

Library of Congress [55c1]

Overshadowed.

M813.5 Griggs, Sutton Elbert, 1872–
G87o Overshadowed. A novel. By Sutton E. Griggs ... Nashville, Tenn., The Orion publishing co., 1901.
219p. 20½cm.

M614 Overton, John.
Ov2b A birth control service among urban Negroes; Study conducted by the Department of Health, City of Nashville, by John Overton and Ivah Uffelman. Reprinted from Human fertility, 7:97-101, August 1942.

1. Birth control.

M323 Ovington, Mary White, 1865–
N214o How the National Association for the Advancement of Colored People began. New York, NAACP, 1945.

5p. 23cm.
White author

1. National Association for the Advancement of Colored People.

Ovington, Mary White, 1865–joint comp.

M810.8 Pritchard, Myron Thomas, 1853– *comp.*
P93 The upward path; a reader for colored children with an introduction by Robert R. Moton ... comp. by Myron T. Pritchard ... and Mary White Ovington ... New York, Harcourt, Brace and Howe [°1920]

xi, [1], 255 p. incl. front., illus. 19½cm.

1. Readers and speakers—1870– I. Ovington, Mary White, 1865– joint comp. II. Title. III. Title: Colored children, Reader for.

20—16516

Library of Congress PE1126.N3P8

Copyright A 597468 [41o1]

M350 Owen, Chandler.
Ow2n Negroes and the war. Washington, D. C., Office of War Information, 194 .

6p. illus. 34cm.

1. World war, 1939-1945. I. Title.

M355 Owens, Don Benn.
Ow2c Chemical warfare simplified. A military handbook for gas officers, noncommissioned officers and enlisted men of the Regular Army and National Guard, by Don Benn Owens and James J. Clark. Chicago, Educational Publications, 1938.

85p. 21cm.

1. Chemical warfare.

M973.8 Owens, Susie Lee
Ow2u Union League of America; Political activities in Tennessee, the Carolinas, and Virginia, 1865-1870, an abridgement. New York, New York University, 1947.

23p. 23cm.

1. U.S. - Hist. 1865-1898.
2. Union League of America. 3. ~~Political parties.~~ 3. Politics and suffrage.

Cameroons, French
M896.3 Owono, Joseph
Ow5tb Tante-Bella; roman d'aujourd'hui et de demain. Yaounde, Librairie au Messager, 1959.

293p. 20cm.
Portrait of author on front of book.

I. Title.

Oxford studies in African affairs.

Nigeria
M966.9 Biobaku, Saburi Oladeni.
B52e The Egba and their neighbours, 1842–1872. Oxford, Clarendon Press, 1957.

vi, 128 p. maps, tables. 22 cm. (Oxford studies in African affairs)

"Based on a Ph. D. thesis submitted to the University of London in May 1951."
Bibliography: p. [108]–118.

1. Egba (African tribe) 2. Nigeria—Pol. & govt. (Series)

DT515.B5 966.92 57–59620

Library of Congress [5]

Oxley, Lawrence G.

M362.7 Sanders, Wiley Britton, 1898– *ed.*
Sa5 Negro child welfare in North Carolina, a Rosenwald study, directed by Wiley Britton Sanders ... under the joint auspices of the North Carolina State board of charities and public welfare and the School of public welfare, the University of North Carolina. Chapel Hill, Pub. for the North Carolina State board of charities and public welfare by the University of North Carolina press, 1933.

xiv p., 2 l., [3]–326 p. 24cm.

1. Negroes—North Carolina. 2. Negroes—Moral and social conditions. 3. Charities—North Carolina. 4. Children—Charities, protection, etc.—North Carolina. 5. Juvenile delinquency—North Carolina. 6. Social surveys I. North Carolina. State board of charities and public welfare. II. North Carolina. University. School of public welfare. III. Title.

33—18006

Library of Congress E185.86.S27 [45t1] 325.260075

Kenya
M967.62 Oyende, J P
Oy3
Chifu hodari wa kiafrika. The ideal African chief. Nairobi, Eagle Press, 1951.
14p. 18cm. (Mawazo ya wenzenu. Your friends are thinking series)
Written Swahili and English.
1. Leadership. 2. Africa - Native races. I. Title. II. Title: The ideal African chief. III. Series. IV. Series: Your friends are thinking series.

Kenya
M967.62 Oyende, J P
Oy3p
Paro mako kuom dohini e Kenya [Some thoughts on native tribunals in Kenya] Nairobi, Eagle Press, 1950.
27p. 18cm. (Paro mag jowadi. Your friends are thinking series)
Written in Luo and English
1. Justice, Administration of - Kenya Colony and Protectorate. 2. Kenya Colony and Protectorate. I. Title. II. Title: Some thoughts on native tribunals in Kenya. III. Series. IV. Series: Your friends are thinking series.

Nigeria
M966.9 Oyenuga, V A
Ac85
The latest development in Marxist ideology.
Pp. 19-27.
(In: Action Group of Nigeria. 1956 summer school lectures. Ibadan, Action Group Bureau of Information, 1957)

Nigeria
M530 Oyewole, 'Dotun.
Oy3
An introduction to physics. London, Macmillan and Co., 1964.
460p. illus., 21½cm.
1. Physics. I. Title.

Nigeria
M540 Oyewole, 'Femi.
Oy3
An introduction to Chemistry. London, Macmillan and Co., 1964.
440p. illus. 21½cm.
1. Chemistry. I. Title.

Oyinza okutunda edduka?
Uganda
M658 Lumu, Nehemiah Bosa Eryan, 1912-
L97
Oyinza okutunda edduka? [Can you run a shop?] Nairobi, Eagle Press, 1957.
59p. illus.
Written in Luganda.
1. Stores, Retail - Uganda. I. Title.

Cameroun
M896.3 Oyono, Ferdinand Léopold, 1929-
Oy4c
Chemin d'Europe, roman. Paris, Julliard [1960]
196 p. 19 cm.
"A Monsieur Francois Laval - Respectieuve hommage de Uautenr. Oyono."
I. Title.
A 61-196
Illinois. Univ. Library for Library of Congress [2]

Cameroons
M896.3 Oyono, Ferdinand Léopold, 1929-
Oy4
Ferdinand Oyono; écrivain camerounais. [Textes commentés par Roger Mercier et M. et S. Battestini. Paris] Fernand Nathan [1964]
62p. 19½cm. (Classiques du monde. Littérature africaine, 8)
"Oeuvres": p. 5.
Portrait of author on book cover.
I. Mercier, Roger, ed. II. Series.

Cameroun
M896.3 Oyono, Ferdinand Léopold, 1929-
Oy4v2
Houseboy; translated from the French by John Reed. London, Heinemann, 1966.
[4], 140 p. 20½ cm. 18/-
(B 66-8890)
Originally published as Une vie de boy. Paris, Julliard, 1956.
Portrait of author on book jacket.
I. Title.
PZ4.O988Ho 66-70765
Library of Congress [5]

Cameroun
M896.3 Oyono, Ferdinand Léopold, 1929-
Oy4v
Une vie de Boy; roman. Paris, Rene Julliard, 1956.
183p. 19cm.
I. Title.

Cameroun
M896.3 Oyono, Ferdinand Léopold, 1929-
Oy4vi
Le vieux Nègre et la médaille; roman. Paris, Rene Julliard, 1956.
209p. 19cm.
1. Cameroons-Fiction

Cameroons
M896.2 Oyono, Guillaume
Oy6t
Trois prétendants; un mari; pièce en quatre actes et un intermède. Yaoundé, [Cameroun] Editions CLE, 1964.
126p. 18cm.
Portrait of author on book cover.
1. African drama. I. Title.

Ozidi.
Nigeria
M896.2 Clark, John Pepper, 1935-
C54oz
Ozidi: a play [by] J. P. Clark. London, Ibadan, Oxford U. P., 1966.
[6], 121 p. 18½ cm. (A Three crowns book) 7/6
(B 66-22209)
Based on the Nigerian Ijaw saga of Ozidi.
I. Title.
PR6053.L3O9 822'.914 67-74851
Library of Congress [3]

M174 Pace, Harry Herbert, 1884-
P11b
Beginning again, by Harry H. Pace. Philadelphia, Dorrance & company, inc. [1934]
72 p. front. 19½cm.
1. Success. 2. Will. I. Title.
35-734
Library of Congress HF5386.P18
Copyright A 78810 [2] 174

M368 Pace, Harry Herbert, 1884-
P11s
The cash value of lives, by Harry H. Pace. Reprinted from Forbes magazine. [Van Wert, Ohio, General mutual life insurance company, c1932.
11 unnumb. p. 21½cm.
1. Insurance. I. Title.

M368 Pace, Harry H[erbert] 1884-
P11c
The contribution of Negro insurance companies towards the economic status of the race, past, present, future. [Chicago, Ill.]
12p. 23cm.
1. Insurance.

M331 Pace, Harry H[erbert] 1884-
P11w
What the Negro has not done in business. An address delivered to the West Virginia State Teachers' Association, by Harry H. Pace. Jamaica, New York, The Lone Star Press, [n.d.]
[7]p. 15cm.
1. Business.

...Le pacte de sang au Dahomey.
Dahomey Hazoumé, Paul.
M966.8
H331
... Le pacte de sang au Dahomey. Paris, Institut d'ethnologie, 1937.
viii, 170 p. 8 pl. (1 col.) diagr. 27cm. (Université de Paris. Travaux et mémoires de l'Institut d'ethnologie.—xxv)
1. Blood covenant. 2. Ethnology—Dahomey. I. Title.
39—16316
Library of Congress DT541.H35
——— Copy 2.
Copyright A—Foreign 35348
[40c2] 572.9668

Uganda Padhola
M967.61 Ooth-Ofumbi, Arphaxed Charles K, 1932-
Ob5
Padhola [History and customs of the Jo Pahdola] Nairobi, Eagle Press, 1960.
84p. 21½cm.
Written in Luo (Ludoma)
1. Jopadhola. 2. Uganda - Native races. I. Title.

Trinidad
M330 Padmore, George, 1903- 1959.
P13af
Africa: Britain's third empire. London, D. Dobson [1949]
266 p. 22 cm.
Bibliographical footnotes.
Errata slip mounted on p. [5]
1. Gt. Brit.—Colonies—Africa. 2. Gt. Brit.—Colonies—Administration. 3. Africa—Nationality. 4. Africa—Econ. condit.
A 50-5014
Rochester. Univ. Libr. for Library of Congress DT32.P8 [3]

Trinidad
M330 Padmore, George, 1903-1959.
P13a
... Africa and world peace, with a foreword by Sir Stafford Cripps ... London, M. Secker and Warburg, ltd., 1937.
xi, 285 p. 18½cm.
Errata slip inserted.
Bibliography: p. 273-278.
1. Africa — Politics. 2. Africa — Colonization. 3. Imperialism. 4. Competition, International. 5. Europe—Politics—1871- I. Title.
38—331
Library of Congress DT21.P3
[43d1] 960

Trinidad
M330
P13g

Padmore, George, 1903–1959.
The Gold Coast revolution; the struggle of an African people from slavery to freedom. London, D. Dobson [1953]
272 p. illus. 22 cm.

1. Gold Coast—Native races. I. Title.

DT511.P3 966.7 53—11820 ‡
Library of Congress [54g5]

Trinidad
M330
P13h

Padmore, George, 1903–1959.
How Britain rules Africa [by] George Padmore. London, Wishart books ltd. [1936]
xiii, 402 p. maps. 22ᶜᵐ.
Bibliography: p. 399–402.

1. Gt. Brit.—Colonies—Africa. 2. Gt. Brit.—Colonies—Administration. I. Title.

36—12945
Library of Congress JQ1890.P3
[a39g2] 325.342096

Trinidad
M330
P131

Padmore, George, 1903-1959.
The life and struggles of Negro toilers, by George Padmore. London, Published by the R.I.L.U. Magazine for the International trade union committee of Negro workers, 1931.

126p. 22cm.

1. Labor and laboring classes. I. Title.
II. International Trade Union Committee of Negro Workers.

Trinidad
M330
P13p

Padmore, George, 1903–1959.
Pan-Africanism or communism? The coming struggle for Africa. New York, Roy Publishers [1956]
463 p. illus. 23 cm.

1. Africa—Politics. I. Title.

DT31.P3 1956a 960 55—9307 ‡
Library of Congress [7]

Trinidad
M330
P13v

Padmore, George, 1903-1959. ed.
The voice of coloured labour; Speeches and reports of colonial delegates to the world trade union conference, 1945. Manchester, Panaf Service [1945]

55p. 22cm.

1. Labor and laboring classes. 2. Trade Unions. I. World Trade Union Conference, 1945- II. Title.

M323
C91w

Padmore, George, 1903-1959.joint author.
Cunard, Nancy, 1896-
The white man's duty, by Nancy Cunard and George Padmore... 2nd edition. Manchester, Panaf service, ltd., 1945.

51p. 21½cm.

M306
P19c2

Padmore, George, 1903-1959, ed.
Pan-African Congress. 5th, Manchester, Eng., 1945.
History of the Pan-African Congress: colonial and coloured unity, a programme of action. Edited by George Padmore. [2d ed. with new material] London, Hammersmith Bookshop [1963]

vi, 74p. 22cm.
"Report of the 1945 Pan-African Congress."

Padmore, George, 1903-1959.

Ghana.
M966.7
N65h

Nkrumah, Kwame, 1909-
Hands off Africa. Some famous speeches by Dr. The Rt. Hon. Kwame Nkrumah, P.C., M.P. (First President of the Republic of Ghana); with a tribute to George Padmore written by Tawia Adamafio, General Secretary of C.P.P. Accra, Kwabena Owusu-Akyem [1960]

62p. ports. 21cm.

Padmore, George. 1903-1959.

M304
P19
v.1, no.2

Ford, James W
World problems of the Negro people. (a reputation of George Padmore.) New York, issued by the Harlem section of the communist party [n.d.]

24p. 15cm. (Series on Negro problems.)

Padmore, George, 1903-1959.

Ghana
M89
N93n

Nkrumah, Kwame, 1909-
Funeral oration ... on the occasion of the interment of the ashes of the late George Padmore at Christiansborg Castle, Osu, Accra, Sunday 4th October 1959. Accra, Government Printers, 1959.

2p. 25cm.

Padmore, George, 1903-1959 ed.

M306
P19c

Pan African Congress.
Colonial and Colored unity, a programme of action; History of the Pan African Congress, ed. by George Padmore, Manchester, England, Pan-African Federation [1945]

79p. 21cm.

Puerto Rico
M864
P14a

Pagán, Bolívar, 1899–
América y otras páginas, por Bolívar Pagán ... San Juan, P. R., 1922.
4 p. l., 5-192 p. 19½ᶜᵐ.
CONTENTS.—En el umbral (prólogo)—Páginas previas.—América.—El arte social.—Hombres e ideas.—Apuntes críticos.—Cuentos de amor.

I. Title. 1. Puerto Rico-literature.

22-12201
Library of Congress AC75.P3
[2]

Puerto Rico
M864
P14h

Pagán, Bolívar, 1899–
Historia de los partidos políticos puertorriqueños, 1898–1956. San Juan, P. R., Librería Campos, 1959.
2 v. illus. 23 cm.

1. Political parties—Puerto Rico. I. Title.

JL1059.A45P2 59—38693 ‡
Library of Congress [1]

Puerto Rico
M864
P14i

Pagán, Bolívar, 1899–
... Ideales en marcha; discursos y artículos. San Juan, Puerto Rico, Biblioteca de autores puertorriqueños, 1939.
3 p. l., [9]-306 p., 3 l. 20ᶜᵐ.
"En homenaje a Bolívar Pagán [discurso pronunciado por Rafael Martínez Nadal, en junio 25, 1937]": p. [7]-19.
"Hablando con Bolívar Pagán [entrevista, de Angela Negrón Muñoz, abril 2, 1933]": p. [21]-38.

1. Puerto Rico—Pol. & govt.—1898– I. Martínez Nadal, Rafael, 1878– II. Negrón Muñoz, Angela. III. Title.

40—2088
Library of Congress F1975.P26
[42c1] 972.95

Puerto Rico
M864
P14l

Pagán, Bolívar, 1899–
... Ley municipal, revisada, anotada y comentada, por Bolívar Pagán. (Contiene la Ley municipal y todas las demás leyes aplicables a los municipios, el acta orgánica, el reglamento de contabilidad municipal, y toda la jurisprudencia del Tribunal supremo sobre cuestiones municipales hasta el tomo 32, incl.) San Juan, Puerto Rico, La Correspondencia de Pto. Rico, inc., 1925.
xi, 13-256, [4] p. 22ᶜᵐ. (Biblioteca de divulgación legal, vol. I)

1. Municipal government—Puerto Rico. 2. Municipal corporations—Puerto Rico. I. Puerto Rico. Laws, statutes, etc. II. Title.

42-51912
Library of Congress JS2024.P3
[3]

Pagan Spain.

M813.5
W93p

Wright, Richard, 1908–
Pagan Spain. [1st ed.] New York, Harper [1957]
241 p. 22 cm.

1. Spain—Descr. & trav.—1951– I. Title.
Full name: Richard Nathaniel Wright.

DP48.W7 914.6 56-11091 ‡
Library of Congress [20]

Pagan Spain.

M813.5
W93pa

Wright, Richard, 1908-1960.
Pagan Spain. London, Bodley Head, [c1957]

191p. 22cm.

Nigeria
M966.9
C88p

Page, Jesse.
The black bishop: Samuel Adjai Crowther, by Jesse Page, F. R. G. S. With preface by Eugene Stock ... with 16 illustrations and map. London, Hodder and Stoughton, 1908.
xv, 440 p. 16 pl. (incl. front., ports.) fold. map. 22ᶜᵐ.

1. Crowther, Samuel Adjai, bp., 1806?-1891. I. Title.
2. Niger mission

10-9742
Library of Congress BV3625.N6C7
[a44c1]

A pageant in seven decades, 1868-1938.

M301
D852ap

Du Bois, William Edward Burghardt, 1868-
A pageant in seven decades, 1868-1938, by William Edward Burghardt Du Bois... An address delivered on the occasion of his seventieth birthday at the University convocation of Atlanta University, Morehouse College and Atlanta, Ga., February 23, 1938.

44p. 25cm.

Pageant of Ghana.

Ghana
M966.7
W83p

Wolfson, Freda.
Pageant of Ghana. London, Oxford University Press, 1958.
266 p. illus. 23 cm. (West African history series)

1. Ghana—Hist. I. Title.

DT510.W6 966.7 58—3099 ‡
Library of Congress [59b5]

Pageants - Sunday school

M268.76
T66s

Townsend, Willa A arr.
A song in the night time: a Christmas pageant-program for Sunday schools, arranged by Mrs. W.A. Townsend. Nashville, Tenn., Sunday school publishing board n.d.
16p. 23cm.
Music included.

Pages de Marie et d'Helene.
Haiti
M844
M82
Morpeau, Hélène M
Pages de Marie et d'Helene. Port-au-Prince, Les Presses Libres, 1954.
XIV, 219p. illus. 22cm. (Collection du tricinquantenaire.)

Painters.
France
M840
D89pe
Dumas, Alexandre, 1802-1870.
La peinture chez les anciens suivee de l'histoire des peintres. Bruxelles, Meline, Cans et cie., 1845.
284p. 16cm.
1. Painters. I. Title.

Le Palais de la Légion d'Honneur.
Martinique
M844
B33p
Beaudza, Louis
Le palais de la légion d'honneur, par Louis Beaudza. Paris, L. Fournier, 1928.
42p. 22½cm.

Pages d'histoire d'Haïti.
Haiti
M972.94
L37p
Laurent, Gérard Mentor.
Pages d'histoire d'Haïti. Port-au-Prince, La Phalange, 1960.
271 p. 21 cm.
A selection from articles published in La Phalange. Cf. p. [5]
Bibliography: p. [269]-271.
1. Haiti—Hist.—Revolution, 1791-1804. 2. Haiti—Hist.—1804-1844. I. Title.
A 61-4316
Florida. Univ. Library for Library of Congress [1]

M813.5
P16r
Paisley, John Walter.
Ras Bravado, by J. W. Paisley. Boston, The Christopher publishing house [°1938]
2 p. l., 7-146 p. 20½cm.
I. Title. 38-12835
Library of Congress PZ3.P1673Ras
——— Copy 2.
Copyright A 117732 [3]

Puerto Rico
M861
P17p
Palés Matos, Luis
Poesía, 1915-1956. Introducción por Federico De Onís. San Juan, Universidad de Puerto Rico, 1957.
305p. 21cm.
I. Title.

Pages from our past.
Jamaica
M823.91
T21p
Taylor, Stanley Arthur Goodwin, 1894–
Pages from our past. Kingston, Jamaica, Pioneer Press [1954]
183 p. 19 cm.
1. Jamaica—Hist.—Fiction. I. Title.
PZ4.T246Pag 55-43678 ‡
Library of Congress [1]

M811.5
P16v
Paisley, John Walter.
The voice of Mizraim, by John Walter Paisley. New York and Washington, The Neale publishing company, 1907.
122 p. 19cm.
Poems.
I. Title. 1. Poetry.
7-33904
Library of Congress PS3531.A29V6 1907
Copyright A 193829 [a36b1] 811.5

Puerto Rico
M861.
P17
Palés Matos, Luis.
... Tuntún de pasa y grifería; poemas afroantillanos. San Juan de Puerto Rico, Biblioteca de autores puertorriqueños, 1937.
183 p., 2 l. 17cm.
I. Title. 1. Puerto Rican poetry.
39-12503
Library of Congress PQ7439.P24T8 [2] 861.6

Pages retrouvees, oeuvres en prose et en vers.
Haiti
M840.9
B796
Brouard, Carl
Pages retrouvees, oeuvres en prose et en vers. (groupees par les soins ducomite soixantieme anniversaire de Carl Brouard). Port-au-Prince, Editions Panorama, 1963.
182p. 22cm.

M967.5
P28h
Paiva Manso, Levy Maria Jordão, 1831-1875.
Historia do Congo; obra posthuma. (Documentos). Lisboa, Typographia da Academia, 1877.
369p. 24½cm.

Puerto Rico
M861
P17v
Palés Matos, Vicente, 1903–
... Viento y espuma, cuentos y poemas ... Mayagüez, P. R., Editorial Puerto Rico, 1945.
2 p. l., 7-252 p., 1 l. 20cm. (*Half-title:* Obras completas, vol. I)
Biblioteca Autores antillanos.
"Printed in Argentine."
Autographed
I. Title. 1. Puerto Rican poetry.
PQ7439.P243V5 868.6 A F 47-3609
Northwestern univ. Libr. for Library of Congress [3]†

Páginas recolhidas.
Brazil
M869.3
M18pag
Machado de Assis, Joaquim Maria, 1839-1908.
Páginas recolhidas. Rio de Janeiro, W. M. Jackson Inc. Editôres, 1957.
298p. 20½cm. (Obras completas de Machado de Assis)

Pakistan-Description and travel.
M910
Ad17
Adams, Effie Kaye.
Experiences of a Fulbright teacher. Boston, Christopher Pub. House [1956]
215 p. 21 cm.
1. Pakistan—Descr. & trav. 2. Voyages and travels—1950- 3. Teachers, Interchange of. I. Title.
DS379.A6 *915.47 56—2860 ‡
Library of Congress [57g5]

Palés Matos, Luis
Latin America
M861.08
F56a
Pp. 204-217. In -
Fitts, Dudley, 1903– ed.
Anthology of contemporary Latin-American poetry, edited by Dudley Fitts. Norfolk, Conn., New directions [1942]
ix, [2], x-xxi, 667 p. 23½ cm.
Added t.-p.: Antología de la poesía americana contemporánea.
English and original text (Spanish, Portuguese or French) on opposite pages.
"Biographical and bibliographical notes, by H. R. Hays": p. 581-641.
1. Spanish-American poetry (Collections) 2. Spanish-American poetry—Translations into English. 3. English poetry—Translations from Spanish. 4. Spanish-American poetry—Bio-bibl. I. Hays, Hoffman Reynolds. II. Title.
PQ7084.F5 861.6082 43—485
Library of Congress [54r43k²7]

Le pagne noir.
Ivory Coast
M966.68
D12p
Dadié, Bernard B
Le pagne noir, contes africains. Paris, Présence africaine [1955]
156 p. 19 cm.
I. Title.
A 56-6019
Illinois. Univ. Library for Library of Congress [1]

Palace of the peacock.
British Guiana
M823.91
H24p
Harris, Wilson.
Palace of the peacock. London, Faber and Faber [1960]
152 p. 19 cm.
I. Title.
Full name: Theodore Wilson Harris.
PZ4.H318Pal 61-24895 ‡
Library of Congress [1]

Palestine-Descr. & trav.
M910
B14m
Bagley, *Mrs.* Caroline.
My trip through Egypt and the Holy Land, by Caroline Bagley. New York, The Grafton press [°1928]
223 p. front. (map) plates, ports. 21cm.
1. Egypt—Descr. & trav. 2. Palestine—Descr. & trav. I. Title.
28-16113
Library of Congress DT55.B25
——— Copy 2.
Copyright A 1077917 [3]

Paid servant.
British Guiana
M823.91
B73p
Braitwaite, Edward Ricardo
Paid servant. London, Bodley Head, 1962.
219p. 21cm.
Portrait of author on book jacket.

Palaces - Yoruba.
Nigeria
M728
Oj5
Ojo, G J Afolabi.
Yoruba palaces: a study of Afins of Yorubaland [by] G. J. Afolabi Ojo. London, University of London P. [1967]
112 p. plates, maps, plans, tables. 21 cm. 12/6
(B 67-2079)
Bibliography: p. 106.
1. Palaces—Yoruba. I. Title.
NA1597.Y6O38 728.8'2 67-75209
Library of Congress [2]

Palestine-Descr. & trav.
M915.69
B 62
Blyden, Edward Wilmot, 1832-1912.
From West Africa to Palestine. By Edward W. Blyden, M. A. Freetown, Sierra Leone, T. J. Sawyer; [etc., etc.] 1873.
viii, [9]-201 p. front. 22cm.
Printed in Great Britain.
1. Palestine—Descr. & trav. 2. Voyages and travels. I. Title.
15-1109
Library of Congress G490.B7

Palestine-Descr. & trav.

Liberia
M966.6
B62f

Blyden, Edward Wilmot, 1832-1912.
From West Africa to Palestine. By Edward W. Blyden, M.A. Freetown, Sierra Leone, T.J. Sawyer; [etc.,etc.] 1873.

viii, [9]-201p. front. 22cm.
Printed in Great Britain.

Palestine-Descr. & trav.

M910
L24s

Lane, James Franklin, 1874–
Some things we saw while abroad; a visit to Europe, the Holy Land and Egypt, by J. F. Lane ... and Mary Edna Lane ... Boston, The Christopher publishing house [°1941]
xv, 17-224 p. plates, ports. 19cm.

1. Europe—Descr. & trav. 2. Palestine—Descr. & trav. 3. Egypt—Descr. & trav. I. Lane, Mrs. Mary Edna (Johnson) 1872– joint author. II. Title.

Library of Congress D975.L34 42-2498
[4] 910.4

Palestine-Descr. & trav.

M286
P87p

Powell, Adam Clayton, 1865–
Palestine and saints in Caesar's household, by A. Clayton Powell, sr. New York, R. R. Smith, 1939.
viii p., 2 l., 13-217 p. 21cm.

1. Palestine — Descr. & trav. 2. Baptists — Sermons. 3. Sermons, American. I. Title.

Library of Congress BX6452.P6 39-25083
——— Copy 2.
Copyright A 131759 [2] 915.69

Palestine—Descr. & trav.

M910
Se1

Seaton, Daniel P.
The Land of promise; or, The Bible land and its revelation. Illustrated with several engravings of some of the most important places in Palestine and Syria. By D. P. Seaton, D. D., M. D. Philadelphia, Pa., Publishing house of the A. M. E. church, 1895.
ix, 443 p. front. (port.) 16 pl., map. 24½cm.

1. Palestine—Descr. & trav. 2. Syria—Descr. & trav.

7—14411

Library of Congress DS107.S45
[38b1]

Palestine and saints in Caesar's household.

M286
P87p

Powell, Adam Clayton, 1865–
Palestine and saints in Caesar's household, by A. Clayton Powell, sr. New York, R. R. Smith, 1939.
viii p., 2 l., 13-217 p. 21cm.

1. Palestine — Descr. & trav. 2. Baptists — Sermons. 3. Sermons, American. I. Title.

Library of Congress BX6452.P6 39-25083
——— Copy 2.
Copyright A 131759 [2] 915.69

Palisirs de Saint-Domingue.

Haiti
M972.94
F82p

Fouchard, Jean, 1912–
Plaisirs de Saint-Domingue; notes sur sa vie sociale, littéraire et artistique. Port-au-Prince, Impr. de l'État. 1955.
181 p. 21 cm.

1. Haiti—Soc. life & cust. 2. Haiti—Intellectual life. I. Title.

F1923.F6 56-58741 ‡

Library of Congress [2]

The Palm-wine drinkard

Nigeria
M896.3
T88p

Tutuola, Amos.
The palm-wine drinkard and his dead palm-wine tapster in the Dead's Town. New York, Grove Press [1953]
130 p. 21 cm.

I. Title.

PZ4.T968Pal 2 53-8397 ‡

Library of Congress [3]

The palm wine drinkard.

Nigeria
M896.3
T88p

Tutuola, Amos.
The palm-wine drinkard and his dead palm-wine tapster in the Deads' Town. London, Faber and Faber [1952]
125 p. 21 cm.

I. Title.

PZ4.T968Pal 52-43382 ‡

Library of Congress [53b1]

Peru
M985
P18

Palma, Ricardo, 1833–1919.
... La monja de la llave; prólogo de P. Matalonga ... México, D. F., Compañía general editora, s. a., 1940.
191, [1] p. 18½cm. (Colección Mirasol. [4])
"Forman este volumen dieciseis 'historias de amor,' extraídas de las 'Tradiciones peruanas'."—p. 11.

1. Legends—Peru. I. Matalonga, P., ed. II. Title.
[Full name: Manuel Ricardo Palma]

42-12800

Library of Congress F3409.P1788
[3] 985

Peru
M985
P18t

Palma, Ricardo, 1833–1919.
... Tradiciones peruanas escogidas (edición crítica) Prólogo, selección y notas de Luis Alberto Sánchez. Santiago de Chile, Ediciones Ercilla, 1940.
3 p. l., [9]-215, [3] p. 18cm. (Half-title: Biblioteca Amauta (Serie América) [V. 1])
"Noticia bibliográfica": p. 14-16.

1. Legends—Peru. 2. Peru—Hist. I. Sánchez, Luis Alberto, 1900– ed. II. Title.
[Full name: Manuel Ricardo Palma]

41—9583

Library of Congress F3409.P1732
[44e1] 985

Une palme et des roses, poèmes.

Haiti
M841
L616p

Libose, Jean
Une palme et des roses, poèmes. Port-au-Prince, Imprimerie du College Vertieres, 1941.

41p. 18cm.

M370
P18r

Palmer Memorial Institute, Sedalia.
Report of the president to the Board of Trustees. 19 -

v. tables. 28cm. annual.
Library has: 1937.

1. Private schools.

Palmer memorial institute, Sedalia, N.C.

M395
B81

Brown, Charlotte (Hawkins) 1883–
The correct thing to do—to say—to wear, by Charlotte Hawkins Brown. ~~Boston, The Christopher publishing house [°1941]~~ Sedalia, N.C. Published by the author, 1940
142 p. 19½cm.
"This book has been almost wholly written out of the ideals, observations and practices growing out of the experiences of the Palmer memorial institute."—p. 138.
Bibliography: p. 138.

1. Etiquette. I. Palmer memorial institute, Sedalia, N. C. II. Title.

41—26722

Library of Congress BJ1853.B73 1941
[44d1] 395

MD9
B797s

Palmer Memorial Institute, Sedalia, N.C.
Saunders, Lucinda Yancey.
An idea that grew into a million; The life story of Charlotte Hawkins Brown...Reprinted from Abbott's monthly, November, 1930.

[4]p. port. illus. 29cm.

M811.5
P182n

Palmer, Vernon Urquhart, 1930–
The new grand army; poems. New York, Vantage Press [1965]
64p. 21cm.

I. Title.

Mauritius
M841
C27p

Les palmiers.
Castellan, Charles
Les palmiers, par Charles Castellan... Paris, Librairie de Charles Gosselin, 1832.

iv, 175p. 18½cm.

M811.5
N98p

Les palmiers.
Nyabongo, Virginia Lee (Simmons)
Les palmiers. La Habana, 1951.
60 p. port. 25 cm.
Poems.

I. Title.

PQ3939.N9P3 51-27375

Library of Congress [1]

M811.08
P18

Palms; Negro poets' number, v. IV, no.1. Guadalajara, Mexico, Idella Purnell, 1926.

32p. 20cm.
Special issue containing the work of Negro poets.
Editor: Countee Cullen.
Contents: The Negro renaissance, by Walter White. -Poems by: Arna Bontemps. Albert Rice. Clarissa Scott. Georgia Douglas Johnson. William Stanley Braithwaite. Waring Cuney. Anne Spencer. Countee Cullen. Lewis Alexander. Jessie Fauset.

M811.08
P18

Palms; Negro poets' number, v. IV, no.1. Guadalajara, Mexico, Idella Purnell, 1926. (card 2)

W.E. DuBois. Bruce Nugent. Gwendolyn Bennett. Helene Johnson, Langston Hughes. -The Weary blues, by Alain Locke.

1. Poetry.
I. Cullen, Countee, 1903-1946 ed.

La paloma de vuelo popular elegias.

Cuba
M861.6
G94p

Guillén, Nicolás, 1902–
La paloma de vuelo popular elegias. Buneos Aires, Editorial Losada, S.A., 1948.

157p. 18½cm.
Portrait of author on cover of book.

1. Cuban poetry. I. Title.

M811.08
P825

Pamphlet poets.
Four Negro poets: Claude McKay, Jean Toomer. Countee Cullen. Langston Hughes. With an introduction by Alain Locke. New York, Simon E. Schuster Publishers, n.d.

31p. 21½cm. (The Pamphlet poets.)

M610
P19
v.1

Pamphlets relating to medicine, nos. 1-15.

1. Steward, S.T. Woman in medicine.
2. Jackson, A.B. The health question of the man next door.
3. Jackson, A.B. Artificial hyperaemia and its therapeutic application.
4. Jackson, A.B. The rcatment of tuberculosis.
5. Jackson, A.B. The injection of magnesium sulphate for acute articular rheumatism.
6. Jackson, A.B. The treatment of rheumatism by injection of magnesium sulphate.

Africa
M960
L527

Pan-Africanism.
Legum, Colin.
Pan-Africanism; a short political guide. London, Pall Mall Press [1962]
296 p. map. 23 cm.
Bibliography: p. 279-285.
Appendices (p. 134-278) Documentary guide to Pan-Africanism.
White author.

1. Pan-Africanism. 2. Africa-Congresses.

DT30.L39 1962b 960 62-5026
Library of Congress [3]

Senegal
M960
T346

Pan-Africanism.
Thiam, Doudou.
The foreign policy of African States: ideological bases, present realities, future prospects. Pref. by Roger Decottignies. [Translation with revisions by the author] New York, Praeger [1965]

xv, 134p. 23cm.
Bibliographical footnotes.

M610
P19
v.1

card. 2

7. Murray, P.M. Hospital provision for the Negro race.
8. Murray, P.M. Harlem's health.
9. Nichols, Franklin O. Some public health problems of the Negro.
10. Manhattan medical society. Open letter to Mr. Edwin R. Embree.
11. Manhattan medical society. Open letter to American legion.
12. Wright, Louis T. Diagnosis and treatment of fractured skulls.

Africa
M960
L527a

Pan-Africanism.
Legum, Colin.
Pan-Africanism; a short political guide. New York, Praeger [1962]
296 p. illus. 21 cm. (Books that matter)
Includes bibliography.
Appendices (p. 134-278) Documentary guide to Pan-Africanism.

1. Pan-Africanism. 2. Africa-Congresses.

DT30.L39 1962a 960 62-13489 ‡
Library of Congress [10]

M960
Am3

Pan Africanism - Addresses, essays, lectures.
American Society of African Culture.
Pan-Africanism reconsidered. Berkeley, University of California Press, 1962.
xix, 376 p. tables. 25 cm.
"Speeches, papers, and comments given at the Third Annual Conference of the American Society of African Culture, which was held in Philadelphia at the University of Pennsylvania from June 22 to June 26, 1960."
Bibliographical footnotes.

1. Pan-Africanism—Addresses, essays, lectures. 2. Africa—Civilization—Addresses, essays, lectures. ~~3. Negro race.~~ I. Title.
3. Negritude. 4. Africa - Social thought.
DT30.A53 301.451 62-11491
Library of Congress [5]

M306
P19c

Pan African Congress.
Colonial and Colored unity, a programme of action; History of the Pan African Congress, ed. by George Padmore. Manchester, England, Pan-African Federation [1945]

79p. 21cm.

1. Padmore, George, 1903 - ed. I. Title.

Kenya
M967.62
M45f3

Pan-Africanism.
Mboya, Tom
Afrika frit - og hvad sa? [n.p.] Fremads Fokusbøger, 1964.

235p. illus., ports. 18½cm.
Translation of Freedom and after.
Autobiographical
Written in Danish

1. Kenya Colony and Protectorate. 2. Africa - Politics. 3. Pan-Africanism. I. Title.

Zambia
M960
F16

Pan-Africanism - Addresses, essays, lectures.
Kaunda, Kenneth David, *Pres., Zambia*, 1924-
A humanist in Africa: letters to Colin M. Morris from Kenneth D. Kaunda. London, Longmans, 1966.
8-136 p. 20½ cm. 16/-
(B 66-16714)

1. Nationalism—Africa—Addresses, essays, lectures. 2. Pan-Africanism—Addresses, essays, lectures. I. Morris, Colin M. II. Title.

DT963.6.K3A45 320.15808 66-76308
Library of Congress [3]

M306
P19c2

Pan-African Congress. *5th, Manchester, Eng., 1945.*
History of the Pan-African Congress: colonial and coloured unity, a programme of action. Edited by George Padmore. [2d ed. with new material] London, Hammersmith Bookshop [1963]
vi, 74 p. 22 cm.
"Report of the 1945 Pan-African Congress."

1. Pan Africanism—Congresses. I. Padmore, George, 1903-1959, ed. II. Title. III. Title: Colonial and coloured unity.

DT30.P28 1945ca 64-54191
Library of Congress [1]

Kenya
M967.62
M45f

Pan-Africanism.
Mboya, Tom.
Freedom and after. [1st ed.] Boston, Little, Brown [1963]
x, 288 p. illus., ports., map (on lining papers) 22 cm.
Autobiographical.

1. Kenya Colony and Protectorate—2. Africa—Politics—1960- 3. Pan-Africanism. I. Title.

DT434.E27M35 967.62 63-20102

G
M960
N65al

Pan-Africanism - Addresses, essays, lectures.
Nkrumah, Kwame, Pres. Ghana, 1909-
All-African People's Conference. Speeches by the Prime Minister of Ghana at the opening and closing sessions on December 8th and 13th, 1958. [at the] Community Centre, Accra. [Accra, Govt. Printer, 1958]
12p. 21½cm.
Cover title.

1. Africa - Politics. I. Title. 2. Pan-Africanism - Addresses, essays, lectures.

Ghana
M960
Ab81

Pan-Africanism.
Abraham, Willie E 1934-
The mind of Africa. ~~Chicago, University of Chicago Press [1962]~~ London, Weidenfeld and Nicholson [1962]
206 p. 23 cm. (The Nature of human society)
Portrait of author on book jacket.

1. Africa—Civilization. 2. Africa—Econ. condit. 3. Pan-Africanism. I. Title.

DT30.A2 916 63-9733 ‡
Library of Congress [5]

Kenya
M967.62
M45f2

Pan-Africanism.
Mboya, Tom.
Freedom and after. ~~[1st ed.] Boston, Little, Brown [1963]~~ [London] A. Deutsch [1963]
~~x, 288 p.~~ illus., ports., map (on lining papers) 22 cm. 271p.
Autobiographical.

1. Kenya Colony and Protectorate—2. Africa—Politics—1960- 3. Pan-Africanism. I. Title.

DT434.E27M35 967.62 63-20102
Library of Congress [5]

M306
P19c2

Pan Africanism - Congresses.
Pan-African Congress. *5th, Manchester, Eng., 1945.*
History of the Pan-African Congress: colonial and coloured unity, a programme of action. Edited by George Padmore. [2d ed. with new material] London, Hammersmith Bookshop [1963]
vi, 74 p. 22 cm.
"Report of the 1945 Pan-African Congress."

1. Pan Africanism—Congresses. I. Padmore, George, 1903-1959, ed. II. Title. III. Title: Colonial and coloured unity.

DT30.P28 1945ca 64-54191
Library of Congress [1]

Ghana
M960
Ab81a

Pan-Africanism.
Abraham, Willie E
The mind of Africa. [Chicago] University of Chicago Press [1962]
206 p. 23 cm. (The Nature of human society)

1. Africa—Civilization. 2. Africa—Econ. condit. 3. Pan-African ism. I. Title.

DT30.A2 916 63-9733 ‡
Library of Congress [63f5]

Ghana
M960
N65

Pan-Africanism.
Nkrumah, Kwame, *Pres. Ghana*, 1909-
Africa must unite. New York, F. A. Praeger [1963]
xvii, 229 p. port., map (on lining papers) 23 cm.
Bibliographical footnotes.

1. Pan-Africanism. 2. Africa—Hist. 3. Ghana—Hist. 4. States, New. I. Title.

DT30.N45 1963 960 63—18462
Library of Congress [64f5]

Trinidad
M330
P13p

Pan-Africanism or communism?
Padmore, George, 1903-
Pan-Africanism or communism? The coming struggle for Africa. New York, Roy Publishers [1956]
463 p. illus. 23 cm.

1. Africa—Politics. I. Title.

DT31.P3 1956a 960 55-9307 ‡
Library of Congress [7]

Haiti
M327.7
D46

Pan Americanism.
Desinor, Yvan M
Tragédies Américaines. Port-au-Prince, Imprimerie de l'Etat, 1962.

171p. 21cm.

1. Pan Americanism. I. Title.

Ghana
M960
Q23

Pan-Africanism.
Quaison-Sackey, Alex.
Africa unbound; reflections of an African statesman. Foreword by Kwame Nkrumah. New York, Praeger [1963]
174 p. 21 cm. (Books that matter)

1. Africa—Politics. 2. Pan-Africanism. 3. Negroes in Africa. I. Title.

DT30.Q3 916 63-10897 ‡
Library of Congress [5]

M960
Am3

Pan-Africanism reconsidered.
American Society of African Culture.
Pan-Africanism reconsidered. Berkeley, University of California Press, 1962.
xix, 376 p. tables. 25 cm.
"Speeches, papers, and comments given at the Third Annual Conference of the American Society of African Culture, which was held in Philadelphia at the University of Pennsylvania from June 22 to June 26, 1960."
Bibliographical footnotes.

1. Pan-Africanism—Addresses, essays, lectures. 2. Africa—Civilization—Addresses, essays, lectures. ~~3. Negro race.~~ I. Title.
3. Negritude. 4. Africa-Social thought.
DT30.A53 301.451 62-11491
Library of Congress [5]

Panama
M986.2
W52f

Panama.

Westerman, George W
Fifty years (1903-1953) of treaty negotiations between the United States and Republic of Panama. Panama, Imprenta de la Academia, 1953?

26p. 21cm.
Spanish text - 26p.

Panama
M986.2
W52m

Panama.
Westerman, George W
A minority group in Panama; Some aspects of West Indian life. 3rd ed. Panama, National Civic League, 1950.

32 p. 21 cm.

Panama
M986.2
W52so

Panama.

Westerman, George W
Sore spots in United States-Panama Relations Address given at International House, Chicago, by George W. Westerman, associate editor, "The Panama Tribune," delegate to the Inter-American Press Association's 8th Annual Meeting on October 16, 1952 under sponsorship of the Labor-Education Division of Roosevelt College, N.Y., The Isthmian Civic Society, 1952.

9p. 21cm.
Spanish - text

Panama
M986.2
W52t

Panama.
Westerman, George W
Toward a better understanding. Preface by Gil Blas Tejeira. 2nd ed. [Panama] 1946.

20 p. 22 cm.
English and Spanish text, separately paged; added t.p. in Spanish.
Inscribed by author: Sincere regards, G.W. Westerman.
______ ______cop. 2. Inscribed by author: To Walter White with compliments. G.W. Westerman.

Panama
MB9
M52w

Panama - History.

Westerman. George W
Carlos Antonio Mendoza father of Panama's Independence Act in commemoration of the Centennial of his birth, October 31, 1856. Panama, Published by the Bellas Artes Department and also Publications from the Educational Department Panama, 19??

83p. illus., port. 21½cm.
Bound with: Carlos Antonio Mendoza padre del acta de independencia de Panama. 83p.

Panama
M986.2
W52u

Panama - Housing.

Westerman, George W
Urban housing in Panama and some of its problems. Panama, Imprenta de la Academia, 1955.

43p. tables 23½cm.

Haiti
M972.94
J98q

Panama canal.
Justin, Joseph
Autour de l'isthme de Panama (questions internationales d'actualité) par Joseph Justin. Port-au-Prince, Imprimerie H. Amblard, 1913.

ii, 43p. 22½cm.

Panama
M986.2
W52sc

Panama Canal - Segregation in education.

Westerman, George W
School segregation on the Panama Canal Zone.

Pp. 276-87 22½cm.
Reprinted from Phylon, The Atlanta University Review of Race and Culture, Third Quarter, 1954.

Panama
M986.2
W52s

Panama Canal Zone.
Westerman, George W
A Study of socio-economic conflicts on the Panama Canal Zone. Panama City, Liga Civica Nacional.

26, 29p. 22cm.

Haiti
M972.94
C29p

... Le panaméricanisme à travers l'histoire...

Chaumette, Max Gustave.
... Le panaméricanisme à travers l'histoire d'Haïti; préface de André Liautaud ... Port-au-Prince, Haïti [Imprimerie Telhomme] 1944.

4 p. l., [5]-126, [2] p. 21cm.
"Bibliographie": p. [125]-126.

1. Haiti—Hist. 2. American republics. I. Title.

44-44784

Library of Congress F1921.C496
[2] 972.94

M780
P19

Panassié, Hugues.
Guide to jazz, by Hugues Panassié and Madeleine Gautier. Translated by Desmond Flower; edited by A. A. Gurwitch. Introd. by Louis Armstrong. Boston, Houghton Mifflin, 1956.

vii, 312 p. illus., ports. 22 cm.
"First published in Paris, May 1954, under the title Dictionnaire du jazz. In its present form the book has been brought up to date and expanded for American publication."

1. Music—Bio-bibl. 2. Jazz music—Dictionaries. I. Gautier, Madeleine, 1905– joint author. II. Title.

ML102.J3P33 *785.42 781.5 56—10291

Library of Congress [57f10]

Bahamas
M332
Sm6a

Panics.
Smith, James Carmichael, 1852–
Abundance and hard times, by Jas. C. Smith ... London, K. Paul, Trench, Trübner & co., ltd., 1908.

30 p. 21½cm.
A plea for the establishment by law of "the wage co-operative system of profit-sharing" and "the double standard money system."

1. Panics. 2. Currency question—Gt. Brit. 3. Profit-sharing. I. Title.

16-7960

Library of Congress HB3723.S55

Russia
M891
P97po

Panin, Ivan, 1855- tr.
Pushkin, Aleksandr Sergieevich, 1799-1837.
Poems by Alexander Pushkin; translated from the Russian, with introduction and notes by Ivan Panin. Boston, Cupples and Hurd, 1888.

179 p. 18cm.

I. Panin, Ivan, 1855– tr.

13-24617

Library of Congress
———— Copy 2.
Copyright 1888: 26862 [a37b1]

Ghana
M700
K98

Panoply of Ghana.
Kyerematen, Alex Atta Yaw, 1916-
Panoply of Ghana. [London] Longmans [1964]

vii, 120p. illus. (part col.) ports. (part col.) 23cm.

Virgin Is.
M811.5
C86p

Panorama.

Creque, Cyril Felix William, 1899–
Panorama; St. Thomas, Virgin Islands. [Poems] [Wauwatosa, Wis., Printed by the Kenyon Press Pub. Co., 1947]

81 p. 24 cm.

I. Title.
PS3093.C7P3 811.5 47-25197*
© 10May47; author, Charlotte Amalie, Virgin Islands; A13732.

Library of Congress [2]

Haiti
M843.91
T35pa

Panorama de l'art haïtien.

Thoby-Marcelin, Philippe, 1904–
Panorama de l'art haïtien. Port-au-Prince, Impr. de l'État, 1956.

75 p. 20 cm.

1. Art—Haiti—Hist. I. Title.

A 57-5914

Florida. Univ. Library
for Library of Congress [1]

Dominican Republic
M860.9
H38p

... Panorama histórico de la literatura dominicana.
Henríquez Ureña, Max, 1885–
... Panorama histórico de la literatura dominicana (conferencias dictadas en la Facultad de filosofía de la Universidad del Brasil) Rio de Janeiro [Companhia brasileira de artes gráficas] 1945.

337 p., 1 l. 24cm.
"Correcciones": slip inserted.
Bibliographical foot-notes.

1. Dominican literature—Hist. & crit. I. Title.

PQ7400.H37 860.9 47-3336

Library of Congress [3]

Haiti
MB9
G94

Pantal a Paris.
Bervin, Antoine
Pantal a Paris. 2nd ed. Port-au-Prince, Imp. de l'Etat, 1953.

252p. 18cm. (Collection du sesquicentenaire de l'indépendance d'Haiti)

M811.5
H87p

The panther and the lash.

Hughes, Langston, 1902–
The panther and the lash; poems of our times. [1st ed.] New York, Knopf, 1967.

101 p. 22 cm.

I. Title.

PS3515.U274P3 811'.5'2 67—16156

Library of Congress [67d25]

Dominican Republic
M398
R61

...Papa Legba.

Rodriguez, Manuel Tomás.
...Papa Legba. Ciudad Trujillo, R.D., Imp. Arte y cine, c. por a., 1945.

3p. l., [1], -190p., 2 l. front. 21cm.
Portrait of author laid in.

Haiti
M200
P19c

Papailler, Hubert
Coup d'ailes. Montreal, Imprimerie Saint-Joseph, 1956.

47p. 15½cm.

1. Haiti - Religion.

Haiti
M843.91
P191

Papailler, Hubert.
Les Laboureurs de la mer. [Canada, n.p.] 1959.
143p. 18cm.

1. Haiti. I. Title.

Haiti
M226.8
P28v

Parables.
Paultre, Hector
La vigne du seigneur et la parabole de l'econome infidele.
23p. 15½cm.

Haiti
M841
P21n

Paret, Timothee, Louis Joseph, 1887-1942.
Nouvelle floraison, poèmes. Paris, Editions de la revue mondiale, 1927.
194 [cxcvii-ccvi]p. 18cm.

1. Haitian poetry. I. Title.

M812.5
G51p

Paper and Pencil, an allegory for young people.
Glover, Leonard Horace.
Paper and Pencil, an allegory for young people. Illustrated by Doris Toby Marie Duncan. [1st ed.] New York, Exposition Press [1957]
54 p. illus. 21 cm.

I. Title.

PN6120.A5G515 812.5 57-14159 ‡
Library of Congress [2]

Congo
(Leopolaville)
M967.5
M42

Parent and child.
Matota, H
Influence des membres masculins de la famille sur l'enfant Mukongo; etude descriptive et interpretative. [Louvain, Institut de Psychologie Appliquee et de Pedagogie, 1958]
261p. tables, map. 27cm.
Mimeographed.
At head of title: Université Catholique de Louvain. Institut de Psychologie Appliquée et de Pedagogie

(Continued on next card)

Haiti
M841
A u4p

Parfums créoles.
Auguste, Jules.
Parfums créoles... Préface par Paul Théodore-Vibert. Paris, Berger-Levrault & co., Editeurs, 1905.
vi, 157p. port. (front.) 23cm.

Haiti
M843.91
P19e

Papillon, Pierre.
L'exile du ciel. Port-au-Prince, Henri Deschamps, 1949.
141p. port. 20cm.

1. Haitian fiction. I. title

Congo
(Leopoldville)
M967.5
M42

Parent and child.
Matota, H
Influence des membres masculins de la famille sur l'enfant Mukongo, 1958. (Card 2)

"Mémoire présenté par H. Matota, S. J., pour l'obtention du grade de licencié en psychologie appliquée."
"Références bibliographiques:" p. 252-256.

1. Congo, Belgian. 2. Family - Congo, Belgian. 3. Parent and child. 4. Children in the Congo. I. Title.

Martinique
M972.98
T36p

Parfums et saveurs des Antilles.
Thomarel, André
Parfums et saveurs des Antilles. Préface de Daniel Thaly, illustré par Ardachés Baldjian. [Paris, Ch. Ebener, 1934]
42p. plates. 32cm.

Cuba
M972.91
Se6

Para blancos y Negros.
Serra y Montalvo, Rafael, 1858–
Para blancos y negros; ensayos políticos, sociales y económicos, por Rafael Serra. 4 ser. Habana, Impr. "El Score," 1907.
215, [4] p. incl. illus., ports., facsim. 21½cm.
"Lecciones de política, escrito en inglés por C. Nordhoff, y vertido al castellano por R. Serra": p. [25]-84.

1. Negroes. 2. Negroes in Cuba. I. Title.
8-1541 Revised
Library of Congress F1789.N3S4
[r44b2]

M370
M76p

Parent-teacher cooperation.
Montgomery, Bishop Marteinne.
Parent-teacher cooperation, by Bishop Marteinne Montgomery ... Birmingham, Ala., Progressive publishing co., 1942, °1946.
xvi, 158 p. diagrs. 20½cm.
Imprint date, 1942, blotted out; "copyright 1946" stamped on t.-p.
Includes bibliographies.

1. Parents' and teachers' associations. 2. Negroes—Education. I. Title.
46—7021
Library of Congress LC225.M6
[47c2] 371.103

Puerto Rico
M863
R524

The pariahs.
Rivera Correa, R R
The pariahs. New York, Carlton Press [1967]
60p. 21cm.
Portrait of author on book jacket.

1. Puerto Rico - History - Fiction.
2. Albizu Campos, Pedro - Fiction.
I. Title.

Dominican Republic
P30.9
[illegible]

Para la historia de los indigenismos.
Henríquez Ureña, Pedro, 1884–
... Para la historia de los indigenismos ... Buenos Aires [Imprenta de la Universidad de Buenos Aires] 1938.
147 p., 1 l. 22½cm. (Facultad de filosofía y letras de la Universidad de Buenos Aires. Instituto de filología. [Biblioteca de dialectología hispanoamericana, director: Amado Alonso. Anejo III])
"Bibliografía": p. [7]-14.
Contents.—Papa y batata.—El enigma del aje.—Boniato.—Caribe.—Palabras antillanas.

1. Spanish language—Foreign words and phrases—Indian. I. Title.
42—5419
Library of Congress PC4822.H4
[44d1] 462.4

M370
M76p

Parents' and teachers' assoc. tions.
Montgomery, Bishop Marteinne.
Parent-teacher cooperation, by Bishop Marteinne Montgomery ... Birmingham, Ala., Progressive publishing co., 1942, °1946.
xvi, 158 p. diagrs. 20½cm.
Imprint date, 1942, blotted out; "copyright 1946" stamped on t.-p.
Includes bibliographies.

1. Parents' and teachers' associations. 2. Negroes—Education. I. Title.
46—7021
Library of Congress LC225.M6
[47c2] 371.103

Haiti
M843.91
M28p

Parias; documentaire.
Magloire-Saint-Aude, Clément
Parias; documentaire. [Port-au-Prince, Imprimerie de l'Etat, 1949]
100p. 21cm.

I. Title.

Haiti
M226.8
P28n

Parables.
Paultre, Hector
Note explicative sur la parabole de l'econome infidele. Preface de Jean-Charles Pressoir. Port-au-Prince, Imprimerie Vertieres, n.d.
24p. 15½cm.

Haiti
M841
P21a

Paret, Timothée, 1887–
... L'âme vibrante, poèmes. 2. éd. Paris, Jouve & cie, 1929.
222 p. front. (port.) 18½ cm. (On cover: Bibliothèque haitienne)
"Notes bio-bibliographiques": p. [11]-12.

I. Title. 1. Haitian poetry.
[Full name: Louis Joseph Timothée Paret]
31—9154
Library of Congress PQ3949.P3A8 1929
[48c½] 841.91

Guadeloupe
M248
P13pa
1854

Paris.
Privat d'Anglemont, Alex[andre] ca1815-1859.
Paris anecdote; Les industries inconnues, la childebert, les oiseaux de nuit, la villa des chiffoniers, por Alex. Privat d'Anglemont. Paris, Chez P. Jannet, Librairie, 1854.
232p. 16cm.

Haiti
M226.8
P28p

Parables.
Paultre, Hector
Les paraboles du Seigneur et la Dette de peche. Port-au-Prince, Haiti [Imprimer par la Presse Evangelique d'Haiti, n.d.]
14p. 15½cm.

Haiti
M972.94
P21

Paret, Timothée, 1887–
... Dans la mêlée ... Pensées, conférences, discours, etc. (1916-1931) ... Paris, Jouve & cie, 1932.
230, [2] p. front. (port.) plates. 19½cm.
Addresses and articles on politics in Haiti.

1. Haiti—Pol. & govt.—1844— 2. Political parties—Haiti. I. Title.
[Full name: Louis Joseph Timothée Paret]
33—5230
Library of Congress F1926.P22
[2] 972.94

Guadeloupe
M248
P13p
1886

Paris.
Privat d'Anglemont, Alexandre, d. ca. 1815-1859
... Paris inconnu, avec une étude sur la vie de l'auteur par A. Delvau. Soixante-trois dessins à la plume, par F. Coindre. Paris, P. Rouquette, 1886.
2 p. l., 355, [1] p. front., illus. 25cm.
First edition, Paris, 1861.
Contents.—Alexandre Privat d'Anglemont, étude par M. Alfred Delvau.—Fragment d'un article publié par M. Victor Cochinat, aussitôt après l'enterrement de Privat d'Anglemont.—Portraits et caractères.—Le cloître Saint-Jean de Latran.—Le camp des barbares de Paris.—Rues Traversine et Clos-Bruneau.—Paris en villages.—Peintures d'histoire, portraits et paysages.—Esquisses parisiennes.—Nouvelles.—Théâtre.—Articles divers.—Lettres.—Poésies. Sonnets.—La closerie des lilas.
1. Paris. I. Delvau, Alfred, 1825-1867.
4—21516
Library of Congress DC715.P97
[a22c1]

Paris.
Guadeloupe
M848 Privat d'Anglemont, Alexandre, 1815-1859.
P13p Paris inconnu, par A. Privat d'Anglemont,
1875 précédé d'une etude sur sa vie par Alfred
Delvau, deuxieme ed., aug... Paris, Adolphe
Delahays, Librairie-Editeur, 1875.

315p. 16cm.

Paris.
Guadeloupe
M848 Privat d'Anglemont Alexandre, ca1815-1859.
P13p Paris inconnu, par A. Privat D'Anglemont.
1861 Précédé d'une étude sur sa vie par M. Alfred
Delvau ... Paris, Adolph Delahays, Librairie-
Editeur, 1861.

283p. 16cm.

Paris.
Guadeloupe
M848 Privat d'Anglemont, Alexandre, 1815-1859.
P13s Les singes de dieu et les hommes du diable;
edited with foreword, notes and vocabulary by
Mercer Cook and Guichard Parris. Atlanta,
Atlanta University, 1936.

152-27½cm. (Atlanta University French
series)
Vocabulary and notes: p. 9-16.
Text taken from 1884 edition of Paris
Inconnu

Paris-Soc. life & cust.
Guadeloupe
M848 Privat d'Anglemont, Alexandre, d.ca. 1815-1859.
P13pa ...Paris anecdote, avec une préface et des
1885 notes par Charles Monselet. Ed. illustrée de
cinquante dessins àla plume par J. Delon, et
d'un portrait de Privat d'Anglemont grave à
l'eau-forte par R. de Los Rios. Paris, P.
Rouquette, 1885.

2p. l., 278p., 1 l. front (port.) illus.
25cm.
Title in red and black

Paris. Exposition coloniale internationale,
1931.
Martinique
M972.98 Philémon, Césaire.
P53g ... Galeries martiniquaises; population, mœurs, activités
diverses et paysages de la Martinique; 3 cartes, 42 illustrations.
1. éd. Fort-de-France, Dans toutes les librairies et chez
l'auteur; Paris, Chez l'auteur [1931]

430 p., 1 l. front., plates, ports., fold. maps. 23cm.
At foot of t.-p.: Exposition coloniale internationale, Paris, 1931.

1. Martinique. I. Paris. Exposition coloniale internationale, 1931.
II. Title.
32-18871
Library of Congress F2081.P53
Copyright A—Foreign 14467
[2]
917.298

Paris. Université. Faculté de droit et des
sciences économiques. Série "Afrique," no. 2.
Senegal
M966.3 Traoré, Bakary.
T688 Forces politiques en Afrique noire, par Bakari Traoré,
Mamadou Lô et Jean-Louis Alibert ... Paris, Presses universitaires de France, 1966.

viii, 312 p. 24 cm. (Travaux et recherches de la Faculté de
droit et des sciences économiques de Paris. Série "Afrique," no 2)
20 F. (F 66-12565)

Includes bibliographies.

1. Political parties—Senegal. 2. Africa, Sub-Saharan—Politics.
I. Title. (Series: Paris. Université. Faculté de droit et des
sciences économiques. Série "Afrique," no 2) II. Lo,
Mamadou. III. Alibert, Jean-Louis. IV. Series.
JQ3396.A979T7 329.9'663 67-74794
Library of Congress [2]

...Paris anecdote.
Guadeloupe
M848 Privat d'Anglemont, Alexandre, d.ca. 1815-1859.
P13pa ...Paris anecdote, avec une préface et des
1885 notes par Charles Monselet. Ed. illustrée de
cinquante dessins à la plume par J. Delon, et
d'un portrait de Privat d'Anglemont grave
à l'eauforte par R. de Los Rios. Paris, P.
Rouquette, 1885.

2p. l., 278p., 1 l. front. (port.) illus.
25cm.

M808.8 The Paris review.
P21 Best short stories. Introd. by William Styron. [1st ed.]
New York, Dutton, 1959.

245 p. 21 cm.

1. Short stories.

PZ1.P215Be 59—10771 ‡
Library of Congress [60k10]

Park, Mungo, 1771-1806.
Senegal
M966.3 Isaaco.
Is1 [The] journal of Isaaco, Mungo Park's guide.

(In: Park, Mungo. The journal of a mission to
the interior of Africa, in the year 1805...
London, John Murray, 1815, v.2, pp.289-335.)

Park, Robert Emory, 1868-1942.
M301 Masuoka, Jitsuichi, 1903- ed.
M39 Race relations: problems and theory; essays in honor of
Robert E. Park. Edited by Jitsuichi Masuoka and Preston
Valien. Chapel Hill, University of North Carolina Press
[1961]

x, 290 p. 24 cm.
Bibliographical footnotes.

1. Race problems—Addresses, essays, lectures. 2. U. S.—Race
question—Addresses, essays, lectures. 3. Park, Robert Emory, 1868-1942. I. Valien, Preston, joint ed. II. Title.

HT1521.M29 301.451 61—66070
Library of Congress [62q5]

M326.99B Parker, Allen.
P22r Recollections of slavery times, by
Allen Parker. Worcester, Mass., Chas.
W. Burbank and Co., 1895.
96p. 18½cm.

1. Slavery in the U.S. 2. Slave narratives

Basutoland Parker, Cecil John Lanham, 1899-
M896.3 Mopeli-Paulus, Attwell Sidwell, 1913-
M79b Blanket boy, by Peter Lanham [pseud.]
Based on an original story by A.S. Mopeli-
Paulus. New York, Crowell [1953.]

309p. 21cm.

Parker, Cecil John Lanham, 1899-
Basutoland
M896.3 Mopeli-Paulus, Attwell Sidwell, 1913-
M79bL Blanket boys's moon, by Peter Lanham pseud.
Based on an original story by A.S. Mopeli-
Paulus. London, Collins, 1953.

320p. 21cm.

Parker, Cecil John Lanham, 1899-
Basutoland
M896.3 Mopeli-Paulus, Attwell Sidwell, 1913-
M79blu Blut hat nur eine farbe, roman (Blanket
boy's moon), [by] Peter Lanham, nach einem
Tatsachenbericht von A.S. Mopeli-Paulus.
Munchen, R. Piper, 1953.

398p. 19cm.

Parker, Cecil John Lanham, 1899-
Basutoland
M896.3 Mopeli-Paulus, Attwell Sidwell, 1913-
M79d Dekenjongen. Door Peter Lanham en
A. S. Mopeli-Paulus, stamhoofd van
Basoetoland, Zuid-Afrika. Amsterdam,
Uitgeverij Nieuwe Wieken [1952]

296p. 23cm.
Title: Blanket boy's moon.

M572 Parker, George Wells
P22c The children of the sun, by George Wells
Parker ... Omaha, Nebraska, The Hamitic league
of the world c1918.

31p. 22cm.

1. Africa. I. Title.

M01 Parker, John W
P22b A bibliography of the published writings
of Benjamin Griffith Brawley. Reprinted
from the North Carolina Historical Review,
Vol. XXXIV, No. 2, April, 1957.

13p. 25cm.

1. Bibliography. 2. Brawley, Benjamin
Griffith, 1822-1939. I. Title.

M616 Parker, John W
P22e The effect of terramycin and aureomycin on
blood coagulation, by John W. Parker, Jr.,
and Louis T. Wright. Science, September 12,
1952.

282-284p. 26cm.
Reprinted from Science. V. 116, September 12
1952.

1. Antibiotics.

M616 Parker, John W.
P22f Further observations on soft tissue infections treated with terramycin, by John W.
Parker, John C. Lord, James C. DiLorenxo,
Louis T. Wright, and Boris A. Shidlovsky.
Antibiotics and chemotherapy, 1953.

123p-150p. tables. 26cm.
Reprinted from Antibiotics and chemotherapy,
February 1953.

1. Antibiotic

M812.5 Parker, John W
P22 Some comments on the A Shrew - The Shrew
controversy.

pp. 178-82 23cm.
Reprinted from CLA Journal, Vol. 2, No. 3,
March 1959.

1. Drama, American - History and Criticism.
2. The Taming of the Shrew - History and
Criticism.

Parker, Thomas, 1830- p. 200-01
M286 Whitted, J A
W61h A history of the Negro Baptists of North
Carolina, by Rev. J.A. Whitted... Raleigh,
Presses of Edwards and Broughton printing co.,
1908.
212p. front. plates & 23½cm.

Parkes, Francis Ernest Kobina.
African heaven, pp. 230-231.
M808.8 New world writing. 1st-
N42 Apr. 1952-
v.15 [New York] New American Library.

v. 18 cm. (N.A.L. Mentor books)

Ghana
M896.1 Parkes, Frank Kobina
P22s Songs from the wilderness. London, University of London Press [1965]

64p. 22cm.

I. Title.

Parkhurst, Henry Martyn, 1825- reporter.
MC10 **Brown, William Wells,** *b.* 1815.
B811 A lecture delivered before the Female anti-slavery society of Salem, at Lyceum hall, Nov. 14, 1847. By William W. Brown, a fugitive slave. Reported by Henry M. Parkhurst ... Boston, Massachusetts anti-slavery society, 1847.

22 p. 19^cm^.

1. Slavery in the U. S.—Controversial literature—1847. I. Female anti-slavery society of Salem. II. Parkhurst, Henry Martyn, 1825- reporter.

Library of Congress E449.B8831 11—6899
[a29b1]

MB9 **Parks, Gordon** Roger, 1912-
P22 A choice of weapons. [1st ed.] New York, Harper & Row [1966]

x, 274 p. 22 cm.

I. Title.

PS3566.A73C5 770.924 (B) 64-25119

Library of Congress [5]

M813.5 **Parks, Gordon** Roger, 1912-
P23Le The learning tree. [1st ed.] New York, Harper & Row [1963]

308 p. 22 cm.

I. Title.

PZ4.P249Le 63-16528 ‡

Library of Congress [5]

MB9 **Parks, Lillian (Rogers)**
P23m My thirty years backstairs at the White House [by] Lillian Rogers Parks in collaboration with Frances Spatz Leighton. New York, Fleet Pub. Corp. [1961]

346 p. 21 cm.
Portrait of author on book jacket.

1. Presidents—U. S.—Biog. 2. Presidents—U. S.—Wives. 3. Washington, D. C. White House. I. Title.

E176.1.P37 923.173 61—7626 ‡

Library of Congress [61f30]

Parnaso antillano;
Dominican
Republic **Bazil, Osvaldo.**
M861.6 Parnaso antillano; compilación completa de los mejores poetas de Cuba, Puerto Rico y Santo Domingo, por Osvaldo
B34p. Bazil. Barcelona, Maucci; [etc., etc., 1918]

2 p. l., viii p., 1 l., [7]-384 p. 19^cm^.

1. Cuban poetry (Selections: Extracts, etc.) 2. Puerto Rican poetry (Selections: Extracts, etc.) 3. Dominican poetry (Selections: Extracts, etc.) I. Title.

Library of Congress PQ7361.B3 18—21077
[42c1]

Parnaso dominicano;
Dominican **Bazil, Osvaldo.**
Republic
M861.6 Parnaso dominicano; compilación completa de los mejores poetas de la república de Santo Domingo, por Osvaldo Bazil.
B34p 3 Barcelona, Maucci; [etc., etc., 1917]

223 p. 18½^cm^.

1. Dominican poetry. I. Title.

18—21988

Library of Congress PQ7451.B3
[a39b1]

Parnaso portorriqueno.
Puerto Rico
M861. **Torres Rivera, Enrique,** *ed.*
T63 Parnaso portorriqueño, antología esmeramamente seleccionada de los mejores poetas de Puerto Rico por Enrique Torres Rivera. Barcelona, Maucci [1920]

351 p. 18½^cm^.

1. Puerto Rican poetry (Collections) I. Title.

41-21069 Revised

Library of Congress PQ7434.T6
[r42c2] 861.0822

M810.8 **The Parnassian;** prose and poetry by sixteen members of the
P24 younger generation, with an introduction by Alphеus Butler. Chicago, Washington [etc.] Laurel publishers, 1930.

64 p. 21^cm^.

"Limited edition."
"First printing September 1930."
Partial contents: Introduction, by Alpheus Butler-Streets. Half-moon lane, by Alpheus Butler. Hands of a brown woman, by Frank Marshall Davis. Clay, by Beatrice M. Murphy.
1. American literature—20th cent. I. Butler, Alpheus.

30-30197

Library of Congress PS536.P3
——— Copy 2.
Copyright A 30295 [2] 810.8

Parny, Evariste Désiré de Forges, vicomte de, 1753-1814.
Guadeloupe
M841 **Barquissau, Raphaël.**
L55b Les poètes créoles du XVIIIe siècle (Parny, Bertin, Léonard) Paris, J. Vigneau, 1949.

249 p. ports. 24 cm.
Bibliography: p. [225]-228.
White author.

1. Parny, Évariste Désiré de Forges, vicomte de, 1753-1814. 2. Bertin, Antoine, chevalier de, 1752-1790. 3. Léonard, Nicolas Germain, 1744-1793. I. Title. II. Leonard, Nicolas, Germain, 1744-1793.

PQ427.B3 841.509 50-20934

Library of Congress [1]

Paro mag jowadi.
Kenya
M967.62 Oyende, J P
Oy3p Paro mako kuom dohini e Kenya [Some thoughts on native tribunals in Kenya] Nairobi, Eagle Press, 1950.

27p. 18cm. (Paro mag jowadi. Your friends are thinking series)
Written in Luo and English
1. Justice, Administration of - Kenya Colony and Protectorate. 2. Kenya Colony and Protectorate. I. Title. II. Title: Some thoughts on native tribunals in Kenya. III. Series. IV. Series: Your friends are thinking seriès.

Paro mako kuom dohini e Kenya.
Kenya
M967.62 Oyende, J P
Oy3p Paro mako kuom dohini e Kenya [Some thoughts on native tribunals in Kenya] Nairobi, Eagle Press, 1950.

27p. 18cm. (Paro mag jowadi. Your friends are thinking series)
Written in Luo and English
1. Justice, Administration of - Kenya Colony and Protectorate. 2. Kenya Colony and Protectorate. I. Title. II. Title: Some thoughts on native tribunals in Kenya. III. Series. IV. Series: Your friends are thinking seriès.

M910 Parris, Guichard, 1903-
C77m Cook, Mercer, 1903- ed.
Madame de Duras' Ourika, followed by Delphine Gay's poem Ourika. Edited with a foreword, notes and vocabulary by Mercer Cook and Guichard Parris. Atlanta, Atlanta University, 1936.

49 p. 28 cm. (Atlanta University french series)

M910 Parris, Guichard, 1903- ed.
C77s Cook, Mercer, 1903- ed.
Saint Lambert's Zimeo. Edited with foreword, notes and vocabulary by Mercer Cook and Guichard Parris. Atlanta, Atlanta University, 1936.

28 p. 28 cm. (The Atlanta University french series)

M976.6 Parrish, Mary E Jones
P24e Events of the Tulsa disaster, by Mrs. Mary E. Jones Parrish.
[n.p., n.p., n.d.]
112p. plates. 22cm.
Cover title.

1. Tulsa, Oklahoma. 2. Riots. I. Title.

M326
P24o Parrott, Russell, 1791-1824.
An oration on the abolition of the slave trade, by Russell Parrott. Delivered on the first of January, 1814, at the African church of St. Thomas. Philadelphia. Printed for the different societies, 1814.

13p. 21cm.

1. Slave trade.

West Indies
M972.9 **Parry, John Horace.**
P24s A short history of the West Indies, by J. H. Parry and P. M. Sherlock. London, Macmillan; New York, St. Martin's Press, 1956.

316 p. illus. 23 cm.
Includes bibliography.

1. West Indies—Hist. I. Sherlock, Philip Manderson, joint author.

F1621.P33 972.9 56—58641 ‡

Library of Congress [57k10]

M512 **Parson, Robinson H**
P25 College algebra. [1st ed.] New York, Vantage Press [1963]

383 p. diagrs., tables. 21 cm.
Portrait of author on book jacket.

1. Algebra. I. Title.

QA154.P32 512 63-25497

Library of Congress [3]

Parson Johnson's lecture...
M811.5 Todd, Walter E
T56p. Parson Johnson's lecture, by Walter E. Todd. Washington, D.C., Murray bros., 1906.
45p. front. 19cm.

Parson Wiggins' son.
M813.5 Williams, Richard L.
W68ip Parson Wiggins' son. New York, Carlton Press [1964]

117p. 21cm. (A Geneva book)

Parsons, Albert Richard, 1848-1887

MB9
P25p

Parsons, Lucy Eldine(Gonzalez)
Life of Albert R. Parsons, with brief history of the labor movement in America ... Chicago, L.E. Parsons, 1889.

4p. l., xxviiip., 2l., 254p. front. plates. ports., facsims., diagr. 22½cm.

Cape Verde
M398
P25fol

Parsons, Elsie Worthington (Clews) 1875–1941.
Folk-lore from the Cape Verde islands ... by Elsie Clews Parsons ... Cambridge, Mass., and New York, American folk-lore society, 1923.

2 v. 25cm. (*Half-title:* Memoirs of the American folk-lore society, vol. xv, pt. I–II)

Contains music.
"Published in co-operation with the Hispanic society of America."
"Bibliography and abbreviations": v. 1, p. xvii–xxv.

1. Folk-lore—Cape Verde islands. I. Hispanic society of America.

24—4017

Library of Congress GR1.A5 vol. xv, pt. I–II
——— Copy 2. GR360.C3P3
[a43h1]

M398
P25

Parsons, (Mrs.) Elsie Worthington (Clews), 1875–1944. (ed.)
Folklore of the Sea islands, South Carolina, by Elsie Clews Parsons. Cambridge, Mass., and New York, American Folklore Society, 1923.

xxx. 219p. illus. (map) 25cm.
(Half- title: Memoirs of the American Folklore society, vol. xvi.)
Contains music.
"List of informants or writers of the tables": p. xxiii-xxvi.

(Continued on next card)

M398
P25

Parsons, (Mrs.) Elsie Worthington (Clews), 1875–1944.(ed.)
Folklore of the Sea islands. 1923.
(Card 2)

"Bibliography and abbreviations" p. xxvii-xxx.

Pages 218–219, Advertising matter.

1. Folklore. 2. Folklore - South Carolina - Sea islands.

Bahamas
M398
P25f

Parsons, Elsie Worthington (Clews) 1875–1944, *ed.*
Folk-tales of Andros island, Bahamas. By Elsie Clews Parsons. Lancaster, Pa., and New York, American folklore society, 1918.

xx, 170 p. illus. (music) 25cm. (*Half-title:* Memoirs of the American folk-lore society. vol. XIII)

"List of informants or writers of the tales": p. xv–xvi.
"Bibliography and abbreviations": p. xvii–xx.
Pages 168–170, advertising matter.

1. Folk-lore—Bahamas.

19—4413

Library of Congress GR1.A5
——— Copy 2. GR121.B3P3
[a45g1]

MB9
P25p

[Parsons, Lucy Eldine (Gonzalez)]
Life of Albert R. Parsons, with brief history of the labor movement in America ... Chicago, L. E. Parsons, 1889.

4 p. l., xxviii p., 2 l., 254 p. front., plates, ports., facsims., diagr. 22½cm.

1. Parsons, Albert Richard, 1848–1887. 2. Labor and laboring classes—U. S.—Hist. 3. Chicago. Haymarket square riot, 1886. I. Title.

15—1424

Library of Congress HX843.P3
[45r42d1]

Parsons, Talcott, 1902- ed.

M301
D122

Dædalus.
The Negro American. Edited and with introductions by Talcott Parsons and Kenneth B. Clark, and with a foreword by Lyndon B. Johnson. Illustrated with a 32 page portfolio of photos. by Bruce Davidson, selected and introduced by Arthur D. Trottenberg. Boston, Houghton Mifflin, 1966.
xxix, 781 p. illus. 24 cm. (The Daedalus library [v. 7])
Most of the essays, some in slightly different form, appeared originally in the Fall 1965 and Winter 1966 issues of Daedalus.
Includes bibliographical references.
1. Negroes—Addresses, essays, lectures. 2. Negroes—Civil rights—Addresses, essays, lectures. I. Parsons, Talcott, 1902- ed. II. Clark, Kenneth Bancroft, 1914- ed. III. Title.

E185.6.D24 301.45196073 66—17174

Library of Congress [67f14]

Parti démocratique de Guinée.

Guinea
M966.52
T64ac

Touré, Sékou, *Pres. Guinea*, 1922–
L'action politique du Parti démocratique de Guinée pour l'émancipation africaine. [Conakry, Impr. nationale, 1959–
v. illus. 24 cm.

1. Nationalism—Guinea, French. 2. Parti démocratique de Guinée. I. Title.

DT543.T6 60-22321 rev ‡

Library of Congress [r62b1]

The party of Negro and white.

M335.4
P42p

Perry, Pettis
The party of Negro and white; from his summation speech to the jury in the thought-control Smith Act trial at Foley Square, New York, Jan. 13,1953. With an introduction by Herbert Aptheker. New York, New Century Publishers, 1953.

15p. 18cm.

Party politics in the West Indies.

Trinidad
M972.9
J23

James, C L R , 1901–
Party politics in the West Indies. San Juan, Vedic Enterprises, n.d.

175p. 22cm.
Portrait of author on back cover.

Martinique
M843.91
R39p

Les passagers du Perwyn.

Richer, Clément.
Les passagers du Perwyn; roman. Paris, Stock, Delamain et Boutelleau, 1944.
212 p. 19 cm.

I. Title.

PQ2635.I 32P3 50-41225

Library of Congress [3]

... Passe-temps, poésies...

Haiti
M841
L61p

Lhérisson, Justin, 1873–
... Passe-temps, poésies ... [Tours, Imp. Deslis frères] 1895.

95, [1] p. front. (port.) 20½cm. [*With his* Les chants de l'aurore ... Port-au-Prince, 1893]

At head of title: Bibliothèque haïtienne ...

I. Title.

25-20888

Library of Congress PQ3949.L5C5

Passing.

M813.5
L32

Larsen, Nella.
Passing, by Nella Larsen. New York & London, A. A. Knopf, 1929.
6 p. l., 3-215, [1] p., 1 l. 19½cm.

I. Title.

29—9090

Library of Congress PZ3.L33Pas
[44e1]

Jamaica
M821.91
M165p

Passing thru
McFarland, Harry Stanley, 1900–
Passing thru; a collection of poems. 1st ed. New York, W. Malliet, 1950.

120p. 21cm.

La passion de Djimé.

Mali
M966.2
S18p

Sissoko, Fily Dabo.
La passion de Djimé. Paris, Éditions de La Tour du guet [1956]
118 p. 19 cm.
Portrait of author on book jacket.

I. Title.

A 57-2634

Illinois. Univ. Library
for Library of Congress [3]

The passport of Mallam Ilia.

Nigeria
M896.3
Ek8pa

Ekwenski, Cyprian
The passport of Mallam Ilia. Cambridge, The University Press, 1960.

80p. 18½cm.

The past, present, and future.

M811.5
C54pt

Clark, B
The past, present, and future;in prose and poetry. Toronot, Adam, Stevenson and Co., 1867.

168p. port. 16½cm.
Pages missing.

The pastor's voice.

M811.5
B79p

Brooks, Walter Henderson, 1851–
The pastor's voice, a collection of poems by Walter Henderson Brooks. Washington, D. C., The Associated publishers, inc. [1945]
xxviii, 391 p. front., ports. 20cm.

I. Title.

45-6354

Library of Congress PS3503.R78P3
[3] 811.5

The path of dreams.

M811.5
M128p

McClellan, George Marion.
The path of dreams, by George Marion McClellan. Louisville, Ky., J. P. Morton & company, incorporated [1916]
2 p. l., 76 p. 20½cm. $1.25
Poems.

I. Title.

16-9044

Library of Congress PS3525.A155P3 1916
Copyright A 428509

The path of Negro liberation.

M335.4
D29p

Davis, Benjamin Jefferson, 1903–
The path of Negro liberation, by Benjamin J. Davis [New York, New Century Publishers, 1947]

22p. 18½cm.

The path of thunder.

S. Africa
M896.3
Ab8p

Abrahams, Peter, 1919–
The path of thunder, by Peter Abrahams. New York, and London . Harper & Brothers, c1948.

278p. 20½cm.

Path to Nigerian freedom.
Nigeria Awolowo, Obafemi.
M966.9 Path to Nigerian freedom; with a foreword by Margery
Aw6p Perham. London, Faber and Faber [1947]
187 p. 23 cm.

1. Nigeria—Pol. & govt. I. Title.
JQ3082.A85 342.66909 47—24937*
Library of Congress [47b1]

M615.4 Patrick, Thomas William, 1872-
P27p Patrick's course in pharmacy, specially designed for preparing drug clerks to pass the Board of Pharmacy... in twenty lessons. Boston, The Blanchard Printing Co., 1906.
20 parts. 28cm.
Missing: Lessons 1, 19, 20.

1. Pharmacy.

Patterns of race relations in the South.
M323. Coleman, Charles C
C67p Patterns of race relations inthe South. New York, Exposition Press [1949]
44p. 21cm.

Pathfinders.
MB Thoms, Adah B.
T38p Pathfinders, a history of the progress of colored graduate nurses, compiled by Adah B. Thoms ... with biographies of many prominent nurses ... [New York, Printed at Kay printing house, inc., °1929]
xvi, 240 p. front., 1 illus., plates, ports. 23½cm.

1. Nurses and nursing. 2. Negroes—Biog. 3. Women, Negro. 4. Nurses and nursing—Study and teaching. I. Title.
[Full name: Adah B. Glassell Thoms]
Library of Congress RT71.T45 29—19412
[41g1]

...Patrie, espérances et souvenirs....
Haiti
M841 Guilbaud, Tertullien, 1856-
G94p ...Patrie, espérances et souvenirs ... Paris, Librairie L. Cerf, 1885.
2p. l., 150p. 16½cm. (With his Feuilles au vent. Paris, 1888)

MB9 Patterson, Floyd.
P26 Victory over myself. With Milton Gross. [New York] B. Geis Associates; distributed by Random House [1962]
244 p. illus. 22 cm.
Portrait of author on book jacket.

I. Title.
GV1132.P3A3 927.9683 62-15657 ‡
Library of Congress [10]

Pathways to democracy.
Trinidad
M323 Maloney, Arnold Hamilton, 1888-
M29p Pathways to democracy, by ... Arnold Hamilton Maloney ... Clarence McDonald Maloney ... [and] Arnold Hamilton Maloney, jr. ... Boston, Meador publishing company [1945]
589 p. 20½cm.

1. Democracy. 2. Minorities. 3. Negroes. I. Maloney, Clarence McDonald, joint author. II. Maloney, Arnold Hamilton, 1916- joint author. III. Title.
45-1864
Library of Congress * JC423.M32
[3] 321.8

Patriotic moments.
M811.5 Brewer, John Mason, 1896- editor.
B75p Patriotic moments: a second book of verse by the Bellerophon quill club of the Booker T. Washington high school, Dallas, Texas. Edited by J.Mason Brewer.
n.p., n.p., 1936.
24p. 19½cm.

Patterson, Frederick Douglas,1901- jt.ed.
MB9 Hughes, William Hardin, 1881- ed.
M85h Robert Russa Moton of Hampton and Tuskegee, edited by William Hardin Hughes [and] Frederick D. Patterson. Chapel Hill, University of North Carolina Press [1956]
238 p. illus. 24 cm.
"Volume of tributes to the life of Dr. Robert Russa Moton."

1. Moton, Robert Russa, 1867-1940. 2. Tuskegee Institute. 3. Hampton Institute, Hampton, Va. I. Patterson, Frederick Douglas, 1901- joint ed.
E185.97.M92H8 923.773 56—14299 ‡
Library of Congress [57i7]

Patrice Lumumba.
Congo
Léopoldville
MB9 Europe; revue mensuelle.
L97e Patrice Lumumba. [Paris] 1962.
173p. 21½cm.

M813.5 Patriotism.
H87m Hughes, Langston, 1902-
My America. Reprinted from the Journal of Educational Sociology, February 1943.
2p. 18cm.
Inscribed: For Arthur Spingarn-Langston Hughes.

MB9 Patterson, Haywood, 1913 or 14- 1952.
P27s Scottsboro boy, by Haywood Patterson [and] Earl Conrad. [1st ed.] Garden City, N. Y., Doubleday, 1950.
viii, 309 p. 22 cm.

ViHaI
1. Scottsboro case. I. Conrad, Earl. II. Title.
343 50-8070
Library of Congress [50]

Congo
(Léopoldville)
MB9 Patrice Lumumba; la verite sur le crime
L97pt odieux des colonialistes. Paris, Editions en Langues Etrangeres, 1961.
268p. 20cm.
Portrait of biographee on front of book.

1. Lumumba, Patrice, 1925-1961.

Patron de New York.
Ivory Coast
M973 Dadie, Bernard B , 1916-
D12p Patron de New York. Paris, Présence Africaine, 1964.
308p. 18½cm.

1. U. S. - Civilization. 2. U. S. - Social life and customs. I. Title.

Jamaica
M823.91 Patterson, Horace Orlando, 1940-
P27ab An absence of ruins, [by] H. Orlando Patterson. London, Hutchinson, 1967.
160 p. 20½ cm. 21/-
(B 67-6532)

I. Title.
PZ4.P3196Ab 67-90010
Library of Congress [3]

Nigeria Patrice Lumumba.
M896.2 Ogali, Ogali Agu, 1931-
Og1p Patrice Lumumba; a drama. Onitsha, Nigeria, Tabansi Printing Press, 1961.
40p. illus. 21½cm.
Portrait of author on book cover.

Patterns of African development.
Kenya
M960 Spiro, Herbert J ed.
M458 Patterns of African development; five comparisons, edited by Herbert J. Spiro. Englewood Cliffs, N. J., Prentice-Hall [1967]
144 p. 21 cm. (A Spectrum book)
Bibliographical footnotes.
CONTENTS.—Introduction, by H. J. Spiro.—Some reflections on constitutionalism for emergent political orders, by C. J. Friedrich.—Nationalism in a new perspective: the African case, by I. Abu-Lughod.—The challenge of change: Japan and Africa, by C. E. Welch.—Borrowed theory and original practice in African politics, by A. A. Mazrui.—Repetition or innovation? By H. J. Spiro.
1. Africa—Politics—1960- —Addresses, essays, lectures. I. Title.
DT30.S675 320.9'6 67-14837
Library of Congress [3]

Jamaica
M823.91 Patterson, Horace Orlando, 1940-
P27c2 The children of Sisyphus, a novel, by H. Orlando Patterson. [1st American ed.] Boston, Houghton Mifflin, 1965 [°1964]
206 p. 21 cm.
Portrait of author on book jacket.

I. Title.
PZ4.P3196Ch 2 65-10682
Library of Congress [3]

M615.4 Patrick, Thomas William, 1872-
P27L A little fun with the U.S.P. (8th revision) before it leaves us. Boston, n.d.
[5]p. 18cm.

I. Title. II. United States Pharmacopoeia.

Patterns of Negro segregation.
M301 Johnson, Charles Spurgeon, 1893-
J63pa Patterns of Negro segregation [by] Charles S. Johnson ... New York, London, Harper & brothers [1943]
xxii, 332 p. 24 cm.
"First edition."
Bibliographical foot-notes.

1. Negroes. 2. U. S.—Race question. I. Title.
43—1802
Library of Congress E185.61.J625
[45k7] 325.260973

Jamaica
M823.91 Patterson, Horace Orlando, 1940-
P27c The children of Sisyphus, a novel [by] H. Orlando Patterson. London, New Authors Limited [1964]
206 p. 21 cm.

I. Title.
PZ4.P3196Ch 65-483
Library of Congress [1]

Jamaica
M823.91
Sa3a

Patterson, Horace Orlander, 1940-
One for a penny.

Pp. 114-120.

In: Salkey, Andrew, comp. Stories from the Caribbean. London, Elek Books, 1965.

Jamaica
M972.92
P27

Patterson, Horace Orlando, 1940-
The sociology of slavery: an analysis of the origins, development and structure of Negro slave society in Jamaica. ⌈London, MacGibbon & Kee⌈1967⌉
310 p. 4 plates (incl. 3 maps), tables. 22½ cm. (Studies in society) 63/- (B 67-8966)
Bibliography: p. 297-301.

1. Slavery in Jamaica. I. Title. (Series)

HT1096.P3 301.45'22'097292 67-86315

Library of Congress ⌈3⌉

Jamaica
M823.91
Sa3a

Patterson, Horace Orlando, 1940-
The very funny man: a tale in two moods.

Pp. 108-113.

In: Salkey, Andrew, comp. Stories from the Caribbean. London, Elek Books, 1965.

M612.68
P27

Patterson, John Andrew, 1875-
The breaking dawn; or, How long may we live in the body? By Rev. J. Andrew Patterson. Being a survey of the doctrines of renewed youth and the perpetuation of life in physical embodiment. Orange, N. J., The Chronicle publishing co., 1910.
ix, 121 p. front. (port.) 23cm. $1.00

1. Hygiene. 2. Longevity. 10-13871

Library of Congress RA776.P3

© Apr. 14, 1910; 2c. June 2, 1910; A 265369; J. A. Patterson, Orange, N. J.

MB9
P264

Patterson, Katheryn
No time for tears. Chicago, Johnson Pub. Co., 1965.

109p. 21cm.

1. Patterson, Katheryn. 2. Handicapped. children. I. Title.

MB9
P264

Patterson, Katneryn.
Patterson, Katheryn
No time for tears. Chicago, Johnson Pub. Co., 1965.

109p. 21cm.

1. Patterson, Katheryn. 2. Handicapped children. I. Title.

MB9
P271

Patterson, Louis H.
Life and works of a Negro detective, by Louis H. Patterson, Jr. Dayton, Ohio, The author n.d.

132p. port. 23cm.

1. Detectives. ~~2. Biographies.~~

M331.88
T371

Patterson, Samuel C
Thompson, Louise.
The IWO and the Negro people; A message and an appeal from Louise Thompson and Samuel Patterson. New York, International Workers Order, n.d.

⌈12⌉p. illus. ports. 15x11cm.

M331.88
T371
1943

Patterson, Samuel C.
Thompson, Louise.
The IWO and the Negro people; A message & an appeal from Louise Thompson and Samuel C. Patterson. New York, International Workers Order, 1943.

22p. illus. ports. 15x23cm.

M323
W73

Patterson, William Lorenzo, 1891-
The battle for America.
Pp. 46-56.

In: Winston, Henry M. Negro freedom. New York, New Current Publishers, 1964.

M335.4
C73

Patterson, William Lorenzo, 1891-
The Communist position on the Negro question ⌈by⌉ William Z. Foster, Benjamin J. Davis, jr., Eugene Dennis ⌈and others⌉ ... Introduction by Nat Ross. New York, New century publishers, 1947.
61, ⌈1⌉ p. 22cm.

1. Negroes. 2. Communism—U. S.—1917- I. Foster, William Zebulon, 1881-

E185.61.C752 325.260973 47-24094

Library of Congress ⌈3⌉

M335.4
C73s

Patterson, William Lorenzo, 1891-
Communists and the Scottsboro case.

M304
P19
V.2
no.2

(In: Communists in the struggle for Negro rights ... New York, New Century, 1945. 19cm. pp. 14-18).

MB9
R321a

Patterson, William Lorenzo, 1891- Introd.
Lawson, Elizabeth,
The gentleman from Mississippi; our first Negro congressman, Hiram R. Revels, by Elizabeth Lawson with an introduction by William L. Patterson. ⌈New York, publisher by author, c 1960⌉

63p. ports. 19cm.
Reference notes: p.54-63.
White author.

Haiti
M972.94
C376m

Paul, Emmanuel Casséus
Dernieres precisions.

pp. 41-64 22cm.
Boundwith: Etienne D. Charlier, En marge de notre. 1955.

I. Title.

Haiti
M398
P28e

Paul, Emmanuel Casséus.
L'ethnographie en Haïti, ses initiateurs, son état actuel, ses tâches et son avenir. Port-au-Prince, Impr. de l'État, 1949.
40, ⌈1⌉ p. ports. 24 cm.
Bibliography: p. ⌈41⌉

1. ~~Ethnology—Haiti—History~~ 1. Haiti - Soc. life & customs
2. Ethnology - Haiti) - ~~History~~
F1916.P3 51-31642

Library of Congress ⌈1⌉

Haiti
M784.4
P28c

Paul, Emmanuel Casséus.
Nos chansons folkloriques et la possibilité de leur exploitation pédagogique. Port-au-Prince, Presses libres, 1951.
38 p. 20 cm. (Collection Notre terre)

Haitian folksongs
1. ~~Folk-songs, Haitian—Hist. & crit.~~

ML3565.P4 52-24912 ‡

Library of Congress ⌈1⌉

Haiti
M398
P28n

Paul, Emmanuel Casséus.
... Notes sur le folk-lore d'Haïti, proverbes et chansons ... Port-au-Prince, Haïti ⌈Imp. Télhomme⌉ 1946.
1 p. l., 5-80 p. illus. (incl. music) 20½cm.

Haitian proverbs Haitian folksongs
1. ~~Proverbs, Haitian~~ 2. ~~Folk-songs, Haitian.~~

PM7854.H3P35 398 47-16942

Library of Congress ⌈3⌉

Paul, Emmanuel Casséus.

Haiti
M786
D41e

Denis, Lorimer.
Essai d'organographie Haitienne, by Lorimer Denis & Emmanuel C. Paul. Port-au-Prince, Imp. Valcin, 1948.

38p. illus. 23½cm.

Publication de Bureau d'Ethnologie de la Republique d'Haiti.

M815
Sp3d

Paul, Nathaniel, 1775?-1839, Speech p. 14-16

Speeches delivered at the anti-colonization meeting in Exeter Hall, London, July 13, 1833, by James Cropper, William Lloyd Garrison, Nathaniel Paul, Daniel O'Connell, Mr. Buckingham, Mr. Hunt, Mr. Abrahams, George Thompson. Boston, Printed by Garrison & Knapp, 1833.

40p. 23½cm.

M813.5
P28s

Paulding, James E., 1935-
Sometime tomorrow. New York, Carlton Press ⌈1965⌉

136p. 21cm.
Portrait of author on book jacket.

I. Title.

Haiti
M972.94
P28c

Pauléus-Sannon, H 1870-1938.
...Le Cap Français vu par une Americaine. ⌈Port-au-Prince⌉ Imp. Aug. A. Heraux, 1936.

1. Cap Français. 2. Haiti.

Haiti
M972.94 **Pauleus-Sannon, H 1870-1938**
P28g ...La guerre de l'independance, par H. Paulius Sannon. Port-au-Prince, Cheraquit, Imp. 1925.

184p. 23½cm.
Presentation copy.
Autographed by the author.

1. Haiti

Haiti
M972.94 **Pauléus-Sannon, H.**, 1870-1938.
P28ha ... Haïti et le régime parlementaire. Examen de la constitution de 1889 ... Paris, A. Fontemoing, 1898.

2 p. l., iv, [5]-180 p. 21½cm.

1. Haiti. Constitution, 1889.

10-21291

Library of Congress [80c1] JL1083.1889.P3

1870-1938

Haiti
MB9 **Pauléus Sannon, H.** 1870-1938.
T64p Histoire de Toussaint-Louverture, par H. Pauléus Sannon ... Port-au-Prince (Haiti) Impr. A. A. Héraux, 1920-

v. port. 24cm.

1. Toussaint Louverture, Pierre Dominique, 1746?-1803. 2. Haiti—Hist.—Revolution, 1791-1804.

20—22229

Library of Congress F1923.T603 [44b1]

Haiti
M972.94 Paultre, Emile
P281e Essai sur M. Price-Mars (Prix de l'alliance Francaise.) Preface D'Etzer Vilaire. [Port-au-Prince] Imprimerie d'etat, 1933.
101p 16cm.

1. Le Comite Haitien. 2. Mars, Jean Price, 1876- 3. Haiti.

Haiti
M841 Paultre, Emile
P28s Le sel de la terre; poems. Port-au-Prince, Haiti, N. A. Theodore, 1956.

30p. 22½cm.

1. Haiti-Poetry.

Haiti
M972.94 Paultre, Hector
P286i ...L'indivisible, 9e article de la collection pour une nouvelle géométrie ... Port-au-Prince, Librarie nouvelle [1943?]

18p. 21cm.

1. Geometry.

Haiti
M972.94 Paultre, Hector.
P28bj ...J'ai Commis le crime. 8e article de la collection pour une nouvelle Géométrie... Port-au-Prince, Librairie Nouvelle, [1943?]

22p. 21cm.

~~1. Haitian author~~
2. Geometry

Haiti
M226.8 Paultre, Hector
P28n Note explicative sur la parabole de l'econome infidele. Preface de Jean-Charles Pressoir. [Port-au-Prince, Imprimerie Vertieres, n.d.]
24p. 15½cm.

~~1. Haitian author.~~ 2. Parables.

Haiti
M226.8 Paultre, Hector
P28p Les paraboles du Seigneur et la Dette de peche. Port-au-Prince, Haiti [Imprime par la Presse Evangelique d'Haiti, n.d.]
14p. 15½cm.

~~1. Haitian author.~~ 2. Parables.

Haiti
M972.94 **Paultre, Hector.**
P286p ...La prudence du serpent interpretation de la parabole de l'econome infidele. Lettre-préface de Dantes Bellegarde. Petion-Ville, Haiti, La Presse Evangelique [1947]

48p. 18cm.

1. Haiti-religion
I. Title

Haiti
M226.8 Paultre, Hector
P28v La vigne du seigneur et la parabole de l'econome infidele.
23p. 15½cm.

~~1. Haitian author.~~ 2. Parables.

Paura.
M813.5 Wright, Richard, 1909-
W93n8 Paura, romanzo. III edizione. Roma, Bompiani, 1951.

582p. 20cm.

Cameroons Le pauvre Christ de Bomba; roman.
MB96.3 Biyidi, Alexandre, 1932-
B65p Le pauvre Christ de Bomba; roman. [by] Mongo Beti [pseud]. Paris, Robert Laffont, 1956.

370p. 19cm.

France La pauvre femme.
M841 Ségálas, Anaïs (Ménard) 1814-1895.
Se3p La pauvre femme. [a poem]
Extract from Athenée des arts, 183[illegible].

[2] p. 20 cm.

M974.7 Payne, Aaron Hamlet
P29n The Negro in New York prior to 1860; The Necessity of the egg cortex for fertilization, by E. E. Just; Typical death-bed scenes in the Victorian novel, by Grace Coleman. The Howard review, June 1923.

95p. 26cm.

I. Just, Ernest Everett, 1883. II. Coleman

Payne, Buckner H., 1799-1883. The negro... 1867.

M572 **Berry, Harrison,** *b.* 1816.
B45 A reply to Ariel. By Harrison Berry ... Macon, Geo., American union book and job office print, MDCCCLXIX [*i. e.* 1869]

36 p. 22½cm.

1. Payne, Buckner H., 1799-1883. The negro ... 1867. 2. Negroes.

13—16791

Library of Congress HT1589.P33 [a38b1]

M326 **Payne, Daniel Alexander, 1811-1893.**
An8s [Address]

(In: Anti-slavery Conference. Paris, 1867. Special report. London. Committee of the British and Foreign Anti-slavery Society 1867 Pp. 24-26)

M287.8 **Payne, Daniel Alexander,** *bp.*, 1811-1893.
P29 History of the African Methodist Episcopal church, by Daniel A. Payne ... Edited by Rev. C. S. Smith ... Nashville, Tenn., Publishing house of the A. M. E. Sunday-school union, 1891.

2 p. l., iii-xvi, 502 p. front., ports. 25cm.

"The present volume will be considered as volume I ... volume II is now in course of preparation."—1st prelim. leaf. No more published?

1. African Methodist Episcopal church—Hist. I. Smith, Charles Spencer, 1832- ed.

37-29687

Library of Congress BX8443.P28 [2] 287.8

M287.8 Payne, Daniel Alexander, 1811-1893
P29m The moral significance of the XVth amendment Xenia, Ohio, Printed by the Xenia Gazette company, 1870]

8p. 21½cm.

1. Fifteenth Amendment. I. Title.

M811.3 **Payne, Daniel Alexander, 1811-1893.**
P29p The pleasures, and other miscellaneous poems. By Daniel A. Payne. Baltimore, Sherwood & Co., 1850.
[8] -43p. 16cm.

1. Poetry. I. Title.

MB9 **Payne, Daniel Alexander, 1811-1893.**
P29r Recollections of seventy years; by Bishop Daniel Alexander Payne ... With an introduction by Rev. F. J. Grimke ... Comp. and arranged by Sarah C. Bierce Scarborough. Ed. by Rev. C. S. Smith. Nashville, Tenn., Publishing house of the A. M. E. Sunday school union, 1888.

335 p. pl., 8 port. (incl. front.) 19cm.

1. African Methodist Episcopal church. I. Scarborough, Sarah C. Bierce, comp. II. Smith, Charles Spencer, 1852- ed. III. Title.

14-12737

Library of Congress E185.97.P34

M287.8 P29r Payne, Daniel Alexander, 1811-1893.
Response of Bishop Payne to Rev. R.C. Ransom. [n.p., n.p., n.d.]

4unnumb. p. 24cm.
Response to an article written by Reverdy C. Ransom and published in the Christian Recorder, Sept. 1890.

1. African Methodist Episcopal Church-Education. 2. Wilberforce University, Ohio. 3. Colleges and Universities.

M287.8 P29t Payne, Daniel Alexander, 1811-1893.
A treatise on domestic education. Cincinnati, Cranston & Stowe, 1889.

184p. 17cm.

1. Education, Religious.

Payne, Daniel Alexander, bp., 1811-1893.

M89 P29d **Coan, Josephus Roosevelt.**
Daniel Alexander Payne, Christian educator, by Josephus Roosevelt Coan ... Philadelphia, Pa., Printed by the A. M. E. book concern [©1935]
viii p., 1 l., 9-139 p. 21cm.
Bibliography: p. 135-139.

1. Payne, Daniel Alexander, bp., 1811-1893.
Library of Congress BX8449.P3C6 35-13104
——— Copy 2.
Copyright A 85040 [2] 922.773

M370 P29e **Payne, Enoch George, 1877–**
An estimate of our Negro schools, by E. George Payne ... New York, N. Y., The American church institute for Negroes [1943?]
26, [2] p. illus. (incl. port.) 21½cm.
White author.

1. Negroes — Education. 2. Protestant Episcopal church in the U. S. A.—Education. I. The American church institute for Negroes.
44-24120
Library of Congress LC2801.P37
[3] 371.974

M89 P294 **Paynter, John Henry,** 1862-1947
Fifty years after, by John H. Paynter ... New York, Margent press, 1940.
vi p., 1 l., 9-224 p. front., ports. 22½cm.

I. Title.
40-13882
Library of Congress PS3531.P37F5 1940
——— Copy 2.
Copyright [2] 818.5

M813.5 P29 **Paynter, John Henry,** 1862-1947
Fugitives of the Pearl, by John H. Paynter ... Washington, D. C., The Associated publishers, inc. [©1930]
xi, 209 p. ports. 19cm.
"Descendants of Paul and Amelia Edmonson": p. [203]-209.

1. Slavery in the U. S.—Fiction. I. Title.
31—1514
Library of Congress PZ3.P2938Fu
——— Copy 2.
Copyright A 33116 [30d1]

M331 P29 **Paynter, John Henry,** 1862-1947
Horse and buggy days with Uncle Sam, by John H. Paynter, A. M. New York, Margent press, 1943.
xiii p., 2 l., 19-190 p. ports. 22½cm.

1. Negroes—Employment. 2. Civil service—U. S. I. Title.
43-9624
Library of Congress E185.8.P38
[6] 923.573

M910 P29 **Paynter, John Henry,** 1862-1947
Joining the navy; or, Abroad with Uncle Sam. By Jno. H. Paynter ... Hartford, Conn., American publishing company, 1895.
298 p. front., plates, ports. 20½cm.

1. Voyages around the world.
Library of Congress [29c1] G440.P34 5-38244†

O pays, mon beau peuple.

Sénégal M896.3 Ou8p **Ousmane, Sembene.** 1923-
Ô pays, mon beau peuple; roman. Paris, Le Livre contemporain [1957]
234 p. 19 cm.

I. Title.
A 58-6146
Illinois. Univ. Library for Library of Congress [1]

Paysages et Paysans au crepuscule du coeur.

Haiti M841 V12p Vilaire, Jean Joseph
Paysages et Paysans au crepuscule du coeur. Poesies. Paris, Albert Messein, editeur. 1930.

96p. 19cm.

Paysages inviolés.

Martinique M841.91 T32p Thaly, Daniel Desiré Alin, 1879-
Paysages inviolés.

(In: Le Beffroi, 74:17-22, Janvier 1908)

M812.5 P29 Payton, Lew, 1873-
Did Adam sin? and other stories of Negro life in comedy-drama and sketches. Los Angeles, Lew Payton, 1937.

132p. 21cm.

1. Drama
I. Title

Uganda M896.3 P29L p'Bitek Okot, J O 1931-
Lak tar miyo kinyero wi lobo [Are your teeth white? The laugh!] Kampala, The Eagle Press, 1953.

137p. illus. 18cm.
A novel depicting life in the towns and villages of East Africa, by an Acholi author. Written in Lwo.

I. Title.

Uganda M896.1 P29s p'Bitek Okot, J O 1931-
Song of lawino. Nairobi, Kenya, East African Publishing House, 1966.

216p. 19cm. (Modern African Library)
Portrait of author on book cover.

I. Title.

M301 M69 Peace, William H
The South reacts.

Pp. 96-127.
In: Mitchell, Glenford E., ed. The angry black south. New York, Corinth Books, 1962.

Peace, William H., jt ed.

M301 M69 **Mitchell, Glenford E** *ed.*
The angry black South. Edited by Glenford E. Mitchell and William H. Peace, III. New York, Corinth Books, 1962.
159 p. 21 cm.
Portraits of authors on back of book.

1. Negroes—Southern States. 2. U. S.—Race question. I. Peace, William H., joint ed. II. Title.
E185.61.M67 301.451 61—15876 ‡
Library of Congress [62f5]

M301 M69 Peace, William H., jt. auth.
Mitchell, Glenford E
The continuing struggle, by Glenford E. Mitchell and William H. Peace.

Pp. 152-159.
In: Mitchell, Glenford E., ed. The angry black south. New York, Corinth Books, 1962.

Peace.

M261.6 A12 **Alford, Neal B**
The invisible road to peace. Boston, Meador Pub. Co. [1957]
96 p. 21 cm.

1. Church and social problems. 2. Peace. I. Title.
HN31.A59 261.6 58-26538 ‡
Library of Congress [1]

Peace.

M815.5 B88u Bunche, Ralph Johnson, 1904-
UN and peace-making. n.p., [1950]

15p. 28cm.
Address delivered in Denver, May 11, 1950.
Mimeographed.

Peace.

M252 H91w Huntley, Thomas Elliott
When people behave like sputniks (as I saw them). New York, Vantage Press, 1960.

112p. 20½cm.

Peace.

M341.1 St41 Stephens, Perry Alexander.
Lasting peace and democracy. [New York, F. Hubner & Co., 1946]

11p. 22cm.

Peace!

Ghana
M966.7
N65p

Nkrumah, Kwame, Pres. Rep. of Ghana, 1909-
Peace! The world from African eyes. Address by the President of the Republic of Ghana, Osgayefo Dr. Kwame Nkrumah, to the 15th session of the United Nation's General Assembly September 28, 1960. [Chicago, Afro-American Heritage Ass'n, 1960]

27p. 21cm.

Peace, the mother of nations.

Basutoland
M968.6
D18p

Damane, Mosebi
Peace, the mother of nations. The "Saga" of the origin of the Protestant church in Basutoland. Basutoland, Morija Printing works of the Paris Evangelical Missionary Society 1947.

54p. 24cm.

Peace, the mother of nations.

M968
D18p

Damane, Mosebi.
Peace, the mother of nations. The "Saga" of the origin of the Protestant church in [Basutoland. Basutoland, Morija Printing works of the Paris Evangelical Missionary Society] 1947.

54p. 24cm.

Peace-corpsism..

Nigeria
M309.22 Obi, Enuenwemba.
Ob3

Peace-corpsism. [1st ed.] New York, Pageant Press [1962]

78 p. 20 cm.
Portrait of author on book jacket.

1. U. S. Peace Corps. I. Title.

HC60.5.O2 309.2206173 62-20947 ‡

Library of Congress [5]

M341.1
P31

Peace on earth by Trygve Lie and others. Introduction by Robert E. Sherwood. New York, Hermitage House, 1949.

251p. 22cm.
Partial contents: The international trusteeship system, by Ralph Bunche.
I. Bunche, Ralph. The International Trusteeship System. 1. United nations.

Peake, Mary Smith Kelsey, 1823-

MB9
P311

Lockwood, Lewis C
Mary S. Peake, the colored teacher at Fortress Monroe. By Rev. Lewis C. Lockwood... with an appendix. Boston, American tract society [n.d.]

64p. front. 15½cm.

Peanut.

M630.7
C25pe

Carver, George Washington, 1864-1943.
The peanut, by George W. Carver and Austin W. Curtis, Jr. Tuskegee Institute, Alabama, Tuskegee Institute press, 1943.

14p. 23cm. (Bulletin no.44, February 1943)

Peanut - Cultivation.

M630.7
C25h5

Carver, George Washington, 1864-1943.
How to grow the peanut and 105 ways of preparing it for human consumption. Eighth edition, January 1942. Tuskegee Institute, Alabama, Tuskegee Institute press, 1942.

30p. 23cm. (Bulletin no.31, June 1925)

Peary, Robert Edwin, 1856-1920.

MB9
H39h

Henson, Matthew Alexander, 1866-
A negro explorer at the North pole, by Matthew A. Henson; with a foreword by Robert E. Peary ... and an introduction by Booker T. Washington; with illustrations from photographs. New York, Frederick A. Stokes company [1912]

xx p., 1 l., 200 p. front., plates, ports. 19½ cm.

1. Arctic regions. 2. North pole. 3. Peary, Robert Edwin, 1856-1920. I. Title.

Library of Congress G670 1909.H5 12-4225

[42m1]

Peau noire, masques blancs.

Martinique
M323
F21p

Fanon, Frantz, 1925-
Peau noire, masques blancs. Préf. de Francis Jeanson. Paris, Éditions du Seuil [1952]

222 p. 19 cm. (Collections Esprit. La condition humaine)
Bibliographical footnotes.

1. Negro race. I. Title.

Harvard Univ. Library for Library of Congress A 53-3621 [1]

La pêche aux filets.

France
M840
D89ca

Dumas, Alexandre, 1802-1870.

Gabriel Lambert, Bruxelles, Meline, Cans et Cie, 1844.

271p. 15cm.

M623.74
P33

Peck, James L H.
Armies with wings, by James L. H. Peck; with illustrations and diagrams. New York, Dodd, Mead & company, 1940.

xiv, 274 p. front., illus., plates, diagrs. 21 cm.
Bibliography: p. 273-274.

1. Aeronautics, Military. I. Title.

Library of Congress UG630.P35 40-5041

[44w8] 623.74

M623.74 Peck, James L H.
P33s

So you're going to fly, by James L. H. Peck ... with official photographs and diagrams by the author. New York, Dodd, Mead & company, 1941.

xiv, 241 p. front., illus., plates, diagrs. 21 cm.
Bibliography: p. 239-241.

1. Aeroplanes—Piloting. 2. Aeronautics, Military. I. Title.

41-51786

Library of Congress TL710.P4 [43f5] 629.1325

M323
P33c

[Peck, Jim]
Cracking the color line; non-violent direct action methods of eliminating racial discrimination. New York, CORE, 1959.

24p. illus. 22½cm.

1. Race relations.

M326.5
P33r

Peck, Nathaniel.
Report of Messrs. Peck and Price, who were appointed at a meeting of the free colored people of Baltimore, held on the 25th November, 1839, delegates to visit British Guiana and the Island of Trinidad; and other information, showing the advantages to be derived by immigrating to those colonies.

32p. 23½cm.

1. British Guiana. 2. Trinidad. 3. Baltimore. I. Price, Thomas S. joint author.

The pecking order.

M813.5 Kennedy, Mark.
K38

The pecking order. New York, Appleton-Century-Crofts [1953]

278 p. 21 cm.

I. Title.

PZ4.K354Pe 53-6723 ‡

Library of Congress [3]

M972.95 Pedreira, Antonio Salvador, 1899-
B23
V1

... Un hombre del pueblo, José Celso Barbosa. San Juan de Puerto Rico, Imprenta Venezuela, 1937.

8 p. l., 9-173 p., 2 l. 21½ cm. (On cover: La obra de José Celso Barbosa, vol. I)

At head of title: Antonio S. Pedreira.

1. *Barbosa, José Celso, 1857-1921. I. Title.

46-30940

Library of Congress F1975.B24 vol. 1

[2] (972.91) 923.1

M972.95 Pedreira, Antonio Salvador, 1899-
B23

Barbosa, José Celso, 1857-1921.
... La obra de José Celso Barbosa ... San Juan de Puerto Rico [Imprenta Venezuela] 1937-39.

4 v. pl., ports., fold. facsim. 22 cm.
Vol. 1 has cover-title and special t.-p.

Contents.—I. Un hombre del pueblo, José Celso Barbosa, por A. S. Pedreira.—II. Post umbra, juicios sobre José Celso Barbosa.—III. Problema de razas.—IV. Orientando al pueblo, 1900-1921.

1. Barbosa, José Celso, 1857-1921. 2. Puerto Rico—Pol. & govt.—1898- 3. Negroes in Puerto Rico. 4. Negroes. I. Pedreira, Antonio Salvador, 1899-

[Full name: José Celso Barbosa y Alcalá]

46-30939

Library of Congress F1975.B24 [47c1] 972.91

Pedreira, Antonio Salvador, 1899-

Puerto Rico
M860
F414

Ferrer-Canales, Jose, 1913-
Antonio S. Pedreira: "Hostos, ciudadano de America." Puerto Rico, 1939.

25p. illus. 18½cm.

The Pedro Gorino...

MB9
D34p

Dean, Harry, 1864-
The Pedro Gorino; the adventures of a Negro sea-captain in Africa and on the seven seas in his attempts to found an Ethiopian empire; an autobiographical narrative by Captain Harry Dean, with the assistance of Sterling North. Boston and New York, Houghton Mifflin company, 1929.

xvi, 262 p. illus. 22½ cm.

1. Seafaring life. 2. Voyages and travels. 3. Africa, South. I. North, Sterling, 1906- II. Title.

29-6322

Library of Congress G530.D4 [a44u1]

Pedroso, Regino, 1898-

Latin America
M861.08
F56a

Pp. 244-249. In -
Fitts, Dudley, 1903- ed.
Anthology of contemporary Latin-American poetry, edited by Dudley Fitts. Norfolk, Conn., New directions [1942]

ix, [2], x-xxi, 667 p. 23½ cm.
Added t.-p.: Antología de la poesía americana contemporánea.
English and original text (Spanish, Portuguese or French) on opposite pages.
"Biographical and bibliographical notes, by H. R. Hays": p. 581-641.

1. Spanish-American poetry (Collections) 2. Spanish-American poetry—Translations into English. 3. English poetry—Translations from Spanish. 4. Spanish-American poetry—Bio-bibl. I. Hays, Hoffman Reynolds. II. Title.

PQ7084.F5 861.6082 43-485

Library of Congress [54r43k[2]7]

Cuba
M861.6
P34a

Pedroso, Regino, 1898–
... Antología poética (1918–1938) ₍Habana₎ Municipio de la Habana, 1939.
2 p. l., 7–144, ₍2₎ p. 21ᶜᵐ.

I. Title. 1. Cuban poetry. 40-13851
Library of Congress PQ7389.P28A6 1939
₍2₎ 861.6

Cuba
M861.6
P34b

Pedroso, Regino, 1898–
... Bolívar; sinfonía de libertad, poema. La Habana, P. Fernández y cía., s. en c., 1945.
5 p. l., 15–40 p., 3 l. port. 24ᶜᵐ.
"Segunda edición."

1. Bolívar, Simón, 1783–1830—Poetry. 2. Cuban poetry.
46-15347
Library of Congress PQ7389.P28B6
₍2₎ 861.6

Cuba
M861.6
P34m

Pedroso, Regino, 1898–
Más allá canta el mar; poema de Regino Pedroso. Premio nacional de poesía, 1938. La Habana, En la Verónica, imprenta de Manuel Altolaguirre, 1939.
5 p. l., 13–63, ₍1₎ p., 2 l. 26½ᶜᵐ. (*On cover:* Ediciones "Heroe")

I. Title. 1. Cuban poetry. A C 40-2435
Harvard univ. Library for Library of Congress ₍2₎

Cuba
M861.6
P34n

Pedroso, Regino, 1898–
... Nosotros, poemas. La Habana, 1933.
2 p. l., 9–70 p. 21ᶜᵐ.

I. Title. 1.Cuban poetry. 38-22228
Library of Congress PQ7389.P28N6
₍2₎ 861.6

Bahamas
M398
P34

Peek, Basil
Bahamian proverbs, arranged and illustrated by Basil Peek. London, John Culmer, 1949.

₍30₎p. illus. 19cm.
Edition is limited to one thousand copies of which fifty are for presentation and review.

1. Bahamas - Folk-lore
I. title

M343.3
Am3v

Peekskill, N. Y. - Riots.
American Civil Liberties Union.
Violence in Peekskill; A report of the violations of civil liberties at two Paul Robeson concerts near Peekskill, N.Y., August 27th and September 4th, 1949. New York,₍1949?₎

51p. illus. 20cm.
Original report issued in multigraphed form December, 1949.

La peinture chez les anciens suivee de l'histoire des peintres.

France
M240
D89pe

Dumas, Alexandre, 1802-1870.
La peinture chez les anciens suivee de l'histoire des peintres. Bruxelles, Meline, Cans et cie., 1845.

284p. 16cm.

Brazil
M869.1
C27o

Peixoto, Afranio, 1876- ed.
Castro Alves, Antonio de, 1847–1871.
... Obras completas de Castro Alves. Introdução e notas de Afranio Peixoto ... 2. ed. São Paulo ₍etc.₎ Companhia editora nacional, 1942.
2 v. fronts. (ports.) facsims. 20½ᶜᵐ. (Livros do Brasil. Vol. 1. Collecção de obras-primas da literatura nacional dirigida por Afranio Peixoto)
"Bibliographia de Castro Alves": v. 2, p. 599–602. Bibliographical foot-notes.
CONTENTS.—t. 1. Espumas fluctuantes. Hymnos do Equador.—t. 2. Os escravos. Gonzaga; ou, A revolução de Minas. Reliquias. Correspondencia.
I. *Peixoto, Afranio, 1876– ed.
A 42–3296
Harvard univ. Library for Library of Congress PQ9697.C35 1942
₍44d1₎† 869.081

M811.5
P33

Pektor, Irene Mari.
Golden banners, by Irene Mari Pektor. Boston, The Christopher publishing house ₍ᶜ1941₎
ix, 11–211 p. 19½ᶜᵐ.
Poems.

I. Title.
41-2848
Library of Congress PS3531.E298G6 1941
——— Copy 2.
Copyright ₍2₎ 811.5

Guadeloupe
M741
P36

Pélage, Al
La Guadeloupe vue ₍gravures et dessins humoristiques de Al Pélage. Préface de E. Isaac. Basse-Terre, Guadelope, Imprimerie Officiele, n.d.₎

22 leaves 23cm.
Cover title.

1. Wit and humor, Pictorial. I. Title.

Guadeloupe
M972.97
F84M

Pélage, Magloire d. 1808.
Frasans, Hippolyte de.
Mémoire pour le chef de brigade Magloire Pélage et pour les habitans de la Guadeloupe, chargés, par cette colonie, de l'administration provisoire, après le départ du capitaine-général Lacrosse ... Paris, Desenne ₍etc.₎ an XI.—1803.
2 v. 20ᶜᵐ.
By H. de Frasans and Jean Thomas Langlois.

1. Guadeloupe—Hist. I. Langlois, Jean Thomas. II. Title.
2-18833 rev.
Library of Congress F2066.F84
₍r37b2₎

Pelee peak - Eruption, 1902.
Martinique
M972.98
P53m

Philémon, Césaire.
... La montagne Pelée et l'effroyable destruction de Saint-Pierre (Martinique) le 8 mai 1902; le brusque réveil du volcan en 1929. Éd. originale. Fort-de-France, Chez l'auteur; Paris, Impressions Printory et G. Courville ₍ᶜ1930₎
4 p. l., ₍11₎–211 p., 1 l. plates, fold. maps. 22½ᶜᵐ.
"Il a été tiré de cet ouvrage cinquante exemplaires sur papier pur fil Lafuma, numérotés de 1 à 50, qui constituent l'édition originale."

1. Pelee peak—Eruption, 1902. 2. Saint-Pierre, Martinique. I. Title.
31-13052
Library of Congress F2081.P54
Copyright A—Foreign 10883
₍2₎ ₍917.298₎ 551.21097298

MB9
P36m

Pelham, Benjamin B., 1862-1948.
Mallas, Aris A
Forty years in politics; the story of Ben Pelham, by Aris A. Mallas, Jr., Rea McCain ₍and₎ Margaret K. Hedden. Detroit, Wayne State University Press, 1957.
92 p. illus. 24 cm.

1. Pelham, Benjamin B., 1862–1948. 2. Finance, Public—Wayne Co., Mich. 3. Wayne Co., Mich.—Pol. & govt. I. Title.
F572.W4P4 923.573 57—10562 ‡
Library of Congress ₍59f5₎

Pelham, Robert A.

M312
Un3n
1915

U. S. Bureau of the census.
... Negroes in the United States. Washington, Govt. print. off., 1915.

207 p. incl. illus. (map) tables. diagr. 31cm. (Its Bulletin 129)

Martinique
M972.98
M61m

Pelee, Mont-Eruption, 1902.
Miller, James Martin, 1859–1939.
The Martinique horror and St. Vincent calamity, containing a full and complete account of the most appalling disaster of modern times ... by J. Martin Miller ... in collaboration with Hon. John Stevens Durham ... Philadelphia, National publishing co. ₍1902₎
8, 17–500 p. 2 front., illus., plates, ports., maps. 23½ᶜᵐ.
Issued also under the title: True story of the Martinique and St. Vincent calamities ... by Prof. John Randolph Whitney.
1. La Soufrière, St. Vincent—Eruption, 1902. 2. Pelée, Mont—Eruption, 1902. 3. St. Vincent. 4. Volcanoes. I. Durham, John Stevens, 1861– joint author. II. Title.
2-17542
Library of Congress F2081.M64
₍a44f1₎

Pellagra.

M614.5
G82p

Green, H M
Pellagra; in monograph, by H. M. Green... Knoxville, Tenn., The author, c 1927
158p. plates. 20½cm.
Inscribed copy: "To Mr. Arthur Spingarn with the complements of the author, H. M. Green.

M286
P36s

Pelt, Owen D
The story of the National Baptists, by Owen D. Pelt and Ralph Lee Smith. ₍1st ed.₎ New York, Vantage Press ₍1960₎
272 p. illus. 22 cm.
Includes bibliography.

1. National Baptist Convention of the United States of America—Hist. I. Smith, Ralph Lee, joint author.
BX6443.P4 286.173 60-15470 ‡
Library of Congress ₍5₎

Pemba, George Milwa, 1915- illus.

South Africa
M398
Oc51

O'Connell, Ruby M Agar -
Iintsomi; Bantu folk stories. Illustrations by G.M. Pemba and others; Xhosa translations by B.A. Bangeni. Lovedale press, [1938?]

47p. illus. 29cm.

Zanzibar
M967.8
Om1

Pemba - History.
Omar, C A Shariff
Kisiwa cha Pemba; historia na masimulizi [History and traditions of the Island of Pemba] Nairobi, Eagle Press, 1951.
21p. illus., port., maps. 21cm.
Written in Swahili.

1. Pemba. - History. 2. Pemba. - Social life and customs. 3. Zanzibar. I. Title.

Zanzibar
M967.8
Om1

Pemba - Social life and customs.
Omar, C A Shariff
Kisiwa cha Pemba; historia na masimulizi [History and traditions of the Island of Pemba] Nairobi, Eagle Press, 1951.
21p. illus., port., maps. 21cm.
Written in Swahili.

1. Pemba. - History. 2. Pemba. - Social life and customs. 3. Zanzibar. I. Title.

The Pen of an African.

Ethiopia
M963
B61p

Blayechettai, Joseph Emanuel
The Pen of an African. [n.p.] 1922.

95p. illus. port. 20½cm.

1. Blayechettai, Joseph Emanuel. 2. Abyssinia. I. Title.

Pen pictures of pioneers of Wilberforce.

MB
B80p
Brown, Hallie Quinn, *ed.*
Pen pictures of pioneers of Wilberforce, compiled and edited by Hallie Q. Brown ... illustrated from photographs from widely different sources. [Xenia, O., The Aldine publishing company, °1937]
96 p. illus. (incl. ports.) 20½cm.

1. Wilberforce university, Wilberforce, O. I. Title. 37-13020
Library of Congress LC2851.W61B7
——— Copy 2.
Copyright A 107185 [3] 378.771

M07
P38
Penn, Irvine Garland, 1867-1910
The Afro-American press and its editors, by I. Garland Penn ... with contributions by Hon. Frederick Douglass, Hon. John R. Lynch [etc.] ... Springfield, Mass., Willey & co., 1891.
5 p. l., [15]-565, [4] p. front., illus. (incl. ports.) fold. facsim. 20½ cm.

1. Press—U. S. 2. ~~Negroes~~—Biog. 10—7631
Library of Congress PN4888.N4P4
[48i1]

M252
P38t
Pennington, James William Charles, 1812-1871.
A two years' absence, or a farewell sermon, preached in the fifth Congregational Church, by J.W.C. Pennington. Nov. 2d., 1845, Hartford, Published by H. T. Wells, 1845.

31p. 22½cm.

1. Sermons. I. Title.

The pencil of God.

Haiti
M843.91
T35p
Thoby-Marcelin, Philippe, 1904-
The pencil of God, by Philippe Thoby-Marcelin and Pierre Marcelin; translated by Leonard Thomas, with an introd. by Edmund Wilson. Boston, Houghton Mifflin, 1951.
xvii, 204 p. 22 cm.

I. Marcelin, Pierre, 1908- joint author. II. Title.
Full name: Émile Philippe Thoby-Marcelin.

PZ3.T35Pe 843.91 50-58334
Library of Congress [3]

M973.8
P38.u
Penn, Irvine Garland, 1867-1910 *ed.*
The united negro: his problems and his progress, containing the addresses and proceedings the Negro young people's Christian and educational congress, held August 6-11, 1902; introduction by Bishop W. J. Gaines ... edited by Prof. I. Garland Penn ... Prof. J. W. E. Bowen ... Atlanta, Ga., D. E. Luther publishing co., 1902.
xxx, 600 p. illus., plates, ports. 21cm.

1. ~~Negroes~~—Moral and social conditions. 2. ~~Negroes~~—Religion. I. Bowen, John Wesley Edward, 1855- joint ed. II. Title.
3—1805
Library of Congress E185.5.P41
[a45e1]

Pennington, James William Charles, 1812-1871.

M326.99B
B22n
Banks, J H 1833-
... A narrative of events of the life of J. H. Banks, an escaped slave, from the cotton state, Alabama, in America ... Written, with introduction, by J.W.C. Pennington, Liverpool, M. Rouke, 1861.

92 [2]p. 17cm.

The pencil of God.

Haiti
M843.91
T35p2
Thoby-Marcelin, Philippe, 1904-
The pencil of God, by Philippe Thoby-Marcelin and Pierre Marcelin; translated by Leonard Thomas, ~~with an introd. by Edmund Wilson. Boston, Houghton Mifflin, 1951.~~ London, Victor Gollancz, 1951.
xvii, 204 p. 22 cm.

I. Marcelin, Pierre, 1908- joint author. II. Title.
Full name: Émile Philippe Thoby-Marcelin.

PZ3.T35Pe 843.91 50-58334
Library of Congress [3]

M304
P19
v.6, no.4
Penn, Irvine Garland, 1867-1930.
Progress of the Afro-American.
The reasons why the colored man is not in the World's Columbian Exposition. The Afro-American's Contribution to Columbian literature. Introduction by Frederick Douglass. [Chicago, Ill., 1893]

81p. 19cm.

M610
P19
v.1
no.14
Pennsylvania. Department of welfare.
Directory of Pennsylvania institutions caring for the sick and the aged.
Prepared by the Bureau of assistance.
Harrisburg, Department of Welfare, 1930.
58p. 23cm.
1. Health - Pennsylvania.
2. Directories - Pennsylvania.
I. Title.
3. Hospitals - Penn. - Direct.
4. Old age homes - Penn. - Direct.

Penciled poems.

M811.5
D19de
Dandridge, Raymond Garfield.
Peneiled poems, by Ray G. Dandridge. Cincinnati, O. [Powell & White, printers] 1917.
51, [1] p. incl. port. 19½cm. $1.00

I. Title. 18-505
Library of Congress PS3601.D3P4
——— Copy 2.
Copyright A 481104

M252
P38a
Pennington, James William Charles, 1812-1871
An address delivered at Newark, N.J. at the first anniversary of West India Emancipation. August 1, 1839. By J.W.C. Pennington. Newark, N.J., Aaron Guest Printer, 1839.

12p. 20cm.

1. West India Emancipation.

M304
P19
v.3,no.6
M974.8
P38m
Pennsylvania. *Dept. of welfare.*
... Negro survey of Pennsylvania. Harrisburg [1928]
97 p. incl. tables, diagrs. 23cm.
At head of title: Commonwealth of Pennsylvania. Department of welfare.

1. ~~Negroes~~—Pennsylvania. I. Title.
28-27371 Revised
Library of Congress E185.93.P41P32
[r31d2]

M323
Su7n
Pendleton, Helen B.
Negro dependence in Baltimore.

(In: Survey midmonthly. The Negro in the cities of the North. New York, The Charity Organization Society, 1905. 26cm. p.50-57).

M326.99B
P38f
Pennington, James William Charles, 1812-1871
The fugitive blacksmith; or, Events in the history of James W. C. Pennington ... formerly a slave in the state of Maryland, United States ... 2nd ed. London, C. Gilpin, 1849.

xv, 87p. 16cm.

1. Slavery in the U. S. - Maryland. 2. Slave narratives.

M974.8
P38m
Pennsylvania.
Pennsylvania. *Dept. of welfare.*
... Negro survey of Pennsylvania. Harrisburg [1928]
97 p. incl. tables, diagrs. 23cm.
At head of title: Commonwealth of Pennsylvania. Department of welfare.
M304
P19
V.3.no.6

1. Negroes—Pennsylvania. I. Title.
28-27371 Revised
Library of Congress E185.93.P41P32
[r31d2]

M973
P37
Pendleton, Leila (Amos) 1860-
A narrative of the negro, by Mrs. Leila Amos Pendleton ... Washington, D. C., Press of R. L. Pendleton, 1912.
217, [3] p. incl. illus., map. pl., port. 22½cm.

1. History. ~~Negroes.~~ 2. Negro race. 12—14104
Library of Congress E185.P39
[a42b1]

M973
P38t
Pennington, James William Charles, 1812-1871.
Text book of the origin and history, &c. &c. of the colored people. By James W.C. Pennington. Hartford, L. Skinner, printer, 1841.

96p. 12½cm.
Inscribed copy: Dr. Graham with the respects of the author.

1. Slavery in the U.S. - Controversial literature - 1841.

Pennsylvania.

M973.6
P83p1
1866
Pennsylvania state equal rights' league, Pittsburg, Pa.
A synopsis of the proceedings of the second annual meeting of the Pennsylvania state equal rights league, at Pittsburg, August 8th, 9th and 10th, 1866. Philadelphia, G.T. Stockdale, printer, 1866.
47p. 21½cm.

Senegal
M610
Sa58
Pene, Pierre, jt. author.
Sankalé, Marc
Médecine sociale au Sénégal, par Marc Sankalé et Pierre Pène. Dakar, Afrique documents, 1960.

104p. illus., map. 24cm. (Cahiers documents, no. 1, March 1960)
Includes bibliography.

M814.4
P69e
Pennington, James William Charles, 1812-1871.
To the reader.

Pp. xvii-xx.

In: Plato, Ann. Essays. Hartford, The Author, 1841.

Pennsylvania.

M973.6
St2
1848
State convention of coloured citizens, Harrisburg, Pa.
Minutes of the state convention of the coloured citizens of Pennsylvania, convened at Harrisburg, December 13th and 14, 1848. Philadelphia, Merrihew and Thompson, 1849.
24p. 21cm.

Pennsylvania.
M973.6 St2h 1865
State equal rights convention, Pennsylvania.
Proceedings of the state equal rights' convention, of the colored people of Pennsylvania, held in the city of Harrisburg, February 8th, 9th and 10th, 1865, together with a few of the arguments presented suggesting the necessity for holding the convention, and an address to the colored state convention, to the people of Pennsylvania [Philadelphia] Printed for and by order of the convention, 1865.
50p. 21cm.

M973.6 P83pi 1866
Pennsylvania state equal rights' league, Pittsburg, Pa.
A synopsis of the proceedings of the second annual meeting of the pennsylvania state equal rights league, at Pittsburg, August 8th, 9th and 10th, 1866. Philadelphia, G. T. Stockdale, printer, 1866.
47p. 21½cm.
1. Congresses and conventions. 2. Equal rights' league. 3. Pennsylvania. I. Pennsylvania state rights. league. [Memorial] to the honorable, (over)

The people one knows, a novel.
M813.5 B638p
Boles, Robert.
The people one knows, a novel. Boston, Houghton Mifflin, 1964.
177 p. 21 cm.
I. Title.
PZ4.B6883Pe 64-17862
Library of Congress [5]

Pennsylvania.
M974.8 W93n
Wright, Richard Robert, 1878–
The Negro in Pennsylvania; a study in economic history ... By Richard R. Wright, jr. [Philadelphia, A. M. E. book concern, printers, 1912]
250 p. 23½cm.
Thesis (PH. D.)—University of Pennsylvania, 1911.
Bibliography: p. 233-250.
1. Negroes—Pennsylvania.
Library of Congress E185.93.P41W9 12—21986
[42b1]

Congo Leopoldville M967.5 L97p
La pensée politique de Patrice Lumumba.
Lumumba, Patrice, 1925-1961
La pensée politique de Patrice Lumumba. Préface de Jean-Paul Sartre. Textes recueillis et présentés par Jean Van Lierde. Bruxelles, le Livre Africain, 1963.
401p. port. 21½cm.

People vs. property.
M331.833 L85p
Long, Herman Hodge.
People vs. property; race restrictive covenants in housing [by] Herman H. Long [and] Charles S. Johnson. Nashville, Fisk Univ. Press, 1947.
ix, 107 p. maps, diagrs. 21 cm.
Bibliographical footnotes.
1. Negroes — Housing. 2. Negroes — Segregation. 3. Real covenants—U. S. I. Johnson, Charles Spurgeon, 1893– joint author. II. Title.
E185.89.H6L7 325.260973 48—5205*
Library of Congress [48x10]

Pennsylvania - History.
M814.3 F77
[Forten, James, 1776-1842]
To the Honourable the Senate and House of Representatives of the Commonwealth of Pennsylvania. The memorial of the people of colour of the city of Philadelphia and its vicinity respectfully sheweth... [n.p. 1832]
8p. 18½cm.
Signed: James Forten, Chairman; William Whipper, Robert Purvis, secretaries.

Haiti M841 V712pe
Pensées et réflexions.
Vilaire, Jean-Joseph, 1881-
Pensées et réflexions. Port-au-Prince, Imp. de l'Etat, 1949.
182p. 15cm.

People's National Party.
Trinidad M329 W67ap
Williams, Eric Eustace, 1911-
The approach of independence; an address to the fourth annual convention of the People's National Movement. [Port-of-Spain, P.N.M. Publishing Co., 1960]
23p. 21cm.
1. People's National Party. 2. Trinidad - Political parties. 3. Political parties - Trinidad. I. Title.

Pennsylvania. University. Henry Phipps institute.
M304 P19 v.1 no.15
Mossell, Sadie Tanner.
... A study of the negro tuberculosis problem in Philadelphia, by Sadie T. Mossell ... Philadelphia, Henry Phipps institute, 1923.
v, 7-29, [3] p. illus. (maps) diagr. 20cm.
At head of title: University of Pennsylvania.
"This study was made under the auspices of the Whittier centre and the Henry Phipps institute; it was revised by the Philadelphia health council and Tuberculosis committee."
1. Tuberculosis—Philadelphia. 2. Negroes—Philadelphia. I. Pennsylvania. University. Henry Phipps institute.
Library of Congress RC313.A57M6 25—20530
[a28c1]

Peonage - U. S.
M06 Am3 no. 15
Hershaw, Lafayette M.
... Peonage, by Lafayette M. Hershaw ... Washington, D. C., The Academy, 1915.
1 p. l., [5]-13 p. 22½cm. (The American negro academy. Occasional papers, no. 15)
1. Peonage—U. S.
Library of Congress E185.5.A51 no. 15 16-7104
——— Copy 2. HD4875.U5H4
——— Copy 3.

Trinidad M329 W67o
People's National Movement.
Williams, Eric Eustace, 1911-
Our fourth anniversary, the last lap; political leader's address on September 24, 1960, at the University of Woodford Square, marking the fourth year of P.N.M.'s first term of office. [Port-of-Spain, P.N.M. Publishing Co., 1960]
15p. 21cm.
Portrait on cover.
1. People's National Movement. 2. Trinidad - Political parties. 3. Political parties.- Trinidad. I. Title.

Pennsylvania Augustine society for the education of the people of colour.
M815.2 Sa8a
Saunders, Prince, 1785-1839
An address delivered at Bethel Church, Philadelphia on the 30th of September, 1818 before the Pennsylvania Augustine society for the education of people of colour. By Prince Saunders. To which is annexed the constitution of the society. Philadelphia, Joseph Rakestraw, 1818.
12 p. 24cm.
1. Pennsylvania Augustine society for the education of the people of colour.

Africa M960 Sch3
The people of Africa.
[Schieffelin, Henry Maunsell, b. 1808, ed.
The people of Africa. A series of papers on their character, condition, and future prospects, by E. W. Blyden, D. D., Tayler Lewis, D. D., Theodore Dwight, esq., etc., etc. New York, A. D. F. Randolph & co., 1871.
8 p. l., 157 p. plates, facsims. (part fold.) 19cm.
"Introductory" signed: H. M. S.
CONTENTS.—I. The Negro in ancient history. By Rev. Edward W. Blyden.—II. The Koran. African Mohammedanism. By Tayler Lewis.—III. Condition and character of Negroes in Africa. By Theodore Dwight, esq.—IV. Condition of education in Liberia.—V. Extracts from Prof. Bly-
(Continued on next card)
14—15131
[42b1]

Trinidad M329 W67p
People's National Movement.
Williams, Eric Eustace, 1911-
Perspectives for our party; address delivered to the third annual convention of the People's National Movement on October 17, 1958. [Port-of-Spain, P.N.M. Publishing Co., 1958]
20p. 22cm.
1. People's National Movement. 2. Trinidad - Political parties. 3. Political parties - Trinidad. I. Title.

M973.6 P83pi 1866
Pennsylvania State Equal Rights League
Memorial to the honorable, the Senate and House of Representatives of the United States. Philadelphia, 1866.
8p. 21½cm.
Bound with: Synopsis of proceedings of the second annual meeting of the League.

The people of Kenya speak for themselves.
Kenya M967.62 K82
Koinange, Mbiyu.
The people of Kenya speak for themselves. Detroit, Kenya Publication Fund, 1955.
115 p. illus. 17 cm.
1. Kenya Colony and Protectorate—Pol. & govt. I. Title.
DT434.E2K64 916.762 55-22305 ‡
Library of Congress [5]

The pepperpot man.
M813.5 J72p
Jones, Ralph H
The pepperpot man. New York, Vantage Press, 1965.
197p. 20½cm.
Portrait of author on book jacket.
I. Title.

M973.6 P83pe 1866
Pennsylvania State Equal Rights League.
Preamble and constitution of the Pennsylvania State Equal Rights' League, acting under the jurisdiction of the National Equal Rights' League of the United States of America and Constitution for Subordinate Leagues... Philadlephia, J. McC.Crummill, 1866.
30p. 14cm.
1. National Equal rights' League. 2. Equal Rights' League.

People of the City.
Nigeria M896.3 Ek8p
Ekwensi, Cyprian
People of the City. London, Andrew Dakers, Ltd., 1954.
237p. 18½cm.
I. Title.

Pequena história de música.
Brazil M869 An2pe
Andrade, Mário de, 1893-1945.
Pequena história de musica. 5ª edicão. São Paulo, Livraria Martins Editôra, 1958.
232p. illus., port. 21½cm.
(Obras Completas de Mário de Andrade)

MB
P34e
Peques, Albert Witherspoon, 1859-
Our Baptist ministers and schools. By A. W. Peques... with an introduction by C. L. Purce... illustrated ͵Springfield, Mass., Springfield printing and binding co., 1892.

622, 18p. plates. 20½cm.

1. Baptists. I. Title.

Nigeria
M784
K58
Percussion music - Hist. & crit.
King, Anthony.
Yoruba sacred music from Ekiti. ͵Nigeria͵ Ibadan University Press, 1961.
ix, 45, xlix p. illus., music. 22 cm.
Music: xlix p. at end.

1. Music, African. 2. Music, Primitive. 3. Yorubas—Music. 4. Percussion music—Hist. & crit. I. Title.

ML3760.K47 62-752
Library of Congress ͵1͵

Cameroun
M896.3
B436p
La perdrix blanche.
Bengono, Jacques, 1938–
La Perdrix blanche, trois contes moraux. Yaoundé, Abbia, Cle, 1966.
80 p. 18 cm. unpriced (F 68-6862)
Illustrated cover.

I. Title.

PQ3989.2.B4P4 66-68212
Library of Congress ͵2͵

Latin America
M861.08
P41a
Pereda Valdés, Ildefonso, 1899– *ed.*
Antología de la poesía negra americana. Santiago de Chile, Ediciones Ercilla, 1936.
155 p., 1 l. 20cm. (Biblioteca América)
Includes bio-bibliographical sketches of the authors.

1. ~~Negro~~ poetry. (collections) ~~2. Negro authors.~~ I. Title.
38—2047
Library of Congress PN6108.P4
͵45d1͵ 808.81

Uruguay
M864.6
P41m
Pereda Valdés, Ildefonso, 1899–
... El negro rioplatense, y otros ensayos. Montevideo, C. García & cía, 1937.
187, ͵1͵ p., 1 l. plates. 17½cm.
CONTENTS.—Contribución al estudio del tema del negro en la literatura castellana hasta fines de la edad de oro.—Contribución al estudio de la música popular brasileña.—Supersticiones africanas del Río de la Plata.—Los pueblos negros del Uruguay y la influencia africana en el habla rioplatense.—Vocabulario de palabras de origen africano en el habla rioplatense.—El diablo mundo y Martín Fierro.—"La mojiganga de la muerte"; una pieza menor poco conocida de Calderón.—Los antiquijotes.—El "no" japonés y la tragedia griega.—Balzac, novelista de una época.—Las ideas ultraconservadoras de Chateaubriand.
1. Negroes in literature and art. 2. Negroes in South America. 3. ~~Literature, Modern—Addresses, essays, lectures.~~ I. Title.
3. Uruguay
39—10565
Library of Congress PQ8519.P26N4
white author
͵42c1͵ 864.6

Haiti
M843.91
P41m
Perez, Jeanne.
La mansarde. Port-au-Prince, Seminaire Adventiste, 1950.

175p. 19cm. (Collection La semeuse)

1. Haitian fiction. I. Title

Performing arts - West Indies, British.
Trinidad
M700
H55
Hill, Errol G., ed.
The artist in West Indian society; a symposium. ͵Mona, Jamaica͵ University of the West Indies, Dept. of Extra-Mural Studies ͵1963?͵
79 p. 21 cm.
"The contributions ... were first delivered in a seminar organised by the University of the West Indies' Department of Extra-Mural Studies during May and June, 1963, in Port-of-Spain, Trinidad."

1. Art — West Indies, British. 2. Performing arts — West Indies, British. 3. Art and society. I. Mona, Jamaica. University of the West Indies. Dept. of Extra-Mural Studies. II. Title.

N6591.H5 65-3616
Library of Congress ͵1͵

Africa
MB9
P41t
Perham, Margery Freda, 1896– *ed.*
Ten Africans, edited by Margery Perham. London, Faber and Faber limited ͵1936͵
356 p. front., plates, ports., fold. map. 23cm.
CONTENTS.—Introduction, by Margery Perham.—The story of Bwembya of the Bemba tribe, northern Rhodesia, recorded by Audrey I. Richards.—The story of Udo Akpabio of the Anang tribe, southern Nigeria, recorded by W. Groves.—The story of Ndansi Kumalo of the Matabele tribe, southern Rhodesia, recorded by J. W. Posselt and Margery Perham.—The story of Rashid Bin Hassani of the Bisa tribe, northern Rhodesia, recorded by W. F. Baldock.—The story of Nosente, the mother of compassion of the Xhosa tribe, South Africa, recorded by

(Continued on next card)
36-24346
͵3͵

Africa
MB9
P41t
Perham, Margery Freda, 1896– *ed.* Ten Africans ... ͵1936͵ (Card 2)
CONTENTS—Continued.
Monica Hunter.—The story of Amini Bin Saidi of the Yao tribe of Nyasaland, recorded by D. W. Malcolm.—The story of Parmenas Mockerie of the Kikuyu tribe, Kenya, written by himself.—The story of Martin Kayamba Mdumi, M. B. E., of the Bondei tribe, written by himself.—The story of Gilbert Coka, of the Zulu tribe of Natal, South Africa, written by himself.—The story of Kofoworola Aina Moore, of the Yoruba tribe, Nigeria, written by herself.

1. Africa—Biog. 2. Bantus. I. Title.
36-24346
Library of Congress DT18.P38 1936
Copyright A ad int. 21868 ͵3͵ 920.06

Periodicals - Indexes.
M016.05
C331
Central State College. Wilberforce, Ohio. Library.
Index to selected Negro periodicals, 1950- Wilberforce, Ohio, The College, 19 -

v. 22cm. quarterly.
See holdings card for issues in library.

Periodicals - Indexes.
M016.05
M351
A Guide to Negro periodical literature. v. 1– Feb. 1941–
Winston-Salem, N. C. ͵etc., 1941–
v. 28cm. quarterly (irregular)
Reproduced from type-written copy.
Compiler: Feb. 1941– A. P. Marshall.

1. Negroes—Bibl.—Period. 2. Periodicals—Indexes. I. Marshall, Albert Prince, 1914– comp.
45-41871
Library of Congress Z1361.N39G8
016.32526

Periquet, Fernando.
M784
J63go
Johnson, James Weldon, 1871-1938. tr.
Goyescas; an opera in three tableaux. The book by Fernando Periquet. The music by Enrique Granados. English version by James Weldon Johnson. New York, G. Schirmer, 1915.

165p. 29½cm.

Periquet, Fernando.
M784
J63g
Johnson, James Weldon, 1871-1938. tr.
Goyescas, or The rival lovers; opera in three tableaux. The book by Fernando Periquet, the music by Enrique Granados, English version by James Weldon Johnson. New York, G. Schirmer ͵c1915͵

42p. 24½cm. (G. Schirmer's collection of opera-librettos)
Inscribed copy: To Captain A.B. Spingarn, Yours sincerely, James Weldon Johnson.
White author.

M616
W93t5
Peritonitis.
Wright, Louis Tompkins, 1891-1952.
Treatment of acute peritonitis with aureomycin, by Louis T. Wright, William I. Metzger, and Edward B. Shapero. Reprinted from the American journal of surgery, 78:15-22, July 1949.

Perkins, Archie Ebenezer, 1879- , p. 60-36.
M378A1
D29p
Davis, Walker Milan, 1908-
Pushing forward; a history of Alcorn A. & M. college and portraits of some of its successful graduates, by W. Milan Davis... Okolona, Miss., The Okolona industrial school, 1938.

x, 124 p. illus. (incl. ports.) 23½cm.

MB
P41w
Perkins, Archie Ebenezer, 1879- ed.
Who's who in colored Louisiana, 1930; A.E. Perkins ... editor. Baton Rouge, La., Douglas Loan Co., Inc. 1930.

153p. illus. plates, ports., facism. 21cm.

M371.91
P419
Perkins, Fannie Lee (LaGrone)
Teaching techniques for cerebral palsied children, by Fannie Lee L. Perkins. ͵1st ed.͵ New York, Vantage Press ͵1964, °1963͵
117 p. 21 cm.
Bibliography: p. 58-60.

1. Cerebral palsied children—Education. I. Title.
2. Handicapped children-education.
LC4580.P4 371.91 64-4181
Library of Congress ͵5͵

M811.5
P42s
Perkins, Minnie Louise, 1932-
A string of pearls. ͵Chicago, Ill. c 1945͵

16p. port. (on cover) 24cm.

1. Poetry. I. Title.

cat.

MB
W53
Perry, C J
White, Charles Frederick.
Who's who in Philadelphia; a collection of thirty biographical sketches of Philadelphia colored people ... together with cuts and information of some of their leading institutions and organizations, by Charles Fred. White ... with an introduction by R. R. Wright, jr., PH. D., and containing additional articles by C. J. Perry, B. F. Lee, jr., R. R. Wright, jr., and Charles Fred. White ... Philadelphia, The A. M. E. book concern ͵°1912͵
206 p., 1 l. incl. illus., plates. 24 cm.
1. Negroes—Philadelphia. I. Title.
12—14969
Library of Congress F158.9.N3W5
͵48b1͵

M813.5
P42p
Perry, Charles.
Portrait of a young man drowning. New York, Simon and Schuster, 1962.
307 p. 22 cm.

I. Title.

PZ4.P462Po 62-7555 ‡
Library of Congress ͵5͵

M813.5
P42p2
Perry, Charles
Portrait of a young man drowning. ͵London͵ A. Deutsch ͵1962͵

307p. 20cm.

I. Title.

M616.12 P42 **Perry, Henry.**
I had heart disease. [1st ed.] New York, Pageant Press [1955]
27 p. 21 cm.
1. Heart—Diseases. I. Title.
RC682.P4 616.12 55-11283 ‡
Library of Congress [3]

M39 P42f **Perry, John Edward, 1870–**
Forty cords of wood; memoirs of a medical doctor ... Jefferson City, Mo., Lincoln university [1947]
xvi, 459 p. illus., ports. 23½cm.
1. Negro physicians. I. Title. 2. National Medical Assoc. 3. Biography.
R154.P43A3 926.1 Med 47-944
© 6Mar47; publisher; A11697.
U. S. Army medical library for Library of Congress [W1045P462f 1947] [4]†

M811.5 P429v **Perry, John Sinclair, 1889–**
Voice of humanity; song of the New World. Boston, Christopher Pub. House [1952]
46 p. 21 cm.
I. Title.
PS3531.E69V6 811.5 52-26306 ‡
Library of Congress [1]

M323 N21a Perry, Leslie Sterling, 1906–
Patterns of discrimination in fundamental human rights.
(In: National Association for the Advancement of Colored People. An appeal to the world; ... New York, 1947. 21cm. p. 62-84).

M335.4 P42c **Perry, Pettis.**
The Communist Party; vanguard fighter for peace, democracy, security, socialism. New York, New Century Publisher[s, 1953]
64 p. illus. 20 cm.
1. Communist Party of the United States of America. 2. Communism—U. S.—1917–
JK2391.C5P4 54-3705 ‡
Library of Congress [2]

M323.4 P42l Perry, Pettis.
Lessons of the civil rights mobilization. Political affairs, v.29, March 1950.
58-67p. 19cm.
Detached copy.
1. Civil rights.

M335.4 P42n Perry, Pettis.
Negro representation - a step towards Negro freedom. Introduction by Betty Gannett. New York, New Century Publishers, 1952.
24 p. 19 cm.
1. Politics and suffrage. I. Title.

M335.4 P42p Perry, Pettis
The party of Negro and white; from his summation speech to the jury in the thought-control Smith Act trial at Foley Square, New York, Jan. 13, 1953. With an introduction by Herbert Aptheker. New York, New Century Publishers, 1953.
15p. 18cm.
1. Communist Party of the United States of America. 2. Communism - U.S. I. Title

---

M335.4 P42ps Perry, Pettis
Pettis Perry speaks to the court, opening statement to the Court and Jury in the case of the sixteen Smith Act victims in the trial at Foley Square, New York. New Century Publishers, 1952.
16 p. 19cm.
1. Communist Party of the United States. 2. Smith Act. 3. Alien Registration Act.

M335.4 P42w Perry, Pettis.
White chauvinism and the struggle for peace. N.Y., New Century, 1952.
5-22p. 20cm.
1. Communist party of the United States. I. Title.

M572. P42 **Perry, Rufus Lewis, 1833–1895.**
The Cushite; or The descendants of Ham as found in the sacred Scriptures, and in the writings of ancient historians and poets from Noah to the Christian era. By Rufus L. Perry ... Springfield, Mass., Willey & co., 1893.
2 p. l., [iii]–x, 11–175 p. 19½cm.
1. Cushites. 2. Negro race.
Library of Congress GN545.P4 [a32b1] 5—39821

M814.5 P41r Persico, George Cecil S ,
Reflective moments, by George C. Persico, [n.p., The Record Press] 1949.
xi, 182p. 22½cm.
1. Essays.

M323 P81p Personal adventures in race relations.
Popel, Esther, 1896–
Personal adventures in race relations [by] Esther Popel Shaw. New York, The Woman's Press [c1946]
24p. 21½cm.

Personality.
M323 D29c **Davis, Allison, 1902–**
Children of bondage; the personality development of Negro youth in the urban South, by Allison Davis and John Dollard, prepared for the American youth commission. Washington, D. C., American council on education, 1940.
xxviii, 299, [1] p., 1 l. diagrs. 23½cm.
Illustration mounted on cover.
1. Negroes—Moral and social conditions. 2. Personality. 3. Social psychology. I. *Dollard, John, 1900– joint author. II. American council on education. American youth commission. III. Title.
[*Full name:* William Allison Davis]
40—13685
Library of Congress E185.86.D38 [a45r41j²10] 325.260975

Personality.
M301 F86ny **Frazier, Edward Franklin, 1894–**
Negro youth at the crossways, their personality development in the middle states, by E. Franklin Frazier; prepared for the American youth commission. Washington, D. C., American council on education, 1940.
xxiii, 301, [2] p. illus. (maps) diagr. 23½ cm.
"This volume ... describes the experiences of Negro boys and girls living in Washington, D. C., and Louisville, Kentucky; these communities were selected as examples of middle-area conditions."—Pref.
1. Negroes—Moral and social conditions. 2. Youth. 3. Personality. 4. Social psychology. 5. Negroes—District of Columbia. 6. Negroes—Louisville, Ky. I. American council on education. American youth commission. II. Title.
40—32764
Library of Congress E185.6.F74 [42z²7] 325.2609753

Personality.
M323 Am3 Johnson, Charles Spurgeon, 1893–
Negro personality changes in a Southern community.
(In: American Sociological Society. Race and culture contacts ... New York, McGraw-Hill, 1934, 23cm. p. 208-127)

Personals.
M811.5 B64p Bontemps, Arna Wendell
Personals. London, Paul Breman, 1963.
44p. 21½cm.
"For Arthur Spingarn - with lasting esteem, Arna Bontemps, 4-17-64."

Personne, tradition et culture en Afrique noire.
Africa M960 As6a Aglemagnon, François N'sougan
Personne, tradition et culture en Afrique noire.
Pp. 22-30.
In: Aspects de la culture noire. 1958.

Personnel service in education.
M370 C12m no.2 **Caliver, Ambrose, 1894–**
... A background study of Negro college students, by Ambrose Caliver, senior specialist in the education of Negroes, Office of education ... Washington, U. S. Govt. print. off., 1933.
vii, 132 p. incl. tables, diagrs. 23cm. (U. S. Office of education. Bulletin, 1933, no. 8)
At head of title: United States Department of the interior. Harold L. Ickes, secretary. Office of education. William John Cooper, commissioner.
Bibliography: p. 116–117.
1. Negroes—Education. 2. Personnel service in education. 3. Negroes—Moral and social conditions. I. Title. II. Title: Negro college students.
E 33-1322
U. S. Off. of educ. Library L111.A6 1933 no. 8
——— Copy 2. LC2801.C32
for Library of Congress L111.A6 1933 no. 8
——— Copy 2. LC2801.C28
[a38t1] (370.6173) 371.9740973

Personnel service in education.
Caliver, Ambrose, 1894–
M371.425 C12 ... Vocational education and guidance of Negroes; report of a survey conducted by the Office of education, by Ambrose Caliver, senior specialist in the education of Negroes ... United States Department of the interior. Harold L. Ickes, secretary. Office of education, J. W. Studebaker, commissioner. Washington, U. S. Govt. print. off., 1938.
x, 137 p. incl. tables, diagrs. 23cm. (U. S. Office of education. Bulletin, 1937, no. 38)
At head of title: Project in vocational education and guidance of Negroes.
On p. [2] of cover: National survey of vocational education and guidance of Negroes.
(Continued on next card)
E 39-3 †
[a46d²3]†

Personnel service in education.
M378 C16 **Canady, Herman George.**
... Individual differences among freshmen at West Virginia state college and their educational bearings, by Herman G. Canady ... Institute, W. Va., West Virginia state college 1936]
42 p. tables, diagrs. 23½cm. (West Virginia state college bulletin, series 23, no. 2. April 1936. Contribution no. 3 of the Department of psychology and philosophy)
Bibliography: p. [40]–42.
1. Mental tests. 2. Personnel service in education. I. Title.
E 39-40
U. S. Off. of educ. Library for Library of Congress LB1131.C28 [2]

Perspectives for our party.
Trinidad
M329 Williams, Eric Eustace, 1911-
W67p Perspectives for our party; address delivered to the third annual convention of the People's National Movement on October 17, 1958. [Port-of-Spain, P.N.M. Publishing Co., 1958]

20p. 22cm.

1. People's National Movement. 2. Trinidad - Political parties. 3. Political parties - Trinidad. I. Title.

Perspectives for the West Indies.
Trinidad
M972.9 Williams, Eric Eustace, 1911-
W67p Perspectives for the West Indies [speech delivered at San Fernando on Monday, May 30th, 1960. Port-of-Spain, P.N.M. Pub. Co., 1960]

12p. 21cm.

1. West Indies - Politics and government.
I. Title

Peru—History.
Peru
M985 Palma, Ricardo, 1833-1919.
P18t ... Tradiciones peruanas escogidas (edición crítica) Prólogo, selección y notas de Luis Alberto Sánchez. Santiago de Chile, Ediciones Ercilla, 1940.

3 p. l., [9]-215, [3] p. 18cm. (Half-title: Biblioteca Amauta (Serie América) [V. 1])

"Noticia bibliográfica": p. 14-16.

1. Legends—Peru. 2. Peru—Hist. I. Sánchez, Luis Alberto, 1900- ed. II. Title.
[Full name: Manuel Ricardo Palma]

Library of Congress PS400.P1732 41—9563
[44e1] 985

Peru - Literature.
Peru
M860 Diez Canseco, José
D56 Lima; coplas y guitarras. Lima, 1949.

140p. illus. 22½cm. (His Obra Completas de, V. 1)

Peruvian literature.
Peru
M863.6 López Albújar, Enrique, 1872-
L88n ... Nuevos cuentos andinos. Santiago de Chile, Ediciones Ercilla, 1937.

4 p. l., [11]-185 p., 1 l. 22cm. (Half-title: Biblioteca América)

Contents.—El brindis de los yayas.—Huayna-pishtanag.—El blanco.—Cómo se hizo pishtaco Calixto.—El trompiezo.—Juan Rabines no perdona.—Una posesión judicial.

I. Title.

Library of Congress PQ8497.L6N8 38—12446
[45d1] 863.6

Peruvian poetry.
Peru
M861 Cruz, Nicomedes Santa, 1925-
D35 Decimas. Primera edicion. Peru, Juan Mejia Baca [1960]

146p. 17cm.
Portrait on cover.

Peruvian poetry.
Peru
M861 Cruz, Nicomedes Santa, 1925-
D35d Decimas. Lima Juan Mejia Baca 1959.

22p. 21cm.
Autographed: "A Mr. Arthur B. Spingarn con todo mi sincero afecto."

MB9 Peskin, Allan, ed.
M29 Malvin, John, 1795-1880.
North into freedom; the autobiography of John Malvin, free Negro, 1795-1880. Edited and with an introd. by Allan Peskin. Cleveland, Press of Western Reserve University, 1966.

vii, 87 p. 23 cm.

"A book from Cleveland State University."
Bibliographical references included in "Notes to the introduction" (p. 22-24)

1. Negroes—Ohio. 2. Negroes—Civil rights. I. Peskin, Allan, ed. II. Title.

E185.97.M26A3 1966 66-28142
301.451960924 (B)

Library of Congress [8]

Haiti Petain, Maréchal,
M972.94 Pluviose, Rosemond N
P74p Parallele historique "Petain-Dessalines." Port-au-Prince, Haiti, Imprimerie de l'etat, 1946.
12p. 20cm.

Pétal par pétale.
Haiti
M841 Wiener, Wanda Ducoste
W634p Pétal par pétale. [Paris, Maitre-Imprimeur, 1962.

29p. 4 plates. 24cm. (Collection "L'ile heureuse.")
"... Toute ma cordialite a Arthur Spingarn, Wanda Ducaster Wiener, New York, 1962".

I. Title.

Pétales et paillons.
Haiti
M841 Ricot, Justinien
R42p Pétales et paillons. Paris Jouve & Cia, 1927.
116p. 18cm.

M811.5 Peters, Ada Tress
P44w War poems, by Peters sisters. [n.p., n. p., 1919]
83p. photo, 18½ cm.

I. Peters, Ethel Pauline, jt. author.
1. Poetry
II. Title

Peters, Ethel Pauline, jt. author.
M811.5 Peters, Ada Tress
P44w War poems, by Peters sisters. [n.p., n. p., 1919]

83p. photo, 18½ cm.

South Africa
M896 Peters, Lenrie, 1932-
M88 'After they put down their overalls'

P. 243

In: Mphahlele, Ezekiel, ed. African writing today. Baltimore, Penguin Books, 1967.

Gambia
M896.1 Peters, Lenrie, 1932-
P94p Poems. Ibadan, Mbari Publications [1964]

44p. 20cm.

I. Mbari Publications.

Gambia
M896.3 Peters, Lenrie, 1932-
P94s The second round. [London] Heinemann [1965]

192p. 19cm.

I. Title.

Peters, William, 1921-
M323.4 Evers, Myrlie
Ev27 For us, the living, by Mrs. Medgar Evers with William Peters. [1st ed.], Garden City, N. Y., Doubleday, 1967.

378 p. 22 cm.

1. Evers, Medgar Wiley, 1925-1963. I. Peters, William, 1921- II. Title.

E185.97.E94E9 323.4'0924 67-22454

Library of Congress [3]

MB9 Peterson, Daniel H.
P441 The looking-glass: being a true report and narrative of the life, travels and labors of the Rev. Daniel H. Peterson, a colored clergyman; embracing a period of time from the year 1812 to 1854, and including his visit to west rn Africa. With engravings,. New York, Wright, Printer, 1854.
X 150p. illus. 15cm.

~~1. Biography~~. 2. Churches.

M230.67 Peterson, Frank Loris.
P44 The hope of the race, by Frank Loris Peterson. Nashville, Tenn., Southern publishing association [c1934]

333 p. incl. front., illus., ports., diagrs. col. pl. 20½cm.

1. Seventh-day Adventists—Doctrinal and controversial works. 2. Negroes—Religion. I. Title.

Library of Congress BX6154.P45 35-1032
——— Copy 2.
Copyright A 77848 [3] 230.67

M812.5 Peterson, Louis Stamford, 1922-
P44 Take a giant step, a drama in two acts. New York, French [1954]

110 p. 19 cm.

I. Title.

PS3531.E867T3 812.5 54-31878 †

Library of Congress [3]

Petion, Alejandro Sabes, pres. Haiti, 1770-1818.
Haiti
M842 Brierre, Jean Fernand, 1909-
B76p Pétion y Bolivar. Buenos Aires, Ediciones Troquel, 1955.

201p. illus. 20cm.

Pétion, Alexandre Sabes, pres. Haiti, 1770-1818

Haiti
M972.94
D15a

Dalencour, Francois Stanislas Ranier, 1880-
Alexandre Pétion devant l'humanité; Alexandre Pétion et Simon Bolivar; Haiti et l'Amerique Latine, par Francois Dalencour et Expedition de Bolivar par le Sénateur Marion. Port-au-Prince, Chez l'Auteur, [1928]

129p. illus. 23cm.

Le petit soldat.

Haiti
MB9
P61b

Brierre, Jean Fernand, 1909-
Le petit soldat, causerie prononcée à l'Association des étudiants en droit. Port-au-Prince, Impr. haïtienne, 1934.

cover-title, 20 p. 21 cm.

1. Pierre, Joseph, also known as Pierre Sully, d. 1915. I. Title.

F1926.P6B7 923.57294 45-31263 rev*

Library of Congress [r47c1]

MB9
T79p

Petry, Ann (Lane), 1912-
The girl called Moses; the story of Harriet Tubman. London, Methuen & Co., 1960.

205p. 19½cm.

1. Tubman, Harriet (Ross), 1815?-1913.
I. Title.

Pétion, Alexandre Sabés, pres. Haiti, 1770-1818.

Haiti
M972.94
D15f

Dalencour, François Stanislas Ranier, 1880-
... La fondation de la république d'Haïti par Alexandre Pétion, par le docteur François Dalencour ... Port-au-Prince, Haïti, L'auteur, 1944.

2 p. l., 344 p. port. 23½cm. (Collection historique du dr. François Dalencour: Recherches techniques sur l'histoire d'Haïti)

"Œuvres du docteur François Dalencour": verso of 2d prelim. leaf.

1. Haiti—Hist.—1804-1844. 2. Pétion, Alexandre Sabés, pres. Haiti, 1770-1818.

Library of Congress F1924.D3 45-14911
[2] 972.94

M306
N21pe

A petition...
[National Negro Congress]
A petition ... to the United Nations on behalf of 13 million oppressed Negro citizens of the United States of America. New York, 1946.

1*p. 23cm.
Contains also: The oppression of the American Negro: the facts, by Herbert Aptheker: p. 8-14.

M813.5
P44h

Petry, Ann (Lane), 1912-
Harriet Tubman, conductor on the Underground Railroad. New York, Crowell [1955]

247 p. 21 cm.

1. Tubman, Harriet (Ross) 1815?-1913—Fiction.

PZ3.P44904Har 55—9215 ‡

Library of Congress [56u7]

Pétion, Alexandre Sabes, Pres. Haiti, 1770-1818.

Haiti
MB
D15f

Dalencour, François Stanislas Ranier, 1880-
Francisco de Miranda et Alexandre Pétion l'expédition de Miranda; le premier effort de libération Hispano-Américaine le premier vagissement du Panaméricanisme. Port-au-Prince, Librairie Berger-Levrault, 1955.

325p. ports. illus. 23cm.

Petition of the Universal Negro Improvement Association...

M341.1
Un3p

Universal Negro Improvement Association.
Petition of the Universal Negro Improvement Association and African Communities League, representing the interest of the four hundred million Negroes Indiginies of Africa, the British subjects in the West Indies, South and Central America, and the citizens, and other Negro inhabitants of the United States of America and those of Asia and Europe, to the League of Nations. [New York, The Association, 1922?]
7 leaves. 28cm.

M813.5
Se1c

Petry, Ann (Lane), 1912-
In darkness and confusion.

pp. 98-128.
In: Cross section 1947, ed. by Edwin Seaver. 1947.

I. Title.

Petion, Alexandre Sabes, pres. Haiti, 1770-1818.

Haiti
M972.94
L56g

Lespinasse, Pierre Eugène de.
... Gens d'autrefois. Vieux souvenirs ...
Paris, La Revue mondiale, 1926-

v. ports. 19cm. (Collection haïtienne d'expression française)

1. Haiti—Hist.—1804- 2. Boyer, Jean Pierre, pres. Haiti, 1776-1850. 3. Pétion, Alexandre Sabés, pres. Haiti, 1770-1818. 4. Christophe, Henri, king of Haiti, 1767-1820. I. Title.

Library of Congress F1924.L63 28-25703
——— Copy 2. [3]

M342.73
M615

The petitioners.

Miller, Loren.
The petitioners; the story of the Supreme Court of the United States and the Negro. New York, Pantheon Books [1966]

xv, 461 p. 22 cm.
Bibliographical references included in "Notes" (p. [435]-455)

1. U. S. Supreme Court. 2. Negroes—Legal status, laws, etc. I. Title.

342.73 65-14582

Library of Congress [5]

M813.08
B46a

Petry, Ann (Lane), 1912-
Like a winding street.

(In: The Best American Short stories...1946. Boston, Houghton Mifflin, 1946. 21cm. p. 302-315.)

Haiti
M972.94
M31p

Pétion, Alexandre Sabès., Pres. Haiti, 1770-1818.

Manigat, Leslie F
La politique agraire du gouvernement D'Alexandre Pétion (1807-1818). Port-au-Prince, Imp. La Phalange, 1962.

74p. 20½cm.

Les petits.

Haiti
M972.94
D38p

Delorme, Desmesvar, 1833-1901.
Les petits. La Hollande, par Demesvar Delorme (de la Republique d'Haiti). Treurenberg, Bruxelles, Edité par la SociétéBelge de Librairie, 1893.

234p. 23cm.

M813.5
P44n

Petry, Ann (Lane), 1912-
The Narrows. Boston, Houghton Mifflin, 1953.
428 p. 22 cm.

First edition.

I. Title.

PZ3.P44904No 53-5729 ‡

Library of Congress [7]

Petit manuel Francais-

Mali
M496
T69p

Travele, Moussa editor.
Petit manuel Francais-bambara, par Moussa Travele... 2e edition revue et augment.. Paris, Librairie orientaliste Paul Geuthner, 1923.
89p. 19cm.

M813.5
P44c

Petry, Ann (Lane), 1912-
Country place. Boston, Houghton Mifflin Co., 1947.

266p. 22cm.

1. Fiction. I. Title.

M831.5
P44m2

Petry, Ann (Lane), 1912-
The narrows. London, Victor Gollanz, Ltd. 1954.

428p. 19½cm.

I. Title.

Martinique

Le petit roi de Chimérie, conte.

M843.9
M32pc

Maran, René, 1887-
... Le petit roi de Chimérie, conte; préface de Léon Bocquet. Paris, A. Michel [1924]
237, [1] p. 19cm.

I. Bocquet, Léon, 1876- II. Title.

Library of Congress PQ2625.A74P4 1924 24-8818
Copyright A—Foreign 24205
[2]

M813.5
P44c
1950

Petry, Ann (Lane), 1912-
Country place. New York, New American Library, 1950.

190p. 18cm. (Signet books)
Pocket book edition.

I. Title.

M813.5
P44s
1947

Petry, Ann (Lane), 1912-
... The street. London, M. Joseph [1947]

312p. 21cm.
At head of title: Ann Petry.

I. Title

M813.5 P44s
Petry, Ann (Lane), 1912-
The street, New York, New American Library, 1949.
189p. 18cm. (Signet books)
Pocket book edition.
I. Title.

M813.5 P44s 1954
Petry, Ann (Lane), 1912-
The street. New York, New American Library, 1954.
270p. 18cm. (Signet giant, S1123)
Pocket book edition.
"Complete and unabridged."
I. Title

M813.5 P44s 1958
Petry, Ann (Lane), 1912-
The street. London, Harborough Publishing Co., 1958.
203p. 18cm.
I. Title.

M813.5 P44t
Petry, Ann (Lane), 1912-
Tituba of Salem Village, by Ann Petry. New York, Crowell [1964]
254 p. 21 cm.
Portrait of author on book cover.
1. Tituba—Juvenile fiction. 2. Witchcraft—Salem, Mass.—Juvenile literature. I. Title.
PZ7.P4473Ti 64-20691
Library of Congress [7-1]

Pettet, Zellmer Roswell, 1880-
M312 Un3n 1935
U. S. *Bureau of the Census.*
... Negroes in the United States, 1920-32. Prepared under the supervision of Z. R. Pettet, chief statistician for agriculture, by Charles E. Hall, specialist in Negro statistics. Washington, U. S. Govt. print. off., 1935.
xvi, 845 p. incl. maps, tables, diagrs. 30cm.
At head of title: U. S. Department of commerce. Daniel C. Roper, secretary. Bureau of the census. William Lane Austin, director.
"This report supplements the volume, "Negro population in the United States, 1790-1915," published by the Bureau of the census in 1918."—p. iii.
1. Negroes. I. Pettet, Zellmer Roswell, 1880- II. Hall, Charles Edward, 1868-
35—26785
Library of Congress HA205.A33 1920-32
[45w1] 325.260973

U.S. M951.9 P45
Pettigrew, Thomas H
The Kunu-ri (Kumori) incident. [1st ed.] New York, Vantage Press [1963]
55 p. illus. 21 cm.
1. Korean War, 1950-1951—Personal narratives, American. I. Title.
DS921.6.P4 951.9042 63-4031 ‡
Library of Congress [5]

MB9 P46q
Peyton, Thomas Roy, 1897-
Quest for dignity, an autobiography of a Negro doctor. Los Angeles, W. F. Lewis [1950]
vii, 156 p. 24 cm.
I. Title. II. Title: Negro doctor.
R154.P49A3 926.1 50-13642
Library of Congress [a50e2]

Haiti M972.94 P44v
Phareaux, Lallier C
La vie contemporaine. Port-au-Prince, Impr. de l'État, 1953.
630 p. illus. 21 cm. (Collection du Tricinquantenaire de l'indépendance d'Haïti)
1. Haiti—Civilization. I. Title.
F1915.P5 54-34975 ‡
Library of Congress [1]

M614 R66fo
Pharmacopoeias.
Roman, Charles Victor, 1864-1934, comp.
... Formulae supplemental to those in U.S. pharmacopoeia and national formulary, with explanatory notes and appendix, compiled by the chief of the clinic. [Nashville, 1909?]
57p. 13cm.
Cover title: Eye, ear, nose and throat formulary of remedies used in Dr. Roman's Clinic, Meharry Medical College.
Contains: The Deontological orientation of its membership the chief function of a medical society, by C. V. Roman.

M615.4 P27p
Pharmacy.
Patrick, Thomas William, 1872-
Patrick's course in pharmacy, specially designed for preparing drug clerks to pass the Board of Pharmacy... in twenty lessons. Boston, The Blanchard Printing Co., 1906.
20 parts. 28cm.
Missing: Lessons 1, 19, 20.

Haiti M841 P51ec
Phelps, Anthony
Eclats de silence, poèmes. Port-au-Prince, Art Graphique Presses, 1962.
1 v. illus. port., 21cm. (Collection Haiti Litteraire)
I. Title.

Haiti M841 P51e
Phelps, Anthony
Ete... poeme. Port-au-Prince, Imprimerie N.A. Theodore, 1960.
31p. 22cm. (Collection Samba)
1. Haitian poetry. I. Title.

Haiti M841 P51p
Phelps, Anthony
Présence (poème). Illustrations de Luckner Lazard. Port-au-Prince, Art Graphique Presse, 1961.
[9] p. illus. 21½cm. (Collection Haiti Litteraire)
1. Haitian poetry. I. Title.

MB9 B88p
[Phelphs-Stokes Fund]
Ralph Johnson Bunche, peacemaker. New York, 1951.
28p. 22cm.
Addresses delivered at a dinner, given in honor of Dr. Bunche, January 18, 1951.
1. Bunche, Ralph Johnson, 1904-
I. Bunche, Ralph Johnson - Address.

Phelps-Stokes fund.
M03 En1
Encyclopedia of the Negro, preparatory volume with reference lists and reports, by W. E. B. Du Bois ... and Guy B. Johnson ... prepared with the cooperation of E. Irene Diggs, Agnes C. L. Donohugh, Guion Johnson [and others] ... Introduction by Anson Phelps Stokes. New York, The Phelps-Stokes fund, inc., 1945.
207, [1] p. group port. 23½ cm.
1. Negro race—Dictionaries and encyclopedias. 2. Negro race—Bibl. I. Du Bois, William Edward Burghardt, 1868- ed. II. Johnson, Guy Benton, 1901- joint ed. III. Phelps-Stokes fund.
45—3862
Library of Congress HT1581.E5
[47b7] 572.96

Phenomena.
M811.5 At5pn
Atkins, Russell
Phenomena. [Afterword, by Casper Leroy Jordan] Wilberforce, Ohio, The Free Lance Poets and Prose Workshop, Wilberforce University Press, 1961.
79p. 22cm.

Philadelphia.
M301 D853ne5
Du Bois, William Edward Burghardt, 1868-
The Negro south and north, by Professor W.E. Burghardt Du Bois. [Reprinted from the Bibliotheca sacra, July 1905.
500-513p. 22cm.

Philadelphia.
M301 D853p
Du Bois, William Edward Burghardt, 1868-
... The Philadelphia Negro; a social study by W. E. Burghardt Du Bois ... Together with a special report on domestic service by Isabel Eaton ... Philadelphia, Pub. for the University, 1899.
xx, 520 p. incl. diagrs. 2 fold. plans. 23cm. (Publications of the University of Pennsylvania. Series in political economy and public law. no. 14)
Contents.—The Philadelphia Negro.—Appendixes: A. Schedules used in the house-to-house inquiry. B. Legislation, etc., of Pennsylvania in regard to the Negro. C. Bibliography.—Special report on Negro domestic service in the seventh ward, Philadelphia, by I. Eaton.
1. Negroes — Philadelphia. 2. U. S. — Race question. 3. Servants. I. Eaton, Isabel. II. Title.
5—33530
Library of Congress F158.9.N3D8
———— Copy 2. H31.P4 no. 14
[45d1]

Philadelphia.
M289.9 F27
Fauset, Arthur Huff, 1899-
... Black gods of the metropolis; Negro religious cults of the urban North, by Arthur Huff Fauset. Philadelphia, University of Pennsylvania press; London, H. Milford, Oxford university press, 1944.
x, 126 p. plates, ports. 23½cm. (Publications of the Philadelphia anthropological society. Vol. III)
Half-title: ... Brinton memorial series. [No. 2]
Issued also as thesis (PH. D.) University of Pennsylvania.
"A study of five Negro religious cults in the Philadelphia of today."—Pref.
1. Negroes—Religion. 2. Negroes—Philadelphia. 3. Sects—U. S. I. Title.
44—3761
Library of Congress BR563.N4F3 1944 a
[47x3] 289.9

Philadelphia.
M814.3 F77
[Forten, James, 1776-1842]
To the Honourable the Senate and House of Representatives of the Commonwealth of Pennsylvania. The memorial of the people of colour the city of Philadelphia and its vicinity respectfully sheweth... [n.p. 1832]
8p. 18½cm.
Signed: James Forten, Chairman; William Whipper, Robert Purvis, secretaries.

Philadelphia, Pa.
M331 M66
Minton, Henry M.
Early history of Negroes in business in Philadelphia. Read before the American Historical, March,1913, by Henry M. Minton. [Nashville, Tenn.,A.M.E.S.S. Union,1913?]
20p. 22½cm.

Philadelphia.

M304 F19 v.1 no.15

Mossell, Sadie Tanner.
... A study of the negro tuberculosis problem in Philadelphia, by Sadie T. Mossell ... Philadelphia, Henry Phipps institute, 1923.

v, 7–29, ⌐3¬ p. illus. (maps) diagr. 20ᶜᵐ.

At head of title: University of Pennsylvania.
"This study was made under the auspices of the Whittier centre and the Henry Phipps institute; it was revised by the Philadelphia health council and Tuberculosis committee."

1. Tuberculosis—Philadelphia. 2. Negroes—Philadelphia. I. Pennsylvania. University. Henry Phipps institute.

Library of Congress RC313.A57M6 25—20530 ⌐a28c1¬

Philadelphia.

MB9 St5

Still, James, *b*. 1812.
Early recollections and life of Dr. James Still. ⌐Philadelphia¬ Printed for the author by J. B. Lippincott & co., 1877.

274 p. front. (port.) 19ᶜᵐ.

Library of Congress E185.97.S85 14-15948 ⌐37b1¬
Copyright 1877; 3478

Philadelphia.

MB W58

White, Charles Frederick.
Who's who in Philadelphia; a collection of thirty biographical sketches of Philadelphia colored people ... together with cuts and information of some of their leading institutions and organizations, by Charles Fred. White ... with an introduction by R. R. Wright, jr., PH. D., and containing additional articles by C. J. Perry, B. F. Lee, jr., R. R. Wright, jr., and Charles Fred. White ... Philadelphia, The A. M. E. book concern ⌐°1912¬

206 p., 1 l. incl. illus., plates. 24 cm.

1. Negroes—Philadelphia. I. Title.

Library of Congress F158.9.N3W5 12—14969 ⌐48b1¬

M324 P97a

Philadelphia - Politics and government.
Purvis, Robert
Appeal of forty thousand citizens threatened with disfranchisement to the people of Pennsylvania. Philadelphia, Merrihew and Gunn, 1838.

18p. 21½cm.

Philadelphia, Pa.

M973.6 C77 1831.

Convention of the people of colour.
Minutes and proceedings of the first annual meeting of th e people of colour, held by adjournments in the city of Philadelphia, from the sixth to the eleventh of June, inclusive, 1831. Philadelphia, Published by order of the committee of arrangements, 1831.
20p. 19cm.

Philadelphia, Pa.

M973.6 C77 1833

Convention of the people of colour.
Minutes and proceedings of the third annual convention, for the improvement of the free people of colour in these United States, held by adjournments in the city of Philadelphia, from the 3rd to the 13th of June inclusive, 1833. New York, Published by order of the Convention, 1833.
16p. 19cm.

Philadelphia, Pa.

MB9 C79r

Coppin, Fanny Jackson, 1837-1913.
Reminiscences of school life, and hints on teaching, by Fanny Jackson Coppin. Introduction by William C. Bolivar. ⌐Philadelphia, Pa., A.M.E. Book Concern, 1913¬
191p. port (front.) 20½cm.
Introduction by William C. Bolivar.

Philadelphia. First African Baptist Church.

M286 B79o

Brooks, Charles H 1861–
Official history of the First African Baptist church, Philadelphia, Pa., by Charles H. Brooks. Philadelphia, Pa., 1922.

167 p. incl. plates, ports. 21½ᶜᵐ.

Copyright 1923.

1. Philadelphia. First African Baptist church.

Library of Congress BX6445.P5B7 23-8814
——— Copy 2.
Copyright A 704310 ⌐2¬

Philadelphia. First African Presbyterian Church.

M285 C29

Catto, William Thomas
A semi-centenary discourse, delivered in the First African Presbyterian church, Philadelphia, on the fourth Sabbath of May, 1857: with a history of the church from its first organization: including a brief notice of Rev. John Gloucester, its first pastor. By Rev. William T. Catto, pastor. Also, an appendix, containing sketches of all the colored churches in Philadelphia. Philadelphia, J. M. Wilson, 1857.

111 p. 23ᶜᵐ.

1. Philadelphia. First African Presbyterian church. 2. Gloucester, John, 1776 or 7–1822. I. Title.

Library of Congress BX9211.P5A3 13–14590 ⌐a32c1¬

The Philadelphia Negro.

M301 D85 3p

Du Bois, William Edward Burghardt, 1868–
... The Philadelphia Negro; a social study by W. E. Burghardt Du Bois ... Together with a special report on domestic service by Isabel Eaton ... Philadelphia, Pub. for the University, 1899.

xx, 520 p. incl. diagrs. 2 fold. plans. 26ᶜᵐ. (Publications of the University of Pennsylvania. Series in political economy and public law. no. 14)

CONTENTS.—The Philadelphia Negro.—Appendixes: A. Schedules used in the house-to-house inquiry. B. Legislation, etc., of Pennsylvania in regard to the Negro. C. Bibliography.—Special report on Negro domestic service in the seventh ward, Philadelphia, by I. Eaton.

1. Negroes — Philadelphia. 2. U. S. — Race question. 3. Servants. I. Eaton, Isabel. II. Title.

Library of Congress F158.9.N3D8 5—33530
——— Copy 2. H31.P4 no. 14
⌐45d1¬

Martinique
M972.98 P53g

Philémon, Césaire.
... Galeries martiniquaises; population, mœurs, activités diverses et paysages de la Martinique; 3 cartes, 42 illustrations. 1. éd. Fort-de-France, Dans toutes les librairies et chez l'auteur; Paris, Chez l'auteur ⌐1931¬

430 p., 1 l. front., plates, ports., fold. maps. 23ᶜᵐ.

At foot of t.-p.: Exposition coloniale internationale, Paris, 1931.

1. Martinique. I. Paris. Exposition coloniale internationale, 1931. II. Title.

Library of Congress F2081.P53 32-13871
Copyright A—Foreign 14467
⌐2¬ 917.298

Martinique
M972.98 P53m

Philémon, Césaire.
... La montagne Pelée et l'effroyable destruction de Saint-Pierre (Martinique) le 8 mai 1902; le brusque réveil du volcan en 1929. Éd. originale. Fort-de-France, Chez l'auteur; Paris, Impressions Printory et G. Courville ⌐°1930¬

4 p. l., ⌐11¬–211 p., 1 l. plates, fold. maps. 22½ᶜᵐ.

"Il a été tiré de cet ouvrage cinquante exemplaires sur papier pur fil Lafuma, numérotés de 1 à 50, qui constituent l'édition originale."

1. Pelee peak—Eruption, 1902. 2. Saint-Pierre, Martinique. I. Title.

Library of Congress F2081.P54 31-13052
Copyright A—Foreign 10883
⌐2¬ [917.298] 551.21097298

Martinique
M972.98 P53s

Philémon, Césaire
Souvenirs. Préface de F. Thizy. 2ᵉ ed. Paris, Exposition coloniale internationale, 1931.

176p. illus., ports. 22½cm.

1. Martinique-Description and Travel. I. Title.

Martinique
M972.98 P53a

Philip, John Baptist, d. 1829.
An address to the Right Hon. Earl Bathurst, His Majesty's Principal of State for the Colonies, relative to the claims which the coloured population of Trinidad have to the same civil and political privileges with their white fellow-subjects. By a free mulatto of the Island. London, Printed in the year 1824.

298p. 20cm.

1. Trinidad. 2. Williams, Francis. 3. Bathurst, Henry, 3d Earl of, 1762-1834

Philip, John Baptist, d. 1829.

Martinique
M972.98 P53a

An oration, pronounced on the 29th of July, after the funeral dirge of Doctor John Baptista Philip, who died on the 16th of June, 1829, in Trinidad. London, printed by C. Lawler, n.d.

30p. 20cm.
Bound with: Philip, John Baptist - An address to the Right Hon. Earl Bathurst.

MB9 P54f

Phillips, Charles Henry, *bp*., 1858–
From the farm to the bishopric; an autobiography, by Bishop Charles Henry Phillips. Nashville, Tenn., Printed for the author by the Parthenon press ⌐°1932¬

308 p. 19½ᶜᵐ.

I. Title.

Library of Congress BX8469.P5A3 33-1972
——— Copy 2.
Copyright A 58535 ⌐2¬ 922.773

M287.5 P54

Phillips, Charles Henry, *bp*., 1858–
The history of the Colored Methodist Episcopal church in America: comprising its organization, subsequent development, and present status. By C. H. Phillips ... Jackson, Tenn., Publishing house C. M. E. church, 1898.

247 p. incl. plates, ports. front. 19ᶜᵐ.

"Biography of the author. By J. W. Smith ...": p. 7–18.

1. Colored Methodist Episcopal church. 2. Church.

Library of Congress BX8463.P5 C-375 Revised 2
Copyright 1898: 43764 ⌐r33e2¬

Nigeria
M784 P54

Phillips, Ekundayo
Yoruba music (African); fusion of speech and music. Johannesburg, African Music Society, 1953.

58p. diagrs. 24½cm.

1. Yoruba Music. 2. Music - Africa, West.

M811.5 P54f

Phillips, Hilton Alonzo, 1905–
Flames of rebellion (against enthroned tyranny) by Hilton A. Phillips ... ⌐Los Angeles, Printed by the California eagle press, °1936¬

viii, 237 p. port. 22ᶜᵐ.

Prose and poetry.

1. Race problems. 2. Negro race. 3. Negroes. 4. U. S.—Race question. I. Title. 2. Poetry.

Library of Congress HT1521.P5 36-10090
——— Copy 2.
Copyright A 92792 ⌐5¬ 323.1

M910 P54L

Phillips, Hilton Alonzo, 1905–
Liberia's place in Africa's sun, by Hilton Alonzo Phillips ... with a foreword by Hon. Hugh E. MacBeth ... New York, N. Y., The Hobson book press, 1946.

2 p. l., vii–xviii, 156 p. 21½ᶜᵐ.

Reproduced from type-written copy.
Bibliography: p. ⌐153¬–156.

1. Liberia. I. Title.

Library of Congress DT632.P5 46-5061
⌐5¬ 966.6

M813.5 P53m

Phillips, Jane, 1944–
Mojo hand. New York, Trident Press ⌐1966¬

180 p. 22 cm.

Portrait of author on book jacket.

I. Title.

PZ4.P558Mo 66-24834
Library of Congress ⌐3¬

M89 P16p
Phillips, Porter William, 1896–
W. W. Brown, host, by Porter W. Phillips ... New York [etc.] Fleming H. Revell company [°1941]
102 p. pl., ports. 19cm.

1. Brown, Willis W., 1859–1980. 2. Metropolitan Baptist church, N.Y.
Library of Congress BX6455.B7P45 41-5260
——— Copy 2. [2] 922.673

M813.5 P54b
Phillips, Waldo B
Babylon has no exit, by Waldo B. Phillips. [n. p., 1964]
48 p. 22 cm.
Cover title.

1. Negroes—Education. I. Title.
LC2781.P45 64-19764
Library of Congress [3]

M811.5 P55p
Phillips, Waldo B
Poetry in proflection. Los Angeles, Compton Counseling Center [1965]
38p. 21½cm.
I. Title.

M8 W58g
Phillips, Wendell, 1811-1884.
pp. 62-99
In: Laureen White's Giants lived in those days. 1959.

Phillips, Wendell, 1811-1884.
M815.4 D74eq
Douglass, Frederick, 1817-1895.
The equality of all men before the law claimed and defended; in speeches by Hon. William D. Kelley, Wendell Phillips, and Frederick Douglass, and letters from Elizur Wright and Wm. Heighton. Boston, Press of G. C. Rand & Avery, 1865.
43p. 23cm.

M323 W587m
Phillips County, Arkansas.
White, Walter Francis, 1893-
Massacring whites in Arkansas. The Nation, December 6, [19]
2p. 31cm.

M372.4 C35p
Phillis Wheatley, poetess.
Chambers, Lucille Arcola
Phillis Wheatley, poetess. Art by John Neal. New York, C. & S Ventures, 1965.
[23]p. illus. 31cm. (Negro pioneers)
"Compliments of Lucille Arcola Chambers, '67."
I. Title. II. Series.

Phillis Wheatley association.
M89 H91n
Hunter, Jane Edna (Harris) 1882–
A nickel and a prayer, by Jane Edna Hunter. [Nashville, The Parthenon press, °1940]
198 p. 2 pl. (incl. port.) on 1 l. 19½cm.

1. Negroes—Charities. I. Phillis Wheatley association. II. Title.
41-7251
Library of Congress HV3181.H8
[a43f2] 923.673

Haiti M841 P54v
Philoctete, Raymond
Voix dans le soir; poèmes. Port-au-Prince, Edition "La Semeuse," 1945.
20p. 21cm.
1. Haitian poetry. I. title

Haiti M841 M82c
Philoctete, Rene
Promese. [Port-au-Prince] Editions les Araignes du Soir, 1963.
folder ([5]p.) 19½cm.
Printed on verso of Morisseau, Roland. Clef du soleil.
Poem.
I. Title.

Philologie créole.
M447.9 F14p
Faine, Jules.
... Philologie créole; études historiques et étymologiques sur la langue créole d'Haiti. Port-au-Prince, Haiti, Imprimerie de l'État, 1936.
xviii, 303, [1] p. 23½cm.
Each section preceded by half-title, not included in collation (3 l.)
"Bibliographie": p. [xvii]–xviii.

1. Creole dialects—Haiti. I. Title.
40-23085
Library of Congress PM7854.H3F25 1936
[2] 447.9

Cameroun M896.3 P548s
Philombe, René, 1930-
Sola ma chérie. Yaoundé, Editions Abbia avec la collaboration de CLE, 1966.
124p. 18cm.
I. Title.

Philosopher and saint.
M811.5 B97p
Butler, Alpheus.
Philosopher and saint; sonnets and other poems. New York, Exposition Press [1951]
64 p. 23 cm.

I. Title. *Full name:* James Alpheus Butler.
PS3503.U84P5 811.5 51-11835 ‡
Library of Congress [2]

Philosopher or dog?
Brazil M869.3 M18ph
Machado de Assis, Joaquim Maria, 1839-1908.
Philosopher or dog? (Quincas Borba) Translated from the Portuguese by Clotilde Wilson. New York, Noonday Press [°1954]
271 p. 21 cm.
Sequel to Epitaph of a small winner.

I. Title.
PZ3.M1817Ph 54-11195 ‡
Library of Congress [3]

Philosophy.
Brazil M869 B27di
Barreto de Menzes, Tobias, 1839-1889.
... Discursos [Rio de Janeiro, Empreza Graphica Editora, Paulo Pongetti & C., 1926]
xii, 195p. port. 24cm. (Ediçăo do estado de Sergipe)
Obias completas IV.

Philosophy.
Brazil M869 B27es
Barreto de Menzes, Tobias, 1839-1889.
... Estudos Allemães. [Rio de Janeiro, Empreza graphica Editora, Paulo Pongetti & C., 1926]
XXXVIII, 514, IIp. port. 24cm. (Ediçăo do estado de Sergipe)
Obras completas VIII.

Philosophy.
Brazil M869 B27ph
Barreto de Menzes, Tobias, 1839-1889.
... Philosophia e critica. (Rio de Janeiro, Empreza graphica Editora, Paulo Pongetti & C., 1926)
XII, 386p. port. 24cm. (Ediçao do estado de Sergipe)
Obras completas, v.III.

Philosophy.
Brazil M869 B27po
Barreto de Menzes, Tobias, 1839-1889.
... Polemicas. [Rio de Janeiro, Empreza graphica Editora, Paulo Pongetti & C., 1926]
XXXVIII. 426p. port. 24cm. (Edicao do estado de Sergipe)
Obras completas, v.II.

Philosophy.
Brazil M869 B27q
Barreto de Menzes, Tobias, 1839-1889.
... Questões vigentes. [Rio de Janeiro. Empreza graphica Editora, Paulo Pongetti & C., 1926]
XX, 321, [1]p. port. 24cm.
Obras completas, v.IX.

Philosophy.
Brazil M869 B27v
Barreto de Menzes, Tobias, 1839-1889.
... Varios escriptos. [Rio de Janeiro, Empreza graphica Editora, Paulo Pongetti & C., 1926]
LVIII, 346, 11p. port. 24cm. (Ediçăo do estado de Sergipe)
Obras completas v. X.

Philosophy.
M100 J711
Jones, Gilbert Haven, 1881-
Lotye und Bowne. Eine Vergleichung ihrer philosophischen arbeit. Inaugural - Dissertation der Philosophischen fakultät der universität Jena zur erlangung der doktorwürde. Weida i.Th. Druck von Thomas & Hubert, 1909.
117p. 23½cm.

Philosophy.
[illegible] Locke, Alain
[illegible] Values and imperatives.

(In: Kallen, Horace M. ed. American philosophy today and tomorrow. New York, Lee Furman, 1935. cm. p. 313-333)

M191 Philosophy.
M846 Morton, Lena Beatrice.
Man under stress. New York, Philosophical Library ⌊1960⌋
129 p. 22 cm.
Includes bibliography.

1. Philosophy. 2. Religion. I. Title.

B56.M65 101 60-13638 ‡

Library of Congress ⌊5⌋

Philosophy.
M153 Simmons, James W
Si4t Thoughts from the mind. New York, Exposition Press, 1962.

94p. 23cm.
Portrait of author on book jacket.
"An Exposition-Banner book."

Philosophy.
M150 Teague, Wilbur A
T22 Decline in American democracy. New York, Vantage Press ⌊1963⌋

98p. 20½cm.
Portrait of author on book jacket.

Philosophy.
M153 Williams, Herbert L 1917-
W672 Adventure into thought. New York, Exposition Press ⌊1964⌋

69p. 21cm.

1. Philosophy. I. Title.

Ghana Philosophy, African.
M335 Nkrumah, Kwame, Pres. Ghana, 1909-
N65 Consciencism; philosophy and ideology for decolonization and development with particular reference to the African revolution. New York, Monthly Review Press ⌊1965,©1964⌋

vi, 122p. 23cm.

Philosophy, American.
M153 Hopps, Abe Albert
H77 Facts, fantasy and comparison. New York, Vantage Press ⌊1965⌋

99p. 20½cm.
Portrait of author on book jacket.

1. Philosophy, American. I. Title.

Philosophy, Ancient - Hist.
M180 James, George G M
J23 Stolen legacy: the Greeks were not the authors of Greek philosophy, but the people of North Africa, commonly called the Egyptians. New York, Philosophical Library ⌊1954⌋
190 p. 22 cm.

1. Philosophy, Ancient—Hist. I. Title.

B171.J3 180 54-4101 ‡

Library of Congress ⌊7⌋

The philosophy of Booker T. Washington.
M814.4 Boone, Theodore Sylvester, 1896-
W27bo The philosophy of Booker T. Washington, the apostle of progress, the pioneer of the new deal, by Theodore S. Boone ... with introduction by L. K. Williams. ⌊Fort Worth, Tex., Manney printing co., ©1939⌋
xix, 311 p. pl., port. 20cm.
Bibliography: p. vii-xi.

1. Washington, Booker Taliaferro, 1859?-1915. I. Title.

39-17748

Library of Congress E185.97.W14
——— Copy 2.
Copyright A 130418 ⌊3⌋ 923.773

The philosophy of Negro suffrage.

Riley, Jerome R.
M324 The philosophy of negro suffrage. By Jerome R.
R45p Riley, M. D. Hartford, Conn., American publishing company, 1895.
110 p. front. (port.) 20½cm.

1. Negroes—Politics and suffrage. 2. Negroes. I. Title.

12—3518

Library of Congress E185.61.R57
——— Copy 2.
Copyright 1895: 52795 ⌊a36d1⌋

Phonograph records.
M808 Locke, Alain LeRoy, 1886-
R45p ... The Negro and his music, by Alain Locke ... Washington, D. C., The Associates in Negro folk education, 1936.
3 p. l., 142 p. 20½ cm. (Bronze booklet no. 2)
"Reading references" at end of each chapter; "Recorded illustrations" at end of most of the chapters.

1. Negro musicians. 2. Negro songs—Hist. & crit. 3. Music—U. S.—Hist. & crit. 4. Jazz music. 5. Phonograph records. I. Title.

37—10637

Library of Congress E185.5.B85 no. 2
——— Copy 2. ML3556.L8N4
⌊42t2⌋ (325.260973) 784.756

The phony.
M813.5 Fenderson, Harold, 1910-
F35 The phony. New York, Exposition Press, 1959.

139p. 21cm.

Photography - Portraits.
M301 Baldwin, James, 1924-
B19 Nothing personal. Photos. by Richard Avedon and text by James Baldwin. ⌊New York, Atheneum, 1964⌋
1 v. (chiefly illus., ports.) 37 cm.

1. Photography—Portraits. I. Baldwin, James, 1924- II. Title.

TR680.A89 301.2 64-23639

Library of Congress ⌊4-3⌋

Phrenology.

M575 ⌊Sampson, John Patterson, 1839-
Sa4 Mixed races: their environment, temperament, heredity and phrenology. Hampton, Va., Normal school steam press, 1881.

ix, ⌊12⌋ - 159p. front. 22½cm.

M306 The Phylon institute.
P56f The first Phylon institute and twenty-first Atlanta university conference. Preliminary call held in Atlanta, April 17-19, 1941... Reprinted from Phylon, third quarter, 1941.

275-288p. 25½cm.

1. Economic conditions. 2. Atlanta university conference. I. Du Bois, William Edward Burghardt, b 1868-

---

Physical Anthropology

See

Somatology.

Physical anthopology and the Negro in the present crisis.

M610 Cobb, William Montague, 1904-
C63p3 Physical anthopology and the Negro in the present crisis. Reprinted from the Journal of the National Medical Association, 34:181-187, September 1942.

181-187p. 28cm.

Physical anthropology of the American Negro.

M610 Cobb, William Montague, 1904-
C63p 5 Physical anthropology of the American Negro. Reprinted from the American journal of physical anthropology, 29:114-223, June 1942.

114-223p. tables. 26cm.
Literature cited: pp. 189-192.

M610 Physicians.
C63d 6 Cobb, William Montague, 1904-
Discussion of paper, Medical manpower, by Thomas Parran. Reprinted from Journal of Association of American Medical Colleges, v.27, 1948.

27-28p. 27cm.
Mimeographed.

Physicians.
Kenney, John A 1874-
The Negro in medicine, by John A. Kenney ... ⌊Tuskegee
MB Institute, Ala., Printed by the Tuskegee institute press, ©1912⌋
K39n 60 p. front., plates (part fold.) ports. 24½cm.

1. Negro physicians. 2. Negroes—Education. I. Title.

12—25563

Library of Congress E185.82.K36
Copyright A 327638 ⌊a37b1⌋

Physicians.
M304 Lewis, Julian Herman
P19 Number and geographic location of Negro
v.3, no.14 physicians in the United States. Reprinted from the Journal of the American Medical association, v. 104, April 6, 1935, p. 1272-1273.

M39 P42f

Perry, John Edward, 1870–
Forty cords of wood; memoirs of a medical doctor ... Jefferson City, Mo., Lincoln university [1947]
xvi, 459 p. illus., ports. 23½cm.

1. [Negro physicians] I. Title.
R154.P43A3 926.1 Med 47–944
© 6Mar47; publisher; A11697.

U. S. Army medical library for Library of Congress [W104SP462f 1947] [4]†

Physicians.
M39 So5m 1951
Somerville, John Alexander, 1882–
Man of color, an autobiography. With a foreword by P. M. Sherlock. Kingston, Jamaica, Pioneer Press, 1951.

134p. 19cm.
Pocket book edition.

Physicians.
St. Lucia M610 Sp3m
Spencer, Gerald Arthur, 1902–
Medical symphony, a study of the contributions of the Negro to medical progress in New York. [New York, °1947]
120 p. ports. 21 cm.
"References": p. 9.

1. Medicine—New York (City) 2. Negro physicians. I. Title.
R292.N7S63 610.97471 48–8224*
Library of Congress [3]

Physicians.
M973 W86np
Woodson, Carter Godwin, 1875–
The Negro professional man and the community, with special emphasis on the physician and the lawyer, by Carter Godwin Woodson. Washington, D. C., The Association for the study of Negro life and history, inc. [°1934]
1 p. l., v–xviii, 365 p. diagr. 23½cm.
"[This study forms] a part of the effort of the Association for the study of Negro life and history to portray the social and economic conditions obtaining among Negroes in the United States since the civil war."—Foreword.
1. Negroes—Employment. 2. Negroes—Moral and social conditions. 3. Negro physicians. 4. Negro lawyers. I. Association for the study of Negro life and history, inc. II. Title.
34—10066
Library of Congress E185.82.W88 [34f5] 325.260973

Physicians - Women.
M610 P19 v.1 no.1
Steward, S Maria, 1845–
Women in medicine; a paper read before the National association of colored women's clubs at Wilberforce, Ohio, August 6, 1914, by S. Maria Steward... Wilberforce, Ohio The author 1914

24p. ports. 19½cm.

Physicians

See also

Medicine

Physics.
M304 P19 v.4, no.8
Alexis, Lucien V.
The syllabus to fundamentals, in physics and in chemistry. An overthrow of modern scientific thought concerning the basic principles of physics and of chemistry. New Orleans, the McDough 35 Press, 1928.
40p. 21cm.

Physics.
M530 A12f
Alexis, Lucien Victor.
Fundamentals in physics and in chemistry ... by Lucien V. Alexis ... New Orleans, La., L. V. Alexis, 1929–
v. illus., diagrs. 24cm.

1. Physics. 2. Chemistry, Physical and theoretical. 29–18054
Library of Congress QC21.A37
——— Copy 2.
Copyright A 12041 [3]

Nigeria M530 Oy3
Physics.
Oyewole, 'Dotun.
An introduction to physics. London, Macmillan and Co., 1964.

460p. illus. 21½cm.

The Picaroons.

Jamaica M972.92 H55p
Hill, Richard, 1795–1872.
The Picaroons; or, one hundred and fifty years ago: being a history of commerce and navigation in the West Indian seas. By the Honorable Richard Hill...communicated to the Port Royal reading society. Dublin, John Falconer, 1869.

80p.

M811.08 P58
Piccioni, Leone, ed.
Antologia dei poeti Negri d'America [di] Leone Piccioni [e] Perla Cacciaguerra. Introducione e appendice critica di Leone Piccioni. [n.p.] Arnoldo Mondadori Editore [1964]

675p. 22cm.
White editors
English and Italian on opposite pages.

1. Poetry - Collections. I. Title.

M810.9 P581
Piccioni, Leone.
Letteratura dei negri d'America. Milano, Gruppo editoriale "Academia" [1949]
344 p. 22 cm.
Includes bibliographical references.

1. American literature—Negro authors—Hist. & crit. 2. ~~Negro literature (American)—Hist. & crit.~~ 3. ~~Negro poetry (American)~~—Translations into Italian. 4. Italian poetry—Translations from English. I. Title.
PS591.N4P5 50–24617
Library of Congress [1]

Piccola America Negra, romanzo.
M813.5 H87p
Hughes, Langston, 1902–
Piccola America Negra, romanzo. Milano, Italy, Longanesi, 1948.

372 p. 18 cm. (La Gaja scienza, v. 27)
Translation of Not without laughter.

M326.99B P58k 1941
Pickard, Kate E R
The kidnapped and the ransomed, by Kate E. R. Pickard ... New York, Negro publication society of America, inc., 1941.
315, [1] p. 22cm. ([Negro publication society of America. Publications] Series I, History. No. 1)
"The first edition ... appeared in 1856."—Editor's note.
"Appendix. Seth Conklin [by W. H. Furness]": p. 298–315.

1. Still, Peter. 2. Still, Lavinia. 3. Slavery in the U. S.—Kentucky. 4. Slavery in the U. S.—Alabama. 5. Concklin, Seth, 1802–1851. I. Furness, William Henry, 1802–1896. II. Negro publication society of America. III. Title.
43—17835
Library of Congress E444.S855 [45e1] 326.92

M326.99B P58k
Pickard, Kate E R.
The kidnapped and the ransomed. Being the personal recollections of Peter Still and his wife "Vina," after forty years of slavery. By Mrs. Kate E. R. Pickard. With an introduction, by Rev. Samuel J. May; and an appendix, by William H. Furness, D. D. Syracuse, W. T. Hamilton; New York [etc.] Miller, Orton and Mulligan, 1856.
xxiii (i. e. xxi), 25–409 p. 3 pl. (incl. front.) 19 cm.
Pages ix–x omitted in paging.
Added t.-p., engraved.
"Appendix. Seth Concklin [by William H. Furness]": p. 377–409.
1. Still, Peter. 2. Still, Lavinia. 3. Slavery in the U. S.—Kentucky. 4. Slavery in the U. S.—Alabama. 5. Concklin, Seth, 1802–1851. I. Furness, William Henry, 1802–1896. II. Title.
5. Slave narratives. 14—15958
Library of Congress E444.S85 [48g1]

M304 P19 v.5, no.3
Pickens, William, 1881–1954.
Abraham Lincoln, man and statesman (abridged) by William Pickens. [New York] °1930.
cover-title, 15 p. 23cm.

1. Lincoln, Abraham, pres. U. S.—Addresses, sermons, etc.
30-6041
Library of Congress E457.8.P596
——— Copy 2.
Copyright AA 35230 [3]

M323 P58af
Pickens, William, 1881–1954.
Aftermath of a lynching. New York, National Association for the Advancement of Colored People. 1931.

2p. 29cm.
Reprinted from the Nation April 15, 1931.

1. Lynching--Indiana.

M323 P58aml
Pickens, William, 1881–1954.
American Æsop; Negro and other humor, by William Pickens ... Boston, The Jordan & More press, 1926.
xx, 183 p. front. 20 cm.
Inscribed copy: Scribbled for my friend, A. B. Spingarn, by Wm. Pickens- Sept. 13, (for good luck) 1926.

1. Wit and humor. 2. ~~Negro wit and humor.~~ I. Title.
26—12677
Library of Congress PN6161.P58 [48d½]

M323 P58b
Pickens, William, 1881– 1954.
Bursting bonds; enlarged edition, The heir of slaves, by William Pickens ... Boston, The Jordan & More press, 1923.
x, 222 p. 19½cm.

I. Title. 23—12345
Library of Congress E185.97.P592
——— Copy 2.
Copyright A 711698 [38e1]

M304 P19 v.5, no.4
Pickens, William, 1881– 1954.
Frederick Douglass and the spirit of freedom (abridged) by William Pickens. [New York] °1931.
cover-title, 15 p. 23cm.

1. Douglass, Frederick, 1817–1895.
30–33744
Library of Congress E449.D772
——— Copy 2.
Copyright AA 56967 923.673

M323 P58h
Pickens, William, 1881–1954.
The heir of slaves; an autobiography, by William Pickens ... Boston, New York [etc.] The Pilgrim press [1911]
viii, 138 p. 20cm. $0.75

I. Title.
12–885
Library of Congress E185.97.P59
Copyright A 303545

M306
P61p

Pickens, William, 1881- 1954
The Negro and the community.

(In: National Conference of Social Work. Proceedings, 1924. p. 381-86).

M323
P58n

Pickens, William, 1881-1954.
The new negro, his political, civil and mental status, and related essays, by William Pickens ... New York city, The Neale publishing company, 1916.

239 p. 19cm. $1.50

1. ~~Negroes.~~ I. Title.

Library of Congress E185.6.P59 17—2640
——— Copy 2.
Copyright A 455221 [s19d3]

M723
P58v

Pickens, William, 1881- 1954.
The vengeance of the gods, and three other stories of real American color line life, by William Pickens ... introduction by Bishop John Hurst ... Philadelphia, Pa., The A. M. E. book concern [°1922]

125 p. 20cm.

CONTENTS.—The vengeance of the gods.—The superior race.—Passing the buck.—Tit for tat.

I. Title.

Library of Congress PZ3.P5853Ve 22-15210
——— Copy 2.
Copyright A 674947 [3]

Pickens, William, 1881-1954.
Christianity as a basis of common citizenship.

M323
T69

Negro Christian student conference. *Atlanta*, 1914.
The new voice in race adjustments; addresses and reports presented at the Negro Christian student conference, Atlanta, Georgia, May 14-18, 1914. A. M. Trawick, editor ... Pub. by order of the executive committee of the conference. New York city, Student volunteer movement [1914]

1 p. l., [v]-vi p., 1 l., 230 p. 23½cm.

"Best books on the Negro in America and Africa": p. 221-224.

1. Negroes—Congresses. 2. U. S.—Race question. I. Trawick, Arcadius McSwain, 1869- ed. II. Title.

Springfield. Public library for Library of Congress E185.5.N38 A 15-837
[a35f1]

Picket and the pen.

Bahamas
MB9
G68h

Hanna, Hilton E
Picket and the pen; the Pat Gorman story, by Hilton E. Hanna and Joseph Belsky. Yonkers, N. Y., American Institute of Social Science [1960]

416 p. illus. 24 cm.
Includes bibliography.

1. Gorman, Patrick Emmet, 18 2. Amalgamated Meat Cutters and Butcher Workmen of North America. I. Belsky, Joseph, 1902- joint author. II. Title.

HD6509.G6H3 923.3173 60-3982 ‡
Library of Congress [2]

Picketing hell.

M286
P87pi

Powell, Adam Clayton, 1865-
Picketing hell, a fictitious narrative, by A. Clayton Powell... New York, Wendell Malliet and Company, 1942.

254p. front. 22cm.

The Pickling and Curing of Meat in Hot Weather.

M630.7
C25pi

Carver, George Washington, 1864-1943.
The pickling and curing of meat in hot weather. Second edition. Tuskegee Institute, Alabama, Tuskegee Institute press, 1925.

23p. 23cm. (Bulletin no. 23 June 1925)

Puerto Rico
M972.95
P58

Picó, Rafael.
The geographic regions of Puerto Rico. Río Piedras, University of Puerto Rico Press, 1950.

xiii, 256 p. illus., maps. 24 cm.
Based on thesis—Clark University.
Bibliography: p. 233-256.

1. Puerto Rico. I. Title. *Full name:* Rafael Picó Santiago.

F1958.P5 330.97295 51—26021
Library of Congress [52e5]

Pictorial history of the American Negro.

M973
F95

Fuller, Thomas Oscar, 1867–
Pictorial history of the American Negro, by Thomas O. Fuller; a story of progress and development along social, political, economic, educational and spiritual lines. Memphis, Tenn., Pictorial history, inc., 1933.

xxiii, 375 p. col. front., illus. (incl. ports., maps) 28½cm.
Bibliography: p. 361-363.

1. Negroes 2. Negroes — Education. 3. Negroes — Moral and social conditions. 4. Negroes—Biog. I. Title.

33—17185
Library of Congress E185.F97
[43o1] 325.260973

A pictorial history of the Negro in America.

M813.5
H87pi2

Hughes, Langston, 1902–
A pictorial history of the Negro in America, by Langston Hughes & Milton Meltzer. New rev. ed. New York, Crown Publishers [1963]

337, [10] p. illus., ports., maps, facsims. 29 cm.
Bibliography: p. [341]

1. Negroes—Hist.—Pictorial works. I. Meltzer, Milton, 1915- joint author. II. Title.

E185.H83 1963 325.2670973 63-12074
Library of Congress [5]

A pictorial history of the Negro in America.

M813.5
H87pi

Hughes, Langston, 1902–
A pictorial history of the Negro in America, by Langston Hughes & Milton Meltzer. New York, Crown [1956]

316 p. illus., ports., maps, facsims. 29 cm.
Bibliography: p. 318.

1. Negroes—Hist.—Pictorial works. I. Meltzer, Milton, 1915- joint author. II. Title. *Full name:* James Langston Hughes.

E185.H83 325.260973 56—7192
Library of Congress [57f20]

The picture-poetry book.

M811.5
M12

McBrown, Gertrude Parthenia.
The picture-poetry book, by Gertrude Parthenia McBrown; illustrated by Lois Mailou Jones. Washington, D. C., The Associated publishers, inc., 1935.

x, 73 p. incl. front., illus. 22cm.
Verse for children.

I. Title.

36—4191
Library of Congress PZ8.3.M124Pi
[43d1] 811.5

Piel negra.

Uruguay
M861.6
B27p

Barrios, Pilar E
Piel negra, poesias (1917-1947.) Prólogo de Alberto Britos. Caratula de Vicente Martin. Montevideo, Editó Nuestra Raza, 1947.

113 [2]p. port. 20½cm.

M975.8
P61a

Pierce, Joseph Alphonso, 1902-
The Atlanta Negro; A collection of data on the Negro population of Atlanta, Georgia, by Joseph A. Pierce and Marion M. Hamilton, Atlanta, American Council on Education, American Youth Commission in cooperation with the National Youth Administration of Georgia, 1940.

136p. maps, graphs. tables. 28cm.

1. Atlanta, Ga. I. Hamilton, Marion A. ~~II. Title.~~

M331
P61n

Pierce, Joseph Alphonso, 1902–
Negro business and business education, their present and prospective development. [1st ed.] New York, Harper [1947]

xiv, 338 p. tables. 24 cm. (Atlanta University. Publications, no. 24)
"References" at end of most of the chapters.

1. ~~Negroes as~~ businessmen. 2. ~~U. S.~~—Indus. 3. Business education—~~U. S.~~ I. Title. (Series)

E185.5.A88 no. 24 325.260973 47-11352 rev*
——— Copy 2. E185.8.P5
Library of Congress [r48x7]

M301
Eb74

Pierce, Ponchitta
Crime in the suburbs
Pp. 117-123

In: Ebony. The white problem in America. Chicago, Johnson Pub. Co., 1966.

M393
P61e

Pierce, Samuel Henry, 1913-
Excerpts from a morticians's workshop. Atlanta, Georgia, Board of Directors of the Georgia Funeral Directors and Embalmers Assoc., 1958.

144p. illus. 21½cm.
Picture and biographical sketch of the author on the book jacket.

1. Undertakers and undertaking. I. Title.

M393
P61

Pierce, Samuel Henry, 1913–
Morgue guide; a manual of embalming. [Atlanta?] °1954.

94 p. illus. 23 cm.

1. Embalming. I. Title.

RA623.P5 55-15209 ‡
Library of Congress [3]

Pierre, Joseph, also known as Pierre Sully, d. 1915.

Haiti
MB9
P61b

Brierre, Jean Fernand, 1909–
Le petit soldat, causerie prononcée à l'Association des étudiants en droit. Port-au-Prince, Impr. haïtienne, 1934.

cover-title, 20 p. 21 cm.

1. Pierre, Joseph, also known as Pierre Sully, d. 1915. I. Title.

F1926.P6B7 923.57294 45-31263 rev*
Library of Congress [r47c1]

Haiti
M610
P61p

Pierre-Louis, Constant.
Pathologie chirurgicale a l'usage de l'etudiant Haitien. Port-au-Prince. Imp. Telhomme, 1948.

386p. illus. 22cm. (Bibliothèque Haitienne)

1. Haiti--Medicine (Surgery). 2. Surgery.

Haiti
M972.94
P66m

Pierre-Louis, Joseph F
Le masque humain; roman politico, social & historique. Port-au-Prince, Imprimerie Oedipe, 1956.

39p. 23cm.

1. Haiti - Fiction.

Haiti
M972.94 **Pierre Louis, Joseph F**
P66p Pied de femmes; un roman d'amour et de caractere. Port-au-Prince, Imp. Edwidg Cqen, 1959.
34p. 22cm.
1. Haiti - Fiction.

Haiti
M972.94 Pierre - Louis, Joseph F
P66s La situation haitienne. Vouloir c'est pouvoir surtout quand un a de la bonne volonté. Port-au-Prince, Haiti, Imprimerie du Commerce, ⌊n.d.⌋
27p. 21cm.
1. Haiti

Haiti
M972.94 Pierre-Louis, Joseph F
P66s La situation haitienne; revue corrigee et augmentee. Port-au-Prince, Active presse, 1950.
1950
44p. 20cm.
1. Haiti.

Haiti
M630 Pierre-Louis, Regnier.
P66p Notes sur la canne à sucre. Port-au-Prince, Barthélemy. ⌊1948?⌋
20p. 20cm.
Haitian author.
1. Sugar cane. 2. Haiti--Agriculture.

Haiti
M398 Pierre-Louis, Ulysse
P612 Sortilèges, Afro-Haitiens (contes et légendes). Préface du Dr. Jean Price-Mars. Port-au-Prince, Imprimerie de l'État, 1961.
120p. 18½cm.
1. Tales, Haitian. 2. Folklore - Haiti. I. Mars, Jean Price, 1876- Preface. II. Title.

Pierre Sully.
Haiti
M841 Dauphin, Marcel, 1910-
D26p Pierre Sully. Port-au-Prince, Imprimerie de l'Etat, 1960.
85p. ports. 21cm.

Pierre Teilhard de Chardin et la politique Africaine.
Sénégal
M966.3 Senghor, Léopold Sédar, 1906-
Se5p Pierre Teilhard de Chardin et la politique Africaine, Pierre Teilhard de Chardin sauvons l'humanite. L'art dans la ligne de l'énergie humaine. Paris, Editions du Seuil, 1962.
102p. illus. 19cm.

Pietro chevalier d'amour (The Saracen Blade)
M813.5 Yerby, Frank, 1916-
Y46pi Pietro chevalier d'amour (The Saracen Blade); roman. Traduit de l'anglais par Michèle Laurent. Paris, Éditions Denoel ⌊1954⌋
411p. 21½cm.

Pigments.
French Guiana
M841 Damas, Leon G. , 1912-
D18p Pigments avec une préface de Robert Desnos et un bois gravé de Frans masereel. Paris, G.L.M., 1937.
42 unnumbered p. front. 19½cm.
Exemplaire numéro 262.

M784 **Pike, Gustavus D**
P63 The Jubilee singers, and their campaign for twenty thousand dollars. By G. D. Pike ... Boston, Lee and Shepard; New York, Lee, Shepard and Dillingham, 1873.
219 p., 1 l. incl. front. ports. 20½ cm.
Includes a brief account of Fisk university, Nashville.
"Jubilee songs": p. ⌊161⌋-219.
1. Jubilee singers. 2. Negro musicians. 3. Fisk university, Nashville. 4. Negro songs. I. Title.
6—8203
Library of Congress ML400.P63
⌊45o1⌋

Guiana, British
M822.91 Pilgrim, Frank
P64m Miriamy; a West Indian play in three acts. ⌊Georgetown, British Guiana, B. G. Lithographic Co., 1963⌋
67p. 20½cm.
I. Title.

The pilgrimage of Harriet Ransom's son.
M89 **Ransom, Reverdy Cassius, Bp., 1861-**
R17p The pilgrimage of Harriet Ransom's son. Nashville, Sunday School Union ⌊1949⌋
336 p. port. 23 cm.
Autobiography.
I. Title.
BX8473.R25A3 922.773 51-27687
Library of Congress ⌊1⌋

A pilgrimage to my motherland.
Jamaica
M966.9 Campbell, Robert
C15p A pilgrimage to my motherland. An account of a journey among the Egbas and Yorubas of Central Africa, in 1859-60. By Robert Campbell ... of the Niger Valley exploring party ... New-York, T. Hamilton; Philadelphia, The author, 1861.
145p. front. (port) double map. 19cm.
1. Lagos - Description and travel. 2. Yoruba - Description and travel. I. Title.

A pilgrimage to my motherland.
Jamaica
M966.9 Campbell, Robert
C15p2 A pilgrimage to my motherland; or, Reminiscences of a sojourn among the Egbas and Yorubas of Central Africa, in 1859-60. By Robert Campbell. With an introduction by Sir Culling E. Eardley. London, William John Johnson, 1861.
116p. front. 19cm. illus.

S. Africa The Pilgrim's Progress.
M896 Soga, Tiyo Burnside, 1829-1871, tr.
So2u Uhambo lo Mhambi ⌊Translation of The Pilgrim's Progress. Part 1 translated by Tiyo Soga. Part II translated by J. Henderson Soga⌋ Lovedale, Lovedale Institution Press, ⌊n.d.⌋
187, 1-190 p. 18½ cm.

The piling of clouds.
British Guiana
M823.91 **Mittelhölzer, Edgar.**
M69p The piling of clouds. London, Putnam ⌊1961⌋
262 p. 21 cm.
I. Title.
Full name: Edgar Austin Mittelhölzer.
PZ3.M6977Pi 62-4037 ‡
Library of Congress ⌊3⌋

Pilot guides-Madagascar.
Mauritius
M969.82 **Lislet-Geoffroy, Jean Baptiste, 1755-1836.**
G29m Memoir and notice explanatory of a chart of Madagascar and the North-Eastern archipelago of Mauritius; drawn up according to the latest observations, under the auspices and government of His Excellency Robert Townsend Farquhar ... By Lislet Geoffroy ... Now first pub. in the original French, with an English translation, together with some observations on the coast of Africa, and a brief notice on the winds on the coast of Madagascar ⌊by M. Barbarin⌋ London, J. Murray, 1819.
v, 57 p. front. (fold. chart.) 28cm.
1. Pilot guides—Madagascar. 2. Pilot guides—Mauritius. I. Farquhar, Sir Robert Townsend, 1776-1830, ed. II. Barbarin, ———.
13—23158
Library of Congress VK891.G34
⌊39b1⌋

Pilot guides-Mauritius.
Mauritius
M969.82 **Lislet-Geoffroy, Jean Baptiste, 1755-1836.**
G29m Memoir and notice explanatory of a chart of Madagascar and the North-Eastern archipelago of Mauritius; drawn up according to the latest observations, under the auspices and government of His Excellency Robert Townsend Farquhar ... By Lislet Geoffroy ... Now first pub. in the original French, with an English translation, together with some observations on the coast of Africa, and a brief notice on the winds on the coast of Madagascar ⌊by M. Barbarin⌋ London, J. Murray, 1819.
v, 57 p. front. (fold. chart.) 28cm.
1. Pilot guides—Madagascar. 2. Pilot guides—Mauritius. I. Farquhar, Sir Robert Townsend, 1776-1830, ed. II. Barbarin, ———.
13—23158
Library of Congress VK891.G34
⌊39b1⌋

Martinique
M972.98 Pilotin, René A Th
P64f Face a l'univers (il faut réformer le conformisme). Paris, Jean D'Halluin, Editeur, 1959.
190p. 19cm. (Collection Alternance)
1. Martinique. I. Title.

M329.6 Pinchback, Pinckney Benton Stewart, 1837-1921.
R29p Address.
(In: Republican Party. National Convention. 8th. Chicago, 1884. Proceedings... p. 119).

M815.4 Pinchbeck, Pickney Benton Stewart, 1837-1921.
P65r ⌊Remarks concerning claim to seat in the U.S. Senate, New Orleans, September, 1875.
4p. 21½cm.
1. Politics.

M815.4
P65s
Pinchback, Pinckney Benton Stewart, 1837-1921.
Remarks of Hon. P.B.S. Pinchback of Louisiana in the House of representatives, Monday June 8th, 1874 on his right to a seat as representative at large from the state of Louisiana, as against the claim of Hon. George E. Sheridan.
15p. 21½cm.

M815.4
P65s
Pinchback, Pinckney Benton Stewart, 1837-1921.
Remarks of Hon. P.B.S. Pinchback of Louisiana in the House of representatives, Monday June 8th, 1874 on his right to a seat as representative at large from the state of Louisiana, as against the claim of Hon. George E. Sheridan.
15p. 21½cm.
Bound with: Speech... on the election bill.
1. Orations.

M815.4
P65s
Pinchback, Pinckney Benton Stewart, 1837-1921.
Speech of Hon. P.B.S. Pinchback on the election bill delivered in the Louisiana state senate, Friday, January 21st, 1870. New Orleans, New Orleans standard print, 1870.
8p. 22cm.
1. Orations. 2. Elections.

M815.4
P65r
Pinchback, Pickney Benton Stewart, 1837-1921.
A statement of the law and facts involved in the case of P.B.S. Pinchback claiming a seat in the U.S. Senate as senator elect from the state of Louisiana ₍1873₎
13p. 24cm.
Bound with - Remarks concerning claim to seat in U.S. Senate.
1. Politics

M973.6
N21t
1879
Pinchback, Pickney Benton Stewart, 1837-1921.
National Conference of Colored Men. Nashville.
Proceedings of the National Conference of Colored Men of the United States, held in the State Capitol at Nashville, Tennessee, May 6, 7, 8, and 9, 1879. Washington, D.C., Rufus H. Darby, 1879.
107p. 19cm.

The pine tree mission.
M266
J63
Johnson, James H A, 1835-
The pine tree mission. By James H.A. Johnson... Baltimore, J. Lanahan, 1893.
114p. port. plates. 18cm.

Piney Woods and its story.
M370
J71p
Jones, Laurence Clifton, 1884-
Piney Woods and its story, by Laurence C. Jones ... with an introduction by S. S. McClure. New York, Chicago ₍etc.₎ Fleming H. Revell company ₍°1922₎
151 p. front., plates, ports. 19½ᶜᵐ.
1. Piney Woods country life school, Braxton, Miss. I. Title.
23—6641
Library of Congress LC2852.B72J6
₍44k1₎

Piney Woods country life school, Braxton, Miss.
M323
J71b
Jones, Laurence Clifton, 1884-
The bottom rail; addresses and papers on the Negro in the lowlands of Mississippi and on inter-racial relations in the South during twenty-five years, by Laurence C. Jones ... with an introduction by Francis S. Harmon ... New York ₍etc.₎ Fleming H. Revell company ₍°1935₎
96 p. front. (port.) 19½ᶜᵐ. Inscribed: To A. B. Spingarn fam.—To Miss Mary White Ovington, in appreciation of her efforts to strengthen the Bottom Rail, Laurence C. Jones, Piney Woods, Miss. 1935.
1. Negroes—Mississippi. 2. U. S.—Race question. 3. Piney Woods country life school, Braxton, Miss. I. Title.
35—4380
Library of Congress E185.93.M6J6
₍45f1₎ 325.2609762

Piney Woods country life school, Braxton, Miss.
M370
J71s
Jones, Laurence Clifton, 1884-
The spirit of Piney Woods, by Laurence C. Jones ... introduction by George Foster Peabody. New York, Chicago ₍etc.₎ Fleming H. Revell company ₍°1931₎
2 p. l., 3-98 p. front., plates, ports. 19½ᶜᵐ.
"Addresses delivered on Sunday evenings to the students of Piney Woods country life school."—Foreword.
1. Piney Woods country life school, Braxton, Miss. I. Title.
31—34338
Library of Congress LC2852.B72J63
——— Copy 2.
Copyright A 41914 ₍30d1₎ 371.97409762

Piney Woods country life school, Braxton, Miss.
M370.
J71p
Jones, Laurence Clifton, 1884-
Piney Woods and its story, by Laurence C. Jones ... with an introduction by S. S. McClure. New York, Chicago ₍etc.₎ Fleming H. Revell company ₍°1922₎
151 p. front., plates, ports. 19½ᶜᵐ.
1. Piney Woods country life school, Braxton, Miss. I. Title.
23—6641
Library of Congress LC2852.B72J6
₍44k1₎

Brazil
M869.4
P65f
Pinheiro, Xavier.
... Francisco Octaviano, Carioca illustre nos letros, no jornalismo, napolitica, na tribuna e na diplomacia. Rio de Janeiro, Edição da Revista de Lingua Portugues a. ₍n.d.₎
477 p. 25 cm.
White author.
I. Octaviano de Almeida Rosa, Francisco, 1825-1889. 1. Brazilian literature.

Brazil
M869.2
N17d
Pinho, José de Morais
Filhos de santo.
Pp. 233-286.
In: Nascimento, Abdias do, ed. Dramas para Negroes e prologo para brancos. Rio de Janeiro, Teatro Experimental do Negro, 1961.
I. Title.

Pinktoes.
M813.5
H57pi2
Himes, Chester B 1909-
Pinktoes, a novel ₍by₎ Chester Himes. New York, Putnam ₍1965₎
256 p. 21 cm.
I. Title.
PZ3.H57Pi 4 65-13972
Library of Congress ₍5₎

Pinktoes.
M813.5
H57pi
Himes, Chester B 1909-
Pinktoes. Paris, Olympia Press ₍1961₎
207 p. 18 cm. (The Traveller's companion series, no. 87)
I. Title.
PZ3.H57Pi 62-3948 ‡
Library of Congress ₍1₎

Pioneer Press series.
W. Indies
M823
C23
Caribbean anthology of short stories, by Ernest A. Carr ₍and others₎ Kingston, Jamaica, Pioneer Press ₍1953₎
146 p. 19 cm. (Pioneer Press series)
Contents: Ernest A. Carr. Lucille Iremonger. Ethel Rovere. Edgar Mittelholzer. C.W. Ogle. R.L.C. Aarons. Samuel Selvon. Vera Bell. John Wickham. W.G. Ogilvie. Clinton V. Black. Neil Cameron. William S. Arthur. Hugh Panton Morrison.
1. Short stories. I. Carr, Ernest A.
PZ1.C18 54-26084 ‡
Library of Congress ₍1₎

Pioneers and patriots.
MB
T629
Toppin, Edgar Allan, 1928-
~~Dobler, Lavinia G~~
Pioneers and patriots: the lives of six Negroes of the Revolutionary era ₍by₎ Lavinia Dobler and Edgar A. Toppin. Illustrated by Colleen Browning. ₍1st ed.₎ Garden City, N. Y., Doubleday, 1965.
118 p. illus., facsims., ports. 22 cm. (Zenith books)
1. Negroes—Biog.—Juvenile literature. I. Toppin, Edgar Allan, 1928- joint author. II. Title.
E185.96.D6 j 920 65-17241
Library of Congress ₍5₎

M979.4
T42
Pioneers of Negro origin in California.
Thurman, Sue Bailey.
Pioneers of Negro origin in California. San Francisco, Acme Publishing Company, 1949.
70 p. 21 cm.

Martinique
M843.9
M32pi
...Les pionniers de l'empire...
Maran, René, 1887-
... Les pionniers de l'empire ... Paris, A. Michel ₍1943₎-
v. port., maps (part double) 20ᶜᵐ.
"Bibliographie": v. 1, p. ₍335₎-339.
Contents.—1. Jean de Béthencourt. Anselme d'Isalguier. Binot le Paulmier de Gonneville. Jacques Cartier. Jean Parmentier. Nicolas Durand de Villegaignon. Jean Ribaut. —v.2 Samuel Champlain Belain d'Esnambuc. Robert Cavelier de la Salle.
1. Explorers, French. 2. France—Colonies—Biog. I. Title.
46—13128
Library of Congress G255.M3
₍47c1₎ 923.944

M323.4
P661
Pipes, William Harrison, 1912-
Death of an "Uncle Tom," by William Pipes. New York, Carlton Press ₍1967₎
118 p. 21 cm. (A Hearthstone book)
Bibliographical footnotes.
Portrait of author on book jacket.
1. Negroes—Civil rights—Addresses, essays, lectures. I. Title.
E185.61.P6 322'.4'0973 67-4682
Library of Congress ₍3₎

M251
P66s
Pipes, William Harrison, 1912-
Say amen, brother! Old-time Negro preaching: a study in American frustration. New York, William-Frederick Press, 1951.
I, 210 p. 24 cm.
Bibliography: p. 201-205.
ViHaI
1. Negroes—Religion. 2. Preaching—~~Hist.~~ I. Title. II. Title: Old-time Negro preaching.
BR563.N4P53 251 51-11631
Library of Congress ₍5₎

M811.5
H87pi
Piquion, René.
... Langston Hughes, un chant nouveau; introduction par Arna Bontemps. Port-au-Prince, Haiti, Imprimerie de l'État ₍1940₎
159 p. ports. 22ᶜᵐ.
At head of title: René-Piquion.
"Bibliographie": p. 159.
1. °Hughes, Langston, 1902- Haitian author
42-48345 Provisional
Library of Congress PS3515.U274Z7
₍2₎ 811.5

Haiti
M972.94 Piquion, René
P662n Négritude. Port-au-Prince, Imprimerie de l'Etat, 1961.

501p. 21½cm.
" À M. Arthur Spingarn hommage de l'auteur. René Piquion."

1. Haiti. I. Title.

Piquion, René, joint author.

Haiti
M972.94 Blanchet, Jules.
B59e ... Essais sur la culture; préface har [!] Dumayric Charlier. [Port-au-Prince] V. Valcin, imprimeur [194-?]

1 p. l., iv, 74 p. 18½cm.
At head of title: Jules Blanchet et René Piquion.

1. Civilisation—Philosophy. 2. Culture. I. Piquion, René, joint author.

45-29695
Library of Congress CB19.B54
[2] 901

Pissarro, Camille, 1830-1903.

Virgin Is.
M89 Jarvis, Jose Antonio, 1901-
P57j Camille Pissarro (painter from the Virgin islands) by J. Antonio Jarvis. Charlotte Amalie, V. I., The Art league of St. Thomas [1947]

31 p. incl. port. 20 x 15½cm.
Bibliography: p. 31.

1. Pissarro, Camille, 1830-1903.

ND553.P55J3 927.5 47-24605
Library of Congress [2]

Uganda Pit ki gwoko lotino.
M649.1 Davies, H F
D28 Pit ki gwoko lotino [Infant welfare] Aye okobo Erica Lakor. [Revised by C. Moore and Labeka Auma] Kampala, Eagle Press, 1953.

20p. 18cm.
Written in Lwo. (Acoli)

1. Infants - Care and hygiene. I. Title. II. Lakor, Erica, tr.

M811.5 Pitcher, Oliver, 1923-
P68d Dust of silence. With an introduction by Robert Grantham. New York, Troubador Press, 1958.

30p. port. 18½cm.
Portrait of author on book jacket.

I. Title.

Dominican
Republic A pitcher's story.
M796.357 Marichal, Juan.
M337 A pitcher's story, by Juan Marichal with Charles Einstein. [1st ed.] Garden City, N. Y., Doubleday, 1967.

215 p. illus. 22 cm.

1. Einstein, Charles, joint author. II. Title.

GV865.M335A3 796.357'2'0924 67-19069
Library of Congress [5]

The pitiful and the proud.
M910 Rowan, Carl Thomas.
R78p The pitiful and the proud. New York, Random House [1956]

432 p. 22 cm.

1. Asia—Politics. 2. Asia—Soc. condit. 3. Race. I. Title.

DS35.R6 950 56-5220 ‡
Library of Congress [57q²10]

Pitsong.
Basutoland
M269.3 Mofolo, Thomas, 1875?-
M72p Pitsong [by] Thomas Mofolo. Morija, Sesuto book depot, 1930.

433p. 16cm.

M784 Pittman, Evelyn LaRue
P68r Rich heritage; songs about American Negro heroes. Oklahoma City, Oklahoma, Harlow Publishing Corporation, 1944.

48p. illus. ports. 30cm.

1. Music and musicians. 2. Biographies. I. Title.

M813.5 Pitts, Gertrude.
P68t Tragedies of life; takes place in the United States, by Gertrude Pitts ... Newark, N. J., ©1939.

62 p. 18cm.

I. Title. 39-25324

Library of Congress PZ3.P680Tr
——— Copy 2.
Copyright A 133698 [2]

Pitts, Lucia Mae jt. author.

M811.5 Harris, Helen C
H24t Triad. Poems by Helen C. Harris, Lucia Mae Pitts [and] Tomi Carolyn Tinsley. Privately published, December, 1945.
95p. 21cm.

M334 Pitts, Nathan Alvin, 1913-
P68c The cooperative movement in Negro communities of North Carolina. Washington, Catholic University of America Press, 1950.

xii, 201 p. maps. 28 cm. (The Catholic University of America. Studies in sociology, v. 33)

Thesis—Catholic University of America.
Bibliography: p. [193]-196.

ViHaI

1. ~~Negroes~~—North Carolina. 2. Cooperation—~~North Carolina~~. I. Title. (Series)
HD3446.A3N85 334 A 50-9075
Catholic Univ. of America. Library for Library of Congress [3]†

M811.5 Pitts, Richard Wesley, 1910-
P68e Excelsior., Book of Poems, by Richard W. Pitts. Holly Springs, Miss., The author, c19 4
20 p. port. 19cm.
1. Poetry

M811.5 Pitts, Richard Wesley, 1910-
P68t Thy kingdom come, thy will be done on earth, as it is in heaven. Post war meditations. A book of poems by Richard W. Pitts. Holly Springs, Miss., The author, 1944
37p. port 22cm.
1. Poetry

Pittsburgh.
M974.8 Moore, Martha Edith (Bannister) 1910-
M78 Unmasked; the story of my life on both sides of the race barrier, by Martha B. Moore. [1st ed.] New York, Exposition Press [1964]

106 p. 21 cm.

1. Discrimination—Pittsburgh. 2. Pittsburgh. I. Title.

E185.97.M8A3 301.451 64-4395
Library of Congress [5]

M301
R27so Pittsburgh.
Reid, Ira DeAugustine, 1901-
Social conditions of the Negro in the hill district of Pittsburgh; survey conducted under the direction of Ira DeA. Reid. [Pittsburgh] General Committee on the Hill Survey, 1930.

117p. diagrs. 24½cm.
Bibliography: p. 116-117.

M301 Pittsburgh. General Committee on the Hill
R27so Survey

Reid, Ira DeAugustine, 1901-
Social conditions of the Negro in the hill district of Pittsburgh; survey conducted under the direction of Ira DeA. Reid. [Pittsburgh] General Committee on the Hill Survey, 1930.

117p. diagrs. 24½cm.
Bibliography: p.116-117.

M286 Pius, N H
P68o An outline of Baptist history; a splendid reference work for busy workers; a record of the struggles and triumphs of Baptist pioneers and builders by N. H. Pius... Nashville, Tenn., National Baptist publishing board, 1911.
154p. 19cm.

1. Baptists.

South
Africa
M968 Plaatje, Solomon Tshekisho, 1878-1932, tr.
P69d Dintšhontšho tsa bo-Juliuse Kesara; e leng lokwalô lwa "Julius Caesar" lo lo kwadilweng, kê William Shakespeare. Lo siamisitšwe e bile lo relagantšwe kê G. P. Lestrade. [4th ed.] Johannesburg, Witwatersrand University Press, 1954.

75p. 18cm. (Bantu Treasury, edited by C. M. Doke, III)
Written in Sechuana.
I. Shakespeare, William. II. Title. III. Series.

S. Africa
M968 Plaatje, Solomon Tshekisho, 1878-1932, tr.
P69d Dintshontsho tsa Bo-Juliuse Kesara, kê
1879/4 William Shakespeare [Translated by S. T. Plaatje; foreward by G. P. Lestrade] Johannesburg, University of Witwatersrand Press, 1942.

75 p. 17½ cm.
Shakespeare's-Julius Caesar translated into Tswana.

I. Shakespeare, William.

S. Africa
M968 Plaatje, Solomon Tshekisho, 1878-1932
P69mh Mhudi; an epic of South African native life a hundred years ago. Lovedale, Lovedale Press [1930]

225 p. 19 cm.

I. Title.

S. Africa
M968
P69m
Plaatje, Solomon Tshekisho, 1878-1932
The mote and the beam. An epic on sex-relationship 'twixt white and black in British South Africa. New York, Young's Book Exchange, n.d.

11 p. 23 cm.

1. Africa, South-race relations.

The place of wrath.
M812.5
Am57
Amis, Lola (James)
3 plays: The other side of the wall, The place of wrath, Helen. New York, Exposition Press [1965]

88p. 21cm.

I. Title: The other side of the wall. II. Title: The place of wrath. III. Title: Helen.

Plantation life.
M973.5
L95j
Jones, Katharine M , 1900- ed.
The plantation South. [1st ed.] Indianapolis, Bobbs-Merrill [1957]

412p. illus. 22cm.
Includes bibliography.
White author.

S. Africa
M968
P69m
Plaatje, Solomon Tshekisho, 1878-1932.
Native life in South Africa, before and since the European war and the Boer rebellion, by Sol. T. Plaatje. Fourth edition. Kimberley, South Africa, New York. The Crisis.

382 p. illus. $18\frac{1}{2}$ cm.

1. Africa, South. 2. Jabavu, John Tengo, 1859-1921. 3. Land tenure - Africa, S. - Law.

Placido

see

Valdes, Gabriel de la Concepcion, 1809-1844

Plantation life.
M975
N31
Laws, J Bradford.
The Negroes of Cinclare Central Factory and Calumet Plantation, Louisiana. [Bulletin of the Labor Dept. no. 38, 1902] pp. 95-120.

In: The Negro in the black belt... Washington, D.C., Dept. of Labor, [189 - 190]

S. Africa
M968
P69n
1916
Plaatje, Solomon Tshekisho, 1878-1932
Native life in South Africa, before and since the European war and the Boer rebellion, by Sol. T. Plaatje ... London, P. S. King & son, ltd. [1916]
xxxii, 352 p. 2 port. (incl. front.) $18\frac{1}{2}$ cm.

1. Africa, South--Native races. 2. Land tenure—Africa, South—Law. 3. Africa, South—Hist.—Rebellion, 1914-
17-13382
Library of Congress DT763.P7 1916

Plain talks to colored people.
M252
B67w
Bowen, John Wesley Edward, 1855-
What shall the harvest be? A national sermon; or, A series of plain talks to the colored people of America, on their problems, by the Rev. J. W. E. Bowen, Ph. D., in the Asbury Methodist Episcopal church. Washington, D.C., Press of the Stafford printing co., 1892.

87p. front. (port) $22\frac{1}{2}$cm/

M326.99B
N81
1853
Plantation life.
Northup, Solomon, b. 1808.
... Twelve years a slave. Narrative of Solomon Northup, a citizen of New-York, kidnapped in Washington city in 1841, and rescued in 1853, from a cotton plantation near the Red river, in Louisiana. Auburn, Derby and Miller; Buffalo, Derby, Orton and Mulligan; [etc., etc.] 1853.
xvi, [17]-336 p. front., pl. $19\frac{1}{2}$ cm.
At head of title: Tenth thousand.
Preface signed: David Wilson.

1. Plantation life. 2. Slavery in the U. S.—Louisiana. I. Wilson, David, 1818-1887, ed.
10—34503
Library of Congress E444.N87
[39h1]

S. Africa
M968
P69s
Plaatje, Solomon Tshekisho, 1878-1932
Sechuana proverbs with literal translations and their European equivalents. Diane tsa secoana le maele a sekgooa a a dumalanang naco. By Solomon T. Plaatje ... London, K. Paul, Trench, Trubner & co., ltd., 1916.
3 p. l., ix-xii, 98 p. front., ports. $12\frac{1}{2} \times 19^{cm}$.

1. Sechuana proverbs. 2. Bechuana people.
17-4470
Library of Congress

The Plaindealer.
MB9
P36m
Mallas, Aris A
Forty years in politics; the story of Ben Pelham, by Aris A. Mallas, Jr., Rea McCain [and] Margaret K. Hedden. Detroit, Wayne State University Press, 1957.

92p. illus. 24cm.

Plantation life.
M326.99B
R15f
Randolph, Peter.
From slave cabin to the pulpit. The autobiography of Rev. Peter Randolph: the southern question illustrated and sketches of slave life. Boston, James H. Earle, 1893.

220p. front. $19\frac{1}{2}$cm.

S. Africa
M968
P69se
Plaatje, Solomon Tshekisho, 1878-1932
A Sechuana reader in international phonetic orthography, with English translations, by Daniel Jones and Solomon Tshekisho Plaatje. London, The University of London Press, 1916.

xxxi, 45 p. 19 cm.

1. Sechuana grammar.

Planning together...
M370
W58pl
Whiting, Helen Adele
Planning together and following through, being ways of cooperating for inservice growth of Jeanes supervising teachers of Georgia Negro elementary schools.
n.p., n.p., c 1945
46p. 23cm.

Plantation life.
M326.99B
R15s
1855
Randolph, Peter.
Sketches of slave life: or, Illustrations of the 'peculiar institution.' By Peter Randolph, an emancipated slave. Boston, Pub. for the author, 1855.
35 p. 20^{cm}.

1. Plantation life.
10-34660
Library of Congress [35b1] E444.R19

Place : America.
M812.5
R38p
Richardson, Thomas.
Place: America (a theatre piece) by Thomas Richardson, based on the history of the National association for the advancement of colored people, foreword by Sterling A. Brown. New York, National association for the advancement of colored people [c1939]
51 p. 20^{cm}.

1. National association for the advancement of colored people. II. Title.
40-8718
Library of Congress PN6120.N4R45
——— Copy 2.
Copyright D pub. 60098 [2] 812.5

Plantation echoes.
M811.5
H38
Henderson, Elliott Blaine.
Plantation echoes; a collection of original Negro dialect poems, by Elliott Blaine Henderson. Columbus, O., Press of F. J. Heer, 1904.
95 p. $19\frac{1}{2}^{cm}$.

1. Negro-English dialects. I. Title.
5—36529
Library of Congress PS3515.E484P6 1904
[a37b1]

Plantation recipes.
M641.5
B67p
Bowers, Lessie.
Plantation recipes. [1st ed. New York, R. Speller, 1959.
194 p. 22 cm.

1. Cookery, American—Southern States. I. Title.
TX715.B76 641.5975 59-13903 ‡
Library of Congress [5]

A place of adventure; essays and sermons.
M252
J63p
Johnson, John Howard, 1897-
A place of adventure; essays and sermons. Foreword by Hughell E. W. Fosbroke. [Rev. ed.] Greenwich, Conn., Seabury Press, 1955.
130 p. 19 cm.

1. New York. St. Martin's Church. 2. Protestant Episcopal Church in the U. S. A.—Sermons. 3. Sermons, American. I. Title.
BX5980.N5M34 1955 283.747 55-13760 ‡
Library of Congress [3]

Plantation life.
M301
J63s
Johnson, Charles Spurgeon, 1893-
Shadow of the plantation, by Charles S. Johnson ... Chicago, Ill., The University of Chicago press [1934]
xxiv, 214, [1] p. front., plates, diagr. 22 cm.
Macon county, Alabama, was the area chosen for this survey. cf. Introd.

1. Plantation life. 2. Negroes—Macon co., Ala. I. Title.
34—19995
Library of Congress E185.93.A3J6
[44h1] 325.2609761

Plantation songs.
M784
H15
Hallowell, Emily, ed.
Calhoun plantation songs, collected and edited by Emily Hallowell. Boston, C. W. Thompson & Co., 1901.

61p. 27cm.

1. Songs, Plantation. I. Title. II. Title: Plantation songs.

Les plantes et les legumes d'Haiti qui guerissent.

Haiti
M972.94
B83p

Brutus, Timoléon C

Les plantes et les legumes d'Haiti qui guerissent; mille et une recettes pratiques. Port-au-Prince, Imprimerie de l'Etat, 1960.

v. 24cm.

Lib. has: v. 2.

M814.4
P69e

Plato, Ann.

Essays; including biographies and miscellaneous pieces, in prose and poetry. By Ann Plato. Hartford, Printed for the author, 1841.

3 p. l., [xvii]–xx, [19]–122 p. 15 cm.

1. Negro authors. I. Title.

16-18674

Library of Congress PS2593.P947 1841

M813.3
P69m

Platt, S H

The martyrs and the fugitive; or a narrative of the captivity, sufferings and death of an African family and the slavery and escape of their son. By Rev. S.H. Platt... New York, Printed by Daniel Fanshaw, 1859.

95p. 19½cm.

I. Title.

Play songs of the deep south.

M784
J61

Johns, Altona (Trent)

Play songs of the deep south. Illustrated by James A. Porter. Washington, D.C., The Associated Publishers, Inc., [1944]

33p. illus. 27½cm.

Plays and pageant...

M812.08
R39

Richardson, Willis, 1889- comp.

Plays and pageants from the life of the Negro [compiled by] Willis Richardson. Washington, D. C., The Associated publishers, inc. [°1930]

x, 373 p. incl. front., illus., plates. 22½cm.

CONTENTS.—Plays: Sacrifice, by Thelma M. Duncan. Antar of Araby, by Maud Cuney-Hare. Ti Yette, by John Matheus. Graven images, by May Miller. Riding the goat, by May Miller. The black horseman, by Willis Richardson. The king's dilemma, by Willis Richardson. The house of sham, by Willis Richardson.—Pageants: Two races, by Inez M. Burke. Out of the dark, by Dorothy C. Guinn. The light of the women, by Frances Gunner. Ethiopia at the bar of justice, by Edward J. McCoo.

1. Negro drama. 2. Negroes in literature and art. I. Title.

30—7094

Library of Congress PS627.N4R5

[43n1]

Plays for a Negro theatre.

M812.5
Ed5s

Edmonds, Randolph, 1900-

Six plays for a Negro theatre, by Randolph Edmonds ... foreword by Frederick H. Koch ... Boston, Walter H. Baker company [°1934]

3 p. l., 5-155 p. 19½cm.

CONTENTS.—Bad man.—Old man Pete.—Nat Turner.—Breeders.—Bleeding hearts.—The new window.

1. Negro drama. 2. Negroes in literature and art. I. Title: Plays for a Negro theatre.

[Full name: Sheppard Randolph Edmonds]

34—10819

Library of Congress PS3500.D5036 1934

[44d1] 812.5

Plays of Negro life...

M812.08
L79

Locke, Alain Le Roy, 1886- ed.

Plays of Negro life; a source-book of native American drama, selected and edited by Alain Locke ... and Montgomery Gregory ... decorations and illustrations by Aaron Douglas. New York and London, Harper & brothers, 1927.

10 p. l., 3-430 p. front., plates. 22½ cm.

"Bibliography of Negro drama": p. 424-430.

1. Negroes in literature and art. 2. American drama (Collections) 3. Negro literature. I. Gregory, Montgomery, 1887- joint ed. II. Title. III. Title: Negro life, Plays of.

27—22553

Library of Congress PS627.N4L6

[45x²1]

Playtime in Africa.

Ghana
M896.1
Su8p

Sutherland, Efua.

Playtime in Africa. Text by Efua Sutherland. Photos. by Willis E. Bell. [1st ed.] New York, Atheneum, 1962.

56 p. illus. 24 cm.

1. Children in Africa—Juvenile literature. 2. Games. I. Bell, Willis E., illus. II. Title.

PZ9.S9476Pl j916 62—7368 ‡

Library of Congress [62k5]

A plea for social justice fro the Negro women.

M396
F95p

[Fulton, David Bryant] 1863-

... A plea for social justice for the negro woman ... Issued by the Negro society for historical research, Yonkers, N. Y. [New York] Lincoln press ass'n., 1912.

cover-title, 11 p. 17½cm. (Negro society for historical research. Occasional paper no. 2)

Signed: Jack Thorne [pseud.]

1. Women, Negro. I. Title.

30-28450

Library of Congress E185.5.N4 no. 2

[2] 325.26

M814.5
Yo8p

A plea for understanding.

Young, Plummer Bernard, 1884-

A plea for understanding, editorials reprinted from the Norfolk Journal and guide. Norfolk, Va. Guide Publishing co., 1935.

2 fold, l., 6 columns. 25cm.

Contents: -Our educational dilemma and proposed court action as a remedy; -Let us understand each other.

A plea for unity among American Negroes.

M304
P19
v.4,no2

Barrett, Samuel.

A plea for unity among American negroes and the negroes of the world; a book dealing with one of the phases of the negro problem as it effects the negroes themselves. By Dr. Samuel Barrett ... (3d ed.—enl. and rev.) [Cedar Falls, Ia., Woolverton printing co., °1926]

67 p. 17½cm.

1. Negroes. I. Title.

26-14842

Library of Congress E185.6.B27

——— Copy 2.

Copyright A 904979 [2]

Plea of the Negro soldier.

M811.5
W58p

White, Charles Fred, 1876-

Plea of the negro soldier, and a hundred other poems, by Corporal Charles Fred. White ... Easthampton, Mass., Press of Enterprise printing company [°1908]

170, [2] p. front. (port.) 19cm.

I. Title.

8—18064

Library of Congress PS3174.W58

Copyright A 203554 [a31d1]

A pleasant encounter and other poems.

M811.5
J714p

Jones, Elois Murry (Redmond)

A pleasant encounter and other poems, by E. H. Jones. New York, Vantage Press, 1964.

59p. 20½cm.

Portrait of author on book jacket.

1. Poetry. I. Title.

M634
P72

Pleasants, Clarence

Galveston, the Oleander City; an appreciation. New York, Exposition Press [1966]

31 p. 21 cm.

1. Oleander. 2. Galveston, Tex. - Description.

The pleasures.

M811.3
P29p

Payne, Daniel Alexander, 1811-1894.

The pleasures, and other miscellaneous poems. By Daniel A. Payne. Baltimore, Sherwood & Co., 1850.

[8]-43p. 16cm.

The pleasures of exile.

Barbados
M823
L18p

Lamming, George, 1927-

The pleasures of exile. London, M. Joseph [1960]

232 p. 23 cm.

1. Colonies. 2. West Indies, British. I. Title.

PR6023.A518P5 828.91 60-51766 ‡

Library of Congress [2]

The pleasures of life.

M811.5
M 553

Merriweather, Claybron W.

The pleasures of life, lyrics of the lowly, essays, and other poems, by Claybron W. Merriweather ... [Hopkinsville, Ky., The New era printing company, 1931]

156 p. 20cm.

I. Title.

31-17719

Library of Congress PS3525.E687P6 1931

Copyright A 39248 [2] 810.81

The pleasures of smoking as expressed by those poets...

M394.1
W32p

Watkins, Sylvestre Cornelius, 1911- comp.

The pleasures of smoking as expressed by those poets, wits and tellers of tales who have drawn their inspiration from the fragrant weed. New York, H. Schuman [1948]

xii, 208 p. illus. 25 cm.

1. Smoking. I. Title.

GT3020.W37 394.1 48-9635*

Library of Congress [5]

South Africa
M896
M88

Pliya, Jean

The Fetish Tree

Pp. 226-240.

In: Mphahlele, Ezekiel, ed. African writing today. Baltimore, Penguin Books, 1967.

The plot that failed.

Liberia
M966.6
T79p

Liberian Information Service.

The plot that failed; the story of the attempted assisination of President Tubman. Monrovia, Liberian Information Service [1959]

68p. ports. 21cm.

Autographed: "This was stolen from my house John B. Falconer by Arthur Spingarn."

Plum bun.

M813.5
F27p2

Fauset, Jessie Redmon, 1882-1961.

Plum bun, a novel without a moral, by Jessie Redmon Fauset... New York, Frederick A. Stokes company, 1929.

379p. 20cm.

I. Title.

Plum bun.

M813.5 Fauset, Jessie Redmon, 1882-1961.
F27p Plum bun, ‹by› Jessie Redmon Fauset ... New York, Frederick A. Stokes company ‹1929›
381p. 20cm.

Inscribed copy: "For Arthur & Marion, With love - Jessie Fauset. January 21, 1929, New York.

Haiti
M972.94 Pluviose, Rosemond N
P74p Parallele historique "Petain-Dessalines." Port-au-Prince, Haiti, Imprimerie de l'etat, 1946.
12p. 20cm.

1. Haiti--History. 2. Petain, Maréchal, 3. Dessalines, Jean Jacques, emperor of Haiti, 1758-1806.

Brazil Poemas escolhidos.
M869.1 Cruz e Souza, João da, 1861-1898.
C88po Poemas escolhidos. Seleção e introduc‹ão› de Massaud Moises. São Paulo, Editôra Cultrix ‹1961›
158p. 19½cm.

Plumes.

M812.5 Johnson, Georgia Douglas.
J63p Plumes, a play in one act, by Georgia Douglas Johnson... New York, Samuel French, c 1927.
15p. 18½cm.

Pocahontas, d. 1617-Fiction.
M813.5 Graham, Shirley.
G76s3 The story of Pocahontas; illustrated by Mario Cooper. Enid La Monte Meadowcroft, supervising editor. New York, Grosset & Dunlap ‹1953›
180 p. illus. 22 cm. (Signature books, 21)

1. Pocahontas, d. 1617—Fiction.
Full name: Lola Shirley (Graham) McCanns.

PZ7.G757Sv 52—13749 ‡
Library of Congress ‹54c2›

Senegal Poèmes Africains.
M896.1 M'baye, Annette
M45p Poèmes Africains. ‹Paris› Centre d'Art National Français ‹1965›
‹10›p. 19cm. (Collection Art et Poesie)

I. Title.

M616 Plummer, Jewel I.
P73 Triethylene melamine in vitro studies; I. Mitotic alterations produced in chick fibroblast tissue cultures, by Jewel I. Plummer, Louis T. Wright, Grace Antikajian, and Solomon Weintraub. Cancer Research, Inc., 1952.
796-800p. tables graphs 27cm.
Reprinted from Cancer Research, November 1952.

I. Wright, Louis Tompkins, 1891-1952.
1. Tissues - Culture.

The pocket book of Negro facts.

M03 Watkins, Sylvestre Cornelius, 1911-
W32 The pocket book of Negro facts. Chicago, Bookmark Press ‹1946›
24p. 21cm.
Cover title.
"Books by and about Negroes":p. 21-22.

Poèmes de l'Afrique noire.

Mali
M896.1 Sissoko, Fily Dabo
Si83 Poèmes de l'Afrique noire; feux de brousse harmakhis fleurs et chardons. Paris, Debresse-Poésie, 1963.
170p. 19cm.

Plummer, Jewel I.
M616 Wright, Jane Cooke
W928i In vivo and in vitro effects on chemotherapeutic agents on human neoplastic diseases; A preliminary report on the comparison of the effects of chemotherapeutic agents on human tumors in tissue culture and the effects of each such agent in the patient from whom the tissue for culture was taken, by Jane C. Wright, Jewel I, Plummer, Rosette Spoerri Coidan and Louis T. Wright. New York, Harlem Hospital bulletin, 1953.
58-63p. 23cm.
Reprinted from the Harlem Hospital bulletin, September 1953.

Poe, Edgar Allan, 1809-1849-Fiction.
M813.5 Williams, Chancellor.
W67 The raven, by Chancellor Williams. Philadelphia, Dorrance and company ‹1943›
2 p. l., iii-iv p., 1 l., 7-562 p. 23½ cm.
A novel.

1. Poe, Edgar Allan, 1809-1849—Fiction. I. Title.
43-17566
Library of Congress PZ3.W67148Rav
‹5›

Poemes d'Haiti et de France.
Haiti
M841 Roumer, Émile.
R76p ... Poèmes d'Haïti et de France. Paris, Éditions de la Revue mondiale, 1925.
92 p., 1 l. 19cm. (Collection haïtienne d'expression française, sous la direction de m. Louis Morpeau)

I. Title.

PQ3949.R74P6 47-38523
Library of Congress ‹3›

Plums.
M630.7 Carver, George Washington, 1864-1943.
C25f 43 ways to save the wild plum crop, by G. W. Carver...‹Tuskegee Institute, Alabama› Tuskegee Normal and Industrial Institute experiment station ‹1917.
12p. 23cm. (Bulletin 34, April 1917)

A poem - Abraham Lincoln.
M811.5 ‹Fulton, David B.›
F95p A poem - Abraham Lincoln, by "Jack Thorne" ... ‹New York, 1909›
‹4› p. port. 24cm.

...Poemes de la mort, 1898-1905.
Haiti
M841. Vilaire, Etzer, 1872-
V71po ... Poèmes de la mort, 1898-1905. Paris, Fischbacher, 1907.
2 p. l., xxxiv, 306 p. incl. front. (port.) 18cm. (Collection des poètes français de l'étranger ...)

I. Title.
25-24082
Library of Congress PQ3949.V55P6

M910 The plunder of Ethiopia.
Im2p Imes, William Lloyd, 1889-
The plunder of Ethiopia by William Lloyd Imes... and Liston M. Oak... Preface by Captain Guesseppe Altieri. ‹N. Y. American league against war and fascism n.d.›
11 unnumb. p. 15½cm.

Poem counterpoem.
M811.5 Danner, Margaret
D23p Poem counterpoem, by Margaret Danner and Dudley Randall. Detroit, Broadside Press, 1966.
24p. 16cm.

I. Randall, Dudley. II. Title.

Poems.
Panama
M811.5 Johnson, Hugh G , 1910-
J87pm Poems. New York, Comet Press Books, 1961.
41p. 20½cm.
Portrait of author on back of book jacket.

Africa
M896.3 Les plus beaux écrits de l'union française
P741 et du Maghreb, Présentées par Mohamed El Kholti, Léopold Sédar Senghor, ‹and others› Paris, Editions du Vieux, Colombier, 1947.
455p. 21cm.

1. Africa - Literature. 2. Literature - Africa. I. Senghor, Léopold Sédar, 1906- II. Madagascar.

Dominican Poemas de una sola angustia.
Republic
M861.6 Inchaustegui Cabral, Hector, 1912-
In2 Poemas de una sola angustia. Ciudad Trujillo, Imp. "La Opinion, C. por A.", 1940.
92p. 19cm.

Poems.
M811.5 McClellan, George Marion, 1860-1934.
M128po Poems. Nashville, Tenn., Publishing House A.M.E. Church Sunday School Union, 1895.
145p. 19cm.

Poems by a slave in the island of Cuba.
Cuba
M861.6 [Manzano, Juan Francisco] 1797-1854.
M26 Poems by a slave in the island of Cuba, recently liberated; translated from the Spanish, by R.R. Madden, M.D., with the history of the early life of the negro poet, written by himself; to which are prefixed two pieces descriptive of Cuban slavery and the slave-traffic, by R.R.M. London, T. Ward & co., 1840.
4p. l., v p., 1 l., [9]-188p. 22½cm.

Poems of a singer.
M811.5 Lovingood, Penman
L95p Poems of a singer. Compton, Lovingood Company [1963]
68p. 16½cm.

Poems of the four seas.
M811.5 Jones, Joshua Henry.
J713p Poems of the four seas, by Joshua Henry Jones. Boston, The Cornhill publishing co. [1921]
4 p. l., 3-52 p. 19cm.
I. Title.
Library of Congress PS3519.O445P6 1921 22-1238
Copyright A 654223 [2]

Poems by candelight and the flare of a match.
M811.5 Morgan, James H , 1916-
M82p. Poems by candelight and the flare of a match. New York, Vantage Press, 1967.
152p. 22cm.
Portrait of author on book jacket.
I. Title.

Poems of a West-Indian.
Trinidad Lambert, Calvin Stollmeyer, 1913?-
M821.91 Poems of a West-Indian. London, "Poetry
L17p of to-day", 1938.
35p. 20cm.

Poems of thought and cheer.
M811.5 McCorkle, George Washington
M13po Poems of thought and cheer, by George Washington McCorkle. Washington, D.C., Published under the auspices of the National bureau of Negro writers and entertainers n.d.
21p. 23½cm.

Jamaica
M821.91 Poems for Easter, 1959.
H14 Devon, Arthur H. Stockwell, 1959.
30p. 18cm.
Partial contents.- [Poems] by Vivian Hazell.
I. Hazel, Vivian. Poems. p. 20-21.

Poems of cabin and field.
M811.4 Dunbar, Paul Laurence, 1872-1906.
D 91p Poems of cabin and field, by Paul
1900 Laurence Dunbar, illustrated with photographs by the Hampton Institute Camera Club and decorations by Alice Morse. New York, Dodd, Mead & Co., 1900.
125p. illus. pl. 22cm.

Poems sacred and profane.
Jamaica
M821.91 Hazel, Vivian B
H33p Poems sacred and profane. Devon, Arthur H. Stockwell, 1961.
31p. port. 18½cm.
Portrait of author in book.
I. Title.

Poems for niggers and crackers.
M811.5 Ibrahim ibn Ismail, 1934-
Ib7p Poems for niggers and crackers, by Ibrahim ibn Ismail [and] James V. Hatch. Illustrations Camille Billops. [Cairo, n.p., 1965]
54p. 21cm.

Poems of cabin and field.
M811.4 Dunbar, Paul Laurence, 1872-1906.
D91p Poems of cabin and field ... illustrated with photographs by the Hampton institute camera club and decorations by Alice Morse. New York, Dodd, Mead & co., 1899.
125 p. illus., pl. 8°.
I. Title.
99-5826
Library of Congress (PS1556.P6 1899)
[45k1]

Poems to remember always.
M811.5 Sheperd, John H 1930-
Sh47p Poems to remember always [by] John H. Sheperd. [1st ed.] New York, Greenwich Book Publishers [c1965]
31p. 22cm.

Poems for the day.
M811.5 Lee, Harrison Edward.
L51p Poems for the day. New York, Comet Press Books [1954]
28 p. 23 cm.
I. Title.
PS3523.E334P6 811.5 54-9548 ‡
Library of Congress [2]

Poems of inspiration for better living.
M811.5 Reason, Arthur Wesley, 1887-
R23p Poems of inspiration for better living. New York, Exposition Press, 1959.
97p. 20½cm.

Poesía, 1915-1956.
Puerto Rico
M861 Palés Matos, Luis
P17p Poesía, 1915-1956. Introducción por Federico De Onís. San Juan, Universidad de Puerto Rico, 1957.
305p. 21cm.

Poems from Black Africa.
U.S.
M896.1 Hughes, Langston, 1902- ed.
H874 Poems from Black Africa: Ethiopia, South Rhodesia, Sierra Leone, Madagascar, Ivory Coast, Nigeria, Kenya, Gabon, Senegal, Nyasaland, Mozambique, South Africa, Congo, Ghana, Liberia. Bloomington, Indiana University Press [1963]
158 p. illus. 22 cm. (UNESCO collection of contemporary works)
1. African poetry—Translations into English. 2. English poetry—Translations from African. I. Title.
Full name: James Langston Hughes.
PL8013.E5H8 896 62-8972 ‡
Library of Congress [5]

M808.81 Poems of 1958. Devon, Arthur H. Stockwell,
P75 1958.
136p. 18½cm.
"With compliments - V. H., page 77."
1. Poetry - Anthology.

Poesia dei popoli primitivi.
Africa
M896.1 Sydow, Eckart von, 1885-1942, ed.
Sy25 Poesia dei popoli primitivi; lirica religiosa, magica e profana. Scelta, introd. e note di Eckart v. Sydow. [Traduzione di Roberto Bazlen. Modena, Guanda, 1951.
197 p. 24 cm. (Collezione Fenice; edizione fuori serie, 15)
Includes selected African poems translated into Italian from African languages.
1. Literature, Primitive. 2. Poetry—Collections. 3. Italian poetry—Translations from foreign literature. I. Title.
[PN1347.S] A 52-7577
Illinois. Univ. Library for Library of Congress [1]

Poems in all moods.
Trinidad
M821 Cruickshank, Alfred M.
C88p Poems in all moods, by Alfred M. Cruickshank ... Port of Spain, Trinidad, Belle Eau Road, 1937.
viii, [10] - 203p. 19½cm.

Poems of simplicity.
Graves, Linwood D.
M811.5 Poems of simplicity, and The living dead, a short true story,
G78 by Linwood D. Graves. [Kingsport, Tenn.] Priv. print. [Kingsport press, inc.] 1938.
x, 116 p. incl. front. (port.) 20cm.
I. Title. II. Title: The living dead.
Library of Congress PS3501.G7P6 1938 40-8863
——— Copy 2.
Copyright [2] 811.5

Dominican
Republic ... La poesía folklórica en Santo Domingo.
M861.6 Nolasco, Flérida de.
N71p ... La poesía folklórica en Santo Domingo. Santiago, República dominicana, Editorial El Diario [1946]
4 p. l., [11]-307, [1] p. 23cm.
Contents.—Conferencia.—Provincia de Azua.—Provincia de Barahona.—Cabral.—Enriquillo.—Provincia Bahoruco.—Provincia Benefactor.—Las Matas de Farfán.—Provincia Trujillo Valdez.—Distrito de Santo Domingo.—Provincia del Seibo.—Higuey.
1. Dominican poetry (Collections) 2. Folk-lore, Dominican. 3. Dominican poetry—Hist. & crit. I. Title.
PQ7406.N6 47-844
Library of Congress [4]

Poesia Negro-Americana.
M811.08 Izzo, Carlo, comp.
I29 Poesia Negro-Americana, a cura di Carlo Izzo presentazione e traduzioni di Gianna Menarini [Milano] Nuova Accademia [1963]

263p. illus. 20cm.
Bibliografia generale: p. 253-256.

1. Poetry. I. Title.

Sudan Poesia Sudanese.
M896.1 Tescaroli, Livio, comp.
T28 Poesia Sudanese. [Bologna] Editrice Nigrizia, 1961.

119p. illus. 21½cm. (Museum Combonianum, No. 12)
Appendice musicale: p. 87-117.
White compiler.

Poésie commune, 6
French Guiana
M841 Damas, Leon Gontran tr. 1912-
D18pe Poèmes nègres sur des airs africains. [Paris] GLM [1948]
28 p. illus. 26 cm. (Poésie commune, 6)

1. African languages—Texts. (Series)
A 49-2796 rev*

New York. Public Libr. for Library of Congress [r49b1]

Poesie cosmique (prèmiere séries).
Haiti
M841 Drouinaud, Lapierre
D839p Poeme cosmique (première séries). Port-au-Prince, Imprimerie des Antilles, n.d.

24p. 20cm.

1. Haitian poetry. I. Title.

...La poésie francaise chez les noirs d'Haïti;
Haiti Valmy-Baysse, Jean, 1874-
M840.9 ... La poésie française chez les noirs d'Haïti; confé-
V24p rence faite le 4 juin 1903 ... sous les auspices de la Nouvelle revue moderne. Paris, Nouvelle revue moderne [1903?]
46 p., 1 l. 22½ cm.
At head of title: J. Valmy-Baysse.
With this is bound: Lespès, P. Haïti devant la France. Port-au-Prince, 1891.

1. Haitian poetry (French) 2. French poetry—Haitian authors. I. Title.
Library of Congress PQ3942.V3 25—24084
[a48b½]

Poesies completes.
Haiti
M841. Vilaire, Etzer, 1872—
V71p ...Poesies completes... Ed. definitive. Paris, A. Messein, 1914—19.

3v. 19cm.

Poesies nationales (premiere serie)
Haiti
M841. Coicou, Massillon, 1867-
C66p ... Poésies nationales (première série) Par Massillon Coicou, avec une préface de M. Charles-D. Williams. Paris, Imprimerie V. Goupy et Jourdan, 1892.
4 p. l., [11]-274 p. 18cm. (Bibliothèque haïtienne)

I. Title.
25-20882
Library of Congress PQ3949.C6P6 1st ser.

The poet and other poems.
M811.5 Dandridge, Raymond Garfield.
D 19p The poet and other poems, by Raymond Garfield Dandridge. Cincinnati, O. [Powell & White] 1920.
6 p. l., 15-64 p. 19½cm.

I. Title.
Library of Congress PS3601.D3P6 1920 20-15360
——— Copy 2.
Copyright A 576134 [2]

Poetas de color.
Cuba
MB Calcagno, Francisco, 1827-1903.
C12p Poetas de color, por Francisco Calcagno.
1887 Placido, Manzano, Rodriguez, Echemendia, Silveira, Medina. Cuarta edicion. Habana, Imp. Mercantil de los Herederos de Santiago S. Spencer, 1887.

7-110p. 19½cm.

Poetas de color.
Cuba
MB
C12p Calcagno, Francisco, 1827-1903.
Poetas de color, por Francisco Calcagno. Plácido, Manzano, Rodriguez, Echemendía, Silveira, Medina. Habana, Imp. militar de la v. de Soler y compañia, 1878.
1 p. l., [5]-54 p. 23½cm.

1. Poets, Cuban. 2. Negro authors. I. Title.
22-9233
[34b1]
Library of Congress PQ7380.C3

Poetas e contistas Africanos de expressão Portuguesa.
Africa
M896 Neves, João Alves das, ed.
N297 Poetas e contistas Africanos de expressão Portuguesa: Cabo verde, Guiné, São Tomé e príncipe, Angola, Moçambique. [São Paulo] Editôra Braziliense [1963]
211p. 20½cm.
White editor

1. Portuguese literature - Africa.
2. African literature. I. Title.

Les poétes créoles du xviiie siècle.
Guadeloupe
M841 Barquissau, Raphaël.
L55b Les poètes créoles du XVIIIe siècle (Parny, Bertin, Léonard) Paris, J. Vigneau, 1949.
249 p. ports. 24 cm.
Bibliography: p. [225]-238.
White author.

1. Parny, Évariste Désiré de Forges, vicomte de, 1753-1814. 2. Bertin, Antoine, chevalier de, 1752-1790. 3. Léonard, Nicolas Germain, 1744-1793. I. Title. II. Léonard, Nicolas Germain, 1744-1793.
PQ427.B3 841.509 50-20934
Library of Congress [1]

Cuba Poétes d'aujourd'hui, 111.
M861.6 Guillén, Nicholas, 1904-
G94n Nicolas Guillen, presentation, choix de textes, traduction, par Claude Couffin. [Paris] Editions Pierre Seghers, 1964.
191p., ports. 16cm. (Poétes d'aujourd'hui, 111)

Poètes d'Aujourd'hui, 114.
M811.5 Hughes, Langston, 1902-
H87La Langston Hughes, présentation par Francois Dodat. Choix de textes. Bibliographie, portraits, fac-similés. Paris, Editions Pierre Seghers,

191p. 16cm.

French Guiana
M841.08 Poètes d'expression française.
D18 Damas, Leon G ed., 1912-
Poètes d'expression française [d'Afrique Noire, Madagascar, Réunion, Guadeloupe, Martinique, Indochine, Guyane] 1900-1945. Paris, Éditions du Seuil [1947]
322 p. (Latitudes françaises, 1)
Collection "Pierres vives."

1. French poetry—20th cent. I. Title. (Series. Series: Collection "Pierres vives")
A 49-2183*
Illinois. Univ. Library for Library of Congress [1]

Poeti d'Africa nera.
Africa
M896.1 Brambilla, Cristina, ed.
B73 Poeti d'Africa nera. A cura di Cristina Brambilla. [Roma] Carucci [1958]

150p. 17cm. (Collana di poesia, 7)
Bibliography: p. 147.
White editor.

1. African poetry. I. Title.

Poetic creations.

M811.5 Kirton, St. Clair.
K63p Poetic creations, by St. Clair Kirton. [Boston, Mass., Lester Benn, c1943]

36p. 22cm.

Poetic pearls...
M811.5 Figgs, Carrie Law Morgan.
F46p Poetic pearls, by Carrie Law Morgan Figgs ... Jacksonville, Florida, Edward Waters College Press, 1920.

32p. front (port) 15½cm.

Poetical reports of life.
M811.5 Henderson, George S
H383 Poetical reports of life. New York. Printed for the author by the Gunther Press. 1938.

136 p. 19cm.

Poetically speaking.
M811.5
En6p Ennis, Willie, 1933-
Poetically speaking. [1st ed.] New York, Exposition Press [1957]
56 p. 21 cm.

I. Title.
PS3509.N55P6 811.5 57-4700 ‡
Library of Congress [2]

Poetry.
M808.81 Afrikanische lyrik aus zwei kontinenten.
Af8 Ausgewahlt von Franz-Josef Klemisch, mit einer einletung von Janheinz Jahn. Stuttgart, Philipp Reclam [1966]

95p. 15cm.
"For Arthur - Sincerely, Langston, New York, Dec. 16, 1966."

Poetry.
M811.5 Ah3f
Aheart, Andrew Norwood.
Figures of fantasy, poems. New York, Exposition Press [c1949]
54p. 22cm.

Poetry.
M808.81 A12
Aladár, Komlós, ed.
Harlemi Arnyak, eszak-amerikai neger koltok versei. Budapest, Magveto Konyvkiado, 1959.
82p. illus. 25cm.

Poetry.
M811.5 A15r
Allen, J. Mord, 1875-
Rhymes, tales and rhymed tales, by J. Mord Allen. Topeka, Kansas, Monotyped by Crane & Co., 1906.
153p. 18cm.

Poetry.
M811.5 A87pz
Americka poezia 20; storocia. Bratislava, Slovenske Vydavatel'stvo Krasnej Literatury, 1959.
230p. 20cm.
"For Arthur Springarn, Sincerely, Langston Hughes - New York, April 25, 1960."
Partial contents.- [Poems] by Langston Hughes, translated into Czech.
1. Poetry.

Poetry.
M811.5 An2gr
Anderson, Charles Louis, 1938-
Frustration; a Negro poet looks at America. [Brief biography of the author, by Dorothy Durem] Puebla, Puebla, Mexico, Published by El Grupo Literario of the United Nations School, 197?
Unp. 21cm.

Poetry.
M811.5 An21
Andrews, Henry Herz.
Idle moments, by Henry H. Andrews. New York, The Poets Press [c 1941]
49p. 22cm.

Poetry.
M811.5 An2v
Andrews, Henry Herz.
Vicious youth. A poem by Henry Andrews (dedicated to girls who have been the victims of ungrateful men). Boston, Popular Poetry Publishers [c1940]
34p. 17cm.

Poetry.
M811.5 At5pn
Atkins, Russell
Phenomena. [Afterword, by Casper Leroy Jordan] Wilberforce, Ohio, The Free Lance Poets and Prose Workshop, Wilberforce University Press, 1961.
79p. 22cm.

Poetry.
M811.5 At5e
Atkins, Thomas.
The eagle, by Thomas Atkins... St. Louis, Missouri, St. Louis, Argus, 1936.
87p. 22cm.

Poetry.
M811.5 B15a
Bailey, Edna Shans
Autumn leaves; a family book of poems, facts and fiction. Martha, Tenn., 1955.
93p. illus. 22½cm.
1. Poetry.

Poetry.
M811.5 B22g
Banks, William Augustus.
Gathering dusk, by William Augustus Banks. Chattanooga, Tenn., The Wilson Printing, Co., [c1935.]
8p. 20½cm.

Poetry.
M811.5 B221
Banks, William Augustus.
"Lest we forget," by William Augustus Banks. Chattanooga, Tenn., Central High press [c1930]
11p. 20cm.

Poetry.
Uruguay M861.6 B27p
Barrios, Pilar E
Piel negra, poesias (1917-1947.) Prólogo de Alberto Britos. Caratula de Vicente Martin. Montevideo, Editó Nuestra Raza, 1947.
113 [2]p. port. 20½cm.

Poetry.
M811.5 B321
Batipps, Percy Oliver.
Lines of life, by Percy Oliver Batipps. Media, Penna., American publishing company, 1924.
118 p. 17½cm.
Verse.
I. Title.
Library of Congress PS3503.A86L5 1924 24-31320
Copyright A 814202 [2]

Poetry.
M811.5 B32g
Battle, Effie T
Gleanings from Dixie land. [Alabama, Tuskegee institute, 1914]
24p. 25cm.

Poetry.
M811.5 B33t
Baxter, Joseph Harvey Lowell.
That which concerneth me; sonnets and other poems, by J. Harvey L. Baxter. Roanoke, Va., The Magic city press, 1934.
viii, 87 p. 20cm.
I. Title. 1. Poetry.
Library of Congress PS3503.A929T5 1934 34-33084
——— Copy 2.
Copyright A 75642 [2] 811.5

Poetry.
M811.5 B35l
Beadle, Samuel Alfred.
Lyrics of the under world, by S. A. Beadle ... Jackson, Miss., W. A. Scott, 1912.
v, [2], 148, [3] p. incl. illus., plates. plates (1 col.) port. 22cm. $1.50
I. Title.
12-2948
Library of Congress PS3503.E15L8 1912
Copyright A 309190

Poetry.
M811.4 B41po
Bell, James Madison, 1826-1902.
A poem, entitled the Triumph of Liberty, delivered April 7, 1870, at Detroit Opera House, by J. Madison Bell, on the occasion of The grand celebration of the final ratification of the fifteenth amendment to the constitution of the United States. Detroit, Printed by the Tunis Steam Printing Co., 187.
32p. port. 21cm.

Poetry.
M811.4 B41p
Bell, James Madison, 1826-1902.
A poem entitled the day and the war, delivered January 1, 1864, at Platt's Hall, by J. Madison Bell, at the celebration of the first anniversary of President Lincoln's Emancipation Proclamation. San Francisco, Agnew & Deffebach, 1864.
27p. 21½cm.

Poetry.
M811.4 B41
Bell, James Madison, 1826-1902.
The poetical works of James Madison Bell ... Lansing, Mich., Press of Wynkoop, Hallenbeck, Crawford co, [1904?]
221 p., 1 l. front., ports. 20cm.
"Second edition."
"Biographical sketch of J. Madison Bell ... by Bishop B. W. Arnett": p. [3]-14.
I. Arnett, Benjamin William, bp., 1838-1906. 40-37868
Library of Congress PS1085.B5 1904
[2] 811.49

Poetry.
M811.5 B438an
Benjamin, Joseph Louis
And the truth shall make us free, by Joseph Louis Benjamin and Anita Honis. New York, Carlton Press, 1964.
67p. 20½cm.
Portrait of authors on book jacket.
1. Poetry. I. Honis, Anita, jt. auth. II. Title.

Poetry.
M811.5 Berry, Lloyd Andrew
B45h Heart songs and by gones, by Lloyd Andrew Berry. Dayton, Ohio, The author, 1926.
40p. port. 24cm.

Poetry.
M811.5 Beverly, Katharine
B46 A distant spring and other poems. Texas, Artes Graficas, 1952.
62p. 24cm.

Poetry.
M811.4 Bibb, Eloise.
B47p Poems, by Eloise Bibb. Boston, Mass., The Monthly review press, 1895.
107 p. 18cm.

Poetry.
M811.5 Bird, Bessie Calhoun,
B53a Airs from the wood-winds by Bessie Calhoun Bird. With an introduction by Arthur Huff Fauset. Philadelphia, Pa., Alpress [c1935]
23p. 23cm.

Poetry.
M811.5 Blake, Alfred Egbert, 1906-
B58p Poetic facts and philosophy, by Al Ethelred Bladeley, pseud. New York, N.Y., Al Ethelred Blakeley & co., c1936.
23p. 22½cm.

Poetry
M811.08 Bontemps, Arna Wendell, 1902- comp.
B64 Golden slippers, an anthology of Negro poetry for young readers, compiled by Arna Bontemps, with drawings by Henrietta Bruce Sharon. New York and London, Harper & brothers [c1941]
viii, 220 p., 1 l. incl. illus., plates. 21½ cm.
"First edition."
"Biographies": p. 209-215.
1. Negro poetry (American) I. Title.
41—22155
Library of Congress PS591.N4B6
[45w2] 811.0822

Poetry.
M811.5 Bontemps, Arna Wendell
B64p Personals. London, Paul Breman, 1963.
44p. 21½cm.
"For Arthur Spingarn - with lasting esteem, Arna Bontemps, 4-17-64."

Poetry.
M811.5 Borders, William Holmes, 1905-
B64t "Thunderbolts" [by] William Holmes Borders. [Atlanta, Morris Brown college press, c1942]
50 p. illus. 23½cm.
Poems
I. Title.
44-204
Library of Congress PS3503.O548T5
[2] 811.5

Poetry.
M811.5 Boyd, Raven Freemont, 1901-
B69h ... Holiday stanzas. New York, Fortuny's [c1940]
98 p. front. (port.) 22½cm.
At head of title: R. F. Boyd.
"First edition."
1. Holidays—Poetry. I. Title.
41-2848
Library of Congress PS3601.B6H6 1940
——— Copy 2.
Copyright A 148960 [2] 811.5

Poetry.
M811.5 Bradley, Henry T.
B720 Out of the depths, by Henry T. Bradley. New York, The Avondale press incorporated [c1928]
113, [1] p. 20cm.
Poems.
I. Title.
29-596
Library of Congress PS3503.R22108 1928
——— Copy 2
Copyright A 3405 [2]

Poetry.
M811.08 Braithwaite, William Stanley Beaumont, 1878- ed.
B73a Anthology of Massachusetts poets, by William Stanley Braithwaite. Boston, Small, Maynard & company [c1922]
9 p. l., 3-145 p. 17cm.
1. American literature — Massachusetts. 2. American poetry—20th cent. I. Title.
22—7304
Library of Congress PS548.M4B7
——— Copy 2.
Copyright A 661216 28f2]

Poetry.
M811.5 Braithwaite, William Stanley Beaumont, 1878-
B73h The house of falling leaves, with other poems, by William Stanley Braithwaite ... Boston, J. W. Luce and company, 1908.
xi, 13-112 p. 20cm.
Partly reprinted from various periodicals.
I. Title.
8—27527
Library of Congress PS3503.R246H7 1908
Copyright A 217225 [31f1]

Poetry.
M811.5 Braithwaite, William Stanley Beaumont, 1878-
B73s Selected poems. New York, Coward-McCann, Inc. c 1948.
96p. 20½cm.

Poetry.
M811.08 Braithwaite, William Stanley Beaumont, 1878- comp.
B73v Victory! celebrated by thirty-eight American poets, brought together by William Stanley Braithwaite, with an introduction by Theodore Roosevelt. Boston, Small, Maynard & company [c1919]
viii, 84 p. 24cm.
1. European war, 1914-1918—Poetry. I. Title.
19—26576
Library of Congress D526.2.B66
[43q1]

M810 Poetry.
B73d Brawley, Benjamin Griffith, 1882-1939.
The desire of the moth for the star, by Benjamin Griffith Brawley. [eight lines of quotation]. Atlanta, The Franklin - Turner Co.,
14p. 17cm.

M810 Poetry.
B73p Brawley, Benjamin Griffith, 1882-1939.
A prayer. Words by B. G. Brawley... Music by A. H. Ryder... [Atlanta, Ga.] Atlanta Baptist college press [1899]
2p. 23½cm.
Music: p.2

M810 Poetry.
B73t Brawley, Benjamin Griffith, 1882-1939.
A toast to love and death, by Benjamin Griffith Brawley. [eight lines of verse] [Atlanta] Atlanta Baptist College Print, 1902.
29p. 17cm.

Poetry.
M811.08 Breman, Paul, [ed]
B74 Sixes and sevens; an anthology of new poetry. London, P. Breman, 1962.
96p. 21½cm. (Heritage, 2)
Includes biographical references.
White editor.

Poetry.
M811.08 Brewer, John Mason, 1896- ed.
B75h Heralding dawn; an anthology of verse, by [!] selected and edited, with a historical summary on the Texas Negroes' verse-making, by J. Mason Brewer, and with a preface by Henry Smith. [Dallas, Tex., June Thomason, printing, c1936]
7 p. l., 45 p. illus. (ports.) 22½cm.
Includes biographical sketches of the authors.
"Bibliography and acknowledgment": 3d prelim. leaf.
1. Negro poetry (American) 2. American literature—Texas. 3. Negro authors. I. Title.
41-20467
Library of Congress PS591.N4B65
[2] 811.50822

Poetry.
M811.5 Brewer, John Mason, 1896-
B75 Negrito, Negro dialect poems of the Southwest, by J. Mason Brewer; illustrations by Tom Smith. San Antonio, Tex., Naylor printing company, 1933.
3 p. l., 9-97 p., 1 l. illus. 20 cm.
I. Title.
33-28762
Library of Congress PS3503.R496N4 1933
[2] 811.5

Poetry.
M811.5 Brewer, John Mason, 1896- editor.
B75p Patriotic moments: a second book of verse by the Bellerophon quill club of the Booker T. Washington high school, Dallas, Texas. Edited by J. Mason Brewer.
n.p., n.p. 1936.
24p. 19½cm.

Poetry.

M811.5 Brewer, John Mason, 1896- editor.
B75s Senior sentiments and junior jotttings: a first book of verse, by the Bellerophon quill club of the Booker T. Washington high school, Dallas, Texas... Edited by J. Mason Brewer., 1934

24p. 20½cm.

1. Poetry.

Poetry.

M811.5 Britt, Nellie.
B77m My master and I; poems that will encourage, inspire and strengthen. New York, Carlton Press c1964,

48p. 20½cm. (A Lyceum book)
Portrait of author on book jacket.

Poetry.

M811.5 Brooks, Gwendolyn.
B791s A street in Bronzeville, by Gwendolyn Brooks. New York and London, Harper & brothers, 1945.

vi, 57, [1] p. 19½cm.
Poems.
"First edition."

I. Title.

Library of Congress * PS3503.R7244S8 45—7550
[46h5] 811.5

Poetry.

M811.5 Brooks, Walter Henderson, 1851-
B79o Original poems, by Rev. Walter H. Brooks... Published by the sunday school of the church in connection with the fifieth anniversary of his service as pastor. Washington, 1932.
39p. front. 20½cm.

Poetry.

M811.5 Brown, Samuel E
B811o Love letters in rhyme, by Samuel E. Brown. New York, Samuel E. Brown c 1930
29p. 19½cm.
copy no.3 First edition.
Autographed copy: Samuel E. Brown To Edward from your friend, Samuel. September 22nd, nineteen-thirty.

M811.5
B715d Poetry.
Brown, Sterling Allen, 1901-
The devil and the black man.

(In: Folk-say, a regional miscellany... 1929-32. Norman, University of Oklahoma Press, 1929-32. 23½cm. pp. 246-56).

M811.5
B715e Poetry.
Brown, Sterling Allen, 1901-
[Eight poems].

Contents: Transfer. -Old Lem. -Conjured. Colloquy. -Bitter fruit of the tree. -Slim in hell. Break of day. Glory, glory.
Inscribed by Sterling Brown.

(In: Anderson, George Kumler., ed. This generation; a sélection of British and American literature ... New York, Scott, Foresman, 1939. 25½cm. p. 762-763).

Poetry.

M811.5 Brown, Sterling Allen, 1901-
B815 Southern road, poems by Sterling A. Brown; drawings by E. Simms Campbell. New York, Harcourt, Brace and company [c1932]

xv, 135 p. incl. plates. 21cm.
"First edition."

I. Title.

Library of Congress PS3503.R833S6 1932 32-13137
——— Copy 2.
Copyright A 51325 [38g1] 811.5

Poetry

M811.08 The Brown thrush, anthology of verse by Negro students ...
B81 Bryn Athyn, Pa., Claremont, Calif., Lawson-Roberts publishing company [c1932-1935

2v. illus. 23cm.
Vol. 1, edited by Lillian W. Voorhees, Robert W. O'Brien; v. 2, edited by Helen M. O'Brien, Lillian W. Voorhees, Hugh M. Gloster.
Vol. 2, published Memphis, Tenn., The Malcolm-Roberts publishing co.

1. College verse. 2. Negro poetry (American) I. Voorhees, Lillian Welch, ed. II. O'Brien, Robert Welch, ed. III. O'Brien, Helen M., ed. IV. Gloster, Hugh Morris, ed.

Library of Congress PS591.N4B67 32—18258
——— Copy 2.
Copyright A 52920 [37r36e1] 811.50822

Poetry.

M811.5 Browne, Lambert W
B818p Poems. n.p., n.d.

6p. 16cm.

Poetry.

M811.5 Bryant, Joseph G
B84s Stepping back. Philadelphia, A.M.E. Book Concern, n.d.

16p. ports. 15cm.

1. Poetry. I. Title.

Poetry.

M811.5 Bush, Olvia Ward.
B96d Driftwood. [Providence, R.I., Atlantic Printing Co., c1914]
86p. port. 18cm.

Poetry.

M811.5 Butler, Alpheus.
B97 Make way for happiness, by Alpheus Butler. Boston, The Christopher publishing house [c1932]

x p., 1 l., [13]-188 p. 21cm.
Poems.

I. Title. [Full name: James Alpheus Butler]

Library of Congress PS3503.U84M3 1932 32-19489
Copyright A 53240 [2] 811.5

Poetry.

M811.5 Butler, Alpheus.
B97 Make way for happiness, by Alpheus Butler. Boston, The Christopher publishing house [c1932]

x p., 1 l., [13]-188 p. 21cm.
Poems.

I. Title. [Full name: James Alpheus Butler]

Library of Congress PS3503.U84M3 1932 32-19489
Copyright A 53240 [2] 811.5

Poetry.

M811.5 Butler, Alpheus.
B97s Sepia vistas, by Alpheus Butler ... New York, The Exposition press [c1941]

68, [1] p. 19cm.
Poems.

I. Title. [Full name: James Alpheus Butler]

Library of Congress PS3503.U8484 42-8440
[2] 811.5

Poetry.

M811.5 Butler, Anna Land
B977t Touch stone. Wilmington, Delaware Poetry Center, 1961.

29p. 23cm.

1. Poetry. I. Title.

Poetry.

M811.5 Byer, D P ,pseud.
B99c Conquest of Coomassie; an epic of the Mashanti nation, by Aldebaron. With illustrations by Henry M. Brooks. Long Beach, Califronia, publishers [c1923]
103p. port. 16cm.

Poetry.

M811.5 Byer, Dabron P , pseud.
B99c Conquest of Coomassie; an epic of the Mashanti nation, by Aldebaron. With illustrations by Henry M. Brooks. Long Beach, California, publishers [c1923]

103p. port. 16cm.

Poetry.

M811.4 Campbell, Alfred Gibbs.
C15p Poems. By Alfred Gibbs Campbell. Newark, N. J., Advertiser printing house, 1883.

vii, 120 p. 21cm.

I. Title.

Library of Congress PS1252.C2P6 21-17735
Copyright 1883: 8111 [36b1]

Poetry.

M811.5 Cannon, David Wadsworth, 1910-1938.
C16 Black labor chant, and other poems, by David Wadsworth Cannon, jr., 1910-1938; illustrations by John Borican. [New York] The National council on religion in higher education [c1939]

56 p. front. (port.) illus. 24cm.

I. Title. 40—3918

Library of Congress PS3501.O28B55 1939
——— Copy 2.
Copyright A 137179 [40c2] 811.5

Poetry.

M811.5 Carmichael, Waverly Turner.
C21f From the heart of a folk, a book of songs, by Waverly Turner Carmichael, with an introduction by James Holly Hanford. Boston, The Cornhill company . c1918.

ix, 60p. 19½cm.

Poetry.
M811.5 C23r
Carrigan, Nettie W.
Rhymes and jingles for the children's hour, by Nettie W. Carrigan ... Boston, The Christopher publishing house [c1940]
3 p. l., v-vi p., 1 l., 9-57 p. 19cm.
I. Title.
40-29658
Library of Congress PZ8.3.C23Rh
—— Copy 2.
Copyright [3]

Poetry.
M811.5 C55r
Clarke, John Henrik.
Rebellion in rhyme, by John Henrik Clarke. Prairie City, The Decker press [c1948]
105p. 22cm.

Poetry.
M811.5 C69e
Collins, Leslie M
Exile, by Leslie M. Collins. A book of verse. [Atlanta, Ga., The B. F. Logan press, 1938.
39p. 19cm.

Poetry.
Martinique M841.91 C33c
Césaire, Aimé, 1913-
Cadastre; poèmes. Paris, Editions du Seuil, 1961.
91p. 19cm.

Poetry.
M811.5 C59r
Clem, Charles Douglass, 1875-
Booker T. Washington [a poem].
Broadside 16½ x 27½cm.

Poetry.
M811.5 C81h
Corbett, Maurice N
The harp of Ethiopia, by Maurice N. Corbett. Nashville, Tenn., National Baptist publishing board, 1914.
276p. 20cm.

Poetry.
M811.5 C471
Chumbly, Harold A
It may be poetry. 1st ed. [n.p.] 1943.
62p. 23cm.
Author may not be Negro

Poetry.
M811.5 C59r
Clem, Charles Douglass, 1875-
A little souvenir, by Chas. D. Clem. [n.p.n.p.] c1908.
[8] p. port. 19½cm.

Poetry.
M811.5 C82b
Cotter, Joseph S eamon , jr. 1895-1919.
The band of Gideon and other lyrics, by Joseph S. Cotter, Jr., Boston, THe Cornhill company [c1918.]
x, 29, 1 p. 19½cm.

Poetry.
M861.6 C86c
Cinq poemes. Nicolas Guillen, Robin Wilson, Brian Howard, Randall Swingler, Hans Gebser. Les poetes du mon e defendent le peuple espagnol... madrid, n.d.
8 p. 25½cm.

Poetry.
M811.5 C59r
Clem, Charles Doiglass, 1875- Rhymes of a rhymster. Edmond, Oklahoma, The author, 1901.
52p. port. 17½cm.

Poetry.
M811.5 C82co
Cotter, Joseph Seamon, 1861-
Collected poems of Joseph S. Cotter, sr. New York, H. Harrison [c1938]
78 p. incl. front. (port.) 21½cm.
38-17934
Library of Congress PS3505.O862A17 1938
—— Copy 2.
Copyright A 119429 [3] 811.5

Poetry.
M811.5 C54pt
Clark, B
The past, present, and future; in prose and poetry. Toronot, Adam, Stevenson and Co., 1867.
168p. port. 16½cm.
Pages missing.

Poetry.
M811.5 C61w
Clifford, Carrie Williams,
The widening light, by Carrie Williams Clifford. Boston, Walter Reid Co., c1922
ix, 65p. 23cm.

Poetry.
M811.5 C82w
Cotter, Joseph Seamon, 1861-
A white song and a black one, by Joseph S. Cotter. Louisville, Ky., The Bradley & Gilbert co., 1909.
64 p. incl. front. (port.) 18cm.
I. Title.
9-22188
Library of Congress PS1449.C4W5
Copyright A 244598 [a38b1]

Poetry.
M811.5 C54g
Clark, *Mrs.* Mazie Earhart.
Garden of memories, by Mazie Earhart Clark ... Cincinnati, O., Eaton publishing company, c1932.
1 p. l., 7-62 p. 1 illus., mounted port. 23cm.
Poems.
I. Title.
33-3626
Library of Congress PS3505.L3654G3 1932
Copyright A 60186 [3] 811.5

Poetry.
M811.5 C65m
Coffey, John
A Negro speaks of life. Karlsruhe, Germany, Printed by Engelhardt and Bauer, 1961.
31p. 18cm.

Poetry.
M811.5 C83w
Cowdery, Mae V.
We lift our voices, and other poems, by Mae V. Cowdery. With a frontispiece for the title poem, by Allan Freelon and an introduction by William Stanley Braithwaite. Philadelphia, Alpress, 1936.
68p. front. 21cm.
This is no. 291 of 350 numbered copies.

Poetry (American)
M811.5 C541a
Clark, Peter Wellington, *ed.*
Arrows of gold; an anthology of Catholic verse from "America's first Catholic college for colored youth," edited by Peter Wellington Clark. New Orleans, La., Xavier university press, 1941.
x, 85, [1] p. pl. 21cm.
1. Negro poetry (American) 2. College verse—Xavier university, New Orleans. 3. American literature—Catholic authors. 4. American literature—Southern states. I. Xavier university, New Orleans. II. Title.
41—10132
Library of Congress PS591.N4C5
[41c2] 811.50822

Poetry.
M811.5 C69b
Collins, Leslie M
Biography portraits in verse. [Nashville, Fisk University, n.d.]
17p. 22cm.

Poetry.
M811.5 C831
Cox, Ollie
Last call for peace. New York, Arlain Printing Company, 1959.
87p. port. 21cm.

Poetry.
M811.5 Crowder, Henry
C88h
Henry - Music; poems. Poems by various authors, music arranged by Henry Crowder. Paris, Hours Press, 1930.

20p. illus. 32p.
Contents: Equatorial Way, by Nancy Cunard.-Madrigal, by Richard Aldington.-Creed, by Walter Lowenfels.-From the Only Poet to a Shining Whore, by Samuel Backett.-From Tiresias, by Harold Acton.-Memory Blues, by Nancy Cunard.

Poetry.
M811.5 Cullen, Countee, 1903–
C89ba
The ballad of the brown girl, an old ballad retold, by Countee Cullen, with illustrations and decorations by Charles Cullen. New York and London, Harper & brothers, 1927.
4 p. l., 11 p. double pl. 20cm.

I. Title.
Library of Congress PS3505.U287B3 1927 27-18068
——— Copy 2.
Copyright A 990537 [33e2]

Poetry.
M811.5 Cullen, Countee, 1903–
C89b
The black Christ & other poems, by Countee Cullen, with decorations by Charles Cullen. New York and London, Harper & brothers, 1929.
xiii, 110 p., 1 l. incl. front., illus., plates. 20cm.
"First edition."

I. Title.
29-24220
Library of Congress PS3505.U287B6 1929
[44p1]

Poetry.
M811.08 Cullen, Countee, 1903– ed.
C89ca
Caroling dusk; an anthology of verse by Negro poets, edited by Countee Cullen; decorations by Aaron Douglas. New York and London, Harper & brothers, 1927.

xxii p., 1 l., 237, [1] p. 21½cm.

Poetry.
M811.5 Cullen, Countee, 1903–
C89
Color, by Countee Cullen. New York and London, Harper & brothers, 1925.
xvii, 108 p. 19½cm.
Poems.
"First edition."

I. Title.
25-21678
Library of Congress PS3505.U287C6 1925
[44g1]

Poetry.
M811.5 Cullen, Countee, 1903-
C89c
Copper sun, by Countee Cullen... with decorations by Charles Cullen. New York and London, Harper & brothers, 1927.
xi, 89p. illus. 20cm.
"First edition G-B".

Poetry.
M811.5 Cullen, Countee, 1903–
C89c
Copper sun, by Countee Cullen ... with decorations by Charles Cullen. New York and London, Harper & brothers, 1927.
xi, 89 p. illus. 20cm.
Poems.

I. Title.
27-16151
Library of Congress PS3505.U287C65 1927
[44d1]

Poetry.
M811.5 Cullen, Countee, 1903–
C891
The lost zoo (a rhyme for the young, but not too young) by Christopher Cat and Countee Cullen, with illustrations by Charles Sebree. New York and London, Harper & brothers [°1940]
6 p. l., 72 p., 1 l. col. front., col. plates. 24cm.
Illustrated lining-papers in colors.
"First edition."

I. Sebree, Charles, illus. II. Title.
40-34870
Library of Congress PZ8.3.C889Lo
[45k1]

Poetry.
M811.5 Cullen, Countee, 1903–
C89m
The Medea and some poems, by Countee Cullen. New York and London, Harper & brothers, 1935.
vi p., 2 l., 3-97 p., 1 l. 21cm.
"The Medea of Euripides, a new version by Countee Cullen": p. 1-64.
"First edition."

I. Euripides. Medea. II. Title.
35-13206
Library of Congress PS3505.U287M4 1935
[43i1] 811.5

Poetry.
M811.5 Cullen, Countee, 1903-1946.
C89o
On these I stand; an anthology of the best poems of Countee Cullen. Selected by himself and including six new poems never before published. New York and London, Harper & brothers [1947]
x, 197, [1] p. 21cm.
"First edition."
I. Title.
PS3505.U287A6 1947 811.5 47-30109
© 22Jan47; publisher, New York; A10416.

Library of Congress [20]

Poetry.
M811.5 Cuney, Waring, 1906-
C91p
Puzzles. Selected and introduced by Paul Breman. With 8 two-color woodcuts by Ru van Rossem. Utrecht, De Roos, 1960.

79p. illus. 32cm.
"175 copies were printed on Darwin paper for members of Stichting 'De Roos'. This is number 83."

Poetry.
M811.5 Cuthbert, Marion Vera, 1896–
C97
April grasses, by Marion Cuthbert. New York, The Womans press [°1936]
3 p. l., 30 p. 19½cm.
Poems.

I. Title.
36-8483 rev
Library of Congress PS3505.U963A8 1936
[r43d2] 811.5

Poetry.
M811.5 Cuthbert, Marion Vera, 1896-
C97s
Songs of creation. New York, Woman's Press [1949]

46p. 19cm.

Poetry.
M811.5 Dancer, W E
D19s
Sunshine and shadows. A concert book of Easter, Christmas and exhibition speeches for an occasion, by W.E. Dancer...Jacksonville, Florida, Sentinel Print [1930?]

130p. port. 18½cm.
Fifth edition.

Poetry.
M811.5 Dandridge, Raymond Garfield.
D19de
Penciled poems, by Ray G. Dandridge. Cincinnati, O. [Powell & White, printers] 1917.
51, [1] p. incl. port. 19½cm. $1.00

I. Title.
18-505
Library of Congress PS3501.D3P4
——— Copy 2.
Copyright A 481104

Poetry.
M811.5 Dandridge, Raymond Garfield.
D19p
The poet and other poems, by Raymond Garfield Dandridge. Cincinnati, O. [Powell & White] 1920.
6 p. l., 15-64 p. 19½cm.

I. Title.
20-15360
Library of Congress PS3501.D3P6 1920
——— Copy 2.
Copyright A 576134 [2]

Poetry.
M811.5 Dandridge, Raymond Garfield.
D19z
Zalka Peetruza and other poems, by Raymond Garfield Dandridge. Cincinnati, The McDonald Press, 1928.
xiii, 107p. port. 24cm.
autographed presentation copy.

Poetry.
M821.91 Darlington, Levi A.
D24c
Calliope, by Levi A. Darlington. Trinidad, Cosmopolitan Printing Works, 1938.
124p. 19½cm.

Poetry.
M811.08 Davidman, Joy, *ed.*
D28w
... War poems of the United nations; three hundred poems, one hundred and fifty poets from twenty countries. Sponsored by the League of American writers. Edited by Joy Davidman. New York, Dial press, 1943.
ix, 395 p. 21cm.
At head of title: The songs and battle cries of a world at war.

1. World war, 1939– —Poetry. 2. English poetry—20th cent. 3. American poetry—20th cent. 4. English poetry—Translations from foreign literature. I. Title.
43-18223
Library of Congress D745.2.D3
[40] 940.5401

Poetry.
M811.4 Davis, Daniel Webster, 1862–
D29i
Idle moments, containing Emancipation and other poems, by D. Webster Davis. With an introduction by John H. Smythe ... Baltimore, Md., The Educator of Morgan college, 1895.
81 p. 2 pl., port. 17 cm.

I. Title.
24-11130
Library of Congress PS1514.D55
[48b½]

Poetry.
M811.4 Davis, Daniel Webster, 1862–
D29
'Weh down souf, and other poems [by] Daniel Webster Davis. Illustrations [by] William L. Sheppard ... Cleveland, The Helman-Taylor company, 1897.
vi, 7-136 p. front., 3 pl. 18½cm.
Appendix: Introduction to the author's first volume of poems [Idle moments] by John H. Smythe.
Glossary.

I. Title.
24-11131
Library of Congress PS1514.D56
Copyright 1897: 67169 [32b1]

Poetry.

M811.5 D28b
Davis, Frank Marshall, 1905–
Black man's verse, by Frank Marshall Davis. Chicago, Ill., The Black cat press, 1935.
5 p. l., 13–83 p., 1 l. 25½cm.

I. Title.
35-16597
Library of Congress PS3507.A727B6 1935
——— Copy 2.
Copyright A 85803 [37c1] 811.5

Poetry.

M811.5 D28
Davis, Frank Marshall, 1905–
I am the American Negro, by Frank Marshall Davis. Chicago, Ill., Black cat press, 1937.
5 p. l., 13–69, [1] p. 24cm.
Illustration on t.-p.
Poems.
"First edition."

I. Title.
37–2962
Library of Congress PS3507.A727I2 1937
——— Copy 2.
Copyright A 103600 [37d2] 811.5

Poetry.

M811.5 D29t
Davis, Frank Marshall
Through sepia eyes, by Frank Marshall Davis. Decorations by William Fleming. Chicago, Black cat press, 1938.
10p. illus. 24½cm.

Poetry.

M811.5 D29m
Davis, Walter Max.
The man with the pipe, by Walter Max Davis. Atlantic City, N.J., W. M. Davis, c 1945.
60p. 20½cm.

M811.5 D34l
Poetry.
Deas, Katherine.
Life line poems. Chicago, Edward C. Deas.
32p. port. 18cm.

Martinique M841.91 D46s
Poetry.
Desportes, George, 1921-
Sous l'oeil fixe du soleil; poèmes masqués. Paris, Debresse-Poèsie, 1958.
127p. 19cm.

Africa M896.1 D55
Poetry.
Dick, A J B ed.
The Cambridge book of verse for African schools. Cambridge, The University Press, 1966.
100p. 21½cm.
White editor.

1. African poetry. 2. Poetry. I. Title.

Poetry.

M811.5 D550
Dickerson, Noy Jasper
Original poetry, by Noy Jasper Dickerson. Bluefield, W. Va, The author c1927
33p. 17cm.

Poetry.

M811.5 D55s
Dickerson, Noy Jasper.
A scrap book, by Noy Jasper Dickerson. Boston, The Christopher publishing house [c1931]
48 p. 20½cm.
Prose and verse.

I. Title.
31-35186
Library of Congress PS3507.I 2683 1931
Copyright A 41823 [3] 818.5

Poetry.

M811.5 D611
Dinkins, Charles Roundtree.
Lyrics of love, by Charles R. Dinkins. Columbia, S. C., The State company [1904]
280 p. 2 port. (incl. front.) 19cm.

I. Title.
4–11500
Library of Congress PS3507.I 647L5 1904
Copyright [a39b1]

Poetry.

M811.5 D66p
Dodson, Owen, 1914–
Powerful long ladder, by Owen Dodson ... New York, Farrar, Straus and company, inc., 1946.
4 p. l., 103 p. 21cm.
Poems.

I. Title.
46–6372
Library of Congress PS3507.O364P6 [47f3] 811.5

Poetry.

M811.5 D73t
Dorsey, Thomas A.
Thomas A. Dorsey's poem book for all occasions Chicago, Ill, The author, [c1945]
36p. 22cm.

Poetry.

M811.4 D91c
Dunbar, Paul Laurence, 1872–1906.
Candle-lightin' time, by Paul Laurence Dunbar; illustrated with photographs by the Hampton institute camera club and decorations by Margaret Armstrong. New York, Dodd, Mead & co., 1901.
127 p. incl. front., illus., plates. 22½cm.
Title within ornamental border; text within floreated oval borders, in green.
Poems.
"First edition published October, 1901."

I. Title.
1–25641
Library of Congress PS1556.C2 1901 [40f1]

Poetry.

M811.4 D91ch 1907
Dunbar, Paul Laurence, 1872-1906.
Chris'mus is a' comin' & other poems by Paul Laurence Dunbar. New York, Dodd, Mead & Co., 1907.
48p. 14½cm.

Poetry.

M811.4 D91ch
Dunbar, Paul Laurence, 1872-1906.
Chris' mus' is a' comin' & other poems, by Paul Laurence Dunbar. New York, Dodd, Mead & Co. [1905]
48p. 14½cm.

Poetry.

M811.4 D91co
Dunbar, Paul Laurence, 1872–1906.
The complete poems of Paul Laurence Dunbar, with the introduction to "Lyrics of lowly life," by W. D. Howells. New York, Dodd, Mead and company, 1913.
xxxii, 289 p. front. (port.) 21cm.

13—25781
Library of Congress PS1556.A1 1913 [43h1]

Poetry.

M811.4 D91h
Dunbar, Paul Laurence, 1872–1906.
Howdy, honey, howdy, by Paul Laurence Dunbar; illustrated with photographs by Leigh Richmond Miner, decorations by Will Jenkins. New York, Dodd, Mead and company, 1905.
[125] p. incl. front., illus., pl. 22½cm.

I. Title.
5—33661
Library of Congress PS1556.H6 1905 [a35b1]

Poetry.

M811.4 D91j
Dunbar, Paul Laurence, 1872–1906.
Joggin' erlong, by Paul Laurence Dunbar; illustrated with photographs by Leigh Richmond Miner and decorations by John Rae. New York, Dodd, Mead & company, 1906.
119 p. incl. front., illus., plates. 22½ cm.
Plates printed on both sides. Ornamental borders.

I. Title. 1. Poetry.
6—37888
Library of Congress [38g1]

Poetry.

M811.4 D91Lig
Dunbar, Paul Laurence, 1872–1906.
Li'l' gal, by Paul Laurence Dunbar; illustrated with photographs by Leigh Richmond Miner ... decorations by Margaret Armstrong. New York, Dodd, Mead and co., 1904.
123, [1] p. incl. front., illus. 22½cm.
Ornamental borders.

I. Title.
4—30974
Library of Congress PS1556.L5 1904 [45f1]

Poetry.

M811.4 D91 li
Dunbar, Paul Laurence, 1872–1906.
Little brown baby [by] Paul Laurence Dunbar; poems for young people. Selections, with biographical sketch by Bertha Rodgers; illustrated by Erick Berry [pseud.] New York, Dodd, Mead & company, 1940.
xiv, 106 p. incl. plates. 21 cm.

1. Poetry.
I. Rodgers, Bertha, ed. II. *Best, Allena (Champlin) 1892– illus. III. Title.
40—4721
Library of Congress PZ8.3.D918Li [45t1]

Poetry.

M811.4 D91ly
Dunbar, Paul Laurence, 1872–1906.
Lyrics of love and laughter, by Paul Laurence Dunbar. New York, Dodd, Mead and company, 1903.
xi, 180 p. front. 17cm.

I. Title.
3—7777
Library of Congress PS1556.L55 1903 [44b1]

Poetry.
M811.4 D91 lyl
Dunbar, Paul Laurence, 1872-1906.
Lyrics of lowly life, by Paul Laurence Dunbar, with an introduction by W. D. Howells. New York, Dodd, Mead and company, 1896.
xx, 208 p. front. (port.) 17cm.
1. Title. 1. Poetry.
4-13820
Library of Congress PS1556.L6 1896
——— Copy 2. 16cm. (p. 199-208 wanting)
[42u2]

Poetry.
M811.4 D91lyr
Dunbar, Paul Laurence, 1872-1906.
Lyrics of sunshine and shadow, by Paul Laurence Dunbar. New York, Dodd, Mead & company, 1905.
x p., 1 l., 109 p. front. 17cm.
1. Title.
5-12695
Library of Congress PS1556.L65 1905
Copyright [86h1]

Poetry.
M811.4 D91lyh
Dunbar, Paul Laurence, 1872-1906.
Lyrics of the hearthside, by Paul Laurence Dunbar. New York, Dodd, Mead and company, 1899.
x, 227 p. front. (port.) 16cm.
1. Title.
99-1025
Library of Congress PS1556.L7 1899
[43f1]

Poetry.
M811.4 D91m
Dunbar, Paul Lawrence, 1872 - 1906
Majors and minors; poems, by Paul Lawrence Dunbar, [Toledo, Ohio, Hadley and Hadley, printers, c 1895]
148p. port.

Poetry.
M811.4 D91o
Dunbar, Paul Lawrence, 1872-1906.
Oak and ivy, by Paul Dunbar. Dayton, Ohio, Press of United brethen publishing house, 1893.
[5]-62p. 19½cm.

Poetry.
M811.4 D91p 1900
Dunbar, Paul Laurence, 1872-1906.
Poems of cabin and field, by Paul Laurence Dunbar, illustrated with photographs by the Hampton Institute Camera Club and decorations by Alice Morse. New York, Dodd, Mead & Co., 1900.
125p. illus. pl. 22cm.

Poetry.
M811.4 D91p
Dunbar, Paul Laurence, 1872-1906.
Poems of cabin and field ... illustrated with photographs by the Hampton institute camera club and decorations by Alice Morse. New York, Dodd, Mead & co., 1899.
125 p. illus., pl. 8°.
1. Title.
99-5828
Library of Congress (a) (PS1556.P6 1899)
[45k1]

Poetry.
M811.4 D91s
Dunbar, Paul Laurence, 1872-1906.
Speakin' o' Christmas, and other Christmas and special poems, by Paul Laurence Dunbar; with numerous illustrations. New York, Dodd, Mead and company, 1914.
96 p. front., plates. 18cm $1.00
1. Title.
14-18594
Library of Congress PS1556.S6 1914
Copyright A 387181 [37b1]

M811 D91w
Poetry.
Dunbar, Paul Laurence, 1872-1906.
When Malindy sings poems by Paul Laurence Dunbar; illustrated with photographs by the Hampton institute camera club; decorations by Margaret Armstrong. New York, Dodd, Mead and co., 1903.
3p. l., 9-144p. incl. front. illus. 22cm.
Blue ornamental borders.

M811.08 D91d
Poetry.
Dundo, anthology of poetry by Cleveland Negro youth, edited by Clarence F. Bryson and James N. Robinson, Cleveland, The January Club, 1931.
26p. 17cm.

Poetry.
M811.5 D91
Dungee, John Riley, 1860-
Random rhymes, formal and dialect, serious and humorous, racial, religious, patriotic and sentimental, by J. Riley Dungee. [Norfolk, Va., Guide publishing company, inc., printers] 1929.
101 p., 1 l. ports. 22cm.
1. Title. 1. Poetry.
29-10058
Library of Congress PS3507.D8R3 1929
Copyright A 6723 [2]

Poetry.
M811.5 Ea7
Eastmond, Claude T.
Light and shadows, by Claude T. Eastmond. Boston, The Christopher publishing house [c1934]
1 p. l., [5]-66 p. 21cm.
Poems.
1. Title. 1. Poetry.
34-1969
Library of Congress PS3509.A754L5 1934
Copyright A 69220 [2] 811.5

Poetry.
M811.08 Ee1
Eekhout, Jan H., comp.
De Neger zingt; Amerikaansche Negerlyriek. Amsterdam, Derde Druk Uitgeversmaatschappuholland, n.d.
67p. 19cm.
White compiler.

Poetry.
M811.5 E149s
Elliot, Emily I
Still waters and other poems. Cambridge, The author, 1949.
28p. 19cm.
Portrait attached.

Poetry.
M811.5 E151
Elliott, James A O
"I amwith you always" and other poems - religious, romantic and humorous, by James A.O. Elliott. London, Arthur H. Stockwell, Ltd. [n.d.]
88p. front., plates. 19cm.

Poetry.
M811.5 Ep7
Epperson, Aloise (Barbour)
The hills of yesterday, and other poems by Aloise Barbour Epperson. Norfolk, Va. [Washington, Printed by J. A. Brown] 1943.
74 p. front. (port.) 23½cm.
1. Title.
44-12849
Library of Congress PS3509.P67H5
[2] 811.5

Poetry.
M811.5 F45c
Fields, Maurice C 1915-1938.
The collected poems of Maurice C. Fields. New York, N. Y., The Exposition press [c1940]
5 p. l., 13-64 p. 21½cm.
42-2627
Library of Congress PS3511.I3 1940
——— Copy 2. [3] 811.5

Poetry.
M811.5 F45t
Fields, Maurice C 1915-1938.
... Testament of youth. New York, Pegasus publishing company [c1940]
82 p. 20cm.
Poems.
"First edition."
1. Title.
41-6400
Library of Congress PS3511.I3T4 1940
[2] 811.5

Poetry.
M811.5 F46p
Figgs, Carrie Law Morgan.
Poetic pearls, by Carrie Law Morgan Figgs... Jacksonville, Florida, Edward Waters College Press, 1920.
32p. front (port) 15½cm.

Poetry.
M811.5 F525
Fisher, Gertrude Arquene.
Original poems, by Gertrude Arquene Fisher. Parsons, Kansas.. Parsons, Kansas, Foley Railway Printing Co., c1910
11p. port. 17½cm.

Poetry.
M811.5 F61c
Flanagan, Thomas Jefferson, 1890-
The canyons at Providence (the lay of the clay minstrel) by Thomas Jefferson Flangan.
21 3 p. illus. 22½cm.

M811.5
F61r

Poetry.
Flanagan, Thomas Jefferson, 1890-
The road to Mount McKeithan, by Thomas Jefferson Flanagan. Atlanta, Ga., The independent Publishers, 1927.

38p. [5] leaves. port. (front.) 17cm.

M811.5
F77

Poetry.
Fortune, Timothy Thomas
Dreams of life miscellaneous poems, by Timothy Thomas Fortune.
New York, Fortune and Peterson, 1905.
192p. front. 20½cm.

Martinique
M841.91
G49sa

Poetry.
Glissant, Edouard, 1928-
Le sang rivé; poèmes. Paris, Présence Africaine, 1961.

68p. 18½cm.

M811.5
F61s

Poetry.
Flangan, Thomas Jefferson
Smilin' thru the corn and other verse.
Atlanta Ga., Published by the Independent Publishers corporation [c1927]
68p. 18cm.

M811.08
F82

Poetry.
Four Lincoln University poets. Foreword by President William Hallock Johnson.
Waring Cuney, William Allyn Hill, Edward Silvera, Langston Hughes.
16 p. 21½cm. (Lincoln university Herald, v. 33, no.33, March 1930.)

M811.5
G63m

Poetry.
Goodwin, Ruby Berkley.
From my kitchen window; the poems of Ruby Berkley Goodwin, with an introduction by Margeret Widdemer... New York, W. Malliet and company, 1942.

5p. l., 13-66p. 23½cm.
"First edition"

M811.5
F62c

Poetry.
Fleming, Sarah Lee Brown.
Clouds and sunshine, by Sarah Lee Brown Fleming ... Boston, The Cornhill company [1920]
5 p. l., 53 p. 19½cm.
Poems.

I. Title.
Library of Congress PS3511.L445C6 1920 20-22035
Copyright A 604407

M811.5
F95p

Poetry.
[Fulton, David N.]
A poem - Abraham Lincoln, by "Jack Thorne" ... [New York, 1909]
[4] p. port. 24cm.

M811.5
G65p

Poetry.
Gordon, Selma.
Poems. [lacks imprint]
19p. 15cm.

M811.5
F75s

Poetry.
Ford, Nick Aaron.
Songs from the dark, by Nick Aaron Ford. Boston, Meador publishing company, 1940.
40 p. 20½cm.
Poems.

I. Title.
40-35665
Library of Congress PS3601.F686 1940
——— Copy 2.
Copyright [2] 811.5

M811.5
G17

Poetry.
Gardner, Benjamin Franklin, 1900-
Black [by] Benjamin Franklin Gardner. Caldwell, Id., The Caxton printers, ltd., 1933.
79 p. 19½cm.
Poems.

I. Title.
34-29
Library of Congress PS3513.A6815B5 1933
[2] 811.5

M811.5
G65h

Poetry.
Gordon, Selma.
Shall we live without a sorrow? [poems] [lacks imprint]

Broadside 16½x10

M811.5
F75b

Poetry.
Ford, Robert Edgar.
Brown chapel, a story in verse, by Rev. Robert E. Ford. [Baltimore?] 1905.
307 p. front. (port.) 24 cm.

5-40387
Library of Congress

Jamaica
M821.91
G19se

Poetry.
Garvey, Marcus
Selections from The Poetic meditations of Marcus Garvey.New York, Published by Any Jacques Garvey, c1927.
30p. 20cm.

M811.5
G65s

Poetry.
Gordon, Selma.
Special poems, by Selma Gordon. Book no.3, [Omaha, Nebraska, The author, 1940?]
19p. 17cm.

M811.5
F77o

Poetry.
Fortson, Bettiola Heloise, 1890-
Original poems and essays of Bettiloa Heloise Fortson... [lacks imprint]
62p. port. 17½cm.
contains some prose

M811.5
G34m

Poetry.
Gholson, Edward.
Musings of a minister, by Rev. Edward Gholson. Boston, The Christopher publishing house [1943]
viii, 9-101 p. 19cm.
Poems.

I. Title.
43-11475
Library of Congress PS3513.H6M8
[2] 811.5

M811.5
G65su

Poetry.
Gordon, Selma.
The summerland of God [poem] [lacks imprint]
Broadside 16½ x 10

M815.2
J71t

Poetry.
Fortune, Michael
New Year's anthem, sung in the African episcopal church of St. Thomas, Jan. 1, 1808.
[23] - 24p.
Bound in Absalom Jones, a Thanksgiving sermon, preached January 1, 1808 in St. Thomas's or the African episcopal church, Philadelphia.

M811.5
G42m

Poetry.
Gilmore, F. Grant.
Masonic and other poems. [n.p. n.p.] 1908.

[21] p. port. (front) 18cm.

M811.5
G74d

Poetry.
Govern, Rena Greenlee
Democracy's task, by Rena Greenlee Geovern.
[New York The author 1945]
36p. 23cm.

Poetry.
M398 G76h
Graham, Lorenz B
How God fix Jonah, by Lorenz Graham; wood engravings by Letterio Calapai. New York, Reynal & Hitchcock [1946]
3 p. l., ix-xvi, 171 p. illus. 22½cm.
"Stories [in verse] from the Bible ... in the idiom of the West African native."—Introd.
1. Folk-lore—African, West. 2. Bible—History of Biblical events—Poetry. I. Title.
GR350.G7 398.21 46-8692
© 18Nov46; author, New York; A8388.
Library of Congress [8]

Poetry.
M811.5 G78m
Graves, Linwood D
"Mother", also "the hidden flower... by Linwood D. Graves. [Big Stone Gap, Va., the author, n.d.]
4 unnumb. p. 21½cm.

M811.5 H18t
Poetry.
[Hamilton Junior]
Tales (tails) of the Tigers. World series edition. Detroit, The author, 1940.
16p. 22cm.
Autographed.

Poetry.
M811.5 H18ot
Hamilton, Sarah B Edmonds
Out of my heart; poems. New York, Exposition Press, 1961.
96p. 20½cm.
Portrait of author on back of book jacket.

Poetry.
M811.5 H18s
Hammond, Basil Calvin
Something to remember; poems. New York, Exposition Press, 1960.
87p. 20cm.
Portrait of author on book jacket.

M811.5 H19m
Poetry.
Handy, Olive Lewis.
My deeply solemn thoughts. n.p. 1939.
35p. 19cm.
Autographed.

Poetry.
M811.5 H22
Harleston, Edward Nathaniel, 1869–
The toiler's life; poems, by Edward Nathaniel Harleston; with an introduction by L. S. Crandall. Philadelphia, The Jenson press, 1907.
xv, 238 p. front. (port.) 19½cm.
Introduction (biographical) by L. S. Crandall.
I. Title.
7–32335
Library of Congress PS3515.A6T6
Copyright A 182881 [a39b1]

Poetry.
M811.4 H23a
Harper, Francis Ellen Watkins, 1825-1911.
Atlanta offering; poems, by Frances E.W. Harper. Philadelphia, 1006 Bainbridge Street, 1895.
70p. 17cm.

Poetry.
M811.4 H23i
Harper, Francis Ellen Watkins, 1835-1911.
Idylls of the Bible, by Mrs. F.E.W. Harper. Philadelphia, 1006 Bainbridge Street, 1901.
64p. port. 16½cm.

Poetry.
M811.4 H23m
Harper, Frances Ellen Watkins, b. 1825.
Moses: a story of the Nile, by Mrs. F.E.W. Harper. Second edition. Philadelphia, Merrihew and son, 1869.
47p. 15cm.

M811.4 H23p 1900
Poetry.
Harper, Frances Ellen Watkins, b. 1825.
Poems, by Frances E. Watkins Harper. Philadelphia, 1006 Bainbridge Street, 1900.
vi, 90p. front. (port.) 17cm.

Poetry.
M811.4 H23p 1898
Harper, Francis Ellen Watkins, 1825-1911.
Poems, by Francis E.W. Harper. Philadelphia, 1006 Bainbridge Street, 1898.
74p. 14cm.

Poetry.
M811.4 H23p 1896
Harper, Francis Ellen Watkins, 1825-1911.
Poems, by Frances E.W.Harper. Philadelphia, 1006 Bainbridge Street, 1896.
vi, 74p. port. (front) 17cm.

Poetry.
M811.4 H23p
Harper, Frances Ellen Watkins, *b.* 1825.
Poems. [By] Frances E. Watkins Harper. Philadelphia, Merrihew & son, printers, 1871.
48 p. 15cm.
Cover has imprint: Providence, A. C. Greene, printer, 1876.
Library of Congress PS1799.H7P6 1871 1-987
[a33b1]

Poetry.
M811.4 H23po 1874
Harper, Mrs. Frances Ellen (Watkins), 1825-
Poems on miscellaneous subjects, by Frances Ellen Watkins. Twentieth edition. Philadelphia, Merrihew & Son, 1874.
56p. 14½cm.
Miscellaneous writings prose: 48-56.
Preface signed: W.L.G. [i.e. Wm L. Garrison?]

Poetry.
M811.4 H23pd
Harper, *Mrs.* Frances Ellen (Watkins) *b.* 1825.
Poems on miscellaneous subjects, by Frances Ellen Watkins. 10th thousand. Philadelphia, Merrihew & Thompson, printers, 1857.
56 p. 16½cm.
"Miscellaneous writings [prose]": p. 48-56.
Preface signed: W. L. G. (*i. e.* Wm. L. Garrison?)
26-20586
Library of Congress PS1799.H7P7 1857

Poetry.
M811.4 H23s
Harper, Frances Ellen Watkins, b. 1825.
Sketches of southern life, by Frances E. Watkins Harper. Philadelphia, Merrihew and son, 1888.
58p. 15½cm.

Poetry.
M811.4 H23sp
Harper, Frances Ellen Watkins, b. 1825,
The sparrow's fall... and other poems, by Frances E.W. Harper. [n.p., n.p., n.d.]
22p. port. 16cm.

M811.5 H23r
Poetry.
Harreld, Claudia White, -1952.
Remembered encounters. Atlanta, Logan Press, 1951.
44p. 24cm.
Inscribed by author.

Poetry.
M811.5 H24t
Harris, Helen C.
Triad. Poems by Helen C. Harris, Lucia Mae Pitts [and] Tomi Carolyn Tinsley. Privately published, December, 1945.
95p. 21cm.

Poetry.
M811.5 H24l
Harris, Leon R
Locomotive puffs from the back shop, by Leon R. Harris. Boston, B. Humphries, inc. [1946]
56 p. 19½cm.
1. Railroads—Poetry. I. Title.
46-18741
Library of Congress PS3515.A755L6
[3] 811.5

Poetry.
M811.5 H24st
Harris, Leon R
The steel makers and other war poems ... by Leon R. Harris. Portsmouth, Ohio T.C. McConnell printery c1918.
15p. 21cm.

Poetry.
M811.4 H35m
Heard, Josephine D. (Henderson), 1861-
Morning glories, by Josephine D. (Henderson) Heard, Philadelphia, Penna. March 17, 1890.
108p. port. 18cm.

Poetry.
M910 H43v
Hershaw, Fay McKeene.
Verse along the way. 1st ed. New York, Exposition Press 1954
48p. 21cm.

Poetry.
M811.5 H25h
Harrison, Eunice B
Here is my heart. New York, Carlton Press, 1962.
55p. 21cm.
Portrait of author on book jacket.

Poetry.
M811.5 H38d
Henderson, Elliott Blaine
Darkey ditties; poems. Columbus, Ohio, 1915.
54p. 20cm.

Poetry.
M811.5 H53
Higgs, Oliver F
Into the realm, a collection of poems. Connecticut, The Poet's Press, 1954.
37 p. 23 cm.
Inscribed by author.

Poetry.
M811.5 H24s
Harrison, James Minnis, 1873-
Southern sunbeams, a book of poems by James M. Harrison. Richmond, Virginia, The Saint Luke press, 1926.
100p. port. 20cm.

Poetry.
M811.5 H38h
Henderson, Elliott Blaine.
Humble folks; poems composed by Elliott Blaine Henderson... Springfield , Ohio, Published by the author, 1909.
65p. 21cm.

Poetry.
M811.5 H55a
Hill, Anne K
Aurora, poems. New York, The author, 1948.
53p. front. (port.) 20cm.

Poetry.
M811.5 H32f
Hayden, Robert Earl.
Flying shadow, poems. n.p., n.d.
41 l. 29cm.
Type-written.

Poetry.
M811.5 H38j
Henderson, Elliott Blaine.
Jes' Plain Black Fo'ks; Blain Henderson... Springfield, Ohio, n.p. n.d.
51p. port. (front.) 21cm.

Poetry.
M811.5 H55s
Hill, Julious C.
A song of magnolia, by Julious C. Hill ... Boston, Meador publishing company, 1937.
88 p. 20½cm.
1. Title.
37-10960
Library of Congress PS3515.I 4988S 1937
——— Copy 2.
Copyright A 105846 [3]
811.5

Poetry.
M811.5 H32h
Hayden, Robert Earl.
Heart-shape in the dust; poems by Robert E. Hayden. Detroit, Mich., The Falcon press [c1940]
1 p. l., [5]-63 p. 23cm.
1. Title.
41-2241
Library of Congress PS3515.A9363H4 1940
——— Copy 2.
Copyright [3]
811.5

Poetry.
M811.5 H38o
Henderson, Elliott Blaine.
Old fashioned black fo'ks; poems, by Elliott Blaine Henderson. Columbus, Ohio, Published by the author, 1913.
54p. 18½cm.

Poetry.
M811.5 H55so
Hill, Julius C
A sooner song, by Julius C. Hill. New York, Empire books [c1935]
63p. 19½cm.

Poetry.
M811.5 H32k
Hayden, Robert Earl, comp.
Kaleidoscope; poems by American Negro poets, edited and with an introd. by Robert Hayden. [1st ed.] New York, Harcourt, Brace & World [1967]
xxiv, 231p. ports. (on lining papers) 20cm. (Curriculum-related books)
Portrait of author on book jacket.

Poetry.
M811.5 H38
Henderson, Elliott Blaine.
Plantation echoes; a collection of original Negro dialect poems, by Elliott Blaine Henderson. Columbus, O., Press of F. J. Heer, 1904.
95 p. 19½cm.
1. Negro-English dialects. I. Title.
5-26529
Library of Congress PS3515.E434P6 1904
[a37b1]

Poetry.
M811.5 H55w
Hill, Leslie Pinckney, 1880-
The wings of oppression, by Leslie Pinckney Hill. Boston, The Stratford co., 1921.
5 p. l., 124 p. 19½cm.
Poems.
I. Title.
21-15940
Library of Congress PS3515.I 496W5 1921
[42c1]

Poetry.
M811.5 H32L
Hayden, Robert Earl
The lion and the archer: poems [by Robert Hayden and Myron O'Higgins. Nashville, Tenn., Mills Book Store, 1948.
28p. 24cm.

Poetry.
M811.5 H39o
Henry, Thomas Millard.
The optimist, by Thomas Millard Henry. [New York, Hebbons press, c1928]
1 p. l., v-xii, 49 p. incl. port. 16½cm.
Poems.
I. Title.
28-14449
Library of Congress PS3515.E579O7 1928
——— Copy 2.
Copyright A 1077617 [3]

Poetry.
M811.5 H55t
Hill, Mildred Martin.
A traipsin' heart, by Mildred Martin Hill. New York, W. Malliet and company, 1942.
4 p. l., 7-81 p. 23½cm.
Poems.
I. Title.
42-22604
Library of Congress PS3515.I 4976T7
[2]
811.5

Poetry.
M808.81 Hollo, Anselm, comp.
H728 Negro verse. London, Vista Books, 1964.
48p. 18½cm.
White compiler.

Poetry.
M811.5 Horne, Frank
H78 Haverstraw. London, Paul Breman, 1963.
40p. 21½cm. (Heritage, 3)

Poetry.
M811.5 Hughes, Langston, 1902-
H87fi Fields of wonder [by] Langston Hughes. New York, A. A. Knopf, 1947.
xiii, 114, [1] p., 1 l. 22cm.
Poems.
"First edition."
I. Title.
[Full name: James Langston Hughes]
PS3515.U274F45 811.5 47—2075
© 24Feb47; author, Atlanta; A11146.
Library of Congress [47k5]

Poetry.
M811.5 Holloway, John Wesley
H72b Bandanas. [n.p.n.p. n.d.]
119p. 18½cm.

Poetry.
M811.5 Howard, Alice Henrietta.
H83 Onion to orchid; poems by Alice Henrietta Howard. New York, The William-Frederick press, 1945.
32 p. 19½cm. (On cover: The William-Frederick poets. (No. 18))
I. Title.
46-1304
Library of Congress PS3515.O81505
[3] 811.5

Poetry.
M811.5 Hughes, Langston, 1902-
H87fin Fine clothes to the Jew, by Langston Hughes. New York, A. A. Knopf, 1927.
89p., 1 l. 19½cm.

Poetry.
M811.5 Holloway, John Wesley.
H72f From the desert, by John Wesley Holloway ... New York, The Neale publishing company, 1919.
ix, 11-147 p. 19½cm.
Poems.
I. Title.
20—1246
Library of Congress PS3515.O424F7 1919
Copyright A 561241 [38d1]

Poetry.
M811.5 Howell, Wilbert R.
H839r The rhyme of the devil-germs. New York, Pageant Press, 1963.
28p. illus. 20cm.

Poetry.
M811.5 Hughes, Langston, 1902-
H87fr ... Freedom's plow. New York, Musette publishers [1943]
14 p. 19½cm.
A poem.
Inscribed copy: For Arthur Spingarn, Sincerely, Langston Hughes. New York, May 30, 1943.
I. Title.
[Full name: James Langston Hughes]
43-17249
Library of Congress PS3515.U274F7
[3] 811.5

Poetry.
M811.4 Holly, Joseph Cephas, 1825-1854.
H72f Freedom's offering, a collection of poems. By Joseph C. Holly ... Rochester, C. H. McDonnell, printer, 1853.
38 p., 1 l. 20cm.
I. Title.
27-7631 Revised
Library of Congress PS1949.H58
[r45b2]

Poetry.
M811.5 Huff, William Henry, 1887-
H86f From deep within. Chicago, Dierkes, 1951.
40p. 20cm.

Poetry.
M811.5 Hughes, Langston.
H87fr Freedom's plow. New York, Musette
1943 publishers [c1943]
14p. 19½cm.

Poetry.
M811.5 Holmes, B L
H73i The idol hour. Poetic Works of B. L. Holmes... Edgefield, S.C. [n.d.]
47p. 23cm.

Poetry.
M811.5 Huff, William Henry, 1887-
H86s Sowing and reaping and other poems. Avon Illinois, Hamlet press, 1950.
77p. 22cm.

Poetry.
M811.5 Hughes, Langston, 1902-
H87g Gedichte. Herausgegeben von Eva Hesse und Paridam van dem Knesebeck. Munchen, Langewiesche-Brandt 1960.
1 v. (unpaged) 21cm.
Bibliography included.
Portrait on cover.

Poetry.
M811.5 Horn, Max T ed.
H78 Stories in verse. New York, Odyssey Press [1943]
430p. 20cm.
Partial contents.- The creation, by James Weldon Johnson.- De Boll Weevil.
1. Poetry. I. Title. II. De Boll Weevil.

Poetry.
M811.5 Hughes, Langston, 1902-
H87d Dear lovely death, by Langston Hughes. Amenia, N.Y., Priv. print. at the Troutbeck press, 1931.
[18]p. mounted front. (port) 21½cm.

Poetry.
M811.5 Hughes, Langston, 1902-
H87negm The Negro mother and other dramatic recitations by Langston Hughes. With decorations by Prentiss Taylor. New York The Golden Stair press 1931
20p. illus. 24cm.
"One of 17 signed copies bound in Robin's paper for presentations only.

Poetry.
M811.5 Horne, Frank, 1899-
H87a Haverstraw; lyrics for the halt. [n.p., n.p., 1960]
16 leaves. 28½cm.
Mimeographed.
"For Arthur Spingarn in appreciation for your warm friendliness through the years. Frank Horne, 5/26/61."
-. Poetry, American. I. Title.

Poetry.
M811.5 Hughes, Langston, 1902-
H87dr The dream keeper and other poems [by] Langston Hughes; with illustrations by Helen Sewell. New York, A. A. Knopf, 1932.
9 p. l., 3-77 p. front., illus. 21cm.
"First edition."
I. Title.
[Full name: James Langston Hughes]
32-19486
Library of Congress PS3515.U274D7 1932
[a46d1] 811.5

Poetry
M811.5 Hughes, Langston, 1902-
H87negm The Negro mother and other dramatic
1931 recitations, by Langston Hughes. With decorations by Prentiss Taylor. New York The Golden Stair Press c1931
20p. 24cm.

Poetry.
M811.08 H87 Hughes, Langston, 1902- ed.
New Negro poets U. S. A. Forward by Gwendolyn Brooks. Bloomington, Indiana University Press ₍1964₎
127p. 21cm.

Poetry.
M811.5 H87w Hughes, Langston, 1902–
The weary blues, by Langston Hughes; with an introduction by Carl Van Vechten. New York, A. A. Knopf, 1926.
109 p. 19½cm.
Poems.
I. Title.
Library of Congress PS3515.U274W4 1926 26—4780 ₍39k1₎

Poetry.
M811.5 J41t Jenkins, Welborn Victor
Trumpet in the new moon and other poems, by Welborn Victor Jenkins. Foreword by E.H. Webster. Boston, The Peabody Press, 1934.
62p. 19cm.

Poetry.
M811.5 H87py Hughes, Langston, 1902-
Poems.
(In: Yoseloff, Thomas. Seven poets in search of an answer... New York, B. Ackerman, 1944.) pp. 41-52.

Poetry.
M811.08 Iz9 Izzo, Carlo, comp.
Poesia Negro-Americana, a cura di Carlo Izzo presentazione e traduzioni di Gianna Menarini ₍Milano₎ Nuova Accademia ₍1963₎
263p. illus. 20cm.
Bibliografia generale: p. 253-256.
1. Poetry. I. Title.

Poetry.
M811.5 J41b Jenkins, William H.
"Blossoms" (dedicated to my mother) by William H. Jenkins.
35p. 17½cm.

Poetry.
M811.5 H87sh Hughes, Langston, 1902-
Shakespeare in Harlem, by Langston Hughes, with drawings by E. McKnight Kauffer. New York, A. A. Knopf, 1942.
7p. l., 3-124p., 1 l. incl. front. illus. 22cm.

Poetry.
M811.4 J13v Jackson, A J
A vision of life and other poems. By A. J. Jackson. Hillsborough, O., Printed at the Highland news office, 1869.
52 p. 20cm.

Poetry.
M811.5 J62s Johnson, Adolphus.
The silver chord; poems by Adolphus Johnson. Philadelphia, Pa., ₍n.p.n.d.₎
48p. 19½cm.

Poetry.
M811.5 H87si2 Hughes, Langston, 1902-
₍Six broadsides, poem₎ Illus. by Aaron Douglas, n.p.,n.d.
6 broadsides. 41 x 29cm.
Contents: Hard luck. - Down an' out. - Misery. Bound no'th blues. - Lonesome place. - Feet o' Jesus.
Inscribed by author: For my friend - Arthur Spingarn - Sincerely, Langston Hughes. March 1931.

Poetry.
M811.5 J15s Jacobson, Harriet Price
...Songs in the night. New York, the Exposition press c1947
63p. 22cm.
At head of title: Poems by Harriet Price Jacobson.
Inscribed copy: To the Hon. Arthur B. Spingarn, from the author Harriet Price Jacobson.

Poetry.
M811.5 J624m Johnson, Charles Bertram
The mantle of Dunbar and other poems. ₍by₎ Chas. Bertram Johnson. ₍Kirksville, Missouri, The author, 1917?₎
32p. 20cm.

Poetry.
M811.5 H87j Hughes, Langston, 1902-
Jim Crow's last stand. New York Negro publications society of America, c 1943.
30p. 19cm. (Race and culture series, no. 2)
Inscribed copy: For Arthur Spingarn, my first booklet published by a Negro publisher. Sincerely, Langston Hughes. New York, May 15, 1944.

Latin America Poetry.
M808.8 J19 Jahn, Janheinz, comp. and tr.
Rumba macumba; Afrocubanishe lyrik. Munchen, Carl Henser Verlag, 1957.
79p. 20cm.

Poetry.
M811.5 J624s Johnson, Charles Bertram.
Songs of my people ₍by₎ Charles Bertram Johnson. Boston, The Cornhill company ₍1918₎
vi, 55 p., 1 l. 19½cm.
I. Title.
Library of Congress PS3601.J55S6 1918 19-5146
——— Copy 2.
Copyright A 512775 ₍2₎

Poetry.
M811.08 H87p Hughes, Langston, 1902- ed.
The poetry of the Negro, 1746-1949; an anthology ed. by Langston Hughes and Arna Bontemps. ₍1st ed.₎ Garden City, N. Y., Doubleday, 1949.
xviii, 429 p. 22 cm.
1. Negro poetry. 2. Negro poetry (American) 3. Negro race—Poetry. I. Bontemps, Arna Wendell, 1902- joint ed. II. Title.
Full name: James Langston Hughes.
PN6109.7.H8 811.082 49—7193*
Library of Congress ₍50g¹10₎

Poetry.
M811.5 J24n Jamison, Roscoe C
The Negro business league of St. Joseph, Mo.
2p. 19cm.
Bound with: Roscoe C. Jamison's Negro soldiers.

Poetry.
M811.5 J628a Johnson, Charles R H
An afterthought. n.p., ₍194 ₎
₍4₎p. 20cm.

Poetry.
M811.5 H87so Hughes, Langston
A song of spain poem In: Deux poemes par Federico Garcia Lorca et Langston Hughes. Les poetes du monde defendent le peuple espagnol 3... 1937
4 p. 21cm.
Inscribed: To author Spingarn. Sincerely, Langston Hughes

Poetry.
M811.5 J24n Jamison, Roscoe C
Negro soldiers ("these truly are the brave") and other poems, by Roscoe C. Jamison. Second edition. St. Joseph, Mo., William F. Neil, 1918.
12 unnumb. p. port. 21½cm.

Poetry.
M811.5 J6321 Johnson, Fenton.
A little dreaming, by Fenton Johnson. Chicago, The Peterson linotyping company, 1913.
80 p. front. (port.) pl. 20cm. $0.75
Poems.
I. Title.
Library of Congress PS3519.O245L5 1913 13-15814
Copyright A 347983

Poetry.

M811.5 J632s

Johnson, Fenton, 1888–

Songs of the soil, by Fenton Johnson ... New York, F. J. [°1916]

3 p. l., iii, [1], 39 p. 16½cm. $0.50

Reprinted in part from the Citizen.

I. Title.

Library of Congress PS3519.O245S6 1916 16-6071

Copyright A 427114

Poetry

M811.08 J63b

Johnson, James Weldon, 1871–1938, *ed.*

The book of American Negro poetry, chosen and ed. with an essay on the Negro's creative genius, by James Weldon Johnson ... New York, Harcourt, Brace and company [1922]

xlviii, 217 p. 20cm.

1. Negro poetry (American) I. Title.

Library of Congress PS591.N4J6 22-5616 [42y2]

Poetry.

M811.5 J63s

Johnson, James Weldon, 1871–1938.

Saint Peter relates an incident, selected poems by James Weldon Johnson. New York, The Viking press, 1935.

ix p., 1 l., 13-105 p. 24cm.

I. Title.

Library of Congress PS3519.O2625A6 1935 35-22363 [a42d1] 811.5

Poetry.

M811.5 J632v

Johnson, Fenton, 1888–

Visions of the dusk, by Fenton Johnson ... New York, F. J. [°1915]

4 p. l., [1], 71 p. front. (port.) 16½cm. $1.00

Poems.

I. Title.

Library of Congress PS3519.O245V5 1915 15-11835

Copyright A 406052

Poetry.

M811.5 J63fi

Johnson, James Weldon, 1871-1939.

... Fifty years; a poem, written by James W Johnson, a graduate of Atlanta university and published in the New York Times, J anuary 1, 1913; with an estimate of its merit and a sketch of the author. [Atlanta, Ga., The Atlanta university press, n.d.]

8p. 14cm. (Atlanta university leaflet, no.27)

Poetry.

M811.5 J63s

Johnson, James Weldon, 1871-1938.

Saint Peter relates an incident of the resurrection day by James Weldon Johnson. New York, The Viking press, 1930.

14p. 26cm.

Poetry.

M811.5 J629a

Johnson, Georgia (Douglas)

An autumn love cycle [by] Georgia Douglas Johnson. New York, H. Vinal, limited, 1928.

xix, 70 p., 1 l. incl. front. 19½cm.

Poems.

I. Title.

Library of Congress PS3519.O258A8 1928 29-1478 [3]

Poetry.

M811.5 J63f

Johnson, James Weldon, 1871–

Fifty years & other poems, by James Weldon Johnson ... with an introduction by Brander Matthews. Boston, The Cornhill company [°1917]

xiv p., 1 l., 92, [2] p. 19½cm.

Reprinted in part from various periodicals.

I. Title. 1. Poetry.

Library of Congress PS3519.O2625F5 18-10300 [38d1]

Poetry.

M811.5 J64c

Johnston, Percy Edward, 1930-

Concerto for girl and convertible, opus no.5, and other poems. [Washington, D.C., Continental Press, c 1960]

19p. 22cm.

Poetry.

M811.5 J629h

Johnson, Georgia (Douglas)

The heart of a woman, and other poems, by Georgia Douglas Johnson, with an introduction by William Stanley Braithwaite. Boston, The Cornhill company, 1918.

xii, 62 p. 19 cm.

I. Title.

Library of Congress PS3601.J6H4 1918 18-19164

Poetry.

M811.5 J63g Lond.ed.

Johnson, James Weldon, 1871-1938.

God's trombones; some Negro sermons in verse, by James Weldon Johnson. London, George Allen & Unwin Ltd., Museum Street.

58p. 22½cm.

Poetry.

M811.5 J99s 1915

Jones, Edward Smyth, 1881-

The sylvan cabin, a centenary ode on the birth of Lincoln, by Edward Smyth Jones; with introduction taken from the N.Y. Times, San Francisco, published by the author, 1915.

9 unnumb. leaves port. (front.) 20½cm.

On cover: Panama-Pacific International Exposition Edition.

Poetry.

M811.5 J629s

Johnson, Georgia (Douglas)

Share my world; a book of poems. [Washington, D.C., Halfway House] 1962.

32p. 15cm.

Poetry.

M811.5 J63g London ed.

Johnson, James Weldon, 1871-1938.

God's trombones; some Negro sermons in verse, by James Weldon Johnson. London, George Allen & Unwin, Ltd. [1929]

58p. 22cm.

Poetry.

M811.5 J714p

Jones, Elois Murry (Redmond)

A pleasant encounter and other poems, by E. H. Jones. New York, Vantage Press, 1964.

59p. 20½cm.

Portrait of author on book jacket.

1. Poetry. I. Title.

Poetry.

M811.5 J629br

Johnson, *Mrs.* **Georgia Douglas (Camp)** 1886–

Bronze: a book of verse, by Georgia Douglas Johnson ... with an introduction by Dr. W. E. B. DuBois. Boston, B. J. Brimmer company, 1922.

3 p. l., 5-101 p. 16cm.

I. Title.

Library of Congress PS3519.O248B7 1922 22-1123 [a42d1]

Poetry.

M811.5 J630

Johnson, James Weldon, 1871–1938.

God's trombones; seven Negro sermons in verse, by James Weldon Johnson, drawings by Aaron Douglas, lettering by C. B. Falls. New York, The Viking press, 1927.

4 p. l., 56 p. plates. 28cm.

I. Title. II. Title: Negro sermons in verse.

Library of Congress PS3519.O2625G6 1927 27-12269 [a41j2]

Poetry.

M811.5 J71b

Jones, Harold R.

Broadway and other poems, by Harold R. Jones. Montclair, New Jersey. n.d.

59p. port. 20cm.

Poetry.

Panama M811.5 J87pm

Johnson, Hugh G , 1910-

Poems. New York, Comet Press Books, 1961.

41p. 20½cm.

Portrait of author on back of book jacket.

Poetry.

M811.5 J63hu

Johnson, James Weldon, 1871-1938.

Huit sermons nègres, par James Weldon Johnson; traduits par J. Roux-Delimal.

Contents: No. 125 Seigneur, écoute; La création du monde; Le fils prodigue; Oraison funèbre. No. 126 Noe construit l'arche; Libère mon peuple; La crucifixion; Jugement dernier.

Inscribed: A mon ami - Arthur B. Spingarn, Hommage cordiale, James Weldon Johnson.

Poetry.

M811.5 J713h

Jones, Joshua Henry, *jr.*

The heart of the world, by Joshua Henry Jones, jr. Boston, The Stratford co., 1919.

2 p. l., 82 p. 19cm.

Poems.

I. Title.

Library of Congress PS3519.O445H3 1919 19-16027

——— Copy 2.

Copyright A 536217 [2]

Poetry.

M811.5 Jones, Joshua Henry.
J713p Poems of the four seas, by Joshua Henry Jones. Boston, The Cornhill publishing co. [°1921]

4 p. l., 3-52 p. 19cm.

I. Title.

Library of Congress PS3519.O445P6 1921 22-1238
Copyright A 654223 [2]

Poetry.

M811.5 Jones, LeRoi.
J72pr Preface to a twenty volume sucide note; [poems] New York, Totem Press in association with Corinth Books [1961]

47p. 21cm.

Poetry.

Martinique
M841.91 Joyau-Dormoy, Alice.
J84c Chant des isles. Paris, Bellenand [1953]

101 p. 20 cm.

I. Title.

PQ2619.O704C5 841.91 A 53-7796

Illinois. Univ. Library for Library of Congress [3]†

Poetry.

M811.08 Kerlin, Robert Thomas, 1866-
K45 Negro poets and their poems, by Robert T. Kerlin ... Washington, D. C., Associated publishers, inc. [°1923]

xv, 285 p. front., illus. (incl. ports.) 19½cm.

1. Negro authors. 2. Negro poetry (American) I. Title.

Library of Congress PS591.N4K4 24-1295
[44e1]

Poetry.

M811.5 King, Bert Roscoe, 1887-
K58 The wise fool. New York Exposition Press, 1959.

79p. 20½cm.

Poetry.

M811.5 Kirton, St. Clair.
K63p Poetic creations, by St. Clair Kirton. [Boston, Mass., Lester Benn, c1943]

36p. 22cm.

Poetry.

M811.5 Knox, Jacqueline Lloyd.
K77b Bittersweets; a book of verse, by Jacqueline Lloyd Knox. [Philadelphia, Dorrance & co., inc. [1938]

50 p. 19½cm.

I. Title.

Library of Congress PS3521.N82B5 1938 38-33362
——— Copy 2.
Copyright A 123192 [2] 811.5

Poetry.

M811.5 LaGrone, Oliver,
L13f Footfalls; Poetry from America's becoming. Detroit, Darel press, 1949.

x, 37p. illus. 22cm.
Biographical sketch by Yale Soifer.

M811.08
L29c Poetry.
1845 Lanusse, Armand, 1812-1867, comp.
Les Cenelles, choix de poesies indigenes... Nouvelle Orleans, Imprime par H. Lauve et compagnie. 1845.

214p. 16½cm.

Poetry.

M811.08 Lanusse, Armand, 1812-1867, comp.
L29c Creole voices; poems in French by free men of color, first
1945 published in 1845, edited by Edward Maceo Coleman ... with a foreword by H. Carrington Lancaster ... A Centennial ed. Washington, D. C., The Associated publishers, inc., 1945.

2 p. l., xlvi, 130 p. 19½cm.

This anthology, compiled by Armand Lanusse, who was also one of the principal contributors, was originally published in New Orleans under title: Les cenelles, choix de poésies indigènes.

Present edition includes poems of V. E. Rillieux and P. A. Desdunes, two later poets (p. [109]-128)

1. American poetry (French)—Louisiana. 2. French poetry—American authors. 3. Negro poetry (American) I. Coleman, Edward Maceo, ed. II. Title.

Library of Congress * PQ3937.L8L32 46-352
[10] 841.082

Poetry.

M808.8 Letteratura Negra. Prefazione di Pier Paolo
L718 Pasolini. [Roma] Editori Ruinti [1961]

2v. 22½cm.

Poetry.

M811.5 Lewis, Carrie Louise, 1932-
L58p Polished pebbles; poems. New York, Exposition Press, 1960.

48p. 20½cm.
Portrait of author on book jacket.

Poetry.

M811.5 Lewis, Robert V
L58 Selected poems. Detroit, Seminary Press, c1948.

22p. 22cm.

Poetry.

M811.5 McBrown, Gertrude Parthenia.
M12 The picture-poetry book, by Gertrude Parthenia McBrown; illustrated by Lois Mailou Jones. Washington, D. C., The Associated publishers, inc., 1935.

x, 73 p. incl. front., illus. 22cm.

Verse for children.

I. Title.

Library of Congress PZ8.3.M124Pi 36-4191
[43d1] 811.5

Poetry.

M811.5 McClellan, George Marion.
M128p The path of dreams, by George Marion McClellan. Louisville, Ky., J. P. Morton & company, incorporated [°1916]

2 p. l., 76 p. 20½cm. $1.25

Poems.

I. Title.

Library of Congress PS3525.A155P3 1916 16-9044
Copyright A 428509

Poetry.

M811.5 McClellan, George Marion, 1860-1934.
M128s Songs of a southerner, by George Marion McClellan. Boston, Press of Rockwell and Chruchill, 1896.

16p. front. 22cm.

Poetry

M811.5 McCorkle, George Washington
M13p. Poems of thought and cheer, by George Washington McCorkle. Petersburg, Va. n.d.

8p. 20½ cm.
autographed by author

Poetry.

M811.5 McCorkle, George Washington
M13po Poems of thought and cheer, by George Washington McCorkle. Washington, D.C., Published under the auspicesof the National bureau of Negro writers and enterainers n.d.

21p. 23½cm.

Poetry.

M811.4 McGirt, James Ephraim.
M17 Avenging the Maine, A drunken A. B., and other poems. By James Ephraim McGirt. Raleigh, Edwards & Broughton, printers, 1899.

86 p. front. (port.) 18cm.

I. Title.

Library of Congress PS3525.A235A8 1899 0-351
Copyright 1899: 68204 [a27f1]

Poetry.

M811.4 McGirt, James Ephraim.
M17 Avenging the Maine, A drunken A. B., and other poems.
1901 By James Ephraim McGirt. Raleigh, Edwards & Broughton, printers, 1899.

86 p. front. (port.) 18cm.

I. Title.

Library of Congress PS3525.A235A8 1899 0-351
Copyright 1899: 68204 [a27f1]

Poetry.

M811.4 McGirt, James Ephraim.
M17f For your sweet sake; poems, by James E. McGirt. Philadelphia, The John C. Winston co. [°1906]

2 p. l., 79 p. front. (port.) 20cm.

Ornamental borders.

I. Title.

Library of Congress PS3525.A235F6 1906 7-4786 Revised
Copyright A 165080 [r30d2]

Poetry.
M811.4 M17s
McGirt, James Ephraim
Some simple songs and a few more ambitious attempts. By James E. McGirt... Philadelphia, George F. Lasher c 1901
72p. front. plates. 18cm.

Poetry.
M811.4 M17t
McGirt, James Ephraim.
The triumphs of Ephraim by James E. McGirt. Philadelphia [The McGirt Publishing Co.] 1907.
131p. front. (port.) illus. 20cm.

Jamaica
Poetry.
M821.91 M19c
McKay, Claude, 1890-
Constab ballads, by Claude McKay. London, Watts & co., 1912.
94p. 20cm.

Poetry.
Jamaica
M821.91 M19h
McKay, Claude, 1890-
Harlem shadows; the poems of Claude McKay, with an introduction by Max Eastman. New York, Harcourt, Brace and company [°1922]
xxi, 95 p. 19½cm.

I. Title.
22—8810
Library of Congress PS3525.A24785H3 1922
——— Copy 2
Copyright A 659695 [38g2]

Jamaica
Poetry
M821.91 M19p
McKay, Claude, 1890-
Poems. In: The Cambridge Magazine. Summer 1920, p. 55-59.

Jamaica
Poetry.
M821.91 M19so
McKay, Claude, 1890-
Songs of Jamaica, by Claude McKay. With an introduction by Walter Jekyll... Kingston, Jamaica, Aston W. Gardner & co., 1912.
140p. front. 18½cm
Music.

Jamaica
Poetry.
M821.91 M19sp
McKay, Claude, 1890-
Spring in New Hampshire and other poems, by Claude McKay. London, Grant Richards, 1920.
40p. 20cm.

Poetry.
M896.2 M28r
Maile, Mallane L.
Ramasoabi le potse. Morija, Sesuto depot, 1947.
30p. 18cm.
"Father of weeping" in Sotho

Poetry.
M811.5 M33e
Margetson, George Reginald
England in the West Indies; a neglected and degenerating empire, by George Reginald Margetson. Cambridge, Mass., The author c1906.
35p. 23½cm.

Poetry.
M811.5 M33e
Margetson, George Reginald
Ethiopia's flight; the Negro question, or, the white man's fear, by George Reginald Margetson, c. Cambridge, Mass., George Reginald Margetson, c1907.
22p. 23cm.

Poetry.
M811.5 M33f
Margetson, George Reginald.
The fledgling bard and the poetry society, by George Reginald Margetson ... Boston, R. G. Badger; [etc., etc., °1916]
111 p. 19½ cm.
In verse.

I. Title.
16—10921
Library of Congress PS3525.A633F6 1916

Poetry.
M811.5 M33s
Margetson, George Reginald.
Songs of life, by George Reginald Margetson. Boston, Sherman, French & company, 1910.
3 p. l., 57 p. 19½cm. $1.00

10-13842
Library of Congress
© June 7, 1910; 2c. June 10, 1910; A 265594; Sherman, French & co., Boston, Mass.

Poetry.
M811.5 M35a
Marshall, Florence E.
Are you awake? by Florence E. Marshall. Lansing, Michigan, Shaw Publishing Co., c1936.
96p. 22½cm.

Poetry.
M811.5 M38n
Mason, Mason Jordon
Notebook 1, 3-4, 23.
New Mexico, Motive Book Shop, n.d.,
v. illus. 21cm.

Poetry.
M811.5 M38n
Mason, Jordan Mason.
Notebook # 23. New Mexico, Motive Book Shop, n.d.
13p. illus. 21cm.

Poetry.
M811.5 M38n
Mason, Mason Jordan
Notebook 23. New Mexico, Motive Book Shop, n.d.
13p. illus. 21cm.

Poetry.
M811.5 M38y
Mason, Mason Jordan
The yardarm of Murphey's kite. Ranches of Taos, New Mexico, Motive Press, 1956.
58p. illus. 24½cm.

Poetry.
M811.5 M46p
Means, St. Elmo.
Rev. St. Elmo Means' poems, essays, musings and quotations, ed. by Rev. St. Elmo Means. [Columbia, S. C., University press, °1920]
3 p. l., 5-97 p. front. (port.) 15½cm.

Library of Congress PS3501.M4A16 1920 20-15164
Copyright A 571832 [3]

Poetry.
M811.5 M46b
Means, Sterling M
The black devils and other poems, by Sterling M. Means. Louisville, Ky., Pentecostal publishing co., 1919.
56p. 19cm.

Poetry.
M811.5 M46d
Means, Sterling M.
The deserted cabin, and other poems, by Rev. Sterling M. Means. Atlanta, Ga., A. B. Caldwell, 1915.
2 p. l., 13-96 p. 20½cm. $0.50

I. Title.
Library of Congress PS3377.M8D4 1915 15-9551
Copyright A 398657

Poetry.
M808.81 M479
Los Mejores versos de la poesía negra. [Buenos Aires, 1943]
40 p. illus. 22 x 10 cm. (Cuadernillos de poesía, 23)
Cover title.

1. Negro poetry.
PN6109.7.M4 57-32519
Library of Congress [8]

Poetry.

M811.4 M521 Menard, John Willis
Lays in summer lands. Poems, by J. Willis Menard. With the press notices of his speech and his appearance in Congress. Washington, Enterprise publishing company, 1879.
vii, 84p. 18cm.
1st edition.

Poetry.

M811.5 M78 Moorer, Lizelia Augusta Jenkins.
Prejudice unveiled, and other poems, by Lizelia Augusta Jenkins Moorer. Boston, Roxburgh publishing company, 1907.
170 p. front. (port.) 19cm.

I. Title.

Library of Congress PS3525.O582P7 1907 7-29524
Copyright A 178092 [a36b1]

Poetry.

M811.5 N47 Newsome, Effie Lee.
Gladiola garden; poems of outdoors and indoors for second grade readers, by Effie Lee Newsome; illustrations by Lois Mailou Jones. Washington, D. C., The Associated publishers, 1940.
xv, [1], 167 p. incl. front., illus. 23½cm.
Illustrated lining-papers in color.

I. Title.

[Full name: Mary Effie (Lee) Newsome]
41-8081
Library of Congress PZ8.3.N467G1
[a45d1]

Poetry.

M813.5 M55d Merritt, Alice Haden.
... Dream themes, and other poems, by Alice Haden Merritt. Philadelphia, Dorrance and company [°1940]
57 p. 20cm. (Contemporary poets of Dorrance (204))

I. Title.

40-8084
Library of Congress PS3525.E677D7 1940
——— Copy 2.
Copyright A 139154 [2] 811.5

Poetry.

M808.81 M83 Morris, Tina, ed.
Victims of our fear. [Blackburn, Eng.] Screeches Publication, n.d.
[36]p. 25½cm.
Mimeographed.
White editor.

Poetry.

M811.5 N51v Nichols, James Emanuel
Verse fragments. New York Vantage Press, 1958.
77p. 21cm.

Poetry.

M811.5 M553G Merriweather, Claybron W.
Goober peas, by Claybron W. Merriweather .. Boston, The Christopher publishing house [°1932]
xii, 13-174 p. 21cm.
Poems.

I. Title.

32-19484
Library of Congress PS3525.E687G6 1932
Copyright A 53239 [2] 811.5

Poetry.

M811.5 M83d Morrison, William Lorenzo.
Dark rhapsody; poems by William Lorenzo Morrison. New York, H. Harrison [1945]
62 p. 20½cm.

I. Title.

46-796
Library of Congress PS3525.O7594D3
[2] 811.5

Poetry.

M811.5 N66g Noad, Emma M
Golden sunshine and other poems, by Emma M. Noad. London, Arthur H. Stockwell, n.d.
24p. 19cm.

Poetry.

M811.5 M58d Middleton, Henry Davis.
Dreams of an idle hour, by Henry Davis Middleton ... [Chicago, Advocate publishing co., °1908]
70 p., 1 l. 21½cm.

9-5468
Library of Congress (Copyright 1908 A 224562)

Poetry.

M811.08 M84 Morton, Lena Beatrice.
Negro poetry in America, by Lena Beatrice Morton. Boston, Mass., The Stratford company, 1925.
4 p. l., 71 p. illus. (music) 18cm.
"The tragedy": p. 57-71.
Bibliography: p. 36; "References used": p. 71.

1. Negro poetry (American)—Hist. & crit. 2. Tragedy. I. Title.
25—15783
Library of Congress PS310.N4M6
——— Copy 2.
Copyright A 861050 [41g1]

Poetry.

M811.08 N94 Nussbaum, Anna, ed.
Afrika singt, eine auslese neuer afro-amerikanischer lyrik, herausgegeben von Anna Nussbaum. Wien und Leipzig, F. G. Speidel [1929]
2 p. l., [7]-169, [3] p., 1 l. 22cm.
"Die nachdichtungen und übertragungen stammen von Hermann Kesser, Josef Luitpold, Anna Siemsen, Anna Nussbaum."

1. Negro poetry (American) I. Kesser, Hermann, 1880- tr. II. Luitpold, Josef, tr. III. Siemsen, Anna, 1882- tr.
29-21778
Library of Congress PS591.N4N8
[2]

Poetry.

M811.5 M591 Miller, Clifford L.
Imperishable the temple: a collection of verse. Mexico City, 1962.
[69]p. 21cm.

Poetry

M811.08 M951 Murphy, Beatrice M ed.
Ebony rhythm, an anthology of contemporary Negro verse. New York, Exposition Press [1948]
162 p. 23 cm.

1. Negro poetry (American) I. Title.
PS591.N4M76 811.5082 48-1162 rev*
Library of Congress [r48f2]

Poetry.

M811.5 N98w Nyabongo, Virginia Lee (Simmons)
Whitecaps [by] Virginia Simmons. [Yellow Springs, O., The Antioch press, 1942]
79p. illus. 21cm.

Poetry.

M811.5 M61i Miller, May
Into the clearing. Washington, The Charioteer Press, 1959.
24p. 19cm.

Poetry.

M811.08 M95 Murphy, Beatrice M ed.
... Negro voices, edited by Beatrice M. Murphy; illustrations by Clifton Thompson Hill. New York, H. Harrison [°1938]
173, [3] p. illus. 21½cm.
At head of title: An anthology of contemporary verse.

1. Negro poetry (American) I. Title.
39—2667
Library of Congress PS591.N4M8
[43d1] 811.50822

Poetry.

M811.5 P16v Paisley, John Walter.
The voice of Mizraim, by John Walter Paisley. New York and Washington, The Neale publishing company, 1907.
122 p. 19cm.
Poems.

I. Title.

7-36904
Library of Congress PS3531.A29V6 1907
Copyright A 190329 [a36b1] 811.5

Poetry.

M814.5 M78p Moore, S Benjamin editor.
..."Poor Ben's choice pebbles, edited by S. Benj. Moore...Durham, N.C., The Moore Print, 1908.
28p. port. 20½cm.

Poetry.

M811.5 M951 Murphy, Beatrice M
Love is a terrible thing, By Beatrice M. Murphy. New York, The Hobson book press, 1945.
ix, 65p. 21½cm.

M811.08 P18 Poetry.
Palms; Negro poets' number, v.IV. no.1. Guadalajara, Mexico, Idella Purnell, 1926.
32p. 20cm.
Special issue containing the work of Negro poets.
Editor: Countee Cullen.
Contents: The Negro renaissance, by Walter White. -Poems by: Arna Bontemps. Albert Rice. Clarissa Scott. Georgia Douglas Johnson. William Stanley Braithwaite. Waring Cuney. Anne Spencer. Countee Cullen. Lewis Alexander. Jessie Fauset.

M811.08
P13
Poetry.
Palms; Negro poets' number, v.IV, no. 1.
Guadalajara, Mexico, Idella Purnell. 1926.
(card 2)

W.E. DuBois, Bruce Nugent. Gwendolyn Bennett.
Helene Johnson. Langston Hughes. -The Weary
blues, by Alain Locke.

Poetry.
M811.3
P29p
Payne, Daniel Alexander, 1811-1894.
The pleasures, and other miscellaneous
poems. By Daniel A. Payne. Baltimore,
Sherwood & Co., 1850.
[8] -43p. 16cm.

Poetry.
M861.08 Pereda Valdés, Ildefonso, 1899- *ed.*
P41a
... Antología de la poesía negra americana. Santiago de
Chile, Ediciones Ercilla, 1936.
155 p., 1 l. 20ᶜᵐ. (Biblioteca América)
Includes bio-bibliographical sketches of the authors.

1. Negro poetry. 2. Negro authors. I. Title.
38-2047
Library of Congress PN6108.P4
[45d1] 808.81

Poetry.
M811.5
P42s
Perkins, Minnie Louise, 1932-
A string of pearls. [Chicago, Ill. c 1945]
16p. port. (on cover) 24cm.

Poetry.
M811.5
P44w
Peters, Ada Tress
War poems, by Peters sisters. [n.p.,
n. p., 1919]
83p. photo, 18½ cm.

Poetry.
M811.5
P54f
Phillips, Hilton Alonzo, 1905-
Flames of rebellion (against enthroned tyranny) by Hilton
A. Phillips ... [Los Angeles, Printed by the California eagle
press, ᶜ1936]
viii, 237 p. port. 22ᶜᵐ.
Prose and poetry.

1. Race problems. 2. Negro race. 3. Negroes. 4. U. S.—Race question.
I. Title.
36-10080
Library of Congress HT1521.P5
——— Copy 2.
Copyright A 92792 [3] 323.1

M811.5
P68e
Poetry
Pitts, Richard Wesley, 1910-
Excelsior., Book of Poems, by Richard
W. Pitts. Holly Springs, Miss., The author,
c1944
20 p. port. 19cm.

Poetry.
M811.5
P68t
Pitts, Richard Wesley, 1910-
Thy kingdom come, thy will be done on
earth, as it is in heaven. Post war
meditations. A book of poems by Richard W.
Pitts. Holly Springs, Miss., The author,
1944
37p. port 22cm.

Poetry.
M811.08
P78
Pool, Rosey E comp.
Beyond the blues; new poems by American
Negroes. Kent, Hand and Flower Press [1962]
188p. 18cm.
"Selected bibliography": p. 186-188.

White editor.

Poetry.
M811.08
P781k
Pool, Rosey Eva, 1905- , ed and tr.
Ik zag hoe zwart ik was; verzen van Noord-
Amerikaanse Negers. Versameld Ingeleid en
van vertalingen voorzien door Rosey E. Pool
en Paul Breman, Den Haag, Bert Bakker,
1958.
203p. 18½cm.
English and Dutch on opposite pages.
"December 20th, 1958, London: Very happy to
be allowed to inscribe this copy for my friend,
Arthur B. Spingarn, Rosey E. Pool."
White editors.
1. Poetry. 2. Biography. I. Breman, Paul,
jt. ed. and tr. II. Title.

Poetry.
M811.5
P81f
Popel, Esther, 1896-
A forest pool, by Esther Popel. Washing-
ton, D. C., Priv. print. Modernistic press
1934.
6p. l., 42p. 22cm.
"Gift edition."
Inscribed copy: "To Mr. Spingarn, Sincerely
and with cordial good wishes—Esther Popel,
1940.

Poetry.
M811.5
P81f
Popel, Esther, 1896-
A forest pool, by Esther Popel. Washington, D. C., Priv.
print. [Modernistic press] 1934.
6 p. l., 42 p. 22ᶜᵐ.
"Gift edition."
Poems.

I. Title.
[Full name: Mrs. Esther (Popel) Shaw]
35-34780
Library of Congress PS3531.O628F6 1934
[3] 811.5

M811.5
P81t
Poetry.
Popel, Esther, 1896-
Thoughtless thinks by a thinkless thought-
er.. Dedicated to my mother and my six best
friends, by Esther A. B. Popel. Lacks imprint
16p. port. 16cm.
Inscribed on title page: "A first venture
to raise money for college expenses! It
netted $100! Esther Popel.

Poetry.
M811.08
P83d
Porter, Edna, comp.
Double blossoms, Helen Keller anthology,
compiled by Edna Porter. New York, L.
Copeland, 1931.
96p. front. (port.) 20cm.

Poetry.
M811.5
P83s
Porter, George W
Streamlets of poetry, by George W. Porter ..
Memphis, Tenn., The author, c1912.
87p. front. 19cm.

Poetry.
M811.5
P83i
Porter, John Thomas
In spite of handicaps; a book of verse.
New York, Comet Press Books, 1959.
50p. 20cm.
Portrait of author on book jacket.

Poetry.
M8115
P91va
Prentice, Bessie Elizabeth
"Various moods" with Marie. Volume
II. Los Angeles, Burris, printer,
c1944.
27p. 16cm.
cover title.

Poetry.
M811.5
P91v
Prentice, Bessie Elizabeth
"Various Moods" with Marie. Los
Angeles, n.p., c 1940
26p. port. 16½cm.
Autographed copy: Marie Prentice.
D.E.S. no. 37 Victory chapter."

Poetry.
M813.4
P97h
Purvis, T T
Hagar; the singing maiden, with other
stories and rhymes, by T. T. Purvis.
Philadelphia, Walton and co., 1881.
28p. 19½cm.

Poetry.
Madagascar
M841.91
R11at
Rabemananjara, Jacques, 1913-
Antidote; poèmes. Paris, Présence
Africaine, 1961.
46p. 19½cm.

Madagascar
M969
R11n
Poetry.
Rabemananjara, Jacques, 1913-
Nationalisme et problèmes Malgaches. Paris,
Presence Africaine, 1958.
219p. 22½cm.

1. Madgascar - Politics and government.
2. Poetry. I. Title.

Poetry.
Madagascar
M969 R11n
Rabemananjara, Jacques, 1913-
Nationalisme et problèmes Malgaches.
Paris, Presence Africaine, 1958.

219p. 22½cm.

1. Madagascar-Politics and government.
2. Poetry. I. Title.

Poetry.
M811.5 R12r
Ragland, J Farley
Rhymes of the times, The Poems of J. Farley Ragland with a foreword by Dr. Arthur Paul Davis. New York, Wendell Malliet and Co., 1946.
110p. 21cm.

Poetry
M811.5 R12h
Ragland, James Farley.
The Home Town Sketch Book. "It happened here." A Souvenir of Brunswick incidents; of dale and hill in Lawrenceville, Ant St. Paul School events, by J. Farley Ragland. Lawrenceville, Va., The Brunswick Times-Gazette Press., 1940.
76p. 21½cm.

Poetry.
M811.5 R12l
Ragland, James Farley.
Lyrics and laughter, a volume of contempory [!] verse by J. Farley Ragland. [Lawrenceville, Va., The Brunswick Times-Gazette press, °1939]
5 p. l., 13-90 p. incl. port. 21cm.

I. Title.
40-4965
Library of Congress PS3601.R27L9 1939
——— Copy 2.
Copyright A 130629 [2] 811.5

Poetry.
M811.5 R21s
Ragland, James Farley, 1904-
Stepping stones to freedom; poems of pride and purpose. Richmond, Virginia, Quality Printing, c 1960.

30p. port. 23cm.

Poetry.
M811.5 R125b
Ratcliff, Theodore P.
Black forever more by Theodore P. Ratcliff... Okolona, Miss., Okolona industrial school, 1939.

36p. port. 23cm.
Inscribed copy: Compliments, T.P. Ratcliff.

Poetry.
M811.4 R21
Ray, Henriette Cordelia, d. 1916.
Poems, by H. Cordelia Ray. New York, The Grafton press, 1910.
ix, [5]-169 p. 19½cm. $1.00

11-9931 Revised
Library of Congress PS3535.A87P6 1910
Copyright A 286137 [r22d2]

Poetry.
M811.5 R23p
Reason, Arthur Wesley, 1887-
Poems of inspiration for better living.
New York, Exposition Press, 1959.

97p. 20½cm.

Poetry.
M811.5 R33m
Reynolds, Evelyn Crawford.
...No alabaster box and other poems, by Eve Lynn, [pseud.] with an introduction by Gene Rhodes. Philadelphia, Alpress, 1936.

37p. 24cm.
Limited edition of 350 copies.

Poetry.
M811.5 R43v
Ridout, Daniel Lyman.
Verses from a humble cottage, by Daniel Lyman Ridout. [Hampton, Va., Hampton institute press, 1924]
28 p. 19cm.

I. Title.
24-18782
Library of Congress PS3535.I 4365V4 1924
Copyright A 802879 [2]

Poetry.
M811.5 R51t
Ritch, Manly.
Thoughts of a postman, by Manly Ritch. 3d ed. Boston, The Christopher publishing house [°1926]
ix, 101 p. front. (port.) 21cm.
Poems.

I. Title.
26-14051
Library of Congress PS3535.I 84T5 1926
Copyright A 901276 [2]

Poetry.
M811.5 R52
Rivers, Conrad Kent, 1933-
These black bodies and this sunburnt face.
Cleveland, Free Lance Press, 1962.

28p. 22cm.

Poems.

Poetry.
M811.5 R632l
Rogers, James Overton, 1933-
Blues and ballads of a black Yankee; a journey with Sad Sam, by J. Overton Rogers. Foreword by Whitney M. Young, Jr. [1st ed.] New York, Exposition Press [1965]
63 p. 21 cm.
Poems.

1. Negroes—Poetry. I. Title.
PS3568.O44B5 811.54 65-5026
Library of Congress [5]

Poetry.
M811.4 R79t
Rowe, George Clinton, 1853-1903.
Thoughts in verse. A volume of poems, by George Clinton Rowe ... Charleston, S. C., Kahrs, Stolze & Welch, printers, 1887.
118 p. port. 18½cm.

I. Title.
29-30827
Library of Congress PS2736.R55T5
Copyright 1887: 13869

Poetry
M811.5 R79
Rowland, Ida.
... Lisping leaves, by Ida Rowland. Philadelphia, Dorrance and company [°1939]
55 p. 20cm. (Contemporary poets of Dorrance. (191))

I. Title.
40-1972
Library of Congress PS3535.O9658L5 1939
——— Copy 2.
Copyright A 135684 [2] 811.5

Poetry.
M808.8 Sa59
Sanz y Díaz, José, 1907- ed.
Lira negra (selecciones españolas y afroamericanas) [Madrid, M. Aguilar, 1945]
380 p. front. 12 cm. (Colección Crisol, núm. 31)
White editor.

1. Negro poetry. 2. Negro authors. 3. Negroes in literature. I. Title. (Series)
A 48-5448*
Yale Univ. Library
for Library of Congress [3]

M811.08 Sc8
Poetry.
Schwarzer bruder; lyrik Amerikanischer neger; gedichte, spirituals, work songs, protestlieder. Enlisch und Deutsch. Leipzig, Verlag Philipp Reclam c1966.

206p. 17cm.
"For Arthur - Sincerely, Langston. New York, August 25, 1966. See pages 37-59."

1. Poetry.

Poetry.
M811.5 Sc81
Scott, Emory Elrage.
Lyrics of the Southland, by Emory Elrage Scott. [Chicago, Printed by Wilton press, °1913]
3 p. l., 9-93 p. 18cm. $1.00

I. Title.
13-8600
Library of Congress PS3537.C88L8 1913
Copyright A 343964

Poetry.
M811.08 S16
The Scribes, St. Louis.
Sing, laugh, weep; a book of poems by the Scribes. With illustrations by Theopolus Williams. St. Louis, Press publishing co., 1944.
126 p. illus. 20cm.

1. American poetry—20th cent. 2. American literature—Missouri—St. Louis. I. Title. 3. Poetry.
44-9876
Library of Congress PS572.S25S35
[46d1] 811.5082

Poetry.
M811.5 Se8b
Seuell, Malchus M , 1911-
The black Christ and verse. Downey, Calif., The Author, 1957.
77p. 21cm.

Poetry.
M811.5 Se8m
Seuell, Malchus M , 1911-
The mad pagan and verse. Downey, California, Elena Quinn, 1959.

72p. 22cm.

Poetry.

M811.5 Se9b

Seymour, Alexander.
Brighter Christmas; Christmas poems, by Alexander Seymour. New York, Cr st publishing co. ⌊1945⌋

16p. 20½cm.

Poetry.

M811.5 Se91

Seymour, Alexander.
Love lighters; love poems, by Alexander Seymour. ⌊New York, Crest publishing co., c1945⌋

15p. 13½cm.

Poetry.

M811.5 Sh1

Shackelford, Theodore Henry.
My country, and other poems, by Theodore Henry Shackelford, illustrated by the author, introduction by Charles Hastings Dodd ... ⌊Philadelphia, Press of I. W. Klopp co., °1918⌋

216 p. front. (port.) plates. 19½cm.

"Contains all the poems included in ... 'Mammy's cracklin' bread'."
Music: p. ⌊158⌋–⌊161⌋

I. Title. 1. Poetry.

18—12942

Library of Congress PS3601.S5M8 1918 ⌊43b1⌋

Poetry.

M811.5 Sh7d

Shoeman, Charles Henry
A dream, and other poems. By Charles Henry Shoeman. Sedond edition. Ann Arbor, Mich., George Wahr, 1899-1900.
viii 9 202p. 15½cm.

Poetry.

M811.5 Si[illegible]r3

Simpkins, Thomas V.
Rhymes of puppy love and others, including Negro dialect, by Thomas V. Simpkins ... Boston, The Christopher publishing house ⌊°1935⌋

x, 13-60 p. 20½cm.

I. Title.

35–876

Library of Congress PS3537.I 7R5 1935
Copyright A 79074 ⌊3⌋ 811.5

Poetry.

M811.4 Su7s

Sluby, M F
Satire. Lines suggested on reading the confession of Dr. B.T. Tanner, editor of the "Christian Recorder", by M.F. Sluby. December 8th, 1881 and May 11th, 1883, Philadelphia, Pa ⌊lacks imprint⌋
8p. 19cm.

Poetry.

M811.5 Sm5p

Smith, John Windsor.
Parted and other poems, by John Windsor Smith. ⌊New York, The author, c1942⌋

16p. port. 19cm.

M811.5 Sm6

Poetry.

Smith, Lucy.
No middle ground, a collection of poems by Philadelphia, The Phila. Council Arts, Sciences and Professions, 1952.

29 p. 22 cm.

Poetry.

M811.5 Sp31w

Spearman, Aurelia L.P. (Childs)
What Christ means to us; a book of religious verse. New York, Carlton Press ⌊1964⌋

99p. 20½cm.

Poetry.

M811.5 St2

Stanford, Theodore Anthony.
Dark harvest, by Theodore Anthony Stanford, with an introduction by Joseph V. Baker. Philadelphia, Pa. ⌊Bureau of Negro affairs⌋ 1936.

ix, 32 ⌊1⌋ p. 23½cm.
Inscribed copy: Theodore Anthony Stanford.

Poetry.

M811.5 St7c

Stone, Leroy Owen,
Continental streamlets (a joint poetical premiere). Poems by Leroy Owen Stone and Percy Edward Johnston. ⌊Washington, D.C., Continental Press, c 1960⌋

7p. 18cm.

Poetry.

M811.5 Sw3e

Sweetwine, Charles.
The earth shall conquer you, an epic poem, by Charles Sweetwine. N.Y.C., Charles Sweetwine, ⌊c 1945⌋

10 unnumb. p. 23cm.

Poetry.

M811.5 T36b

Thomas, Charles Cyrus, 1909–
A black lark caroling, by Charles Cyrus Thomas. Dallas, Tex., The Kaleidograph press ⌊°1936⌋

xii p., 2 l., 17–73 p. 20cm.

Poems.

I. Title. 1. Poetry.

37–4734

Library of Congress PS3539.H566B6 1936
——— Copy 2.
Copyright A 104348 ⌊2⌋ 811.5

Poetry.

M811.5 T36s

Thomas, Charles Cyrus, 1909–
Sweet land of liberty, by Charles Cyrus Thomas ... Dallas, Texas, The Kaleidograph press ⌊n.d.⌋
8p. 21½cm.

Poetry.

M811.5 T371e

Thompson, Aaron Belford.
Echoes of spring. By Aaron Belford Thompson ... Rossmoyne, O., The author, 1901.

2 p. l., 76, ⌊2⌋ p. port. 17½cm.

I. Title.

1–22913

Library of Congress PS3539.H63E4 1901
Copyright A 9503 ⌊a19b1⌋

Poetry.

M811.5 T371 h

Thompson, Aaron Belford.
Harvest of thoughts. By Aaron Belford Thompson ... With an introduction by James Whitcomb Riley. Illustrated by G. T. Haywood. Indianapolis, Ind., The author, °1907.

8 p. l., 110 p. plates, port., facsim. 18cm.

I. Title.

7–28263 Revised

Library of Congress PS3539.H63H3 1907
⌊r42b2⌋ 811.5

Poetry.

M811.5 T371h

Thompson, Aaron Belford.
Morning songs. By Aaron Belford Thompson. Rossmoyne, O., The author, 1899.

82 p., 1 l. port. 18cm.

I. Title.

0–77 Revised

Library of Congress PS3539.H63M6 1899
Copyright 1899; 70950

Poetry.

M811.5 T37g

Thompson, Clara Ann.
A garland of poems, by Clara Ann Thompson ... Boston, The Christopher publishing house ⌊°1926⌋

96 p. 20½cm.

I. Title.

26–15258

Library of Congress PS3539.H645G3 1926
Copyright A 901617 ⌊2⌋

Poetry.

M811.5 T37so

Thompson, Clara Ann
Songs from the wayside. By Clara Ann Thompson. Rossmoyne, Ohio, Published and sold by the author, 1908.
96p. 17½cm.

Poetry.

M811.5 T372w

Thompson, Clara Ann.
What means this beating of the sheep? Poem by Clara Ann Thompson. ⌊Rossmoyne, Ohio, Box 17, 1921⌋
⌊8⌋ p. 17cm.

Poetry.

M811.5 T37s

Thompson, Joseph
Songs of Caroline, by Joseph Thompson. Chicago, Ill., Joseph Thompson 1936
30p. front. 20x11cm.

M811.5 T375a
Poetry.
Thompson, Minnie E. Coleman.
Amateur efforts of Minnie E. Coleman Thompson. n.p. n.d.
29p. 22cm.
Mimeographed.

M811.5 T37g
Poetry.
Thompson, Priscilla Jane.
Gleanings of quiet hours. By Priscilla Jane Thompson ... Rossmoyne, O., The author, °1907.
3 p. l., 100 p. front. (port.) 17½ cm.
I. Title.
Library of Congress PS3539.H68G5 1907 8—6633
[a48b1]

M811.5 T39b
Poetry.
Thornton, George Bennett, 1881–
Best poems, containing all the poetical works of George B. Thornton. 2d ed. Wilberforce, Ohio [1949]
86 p. port. 22 cm.
PS3539.H833 1949 811.5 50-1402
Library of Congress [2]

M811.5 T39b
Poetry.
Thornton, George Bennett, 1881–
Best poems of George B. Thornton ... [Orangeburg, S. C., G. B. Thornton] 1937.
cover-title, 28 p. illus. (port.) 21½cm.
Blank page for "Autographs" (p. 28)
"Biographical sketch": p. [1]
Library of Congress PS3601.T5B4 1937 38-31017
[3] 811.5

M811.5 T39g
Poetry.
Thornton, George Bennett
Great poems. First edition. Wilberforce, Ohio, George B. Thornton [c1946] ix, 41p. front. 22cm.

M811.5 T39s
Poetry.
Thornton, George Bennett, 1881-
Selections from Thornton with notes; a collection of classical poetry... 1st ed. Wilberforce, Ohio. The Author. 1954.
60p. 21cm.

M811.5 T56f
Poetry.
Todd, Walter E.
Fireside musings [poems] by Walter E. Todd. Washington, D. C., Murray brothers, ~~1908~~. 1909 *second edition*
52 p., 1 l. port. 18cm.
Library of Congress (Copyright 1908 A 209240) 8-20855

M811.5 T56f
Poetry.
Todd, Walter E.
Fireside musings [poems] by Walter E. Todd. Washington, D. C., Murray brothers, 1908.
52 p., 1 l. port. 18cm.
Library of Congress (Copyright 1908 A 209240) 8-20855

M811.5 T56a
Poetry.
Todd, Walter E.
A little sunshine, by Walter E. Todd. Washington, D. C., Murray bros. printing co. [°1917]
61 p., 1 l. front. (port.) 16cm. $0.50
Poems.
I. Title.
Library of Congress PS3601.T7L5 1917 17-30029
——— Copy 2.
Copyright A 477525

M811.5 T56b
Poetry.
Todd, Walter E.
A little sunshine, by Walter E. Todd. [n.p., n.p., n.d.]
61p. front. (port.) 15cm.
Poems.

M811.5 T56p.
Poetry.
Todd, Walter E
Parson Johnson's lecture, by Walter E. Todd. Washington, D.C., Murray bros., 1906
45p. front. 19cm.

Venezuela M869.1 T59h
Poetry.
Tomás, Benito Luciano.
Harlemitta dreams, by Benito Luciano Tomás. New York, 1934.
95 p. illus. (port.) 23½cm.
I. Title.
Library of Congress PS3539.O34H3 1934 34-31685
——— Copy 2.
Copyright A 76039 [2] 811.5

M811.5 T59v
Poetry.
Tomlin, J Henri
Varied verses, a book of poems, by J Henri Tomlin. Tampa, Fla., The author, c1937
92p. 16½cm.

M811.5 T61e
Poetry.
Toomer, Jean, 1894–
Essentials, by Jean Toomer. Definitions and aphorisms. Private ed. Chicago [The Lakeside press] 1931.
4 p. l., lxiv p. 18½cm.
"This edition is limited to one thousand numbered copies." This copy is not numbered.
1. Aphorisms. I. Title.
Library of Congress PN6271.T55 32-14189
——— Copy 2.
Copyright A 52188 [2] 818.5

M811.5 T72m
Poetry.
Trent, Hattie Covington
My memory gems. North Carolina, Livingstone College, 1948.
87p. ports. 22cm.
Autographed.

M811.5 T84s
Poetry.
Turner, Adolph John.
The song I sing. New York, Exposition Press [1964]
64p. 20cm.
Portrait of author on book jacket.

M811.5 T85
Poetry.
Turner, Lucy Mae.
'Bout cullud folkses; poems by Lucy Mae Turner. New York, H. Harrison [1938]
64 p. 22cm.
I. Title.
Library of Congress PS3601.T8B6 1938 38-31464
——— Copy 2.
Copyright A 120907 [3] 811.5

M811.5 UN2b
Poetry.
Underhill, Irvin W 1868-
The brown madonna and other poems, by Irvin W. Underhill, Sr. Philadelphia, Pa. [c1929]
95p. 18cm.

M811.5 Un2
Poetry.
Underhill, Irvin W 1868–
Daddy's love, and other poems, by Irvin W. Underhill ... Philadelphia, Pa. [A. M. E. book concern, printers, 1916]
87 p. 19cm. $0.60
I. Title.
Library of Congress PS3541.N4D3 1916 17-548
Copyright A 453468

M811.5 V27c
Poetry.
Vance, Hart.
Cui bono? Dallas, Texas, The author, 1919
12p. 18½cm.

M811.5 V28r
Poetry.
Vandyne, William Johnson
Revels of fancy, by William Johnson Vandyne two lines of verse Boston A.F. Grant, publishers, 1891.
50p. 17½cm.

Poetry.
M811.4 W14 Walden, Islay, 1849-1884.
Walden's miscellaneous poems, which the author desires to dedicate to the cause of education and humanity. Washington, Reed & Woodward, printers, 1872.
4 p. l., [5]-50 p. 14½cm.
Library of Congress PS3129.W49 32-919
Copyright 1872: 8176

Poetry.
M811.5 W152me Walker, James Robert.
Menus of love. New York, Carlton Press, 1963.
130p. 20cm. (A Lyceum book)

Poetry.
M811.5 W152m Walker, James Robert.
Musings of childhood. New York, Comet Press Books, 1960.
115p. 21cm.
Portrait of author on book jacket.

Poetry.
M811.5 W153 Walker, Margaret, 1915-
For my people, by Margaret Walker, with a foreword by Stephen Vincent Benét. New Haven, Yale university press, 1942.
58 p. 24½cm. (Half-title: The Yale series of younger poets, ed. by S. V. Benét. [41])
Poems.
I. Title.
Yale univ. Library for Library of Congress PS3545.A517F6 A 42-4985
[45q4] 811.5

Poetry.
Walker, William
M811.5 W154e Poem book no.8 of everyday life poetry, by William Walker... Chicago, Ill., Wm. Walker, c1942.
16p. port. 22cm.

Poetry.
Walker, William
M811.5 W154ed Poem book number ten by W.M. Walker... Chicago. Ill., The author, c1943.
20p. front. 21cm.

Poetry.
M811.5 W154t Walker, William
This race of mine, by William Walker... Chicago, Ill., Wm. Walker, c 1938.
23p. port. 21½cm.

Poetry.
Walker, William
M811.5 W154el Walker's book no.9 of everyday life poetry [by] Wm. Walker. Chicago. Ill., Wm. Walker, c1943.
16p. port. 21½cm.

Poetry.
M811.5 W154a Walker, William
Walker's no.2 all occasion poem book, every day life poetry, by William Walker... Chicago, William Walker [c1944]
206p. front. 19½cm.

Poetry.
M811.08 W166 Walrond, Eric, 1898- comp.
Black and unknown bards; a collection of Negro poetry, selected by Eric Walrond and Rosey Pool. Kent [England] The Hand & Flower Press [1958]
43p. 21cm.
1. Poetry. I. Pool, Rosey, jt. comp. II. Title.

Poetry.
M811.5 W25t Warren, Samuel Enders, 1903-
The teacher and other poems. Houston, Texas, privately printed, 1953.
23p. 22cm.

Poetry.
M811.5 W25t Warrick, Calvin Horatio.
The true criteria and other poems, by C. Horatio Warrick. Kansas City, Mo., The Sojourner press, 1924.
120 p. port. 20½cm.
I. Title.
Library of Congress PS3545.A763T7 1924 24-22084 Revised
[r41c2]

M811.1 W56e 1770 Poetry.
Wheatley, Phillis, afterwards Phillis Peters, 1753?-1784.
An elegiac poem, on the death of the celebrated divine and eminent servant of Jesus Christ, the Reverend and learned George Whitefield, chaplain to the Right Honourable the Countess of Huntingdon, &c. &c. who made his exit from this transitory state, to dwell in the celestial realms of bliss, on Lord's-day, 30th September, 1770, when he was siez'd with a fit of the asthma, at Newbury-Port, near Boston, New England. In which is a condolatory address

M811.1 W56e 1770 Wheatley, Phillis, afterwards Phillis Peters, 1753?-1784.
An elegiac poem ... (card 2)
to his truly noble benefactress the worthy and pious Lady Huntingdon; and the orphan-children in Georgia, who, with many thousands are left, by the death of this great man, to lament the loss of a father, friend, and benefactor. By Phillis, a servant girl, of 17 years of age, belonging to Mr. J. Wheatley, of Boston;--She has been but 9 years in this country from Africa.

M811.1 W56e 1770 Wheatley, Phillis, afterwards Phillis Peters, 1753?-1784.
An elegiac poem ... (card 3)
Boston: Printed and sold by Ezekiel Russell, in Queen-street, and John Boyles, in Marlboro'-street [1770]
8 p. 19½cm.
Added to.-p., illus.

Broadside
M811.1 W56e 1770 Poetry.
Wheatley, Phillis, afterwards Phillis Peters, 1753?-1784.
An elegiac poem, on the death of that celebrated divine, and eminent servant of Jesus Christ, the late Reverend, and pious George Whitefield, Chaplain to the Right Honourable the Countess of Huntingdon, &c. &c. who made his exit from this transitory state, to dwell in the celestial realms of bliss, on Lord's-day, 30th of September, 1770, when he was seiz'd with a fit of asthma, at Newbury-Port, near Boston, in New England.

Broadside
M811.1 W56e 1770 Wheatley, Phillis ...
An elegiac poem. (card 2)
In which is a condolatory address to his truly benefactress the worthy, and pious Lady Huntingdon, and the orphan-children in Georgia; who, with many thousands, are left, by the death of this great man, to lament the loss of a father, friend, and benefactor. By Phillis, a servant girl, of 17 years of age, belonging to Mr. J. Wheatley, of Boston: -and has been but 9 years in this country from Africa.

Broadside
M811.1 W56e 1770 Wheatley, Phillis ...
An elegiac poem. (card 3)
Boston, Sold by Ezekiel Russell, in Queen-Street, and John Boyles, in Marlboro Street. 1770.
Broadside. 40½ x 33cm.
Framed.
1. Whitefield, George, 1714-1770.
2. Poetry.

Poetry.
M811.1 W56e 1771 Wheatley, Phillis, afterwards Phillis Peters, 1753?-1784.
An elegiac poem on the death of that celebrated Divine and eminent servant of Jesus Christ, the Reverend and learned Mr. George Whitefield...Bp. [29]-31. In: Ebenezer Pemberton Heaven the residence of saints. A sermon occasioned by the sudden and much lamented death of the Rev. George Whitefield...Boston, Printed: London, reprinted, for E. and C Dilly in the Poultry; and sold at the chapel in Tottenham-Court Road, and at the Tabernacle near Moorfields, 1771.
31p. 20cm.

Poetry.
M811.1 W56el 1784 Wheatley, Phillis, afterwards Phillis Peters, 1753?-1784.
An elegy, sacred to the memory of that great divine, the Reverend and learned Dr. Samuel Cooper, who departed this life December 29, 1783 aetatis 59. By Phillis Peters. Boston, Printed and sold by E. Russell, in Essex-Street, near Liberty-Pole, M,DCC, LXXIV.
8p. 18cm.

Poetry.
M811.1 W56m 1838 Wheatley, Phillis, afterwards Phillis Peters, 1753?-1784.
Memoir and poems of Phillis Wheatley, a native African and a slave. Also, poems by a slave...Third edition. Boston, Published by Isaac Knapp, 1838.
155p. 16½cm.

Poetry.

M811.1 W56o

Wheatley, Phillis, afterwards Phillis Peters, 1753?-1784.
An Ode, on the birthday of Pompey Stockbridge
[n.p. n.d.]
Broadside. 10. 5 X 9.5 cm.

Poetry.

M811.1 W56po

Wheatley, Phillis, *afterwards* Phillis Peters, 1753?-1784.
... Poems and letters; first collected edition, ed. by Chas. Fred. Heartman; with an appreciation by Arthur A. Schomburg. New York, C. F. Heartman [1915]
111 p. incl. front. (port.) 24½cm. (*Verso of half-title:* Heartman's historical series, no. 8)
At head of title: Phillis Wheatley (Phillis Peters)
No. 29 of 350 copies printed on Ben Day paper.
I. Heartman, Charles Frederick, 1883- II. Schomburg, Arthur Alfonso, 1874-
15—22732
Library of Congress PS866.W5 1915 [38b1]

Poetry.

M811.1 W56poem 1773

Wheatley, Phillis, afterwards Phillis Peters, 1753?-1784.
Poems on comic, serious, and moral subjects. By Phillis Wheatley, Negro-servant to Mr. John Wheatley, of Boston in New England. The second edition, corrected. London, J. French, bookseller [1773]
124p. front. (port) 18cm.
A unique edition of the first edition-"Poems on various subjects, religious and moral, by Phillis Wheatley, with variant title page.

Poetry,

M811.1 W56po 1816

Wheatley, Phillis, afterwards Phillis Peters, 1753?-1784.
Poems on various subjects, religions and moral. By Phillis Wheatley, Negro servant to Mr. John Wheatley, of Boston, in New-England, London, printed. Re-printed in New-England, 1816.
120 p. 17cm.

Poetry.

M811.1 W56po 1802

Wheatley, Phillis, afterwards Phillis Peters, 1753?-1784.
Poems on various subjects, religious and moral. By Phillis Wheatley, negro servant to Mr. John Wheatley of Boston, in New England. Dedicated to the Countess of Huntingdon. Walpole, N. H. Printed for Thomas & Thomas, By David Newhall, 1802.
86p. 15cm.

Poetry.

M811.1 W56po 1793

Wheatley, Phillis, *afterwards* Phillis Peters, 1753?-1784.
Poems on various subjects, religious and moral. By Phillis Wheatley, negro servant to Mr. John Wheatley, of Boston, in New-England. Albany: Re-printed, from the London edition, by Barber & Southwick, for Thomas Spencer, book-seller, Market-street, 1793.
viii, 9-80, [3] p. 15½ cm.
Signatures: [A]-L⁴, M².
30—20912
Library of Congress PS866.W5 1793 [48b1]

Poetry.

M811.1 W56po

Wheatley, Phillis, *afterwards* Phillis Peters, 1753?-1784.
Poems on various subjects, religious and moral. By Phillis Wheatley, negro servant to Mr. John Wheatley, of Boston, in New-England. Philadelphia: Printed by Joseph James, in Chesnut-street. 1787.
55, [2] p. 16½cm.
Book-plate: Thomas Hornsby, 1793.
26-374
Library of Congress PS866.W5 1787 [2]

Poetry.

M811.1 W56po

Wheatley, Phillis, *afterwards* Phillis Peters, 1753?-1784.
Poems on various subjects, religious and moral. By Phillis Wheatley, negro servant to Mr. John Wheatley, of Boston, in New-England. London: Printed. Philadelphia: Re-printed, and sold by Joseph Crukshank, in Market-street, between Second and Third-streets. 1786.
vi, [2], [9]-66, [2] p. 15½cm.
26-376
Library of Congress PS866.W5 1786 [2]

Poetry.

M811.1 W56po

Wheatley, Phillis, afterwards Phillis Peters, 1753?-1784.
Poems on various subjects, religious and moral. By Phillis Wheatley, Negro servant to Mr. John Wheatley, of Boston, in New England. With memoirs, by W. H. Jackson. Cleveland, Ohio, The Rewell publishing co, [c1886]
149p. front. (Port) 17½cm.

Poetry.

M811.1 W56po

Wheatley, Phillis, *afterwards* Phillis Peters, 1753?-1784.
Poems on various subjects, religious and moral. By Phillis Wheatley, Negro servant to Mr. John Wheatley, of Boston, in New England. London: Printed for A. Bell, bookseller, Aldgate; and sold by Messrs. Cox and Berry, King-street, Boston. MDCCLXXIII.
v, [1] p., 1 l., [9]-124, [3] p. front. (port.) 17½cm.
Signatures: [A]-Q⁴.
30—20911
Library of Congress PS866.W5 1773 [39b1]
———— Copy 2.

Poetry.

M811.1 W56s 1915 oversize

Wheatley, Phillis, afterwards Phillis Peters, 1753?-1784.
Six broadsides relating to Phillis Wheatley (Phillis Peters) with portrait and facsimile of her handwriting. New York, printed for Chas. Fred Heartman, 1915.
8 leaves, facsims. front. (port.) 38cm.

Poetry.

M811.08 W56

Wheeler, Benjamin Franklin, 1854-1919, *comp.*
Cullings from Zion's poets, by B. F. Wheeler, D. D. [Mobile? Ala., ©1907]
384 p. front., ports. 20cm.
1. Religious poetry, American. 2. Negro poetry (American) I. Title.
8—20853
Library of Congress PS595.R4W5
Copyright A 178145 [a37b1] 811.0822

Poetry.

M811.5 W58p

White, Charles Fred, 1876-
Plea of the negro soldier, and a hundred other poems, by Corporal Charles Fred. White ... Easthampton, Mass., Press of Enterprise printing company [©1908]
170, [2] p. front. (port.) 19cm.
I. Title.
8—18094
Library of Congress PS3174.W58
Copyright A 203554 [a31d1]

Poetry

M811.08 W58

White, Newman Ivey, 1892- *ed.*
An anthology of verse by American Negroes, edited with a critical introduction, biographical sketches of the authors, and bibliographical notes by Newman Ivey White ... and Walter Clinton Jackson ... with an introduction by James Hardy Dillard ... Durham, N. C., Trinity college press, 1924.
2 p. l., iii-xi, 250 p. 20½cm. (*Half-title:* Trinity college publications)
"Bibliographical and critical notes": p. 214-237.
1. Negro poetry (American) I. Jackson, Walter Clinton, 1879- joint ed. II. Title.
24—8308
Library of Congress PS591.N4W5 [42k1]

Poetry.

M811.4 W58a

Whitfield, J M.
America and other poems. By J. M. Whitfield. Buffalo, J. S. Leavitt, 1853.
2 p. l., [vii]-viii, [9]-85 p. 15½cm.
I. Title.
31-36846
Library of Congress PS3190.W45
———— Copy 2.

M811.4 W59L

Poetry.
Whitman, Albery Allson, 1851-1901.
Leelah misled; a poem. By A. A. Whitman. Elizabeth-town [Ky.], Richard Larue, printer. 1873.
39p. 14cm.

Poetry.

M811.4 W59n

Whitman, Albery Allson, 1851-1901.
Not a man, and yet a man: by A. A. Whitman. Springfield, O., Republic printing company, 1877.
254 p. front. (port.) 19½cm.
Poems.
1. Slavery in the U. S.—Poetry. I. Title.
31-28854 Revised
Library of Congress PS3187.W2N6 [r42b2]

M811.4 W59r

Poetry.
Whitman, Albery Allson, 1851-1901.
The rape of Florida, by Albery A. Whitman. St. Louis, Nixon - Jones Printing Co. 1884.
95p. front. 19cm.

Poetry.

M811.4 W59t 1890

Whitman, Albery Allson, 1851-1901.
Twasinta's Seminoles; or Rape of Florida. By Albery A. Whitman. Third ed. carefully rev. St. Louis, Nixon-Jones printing co., 1890.
96p. incl. front. (port.) 26cm.

Poetry.

M811.4 W59t

Whitman, Albery Allson 1851- 1901
Twasinta's Seminoles; or, Rape of Florida. By Albery A. Whitman. Rev. ed. St. Louis, Nixon-Jones printing co., 1885.
97 p. incl. front. (port.) 19½cm.
1. Seminole Indians—Poetry. I. Title.
31-28855
Library of Congress PS3187.W2T3
Copyright 1885: 19359 [37b1]

Poetry.

M811.5 W61

Whitney, Salem Tutt
Mellow musings, by Salem Tutt Whitney, with an introduction by Thomas L. G. Oxley ... Boston, Mass., The Colored poetic league of the world, 1926.
XXV, 126p. plates. 19cm.

Poetry.

M811.5 **Wiggins, Bernice Love, 1897–**
W63t Tuneful tales, by Bernice Love Wiggins. El Paso, Tex., 1925.

174 p. 20cm.

In verse.

I. Title.

Library of Congress PS3545.I 246T8 1925 26–1848

Copyright A 875896 ₍2₎

Poetry.

M811.5 **Wilds, *Mrs.* Myra Viola.**
W64t Thoughts of idle hours, by Myra Viola Wilds ... illustrations by Lorenzo Harris ... Nashville, Tenn., National Baptist publishing board, 1915.

81 p. front. (port.) illus. 16cm. $0.65

I. Title.

15–19093

Library of Congress PS3545.I 358T5 1915

Copyright A 410560

Poetry.

M811.5 **Wilkinson, Henry Bertram, 1889–**
W65d Desert sands, a volume of verse touching various topics, by Henry B. Wilkinson ... London, A. H. Stockwell, ltd. ₍1933₎

108 p., 2 l. 18½cm.

I. Title.

A 40–3142

No. Carolina. Univ. Libr. for Library of Congress PS3545.D ₍2₎

Poetry.

M811.5 **Wilkinson, Henry Bertram, 1889–**
W65i Idle hours, by Henry B. Wilkinson. New York, F. H. Hitchcock ₍°1927₎

5 p. l., 86 p. 19½cm.

Poems.

"Only two hundred and fifty copies of this book have been printed and the type distributed."

I. Title.

Library of Congress PS3545.I 398 I 4 1927 28–5706

Copyright A 1013904 ₍3₎

Poetry.

M811.5 **Wilkinson, Henry Bertram, 1889–**
W65s Shady-rest, by Henry B. Wilkinson ... New York, F. H. Hitchcock ₍°1928₎

5 p. l., 69 p. 19½cm.

Poems.

"Only two hundred and fifty copies of this book have been printed and the type distributed."

I. Title.

Library of Congress PS3545.I 398S5 1928 28–21570

Copyright A 1054264 ₍2₎

Poetry.

M811.5 Wilkinson, Henry Bertram, 1889–
W65t Transitory, a poem by Henry B. Wilkinson. Dedicated to a peaceful world. Boston, privately printed for the author by the Popular Poetry Publishers, ₍c1941₎

20p. 16cm.

autographed copy

Poetry.

M811.5 **Williams, Henry Roger, 1869–**
W67 Heart throbs—poems of race inspiration—written by H. Roger Williams ... Mobile, Ala., Gulf city printing co., inc., 1923.

80 p. incl. port. 21cm.

I. Title.

Library of Congress PS3545.I 5282H4 1923 23–6889

——— Copy 2.

Copyright A 698788 ₍2₎

Poetry.

M811.5 **Williams, Louis Albion.**
W6731 In memory of George Washington Carver (a funeral sermon) by Louis Albion Williams; frontispiece by Fred Carlo. Cleveland, O., The American weave magazine ₍1944₎

15 p. illus. (port.). 20½cm.

In verse.

1. Carver, George Washington, 1864?–1943.

44–30848

Library of Congress S417.C3W5 ₍2₎ 811.5

Poetry.

M811.5 **Wilson, William Green, 1867–**
W69r Rhymes & sketches from the cabin fireside, by William Green Wilson. ₍Selma, Ala., Lloyd printing company, °1931₎

2 p. l., 62, ₍2₎ p. 21½cm.

I. Title.

CA 31–1104 Unrev'd

Library of Congress PS3545.I 643R5 1931

——— Copy 2.

Copyright A 45078 811.5

Poetry.

M811.5 Winston, Bessie Brent.
W731 Life's red sea and other poems. Washington, Review and Herald publishing association, 1950.

32p. 14cm.

Poetry.

M811.5 Witherspoon, James William, 1893–
W77b A breath of the muse, a volume of poetic browsings containing several prose writings, by J. William Witherspoon. Illustrated. Columbia, S.C., Hampton publishing company, 1927.

132p. plates. 20cm.

Poetry.

M811.5 **Wood, Odella Phelps.**
W85 Recaptured echoes, by Odella Phelps Wood. New York, The Exposition press ₍1944₎

64 p. 19½cm. ₍Poets of America. Series four₎

I. Title.

45–193

Library of Congress PS3545.O484R4 ₍3₎ 811.5

Poetry.

M811.5 Wright, Bruce McMarion, 1917–
W93b ... From the shaken tower, Poems by Bruce McM. Wright. Cardiff ₍England₎ William Lewis (printers), 1944

38p. 18½cm.

Poetry.

M811.5 **Yancey, Bessie (Woodson) 1882–**
Y15 Echoes from the hills; a book of poems, by Bessie Woodson Yancey. Washington, D. C., The Associated publishers, inc. ₍°1939₎

vi, 62 p. 19½cm.

I. Title.

40–520

Library of Congress PS3547.A5E3 1939 ₍a45c1₎ 811.5

Poetry.

M811.5 Yeiser, Idabelle.
Y361 Lyric and legend. Boston, Christopher Pub. House, ₍1947₎

77p. 21cm.

Poetry - Anthologies.

M811.5 Hughes, Langston, 1902–
H871o Io sono un Negro. A cura di Stefania Piccinato. Milano, Edizioni Avanti, 1960.

103p. 16½cm.

Poetry - Anthologies.

M808.81 Vojáka, Knihovna, comp.
V85 Černošská poesie; světová antologie. Praha, Naše Vojsko, 1958.

371p. illus. 21cm.
Biographies: pp. 361-371.
Czech translations.
White author.

Poetry - anthologies.

M811.08 Works Progress Administration. New Jersey.
W89a An Anthology of Negro poetry by Negroes and others, arranged by Beatrice F. Wormley, and Charles Carter, under the supervision of Benjamin F. Seldon ₍Newark, N.J. n.d.₎

135p. 28cm.

Poetry - Anthology.

M808.81 Poems of 1958. Devon, Arthur H. Stockwell,
P75 1958.

136p. 18½cm.

Poetry - Bibliography.

M01 **Porter, Dorothy (Burnett) 1905–**
P83n North American Negro poets, a bibliographical checklist of their writings, 1760–1944, by Dorothy B. Porter. Hattiesburg, Miss., The Book farm, 1945.

90 p. 23½ cm. ₍Heartman's historical series no. 70₎

"An expansion of the Schomburg checklist."—Pref.

1. Negro poetry (American)—Bibl. I. Schomburg, Arthur Alfonso, 1874–1938. A bibliographical checklist of American Negro poetry. II. Title.

Full name: Dorothy Louise (Burnett) Porter.

Z1361.N39P6 016.811 45—4014

Library of Congress ₍a58n½₎

Poetry - Bibliography

Puerto Rico
M864 **Schomburg, Arthur Alfonso, 1874–**
Sch6b A bibliographical checklist of American Negro poetry, comp. by Arthur A. Schomburg. New York, C. F. Heartman, 1916.

57 p. 25cm. (*Added t.-p.:* Bibliographica americana; a series of monographs ed. by Charles F. Heartman. vol. II)

Printed on one side of leaf only.

"Bibliography of the poetical works of Phillis Wheatley (copyrighted by Charles F. Heartman) ₍reprinted from Heartman's 'Phillis Wheatley (Phillis Peters)'₎": p. 47–57.

1. Negro poetry (American)—Bibl. 2. Wheatley, Phillis, afterwards Phillis Peters, 1753?–1784—Bibl. I. Heartman, Charles Frederick, 1883–

17—7194

Library of Congress Z1231.P7S3 ₍a40b1₎

Poetry—Children.

M811.5 W58a Whiting, Helen Adele.
Along the road (verse for children) by Helen Adele Whiting. [Atlanta, Ga., Superior printing company, 1938]

19p. illus. 19cm.

Poetry - Collections.

M811.08 C91 Cuney, Waring, 1906- ed.
Lincoln University poets; centennial anthology [1854-1954] Edited by Waring Cuney, Langston Hughes, and Bruce McM. Wright. Foreword by Horace Mann Bond; introd. by J. Saunders Redding. [1st ed.] New York, Fine Editions Press [1954]

72 p. 21 cm.
Inscribed by Langston Hughes.
Autographed by authors.

1. Negro poetry (American) I. Title.

PS591.N4C84 811.5082 54-2461 ‡

Library of Congress [2]

Poetry - Collections.

M811.08 Sc9 Schwarzer orpheus, moderne dichtung Afrikanischer völker beider hemisphären.
Ausgewählt und übertragen von Janheinz Jahn. Munchen, Charl Hanser Verlag, 1954.

193p. 23cm.

Poetry - Collections.

M811.08 B14g Bagish, Zishe, ed.
Das gesang von neger volk, überdicht von Zishe Bagish [anthology of Negro poetry translated into Yiddish] Bucharest, 1936.

44p. 13cm.

Poetry - Collections.

M811.08 H42a Hermlin, Stephen, ed.
Auch ich bin Amerika. Dichtingen Amerikanischer neger. Berlin, Volk und Welt, 1948.

144p. 20½cm.

Poetry - Collections.

Africa M896.1 Sy25 Sydow, Eckart von, 1885-1942, ed.
Poesia dei popoli primitivi; lirica religiosa, magica e profana. Scelta, introd. e note di Eckart v. Sydow. [Traduzione di Roberto Bazlen. Modena, Guanda, 1951.

197 p. 24 cm. (Collezione Fenice; edizione fuori serie, 15)

1. Literature, Primitive. 2. Poetry—Collections. 3. Italian poetry—Translations from foreign literature. I. Title.

[PN1347.S] A 52-7577

Illinois. Univ. Library for Library of Congress [1]

Poetry - Collections.

Lat. American M861.08 B21m Ballagos, Emilio, 1910- ed.
Mapa de la poesia Negra Americana. Ilustraciones de Ravenet. Buenos Aires, Editorial Pleamar, 1946.

324p. cm.

Poetry - Collections.

M811.08 M47 Meine dunklen Hände, moderne Negerlyrik in orginal und nachdichtung. Mûchen, Nymphenburger Verlagshandlung, 1953.

90p. 20cm.

Poetry - Collections.

M811.08 Z44p Zenkevitch, Ivan Kushkeen Michael, ed.
Poets of America. XX century, an anthology. Moscow, Literary Art State Publishing House, 1939.

288p. 22cm.
Text in Russian.

Poetry - Collections.

M811.08 B98b Byars, J C
Black and white; compiled and edited by J. C. Byars, Jr. 1st ed. Washington, D. C., Crane Press, 1927.

96p. illus. 24cm.
"First edition limited to 1000 copies."

Poetry - Collections.

M811.08 N92 Nuovissima poesia Americana e Negra con testo a fronto, 1949-1953. Introduzione versione e note c cura di Carlo Izzo. Parma, Ugo Guanda Editore, 1953.

XXVII, 419p. 24cm.

Poetry - Criticism.

Martinique M89 C33j Juin, Hubert
Aimé Césaire; poète noir. Préface de Claude Roy. Paris, Présence Africaine, 1956.

105p. 19cm.

Poetry - Collections.

Africa M808.81 B75 Brent, P L ed.
Young Commonwealth poets '65. London, Heinemann in assocation with Cardiff Commonwealth Arts Festival [1965]

216p. 22½cm.
White editor.

1. Poetry - Collection. 2. African poetry. 3. West Indian poetry. I. Title.

Poetry - Collection.

Latin America M861.08 P41a Pereda Valdes, Ildefonso, 1899- ed.
.. Antología de la poesía negra americana. Santiago de Chile, Ediciones Ercilla, 1936.

155p., 11. 20cm. (Biblioteca America)

Poetry - History and criticism.

M810.9 B81n Brown, Sterling Allen, 1901-
... Negro poetry and drama, by Sterling A. Brown ... Washington, D. C., The Associates in Negro folk education, 1937.

8 p. l., 142 p. 21½cm. (Bronze booklet no. 7)
"Reading references" at end of each chapter.

1. Negroes in literature and art. 2. Negro poetry (American)—Hist. & crit. 3. Negro drama. I. Title.

Library of Congress E185.5.B85 no. 7 38-20046
——— Copy 2. PS153.N5B68
[42n2] (825.260973) 811.09

M811.08 B46 Poetry - Collections.

Berti, Luigi, ed.
Canti negri. Firenze, Fussi [1949]

173p. 17cm. (Il Melagrano, scritti rari e rappresentativi di poesia e pensiero in versioni d'arte con testo a fronte, 52-54).

English, Spanish, or French with Italian translation; added t.p. in English.
Includes bibliographical references.

Poetry - Collections.

M811.08 P58 Piccioni, Leone, ed.
Antologia dei poeti Negri d'America [di] Leone Piccioni [e] Perla Cacciaguerra. Introducione e apprendice critica di Leone Piccioni. [n.p.] Arnoldo Mondadori Editore [1964]

675p. 22cm
White editors.
English and Italian on opposite pages.

Poetry - periodicals.

Rough weather, 1950
Los Angeles, 1950-

v. 22cm.
Frequency varies.

See holdings card for issues in library.

Poetry - Collections.

810.8 C76 Constelación Negra, antologia de la literatura Negro Americana. Traducción del ingles, selección y pórtico de Julio Gómez de la Serna. Barcelona, Ediciones Ayma, 1942.

142p. 19cm.

Poetry - Collections.

Latin America M861.08 Sa Sanz y Diaz, José
Lira Negra (Selecciones espanõlas y Afroamericanas.) Recopilacion prólogo y notas de José Sanz y Diaz. [Madrid, M. Aguilar, 1945]

380p. 12½cm.

Poetry- periodicals.

Suck egg mule; A recalcitrant beast, New Mexico, Ranches of Taos, 1951.

v. illus. 18cm.
See holdings card for issues in library.

Poetry - Segration in transportation - Montgomery, Ala.

M811.5 Morris, Joseph C
M83m Montgomery on the march; a symbol, the bus boycott in Montgomery, Ala. and its meaning, 1955-1956. [New York] Joseph C. Morris, 1956.

9p. 13cm.

1. Poetry - Segration in transportation - Montgomery, Ala. 2. Montgomery, Ala. - Race question - Poetry. I. Title.

British Guiana Poetry - British Guiana.
M821 Gibson, Rufus
G35L Lyrics of life and love. New York, Carlton Press [1964]

96p. 20½cm. (A Lyceum book)

Poetry-Portuguese.

Angola
M896.08 Andrade, Mário Pinto de, 1928-
An2a Antologia da poesia Negra de expressão Portuguesa. Precedida de Cultura Negro-Africana e Assimila, cão. Paris, Pierre

106p. 19cm.
Bibliographical notes.

Poetry - Somali authors.

Somalia
M896.1 Syad, William J F
Sy11k Khamsine; poèmes. Preface de Léopold S. Senghor. Paris, Présence Africaine [1959]

70p. 20cm.
Text in English or French.

Poetry - Congo.

Congo(Leopoldville)
M709 Italiaander, Rolf, 1913-
It1 Kongo; builder und verse. [Gütersloh] C. Bertelsman [©1959]

43p. illus. 19cm.

Poetry-Ruanda.

Rwanda
M967.5 Kagame, Alexis, 1912-
K10d La divine pastorale, traduction français, par l'auteur, de la première Veillée d'une épopée écrite en langue Ruandaise. Bruxelles, Editions du Marais, 1952.

108p. port. plates, 25cm.

Poetry - Study and teaching.

M810.9 Brown, Sterling Allen, 1901-
B81o Outline for the study of the poetry of American Negroes, by Sterling A. Brown... prepared to be used with the book of American Negro poetry, edited by James Weldon Johnson. New York, Harcourt Brace & co., c1931.

52p. 19cm.

Poetry - Ghana.

Ghana
M896.1 Stewart, MacNeill
St4a Appeal to reason -- to the political leaders of the country this poem is respectfully dedicated --. Accra, 1951.

4p. ports. 18cm.

Poetry-Ruanda.

Rwanda
M967.5 Kagame, Alexis, 1912-
K10n La naissance de l'univers. Illustrations par Ant. de Vinck. Bruxelles, Editions du Marais, 1955.

85p. illus. 25cm.

Poetry - Translations into Italian.

M810.9 Piccioni, Leone.
P581 Letteratura dei negri d'America. Milano, Gruppo editoriale "Academia" [1949]

344 p. 22 cm.
Includes bibliographical references.

1. American literature—Negro authors—Hist. & crit. 2. Negro literature (American)—Hist. & crit. 3. Negro poetry (American)—Translations into Italian. 4. Italian poetry—Translations from English. I. Title.

PS591.N4P5 50-24617
Library of Congress [1]

Poetry - Guadeloupe.

Guadeloupe
M841 Béville, Albert
B46 Initation, by Paul Niger [pseud.] Paris, Pierre Seghers, 1954.

45p. 18cm.

Poetry-Ruanda.

Rwanda
M967.5 Kagame, Alexis, 1912-
K10p La poésie dynastique au Rwanda, par Alexis Kagame... Bruxelles, Institut Royal Colonial Belge, 1951.

240p. 24cm.

Poetry - 20th century.

M811.08 Braithwaite, William Stanley Beaumont, 1878- ed.
B73 Anthology of magazine verse for 1913-29 and yearbook of American poetry, edited by William Stanley Braithwaite. New York, G. Sully and company, inc. [1913]-29.

17 v. 22 cm.

1926: Sesqui-centennial edition.
Imprint varies: 1913-14, Cambridge, Mass., Issued by W. S. B.—1915, New York, Gomme & Marshall.—1916, New York, L. J. Gomme.—1917-22, Boston, Small, Maynard & company.—1923-27, Boston, B. J. Brimmer company.—1928, New York, H. Vinal, ltd.—1929, New York, G. Sulley and company, inc.

1. American poetry—20th cent. I. Title. II. Title: Magazine verse. III. Title: Yearbook of American poetry.

Library of Congress PS614.B7 15—26325
[47r36m1]

Poetry - Guadeloupe.

Guadeloupe
M84 Tirolien, Guy
T51b Balles d'or; poemes. [Paris, Présence Africaine, 1960]

91p. 16½cm.

Poetry - St. Lucia.

St. Lucia
M821.91 Walcott, Derek, 1930-
W14i In a green night, poems 1948-1960. London, Jonathan Cape [1962]

79p. 21cm.

Poetry—20th cent.

M811.08 Braithwaite, William Stanley Beaumont, 1878- ed.
B73o Our Lady's choir, a contemporary anthology of verse by Catholic sisters, edited by William Stanley Braithwaite; with a foreword by the Rev. Hugh Francis Blunt and an introduction by Ralph Adams Cram, LITT. D. Boston, B. Humphries, inc., 1931.

xxx, 213, [1] p. 21^{cm}.

2575 copies printed. One of 2000 numbered copies on Hamilton's mellow book.

1. American literature—Catholic authors. 2. American poetry—20th cent. I. Title.

Library of Congress PS591.C3B7 32—26225
[44i1] 811.508

Poetry - Jamaica.

Jamaica
M821.91 McFarland, Harry Stanley, 1900-
M165m Missing pages; poems. Boston, Forum Publishing Co., 1962.

72p. 18cm.

Poetry - Swahili.

Tanganyika
M967.82 Abedi, K Amri
Ab3 Sheria za kutunga mashairi na diwani ya Amri [The poems of Amri with an essay on Swahili poetry and the rules of versification] Kampala, The Eagle Press, 1954.

148p. 21½cm.

British Guiana Poetry - British Guiana.
M821 Carter, Martin
C24 Poems of resistance from British Guiana. London, Lawrence and Wishart, 1954.

18p. 18½cm.

Poetry - Martinique.

Martinique
M841.91 Morand, Florette
M79c Chanson pour ma Savane. Préface de Pierre Mac Orlan. Paris, Librairie de L'Escalier, 1958.

79p. port. 19cm.

Poetry - Swahili.

M896.1 Muyaka bin Haji al-Ghassaniy.
M98d Diwani ya Muyaka bin Haji al-Ghassaniy; pamoja na khabari za maisha yake ambazo zimehadithiwa ni W. Hichens. Johannesburg, University of Witwatersrand press, 1940.

115p. 18cm. (Bantu treasury, no.4)

Swahili poems of Muyaka

Poetry - Trinidad.

Trinidad
M821.91 J77

Joseph, Fitzroy G
A living expression. New York, Pageant Press, Inc., [1958]

60p. 20cm.
Picture and biographical sketch of the author on the book jacket.

Poetry, African.

Ivory Coast
M896.1 B63c

Bognini, Joseph Miezan, 1936-
Ce dur appel de l'espoir, poemes. Paris, Presence Africaine, 1960.

126p. 19cm.
Portrait of author on back of book.

Poetry, African.

S. Africa
M896 J68u

Jolobe, James J R 1902-
Umyezo [by] James J.R. Jolobe, B.A. Amazwi okugabula izigcawu enziwe ngu W.G. Bennie. Johannesburg, The University of the Witwatersrand press, 1944.

viii, 71, [1]p. 18cm. [The Bantu treasury, edited by C.M.Doke. II]
"Xhosa poems... War-time reprint, revised and altered."--p. [ii]

Poetry-Virgin Islands.

M811.5 An29r

Anduze, Aubrey
Reminiscence, by Aubrey Anduze. St. Thomas, Virgin Islands. The art Shop, 1940.
89p. 22½cm.

Poetry, African.

Nigeria
M896.1 C54

Clark, John Pepper, 1935-
Poems. [Pictures by Susanne Wenger. Ibadan, Mbari Publications, 1962]

51p. 26½cm.

Poetry, African.

Africa
M896 M31l

Mangoaela, Zekea D.
Lithoko tsa Marena a Basotho, tse bokeletsoeng ke Z. D. Mangoaela. Morija, Sesuto Book Depot, 1928.

246p. 17½cm.

Poetry - West Indies.

West Indies
M821 H33p

Hazell, Vivian
Poems. Devon, Arthur H. Stockwell, Ltd., [1956]

30p. 18½cm.

Poetry, African.

Sénégal
M896.1 D6221

Diop, Birago, 1906-
Leurres et lueurs; poèmes. Paris, Présence Africaine, [1960]

86p. 19cm.

Poetry, African.

Africa
M896.1 R25

Reed, John, comp. and ed.
A book of African verse, compiled and edited by John Reed and Clive Wake. London, Heinemann Educational Books, 1964.

119p. 18cm.
White compilers.

1. African poetry. 2. Poetry - Africa. I. Title.

Poetry - West Indies.

West Indies
M821.08 K98

Kyk-over-al anthology of West Indian poetry.
Revised by A. J. Seymour. Georgetown, British Guiana, 1957.

99p. 23cm. (Kykoveral 22)

Poetry, African.

Ghana
M896.1 D36a

Dei-Anang, Michael F , 1909-
Africa speaks; a collection of original verse with an introduction on "Poetry in Africa." Accra, Guinea Press, 1959.

99p. 19cm.

Poetry, African.

Senegal
M896.1 Se5a

Senghor, Léopold Sédar, 1906- ed.
Anthologie de la nouvelle poésie nègre et malgache de langue française, par Léopold Sédar Sédar Senghor, précédée de Orphée noir, par Jean-Paul Sartre. [1. éd.] Paris, Presses universitaires de France, 1948.

xliv, 227p. 23cm.

Poetry - Xhosa.

South Africa
M896 M87in2

Mqhayi, Samuel Edward Krune, 1875-
Inzuzo [Reward] Amazwi okugabula izigcawu enziwe ngu Rev. R. Godfrey. [Reprinted in new orthography] Johannesburg, Witwatersrand University Press, 1957.
96p. 18cm. (Bantu treasury, edited by D. T. Cole, VII)
Written in Zhosa.

1. Poetry - Xhosa. 2. Xhosa Poetry. I. Title.

Poetry, African.

S. Africa
M896 J68L

Jolobe, James J R , 1902-
Lovedale Xhosa rhymes (IziGengcelezo zose Dikeni) azilungele la Kabanga: Sub A, Sub B, Std 1, Std 11 ngu James J. Jolobe. Lovedale, The Lovedale Press, 1952.

44p. 19cm.

Poetry, African.

Sénégal
M896.1 Se5n

Senghor, Léopold Sédar, 1906-
Nocturnes; poèmes. Paris, Éditions de Seuil, [1961].

94p. 18½cm.
"A Monsieur Spingarn en hommage".

Poetry - Yoruba.

Nigeria
M896.1 G25y

Gbadamosi, Bakare, comp.
Yoruba poetry, collected and translated by Bakare Gbadamosi and Ulli Beier. Eight silkscreen prints and ten vignetts by Susanne Wenger. Ibadan, Nigeria Printing and Publishing Co., 1959.
68p. illus. 26½cm.
A Special publication of "Black Orpheus"

Poetry, African.

S. Africa
M896 J86p

Jolobe, James J R 1902
Poems of an African. Capetown, Lovedale press, 1946.

34p.

1. Poetry, African 48-21405

Poetry, African.

Africa
M896 Su5c

Sulzer, Peter, comp.
Christ esrscheint am Kongo; Afrikanische Erzählungen und Gedichte gesammelt und Gedichte gesammelt und ubertragen von Peter Sulzer. Heilbronn, Eugen Salzer. [1958,

255p. 20cm.
Biography: p. 248-251.

Poetry - Zulu.

South Africa
M896 V71i3

Vilakazi, Benedict Wallet, 1906-1947.
Inkondlo Kazulu [Zulu poems] Namazwi ebika alotshwe ngu Dr. Innes B. Gumede. [4th ed.] Johannesburg, Witwatersrand University Press, 1955.
63p. illus. 18cm. (Bantu treasury, edited by C. M. Doke, I)

1. Poetry - Zulu. 2. Zulu - Poetry. I. Title.

Poetry, African.

South Africa
M896 J68u2

Jolobe, James J R
Umyezo. [Xhosa poems] Amazwi okugabula izigcawu enziwe ngu Dr. W. G. Bennie. [Reprinted in new orthography] Johannesburg, Witwatersrand Press, 1957.
87p. 18cm. (The Bantu treasury, ed. by D. T. Cole, II)

1. Xhosa Poetry. 2. Poetry, African. I. Title. II. Series.

Haiti
M841 B38c

Poetry, Haitian.
Beauge, Jacqueline
Climats en Marche. Port-au-Prince, Imprimerie des Antilles, 1962.

29p. port. 21cm. (Collection Haiti littéraire)

Haiti
M841
B76c

Poetry, Haitian.

Brierre, Jean Fernand, 1909-
Cantique à trois voix pour une Poupée d'ébène; poeme. [Paris] Collection Librairie Indigene, 1960.

21p. port. 13½cm.

Haiti
M841
M58am

Poetry, Haitian.

Michel, Jacques P
Amour immorte'elle; poèmes. «Port-au Prince, Imprime au Centre Audio Visuel, n.d.»

41p. leaves illus., port. 20½cm.
Cover title.
Portrait of author in book.

Poetry of places - Bahamas.

Bahamas
M821
C89

Culmer, Jack, *comp.*
A book of Bahamian verse. [2d ed.] London, J. Culmer [1948]

41 p. 28 cm.
Contents: Bliss Carman. H.C. Christie. Pennington Haile. Richard Kent. Richard Le Gallienne. Julia Warner Michael. Margaret Joyce Scott. Iris Tree.

1. Bahamas—Descr. & trav.—Poetry. 2. Poetry of places—Bahamas.

PN6110.P7B3 1948 808.81 49-29929*

Library of Congress [3]

Haiti
M841
B76ch

Poetry - Haitian.

Brierre, Jean Fernand, 1909-
Aux champs pour occide; sur un clavier bleu et rouge; hommage au maître Occilius Jeanty. Port-au-Prince, Imprimerie N. A. Theodore, 1960.

43p. 18½cm.

Haiti
M841
M82f

Poetry, Haitian.

Morisseau, Roland
5 poèmes de reconnaissance. Port-au-Prince, Imprimerie Theodore, 1961.

29p. 18½cm.
Portrait of author on back of book.

Haiti
M841
D734

Poetry of places-Caribbean area.

Dorismond, Jean Baptiste.
Sur les traces de Caonabo et de Toussaint-Louverture; poèmes caraïbes [par] Félix Desroussels [pseud.] Préf. de Jean-Baptiste Dorismond. Port-au-Prince, Impr. de l'État, 1953.

246 p. 21 cm. (Collection du cent-cinquantenaire)

1. Caribbean area—Hist.—Poetry. 2. Poetry of places—Caribbean area. I. Title.

PQ3607.O6473S8 54-32879 ‡

Library of Congress [1]

Haiti
M841
D26r

Poetry, Haitian.

Dauphin, Marcel, 1910-
Reflet des heures, poèmes. Port-au-Prince, Achevé d'imprimer sur les Presses de la Compagnie Lithographique d'Haiti, 1961.

52p. 18½cm.

Haiti
M841
Sa3c

Poetry, Haitian.

St. Hilaire, Paul
Chants du Paria. «Cap Haitien» Campagnie Lithographique d'Haiti, 1962.

30p. port. 21½cm.
Portrait of author in book.

Poetry of places - Harlem, New York (City)

M811.5
T58h

Tolson, Melvin Beaunorus.
Harlem gallery, by M. B. Tolson. With an introd. by Karl Shapiro. New York, Twayne [1965-

v. 21 cm.
Poetry.
CONTENTS.—book 1. The curator.

1. Negroes—New York (City)—Poetry. 2. Harlem, New York (City)—Descr.—Poetry. 3. Poetry of places—Harlem, New York (City) I. Title.

PS3539.O334H3 811.52 64-25063

Library of Congress [5]

Haiti
M841
D46ai

Poetry, Haitian.

Despeognes, Henri-Guy Louis.
Les ailes du sourire; poemes. Port-au-Prince, Imprimerie Union, 1962.

30p. 17½cm.

Poetry, Russian.

Russia
M891
P97s

Pushkin, Alexander Sergĕevich, 1799-1837.
Selections from the prose and poetry of Pushkin. Edited and introduced by Ernest J. Simmons. New York, Dell Publishing Co., 1961.

382p. 17cm. (A Laurel reader)
Sketch of author on book.
Cover title.

The poetry of the Negro.

M811.08
H87p

Hughes, Langston, 1902- *ed.*
The poetry of the Negro, 1746-1949; an anthology ed. by Langston Hughes and Arna Bontemps. [1st ed.] Garden City, N. Y., Doubleday, 1949.

xviii, 429 p. 22 cm.

1. Negro poetry. 2. Negro poetry (American) 3. Negro race—Poetry. I. Bontemps, Arna Wendell, 1902- joint ed. II. Title.
Full name: James Langston Hughes.

PN6109.7.H8 811.082 49-7193*

Library of Congress [50r10]

Haiti
M841
F82s

Poetry, Haitian.

Fouche, Franck
Symphonie en noir majeur poeme; pour Roussan Camille in memoriam. Port-au-Prince, Art Graphique Presse, 1962.

13p. 21½cm.

Jamaica
M821.91
P75

Poetry for children by poets of Jamaica.
Cover design and illus. by Lisa Salmon. Kingston, Jamaica, Pioneer Press, 1950.

100p. 19cm.

1. Jamaican poetry.

Cuba
MB
C12p

Poets, Cuban.

Calcagno, Francisco, 1827-1903.
Poetas de color, por Francisco Calcagno. Plácido, Manzano, Rodríguez, Echemendía, Silveira, Medina. Habana, Imp. militar de la v. de Soler y compañía, 1878.

1 p. l., [5]-54 p. 23½cm.

1. Poets, Cuban. 2. Negro authors. I. Title.

22-9233

Library of Congress [34b1] PQ7380.C3

Haiti
M841
L93o

Poetry, Haitian.

Louis, Janine Tavernier
Ombre ensoleillée. Preface de Roland Morisseau. Illustration de Villard Denis. Port-au-Prince, Imprimerie Gervais Louis, 1961.

21p. 19½cm.
Portrait of author on back of book.

M811.5
P55p

Poetry in proflection.

Phillips, Waldo B
Poetry in proflection. Los Angeles, Compton Counseling Center [1965]

38p. 21½cm.

I. Title.

Cuba
MB
C12p
1887

Poets, Cuban.

Calcagno, Francisco, 1827-1903.
Poetas de color, por Francisco Calcagno. Placido, Manzano, Rodriguez, Echemendia, Silveira, Medina. Cuarta edicion. Habana, Imp. Mercantil de los Herederos de Santiago S. Spencer, 1887.

7-110p. 19½cm.

Haiti
M841
L96p

Poetry, Haitian.

Lubin, Maurice A
Poesies Haitiennes. Rio de Janeiro, Livraria Editora da Casa, 1956.

147p. 22cm.

Jamaica
M784
P75

Poetry League of Jamaica
Jamaican school songs. Kingston, 1963.

43p. 17½cm.

1. Jamaican songs. I. Title.

Dominican Republic
M861.5
C76a

Poets, Dominican.

Contín Aybar, Pedro René, *comp.*
Antología poética dominicana; selecciones, prólogo y notas críticas, por Pedro René Contín y Aybar. Ciudad Trujillo, Librería dominicana, 1943.

9 p. l., xvii, 310 p., 1 l. 22½ cm.
Imprint on cover: Editorial El Diario, Santiago, República dominicana, 1943.
Includes biographical sketches of the poets whose works are here given.

1. Dominican poetry (Collections) 2. Poets, Dominican. I. Title.

PQ7406.C63 861.5082 A 44-765

Harvard Univ. Library for Library of Congress [a48c1]†

The poet's doorway; poems.
M811.5 G223p
Gates, Eddie
The poet's doorway; poems. New York, Carlton Press [1964]
64p. 21cm. (A Lyceum book)
Protrait of author on book.
I. Title.

Poitier, Sidney, 1927-
Pp. 371-394. In-
MB9 P83a
Funke, Lewis, 1912- ed.
Actors talk about acting; fourteen interviews with stars of the theatre [by] Lewis Funke and John E. Booth. New York, Random House [1961]
469 p. 24 cm.
White author.
1. Actors. 2. Acting. I. Booth, John Erlanger, joint ed. II. Title. III. Funke, Lewis, 1912- , ed.
PN2285.F8 792.028 61-6268 ‡
Library of Congress [61q15]

MB9 M358p
Poling, James
Thurgood Marshall and the 14th Amendment. New York, Committee of 100, 1952.
29-[32]p. port. 31cm.
Reprinted from Collier's February 23, 1952.
White author?
1. Marshall, Thurgood, 1908-
2. Fourteenth amendment.

Haiti M841 Un2p
The poets of Haiti, 1782-1934.
Underwood, Edna (Worthley) 1873- tr.
The poets of Haiti, 1782-1934, translated by Edna Worthley Underwood; woodcuts by Pétion Savain, glossary by Charles F. Pressoir. Portland, Me., The Mosher press, 1934.
xiii, 159 p., 1 l. incl. illus., pl. 19cm.
Includes biographical matter.
1. Haitian poetry (French)—Translations into English. 2. English poetry—Translations from Haitian (French) I. Title.
Library of Congress PQ3946.Z5E5 1934 34-22300
[a42e1] 841.0822

M343.3 Sh6k
Police.
Shields, Art.
The killing of William Milton; Introduction by Simon W. Gerson. New York, Daily Worker, 1948.
14p. 18cm.

Polished pebbles;
M811.5 L58p
Lewis, Carrie Louise, 1932-
Polished pebbles; poems. New York, Exposition Press, 1960.
48p. 20½cm.
Portrait of author on book jacket.

Poets of today.
M811.08 L95
Lowenfels, Walter, 1897- ed.
Poets of today; a new American anthology. With a prologue poem by Langston Hughes. New York, International Publishers [1964]
143 p. 21 cm.
White editor.
Includes poems by 20 Negro authors.
1. American poetry—20th cent. I. Title.
PS614.L75 811.5082 64-8443
Library of Congress [5]

Police - Mississippi.
M352.2 M69
Mississippi black paper; fifty-seven Negro and white citizens' testimony of police brutality, the breakdown of law and order and the corruption of justice in Mississippi. Foreword by Reinhold Niebuhr. Introd. by Hodding Carter III. New York, Random House [1965]
92 p. illus. 28 cm.
1. Police — Mississippi. 2. Law enforcement — Mississippi. 3. Negroes—Mississippi. I. Title: Fifty-seven Negro and white citizens' testimony of police brutality. II. Niebuhr, Reinhold, 1892-
HV8145.M7M5 323.11960762 65-18103
Library of Congress [8]

M813.5 P759f
Polite, Carlene Hatcher.
The flagellants. New York [Farrar, Straus & Giroux, 1967]
214 p. 21 cm.
Portrait of author on book jacket.
I. Title.
PZ4.P7674Fl 67-15013
Library of Congress [5]

M286 P75
Poinsett, Alex
Common folk in an uncommon cause. With photographs by Francis Mitchell. Chicago, Liberty Baptist Church, 1962.
63p. illus. ports. 20½cm.
1. Chicago. Liberty Baptist Church.
2. Churches - Chicago. I. Title.

Tobago M352.2 Ot5
Police - Trinidad and Tobago.
Ottley, Carlton Robert
A historical account of the Trinidad and Tobago police force from the earliest times. Trinidad, The Author, 1964.
152p. illus., port. 18½cm.
1. Police - Trinidad and Tobago.
2. Trinidad and Tobago. I. Title.

Political agitation in the Gold Coast.
Ghana M966.7 D234p
Danquah, Moses E
Political agitation in the Gold Coast; a critique of its principles and methods. Accra, published by the Author, 1949.
31p. 18cm.

M301 Eb74
Poinsett, Alex
Poverty amidst plenty
Pp. 93-103
In: Ebony. The white problem in America. Chicago, Johnson Pub. Co., 1966.

M343.3 M35p
Police brutality.
Marshall, Horace.
Police brutality; Lynching in the Northern style, with a special message from Councilman Benjamin J. Davis. New York, Office of Councilman Benjamin J. Davis, [1947]
21p. illus. 21cm.

The political and constitutional problems of Nigeria.
Nigeria M966.9 Ak52
Akinyede, Gilbert Benjamin Akinyemi
The political and constitutional problems of Nigeria. [Lagos, Nigerian Print. and Pub. Co., 1957]
88p. port. 21½cm.
Portrait of author in book.
References: p. [2]

Pointe de Sable, Jean Baptiste, 1745?-1818-Fiction.
M813.5 G76j
Graham, Shirley.
Jean Baptiste Pointe de Sable, founder of Chicago. New York, J. Messner [1953]
180 p. 22 cm.
1. Pointe de Sable, Jean Baptiste, 1745?-1818—Fiction.
Full name: Lola Shirley (Graham) McCanns.
PZ7.G757Je 53-9746 ‡
Library of Congress [54n7]

The policy king.
M813.5 C127p
Caldwell, Lewis A H
The policy king, by Lewis A. H. Caldwell. Chicago, Ill., New vistas publishing house [1945]
2 p. l., iv, 808 p. illus., pl. 22½cm.
I. Title.
46-2017
Library of Congress PZ3.C127424Po
[47c1]

Political consciousness.
Ghana M966.7 W83p
Hayford, Casely, 1866-1930.
Political consciousness.
pp. 209-210.
In: Pageant of Ghana, by Freda Wolfson. 1958.

Pointing the way.
M813.5 G87p
Griggs, Sutton Elbert, 1872-
Pointing the way, by Sutton E. Griggs. Nashville, Tenn., The Orion publishing company, 1908.
233 p. 20cm.
I. Title.
8-22561
Library of Congress PZ3.G888P
Copyright A 218463 [a38b1]

M252 P75t
Poling, Daniel Alfred, 1884- ed.
A treasury of great sermons, selected by Daniel A. Poling, with biographical notes and comments. New York, Greenberg [1944]
ix, 198 p. 21cm.
White author.
1. Sermons. I. Title. II. Imes. William Lloyd, 1889- Faith versus success, p. 181-85. 44-51172
Library of Congress BV4241.P58
[25] 252.0082

Political conventions - West Indies.
Trinidad M972.98 W67r
Williams, Eric Eustace, 1911-
Responsibilities of the party member by Dr. Eric Williams, premier of Trinidad and Tobago; full text of the political leader's address to the fifth annual convention on Friday, September (1960). [Port-of-Spain, P.N.M., 1960]
16p. 21cm.

Political parties
see also
Politics and suffrage

Political parties - West Indies.
Trinidad
M972.98 Williams, Eric Eustace, 1911-
W67r Responsibilities of the party member by Dr. Eric Williams, premier of Trinidad and Tobago; full text of the political leader's address to the fifth annual convention on Friday, September (1960). [Port-of-Spain, P.N.M., 1960]

16p. 21cm.

Politics.

M815.5 Bruce, John Edward, 1856-
B83 Occasional political tracts.
No.10

3 p. 21cm.

Political parties - Puerto Rico.
Puerto Rico
M864 Pagán, Bolívar, 1899-
P14h Historia de los partidos políticos puertorriqueños, 1898-1956. San Juan, P. R., Librería Campos, 1959.

2 v. illus. 23 cm.

1. Political parties—Puerto Rico. I. Title.

JL1059.A45P3 59-38693 ‡

Library of Congress [8]

...The political plight of the Negro...
Miller, Kelly, 1863-
M329 ...The political plight of the Negro,
M61p by Kelly Miller. Washington, D.C., Murray bros. printing co., inc., 1913.
21 3 p. 23cm. (Kelly Miller's mongraphic magazine, vol. 1 May 1913)

Politics.

M815.5 Bruce, John Edward, 1856-
B83 Reply to Senator Wade Hampton's article in
No.8 the Forum for June, on ... What Negro Supremacy means." by John E. Bruce... Washington, D.C., 1888.

17p. 21½cm.

Senegal Political parties - Sénégal.
M966.3 Traoré, Bakary.
T688 Forces politiques en Afrique noire, par Bakari Traoré, Mamadou Lô et Jean-Louis Alibert ... Paris, Presses universitaires de France, 1966.

viii, 312 p. 24 cm. (Travaux et recherches de la Faculté de droit et des sciences économiques de Paris. Série "Afrique," no 2) 20 F. (F 66-12565)

Includes bibliographies.

1. Political parties—Senegal. 2. Africa, Sub-Saharan—Politics. I. Title. (Series: Paris. Université. Faculté de droit et des sciences économiques. Série "Afrique," no 2) II. Lo, Mamadou. III. Alibert, Jean-Louis. IV. Series.

JQ3396.A979T7 329.9'663 67-74794

Library of Congress [4]

Haiti Political remarks on some French works...
M972.94 Vastey, Pompée Valentin, baron de, d. 1820?
V44p Political remarks on some French works and newspapers, concerning Haiti, by the Baron de Vastey... at Sans Souci, from the King's printing office, 1817, the 14th of Independence. Translated exclusively for the Pamphletier. London, 1818.

[165] - 239p. 21½cm.

Politics.
MB9 Coleman, Lucretia H. Newman
Ar6 Poor Ben: a story of real life...
Nashville, Tenn., A.M.E. Sunday school union, 1890.
220p. port. (front.) illus. 19cm.

Political parties - Trinidad.
Trinidad
M329 Williams, Eric Eustace, 1911-
W67ap The approach of independence; an address to the fourth annual convention of the People's National Movement. [Port-of-Spain, P.N.M. Publishing Co., 1960]
23p. 21cm.

1. People's National Party. 2. Trinidad - Political parties. 3. Political parties - Trinidad. I. Title.

Uganda Political rights.
M323 Lucas, Eric, ed.
B31 What is freedom. London, Oxford University Press, 1963.

136p. 18cm.

Politics.

M324 Equal suffrage. Address from the colored citizens of
Eq2a Norfolk, Va., to the people of the United States. Also an account of the agitation among the colored people of Virginia for equal rights. With an appendix concerning the rights of colored witnesses before the state courts. New Bedford, Mass., E. Anthony & sons, printers, 1865.

cover-title, 26 p. 22cm.

1. Negroes—Virginia—Politics and suffrage.

[30d1] 9-32794†

Library of Congress JK1929.V6E6

Political parties - Trinidad.
Trinidad
M329 Williams, Eric Eustace, 1911-
W67o Our fourth anniversary, the last lap; political leader's address on September 24, 1960, at the University of Woodford Square, marking the fourth year of P.N.M.'s first term of office. [Port-of-Spain, P.N.M. Publishing Co., 1960]
15p. 21cm.
Portrait on cover.
1. People's National Movement. 2. Trinidad - Political parties. 3. Political parties - Trinidad. I. Title.

Political science—Addresses, essays, lectures.

M283. Crummell, Alexander, 1819-1898.
C88d The duty of a rising Christian state to contribute to the world's well-being and civilization, and the means by which it may perform the same. The annual oration before the Common council and the citizens of Monrovia, Liberia—July 26, 1855: being the day of national independence. By the Rev. Alex. Crummell ... London, Wertheim & Macintosh, 1856; reprinted by the Massachusetts colonization society, 1857.

31, [1] p. 21½cm.

1. Political science—Addresses, essays, lectures.

15-9591

Library of Congress JC341.C3

Politics.

MB9 Mallas, Aris A
P36m Forty years in politics; the story of Ben Pelham, by Aris A. Mallas, Jr., Rea McCain [and] Margaret K. Hedden. Detroit, Wayne State University Press, 1957.

92 p. illus. 24 cm.

1. Pelham, Benjamin B., 1862-1948. 2. Finance, Public—Wayne Co., Mich. 3. Wayne Co., Mich.—Pol. & govt. I. Title.

F572.W4P4 923.573 57-10562 ‡

Library of Congress [59f5]

Political parties - Trinidad.
Trinidad
M329 Williams, Eric Eustace, 1911-
W67p Perspectives for our party; address delivered to the third annual convention of the People's National Movement on October 17, 1958. [Port-of-Spain, P.N.M. Publishing Co., 1958]
20p. 22cm.

1. People's Nati nal Movement. 2. Trinidad - Political parties. 3. Politica. parties - Trinidad. I. Title.

Politics.

M06 American Negro academy, *Washington, D. C., ed.*
Am3 ... The Negro and the elective franchise. A series of
no.11 papers and a sermon ... Washington, D. C., The Academy, 1905.

2 p. l., [3]-85 p. 23 cm. (Occasional papers, no. 11)

CONTENTS.—1. Meaning and need of the movement to reduce southern representation [by] Mr. A. H. Grimke.—2. The penning of the Negro (the Negro vote in the states of the revised constitutions) [by] Mr. C. C. Cook.—3. The Negro vote in the states whose constitutions have not been specifically revised [by] Mr. John Hope.—4. The potentiality of the Negro vote, North and West [by] Mr. John L. Love.—5. Migration and distribution of the Negro population as affecting the elective franchise [by] Mr. Kelly Miller.—6. The Negro and his citizenship [by] Rev. F. J. Grimke.

1. Negroes—Politics.

Library of Congress E184.N3A5 5-38801
[48b1]

Politics.

M304 Miller, George Frazier
P19 A reply to the political plea of Bishop
v.6, no.13 Cleland K Nelson and Bishop Thomas F. Gailor at the Cathedral of St. John the Divine in the city of New York, Sunday evening, October 19, 1913. A sermon by Reverend George Frazier Miller...October 26, 1913. Brooklyn, The interboro Press, 1913.
[18 p] 22cm.

Political parties - West Indies.
Trinidad
M972.9 James, C L R , 1901-
J23 Party politics in the West Indies. San Juan, Vedic Enterprises, n.d.

175p. 22cm.
Portrait of author on back cover.

Politics.

M815.5 Bruce, John Edward, 1856-
B83 Occasional political tracts. no.1.
No.9

3 p. 21cm.

Politics.

M329 Miller, Kelly, 1863-
M61p ...The political plight of the Negro, by Kelly Miller. Washington, D.C., Murray bros printing co., inc., 1913.

21 3 p. 23cm. (Kelly Miller's mongraphic magazine, vol. 1, May 1913)

Politics.
M304 Morris, Charles S.
P19 The [illegible] and the Negro. Lacks
v.4, no.14 imprint
24p. 21cm.

Politics
M324 Murray, George Washington, 1853-1926.
M96s Speech of Hon. G.W. Murray of South Carolina, on the Repeal of the Federal election laws, in the House of Representatives, October 5, 1893. ⌊Lacks imprint⌋

14p. 24cm.

Politics.
M815.4 Pinchback, Pinckney Benton Stewart, 1837-1923.
P65r ⌊Remarks concerning claim to seat in the U.S. Senate, New Orleans, September, 1875.

4p. 21½cm.

Politics.
M815.4 Pinchback, Pickney Benton Steuart, 1837-1923.
P65r A statement of the law and facts involved in the case of P.B.S. Pinchback claiming a seat in the U.S. senate as senator elect from the state of Louisiana ⌊1873⌋

13p. 24cm.

Politics
M329.6 Rivers, Francis E
R52a An appeal to the common sense of colored citizens, by Francis E. Rivers. New York, Republican national committee, 1940.

32p. 21½cm.

M973 Politics.
R54 Robertson, L O
We want Roosevelt again because of facts and figures; a brief review of part of the achievements by L. O. Robertson... Washington, D.C. ⌊1946⌋

24p. tables. 23cm.

Politics.
M304 White, Walter Francis.
P19 Election by terror in Florida, by Walter F.
V.7 White. Reprinted from the New Republic of
no.1 January 12, 1921. N.Y.C., National association for the advancement of the colored people, 1921.

11p. 20½cm.

Politics and government.
Langston, John Mercer, 1829-1897.
M815 Freedom and citizenship. Selected lectures
L26 and addresses of Hon. John Mercer Langston... With an introductory sketch by Rev. J. E. Rankin... Washington, D. C., R. H. Darby, 1883.
286 p. front. (port.) 20cm.

Politics and government.
M324 Ross, Hilliard Franklin
R73e The election of 1936, by Hilliard Franklin Ross. New York, N.Y. The author 1936.
36p. 22cm.

Politics and government - Africa.
Northern Rhodesia
M968.94
K16 Kaunda, Kenneth, 1924-
Black government; a discussion between Colin Morris and Kenneth Kaunda. Lusaka, Northern Rhodesia, United Society for Christian Literature, 1960.

116p. ports. 22cm.
Biographies included.

Panama Politics and government - 1945-
M327.73 Schollianos, Alva.
Sc65 Call to greatness; shaping recommendations into programs of action. New York, William-Frederick Press, 1963.

viii, 191 p. 23 cm. (*His* Prospects for America, 2)

1. U. S.—Pol. & govt.—1945- 2. U. S.—For. rel.—1945- I. Title.

E743.S37 327.73 61-18292

Library of Congress ⌊5⌋

Politics and suffrage.
M324 Brewer, John Mason, 1896-
B75n Negro legislators of Texas and their descendants; a history of the Negro in Texas politics from reconstruction to disfranchisement, by J. Mason Brewer ... with an introduction by Herbert P. Gambrell ... Dallas, Tex., Mathis publishing co. ⌊°1935⌋

x, 134 p. ports. (1 fold.) map. 20cm.

1. Negroes—Texas. 2. Negroes—Politics and suffrage. 3. Texas—Pol. & govt.—1865- 4. Negroes—Biog. I. Title. II. Title: Negro in Texas politics.

35-17051

Library of Congress E185.93.T4B7

——— Copy 2.

Copyright A 86409 ⌊36d3⌋ 325.2609764

Politics and suffrage.
M324 Butcher, Margaret Just, 1913-
B97noi Le Noir Americain et les elections. ⌊Maroc, le Service Americain d'Information, 1960?⌋

8p.; 8p. 21cm.
In French and Arabic.
Autographed.

Politics and suffrage.
M323.4 Carmichael, Stokely.
C212 Black power; the politics of liberation in America ⌊by⌋ Stokely Carmichael & Charles V. Hamilton. New York, Random House ⌊1967⌋

xii, 198 p. 22 cm.

Bibliography: p. 187-189.

1. Negroes—Civil rights. 2. Negroes—Politics and suffrage. I. Hamilton, Charles V., joint author. II. Title.

E185.615.C32 323.4'0973 67—22656

Library of Congress ⌊68f5⌋

Politics and suffrage.
M324 Clayton, Edward Taylor, 1921-
C579 The Negro politician, his success and failure ⌊by⌋ Edward T. Clayton. With an introd. by Martin Luther King, Jr. Chicago, Johnson Pub. Co., 1964.

xiv, 213 p. 22 cm.

1. Negroes—Politics and suffrage. I. Title.

E185.6.C637 62—21536

Library of Congress ⌊65d4⌋

Politics and suffrage
M973.6
C83 Coloured Citizens of New Jersey.
1849 Proceedings and address of the coloured citizens of N.J. convened at Trenton, August 21st and 22nd, 1849, for the purpose of taking the initiatory measure for obtaining the right of suffrage, in this our native state. ⌊Lacks imprint, 1849⌋

9p. 14½cm.

M324 Politics and suffrage
C73v Committee of Editors and Writers of the South
Voting restrictions in the 13 southern states. Atlanta, The Committee, 1944.

⌊12⌋p. illus. graphs. 23cm.

Politics and suffrage.
M06 Cromwell, John Wesley, 1846-
Am3 ... The challenge of the disfranchised; a plea for the en-
no.22 forcement of the 15th amendment, by John W. Cromwell. Washington, D. C., The Academy, 1924.

10 p. 23cm. (American Negro academy. Occasional papers, no. 22)

1. Negroes—Politics and suffrage. I. Title.

37-18058

Library of Congress E185.5.A51 no. 22

⌊3⌋ (325.260973) 325.260973

Politics and suffrage.
M815.4 Douglass, Frederick, 1817-1895.
D74eq The equality of all men before the law claimed and defended; in speeches by Hon. William D. Kelley, Wendell Phillips, and Frederick Douglass, and letters from Elizur Wright and Wm. Heighton. Boston, Press of G. C. Rand & Avery, 1865.

43p. 23cm.

Politics and suffrage.
M815.4 Douglass, Frederick, 1817?-1895.
D739f2 Frederick Douglass, selections from his writings. Edited, with an introd., by Philip S. Foner. New York, International Publishers ⌊1964, °1945⌋

96 p. 21 cm.

Cover title: Selections from the writings of Frederick Douglass.

1. Slavery in the U. S.—Anti-slavery movements. 2. Negroes—Politics and suffrage. I. Foner, Philip Sheldon, 1910- ed.

E449.D737 1964 326.4 64-6594

Library of Congress ⌊5⌋

M815.4 Politics and suffrage.
D739u ⌊Douglass, Frederick⌋ 1817-1895.
U. S. Grant and the colored people. His wise, just, practical, and effective friendship thoroughly vindicated by incontestable facts in his record from 1862 to 1872. Words of truth and soberness! He who runs may read and understand!! Be not deceived, only truth can endure!!! ⌊Washington, 1872⌋

8 p. 24cm.

Caption title.
Signed: Frederick Douglass.

1. Grant, Ulysses Simpson, pres. U. S., 1822-1885. 2. Negroes—Politics and suffrage. 3. Campaign literature, 1872—Republican. I. Title.

12—6966

Library of Congress E185.2.D73

⌊32b1⌋

Politics and suffrage.

M301 D85 Du Bois, William Edward Burghardt, 1868–
Black reconstruction; an essay toward a history of the part which black folk played in the attempt to reconstruct democracy in America, 1860–1880, by W. E. Burghardt Du Bois ... New York, Harcourt, Brace and company [°1935]
6 p. l., 3–746 p. 22cm.
"First edition."
Bibliography: p. 731–737.
1. Reconstruction. 2. Negroes. 3. Negroes—Politics and suffrage. 4. Negroes—Employment. 5. U. S.—Pol. & govt.—1865–1877. I. Title.
35–8545
Library of Congress E668.D83 [45g*2] 325.260973

Politics and suffrage.

M324 Ed57n Edmonds, Helen G
The Negro and fusion politics in North Carolina, 1894–1901. Chapel Hill, University of North Carolina Press [1951]
viii, 260 p. illus., maps. 25 cm.
Bibliography: p. 239–247.
1. Negroes—North Carolina. 2. North Carolina—Pol. & govt.—1865– 3. Negroes—Politics and suffrage. I. Title.
E185.93.N6E4 325.2609756 51—4106
Library of Congress [53q5]

Politics and suffrage.

M06 Am3 no. 16 Grimke, Archibald Henry, 1849–
... The ballotless victim of one-party governments. Annual address by Archibald H. Grimke ... Washington, D. C., The Academy, 1913.
18 p. 21½cm. (The American negro academy. Occasional papers, no. 16)
1. Negroes—Politics and suffrage. 2. Negroes—Legal status, laws, etc. I. Title.
13-18319
Library of Congress E185.5.A51 no. 16
——— Copy 2. JK1929.A2G8
——— Copy 3. JK1929.A2G8 copy 2

Politics and suffrage

M304 P19 v.4,no.7 Grimké, Archibald Henry, 1849–1930.
Why disfranchisement is bad, by Archibald H. Grimké. Philadelphia, Press of E. A. Wright, 1904?]
[12] p. 23cm.
"From July, 1904 number the Atlantic monthly."
1. Negroes—Politics and suffrage.
Library of Congress JK1924.G8 [a33b1] 6—25943

Politics and suffrage.

M304 P19 V.5, no.11. Grimke, Archibald Henry, 1849–1930.
Why disfranchisement is bad. Reprinted from the Atlantic Monthly, July 1904.
[10]p.

Politics and suffrage.

M973 L82 at Logan, Rayford Whittingham, ed.
The attitude of the southern white press toward Negro suffrage, 1932–1940; edited by Rayford W. Logan, PH. D., with a foreword by Charles H. Wesley, PH. D. Washington, D. C., The Foundation publishers, 1940.
cover-title, xii, 115 p. 23cm.
1. Negroes—Politics and suffrage. 2. Press—Southern states. I. Title.
40—30270
Library of Congress JK1929.A21.6 [42f2] 324.15

Politics and suffrage.

M973.8 L99s Lynch, John Roy, 1847–
Some historical errors of James Ford Rhodes, by Major John R. Lynch. Boston, New York, The Cornhill publishing company [°1922]
xx, 115 p. front., ports. 19cm.
1. Rhodes, James Ford, 1848– History of the United States from the compromise of 1850 ... 2. Negroes—Politics and suffrage. I. Title.
22—23557
Library of Congress E415.7.R479
——— Copy 2.
Copyright A 690307 [37d1]

Politics and suffrage.

M324 M77b Moon, Henry Lee, 1901–
Balance of power: the Negro vote. [1st ed.] Garden City, N. Y., Doubleday, 1948.
256 p. 22 cm.
Bibliographical footnotes.
1. Negroes—Politics and suffrage. 2. Elections—U. S. I. Title.
JK2275.N4M6 324.15 48—6926*
Library of Congress [50d*15]

Politics and suffrage.

M324 N86 Nowlin, William Felbert, 1897–
The Negro in American national politics, by William F. Nowlin, A. M. Boston, Mass., The Stratford company [°1931]
4 p. l., 148 p. 19½ cm.
Bibliography: p. 145–148.
1. Negroes—Politics and suffrage. I. Title.
Library of Congress JK2275.N4N8 [49e½] 32—5242 325.26

Politics and suffrage

M973.8 Ow2u Owens, Susie Lee
Union League of America; Political activities in Tennessee, the Carolinas, and Virginia, 1865–1870, an abridgement. New York, New York University, 1947.
23p. 23cm.

M335.4 P42n Politics and suffrage.
Perry, Pettis.
Negro representation - a step towards Negro freedom. Introduction by Betty Gannett. New York, New Century Publishers, 1952.
24 p. 19 cm.

Politics and suffrage.

M324 R45p Riley, Jerome R.
The philosophy of negro suffrage. By Jerome R. Riley, M. D. Hartford, Conn., American publishing company, 1895.
110 p. front. (port.) 20½cm
1. Negroes—Politics and suffrage. 2. Negroes. I. Title.
12—3518
Library of Congress E185.61.R57
——— Copy 2.
Copyright 1895: 52795 [36d1]

Politics and suffrage.

M324 S m5n Smith, Arthur J.
The Negro in the political classics of the American government, by Arthur J. Smith. Washington, D. C. [°1937]
cover-title, 25 l. 12 x 18½cm.
"A short biography of each Negro United States senator and representative, elected and seated ... since 1870."
1. Negroes—Biog. 2. Negroes—Politics and suffrage. I. Title.
39-33068
Library of Congress E185.96.S65
——— Copy 2.
Copyright AA 232559 [2] 923.273

Politics and suffrage.

M323 W58d White, George Henry, 1852–1918.
Defense of the Negro race—charges answered ... Speech of Hon. George H. White, of North Carolina, in the House of representatives, January 29, 1901. Washington [Govt. print. off.] 1901.
14 p. 24cm.
1. Negroes—Politics and suffrage.
12—11526
Library of Congress E185.6.W56 [a41b1]

Politics and suffrage.

M324 W67a Williams, Franklin Hall, 1917–
An American principle realized. Reprinted from The Pacific spectator, v.6, no.4, Autumn 1952.
[7]p. 23cm.

The politics and administration of Nigerian government.

Nigeria M966.9 B619 Blitz, L Franklin, ed.
The politics and administration of Nigerian government, edited by Franklin Blitz. Contributors: M. J. Campbell [and others] New York, Praeger, 1965.
xiv, 281p. illus. 22cm.
Partial contents.- Land, people and tradition in Nigeria, by Akin L. Mabogunje.- Constitutional development, by Oluwole Idowu Odumosu.
Bibliography: p. 265-271.
White editor.

Politics in West Africa.

St. Lucia M966 L589 Lewis, William Arthur, 1915–
Politics in West Africa [by] W. Arthur Lewis. Toronto, New York, Oxford University Press, 1965.
90 p. map. 19 cm. (The Whidden lectures, 1965)
1. Africa, West—Politics. 2. States, New. I. Title. (Series)
DT471.L57 320.966 65—8469
Library of Congress [66c2]

Haiti M972.94 M31p La politique agraire du gouvernement.
Manigat, Leslie F
La politique agraire du gouvernement d'Alexandre Pétion (1807-1818). Port-au-Prince, Imp. La Phalange, 1962.
74p. 20½cm.

M811.5 P75d Polk, Elaine D R
Dreams at twilight; religious meditations in verse and prose. [1st ed.] New York, Exposition Press [1956]
96 p. 21 cm.
I. Title.
PS3531.O26D7 811.5 56-10976 ‡
Library of Congress [3]

M813.5 P76s Pollard, Freeman, 1922–
Seeds of turmoil; a novel of American PW's brainwashed in Korea. [1st ed.] New York, Exposition Press [1959]
264 p. 21 cm.
Portrait of author on book jacket.
1. Korean War, 1950–1953—Fiction. I. Title.
PZ4.P774Se 59–65501 ‡
Library of Congress [2]

Haiti M972.94 P77c Pommayrac [Alcibiade] 1844–1910.
Un conseil a mon pays (Republique d'Haiti) Paris, Librairie E. Bernard & Cie, 1894.
98p. 17½cm.
1. Haiti.

Haiti
M972.94 P79h
Pompee, Arsene
Haiti devant les problemes interamericains. Port-au-Prince, Imprimerie de l'etat, [1947]
79p. 21cm.

1. Haiti

M811.08 P78
Pool, Rosey Eva, 1905- , comp.
Beyond the blues; new poems by American Negroes. Kent, Hand and Flower Press [1962]
188p. 18cm.
"Selected bibliography": p.186-188.
"To Arthur Spingarn in friendship and gratitude, Rosey E. Pool, Salisbury, N.C. October, 1962."
White editor.

1. Poetry. I. Title.

M301 R27p
Poor land and peasantry.
Reid, Ira DeAugustine, 1901-
Poor land and peasantry, by Arthur Raper and Ira DeA. Reid. pp. 15-17, 41-42.

In: North Georgia review; A magazine of the southern regions, winter, 1939-1940.

Haiti
M840.9 P77d
Pompilius, Pradel.
Destin de la langue Française en Haiti; Conférence prononcée à l'Institut Français d'Haiti, le 19 février 1952. Port-au-Prince, Les Presses Libres, 1952.
5-20p. 22cm.

1. French language in Haiti ~~Haitian language~~ I. Title.

M811.08 P78i
Pool, Rosey Eva, 1905- ed.
Ik ben de nieuwe Neger. Gedichten, rijmen, liedjes en dokumenten uit 300 jaar verzet van de Americaanse Neger, bijeengebracht, ingeleid en van vertalingen en kommentaar voorzien door Rosey E. Pool met een woord vooraf van J. W. Schulte Nordholt. Den Haag, Bert Bakker [1965]
264p. 17cm.
English and Dutch. White editor.
"For my dear friend, Arthur B. Spingarn, horticulturist, par excellence, a bunch of ... as I like it from your humble & most devoted botanist. Rosey E. Pool, August, '65."
I. Title.

The poor man with a million shillings.
Tanganyika
M967.82 Om1m
Omari, Dunstan Alfred, 1922- . jt. auth.
Mtu maskini mwenye sh.1,000,000. The poor man with a million shillings. [By C. W. W. Ryan and D. A. Omari] Dar es Salaam, Eagle Press, 1954.
16p. 18cm. (Mazungumzo ya uraia. Talks on citizenship, no.2)
Writtn in Swahili and English.
1. Money. I. Title. II. Title: The poor man with a million shillings. III. Series: Mazungumzo ya uraia, no. 2. IV. Talks on citizenship, no. 2. V. Ryan, C. W. W.

Haiti
M840.9 P77m
Pompilus, Pradel
Manuel illustré d'histoire de la littérature Haitienne. Port-au-Prince, Editions Henri Deschamps, 1961.
613p. illus., ports. 19½cm.

1. Haiti-Literature-History. 2. Literature-Haiti-History. 3. Haiti-Biographies. 4. Biographies-Haiti. I. Title.

M811.08 P78ik
Pool, Rosey Eva, 1905- , ed and tr.
Ik zag hoe zwart ik was; verzen van Noord-Amerikaanse Negers. Versameld Ingeleid en van vertalingen voorzien door Rosey E. Pool en Paul Breman, Den Haag, Bert Bakker, 1958.
203p. 18½cm.
English and Dutch on opposite pages.
"December 20th, 1958, London: Very happy to be allowed to inscribe this copy for my friend, Arthur B. Spingarn, Rosey E. Pool."
White editors.
1. Poetry. 2. Biography. I. Breman, Paul, jt. ed. and tr. II. Title.

M811.5 P81f
Popel, Esther, 1896-1958
A forest pool, by Esther Popel. Washington, D. C., Priv. print. Modernistic press 1934.
6p. 1., 42p. 22cm.
"Gift edition."
Inscribed copy: "To Mr. Spingarn, Sincerely and with cordial good wishes—Esther Popel, 1940.

1. Poetry. I. Title

Haiti
M840.9 P77p
Pompilus, Pradel, *ed.*
Pages de littérature haïtienne commentées et mises en place avec un tableau de la littérature haïtienne, à l'usage des classes d'humanités. Port-au-Prince, Impr. de l'État, 1951-
v. 24 cm.
Errata slip inserted.
Contents.—[1] 1. ptie. La poésie. 2. ptie. Le roman.

1. ~~French literature—Haitian authors.~~ 2. Haitian literature—Hist. & crit. 3. Haitian poetry
PQ3945.P6 51-28005
Library of Congress [1]

Pool, Rosey Eva, 1905- , jt. comp.
M811.08 W166
Walrond, Eric, 1898- comp.
Black and unknown bards; a collection of Negro poetry, selected by Eric Walrond and Rosey Pool. Kent [England] The Hand & Flower Press [1958]
43p. 21cm.

1. Poetry. I. Pool, Rosey, jt. comp. II. Title.

M323 P81p
Popel, Esther, 1896-1958
Personal adventures in race relations [by] Esther Popel Shaw. New York, The Woman's Press [c1946]
24p. 21½cm.

1. Race relations. I. Title.

Pondo - History.
S. Africa
M968 N23a
Ndamase, Victor Poto.
Ama-Mpondo: Ibali ne -Ntalo, ngu Victor Poto Ndamase. Lovedale, Ishicilelwe e- Lovedale 1925?
xiv, 158p. illus. ports. 19½cm.
Pondo history.

M297 P782
Poole, Elijah, 1897-
Message to the blackman in America, by Elijah Muhammad. Chicago, Muhammad Mosque of Islam No. 2 [1965]
xxvii, 355 p. 22 cm.

1. Black Muslims—Doctrinal and controversial works. ~~2. Negroes.~~ I. Title.
BP222.P6 297.87 65-9686
Library of Congress [3]

M811.5 P81t
Popel, Esther, 1896-1958
Thoughtless thinks by a thinkless thought-er.. Dedicated to my mother and my six best friends, by Esther A. B. Popel. Lacks imprint
16p. port. 16cm.
Inscribed on title page: "A first venture to raise money for college expenses! It netted $100! Esther Popel.

1. Poetry. I. Title.

Pong'o ic ok e gago ringruok.
Kenya
M613.2 H55f
Humphrey, Norman
Pong'o ic ok e gago ringruok [Feeding the body is more than filling the stomach. [Tr. by C. J. Amenya] Nairobi, Eagle Press, 1950.
14p. 21½cm. (Como ngima. Aim at healthy living series)
Written in Luo.
1. Nutrition. I. Title. II. Series. III. Aim at healthy living series. IV. Amenya, C. J., tr.

Poor-Europe.
M814.4 W272m
Washington, Booker Taliaferro, 1859?-1915.
The man farthest down; a record of observation and study in Europe, by Booker T. Washington, with the collaboration of Robert E. Park. Garden City, New York, Doubleday, Page & company, 1912.
4 p. l., 3-390 p., 1 l. fold. map. 20½cm.

1. Labor and laboring classes—Europe. 2. Poor—Europe. I. Park, Robert E., joint author. II. Title.
12-23003
Library of Congress HD4851.W3
——— Copy 2.
Copyright A 320588 [a39k1]

Popo and Fifina, children of Haiti.
M813.5 B64p
Bontemps, Arna.
Popo and Fifina, children of Haiti, by Arna Bontemps and Langston Hughes; illustrations by E. Simms Campbell. New York, The Macmillan company, 1932.
5 p. l., 100 p. incl. illus., plates. front. 22cm.

I. Hughes, Langston, 1902- joint author. II. Title.
32-24066
Library of Congress PZ7.B644SPo [45m1]

MB9 T85p
Ponton, Mongo Melancthon , 1860-
Life and times of Henry M. Turner... by M. M. Pontan... Atlanta, Ga., A.B. Caldwell Pub. Co., 1917.
[24] - 173p. front. (port.) 20cm.

1. ~~Biography.~~ I. Turner, Henry Mc Neal, 1834-1915.

...."Poor Ben's choice pebbles.
M814.5 M78p
Moore, S Benjamin editor.
..."Poor Ben's choice pebbles, edited by S. Benj. Moore...Durham, N.C., The Moore Print, 1908.
28p. port. 20½cm.

Population.
M312 Un3er
U. S. *Bureau of the census.*
... Negro population 1790-1915. Washington, Govt. print. off., 1918.
844 p. incl. maps, tables, diagrs. 30cm.
At head of title: Department of commerce. Bureau of the census. Sam. L. Rogers, director.
"Prepared by Dr. John Cummings in the Division of revision and results, under the general supervision of Dr. Joseph A. Hill."—"Letter of transmittal," p. 13.

1. Negroes. I. Cummings, John, 1868-1936. II. Hill, Joseph Adna, 1860- III. Title.
18-26864
Library of Congress HA205.A33 [42t2]

Population

M312
Un3n
1935

U. S. Bureau of the Census
... Negroes in the United States, 1920-32. Prepared under the supervision of A. R. Pettet, chief statistician for agriculture, by Charles E. Hall, specialist in Negro statistics. Washington, U.S. Govt. Print. Off., 1935.

xvi, 845p. incl. maps, talbes, diagrs. 30cm.

Population.

M312
Un3n
1915

U. S. *Bureau of the census.*
... Negroes in the United States. Washington, Govt. print. off., 1915.

207 p. incl. illus. (maps) tables. diagrs. 31cm. (*Its* Bulletin 129)

At head of title: Dept. of commerce. Bureau of the census. Wm. J. Harris, director.

To be followed by a more complete and comprehensive report on the same subject. *cf.* Letter of transmittal.

"Prepared in the Division of revisions and results under the general supervision of Dr. Joseph A. Hill, expert special agent. The statistical tables were planned and arranged by ... Charles E. Hall, William Jennifer, and Robert A. Pelham."—Letter of transmittal, p. 5.

1. Negroes. I. Hill, Joseph Adna, 1860-1938.

15-26297 Revised 2

Library of Congress HA201.1900.A12 no. 129
——— 2d set. E185.6.U585
[r43d2]

Population

M312
Un3n

U.S. Bureau of the Census.
... Negroes in the United States. Washington, Govt. Print. Off., 1904.

333p. incl. charts, diagrs. 29x22½cm.

Por allá.

Cuba
M863.6
J56p

Jiménez, Chiraldo, 1892-
...Por allá, novela. Manzanillo [Cuba] Editorial El Arte, 1931.

175p. 19½cm.

Haiti
M972.94
P83b

[Port-au-Prince, Haiti.]
Bulletin de la commune de Port-au-Prince. Port-au-Prince, Service National de l'Enseignement Professionnel, 1932.

70, [50]p. illus. 27cm.
Cover title: Ville de Port-au-Prince.

1. Haiti - Description and Travel.
2. Haiti - History.

Port-au-Prince, Haiti - History.

Haiti
M972.94
D49c

Devauges, Roland
Une capitale antillaise: Port-au-Prince (Haiti)

40p. illus. maps 24cm.
Extrait de la revue Les Cashiers d'Outre-Mer, Tome VII (1954)

Port-au-Prince, Haiti—Hist.—Chronology.

Haiti
M972.94
L16v

Lamaute, Emmanuel.
... Le vieux Port-au-Prince (une tranche de la vie haïtienne) suivi de quelques faits et dates ... Port-au-Prince, Haïti, Imprimerie de la Compagnie lithographique d'Haïti, 1939.

4 p. l., 7-256 p. front., plates (incl. music) ports. (part fold.) 22½cm.
"Errata": slip inserted.

1. Port-au-Prince, Haiti—Descr. 2. Port-au-Prince, Haiti—Soc. life & cust. 3. Port-au-Prince, Haiti—Hist.—Chronology. I. Title.

41-51912

Library of Congress F1929.P8L3
[2] 917.294

Port-au-Prince, Haiti—Soc. life & cust.

Haiti
M972.94
L16v

Lamaute, Emmanuel.
... Le vieux Port-au-Prince (une tranche de la vie haïtienne) suivi de quelques faits et dates ... Port-au-Prince, Haïti, Imprimerie de la Compagnie lithographique d'Haïti, 1939.

4 p. l., 7-256 p. front., plates (incl. music) ports. (part fold.) 22½cm.
"Errata": slip inserted.

1. Port-au-Prince, Haiti—Descr. 2. Port-au-Prince, Haiti—Soc. life & cust. 3. Port-au-Prince, Haiti—Hist.—Chronology. I. Title.

41-51912

Library of Congress F1929.P8L3
[2] 917.294

Port-of-Spain, Trinidad.

Trinidad
M972.98
Ac4m

Achong, Tito Princilliano.
... The Mayor's annual report. A review of the activities of the Port-of-Spain City council, with discourses on social problems affecting the Trinidad community, for the municipal year 1942-43, by his worship the Mayor Alderman Tito Pachong. Boston, Meador Publishing Co., [1944]

343p.

Porte ouverte sur la communaute Franco-Africaine.

Guinea, French
M966.52
D54

Diabate, Boubacar
Porte ouverte sur la communaute Franco-Africaine. [Bruxelles, Editions Remarques Congolaises, 1961]

169p. illus, maps. 19cm. (Collection "Perspective Africaines", no. 1)
Port. of author in book.

Haiti
M843.91
G26

Le portefeuille, roman, au service de l'ordre.
Gédéon, Max.
...Le portefeuille, roman, au service de l'ordre.- Port-au-Prince, Impre. de "La Presse," 1934.

vii, 169p., 1 l. 20 x 15½ cm.
(Bibliothèque haïtienne)

Sierra Leone
M966.4
P83

Porter, Arthur T
Creoledom; a study of the development of Freetown society. London, Oxford University Press, 1963.

xii, 151 p. illus., ports., maps (part fold.) 23 cm.

Revision of thesis, Boston University, submitted under title: The development of the Creole society of Freetown, Sierra Leone.
Bibliography: p. 142-146.

Portrait of author on book jacket.

1. Freetown, Sierra Leone—Soc. condit. I. Title.

HN800.F7P6 1963 301.44 63-4297

Library of Congress [5]

M89
R84

Porter, Dorothy Burnett, 1905-
David Ruggles, an apostle of human rights. Reprinted from the Journal of Negro history, 28:23-50, January 1943.

23-50p. 24½cm.
Inscribed by author: To Mr. Arthur B. Spingarn, from Dorothy Porter.

1. Ruggles, David, 1811-1849
2. Abolitionists

M01
P83h

Porter, Dorothy Burnett, 1905- comp.
Howard University masters' theses submitted in partial fulfillment of the requirements for the master's degree at Howard University, 1918-1945, compiled by Dorothy B. Porter. Washington, D.C., The Graduate school, Howard University, 1946.

44p. 23cm.

1. Dissertations, Academic.

M026
P831

Porter, Dorothy Burnett, 1905-
A library on the Negro. The American scholar, 7:115-117, Winter 1938.

115-117p. 25cm.
Detached copy.

1. Libraries - Special collections
I. title

M01
P83n

Porter, Dorothy (Burnett) 1905-
North American Negro poets, a bibliographical checklist of their writings, 1760-1944, by Dorothy B. Porter. Hattiesburg, Miss., The Book farm, 1945.

90 p. 23½ cm. (Heartman's historical series no. 70)

"An expansion of the Schomburg checklist."—Pref.

1. Negro poetry (American)—Bibl. I. Schomburg, Arthur Alfonso, 1874-1938. A bibliographical checklist of American Negro poetry. II. Title.

Full name: Dorothy Louise (Burnett) Porter.

Z1361.N39P6 016.811 45-4014

Library of Congress [a58n½]

M806
P83o

Porter, Dorothy Burnett, 1905-
The organized educational activities of Negro literary societies, 1828-1846.
Reprinted from The Journal of Negro education, October, 1936.
555 - 576p. 25cm.
1. Societies, Literary
2. Free Negroes
I. Title

M378
P83p

Porter, Dorothy Burnett, 1905-
The preservation of university documents: with special reference to Negro colleges and universities. Washington, D.C., 1942.
"Reprinted from the Journal of Negro Education, October, 1942, p. 527-528."
527-528p. 25cm.

Porter, Dorothy (Burnett) 1905-

M01
H83

Howard university, *Washington, D. C. Founders library. Moorland foundation.*
A catalogue of books in the Moorland foundation, compiled by workers on projects 271 and 328 of the Works progress administration, Margaret R. Hunton and Ethel Williams, supervisors, Dorothy B. Porter, director. Washington, D. C., Howard university, 1939.

2 p. l., ii numb. l., 94, 166, 159, 23, 33, 19 p. 27½ x 21½cm.

Each part preceded by leaf with half-title not included in paging (6 leaves)

Mimeographed.

1. Negroes—Bibl. 2. Negro literature—Bibl. I. *Porter, Dorothy (Burnett) 1905- II. Hunton, Margaret R. III. Williams, Ethel. IV. U. S. Work projects administration.

39-14329 Revised

Library of Congress Z1361.N39H8
[r44f2] 016.325260973

M811.08
P83d

Porter, Edna, *comp.*
Double blossoms, Helen Keller anthology, compiled by Edna Porter. New York, L. Copeland, 1931.

96 p. front. (port.) 20cm.
White compiler.
Partial contents: Helen Keller, by Langston Hughes. -Courage. He said. by Jessie Fauset. Spirit vision. by Countee Cullen. -Mother night. by James Weldon Johnson. -Helen Keller. by W.E.B. DuBois. III. a.t. Fauset IV. a.t. Cullen

1. Keller, Helen Adams, 1880- —Poetry. I. Title. V. a.t. John[son]
2. Poetry - II. Hughes, Langston. Helen Keller-p. 19 (over)

31—34592

V. a.t. DuBois
Library of Congress HV1624.K4P6

[41c1] 811.508

M646.7
P83

Porter, Gladys L
Three Negro pioneers in beauty culture, by Gladys L. Porter. [1st ed.] New York, Vantage Press [1966]

48 p. ports. 21 cm.
Bibliography: p. 48.

Portrait of author on book jacket.

1. Beauty operators. I. Title.

TT955.A1P6 646.720922 65-28009

Library of Congress [2]

M811.5
P83s
Porter, George Wellington,
Streamlets of poetry, by G. W. Porter ...
Memphis, Tenn., The author, c1912.
87 p. front. 19cm.

1. Poetry. I. Title.

Africa
M960
Am3
Porter, James Amos, 1905-1970
The American Negro artist looks at Africa.

Pp. 293-296.

In: American Society of African Culture.
Pan-Africanism reconsidered. Berkeley,
University of California Press, 1962.

M709
P83m
Porter, James Amos, 1905- 1970
Modern Negro art, by James A. Porter ... With eighty-five halftone plates. New York, The Dryden press, 1943.
viii, 272 p. incl. plates. 21cm.
Bibliography: p. 183-192.

Inscribed copy: To Mr. Arthur Spingarn
with thanks for encouragement in the past.
J. A. Porter/43.

1. Negro art. 2. Negro artists. I. Title.

43-16044 Revised
Library of Congress N6538.N5P6
r45i2l0 706.9

M815.5
H83n
Porter, James Amos, 1905- 1970
The Negro in modern art.

(In: Howard University, Washington, D.C.
Graduate School Div. of Social Sciences. The
New Negro thirty years afterward ... Washington,
Howard University, 1956. 23cm. pp. 48-56.)

M973.9
F46
No.15
Porter, James Amos, 1905- 1970
Progress of the Negro in art during the
past fifty years. Pittsburgh, Pittsburgh
Courier, 1950.

7p. port. illus. 24cm. (Fifty years of
progress)

Porter, James Amos, 1905-1970, illus.
M784
J61
Johns, Altona (Trent)
Play songs of the deep south. Illustrated by
James A. Porter. Washington, D.C., The Associated Publishers, Inc., [1944]

33p. illus. 27½cm.

M740
P82
Porter, James Amos, 1905-1970 illus.
Talking animals, by Wilfrid D. Hambly;
illus. by James A. Porter. Washington, D. C.,
Associated Publishers. 1949.

x, 100p. illus. 26cm.

1. Animals, Legends and stories of
2. Tales, African. I. title
II. Hambly, Wilfrid Dyson, 1886-

M811.5
P831
Porter, John Thomas
In spite of handicaps; a book of verse.
New York, Comet Press Books, 1959.

50p. 20cm.
Portrait of author on book jacket.

1. Poetry (American). I. Title.

M323
P83r
Porter, Kenneth Wiggins.
Relations between Negroes and Indians within the present limits of the United States, by Kenneth W. Porter ... Washington, D. C., The Association for the study of Negro life and history, inc. [193-]
1 p. l., 81 p. 24½cm.
White author.

Race relations.
1. Negroes. 2. Indians of North America. I. Association for the study of Negro life and history, inc. II. Title.

37-14789
Library of Congress E185.4.P67
[3] [970.1] 325.260973

Porters - Correspondence, reminiscences, etc.
MB9
T857
Turner, Robert Emanuel, 1875-
Memories of a retired Pullman porter. [1st ed.] New York, Exposition Press [1954]
191 p. illus. 21 cm.

1. Porters—Correspondence, reminiscences, etc. I. Title.
Full name: Robert Emanuel Hammond Turner.

HD8039.R37T8 923.873 54-10978 ‡
Library of Congress [2]

Portland.
M979
R24r
Reddick, Lawrence Dunbar, 1910- ed.
Race relations on the Pacific coast.
New York, Journal of educational sociology,
1945.

129-208p. 23cm.
Special issue of The Journal of educational
sociology, November 1945.
Partial contents: -The new race-relations
frontier, by L. D. Reddick. -Portland, by
E. C. Berry.

Portrait of a decade.
M323.4
L58
Lewis, Anthony, 1927-
Portrait of a decade; the second American revolution [by] Anthony Lewis and the New York times. New York, Random House [1964]
322 p. illus. 25 cm.
White author.
Partial contents.- A Negro assays the Negro
mood, by James Baldwin.- Explanation of the
'Black psyche', by John Oliver Killens.
1. Negroes—Civil rights. I. New York times. II. Title. III. Title: The second American revolution.

E185.61.L52 1964 323.40973 64-14832
Library of Congress [4-1]

Portrait of a man.
M811.5
F84p
Franklin, Carl.
Portrait of man, a love poem. [1st ed.] New York, Exposition Press [1952]
47 p. 21 cm.

I. Title.

PS3511.R273P6 811.5 52-11485 ‡
Library of Congress [5]

Portrait of a young man drowning.
M813.5
P42p
Perry, Charles.
Portrait of a young man drowning. New York, Simon and Schuster, 1962.
307 p. 22 cm.

I. Title.

PZ4.P462Po 62-7555 ‡
Library of Congress [5]

Portrait of a young man drowning.
M813.5
P42p2
Perry, Charles
Portrait of a young man drowning. [London]
A. Deutech [1962]

307p. 20cm.

Portraitins; lere serie.
Haiti
MB
L61p
Lherisson, Justin
Portraitins; lere serie. Port-au-Prince,
Imp., H. Amblard, 18?4.

44p. 18cm.

Portraits.
M757
C78
Cooper, William Arthur, 1895-
A portrayal of Negro life, by William Arthur Cooper. Published under the auspices of the Division of coöperation in education and race relations; coöperating organizations: State department of public instruction, Raleigh, N. C., University of North Carolina, Chapel Hill, N. C., Duke university, Durham, N. C. [Durham, N. C., The Seeman printery, inc.] 1936.
xi, 110 p. incl. plates, ports. 23½ cm.
"Portraits ... all of real people ... painted to portray some phase or mood of Negro life."—Pref.
1. Negroes in literature and art. I. Title.

36—10959
Library of Congress ND237.C68A4
[48f½] 757

Portraits in color.
MB
C42
Cherry, Gwendolyn S
Portraits in color; the lives of colorful
Negro women, by Gwendolyn Cherry, Ruby Thomas,
and Pauline Willis. [1st ed.] New York,
Pageant Press [1962]

224p. illus. 21cm.
Includes bibliography.

A portrayal of Negro life.
M757
C78
Cooper, William Arthur, 1895-
A portrayal of Negro life, by William Arthur Cooper. Published under the auspices of the Division of coöperation in education and race relations; coöperating organizations: State department of public instruction, Raleigh, N. C., University of North Carolina, Chapel Hill, N. C., Duke university, Durham, N. C. [Durham, N. C., The Seeman printery, inc.] 1936.
xi, 110 p. incl. plates, ports. 23½ cm.
"Portraits ... all of real people ... painted to portray some phase or mood of Negro life."—Pref.
1. Negroes in literature and art. I. Title.

36—10959
Library of Congress ND237.C68A4
[48f½] 757

Portuguese language - Foreign words and phrases -
Africans.
Brazil
M869
R13e
Raimundo, Jacques.
... O elemento afro-negro na lingua portuguesa. Rio [de Janeiro] Renascença editora, 1933.
191, [2] p., 1 l. 18½cm. (*On cover:* Biblioteca pedagogica "Renascença")
"Bibliografia": p. [181]-191.

1. Portuguese language—Foreign words and phrases—African.
I. Title.

37-19669
Library of Congress PC5307.A6R3
[2] 469.24

Portuguese literature - Africa.
Africa
M896
N297
Neves, João Alves das, ed.
Poetas e contistas Africanos de expressão
Portuguesa: Cabo verde, Guiné, São Tomé e
príncipe, Angola, Moçambique. [São Paulo]
Editôra Brazilienae [1963]

211p. 20½cm.
White editor

1. Portuguese literature - Africa.
2. African literature. I. Title.

Portuguese poetry.

Portugal
M869
C82v
Costa Alegre, Caetano da, 1864-1890.
Versos. Lisboa, Livraria Ferin, 1916.

167p. port. 19cm.

M323
P84wy
Posey, Barbara Ann
Why I sit-in; the girl who started a nationwide civil-rights movement tells how and why she sits and waits. New York, NAACP, 1960.

4p. port. 22cm.
Reprinted from Datebook magazine.

1. Civil rights. 2. Race relations. 3. Sit-in demonstration. I. Title.

M975.4
P84n
Posey, Thomas Edward, 1901–
The Negro citizen of West Virginia, by Thomas E. Posey ... Institute, W. Va., Press of West Virginia state college ⌊1934⌋
1 p. l., ⌊5⌋-119 p. plates, ports., diagrs. 24cm.
Bibliography: p. ⌊110⌋-112.

1. Negroes—West Virginia. I. Title.

Library of Congress E185.93.W5P6 37-27796
⌊2⌋ 325.2609754

La posie est dans l'histoire.

Africa, Central
M896.1
B219
Samboté, Pierre
La posie est dans l'histoire. Paris, P. J. Oswald ⌊1960⌋

40p. 19cm. (Collection Janus)

The position of Negro women.

M304
P19
v.1, no.3
Gordon, Eugene, 1890–
The position of Negro women, by Eugene Gordon and Cyril Briggs ... ⌊New York, Workers library publishers, 1935⌋
15, ⌊1⌋ p. 15½cm.
Caption title: Negro women workers in the U. S. A.
Illustration on t.-p.

1. Women, Negro. 2. Woman—Employment. I. Briggs, Cyril V., 1888– joint author. II. Title. III. Title: Negro women workers in the U. S. A.

Library of Congress E185.8.G67 45-48860
⌊2⌋

Post-war.

M323.
Im1
Imbert, Dennis I
The Negro after the war, by D. I. Imbert ... 1st ed. New Orleans, La., Williams printing service, 1943.
3 p. l., 74 p., 2 l. 21½cm.

1. Negroes. I. Title.

Library of Congress E185.61.I 5 44-27088
⌊3⌋ 325.260973

M331
H87p
The post-war industrial outlook for Negroes.
Howard University, Washington D.C. Division of Social Science.
The post-war industrial outlook for Negroes; Papers and proceedings of the eighth annual Conference of the Division of the Social Sciences. Co-sponsor: The A. Philip Randolph Fund, October 18-20, 1944 ..., edited by Kurt Braun. Washington, D.C., Published by the Howard University Press for The Graduate School, Howard University, 1945.

M331
H87p
Howard University, Washington D.C. Division of Social Science. The post-war industrial outlook for Negroes. (card 2)

VI, 219p. 23 cm. (Howard University Studies in the social sciences)

1. Labor and laboring classes. I. Title. II. Series.

Post-war jobs for veterans, Negroes, women.

M331
H86
Hudson, Roy.
Post-war jobs for veterans, negroes, women, by Roy Hudson. New York, Workers library publishers, 1944.
24 p. illus. 19cm.

1. Veterans—Employment—U. S. 2. Negroes—Employment. 3. Woman—Employment—U. S. I. Title.

A 45-2552

Harvard univ. Library for Library of Congress HD5724.H83
⌊3⌋† 331.137

Post-war struggle for domestic peace.

M815.5
G76t
Granger, Lester Blackwell, 1896-
...to the unfinished struggle; three addresses to American college youth. New York, National Urban League, ⌊1944⌋.

2, 5-7p. 15½cm.

Postage stamps - Haiti.

Haiti
M383
M76
Montès, Léon
La timbrologie Haitienne, 1881-1954. Port-au-Prince, Henri Deschamps, 1954.

iv, 205p. illus. 21cm.

M05
R29
Poston, Theodore Roosevelt, 1906-
The Negro press. (The Reporter, 1:14-17, December 6, 1949.)

(In: The Reporter, 1:14-17, December 6, 1949.)

1. Newspapers.

M810.8
M77p
Poston, Theodore, Roosevelt, 1906-
The revolt of the evil fairies.

(In: Moon, Bucklin, ed. Primer for white folks. Garden City, N. Y. Doubleday, Doran, 1945. 21½cm. pp. 193-197).

Haiti
M89
C14p
Posy, Bonnard
Roussan Camille, le poète d'assaut a la nuit. ... Port-au-Prince, Imprimerie des Antilles, 1962.

39p. port. 21cm.

1. Camille, Roussan, 1915- 2. Haitian, poetry.

The Potential Negro Market.

M658
J63
Johnson, Joseph T 1909–
The potential Negro market. ⌊1st ed.⌋ New York, Pageant Press ⌊1952⌋
185 p. 24 cm.

1. Negroes. 2. Consumers—U. S. 3. U. S.—Comm. I. Title.

HF3031.J6 52-14925 ‡
*658.83 658.8072

Library of Congress ⌊10⌋

Potter, Henry Codman, bp., 1834-1908

M814.4
W272bi
Washington, Booker Taliaferro, 1859?-1915
⌊Bishop Potter and the Negro, address⌋

(In: New York. People's Institute. Memorial to Henry Codman Potter by the People's Institute, Cooper Union,... December twentieth, MCMVIII. New York, ⌊Cheltenham Press⌋ 1909. 21cm. pp.60-67)

Uganda
M367
P85
Potts, C W K
Social club mu Afrika ⌊Social club in East Africa⌋ Kyakyusibwa F. B. Lubwama. Nairobi, Eagle Press, 1953.

32p. 22½cm.
Written in Luganda.
White author.

1. Africa, East - Clubs. 2. Clubs. I. Title. II. Lubwama, F. B., tr.

Pouget, Louis-Edouard.

Haiti
M89
P86b
Bervin, Antoine.
...Louis-Edouard Pouget. Port-au-Prince, Societe d'Editions et de Librairie [n.d.]

183p. port. 18½cm. (Bibliotheque Haitienne)

Pour la révolution Africaine.

Martinique
M960
F217
Fannon, Frantz, 1925-1962.
Pour la révolution Africaine; ecrits politiques Paris, Francois Maspero, 1964.
223p. 21½cm. (Cahiers Libnes, nos. 53-54.)

Pour notre libération économique et financière.

Haiti
M972.94
H86p
Hudicourt, Pierre Lelio
Pour notre libération économique et financière. ⌊Port-au-Prince, Édition du Parti socialiste populaire, 1946⌋
25 p. 21 cm.

1. Haiti—Economic policy. 2. Finance—Haiti. 3. Haiti—For. rel.—U. S. 4. U. S.—For. rel.—Haiti. I. Title.

A 48-6316*

Harvard Univ. Library for Library of Congress ⌊1⌋

Pour toi, Nègre mon frère ...

Dahomey
M896.2
V66p
Viderot, Toussaint.
Pour toi, nègre mon frère ... "Un homme comme les autres." ⌊Par⌋ Toussaint Viderot "Mensah." Monte Carlo, Éditions Regain ⌊1960⌋
154 p. 19 cm.
A play.

I. Title.

A 61-4375

Illinois. Univ. Library for Library of Congress ⌊1⌋

Pour un coumbite; poemes 1962-1963.

Haiti
M841
Ad72p

Adolphe, Armand
Pour un coumbite; poemes 1962-1963. Preface de Gerard Campfort. Port-au-Prince, Imprimerie M. Rodriquez, 1963.

28p. 21½cm.

Cuba
M863.6
P86n

Poveda Ferrer, Simeon.
Nydia y Fidel; novela cubana por Simeon Poveda Ferrer. Habana, Imprenta "La Prueba", 1920.

274p. port. 19½cm.

1. Cuban fiction. I. Title.

M286
P87

Powell, Adam Clayton, 1865-1953
Against the tide; an autobiography, by A. Clayton Powell, sr. ... New York, R. R. Smith, 1938.
x p., 2 l., 327 p. front. (port.) 22½ᶜᵐ.

I. Title.

38—38019

Library of Congress BX6455.P63A3
[43d1]
922.673

M286
P87p

Powell, Adam Clayton, 1865-1953
Palestine and saints in Caesar's household, by A. Clayton Powell, sr. New York, R. R. Smith, 1939.
viii p., 2 l., 13-217 p. 21ᶜᵐ.

1. Palestine—Descr. & trav. 2. Baptists—Sermons. 3. Sermons, American. I. Title.

39-25033

Library of Congress BX6452.P6
——— Copy 2.
Copyright A 131759 [2]
915.69

M286
P87pi

Powell, Adam Clayton, 1865-1953.
Picketting hell, a fictitious narrative, by A. Clayton Powell... New York, Wendell Malliet and Company, 1942.

254p. front. 22cm.

I. Title.

M286
P97r

Powell, Adam Clayton, 1865-1953
Riots and ruins, by A. Clayton Powell, sr. ... New York, R. R. Smith, 1945.
xiv p., 1 l., 17-171 p. 22½ᶜᵐ.

1. Race relations 2. Riots. I. Title.

45-8935

Library of Congress • E185.61.P78
[20]
325.260973

M380
P87

Powell, Adam Clayton, 1908-
Comparative wage costs and trade advantage: the European economic community, Great Britain, and the United States. Committee on Education and labor, House of Representatives, Eighty-eighth Congress, first session. Washington, U. S.Govt. Print. Off., 1963.

vi, 103p. 24cm.

1. Competition, International. 2. Labor costs - European Economic Community countries. 3. Labor costs - Gt. Brit. 4. Labor costs - U.S. I. Title.

M252
P87

Powell, Adam Clayton, 1908-
Keep the faith, baby! New York, Trident Press, 1967.
293 p. 22 cm.

1. Baptists—Negro—Sermons. 2. Sermons, American I. Title.

BX6452.P59 252.06 67-16402

Library of Congress [12]

M973
P87

Powell, Adam Clayton, 1908-
Marching blacks, an interpretive history of the rise of the black common man, by Adam Clayton Powell, jr. New York, Dial press, 1945.
4 p. l., 3-218 p. 21ᶜᵐ.
Bibliography: p. 215-218.

1. Negroes. 2. Negroes—Hist. I. Title.

46-1158

Library of Congress • E185.6.P8
[35]
325.260973

Powell, Adam Clayton, 1908-

MB9
P87L

Lewis, Claude.
Adam Clayton Powell. Greenwich, Conn., Fawcett Publications [1963]
127 p. 18 cm. (Gold medal books)
"K1361."

1. Powell, Adam Clayton, 1908-

E748.P86L4 64-703

Library of Congress [5]

M248
P87

Powell, Raphael Philemon.
The prayer for freedom; a memorial of the prayer pilgrimage, May 17, 1957. New York, 1957.

16p. 22cm.

I. Title.

M304
P19
v.3, no.9

Powell, W H R
The Negro and the bread line. The danger of his remaining. Some things he should do to get out, and Is Negro womanhood equal to its task of constructive leadership in these days of distressing unemployment. [Philadelphia, James Printing Co. 1931]
[22]p. 22cm.
1. Women

M223.2
P87

Powell, W H R
A supervised life; or, Impressions from the Twenty-third psalm, by W. H. R. Powell ... [Philadelphia, Press of B. F. Emery company, 1945]
xiii, 145 p. plates. 19ᶜᵐ.

1. Bible. O. T. Psalms XXIII—Sermons. 2. Baptists—Sermons. 3. Sermons, American. I. Title.

45-5226

Library of Congress BS1450 23d.P6
[3]
223.2

M629.13
P87

Powell, William J.
Black wings [by] Lieut. William J. Powell. Los Angeles, I. Deach, jr., 1934.
2 p. l., iii-xiii, [1], 15-218 p. front. (port.) illus. (incl. ports.) 23½ᶜᵐ.
"Autograph first edition."

1. Negroes in aeronautics. 2. Aeronautics. I. Title.

34-38845

Library of Congress TL553.P6
[45d1]
629.13

Barbados The power of Negro action.
M942
M45

Maxwell, Neville George Anthony.
The power of Negro action, by Neville Maxwell. [London] N. G. A. Maxwell [1966]
1-80 p. 22 cm. 8/-
(B 66-5466)
Bibliography: p. 57-58.

1. West Indians in Great Britain. 2. Negroes in Great Britain. 3. Gt. Brit.—Race question. I. Title.

DA125.W4M3 301.45196042 66-70698

Library of Congress [5]

Powerful long ladder.

M814.5
D66p

Dodson, Owen, 1914-
Powerful long ladder, by Owen Dodson ... New York, Farrar, Straus and company, inc., 1946.
4 p. l., 103 p. 21ᶜᵐ.
Poems.

I. Title.

46—6872

Library of Congress PS3507.O364P6
[47f3]
811.5

Senegal Poyas, B., joint author.
M973
N23

N'Diaye, Jean Pierre.
Les noirs aux États-Unis pour les africains, par J. P. N'Diaye, J. Bassene, B. Poyas. [Paris, 1964]
184 p. illus. 21 cm. (Réalités africaines, no 7)
Includes bibliographical references.

1. Negroes—Hist. 2. Black Muslims. I. Bassene, J., joint author. II. Poyas, B., joint author. III. Title. (Series)

E185.R38 no. 7 65-44441

Library of Congress [1]

Practical farming for the South.

M630
B87p

Bullock, Benjamin Franklin, 1888-
Practical farming for the South, by B. F. Bullock ... Chapel Hill, The University of North Carolina press, 1944.
xvii, [3], 3-510 p. illus. 21ᶜᵐ.
"Farm publications": p. 480-486. Bibliography [on mulching and sub-surface tillage]: p. 498.

1. Agriculture—Handbooks, manuals, etc. 2. Agriculture—Southern states. [2. Southern states—Agriculture] 3. Faulkner, Edward Hubert, 1886- Plowman's folly. I. Title. II. Title: Farming for the South.

Agr 44-211

U. S. Dept. of agr. Library for Library of Congress 31.3B87 S505.B8
[50]†
630.2

Practical theology.

M230
C68

Collins, Judge Gould.
Practical theology. New York, Comet Press Books [1959, °1960]
75 p. 21 cm. (A Reflection book)

1. Christian Methodist Episcopal Church—Doctrinal and controversial works. I. Title.

BX8467.C6 230.78 59-65287 ‡

Library of Congress [5]

Prairie View Agricultural and Mechanical College

see

Texas. Agricultural and Mechanical College, Prairie View

Praise-poems of Tswana chiefs.

South Africa
M896.1
Sch16

Schapera, Isaac, 1905- ed. and tr.
Praise-poems of Tswana chiefs. Translated and edited with an introd. and notes, by I. Schapera. Oxford, Clarendon Press, 1965.
vi, 255 p. geneal. tables, map. 23 cm. (Oxford library of African literature)
Bibliography: p. [246]-247.

1. Sechuana poetry. 2. Tswana (Bantu tribe)—Kings and rulers. I. Title.

PL8651.7.S3 896.3 65-8539

Library of Congress [2]

Mali
M966.2
Oulp

La pratique du droit Musulman.
Ouane, Ibrahima Mamadou, 1908-
La pratique du droit Musulman. Loire, Société d'exploitation imprimerie moderne a Andrezieux, 1958.
43p. port. 18cm.

Rhodesia
M968.9
C43

Pratt, Cranford, joint editor.
Leys, Colin, *ed.*
A new deal in Central Africa, edited by Colin Leys and Cranford Pratt. New York, Praeger [1960]
226 p. illus. 22 cm. (Books that matter)
Includes bibliography.
1. Rhodesia and Nyasaland. I. Pratt, Cranford, joint ed. II. Title.
DT856.L4 968.9 60-12201 ‡
Library of Congress [20]

M264
B54

Prayer.
Bishop, Shelton Hale.
The wonder of prayer. Greenwich, Conn., Seabury Press, 1959.
95 p. 20 cm.
1. Prayer. I. Title.
BV210.2.B57 264.1 59-5700 ‡
Library of Congress [5]

M248
M38wt

Prayer.
Massey, James Earl.
"When thou prayest"; an interpretation of Christian prayer according to the teachings of Jesus. Anderson, Ind., Warner Press [1960]
64 p. 19 cm.
1. Prayer. I. Title.
BV215.M37 248.32 60-11408 ‡
Library of Congress [2]

M810
B73p

A prayer.
Brawley, Benjamin Griffith, 1882-1939.
A prayer. Words by B. G. Brawley... Music by A. H. Ryder... [Atlanta, Ga.] Atlanta Baptist college press [1899]
2p. 23½cm.
Music: p. 2

M248
P87

The prayer for freedom.
Powell, Raphael Philemon.
The prayer for freedom; a memorial of the prayer pilgrimage, May 17, 1957. New York, 1957.
16p. 22cm.
I. Title.

M266.58
C67p

Preacher with a plow.
Coles, Samuel B *d.* 1957.
Preacher with a plow. Boston, Houghton Mifflin [1957]
241 p. illus. 21 cm.
1. Missions—Angola. I. Title.
BV3625.A6C57 [266.58] 276.73 57-8223 ‡
Library of Congress [15]

M251
J63t

Preaching.
Johnson, Henry Theodore, 1857-
Tuskegee talks. Ministerial training and qualification, by H.T. Johnson... Philadelphia, Press of international printing co. c1902
viii, 49p. front. 23cm.

M251
P66s

Preaching
Pipes, William Harrison, 1912-
Say amen, brother ! Old-time Negro preaching: a study in American frustration. New York, William-Frederick Press, 1951.
i, 210p. 24cm.
Bibliograhy: p. 201-205.

M251
R56a

Preaching.
Robinson, James Herman.
Adventurous preaching. [1st ed.] Great Neck, N. Y., Channel Press [1956]
188 p. 21 cm. (The Lyman Beecher lectures at Yale, 1955)
1. Preaching. 2. Theology, Pastoral. I. Title.
BV4211.2.R6 251 56-13819 ‡
Library of Congress [7]

Haiti
M920
T49pr

La préconnaissance du futur.
Tippenhauer, Louis Gentil, 1867-
La préconnaissance du futur; interview relative a la decouverte de la loi du temps. Port-au-Prince, Fondation Internationale de Meterologie de Port-au-Prince, 1950.
32p. illus. 23cm.
Interview de Pierre Moraviah Morpeau avec ... Docteur Louis Gentil Tippenhauer.

M811.5
J72pr

Preface to a twenty volume suicide note.
Jones, LeRoi.
Preface to a twenty volume suicide note; [poems] New York, Totem Press in association with Corinth Books [1961]
47 p. 21 cm.
I. Title.
PS3519.O4545P7 811.54 61-14982 ‡
Library of Congress [2]

M301
J63p r

... A preface to racial understanding.
Johnson, Charles Spurgeon, 1893-
... A preface to racial understanding. New York, Friendship press [°1936]
ix, 206 p. 19½cm.
At head of title: By Charles S. Johnson.
"Bibliographical notes": p. 193-201.
1. Negroes. 2. U. S.—Race question. I. Title.
36—14692
Library of Congress E185.61.J68
[45x2] 325.260973

Nigeria
M618.2
Ad35

Pregnancy.
Adeniyi-Jones, O., jt auth.
You and your baby [by] W. R. F. Collis [and] O. Adeniyi-Jones. Lagos, African Universities Press [1964]
94p. 18½cm. illus.

M618.2
Se4p

Pregnancy spacing in the rural public health...
Seibels, Robert E
Pregnancy spacing in the rural public health, by Robert E. Seibels... Columbia, South Carolina, The South Carolina state board of health, 1942.
20p. tables. 23cm.

Uruguay
M861.6
B77p

Pregón de marimorena...
Brindis de Salas, Virginia.
Pregón de marimorena (poemas) Prólogo de Julio Guadalupe. 1. ed. Montevideo, Sociedad Cultural Editora Indoamericana, 1946.
59p. port. 20cm.

M323.2
C54p

Prejudice and your child.
Clark, Kenneth Bancroft, 1914-
Prejudice and your child. Boston, Beacon Press [1955]
151 p. 22 cm.
Includes bibliography.
1. U. S.—Race question. 2. Prejudices and antipathies. 3. Child study. 4. Segregation in education. I. Title.
BF723.R3C5 157.3 55—9502 ‡
Library of Congress [55q30]

M811.5
M78

Prejudice unveiled.
Moorer, Lizelia Augusta Jenkins.
Prejudice unveiled, and other poems, by Lizelia Augusta Jenkins Moorer. Boston, Roxburgh publishing company, 1907.
170 p. front. (port.) 19cm.
I. Title.
Library of Congress PS3525.O582P7 1907 7—28684
Copyright A 178092 [a36b1]

M323
A17r

Prejudices and antipathies.
Allport, Gordon W
Roots of prejudice, by Gordon W. Allport & Bernard M. Kramer. New York, American Jewish Congress, 1946.
22p. illus. tables. 19cm.
Special number of Jewish Affairs, December 1, 1946.

M323.2
C54p

Prejudices and antipathies.
Clark, Kenneth Bancroft, 1914-
Prejudice and your child. Boston, Beacon Press [1955]
151 p. 22 cm.
Includes bibliography.
1. U. S.—Race question. 2. Prejudices and antipathies. 3. Child study. 4. Segregation in education. I. Title.
BF723.R3C5 157.3 55—9502 ‡
Library of Congress [55q30]

M323
C831

Prejudices and antipathies.
Council against intolerance in America.
An American answer to intolerance. Teacher's manual no. 1, junior and senior high schools. Experimental form, 1939. New York city, Council against intolerance in America, 1939.
130 p., 1 l. 23 cm.
"Prepared by Frank Walser, with the assistance of Annette Smith and Violet Edwards."
"Bibliography of plays suitable for high school production": p. 117-118.
Bibliography: p. 119-130.
1. Propaganda. 2. Prejudices and antipathies. 3. Toleration. I. ~~Walser, Frank. II. Smith, Annette. III. Edwards, Violet.~~ IV. Title. V. Title: Intolerance. I. Race relations. II. White, Walter, 1893-1955.
A 40—2271
New York Univ. Wash. Sq. Library HM263.C7
for Library of Congress HM263.C6
[a50m1] 301.1523

Prejudices and antipathies.

M323 Et3w Etheridge, Frank Oscar
"What became of race prejudice?. By Frank Oscar Etheridge. New York, William-Frederocl press, 1943.
23p. 13½cm.

Prejudices and antipathies.

Ghana M301 G166 Gardiner, Robert Kweku Atta, 1914-
A world of peoples ₍by₎ Robert Gardiner. London, British Broadcasting Corporation, 1966.
93p. 22cm. (The Reith lectures, 1965)

Prejudices and antipathies.

M815.5 G88 v.1, no. 9 **Grimke, Francis James, 1850–**
Christianity and race prejudice; two discourses delivered in the Fifteenth street Presbyterian church, Washington, D. C. May 29th, and June 5th, 1910. By the pastor Rev. Francis J. Grimke ... ₍Washington, Press of W. E. Cobb, 1910₎
29 p. 22½cm.

10-16329

Library of Congress

Prejudices and antipathies.

M304 F19 v.5, no.13 ₍Harris, James E. ₎
Black justice. New York, American Civil Liberties union, 1931.

M323.4 H24b 27p. 23cm.

Prejudices and antipathies.

M323. W93m The Writers' Board.
The myth that threatens America. New York, The Board.
3-35p. 21cm.

Prejudices and antipathies (Child psychology)

M649.1 Y86 **Young, Margaret B**
How to bring up your child without prejudice, by Margaret B. Young. ₍1st ed. New York, Public Affairs Committee, 1965₎
20 p. col. illus. 18 cm. (Public affairs pamphlet no. 373)
Cover title.
Bibliography: p. 20.

1. Prejudices and antipathies (Child psychology) I. Title.

BF723.P75Y6 65-5635

Library of Congress ₍10₎

Prelude to Ghana's industrialisation.

Ghana M966.7 Ak8p **Akwawuah, Kwadwo Asafo,** 1930
Prelude to Ghana's industrialisation. London, Mitre Press ₍1960₎
96 p. 23 cm.

1. Ghana—Econ. condit. I. Title.

HC517.G6A65 330.9667 60-35912 ‡

Library of Congress ₍1₎

Haiti M841 H41p **Les préludes;**
Héraux, Edmond, 1858–
Les préludes; poésies, par Edmond Heraux... Paris, Grassart, Librairie-Editeur, 1888.
xvii, 318, iiip. 18cm.

Premières notions de lectures.

Haiti M972.94 L61p Lhérisson, Lélia J
Premières notions de lectures, Cours préparatoire 1re. partie, par Lélia J. Lhérosson... Port-au-Prince, Haiti Imprimerie du college vertiers, 1929.
70 2p. illus. 22cm.

Haiti M972.94 N34pr Les premiers citoyens et les premiers députés noirs et de couleur.
Nemours, Alfred, 1883–
... Les premiers citoyens et les premiers députés noirs et de couleur; la loi du 4 avril 1792, ses précédents, sa première application à Saint-Domingue, d'après des documents inédits de l'époque. Suivi de: Le Cap Français en 1792, à l'arrivée de Sonthonax, d'après des documents inédits de l'époque. Port-au-Prince, Haiti, Imprimerie de l'état, 1941.
2 p. l., 170 p. plates. 23cm.
At head of title: Général Nemours.
"Bibliographie": p. 167–168.

1. Haiti — Pol. & govt.—1791–1804. 2. France — Colonies — Santo Domingo. I. Title. II. Title: Le Cap Français en 1792.

42-4818

Library of Congress F1928.N45

₍2₎ 972.94

Ghana M398 P91h Prempeh, Albert Kofi
~~Courlander, Harold, 1908–~~
The hat-shaking dance, and other tales from the Gold Coast, by Harold Courlander, with Albert Kofi Prempeh. Illustrated by Enrico Arno. ₍1st ed.₎ New York, Harcourt, Brace ₍1957₎
115 p. illus. 21 cm.

1. Tales, Ashanti. I. Title. II Courlander, Harold, 1908
2. Ghana - Folktales

PZ8.1.C8Hat 56-5872 ‡

Library of Congress ₍57h5₎

M8115 P91va Prentice, Bessie Elizabeth
"Various moods" with Marie. volume II. Los Angeles, Burris, printer, c1944.
27p. 16cm.
cover title.

1. Poetry I. Title

M811.5 P91v **Prentice, Bessie Elizabeth**
"Various Moods" with Marie. Los Angeles, n.p., c 1940
26p. port. 16½cm.
Autographed copy: "Marie Prentice. D.E.S. no. 37 Victory chapter."

1. Poetry I. Title

M378FB F54p Preparing Negro youth for life in one world. Fisk University. Nashville.
Preparing Negro youth for life in one world. Nashville, 1949?
₍20₎p. illus. 30cm.

Presbyterian church.

M815.5 G88 v.1, no.5 Grimke, Francis James, 1850-
Organic union between the Cumberland Presbyterian church, and the Presbyterian church in the United States.
16p. 23cm.

Presbyterian church— Collected works.

M208.1 G88 **Grimké, Francis James, 1850–1937.**
The works of Francis J. Grimké, edited by Carter G. Woodson ... Washington, D. C., The Associated publishers, inc. ₍1942₎
4 v. 23½cm.
CONTENTS.—I. Addresses mainly personal and racial.—II. Special sermons.—III. Stray thoughts and meditations.—IV. Letters.

1. Presbyterian church — Collected works. 2. Theology — Collected works—20th cent. 3. U. S.—Race question. I. Woodson, Carter Godwin, 1875– ed.

42—18902

Library of Congress BX8915.G78

₍43d2₎ 208.1

M285 B23 Presbyterian Church-Missions.
Barber, Jesse Belmont.
Climbing Jacob's ladder; story of the work of the Presbyterian Church U. S. A. among the Negroes. New York, Board of National Missions, Presbyterian Church in the U. S. A. ₍1952₎
108 p. 23 cm.
"Originally prepared and published as a master's thesis in the Department of Church History of Auburn Theological Seminary ... revised and brought down to date."
Includes bibliography.

1. Negroes—Missions. 2. Presbyterians, Negro. 3. Presbyterian Church—Missions. I. Title.

BX8946.N4B3 [266.5] 277.3 52-11209 ‡

Library of Congress ₍2₎

Presbyterian Church - Sermons.

M252 Im2b **Imes, William Lloyd, 1889–**
The black pastures, an American pilgrimage in two centuries; essays and sermons. ₍1st ed.₎ Nashville, Hemphill Press, 1957.
146 p. illus. 24 cm.

1. Presbyterian Church—Sermons. 2. Sermons, American. 3. U. S.—Race question. I. Title.

BX9178.I 5B5 252.051 57-11472 ‡

Library of Congress ₍8₎

Presbyterian Church in the U.S.

M285 An2 Anderson, Matthew, 1848-1928.
Presbyterianism. Its relation to the Negro. Illustrated by the Berean Presbyterian church, Philadelphia, with sketch of the church and autobiography of the author, by Matthew Anderson ... with introductions by Francis J. Grimke ... and John B. Reeve ... Philadelphia, John McGill White & Co. ₍1897₎
263p. front. 19½cm.

Presbyterian Church in the U.S.A.

M285 W15 Walker, James Garfield
Presbyterianism and the Negro, by Rev. James Garfield Walker... Greensboro, N.C.
₍n.p., n.d.₎
92p. front. 23cm.

Presbyterian Church in the U.S.A. - Missions.

M285 D79f Draper, Charlotte
For the Presbyterian female of color's enterprising society in Baltimore. A free-will offering by Charlotte Draper. For the benefit of Africa. The Island of Corsica, in Western Africa. January 25, 1860... Baltimore, Printed by Frederick A. Hanzsche.
96p. port. 23cm.

Presbyterian church in the U. S.—Missions.

M285
Sh4p

Sheppard, William Henry, 1865–1927.
Presbyterian pioneers in Congo, by William H. Sheppard. Introduction by Rev. S. H. Chester, D. D. Richmond, Va., Presbyterian committee of publication [1917]
157 p. incl. front., illus. (incl. map) ports. 19½cm.

1. Missions—Kongo, Belgian. 2. Kongo, Belgian—Descr. & trav. 3. Presbyterian church in the U. S.—Missions. I. Title.

44-34996

Library of Congress BV3625.K6S48
[2]

The Presbyterian female of color's enterprising society.

M285
D79f

Draper, Charlotte
For the Presbyterian female of color's enterprising society in Baltimore. A free-will offering, by Charlotte Draper. For the benefit of Africa. The Island of Corsica, in Western Africa. January 25, 1860... Baltimore, Printed by Frederick A. Hanzsche.
96p. port. 23cm.

Presbyterian pioneers in Congo.

M285
Sh4p

Sheppard, William Henry, 1865–1927.
Presbyterian pioneers in Congo, by William H. Sheppard. Introduction by Rev. S. H. Chester, D. D. Richmond, Va., Presbyterian committee of publication [1917]
157 p. incl. front., illus. (incl. map) ports. 19½cm.

1. Missions—Kongo, Belgian. 2. Kongo, Belgian—Descr. & trav. 3. Presbyterian church in the U. S.—Missions. I. Title.

44-34996

Library of Congress BV3625.K6S48
[2]

Presbyterianism and the Negro

M285
W15

Walker, James Garfield
Presbyterianism and the Negro, by Rev. James Garfield Walker ... Greensboro, N.C. [n.p., n.d.]

92p. front. 23cm.

Presbyterians.

M285
B23

Barber, Jesse Belmont.
Climbing Jacob's ladder; story of the work of the Presbyterian Church U. S. A. among the Negroes. New York, Board of National Missions, Presbyterian Church in the U. S. A. [1952]
108 p. 23 cm.
"Originally prepared and published as a master's thesis in the Department of Church History of Auburn Theological Seminary ... revised and brought down to date."
Includes bibliography.

1. Negroes—Missions. 2. Presbyterians, Negro. 3. Presbyterian Church—Missions. I. Title.

BX8946.N4B3 [266.5] 277.3 52-11209 ‡

Library of Congress [2]

M345
P92d

Prescott, Patrick B
The doctrine of lateral support in Illinois; Being a treatise on the law in Illinois,.... particularly as it affects property abutting a subway in Chicago, now being built for purposes of local transportation. Reprinted from the John Marshall law quarterly, September 1940.

17p. 25cm.

1. Property--Law.

Présence.

Haiti
M841
P51p

Phelps, Anthony
Présence (poème). Illustrations de Luckner Lazard. Port-au-Prince, Art Graphique Presse, 1961.

[9] p. illus. 21½cm. (Collection Haiti Litteraire)

Présence africaine.

Africa
M916
Af8

Africa seen by American Negroes. [Paris, Présence africaine [1958]
418 p. illus. 22 cm.
Includes bibliography.

1. Africa — Civilization. 2. Africa — Civilization — American influences. 3. Negroes in Africa. I. Présence africaine.

DT14.A35 916 59-49517 ‡

Library of Congress [60b1]

Africa
M960
P92
no.10-11

Présence Africaine.
L'art Negre. Paris, Aux Éditions du Seuil, 1951.

254p. illus. plates. 19cm. (Cahiers speciaux, no. 10-11)

1. Art, African.

Africa
M960
P92
no.14

Présence Africaine.
Les etudiants noirs parlent. Paris, Présence Africaine, 1953.
311p. 19cm. (Cahiers speciaux, no. 14)

1. Africa. 2. African students.

Africa
M960
P92
no.15

Présence Africaine.
Hommage à Jacques Richard-Molard, 1913-1951. Paris, Présence Africaine, 1953.

383p. 19cm. (Cahiers speciaux, no. 15)

1. Africa.

Africa
M960
P92
no.8-9

Présence Africaine.
Le monde noir. Paris, Présence Africaine, 1950.

443p. illus. plates. 21½cm. (Cahiers speciaux, no. 8-9)

1. Art, African. 2. African literature.
I. Monod, Theodore, ed.

Presence africaine, 1947-
[Paris], Editions du Seuil, 1947-

no. illus. 23cm.
Frequency varies.
Editor: Alioune Diop.

See holdings card for issues in library.

1. Africa.

Africa
M960
P92

Présence Africaine.
Le 1er congrès international des ecrivains et artistes noirs. No. special. Paris, Présence Africaine, 1956.

408p. illus. 22½cm.

1. African authors. 2. Authors, African.

Africa
M960
P92
no.13

Présence Africaine.
Le travail en Afrique noire. Paris, Aux Éditions du Seuil, 1952.
427p. 19cm. (Cahier speciaux, no. 13)

Africa-Labor and laboring classes.

Africa
M960
P92
no.16

Présence Africaine.
Trois ecrivains noirs. Paris, Présence Africaine, 1954.
426p. 19cm. (Cahiers speciaux, no. 16)

1. African literature.

M378
H73p

The present problems involved in graduate and professional training for Negroes in the South.
Holmes, Dwight Oliver Wendell, 1877-
The present problems involved in graduate and professional training for Negroes in the South; An address before... the Association of Colleges as Secondary Schools for Negroes. Reprinted from the Proceedings of the Association of Colleges and Secondary Schools for Negroes, 1939.

7p. 23cm.

Present-day Brazilian race relations.

M015
Iv9p

Ivy, James Waldo
Present-day Brazilian race relations - a brief bibliography with an introduction. New York, The Crisis, 1958.

27p. 20cm.

The preservation of university documents;

M378
P83p

Porter, Dorothy Burnett, 1905-
The preservation of university documents: with special reference to Negro colleges and universities. Washington, D.C., 1942.
"Reprinted from the Journal of Negro Education, October, 1942, p. 527-528."
527-528p. 25cm.

Presidents - U. S.

M575.1
R616

Rogers, Joel Augustus, 1880-
The five Negro presidents according to what people said they were. New York, J. A. Rogers, 1965.

19p. ports. 20cm.

1. Heredity. 2. Presidents - U.S.
I. Title.

Presidents - U.S. - Biography.

MB9
F46m

Fields, Alonzo.
My 21 years in the White House. New York, Coward-McCann [1961]
223 p. 22 cm.
Portrait of author on book jacket.

1. Washington, D. C. White House. 2. Washington, D. C.—Soc. life & cust. 3. Presidents—U. S.—Biog. 4. Presidents—U. S.—Wives. 5. Visits of state—U. S. I. Title.

F204.W5F5 923.173 61-15068 ‡

Library of Congress [62b5]

Presidents-U.S.-Biography.

MB9
P23m

Parks, Lillian (Rogers)
My thirty years backstairs at the White House ₍by₎ Lillian Rogers Parks in collaboration with Frances Spatz Leighton. New York, Fleet Pub. Corp. ₍1961₎
346 p. 21 cm.
Portrait of author on book jacket.

1. Presidents—U. S.—Biog. 2. Presidents—U. S.—Wives. 3. Washington, D. C. White House. I. Title.

E176.1.P37 923.173 61—7626 ‡

Library of Congress ₍61t³30₎

Presidents - U. S. - Staff.

M973.92
M83

Morrow, Everett Frederic, 1909–
Black man in the White House; a diary of the Eisenhower years by the administrative officer for special projects, the White House, 1955–1961. New York, Coward-McCann ₍1963₎
308 p. 22 cm.

1. U. S.—Pol. & govt.—1953–1961. 2. Negroes—Civil rights. 3. Presidents—U. S.—Staff. 4. Eisenhower, Dwight David, Pres. U. S., 1890– I. Title.

E835.M58 328.40973 63—13310 ‡

Library of Congress ₍64f14₎

Presidents - U.S. - Wives.

MB9
F46m

Fields, Alonzo.
My 21 years in the White House. New York, Coward-McCann ₍1961₎
223 p. 22 cm.
Portrait of author on book jacket.

1. Washington, D. C. White House. 2. Washington, D. C.—Soc. life & cust. 3. Presidents—U. S.—Biog. 4. Presidents—U. S.—Wives. 5. Visits of state—U. S. I. Title.

F204.W5F5 923.173 61—15068 ‡

Library of Congress ₍62b³5₎

Presidents- U.S.-Wives.

MB9
P23m

Parks, Lillian (Rogers)
My thirty years backstairs at the White House ₍by₎ Lillian Rogers Parks in collaboration with Frances Spatz Leighton. New York, Fleet Pub. Corp. ₍1961₎
346 p. 21 cm.
Portrait of author on book jacket.

1. Presidents—U. S.—Biog. 2. Presidents—U. S.—Wives. 3. Washington, D. C. White House. I. Title.

E176.1.P37 923.173 61—7626 ‡

Library of Congress ₍61t³30₎

M331.833
P92

President's conference on home building and home ownership, *Washington, D. C.*, 1931.
Negro housing; report of the Committee on Negro housing, Nannie H. Burroughs, chairman; prepared for the committee by Charles S. Johnson; edited by John M. Gries and James Ford. Washington, D. C., The President's conference on home building and home ownership ₍°1932₎
xiv, 282 p. front., plates. 23½ᶜᵐ.
On cover: Physical aspects; social and economic factors; home ownership and financing.
(Continued on next card)

32—26908

₍43t2₎

M331.833
P92

President's conference on home building and home ownership, *Washington, D. C.*, 1931. Negro housing ... ₍°1932₎ (Card 2)
Bibliography: p. 260–271.

1. Housing—~~U. S.~~ 2. Labor and laboring classes—Dwellings. ~~3. Negroes.~~ ~~4. Negroes~~—Moral and social conditions. 5. U. S.—Race question. I. Burroughs, Nannie Helen, 1879– II. Johnson, Charles Spurgeon, 1893– ed. III. Gries, John Matthew, 1877– ed. IV. Ford, James, 1884– joint ed. V. Title.

32—26908

Library of Congress E185.86.P87
——— Copy 2. HD7286.P8 1931 b vol. 6
₍43t2₎ ₍325.26₎ 331.8330973

M331.833
P92r

President's Conference on Home Building and Home Ownership. Washington, D.C. 1931.
Report. Washington, D. C. Committee on Negro Housing. 1931.

4v. 27cm.
Contents: -Report on social and economic factors in housing for Negroes. -Study of economic and social factors in housing conditons among Negroes in Chicago...., by Earl R. Moses. -Bibliography. -Appendices.

The presidents of Liberia.

M910.
W15p

Walker, Thomas Hamilton Beb 1873–
The presidents of Liberia. A biographical sketch for students. Containing biographies of the presidents and some of the leaders in the making of the republic. With portraits, by Thos. H. B. Walker ... Jacksonville, Fla. ₍Mintz printing co.₎ 1915.
4 p. l., 11–96, ₍7₎ p. incl. plates, ports. 19½ᶜᵐ. $1.25

1. Liberia—Presidents. I. Title.

15-8010

Library of Congress DT636.A3W3
——— Copy 2.
Copyright A 398286

Presidents of Negro Land Grant Colleges.

See
Conference of Presidents of Negro Land Grant Colleges.

Africa
M809
P912

Press, John, ed.
Commonwealth literature: unity and diversity in a common culture; extracts from the proceedings of a Conference held at Bodington Hall, Leeds, 9-12 September 1964, under the auspices of the University of Leeds. ₍London₎ Heinemann ₍1965₎

223p. 22cm.
White editor
Partial contents.- Some provisional
(Continued on next card)

Africa
M809
P912

Press, John, ed. Commonwealth literature. ₍1965₎ (Card 2)

Partial contents.- Continued.
comments on West Indian novels, by John J. M. Figueroa.- The use of English in Nigeria, by J. O. Ekpenyong.- Nationalism and the writer, by Eldred D. Jones.- The novelist as teacher, by Chinua Achebe.
1. Literature - Study and teaching.
I. Leeds, Eng. University. I. Title.

Press.

MO7
B79n

Brooks, Maxwell R
The Negro press re-examined; political content of leading Negro newspapers. Boston, Christopher Pub. House ₍1959₎
125 p. 21 cm.
Includes bibliographies.

1. Negro press. I. Title.

PN4888.N4B7 071.3 59—8809 ‡

Library of Congress ₍60d5₎

Press.

MO7
H55w

Hill, Roy L
Who's who in the American Negro press. Dallas, Royal Pub. Co. ₍1960₎
80 p. 21 cm.
Bibliography: p. 70.

1. Negro press. 2. Negroes—Biog. I. Title.

PN4888.N4H5 071.3 60—4017

Library of Congress ₍61d3₎

Press

MO7
P38

Penn, Irvine Garland, 1867–
The Afro-American press and its editors, by I. Garland Penn ... with contributions by Hon. Frederick Douglass, Hon. John R. Lynch ₍etc.₎ ... Springfield, Mass., Willey & co., 1891.
5 p. l., ₍15₎–565, ₍4₎ p. front., illus. (incl. ports.) fold. facsim. 20½ cm.

1. Press—U. S. 2. Negroes—Biog.

10—7631

Library of Congress PN4888.N4P4
₍48l1₎

Press.

MO70
Sh26

Shaw, O'Wendell.
Writing for the weeklies: how to earn sparetime money as a weekly newspaper correspondent. Columbus, Ohio, Russwurm Press, °1962.
28 p. 23 cm.

1. Journalism—Authorship. 2. Negro press. I. Title.

PN147.S47 61—18806 ‡

Library of Congress ₍3₎

Press.

MO7
W65

Wilkins, Roy.
The Negro press hits back. Toronto, Reprinted from the Magazine digest, April 1943.

3-7p. 19cm.

Press-Guadeloupe.

Guadeloupe
M972.97
B59c

Blanche, Lenis.
... Contribution à l'histoire de la presse à la Guadeloupe, par Lenis Blanche ... ₍Basse-Terre, Imprimerie catholique₎ 1935.
xiv, 85 p., 2 l. 23ᶜᵐ.
At head of title: Gouvernement de la Guadeloupe et dépendances.
"Publié à l'occasion du Tricentenaire des Antilles."

1. Press—Guadeloupe. 2. Liberty of the press—Guadeloupe. I. Guadeloupe.

37-7918

Library of Congress PN4969.G82B6
₍3₎ 071.297

Press—Guadeloupe.

Guadeloupe
M972.97
B59h

Blanche, Lénis.
... Histoire de la Guadeloupe; préface de m. Henry Bérenger ... Paris, M. Lavergne, imprimeur, 1938.
5 p. l., ₍5₎–191 p. 25½ᶜᵐ.
Contents.—Introduction.—La Guadeloupe française.—Quatre études sur l'histoire des Antilles: Christophe Colomb ou le baptême de l'île. Du Tertre, historien. Pierre Belain d'Esnambuc. Petite histoire de l'imprimerie et de la presse à la Guadeloupe.

1. Guadeloupe—Hist. 2. Antilles, Lesser—Hist. 3. Press—Guadeloupe.

39-10124

Library of Congress F2066.B65
₍2₎ 972.97

Press-Southern states.

M973
L82at

Logan, Rayford Whittingham, *ed.*
The attitude of the southern white press toward Negro suffrage, 1932–1940; edited by Rayford W. Logan, PH. D., with a foreword by Charles H. Wesley, PH. D. Washington, D. C., The Foundation publishers, 1940.
cover-title, xii, 115 p. 23ᶜᵐ.

1. Negroes—Politics and suffrage. 2. Press—Southern states. I. Title.

40—30270

Library of Congress JK1929.A2L6
₍42f2₎ 324.15

Nigeria
MO70
A13

The press in Africa.
Ruth Sloane Associates, Washington, D. C.
The press in Africa. Edited by Helen Kitchen. Washington, 1956.

96p. 29cm.

Haiti
M972.94
P92m

Pressoir, Catts.
... La médecine en Haiti. Port-au-Prince (Haiti) Imprimerie modèle, 1927.
3 p. l., ₍v₎–xii, 254 p., 1 l. 22ᶜᵐ.
At head of title: Dʳ C. Pressoir.

1. ~~XXXXXXXXXXX~~. I. Title. 2. Haiti—Medicine.

28-16277

Library of Congress R475.H2P7

Haiti
M972.94
P92p

Pressoir, Catts.
... Le protestantisme haïtien ... ₍Port-au-Prince?₎, Impr. de la Société biblique et des livres religieux d'Haïti, 1945- 44
2 v. 23 cm.
At head of title: Docteur C. Pressoir.
Vol. 1 issued in parts, 1945-
"Ce volume rentre dans la deuxième partie du treizième volume de l'Histoire de la nation haïtienne, publiée sous la direction du dr. François Dalencour; section d'histoire religieuse."—v. 1, verso of 2d prelim. leaf.
1. Protestant churches—Haiti. I. Title. 2. Haiti-Religion
BX4835.H3P73 277.294 47-6079
Library of Congress ₍2₎

Haiti
M972.94
P926b

Pressoir, Charles Fernand
...Debats sur le creole et le folklore. Afriques grises ou Frances brunes? Langue, races, religion et culture populaires, avec des textes. Port-au-Prince, Imprimerie de l'Etat, 1947.
80p. 22cm.
1. Creole dialects. 2. Haiti-Creole dialects. 3. Santo Domingo - Creole dialects. I. Title.

Pressure groups.
M323
Sa2

St. James, Warren D 1921-
The National Association for the Advancement of Colored People: a case study in pressure groups. Foreword by Ulysses S. Donaldson. ₍1st ed.₎ New York, Exposition Press ₍1958₎
252 p. 21 cm. (An Exposition-university book)
Bibliography: p. ₍248₎-252.
1. National Association for the Advancement of Colored People. 2. Pressure groups.
E185.5.N276S3 57—10668
*301.451 325.260973
Library of Congress ₍59h7₎

Rwanda
M967.5
K11p2

Des prêtres noirs s'interrogent, par A. Abble ₍et al.₎ Preface de S. Exc. Mgr. Lefebvre. 2d ed. Paris, Les Editions du Cerf, 1957.
283p. 19cm. (Recontres, 47)
Partial contents.- La literature orale au Ruanda ₍par₎ Alexis Kagame.
1. Congo, Belgian. I. Title.

Rwanda
M967.5
K11p

Des prêtes noirs s'interragent.
Des prêtes noirs s'interragent, par A. Abble ₍et al.₎ Preface de S. Exc. Mgr., Lefebvre. Paris, Les Editions du Cerf, 1956.
281p. 19cm. (Recontres, 47)

Portugal
M869
D71p

O preto do Charleston (novela) Lisboa.
Dominiguos, Mario.
O preto do Charleston (novela) Lisboa, Livraria editora Guimaraes ₍1932?₎
276 p. 18 cm.

Virgin Islands
M813.5
P92

Pretto, Clarita C ₍1934?-
The life of Autumn Holliday; a novel. New York, Exposition Press, ₍1958₎
95p. 20cm.
Picture and biographical sketch of the author on the book jacket.
I. Title.

Preuve de la recidive et police scientifique.
Haiti
M972.94
B54p

Bistoury, André F
... Preuve de la récidive et police scientifique. Port-au-Prince, Haïti, 1946.
3 p. l., 9-152 p., 4 l. illus. (incl. ports.) diagrs. 21½cm.
1. Recidivists—Haiti. I. Title.
HV6049.B5 364.32 47-23196
Library of Congress ₍1₎

Liberia
M966.6
P93L

Price, Frederick A
Liberian odyssey "by hammock and surfboat"; the autobiography of F. A. Price. ₍1st ed.₎ New York, Pageant Press ₍1954₎
260 p. illus. 26 cm.
Author a Liberian citizen who was born in Barbados. B.W.I.
1. Missions—Liberia. I. Title.
BV3625.L6P7 922.7666 54-9267 ‡
Library of Congress ₍3₎

Haiti
M972.94
P93c

Price, Hannibal, 1842-1893.
...Cours de droit administratif contenant l'exposé des principes, le resumé de la législation administrative dans son dernier etat...par Hannibal Price... 2d ed. Havre, Imprimerie-Lithographie Duval & Davonet, 1910.
xxxix, 516p. 22½cm.
1. Haiti--Laws.

Haiti
M972.94
P93r

Price, Hannibal, *d.* 1893.
De la réhabilitation de la race noire par la république d'Haïti, par Hannibal Price ... Port-au-Prince, J. Verrollot, 1900.
1 p. l., xvii, 736 p. 24½cm.
1. Haiti—Hist. ~~2. Negroes in Haiti.~~ 3. Monogenism and polygenism.
8—32097
Library of Congress F1921.P94
₍44d1₎

Price, Joseph Charles, 1854-1893.
MB9
P93

Walls, William Jacob, *bp.*, 1885-
Joseph Charles Price, educator and race leader, by William Jacob Walls. Boston, The Christopher publishing house ₍1943₎
xx p., 1 l., 23-568 p. plates, ports. 20½cm.
Bibliography: p. 537-540.
d. Oct '93
1. Price, Joseph Charles, 1854-1893.
43—7930
Library of Congress E185.97.P9W3
₍45f1₎ 923.773

Price, Thomas.
M326.99B
R68
1840

Roper, Moses.
A narrative of the adventures and escape of Moses Roper, from American slavery; with a preface, by the Rev. T. Price ... 4th ed. London, Harvey and Darton, ~~1840.~~ 1838 2ed.
xii, 120 p. front. (port.) illus. 15cm.
1. Slavery in the U. S.—South Carolina. I. Price, Thomas.
17-24785
Library of Congress E444.R785

M326.5
P33r

Price, Thomas S. joint author.
Peck, Nathaniel.
Report of Messrs. Peck and Price, who were appointed at a meeting of the free colored people of Baltimore, held on the 25th November, 1839, delegates to visit British Guiana and the Island of Trinidad; and other information, showing the advantages to be derived by immigrating to those colonies.
32p. 23½cm.

M973
P93

Price, Willard.
The negro around the world, by Willard Price ... pictorial maps by George Annand. New York, George H. Doran company ₍©1925₎
75 p. incl. front., maps. 19½cm.
~~1. Negro race.~~ I. Title. 2. Travel books.
25—9188
Library of Congress HT1581.P7
₍a25d8₎

Price of freedom.
M378Te
J63

Johnson, Ozie Harold.
Price of freedom. ₍Houston? Tex.₎ ©1954.
117 p. 24 cm.
1. Texas Southern University. School of Law. 2. Negroes—Texas. 3. Discrimination in education. 4. Law—Study and teaching—Texas. I. Title.
371.974 54-31912 ‡
Library of Congress ₍1₎

Price policy.
St. Lucia
M330
L58o

Lewis, William Arthur, 1915-
Overhead costs; some essays in economic analysis. London, G. Allen & Unwin ~~₍1949₎~~ 1951
200 p. diagrs. 23 cm. (The Library of economics. Sect. 2: New works, 3)
Bibliographical footnotes.
1. Cost. 2. Price policy. 3. Monopolies. I. Title. (Series)
HB221.L54 338.52 49—6466*
Library of Congress ₍55c½₎

Nigeria
M966.9
N916

The pride of Urhobo nation.
Numa, Frederick Yamu, 1916-
The pride of Urhobo nation. Lagos, Ribway Press ₍1950₎
56p. illus., port. 18cm.
Portrait of author in book.

M813.5
Y46p

Pride's castle.
Yerby, Frank, 1916-
Pride's castle. New York, Pocket Books, Inc., 1952.
382p. 16cm. (Cardinal edition C 21)
Pocket book edition.

Sudan French
M966.2
Ou1

Le principe du droit Musulman.
Ouane, Ibrahima Mamadou, 1908-
Le principe du droit Musulman. Paris, Les Presses Universelles, 1957.
91p. port. 19cm.

Nigeria
M496
Og2

Prima I. Ogbe Edo (Benin reader. Book I) Lagos, Church Missionary Society Bookshop, 1934.
24p. 19cm.
1. Benin, readers.

Nigeria
M496
Og2
Prima 11. Oghe Edo (Benin reader Book II) Lagos, Church Missionary Society Bookshop, 1934.
32p. 19cm.
1. Benin, readers.

Nigeria
M496
Og2
Prima 11. Oghe Edo (Benin reader Book II) Lagos, Church Missionary Society Bookshop, 1934.
32p. 19cm.
1. Benin, readers.

M496
Og2
Bk I
Prima I. Oghe Edo Benin reader. Lagos, Church Missionary Society Bookshop, 1934.
24p. 19cm.
1. Benin, reader.

Africa
M498
Og2
Bk II
Prima 11. Oghe Edo Benin reader. Lagos, Church Missionary Society Bookshop, 1934.
32p. 19cm.
1. Benin - reader.

Primary education.
M370
W58pr
Whiting, *Mrs.* Helen Adele (Johnson) 1885–
Primary education. 2d ed. By Helen Adele Whiting. Boston, The Christopher publishing house [1927]
148 p. illus. 20½cm.
Contains references.
1. Education of children. I. Title.
27-18410 Revised
Library of Congress LB1511.W5 1927
Copyright A 996915 [r39c2]

The Prime Minister of Kenya's speeches, 1963-1964.
Kenya
M967.65
K42
Kenyatta, Jomo.
Harambee! The Prime Minister of Kenya's speeches 1963–1964, from the attainment of internal self-government to the threshold of the Kenya Republic. Foreword by Malcolm MacDonald. The text edited and arr. by Anthony Cullen on instructions of the Permanent Secretary, Prime Minister's Office. Nairobi, New York, Oxford University Press, 1964 [i. e. 1965]
xi, 114 p. illus., ports. 22 cm.
1. Kenya—Pol. & govt.—Addresses, essays, lectures. I. Title. II. Title: The Prime Minister of Kenya's speeches, 1963–1964.
DT434.E26K4 354.6762035 65-4596
Library of Congress [2]

Primeiras trovas burlescas de Getulino.
Brazil
M869.1
G143p
[Gama, Luiz Gonzaga Pinto da] 1830-1882.
Primeiras trovas burlescas de Getulino. 2ª ed. correcta e augmentada ... Rio de Janeiro, Typ. de Pinheiro & c a; 1861.
252p. 18½cm.

Primer for white folks.
M810.8
M77p
Moon, Bucklin, 1911– *ed.*
Primer for white folks, edited by Bucklin Moon. Garden City, New York, Doubleday, Doran and co., inc., 1945.
xiv p., 1 l., 491 p. 21½ cm.
"First edition."
1. Negroes. I. Title.
45-7185
Library of Congress E185.5.M72
[47q5]
325.260973

Nigeria
M372.4
At47
Bk 1
Primers, African.
Atilade, Emmanuel Adekunle, 1911-
Akoka Yoruba, Apa I. [Lagos, Ife Olu Printing Works [n.d.]
32p. illus. 18cm.

Primers, African.
Nigeria
M372.4
Od8
Bk. 1
Odujinrin, J S A
ABD asiko; apa kin-ni. Lagos, Olufunmiso Printing Works, 1963?
56p. illus. 18cm.

Primers, African.
Nigeria
M372.4
Od831
Odunjo, J Folahan
Iwe-kini Alawiye; fun alakòbèrè èkó Yoruba l'omode ati l'agbà. Eni ti o ya àwòran rè ni Tayo Aiyegbusi. Ikeja [Nigeria] Longmans of Nigeria, 1963.
62p. illus. 18½cm.
Translated title: Alawiye primer and reader. Written in Yoruba.

The primitive.
M813.5
H57p
Himes, Chester B 1909–
The primitive. [New York] New American Library [1955]
151 p. 19 cm. (A Signet book, 1264)
I. Title.
PZ3.H57Pr 56-6204 ‡
Library of Congress [3]

Senegal
M896.1
D54
Primordiale du sixième jour.
Diakhaté, Lamine
Primordiale du sixième jour. Paris, Présence Africanine, 1963.
57p. 19½cm.
I. Title.

MB9
P93n
Prince, *Mrs.* Nancy (Gardener) [, 1799-ca,1860
A narrative of the life and travels of Mrs. Nancy Prince. Boston, The author, 1850.
87, [1] p. 16cm.
1. Russia—Soc. life & cust. 2. West Indies—Descr. & trav.
[29b1]
20-18619
Library of Congress CT275.P848A3

M326.99B
P93
[Prince, Mary].
The history of Mary Prince, a West Indian slave. Related by herself. With a supplement by the Editor. To which is added, the narrative of Asa-Asa, a captured African... London, Published by F. Westley and A. H. Davis, 1831.
44p. 22½cm.
1. Slavery in the West Indies. I. Asa-Asa, Louis. Narrative. 2. Slave narratives.

M326.99B
P93
Prince, Mary.
Prince, Mary,
The history of Mary Prince, a West Indian slave. Related by herself. With a supplement by the author. To which is added the narrative of Asa-Asa, a captured African ...2ed. London: F.Westley and A.H.Davis. 1831.
43p.22cm.

The prince and the singer.
M812.5
V94r
Voteur, Ferdinand.
A right angle triangle. The prince and the singer. By Ferdinand Voteur. [New York, Ardsley publishing company, °1938]
4 p. l., 11-213 p. 20½cm.
Plays.
I. Title. II. Title: The prince and the singer.
39-11806
Library of Congress PS3543.O68R5 1938
——— Copy 2.
Copyright D pub. 62986 [2] 812.5

Prince Hall and his followers.
M366
C85p
Crawford, George Williamson.
Prince Hall and his followers; being a monograph on the legitimacy of negro masonry, by George W. Crawford ... New York, The Crisis [1914]
95, [1] p. incl. front. (port.) 22½cm. $1.00
Bibliography: last page.
Inscribed copy: To my good friend Arthur Spingarn, George Crawford.
1. Freemasons, Negro. I. Title.
15-293
Library of Congress HS883.C7
Copyright A 387936 [31d1]

The Prince Hall primer.
M366.1
W67p
1946
Williamson, Harry A.
The Prince Hall primer. rev. ed. New York. The author, 1946.
59p. 19½cm.

The Prince Hall primer.
M366.1
W67p
1925
Williamson, Harry A.
The Prince Hall primer, a historical quiz. New York, Prince Hall Masonic Publishing co., 1925.
24p. 18½cm. (Midget Library no.1)

The prince of thieves.
France
M840
D89pr
Dumas, Alexandre, 1802–1870.
... The prince of thieves, newly tr. by Alfred Allinson; with three coloured illustrations by Frank Adams. London, Methuen & co. [1904]
3 p. l., 126 p. 3 col. pl. (incl. front.) 24cm. (The novels of Alexandre Dumas)
Sequel: Robin Hood.
1. Robin Hood. I. Allinson, Alfred Richard, tr. II. Title.
4-37080
Library of Congress PZ3.D89Pr6
[a37c1]

The Prince of Washington square.

M813.5 Liscomb, Harry F.
L68p The Prince of Washington square; an up-to-the-minute story, by Harry F. Liscomb. New York, Frederick A. Stokes company, 1925.

ix p., 1 l., 180 p. 19cm.

I. Title.

25—6703

Library of Congress PZ3.L684Pr

[44d1]

Princess Malah.

M813.1 Hill, John H.
H55 Princess Malah, by John H. Hill. Washington, D. C., The associated publishers, inc. [c1933]

vii p., 1 l., 330 p. 21cm.

1. Washington, George, pres. U. S.—Fiction. 2. Washington, Mrs. Martha (Dandridge) Custis, 1731-1801 — Fiction. 3. Slavery in the U. S.—Virginia—Fiction. I. Title.

33—3600

Library of Congress PZ3.H5521Pr
——— Copy 2.
Copyright A 60229 [a33e1]

The princess of Naragpur.

M813.5 Durant, E Elliot.
D93p The princess of Naragpur; or, A daughter of Allah, by E. Elliot Durant ... and Cuthbert M. Roach. New York, The Grafton press [c1928]

3 p. l., 5-191 p. 21½cm.

1. Roach, Cuthbert M., joint author. II. Title.

29-698

Library of Congress PZ3.D9319Pr
——— Copy 2.
Copyright A 3384 [2]

Princesses creoles.

Haiti
M972.94 Nemours, Alfred, 1883-
N34p Princesses creoles. Lettre-preface de M. Claude Farrere. Paris, Berger-Levrouet, editeurs, 1927.

69 1 p. 15cm.

Le principe du droit Musulman.

Mali
M966.2 Ouane, Ibrahima Mamadou, 1908-
Ou1 Le principe du droit Musulman. Paris, Les Presses Universelles, 1957.

91p. port. 19cm.

Haiti Principes de l'unite.
M110 Lemoine, Raoul Fanini
L54 Principes de l'unite. [Port-au-Prince, Haiti, Imprimerie Théodore, n.d.]

31p. port. 21cm. (Serie des Saintes-Ecritures)
Portrait of author in book.

M610 Pringle, Henry F
P93c The color line in medicine, by Henry F and Katharine Pringle. New York, Committee of 100, 1948.

12p. graphs. 23cm.
Reprinted from Saturday Evening Post, Jan. 24, 1948.

1. Medicine. 2. Discrimination.

Prisoners - Personal narratives.

M364 Williamson, Henry, *pseud.*
W674 Hustler! [By] Henry Williamson. Edited by R. Lincoln Keiser. With a commentary by Paul Bohannan. [1st ed.] Garden City, N. Y., Doubleday, 1965.

xi, 222 p. 22 cm.
Autobiographical.

1. Prisoners—Personal narratives. I. Keiser, R. Lincoln, 1937- ed. II. Title.

HV6248.W49A3 364.15 65-10686

Library of Congress [5]

Cuba Prisoners - Personal narratives - Cuba.
M365 Morales Rodríquez, René, 1923-
R618 Dos cruces (Two crosses). La Habana, 1958.

xx, iii, 332p. 22cm.
Autographed.

1. Prisoners - Personal narratives - Cuba. I. Title.

M811.5 Pritchard, Gloria Clinton.
P93 Trees along the highway. New York, Comet Press Books [1953]

26 p. 22 cm.
Poems.

I. Title.

PS3531.R67T7 811.5 54-1228 rev ‡

Library of Congress [r54d2]

M81018 Pritchard, Myron Thomas, 1853- *comp.*
P93 The upward path; a reader for colored children with an introduction by Robert R. Moton ... comp. by Myron T. Pritchard ... and Mary White Ovington ... New York, Harcourt, Brace and Howe [c1920]

xi, [1], 255 p. incl. front., illus. 19½cm.

1. Readers and speakers—1870- I. Ovington, Mary White, 1865- joint comp. II. Title. III. Title: Colored children, Reader for.

20—16518

Library of Congress PE1126.N3P8
Copyright A 507468 41e1]

Guadeloupe
M944.36 Privat d'Anglemont, Alexandre, d. ca. 1815-1859
P13p ... Paris anecdote, avec une préface et des notes par Charles
1885 Monselet. Éd. illustrée de cinquante dessins à la plume par J. Belon, et d'un portrait de Privat d'Anglemont grave à l'eau-forte par R. de Los Rios. Paris, P. Rouquette, 1885.

2 p. l., 278 p., 1 l. front. (port.) illus. 25cm.
Title in red and black.
1st edition Paris, 1854.
CONTENTS.—Alexandre Privat d'Anglemont.—Les industries inconnues.—La Childebert.—Les oiseaux de nuit.—La villa des chiffoniers.—Voyage de découverte du boulevard à la Courtille par le faubourg du Temple.—Paris inconnu.

1. Paris—Soc. life & cust. I. Monselet, Charles, 1825-1888, ed. II. Title.

4—21517

Library of Congress DC715.P96

[a42b1]

Guadeloupe
M848 Privat d'Anglemont, Alexandre, ca1815-1859.
P13pa Paris anecdote; Les industries inconnues,
1854 la childebert, les oiseaux de nuit, la villa des chiffoniers, par Alex. Privat d'Anglemont. Paris, Chez P. Jannet, Librairie, 1854.

232p. 16cm.

1. Paris.

Guadeloupe
M848 Privat d'Anglemont, Alexandre, c. da. 1815-1859
P13p ... Paris inconnu, avec une étude sur la vie de l'auteur
1886 par A. Delvau. Soixante-trois dessins à la plume, par F. Coindre. Paris, P. Rouquette, 1886.

2 p. l., 355, [1] p. front., illus. 25cm.
1st edition, Paris, 1861.
CONTENTS.—Alexandre Privat d'Anglemont, étude par M. Alfred Delvau.—Fragment d'un article publié par M. Victor Cochinat, aussitôt après l'enterrement de Privat d'Anglemont.—Portraits et caractères.—Le cloitre Saint-Jean de Latran.—Le camp des barbares de Paris.—Rues Traversine et Clos-Bruneau.—Paris en villages.—Peintures d'histoire, portraits et paysages.—Esquisses parisiennes.—Nouvelles.—Théâtre.—Articles divers.—Lettres.—Poésies. Sonnets.—La closerie des lilas.

1. Paris. I. Delvau, Alfred, 1825-1867.

4-21516

Library of Congress DC715.P97

Guadeloupe
M848 Privat d'Anglemont, Alexandre, c. da. 1815-1859
P13p ... Paris inconnu, avec une étude sur la vie de l'auteur
1886 par A. Delvau. Soixante-trois dessins à la plume, par F. Coindre. Paris, P. Rouquette, 1886.

2 p. l., 355, [1] p. front., illus. 25cm.
First edition, Paris, 1861.
CONTENTS.—Alexandre Privat d'Anglemont, étude par M. Alfred Delvau.—Fragment d'un article publié par M. Victor Cochinat, aussitôt après l'enterrement de Privat d'Anglemont.—Portraits et caractères.—Le cloitre Saint-Jean de Latran.—Le camp des barbares de Paris.—Rues Traversine et Clos-Bruneau.—Paris en villages.—Penitures d'histoire, portraits et paysages.—Esquisses parisiennes.—Nouvelles.—Théâtre.—Articles divers.—Lettres.—Poésies. Sonnets.—La closerie des lilas.

1. Paris. I. Delvau, Alfred, 1825-1867.

4—21516

Library of Congress DC715.P97

[22c1]

Guadeloupe
M848 Privat d'Anglemont, Alexandre, 1815-1859.
P13p Paris inconnu, par A. Privat d'Anglemont,
1875 précéde d'une etude sur sa vie par Alfred Delvau, deuxieme ed., aug... Paris, Adolphe Delahays, Librairie-Editeur, 1874.

315p. 16cm.

1. Paris. I. Cochinat, Victor. Fragment d'un article, p. 17-22.

Guadeloupe
M848 Privat d'Anglemont Alexandre, ca1815-1859.
P13p Paris inconnu, par A. Privat D'Anglemont.
1861 Précédé d'une etude sur sa vie par M. Alfred Delvau ... Paris, Adolph Delahays, Librairie-Editeur, 1861.

283p. 16cm.

1. Paris. I. Delvau, Alfred, 1825-1867.

Guadeloupe
M848 Privat d'Anglemont, Alexandre, 1815-1859.
P13s Les singes de dieu et les hommes du diable; edited with foreword, notes and vocabulary by Mercer Cook and Guichard Parris. Atlanta, Atlanta University, 1936.

15l 27½cm. (Atlanta University French series)

Vocabulary and notes: p. 9-16.
Text taken from 1884 edition of Paris Inconnu.

1. Paris. I. Cook, Mercer, 1903- ed.
I. Title.

M370 Private schools.
P18r Palmer Memorial Institute. Sedalia.
Report of the president to the Board of Trustees. 19 -

v. tables. 28cm. annual.
Library has: 1937.

The problem.

M813.5 Gilmore, F Grant.
G422p "The problem," a military novel, by F. Grant Gilmore ... [Rochester, N. Y., Press of H. Conolly co., c1915]

99 p. port. 18½cm. $0.75

I. Title.

15-20986

Library of Congress PZ3.G422P
Copyright A 411448

The problem of Nigerian students over-seas.

Nigeria
M378.3 Olugboji, Dayo
OL9 The problem of Nigerian students over-seas. [Lagos, C. M. S. Press, 1959]

28p. 21½cm.

Problemas sociales; el Negro.
Puerto Rico
M301
R72
Rosario, Jose Colomban
Problemas sociales; el Negro: Haiti-Estados Unidos-Puerto Rico, por Jose Colomban Rosario y Justina Carrion. San Juan, Negociado de Materiales, Imprenta y Transporte, 1940.
174p. 21cm. (Universidad de Puerto Rico. Boletim, series X, no. 2, December 1939)
Bibliography: p. 161-165.

Probleme des classes a travers l'histoire d'Haiti;
M972.94
D42p
Denis, Lorimer.
Problème des classes à travers l'histoire d'Haïti; sociologie politique ₍par₎ Lorimer Denis et François Duvalier. ₍Port-au-Prince?₎ Au Service de la Jeunesse, 1948.
xii, 128 p. 19 cm. (Collection "Les Griots")
"Bibliographie": p. ₍127₎-128.
1. Haiti—Hist. 2. Haiti—Soc. condit. I. Duvalier, François, joint author. II. Title.
F1921.D4 972.94 49-21310*
Library of Congress ₍1₎

Problems and opportunities confronting Negroes in the field of business.
M658
F57
Fitzhugh, H Naylor, ed.
Problems and opportunities confronting Negroes in the field of business; report on the National Conference on Small Business. Washington, D. C., U. S. Dept. of Commerce, 1962.
103p. 23½cm.

... Problems in the collegiate education of Negroes.
M378
D29
Davis, John Warren, 1888-
... Problems in the collegiate education of Negroes, by President John W. Davis ... Institute, W. Va., 1937.
56 p. 23cm. (West Virginia state college bulletin, June 1937. Ser. 24, no. 4)
Contribution no. 8 of the Department of education. Publications of West Virginia State college.
1. Negroes—Education. 2. Universities and colleges—U. S. I. Title. II. Title: Collegiate education of Negroes.
U. S. Off. of educ. Library for Library of Congress LC2781.D35 E 37-208 Revised
₍r44d2₎† 378.73

M323
W89p
Problems of adjustment of race and class in the South.
Work, Monroe Nathan, 1866-1945.
Problems of adjustment of race and class in the South. Reprinted from Social forces, 16:108-117, October 1937.

M323
T61
Problems of civilization.
Toomer, Jean, 1894-
Race problems and modern society.
(In: Problems of civilization ... New York, D. Van Nostrand company, 1929. 18 cm. p. 67-114).

Problems of industrial planning and management in Nigeria.
Nigeria
M338
On9
Onyemelukwe, Clement Chukwukadibia.
Problems of industrial planning and management in Nigeria ₍by₎ C. C. Onyemelukwe. London, Longmans, 1966.
vii, 330 p. tables, diagrs. 22½ cm. 42/-
(B 66-14802)
Bibliography: p. 319-322.
1. Nigeria—Economic policy. 2. Nigeria—Indus. I. Title.
HC517.N48O55 338.9669 66-74020
Library of Congress ₍3₎

MB9
W67
Proctor, Charles Hayden, 1848?-1890.
The life of James Williams, better known as Professor Jim, for half a century janitor of Trinity college. By C. H. Proctor ... Hartford, Case, Lockwood and Brainard, printers, 1873.
79 p. front. (port.) 17½ cm.
1. Williams, James, b. 1790? 2. Trinity college, Hartford, Conn.
13—33803
Library of Congress E185.97.W72
₍48b1₎

MB9
P94
Proctor, Henry Hugh, 1868-1933.
Between black and white; autobiographical sketches, by Henry Hugh Proctor. Boston, Chicago, The Pilgrim press ₍°1925₎
xi, 189 p. front., pl., ports. 19½cm.
I. Title.
25—556
Library of Congress E185.97.P95
₍a42d1₎

M973
P942
Proctor, Samuel Dewitt, 1921-
The young Negro in America, 1960-1980, by Samuel D. Proctor. New York, Association Press ₍1966₎
160 p. 21 cm.
Bibliographical references included in "Notes by chapters" (p. 159-160)
1. Negroes—Civil rights. 2. Negroes—Hist. I. Title.
E185.61.P76 301.451960973 66-18750
Library of Congress ₍5₎

Profession, Choice of.
M370.
C12 v
Caliver, Ambrose, 1894-
... Vocational education and guidance of Negroes; report of a survey conducted by the Office of education, by Ambrose Caliver, senior specialist in the education of Negroes ... United States Department of the interior. Harold L. Ickes, secretary. Office of education, J. W. Studebaker, commissioner. Washington, U. S. Govt. print. off., ~~1938.~~ 1937.
x, 137 p. incl. tables, diagrs. 23cm. (U. S. Office of education. Bulletin, 1937, no. 38)
At head of title: Project in vocational education and guidance of Negroes.
On p. ₍2₎ of cover: National survey of vocational education and guidance of Negroes.
~~(Continued on next card)~~
E 39-3 †
₍a46d²3₎†

Profession, Choice of.
M378.3a
C85
Crawford, George Williamson, 1877-
The Talladega manual of vocational guidance (The red book) written and compiled by George W. Crawford ... ₍Talladega, Ala.₎ Pub. under the auspices and official sponsorship of the Board of trustees of Talladega college ₍°1937₎
x, 146 p. incl. illus. (map) tables, diagrs. 23½cm.
"A bibliography on vocational guidance": p. 141-146.
1. Negroes — Employment. 2. Negroes — Education. 3. Profession, Choice of. 4. Talladega college, Talladega, Ala. I. Title.
37—5167
Library of Congress E185.8.C86
——— Copy 2.
Copyright A 105261 ₍38d3₎ [371.425] 325.260973

Profession, Choice of
M370.
Ev2 e
Everett, Faye Philip, ed.
The colored situation; a book of vocational and civic guidance for the Negro youth, by Faye Philip Everett ... Boston, Meador publishing company, 1936.
312 p. illus. (ports.) 20½cm.
On cover: The colored situation ₍by₎ Faye P. Everett & others.
"Articles and books written by Dr. A. B. Jackson": p. 242-243.
1. Negroes—Employment. 2. Profession, Choice of. 3. Negroes—Moral and social conditions. I. Title. II. Title: Vocational and civic guidance for the Negro youth.
36—9272
Library of Congress E185.8.E94
₍42l2₎ [371.425] 325.260973

M973.9
F46
No.16
Professions.
Reid, Ira De Augustine, 1901-
Fifty years of progress in the professions. Pittsburgh, Pittsburgh Courier, 1950.
7p. port. illus. 24cm. (Fifty years of progress)

Profit-sharing.
Bahamas
M332
Sm6a
Smith, James Carmichael, 1852-
Abundance and hard times, by Jas. C. Smith ... London, K. Paul, Trench, Trübner & co., ltd., 1908.
30 p. 21½cm.
A plea for the establishment by law of "the wage co-operative system of profit-sharing" and "the double standard money system."
1. Panics. 2. Currency question—Gt. Brit. 3. Profit-sharing. I. Title.
16-7960
Library of Congress HB3723.S55

Profit-sharing.
Bahamas
M332
Sm6m
Smith, James Carmichael, 1852-
Money and profit-sharing; or, The double standard money system, by Jas. C. Smith ... London, K. Paul, Trench, Trübner & co., l^td, 1908.
xix, 232 p. incl. tables. fold. tab., fold. diagr. 22cm.
1. Money. 2. Profit-sharing. 3. Currency question—Gt. Brit. 4. Value. I. Title. II. Title: Double standard money system.
9—3071
Library of Congress HG221.S62

Bahamas
M332
Sm6d
Profits.
Smith, James Carmichael, 1852-
The distribution of the produce, by James C. Smith. London, Kegan Paul, Trench, Trübner & Co., 1892.
77 p. 19 cm.

Progress.
M815.5
G86
v.1,no.7
Grimke, Francis James, 1850-
The progress and development of the colored people of our nation; an address delivered before the American missionary association, Wednesday evening, October 21, 1908, at Galesburg, Illinois. By Rev. Francis J. Grimke ... ₍Washington?₎ 1909₎
14 p. 23½cm.
1. Negroes.
9—12228
Library of Congress E185.6.G86
₍37d1₎

Progress.
M370
G98s
Gusman, Jessie Parkhurst, 1898-
Some achievements of the Negro through education. Rev. ed. Tuskegee, Alabama, Tuskegee Institute, Dept. of Records and Research, 1950.
34p. 28cm. (Records and research pamphlet no.1)

Progress.
M304
P19
V.5, no.12
Hope, John, 1868-1936.
A message for New Year's day, 1932. (lacks imprint)
7p. 22cm.

Progress and achievements of the colored people.
M973
M61p
Miller, Kelly, 1863-1939
Progress and achievements of the colored people ... Kelly Miller and Joseph R. Gay ... Washington, D. C., Austin Jenkins Co. ₍c1917₎
490p. plates. 21½cm.

Progress & perspiration.
Tanganyika
M967.82 Omari, Dunstan Alfred, 1922- jt. auth.
Om1ma Maendeleo na jasho. Progress & perspiration. [By C. W. Ryan and D. A. Omari] Dar es Salaam, Eagle Press, 1954.
19p. 18cm. (Mazungumzo ya uraia. Talks on citizenship, no. 3)
Written in English and Swahili.
1. Tanganyika. I. Title. II. Title: Progress & perspiration. III. Series: Mazungumzo ya uraia, no. 3. IV. Series: Talks on citizenship, no. 3. V. Ryan, C. W. W.

Progress and portents for the Negro in medicine.
M610 Cobb, William Montague, 1904-
C63p Progress and portents for the Negro in medicine. New York, National Assn. for the Advancement of Colored People, 1948.
53p. illus. ports. map. 22cm.

Progress of a race;
M973.8 [Gibson, John William] 1841- ed.
G35 Progress of a race; or, The remarkable advancement of the American Negro, from the bondage of slavery, ignorance, and poverty to the freedom of citizenship, intelligence, affluence, honor and trust. Rev. and enl. by J. L. Nichols ... and William H. Crogman ... With special articles by well known authorities, Mrs. Booker T. Washington, Charles M. Melden ... M. W. Dogan ... Albon L. Holsey ... and an introduction by Robert R. Moton ... Naperville, Ill., J. L. Nichols & company [°1920]
480 p. front., illus., ports. 21½cm.
(Continued on next card)
20—22088
[4411]

Progress of a race;
M973.8 [Gibson, John William] 1841- ed. Progress of a race
G35 ... [°1920] (Card 2)
"Who's who in the Negro race": p. 329-460.
Published in 1912 by John William Gibson and William H. Crogman. First edition published under title: The colored American.
1. Negroes. I. Nicholas, James Lawrence, 1890- II. Crogman, William Henry, 1941- III. Title.
20—22088
Library of Congress E185.G452
[4411]

M614 Progress of the Negro.
R66a Roman, Charles Victor, 1864-1934.
After fifty years— what and whither. Reprinted from the Journal of the National Medical Association, 6: [1925]
8p. 21cm.

The progression of the race in the United States and Canada
MB
B85p Buck, D D
The progression of the race in the United States and Canada treating of the great advancement of the colored race. Chicago, Atwell Printing and Binding Co., 1907.
xii, [16]- 540p. plates 23cm.

Progressive missions in the south.
MB
D91p Duncan, Sara J
Progressive missions in the south and addresses with illustrations and sketches of missionary workers and ministers and bishops' wives. Atlanta, Ga., The Franklin Printing and Publishing Co., 1906.
[8]-299p. 20½cm.

Project de constitution conforme a la destinée glorieuse du peuple Haitien.
Haiti
M972.94 Dalencour, François Stanislas Ranier, 1880-
D15pr Project de constitution conforme a la qu'elle fut forgée par nos aieux de 1790 a 1803 d'ogé et chavannes a pétion et dessalines et discours prononcée 27 Décembre 1945 a l'occasion du 139 me anniversaire de la fondation de la République d'Haiti. 2d édition amendée et augmentée. Port-au-Prince, Chez L'auteur, 1957.
103p. 21cm.

Project method in teaching.
Whiting, Helen Adele (Johnson) 1885-
M370 For human welfare, being notes from records of some phases
W58f of the Georgia program of Negro rural elementary schools and communities, 1935-1943, by Helen Adele Whiting. [Atlanta, Morris Brown college press, 1946]
68 p. incl. illus., forms. 28cm.
Errata slip inserted.
1. Negroes—Education. 2. Project method in teaching. 3. Education—Georgia. I. Title.
46-7025
Library of Congress LC2802.G4W47
[5] 371.974

Proletariat.
M810.8 American writers' congress, *New York*, 1935.
Am3w American writers' congress, edited by Henry Hart. New York, International publishers [°1935]
viii, 9-192 p. 20cm.
"A congress of American revolutionary writers ... held in New York city on April 26, 27 and 28, 1935."—p. 10.
1. Authors, American — Congresses. 2. American literature — 20th cent.—Hist. & crit. 3. Proletariat. 4. Social problems in literature. I. Hart, Henry, 1903- ed.
35—36744
Library of Congress PS7.A6 1935
———— Copy 2.
Copyright A 88480 [36f5] 810.6373

La promenade amoureuse...
Martinique
M841.91 Coridun, Victor
C81p La promenade amoureuse "Vers le bonchur". sextour. Fort-de-France, Imp. R. Illemay, 1933.
121 22cm.
At head of title: Pour la propagande. Allons! ... Femme, en avant! ...

Promese.
Haiti
M841 Philoctete, Rene
M82o Promese. [Port-au-Prince] éditions les Araignes du Soir, 1963.
folder ([5]p.) 19½cm.
Printed on verso of Morisseau, Roland. Clef du soleil.
Poem.
I. Title.

The promised land.
M813.5 Lubin, Gilbert.
L962 The promised land, by Gilbert Lubin. Boston, The Christopher publishing house [°1930]
59 p. 20½cm.
I. Title.
30-22030
Library of Congress PZ3.L9697Pr
———— Copy 2.
Copyright A 26029 [3]

The promise of Nigeria.
Nigeria
M966.9 Epelle, Sam, 1930-
Ep2p The promise of Nigeria. London, Pan Books Ltd., 1960.
252p. 17½cm.
Portrait of author on book cover.

M813.5 The promised land.
F53p Fisher, Rudolph, 1897-1934.
The promised land. The Atlantic monthly, January 1927.
37-45p. 24cm.

Bahamas
M332
Sm6n Property.
Smith, James C.
The National providence: essays by Jas. C. Smith... London, Kegan Paul, Trench, Trubner & Co., 1910.
vi, 1 l. 103p. 21½cm.

M345 Property--Law.
P92d Prescott, Patrick B
The doctrine of lateral support in Illinois; Being a treatise on the law in Illinois... particularly as it affects property abutting a subway in Chicago, now being built for purposes of local transportation. Reprinted from the John Marshall law quarterly, September 1940.
17p. 25cm.

Nigeria Property (Ibo law)
M340 Obi, Samuel Nwanko Chinwuba.
Ob3 The Ibo law of property. London, Butterworths, 1963.
239 p. illus. 23 cm. (Butterworth's African law series, no. 6)
Includes bibliography.
1. Property (Ibo law) I. Title.
347.209669 64-3942 ‡
Library of Congress [3]

Propaganda.
M323 Council against intolerance in America.
C831 An American answer to intolerance. Teacher's manual no. 1, junior and senior high schools. Experimental form, 1939. New York city, Council against intolerance in America, 1939.
130 p., 1 l. 28 cm.
"Prepared by Frank Walser, with the assistance of Annette Smith and Violet Edwards."
"Bibliography of plays suitable for high school production": p. 117-118.
Bibliography: p. 119-130.
1. Propaganda. 2. Prejudices and antipathies. 3. Toleration. I. ~~Walser, Frank~~ ~~II. Smith, Annette~~ ~~III. Edwards, Violet.~~ IV. Title. V. Title: Intolerance. 4. Race relations. II. White, Walter, 1893 - 1955
A 40—2271
New York Univ. Wash. Sq. Library HM263.C7
for Library of Congress HM263.C6
[a50m1] 301.1523

Prophete, Raoul
Haiti
M972.94 Chauvet, Henri, 1863-1928.
C39t ...A travers la republique d'Haiti. Relations de la tournée presidentielle dans le nord. (Première série) par Henri Chauvet et Raoul Prophète. Paris, Imp. Vve Victor Goupy, 1894.
454p. 19cm.

Prosa de prisa; cronicas.
Cuba
M861 Guillén, Nicolás, 1902-
G945 Prosa de prisa; cronicas. [Santa Clara, Cuba] Universidad Central de Las Villas, Direccion de Publicaciones, 1962.
343p. 21cm. (Santa Clara, Cuba (City) Universidad Central de Las Villas. Nuevo plan de publiociones, 35)
Errata slip mounted on inside of front cover.
1. Title.

2

Nicaragua
Prosas profanas and other poems.
M861.6 Darío, Rubén, 1867-1916.
D248 Prosas profanas and other poems, by Ruben Dario; tr. from the Spanish by Charles B. McMichael. New York, Nicholas L. Brown, 1922.
4 p. l., 11-60 p. 19½cm.
I. McMichael, Charles Barnsley, 1850- tr. II. Title.
22-3798
Library of Congress PQ7519.D8P73
[42c1]

Protestant Episcopal church in the U.S.A. - Education.
M370 Payne, Enoch George, 1877-
P29e An estimate of our Negro schools, by E. George Payne ... New York, N. Y., The American church institute for Negroes [1943?]
26, [2] p. illus. (incl. port.) 21½cm.
1. Negroes — Education. 2. Protestant Episcopal church in the U. S. A.—Education. I. The American church institute for Negroes.
44-24120
Library of Congress LC2801.P37
[3] 371.974

Nigeria Protestants.
M200 Christian Council of Nigeria.
C46 Building for tomorrow; a pictorial history of the protestant church in Nigeria. Lagos, Christian Council of Nigeria, 1960.
35p. illus., ports. 28cm.

Prose.
M811.5 Clark, B
C54pt The past, present, and future; in prose and poetry. Toronot, Adam, Stevenson and Co., 1867.
168p. port. 16½cm.
Pages missing.

Protest Episcopal Church in the U.S.A. - Sermons
M252 Johnson, John Howard, 1897-
J63p A place of adventure; essays and sermons. Foreword by Hughell E. W. Fosbroke. [Rev. ed.] Greenwich, Conn., Seabury Press, 1955.
190 p. 19 cm.
1. New York. St. Martin's Church. 2. Protestant Episcopal Church in the U. S. A.—Sermons. 3. Sermons, American. I. Title.
BX5980.N5M34 1955 283.747 55-13760 ‡
Library of Congress [5]

Proud shoes; the story of an American family.
MB9 Murray, Pauli, 1910-
M96p Proud shoes; the story of an American family. [1st ed.] New York, Harper [1956]
276 p. 22 cm.
I. Title.
E185.97.M95 920 56-10698 ‡
Library of Congress [15]

Senegal Prose and poetry.
M896 Senghor, Léopold Sédar, 1906-
Se5p Prose and poetry. Selected and translated by John Reed and Clive Wake. London, Oxford University Press, 1965.
181p. 18½cm.
Includes bibliography.
1. African literature. I. Title. II. Reed, John, comp. III. Wake, Clive, jt. comp.

Protestant Episcopal church in the U. S. A.- Sermons.
M252 Johnson, John Howard, 1897-
J63h Harlem, The war, and other addresses, by John Howard Johnson ... New York, W. Malliet and company, 1942.
6 p. l., 163 p. front. (port.) 22cm.
"First edition."
1. Protestant Episcopal church in the U. S. A.—Sermons. 2. Sermons, American. I. Title.
42-22629
Library of Congress BX5937.J4H3
[5] 252.03

M398 Proverbs.
B75o Brewer, John Mason, 1896-
Old-time Negro proverbs.
(In: Dobie, James Frank. ed. Spur-of-the-cock ... Austin, Texas, Texas Folk-lore Society, 1933. 22½cm. pp. 101-105.

Protestant churches-Haiti.
Haiti
M972.94 Pressoir, Catts.
P92p ... Le protestantisme haïtien ... [Port-au-Prince?] Impr. de la Société biblique et des livres religieux d'Haïti, 1945-
v. 23 cm.
At head of title: Docteur C. Pressoir.
Vol. 1 issued in parts, 1945-
"Ce volume rentre dans la deuxième partie du troisième volume de l'Histoire de la nation haïtienne, publiée sous la direction du dr. François Dalencour; section d'histoire religieuse."—v. 1, verso of 2d prelim. leaf.
1. Protestant churches—Haiti. I. Title.
BX4835.H3P73 277.294 47-6079
Library of Congress [2]

Protestant Episcopal Church in the U.S.A. - Sermons.
M525 Wright, Nathan.
W93r The riddle of life, and other sermons. Boston, Bruce Humphries [1952]
98p. 24cm.

Proverbs, African.
Cameroon
M398.9 Akwa, Dika Guillaume Betoté
Ak88b Bible de la sagesse Bantoue; [choix d'aphorismes, devinettes et mots d'esprit du Cameroun et du Gabon. Collectés par: Le Prince Dika-Akwa Guillaume Betoté de Bonambéla, avec l'aide de: Michel Doo-Kingué et M'Barga N'Goumou Manga Fabien. Présentés par: Madeleine Rousseau. Illustration de: Devi Tuszynski. Paris [Centre Artistique et Culturel Camerounais] 1955.
147p. 19½cm. (Collection Centraccam Série A)

M261 Protestant churches-U. S.
H77 Haynes, Leonard L 1923-
The Negro community within American Protestantism, 1619-1844. Boston, Christopher Pub. House [1953]
264 p. 21 cm.
1. Negroes—Religion. 2. Protestant churches—U. S. I. Title.
BR563.N4H38 *261.8 53-4230 ‡
Library of Congress [54d2]

Protestant Episcopal church in the U.S.A.— Virginia.
M283 Brydon, George Maclaren, 1875-
B84 The Episcopal church among the Negroes of Virginia, by G. Maclaren Brydon ... Richmond, Va., Virginia diocesan library, 1937.
25, [1] p. 23cm.
"Statistics; the colored work in the diocese of Virginia, 1937": [4] p. inserted at end.
1. Episcopalians, Negro. 2. Protestant Episcopal church in the U. S. A.—Virginia.
37-20872
Library of Congress BX5979.B78
——— Copy 2. E185.7.B78
[2] 283.755

Proverbs, African.
Kenya
M398 Barra, G
B27 1,000 Kikuyu proverbs with translations and English equivalents. [2d ed.] London, Macmillan and Co., Ltd., 1960.
123p. 18½cm.

Protestant churches-U.S.
M277.3 Johnston, Ruby Funchess.
J64r The religion of Negro Protestants; changing religious attitudes and practices. New York, Philosophical Library [1956]
xxvi, 224 p. tables. 24 cm.
Bibliography: p. 214-217.
1. Negroes—Religion. 2. Protestant churches—U. S. I. Title.
BR563.N4J62 277.3 56-13828
Library of Congress [56h7]

Protestant Episcopal Church in the U.S.A. Book of common prayer. Communion service.
M740 Crite, Allan Rohan, 1910- illus.
C86a All glory; brush drawing meditations on the Prayer of consecration. Cambridge, Mass., Society of Saint John the Evangelist, 1947.
[28] l. illus. 24 cm.
1. Lord's supper—Art. I. Protestant Episcopal Church in the U. S. A. Book of common prayer. Communion service. II. Title.
N8054.C7 741.6382 48-3019*
Library of Congress [3]

Proverbs, African.
Uganda
M398 East African Literature Bureau
Ea67 Engero eximu [Proverbs. Illustrated by L. N. Sekaboga] Kampala, Eagle Press, 1951.
11p. illus. 18cm. (Eagle improve your reading series, no. I)
Written in Luganda.

Protestant Episcopal church in the U.S.A.
M283 Convocation of the Colored Clergy.
C76p Proceedings of the first Convocation of the colored clergy of the Protestant Church in the United States of America, held at the church of the Holy Communion, 6th Avenue and 20th Street, New York City, Sept. 12th, 13th and 14th, 1883. Newark, N.J., Starbuck and Dunham, 1883.
24p. 23cm.

Le protestantisme haïtien...
Haiti
M972.94 Pressoir, Catts.
P92p ... Le protestantisme haïtien ... [Port-au-Prince?] Impr. de la Société biblique et des livres religieux d'Haïti, 1945-
v. 23 cm.
At head of title: Docteur C. Pressoir.
Vol. 1 issued in parts, 1945-
"Ce volume rentre dans la deuxième partie du troisième volume de l'Histoire de la nation haïtienne, publiée sous la direction du dr. François Dalencour; section d'histoire religieuse."—v. 1, verso of 2d prelim. leaf.
1. Protestant churches—Haiti. I. Title.
BX4835.H3P73 277.294 47-6079
Library of Congress [2]

Proverbs, African.
Kenya
M398 Kabetu, M N.
K112 Kagurarũ na waithĩra. London, New York, T. Nelson [1961]
88p. illus. 18cm.

Proverbs, African.
Uganda
M398
K119
Kagoro, E D
Ezimu ha afumo z'abatooro hali Nyinanyowe, N'abagenzi Bange [Batooro proverbs] Kampala. Eagle Press, 1956.
iv, 15p. 21cm.
Written in Nyora-Tooro.

1. Proverbs, African. 2. Uganda - Proverbs. I. Title.

Proverbs, Hebrew.
M296
R91
Russell, Charles L ed. and tr.
Light from the Talmud... by Charles L. Russell. New York, Bloch Publishing Co., 1942.
iv, 200p. incl. tab. 20cm.
Hebrew and English on opposite pages.

M309
P949
Provost, C Antonio, 1910-
The birth of the modern renaissance (and the rise of the U. S. A.) by C. Antonio Provost. Illus. [by] Art Henkel. [1st ed.] New York, Pageant Press [1965-
v. illus. 21 cm.
Bibliographical footnotes.
Portrait of author on book jacket.

1. U. S.—Moral conditions. 2. U. S.—Soc. condit. I. Title.
HN65.P7 309.173 65-29725
Library of Congress

Africa
M398
L56
Proverbs, African.
Leslau, Charlotte, comp.
African proverbs. Compiled by Charlotte and Wolf Leslau. With decorations by Jeff Hill. Mount Vernon, N. Y., Peter Pauper Press [1962]
61 p. col. illus. 19 cm.
White comp.

1. Proverbs, African. I. Leslau, Wolf, joint comp.
PN6519.A6L4 62-6237
Library of Congress [5]

Proverbs, Jabo.
Liberia
M398
B62
Blooah, Charles G
Jabo proverbs from Liberia; maxims in the life of a native tribe, by George Herzog... with the assistance of Charles G. Blooah. London, Pub. for the International institute of African languages & cultures by Oxford Univ. press, H. Milford, 1936.
xiii p., 1 l., 272p. 22½cm.

...La prudence du serpent interpretation de la parabole...
Haiti
M972.94
P286p
Paultre, Hector.
...La prudence du serpent interpretation de la parabole de l'econome infidele. Lettre-préface de Dantes Bellegarde. Petion-Ville, Haiti, La Presse Evangelique [1947]
48p. 18cm.

Proverbs, African.
Mali
M966.2
S18
Sissoko, Fily Dabo.
Sagesse noire (sentences et proverbes malinkés) Paris, Editions de la Tour du guet [1955]
xviii, 62 p. port. 21 cm.

1. Proverbs, African. I. Title.
A 56-984
Illinois. Univ. Library for Library of Congress [3]

Nigeria
M398
D156
Proverbs, Nigerian.
Dalegan, Ibrahim Agboola
Iwe owe tuntun. [New book of proverbs] Aka rerin. [Ilorin, Dalegan Trading Services, 1960]
45p. 18cm.
Written in Yoruba.

Pryde, Marion (Jackson) 1911- joint author.
MB
F629
Fleming, Beatrice (Jackson) 1902-
Distinguished Negroes abroad, by Beatrice J. Fleming and Marion J. Pryde. Washington, D. C., The Associated publishers [1946]
viii, 272 p. illus. (incl. ports.) 20½ cm.

1. Negroes in foreign countries. I. Pryde, Marion (Jackson) 1911- joint author. II. Title.
CT2750.A1F54 325.26 47-2301
© 6Mar47; The Associated publishers, inc.; A10979.
Library of Congress [47e8]

Africa
M398.9
W61
Proverbs, Fulah.
Whitting, Charles Edward Jewel, comp.
Hausa and Fulani proverbs. Lagos, Government Printer, 1940.
192p. 26cm.
Hausa and English.
White compiler.

1. Proverbs, Hausa. 2. Proverbs, Fulah. I. Title.

Haiti
M398
P94p
Proverbs haitien avec leur traduction litterale ou leurs equivalents en Francais. [n.p., n. p., n.d.]
205p. 19cm.
Lacks title page.

1. Haitian proverbs

Jamaica
M823.91
D37p
Psyche.
De Lisser, Herbert George, 1878-1944.
Psyche. London, Ernest Benn [1961]
224p. 17½cm.
"First published 1952."

I. Title.

Haiti
M398
B29
Proverbs, Haitian.
Bastien, Rémy
Anthologie du folklore Haïtien. Mexico, [Sociedad de Alumnos, de la Escuela Nacional de Antropologia] 1946.
118p. 23cm. (Acta antropologica. I:4)
White author.

1. Folk-lore - Haiti. 2. Haiti - Folk-lore. 3. Proverbs, Haitian 4. Riddles, Haitian. I. Title.

The Proverbs of our land.
Nigeria
M398
L14p
Lakeru, J A , comp.
Awọn owe ilẹ wa. Abeokuta, E.N.A. Press, 1916.
32p. 18½cm.
Translation: The proverbs of our land (Yoruba proverbs)

The psychiatrist.
Brazil
M869.3
M18p
Machado de Assis, Joaquim Maria, 1839-1908.
The psychiatrist, and other stories. Translated by William L. Grossman and Helen Caldwell. Berkeley, University of California Press, 1963.
147p. 22cm.

Nigeria
M398
J64
Proverbs, Hausa.
Johnston, Hugh Anthony Stephens, ed. & tr.
A selection of Hausa stories; compiled and translated by H. A. S. Johnston. Oxford, Clarendon P., 1966.
l, 241 p. 22½ cm. (Oxford library of African literature) 35/-
(B 66-16883)
Appendix in Hausa.

1. Tales, Hausa. 2. Proverbs, Hausa. I. Title.
PL8234.Z95E5 1966 398.2 66-75454
Library of Congress [3]

M974.52
P94a
Providence, R. I., Africa union meeting and school house.
A short history of the African union meeting and school house erected in Providence (R.I.) in the years 1819, 20, 21, with rules for its future government... Providence, Brown & Danforth, 1821.
32p. 22cm.
1. African union meeting and school house.
2. Education - Providence, R. I.

Psychiatry.
Haiti
M972.94
M352c
Mars, Louis.
...La crise de possession dans le voudou, essais de psychiatrie comparee [by] Louis Mars... Port-au-Prince, Haiti, Imprimerie de l'Etat, 1946.
XV, 103p. 20cm. (Bibliotheque de l'Institut d'Ethnologie de Port-au-Prince).

Africa
M398.9
W61
Proverbs, Hausa.
Whitting, Charles Edward Jewel, comp.
Hausa and Fulani proverbs. Lagos, Government Printer, 1940.
192p. 26cm.
Hausa and English.
White compiler.

1. Proverbs, Hausa. 2. Proverbs, Fulah. I. Title.

Providing adequate health service to Negroes.
M610
D29
Davis, Michael M.
Providing adequate health service to Negroes, by Michael M. Davis and Hugh M. Smythe. N.Y., Committee on Research in Medical Economics, 1949.
13p. 21½cm.

A psychological study of delinquent.
M136.7
D22
Daniel, Robert Prentiss, 1902-
A psychological study of delinquent and non-delinquent negro boys, by Robert P. Daniel ... Published with the approval of Professor Rudolf Pintner, sponsor ... New York city, Teachers college, Columbia university, 1932.
vi, 59 p. 23½cm. (Teachers college, Columbia university. Contributions to education, no. 546)
Issued also as thesis (PH. D.) Columbia university.
Bibliography: p. 56-59.

1. Boys. 2. Negroes. 3. Character tests. 4. Children, Abnormal and backward. 5. Juvenile delinquency. I. Title.
Library of Congress E185.65.D23 32-34641
——— Copy 2. LB5.C8 no. 546
[15] [159.922763] 136.763

Psychologie et education.
Haiti
M370.15 Boigris, Oscar
B63p
Psychologie et education, par Oscar Boigris. Haiti, Henri Deschamps [n.d.]

73p. 19cm.

Psychology.
MSS Wright, Nathan.
W93
Black Power. New York, Hawthorne Books [1967]

185 leaves. 28cm.
"Uncorrected proofs."

Public law - Bamiléké, Cameroun.
Cameroons, French
M967.11 Kwayeb, Enock Katté.
K971
Les institutions de droit public du pays Bamiléké, Cameroun; évolution et régime actuel. Paris, Librairie générale de droit et de jurisprudence, 1960.

199 p. illus. 26 cm. (Bibliothèque d'histoire du droit et droit romain, t. 5)

1. Public law—Bamiléké, Cameroun. I. Title.

61-26999 ‡

Library of Congress [5]

M323 Psychology.
C38o Charles, Charles V
Optimism and frustration in the American Negro. Reprinted from the Psychoanalytic review, 29:270-299, July, 1942.

270-299p. 24cm. (Psychogenetic studies in race psychology, no.6)

Psychology—[Study and] teaching.
M378 Canady, Herman George, 1901-
C16p
... Psychology in Negro institutions, by Herman G. Canady ... Institute, W. Va., West Virginia state college [1939]

24 p. tables. 23cm. (West Virginia state college bulletin. Series 26, no. 3. June, 1939)

"Contribution no. 1 of the Research council at West Virginia state college—curricula studies."

1. Psychology—[Study and] teaching. 2. Universities and colleges—U. S.—Curricula. 3. Negroes—Education. I. Title. II. Title: Negro institutions.

E 39-308

U. S. Off. of educ. Library for Library of Congress LC2801.C4 [4]

Public opinion.
M306 Johnson, Charles Spurgeon, 1893-
M21p
Public opinion and the Negro.

(In: National Conference of Social Work. Proceedings, 1923. Chicago, University of Chicago, 1923. 22cm. p. 497-502)

Psychology.
M301 Cleaver, Eldridge, 1935-
C58
Soul on ice. With an introd. by Maxwell Geismar. [1st ed.] New York, McGraw-Hill [1967, °1968]

xv, 210 p. 22 cm.
"A Ramparts book."

1. Negroes—Psychology. I. Title.

E185.97.C6 301.451'96'073 (B) 67-27277

Library of Congress [10-2]

... Psychology in Negro institutions.
M378 Canady, Herman George, 1901-
C16p
... Psychology in Negro institutions, by Herman G. Canady ... Institute, W. Va., West Virginia state college [1939]

24 p. tables. 23cm. (West Virginia state college bulletin. Series 26, no. 3. June, 1939)

"Contribution no. 1 of the Research council at West Virginia state college—curricula studies."

1. Psychology—[Study and] teaching. 2. Universities and colleges—U. S.—Curricula. 3. Negroes—Education. I. Title. II. Title: Negro institutions.

E 39-308

U. S. Off. of educ. Library for Library of Congress LC2801.C4 [4]

Public opinion on lovers.
Nigeria
M896.3 Maxwell, Highbred
M45p
Public opinion on lovers. Onitsha, Nigeria, Students' Own Bookshop [n.d.]

46p. 21cm.

Psychology.
M301 Hernton, Calvin C
H43w
White papers for white Americans [by] Calvin C. Hernton. [1st ed.] Garden City, N. Y., Doubleday, 1966.

155 p. 22 cm.

1. U. S.—Race question. 2. Negroes—Psychology. I. Title.

E185.61.H53 301.45196073 66-12244

Library of Congress [5]

Public administration in Ethiopia.
M910 Howard, William Edward Harding.
H83p
Public administration in Ethiopia; a study in retrospect and prospect. Groningen, J. B. Wolters, 1955.

viii, 204 p. map. 23 cm.
Proefschrift—Amsterdam.
"The written Constitution of 1931": p. 187-196.
"Stellingen" inserted.
Bibliography: p. 197-199.

1. Ethiopia—Pol. & govt. I. Ethiopia. Constitution. II. Title.

JQ3754.H6 *320.963 342.63 55-58722

Library of Congress [57d1]

Nigeria
M966.9 Public Relations Department.
P96
100 facts about Nigeria. Lagos, Public Relations Department, n.d.

8p. map 20½cm.

1. Nigeria - history.

Psychology.
M301 Killens, John Oliver, 1916-
K55
Black man's burden. New York, Trident Press, 1965.

176 p. 21 cm.

1. Negroes—Segregation. 2. Negroes—Psychology. I. Title.

E185.61.K487 301.45196073 65-24155

Library of Congress [66f7]

Public Affairs pamphlet no. 209.
M323 National Association for the Advancement of Colored People.
N21
Segregation and the schools, with the cooperation of the National Association for the Advancement of Colored People. New York, Public Affairs Committee, 1954.

28p. 18cm. (Public Affairs pamphlet no. 209)

Nigeria
M966.9 Public Relations Department
P96o
Our delegates in London. Lagos, Public Relations Department, n.d.

14p. illus. 20½cm. (Crownvird Series No.34)

1. Nigeria.

Psychology.
M301 Thorpe, Earl E
T39m
The mind of the Negro; an intellectual history of Afro-Americans. Baton Rouge, La., Printed by Ortlieb Press [1961]

562 p. 24 cm.
Includes bibliography.

1. Negroes—Intellectual life. 2. Negroes—Psychology. I. Title.

E185.82.T5 325.2670973 61-16125 ‡

Library of Congress [62k5]

Public finance - Ghana.
Ghana
M336.2 Goka, F K D 1919-
G56
Budget statement, 1961/62. [Accra, Ministry of Information, 1962]

14p. 24½cm.

1. Ghana - Public finance. 2. Public finance - Ghana. 3. Ghana - Economic conditions

---

Nigeria
M966.9 Public Relations Department
P96ou
Our ministers speak. Lagos, Public Relations Department, n.d.

20p. illus. 20½cm. (Crownbird Series No.24)

1. Nigeria - Politics and government.

Psychology.
M323.4 Wright, Nathan.
W934
Black power and urban unrest; creative possibilities. [1st ed.] New York, Hawthorn Books [1967]

200 p. 22 cm.
Bibliographical references included in "Notes" (p. 195)

1. Negroes—Civil rights. 2. U. S.—Race question. 3. Negroes—Psychology. I. Title.

E185.615.W7 323.4'0973 67-15556

Library of Congress [68t10]

Public health

See

Hygiene, Public.

Public school segregation and integration in the North.
M371.974 National Association of Intergroup Relations Officials. Commission on School Integration.
W65
Public school segregation and integration in the North; analysis and proposals of the [NAIRO] Commission on School Integration [prepared by Doxey A. Wilkerson] Washington, 1963.

vi, 104p. tables. 22cm.
Special issue of the Journal of Intergroup Relations.
Bibliography: p. 87-104.
(Continued on next card)

Public school segregation and integration in the North.
M371.974 W65
National Association of Intergroup Relations Officials. Commission on School Integration. Public school. 1963. (Card 2)

1. Segregation in education. I. Wilkerson, Doxey Alphonso, 1905- II. Journal of intergroup relations. III. Title.

Public schools.
M301 D853h
DuBois, William Edward Burghardt
Heredity and the public schools, a lecture delivered under the auspices of the Principals' Association of the Colored Schools of Washington, Friday, March 25, 1904. Washington, D. C., 1904.

11p. 22cm.

Public schools.
M370 M83f
Morton, Lena Beatrice
Farewell to the public schools, I'm glad we met. Boston, Meador Publishing Company, 1952.

223 p. 21cm.

Public schools-U. S.-Finance.
M370 W65f
Wilkerson, Doxey Alphonso, 1905–
Federal aid to education; to perpetuate or diminish existing educational inequalities? By Doxey A. Wilkerson. Issued April, 1937. Chicago, American federation of teachers [1937]
12 p. incl. tables. $21\frac{1}{2}$cm.

1. Education and state—U. S. 2. Education—U. S.—Finance. 3. Public schools—U. S.—Finance. 4. Negroes—Education—[Finance] I. Title.

U. S. Off. of educ. Library for Library of Congress LB2825.W65 [2] E 40-446

Public schools—West Virginia— Kanawha co.
M370 G61r
Goodlett, Carlton Benjamin.
... The reading abilities of the Negro elementary school child in Kanawha county, West Virginia ... [by] Carlton B. Goodlett ... and Andrew H. Calloway ... Institute, W. Va. [1940]
47 p. incl. tables. 23cm. (West Virginia state college [bulletin] Aug.-Nov. 1940. Ser. 5)
"Contribution no. 10, the Department of education."
"Publication of West Virginia state college."
1. Reading (Elementary) [1. Reading—Tests and scales] 2. Negroes—Education. 3. Public schools—West Virginia—Kanawha co. [3. Kanawha co., W. Va.—Schools] I. Calloway, Andrew H., joint author. II. Title.
E 41-54
U. S. Off. of educ. Library for Library of Congress LB1573.G57 [3] 371.974

Public secondary education for Negroes in North Carolina.
M370 L85p
Long, Hollis Moody, 1900–
... Public secondary education for Negroes in North Carolina, by Hollis Moody Long ... Published with the approval of Professor Grayson N. Kefauver, sponsor. New York city, Teachers college, Columbia university, 1932.
xi, 115 p. illus. (map) diagr. $23\frac{1}{2}$ cm. (Teachers college, Columbia university. Contributions to education, no. 529)
Issued also as thesis (PH. D.) Columbia university.
Bibliography: p. 114-115.
1. Negroes — Education. 2. Negroes — North Carolina. 3. High schools—North Carolina. 4. Education, Secondary. 5. Education — North Carolina. I. Title.
Library of Congress LC2802.N8L6 1932a 32—23749
——— Copy 2. LB5.C8 no. 529
[42q1] 371.974

Sierra Leone Public utilities - Nigeria.
M338 C217
Carney, David Edward.
Government and economy in British West Africa; a study of the role of public agencies in the economic development of British West Africa in the period 1947-1955. New York, Bookman Associates [1961]
207 p. 22 cm.
Issued in 1950 in microfilm form, as thesis, University of Pennsylvania, under title: Public agencies and economic development in British West Africa.
Bibliography: p. 197-201.
1. Africa, West—Econ. condit. I. Title.
HC517.W5C3 1961 338.966 61-9845
Library of Congress [10]

Public welfare.
M306 N21p
National conference of social work.
Proceedings ... Selected papers [of the] ... annual meeting. 1st-
1874- Library has: 1919, 1924
New York [etc.] 1874-19
v. ports., tables (part fold.) diagrs. 22-24 cm.
Issued under earlier names of the conference as follows: 1874, Conference of boards of public charities; 1875-79, Conference of charities; 1880-81, Conference of charities and corrections; 1882-1916, National conference of charities and correction (varies slightly)
Title varies slightly.
Vol. for 1874 (originally published in the Journal of social science, no. 6) was issued without title by the American social science association; reprinted in 1885 under title Proceedings of the first Conference of charities and correction.
(Continued on next card)
8-35377 rev 2
[r46p²20]

M813.5 P96
Puckett, G Henderson
One more tomorrow. New York, Vantage Press, 1959.

288p. 21cm.
Portrait of author on jacket.

I. Title.

Pudd'nhead Wilson.
M813.5 H87clp
Clemens, Samuel Langhorne, 1835-1910.
Pudd'nhead Wilson, by Mark Twain pseud. With an introduction by Langston Hughes. New York, Bantam Books, 1959.

143p. 18cm.

M370 W67p
Pudge grows up.
Williams, Frances Harriet.
Pudge grows up; Series of meetings for high school girls, by Frances Williams and Wenonah Logan. New York, Womans press, 1936.

28p. 28cm.

Puerto Rican essays.
Puerto Rico M864 C23t
Carrion, Madura Tomás
"Ten con ten." Impresiones de un Viaje á la América de Norte. Puerto Rico, "La Republica Española," 1906.

4-200p. 17cm.
Presentation copy inscribed by author, 1906.

Puerto Rican Fiction.
Puerto Rico M863 L13t
Laguerre, Enrique A
... El 30 de febrero (vida de un hombre interino) San Juan de Puerto Rico, Biblioteca de autores puertorriqueños, 1943.
333 p., 2 l. $20\frac{1}{2}$cm.
A novel.

I. Title.
A 43-3163
Harvard univ. Library for Library of Congress PQ7439.L3T7 [3] 863.6

Puerto Rican fiction.
Puerto Rico M863 L13l
Laguerre, Enrique A
...La llamarada novela,. 3rd ed. San Juan, Puerto Rico, Bibliotica de autores Puertorriquenos, 1945.

406p. $20\frac{1}{2}$cm.

Puerto Rican fiction.
Puerto Rico M864 T48c
Timothée, Pedro Carlos, 1864-
Cuentos populares por Pedro C. Timothée. 2d. ed. San Juan, Puerto Rico, 1923.

223p. 20cm.

Puerto Rico
M917.417 C71p
A Puerto Rican in New York.
Colon, Jesus, 1901-
A Puerto Rican in New York, and other sketches. New York, Mainstream Publishers, 1961.
202 p. 21 cm.
Portrait of author on back of book.

1. Puerto Ricans in New York (City) I. Title.
F128.9.P8C6 917.471 61-19786 ‡
Library of Congress [3]

Puerto Rican literature.
Puerto Rico M864 C23c
Carrión, Maduro Tomás.
... Cumba ... Puerto-Rico, Tip. boletin mercantil, 1903-
xv, 201p. 18cm.

Puerto Rican literature.
Puerto Rico M864 P14a
Pagán, Bolívar, 1899-
América y otras páginas, por Bolívar Pagán ... San Juan, P. R., 1922.

4p. l., 5-192p. $19\frac{1}{2}$cm.

Puerto Rico M860 F39
Puerto Rican literature (Slections: Extracts, etc.)
Fernandez Junos, Manual, 1846-1928
Antología Portorriqueña; prosa y verso; para lectura escolar. New York, Barnes and Noble, Inc. [1959]

iv, 343p. 18½cm.
White author.

Dominican Republic
Puerto Rican poetry.
M861.6 B34p.
Bazil, Osvaldo.
Parnaso antillano; compilación completa de los mejores poetas de Cuba, Puerto Rico y Santo Domingo, por Osvaldo Bazil. Barcelona, Maucci; [etc., etc., 1918]
2 p. l., viii p., 1 l., [7]-884 p. 19cm.

1. Cuban poetry (Selections: Extracts, etc.) 2. Puerto Rican poetry (Selections: Extracts, etc.) 3. Dominican poetry (Selections: Extracts, etc.) I. Title.
Library of Congress PQ7361.B3 [42c1] 18—21077

Puerto Rican poetry.
Puerto Rico M861. D44p
Derkes, Eleuterio, 1863-1883.
Poesias por Eleuterio Derkes. Puerto Rico. Imprenta del Comercio, 1871.

135 p. $17\frac{1}{2}$cm.

Puerto Rican poetry.
Puerto Rico
M861
D47f
Dessús, Luis Felipe
... Flores y balas (estados de alma)
Guayama, P. R., Tip. Union guayamesa, 1916.

264p. 22cm.
Portrait of author on cover.
Contents - libre I. Versos. - libro II. [Prosa]

Puerto Rico.
Puerto Rico
M972.95
C27m
Castrillo, Valentin
Mis experiencias a través de 70 años.
Caguas, Puerto Rico, 1960.

Unpaged port. 20½cm.

Puerto Rico
M864
P141
Puerto Rico - Politics and government - 1898-
Pagán, Bolívar, 1899-
... Ideales en marcha; discursos y artículos. San Juan, Puerto Rico, Biblioteca de autores puertorriqueños, 1939.
8 p. l., [9]-308 p., 8 l. 20cm.
"En homenaje a Bolívar Pagán [discurso pronunciado por Rafael Martínez Nadal, en junio 25, 1937]": p. [7]-19.
"Hablando con Bolívar Pagán [entrevista, de Angela Negrón Muñoz, abril 2, 1933]": p. [21]-33.

1. Puerto Rico—Pol. & govt.—1898- I. Martínez Nadal, Rafael, 1878- II. Negrón Muñoz, Angela. III. Title.
40-2968
Library of Congress F1975.P26
[42c1] 972.95

Puerto Rico
Puerto Rican poetry.
M861
P17
Palés Matos, Luis.
... Tuntún de pasa y grifería; poemas afroantillanos. San Juan de Puerto Rico, Biblioteca de autores puertorriqueños, 1937.
133 p., 2 l. 17cm.

I. Title.
39-12503
Library of Congress PQ7439.P24T8
[3] 861.6

Puerto Rico Puerto Rico.
M972.95
P58
Picó, Rafael.
The geographic regions of Puerto Rico. Río Piedras, University of Puerto Rico Press, 1950.
xiii, 256 p. illus., maps. 24 cm.
Based on thesis—Clark University.
Bibliography: p. 233-256.

1. Puerto Rico. I. Title.
Full name: Rafael Picó Santiago.
F1958.P5 330.97295 51-26021
Library of Congress [52e5]

Puerto Rico. University. Boletim, December 1939.
Puerto Rico
M301
R72
Rosario, Jose Colomban
Problemas sociales; el Negro: Haiti-Estados Unidos-Puerto Rico, por Jose Colomban Rosario y Justina Carrion. San Juan, Negociado de Materiales, Imprenta y Transporte, 1940.

174p. 21cm. (Universidad de Puerto Rico. Boletim, series X, no. 2, December 1939)
Bibliography: p. 161-165.

Puerto Rican poetry.
Puerto Rico
M861
P17v
Palés Matos, Vicente, 1903-
...Viento y espuma, cuentos y poemas ...
Mayagüez, P. R., Editorial Puerto Rico, 1945.

2p. l., 7-252 p., 1 l. 20cm. (Half-title: Obras completas, vol. I)
Biblioteca Autores antillanos.
"Printed in Argentine."

Puerto Rico.
Puerto Rico
M301
R72
Rosario, Jose Colomban
Problemas sociales; el Negro: Haiti-Estados Unidos-Puerto Rico, por Jose Colomban Rosario y Justina Carrion. San Juan, Negociado de Materiales, Imprenta y Transporte, 1940.

174p. 21cm. (Universidad de Puerto Rico. Boletim, series X, no. 2, December 1939)
Bibliography: p. 161-165.

Les puissants.
Guadeloupe
M843
B46p
Béville, Albert
Les puissants [par] Paul Niger [pseud.]
Paris, Les Editions du Scorpion [1958]

221p. 19cm. (Collection Alternance)

Puerto Rican poetry (Collections)
Puerto Rico
M861.
T63
Torres Rivera, Enrique, ed.
Parnaso portorriqueño, antología esmeramamente seleccionada de los mejores poetas de Puerto Rico por Enrique Torres Rivera. Barcelona, Maucci [1920]
351 p. 18½cm.

1. Puerto Rican poetry (Collections) I. Title.
41-21059 Revised
Library of Congress PQ7434.T6
[r42c2] 861.0822

Puerto Rico - Directory.
Puerto Rico
M864.
T48
Timotheo, Pedro C.
El consultor, folleto de amena literatura, con informacion utilisima para padres, maestros y estudiantes, relacion de professonale y altos funcionarios, comerciantes de San Juan, etc. Compilado por Pedro C. Timothee. San Juan, P. R., 1929.

112p. 19cm.

M304
P19
V.4, no.9
The Pullman Porter.
Issued by the Brotherhood of Sleeping Car Porters, 2311 Seventh avenue, New York, 1927.
15p. 20cm.
1. Brotherhood of Sleeping Car Porters.

Puerto Rico
M917.417
C71p
Puerto Ricans in New York (City)
Colon, Jesus, 1901-
A Puerto Rican in New York, and other sketches. New York, Mainstream Publishers, 1961.
202 p. 21 cm.
Portrait of author on back of book.

1. Puerto Ricans in New York (City) I. Title.
F128.9.P8C6 917.471 61-19788 ‡
Library of Congress [3]

Puerto Rico
M863
R524
Puerto Rico - History - Fiction.
Rivera Correa, R R
The pariahs. New York, Carlton Press [1967]

60p. 21cm.
Portrait of author on book jacket.

1. Puerto Rico - History - Fiction.
2. Albizu Campos, Pedro - Fiction.
I. Title.

Pulpit and platform efforts.
M234.8
Ea7p
Eason, James Henry, 1866-
Pulpit and platform efforts. Sanctifications vs. fanaticism, by Rev. J. H. Eason... with introduction by Rev. C. L. Fisher... Nashville, Tenn., National Baptist publishing board, 1899.

120p. front. 19½cm.

Puerto Ricans in New York (City) - Personal narratives.
MB9
T366
Thomas, Piri, 1928-
Down these mean streets. [1st ed.] New York, Knopf, 1967.
xiii, 333 p. 22 cm.
Autobiographical.

1. Puerto Ricans in New York (City)—Personal narratives. I. Title.
F128.9.P8T5 301.451'67'97471 66-19402
Library of Congress [5]

Puerto Rico - Politics and government.
Puerto Rico
M972.95
B23
Barbosa, José Celso, 1857-1921.
...La obra de José Celso Barbosa ... San Juan de Puerto Rico [Imprenta Venezuela] 1937-39.

4v. pl., ports., fold. facism. 22cm.
vol. 1 has cover-title and special t.-p.

Kenya
M376
R112
Puonjrwok mar nyako.
Rabuku, Martin A
Puonjrwok mar nyako [A girl's education]
Nairobi, Eagle Press, 1950.

23p. 18cm. (Paro mag jowadu. Your friends are thinking series)
Written in Luo and English.

1. Education of women. I. Title.
II. Title: A girl's education. III. Series.

Puerto Rico. Laws, statutes, etc.
Puerto Rico
M864
P142
Pagán, Bolivar, 1899-
...Ley municipal, revisada, anotada y comentada, por Bolívar Pagán. (Contiene la Ley municipal y todas las demás leyes aplicables a los municipios, el acta orgánica, el reglamento de contabilidad municipal, y toda la jurisprudencia del Tribunal supremo ... San Juan, Puerto Rico, La Correspondencia de Pto. Rico, inc., 1925.
xi, 13-256 [4] p. (Biblioteca de divulgación legal, vol. I)

Puerto Rico - Politics and government.
Puerto Rico
M864
Ca3a
Carrion, Madura Tomás.
Alma Latina. San Juan, Puerto Rico, Tipografía del Boletin Mercantel, 1905.

100p. 18cm.

A Puritan, pseud.
M326.
R84ab
Ruggles, David
The abrogation of the Seventh commandment, by the American churches ... New-York, D. Ruggles, 1835.
23 p. 18½cm.
[Markoe pamphlets, v. 57, no. 15]
Signed: A Puritan.

1. Slavery in the U. S.—Controversial literature—1835. I. A Puritan, pseud.
Library of Congress AC901.M3 vol. 57 28-18699
[3]

Purlie victorious.
M812.5 D29p
Davis, Ossie.
Purlie victorious; a comedy in three acts. New York, S. French [°1961]
90 p. 19 cm.

I. Title.

PS3507.A7444P8 812.54 62-51166 ‡
Library of Congress [2]

M200 P97
Purnell, J M , 1927-
In his pavilion; reflections upon religion and modern society. New York, Exposition Press, 1959.
162p. 21½cm.

1. Religion. I. Title.

Ghana M370 B96
Purposeful education for Africa.
Busia, Kofi Abrefa, 1913
Purposeful education for Africa, by K. A. Busia. The Hague, Mouton, 1964.
107 p. 20 cm. (Publications of the Institute of Social Studies. Series minor, v. 4)
Erratum slip inserted.
Bibliographical footnotes.

1. Education—Africa. I. Title. (Series: Hague. Institute of Social Studies. Publications: series minor, v. 4)

LA1501.B8 65-4146
Library of Congress [65b1]

M324 P97a
Purvis, Robert, 1810-1898
Appeal of forty thousand citizens threatened with disfranchisement to the people of Pennsylvania. Philadelphia, Merrihew and Gunn, 1838.
18p. 21½cm.

1. Philadelphia - Politics and government.

M815.3 P97s
Purvis, Robert, 1810-1898
Speeches and letters by Robert Purvis [Published by the request of the "Afro-American League." Correspondence between Robert Purvis and Bayard Taylor. [n.p. 1860?]
23p. front (port) 23½cm.
1. Speeches 2. Slavery
3. Colonization

M817.4 P97h
Purvis, T T
Hagar; the singing maiden, with other stories and rhymes, by T. T. Purvis. Philadelphia, Walton and co., 1881.
298p. 19½cm.

1. Short stories. 2. Poetry. I. Title.

Pushing forward;
M378A1 D29p
Davis, Walker Milan, 1908-
Pushing forward; a history of Alcorn A. & M. college and portraits of some of its successful graduates, by W. Milan Davis ... Okolona, Miss., The Okolona industrial school, 1938.
x, 124 p. illus. (incl. ports.) 23½cm.

1. Alcorn agricultural and mechanical college, Alcorn, Miss. 2. Negroes—Biog. I. Title.

38-9709
Library of Congress S537.A39D35
——— Copy 2.
Copyright A 114827 [3] 630.711

Russia M891 P97a
Pushkin, Aleksandr Sergeevich, 1799-1837.
An amateur peasant girl. Illustrated by Ian Ribbons. [London] Rodale Press [1955]
48 p. col. illus. 19 cm. (Miniature books)
Translation of Барышня-крестьянка (transliterated: Baryshnia-krest'ianka)

I. Title.

PG3347.B3R5 °891.733 56-35144
Library of Congress [5]

Temporary card
M891 P97t
Pushkin, Alexander Sergieevich, 1799-1837.
Complete works published under the direction of M. A. Tsiavlovski. Moscow-Leningrad, Academia, 1936.
6 vols. 26 x 18cm.
Printed in Russian.

Russia M891 P97e
Pushkin, Aleksandr Sergieevich, 1799-1837.
... Eugeny Onegin, translated by Oliver Elton and illustrated by M. V. Dobujinsky, with a foreword by Desmond MacCarthy. London, The Pushkin Press, 1946.
xxxiii, 3-255p. illus. 21cm.

I. Title.

Russia M891 P97po
Pushkin, Aleksandr Sergieevich, 1799-1837.
Poems by Alexander Pushkin; translated from the Russian, with introduction and notes by Ivan Panin. Boston, Cupples and Hurd, 1888.
179 p. 18cm.

I. Panin, Ivan, 1855- tr. 13-24617
Library of Congress
——— Copy 2.
Copyright 1888: 26902 [a37b1]

Russia M891 P97pr
Pushkin, Aleksandr Sergieevich, 1799-1837.
The prose tales of Alexander Poushkin, translated from the Russian by T. Keane. London, G. Bell and sons, ltd., 1914.
4 p. l., [3]-466 p. 17cm. (*On cover:* Bohn's popular library)
Contents. — The captain's daughter. — Doubrovsky. — The queen of spades.—An amateur peasant girl.—The shot.—The snowstorm. — The postmaster.—The coffin-maker.—Kirdjali.—The Egyptian nights.—Peter the Great's negro.

I. Keane, T., tr.
15-18915
Library of Congress PZ3.P979A
[42c1]

Russia M891 P97r
Pushkin, Aleksandr Sergieevich, 1799-1837.
The Russian wonderland: coq d'or, the tale of the fisherman and the fish, the tale of Czar Saltan. A metrical translation from the Russian of Alexander Poushkin, by Boris Brasol Manning... New York, The Paisley press, 1936.
ix, 62p. 21½cm.

1. Russian short stories. I. Brasol, Boris, trans. II. Title. III. Coq d'or. IV. The tale of Czar Saltan. V. The tale of the fisherman.

Russia M891 P97s
Pushkin, Alexander Sergieevich, 1799-1837.
Selections from the prose and poetry of Pushkin. Edited and introduced by Ernest J. Simmons. New York, Dell Publishing Co., 1961.
382p. 17cm. (A Laurel reader)
Sketch of author on book.
Cover title.

1. Russia - Poetry. 2. Poetry, Russian. I. Simmons, Ernest J., ed.

M326.5 P98r
Putnam, Lewis H.
A review of the cause and the tendency of the issues between the two sections of the country, with a plan to consolidate the views of the people of the United States in favor of emigration to Liberia, as the initiative to the efforts to transform the present system of labor in the southern states into a free agricultural tenantry, by the respective legislatures with the support of Congress to make it a national measure. By (cont'd)

Card 2
M326.5 P98r
By Lewis H. Putnam... Albany, N.Y., Weed, Parsons & co., 1859.
29p. 24cm.

1. Colonization. 2 Liberia

M973.8 P98r
Putnam, Lewis H
The review of the revolutionary elements of the rebellion, and of the aspect of reconstruction; with a plan to restore harmony between the two races in the southern states. By a colored man. Brooklyn, 1868.
44 p. 23cm.
Introduction signed: L. H. Putnam.

1. Reconstruction. I. Title.

4-15582
Library of Congress E668.P98
[a29d1]

Putnam, Samuel, 1892- tr.
Brazil M869.3 Am1v
Amado, Jorge, 1912-
The violent land, by Jorge Amado, translated from the Portuguese (Terras do sem fim) by Samuel Putnam. New York, A. A. Knopf, 1945.
6 p. l., 335, [1] p. 19cm.
"First American edition."

I. °Putnam, Samuel, 1892- tr. II. Title.
45-4925
Library of Congress ° PZ3.A478Vi
[20]

Putting the most into life.
M814.4 W272p
Washington, Booker Taliaferro, 1859?-1915.
Putting the most into life, by Booker T. Washington ... New York, T. Y. Crowell & co. [1906]
4 p. l., 35, [1] p. front. (port.) 19½cm.
"The chapters in this little book were originally part of a series of Sunday evening talks given by the principal to the students of the Tuskegee normal and industrial institute."

1. Negroes. I. Title.
6-36185
Library of Congress E185.6.W318
Copyright [a30g1]

Puzzles.
M811.5 C91p
Cuney, Waring, 1906-
Puzzles. Selected and introduced by Paul Breman. With 8 two-color woodcuts by Ru van Rossem. Utrecht, De Roos, 1960.
79p. illus. 32cm.
"175 copies were printed on Darwin paper for members of Stichting 'De Roos'. This is number 83."

Pwonye me pur.
Uganda M630 St1
Staples, E G
Pwonye me pur [Lectures in elementary agriculture. Translated by Lakana Otim and T. L. Lawrence. Rev. by Tomasi Otim and others] Nairobi, Eagle Press, 1949.
25p. 18½cm.
Written in Acoli.
White author.
1. Agriculture. I. Title. II. Otim, Lakana, tr.

Africa
M960 Quaison-Sackey, Alex
J88 Africa and the United Nations.
Pp. 354-377.

In: Judd, Peter, ed. African independence. New York, Dell Pub. Co., 1963.

M973 Quarles, Benjamin Arthur, 1905-
Qu2n The Negro in the American Revolution. Chapel Hill, Published for the Institute of Early American History and Culture, Williamsburg, Va., by University of North Carolina Press [1961]
xiii, 231 p. front. 24 cm.
Bibliography: p. [201]-223.
1. U. S.—Hist.—Revolution—Negroes. I. Institute of Early American History and Culture, Williamsburg, Va. II. Title.
Full name: Benjamin Arthur Quarles.
E269.N3Q3 973.315967 61—66795
Library of Congress [62k10]

Quarto de despejo.
Brazil
MB9 Jesus, Carolina Maria de
J49 Quarto de despejo. 4.ª edição. 40.º milheiro. Favelada, Diario de Uma, 196?

182p. illus. 25cm.

Ghana
M960 Quaison-Sackey, Alex.
Q23 Africa unbound; reflections of an African statesman. Foreword by Kwame Nkrumah. New York, Praeger [1963]
174 p. 21 cm. (Books that matter)
1. Africa—Politics. 2. Pan-Africanism. ~~3. Negroes in Africa.~~ I. Title.
DT30.Q3 916 63-10827 ‡
Library of Congress [5]

M973 Quarles, Benjamin Arthur, 1905-
Q25 The Negro in the Civil War. [1st ed.] Boston, Little, Brown [1953]
xvi, 379 p. illus. 21 cm.
Bibliography: p. [349]-360.
1. U. S.—Hist.—Civil War—~~Negroes.~~ I. Title.
E540.N3Q3 973.715 53—7309
Library of Congress [54k10]

Quash, Eugene T. jt. author.
M616 Wright, Louis Tompkins, 1891-1952
W93v A vehicle for the tropical use of certain therapeutic agents, by Aaron Prigot, Louis T. Wright, and Eugene T. Quash. Reprinted from Antibiotics and chemotherapy, 1953.

418-420p. illus. 25cm.
Reprinted from the Antibiotics and chemotherapy, April 1953.

Ghana A qualitative analysis for school certificate.
M540.7 Adu-Ampoma, Samuel H
Ad8 A qualitative analysis for school certificate. Cambridge, University Press, 1962.

29p. tables 17cm.

M973 Quarles, Benjamin Arthur, 1905-
Q25n The Negro in the making of America. [1st ed.] New York, Collier Books [1964]
288 p. 18 cm. (A Collier books original)
"AS 584."
Bibliography: p. 267-271.
1. Negroes—Hist. I. Title.
E185.Q2 301.451 64-21833
Library of Congress [4-1]

Le quatrième siècle; roman.
Martinique
M843.9 Glissant, Édouard, 1928-
G49q Le quatrième siècle; roman. Paris, Éditions du Seuil [1964]

290p. 21cm.
Portrait of author on back of book.

I. Title.

M815.4 Quarles, Benjamin Arthur, 1905-
D739q Frederick Douglass. Washington, Associated Publishers [1948]
xi, 378 p. illus., ports. 21 cm.
Bibliography: p. 351-362.
1. Douglass, Frederick, 1817?-1895.
E449.D774 923.673 48—2544*
Library of Congress [49f5]

Quarles, Benjamin Arthur, 1905- , ed.
MB9 Douglass, Frederick, 1817?-1895.
D74n Narrative of the life of Frederick Douglass, an American slave, written by himself. Edited by Benjamin Quarles. Cambridge, Mass., Belknap Press, 1960.

xxvi, 163p. port., map. 22cm. (The John Harvard library)

La xive. législature.
Haiti Michel, Antoine.
M972.94 ... La xive. législature ... Port-au-Prince, Haiti, Imprimerie "La Presse", 1932-
M58d v. 23½^cm.
At head of title, v. 1- : Au service de la jeunesse haïtienne.
1. Haiti (Republic) Assemblée nationale, 1873-1874. 2. Haiti—Pol. & govt.—1844- I. Title.
Library of Congress F1926.M63 33-12850
[2] 972.94

Quarles, Benjamin Arthur, 1905- , jt. author
MB ~~Sterling, Dorothy, 1913-~~
Qu26 Lift every voice; the lives of Booker T. Washington, W. E. B. Du Bois, Mary Church Terrell, and James Weldon Johnson [by] Dorothy Sterling and Benjamin Quarles. Illustrated by Ernest Crichlow. [1st ed.] Garden City, N. Y., Doubleday, 1965.
116 p. illus., ports. 22 cm. (Zenith books)
1. Washington, Booker Taliaferro, 1859-1915—Juvenile literature. 2. Du Bois, William Edward Burghardt, 1868-1963—Juvenile literature. 3. Terrell, Mary (Church) 1863-1954—Juvenile literature. 4. Johnson, James Weldon, 1871-1938—Juvenile literature. I. Quarles, Benjamin, joint author. II. Title.
E185.96.S77 920.073 65-17237
Library of Congress [5]

Quartet.
Africa, South
M896.3 Rive, Richard, 1931- *ed.*
R52 Quartet; new voices from South Africa: Alex La Guma, James Matthews, Alf Wannenburgh, Richard Rive. New York, Crown Publishers [1963]
223 p. 22 cm.
Short stories.
1. Short stories, South African. I. Title. II. Title: New voices from South Africa. 2. Africa, South - Short stories.
PZ1.R44Qar 63-21106
Library of Congress [5]

Queen of Persia.
M813.5 Cotton, Ella Earls.
C82q Queen of Persia, the story of Esther who saved her people. Illustrated by Stina Nagel. [1st ed.] New York, Exposition Press [1960]
150 p. illus. 22 cm.
Portrait of author on book jacket.
1. Esther, Queen of Persia—Fiction. I. Title.
PZ4.C848Qe 60-4670 ‡
Library of Congress [2]

M973.7 Quarles, Benjamin Arthur, 1905-
Qu2 Lincoln and the Negro. New York, Oxford University Press, 1962.
275 p. illus. 21 cm.
Includes bibliography.
1. Lincoln, Abraham, Pres. U. S.—Relations with Negroes. 2. Lincoln, Abraham, Pres. U. S.—Views on slavery. I. Title.
Full name: Benjamin Arthur Quarles.
E457.2.Q3 923.173 62—9829 ‡
Library of Congress [63i5]

Quartier noir.
Jamaica
M823.91 McKay, Claude, 1890-
M19h6 Quartier noir (Home to Harlem) traduit du Negre Americain par Louis Guilloux. Paris, Les Editions Rieder, 1932.
287p. 19cm.

Egypt The Queen of Sheba and her only son Menyelek.
M962 Kebra nagast.
K23q The Queen of Sheba & her only son Menyelek; being the history of the departure of God & His Ark of the covenant from Jerusalem to Ethiopia, and the establishment of the religion of the Hebrews & the Solomonic line of kings in that country. A complete translation of the Kebra nagast with introduction by Sir E. A. Wallis Budge ... Now first pub. with 31 illustrations from Ethiopic mss. in the British museum. London, Boston, Mass. [etc.] The Medici society, limited, 1922.
xc, 241, [1] p. xxxi pl. (incl. front., facsim.) 23^cm.
(Continued on next card)
22—13424
[32d2]

M973 Quarles, Benjamin Arthur, 1905- , jt. author
Qu25ne The Negro American; a documentary history [by] Leslie H. Fishel, Jr. [and] Benjamin Quarles. Glenview, Ill., Scott, Foresman [1967]
536 p. illus., facsims., maps, ports. 24 cm.
Bibliographical footnotes.
1. Negroes—Hist.—Sources. ~~I. Quarles, Benjamin, joint author.~~ II. Title. I. Fishel, Leslie H.
E185.F5 973 67—26184
Library of Congress [68f5]

MB9 Quarto - centennial of H.M. Turner as bishop
T85q in the A.M.E. church, celebrated in St. Paul A.M.E. church, Saint Louis, Missouri. Nashville, Tenn., A.M.E. Sunday School union, 1905.

143p. 19cm.

1. Turner, Henry McNeil, 1834-1915.
2. African methodist episcopal church.

Haiti Quelques aspects du problème de la population..
M572 Aristide, Achille.
Ar4q Quelques aspects du problème de la population en Haïti. Communication présentée à la "Première Conférence de l'hémisphère occidental sur les problèmes de la population et de la planification de la famille" tenue à San Juan, Porto-Rico, du 12 au 15 mai 1955. Port-au-Prince, Impr. de l'État, 1955.
61 p. 21 cm.
Bibliography: p. 35.
1. Haiti—Population. I. Title.
HB3551.A7 56-26123
Library of Congress [1]

Quelques moeurs et coutumes des paysans Haitiens...
Haiti
M972.94 Romain, J B
R66q
Quelques moeurs et coutumes des paysans Haitiens; travaux pratiques d'ethnographie sur la region de milot a l'usage des etudiants. Port-au-Prince, Imprimerie de l' Etat, 1958.
264p. illus. 23cm.
1. Haiti - Social life and customs. I. Title.

Quest for dignity.
MB9 Peyton, Thomas Roy, 1897-
P46q
Quest for dignity, an autobiography of a Negro doctor. Los Angeles, W. F. Lewis [1950]
vii, 156 p. 24 cm.
I. Title. II. Title: Negro doctor.
R154.P49A3 926.1 50-13642
Library of Congress [a50c2]

M973 Quick, Charles Whitted,
R72
Legal concepts in the quest for equality, by Charles W. Quick and Donald B. King.
Pp. 147-162.
In: Rose, Arnold Marshall, ed. Assuring freedom to the free. Detroit, Wayne State University, 1964.

Quelques vues politiques et morales (questions haitiennes)
M972.94 Dorsainvil, Justin Chrysostome, 1880-
D739
... Quelques vues politiques et morales (questions haitiennes) Port-au-Prince (Haiti) Imprimerie modèle, 1934.
cover-title, 1 p. l., vi, [9]-132 p., 1 l. 24½cm.
At head of title: Dr. J. C. Dorsainvil.
Errata slip inserted.
1. Haiti—Pol. & govt.—1844- 2. Haiti—Soc. condit. I. Title.
35-29263
Library of Congress F1928.D67
[2] 972.94

The quest of the silver fleece.
M301 Du Bois, William Edward Burghardt, 1868-
D85q
The quest of the silver fleece; a novel, by W. E. Burghardt Du Bois ... illustrated by H. S. DeLay. Chicago, A. C. McClurg & co., 1911.
434 p. front., plates. 21½cm.
I. Title.
11-27912
Library of Congress PZ3.D8523Q
[42l1]

MB Quick, William Harvey, 1856-
Q4n
Negro stars in all ages of the world, by W. H. Quick ... 2nd ed. Richmond, Va., S.B. Adkins & Co., 1898.
272p. 22cm.
1. Biography. I. Title.

Dahomey
M966.8 Quénum, Maximilien.
Que 3
Au pays des fons (us et coutumes du Dahomey). 2 me édition revue et corrigée. Paris, Larose éditeurs, 1938.
170p. port. (front.) plates. illus. 24cm.
1. Dahomey. I. Title.

The question before Congress.
M973 Mitchell, George Washington, 1865-
M69q
The question before Congress, a consideration of the debates and final action by Congress upon various phases of the race question in the United States, by Geo. W. Mitchell. Philadelphia, Pa., The A. M. E. book concern [°1918]
247 p. 23½cm.
1. Slavery in the U. S. 2. Negroes. 3. U. S.—Race question. I. Title.
18-21546
Library of Congress E441.M68
[43g1]

Quicksand.
M813.5 Larsen, Nella.
L32q
Quicksand, by Nella Larsen. New York & London, A. A. Knopf, 1928.
4 p. l., 301, [1] p., 1 l. 19½cm.
I. Title.
28-6740
Library of Congress PZ3.L323Qu
[48d1]

Dahomey
M960 Quenum, Maxmillien Possy Berry
Qu3
L'Afrique noire (rencontre avec l'Occident). [Paris] Fernand Nathan, Éditeur [1958]
172p. ports. 21cm.
1. Africa - Social life and conditions. I. Title.

Senegal La question des salaires au Sénégal, 1965.
M966.3 Diouf, Coumba N'Doffène
D63
La question des salaires au Sénégal, 1965; notes et commentaires mis en ordre et présentés par Coumba N'Doffène Diouf, Georges Vermot-Gauchy et Charles Francis Brun. [Dakar] Librairie Clairafrique [1966]
82p. illus. 24cm. (Dossiers Africains, no. 2)

Africa Quigg, Philip W., ed.
M960 Foreign affairs (*New York*)
F76
Africa; a Foreign affairs reader, edited by Philip W. Quigg. Foreword by Hamilton Fish Armstrong. [1st ed.] New York, Published for the Council on Foreign Relations by Praeger [1964]
xii, 346 p. 25 cm.
1. Africa, Sub-Saharan—Politics—Addresses, essays, lectures. 2. Nationalism—Africa, Sub-Saharan. 3. Africa, South—Native races—Addresses, essays, lectures. I. Quigg, Philip W., ed. II. Title.
DT352.F6 1964 960.3082 64-12589
Library of Congress [5]

Dahomey
M966.8 Quénum, Maximilien Possy Berry
Que 31
Légendes Africaines; Côte d'Ivoire - Soudan-Dahomey. Illustrations de P. Tardy. Rochefort-Sur-Mer, Imprimerie A. Thoyon-Thèze, 1956.
101p. illus. 28cm.
1. Dahomey - Legends. 2. Africa - Legends. I. Title.

A question of life.
M248 Henry, Romiche.
H39
A question of life. New York, Vantage Press. [1963]
79p. 20½cm.

Quincas Borba.
Brazil Machado de Assis, Joaquim Maria. 1839-1908.
M869.3
M18q
... Quincas Borba. Rio de Janeiro. Paris. Garnier [1923?]
3 p. l., 360p. 19cm. (Collecção dos autores celebres da litteratura brasileira)
At head of title: Machado de Assis.
A continuation of the author's Memorias posthumas de Braz Cubas.

Brazil
M981 Querino, Manuel Raymundo, 1851-
Q3a
A arte culinaria na Bahia. Prefácio Bernardino de Souza. Bahia, Livraria Progresso Editora, 1957.
86p. 16½cm.
1. Cookery-Brazil. I. Title.

Questions and answers.
M220 Jackson, Olive Scott.
J13
God in the flesh; questions and answers about women, Jews, Negroes, and the church. New York, William-Frederick Press, 1958.
29 p. 22 cm.
1. Questions and answers. I. Title.
AG195.J2 220.76 57-12709 ‡
Library of Congress [1]

M811.5 Quintot, Raymond
H87
Langston Hughes; ou, L' etoile noire. Poemes traduits par Georges Peleman et Raymond Quintot. Ixelies, Bruxelles, aux Editions du C.E.L.F., 1964.
82p. 18cm. (Les Cahiers de la Tour de Babel, no. 225).
"Prix Interfrance de l'essai."
White author.
"For Arthur - this first book entirely about me by someone not me - Sincerely, Langston. Harlem, U.S.A., June, 1964"
1. Hughes, Langston, 1902-
I. Hughes, Langston, 1902-

Brazil Querino, Manuel Raymundo, 1851-
M981
Q3c
... Costumes africanos no Brasil. Prefacio e notas de Arthur Ramos. Rio de Janeiro, Civilizacao Brasileira, 1938.
351p. 18½cm. (Bibliotheca de divulgacao scientifica, vol. XV.)
1. Brazil - African customs. I. title

Questions and answers on twelfth night.
Nigeria
M820.7 Oguine, O D M
Og9
Questions and answers on twelfth night, with summaries. Onitsha [Nigeria, Etudo, 1962.
58p. 21cm.

Quinze jours au sinai.
France
M840 Dumas, Alexandre, 1802-1870.
D89q
Quinze jours au sinai. Bruxelles, Meline, Cans et Cie., 1839.
2 vols. in 1 16cm.

Quotations.
M304 Davis, Mitchell, compiler.
P19 One hundred choice quotations by
v.4, no.3 prominent men and women of the Negro race.
A valuable little gift book collected during spare moments and compiled by Mitchell Davis. [n.p. n.d.]
34p. 15cm.

Quotations.
M814.4 Washington, Booker Taliaferro, 1859?-1915.
W272b Black-belt diamonds; gems from the speeches, addresses, and talks to students of Booker T. Washington ... selected and arranged by Victoria Earle Matthews; introduction by T. Thomas Fortune. New York, Fortune and Scott, 1898.
xii, 115 p. front. (port.) 15cm.

1. Negroes. I. Matthews, Victoria Earle.

Library of Congress E185.6.W3 98-552 Revised
Copyright 1898: 40048 [r32c2]

R., J. B.
MB9 Jennings, Paul, b. 1799.
M26j A colored man's reminiscences of James Madison. By Paul Jennings. Brooklyn, G. C. Beadle, 1865.
vi, [7]-21 p. front. (facsim.) 30cm. (Half-title: Bladensburg series. no. 2)
"Reprinted 1865. Seventy-five copies."
"Preface signed J. B. R."

1. Madison, James, pres. U. S., 1751-1836. I. J. B. R. II. R., J. B. III. Title.

Library of Congress E342.J54 13-20475
[a37b1]

M301 Raab, Earl, ed.
R11 American race relations today. [1st ed.] Garden City, N. Y., Doubleday, 1962.
195 p. 18 cm. (Anchor books, A318)
Partial contents.-Changing social roles in the new south, by Joseph S. Himes.-The sit-ins and the new Negro students, by Charles U. Smith (abridged).-The Black muslims in America, by C. Eric Lincoln.
White editor.

1. U. S.—Race question. 2. Minorities—U. S. I. Title.

E184.A1R19 301.451 62-15926 ‡
Library of Congress [5]

Råb det fra bjergene.
M813.5 Baldwin, James, 1924-
B18g5 Råb det fra bjergene [Go tell it on the mountain] Overstat fra Amerikansk af Gudrun Vergmann. [Copenhagen] Steen Hasselbalchs Forlag, 1965.
263p. cm.
Written in Danish.

I. Title.

Madagascar
M841 Rabéarivelo, Jean Jospeh, 1901-1937.
R11v Sylves; nobles dedaens, fleurs mêlees, Destinée, Dixains, Sonnets & poèmes d'Iarive. Tananarive, Imprimerie de l'Imerina, 1927.
[102]p. 24cm.
Bound with volumes by same author.

1. French literature - Madagascan author.
I. Title.

Malagasy
M841 Rabéarivelo, Jean-Joseph, 1901-1937.
R11tw 24 poems. [Translated by Gerald Moore and Ulli Beier] Designed and illustrated by M. E. Betts. Ibadan, Mbari Publications, 1962.
[40]p. illus. 21-1/2cm.

I. Title. II. Mbari Publications.

Madagascar
M841 Rabéarivelo, Jean Joseph, 1901-1937.
R11v Volumes; vers le bonheur, la guirlande a l'amitié, Interlude rythmique, sept quatrains, arbres, au soleil estival, coeur & ciel d'Iarive. Tannanrive, Imprimerie de l'Imerina, 1928.
[109]p. 24cm.

1. French literature - Madagascan author.

Rabéarivelo, Jean Joseph, 1901-1937.
Madagascar
MB9 Boudry, Robert, 1893-
R11b Jean-Joseph Rabéarivelo et la mort. Préface de Jean Amrouche. Paris, Présence Africaine, 1958.
84p. 19cm.

French Guiana
M841.08 Rabearivelo, Jean Joseph, 1901-1937.
D18 Damas, Leon G ed., 1912-
Poètes d'expression française [d'Afrique Noire, Madagascar, Réunion, Guadeloupe, Martinique, Indochine, Guyane] 1900-1945. Paris, Éditions du Seuil [1947]
322p. (Lattitudes françaises, 1)
Collection "Pierres vives."

Rabel, Jean.
Haiti
M972.94 Sylvain, Georges, 1866-1925
Sy58a Allocution de Me. Georges Sylvain, administrateur délégue de l'union patriotique, prononcée a Jean Rabel le 19 Août 1923.
4p. 25½cm.

Madagascar
M842.91 Rabemananjara, Jacques, 1913-
R11ag Agapes des dieux; Tritriva; tragédie malgache. Paris, Présence Africaine [1962]
265p. 19cm.

1. Madagascar - Drama. I. Title.
II. Title: Tritriva.

Madagascar
M841.91 Rabemananjara, Jacques, 1913-
R11at Antiodote; poèmes. Paris, Présence Africaine, 1961.
46p. 19½cm.

1. Poetry. I. Title.

Madagascar
M841.91 Rabemananjara, Jacques, 1913-
R11an Antsa, poème. Préf. de François Mauriac. Paris, Présence africaine ~~1956~~, Nouvelle ed. [1961]
~~66 p.~~ 20 cm. 67p.
"Paru à l'occasion du Premier Congrès international des écrivains et artistes noirs."

I. Title.

Illinois. Univ. Library for Library of Congress A 57-1468 [5]

Madagascar
M841.91 Rabemananjara, Jacques, 1913-
R11a Antsa, poème. Préf. de François Mauriac. Paris, Présence africaine [1956]
66 p. 20 cm.
"Paru à l'occasion du Premier Congrès international des écrivains et artistes noirs."

I. Title.

Illinois. Univ. Library for Library of Congress A 57-1468 [5]

Madagascar
M842.91 Rabemananjara, Jacques, 1913-
R116 Les boutriers de l'aurore; tragédie malgache en 3 actes, 6 tableaux. Paris, Présence Africaine, 1957.
231p. 19½cm.

1. Madagascar - Drama. I. Title.

Madagascar
M841.91 Rabemananjara, Jacques, 1913-
R11 Jacques Rabemananjar. Présentation par Elaine Boucquey-de Schutter. Choix de textes bibliographie, portraits, facsimilés. [Paris] Editions Pierre Seghers, 1964.
185p. illus. 16cm. (Poètes d'aujourd'hui, 112)
Portrait of author on front cover.
1. Rabemananajar, Jacques, 1913-
I. Boucquey-de Schutter, Elaine.

Madagascar
M841.91 Rabemananjara, Jacques, 1913-
R11 l Lamba, poème. Paris, Présence africaine [1956]
78 p. 20 cm.

I. Title.

Illinois. Univ. Library for Library of Congress A 57-2128 [5]

Madagascar
M969 Rabemananjara, Jacques, 1913-
R11n Nationalisme et problemes Malgaches. Paris, Presence Africaine, 1958.
219p. 22½cm.

1. Madgascar - Politics and government.
2. Poetry. I. Title.

Madagascar
M969 Rabemananjara, Jacques, 1913-
R11t Témoignage malgache et colonialisme. Paris, Présence africaine [1956]
46 p. 19 cm. (Collection "Le Colonialisme," 2)
First ed. published in 1946 under title: Un Malgache vous parle.

1. Madagascar—Pol. & govt. I. Title.

JQ3453 1956.R3 57-30796 ‡
Library of Congress [5]

Rabemananjara, Jacques, 1913-
Congo(Leopoldville)
M840.8 Mushiete, Paul
M971 La littérature française africaine; petite anthologie des écrivains noirs d'expression francaise. Leverville, Bibliothèque de l'Étoile, 1957.
40p. 17½cm.

Rabemananjar, Jacques, 1913-
Madagascar
M841.91 Rabemananjara, Jacques, 1913-
R11 Jacques Rabemananjar. Présentation par Elaine Boucquey-de Schutter. Choix de textes bibliographie, portraits, fac-similés. [Paris] Editions Pierre Seghers, 1964.
185p. illus. 16cm. (Poètes d'aujourd'hui, 112)
Portrait of author on front cover.
1. Rabemananajar, Jacques, 1913- I. Boucquey-de Schutter, Elaine.

Kenya
M376 Rabuku, Martin A
R112 Puonjrwok mar nyako [A girl's education] Nairobi, Eagle Press, 1950.
23p. 18cm. (Paro mag jowadu. Your friends are thinking series)
Written in Luo and English.
1. Education of women. I. Title. II. Title: A girl's education. III. Series.

Race
Haiti
M572 Aristide, Achille.
Ar4 ... Le racisme et le métissage devant la science. 2. éd. ... [n. p.] Haiti, Compagnie lithographique, 1945.
21 p. 20½cm.
1. Race. I. Title.
GN62.A7 572 47-18368
Library of Congress [2]

Race.
M573 Armattoe, Raphael Ernest Grail.
Ar5s Space, Time and race; or, the age of man in America. An address to great James St. Women's Guild. [Londonderry, 1946]

Race.
Gold Coast
M966.7 De Graft-Johnson, John Coelman, 1919-
D36a African glory; the story of vanished Negro civilizations. London, Watts [1954]
209p. illus. 23cm.

Race.
M573.5 Delany, Martin Robison, 1812-1885.
D37 Principia of ethnology: the origin of races and color, with an archeological compendium of Ethiopian and Egyptian civilization, from years of careful examination and enquiry, by Martin R. Delany ... Philadelphia, Harper & brother, 1879.
viii, [9]-95 p. incl. illus., pl., map. 2 pl. 20½cm.
1. Monogenism and polygenism. 2. Color of man. 3. Egypt—Civilization. 4. Negro race.
Library of Congress GN370.D33 5—29787
[a33b1]

Race.
M301 Du Bois, William Edward Burghardt, 1868-
D853su3 The superior race (an essay) by W.E. Burghardt Du Bois, [n.p., n.p., n.d.]
55-60p. 24½cm.

Martinique Race.
M323 Fanon, Frantz, 1925-1961.
F21p3 Black skin, white masks. Translated by Charles Lam Markmann. New York, Grove Press [1967]
232p. 21cm.
Translation of Peau noire, masques blancs.
Bibliographical footnotes.
1. Negro race. I. Title.

Race.
Martinique
M323. Fanon, Frantz, 1925-
F21p Peau noire, masques blancs. Préf. de Francis Jeanson. Paris, Éditions du Seuil [1952]
222 p. 19 cm. (Collections Esprit. La condition humaine)
Bibliographical footnotes.
1. Negro race. I. Title.
A 53-3681
Harvard Univ. Library for Library of Congress [1]

Race.
M572 Ford, Theodore P.
F75 God wills the Negro; an anthropological and geographical restoration of the lost history of the American Negro people, being in part a theological interpretation of Egyptian and Ethiopian backgrounds. Compiled from ancient and modern sources, with a special chapter of eight Negro spirituals. By Theodore P. Ford, PH. B. Chicago, Ill., The Geographical institute press, 1939.
159 p. incl. front., illus. 23cm.
Includes music.
Bibliographical foot-notes.
1. Negro race. 2. Negro songs. I. Title.
Library of Congress GN545.F6 39-2105
——— Copy 2.
Copyright A 124575 [3] 572.96

Race.
M573.2 Johnson, Edward Augustus, 1860-
J63a Adam vs. ape-man, and Ethiopia, by Edward A. Johnson ... [New York, Printed by J. J. Little & Ives company, 1931.
x, 7-293 p. front., plates, ports., map. 19½cm.
1. Ethiopia—Hist. 2. Negro race. I. Title. 31-10249
Library of Congress GN350.J6
——— Copy 2.
Copyright A 36363 [3] 573.2

Race.
M213 Lewis, Robert Benjamin
L58 Light and truth; collected from the Bible
1851 and ancient and modern history, containing the universal history of the colored an the Indian race, from the creation of the world to the present time. By R.B. Lewis...Boston, published by Moses N. Taylor, 1851.
viii, 9-400p. 19cm.

Race.
M808 Locke, Alain Le Roy, 1886-
L79r Le role du Nègre dans la culture des Amériques, conférences. Port-au-Prince, Haiti, Impr. de l'Etat, 1943.
141p. 21cm.

Race.
Africa, South
M960 Mphahlele, Ezekiel.
M87 The African image. ~~New York, Praeger, 1962.~~ London, Faber and Faber [1962]
240 p. 21 cm. ~~(Books that matter)~~
Includes bibliography.
1. Negro Race. 2. Literature - Africa ~~2. Negroes in literature.~~ I. Title. 3. Negritude. 4. Africa - Native races.
GN645.M7 1962a 809.93 62-19061 ‡
Library of Congress [5]

Race.
M930 Norris, John William.
N79e The Ethiopian's place in history, and his contribution to the world's civilization; the negro—the Hamite, the stock, the stems and the branches of the Hamitic people. By Rev. John William Norris ... Baltimore, The Afro-American co., 1916.
5 p. l., 60 p. 23½cm. $0.75
1. Negro race. I. Title.
Library of Congress HT1589.N57 16-6281
——— Copy 2.
Copyright A 427196

Race.
M200 Oliver, C Herbert, 1925-
O13n No flesh shall glory. [Nutley, N. J.] Presbyterian and Reformed Pub. Co., 1959.
96 p. 21 cm.
1. Race. 2. Segregation—Religious aspects. 3. Sociology, Biblical. I. Title.
BT734.O4 261.83 59-14513 ‡
Library of Congress [2]

Race.
M572 Parker, George Wells
P22c The children of the sun, by George Wells Parker...Omaha Nebraska, The Hamitic league of the world c 1918
31p. 22cm.

Race.
M572.893 Perry, Rufus Lewis, 1833-1895.
P42 The Cushite; or The descendants of Ham as found in the sacred Scriptures, and in the writings of ancient historians and poets from Noah to the Christian era. By Rufus L. Perry ... Springfield, Mass., Willey & co., 1893.
2 p. l., [iii]-x, 11-175 p. 19½cm.
1. Cushites. 2. Negro race.
Library of Congress GN545.P4 5—29821
[a32b1]

Race.
M910 Rowan, Carl Thomas.
R78p The pitiful and the proud. New York, Random House [1956]
432 p. 22 cm.
1. Asia—Politics. 2. Asia—Soc. condit. 3. Race. I. Title.
DS35.R6 950 56—5220 ‡
Library of Congress [57q²10]

Race.
M973.2 Tyndall, John William, 1877-
T97 The origin of the black man, by John W. Tyndall ... St. Louis, Mich., Metropolitan correspondence Bible college [°1927]
3 p. l., 114, [1] p. 19cm.
1. Negro race. I. Title.
27-15666
Library of Congress HT1589.T8
[2]

Race - History.
M813.5 Bontemps, Arna Wendell, 1902-
B64st Story of the Negro; illustrated by Raymond Lufkin. 2d
1955 ed., enl. New York, Knopf, 1955.
243 p. illus. 22 cm.
1. Negro race—Hist. 2. Negroes in America. 3. Slavery—Hist.
E29.N3B6 1955 325.26097 56-142 ‡
Library of Congress [10]

Race-question.

M323 B26d

Barnett, Horace Edward, 1854-

Democracy a misnomer, by Horace E. Barnett. Richmond, The Saint Luke press, 1924.

100 p. 19cm.

1. Negroes. 2. U. S.—Race question. I. Title.

Library of Congress E185.61.B24 24-24150

——— Copy 2.

Copyright A 807251 [2]

Race and runners.

M572 C63r

Cobb, William Montague, 1904-

Race and runners. Reprinted from the Journal of health and physical education, January 1936.

[8]p. illus. 30cm.

Inscribed: With the author's compliments.

... La race noire dans la democratie américaine.

M973 N33

Nelson, William Stuart, 1895-

... La race noire dans la démocratie américaine. Paris, Groupe d'études en vue du rapprochement international [L'émancipatrice imprimerie] 1922.

x, 84, [2] p. illus. 18cm.

1. Negroes. I. Title.

Library of Congress E185.N43 [41b1] 24-195

M323 F63c

Race--Terminology.

Fletcher, Otis Gaus.

Colored Americans ask for a good name, and for an investigation of dictionaries and encyclopedias published and circulated in the United States of America with a view to delete evil designed names. Lexington, Kentucky, The author, 1946.

32p. port. 19cm.

Autographed.

M610 C63r

Race and runners.

Cobb, William Montague, 1904-

Race and runners. Reprinted from the Journal of health and physical education, January 1936.

[8]p. illus. 30cm.

Inscribed: With the author's compliments.

Race prejudice and discrimination.

M323 R72

Rose, Arnold Marshall, 1918- ed.

Race prejudice and discrimination; readings in intergroup relations in the United States. 1st ed. New York, Knopf, 1951.

xi, 605, vi p. 22cm.

Race adjustment.

M323 M61r

Miller, Kelly, 1863-1939.

Race adjustment; essays on the Negro in America, by Kelly Miller. New York and Washington, The Neale publishing company, 1908.

306 p. 21cm.

CONTENTS.—Radicals and conservatives.—As to The leopard's spots.—An appeal to reason on the race problem.—The Negro's part in the Negro problem.—Social equality.—The city Negro.—Religion as a solvent of the race problem.—Plea of the oppressed.—The land of Goshen.—Surplus Negro women.—Rise of the professional class.—Eminent Negroes.—What Walt Whitman means to the Negro.—Frederick Douglass.—Jefferson and the Negro.—The artistic gifts of the Negro.—The early struggle for education.—A brief for the higher education of the Negro.—Roosevelt and the Negro.

1. Negroes. I. Title.

Library of Congress E185.5.M64 [a42g1] 8-24845

Race discrimination.

M261.8 K299

Kelsey, George D

Racism and the Christian understanding of man, by George D. Kelsey. New York, Scribner [1965]

178 p. 24 cm.

Bibliographical footnotes.

1. Church and race problems. 2. Race discrimination. I. Title.

BT734.2.K42 261.83 65-27241

Library of Congress [5]

Race Prejudice and the Negro Artist.

M323 J632r

Johnson, James Weldon, 1871-1938.

Race prejudice and the Negro artist, by James Weldon Johnson. Harpers monthly, November, 1928.

770-776p. 24½cm.

Race and conscience in America.

M323 F91

Friends, Society of. American Friends Service Committee.

Race and conscience in America; a review... Norman, University of Oklahoma Press, 1959.

53p. 23cm.

Race discrimination - U.S.

M323.4 M96s

Murray, Pauli, 1910- *ed.*

States' laws on race and color, and appendices containing international documents, federal laws and regulations, local ordinances and charts. [Cincinnati, Woman's Division of Christian Service, Board of Missions and Church Extension, Methodist Church, 1950 [i. e. 1951]

x, 746 p. forms. 24 cm.

1. Negroes—Legal status, laws, etc. 2. Race discrimination—U. S. I. Title.

Library of Congress 325.260973 [51u10] 51—2354

The Race Problem and Peace.

M323 J632 no. 5

Johnson, James Weldon, 1871-1938.

The race problem and peace, by James Weldon Johnson. Presented to the VI international summer school of the Women's International League for Peace and Freedom, Chicago, May, 1924. Reprinted for the advancement of colored people, 1924.

M304 P19 V.5no.10

7p. 23cm.

Race and culture contacts.

M323 Am3

[American sociological society]

Race and culture contacts; E. B. Reuter, editor ... 1st ed. New York and London, McGraw-Hill book company, inc., 1934.

viii, 253 p. 23cm.

Papers selected from the proceedings of the twenty-eighth annual meeting of the American sociological society, at the request of the Executive committee. *cf.* Pref.

1. Race problems. I. Reuter, Edward Byron, 1880- ed. II. Title.

Library of Congress HT1521.A5 [45r35k1] 34—38508 323.1062

Race discrimination - U.S.

M796 R56

Robinson, John Roosevelt, 1919-

Baseball has done it, by Jackie Robinson. Edited by Charles Dexter. [1st ed.] Philadelphia, Lippincott [1964]

216 p. 21 cm.

1. Negro athletes. 2. Race discrimination—U. S. I. Title.

GV865.R6A2 301.451 64—14467

Library of Congress [64k7]

Race problems.

M06 Am35

American academy of political and social science, ***Philadelphia.***

The American Negro ... Editor in charge of this volume: Donald Young ... Philadelphia, The American academy of political and social science, 1928.

viii, 359 p. front., illus. (maps) diagrs. 24cm. (*Its* Annals. vol. cxxxx [no. 229] November, 1928)

Contains bibliographies.

CONTENTS.—Foreword.—Race relations.—The Negro as an element in the population of the United States.—The legal status of the Negro.—The economic achievement of the Negro. — The mental ability and achievement of the Negro.—Organzations for social betterment.—Race relations in other lands.

1. Negroes. 2. Negro race. 3. U. S.—Race question. 4. Race problems. I. Young, Donald Ramsey, 1898- ed. II. Title.

Library of Congress H1.A4 vol. cxxxx 28—29716

——— Copy 2. E185.6.A38 [41k3]

Race and culture contacts in the modern world.

M301 F86ra

Frazier, Edward Franklin, 1894-

Race and culture contacts in the modern world. [1st ed.] New York, Knopf, 1957.

338 p. 22 cm.

1. Race problems. 2. Acculturation. 3. Class distinction. I. Title.

HT1521.F7 *301.45 323.1 57—5051 ‡

Library of Congress [58r10]

Race fear and housing in a typical American community.

M331.833 Evlr

Evans, William Leonard, 1886-

Race fear and housing in a typical American community, by William L. Evans ... New York, N. Y., Pub. for the Memorial center and urban league, inc., by the National urban league [1946]

44 p. 21½cm.

1. Housing—Buffalo. 2. Negroes—Buffalo. 3. U. S.—Race question. I. Title.

HD7304.B9E9 331.833 46-7927

Library of Congress [5]

Race problems

M323 Am3a

American Academy of Political and Social Science

America's race problems, addresses at the annual meeting ... Philadelphia, April 12, 1901. New York, Published for the Academy by McClure, Phillips & Co., 1901.

187p. 23½cm.

M301 J63ra

Race and race relations.

Johnson, Charles S

Race and race relations. New York City, American missionary association, 1943.

9p. 23cm.

Race ideals.

M304 P19 V.5, no.14

Hill, Leslie Pinckney, 1880-

Negro ideals, their effect and their embarrassments. Reprinted from the Journal of Race Development, v.6, no.1, July 1915, p. 91-103.

Race problems.

M304 P19 v.4,no2

Barrett, Samuel.

A plea for unity among American negroes and the negroes of the world; a book dealing with one of the phases of the negro problem as it effects the negroes themselves. By Dr. Samuel Barrett ... (3d ed.—enl. and rev.) [Cedar Falls, Ia., Woolverton printing co., °1926]

67 p. 17½cm.

1. Negroes. I. Title.

Library of Congress E185.6.B27 26-14842

——— Copy 2.

Copyright A 904979 [2]

M323 B64c
Race problems.
Bonner, Harry G
The Corundum people; the race of many complexions and varied personalities. N.Y., William-Frederick press, 1948.
16p. 21cm.

M610 C63ne3
Race problem.
Cobb, William Montague, 1904-
The Negro as a biological element in the American population. Reprinted from the Journal of Negro education. 8:336-348, July 1939.
336-348p. 25cm.

M323 C83c
Race problems.
Cox, Oliver Cromwell, 1901-
Caste, class, & race; a study in social dynamics. Introd. by Joseph S. Roucek. [1st ed.] Garden City, N. Y., Doubleday, 1948.
xxxviii, 624 p. diagrs. 24 cm.
Bibliography: p. [585]-600.
1. Caste. 2. Class distinction. 3. Race problems. I. Title.
HT609.C7 323.3 48-338*
Library of Congress [50r*10]

M301 B81r
Race problems.
Browne, Robert S
Race relations in international affairs. Introd. by Roger N. Baldwin. Washington, Public Affairs Press [1961]
62 p. 23 cm.
Includes bibliography.
1. Race problems. 2. International relations. 3. U. S.—Race question. I. Title.
HT1521.B7 301.451 61-11688 ‡
Library of Congress [10]

M610 C63ne5
Race problems.
Cobb, William Montague, 1904-
Negro survival. Reprinted from the Journal of Negro education. 7:564-566, October 1938.
[564-566p. 25cm.

M323 C88d
Race problems.
Crosswaith, Frank Rudolph, 1892-
Discrimination incorporated, by Frank R. Crosswaith and Alfred Baker Lewis. Social action, 8:4-39, January 15, 1942.

M308 F19 V.4, no.5
Race problems.
Bruce, John Edward, 1856-
The blot on the escutcheon. An address delivered before Afro-American League, Branch no.1, at the Second Baptist Church, Washington, D.C., April 4th, 1890, by J. E. Bruce. Washington, R. L. Pendleton, Printer, 1890.
18p. 16cm.

M610 C63p3
Race problems.
Cobb, William Montague, 1904-
Physical anthropology and the Negro in the present crisis. Reprinted from the Journal of the National Medical Association, 34: 181-187, September 1942.
181-187p. 28cm.

M323 C88r
Race problems.
Crummell, Alexander, 1819-1898.
The race problem in America, by Alex. Crummell... Washington, D.C., William R. Morrison, 1889.
19p. 19cm.
"A paper read at the church congress (Protestant episcopal church). Buffalo, N.Y., November 20, 1888."

M323 B88w
Race problems.
Bunche, Ralph Johnson.
A World view of race, by Ralph J. Bunche. Washington, D.C., The Associates in Negro Folk Education, 1936.
98p. 20cm.

M610 C63r
Race question.
Cobb, William Montague, 1904-
Race and runners. Reprinted from the Journal of health and physical education, January 1936.
[8]p. illus. 30cm.
Inscribed: With the author's compliments.

M815.4 D741o
Race problems.
Douglass, Frederick, 1817-1895.
Address delivered in the Metropolitan A.M.E. church, Washington, D.C. Tuesday, January 9th, 1894, on the lessons for the hour. In which he discusses the various aspects of the so-called, but miscalled, Negro problem. Baltimore, Press of Thomas and Evans, 1894.
36p. 22cm.
Cover title: Lessons of the hour.

MB9 C31b
Race problems.
Cayton, Horace Roscoe, 1903-
The bitter crop. New York, 1948.
(In: Northwest harvest; A regional stock-taking. Ed. by V.L.O. Chittick. New York, Macmillan, 1948. 21cm. pp.174-193.)

M610 C63s tr
Race problems.
Cobb, William Montague, 1904-
Strictly on our own. The Oracle, 1947.
12,13-14p. 28cm.

M973.9 F46 No.5
Race problems.
DuBois, William Edward Burghardt, 1898-
20th century; The Century of the color line. Pittsburgh, Pittsburgh Courier, 1950.
7p. illus. 24cm. (Fifty years of progress)

M34313 C49w
Race problems.
Civil Rights Congress.
We charge genocide; The historic petition to the United Nations for relief from a crime of the United States government against the Negro people. New York, Civil Rights Congress, 1951.
239p. 24cm.

M610 C63y
Race problems.
Cobb, William Montague, 1904-
Your nose won't tell. Reprinted from the Crisis, 45:332, 336, October 1938.
one lead, columns. 30cm.

M301 F86ra
Race problems.
Frazier, Edward Franklin, 1894-
Race and culture contacts in the modern world. [1st ed.] New York, Knopf, 1957.
338 p. 22 cm.
1. Race problems. 2. Acculturation. 3. Class distinction. I. Title.
HT1521.F7 *301.45 323.1 57-5051 ‡
Library of Congress [58r*10]

MB9 C55
Race problems.
Clark, Septima (Poinsette) 1898-
Echo in my soul, by Septima Poinsette Clark with LeGette Blythe. Foreword by Harry Golden. [1st ed.] New York, Dutton, 1962.
243 p. illus. 21 cm.
An autobiography.
1. Negro teachers—Correspondence, reminiscences, etc. I. Blythe, LeGette, 1900- II. Title.
E185.97.C59A3 923.773 62-14718 ‡
Library of Congress [10]

Trinidad M796.358 C76co
Race problems.
Constantine, Learie Nicholas, 1902-
Colour bar. London, Stanley Paul and Co., 1954.
xxi, 193p. illus. 22cm.

Ghana M301 G166
Race problems.
Gardiner, Robert Kweku Atta, 1914-
A world of peoples [by] Robert Gardiner. London, British Broadcasting Corporation, 1966.
93 p. 22 cm. (The Reith lectures, 1965) 15/-
(B 66-7752)
Includes bibliographies.
1. Race problems. 2. Prejudices and antipathies. I. British Broadcasting Corporation. II. Title. (Series)
HT1521.G3 1966 301.45 66-71229
Library of Congress [67f5]

Race problems.
M323 F91
Friends, Society of. American Friends Service Committee.
Race and conscience in America; a review... Norman, University of Oklahoma Press, 1959.
53p. 23cm.

Race problems.
Trinidad M323 H41
Hercules, Eric E L
Democracy limited, by Eric E. L. Hercules. Cleveland, O., Central publishing house 1945
183p. 20½cm.
"First printing."

M815.5 M12c
Race problems.
Macbeth, Hugh E
Colored America answers the challenge of Pearl S. Buck. Los Angeles, The author, 1942.
29p. 24cm. (Interracial reference series)
At head of title: Justice for all humanity.
Contents on author card.

Race problem.
M304 P19 v.5, no.17
Garvey, Marcus, 1887-1940.
Aims and objects of Movement for solution of Negro problems outlined... New York, Press of the Universal Negro Improvement Association, 1924
[12] p. 22cm.

M323 H73n
Race problems.
Holmes, Dwight Oliver Wendell, 1877-
The Negro chooses democracy. Reprinted from the Journal of Negro education. [8:620-633] October, 1939.
Dedicatory address, The Savery Library, Talladega College, April 16, 1939.

Race problems.
M260 M45s
Mays, Benjamin Elijah, 1895-
Seeking to be Christian in race relations. New York, Friendship Press, 1957.
84 p. 20 cm.
1. Race problems. 2. Church and social problems. I. Title.
BR115.R3M3 1957 *261.8 57—6580 ‡
Library of Congress [58k10]

Race problems.
Jamaica M323 G19
Garvey, Marcus, 1887-1940.
An appeal to the soul of white America... by Marcus Garvey. New York, Press of the Universal Negro Improvement Association, 1924.
[8]p. 21cm.

Race problems.
M323 Im1
Imbert, Dennis I
The stranger within our gates; a South American's impression of America's social problems, by D.I. Imbert. First edition... New Orleans, La., Watson bros. press, 1945.
102 p. plate. 15cm.

Race problems.
M323 M59b
Miller, Henry Jefferson, 1877 -
Blasted barriers; views of a reporter in story and song. Boston, Christopher Pub. House [1950]
140p. 21cm.

Race problems.
Grimke, Francis James, 1850-
M815.5 G88 v.1, no. 11
Gideon bands for work within the race and for work without the race, a message to the colored people of the United States; a discourse delivered in the Fifteenth street Presbyterian church, Washington, D. C., Sunday, March the 2nd, 1913, by the pastor Rev. Francis J. Grimke ... [Washington, D. C., R. L. Pendleton, 1913]
21 p. 22cm.
1. Negroes. I. Title.
Library of Congress E185.6.G83 13-12039
——— Copy 2.

Race Problems.
M323 J632a
Johnson, James Weldon, 187-1938.
[Articles on the Negro in America]
Contents: The American Negro. -The Negro and racial conflicts. -The contribution of the Negro.
(In: Brown, Francis J. and Joseph Slavey Roucek. ed. Our racial and national minorities. New York, Prentice-Hall, 1937. 21cm. p. 56-66, 549-560, 739-748)
Inscribed by F.J. Brown.

M323 M690
Race problems.
Mitchell, Arthur W , 1883-
Overcoming difficulties under adverse conditions, address...in the House of Representatives, Thursday, April 6, 1939. Washington, Govt. Print. Off. 1939.
15p. 23cm.
Founder's Day address delivered at Tuskegee Institute, Alabama, April 2, 1939.

Race problems.
M815.5 G88 v.1, no.17
Grimke, Francis James, 1850-1937
The race problem - two suggestions as to its solution, by Rev. Frances Grimke [Washington, 1919]
8p. 23cm.

Race problems.
M323 L14
Laidler, Harry Wellington, 1884- ed.
The role of the races in our future civilization; symposium edited by Harry W. Laidler. Participants: Sir Norman Angell, Pearl S. Buck, Hon. Lawrence W. Cramer [and others] ... New York city, League for industrial democracy [1942]
112 p. 23cm. (On cover: L. I. D. Pamphlet series)
"All ... articles except those of Pearl S. Buck and Lester B. Granger were prepared for the L. I. D. conference, May 8-9, 1942."
1. Race problems. I. Title.
42—24499
Library of Congress HT1521.L2 [43h3] 323.1082

M323 N21
Race problems.
National Association for the Advancement of Colored People.
Let's be honest about democracy. New York, NAACP, 1939.
23p. illus. 22cm.

Race problems.
M815.5 G88 v.1, no.18
Grimke, Francis Jones, 1850-1937.
The race problem as it respects the colored people and the Christian Church, in the light of the developments of the last year. A discourse, delivered at a Union Thanksgiving service held at the Plymouth Congregational Church, by Rev. Francis J. Grimke. Washington, 1919
16p. 23cm.

Race problems.
M335.4 L62
Lightfoot, Claude
Turning point in freedom road; the fight to end jim crow now. New York, New Century Publishers, 1962.
32p. 18½cm.
1. Communism. 2. Race problems. I. Title.

M323 N217
Race problems.
National Conference on the Problems of the Negro and Negro Youth.
Report. Washington, D.C. 1937.
48p. 27cm.
Mimeographed.

M323 H33m
Race problems.
Hayward, Ernest, 1927-
Mr. Charlie, let's you and I talk. New York, Vantage Press [1966]
173p. 21cm.

Race problems.
M308 L79w
Locke, Alain Le Roy, 1886- ed.
When peoples meet; a study in race and culture contacts, edited by Alain Locke ... and Bernhard J. Stern ... New York, Committee on workshops, Progressive education association [1942]
xii, 756 p. 24½ cm. (Half-title: Progressive education association publications. Committee on workshops)
1. Acculturation. 2. Minorities. 3. Race problems. I. Stern, Bernhard Joseph, 1894- joint ed. II. Title.
42—326
Library of Congress CB5.L6 [45g5] 901

Race problems.
M306 N21pe
[National Negro Congress]
A petition... to the United Nations on behalf of 13 million oppressed Negro citizens of the United States of America. New York, 1946.
15p. 23cm.

Race Problems.
M05
R29
The Negro citizen. New York, The Reporter, 1949.

2-19, 35-37p. 29cm.
Special feature of the Reporter, December 6 1949.

Race problems.
M811.5
P54f
Phillips, Hilton Alonzo, 1905–
Flames of rebellion (against enthroned tyranny) by Hilton A. Phillips ... ⌊Los Angeles, Printed by the California eagle press, ©1936⌋
viii, 237 p. port. 22cm.
Prose and poetry.

1. Race problems. 2. Negro race. 3. Negroes. 4. U. S.—Race question. I. Title.
36-10090
Library of Congress HT1521.P5
——— Copy 2.
Copyright A 92792 ⌊5⌋ 323.1

Race problems.
M323
R54b
Robertson, Julius Winfield.
This bird must fly, by Julius Winfield Robertson. Washington, D. C., Unity press and pamphlet service ⌊©1944⌋
113 p. 22cm.

1. Negroes. I. Title.
45-14337
Library of Congress E185.61.R67
⌊2⌋ 325.260973

Race problems.
M973.
R63s
Rogers, Joel Augustus, 1880–
Sex and race; Negro-Caucasian mixing in all ages and all lands, by J. A. Rogers ... New York city, J. A. Rogers publications ⌊1940–44⌋
3 v. fronts. (v. 1-2) illus. (incl. ports., map, facsims.) 23½cm.
Vol. 2 has subtitle: A history of white, Negro and Indian miscegenation in the two Americas.
Includes bibliographies.
CONTENTS.—v. 1. The old world.—v. 2. The new world.—v. 3. Why white and black mix in spite of opposition.
1. Race problems. 2. Negroes. 3. Miscegenation. I. Title.
41—20
Library of Congress GN237.R6 1940
⌊45r45e2⌋ 572

Race problem.
Cuba
M723
R95
Ruiz Suarez, Bernardo
The color question in the two Americas, by Dr. Bernardo Ruez Suarez. Translated by John Crosby Gordon. New York, Hunt publishing co., 1922.

111p. 18cm.

Race problems.
Jamaica
M325
Sch6g
Scholes, Theophilus E Samuel, 1856-1906.
Glimpses of the ages; or, The "superior" and "inferior" races, so-called, discussed in the light of science and history, by Theophilus E. Samuel Scholes ... London, J. Long, 1905–08.
2 v. 22½cm.
Vol. 2 wanting in L. C.

1. Ethnology. 2. Race problems. I. Title.
Library of Congress CB195.S3 6-5684 Revised
⌊r33b2⌋

Race problems.
M323
Sch9
Schuyler, George Samuel, 1895-
Some unsweet truths about race prejudice.

Pp. 89-106. 24cm.

In: Schmalhausen, Samuel D., ed. Behold America. New York, Farrar and Rinehart, 1931.

Race problems.
M323
Sh2
Shaw, Alexander P.
Christianizing race relations as a negro sees it ⌊by⌋ Reverend A. P. Shaw ... ⌊Los Angeles, Wetzel publishing company, ©1928⌋
88 p. 20½cm.

1. Negroes. 2. U. S.—Race question. I. Title.
28-18116
Library of Congress E185.61.S53
——— Copy 2.
Copyright A 1077285 ⌊2⌋

Race problem.
MB9
So5m
Somerville, John Alexander, 1882-
Man of color, an autobiography. A factual report on the status of the American Negro today. ⌊1st ed.⌋ Los Angeles, L. L. Morrison ⌊1949⌋

170p. port. 24cm. (The Publisher's library, no.5)

Race problems.
M306
Sol
1913
Southern Sociological Congress, 2d, Atlanta, 1913.
The South mobilizing for social service; addresses delivered at the Southern Sociological Congress, Atlanta, Georgia, April 25-29, 1913. Ed. by James E. McCulloch. Nashville, 1913.

702p. 24cm.

Race problems.
M323
St4
Stemons, James Samuel.
As victim to victims; an American Negro laments with Jews, by James Samuel Stemons. New York, Fortuny's ⌊©1941⌋
268 p. 22½cm.
"First edition."

1. Negroes—Moral and social conditions. 2. Jewish question. 3. Race problems. I. Title. II. Title: An American Negro laments with Jews.
41—9105
Library of Congress E185.61.S8
⌊42d2⌋ 325.260973

Race problemS.
M323
St7n
Storey, Moorfield.
The Negro question; An address delivered before the Wisconsin Bar Association, June 27, 1918. New York, NAACP ⌊1918⌋

30p. 23cm.

Race problems.
Africa
M323
T139
Tajfel, Henri, *ed.*
Disappointed guests; essays by African, Asian, and West Indian students. Edited by Henri Tajfel and John L. Dawson. London, New York, Oxford University Press, 1965.
158, ⌊1⌋ p. 23 cm.
"Issued under the auspices of the Institute of Race Relations."
Bibliography: p. ⌊159⌋

1. Students, Foreign—Gt. Brit. 2. Gt. Brit.—Race question. 3. Race problems. I. Dawson, John L. M., joint ed. II. Institute of Race Relations. III. Title.
LA637.7.T3 370.196 65-8757
Library of Congress ⌊2⌋

Race problems.
M323
T37
Thompson, Edgar Tristram, 1900– *ed.*
Race relations and the race problem, a definition and an analysis. Edgar T. Thompson, editor; contributors: Robert E. Park, Edward B. Reuter, S. J. Holmes ⌊and others⌋ ... Durham, N. C., Duke university press, 1939.
xv, 338 p. incl. illus. (maps) tables, diagrs. 23½cm. (*Half-title:* Duke university publications)
"A Duke university centennial publication."
CONTENTS.—Introduction, by E. T. Thompson.—The nature of race relations, by R. E. Park.—Competition and the racial division of labor, by E. B. Reuter.—The trend of the racial balance of births and deaths, by S. J. Holmes.—Racial competition for the land, by R. B. Vance.—Patterns of race conflict, by G. B. Johnson.—The Negro as a contrast conception,

(Continued on next card)
39—21842
⌊45f3⌋

Race problemS.
M304
P19
V.5, no.15

M323
T41
Three articles on the Negro race problem. Published in September 1923 number of Current History. Should the color line go. By Hon. Robert Warson Winston; The Negro's greatest enemy, by Marcus Garvey; The Negro exodus from the South, by Eric D. Waldron. ⌊New York Press of the Universal Negro Improvement Association 1924⌋

29p. 22cm.

M323
T61
Race problems.
Toomer, Jean, 1894-
Race problems and modern society.

(In: Problems of civilization ... New York. D. Van Nostrand company. 1929. 18cm. p. 67-114).

Race problems.
M341.1
Un3p
Universal Negro Improvement Association.
Petition of the Universal Negro Improvement Association and African Communities League, representing the interest of the four hundred million Negroes Indiginies of Africa, the British subjects in the West Indies, South and Central America, and the citizens, and other Negro inhabitants of the United States of America and those of Asia and Europe, to the League of Nations.
⌊New York, The Association, ⌊1922⌋
7 leaves. 28cm.

Race problems.
M323.
Sp4p
Universal races congress. 1st London, 1911.
Papers on inter-racial problems, communicated to the first Universal races congress, held at the University of London, July 26-29, 1911, ed., for the Congress executive, by G. Spiller, Hon. organiser of the Congress, Pub. for the World peace foundation, Ginn and company, Boston, London, P. S. King & son, 1911.

xvi, 485p., 1 l. 25½cm.

M323
W587a
Race problems.
White, Walter Francis, 1893-
...The American Negro and his problems, a comprehensive picture of a serious and pressing situation... Girard, Kansas, Haldeman-Julius publications, 1927.

64p. 12cm. (Little blue book no. 758, edited by E. Haldeman-Julius).

M323
W89p
Race problems.
Work, Monroe Nathan, 1866-1945.
Problems of adjustment of race and class in the South. Reprinted from Social forces, 16:108-117, October 1937.

M323
Y4d
Race problems.
Yergan, Max, 1894-
Democracy and the Negro people today. Washington, D.C., National Negro Congress, 194 .

3-15p. 19cm.

Race problems - Addresses, essays, lecture.
South Africa
M968 N65
Nkosi, Lewis, 1935-
Home and exile. [London] Longman's [1965]
136p. 20½cm.
1. South Africa. 2. Literature - Africa. 3. Race problems - Addresses, essays, lecture. I. Title.

Race question.
M323 B19n
Baldwin, James, 1924-
Nobody knows my name; more notes of a native son. New York, Dial Press, 1961.
241 p. 22 cm.
1. Negroes. 2. U. S.—Race question. I. Title.
E185.61.B197 301.451 61—11596 ‡
Library of Congress [61o20]

Race question
M810 B73so
Brawley, Benjamin Griffith, 1882-1939.
A social history of the American Negro, being a history of the Negro problem in the United States, including a history and study of the republic of Liberia, by Benjamin Brawley. New York, The Macmillan company, 1921.
xv, 420 p. 22½cm.
"Select bibliography": p. 390-406.
1. Negroes. 2. Slavery in the U. S. 3. U. S.—Race question. 4. Liberia. I. Title.
21—15578
Library of Congress E185.61.B82 [a43g1]

Race problems - Addresses, essays, lectures.
M301 M39
Masuoka, Jitsuichi, 1903- ed.
Race relations: problems and theory; essays in honor of Robert E. Park. Edited by Jitsuichi Masuoka and Preston Valien. Chapel Hill, University of North Carolina Press [1961]
x, 290 p. 24 cm.
Bibliographical footnotes.
1. Race problems—Addresses, essays, lectures. 2. [Negroes]—Race question—Addresses, essays, lectures. 3. Park, Robert Emory, 1868-1942. I. Valien, Preston, joint ed. II. Title.
HT1521.M29 301.451 61—66070
Library of Congress [62g2]

Race question.
M813.5 B19n2
Baldwin, James, 1924-
Notes of a native son. ~~New York, Dial Press, 1963 [1955]~~ London, M. Joseph [1964]
165p. 21½cm.
Essays.
1. Negroes. 2. U. S.—Race question. I. Title.
E185.61.B2 1963 64-115
Library of Congress [5]

Race question.
M323. B81w
Brown, Earl Louis, 1900-
... Why race riots! Lessons from Detroit, by Earl Brown ... [New York, Public affairs committee, inc.] 1944.
cover-title, 31, [1] p. illus., diagrs. 21cm. (Public affairs pamphlets, no. 87)
"First edition, January, 1944."
"For further reading": p. 31.
1. Detroit—Riot, 1943. 2. Negroes—Detroit. 3. U. S.—Race question. I. Title.
44—5826
Library of Congress F574.D4B58 [46g5] 977.434

Race psychology.
M614 R66n3
Roman, Charles Victor, 1864-1934.
The Negro's psychology and his health. Reprinted from Hospital Social Service, 11:89-95, 1925.

Race question.
M813.5 B19n
Baldwin, James, 1924-
Notes of a native son. Boston, Beacon Press [1955]
175 p. 22 cm.
Essays.
1. Negroes. 2. U. S.—Race question. I. Title.
E185.61.B2 *301.451 325.260973 55—11325 ‡
Library of Congress [12]

Race question.
M323.4 B93a4
Burns, W Haywood
Sort protest; de Amerikanske Negeres kamp for ligeberettigelse. Glostrup, Det Danske Forlag [1964]
119p. 21cm.
Translation of The voices of Negro protest in America.
Written in Danish.
1. Civil rights. 2. Race question. I. Title.

Race question.
M06 Am35
American academy of political and social science, *Philadelphia.*
The American Negro ... Editor in charge of this volume: Donald Young ... Philadelphia, The American academy of political and social science, 1928.
viii, 359 p. front., illus. (maps) diagrs. 24cm. (*Its* Annals. vol. CXXXX [no. 229] November, 1928)
Contains bibliographies.
CONTENTS.—Foreword.—Race relations.—The Negro as an element in the population of the United States.—The legal status of the Negro.—The economic achievement of the Negro. — The mental ability and achievement of the Negro.—Organizations for social betterment.—Race relations in other lands.
1. Negroes. 2. Negro race. 3. U. S.—Race question. 4. Race problems. I. Young, Donald Ramsey, 1898- ed. II. Title.
Library of Congress H1.A4 vol. CXXXX 28—29716
——— Copy 2. E185.6.A58 [41k3]

Race question.
M267.5 B411
Bell, Juliet Ober, 1895-
Interracial practices in community Y. W. C. A.'s; a study under the auspices of the Commission to gather interracial experience, as requested by the sixteenth National convention of the Y. W. C. A.'s of the U. S. A., conducted by Juliet O. Bell, PH. D., and Helen J. Wilkins. New York, N. Y., National board, Y. W. C. A., 1944.
3 p. l., 116 p. 21½cm.
"Recommendations related to interracial practices in community Y. W. C. A.'s to be submitted for action to the seventeenth National convention" (8 p.) inserted.
1. U. S.—Race question. 2. Negroes. 3. Young women's Christian associations. I. Wilkins, Helen J., joint author. II. Young women's Christian associations. U. S. National board. Commission to gather interracial experience. III. Title.
Library of Congress E185.61.B4 44-7133
[4] 267.43265

Race question.
M323.4 B93
Burns, W Haywood.
The voices of Negro protest in America. With a foreword by John Hope Franklin. London, New York, Oxford University Press, 1963.
88 p. 19 cm.
"Issued under the auspices of the Institute of Race Relations, London."
Bibliography: p. [85]-88.
1. Negroes—Civil rights. 2. U. S.—Race question. I. Title.
E185.61.B96 323.40973 63-6378
Library of Congress [5]

Race question.
M323 B19f
Baldwin, James, 1924-
The fire next time. New York, Dial Press, 1963.
120 p. 21 cm.
1. Negroes. 2. U. S.—Race question. 3. Mohammedans in the U. S. I. Title.
E185.61.B195 301.451 63—11713 ‡
Library of Congress [63g10]

Race question.
M973 B43c
Bennett, Lerone, 1928-
Confrontation: black and white. Foreword by A. Philip Randolph. Chicago, Johnson Pub. Co., 1965.
xii, 321 p. 22 cm.
Bibliography: p. [305]-312.
1. Negroes—Hist. 2. U. S.—Race question. I. Title.
E185.B42 301.45196073 65-21952
Library of Congress [5]

Race question.
M323 C12e
Caliver, Ambrose, 1894-
Education of teachers for improving majority-minority relationships. Course offerings for teachers to learn about racial and national minority groups. By Ambrose Caliver ... Federal security agency. Paul V. McNutt, administrator. U. S. Office of education, John W. Studebaker, commissioner. Washington, U. S. Govt. print. off., 1944.
iv, 64 p. incl. illus., tables. 23cm. (U. S. Office of education. Bulletin 1944, no. 2)
"Selected references and sources of information": p. 60-64.
1. U. S.—Race question. 2. Minorities. 3. Teachers, Training of—U. S. 4. Universities and colleges—Curricula. I. Title.
E 45—7
U. S. Off. of educ. Library for Library of Congress L111.A6 1944, no. 2
——— Copy 2. E184.A1C3
[46k3]† (370.6173) 325.73

Race question.
M323 B19f2
Baldwin, James, 1924-
The fire next time. ~~New York, Dial Press, 1963.~~ London, M. Joseph [1963]
112p. 21 cm.
1. Negroes. 2. U. S.—Race question. 3. Mohammedans in the U. S. I. Title.
E185.61.B195 301.451 63—11713 ‡
Library of Congress [63g10]

Race question.
M301 B439
Bennett, Lerone, 1928-
The Negro mood, and other essays. Chicago, Johnson Pub. Co., 1964.
ix, 104 p. 22 cm.
1. U.S.—Race question. 2. Negroes. I. Title.
E185.61.B43 301.451 64-8370
Library of Congress [5]

Race question.
M323 C17
Capponi, Joseph Burritt Sevelli.
Ham and Dixie. A just, simple and original discussion of the southern problem: by J. B. Sevelli-Capponi ... [St. Augustine, Fla., 1895]
371 p. 16½cm.
1. ~~Negroes. 2. U. S.~~—Race question.
12-14310
Library of Congress E185.6.S49
Copyright 1896: 52126

Race question.
M323 B19n2
Baldwin, James, 1924-
Nobody knows my name; more notes of a native son. ~~New York, Dial Press, 1961.~~ London, Michael Joseph, [1964]
196p. 22cm.
1. ~~Negroes. 2. U. S.~~—Race question. I. Title.
E185.61.B197 301.451 61—11596 ‡
Library of Congress [63o5]

Race question.
M89 G87b
Branson, Helen Kitchen, 1916-
Let there be life: the contemporary account of Edna L. Griffin, M. D. Pasadena, Calif., M. S. Sen [1947]
135 p. port. 24 cm.
1. Griffin, Edna La Fiore, 1905- 2. U. S.—Race question. I. Title.
R154.G7678B7 926.1 48-2438*
Library of Congress [2]

Race question.
M323.4 C54
Clark, Kenneth Bancroft, 1914-
The Negro protest: James Baldwin, Malcolm X, Martin Luther King talk with Kenneth B. Clark. Boston, Beacon Press [1963]
56 p. 21 cm.
1. Negroes. 2. U. S.—Race question. I. Title.
E185.61.C69 323.40973 63—21975
Library of Congress [64f20]

Race question.

M323.2 C54p

Clark, Kenneth Bancroft, 1914–
Prejudice and your child. Boston, Beacon Press [1955]
151 p. 22 cm.
Includes bibliography.

1. U. S.—Race question. 2. Prejudices and antipathies. 3. Child study. 4. Segregation in education. I. Title.

BF723.R3C5 157.3 55—9502 ‡
Library of Congress [55q30]

Race question.

M06 Am3 no.4

Cook, Charles C
... A comparative study of the Negro problem, by Mr. Charles C. Cook ... Washington, D. C., The Academy, 1899.
11 p. 23cm. (The American Negro academy. Occasional papers. no. 4)

1. Negroes. 2. U. S.—Race question.

Library of Congress E185.5.A51 10-7971
——— Copy 2. E185.61.C77
[a46b1]

Race question.

M323. C78

[**Cooper, Anna Julia (Haywood)**] 1859–
A voice from the South. By a black woman of the South. Xenia, O., The Aldine printing house, 1892.
3 p. l., iii p., 1 l., [9]–304 p. front. (port.) 18cm.
CONTENTS.—Womanhood a vital element in the regeneration and progress of a race.—The higher education of woman.—"Woman vs. the Indian."—The status of woman in America.—Has America a race problem; if so, how can it best be solved?—The Negro as presented in American literature.—What are we worth?—The gain from a belief.

1. Negroes. 2. U. S.—Race question. 3. Women in the U. S. I. A black woman of the South. II. Title.

12—2877
Library of Congress E185.6.C77
[a43r37g1]

Race question

M323.1 C87

Crogman, William Henry, 1841–
Talks for the times; by W. H. Crogman, South Atlanta, Ga. [Atlanta, Press of Franklin prtg. & pub. co., 1896]
xxiii, 9–330 p. front. (port.) 20cm.
CONTENTS.—Biographical sketch.—Frederick Douglass.—Life's deeper meanings.—Negro education: its helps and hindrances.—President Edmund Asa Ware.—Unveiling of monument to President Ware.—Wholesome effects of Christian education.—Bishop Atticus G. Haygood.—The negro's needs.—The negro's claims.—Twenty-sixth anniversary of emancipation proclamation.—Laying of the corner-stone of the library of Gammon theological seminary.—The negro problem.—Importance of correct ideals.—Christian scholars for negro pulpits.—Thirty-second anniversary of emancipation proclamation.
1. Negroes. 2. U. S.—Race question. 2nd ed.

12—2896
Library of Congress E185.5.C94
[44c1]

-Race question.

M323. C88a

Crummell, Alexander, 1819–1898.
Africa and America; addresses and discourses by Alex Crummell ... Springfield, Mass., Willey & co., 1891.
vii, [1] p., 2 l., [13]–466 p. front. (port.) 20½cm.

1. Negroes. 2. Negroes—Colonization—Africa. 3. U. S.—Race question.

12—2895
Library of Congress E185.5.C95
[37f1]

Race question.

M323 D44c

Derricks, Cleavant, 1910–
Crumbs from the master's table. [1st ed.] New York, Pageant Press [°1955]
93 p. 21 cm.

1. Negroes. 2. U. S.—Race question. I. Title.

E185.61.D45 325.260973 55-12424 ‡
Library of Congress [2]

Race question.

M815.4 D74t

Douglass, Frederick, 1817?–1895.
Three addresses on the relations subsisting between the white and colored people of the United States, by Frederick Douglass. Washington [D. C.] Gibson bros., printers, 1886.
68 p. 23 cm.

1. U. S.—Race question. 2. Negroes—Civil rights.
[*Name originally:* Frederick Augustus Washington Bailey]

E185.61.D734 325.260973 34-7727
Library of Congress [a48b1]

Race question.

M323 D77

Doyle, Bertram Wilbur, 1897–
The etiquette of race relations in the South; a study in social control, by Bertram Wilbur Doyle ... Chicago, Ill., The University of Chicago press [°1937]
xxv, 249 p. 22 cm.
Bibliography: p. 173–190.

1. Negroes. 2. U. S.—Race question. 3. Negroes—Moral and social conditions. 4. Slavery in the U. S. I. Title. II. Title: Race relations in the South.

37—20152
Library of Congress E185.61.D764
[39u4] 325.260975

Race question.

M301 D853a8

Du Bois, William Edward Burghardt, 1868–
The Amenia conference, an historic negro gathering. By W. E. Burghardt Du Bois ... Amenia, N. Y., Priv. print. at the Troutbeck press, 1925.
18 p., 1 l. 23cm. (Troutbeck leaflets, no. 8)
"Of this eighth number ... two hundred copies have been printed for private distribution."

1. Negroes. 2. U. S.—Race question. I. Title.

25-21506
Library of Congress E185.61.D8
[2]

Race question

M06 Am3 no.2

Du Bois, William Edward Burghardt. 1868–
... The conservation of races, by W. E. Burghardt Du Bois. Washington, D. C., The Academy, 1897.
15p. 23cm. (American Negro Academy. Occasional papers, no.2)

Race question.

M301 D852d

DuBois, William Edward Burghardt, 1868–
Dusk of dawn; an essay toward an autobiography of a race concept, by W. E. Burghardt DuBois. New York, Harcourt, Brace and company [°1940]
viii p., 2 l., 3–334 p. 22cm.
"First edition."

1. Negroes. 2. U. S.—Race question. I. Title.

40—27643
Library of Congress E185.97.D73
[45r°2] 923.1

Race question.

M301 D853g

Du Bois, William Edward Burghardt, 1868–
The gift of black folk; the Negroes in the making of America, by W. E. Burghardt Du Bois ... introduction by Edward F. McSweeney ... Boston, Mass., The Stratford co., 1924.
2 p. l., iv, 349 p. 19½cm. (*On cover:* Knights of Columbus racial contribution series)

1. Negroes. 2. U. S.—Race question. I. Title. II. Title: Negroes in the making of America.

24—17975
Library of Congress E185.D83
[45v1]

Race question.

M301 D853p

Du Bois, William Edward Burghardt, 1868–
... The Philadelphia Negro; a social study by W. E. Burghardt Du Bois ... Together with a special report on domestic service by Isabel Eaton ... Philadelphia, Pub. for the University, 1899.
xx, 520 p. incl. diagrs. 2 fold. plans. 26cm. (Publications of the University of Pennsylvania. Series in political economy and public law. no. 14)
CONTENTS.—The Philadelphia Negro.—Appendixes: A. Schedules used in the house-to-house inquiry. B. Legislation, etc., of Pennsylvania in regard to the Negro. C. Bibliography.—Special report on Negro domestic service in the seventh ward, Philadelphia, by I. Eaton.
1. Negroes—Philadelphia. 2. U. S.—Race question. 3. Servants. I. Eaton, Isabel. II. Title.

5—33530
Library of Congress F158.9.N3D8
——— Copy 2. H31.P4 no. 14
[45d1]

Race question.

M301 Eb74

Ebony.
The white problem in America, by the editors of Ebony. Chicago, Johnson Pub. Co., 1966.
v, 181 p. 22 cm.
"First published as a special issue of Ebony magazine, August, 1965."

1. U. S.—Race question. 2. Negroes—Civil rights. I. Title.

E185.615.E2 323.40973 66-24412
Library of Congress [5]

Race question.

M323.4 M615

Equality [by] Robert L. Carter [and others] With a foreword by Charles Abrams. New York, Pantheon Books [1965]
xxv, 191 p. 22 cm.

1. ~~U. S.~~—Race question. 2. ~~Negroes~~—Civil rights. ~~3. Civil rights—U. S.~~ I. Carter, Robert L., 1917– II. Abrams, Charles, 1901–

E185.61.E55 301.451 65-10210
Library of Congress [5]

Race question.

Nigeria M297 Es77

Essien-Udom, Essien Udosen.
Black nationalism; a search for an identity in America. [Chicago] University of Chicago Press [1962]
xiii, 367 p. illus., ports. 25 cm.
Bibliography: p. 351–360.

1. Mohammedans in the U. S. 2. Negroes. 3. U. S.—Race question. I. Title.

E185.61.E75 297.0973 62—12632
Library of Congress [62x5]

Race question.

M331.833 Evlr

Evans, William Leonard, 1886–
Race fear and housing in a typical American community, by William L. Evans ... New York, N. Y., Pub. for the Memorial center and urban league, inc., by the National urban league [1946]
44 p. 21½cm.

1. Housing—Buffalo. 2. Negroes—Buffalo. 3. U. S.—Race question. I. Title.

HD7304.B9E9 331.833 46-7927
Library of Congress [5]

Race question.

M323. F77

Fortune, Timothy Thomas.
Black and white: land, labor, and politics in the South. By T. Thomas Fortune ... New York, Fords, Howard, & Hulbert, 1884.
iv p., 2 l., [9]–310 p. 17½cm. (*On cover:* American questions)

1. Negroes. 2. U. S.—Race question. 3. Southern states—Econ. condit.

Library of Congress E185.61.F74 12—2876
——— Copy 2.
Copyright 1884: 16803 [38g1]

Race question.

M301 F84

Frazer, Charles Rivers, 1879–
White man, black man. [1st ed.] New York, Exposition Press [1965]
69 p. 21 cm.

1. ~~U. S.~~—Race question. 2. ~~Negroes.~~ 3. Toleration. I. Title.

E185.61.F826 301.45196073 65—8471
Library of Congress [66d4]

Race question.

M301 F86b 1962

Frazier, Edward Franklin, 1894–1962.
Black bourgeoisie. With a new pref. by the author. New York, Collier Books [1962]
222 p. illus. 18 cm. (Collier books, AS347)

1. Negroes. 2. U. S.—Race question. 3. Middle classes—U. S. I. Title.

E185.61.F833 1962 325.2670973 A 62-8728 ‡
Library of Congress [5]

Race question.

M301 F86b1

Frazier, Edward Franklin, 1894–
Black bourgeoisie. Glencoe, Ill., Free Press [1957]
264 p. 22 cm.
Includes bibliographies.

1. Negroes. 2. U. S.—Race question. 3. Middle classes—U. S. I. Title.

E185.61.F833 325.260973 56—11964 ‡
Library of Congress [57o20]

Race question.

M301
G86b

Frazier, Edward Franklin, 1894–
Bourgeoisie noire. Paris, Librairie Plon ͵1955͵
233 p. illus. 20 cm. (Recherches en sciences humaines, 7)

1. Negroes. 2. U. S.—Race question. 3. Middle classes—U. S. I. Title.
E185.61.F83 56-27366 ‡
Library of Congress ͵8͵

Race question

M323
F95b

Fuller, Thomas Oscar, 1867–
"Bridging the racial chasms"; a brief survey of inter-racial attitudes and relations, by T. O. Fuller ... Memphis, Tenn., T. O. Fuller ͵°1937͵
4 p. l., 73 p. incl. front., illus. 23½ cm.

1. U. S.—Race question. 2. Negroes. I. Title.
Library of Congress E185.61.F96 38-7817
——— Copy 2.
Copyright A 112966 ͵3͵ 325.260973

Race question.

M323.
G12

Gaines, Wesley John, *bp.*, 1830–
The negro and the white man. By Bishop W. J. Gaines ... Philadelphia, A. M. E. publishing house, 1897.
218 p. 20 cm.

1. Negroes. 2. U. S.—Race question.
12-2865
Library of Congress E185.6.G14
Copyright 1897: 52762

Race question.

M06
J61
no. 11

Galloway, Charles Betts, *bp.*, 1849–1909.
... The South and the Negro; an address delivered at the seventh Annual conference for education in the South, Birmingham, Ala., April 26, 1904, by the Rev. Bishop Charles B. Galloway ... New York, The Trustees, 1904.
16 p. 23 cm. (Trustees of the John F. Slater fund. Occasional papers. no. 11)

1. Negroes. 2. U. S.—Race question. I. Title.
Library of Congress E185.5.J65 no. 11 5-30400
——— Copy 2. E185.61.G17
͵30e1͵

Race question.

M06
J61
no.10

Gilman, Daniel Coit, 1831–1908.
... A study in black and white; an address at the opening of the Armstrong-Slater trade school building, November 18, 1896, by Daniel C. Gilman. Baltimore, The trustees ͵J. Murphy & co., printers͵ 1897.
14 p. 24½ cm. (Trustees of the John F. Slater fund. Occasional papers, no. 10)
"Reported by the 'Southern workman', and printed in that journal, December, 1896."—p. 5.

1. Negroes. 2. U. S.—Race question.
6-10235
Library of Congress E185.5.J65
͵30f1͵

MB9
G76w

Race question.

Grant, Daniel T 1914–
When the melon is ripe; the autobiography of a Georgia Negro high school principal and minister. ͵1st ed.͵ New York, Exposition Press ͵1955͵
174 p. 21 cm.

1. U. S.—Race question. I. Title.
E185.97.G7A3 325.260973 55-12465 ‡
Library of Congress ͵2͵

Race question.

M323
G87w

Griggs, Sutton Elbert, 1872–
Wisdom's call, by Sutton E. Griggs ... Nashville, Tenn., The Orion publishing co., 1911.
2 p. l., vii-viii p., 1 l., 11-193 p. 19 cm.

1. U. S.—Race question. I. Title.
11-30416
Library of Congress E185.61.G85
͵48g½͵

Race question.

M06
Am3
no.21

Grimké, Archibald Henry, 1849–
The shame of America, or, The negro's case against the republic, by Archibald H. Grimke. Washington, D. C., The Academy, 1924.
18 p. 23 cm. (American negro academy. Occasional papers, no. 21)

1. Negroes. 2. U. S.—Race question. I. Title.
Library of Congress E185.A51 no. 21 24-13777
͵a24b2͵

Race question.

M815.5
G88
v.1,no.
13

Grimke, Francis James, 1850–
Excerpts from a thanksgiving sermon by Francis J. Grimke ... Delivered November 26, 1914, and Two letters addressed to Hon. Woodrow Wilson ... ͵Washington, Printed by R. L. Pendleton, 1914͵
8 p. 22½ cm.

1. U. S.—Race question. 2. Thanksgiving day addresses.
18-4034
Library of Congress E185.61.G8754
——— Copy 2.

Race question.

M815.5
G88
v.1,no.
4

Grimke, Francis James, 1850–
God and the race problem. A discourse delivered in the Fifteenth street Presbyterian church, Washington, D. C. By the pastor, Rev. Francis J. Grimke, May 3rd, 1903. ͵Washington, 1903͵
12 p. 23½ cm.
Caption title.

1. Negroes. 2. U. S.—Race question. I. Title.
18-15158
Library of Congress E185.61.G88
͵37b1͵

Race question.

M208.1
G88

Grimké, Francis James, 1850–1937.
The works of Francis J. Grimké, edited by Carter G. Woodson ... Washington, D. C., The Associated publishers, inc. ͵1942͵
4 v. 23½ cm.
CONTENTS.—I. Addresses mainly personal and racial.—II. Special sermons.—III. Stray thoughts and meditations.—IV. Letters.

1. Presbyterian church — Collected works. 2. Theology — Collected works—20th cent. 3. U. S.—Race question. I. Woodson, Carter Godwin, 1875– ed.
42-18902
Library of Congress BX8915.G73
͵43d2͵ 208.1

Race question.

M331
H24b

Harris, Abram Lincoln, 1899–
The black worker; the Negro and the labor movement, by Sterling D. Spero and Abram L. Harris. New York, Columbia university press, 1931.
x, 509 p., 1 l. 22½ cm.
Issued also as A. L. Harris's thesis (PH. D.) Columbia university. Mr. Harris wrote chapters 2-5, 10, 14-15, 17-19.
"Bibliography of works cited": p. 485-490.

1. Negroes—Employment. 2. Trade-unions—U. S. 3. Labor and laboring classes—U. S. 4. Negroes—Civil rights. 5. U. S.—Race question. I. Harris, Abram Lincoln, 1899– joint author. II. Title. III. Title: The Negro and the labor movement.
31-3610
Library of Congress E185.8.S74
͵44p²2͵ [325.26] 331.6

Race question

M323
H24n

Harrison, Hubert H.
The Negro and the nation, by Hubert H. Harrison. New York, Cosmo-advocate publishing co. ͵pref. 1917͵
64 p. 16½ cm.

1. Negroes. 2. U. S.—Race question. I. Title.
22-18697
Library of Congress E185.61.H28
͵41b1͵

Race question.

M973
H237w

Harrison, Hubert H.
When Africa awakes; the "inside story" of the stirrings and strivings of the new negro in the western world, by Hubert H. Harrison ... New York city, The Porro press, 1920.
146 p. illus. (port.) 18½ cm.

1. Negroes. 2. U. S.—Race question. I. Title.
Library of Congress E185.61.H31 22-4902
͵2͵

Race question.

M323.2
H33c

Haynes, George Edmund, 1880–
The clinical approach to race relations; how to promote interracial health in your community, by George Edmund Haynes. ͵New York, Dept. of race relations, the Federal council of the churches of Christ in America, 1946͵
cover-title, 36 p. diagr. 22 cm.

1. U. S.—Race question. I. Title.
E184.A1H38 572 46-7809
Library of Congress ͵5͵

Race question.

M323.2
H33t

Haynes, George Edmund, 1880–
The trend of the races ͵by͵ George Edmund Haynes ... with an introduction by James H. Dillard. New York, Council of women for home missions and Missionary education movement of the United States and Canada ͵°1922͵
xvi p., 1 l., 205 p. front., plates. 19½ cm.
"A select reading list": p. 201-205.

1. Negroes. 2. U. S.—Race question. I. Title.
22-15670
Library of Congress E185.61.H43
͵38d1͵

Race question.

M301
H43

Hernton, Calvin C
Sex and racism in America ͵by͵ Calvin C. Hernton. ͵1st ed.͵ Garden City, N. Y., Doubleday, 1965.
180 p. 22 cm.
Bibliographical footnotes.

1. ~~U. S.~~—Race question. 2. Sex (Psychology) 3. Miscegenation. I. Title.
E185.62.H4 301.451 64-20576
Library of Congress ͵5͵

Race question.

M301
H43w

Hernton, Calvin C
White papers for white Americans «by» Calvin C. Hernton. «1st ed.» Garden City, N.Y., Doubleday, 1966.
155 p. 22 cm.
Portrait of author on book jacket.

Race question

MB9
L63hu

Hubert, James Henry, 1885–
The life of Abraham Lincoln, its significance to Negroes and Jews; an address delivered before Gad lodge, no. 11, Free sons of Israel, February 15, 1939. ... with an introduction by Dr. William Heard Kilpatrick ... and an extract from the presidential address on the test of American democracy delivered before the sixty-fifth annual session of the National Conference of social work, by Dr. Solomon Lowenstein. N.Y. Malliet & Co., 1939.
22p. 23cm.

Race question.

M252
H91a

Huntley, Thomas Elliott.
As I saw it, not commUnism but commOnism; a prophetic appraisal of the status quo, a message for our times and for all times, for America and for all nations. New York, Comet Press Books ͵1955, °1954͵
146 p. 23 cm.
"The Central Baptist Church on Wheels": p. 119-146.

1. Communism and religion. 2. U. S.—Race question. 3. St. Louis. Central Baptist Church. 4. Baptists—Sermons. 5. Sermons, American. I. Title.
BX6452.H8 252.06 55-874 ‡
Library of Congress ͵2͵

Race question.

M813.5
Im1c

Imbert, Dennis I.
The colored gentleman, a product of modern civilization, by D. I. Imbert. 1st ed. New Orleans, La., Williams printing service, 1931.
2 p. l., 86 p., 3 l. front., ports. 21½ cm.
"Supplement: Prominent leaders of the colored race in New Orleans who have achieved success" (3 l. and 12 port. at end)

1. U. S.—Race question. 2. Negroes—New Orleans. I. Title.
Library of Congress PZ3.I 313Co 31-13090
——— Copy 2.
Copyright A 38301 ͵3͵

Race question.

M252
Im2b

Imes, William Lloyd, 1889–
The black pastures, an American pilgrimage in two centuries; essays and sermons. [1st ed.] Nashville, Hemphill Press, 1957.
146 p. illus. 24 cm.

1. Presbyterian Church—Sermons. 2. Sermons, American. 3. U. S.—Race question. I. Title.

BX9178.I 5B5 252.051 57-11479 ‡
Library of Congress [3]

Race question.

M323.
J13

Jackson, Algernon Brashear, 1878–
Jim and Mr. Eddy; a Dixie motorlogue, by Algernon Brashear Jackson ... Washington, D. C., The Associated publishers, inc. [°1930]
vii, 199 p. 19½ cm.

1. Negroes. 2. U. S.—Race question. I. Title.
31-6317
Library of Congress E185.61.J12
——— Copy 2.
Copyright A 33931 [35c1] 325.26

Race question.

M323
J13m

Jackson, Algernon Brashear, 1878–
The man next door, by Algernon Brashear Jackson ... Philadelphia, Neaula publishing company [°1919]
253 p. 19 cm.

1. Negroes. 2. U. S.—Race question. I. Title.
20-3860
Library of Congress E185.6.J12
——— Copy 2.
Copyright A 565003 [4]

Race question.

M323
J63n

Johnson, James Weldon, 1871–1938.
Negro Americans, what now? By James Weldon Johnson. New York, The Viking press, 1934.
viii, 103 p. 19½ cm.

1. Negroes. 2. U. S.—Race question. 3. Negroes—Civil rights. 4. Negroes—Moral and social conditions. I. Title.
34-35660
Library of Congress E185.61.J69
[44g²2] 325.260973

M301
J63ne6

Race question.
Johnson, Charles Spurgeon, 1893–
The Negro in American civilization; a study of Negro life and race relations in the light of social research, by Charles S. Johnson... London, Constable and co., 1931.

xiv, 538 p. diagrs. 22½cm.
Results of social research for the National interracial conference and problems discussed at its meeting in Washington, D.C., December 16-19, 1928.
Bibl. p. 485-509

Race question.

M301
J63pa

Johnson, Charles Spurgeon, 1893–
Patterns of Negro segregation [by] Charles S. Johnson ... New York, London, Harper & brothers [1943]
xxii, 332 p. 24 cm.
"First edition."
Bibliographical foot-notes.

1. Negroes. 2. U. S.—Race question. I. Title.
43-1802
Library of Congress E185.61.J625
[45k²7] 325.260973

Race question.

M301
J63pr

Johnson, Charles Spurgeon, 1893–
... A preface to racial understanding. New York, Friendship press [°1936]
ix, 206 p. 19½ cm.
At head of title: By Charles S. Johnson.
"Bibliographical notes": p. 198–201.

1. Negroes. 2. U. S.—Race question. I. Title.
36-14802
Library of Congress E185.61.J63
[45x2] 325.260973

Race question.

M301
J63t

Johnson, Charles Spurgeon, 1893–
To stem this tide, a survey of racial tension areas in the United States [by] Charles S. Johnson and associates. Boston and Chicago, The Pilgrim press, 1943.
x, 142 p. 20 cm.
"The Julius Rosenwald fund of Chicago sponsored this study ... [which was] made by the Institute of social studies at Fisk university ... under the direction of Dr. Charles S. Johnson."—Pref.
Bibliographical foot-notes.

1. Negroes. 2. U. S.—Race question. I. Fisk university, Nashville. Social science institute. II. Title.
44-247
Library of Congress E185.61.J635
[46d²7] 325.260973

Race question.

M323
J71b

Jones, Laurence Clifton, 1884–
The bottom rail; addresses and papers on the Negro in the lowlands of Mississippi and on inter-racial relations in the South during twenty-five years, by Laurence C. Jones ... with an introduction by Francis S. Harmon ... New York [etc.] Fleming H. Revell company [°1935]
96 p. front. (port.) 19½ cm. Inscribed: To A. B. Spingarn fam.—To Miss Mary White Ovington, in appreciation of her efforts to strengthen the Bottom Rail, Laurence C. Jones, Piney Woods, Miss. 1938.
1. Negroes—Mississippi. 2. U. S.—Race question. 3. Piney Woods country life school, Braxton, Miss. I. Title.
35-4380
Library of Congress E185.93.M6J6
[45f1] 325.2609762

Race question.

M301
J94d

Julius Rosenwald fund.
Directory of agencies in race relations, national, state and local. Chicago, Ill., Julius Rosenwald fund, 1945.
124 p. 23 cm.
"The burden of the responsibility for compilation and editing ... has been upon Elizabeth Linn Allen."—Introd.

1. U. S.—Race question. 2. Association and associations—U. S.—Direct. I. Allen, Elizabeth Linn, ed.
46-6079
Library of Congress E184.A1J8
[47h3] 572

Race question.

M323
K45

Kerlin, Robert Thomas, 1866–
The voice of the Negro, 1919, by Robert T. Kerlin ... New York, E. P. Dutton & company [°1920]
xii p., 1 l., 188 p. front. (ports.) 19½ cm.
"A compilation from the colored press of America for the four months immediately succeeding the Washington riot. It is designed to show the Negro's reaction to that and like events following, and to the world war and the discussion of the treaty."—Pref.

1. Negroes 2. U. S.—Race question. I. Title.
20-13602
Library of Congress E185.61.K4
[48e1]

Race question.

M323
K58

King, Willis J.
... The Negro in American life; an elective course for young people on Christian race relationships, by Willis J. King ... New York, Cincinnati, The Methodist book concern [°1926]
154 p. illus. (map) 19 cm. (World friendship series)
"Approved by the Committee on curriculum of the Board of education of the Methodist Episcopal church."

1. Negroes. 2. U. S.—Race question.
26-11637
Library of Congress E185.6.K54
[a38d1]

Race question.

M323.3
L33

Larsson, Clotye Murdock, ed.
Marriage across the color line, edited by Clotye M. Larsson. Chicago, Johnson Pub. Co., 1965.
xi, 204 p. 22 cm.

1. Miscegenation. 2. ~~U. S.~~—Race question. I. Title.
HQ1031.L3 301.422 65-21549
Library of Congress [3]

Race question.

M335
L62

Lightfoot, Claude
The Negro question in the U.S.A.; resolution adopted by the 17th convention of the Communist party, U.S.A. together with the address to the convention by Claude Lightfoot. [New York, New Century Publishers, 1960]
23p. 20cm.

1. Race question. 2. Communism - U.S. I. Title.

Race question.

M301
L63

Lincoln, Charles Eric.
My face is black, by C. Eric Lincoln. Boston, Beacon Press [1964]
137 p. 21 cm.
Bibliographical references included in "Notes" (p. [134]–137)

1. ~~Negroes.~~ 2. ~~U. S.~~—Race question. 3. Black Muslims. I. Title.
E185.61.L57 301.451 64–22695
Library of Congress [65f9]

Race question.

M301
L726m

Little, Malcolm, 1925-1965.
Malcolm X speaks; selected speeches and statements. Edited with prefatory notes, by George Breitman. New York, Merit Publishers, 1965.

xiii, 242p. illus., ports. 22cm.

1. Race question. 2. Civil rights. 3. Black Muslims. I. Breitman, George, ed. II. Title.

Race question.

M323.2
L83a

Lomax, Louis E 1922–
The Negro revolt. [1st ed.] ~~New York, Harper [1962]~~ London, H. Hamilton [1963]
271 p. 22 cm.
Includes bibliography.

1. Negroes—Civil rights. 2. ~~U. S.~~—Race question. I. Title.
E185.61.L668 301.451 62-7911 ‡
Library of Congress [10]

Race question.

M323.2
L83

Lomax, Louis E 1922–
The Negro revolt. [1st ed.] New York, Harper [1962]
271 p. 22 cm.
Includes bibliography.

1. Negroes—Civil rights. 2. U. S.—Race question. I. Title.
E185.61.L668 301.451 62-7911 ‡
Library of Congress [10]

Race question.

M323.3
M21a

McKinney, Thomas Theodore, 1869–
All white America; a candid discussion of race mixture and race prejudice in the United States, by T. T. McKinney ... Boston, Meador publishing company, 1937.
214 p. 21 cm.
Bibliographical notes: p. 213–214.

1. U. S.—Race question. 2. Miscegenation. 3. Negroes. I. Title.
37-2557
Library of Congress E185.61.M156
[5] 325.260973

Race question.

M323
M26k

Maffett, Robert Lee, 1920–
The kingdom within; a study of the American race problem and its solution. Foreword by Gaius Jackson Slosser. [1st ed.] New York, Exposition Press [1955]
182 p. 21 cm.

1. U. S.—Race question. 2. Negroes. I. Title.
E185.61.M2 325.260973 55-11124 ‡
Library of Congress [5]

Trinidad
Race question.

M323.
M29s

Maloney, Arnold Hamilton.
Some essentials of race leadership, by Arnold Hamilton Maloney ... Xenia, O., The Aldine publishing house, 1924.
180, [4] p. 20 cm.

1. Negro race. 2. U. S.—Race question. I. Title.
24-6120
Library of Congress E185.61.M25
——— Copy 2.
Copyright A 777566 [2]

Race question.

M323. M61a

Miller, Kelly, 1863–1939.
An appeal to conscience; America's code of caste a disgrace to democracy, by Kelly Miller ... with an introduction by Albert Bushnell Hart. New York, The Macmillan company, 1918.
108 p. 17cm.

1. Negroes. 2. U. S.—Race question. I. Title.
18—12468
Library of Congress E185.61.M63
[a44b1]

Race question.

M304 P19 v.7 no.16

Miller, Kelly, 1863–
As to The leopard's spots; an open letter to Thomas Dixon, jr., by Kelly Miller ... Washington, D. C., K. Miller [°1905]
21 p. 23cm.

1. Dixon, Thomas, 1864– 2. Negroes. 3. U. S.—Race question. I. Title.
5—33680
Library of Congress E185.61.M643
Copyright [30b1]

Race question.

M323 M61d

Miller, Kelly, 1863–
The disgrace of democracy; open letter to President Woodrow Wilson, by Kelly Miller ... [Washington, 1917]
cover-title, 3-18 p. 21cm.

1. Negroes. 2. U. S.—Race question. I. Title.
17—28905
Library of Congress E185.61.M644

Race question.

M323 M51e

Miller, Kelly, 1863–1939.
The everlasting stain, by Kelly Miller ... Washington, D. C., The Associated publishers [°1924]
xiii p., 1 l., 352 p. 19½cm.
"The essays in this collection center about the issues growing out of the world war and the Negro's relation to them."—Pref.

1. Negroes. 2. U. S.—Race question. I. Title.
25—2354
Library of Congress E185.61.M6442
[a41e1]

Race question.

M323. M610

Miller, Kelly, 1863–1939.
Out of the house of bondage, by Kelly Miller ... New York, The Neale publishing company, 1914.
242 p. 19½cm.
Reprinted from various periodicals.
CONTENTS.—Oath of Afro-American youth.—A moral axiom.—Out of the house of bondage.—The physical destiny of the American negro.—Education for manhood.—Crime among negroes.—The American negro as a political factor.—Fifty years of negro education.—Negroes in professional pursuits.—"The negro in the New world" and "The conflict of color."—The ministry.—The ultimate race problem.—I see and am satisfied.

1. Negroes. 2. U. S.—Race question. I. Title.
14—9858
Library of Congress E185.6.M633
[a43f1]

Race question

M973 M69q

Mitchell, George Washington, 1865–
The question before Congress, a consideration of the debates and final action by Congress upon various phases of the race question in the United States, by Geo. W. Mitchell. Philadelphia, Pa., The A. M. E. book concern [°1918]
247 p. 23½cm.

1. Slavery in the U. S. 2. Negroes. 3. U. S.—Race question. I. Title.
18—21546
Library of Congress E441.M68
[43g1]

Race question.

M301 M69

Mitchell, Glenford E *ed.*
The angry black South. Edited by Glenford E. Mitchell and William H. Peace, III. New York, Corinth Books, 1962.
159 p. 21 cm.
Portraits of authors on back of book.

1. Negroes—Southern States. 2. U. S.—Race question. I. Peace, William H., joint ed. II. Title.
E185.61.M67 301.451 61—15876 ‡
Library of Congress [62f5]

Race question.

M323 M76n

Montgomery, Leroy J
The Negro problem; its significance, strength and solution. New York, Island Press [1950]
87 p. 22 cm.

1. Negroes. I. Title.
E185.61.M7 325.260973 50—10696
Library of Congress [3]

Race question.

M323.1 M85s

Moton, Robert Russa, 1867-1940.
Some elements necessary to race development [an address delivered at the Tuskegee Commencement, May 1912] Hampton, Press of the Hampton Normal and Agricultural Institute, 1913.
22p. 13cm.
"Reprinted from the Southern workman for July, 1912."

1. Race question. I. Title.

Race question.

M323.1 M85

Moton, Robert Russa, 1867–1940.
What the Negro thinks, by Robert Russa Moton. Garden City, N. Y., Doubleday, Doran and company, inc., 1929.
vii p., 2 l., 267 p. 21½cm.
"First edition."

1. Negroes. 2. U. S.—Race question. I. Title.
29—9727
Library of Congress E185.61.M934
[45y1]

Race Question.

M323 N21

National Association for the Advancement of Colored People.
How about a decent school for me? New York.
20p. illus. 20cm.

M323 N21

Race question.
National association for the advancement of colored people.
Racial inequalities in education. New York, The national association for the advancement of colored people., 1938.
cover-title. 24p. tables. 22½cm.
Illustrations on cover.
Foreword signed: Walter White.

Race question.

M323 T69

Negro Christian student conference. *Atlanta, 1914.*
The new voice in race adjustments; addresses and reports presented at the Negro Christian student conference, Atlanta, Georgia, May 14–18, 1914. A. M. Trawick, editor ... Pub. by order of the executive committee of the conference. New York city, Student volunteer movement [1914]
1 p. l., [v]–vi p., 1 l., 230 p. 23½cm.
"Best books on the Negro in America and Africa": p. 221–224.

1. Negroes—Congresses. 2. U. S.—Race question. I. Trawick, Arcadius McSwain, 1869– ed. II. Title.
A 15—837
Springfield. Public library for Library of Congress E185.5.N38
[a35f1]

Race question.

M261 N33c

Nelson, William Stuart, 1895– *ed.*
The Christian way in race relations. [1st ed.] New York, Harper [1948]
ix, 256 p. 21 cm.
"The result of a co-operative enterprise on the part of the members of the Institute of Religion."

1. U. S.—Race question. 2. Church and social problems—U. S. I. Institute of Religion, Howard University, Washington, D. C. II. Title.
BR115.R3N4 261 48—5726*
Library of Congress [40d10]

Race question.

M811.5 P54f

Phillips, Hilton Alonzo, 1905–
Flames of rebellion (against enthroned tyranny) by Hilton A. Phillips ... [Los Angeles, Printed by the California eagle press, °1936]
viii, 237 p. port. 22cm.
Prose and poetry.

1. Race problems. 2. Negro race. 3. Negroes. 4. U. S.—Race question. I. Title.
36—10090
Library of Congress HT1521.P5
——— Copy 2.
Copyright A 92792 [5] 323.1

Race question.

M331.833 P92

President's conference on home building and home ownership, *Washington, D. C.,* 1931.
Negro housing; report of the Committee on Negro housing, Nannie H. Burroughs, chairman; prepared for the committee by Charles S. Johnson; edited by John M. Gries and James Ford. Washington, D. C., The President's conference on home building and home ownership [°1932]
xiv, 282 p. front., plates. 23½cm.
On cover: Physical aspects; social and economic factors; home ownership and financing.
(Continued on next card)
32—26008
[48t2]

Race question.

M301 R11

Raab, Earl, *ed.*
American race relations today. [1st ed.] Garden City, N. Y., Doubleday, 1962.
195 p. 18 cm. (Anchor books, A318)
Partial contents. Changing social roles in the new south, by Joseph S. Himes.-The sit-ins and the new Negro students, by Charles U. Smith (abridged).-The Black muslims in America by C. Eric Lincoln.
White editor.

1. U. S.—Race question. 2. Minorities—U. S. I. Title.
E184.A1R19 301.451 62—15926 ‡
Library of Congress [3]

Race question.

MB R24

Redding, Jay Saunders, 1906–
The lonesome road; the story of the Negro's part in America. [1st ed.] New York, Doubleday, 1958.
355 p. 24 cm. (Mainstream of America series)
Includes bibliography.

1. Negroes. 2. Negroes—Biog. 3. U. S.—Race question. I. Title.
E185.61.R298 58—6647 ‡
*301.451 325.260973
Library of Congress [58f30]

M301 R27c

Race question.
Reid, Ira DeAugustine, 1901–
The church and education for Negroes.
(In: Bowen, Trevor. Divine white right: a study of race segregation and interracial cooperation in religious organizations and institutions in the United States. New York and London, Pub. for the Institute of Social and Religious Research by Harper c1934, p.235-310).

Race question.

M301 R27n4

Reid, Ira De Augustine, 1901–
The Negro immigrant, his background, characteristics and social adjustment, 1899–1937, by Ira De A. Reid ... New York, Columbia university press; London, P. S. King & son, ltd., 1939.
261 p. incl. tables. 23cm. (*Half-title:* Studies in history, economics and public law, ed. by the Faculty of political science of Columbia university. no. 449)
Issued also as thesis (PH. D.) Columbia university.
Bibliography: p. 253–258.

1. Negroes. 2. U. S.—Race question. 3. U. S.—Emig. & immig. I. Title.
39—19909
Library of Congress H31.C7 no. 449
——— Copy 2. JV6895.N44R4 1939 a
Copyright A 126486 [40k5] (308.2) 325.260973

M323 R32n

Race question.
Revolutionary Workers League.
The Negro under capitalism; Resolution adopted by the fourth plenum of the Central Committee of the Revolutionary Workers League of the United States, September 3-4, 1930. Detroit, Demos Press, 193 .
12p. 27cm.
Mimeographed.

M323 R561
Race question.
Robinson, James Herman, ed.
Love of this land; progress of the Negro in the United States. Illustrated by Elton C. Fax. Philadelphia, Christian Education Press [1956]
76 p. illus. 23 cm.
1. Negroes. 2. U. S.—Race question. I. Title.
E185.61.R68 325.260973 56-9483 ‡
Library of Congress [2]

M323 R78
Race question.
Rowan, Carl Thomas.
South of freedom. [1st ed.] New York, Knopf, 1952.
270 p. 22 cm.
1. Negroes. 2. U. S.—Race question. I. Title.
E185.61.R86 *301.451 325.260975 51—11990 ‡
Library of Congress [53r7]

M323 T55w
Race question.
Tobias, Channing H , 1882-
World implications of race. New York, Foreign Missions Conference of North America, 1944.
11-15p. 23cm.
Bound with Redfield, Robert. Race and human nature: an anthropologists view.
At head of title: Challenge of race.

M973. R63a
Race question
Rogers, Joel Augustus, 1880-
As nature leads; an informal discussion of the reason why Negro and Caucasian are mixing in spite of opposition. By J. A. Rogers ... [Chicago, Printed by M. A. Donohue & co., °1919]
2 p. l., [7]-207 p. 20 cm.
Errata slip attached to fly-leaf.
1. U. S.—Race question. 2. Negroes. 3. Miscegenation. I. Title.
19—9528
Library of Congress E185.62.R72 [48d½]

M326. Sc71
Race question.
Scarlett, George Chandler, 1880-
Laws against liberty, by George C. Scarlett ... New York, N. Y. [Cosmos printing co., inc., °1937]
135 p. 21cm.
1. Liberty. 2. Negroes. 3. U. S.—Race question. 4. Slavery in the U. S. I. Title.
Yale law school. Library for Library of Congress A 39—1029 [40c1]

M261.8 T64
Race question.
Totiress, Richard E
Heaven's entrance requirements for the races. [Rev. ed.] New York, Comet Press Books, 1957.
50 p. 21 cm. (A Reflection book)
1. U. S.—Race question. I. Title.
BR115.R3T6 1957 *261.8 57-3115 ‡
Library of Congress [3]

M973 R63f 1924
Race question.
Rogers, Joel Augustus, 1880-
From superman to man, by J. A. Rogers ... New York, Lenox Pub. co., [1924]
128 p. 19cm. $1.00
Fourth edition.
1. U. S.—Race question. I. Title.
Library of Congress E185.61.R71 17-13073 Revised
——— Copy 2.
Copyright A 460096 [r30c2]

M323 Sh2
Race question.
Shaw, Alexander P.
Christianizing race relations as a negro sees it [by] Reverend A. P. Shaw ... [Los Angeles, Wetzel publishing company, °1928]
88 p. 20½cm.
1. Negroes. 2. U. S.—Race question. I. Title.
28-13116
Library of Congress E185.61.S53
——— Copy 2.
Copyright A 1077235 [2]

M06 J61 no. 24
Race question.
University commission on southern race questions.
Five letters of the University commission on southern race questions. [Charlottesville, Va., 1927.
22 p. 23cm. (On cover: The Trustees of the John F. Slater fund. Occasional papers no. 24)
The first four letters appeared in 1916-19 under title: Four open letters from the University commission on race questions to the college men of the South.
CONTENTS.—Lynching.—Education.—Migration.—A new reconstruction.—Interracial cooperation.—Introductory address (Knoxville, Tenn., 1919)—Southern educators appeal for enforcement of law.
1. U. S.—Race question.
Library of Congress E185.5.J65 no. 24 28—28327
——— Copy 2. E185.61.U588
[39d1]

M973. R63f
Race question.
Rogers, Joel Augustus, 1880-
From superman to man, by J. A. Rogers ... [Chicago, M. A. Donohue & co., printers, °1917]
128 p. 19cm. $1.00
1. U. S.—Race question. I. Title.
Library of Congress E185.61.R71 17-13073 Revised
——— Copy 2.
Copyright A 460096 [r30c2]

M323 St4k
Race question.
Stemons, James Samuel.
The key; a tangible solution of the negro problem, by James Samuel Stemons ... New York, The Neale publishing company, 1916.
156 p. 19cm. $1.00
1. Negroes. 2. U. S.—Race question. I. Title.
17-2334
Library of Congress E185.61.S82
——— Copy 2. [36b1]
Copyright A 455220

M323. W279
Race question.
Washington conference on the race problem in the United States, Washington, D. C., 1903.
How to solve the race problem. The proceedings of the Washington conference on the race problem in the United States under the auspices of the National sociological society, held at the Lincoln temple Congregational church; at the Nineteenth street Baptist church and at the Metropolitan A. M. E. church, Washington, D. C., November 9, 10, 11, and 12, 1903. Addresses, resolutions and debates by eminent men of both races and in every walk of life. Washington, D. C., Beresford, printer, 1904.
1 p. l., 286 p. front., illus. (port.) 23½cm.
Edited by Jesse Lawson. [45p1]
1. Negroes. 2. U. S.—Race question. I. Lawson, Jesse, ed. II. National sociological society.
Library of Congress E185.5.W32 4—14581

M614 R66a2
Race question
Roman, Charles Victor, 1864-
American civilization and the Negro; the Afro-American in relation to national progress, by C. V. Roman ... Illustrated with half-tone engravings. Philadelphia, F. A. Davis company, 1916.
xii, 434 p. front., plates, ports., diagr. 24cm.
1. Negroes. 2. U. S.—Race question. I. Title.
16—2965
Library of Congress E185.61.R75 [39f1]

M323 T21c
Race question.
Taylor, Cæsar Andrew Augustus P.
The conflict and commingling of the races; a plea not for the heathens by a heathen to them that are not heathens. By Cæsar A. A. P. Taylor. New York, Broadway publishing company, 1913.
3 p. l., xv, 119 p. 20cm.
1. U. S.—Race question. 2. Negroes. I. Title.
13—10926
Library of Congress E185.61.C22
Copyright A 347353 [a37b1]

M323 W37
Race question.
Weatherford, Willis Duke, 1875-
Race relations; adjustment of whites and Negroes in the United States, by Willis D. Weatherford ... and Charles S. Johnson ... Boston, New York [etc.] D. C. Heath and company [°1934]
x, 590 p. 22½ cm. (On cover: Social relations series)
Bibliography: p. 556-576.
1. Negroes. 2. U. S.—Race question. 3. Negroes—Moral and social conditions. 4. Slavery in the U. S. I. Johnson, Charles Spurgeon, 1893- joint author. II. Title.
34—36788
Library of Congress E185.W42 [40h°3] 325.260973

M323 R72
Race question.
Rose, Arnold Marshall, 1918- ed.
Race prejudice and discrimination; readings in intergroup relations in the United States. 1st ed. New York Knopf, 1951.
xi, 605, vip. 22cm.

M323 T37
Race question.
Thompson, Edgar Tristram, 1900- ed.
Race relations and the race problem, a definition and an analysis. Edgar T. Thompson, editor; contributors: Robert E. Park, Edward B. Reuter, S. J. Holmes [and others] ... Durham, N. C., Duke university press, 1939.
xv, 338 p. incl. illus. (maps) tables, diagrs. 23½cm. (Half-title: Duke university publications)
"A Duke university centennial publication."
CONTENTS.—Introduction, by E. T. Thompson.—The nature of race relations, by R. E. Park.—Competition and the racial division of labor, by E. B. Reuter.—The trend of the racial balance of births and deaths, by S. J. Holmes.—Racial competition for the land, by R. B. Vance.—Patterns of race conflict, by G. B. Johnson.—The Negro as a contrast conception,
(Continued on next card)
39—21842
[45i°3]

M323 F587h
Race question.
White, Walter Francis, 1893-1955.
How far the promised land? New York, Viking Press, 1955.
244 p. 22 cm.
1. U. S.—Race question. 2. Negroes. I. Title.
E185.61.W6 325.260973 55—9638 ‡
Library of Congress [56r°15]

M301 R76d
Race question.
Roussève, Ronald J 1932-
Discord in brown and white; nine essays on intergroup relations in the United States by a Negro American. [1st ed.] New York, Vantage Press [1961]
89 p. 22 cm.
Includes bibliography.
1. Negroes. 2. U. S.—Race question. I. Title.
E185.61.R82 301.451 61-4684 ‡
Library of Congress [5]

M323 T39
Race question.
Thornton, M W 1873-
The white Negro; or, A series of lectures on the race problem. By Rev. M. W. Thornton ... Burlington, Ia., C. Lutz printing and publishing co., 1894.
99 p. front. (port.) 19½cm.
1. Negroes. 2. U. S.—Race question.
12—5302
Library of Congress E185.5.T61
Copyright 1894: 8396 [a38b1]

M323 W587ro
Race question.
White, Walter Francis, 1893-
Rope & faggot; a biography of Judge Lynch, by Walter White. New York & London, A. A. Knopf, 1929.
xiii p., 2 l., [3]-272, iv p., 1 l. incl. tables. front. 21½cm.
Bibliography: p. 260-272.
1. Lynch law. 2. Negroes. 3. U. S.—Race question. I. Title. II. Title: A biography of Judge Lynch.
29—10015
Library of Congress HV6457.W45 [44e1]

Race question

M323
W67

Williams, Frances Harriet.
The business girl looks at the Negro world, a study course, by Frances Harriet Williams ... New York, The Womans press, 1937.
3 p. l., 55 p. illus. (maps) 21½cm.
1. Negroes—Moral and social conditions. 2. Negroes—Stat. 3. U. S.—Race question. I. Title.
37—4315
Library of Congress E185.61.W73 [42d1] 325.260973

Race question.

M301
W673

Williams, John Alfred, 1925–
This is my country too [by] John A. Williams. [New York] New American Library [1965]
xix, 169 p. 21 cm. (An NAL-World book)
1. ~~Negroes~~—Race question. 2. U. S.—Desc. & trav.—1960– I. Title.
E185.61.W734 301.451 65–17842
Library of Congress [5]

Race question.

M323.4
W934

Wright, Nathan.
Black power and urban unrest; creative possibilities. [1st ed.] New York, Hawthorn Books [1967]
200 p. 22 cm.
Bibliographical references included in "Notes" (p. 195)
1. Negroes—Civil rights. 2. U. S.—Race question. 3. Negroes—Psychology. I. Title.
E185.615.W7 323.4'0973 67—15556
Library of Congress [68t10]

Race Question.

MSS
W93

Wright, Nathan.
Black power ~~and urban unrest; creative possibilities.~~ [1st ed.] New York, Hawthorn Books [1967]
~~200 p. 22 cm.~~ 185 leaves. 28cm.
~~Bibliographical references included in "Notes" (p. 195)~~
"Uncorrected proofs."
1. ~~Negroes~~—Civil rights. 2. ~~U. S.~~—Race question. 3. ~~Negroes~~—Psychology. I. Title.
E185.615.W7 323.4'0973 67—15556
Library of Congress [7]

Race question.

M323
W93n

Wright, Richard Robert, 1878–
The negro problem; being extracts from two lectures on "The sociological point of view in the study of race problems," and "The negro problem; what it is not and what it is," by R. R. Wright, jr. [Philadelphia, Printed by the A. M. E. book concern, °1911]
47 p. 18cm. $0.25
1. Negroes. 2. U. S.—Race question. I. Title.
12–1050
Library of Congress E185.61.W95
Copyright A 305268

Race question - Addresses, essays, lectures.

M323
D22

Daniel, Bradford, ed.
Black, white, and gray; twenty-one points of view on the race question. New York, Sheed and Ward [1964]
xii, 308 p. 22 cm.
1. U. S.—Race question—Addresses, essays, lectures. 2. Negroes—Addresses, essays, lectures. I. Title.
E185.61.D26 301.451 64—13575
Library of Congress [64f7]

M301
J72

Race question - Addresses, essays, lectures.
Jones, LeRoi.
Home; social essays. New York, Morrow, 1966.
252 p. 22 cm.

Race question - Addresses, essays, lectures.

M301
M39

Masuoka, Jitsuichi, 1903– ed.
Race relations: problems and theory; essays in honor of Robert E. Park. Edited by Jitsuichi Masuoka and Preston Valien. Chapel Hill, University of North Carolina Press [1961]
x, 290 p. 24 cm.
Bibliographical footnotes.
1. Race problems—Addresses, essays, lectures. 2. ~~U. S.~~—Race question—Addresses, essays, lectures. 3. Park, Robert Emory, 1868–1942. I. Valien, Preston, joint ed. II. Title.
HT1521.M29 301.451 61—66070
Library of Congress [62q5]

Race question - Addresses, essays, lectures.

M973
R72

Rose, Arnold Marshall, 1918– ed.
Assuring freedom to the free; a century of emancipation in the USA. With an intro. by Lyndon B. Johnson. Detroit, Wayne State University Press, 1964.
306p. 21cm.

Race question - Addresses, essays, lectures.

M973
W75

Wish, Harvey, 1909– ed.
The Negro since emancipation. Englewood Cliffs, N. J., Prentice-Hall [1964]
vi, 184 p. 21 cm. (A Spectrum book)
Bibliography: p. 183–184.
White editor.
An anthology of excerpts from the writings of 15 Negro leaders.
1. ~~Negroes~~—Hist.—Addresses, essays, lectures. 2. ~~U. S.~~—Race question—Addresses, essays, lectures. I. Title.
E185.61.W79 301.451 64–23550
Library of Congress [5]

Race question - Bibliography

M01
W36

Waxman, Julia.
Race relations, a selected list of readings on racial and cultural minorities in the United States, with special emphasis on Negroes, by Julia Waxman. Chicago, Ill., Julius Rosenwald fund, 1945.
47 p. 22½cm.
Classified and annotated.
1. Negroes—Bibl. 2. U. S.—Race question—Bibl. 3. Minorities—U. S.—Bibl. I. Julius Rosenwald fund. II. Title.
45–7918
Library of Congress Z1361.N39W3 [20] 016.3251

Race question—Fiction.

M813.5
Sh1

Shackelford, Otis M 1871–
Lillian Simmons; or, The conflict of sections; a story by Otis M. Shackelford ... illustrated by William Hamilton. Kansas City, Mo., Burton publishing company [°1915]
2 p. l., 7–210 p. incl. plates. pl. 21cm. $1.50
1. U. S.—Race question—Fiction. I. Title.
15–16441
Library of Congress PZ3.S5228L
Copyright A 411052

Race question - Poetry.

M811.5
C46h

Christian, Marcus Bruce, 1900–
High ground; a collection of poems published in commemoration of the United States Supreme Court's decision of May 17, 1954, and its final decree of May 31, 1955, abolishing racial segregation in the nation's public schools. New Orleans [Southern Pub. Co.] 1958.
20p. 27cm.
Portrait of author on book cover.
"Sincerely Marcus B. Christian."

Race question - Gt. Brit.

Jamaica
M325
D29

Davison, Robert Barry.
Commonwealth immigrants. London, Oxford University Press, 1964.
xi, 87p. 19cm.
"Issued under the auspices of the Institute of Race Relations, London."

Race relations.

M813.5
Ad1s

Adams, Frankie V
Soulcraft; sketches on Negro-white relations designed to encourage friendship, by Frankie V. Adams. Atlanta, Ga., Morris Brown college press, Morris Brown college [1944]
5 p. l., 13–65 p. 22cm.
1. Negroes. I. Title.
45–109
Library of Congress E185.61.A23 [3] 325.26

Race relations.

Cuba
M972.91
B46n

Betancourt, Juan René
El Negro: ciudadano del futuro. La Habana, Impreso en los Talleres Tipograficos de Cardenas y Cia, 1959.
248p. illus. 23½cm.

Race relations.

M301
B64

Booker, Simeon.
Black man's America. Englewood Cliffs, N. J., Prentice-Hall [1964]
230 p. 22 cm.
~~1. Negroes.~~ I. Title. 1. Race relations. 2. History.
E185.6.B76 301.451 64–14541
Library of Congress [5]

Race relations.

M323
B81m

Browning, Matthew.
My tour through Dixie. Minneapolis, Martin Brown, 1947.
[9]p. 20cm.

Race relations.

M815.5
B881

Bunche, Ralph Johnson, 1904–
International significance of race relations. n.p., 1950.
7p. 28cm.
Address delivered by Dr. Bunche, May 10, 1950, at the Denver Unity Council luncheon.
Mimeographed.

Race relations.

M815.5
B88m

Bunche, Ralph Johnson, 1904–
More powerful than the a-bomb. American Association for the United Nations, [195]
[4]p. 28cm.
Reprinted from the Progressive, but originally adapted from a speech presented at the World Affairs Institute at the University of Denver.

Race relations.

M817.5
C22

Carpenter, Ben
Simple Simon; a portfolio. Los Angeles, Calif., Carpto Publishing Co., 1962.
61p. 24cm.

Race relations.
M323 C43
Chicago. Mayor. Conference on Race Relations. February, 1944.
Proceedings... Chicago, The Committee, 1944.
64p. 28cm.

Race relations.
M323. D11
Dabney, Wendell Phillips, 1865
The wolf and the lamb, by Wendell P. Dabney. Cincinnati, O., The author, c 1913.
Cover-title. 16p. illus. 23cm.

Race relations.
M323 H18
Hamilton, Mary
Freedom riders speak for themselves [by] Mary Hamilton, Louise Inghram, and others. [Detroit, News & letters, 1961]
62p. illus. 18½cm.
"A News & letters pamphlet."

Race relations.
M323.2 C49
Citizens Emergency Conference for Internacial Unity. Hunter College, 1943.
Report of the Citizens Emergency Conference for Interracial unity held at Hunter College... September 25, 1943. New York, The Conference, [1943]
30p. 22½cm.

M323.2 D34m
Race relations.
De Hueck, Catherine
Manifesto of Friendship House. New York, Friendship House, 1943.
3 p. 16cm.
Reprinted from Friendship House news. Dec. 1943.

Race relations.
M323 H24r
Harris, Leon R
Run, Zebra, run. New York, Exposition Press, 1959.
260p. 21cm.
Portrait of author on book jacket.

Race relations.
M301 C58
Cleaver, Eldridge, 1935–
Soul on ice. With an introd. by Maxwell Geismar. [1st ed.] New York, McGraw-Hill [1967, °1968]
xv, 210 p. 22 cm.
"A Ramparts book."
1. Negroes—Psychology. I. Title. 2. Race relations.
E185.97.C6 301.451'96'073 (B) 67-27277
Library of Congress [10-2]

M973.9 F46 No.6
Race relations.
Embree, Edwin Rogers, 1883-1950.
Fifty years of progress in human relations. Pittsburgh, Pittsburgh Courier, 1950.
7p. port. illus. 24cm. (Fifty years of progress)

M323.2 H33ch
Race relations.
Haynes, George Edmund, 1880–
Changing racial attitudes and customs. Reprinted from Phylon, First quarter, 1941.
16p. 25cm.

Race relations.
M323. C67p
Coleman, Charles C
Patterns of race relations in the South. New York, Exposition Press [1949]
44p. 21cm.

M323.2 F31t
Race relations.
Federal Council of the Churches of Christ in America. Dept. of Race Relations.
Toward interracial fellowship. New York, 1939.
7p. 22cm. (Interracial publications, no.42)
18th annual report.

Race relations.
M323.2 H33e
Haynes, George Edmund.
Enlistment for brotherhood in your community, by George Edmund Haynes. New York, Department of Race Relations, The Federal Council of the Churches of Christ in America, 1947.
36p. 21½cm.

Race relations.
M323 C82f
Coston, William Hilary.
A freeman and yet a slave. By W. H. Coston ... Burlington [Ia.] Wohlwend bros., printers [1888] 1884.
84 p. front. (port.) 17cm.
1. Negroes. I. Title.
Library of Congress E185.61.C8 7—21497
Copyright 1888: 12419 [a30c1]

Race relations.
M323.2 F31y
Federal Council of the Churches of Christ in America. Dept. of Race Relations.
Your community and its unity; How you can help improve race relations. New York, the Council, 1944.
31p. illus. 18cm. (Interracial publication, no.34)

Race relations.
M323.2 H33p
Haynes, George Edmund, 1880–
Public approbation as a means of changing interracial attitudes and customs. Reprinted from Social Forces, 24:105-110, October 1945.
105-110p. 25cm.

Race relations.
M323 C831
Council against intolerance in America.
An American answer to intolerance. Teacher's manual no. 1, junior and senior high schools. Experimental form, 1939. New York city, Council against intolerance in America, 1939.
130 p., 1 l. 23 cm.
"Prepared by Frank Walser, with the assistance of Annette Smith and Violet Edwards."
"Bibliography of plays suitable for high school production": p. 117-118.
Bibliography: p. 119-130.
1. Propaganda. 2. Antipathies and prejudices. 3. Toleration. I. ~~Walser, Frank, ir. Smith, Annette, ill. Edwards, Violet.~~ IV. Title. v. Title: Intolerance. 4. Race relations. II. White, Walter, 1893-1955.
New York Univ. Wash. Sq. Library HM268.C7 A 40—2271
for Library of Congress HM263.C8 [a49k1] 301.1523

Race relations.
M813.5 F34f
Felton, James A 1919–
Fruits of enduring faith; a story of racial unity. New York, Exposition Press [1965]
96p. 21cm.
Portrait of author on book jacket.
1. Race relations. I. Title.

Race Relations.
M323 H831
Howell, Charles Garfield.
It could happen here, the menace of native facism in America after World War II, by Charles Garfield Howell. New York, The William-Frederick press, 1945.
59 p. 19½cm.

Race relations.
M323 C97d
Cuthbert, Marion
Democracy and the Negro, by Marion Cuthbert. New York, Council for social action, 1936.
31p. illus. 20cm.
Social action, vol. II, no. 14, September 15, 1936.

Race relations.
M323.4 G98d
Guzman, Jessie Parkhurst, 1898–
Desegregation and the Southern states 1957; legal action and voluntary group action. Tuskegee, Ala., Tuskegee Institute, Dept. of Records and Research, 1958.
59p. 23½cm.

Race relations.
M323 J132
Jackson, James Edward
3 brave men tell how freedom comes to an old South City, Nashville, Tenn. [New York, Publisher's New Press, 1963]
27p. 22½cm
1. Race relations. 2. Nashville, Tenn. I. Title.

Race relations.
M304 Johnson, James Weldon
P19 Legal aspects of the Negro problem, by
V.7 James Weldon Johnson and Herbert J. Seligmann.
No.12 Reprinted from the Annals of the American Academy of Political and Social Science, November, 1928.

8p. 23½cm.

Race relations.

M260 Mays, Benjamin Elijah, 1895-
M45s ... Seeking to be Christian in Race Relations, by Benjamin E. Mays. New York, Friendship Press [1946]

48p. 18cm. (Study and action pamphlets on race relations)

Race relations.

M323 [Peck, Jim]
P33c Cracking the color line; non-violent direct action methods of eliminating racial discrimination. New York, CORE, 1959.

24p. illus. 22½cm.

1. Race relations.

Race relations.
M323 Johnson, James Weldon, 1871-1938.
J632 The race problem and peace, by James Weldon
no. 5 Johnson. Presented to the VI international summer school of the Women's international
M304 League for Peace and Freedom, Chicago, May,
P19 1924. Reprinted for the advancement of colored
V.5 no.10 people, 1924.

7p. 23cm.

Race relations.
M304 Miller, Kelly, 1863-1939.
P19 As to the leopard's spots. An open
v.5, no.7 letter to Thomas Dixon, Jr. By Kelly Miller. Washington, D.C., The author, 1905.
21p. 23cm.

Race relations.
M323 Popel, Esther, 1896-
P81p Personal adventures in race relations [by] Esther Popel Shaw. New York, The Woman's Press [c1946]

24p. 21½cm.

Race relations.
M301 Johnson, Charles S
J63ra Race and race relations New York City, American missionary association, 1943
9p. 23cm.

M323.2 Race relations.
M84a Morton, James.
The Atlanta plan of inter-racial co-operation. Atlanta, Inter-racial Committee, n.d.

8p. diagr. 23cm.

Race relations.

M323 Porter, Kenneth Wiggins.
P83r Relations between Negroes and Indians within the present limits of the United States, by Kenneth W. Porter ... Washington, D. C., The Association for the study of Negro life and history, inc. [193-]

1 p. l., 81 p. 24½cm.

1. Negroes. 2. Indians of North America. I. Association for the study of Negro life and history, inc. II. Title.

37-14790

Library of Congress E185.4.P67

[3] [970.1] 325.260973

Race relations.
M323.2 Laura Spelman Rockfeller Memorial.
L37p Proceedings of the inter-racial conference. Laura Spelman Rockfeller memorial. New Haven, Conn., Zeta Psi fraternity house, December 19-21, 1927.
ii, 280p. 28cm.
Mimeographed.

M323 Race relations.
N21 National Association for the Advancement of Colored People.
Civil rights in the United States; A balance sheet of group relations, 194-
New York, American Jewish Congress and the National Association for the Advancement of Colored People, 194-

v. 23 cm. annual.
See holdings card for issues in library.

Race relations.

M323 Posey, Barbara Ann
P84wy Why I sit-in; the girl who started a nationwide civil-rights movement tells how and why she sits and waits. New York, NAACP, 1960.

4p. port. 22cm.

Race relations.

M306 Lewis, Edward Shakespeare, 1901-
N21p Progress in interracial relationships. New York, 1943.

In: National Conference of Social Work. Selected papers at seventieth annual meeting... 1943. New York, Columbia University for the Conference, 1943. 23cm. pp. 277-289.

M323 Race relations.
N21 National Association for the Advancement of Colored People.
Report.
New York, 19-

v. illus. (map) ports. 16-23 cm. annual.
Each report has a special title.
See holdings card for reports in library.

1. Race relations. 2. Civil rights.

Race relations.
M286 Powell, Adam Clayton, 1865-
P87r Riots and ruins, by A. Clayton Powell, sr. ... New York, R. R. Smith, 1945.

xiv p., 1 l., 17-171 p. 22½cm.

1. Negroes. 2. Riots. I. Title.

45-5935

Library of Congress E185.61.P78

[20] 325.260073

Race relations.
M323 Long, Herman Hodge
L85c Race relations in the United States.

pp. 181-217. 25cm.
In: Coloured immigrants in Britain, by J. A. G. Griffith, et al. London, Oxford University Press, 1960.

M306
N213p Race relations.
National Negro Congress.
Proceedings.
Washington, 1936-
v. 20cm.
See holdings card for proceedings in library.

M323.2
R24e Race relations.
Reddick, Lawrence Dunbar, 1910-
Educational programs for the improvement of race relations: Motion pictures, radio, the press, and libraries. Washington, D.C. Journal of Negro education, 1944.

267-289p. 25cm.
Reprinted from the Journal of Negro education, Summer, 1944.

Race relations.

M214.5 Mason, Madison Charles Butler, 1859-1915.
M38 Solving the problem; a series of lectures by the late Rev. M. C. B. Mason ... comp. by Mrs. M. C. B. Mason ... [Mt. Morris, Ill., Kable brothers company] 1917.

142 p. front. (port.) 20cm. $1.25

1. Mason, Mary E., "Mrs. M. C. B. Mason," comp.

17-30911

Library of Congress AC8.M384
Copyright A 477487

Race relations.
M323 Norman, Dorothy, ed.
N78t Twice a year. A book of literature, the arts and civil liberties. New York, Twice A Year Press, 1946.

513p. 23cm.
Double Number - Fourteen - Fifteen
Fall - Winter - 1946-1947.
Richard Wright, Association editor.

Race relations.
M979
R24r Reddick, Lawrence Dunbar, 1910- ed.
Race relations on the Pacific coast.
New York, Journal of educational sociology, 1945.

129-208p. 23cm.
Special issue of The Journal of educational sociology, November 1945.
Contents: -The new race-relations frontier, by L. D. Reddick. -Seattle, by R. W. O'Brien. -Portland, by E. C. Berry. -San Francisco, by Joseph James. -Los Angeles, by Charles Bratt.

M979
R24r
Reddick, Lawrence Dunbar
Race relations on the Pacific coast. (card 2)

-Critical summary, by Carey McWilliams.
-Select bibliography, by Miriam Matthews.

Race relations.
M323
W379
Weaver, Robert Clifton, 1907-
Summary of conference and plans for future. [Conference on Research in Race Relations, University of Chicago, July 26-30, 1952]
Reprinted from Inventory of research in racial and cultural relations, v.5, no.2-3, Winter-spring, 1953.

204-213p. 24cm.

Race relations.
M323
W73n
Winston, Henry M.
Negro freedom, a goal for all Americans, by Henry M. Winston [and others. New York, New Currents Publishers, 1964.

56p. 18½cm.

M815.5
R55r
Race relations.
Robeson, Paul, 1898-
Racial responsibility.

Pp. 42-47 port. 24cm.
In: Pioneering for a Civilized World. Report of the New York Herald Tribune Twelfth Forum on Current Problems. At the Waldorf-Astoria New York City, November 16 and 17, 1943. New York, Herald Tribune, 1943. 267p.

Race relations.
M323
W46f
Wells, Moses Peter
Faults of the world. New York, Carlton Press, 1962.

150p. 23cm.
"A Reflection book."
Portrait of author on book jacket.

Race relations.
M813.5
W93ec
Wright, Richard, 1909-
Ecoute, homme blanc (White man, listen!) Traduit de l'Américan,par Dominique Guillet. Paris, Calmann-Lévy, Editeurs, 1959.

225p. 19cm.

1. Race relations. I. Title. II. Title: White man, listen!

Race relations.
M815.5
Sh4r
Shepard, James Edward, 1875-
Racial and inter-racial relations in North Carolina and the south; Speech delivered by, on the twentieth anniversary of the Michigan avenue Y.M.C.A., Buffalo, N.Y., October 22, 1943.

20 leaves. 28cm.
Mimeographed.

Race relations
M323.2
W58r
White Plains, New York. Human Relations Center.
Report to the White Plains schools, 1948.
White Plains, N.Y., 1948.

25p. 28cm.
Mimeographed.

Race relations.
M813.5
W93es
Wright, Richard, 1909-
¡Escucha, hombre blanco! (White man, listen!) Traducción de Floreal Mazía. Buenos Aires, Editorial Sudamericana, 1959.

178p. 20½cm.

1. Race relations. I. Title. II. Title: ¡Escucha,hombre blanco!

Race relations.
M306
Sold
Southern Sociological Congress, Knoxville, Tenn.
"Distinguished service citizenship". Edited by J. E. McCulloch. Washington, D.C., Southern Sociological Congress [1919]

M323.2
W65p
Race relations.
Wilkins, Marjorie V
Pioneer in human relations. Reprinted from New York State education, February 1949.

4p. 25cm.

Race relations.
M323
Z65
Zilton, A W
The negative forces vs. the positive qualities. [n.p., n.p., 1942]

40p. illus. (ports) 23cm.
Cover title.

M306
Sol
1919
Race relations.
Southern Sociological Congress. Knoxville. 1919
Distinguished service citizenship. Ed. by J. E. McCulloch. Washington, D. C., Southern Sociological Congress, 1919.

170 p. 23 cm.
Partial contents: Interracial co-operation and the south's new economic conditions, by Monroe Work.

Race relations.
M323
W651
Wilkins, Roy, 1901-
Integration crisis in the South; an address delivered at the 14th annual State convention of the NAACP in Charlotte, N. C., October 11th, 1957, and broadcast over radio network facilities of the American Broadcasting Company. New York, National Association for the Advancement of Colored People [1957]
11p. 21½cm.
1. Race relations. 2. Southern states. I. Title.

Race relations - Caricatures and cartoons.
M741
B734
Brandon, Brumsic
Some of my best friends. [Westbury, N. Y., 1963]

[12]p. (Chiefly illus.) 21cm.

Race relations.
M323
Su6
Summit Meeting of National Negro Leaders, Washington, D. C., 1958.
Report of proceeding [of] Summit Meeting of Negro Leaders, Washington, D.C., May 12, 13, 1958. Sponsored by National Newspaper Publishers Association. [Washington, National Newspaper Publishers Association] 1958.
137p. illus. 33cm.
Contents.- Speech, by William O. Walker.- Speech, by A. Philip Randolph.- Speech, by Paul H. Cooke.- Address, by Roy Wilkins.-
(Continued on next card)

Race relations.
M323
W67a
Williams, Chancellor.
And if I were white, a reply to the if I were a Negro series by prominent white writers. By Chancellor Williams. Washington, D.C., Shaw Publishing Co. [c1946]

63p. front (port.) 19½cm.

Race relations - Churches.
M261.2
R27
Religious Leadership Conference on Equality of Opportunity, Harriman, N.Y.
Discrimination, what can churches do? A Handbook and report on the religious leadership conference on equality of opportunity, Arden House, Harriman, N.Y., April 28-29, 1958. New York, Commission Against Discrimination, 1958.

38p. 21½cm.

Race relations.
M323
Su6
Summit Meeting on National Negro Leaders, Washington, D. C., 1958. Report of proceedings. 1958. (Card 2)
Contents - Continued.
Speech by Thurgood Marshall.- How shall we travel the road of freedom together, by F. L. Shuttleworth.
At head of title: Lighting the way to freedom.
Mimeographed.
1. Race relations. 2. Civil rights. 3. Freedom. I. Title. II. National Newspaper Publishers Association.

Race relations.
M335.4
W73n
Winston, Henry.
Negro-white unity. New York, New Outlook Publishers, 1967.

31p. 20cm.

1. Race relations. 2. Communism. I. Title.

Race relations - Drama.
M812.5
B73f
Branch, William Blackwell
"Fifty steps toward freedom." A Dramatic presentation in observance of the fiftieth anniversary of the National Association for the Advancement of Colored People 1909-1959. Premier performance, July 14, 1959, during NAACP Golden Anniversary Convention at New York Coliseum, New York, N. Y. Produced and directed by Dick Campbell. Music by the Edna Gay Chorus. Balladeer, Johnny Barracuda. Narration by Ossie Davis. [New York, N.A.A.C.P. 1959]
26p. 21½cm.

Race relations - Drama.
MSS B73
Branch, William Blackwell
"Fifty steps toward freedom." A dramatic presentation in observance of the fiftieth anniversary of the National Association for the Advancement of Colored People, 1909-1959.

48p.
"Corrected Proof."
"For Arthur Spingarn."

Race relations - Fiction.
M813.5 J62m
Johnson, Evelyn Allen
My neighbor's island. New York, Exposition Press [1965]

55p. 21cm.

1. Race relations - Fiction. 2. Discrimination in housing - Fiction. I. Title.

Race relations - Europe.
M304 P19 v.7 no.8
White, Walter Francis, 1893-
The color line in Europe. Reprinted from the Annals of the American academy of political and social science, November, 1928.

6p. 23½cm.

Race relations - New Jersey.
M304 P19 V.7,no.3
New Jersey Conference of Social Work. Interracial Committee.
New Jersey's twentieth citizen; The Negro. Newark, Interacial Committee of the New Jersey Conference of Social Work, 1932.

18p. illus. 23cm.

Race relations...
Mol W36
Waxman, Julia.
Race relations, a selected list of readings on racial and cultural minorities in the United States, with special emphasis on Negroes, by Julia Waxman. Chicago, Ill., Julius Rosenwald fund, 1945.
47 p. 22½ᶜᵐ.
Classified and annotated.

1. Negroes—Bibl. 2. U. S.—Race question—Bibl. 3. Minorities—U. S.—Bibl. I. Julius Rosenwald fund. II. Title.
45-7918
Library of Congress * Z1361.N39W3 [20] 016.3231

Race relations.
M323 W37
Weatherford, Willis Duke, 1875-
Race relations; adjustment of whites and Negroes in the United States, by Willis D. Weatherford ... and Charles S. Johnson ... Boston, New York [etc.] D. C. Heath and company [°1934]
x, 590 p. 22½ cm. (On cover: Social relations series)
Bibliography: p. 556-576.

1. Negroes. 2. U. S.—Race question. 3. Negroes—Moral and social conditions. 4. Slavery in the U. S. I. Johnson, Charles Spurgeon, 1893- joint author. II. Title.
34—36788
Library of Congress E185.W42 [40h³3] 325.260973

Race relations: problems and theory.
M301 M39
Masuoka, Jitsuichi, 1903- ed.
Race relations: problems and theory; essays in honor of Robert E. Park. Edited by Jitsuichi Masuoka and Preston Valien. Chapel Hill, University of North Carolina Press [1961]
x, 290 p. 24 cm.
Bibliographical footnotes.

1. Race problems — Addresses, essays, lectures. 2. U. S. — Race question—Addresses, essays, lectures. 3. Park, Robert Emory, 1863-1942. I. Valien, Preston, joint ed. II. Title.
HT1521.M29 301.451 61—66070
Library of Congress [62q5]

Race relations and the race problem.
M323 T37
Thompson, Edgar Tristram, 1900- ed.
Race relations and the race problem, a definition and an analysis. Edgar T. Thompson, editor; contributors: Robert E. Park, Edward B. Reuter, S. J. Holmes [and others] ... Durham, N. C., Duke university press, 1939.
xv, 338 p. incl. illus. (maps) tables, diagrs. 23½ᶜᵐ. (Half-title: Duke university publications)
"A Duke university centennial publication."
CONTENTS.—Introduction, by E. T. Thompson.—The nature of race relations, by R. E. Park.—Competition and the racial division of labor, by E. B. Reuter.—The trend of the racial balance of births and deaths, by S. J. Holmes.—Racial competition for the land, by R. B. Vance.—Patterns of race conflict, by G. B. Johnson.—The Negro as a contrast conception,
(Continued on next card)
39—21842
[45f³3]

Race relations in international affairs.
M301 B81r
Browne, Robert S
Race relations in international affairs. Introd. by Roger N. Baldwin. Washington, Public Affairs Press [1961]
62 p. 23 cm.
Includes bibliography.

1. Race problems. 2. International relations. 3. U. S.—Race question. I. Title.
HT1521.B7 301.451 61-11688 ‡
Library of Congress [10]

Race relations in the South.
M323 D77
Doyle, Bertram Wilbur, 1897-
The etiquette of race relations in the South; a study in social control, by Bertram Wilbur Doyle ... Chicago, Ill., The University of Chicago press [°1937]
xxv, 249 p. 22 cm.
Bibliography: p. 173-190.

1. Negroes. 2. U. S.—Race question. 3. Negroes—Moral and social conditions. 4. Slavery in the U. S. I. Title. II. Title: Race relations in the South.
37—20152
Library of Congress E185.61.D764 [39u4] 325.260975

Race relations in the United States.
M323 L85c
Long, Herman Hodge
Race relations in the United States.

pp. 181-217. 25cm.
In: Coloured immigrants in Britain, by J. A. G. Griffith, et al. London, Oxford University Press, 1960.

A race with a history and a country.
MB B73r
Bragg, George Freeman, 1863-1940.
A race with a history and a country [by] The Rev. George Freeman Bragg... Baltimore, Md., C. M. Dofsey & sons [n.d.]
31 [5] p. 17½cm.

Racial adjustments in the Methodist Episcopal...
M323 R25
Reed, John Hamilton.
Racial adjustments in the Methodist Episcopal church, by John H. Reed ... with an introduction by Adna B. Leonard ... New York, The Neale publishing company, 1914.
198 p. 19ᶜᵐ.

1. Methodist Episcopal church—Government. 2. Methodists, Negro. I. Title.
14-17108 Revised
Library of Congress BX8435.R4
Copyright A 380509 [r40b2]

Racial and inter-racial relations in North Carolina and the south.
M815.5 Sh4r
Shepard, James Edward, 1875-
Racial and inter-racial relations in North Carolina and the south; Speech delivered by, on the twentieth anniversary of the Michigan avenue Y.M.C.A., Buffalo, New York, October 22, 1943.

20 leaves. 28cm.
Mimeographed.

Racial cooperation.
M815.5 G88 V.1, no.20
Grimke, Francis James, 1850-1937.
The next step in racial cooperation. A discourse delivered in the Fifteenth Street Presbyterian Church, Washington, D.C. November 20, 1921, by the Pastor, Rev. Francis J. Grimke. Washington, 1921

12p. 23cm.

Racial equality.
M815.5 Sp47r
Spingarn, Joel Elias, 1875-1939.
Racial equality; Address delivered at the twenty-third annual conference of the National Association for the Advancement of Colored People, held at Washington, D.C., May 17, 1932. N.Y., National Association for the Advancement of Colored, 1932.

8p. 27cm.

Racial inequalities in education.
M323 N21
National association for the advancement of colored people.
Racial inequalities in education. New York, The national association for the advancement of colored people, 1938.
cover-title, 24 p. tables. 22½ᶜᵐ.
Illustrations on cover.
Foreword signed: Walter White.

1. Negroes—Education. 2. U. S.—Race question. I. Title.
A 40-2768
Duke univ. Library for Library of Congress [2]

Racial integrity;
M304 P19 v.5, no.18
Schomburg, Arthur Alfonso, 1874-1938.
Racial integrity; a plea for the establishment of a chair of Negro history in our schools and colleges, etc. Read before the teachers' summer class at Cheney Institute, July 1913. [n. p.] A. V. Bernier [1913?]
19 p. 23 cm. (Negro Society for Historical Research. Occasional paper no. 3)

1. Negroes—Hist. 2. Negro literature. I. Title. II. Series.
E185.5.N4 no. 3 48-32619*
Library of Congress [1]

Racial problems in housing.
M331.833 N21r
National urban league.
Racial problems in housing. [New York] National urban league [1944]
30p. illus. 27½cm. (Interacial planning for community organization. Bulletin no.2)

Racial solidarity.
M614 R66k
Roman, Charles Victor 1864-1934.
A knowledge of history is conducive to racial solidarity, and other writings, by C. V. Roman ... Nashville, Tenn., Sunday school union print, 1911.
54 p. incl. front. (port.) 18½ᶜᵐ.
Cover title: Racial solidarity.

1. Negroes.
11-29624
Library of Congress E185.R75
Copyright A 300358

A racial survey of the British people.
M942 Ar5r
Armattoe, Raphael Ernest,Grail.
A racial survey of the British people. Reprinted from The Londonderry Sentinel, Tuesday, 4th April, 1944. Pp. 1-8.

Racism and the Christian understanding of man.

M261.8 K299 Kelsey, George D
Racism and the Christian understanding of man, by George D. Kelsey. New York, Scribner [1965]
178 p. 24 cm.
Bibliographical footnotes.
1. Church and race problems. 2. Race discrimination. I. Title.
BT734.2.K42 261.83 65-27241
Library of Congress [5]

Radio operator.

M304 P19 v.7 no.29 Carter, Elmer A
Not in the headlines, a story of a Negro radio operator, by Elmer A. Carter. Reprinted from Opportunity, November, 1931. New York, National urban league, 1931.
4p. 28½cm.

The raft.

Nigeria M896.2 C54 Clark, John Pepper, 1935-
Three plays: Song of a goat; The masquerade; The raft. London, Oxford University Press, 1964.
134p. 18½cm.

...Le racisme et le métissage devant science.

Haiti M572 Ar4 Aristide, Achille.
... Le racisme et le métissage devant la science. 2. éd. ... [n. p.] Haïti, Compagnie lithographique, 1945.
21 p. 20½cm.
1. Race. I. Title.
GN62.A7 572 47-18868
Library of Congress [2]

Radio plays

M812.08 B26r Barnouw, Erik, 1908- ed.
Radio drama in action; twenty-five plays of a changing world, edited by Erik Barnouw ... New York, Toronto, Farrar & Rinehart, inc. [1945]
xii, 397p. 21cm.
Partial contents: -Booker T. Washington in Atlanta, by Langston Hughes. -The Negro domestic, by Roi Ottley.

Ragazzo Negro.

M813.5 W93a2 Wright, Richard, 1909-
Ragazzo Negro. Einaudi, 1952.
359p. 19cm.

The radiance of the king.

French Guinea M965.52 L45ra Laye, Camara, 1928-
The radiance of the king. Translated from the French by James Kirkup. London, Collins, 1956.
319p. 20½cm.

Radio plays.

M792 B26r Barnouw, Erik, 1908- ed.
Radio drama in action; twenty-five plays of a changing world, edited by Erik Barnouw ... New York, Toronto, Farrar & Rinehart, inc. [1945]
xii, 397 p. 21 cm.
White author.
1. Radio plays. I. Title.
PN6120.R2B35 792 45-9883
Library of Congress [a55w2]

M811.5 R12h Ragland, James Farley, 1904-
The Home Town Sketch Book. "It happened here." A Souvenir of Brunswick incidents; of dale and hill in Lawrenceville, Ant St. Paul School events, by J. Farley Ragland. Lawrenceville, Va., [The Brunswick Times-Gazette Press], 1940.
76p. 21½cm.
1. Poetry

Un radiante spiritual.

M89 An24u Anderson, Marian, 1902-
Un radiante spiritual. [Traducción de Luisa Rivaud] Buenos Aires, Compania General Fabril Editora, 1958.
309p. 19½cm.
Title: My Lord, What a Morning.
Portrait of author on book jacket.

Radio plays.

M813.5 G760 Graham, Shirley
Track thirteen.
(In: Welch, Constance, ed. Yale radio plays; ... Boston, Mass., Expression company, c1940. 21cm. p.171-63.)

M811.5 R12l Ragland, James Farley, 1904-
Lyrics and laughter, a volume of contempory [!] verse by J. Farley Ragland. [Lawrenceville, Va., The Brunswick Times-Gazette press, °1939]
5 p. l., 13-60 p. incl. port. 21cm.
I. Title. 1. Poetry.
Library of Congress PS3601.R27L9 1939 40-4965
——— Copy 2.
Copyright A 130629 [3] 811.5

Radiesthesie.

Haiti M133 H72n Holly, Théodose A
... Notions méthaphysiques [!] et autres, révélées ou confirmées par la radiesthésie ... Port-au-Prince, Haïti, Imp. V. Valcin [194-?-
v. 23cm.
Contents.—I. Dieu et l'univers (mécanisme du monde)
1. Radiesthesia. I. Title.
44-30292
Library of Congress BF1142.H6
[2] 133

Botswana M896.2 R119m Raditladi, Leetile Disang, 1910-
Motšwasele II. Third edition. Johannesburg, South Africa, Witwatersrand University Press, 1954.
65p. 17cm. (The Bantu Treasury, edited by D. T. Cole - #IX.)
Written in Tswana.
I. Title.

M811.5 R12r Ragland, James Farley, 1904-
Rhymes of the times, The poems of J. Farley Ragland with a foreword by Dr. Arthur Paul Davis. New York, Wendell Malliet and Co., 1946.
110p. 21cm.

Radio.

M814.5 W93u Writers' congress, *University of California at Los Angeles*, 1943.
Writers' congress; the proceedings of the conference held in October 1943 under the sponsorship of the Hollywood writers' mobilization and the University of California. Published in coöperation with the Writers' congress continuations committee of the Hollywood writers' mobilization. Berkeley and Los Angeles, University of California press, 1944.
xx, 663 p. incl. front. (facsim.) 23cm.
1. Authors. 2. World war, 1939- —Addresses, sermons, etc. I. Hollywood writers' mobilization. II. California. University. University at Los Angeles.
A 44-3485
California. Univ. Libr. for Library of Congress [12]

Botswana M896.2 R11m Raditladi, Leetile Disang, 1910-
Motšwasele II. Johannesburg, South Africa, University of the Witwatersrand Press, 1945.
65p. 18cm. (The Bantu Treasury, edited by C. M. Doke - #IX.)
Historical drama in Tswana.
I. Motšwasele II.

M811.5 R21s Ragland, James Farley, 1904-
Stepping stones to freedom; poems of pride and purpose. Richmond, Virginia, Quality Printing, c 1960.
30p. port. 23cm.
Autographed: "With best wishes."
1. Poetry. I. Title.

Radio drama in action.

M812.08 B26r Barnouw, Erik, 1908- ed.
Radio drama in action; twenty-five plays of a changing world, edited by Erik Barnouw ... New York, Toronto, Farrar & Rinehart, inc. [1945]
xii, 397 p. 21cm.
1. Radio plays. I. Title.
Library of Congress PN6120.R2B35 45-9883
[47f7] 792

Rafina, Gesner.

Haiti M841. B32s Battier, Alcibiade Fleury, 1841-
Sous les Bambous, poésies par Alcibiade Fleury-Battier ... accompagnées d'un avant-propos de M. Gesner Rafina ... Paris, Imprimerie typographique Kugelmann, 1881.
319 p. 25cm.
"Coup-d'œil sur le livre des poésies publié par M. A.-F. Battier", signed Edgar La Selve: p. [313]-319.
1. Rafina, Gesner. II. Title.
25-20890
Library of Congress PQ3949.B3S6

The ragtime songbook.

M784 C38 Charters, Ann, *ed.*
The ragtime songbook; songs of the ragtime era by Scott Joplin ... and others. Compiled and edited, with historical notes concerning the songs and the times, by Ann Charters. New York, Oak Publications [1965]
112 p. illus. 28 cm.
Principally unacc., with chord symbols.
"Introduction": p. 8-34.
White editor.
1. Music, Popular (Songs, etc.)—U. S. 2. Music, Popular (Songs, etc.)—U. S.—Hist. & crit. I. Title.
M1630.18.C515R3 784.7 65-22694/M
Library of Congress [3]

M252
R13m

Raikes, John W 1850-
Man, know thyself. By John W. Raikes. 2d ed., rev. and enl. Wilmington, Del., H. A. Roop, printer, 1913.
92 p. 17½cm. $0.50

1. Title. 1. Sermons

Library of Congress 13-8366
Copyright A 343851

Railroads—Poetry.

M811.5
H241

Harris, Leon R
Locomotive puffs from the back shop, by Leon R. Harris. Boston, B. Humphries, inc. ₍1946₎
56 p. 19½cm.

1. Railroads—Poetry. I. Title.

Library of Congress PS3515.A755L6 46-18741
₍3₎ 811.5

Railroads—U.S.— Sleeping-cars.

M331
R73b

Brazeal, Brailsford Reese.
The Brotherhood of sleeping car porters, its origin and development, by Brailsford R. Brazeal ... Foreword by Leo Wolman ... New York and London, Harper & brothers ₍1946₎
xiv, 258 p. incl. tables. front., pl., ports. 22cm.
"This study has been undertaken ... to qualify for a doctorate at Columbia university."—Pref.
Bibliography: p. 245-250.

1. Brotherhood of sleeping car porters. 2. Railroads—U. S.—Sleeping-cars.

Library of Congress HD6515.R36B83 46-2727
₍15₎ 331.88156

M784
R13

Raim, Walter, *ed.*
The Josh White song book. Biography and song commentaries by Robert Shelton. Illus. by Stu Gross. Chicago, Quadrangle Books ₍1963₎
191 p. illus. 32 cm.
For voice and piano, with chord symbols for guitar.
Discography: p. 190-191.
White editor.

1. Folk-songs, American. 2. Ballads, American. 3. Negro spirituals. 4. Folk-songs, American—Discography. I. White, Josh. II. Title.

M1629.R16J7 784.4973 63-18475/M
Library of Congress ₍5₎

Raimond, Julian, 1743-1802.

Haiti
M972.94
As7ac
1790

Assemblée des Citoyens de Couleur des Isles, & Colonies Françoises. Paris.
Adresse des Citoyens de Couleur des Isles, & Colonies Françoises; a l'Assemblée Génerale des Représentans de la Commune de Paris; prononcée, le premier Février 1790, par M. de Joly ... Paris, 1790.
15p. 21½cm.
Signed by De Joly, Raimond, Oge, etc.

Raimond, Julian, 1743-1802.

Haiti
M972.94
As7ad
1790

Assemblée des Citoyens de Couleur des Isles, et Colonies Françoises. Paris.
Adresse des Citoyens de Couleur residans a Paris, a l'Assemblée nationale, suivie de la réponse de M. le President, du 7 Septembre 1992 ₍sic₎ l'an 4e de la liberté, & le premier de l'égalité; imprimées & envoyées aux 83 departmens & aux armées, par ordre de l'Assemblée.
₍Paris, De l'Imprimerie Nationale, 1792₎
3p. 19cm.

Haiti
M972.94
As7ad
1790

Assemblée des Citoyens des Couleur des Isles, et Colonies Françoises.(Card 2)

Signed by Raimond.

Bound in: Adresse a l'Assemblée Nationale...du e Juillet 1790.

Haiti
M972.94
R13c
1794

Raimond, Julien, 1743?-1802?
Correspondance de Julien Raimond, avec ses frères de Saint-Domingue, et les pièces qui lui ont été adressées par eux. Paris, Imprimerie du Cercle Social ₍1794₎.
vii, ₍3₎ - 136p. 25cm.

1. Santo Domingo (French Colony). 2. Haiti History.

Haiti
M972.94
R13L
1791

Raimond, Julien,1743?-1802.
Lettres de J. Raimond, a ses freres les hommes de couleur. Et comparaison des originaux de sa correspondance, avec les extraits perfides qu'en ont fait MM. Page et Brulley, dans un libelle intitulé: Développement des causes, des troubles et des désastres des colonies françaises. Paris, De L'Imprimerie Cercle Social₍1791₎
20,8p. 25½cm.

Haiti
M972.94
R13r
1790

₍Raimond, Julien, 1743?-1802?₎
Reclamations adressées à l'Assemblée Nationale, par les personnes de couleur, propriétaires & cultivateurs de la colonie françoise de Saint Domingue ₍1790₎
8p. 20cm.
₍Signé Raimond₎

1. Haiti - History. 2. Santo Domingo (French Colony).

Haiti
M972.94
R13re
1791

Raimond, Julien, 1743?-1802?
Reponse aux considerations de M. Moreau, dit Saint-Méry, député a l'assemblée nationale, sur les colonies; par M. Raymond, citoyen de couleur de Saint-Domingue ... A Paris, De l'Imprimerie de Patriote François, 1791.
68p. 20½cm.

Haiti
M972.94
R13v
1792

Raimond, Julien, 1743?-1802?
Véritable origine des troubles de S. Domingue, et des différentes causes qui les ont produits; par M. Julien Raimond. Paris, Chez Desenne ₍etc.₎ 1792.
55p. 21½cm.

1. Santo Domingo (French Colony).
2. Haiti - History.

Raimond, Julien, 1743?-1802?

M910
C77f

Cook, Mercer.
Five French Negro authors, by Mercer Cook ... Washington, D. C., The Associated publishers, inc. ₍1943₎
xiv, 164 p. incl. front. ports. 19½ cm.
Bibliographical references included in "Notes" (p. 151-161)
CONTENTS.—Julien Raimond.—Charles Bissette.—Alexandre Dumas.—Auguste Lacaussade.—Rene Maran.

1. Raimond, Julien, 1743?-1802? 2. Bissette, Cyrille Charles Auguste, 1795-1858. 3. Dumas, Alexandre, 1802-1870. 4. Lacaussade, Auguste, 1817-1897. 5. Maran, René, 1887- 6. French literature—Hist. & crit. 7. Negro authors. I. Title.
₍Full name: Will Mercer Cook₎

Library of Congress PQ150.N4C6 43—13504
₍44j5₎ 840.903

Raimond, Julien, 1743?-1802?

Haiti
M972.94
M82d

₍Morpeau, Moravia₎ ed.
Documents inedits pour l'histoire. Correspondance concernant l'emprisonnement et la mort de Toussaint Louverture. Procesverbal de l'autopsie de son cadavre au Fort de Jouv (Jura) France et rapport des médecin et chirurg en memoire du commissaire Julien Raymond sur la colonie de Saint-Domingue au premier consul Bonaparte publiés par M. Morpeau. Port-au-Prince, Imprimerie et Librairie der Sacre Coeur, 1920.
16p. 23cm.

Raimond, Julien, 1743?-1802?

M972.94
N34p

Nemours, Alfred, 1883-
... Les premiers citoyens et les premiers députés noirs et de couleur; la lou du 4 avril 1792, ses précédents, sa première application à Saint-Domingue, d'après des documents inédits de l'époque. Suivi de : Le Cap Français en 1792, à l'arrivée de Sonthonax, d'après des documents inédits de l'époque. Port-au-Prince, Haiti, Impreimerie de l'état, 1941.
2p. l., 170p. plates. 23cm.

Brazil
M869.
R13e

Raimundo, Jacques.
... O elemento afro-negro na lingua portuguesa. Rio ₍de Janeiro₎ Renascença editora, 1933.
191, ₍2₎ p., 1 l. 18½cm. (*On cover:* Biblioteca pedagogica "Renascença")
"Bibliografia": p. ₍181₎-191.

1. Portuguese language—Foreign words and phrases—African. 2. Title.

Library of Congress PC5307.A6R3 37-19669
₍2₎ 469.24

Brazil
M869
R13n

Raimundo, Jacques.
... O negro brasileiro, e outros escritos. Rio ₍de Janiero₎ Record. 1936.
188p., 21 incl. front. 18½cm.

1. Brasil

Rain for the plains.

Jamaica
M823.91
H84r

Howland, Cicely.
Rain for the plains, and other stories by Cicely Howland. Kingston, Ja., Printed by the Gleaner co., ltd., 1943.
2 p. l., 189 p. 18cm.

I. Title.

New York. Public library for Library of Congress ₍2₎ A 45-4777

MB9
Su6c

Rainey, Joseph H ayne, 1832-1887
Eulogy on Charles Sumner.

(In: William M. Cornell. Charles Sumner: memoir and eulogies. Boston, J. H. Earles, 1874. pp.291-300.)

Africa, South
M896.2
H97r

The rain-killers.

Hutchinson, Alfred, 1924-
The rain-killers; a play in four acts. London, University of London Press ₍1964₎
80p. 19cm.

I. Title.

M326
An8s

Rainy, William
₍Address₎

(In: Anti-slavery Conference, Paris, 1867. Special report. London, Committee of the British and Foreign Anti-slavery Society 1867 Pp. 45-49)

M812.5 H19r3
Un raisin au soleil.
Hansberry, Lorraine, 1930-1965.
Un raisin au soleil. [A raisin in the sun]. Adaptation d'Emmanuel Robles d'après le texte français de Philippe Bonnière. Paris, Éditions Seghers, 1959.
216p. illus. 17½cm.
Portrait of author on back of book.
"For Arthur - Harlem, Langston Hughes, Paris, November 6, 1964"
I. Title.

Raleigh, North Carolina.
M301 C24
Carter, Wilmoth Annette, 1916-
The urban Negro in the South. [1st ed.] New York, Vantage Press [1962]
272 p. illus. 22 cm.
Includes bibliography.
1. Negroes—Raleigh, N. C. 2. Negroes as businessmen. I. Title.
F264.R1C3 301.451 62-4678 ‡
Library of Congress [5]

Trinidad
M972.9 T737
Rampersad, Frank
Growth and structural change in the economy of Trinidad and Tobago, 1951-1961.
Pp. 82-176.
In: Trinidad and Tobago. Central Statistical Office. Research paper, no. 1. Port-of-Spain, 1963.

M812.5 H19r
A raisin in the sun.
Hansberry, Lorraine, 1930-
A raisin in the sun; a drama in three acts. New York, Random House [1959]
142 p. illus. 21 cm. (A Random House play)
I. Title.
PS3515.A515R3 812.54 59-10834 ‡
Library of Congress [60x10]

Madagascar
M969.1 R142
Ramandraivonona, Désiré.
Le Malgache; sa langue, sa religion. Paris, Présence africaine [1959]
241 p. 9 illus. 25 cm.
"Bibliographie": p. [239]-241.
1. Malagasy language. 2. Madagascar—Religion. I. Title.
PL5379.R3 A 59-8219
Chicago. Univ. Libr. for Library of Congress [a60b½]†

Africa
M896 J193
Ramsaran, John.
Jahn, Janheinz
Approaches to African literature. Non-English writings, by Janheinz Jahn and English writings in West Africa, by John Ramsaran with reading lists. Ibadan, Ibadan University Press, 1959.
31p. 21½cm.
Includes bibliography.
White author.

M812.5 H19r 1959
A raisin in the sun.
Hansberry, Lorraine, 1930-
A raisin in the sun. New York, The New American Library, 1959.
126p. 18cm.

West Indies
M823 R144
Ramchand, Kenneth, *comp.*
West Indian narrative: an introductory anthology. London, Nelson, 1966.
xii, 226 p. illus. (ports.) 19½ cm. 12/6 (B 66-9785)
Includes excerpts from English novelists dealing with the West Indies.
Col. maps on endpapers.
White compiler.
Includes extracts from works by West Indian writers.
1. English fiction (Collections) 2. West Indies in literature. I. Title. II. Sherlock, Philip M Preface.
PZ1.R138We 66-74111
Library of Congress [5]

W. Indies
M523 R14s
Ramsay, Obadiah Anderson.
The sun has no heat, by Obadiah Anderson Ramsay. [New York, °1939]
5 p. l., 204 p. chart. 22cm.
1. Cosmology—Curiosa and miscellany. 2. Heat. 3. Sun. I. Title. 39-33950
Library of Congress QB52.R35
——— Copy 2.
Copyright A 134352 [2] 523.0683

M812.5 H19ra
A raisin in the sun.
Hansberry, Lorraine, 1930-
A raisin in the sun; a drama in three acts. London, Methuen & Co., Ltd., 1959.
107p. illus. 21cm. (A Random House play)

M973 R14
Ramos, Arthur, 1903-1949
... As culturas negras no novo mundo ... Rio de Janeiro, Civilização brasileira, s/a., 1937.
399p. illus. (maps) plates, diagr. 18½cm. (Bibliotheca de divulgação scientifica, sob a direcção de Arthur Ramos. vol. XII)
1. Soc. life & cust. 2. Religion. 3. Folk-lore
I. title

M781 R14br
Ramsey, Frederic, 1915-
Been here and gone. New Brunswick, N. J., Rutgers University Press [1960]
177 p. illus. 24 cm.
White author.
1. Music—~~Negroes~~ 2. ~~Negroes~~—Southern States. 3. Southern States—Soc. life & cust.—1865- —Illustrations. I. Title.
Full name: Charles Frederic Ramsey.
ML3556.R3 781.775 59—7514
Library of Congress [61e20]

M812.5 B46
A raisin in the sun.
Hansberry, Lorraine, 1930-
A raisin in the sun.
Pp. 232-254.
(In: The Best Plays. New York, Dodd, Mead, 1958-1959. 21cm.)

Brazil
M869 C21ar
Ramos, Arthur, 1903-1949.
Carneiro de Souza, Edison, 1912-
Arthur Ramos: Brazilian anthropologist (1903-1949). Tr. by James Ivy. Reprinted from Phylon, 12:73-81, first quarter, 1951.
73-81 p. 24 cm.

M781 R14j
Ramsey, Frederic, 1915- *ed.*
Jazzmen, edited by Frederic Ramsey, jr., and Charles Edward Smith. With 32 pages of illustrations. New York, Harcourt, Brace and company [1939]
xv, 360 p. plates, ports. 22 cm.
Contributors (in addition to the editors): William Russell, S. W. Smith, E. Simms Campbell, E. J. Nichols, Wilder Hobson, Otis Ferguson and R. P. Dodge.
"First edition."
White author.
1. Jazz music. 2. Negro musicians. 3. Musicians, American. I. Smith, Charles Edward, joint ed. II. Title.
Full name: Charles Frederic Ramsey.
ML3561.R24J2 780.973 39—31807
Library of Congress [59f2]

M630.7 C25r
The raising of hogs, one of the best ways to fill the empty dinner pail.
Carver, George Washington, 1864-1943.
The raising of hogs, one of the best ways to fill the empty dinner pail. Second edition, February 1940. Tuskegee Institute, Alabama, Tuskegee Institute press, 1935.
7p. 23cm. (Bulletin no.40, October 1935)

Brazil
M981 R14p
Ramos, Guerreiro
O problema nacional do Brasil. 2.ª edição. Rio, Editôra Saga, 1960.
262p. 23½cm.
1. Brazil. I. Title.

M813.5 R149
Ramsey, LeRoy L.
The trial and the fire. New York, Exposition Press c1967.
160p. 21cm.
Portrait of author on book cover.
I. Title.

Madagascar
M841 R13c
Rajaona, Henri
Cahnts des écoliers Malgaches, paroles de H. Rajaona, musique de J. Landeroin. Paris, Librairie Armand Colin, 1904.
41p. 16½cm.
1. French literature-Madagascan author.
2. Music-Madagascar.

Trinidad
M917.298 R14
Rampersad, Felix Alban
Trinidad, gem of the Caribbean. Port-of-Spain, Quick-Service Printing Co., n.d.
128p. illus. 21cm.
1. Trinidad - Description and Travel.
I. Title.

Madagascar
M843 B69s
Ranavalo III, Queen of Madagascar.
Boyer, Danika.
Sa majeste Ranavalo III, ma reine. Paris, Fasquelle Editeurs, 1946.
255 p. front (port.) 19 cm.

Ranch life.

MB9
W15b
Branch, Hettye (Wallace)
The story of "80 John," a biography of one of the most respected Negro ranchmen in the Old West. [1st ed.] New York, Greenwich Book Publishers [1960]
59 p. 22 cm.
Portrait on back of book jacket.

1. Wallace, Daniel Webster, 1860-1939. 2. Cattle trade—Mitchell Co., Tex. 3. Ranch life.
F392.M6B7 60-11709 ‡
Library of Congress [5]

M323
Su6
Randolph, Asa Philip, 1889-
Speech.
Pp. 29-34.
In: Summit Meeting of National Negro Leaders, Washington, D.C. Report. Washington, National Newspaper Publishers Association, 1958.

Random reveries.

Jamaica
M821.91
W15r
Wallace, George B.
Random reveries, by George B. Wallace. With an introduction by Hon. B. H. Easter... Jamaica, n.p., 1944.
98p. 20½cm.

Rançon du génie...

Haiti
MB9
T64b
Brutus, Timoléon C
Rançon du génie; ou, La leçon de Toussaint Louverture, par Timoléon C. Brutus ... Port-au-Prince, Haiti, N. A. Théodore, 1945-
v. plates, port. 22½cm. (On cover: Collection "Pro patria")
"Bibliographie des ouvrages lus ou consultés pour écrire Rançon du génie."—v. 1, p. [i]-iii (1st group)

1. Toussaint Louverture, Pierre Dominique, 1746?-1803. I. Title.
46-20686
Library of Congress F1923.T785
[2] 923.27294

MO6
N21r
Randolph, Asa Philip, 1889-
National Negro Congress.
Resolutions of the National Negro Congress held in Chicago, Ill. February 14, 15, 16, 1936. [n.p.] 1936.
19p. 21cm.

Random rhymes.

M811.5
D91
Dungee, John Riley, 1860-
Random rhymes, formal and dialect, serious and humorous, racial, religious, patriotic and sentimental, by J. Riley Dungee I. [Norfolk, Va., Guide publishing company, inc., printers] 1929.
101 p., 1 l. ports. 22cm.

I. Title.
Library of Congress PS3601.D6R3 1929 29-10055
Copyright A 6723 [2]

M811.08
R153
Randall, Dudley, 1914- comp.
For Malcolm; poems on the life and the death of Malcolm X. Edited by Dudley Randall and Margaret G. Burroughs. Pref. and eulogy by Ossie Davis. [1st ed.] Detroit, Broadside Press, 1967.
xxvi, 127 p. ports. 21 cm.
Bibliography: p. 113-120.

1. Little, Malcolm, 1925-1965—Poetry. I. Burroughs, Margaret G., 1917- joint comp. II. Title.
PS3568.A49F6 811'.008'03 66-28244
Library of Congress [3]

Randolph, Asa Philip, 1889-
The March on Washington Movement during World War II. pp. 75-78.

M323.4
W52
Westin, Alan F ed.
Freedom now! The civil-rights struggle in America. Edited by Alan F. Westin. New York, Basic Books [1964]
xv, 346 p. 22 cm.
Bibliography: p. [329]-341.

1. Negroes — Civil rights — Addresses, essays, lectures. 2. Civil rights—U. S.—Addresses, essays, lectures. I. Title.
E185.61.W54 301.451 64-17401
Library of Congress [5]

M252
R16
Rankin, Arthur Edward, 1879-
The call of the age; sermons and addresses, by Arthur E. Rankin ... Kansas City, The press of Thomas & Williams c1926
112p. port. 19cm.

1. Sermons.

Randall, Dudley, 1914-

M811.5
D23p
Danner, Margaret.
Poem counterpoem, by Margaret Danner and Dudley Randall. Detroit, Broadside Press, 1966.
24p. 16cm.

I. Randall, Dudley. II. Title.

MB9
J31
Randolph, Edwin Archer, 1854-
The life of Rev. John Jasper, pastor of Sixth Mt. Zion Baptist church, Richmond, Va.; from his birth to the present time, with his theory on the rotation of the sun. By E. A. Randolph, LL. B. Richmond, Va., R. T. Hill & co., 1884.
xii, 167 p. front. (port.) 19½cm.

1. Jasper, John, 1812-1901. 2. Negroes—Virginia.
12—10718
Library of Congress E185.97.J39
Copyright 1884: 7138 [a26c1]

MB9
L76r
Rankin, Arthur Edward, 1879-
Livingstone returned; the story of a measureless labor of love. With an introd. by G. Lake Imes. [1st ed.] New York, Exposition Press [1955]
131 p. 21 cm.

1. Livingstone, David, 1813-1873. I. Title.
DT731.L8R3 923.942 55-9409 ‡
Library of Congress [2]

M342
R15
Randolph, Asa Philip, 1889-
Chart and compass.
(In: Wiso, James W. Our Bill of rights: what it means to me, ... New York, Bill of Rights Sesqui-centennial Committee, 1941. pp. 112-113.)

I. a.t. Wiso. II. t. Our Bill of rights. 1. Liberty III. Bill of Rights Sesqui-Centennial Committee, 1941.

M176
R15
Randolph, Paschal Beverly, 1825-1874.
... Magia sexualis. Traduction français, par Maria de Naglowska. Edition originale. Paris, R. Télin, 1931.
218p., 1 l. illus., plates (incl. music, port. col.) port., fold. tables. 23cm.
At head of title: P.B. Randolph.
1. Sexuals ethics. 2. Occult sciences.
I. Naglooskaea, tr. II. Title.

Rankin, Jeremiah Eames, 1828-1904.

M815.4
L26
Langston, John Mercer, 1829-1897.
Freedom and citizenship. Selected lectures and addresses of Hon. John Mercer Langston ... With an introductory sketch by Rev. J. E. Rankin ... Washington, D. C., R. H. Darby, 1883.
286 p. front. (port.) 20cm.

1. Negroes. 2. U. S.—Pol. & govt.—1865-1898. I. Rankin, Jeremiah Eames, 1828-1904. II. Title.
15—10680
Library of Congress E185.6.L28
Copyright 1883: 19154 [40b1]

M346
R21p
Randolph, Asa Philip, 1889-
Conciliation and arbitration.
(In: Proceedings of the National Conference of Social Work, 1939. New York, Columbia University, 1939. 24cm. p.216-225)

1. Industrial relations.

M326.99B
R15f
Randolph, Peter, d.1897
From slave cabin to the pulpit. The autobiography of Rev. Peter Randolph: the southern question illustrated and sketches of slave life. Boston, James H. Earle, 1893.
220p. front. 19½cm.

1. Slave narratives. 2. Plantation. I. Title.

M812.5
R160
Rankin, Wilfred.
Ovans L. aemilius paulus urbem ingreditur, a play in two acts. n.p. [193]
10p. 28cm.
Mimeographed.

1. Latin drama.

M323.4
W52
Randolph, Asa Philip, 1889-
Jobs for Negroes - the unfinished revolution.
pp. 104-110.
In: Westin, Alan F. Freedom now. New York, Basic Books, 1964.

M326.99B
R15s
1855
Randolph, Peter, d.1897.
Sketches of slave life: or, Illustrations of the 'peculiar Institution.' By Peter Randolph, an emancipated slave. Boston, Pub. for the author, 1855.
35p. 20cm.

1. Plantation life. 2. Slave narratives. I. Title.

M343.3
R17b
Ransom, Leon Andrew, 1898-
Brief submitted to the United States Department of Justice in order to persuade the Federal government to take action against those guilty of the lynching of Dan Pippen and A. T. Harden at Tuscaloosa, Alabama, in August 1933, after the State authorities failed to do so, signed by Leon A. Ransom, Charles H. Houston, and Edward P. Lovett. New York, National Association for the Advancement of Colored People, 1933.
47p. 23cm.
1. Lynching-- Alabama.

M323
R14m
Ransom, Reverdy Cassius, bp., 1861-
The Negro; the hope or the despair of Christianity, by Bishop Reverdy C. Ransom ... Boston, Mass., Ruth Hill, publisher [°1935]
7 p. l., 98 p. 20½cm.
"A word" signed: W. E. B. Du Bois. "Preface" signed: R. R. Wright, jr.
Several of the articles are addresses.
1. Negroes. A 38—540
New York. Public library for Library of Congress BR563.N4R3
[a48c1]† 325.260973

M815.5
R17s
Ransome, Reverdy Cassius, 1861-
The spirit of freedom and justice; orations and speeches, by Reverdy C. Ransom. Nashville, Tenn., A.M.E. Sunday School Union, 1926.
175p. portraits, 23cm.
1. Orations. I. Title.

Ras Bravado.
M813.5
P16r
Paisley, John Walter.
Ras Bravado, by J. W. Paisley. Boston, The Christopher publishing house [°1938]
2 p. l., 7-146 p. 20½cm.
I. Title. 38-12835
Library of Congress PZ3.P1673Ras
——— Copy 2.
Copyright A 117732 [3]

M814.5
W89
Ransom, Reverdy Cassius, 1861-
The Negro, the hope or despair of Christianity.
(In: World Fellowship of Faiths. International Congress. 1st, Chicago and New York, 1933-1934. Addresses... New York, Liveright Publishing Corporation [1935] cm. p. 316-322.)

M286
R17c
Ransome, William Lee, 1879-
Christian stewardship and Negro Baptists, by W. L. Ransome ... Richmond, Virginia, National ministers' institute, Virginia union university. Richmond, Va., Brown print shop, inc., 1934.
198 p. 20cm.
"A short bibliography": p. 190.
1. Stewardship, Christian. 2. Baptists, Negro. 3. Baptists—Missions. I. National ministers' institute, Virginia. Union university, Richmond. II. Title.
36-30056
Library of Congress BV772.R25
——— Copy 2. [3] 254

Rapport sur la doctrine et le programme du parti.
Sénégal
M966.3
Se5ra
Senghor, Léopold Sédar, 1906-
Rapport sur la doctrine et le programme du parti. Paris, Présence Africaine, 1959.
90p. 20cm. (Congrès Constitutif Du P.F.A. Dakar, 1-3 Juillet 1959).

MB9
D91d
Ransom, Reverdy Cassius, 1861-
The New Negro [poem]
23 x 14cm.
Broadside.
Bound with - Dunbar, A.R.M.-
Paul Laurence Dunbar...

M252
R17o
Ransome, William Lee, 1879-
An old story for this new day and other sermons and addresses. Richmond, Central Publishing co., 1954.
207p. 20cm.
1. Sermons. I. Title.

Virgin Is.
M813.5
R18f
Rasmussen, Emil Michael, 1893-
The first night. New York, W. Malliet, 1947.
278 p. 24 cm.
I. Title.
PZ3.R1848Fi 50-55519
Library of Congress [2]

MB9
R17p
Ransom, Reverdy Cassius, Bp., 1861-
The pilgrimage of Harriet Ransom's son. Nashville, Sunday School Union [1949]
336 p. port. 23 cm.
Autobiography.
I. Title.
BX8473.R25A3 922.773 51-27687
Library of Congress [1]

Nigeria
M784
R17a
Ransome-Kuti, Josaiah Jesse, 1855-1930.
Awọn orin mimọ ni ede ati Ohùn Ilẹ Wa. Yoruba sacred songs. Lagos, C.M.S. Bookshop, 1925.
Pp. 556-617 18½cm.
Translation: A series of sacred songs in the language and the tone of our land.
1. Nigeria-Songs. 2. Yoruba-Songs. I. Title: A series of sacred songs.

M811.5
R125b
Ratcliff, Theodore P.
Black forever more by Theodore P. Ratcliff... Okolona, Miss., Okolona industrial school, 1939.
36p. port. 23cm.
Inscribed copy: Compliments, T.P. Ratcliff.
1. Poetry. I. Title.

M378W
R17s
Ransom, Reverdy Cassius, bp, 1861-
School days at Wilberforce, by Reverdy C. Ransom. [Springfield Ohio, The New Era Co., 1892]
66p. front., port. 20½cm.
1. Wilberforce University, Xenia, Ohio.

Nigeria
MB9
R17
Ransome-Kuti, Josaiah Jesse, 1855-1930.
Delano, Isaac O
The singing minister of Nigeria; the life of the Rev. Canon J. J. Ransome-Kuti, by Isaac O. Delano ... London, United society for Christian literature [1942]
63, [1] p. 18½cm. (Half-title: Africa's own library, no. 2)
1. Ransome-Kuti, Josaiah Jesse, 1855-1930. 2. Missions — Nigeria. I. United society for Christian literature, London. II. Title.
44-35818
Library of Congress BV3625.N6R3
[2] 922

Ratoon.
Guyana
M823.91
N54r
Nicole, Christopher.
Ratoon. New York, St. Martin's Press [1962]
256 p. 22 cm.
I. Title.
PZ4.N6425Rat 62-11111 ‡
Library of Congress [5]

Ransom, Reverdy Cassius, bp., 1861- ed.
M280
Y33
Year book of Negro churches, with statistics and records of achievements of Negroes in the United States ... 1935/36-
Wilberforce, O., Printed at Wilberforce university [19
v. 22½cm.
Editor: 1935/36- Reverdy C. Ransom.
"Published by authority of the bishops of the A. M. E. church."
1. Negroes. 2. Negroes—Religion. 3. Churches—U. S. 4. Negroes—Stat. I. Ransom, Reverdy Cassius, bp., 1861- ed. II. African Methodist Episcopal church. III. Title: Negro churches, Year book of.
37—22490
Library of Congress E185.7.Y43
[44e1] 325.260973

M811.4
W59r
The rape of Florida.
Whitman, Albery Allson, 1851-1901.
The rape of Florida, by Albery A. Whitman. St. Louis, Nixon - Jones Printing Co. 1884.
95p. front. 19cm.

Rauschenbusch, Walter, 1861-1918.
M260
M45g
Mays, Benjamin Elijah, 1895- comp.
A gospel for the social awakening; selections from the writings of Walter Rauschenbusch, compiled by Benjamin E. Mays, with an introd. by C. Howard Hopkins. New York, Association Press, 1950.
187p. 20cm. (A. Haddam House book)
Bibliography: p. [6]

Ransom, Reverdy Cassius, 1861-
M811.4
D899d
Dunbar, Alice Ruth Moore, 1875-
Paul Laurence Dunbar, poet Laureate of the Negro race, by Mrs. Paul Laurence Dunbar, W. S. Scarborough and Reverdy C. Ransom. Reprinted from The A.M.E. Church Review. Philadelphia, Pa.
32p. portraits. 23cm.

M301
R27sh
Raper, Arthur Franklin, 1899- jt. auth.
Reid, Ira DeAugustine, 1901-
Sharecroppers all by Arthur F. Raper and Ira DeA. Reid. Chapel Hill, The University of North Carolina press, 1941.
xp., 2l., 3-281p. front. plates. 21½cm.

The raven.
M813.5
W67
Williams, Chancellor.
The raven, by Chancellor Williams. Philadelphia, Dorrance and company [1943]
2 p. l., iii-iv p., 1 l., 7-562 p. 28½ cm.
A novel.
1. Poe, Edgar Allan, 1809-1849—Fiction. I. Title.
43-17566
Library of Congress PZ3.W67143Rav
[5]

M974.7 R21
Ray, Archibald
All shook up, as told to Archibald Ray. New York, Agapé Books, 1958.

96p. 15½cm.

1. Harlem, New York - Politics and government. I. Title.

Ray, Charles B.

M974.7 W93a
Wright, Theodore Sedgewick.
An address to the three thousand colored citizens of New York who are the owners of one hundred and twenty thousand acres of land in the state of New York, given to them by Gerrit Smith... September 1, 1846. New York n.p. 1846.

20p. 23cm.

M811.4 R21
Ray, Henriette Cordelia, 1850-1916
Poems, by H. Cordelia Ray. New York, The Grafton press, 1910.
ix, [5]-169 p. 19½cm. $1.00

1. Poetry.

11-9931 Revised
Library of Congress PS3535.A87P6 1910
Copyright A 286137 [r22d2]

M323. R21
Raymond, Harry.
Dixie comes to New York; Story of the Freeport GI slayings. Introduction by Benjamin J. Davis, Jr. New York, Daily Worker, 1946.

14p. illus. 19cm.

1. New York, I. Davis, Benjamin Jefferson, 1903- II. Title.

M343.3 R21i
Raymond, Harry.
The Ingrams shall not die! story of Georgia's new terror; introduction by Benjamin J. Davis. N.Y., Daily Worker, 1948.

14p. ports. 18cm.

White author

1. Ingram, Rosa Lee. 2. Georgia. 3. Civil rights, Denial of. I. Davis Benjamin Jefferson, 1903-

---

M343.3 R21s
Raymond, Harry.
Save Willie McGee. New York, New Century, 1951.

14p. 19cm.

White author.

1. McGee, Willie. 2. Mississippi. 3. Civil rights, Denial of. I. Title.

Rays of heavenly light, Church of God...

M245 R56r
Robinson, Archibald Boaz, 1900-

Rays of heavenly light, Church of God holiness hymnal; written for the national convention of Churches of God, Holiness, by Elder A. B. Robinson ... Asheville, N. C., 1941.
xi, 2-75, xii-xxvii, [84] p. 21cm.
Music: [84] p. at end.

1. Churches of God, Holiness—Hymns. 2. Hymns, English. I. Title

42-684
Library of Congress M2131.C8R6 [2] 783.9

The reaction of Negro publications and organizations to German anti-Semitism.

M07 W41
Wedlock, Lunabelle.
... The reaction of Negro publications and organizations to German anti-Semitism, by Lunabelle Wedlock, M. A. Washington, D. C., The Graduate school, Howard university, 1942.
4 p. l., [7]-208 p. 23½ cm. (The Howard university studies in the social sciences, vol. III, no. 2)

1. Negroes. 2. Jewish question. 3. Jews in Germany. I. Title.

43-431
Library of Congress H31.H66 vol. 3, no. 2
[48f1] (308.2) 325.260973

M89 B23r
Reade, Aleyn Lyell, 1876-
Johnsonian gleanings, by Aleyn Lyell Reade. Pt. II. Francis Barber, The doctor's Negro servant. London, Privately printed for the author at the Arden Press, 1912.

10p. 1 132p. front. ports. 22cm.
Contains letters written by Francis Barber.

1. Johnson, Samuel, 1709-1784. 2. Barber, Francis, d 1801.

Nigeria M896.3 Aj74
Readers - 1950-
Ajose, Audrey.
Yomi in Paris; with drawings by Mick Pilcher. Cambridge, Cambridge U. P., 1966.
87 p. illus. 18½ cm. 4/-
(B 66-12458)

1. English language—Text-books for foreigners. 2. Readers—1950- I. Title.

PE1128.A43 428.644 66-73973
Library of Congress [5]

Nigeria M896.3 Ek8t
Readers-1950-
Ekwensi, Cyprian. Odiatu Duaka, 1921-
Trouble in Form Six; drawings by Prue Theobalds. Cambridge, Cambridge U. P., 1966.
78 p. illus. 18½ cm. 3/6
(B 66-4075)

1. Readers—1950- I. Title.

PE1121.E55 428.64 66-10246
Library of Congress [5]

Readers - 1950-

Jamaica M327.4 Sa34
Salkey, Andrew.
The shark hunters; illustrated by Peter Kesteven. London, Nelson, 1966.
vi, 74 p. illus. 21½ cm. (Rapid reading) 4/-
(B 67-4805)

1. Readers—1950- I. Title.

PE1121.S28 67-88098
Library of Congress [3]

Readers and speakers—1870-

M313.5 C16
Cannon, Elizabeth Perry.
Country life stories, some rural community helpers, by Elizabeth Perry Cannon ... & Helen Adele Whiting ... introduction by Mabel Carney ... illustrated by Vernon Winslow ... New York, E. P. Dutton & co., inc., 1938.
xiii, [2], 17-95 p. incl. col. front., illus. (part col.) 19½cm.
"This book is intended to serve as a social studies reader for pupils on the elementary level in small rural schools."—Foreword.
"First edition."

1. Readers and speakers—1870- I. Whiting, Helen Adele, joint author. II. Title.

38-9190
Library of Congress PE1127.F4C3
[3] [323.354] 372.4

Readers and speakers-1870-

M815 N33d
Nelson, Alice Ruth (Moore) Dunbar, 1875-1930, *ed.*
The Dunbar speaker and entertainer, containing the best prose and poetic selections by and about the Negro race, with programs arranged for special entertainments ed. by Alice Moore Dunbar-Nelson, with an introduction by Leslie Pinckney Hill ... Naperville, Ill., J. L. Nichols & co. [°1920]
288 p. front., illus., plates, ports. 21½ cm.

1. Readers and speakers—1870-

20—21507
Library of Congress PN4305.N5N4
[41f1]

Readers and speakers-1870-

M810.8 P93
Pritchard, Myron Thomas, 1853- *comp.*
The upward path; a reader for colored children with an introduction by Robert R. Moton ... comp. by Myron T. Pritchard ... and Mary White Ovington ... New York, Harcourt, Brace and Howe [°1920]
xi, [1], 255 p. incl. front., illus. 19½cm.

1. Readers and speakers—1870- I. Ovington, Mary White, 1865- joint comp. II. Title. III. Title: Colored children, Reader for.

20—16516
Library of Congress PE1126.N3P8
Copyright A 597468 [41o1]

Readers and speakers—1870-

M973. W86 am
Woodson, Carter Godwin, 1875-
African myths, together with proverbs; a supplementary reader composed of folk tales from various parts of Africa, adapted to the use of children in the public schools, by Carter Godwin Woodson ... Washington, D. C., The Associated publishers, inc. [°1928]
xv, 184 p. incl. front., illus. 19½cm.

1. Tales, African. 2. Readers and speakers—1870- I. Title.

29—1210
Library of Congress PE1127.G4W7
[44o2]

Senegal M808.8 D67
Readers and speakers - Text-books - Africa.
Diboti, Max Ekoka, ed.
Voix d'Afrique ... échos du monde; livre de lecture, cours moyen classes terminales [par] M. Diboti Ekoka [et] Richard Dogbeh. Illustrations de Tanguy de Rémur. Paris, Librairie Istra [1965]

255p. illus. 21½cm.

1. Readers and speakers - Text-books - Africa. 2. French language - Readers and speakers - Africa. I. Dogveh, Richard, jt. ed. II. Title.

Nigeria M372.4 At47 Bk 1
Readers and speakers - Yoruba language.
Atilade, Emmanuel Adekunle, 1911-
Akoka Yoruba, Apa I. [Lagos, Ife Olu Printing Works [n.d.]

32p. illus. 18cm.

Nigeria M372.4 At47 Bk. 3
Readers and speakers - Yoruba language.
Atilade, Emmanuel Adekunle, 1911-
Akoka Yoruba, Apa keta. Lagos, New Nigeria Press [1962]

96p. illus. 21cm.
Written in Yoruba.

M810.8 R26
The Reader's companion to world literature. Editor: Lillian Herlands Hornstein; co-editor: G. D. Percy [and others] General editor: Calvin S. Brown. [New York] New American Library [1956]
493 p. 18 cm. (A Mentor book, MD179)

1. Literature—Dictionaries. 2. Literature—Bio-bibl. 3. Literature—Hist. & crit. ~~I. Hornstein, Lillian Herlands, 1909- ed.~~ I. Brown, Sterling, 1901-

PN41.R4 803 56—13345 ‡
Library of Congress [57o5]

M808.81 R228
The Reader's digest.
Reader's digest condensed books. spring 1950-

Pleasantville, N. Y.
v. 20 cm. quarterly.
Partial contents.- Up from slavery, by Booker T. Washington, Autumn, 1960.- To Sir with love, by E. R. Braithwaite, Spring, 1963.

I. Title.

AP2.R2553 051 50—19721
Library of Congress [57r*2]

M808.81
R228

Reader's digest condensed books.

The Reader's digest.
Reader's digest condensed books. spring 1950–
Pleasantville, N. Y.
v. 20 cm. quarterly.

I. Title.

AP2.R2553 051 50—12721
Library of Congress ₍67f²8₎

M370.
G61r

₍Reading—Tests and scales₎

Goodlett, Carlton Benjamin.
... The reading abilities of the Negro elementary school child in Kanawha county, West Virginia ... ₍by₎ Carlton B. Goodlett ... and Andrew H. Calloway ... Institute, W. Va. ₍1940₎
47 p. incl. tables. 23ᶜᵐ. (West Virginia state college ₍bulletin₎ Aug.–Nov. 1940. Ser. 5)
"Contribution no. 10, the Department of education."
"Publication of West Virginia state college."
1. Reading (Elementary) ₍1. Reading—Tests and scales₎ 2. Negroes—Education. 3. Public schools—West Virginia—Kanawha co. ₍3. Kanawha co., W. Va.—Schools₎ I. Calloway, Andrew H., joint author. II. Title.
E 41-54
U. S. Off. of educ. Library for Library of Congress LB1573.G57 ₍3₎† 371.974

M370.
G61r

Reading (Elementary)

Goodlett, Carlton Benjamin.
... The reading abilities of the Negro elementary school child in Kanawha county, West Virginia ... ₍by₎ Carlton B. Goodlett ... and Andrew H. Calloway ... Institute, W. Va. ₍1940₎
47 p. incl. tables. 23ᶜᵐ. (West Virginia state college ₍bulletin₎ Aug.–Nov. 1940. Ser. 5)
"Contribution no. 10, the Department of education."
"Publication of West Virginia state college."
1. Reading (Elementary) ₍1. Reading—Tests and scales₎ 2. Negroes—Education. 3. Public schools—West Virginia—Kanawha co. ₍3. Kanawha co., W. Va.—Schools₎ I. Calloway, Andrew H., joint author. II. Title.
E 41-54
U. S. Off. of educ. Library for Library of Congress LB1573.G57 ₍3₎† 371.974

M370.
G61r

... The reading abilities of the Negro elementary child...
Goodlett, Carlton Benjamin.
... The reading abilities of the Negro elementary school child in Kanawha county, West Virginia... ₍by₎ Carlton B. Goodlett... and Andrew H. Calloway... Institute, W. Va. ₍1940₎
47p. incl. tables. 23cm. (West Va. state college ₍bulletin₎ Aug.- Nov. 1940. Ser. 5)

M378.
D22

The reading interests and needsof Negro college.

Daniel, Walter Green, 1905–
The reading interests and needs of Negro college freshmen regarding social science materials, by Walter Green Daniel ... New York, Teachers college, Columbia university, 1942.
2 p. l., vii–xii p., 1 l., 128 p. incl. tables. 23½ᶜᵐ. (Teachers college, Columbia university. Contributions to education, no. 862)
Bibliography: p. ₍101₎–105. "Titles with authors included in the check list of books relating to social science problems": p. 125–128.
1. Books and reading. 2. Social sciences. 3. Negroes—Education. I. Title.
43—3715
Library of Congress H62.D23
——— Copy 2. LB5.C8 no. 862
₍43k5₎ 307.11753

M810.8
C88

Readings from Negro authors...

Cromwell, Otelia ed.
Readings from negro authors, for schools and colleges, with a bibliography of negro literature, by Otelia Cromwell ... Lorenzo Dow Turner ... Eva B. Dykes ... New York, Harcourt, Brace and company ₍°1931₎
xii, 388 p. 21ᶜᵐ.
"A bibliography of negro literature": p. 371–383; contains "Collateral reading."
1. Negro literature (American) 2. Negro literature (American)—Bibl. 3. American literature—Negro authors. I. Turner, Lorenzo Dow, joint ed. II. Dykes, Eva Beatrice, joint ed. III. Title.
31—31497
Library of Congress PS508.N3C7 ₍a45m1₎ 810.8

M309.1
W934

Ready to riot.

Wright, Nathan.
Ready to riot. ₍1st ed.₎ New York, Holt, Rinehart and Winston ₍1968₎
148 p. illus., maps. 22 cm.
Bibliographical footnotes.
1. Newark, N. J.—Soc. condit. 2. Negroes—Newark, N. J. I. Title.
HN80.N685W74 309.1'749'32 68-12218
Library of Congress ₍15-2₎

M813.5
H57r

The Real cool killers.
Himes, Chester B , 1909-
The real cool killers. Avon original.
New York, Avon Publications, Inc., 1959.

160p. 18cm.

I. Title.

M331.833
L85p

Real covenants - U.S.

Long, Herman Hodge.
People vs. property; race restrictive covenants in housing ₍by₎ Herman H. Long ₍and₎ Charles S. Johnson. Nashville, Fisk Univ. Press, 1947.
ix, 107 p. maps, diagrs. 21 cm.
Bibliographical footnotes.
1. Negroes — Housing. 2. Negroes — Segregation. 3. Real covenants—U. S. I. Johnson, Charles Spurgeon, 1893– joint author. II. Title.
E185.89.H6L7 325.260973 48—5905*
Library of Congress ₍48x10₎

Nigeria
M333
Ek34

Real property - Nigeria.
Ekineh, Aliyi.
You and your landlord and you and the law of libel and slander. Lagos, Megida Printers and Publishers ₍c1961.

50p. 22½cm. (Megida legal guide series, no.1)

Nigeria
M966.9
E14n
1962

Real property - Nigeria.

Elias, Taslim Olawale. 3d ed.
Nigerian land law and custom. ₍London, Routledge & K. Paul ₍~~1951~~₎ 1962
xxvii, ~~326~~ 386 p. map. 23 cm.
Thesis—University of London.
Includes legislation.
Bibliography: p. 316–319.
1. Land tenure—Nigeria—Law. 2. Real property—Nigeria. I. Nigeria. Laws, statutes, etc. II. Title.
333.3 52—28040
Library of Congress ₍53e3₎

Nigeria
M966.9
E14n

Real Property - Nigeria .

Elias, Taslim Olawale.
Nigerian land law and custom. London, Routledge & K. Paul ₍1951₎
xxvii, 326 p. map. 23 cm.
Thesis—University of London.
Includes legislation.
Bibliography: p. 316–319.
1. Land tenure—Nigeria—Law. 2. Real property—Nigeria. I. Nigeria. Laws, statutes, etc. II. Title.
333.3 52—28040
Library of Congress ₍53e3₎

Malawi
M968.97
C44r

Realities of African independence.

Chisiza, Dunduza Kaluli.
Realities of African independence. ₍London₎ Africa Publications Trust ₍1961₎
24 p. 22 cm.
1. Africa. I. Title.
DT30.C5 61–65260 ‡
Library of Congress ₍2₎

M811.5
W33

Reap the Harvest.

Watson, Nana.
Reap the harvest. New York, William-Frederick Press, 1952.
31 p. 22 cm. (The William-Frederick poets: 95)
I. Title.
PS3545.A8728R4 811.5 52-11783 ‡
Library of Congress ₍1₎

M811.5
R23p

Reason, Arthur Wesley, 1887-
Poems of inspiration for better living.
New York, Exposition Press, 1959.

97p. 20½cm.
Portrait of author on book jacket.

1. Poetry, American. I. Title.

M326
G87a
1854

Reason, Charles Lewis, 1818-1893
The colored people's industrial college.

(In: Griffiths, Julia ed. Autographs for freedom. Auburn, Alden, Beardsley, 1854. 19½cm. Pp. 11-15).

MB9
C56c

Reason, Charles L. Freedom, a poem.
Crummell, Alexander.
The man, the hero, the christian! A eulogy on the life and character of Thomas Clarkson, delivered in the city of New York, December, 1846, by the Rev. Alexander Crummell, together with Freedom, a poem, read in the same occasion by M. Charles L. Reason. New York, Egbert, Hovey E. King, printers, 1847.

M326
G87a
1854

Reason, Charles Lewis, 1818-1893
Hope and confidence, ₍poem₎ .

(In: Griffiths, Julia ed. Autographs for freedom. Auburn, Alden, Beardsley, 1854. 19½cm. Pp. 226-229).

MB9
C79r

Reason, Charles Lewis, 1818-1893
Coppin, Fanny Jackson, 1837-1913
Reminiscences of school life, and hints on teaching, by Fanny Jackson Coppin. Introduction by William C. Bolivar. ₍Philadelphia, Pa., A.M.E. Book Concern, 1913₎

191p. port (front.) 20½cm.
Introduction by William C. Bolivar.

MB9
Sh2s

Reason, Patrick.
Stuart, Charles.
A memoir of Granville Sharp, to which is added Sharp's "Law of retribution," By Charles Stuart. New York, American anti-slavery society ₍1836₎

156p. front. 19cm.

M326.
L61

Reason, Patrick, Truth shall make you free. (Engraving)
The Liberty bell. By friends of freedom .. Boston, Massachusetts anti-slavery fair, 1839–46; National anti-slavery bazaar, 1847–58.
15 v. plates, ports. 17½–20ᶜᵐ.
"Edited and published annually in Boston, by Maria Weston Chapman, 1848 to 1858 (one or two years being omitted)"—Samuel May, Catalogue of anti-slavery publications in America.
No volumes issued for 1840, 1850, 1854–55, 1857. *cf.* Faxon, Literary annuals and gift books.
Volume for 1841 wanting in L. C. set.
1. Slavery in the U. S. 2. Gift-books (Annuals, etc.) I. Chapman, Maria (Weston) 1806–1885, ed. II. Massachusetts anti-slavery fair. III. National anti-slavery bazaar, Boston.
5—22887
Library of Congress E449.L69 ₍43l1₎

M304
P19
v.6, no.4

The reasons why the colored man is not in the World's Columbian Exposition. The Afro-American's contribution to Columbian literature. Introduction by Frederick Douglass. ⌜Chicago, Ill., 1893⌟
81p. 19cm.

Nigeria
M896.4
Ok5r

The rebel line.
Okoye, Mokwugo, 1926-
The rebel line; memoirs of revolutionary struggle and a penetrating study of life and literature with moving panegyrics on love and liberty. ⌜Onitsha, Nigeria, Etudo Limited, 1962⌟
111p. 21cm.

M811.5
C55r

Rebellion in rhyme.
Clarke, John Henrik.
Rebellion in rhyme, by John Henrik Clarke. Prairie City, The Decker press ⌜1948⌟
105p. 22cm.

M910
W67r

The rebirth of African civilization.
Williams, Chancellor.
The rebirth of African civilization. Washington, Public Affairs Press ⌜1961⌟
328 p. 24 cm.
Includes bibliography.

1. Africa, Sub-Saharan—Civilization. I. Title.

DT352.W5 916.7 61-11689 ‡
Library of Congress ⌜5⌟

M811.5
W85

Recaptured echoes.
Wood, Odella Phelps.
Recaptured echoes, by Odella Phelps Wood. New York, The Exposition press ⌜1944⌟
64 p. 19½cm. (Poets of America. Series four)

I. Title.

Library of Congress * PS3545.O484R4 45-166
⌜3⌟ 811.5

M640
R54h
1843

Receipts.
Roberts, Robert.
The house servant's directory. Or, A monitor for private families: comprising hints on the arrangement and performance of servants' work ... and upwards of 100 useful receipts, chiefly comp. for the use of house servants ... By Robert Roberts ... ⌜2d ed.⌟ Boston, Munroe and Francis; New York, C. S. Francis, 1828.
xiv, ⌜15⌟-180 p. 18½cm.

1. Servants. 2. Receipts. I. Title.

Library of Congress TX331.R64 7—28299
⌜a23c1⌟.

M640
R54h
1828

Receipts.
Roberts, Robert
The house servant's directory. Or, a monitor for private families: comprising hints on the arrangement and perfprmance of servant's work... and upwards of 100 useful receipts, chiefly compiled for the use of house servants... Boston, Munroe and Francis; New York, Charles S. Francis, 1828.
180p. 17½cm.

M640
R54h
1827

Receipts.
Roberts, Robert.
The house servant's directory. Or, A monitor for private families: comprising hints on the arrangement and performance of servants' work ... and upwards of 100 useful receipts, chiefly comp. for the use of house servants ... By Robert Roberts ... ⌜2d ed.⌟ Boston, Munroe and Francis; New York, C. S. Francis, 1828.
xiv, ⌜15⌟-180 p. 18½cm.

1. Servants. 2. Receipts. I. Title.

Library of Congress TX331.R64 7—28299
⌜a23c1⌟

Senegal
M641.5
Sa18

Recettes culinaires Sénégalaises.
Sagna, Anna
Recettes culinaires Sénégalaises. Dakar, Société Africaine d'Édition ⌜n.d.⌟
48p. 21½cm.

1. Cookery, Senegalese. I. Title.

Dahomey
M960
V66

A la recherche de la personnalité Négro-Africaine...
Viderot, Toussaint
A la recherche de la personnalité Négro-Africaine; Tu gagneras ton pain à la sueuer de ton front. Monte-Carol, Éditions Regain ⌜1960⌟
216p. illus. 21½cm.

Africa
M960
As6a

Recherches et debats du Centre Catholique des Intellectuels Francais. Nouvelle série, no.24.
Aspects de la culture noire ⌜by⌟ Genevieve Calame-Griaule, François Agblemagnon ⌜and others⌟ Paris, Librairie Arthème Fayard ⌜1958⌟
218p. 19½cm.

Guinea
M966.24
N51r

Recherches sur l'empire du Mali au Moyen Âge.
Niane, Djibril Tamsir
Recherches sur l'empire du Mali au Moyen Âge. Conakry, Institut National de Recherches et de Documentation, 1962.
70p. 24cm.

1. Mai - History. I. Title.

Haiti
M972.94
B54p

Recidivists—Haiti.
Bistoury, André F
... Preuve de la récidive et police scientifique. Port-au-Prince, Haïti, 1946.
8 p. l., 9-152 p., 4 l. illus. (incl. ports.) diagrs. 21½cm.

1. Recidivists—Haiti. I. Title.

HV6049.B5 364.32 47-22196
Library of Congress ⌜1⌟

Jamaica
M822.91
R24y

Reckford, Barry
You in your small corner; a play. London ⌜n.p., n.d.⌟
⌜56⌟ leaves. 22cm.
"To Arthur Spingarn with great respect & affection. Barry Reckford."
Mimeographed.

I. Title.

Haiti
M842.
H52r

...La reclamation Hopton...
Hibbert, Fernand.
...La reclamation Hopton, Comédie en deux actes, par Fernand Hibbert. Port-au-Prince, Imprimerie de l'abeille, 1916.
68p. 19cm. (:Supplément de la revue de la ligue de la jeunesse Haitienne, 20 avril 1916)

M972.9A
As70
1789

Réclamations des Nègres libres, colons Américains. ⌜Lacks imprint⌟
3p. 21cm.
Signed: Les Nègres libres, Colons Américains.

1. Santo Domingo - French colonies.
I. Assemblée des Citoyens de Couleur, des Isles et Colonies Françoises, Paris.
II. Les Negres Libres, Colons Américains.

MB9
P29r

Recollections of seventy years.
Payne, Daniel Alexander, 1811-1893.
Recollections of seventy years; by Bishop Daniel Alexander Payne ... With an introduction by Rev. F. J. Grimke ... Comp. and arranged by Sarah C. Bierce Scarborough. Ed. by Rev. C. S. Smith. Nashville, Tenn., Publishing house of the A. M. E. Sunday school union, 1888.
335 p. pl., 8 port. (incl. front.) 19cm.

1. African Methodist Episcopal church. I. Scarborough, Sarah C. Bierce, comp. II. Smith, Charles Spencer, 1852- ed. III. Title.

14-12737
Library of Congress E185.97.P34

Haiti
M843.91
M83r

Recolte.
Morisseau-Leroy, Felix, 1912-
Recolte, Port-au-Prince, Les Editions Haitiennes, 1946.
146p. 20cm.

M973.8
B439

Reconstruction.
Bennett, Lerone, 1928-
Black Power, U. S. A., the human side of Reconstruction, 1867-1877. ⌜1st ed.⌟ Chicago, Johnson Pub. Co., 1967.
401 p. illus., ports. 24 cm.
Bibliography: p. 390-393.
Portrait of author on book jacket.

1. ~~Negroes~~—Hist.—1863-1877. I. Title.
2. Reconstruction.
E185.2.B38 973.8 67—28229
Library of Congress ⌜68f5⌟

M301
D853b

Reconstruction.
Du Bois, William Edward Burghardt, 1868-
Black reconstruction; an essay toward a history of the part which black folk played in the attempt to reconstruct democracy in America, 1860-1880, by W. E. Burghardt Du Bois ... New York, Harcourt, Brace and company ⌜1935⌟
6 p. l., 3-746 p. 22cm.
"First edition."
Bibliography: p. 731-737.

1. Reconstruction. 2. Negroes. 3. Negroes—Politics and suffrage. 4. Negroes—Employment. 5. U. S.—Pol. & govt.—1865-1877. I. Title.

35—8545
Library of Congress E668.D83 325.260973
⌜45g^2⌟

M973
F85r

Reconstruction.
Franklin, John Hope, 1915-
Reconstruction: after the Civil War. ⌜Chicago⌟ University of Chicago Press ⌜1961⌟
258 p. illus. 21 cm. (The Chicago history of American civilization)
Includes bibliography.

1. Reconstruction.

E668.F7 973.8 61-15931 ‡
Library of Congress ⌜10⌟

Reconstruction.
M973.8 F854
Franklin, John Hope
Reconstruction and the Negro.

Pp. 59-86.

In: Hyman, Harold M. New frontiers of the American reconstruction. Urbana, University of Illinois Press, 1966.

1. Reconstruction.

Reconstruction.
M975.7 G92r
Gruening, Martha , comp.
Reconstruction and the Ku Klux in South Carolina, compiled by Martha Gruening. New York, National Association for the Advancement of Colored People, Dept. of Publications and Research.

[3]p. 25cm. (Bulletin, no.1)

Reconstruction.
M973.8 F854
Hyman, Harold Melvin, 1924- , ed.
New frontiers of the American Reconstruction, edited by Harold M. Hyman. Urbana, University of Illinois Press, 1966.

x, 156p. 24cm.
Papers presented at a conference held at the University of Illinois in April 1965.
Includes bibliographical footnotes.
White editor.
Partial contents.- Reconstruction and the Negro, by John Hope Franklin.

Reconstruction.
M815 L26
Langston, John Mercer, 1829-1897.
Freedom and citizenship. Selected lectures and addresses of Hon. John Mercer Langston... With an introductory sketch by Rev. J. E. Rankin... Washington, D. C., R. H. Darby, 1883.
286 p. front. (port.) 20cm.

Reconstruction.
M973.8 L26o
Langston, John Mercer, 1829–1897.
The other phase of reconstruction. Speech of Hon. John Mercer Langston, delivered at Congregational tabernacle, Jersey City, New Jersey, April 17, 1877. Peaceful reconstruction possible ... Washington, D. C., Gibson brothers, printers, 1877.
16 p. 23½cm.

1. Reconstruction.

18-5993
Library of Congress E668.L28

Reconstruction.
M973.8 L99
Lynch, John Roy, 1847–1936.
The facts of reconstruction, by John R. Lynch ... New York, The Neale publishing company, 1913.
325 p. front., ports. 19½cm.
"The state of Mississippi is made the pivotal one in the presentation of the facts and historical points touched upon in this work."—Pref.

1. Reconstruction. 2. Reconstruction—Mississippi. I. Title.
14—471
Library of Congress E668.L98
[a41c1]

Reconstruction.
M973.8 P98r
[Putnam, Lewis H]
The review of the revolutionary elements of the rebellion, and of the aspect of reconstruction; with a plan to restore harmony between the two races in the southern states. By a colored man. Brooklyn, 1868.
44 p. 23cm.
Introduction signed: L. H. Putnam.

1. Reconstruction. I. Title.
4—15582
Library of Congress E668.P98
[n29d1]

Reconstruction.
M973.8 R81r
Rozwenc, Edwin Charles, 1915– ed.
Reconstruction in the South. Boston, Heath [1952]
100 p. 24 cm. (Problems in American civilization; readings selected by the Dept. of American Studies, Amherst College)
Bibliography: p. [108]–109.
White author.

1. Reconstruction. 2. Southern States—Hist.—1865-1877. I. Title.
E668.R83 973.8 52—1818 ‡
Library of Congress [60q2]

Reconstruction.
M325 Un3n
U.S. Department of labor. Division of Negro economics.
The Negro at work during the world war and during reconstruction. Statistics, problems and policies relating to the greater inclusion of Negro wage earners in American industry and agriculture... Washington, Government printing office, 1921.
144p. diagrs., tables 22½cm.

Reconstruction - Addresses, essays, lectures.
M973 C886
Crowe, Charles Robert, 1928– ed.
The age of Civil War and Reconstruction, 1830–1900; a book of interpretative essays, edited by Charles Crowe. Homewood, Ill., Dorsey Press, 1966.
x, 479 p. 26 cm. (The Dorsey series in American history)
Includes bibliographies.

1. Southern States—Hist.—Addresses, essays, lectures. 2. U. S.—Hist.—Civil War—Addresses, sermons, etc. 3. Reconstruction—Addresses, essays, lectures. I. Title.
F209.C7 973.08 66–27454
Library of Congress [5]

Reconstruction-Fiction.
M813.4 T64f 1961
Tourgée, Albion Winegar, 1838–1905.
A fool's errand. Edited by John Hope Franklin. Cambridge, Belknap Press of Harvard University Press, 1961.
404 p. 22 cm. (The John Harvard library)

1. Reconstruction—Fiction. 2. Ku-Klux Klan. I. Title.
PZ3.T64Fo7 61—18744 ‡
Library of Congress [62f5]

Reconstruction - Fiction.
M813.5 Y46v
Yerby, Frank, 1916–
The vixens, a novel by Frank Yerby. New York, The Dial press, 1947.
347 p. 21 cm.

1. Reconstruction—Fiction. I. Title.
PZ3.Y415Vi 47—3065
© 23Apr47; Frank Yerby, Valley Stream, L. I.; A12200.
Library of Congress [48k5]

Reconst uction - Alabama.
M973.8 R81r
Bond, Horace Mann, 1904-
Social and economic forces in Alabama reconstruction.

pp. 32-50.
In: Reconstruction in the South, by Edwin Charles Rozwenc. 1952.

Reconstruction-Mississippi.
M973.8 L99
Lynch, John Roy, 1847–1936.
The facts of reconstruction, by John R. Lynch ... New York, The Neale publishing company, 1913.
325 p. front., ports. 19½cm.
"The state of Mississippi is made the pivotal one in the presentation of the facts and historical points touched upon in this work."—Pref.

1. Reconstruction. 2. Reconstruction—Mississippi. I. Title.
14—471
Library of Congress E668.L98
[a41c1]

Reconstruction - South Carolina
M973.8 T21
Taylor, Alrutheus Ambush
The Negro in South Carolina during the reconstruction by Alrutheus Taylor. Wash., D.C., The Association for the Study of Negro Life and History, c1924.

1v. 341p. 24cm.

Reconstruction-Virginia.
M973.8 T21n
Taylor, Alrutheus Ambush.
The Negro in the reconstruction of Virginia, by Alrutheus Ambush Taylor ... Washington, D. C., The Association for the study of Negro life and history [°1926]
iv, 300 p. 24½cm.
Bibliography: p. 287–292.

1. Negroes—Virginia. 2. Reconstruction—Virginia. I. Association for the study of Negro life and history, inc. II. Title.
27—5705
Library of Congress E185.93.V8T3
[43g1]

Reconstruction (1939-)--Africa.
Nigeria M966.9 Or 1w
Orizu, Akweke Abyssinia Nwafor, 1920–
Without bitterness; western nations in post-war Africa, by A. A. Nwafor Orizu. New York, N. Y., Creative age press, inc. [1944]
xiv, 395 p. 21cm.

1. Africa—Civilization. 2. Africa—Native races. 3. Nigeria—Soc. condit. 4. Reconstruction (1939–)—Africa. I. Title.
44—7985
Library of Congress DT14.O7
[46q7] 960

Reconstruction in the South.
M973.8 R81r
Rozwenc, Edwin Charles, 1915– ed.
Reconstruction in the South. Boston, Heath [1952]
100 p. 24 cm. (Problems in American civilization; readings selected by the Dept. of American Studies, Amherst College)
Bibliography: p. [108]–109.
White author.

1. Reconstruction. 2. Southern States—Hist.—1865-1877. I. Title.
E668.R83 973.8 52—1818 ‡
Library of Congress [60q2]

Africa M960 R245
Recontres internationales, Bouaké, Ivory Coast, 1962.
Tradition et modernisme en Afrique noire. Paris, Editions du Seuil [1965]
317p. 21cm.
"Organisées par le Centre cultural du Monastère bénedictin de Bouaké (Cote d'Ivoire)
Partial contents.- Les traditions africaines, gages de progrès, by Amadou Hampaté Ba.-
(Continued on next card)

Africa M960 R245
Recontres internationales, Bouaké, Ivory Coast, 1962. Tradition et modernisme en Afrique noire, 1965. (Card 2)
(Partial contents.- Continued)
La crise actuelle de la civilisation africaine, by Joseph Ki Zerbo.

1. Africa - Social condition. I. Bouaké, Ivory Coast. Monastere bénédictin. II. Title.

Recording and registry acts.
M347.2 C82a
Cosey, Alfred Bonito.
American and English law on title of record, with practice and procedure supported by American and English decisions, by Alfred Bonito Cosey ... 1st ed. New York, Isaac Goldmann co., 1914.
415 p. 23½cm. $3.75

1. Land titles—Registration and transfer—U. S. 2. Land titles—Registration and transfer—Gt. Brit. [3. Recording and registry acts] I. Title.
14-20229
Library of Congress
——— Copy 2.
Copyright A 387454

M975.3
J71

Recreation and amusement among Negroes in Washington, D. C.
Jones, William Henry 1896-
Recreation and amusement among Negroes in Washington, D.C.; a sociological analysis of the Negro in an urban environment, by William H. Jones ... Washington, D.C., Howard University Press, 1927.

xi-xv, 17-216p. plates, map, diagr. 21½cm. (Half-title: Howard University studies in urban sociology)
Bibliography: p.203-207.

M610.
C65me5

Recruiting and enlistment.
Cobb, William Montague, 1904-
Medico-Chi and the national selective service. Reprinted from the Journal of the National Medical Association 37:192-197, November, 1945.

Africa
M896.1
Es58

Recueil de poésies.
Esomba Atangana, Henri, comp.
Recueil de poésies. Paris, Les Éditions Domat-Monchrestien, 1939.

24p. 28½cm.
White compiler.

The red badge of courage and four great stories.

M813.5
C85el

Crane, Stephen
The red badge of courage and four great stories. With an introduction by Ralph Ellison. New York, Dell Publishing Co., 1960.

351p. 16½cm.
White author.

M06
J61
No.29

[Redcay, Edward Edgeworth] *comp.*
Public secondary schools for Negroes in the Southern states of the United States; a complete list of all public schools for Negroes in the Southern states of the United States that offer any instruction at all on the secondary level, as of October 1, 1933. [Washington, D. C.] 1935.

72 p. incl. tables. 22½cm. (*On cover:* The Trustees of the John F. Slater fund. Occasional papers, no. 29)

"At the annual meeting of the Board of trustees of the John F. Slater fund in April, 1933, it was voted to have a study made to ascertain just what development had taken place in the field of secondary education

(Continued on next card)

35-12488

[36d2]

251828

M06
J61
No.29

[Redcay, Edward Edgeworth] *comp.* Public secondary schools for Negroes in the Southern states of the United States ... 1935. (Card 2)

for Negroes since 1911. Mr. Edward E. Redcay was engaged to make this study and within a short time his findings will be available in printed form. In the meantime ... it seemed wise to publish the raw data that had been collected for this purpose. This Occasional paper is the outcome of that decision."—Foreword.

1. High schools—Southern states—Direct. 2. Negroes—Education.

Library of Congress — E185.5.J65 no. 29 — 35-12488
[36d2] (825.260973) 371.9740975

M813.5
As3r

Redder blood.
Ashby, William Mobile, 1889-
Redder blood; a novel, by William M. Asby. New York, The Cosmopolitan press, 1915.

188p. 19cm.

M306
H431

Reddick, Lawrence Dunbar, 1910-
Bibliographical problems in Negro research.

(In: Herskovits, M. J. The interdisciplinary aspects of Negro studies. Bulletin of the American Council of Learned Societies, no. 32, September 1941, pp. 26-30.)

M89
K58r

Reddick, Lawrence Dunbar, 1910-
Crusader without violence; a biography of Martin Luther King, Jr. [1st ed.] New York, Harper [1959]

243 p. illus. 22 cm.

1. King, Martin Luther. 2. Negroes—Civil rights. 3. Segregation in transportation—Montgomery, Ala. I. Title.

E185.97.K5R4 — 922.673 — 59-7160 ‡

Library of Congress [60]

M323.2
R24e

Reddick, Lawrence Dunbar, 1910-
Educational programs for the improvement of race relations: Motion pictures, radio, the press, and libraries. Washington, D.C. Journal of Negro Education, 1944.

267-289p. 25cm.
Reprinted rom the Journal of Negro education, Summer, 1944.

1. Race relations I. Title

M814.5
R24

Reddick, Lawrence Dunbar, 1910-
Introductory note.

(In: Beethoven, II. Emancipation symphony. Atlanta, George, The Fuller Press, 1953. 24cm. pp.5-22)

I. Beethoven II, pseud.
II. t. - Emancipation symphony.

M323
N78t

Reddick, Lawrence Dunbar, 1910-
Letters from a Jim Crow Army.

pp. 371-382.
In: Twice a year, ed. by Dorothy Norman. 1946.

1. U. S. Army. 2. Soldiers. I. Title.

M973
R24n

Reddick, Lawrence Dunbar, 1910-
The Negro in the building of America. New York, National Committee for the Participation of Negroes in the American Common World's Fair of 1940 in New York, 1940.

4-7p. 23cm.
In: Souvenir program of Negro week on the American Common, World's Fair of 1940 in New York.

1. U.S. - History. I. Title.

M977
R24n

Reddick, Lawrence Dunbar, 1910- ed.
The Negro in the north during wartime. New York, Journal of educational sociology. 1944.

257-320p. 23cm.
Special issue of The Journal of educational sociology, January 1944.
Contents: -Chicago, by J. G. St. Clair Drake. -New York, by W. M. Banner. -Detroit, by L. E. Martin. -Baltimore, by E. S. Lewis.

M977
R24n

Reddick, Lawrence Dunbar, 1910-
The Negro in the north during wartime. (card 2)

-What the northern Negro thinks about democracy, by L. D. Reddick. -Critical summary by E. Frazier and A. D. Black. -Select bibliography, by M. E. Anthony.

1. Chicago. 2. New York (City). 3. Detroit. 4. Baltimore.

M979
R24r

Reddick, Lawrence Dunbar, 1910- ed.
Race relations on the Pacific coast. New York, Journal of educational sociology, 1945.

129-208p. 23cm.
Special issue of The Journal of educational sociology, November 1945.
Contents: -The new race-relations frontier, by L. D. Reddick. -Seattle, by R. W. O'Brien. -Portland, by E.C. Berry. -San Francisco, by Joseph James. -Los Angeles, by Charles Bratt.

M979
R24r

Reddick, Lawrence Dunbar, 1910- ed.
Race relations on the Pacific coast. (card 2)

-Critical summary, by Carey McWilliams.
-Select bibliography, by Miriam Matthews.

1. Seattle 2. Portland. 3. San Francisco. 4. Los Angeles. 5. Race relations.

M973
R24w

Reddick, Lawrence Dunbar, 1910- jt. auth.
Worth fighting for; a history of the Negro in the United States during the Civil War and Reconstruction [by] Agnes McCarthy and Lawrence Reddick. Illustrated by Colleen Browning. [1st ed.] Garden City, N. Y., Doubleday, 1965.

118 p. col. illus., ports. 22 cm. (Zenith books)

1. ~~Negroes~~—History, Juvenile. 2. U. S.—Hist.—Civil War—~~Negroes~~—Juvenile literature. ~~3. Reddick, Lawrence Dunbar, 1910- joint author.~~ II. Title. I. McCarthy, Agnes.

E185.2.M23 — 973.715 — 65-10281

Library of Congress [5]

Reddick, Lawrence Dunbar, 1910-
The Negro as southerner and American, pp. 130-147.

M301
Se4s

Sellers, Charles Grier, ed.
The southerner as American. [By] John Hope Franklin [and others] Chapel Hill, University of North Carolina Press [1960]

216p. 24cm.
Includes bibliography.

M810
R24a

Redding, Jay Saunders, 1906-
An American in India; a personal report on the Indian dilemma and the nature of her conflicts. [1st ed.] Indianapolis, Bobbs-Merrill [1954]

277 p. 23 cm.

1. India—Intellectual life. 2. India—Soc. life & cust. I. Title.

DS414.R35 — 915.4 — 54-9489 ‡

Library of Congress [54q15]

M8
R24

Redding, Jay Saunders, 1906-
The lonesome road; the story of the Negro's part in America. [1st ed.] New York, Doubleday, 1958.

355 p. 24 cm. (Mainstream of America series)
Includes bibliography.

~~1. Negroes.~~ ~~2. Negroes—Biog.~~ 3. U. S.—Race question. I. Title.

E185.61.R298 — *301.451 325.260973 — 58-6647 ‡

Library of Congress [58r30]

M817
St45
Redding, Jay Saunders, 1906- Introd. essay.
Sterling, Philip, ed.
Laughing on the outside; the intelligent whiter reader's guide to Negro tales and humor. Introductory essay by Saunders Redding. Cartoons by Ollie Harrington. New York, Grosset & Dunlap ⌈1965⌉
254 p. illus. 22cm.
Bibliography: p. ⌈251⌉-254.
Includes selections from writings by American Negro authors.

M810
R24h
Redding, Jay Saunders, 1906-
The meaning of Bandung.
Pp. 417-433.
In: The American Scholar. The American scholar reader. New York, Atheneum, 1960.
1. Bandung Conference.

M973
R246
Redding, Jay Saunders, 1906-
The Negro, by Saunders Redding. Washington, Potomac Books, 1967.
xii, 101 p. illus. 22 cm. (The U. S. A. survey series)
Bibliography: p. 91-94.
Portrait of author on book jacket.
1. Negroes—Hist. I. Title.
E185.R42 301.451'96'073 66-19024 rev
Library of Congress ⌈r68f5⌉

M810.9
H55an
Redding, Jay Saunders, 1906-
The Negro writer and American literature.
Pp. 1-19.
In: Hill, Herbert, ed. Anger and beyond. New York, Harper & Row, 1966.

M810
R24n
Redding, Jay Saunders, 1906-
No day of triumph, by J. Saunders Redding, with an introduction by Richard Wright ... New York and London, Harper & brothers ⌈1942⌉
6 p. l., 3-342 p. 22½cm.
"First edition."
Portrait on jacket.
1. Negroes. I. Title.
Library of Congress E185.6.R42 42—22760
⌈44x5⌉ 325.260973

M810
R24o
Redding, Jay Saunders, 1906-
On being Negro in America. ⌈1st ed.⌉ Indianapolis, Bobbs-Merrill ⌈1951⌉
156 p. 21 cm.
1. Negroes. I. Title.
E185.61.R3 325.260973 51—13473 ‡
Library of Congress ⌈52x7⌉

M810
R24s
Redding, Jay Saunders, 1906-
Stranger and alone, a novel. ⌈1st ed.⌉ New York, Harcourt, Brace ⌈1950⌉
308 p. 21 cm.
I. Title.
PZ3.R246533St 50-5405
Library of Congress ⌈5⌉

M810
R24th
Redding, Jay Saunders, 1906-
They came in chains; Americans from Africa. ⌈1st ed.⌉ Philadelphia, Lippincott ⌈1950⌉
320 p. 22 cm. (The Peoples of America series)
Bibliography: p. 304-308.
1. Negroes—Hist. I. Title. (Series) ViHaI
E185.R4 325.260973 50-8476
Library of Congress ⌈15⌉

M810.
R24to
Redding, Jay Saunders, 1906-
To make a poet black ⌈by⌉ J. Saunders Redding. Chapel Hill, The University of North Carolina press, 1939.
x p., 2 l., ⌈3⌉-142 p. 22cm.
"Factual material and critical opinion on American Negro literature."—Pref.
Bibliography: p. ⌈131⌉-136.
1. Negro literature—Hist. & crit. I. Title.
39—27275
Library of Congress PS153.N5R4
——— Copy 2.
Copyright A 127398 ⌈41k2⌉ 810.9

Trinidad
M822.91
H55
Redhead, Wilfred
Goose and gander.
Pp. 97-118.
In: Hill, Erroll G., ed. Caribbean plays, v.2. Mona, Jamaica, Mona, University of the West Indies, 1965.

Rediscovery and other poems.
Ghana
M896.1
W672r
Williams, George Awoonor, 1935-
Rediscovery and other poems. Ibadan, Mbari Publications ⌈1964⌉
36p. 20cm.

Redmond, Sidney Dillion, 1871-1948.
MB9
R24g
Wilson, Charles H 1905-
God! Make me a man! A biographical sketch of Dr. Sidney Dillion Redmond. Boston, Meador Pub. Co. ⌈1950⌉
61 p. port. 21 cm.
1. Redmond, Sidney Dillion, 1871-1948. I. Title.
E185.97.R4W5 920 50-7842
Library of Congress ⌈5⌉

Redmond, Sidney Dillion, 1871-1948
MB9
R24g
Wilson, Charles H 1905-
God! Make me a man! A biographical sketch of Dr. Sidney Dillion Redmond. Boston, Meador Pub. Co. 1950 .
61p. port. 21cm.

Ao redor de Machado de Assis.
Brazil
M869.3
M18r
Machado de Assis, Joaquim Maria, 1839-1908.
Ao redor de Machado de Assis (pesquisas e comemorativa do cinqüentenário da morte de Joaquim Maria Machado de Assis - 1839-1908). ⌈ed. by Raymundo Magalhaes, Junior⌉ Rio de Janeiro, Editôra Civilização Brasileira, 1958.
285p. port. illus. 21½cm.

M813.5
R251
Reed, Ishmael, 1938-
The free-lance pallbearers. ⌈1st ed.⌉ Garden City, N. Y., Doubleday, 1967.
155 p. 22 cm.
Portrait of author on book jacket.
I. Title.
PZ4.R323Fr 67-19084
Library of Congress ⌈5⌉

Africa
M896.1
R25
Reed, John, comp. and ed.
A book of African verse, compiled and edited by John Reed and Clive Wake. London, Heinemann Educational Books, 1964.
119p. 18cm.
White compilers.
1. African poetry. 2. Poetry - Africa. I. Title.

Reed, John, comp.
Senegal
M896
Se5p
Senghor, Léopold Sédar, 1906-
Prose and poetry. Selected and translated by John Reed and Clive Wake. London, Oxford University Press, 1965.
181p. 18½cm.
Includes bibliography.
1. African literature. I. Title. II. Reed, John, comp. III. Wake, Clive, jt. comp.

M323
R25
Reed, John Hamilton.
Racial adjustments in the Methodist Episcopal church, by John H. Reed ... with an introduction by Adna B. Leonard ... New York, The Neale publishing company, 1914.
193 p. 19cm.
1. Methodist Episcopal church—Government. 2. Methodists, Negro. I. Title.
Library of Congress BX8435.R4 14-17103 Revised
Copyright A 380509 ⌈r40b2⌉

A reed in the tide.
Nigeria
M896.1
C54r
Clark, John Pepper, 1935-
A reed in the tide. ⌈London⌉ Longmans ⌈1965⌉
40p. 20½cm.
I. Title.

M813.5
R54r
Reefer club.
Roberts, Luke
Reefer club. New York, Universal, 1953.
124p. 18cm. (Uni-Book No. 49)

Reese, David Meredith, 1800-1861. A brief review of the "First annual report ... anti-slavery society.
M326.
R84e
Ruggles, David.
The "extinguisher" extinguished! or, David M. Reese, M. D., "used up." By David Ruggles, a man of color. Together with some remarks upon a late production, entitled "An address on slavery and against immediate emancipation with a plan of their being gradually emancipated and colonized in thirty-two years. By Heman Howlett." New-York, D. Ruggles, 1834.
1v, ⌈5⌉-48 p. 19½ cm.
⌈Markoe pamphlets, v. 14, no. 14⌉
(Continued on next card)
19—17294
⌈48c1⌉

Reese, David Meredith, 1800-1861. Humbugs of New-York.
M326. R84an
Ruggles, David.
An antidote for a poisonous combination recently prepared by a "citizen of New-York," alias Dr. Reese, entitled, "An appeal to the reason and religion of American Christians," &c. Also, David Meredith Reese's "Humbugs" dissected, by David Ruggles ... New-York, W. Stuart, 1838.
cover-title, 32 p. 22½cm.
1. An appeal to the reason ... of American Christians, against the American anti-slavery society. 2. Reese, David Meredith, 1800-1861. Humbugs of New-York. 3. American anti-slavery society. 4. Slavery in the U. S.—Controversial literature—1838.
11—11642
Library of Congress E449.R93 [44e1]

Haiti M972.94 R26
Refutation de faits controuvés et d'appreciations contradictoires que contient l'oeuvre intitulé: souvenirs historiques de Guy Joseph Bonnet. Port-au-Prince, Imprimerie de T. Bouchereau [1868]
113p. 23cm.
Supposed author - Saladin, Lamour
1. Bonnet, Guy Joseph, 1773-1843.
2. Haiti-history.
3. Lamour, Saladin, Supposed author

Rehearsals of discompesure.
M808.4 Sc8
Scott, Nathan A
Rehearsals of discomposure; alienation and reconciliation in modern literature: Franz Kafka, Ignazio Silone, D. H. Lawrence [and] T. S. Eliot. New York, King's Crown Press, 1952.
xv, 294 p. 21 cm.
Bibliography: p. [273]-288.
1. Religion and literature. 2. Literature, Modern—20th cent.—Hist. & crit. I. Title.
PN49.S33 809.04 52—13349
Library of Congress [53h7]

Africa, South M968 R25
Reeves, Richard Ambrose, *Bp.*, 1899–
Shooting at Sharpeville; the agony of South Africa. With a foreword by Chief Luthuli. [1st American ed.] Boston, Houghton Mifflin, 1961 [°1960]
xvi, 141 p. illus., map. 23 cm.
White author.
1. Sharpeville, South Africa—Massacre, 1960. I. Title.
II. Luthuli, Albert John, 1898- Foreword.
DT944.S5R4 1961 323.2 61—5373
Library of Congress [61k10]

Ghana M700 K98
Regalia (Insignia) - Ghana.
Kyerematen, Alex Atta Yaw, 1916-
Panoply of Ghana. [London] Longmans [1964]
viii, 120p. illus. (part col.) ports. (part col.) 23cm.

M260 R27
Reid, Gaines S 1890–
The church and the layman: man's duty to God; a plea for positive and dynamic support of the Christian church. Foreword by George W. Baber. [1st ed.] New York, Exposition Press [1959]
86 p. 21 cm.
Portrait of author on book jacket.
1. Laity. I. Title.
BV4525.R43 241 59-3720 ‡
Library of Congress [2]

...Reference list of southern colored schools.
M06 J61 no. 20
John F. Slater fund.
... Reference list of southern colored schools. 2d ed. Lynchburg, Va., J. P. Bell company, inc., printers, 1921.
15 p. 23½cm. (The trustees of the John F. Slater fund. Occasional papers, no. 20)
1. Negroes—Education. 2. Education—Southern states—Direct. I. Title.
21-7358
Library of Congress E185.5.J65 no. 20 [32c1]

Le regard du roi, roman.
French Guinea M966.52 L45r
Laye, Camara, 1928–
Le regard du roi, roman. Paris, Plon [1954]
254 p. 19 cm.
I. Title.
Illinois. Univ. Library for Library of Congress A 55-3692 [1]

M301 R27a
Reid, Ira De Augustine, 1901– 1968
... Adult education among Negroes, by Ira De A. Reid ... Washington, D. C., The Associates in Negro folk education, 1936.
3 p. l., 73 p. 20½cm. (Bronze booklet no. 1)
Bibliography: p. 70–73.
1. Negroes—Education. 2. Education of adults. I. Title.
37—7110
Library of Congress E185.5.B85 no. 1
——— Copy 2. E185.82.R45
[42r40i2] (325.260973) 371.9740973

Reflections; Nigerian prose and verse.
Ghana M896 Ad34
Ademola, Frances, ed.
Reflections; Nigerian prose and verse. [Preface by Ezekiel Mphahlele] Lagos [Nigeria] African Universities Press [1962]
123p. 18½cm.
Ghanaian editor.

La régence.
France M840 D89re
Dumas, Alexandre, 1802-1870.
La régence. Bruxelles, Meline, Cans et cie., 1849.
2 vols. in 1 15cm.

M323 G44a
Reid, Ira De Augustine, 1901-1968
The American Negro.
(In: Gittler, Joseph Bertram. Understanding minority groups. New York, Wiley, 1956. 24cm. pp. 70-83)

Reflections on the review of the Nigerian constitution.
Nigeria M966.9 N98
Nwabueze, B O
Reflections on the review of the Nigerian constitution. [Lagos, Times Press, 1963]
32p. 24cm.

Trinidad M220 C86n
Regeneration (Theology)
Crichlow, Cyril A 1889–
The new birth; a handbook of Scriptu[r]al documentation. [1st ed.] New York, Pageant Press [1956]
143 p. 21 cm.
1. Regeneration (Theology) I. Title.
BT790.C7 234.4 56-11348 ‡
Library of Congress [2]

M301 R27c
Reid, Ira DeAugustine, 1901-1968
The church and education for Negroes.
(In: Bowen, Trevor. Divine white right: a study of race segregation and interracial co-operation in religious organizations and institutions in the United States. New York and London, Pub. for the Institute of Social and Religious Research by Harper c1934. p.235-310).
I. Bowen, Trevor. II. Institute of Social and Religious Research. III. Title. 1. Religion. 2. Race question. 3. Employment. 4. Education.

Haiti M841 D26r
Reflet des heures.
Dauphin, Marcel, 1910-
Reflet des heures, poèmes. Port-au-Prince, Achevé d'imprimer sur les Presses de la Compagnie Lithographique d'Haiti, 1961.
52p. 18½cm.

Regnum montis and its contemporary...
M232 H72
Holley, Joseph Winthrop, 1874–
Regnum montis and its contemporary; heralding the second coming of Christ in the decade, 1995–2005, and the end of the world of things material. New York, William-Frederick Press, 1958.
141 p. 23 cm.
1. Second Advent. I. Title.
BT885.H713 232.6 57-12740 ‡
Library of Congress [1]

M371.974 So13
Reid, Ira De Augustine, 1901-1968
Desegregation and social change.
Pp. 198-20.
Negro author.
In: Social problems. Desegregation in the public schools. New York, Society for the Study of Social Problems, 1955.

Reformers.
M301 H24e
Harris, Abram Lincoln, 1899–
Economics and social reform. New York, Harper [1958]
357 p. 22 cm.
1. Reformers. 2. Economics—Hist. I. Title.
HN15.H3 301.1535 58-5102 ‡
Library of Congress [30]

...Regrets et tendresses.
Martinique M972.98 T36r
Thomarel, André
...Regrets et tendresses. Préface de Robert Chauvelot, 1936.
76p. 19cm.
At head of title: Sous le ciel des Antilles.

M973.9 F46 No.16
Reid, Ira De Augustine, 1901-1968
Fifty years of progress in the professions. Pittsburgh, Pittsburgh Courier, 1950.
7p. port. illus. 24cm. (Fifty years of progress)
1. Professions. I. Series.

M301
R27i

Reid, Ira DeAugustine, 1901- 1968
In a minor key; Negro youth in story and fact, by Ira DeA. Reid; prepared for the American youth commission. Washington, D. C., American council on education, 1940.
8 p. l., 3-134 p., 1 l. diagrs. 26cm.
"Authorities for the facts": p. [121]-134.
1. Negroes—Moral and social conditions. 2. Negroes—Education. I. American council on education. American youth commission. II. Title. III. Title: Negro youth in story and fact.
40-10435
Library of Congress E185.6.R45
[10] 325.260973

M306
N21m

Reid, Ira De Augustine, 1901-1968
Social change, Social relations, and Social work.
(In: National Conference of Social Work. Minority groups... New York, Columbia University, 1955. 24cm. pp.?-12)

Jamaica
M823.91
R271

Reid, Victor Stafford, 1913-
The leopard. London, Heinemann, 1958.
185p. 18½cm.
1. Africa - Fiction. 2. Kenya - Fiction. I. Title.

M301.
R27n2

Reid, Ira de Augustine, 1901-1968
The Negro community of Baltimore, a summary report of a social study conducted for the Baltimore urban league through the department of research, National urban league, by Ira de A. Reid. Drawings by Wilmer Jennings. Baltimore Md., The Baltimore urban league, 1935.
47p. charts. 27cm.
Inscribed copy: For Arthur B. Spingarn, with the compliments of Ira de A. Reid, February 9, 1940.

M301
R27so

Reid, Ira DeAugustine, 1901-1968
Social conditions of the Negro in the hill district of Pittsburg; survey conducted under the direction of Ira DeA. Reid. [Pittsburgh] General Committee on the Hill Survey, 1930.
117p. diagrs. 24½cm.
Bibliography: p.116-117.
1. Pittsburgh. I. National Urban League II. General Committee on the Hill Survey, (Pittsburgh)

Jamaica
M823.91
R271

Reid, Victor Stafford, 1913-
The leopard. New York, Viking Press, 1958.
159 p. 21 cm.
I. Title.
PZ3.R2739Le 58-7064 ‡
Library of Congress [5]

M301
R27n4

Reid, Ira De Augustine, 1901- 1968
The Negro immigrant, his background, characteristics and social adjustment, 1899-1937, by Ira De A. Reid ... New York, Columbia university press; London, P. S. King & son, ltd., 1939.
261 p. incl. tables. 23cm. (*Half-title:* Studies in history, economics and public law, ed. by the Faculty of political science of Columbia university. no. 449)
Issued also as thesis (PH. D.) Columbia university.
Bibliography: p. 253-258.
1. Negroes. 2. U. S.—Race question. 3. U. S.—Emig. & immig. I. Title.
39-19909
Library of Congress H31.C7 no. 449
——— Copy 2. JV6895.N44R4 1939 a
Copyright A 126486 [40k5] (308.2) 325.260973

Reid, Ira DeAugustine, 1901-1968
Symposium: the new south and higher education discussion, pp. 68-75.

M371.974
T87n

Tuskegee Institute.
The new south and higher education: what are the implications for higher education of the changing socio-economic conditions of the south? A symposium and ceremonies held in connection with the inauguration of Luther Hilton Foster, fourth president of Tuskegee Institute[October 31 and November 1, 1953. Tuskegee, Ala.] Dept. of Records and Research, Tuskegee Institute, 1954
x, 145p. map. 24cm.

West Indies
M808.8
H839

Reid, Victor Stafford (1913-)
My father's house.
Pp. 68-75.
In: Howes, Barbara, ed. From the green Antilles. New York, Macmillan, 1966.

M301
R27n5

Reid, Ira DeAugustine, 1901- 1968
The Negro in New Jersey; report of a survey by the Interracial committee of the New Jersey Conference of Social Work in cooperation with the state Department of Institutions and Agencies. [Ira DeA. Reid, director] [Newark] 1932.
116p. incl. front. (map) diagrs. 28cm.
1. New Jersey. I. New Jersey, Dept. of Institutions and Agencies. II. Valentine, William Robert, 1879- . III. New Jersey Conference of Social Work. Interracial Committee.

M301
R27t

Reid, Ira DeAugustine, 1901-1968
Two hundred families of small wage earners-An analysis of their economic status as it relates to problems of housing, Newark, N.J. n.p., 1931.
4p. graphs. 27cm.
Mimeographed.
1. Labor and laboring classes. 2. Newark, N.J.

Jamaica
M823
F82

Reid, Victor Stafford, 1913-
Mr. Quinton.
Pp. 122-128.
In: 14 Jamaican short stories. Jamaica, Pioneer Press, 1950.

M301.
R27n6

Reid, Ira De Augustine, 1901-1968
The Negro population of Denver, Colorado, a survey of its economic and social status, by Ira De A. Reid ... N. Y., The Denver interracial committee, 1929.
46 p. tables. 23½cm.
1. Denver, Colorado.

M301
R27u

Reid, Ira De Augustine, 1901- 1968
The urban Negro worker in the United States, 1925-1936; An analysis of the training types, and conditions of employment and the earnings of 200,000 skilled and white-collar Negro workers. Volume I, statistics by regions, by Ira De A Reid, Preston Valien, and Charles S. Johnson... Washington, D. C., Govt. Print. Off. 1938.
127p. tables. 25cm.
1. Labor and laboring classes. I. Title. II. Johnson, Charles Spurgeon, 1893-

---

Jamaica
M823.91
R27n
1950

Reid, Victor Stafford, 1913-
New day. London, William Heinemann, 1950.
344p. 19cm.
1. Jamaica - Fiction
1. title

M301
R27p

Reid, Ira DeAugustine, 1901-1968
Poor land and peasantry, by Arthur Raper and Ira DeA. Reid. pp. 15-17, 41-42.
In: North Georgia review; A magazine of the southern regions, winter, 1939-1940.
I. Title.
1. Southern states-Econ. condit.
2. Sharecropping.

Reid, Ira de Augustine, 1901-1968.

M973
C73a
1943

Commission on Interracial Cooperation.
America's tenth man; A brief survey of the Negro's part in American history. 22ed. rev. Atlanta, The Commission, 1943.
31p. illus. 23cm.

Jamaica
M823.91
R27n

Reid, Victor Stafford, 1913-
New day. [1st ed.] New York, A. A. Knopf, 1949.
viii, 374 p. 20 cm.
I. Title. 1. Jamaican fiction
PZ3.R2739Ne 49-1576*
Library of Congress [7]

M301
R27sh

Reid, Ira DeAugustine, 1901-1968
Sharecroppers all by Arthur F. Raper and Ira DeA. Reid. Chapel Hill, The University of North Carolina press, 1941.
xp., 21., 3-281p. front. plates. 21½cm.
1. Southern states - Econ. condit. - 1919-
2. Southern states - Soc. condit.
3. Share-cropping.
I. Raper, Arthur Franklin, 1899- jt. auth.
II. Title.

Jamaica
M823.91
R271u

Reid, Victor Stafford, 1913-
Het luipaard; roman (The leopard). [Translated by Rosey E. Pool]. Amsterdam, Wereld-Bibliotheek, 1959.
133p. 20cm.
I. Title.

Jamaica
M823
F82

Reid, Victor Stafford, 1913-
No mourning in the valley.
Pp. 1-13.
In: 14 Jamaican short stories. Jamaican, Pioneer Press, 1950.

West Indies
M808.8 Reid, Victor Stafford (1914-)
H839 A requiem for Dan'l Moore.

Pp. 63-67.

In: Howes, Barbara, ed. From the green Antilles. New York, Macmillan, 1966.

Jamaica
M823.91 Reid, Victor Stafford, 1913-
Sa3w Waterfront bar.

pp. 189-192

In Andrew Salkey's West Indian Stories. 1960.

The reign of terror.
M813.5 Brown, Mattye Jeanette
B814r The reign of terror. New York, Vantage Press [1962]

119p. 21cm.

Ghana
M966.7 Reindorf, Carl Christian, 1834-1917.
W83p The battle of Asamankow.

pp. 115-119.
In: Pageant of Ghana, by Freda Wolfson. 1958.

1. Asamankow. I. Title.

Gold Coast
M966.7 Reindorf, Carl Christian, 1834-1917.
R27h History of the Gold Coast and Asante, based on traditions and historical facts comprising a period of more than three centuries from about 1500 to 1860. With a biographical sketch by Dr. C. E. Reindorf. 2nd ed. Basel, Switzerland, Basel Mission Book Depot, n.d.

XII, 349p. illus. front.(port.) 21cm.
1. Gold Coast - Hist. 2. Asjanto - Hist. 3. Missions - Gold Coast. I. Christaller, Johann Gottlieb, 1827-1895, ed.

Gold Coast Reindorf, Carl Christian, 1834-1917.
M966.7 Reindorf, Carl Christian, 1834-1917.
R27h The history of the Gold Coast and Asante. Based on traditions and historical facts comprising a period of more than three centuries from about 1500 to 1860. By Rev. Carl Christian Reindorf, with a biographical sketch by Dr. C.E. Reindorf. 2nd ed. Basel, Switzerland, Basel Mission Book Depot [n.d.]

XII, 349p. front. (port.) illus. 21cm.

La reine des pommes.
M813.5 Himes, Chester B , 1909-
H57rei La reine des pommes. (The five cornered square). Paris, Gallimard 1958.

248p. 18cm.

M781 Reisner, Robert George.
R271 The literature of jazz, a selective bibliography. With an introd. by Marshall W. Stearns. [2d ed. rev. and enl.] New York, New York Public Library, 1959.

63 p. 26 cm.

1. Jazz music—Bibl. I. Title.

ML128.J3R4 1959 016.78157 59-9577

Library of Congress [2]

The Reith lectures, 1965.
Ghana
M301 Gardiner, Robert Kweku Atta. 1914-
G166 A world of peoples [by] Robert Gardiner. London, British Broadcasting Corporation, 1966.

93 p. 22 cm. (The Reith lectures, 1965) 15/-
(B 66-7752)
Includes bibliographies.
Portrait of author on book jacket.

1. Race problems. 2. Prejudices and antipathies. I. British Broadcasting Corporation. II. Title. (Series)

HT1521.G3 1966 301.45 66—71229

Library of Congress [67f5]

Relations between Negroes and Indians...
M323 Porter, Kenneth Wiggins.
P83r Relations between Negroes and Indians within the present limits of the United States, by Kenneth W. Porter ... Washington, D. C., The Association for the study of Negro life and history, inc. [193-]

1 p. l., 81 p. 24½cm.

1. Negroes. 2. Indians of North America. I. Association for the study of Negro life and history, inc. II. Title.

37-14799

Library of Congress E185.4.P67
[3] [970.1] 325.260973

Relativity.
M304 Alexis, Lucien V.
P19 An empiracal disclosure of the fallacies
v.4, no.7 of relativity. New Orleans, La., The McDough 35 Press [1931]

Cuba Relatos de Marcos Antilla.
M863.6 [Rodríguez, Luis Felipe] 1888-
R61r Relatos de Marcos Antilla; la tragedia del cañaveral. La Habana, Impresora cubana, s. a. [1932?]
3 p. l., iii-xvii, 106 p. 22½cm.
Author's name on cover.
First published 1928.
CONTENTS.—Americanismo y cubanismo literarios, por Juan Marinello.—Marcos Antilla contado por si mismo.—La chimenea.—Cama no. 13.—Fantasmas en el cañaveral.—El Pelirrojo.—La guardarraya.—Míster Lewis.—Los Almarales.—El ego de Nicolás.—Los subalternos.—El haz de caña.—La danza lucumí.—El nacimiento de Margarito.
I. *Marinello, Juan, 1899- Americanismo y cubanismo literarios. II. Title.
[Full name: Luis Felipe Rodríguez Rodríguez]

41-16681

Library of Congress PQ7389.R6M3 1932 a
[2] 863.6

La Relève, politique, littéraire.

Port-au-Prince, Haïti [1933-
M05 v. illus., ports. 23½cm. monthly.
R27 Library has: 1933-1938. (incomplete)
1935 complete.

44-42921

Library of Congress AP21.R33
[2] 054

Senegal Reliefs; poemes.
M896.1 Fall, Malick
F19r Reliefs; poèmes. Préface de Léopold Sédar Senghor. Paris, Présence Africaine, 1964.

101p 19½cm.

... Religiões Negras.
Brasil
M569 Carneiro de Souza, Edison, 1912
C21r ... Religiões negras; notas de etnografia religiosa ... Rio de Janeiro, Civilização brasileira s. a., 1936.

188 p., 2 l. 1 illus., plates. 18½cm. (Biblioteca de divulgação scientifica, dirigida pelo prof. dr. Arthur Ramos. vol. VII)

1. Negro race—Religion. 2. Negroes in Brazil. 3. Folk-lore, Negro. I. Title.

38-33447

Library of Congress BL2490.C3
[2] 291.14

Religion.
M200 Anderson, E Hutto
An23 Adjustment. New York, Carlton Press [1965]

73p. 21cm.
Portrait of author on book jacket.

1. Religion. I. Title.

Religion.
M220 Banks, William L.
B226 Jonah, verse by verse. New York, Vantage Press [1963]

103p. 21cm.

Religion.
M252 Borders, William Holmes, 1905-
B64g God is real. [Atlanta, Georgia, Fuller Press, [©1951]

210p. port. 21½cm.

Religion.
M398 Brewer, John Mason, 1896-
B75w The Word on the Brazos; Negro preacher tales from the Brazos bottoms of Texas. Foreword by J. Frank Dobie; illus. by Ralph White, Jr. Austin, University of Texas Press, 1953.

100 p. illus. 24 cm.
First edition.
Autographed by authors.

1. Folk-lore, Negro. 2. Folk-lore—Brazos Valley. ~~3. Negroes—~~ Religion. I. Title.

GR103.B7 398.21 53—10834 ‡

Library of Congress [54k5]

Religion
Jamaica
M824 Brown, Ethelred
B81j Jesus of Nazareth the world's greatest religious teacher was unitarian ... a sermon delivered on Sunday evening, March 14, 1943 and repeated on Sunday evening April 11, 1943 at the Harlem Unitarian Church ... New York, City.

10p. 19cm.

Religion.

M261 Burroughs, Nannie Helen, 1879-
B94m Making your community Christian, by Nannie H. Burroughs. Washington, D. C., Woman's Convention [n.d.]

100p. 19cm.

Religion.
Brazil
M309
C21r
Carneiro de Sousa, Edison, 1912-
... Religiões negras; notas de etnografia religiosa ... Rio de Janeiro, Civilização brasileira s. a., 1936.
188 p., 2 l. 1 illus., plates. 18½cm. (Biblioteca de divulgação scientifica, dirigida pelo prof. dr. Arthur Ramos. vol. VII)
1. Negro race—Religion. 2. Negroes in Brazil. 3. Folk-lore, Negro. I. Title.
Library of Congress BL2490.C3 38-33447
[2] 291.14

Religion.
M234.8
Ea7p
Eason, James Henry, 1866-
Pulpit and platform efforts. Sanctifications vs. fanaticism, by Rev. J. H. Eason... with introduction by Rev. C. L. Fisher... Nashville, Tenn., National Baptist publishing board, 1899.
120p. front. 19½cm.

Religion.
M289.9
F27
Fauset, Arthur Huff, 1899-
... Black gods of the metropolis; Negro religious cults of the urban North, by Arthur Huff Fauset. Philadelphia, University of Pennsylvania press; London, H. Milford, Oxford university press, 1944.
x, 126 p. plates, ports. 23½cm. (Publications of the Philadelphia anthropological society. Vol. III)
Half-title: ... Brinton memorial series. [No. 2]
Issued also as thesis (PH. D.) University of Pennsylvania.
"A study of five Negro religious cults in the Philadelphia of today."—Pref.
1. Negroes—Religion. 2. Negroes—Philadelphia. 3. Sects—U. S. I. Title.
Library of Congress BR563.N4F3 1944 a 44-3761
[47x3] 289.9

Religion.
MB9
F73
Foote, *Mrs.* Julia A J 1823-
A brand plucked from the fire. An autobiographical sketch, by Mrs. Julia A. J. Foote ... Cleveland, O., Printed for the author by W. F. Schneider, 1879.
124 p. 17½cm.
1. Evangelistic work. 2. Negroes—Religion. I. Title.
Library of Congress E185.97.F6F6 12-16485
Copyright 1879: 8296

Religion.
M277
F86
Frazier, Edward Franklin, 1894-1962.
The Negro church in America. New York, Schocken Books [1964, °1963]
xii, 92 p. 23 cm. (Studies in sociology)
Bibliographical footnotes.
1. ~~Negroes~~—Religion. I. Title. 2. Church history.
BR563.N4F7 277.3 62-19390
Library of Congress [5]

Religion.
M204
G35b
Gibson, Bertha Askew
The big three then the big job. New York, Vantage Press, 1960.
191p. 20½cm.
Portrait of author on back of book jacket.

Religion.
M261
H33
Haynes, Leonard L 1923-
The Negro community within American Protestantism, 1619-1844. Boston, Christopher Pub. House [1953]
264 p. 21 cm.
1. Negroes—Religion. 2. Protestant churches—U. S. I. Title.
BR563.N4H38 *261.8 53-4230 ‡
Library of Congress [54d2]

Religion.
M209
J64
Johnston, Ruby F
The development of Negro religion. New York, Philosophical Library [1954]
202 p. illus. 23 cm.
1. Negroes—Religion. I. Title.
BR563.N4J6 277.3 54-7966 ‡
Library of Congress [54k10]

Religion.
M277.3
J64r
Johnston, Ruby Funchess.
The religion of Negro Protestants; changing religious attitudes and practices. New York, Philosophical Library [1956]
xxvi, 224 p. tables. 24 cm.
Bibliography: p. 214-217.
1. Negroes—Religion. 2. Protestant churches—U. S. I. Title.
BR563.N4J62 277.3 56-13828
Library of Congress [56h7]

Religion.
M261.8
J717
Jones, Howard O
Shall we overcome? A challenge to Negro and white Christians [by] Howard O. Jones. Westwood, N. J., F. H. Revell Co. [1966]
146 p. 21 cm.
1. Church and race problems—U. S. 2. Negroes—Religion. I. Title.
BT734.2.J6 261.83 66-17048
Library of Congress [5]

Religion.
M209
J73
Jones, Raymond Julius, 1910-
... A comparative study of religious cult behavior among Negroes, with special reference to emotional group conditioning factors, by Raymond Julius Jones ... Washington, D. C., Pub. by the Graduate school for the Division of the social sciences, Howard university, 1939.
cover-title, 2 p. l., v, 125 p. 23½cm. (The Howard university studies in the social sciences, vol. II, no. 2)
Thesis (M. A.)—Howard university, 1939.
1. Negroes—Religion. I. Title. II. Title: Cult behavior among Negroes.
Library of Congress H31.H66 vol. 2, no. 2 40-6600
[a43f2] 325.260973

Religion.
Cuba
M972.91
L11
Lachatañeré, Rómulo.
... Manual de santería; el sistema de cultos "lucumís." La Habana, Cuba, Editorial Caribe, 1942.
88, [7] p. incl. illus. (facsim.) map, tables. 20½cm. (*On cover:* Estudios afro-cubanos)
At head of title: R. Lachatañeré.
1. Cuba—Religion. 2. Negro race—Religion. 3. Negroes in Cuba. I. Title.
Library of Congress BL2530.C9L3 42-25316
[44c1] 299.64

Religion.
Gold Coast
M200
L14k
Laing, George E. F
A king for Africa. London and Redhill, United Society for Christian Literature, 1945.
63p. 18cm.

Religion.
M260
M45nc
Mays, Benjamin Elijah, 1895-
The Negro's church, by Benjamin Elijah Mays and Joseph William Nicholson. New York, Institute of social and religious research [°1933]
xiii, 321 p. illus. (maps) 19½cm.
"The Institute of social and religious research ... is responsible for this publication."—p. [ii]
1. Negroes—Religion. 2. Churches—U. S. I. Nicholson, Joseph William, joint author. II. Institute of social and religious research. III. Title.
Library of Congress BR563.N4M3 33-6349
——— Copy 2.
Copyright A 59858 [a40q2] [261] 325.260973

Religion.
M260
M45ng
Mays, Benjamin Elijah, 1895-
The Negro's God as reflected in his literature [by] Benjamin E. Mays ... lithographs by James L. Wells. Boston, Chapman & Grimes, inc. [°1938]
viii p., 1 l., 269 p. 20cm.
Bibliography: p. 257-263.
1. Negro literature—Hist. & crit. 2. Negroes—Religion. 3. God. 4. Religion in literature. I. Title.
Library of Congress PS153.N5M3 38-37550
[43i1] [231] 810.9

Religion.
M378
M21r
McKinney, Richard Ishmael, 1906-
Religion in higher education among Negroes, by Richard I. McKinney ... New Haven, Yale university press; London, H. Milford, Oxford university press, 1945.
xvi, 165, [1] p. incl. tables. 23½cm. (*Half-title:* Yale studies in religious education, XVIII)
"The complete results of this study were presented as a dissertation ... for the degree of doctor of philosophy in Yale university [1942]."—p. xii.
Bibliography: p. [149]-161.
1. Negroes—Education. 2. Negroes—Religion. 3. Universities and colleges—Religion. I. Title.
Yale univ. Library for Library of Congress BV1610.M33 A 45-4633
[46i7]†

Religion.
M304
P19
v.6, no.15
Miller, George Frazier.
A discussion. Is religion reasonable? Mr. Clarence Darrow says no and the Black man it is self-stultification. Bishop Jones says yes it is the Universal Ground of Hope. A challenge by Dr. Du Bois, Editor of The Crisis. The objection and the challenge met, by George Frazier Miller. [Brooklyn, The Henne Press, n.d.]
[8] p. 22cm.

Religion.
M304
P19
v.6, no. 14
Miller, George Frazier.
The sacredness of humanity, annual sermon of the conference of church workers (Episcopal) among colored people at St. Philip's church, New York, October 6-9, 1914. Brooklyn, Frank R. Chisholm, printer, 1914.
15p. 23p.

Religion.
M210
M76a
Montgomery, Leroy Jeremiah
An analysis of two distinct religions: organized christianity and the religion of Jesus Christ. New York, New Voices Publishing Co., 1956.
32p. 21½cm.

Religion.
M210
M76t
Montgomery, Leroy Jeremiah
Two distinct religions, Christanity and the religion of Jesus Christ, by Leroy Jeremiah Montgomery... Houston, Texas, Informer publishing company n.d.
69p. 17½cm.

Religion.
M200
M77
Moon, Bertha Louise Hardwick
The bird on the limb. New York Comet Press, 1959.
40p. 21cm.

M191
M846
Religion.
Morton, Lena Beatrice.
Man under stress. New York, Philosophical Library [1960]
129 p. 22 cm.
Includes bibliography.
1. Philosophy. 2. Religion. I. Title.
B56.M65 101 60-13638 ‡
Library of Congress [5]

M301
R27c
Religion.
Reid, Ira DeAugustine, 1901-
The church and education for Negroes.
(In: Bowen, Trevor. Divine white right: a study of race segregation and interracial co-operation in religious organizations and institutions in the United States. New York and London, Pub. for the Institute of Social and Religious Research by Harper c1934. p.235-310).

Religion.
M280
Y33
Year book of Negro churches, with statistics and records of achievements of Negroes in the United States ... 1935/36-
Wilberforce, O., Printed at Wilberforce university [19
v. 22½cm.
Editor: 1935/36- Reverdy C. Ransom.
"Published by authority of the bishops of the A. M. E. church."
1. Negroes. 2. Negroes—Religion. 3. Churches—U. S. 4. Negroes—Stat. I. Ransom, Reverdy Cassius, bp., 1861- ed. II. African Methodist Episcopal church. III. Title: Negro churches, Year book of.
37-22400
Library of Congress E185.7.Y43
[44e1] 325.260073

Religion.
M230
Of4g
[Offley, Greensbury W.] 1808-
God's immutable declaration of his own moral and assumed natural image and likeness in man, declared (Genesis 1:26-27,) and revealed to the Prophet Daniel, 7-9, and to St. John Rev. 1:13-14; or, The Nations weighed in the balance. New Bedford, Mercury Stean printing House, 1875.
30p. illus. 22½cm.

Religion.
M280
R35d
Richardson, Harry Van Buren.
Dark glory, a picture of the church among Negroes in the rural South. New York, Pub. for Home Missions Council of North America and Phelps-Stokes Fund by Friendship Press [1947]
xiv, 209 p. 19 cm.
"A selected reading list": p. 194-197.
1. Negroes—Religion. I. Title.
BR563.N4R5 277.5 47-24753*
Library of Congress [49h1]

M270
M85w
Religion - History.
Moses, W H
The white peril, by W. H. Moses...
[Philadelphia, Pa., Lisle - Carey press, 1919]
xxxii, 260p. 19cm.

Religion.
M973.8
P38u
Penn, Irvine Garland, 1867- ed.
The united negro: his problems and his progress, containing the addresses and proceedings the Negro young people's Christian and educational congress, held August 6-11, 1902; introduction by Bishop W. J. Gaines ... edited by Prof. I. Garland Penn ... Prof. J. W. E. Bowen ... Atlanta, Ga., D. E. Luther publishing co., 1902.
xxx, 600 p. illus., plates, ports. 21cm.
1. Negroes—Moral and social conditions. 2. Negroes—Religion. I. Bowen, John Wesley Edward, 1855- joint ed. II. Title.
3-1895
Library of Congress E185.5.P41
[a45e1]

Religion.
M220
Sm7i
Smothers, Felton C 1926-
I am the beginning and the ending; a book of excerpts from Genesis and the Revelations of St. John, The Divine. Edited and illustrated by Felton Smothers. New York, Carlton Press, 1961.
34p. illus. 21cm.
Portrait of author on book jacket.

Religion - Congo (Leopoldville)
Congo (Leopoldville)
M200
L96
Lufuluabo, Francois-Marie
Vers une théodicée bantoue. Mechliniae, Imprimi potest, 1961.
50p. 22½cm.

Religion.
M230.67
P44
Peterson, Frank Loris.
The hope of the race, by Frank Loris Peterson. Nashville, Tenn., Southern publishing association [°1934]
333 p. incl. front., illus., ports., diagrs. col. pl. 20½cm.
1. Seventh-day Adventists—Doctrinal and controversial works. 2. Negroes—Religion. I. Title.
35-1082
Library of Congress BX6154.P45
——— Copy 2.
Copyright A 77848 [3] 230.67

Religion.
M200
T42c
Thurman, Howard, 1899-
The creative encounter; an interpretation of religion and the social witness. [1st ed.] New York, Harper [1954]
153 p. 20 cm.
"The substance ... in essentially the present form, was given as the Merrick lectures at Ohio Wesleyan University in March, 1954."
1. Experience (Religion) 2. Religion. I. Title.
BR110.T48 248 54-11664 ‡
Library of Congress [25]

Religion, African.
Ghana
M966.7
W83p
Crowther, Samuel Adjai, -1891.
Christian worship, 1841.
pp. 122-123.
In: Pagaent of Ghana, by Freda Wolfson.

Religion
M251
P66s
Pipes, William Harrison, 1912-
Say amen, brother! Old-time Negro preaching: a study in American frustration. New York, William-Frederick Press, 1951.
1, 210p. 24cm.

Religion.
M277
W27
Washington, Joseph R
Black religion; the Negro and Christianity in the United States [by] Joseph R. Washington, Jr. Boston, Beacon Press [1964]
ix, 308 p. 22 cm.
Bibliographical references included in "Notes" (p. 298-308)
1. ~~Negroes~~—Religion. I. Title. II. Title: The Negro and Christianity in the United States. 2. Church history.
BR563.N4W3 277.3 64-13529
Library of Congress [5]

Religion, diet, and health of Jews.
M296
J56r
Jiggetts, J Ida.
Religion, diet, and health of Jews. With a pref. by Abraham I. Katsh. New York, Bloch Pub. Co., 1949.
xiii, 125p. map, diagr. 21cm.
Bibliographies: p. 111-121.

Religion.
M200
P97
Purnell, J M , 1927-
In his pavilion; reflections upon religion and modern society. New York, Exposition Press, 1959.
162p. 21½cm.

Religion.
M242
W58c
Whittier, A Gerald
Christian meditations. New York, Carlton Press, 1961.
178p. 23cm.
Portrait of author on book jacket.

Religion and literature.
M808.4
Sc8m
Scott, Nathan A
Modern literature and the religious frontier. [1st ed.] New York, Harper [1958]
138 p. 22 cm.
Includes bibliography.
1. Religion and literature. 2. Literature, Modern—20th cent.—Hist. & crit. I. Title.
PN1077.S39 809.04 58-7476 ‡
Library of Congress [25]

Religion.
M973
R14
Ramos, Arthur, 1903- 1949.
... As culturas negras no novo mundo ... Rio de Janeiro, Civilização brasileira, s/a., 1937.
399, [1] p. illus. (maps) plates, diagr. 18½cm. (Bibliotheca de divulgação scientifica, sob a direcção de Arthur Ramos. vol. XII)
1. Negroes in America. 2. Negro race—Soc. life & cust. 3. Negro race—Religion. 4. Folk-lore, Negro. I. Title.
[Full name: Arthur Ramos de Araujo Pereira]
38-12715
Library of Congress E29.N3R3
[a44e1] 325.26097

Religion.
M973
W86r
Woodson, Carter Godwin, 1875-
The history of the Negro church, by Carter G. Woodson ... Washington, D. C., The Associated publishers [°1921]
x, 330 p. front., plates, ports. 20½cm.
1. Negroes—Religion. I. Title. II. Title: Negro church, The history of the.
22-985
Library of Congress BR563.N4W6
[44q1]

Religion and literature.
M808.4
Sc8
Scott, Nathan A
Rehearsals of discomposure; alienation and reconciliation in modern literature: Franz Kafka, Ignazio Silone, D. H. Lawrence [and] T. S. Eliot. New York, King's Crown Press, 1952.
xv, 294 p. 21 cm.
Bibliography: p. [273]-288.
1. Religion and literature. 2. Literature, Modern—20th cent.—Hist. & crit. I. Title.
PN49.S33 809.04 52—13349
Library of Congress [53h7]

M614
R66sc
Religion and science.
Roman, Charles Victor, 1864-1934.
Science and Christian ethics...n.p., c1912.
58p. 20cm.
Contents: -. Part I. Statement of principles.--. Part II. Religion a necessity to man...--. Part III. Racial self respect and racial antagonism.

Religion in higher education among Negroes.
M378
M21r
McKinney, Richard Ishmael, 1906-
Religion in higher education among Negroes, by Richard I. McKinney ... New Haven, Yale university press; London, H. Milford, Oxford university press, 1945.
xvi, 165, [1] p. incl. tables. 23½cm. (*Half-title:* Yale studies in religious education, XVIII)
"The complete results of this study were presented as a dissertation ... for the degree of doctor of philosophy in Yale university [1942]."—p. xii.
Bibliography: p. [149]-161.
1. Negroes—Education. 2. Negroes—Religion. 3. Universities and colleges—Religion. I. Title.
Yale univ. Library for Library of Congress BV1610.M33 A 45—4633
[461⁷]†

Religion in literature.
M200
M45ng
Mays, Benjamin Elijah, 1895-
The Negro's God as reflected in his literature [by] Benjamin E. Mays ... lithographs by James L. Wells. Boston, Chapman & Grimes, inc. [°1938]
viii p., 1 l., 269 p. 20cm.
Bibliography: p. 257-268.
1. Negro literature—Hist. & crit. 2. Negroes—Religion. 3. God. 4. Religion in literature. I. Title.
Library of Congress PS153.N5M3 [43i1] 38—37550 [231] 810.9

Religion in literature.
M808.4
Sc8t
Scott, Nathan A ed.
The tragic vision and the Christian faith. New York, Association Press [1957]
346 p. 21 cm. (A Haddam House book)
Includes bibliography.
1. Religion in literature. 2. Tragic, The. 3. Christianity—Philosophy. I. Title.
PN49.S34 801 57—11604 ‡
Library of Congress [58x10]

M248
W67
Religion in poetry.
Williams, Florence B
The guiding light. Baltimore, National Baptist Training Union Board Publisher, 1962.
94p. 21½cm.

M200.
T42r
The religion of Jesus and the disinherited.
Thurman, Howard, 1899-
(In: Johnson, Thomas Herbert, ed. In defense of democracy. New York, Putnam, 1949. 21cm. p.125-135.)

The religion of Negro Protestants...
M277.3
J64r
Johnston, Ruby Funchess.
The religion of Negro Protestants; changing religious attitudes and practices. New York, Philosophical Library [1956]
xxvi, 224 p. tables. 24 cm.
Bibliography: p. 214-217.
1. ~~Negroes~~—Religion. 2. Protestant churches—U. S. I. Title.
BR563.N4J62 277.3 56—13828
Library of Congress [56h7]

Religions - Congresses.
M814.5
W89
World fellowship of faiths. *International congress. 1st, Chicago and New York,* 1933-1934.
World fellowship; addresses and messages by leading spokesmen of all faiths, races and countries, edited by Charles Frederick Weller ... New York, Liveright publishing corporation [°1935]
xviii, 986 p. 22 cm.
"This book ... condenses and co-ordinates the 242 addresses delivered by 199 spokesmen ... in the 83 meetings held ... by the first International congress of the World fellowship of faiths."—p. v.
1. Religions—Congresses. 2. Religions—Addresses, essays, lectures. I. Weller, Charles Frederick, 1870- ed.
Library of Congress BL21.W6 1933-1934 36—2382
[48k½] 290.631

M200
V44
Religions - Hist.
Vassall, William F
The origin of Christianity; a brief study of the world's early beliefs and their influence on the early Christian church, including an examination of the lost books of the Bible. [1st ed.] New York, Exposition Press [1952]
183 p. 21 cm.
1. Religions—Hist. 2. Christianity—Origin. 3. Bible. N. T. Apocryphal books—Criticism, interpretation, etc. I. Title.
BL80.V27 290 52—10685 ‡
Library of Congress [5]

Religious education.
M06
Am3
no. 13
Moorland, Jesse Edward, 1863-1940.
... The demand and the supply of increased efficiency in the negro ministry. By Jesse E. Moorland ... Washington, D. C., The Academy, 1909.
14 p. 22cm. (Occasional papers, no. 13. American negro academy)
1. Negroes—Education. 2. Religious education.
Library of Congress E185.5.A51 no. 13 10—3009
——— Copy 2. E185.82.M82
[a42d1]

M268
T97
Religious education.
Tyms, James Daniel
The rise of religious education among Negro Baptists; a historical case study, by James D. Tyms. [1st ed.] New York, Exposition Press [1966, °1965]
xiv, 409p. 21cm. (An Exposition-university book)
Bibliography: p. [397]-403.

M220
V44p
Religious education.
Vass, S[amuel] N
Principle and methods of religious education. Nashville, Tenn. Sunday School Publishing Board, c1932.
378, 2p. illus. 20cm.

M784
D48
Religious folk-songs of the Negro.
Dett, Robert Nathaniel, 1882- ed.
Religious folk-songs of the Negro as sung at Hampton institute, edited by R. Nathaniel Dett ... Hampton, Va., Hampton institute press, 1927.
xxvii, 236, [1], ii, xiii p. 24cm.
1. Negro songs. I. Hampton, Va. Normal and agricultural institute. II. Title.
Library of Congress M1670.H3 1927 27—10635
[45m1]

M784
F36r
Religious folk songs of the Negro, as sung on the plantations.
Fenner, Thomas P
Religious folk songs of the Negro, as sung on the plantations. New ed. Arranged by the musical directors of the Hampton Normal and Agricultural Institute. From the original edition. Hampton, Va., The Institute Press, 1916.
178p. 21½cm.

M261.2
R27
Religious Leadership Conference on Equality of Opportunity, Harriman, N. Y.
Discrimination, what can churches do? A Handbook and report on the religious leadership conference on equality of opportunity, Arden House, Harriman, N.Y., April 28-29, 1958. New York, Commission Against Discrimination, 1958.
38p. 21½cm.
1. Churches-Race relations. 2. Race relations -Churches. I. Title.

M811.5
Sp31w
Religious poetry.
Spearman, Aurelia L. P. (Childs)
What Christ means to us; a book of religious verse. New York, Carlton Press [1964]
99p. 20½cm.

M811.08
W56
Religious poetry, American.
Wheeler, Benjamin Franklin, 1854-1919, *comp.*
Cullings from Zion's poets, by B. F. Wheeler, D. D. [Mobile? Ala., °1907]
384 p. front., ports. 20cm.
1. Religious poetry, American. 2. Negro poetry (American) I. Title.
Library of Congress PS595.R4W5 8—20853
Copyright A 178145 [a37b1] 811.0822

M200
Ev1b
Religious Principles.
Evans, Luther, 1915-
The book of Thoth. New York, Comet Press Books, 1960.
56p. 20½cm.
Portrait of author on book jacket.

Malawi
M968.97
N87m
Religious tract society, London.
Ntara, Samuel Yosia, 1904 *or* 5-
Man of Africa, by Samuel Yosia Ntara; translated and arranged from the original Nyanja by T. Cullen Young. Foreword by Professor Julian Huxley ... London, The Religious tract society [1934]
180, [1] p. front., plates. 19cm.
"Prize-winning biography under authority of the International institute of African languages and cultures ... 1933."—p. [2]
1. Ethnology—Nyasaland. I. Young, T. Cullen, tr. II. Religious tract society, London. III. International institute of African languages and cultures.
Library of Congress DT864.N8 35-6977
[5] 572.96897

Brazil
M869.3
M18re2
Reliquias de casa velha.
Machado de Assis, Joaquim Maria, 1839-1908.
... Reliquias de casa velha, por Machado de Assis ... Rio de Janeiro, Paris, Garnier [1921?]
5 p. l., [3]-264 p., 1 l. 19cm. (Collecção dos autores celebres da litteratura brasileira)
CONTENTS.—A Carolina.—Pae contra mãe.—Maria Cora.—Marcha funebre.—Um capitão de voluntarios.—Suje-se gordo!—Umas ferias.—Evolução.—Pylades e Orestes.—Anecdota do cabriolet.—Paginas criticas e commemorativas.—Não consultes medico.—Lição de botanica.
I. Title.
Library of Congress PQ9697.M18R4 31-29718 869.8

Reliquias de casa velha.
Brazil
M869.3
M18re2
1957
Machado de Assis, Joaquim Maria, 1839-1908.
Reliques de casa velha. Rio de Janeiro, W. M. Jackson Inc. Editôres, 1957.
2v. 20½cm. (Obras completas de Machado de Assis)

The reluctant African.

M910
L83r
Lomax, Louis E 1922-
The reluctant African. [1st ed.] New York, Harper [1960]
117 p. illus. 22 cm.
Portrait of author on book jacket.

1. Africa—Native races. 2. Africa—Politics. I. Title.

DT15.L65 323.1096 60-16472 ‡
Library of Congress [80]

Reminiscene II.

Virgin Islands
M811.5
An29re
Anduze, Aubrey
Reminiscene II. [St. Thomas, Virgin Islands, 1944]

68p. 21cm.

Report of proceedings [of] Summit Meeting of Negro Leaders, Washington, D.C.

M323
Su6
Summit Meeting of National Negro Leaders, Washington, D. C., 1958.
Report of proceedings [of] Summit Meeting of Negro Leaders, Washington, D.C., May 12, 13, 1958. Sponsored by National Newspaper Publishers Association. [Washington, National Newspaper Publishers Association] 1958.

137p. illus. 33cm.

Contents.- Speech, by William O. Walker.- Speech, by A. Philip Randolph.- Speech, by Paul H. Cooke.- Address, by Roy Wilkins.-

(Continued on next card)

Remarques.

Haiti
M844
M27r
Magloire, Jean.
... Remarques; préface de Léon Laleau. Port-au-Prince, Haïti, Impr. du Collège Vertières [1940?]
3 p. l., 5-103 p. 18cm.

1. Journalists—Correspondence, reminiscences, etc. I. Title.
44-53541
Library of Congress PQ3949.M15R4
[2] 848.91

Nigeria
M966.9
Az2r
Renascent Africa.
Azikiwe, Benjamin Nnamdi, 1904-
Renascent Africa, by Nnamdi Azikiwe...Accra, Gold Coast, West Africa, The author [1937]

313p. port. 22cm.

Report of proceedings [of] Summit Meeting of Negro Leaders, Washington, D.C.

M323
Su6
Summit Meeting on National Negro Leaders, Washington, D. C., 1958. Report of proceedings. 1958. (Card 2)

Contents - Continued.
Speech by Thurgood Marshall.- How shall we travel the road of freedom together, by F. L. Shuttleworth.
At head of title: Lighting the way to freedom.
Mimeographed.
1. Race relations. 2. Civil rights.
3. Freedom. I. Title. II. National Newspaper Publishers Association.

M811.5
H23r
Remembered encounters.
Harreld, Claudia White, -1952.
Remembered encounters. Atlanta, Logan Press, 1951.

44p. 24cm.

Inscribed by author.

Rendezvous with America.

M811.5
T58
Tolson, Melvin B
Rendezvous with America, by Melvin B. Tolson. New York, Dodd, Mead & company, 1944.
xii, 121 p. 19cm.
Poems.

I. Title.
Library of Congress PS3539.O334R4 44-7183
[45h5] 811.5

...Report of the United States Commission.

M972.94
Un3r
U. S. *Commission on education in Haiti.*
... Report of the United States Commission on education in Haiti. October 1, 1930. Washington, U. S. Govt. print. off., 1931.
vii, 74, [2] p. incl. map, tables. 24½cm. ([Publication, no. 166] Latin American series, no. 5)
R. R. Moton, chairman.

1. Education—Haiti. I. Moton, Robert Russa, 1867- II. U. S. Dept. of state. [Publication, no. 166] III. U. S. Dept. of state. Latin American series, no. 5. IV. Title.
31-26635
Library of Congress LA491.U6 1930
——— Copy 2. F1401.U65 no. 5
[33f3] 379.7294

Virgin Is.
M811.5
An29r
Reminiscence.
Anduze, Aubrey
Reminiscence. St. Thomas, Virgin Islands, The Art Shop, 1940.

89p. 22½cm.

Renfro, Gloster Herbert, 1867-1894.

M811.1
W561
1916
Wheatley, Phillis, afterwards Phillis Peters, 1753?-1784.
Life and works of Phillis Wheatley, containing her complete poetical works. Numerous letters, and a complete biography of the famous poet of a century and a half ago, by G. Herbert Renfro. Also a sketch of the life of Mr. Renfro by Leila Amos Pendleton. Washington, D. C. 1916.

112p. portrait, 19cm.

M366.1
R29
Report on Negro freemasonry. A consideration of the subject of Negro freemasonry by the Most Worshipful Grand Lodge of Masons in Massachusetts. Decrees of the Superior Court of Pennsylvania - October term 1946, favoring the W.M. Prince Hall Grand Lodge F. & A.M. of Pennsylvania.

29p. 23½cm.

1. Freemasons.

Reminiscences of Abraham Lincoln.

MB9
L63ri
Rice, Allen Thorndike, 1851-1889, ed.
Reminiscences of Abraham Lincoln by distinguished men of his time, collected and edited by Allen Thorndike Rice... New York, North American publishing company, 1886.

Repartition des groupessanguins Abo et Rh en Haiti.

Haiti
M612.1
R66
Romain, J B
Repartition des groupes sanguins Abo et Rh en Haiti. Port-au-Prince, Imprimerie de l'Etat, 1964.

[illegible]p. map. 23½cm.
Includes bibliography.

1. Blood. I. Title.

Report on Negro universities and colleges...

M06
J61
no. 21
Williams, William Taylor Burwell, 1866-1941.
Report on negro universities and colleges, by W. T. B. Williams ... [Baltimore?] 1922.
28 p. incl. tables. 23cm. (*On cover:* The Trustees of the John F. Slater fund. Occasional papers, no. 21)

1. Negroes—Education. 2. Universities and colleges—Southern states. I. Title.
23-7445
Library of Congress E185.5.J65 no. 21
——— Copy 2. E185.82.W72
[a44f1]

Reminiscences of college days.

MB9
F73r
Fonvielle, W F
Reminiscences of college days, by W. F. Fonvielle ... Goldsboro, N. C., Printed for the author by Edwards & Broughton, 1904.
143p. front. portraits. 20cm.

M324
M96s
Repeal of the Federal Election laws.
Murray, George Washington, 1853-1926.
Speech of Hon. G.W. Murray of South Carolina, on The Repeal of the Federal election laws, in the House of Representatives, October 5, 1893. [Lacks imprint]

14p. 24cm.

Haiti
M844
C23s
Representative government and representation.
Carrie, Francois Eugene.
Synthèse de la "jouissance effective" des droits de l'homme et des droits du peuple. Port-au-Prince, Haiti, 1943-1944.

vii, 137, iiip. 21cm.
At head of title: La Croisade démocratique; organe de défense des principes et des idéaux démocratiques, autorisé par le Département de l'Intérieur.
Mimeographed.
Haitian author.

Reminiscences of my life in camp...

M350
T21
Taylor, Susie King, 1848-
Reminiscences of my life in camp with the 33d United States colored troops, late 1st S. C. volunteers, by Susie King Taylor ... Boston, The author, 1902.
xii p., 1 l., 82 p. front., pl., ports. 19½cm.

1. U. S.—Hist.—Civil war—Regimental histories—U. S. inf.—33d. 2. U. S. infantry. 33d regt., 1862-1866. I. Title.
2-30128
Library of Congress E492.94.33dT
[a44b1]

A reply to Ariel.

M572
B45
Berry, Harrison, *b.* 1816.
A reply to Ariel. By Harrison Berry ... Macon, Geo., American union book and job office print, MDHIILXIX [*i. e.* 1869]
36 p. 22½cm.

1. Payne, Buckner H., 1799-1883. The negro ... 1867. 2. Negroes.
12-16791
Library of Congress HT1589.P33
[a38b1]

Republican party.

M329.6
R52a
Rivers, Francis E.
An appeal to the common sense of colored citizens, by Francis E. Rivers. New York, Republican national committee, 1940.

32p. 21½cm.

M329.6 Republican Party - Hist.
B79 **Brooke, Edward William, 1919–**
The challenge of change; crisis in our two-party system, by Edward W. Brooke. ₍1st ed.₎ Boston, Little, Brown ₍1966₎
xviii, 269 p. 22 cm.
Bibliography: p. 267–269.

1. U. S.—Pol. & govt.—20th cent. 2. Republican Party—Hist. 3. U. S.—Social policy. I. Title.

E743.B77 329.6 66–16557
Library of Congress ₍5₎

M329.6 Republican Party. National Convention. 8th
R29p Chicago, 1884.
Proceedings ... held at Chicago, Illinois June 3,4,5, and 6, 1884.
v.3 - 207p. 22½cm.
Partial contents: Addresses by -John R. Lynch, P.B.S. Pinchback, John C. Dancy, and Samuel Lee.

I.a.t. Lynch, John R. II.a.t. Pinchback, P.B.S. III.a.t. Dancy, John C. IV. a.t.Lee, Samuel.

The Republic of Liberia.
Liberia
M966.6 Yancy, Ernest Jerome
Y15re The Republic of Liberia. London, George Allen & Unwin, 1959.

144p. port. illus. 18½cm.

La resaca (bionovela).
Puerto Rico
M863 Laguerre, Enrique A
L63r La resaca (bionovela). San Juan de Puerto Rico, Biblioteca de Autores Puertorriquenos, 1949.

452p. 18½cm.

Le rescapé de l'Ethylos.
Mali
M132.161 Gologo, Mamadou
G58 Le rescapé de l'Ethylos. Paris, Présence Africaine ₍1963₎

378p. 18½cm.

Research.
M378 **West Virginia. State college, *Institute. Research council.***
W52a ... An adventure in cooperative research; Harry W. Greene, editor; associate editors: Herman G. Canady, Harrison H. Ferrell ₍and others₎ ... Personnel of Research council: Harry W. Greene, chairman; Hillery C. Thorne, executive secretary ₍and others₎ ... Institute, W. Va., West Virginia State college ₍1944₎
74 p. 23ᶜᵐ. (West Virginia state college bulletin. Ser. 31, no. 1. Feb. 1944)
Cover-title: The Research council at West Virginia State college publishes An adventure in cooperative research.
"Fourth contribution of the Research council."—Introd.
"The second of a series ... in connection with the semi-centennial celebration (1941) of the West Virginia State college."—Introd.
(Continued on next card)
44–42483
₍4₎

Research.
M378 West Virginia. State college, *Institute. Research council.*
W52a ... An adventure in cooperative research ... ₍1944₎ (Card 2)
CONTENTS.—The conference in review, by H. C. Thorne.—The theory of educational research, by J. S. Price.—The newer Negro and his education, by F. C. Sumner.—Some suggestions for research in the contribution of the Negro to American life, by John Lovell, jr.—The promotion of biological research, by H. E. Finley.—South America, a new frontier, by V. B. Spratlin.

1. Negroes. 2. Negroes—Education. 3. Negroes in South America. I. Greene, Harry Washington, 1896– ed. II. Title.
44–42483
Library of Congress E185.5.W5
₍4₎ 325.260073

Research and creative writings at West Virginia state college.
M378 **Greene, Harry Washington, 1896–**
G83t ... Two decades of research and creative writings at West Virginia state college, compiled by Harry W. Greene ... Institute, W. Va., West Virginia state college ₍1939₎
iv p., 1 l., ₍7₎–24 p. 23ᶜᵐ. (West Virginia state college bulletin. Ser. 26, no. 4. Aug.–Nov. 1939)
Contribution no. 2 of the Research council at West Virginia state college.
Publications of West Virginia state college.
Z5055.U5W45
(Continued on next card)
E 40–5 rev
₍r46e2₎†

Research company of America, New York.
M658.7 **Baltimore Afro-American.**
B21 Baltimore, America's 5th largest Negro market; a report on the characteristics of the Baltimore Negro market, its buying habits and brand preferences in 1945, from a survey by the Research company of America, N. Y., analyzed and projected by the Harry Hayden company, N. Y., compiled and published by the Baltimore Afro-American. ₍Baltimore₎ °1946.
1 p. l., 100 p. illus., diagrs. 28 x 22ᶜᵐ.

1. Market surveys—Baltimore. 2. Negroes—Baltimore. I. Research company of America, New York. II. Hayden (Harry) company, New York. III. Title.

HF3163.B2B3 658.8 47–16240
Library of Congress ₍3₎

Research Company of America, N. Y.
M658.7 Baltimore Afro-American.
B21 Baltimore, America's 5th largest Negro market; a report on the characteristics of the Baltimore Negro market, its buying habits and brand preferences in 1945, from a survey by the Research company of America, N. Y. analyzed and projected by the Harry Hayden Company, N. Y. Compiled and published by the Baltimore Afro-American ₍Baltimore₎ c1946.

1p. 100p. illus. diagr. 28x22cm.

Research company of America, N. Y.
M658.7 Washington Afro-American.
W27 The Washington Afro-American report on characteristics of the Washington Negro market...its product buying and brand preferences in 1945, compiled by the Washington Afro-American, from a survey conductedby the Research company of America. Washington, D.C. c1945.

92p. illus., diagrs. 28x22cm.

A resemblance and a contrast between the American Negro
M815.5 **Grimke, Francis James, 1850–**
G88 A resemblance and a contrast between the American
v.1,no.2 negro and the children of Israel in Egypt, or The duty of the negro to contend earnestly for his rights guaranteed under the Constitution. This discourse was delivered in the Fifteenth street Presbyterian church. By the pastor, Rev. Francis J. Grimke, D. D., October 12th, 1902 ... ₍Washington, 1902₎
14 p. 23ᶜᵐ.
Caption title.
1. Negroes—Civil rights. I. Title.
18–15157
Library of Congress E185.61.G885
₍37₍1₎

The resentment .
M813.5 **Spencer, Mary Etta.**
Sp3r The resentment, by Mary Etta Spencer. ₍Philadelphia, Printed by A. M. E. book concern, 1921₎
4 p. l., ₍7₎–216 p. 20½ cm.

I. Title.
21–20882
Library of Congress PZ3.S7466Re
₍48c1₎

The reservoir.
Nigeria
M966.9 Akpan, Ntieyong U ,1924–
Ak6r The reservoir. Abridged and adapted by G. Plummer. Illustrated by E.F. Gibbons. London, Longmans, Green and Co., 1959.

86p. 18cm. (New English Supplementary Reader. Stage 5)

Haiti La resistance haitienne.
M972.94 **Bellegarde, Dantès, 1877–**
B41re ... La résistance haïtienne (l'occupation américaine d'Haïti); récit d'histoire contemporaine. Montréal, Éditions Beauchemin, 1937.
2 p. l., ₍9₎–175 p., 2 l. incl. front. (map) plates. 20½ᶜᵐ.
Bibliographical foot-notes.

1. Haiti—Hist.—1844– 2. U. S.—For. rel.—Haiti. 3. Haiti—For. rel.—U. S. I. Title.
₍Full name: Louis Dantès Bellegarde₎
A C 38–1300
New York. Public library for Library of Congress F1926.B44
₍a43c1₎

Resolutions.
Africa
M960 Conference of Independent African States.
C76d Declaration and resolutions, 22nd April, 1958. Accra, Parliament House, 1958.

16p. 21cm.

1. Africa - Politics and govt. 2. Resolutions. I. Title.

Resolutions of the National Negro Congress held in Chicago, Ill...
M06 National Negro Congress.
N21r Resolutions of the National Negro Congress held in Chicago, Ill. February 14, 15, 16, 1936. ₍n.p.₎ 1936.
19p. 21cm.

Resources in Negro youth.
M323 National association for the advancement
N21 of colored people.
Resources in Negro youth. New York city, National association for the advancement of colored people, 1940.
13p. 20cm.

Respect for human dignity.
Nigeria
M966.9 Azikiwe, Nnamdi, 1904–
Az2re Respect for human dignity; an inaugural address delivered by His Excellency Dr. Nnamdi Azikiwe, Governor General and Commander-in-Chief ₍of the₎ Federation of Nigeria, 16 November, 1960. ₍Enugu, Government Printer₎ 1960.

25p. ports. 25cm.
Biographical data: pp. 19-25.

Nigeria Respect for human dignity.
M966.9 Azikiwe, Benjamin Nnamdi, 1904–
Az2zi Zik on African unity; opening address to the heads of African and Malagasy States Conference in Lagos, 25th Jan. 1962 & Respect for human dignity; inaugural address delivered on 16th November 1960. Lagos, Udo-Na-Meche Stores, 1962.

21p. 22½cm
Cover title.

Responsibilities of the party member.
Trinidad
M972.98 Williams, Eric Eustace, 1911–
W67r Responsibilities of the party member by Dr. Eric Williams, prèmier of Trinidad and Tobago; full text of the political leader's address to the fifth annual convention on Friday, September (1960). ₍Port-of-Spain, P.N.M., 1960₎

16p. 21cm.

Restless nations.
M909.82 C76a
Conference on Tensions in Development, *Oxford University, 1961.*
Restless nations; a study of world tensions and development. Foreword by Lester B. Pearson. ~~New York, Dodd, Mead, 1962.~~ London, Allen and Unwin [1962]
217 p. 22 cm.
Sponsored by the Council on World Tensions.
1. Underdeveloped areas. 2. Economic assistance. 3. World politics—1955– I. Council on World Tensions. II. Title.
HC60.C63 1961 338.91 62—16328 ‡
Library of Congress [64v7]

Rethinking our Christianity.
M230 H87r
Hughley, Judge Neal, 1907–
Rethinking our Christianity, by J. Neal Hughley ... Philadelphia, Dorrance and company [°1942]
8 p. l., 15-242 p. 19½ cm.
Bibliographical foot-notes.
1. Christianity—Essence, genius, nature. I. Title.
42-8142
Library of Congress BR121.H76
[3] 230

Revels, Hiram Rhoades, 1827-1901.
M89 R321a
Lawson, Elizabeth,
The gentleman from Mississippi; our first Negro congressman, Hiram R. Revels, by Elizabeth Lawson with an introduction by William L. Patterson. [New York, published by author, c 1960]
63p. ports. 19cm.
Reference notes: p. 54-63.
White author.

Restless nations; a study of world tensions and development.
M909.82 C76
Conference on Tensions in Development, *Oxford University, 1961.*
Restless nations; a study of world tensions and development. Foreword by Lester B. Pearson. New York, Dodd, Mead, 1962.
217 p. 22 cm.
Sponsored by the Council on World Tensions.
1. Underdeveloped areas. 2. Economic assistance. 3. World politics—1955– I. Council on World Tensions. II. Title.
HC60.C63 1961 338.91 62—16328 ‡
Library of Congress [64v7]

Retour de Guyane.
French Guiana
M841 D18r
Damas, Leon G., 1912-
Retour de Guyane. Paris, Librairie José Corti [1938]
203p. 18½cm.

Revels of fancy.
M811.5 V28r
Vandyne, William Johnson
Revels of fancy, by William Johnson Vandyne two lines of verse Boston A.F. Grant, publishers, 1891.
50p. 17½cm.

Restoration verse.
M811.08 B73b4
Braithwaite, William Stanley Beaumont, 1878– *comp.*
The book of restoration verse; chosen and ed. with notes by William Stanley Braithwaite ... New York, Brentano's, 1910.
3 p. l., xiii-xv, 864 p. 17cm.
Title vignette.
Forms the second in a series of four volumes to cover British poetry from the publications of Tottel's miscellany, 1557; the other volumes being The book of Elizabethan verse, The book of Georgian verse, and The book of Victorian verse (not yet published?)
1. English poetry—Early modern (to 1700) I. Title. II. Title: Restoration verse.
9—29554
Library of Congress PR1173.B5 vol. 2
Copyright A 251718 [3711]

Return of the sun.
M301 B81
Brown, Eugene, 1919-
Return of the sun. [New York, The Michromac Publishing Company, 1959]
52p. 20cm.

Revenants.
France
M840 D891re
Dumas, Alexandre, 1824-1895.
Revenants, par Alexandre Dumas, fils. Bruxelles, Meline, Cans et Cie., 1851.
278p. 16cm.

Restoration verse.
M811.08 B73b
Braithwaite, William Stanley Beaumont, 1878– *comp.*
The book of restoration verse; chosen and ed. with notes by William Stanley Braithwaite ... London, Duckworth, 1909.
xv, 864p. 19cm.
Title vignette.
Forms the second in a series of four volumes to cover British poetry from the publications of Tottel's miscellany, 1557; the other volumes being The book of Elizabethan verse, The book of Georgian verse, and The book of Victorian verse (not yet published?)
1. English poetry—Early modern (to 1700) I. Title. II. Title: Restoration verse.
9—29554
Library of Congress PR1173.B5 vol. 2
Copyright A 251718 [3711]

Return to Goli.
South Africa
M896.3 Ab8r
Abrahams, Peter, 1919–
Return to Goli. London, Faber and Faber [1953]
224 p. 19 cm.
Autobiographical.
1. Africa, South—Native races. 2. Johannesburg—Descr. I. Title.
DT763.A62 1953 *301.451 325.260968 53—30755 ‡
Library of Congress [54c1]

Rêves de feu.
Haiti
M841 D47r
Desroches, Luc L.
Rêves de feu, poèmes. Haiti, Les Presses Libres, [1951?]
30p. 20cm. (Collection Nos poètes)

Restrepo, Antonio Jose, jt. auth.
Colombia
M89 Ob2u
Uribe, Juan De D.
Candelario Obeso, por Juan de D. Uribe y Antonio J. Restrepo. Bogota, Imprenta de Vapor de Zalamea Hermanes, 1886.
28p. 17cm.

Réunion
M398 H44f
Réunion
Hery, Louis-Emile
Fables créoles et explorations dans l'intérieur de l'Île Bourbon. nouvelle edition. Paris, Typographie et Lithographie J. Rigal. 1883.
193p. 25cm.

Reves et chant...
Haiti
M841 C46r
Chrisphonte, Prosper.
Reves et chants, preface d M. le Colonel Nemours. Paris, Jouve & cie, 1929.

The resurrection & other poems.
M811.5 B78r
Brooks, Jonathan Henderson, 1905–1945.
The Resurrection & other poems. Dallas, Kaleidograph Press [1948]
55 p. 20 cm.
I. Title.
PS3503.R725R4 811.5 49-18197*
Library of Congress [1]

The revelation of Saint Orgne the damned...
M301 D85r7
Du Bois, William Edward Burghardt, 1868–
The revelation of Saint Orgne the damned, by W. E. Burghardt Du Bois. Commencement, 1938, Fisk university. [Nashville, Hemphill press [°1939]
16 p. 23cm.
Copy number: 64
Autographed: W.E.B. DuBois
1. Negroes—Education. 2. Negroes—Moral and social conditions. I. Title.
39-8222
Library of Congress E185.6.D705
——— Copy 2.
Copyright A 126710 [2] 825.26

Review of the revolutionary elements of the rebellion.
M973.8 P98r
Putnam, Lewis H
The review of the revolutionary elements of the rebellion, and of the aspect of reconstruction; with a plan to restore harmony between the two races in the southern states. By a colored man. Brooklyn, 1868.
44p. 23cm.
Introduction signed: L.H. Putnam.

Resurreição.
Brazil
M869.3 M18re7
Machado de Assis, Joaquim Maria, 1839–1908.
... Resurreição. Rio de Janeiro [etc.] W. M. Jackson inc., 1937.
235 p., 1 l. front. (port.) 20cm.
At head of title: Machado de Assis.
First published 1872.
I. Title.
38-32243
Library of Congress PQ9697.M18R45 1937
[2] 869.3

Revelations.
M231.74 Yo8s
Young, Lucinda Smith.
The seven seals. " A sinner's dream", " conversion," "Daniel in the lion's den," "meditation," "distance of falling ," vision of the judgement," vision of after the judgement,".
By Madame Lucinda Smith-Young. Philadelphia, Pa., J. Gordan Baugh, 1903.
199p. front. plates. 18½cm.

A review of Zulu literature.
South Africa
M896 N98r
Nyembezi, Cyril Lincoln Sibusiso, 1919-
A review of Zulu literature. University lecture delivered in the University of Natal, Pietermaritzburg, 7th June, 1961. Pietermaritzburg, University of Natal Press, 1961.
10p. 21½cm.
1. Zulu literature - History and criticism.

The review or the revolutionary elements ...

M973.8 P98r
Putnam, Lewis H
The review of the revolutionary elements of the rebellion, and of the aspect of reconstruction; with a plan to restore harmony between the two races in the southern states. By a colored man. Brooklyn, 1868.
44 p. 23cm.
Introduction signed: L. H. Putnam.
1. Reconstruction. I. Title.
Library of Congress E668.P98 4—15532 [a29d1]

M811.5 R33
Reynolds, Evelyn Crawford.
To no special land; a book of poems, by Eve Lynn [pseud.] With a foreword by Mary McLeod Bethune. [1st ed.] New York, Exposition Press [1953]
64 p. 21 cm.
I. Title.
PS3535.E945T6 811.5 53-7871 ‡
Library of Congress [2]

Rhodes, Cecil John, 1853-1902-Fiction.
Rhodesia
M896.3 Sa46o
Samkange, Stanlake John Thompson, 1922–
On trial for my country [by] Stanlake Samkange. London, Heinemann, 1966.
viii, 160 p. 20½ cm. 18/- (B 66-17472)
Map on endpapers.
1. Lobengula, King of the Matabele, 1833 (ca.)-1893?—Fiction. 2. Rhodes, Cecil John, 1853-1902—Fiction. I. Title.
PZ4.S188On 67-70814
Library of Congress [3]

Revised search light on the seventh day...

M220.7 B69r
Boyd, Boston Napoleon Bonapart, 1860–
Revised search light on the seventh day Bible and x-ray, by organic, supernatural and artificial science; discoveries of the twentieth century, by Boston Napoleon Bonapart Boyd. Greenville, N. C., 1924.
250 p. front. (port.) 20½cm.
Revised edition of "Search light on the seventh wonder".
I. Title.
Library of Congress BS530.B6 1924 25-520
——— Copy 2.
Copyright A 815029 [2]

Rhapsodie caribe.
Guadeloupe
M841 D37r
Delisle, Gérard, 1927–
Rhapsodie caribe. [Paris, Gallimard [1960]
81 p. 19 cm. (Jeune poésie NRF)
I. Title.
Illinois. Univ. Library for Library of Congress A 61-1869 [8]

M973 R34n
Rhodes, Jacob
The national history of the colored people, containing a collection of facts respecting the origin, character and prospects of the African race, by Rev. Jacob Rhodes... New York, Published for the author, 1850.
32p. 14cm.
1. History.

La révolution de 1843.
Haiti
M972.94 M31r
Manigat, Leslie
La révolution de 1843; essai d'analyse historique d'une conjoncture de crise. [Port-au-Prince] le Normalien [1959]
31p. 23cm.
Bibliography.

Rheumatism.
M610 P19 v.1 no.5
Jackson, Algernon Brashear, 1878-
The injection of magnesium sulphate for acute articular rheumatism, by Algernon Brashear Jackson... Reprinted from the New York medical jlurnal for June 24, 1911.
8p. 20½cm.

Rhodes, James Ford, 1848-
History of the United States from the compromise of 1850 ...
M973.8 L99s
Lynch, John Roy, 1847–
Some historical errors of James Ford Rhodes, by Major John R. Lynch. Boston, New York, The Cornhill publishing company [1922]
xx, 115 p. front., ports. 19cm.
1. Rhodes, James Ford, 1848– History of the United States from the compromise of 1850 ... 2. Negroes—Politics and suffrage. I. Title.
22—23557
Library of Congress E415.7.R479
——— Copy 2.
Copyright A 690397 [37d1]

Revolution of color series.
South Africa
M968.91 M879
Mtshali, Benedict Vulindlela
Rhodesia: background to conflict [by] B. Vulindlela Mtshali. New York, Hawthorn Books [1967]
255 p. 24 cm. (Revolution of color)
Bibliographical references included in "Notes": p.203-211. "The politics of southern Africa, 1960-1966, a selective bibliography": p. 215-244.
1. Rhodesia-Pol. & govt. I. Title. (Series Revolution of color series)

Rheumatism.
M610 P19 v.1 no.6
Jackson, Algernon Brashear, 1878-
The treatment of rheumatism by injection of magnesium sulphate, by Algernon Brashear Jackson... Reprinted from "The Practitioner for January, 1912.
3p. 24½cm.
Bound in: Medical pamphlets.

Haiti
M843.91 T35b
Rhodes, Peter C., tr.
Thoby-Marcelin, Philippe, 1904–
The beast of the Haitian hills, by Philippe Thoby-Marcelin and Pierre Marcelin, translated from the French, La bête du Musseau, by Peter C. Rhodes. New York, Toronto, Rinehart & company, inc. [1946]
5 p. l., 3-210 p. 19½cm.
I. Marcelin, Pierre, 1908– joint author. II. Rhodes, Peter C., tr. III. Title.
[Full name: Émile Philippe Thoby-Marcelin]
PZ3.T35Be 843.91 46-8130
© 7Nov46; 2c 12Oct46; publisher, New York; A8804.
Library of Congress [5]

Revolutions.
Trinidad
M320 J23w
James, Cyril Lionel Robert, 1901–
... World revolution, 1917-1936; the rise and fall of the Communist International. London, M. Secker and Warburg, ltd. [1937]
xii, 9-429 p. 22cm.
At head of title: C. L. R. James.
"How much the book owes to the writings of Trotsky, the text can only partially show."—p. xii.
1. Communist International. 2. Communism. 3. Revolutions. 4. World politics. 5. Russia—Pol. & govt.—20th cent. 6. Trotskil, Lev, 1879-1940. 7. Stalin, Iosif, 1879– I. Title.
37—23067
Library of Congress HX11.I 5J25 [45g1] 335.40621

Rhode Island.
MB9 B818L
Brown, William J b. 1814.
The life of William J. Brown, of Providence, R. I. With personal recollections of incidents in Rhode Island. Providence, Angell & co., printers, 1883.
230 p. 19½cm.
1. Negroes—Rhode Island. 2. Rhode Island—Soc. life & cust.
16—14559
Library of Congress E185.97.B88 [37b1]

Rhodesia.
Rhodesia
M968.91 Sh17
Shamuyarira, Nathan M 1929–
Crisis in Rhodesia. With a foreword by Sir Hugh Foot. [London] Andre Deutsch [1965]
240p. map. 22½cm.
Portrait of author on book jacket.
I. Rhodesia. I. Title.

M323 R32n
Revolutionary Workers League.
The Negro under capitalism; Resolution adopted by the fourth plenum of the Central Committee of the Revolutionary Workers League of the United States, September 3-4, 1930. Detroit, Demos Press, 193 .
12p. 27cm.
Mimeographed.
1. Race question. 2. Labor and laboring classes. I. Title.

Rhode Island.
M366.1 F87r
Freemasons. rRhode Island. Grand Lodge.
Proceedings. 1st- 1876-
Providence, 1878-
v. 22cm. annual
1st, 2nd, 3rd, proceedings published together with the constitution, by-laws and rurles of order.
See holdings card for proceedings in library.

Rhodesia - Politics & government.
South Africa
M968.91 M879
Mtshali, Benedict Vulindlela
Rhodesia: background to conflict [by] B. Vulindlela Mtshali. New York, Hawthorn Books [1967]
255 p. 24 cm. (Revolution of color)
Bibliographical references included in "Notes": p. 203-211. "The politics of southern Africa, 1960-1966, a selective bibliography": p. 215-244.
1. Rhodesia—Pol. & govt. I. Title. (Series: Revolution of color series)
DT948.M7 968.9'1 67-15557
Library of Congress [5]

M811.5 R33m
Reynolds, Evelyn Crawford.
... No alabaster box and other poems, by Eve Lynn, [pseud.] with an introduction by Gene Rhodes. Philadelphia, Alpress, 1936.
37p. 24cm.
Limited edition of 350 copies. This copy is number 264.
1. Poetry. I. Title.

Rhode Island-Soc. life & cust.
MB9 B818L
Brown, William J b. 1814.
The life of William J. Brown, of Providence, R. I. With personal recollections of incidents in Rhode Island. Providence, Angell & co., printers, 1883.
230 p. 19½cm.
1. Negroes—Rhode Island. 2. Rhode Island—Soc. life & cust.
16—14559
Library of Congress E185.97.B88 [37b1]

Rhodesia, Northern - Fiction.
Zambia
M896.3 M38L
Massiye, A Sylvester
The lonely village. London, Thomas Nelson, 1951.
48p. map. 18½cm. (Eagle fiction library)

Rhodesia, Northern - Native races.
Zambia
M968.94 Mupatu, Y W
M93 Mulambwa Santulu u amuhela bo mwene. [Mulambwa Santulu welcomes the Mbunda chiefs] London, Macmillan, 1958.
37p. 18cm. (Bantu heritage series)
Written in Lozi.

Rhodesia, Northern - Politics and government.
Northern Rhodesia
MB9 Kaunda, Kenneth D 1924-
K16 Zambia shall be free; an autobiography. ~~New York, Praeger [1963, °1962]~~ London, Heinemann, 1962.
202 p. illus. 19 cm. (Books that matter)
1. Rhodesia, Northern—Pol. & govt. I. Title.
DT963.K3 968.94 63-8622 ‡
Library of Congress [5]

Rhodesia, Northern - Politics and government.
Rhodesia, Northern
MB9 Kaunda, Kenneth D 1924-
K16a Zambia shall be free; an autobiography. New York, Praeger [1963, °1962]
202 p. illus. 19 cm. (Books that matter)
1. Rhodesia, Northern—Pol. & govt. I. Title.
DT963.K3 968.94 63-8622 ‡
Library of Congress [5]

Rhodesia, Southern - Grammar.
Rhodesia, S.
M496 Chitepo, H W
C44s Soko risina musoro. Translated and edited with notes by Hazel Carter. London, Oxford University Press, 1958.
61p. 21½cm.

Rhodesia and Nyasaland.
Rhodesia
M968.9 Leys, Colin, ed.
C43 A new deal in Central Africa, edited by Colin Leys and Cranford Pratt. New York, Praeger [1960]
226 p. illus. 22 cm. (Books that matter)
Includes bibliography.
1. Rhodesia and Nyasaland. I. Pratt, Cranford, joint ed. II. Title.
DT856.L4 968.9 60-12201 ‡
Library of Congress [20]

Rhodesia and Nyasaland - Native races.
Malawi
M968.9 Chiume, Kanyama, 1929-
C44 The Federation of Rhodesia and Nyasaland: the future of the dilemma [by] Channing Richardson, Kanyama Chiume, Joshua Nkomo [and others. New York] American Committee on Africa [°1959]
38p. 22cm. (Africa today pamphlets, 4)

Rhodesia and Nyasaland - Pol. & govt.
Malawi
M968.9 Chiume, Kanyama, 1929-
C44 The Federation of Rhodesia and Nyasaland: the future of the dilemma [by] Channing Richardson, Kanyama Chiume, Joshua Nkomo [and others. New York] American Committee on Africa [°1959]
38p. 22cm. (Africa today pamphlets, 4)

Rhodesia: background to conflict.
South Africa
M968.91 Mtshali, Benedict Vulindlela
M879 Rhodesia: background to conflict [by] B. Vulindlela Mtshali. New York, Hawthorn Books [1967]
255 p. 24 cm. (Revolution of color)
Bibliographical references included in "Notes": p. 208-211. "The politics of southern Africa, 1960-1966, a selective bibliography": p. 215-244.
1. Rhodesia—Pol. & govt. I. Title. (Series: Revolution of color series)
DT948.M7 968.9'1 67-15557
Library of Congress [5]

Rhyme and reason.
M811.5 Simpkins, Thomas V
S158r Rhyme and reason. Boston, Christopher Pub. House [1949]
95 p. 21 cm.
Poems.
I. Title.
PS3537.I 7R45 811.5 49-1799*
Library of Congress [2]

The rhyme of the devil-germs.
M811.5 Howell, Wilbert R.
H839r The rhyme of the devil-germs. New York, Pageant Press, 1963.
28p. illus. 20cm.

Rhymes, tales and rhymed tales.
M811.5 Allen, J Mord, 1875-
A15r Rhymes, tales and rhymed tales, by J. Mord Allen. Topeka, Kansas, Monotyped by Crane & Co., 1906.
153p. 18cm.

Rhymes and jingles for the children's hour.
M811.5 Carrigan, Nettie W.
C23r Rhymes and jingles for the children's hour, by Nettie W. Carrigan ... Boston, The Christopher publishing house [c1940]
3p. l., v-vip., 1 l., 9-57p. 19cm.

Rhymes & sketches...
M811.5 Wilson, William Green, 1867-
W69r Rhymes & sketches from the cabin fireside, by William Green Wilson. [Selma, Ala., Lloyd printing company, °1931]
2 p. l., 62, [2] p. 21½cm.
I. Title.
CA 31-1104 Unrev'd
Library of Congress PS3545.I 643R5 1931
——— Copy 2.
Copyright A 45073 811.5

Rhymes of a rhymster.
M811.5 Clem, Charles Douglass, 1875-
C59r Rhymes of a rhymster. Edmond, Oklahoma, The author, 1901.
52p. port. 17½cm.

Rhymes of puppy love and others.
M811.5 Simpkins, Thomas V.
S158r3 Rhymes of puppy love and others, including Negro dialect, by Thomas V. Simpkins ... Boston, The Christopher publishing house [°1935]
x, 13-60 p. 20½cm.
I. Title.
35-876
Library of Congress PS3537.I 7R5 1935
Copyright A 79074 [3] 811.5

Rhythm.
M813.5 Hughes, Langston, 1902-
H87fibr The first book of rhythms. Pictures by Robin King. New York, F. Watts [1954]
63 p. illus. 23 cm. ([First books] 49)
Inscribed by author.
1. Rhythm. I. Title.
BH301.R5H8 *101 701.17 54-5991 ‡
Library of Congress [20]

The rhythm of violence.
Africa, South
M896.2 Nkosi, Lewis
N65 The rhythm of violence. London, Oxford University Press, 1964.
69p. 18½cm.
"A three crowns book"

Riathana ria ikumi na rimwe kana umenyeeri bwa muthetu.
Kenya
M630 Lowdermilk, Walter C
L95e Riathana ria ikumi na rimwe kana umenyeeri bwa muthetu [The eleventh commandment or Care of the land] [Tr. by Samson Mzee] [London, W. & J. Mackay, n.d.]
16p. 18cm.
Written in Meru.
White author.
1. Agriculture - Kenya. I. Title.

Brazil
M869.2 Ribeiro, Joaquim.
N17d Aruanda.
Pp. 287-307.
In: Nascimento, Abdias do, ed. Dramas papa Negroes e prologo pars brancos. Rio de Janeiro, Teatro Experimental do Negro, 1961.
I. Title.

MB9 Rice, Allen Thorndike, 1851-1889, ed.
L63ri Reminiscences of Abraham Lincoln by distinguished men of his time, collected and edited by Allen Thorndike Rice ... New York, North American publishing company, 1886.
lxix, 2-13, 656 p. incl. facsims. front., plates, ports., fold. facsim. 23½cm.
Biographical sketches [of authors]: p. 609-649.
1. Lincoln, Abraham, pres. U. S., 1809-1865. [Full name: Charles Allen Thorndike Rice]
12-17395 rev
Library of Congress E457.15.R49 1886
[r45b2]

Richard Allen from a slave boy...
M812.5 Baxter, Daniel Minort
B33r Richard Allen from a slave boy to the first bishop of African methodist episcopal church, 1760-1816; a drama in four acts, by Rev. Daniel Minort Baxter... [Philadelphia, Pa., the A.M.E. book concern, 1934]
59p. 15½cm.

Richard III, King of Eng., 1452-1485-Drama.

M812.3 Séjour, Victor, 1816-1874.
Se4m Richard III, Drame en cinq actes, en prose.
no.3 Nouvelle édition. Paris, Michel Lévy Frères, 1870.

108p. 19cm.

Richard Wright's blues.

M813.5 The Antioch review.
E14r The Antioch review anthology; essays, fiction, poetry, and reviews from the Antioch review. Edited by Paul Bixler. [1st ed.] Cleveland, World Pub. Co. [1953]

470p. 22cm.

M323 **Richards, Eugene S**
R38 Ethnic relations in the United States [by] Edward C. McDonagh and Eugene S. Richards. New York, Appleton-Century-Crofts [1953]

xiv, 408 p. illus. 25 cm. (Appleton-Century-Crofts sociology series)

Includes bibliographies.

1. Minorities—U. S. 2. U. S.—Race question. I. ~~Richards, Eugene S., joint author~~ II. Title.
I. McDonagh, Edward C jt. auth.

E184.A1M137 325.73 52-13692

Library of Congress [20]

MB **Richardson, Ben Albert.**
R39g Great American Negroes; rev. by William A. Fahey, illustrated by Robert Hallock. New York, Crowell [1956]
1956

339 p. illus. 21 cm.

1. ~~Negroes~~—Biog. I. Title.

E185.96.R5 1956 325.260973 56—9808 ‡

Library of Congress [57r°10]

MB **Richardson, Ben Albert.**
R39g Great American Negroes [by] Ben Richardson, illustrated by Louise Costello. New York, Thomas Y. Crowell company [1945]

viii, 223 p. illus., ports. 21cm.

CONTENTS.—Popular music: Duke Ellington. William C. Handy. Fats Waller.—The orchestra: Dean Dixon.—Classical music: William Grant Still.—Singers: Marian Anderson.—The theater: Paul Robeson. Katherine Dunham.—Boxers: Joe Louis.—Track stars: Jesse Owens.—Education: Mordecai W. Johnson. Mary McLeod Bethune.—Science and invention: George Washington Carver. Charles Drew.—Literature: Langston Hughes.—The church: Adam Clayton Powell, sr.—Politics: Adam Clayton Powell, jr. Walter White.—The military: Crispus Attucks. Benjamin O. Davis, sr. Benjamin O. Davis, jr.

1. Negroes—Biog. I. Title.

Library of Congress E185.96.R5 45—9710

[46v²10] 325.260973

Richardson. Clement, 1878- ed.

MB **The National cyclopedia of the colored race;** editor-in-chief,
R39 Clement Richardson ...
Montgomery, Ala., National publishing company, inc., 1919-

v. illus., ports. 31cm.

1. Negroes. 2. Negroes—Biog. I. Richardson, Clement, 1878- ed.

Library of Congress E185.N27 19—15870

[a41f1]

Trinidad
M972.98 Richardson, E C
R39 Onward Trinidad; the solution to our economic and social problems. [Port-of-Spain, Enterprise Electric Printery, n.d.]

25p. 22½cm.

1. Trinidad - Economic condition.
2 Trinidad - Social conditions. I. Title.

M280 **Richardson, Harry Van Buren,** 1901-
R36d Dark glory, a picture of the church among Negroes in the rural South. New York, Pub. for Home Missions Council of North America and Phelps-Stokes Fund by Friendship Press [1947]

xiv, 209 p. 19 cm.

"A selected reading list": p. 194-197.

1. ~~Negroes~~—Religion. I. Title.

BR563.N4R5 277.5 47—24753*

Library of Congress [49h1]

M231 Richardson, Harry Van Buren, 1901-
W62 Why I believe there is a God.

Pp. 74-80.

In: Why I believe there is a God. Chicago, Johnson Pub. Co, 1965.

Liberia
M966.6 Richardson, Nathaniel R
R391 Liberia's past and present. London, The Diplomatic Press and Publishing Company, 1959.

348p. illus. ports. 28cm.

1. Liberia - History. 2. Liberia - Biographies.

M812.5 **Richardson, Thomas.**
R38p Place: America (a theatre piece) by Thomas Richardson, based on the history of the National association for the advancement of colored people, foreword by Sterling A. Brown. New York, National association for the advancement of colored people [°1939]

51 p. 20cm.

I. National association for the advancement of colored people. II. Title. 1. Drama.

Library of Congress PN6120.N4R45 40-8718

——— Copy 2.

Copyright D pub. 69096 [2] 812.5

M812.08 Richardson, Willis, 1889-
Sh2 The Chip woman's fortune.

(In: Shay, Frank, ed. Fifty more comtemporary one-act plays. N.Y., D. Appleton and company, 1928. 21cm. p.413-424.)

M812.5 **Richardson, Willis, 1889-**
R38K The king's dilemma, and other plays for children; episodes of hope and dream. [1st ed.] New York, Exposition Press [1956]

71 p. 21 cm.

1. Children's plays. I. Title.

PN6120.A5R492 812.5 56-11597 ‡

Library of Congress [2]

M812.08 **Richardson, Willis, 1889-** *ed.*
R39n Negro history in thirteen plays, by Willis Richardson and May Miller. Washington, D. C., The Associated publishers, inc. [°1935]

vii, 333 p. 21½cm.

1. Negro drama. 2. Negroes in literature and art. I. Miller, May, joint ed. II. Title.

Library of Congress PS627.N4R47 36—17

[43u2] 812.50822

M812.08 **Richardson, Willis, 1889-** *comp.*
R39 Plays and pageants from the life of the Negro [compiled by] Willis Richardson. Washington, D. C., The Associated publishers, inc. [°1930]

x, 373 p. incl. front., illus., plates. 22½cm.

CONTENTS.—Plays: Sacrifice, by Thelma M. Duncan. Antar of Araby, by Maud Cuney-Hare. Ti Yette, by John Matheus. Graven images, by May Miller. Riding the goat, by May Miller. The black horseman, by Willis Richardson. The king's dilemma, by Willis Richardson. The house of sham, by Willis Richardson.—Pageants: Two races, by Inez M. Burke. Out of the dark, by Dorothy C. Guinn. The light of the women, by Frances Gunner. Ethiopia at the bar of justice, by Edward J. McCoo.

1. Negro drama. 2. Negroes in literature and art. I. Title.

Library of Congress PS627.N4R5 30—7094

[43n1]

Rich heritage; songs about American Negro heroes.

M784 Pittman, Evelyn LaRue
P68r Rich heritage; songs about American Negro heroes. Oklahoma City, Oklahoma, Harlow Publishing Corporation, 1944.

48p. illus. ports. 30cm.

Martinique Richer, Clément, 1915-
M843.9 La croisiere de "La Priscilla," roman.
R39c Paris, Plon, [1947]

247p. 19cm.

I. Title

Martinique Richer, Clément
M843.9 Le dernier voyage du "Pembroke", roman.
R39d Paris, Plon, 1940.

248p. 19cm.
"Prix Marianne 1939."

I. Title

Martinique Richer, Clément
M843.9 Les femmes preferent les brutes. Paris.
R39fe Roger Seban, 1949.

179p. 19cm.

I. Title

Martinique Richer, Clement
M843.9 Le fils de Ti-Coyo, roman. Paris,
R39fi Plon, 1954.

254p. 19cm.

I. title

Martinique **Richer, Clément.**
M843.9 L'homme de la caravelle, roman. Paris, Plon [1952]
R39h 254 p. 19 cm.

I. Title.

A 53-2759

Illinois. Univ. Library for Library of Congress [2]

Martinique
M843.91 Richer, Clément.
R39l Len Sly, roman. Paris, Plon [1949]
245 p. 19 cm.

I. Title.

Illinois. Univ. Library for Library of Congress [1] A 50-3150

Martinique
M843.91 Richer, Clément.
R39p Les passagers du Perwyn; roman. Paris, Stock, Delamain et Boutelleau, 1944.
212 p. 19 cm.

I. Title.

PQ2635.I 39P3 50-41225
Library of Congress [2]

Richer, Clément.
Martinique Son of Ti-Coyo; translated from the French by Gerard
M843.91 Hopkins. London, R. Hart-Davis, 1954.
R39s 143 p. 21 cm.
"First published in French under the title of Nouvelles aventures de Ti-Coyo et de son requin."

I. Title.

PZ3.R404So 843.91 54-26080 ‡
Library of Congress [1]

Richer, Clément.
Martinique Son of Ti-Coyo. [Translated from the French by Gerard
M843.91 Hopkins. 1st American ed.] New York, Knopf, 1954.
R39s2 245 p. illus. 21 cm.

I. Title.

PZ3.R404So 2 843.91 54-7200 ‡
Library of Congress [8]

Martinique
M843.91 Richer, Clément.
R39t Ti-Coyo and his shark: an immoral fable. [Translated from the French by Gerard Hopkins. 1st American ed.] New York, Knopf, 1951.
235 p. illus. 21 cm.

I. Title.

PZ3.R404Ti 51—11057
Library of Congress [53g2]

Martinique
M843.91 Richer, Clément.
R39t2 ... Ti-coyo et son requin. Paris, Plon [1941]
2 p. l., 248 p., 1 l. 18½ cm.

I. Title.

Library of Congress PQ2635.I 32T5 45-34517
[2] 843.91

Martinique
M843.91 Richer, Clément, 1915-
R39t3 Ti-Coyo und sein hai (Ti-Coyo et son requin.) Darmstadt und Genf, Holle, 1953.
231p. 19cm.
I. Title.

West Indies
M808.8 Richer, Clément, (1914-)
H839 Up in smoke. Translated by Patrick Bowles.
Pp. 184-194.
In: Howes, Barbara, ed. From the green Antilles. New York, Macmillan, 1966.

West Indies
M808.8 Richer, Clément, (1914-)
H839 Up in smoke. Translated by Patrick Bowles.
Pp. 184-194.
In: Howes, B rbara, ed. From the green Antilles. New York, Macmillan, 1966.

M973.8 Richings, G F.
R39 Evidences of progress among colored people. By G. F. Richings ... 12th ed. Philadelphia, G. S. Ferguson co., 1905.
xvi, 17-595 p. illus. (incl. ports.) 19½ cm.

1. Negroes. I. Title.

Library of Congress E185.6.R532 6—10835
Copyright A 20946 [a37b1]

Haiti
M841 Ricot, Justinien
R42p Pétales et paillons. Paris, Jouve & Cia, 1927.
116p. 18cm.

1. Haitian poetry. I. Title.

The Riddle of Life, and other Sermons.

M252 Wright, Nathan.
W93r The riddle of life, and other sermons. Boston, Bruce Humphries [1952]
98 p. 24 cm.

1. Protestant Episcopal Church in the U. S. A.—Sermons. 2. Sermons, American. I. Title.

BX5937.W7R5 252.03 52-14342 ‡
Library of Congress [2]

Ghana Riddles, African.
M398.6 Amartey, A A
Am18 Adzenuloo. [Riddles] Accra, Bureau of Ghana Languages, 1961.
77p. 20cm.
Written in Ga.

1. Riddles, African. I. Title.

Zanzibar Riddles, African.
M398 Farsi, Shaaban Saleh
F25 Swahili sayings from Zanzibar. Book 2
Bk.2 Riddles and superstitions. Dar es Salaam, East African Literature Bureau, 1963.
32p. 18cm.
Written in Swahili.
1. Riddles, African. 2. Folk-lore,-Zanzibar. I. Title.

Riddles, African.
Zanzibar
M398 Farsi, Shaaban Saleh
F25 Swahili sayings from Zanzibar. Book 2, Riddles and superstitions. Dar es Salaam, East African Lieteature Bureau, 1963.
32p. 18cm.
Written in Swahili.
1. Riddles, African. 2. Folk-lore - Zanzibar. I. Title.

Riddles, African.
Kenya
M398 Gecaga, Bethuel Mareka
G26 Gwata ndaĩ, ndaĩ na ng'ano. [Riddles and stories, a miscellany. Illustrated by W. S. Agutu] Nairobi, Eagle Press, 1950.
39p. illus. 18½cm. (Mabuku ma kuiga muthithu wa maundu maitu. [A treasury of East African literature])
Written in Kikuyu.
1. Riddles, African. 2. Folk-lore - Kenya. I. Title. II. Series: A treasury of East African literature. III. Agutu, W. S., illus.

Tanganyika Riddles, African.
M398.6 Meena, E K
M47 Vitendawili [Riddles] Kutoka makabila mbalimbali ya Tanganyika, kimetungwa na E. K. Meena, G. V. Mmari na H. H. Sangiwa. London, Oxford University Press, 1960.
27p. illus. 18½cm.
Written in Swahili.

1. Riddles, African. I. Mmari, G. V., jt. auth. II. Sangiwa, H. H., jt. auth. III. Title.

Riddles, Haitian.
Haiti
M398 Bastien, Rémy
B29 Anthologie du folklore Haïtien. Mexico, [Sociedad de Alumnos, de la Escuela Nacional de Antropologia] 1946.
118p. 23cm. (Acta antropologica. I:4)
White author.

1. Folk-lore - Haiti. 2. Haiti - Folk-lore. 3. Proverbs, Haitian. 4. Riddles, Haitian. I. Title.

Riddles, Haitian.

M398 Hon, Addin.
H75t Torias; contes et proverbes creoles. Port-au-Prince, Imp. du College Certieres, 1945.
50p. 20cm.

M811.5 Ridout, Daniel Lyman.
R43v Verses from a humble cottage, by Daniel Lyman Ridout. [Hampton, Va., Hampton institute press, 1924]
28 p. 19 cm.
Inscribed copy: To Professor Robert T. Kerlin, In grateful appreciation of his unfailing heroism in the defense of a struggling race. From Daniel Lyman Ridout, July 15, 1924.

I. Title. 1. Poetry.

Library of Congress PS3535.I 4365V4 1924 24-18782
Copyright A 802879 [2]

Nigeria Ridout, Ronald.
M372.6 Ogunlesi, Josiah Soyemi, 1904- jt. auth.
Og9 English for Africans, 1, by Ronald Ridout
Bk.1 and J. S. Ogunlesi. Illustrated by J. D. Akeredolu. London, Ginn, 1960.
32p. illus. 26cm.

Nigeria
M372.6
Og9
Bk 2
Ridout, Ronald.
Ogunlesi, Josiah Soyemi, 1904- jt. auth.
English for Africans, 2, by Ronald Ridout and J. S. Ogunlesi. Illustrated by A. Adenuga. London, Ginn, 1955.
32p. illus. 26cm.

The right to live.
M813.5
W21r
Ward, Thomas Playfair, 1895-
The right to live. [1st ed.] New York, Pageant Press [1953]
249 p. 21 cm.
I. Title.
PZ7.W216Ri 53-10079 ‡
Library of Congress [2]

Riley, John W., joint author.
M378F
N49
Neyland, Leedell W.
The historyof Florida Agricultural and Mechanical University, by Leedell W. Neyland and John W. Riley. Gainesville, University of Florida Press, 1963.
xi, 303p. illus., ports. 24cm.
Bibliography: p. 281-282.

Nigeria
M372.6
Og9
Bk3
Ridout, Ronald.
Ogunlesi, Josiah Soyemi, 1904- jt. auth.
English for Africans, 3, by Ronald Ridout and J. S. Ogunlesi. Illustrated by A. Adenuga. London, Ginn, 1959.
32p. illus. 26cm.

Rights and responsibilities.
M323
C43
Chicago. Mayor. Conference on Race Relations. February 1944.
Proceedings... Chicago, The Committee, 1944.
64p. 28cm.

M910
R45
Riley, Willard D
Wisdom in Ethiopia. [1st ed.] New York, Vantage Press [1959]
66 p. 22 cm.
Ethiopia-
1. ~~XXXXXX~~—Religion. I. Title.
BR563.N4R54 241 59-3659 ‡
Library of Congress [2]

Cameroun
M967.11
R629
Rifoe, Simon, 1943-
Le tour du Cameroun en 59 jours. Yaounde, Editions CLE, 1965.
58p. illus., map. 18cm.
Portrait of author on book jacket.
1. Cameroun - Description and travel.
I. Title.

Rights of passage.
Barbados
M821.91
B737
Brathwaite, Edward, 1930-
Rights of passage. London, New York [etc.] Oxford U. P., 1967.
[8], 86 p. 22½ cm. 21/- (B 67-8102)
I. Title.
PR6052.R29R5 811 67-75397
Library of Congress [67d3]

M813.5
R46o
Rimanelli, Giose, 1926-
Original sin. Translated from the Italian by Ben Johnson. New York, Random House [1957]
179 p. 21 cm.
A novel.
I. Title. II. Johnson, Ben, tr.
PZ3.R4568Or 57-5876 ‡
Library of Congress [5]

Haiti
M841
R44r
Rigaud, Milo, 1909-
Rythmes et rites. Fontenay, n.d.
25p. 19cm.
I. Title.

Haiti
M972.94
R44
Riguad, Candelon
Promenades dans les campagnes d'Haiti agriculture, industrie, légendes religions, superstitions La Plaine de la Croix des Bouquets dite: "Cul de Sac" 1789-1928. Paris, L'Edition Française Universelle, n.d.
220p. illus. 21cm.
1. Haiti-Industry.

...Rimes haïtiennes;
Haiti
M841
Ed6r
Edouard, Emmanuel,
...Rimes haïtiennes; poésies, par Emmanuel Edouard, 1874-1881. Paris, E. Dentu, Libraire-Editeur, 1882.
157p. 18½cm.

Haiti
M133
R44
Rigaud, Milo, 1904-
La tradition voudoo et le voudoo haïtien: son temple, ses mystères, sa magie. Photos. de Odette Mennesson-Rigaud. Paris, Niclaus, 1953.
433 p. illus., port., map. 23 cm.
1. Voodooism. 2. Folk-lore—Haiti. I. Title.
BL2490.R53 133.4 53-33161
Library of Congress [54c1]

Haiti
M972.94
R44s
Rigaud, Milo, 1904-
Sténio Vincent révélé par la justice et par l'opinion publique. Port-au-Prince, H. Deschamps [1957]
97 p. illus. 27 cm.
1. Vincent, Sténio, Pres. Haiti, 1874-
A 58-2090
Florida. Univ. Library for Library of Congress [1]

M973
R47
Ringel, Frederick Julius, 1904- ed.
America as Americans see it, edited by Fred J. Ringel; illustrated by over 100 American artists. New York, Harcourt, Brace and co. [c1932]
xviii, 365p. front., illus. (incl. facsim.) plates, ports. 22cm.
First edition.
Partial contents: -Black America, by W.E.B. DuBois: Introduced by Walter White. -Back to Africa, by Robert L. Ephraim. -The creative Negro, by James Weldon Johnson: Introduced by Countee Cullen.

A right angle triangle.
M812.5
V94r
Voteur, Ferdinand.
A right angle triangle. The prince and the singer. By Ferdinand Voteur. [New York, Ardsley publishing company, °1938]
4 p. l., 11-213 p. 20½ᶜᵐ.
Plays.
I. Title. II. Title: The prince and the singer.
Library of Congress PS3543.O68R5 1938 39-11806
——— Copy 2.
Copyright D pub. 62986 [2] 812.5

M06
N214r
Riis, Roger William.
The answer to the Negro problem. Reprinted from Coronet, April 1949.
4p. 19cm.
1. National Urban League. I. Title.

M813.5
F53r
Ringtail.
Fisher, Rudolph, 1897-1934.
Ringtail. Atlantic monthly, May 1925.
652-660p. 24cm.

The right to equal opportunity in employment.
M323
N78t
Murray, Pauli, 1910-
The right to equal opportunity in employment.
pp. 383-407.
In: Twice a year, ed. by Dorothy Norman. 1946.

M324
R45p
Riley, Jerome R.
The philosophy of negro suffrage. By Jerome R. Riley, M. D. Hartford, Conn., American publishing company, 1895.
110 p. front. (port.) 20½ᶜᵐ.
1. Negroes—Politics and suffrage. ~~2. Negroes.~~ I. Title.
12-3518
Library of Congress E185.61.R57
——— Copy 2.
Copyright 1895. 52795 [36d1]

Rio de Janeiro-Hist.
Brazil
M869
L62a
Lima, Jorge de, 1893-
... Anchieta. Rio de Janeiro, Civilização brasileira, s. a., 1934.
211 p., 2 l. 18½ᶜᵐ. (Biblioteca brasileira de cultura, dirigida por Tristão de Athayde)
Contents. — Anchieta.—Escola de Piratininga.—As reducções. — Iperoig.—Fundação do Rio de Janeiro.—Reritiba.—Bibliographia (p. [209]-211)
1. Anchieta, José de, 1534-1597. 2. Jesuits in Brazil. 3. Rio de Janeiro—Hist.
35-18715
Library of Congress F2528.A536 [a42c1] 922.281

Rio de la Plata.

M910 Diggs, Irene.
D56n The Negro in the viceroyalty of the Rio de la Plata. Reprinted from the Journal of Negro History, 36:281-301, July 1951.

281-301p. 25cm.

Jamaica Riot.
M823.91 Salkey, Andrew
Sa3r Riot. Illustrated by William Papas. Lonson, Oxford University Press, 1967.

196p. illus. 23cm.
"For Arthur, from Andrew, 28-5-67."

I. Title.

Riots.
M976.6 Parrish, Mary E Jones
P24e Events of the Tulsa disaster, by Mrs. Mary E. Jones Parrish.
[n.p., n.p., n.d.]
112p. plates. 22cm.

Cover title.

Riots.
M286 **Powell, Adam Clayton, 1865–**
P87r Riots and ruins, by A. Clayton Powell, sr. ... New York, R. R. Smith, 1945.
xiv p., 1 l., 17-171 p. 22½ᶜᵐ.

1. Negroes. 2. Riots. I. Title.

Library of Congress E185.61.P78 45-5935
[20] 325.260973

M323 Riots--Arkansas.
W587m White, Walter Francis, 1893-
Massacring whites in Arkansas. The Nation, December 6, [19]

2p 31cm.

Riots - Detroit.

M323. White, Walter Francis, 1893-
W587w What caused the Detroit riot? An analysis by Walter White and Thurgood Marshall. New York, NAACP, 1943.

37p. 22½cm.

M323 Riots--East St. Louis.
N21 National Association for the Advancement of Colored People.
The Massacre of East St. Louis, compiled from facts and pictures collected by Martha Gruening and W. E. Burghardt Du Bois. Reprinted from The Crisis.

20p. illus. 25cm.

M323 Riots--Florida.
N21 National Association for the Advancement of Colored People.
Groveland U.S.A. New York, 1949.

[6]p. 20cm.

M343.3 Riots--New York.
Am3v American Civil Liberties Union.
Violence in Peekskill; A report of the violations of civil liberties at two Paul Robeson concerts near Peekskill, N.Y., August 27th and September 4th, 1949. New York, [1949?]

51p. illus. 20cm.
Original report issued in multigraphed form December, 1949.

M974.71 Riots--New York (City).
N42s New York (City) Mayor's Commission to Inquire into Conditions in Harlem following the March, 1935, Rioting.
Social and economic s tudy of Harlem. New York, Amsterdam News, 193 .

58p. 28cm.
Mimeographed.

M343.3 Riots--Tennessee.
H22t3 Harrington, Oliver W
It happened in Columbia Tennessee. New York, National Committee for Justice in Columbia, [1946?]

8p. illus. 21cm.
Published also under title Terror in Tennessee.

M343.3 Riots--Tennessee.
H23t2 Harrington, Oliver W
Terror in Tennessee. New York, National Association for the Advancement of Colored People. Legal Defense and Education Fund, 1946.

10p. illus. 21cm.

M343.3 Riots--Tennessee.
H23t Harrington, Oliver W
Terror in Tennessee; The truth about the Columbia outrages. New York, Committee of 100, [1946?]

10p. illus. 21cm.
Reprint of pamphlet issued by NAACP.

M343.3 Riots--Tennessee.
H23t4 Harrington, Oliver W.
Terror in Tennessee. The truth about the Columbia outrages. New York, Nat'l Comm. for Justice in Columbia, Tennessee. [1946?]

8p. 25cm.

M343.3 Riots - Washington, D.C.
K63w Kirksey, Thomas
Who stopped the race riots in Washington; real causes and effects of race clashes in the District of Columbia, T. Kirksey... J. Henry Hewlett... Washington, D.C., Murray bros., n.d.
12p. 23½cm.

Riots and ruins.

M286 **Powell, Adam Clayton, 1865–**
P87r Riots and ruins, by A. Clayton Powell, sr. ... New York, R. R. Smith, 1945.
xiv p., 1 l., 17-171 p. 22½ᶜᵐ.

1. Negroes. 2. Riots. I. Title.

Library of Congress E185.61.P78 45-5935
[20] 325.260973

... The ripening.

France
M843 **Colette, Sidonie Gabrielle, 1873–**
C67r ... The ripening; translated from the French by Ida Zeitlin. New York, Farrar & Rinehart, incorporated [°1932]
3 p. l., 3-244 p. 20ᶜᵐ.
At head of title: Colette.

1. Zeitlin, Ida, tr. II. Title. *Translation of Le blé en herbe.*
32-21436 Revised
Library of Congress PZ3.C678984Ri
——— Copy 2.
Copyright A 53725 [r36d2] 843.91

The ripening.

Martinique
M843.9 **Glissant, Édouard, 1928–**
G49r The ripening. Translated by Frances Frenaye. New York, G. Braziller, 1959.
253 p. 22 cm.
Translation of La lézarde.

I. Title.

PZ4.G559Ri 843.914 59-12068 ‡
Library of Congress [2]

Rip Van Winkle.

Uganda
M967.61 Ntungwerisho, Yemima K tr.
N88r Ruhondeza mwene busasi [Rip Van Winkle] Nairobi, The Eagle Press, 1950.

22p. 18cm.
Written in Runyankore.

Ripley, Dorothy.

M815.2 Letters addressed to Dorothy Ripley, from
J711 several Africans and Indians, on subjects of
2d ed Christian experience, &c...Second edition... Bristol, printed by Philip Rose [n.d.]

38p. 18cm.
Bound with edition of 1807.

Ripley, Dorothy.

M815.2 Letters addressed to Dorothy Ripley, from
J711 several Africans & Indians, on subjects of
1807 Christian experience, &c... Chester, printed by J. Hemingway, 1807.

52p. 16cm.

Haiti M841 D93r
Rires et pleurs, poésies ...
Durand, Oswald, 1840-
... Rires et pleurs, poésies ... Corbeil, É. Crété, impr., 1896.
2 v. 17cm.
CONTENTS.—pt. 1. Poèms. Élégies. Satires. Odelettes.—pt. 2. Fleurs des mornes. Refrains. Nos payses. Contes créoles.
1. Title.
25-20885
Library of Congress PQ3949.D9R5

M811.5 R51t
Ritch, Manly.
Thoughts of a postman, by Manly Ritch. 3d ed. Boston, The Christopher publishing house [1926]
ix, 101 p. front. (port.) 21cm.
Poems.
1. Title. 1. Poetry.
Library of Congress PS3535.I 84T5 1926 26-14061
Copyright A 901278 [2]

Africa, South
M896.3 R52af
Rive, Richard, 1931-
African songs. Berlin, Seven Seas Publishers, 1963.
149p. 19cm.
1. Africa, South - Short stories. I. Title.

M813.4 B56r
The rise and progress of the kingdoms of light and darkness.
Blackson, Lorenzo D 1817
The rise and progress of the kingdoms of light and darkness; or, The reign of Kings Alpha and Abadon. By Lorenzo D. Blackson ... Philadelphia, J. Nicholas, 1867.
288 p. plates. 18cm.

M815.4 D739aL 1966
Ritchie, Barbara.
Douglass, Frederick, 1817?-1895.
Life and times of Frederick Douglass. Adapted by Barbara Ritchie. New York, Crowell [1966]
viii, 210 p. 21 cm.
Shortened version, adapted from the 2d rev. ed. of the author's autobiography: Life and times, published in 1892, as enlarged from his My bondage and my freedom, 1855.
1. Slavery in the U. S.—Anti-slavery movements. 2. Slavery in the U. S.—Maryland. I. Ritchie, Barbara.
E449.D744 1966 326.092 66-7048
Library of Congress [67d5]

South Africa
M896 M88
Rive, Richard, 1931-
Dagga-Smoker's Dream
Pp. 264-267.
In: Mphahlele, Ezekiel, ed. African writing today. Baltimore, Penguin Books, 1967.

M268 T97
The rise of religious education among Negro Baptists.
Tyms, James Daniel.
The rise of religious education among Negro Baptists; a historical case study, by James D. Tyms. [1st ed.] New York, Exposition Press [1966, °1965]
xiv, 408 p. 21 cm. (An Exposition-university book)
Bibliography: p. [397]-408.
1. Baptists, ~~Negro~~—Education. I. Title. 2. Religious education.
BX6450.T93 268.86133 66-1120
Library of Congress [8]

Ghana
M343 Of6
Rites and ceremonies - Ghana.
Ofori, David
Why kibi ritual murder? An inside story of a sensational so-called "ritual murder" case. [Accra, Heal Press, 1954]
36p. illus., port. 21cm.
Portrait of author on t.p.

South Africa.
M896.3 R52e
Rive, Richard, 1931-
Emergency; a novel. London, Faber and Faber [1964]
251p. 19cm.
Portrait of author on book jacket.
1. Africa, South - History - Fiction. I. Title.

Barbados
M972.9 H85
The rise of West Indian democracy.
Hoyos, F A
The rise of West Indian democracy; the life and times of Sir Grantley Adams. [n.p.] Advocate Press, 1963.
228, x p. ports. 21cm.
1. Adams, Sir Grantley Herbert, 1898- 2. West Indians - History. I. Title.

Cuba
M861.6 C571r
A ritmo de tambor.
Clavijo Tisseur, Arturo, 1886-
A ritmo de tambor. Santiago de Cuba, Editorial "Ros", 1937.
105p. 19cm.

South Africa
M896.3 R52m
Rive, Richard, 1931- ed.
Modern African prose; an anthology compiled and edited by Richard Rive. Illustrated by Albert Adams. London, Heinemann Educational Books [1964]
214p. illus. 19cm.
"Arthur Spingarn from Richard Rive (South Africa). 16th September, 1965."
Partial contents.- As the night the day, by Abioseh Nicol.- Resurrection, by Richard Rive.- New life at Kyerafaco, by Efua Sutherland.- Her warrior, by Jonathan Kariara.- Eleven
(Continued on next card)

M89 L91r
... Rising above color.
Lotz, Philip Henry, 1889- ed.
... Rising above color, edited by Philip Henry Lotz ... New York, Association press; New York, Fleming H. Revell company, 1943.
viii, 112 p. 21 cm. (*His* Creative personalities. Vol. v)
"For further reading" at end of each chapter except one.
CONTENTS.—George Washington Carver, man with a magic wand, by F. G. Lankard.—Marian Anderson, singer, by H. B. Hunting.—W. E. B. DuBois, scholar and fighter, by H. B. Hunting.—Robert Russa Moton, co-operator and educator, by H. B. Hunting.—Samuel Coleridge-Taylor, musician, by F. W. Clelland.—Richard Allen, first
(Continued on next card)
44-40017
[49w²5]

Ghana
M343 Of6
Ritual murder.
Ofori, David
Why kibi ritual murder? An inside story of a sensational so-called "ritual murder" case. [Accra, Heal Press, 1954]
36p. illus., port. 21cm.
Portrait of author on t.p.

South Africa
M896.3 R52m
Rive, Richard, 1931- ed. Modern African prose; an anthology compiled and edited by Richard Rive. [1964]
(Card 2)
Partial contents.- Continued.
o'clock: the wagons, the share, by Peter Clarke.- Papa, the snake and I, by Luis Bernardo Honwana.- The martyr, by James Ngugi.
1. African literature. I. Title.

M810 B81r
The rising sun.
Brown, William Wells, b. 1815.
The rising sun; or, The antecedents and advancement of the colored race. By Wm. Wells Brown ... Boston, A. G. Brown & co., 1874.
ix, 9-552 p. front. (port.) 21cm.
"Representative men and women": p. 418-552.
1. Negroes. 2. Negro race. 3. Slavery in the U. S. 4. Negroes—Biog. I. Title.
29-8376
Library of Congress E185.B884
[42d1]

M784 J63g
The rival lovers.
Johnson, James Weldon, 1871-1938. tr.
Goyescas, or The rival lovers; opera in three tableaux. The book by Fernando Periquet, the music by Enrique Granados, English version by James Weldon Johnson. New York, G. Schirmer [c1915]
42p. 24½cm. (G. Schirmer's collection of opera-librettos)
Inscribed copy: To Captain A. B. Spingarn, Yours sincerely, James Weldon Johnson.
White author.

Africa, South
M896.3 R52
Rive, Richard, 1931- ed.
Quartet; new voices from South Africa: Alex La Guma, James Matthews, Alf Wannenburgh, Richard Rive. New York, Crown Publishers [1963]
223 p. 22 cm.
Short stories.
1. Short stories, South African. I. Title. II. Title: New voices from South Africa. 2. Africa, South - Short stories.
(Over)
PZ1.R44Qar 63-21108
Library of Congress [5]

M323. W587ri
... A rising wind.
White, Walter Francis, 1893-
... A rising wind. Garden City, New York, Doubleday, Doran and company, inc., 1945.
155 p. 19½cm.
At head of title: Walter White.
"First edition."
1. World war, 1939-1945—Negroes. I. Title.
45-2285
Library of Congress D810.N4W48
[47i7] 940.5403

M784 J63go
The rival lovers.
Johnson, James Weldon, 1871-1938. tr.
Goyescas; an opera in three tableaux. The book by Fernando Periquet. The music by Enrique Granados. English version by James Weldon Johnson. New York, G. Schirmer, 1915.
16p. 29½cm.

South Africa
M896.3 R52m
Rive, Richard, 1931-
Resurrection.
Pp. 53-65.
In: Rive, Richard, ed. Modern African prose. London, Heinemann Educational Books, 1964.

Rive, Richard, 1931-

Africa, South
M896.3
R52

Rive, Richard, 1931- ed.
Quartet; new voices from South Africa: Alex La Guma, James Matthews, Alf Wannenburgh, Richard Rive. New York, Crown Publishers [1963]
223p. 22cm.
Short stories.

Guadeloupe
M843.91
R52

Rivel, Mount de
Kiroa; contes. Paris, Présence Africaine [1960]
37p. illus. port. 18½cm.
1. Guadeloupe - Short stories. I. Title.

River, face homeward.

U.S.
M966.7
An24

Anderson, Rosa Claudette.
River, face homeward (Suten dan wani hwe fie); an Afro-American in Ghana. [1st ed.] New York, Exposition Press [1966]
120, [1] p. illus., ports. 21 cm.
"References": p. [121]
1. Ghana—Soc. life & cust. I. Title. II. Title: Suten dan wani hwe fie.
DT510.4.A58 916.67 66-8809
Library of Congress [3]

The river between.

Kenya
M896.3
N49r

Ngugi, James, 1938-
The river between. London, Heinemann [1965]
174p. 18½cm.
1. Kenya - Fiction. I. Title.

River George.

M813.5
L51r

Lee, George Washington, 1894-
River George, by George W. Lee. New York, The Macaulay company [°1937]
275 p. 19½cm.
I. Title.
37-6127
Library of Congress PZ3.L5123Ri
——— Copy 2.
Copyright A 105535 [3]

Puerto Rico
M863
R524

Rivera Correa, R R
The pariahs. New York, Carlton Press [1967]
60p. 21cm.
Portrait of author on book jacket.
1. Puerto Rico - History - Fiction. 2. Albizu Campos, Pedro - Fiction. I. Title.

M811.5
R52

Rivers, Conrad Kent, 1933-
These black bodies and this sunburnt face. Cleveland, Free Lance Press, 1962.
28 p. 22 cm.
Poems.
I. Title. 1. Poetry.
PS3535.I 895B5 62-21042 ‡
Library of Congress [5]

M329.6
R52a

Rivers, Francis E , 1893-
An appeal to the common sense of colored citizens, by Francis E. Rivers. New York, Republican national committee, 1940.
32p. 21½cm.
1. Politics. 2. Republican party. I. Title.

Rivers, William Napoleon, 1897- ed.

France
M840.
D89ge

Dumas, Alexandre, 1802-1870.
Dumas' Georges; an intermediate French reader; edited with introduction, notes, and vocabulary by W. Napoleon Rivers ... and John Frederic Matheus ... Washington, D. C., The Associated publishers [°1936]
2 p. l., vii-xi p., 1 l., 233 p. 17cm.
Attributed by Mirecourt to Mallefille. cf. A. F. Davidson, Alexandre Dumas, 1902, p. 397.
1. French language—Chrestomathies and readers. I. Rivers, William Napoleon, 1897- ed. II. Matheus, John Frederic, joint ed. III. Mallefille, Jean Pierre Félicien, 1813-1868, supposed author. IV. Title: Georges.
36-37277
Library of Congress PQ2227.G4 1936
——— Copy 2.
Copyright A 100066 [3] 843.76

Tanganyika
M967.82
R52h

Riwa, R L
Hadithi za rafiki saba; Hadithi tamu za zamani. [Tales told by seven friends] Nairobi, The Eagle Press, 1951.
45p. illus. 21½cm.
Written in Swahili.
1. Tanganyika.

Roach, Cuthbert M., joint author.

M813.5
D93p

Durant, E Elliot.
The princess of Naragpur; or, A daughter of Allah, by E. Elliot Durant ... and Cuthbert M. Roach. New York, The Grafton press [°1928]
3 p. l., 5-191 p. 21½cm.
1. Roach, Cuthbert M., joint author. II. Title.
28-698
Library of Congress PZ3.D9319Pr
——— Copy 2.
Copyright A 3384 [2]

M910
R53v

Roach, Thomas E
Victor, by Thomas E. Roach ... Boston, Meador publishing company [1943]
143 p. 20½cm.
"A story of the life and mission of the author."—Pref.
I. Title.
43-6662
Library of Congress BR1725.R6A3
[2] 922

The road.

Nigeria
M896.2
So3r

Soyinka, Wole
The road. London, Oxford University Press, 1965.
101p. 18½cm.

"The road ... is too little travelled."

M815.5
B88r

Bunche, Ralph Johnson, 1904-
"The road ... is too little travelled," [address delivered by Dr. Ralph Bunche at Lincoln birthday observation of the Mid-day Luncheon Club at Springfield, Illinois, February 12, 1951] [Springfield, Illinois, 1951]

The road to Birmingham.

M813.5
J23r

James, Beauregard, pseud.
The road to Birmingham. New York, Published for Society for Racial Peace of Washington, D. C., by Bridgehead Books, 1964.
191 p. 22 cm.
I. Title.
PZ4.J2815Ro 64-12721
Library of Congress [5]

The road to brotherhood.

M204
N81r

Northern Baptist convention. *Board of education.*
The road to brotherhood, compiled and edited by the Department of missionary education of the Baptist board of education. New York city, Baptist board of education, Dept. of missionary education [1924]
xiv, 163 p. front., plates, ports. 19½cm.
1. Baptists—Missions. I. Title.
26-15433 Revised
Library of Congress BV2520.N6
[r43c2]

Africa, S.
M968
H97r

Road to Ghana.

Hutchinson, Alfred, 1924-
Road to Ghana. [1st American ed.] New York, John Day Co. [1960]
190 p. 22 cm.
Autobiographical
Portrait of author on book jacket.
1. Africa, South—Native races. 2. Africa, East—Native races. I. Title.
DT763.H68 1960 968 60-16051 ‡
Library of Congress [61x20]

The road to happiness, and other essays.

M248
N48

Newton, Percy John.
The road to happiness, and other essays. Boston, Chapman & Grimes [1955]
158 p. illus. 22 cm.
1. Christian life. I. Title.
BV4501.N46 248 54-7551 ‡
Library of Congress [2]

M811.5
F61r

The road to Mount McKeithaw...
Flanagan, Thomas Jefferson, 1890-
The road to Mount McKeithaw, by Thomas Jefferson Flanagan. Atlanta, Ga., The Independent Publishers, 1927.
38p. leaves. port. (front.) 17cm.
~~174777~~

The road to Negro liberation;

M304
P19
v.1, no.5

Haywood, Harry.
The road to Negro liberation; the tasks of the Communist party in winning working class leadership of the Negro liberation struggles, and the fight against reactionary nationalist-reformist movements among the Negro people. By Harry Haywood. Report to the eighth convention of the Communist party of the U. S. A., Cleveland, April 2-8, 1934. New York city, Workers library publishers, 1934.
63 p. 17½cm.
1. Negroes. 2. Communist party of the United States of America. I. Title.
44-31795
Library of Congress E185.61.H44
[2] 325.26

Road without turning.

M89
R559

Robinson, James Herman.
Road without turning, the story of Reverend James H. Robinson; an autobiography. New York, Farrar, Straus [c1950]
312p. 21cm.

Ghana M966.7 Su8
The roadmakers.
Sutherland, Efua.
The roadmakers. Photos. by William E. Bell. Planned and written by Efua Sutherland. Accra, Ghana Information Services [1961]
unp. (chiefly illus.) 32cm.
1. Ghana-Description and travel. I. Bell, William E. II. Title.

M975.5 R74
Roberts, Harry Walter, 1902
A study of the Sutherland community, Dinwiddie County, Virginia. A contribution on behalf of Virginia State College to a cooperative research project of the Conference of Presidents of Negro Land-Grant Colleges and the Tennessee Valley Authority. Petersburg, Virginia State College, 1959.
74p. 23cm. (Virginia State College gazette, v.65, no.3 September 1959)
1. Dinwiddie County, Virginia. 2. Virginia. 3. Sutherland Community, Virginia. I. Title.

M326.5 Am3r
Roberts, Joseph Jenkins, pres. of Liberia, 1809-1876.
Inaugural address.
(In: American Colonization Society. Memorial of the semi-centennial anniversary... January 15, 1867. With documents concerning Liberia. Washington, The Society, 1867. 24cm. p. 150-61).

M811.5 R53e
Robbin, William Allston, 1940-
Elbowroom! Elbowroom! New York, Vantage Press [1965]
68p. 20½cm.
Portrait of author on book jacket.
I. Title.

Jamaica M398 B38
Roberts, Helen Heffron, 1888-
Beckwith, Martha Warren, 1871-
Jamaica Anansi stories, by Martha Warren Beckwith; with music recorded in the field by Helen Roberts. New York, American folk-lore society, 1924.
xiii, 295 p. 25cm. (*Half-title:* Memoirs of the American folk-lore society, vol. XVII)
1. Folk-lore—Jamaica. 2. Negro-English dialects. I. Roberts, Helen Heffron, 1888- II. Title. III. Title: Anansi stories.
25—10866
Library of Congress GR1.A5 vol. XVII [42e1]

M326.5 Ar5
Roberts, Joseph Jenkins, pres. of Liberia, 1809-1876.
[Armistead, Wilson] 1819?-1868.
Calumny refuted by facts from Liberia; with extracts from the inaugural address of the coloured President Roberts; an eloquent speech of Hilary Teage, a coloured senator; and extracts from a discourse by H. H. Garnett, a fugitive slave, on the past and present condition, and destiny of the coloured race. Presented to the Boston Anti-slavery bazaar, U. S., by the author of "A tribute for the negro". London, C. Gilpin; New York, W. Harned, Anti-slavery office; [etc., etc.] 1848.
46 p. 18cm.
1. Liberia. 2. Negroes — Colonization—Africa. I. Roberts, Joseph Jenkins, pres. of Liberia, 1809-1876. II. Teage, Hilary. III. Garnett, H. H. IV. Title.
[33b1] 24-3758
Library of Congress DT632.A3

France M840 D89ro
La robe de noce.
Dumas, Alexandre, 1802-1870.
La robe de noce. Bruxelles, Meline, Cans et Cie., 1846.
305p. 15cm.

Jamaica M398 B38j
Roberts, Helen Heffron, 1888-
Beckwith, Martha Warren, 1871-
Jamaica folk-lore, collected by Martha Warren Beckwith, with music recorded in the field by Helen H. Roberts. New York, The American folk-lore society, G. E. Stechert & co. [1928]
4 p. l., [3]-95, 67, [3]-187, 47 p. front., illus., plates. 25cm. (*Half-title:* Memoirs of the American folk-lore society. Vol. XXI)
Each part also published separately as Publications of the Folk-lore foundation, Vassar college, no. 1, 2, 6 and 8.
Includes "References."
CONTENTS.—Folk games of Jamaica.—Christmas mummings in Jamaica.—Jamaica proverbs.—Notes on Jamaican ethnobotany.
1. Folk-lore—Jamaica. I. Roberts, Helen Heffron, 1888-
30—18643
Library of Congress GR1.A5 vol. XXI [45g1] 398.097292

Jamaica M820 H38
Roberts, Leslie
Good brown earth.
Pp. 17-20.
In: Hendriks, A. L., ed. The independence anthology of Jamaican literature. Kingston, Arts Celebration Committee, Ministry of Development and Welfare, 1962.

M813.5 R54h
Robert, Luke
Harlem doctor. New York, Universal, 1953.
126p. 18½cm. (Uni-Book No. 75)
I. Title.

Ghana M784 R54
Roberts, J T
A hymn of thanksgiving and other songs. Accra, Accra High School, 1953.
10p. port. 25cm.
1. Music. 2. Songs. I. Title.

M813.5 R54
Roberts, Luke.
Harlem model. New York, Designs Publishing Corporation, 1952.
124 p. 18 cm. (Bronze Book, no. 1)
I. Title.

Tanganyika M896.4 R54
Robert, Shaaban
Kielezo cha insha [model essays] Johannesburg, Witwatersrand University Press, 1961.
111p. 18½cm. (The Bantu Treasury, xiii) "First published 1954". Written in Swahili.
1. Swahili language - Addresses, essays, lectures. I. Cole, D T ed.

Gold Coast M966.7 Ac2s
Roberts, J T Sermon, p. 13-15.
Accra, Gold Coast. High School.
Report for the year 1924-1925, with the sermon preached by the principal. Accra, Gold Coast, 1925.
15p. illus. 20cm.
At head of title: Souvenir of second founder's day celebration.

M813.5 R54r
Roberts, Luke
Reefer club. New York, Universal, 1953.
124p. 18cm. (Uni-Book No. 49)
I. Title.

Tanganyika M896.3 R54k
Robert, Shaaban
Kielezo cha insha [Model essays] Johannesburg, Witwatersrand University Press, 1957.
111p. 18cm. (Bantu treasury, XIII) Written in Swahili.
1.Swahili essays. I. Title.

M326.99B R54n
Roberts, James, b. 1753.
The narrative of James Roberts, soldier in the revolutionary war and at the battle of New Orleans. Chicago: printed for the author, 1858. Hattiesburg, Miss., The Book farm, 1945.
cover-title, viii, [9]-32 p. 21½cm. [Heartman's historical series, no. 71]
"Photo-lithoprint reproduction."
"One hundred and thirty-six copies reprinted from the apparently unique copy in the Charles E. Heartman collection of material relating to Negro culture."
1. Slavery in the U. S.—Condition of slaves. 2. New Orleans, Battle of, 1815. 3. Slave narratives
45-9855
Library of Congress E444.R7 [4] 326.92

M286 W61h
Roberts, Nicholas Franklin, 1849- p.204.
Whitted, J A
A history of the Negro Baptists of North Carolina, by Rev. J.A. Whitted... Raleigh, Presses of Edwards and Broughton printing co., 1908.
212p. front. plates - 22½cm.

Tanganyika M967.82 R54r
Robert, Shaaban
Kusadikika. Nchi Iloyo Angani. London, Thomas Nelson and sons, ltd. 1951.
57p. illus. 18½cm.
1. Tanganyika.

Liberia M966.6 R54a
Roberts, Joseph Jenkins, 1809-1876.
An address delivered at the fifty-second annual meeting of the American Colonization Society held in Washington, D. C., January 19, 1869. New York, American Colonization Society, [1869]
16 p. 23 cm.
1. Liberia.

M640 R54h 1843
Roberts, Robert.
The house servant's directory. Or, A monitor for private families: comprising hints on the arrangement and performance of servants' work ... and upwards of 100 useful receipts, chiefly comp. for the use of house servants ... By Robert Roberts ... [2d ed.] Boston, Munroe and Francis; New York, C. S. Francis, 1828. 1843.
xiv, [15]-180 p. 18½cm.
1. Servants. 2. Receipts. I. Title.
7—28299
Library of Congress TX331.R64 [a23c1]

M640
R54h
1828

Roberts, Robert
The house servant's directory. Or, a monitor for private families: comprising hints on the arrangement and performance of servant's work... and upwards of 100 various and useful receipts, chiefly compiled for the use of house servants... Boston, Munroe and Francis; New York, Charles S. Francis, 1828/

180p. 17½cm.

1. Servants. 2. Receipts. I. Title.

M910
R54a

Robeson, Eslanda (Goode), 1896-1965
African journey [by] Eslanda Goode Robeson, with 64 pages of illustrations. New York, The John Day company [1945]

154 p., 1 l. illus. (incl. maps) plates, ports. 22cm.
Bibliographical foot-notes.

1. Africa—Descr. & trav. 2. Africa—Native races. I. Title.
[Full name: Eslanda Cardoza (Goode) Robeson]
45—6978
Library of Congress DT12.R54
[46v7] 916

M335.4
R54f

Robeson, Paul, 1898-
Foreword.

(In: Taruc, Luis. Born of the people. New York, International Publishers 1953. 21cm. pp. 7-10)

M640
R54h
1827

Roberts, Robert.
The house servant's directory. Or, A monitor for private families: comprising hints on the arrangement and performance of servants' work ... and upwards of 100 useful receipts, chiefly comp. for the use of house servants ... By Robert Roberts ... ~~2d ed.~~ Boston, Munroe and Francis; New York, C. S. Francis, ~~1828~~. 1827.
xiv, [15]-180 p. 18½cm.

1. Servants. 2. Receipts. I. Title.
7—28399
Library of Congress TX331.R64
[a23c1]

M973
R543a

Robeson, Eslanda (Goode) 1896-1965jt. auth.
American argument, Pearl S. Buck with Eslanda Goode Robeson. New York, J. Day Co. [1949]
xii, 206 p. 21 cm.

1. National characteristics, American. ~~2. U. S.~~—Civilization. ~~3. Negroes.~~ ~~I. Robeson, Eslanda (Goode) 1896-~~ II. Title.
E169.1.B92 917.3 49-7264*
Library of Congress [25]

M331
R54f

Robeson, Paul, 1898-
Forge Negro-labor unity for peace and jobs. N.Y., Harlem Trade Union Council, 1950.

15p. 18½cm.

1. Labor and laboring classes. I. Title.

Roberts, Robert, p. 17-21.

M326.53
G19

Garrison, William Lloyd, 1805-1879.
Thoughts on African colonization: or, An impartial exhibition of the doctrines, principles and purposes of the American colonization society. Together with the resolutions, addresses and remonstrances of the fee people of color... By Wm. Lloyd Garrison. Boston, Printed and pub. by Garrison and Knapp, 1832.

iv, 160, 76p. 23cm.

MB9
R54r

Robeson, Eslanda (Goode), 1896-1965
Paul Robeson, Negro. New York, Harper & brothers, 1930.

178p. front., ports. 23cm.
First edition.

MB9
R54h

Robeson, Paul, 1898-
Here I stand. New York, Othello Associates [1958]
128 p. 22 cm.
Autobiographical.

I. Title.
E185.97.R62 *301.451 325.260973 58-2066
Library of Congress [2]

M323
R54b

Robertson, Julius Winfield.
This bird must fly, by Julius Winfield Robertson. Washington, D. C., Unity press and pamphlet service [°1944]
113 p. 22cm.

Race problems
~~1. Negroes.~~ I. Title.
45-14337
Library of Congress E185.61.R67
[2] 325.260973

MB9
R54r
Lon. ed.

Robeson, Eslanda (Goode), 1896-1965
Paul Robeson, Negro, by Eslanda Goode Robeson. ~~New York and~~ London, ~~Harper & brothers, 1930.~~ Victor Gollancz Ltd. 1930.
~~5 p. l., 178 p. front., ports. 23 cm.~~ 153p.
"First edition."

1. Robeson, Paul, 1898-
[Full name: Eslanda Cardoza (Goode) Robeson]
30—18186
Library of Congress E185.97.R65
[a45u1] 920

MB9
R54h2

Robeson, Paul, 1898-
Here I stand. London, Dobson [c1958].

128p. 22cm.
Autobiographical.

I. Title.

M973
R54

Robertson, L O
We want Rossevelt again because of facts and figures; a brief review of part of the achievements of the Roosevelt administration, compiled by L. O. Robertson... Washington, D.C., Colored National Democratic League [1936]

24p. tables. 23cm.

1. Roosevelt, Franklin Delano. 2. Politics.

M910
R54w

Robeson, Eslanda (Goode), 1896-1965
What do the people of Africa want? By Mrs. Paul Robeson. N.Y., Council on African affairs, 1945.

23p. illus. map. 20cm.

1. Africa I. Title

MB9
R54i

Robeson, Paul, 1898-
Itt állok... (Here I stand). Budapest, Európa Könyvkiado, 1958.

191p. illus. 21½cm.

I. Title.

M813.5
R53k

Roberson, Sadie L.
Killer of the dream; short stories. New York, Carlton Press [1963]

95p. 21cm.

Portrait of author on book jacket.

1. Title. 1. Short stories.

M910
H92a

Robeson, Eslanda (Goode), 1896-1965
Hunton, William Alphaeus, 1903-
Africa fights for freedom, by Alphaeus Hunton, with an introduction by Eslanda Goode Robeson. N.Y., New Century, 1950.

15 p. 20 cm.

M335.4
R54n

Robeson, Paul, 1898-
The Negro people and the Soviet Union. New York, New Century Publishers, 1950.

15p. 13cm.

1. Communism.

M910
R54a
1946

Robeson, Eslanda (Goode) 1896- 1965
African journey, by Eslanda Goode Robeson. London, V. Gollancz ltd, 1946.
187 p. illus. (maps) plates, ports. 20½cm.
Bibliographical foot-notes.

1. Africa—Descr. & trav. 2. Africa—Native races. I. Title.
[Full name: Eslanda Cardoza (Goode) Robeson]
46-21337
Library of Congress DT12.R54 1946
[2] 916

M815.5
R55f

Robeson, Paul, 1898-
For freedom and peace, address at Welcome home rally, New York, June 19, 1949. New York, Council on African Affairs, [1949]

14p. 22cm.

I. Title.

M910
C759

Robeson, Paul, 1898-
Opening statement of the conference.

(In: Council on African Affairs. Conference on Africa - New Perspectives. Proceedings. New York, 1944. 21cm. p.10-12)

M815.5
R54p
Robeson, Paul, 1898-
Paul Robeson speaks to youth. New York, Challenge, 1951.

[21]p. illus. 13cm.
Address delivered to the first national convention of the Labor Youth League, Nov. 24, 1950.

I. Labor Youth League.

M815.5
R55r
Robeson, Paul, 1898-
Racial responsibility.

Pp. 42-47 port. 24cm.
In: Pioneering for a Civilized World. Report of the New York Herald Tribune Twelfth Forum on Current Problems. At the Waldorf-Astoria New York City, November 16 and 17, 1943. New York, Herald Tribune, 1943. 267p.

1. Race relations.

M343.3
Am3v
Robeson, Paul, 1898-
American Civil Liberties Union.
Violence in Peekskill; A report of the violations of civil liberties at two Paul Robeson concerts near Peekskill, N.Y., August 27th and September 4th, 1949. New York, [1949?]

51p. illus. 20cm.
Original report issued in multigraphed form December, 1949.

M817.5
G76p
Robeson, Paul, 1898-
Graham, Shirley.
Paul Robeson, citizen of the world, by Shirley Graham; foreword by Carl Van Doren ... New York, J. Messner, inc. [1946]
4 p. l., 264 p. front., ports. 22cm.
Bibliography: p. 259.

1. Robeson, Paul, 1898-
[Full name: Lola Shirley (Graham) McCanns]
46—5096
Library of Congress E185.97.R64
[47y7] 920

MB9
R54r
Robeson, Paul, 1898-
Robeson, Eslanda (Goode)
Paul Robeson, Negro, by Eslanda Goode Robeson. New York and London, Harper & brothers, 1930.
5 p. l., 178 p. front., ports. 23 cm.
"First edition."

1. Robeson, Paul, 1898-
[Full name: Eslanda Cardoza (Goode) Robeson]
30—18186
Library of Congress E185.97.R65
[a45u1] 920

MB9
R54r
Robeson, Paul, 1898-
Robeson, Eslanda (Goode)
Paul Robeson, Negro, by Eslanda Goode Robeson. New York and London, Harper & brothers, 1930.
5 p. l., 178 p. front., ports. 23 cm.
"First edition."

1. Robeson, Paul, 1898-
[Full name: Eslanda Cardoza (Goode) Robeson]
30—18186
Library of Congress E185.97.R65
[a45u1] 920

MB9
B799n
Robeson, Paul, 1898-
Yergan, Max, 1894-
The Negro and justice; A plea for Earl Browder, by Max Yergan and Paul Robeson. New York, Citizens' Committee to Free Earl Browder, 1941.

11p. illus. 19cm.

France
M840
D89pr
Robin Hood.
Dumas, Alexandre, 1802-1870.
... The prince of thieves, newly tr. by Alfred Allinson; with three coloured illustrations by Frank Adams. London, Methuen & co. [1904]
3 p. l., 126 p. 3 col. pl. (incl. front.) 24cm. (The novels of Alexandre Dumas)
Sequel: Robin Hood.

1. Robin Hood. I. Allinson, Alfred Richard, tr. II. Title.
4—37050
Library of Congress PZ3.D89Pr6
[a37c1]

M245
R56r
Robinson, Archibald Boaz, 1900-
Rays of heavenly light, Church of God holiness hymnal; written for the national convention of Churches of God, Holiness, by Elder A. B. Robinson ... Asheville, N. C., 1941.
xi, 2-75, xii-xxvii, [84] p. 21cm.
Music: [84] p. at end.

1. Churches of God, Holiness—Hymns. 2. Hymns, English. I. Title
42-564
Library of Congress M2131.C8R6
[2] 783.9

M784
R56w
Robinson, Archibald Boaz, 1900-
A weary stranger without a home. Asheville, North Carolina, The author, [1941].

[2]p. 24cm. (Trumpets of Gabriel, Jubilee anthems, no.2)

I. Title.

Trinidad
M972.98
R56
Robinson, Arthur N R
Budget speech, 1965. Friday, 15th January, 1965. [Trinidad, Government Printery] 1965.

40p. 23cm.

1. Trinidad - Economic conditions.
2. Budget - Trinidad.

Trinidad
M330
R56
Robinson, Arthur N R
Economic development in Trinidad and Tobago; a lecture. [Port-of-Spain, P. N. M. Pub. Co., n.d.]

15p. 21cm.
Portrait of author on front cover.

1. Trinidad and Tobago - Economic policy.
I. Title.

Nigeria
M496
R56
Robinson, Charles Henry, 1861-
Specimens of Hausa literature, by Charles Henry Robinson ... Cambridge [Eng.] University press, 1896.
xix, 112 p., 1 l. facsims. 24½cm.
Bibliography: p. [xvii]-xix.
White author.

1. Hausa literature.

Library of Congress 20—8155
——— Copy 2. [28b1]

M973
R56d
Robinson, Donald B 1913- ed.
The day I was proudest to be an American. [1st ed.] Garden City, N. Y., Doubleday, 1958.
288 p. 22 cm.

1. U. S.—Civilization—Addresses, essays, lectures. 2. U. S.—Hist.—Anecdotes. I. Title.
E169.1.R722 917.3 58-10037 ‡
Library of Congress [30]

M01
H75
Robinson, Evelyn R., jt. auth.
Homer, Dorothy R , comp.
The Negro, a selected bibliography. Compiled by Dorothy R. Homer and Evelyn R. Robinson. 7th ed. rev. New York, New York Public Library, 1955.
23p. 25cm.
Reprinted from the New York Public Library Bulletin, March 1955.
1. Bibliographies. I. Title.
II. Robinson, Evelyn R., jt. auth.

M372.4
R562
Robinson, Florine.
Ed and Ted; a story about two boys who became friends. Illustrated by Omar Davis. [1st ed.] New York, Exposition Press [1965]
60 p. col. illus. 22 cm.

I. Davis, Omar, illus. II. Title.
PZ7.R5657Ed 65-29735
Library of Congress [2]

M811.5
R55
Robinson, Golia W
Twenty-five; a collection of poems and lyrics. New York, William-Frederick Press, 1953.
22 p. 22 cm. (The William-Frederick poets, 98)

I. Title.
PS3535.O25645T9 811.5 53-5208 ‡
Library of Congress [2]

M304
P19
v.6, no.9
Robinson, J G
Why I am an exile, a pamphlet containing J.G. Robinsons letters to President Wilson asking for legislation against mob violence... [lacks imprint] [16] p. 18cm.

1. World War I. 2. Soldiers.

Robinson, Jackie
see
Robinson, John Roosevelt, 1919-

M251
R56a
Robinson, James Herman, 1907-
Adventurous preaching. [1st ed.] Great Neck, N. Y., Channel Press [1956]
186 p. 21 cm. (The Lyman Beecher lectures at Yale, 1955)

1. Preaching. 2. Theology, Pastoral. I. Title.
BV4211.2.R6 251 56-13819 ‡
Library of Congress [7]

M323
R561
Robinson, James Herman, 1907- , ed.
Love of this land; progress of the Negro in the United States. Illustrated by Elton C. Fax. Philadelphia, Christian Education Press [1956]
76 p. illus. 23 cm.

1. Negroes. 2. U. S.—Race question. I. Title.
E185.61.R68 325.260973 56-9433 ‡
Library of Congress [2]

MB9
R559

Robinson, James Herman, 1907-
Road without turning, the story of Reverend James H. Robinson; an autobiography. New York, Farrar, Straus [1950]
312 p. 21 cm.

VIHaI

I. Title.
BX9225.R715A3 922.573 50-9789
Library of Congress [15]

M301
R56t

Robinson, James Herman, 1907-
Tomorrow is today. Philadelphia, Christian Education Press [1954]
127 p. 22 cm.

1. Social conditions. I. Title.
HN18.R57 *301.23 301.153 54-11556 ‡
Library of Congress [2]

M231
W62

Robinson, James Herman, 1907-
Why I believe there is a God.
Pp. 14-19.
In: Why I believe there is a God. Chicago, Johnson Pub. Co., 1965.

Robinson, James Herman, 1907-
Foreword, pp. 7-11.

M370
Isle

Isaacs, Harold Robert, 1910-
Emergent Americans; a report on "Crossroads Africa." With a foreword by James H. Robinson. New York, John Day Co. [1961]
158p. 21cm.
White author.

M323
N21

Robinson, James Herman, 1907-
National association for the advancement of colored people.
Resources in Negro youth. New York city, National association for the advancement of colored people, 1940.
18p. 20cm.

M973
R63af

Rogers, Joel Augustus, 1880-1966
Africa's gift to America; the Afro-American in the making and saving of the United States. [1st ed.] New York [1959]
254 p. illus. 29 cm.
Includes bibliography.

1. Negroes—Hist. 2. Negroes in Africa. I. Title.
E185.R74 325.2670973 60-602 ‡
Library of Congress [5]

M973
R63 a

Rogers, Joel Augustus, 1880- 1966
As nature leads; an informal discussion of the reason why Negro and Caucasian are mixing in spite of opposition. By J. A. Rogers ... [Chicago, Printed by M. A. Donohue & co., °1919]
2 p. l., [7]-207 p. 20 cm.
Errata slip attached to fly-leaf.

1. U. S.—Race question. 2. Negroes. 3. Miscegenation. I. Title.
19—9528
Library of Congress E185.62.R72
[48d½]

M575.1
R616

Rogers, Joel Augustus, 1880-1966
The five Negro presidents according to what people said they were. New York, J. A. Rogers, 1965.
19p. ports. 20cm.

1. Heredity. 2. Presidents - U.S.
I. Title.

M973
R63f
1924

Rogers, Joel Augustus, 1880- 1966
From superman to man, by J. A. Rogers ... [~~Chicago, M. A.~~ New York, ~~Donohue & co., printers, °1917~~] Lenox Pub. co., [1924]
128 p. 19ᶜᵐ.
Fourth edition.

1. U. S.—Race question. I. Title. 17-13073 Revised
Library of Congress E185.61.R71
———— Copy 2.
Copyright A 460096 [r30c2]

M973
R63f

Rogers, Joel Augustus, 1880- 1966
From superman to man, by J. A. Rogers ... [Chicago, M. A. Donohue & co., printers, °1917]
128 p. 19ᶜᵐ. $1.00
First edition.
Inscribed copy: To Arthur B. Spingarn
Sincerest good wishes of J. A. Rogers.

1. U. S.—Race question. I. Title. 17-13073 Revised
Library of Congress E185.61.R71
———— Copy 2.
Copyright A 460096 [r30c2]

M973
R63k

Rogers, Joel A ugustus, 1880- 1966
The Ku Klux spirit. A brief outline of the history of the Ku Klux Klan past and present, by J.A. Rogers. New York, The Messenger Publishing Co., c1923.
48p. 17cm.
Inscribed: To Arthur B. Spingarn with high regard. J.A. Rogers.

1. Ku Klux Klan.

M973
R63r

Rogers, Joel Augustus, 1880-1966
The real facts about Ethiopia, by J. A. Rogers...3d. and enl. ed. N.Y., J. A. Rogers publications, 1936.
31, 2p. 23cm.

1. Ethiopia.

M973
R63s

Rogers, Joel Augustus, 1880-1966
Sex and race; Negro-Caucasian mixing in all ages and all lands, by J. A. Rogers ... New York city, J. A. Rogers publications [1940-44]
3 v. fronts. (v. 1-2) illus. (incl. ports., map, facsims.) 23½ᶜᵐ.
Vol. 2 has subtitle: A history of white, Negro and Indian miscegenation in the two Americas.
Includes bibliographies.
CONTENTS.—v. 1. The old world.—v. 2. The new world.—v. 3. Why white and black mix in spite of opposition.

1. Race problems. 2. ~~Negroes~~. 3. Miscegenation. I. Title.
(over)
41—20
Library of Congress GN237.R6 1940
[45r45e2] 572

M813.5
R63

Rogers, Joel Augustus, 1880- 1966
She walks in beauty. Los Angeles, Western Publishers, 1963.
316 p. 23 cm.

I. Title.
PZ4.R727Sh 63-22256
Library of Congress [5]

M973
R63w

Rogers, Joel Augustus, 1880-1966
World's great men of color ... By J. A. Rogers ... New York, N. Y., J. A. Rogers [1946-47]
2 v. illus. (incl. ports.) 23½ᶜᵐ.
On cover: 3000 B. C. to 1946 A. D.
Paged continuously.
"First edition."
Includes bibliographies.
Inscribed copy: To Arthur B. Spingarn with every good wish of J.A. Rogers.

1. Negro race—Biog. I. Title.
DT18.R59 325.26 46-8140 rev
Library of Congress [r47b2]

M973
R63w3
1935

Rogers, Joel Augustus, 1880- 1966
World's greatest men and women of African descent. Small ed. By J. A. Rogers ... New York city, J. A. Rogers, °1935.
71 p. illus. (incl. ports.) 28ᶜᵐ.
"Limited edition."

1. ~~Negroes—Biog.~~ Biography I. Title.
CA 35—132 Unrev'd
Library of Congress DT18.R6 1935
[43b1] 325.26

M973
R63w5

Rogers, Joel Augustus, 1880- 1966
World's greatest men of African descent... by J. A. Rogers...N. Y. C., J. A. Rogers, 1931.
iv, 79p. illus. 23cm.

1. Biography. I. Title.

M973
R63y

Rogers, Joel Augustus, 1880- 1966
Your history from the beginning of time to the present, by J.A. Rogers. Pittsburgh, Pa., Pittsburgh Courier, 1940.
96 unnumb. p. illus. 30cm.

1. History. I. Title.

M796
R56

Robinson, John Roosevelt, 1919-
Baseball has done it, by Jackie Robinson. Edited by Charles Dexter. [1st ed.] Philadelphia, Lippincott [1964]
216 p. 21 cm.

1. ~~Negro~~ athletes. 2. Race discrimination—U. S. I. Title.
GV865.R6A2 301.451 64—14467
Library of Congress [64k7]

MB9
R56

Robinson, John Roosevelt, 1919-
Breakthrough to the big league; the story of Jackie Robinson, by Jackie Robinson and Alfred Duckett. New York, Harper & Row [1965]
xiii, 178 p. ports. 22 cm. (A Breakthrough book)

I. Duckett, Alfred. II. Title. 1. Baseball.
GV865.R6A27 927.96357 64-19719
Library of Congress [4-3]

MB9
R56r

Robinson, John Roosevelt, 1919-
Jackie Robinson, my own story, as told to Wendell Smith; foreword by Branch Rickey. New York, Greenberg [1948]
170 p. illus., ports. 21 cm.

I. Smith, Wendell. II. Title.
GV865.R6A3 927.96357 48—6600*
Library of Congress [49u7]

M796
K12
Robinson, John Roosevelt, 1919-
Tips on watching baseball. The second baseman.

(In: Kahn, Roger, ed. The mutual baseball almanac. Garden City, Doubleday, 1954. 22cm. pp. 22-24.)

M910
R56
Robison, Lois
Let's go; teacher's book, Junior. Greenwich, Connecticut, The Seabury Press, 1952.

48p. illus. 21cm.

1. Liberia - Juvenile literature. 2. Juvenile literature. I. Title.

Haiti
M843.91
R581
Rochemont, Serge F
Ivraie ou Sénevé; contes - maximes et nouvelles. Grand'rue, Port-au-Prince, Les Presses Libres, 1956.

120p. 21cm.

1. Haiti-Fiction.

Robinson, John Roosevelt, 1919-

MB9
R56w
Rowan, Carl Thomas.
Wait till next year; the life story of Jackie Robinson, by Carl T. Rowan with Jackie Robinson. New York, Random House [1960]

339 p. illus. 24 cm.

1. Robinson, John Roosevelt, 1919- I. Title.

GV865.R6R64 927.96357 60—5566 ‡

Library of Congress [61r15]

M301
M69
Robson, Charles Benjamin.
The long struggle.

Pp. 7-29.
In: Mitchell, Glenford E., ed. The angry black south. New York, Corinth Books, 1962.

Rochester, N.Y.

M974.7
C67
Coles, Howard W
City directory of Negro business and progress, 1939-40. Howard W. Coles, compiler and publisher. Rochester, N.Y., the author, 1940.
12 unnumb. p. illus. $22\frac{1}{2}$cm.

M813.5
R56w
Robinson, John Terry
White horse in Harlem. New York, Pageant Press [1965]

159p. 21cm.

I. Title.

M812.08
B26r
Robson, William N
Open letter on race hatred.

White author.
(In: Barnouw, Erik, ed. Radio drama in action; ... N.Y., Farrar & Rinehart, 1945. 21cm. p.62-77)

Rochester, N. Y.

M974.7
C67c
Coles, Howard W
The cradle of freedom; a history of the Negro in Rochester, western New York and Canada ... by Howard W. Coles ... Sketches and illustrations by Claude Paul, engravings by Photo-cast, inc., Rochester, New York. Rochester, N. Y., Oxford press, 1941-
v. illus. (incl. ports., facsims.) 24cm.

1. Negroes. 2. Negroes in Rochester, N. Y. 3. Slavery in the U. S.—Anti-slavery movements. I. Title.
42-25474

Library of Congress E185.6.C68
[5] 325.26

Robinson, Josephine.

M245
T21c
Taylor, Marshall W
A collection of revival hymns and plantation melodies, by Marshall W. Taylor... Musical composition by Miss Josephine Robinson. Copied by Miss Amelia C. and Hettie C. Taylor. Cincinnati: Marshall W. Taylor and W.C. Echols, 1883.
276p. front. $16\frac{1}{2}$cm.

M792
B26r
Robson, William N., 1906-
Open letter on race hatred (radio script).

White author.

(In: Barnouw, Erik. Radio drama in action... New York, Farrar & Rinehart, Inc. [1945] 21cm. pp.60-77)

Rochester, N. Y. Douglass monument.

M815.4
D73at
Thompson, John W.
An authentic history of the Douglass monument; biographical facts and incidents in the life of Frederick Douglass ... By J. W. Thompson ... Rochester, N. Y., Rochester herald press, 1903.
204 p., 1 l. 4 pl., 12 port. (incl. front.) 22cm.

1. Douglass, Frederick, 1817-1895. 2. Rochester, N. Y. Douglass monument.
3—15416

Library of Congress E449.D78
[44b1]

Jamaica
M823.91
Sa3a
Robinson, R O
A free country.

Pp. 70-84.

In: Salkey, Andrew, comp. Stories from the Caribbean. London, Elek Books, 1965.

M792
B26r
Robson, William N., 1906-
Open letter on race hatred (radio script).

White author.

(In: Barnouw, Erik. Radio drama in action... New York, Farrar & Rinehart, Inc. [1945] 21cm. pp.60-77)

M326
G87a
1853
Rochester Ladies' Anti-slavery Society.
Griffiths, Julia ed.
Autographs for freedom. Boston, J.P. Jewett and co.; Cleveland, O., Jewett, Proctor, and Worthington; etc., 1853.

viii, 263p. incl. front. 2pl. $19\frac{1}{2}$cm.
A collection of signed articles, poems, etc., by men and women prominent in the anti-slavery movement. Most of the signatures are in facsimile.
(For other editions of this title, see entries under editor's name).

Robinson, Rowland Evans.

Puerto Rico
M864
Sch6f
Schomburg, Arthur Alfonso, 1874-
Foreword.

(In: Robinson, Rowland Evans. Out of bondage and other stories; foreword by Arthur Schomburg,... Rutland, Vt., C.E. Tuttle company [c1936] 24cm. pp. [5]-9.)

Haiti
M972.94
R58h
Roche-Grellier,
Haiti, la politique a suivre, par Roche-Grellier. Paris, Librairie Arthur Rousseau, 1892.
98p. $23\frac{1}{2}$cm.

1. Haiti—Politics and government.

(cat.)

The rock of wisdom.

M220
C16
Cannon, Noah Calwell
The rock of wisdom; an explanation of the sacred scriptures, by the Rev. N. C. Cannon, (a man of color.) To which are added several interesting hymns. [New York] 1833.
2p. l., 3-144p. port. 18cm.

MB9
R57
Robinson, W H, 1848-
From log cabin to the pulpit; or fifteen years in slavery by W. H. Robinson. [Eau Claire, Wis., James H. Tifft, 1913.]

200p. illus. $19\frac{1}{2}$cm.

1. Slave narratives. 2. U.S. History - Personal narrative.

Haiti
M972.94
R58ha
Roche-Grellier,
Haiti son passé, son avenir, par Roche-Grellier. Paris, Arthur Rousseau, 1891.
152p. 23cm.

1. Haiti—History.

Rodgers, Bertha, ed.

M811.4
D91 li
Dunbar, Paul Laurence, 1872-1906.
Little brown baby [by] Paul Laurence Dunbar; poems for young people. Selections, with biographical sketch by Bertha Rodgers; illustrated by Erick Berry [pseud.] New York, Dodd, Mead & company, 1940.
xiv, 106 p. incl. plates. 21 cm.

1. Poetry.
I. Rodgers, Bertha, ed. II. *Best, Allena (Champlin) 1892- illus. III. Title.
40—4721

Library of Congress PZ8.3.D918Li
[45t1]

Brazil
M869.2
N17d
Rodrigues, Nélson.
Anjo Negro.

Pp. 309-374.

In: Nascimento, Abdias do, ed. Dramas para Negroes e prologo para brancos. Rio de Janeiro, Teatro Experimental do Negro, 1961.

I. Title.

Rodriques Lapa, Manuel, 1897- ed.

Brazil
M869.1
G589
Gonzaga, Thomaz Antonio, 1744–1807?
... Obras completas de Tomás Antonio Gonzaga. Edição critica de Rodrigues Lapa. São Paulo ₍etc.₎ Companhia editora nacional, 1942–

v. 20cm. (Livros do Brasil, v. 5)

CONTENTS.—₍1₎ Poesias.—Cartas chilenas.—Tratado de direito natural, livro primeiro.

I. Rodrigues Lapa, Manuel, 1897- ed.

Library of Congress PQ9696.G6 1942 45-16885
₍2₎ 869.081

Rodriquez, Agustin Baldomero.

MB
C12p
Calcagno, Francisco, 1827-1903.
Poetas de color, por Francisco, Calcagno. Plácido, Manzano, Rodriguez, Echemendía, Silveira, Medina. Habana, Imp. militar de la v. de Soler y compañia, 1878.
1 p. l., ₍5₎-54 p. 23½cm.

Rodriquez, Agustin Baldomero.

MB
C12p
Calcagno, Francisco, 1827-1903.
Poetas de color, por Francisco Calcagno. Placído, Manzano, Rodriguez, Echemendía, Silveira, Medina. Habana, Imp. militar de la v. de Soler y compañia, 1878.
1 p. l., ₍5₎-54 p. 23½cm.

Cuba
M863.6
R61c
Rodríguez, Luis Felipe, 1888–
... Ciénaga. La Habana, Editorial Trópico, 1937.
233 p., 1 l. 20½cm. (Novela cubana, 1)

I. Title. 1. Cuban fiction.

Library of Congress PQ7389.R6C5 39—4814
₍43c1₎

Cuba
M863.6
R61m
₍Rodríguez, Luis Felipe₎ 1888–
Marcos Antilla; relatos de cañaveral. La Habana, Editorial Hermes ₍1932₎

4 p. l., iii–xxvi p., 1 l., 9–155 p. 20½cm.

Author's name on cover.

CONTENTS.—Marcos Antilla contado por sí mismo.—Cama 1 y 3.—Fantasmas en el cañaveral. — El Pelirrojo. — La guardarraya. — Míster Lewis.—Los Almarales.—El ego de Nicolás.—Los subalternos.—El haz de cañas.—La danza lucumí.

I. Title. 1. Cuban fiction.

Library of Congress PQ7389.R6M3 36-16065
863.6

Cuba
M863.6
R61r
₍Rodríguez, Luis Felipe₎ 1888–
Relatos de Marcos Antilla; la tragedia del cañaveral. La Habana, Impresora cubana, s. a. ₍1932?₎
3 p. l., iii–xvii, 106 p. 22½cm.
Author's name on cover.
First published 1928.
CONTENTS. — Americanismo y cubanismo literarios, por Juan Marinello.—Marcos Antilla contado por sí mismo.—La chimenea.—Cama no. 13.—Fantasmas en el cañaveral.—El Pelirrojo.—La guardarraya.—Míster Lewis.—Los Almarales.—El ego de Nicolás.—Los subalternos.—El haz de caña.—La danza lucumí.—El nacimiento de Margarito.
I. *Marinello, Juan, 1899– Americanismo y cubanismo literarios. II. Title. 1. Cuban fiction.
₍Full name: Luis Felipe Rodríguez Rodríguez₎

Library of Congress PQ7389.R6M3 1932 a 41-16081
₍2₎ 863.6

Dominican
Republic
M398
R61
Rodríguez, Manuel Tomás.
...Papa Legba. Ciudad Trujillo, R.D., Imp. Arte y cine, c. por a., 1945.

3p. l., ₍11₎ -190p., 2 l. front. 21cm.
Portrait of author laid in.

1. Haitian folk-lore. 2. Haiti-Voodooism.
I. Title.

Rodriguez, René Morales
see
Morales Rodriguez, René

M811.5
R62t
Roe, Helene
Teach me to live; a selection of prose poems. ₍n.p.₎ 1963

19p. illus. 23cm.
Portrait of author in book.

I. Title.

Roger de Beauvoir

See

Beauvoir, Eugène Auguste Roger de Bully.

Rogers, Elymas Payson, d. 1861.

M326.99B
L82
Loguen, Jermain Wesley, 1814–1872.
The Rev. J. W. Loguen, as a slave and as a freeman. A narrative of real life. Syracuse, N. Y., J. G. K. Truair & co., printers, 1859.

x, ₍11₎–454 p. front. (port.) 18cm.

Written in the third person, but apparently the work of Loguen.
Two letters at end of volume are dated 1860.
"Testimony of Rev. E. P. Rogers," including a poem "Loguen's position": p. 445–450.

1. Slavery in the U. S.—Fugitive slaves. 2. Slavery in the U. S.—Anti-slavery movements. 3. Underground railroad. I. Rogers, Elymas Payson, d. 1861.

Library of Congress E444.L83 14—15518
₍48r42d1₎

M811.5
R632b
Rogers, James Overton, 1933–
Blues and ballads of a black Yankee; a journey with Sad Sam, by J. Overton Rogers. Foreword by Whitney M. Young, Jr. ₍1st ed.₎ New York, Exposition Press ₍1965₎

63 p. 21 cm.

Poems.

1. ~~Negroes~~—Poetry. I. Title.

PS3568.O44B5 811.54 65-5026

Library of Congress ₍3₎

Le roi miracule.

Cameroons
M896.3
B55r
Biyidi, Alexandre, 1932–
Le roi miracule; cronique des essazam; roman by Mongo Beti ₍pseud.₎ Paris, Buchet & Chastel, 1958.

254p. 18½cm
At head of title: mongo Beti

Haiti
M841
R74
Roker, Samuel J
Vox Nigri. Port-au-Prince, Editions Panorama, 1963.

31p. 22cm.
"To Mr. Roy Wilkins who deeply loves his race and the Negroes all over the world. Cordially from the author, Port-au-Prince, June 27, 1963."

1. Haitian poetry. I. Title.

M780.9
C83
Roldan, Amadeo.
The artistic position of the American composer. Pp. 175-77.

In: Cowell, Henry, ed. American composers on American music. Stanford University, Calif., Stanford University Press, 1933.

Le role du Nègre dans la culture des Amériques, conférences.

Locke, Alain Le Roy, 1886–

M308
L79r
Le role du Nègre dans la culture des Amériques, conférences. Port-au-Prince, Haïti, Impr. de l'État, 1943.

141 p. 21 cm.

"La traduction française du texte anglais original est due à la précieuse collaboration du docteur et de madame Camille Lhérisson."

1. Negroes. 2. Negroes in America. 3. America—Civilization. I. Title.

E185.6.L78 325.26097 48-37282*‡

Library of Congress ₍1₎

The Rôle of the missionaries in conquest.

S. Africa
M266
M28r
Majeke, Nosipho
The Rôle of the missionaries in conquest. Johannesburg, Society of Young Africa, 195?

140p. 21½cm.

1. Africa, South - Missionaries. 2. Missionaries - Africa, South. I. Title.

The role of the races in our future civilization;

M323
L14
Laidler, Harry Wellington, 1884– *ed.*
The role of the races in our future civilization; symposium edited by Harry W. Laidler. Participants: Sir Norman Angell, Pearl S. Buck, Hon. Lawrence W. Cramer ₍and others₎ ... New York city, League for industrial democracy ₍1942₎

112 p. 23cm. (*On cover:* L. I. D. Pamphlet series)

"All ... articles except those of Pearl S. Buck and Lester B. Granger were prepared for the L. I. D. conference, May 8–9, 1942."

1. Race problems. I. Title.

Library of Congress HT1521.L2 42—24499
₍43h3₎ 323.1082

Rollin, Frank A , pseud.

see

Whipper, Frances E Rollin

Rolling along in song.

M784
J63r
Johnson, John Rosamond, 1873– *ed.*

Rolling along in song; a chronological survey of American Negro music, with eighty-seven arrangements of Negro songs, including ring shouts, spirituals, work songs, plantation ballads, chain-gang, jail-house, and minstrel songs, street cries, and blues, edited and arranged by J. Rosamond Johnson. New York, The Viking press, 1937.

224 p. 26cm.

1. Negro songs. I. Title.

Library of Congress M1670.J65R6 37—27426
₍46u2₎ 784.756

M813.5
R64d
Rollins, Bryant.
Danger song. [1st ed.] Garden City, N. Y., Doubleday, 1967.
280 p. 22 cm.
Portrait of author on book jacket.

I. Title.
PZ4.R758Dan 67-10370
Library of Congress [5]

M810.8
R65
Rollins, Charlemae, *comp.*
Christmas gif'; an anthology of Christmas poems, songs, and stories, written by and about Negroes. Line drawings by Tom O'Sullivan. Book design by Stan Williamson. Chicago, Follett Pub. Co. [1963]
119 p. illus. 25 cm.

1. Christmas—Poetry. 2. Christmas stories. 3. American literature—Negro authors. 4. Negro literature—U. S. I. Title.
PS509.C56R6 810.89 63-17805
Library of Congress [5]

MB
R652
Rollins, Charlemae Hill.
Famous American Negro poets, by Charlemae Rollins. New York, Dodd, Mead [1965]
95 p. ports. 22 cm. (Famous biographies for young people)
Portrait of author on book jacket.
Langston Hughes (p. 69-74) has autograph "March 10, 1965, For Arthur - Sincerely - Langston.

1. Negro authors—Juvenile literature. I. Title.
2. Biography.
PS153.N5R6 928.1 65-11811
Library of Congress [4-1]

M792
R65
Rollins, Charlemae Hill.
Famous Negro entertainers of stage, screen, and TV, by Charlemae Rollins. New York, Dodd, Mead [1967]
122 p. ports. 22 cm. (Famous biographies for young people)
CONTENTS.—Ira Aldridge.—Marian Anderson.—Louis "Satchmo" Armstrong.—Josephine Baker.—Harry Belafonte.—Nat "King" Cole.—Sammy Davis, Jr.—"Duke" Ellington.—Lena Horne.—Eartha Kitt.—Sidney Poitier.—Leontyne Price.—Paul Robeson.—Bill "Bojangles" Robinson.—"Bert" Williams.—Thomas "Fats" Waller.

1. Negro actors. I. Title.
PN2286.R6 792'.028'0922 67-14305
Library of Congress [5]

MB
R65
Rollins, Charlemae Hill.
They showed the way; forty American Negro leaders. New York, Crowell [1964]
165 p. 21 cm.

1. Negroes—Biog. I. Title.
E185.96.R6 920.073 64-20692
Library of Congress [65k9]

M813.5
R65h
Rollins, Lanier
The human race is a gang. New York, Carlton Press [1964]
85p. 20½cm.
Portrait of author on book jacket.

I. Title.

Haiti
M972.94
R66me
Romain, Jean-Baptiste, 1916-
Memoire sur l'anthropometrie en Haiti. Preface du Professeur Jacques Butterlin. Port-au-Prince, Haiti, Imprimerie Vertieres, 1946.
35p. 22cm.

1. Haiti-Anthropology.

Haiti
M972.94
R66i
Romain, Jean-Baptiste, 1916-
Introduction à l'anthropoligie physique des Haitiens; stature, indice cormique, indice cephalique. Port-au-Prince, Imprimerie N. A. Theodore, 1962.
140p. illus.

1. Anthropology - Haiti. I. Title.

Haiti
M972.94
R66n
Romain, Jean-Baptiste, 1916-
Noms de lieux d'époque coloniale en Haiti; essai sur la toponymie du nord a l'usage des etudiants. Port-au-Prince, Imprimerie de l'Etat, 1960.
205p. illus. 23½cm. (Revue de la Faculte d'Ethnologie No. 3).

1. Haiti. I. Title.

Haiti
M972.94
R66q
Romain, Jean-Baptiste, 1916-
Quelques moeurs et coutumes des paysans Haitiens; travaux pratiques d'ethnographie sur la region de milot a l'usage des etudiants. Port-au-Prince, Imprimerie de l'Etat, 1958.
264p. illus. 23cm.

1. Haiti - Social life and customs. I. Title.

Haiti
M612.1
R66
Romain, Jean-Baptiste, 1916-
Repartition des groupes sanguins Abo et Rh en Haiti. Port-au-Prince, Imprimerie de l'Etat, 1964.
12p. map. 23½cm.
Includes bibliography.

1. Blood. I. Title.

M614
R66a
Roman, Charles Victor, 1864-1934.
After fifty years-- what and whither. Reprinted from the Journal of the National Medical Association, 6: [1925]
8p. 21cm.

1. Progress of the Negro.

M614
R66 a2
Roman, Charles Victor, 1864-1934
American civilization and the Negro; the Afro-American in relation to national progress, by C. V. Roman ... Illustrated with half-tone engravings. Philadelphia, F. A. Davis company, 1916.
xii, 434 p. front., plates, ports., diagr. 24cm.
Inscribed copy: To Capt. Arthur B. Spingarn in testimony of gratitude for his effective, wholehearted and disintered service to my race and mankind. Aug. 8/18 C. V. Roman.
1. Negroes. 2. U. S.—Race question. I. Title.
16-2965
Library of Congress E185.61.R75
[39f1]

M614
R66a4
Roman, Charles Victor, 1864-1934.
The American Negro and social hygiene. Reprinted from Social Hygiene, 7:41-47, January 1921.

1. Hygiene, Public.

M614
R66c
Roman, Charles Victor, 1864-1934.
The cultural background of modern medicine. Reprinted from the Journal of the National Medical Association, July-September, 1924.
4p. 26cm.

1. Medicine.

M614
R66fo
Roman, Charles Victor, 1864-1934.
The deontological orientation of its membership, the chief function of a medical society.
(In: Roman, Victor. Formulae supplemental to those in U.S. pharmacopoeia and national formulary. [Nashville, 1909] pp.47-57).

M614
R66d
Roman, Charles Victor, 1864-1934.
The dethronement of a king. Reprinted from the Journal of the National Medical Association, April-June, 1913.
12p. 19cm.

1. Temperance.
814.5

M614
R66fo
Roman, Charles Victor, 1864-1934. comp.
... Formulae supplemental to those in U.S. pharmacopoeia and national formulary, with explanatory notes and appendix, compiled by the chief of the clinic. [Nashville 1909]
57p. 13cm.
Cover title: Eye, ear, nose and throat formulary of remedies used in Dr. Roman's Clinic, Meharry Medical College.

M614
R66fo
Roman, Charles Victor, Formulae supplemental ... (card 2)
Contains: The Deontological orientation of its member ship the chief function of a medical society, by C.V. Roman.

1. Paharmacopoeias. 2. Medicine - Formulas
I. Meharry Medical College, Nashville. Dr. Roman's Clinic.

M614
R66fr
Roman, Charles Victor, 1864-1934.
Fraternal message from the African Methodist Episcopal Church to the Methodist Church of Canada, together with comments by reporters and editors. Nashville, Hemphill press, 1920.
36p. port. 19cm.

I. African Methodist Episcopal Church.
II. Methodist Church (Canada).

M614
R66k
Roman, Charles Victor 1864-1934.
A knowledge of history is conducive to racial solidarity, and other writings, by C. V. Roman ... Nashville, Tenn., Sunday school union print, 1911.
54 p. incl. front. (port.) 18½cm.
Cover title: Racial solidarity.

I. Racial solidarity.
1. Negroes.
11-29624
Library of Congress E185.R75
Copyright A 300358

M614
R66m
Roman, Charles Victor, 1864-1934.
The medical phase of the South's ethnic problem. Reprinted from the Journal of the National Medical Association. 8:150-152. [1916]

1. Medicine.

M614
R66pe
Roman, Charles Victor, 1864-1934.
Personality in progress. Reprinted from the Journal of the National Medical Association, April-June, 1922.

broadside 32cm.

1. National Medical Association

M614
R66se
Roman, Charles Victor, 1864-1934.
Some ramifications of the sexual impulse. Reprinted from the Journal of the National Medical Association, October-December, 1920.

4p. 28cm.

1. Sex--Cause and determination.

M378M
R66
Roman, Charles Victor, 1864-1934.
Meharry medical college, a history, by Charles Victor Roman ... Nashville, Sunday School publishing board of the National Baptist convention, inc., 1934.

xi, 41, 224p. plates. 23½cm.

1. Medical schools. I. Title.
2. Meharry Medical College, Nashville.

M614
R66pr
Roman, Charles Victor, 1864-1934.
A preventable death rate. Reprinted from the Journal of the National Medical Association, 7:88-94, April-June, 1915.

Health.

M614.
R66su
Roman, Charles Victor, 1864-1934.
Survival values diminishing returns and the margin of safety. Tuskegee, Tuskegee Institute, 1932.

14p. 23cm.

I. Title.

M614
R66n2
Roman, Charles Victor, 1864- 1934
Negro health problems. Reprinted from Cincinnati medical bulletin, February, 1922.

3p. 27cm.

1. Health.

M306
Sol
1913
Roman, Charles Victor, 1864-1934
Racial self-respect and racial antagonism.

(In: Southern Sociological Congress. 2d. Atlanta, 1913. The human way. ... Nashville, 1913. 24cm. p.102-112)

M614.
R66u
Roman, Charles Victor, 1864-1934
The unsatisfied valence. Reprinted from Journal of the National Medical Association, v.9, no.4.

I. Title.

M306
Sol
1919
Roman, Charles Victor, 1864-1934
The Negro woman and the health problem.

(In: Southern Sociological Congress. Houston 1915. The New chivalry - health. Nashville, Southern Sociological Congress, 1915. 24cm. pp. 392-405)

M306
Sol
1913
Roman, Charles Victor, 1864-1934.
Racial self-respect and racial antagonism.

(Southern Sociological Congress. 2d, Atlant, 1913. The South mobilizing for social service,... Nashville, 1913. 24cm. pp. 444-454).

Roman, Charles Victor, 1864-1934. The church in relation to a growing race pride.

M323
T69
Negro Christian student conference. *Atlanta*, 1914.
The new voice in race adjustments; addresses and reports presented at the Negro Christian student conference, Atlanta, Georgia, May 14-18, 1914. A. M. Trawick, editor ... Pub. by order of the executive committee of the conference. New York city, Student volunteer movement [1914]

1 p. l., [v]-vi p., 1 l., 280 p. 23½cm.

"Best books on the Negro in America and Africa": p. 221-224.

1. Negroes—Congresses. 2. U. S.—Race question. I. Trawick, Arcadius McSwain, 1869- ed. II. Title.

A 15-837

Springfield. Public library for Library of Congress E185.5.N38 [a35f1]

M306
Sol
1919
Roman, Charles Victor, 1864-1934.
The Negro woman and the health problem.

(In: Southern Sociological Congress. Houston 1915. The New chivalry - health. Nashville, Southern Sociological Congress, 1915. 24cm. pp. 392-405)

M614
R66r
Roman, Charles Victor, 1864-1934.
The relation of prevalent diseases to physical stamina. Reprinted from the Journal of the National Medical Association, April-June, 1914.

8p. 22cm.

1. Health.

Roman, Charles Victor, 1864-1934. The Negro's psychology and his health. p. 270-273. 1924.

M306
N21p
1924
National conference of social work.
Proceedings... Selected papers of the ... annual meeting.

1st - 1874- Library has: 1919, 1924
New York etc. 1874-19

M614
R66n3
Roman, Charles Victor, 1864-1934.
The Negro's psychology and his health. Reprinted from Hospital Social Service, 11:89-95, 1925.

1. Health. 2. Race psychology.

M614
R66sc
Roman, Charles Victor, 1864-1934.
Science and Christian ethics...n.p., [1912].

58p. 20cm.

Contents: -. Part I. Statement of principles.--. Part II. Religion a necessity to man...--. Part III. Racial self respect and racial antagonism.

1. Religion and science. I. Title.

A
M280
M91u
Roman Catholic Church.
Müller, Edward.
Umlando weBandhla. Mariannhill, Mission press, 1929.

57p. front (port.) 18½cm.
History of the Roman Catholic Church in Zulu.

M614
R66n4
Roman, Charles Victor, 1864-1934.
The Negro woman and the health problem. Reprinted from the Journal of the National Medical Association, 7:182-191, July-Sept. 1915.

1. Women. 2. Health.

M614.
R66sk
Roman, Charles Victor, 1864-1934.
Skeletology. Reprinted from the Journal of the National Medical Association, Oct.-Dec. 1922.

2p. 27cm.

1. Medicine--Study and teaching. I. Title.

Le roman d'Antar d' apres les anciens textes arabes.

Arabia
M892.8
An8r
Antar, 525?-615? or Antarud Ibn Shaddad
... Le roman d' Antar d'après les anciens textes arabes. Paris, L'Édition d'art [°1923]

2 p. l., vi, 218 p., 1 l. 19cm. [Épopées et légendes]

Adapted and abridged by Gustave Rouger, whose name appears at head of title.

I. Rouger, Gustave. II. Title.

24-14472

Library of Congress
Copyright A—Foreign 24070 [2]

Le roman de Bouqui.
Haiti M843.91 C73r
Comhaire-Sylvain, Suzanne.
Le roman de Bouqui, par Suzanne Comhaire-Sylvain; couverture de V. Pierre-Noël et 18 dessins originaux de l'auteur. Port-au-Prince, Haiti [Impr. du Collège Vertières] 1940.
1 p. l., v, 116 p. 25cm.
Without the "18 dessins originaux de l'auteur."
I. Title.
Library of Congress PQ3949.C63R6 43-411 [2] 843.91

The romantic adventures of Rosy, the octoroon.
M813.4 C67
Coleman, Albert Evander.
The romantic adventures of Rosy, the octoroon, with some account of the persecution of the southern negroes during the reconstruction period, by Albert Evander Coleman. Boston, Mass., Meador publishing company [c1929]
121 p. 20½cm.
I. Title.
Library of Congress PZ3.C677Ro 29-29022
——— Copy 2.
Copyright A 16363 [2]

M813.5 J13r
Room for Randy.
Jackson, Jesse.
Room for Randy. Illustrated by Frank C. Nicholas. New York, Friendship Press [1957]
136 p. illus. 22 cm.
I. Title.
PZ7.J13624Ro 57-6164 ‡
Library of Congress [7]

M841.5 A 16 1771
Romance.
Leonard, Nicolas Germain, 1744-1793
Romance. In: Almanach des Muses, 1771. (Paris, Delalain, 1771) p. 136.

Romanticism—England.
M808 D98
Dykes, Eva Beatrice.
The Negro in English romantic thought; or, A study of sympathy for the oppressed, by Eva Beatrice Dykes. Washington, D. C., The Associated publishers, inc., 1942.
5 p. l., 197 p. 23½cm.
Bibliography: p. 157-166.
1. Romanticism—England. 2. Negroes in literature and art. 3. English literature—18th cent.—Hist. & crit. 4. English literature—19th cent.—Hist. & crit. I. Title.
42-6447
Library of Congress PR447.D9 [45j2] 820.903

Roosevelt, Franklin Delano, pres. of U. S., 1882-1945.
MB9 R571
Law, John
Franklin Delano Roosevelt, a friend to man. A tribute in verse by John Law. New York, William - Frederick press, 1946.
15p. 20cm.

The Romance of African Methodism.
M287.8 S16
Singleton, George A
The romance of African Methodism; a study of the African Methodist Episcopal Church. New York, Exposition Press [1952]
251 p. illus. 22 cm.
1. African Methodist Episcopal Church—Hist. I. Title.
BX8443.S45 287.8 51-13284 ‡
Library of Congress [1]

Rome-Hist.-Nero, A.D. 54-68-Fiction.
France M840 D89ac
Dumas, Alexandre, 1802-1870.
Acté. Bruxelles Société Typographique Belge, 1838.
2 vols. in 1. 15½cm.

M973 R54
Roosevelt, Franklin Delano.
Robertson, L O
We want Roosevelt again because of facts and figures; a brief review of part of the achievements of the Roosevelt administration, compiled by L.O. Robertson... Washington, D.C. [1946]
24p. tables. 23cm.

Romancero aux étoiles.
Haiti M843.91 A13r
Alexis, Jacques Stephen, 1922-
Romancero aux étoiles; contes. Paris, Gallimard [1960]
271 p. 19 cm.
CONTENTS.—Dit de Bouqui et de Malice.—Dit d'Anne aux longs cils.—Fable de Tatez'o-Flando.—Chronique d'un faux-amour.—Dit de la Fleur d'Or.—Le sous-lieutenant enchanté.—Romance du Petit-Viseur.—Le Roi des Songes.—La rouille des ans.
I. Title.
A 60-3555
Illinois. Univ. Library for Library of Congress [1]

M366.1 R66m
Romeo, Frank J
Masonic collection of odes, compiled from the Masonic concordia, by Frank J. Romeo. n.p., n.d.
5p. 15cm.
At head of title: To David W. Parker, most worshipful grand master and the Prince Hall Grand Lodge of the State of New York.
1. Freemasons.

Roosevelt, Franklin Delano, Pres. of U.S. 1882-1945.
Panama M986.2 W523
Westerman, George W ed.
In memoriam; The tribute of a sorrowing group on the passing of the late Franklin Delano Roosevelt. Panama, Isthmian Negro Youth Congress, 1945.
36p. 22cm.
Inscription: To A.B. Spingarn, President NAACP from ?

Romances pour ninoche.
Haiti M841.1 Au4
Auguste, Gérard Bonaparte
Romances pour ninoche; poèmes. Louvain, Editions Arta, 1953.
38p. 20cm.

Romulus.
Haiti M843.91 H52sc
Hibbert, Fernand.
... Scènes de la vie haïtienne. Romulus. Port-au-Prince, Imprimerie de l'Abeille, 1908.
3 p. l., [9]-120 p., 1 l. 21cm.
I. Title. II. Title: Romulus.
25-20830
Library of Congress PQ3949.H5S3

Roosevelt, Theodore, pres. U.S., 1858-1919.
MB9 R672
Amos, James E 1879-
Theodore Roosevelt: hero to his valet, by James E. Amos. New York, The John Day company, 1927.
6 p. l., 3-162 p., 1 l. front., ports., facsim. 19½cm.
1. Roosevelt, Theodore, pres. U. S., 1858-1919.
27-7592
Library of Congress E757.A52 [39k1]

Martinique M841.91 R66s
Romanette, Irmine
Sonate, poésies, Dessins de Georges Guiraud. Paris, Jouve, 1951, c1950.
190p. port, illus. 19cm.
1. Martinican poetry. I. Title.

Romulus.
Haiti M843.91 H52sc 1907
Hibbert, Fernand, 1873-1928.
Scènes de la vie Haitienne. Les Thezar. Port-au-Prince, Imp. de l'Abeille, 1907.
253p. 19cm.

Roosevelt, Theodore, pres.U.S., 1858-1919.
Haiti M972.94 F51r
Firmin, Anténor, 1850-1911.
M. Roosevelt, président des États-Unis et la République d'Haïti, par A. Firmin ... New York, Hamilton bank note engraving and printing company; Paris, F. Pichon et Durand-Auzias, 1905.
x, 501, [1] p. front. (port.) 19cm.
1. Haiti—For. rel.—U. S. 2. U. S.—For. rel.—Haiti. 3. Haiti—Pol. & govt.—1844- 4. Roosevelt, Theodore, pres. U. S., 1858-1919.
6-26
Library of Congress F1921.F52 [43f1]

Martinique M841.91 R66so
Romanette, Irmine
...Sonson de la Martinique, roman. Paris, Société Française d'Editions littéraires et Techniques, 1932.
248p. 18½cm.
At head of title: Bibliothèque du Hérisson.
1. Martinique-Fiction. 2. Martinican fiction. I. Title.

La ronde des jours.
Ivory Coast M896.1 D12r
Dadié, Bernard B
La ronde des jours. Paris, P. Seghers [1956]
56 p. 18 cm. (Collection P. S., no 476)
On cover: Poésie 56.
I. Title. (Series)
[PQ1184.C57 no. 476] A 57-1627
Illinois. Univ. Library for Library of Congress [1]

The rootless.
M813.5 T86r
Turpin, Waters Edward, 1910-
The rootless. [1st ed.] New York, Vantage Press [1957]
340 p. 21 cm.
I. Title.
PZ3.T867Ro 56-12795 ‡
Library of Congress [2]

M323
Al7r
Roots of prejudice.
Allport, Gordon W
Roots of prejudice, by Gordon W. Allport & Bernard M. Kramer. New York, American Jewish Congress, 1946.

22p. illus. tables. 19cm.
Special number of Jewish Affairs, December 1, 1946.

Rope & faggot.
M323.
W587ro
White, Walter Francis, 1893-
Rope & faggot; a biography of Judge Lynch, by Walter White. New York & London, A. A. Knopf, 1929.

xiii p., 2 l., [3]-272, iv p., 1 l. incl. tables. front. 21½cm.
Bibliography: p. 269-272.

1. Lynch law. 2. Negroes. 3. U. S.—Race question. I. Title. II. Title: A biography of Judge Lynch.

29—10015

Library of Congress HV6457.W45
[44e1]

M326.99B
R68
1838
Roper, Moses, 1816-
A narrative of the adventures and escape of Moses Roper, from American slavery; with a preface, by the Rev. T. Price... Second edition. London, Harvey and Darton, 1838.

xii, 108p. 15cm.

M326.99B
R68
1840
Roper, Moses, 1816-
A narrative of the adventures and escape of Moses Roper, from American slavery; with a preface, by the Rev. T. Price ... 4th ed. London, Harvey and Darton, 1840.

xii, 120 p. front. (port.) illus. 15cm.

2. Slave narratives.
1. Slavery in the U. S.—South Carolina. I. Price, Thomas.

17-24785

Library of Congress E444.R785

M326.99B
R68
1846
Roper, Moses, 1816-
Narratives of the adventures and escape of Moses Roper from American Slavery. 33rd thousand. Berwick-Upon-Tweed, The Author, 1846.

88p. illus. 17cm.

1. Slave narratives.

Puerto Rico
M861
R71a
Rosa-Nieves, Cesáreo, 1904-
Aguinaldo lírico de la poesía Puertorriqueña. Prólogo, selección, ordenación y notas de Cesáreo Rosa-Nieves. Puerto Rico, Liberia Campos, 1957.

3v. 20cm.

continued on next card.

Puerto Rico
M861
R71a
Rosa-Nieves, Cesáreo, 1904-
Aguinaldo lírico de la poesía Puertorriqueña. Puerto Rico, Liberia Campos, 1957. (Card 2)

Contents-v.1-Románticos y Parnasianos (ciclos) generacionales 1843-1880 y 1880-1907). -v.2-Los modernistas (ciclo generacional: 1907-1921).-v.3-Postmoderniastas y vanguardistas (ciclo generacional: postmodernismo: 1921-1945, y vanguardismo: 1945-1956).

1. Literature-Puerto Rico. I. Title.

Rosa-Nieves, Cesáreo. 1904-
Puerto Rico
M861
R71a
Rosa-Nieves, Cesáreo, 1904-
Aguinaldo lírico de la poesía Puertorriqueña. Prólogo, selección, ordenación y notas de Cesáreo Rosa-Nieves. Puerto Rico, Liberia Campos, 1957.

3v. 20cm.

Puerto Rico
MB9
Ay2
Rosa-Nieves, Cesáreo, 1904-
Francisco de Ayerra Santa María, poeta Puertorriqueño, 1630-1708. Suan Juan, Universidad de Puerto Rico, 1948.

30p. 23cm.

1. Ayerra Santa Maria, Francisco de, 1630-1708.

Puerto Rico
M861
R71s
Rosa-Nieves, Cesáreo, 1904-
Siete caminos en luna de sueños; poemas. San Juan, Biblioteca de Autores Puertorriqueños, 1957.

121p. 20cm.

I. Title.

Puerto Rico
M301
R72
Rosario, Jose Colomban
Problemas sociales; el Negro: Haiti-Estados Unidos-Puerto Rico, por Jose Colomban Rosario y Justina Carrion. San Juan, Negociado de Materiales, Imprenta y Transporte, 1940.

174p. 21cm. (Universidad de Puerto Rico. Boletim, series X, no. 2, December 1939)
Bibliography: p. 161-165.

1. Social life and conditions. 2. Puerto Rico. 3. Haiti. I. Carrion, Justina. II. Title. III. Series: Puerto Rico. University. Bolemtim, December 1939.

Roscoe, John, 1861-1932. The Baganda.
Uganda
M967.61
K11c
Kagwa, *Sir* Apolo, 1864?-1927.
The customs of the Baganda, by Sir Apolo Kagwa, translated by Ernest B. Kalibala, edited by May Mandelbaum Edel. New York, Columbia university press, 1934.

199 p. 24cm. (*Half-title:* Columbia university contributions to anthropology. Vol. XXII)
"What is presented here is ... essentially an annotation and expansion of The Baganda [by John Roscoe]"—Pref.

1. Baganda. 2. Ethnology—Uganda. I. Kalibala, Ernest B., tr. II. Edel, May (Mandelbaum) 1909- ed. III. Roscoe, John, 1861-1932. The Baganda.

A 40-1824

Brown univ. Library for Library of Congress E51.C7 vol. 22
[a44g1]† (572.97) 572.96761

M973
R72
Rose, Arnold Marshall, 1918- *ed.*
Assuring freedom to the free; a century of emancipation in the USA. With an introd. by Lyndon B. Johnson. Detroit, Wayne State University Press, 1964.

306 p. 21 cm.
Bibliographical footnotes.
White editor.
Partial contents.- The Emancipation Proclamation: 1863-1963, by John Hope Franklin.-

~~1. Negroes—Hist.—Addresses, essays, lectures. 2. U. S.—Race question—Addresses, essays, lectures. I. Title.~~
(Continued on next card)

E185.6.R74 301.451 63—14634

Library of Congress [64d7]

M973
R72
Rose, Arnold Marshall, 1918- ed.
Assuring freedom to the free; a century of emancipation in the USA. Detroit, Wayne State University Press, 1964. (Card 2)
Contents - Continued.
Religious roots of the Negro protest, by Carleton L. Lee.- The city of Detroit and the Emancipation Proclamation, by Broadus N. Butler.- Changes in occupation as they affect the Negro, by G. Franklin Edwards.- The changing structure of the American City and the Negro, by Robert C. Weaver.-
(Continued on next card)

M973
R72
Rose, Arnold Marshall, 1918- ed.
Assuring freedom to the free; a century of emancipation in the USA. Detroit, Wayne State University Press, 1964. (Card 3)
Contents - Continued.
Legal concepts in the quest for equality, by Charles W. Quick and Donald B. King.- Educational changes affecting American Negroes, by Rayford W. Logan.- Civil rights action and the Urban League, by Whitney M. Young, Jr.- The Black Muslims as a protest movement, by C. Eric Lincoln. - The Transformation of the Negro intellectual, by John Hope Franklin.

M323
R72
Rose, Arnold Marshall, 1918- ed.
Race prejudice and discrimination; readings in intergroup relations in the United States. 1st ed. New York, Knopf, 1951.

xi, 605, vi p. 22cm.
Partial contents: Three centuries of discrimination against the Negro, by W.E.B. DuBois. Negro labor since 1929, by Robert C. Weaver. The Negro in the political life of the United States, by Ralph J. Bunche. -The psychology of the Negro under discrimination, by Horace R. Cayton. The Negro's vested interest in

---

M323
R72
Rose, Arnold Marshall. Race prejudice and discrimination... 195. (card 2)

segregation, by E. Franklin Frazier. -A new problem for Negroes: Integration, by Lester B. Granger.
White author.
1. Race question . I. Title. II. a.t. DuBois. III. a.t. Bunche. IV. a.t. Cayton. V. a.t. Weaver. VI. a.t. Frazier. VII. a.t. Granger.

Rose only loved my money.
Nigeria
M896.2
Og9r
Ogu, H O
Rose only loved my money. Aba [Nigeria] Treasure Press [n.d.]

32p. 18cm. (Treasure series, no. 1)

M813.5
R72
Rosebrough, Sadie Mae
Wasted travail. New York, Vantage Press, Inc., 1951.

90p. 21½cm.

I. Title.

Haiti
M972.94
R72 h
Rosemond, Henri Chrysostome
Haiti, our neighbor (a play in two acts and twelve scenes) by Henri Ch. Rosemond ... Brooklyn, N. Y., The Haitian publishing company [1944]

95 p. plates, ports., coat of arms. 20 cm.
Inscribed copy: Expression d'une grande admiration à Mr. Arthur B. Spingarn Ce 28 September 1944, Henri Rosemond.

I. Title. 1. Haitian drama

44-12517

Library of Congress PR9900.H4R6
[2] 822.91

Haiti
M972.94
R72t
Rosemond, Henri Chrysostome.
The truth about Haiti and the new deal government with Colonel Paul E. Magloire. N.Y., Haitian publishing co., 1950.

11p. 23cm.

1. Haiti - Pol. & govt. 2. Magloire, Paul Eugene, pres., of Haiti, 1907-

Haiti
M972.94 Rosemond, Jules
R722c ...La Crête-à-Pierrot luttes pour l'indépendance d'Haiti, Fevrier et Mars 1802, par Jules Rosemond... Port-au-Prince, Imprimerie Bernard, 1913.

76 [2]p. 19cm.

1. Haiti-history. I. Title.

Rosskam, Edwin, 1903-

M813.5 Wright, Richard, 1909-
W93t 12 million black voices; a folk history of the Negro in the United States; text by Richard Wright, photo-direction by Edwin Rosskam. New York, The Viking press, 1941.

152 p. illus. 26cm.

"First published in October 1941."

1. Negroes—Moral and social conditions. I. *Rosskam, Edwin, 1903- II. Title.

[Full name: Richard Nathaniel Wright]

41—25589

Library of Congress E185.6.W9

[45n2] 325.260973

Haiti
M843.91 Roumain, Jacques, 1907-1944.
R76m ... Les fantoches... [Port-au-Prince, Collection Indigene, 1931.

152p. 18cm.

Inscribed copy: A Monsieur Arthur B. Spingarn, Témoignagede sympathie, Jacques Roumain.

Bound with : La Montague Ensorcelée, by Jacques Roumain.

1. Haitian fiction. n. I. Title.

Rosenwald, Julius.

M323 Johnson, James Weldon, 1871-1938.
J632e The shining life, by James Weldon Johnson... An appreciation of Julius Rosenwald delivered at a memorial service in Fisk Memorial Chapel, Nashville, Tennessee, February 14, 1932. Fisk University bulletin, vol. 8, 1932.

11p. 23cm.

Rotberg, Robert I., ed.

Malawi
M968.97 Mwase, George Simeon, ca. 1880-1962.
M98 Strike a blow and die; a narrative of race relations in colonial Africa. Edited and introduced by Robert I. Rotberg. Cambridge, Mass., Harvard University Press, 1967.

xiii, 135 p. map, ports. 22 cm.

Bibliographical footnotes.

1. Chilembwe, John, d. 1915. 2. Malawi—Hist. I. Rotberg, Robert I., ed. II. Title.

DT862.M68 968.97'020924 (B) 66-21342

Library of Congress [5]

Haiti
M843.91 Roumain, Jacques, 1907-1944.
R76g ... Gouverneurs de la rosée, roman. [Port-au-Prince, Imprimerie de l'état, 1944]

xiv, 321 p., 1 l. incl. port. 20cm. (Collection indigène)

"Notice biographique": p. vii-xiii.

"L'oeuvre littéraire et scientifique de Jacques Roumain": p. xiv.

I. Title. 1. Haitian fiction

New York. Public library for Library of Congress A 45-3118

PQ3949.R73G6

[2]† 863.6

... Roses et camélias.

Haiti
M841 Moravia, Charles, 1876-
M79r ... Roses et camélias, poésies par Charles Moravia. Port-au-Prince, Impr. Madame F. Smith, 1903.

3 p. l., 127, [1] p. 16cm.

At head of title: Bibliothèque haïtienne.

I. Title.

Library of Congress PQ3949.M6R6 1903 26-3538

——— Copy 2.

With this are bound: Heine, H. L'intermezzo. 1917. Copy 2, and Heine, H. Autres poèmes. 1918. Copy 4.

M301 Rouček, Joseph Slabey, 1902- ed.
R75 Contemporary sociology. New York, Philosophical Library [1958]

xii, 1209 p. illus. 24 cm.

Includes bibliographies and bibliographical references.

White author.

1. Sociology—Hist.

HM19.R6 301 58—59414

Library of Congress [60q10]

Haiti
M843.91 Roumain, Jacques, 1907-1944.
R76h Herr über den tau. Berlin, Rowohlt Hamburg. 1950.

163p. 17½cm.

1. Haitian fiction. I. Title.

M324 Ross, Hilliard Franklin
R73e The election of 1936, by Hilliard Franklin Ross. New York, N.Y. The author 1936.

36p. 22cm.

1. Voting. 2. Politics and government.
I. Title.

Rouge est le sang des Noirs.

S. Africa
M896.3 Abrahams, Peter, 1909-
Ab8ro Rouge est le sang des Noirs. (Mine boy). Roman. Traduit de l'anglais par Denise Shaw-Mantoux. [Paris] Casterman, 1960.

226p. 20cm. (Collection l'élienne)

Haiti
M843.91 Roumain, Jacques, 1907-1944.
R76ma Masters of the dew. Translated by Langston Hughes and Mercer Cook. New York, Reynal & Hitchcock, [1947]

180 p. 19cm.

I. Title III. Cook, Mercer.
II. Hughes, Langston. 1. Haitian fiction

Africa, South
M968 Ross, Richard Ernest van der, 1921-
Sp6s Through coloured glasses.

pp. 237-248.

In: South Africa the road ahead, comp. by Hildegarde Spottiswoode. 1960.

I. Title.

Rouger, Gustave.

Arabia
M892.8 Antar, 525?-615? or Antarad Ibn Shaddad
An8r ... Le roman d'Antar d'après les anciens textes arabes. Paris, L'Édition d'art [1923]

2 p. l., vi, 218 p., 1 l. 19cm. [Épopées et légendes]

Adapted and abridged by Gustave Rouger, whose name appears at head of title.

I. Rouger, Gustave. II. Title.

Library of Congress 24-14472

Copyright A—Foreign 24070

[2]

Haiti
M843.91 Roumain, Jacques, 1907-1944.
R76m La montagne ensorcelée. Preface du Dr. Price Mars. [Port-au-Prince, Haiti] Collection Indigene, 1931.

113p. 18cm.

Inscribed copy: A Monsieur Arthur B. Spingarn, Hommage empressé, Jacques Roumain.

1. Haitian fiction. I. Title.

Ross, Mrs. Solomon D.
MB The minister's wife, by Mrs. S.D.Ross.
R73m [Detroit, Arbora publishing co., c1946]
78p.

1. Biography. I. Title.

MB9 Rough steps on my stairway.
Sp32 Spellman, Cecil Lloyd, 1906-
Rough steps on my stairway; the life history of a Negro educator. [1st ed.] New York, Exposition Press [1953]

273 p. 21 cm.

1. Negro teachers—Correspondence, reminiscences, etc. I. Title.

LC2731.S65 923.773 53-5639 ‡

Library of Congress [5]

Haiti
M843.91 Roumain, Jacques, 1907-1944.
R76m La montagne ensorcelée. Preface du Dr. Price Mars. [Port-au-Prince, Haiti] Collection Indigene, 1931.

113p. 18cm.

Inscribed copy: A Monsieur Arthur B. Spingarn, Hommage empressé, Jacques Roumain.

1. Haitian fiction. I. Title.

Argentina
M982. Rossi, Vicente.
R73 ... Cosas de negros; los orijenes del tango y otros aportes al folklore rioplatense. Rectificaciones históricas. Rio de la Plata [Córdoba, Imprenta argentina] 1926.

436 p., 2 l., 7 p. illus. (music) 26cm.

1. Negroes in Argentine republic. 2. Negroes in Uruguay. 3. Folklore, Negro. 4. Negroes—Dancing. 5. Tango (Dance) I. Title.

27—25000

Library of Congress F3021.N3R8

[a45d1]

Haiti
M841. Roumain, Jacques, 1907-1944.
R76b ... Bois-d'ébène [par] Jacques Roumain. Port-au-Prince, Haiti, Imp. H. Deschamps [1945]

2 p. l., 20 p. 20cm.

At head of title: Poèmes.

1. Haitian Poetry. I. Title.

A 46-2605

New York. Public library for Library of Congress PQ3949.R73B6

[2]† 841.91

Roumain, Jacques, 1907-1944 - Poems.

Latin America Pp. 290-293. In -
M861.08 Fitts, Dudley, 1903- ed.
F56a Anthology of contemporary Latin-American poetry, edited by Dudley Fitts. Norfolk, Conn., New directions [1942]

ix, [2], x-xxi, 667 p. 23½ cm.

Added t.-p.: Antología de la poesía americana contemporánea. English and original text (Spanish, Portuguese or French) on opposite pages.

"Biographical and bibliographical notes, by H. R. Hays": p. 581-641.

1. Spanish-American poetry (Collections) 2. Spanish-American poetry—Translations into English. 3. English poetry—Translations from Spanish. 4. Spanish-American poetry—Bio-bibl. I. Hays, Hoffman Reynolds. II. Title.

PQ7084.F5 861.6082 43—485

Library of Congress [54r43k*7]

Roumain, Jacques, 1907-1944 - Poetry.

Haiti
M841
B76d

Brierre, Jean Fernand, 1909–
... Nous garderons le dieu. En hommage au grand leader haïtien de gauche: Jacques Roumain. Port-au-Prince, Imprimerie H. Deschamps, 1945.
1 p. l., 27 p. 20 x 15 cm.
At head of title: Jean F. Brierre.
Poems.
1. Roumain, Jacques, 1907–1944—Poetry. I. Title.
PQ3949.B67N6 A 47-4363
New York. Public library for Library of Congress ₍2₎†

Roux, P.

Haiti
M972.94
A16

Almanach royal d'Hayti pour l'année 18 ...
presenté au roi par P. Roux. Cap-Henry, P. Roux, impr. de Sa Majesté ₍18
v. 18½–20ᶜᵐ.
1. Haiti—Registers. I. Roux, P.
ca 12-1228 Unrev'd
Library of Congress JL1080.A4 ₍a45b1₎

M323
R78

Rowan, Carl Thomas, 1925–
South of freedom. ₍1st ed.₎ New York, Knopf, 1952.
270 p. 22 cm.
1. Negroes. 2. U. S.—Race question. I. Title.
E185.61.R86 *301.451 325.260975 51—11990 ‡
Library of Congress ₍53f7₎

Haiti
M841
R76p

Roumer, Émile.
... Poèmes d'Haïti et de France. Paris, Éditions de la Revue mondiale, 1925.
92 p., 1 l. 19ᶜᵐ. (Collection haïtienne d'expression française, sous la direction de m. Louis Morpeau)
I. Title. 1. Haitian poetry.
PQ3949.R74P6 47-38523
Library of Congress ₍1₎

Haiti
M841.1
R76

Rouzier, Mona.
Sur les vieux thèmes. Port-au-Prince, N. A. Théodore ₍1958₎
57 p. 18 cm.
Poems.
I. Title.
A 59-2240
Florida. Univ. Library for Library of Congress ₍1₎

MB9
R56w

Rowan, Carl Thomas, 1925–
Wait till next year; the life story of Jackie Robinson, by Carl T. Rowan with Jackie Robinson. New York, Random House ₍1960₎
339 p. illus. 24 cm.
Portrait of author on book jacket.
1. Robinson, John Roosevelt, 1919– I. Title.
GV865.R6R64 927.96357 60—5566 ‡
Library of Congress ₍61f15₎

Roumer, Emile
Pp. 502-503. In -

Latin
America
M861.08
F56a

Fitts, Dudley, 1903– ed.
Anthology of contemporary Latin-American poetry, edited by Dudley Fitts. Norfolk, Conn., New directions ₍1942₎
ix, ₍2₎, x-xxi, 667 p. 23½ cm.
Added t.-p.: Antología de la poesía americana contemporánea.
English and original text (Spanish, Portuguese or French) on opposite pages.
"Biographical and bibliographical notes, by H. R. Hays": p. 581-641.
1. Spanish-American poetry (Collections) 2. Spanish-American poetry—Translations into English. 3. English poetry—Translations from Spanish. 4. Spanish-American poetry—Bio-bibl. I. Hays, Hoffman Reynolds. II. Title.
PQ7084.F5 861.6082 43—485
Library of Congress ₍54r43k5 7₎

W. Indies
M823
C23

Rovere, Ethel
Only white people cry.

(In: Caribbean anthology of short stories,... Kingston, Jamaica, Pioneer Press 1953. 19cm. pp. 98-105.)

Rowan, Levi John p. 64 - 69.

M378A1
D29p

Davis, Walker Milan, 1908–
Pushing forward; a history of Alcorn A. & M. college and portraits of some of its successful graduates, by W. Milan Davis ... Okolona, Miss., The Okolona industrial school, 1938.
x, 124 p. illus. (incl. ports.) 23½ᶜᵐ.
1. Alcorn agricultural and mechanical college, Alcorn, Miss. 2. Negroes—Biog. I. Title.
Library of Congress S537.A39D35 38-9709
——— Copy 2.
Copyright A 114827 ₍3₎ 630.711

M976.3
R76

Roussève, Charles Barthelemy.
The Negro in Louisiana; aspects of his history and his literature, by Charles Barthelemy Roussève, M. A. New Orleans, The Xavier university press, 1937.
xvii, 212 p. front., illus. (music) plates, diagrs. 20½ᶜᵐ.
"This work, prepared in 1935 in partial fulfillment of the requirements for the degree of master of arts, makes its appearance ... substantially as it was originally written, save for ... several minor alterations and the addition of a few details."—p. vii.
Bibliography: p. 193-201.
1. Negroes—Louisiana. 2. Negroes in literature and art. 3. Negro authors. I. Title.
38-525
Library of Congress E185.93.L6R6 ₍42h2₎ 325.2609763

W. Indies
M823
C23

Rovere, Ethel
Spanish jar.

(In: Caribbean anthology of short stories,... Kingston, Jamaica, Pioneer Press 1953. 19cm. pp. 27-34.)

M811.4
R79t

Rowe, George Clinton, 1853–1903.
Thoughts in verse. A volume of poems, by George Clinton Rowe ... Charleston, S. C., Kahrs, Stolze & Welch, printers, 1887.
118 p. port. 18½ᶜᵐ.
I. Title. 1. Poetry.
29-30627
Library of Congress PS2735.R55T5
Copyright 1887: 13869

M301
R76d

Roussève, Ronald J 1932–
Discord in brown and white; nine essays on intergroup relations in the United States by a Negro American. ₍1st ed.₎ New York, Vantage Press ₍1961₎
89 p. 22 cm.
Includes bibliography.
Portrait of author on book jacket.
1. Negroes 2. U. S.—Race question. I. Title.
E185.61.R82 301.451 61-4684 ‡
Library of Congress ₍5₎

M323
R78g

Rowan, Carl Thomas, 1925–
Go South to sorrow. New York, Random House ₍1957₎
246 p. 21 cm.
1. Negroes—Segregation. 2. Negroes—Southern States. I. Title.
E185.61.R855 325.260975 57-5878 ‡
Library of Congress ₍25₎

M811.5
R79

Rowland, Ida.
... Lisping leaves, by Ida Rowland. Philadelphia, Dorrance and company ₍©1939₎
55 p. 20ᶜᵐ. (Contemporary poets of Dorrance. (191))
I. Title. 1. Poetry.
40-1973
Library of Congress PS3535.O9658L5 1939
——— Copy 2.
Copyright A 135884 ₍2₎ 811.5

La route du Ghana. (Road to Ghana).

Africa,
South
M968
H97ro

Hutchinson, Alfred, 1924-
La route du Ghana. (Road to Ghana). Traduit de l'anglais par Jean Fillion. Paris, Editions Albin Michel, 1961.
263p. 20½cm.

M301
Eb74

Rowan, Carl Thomas, 1925-
No whitewash for U. S. abroad
Pp. 31-37

In: Ebony. The white problem in America. Chicago, Johnson Pub. Co., 1966.

MB9
W671r

Rowland, Mabel, ed.
Bert Williams, son of laughter; a symposium of tribute to the man and to his work, by his friends and associates, with a preface by David Belasco; edited by Mabel Rowland. New York city, The English crafters ₍©1923₎
xvii p., 1 l., 218 p. front., plates, ports., facsim. 19½ cm.
1. Williams, Egbert Austin, 1875–1922.
23-8622
Library of Congress PN2287.W46R6 ₍8₎

... La route ensoleillée...

Haiti
M841
H61r

Hippolyte, Dominique, 1889–
... La route ensoleillée ... Paris, Éditions de la Pensée latine, 1927.
171 p., 1 l. 19½ᶜᵐ.
Poems.
I. Title.
45-43006
Library of Congress PQ3949.H54R6 ₍2₎

M910
R78p

Rowan, Carl Thomas, 1925–
The pitiful and the proud. New York, Random House ₍1956₎
432 p. 22 cm.
1. Asia—Politics. 2. Asia—Soc. condit. 3. Race. I. Title.
DS35.R6 950 56—5920 ‡
Library of Congress ₍57q10₎

Haiti
M841
R81v

Roy, Herard C L.
... Les variations tropicales et Les mandragores. Port-au-Prince, Haiti, Imprimerie de l'état ₍193–?₎
101 p. 19½ᶜᵐ.
Poems.
I. Title. II. Title: Les mandragores. 1. Haitian poetry.
42-12373
Library of Congress PQ3949.R75V3 ₍2₎ 841.91

Roy, Jessie Hailstalk, 1896- , jt. author

MB
D44w

Derricotte, Elise Palmer.
Word pictures of the great, by Elise Palmer Derricotte ... Geneva Calcier Turner ... [and] Jessie Hailstalk Roy ... illustrated by Lois Mailou Jones. Washington, D. C., The Associated publishers inc. [°1941]

xiii, 280 p. incl. front., illus. 21½cm.
Illustrated lining-papers in color.
"Books to read" at end of each section.

1. Negroes—Biog. I. Turner, Geneva Calcier, joint author. II. Roy, Jessie Hailstalk, joint author. III. Title.

41—13255

Library of Congress E185.96.D4
[a44g2] [325.260973] 920.073

Jamaica
M823.91
R812b

Roy, Namba.
Black Albino. [London] New Literature, 1961.

196p. 21cm.

1. Jamaica - Fiction. I. Title.

M973.8
R81r

Rozwenc, Edwin Charles, 1915- *ed.*
Reconstruction in the South. Boston, Heath [1952]

109 p. 24 cm. (Problems in American civilization; readings selected by the Dept. of American Studies, Amherst College)
Bibliography: p. [108]-109.
White author.

1. Reconstruction. 2. Southern States—Hist.—1865-1877. I. Title.

E668.R83 973.8 52—1818 ‡
Library of Congress [60q2]

Ruanda-Urundi-History.

Rwanda
M967.5
K10h

Kagame, Alexis, 1912-
L'Histoire des armées-bovines dans l'ancien Rwanda. [Bruxelles, 1961]

147p. 24cm. (Académie royale des sciences d'outre-mer. Classe des sciences morales et politiques. Mémoires in-8°, Nouv. sér, t. 25, f.4)

Ruanda-Urundi-History.

Rwanda
M967.5
K10no

Kagame, Alexis, 1912-
La notion de génération appliquée à la généalogie dynastique et à l'historie du Rwanda des Xe - XIe siecles a nos jours. Bruxelles, Academie Royale des Sciences Coloniales, 1959.

117p. 24½cm.

Ruanda-Urundi - History, Military.

Rwanda
M967.57
K11m

Kagame, Alexis, 1912-
Les milices du Rwanda précolonial. [Bruxelles, 1963]

196 p. 25 cm. (Académie royale des sciences d'outre-mer. Classe des sciences morales et politiques. Mémoires in 8°. Nouv. sér., t. 28, fasc. 3)

1. Ruanda-Urundi—Soc. life & cust. 2. Ruanda-Urundi—History, Military. I. Title. (Series)

[DT641.A27 n. s., t. 28, fasc. 3] A 63-770

Yale Univ. Library
for Library of Congress [1]

Ruandi - Urundi - Language and languages.

Rwanda
M496
K11

Kagame, Alexis, 1912-
La langue du Rwanda et du Burundi expliquée aux autochtones. [Kabgayi, 1960]

252p. 20cm.

Ruanda-Urundi-Literature.

Rwanda
M896.9
K11b

Kagame, Alexis, 1912-
Bref apercu sur la poésie dynastique du Rwanda. Bruxelles, Editions Universitaires, n.d.

30p.
[Extrait de la revue Zaire]

Ruanda-Urundi - Proverbs.

Ruanda-Urundi
M398.9
N65

Nkongori, Laurent
Proverbes du Rwanda, par Laurent Nkongori. Avec la collaboration de Thomas Kamanzi. Tervuren, Annales du Musée Royal du Congo Belge, 1957.

79p. 27cm.

Ruanda-Urundi - Social life and customs.

Rwanda
M967.57
K11m

Kagame, Alexis, 1912-
Les milices du Rwanda précolonial. [Bruxelles, 1963]

196 p. 25 cm. (Académie royale des sciences d'outre-mer. Classe des sciences morales et politiques. Mémoires in 8°. Nouv. sér., t. 28, fasc. 3)

1. Ruanda-Urundi—Soc. life & cust. 2. Ruanda-Urundi—History, Military. I. Title. (Series)

[DT641.A27 n. s., t. 28, fasc. 3] A 63-770

Yale Univ. Library
for Library of Congress [1]

Ruanda language - Texts.

Rwanda
M896.1
K11iy

Kagame, Alexis, 1912- comp.
Iyo wiliwe nta rungu. Kabgayi, Les Editions Royales, 1949.

232p. 13cm
Written in Ruanda.

Nyasaland
M967.61
H34

Rubadiri, J., tr.
Head, M E
Ensi mwe tuli n'abanti Nga bwe bagyeyambisa. The land and how men use it. Ebifaananyi bya J. Rubadiri. Nairobi, Eagle Press, 1953.

8 p. illus. 18 cm.
Written in Luganda.
White author.

Africa
M266
St29t

Rubusane, Walter Benson, 1858-1936
Cooperation from the West.

Pp. 147-156.

In: Stauffer, Milton Theobald, ed. Thinking with Africa: chapters by a group of nationals interpreting the Christian movement. New York, Published for the Student Volunteer Movement for

---

Africa
M266
St29t

Rubusana, Walter Benson, 1858-1936.
Cooperation from... (card 2)

Foreign Missions by the Missionary Education Movement of the United States and Canada, 1927.

M326
R82

Ruchames, Louis, 1917- *ed.*
The abolitionists; a collection of their writings. New York, Putnam [1963]

259 p. 22 cm.
Contains selections from the writings of David Ruggles, Theodore S. Wright, Charles Lenox Remond and Frederick Douglass.
White editor.

1. Abolitionists. 2. Slavery in the U. S.—Controversial literature. 3. Slavery in the U. S.—Anti-slavery movements. I. Title.

E449.R88 326.4 63—16184 ‡
Library of Congress [63f5]

MB9
B64r

Rudd, Daniel Arthur, 1854-
From slavery to wealth, the life of Scott Bond; the rewards of honesty, industry, economy and perseverance, by Dan A. Rudd and Theo. Bond; with preface by Hon. J. C. Napier ... Madison, Ark., The Journal printing company, 1917.

383 p. incl. front., plates, ports. plates, ports. 24cm.

1. Bond, Scott. I. Bond, Theophilus, 1879- joint author. II. Title.

18—11070

Library of Congress E185.97.B7
[45b1]

The rudiments of music, step by step.

M781
Sm64

Smith, Ruby R
The rudiments of music, step by step, by Ruby R. Smith. [1st ed.] New York, Vantage Press [1965]

71 p. illus., music. 21 cm.
Portrait of author on book jacket.

1. Music—Theory, Elementary. I. Title.

MT7.S673R8 781.2 64-24743/MN
Library of Congress [5]

La rue Cases-Nègres.

Martinique
M843.91
Z71r

Zobel, Joseph.
La rue Cases-Nègres. [Roman. Paris] Les Quatre Jeudis [1955]

240 p. 21 cm.

I. Title.

A 56-3135

Illinois. Univ. Library
for Library of Congress [3]

MB9
At8c

Ruffin, George Lewis, 1834-1885
Crispus Attucks, by George L. Ruffin. Phila[delphia] Pa., The Langston civic club of America, °1942.

[16] p. 14½cm.

1. Attucks, Crispus, d. 1770. I. Langston civic club of America.

42-12911

Library of Congress E215.4.A8R8
[2] 973.3113

Ruffin, George Lewis, 1834-1885

MB9
St4s

Stevens, Walter James, 1877-
Chip on my shoulder, autobiography of Walter J. Stevens. Boston, Meador publishing Company, [1946]

315p. front. (port.) 20½cm.

Rugambwa, Laurian
Introduction; a word from Africa. Pp.9-11. In-

Tanganyika
M967.82
R84w

Kittler, Glenn D
The White Fathers. Introd. by Bishop Laurian Rugambwa. [1st ed.] London, W. H. Allen, 1957.

319 p. illus. 22 cm.

1. White Fathers. I. Kittler, Glenn D.
I. Title: A word from Africa.

BV2300.W5K5 [266.2] 276 57-6134 ‡
Library of Congress [20]

M326. R84ab
Ruggles, David, 1811-1849.
The abrogation of the Seventh commandment, by the American churches ... New-York, D. Ruggles, 1835.
23 p. 16½cm.
[Markoe pamphlets, v. 57, no. 15]
Signed: A Puritan.
1. Slavery in the U. S.—Controversial literature—1835. I. A Puritan, pseud.
Library of Congress AC901.M2 vol. 57 22-18699
[2]

Latin America M808.8 J19
Rumba macumba.
Jahn, Janheinz, comp. and tr.
Rumba macumba; Afrocubanische lyrik. Munchen, Carl Henser Verlag, 1957.
79p. 20cm.

M370 C12 r
Rural elemenary education among Negroes.
Caliver, Ambrose, 1894-
... Rural elementary education among Negroes under Jeanes supervising teachers. By Ambrose Caliver, senior specialist in the education of Negroes, U. S. Office of education. United States Department of the interior. Harold L. Ickes, secretary. Office of education, William John Cooper, commissioner. Washington, U. S. Govt. print. off., 1933.
v, 57 p. incl. tables, diagrs. pl. 23cm. (U. S. Office of education. Bulletin, 1933, no. 5)
1. Negroes—Education. I. Title.
E 33-1198
U. S. Off. of educ. Library L111.A6 1933, no. 5
——— Copy 2. LC2801.C34
for Library of Congress L111.A6 1933, no. 5
——— Copy 2. LC2801.C33
[43n1] (370.61) 371.9740975

M326. R84an
Ruggles, David, 1811-1849
An antidote for a poisonous combination recently prepared by a "citizen of New-York," alias Dr. Reese, entitled, "An appeal to the reason and religion of American Christians," &c. Also, David Meredith Reese's "Humbugs" dissected, by David Ruggles ... New-York, W. Stuart, 1838.
cover-title, 32 p. 22½cm.
1. An appeal to the reason ... of American Christians, against the American anti-slavery society. 2. Reese, David Meredith, 1800-1861. Humbugs of New-York. 3. American anti-slavery society. 4. Slavery in the U. S.—Controversial literature—1838.
11-11642
Library of Congress E449.R93
[44c1]

M813.5 H57ru
Run man, run.
Himes, Chester B 1909-
Run man, run [by] Chester Himes. New York, Putnam [1966]
192 p. 22 cm.
I. Title.
PZ3.H57Ru 66-20282
Library of Congress [67c8]

M973 W86 r
The rural Negro.
Woodson, Carter Godwin, 1875-
The rural Negro, by Carter Godwin Woodson. Washington, D.C., The Association for the study of Negro life and history, inc. [c1930]
xvi p., 1 l., 265p. illus. (incl. map) 22cm.

M326. R84e
Ruggles, David, 1811-1849
The "extinguisher" extinguished! or, David M. Reese, M. D., "used up." By David Ruggles, a man of color. Together with some remarks upon a late production, entitled "An address on slavery and against immediate emancipation with a plan of their being gradually emancipated and colonized in thirty-two years. By Heman Howlett." New-York, D. Ruggles, 1834.
iv, [5]-48 p. 19½ cm.
[Markoe pamphlets, v. 14, no. 14]
(Continued on next card)
19-17294
[48e1]

M323 H24r
Run, Zebra, run.
Harris, Leon R
Run, Zebra, run. New York Exposition Press, 1959.
260p. 21cm.
Portrait of author on book jacket.

M610 B44
Rural Negro health;
Joint health education committee, *Nashville.*
Rural Negro health; a report on a five-year experiment in health education in Tennessee, by Michael J. Bent, M. D., and Ellen F. Greene, M. A., for the Joint health education committee. Nashville, Tenn., Julius Rosenwald fund, 1937.
85 p. diagrs. 23cm.
"General references": p. 79-83.
1. Negroes—Tennessee. 2. Hygiene—Study and teaching. 3. Hygiene, Public—Tennessee. I. Bent, Michael James, 1885- II. Greene, Ellen F. III. Title.
38-21257
Library of Congress RA420.J73
[41m2] 613.07

M326. R84e
Ruggles, David, 1811-1849 The "extinguisher" extinguished ... 1834. (Card 2)
1. Reese, David Meredith, 1800-1861. A brief review of the "First annual report of the American anti-slavery society." 2. Howlett, Heman. An address on slavery and against immediate emancipation. 3. Slavery in the U. S.—Controversial literature—1834. I. Title.
19-17294
Library of Congress AC901.M2 vol. 14
——— Copy 2. [Miscellaneous pamphlets, v. 859, no. 6] AC901.M5 vol. 859
[48e1]

M813.5 T17r
The runaway elephant.
Tarry, Ellen, 1906-
The runaway elephant. Pictures by Oliver Harrington. New York, Viking Press, 1950.
37p. col. illus. 25cm.

M370 T36s
Rural Negroes.
Thomasson, Maurice Ethan, 1892-
A study of special kinds of education for rural Negroes [by] Maurice E. Thomasson ... Charlotte, N. C., 1936.
vi, 104 p., 1 l., 23cm.
Thesis (PH. D.)—Columbia university, 1936.
Vita.
"This study was concerned with agencies which offered instruction in fields other than those ordinarily included in the regular public school program ... Researches were conducted ... in the state of Virginia."—p. 2.
Bibliography: p. [103]-104.
1. Negroes—Education. 2. Negroes—Virginia. 3. Sociology, Rural. I. Title: Education for rural Negroes. II. Title: Rural Negroes.
36-21306
Library of Congress LC2802.V8T5 1936
Columbia Univ. Libr. [37c2] 371.97409755

MB9 R84
Ruggles, David, 1811-1849
Porter, Dorothy Burnett, 1905-
David Ruggles, an apostle of human rights. Reprinted from the Journal of Negro history, 28:23-50, January 1943.
23-50p 24½cm.
Inscribed by author: To Mr. Arthur B. Spingarn, from Dorothy Porter.

MB9 C77r
The rungless ladder.
Cooke, W C
The rungless ladder; a story of how failures led to successful living. New York, Exposition Press, 1960.
49p. illus. 20½cm.
Portrait of author on book jacket.

MB9 D58b
Rural school fund, inc.
Brawley, Benjamin Griffith, 1882-
Dr. Dillard of the Jeanes fund, by Benjamin Brawley ... with an introduction by Anson Phelps Stokes ... New York, Chicago [etc.] Fleming H. Revell company [c1930]
2 p. l., 151 p. front., pl., ports. 21cm.
1. Dillard, James Hardy, 1856- 2. Negroes—Education. 3. Negro rural school fund, inc. 4. John F. Slater fund.
30-24877
Library of Congress LC2801.B75
[45j1] 923.673

Cuba M323 R85
Ruiz Suarez, Bernardo
The color question in the two Americas, by Dr. Bernardo Ruez Suarez. Translated by John Crosby Gordon. New York, Hunt publishing co., 1922.
111p. 18cm.
1. Race problem. 2. Cuba. 3. Color. I. Title.

M326.99B C84r
Running a thousand miles for freedom...
Craft, William.
Running a thousand miles for freedom; or, the escape of William and Ellen Craft from slavery. London, William Tweedie, 1860.
111p. front. 17½cm.

M287.8 R89s
Rush, Christopher, 1777-1873.
A short account of the rise and progress of the African M. E. church in America, written by Christopher Rush ... with the aid of George Collins. Also, a concise view of church order or government, from Scripture, and from some of the best authors on the subject of church government relative to episcopacy. New York, Pub. by the author in 1843, republished by C. Rush, C. W. Robinson, A. Cole, and J. Simmons, 1866.
106 p., 1 l. 19½cm.
I. Collins, George.
1. African Methodist Episcopal Church - History
5-1557
Library of Congress

Cuba M861.6 R85v
Ruiz Suarez, Bernardo
Vibraciones, producciones poeticas. Habana, casa Editoria: Gutierrez y compania, [n.d.]
145p. port. 17cm.
1. Cuban poetry. I. Title.

M975.5 EL59
Rural conditions.
Ellison, John Malcus, 1889- jt. auth.
Negro life in rural Virginia, 1865-1934, by William Edward Garnett and John Malcus Ellison. [Blacksburg, Va., Virginia Polytechnic Institute, 1934]
35p. illus., maps. 23cm. (Virginia Polytechnic Institute Bulletin 295)
1. Virginia - Rural conditions. 2. Rural conditions. I. Garnett, William Edward. II. Title.

M296 R91
Russell, Charles L ed. and tr.
Light from the Talmud ... by Charles L. Russell. New York, Bloch Publishing Co., 1942.
iv, 200p. incl. tab. 20cm.
Hebrew and English on opposite pages.
1. Proverbs, Hebrew. 2. Talmud Selections. I. Title.

Russia.
U.S. M947 Sm58
Smith, Homer.
Black man in Red Russia; a memoir. With an introd. by Harrison Salisbury. Chicago, Johnson Pub. Co., 1964.
xvi, 221 p. illus. (on lining papers) 22 cm.
1. Russia. I. Title.
DK267.S587 914.7 64-23261
Library of Congress [8]

Rust college, Holly Springs, Miss.
M378R B17h
Baker, Webster B
History of Rust college, by Webster B. Baker ... Greensboro, N. C., The author, c 1924.
viii, [9]-221p. front., plates. 22cm.

Africa M896 R93d
Rutherfoord, Peggy, ed.
Darkness and light; an anthology of African writing. With a pref. by Trevor Huddleston. London, Faith Press [1958]
208 p. 23 cm.
White editor.
1. Negro literature—Africa. 2. English literature—Translations from foreign literature. I. Title.
PN6014.R79 808.89 59-2791 ‡
Library of Congress [2]

Russia - Foreign relation - Haiti.
M972.94 El4p
Elie, Louis E
... Le président Boyer et l'empereur de Russie Alexandre Ier. (Une mission diplomatique à Saint-Pétersbourg en 1821.) Port-au-Prince, Haïti, Imprimerie du Collège Vertières [1942?]
51 p., 1 l. 21cm.
Introductory letter dated 1942.
1. Haiti—Hist.—1804-1844. 2. Haiti—For. rel.—Russia. 3. Russia—For. rel.—Haiti. 4. Boyer, Jean Pierre, pres. Haiti, 1776-1850. 5. Alexander I, emperor of Russia, 1777-1825.
48-14548
Library of Congress F1924.E5 [44d1] 972.94

M301 G623
Rustin, Bayard
The meaning of Birmingham.
Pp. 317-324.
In: Goodman, Paul, 1911- ed. Seeds of liberation. New York, G. Braziller, 1965.

M301 R93
Ruthland, Eva.
The trouble with being a mama. New York, Abingdon Press [1964]
143p. 21cm.
Autobiographical.
1. Segregation. 2. Children-Management. I. Title.

Russia - Poetry.
Russia M891 P97s
Pushkin, Alexander Sergeevich, 1799-1837.
Selections from the prose and poetry of Pushkin. Edited and introduced by Ernest J. Simmons. New York, Dell Publishing Co., 1961.
382p. 17cm. (A Laurel reader)
Sketch of author on book.
Cover title.

M301 G623
Rustin, Bayard, jt. auth.
Mississippi muddle, by Dave Dellinger and Bayard Rustin.
Pp. 306-316.
In: Goodman, Paul, 1911- ed. Seeds of liberation. New York, G. Braziller, 1965.

Kenya M967.62 R93m
Ruthuku, J M translator.
Mundu Murimu muugi muno; George Washington Carver; a great Negro scientist by Janet H. Schwab. Translated by J. M. Ruthuku. London, The English Press, ltd., 1950.
16p. 18cm.
Written in Kikuyu.
1. Carver, George Washington.

Russia - Politics and government - 20th century.
Trinidad M820 J23w
James, Cyril Lionel Robert, 1901-
... World revolution, 1917-1936; the rise and fall of the Communist International. London, M. Secker and Warburg, ltd. [1937]
xii, 9-429 p. 22cm.
At head of title: C. L. R. James.
"How much the book owes to the writings of Trotsky, the text can only partially show."—p. xii.
1. Communist International. 2. Communism. 3. Revolutions. 4. World politics. 5. Russia—Pol. & govt.—20th cent. 6. Trotskii, Lev, 1879-1940. 7. Stalin, Iosif, 1879- I. Title.
37-22067
Library of Congress HX11.I 5J25 [45g1] 335.40621

M301 G623
Rustin, Bayard, jt. auth.
Struggle for integration, 1960, by A. J. Muste and Bayard Rustin.
Pp. 287-299.
In: Goodman, Paul, 1911- ed. Seeds of liberation. New York, G. Braziller, 1965.

Ruthuku, J. M., tr.
Kenya M613.2 H88f3
Humphrey, Norman
Kũiyũria nda tikou gũthodeka mwĩrĩ [Feeding the body is more than filling the stomach. Tr. by J. M. Ruthuku] Nairobi, Eagle Press, 1950.
16p. 22cm. (Taanya Ũgima-ini. Aim at healthy living series)
Written in Kikuyu.
White author.
1. Nutrition. I. Title. II. Series. III. Aim at healthy living series. IV. Ruthuku, J. M., tr.

Russia - Social life and customs.
M89 P93m
Prince, Mrs. Nancy (Gardener) b. 1799.
A narrative of the life and travels of Mrs. Nancy Prince. Boston, The author, 1850.
87, [1] p. 16cm.
1. Russia—Soc. life & cust. 2. West Indies—Descr. & trav.
20-18619
[29b1] CT275.P848A3
Library of Congress

M323 R92
Rustin, Bayard
We challenged Jim Crow! A report on the journey of reconciliation April 9-23, 1947. by George Houser and Bayard Rustin. New York, Fellowship of Reconciliation; Congress of Racial Equality, 1947.
15p. 22cm.
1. Transportation - Segregation. I. Title

Ruthuku, J. M., tr.
Kenya M613.2 H88w3
Humphrey, Norman
Ũkwenda ng'aragũ kana buthi? [Which do you want: starvation or nourishment? Tr. by J. M. Ruthuku] Nairobi, Eagle Press, 1949.
9p. 21½cm. (Taanya Ũgimaini. Aim at healthy living series)
Written in Kikuyu.
White author.
1. Nutrition. I. Title. II. Series. III. Ruthuku, J. M., tr.

Russian short stories.
Russia M891 P97r
Pushkin, Aleksandr Sergieevich, 1799-1837.
The Russian wonderland: coq d'or, the tale of the fisherman and the fish, the tale of Czar Saltan. A metrical translation from the Russian of Alexandr Pouskin, by Boris Brasol Manning... New York, The Paisley press, 1936.
ix, 62p. 21½cm.

Nigeria M070 A13
Ruth Sloane Associates, Washington, D. C.
The press in Africa. Edited by Helen Kitchen. Washington, 1956.
96p, 29cm.
Partial contents.- Introduction: A Nigerian journalists looks at African newspapers, by Abiodun Aloba.
1. African newspapers. 2. African periodicals. I. Kitchen, Helen A., ed. II. Title.

Rwanda - Family life.
Rwanda M967.5 K10o
Kagame, Alexis, 1912-
Les organisations socio-familia-les de l'ancien Rwanda. Bruxelles, Académie royale des Sciences Coloniales. 1954.
355p. plates, 24cm.

The Russian wonderland.
Russia M891 P97r
Pushkin, Aleksandr Sergieevich, 1799-1837.
The Russian wonderland: coq d'or, the tale of the fisherman and the fish, the tale of Czar Slatan A metrical translation from the Russian of Alexander Pouskin, by Boris Brasol Manning... New York, The Paisley press, 1936.
ix, 62p. 21½cm.

Africa M896 R93d2
Rutherfoord, Peggy, ed.
African voices; an anthology of native African writing. New York, Vanguard Press [1960, °1958]
208 p. 22 cm.
First published in 1958 under title: Darkness and light.
White editor.
1. Negro literature—Africa. 2. English literature—Translations from foreign literature. I. Title.
PN6014.R79 1960 808.89 60-9719 ‡
Library of Congress [60q15]

Rwanda M967.57 K11h
Rwanda - History.
Kagame, Alexis, 1912-
Histoire du Rwanda. 2me édition. Leverville, Congo Belge, Bibliothè de L'ethiole [n.d.]
61p. 17½cm.

Rwanda
M896.1
K11in

Rwanda - Literature.
Kagame, Alexis, 1912-
Indyohesha-Birayi. Kabgayi, Les Editions Royales, 1949.

60p. 12½cm.

Rwanda-Social life and cust.

Rwanda
M967.5
K10o

Kagame, Alexis, 1912-
Les organisations socio-familia- les de l'ancien Rwanda. Bruxelles, Académie royale dos Sciences Coloniales. 1954.

355p. plates. 24cm.

Rythmes et rites.

Haiti
M841
R44r

Rigaud, Milo
Rythmes et rites. Fontenay, n.d.

25p. 19cm.

Rwanda
M896.1
K11is

Rwanda - Literature.
Kagame, Alexis, 1912-
Isoko Y'amajyambere. Kabgayi, Rwanda; Ibitabo By'Injijura Muco (Editions Morales) 1949-1951.
3v. 12½cm.

Ryan, C. W. W.

Tanganyika
M967.82
Om1k

Omari, Dunstan Alfred, 1922- jt. auth.
Kwa nini tuna haja ya serikali? Why do we have government? [By C. W. W. Ryan and D. A. Omari] Dar es Salaam, Eagle Press, 1954.

17p. 18cm. (Mazungumzo juu ya uraia. Talks on citizenship no.1)
Written in Swahili and English.

1. Tanganyika. I. Title. II. Title: Why do we have government? III. Series: Mazungumzo ya uraia, no.1. IV. Series: Talks on citizenship, no. 1. V. Ryan, C. W. W.

Haiti
M841
B44r

Rythmes Négres.
Benoit, Clément
Rythmes Négres. Port-au-Prince, Haiti, Editions Henri Deschamps, 1945.

41p. 23½cm.

Rwanda - Poetry.

Rwanda
M896.1
K11a

Kagame, Alexis, 1912-
Avec un troubadour du Rwanda. Bruxelles, Editions Universitaires, 1949.

7p. 24cm.
Extrait de Zaire, Juillet 1949.
"A Monsieur le Ministre De Brinyne bien respeitnensement. Al Kagame."

1. Rwanda - Poetry. I. Title.

Ryan, C. W. W.

Tanganyika
M967.82
Om1ma

Omari, Dunstan Alfred, 1922- jt. auth.
Maendeleo na jasho. Progress & perspiration. [By C.W. W. Ryan and D. A. Omari] Dar es Salaam, Eagle Press, 1954.

19p. 18cm. (Mazungunmzo ya uraia. Talks on citizenship, no. 3)
Written in English and Swahili.

1. Tanganyika. I. Title. II. Title: Progress & perspiration. III. Series: Mazungunmzo ya uraia, no. 3. IV. Series: Talks on citizenship, no. 3. V. Ryan, C. W. W.

Sabbath.

M263
Sc8s

Scott, Timothy D
Sunday, The Christian sabbath, a brief discussion of the Sunday question, by the Reverend Timothy D, Scott... Springfield, Ohio, The Whyte printing co. n.d.

137p. front 20½cm.

Rwanda - Poetry.

Rwanda
M967.5
K10d

Kagame, Alexis, 1912-
La divine pastorale, traduction français, par l'auteur, de la première Veillée d'une épopée écrite en langue Ruandaise. Bruxelles, Editions du Marais, 1952.

108p. port. plates. 25cm.

Ryan, C. W. W.

Tanganyika
M967.82
Om1m

Omari, Dunstan Alfred, 1922- jt. auth.
Mtu maskini mwenye sh.1,000,000. The poor man with a million shillings. [By C. W. W. Ryan and D. A. Omari] Dar es Salaam, Eagle Press, 1954.

16p. 18cm. (Mazungunmzo ya uraia. Talks on citizenship, no.2)
Writtn in Swahili and English.

1. Money. I. Title. II. Title: The poor man with a million shillings. III. Series: Mazungunmzo ya uraia, no. 2. IV. Talks on citizenship, no. 2. V. Ryan, C. W. W.

M813.5
W147s

Sabih.
Walker, Claudius Roland
Sabih. New York, Carlton Press [1965]

147p. 21cm.
Portrait of author on book cover.

Rwanda - Poetry.

Rwanda
M967.5
K10n

Kagame, Alexis, 1912-
La naissance de l'univers. Illustrations par Ant. de Vinck. Bruxelles, Editions, du Marais, 1955.

85p. illus. 25cm.

Ryan, C. W. W.

Tanganuika
M967.82
Om1t

Omari, Dunstan Alfred, 1922- jt. auth.
Tanganyika, tajiri au maskini? Tanganyika - rich or poor? [By C. W. W. Ryan and D. A. Omari] Dar es Salaam, 1954.

17p. 18cm. (Mazungumzo ya uraia. Talks on citizanship, no. 4)
Written in Swahili and English.

1. Tanganyika. I. Title. II. Tanganyika - rich or poor? III. Mazungumzo ya uraia, no. 4. IV. Talks on citizenship. no. 4. V. Ryan, C. W. W.

M323
Sa13

Sabourin, Clemence.
Let the righteous speak! Travel memoirs. [1st ed.] New York, Pageant Press [1957]
89 p. 21 cm.

1. Negroes—Segregation. 2. Southern States—Descr. & trav. I. Title.
E185.61.S25 325.260975 57-8311 ‡
Library of Congress

Rwanda - Poetry.

Rwanda
M967.5
K10p

Kagame, Alexis, 1912-
La poésie dynastique au Rwanda, par Alexis Kagame... Bruxelles, Institut Royal Colonial Belge, 1951.

240p. 24cm.

M810
B73p

Ryder, A H
Brawley, Benjamin Griffith, 1882-1939.
A prayer. Words by B. G. Brawley... Music by A. H. Ryder... [Atlanta, Ga.] Atlanta Baptist college press [1899]

2p. 23½cm.
Music: p.2

Sackey, Alex Quaison-
see
Quaison-Sackey, Alex

Rwanda - Politics.

Rwanda
M967.5
K10c

Kagame, Alexis, 1912-
Le code des institutions politiques du Rwanda précolonial, par Alexis Kagame. Bruxelles, Institut Royal Colonial Belge, 1952.

136p. 24cm.

Rythmes du Khalam

Senegal
M896.1
D62r

Diop, Ousmane Socé, 1911-
Rythmes du Khalam [par] Ousmane Socé [pseud.] Préface de Georges Larché. Paris, Nouvelles Editions Latines [1962]

60p. 18½cm.

I. Title.

Le sacré paîen et le sacré chrêtien.

Africa
M960
As6a

Kagame, Alexis, 1912-
Le sacré paîen et le sacré chrêtien.

Pp. 126-145.
In: Aspects de la culture noire. 1958.

Nigeria
M896.3 The sacrificial egg.
Ac4s Achebe, Chinua
The sacrificial egg, and other stories. Onitsha «Nigeria» Etudo «1962»

31p. illus. 22cm.

I. Title.

Sad-faced boy.

M813.5 **Bontemps, Arna.**
B64s3 Sad-faced boy, by Arna Bontemps; illustrated by Virginia Lee Burton. Boston, Houghton Mifflin company, 1937.

4 p. l., 118, ⌊1⌋ p. col. front., plates (part col.) 21 cm.

Illustrated lining-papers.

I. Title.

Library of Congress PZ7.B6443Sad 37—5361
⌊45e1⌋

Senegal
M966.3 Sadji, Abdoulaye, 1910-
Sa15 Education Africaine et civilisation. ⌊Dakar, Imprimerie A. Diop, 1964⌋

92p. 24cm.

1. Education - Senegal. 2. Africa - Civilization. 3. Senegal. I. Title.

Sénégal
M896.3 Sadji, Abdoulaye, 1910-
Sa1m Maïmouna; roman. Paris, Présence Africaine, 1958.

251p. 18½cm.

I. Title.

Senegal
M896.3 Sadji, Abdoulaye, 1910-
Sa15m Modou Fatim. ⌊Dakar, Imprimerie A. Diop, n.d.⌋

54p. 16cm. (Collection "Mer-Gaddou")

I. Title.

Africa
M060 Sadji, Abdoulaye, 1910-
P92 Nini, mulâtresse du Sénégal.
no.16

(In: Présence Africaine. Trois ecrivains noirs. Paris, Présence Africaine, 1954. 19cm. pp.286-415)

Senegal Sadji, Abdoulaye, 1910-
M896.3 Tounka, nouvelle. Paris, Présence
Sa1t Africaine ⌊1965⌋

90p. 17½cm.

I. Title.

M323.4 Safeguard our rights; Stories based on the
Sa1 report of the President's Committee on Civil Rights. New York, Anti-Defamation League of B'Nai B'rith, n.d.

3-31p. illus. 18½cm.

1. Civil rights.

M287.1 The Saga of the Church ⌊Poem⌋
J62h Johnson, Charlest R.H. comp.
A history of the Wesleyan Methodist Church of America. The story of one hundred years, 1842-1942 of the First Wesleyan Methodist church at Dayton, Ohio. Compiled and edited by Charlest R.H. Johnson.

74p. illus. 24cm.

Sagesse noire (sentences et proverbes malinkés)

Mali
M966.2 **Sissoko, Fily Dabo.**
Si8 Sagesse noire (sentences et proverbes malinkés) Paris, Editions de la Tour du guet ⌊1955⌋

xviii, 62 p. port. 21 cm.

1. Proverbs, African. I. Title.

A 56-984

Illinois. Univ. Library for Library of Congress ⌊8⌋

Senegal
M641.5 Sagna, Anna
Sa18 Recettes culinaires Sénégalaises. Dakar, Société Africaine d'Édition «n.d.»

48p. 21½cm.

1. Cookery, Senegalese. I. Title.

Cameroons Sahara.
M966.1 Afana, Osende
Af78 Sahara, Hiroshima Africain! ⌊Le Caire, Imprimerie des Auteurs, 1958⌋

48p. ports., map. 21½cm.
Portrait of author in book.

1. Sahara.

Haiti
M843.91 **Saint-Amand, Edris,** 1918-
Sa22b Bon Dieu rit, roman. Paris, Domat ⌊1952⌋

319 p. 19 cm.

I. Title.

A 53-3454

Illinois. Univ. Library for Library of Congress ⌊8⌋

Réunion
M841 Saint-Amand, François
Sa2 Les bourbonnaises, poésies par François Saint-Amand. Maurice, imprimerie de L.A. Denry, 18[illegible]8.
v, 200, 2p. 20cm.

I. Title.

St. Augustine, b. 354-430 A.D.
Zanzibar
M89 Sehoza, Samuel
Sa2s St. Augustine. Translated from the Swahili. London, Society for Promoting Christian Knowledge, 1927.

47p. 18½cm. (Little books for Africa)

St. Augustine's college, Raleigh, N.C.

M378sa **Halliburton, Cecil D.**
H15 A history of St. Augustine's college, 1867-1937, by Cecil D. Halliburton. Raleigh, N. C., St. Augustine's college, 1937.

4 p. l., 97, ⌊1⌋ p. 2 pl. (1 fold.) 23½cm.

"Notes on bibliography": p. ⌊98⌋

1. St. Augustine's college, Raleigh, N. C.

38-35117

Library of Congress LC2851.S322H3
——— Copy 2. ⌊3⌋ 378.756

Haiti
M841 St-Cyr, Frantz Colbert.
Sa2b Berbe de fleurs. Imp. V. Valcin, 1949.

88p. port. 22½cm.
Poème

1. Haitian poetry. I. Title.

Saint-Domingue.

M972.94 **Lepelletier de Saint-Remy, R.**
L55 Saint-Domingue. Étude et solution nouvelle de la question haïtienne. Par m. R. Lepelletier de Saint-Remy ... Paris, A. Bertrand, 1846.

2 v. plan. 8°.

"Annexe bibliographique": v. 2, p. 537-548.
White author.

1. Haiti—Hist. 2. Finance—Haiti (Republic) 3. Finance—Dominican republic. I. Title.

2-12854

Library of Congress F1931.L59
⌊a27d1⌋

Saint Domingue.

Haiti
M972.94 Trouillot, Hencock
T75c La condition des Negres domestiques a Saint-Domingue. Port-au-Prince, Haiti, 1955.

30p. 23cm.

St. Fleur, Ménélick.

Haiti
M704 ... Choses d'art et de pensée. Port-au-Prince, Haïti, Imprimerie du College Vertières ⌊1939⌋
C45 58, ⌊1⌋ p. ports. 27cm.

Addresses by Justin J. Kénol, Joseph Evelliard, Ménélick St. Fleur and Lynch Kénol.
Includes music.

1. Art—Addresses, essays, lectures. 2. Art—Haiti. I. Kénol, Justin J. II. Evelliard, Joseph. III. St. Fleur, Ménélick. IV. Kénol, Lynch.

42-48470

Library of Congress N6606.C5
⌊3⌋ 704

Haiti
M841 St. Hilaire, Paul
Sa3c Chants du Paria. «Cap Haitien» Campagnie Lithographique d'Haiti, 1962.

30p. port. 21½cm.
Portrait of author in book.

1. Poetry, Haitian. I. Title.

M323
Sa2
St. James, Warren D 1921-
The National Association for the Advancement of Colored People: a case study in pressure groups. Foreword by Ulysses S. Donaldson. ₍1st ed.₎ New York, Exposition Press ₍1958₎
252 p. 21 cm. (An Exposition-university book)
Bibliography: p. ₍248₎-252.
1. National Association for the Advancement of Colored People. 2. Pressure groups.
E185.5.N276S3 57—10668
*301.451 325.260973
Library of Congress ₍59h7₎

St. James' First African Church, Balt., Md.
M283
B73p
No.6
Bragg, George Freeman, 1863-1940.
St. James' First African church, ₍Baltimore, Md.
Baltimore, Md., 1921₎
₍15₎ p. 19cm.

Haiti
M841
Sa334
St. Jean, Serge.
Du sombre au clair; poèmes, 1963-1964. Port-au-Prince, Impr. Panorama ₍1964₎
84 p. 21 cm. (Collection Houngénikon)
I. Title.
PQ3949.2.S23D6 65-46747
Library of Congress ₍1₎

M285.7
Sa2s
St. John's Congregational Church. Springfield, Mass.
St. John's institutional activities. Springfield, 1926.
20p. illus. 23cm.
1.Congregational churches.

M910
C77s
Saint-Lambert, Jean François de, 1716-1803.
Cook, Mercer, 1903- ed.
Saint Lambert's Zimeo. Edited with foreword, notes and vocabulary by Mercer Cook and Guichard Parris. Atlanta, Atlanta University, 1936.
28 p. 28 cm. (The Atlanta University french series)

Haiti
M841.08
Sa2p
Saint-Louis, Carlos, 1923- *ed.*
Panorama de la poésie haïtienne ₍par₎ Carlos St.-Louis & Maurice A. Lubin. Port-au-Prince, H. Deschamps, 1950.
vi, 635 p. fold. col. map. 20 cm. (Collection Haïtiana)
Includes bio-bibliographical sketches.
Bibliography: p. 634-635.
1. Haitian poetry (French) 2. French poetry—Haitian authors. I. Lubin, Maurice A., ed. (Series)
PQ3946.S3 52-18659
Library of Congress ₍1₎

St. Louis - Segregation in education.
M371.974
V23
Valien, Bonita H
The St. Louis story: a study of desegregation. New York, Anti-Defamation League of B'nai B'rith, 1956.
72p. 23cm.

St. Louis, Mo.
M977.8
Yo8y
Young, N B editor.
Your St. Louis and Mine."
St. Louis, N.B. Young ₍1937₎
80p. illus 25½cm.

St. Louis, Missouri - Economic conditions.
M330
H24
Harris, Harry C
The Negro in the St. Louis Economy, 1954, by Irwin Sobel, Werner Z. Hirsch and Harry C. Harris St. Louis, Urban League of St. Louis, Inc., 1954.
95p. tables 23cm.

St. Louis. Central Baptist Church.
M252
H91a
Huntley, Thomas Elliott.
As I saw it, not commUnism but commOnism; a prophetic appraisal of the status quo, a message for our times and for all times, for America and for all nations. New York, Comet Press Books ₍1955, °1954₎
146 p. 23 cm.
"The Central Baptist Church on Wheels": p. 119-146.
1. Communism and religion. 2. U. S.—Race question. 3. St. Louis. Central Baptist Church. 4. Baptists—Sermons. 5. Sermons, American. I. Title.
BX6452.H8 252.06 55-874 ‡
Library of Congress ₍2₎

St. Louis woman was a wolf.
M814.5
H19s
Handy, Willliam Christopher, 1873-
St. Louis woman was a wolf. New York, 1945.
(In Silver, Abner. All women are wolves. New York, Readers' press, 1945. 28cm. p. 10)

St. Lucia - Poetry.
St. Lucia
M821.91
W14i
Walcott, Derek, 1930-
In a green night, poems 1948-1960. London, Jonathan Cape ₍1962₎
79p. 21cm.

St. Luke's Episcopal Church, Washington, D.C.
M283
B73p
no.7
Bragg, George F₍reeman₎ 1863-1940.
Afro-American church work. Historical addresses. By the Rev. George F. Bragg. ₍Baltimore, Md., 1918₎
41p. 20cm.

St. Luke's Episcopal Church, Washington, D.C.
M283
B73p
No.7
Bragg, George Freeman, 1863-1940.
Afro-American church work. Historical address. By the Rev. George F. Bragg. ₍Baltimore, Md., 1918₎
41p. 20cm.

Saint Mars, Gabrielle Anne Cisterne de Courtiras, vicomtesse de 1804-1872, supposed author.
France
M840
B89jo
Dumas, Alexandre, 1802-1870.
The journal of Madame Giovanni, by Alexandre Dumas, translated from the French edition (1856) by Marguerite E. Wilbur. London, Hammond, Hammond & co. ltd ₍°1944₎
305 p. 22½cm.
Has been attributed to Vicomtesse de Saint Mars. cf. Bibl. nat. Cat. gén., and Quérard, J. M. Les supercheries littéraires dévoilées.
French edition, 1856, has title: Taïti-Marquises-Californie; journal de madame Giovanni, rédigé et publié par Alexandre Dumas.
I. Saint Mars, Gabrielle Anne Cisterne de Courtiras, vicomtesse de, 1804-1872, supposed author. II. Wilbur, Marguerite Knowlton (Eyer) tr. III. Title.
45-6309
Library of Congress PZ3.D89Jo 2
₍3₎ 843.76

Saint Mars, Gabrielle Anne Cisterne de Courtiras, vicomtesse de, 1804-1872, supposed author.
France
M843
D89j
Dumas, Alexandre, 1802-1870.
The journal of Madame Giovanni, by Alexandre Dumas, translated from the French edition (1856) by Marguerite E. Wilbur, with a foreword by Frank W. Reed. New York, Liveright publishing corporation ₍1944₎
xxxi p., 1 l., 404 p. 22½ cm.
Has been attributed to Vicomtesse de Saint Mars. cf. Bibliothèque nationale, Catalogue général, and Quérard, J. M., Les supercheries littéraires dévoilées.
French edition, 1856, has title: Taïti-Marquises-Californie; journal de madame Giovanni, rédigé et publié par Alexandre Dumas.
I. Saint Mars, Gabrielle Anne Cisterne de Courtiras, vicomtesse de, 1804-1872, supposed author. II. Wilbur, Marguerite Knowlton (Eyer) tr. III. Title.
PZ3.D89Jo 843.76 44—1899
Library of Congress ₍59q1₎

St. Lucia
M823.91
Sa22s
St. Omer, Garth, 1931-
Syrop.
Pp. 139-187.
In: Introduction 2. London, Faber and Faber, 1964.

Saint Peter relates an incident.
M811.5
J63s
Johnson, James Weldon, 1871-1938.
Saint Peter relates an incident, selected poems by James Weldon Johnson. New York, The Viking press, 1935.
ix p., 1 l., 13-105 p. 24cm.
I. Title.
35—22368
Library of Congress PS3519.O2625A6 1935
₍a42d1₎ 811.5

Saint Peter relates an incident of the resurrection.
M811.5
J63s
Johnson, James Weldon, 1871-1938.
Saint Peter relates an incident of the resurrection day by James Weldon Johnson. New York, The Viking press, 1930.
14pp 28cm.

Saint-Pierre, Martinique.
Martinique
M972.98
P53m
Philémon, Césaire.
... La montagne Pelée et l'effroyable destruction de Saint-Pierre (Martinique) le 8 mai 1902; le brusque réveil du volcan en 1929. Éd. originale. Fort-de-France, Chez l'auteur; Paris, Impressions Printory et G. Courville ₍°1930₎
4 p. l., ₍11₎-211 p., 1 l. plates, fold. maps. 22½cm.
"Il a été tiré de cet ouvrage cinquante exemplaires sur papier pur fil Lafuma, numérotés de 1 à 50, qui constituent l'édition originale."
1. Pelee peak—Eruption, 1902. 2. Saint-Pierre, Martinique. I. Title.
31-13052
Library of Congress F2081.P54
Copyright A—Foreign 10883
₍2₎ [917.298] 551.21097298

Haiti
MB9
T64re
Saint-Rémy, Joseph, 1815-1856
Vie de Toussaint-L'Ouverture. Par Saint-Remy. Paris, Moquet, 1850.
xl, 408 p. front. (port.) 22½cm.
1. Toussaint-Louverture, Pierre Dominique, 1746?-1803. 2. Haiti—Hist.—Revolution, 1791-1804.
14—8387
Library of Congress F1923.T9
₍35b1₎

St. Stephen's, Petersburg, Va.

M283 Bragg, George F[reeman] 1863-1940.
B73p The story of Old St. Stephens, Petersburg, Va.,
no.3 and the Origin of the Bishop Payne Divinity School, by the Rev. George F. Bragg. [Baltimore, Md., 1917]

16p. 18½cm.

St. Stephens's, Petersburg, Va.

M283 Bragg, George Freeman, 1863-1940.
B73p The story of Old St. Stephens, Petersburg, Va.,
No.3 and the Origin of the Bishop Payne Divinity School. By the Rev. George F. Bragg. [Baltimore, Md.] 1917.

16p. 18½cm.

Martinique St. Vincent.
M972.98 Miller, James Martin, 1859-1939.
M61m The Martinique horror and St. Vincent calamity, containing a full and complete account of the most appalling disaster of modern times ... by J. Martin Miller ... in collaboration with Hon. John Stevens Durham ... Philadelphia, National publishing co. [1902]

8, 17-560 p. 2 front., illus., plates, ports., maps. 23½cm.

Issued also under the title: True story of the Martinique and St. Vincent calamities ... by Prof. John Randolph Whitney.

1. La Soufrière, St. Vincent—Eruption, 1902. 2. Pelée, Mont—Eruption, 1902. 3. St. Vincent. 4. Volcanoes. I. Durham, John Stevens, 1861- joint author. II. Title.

2-17542

Library of Congress F2081.M64 [a44f1]

Les Saintes, French West Indies.
Guadeloupe
M972.97 Bréta, Félix, 1872-1938.
B75s ... Les Saintes (dépendances de la Guadeloupe) Recueil de notes et observations générales. Paris, Larose, 1939.

4 p. l., [11]-156 p., 1 l. plates, fold. map. 18½cm.

Edited by Évélie Bréta.

1. Les Saintes, French West Indies. I. Bréta, Évélie, ed.

46-26005

Library of Congress F2151.B74 1939 [2] 917.297

Saints.
MB9 Tarry, Ellen, 1906-
M37t Martin de Porres, saint of the New World. Illustrated by James Fox. London, Burns and Oates; New York, Vision Books [1963]

173p. illus. 22cm. (Vision books, 57)

Martinique
M808.8 Sainville, Léonard.
Sa28 Anthologie de la littérature Négro-Africaine. [Paris, Présence Africaine, 1963-]

v. 24cm.

Contents.- I. Romanciers et conteurs.

1. Literature. 2. African literature.

Martinique
M843.91 Sainville, Léonard
Sa28f Au fond du bourg. [Paris] Ecrivains Noirs du Monde [n.d.]

216p. 19cm.

I. Title.

Martinique
M843.91 Sainville, Léonard.
Sa2d Dominique, Nègre esclave. Paris, Fasquelle, 1951.

327p. 19cm.

1. French fiction. I. Title.
2. West Indian fiction.

Sainville, Léonard.
M808.8 Letteratura Negra. Prefazione di Pier Paolo
L718 Pasolini. [Roma] Editori Ruinti [1961]

2v. 22½cm.

Sainville, Léonard.
Martinique Victor Schœlcher, 1804-1893. Paris, Fasquelle, 1950.
M843.91 269 p. ports. 20 cm.
Sa2v "Bibliographie": p. [261]-269.

1. Schœlcher, Victor, 1804-1893.

A 51-1381

Harvard Univ. Library for Library of Congress [1]

Une saison au Congo; théâtre.
Martinique
M842.91 Césaire, Aimé
C33s Une saison au Congo; théâtre. Paris, Editions du Seuil, 1966.

127p. 18½cm.

I. Title.

Sudan, Egyptian
M741 Salahi, Ibrahim
Sa3 Drawings. [Ibadan, Nigeria, Mbari Publications, 1962]

[19]p. illus. (African Artists series, no. 2)

1. Drawings. I. Series.

Tanganyika
M392 Saleh el-Busaidy, Hamed
Sa32 Ndoa na talaka [Marriage and divorce] Nairobi, Eagle Press, 1958.

45p. 21½cm.
Written in Swahili.

1. Marriage. 2. Divorce. I. Title.

Africa
M808.83 Salkey, Andrew, 1928-
B396 Anancy.

Pp. 94-100.

In: Black Orpheus. Black Orpheus; an anthology of African and Afro-American prose. New York, McGraw-Hill, 1965.

Jamaica
M823.91 Salkey, Andrew, 1928-
Sa3d Drought. Illustrated by William Papas. London, Oxford University Press, 1966.

144p. illus. 22cm.
"For Arthur from Andrew. 9.5.66."

I. Title.

Jamaica
M823.91 Salkey, Andrew, 1928-
Sa3ea Earthquake. Illustrated by William Papas. London, Oxford University Press 1965.

123p. 22½cm.
"For Arthur from Andrew Salkey, 16.11.65."

I. Title.

Jamaica
M823.91 Salkey, Andrew, 1928-
Sa3e2 Escape to an autumn pavement. [London, New English Library, 1966]

190p. 18cm.
"A four square book."
"For Arthur from Andrew, 9.5.1966."

I. Title.

Jamaica
M823.91 Salkey, Andrew, 1928-
Sa3e Escape to an autumn pavement. London, Hutchinson, 1960.

207p. 20cm.
Inscribed: "For Arthur B., Affectionately Andrew, 7-4-'61."

I. Title.

Jamaica
M823.91 Salkey, Andrew, 1928-
Sa3h Hurricane. Illustrated by William Papas. London, Oxford University Press, 1964.

118p. illus. 21½cm.

I. Title.

Jamaica
M823.91 Salkey, Andrew, 1928-
Sa3L The late emancipation of Jerry Stover. London, Hutchinson, 1968.

[7], 246 p. 21 cm. 30/-
(SBN 09 085 530 2) (B 68-02620)
Portrait of author on book jacket.
"A little 'previous', I know, Arthur, but allow me to inscribe this new novel to you in celebration of your forthcoming 90th Birthday, in March this year... Andrew Salkey, 9-2-1968."
I. Title.

PZ4.S1687Lat 68-91611

Library of Congress [2]

Jamaica
M823.91 Salkey, Andrew, 1928-
Sa3q A quality of violence. London, New Authors, Ltd., 1959.

205p. 20½cm.
Portrait of author on book jacket.

I. Title.

Jamaica
M823.91
Sa3r

Salkey, Andrew, 1928-
Riot. Illustrated by William Papas. Lonson, Oxford University Press, 1967.

196p. illus. 23cm.
"For Arthur, from Andrew, 28-5-67.

I. Title

Jamaica
M372.4
Sa34

Salkey, Andrew, 1928-
The shark hunters; illustrated by Peter Kesteven. London, Nelson, 1966.

vi, 74 p. illus. 21½ cm. (Rapid reading) 4/-
(B 67-4895)

1. Readers—1950- I. Title.

PE1121.S28 67-88093

Library of Congress [5]

Jamica
M823.91
Sa3a

Salkey, Andrew, comp.
Stories from the Caribbean, an anthology. Selected and introduced by Andrew Salkey. London, Elek Books [1965]

256p. 21cm.
"For Arthur from Andrew, 5/22/65."
Partial contents.- Man, in England, you've just got to love animals, by Samuel Selvon.- When Greeks meets Greek, by Samuel Selvon.- Gussy and the boss, by Samuel Selvon.- Cane is better, by Samuel Selvon.-
(Continued on next card)

Jamaica
M823.91
Sa3a

Salkey, Andrew, comp.
Stories from the Caribbean, an anthology. [1965] (Card 2)

Partial contents - Continued.
A free country, by R. O. Robinson.- A shirt apiece, by R. O. Robinson.- Small islan complex, by Donald Hinds.- Busman blues, by Donald Hinds.- Any lawful impediment, by Donald Hinds.- The very funny man: a tale in two moods, by H. Orlando Patterson.- One for a penny, by H. Orlando Patterson.-
(Continued on next card)

Jamaica
M823.91
Sa3a

Salkey, Andrew, comp.
Stories from the Caribbean, an anthology. [1965] (Card 3)

Partial contents - Continued.
The valley of cocoa, by Michael Anthony.- Pita of the deep sea, by Michael Anthony.- Triumph, by C. L. R. James.- La divina pastora, by C. L. R. James.- Village tragedy, by John Hearne.- The lost country, by John Hearne.- Birds of a feather, by George Lamming.- Hunters and hunted, by
(Continued on next card)

Jamaica
M823.91
Sa3a

Salkey, Andrew, comp.
Stories from the Caribbean, an anthology. [1965] (Card 4)

Partial contents - Continued.
Jan Carew.- The stragglers, by Claude Thompson.- The house of many doors, by Claude Thompson.- Miss Clarke is dying, by Edgar Mittelholzer.- A long long pause, by Denis Williams.- The wintering of Mr. Kolawole, by O. R. Dathorne.- The black angel, by Edward Braithwaite.- The silk-cotton tree, by
(Continued on next card)

Jamaica
M823.91
Sa3a

Salkey, Andrew, comp.
Stories from the Caribbean, an anthology. [1965] (Card 5)

Partial contents - Continued.
A. N. Forde.- Set down this, by Cecil Gray.

1. West Indian literature. 2. Short stories, West Indian. I. Title.

Jamaica
M823.91
Sa3w

Salkey, Andrew, 1928- , ed.
West Indian stories. London, Faber and Faber, 1960.

224p. 20cm.
Inscribed: "For Arthur B., affectionately, Andrew, 7-4-'61."

Contents.- A morning at the office, by Edgar Mittelholzer.- We know not whom to mourn, by Edgar Mittelholzer.- A wedding in spring, by George Lamming.- Of thorns and thistles, by George Lamming.- At the
(Continued on next card)

Jamaica
M823.91
Sa3w

Salkey, Andrew, 1928- , ed. West Indian stories. 1960. (Card 2)

Contents continued.
stelling, by John Hearne.- The wind in this corner, by John Hearne.- Knock on wood, by Samuel Selvon.- My girl and the city, by Samuel Selvon.- Calypsonian, by Samuel Selvon.- Waiting for Aunty to cough, by Samuel Selvon.- The coming of Amalivaca, by Jan Carew.- Mr. Dombey, the Zombie, by Geoffrey Drayton.- The Covenant, by
(Continued on next card)

Jamaica
M823.91
Sa3w

Salkey, Andrew, 1928- , ed. West Indian stories. 1960. (Card 3)

Contents continued.
Wilson Harris.- Jamaican Fragment, by A. L. Hendricks.- Arise, My Love, by Jan Williams.- There's always the Angels, by F. A. Collymore. - The Fig-tree and the villager, by Roy Henry.- My fathers before me, by Karl Sealey.- The Tallow Pole, by Barnabas J. Ramon Fortune.- Blackout, by Roger Mais.- Crossroads Nowhere, by Stuart Hall.- Waterfront Bar, by
(Continued on next card)

Jamaica
M823.91
Sa3w

Salkey, Andrew, 1928- , ed. West Indian stories. 1960. (Card 4)

Contents continued.
V. S. Reid.- Drunkard of the River, by Michael Anthony.- Minutes of Grace, by E. R. Braithwaite.- Ars Longa; Vita Brevis, by John Figueroa.-

1. Short stories - West Indies. 2. West Indies - Short stories. I. Title.

Jamaica
M821.91
Sa3

Salmon, Lisa
Frankie frog, nonsense rhymes and sketches. Kingston, Jamaica, The Pioneer Press, 1952.

30p. illus. 24cm.

1. Nonsense verses
I. title 2. Children's poetry

Haiti
M842
Sa3t

Salnave, Théophile.
Trois noms, trois marques, trois papas; mélodrame en Créole. Imp. Duchemin, [1951]

32p. 20cm.

1. Creole dialects--Drama. 2. Haitian drama. I. Title.

Salud y belleza;

M613
L32s

Lara Mena, Maria Julia de.
Salud y belleza; divulgaciones cientificas sobre anatomia, fisiologia, patologia, higiene y estetica de la mujer, por la dra. Maria Julia de Lara... Con un juicio critico del profesor dr. W. H. Hoffmann... Con 260 ilustraciones. La Habana, Cuba, Casa editora "La Propagandista," s.a., 1940.
xxxv, 663 p. illus. (incl. ports., facsim.) col. pl., tables, diagrs. 24cm.

Le salut par la terre..

Haiti
M972.94
D15sa
no.5

Dalencour, François Stanislas Ranier, 1880-
Le salut par la terre et le programme économique de l'avenir, par le dr François Dalencour ... Port-au-Prince, L'auteur [1935?]

cover-title, 39 p. 22½cm.
"Bibliographie": p. 25.

1. Agriculture—Economic aspects—Haiti. I. Title.
44-33351

Library of Congress HD1842.D8
[2]

Le salut par la terre et le programme economique de l'avenir..

Haiti
M972.94
D15s

Dalencour, François Stanislas Ranier, 1880-
Le salut par la terre et le programme économique de l'avenir, par le dr François Dalencour ... Port-au-Prince, L'auteur [1935?]

cover-title, 39 p. 22½cm.
"Bibliographie": p. 25.

1. Agriculture—Economic aspects—Haiti. I. Title.
44-33351

Library of Congress HD1842.D8
[2]

Ghana
M896.3
Sa41ab

Sam, Gilbert A
The absconding bridegroom. [Accra, Gillian Syndicate, 1952]

24p. 20½cm. (Kanzaar series, 3)

I. Title.

Ghana
M896.3
Sa41as

Sam, Gilbert A
Asaabea's revenge. Somanya, The Ayerh Printing Works [n.d.]

21p. 15½cm. (Kanzaar series, no. 2)
Cover title.

I. Title.

Sam McDonald's farm.

MB9
M23

McDonald, Emanuel B 1884-
Sam McDonald's farm; Stanford reminiscences by Emanuel B. "Sam" McDonald. Stanford, Calif., Stanford University Press, 1954.

422 p. illus. 24 cm.

1. Stanford University—Hist. I. Title.

LD3027.M2 378.794 54-7166 ‡

Library of Congress [5]

Sam Patch, the high, wide, & handsome jumper.

M813.5
B64s5

Bontemps, Arna Wendell, 1902-
Sam Patch, the high, wide, & handsome jumper, by Arna Bontemps and Jack Conroy; illustrated by Paul Brown. Boston, Houghton Mifflin, 1951.

89 p. illus. (part col.) 22 cm.

I. Conroy, Jack, 1899- joint author. II. Title.

PZ7.B6443Sam 51-247

Library of Congress [7]

Senegal
M966.3
Sa44

Samb, El-Hadj Assane Marokhaya
"Cadior demb": essai sur l'histoire du Cayor. [Préface de Bathie Samb. Introd. de M. Issa Diop. Seconde édition, revue et corrigée] Dakar [Edition Diop] 1965.

64p. illus. 23cm.

1. Senegal - History. I. Title.

Rhodesia
M896.3
Sa46o
Samkange, Stanlake John Thompson, 1929-
On trial for my country [by] Stanlake Samkange. London, Heinemann, 1966.
viii, 160 p. 20½ cm. 18/- (B 66-17472)
Map on endpapers.
1. Lobengula, King of the Matabele, 1833 (ca.)-1893?—Fiction. 2. Rhodes, Cecil John, 1853-1902—Fiction. I. Title.
PZ4.S188On 67-70814
Library of Congress [3]

M341.1
H85f
Sampson, Edith Spurlock 1901-
World security begins at home.
(In: Hoxie, R. G. ed. Frontiers for freedom. Denver, University of Denver, 1952, 24cm. p. 234-239.

M818.5
Sa4j
Sampson, John Patterson, 1837-
Jolly people. The author, n.d.
11. 5 p. 27cm.
I. title
1. Maxims

M575
Sa4
[Sampson, John Patterson, 1837-
Mixed races: their environment, temperament, heredity and phrenology. Hampton, Va., Normal school steam press, 1881.
ix, [12] - 159p. front. 22½cm.
1. Phrenology. 2. Miscegenation. I. Title.

MB9
L51s
1958
Sams, Jessie (Bennett)
White mother. [1st ed.] London, Michael Joseph, 1958.
224p. 21cm.
Autobiographical.
1. Lee, Rossie. I. Title.

MB9
L51s
Sams, Jessie (Bennett)
White mother. [1st ed.] New York, McGraw-Hill [1957]
241 p. 21 cm.
Autobiographical.
1. Lee, Rossie. I. Title.
CT275.L344S3 920.7 57-12911 ‡
Library of Congress [25]

MB18
Sa49
Samuels, Calvin Henry McNeal.
Me. New York, Comet Press Books [c1954]
41 p. 22 cm.
Anecdotes, essays, and poetry.
I. Title.
PS3537.A58M4 818.5 55-578 ‡
Library of Congress [2]

Panama
M986.2
W521
Samuels, Linda R
Westerman, George W
Introduction.
(In: An exhibit on the races of mankind, prepared by Linda Samuels. Panama, Isthmian Negro Youth Congress, 1946. 21 cm. pp.)
Inscribed by Linda R. Samuels: Very truly yours.

San Francisco.
M301.
J63ne8
Johnson, Charles Spurgeon, 1893-
The Negro war worker in San Francisco, a local self-survey. Technical staff: Charles S. Johnson, Herman H. Long [and] Grace Jones ... A project, financed by a San Francisco citizen, administered by the Y. W. C. A., and carried out in connection with the Race relations program of the American missionary association, Dr. Charles S. Johnson, director, and the Julius Rosenwald fund. [San Francisco?] 1944.
2 p. l., 98 p. 28cm.
Reproduced from type-written copy.
1. Negroes—San Francisco. I. American missionary association. II. Julius Rosenwald fund. III. Title.
45-2530
Library of Congress F869.S3J57 [3] 331.98

San Francisco.
M979
R24r
Reddick, Lawrence Dunbar, 1910- ed.
Race relations on the Pacific coast. New York, Journal of educational sociology, 1945.
129-208p. 23cm.
Special issue of The Journal of educational sociology, November 1945.
Partial contents: -The new race-relations frontier, by L. D. Reddick. -San Francisco, by Joseph James.

M979.4
Sa5r
San Francisco,
San Francisco. Interim Steering Committee of the Johnson Survey.
Report. n.p., 1944.
11p. 28cm.
Mimeographed.

San Francisco. Church for the Fellowship of All Peoples.
M200
T42f
Thurman, Howard, 1899-
Footprints of a dream; the story of the Church for the Fellowship of All Peoples. New York, Harper [1959]
157 p. illus. 20 cm.
1. San Francisco. Church for the Fellowship of All Peoples. I. Title.
BX9999.S3C5 289.9 59-11412 ‡
Library of Congress [20]

M979.4
Sa5r
San Francisco. Interim Steering Committee of the Johnson Survey.
Report. n.p., 1944.
11p. 28cm.
Mimeographed.
1.San Francisco, Calif. I. Johnson, Charles Spurgeon, 1893- . II. Julius Rosenwald Fund. III. American Missionary Association. Race Relations Division.

San Juan, Famous charge of the Black Regiment.at- July 1, 1898- (illus.)
M304
P19
V.5, no.6
Dabney, Wendell Phillips.
The wolf and the lamb... Cincinnati, Ohio, The author, 1913.
14p. illus.
M323
D11

Sánchez, Luis Alberto, 1900- ed.
Peru
M985
P18t
Palma, Ricardo, 1833-1919.
... Tradiciones peruanas escogidas (edición crítica) Prólogo, selección y notas de Luis Alberto Sánchez. Santiago de Chile, Ediciones Ercilla, 1940.
3 p. l., [9]-215, [3] p. 18cm. (*Half-title:* Biblioteca Amauta (Serie América) [V. 1])
"Noticia bibliográfica": p. 14-16.
1. Legends—Peru. 2. Peru—Hist. I. Sánchez, Luis Alberto, 1900- ed. II. Title.
[*Full name:* Manuel Ricardo Palma]
41-9583
Library of Congress F3409.P1752 [44e1] 985

MB9
Sa51
1784
Sancho, Ignatius, 1729-1780.
Letters of the late Ignatius Sancho, an African. To which are prefixed, memoirs of his life. The third edition. London, Printed by J. Nichols and sold by C. Dilly, in the Poultry, 1784.
xiv, 393p. front (port) 16½cm.

MB9
Sa51
1783
Sancho, Ignatius, 1729-1780.
Letters of the late Ignatius Sancho, an African... To which are prefixed, memoirs of his life... The second edition. London, Printed for J. Nichols and C. Dilly, in the Poultry, 1783.
2v. fronts. (v.1 port.) 16cm.

MB9
Sa51
1782
Sancho, Ignatius, 1729-1780.
Letters of the late Ignatius Sancho, an African ... To which are prefixed, memoirs of his life ... London, Printed by J. Nichols, and sold by J. Dodsley [etc.] 1782.
2 v. fronts. (v. 1: port.) 18cm.
"The life of Ignatius Sancho" (v. 1, p. [i]-xvi) was written by Joseph Jekyll. *cf.* Dict. nat. biog. v. 29, p. 289.
First edition. In orėginal boards. Uncut.
I. Jekyll, Joseph, 1754-1837.
44-53571
Library of Congress CT788.S168A3 [2]

Sancho, Ignatius, 1729-1780.
Africa
M896
B36
Dathorne, Ronald
African writers of the Eighteenth Century: Ignatius Sancho; Ottobah Cugoano: Olaudah Equiano.
Pp. 234-240.
In: Beier, Ulli, Comp. Introduction to African literature. London, Longmans, 1967.

Sanctification vs. fanaticism.
M234.8
Ea7p
Eason, James Henry, 1866-
Pulpit and platform efforts. Sanctifications vs. fanaticism, by Rev. J.H. Eason...with introduction by Rev. C.L. Fisher...Nashville, Tenn., National Baptist publishing board, 1899.
120p. front. 19½cm.

Sanda, pseud.
see
Stowers, Walter H

M813.5
Sa5h
Sanders, Tom
Her Golden Hour, by Tom Sanders. Houston, Texas, 1929.
167p. illus. 19cm.
I. Title

Sangenis, Miguel, tr.
Haiti
M972.9 Morisseau-Leroy, Felix, 1912-
M819d
...Le destin des Caraibes. El destino del Caribe. Port-au-Prince, Haiti ⌊Imprimerie Telhomme⌋ 1941.
1p. l., ⌊1⌋, 6-107, ⌊1⌋p. 21cm.
French and Spanish on opposite pages, numbered in duplicate.

Senegal
M610
Sa58
Sankalé, Marc
Médecine sociale au Sénégal, par Marc Sankalé et Pierre Pène. Dakear, Afrique documents, 1960.
104p. illus., map. 24cm. (Cahiers documents, no. 1, March 1960)
Includes bibliography.
1. Medicine - Senegal. 2. Social medicine. I. Pene, Pierre, jt. author. II. Title.

M362.7
Sa5
Sanders, Wiley Britton, 1898- ed.
Negro child welfare in North Carolina, a Rosenwald study, directed by Wiley Britton Sanders ... under the joint auspices of the North Carolina State board of charities and public welfare and the School of public welfare, the University of North Carolina. Chapel Hill, Pub. for the North Carolina State board of charities and public welfare by the University of North Carolina press, 1933.
xiv p., 2 l., 3-326 p. 24cm.
1. Negroes—North Carolina. 2. Negroes—Moral and social conditions. 3. Charities—North Carolina. 4. Children—Charities, protection, etc.—North Carolina. 5. Juvenile delinquency—North Carolina. 6. Social surveys I. North Carolina. State board of charities and public welfare. II. North Carolina. University. School of public welfare. III. Title. I. Oxley, Lawrence C.
Library of Congress E185.86.S27 33-18906
⌊45t1⌋ 325.2600756

Sangiwa, H. H., jt. auth.
Tanganyika
M398.6 Meena, E K
M47
Vitendawili ⌊Riddles⌋ Kutoka makabila mbalilbali ya Tanganyika, kimetungwa na E. K. Meena, G. V. Mmari na H. H. Sangiwa. London, Oxford University Press, 1960.
27p. illus. 18½cm.
Written in Swahili.
1. Riddles, African. I. Mmari, G. V., jt. auth. II. Sangiwa, H. H., jt. auth. III. Title.

Haiti
M843.91
B83s
Sans pardon.
Brun, Amedée, 1868-1896.
Sans pardon. Port-au-Prince, Imprimerie de l'Abeille, 1909.
⌊8⌋ 404p. 20cm.

Sanderson, Meredith, tr.
Malawi
M496.3
Ab32
Abdallah, Yohanna B
Chikala cha wayao, uwulembile ndo Yohanna B. Abdallah. Soni uwalundenye ndo Meredith Sanderson. Zomba, Nyasaland, Government Printing Office, 1919.
60, 60p. 21½cm.
Yao and English; added t.p. in English.
1. Yao language - Grammar. I. Title. II. Sanderson, Meredith, tr.

Les sangliers; roman.
Martinique
M843.9
J93
Junin, Hubert
Les sangliers; roman. Paris, Editions du Seuill, 1958.
170p. 18½cm.
I. Title.

Congo (Leopoldville)
M896.3
K139s
Sans rancune; roman.
Kanza, Thomas R
Sans rancune; roman. London, Scotland ⌊1965⌋
143p. 21½cm.

M784
Sa5
Sandilands, Alexander
A hundred and twenty Negro spirituals; selected chiefly with a view to their being used by Africans in Africa. Morija, Basutoland, Morija Sesuto Book Depot, 1951.
158p. 20cm.
White author.
1. Spirituals. I. Title.

Sango language - Dictionary.
Fr.Guiana
A
M496
Eb71
Éboué, Adolphe Felix Sylvestre, 1884-1944.
...Langues Sango, Banda, Baya, Mandjia. Notes grammaticales. Mots groupés d'après le sens. Phrases usuelles. Vocabulaire, par A. F. Éboué. Preface de M. Gaudefroy-Demombynes. Paris, Emile Larose, 1918.
iii, 109p. 10 x 11cm.

Santa Maria, Francisco de Ayerra, 1630-1708.
see
Ayerra Santa Maria, Francisco de, 1630-1708

M813.5
H87s
Sandy.
Hughes, Langston, 1902-
... Sandy; Not without laughter, traduit de L'American par Gabriel Beauroy. Paris, Les Editions Rieder, 1934.
⌊8⌋ 304 p. 19 cm.

Nigeria
M900
Sa58
Sangowawa, Bennett Adetola Oluwole (1915-)
Scholars' handbook of history, Part II. Rev. and enl. ed., Ijebu-Ode, Nigeria, Benson House of Commerce ⌊1958⌋
121p. 18cm.
1. History. 2. Nigeria - History.

Haiti
M972.94
P926b
Santo Domingo-Creole dialects.
Pressoir, Charles Fernand
...Debats sur le creole et le folklore. Afriques grises ou Frances brunes? Langue, races, religion et culture populaires, avec des textes. Port-au-Prince, Imprimerie de l'Etat, 1947.
80p. 22cm.

Sandy Spring, Maryland.
M975
N31
Thom, William Taylor.
The Negroes of Sandy Spring, Maryland: A social study, Bulletin of the Labor Dept., no.32, 1901. pp. 43-102.
In: The Negro in the black belt... Washington, D.C., Dept. of Labor, ⌊1897-1902⌋

M813.5
W93s
Sangre Negra.
Wright, Richard, 1909-1960.
Sangre Negra (Native son). Traducción de Pedro Lecuona. Buenos Aires, Editorial Sudamericana, 1959.
567p. 18½cm.

Haiti
M972.94
As7ada
1789
Santo Domingo -(French Colony).
Assemblée des Citoyens de Couleur, des Isles et Colonies Françoises. Paris.
Adresse à l'Assemblée-Nationale, pour les Citoyens-libres de Couleur, des Isles & Colonies Françoises, 18 Octobre 1789 ⌊Lacks imprint⌋
9p. 19cm.
Signed by De Joly; Raimond; Oge, etc.

Martinique
M841.91
G49sa
Le sang rivé.
Glissant, Edouard, 1928-
Le sang rivé; poèmes. Paris, Présence Africaine, 1961.
68p. 18½cm.

M813.5
W93s
... Sangre negra.
Wright, Richard, 1909-
... Sangre negra ("Native son") Traducción de Pedro Lecuona. Buenos Aires, Editorial sudamericana ⌊1941⌋
4 p. l., 11-566, ⌊1⌋ p., 2 l. 18cm. (On cover: Colección Horizonte)
I. Lecuona, Pedro, tr. II. Title.
⌊Full name: Richard Nathaniel Wright⌋
Library of Congress PS3545.R815N28 42-18505
⌊2⌋

Haiti
M972.94
As7ad
1790
Santo Domingo - (French Colony).
Assemblée des Citoyens de Couleur des Isles, et Colonies Françoises. Paris.
Adresse des Citoyens de Coulour residans a Paris, a l'Assemblée nationale, suivie de la réponse de M. le President, du 7 Septembre 1992 ⌊sic⌋ l'an 4e de la liberté, & le premier de l'égalité; imprimées & envoyées aux 83 departmens & aux armées, par ordre de l'Assemblée.
⌊Paris, De l'Imprimerie Nationale, 1792⌋
3p. 19cm.

Santo Domingo - (French colony).

Haiti
M972.94
As7ca
1789

Assemblée des Citoyens des Isles & Colonies Françoises. Paris.
Cahier, contenant les plaintes, doléances & reclamations des Citoyens-libres & proprietaires de couleur, des Isles & Colonies françoises. [Paris, 1789].

15p. 20cm.

Santo Domingo-(French Colony).

Haiti
M972.94
As7de
1789

Assemblée des Citoyen de Couleur,des Isles,& Colonies Françoises. Paris.
Dernieres observations des citoyen de couleur des isles et colonies Françoises, du 27 Novembre 1789. [Paris,1789]

19p. 20cm.

Santo Domingo - (French colony).

Haiti
M972.94
As7ex

Assemblée des Citoyens de Couleur, des isles et Colonies françoises, Paris.
Extrait du Procès-verbal de l'Assemblée des Citoyens-Libres de Couleur, & propriétaires des Isles & colonies françoises, constituée sous le titre de colons Americains, du 12 Septembre 1789. [Paris, 1789]

16p. 19½cm.

Santo Domingo-(French Colony).

Haiti
M972.94
As7o
1789

Assemblée des Citoyens de Couleur, des Isles & Colonies Françoises. Paris.
Observations adressées, a l'Assemblée Nationale, par un député des colons Amériquains. [Paris, 1789?]

15p. 19½cm.

Santo Domingo - (French Colony).

Haiti
M972.94
As7pc

Assemblée des Citoyens de Couleur des Isles & Colonies Françoises. Paris.
Petition des citoyens de couleurs des colonies sur la conspiration et la coalition des colons avec les Anglais. Lue, le 5 Vendémaiaire, à la barre de la convention. Paris, De l'Imprimerie de Pain, Passage-Honorè. [n.d.]

12p. 19½cm.

Santo Domingo - (French colony).

Haiti
M972.94
As7p
1791

Assemblée des Citoyens de Couleur des Isles & Colonies Francoises. Paris.
Pétition Nouvelle des Citoyens de Couleur des Isles Françoises, a l'Assemblée Nationale; précédée d'un advertissement sur les manoeuvres employées pour faire échouer cette pétition, et suive de pièces justificatives... Paris, Chez Desenne, libraire, Bailly, Libraire, et au Bureau du Patriote François, 1791.

19p. 22cm.

Santo Domingo - (French colony).

Haiti
M972.94
As7rec

Assemblée des Citoyens de Couleur, des isles & Colonies Françoises. Paris.
Reclamation des Citoyens de Couleur, des Isles & colonies Françoises; sur le Décret du 8 Mars 1790.

23p. 20cm.
Signed by De Joly; Raimond; Oge, etc.

Santo Domingo - (French Colony).

Haiti
M972.94
As7o
1789

Assemblée des Citoyens de Couleur des Isles, & Colonies Françoises. Paris.
Réclamations des Nègres libres, colons Americains. [Lacks imprint]

3p. 19½cm.

Bound with Observations adressées, a l'Assemblée Nationale...1789.

1. Santo Domingo (French Colony)
2. Haiti-Hist.

Santo Domingo-(French Colony).

Haiti
M972.94
As7s
1789

Assemblée des Citoyens de Couleur des Isles, & Colonies Françoises. Paris.
Supplique et petition des citoyens de couleur des Isles & colonies Françoises, tendante à obtenir un judgement. 30 Janvier 1790.

4p. 19½cm.
Signed:DeJoly,Raimond, Ogé,etc.
Bound in with: Supplique et petition... 1789.

Santo Domingo - (French Colony).

Haiti
M972.94
As7s
1789

Assemblée des Citoyens de Couleur des Isles & Colonies Françoises. Paris.
Supplique et petition des citoyens de Couleur des Isles & colonies Françoises sur le motion faite le 27 Novembre 1789, par M. de Curt, Député de la Guadeloupe, au nom des colonies reunies ... 1789. Paris, 1789.

21p. 19½cm.
Signed: De Joly; Raimond; Oge, etc.

Santo Domingo-(French Colony).

Haiti
M972.94
C73m
1792

Commissaires des Citoyens de Couleur de Saint Marc.
Réflexions politiques sur les troubles et la situation de la partie Françoise de Saint-Domingue, publiées par les commissaires des citoyens de couleur de Saint Marc et de plussieurs paroisses de cette colonie,auprés de l'assemblée nationale et du roi. Paris, De L'Imprimeries du Patriote François,1792.
19p. 21cm.
Bound with: Commissaires des Citoyens... Memoire..1792.

Santo Domingo - (French Colony).

Haiti
M972.94
L71r
1791

Littey, Janvier.
Réponse de Janvier Littey. Homme de couleur de la Martinque, et député à la Covention nationale, A. P. J. Leborgne. [Paris; De l'Imprimerie de Cuffroy, [1791?]

10p. 22cm.

Santo Domingo -(French Colony).

Haiti
M972.94
R13L
1791

Raimond, Julien, 1743? - 1802?
Lettres de J. Raimond, a ses frères les hommes de couleur. Et comparaison des originaux de sa correspondance, avec les extraits perfides qu'en ont fait MM. Page et Brulley, dans un libelle intitulé: Développement des causes, des troubles et des desastres des colonies françaises. Paris, Cercle Social [1791]

20,.8p. 25½cm.

Santo Domingo - (French Colony).

Haiti
M972.94
R13re
1791

Raimond, Julien, 1743?-1802?
Reponse aux considerations de M. Moreau, dit Saint-Méry, député a l'assemblée nationale, sur les colonies; par M. Raymond, citoyen de couleur de Saint-Domingue ... A Paris, De l'Imprimerie de Patriote François, 1791.

68p. 20½cm.

Santo-Domingo-History.

Haiti
M972.94
J34h

Jean-Baptiste, Saint-Victor, 1910-
Haiti sa lutte pour l'Émancipation; deux concepts d'Indépendance a Saint-Domingue. Paris, La Nef de Paris Editions, 1957.

286p. 22½cm.

1. Haiti - History. 2. Santo-Domingo-History.

Santo Domingo (French Colony).

Haiti
M972.94
As7ad
1790

Assemblée des Citoyens de Couleur des Isles, et Colonies Françoises. Paris.
Adresse a l'Assemblée Nationale des Citoyens de Couleur, réunis a Paris. Sous le titre de Colons Américains, du 5 Juillet 1790. [Lacks imprint]

16p. 19cm.

Santo Domingo(French Colony)

Haiti
M972.94
As7ac
1790

Assemblée des Citoyens de Couleur des Isles,& Colonies Françoises. Paris.
Adresse des Citoyens de Couleur des Isles, & Colonies Françoises; a L'Assemblée Genérale des prononcée, le premier Fevrier 1790, par M. de Joly...Paris, 1790.

15p. 21½cm.
Signed by De Joly, Raimond,Ogé,etc.

Santo Domingo (French Colony)

Haiti
M972.94
As7ad
1790

Assemblée des Citoyens de Couleur des Isles & Colonies Françoises. Paris
Lettre des Citoyens de Couleur, A. M. Le President de l'Assemblée nationale. Du premier août 1790. [Paris, De l'Imprimerie de Patriote Francois, 1790.]

3p. 19cm.

Santo Domingo (French Colony).

Haiti
M972.94
As7ad
1790

Assemblée des Citoyens de Couleur des Isles & Colonies Françoises. Paris.
Lettre des Citoyens de Couleur, A. M. Le President de l'Assemblée nationale. Du premier août 1790. [Paris, De l'Imprimerie de Patriote Francois, 1790.]

3p. 19cm.
Bound with Adresse a l'Assemblée nationale.

Santo Domingo (French Colony)

Haiti
M972.94
As71
1789

Assemblée des Citoyens de Couleur, des Isles & Colonies Françoises. Paris.
Lettre des Citoyens de Couleur, des isles & colonies, francoises, a MM. les membres du Comité de Vérification de l'Assemblée Nationale, du 23 Novembre 1789. Paris, De l'Imprimerie de Lottin l'ainé & Lottin de S.Germain, Imprimeurs-Libraires Ordinaires de la Ville, 1789.

24p. 20½cm.
Signed by: De Joly, Raimond; Oge, etc.

Santo Domingo (French Colony).

Haiti
M972.94
As7pet
1790

Assemblée des Citoyens de Couleur des Isles, & Colonies Françoises. Paris.
Petition a la convention nationale, par les patriotes, citoyens de couleur, déportés par les Anglais et débarqués à Rochefort, après s'être rendus maîtres des Transports No. 34 et 42 par le 41 me degré de latitude Nord. [Paris,] De l'Imprimerie du tribunal criminel du departement de Paris [1790]

19p. 26½cm.

Haiti
M972.94
C73m
1792

Santo Domingo (French Colony).
Commissaires des Citoyens de Couleur de Saint Marc.
Mémoire historique des dernières revolutions des provinces de l'ouest et du sud de la partie, Françoise de Saint-Domingue. Publié par les Commissaires des Citoyens de Couleur de Saint Marc et le plusieurs Paroisses de la colonie, auprès de l'Assemblée Nationale et du Roi. Paris, De l'Imprimerie du Patriote François, 1792.
114p. 21cm.

Haiti
M972.94
R13c
1794

Santo Domingo (French Colony).
Raimond, Julien, 1743?-1802?
Correspondance de Julien Raimond, avec ses frères de Saint-Domingue, et les pièces qui lui ont été adressées par eux. Paris, Imprimerie du Cercle Social [1794].
vii, [3] - 136p. 25cm.

Haiti
M972.94
R13r
1790

Santo Domingo (French Colony).
[Raimond, Julien, 174?-1802?]
Reclamations adressées à l'Assemblée Nationale, par les personnes de couleur, propriétaires & cultivateurs de la colonie françoise de Saint Domingue [1790]
8p. 20cm.
[Signé Raimond]

Haiti
M972.94
R13v
1792

Santo Domingo (French Colony).
Raimond, Julien, 1743?-1802?
Véritable origine des troubles de S. Domingue, et des différentes causes qui les ont produits; par M. Julien Raimond. Paris, Chez Desenne [etc.] 1792.
55p. 21½cm.

M808.8
Sa59

Sanz y Díaz, José, 1907- *ed.*
Lira negra (selecciones españolas y afroamericanas) [Madrid, M. Aguilar, 1945]
380 p. front. 12 cm. (Colección Crisol, núm. 21)
White editor.
1. Negro poetry. 2. Negro authors. 3. Negroes in literature. I. Title. (Series)
A 48-5448*
Yale Univ. Library for Library of Congress [1]

Brazil
M869.3
Am1sa

São Jorge dos Ilhéus.
Amado, Jorge, 1912-
São Jorge dos Ilhéus. 5. ed. São Paulo, Livraria Martins ~~1944~~ 1957
~~369~~ p. 22 cm. (*His* Obras, 9)
360
I. Title.
A 49-6486*
New York. Public Libr. for Library of Congress [1]

Brazil
MB9
J49a

São Paulo, Brazil (City) - Poor.
Jesus, Carolina Maria de.
Child of the dark; the diary of Carolina Maria de Jesus. Translated from the Portuguese by David St. Clair. [1st ed.] New York, Dutton, 1962.
190 p. illus. 21 cm.
Translation of Quarto de despejo.
Picture of author on book jacket.
1. São Paulo, Brazil (City)—Soc. condit. 2. São Paulo, Brazil (City)—Poor. I. Title.
HN290.S33J43 920.7 62—14719 ‡
Library of Congress [62k3]

Brazil
MB9
J49a3

Sao Paulo, Brazil (City) - Social condition.
Jesus, Carolina Maria de
Beyond all pity. Translated by David St. Clair. London, Souvenir Press [1962]
190p. illus. 22cm.
Translation of Quarto de despejo.
American ed. (New York, Dutton) has title: Child of the dark.
1. Sao Paulo, Brazil (City) - Social condition. I. Title.

Brazil
MB9
J49a4

São Paulo, Brazil (City) - Social conditions.
Jesus, Carolina Maria de
Casa de alvenaria, diáro de uma ex-favelada. [Rio de Janeiro, P. de Azevedo, 1961]
183p. 24cm. (Coleção Contrastes e confrontos, 4)

Brazil
MB9
J49a

São Paulo, Brazil (City) - Soc. condit.
Jesus, Carolina Maria de.
Child of the dark; the diary of Carolina Maria de Jesus. Translated from the Portuguese by David St. Clair. [1st ed.] New York, Dutton, 1962.
190 p. illus. 21 cm.
Translation of Quarto de despejo.
Picture of author on book jacket.
1. São Paulo, Brazil (City)—Soc. condit. 2. São Paulo, Brazil (City)—Poor. I. Title.
HN290.S33J43 920.7 62—14719 ‡
Library of Congress [62k3]

M843.91
L11s

Guadeloupe Sapotille et le serin d'argile.
Lacrosil, Michèle
Sapotille et le serin d'argile; roman. Paris, Gallimard [1960]
240p. 19cm.
1. Guadeloupe - Fiction. I. Title.

M813.5
Y46s
1954

The Saracen blade.
Yerby, Frank, 1916-
The Saracen Blade. New York, Pocket Books, inc., 1954.
418p. 16cm.
Cardinal edition.

M813.5
Y46s

The Saracen blade.
Yerby, Frank, 1916-
The Saracen blade, a novel. New York, Dial Press, 1952.
406 p. 21 cm.
I. Title.
Full name: Frank Garvin Yerby.
PZ3.Y415Sar 52-5616 ‡
Library of Congress [12]

Ghana
M966.7
W83p

Sarbah, John Mensah, 1864-1910.
The Akan community.
pp. 201-202.
In: Pageant of Ghana, by Freda Wolfson. 1958.
1. Akan. I. Title.

Gold Coast
M966.7
Sa7f

Sarbah, John Mensah, 1864-1910.
Fanti customary laws. A brief introduction to the principles of the native laws and customs of the Fanti and Akan districts of the Gold coast, with a report of some cases thereon decided in the law courts. By John Mensah Sarbah ... London, W. Clowes and sons, limited, 1897.
xxiii, 295, [1] p. 22cm.
1. Law, Fanti. 2. Gold Coast. 3. Gold Coast—Customary law.
5-32343
Library of Congress GN493.4.A9S3 [a44c1]

Gold Coast
M966.7
Sa7fa

Sarbah, John Mensah, 1864-1910.
Fanti law report of decided cases on Fanti customary laws. Second selection, by John Mensah Sarbah. Long, William Clowes and Sons, limited, 1904.
189p. 22cm.
1. Law, Fanti. 2. Gold Coast - Customary Law. 3. Law Primitive.

M630.71
Sa7v

Sargent, Harvey Owen, 1876?-1936.
... Vocational education in agriculture for negroes; recommendations for the establishment of agricultural schools and programs for Negroes. May, 1926. Issued by the Federal board for vocational education, Washington, D. C. Washington, Govt. print. off., 1926.
ix, 92 p. incl. tables, diagrs. 23cm. (U. S. Federal board for vocational education. Bulletin no. 111. Agricultural series no. 28)
"Prepared ... by H. O. Sargent."—p. ix.
1. Agricultural education. 2. ~~Negroes~~—Vocational, education. I. Title.
E 26-235 rev
U. S. Off. of educ. Library for Library of Congress LC1045.A28 no. 111 LC1045.A25 no. 111 [r30f2]

Martinique
M965.
F21d

Sartre, Jean Paul.
Fanon, Frantz, 1925-1962.
Les damnés de la terre. Préface de Jean-Paul Sartre. Paris, François Maspero, 1961.
242p. 22cm.

Congo
Leopoldville
M967.5
L97p

Sartre, Jean-Paul, 1905- Preface.
Lumumba, Patrice, 1925-1961
La Pensée politique de Patrice Lumumba. Préface de Jean-Paul Sartre. Textes recueillis et présentés par Jean Van Lierde. Bruxelles, le Livre Africain, 1963.
401p. port. 21½cm.

Senegal
M896.1
Se5a

Sartre, Jean Paul, 1905-
Orphee noir.
Senghor, Léopold Sédar, 1906- ed.
Anthologie de la nouvelle poésie nègre et malgache de langue française, par Léopold Sédar Senghor, précédée de Orphée noir, par Jean-Paul Sartre. [1. éd.] Paris, Presses Universitaires de France, 1948.
xliv. 227p. 23cm.

M813.5
W38s

Sasebo diary.
Webb, Charles Lewis.
Sasebo diary. New York, Vantage Press [1964]
129p. 20½cm.
Portrait of author on book jacket.

M780 Satchmo.
Ar5 **Armstrong, Louis, 1900–**
Satchmo; my life in New Orleans. New York, Prentice-Hall ₍1954₎
240 p. illus. 21 cm.

1. Musicians—Correspondence, reminiscences, etc. 2. Jazz music. I. Title.

ML419.A75A3 927.8 54–9628 ‡
Library of Congress ₍54d30₎

M780 Satchmo; my life in New Orleans.
Ar5s Armstrong, Louis, 1900-
Satchmo; my life in New Orleans. London, The Harborough Publishing Co., Ltd., 1954.

157p. 18cm.
Paper back edition.

Guadeloupe
Satineau, Maurice, 1891–
M972.97 ... **Histoire de la Guadeloupe sous l'ancien régime, 1635–1789.**
Sa8h Paris, Payot, 1928.
3 p. l., 400 p. plates, map. $22\frac{1}{2}$ cm. (Bibliothèque historique)
On cover: Bibliothèque coloniale.
"Corrections supplémentaires de l'auteur après le tirage": 1 leaf inserted.
Bibliography: p. ₍386₎–400.

1. Guadeloupe—Hist. 2. Guadeloupe—Econ. condit.
3. Martinican authors
Library of Congress F2066.S25 28–22485
Copyright A—Foreign 39222
₍2₎

Guadeloupe
M89 **Satineau, Maurice.**
Sch6s Schoelcher. Heros de l'abolition de l'esclavage dans les possessions Francaises. Paris, Editions Mellottee 1948

149p. front (port) 19cm.
Guadeloupean author

1. Schoelcher, Victor, 1804-1893.
2. Slavery - French colonies. 3. French literature - Guadeloupean author.

Satire.
M811.4 Sluby, M F
Su7s Satire. Lines suggested on reading the confession of Dr. B.T. Tanner, editor of the "Christian Recorder", by M.F. Sluby. December 8th, 1881 and May 11th, 1883, Philadelphia, Pa. ₍lacks imprint₎

8p. 19cm.

M323.4 **Saunders, Doris E ed.**
Sa87 The day they marched. With an introd. by Lerone Bennett, Jr. Designed by Herbert Temple. Chicago, Johnson Pub. Co. ₍°1963₎
viii, 88 p. illus., ports. 28 cm.

1. March on Washington for Jobs and Freedom, 1963. I. Title.

F200.S2 323.41 63–23081
Library of Congress ₍5₎

M973 **Saunders, Doris E ed.**
Sa87 The Kennedy years and the Negro, a photographic record. Edited by Doris E. Saunders. Introd. by Andrew T. Hatcher. Designed by Herbert Temple. Chicago, Johnson Pub. Co., 1964.
xiii, 143 p. illus., ports. 29 cm.

1. ~~Negroes~~—Hist. 2. ~~Negroes~~—Civil rights. 3. Kennedy, John Fitzgerald, Pres. U. S., 1917–1963. I. Title.

E185.6.S3 973.922 64–20179
Library of Congress ₍64f14₎

M335.4 **Saunders, John.**
Sa8s The struggle for Negro equality; Programs of the Socialist Workers Party, by John Saunders and Albert Parker. New York, Pioneer Publishers for the Socialist Workers Party, 1943.

30p. 22cm.

I. Socialist Workers Party. II. Title.

M89 Saunders, Lucinda Yancey.
B797s An idea that grew into a million; The life story of Charlotte Hawkins Brown... Reprinted from Abbott's monthly, November, 1930.

₍4₎p. port. illus. 29cm.

1. Brown, Charlotte Hawkins, 1883-
2. Palmer Memorial Institute, Sedalia, N.C.

M815.2 **Saunders, Prince, 1755-1839.**
Sa8a An address delivered at Bethel Church, Philadelphia on the 30th of September, 1818 before the Pennsylvania Augustine society for the education of people of colour. By Prince Saunders. To which is annexed the constitution of the society. Philadelphia, Joseph Rakestraw, 1818.

12p. 24cm.
1. Pennsylvania Augustine society for the education of the people of colour.

M815.2 **Saunders, Prince,** 1755-1839, ed.
Sa8h ... **Haytian papers. A collection of the very interesting**
1816 **proclamations, and other official documents; together with some account of the rise, progress, and present state of the kingdom of Hayti. With a preface by Prince Sanders, esq. London, Printed for W. Reed, 1816.**
2 p. l., xv, 228 p. front. (port.) 1 illus. 21cm.
At head of title: By authority.
Head-piece: Coat of arms.

(Continued on next card)
10–8117
₍42d1₎

M815.2 **Saunders, Prince,** 1755-1839, ed. ... **Haytian papers ...**
Sa8h **1816. (Card 2)**
1816 CONTENTS.—Editor's address.—Code Henri. Law respecting the culture ₍of the land₎.—Extracts from the registers of the deliberations of the consuls of the ₍French₎ republic.—Narrative of the accession of Their Royal Majesties to the throne of Hayti.—State of Hayti. Proclamation. Henry Christophe, president ... to the land and naval armaments.—Constitutional law of the Council of state which establishes royalty in Hayti. April 4, 1811.—Kingdom of Hayti. Manifesto of the King. Sept. 18, 1814.—Reflections of the editor. —Royal gazette of Hayti.—Proclamation. Jan. 1, 1816.—Reflections on the abolition of the slave trade.

1. Haiti—Hist.—1804–1844—Sources. 2. Haiti—Pol. & govt.—1804–1844. I. Haiti. Sovereigns, etc., 1807–1820 (Henri I) II. Title.
10–8117
Library of Congress F1924.S22
₍a42d1₎

M815.2 **Saunders, Prince,** 1755-1839, ed.
Sa8h Haytian papers. A collection of the very interesting
1818 proclamations and other official documents, together with some account of the rise, progress, and present state of the kingdom of Hayti. By Prince Sanders. Boston, C. Bingham and co., 1818.
xix, ₍20₎–156 p. 20 cm.
CONTENTS.—Advertisement.—Preface to the English edition.—Code Henri.—Extracts from the registers of the deliberations of the consuls of the ₍French₎ republic.—Narrative of the accession of their royal majesties to the throne of Hayti.—Proclamation. Henry Christophe, president ... to the land and naval armaments of ... Hayti.—Constitutional law of the Council of state which establishes

(Continued on next card)
1—27959
₍48c½₎

M815.2 **Saunders, Prince,** 1755-1839, ed. **Haytian papers ... 1818.**
Sa8h **(Card 2)**
1818 CONTENTS—Continued.
royalty in Hayti. Apr. 4, 1811.—Manifesto of the king. Sept. 18, 1814.—Proclamation. Jan. 1, 1816. Reflections on the abolition of the slave trade.

1. Haiti—Hist.—1804–1844—Sources. 2. Haiti—Pol. & govt.—1804–1844. I. Haiti. Sovereigns, etc., 1811–1820 (Henri I) II. Title.
1—27959
Library of Congress F1924.S23
₍48c½₎

M815.2 Saunders, Prince, 1755-1839.
Sa8m A memoir presented to the American convention for promoting the abolition of slavery and improving the condition of the African race, December 11th, 1818; containing some remarks upon the civil dissentions of the hitherto afflicted people of Hayti... by Prince Saunders. Philadelphia, Dennis Heartt, 1818.

19p. $23\frac{1}{2}$cm.
I. American convention for promoting the abolition of slavery and improving the condition of the African race.

France
M848
Sa8m **Sauvage, Roger, 1917–**
Un du Normandie-Niémen. Préf. du colonel Pouyade. ₍Givors, A. Martel ₍1950₎
316 p. illus., ports. 21 cm.
"Il a été tiré ... 500 exemplaires sur Alfa Mousse des Papeteries Navarre numérotés 1 à 450 et H-C1 à H-C... 181."

French author, b. Paris.

1. France combattante. Forces aériennes françaises libres. Régiment ~~Normandie-Niémen~~. 2. World War, 1939–1945—Aerial operations, French. 3. World War, 1939–1945—Personal narratives, French. I. Title.

D788.S39 940.544944 51–17012
Library of Congress ₍1₎

Guadeloupe Sauvage a Paris.
M843.91
A116s Alcandre, Slyvère, 1913-
Sauvage a Paris; roman. Paris, La Nef de Paris Editions, 1957.

166p. 19cm.

M811.5 **Savage, Eudora V**
Sa9v Vibrations of my heartstrings, by Eudora V. Savage. New York, The Exposition press ₍1944₎
4 p. l., 11–64 p. $19\frac{1}{2}$cm. ₍Poets of America. Series four₎

I. Title.
44–41841
Library of Congress PS3537.A9267V5
₍46c1₎ 811.5

M89 **Savage, Horace C**
L24s Life and times of Bishop Isaac Lane. Nashville, National Publication Co., 1958.
240 p. illus. 20 cm.

1. Lane, Isaac, Bp., 1834–1937.

BX8473.L3S3 922.773 58–30008 ‡
Library of Congress ₍1₎

M326.9 **Savage, William Sherman.**
Sa92 The controversy over the distribution of abolition literature, 1830–1860, by W. Sherman Savage ... ₍Washington, D. C.₎ The Association for the study of Negro life and history, inc., 1938.
xv, 141 p. $23\frac{1}{2}$ cm.
Bibliography: p. 127–134.

1. Slavery in the U. S.—Anti-slavery movements. 2. Slavery in the U. S.—Controversial literature. I. Association for the study of Negro life and history, inc. II. Title.
39—2080
Library of Congress E449.S257
₍40f3₎ 326.4

M378Li **Savage, William Sherman.**
Sa9 The history of Lincoln university ₍by₎ W. Sherman Savage ... Published under the direction of Lincoln university. Jefferson City, Mo., ₍°1939₎
xii, 302 p. illus. (incl. ports., maps, plan) diagrs. $23\frac{1}{2}$cm.
Bibliography: p. 295–296.

1. Lincoln university, Jefferson City, Mo.—Hist.
40–6814
Library of Congress LC2851.L64S3
₍2₎ 378.778

Savage destiny.

British Guiana M823.91
Mittelholzer, Edgar, 1909-
Savage destiny. Original title: Children of Kayana. Abridged. New York, Dell Printers, 1960.

384p. 16½cm.

Savage holiday.

M813.5 W93in
Wright, Richard, 1909-1960.
De la inocencia a la pesadilla. (Savage holiday). Traduccion de Leon Mirlas. Buenos Aires, Editorial Sudamericana, 1956.

252p. 18½cm.

Savage holiday.

M813.5 W93sa
Wright, Richard, 1909-
Savage holiday. New York, Avon Publications, 1954.

220p. 18cm. (Avon red & gold edition T-86)
Pocket book edition.
"Complete and unabridged."

Haiti M843.91 Sa9
Savain, Pétion.
... La case de Damballah, roman. Linogravures originales de l'auteur. Port-au-Prince, Haiti, Imprimerie de l'État, 1939.

4 p. l., [11]-215 p., 1 l. incl. illus., plates. 22cm.

I. Title. 1. Haitian fiction.

41-21964 Provisional

Library of Congress PQ3949.S3C3 1939
[2] 843.91

La savane rouge.

Mali M896.3 S183s
Siscoko, Fily Dabo (d. 1964)
La savane rouge. [n.p.] Les Presses Universelles [1962]

139p. 19cm.

I. Title.

Savannah-Siege, 1779.

M06 Am3 no.5
Steward, Theophilus Gould, 1843-
... How the black St. Domingo legion saved the patriot army in the siege of Savannah, 1779, by T. G. Steward ... Washington, D. C., The Academy, 1899.

15 p. illus. (maps) 23cm. (American negro academy. Occasional papers, no. 5)

1. Savannah—Siege, 1779. 2. U. S.—Hist.—Revolution—Negro troops. 3. France—Army—Infantry—Fontage's legion.

9-24043 Revised

Library of Congress E185.5.A51 no. 5
——— Copy 2. E241.S2S88
[r32e2]

Savannah. First African Baptist church.

M286 L94
Love, Emanuel King, 1850-1900.
History of the First African Baptist church, from its organization, January 20th, 1788, to July 1st, 1888. Including the centennial celebration, addresses, sermons, etc. By Rev. E. K. Love ... Savannah, Ga., The Morning news print., 1888.

7 p. l., iii-v, 360 p. front., illus. 21cm.

1. Savannah. First African Baptist church. I. Title.

26-5886

Library of Congress BX6480.S45F5
Copyright 1888: 24385 [37b1]

Savannah. First African Baptist church.

M286 T36t
Thomas, Edgar Garfield, 1880-
The first African Baptist church of North America, by Rev. Edgar Garfield Thomas ... Savannah, Ga. [1925]

144 p. front., illus. 19cm.

1. Savannah. First African Baptist church. I. Title.

26-4814

Library of Congress BX6480.S45F53
[a45c1]

Savannah. First Bryan Baptist church.

M286 S14
Simms, James Meriles.
The first colored Baptist church in North America. Constituted at Savannah, Georgia, January 20, A. D. 1788. With biographical sketches of the pastors. Written for the church by Rev. James M. Simms. Philadelphia, J. B. Lippincott company, 1888.

264 p. front., plates, ports. 19½cm.

1. Savannah. First Bryan Baptist church.

8-14432 Revised

Library of Congress BX6480.S45F55
Copyright [r31c2]

M343.3 R21s
Save Willie McGee.
Raymond, Harry.
Save Willie McGee. New York, New Century, 1951.

14p. 19cm.

M323 H73n
Savory, William.
Holmes, Dwight Oliver Wendell, 1877-
The Negro chooses democracy. Reprinted from the Journal of Negro education. [8:620-633]. October, 1939.

Dedicatory address, The Savery Library, Talladega College, April 16, 1939.

Savorgnan de Brazza, Pierre Paul François Camille, comte, 1852-1905.

Martinique M843.9 M32s
Maran, René, 1887-
Savorgnan de Brazza. Éd. définitive. Paris, Éditions du Dauphin [1951]

246 p. illus. 21 cm.

1. Savorgnan de Brazza, Pierre Paul François Camille, comte, 1852-1905.

DC342.8.S27M37 52-29890 ‡
Library of Congress [3]

M813.5 Sa9a 1950
Savoy, Willard W , 1916-
Alien land. New York, New American Library, 1950.

192p. 18cm. (Signet books)

Pocket book edition.

I. Title.

M813.5 Sa9a
Savoy, Willard W 1916-
Alien land. [1st ed.] New York, E. P. Dutton, 1949.

320 p. 21 cm.

I. Title. 1. Fiction

PZ3.S2695Al 49-8176*
Library of Congress [7]

Say amen, brother!

M251 P66s
Pipes, William Harrison, 1912-
Say amen, brother! Old-time Negro preaching: a study in American frustration. New York, William-Frederick Press, 1951.

i, 210 p. 24cm.
Bibliography: p. 201-205.

Scan-spans.

M811.5 D349s
Dease, Ruth Roseman
Scan-spans. New York, Vantage Press, [1967]

79p. 21cm.
Portrait of author on book jacket.

I. Title.

M910 B79lw
Scandanavia - Description and travel.
Brooks, William Sampson, 1865-
What a black man saw in a white man's country. Some account of a trip to the land of the midnight sun. 3d ed. Minniapolis, Minn., 1899.

89p. port., illus. 19cm.

Scanlon, David G., joint ed.

Africa M370 C83
Cowan, Laing Gray, ed.
Education and nation-building in Africa. Edited by L. Gray Cowan, James O'Connell [and] David G. Scanlon. New York, F. A. Praeger [1965]

x, 403 p. 21 cm.
Bibliography: p. 397-403.

1. Education—Africa—Addresses, essays, lectures. 2. Nationalism—Africa—Addresses, essays, lectures. I. O'Connell, James, 1925- joint ed. II. Scanlon, David G., joint ed. III. Title.

LA1501.C6 1965 370.96 65-12193
Library of Congress [5]

M784 Sc7
Scarborough, Dorothy, 1878-1935.
On the trail of Negro folk-songs, by Dorothy Scarborough, assisted by Ola Lee Gulledge. Cambridge, Harvard university press, 1925.

5 p. l., [3]-289 p. illus. (music) 24½ cm.
White author.

1. Folk songs. I. Gulledge, Ola Lee. II. Title.

M1670.S3 25—19922
Library of Congress [50z1]

Scarborough, Sarah C. Bierce, comp.

M89 P29r
Payne, Daniel Alexander, 1811-1893.
Recollections of seventy years; by Bishop Daniel Alexander Payne ... With an introduction by Rev. F. J. Grimke ... Comp. and arranged by Sarah C. Bierce Scarborough. Ed. by Rev. C. S. Smith. Nashville, Tenn., Publishing house of the A. M. E. Sunday school union, 1888.

335 p. pl., 8 port. (incl. front.) 19cm.

1. African Methodist Episcopal church. I. Scarborough, Sarah C. Bierce, comp. II. Smith, Charles Spencer, 1852- ed. III. Title.

14-12737

Library of Congress E185.97.P34

M814.4 Sc7b
Scarborough, William Saunders, 1852-1926
The birds of Aristophanes: a theory of interpretation. A paper read before the American Philological Association at its annual meeting at Sage College, Cornell university, Ithaca, N. Y., July 13, 1886. By W.S. Scarborough...Boston, Published for the author by J.S. Cushing & co., 1886.

36p. 18½cm.
Inscribed copy: With compliments, W. S. Scarborough.

M06
Am3
no.8
Scarborough, William Saunders, 1852-1926
... The educated Negro and his mission. By W. S. Scarborough ... Washington, D. C., The Academy, 1903.
11 p. 23cm. (The American Negro academy. Occasional papers. no. 8)
1. Negroes—Education.
Library of Congress E185.82.S38 10—7070
——— Copy 2. E185.5.A51 no. 8
[a40b1]

... Scènes de la vie haïtienne.
Haiti
M843.91 Hibbert, Fernand.
H52sc
... Scènes de la vie haïtienne. Romulus. Port-au-Prince, Imprimerie de l'Abeille, 1908.
3 p. l., [9]-120 p., 1 l. 21cm.
I. Title. II. Title: Romulus.
25-20880
Library of Congress PQ3949.H5S3

Haiti
M972.94
Sclt
Scharon, Faine.
Toussaint Louverture et la Révolution de St-Domingue. Port-au-Prince, Impr. de l'État [1957–
v. 24 cm.
Includes bibliography.
Library has: v.2
1. Haiti—Hist.—Revolution, 1791-1804. 2. Toussaint Louverture, François Dominique, 1743-1803. 3. Haiti—Hist.—To 1791.
F1923.S35 60-43228 ‡
Library of Congress [3]

M480
Sc7f
Scarborough, William Saunders, 1852-1926
First lessons in Greek; adapted to the Greek grammars of Goodwin and Hadley, and designed as an introduction to Xenophon's Anabasis and similar Greek. By William S. Scarborough ... New York and Chicago, A. S. Barnes & company [°1881]
ix p., 1 l., [3]-147 p. 19cm.
1. Greek language—Composition and exercises.
10—28964
Library of Congress PA258.S3
Copyright 1881: 12064 [38b1]

Scènes de la vie Haitienne.
Haiti
M843.91
H52Sc
1907
Hibbert, Fernand, 1873-1928.
Scènes de la vie Haitienne. Les Thezar. Port-au-Prince, Imp. de l'Abeille, 1907.
253p. 19cm.

Schererei mit den Engeln.
M813.5 Hughes, Langston, 1902-1967
H87tro
Schererei mit den Engeln. Kurzgeschichten. »Trouble with the angels«. Short storeis. Herausgegeben von Gunter Klotz. Aus dem Amerikanischen Ubertragen von Paridam von dem Knesebeck, Sigrid Klotz und Horst Wolf.
109p. 17cm. (Reclam Universal Bibliothek, 120)
Written in German.
"For Arthur - another book - Sincerely, Langston, New York, May 1, 1964"

M304
P19
v.7
no.2
Scarborough, William Saunders, 1852-1926
... Tenancy and ownership among negro farmers in Southampton County, Virginia. By W. S. Scarborough ... Washington [Govt. print. off.] 1926.
27 p. map. 23cm. (U. S. Dept. of agriculture. Department bulletin no. 1404)
Contribution from Bureau of agricultural economics.
1. Agriculture—Virginia—Southampton. Co. 2. Negroes—[Agriculture]
Agr 26-670
Library, U. S. Dept. of Agriculture 1Ag84B no. 1404
[6]

Scènes de la vie noire.
Congo(Leopoldville)
M896.3 Edme, Philibert
Ed54
Scènes de la vie noire; Nkoya Kalambwa. Paris, Éditions du Scorpion [1959]
188p. 19cm. (Collection alternance)

Schickel, Richard, joint author.
MB9 Horne, Lena.
H784
Lena, by Lena Horne and Richard Schickel. [1st ed.] Garden City, N. Y., Doubleday, 1965.
300 p. illus., ports. 22 cm.
1. Musicians—Correspondence, reminiscences, etc. I. Schickel, Richard, joint author. II. Title.
ML420.H65A35 792.7 (B) 65-18388/MN
Library of Congress [3]

Scarborough, William Saunders, 1852-1926
M811.4
D899d Dunbar, Alice Ruth Moore, 1875-1935
Paul Laurence Dunbar, poet Laureate of the Negro race, by Mrs. Paul Laurence Dunbar, W. S. Scarborough and Reverdy C. Ransom. Reprinted from The A.M.E. Church Review. Philadelphia, Pa.
32p. portraits. 23cm.

Scenes in the life of Harriet Tubman.
MB9
T79s
Bradford, Sarah Elizabeth (Hopkins) "Mrs. J. M. Bradford," b. 1818.
Scenes in the life of Harriet Tubman. By Sarah H. Bradford. Auburn [N. Y.] W. J. Moses, printer, 1869.
2 p. l., 132 p. front. (port.) 18½cm.
1. Tubman, Harriet (Ross) I. Title.
7-31857
Library of Congress E444.T89
[35g1]

Africa
M960
Sch3
[Schieffelin, Henry Maunsell] b. 1808, ed.
The people of Africa. A series of papers on their character, condition, and future prospects, by E. W. Blyden, D. D., Tayler Lewis, D. D., Theodore Dwight, esq., etc., etc. New York, A. D. F. Randolph & co., 1871.
8 p. l., 157 p. plates, facsims. (part fold.) 19cm.
"Introductory" signed: H. M. S.
CONTENTS.—I. The Negro in ancient history. By Rev. Edward W. Blyden.—II. The Koran. African Mohammedanism. By Tayler Lewis.—III. Condition and character of Negroes in Africa. By Theodore Dwight, esq.—IV. Condition of education in Liberia.—V. Extracts from Prof. Bly-
(Continued on next card)
14—15131
[42b1]

M326.
Sc71
Scarlett, George Chandler, 1880–
Laws against liberty, by George C. Scarlett ... New York, N. Y. [Cosmos printing co., inc., °1937]
135 p. 21cm.
1. Liberty. 2. Negroes. 3. U. S.—Race question. 4. Slavery in the U. S. I. Title.
Yale law school. Library for Library of Congress A 39—1029
[40c1]

South Africa
M896.1 Schapera, Isaac, 1905– ed. and tr.
Sch16
Praise-poems of Tswana chiefs. Translated and edited with an introd. and notes, by I. Schapera. Oxford, Clarendon Press, 1965.
vi, 255 p. geneal. tables, map. 23 cm. (Oxford library of African literature)
Bibliography: p. [246]-247.
White editor.
1. Sechuana poetry. 2. Tswana (Bantu tribe)—Kings and rulers. I. Title.
PL8651.7.S3 896.3 65-8559
Library of Congress [2]

M960
Sch3
[Schieffelin, Henry Maunsell] b. 1808, ed. The people of Africa ... 1871. (Card 2)
CONTENTS—Continued.
den's journal of a visit to Sierra Leone, in February, 1871.—VI. The Syrian (Arabic) college.—VII. Arabic manuscript in Western Africa.—VIII. Mohammedanism in Western Africa ... By Rev. E. W. Blyden.—IX. Remarkable conditions of the African field.—X. A letter from the King of Musadu.—XI. Extracts from N. Y. state colonization journal, April, 1871.
Address by Alexander Crummell.
1. Negroes. 2. Africa—Native races. 3. Africa—Colonization. History I. Blyden, Edward Wilmot, 1832-1912. II. Lewis, Tayler, 1802-1877. III. Dwight, Theodore, 1796-1866. IV. Title.
African literature
Crummell, Alexander
Library of Congress DT15.S4 14—15131
[42b1]

The scene.
M813.5 Cooper, Clarence L
C783sc
The scene. New York, Crown Publishers [1960]
310 p. 22 cm.
I. Title.
PZ4.C7772Sc 59-14031 ‡
Library of Congress [5]

Africa
M896
B36
Scharfe, Don
Hausa poetry, by Don Scharfe and Yahaya Aliyi.
Pp. 34-40
In: Beier, Ulli, comp. Introduction to African literature. London, Longmans, 1967.
1. Hausa poetry. I. Aliyi, Yahaya, jt. auth.

M967.6 Schillings, C G
Sc3f
Flashlights in the jungle; a record of hunting adventures and of studies in wild life in Equatorial East Africa. Translated by Frederic Whyte. With an introduction by Sir H. H. Johnston. Illustrated with 302 of the author's "untouched" photographs taken by day and night. New York, Doubleday, Page and Co., 1905.
782p. illus., port. 23½cm.

Scenes de la vie creole.
Guadeloupe
M843.91 Blancan, André.
B59j
Scènes de la vie créole; Jacques Danglemont, par André Blancan. Paris, Martory & cie, 1917.
4 p. l., 408 p. 18½cm. fr. 3.50
I. Title. II. Title: Jacques Danglemont.
17-25353
Library of Congress PQ2603.L3S4 1917
Copyright A—Foreign 14764

Haiti
MB9
L93s
Scharon, Faine
Toussaint Louverture et la révolution de St.-Domingue. Port-au-Prince, Imprimerie de l'Etat, 1957.
217p.
1. Toussaint Louverture, Pierre Dominique, 1746?-1803.

Martinique Schoelcher, Victor, 1804-1893.
M843.91 Sainville, Léonard.
Sa2v
Victor Schoelcher, 1804-1893. Paris, Fasquelle, 1950.
269p. ports. 20cm.
"Bibliographie": p. [261]-269.

Schoelcher, Victor, 1804-1893.
Guadeloupe
MB9 Satineau, Maurice.
Sch6s Schoelcher. Heors de l'abolition de l'esclavage dans les possessions Francaises. Paris, Editions Mellottee 1948
149p. front (port) 19cm.

M026 Schomburg, Arthur Alfonso, 1874-1938, comp.
Sch64 Exhibition catalogue. 1918. Compiled by Arthur A. Schomburg. [New York, The Poole Press Association Printers, 1918. (Card 2)
23p. 23cm.
"A. B. Spingarn with the sincere appreciation of this compiler."
1. Exhibitions - Catalogs. I. The Negro Library Association. II. Browne, Robert T.

Schomburg, Arthur Alfonso, 1874-1938. A bibliographical checklist of American Negro poetry.
M01 Porter, Dorothy (Burnett) 1905-
P83n North American Negro poets, a bibliographical checklist of their writings, 1760-1944, by Dorothy B. Porter. Hattiesburg, Miss., The Book farm, 1945.
90 p. 23½ cm. (Heartman's historical series no. 70)
"An expansion of the Schomburg checklist."—Pref.
1. Negro poetry (American)—Bibl. I. Schomburg, Arthur Alfonso, 1874-1938. A bibliographical checklist of American Negro poetry. II. Title.
Full name: Dorothy Louise (Burnett) Porter.
Z1361.N39P6 016.811 45-4014
Library of Congress (a58n1)

Schoelcher, Victor, 1804-1893.
Martinique
M993.9 Tardon, Raphaël, 1911-
T17co Le combat de Schoelcher. Paris, Fasquelle Editeurs, 1948.
127p. 19cm.

Puerto Rico
M864 Schomburg, Arthur Alfonso, 1874- 1938
Sch6f Foreword.
(In: Robinson, Rowland Evans. Out of bondage and other stories; foreword by Arthur Schomburg,... Rutland, Vt., C.E. Tuttle company [c1936] 24cm. pp. [5]-9.)
I. Title. -Out of Bondage. II. a.t.-Robinson.

Schomburg, Arthur Alfonso, 1874-1938.
Puerto Rico
M864 Robinson, Rowland Evans, 1833-1900.
Sch6f ... Out of bondage and other stories; foreword by Arthur Schomburg, Robinson biography by Mary Robinson Perkins. Rutland, Vt., C.E. Tuttle company [c1936]
255p. front. (ports.) illus. 24cm.

Jamaica
M325 Scholes, Theophilus E Samuel, 1856-1906.
Sch6b The British empire and alliances; or, Britain's duty to her colonies and subject races. By Theophilus E. S. Scholes ... London, E. Stock, 1899.
viii, 415 p. front. (fold. map) 23cm.
1. Gt. Brit.—Colonies.
9-32469†
Library of Congress JV1026.S4

M304 Schomburg, Arthur Alfonso, 1874-1938
P19 Masonic truths, a letter and document.
V.6, no.7 [lacks imprint]
43p. 20½cm.
1. Masonry.

Schomburg, Arthur Alfonso, 1874-1938
M811.1 Wheatley, Phillis, *afterwards* Phillis Peters, 1753?-1784.
W56po ... Poems and letters; first collected edition, ed. by Chas. Fred. Heartman; with an appreciation by Arthur A. Schomburg. New York, C. F. Heartman [1915]
111 p. incl. front. (port.) 24½cm. (*Verso of half-title:* Heartman's historical series, no. 8)
At head of title: Phillis Wheatley (Phillis Peters)
No. 20 of 350 copies printed on Ben Day paper.
I. Heartman, Charles Frederick, 1883- II. Schomburg, Arthur Alfonso, 1874-
15-22732
Library of Congress PS866.W5 1915
(36b1)

Jamaica
M325 Scholes, Theophilus E Samuel, 1856-1906.
Sch6g Glimpses of the ages; or, The "superior" and "inferior" races, so-called, discussed in the light of science and history, by Theophilus E. Samuel Scholes ... London, J. Long, 1905-08.
2 v. 22½cm.
~~Vol. 2 wanting in L. C.~~
1. Ethnology. 2. Race problems. I. Title.
6-5684 Revised
Library of Congress CB195.S3
(r33b2)

Puerto Rico
M864 Schomburg, Arthur Alfonso, 1874-1938.
Sch6 Placido; an epoch in Cuba's struggle for liberty. Reprinted from The New Centure. Norfolk, Va., Dec. 25, 1909.
Inscribed: "To A.B. Spingarn Esq. Many thanks for 'Darkwaters'.
1. Valdes, Gabriel de la Concepcion, 1809-1844.

Schon, James Frederick.
Nigeria
M966.9 Crowther, Samuel Adjai, 1806-1894.
C88j Journals of the Rev. James Frederick Schon and Mr. Samuel Crowther, who, with the sanction of her majesty's government, accompanied the expedition up the Niger in 1841 in behalf of the church missionary society. With appendices and map. London, Hatchard and sons, 1842.
xxii, 393p. map. 20½cm.

Panama
M327.73 Schollianos, Alva.
Sc65 Call to greatness; shaping recommendations into programs of action. New York, William-Frederick Press, 1963.
viii, 191 p. 23 cm. (*His* Prospects for America, 2)
1. U. S.—Pol. & govt.—1945- 2. U. S.—For. rel.—1945- I. Title.
E743.S37 327.73 61-18292
Library of Congress (5)

Schomburg, Arthur Alfonso, 1874-1938.
M304 Racial integrity; a plea for the establishment of a chair of
P19 Negro history in our schools and colleges, etc. Read before
v.5, no.18 the teachers' summer class at Cheney Institute, July 1913. [n. p.] A. V. Bernier [1913?]
19 p. 23 cm. (Negro Society for Historical Research. Occasional paper no. 3)
"To A.B. Spingarn with highest regards. From a Schomburg
1. ~~Negroes—Hist.~~ 2. Negro literature. I. Title. II. Series.
E185.5.N4 no. 3 48-32619*
Library of Congress (1)

The school comes to the farmer.
MB9 Campbell, Thomas Monroe, 1883-
C154 The school comes to the farmer; the autobiography of T. M. Campbell, with foreword by Jackson Davis. Illus. with photographs. New York, Longmans, Green, 1947.
7-64p. illus. 18½cm.

Puerto Rico
M864 Schomburg, Arthur Alfonso, 1874-1938
Sch6b A bibliographical checklist of American Negro poetry, comp. by Arthur A. Schomburg. New York, C. F. Heartman, 1916.
57 p. 25cm. (*Added t.-p.:* Bibliographica americana; a series of monographs ed. by Charles F. Heartman. vol. II)
Printed on one side of leaf only.
"Bibliography of the poetical works of Phillis Wheatley (copyrighted by Charles F. Heartman) reprinted from Heartman's 'Phillis Wheatley (Phillis Peters)';": p. 47-57.
Poetry-Bibl.
~~1. Negro poetry (American)—Bibl.~~ 2. Wheatley, Phillis, afterwards Phillis Peters, 1753?-1784—Bibl. I. Heartman, Charles Frederick, 1883-
(over)
17-7194
Library of Congress Z1231.P7S3
(a40b1)

Puerto Rico
M864 Schomburg, Arthur Alfonso, 1874-1938.
Sch6s Some interesting facts [program notes].
Contents: Early Negro bands. -Some notable colored men from the West Indies. Alessandro de Medici, Duke of Florence and Benvenuto Cellini.
(In: Business and Professional Men's Forum, Inc. Program of second annual entertainment and dance. New York, 1936. 27cm.)
I. Business and Professional Men's Forum, Inc. New York. 1. Bands(music). 2. West Indies-Biography.

Ghana The school days of Shango Salomon.
M896.3 Tetteh-Lartey, A. C. V. B
T29s The school days of Shango Salomon. Cambridge, University Press, 1965.
78p. illus. 18cm.

M026 Schomburg, Arthur Alfonso, 1874-1938, comp.
Sch64 Exhibition catalogue, first annual exhibition of books, manuscripts, paintings, engravings, sculptures, et cetera, by The Negro Library Association at the Carlton Avenue Young Men's Christian Association, Brooklyn, August 7 to 16, 1918 ... Compiled by Arthur A. Schomburg ... [New York, The Poole Press Association Printers, 1918]
Continued on next card.

Schomburg, Arthur Alfonso, 1874- 1938
American Negro academy, *Washington, D. C.*
M06 Papers of the American Negro academy ... read at the nine-
Am3 teenth annual meeting of the American Negro academy ...
no.18, Washington, D. C., December 28th and 29th, 1915. [Washing-
19 ton, 1916]
78 p. 22cm. (Occasional papers, no. 18/19)
CONTENTS.—The sex question and race segregation, by A. H. Grimke.—Message of San Domingo to the African race, by T. G. Steward.—Status of the free Negro prior to 1860, by L. M. Hershaw.—Economic contribution by the Negro to America, by A. A. Schomberg [!]—The status of the free Negro from 1860 to 1870, by William Pickens.—American Negro bibliography of the year, by J. W. Cromwell.
1. Negroes—Societies. 2. Negroes—Bibl. I. Grimke, Archibald Henry, 1849-1930. II. Steward, Theophilus Gould, 1843- III. Hershaw, Lafayette M. IV. Schomburg, Arthur Alfonso, 1874- V. Pickens, William, 1881- VI. Cromwell, John Wesley, 1846-
(r42b2) 16-17783 Revised
Library of Congress E185.5.A51 no. 18/19
——— Copy 2. E185.5.A525

A school history for Western Nigeria.
Nigeria
M909 Adetoro, J E
Ad36 A school history for Western Nigeria. Book I. London, Macmillan and Co., 1964.
195p. illus. 18½cm.

Schroedinger, Erwin, 1887-

Gold Coast M966.7 Ar5h
Armattoe, Raphael Ernest Grail. -1954
Homage to three great men-Schweitzer, Schroedinger, De Gennaro, by Dr. R.E.G. Armattoe. Reprinted from "The Londonderry Sentinel, of 30th January, 1st February, and 3rd February, 1945., p. 1-11.

M335.4 Sc8st
Schuyler, George Samuel, 1895-
Stalin's blueprint for a Soviet Black Belt in the U.S.A.

pp. 3-9. maps. 23cm.
In: Plain Talk, vol. 9, no. 9, June 1947, pp. 3-9.

1. Communism. I. Title.

Schwarze fanfare.

Ghana MB9 N65s
Nkrumah, Kwame, 1909-
Schwarze fanfare. München, Paul List Verlag, 1958.

268p. 18½cm.

1. Ghana. I. Title.

M813.08 Sch81
Schulman, L M , ed.
Come out the wilderness. New York, Popular Library [1965]

125p. 18cm.
White editor.
Partial contents.- Come out the wilderness, by James Baldwin.- The summer fire, by Owen Dodson.- The sky is gray, by Ernest J. Gaines.- Almos a man, by Richard Wright.- The necessary knocking at the door, by Ann Petry.
(Over)

MB9 V37s
Schuyler, George Samuel, 1895-
The Van Vechten revolution. Reprinted from Phylon, fourth quarter, 1950.

8p. 23cm.

1. Van Vechten, Carl, 1880-

Die schwarze nation (Negro liberation).

M331 H35n2
Haywood, Harry, 1898-
Die schwarze nation (Negro liberation). Lager und Kamp der Neger in den U.S.A. Berlin, Dietx, 1952.

296p. chart. 20½cm.

MB9 Sc87
Schuyler, George Samuel, 1895-
Black and conservative; the autobiography of George S. Schuyler. New Rochelle, N. Y., Arlington House [1966]
362 p. 22 cm.

Portrait of author on book jacket.

I. Title.

PN4874.S35A3 070.10924 (B) 66-23140

Library of Congress [3]

Schuyler, Josephine, joint author.

M154 Sc89
Schuyler, Philippa Duke.
Kingdom of dreams, by Philippa and Josephine Schuyler. [1st ed.] New York, R. Speller [1966]
ix, 217 p. illus. 23 cm.
Bibliography: p. 215-217.

1. Dreams. I. Schuyler, Josephine, joint author. II. Title.

BF1078.S35 154.63 66-16970

Library of Congress [3]

M811.08 Sc8
Schwarzer bruder; lyrik Amerikanischer neger; gedichte, spirituals, work songs, protest-lieder. Enlisch und Deutsch. Leipzig, Verlag Philipp Reclam [1966]

206p. 17cm.
"For Arthur - Sincerely, Langston. New York, August 25, 1966. See pages 37-59."

1. Poetry. I. Hughes, Langston, 1902-1967.

M813.5 Sc8b
Schuyler, George Samuel, 1895-
Black no more; being an account of the strange and wonderful workings of science in the land of the free, A. D. 1933-1940, by George S. Schuyler. New York, The Macaulay company [°1931]
ix p., 1 l., 250 p. 19½cm.

I. Title.

Library of Congress PZ3.S3972Bl 31-2174
——— Copy 2.
Copyright A 33252 [3]

MB9 Sc8a
Schuyler, Philippa Duke, 1932-1967
Adventures in black and white. Foreword by Deems Taylor. [1st ed.] New York, R. Speller [1960]
302 p. illus. 22 cm.
An account of the author's travels in sixty countries.

1. Voyages and travel—1951- I. Title.

ML417.S42A3 927.8 60-9609 ‡

Library of Congress [10]

811.08 Sc9
Schwarzer orpheus, moderne dichtung Afrikanischer völker beider hemisphären. Ausgewählt und übertragen von Janheinz Jahn. München, Charl Hanser Verlag, 1954.

193p. 23cm.

1. Poetry - Collections.

M973.9 F46 No.17
Schuyler, George Samuel, 1895-
Fifty years of progress in Negro journalism. Pittsburgh, Pittsburgh Courier, 1950.

7p. port. 24cm. (Fifty years of progress)

1. Journalism. I. Series.

U.S. M960 Sch89
Schuyler, Philippa Duke 1932-1967
Jungle saints; Africa's heroic Catholic missionaries. [Rome] Herder [1963]

223p. photos. 21cm.
"To Arthur Spingarn with sincere regards and profound respect, from Philippa Schuyler, 12/12/63."

1. Catholic Church in Africa. 2. Missions-Africa. 3. Catholic Church - Missions. I. Title.

Schweitzer, Albert, 1875-

Gold Coast M966.7 Ar5h
Armattoe, Raphael Ernest Grail. -1954.
Homage to three great men- Schweitzer, Schroedinger, De Gennaro, by D. R.E. Armattoe. Reprinted from "The Londonderry Sentinel, of 30th January, 1st February, and 3rd February, 1945, pp. 1-11.

M813.5 Sc8s
Schuyler, George Samuel, 1895-
Slaves today; a story of Liberia, by George S. Schuyler. New York, Brewer, Warren & Putnam, 1931.
3 p. l., 5-290 p. 19½cm.

1. Slavery in Liberia—Fiction. I. Title.

Library of Congress PZ3.S3972Sl 31—32949
——— Copy 2.
Copyright A 44840 [37c1]

M154 Sc89
Schuyler, Philippa Duke, 1932-1967
Kingdom of dreams, by Philippa and Josephine Schuyler. [1st ed.] New York, R. Speller [1966]
ix, 217 p. illus. 23 cm.
Bibliography: p. 215-217.
"To Mr. Moon, hoping he will like our book and wishing him sweet dreams forever. The authors, Josephine & Philippa Schuyler".

1. Dreams. I. Schuyler, Josephine, joint author. II. Title.

BF1078.S35 154.63 66-16970

Library of Congress [3]

Science-Addresses, essays, lectures.

M500 M36n
Maryland. Morgan State College, *Baltimore.*
The Negro in science, by the Calloway Hall editorial committee: Julius H. Taylor, editor [and others. Baltimore, Morgan State College Press [1955]
viii, 192 p. illus. 26 cm.
Includes bibliographies.

1. Science—Addresses, essays, lectures. 2. Negro scientists. I. Taylor, Julius H., ed. II. Title.

Q171.M312 504 55—63107

Library of Congress [56e2]

M323 Sch9
Schuyler, George Samuel, 1895-
Some unsweet truths about race prejudice.

Pp. 89-106. 24cm.
In: Schmalhausen, Samuel D., ed. Behold America. New York, Farrar and Rinehart, 1931.

1. Race problems.

M910 Sc8
Schuyler, Philippa Duke, 1932-1967
Who killed the Congo? New York, Devin-Adair Co., 1962.
310 p. illus. 21 cm.

1. Congo (Leopoldville) I. Title.

DT652.S8 967.5 62-13468 ‡

Library of Congress [10]

Science - Social aspects.

M338.9 G92s
International Conference on Science in the Advancement of New States, *Rehovot, Israel, 1960.*
Science and the new nations, proceedings. Edited by Ruth Gruber. New York, Basic Books [1961]
xv, 314 p. illus., ports. 24 cm.
Sponsored by the Weizmann Institute of Science.

1. Underdeveloped areas. 2. Technical assistance. 3. Science—Social aspects. I. Gruber, Ruth, 1911- ed. II. Title.

HC60.I 545 1960 338.9 61-11992

Library of Congress [15]

Science, men, and money.
M338.9 G92s Lewis, William Arthur, 1915-
Science, men, and money.

Pp. 24-33.
In: Science and the new nations, edited by Ruth Gruber. 1961.

M813.5 Sco8 Scott, Anne, 1900-
George Sampson Brite, by Anne Scott. Boston, Meador publishing company, 1939.

154 p. 20½cm.

I. Title.

39-32045

Library of Congress PZ7.S414Ge
——— Copy 2.
Copyright A 134885 [3]

M811.5 Sc81 Scott, Emory Elrage.
Lyrics of the Southland, by Emory Elrage Scott. [Chicago, Printed by Wilton press, °1913]

3 p. l., 9-93 p. 18cm. $1.00

I. Title. I. Poetry

Library of Congress PS3537.C88L8 1913 13-8600
Copyright A 343964

M614 R66sc Science and Christian ethics...
Roman, Charles Victor, 1864-1934.
Science and Christian ethics...n.p.,[1912].

58p. 20cm.

Contents: -. Part I. Statement of principles.--. Part II. Religion a necessity to man...--. Part III. Racial self respect and racial antagonism.

Scott, Dred.

M815.4 D47tw Douglass, Frederick, 1817-1895.
Two speeches by Frederick Douglass; one on West India emancipation, delivered at Canandaigua, Aug. 4th, and the other on the Dred Scott decision, delivered in New York, on the occasion of the anniversary of the American abolition society, May 1857. Rochester, N. Y., C. P. Dewey, printer [1857]

46 p. 22cm.
The speeches are paged continuously.
The second speech has a half-title which reads: "The Dred Scott decision; speech delivered in part, at the anniversary of the American abolition society, held in New York, May 14th, 1857."

1. Slavery in the U. S.—Emancipation. 2. Scott, Dred. I. American abolition society.

A 17-1159

Title from Harvard Univ. Printed by L. C.

M341.4 Sc81 Scott, James Alexander, 1864-
The law of interstate rendition, erroneously referred to as interstate extradition; a treatise on the arrest and surrender of fugitives from the justice of one state to another; the removal of federal prisoners from one district to another; and the exemption of persons from service of civil process; and with an appendix of the statutes of the states and territories on fugitives from justice, by James A. Scott ... Chicago, Ill., S. Hight, 1917.

xiv, 584 p. 24cm.

1. Extradition—U. S. I. Title. II. Title: Interstate rendition.

Library of Congress 17—20646
——— Copy 2.
Copyright A 470090 [a40b1]

Science and the new nations.

M338.9 G92s Imoke, S E
Nigeria.

Pp. 33-34.
In: Science and the new nations, edited by Ruth Gruber. 1961.

M814.4 W27s Scott, Emmett Jay, 1873-1957
Booker T. Washington, builder of a civilization, by Emmett J. Scott and Lyman Beecher Stowe; illustrated from photographs. Garden City, N.Y., Doubleday, Page & company, 1916.

xx, 331, [1]p; front., plates, ports. 24½cm.
Inscribed by author: To Capt. Arthur B. Spingarn with the cordial regards of his friend...

1. Washington, Booker Taliaferro, 1859?-1915.
I. Stowe, Lyman Beecher, 1880- joint author.

M370 Sc8f Scott, John Irving E
Finding my way. Boston, Meador [1949]

344 p. 21 cm.
Includes "Recommended readings."

1. Students. I. Title.

LB2343.S38 371.8 49-11682*

Library of Congress [15]

Science and the new nations.

M338.9 G92s International Conference on Science in the Advancement of New States, *Rehovot, Israel, 1960.*
Science and the new nations, proceedings. Edited by Ruth Gruber. New York, Basic Books [1961]

xv, 314 p. illus., ports. 24 cm.
Sponsored by the Weizmann Institute of Science.

1. Underdeveloped areas. 2. Technical assistance. 3. Science—Social aspects. I. Gruber, Ruth, 1911- ed. II. Title.

HC60.I 545 1960 338.9 61-11992

Library of Congress [15]

M325 Sco84m Scott, Emmett Jay, 1873-1957
... Negro migration during the war, by Emmett J. Scott ... New York [etc.] Oxford university press, 1920.

v p., 2 l., 3-189 p. 25cm. (Preliminary economic studies of the war, ed. by David Kinley ... no. 16)
At head of title: Carnegie endowment for international peace. Division of economics and history.
Bibliography: p. 175-183.

1. Negroes. 2. European war, 1914-1918—Economic aspects—U. S. I. Title. II. Title: Migration during the war, Negro.

20—9134

Library of Congress HC56.P7 no. 16
[41v2]

M370. Sc81 Scott, John Irving E.
Living with others; a foundation guidance program for junior high and upper elementary grades, by J. Irving E. Scott ... Boston, Meador publishing company, 1939.

110 p. incl. diagr., form. 21cm.
Includes bibliographies.

1. Education of children. I. Title.

39—10724

Library of Congress LB1027.S37
[42d1] 370.15

Scientists.

M500 M36n Maryland. Morgan State College, *Baltimore.*
The Negro in science, by the Calloway Hall editorial committee: Julius H. Taylor, editor [and others. Baltimore] Morgan State College Press [1955]

viii, 192 p. illus. 26 cm.
Includes bibliographies.

1. Science—Addresses, essays, lectures. 2. Negro scientists. I. Taylor, Julius H., ed. II. Title.

Q171.M312 504 55—63107

Library of Congress [56e2]

M330. Sco84 Scott, Emmett Jay, 1873-1957
Scott's official history of the American Negro in the world war, by Emmett J. Scott ... a complete and authentic narration, from official sources, of the participation of American soldiers of the Negro race in the world war for democracy ... a full account of the war work organizations of colored men and women and other civilian activities, including the Red cross, the Y. M. C. A., the Y. W. C. A. and the War camp community service, with official summary of treaty of peace and league of nations covenant. Prefaced with highest trib-

(Continued on next card)

19—11646

[45k1]

M378 Sc8n Scott, John Irving E
Negro students & their colleges. Boston, Meador Pub. Co. [1949]

179 p. 21 cm.

1. Negroes—Education. 2. Universities and colleges—U. S.—Direct. I. Title.

L901.S48 378.73 49-6113*

Library of Congress [15]

Sclaverei und freiheit.

M315.4 D739as Douglass, Frederick, 1817-1895.
Sclaverei und freiheit. Autobiographie von Frederick Douglass. Aus dem Englischen übertragen von Ottifie Uffing. Hamburg, Hoffman und Campe, 1860.

xiv, [2] 366p. 18cm.

M330 Sco84 Scott, Emmett Jay, 1873-1957 Scott's official history of the American Negro in the world war ... (Card 2)
utes to the American Negro by Hon. Newton D. Baker ... Gen. John J. Pershing ... and the late Theodore Roosevelt. [Chicago, Homewood press, °1919]

511, [1] p. front., illus., plates, ports. 23½cm.

1. European war, 1914-1918—Negroes. I. Title: American Negro in the world war.

19—11646

Library of Congress D639.N4S8
[45b1]

Bahamas M821 C89 Scott, Margaret Joyce
The returning, [poem].

(In: Culmer, Jack, comp. A book of Bahamian verse. 2d ed. London, J. Culmer, 1948. 23cm. p.40.)

M813.5 Sco8c Scott, Anne, 1900-
Case 999, a Christmas story. Boston, Meador Pub. Co. [1953]

27 p. illus. 21 cm.

I. Title.

PZ3.S42352Cas 53-39587 ‡

Library of Congress [3]

Scott, Emmett Jay, 1873-1957, ed.

M814.4 W272t Washington, Booker Taliaferro, 1859?-1915, *ed.*
Tuskegee & its people: their ideals and achievements, ed. by Booker T. Washington. New York, D. Appleton and company, 1905.

xiv, 354 p. front., plates, ports. 21cm.
The volume here presented has been edited by Mr. Emmett J. Scott, executive secretary of the Tuskegee institute. The task of editing which the principal had expected to perform has been so well done that it has only been necessary to review the manuscript after its preparation for the publishers, and to forego the strict editorial revisioning planned. *cf.* General introduction.
CONTENTS.—I. The school and its purposes.—II. Autobiographies by graduates of the school.

1. Tuskegee, Ala. Normal and industrial institute. I. Scott, Emmett Jay, 1873- ed. II. Title.

5—17294

Library of Congress LC2851.T82W2
[44j1]

M808.4 Sc8m Scott, Nathan Alexander, 1925-
Modern literature and the religious frontier. [1st ed.] New York, Harper [1958]

138 p. 22 cm.
Includes bibliography.

1. Religion and literature. 2. Literature, Modern—20th cent.—Hist. & crit. I. Title.

PN1077.S39 809.04 58-7476 ‡

Library of Congress [25]

M808.4 Sc8

Scott, Nathan Alexander, 1925-
Rehearsals of discomposure; alienation and reconciliation in modern literature: Franz Kafka, Ignazio Silone, D. H. Lawrence [and] T. S. Eliot. New York, King's Crown Press, 1952.
xv, 294 p. 21 cm.
Bibliography: p. [273]-288.

1. Religion and literature. 2. Literature, Modern—20th cent.—Hist. & crit. I. Title.

PN49.S38 809.04 52—13349
Library of Congress [58b7]

M808.4 Sc8t

Scott, Nathan Alexander, 1925-
The tragic vision and the Christian faith. New York, Association Press [1957]
346 p. 21 cm. (A Haddam House book)
Includes bibliography.

1. Religion in literature. 2. Tragic, The. 3. Christianity—Philosophy. I. Title.

PN49.S34 801 57—11604 ‡
Library of Congress [58x10]

MB9 L93s

Scott, Neil.
Joe Louis, a picture story of his life. New York, Greenberg [1947]
[126] p. illus., ports. 21cm.

1. Louis, Joe, 1914-
GV1132.L6S35 927.9683 47-5025*
© Greenberg: Publisher; 25Jun47; A14096.

Library of Congress [15]

M263 Sc8s

Scott, Timothy Dwight, 1860-
Sunday, The Christian Sabbath, a brief discussion of the Sunday question, by the Reverend Timothy D. Scott... Springfield, Ohio, The Whyte printing co. [n.d.]
137p. front(port) 20½cm.
1. Sabbath
I. Title

Jamaica MB9 Se2s

Scott., William J., ed.
Seacole, Mary.
Wonderful adventures of Mrs. Seacole in many lands. Edited by W.J.S. With an introductory preface by W.H. Russell... London, J. Blackwood, 1857.
xii, 200 p. double front. 17cm.

Largely devoted to an account of the author's experiences as a sutler during the Crimean war.

M290 Sc8

Scott-Bey, R
The door to God-Allah's kingdom is open, who will enter? Broklyn, N.Y. Moorish Science Temple, the Divine and National Movement of North America, Inc., n.d.

6p. 22cm.
Inscribed by author.

1. Moorish Science Temple, the Divine and National Movement of North America, Inc.

M310 Sco8

Scott's blue book a standard classified business and service directory of greater Chicago's colored citizens' commercial, industrial, professional, religious and other activities ... Chicago, Ill., Scott's business and directory service, °19
v. illus. (incl. ports.) 28cm.
Library has: 1937

1. Negroes—Chicago. 2. Chicago—Direct. 3. Negroes—Direct.
40-16153
Library of Congress F548.9.N3S4
——— 2d set.
Copyright [2] 325.26097731

The Scottsboro boys.

M304 P19 v.1, no.15

Herndon, Angelo.
The Scottsboro boys, Four Freed! Five to go. New [York, Published by the workers Library Publishers. 1937]
15p. 15cm.

M343.3 H43s

Scottsboro case.
Herndon, Angelo, 1913-
The Scottsboro boys, four freed! five to go! New York, Workers Library Publishers, 1937.

15p. 17cm.

M304 P19 v. 1, no.16

Scottsboro case.
[International Labor Defense]
Mr. President: Free the Scottsboro boys ! [New York, International Labor Defense, 1934.]

3-30p. 19cm.

M304 P19 v.1,no.13

Scottsboro case.
North, Joseph.
Lynching Negro children in Southern courts (The Scottsboro case). New York, issued by International Labor Defense [n.d.]
15p. illus. 15cm.

MB9 P27s

Scottsboro case.
Patterson, Haywood, 1913-or 14 - 1952.
Scottsboro boy, by Haywood Patterson [and] Earl Conrad. [1st ed.] Garden City, N.Y., Doubleday, 1950.

vii,309p. 22cm.

M304 P19 v.1, no.17

Scottsboro case.
Scottsboro Defense Committee.
Scottsboro: The shame of America. The true story and the true meaning of this famous case. New York, Scottsboro Defense Committee, 1936
30p. illus, 15cm.

M304 P19 v.1, no.17

Scottsboro Defense Committee.
Scottsboro: The shame of America. The true story and the true meaning of this famous case. New York, Scottsboro Defense Committee, 1936
30p. illus, 15cm.

1. Scottsboro case

Scottsboro limited.

M811.5 H87s

Hughes, Langston, 1902-
Scottsboro limited; four poems and a play in verse by Langston Hughes; with illustrations by Prentiss Taylor. New York city, The Golden stair press, 1932.
[20] p. illus. 24½cm.

I. Title.

Library of Congress PS3515.U274S3 1932 32-19487
Copyright AA 99052 [3] 811.5

The scourging of a race.

M252 J63⁴

Johnson, William Bishop, 1858-
The scourging of a race, and other sermons and addresses by W. Bishop Johnson ... Washington, Beresford, printer, 1904.
viii, 228 p. front. (port.) 19½cm.

1. Baptists—Sermons. 2. Sermons, American. I. Title.
4-26231
Library of Congress BX6452.J6 [a44c1]

M813.5 Sc2w

Screen, Robert Martin
We can't run away from here. New York, Vantage Press, 1958.

55p. 21cm.
Portrait of author on book jacket.

I. Title.

M811.08 S16

The Scribes, *St. Louis.*
Sing, laugh, weep; a book of poems by the Scribes. With illustrations by Theopolus Williams. St. Louis, Press publishing co., 1944.
126 p. illus. 20cm.

1. American poetry—20th cent. 2. American literature—Missouri—St. Louis. I. Title. 3. Poetry.
44—9876
Library of Congress PS572.S2S35 [46d1] 811.5082

Scriptology.

Brit.Guiana M821 M36s

Martin, Egbert, 1862-1890.
Scriptology. A series of four short narratives by Leo. Demorara, Printed by Baldwin & Co., 1885.

58p. 18cm.

Sculpture.

M730 M96e

Murray, Freeman Henry Morris.
... Emancipation and the freed in American sculpture; a study in interpretation, by Freeman Henry Morris Murray, introduction by John Wesley Cromwell ... Washington, D. C., The author, 1916.
xxviii p., 2 l., 239, [1] p. plates. 19 cm. (Black folk in art series)
"This monograph is chiefly the expansion of papers which were read as lectures ... at the Summer school and Chautauqua of the National religious training school at Durham, N. C., in 1913. Some of the matter has also appeared in the A. M. E. church review."—Pref.

1. Negroes—Iconography. 2. Sculpture, American. I. Title.
19—2859
Library of Congress E185.89.I 2M9 [36d1]

The sea at dauphin.

St. Lucia M822.91 W14s

Walcott, Derek
The sea at dauphin. [Jamaica] Extra-Mural Dept., University College of the West Indies, 1958.

23p. 21cm. (Caribbean plays no. 4)

I. Title.

Sea-power.
Guadeloupe
M325
C16m
Candace, Gratien, 1873–
... La marine de la France. Marine militaire.—Marine marchande. Paris, Payot, 1938.
2 p. l., [7]–190 p., 1 l. incl. tables. 22½cm. (Bibliothèque politique et économique)
1. France—Navy. 2. Merchant marine—France. 3. Sea-power. I. Title.
New York. Public library for Library of Congress A 39-675 [2]

Seamen.
M359
N331
1948
Nelson, Dennis Denmark, 1907–
The integration of the Negro into the United States Navy, 1776–1947, with a brief historical introduction. [Washington] 1948.
1 v. (various pagings) illus., ports. 27 cm.
Cover title.
"A monograph from the thesis by the same title submitted to the Department of Sociology, Howard University, in partial fulfillment of the requirements for the degree of master of arts."
Seal of Navy Department, United States of America, on cover.
"Navexos–P–526."
Bibliography: p. 209–212.
1. U. S. Navy—Negroes. 2. Negroes as seamen. I. U. S. Navy Dept. II. Title.
E185.63.N4 1948 325.260973 48–46195*
Library of Congress [48c2]

Seattle
M979
R24r
Reddick, Lawrence Dunbar, 1910– ed.
Race relations on the Pacific coast.
New York, Journal of educational sociology, 1945.
129–208p. 23cm.
Special issue of The Journal of educational sociology, November 1945.
Partial contents: -The New race-relations frontier, by L.D. Reddick. -Seattle, by R. W. O'Brien.

Jamaica
M39
Se2e
Seacole, Mary. -1881.
Wonderful adventures of Mrs. Seacole in many lands. Edited by W. J. S. With an introductory preface by W. H. Russell ... London, J. Blackwood, 1857.
xii, 200 p. double front. 17cm.
Largely devoted to an account of the author's experiences as a sutler during the Crimean war.
1. Crimean war, 1853–1856—Personal narratives. I. S[tewart], W. J., ed. II. Title.
H. E. Huntington library for Library of Congress A 25–224

Sean Pendragon requiem.
M811.5
J64s
Johnston, Percy Edward, 1930–
Sean Pendragon requiem. Poetical texture by Percy Edward Johnston. Artistical texture by William A. White. [1st ed.] New York, Dasein-Jupiter Hammon [1964]
27 p. illus. 18 cm. (Black star book, no. B–4)
1. Kennedy, John Fitzgerald, Pres. U. S., 1917–1963—Poetry. I. Title.
PS3560.O39S4 811.54 64–56956
Library of Congress [2]

M810.8
C884
1944
Seaver, Edwin, 1900– ed.
Cross section ... A collection of new American writing.
New York, L. B. Fischer, 1944.
559p. 22cm.
Partial contents: The man who lived underground, by Richard Wright. -Low sky, by Carl Ruthven Offord. -Three poems, by Langston Hughes. -Flying home, by Ralph Ellison.

Seafaring life.
M39
D34p
Dean, Harry, 1864–
The Pedro Gorino; the adventures of a Negro sea-captain in Africa and on the seven seas in his attempts to found an Ethiopian empire; an autobiographical narrative by Captain Harry Dean, with the assistance of Sterling North. Boston and New York, Houghton Mifflin company, 1929.
xvi, 262 p. illus. 22½cm.
1. Seafaring life. 2. Voyages and travels. 3. Africa, South. I. North, Sterling, 1906– II. Title.
29–6322
Library of Congress G530.D4 [a44u1]

The search for America.
M323
M45
Smith, Huston, ed.
The search for America. Edited by Huston Smith, with Richard T. Heffron and Eleanor Wieman Smith. [Englewood Cliffs, N. J.] Prentice-Hall [1959]
176 p. 21 cm. (Spectrum paperbacks, S-9)
"Based on the National educational television series [The search for America]"
1. U. S.—Civilization—Addresses, essays, lectures. 2. U. S.—Relations (general) with foreign countries. I. Title.
E169.1.S62 917.3 59–15720 ‡
Library of Congress [30]

M810.8
C284
1945
Seaver, Edwin, 1900–
Cross section... A collection of new American writing. 1944.
New York, L.B. Fischer, 1945.
xi, 362p. 22cm.
Partial contents: Three poems, by Gwendolyn Brooks. -Middle passage, by Robert E. Hayden. -Early days in Chicago, by Richard Wright.

Trinidad
M700
H55
Sealy, Clifford
Art and the community.
Pp. 55–68.
In: Hill, Errol G., ed. The artist in West Indian society. Mona, Jamaica, University of the West Indies, 1963?.

Search light on the seventh wonder.
M220.7
B69s
Boyd, Boston Napoleon Bonapart, 1860–
Search light on the seventh wonder; x-ray and search light on the Bible with natural science; discoveries of the twentieth century, by Bonaparte Napoleon Boyd. Greenville, N. C., 1905.
260 p. front. (port.) 21cm.
I. Title.
Library of Congress BS530.B6 6-6894 Revised
Copyright A 129446 [r25g2]

Sebree, Charles, illus.
M811.5
C891
Cullen, Countee, 1903–
The lost zoo (a rhyme for the young, but not too young) by Christopher Cat and Countee Cullen, with illustrations by Charles Sebree. New York and London, Harper & brothers [°1940]
6 p. l., 72 p., 1 l. col. front., col. plates. 24cm.
Illustrated lining-papers in colors.
"First edition."
1. Sebree, Charles, illus. II. Title.
40–34870
Library of Congress PZ8.3.C889Lo [45k1]

Trinidad
M822.91
H55
Sealy, Clifford.
The professor.
Pp. 119–148.
In: Hill, Erroll G., ed. Caribbean plays, v.2. Mona, Jamaica, Mona, University of the West Indies, 1965.

Seare vermelha.
Brazil
M869.3
Am1s
Amado, Jorge, 1912–
Seare vermelha. Capa de Clóvis Graciano. São Paulo, Livraria Martins Editôra, 1946.
319p. 22cm. (Obras v. 12)

Secession.
M975.6
B69n
Boykin, James H
North Carolina in 1861. New York, Bookman Associates [1961]
237 p. 21 cm.
Includes bibliography.
1. North Carolina—Soc. condit. 2. Secession. 3. North Carolina—Pol. & govt.—1775–1865.
F258.B6 975.603 61–15678 ‡
Library of Congress [2]

Jamaica
M823.91
Sa3w
Sealey, Karl,
My fathers before me.
pp. 169–175
In Andrew Salkey's West Indian Stories. 1960.

Season of adventure.
Barbados
M823
L18s
Lamming, George, 1927–
Season of adventure. London, M. Joseph [1960]
366 p. 21 cm.
Portrait of author on book jacket.
I. Title.
PZ4.L232Se 60–52320 ‡
Library of Congress [2]

Sechuana poetry.
South Africa
M896.1
Sch16
Schapera, Isaac, 1905– ed. and tr.
Praise-poems of Tswana chiefs. Translated and edited with an introd. and notes, by I. Schapera. Oxford, Clarendon Press, 1965.
vi, 255 p. geneal. tables, map. 23 cm. (Oxford library of African literature)
Bibliography: p. [246]–247.
1. Sechuana poetry. 2. Tswana (Bantu tribe)—Kings and rulers. I. Title.
PL8651.7.S3 896.3 65–8539
Library of Congress [2]

West Indies
M808.8
H839
Sealy, Karl
The sun was a slaver.
Pp. 117–120.
In: Howes, Barbara, ed. From the green Antilles. New York, Macmillan, 1966.

M910.
Se1
Seaton, Daniel P.
The Land of promise; or, The Bible land and its revelation. Illustrated with several engravings of some of the most important places in Palestine and Syria. By D. P. Seaton, D. D., M. D. Philadelphia, Pa., Publishing house of the A. M. E. church, 1895.
ix, 443 p. front. (port.) 16 pl., map. 24½cm.
1. Palestine—Descr. & trav. 2. Syria—Descr. & trav.
7–14411
Library of Congress DS107.S45 [38b1]

S. Africa
M968
P69s
Sechuana proverbs.
Plaatje, Solomon Tshekisho, 1878–1936.
Sechuana proverbs with literal translations and their European equivalents.
Diane tsa secoana le maele a sekgooa a a dumalanang naco. By Solomon T. Plaatje ... London, K. Paul, Trench, Trubner & co., ltd., 1916.
3 p. l., ix-xii, 98 p. front., ports. 12½ x 19 cm.

Senegal
M916.63 Seck, Charles Babacar
Se3 Goree guide touristique. [Dakar] Societe Africaine d'Editions et de Publications [1966]

46p. illus. 22cm.
"Bibliographie sommaire": p.45.

1. Goree, Senegal. I. Title.

The second round.

Gambia
M896.3 Peters, Lenrie, 1932-
P94s The second round. [London] Heinemann [1965]

192p. 19cm.

Secret societies.

M366.7 Dickson, Moses, 1824-
D56m Manual of the International order of twelve of Knights and daughters of Tabor containing general laws, regulations, ceremonies, drill and landmarks, by Moses Dickson. 11th ed. Glasgow, Mo., Published by the Moses Dickson Publishing Co., 1920.

376p. front. (port.) 19½cm.

Second Advent.

M232 Holley, Joseph Winthrop, 1874-
H72 Regnum montis and its contemporary; heralding the second coming of Christ in the decade, 1995-2005, and the end of the world of things material. New York, William-Frederick Press, 1958.

141 p. 23 cm.

1. Second Advent. I. Title.

BT885.H713 232.6 57-12740 ‡

Library of Congress [1]

...Secondary education for Negroes.

M370 Caliver, Ambrose, 1894-
C12m ... Secondary education for Negroes, by Ambrose Caliver ... Washington, U. S. Govt. print. off., 1933.
no.1

ix, 121 p. incl. tables, diagrs. 23cm. (U. S. Office of education. Bulletin, 1932, no. 17)

At head of title: United States Department of the interior. Harold L. Ickes, secretary. Office of education. William John Cooper, commissioner.
William John Cooper, director; Leonard V. Koos, associate director. National survey of secondary education. Monograph no. 7.

1. Negroes—Education. I. Cooper, William John, 1882-1935. II. Koos, Leonard Vincent, 1881- III. Title.

E 33—1447

U. S. Off. of educ. Library L111.A6 1932, no. 17
——— Copy 2. LA222.A14 no. 17
for Library of Congress [L111.A6 1932, no. 17]
[44u2] (370.6173)

Secret societies.

M366.1 Freemasons. Alabama. Grand Lodge. 1879-
F87a2 Proceedings. 1st-
Mobile [etc.] 18 -

v. 20½cm. annual
Place of publication varies.
See holdings card for proceedings in library.

Second American Caravan.

M810.8 The American caravan, a yearbook of American
Am29 literature...New York, The Macaulay company,
1928 1928.

xii, 872p. 24cm.
Title varies: The Second American Caravan.

Partial contents: Winter on earth, by Jean Toomer

The secret.

M89 Jones, Thomas Alfred, 1904-
J71 The secret. New York, Comet Press Books [1958]

127 p. 21 cm. (A Reflection book)
Autobiography.

1. Gambling—Washington, D. C. I. Title.

HV6721.W3J6 *332.68 174.6 58-14959 ‡

Library of Congress [3]

Secret societies.

M366.1 Freemasons. Cleveland. Excelsior Lodge No.11.
F87c34 History, constitution and by-laws... with the masonic directory of the City of Cleveland, of Prince Hall Lodges. The Lodge, 1926.

21p. 13½cm.

The second American revolution.

M323.4 Lewis, Anthony, 1927-
L58 Portrait of a decade; the second American revolution [by] Anthony Lewis and the New York times. New York, Random House [1964]

322 p. illus. 25 cm.
White author.
Partial contents.- A Negro assays the Negro mood, by James Baldwin.- Expalanation of the 'Black psyche', by John Oliver Killens.

1. Negroes—Civil rights. I. New York times. II. Title. III. Title: The second American revolution.

E185.61.L52 1964 323.40973 64-14832

Library of Congress [4-1]

British The secret ladder.
Guiana
M823.91 Harris, Wilson
H24s The secret ladder. London, Faber and Faber [1963]

127p. 19cm.

Secret societies.

M366.1 Freemasons. Connecticut. Grand Lodge.
F87c5 Proceedings. 1st- 1874-
Hartford [etc.] 1875-

v. 23cm. annual
Place of publication varies.
Proceedings were not printed for 1912, 1913.
See holdings card for proceedings in library.

Second April.

M811.5 Kaufman, Bob
K162s Second April. [San Francisco, City Lights Books, 1959]

6 fold l. 69x19cm fold. to 15x19cm.

I. Title.

Secret Societies.

M315.5 Bruce, John Edward, 1856-
B83 Prince Hall, the pioneer of Negro masonry.
No.6 Proofs of the legitimacy of Prince Hall masonry. by John Edard Bruce. New York, 1921.

12p. 17cm.

Secret societies.

M366.1 Freemasons. Delaware. Hiram Grand Lodge.
F87d2 Proceedings. 1st- 1850-
Wilmington [etc.] 18 -

v. 22cm. annual
See holdings card for proceedings. in library.

The second book of Negro spirituals.

M784 Johnson, James Weldon, 1871-
J63s The second book of negro spirituals, edited with an introduction by James Weldon Johnson; musical arrangements by J. Rosamond Johnson. New York, The Viking press, 1926.

189 p. 26 x 19½cm. $3.50

1. Negro songs. I. Johnson, J. Rosamond, 1873- II. Title: Spirituals.

26-27592

Library of Congress M1670.J672
——— Copy 2.
Copyright E 651256 [3-2]

Secret societies.

M366.5 Burrell, William Patrick, 1865-
B95 Twenty-five years history of the grand fountain of the united order of true reformers, 1881-1905. Illustrated. By W. P. Burrell and D. E. Johnson, Sr., Richmond, Va., 1909.

513p. front. ports. 22cm.

Secret societies.

M366.1 Freemasons. Illinois. Grand Lodge.
F87I3 Proceedings. 1st- 1867-
Chicago, 18 -

v. 23cm.
See holdings card for proceedings in library.

... Second report of the New York State Temporary commission on the condition...

M323.5 New York (*State*) *Temporary commission on the condition*
N42 *of the urban colored population.*
... Second report of the New York state Temporary commission on the condition of the colored urban population to the Legislature of the state of New York, February, 1939. Created by chapter 858, Laws of 1937, continued by Chapter 677, Laws of 1938. Albany, J. B. Lyon company, printers, 1939.

190 p. 23cm.
At head of title: Legislative document (1939) no. 69. State of New York.
1. Negroes—New York (State) 2. Negroes—New York (City) 3. Negroes—Employment. 4. Negroes—Health and hygiene. 5. Housing—New York (State) I. Title.

40-30459

Library of Congress E185.93.N56N472
[42c1] 325.2600747

Secret societies.

M366.7 Bush, A E
B96h History of the mosaic templars of America its founders and officials, edited by A. E. Bush and P. L. Dorman. Little Rock, Central printing company, 1924.

291p. front. plates. 19½cm.

Secret societies.

M366.1 Freemasons. Kentucky. Grand Lodge.
F87k3 Proceedings. 1st- 1867-
Louisville [etc.] 1867-

v. 22½cm. annual
Place of publication varies.
Proceedings of a special communication held Nov. 9,10, 1875 bound with 1875 bound with 1875 proceedings.
See holdings card for proceedings in library.

Secret societies.

M366.1 F87m4 Freemasons. Massachusetts. Prince Hall Grand Lodge.
Proceedings. 1st- [1791?]
17 -

v. 23cm. annual
Proceedings of special communications for 1908 and 1909 bound with 1909.
See holdings card for proceedings in library.

Secret societies.

M366.1 F87o5 Freemasons. Ontario. Grand Lodge.
Proceedings. 1st- 1874-
Windsor, 1874-

v 21cm. annual
See holdings card for proceedings in library.

Secret societies.

M366.3 W69o Wilson, Charles B.
The official manual and history of the Grand United Order of Odd Fellows in America... prepared by Charles B. Wilson. Philadelphia, George F. Washer, 1894.

357p. port. 20½cm.

Secret societies.

M366.1 F87m8 Freemasons. Missouri. Grand Lodge.
Proceedings. 1st- 1867-
St. Louis, 1867-

v. 22cm. annual
See holdings card for proceedings in library.
Special communication held Dec. 20, 1866 in St. Louis bound with the 1867 proceedings.

Secret societies.

M366.1 F87r Freemasons. Rhode Island. Grand Lodge.
Proceedings. 1st- 1876-
Providence, 1878-

v. 22cm annual
1st, 2nd, 3rd, proceedings published together with the constitution, by-laws, and rules of order.

See holdings card for proceedings in library.

Upper Volta Les secrets des sorciers noirs.

M966.25 D59s Dim Delobsom, A A.
... Les secrets des sorciers noirs. Avec une préface de Robert Randau [pseud.] ... Paris, Librairie Émile Nourry, 1934.

298 p., 1 l. illus., plates. 22½cm. (Collection science et magie. nº 5)

At head of title: Dim Delobsom A. A.
"Cet ouvrage a obtenu le Grand prix de l'Afrique occidentale française (1934)"

1. Magic—Africa. I. Arnaud, Robert, 1873- II. Title.

A C 35-2867

Title from N. Y. Pub. Libr. Printed by L. C.

[2]

Secret societies.

M366.1 F87n7 Freemasons. New York (State) Grand Lodge.
Proceedings. 1st - 1845-
New York, 18 -

v. 24, 20 22cm. annual
See holdings card for proceedings in library.

Secret societies.

M366.1 F87s Freemasons. South Carolina. Grand Lodge.
Proceedings. 1st- 1867-
Columbia, S.C., 18 -

v. 22cm. annual
See holdings card for proceedings in library.

M794 B56s The secrets of Spanish pool checkers.

Black, Clyde, 1912-
The secrets of Spanish pool checkers, also known as pool checkers or Polish minor checkers, by Clyde "Kingrow" Black and Archie "Checkerboard" Waters. New York [1948-

v. illus. 23 cm.

1. Checkers. I. Waters, Archie, 1918- joint author. II. Title.

GV1463.B57 794.2 48-19338*

Library of Congress [1]

Secret Societies.

M366.1 F87n7 Freemasons. New York (State). United Grand Lodge.
Constitution and Statutes. rev. New York, Tobitt & Bunce, printers, 1876.

43p. 18cm.

Secret societies.

M366.1 F87t5 Freemasons. Tennessee. Grand Lodge.
Proceedings. 1st- 1870-
Nashville, 18 -

v. 22½cm. annual
See holdings card for proceedings in library.

Sects-U.S.

M289.9 F27 Fauset, Arthur Huff, 1899-
... Black gods of the metropolis; Negro religious cults of the urban North, by Arthur Huff Fauset. Philadelphia, University of Pennsylvania press; London, H. Milford, Oxford university press, 1944.

x, 126 p. plates, ports. 23½cm. (Publications of the Philadelphia anthropological society. Vol. III)

Half-title: ... Brinton memorial series. [No. 2]
Issued also as thesis (PH. D.) University of Pennsylvania.
"A study of five Negro religious cults in the Philadelphia of today."—Pref.

1. Negroes—Religion. 2. Negroes—Philadelphia. 3. Sects—U. S. I. Title.

Library of Congress BR563.N4F3 1944 a 44—3761
[47x3] 289.9

Secret societies.

M366.1 F87o3 Freemasons. Ohio. Grand Lodge.
Proceedings. 1st- 1850-
Cleveland, 18 -

v. 22cm. annual.
Place of publication varies.
See holdings card for proceedings in library.

Secret societies.

M366.1 F87v Freemasons. Virginia. Grand Lodge.
Minutes. 1st- 1875-
Petersburg, 18 -

v. 22cm annual
Place of publication varies.
See holdings card for proceedings in library.

See how they play.

M785 G74 Goward, Gladys McFadden.
See how they play; a pictorial tour through the orchestra. New York, Exposition Press [1953]

50 p. illus. 21 cm.

1. Musical instruments—Juvenile literature. I. Title.

ML3930.A2G7 785 53-10540 ‡

Library of Congress [2]

Secret societies.

M366.1 F88o Freemasons. Ohio. Knights Templars. Grand Commandery.
Proceedings. 1st- 1871?-
Chillicothe, etc. 18 -

v. 23cm. annual
Place of publication varies.
Constitution, statutes, regulations and by-laws included in the 1875 proceedings.

Secret societies.

M366.1 F87w2 Freemasons. Washington. Grand Lodge.
The book of laws, containing the constitution and by-laws of comp. by E. H. Holmes under the authority of 1916 Grand Lodge session. n.p. 1919.

92p. 22½cm.

Seeds of liberation.

M301 G623 Goodman, Paul, 1911- ed.
Seeds of liberation. New York, G. Braziller [1965]
xviii, 551 p. 22 cm.

1. World politics—1945- —Addresses, essays, lectures. 2. Civilization, Modern—1950- —Addresses, essays, lectures. I. Title.

D839.3.G56 081 65-12888

Library of Congress [20]

Secret societies.

M366.1 F89o Freemasons. Ohio. Royal Arch Masons.
Transactions. 1st - 1871-
Cleveland, etc. 1872-

v. 22cm. annual
Place of publication varies.
Constitution and by-laws included in 1870 transactions.
See holdings card for proceedings.

M366.1 Am3 Secret societies.

Williamson, Harry A.
Negroes and freemasonry [part 2] The American freemason. 7:153-196 February 1916.

Seeds of turmoil.

M813.5 P76s Pollard, Freeman, 1922-
Seeds of turmoil; a novel of American PW's brainwashed in Korea. [1st ed.] New York, Exposition Press [1959]
264 p. 21 cm.
Portrait of author on book jacket.

1. Korean War, 1950-1953—Fiction. I. Title.

PZ4.P774Se 59-65501 ‡

Library of Congress [2]

The seeking.

M813.5 T36s **Thomas, Will, 1905–**
The seeking. New York, A. A. Wyn ⌊1953⌋
290 p. 22 cm.
Autobiographical.

1. ~~Negroes.~~ I. Title.
E185.97.T52A3 *301.451 325.2609743 53—6928 ‡
Library of Congress ⌊53h10⌋

Seeking the best.

MB9 Shls **Shackelford, Otis M 1871–**
Seeking the best. Dedicated to the negro youth. By Otis M. Shackelford, A. B. Kansas City, Mo., ~~Franklin Hudson publishing co., 1909~~. Burton Publishing Co., 1911.
177 p. incl. front. (port.) 20cm. $1.00

I. Title.
Library of Congress 9—22716
Copyright A 245989 ⌊28d1⌋

M260 M45s Seeking to be Christian in race relations.
Mays, Benjamin Elijah, 1895–
Seeking to be Christian in race relations. New York, Friendship Press, 1957.
84 p. 20 cm.

1. Race problems. 2. Church and social problems. I. Title.
BR115.R3M3 1957 *261.8 57—6580 ‡
Library of Congress ⌊58k10⌋

France M841 Se3m Ségalas, Anaïs (Ménard) 1814–1895.
Mère et jeune fille. ⌊a poem⌋ Extract from Journal des Demoiselles, 1840.
⌊2⌋ p. 20 cm.

1. French poetry. I. Title.

France M841 Se3p Ségalas, Anaïs (Ménard) 1814–1895.
La pauvre femme. ⌊a poem⌋
Extract from Athenée des arts, 1833.
⌊2⌋ p. 20 cm.

1. French poetry. I. Title.

France M841 Se3po Ségalas, Anaïs (Ménard) 1814–1895.
Poésies pour tous. Paris, Alphonse Lemerre, éditeur, 1886.
175 p. 18½ cm.

1. French poetry.

France M841 Se3t Ségalas, Anaïs (Ménard) 1814–1895.
Le trembleur, comedie en deux actes, mêlée de couplets, par mme Anaïs Ségalas, représentée, pour la première fois, à Paris, sur le Second Theatre.- Français le 8 septembre 1849.
14 p. 23½ cm.

I. Title. 1. French drama.

Segalony, J. Marrand de - L'Oasis.

M972.98 D87m **Dufougeré, William, 1878–**
... Madinina, "Reine des Antilles", étude de mœurs martiniquaises; préface de M. le professeur A. Lacroix ... Avec 61 réproductions photographiques, couverture de Pierre Bodard ... frontispice en coleurs de Maurice Millière, bandeaux et culs-de-lampe d'après les dessins originaux de Colmet d'Aage. Paris, Berger-Levrault, 1929.
viii p., 1 l., 258 p., 1 l. col. front., illus., plates, fold. map. 24cm.
"Bibliographie": p. ⌊241⌋–252.
1. Martinique—Descr. & trav. I. Title.
⌊*Full name:* William Marie Barbe Dufougeré⌋
30-14516
Library of Congress F2081.D86
Copyright A—Foreign 6543 ⌊2⌋

Uganda M896.3 Se3s Segganyi, Edward A K
Ssebato bafuma. (Short stories and folklore). ⌊By⌋ Edward A. K. Segganyi, Erasmus K. Kizito ne Jechoada K. S. Mukalazi. ... Nairobi, The Eagle Press, 1959.
164p. illus. 18½cm.
Text in: Luganda.

continued on next card.

Uganda M896.3 Se3s Segganyi, Edward A K
Ssebato bafuma. (Short stories and folklore). ⌊By⌋ Edward A. K. Segganyi, Erasmus K. Kizito ne Jechoada K. S. Mukalazi. ... Nairobi, The Eagle Press, 1959. (Card 2)

1. Uganda-Short stories. 2. Uganda-Folklore. I. Kizito, Erasmus K., jt. auth. II. Mukalazi, Jechoada K.S., jt. auth.

Basutoland M896 Se3m Segoete, Everitt Lechesa.
Monono, Ke moholi, ke mouoane. Morija, Sesuto Book Depot, 1926.
viii, 227p. 15½cm.
Title: Riches, their worthlessness.
Stories about Basutoland.
Written in Sotho.

1. Basutoland. 2. Africa, South.

Basutoland M896 Se3m2 Segoete, Everitt Lechesa
Monono ke moholi ke mouoane. ⌊Riches, their worthlessness⌋ Morija, Basutoland, Morija Book Depot, 1948.
107p. 17½cm.
Written in Sotho.

I. Title.

Basutoland M896 Se3r Segoete, Everitt Lechesa.
Raphepheng. Morija, Sesuto Book Depot, 1913.
122 p. 16 cm.
"Chapters on the life of the old BaSotho cast in the form of descriptions by an old Mo Sotho who is very sarcastic about modern degenerates, and who is given the characterizing name he bears in consequence."

1. Africa, South. 2. Basutoland.

Segregation.

M974.7 C54 **Clark, Kenneth Bancroft, 1914–**
Dark ghetto; dilemmas of social power, by Kenneth B. Clark. Foreword by Gunnar Myrdal. ⌊1st ed.⌋ New York, Harper & Row ⌊1965⌋
xxix, 251 p. illus. 22 cm.

1. Negroes—New York (City) 2. Negroes—Segregation. 3. Harlem, New York (City)—Soc. condit. I. Title.
F128.9.N3C65 301.451 64—7834
Library of Congress ⌊65a14⌋

Segregation.

MB9 W26h **Hawkins, Hugh, *ed.***
Booker T. Washington and his critics; the problem of Negro leadership. Boston, Heath ⌊1962⌋
113 p. 24 cm. (Problems in American civilization)
Includes bibliography.
Contains selections from the writings of Booker T. Washington, Rayford W. Logan, W. B. E. DuBois, Kelly Miller and H. M. Bond.

1. Washington, Booker Taliaferro, 1859?–1915. 2. Negroes—Segregation.
E185.97.W235 923.778 62–4235 ‡
Library of Congress ⌊10⌋

Segregation.

M370 H72e **Holley, Joseph Winthrop, 1874–**
Education and the segregation issue; a program of education for the economic and social regeneration of the Southern Negro. New York, William-Frederick Press, 1955.
62 p. illus. 22 cm.

1. Negroes—Education. 2. Negroes—Segregation. I. Title.
E185.97.H714 371.974 55—5471 ‡
Library of Congress ⌊56f5⌋

Segregation.

M301 K55 **Killens, John Oliver, 1916–**
Black man's burden. New York, Trident Press, 1965.
176 p. 21 cm.

1. Negroes—Segregation. 2. Negroes—Psychology. I. Title.
E185.61.K487 301.45196073 65—24155
Library of Congress ⌊66f7⌋

Segregation.

M331.833 L85p **Long, Herman Hodge.**
People vs. property; race restrictive covenants in housing ⌊by⌋ Herman H. Long ⌊and⌋ Charles S. Johnson. Nashville, Fisk Univ. Press, 1947.
ix, 107 p. maps, diagrs. 21 cm.
Bibliographical footnotes.

1. Negroes — Housing. 2. Negroes — Segregation. 3. Real covenants—U. S. I. Johnson, Charles Spurgeon, 1893– joint author. II. Title.
E185.89.H6L7 325.260973 48—5205*
Library of Congress ⌊48x10⌋

M323 M13s Segregation.
McCulloch, Margaret Callender, 1901–
Segregation, a challenge to democracy. Nashville, Race Relations Dept., American Missionary Association Division, Board of Home Missions, Congregational Christian Churches, Fisk University ⌊1950⌋
39 p. 23 cm.

1. Negroes—Segregation. I. Title.
E185.61.M126 325.260973 50–2114
Library of Congress ⌊3⌋

Segregation.

M323 R78g **Rowan, Carl Thomas.**
Go South to sorrow. New York, Random House ⌊1957⌋
246 p. 21 cm.

1. Negroes—Segregation. 2. Negroes—Southern States. I. Title.
E185.61.R855 325.260975 57–5378 ‡
Library of Congress ⌊25⌋

Segregation.

M301 R93 **Rutland, Eva.**
The trouble with being a mama. New York, Abingdon Press ⌊1964⌋
143 p. 21 cm.
Autobiographical.

1. Segregation.
~~1. Negroes.~~ 2. Children—Management. I. Title.
E185.625.R8 301.451 64–21136
Library of Congress ⌊4-1⌋

Segregation.

M323 Sa13 Sabourin, Clemence.
Let the righteous speak! Travel memoirs. [1st ed.] New York, Pageant Press [1957]
89 p. 21 cm.

1. Negroes—Segregation. 2. Southern States—Descr. & trav. I. Title.
E185.61.S25 325.260975 57-8311 ‡
Library of Congress [2]

Segregation - Africa, South.

S. Africa M968 N51af Ngubane, Jordan K
An African explains apartheid. New York, Praeger [1963]
243 p. illus. 22 cm. (Books that matter)

1. Africa, South—Hist. 2. Segregation—Africa, South. 3. Communism—Africa, South. I. Title.
DT763.N45 968.06 63-7569 ‡
Library of Congress [5]

Segregation in education.

M371.974 K77de Knox, Ellis O'Neal
Democracy and the District of Columbia Public Schools (a brief report of a complete study under the same title by the author). A study of recently integrated public schools. Washington, D.C., NAACP, 1957.

32p. 23cm.

Segregation.

M301 T426 Thurman, Howard, 1899-
The luminous darkness; a personal interpretation of the anatomy of segregation and the ground of hope. [1st ed.] New York, Harper & Row [1965]
xi, 113 p. 20 cm.

1. Negroes—Segregation. 2. Church and race problems. I. Title.
E185.61.T47 301.45196073 65-20445
Library of Congress [5]

Segregation - Africa, South.

S. Africa M968 N51af2 Ngubane, Jordan K
An African explains apartheid. London, Pall Mall [1963]

243p. illus. 22cm.

Segregation in education.

M371.974 W65 National Association of Intergroup Relations Officials. Commission on School Integration.
Public school segregation and integration in the North; analysis and proposals of the [NAIRO] Commission on School Integration [prepared by Doxey A. Wilkerson] Washington, 1963.
vi, 104p. tables. 22cm.
Special issue of the Journal of Intergroup Relations.
Bibliography: p. 87-104.
(Continued on next card)

Segregation.

M323 W73 Winston, Henry.
Old jim crow has got to go. New York, New Age Publishers, 1941.

15p. 19cm.

Segregation-U.S.

M306 N21m National Conference of Social Work.
Minority groups: segregation and integration. Papers presented at the 82d annual forum of the National Conference of Social Work. [Editorial Committee: Irving Weissman, chairman, Lois Clarke and others. Editorial work: Dorothy Swart] New York, Published for the National Conference of Social Work by Columbia University Press, 1955.
vi, 110 p. 24 cm.

1. Segregation—U. S. 2. Social case work. I. Title.
HV95.N35 1955 *301.45 325.73 56-5879
Library of Congress [56f15]

Segregation in education.

M371.974 W65 National Association of Intergroup Relations Officials. Commission on School Integration. Public school. 1963. (Card 2)

1. Segregation in education. I. Wilkerson, Doxey Alphonso, 1905- II. Journal of intergroup relations. III. Title.

Segregation - Anecdotes, facetiae, satire, etc.

M817.5 G86f Gregory, Dick.
From the back of the bus. Photos. by Jerry Yulsman. Introd. by Hugh M. Hefner. Edited by Bob Orben. [1st ed.] New York, Dutton, 1962.
125 p. illus. 23 cm.

1. Negroes—Segregation—Anecdotes, facetiae, satire, etc. I. Title.
PN6231.S485G7 817.54 62-14718 ‡
Library of Congress [3]

M323 M13s Segregation, a challenge to democracy.
McCulloch, Margaret Callender, 1901-
Segregation, a challenge to democracy. Nashville, Race Relations Dept., American Missionary Association Division, Board of Home Missions, Congregational Christian Churches, Fisk University [1950]
89 p. 23 cm.

1. Negroes—Segregation. I. Title.
E185.61.M126 325.260973 50-2114
Library of Congress [3]

Segregation in education.

M323 Un301 U. S. Supreme Court. Brief for appellants in Nos. 1, 2 and 3 and for respondents in no. 5 ... October Term, 1954.

31p. 23cm.

Segregation - Religious aspects.

M200 O13n Oliver, C Herbert, 1925-
No flesh shall glory. [Nutley, N. J.] Presbyterian and Reformed Pub. Co., 1959.
96 p. 21 cm.

1. Race. 2. Segregation—Religious aspects. 3. Sociology, Biblical. I. Title.
BT734.O4 261.83 59-14513 ‡
Library of Congress [2]

Segregation and the schools.

M323 N21 National Association for the Advancement of Colored People.
Segregation and the schools, with the cooperation of the National Association for the Advancement of Colored People. New York, Public Affairs Committee, 1954.

28p. 18cm. (Public affairs pamphlet no. 209)

Segregation in education.

M323 Un30 U. S. Supreme Court. Brief for appellants in Nos. 1, 2 and 4 and for respondents in No. 10 ... October Term, 1953.

235p. 23½cm.

Segregation - Africa, South.

South Africa M968 M313 Mandela, Nelson Rolihlahla, 1918-
No easy walk to freedom: articles, speeches, and trial addresses. Foreword by Ahmed Ben Bella. Introd. by Oliver Tambo. Edited by Ruth First. [London] Heinemann [1965]
xiv, 189p. ports. 22cm.

1. Segregation - Africa, South. 2. Africa, South - Race question. I. First, Ruth, ed. II. Title.

Segregation in education.

M323.2 C54p Clark, Kenneth Bancroft, 1914-
Prejudice and your child. Boston, Beacon Press [1955]
151 p. 22 cm.
Includes bibliography.

1. U. S.—Race question. 2. Prejudices and antipathies. 3. Child study. 4. Segregation in education. I. Title.
BF723.R3C5 157.3 55-9502 ‡
Library of Congress [55q30]

Segregation in education.

M323 Un3h U.S. Supreme Court.
Reply brief for appellants on reargument. No. 2 - Harry Briggs, Jr., et al., appellants, vs. R.W. Elliott, et al., appelles. No. 4 - Dorothy E. Davis, et al., appellants, vs. County School Board of Prince Edward County, appelles. Appeal from the United States District Court for the Eastern District of South Carolina and the Eastern District of Virginia. In the Supreme Court of the United States, October Term, 1953.

40p. 23cm.

Segregation - Africa, South.

South Africa M968 M313a Mandela, Nelson Rolihlahla, 1918-
No easy walk to freedom: articles, speeches, and trial addresses. Foreword by Ahmed Ben Bella. Introd. by Oliver Tambo. Edited by Ruth First. New York, Basic Books [1965]
xiv, 189 p. ports. 22 cm.

1. Segregation—Africa, South. 2. Africa, South—Race question. I. First, Ruth, ed. II. Title.
DT779.7.M35 301.45196068 65-18219
Library of Congress [5]

M371.974 K77d Segregation in education.
Knox, Ellis O
Democracy and the District of Columbia public schools; a study of recently integrated public schools. Washington, Judd & Detweiler, 1957.
viii, 131 p. tables. 24 cm.
Bibliography: p. 123-128.

1. Washington, D. C.—Public schools. 2. Segregation in education. I. Title.
LA255.K6 371.974 57-2405
Library of Congress [2]

Segregation in education.

M371.974 V23 Valien, Bonita H
The St. Louis story: a study of desegregation. New York, Anti-Defamation League of B'nai B'rith, 1956.

72p. 23cm.

Segregation in education.

M370
W65p
Wilkerson, Doxey Alphonso, 1905-
The people versus segregated schools. New York, New Century Publishers, 1955.

15p. 18cm.

Segregation in education - Cases - Digests.

M371.974
G93
Guzman, Jessie Parkhurst, 1898-
Twenty years of court decisions affecting higher education in the South, 1938-1958. Tuskegee, Alabama, Tuskegee Institute, Department of Records and Research, 1960.

36p. 23cm.

1. Segregation in education - Cases - Digests. I. Title.

Segregation in transportation-Montgomery, Ala.

M976.14
F46
Fields, Uriah J 1930-
The Montgomery story; the unhappy effects of the Montgomery bus boycott. [1st ed.] New York, Exposition Press [1959]

87 p. 21 cm.

1. Segregation in transportation—Montgomery, Ala. 2. Negroes—Montgomery, Ala. 3. Montgomery, Ala.—Race question. I. Title.

E185.89.T8F5 301.451 59-4227 ‡

Library of Congress [5]

Segregation in transportation - Montgomery, Ala.

M323
K58s
King, Martin Luther.
Stride toward freedom; the Montgomery story. [1st ed.] New York, Harper [1958]

230 p. illus. 21 cm.

1. Segregation in transportation—Montgomery, Ala. 2. Negroes—Montgomery, Ala. 3. Montgomery, Ala.—Race question. I. Title.

E185.89.T8K5 *301.451 325.2609761 58-7099 ‡

Library of Congress [59d30]

Segregation in transportation - Montgomery, Ala.

MB9
K58r
Reddick, Lawrence Dunbar, 1910-
Crusader without violence; a biography of Martin Luther King, Jr. [1st ed.] New York, Harper [1959]

243 p. illus. 22 cm.

1. King, Martin Luther. 2. Negroes—Civil rights. 3. Segregation in transportation—Montgomery, Ala. I. Title.

E185.97.K5R4 922.673 59-7160 ‡

Library of Congress [60]

Zanzibar
MB9
Sa2s
Sehoza, Samuel
St. Augustine. Translated from the Swahili. London, Society for Promoting Christian Knowledge, 1927.

47p. 18½cm. (Little books for Africa)

1. St. Augustine, b. 354-430 A.D.

M618.2
Se4p
Seibels, Robert E
Pregnancy spacing in the rural public health, by Robert E. Seibels... Columbia, South Carolina, The South Carolina state board of health, 1942.

20p. tables. 23cm.

1. Health. I. Title
2. Birth control.

Chad
M398
Se4
Seid, Joseph Brahim
Au Tchad sous les étoiles. [Paris] Présence Africaine, [1962]

101p. 19cm.

1. Tales, Chad. I. Title.

MB9
Se4d
Seifert, Charles Christopher
Dean, Elmer Wendell
An elephant lives in Harlem, by Elmer Wendell Dean. New York, Ethiopic press.

33p. 19½cm.

Le seige de Paris.

Réunion
M841
L11s
Lacaussade, Auguste, 1817-1897.
Le seige de Paris. Paris, Alphonse Lemerre, 1871.

31p. 18cm.

M812.3
Se4
no.1
Séjour, Victor, 1816-1874.
Les aventuriers; drame en cinq actes et un prologue. Paris, Michel Lévy, Frères, 1860.

136p. 19cm.

I. Title. 1. French drama.

M812.3
Se4c
No.1
Séjour, Victor, 1816-1874.
La chute de Séjan; drame en cinq actes et en vers. Paris, Michel Lévy Frères, 1849.

112p. 19cm.
Clipping laid in
Autographed by author (partly destroyed)

1. French drama. I. Title.

M812.3
Se4
no.2
Séjour, Victor, 1816-1874.
Le compère Guillery; drame en cinq actes et neuf tableaux. Paris, Michel Lévy Frères, 1860.

126p. 19cm.

1. French drama. I. Title.

M812.3
Se4
no.2
Séjour, Victor, 1816-1874.
Le compère Guillery; drame en cinq actes et neuf tableaux. Paris, Michel Lévy Frères, 1860.

126p. 19cm.

M812.3
Se4d
Séjour, Victor, 1816-1874.
Diégarias, drame en cinq actes et en vers. Paris, Doulo, [184-]

31p. 25cm.

1. French drama. I. Title.

M812.3
Se4q
No.5
Séjour, Victor, 1816-1874.
Les enfants de la louve, drame en cinq actes et un prologue. Paris, Michel Lévy Frères, [1865]

27p. 31cm.
No. 5 in a collection of five plays with binder's title: Quatre drames et une comedie.

1. French drama. I. Title.

M812.3
Se4q
No.4
Séjour, Victor, 1816-1874.
Les fils de Charles-Quint, drame en cinq actes, et un prologue en deux tableaux. Paris, Michel Lévy Frères, [1864].

26p. 31cm. (Théatre contemporain illustré)
No.4 in a collection of five plays with binder's title: Quatre drames et une comedie.

1. French drama. I. Title.

M812.3
Se4q
No.1
Séjour, Victor, 1816-1874.
Le fils de la nuit, drame en trois journées et un prologue. Paris, Michel Lévy Frères, [1856].

28p. 31cm. (Théatre contemporain illustré)
No.1 in a collection of five plays with binder's title: Quatre drames et une comedie.

1. French drama. I. Title.

M812.3
Se4n
no.2
Séjour, Victor, 1816-1874.
Les grands vassaux; drame en trois époques et en prose. Paris, Michel Lévy, Frères, 1859.

108p. 19cm.

1. French drama. I. Title.

M812.3
Se4m
No.2
Séjour, Victor, 1816-1874.
La madone des roses, drame en cinq actes, en prose. Paris, Michel Lévy Frères, 1869.

149p. 19cm.

1. French drama. I. Title.

M812.3
Se4m
No.2
Séjour, Victor, 1816-1874.
La madone des roses, drame en cinq actes, en prose. Paris, Michel Lévy Frères, 1869.

149p. 19cm.

1. French drama. I. Title.

M812.3 Se4m no.1
Séjour, Victor, 1816-1874.
Le marquis Caporal, drame en cinq actes, en sept tableaux. Paris, Michel Lévy Frères, 1865.
130p. 19cm.
1. French drama. I. Title.

M812.3 Se4n No.3
Séjour, Victor, 1816-1874.
La tireuse de cartes; drame en cinq actes et un prologue, en prose, par Victor Séjour. 2. éd. Paris, Michel Lévy frères, 1860.
2 p. l., iii, 131 p. 19½cm.
I. Title. 1. French ~~literature~~ drama.
Library of Congress PQ1223.Z76 no.1 34-19717
(842.80822) 842.89

Gold Coast M966.7 B96r
Sekondi, Gold Coast - Soc. Condit.
Busia, Kofi Abrefa.
Report on a social survey of Sekondi-Takoradi. London, Crown Agents for the Colonies on behalf of the Govt. of the Gold Coast, 1950.
164 p. 2 col. maps (1 fold.) 22 cm.
1. Sekondi, Gold Coast—Soc. condit. 2. Takoradi, Gold Coast—Soc. condit.
HN800.G6S43 309.1667 51—20972
Library of Congress [a52b½]

M812.3 Se4c no.3
Séjour, Victor, 1816-1874.
Le martyre du coeur; drame en cinq actes, en prose, par Victor Séjour et Jules Brésil. Paris, Michel Lévy Frères, 1858.
144p. 19cm.
1. French drama. I. Brésil, Jules, jt. auth. II. Title.

M812.3 Se4 no.3
Séjour, Victor, 1816-1874.
Les volontaires de 1814; drame en cinq actes et quatorze tableaux. Paris, Michel Lévy Frères, 1862.
130p. 19cm.
1. French drama. I. Title.

Martinique M841.91 G49s
Le Sel Noir.
Glissant, Édouard, 1928–
Le sel noir; poème. Paris, Éditions du Seuil [1960]
108 p. 19 cm.
Portrait of author on book jacket.
I. Title.
Illinois. Univ. Library for Library of Congress [1] A 60-4939

M812.3 Se4c No.2
Séjour, Victor, 1816- 1874.
Les Massacres de la syrie; drame en huit tableaux. Paris, J. Barbré, n.d.
136p. 19cm.

M811.08 L29c 1845
Séjour, Victor.
Lanusse, Armand, 1812-1867, comp.
Les Cenelles, choix de poesies indigenes ... Nouvelle Orleans, Imprime par H. Lauve et compagnie, 1845.
214p. 16½cm.

Selassie, Haile
see
Haile Selassie I, Emperor of Ethiopia, 1901-

M812.3 Se4c No.2
Séjour, Victor, 1816-1874.
Les Massacres de la syrie; drame en huit tableaux. Paris, J. Barbré, n.d.
136p. 19cm.
1. French drama . I. Title.

Haiti M330 Se4e
Séjourne, Georges.
Essai sur le problème économique d'Haiti; remèdes urgents. Port-au-Prince, Imp. du Séminaire Adventiste, 1948.
59p. tables. 19cm.
1. Haiti--Economic conditions.

M326.99B Sm6n 1897
Selden, Henry M.
Smith, Venture, 1729-1805.
A narrative of the life and adventures of Venture, a native of Africa, but resident above sixty years in the United States of America. Related by himself, New London: Printed in 1798. Reprinted A. D. 1835, and published by a descendant of Venture. Rev. and republished with traditions by H. M. Selden, Haddam, Conn., 1896. Middletown, Conn., J. S. Stewart, printer, 1897.
iv, [5]-41 p. 23½cm.
1. Slavery in the U. S.—Connecticut. I. Selden, Henry M. II. Title.
Library of Congress E444.S66 4—17888
[a29c1]

M812.3 Se4q No.2
Séjour, Victor, 1816-1874.
Le paletot brun, comédie en un acte et en prose. Paris, Michel Lévy Frères, [1859].
7p. 31cm. (Théatre contemporain illustré)
No.2 in collection of five plays with binder's title: Qautre drames et une comedie.
1. French drama. I. Title.

Uganda M398 Ea67
Sekaboga, L. N., illus.
East African Literature Bureau
Engero ezimu [Proverbs. Illustrated by L. N. Sekaboga] Kampala, Eagle Press, 1951.
11p. illus. 18cm. (Eagle improve your reading series, no. I)
Written in Luganda.
1. African. 2. Uganda - Proverbs. I. Title. II. Series. III. Sekaboga, L. N., illus.

M326.99B Sm6n 1835
Selden, Henry M.
Smith, Venture, 1729-1805.
A narrative of the life and adventures of Venture, a native of Africa, but resident above sixty years in the United States of America. Related by himself, New London: Printed in 1798. Reprinted A.D. 1835, and published by a descendant of Venture.
24p. 20cm.

M812.3 Se4m no.3
Séjour, Victor, 1816-1874.
Richard III. Drame en cinq actes, en prose. Nouvelle édition. Paris, Michel Lévy Frères, 1870.
108p. 19cm.

Basutoland M896 Se4p
Sekese, Azariele M
Bukana ea tsomo tsa pitso ea linonyana le tseko ea sefofu le seritsa. Morija, Sesuto Book Depot, 1931.
113 p. 16½ cm.

M252 St67 1924
Select sermons...
Stokes, Andrew Jackson, 1859–
Select sermons, by Rev. A. J. Stokes ... [Nashville, Natl. Baptist pub. board, ~~1920~~] 1924
152 p. front. (port.) plates. 20cm.
Revised edition.
I. Title.
Library of Congress 20-8017
——— Copy 2.
Copyright A 566649 [2]

M812.3 Se4m no.3
Séjour Victor, 1816-1874.
Richard III. Drame en cinq actes, en prose. Nouvelle édition. Paris, Michel Lévy Frères, 1870.
108p. 19cm.
1. Richard III, king of Englan, 1452-1485--Drama. 1. French drama.

Basutoland M896 Se4m
Sekese, Azariele M
Mekhoa le maele a Ba-Sotho. A Hlalosit-soeng ke Azariele Sekese. Morija, Sesuto Book Depot, 1931.
408 p. 20 cm.
Customs and proverbial sayings of the Basutos.
1. Basutoland. 2. Africa, South - Proverbs.

M811.5 G37
Selected gems of poetry.
Gilbert, Mercedes.
Selected gems of poetry, comedy and drama, by Mercedes Gilbert. Boston, The Christopher publishing house [c1931]
7, 11-89 p. 20½cm.
I. Title.
Library of Congress PS3513.I 428S4 1931 31-10590
——— Copy 2.
Copyright A 36566 [2] 818.5

Selected poems.

M811.5 Lewis, Robert V
L58 Selected poems. Detroit, Seminary Press, c1948.

22p. 22cm.

Senegal Selected poems.
M896.1 Senghor, Léopold Sédar.
Se5s Selected poems. Translated and introduced by John Reed and Clive Wake. ~~1st American ed., New York, Atheneum,~~ 1964. London, Oxford University Press, 1964.

xix, 99 p. 22 cm.

I. Title.

PQ2637.E46A6 1964 841.914 64-18302

Library of Congress [5]

Senegal Selected poems.
M896.1 Senghor, Léopold Sédar.
Se5s2 Selected poems. Translated and introduced by John Reed and Clive Wake. [1st American ed.] New York, Atheneum, 1964.

xix, 99 p. 22 cm.

I. Title.

PQ2637.E46A6 1964 841.914 64-18302

Library of Congress [5]

Selected poems.

St. Lucia
M821.91 Walcott, Derek.
W14s Selected poems. New York, Farrar, Straus [1964]

x, 85 p. 22 cm.

I. Title.

PR6045.A26A17 1964 821.914 64-17919

Library of Congress [5]

Selected shorter poems.

Jamaica
M821.91 McFarlane, John Ebenezer Clare, 1894-1962
M167 Selected shorter poems. Kingston, Pioneer Press [1954]

93p. 18cm.
Portrait of author on back cover of book.

M331 Selected studies of Negro employment in
M77t the South.
Hope, John, 1909-
3 southern plants of International Harvester Company, prepared for the NPA Committee of South. Washington, D. C., National Planning Association, 1953.

143 p. tables 23 cm. (National Planning Association. Committee of the South. Report no. 1)
At head of title: Selected studies of Negro employment in the south.

Selected studies of Negro employment in the South.

M331.1 National Planning Association. Committee of
N21s the South.
Selected studies of Negro employment in the South, prepared for the NPA Committee of the South. Washington, National Planning Association [1953-54]

5v. (x, 483, a-i p.) illus. 23cm.
(Its Report no.6)

Selected works of Langston Hughes.

M811.5 Hughes, Langston, 1902-
H87sp Selected works of Langston Hughes. Translated by Shojo Kojima. Japanese edition. Toyko, 1959.

300? p. port. 18½cm.

Africa A selection of African prose.
M896 Whiteley, W H. comp.
W58 A selection of African prose. Oxford, Clarendon Press, 1964.

2v. 22cm.
Contents.- v.1. Traditional oral texts.- v.2. Written prose.

White compiler.

Nigeria A selection of Hausa stories.
M398 Johnston, Hugh Anthony Stephens, ed. & tr.
J64 A selection of Hausa stories; compiled and translated by H. A. S. Johnston. Oxford, Clarendon P., 1966.

I, 241 p. 22½ cm. (Oxford library of African literature) 35/- (B 66-16882)

Appendix in Hausa.

1. Tales, Hausa. 2. Proverbs, Hausa. I. Title.

PL8234.Z95E5 1966 398.2 66-75454

Library of Congress [5]

Self-determining Haiti.

M323 Johnson, James Weldon, 1871-1938.
J632a Self-determining Haiti, by James Weldon Johnson. Four articles reprinted from the Nation embodying a report of an investigation made for the National association for the advancement of colored people, together with official documents ... [New York, The Nation, °1920]

48 p. 23cm.

1. Haiti—For. rel.—U. S. 2. U. S.—For. rel.—Haiti. 3. Haiti—Pol. & govt. I. The Nation, New York. II. National association for the advancement of colored people. III. Title.

A 21—1238

Stanford univ. Library for Library of Congress [a41d1]

M323
J632s Self-determining Haiti...
Johnson, James Weldon, 1871-1938.
Self-determining Haiti, by James Weldon Johnson. Four articles reprinted from the National embodying a report of an investigation made for the National association for the advancement of colored people. N.Y., The Nation, c1920

M323
J632e
no.3 48p. 23cm.

Self-made men.

M815.4 Douglass, Frederick, 1817-1895.
D74se Self-made men. An address before the students of the Indian industrial school, Carlisle, Pa. By Honorable Frederick Douglass. Carlisle, Indian print. [n.d.]
39p. 21cm.

Ethiopia
M896.3 Sellassie, Sahle, 1936-
Se48 Shinega's village; scenes of Ethiopian life. Translated from Chaha by Wolf Leslau. Illus. by Li Gelpke. Berkeley, University of California Press, 1964.

xi, 112 p. illus. 22 cm.

1. Ethiopia—Soc. life & cust. I. Leslau, Wolf, tr. II. Title.

PZ4.S4653Sh 64-12607

Library of Congress [5]

M301 Sellers, Charles Grier, *ed.*
Se4s The southerner as American. [By] John Hope Franklin [and others] Chapel Hill, University of North Carolina Press [1960]

216 p. 24 cm.

Includes bibliography.

1. National characteristics, American. 2. Southern States—Civilization. 3. Southern States—Hist.—Historiography. 4. Southern States—Race question. I. Title.

F209.S44 917.5 60—4104 ‡

Library of Congress [61v⁵30]

Ghana
M896.3 Selormey, Francis, 1927-
Se49n The narrow path. [London] Heinemann [1966]

183p. 20cm.
Portrait of author on book jacket.

I. Title.

Seltzer, Mrs. Adele Szold, 1876— tr.

Martinique
M843.9 Maran, René, 1887-
M32ba Batouala, by René Maran. New York, T. Seltzer, 1922.
1922 4 p. l., 7-207 p. 19½cm.
N.Y. ed. Translated from the French by Adele Szold Seltzer.

I. Seltzer, Mrs. Adele Szold, 1876- tr. II. Title.

22—19479

Library of Congress PZ3.M33Ba [45j1]

Uganda Semambo, Yusufu Balirwana, tr.
M823 Stevenson, Robert Louis
St48 Ekizinga Ky'Obugagga [Treasure Island] Kyakyusibwa Y. B. Semambo. Kampala, Eagle Press, 1951.

156p. 18cm.
Written in Luganda.

I. Title. II. Semambo, Yusufu Balirwana, tr.

A Semana.

Brazil
M869.3 Machado de Assis, Joaquim Maria, 1839-1908.
M18se A Semana. Rio de Janeiro, W. M. Jackson Inc. Editôres, 1957.

3v. 20½cm. (Obras completas de Machado de Assis).

Uganda
M967.61 Sembeguya, F G
Se5g Genda olabe omuisawo [Go and see the doctor] Nairobi, East African Literature Bureau, 1956.

42p. 21cm.
Written in Luganda.

1. Uganda - medicine.

Haiti
M843.91 Les semences de la colère.
L56s Lespes, Anthony.
Les semences de la colère. Port-au-Prince, Henri Deschamps, 1949.

215p. 19cm.

M285
C29
A semi-centenary discourse...
Catto, William T.
A semi-centenary discourse, delivered in the First African Presbyterian church, Philadelphia, on the fourth Sabbath of May, 1857: with a history of the church from its first organization: including a brief notice of Rev. John Gloucester, its first pastor. By Rev. William T. Catto, pastor. Also, an appendix, containing sketches of all the colored churches in Philadelphia. Philadelphia, J. M. Wilson, 1857.
111 p. 23cm.
1. Philadelphia. First African Presbyterian church. 2. Gloucester, John, 1776 or 7–1822. I. Title.
Library of Congress BX9211.P5A3 13–14590 [a32c1]

Senegal
M796.81
Se5
Sène, Moustapha
La Lutte Sénégalaise [n.p., 1966]
18p. ports. 21cm.
"Comité de participation du Sénégal au premier festival mondial des arts Nègres."
Portrait of author on t.p.
1. Wrestling. I. Title.

Senegal
M960
N23
Senegal.
N'diaye, Massata Abdou
Le Sénégal a l'heure de indépendence. [Doullens, France, Imprimerie Dessaint, n.d.]
Pp. 69-168. 19cm.
Bound with the author's Afrique unie et rénovation mondiale. Doullens, France, n.d.
1. Senegal. I. Title.

M811.4
W59t
1890
Seminole Indians - Poetry.
Whitman, Albery Allson, 1851-1901.
Twasinta's Seminoles; or Rape of Florida. By Albery A. Whitman. Third ed. carefully rev. St. Louis, Nixon-Jones printing co., 1890.
96p. incl. front. (port.) 26cm.

Sénégal
M966.3
L98c
Sénégal.
Ly, Abdoulaye.
La Compagnie du Sénégal. [Paris] Présence africaine [1958]
310p. illus. 23cm. (Enquêtes et études)

Senegal
M960
N23
Senegal.
N'diaye, Massata Abdou
Le Sénégal a l'heure de indépendence. [Doullens, France, Imprimerie Dessaint, n.d.]
Pp. 69-168. 19cm.
Bound with the author's Afrique unie et rénovation mondiale. Doullens, France, n.d.

M811.4
W59t
Seminole Indians-Poetry.
Whitman, Albery A 1851–
Twasinta's Seminoles; or, Rape of Florida. By Albery A. Whitman. Rev. ed. St. Louis, Nixon-Jones printing co., 1885.
97 p. incl. front. (port.) 19½cm.
1. Seminole Indians—Poetry. I. Title.
Library of Congress PS3187.W27S 31–28855
Copyright 1885: 19359 [37b1]

Sénégal
M966.3
L98e
Sénégal.
Ly, Abdoulaye
L'etat et la production paysanne ou l'etat et la révolution au Sénégal 1957-1958. Paris, Présence Africaine, 1958.
79p. 19cm.

Senegal
M966.3
Sa15
Senegal.
Sadji, Abdoulaye, 1910-
Education Africaine et civilisation. [Dakar, Imprimerie A. Diop, 1964]
92p. 24cm.
1. Education - Senegal. 2. Africa - Civilization. [3]. Senegal. I. Title.

Uganda
M967.61
Se5b
Sempa, Kalule A
The Buganda government and its constitutional functions [Gaumenti ya Buganda n'emirimu gyayo] Kampala, The Eagle Press, 1953.
55p. 18cm.
Written in English and Luganda
1. Buganda.

Senegal
M966.3
L98m
Sénégal.
Ly, Abdoulaye
Mercenaires noirs; notes sur une forme de l'exploitation des Africains. Paris, Présence Africaine, 1957.
67p. 19cm.

Sénégal
M966.3
Se5afr
Senegal.
Senghor, Léopold Sédar, 1906-
L'Afrique a l'O.N.U., XVI° session. [Paris] Présence Africaine, 1961.
55p. 18cm.
French and English.
1. United Nations - Senegal. 2. Senegal. I. Title.

Haiti
M843.91
Se5c
Senat, Franck
Confidences des ondes. [Port-au-Prince, Imp. H. Deschamps] 1949.
59p. 19½cm.
1. Haitian literature. I. Title.

Senegal
M966.3
M26s
Senegal.
Mademba, Abd-el-Kader.
Au Senegal et au Soudan Français, Paris, Librairie Larose, 1931.
116p. plates. map. 25½cm.
9KH

Sénégal
M966.3
Se5ra
Sénégal.
Senghor, Léopold Sédar, 1906-
Rapport sur la doctrine et le programme du parti. Paris, Présence Africaine, 1959.
90p. 20cm. (Congrès Constitutif Du P.F.A. Dakar, 1-3 Juillet 1959)

Haiti
M841
Se55g
Senat, Franck Charles
Les gloses et les rythemes sales. [n.p.] Imprimerie T. Michel, 1963.
38p. 20cm.
1. Haitian poetry. I. Title.

Senegal
M966.3
M26s
Senegal.
Mademba, Abd-el-Kader.
Au Senegal et au Soudan Français. Paris, Librairie Larose, 1931.
116p. plates. map. 25½cm.

Senegal
M916.63
T145
Senegal - Description and travel.
Tall, Ibra
Un voyage au Senegal. [Tanger, Editions Marocaines et Internationales, 1965.]
[70]p. 15½cm.

M973
L82s
The Senate and the Versailles mandate system.
Logan, Rayford Whittingham, 1897–
The Senate and the Versailles mandate system, by Rayford W. Logan ... Washington, D. C., The Minorities publishers, 1945.
vi p., 1 l., 112 p. 22½cm.
Bibliography: p. 105–106.
1. U. S. Senate. 2. Mandates. I. Title.
Library of Congress JX4021.L6 45—8821 [46g2] 321.027

Senegal
M966.3
N23
Senegal.
N'Diaye, Massata Abdou
Le Sénégal a l'heure de l'independence. [Doullens, France, Imprimerie Dessaint, n.d.]
104p. port. 19cm.
1. Senegal. I. Title.

Senegal
M966.3
Se5pr
Senegal - Description and travel.
Touze, R L
Bignona en Casamance. Préface de Léopold Sédar Senghor. Dakar, Editions Sepa [1963]
214p. illus., maps. 18cm.
White author.
1. Senegal - Description and travel. I. Title. II. Senghor, Léopold Sédar, 1906- Preface.

Senegal - Fiction.
Senegal
M896.3 **Dia, Cheik**
D53av Avant liberte I; roman. Paris, Les Editions du Scorpion, 1964.

92p. 19cm.

Senegal - Fiction.
Senegal
M896.3 Dia, Cheik
D53av Avant liberté I; roman. Paris, Les Editions du Scorpion, 1964.

92p. 19cm.

1. Senegal - Fiction. I. Title.

Senegal - Fiction.
Senegal
M896.3 **Diop, Ousmane Socé, 1911-**
D62k Karim; roman Senegalais [par] Ousmane Soce [pseud] [Paris, Imprimerie Marcel Puyfourcat, 1935]

125p. illus. 22¼cm.
Auto graphed.

Senegal - Fiction.
Senegal
M896.3 Diop, Ousmane Socé, 1911-
D62k Karim; roman Senegalais [par] Ousmane Socé [pseud] [Paris, Imprimerie Marcel Puyfourcat, 1935]

125p. illus. 22½cm.
Autographed.

1. Senegal - Fiction. I. Title.

Sénégal - Fiction.
Senegal
M896.3 Diop, Ousmane Socé, 1911-
D62k3 Karim; roman Sénégalais. Suivi de contes et légendes d'Afrique noire. [par] Ousmane Socé [pseud.] Préface de Robert Delavignette. 3 éd. Paris, Nouvelles Éditions Latines, 1948.

238p. 19cm. (Bibliothèque de l'Union Française)

1. Sénégal - Fiction. I. Title.

Sénégal-Fiction.
Sénégal
M896.3 **Ousmane, Sembene, 1923-**
Ou8b Les bouts de bois de Dieu; Banty Mam Yall. Marseille, Le Livre Contemporain, 1960.

380p. 21cm.
Portrait of author on front of book jacket.

Senegal - Fiction.
Senegal
M896.3 **Ousmane, Sembene**
Ou8b2 God's bits of wood. Translated by Francis Price. [1st ed.] Garden City, N. Y., Doubleday, 1962.

333p. 22cm.

Senegal Senegal - Fiction.
M896.3 **Ousmane, Sembene.**
Ou8b2 God's bits of wood. Translated by Francis Price. [1st ed.] Garden City, N. Y., Doubleday, 1962.

333 p. 22 cm.

I. Title.

PZ4.O935Go 62-11996 ‡

Library of Congress [5]

Senegal - Fiction.
Senegal
M896.3 Ousmane, Sembene, 1923-
Ou8h L'hartmattan. Paris, Présence Africaine [1964]

299p. 18½cm. (Référendum I)

Senegal - History.
Senegal
M966.3 Ndiaye, H jt. auth.
N22 Sénégal; récits historiques, cours élémentaire [par] M. Guilhem [et] H. Ndiaye. Paris, Ligel [1964]

107p. illus., maps. 22cm.

1. Senegal - History. I. Guilhem, M

Senegal - History.
Senegal
M966.3 Samb, El-Hadj Assane Marokhaya
Sa44 "Cadior demo": essai sur l'histoire du Cayor. [Préface de Bathie Samb. Introd. de M. Issa Diop. Seconde édition, revue et corrigée] Dakar [Edition Diop] 1965.

64p. illus. 23cm.

1. Senegal - History. I. Title.

Senegal Senegal - Native races.
M966.3 Ba, Oumar
B12 Notes sur la democratie en pays Toucouleur. [Dakar, Imprimerie A. Diop, n.d.]

52p. 22cm.

1. Toucouleurs. 2. Senegal - Native races. I. Title.

Senegal Senegal - Officials and employees - Salaries, allowances, etc.
M966.3 Diouf, Coumba N'Doffène
D63 La question des salaires au Sénégal, 1965; Notes et commentaires mis en ordre et présentés par Coumba N'Doffène Diouf, Georges Vermot-Gauchy et Charles Francis Brun. [Dakar] Librairie Clairafrique [1966]

82p. illus. 24cm. (Dossiers Africains, no. 2)

Senegal - Poetry.
Sénégal
M896.1 Sourang, Ibrahima
So84au **Aureles. Prêface de Camille Souyris. Palais Miami, Monte-Carlo [1961]**

60p. 18cm. (Cahiers des poetes de notre temps, no. 255)

Senegal - Poetry.
Sénégal
M896.1 Sourang, Ibrahima
So84au Aurêles. Préface de Camille Souyris. Palais Miami, Monte-Carlo [1961]

60p. 18cm. (Cahiers des poetes de notre temps, no. 255)

Sénégal - Politics and government.
Sénégal
M966.3 Diop, Majhemout
D624 Contribution à l'étude des problèmes politiques en Afrique noire. Paris, Présence Africaine, 1958.

267p. 23cm.

1. Sénégal - Politics and government.

Sénégal-Politics and government.
Sénégal
M966.3 **Senghor, Léopold Sédar, 1906-**
Se5p Pierre Teilhard de Chardin et la politique Africaine, Pierre Teilhard de Chardin sauvons l'humanite. L'art dans la ligne de l'énergie humaine. Paris, Éditions du Seuil, 1962.

102p. illus. 19cm.

Senegal - Politics and government - Addresses, essays, lectures.
Senegal
M335 **Senghor, Léopold Sédar.**
Se5 On African socialism. Translated and with an introd. by Mercer Cook. New York, Praeger [1964]

xv, 173 p. 21 cm.

Bibliographical references included in "Notes" (p. 167-173)

CONTENTS.—Nationhood: report on the doctrine and program of the Party of African Federation.—The African road to socialism.—The theory and practice of Senegalese socialism.

1. Senegal—Pol. & govt.—Addresses, essays, lectures. 2. Mali—Pol. & govt.—Addresses, essays, lectures. 3. Socialism in Africa—Addresses, essays, lectures. I. Title.

JQ3396.A91S4 1964 64—16419

Library of Congress [64f4]

Le Sénégal a l'heure de indépendence.
Senegal
M960 N'diaye, Mossata Abdou
N23 Le Sénégal a l'heure de indépendence. [Doullens, France, Imprimerie Dessaint, n.d.]

Pp. 69-168. 19cm.
Bound with the author's Afrique unie et rénovation mondiale. Doullens, France, n.d.

1. Senegal. I. Title.

Le Sénégal a l'heure de l'independance.
Senegal
M966.3 N'Diaye, Massata Abdou
N.. Le Sénégal a l'heure de l'independance. [Doullens, France, Imprimerie Dessaint, n.d.]

104p. port. 19cm.

1. Senegal. I. Title.

Sénégal
M966.3 Senghor, Léopold Sédar, 1906-
Se5af African socialism; a report to the constitutive Congress of the Party of African Federation. Translated and edited by Mercer Cook. New York, American Society of African Culture, 1959.

49p. 21½cm.

1. Africa - Socialism. I. Cook, Mercer, 1903- tr. and ed. II. Title.

Sénégal
M966.3
Se5afr

Senghor, Léopold Sédar, 1906-
L'Afrique a l'O.N.U., XVI° session. [Paris] Présence Africaine, 1961.

55p. 18cm.
French and English.

1. United Nations - Senegal. 2. Senegal. I. Title.

Africa
M960
As6a

Senghor, Léopold Sédar, 1906-
Elégie des Eaux.

Pp. 81-83.
In: Aspects de la culture noire. 1958.

I. Title.

Senegal
M966.3
Se5nt2

Senghor, Léopold Sédar, 1906-
Nationhood and the African road to socialism. Translated by Mercer Cook. Paris, Presence Africaine [1962]

130p. 21½cm.
Includes bibliography.

1. Africa. 2. Socialism. I. Title. II. Cook, Mercer, tr.

Senegal
M896.1
Se5a

Senghor, Leopold Sedar, 1906- ed.
Anthologie de la nouvelle poésie nègre et malgache de langue française, par Léopold Sédar Senghor, précédée de Orphée noir, par Jean-Paul Sartre. [1. éd.] Paris, Presses universitaires de France, 1948.

xliv, 227p. 23cm. (Colonies et empires. 5. sér.: Art et littérature, 1)
Includes biobibliographical sketches of the authors.

Senegal
M896.1
So5e

Senghor, Léopold Sédar, 1906-
Éthiopiques; poèmes. Paris, Éditions du Seuil, 1956.

125p. 19½cm.

I. Title.

South Africa
M896
M88

Senghor, Leopold Sedar, 1906-
Negro Mask.

Pp. 174-175.

In: Mphahlele, Ezekiel, ed. African writing today. Baltimore, Penguin Books, 1967.

Senegal
M896.1
Se5a

Senghor, Léopold Sédar, 1906- ed.
Anthologie de la nouvelle poésie nègre et malgache de langue française, par Léopold Sédar Senghor, précédée de Orphée noir, par Jean-Paul Sartre. [1. éd.] Paris, Presses universitaires de France, 1948.

xliv, 227 p. 23 cm. (Colonies et empires. 5. sér.: Art et littérature, 1)

Includes biobibliographical sketches of the authors.

1. French literature—Colonies. 2. Negro poetry (French) I. Sartre, Jean Paul, 1905- II. Title. (Series)

PQ3899.S4 49-22791*

Library of Congress [1]

Senegal
M896.1
Sc5h

Senghor, Léopold Sédar, 1906-
Hosties noires. Paris, Seuil, [1948].

86P. 19cm. (Collection "Pierres vives")

1. French poetry. I. Title.

Sénégal
M896.1
Se5n

Senghor, Léopold Sédar, 1906-
Nocturnes; poemes. Paris, Éditions de Seuil, [1961]

94p. 18½cm.
"A Monsieur Spingarn en hommage".

1. Poetry, African. I. Title.

Senegal
M896.1
Se5c

Senghor, Léopold Sédar, 1906-
Chants d'ombre. Paris, Éditions du Seuil [1945]

78 p. front. 20 cm. (Collection "Pierres vives")

I. Title. (Series)

PQ2637.E46C5 A F 48-4140*

California. Univ. Libr. for Library of Congress [1]†

Senegal
M896.1
Se5

Senghor, Leopold Sédar, 1906-
L. S. Senghor, poète Sénégalais. [Textes commentés par Roger Mercier et M. et S. Battestini. Paris] Fernand Nathan [1964]

63p. 19½cm. (Classiques du monde. Littérature africaine, 3)
Bibliographie: p. 6-7.
Portrait of author on book cover.

I. Mercier, Roger, ed. II. Series.

Sénégal
M896.1
Se5n

Senghor, Léopold Sédar, 1906-
Nocturnes; poèmes. Paris, Éditions de Seuil, [1961].

94p. 18½cm.
"A Monsieur Spingarn en hommage".

1. Poetry, African. I. Title.

Senegal
M896.1
Se5ch

Senghor, Léopold Sedár, 1906-
Chants pur Naëtt. Paris, Pierre Seghers, Editeur, 1949.

48p. 17½cm.

1. Title.

Senegal
M960
Se5

Senghor, Léopold Sédar, 1906-
Liberte. Paris, Éditions du Seuil, 1964-

v. 20½cm.
Contents.- v.1. Negritude et humanisme.

I. Liberté. II. Title: Negritude and humanisme.

Senegal
M335
Se5

Senghor, Léopold Sédar.
On African socialism. Translated and with an introd. by Mercer Cook. New York, Praeger [1964]

xv, 173 p. 21 cm.

Bibliographical references included in "Notes" (p. 167-173)

CONTENTS.—Nationhood: report on the doctrine and program of the Party of African Federation.—The African road to socialism.—The theory and practice of Senegalese socialism.

1. Senegal—Pol. & govt.—Addresses, essays, lectures. 2. Mali—Pol. & govt.—Addresses, essays, lectures. 3. Socialism in Africa—Addresses, essays, lectures. I. Title. II. Cook, Mercer; tr.

JQ3396.A91S4 1964 64—16419

Library of Congress [64f4]

Senegal
M896.1
Se5ch

Senghor, Léopold Sedár, 1906-
Chants pur Naëtt. Paris, Pierre Seghers, Editeur, 1949.

48p. 17½cm.

1. Title.

Senegal
M896
Se5

Senghor, Léopold Sédar.
Léopold Sédar Senghor; présentation par Armand Guibert, choix de textes bibliographie, portraits, fac-similés. [Paris] Editions Pierre Seghers [1961]

215p. ports. 16cm. (Poétes d'Ajourd'hui, 82)
Portrait of author on front cover.

1. Senghor, Léopold Sédar. I. Guibert, Armand.

Sénégal
M966.3
Se5p

Senghor, Léopold Sédar, 1906-
Pierre Teilhard de Chardin et la politique Africaine, Pierre Teilhard de Chardin sauvons l'humanite. L'art dans la ligne de l'énergie humaine. Paris, Éditions du Seuil, 1962.

102p. illus. 19cm.

1. Sénégal-Politics and government. 2. Chardin, Pierre Teilhard de. I. Title.

South Africa
M896
M88

Senghor, Leopold Sedar, 1906-
Death of the Princess.

Pp. 173-174.

In: Mphahlele, Ezekiel, ed. African writing today. Baltimore, Penguin Books, 1967.

Sénégal
M966.3
Se5nt

Senghor, Léopold Sédar, 1906-
Nation et voie Africaine du socialisme. Paris, Présence Africaine, 1961.

138p. 21½cm.

1. Africa. 2. Socialism. I. Title.

Africa
M896.3
P741

Senghor, Léopold Sédar, 1906-

Les plus beaux écrits de l'union française et du Maghreb, Présentés par Mohamed El Kholti, Leopold Sédar Senghor, [and others] Paris, Editions du Vieux, Colombier, 1947.

455p. 21cm.

Senegal
M896
Se5p
Senghor, Léopold Sédar, 1906-
Prose and poetry. Selected and translated by John Reed and Clive Wake. London, Oxford University Press, 1965.

181p. 18½cm.
Includes bibliography.

1. African literature. I. Title. II. Reed, John, comp. III. Wake, Clive, jt. comp.

Sénégal
M966.3
Se5ra
Senghor, Léopold Sédar, 1906-
Rapport sur la doctrine et le programme du parti. Paris, Présence Africaine, 1959.

90p. 20cm. (Congrès Constitutif Du P.F.A. Dakar, 1-3 Juillet 1959)

1. Sénégal. I. Title.

Senegal
M896.1
Se5s
Senghor, Léopold Sédar.
Selected poems. Translated and introduced by John Reed and Clive Wake. ~~1st American ed., New York, Atheneum, 1964.~~ London, Oxford University Press, 1964.
xix, 99 p. 22 cm.

I. Title. 1. African poetry.
PQ2637.E46A6 1964 841.914 64-18302

Library of Congress [5]

Senegal
M896.1
Se5s2
Senghor, Léopold Sédar.
Selected poems. Translated and introduced by John Reed and Clive Wake. [1st American ed.] New York, Atheneum, 1964.
xix, 99 p. 22 cm.

I. Title. 2. African poetry.
PQ2637.E46A6 1964 841.914 64-18302

Library of Congress [5]

Senegal
M896.1
Se5t
Senghor, Léopold Sédar, 1906-
Tam-Tam schwarz; gesänge vom Senegal. Ausgewählt und übertragen von Janheinz Jahn. Heidelberg, Wolfgang Rothe, 1955.

63p. 24cm.
Biography: p.60-62

I. Title.

Africa
M960
F76
Senghor, Léopold Sédar, 1906-
West Africa in evolution.

Pp. 283-291.

In: Foreign Affairs (New York). Africa. New York, Praeger, 1964.

Senghor, Léopold Sédar, 1906-
Sénégal
M896.3
C68c
Colin, Roland
Les contes noirs de l'Ouest Africain. Témoins majeurs d'un humanisme. Préface de Léopold S. Senghor. Paris, Présence Africaine, 1957.

204p. 18½cm.

French Guiana
M841.08
D18
Senghor, Léopold Sédar..
Damas, Leon G ed., 1912-
Poètes d'expression française [d'Afrique Noire, Madagascar, Réunion, Guadeloupe, Martinique, Indochine, Guyane] 1900-1945. Paris, Éditions du Seuil [1947]

322 p. (Latitudes françaises, 1)
Collection "Pierres vives."

1. French poetry—20th cent. I. Title. (Series. Series: Collection "Pierres vives")

A 49-2183*

Illinois. Univ. Library for Library of Congress [1]

Sénégal
M896.3
D59n
Senghor, Léopold Sédar, 1906.
Diop, Birago, 1906-
Les nouveaux contes d'Amadou Koumba. Préface de Léopold Sédar. Paris, Présence Africaine, 1958.

173p. 18½cm.

Senghor, Léopold Sédar, 1906-
Somalia
M896.1
Syllk
Syad, William J F
Khamsine; poemes. Preface de Léopold S. Senghor. Paris, Présence Africaine [1959]

70p. 20cm.
Text in English or French.

Senghor, Léopold Sédar, 1906-
Sénégal
MB9
Se5g
Guibert, Armand
Léopold Sédar Senghor. Choix de testes, bibliographie, portraits, fac-similés. Paris, Editions Pierre Seghers, 1961.

215p. illus., ports. 16cm. (Poètes d'Aujour'd hui 82)
Portrait of biographee on front cover of book.

Senghor, Léopold Sédar, 1906-
Congo (Leopoldville)
M840.8
M971
Mushiete, Paul
La litterature française africaine; petite anthologie des ecrivains noirs d'expression française. Leverville, Bibliotheque de l'Étoile, 1957.

40p. 17½cm.

Senghor, Léopold Sédar, 1906-
Congo (Leopoldville)
M840.8
M971
Mushiete, Paul
La littérature française africaine; petite anthologie des écrivains noirs d'expression française. Leverville, Bibliothèque de l'Étoile, 1957.

40p. 17½cm.

Senegal
M896
Se5
Senghor, Léopold Sédar.
Senghor, Léopold Sedar.
Léopold Sédar Senghor; présentation par Armand Guibert, choix de textes bibliographie, portraits, fac-similés. [Paris] Editions Pierre Seghers [1961]

215p. ports. 16cm. (Poètes d'Ajourd'hui, 82)

Senegal
M966.3
Se5pr
Senghor, Léopold Sédar, 1906- Preface.
Touze, R L
Bignona en Casamance. Préface de Léopold Sédar Sénghor. Dakar, Editions Sepa [1963]

214p. illus., maps. 18cm.
White author.

1. Senegal - Description and travel. I. Title. II. Senghor, Léopold Sédar, 1906- Preface.

Basutoland
M896.2
M72s2
Senkata.
Mofokeng, Sophonia Machabe
Senkata. [Reprinted in new orthography] Johannesburg, Witwatersrand University Press, 1962.

71p. 17cm. (The Bantu treasury, ed. by D. T. Cole)
Written in Sotho.

Basutoland
M896.2
M72s
Senkatana.
Mofokeng, Sophonia Machabe
Senkatana. Johannesburg, Witwatersrand University Press, 1952.

71p. 17cm. (The Bantu treasury, XII, ed. by C. M. Doke)
Written in Sotho.

Uganda
M640
Se6am
Senkatuka, Mary E 1929-
Idwewok [Our homes] Loejulete Y. Emudon ka N. C. Wiggins. Kampala, Eagle Press, 1957.

14p. illus. 18cm.
Written in Ateso.
Translation of Amaka Goffee. Translated from Luganda.

1. Home economics. I. Emudon, Y., tr. II. Title.

Senior sentiments and junior jottings...
M811.5
B75s
Brewer, John Mason, 1896- editor.
Senior sentiments and junior jottings: a first book of verse, by the Bellerophon quill club of the Booker T. Washington high school, Dallas, Texas... Edited by J. Mason Brewer, 1934.

24p. 20½cm.

Le sentier du tonnerre (Path of thunder)
S. Africa
M896.3
Ab8se
Abrahams, Peter, 1919-
Le sentier du tonnerre (Path of thunder) Traduit de l'anglais par Amélie Audiberti. Roman. Quatorzième édition, Paris, Gallimard, 1950.

286p. 19cm.

...Le sentiment de la valeur personnelle.
Haiti
MB9
C46m
Mars, Jean Price, 1876-
...Le sentiment de la valeur personnelle chez Henry Christophe en fonction de son role de chef psychologie d'un homme d'etat... Port-au-Prince, Haiti, V. Valcin, 1933.
21p. 24cm.

Sentiments of people of color, p. 1-78.

M326.8
G19
Garrison, William Lloyd, 1805-1879.
Thoughts on African colonization: or, An impartial exhibition of the doctrines, principles and purposes of the American colonization society. Together with the resolutions, addresses and remonstrances of the free people of color ... By Wm. Lloyd Garrison. Boston, Printed and pub. by Garrison and Knapp, 1832.
iv, 160, 76 p. 23cm.
1. American colonization society. 2. Negroes—Colonization—Africa.
11-8718
Library of Congress E448.G24
[42c1]

Haiti
M972.94
N14s
Sentinelle perdue...
Nazaire, D
Sentinelle perdue, ouvrage apologetique des dogmes de la doctrine du Roi de l'humanité par D. Nazaire. Port-au-Prince, Imprimerie du Commence [1947].
133p. 22½cm.

M976.3
Se6
The Sepia socialite.
... The Negro in Louisiana, seventy-eight years of progress. Fifth anniversary edition ... New Orleans, Sepia socialite pub. co., 1942.
168 p. illus. 38cm.
Dated on cover, July 1942; on t.-p., Apr. 1942.
1. Negroes—Louisiana.
42-24696
Brief cataloging
Library of Congress E185.93.L6S5
[3] 325.2609763

Sepia vistas.
M811.5
B97s
Butler, Alpheus.
Sepia vistas, by Alpheus Butler ... New York, The Exposition press [°1941]
63, [1] p. 19cm.
Poems.
I. Title.
[Full name: James Alpheus Butler]
42-8440
Library of Congress PS3503.U8484
[2] 811.5

Sequel to the "Pied Piper of Hamelin".
M811.5
C82s
Cotter, Joseph Seamon, 1861-
Sequel to the "Pied Piper of Hamelin", and other poems, by Joseph S. Cotter, sr. New York, H. Harrison [°1939]
93 p. incl. front. (port.) 21½cm.
I. Browning, Robert. The pied piper of Hamelin. II. Title.
40-2545
Library of Congress PS3505.O8684 1939
——— Copy 2.
Copyright A 136033 [2] 811.5

Seraph on the Suwanee.
M810.
H94se
Hurston, Zora Neale.
Seraph on the Suwanee, a novel. New York, C. Scribner's Sons, 1948.
311 p. 21 cm.
I. Title.
PZ3.H9457Se 48-8745*
Library of Congress [12]

Sereres.
Senegal
M966.3
D62n
Diop, Cheikh Anta
Nations Nègres et culture. Paris, Éditions Africaines, 1955.
390p. illus. plates 25cm.

Sermons.
M252
B17p
Baker, William H
Plain pointed practical preaching; old fashioned Bible Chautauqua sermons. New York, Greenwich Book Publishers, [1956]
312p. 20½cm.
Picture of the author on the book jacket.
1. Sermons.

Sermons.
M252
C23b
Best sermons. 1944-
Chicago, New York, Ziff-Davis publishing company [1944-
v. 24 cm.
Editor: 1944- G. P. Butler.
1. Sermons. I. Butler, George Paul, 1900- ed.
BV4241.B38 252.0082 44-51581
Library of Congress [58y²5]

Sermons.
M252
B64g
Borders, William Holmes, 1905-
God is real. [Atlanta, Georgia, Fuller Press, [°1951]
210p. port. 21½cm.

Sermons,
M252.
B64
Borders, William Holmes.
Sermons, by William Holmes Borders ... Philadelphia, Dorrance and company [°1939]
90 p. 20cm.
1. Baptists—Sermons. 2. Sermons, American.
40-131
Library of Congress BX6333.B54S4
——— Copy 2.
Copyright A 134388 [2] 252.061

Sermons.
M252
B64t
Borders, William Holmes, 1905-
Trial by fire and 25 other full length sermons. Atlanta, Georgia, Author, 1957
127p. port. 23cm.

Barbados
M252
B69
Sermons,
Boyce, Edward H
With Christ in the mount; mountain experiences in the life of Christ. [Sermons] New York, Exposition Press [1951]
128 p. 23 cm.
1. Sermons, American. I. Title.
BV4253.B64 252 51-5040
Library of Congress [2]

Sermons.
M286
B73n
Brawley, Edward M, editor.
The Negro Baptist pulpit. A collection of sermons and papers on Baptist doctrine and missionary and educational work. By colored Baptist ministers. Edited by E. M. Brawley... Philadelphia, American Baptist publication society [1890]
300p. 19½cm.

Sermons.
Gold Coast
M966.7
C17u
Capitein, Jacobus Elisa Joannes, 1717-1747.
Uitgewrogte predikatien, de trouwhertige vermaaninge van den apostel der Heydenen Paulus,... Te Amsterdam, By Bernardus Mourik, in de Nes, Jacobus Haffman, op't Rustland, Boeverkoopers.
[16] 115p. 20½cm.

Sermons.
M252
C24g
Carter, Randall Albert, bp., 1867-
Gathered fragments, by Bishop Randall Albert Carter ... Nashville, Tenn., The Parthenon press [°1939]
278 p. 21cm.
1. Methodist church—Sermons. 2. Sermons, American. I. Title.
39-32500
Library of Congress BX8333.C35G3
——— Copy 2.
Copyright A 134070 [2] 252.076

Sermons.
M252
C36
Chappelle, E. E.
The voice of God. New York, Carlton Press [1963]
119p. 20cm.

Sermons.
M252
C59b
Clement, George Clinton, bp., 1871-
Boards for life's building, by George Clinton Clement ... introduction by Rev. Thos. W. Wallace ... Cincinnati, O., Printed for the author, The Caxton press [°1924]
156 p. front. (port.) 20 cm.
I. Title.
24-10716
Library of Congress E185.7.C62
[48c1]

Sermons.
M252
C67s
Cole, Arthur A, 1895-
Seven sermons that can change your life. New York, Exposition Press, [1958]
80p. 21cm.

Sermons.
M252
C78
Cooper, William Arthur.
The awkening; sermons and sermonettes on special occasions. New York, Exposition Press [1963]
120p. 21cm.

Sermons.
M283
C88s
Mss
Crummell, Alexander, 1819-1898.
[Sermon] by Alexander Crummell.
21p. 24cm.
Manuscript.

Sermons.

M252 D74
Douglass, William, *of Philadelphia.*
Sermons preached in the African Protestant Episcopal church of St. Thomas', Philadelphia. By William Douglass, rector. Philadelphia, King & Baird, 1854.
251 p. 19½cm.
9-16546

Library of Congress, no.

Sermons.

M252 G65s
Gordon, Charles B W
Select sermons, by Rev. Charles B.W. Gordon, with an introductory sketch, by Mrs. Rev. Charles B.W. Gordon... volume 1, Third edition. Petersburg Virginia, C.B.W. Gordon, 1918.
xi, 420p. front. 20cm.

Sermons.

M815.5 G88 V.1
Grimke, Francis James, 1850-1937.
Addresses and sermons. (bound volume of pamphlets. no.1-23.

Sermons.

M815.5 G88 V.1 no.1
Grimke, Francis James, 1850-
Some lessons from the assassination of President Wil iam McKinley, by Rev. Francis J. Brimke... delivered Spetember, 1901.
15p. 23cm.

Sermons.

M815.5 G88
Grimke, Francis James, 1850-
Some lessons from the assassination of President William McKinley, by Rev. Franci J. Grimke...delivered September 22, 1901.
15p. 23cm.

Sermons.

M815.5 G88 V.1, no.3
Grimke, Francis James, 1850-
The things of paramount importance in the development of the Negro race. A discourse delivered in the Fifteenth Street Presbyterian Church, Washington, D.C., March 29, 1903, by the pastor Rev. Francis J. Grimke.
13p. 23cm.

Sermons.

M323 G88
Grimke, Francis James, 1850-1937.
The Negro: his rights and wrongs, the forces for him and against him. By Rev. Francis J. Grimke ... [Washington, 1898?]
2 p. l., 100 p. 18cm.
"These sermons were delivered in the Fifteenth street Presbyterian church, Washington, D. C., November 20th and 27th, and December 4th and 11th" [1898]

1. ~~Negroes~~ Sermons.

Library of Congress E185.6.G85 12-11519
[a43b1]

Sermons.

M252 H33d
Haynes, Lemuel, 1753-1833.
Divine decrees, an encouragement to the use of means. A sermon, delivered at Granville (N.Y.) June 25, 1805, before the Evangelical Society, instituted for the purpose of aiding pious and needy young men in acquiring education for the work of the gospel ministry, by Lemuel Haynes. Utica, Printed by Seward and Williams, 1810.
23p. 17cm.

Sermons.

M252 H33s
Haynes, Lemuel, 1753-1833.
[A sermon] delivered at Rutland, (West Parish), October 28th, 1804. Occasioned by the sudden and much lamented death of the late Rev. Job Swift.
pp. [23] -32, in: Job Swift, Discourses on religious subjects...Middlebury, Vermont, Printed by Huntington and Fitch, Nov. 1805.

Sermons.

M252 H74a
Holsey, Lucius H , 1842-
Autobiography, sermons, addresses and essays of Bishop L.H. Holsey... Atlanta, Georgia, Franklin printing and publishing co., 1898.
v, 288p. front. 21cm.

Sermons.

M287.8 H76n
Hood, James Walker, bp., 1831-
The Negro in the Christian pulpit; or the two characters and two destines, as delineated in twenty-one practical sermons. By J. W. Hood... with an appendix containing specimen sermons by other bishops of the same church. Introduction by Rev. A. G. Haygood... Raleigh, Edwards, Broughton & co., 1884.
363p. plates. 19cm.

Sermons.

M252 H78
Horace, J Gentry
None good but God; a general introduction to scientific christianity in the form of a spiritual key to Matthew 19:16-22. New York, Exposition Press [1962]
105p. 21cm.
"An Exposition-testament book."
Portrait of author on book jacket.

Sermons.

M252 H91a
Huntley, Thomas Elliott.
As I saw it, not commUnism but commOnism; a prophetic appraisal of the status quo, a message for our times and for all times, for America and for all nations. New York, Comet Press Books [1955, °1954]
146 p. 23 cm.
"The Central Baptist Church on Wheels": p. 119-146.

1. Communism and religion. 2. U. S.—Race question. 3. St. Louis. Central Baptist Church. 4. Baptists—Sermons. 5. Sermons, American. I. Title.

BX6452.H8 252.06 55-874 ‡
Library of Congress [2]

Sermons.

M252 Im2b
Imes, William Lloyd, 1889-
The black pastures, an American pilgrimage in two centuries; essays and sermons. [1st ed.] Nashville, Hemphill Press, 1957.
146 p. illus. 24 cm.

1. Presbyterian Church—Sermons. 2. Sermons, American. 3. U. S.—Race question. I. Title.

BX9178.I 5B5 252.051 57-11472 ‡
Library of Congress [2]

Sermons.

M252 Im2f
Imes, William Lloyd, 1889-
Faith versus success.
(In: Poling, Daniel A. ed. A treasury of great sermons. New York, Greenberg, 1944. p. 181-185)

Sermons.

M252 Im2g
Imes, William Lloyd, 1889-
God's guiding hand in our history; A sermon for the Dundee centennial. New York, Dundee observer, 1947.
Broadside.

Sermons.

M815.5 J13e
Jackson, Algernon Brashear, 1878-
Evolution and life: a series of lay sermons. By Algernon Brashear Jackson... Philadelphia, Pa., A.M.E. book concern, 1911.
xiv, 15-109p. front. 19cm.

Sermons.

M252 J62p
Johnson, H[enry] T[heodore] 1857-
Pulpit, pew and pastorate. By H. T. Johnson... [n. p., 1902]
139 p. 20cm.
Preface by Edgar J. Penney; Foreword by Bishop B. F. Lee.

Sermons.

M252 J63h
Johnson, John Howard, 1897-
Harlem, The war, and other addresses, by John Howard Johnson ... New York, W. Malliet and company, 1942.
6 p. l., 168 p. front. (port.) 22cm.
"First edition."

1. Protestant Episcopal church in the U. S. A.—Sermons. 2. Sermons, American. I. Title.

Library of Congress BX5937.J4H3 42-22829
[3] 252.03

Sermons,

M252 J63p
Johnson, John Howard, 1897-
A place of adventure; essays and sermons. Foreword by Hughell E. W. Fosbroke. [Rev. ed.] Greenwich, Conn., Seabury Press, 1955.
180 p. 19 cm.

1. New York. St. Martin's Church. 2. Protestant Episcopal Church in the U. S. A.—Sermons. 3. Sermons, American. I. Title.

BX5980.N5M34 1955 283.747 55-13760 ‡
Library of Congress [2]

Sermons,

M252 J634
Johnson, William Bishop, 1858-
The scourging of a race, and other sermons and addresses by W. Bishop Johnson ... Washington, Beresford, printer, 1904.
viii, 228 p. front. (port.) 19½cm.

1. Baptists—Sermons. 2. Sermons, American. I. Title.

Library of Congress BX6452.J6 4-26231
[a44c1]

Sermons.

M252
K58

King, Martin Luther.
Strength to love. [1st ed.] New York, Harper & Row [1963]

146 p. 22 cm.

1. Baptists, Negro—Sermons. 2. Sermons, American. I. Title.

BX6452.K5 252.06 63-12051 ‡

Library of Congress [5]

Sermons.

MB9
M34j

Marrant, John, 1755-1791.
A journal of the Rev. John Marrant, from Aug. the 18th, 1785 to the 16th of March 1790. To which are added, Two sermons; one preached on Ragged Island on Sabbath day, the 27th day of Oct. 1787; the other at Boston, in New England, on Thursday, the 24th of June, 1787. London: Printed for the author: Sold by J. Taylor and Co. at the Royal Exchange; and Mr. Marrant, No. 2 Black Horse Court, in Aldergate-Street. 1790.
106p. 20cm.

Sermons.

M304
P19
v.6,no.14

Miller, George Frazier.
The sacredness of humanity, annual sermon of the conference of church workers (Episcopal) among colored people at St. Philip's church, New York, October 6-9, 1914. Brooklyn, Frank R. Chisholm, printer, 1914.

12p. 22p.

Sermons.

M252
M85f

Moses, W H
Five commandments of Jesus, Matthew 5: 21-48... Study daily each in the light of all by W.H. Moses.

162p. 16cm.

Sermons.

M252
P38t

Pennington, James William Charles, 1812-1871.
A two years' absence, or a farewell sermon, preached in the fifth Congregational Church, by J.W.C. Penington. Nov. 2d., 1845. Hartford, Published by H. T. Wells, 1845.

31p. 22½cm.

Sermons.

M252
P87

Powell, Adam Clayton, 1908-
Keep the faith, baby! New York, Trident Press, 1967.

298 p. 22 cm.

1. Baptists, Negro—Sermons. 2. Sermons, American I. Title.

BX6452.P59 252.06 67-16402

Library of Congress [12]

Sermons.

M286.
P87p

Powell, Adam Clayton, 1865-
Palestine and saints in Caesar's household, by A. Clayton Powell, sr. New York, R. R. Smith, 1939.

viii p., 2 l., 13-217 p. 21cm.

1. Palestine—Descr. & trav. 2. Baptists—Sermons. 3. Sermons, American. I. Title.

Library of Congress BX6452.P6 39-25033

——— Copy 2.

Copyright A 131759 [2] 915.69

Sermons.

M223.2
P87

Powell, W H R
A supervised life; or, Impressions from the Twenty-third psalm, by W. H. R. Powell ... [Philadelphia, Press of B. F. Emery company, 1945]

xiii, 145 p. plates. 19cm.

1. Bible. O. T. Psalms XXIII—Sermons. 2. Baptists—Sermons. 3. Sermons, American. I. Title.

45-5226

Library of Congress BS1450 23d.P6

[3] 223.2

Sermons.

M252
R13m

Raikes, John W 1850-
Man, know thyself. By John W. Raikes. 2d ed., rev. and enl. Wilmington, Del., H. A. Roop, printer, 1913.

92 p. 17½cm. $0.50

I. Title.

Library of Congress 13-8365

Copyright A 343851

Sermons.

M252
R16

Rankin, Arthur E
The call of the ag e; sermons and addresses, by Arthur E. Rankin ... Kansas City, The press of Thomas & Williams c1926
112p. port. 19cm.

Sermons.

M252
R17o

Ransome, William Lee
An old story for this new day and other sermons and addresses. Richmond, Central Publishing co., 1954.

207p. 20cm.

Sermons.

M252
Se89

Sewell, George A.
A motif for living and other sermons. New York, Vantage Press c1963

66p. 21cm.

Sermons.

M252
Sp3s

Spearman, Henry Kuhns.
Soul magnets; twelve sermons from Testament texts, by Rev. Henry Kuhns Spearman, compiled by a memorial by Miss Elizabeth F. Spearman. [Philadelphia, A.M.E. Book Concern, 1929]

116p. front.(port.) 19cm.

Sermons.

M252
St67
1924

Stokes, Andrew Jackson, 1859-
Select sermons, by Rev. A. J. Stokes ... [Nashville, Natl. Baptist pub. board, ~~1920~~] c1924
152 p. front. (port.) plates. 20cm.

Revised edition.

I. Title.

Library of Congress 20-8017

——— Copy 2.

Copyright A 566649 [2]

Sermons.

M200
T42gr

Thurman, Howard, 1899-
The growing edge. [1st ed. New York] Harper [1956]

181 p. 22 cm.

1. Baptists—Sermons. 2. Sermons, American. I. Title.

BX6333.T5G7 252.06 56-12058 ‡

Library of Congress [10]

Sermons.

M252
T49b

Tindley, Charles Albert.
A book of sermons, by Rev. Charles Albert Tindley... with introductory remarks by Rt. Rev. J.S. Caldwell... A brief sketch of the writer's life, in his own words to Dr. S. W. Thomas ... Philadelphia, Pa., Edward T. Duncan [n.d.]

151p. front. 20½cm.

Sermons.

M252
T49b
1932

Tindley, Charles Albert, 1859-1933.
Book of sermons, by Rev. Chas. A. Tindley, with an introduction, by Bishop J.S. Caldwell. Philadelphia, Published by Charles A. Tindley, 1932.

viii, 153p. front (port.) 19½cm.

Sermons.

M304
P19
v.3, no.1

Walker, Charles Thomas, 1858-
The Negro Problem. Its scriptural solution, by Rev. Charles T. Walker, delivered at Tabernacle Baptist Church, Augusta Georgia, Sunday, June 4, 1893. Augusta, Ga., Chronicle Job Printing Co.,
16p. 23cm.

Sermons.

M252
W69

Wilson, William Green
From son-lit skies. New York, Carlton Press, 1964.

58p. 21cm.
Portrait of author on book jacket.

1. Sermons, American. I. Title.

Sermons.

M252
W75e

Wisher, Daniel W
Echoes from the gospel trumpet; three sermons and a paper, by Daniel W. Wisher ,.. New York, E. Scott Co., c1896
109p. port. (front.) 17½cm.

Sermons.

M252
W93r

Wright, Nathan.
The riddle of life, and other sermons. Boston, Bruce Humphries [1952]

98 p. 24 cm.

1. Protestant Episcopal Church in the U. S. A.—Sermons. 2. Sermons, American. I. Title.

BX5937.W7R5 252.03 52-14342 ‡

Library of Congress [2]

Sermons.
M252
W98
Wynn, Daniel Webster, 1919-
Timeless issues ₍by₎ Daniel W. Wynn. New York, Philosophical Library ₍1967₎
x, 144 p. 22 cm.
1. Methodist Church—Sermons. 2. Sermons, American. I. Title.
BX8472.W9 252.07 66-20219
Library of Congress ₍5₎

Servants.
M640
R54h
1828
Roberts, Robert
The house servant's directory. Or, a monitor for private families: comprising hints on the arrangement and performance of servant's work... and upwards of 100 various and useful receipts, chiefly compiled for the use of house servants... Boston, Munroe and Francis; New York, Charles S. Francis, 1828.
180p. 17½cm.

S. Africa
M896.1
Se7
Setsoto; Recitations for the elementary schools. Morija. Sesuto Book Depot, 1946.
44p. 15½cm.
1. Sotho language.

The serpent and the staff.
M813.5
Y46se
Yerby, Frank, 1916-
The serpent and the staff. New York, Dial Press, 1958.
377 p. 21 cm.
I. Title.
Full name: Frank Garvin Yerby.
PZ3.Y415Se 58-12773 ‡
Library of Congress ₍12₎

Servants.
M640
R54h
1843
Roberts, Robert.
The house servant's directory. Or, A monitor for private families: comprising hints on the arrangement and performance of servants' work ... and upwards of 100 useful receipts, chiefly comp. for the use of house servants ... By Robert Roberts ... ₍2d ed.₎ Boston, Munroe and Francis; New York, C. S. Francis, 1828.
xiv, ₍15₎-180 p. 18½cm.
1. Servants. 2. Receipts. I. Title.
7-28299
Library of Congress TX331.R64
₍a23c1₎

M811.5
Se8b
Seuell, Malchus M , 1911-
The black Christ and verse. Downey, Calif., The Author, 1957.
77p. 21cm.
"To National Association for the Advancement of Colored People from Malchus M. Seuell, author and publisher, Oct. '57."
1. Poetry, American. I. Title.

Cuba
M972.91
Se6e
Serra y Montalvo, Rafael, 1858-1909.
...Ensayos politicos. New York, n.p. 1899.
224p. port. illus. 23cm.
Tercera serie.
1. Cuban question-1895-1898.
I. Benjamin, R.O.C. - Los Negros Americanos, p.135-42.

Servants.
M640
R54h
1827
Roberts, Robert.
The house servant's directory. Or, A monitor for private families: comprising hints on the arrangement and performance of servants' work ... and upwards of 100 useful receipts, chiefly comp. for the use of house servants ... By Robert Roberts ... ₍2d ed.₎ Boston, Munroe and Francis; New York, C. S. Francis, 1828.
xiv, ₍15₎-180 p. 18½cm.
1. Servants. 2. Receipts. I. Title.
7-28299
Library of Congress TX331.R64
₍a23c1₎

M811.5
Se8m
Seuell, Malchus M , 1911-
The mad pagan and verse. Downey, California, Elena Quinn, 1959.
72p. 22cm.
"To Mr. Spingarn's Collection of books on Negro leiterature at Howard University from Malchus M. Seuell, a - Negro. 10/8/62. For the record let me say Firstly - I am an American - a - Negro - a Poet and last but not least an Individual. Malchus M. Seuell. 10/8/62."
1. Poetry. I. Title.

Cuba
M972.91
Se6
Serra y Montalvo, Rafael, 1858-
Para blancos y negros; ensayos políticos, sociales y económicos, por Rafael Serra. 4 ser. Habana, Impr. "El Score," 1907.
215, ₍4₎ p. incl. illus., ports., facsim. 21½cm.
"Lecciones de política, escrito en inglés por C. Nordhoff, y vertido al castellano por R. Serra": p. ₍25₎-34.
1. Negroes. 2. Negroes in Cuba. I. Title.
8-1541 Revised
Library of Congress F1789.N3S4
₍r44b2₎

Services of colored Americans...
M350
N32
1851
Nell, William C.
Services of colored Americans, in the wars of 1776 and 1812. By William C. Nell. Boston, Printed by Prentiss & Sawyer, 1851.
24 p. 231/2 cm.

Brazil
M869.3
M18seu
Seus 30 melhores contos.
Machado de Assis, Joaquim Maria, 1839-1908.
Seus 30 melhores contos. Precedidos de uma introdução geral. Rio de Janeiro, Editora Jose Aguilar, 1961.
478p. illus. 16cm.
Portrait of author.

Uganda
M916
Se6
Serunkuma, J N B
Omuseveni eyagenda okusevena ₍One of the seventh (K. A. R.) goes 'a-severing'₎ Kampala, Eagle Press, 1959.
68p. 21½cm.
Written in Luganda.
1. Africa - Description and travel.
I. Title.

M267.3
Ar7
Sessions, J A
Dayton public affairs commissions.
(In: Young Men's Christian Associations. Association of Secretaries. Men working; the Y.M.C.A. program ... New York, Association, Press, c1936. 24cm. p. 32-34)

Arabia
M892.8
M88s
The seven odes; the first chapter in Arabic literature.
Mu'allakat. English.
The seven odes; the first chapter in Arabic literature ₍by₎ A. J. Arberry. London, G. Allen & Unwin; New York, Macmillan ₍1957₎
258 p. 22 cm.
I. Arberry, Arthur John, 1905- tr. II. Title.
PJ7642.E5A7 892.71 57-13803 ‡
Library of Congress ₍20₎

Servants.
M301
D853p
Du Bois, William Edward Burghardt, 1868-
... The Philadelphia Negro; a social study by W. E. Burghardt Du Bois ... Together with a special report on domestic service by Isabel Eaton ... Philadelphia, Pub. for the University, 1899.
xx, 520 p. incl. diagrs. 2 fold. plans. 20cm. (Publications of the University of Pennsylvania. Series in political economy and public law. no. 14)
Contents.—The Philadelphia Negro.—Appendixes: A. Schedules used in the house-to-house inquiry. B. Legislation, etc., of Pennsylvania in regard to the Negro. C. Bibliography.—Special report on Negro domestic service in the seventh ward, Philadelphia, by I. Eaton.
1. Negroes — Philadelphia. 2. U. S. — Race question. 3. Servants. I. Eaton, Isabel. II. Title.
5-33580
Library of Congress F158.9.N3D8
——— Copy 2. H31.P4 no. 14
₍45d1₎

Set my people free.
M89
L63l1
Lilly, William E.
Set my people free; a Negro's life of Lincoln, by William E. Lilly. New York, Farrar & Rinehart, incorporated ₍°1932₎
viii, 269 p. front. (port.) 22½cm.
1. Lincoln, Abraham, pres. U. S., 1809-1865. I. Title.
32-4497
Library of Congress E457.L732
₍43h1₎ 923.173

Seven poets in search of an answer.
M811.5
H87p
Yoseloff, Thomas, 1913- ed.
Seven poets in search of an answer: Maxwell Bodenheim, Joy Davidman, Langston Hughes, Aaron Kramer, Alfred Kreymborg, Martha Millet, Norman Rosten. A poetic symposium edited by Thomas Yoseloff, with an introductory note by Shaemas O'Sheel. New York, B. Ackerman, incorporated ₍1944₎
8 p. l., 15-118 p. illus. (ports.) 24cm.
1. American poetry—20th cent. I. Bodenheim, Maxwell, 1893- II. Davidman, Joy. III. Hughes, Langston, 1902- IV. Kramer, Aaron. V. Kreymborg, Alfred, 1883- VI. Millet, Martha. VII. Rosten, Norman. VIII. Title.
44-4241
Library of Congress PS614.Y58
₍10₎ 811.5082

M331
H334
Servants.
Haynes, Elizabeth Ross.
Negroes in domestic service in the United States, by Elizabeth Ross Haynes. Washington, D. C., Association for the study of Negro life and history, 1923.
384-442p. 25½cm.
Reprinted from the Journal of Negro History, vol. 8, no. 4, Oct. 1923.

M973
S87n
Seton, Julia.
The Negro race, its origins, its work, its destiny ₍by₎ Julia Seton... Los Angeles, Cal., Seton publishers ᶜ1919₎
35p. 18cm.

The seven seals.
M231.74
Yo8s
Young, Lucinda Smith.
The seven seals. "A sinner's dream," "conversion," "Daniel in the lion's den," "meditation," "distance of falling," "vision of the judgement," "vision of after the judgement," By Madame Lucinda Smith-Young. Philadelphia, Pa., J. Gordon Baugh, 1903.
199p. front. plates. 18½cm.

The seven words from the cross.
M232.963 Hood, Solomon Porter
H76s The seven words from the cross [by] Solomon Porter Hood ... Nashville, A. M. E. Sunday School Union Publishing House [n.d.]
128 p. 19cm.

M252 Sewell, George A.
Se89 A motif for living and other sermons. New York, Vantage Press [1963]
66p. 21cm.
Portrait of author on book jacket.
1. Sermons. I. Title.

Sexual ethics
M176 Randolph, Paschal Beverly, 1825-1874.
R15 ... Magia sexualis. Traduction français par Maria de Naglowska. Edition originale. Paris, R. Télin, 1931.
218p., 1 l. illus., plates. (incl. music, port. col.) port. fold. tables. 23cm.
At head of title: P. B. Randolph.

Seventh Day Adventists
Nigeria
M966.9 Babamuboni, I E
B11o Ojo Oluwa (Sunday) lati owo Mr. I. E. Babamuboni. Lagos, Tanimola printing and bookbinding works, 1927.
12p. 18½cm.
In Yoruba.

Sex
Jamaica
M824 McFarlane, J E Clare, 1894-1962
M16s Sex and Christianity; or the case against the system of monogamous marriage ... Kingston, Jamaica. Printed for the author by the Gleaner co., 1932.
116p. 20cm.
Autographed copy.

M811.5 Seymour, Alexander.
Se9b Brighter Christmas; Christmas poems, by Alexander Seymour. New York, Crest publishing co. [1945]
16p. 20½cm.
1. Poetry. I. Title.

Seventh-day Adventists.
M286.7 Miller, George Frazier.
M61a Adventism answered (the Sabbath question) Part first: Passing of the law and the introduction of grace. Part second: Some phases of the gospel liberty. By George Frazier Miller ... Brooklyn, N. Y., Guide printing and publishing company, 1905.
214 p. 20½cm.
1. Seventh-day Adventists. I. Title. 6-5699 Revised
Library of Congress BX6124.M46
[r41b2] 286.7

M614 Sex--Cause and determination.
R66s Roman, Charles Victor, 1864-1934.
Some ramifications of the sexual impulse. Reprinted from the Journal of the National Medical Association, October-December, 1920.
4p. 28cm.

M811.5 Seymour, Alexander.
Se91 Love lighters; love poems, by Alexander Seymour. [New York, Crest publishing co., c 1945]
15p. 13½cm.
1. Poetry.

Seventh-day Adventists-Doctrinal and controversial works.
M286.67 Peterson, Frank Loris.
P44 The hope of the race, by Frank Loris Peterson. Nashville, Tenn., Southern publishing association [°1934]
333 p. incl. front., illus., ports., diagrs. col. pl. 20½cm.
1. Seventh-day Adventists—Doctrinal and controversial works. 2. Negroes—Religion. I. Title. 35-1032
Library of Congress BX6154.P45
——— Copy 2.
Copyright A 77848 [3] 230.67

Sex (Psychology)
M301 Hernton, Calvin C
H43 Sex and racism in America [by] Calvin C. Hernton. [1st ed.] Garden City, N. Y., Doubleday, 1965.
180 p. 22 cm.
Bibliographical footnotes.
1. ~~U. S.~~—Race question. 2. Sex (Psychology) 3. Miscegenation. I. Title.
E185.62.H4 301.451 64-20576
Library of Congress [5]

Seymour, Arthur James, 1914-
West Indies
M21.08 Kyk-over-al anthology of West Indian poetry.
K98 Revised by A. J. Seymour. Georgetown, British Guiana, 1957.
99p. 23cm. (Kykoveral 22)

Seventy Negro spirituals.
M784 Fisher, William Arms, 1861- ed.
F52 Seventy Negro spirituals, edited by William Arms Fisher ... Boston, Oliver Ditson company; New York, C. H. Ditson & co.; [etc., etc., °1926]
xxxiv, [2], 212 p. ports. 32 x 24½cm. (The musicians library)
Edition for high voice.
Bibliography: p. [xxxiii]-xxxiv.
1. Negro songs. I. Title. II. Title: Spirituals. 26-18007
Library of Congress M1.M9F43H
——— Edition for low voice. M1.M9F43L
Copyright A 950085 [a39q1]

Sex and race...
M973 Rogers, Joel Augustus, 1880-
R63s Sex and race; Negro-Caucasian mixing in all ages and all lands, by J. A. Rogers ... New York city, J. A. Rogers publications [1940-44]
3 v. fronts. (v. 1-2) illus. (incl. ports., map, facsims.) 23½cm.
Vol. 2 has subtitle: A history of white, Negro and Indian miscegenation in the two Americas.
Includes bibliographies.
CONTENTS.—v. 1. The old world.—v. 2. The new world.—v. 3. Why white and black mix in spite of opposition.
1. Race problems. 2. Negroes. 3. Miscegenation. I. Title. 41-20
Library of Congress GN237.R6 1940
[45r45e2] 572

M973 Shackelford, Jane Dabney.
Sh1 The child's story of the Negro, by Jane Dabney Shackelford ... illustrated by Lois Mailou Jones. Washington, D. C., The Associated publishers, inc. [°1938]
xi, [1], 219 p. illus. (incl. ports.) 20cm.
Includes bibliographies.
History. ~~1. Negroes.~~ I. Title. 38-27221
Library of Congress GN645.S5
[45f1] [572.96] 372.4

75 years of freedom;
M973 U. S. *Library of Congress.*
Un3s 75 years of freedom; commemoration of the 75th anniversary of the proclamation of the 13th amendment to the Constitution of the United States. The Library of Congress. [Washington, U. S. Govt. print. off., 1943]
cover-title, vi, 108 p. col. pl. 26cm.
"The contribution of the American Negro to American culture was the theme of a series of exhibits and concerts in the Library of Congress commencing on December 18th, the 75th anniversary of the proclamation of the Thirteenth amendment, which ended slavery in the United States."—p. v.
1. Negroes. 2. Negro songs. 3. Negro art. 4. Negro literature (American) I. Title. 43-52457
Library of Congress E185.6.U597
[15] 325.260973

Sex and racism in America.
M301 Hernton, Calvin C
H43 Sex and racism in America [by] Calvin C. Hernton. [1st ed.] Garden City, N. Y., Doubleday, 1965.
180 p. 22 cm.
Bibliographical footnotes.
1. ~~U. S.~~—Race question. 2. Sex (Psychology) 3. Miscegenation. I. Title.
E185.62.H4 301.451 64-20576
Library of Congress [5]

M813.5 Shackelford, Otis M 1871-
Sh1 Lillian Simmons; or, The conflict of sections; a story by Otis M. Shackelford ... illustrated by William Hamilton. Kansas City, Mo., ~~Burton publishing company~~ [°1915] R. M. Rigby printing co.
~~[xxxxxxxxxxxxxxxx]~~ $1.50
7-204p. illus. 21cm.
1. U. S.—Race question—Fiction. I. Title. 15-16441
Library of Congress PZ3.S5228L
Copyright A 411052

Seward, Theodore Frelinghuysin, 1835-1902, comp.
M784 Jubilee songs: as sung by the Jubilee
J87 singers... enlarged, compiled by Theodore F. Seward, and George L. White. New York, Biglow and Main [c1872]
160p. 23cm.
Contains Part I and II.

Sex instruction.
Kenya
M376 Inoti, F M
In7 Mwari uri muuno uti nda [A story for girls] Nairobi, Eagle Press, 1949.
17p. 18cm.
Written in Meru.
1. Sex instruction.

M89 Shackelford, Otis M 1871-
Sh1s Seeking the best. Dedicated to the negro youth. By Otis M. Shackelford, A. B. Kansas City, Mo., ~~Franklin Hudson publishing co., 1909.~~ Burton Publishing Co., 1911.
177 p. incl. front. (port.) 20cm. $1.00
I. Title. 9-22716
Library of Congress
Copyright A 245889 [28d1]

M811.5
Shlm
Shackelford, Theodore Henry, 1888-1923
Mammy's cracklin' bread, and other poems, by Theodore Henry Shackelford; cover illustration by the author ... [Philadelphia, Press of I. W. Klopp co., °1916]
58 p., 1 l. front. (port.) 18cm. $0.50
Contains - When Daddy Hol's Got Ham'. A Supplement to Mammy's Cracklin' Bread and other Poems. [Philadelphia Press of I. W. Klopp Co., c 1917]
I. Title. 1. Poetry.
Library of Congress PS3601.S5M3 1916 16-13167
Copyright A 433159

M811.5
Shl
Shackelford, Theodore Henry, 1888-1923
My country, and other poems, by Theodore Henry Shackelford, illustrated by the author, introduction by Charles Hastings Dodd ... [Philadelphia, Press of I. W. Klopp co., °1918]
216 p. front. (port.) plates. 19½cm.
"Contains all the poems included in ... 'Mammy's cracklin' bread'."
Music: p. [158]-[161]
I. Title. 1. Poetry.
Library of Congress PS3601.S5M8 1918 18-12942
[43b1]

M370
B818t
Shackled still.
Brownlee, Fred L
Toward the elimination of American racism, by Fred L. Brownlee and Ruth A. Morton. New York, American Missionary Association, 1942.
22p. port. tables. 23cm.
White authors.
Partial reprint of 1940-42 biennial report of the American Missionary Association.
Cover title: Shackled still.

M814.5
Shla
Shackleford, William H.
Along the highway, by Wm. H. Shackleford... Nashville, Tenn., African M. E. Sunday School Union n.d.
v. front. 19½cm.
I. Title.

M268
Shls
Shackleford, William H
Sunday school problems, written especially for Sunday school workers, by Wm. H. Shackleford. [n.p.] A.M.E. Sunday school union [n.d.]
v. 19½cm.
volume 1 and 2 bound together.
1. Sunday school.
2. Churches.

M812.5
Ed5sh
Shades and shadows.
Edmonds, Randolph.
Shades and shadows, by Randolph Edmonds. Boston, Meador publishing company, 1930.
171 p. 20 cm.
CONTENTS.—The devil's price.—Hewers of wood.—Shades and shadows.—Everyman's land.—The tribal chief.—The phantom treasure.
I. Title.
[Full name: Sheppard Randolph Edmonds]
Library of Congress PS3509.D5685 1930 30-28709
[2] 812.5

M814.5
E159
Shadow and act.
Ellison, Ralph.
Shadow and act. New York, Random House [1964]
xxii, 317 p. 22 cm.
1. ~~Negroes in~~ literature. 2. ~~Negro~~ authors. I. Title.
PS153.N5E4 1964 809.8 64-18926
Library of Congress [4-1]

MB9
G35g
Shadow and light.
Gibbs, Mifflin Wistar.
Shadow and light; an autobiography with reminiscences of the last and present century. By Mifflin Wistar Gibbs, with an introduction by Booker T. Washington ... Washington, D. C., 1902.
xv, [2], 4-372 p. front., pl., port. 20cm.
1. Negroes. I. Title.
Library of Congress E185.97.G44 2-4974
Copyright [32b1]

M301
J63s
Shadow of the plantation
Johnson, Charles Spurgeon, 1893-
Shadow of the plantation, by Charles S. Johnson ... Chicago, Ill., The University of Chicago press [1934]
xxiv, 214, [1] p. front., plates, diagr. 22 cm.
Macon county, Alabama, was the area chosen for this survey. cf. Introd.
1. Plantation life. 2. Negroes—Macon co., Ala. I. Title.
34-19995
Library of Congress E185.93.A3J6
[44h1] 325.2609761

M323.4
G862
The shadow that scares me.
Gregory, Dick, 1932-
The shadow that scares me. Edited by James R. McGraw. [1st ed.] Garden City, N. Y., Doubleday, 1968.
213 p. 22 cm.
1. ~~Negroes~~—Civil rights. I. Title.
E185.615.G7 323.4 68-10561
Library of Congress [25-2]

Brit. Guiana
M823.91
M69s
Shadows move among them.
Mittelholzer, Edgar, 1909-
Shadows move among them. London, Peter Nevill, 1951.
334p. 18cm.

M811.5
W65s
Shady-rest.
Wilkinson, Henry Bertram, 1889-
Shady-rest, by Henry B. Wilkinson ... New York, F. H. Hitchcock [°1928]
5 p. l., 69 p. 19½cm.
Poems.
"Only two hundred and fifty copies of this book have been printed and the type distributed."
I. Title.
Library of Congress PS3545.I 39S5 1928 28-21570
Copyright A 1054264 [3]

South Africa
M968
P69d
Shakespeare, William, 1564-1616.
Plaatje, Solomon Tshekisho (1878-1932)
Dintšhontšho tsa bo-Juliuse Kesara; e leng lokwalô lwa "Julius Caesar" lo lo kwadilweng, kê William Shakespeare. Lo siamisitšwe e bile lo relagantšwe kê G. P. Lestrade. [4th ed.] Johannesburg, Witwatersrand University Press, 1954.
75p. 18cm. (Bantu Treasury, edited by C. M. Doke, III)
I. Shakespeare, William. II. Title. III. Series.

S. Africa
M968
P69d
1879½
Shakespeare, William, 1564-1616.
Plaatje, Solomon Tshekisho, 1878-1936. tr.
Dintshontsho tsa Bo-Juliuse Kesara, kê William Shakespeare [Translated by S. T. Plaatje; foreward by G. P. Lestrade] Johannesburg, University of Witwatersrand Press, 1942.
75 p. 17½ cm.
Shakespeare's-Julius Caesar translated into Tswana.

U.S.
M822.3
D35
Shakespeare, William, 1564-1616 - Criticism and interpretation.
DeBerry, Frances C 1882-
All the world's a stage for Shakespeare's comedies; a modern interpretation of the Bard's humor. New York, Exposition Press, [1958]
139p. 20cm.
Picture and biographical sketch of author on the book jacket.

Nigeria
M820.7
Og9
Shakespeare, William, 1564-1616 - Study.
Oguine, O D M
Questions and answers on twelfth night, with summaries. Onitsha [Nigeria, Etudo, 1962]
58p. 21cm.

Nigeria
M820.7
Uz7m
Shakespeare, William, 1564-1616 - Study.
Uzodinma, Eddy C C
Shakespeare: Macbeth. Questions and answers with summaries and critical appreciation. Onitsha, Nigeria, Etudo [1962]
68p. 20½cm.

Nigeria
M820.7
Uz7
Shakespeare, William, 1564-1616 - Study.
Uzodinma, Eddy C C
The tragedy of Prince Hamlet. Questions and answers; running analysis and critical essay; Macbeth and Hamlet contrasted. [Onitsha, Nigeria, Etudo, 1963]
83p. 21cm.

Nigeria
M820.7
Uz7m
Shakespeare: Macbeth.
Uzodinma, Eddy C C
Shakespeare: Macbeth. Questions and answers with summaries and critical appreciation. Onitsha, Nigeria, Etudo [1962]
68p. 20½cm.

M811.5
H87sh
Shakespeare in Harlem.
Hughes, Langston, 1902-
Shakespeare in Harlem, by Langston Hughes, with drawings by E. McKnight Kauffer. New York, A. A. Knopf, 1942.
7 p. l., 3-124 p., 1 l. incl. front., illus. 22cm.
"A book of light verse."—4th prelim. leaf.
"First edition."
I. Title.
[Full name: James Langston Hughes]
Library of Congress PS3515.U274S5 42-6325
[47o2] 811.5

M301
D853r5
Shall the Negro be encouraged to seek cultural equality?
Du Bois, William Edward Burghardt, 1868-
Report of debate conducted by the Chicago forum "Shall the Negro be encouraged to seek cultural equality?" Affirmative: W.E. Burghardt Du Bois... Negative: Lothrop Stoddard ... Chicago, [Chicago forum council, °1929]
24p. 19cm.

Shall we live without a sorrow?

M811.5 G65sh Gordon, Selma.
Shall we live without a sorrow? [poem]
[lacks imprint]

Broadside 16½x10

M301 R27sh Share-cropping.
Reid, Ira DeAugustine, 1901-
Sharecroppers all by Arthur F. Raper and Ira DeA. Reid. Chapel Hill, The University of North Carolina press, 1941.

xp., 21., 3-281p. front. plates. 21½cm.

Sharpeville, South Africa-Massacre, 1960.

Africa, South
M968 R25 **Reeves, Richard Ambrose, *Bp.*, 1899-**
Shooting at Sharpeville; the agony of South Africa. With a foreword by Chief Luthuli. [1st American ed.] Boston, Houghton Mifflin, 1961 [°1960]
xvi, 141 p. illus., map. 23 cm.

1. Sharpeville, South Africa—Massacre, 1960. I. Title.

DT944.S5R4 1961 323.2 61-5373

Library of Congress [61k10]

Shall we overcome?

M261.8 J717 **Jones, Howard O**
Shall we overcome? A challenge to Negro and white Christians [by] Howard O. Jones. Westwood, N. J., F. H. Revell Co. [1966]
146 p. 21 cm.

1. Church and race problems—U. S. 2. Negroes—Religion. I. Title.

BT734.2.J6 261.83 66-17048

Library of Congress [5]

Share my world.

M811.5 J629s Johnson, Georgia Douglas
Share my world; a book of poems. [Washington, D.C., Halfway House, 1962].

32p. 15cm.

I. Title.

M323 Sh2 **Shaw, Alexander P.**
Christianizing race relations as a negro sees it [by] Reverend A. P. Shaw ... [Los Angeles, Wetzel publishing company, °1928]
88 p. 20½cm.

Race problems.
1. Negroes. 2. U. S.—Race question. I. Title.

28-13116

Library of Congress E185.61.S53
——— Copy 2.
Copyright A 1077235 [2]

The shame of America...

M06 Am3 no. 21 **Grimké, Archibald Henry, 1849-**
The shame of America, or, The negro's case against the republic, by Archibald H. Grimke. Washington, D. C., The Academy, 1924.
18 p. 23cm. (American negro academy. Occasional papers, no. 21)

1. Negroes. 2. U. S.—Race question. I. Title.

Library of Congress E185.A51 no. 21 24-13777
[a24b2]

M301 R27sh Sharecroppers all.
Reid, Ira DeAugustine, 1901-
Sharecroppers all by Arthur F. Raper and Ira DeA. Reid. Chapel Hill, The University of North Carolina press, 1941.

xp., 21., 3-281p. front. plates. 21½cm.

Shaw, Esther Popel

See

Popel, Esther

Rhodesia
M968.91 Sh17 Shamuyarira, Nathan M 1929-
Crisis in Rhodesia. With a foreword by Sir Hugh Foot. [London] Andre Deutsch [1965]

240p. map. 22½cm.
Portrait of author on book jacket.

I. Rhodesia. I. Title.

M301 R27p Sharecropping.
Reid, Ira DeAugustine, 1901-
Poor land and peasantry, by Arthur Raper and Ira DeA. Reid. pp. 15-17, 41-42.

In: North Georgia review; A magazine of the southern regions, winter, 1939-1940.

MB9 C39j **Shaw, George Clayton, 1863-**
John Chavis, 1763-1838, a remarkable negro who conducted a school in North Carolina for white boys and girls, by G. C. Shaw ... [Binghamton, N. Y., Printed by the Vail-Ballou press, inc., °1931]
xv, 60 p. front., ports. 21cm.

1. Chavis, John, 1763 (ca.)-1838.

31-21510

Library of Congress E185.97.C43
——— Copy 2.
Copyright A 40816 [2] [922.573] 923.773

Shape them into dreams.

M811.5 H71s **Holloway, Ariel (Williams) 1905-**
Shape them into dreams; poems. [1st ed.] New York, Exposition Press [1955]
48 p. 21 cm.

I. Title.

PS3515.O42S5 811.5 55-12126 ‡

Library of Congress [2]

Sharecropping.

M631.114 So8p Southern tenant farmer's union.
Proceedings... annual convention 19 .
Memphis, Tenn., Southern tenant farmers' union, 19

v. 23cm.
Library has: 3rd. annual convention proceedings (Jan., 1937)

M813.5 Sh21a **Shaw, Letty M 1926-**
Angel Mink; a novel. New York, Comet Press Books, 1957.
187 p. 21 cm. (A Nobel book)
Autographed.

I. Title.

PZ4.S5352An 57-7023 ‡

Library of Congress [2]

Shaped to its purpose: Delta Sigma Theta - the first fity years.

M371.85 V966 **Vroman, Mary Elizabeth.**
Shaped to its purpose: Delta Sigma Theta—the first fifty years. New York, Random House [1965]
x, 213 p. 22 cm.

1. Delta Sigma Theta. I. Title.

LJ145.D58V7 371.856 64-8777

Library of Congress [8]

The shark hunters.

Jamaica
M372.4 Sa34 **Salkey, Andrew.**
The shark hunters; illustrated by Peter Kesteven. London, Nelson, 1966.
vi, 74 p. illus. 21½ cm. (Rapid reading) 4/-
(B 67-4805)

1. Readers—1950- I. Title.

PE1121.S28 67-88098

Library of Congress [3]

Shaw, Oliver W.

See

Shaw, O'Wendell, pseud.

M785 Sh2 **Shapiro, Nat, *ed.***
Hear me talkin' to ya; the story of jazz by the men who made it, edited by Nat Shapiro & Nat Hentoff. New York, Rinehart [1955]
432 p. 21 cm.
White editor. Contributors Negro.

1. Jazz music. I. Hentoff, Nat, joint ed. II. Title.

ML3561.J3S46 *785.42 780.973 55-5306 ‡

Library of Congress [30]

Sharp, Granville, 1735-1813.

MB9 Sh2s **Stuart, Charles.**
A memoir of Granville Sharp, to which is added Sharp's "Law of retribution." By Charles Stuart. New York, American anti-slavery society, 1836.

156p. front. 19cm.

M813.5 Sh2g **Shaw, O'Wendell.**
Greater need below, by O'Wendell Shaw. Columbus, O., The Bi-monthly Negro book club [°1936]
2 p. l., 7-161 p. 20cm.

I. Title.

39-16746

Library of Congress PZ3.S5364Gr
[2]

M070
Sh26
Shaw, O'Wendell.
Writing for the weeklies: how to earn sparetime money as a weekly newspaper correspondent. Columbus, Ohio, Ruswurm Press, °1962.
28 p. 23 cm.

1. Journalism—Authorship. 2. Negro press. I. Title.
PN147.S47 61-18806 ‡
Library of Congress [2]

Shepard, Marshall L.
Invocation
M329.2
D32a
Dawson, William Levi, 1886-
Address.

(In: Democracy at work, being the official report of the Democratic National Convention, Philadelphia, Pennsylvania, 1948. Philadelphia, Local Democratic Political Committee of Pennsylvania, 1948. 24cm. p. 150-155)

MB9
T27s
Shepperd, Gladys Byram
Mary Church Terrell respectable person. Baltimore, Human Relations Press, 1959.

125p. port. 23 ½cm.

1. Terrell, Mary Church, 1863-1954.

Shaw, Robert Gould, 1837-1863.
M324.4
W272a
Washington, Booker Taliaferro, 1859-1915.
An address by Booker T. Washington... delivered on the occasion of the unveiling of the Shaw Monument, Boston, Mass., May 31, 1897.

"Cover title. 10p. 9x16cm.
"From The Boston evening transcript of June 1."

M811.5
Sh47p
Sheperd, John H 1930-
Poems to remember always [by] John H. Sheperd. [1st ed.] New York, Greenwich Book Publishers [°1965]
31 p. 22 cm.

PS3537.H6955P6 65-26442
Library of Congress [3]

Sherbro language-Grammar.
Sierra Leone
M496
Su6h
Sumner, A T
A handbook of the Sherbro language, by Rev. A. T. Sumner. London, The Crown Agents for the colonies, 1921.
xii, 132p. 21½cm.

M812.08
Sh2
Shay, Frank, 1888- *ed.*
Fifty more contemporary one-act plays, selected and edited by Frank Shay. New York, D. Appleton and company, 1928.
viii, 510 p. 21cm.
White editor.
Partial contents: Blue blood, by Georgia Douglass Johnson. -The Chip woman's fortune, by Willis Richardson.

1. Drama—Collections. I. Title. II. Title: One-act plays.
II. a.t. Johnson III. a.t. Richardson 28-8719
Library of Congress PN6112.S515
[42e2]

Brazil
M896.3
Am1sh
Shepherds of the night.
Amado, Jorge, 1912-
Shepherds of the night. Translated from the Portuguese by Harriet de Onís. [1st American ed.] New York, Knopf, 1967 [°1966]
xii, 364 p. 22 cm.

I. Title.
PZ3.A478Sh 66-19366 rev
Library of Congress [r67f5]

Jamaica
M398
Sh5
Sherlock, Philip Manderson, 1902-
Anansi the spider man: Jamaican folk tales. Illustrated by Marcia Brown. London, Macmillan, 1962.

vii, 85p. illus. 22cm.

1. Folk tales, Jamaican. I. Title.

Nigeria
M896.3
An96s
She died in the bloom of youth.
Anya, Emmanyel Udegbunem, 1934-
She died in the bloom of youth. Onitsha, Nigeria, Tabansi Bookshop [1958]

39p. 17cm.

M285
Sh4e
Sheppard, William Henry, 1865-1927.
Experiences of a pioneer missionary on the Congo.

(In: Student Volunteer Movement for Foreign Missions. International Convention. 5th, Nashville, 1906. Students and the modern missionary crusade; addresses... New York, Student Volunteer Movement for Foreign Missions, 1906. 24cm. p. 291-296).

1. Missions - Kongo, Belgian. 2. Kongo, Belgian - Descr. & trav. I. Student Volunteer Movement for Kongo, Belgian.

Jamaica
M972.9
Sh54
Sherlock, Philip Manderson, 1902-
Caribbean citizen. London, New York, Longmans, Green [1957]
158 p. illus. 19 cm.

1. West Indies, British. I. Title.
A 58-4133 ‡
Wisconsin. Univ. Libr. for Library of Congress [2]

She knew no evil.
M813.5
Ar6
Arnold, Ethel Nishua.
She knew no evil. New York, Vantage Press [°1952]
76 p. 23 cm.

I. Title.
PZ4.A753Sh 52-11888 ‡
Library of Congress [2]

M285
Sh4p
Sheppard, William Henry, 1865-1927.
Presbyterian pioneers in Congo, by William H. Sheppard. Introduction by Rev. S. H. Chester, D. D. Richmond, Va., Presbyterian committee of publication [1917]
157 p. incl. front., illus. (incl. map) ports. 19½cm.

1. Missions—Kongo, Belgian. 2. Kongo, Belgian—Descr. & trav. 3. Presbyterian church in the U. S.—Missions. I. Title.
44-34906
Library of Congress BV3625.K6S43
[2]

Jamaica
M972.92
Sh54
Sherlock, Philip Manderson, 1902-
Jamaica way. [London] Longmans [1962]
104 p. illus. 19 cm.

1. Jamaica. I. Title.
F1869.S55 64-1067
Library of Congress [1]

She walks in beauty.
M813.5
R63
Rogers, Joel Augustus, 1880-
She walks in beauty. Los Angeles, Western Publishers, 1963.
316 p. 23 cm.

I. Title.
PZ4.R727Sh 62-22256
Library of Congress [3]

M285
Sh4y
Sheppard, William Henry, 1865-1927.
A young hunter, a true story of Central Africa. By Rev. W.H. Sheppard... [Louisville, Ky., The author, n.d.]

7p. illus. 17½cm.

1. Africa, Central. I. Title.

Jamaica
M823.91
Sh54t
Sherlock, Philip Manderson, 1902-
Three Finger Jack's treasure. Illustrated by William Reeves. London, New York, Macmillan, 1961 [i. e. 1962]
176 p. illus. 21 cm.

I. Title.
PZ7.S5452Th 2 62-612 ‡
Library of Congress [5]

M815.5
Sh4r
Shepard, James Edward, 1875-
Racial and inter-racial relations in North Carolina and the south; Speech delivered by on the twentieth anniversary of the Michigan avenue Y.M.C.A., Buffalo, New York, October 22, 1943.

20 leaves. 28cm.
Mimeographed.

I. Title. 1. Race relations. 2. North Carolina.

M285
Sh4y
Sheppard, William Henry, 1865-1927.
A young hunter, a true story of Central Africa By Rev. W. H. Sheppard... [Louisville, Ky., The author, n.d.]

7p. illus. 17½cm.

Spingarn

Jamaica
M398
Sh54
Sherlock, Philip Manderson, 1902-
West Indian folk-tales, retold by Philip Sherlock; illustrated by Joan Kiddell-Monroe. London, Oxford U. P., 1966.
[7], 151 p. col. front., illus., col. plates. 22½ cm. (Oxford myths and legends) 17/6
(B 66-637)

1. Tales, West Indian. I. Kiddell-Monroe, Joan, illus. II. Title.
GR120.S5 1966a 398.24 66-70268
Library of Congress [5]

Jamaica
M972.9
Sh54w

Sherlock, Philip Manderson, 1902-
West Indian story. London, Longmans, 1960.
vii, 134p. illus. 19cm.
Map of the West Indies and British Caribbean Federation Territories on lining papers.
1. West Indies - History. I. Title.

Jamaica
M972.9
Sh54we

Sherlock, Philip Manderson, 1902-
West Indies ⌊by⌋ Philip Sherlock. London, Thames & Hudson ⌊1966⌋
215 p. illus. (incl. ports.) 8 maps, facsims., table. 21½ cm. (New nations and peoples) 35/-
(B 66-22285)
Bibliography: p. 194-196.
1. West Indies—Hist. I. Title.
F1621.S5 972.9 66-66328
Library of Congress ⌊2⌋

Jamaica
M972.92
In3j

Sherlock, Philip Manderson, 1902- ed.
⌊Institute of Jamaica, *Kingston*⌋
Jamaica to-day, a handbook of information for visitors and intending residents, with some account of the colony's history, being a new and revised edition of the late Mr. Frank Cundall's "Jamaica in 1928" ... ⌊London, Printed by Hazell, Watson & Viney ltd.⌋ 1940.
xii, 204, ⌊5⌋ p. front., illus., plates, fold. map. 21cm.
On spine: The Institute of Jamaica.
Five blank pages for "Notes" at end.
"Edited by Philip M. Sherlock with the assistance of Mr. D. M. Gick, Mr. George Goode ⌊and others⌋."—p. ⌊v⌋
"A bibliography of Jamaica": p. 199-204.
1. Jamaica. I. Cundall, Frank, 1858-1937. II. Sherlock, Philip M., ed. III. Title.
Library of Congress F1869.I 55 1940 42-4383
⌊2⌋ 917.292

West Indies
M972.9
P24s

Sherlock, Phillip Manderson, 1902- joint author.
Parry, John Horace.
A short history of the West Indies, by J. H. Parry and P. M. Sherlock. London, Macmillan; New York, St. Martin's Press, 1956.
316 p. illus. 23 cm.
Includes bibliography.
1. West Indies—Hist. I. Sherlock, Philip Manderson, joint author.
F1621.P33 972.9 56-58641 ‡
Library of Congress ⌊57k10⌋

Sherlock, Philip Manderson, 1902- Preface.
West Indies.
M823
R144

Ramchand, Kenneth, comp.
West Indian narrative: an introductory anthology. London, Nelson, 1966.
xii, 226p. illus. (ports.) 19½cm. 12/6
Includes excerpts from English novelists dealing with the West Indies.
Col. maps on endpapers.
White compiler.
Includes extracts from works by West Indian writers.

M814.5
Sh5

Sherman, Ellen Burns, 1867-
Balm for men's souls. Boston, Christopher Pub. House ⌊1953⌋
86 p. 21 cm.
I. Title.
PS3537.H738B3 814.5 53-11753 ‡
Library of Congress ⌊1⌋

M304
T19
v.6,no.10

Sherrod, Fletcher.
Geometry; the trisection of the angle and theorems and corollaries leading to it. Revised, 1933. Fletcher Sherrod, author and publisher. New Orleans, La., ©1932-1933.
⌊14⌋ p. diagrs. 21½cm.
1. Trisection of angle. I. Title. 2 Geometry 3 Mathematics
CA 33-572 Unrev'd
Library of Congress QA468.S45 1933
Copyright AA 122420 513.9

MB9
G65s

Sherwood, William Henry
Life of Charles P. W. Gordon, pastor of the First Baptist church, Petersburg, Virginia, and history of the church, by Rev. William Henry Sherwood... Petersburg, Va., John B. Ege, 1885.
102p. illus. 21½cm.
1. Gordon, Charles B. W
2. First Baptist church, Petersburg, Va.

Sudan
Egyptian
M962.4
Sh61

Shibeika, Mekki.
British policy in the Sudan, 1882-1902. London, New York, Oxford University Press, 1952.
439 p. maps. 23 cm.
Bibliography: p. ⌊426⌋-430.
1. Sudan, Egyptian—Hist. 2. British in the Sudan. I. Title.
DT108.3.S4 962.4 53-766
Library of Congress ⌊2⌋

M813.5
Sh61

Shiel, M⌊atthew⌋ P⌊hipps⌋
The lord of the sea; a romance ... New York, F. A. Stokes co. ⌊1901⌋
viii, 474 p. 12°.
Library of Congress Copyright 1-7319

M343.3
Sh6k

Shields, Art.
The killing of William Milton; Introduction by Simon W. Gerson. New York, Daily Worker, 1948.
14p. 18cm.
White author.
1. Milton, William. 2. Brooklyn, N. Y. 3. Civil rights, Denial of. 4. Police.

Shields, Emma L.
M331.
Un3

U. S. *Women's bureau.*
... Negro women in industry. Washington, Govt. print. off., 1922.
v, 65, ⌊1⌋ p. front. 23cm. (Bulletin no. 20)
At head of title: U. S. Department of labor. James J. Davis, secretary. Women's bureau. Mary Anderson, director.
"This investigation was made by Miss Emma L. Shields ... in conjunction with the Division of Negro economics in the Department of labor."—Letter of transmittal.
1. Negroes—Employment. 2. Woman—Employment—U. S. 3. Women, Negro. I. U. S. Dept. of labor. Division of Negro economics. II. Shields, Emma L. III. Title.
L 22-164
U. S. Dept. of labor. Libr. for Library of Congress HD6093.A35 no. 20
⌊a41n1⌋

Uganda
M910
Sh61

Shillito, James
Ensi gye tulimu ⌊The world in which we live⌋ Kya kyucibwa Aloni Lubwama. Nairobi, Eagle Press, 1950.
39p. illus. 18½cm.
Written in Luganda.
White author.
1. Title. 1. Geography. II. Lubwama, Aloni, tr.

Shiloh Baptist Church, Newport, R. I.
MB9
J51p

Jeter, Henry N
Pastor Henry N. Jeter's twenty-five years experience with The Shiloh Baptist church and her history ... Providence, R. I., Remington printing co., 1901.
98p. plates. 23½cm.

MB9
As3a

Shiloh Baptist church, Philadelphia, Pa.
Articles of faith and covenant of the Shiloh Baptist church, worshipping corner of Clifton and South, between 10th and 11th Streets, Philadelphia... Philadelphia, W.G. P. Brinckloe, 1861.
15p. 15½cm.
Bound with: Jeremiah Asher's An autobiography with details of a visit to England.
I. Title.

Shiloh Baptist Church, Philadelphia, Pa.
MB9
As3a

Asher, Jeremiah, 1812-
An autobiography with details of a visit to England, and some account of the history of the Meeting Street Baptist Church, Providence, R.I., and of the Shiloh Baptist Chruch, Philadelphia, Pa., by Rev. Jeremiah Asher, with an introduction by Rev. J. Wheaton Smith. Philadelphia, the author, 1862.
x, 227p. front. 17½cm.

Shinega's village.
Ethiopia
M896.3
Se48

Sellassie, Sahle, 1936-
Shinega's village; scenes of Ethiopian life. Translated from Chaha by Wolf Leslau. Illus. by Li Gelpke. Berkeley, University of California Press, 1964.
xi, 112 p. illus. 22 cm.
1. Ethiopia—Soc. life & cust. I. Leslau, Wolf, tr. II. Title.
PZ4.S4653Sh 64-12607
Library of Congress ⌊5⌋

The Shining Life.
M323
J632e

Johnson, James Weldon, 1871-1938.
The Shining life, by James Weldon Johnson... An appreciation of Julius Rosenwald delivered at a memorial service in Fisk memorial chapel, Nashville, Tennessee, February 14, 1932. Fisk University bulletin, vol. 8, 1932.
11p. 23cm.

Shipard, Augustus, 1846-08. p. 207-
M286
W61h

Whitted, J A
A history of the Negro Baptists of North Carolina, by Rev. J.A.Whitted... Raleigh, Presses of Edwards and Broughton printing co., 1908.
212p. front. plates - 22½cm.

Guadeloupe Shipping bounties and subsidies.
M325.
G32m

Gerville-Réache, Maxime.
La marine marchande en France et en Allemagne; subventions et primes, par Maxime Gerville-Réache ... Paris, A. Pedone, 1909.
114 p., 1 l. 25cm.
"Bibliographie": p. ⌊5⌋-6.
1. Merchant marine—France. 2. Merchant marine—Germany. 3. Shipping bounties and subsidies.
10-24538
Library of Congress HE743.F8G5

M780
Sh66

Shirley, Kay, *ed.*
The book of the blues. Annotated by Frank Driggs. Record research by Joy Graeme. Music research by Bob Hartsell. New York, Leeds Music Corp. ⌊1963⌋
301 p. 32 cm.
Unacc., with guitar chords.
Background notes, list of recordings, and chord diagrams for guitar and tenor banjo, precede each song.
White editor.
1. Music, Popular (Songs, etc.)—U. S. 2. Folk-songs, American. 3. Negro songs. I. Title.
M1629.S557B6 63-18895/M
Library of Congress ⌊3⌋

Shock.
M616 C81 Cordice, John W V
Polyvinylpyrrolidone in acute traumatic and hemmorrhagic shock, by John W. V. Cordice, Josephine E. Suess, and John Scudder. The Franklin H. Martin Memorial Foundation [1953]
79p. tables 26cm.
Reprinted from Surgery, gynecology and obstetrics, September 1953.

A short history of the Baptist denomination.
M286 F53s Fisher, Miles Mark, 1899–
A short history of the Baptist denomination, by Miles Mark Fisher ... Nashville, Tenn., Sunday school publishing board [1933]
ix, 188 p. 19½cm.
"Collateral reading": p. 180.
1. Baptists—Hist. I. Title.
Library of Congress BX6231.F48 33—19280
——— Copy 2.
Copyright A 63505 [40c1] 286.09

Short stories.
M813.5 M26f Madden, Will Anthony.
Five more short stories. New York, Exposition Press [1963]
64p. 21cm.

Shoe shining.
M685 C69 Collins, Fred
Fred Collins shine book on shoe shining in the home. Washington, D.C., Johnson Doell & Co., 1941.
83p. illus. 20cm.

Short stories.
M813.08 B21b Baltimore Afro-American.
Best short stories by Afro-American writers, 1925–1950, selected and edited by Nick Aaron Ford and H. L. Faggett. Boston, Meador Pub. Co. [1950]
307 p. 21 cm.
1. Negro fiction (American) 2. Short stories, American. I. Ford, Nick Aaron, ed. II. Faggett, Harry Lee, 1911– ed. III. Title.
PZ1.B23Be 50–12374
Library of Congress [5]

Short stories.
M813.5 M26tw Madden, Will Anthony
Two and one; two short stories and a play. New York, Exposition Press, 1961.
50p. 21cm.
Portrait of author on back of book jacket.

M811.5 Sh7d Shoeman, Charles Henry
A dream, and other poems. By Charles Henry Shoeman. Second edition. Ann Arbor, Mich., George Wahr, 1899–1900.
viii[9] 202p. 15½cm.
Poetry. I. Title

Short stories.
Africa M808.83 B396 Black Orpheus.
Black Orpheus; an anthology of new African and Afro-American stories. Edited by Ulli Beier. ~~New York, McGraw-Hill Book Co. [1965, °1964]~~ [London] Longmans [1964]
156 p. 21 cm.
1. Short stories, African—Translations into English. 2. Short stories—Negro authors. I. Beier, Ulli, ed.
PZ1.B552Bl 65–16755
Library of Congress [3]

Short stories.
M808.8 P21 The Paris review.
Best short stories. Introd. by William Styron. [1st ed.] New York, Dutton, 1959.
245 p. 21 cm.
1. Short stories.
PZ1.P215Be 59–10771 ‡
Library of Congress [60k10]

M814.5 Sh7s Shokunbi, Mae (Gleaton)
Songs of the soul, by Mae Gleaton Shokunbi. Philadelphia, Dorrance & company [1945]
viii, 9–76 p. 19cm.
Essays.
I. Title.
Library of Congress PS3537.H95S6 45–17728
[2] 818.5

Short stories.
W. Indies M823 C23 Caribbean anthology of short stories, by Ernest A. Carr [and others] Kingston, Jamaica, Pioneer Press [1953]
146 p. 19 cm. (Pioneer Press series)
Contents: Ernest A. Carr. Lucille Iremonger. Ethel Rovere. Edgar Mittelholzer. C.W. Ogle. R.L.C. Aarons. Samuel Selvon. Vera Bell. John Wickham. W.G. Ogilvie. Clinton V. Black. Neil Cameron. William S. Arthur. Hugh Panton Morrison
1. Short stories. I. Carr, Ernest A.
PZ1.C18 54–26084 ‡
Library of Congress [1]

Short stories.
M813.4 P97h Purvis, T T
Hagar; the singing maiden, with other stories and rhymes, by T. T. Purvis. Philadelphia, Walton and co., 1881.
28p. 19½cm.

Shooting at Sharpeville.
Africa, South M968 R25 Reeves, Richard Ambrose, Bp., 1899–
Shooting at Sharpeville; the agony of South Africa. With a foreword by Chief Luthuli. [1st American ed.] Boston, Houghton Mifflin, 1961 [°1960]
xvi, 141 p. illus., map. 23 cm.
1. Sharpeville, South Africa—Massacre, 1960. I. Title.
DT944.S5R4 1961 323.2 61–5373
Library of Congress [61k10]

Short stories.
M813.08 C554 Clarke, John Henrik, 1915– ed.
American Negro short stories. [1st ed.] New York, Hill and Wang [1966]
xix, 355 p. 21 cm.
1. Short stories, American. 2. American literature—Negro authors. 3. Negro literature (American) I. Title.
PZ1.C563Am 66–23863
Library of Congress [3]

Short stories.
M813.5 R53k Roberson, Sadie L.
Killer of the dream; short stories. New York, Carlton Press [1963]
95p. 21cm.
Portrait of author on book jacket.
1. Title. 1. Short stories.

Shop and class at Tuskegee...
M378 Tu W58 Whiting, Joseph Livingston, 1877–
Shop and class at Tuskegee; a definitive story of the Tuskegee correlation technique, 1910–1930, by J. L. Whiting. Boston, Chapman & Grimes [°1941]
114 p. front., plates, map, tables, diagrs. 21cm.
1. Tuskegee normal and industrial institute. I. Title.
Library of Congress LC2851.T82W5 42–4090
[4] 378.761

Short stories.
M813.08 H52s Hibbard, Clarence Addison, 1887– ed.
Stories of the South, old and new, edited by Addison Hibbard, with an introduction, biographical notes, and bibliography by the editor. Chapel Hill, The University of North Carolina press; New York, W. W. Norton & company [°1931]
xvii, 520 p. 22cm.
1. Short stories, American. 2. American literature—Southern states. I. Title.
Library of Congress PZ1.H522St 31–8683
[44j²1]

Short stories.
M813.08 Sch81 Schulman, L M, ed.
Come out the wilderness. New York, Popular Library [1965]
125p. 18cm.
Partial contents.- Come out the wilderness, by James Baldwin.- The summer fire, by Owen Dodson.- The sky is gray, by Ernest J. Gaines.- Almos a man, by Richard Wright.- The necessary knocking at the door, by Ann Petry.

M813.5 Sh7p Shores, Minnie T
Publicans and sinners. New York, Comet Press Books, 1960.
172p. 20cm.
Portrait of author on book jacket.
I. Title.

Short stories.
M813.08 H874 Hughes, Langston, 1902– ed.
The best short stories by Negro writers; an anthology from 1899 to the present. [1st ed.] Boston, Little, Brown [1967]
xvii, 508 p. 22 cm.
1. Short stories, American. I. Title.
PZ1.H849Be 67–11221
Library of Congress [67f5]

Short stories.
Africa M896 Su5c Sulzer, Peter, comp.
Christ erscheint am Kongo; Afrikanische Erzählungen und Gedichte gesammelt und Gedichte gesammelt und übertragen von Peter Sulzer. Heilbronn, Eugen Salzer. [1958]
255p. 20cm.
Biography: p. 248-251.

Short stories.

M813.5 Wells, Moses Peter
W46t Three adventurous men. New York, Carlton Press, 1963.

55p. 20cm. (A Geneva book)
Portrait of author on book jacket.

Short stories, African - Translations into English.

Africa
M808.83 Black Orpheus.
B496 Black Orpheus; an anthology of new African and Afro-American stories. Edited by Ulli Beier. ~~New York, Mc-Graw-Hill Book Co. [1965, °1964]~~ [London] Longmans [1964]
158 p. 21 cm.

1. Short stories, African—Translations into English. 2. Short stories—Negro authors. I. Beier, Ulli, ed.

PZ1.B552Bl 65-16755

Library of Congress [3]

Shoulder to shoulder.

M973 Granger, Lester Blackwell, 1896-
R56d Shoulder to shoulder.

pp. 238-240.
In: The day I was proudest to be an American, by Donald B. Robinson. 1958.

Short stories.

Africa
M896.3 [Young, T Cullen] ed.
Yo8a African new writing; short stories by African authors. London, Lutterworth Press [1947]
126 p. 19 cm.

1. Short stories. I. Title.

PZ1.Y85Af 48-13317*

Library of Congress [1]

Short stories, Brazilian.

Brazil
M869.3 Machado de Assis, Joaquim Maria, 1839-1908.
M18p The psychiatrist, and other stories. Translated by William L. Grossman & Helen Caldwell. Berkeley, University of California Press, 1963.
147 p. 22 cm.

I. Title.

PZ3.M1817Ps 63-9407 ‡

Library of Congress [5]

A Shropshire lad.

M811.08 Braithwaite, William Stanley, 1878-
B731 Introduction.

(In: Housman, Alfred Edward. A Shropshire lad. Boston, The Four Seas Company, c1919. 15½cm.)

Short stories - Race relations.

M813.08 Williams, John Alfred, 1925- ed.
W67 The angry black [stories and articles by James Baldwin and others] New York, Lancer Books [1962]

160p. 18cm. (Lancer original, 172 625)

Short stories, English-Translations from Italian.

M813.5 Johnson, Ben, ed.
J63s Stories of modern Italy, from Verga, Svevo and Pirandello to the present. Edited, with an introd., by Ben Johnson. New York, Modern Library [1960]
518 p. 19 cm. (The Modern library, 118)

1. Short stories, Italian—Translations into English. 2. Short stories, English—Translations from Italian.

PZ1.J57St 60-10264 ‡

Library of Congress [61f5]

M323 Shuttleworth, F L
Su6 How shall we travel the road of freedom together.

Pp. 115-117.

In: Summit Meeting of National Negro Leaders, Washington, D.C. Report. Washington, National Newspaper Publishers Association, 1958.

Short stories - Haiti.

Haiti
M843.91 Lamothe, Leduc B
L193 Sur la route de la vie; quelques pages de Cudel au coin des amateurs d'art. Préface de Me. J. B. Cinéas. Port-au-Prince, Editions Henri Deschamps, 1960.

112p. 21cm.
Portrait of author in book.

Short stories, Italian-Translations into English.

M813.5 Johnson, Ben, ed.
J63s Stories of modern Italy, from Verga, Svevo and Pirandello to the present. Edited, with an introd., by Ben Johnson. New York, Modern Library [1960]
518 p. 19 cm. (The Modern library, 118)

1. Short stories, Italian—Translations into English. 2. Short stories, English—Translations from Italian.

PZ1.J57St 60-10264 ‡

Library of Congress [61f5]

Si quelqu'un ... chemin de croix.

Cameroun
M896.1 Mveng, Engelbert.
M98s Si quelqu'un ... chemin de crois. [Paris] Mame [1962]

[29]p. illus. 19cm.

1. Jesus Christ - Poetry. I. Title.

Short stories - Kenya.

Kenya
M896.3 Malo, S
M29s Sigend Luo ma duogo chuny [Kerry stories] Ogor gi W. S. Agutu. Nairobi, Eagle Press, 1951.

42p. illus. 21½cm. (Treasury of East African stories)
Written in Luo.
1. Short stories - Kenya. I. Title. II. Agutu, W. S., illus. III. Series.

Short stories, South African.

Africa, South
M896.3 Rive, Richard, 1931- ed.
R52 Quartet; new voices from South Africa: Alex La Ouma, James Matthews, Alf Wannenburgh, Richard Rive. New York, Crown Publishers [1963]

223p. 22cm.
Short stories.

Siasa hapo kale.

Tanganyika
M967.82 Thonya, Lucius Mbasha
T38 Siasa hapo kale [Wisdom of the past] methali katika hadithi, Kingoni kimefasiriwa kwa kiswahili. Dar es Salaam, Eagle Press, 1960.

95p. illus. 21½cm.

1. Tanganyika. 2. Angoni. I. Title.

Short stories - West Indies.

Jamaica
M823.91 Salkey, Andrew, 1928- , ed.
Sa3w West Indian stories. London, Faber and Faber, 1960.

224p. 20cm.

Short stories, West Indian.

Jamaica
M823.91 Salkey, Andrew, comp.
Sa3a Stories from the Caribbean, an anthology. Selected and introduced by Andrew Salkey. London, Elek Books [1965]

256p. 21cm.
"For Arthur from Andrew, 5/22/65."

Nigeria
M398 Sidahome, Joseph E ,1917-1963.
S113 Stories of the Benin Empire. London, Oxford University Press, 1964.

196p. illus. 21½cm.

1. Tales, Nigerian. I. Title.

Short stories, African.

Africa
M896.3 Komey, Ellis Ayitey, ed.
K83 Modern African stories, edited by Ellis Ayitey Komey and Ezekiel Mphahlele. London, Faber and Faber, 1964.

227p. 20cm.
Ghanaian and South African editors.

1. Short stories, African. I. Mphahlele, Ezekiel, jt. ed. II. Title.

Shorter, James Alexander, 1817-1887.

MB9 Wayman, Alexander Walker, bp., 1821-1895.
Sh8w The life of Rev. James Alexander Shorter, one of the bishops of the African M. E. church, by Alexander W. Wayman. With an introduction by Rev. James H. A. Johnson... Baltimore, J. Lanahan, 1890.

50p. front. 19½cm.

Sidelights on Negro soldiers.

M350 Williams, Charles Halston, 1886-
W67 Sidelights on Negro soldiers, by Charles H. Williams ... with an introduction by Benjamin Brawley. Boston, B. J. Brimmer company, 1923.
248 p. 22cm.
"First edition."

1. European war, 1914-1918—Negroes. I. Title.

Library of Congress D639.N4W5 24-2179
——— Copy 2.
Copyright A 766790 [30e1]

M326 S11o **Sidney, Joseph.**
An oration, commemorative of the abolition of the slave trade in the United States; delivered before the Wilberforce philanthropic association, in the city of New-York, on the second of January, 1809. By Joseph Sidney. New-York, Printed for the author, J. Seymour, printer, 1809.
20 p. 20cm.
1. Slavery in the U. S.—Controversial literature—1809. 2. Slave-trade—U. S. I. Wilberforce philanthropic association, New York.
10-32480
Library of Congress E446.S56

Sierra Leone.
M973 W67 **Williams, George Washington, 1849-1891.**
History of the Negro race in America from 1619 to 1880. Negroes as slaves, as soldiers, and as citizens; together with a preliminary consideration of the unity of the human family, an historical sketch of Africa, and an account of the Negro governments of Sierra Leone and Liberia. By George W. Williams ... Popular ed. ... New York & London, G. P. Putnam's sons [°1882]
2 v. in 1. front. (port.) 24cm.
Vol. 2 has half-title only.
1. Negroes. 2. Sierra Leone. 3. Liberia.
26—4249
Library of Congress E185.W69 [43d1]

Sierra Leone-Social life and customs.
M910. H22a **Hargrave, Carrie Guerphan.**
African primitive life, as I saw it in Sierra Leone, British West Africa, by Carrie Guerphan Hargrave. [Wilmington, N. C., Wilmington printing company, 1944]
115 p. incl. front. (port.) plates. 22cm.
1. Sierra Leone—Soc. life & cust. I. Title.
45-2525
Library of Congress DT516.H27 [3] 916.64

Siemsen, Anna, 1882- tr.
M811.08 N94 **Nussbaum, Anna,** *ed.*
Afrika singt, eine auslese neuer afro-amerikanischer lyrik, herausgegeben von Anna Nussbaum. Wien und Leipzig, F. G. Speidel [1929]
2 p. l., [7]-160, [3] p., 1 l. 22cm.
"Die nachdichtungen und übertragungen stammen von Hermann Kesser, Josef Luitpold, Anna Siemsen, Anna Nussbaum."
1. Negro poetry (American) I. Kesser, Hermann, 1880- tr. II. Luitpold, Josef, tr. III. Siemsen, Anna, 1882- tr.
29-21778
Library of Congress PS591.N4S N8 [2]

Sierra Leone - Constitutional history.
Nigeria M966 EL4 **Elias, Taslim Olawale.**
Ghana and Sierra Leone: the development of their laws and constitutions. London, Stevens, 1962.
xii, 334 p. 25 cm. (The British Commonwealth: the development of its laws and constitutions, v. 10)
Bibliography: p. 311-312.
1. Law—Ghana—Hist. & crit. 2. Law—Sierra Leone—Hist. & crit. 3. Ghana—Constitutional history. 4. Sierra Leone—Constitutional history. (Series)
63-2173
Library of Congress [5]

Sierra Leone inheritance.
Sierra Leone
M966.4 F98 **Fyfe, Christopher,** *ed.*
Sierra Leone inheritance. London, Oxford University Press, 1964.
xi, 352 p. illus., facsim., maps, ports. 23 cm. (West African history series)
A book of documents to supplement the author's History of Sierra Leone and Short history of Sierra Leone.
1. Sierra Leone—Hist. 2. Sierra Leone—Hist.—Sources. I. Title.
DT516.A3F9 966.4 64-4656
Library of Congress [3]

Sierra Leona country cloths.
Sierra Leone
M677 Ea77 Easmon, McCormack Charles Farrell.
Sierra Leona country cloths. London, Waterlow & Sons, 1924.
34p. illus. 24½cm.
At head of title: British empire exhibition, 1924 (Sierra Leone section)
"To Mr. Spingarn with best wishes from the author, Yours sincerely, M. C. F.Easmon, 13-10-60."
1. Cloth - Sierra Leone. I. Title.

Sierra Leone - Education.
Sierra Leone
M966.4 T37j Thompson, T J
The jubilee and centenary volume of Fourah Boy College, Freetown, Sierra Leone, by T. J. Thompson. Sierra Leone, The Elsiemay Printing Works, 1930.
173, vi, i-xxiv p. portraits, illus. 24½cm.

Sierra Leone
M966.4 Sily Sierra Leone Year Book, 1960.
[Sierra Leone] Daily Mail [1960],
v. ports. 18cm.
1. Yearbooks - Sierra Leone.

Sierra Leone.
Liberia
M966.6 B62c 1888 Blyden, Edward Wilmot, 1832-1912.
Christianity, Islam and the Negro race. By Edward W. Blyden... With an introduction by the Hon. Smauel Lewis... 2d ed. London, W.B. Whittingham & co., 1888.
3p. L., xv, 432p. front. (port.) 21½cm.

Sierra Leone - Hist.
Sierra Leone
M966.4 F98 **Fyfe, Christopher,** *ed.*
Sierra Leone inheritance. London, Oxford University Press, 1964.
xi, 352 p. illus., facsim., maps, ports. 23 cm. (West African history series)
A book of documents to supplement the author's History of Sierra Leone and Short history of Sierra Leone.
1. Sierra Leone—Hist. 2. Sierra Leone—Hist.—Sources. I. Title.
DT516.A3F9 966.4 64-4656
Library of Congress [3]

Siete caminos en luna de sueños; poemas.
Puerto Rico
M861 R71s Rosa-Nieves, Cesáreo, 1904-
Siete caminos en luna de sueños; poemas. San Juan, Biblioteca de Autores Puertorriqueños, 1957.
121p. 20cm.
I. Title.

Sierra Leone.
Liberia
M966.6 B62c 1887 Blyden, Edward Wilmot, 1832-1912.
Christianity, Islam and the Negro race. By Edward W. Blyden... With an introduction by the Hon. Samuel Lewis. London, W.B. Whittingham & co., 1887.
vii, 423p.
Blyden's own copy containing his signature and corrections in his handwriting.

Sierra Leone - Hist. - Sources.
Sierra Leone
M966.4 F98 **Fyfe, Christopher,** *ed.*
Sierra Leone inheritance. London, Oxford University Press, 1964.
xi, 352 p. illus., facsim., maps, ports. 23 cm. (West African history series)
A book of documents to supplement the author's History of Sierra Leone and Short history of Sierra Leone.
1. Sierra Leone—Hist. 2. Sierra Leone—Hist.—Sources. I. Title.
DT516.A3F9 966.4 64-4656
Library of Congress [3]

Zambia Sifuniso, Kay, jt. auth.
M392 M11 Maango, David
"Tell me, Josephine." [By David Maango, Barbara Hall and Kay Sifuniso] edited by Barbara Hall. [Foreword by Kenneth D. Kaunda] New York, Simon and Schuster, 1964.
142p. 21cm.
Selections from the Tell me, Josephine column started in February, 1960, by the Central African mail, a weekly paper in Northern Rhodesia.
(Over)

Sierra Leone.
Africa, West
M966 G78c Graves, Anna Melissa, ed.
Benvenuto Cellini had no prejudice against bronze; letters from West Africans, edited by Anna Melissa Graves. [Baltimore, Waverly press, inc., 1943]
lxvi, 176p. front., plates, ports. 23½cm.

Sierra Leone-Politics and government.
Africa M966.4 T37p Thompson, T J
The people's appeal for an intermediate court of appeal and an efficient system for the administration of justice in the colony and protectorate of Sierra Leone, by T.J. Thompson... London The Caxton press, 1911.
34p. 21cm. (The people's series)

Kenya Sigend Luo ma duogo chuny.
M896.3 M29s Malo, S
Sigend Luo ma duogo chuny [Kerry stories] Ogor gi W. S. Agutu. Nairobi, Eagle Press, 1951.
42p. illus. 21½cm. (Treasury of East African stories)
Written in Luo.
1. Short stories - Kenya. I. Title. II. Agutu, W. S., illus. III. Series.

Sierra Leone
Sierra Leone
M89 K89i Kamara, Issa.
Benga, by Elizabeth Hirst and Issa Kamara. London, University of London Press, ltd., 1958.
80p. illus., map. 18½cm.
1. Sierra Leone. 2. Bureh, Bai. I. Title.

Sierra Leone-Social life and customs
Sierra Leone
M966.4 G68o **Gorvie, Max.**
Old and new in Sierra Leone, by Max Gorvie ... London and Redhill, United society for Christian literature [1945]
79, [1] p. 18cm. (*Half-title: Africa's own library, no. 9*)
"First published 1945."
1. Ethnology—Sierra Leone. 2. Sierra Leone—Soc. life & cust. I. Title.
S D 46-13 Revised
U. S. Dept. of state. Libr. for Library of Congress DT516.G6 [r46d2]

The sight of dawn-poems.
M811.5 M96 Murray, Henry Clifford
The sight of dawn-poems. New York, Exposition Press, 1959.
61p. 21cm.

S. Africa
M968 Sigila, C A W
S12n Ndalikhenketha elasentla (a long journey up-country). Ibhalwe ngu. Headltown, The Lovedale Press, 1953.

59p. 18cm.

1. Africa, South - Descr. & travel.

The sign in Sidney Brustein's window.

M812.5 Hansberry, Lorraine, 1930-1965.
H19s The sign in Sidney Brustein's window, a drama in three acts. New York, Random House [1965]

lxi, 143 p. ports. 22 cm.

I. Title.

PS3515.A515S5 1965 812.54 65-18311

Library of Congress [5]

The sign of Kelos.

M813.5 Wilson, Pat
W69sk The sign of Kelos. New York, Carlton Press, 1961.

36p. 21cm.
Portrait of author on back of book jacket.

S'il braille, lâche-le....

M813.5 Himes, Chester B 1909-
H5711 S'il braille, lâche-le ... (If he hollers let him go) Tr. de l'américain par Renée Vavasseur et Marcel Duhamel. Paris, A. Michel [1948]

386 p. 21 cm.

I. Title.

PS3515.I 713 I 33 49-24314*

Library of Congress [1]

M811.5 Silence.
W89s Wortham, Anne, 1941-
Silence. New York, Pageant Press [1965]

51p. 21cm.
Poems and essays.

I. Title.

Silhouettes de Nègres et de Négrophiles.

Haiti
M972.94 Mars, Jean Price, 1876-
M35s Silhouettes de Nègres et de Négrophiles. Paris, Présence Africaine, 1959.

210p. illus., ports. 19cm.

Silva Castro, Raúl, comp.

Nicaragua
M861.6 Darío, Rubén, 1867-1916.
D24a ... Antología poética; selección y prólogo de Raúl Silva Castro. [Santiago de Chile, Edición Zig-zag [1936]

283 p., 2 l. 19½ᶜᵐ. (Antologías poéticas, I)

I. Silva Castro, Raúl, comp.

38-12190

Library of Congress PQ7519.D3A6 1936

[3] 861.6

Brazil
M869.2 Silveira, Tasso da
N17d O emparedado.

Pp. 375-417.

In: Nascimento, Abdias do, ed. Dramas para Negroes e prologo para brancos. Rio de Janeiro, Teatro Experimental do Negro, 1961.

I. Title.

Cuba
M861.6 Silveira, Vicente.
Si3f Florscencias de invierno. Colección de versos de Vicente Silveira. Guanajay-1910. Guanajay [Cuba] Papeleria é Imprenta "La 2a Prueba" de Alberto Miranda y Urquiza [1910]

229 [1]p. 23cm.

1. Cuban poetry. I. Title.

The silver chord;

M811.5 Johnson, Adolphus.
J62s The silver chord; poems by Adolphus Johnson. Philadelphia, Pa., [n.p.n.d.]

48p. 19½cm.

M784 Silverman, Jerry
Si3f Folk blues; one hundred and ten American folk blues; compiled, edited, and arranged for voice, piano, and guitar. With a chart of basic guitar chord fingering patterns and a full bibliography and discography. New York, The Macmillan Co., 1958.

297p. 28cm.
White author.
1. Blues. I. Title.

M811.08 Silvera, Edward
F82 [Poems].

(In: Four Lincoln University poets: ... Lincoln University herald. v.33. no.3. March 1930. p. 11-12).

M350 Silvera, John Douglas, 1909-
Si3n The Negro in World War II, by John D. Silvera. Baton Rouge, La. Military press of Louisiana, 1946.

140 unnumbered p. illus. 27cm.

1. World War, 1939-1945. I. Title.

Tanganyika
M967.82 Silvertand, J H
Si3 Probation. Nairobi, The Eagle Press, 1947.

36p. illus. 18½cm.
White author- Translated by African.
Bi-lingual - Swahili and English.

Simango, C. Kamba.

Africa
M784 Burlin, Natalie (Curtis) 1875-1921, *ed.*
B92 Songs and tales from the dark continent, recorded from the singing and the sayings of C. Kamba Simango ... and Madikane Cele ... by Natalie Curtis. New York, Boston, G. Schirmer [©1920]

xxv p., 1 l., 170 p. front., illus., 4 pl., 2 port. 27 cm.
CONTENTS.—Introduction.—C. Kamba Simango.—Simango's letter to the reader.—Proverbs, beliefs and customs, songs and tales of the Ndau tribe, East Africa.—Madikane Čele.—Songs and tales of the Zulin tribe, South Africa.—Simango's farewell to the reader.—Chindau's songs [with the music] (p. [79]-129)—Zulu songs [with the music] (p. [131]-140)—Appendix.
1. Folk-songs, African. 2. Folk-lore—Africa. I. Simango, C. Kamba. II. Čele, Madikane Qaŋdeya. III. Title.

ML3760.B98 21—5086

Library of Congress [a51q1]

Simba, Ng'ombe na jogoo na hadith nyingine
Tanganyika za kiirangi.
M896.3 Issa, N M Hasani
Is7s Simba, Ng'ombe na jogoo na hadith nyingine za kiirangi [Lion, the cow and the cock, and other tales of the Irangi people. Dar es Salaam, Eagle Press, 1960.

14p. 18cm. illus. (Hadith za Tanganyika, Kitabu cha Kwanza)
Written in Swahili.

I. Title. II. Series.

Simbi and the satyr of the dark jungle.

Nigeria.
M896.3 Tutuola, Amos.
T88s Simbi and the satyr of the dark jungle. London, Faber and Faber, 1955.

136p. 20½cm.

Jamaica
M820 Simmonds, Ulric.
H38 Grannie bell.

Pp. 21-27.

In: Hendriks, A. L., ed. The independence anthology of Jamaican literature. Kingston, Arts Celebration Committee, Ministry of Development and Welfare, 1962.

Jamaica
M823 Simmonds, Ulric
F82 Grannie bell.

Pp. 36-45.

In: 14 Jamaican short stories. Jamaica, Prioneer Press, 1950

Simmons, Caesar Felton, 1866-

M304 Johnson, N J
P19 Caesar F. Simmons, his life and
v.4,no.16 accomplishments, Oklahoma's foremost member of the Negro race - 1953.

32p. portraits, 21cm.

Simmons, Ernest J., ed.

Russia
M891 Pushkin, Alexander Sergeevich, 1799-1837.
P97s Selections from the prose and poetry of Pushkin. Edited and introduced by Ernest J. Simmons. New York, Dell Publishing Co., 1961.

382p. 17cm. (A Laurel reader)
Sketch of author on book.
Cover title.

M813.5 Si4c
Simmons, Herbert
Corner boy. New York, Dell Publishing Co., 1957.
224p. 16½cm.
I. Title.

M813.5 Si4c
Simmons, Herbert.
Corner boy, a novel. Boston, Houghton Mifflin, 1957.
208 p. 21 cm.
I. Title.
PZ4.S593Co 57-12108 ‡
Library of Congress [5]

M813.5 Si4m
Simmons, Herbert.
Man walking on eggshells. Boston, Houghton Mifflin, 1962.
250 p. 21 cm.
I. Title.
Full name: Herbert Alfred Simmons.
PZ4.S593Man 62-7389 ‡
Library of Congress [5]

M153 Si4t
Simmons, James W
Thoughts from the mind. New York, Exposition Press, 1962.
94p. 23cm.
Portrait of author on book jacket.
"An Exposition-Banner book."
1. Philosophy. I. Title.

Simmons, Virginia Lee
See
Nyabongo, Virginia Lee (Simmons)

MB Si4
Simmons, William Johnson, 1849-1890
Men of mark: eminent, progressive and rising. By Rev. William J. Simmons ... With an introductory sketch of the author by Rev. Henry M. Turner ... Cleveland, O., G. M. Rewell & co., 1887.
1138 p. front., ports. 23½ cm.
1. Biography 1. Turner, Henry McNeal, 1834-1915.
6—5585
Library of Congress E185.96.S45 [a36d1]

M286 Si4
Simms, James Meriles.
The first colored Baptist church in North America. Constituted at Savannah, Georgia, January 20, A. D. 1788. With biographical sketches of the pastors. Written for the church by Rev. James M. Simms. Philadelphia, J. B. Lippincott company, 1888.
264 p. front., plates, ports. 19½cm.
1. Savannah. First Bryan Baptist church.
8-14482 Revised
Library of Congress BX6480.S45F55
Copyright [r31c2]

M331 Si5
Simms' blue book and national negro business and professional directory. Chicago, Ill., J. N. Simms, 1923-
v. illus. (incl. ports.) 24cm.
1. ~~Negroes~~—Direct. 2. Business. 1. Simms, James N., comp.
23-6597
Library of Congress E185.96.S59
—— 2d set.
Copyright [2]

M331 Si5
Simms, James Nelson, 1871-
Simms' blue book and national negro business and professional directory. Chicago, Ill., J. N. Simms, 1923-
v. illus. (incl. ports.) 24cm.
1. Negroes—Direct. 1. Simms, James N., comp.
23-6597
Library of Congress E185.96.S59
—— 2d set.
Copyright [2]

M973 Si5t
Simons, R E
The three day Negro, yesterday, today, tomorrow, by R.E. Simons.
n.p., n.p., n.d.
25p. 15cm.
1. History
I. Title

M813.5 H83sit3
Simpel nimmt ne frau.
Hughes, Langston, 1902-
Simpel nimmt ne frau. [Simple takes a wife] Berlin, Aufbau-Verlag, 1965.
329p. illus. 19½cm.
Translated from the English.
"This buch for Arthur - Sincerely, Langston. Harlem, U.S.A., July, 1965."
I. Title.

M813.5 H87simp
Simpel spricht sich aus.
Hughes, Langston, 1902-
Simpel spricht sich aus (Simple speaks his mind). Berlin, Aufbau, 1960.
278p. maps. 20cm.

M811.5 Si58ab
Simpkins, Thomas V
ABC's of birds and beasts. New York Vantage Press, [1965]
60p. illus. 21cm.
I. Title.

M811.5 Si58r
Simpkins, Thomas V
Rhyme and reason. Boston, Christopher Pub. House [1949]
95 p. 21 cm.
Poems.
I. Title.
PS3537.I 7R45 811.5 49-1799*
Library of Congress [2]

M811.5 Si58r3
Simpkins, Thomas V.
Rhymes of puppy love and others, including Negro dialect, by Thomas V. Simpkins ... Boston, The Christopher publishing house [c1935]
x, 13-60 p. 20½cm.
I. Title. 1. Poetry.
35-876
Library of Congress PS3537.I 7R5 1935
Copyright A 79074 [3] 811.5

M813.5 H87sim
Simple siger sin mening.
Hughes, Langston, 1902-
Simple siger sin mening: pa dansk ved Michael Tejn. Kobenhavn, Gyldendal, 1954.
227 p. 20 cm.

M817.5 C22
Simple Simon.
Carpenter, Ben
Simple Simon; a portfolio. Los Angeles, Calif., Carpto Publishing Co., 1962.
61p. 24cm.

M813.5 H87sim
Simple speaks his mind.
Hughes, Langston, 1902-
Simple siger sin mening: pa dansk ved Michael Tejn. Kobenhavn, Gyldendal, 1954.
227 p. 20 cm.

M813.5 H87si 1951
Simple speaks his mind.
Hughes, Langston, 1902-
Simple speaks his mind. London, Victor Gollancz, 1951.
231p. 20cm.

M813.5 H87si
Simple speaks his mind.
Hughes, Langston, 1902-
Simple speaks his mind. [New York] Simon and Schuster [1950]
231 p. 20 cm.
I. Title.
Full name: James Langston Hughes.
PS3515.U274S53 813.5 50-7299 rev
Library of Congress [r50q10]

M813.5 H87sis 1958
Simple stakes a claim.
Hughes, Langston, 1902-
Simple stakes a claim. London, Victor Gollancz Ltd., 1958.
191p. 19cm.

Simple stakes a claim.

M813.5 H87sis
Hughes, Langston, 1902-
Simple stakes a claim. New York, Rinehart [1957]
191 p. 20 cm.

I. Title.
Full name: James Langston Hughes.
PS3515.U274S54 817.5 57-9628 ‡
Library of Congress [15]

Les simulacres.

Haiti M843.91 H52s
Hibbert, Fernand.
... Les simulacres; l'aventure de M. Hellénus Caton. Port-au-Prince, Imprimerie Chéraquit, 1923.
102 p. 23cm.
With this is bound the author's Le manuscrit de mon ami, 1923.

I. Title. II. Title: L'aventure de M. Hellénus Caton.
25-20877
Library of Congress PQ3949.H5S5

Sing, laugh, weep.

M811.08 S16
The Scribes, St. Louis.
Sing, laugh, weep; a book of poems by the Scribes. With illustrations by Theopolus Williams. St. Louis, Press publishing co., 1944.
126 p. illus. 20cm.

1. American poetry—20th cent. 2. American literature—Missouri—St. Louis. I. Title. 3. Poetry.
44-9876
Library of Congress PS572.S25S35 [46d1] 811.5082

Simple takes a wife.

M813.5 H87sit
Hughes, Langston, 1902-
Simple takes a wife. [New York] Simon and Schuster, 1953.
240 p. 21 cm.
First edition.
Inscribed by author: Especially for my friend of many years, Arthur Spingarn, these tales with a Harlem blackground, Sincerely, Langston, New York, April 15, 1953.
I. Title.
Full name: James Langston Hughes.
PS3515.U274S57 813.5 53-1553 ‡
Library of Congress [5]

Sin.

M233.2 C55w
Clarke, Andral Wellington, 1896-
What is the unpardonable sin? By A. Wellington Clarke, TH. B. Boston, Mass., Meador publishing company [1929]
64 p. 19½cm.

1. Sin. I. Title.
30-5786
Library of Congress BT721.C6
Copyright A 17468 [3]

Les singes de dieu et les hommes du diable.

Guadeloupe M848 P13s
Privat d'Anglemont, Alexandre, 1815-1859.
Les singes de dieu et les hommes du diable; edited with foreword, notes and vocabulary by Mercer Cook and Guichard Parris. Atlanta, Atlanta University, 1936.
152 27½cm. (Atlanta University French series)
Vocabulary and notes: p. 9-16.
Text taken from 1884 edition of Paris Inconnu.

Simple's Uncle Sam.

M813.5 H87siu
Hughes, Langston, 1902-
Simple's Uncle Sam. [1st ed.] New York, Hill and Wang [1965]
x, 180 p. 21 cm.
"Simple - one more time once - to Arthur - Sincerely, Langston, Harlem, U.S.A., October, 1965."

I. Title.
PS3515.U274S6 817.52 65-24717
Library of Congress [65f20]

Sin and salvation.

M304 P19 v.3, no.7
Brawley, Edward M.
Sin and salvation. A text-book on evangelism. By Edward M. Brawley. Revised by Benjamin Brawley Philadelphia. The Judson Press [1927]
55p. 22cm.

Nigeria
The singing minister of Nigeria.

MB9 D37
Delano, Isaac O
The singing minister of Nigeria; the life of the Rev. Canon J. J. Ransome-Kuti, by Isaac O. Delano ... London, United society for Christian literature [1942]
63, [1] p. 18½cm. (Half-title: Africa's own library, no. 2)

1. Ransome-Kuti, Josiah Jesse, 1855-1930. 2. Missions — Nigeria. I. United society for Christian literature, London. II. Title.
44-35518
Library of Congress BV3625.N6R8 [3] 922

Simply heavenly.

M813.5 H87sip
Hughes, Langston, 1902-
Simply heavenly; a comedy with music. Books and lyrics by Langston Hughes. Music by David Martin. New York, Dramatics Play Service, Inc., 1959.
87p. illus. 20cm.

Sin corner and Joe Smith.

M364 Sm42
Smith, Joseph.
Sin corner and Joe Smith; a story of vice and corruption in Chicago. Forewords by Alderman Leon M. Depres and Jack Mabley. New York, Exposition Press [1963]
119p. 21cm.

The singing teakettle; poems for children.

M811.5 W58s
Whitaker, Christine D
The singing teakettle; poems for children. [1st ed.] New York, Exposition Press [1956]
40 p. 21 cm.

I. Title.
PZ8.3.W58 55-11838 ‡
Library of Congress [3]

Liberia MB9 Si5me
Simpson, Clarence Lorenzo, 1896-
The memoirs of C. L. Simpson, former Liberian Ambassador to Washington and to the Court of St. James's; the symbol of Liberia. London, Diplomatic Press and Pub. Co. [1961]
298 p. illus. 23 cm.

1. Liberia—Hist. I. Title.
DT636.S5A3 966.6 61-65820 ‡
Library of Congress [2]

Sinclair, Cecilia, joint author.

Gold Coast M966.7 B24w
Barker, William Henry, 1882-
West African folk-tales, collected and arranged by W.H. Barker...and Cecilia Sinclair. London, George G. Harrap & Co., 1917.
184p. front., plates. 19cm.
Printed in Great Britain.

MB9 Si64
Singleton, George Arnett, 1894-
The autobiography of George A. Singleton. Boston, Forum Pub. Co. [1964]
272 p. illus., ports. 22 cm.
Portrait of author on book jacket.

BX8449.S5A3 922.773 64-56507
Library of Congress [2]

M07 Si5
Simpson, George Eaton, 1904-
The Negro in the Philadelphia press ... [by] George Eaton Simpson. Philadelphia, 1936.
xv, 158 p. incl. illus. (map) tables, diagrs. 23cm.
Thesis (PH. D.)—University of Pennsylvania, 1934.
"Planoprinting."
An analysis of Negro material published in the Philadelphia record, Public ledger, Evening bulletin and Philadelphia inquirer during 1908-1932.
Bibliography: p. [153]-156.

1. ~~Negroes.~~ 2. ~~Negroes~~—Stat. 3. American newspapers—Philadelphia. I. Title.
37-1807
Library of Congress PN4899.P48S5 1934
Univ. of Pennsylvania Libr.
——— Copy 2. [38g5] 071.4811

M973.8 Si6
Sinclair, William Albert, 1858-
The aftermath of slavery; a study of the condition and environment of the American Negro, by William A. Sinclair ... with an introduction by Thomas Wentworth Higginson, LL. D. Boston, Small, Maynard & company, 1905.
xiii, 358 p. 20cm.

1. Negroes. I. Title.
5-15562
Library of Congress E185.6.S61 [45g1]

M287.8 Si6
Singleton, George Arnett, 1894-
The romance of African Methodism; a study of the African Methodist Episcopal Church. New York, Exposition Press [1952]
251 p. illus. 22 cm.

1. African Methodist Episcopal Church—Hist. I. Title.
BX8443.S45 287.8 51-12284 ‡
Library of Congress [1]

Simu ya kifo [Trail of death]

Tanzania M896.3 K155
Katalambula, Faraji, H. H.
Simu ya kifo [Trail of death] Dar es Salaam, East African Literature Bureau, 1965.
76p. illus. 22cm.
Written in Swahili.

I. Title.

M306 N212
Sinclair, William Albert, 1858-
The Negro and the nations.

(In: National Negro Conference. Proceedings. New York, [1909] p.211-213)

M231 W62
Singleton, Hubert
Why I belive there is a God.

Pp. 58-64.

In: Why I believe there is a God. Chicago, Johnson Pub. Co., 1965.

S. Africa
M896.3
Si6n

Sinxo, Guybon Budlwana, 1902-1962
U-Nomsa (a novel). Lovedale, South Africa, Lovedale Press, 1922? Second printing.

84p. 18cm.
Bound with the author's Umfundisi wase-Mtuqwasi. (I-Noveli.). Lovedale, 1927.

I. Title. 1. Africa, South - Fiction.

S. Africa
M896.3
Si6n

Sinxo, Guybon Budlwana, 1902-1962
Umfundisi wase-Mtuqwasi. (I-Noveli). Lovedale, Lovedale Institution Press, 1927?

89p. 18cm.
Bound with the author's U-Nomsa (a novel). Lovedale, 1922?

S. Africa
M896.3
Si6u

Sinxo, Guybon Budlwana, 1902-1962
Umzali wolahleko (a Novel). Lovedale, Lovedale Press, 1944.

64p. 18½cm.

I. Title.

M326.
Si7o

Sipkins, Henry, 1788-1838
An oration on the abolition of the slave trade; delivered in the African church, in the city of New-York, January 2, 1809. By Henry Sipkins, a descendant of Africa. New-York, Printed by J. C. Totten, 1809.

1 p. l., 21 p. 22cm.

1. Slavery in the U. S.—Controversial literature—1809. 2. Slave-trade—U. S.

10-32479

Library of Congress E446.S61

Sipkins, Henry, 1788-1838. Introductory address
Williams, Peter, 1780?-1840.

M815.2
W37o

An oration on the abolition of the slave trade; delivered in the African church, in the city of New-York, January 1, 1808 ... By Peter Williams, jun., a descendant of Africa. New-York: Printed by Samuel Wood. no. 362 Pearl-street. 1808.

26, [2] p. 22cm.

[Markoe pamphlets, v. 33, no. 14]

1. Slave-trade—U. S.

19—10108

Library of Congress AC901.M2 vol. 33
[31b1]

'Sippi.

M813.5
K55s

Killens, John Oliver, 1916-
'Sippi. New York, Trident Press, 1967.

xiii, 434 p. 22 cm.

I. Title.

PZ4.K48Si 67-16400

Library of Congress [3]

Sirene.

Haiti
M841
Al7s

Alphonse, Raymond Alphée.
Sirene [by] Raymond Alphée Alphonse. Port-au-prince, Haiti, Imprimerie du College Vertieres, 1946.

22p. port. 20½cm.

Sirens, knuckles, boots.

Africa, South
M896.1
B83s

Brutus, Dennis
Sirens, knuckles, boots; poems. [Ibadan, Mbari Publications, 1963]

[34]p. 20cm.

Haiti
M972.94
V44r

Sismonde de Sismondi, J.C.L.
Vastey, Pompée Valentin, baron de, c. 1820?
Reflexions on the blacks and whites. Remarks upon a letter addressed by M. Mazeres, a French ex-colonist, to J.C.L. Sismonde de Sismondi, containing observations on the blacks and whites, the civilization of Africa, the kingdom of Haiti, & c. Translated from the French of the Baron DeVastey by W.H.M.B. London, Sold by J. Hatchard, 190 Piccadilly, and may be had of the Booksellers in general [1817]

83p. 17cm.

Sissie.

M813.5
W68s

Williams, John Alfred, 1925-
Sissie. New York, Farrar, Straus and Cudahy [1963]

277 p. 22 cm.

I. Title.

PZ4.W72624Si 63-8551 ‡

Library of Congress [5]

Mali
M966.2
Si8co

Sissoko, Fily Dabo, 1900-1964.
Coups de Sagaie (controverses sur l'Union Française). Paris, Editions de Latovr Dvgvet, 1957.

142p. 19cm.

I. Title.

Mali
M398
Si8

Sissoko, Fily-Dabo, 1900-1964.
Crayons et portraits. Paris, Imprimerie Union Mulnouse, n.d.

79p. 23cm.

1. Sudan, French - Folktales. I. Title.

Mali
M301
Si8

Sissoko, Fily-Dabo, 1900-1964.
Les noirs et la culture (introduction au probleme de l'evolution culturelle des peuples Africains). New York, 1950.

71p. 20cm.

1. Africa - Social life and customs. 2. Culture - Africa. I. Title.

Mali
M966.2
Si8p

Sissoko, Fily-Dabo, 1900-1964.
La passion de Djimé. Paris, Éditions de La Tour du guet [1956]

113 p. 19 cm.
Portrait of author on book jacket.

I. Title.

A 57-2634

Illinois. Univ. Library for Library of Congress [3]

Mali
M896.1
Si83

Sissoko, Fily Dabo, 1900-1964.
Poèmes de l'Afrique noire; feux de brousse harmakhis fleurs et chardons. Paris, Debresse-poésie, 1963.

170p. 19cm.

1. African poetry. I. Title.

Mali
M966.2
Si8

Sissoko, Fily Dabo, 1900-1964.
Sagesse noire (sentences et proverbes malinkés) Paris, Editions de la Tour du guet [1955]

xviii, 82 p. port. 21 cm.

1. Proverbs, African. I. Title.

A 56-984

Illinois. Univ. Library for Library of Congress [3]

Mali
M896.3
Si83s

Sissoko, Fily Dabo, 1900-1964.
La savane rouge. [Avignon] Les Presses Universelles [1962]

139p. 19cm.

I. Title.

Sit-in demonstrations.

M301
M69

Mitchell, Glenford E ed.
The angry black South. Edited by Glenford E. Mitchell and William H. Peace, III. New York, Corinth Books, 1962.

159 p. 21 cm.
Portraits of authors on back of book.

1. Negroes—Southern States. 2. U. S.—Race question. I. Peace, William H., joint ed. II. Title.

E185.61.M67 301.451 61—15876 ‡

Library of Congress [62f5]

Sit-in demonstrations.

M323
P84wy

Posey, Barbara Ann
Why I sit-in; the girl who started a nationwide civil-rights movement tells how and why she sits and waits. New York, NAACP, 1960.

4p. port. 22cm.

Sit-in demonstrations.

M323
W65m

Wilkins, Roy, 1901-
The meaning of the sit-ins. New York, National Association for the Advancement of Colored People, 1960]

11p. 23cm.

1. Sit-in demonstrations. 2. Civil rights. I. Title.

Rhodesia
M968.91
Si8a

Sithole, Ndabaningi, 1920-
African nationalism. With a foreword by R. S. Garfield Todd. Cape Town, New York, Oxford University Press, 1959.

174 p. 19 cm.

1. Nationalism—Africa. I. Title.

DT31.S55 960.3 59—16995 ‡

Library of Congress [60f5]

Africa
M961 Sithole, Ndabaningi, 1920-
O45 Albert Schweitzer, an African image.
Pp. 103-106.

In: Desai, Ram, ed. Christianity in Africa as seen by the Africans, Denver, A. Swallow [1962]

La situation économique et sociale des États-Unis à la fin du xviiie siècle.

Guadeloupe
M910 Capitaine, Alexandre, 1894-
C17s La situation économique et sociale des États-Unis à la fin du xviiie siècle (d'après les voyageurs français) par Alexandre Capitaine ... Paris, Les Presses universitaires de France, 1926.

xx, 162 p., 1 l. 25½[cm].

1. U. S.—Descr. & trav. 2. U. S.—Soc. condit. 3. U. S.—Econ. condit. I. Title.

26—18783

Library of Congress E164.C28
[42c1]

Siwa muto lugero.

Uganda
M967.61 Nsimbi, Michael B
N87s Siwa muto lugero. London, Longmans, Green and Co., 1957.

80p. 18½cm.

I. Title.

S. Africa
M968 Siwisa, L K
Si96 Imi Zekeliso namama Qhalo esi Xhosa, Ibalwe ngu L.K. Siwisa. Lovedale, The Lovedale Press, 1950.

62p. 18cm.

Six cylinder olympus.

M811.5 Johnston, Percy Edward, 1930-
J64s Six cylinder olympus. [Chicago, Jupiter Hammon Press, 1964]

36p. 17½cm.
"5-18-64 - To A. B. Spingarn - Because you've preserved so much of our work. Percy."

Sixes and sevens; an anthology of new poetry.

M811.08 Breman, Paul, [ed]
B74 Sixes and sevens; an anthology of new poetry. London, P. Breman, 1962.

96p. 21½cm. (Heritage, 2)
Includes biographical references.
White editor.

Sixty years in Congress and twenty-eight out.

MB Moseley, J H 1882-
M85s Sixty years in Congress and twenty-eight out. [1st ed.] New York, Vantage Press [1960]

99 p. illus. 22 cm.

1. Legislators—U. S. 2. Negroes—Biog. I. Title.

JK1021.M75 923.273 60-3728 ‡

Library of Congress [2]

M614
R66sk Skeletology.
Roman, Charles Victor, 1864-1934.
Skeletology. Reprinted from the Journal of the National Medical Association. Oct.-Dec., 1922.

2p. 27cm.

A sketch-map atlas of Nigeria.

Nigeria
M912 Oboli, Herbert Oguejiofo Nkemba
Ob5 A sketch-map atlas of Nigeria, with notes and exercises. New ed. rev. London, George G. Harrap [1962]

46p. maps. 21½cm.

Sketches of slave life: or, Illustrations of...

M326.99B Randolph, Peter.
R15s Sketches of slave life: or, Illustrations of the 'peculiar
1855 institution.' By Peter Randolph, an emancipated slave. Boston, Pub. for the author, 1855.

35 p. 20[cm].

1. Plantation life. I. Title.
2. Slave narratives.

10-34660

Library of Congress [36b1] E444.R19

Sketches of southern life.

M811.4 Harper, Frances Ellen Watkins, b. 1825.
H23s Sketches of southern life, by Frances E. Watkins Harper. Philadelphia, Merrihew and son, 1888.

58p. 15½cm.

Skin - Diseases.

St. Lucia
M610 Spencer, Gerald Arthur, 1902-
Sp3c Cosmetology in the Negro; a guide to its problems, by Gerlad A. Spencer... [New York, The Arlain printing co., 1944]

viii, 9-127p. illus. 19½cm.

M616 Skin-Homeopathic treatment.
W93py Wright, Louis Tompkins, 1891-1952.
Pyoderma gangrenosum in chronic non-specific ulcerative colitis treated with aureomycin, by Louis T. Wright, and Selig Strax. Reprinted from the Harlem Hospital bulletin, 1:99-112, December 1948.

U. S.
M966.1 Skinner, Elliott Percival, 1927-
Sk34 The Mossi of the Upper Volta; the political development of a Sudanese people. Stanford, Calif., Stanford University Press, 1964.

ix, 236 p. illus., map. 24 cm.
Bibliography: p. [225]-227.

1. Mossi (African people) I. Title.

GN655.M6S55 916.61 64—12074

Library of Congress [a64c2]

U.S.
M960 Skinner, Elliott Percival, 1927-
Sk34 ~~Chu, Daniel.~~
A glorious age in Africa; the story of three great African empires [by] Daniel Chu and Elliott Skinner. Illustrated by Moneta Barnett. [1st ed.] Garden City, N. Y., Doubleday, 1965.

120 p. col. illus., col. maps. 22 cm. (Zenith books)

1. Africa—History, Juvenile. I. Chu, Daniel. ~~I. Skinner, Elliott Percival, 1927- joint author.~~ II. Title. 2. Mali. 3. Songhay.

DT23.C5 1965 j 960 65-10280

Library of Congress [5]

M813.5 Skinner, Theodosia B
Sk34i Ice cream from heaven. [1st ed.] New York, Vantage Press [1962]

83p. 20½cm.
Portrait of author on book jacket.

I. Title.

S. Africa
MB9 Skota, T D Mweli, ca.1890- ,
Sk5 comp. and ed.
The African yearly register. Being an illustrated national biographical dictionary (Who's who) of Black folks in Africa. Contributions by the leading native ministers, professors, teachers and doctors. Johannesburg, South Africa, R. L. Esson and Co., Ltd., n.d. (1932?).

xvii, 450p. (Errata sheet on p. 450

S. Africa
MB9 Skota, T. D Mweli, ca.1890-
Sk5 comp. and ed. (card 2)

covers the page number, otherwise, 449p. plus Errata slip - p. 450.)

22cm.

1. Africa, South - Biography.

S. Africa
MB Skota, T D Mweli, ca.1890 ed.
Sk5a The African yearly register; being an illustrated national biographical dictionary (Who's Who) of black folks in Africa. Johannesburg, R.L. Esson & Co., [1932]

449p. illus. portraits. 21½cm.

1. Africa, South - Biographies. 2. Africa - Biographies.

The Slabtown district convention.

M812.5 Burroughs, Nannie Helen, 1879-
B94s The Slabtown district convention: a comedy in one act, by Miss Nannie H. Burroughs. Washington, D.C., the author [c1926]

44p. 18½cm.
Seventh edition.

Slappy Hooper.

M813.5 Bontemps, Arna Wendell, 1902-
B64s1 Slappy Hooper, the wonderful sign painter, by Arna Bontemps and Jack Conroy; pictures by Ursula Koering. Boston, Houghton Mifflin company, 1946.

2 p. l., 44 p. incl. col. front., col. illus. 22 x 24[cm].

I. Conroy, Jack, 1899- joint author. II. Koering, Ursula, illus. III. Title.

PZ7.B6443Sl 46—8242

© 12Nov46; 2c 4Nov46; authors, Nashville and Chicago; A8500.

Library of Congress [47f5]

Slater, John Fox, 1815-1834.

M06
J61
no.2

Howe, Samuel H 1837-
... A brief memoir of the life of John F. Slater of Norwich, Connecticut, 1815 to 1884, by Rev. S. H. Howe ... Baltimore, The Trustees, 1894.

16 p. front. (port.) 25cm. (The trustees of the John F. Slater fund. Occasional papers, no. 2)

1. Slater, John Fox, 1815-1834.

Library of Congress E185.5.J65 7—18171
———— Copy 2. [a32b1]

Kenya
M967.65
S11t

Slater, Montagu
The Trial of Jomo Kenyatta. London, Secker & Warburg, 1955.

255p. 21cm.
White Author

1. Kenya - Politics and government. I. Kenyatta, Jomo. II. Title.

The slave.

M812.5
J72d

Jones, LeRoi.
Dutchman and The slave, two plays. New York, Morrow, 1964.

88 p. 22 cm.

I. Title. II. Title: The slave.

PS3519.O4545D8 812.54 64-22907
Library of Congress [5]

Slave insurrections in the United States...

M326.
C23

Carroll, Joseph Cephas.
Slave insurrections in the United States, 1800-1865, by Joseph Cephas Carroll, PH. D. Boston, Chapman & Grimes, inc. [c1938]

229 p. 20½cm.
"References" at end of each chapter. Bibliography: p. 217-229.

1. Slavery in the U. S.—Insurrections, etc. I. Title.

Library of Congress E447.C27 39—2692
[43g1] 326.973

Slave narratives

M326.99B
A11h

Albert, Mrs. Octavia Victoria (Rogers) 1853-1889?
The house of bondage; or, Charlotte Brooks, and other slaves, original and life-like, as they appeared in their old plantations and city slave life; together with pen-pictures of the peculiar institution, with sights and insights into their new relations as freedmen, freemen, and citizens ... with an intro. by Rev. Bishop Willard F. Mallalien. New York, Hunt & Eaton; Cranston & Stowe, 1890;
xiv, 161p. incl. front. (port.) 19m.

Slave narratives.

M326.99B
An2f

Anderson, Robert, 1843-
From slavery to affluence; memoirs of Robert Anderson, ex-slave ... Hemingford, Neb., The Hemingford ledger, [c1927.

1 p. l., 59 p. plates. 19½cm.
Each plate accompanied by leaf with descriptive letterpress.

I. Title.

Library of Congress E185.97.A54 27-16257
———— Copy 2.
Copyright A 996587 [2]

Slave narratives

M326.99B
Au5

Aunt Sally; or, The cross the way to freedom. A narrative of the slave-life and purchase of the mother of Rev. Isaac Williams, of Detroit, Michigan ... Cincinnati, American Reform Tract and Book Society, ~~1862~~. 1858.

vii, 9-216p. front. (port.) illus., port. group. 15½cm.

Slave narratives

M326.99B
Au8

Autobiography of a female slave. New York, Redfield, 1857.

401, 8p. 19cm.

Slave narratives.

M326.99B
B21f

[Ball, Charles]
Fifty years in chains; or, The life of an American slave ... New York, H. Dayton; Indianapolis, Ind., Dayton & Asher, 1859.

2p. l., [9]-430p. 19cm.

Slave narratives.

M326.99B
B21s

Ball, Charles, negro slave
Slavery in the United States; a narrative of the life and adventures of Charles Ball, a black man, who lived forty years in Maryland, South Carolina and Georgia as a slave ... Lewistown, Pa., J. W. Shugert, 1836.

400p. 18cm.

Slave narratives.

M326.99B
B22n

Banks, J H b1833-
... A narrative of events of the life of J. H. Banks, an escaped slave, from the cotton state, Alabama, in America ... Written, with introduction, by J. W. C. Pennington, Liverpool, M. Rouke, 1861.

92 [2]p. 17cm.

Slave narratives,

M326.99B
B34n

Bayley, Solomon
A narrative of some remarkable incidents in the life of Solomon Bayley, formerly a slave, in the state of Delaware, North America; written by himself, and published for his benefit; to which are prefixed a few remarks, by Robert Hurnardt. 2d ed. London, Printed for Harvey and Darton, 1825.

ix, 48p. 18cm.

Slave narratives.

M326.99B
B47

Bibb, Henry, b. 1815
Narrative of the life and adventures of Henry Bibb, an American slave, written by himself. With an introduction by Lucius C. Matlack. New York, The author, 1849.

1p. l, xii, [13]-204, [3] p. illus. 19cm.

Slave narratives.

M326.99B
B561

Black, Leonard
The life and sufferings of Leonard Black, a fugitive from slavery. Written by himself. New Bedford, Press of Benjamin Lindsey, 1847.

61p. 14cm.

Slave narratives.

M326.99B
B65s

Botkin, Benjamin Albert, 1901-
The slave as his own interpreter.

(In: The Library of Congress quarterly journal of current acquisitions. 2:37-63, November 1944)

White author.

Slave narratives

M326.99B
B815

Brown, John, fl. 1854.
Slave life in Georgia: a narrative of the life, sufferings, and escape of John Brown, a fugitive slave, now in England. Ed. by L. A. Chamerovzow ... London [W.M. Watts] 1855.

1p. l, ii, 250p. front. (port.) 18½cm.

Slave narratives.

M326.99B
C55c
1846

Clark, Lewis Garrard, 1812-1897
Narratives of the sufferings of Lewis and Milton Clarke ... during a captivity of more than twenty years among the slaveholders of Kentucky ... Boston, B. Marsh, 1846.

144p. 18cm.
For other editions of this title, see entries under author's name.

Slave narratives

M326.99B
C78

Cooper, Thomas
Narrative of the life of Thomas Cooper. New York, Published by Isaac T. Hoffer, 1832.

36p. illus. 14cm.

Slave narratives.

M326.99B
C84r

Craft, William
Running a thousand miles for freedom; or, the escape of William and Ellen Craft from slavery. London, William Tweedie, 1860.

111p. front. 17½cm.

Slave narratives.

Ghana
M966.7
C89n

Cugoano, Ottobah
Narrative of the enslavement of Ottobah Cugoano, a native of Africa; published by himself, in the year 1887.

Pp. 120-127 21½cm.
In: The Negro's memorial, or abolitionist's catechism; by an abolitionist. London, Printed for the author and sold by Harchard and Co., 1825.

Slave narratives.

M326.99B
D295

Davis, Noah.
A narrative of the life of Rev. Noah Davis, a colored man. Written by himself, at the age of fifty-four. Printed solely for the author's benefit. Baltimore, Published by John F. Weishampel [1859]

86p. front. (port.) 15½cm.

M326.99B
D91n

Slave narratives.

[Dungy,]
A narrative of the Rev. John Dungy, who was born a slave. Written by his daughter. Rochester, N. Y., Printed for the publisher, 1866.

10p. 21cm.

M326.99B
L24h

Slave narratives

Hawkins, William George, 1823-1909
Lunsford Lane; or, Another helper from North Carolina. Boston, Crosby & Nichols, 1864.

xii, 13-305p. front. (port.) 19½cm.

M326.99B
J15
1861

Slave narratives

Jacobs, Harriet (Brent), 181 -1896
Incidents in the life of a slave girl. Written by herself. ... Edited by Maria Child. Boston, Pub. for the author, 1861.

1p. [5]-306p. 19½cm.
Preface signed: Linda Brent.

M326.99B
H14s

Slave narratives.

Elder, Orville
Samuel Hall, 47 years a slave. A brief story of his life before and after freedom came to him. Washington, Iowa, Journal print, c 1912.

41 unumb. p. 23cm.

M326.99B
H32n

Slave narratives.

[Hayden, William]
Narrative of William Hayden, containing a faithful account of his travels for a number of years, whilst a slave in the South. Written by himself... Cincinnati, Ohio, 1846.

156p. front. (port.) 17½cm.

MB9
J63t

Slave narratives.

Johnson, Thomas L
Twenty - eight years a slave; or the story of my life in three continents, by Thomas L. Johnson... Bourne mouth, W. mate and sons, limited, 1909.
xvi, 266p. front., plates. 19cm.

M326.99B
F31

Slave narratives.

Federal Writers' Project.
Lay my burden down; a folk history of slavery, edited by B. A. Botkin. Chicago, Ill., Univ. of Chicago Press, [1945]

xxi, 285 [1]p. front. plates. 23½cm.

M326.99B
H39t

Slave narratives.

Henson, Josiah 1789-1881
The life of Josiah Henson, formerly a slave, now an inhabitant of Canada, as narrated by himself. Boston, A. D. Phelps, 1849.

iv, 76p. 17cm.
Narrated to S. A. Eliot. cf. Sabin, Bibl. amer.
For other editions of this title, see entries under author's name.

M326.99B
J71e
1855

Slave narratives

Jones, Thomas H
Experience and personal narrative of Uncle Tom Jones: who was for forty years a slave. Also the surprising adventures of Wild Tom, of the island retreat, a fugitive Negro from South Carolina. Boston, J. E. Farwell, 1855.

[7]-54p. 24cm.

Slave narratives.

M326.99B
F31s

Fedric, Francis.
Slave life in Virginia and Kentucky; or, Fifty years of slavery in the southern states of America. By Francis Fedric, an escaped slave. With preface, by the Rev. Charles Lee ... London, Wertheim, Macintosh, and Hunt, 1863.
viii, 115 p. 15½cm.

1. Slavery in the U. S.—Condition of slaves. I. Lee, Charles.

Library of Congress E444.F29 11—11611
[36b1]

M326.99B
H39t
18F2

Slave narratives.

Henson, Josiah, 1789-1881
The life of Josiah Henson, formerly a slave, now an inhabitant of Canada, as narrated by himself. Boston, A.D. Phelps, 1849.
~~iv, 76p.~~ viii 118p. 17cm.

Slave narratives.
Jones, Thomas H.

M326.99B
J71
1871

The experience of Thomas H. Jones, who was a slave for forty-three years. Written by a friend, as related to him by Brother Jones. New Bedford [Mass.] E. Anthony & sons, printers, 1871.
vi, [7]-46 p. front. 19cm.
Portrait on cover.

18—17124

Library of Congress E444.J795
[44b1]

M326.99B
G76

Slave narratives.

Grandy, Moses, b.1786?
Narrative of the life of Moses Grandy; late a slave in the United States of America ... 1st American from the last London ed. ... Boston, O. Johnson, 1844.

iv, [5]-45p., 1 l. 16½cm.

M326.99B
H87

Slave narratives.

Hughes, Louis, 1832-
Thirty years a slave. From bondage to freedom. The institution of slavery as seen on the plantation and in the home of the planter. Autobiography of Louis Hughes. Milwaukee, South Side Printing Co, 1897.

210p. front. (port.) plans (facsims) 21½cm.

M326.99B
J71
1850

Slave narratives.

Jones, Thomas H
The experience of Thomas Jones, who was a slave for forty-three years. Written by a friend as given to him by Brother Jones. Boston, Printed by Daniel Laing, Jr., 1850.

47p. 21½cm.

M326.99B
G81n
1863

Slave narratives.

Green, Jacob D , 1813-
Narrative of the life of J. D. Green, a runaway slave, from, containing an account of his three escapes, in 1839, 1846 & 1848. Seventh thousand. Huddersfield, Printed by Henry Fielding, Kirkgate, 1863.

iv, 42p. 16cm.

M326.99B
J13n

Slave narratives.

Jackson, Andrew, b. 1814
Narrative and writings of Andrew Jackson, of Kentucky; containing an account of his birth, and twenty-six years of his life while a slave; his escape; five years of freedom, together with anecdotes relating to slavery; journal of one year's travels; sketches, etc. Narrated by himself; written by a friend. Syracuse, Daily and Weekly Star Office, 1847.
vi, [7]-120p. 16½cm.

Slave narratives.
Jones, Thomas H

M326.99B
J71e
1880

The experience of Rev. Thomas H. Jones, who was a slave for forty-three years. Written by a friend, as related to him by Brother Jones. Boston, A.T. Bliss and Co., 1880.

83p. 17cm.

Slave narratives.

M326.99B
G881

Grimes, William, b. 1784.
Life of William Grimes, the runaway slave. Written by himself. New Haven, The Author, 1855.

98p. 18cm.

M326.99B
J15
1862

Slave narratives.

Jacobs, Harriet (Brent) 1818-1876.
The deeper wrong; or, Incidents in the life of a slave girl. Written by herself ... Ed. by L. Maria Child. London, W. Tweedie, 1862.

306p. 19½cm.
Preface signed: Linda Brent.

M326.99B
K23

Slave narratives.

Keckley, Elizabeth (Hobbs) 1824-1907
Behind the scenes; or, Thirty years a slave, and four years in the White House. New York, G. W. Carleton & Co., 1868.

[ix]-xvi, [17]-371p. front. (port.) 19cm.

M326.99B L24n
Slave narratives.
Lane, Lunsford, 1803-
The narrative of Lunsford Lane, formerly of Raleigh, N.C., embracing an account of his early life, the redemption, by purchase of himself and family from slavery, and his banishment from the place of his birth for the crime of wearing a colored skin. Published by himself. 4th ed. Boston, Printed for the publisher, Hewes and Watson's Print, 1848.
[5]-54p. 15½cm.

M326.99B P22r
Slave narratives.
Parker, Allen.
Recollections of slavery times, by Allen Parker. Worcester, Mass., Chas. W. Burbank and Co., 1895.
96p. 18½cm.

MB9 R57
Slave narratives.
Robinson, W H , 1848-
From log cabin to the pulpit; or fifteen years in slavery by W. H. Robinson. [Eau Claire, Wis., James H. Tifft, 1913]
200p. illus. 19½cm.

M326.99B L62a
Slave narratives.
The light and truth of slavery. Aaron's history. [Worcester, Mass., 184-?]
48p. illus. 23cm.
Caption title.

M326.99B P38f
Slave narratives.
Pennington, James William Charles, 1812-1871
The fugitive blacksmith; or, Events in the history of James W. C. Pennington ... formerly a slave in the state of Maryland, United States ... 2d ed. London, C. Gilpin, 1849.
xv, 87p. 16cm.

M326.99B R68 1846
Slave narratives.
Roper, Moses
Narratives of the adventures and escape of Moses Roper from American Slavery. 33rd. thousand. Berwick-Upon-Tweed, The Author, 1846.
88p. illus. 17cm.

M326.99B L82
Slave narratives.
Loguen, Jermain Wesley, 1814-1872.
The Rev. J. W. Loguen, as a slave and as a freeman. A narrative of real life. Syracuse, N.Y., J. G. K. Truair & Co, printers, 1859.
x[11]-454p. front. (port.) 18cm.

M326.99B P58k
Slave narratives.
Pickard, Kate E R
The kidnapped and the ransomed. Being the personal recollections of Peter Still and his wife "Vina," after forty years of slavery. By Mrs. Kate E. R. Pickard. With an introduction, by Rev. Samuel J. May; and an appendix, by William H. Furness, D.D. Syracuse, W. T. Hamilton; New York [etc.] Miller, Orton and Mulligan, 1856.
xxiii 25-409p. 3pl. (incl. front.) 19cm.
For other editions, see entries under author's name.

M326.99B R68 1840
Slave narratives.
Roper, Moses
A narrative of the adventures and escape of Moses Roper, from American slavery; with a preface, by the Rev. T. Price ... 4th ed. London, Harvey and Darton, 1840.
xii, 120p. front. (port.) illus. 15cm.

M326.99B M35
Slave Narratives.
Mars, James, b.1790.
Life of James Mars, a slave; born and sold in Connecticut. 4th ed. Written by himself. Hartford, Press of Case, Lockwood & company, 1868.
38p. 19cm.

M326.99B P93
Slave narratives.
[Prince, Mary]
The history of Mary Prince, a West Indian slave. Related by herself. With a supplement by the editor. To which is added, the narrative of Asa-Asa, a captured African ... London, Published by F. Westley and A. H. Davis, 1831.
44p. 22½cm.

M326.99B Sm6
Slave narratives.
Smith, James Lindsay
Autobiography of James L. Smith, including also, reminiscences of slave life, recollections of the war, education of freedmen, causes of the exodus, etc. Norwich [Conn.] Press of the Bulletin Co., 1881.
xiii, 150p. front. 20cm.

M326.99B M35 1864
Slave narratives.
Mars, James b. 1790.
Life of James Mars, a slave born and sold in Connecticut. Written by himself. Hartford, Press of Case Lockwood & company, 1864.
32p. 17½cm.

M326.99B R15f
Slave narratives.
Randolph, Peter.
From slave cabin to the pulpit. The autobiography of Rev. Peter Randolph: the southern question illustrated and sketches of slave life. Boston, James H. Earle, 1893
220p. front. 19½cm.

M326.99B Sm6n 1835
Slave narratives
Smith, Venture, 1729-1805
A narrative of the life and adventures of Venture, a native of Africa, but resident above sixty years in the United States of America. Related by himself, New London: Printed in 1798. ~~XXXXXXXXXXXX~~ Reprinted A.D. 1835, and published by a descendant of Venture.
24p. 20cm.

M326.99B M38
Slave narratives.
[Mason, Isaac] 1822-
Life of Isaac Mason as a slave. Worcester, Mass., 1893.
74 p. incl. front. (port.) 25½cm.
Autobiography.

M326.99B R15s 1855
Slave narratives.
Randolph, Peter.
Sketches of slave life: or, Illustrations of the 'peculiar institution.' By Peter Randolph, an emancipated slave. Boston, Pub. for the author, 1855.
35p. 20cm.

M326.99B Sm6n 1798
Slave narratives
Smith, Venture. 1729-1805
A narrative of the life and adventures of Venture, a native of Africa, but resident above sixty years in the United States of America. Related by himself. New-London. Printed by C. Holt. at the Bee-Office. 1798.
32p. 22½cm.
For other editions of this title, see entries under author's name.

M326.99B Of3
Slave narrative.
Offley, Greensbury W , 1808-
A narrative of the life and labors of the Rev. G. W. Offley, a colored man, and local preacher, who lived twenty-years at the South and twenty-four at the North ... Hartford, Conn., 1860.
52p. 17cm.

M326.99B R54n
Slave narratives.
Roberts, James, b. 1753
The narrative of James Roberts, soldier in the revolutionary war and at the battle of New Orleans. Chicago: printed for the author, 1858. Hattiesburg, Miss., The Book farm, 1945.
viii, 9-32p. 21½cm. (Heartman's historical series, no. 71)

M326.99B St4 1867
Slave narratives
Steward, Austin, b.1794
Twenty-two years a slave, and forty years a freeman; embracing a correspondence of several years, while president of Wilberforce colony, London, Canada West, by Austin Steward. 4th ed. Canadaigua, N.Y. The author, 1867.
xii, [13]-360p. front. (port.) rpl. 18cm.

Slave narratives

M326.99B
St4

Steward, Austin, b. 1794
Twenty-two years a slave, and forty years a freeman; embracing a correspondence of several years, while president of Wilberforce colony, London, Canada West, by Austin Steward. Rochester, N.Y., W. Alling, 1857.

xii, 13 -360p. front. (port.) 4 pl. 19cm.

M326.99B
W24s

Slave narratives.
Strickland, S.
Negro slavery described by a Negro: being the narrative of Ashton Warner, a native of St. Vincent's. With an appendix containing the testimony of four Christian ministers recently returned from the colonies on the system of slavery as it now exists. By S. Strickland... London, Samuel Maunder, 1831.

144p. 15½cm.

MB9
St8

Slave narratives.
Stroyer, Jacob, 1849-
My life in the South. By Jacob Stroyer. New and enl. ed. Salem, Salem observer book and job print, 1889.

83p. 19½cm.

Slave narratives.
M326.99B
T37

Thompson, John, 1812-
The life of John Thompson, a fugitive slave; containing his history of 25 years in bondage, and his providential escape. Written by himself. Worcester, John Thompson, 1856.
143p. 18½cm.

Slave narratives.

M326.99B
T46t

Tilmon, Levin, 1807-1863
A brief miscellaneous narrative of the more early part of the life of L. Tilmon. Written by himself. Jersey City, W. W. & L. A. Pratt, printers, 1853.

97p. 17cm.
Verso of p. 59 unnumbered and blank.

M326.99B
An19t

Slave narratives.
Twelvetrees, Harper, 1823-1881, ed.
The story of the life of John Anderson, the fugitive slave. London, W. Tweedie, 1863.

xv, 182p. front. (port.) 19½cm.

Slave narratives.

M326.99B
V55n

cVeney, Bethany⌋
The narrative of Bethany Veney, a slave woman. With Introduction by Rev. Bishop Mallalieu, and commendatory notices from Rev. V. A. Cooper and Rev. Erastus Spaulding. Worcester, Mass. 1889.

46p. front. (port.) 19½cm.

Slave narratives.

M326.99B
W32s

Watkins, James, 1823(?)
Struggles for freedom; or the life of James Watkins, formerly a slave in Maryland, U.S.; in which is detailed a graphic account of his extraordinary escape from slavery, notices of the fugitive slave law, the sentiments of American divines on the subject of slavery, etc. 19th edition... Manchester, Printed for James Watkins, 1860.
X ⌊11⌋-104p. 18½cm.

Slave narratives.
M326.99B
W33

Watson, Henry
Narrative of Henry Watson, a fugitive slave. Written by himself. Boston, Published by Bela Marsh, 1848.

48p. 18½cm.

Slave narratives.
M326.99B
W67n

Williams, James, b. 1805.
Narrative of James Williams, an American slave. In anti-slavery examiner no. 6
1838
8p. 30cm.

M326.99B
W68

Slave narratives.
Williams, James
Narrative of the cruel treatment of James Williams, a Negro apprentice in Jamaica, from 1st August, 1834, till the purchase of his freedom in 1837, by Joseph Sturge, of Birmingham, by whom he was brought to England. Glasgow: Printed by Aird and Russell, 1837.

20p. 21cm.

Slave songs of the United States.

M784
A15

Allen, William Francis, 1830-1889, comp.
Slave songs of the United States. New York, A. Simpson & Co., 1867.

115p. illus. 22½cm.

Slave trade.

Africa
M966.92
C88s

Crowther, Samuel Adjai, 1806-1891.
Slave trade-African squadron. Lettersfrom the Rev. Samuel Crowther ... and the Rev. Henry Townsend ... London, John MOrtimer, 1850.

16p. 22cm.

Slave-trade.
M301
D853en

Du Bois, William Edward Burghardt, 1868-
The enforcement of the slave-trade laws, by W. E. B. Du Bois.

(*In* American historical association. Annual report ... for the year 1891. Washington, 1892. 24½cm. p. 161-174)

1. Slave-trade. 2. Slavery in the U. S.

O D 17—864

Library of Congress. Card div. E172.A60 1891
⌊42h1⌋

Slave-trade.
M301
D853su6

Du Bois, William Edward Burghardt, 1868-
The suppression of the African slave-trade to the United States of America, 1638-1870, by W. E. Burghardt Du Bois
~~New York, London, etc. Longmans, Green, and co., 1896~~ Third impression. Cambridge, Harvard Univ. Press.
xi, 335 p. diagrs. 23 cm. (*Half-title:* Harvard historical studies, vol. I)

Appendices: A. A chronological conspectus of colonial and state legislation restricting the African slave-trade, 1641-1787.—B. A chronological conspectus of state, national, and international legislation, 1788-1871.—C. Typical cases of vessels engaged in the American slave-trade, 1619-1864.—D. Bibliography (p. ⌊299⌋-325)

1. Slave-trade—U. S. 2. Slave-trade. I. Title.

2—23269

Library of Congress E441.D81
⌊39q1⌋ -326.10973

Slave-trade.

M301
D853so6
1954

Du Bois, William Edward Burghardt, 1868-
The suppression of the African slave-trade to the United States of America, 1638-1870. New York, The Social Science Press, 1954.

339p. 22cm.

Slave trade.

M815.2
J71t

Jones, Absalom, 1746-1818.
A Thanksgiving sermon, preached January 1, 1808, in St. Thomas's or the African Episcopal Church, Philadelphia: an account of the abolition of the African slave trade on that day by the Congress of the United States... Philadelphia, Printed for the use of the congregation, Fry and Kammerer, Printers, 1808.

22 ⌊2⌋p. 21½cm.

M326
P24o

Slave trade.
Parrott, Russell, 1791-1824.
An oration on the abolition of the slave trade, by Russell Parrott. Delivered on the first of January, 1814, at the African church of St. Thomas. Philadelphia. Printed for the different societies, 1814.

13p. 21cm.

Slave trade.

MB9
Sh2s

Stuart, Charles.
A memoir of Granville Sharp, to which is added Sharp's "Law of retribution," By Charles Stuart. New York, American anti-Slavery society, 1836.

156p. front. 19cm.

Slave-trade—Africa.

M326.
F53

Fisher, Ruth Anna *comp.*
Extracts from the records of the African companies, collected by Ruth A. Fisher. Washington, D. C., The Association for the study of Negro life and history, inc. ⌊1930?⌋

1 p. l., 108 p. 24cm.

"These documents ... extracted from the records of the African companies in London ... are from the papers of the Treasury and the Colonial office."—p. 1.

1. Africa—Comm.—Gt. Brit. 2. Gt. Brit.—Comm.—Africa. 3. Slave-trade—Africa. I. Association for the study of Negro life and history, inc. II. Title: African companies.

31—12708

Library of Congress HT1322.F5
———— Copy 2. ⌊38e2⌋ 326.1

Slave trade—Gt. Brit.

Trinidad
M300
W67c

Williams, Eric, 1911-
Capitalism & slavery ⌊by⌋ Eric Williams. Chapel Hill, The University of North Carolina press ⌊1944⌋

ix, 285 p. 22½cm.

Bibliographical references included in "Notes" (p. 213-261) Bibliography: p. 262-270.
"Based on a doctoral dissertation, 'The economic aspect of the abolition of the British West Indian slave trade and slavery,' submitted to the Faculty of modern history of Oxford university in September, 1938."—p. 262.

1. Gt. Brit.—Indus.—Hist. 2. Slave trade—Gt. Brit. I. Title.

44-47876

Library of Congress HC254.5.W5
⌊30⌋ 330.942

Slave-trade--U. S.

M301 D853su6 **Du Bois, William Edward Burghardt, 1868-**
The suppression of the African slave-trade to the United States of America, 1638-1870, by W. E. Burghardt Du Bois ... New York, London etc. Longmans, Green, and co., 1896.
xi, 335 p. diagrs. 23 cm. (*Half-title:* Harvard historical studies, vol. I)

Appendices: A. A chronological conspectus of colonial and state legislation restricting the African slave-trade, 1641-1787.—B. A chronological conspectus of state, national, and international legislation, 1788-1871.—C. Typical cases of vessels engaged in the American slave-trade, 1619-1864.—D. Bibliography (p. [299]-325)

1. Slave-trade—U. S. 2. Slave-trade. I. Title.

2—23269
Library of Congress E441.D81
[39q1] 326.10973

Slave-trade - U. S.

M301 D853so6 1954
Du Bois, William Edward Burghardt, 1868-
The suppression of the African slave-trade to the United States of America, 1638-1870. New York, The Social Science Press, 1954.

339p. 22cm.

Slave-trade—U. S.

M326 Si1o **Sidney, Joseph.**
An oration, commemorative of the abolition of the slave trade in the United States; delivered before the Wilberforce philanthropic association, in the city of New-York, on the second of January, 1809. By Joseph Sidney. New-York, Printed for the author, J. Seymour, printer, 1809.
20 p. 20cm.

1. Slavery in the U. S.—Controversial literature—1809. 2. Slave-trade—U. S. I. Wilberforce philanthropic association, New York.

10-32480
Library of Congress E446.S56

Slave-trade-U. S.

M326 Si70 **Sipkins, Henry.**
An oration on the abolition of the slave trade; delivered in the African church, in the city of New-York, January 2, 1809. By Henry Sipkins, a descendant of Africa. New-York, Printed by J. C. Totten, 1809.
1 p. l., 21 p. 22cm.

1. Slavery in the U. S.—Controversial literature—1809. 2. Slave-trade—U. S.

10-32479
Library of Congress E446.S61

Slave-trade-U.S.

M815.2 W676 **Williams, Peter, 1780?-1840.**
An oration on the abolition of the slave trade; delivered in the African church, in the city of New-York, January 1, 1808 ... By Peter Williams, jun., a descendant of Africa. New-York: Printed by Samuel Wood, no. 362 Pearl-street. 1808.
26, [2] p. 22cm.
[Markoe pamphlets, v. 33, no. 14]

1. Slave-trade—U. S.

10—10108
Library of Congress AC901.M2 vol. 33
[31b1]

Slavery.

Liberia M966.6 B62r
Blyden, Edward Wilmot, 1832-1912.
A voice from bleeding Africa, on behalf of her exiled children, by Edward W. Blyden. Liberia, G. Killian, printed 1856.

33p. 20cm.

Slavery.

Gold Coast M966.7 C17
Capitein, Jacobus Elisa Joannes, 1717-1747.
Staatkundig-Godeleerd Onderzoekschrift over de slaverny, als niet strydig tegen de christelkye vryheid, welk, onder het fehengen van den algenoegzamen God,... Te Leyden, Te Amsterdam, [sic] By Philippus Bonk, By Gerrit de Groot, 1742.

53[18]p. 21cm. portrait opposite p. 22.

Slavery.

Gold Coast M966.7 C89r
Cugoano, Ottobah.
Reflexions sur la traite et l'esclavage des Negres, traduites de l'anglais, d'Ottobah Cugoano afriquain, esclave a la Grenade et libre en Angleterre. Londres; Paris, Chez royez, 1788.

xii, 194p. 21cm.

Gold Coast M966.7 C89t 1791
Slavery.
Cugoano, Ottobah.
Thoughts and sentiments on the evil of slavery; or the nature of servitude as admitted by the law of God, compared to the modern slavery of the Africans in the West Indies; in an answer to the advocates for slavery and oppression. Addressed to the sons of Africa, by a native. London: Printed for, and sold by, the author, no.12, Queen Street, Grosvenor Square. 1791.
[6] - 46 [3]p. 23½cm.

Slavery.

M815.4 D74r
Douglass, Frederick, 1817-1895.
Report the proceedings of the great anti-slavery meeting held in the Rev. Mr. Cairns's church on Wednesday, 23d September, 1846, including the speeches of Wm. Lloyd Garrison and Frederick Douglass. Taken in short hand by Cincinnatus. n.p.,
16p. 17½cm.

Slavery.

M326 H87
Hueston, William C , 1880- , ed.
The John Brown reader, edited, with foreword by William C. Hueston and J. Finley Wilson. Designed by Edward H. Lawson, Sr. Washington, D.C., Murray Brothers, For the I.B.P.O. Elks of the World, 1949.

96p. illus. 22½cm.

Slavery.

M815.3 P97s
Purvis, Robert,
Speeches and letters by Robert Purvis [Published by the request of the "Afro-American League." Correspondence between Robert Purvis and Bayard Taylor. [n.p. 1860?]

23p. front (port) 23½cm.

Slavery.

Haiti M325 Sy5
Sylvain, Benito.
Du sort des indigènes dans les colonies d'exploitation; par Benito Sylvain ... Paris, L. Boyer, 1901.
528 p., 1 l. incl. port. 22½cm.

1. Native races. 2. Slavery. 3. Colonies.

3-3141
Library of Congress JV305.S9

Slavery - Anti - slavery movements.

M816 L26 **Langston, John Mercer, 1829-1897.**
Freedom and citizenship. Selected lectures and addresses of Hon. John Mercer Langston ... With an introductory sketch by Rev. J. E. Rankin ... Washington, D.C., R. H. Darby, 1883.
286 p. front. (port.) 20cm.

1. Negroes. 2. U. S.—Pol. & govt.—1865-1898. I. Rankin, Jeremiah Eames, 1828-1904. II. Title.

15—10680
Library of Congress E185.6.L28
Copyright 1883: 19154 [40b1]

Haiti M972.94 M59
Slavery-Condition of slaves.
[Milescent, Claude Michel Louis]
Essai sur l'amelioration du sort des esclaves. [Paris, 1791].

[1], 26-39 p. 23 cm.
Signed: Milescent, creole.
"Claude Michel Louis Milscent, the author of this pamphlet was a white man & the father of Jules S. Milscent, the Haytian poet."

M326 An8s
Slavery--Congresses.
Anti-slavery conference, Paris, 1867.
Special report of the Anti-slavery conference, held in Paris in the Salle Herz, on the twenty-sixth and twenty-seventh August, 1867. hon. president. M. le duc de Broglie. President. Mons. Edouard Laboulaye ... London, Committee of the British and foreign anti-slavery society [1867]

1 p. l., ii, 166p. 24cm.
Association copy: William Lloyd Garrison with notes in his hand.

Martinique M972.98 B541
Slavery - Emancipation.
Bissette, Cyrille Charles Auguste, 1795-1858.
Lettres politiques sur les colonies, sur l'esclavage et sur les questions qui s'y rattachent, par C. A. Bissette. Paris, Ebrard, Libraire, Passage des Panoramas, 1845.

48p. 23cm.

Slavery - Fiction.

Martinique M843.9 T17s
Tardon, Raphaël, 1911-
Starkenfirst, roman. Paris, Fasquelle Editeurs, 1947.

201p. 22½cm.
Received Prix des Antilles.

Slavery - History.

M813.5 B64st 1955
Bontemps, Arna Wendell, 1902-
Story of the Negro; illustrated by Raymond Lufkin. 2d ed., enl. New York, Knopf, 1955.
243 p. illus. 22 cm.

1. Negro race—Hist. 2. Negroes in America. 3. Slavery—Hist.

E29.N3B6 1955 325.26097 56-142 ‡
Library of Congress [10]

Slavery - History.

M813.5 B64st
Bontemps, Arna Wendell, 1902-
Story of the Negro; illus. by Raymond Lufkin. [1st ed.] New York, A. A. Knopf, 1948.
xii, 239 p. illus. 22 cm.

1. Negro race—Hist. 2. Negroes in America. 3. Slavery—Hist.

E29.N3B6 325.26097 48—6629*
Library of Congress [49r²10]

M326 M61s
Slavery and Catholicism.
Miller, Richard Roscoe.
Slavery and Catholicism. Durham, N. C., North State Publishers [1957]
259 p. illus. 22 cm.

1. Slavery and the church—Catholic Church. 2. Slavery in the U. S. I. Title.

E441.M65 326.973 57—8157 ‡
Library of Congress [57f5]

Slavery and forced labor in the Republic of Liberia.

Liberia
M966.6
In8e

International Commission of Inquiry.
Report ... Slavery and forced labor in the Republic of Liberia, Monrovia, Liberia, Sept. 8, 1930. Washington, D.C., Government Printing Office, 1931.

227p. 23cm.

Slavery in Cuba.

Cuba
M861.6
M26

[Manzano, Juan Francisco] 1797-1854.
Poems by a slave in the island of Cuba, recently liberated; translated from the Spanish, by R. R. Madden, M. D., with the history of the early life of the negro poet, written by himself; to which are prefixed two pieces descriptive of Cuban slavery and the slave-traffic, by R. R. M. London, T. Ward & co., 1840.

4 p. l., v p., 1 l., [9]-188 p. 22½ᶜᵐ.

1. Slavery in Cuba. I. Madden, Richard Robert, 1798-1886, tr. II. Title.

1-13046 Revised

Library of Congress HT1076.M3 [r33b2]

Slavery, in Jamaica.

M326.99B
W67na

Williams, James, b. 1805
A narrative of events, since the first of August, 1834. An apprenticed labourer in Jamaica. London, Printed by John Haddon, 1834.

23p. 17½cm.

M326
M61s

Slavery and the church - Catholic Church.

Miller, Richard Roscoe.
Slavery and Catholicism. Durham, N. C., North State Publishers [1957]

259 p. illus. 22 cm.

1. Slavery and the church—Catholic Church. 2. Slavery in the U. S. I. Title.

E441.M65 326.973 57—8157 ‡

Library of Congress [5715]

Slavery in England.

MB9
Sh2s

Stuart, Charles.
A memoir of Granville Sharp, to which is added Sharp's "Law of retribution," By Charles Stuart. New York, American anti-slavery society, 1836.

156p. front. 19cm.

Slavery in Liberia.

Africa
M966.6
In8e

International Commission of Inquiry into the Existence of Slavery and Forced Labor in the Republic of Liberia.
Report... Monrovia, Liberia, September 8, 1930. Washington, D.C., Govt. Print. Off., 1931.

227p. 23cm.
At head of title: Publications of the Department of State.

Brit. Guiana
M820
C14e

Slavery in Africa.
Cameron, Norman Eustace.
The evolution of the Negro ... By N. E. Cameron ... Georgetown, Demerara, Printed by "The Argosy" company, limited, 1929-34.

2 v. 21ᶜᵐ.

1. Negro race. 2. Negroes in Africa. 3. Slavery in Africa. I. Title.

45-41801

Library of Congress DT15.C3 [2] 960

Slavery in French Colonies.

Haiti
M972.94
C1
1789

C.., J.M.
Précis des gémissemens des Sang-mêlés, les colonies françoises, par J. M. C. Américain, Sang-mêlé. Paris, Chez Baudouin, Imprimeur de l'Assemblée Nationale, 1789.

16p. 21½cm.

Slavery in Liberia —Fiction.

M813.5
Sc8s

Schuyler, George Samuel, 1895-
Slaves today; a story of Liberia, by George S. Schuyler. New York, Brewer, Warren & Putnam, 1931.

3 p. l., 5-290 p. 19½ᶜᵐ.

1. Slavery in Liberia—Fiction. I. Title.

31—32949

Library of Congress PZ3.S3972Sl
——— Copy 2.
Copyright A 44840 [37c1]

Slavery in Africa.

Kenya
M967.6
M45u3

Mbotela, James Juma
The freeing of the slaves in East Africa. London, Evans Bros. [1965]

87p. 19cm.
Translation of Uhuru wa Watumwa.

1. Africa, British East - History.
2. Slavery in Africa. I. Title.

Guadeloupe
MB9
Sch6s

Slavery in French colonies.

Satineau, Maurice
Schoelcher. Heors de l'abolition de l'esclavage dans les possessions Francaises. Paris, Editions Mellottee, 1948.

149p. front. (port.) 19cm.

Slavery in South America.

M980
D56n

Diggs, Irene.
The Negro in the viceroyalty of the Rio de la Plata. Reprinted from the Journal of Negro History, 36:281-301, July 1951.

281-301p. 25cm.

Slavery in Africa.

Kenya
M967.6
M45u

Mbotela, James Juma
Uhuru wa watumwa [The slaves who were brought to Freetown] Nairobi, Eagle Press, 1951.

102p. illus. 18cm.
Written in Swahili.
English ed. has title: The freeing of the slaves in East Africa.

1. Africa, British East - History.
2. Slavery in Africa. I. Title.

Slavery in Haiti.

Haiti
M972.94
J34d

Jean-Baptiste, St. Victor.
... Deux concepts d'indépendance à Saint-Domingue, thèse historique et sociologique présentée au grand Concours latino-américain (année 1943) Préface du dr. Clément Lanier. Port-au-Prince, Haïti [Imprimerie du Collège Vertières] 1944.

308 p., 2 l. incl. port. 22½ᶜᵐ. (On cover: Bibliothèque haïtienne)

At head of title: St. Victor Jn-Baptiste ...
"Bibliographie": p. [305]

1. Haiti—Hist.—To 1791. 2. Haiti—Hist.—Revolution, 1791-1804. 3. Slavery in Haiti. I. Title.

44-52077

Library of Congress F1923.J4 [3] 972.94

Slavery in Surinam.

Surinam
M988
K83

Kom, A de,
Wij slaven van suriname, door A. De Kom. Amsterdam, Uitgevers-Mij. Contact [c1934]

234p. portrait. 20½cm.

Brazil
M869
C21an

Slavery in Brazil.
Carneiro de Souza, Edison, 1912-
Antologia do negro brasileiro. Rio de Janeiro, Editôra Globo [1950]

xix, 432 p. 23 cm.

Slavery in Jamaica.

Jamaica
M972.92
L85h

[Long, Edward] 1734-1813.
The history of Jamaica: or, General survey of the antient and modern state of that island: with reflections on its situation, settlements, inhabitants, climate, products, commerce, laws, and government ... Illustrated with copper plates ... London, T. Lowndes, 1774.

3 v. fold. fronts. (v. 1-2) plates (1 fold.) fold. maps, plan. 28 x 22ᶜᵐ.
Vols. 2-3 paged continuously.

1. Jamaica. 2. Slavery in Jamaica. 3. Natural history—Jamaica. I. Title.

2—11573

Library of Congress F1868.L84 [40e1]

Slavery in the U. S.

M326
Ap84

Aptheker, Herbert, ed.
And why not every man? The story of the fight against Negro slavery. Berlin, Seven Seas Publishers, 1961.

278p. 19cm.
Contains selected documents.
White editor.

Brazil
M981
C76
1934

Slavery in Brazil.

Congresso afro-brasileiro. 1st, Pernambuco, 1934.
Estudos afro-brasileiros; trabalhos apresentados ao 1° Congresso afro-brasileiro reunido no Recife em 1934. Prefacio de Roquette-Pinto. Rio de Janeiro, Ariel, 1935-37.

2 v. plates, port., fold. map, tables. 18½-24ᶜᵐ.
At head of title of v. 2: Gilberto Freyre e outros.
Vol. 2 has title and imprint: Novos estudos afro-brasileiros. (Segundo tomo) Trabalhos apresentados ao 1.° Congresso afro-brasileiro do Recife. Prefacio de Arthur Ramos ... Rio de Janeiro, Civilização brasileira, s. a., 1937.
Vol. 2 has series title: Bibliotheca de divulgação scientifica. vol. 9.
"Toadas de xangô do Recife" (music): v. 1, p. [265]-268.
Includes bibliographies.
1. Negroes in Brazil. 2. Slavery in Brazil. 3. Brazil—Race question. I. *Freyre, Gilberto. II. Title.

36—13058

Library of Congress F2659.N4C6 [44r38g2] 325.260981

Jamaica
M972.92
P27

Slavery in Jamaica.

Patterson, Orlando.
The sociology of slavery: an analysis of the origins, development and structure of Negro slave society in Jamaica. London, MacGibbon & Kee [1967]

310 p. 4 plates (incl. 3 maps), tables. 22½ cm. (Studies in society) 63/-

(B 67-8066)

Bibliography: p. 297-301.

1. Slavery in Jamaica. I. Title. (Series)

HT1096.P3 301.45'22'097292 67-86315

Library of Congress [3]

Slavery in the U. S.

M326.99B
B34n

Bayley, Solomon
A narrative of some remarkable incidents in the life of Solomon Bayley, formerly a slave, in the State of Delaware, North America; written by himself, and published for his benefit; to which are prefixed a few remarks by Robert Hurnardt ...
Second edition. London, Printed for Harvey and Darton, 1825.

ix, 48p. 18cm.

Slavery in the U. S.

M326.99B
B561
Black, Leonard.
The life and sufferings of Leonard Black, a fugitive from slavery. Written by himself. New Bedford, Press of Benjamin Lindsey, 1847.
61p. 14cm.

Slavery in the U.S.

M310
B73s2
Brawley, Benjamin Griffith, 1882–
A short history of the American Negro. Rev. ed., by Benjamin Brawley ... New York, The Macmillan company, 1919.
xvii, 280 p. 20cm.
Bibliography: p. 265–272.

1. Negroes. 2. Slavery in the U. S. 3. Negroes—Education.
19—16297
Library of Congress E185.B82 1919
[43n1]

Slavery in the U.S.

M310
B73so
Brawley, Benjamin Griffith, 1882–1939.
A social history of the American Negro, being a history of the Negro problem in the United States, including a history and study of the republic of Liberia, by Benjamin Brawley. New York, The Macmillan company, 1921.
xv, 420 p. 22½cm.
"Select bibliography": p. 390–408.

1. Negroes. 2. Slavery in the U. S. 3. U. S.—Race question. 4. Liberia. I. Title.
21—15578
Library of Congress E185.61.B82
[a43g1]

Slavery in the U.S.

M326.99B
B80
Brown, Henry Box.
Narrative of Henry Box Brown, who escaped from slavery enclosed in a box 3 feet long and 2 feet wide. Written from a statement of facts made by himself. With remarks upon the remedy for slavery. By Charles Stearns. Boston, Brown & Stearns, 1849.
90p. front. (port.) 18cm.

Slavery in the U.S.

M810
B81m
Brown, William Wells, b. 1814.
My southern home: or, The South and its people. By Wm. Wells Brown ... ~~3d ed.~~ Boston, A. G. Brown & co., ~~1882~~ 1880
vii, 253 p. illus. 19½cm.
Portrait.

1. ~~Negroes~~. 2. Slavery in the U. S. 3. Southern states—Soc. life & cust. I. Title.
2—7807
Library of Congress E185.B88
[37b1]

Slavery in the U. S.

M810
B81r
Brown, William Wells, b. 1815.
The rising sun; or, The antecedents and advancement of the colored race. By Wm. Wells Brown ... Boston, A. G. Brown & co., 1874.
ix, 9–552 p. front. (port.) 21cm.
"Representative men and women": p. 418–552.

1. Negroes. 2. Negro race. 3. Slavery in the U. S. 4. Negroes—Biog. I. Title.
29—8376
Library of Congress E185.B884
[42d1]

Slavery in the U.S.

MB9
C54t
Clark, M M
Tract on American slavery, by the Rev. M.M. Clark, a Colored man, now on a visit to England from the United States of America. Bradford, Printed by H. Wardman, 1847.
23p. 18½cm.

Slavery in the U.S.

M973
C88
Cromwell, John Wesley, 1846–
The Negro in American history; men and women eminent in the evolution of the American of African descent, by John W. Cromwell ... Washington, The American Negro academy, 1914.
xiii, 284 p. front., plates, ports. 23½cm.
Bibliography: p. 257–262.

1. Negroes. 2. Negroes—Biog. 3. Slavery in the U. S. I. Title.
14—7742
Library of Congress E185.C92
——— ——— Copy 2.
Copyright A 369777 [40c1]

Slavery in the U.S.

M326.99B
D295
Davis, Noah.
A narrative of the life of Rev. Noah Davis, a colored man. Written by himself, at the age of fifty-four. Printed solely for the author's benefit. Baltimore, Published by John F. Weishampel. [1859]
86p. front. (port.) 15½cm.

Slavery in the U.S.

M815.4
D74ad2
Douglass, Frederick, 1817–1895.
Address delivered by Hon. Frederick Douglass, at the third annual fair of the Tennessee colored agricultural and mechanical association on Thursday, September 18, 1873 at Nashville, Tenn. Washington, New national era, 1873.
19p. 22cm.

Slavery in the U.S.

M815.4
D74co
Douglass, Frederick, 1817–1895.
The Constitution of the United States: is it pro-slavery or anti-slavery? By Frederick Douglass. A speech delivered in Glasgow, March 26, 1860, in reply to an attack made upon his view by Mr. George Thompson. [Halifax, T. and W. Birtwhistle, printers, 1860?]
16 p. 18½cm.
Caption title.
From the Glasgow daily mail.

1. U. S. Constitution. 2. Slavery in the U. S. 3. Thompson, George, 1804–1878.
A 17-1156
Title from Harvard Univ. Printed by L. C.

Slavery in the U.S.

M815.4
D74cor
Douglass, Frederick, 1817–1895.
Correspondence between the Rev. Samuel H. Cox, of Brooklyn, L.I. and Frederick Douglass, a fugitive slave. New York, American anti-slavery society, 1846.
16p. 22cm.

1. Slavery in the U.S. I. Cox, Samuel H.

Slavery in the U.S.

M815.4
D74a
Douglass, Frederick
Farewell speech of Mr. Frederick Douglass, previously to embarking on board the Cambria, upon his return to America, delivered at the London Tavern on March 30, 1847. Published by order of the Council of the anti-slavery league, from the short-hand notes of Mr. W. Farmer. London, Ward and co., 1847.
24p. 21cm.

Slavery in the U.S.

M323
D77
Doyle, Bertram Wilbur, 1897–
The etiquette of race relations in the South; a study in social control, by Bertram Wilbur Doyle ... Chicago, Ill., The University of Chicago press [c1937]
xxv, 249 p. 22 cm.
Bibliography: p. 173–190.

1. Negroes. 2. U. S.—Race question. 3. Negroes—Moral and social conditions. 4. Slavery in the U. S. I. Title. II. Title: Race relations in the South.
37—20152
Library of Congress E185.61.D764
[39u4] 325.260975

Slavery in the U.S.

M301
D853en
Du Bois, William Edward Burghardt, 1868–
The enforcement of the slave-trade laws, by W. E. B. Du Bois.
(*In* American historical association. Annual report ... for the year 1891. Washington, 1892. 24½cm. p. 161–174)

1. Slave-trade. 2. Slavery in the U. S.
CD 17—864
Library of Congress. Card div. E172.A60 1891
[42h1]

M326
G87a
1853
Slavery in the U.S.
Griffiths, Julia ed.
Autographs for freedom. Boston, J.P. Jewett and co.; Cleveland, O., Jewett, Proctor, and Worthington; etc., 1853.
viii, 263p. incl. front. 2pl. 19½cm.
A collection of signed articles, poems, etc. by men and women prominent in the anti-slavery movement. Most of the signatures are in facsimile.
(For other editions of this title, see entries under editor's name).

Slavery in the U. S.

M326.99B
H39t
1852
Henson, Josiah, 1789–1881.
The life of Josiah Henson, formerly a slave, now an inhabitant of Canada, as narrated by himself. Boston, A. D. Phelps, 1849.
~~iv, 76 p.~~ 17 cm.
Narrated to S. A. Eliot. *cf.* Sabin, Bibl. amer.

I. Eliot, Samuel Atkins, 1798–1862.
11—21827
Library of Congress E444.H52
[48e½]

Slavery in the U.S.

M973
H55f
Hill, Arthur C 1918–
From yesterday thru tomorrow, by Arthur C. Hill and J. W. Miller. New York, Vantage Press [1951]
142 p. 28 cm.

1. Negroes. 2. Slavery in the U. S. I. Miller, Jesse W., 1920– joint author. II. Title.
E185.6.H5 325.260973 51–2475
Library of Congress [10]

Slavery in the U.S.

M326.99B
H87
Hughes, Louis, 1832–
Thirty years a slave. From bondage to freedom. The institution of slavery as seen on the plantation and in the home of the planter. Autobiography of Louis Hughes. Milwaukee, South Side printing company, 1897.
210p. front. (port) plans (facsims) 21½cm.

Slavery in the U.S.

M326.
L61
The Liberty bell. By friends of freedom ... Boston, Massachusetts anti-slavery fair, 1839–46; National anti-slavery bazaar, 1847–58.
15 v. plates, ports. 17½–20cm.
"Edited and published annually in Boston, by Maria Weston Chapman, 1843 to 1858 (one or two years being omitted)"—Samuel May, Catalogue of anti-slavery publications in America.
No volumes issued for 1840, 1850, 1854–55, 1857. *cf.* Faxon, Literary annuals and gift books.
Volume for 1841 wanting in L. C. set.

1. Slavery in the U. S. 2. Gift-books (Annuals, etc.) I. Chapman, Maria (Weston) 1806–1885, ed. II. Massachusetts anti-slavery fair. III. National anti-slavery bazaar, Boston.
5—22887
Library of Congress E449.L69
[4311]

Slavery in the U.S.

M326.99B
M38
Mason, Isaac, 1822–
Life of Isaac Mason as a slave. Worcester, Mass., 1893.
74 p. incl. front. (port.) 23½cm.
Autobiography.

1. Slavery in the U. S.
A 12-61
Title from Univ. of Chicago E444.M39 Printed by L. C.
[a32b1]

M326 M61s
Slavery in the U.S.
Miller, Richard Roscoe.
Slavery and Catholicism. Durham, N. C., North State Publishers [1957]
259 p. illus. 22 cm.
1. Slavery and the church—Catholic Church. 2. Slavery in the U. S. I. Title.
E441.M65 326.973 57-8157 ‡
Library of Congress [57f5]

M326.99B V55n
Slavery in the U.S.
[Veney, Bethany]
The narrative of Bethany Veney, a slave woman. With introd ction by Rev. Bishop Mallalieu, and commendatory notices from Rev. V. A. Cooper and Rev. Erastus Spaulding Worcester, Mass., 1889.
46p. front. (port.) 19½cm.

M973 W86
Slavery in the U.S.
Woodson, Carter Godwin, 1875-
The Negro in our history, by Carter G. Woodson ... Washington, D. C., The Associated publishers, inc. [1922]
xv, 393 p. incl. front., illus. 20cm.
1. Negroes. 2. Slavery in the U. S. I. Title.
22-14504
Library of Congress E185.W89
[a35p2]

M973 M69q
Slavery in the U.S.
Mitchell, George Washington, 1865-
The question before Congress, a consideration of the debates and final action by Congress upon various phases of the race question in the United States, by Geo. W. Mitchell. Philadelphia, Pa., The A. M. E. book concern [1918]
247 p. 23½cm.
1. Slavery in the U. S. 2. Negroes. 3. U. S.—Race question. I. Title.
18-21546
Library of Congress E441.M68
[43g1]

M326.99B W32s
Slavery in the U.S.
Watkins, James, 1823[?]
Struggles for freedom; or the life of James Watkins, formerly a slave in Maryland, U.S.; in which is detailed a graphic account of his extraordinary escape from slavery notices of the fugitive slave law, the sentiments of American divines on the subject of slavery, etc. 19th editions... Manchester, Printed for James Watkins, 1860.
X [1], - 104p. 18½cm.

M973 W86ne
Slavery in the U. S.
Woodson, Carter Godwin, 1875-
Negro makers of history, by Carter G. Woodson ... Washington, D. C., The Associated publishers, inc. [1928]
2 p. l., iii-vi, 362 p. illus. (incl. ports., facsims.) double map. 20 cm.
"An adaptation of [the author's] The Negro in our history to the capacity of children in the elementary schools."—Pref.
1. Negroes. 2. Slavery in the U. S. I. Title.
29-458
Library of Congress E185.W895
[43j1]

M973 N42
Slavery in the U.S.
A new Negro for a new century; an accurate and up-to-date record of the upward struggles of the Negro race. The Spanish-American war, causes of it; vivid descriptions of fierce battles; superb heroism and daring deeds of the Negro soldier ... Education, industrial schools, colleges, universities and their relationship to the race problem, by Prof. Booker T. Washington. Reconstruction and industrial advancement by N. B. Wood ... The colored woman and her part in race regeneration ... by ... Fannie Barrier Williams ... Chicago, Ill., American publishing house [1900]
428 p. front., illus. (ports) 20cm.
(Continued on next card)
0-5252
[44g1]

M326.99B W33
Slavery in the U. S.
Watson, Henry
Narrative of Henry Watson, a fugitive slave. Written by himself. Boston, Published by Bela Marsh, 1848.
48p. 18½cm.

M973 W86s 1959
Slavery in the U. S.
Woodson, Carter Goodwin, 1875-1950.
The story of the Negro retold, by Carter G. Woodson and Charles H. Wesley. 4th ed. rev. and enl. Washington, D.C., The Associated Pub., Inc., 1959.
472p. illus. 20cm.

M326.99B P22r
Slavery in the U.S.
Parker, Allen.
Recollections of slavery times, by Allen Parker. Worcester, Mass., Chas. W. Burbank and Co., 1895.
96p. 18½cm.

M323 W37
Slavery in the U. S.
Weatherford, Willis Duke, 1875-
Race relations; adjustment of whites and Negroes in the United States, by Willis D. Weatherford ... and Charles S. Johnson ... Boston, New York [etc.] D. C. Heath and company [1934]
x, 590 p. 22½ cm. (*On cover: Social relations series*)
Bibliography: p. 556-576.
1. Negroes. 2. U. S.—Race question. 3. Negroes—Moral and social conditions. 4. Slavery in the U. S. I. Johnson, Charles Spurgeon, 1893- joint author. II. Title.
34-36788
Library of Congress E185.W42
[40h³3] 325.260973

M973 W86s
Slavery in the U.S.
Woodson, Carter Godwin, 1875-
The story of the Negro retold, by Carter Godwin Woodson. Washington, D. C., The Associated publishers, inc. [1935]
viii, 369 p. incl. front., illus. (incl. ports., maps) diagr. 20cm.
"The history of the Negro in the United States."—Pref.
Bibliographies at end of each chapter except chapter XII.
1. Negroes. 2. Slavery in the U. S. I. Title.
36-434
Library of Congress E185.W898
[45t1] 325.260973

M326. Sc71
Slavery in the U. S.
Scarlett, George Chandler, 1880-
Laws against liberty, by George C. Scarlett ... New York, N. Y. [Cosmos printing co., inc., 1937]
135 p. 21cm.
1. Liberty. 2. Negroes. 3. U. S.—Race question. 4. Slavery in the U. S. I. Title.
A 39-1029
Yale law school. Library for Library of Congress [40c1]

MB9 W69
Slavery in the U. S.
Wilson, H E
Our Nig; or, sketches from the life of a free black in a two story white house, north. Showing that slavery's shadows fall even there ... By "Our Nig." Boston, Geo. C. Rand, 1859.
140p. 21cm.

M326 B65
Slavery in the U.S. - Anti-slavery movements.
Boston. Citizens.
Proceedings of a crowded meeting of the colored population of Boston... July 15, 1846, for the purpose of bidding farewell to William Lloyd Garrison on his departure for England, with his speech on the occasion. Dublin, Webb and Chapman, 1846.
16p. 18cm.

M326.99B W24s
Slavery in the U.S.
Strickland, S.
Negro slavery described by a Negro: being the narrative of Ashton Warner, a native of St. Vincent's. With an appendix containing the testimony of four Christian ministers recently returned from the colonies on the system of slavery as it now exists. By S. Strickland ... London, Samuel Maunder, 1831.
144p. 15½cm.

M973. W86fo
Slavery in the U. S.
Woodson, Carter Godwin, 1875- *ed.*
Free Negro owners of slaves in the United States in 1830, together with Absentee ownership of slaves in the United States in 1830, compiled under the direction of, and edited by Carter G. Woodson ... Washington, D. C., The Association for the study of Negro life and history [1924]
viii, 78 p. 25cm.
This statistical report was made possible by an appropriation obtained from the Laura Spelman Rockefeller memorial. *cf.* Foreword.
1. Slavery in the U. S. 2. Negroes—Direct. I. Association for the study of Negro life and history, inc. II. Laura Spelman Rockefeller memorial, New York. III. Title. IV. Title: Absentee ownership of slaves in the United States in 1830.
25-28062
Library of Congress E185.W8873
[44n1]

M974.7 C67c
Slavery in the U.S.-Anti-slavery movements.
Coles, Howard W
The cradle of freedom; a history of the Negro in Rochester, western New York and Canada ... by Howard W. Coles ... Sketches and illustrations by Claude Paul, engravings by Photo-cast, inc., Rochester, New York. Rochester, N. Y., Oxford press, 1941-
v. illus. (incl. ports., facsims.) 24cm.
1. Negroes. 2. Negroes in Rochester, N. Y. 3. Slavery in the U. S.—Anti-slavery movements. I. Title.
42-25474
Library of Congress E185.6.C68
[5] 325.26

M326.99B T46t
Slavery in the U. S.
Tilmon, Levin, 1807-1863.
A brief miscellaneous narrative of the more early part of the life of L. Tilmon, pastor of a colored Methodist Congregational church in the city of New York. Written by himself. Jersey City, W. W. & L. A. Pratt, printers, 1853.
1 p. l., 97 p. 17cm.
Verso of p. 59 unnumbered and blank.
1. Slavery in the U. S. I. Title.
37-12163
Library of Congress BX8473.T6A3
[2] 922.773

M973 W86 1928
Slavery in the U.S.
Woodson, Carter Godwin, 1875-
The Negro in our history, by Carter G. Woodson... fifth edition (further revised and enlarged). Washington, D.C., The Associated publishers, inc. [c1928]
xxx, 628p. front. illus. 21½cm.

M815.4 D74an
Slavery in the U.S.- Anti-slavery movements.
Douglass, Frederick, 1817-1895.
The anti-slavery movement. A lecture by Frederick Douglass, before the Rochester ladies' anti-slavery society. Rochester [N. Y.] Press of Lee, Mann & co., 1855.
44 p. 21½cm.
1. Slavery in the U. S.—Anti-slavery movements.
11-7348
Library of Congress E449.D731

Slavery in the U.S.-Anti-Slavery movements.
M815.4 **Douglass, Frederick,** 1817?-1895.
D739f6 Frederick Douglass, selections from his writings. Edited, with an introd., by Philip S. Foner. New York, International Publishers [1964, °1945]
95 p. 21 cm.
Cover title: Selections from the writings of Frederick Douglass.
1. Slavery in the U. S.—Anti-slavery movements. 2. Negroes—Politics and suffrage. I. Foner, Philip Sheldon, 1910- ed.
E449.D737 1964 326.4 64-6594
Library of Congress [5]

Slavery in the U.S.-Anti-slavery movements.
M815.4 Douglass, Frederick.
D739f Frederick Douglass, selections from his writings, edited with an introduction by Phillip S. Foner...New York, International publishers c1945.
95p. 20cm.

Slavery in the U.S. - Anti-slavery movements.
M815.4 **Douglass, Frederick,** 1817?-1895.
D739aL 1966 Life and times of Frederick Douglass. Adapted by Barbara Ritchie. New York, Crowell [1966]
viii, 210 p. 21 cm.
Shortened version, adapted from the 2d rev. ed. of the author's autobiography: Life and times, published in 1892, as enlarged from his My bondage and my freedom, 1855.
1. Slavery in the U. S.—Anti-slavery movements. 2. Slavery in the U. S.—Maryland. I. Ritchie, Barbara.
E449.D744 1966 326.092 66-7048
Library of Congress [67d5]

Slavery in the U.S. - Anti-slavery movements.
M815.4 **Douglass, Frederick,** 1817?-1895.
D739f2 The life and writings of Frederick Douglass [by] Philip S. Foner. New York, International Publishers [1950-
v. ports. 22 cm.
Includes bibliographical references.
CONTENTS.—1. Early years, 1817-1849.—2. Pre-Civil War decade, 1850-1860.
1. Slavery in the U. S.—Anti-slavery movements. I. Foner, Philip Sheldon, 1910-
Name originally: Frederick Augustus Washington Bailey.
E449.D736 923.673 50-7654
Library of Congress [15]

Slavery in the U.S.—Anti-slavery movements.
M815.4 **Douglass, Frederick,** 1817-1895.
D739al 1941 ... Life and times of Frederick Douglass, written by himself. Published for the Frederick Douglass historical and cultural league, in preparation for the one hundredth anniversary of Douglass' first public appearance in the cause of emancipation. New York, N. Y., Pathway press [°1941]
xxx p., 1 l., 31-695 (i. e. 708) p. incl. front. (port.) illus. (facsim.) plates. 23½cm.
At head of title: Centenary memorial subscribers' ed.
"The Life and times is the final form of an autobiography first published as a small Narrative in 1845, expanded in My bondage and my freedom in 1855, further extended in the first edition under the same
(Continued on next card)
41-6875
[7]

Slavery in the U.S.—Anti-slavery movements.
M815.4 Douglass, Frederick, 1817-1895.
D739al 1893 Life and times of Frederick Douglass, written by himself. His early life as a slave, his escape from bondage, and his complete history to the present time, including his connection with the anti-slavery movement...With an introduction, by Mr. George L. Ruffin. New revised edition. Boston, DeWolfe, Fiske & Co., 1893.
752p. port. (front.) 19½cm.
"First edition of final revised edition with long autographed inscription by Frederick Douglass.
(cont.)

Slavery in the U.S.—Anti-slavery movements.
M815.4 **Douglass, Frederick,** 1817-1895.
D739al Life and times of Frederick Douglass, written by himself. His early life as a slave, his escape from bondage, and his complete history to the present time, including his connection with the anti-slavery movement ... With an introduction, by Mr. George L. Ruffin ... Hartford, Conn., Park publishing co., 1881.
xii, xv-xxiii, 13-516 p. 12 pl., 6 port. (incl. front.) 21cm.
Enlarged from the author's My bondage and my freedom, New York, 1855.
1. Slavery in the U. S.—Anti-slavery movements. 2. Slavery in the U. S.—Maryland.
14-3399
Library of Congress E449.D74 [41i1]

Slavery in the U.S.—Anti-slavery movements.
M815.4 **Douglass, Frederick,** 1817-1895.
D739ab My bondage and my freedom ... By Frederick Douglass. With an introduction. By Dr. James M'Cune Smith. New York, Miller, Orton & Mulligan, 1855.
xxxi, [33]-464 p. front. (port.) 2 pl. 18½cm.
Enlarged and published under title: Life and times of Frederick Douglass. Hartford, 1881.
1. Slavery in the U. S.—Anti-slavery movements. 2. Slavery in the U. S.—Maryland. I. Title.
14-4878
Library of Congress E449.D738 [42n1]

M326 Slavery in the U.S.-Anti-slavery movements.
G88a Grimke, Archibald Henry, 1849-1930.
Anti-slavery Boston. The New England magazine. December 1890.
441-459p. illus. 25cm.

Slavery in the U.S.— Anti-slavery movements.
M326.99B **Loguen, Jermain Wesley,** 1814-1872.
L82 The Rev. J. W. Loguen, as a slave and as a freeman. A narrative of real life. Syracuse, N. Y., J. G. K. Truair & co., printers, 1859.
x, [11]-454 p. front. (port.) 18cm.
Written in the third person, but apparently the work of Loguen.
Two letters at end of volume are dated 1860.
"Testimony of Rev. E. P. Rogers," including a poem "Loguen's position": p. 445-450.
1. Slavery in the U. S.—Fugitive slaves. 2. Slavery in the U. S.—Anti-slavery movements. 3. Underground railroad. I. Rogers, Elymas Payson, d. 1861.
14-15518
Library of Congress E444.L83 [43r42d1]

Slavery in the U. S. - Anti-slavery movements.
M326 Ruchames, Louis, 1917- ed.
R82 The abolitionists; a collection of their writings. New York, Putnam c1963.
259p. 22cm.
Contains selections from the writings of David Ruggles, Theordore S. Wright, Charles Lenox Remond and Frederick Douglass.
White editor.
1. Abolitionists. 2. Slavery in the U. S. - Controversial literature. 3. Slavery in the U. S. -Anti-slavery movements. I. Title.

Slavery in the U. S.-Anti-slavery movements.
M326. **Savage, William Sherman.**
Sa92 The controversy over the distribution of abolition literature, 1830-1860, by W. Sherman Savage ... [Washington, D. C.] The Association for the study of Negro life and history, inc., 1938.
xv, 141 p. 23½ cm.
Bibliography: p. 127-134.
1. Slavery in the U. S.—Anti-slavery movements. 2. Slavery in the U. S.—Controversial literature. I. Association for the study of Negro life and history, inc. II. Title.
39-2080
Library of Congress E449.S257 [40f3] 326.4

Slavery in the U. S.-Anti-slavery movements.
MB9 **Ward, Samuel Ringgold,** b. 1817.
W21 Autobiography of a fugitive Negro: his anti-slavery labours in the United States, Canada, & England. By Samuel Ringgold Ward ... London, J. Snow, 1855.
xii, 412 p. front. (port.) 18½ cm.
1. Slavery in the U. S.—Anti-slavery movements.
13-22943
Library of Congress E449.W27 [48b1]

Slavery in the U.S.--Anti-slavery movements.
MB **White, Laureen,** 1908-
W58g Giants lived in those days. [1st ed.] New York, Pageant Press [1959]
188 p. 21 cm.
1. Abolitionists. 2. Slavery in the U. S.—Anti-slavery movements. I. Title.
E449.W58 923.673 59-1450 ‡
Library of Congress [2]

Slavery in the U.S. - Anti-slavery societies
M326. Wesley, Charles Harris, 1891-
W51n The Negro in the organization of abolition. Reprinted from Phylon, 2:223-235, Third quarter 1941.
223-235p. 25cm.
Paper read at the meeting of the American Historical Association, 1940.

Slavery in the U. S. - Bibliography.
M815.4 **Historical records survey.** *District of Columbia.*
D739z Calendar of the writings of Frederick Douglass in the Frederick Douglass memorial home, Anacostia, D. C. Prepared by District of Columbia Historical records survey, Division of professional and service projects, Work projects administration. Sponsored by the Board of commissioners of the District of Columbia. Washington, D. C., District of Columbia Historical records survey, 1940.
7 p. l., 93 numb. l. 27½cm.
Reproduced from type-written copy.
"Publications of District of Columbia Historical records survey": leaves 92-93.
1. Douglass, Frederick, 1817-1895—Bibl. 2. Negroes—Bibl. 3. Slavery in the U. S.—Bibl. I. Washington, D. C. Frederick Douglass memorial home. II. Title.
41-52935
Library of Congress Z8616.D7H57 [5] 012

Slavery in the U.S. - Bibliography
M810.9 **Turner, Lorenzo Dow.**
T85 Anti-slavery sentiment in American literature prior to 1865, by Lorenzo Dow Turner ... Washington, D. C., The Association for the study of Negro life and history, inc. [°1929]
viii, 188 p. 24cm.
"This study ... in 1926, was ... submitted to ... the University of Chicago in candidacy for the degree of doctor of philosophy."—Pref.
Bibliography: p. 153-182.
1. Slavery in the U. S.—Controversial literature. 2. American literature—Hist. & crit. 3. Slavery in the U. S.—Bibl. I. Title.
30-7026
Library of Congress PS310.S6T8
——— Copy 2.
Copyright A 19871 [40j1]

Slavery in the U.S.-Condition of slaves.
M326.99B **Albert,** *Mrs.* **Octavia Victoria (Rogers)** 1853-1889?
Al 1h The house of bondage; or, Charlotte Brooks and other slaves, original and life-like, as they appeared in their old plantation and city slave life; together with pen-pictures of the peculiar institution, with sights and insights into their new relations as freedmen, freemen, and citizens, by Mrs. Octavia V. Rogers Albert, with an introduction by Rev. Bishop Willard F. Mallalieu, D. D. New York, Hunt & Eaton; Cincinnati, Cranston & Stowe, 1890.
xiv p., 1 l., 161 p. incl. front. (port.) 19cm.
1. Slavery in the U. S.—Condition of slaves. 2. Negroes. I. Mallalieu, Willard Francis, bp., 1828-
10-33441
Library of Congress E444.A33 [30d1]

Slavery in the U. S.-Condition of slaves.
M326. **Drew, Benjamin.**
D82 A north-side view of slavery. The refugee: or, The narratives of fugitive slaves in Canada. Related by themselves, with an account of the history and condition of the colored population of Upper Canada. By Benjamin Drew. Boston, J. P. Jewett and company; New York, Sheldon, Lamport and Blakeman; [etc., etc.] 1856.
xii, 387 p. 20cm.
1. Slavery in the U. S.—Fugitive slaves. 2. Slavery in the U. S.—Condition of slaves. 3. Negroes in Canada.
10-34632
Library of Congress E450.D77 [45d1]

Slavery in the U.S. - Condition of slaves
MB Emerson, William Canfield, 1893- ed.
Em3 Stories and spirituals of the Negro slaves. Boston, R.G. Badger c1930.
79p. front. ports. 19½cm.
Includes music.
White author.

Slavery in the U.S.—Condition of slaves.
M326.99B **Federal writers' project.**
F31 Lay my burden down; a folk history of slavery, edited by B. A. Botkin. Chicago, Ill., University of Chicago press [1945]
xxi, 285, [1] p. front., plates. 23½ cm.
Illustrated t.-p.
"A selection and integration of excerpts and complete narratives from the Slave narrative collection of the Federal writers' project."
1. Slavery in the U. S.—Condition of slaves. 2. Negroes—Biog. I. Botkin, Benjamin Albert, 1901- ed. II. Title.
A 45-5576
Chicago. Univ. Library for Library of Congress E444.F26 [47c7] 326.973

Slavery in the U. S.-Condition of slaves.

M326.99B F31s

Fedric, Francis.
Slave life in Virginia and Kentucky; or, Fifty years of slavery in the southern states of America. By Francis Fedric, an escaped slave. With preface, by the Rev. Charles Lee ... London, Wertheim, Macintosh, and Hunt, 1863.

viii, 115 p. 15½cm.

1. Slavery in the U. S.—Condition of slaves. I. Lee, Charles.

Library of Congress E444.F29 11—11611 [30b1]

Slavery in the U.S.—Controversial literature.

M326 W37

Weaver, Robert Bartow.
The struggle over slavery, by Robert B. Weaver ... Chicago, Ill., The University of Chicago press [1938]

vii, 83, [1] p. illus. (incl. ports., map, facsim.) 23cm.

"The major portion of this volume consists of descriptions, statements, and explanations taken from source materials."—Pref.

CONTENTS.—Early slavery in America.—Controversies over the extension of slavery.—The secession movement.—The civil war.—Reconstruction in the South.—Bibliography (p. 83–[84])

1. Slavery in the U. S.—Controversial literature. 2. U. S.—Hist.—1849–1877—Sources. I. Title.

Library of Congress E449.W34 38-17444
——— Copy 2.
Copyright A 119120 [5] 326.973

Slavery in the U. S. - Controversial literature - 1837

M973 Ea7t

Easton, Hosea.
A treatise on the intellectual character, and civil and political condition of the colored people of the U. States; and the prejudice exercised towards them: with a sermon on the duty of the church to them. By Rev. H. Easton ... Boston, I. Knapp, 1837.

54, [2] p. 23cm.

"The sermon, as proposed in our titlepage, is omitted."

1. Negroes. 2. Slavery in the U. S.—Controversial literature—1837.

Library of Congress E185.E14 12—2995 [a44b1]

Slavery in the U. S. - Conditions of slaves.

M326 N515

Nichols, Charles Harold.
Many thousand gone; the ex-slaves' account of their bondage and freedom, by Charles H. Nichols. Leiden, Brill, 1963.

xvi, 229p. 25cm.

Slavery in the U. S.—Controversial literature—1809.

M326 Si1o

Sidney, Joseph.
An oration, commemorative of the abolition of the slave trade in the United States; delivered before the Wilberforce philanthropic association, in the city of New-York, on the second of January, 1809. By Joseph Sidney. New-York, Printed for the author, J. Seymour, printer, 1809.

20 p. 20cm.

1. Slavery in the U. S.—Controversial literature—1809. 2. Slave-trade—U. S. I. Wilberforce philanthropic association, New York.

Library of Congress E446.S56 10-32480

Slavery in the U. S.-Controversial literature-1838.

M326. R84an

Ruggles, David.
An antidote for a poisonous combination recently prepared by a "citizen of New-York," alias Dr. Reese, entitled, "An appeal to the reason and religion of American Christians," &c. Also, David Meredith Reese's "Humbugs" dissected, by David Ruggles ... New-York, W. Stuart, 1838.

cover-title, 32 p. 22½cm.

1. An appeal to the reason ... of American Christians, against the American anti-slavery society. 2. Reese, David Meredith, 1800–1861. Humbugs of New-York. 3. American anti-slavery society. 4. Slavery in the U. S.—Controversial literature—1838.

Library of Congress E449.R98 11—11642 [44e1]

Slavery in the U. S.-Condition of Slaves.

M326.99B R54n

Roberts, James, *b.* 1753.
The narrative of James Roberts, soldier in the revolutionary war and at the battle of New Orleans. Chicago: printed for the author, 1858. Hattiesburg, Miss., The Book farm, 1945.

cover-title, viii, [9]–32 p. 21½cm. (Heartman's historical series, no. 71)

"Photo-lithoprint reproduction."
"One hundred and thirty-six copies reprinted from the apparently unique copy in the Charles E. Heartman collection of material relating to Negro culture."

1. Slavery in the U. S.—Condition of slaves. 2. New Orleans, Battle of, 1815.

Library of Congress E444.R7 45-6855 [4] 326.92

Slavery in the U.S.-Controversial literature-1809.

M326. Si70

Sipkins, Henry.
An oration on the abolition of the slave trade; delivered in the African church, in the city of New-York, January 2, 1809. By Henry Sipkins, a descendant of Africa. New-York, Printed by J. C. Totten, 1809.

1 p. l., 21 p. 22cm.

1. Slavery in the U. S.—Controversial literature—1809. 2. Slave-trade—U. S.

Library of Congress E446.S61 10-32479

Slavery in the U.S.—Controversial literature—1841.

M973 P38t

Pennington, James William Charles, 1812-1871.
Text book of the origin and history, &c. &c. of the colored people. By James W. C. Pennington. Hartford, L. Skinner, printer, 1841.

96 p. 12½cm.

1. Negroes. 2. Slavery in the U. S.—Controversial literature—1841. 3. Negro race.

Library of Congress E185.P41 12—2998 [28c1]

Slavery in the U.S. - Condition of slaves.

M326.99B L62a

The light and truth of slavery. Aaron's history. [Worcester, Mass., 184-?

48p. illus. 23cm.
Caption ti le.

Slavery in the U. S. - Controversial literature - 1830.

M326 W15 1965

Aptheker, Herbert, 1915–
One continual cry; David Walker's Appeal to the colored citizens of the world, 1829–1830, its setting & its meaning, together with the full text of the third, and last, edition of the Appeal. New York, Published for A. I. M. S. by Humanities Press [1965]

150 p. 22 cm.

Bibliography: p. 149–150.

1. Slavery in the U. S.—Controversial literature—1830. I. Walker, David, 1785–1830. Walker's appeal, in four articles; together with a preamble, to the coloured citizens of the world. II. Title.

E446.W2A6 301.4522 65–16708
Library of Congress [5]

Slavery in the U. S.-Controversial literature-1847.

M810 B811

Brown, William Wells, *b.* 1815.
A lecture delivered before the Female anti-slavery society of Salem, at Lyceum hall, Nov. 14, 1847. By William W. Brown, a fugitive slave. Reported by Henry M. Parkhurst ... Boston, Massachusetts anti-slavery society, 1847.

22 p. 19cm.

1. Slavery in the U. S.—Controversial literature—1847. I. Female anti-slavery society of Salem. II. Parkhurst, Henry Martyn, 1825– reporter.

Library of Congress E449.B8831 11—6899 [a29b1]

Slavery in the U. S. - Controversial literature.

M326 R82

Ruchames, Louis, 1917- ed.
The abolitionists; a collection of their writings. New York, Putnam [1963]
259p. 22cm.
Contains selections from the writings of David Ruggles, Theordore S. Wright, Charles Lenox Remond and Frederick Douglass.
White editor.
1. Abolitionists. 2. Slavery in the U. S.- Controversial literature. 3. Slavery in the U. S. - Anti-slavery movements. I. Title.

Slavery in the U.S.-Controversial literaturer 1830.

M326 W15 1829

Walker, David, 1785-1830.
Walker's appeal, in four articles, together with a preamble to the colored citizens of the world, but in particular, and very expressly to those of the United States of America. Written in Boston, in the state of Massachusetts, Sept. 28, 1829. Boston, Published by David Walker, 1829.
76p. 22cm.
First edition.
Bound with Walker's appeal ... 2d ed., 1830.

Slavery in the U. S.-Controversial literature-1847.

M326.99B J13n

Jackson, Andrew, *b.* 1814.
Narrative and writings of Andrew Jackson, of Kentucky; containing an account of his birth, and twenty-six years of his life while a slave; his escape; five years of freedom, together with anecdotes relating to slavery; journal of one year's travels; sketches, etc. Narrated by himself; written by a friend. Syracuse, Daily and weekly star office, 1847.

vi, [7]–120 p. 18½cm.

1. Slavery in the U. S.—Controversial literature—1847.

Library of Congress E444.J13 16-9502

Slavery in the U. S.-Controversial literature.

M326. Sa92

Savage, William Sherman.
The controversy over the distribution of abolition literature, 1830–1860, by W. Sherman Savage ... [Washington, D. C.] The Association for the study of Negro life and history, inc., 1938.

xv, 141 p. 23½ cm.

Bibliography: p. 127–134.

1. Slavery in the U. S.—Anti-slavery movements. 2. Slavery in the U. S.—Controversial literature. I. Association for the study of Negro life and history, inc. II. Title.

Library of Congress E449.S257 39—2080 [40f3] 326.4

Slavery in the U. S.-Controversial literature-1834.

M326. R84e

Ruggles, David.
The "extinguisher" extinguished! or, David M. Reese, M. D., "used up." By David Ruggles, a man of color. Together with some remarks upon a late production, entitled "An address on slavery and against immediate emancipation with a plan of their being gradually emancipated and colonized in thirty-two years. By Heman Howlett." New-York, D. Ruggles, 1834.

iv, [5]–48 p. 19½ cm.

[Markoe pamphlets, v. 14, no. 14]

(Continued on next card)
19—17294 [48e1]

Slavery in the U. S.- Controversial literature-1852.

M815.4 D74o

Douglass, Frederick, 1817–1895.
Oration, delivered in Corinthian hall, Rochester, by Frederick Douglass, July 5th, 1852 ... Rochester, Printed by Lee, Mann & co., 1852.

39 p. 22½cm.

1. Slavery in the U. S.—Controversial literature—1852. 2. Fourth of July orations.

Library of Congress E449.D7526 16-25947

Slavery in the U.S.-Controversial literature.

M810.9 T85

Turner, Lorenzo Dow.
Anti-slavery sentiment in American literature prior to 1865, by Lorenzo Dow Turner ... Washington, D. C., The Association for the study of Negro life and history, inc. [1929]

viii, 188 p. 24cm.

"This study ... in 1926, was ... submitted to ... the University of Chicago in candidacy for the degree of doctor of philosophy."—Pref.
Bibliography: p. 158–182.

1. Slavery in the U. S.—Controversial literature. 2. American literature—Hist. & crit. 3. Slavery in the U. S.—Bibl. I. Title.

Library of Congress PS310.S6T8 30—7026
——— Copy 2.
Copyright A 19871 [40j1]

Slavery in the U.S.- Controversial literature-1835.

M326. R84ab

Ruggles, David.
The abrogation of the Seventh commandment, by the American churches ... New-York, D. Ruggles, 1835.

23 p. 16½cm.

[Markoe pamphlets, v. 57, no. 15]
Signed: A Puritan.

1. Slavery in the U. S.—Controversial literature—1835. I. A Puritan, pseud.

Library of Congress AC901.M3 vol. 57 28-18699 [2]

Slavery in the U. S. - Controversial literature. 1861-

M350 G191

[Garrison, William Lloyd], 1805-1879.
The loyalty and devotion of colored Americans in the revolution and war of 1812. Pub. in Boston, Mass., 1861. New York City, The New York age press, 1918.

24p. 18cm.

M350 G19P 1861

Slavery in the U.S.-Controversial literature-1861.
Garrison, William Lloyd.
The loyalty and devotion of colored Americans in the Revolution and War of 1812. Boston, R. F. Wallcut, 1861.

24p. 18cm.

Slavery in the U. S. - Fiction.

M810 B81c 1853

Brown, William Wells, 1814-1884.
Clotel; or, The President's daughter: a narrative of slave life in the United States. With sketch of the author's life...London, Partridge & Oakey, 1853.

viii, 245p. 17cm.

M326 St5

Slavery in the U.S. - Fugitive slaves.
Still, William, 1821-1902.
The underground railroad. A record of facts, authentic narratives, letters & c., narrating the hardships, hairbreadth escapes and death struggles of the slaves in their efforts for freedom, as related by themselves and others, or witnessed by the author; together with sketches of some of the largest stockholders, and most liberal aiders and advisers of the road. By William Still... Philadelphia, Porter E. Coates, 1872.
2p. l., 780p. front. illus., pl. ports. 24cm.

Slavery in the U.S. - Emancipation

M815.4 D74ad

Douglass, Frederick, 1817-1895
Address by Hon. Frederick Douglass, delivered in the Congregational Church, Washington, D.C., April 16, 1883. On the 21st anniversary of Emancipation in the District of Columbia. Washington, D.C., 1883.

16p. 23½cm.

1. Emancipation day orations. 2. History

Slavery in the U. S.-Fiction.

M813.3 N312

Neilson, Peter, 1795-1861.
The life and adventure of Zamba, an African negro king; and his experience of slavery in South Carolina. Written by himself. Corrected and arranged by Peter Neilson. London, Smith, Elder and co., 1847.
xx, 258 p. front. 20½ cm.
Written by Peter Neilson. cf. Dict. nat. biog.

1. Slavery in the U. S.—Fiction. 2. South Carolina—Soc. life & cust. I. Title.
Library of Congress PZ3.N318L 7—33168
[a28d1]

M326 St5 1886

Slavery in the U.S. - Fugitive slaves.
Still, William, 1821-1902.
Underground railroad records, with a life of the author, narrating the hardships, hairbreadth escapes, and death struggles of the slaves in their efforts for freedom; together with sketches of some of the eminent friends of freedom, and most liberal aiders and advisers of the road. Illus. with 70 fine engravings... and portraits... rev. ed. Phil., William Still, publisher, 1886.
2l, lxiv, 780p. illus. 24cm.

Slavery in the U. S. -Emancipation.

M815.4 D47tw

Douglass, Frederick, 1817–1895.
Two speeches by Frederick Douglass; one on West India emancipation, delivered at Canandaigua, Aug. 4th, and the other on the Dred Scott decision, delivered in New York, on the occasion of the anniversary of the American abolition society, May 1857. Rochester, N. Y., C. P. Dewey, printer [1857]
46 p. 22cm.
The speeches are paged continuously.
The second speech has a half-title which reads: "The Dred Scott decision; speech delivered in part, at the anniversary of the American abolition society, held in New York, May 14th, 1857."
1. Slavery in the U. S.—Emancipation. 2. Scott, Dred. I. American abolition society.
A 17-1159
Title from Harvard Univ. Printed by L. C.

Slavery in the U.S.—Fiction.

M813.3 P29

Paynter, John Henry.
Fugitives of the Pearl, by John H. Paynter ... Washington, D. C., The Associated publishers, inc. [c1930]
xi, 209 p. ports. 19cm.
"Descendants of Paul and Amelia Edmonson": p. [208]-209.

1. Slavery in the U. S.—Fiction. I. Title. 31—1514
Library of Congress PZ3.P2938Fu
——— Copy 2.
Copyright A 33116 [30d1]

Slavery in the U.S. -Hist.

M973 A12

Alexander, William T.
History of the colored race in America. Containing also their ancient and modern life in Africa ... the origin and development of slavery ... the civil war ... Prepared and arranged by Wm. T. Alexander ... Kansas City, Mo., Palmetto publishing co., 1887.
2 p. l., 600 p. front. (port. group) plates, ports. 24cm.

1. Negroes. 2. Slavery in the U. S.—Hist. 3. U. S.—Hist.—Civil war.
4—11144
Library of Congress E185.A4
[a37e1]

Slavery in the U. S.-Emancipation.

M301. F86f

Frazier, Edward Franklin, 1894–
The free Negro family; a study of family origins before the civil war, by E. Franklin Frazier ... Nashville, Tenn., Fisk university press, 1932.
5 p. l., 75 p. illus. (maps) 24 cm. (Half-title: Fisk university social science series)
"Selected bibliography": p. 73–75.

1. Negroes. 2. Freedmen. 3. Mulattoes. 4. Negroes—Moral and social conditions. 5. Slavery in the U. S.—Emancipation. I. Title.
32—14425
Library of Congress E185.F88
[41f1] 325.26

Slavery in the U. S.-Fugitive slaves.

M326. D82

Drew, Benjamin.
A north-side view of slavery. The refugee: or, The narratives of fugitive slaves in Canada. Related by themselves, with an account of the history and condition of the colored population of Upper Canada. By Benjamin Drew. Boston, J. P. Jewett and company; New York, Sheldon, Lamport and Blakeman; [etc., etc.] 1856.
xii, 387 p. 20cm.

1. Slavery in the U. S.—Fugitive slaves. 2. Slavery in the U. S.—Condition of slaves. 3. Negroes in Canada.
10—34632
Library of Congress E450.D77
[45d1]

Slavery in the U.S.-History.

M973 Ep7e 1943

Eppse, Merl R.
An elementary history of America, including the contributions of the Negro race, by Merl R. Eppse ... and A. P. Foster ... Nashville, Tenn., National publication company, 1943.
xi, 350 p. front., illus. (incl. maps, ports.) 20½cm.
"Revised and enlarged."
Bibliography: p. 348-350.

1. Negroes. 2. U. S.—Hist. 3. Slavery in the U. S.—Hist. I. Foster, Austin Powers, 1859– joint author.
43-15927
Library of Congress E185.E684 1943
[3] 325.260973

Slavery in the U.S.—Emancipation.

M89 G18h

Garnet, Henry Highland, 1815–1882.
A memorial discourse; by Rev. Henry Highland Garnet, delivered in the hall of the House of representatives, Washington city, D. C., on Sabbath, February 12, 1865. With an introduction by James McCune Smith, M. D. Philadelphia, J. M. Wilson, 1865.
1 p. l., [15]–91 p. front. (port.) 23cm.
"Sketch of the life and labors of Rev. Henry Highland Garnet": p. 17–68.

1. Slavery in the U. S.—Emancipation. I. Smith, James McCune.
17-8999
Library of Congress E453.G235

Slavery in the U.S.- Fugitive slaves.

M326.99B L82

Loguen, Jermain Wesley, 1814–1872.
The Rev. J. W. Loguen, as a slave and as a freeman. A narrative of real life. Syracuse, N. Y., J. G. K. Truair & co., printers, 1859.
x, [11]–454 p. front. (port.) 18cm.
Written in the third person, but apparently the work of Loguen.
Two letters at end of volume are dated 1860.
"Testimony of Rev. E. P. Rogers," including a poem "Loguen's position": p. 445–450.

1. Slavery in the U. S.—Fugitive slaves. 2. Slavery in the U. S.—Anti-slavery movements. 3. Underground railroad. I. Rogers, Elymas Payson, d. 1861.
14—15518
Library of Congress E444.L83
[43r42d1]

Slavery in the U.S.— Hist.

M973 Ep7e

Eppse, Merl R.
An elementary history of America, including the contributions of the Negro race, by Merl R. Eppse ... and A. P. Foster ... Chicago, Nashville [etc.] National educational publishing co., inc., 1939.
xi, 312 p. front., illus. (incl. ports.) 20½cm.
Includes bibliographies.

1. Negroes. 2. U. S.—Hist. 3. Slavery in the U. S.—Hist. I. Foster, Austin Powers, 1859– joint author. II. Title.
39—1901
Library of Congress E185.E684
[44a2] 325.260973

M973.3 W51n

Slavery in the U.S. - Emancipation
Wesley, Charles Harris, 1891-
The Negroes of New York in the emancipation movement. Reprinted from the Journal of Negro history, 24:65-103, January 1939.
65-103p. 24½cm.

Slavery in the U. S.-Fugitive slaves.

M326. M69 1860

Mitchell, William M.
The underground railroad from slavery to freedom. By the Rev. W. M. Mitchell ... 2d ed. London, W. Tweedie; [etc., etc.] 1860.
ix, [10]–191 p. front. (port.) 16½cm.

1. Underground railroad. 2. Slavery in the U. S.—Fugitive slaves. 3. Negroes—Ontario.
10—34489
Library of Congress E450.M68
[a35b1]

Slavery in the U.S. - Hist.

M973 Ep7n

Eppse, Merl Raymond, 1893–
The Negro, too, in American history. Nashville, National Publication Co., 1949.
xxii, 644 p. illus., ports., maps. 22 cm.
Bibliographical references included in introduction. "Reading material": p. 551–572.

1. Negroes—Hist. 2. Slavery in the U. S.—Hist. I. Title.
E185.E696 1949 325.260973 49–1908 rev*
Library of Congress [r50h3]

Slavery in the U.S.-Emancipation.

M973. W86m

Woodson, Carter Godwin, 1875– *ed.*
The mind of the Negro as reflected in letters written during the crisis, 1800–1860, edited by Carter G. Woodson ... Washington, D. C., The Association for the study of Negro life and history, inc. [c1926]
5 p. l., v–xxxii, 672 p. 24cm.

1. Negroes. 2. Negroes—Moral and social conditions. 3. Slavery in the U. S.—Emancipation. I. Association for the study of Negro life and history, inc. II. Title.
26—14304
Library of Congress E185.W8877
[45m1]

M326 N48

Slavery in the U.S. - Fugitive slaves.
New York committee of vigilance.
... Report of the New York committee of vigilance, with interesting facts relative to their proceedings. [N.Y.] Published by direction of the committee. G. Vale, jun. printer, 1842.
38p. 21cm.
See holdings card.
1842 report signed by W. Johnston.

Slavery in the U.S.—Insurrection, etc.

M326. C23

Carroll, Joseph Cephas.
Slave insurrections in the United States, 1800–1865, by Joseph Cephas Carroll, PH. D. Boston, Chapman & Grimes, inc. [c1938]
229 p. 20½cm.
"References" at end of each chapter. Bibliography: p. 217–229.

1. Slavery in the U. S.—Insurrections, etc. I. Title.
39—2692
Library of Congress E447.C27
[43g1] 326.973

Slavery in the U.S. - History.

M973
Ep7n

Eppse, Merl Raymond, 1893–
The Negro, too, in American history. Nashville, National Publication Co., 1949.
xxii, 644 p. illus., ports., maps. 22 cm.
Bibliographical references included in introduction. "Reading material": p. 551–572.

1. Negroes—Hist. 2. Slavery in the U. S.—Hist. I. Title.

E185.E696 1949 325.260973 49–1908 rev*

Library of Congress r50b3

Trinidad
M320
J23h

Slavery in the U. S.-Insurrections, etc.

James, Cyril Lionel Robert, 1901–
A history of Negro revolt, by C. L. R. James. London, Fact ltd., 1938
97 p. 19cm. (Fact. no. 18. Sept., 1938)
CONTENTS.—San Domingo.—The old United States.—The civil war.—Revolts in Africa.—Marcus Garvey.—Negro movements in recent years.—Light reading (Margaret Cole): The book guide.

1. Negroes. 2. Negro race. 3. Slavery in the U. S.—Insurrections, etc.

A 40–2762

Duke univ. Library for Library of Congress 2

Slavery in the U. S. - Juvenile liteature.

M973.714
St45

Sterling, Dorothy.
Forever free, the story of the Emancipation Proclamation. Illustrated by Ernest Crichlow. 1st ed. Garden City, N. Y., Doubleday 1963
206 p. illus. 22 cm.
Includes bibliography.

1. Emancipation Proclamation—Juvenile literature. 2. Slavery in the U. S.—Juvenile literature. I. Title.

E453.S83 j 973.7 63–7691 ‡

Library of Congress 8

M784
C541

Slavery in the U.S. - Music.
Clark, George W.
The liberty minstrel... by Geo. W. Clark. New York, Leavitt & Alden, etc., 1845.
184 [2]p. 18½cm.
Contains music-

Slavery in the U.S.—Poetry.

M811.08
B81

Brown, William Wells, b. 1814, comp.
The anti-slavery harp: a collection of songs for anti-slavery meetings. Comp. by William W. Brown. 2d ed. Boston, B. Marsh, ~~1849.~~ 1848.
47, 1 p. 17cm.

1. Slavery in the U. S.—Poetry. I. Title.

Library of Congress E449.B888 11–6900
a31c1

Slavery in the U.S.—Poetry.

M811.4
W59n

Whitman, Albery Allson, 1851–1901.
Not a man, and yet a man: by A. A. Whitman. Springfield, O., Republic printing company, 1877.
254 p. front. (port.) 19½cm.
Poems.

1. Slavery in the U. S.—Poetry. I. Title. 31–28854 Revised

Library of Congress PS3187.W2N6
r42b2

Slavery in the U. S.-Societies.

M326.5
Am3r

American colonization society.
Memorial of the semi-centennial anniversary of the American colonization society, celebrated at Washington, January 15, 1867. With documents concerning Liberia. Washington, The Society, 1867.
viii, 9–191, 1 p. 24cm.

1. Slavery in the U. S.—Societies. 2. Liberia. 3. Negroes—Colonization—Africa.

Library of Congress E448.A53 4–19076
44c1

Slavery in the U.S.-Alabama.

M326.99B
Au5

Aunt Sally; or, The cross the way to freedom. A narrative of the slave-life and purchase of the mother of Rev. Isaac Williams, of Detroit, Michigan ... Cincinnati, American reform tract and book society, 1862.
vii, 9–216 p. front. (port.) illus., port. group. 15½cm.
Slave life in North Carolina and Alabama.

1. Williams, Sally, American slave. 2. Slavery in the U. S.—North Carolina. 3. Slavery in the U. S.—Alabama. I. American reform tract and book society, Cincinnati, pub.

15–23529

Library of Congress E444.W79
a37b1

Slavery in the U.S.- Alabama.

M326.99B
P58k
1941

Pickard, Kate E R
The kidnapped and the ransomed, by Kate E. R. Pickard ... New York, Negro publication society of America, inc., 1941.
315, 1 p. 22cm. (Negro publication society of America. Publications; Series I, History. No. 1)
"The first edition ... appeared in 1856."—Editor's note.
"Appendix. Seth Conklin by W. H. Furness": p. 298–315.

1. Still, Peter. 2. Still, Lavinia. 3. Slavery in the U. S.—Kentucky. 4. Slavery in the U. S.—Alabama. 5. Concklin, Seth, 1802–1851. I. Furness, William Henry, 1802–1896. II. Negro publication society of America. III. Title.

43–17335

Library of Congress E444.S855
45e1 326.92

Slavery in the U. S.-Alabama.

M326.99B
P58k

Pickard, Kate E R.
The kidnapped and the ransomed. Being the personal recollections of Peter Still and his wife "Vina," after forty years of slavery. By Mrs. Kate E. R. Pickard. With an introduction, by Rev. Samuel J. May; and an appendix, by William H. Furness, D. D. Syracuse, W. T. Hamilton; New York etc. Miller, Orton and Mulligan, 1856.
xxiii (i. e. xxi), 25–409 p. 3 pl. (incl. front.) 19 cm.
Pages ix–x omitted in paging.
Added t.-p., engraved.
"Appendix. Seth Concklin by William H. Furness": p. 377–409.

1. Still, Peter. 2. Still, Lavinia. 3. Slavery in the U. S.—Kentucky. 4. Slavery in the U. S.—Alabama. 5. Concklin, Seth, 1802–1851. I. Furness, William Henry, 1802–1896. II. Title.

14–15958

Library of Congress E444.S85
48g1

Slavery in the U.S. - Alabama.

M326.99B
W67n

Williams, James, b.1805.
Narrative of James Williams, an American slave. In anti-slavery examiner no. 6
1838
8p. 30cm.

Slavery in the U. S.-Alabama.

M326.99B
W67n
1838

Williams, James, b. 1805.
Narrative of James Williams. An American slave; who was for several years a driver on a cotton plantation in Alabama ... New-York, The American anti-slavery society, 1838.
xxiii, 25–108 p. front. (port.) 15cm.
Written by J. G. Whittier from the verbal narrative of Williams. cf. G. R. Carpenter, John Greenleaf Whittier, 1903, p. 165.

1. Slavery in the U. S.—Alabama. I. Whittier, John Greenleaf, 1807–1892. II. American anti-slavery society, New York. III. Title.

17–5248

Library of Congress E444.W743
39c1

Slavery in the U. S.-Connecticut.

M326.99B
M35

Mars, James, b. 1790.
Life of James Mars, a slave; born and sold in Connecticut. 4th ed. Written by himself. Hartford, Press of Case, Lockwood & company, 1867.
38 p. 19cm.

1. Slavery in the U. S.—Connecticut.

14–17086

Library of Congress E444.M36
a37b1

Slavery in the U.S. - Connecticut.

M326.99B
M35
1864

Mars, James b. 1790.
Life of James Mars, a slave born and sold in Connecticut. Written by himself. Hartford, Press of Case Lockwood & company, 1864.
32p. 17½cm.

Slavery in the U.S.-Connecticut.

M326.99B
Sm6n
1835

Smith, Venture, 1729-1805.
A narrative of the life and adventures of Venture, a native of Africa, but resident above sixty years in the United States of America. Related by himself, New London: Printed in 1798. Reprinted A.D. 1835, and published by a descendant of Venture.
24p. 20cm.

Slavery in the U.S.- Connecticut.

M326.99B
Sm6n
1897

Smith, Venture, 1729–1805.
A narrative of the life and adventures of Venture, a native of Africa, but resident above sixty years in the United States of America. Related by himself, New London: Printed in 1798. Reprinted A. D. 1835, and published by a descendant of Venture. Rev. and republished with traditions by H. M. Selden, Haddam, Conn., 1896. Middletown, Conn., J. S. Stewart, printer, 1897.
iv, 5–41 p. 23½cm.

1. Slavery in the U. S.—Connecticut. I. Selden, Henry M. II. Title.

Library of Congress E444.S66 4–17886
a29c1

Slavery in the U.S. - Connecticut.

M326.99B
Sm6n
1798

Smith, Venture, 1729-1805.
A narrative of the life and adventures of Venture, a native of Africa, but resident above sixty years in the United States of America. Related by himself. New-London. Printed by C. Holt, at the Bee-Office, 1798.
32p. 22½cm.

Slavery in the U. S.-Georgia.

M326.99B
B21f

Ball, Charles.
Fifty years in chains; or, The life of an American slave ... New-York, H. Dayton; Indianapolis, Ind., Dayton & Asher, 1859.
2 p. l., 9–430 p. 19cm.
Prepared by ——— Fisher from the verbal narrative of Ball, a slave. cf. Introd. to the New York ed. of 1837.
Earlier editions published under title: Slavery in the United States ...

1. Slavery in the U. S.—Maryland. 2. Slavery in the U. S.—South Carolina. 3. Slavery in the U. S.—Georgia. I. Fisher, ———. II. Title.

14–4028

Library of Congress E444.B184
45d1

Slavery in the U.S.-Georgia.

M326.99B
B21s

Ball, Charles, negro slave.
Slavery in the United States; a narrative of the life and adventures of Charles Ball, a black man, who lived forty years in Maryland, South Carolina and Georgia as a slave ... Lewistown, Pa., J. W. Shugert, 1836.
400 p. 18cm.
Prepared by ——— Fisher from the verbal narrative of Ball. cf. Introd. to New York edition of 1837.
A later edition (New York, 1859) published under title: Fifty years in chains ...

1. Slavery in the U. S.—Maryland. 2. Slavery in the U. S.—South Carolina. 3. Slavery in the U. S.—Georgia. I. Fisher, ———.

14–4026

Library of Congress E444.B18
44c1

Slavery in the U. S.-Georgia.

M326.99B
B815.

Brown, John, fl. 1854.
Slave life in Georgia: a narrative of the life, sufferings, and escape of John Brown, a fugitive slave, now in England. Ed. by L. A. Chamerovzow ... London W. M. Watts, 1855.
1 p. l., ii, 250 p. front. (port.) 16½cm.

1. Slavery in the U. S.—Georgia. I. Chamerovzow, Louis Alexis, ed.

13–18452

Library of Congress E444.B87
41b1

Slavery in the U.S.—Kentucky.

M326.99B
B47

Bibb, Henry, b. 1815.
Narrative of the life and adventures of Henry Bibb, an American slave, written by himself. With an introduction by Lucius C. Matlack. New York, The author, 1849.
1 p. l., xii, 13–204, 3 p. illus. 19cm.

1. Slavery in the U. S.—Kentucky. I. Matlack, Lucius C.

14–5639

Library of Congress E444.B58
44e1

Slavery in the U. S. -Kentucky.

M326.99B C55c 1845 Clarke, Lewis Garrard, 1815?-1897.
Narrative of the sufferings of Lewis Clarke, suring a captivity of more than twenty-five years, among the Algerines of Kentucky, one of the so called Christian states of North America. Dictated by himself. Boston, David H. Ela, Printer, 1845.
viii, 108p. 23cm.

Slavery in the U.S.—Maryland.

M815.4 D739al 1941 **Douglass, Frederick, 1817-1895.**
... Life and times of Frederick Douglass, written by himself. Published for the Frederick Douglass historical and cultural league, in preparation for the one hundredth anniversary of Douglass' first public appearance in the cause of emancipation. New York, N. Y., Pathway press [°1941]
xxx p., 1 l., 31-695 (i. e. 703) p. incl. front. (port.) illus. (facsim.) plates. 23½cm.
At head of title: Centenary memorial subscribers' ed.
"The Life and times is the final form of an autobiography first published as a small Narrative in 1845, expanded in My bondage and my freedom in 1855, further extended in the first edition under the same
(Continued on next card)
41-6875

Slavery in the U. S.-Maryland.

M815.4 D739an **Douglass, Frederick, 1817-1895.**
Narrative of the life of Frederick Douglass, an American slave. Written by himself. Boston, Pub. at the Anti-slavery office, 1845.
xvi, 125 p. front. (port.) 17cm.
Preface signed: Wm. Lloyd Garrison.

1. Slavery in the U. S.—Maryland. I. Garrison, William Lloyd, 1805-1870.
14-3386
Library of Congress E449.D746 [41i1]

Slavery in the U.S. - Kentucky.

M326.99B P58k 1941 **Pickard, Kate E R**
The kidnapped and the ransomed, by Kate E. R. Pickard ... [New York] Negro publication society of America, inc., 1941.
815, [1] p. 22cm. ([Negro publication society of America. Publications; Series I, History. No. 1])
"The first edition ... appeared in 1856."—Editor's note.
"Appendix. Seth Conklin [by W. H. Furness]": p. 293-815.

1. Still, Peter. 2. Still, Lavinia. 3. Slavery in the U. S.—Kentucky. 4. Slavery in the U. S.—Alabama. 5. Concklin, Seth, 1802-1851. I. Furness, William Henry, 1802-1896. II. Negro publication society of America. III. Title.
42-17835
Library of Congress E444.S855 [45e1] 326.92

Slavery in the U.S.—Maryland.

M815.4 D739al **Douglass, Frederick, 1817-1895.**
Life and times of Frederick Douglass, written by himself. His early life as a slave, his escape from bondage, and his complete history to the present time, including his connection with the anti-slavery movement ... With an introduction, by Mr. George L. Ruffin ... Hartford, Conn., Park publishing co., 1881.
xii, xv-xxiii, 13-516 p. 12 pl., 6 port. (incl. front.) 21cm.
Enlarged from the author's My bondage and my freedom, New York, 1855.

1. Slavery in the U. S.—Anti-slavery movements. 2. Slavery in the U. S.—Maryland.
14-3399
Library of Congress E449.D74 [41i1]

M815.4 D739an2 Slavery in the U.S.—Maryland.
Douglass, Frederick, 1817-1895.
Narrative of the life of Frederick Douglass, an American slave. Written by himself. Dublin, Webb and Chapman, 1845.
xvi, 125p. front. (port.) 17cm.
Preface signed: Wm. Lloyd Garrison.
Letter from Wendell Phillips.
First Dublin edition.
Special preface by Frederick Douglass.

Slavery in the U. S.-Kentucky.

M326.99B P58k **Pickard, Kate E R.**
The kidnapped and the ransomed. Being the personal recollections of Peter Still and his wife "Vina," after forty years of slavery. By Mrs. Kate E. R. Pickard. With an introduction, by Rev. Samuel J. May; and an appendix, by William H. Furness, D. D. Syracuse, W. T. Hamilton; New York [etc.] Miller, Orton and Mulligan, 1856.
xxiii (i. e. xxi), 25-409 p. 8 pl. (incl. front.) 19 cm.
Pages ix-x omitted in paging.
Added t.-p., engraved.
"Appendix. Seth Concklin [by William H. Furness]": p. 377-409.
1. Still, Peter. 2. Still, Lavinia. 3. Slavery in the U. S.—Kentucky. 4. Slavery in the U. S.—Alabama. 5. Concklin, Seth, 1802-1851. I. Furness, William Henry, 1802-1896. II. Title.
14-15958
Library of Congress E444.S85 [48g1]

Slavery in the U.S.—Maryland.

M815.4 D739ab **Douglass, Frederick, 1817-1895.**
My bondage and my freedom ... By Frederick Douglass. With an introduction. By Dr. James M'Cune Smith. New York, Miller, Orton & Mulligan, 1855.
xxxi, [33]-464 p. front. (port.) 2 pl. 18½cm.
Enlarged and published under title: Life and times of Frederick Douglass. Hartford, 1881.

1. Slavery in the U. S.—Anti-slavery movements. 2. Slavery in the U. S.—Maryland. I. Title.
14-4878
Library of Congress E449.D738 [42n1]

Slavery in the U. S.-Maryland.

M326.99B P38f **Pennington, James William Charles, 1812-1871**
The fugitive blacksmith; or, Events in the history of James W. C. Pennington ... formerly a slave in the state of Maryland, United States ... 3d ed. London, C. Gilpin, 1850.
~~xix, [1], 84 p.~~ 16cm.
XV, 87 p.

1. Slavery in the U. S.—Maryland.
12-20358
[37b1]
Library of Congress E444.P41

Slavery in the U.S.-Louisiana.

M326.99B N81 1853 **Northup, Solomon, b. 1808.**
... Twelve years a slave. Narrative of Solomon Northup, a citizen of New-York, kidnapped in Washington city in 1841, and rescued in 1853, from a cotton plantation near the Red river, in Louisiana. Auburn, Derby and Miller; Buffalo, Derby, Orton and Mulligan; [etc., etc.] 1853.
xvi, [17]-336 p. front., pl. 19½ cm.
At head of title: Tenth thousand.
Preface signed: David Wilson.

1. Plantation life. 2. Slavery in the U. S.—Louisiana. I. Wilson, David, 1818-1887, ed.
10-34503
Library of Congress E444.N87 [39h1]

Slavery in the U.S.-Maryland.

MB9 D74n **Douglass, Frederick, 1817?-1895.**
Narrative of the life of Frederick Douglass, an American slave, written by himself. Edited by Benjamin Quarles. Cambridge, Mass., Belknap Press, 1960.
xxvi, 163 p. port., map. 22 cm. (The John Harvard library)

1. Slavery in the U. S.—Maryland. (Series) I. Quarles, Benjamin, ed.
Name originally: Frederick Augustus Washington Bailey.
E449.D74905 326.99 59-11516
Library of Congress [60k15]

Slavery in the U. S.—Missouri.

M810 B799al 1850 **Brown, William Wells, b. 1815.**
Levensgeschiedenis van den Amerikaanschen slaaf, W. Wells Brown, Amerikaansch afgevaardigde bij het vredescongres te Parijs, 1849, door hem zelven beschreven. Naar den 5. Engelschen druk vertaald door M. Keijzer. Zwolle, W. E. J. Tjeenk Willink, 1850.
x, 119, [1] p. front. (port.) 23½cm.
Narrative of the author's experiences as a slave in St. Louis and elsewhere.

1. Slavery in the U. S.—Missouri. I. Keijzer, M., tr. II. Title.
1-6413
Library of Congress E444.B885

Slavery in the U.S.-Maryland.

M326.99B B21f [Ball, Charles]
Fifty years in chains; or, The life of an American slave ... New-York, H. Dayton; Indianapolis, Ind., Dayton & Asher, 1859.
2 p. l., [9]-430 p. 19cm.
Prepared by [———] Fisher from the verbal narrative of Ball, a slave. *cf.* Introd. to the New York ed. of 1837.
Earlier editions published under title: Slavery in the United States ...

1. Slavery in the U. S.—Maryland. 2. Slavery in the U. S.—South Carolina. 3. Slavery in the U. S.—Georgia. I. Fisher, ———. II. Title.
14-4028
Library of Congress E444.B184 [45d1]

Slavery in the U.S. - Maryland.

M815.4 D739an2 1846 Douglass, Frederick, 1817-1895.
Narrative of the life of Frederick Douglass, an American slave. Written by himself. 3rd English edition. Wortley, Neer Leeds, Printed by Joseph Barker, 1846.
170p. port. 16½cm.

Slavery in the U.S. - Missouri.

M810 B799a 1848 Brown, William Wells, b. 1815-
Narrative of William W. Brown, a fugitive slave. Written by himself. Boston, The Anti-slavery, 1848.
xi [13]-144p. front (port.) 17½cm.
Narrative of the author's experiences as a slave in St. Louis and elsewhere.
[Second edition, enlarged.]
Inscribed copy: to Andrew Paton, with the respect of the author, Boston, March 7, 1848.

Slavery in the U.S.—Maryland.

M326.99B B 21s Ball, Charles, *negro slave.*
Slavery in the United States; a narrative of the life and adventures of Charles Ball, a black man, who lived forty years in Maryland, South Carolina and Georgia as a slave ... Lewistown, Pa., J. W. Shugert, 1836.
400 p. 18cm.
Prepared by ——— Fisher from the verbal narrative of Ball. *cf.* Introd. to New York edition of 1837.
A later edition (New York, 1859) published under title: Fifty years in chains ...
1. Slavery in the U. S.—Maryland. 2. Slavery in the U. S.—South Carolina. 3. Slavery in the U. S.—Georgia. I. Fisher, ———.
14-4026
Library of Congress E444.B18 [44c1]

Slavery in the U. S.-Maryland.

M815.4 D739an 1846 **Douglass, Frederick, 1817-1895.**
Narrative of the life of Frederick Douglass, an American slave. Written by himself. Boston, Pub. at the Anti-slavery office, ~~1845~~. 1846.
xvi, 125 p. front. (port.) 17cm.
Preface signed: Wm. Lloyd Garrison.

1. Slavery in the U. S.—Maryland. I. Garrison, William Lloyd, 1805-1879.
14-3386
Library of Congress E449.D746 [41i1]

M810 B799a 1848 Slavery in the U.S. - Missouri
Brown, William Wells, b. 1815-
Narrative of William W. Brown... (card 2)

"This second edition contains much new matter up to p. 108 it is a revision of the first ed. and the last 35 pages are new." ABS.

Slavery in the U. S. - Maryland.

M815.4 D739aL 1966 **Douglass, Frederick, 1817?-1895.**
Life and times of Frederick Douglass. Adapted by Barbara Ritchie. New York, Crowell [1966]
viii, 210 p. 21 cm.
Shortened version, adapted from the 2d rev. ed. of the author's autobiography: Life and times, published in 1892, as enlarged from his My bondage and my freedom, 1855.

1. Slavery in the U. S.—Anti-slavery movements. 2. Slavery in the U. S.—Maryland. I. Ritchie, Barbara.
E449.D744 1966 326.092 66-7048
Library of Congress [67d5]

Slavery in the U. S. - Maryland.

M815.4 D739an2 1846 Douglass, Frederick, 1817-1895.
Narrative of the life of Frederick Douglass, an American slave, Written by himself...2nd Dublin ed. Dublin, Webb & Chapman, 1846.
xviii, 122, cxxiv-cxxxvp. front. (port.) 19cm.
Preface to the 1st American edition, signed: Wm. Lloyd Garrison.
Letter from Wendell Phillips.
"Falsehood refuted," by A.A.C. Thompson in the Delaware Republican. Reply by Frederick Douglass," p. cxxiii-cxxviii.

Slavery in the U. S.-Missouri.

M810 B799a 1847 **Brown, William Wells, b. 1815.**
Narrative of William W. Brown, a fugitive slave. Written by himself. Boston, The Anti-slavery office, 1847.
xi, [13]-110 p. front. (port.) 17½cm.
Narrative of the author's experiences as a slave in St. Louis and elsewhere.

1. Slavery in the U. S.—Missouri.
14-4708
Library of Congress E444B88 [37b1]

Slavery in the U.S.-Missouri.

MB9 B83 **Bruce, Henry Clay,** 1836–1902.
The new man. Twenty-nine years a slave. Twenty-nine years a free man. Recollections of H. C. Bruce. York, Pa., P. Anstadt & sons, 1895.
x, [11]–176 p. front. (port.) 23½cm.
Narrative of slave life, mainly in Missouri.

1. Slavery in the U. S.—Missouri. I. Title.

Library of Congress E444.B9 14—7617
Copyright 1895: 15063 [40f1]

Slavery in the U. S.-New England.

M326. G83n **Greene, Lorenzo Johnston,** 1899–
The Negro in colonial New England, 1620–1776, by Lorenzo Johnston Greene ... New York, Columbia university press; London, P. S. King & Staples, ltd., 1942.
404 p. 23 cm. (*Half-title:* Studies in history, economics and public law, ed. by the Faculty of political science of Columbia university. No. 494)
Issued also as thesis (PH. D.) Columbia university.
Bibliography: p. 361–384.

1. Slavery in the U. S.—New England. 2. Negroes—New England. 3. New England—Hist.—Colonial period. I. Title.

Library of Congress H31.C7 no. 494 43—2384
——— Copy 2. E444.N5G7 1942a
[48x2] (308.2) 326.974

Slavery in the U.S.—New York (State)

M326.99B St4 1867 **Steward, Austin,** *b.* 1794.
Twenty-two years a slave, and forty years a freeman; embracing a correspondence of several years, while president of Wilberforce colony, London, Canada West, by Austin Steward. ~~4th~~ ed. ~~Rochester, N. Y., Allings & Cory, 1861.~~ Canandaigua, N.Y. The Author, 1867.
xii, [13]–360 p. front. (port.) 4 pl. 18cm.

1. Slavery in the U. S.—Virginia. 2. Slavery in the U. S.—New York (State) 3. Wilberforce negro colony, Middlesex Co., Ont. I. Title.

Library of Congress E444.S845 14—17056
[s20f2]

Slavery in the U.S.-North Carolina.

M326.99B Au5 **Aunt Sally;** or, The cross the way to freedom. A narrative of the slave-life and purchase of the mother of Rev. Isaac Williams, of Detroit, Michigan ... Cincinnati, American reform tract and book society, 1862.
vii, 9–216 p. front. (port.) illus., port. group. 15½cm.
Slave life in North Carolina and Alabama.

1. Williams, Sally, American slave. 2. Slavery in the U. S.—North Carolina. 3. Slavery in the U. S.—Alabama. I. American reform tract and book society, Cincinnati, pub.

Library of Congress E444.W79 15—23529
[a37b1]

Slavery in the U. S.-North Carolina.

M326.99B G76 **Grandy, Moses,** *b.* 1786?
Narrative of the life of Moses Grandy; late a slave in the United States of America ... 1st American from the last London ed. ... Boston, O. Johnson, 1844.
iv, [5]–45 p., 1 l. 16½cm.
Introduction signed: George Thompson.

1. Slavery in the U. S.—North Carolina. I. Thompson, George, 1804–1878, ed.

[35b1] 11-6095
Library of Congress E444.G75

MB9 M48 1851 Slavery in the U.S. - North Carolina.
Melbourn, Julius, b. 1790.
Life and opinions of Julius Melbourn; with sketches of the lives and characters of Thomas Jefferson, John Quincy Adams, John Randolph, and several other eminent American Statesmen. Ed. by a late member of Congress. Syracuse, Hall 1851.

xii, 258p. (port.) 20cm.

Slavery in the U.S.-North Carolina.

MB9 M48 **Melbourn, Julius,** *b.* 1790.
Life and opinions of Julius Melbourn; with sketches of the lives and characters of Thomas Jefferson, John Quincy Adams, John Randolph, and several other eminent American statesmen. Ed. by a late member of Congress. Syracuse, Hall & Dickson; [etc., etc.] 1847.
239 p. front. (port.) 20cm.

1. Slavery in the U. S.—North Carolina. 2. U. S.—Descr. & trav. 3. U. S.—Pol. & govt.—1815–1861. I. Hammond, Jabez Delano, 1778–1855, ed.

Library of Congress E338.M51 12—30047
[45c1]

Slavery in the U. S.-South Carolina.

M326.99B B21f **Ball, Charles,**
Fifty years in chains; or, The life of an American slave ... New-York, H. Dayton; Indianapolis, Ind., Dayton & Asher, 1859.
2 p. l., [9]–430 p. 19cm.
Prepared by ——— Fisher from the verbal narrative of Ball, a slave. *cf.* Introd. to the New York ed. of 1837.
Earlier editions published under title: Slavery in the United States ...

1. Slavery in the U. S.—Maryland. 2. Slavery in the U. S.—South Carolina. 3. Slavery in the U. S.—Georgia. I. Fisher, ———. II. Title.

Library of Congress E444.B184 14—4028
[45d1]

Slavery in the U.S.—South Carolina.

M326.99B B21s **Ball, Charles,** *negro slave.*
Slavery in the United States; a narrative of the life and adventures of Charles Ball, a black man, who lived forty years in Maryland, South Carolina and Georgia as a slave ... Lewistown, Pa., J. W. Shugert, 1836.
400 p. 18cm.
Prepared by ——— Fisher from the verbal narrative of Ball. *cf.* Introd. to New York edition of 1837.
A later edition (New York, 1859) published under title: Fifty years in chains ...

1. Slavery in the U. S.—Maryland. 2. Slavery in the U. S.—South Carolina. 3. Slavery in the U. S.—Georgia. I. Fisher, ———.

Library of Congress E444.B18 14—4026
[44c1]

Slavery in the U. S.-South Carolina.

M326.99B R68 1840 **Roper, Moses.**
A narrative of the adventures and escape of Moses Roper, from American slavery; with a preface, by the Rev. T. Price. 4th ed. London, Harvey and Darton, 1840. ~~1838~~ 2d.
xii, 120 p. front. (port.) illus. 15cm.

1. Slavery in the U. S.—South Carolina. I. Price, Thomas.

Library of Congress E444.R785 17-24785

MB9 St8 Slavery in the U.S. - South Carolina.
Stroyer, Jacob, 1849–
My life in the South. By Jacob Stroyer. New and enl. ed. Salem, Salem observer book and job print, 1889.

83p. 19½cm.

Slavery in the U.S.-Virginia.
M326.99B Adln **Adams, John Quincy,** *b.* 1845.
Narrative of the life of John Quincy Adams, when in slavery, and now as a freeman. Harrisburg, Pa., Sieg, printer, 1872.
64 p. 11½cm.
Account of the author's experiences as a slave in Virginia before 1862.

1. Slavery in the U. S.—Virginia.

Library of Congress E444.A2 14—5640
[a41b1]

Slavery in the U. S.—Virginia.

M973. M45 **Mazyck, Walter H.**
George Washington and the Negro, by Walter H. Mazyck ... Washington, D. C., The associated publishers, inc. [©1932]
vii p., 1 l., 180 p. 19½cm.

1. Washington, George, pres. U. S.—Associates and employees. 2. Slavery in the U. S.—Virginia. 3. U. S.—Hist.—Revolution—Negro troops. I. Title.

Library of Congress E312.17.M38 32—4101
——— Copy 2.
Copyright A 47409 [38j2] 923.173

Slavery in the U.S.-Virginia.

M326.99B Sm6 **Smith, James Lindsay**
Autobiography of James L. Smith, including, also, reminiscences of slave life, recollections of the war, education of freedmen, causes of the exodus, etc. Norwich [Conn.] Press of the Bulletin company, 1881.
xiii p., 1 l., 150 p. front. (port.) 2 pl. 20cm.

1. Slavery in the U. S.—Virginia. 2. Freedmen.

Library of Congress E444.S65 14—15959
[44e1]

Slavery in the U.S.— Virginia.

M326.99B St4 1867 **Steward, Austin,** *b.* 1794.
Twenty-two years a slave, and forty years a freeman; embracing a correspondence of several years, while president of Wilberforce colony, London, Canada West, by Austin Steward. ~~4th~~ ed. ~~Rochester, N. Y., Allings & Cory, 1861.~~ Canandaigua, N.Y. The Author, 1867.
xii, [13]–360 p. front. (port.) 4 pl. 18cm.

1. Slavery in the U. S.—Virginia. 2. Slavery in the U. S.—New York (State) 3. Wilberforce negro colony, Middlesex Co., Ont. I. Title.

Library of Congress E444.S845 14—17056
[s20f2]

Slavery in the U. S.-Virginia.

M326.99B St4 **Steward, Austin,** *b.* 1794.
Twenty-two years a slave, and forty years a freeman; embracing a correspondence of several years, while president of Wilberforce colony, London, Canada West, by Austin Steward. Rochester, N. Y., W. Alling, 1857.
xii, [13]–360 p. front. (port.) 4 pl. 19cm.
Narrative of slave life in Virginia and in central New York.

1. Slavery in the U. S.—Virginia. 2. Wilberforce negro colony, Middlesex co., Ont. I. Title.

Library of Congress E444.S84 6—34319
[a27d1]

Slavery in the U.S.— Virginia— Fiction.

M813.1 H55 **Hill, John H.**
Princess Malah, by John H. Hill. Washington, D. C., The associated publishers, inc. [©1933]
vii p., 1 l., 330 p. 21cm.

1. Washington, George, pres. U. S.—Fiction. 2. Washington, Mrs. Martha (Dandridge) Custis, 1731–1801—Fiction. 3. Slavery in the U. S.—Virginia—Fiction. I. Title.

Library of Congress PZ3.H5521Pr 33—3600
——— Copy 2.
Copyright A 60229 [a38e1]

Slavery in the United States.

M326.99B Au8 Autobiography of a female slave.
New York, Redfield, 1857.
401, 8p. 19cm.

Slavery in the United States.

M326.99B C84r Craft, William.
Running a thousand miles for freedom; or, the escape of William and Ellen Craft from Slavery. London, William Tweedie, 1860.

111p. front. 17½cm.

Slavery in the United States.

MB9 D74fo Douglass, Frederick.
Frederick Douglass, selections from his writings, edited with an introduction by Philip S. Foner... New York, International publishers, [c1945]

95p. 20cm.

Slavery in the West Indies.
M326.99 B P93 [Prince, Mary.]
The history of Mary Prince, a West Indian slave. Related by herself. With a supplement by the Editor. To which is added, the narrative of Asa-Asa, a captured African... London, Published by F. Westley and A.H. Davis, 1831.

44p. 22½cm.

M326.99B
W68
Slavery in the West Indies.
Williams, James
Narrative of the cruel treatment of James Williams, a Negro apprentice in Jamaica, from 1st August, 1834, till the purchase of his freedom in 1837, by Joseph Sturge, of Birmingham, by whom he was brought to England. Glasgow: Printed by Aird and Russell. 1837.
20p. 21cm.

M658
F57
Small business.
Fitzhugh, H Naylor, ed.
Problems and opportunities confronting Negroes in the field of business; report on the National Conference on Small Business. Washington, D. C., U. S. Dept. of Commerce, 1962.
103p. 23½cm.

M335.4
P42pe
Smith Act.
Perry, Pettis
Pettis Perry speaks to the court, opening statement to the Court and jury in the case of the sixteen Smith Act victims in the trial at Foley Square, New York. New York, New Century Publishers, 1952.
16 p. 19cm.

Martinique
M972.98
B541
Slavery in the West Indies, French.
Bissette, Cyrille Charles Auguste, 1795-1858.
Lettres politiques sur les colonies, sur l'esclavage et sur les questions qui s'y rattachent, par C. A. Bissette. Paris, Ebrard, Libraire, Passage des Panoramas, 1845.
48p. 23cm.

M728.6
W67s
The small home of tomorrow.
Williams, Paul R 1894-
The small home of tomorrow, by Paul R. Williams, A. I. A. Hollywood, Murray & Gee, incorporated, 1945.
2 p. l., 7-95 p. illus. (incl. port., plans) 28 x 21½ cm.
1. Architecture, Domestic—Designs and plans. I. Title.
45-6335
Library of Congress NA7127.W614
[47i⁵] 728.6

MB 9
Ed9s
Smith, Alice Ward.
Jess Edwards rides again, by Alice Ward Smith ... Boston, The Christopher publishing house [°1934]
3 p. l., 9-145 p. 20cm.
I. Title.
Library of Congress PZ3.S64155Je 34-21154
——— Copy 2.
Copyright A 74321 [3]

M071
V87
Slaves, Fugitive.
Voice of the fugitive, v.1-2, Jan. 1851- Dec. 1852. Sandwich, Canada West, 1851-52.
2v. 49cm. semi-weekly.
H. Bibb, editor.
52 no. in 2v. lacks v.2, no.6,7,8.

M324
Smle
Smalls, Robert, 1839-1915
Elections methods in the south, by Robert Smalls. Excerpt from The North American Review, v. CLI, no. 408, November, 1890.
[593-600p. 22cm.
1. Elections I. title

MB9
C259
Smith, Alvin D
George Washington Carver, man of God. [1st ed.] New York, Exposition Press [1954]
76 p. 21 cm.
1. Carver, George Washington, 1864?-1943.
S417.C3S5 925 54-6185 ‡
Library of Congress [3]

M813.5
Sc8
Slaves today.
Schuyler, George Samuel, 1895-
Slaves today; a story of Liberia, by George S. Schuyler. New York, Brewer, Warren & Putnam, 1931.
3 p. l., 5-290 p. 19½cm.
1. Slavery in Liberia—Fiction. I. Title.
31-32949
Library of Congress PZ3.S3972Sl
——— Copy 2.
Copyright A 41840 [37c1]

M815.5
B83
No.8
Smalls, Robert, 1838-1915
Bruce, John Edward, 1856-
Reply to Senator Wade Hampton's article in the Forum for June, on ... "What Negro Supremacy means." by John E. Bruce... Washington, D.C., 1888.
17p. 21½cm.

MB9
Sm5
Smith, Amanda (Berry) 1837-1915.
An autobiography; the story of the Lord's dealings with Mrs. Amanda Smith, the colored evangelist; containing an account of her life work of faith, and her travels in America, England, Ireland, Scotland, India and Africa, as an independent missionary. With an introduction by Bishop Thoburn ... Chicago, Meyer & brother, 1893.
xvi, 17-506 p. front., plates, ports. 20½cm.
1. Evangelistic work. 2. Voyages and travels.
14-13153
Library of Congress BV3785.S56A3 1893
[34b1]

M371.32
SL52
Sloan, Irving
The Negro in modern American history textbooks: a study of the Negro in selected junior and senior high history textbooks as of September, 1966. [Chicago. American Federation of Teachers [1966]
47p. 20cm.
White author?
1. Textbooks - History. I. Title.

MB9
Sm1s
Smalls, Robert, 1839-1915.
Sterling, Dorothy, 1913-
Captain of the Planter; the story of Robert Smalls. Illustrated by Ernest Crichlow. [1st ed.] Garden City, N. Y., Doubleday, 1958.
264 p. illus. 22 cm.
Includes bibliography.
1. Smalls, Robert, 1839-1915. I. Title.
E185.97.S6S8 923.273 58-5589 ‡
Library of Congress [15]

M324
Sm5n
Smith, Arthur J. , 1877-
The Negro in the political classics of the American government, by Arthur J. Smith. Washington, D. C. [°1937]
cover-title, 25 l. 12 x 18½cm.
"A short biography of each Negro United States senator and representative, elected and seated ... since 1870."
1. Negroes—Biog. 2. Negroes—Politics and suffrage. I. Title.
39-33068
Library of Congress E185.96.S65
——— Copy 2.
Copyright AA 232559 [2] 923.273

M811.4
Su7s
Sluby, M F
Satire. Lines suggested on reading the confession of Dr. B.T. Tanner, editor of the "Christian Recorder", by M.F. Sluby. December 8th, 1881 and May 11th, 1883, Philadelphia, Pa. [lacks imprint]
8p. 19cm.

M813.5
D292s
Smarty-pants and other stories.
Davis, Milburn J
Smarty-pants and other stories. New York, Comet Press, 1962.
28p. 19cm.

MB9
K41s
Smith, C C
The life and work of Jacob Kenoly, by C. C. Smith. Cincinnati ... Methodist Book Company, c1912.
160p. 19cm.
1. Liberia. 2. Kenoly, Jacob, 1876-

Africa
M896.1
S182
Sluneční prudké pochodně. [Translation Jiří Valja a Petr Kopta. Praha, Mladá fronta, 1962.
[24]p. illus. 27cm.
"With birthday greetings to Arthur-Langston, March 28, 1962. The African poems in Czech."
1. African poetry.

M335.4
B81
Smith Act.
Brown, Lloyd Louis, 1913-
Stand up for freedom; The Negro people vs. the Smith Act. New York, New Century Publishers, 1952.
15 p. ports. 19cm.

M814.5
Sm54
Smith, Carl S
Letters from my nephew slim. New York, Vantage Press [1965]
120p. 20½cm.
Portrait of author on book cover.
I. Title.

Smith, Charles Edward, jt. auth.

M781 K14j

Ramsey, Frederic, 1915– *ed.*
Jazzmen, edited by Frederic Ramsey, jr., and Charles Edward Smith. With 32 pages of illustrations. New York, Harcourt, Brace and company [1939]

xv, 360 p. plates, ports. 22 cm.

Contributors (in addition to the editors): William Russell, S. W. Smith, E. Simms Campbell, E. J. Nichols, Wilder Hobson, Otis Ferguson and R. P. Dodge.
"First edition."
White author.

1. Jazz music. 2. Negro musicians. 3. Musicians, American. I. Smith, Charles Edward, joint ed. II. Title.

Full name: Charles Frederic Ramsey.

ML3561.R24J2 780.973 39—31807

Library of Congress [59f2]

M287.8 Sm5h

Smith, Charles Spencer, 1852-1923.
A history of the African methodist episcopal church, being a volume supplemental to a history of the African methodist episcopal church, by Daniel Alexander Payne... Chronicling the principal events in the advance of the African methodist episcopal church from 1856-1922. By Charles Spencer Smith... Philadelphia, Pa., Book concern of the A.M.E. church, 1922.
570p. 23½cm.
1. African methodist episcopal church.

M304 P19 v.4,no.13

Smith, Charles Spencer, 1852-1923.
The relation of the British government to the natives of South Africa. Address of Bishop C.S. Smith, resident bishop of the American Methodist Episcopal Church in South Africa, 1904-1906, delivered at the Negro Young People's Christian and Educational Congress in Convention Hall, Washington, D.C., Wednesday, August 1, 1906.

15p. 21½cm.

1. Africa, South.

Smith, Charles Spencer, 1852-1923 ed.

M287.8 P29

Payne, Daniel Alexander, *bp.*, 1811-1893.
History of the African Methodist Episcopal church, by Daniel A. Payne... Edited by Rev. C. S. Smith ... Nashville, Tenn., Publishing house of the A. M. E. Sunday-school union, 1891.

2 p. l., iii–xvi, 502 p. front., ports. 23cm.

"The present volume will be considered as volume I ... volume II is now in course of preparation."—1st prelim. leaf. No more published?

1. African Methodist Episcopal church—Hist. I. Smith, Charles Spencer, 1852– ed.

Library of Congress BX8443.P28 37-29687

[2] 287.8

Smith, Charles Spencer, 1852-1923, editor

MB9 P29r

Payne, Daniel Alexander, 1811-1893.
Recollections of seventy years; by Bishop Daniel Alexander Payne ... With an introduction by Rev. F. J. Grimke ... Comp. and arranged by Sarah C. Bierce Scarborough. Ed. by Rev. C. S. Smith. Nashville, Tenn., Publishing house of the A. M. E. Sunday school union, 1888.

335 p. pl., 8 port. (incl. front.) 19cm.

1. African Methodist Episcopal church. I. Scarborough, Sarah C. Bierce, comp. II. Smith, Charles Spencer, 1852– ed. III. Title.

14-12737

Library of Congress E185.97.P34

M301 R11

Smith, Charles U.
The sit-ins and the new Negro student.
Pp. 57-67.

(In: Raab, Earl. American race relations today. Garden City, N. Y., Doubleday, 1962)

M309.2 Sm55

Smith, Ed, 1937–
Where to, black man? Chicago, Quadrangle Books, 1967.
221 p. 22 cm.

1. U. S. Peace Corps—Ghana. I. Title. 2. Ghana.

HC60.5.S6 309.2'235'667 67-21640 rev

Library of Congress [r68f3]

Smith, Edwin W.

M910 C73

Committee on Africa, the war, and peace aims.
The Atlantic charter and Africa from an American standpoint; a study by the Committee on Africa, the war, and peace aims. The application of the "eight points" of the charter to the problems of Africa, and especially those related to the welfare of the African people living south of the Sahara, with related material on African conditions and needs. New York city, 1942.

xi, 164 p. fold. map. 23cm.

"Selected African bibliography": p. 144–150.

D754.A34C6 1942

(Continued on next card)

42-18394 Revised

[46c2]

Gold Coast
M39 Ag8s Gold Coast

Smith, Edwin William, 1876–
Aggrey of Africa, a study in black and white, by Edwin W. Smith ... New York, Doubleday, Doran and company, inc., 1929.

xii, 292 p. front., plates, ports. 22 cm.

Maps on lining-papers.

1. Aggrey, James Emman Kwegyir, 1875-1927.

29—18099

Library of Congress E185.97.A26

[48r38j1]

Smith, Elmer, 1909.

M304 P19 v.7 no.29

Carter, Elmer A
Not in the headlines, a story of a Negro radio operator, by Elmer A. Carter.
Reprinted from Opportunity, November, 1931.
New York, National urban league, 1931.

4p. 28½cm.

M810.8 Sm5m

Smith, Elmer Reid, 1904– *ed.*
Meet an American! Edited by Elmer R. Smith ... New York, Chicago, Harcourt, Brace and company [1944]

xiv, 480 p. incl. front., illus. 20½cm.
Partial contents: A college built on faith, by Mary McLeod Bethune. -Let America be America again, by Langston Hughes.

I. Bethune, Mary McLeod. A college built on faith.
II. Hughes, Langston. Let America be America again.
1. ~~American~~ literature ~~(Selections: Extracts, etc.)~~ 2. ~~National characteristics, American.~~ 3. ~~U. S.—Civilization.~~ I. Title.

44-4431

Library of Congress PS500.H5S5

[25] 810.82

Smith, Ezekiel Ezra.

MB N42

Newbold, Nathan Carter, 1871- ed.
Five North Carolina Negro educators; prepared under the direction of N. C. Newbold. Chapel Hill, The University of North Carolina press, 1939.

Xii, 142p. ports. 22cm.

U.S. M947 Sm58

Smith, Homer.
Black man in Red Russia; a memoir. With an introd. by Harrison Salisbury. Chicago, Johnson Pub. Co., 1964.

xvi, 221 p. illus. (on lining papers) 22 cm.
Portrait of author on book jacket.

1. Russia. I. Title.

DK267.S587 914.7 64-23261

Library of Congress [3]

M323 M45

Smith, Huston, *ed.*
The search for America. Edited by Huston Smith, with Richard T. Heffron and Eleanor Wieman Smith. [Englewood Cliffs, N. J.] Prentice-Hall [1959]

176 p. 21 cm. (Spectrum paperbacks, S-9)

"Based on the National educational television series [The search for America]"
White author.
Partial contents.- Race in America: the Negro perspective, by Benjamin Mays.
1. U. S.—Civilization—Addresses, essays, lectures. 2. U. S.—Relations (general) with foreign countries. I. Title.

E169.1.S62 917.3 59-15720 ‡

Library of Congress [20]

Bahamas
M332 Sm6a

Smith, James Carmichael, 1852–
Abundance and hard times, by Jas. C. Smith ... London, K. Paul, Trench, Trübner & co., ltd., 1908.

30 p. 21½cm.

A plea for the establishment by law of "the wage co-operative system of profit-sharing" and "the double standard money system."

1. Panics. 2. Currency question—Gt. Brit. 3. Profit-sharing. I. Title.

16-7960

Library of Congress HB3723.S55

Bahamas
M332 Sm6d

Smith, James Carmichael, 1852-
The distribution of the produce, by James C. Smith. London, Kegan Paul, Trench, Trübner & Co., 1892.

77p. 19cm.

1. Money. 2. Profits.

Bahamas
M332 Sm6e

Smith, James Carmichael, 1852–
Economic reconstruction; a paper read at the Royal colonial institute, on 15th June, 1916, by Jas. C. Smith ... London, P. S. King & son, ltd., 1918.

23, [1] p. 21½cm.

Preface signed: A. H. Mackmurdo.

1. European war, 1914– —Economic aspects—Gt. Brit. 2. Money—Gt. Brit. I. Title.

18-20511

Library of Congress HC256.2.S6

Bahamas
M332. Sm6i

Smith, James Carmichael, 1852–
Inter-temporary values; or, The distribution of the produce in time. By James C. Smith ... London, K. Paul, Trench, Trübner, & co., ltd., 1906.

2 p. l., 136 p. incl. tables. charts (1 fold.) 22cm.

Appendixes: A. Coinage act, 1870.—B. [Miscellaneous charts]—C. Wholesale and retail prices.—D. The double monetary unit.—E. Inter-temporary value.

1. Money. 2. Value.

A 10-1897

Title from National Monetary Commission. Printed by L. C.

Bahamas
M332 Sm61e

Smith, James Carmichael, 1852-
Legal tender, correspondence with the editor of "The bankers' magazine." London, Kegan Paul, Trench, Trubner, 1909.

16p. graphs. 21½cm.

1. Currency question - Gt. Brit. 2. Money.
3. Gt. Brit. - Econ. condit.
I. Title.

Bahamas
M332 Sm6l

Smith, James Carmichael., 1852-
Legal tender; essays, by Jas. C. Smith ... London, K. Paul, Trench, Trübner & co., ltd., 1910.

3 p. l., v–xviii, 285 p. incl. tables. fold. diagr. 21½cm.

Contents.—Economic definitions and illustrations.—Legal tender.—Taxation.—The money of India.—Money and currency.

1. Currency question—Gt. Brit. 2. Money. 3. Gt. Brit.—Econ. condit. I. Title.

13-8350

Library of Congress HG939.S7

Bahamas
M332 Sm6m

Smith, James Carmichael, 1852–
Money and profit-sharing; or, The double standard money system, by Jas. C. Smith ... London, K. Paul, Trench, Trübner & co., ld., 1908.

xix, 232 p. incl. tables. fold. tab., fold. diagr. 22cm.

1. Money. 2. Profit-sharing. 3. Currency question—Gt. Brit. 4. Value. I. Title. II. Title: Double standard money system.

9—3071

Library of Congress HG221.S62

Bahamas
M332
Sm6n

Smith, James Carmichael, 1852-
The National providence; essays, by Jas. C. Smith... London, Kegan Paul, Trench, Trubner & Co., 1910.

vi, 1 l, 103p. 21½cm.

1. Society. 2. Property. 3. Economics. I. Title.

M287.8
Sm6v

Smith, James H. , 1874-
Vital facts concerning the African Methodist Episcopal Church; its origin, doctrines, government, usages, polity progress (a Socratic exposition) by James H. Smith. With an introduction by Sherman L. Greene. [rev. ed.] [n.p., n.p.] 1941.

216p. portraits. 19cm.

1. African Methodist Episcopal Church.

M326.99B
Sm6

Smith, James Lindsay
Autobiography of James L. Smith, including, also, reminiscences of slave life, recollections of the war, education of freedmen, causes of the exodus, etc. Norwich [Conn.] Press of the Bulletin company, 1881.

xiii p., 1 l., 150 p. front. (port.) 2 pl. 20cm.

1. Slavery in the U. S.—Virginia. 2. Freedmen. 3. Civil war 4. Norwich Conn. 5. Slave narratives. 14—15959

Library of Congress E444.S65 [44e1]

M326
G87a
1854

Smith, James McCune, 1813-1865.
Freedom-liberty.

(In: Griffiths, Julia ed. Autographs for freedom. Auburn, Alden, Beardsley, 1854. 19½cm. p. 241).

M326
G87a
1853

Smith, James McCune, 1813-1865.
John Murray of Glasgow.

(In: Griffiths, Julia ed. Autographs for freedom. Boston, Jewett, 1853. 19½cm. Pp. 62-67).

Smith, James McCune, 1813-1865

MB9
G18h

Garnet, Henry Highland, 1815-1882.
A memorial discourse; by Rev. Henry Highland Garnet, delivered in the hall of the House of representatives, Washington city, D. C., on Sabbath, February 12, 1865. With an introduction by James McCune Smith, M. D. Philadelphia, J. M. Wilson, 1865.

1 p. l., [15]-91 p. front. (port.) 23cm.

"Sketch of the life and labors of Rev. Henry Highland Garnet": p. 17-68.

1. Slavery in the U. S.—Emancipation. I. Smith, James McCune. 17-8999

Library of Congress E453.G235

Smith, James McCune, 1813-1865

M974.7
W93a

Wright, Theodore Sedgewick.
An address to the three thousand colored citizens of New York who are the owners of one hundred and twenty thousand acres of land in the state of New York, given to them by Gerrit Smith... September 1, 1846. New York, n.p. 1846

20p. 23cm.

MB9
G58s

Smith, James Wesley.
Goldwater and the Republic that was, by J. Wesley Smith. New York, Carlton Press [1965]

74 p. 21 cm. (A Reflection book)

Portrait of author on book jacket.

1. Goldwater, Barry Morris, 1909- 2. Conservatism—U. S. 3. Negroes—Civil rights. I. Title.

E840.8.G6S6 65-8665

Library of Congress [5]

Virgin Is.
M813.5
Sm5d

Smith, Joe, *pseud.*
Dagmar of Green Hills. [1st ed.] New York, Pageant Press [1957]

124 p. 21 cm.

I. Title.

PZ4.S65Dag 57-8306 ‡

Library of Congress [5]

M813.08
C554

Smith, John Caswell
Fighter
Pp. 135-147

In: Clarke, John Henrik, ed. American Negro short stories. New York, Hill and Wang, 1966.

M811.5
Sm5p

Smith, John Windsor,
Parted and other poems, by John Windsor Smith. [New York, The author, c1942]

16p. port. 19cm.

1. Poetry.

M364
Sm42

Smith, Joseph
Sin corner and Joe Smith; a story of vice and corruption in Chicago. Forewords by Alderman Leon M. Despres and Jack Mabley. New York, Exposition Press [1963]
119p. 21cm.
Portrait of author on book jacket.

1. Chicago - Vice. 2. Vice - Chicago. 3. Chicago - Police-Investigation. 4. Criminal investigation - Chicago. I. Title.

M973
Sm6g

Smith, L T
A great truth in a nutshell. A few ancient and modern facts of the colored people, by one of their number, Rev. L.T. Smith. Part first. [n.p., n.p., n.d.]
vi, [7] 70p. 17½cm.

1. History I. Title

M811.5
Sm6

Smith, Lucy.
No middle ground, a collection of poems by Philadelphia, The Phila. Council Arts, Sciences and Professions, 1952.

29 p. 22 cm.

1. Poetry. I. Title.

Smith, Lucy, jt. auth.

M811.5
W93g

Wright, Sarah E
Give me a child, by Sarah E. Wright and Lucy Smith. Philadelphia, Kraft Publishing Company, 1955.

40p. illus. 27cm.

Nigeria
M966.9
B11

Smith, Mary Felice, 1924-
Baba *of Karo*, 1890 (ca.)-1951.
Baba of Karo, a woman of the Muslim Hausa. [Autobiography recorded] by M. F. Smith. With an introd. and notes by M. G. Smith; pref. by Daryll Forde. London, Faber and Faber [1954]

299 p. illus. 23 cm.

1. Hausas. 2. Women in Nigeria. I. Smith, Mary Felice, 1924-

DT515.B115 1954 54-4526 ‡

Library of Congress [56e2]

M231
Sm63

Smith, Paul Dewey
Man's relationship and duty to God. New York, Carlton press [1964]

546p. illus. 24cm. (A reflection book)

1. Bible - Interpretation (Mystical or spiritual). I. Title.

M370
Sm51e

Smith, Payson, 1873-
Education in the forty-eight states, by Payson Smith, Frank W. Wright and associates ... Prepared for the Advisory committee on education. Washington, U. S. Govt. print. off., 1939.

xv, 199 p. incl. tables. 23cm. ([U. S.] Advisory committee on education. Staff study no. 1)

Bibliographical foot-notes. "Publications of the committee": p. 199.

1. Education—U. S. I. ~~Wright, Frank Watson, 1880-~~ joint author. II. Title.

39—26774

Library of Congress L111.A93 no. 1
—— Copy 2. LA210.S53
[42x3] (370.973) 370.973

Smith, Ralph Lee, jt. auth.

M286
P36s

Pelt, Owen D
The story of the National Baptists, by Owen D. Pelt and Ralph Lee Smith. [1st ed.] New York, Vantage Press [1960]

272 p. illus. 22 cm.

Includes bibliography.

1. National Baptist Convention of the United States of America—Hist. I. Smith, Ralph Lee, joint author.

BX6443.P4 286.173 60-15470 ‡

Library of Congress [5]

Nigeria
M966.9
Aj11y

Smith, Robert Sydney.
Ajayi, J F Ade.
Yoruba warfare in the nineteenth century, by J. F. Ade Ajayi and Robert Smith. Cambridge [Eng.] University Press, 1964.

x, 160 p. maps, plans, plate. 23 cm.

Bibliography: p. 148-151. Bibliographical footnotes.

1. Yorubas. 2. Nigeria—Hist. I. Smith, Robert Sydney. II. Title.

DT513.A48 966.9 64-21522

Library of Congress [5]

M781
Sm64

Smith, Ruby R
The rudiments of music, step by step, by Ruby R. Smith. [1st ed.] New York, Vantage Press [1965]

71 p. illus., music. 21 cm.

Portrait of author on book jacket.

1. Music—Theory, Elementary. I. Title.

MT7.S673R8 781.2 64-24743/MN

Library of Congress [5]

M331 Sm6
Smith, Stanley Hugh.
Freedom to work. New York, Vantage Press [1955]
217 p. illus. 22 cm.
"Taken in part from ... [the author's] doctoral dissertation submitted at the State College of Washington, 1953."
1. Discrimination in employment—Washington (State) I. Title.
2. Employment.
HD4903.5.U6W27 331.11 54—11884 ‡
Library of Congress [55d5]

M326.99B Sm6n 1897
Smith, Venture, 1729–1805.
A narrative of the life and adventures of Venture, a native of Africa, but resident above sixty years in the United States of America. Related by himself, New London: Printed in 1798. Reprinted A. D. 1835, and published by a descendant of Venture. Rev. and republished with traditions by H. M. Selden, Haddam, Conn., 1896. Middletown, Conn., J. S. Stewart, printer, 1897.
iv, [5]–41 p. 23½cm.
1. Slavery in the U. S.—Connecticut. I. Selden, Henry M. II. Title.
Library of Congress E444.S66 4—17688
[a29c1]

M326.99B Sm6n 1835
Smith, Venture, 1729–1805.
A narrative of the life and adventures of Venture, a native of Africa, but resident above sixty years in the United States of America. Related by himself, New London: Printed in 1798. Reprinted A.D. 1835, and published by a descendant of Venture.
24p. 20cm.
1. Slavery in the U.S.-Connecticut. I. Selden, Henry M. II. Title 2. Slave narratives

M326.99B Sm6n 1798
Smith, Venture, 1729–1805.
A narrative of the life and adventures of Venture, a native of Africa, but resident above sixty years in the United States of America. Related by himself. New-London. Printed by C. Holt, at the Bee-Office, 1798.
32p. 22½cm.
1. Slavery in the U.S. - Connecticut. II. Title. 2. Slave narratives.

Smith, Wendell.
MB9 R56r
Robinson, John Roosevelt, 1919–
Jackie Robinson, my own story, as told to Wendell Smith; foreword by Branch Rickey. New York, Greenberg [1948]
170 p. illus., ports. 21 cm.
I. Smith, Wendell. II. Title.
GV865.R6A3 927.96357 48—6600*
Library of Congress [49u7]

M723 S71
Smith, Wilford H.
The Negro and the law.
(In: The Negro problem; a series of articles by representative American Negroes of today ... New York, J. Pott & co., 1903. 19cm. p.125-159)

M813.5 Sm68a
Smith, William Gardner, 1926–
Anger at innocence. New York, New American Library of American literature, 1951.
191p. 18cm.
A Signet book - paper back.
I. Title.
PZ3.S6638An 50—10194
Library of Congress [5]

M813.5 Sm68a
Smith, William Gardner, 1926–
Anger at innocence. New York, Farrar, Straus [1950]
300 p. 21 cm.
I. Title.
PZ3.S6638An 50-10194
Library of Congress [5]

M813.5 Sm681 1949
Smith, William Gardner, 1926–
Last of the conquerors. New York, New American Library, 1949.
191p. 18cm. (Signet books)
Pocket book edition.
I. Title.

M813.5 Sm681
Smith, William Gardner, 1926–
Last of the conquerors. New York, Farrar, Straus, 1948.
262p. 21cm.
I. Title.

M813.5 Sm681 1948
Smith, William Gardner, 1926–
Last of the conquerors. New York, The New American Library, 1948.
191p. 18cm. (A Signet Book)
I. Title.

M813.5 Sm68s
Smith, William Gardner, 1926–
South Street. New York, Farrar, Straus and Young [1954]
312 p. 21 cm.
I. Title.
PZ3.S6638So 54-5687 ‡
Library of Congress [7]

M813.5 Sm68st
Smith, William Gardner, 1926–
The stone face, a novel. New York, Farrar, Straus [1963]
213 p. 21 cm.
I. Title.
PZ3.S6638St 63–11184
Library of Congress [5]

M780 Sm68
Smith, Willie, 1897–
Music on my mind; the memoirs of an American pianist, by Willie the Lion Smith with George Hoefer. Foreword by Duke Ellington. [1st ed.] Garden City, N. Y., Doubleday, 1964.
xvi, 318 p. 22 cm.
Includes bibliographies, list of Willie Smith's compositions, and discography.
1. Musicians—Correspondence, reminiscences, etc. 2. Jazz music. I. Hoefer, George. II. Title.
ML417.S675A3 781.57 64–13840/MN
Library of Congress [5]

Smoking.
M394.1 W32p
Watkins, Sylvestre Cornelius, 1911– *comp.*
The pleasures of smoking as expressed by those poets, wits and tellers of tales who have drawn their inspiration from the fragrant weed. New York, H. Schuman [1948]
xii, 203 p. illus. 25 cm.
1. Smoking. I. Title.
GT3020.W37 394.1 48-9635*
Library of Congress [5]

M220 Sm71
Smothers, Felton C 1926–
I am the beginning and the ending; a book of excerpts from Genesis and the Revelations of St. John, The Divine. Edited and illustrated by Felton Smothers. New York, Carlton Press, 1961.
34p. illus. 21cm.
Portrait of author on book jacket.
1. Religion. I. Title. II. Bible. Selections.

Smuts, Jan Christiaan, 1870–
S. Africa
M968 T11
Tabata, I. B.
8 million demand freedom! What about it, Gen. Smuts? by I. B. Tabata. New York, Council on African Affairs, 1946.
23p. 20½cm.

U.S. M960 C76a
Smyth, John Henry, 1844–1908.
The African in Africa and the African in America.
Pp. 69-84.
In: Congress on Africa, Atlanta, 1895. Africa and the American Negro. Atlanta, Gamma Theological Seminary, 1896.

M301 R75
Smythe, Hugh Heyne, 1913–
Japan, by Keüchi Chikozawa and H.H. Smythe.
Pp. 979-92
In: J. S. Rouček's Contemporary Sociology. 1958.

M910 Sm9n
Smythe, Hugh Heyne, 1913–
The new Nigerian elite [by] Hugh H. Smythe and Mabel M. Smythe. Stanford, Calif., Stanford University Press, 1960.
ix, 196 p. map. 24 cm.
Bibliographical references included in "Notes" (p. [175]–191)
1. Upper classes—Nigeria. 2. Nigeria—Soc. condit. I. Smythe, Mabel M., joint author. II. Title.
HN800.N5S56 301.4409669 60—13870
Library of Congress [61r10]

M301 R75
Smythe, Hugh Heyne, 1913–
Race and intergroup relations.
Pp. 184-200
In: J.S. Rouček's Contemporary Sociology. 1958.

Smythe, Mabel M., jt auth

M910
Sm9n

Smythe, Hugh H
The new Nigerian elite [by] Hugh H. Smythe and Mabel M. Smythe. Stanford, Calif., Stanford University Press, 1960.

ix, 196 p. map. 24 cm.

Bibliographical references included in "Notes" (p. [175]-191)

1. Upper classes—Nigeria. 2. Nigeria—Soc. condit. I. Smythe, Mabel M., joint author. II. Title.

HN800.N5S56 301.4409669 60—13870

Library of Congress [61f10]

Sobel, Louis Harry, joint author.

M331
G76t

Granger, Lester Blackwell, 1896–
Toward job adjustment, with specific reference to the vocational problems of racial, religious and cultural minority groups, by Lester B. Granger ... Louis H. Sobel ... [and] William H. H. Wilkinson ... Prepared under the direction of Committee on minority groups, Section on employment and vocational guidance, Welfare council of New York city. [New York] Welfare council of New York city [°1941]

78 p., 1 l. illus. 21½cm.

Bibliography: 76-78. White author

1. Interviewing. 2. Employment agencies. 3. Minorities. I. Sobel, Louis Harry, joint author. II. Wilkinson, William H. H. III. Welfare council of New York city. Section on employment and vocational guidance. IV. Title.

Library of Congress HD5861.G65 41-16628

[10] 331.11511

Social and economic forces in Alabama reconstruction.

M973.8
R81r

Bond, Horace Mann, 1904–
Social and economic forces in Alabama reconstruction.

pp. 32-50.
In: Reconstruction in the South, by Edwin Charles Rozwenc. 1952.

M813.5
Sm9f

Smythwick, Charles A
False measure; a satirical novel of the lives and objectives of upper middle-class Negroes. New York, William-Frederick Press, 1954.

285 p. 22 cm.

I. Title.

PZ4.S668Fal 53-10280 ‡

Library of Congress [3]

Barbados
M796.358
Sol2c

Sobers, Garfield.
Cricket, advance! [By] Gary Sobers. [London] Pelham Books [1965]

109 p. illus., ports. 26 cm.

1. Cricket. I. Title.

GV917.S6 65-87615

Library of Congress [3]

Social case work.

M306
N21m

National Conference of Social Work.
Minority groups: segregation and integration. Papers presented at the 82d annual forum of the National Conference of Social Work. [Editorial Committee: Irving Weissman, chairman, Lois Clarke and others. Editorial work: Dorothy Swart] New York, Published for the National Conference of Social Work by Columbia University Press, 1955.

vi, 110 p. 24 cm.

1. Segregation—U. S. 2. Social case work. I. Title.

HV95.N35 1955 *301.45 325.73 56—5879

Library of Congress [56f15]

M39
Ed9t

Snow Hill normal and industrial institute, Snow Hill, Ala.
Edwards, William James, 1869–
Twenty-five years in the Black belt, by William J. Edwards ... Boston, The Cornhill company [°1918]

xvii p., 1 l., 143, [1] p. front. (port.) plates (incl. ports.) 19½ cm.

Autobiographical narrative and history of the Snow Hill normal and industrial institute, Snow Hill, Ala.

1. Snow Hill normal and industrial institute, Snow Hill, Ala. I. Title.

E185.82.E25 19—5302

Library of Congress [54e½]

Barbados
M796.358
Sol2

Sobers, Garfield.
Cricket crusader. [London] Pelham Books [1966]

171p. illus., ports. 22cm.

I. Title. 1. Cricket.

Social change - Case studies.

Africa, South
M968
V71

Vilakazi, Absolom.
Zulu transformations: a study of the dynamics of social change. Pietermaritzburg, University of Natal Press, 1962.

x, 168 p. maps, diagrs. 25 cm.

"Originally presented as a Ph. D. thesis to the University of Natal."
Bibliography: p. 163-165.

1. Zulus. 2. Social change—Case studies. I. Title.
3. Africa, South - Social life and customs.

DT878.Z9V5 63-36287

Library of Congress [3]

Snow Hill normal and industrial institute, Snow Hill, Ala.

M39
Ed9t

Edwards, William James, 1869–
Twenty-five years in the Black belt, by William J. Edwards ... Boston, The Cornhill company [°1918]

xvii p., 1 l., 143, [1] p. front. (port.) plates (incl. ports.) 19½cm.

Autobiographical narrative and history of the Snow Hill normal and industrial institute, Snow Hill, Ala.

1. Snow Hill normal and industrial institute, Snow Hill, Ala. I. Title.

Library of Congress E185.82.E25 19—5302

[44d1]

Sobers, Gary
see
Sobers, Garfield

Social-class influences upon learning.

M370
D29s

Davis, Allison, 1902–
Social-class influences upon learning. Cambridge, Harvard Univ. Press, 1948.

100 p. 18 cm. (The Inglis lecture, 1948)

1. Educational sociology. I. Title. (Series: The Inglis lectures, Harvard University, 1948)

Full name: William Allison Davis.

LC191.D36 370.193 48—9626*

Library of Congress [50z7]

U.S.
M839
Iv3s

The snow queen and other tales.
Andersen, Hans Christian
The snow queen and other tales. A new selection and translation with an introd. by Pat Shaw Iversen. Illustrated by Sheila Greenwold. New York, New American Library c1966.

318p. 18cm.
"A Signet book."

Nigeria
M966.9
N916

Sobo (African people).
Numa, Frederick Yamu, 1916–
The pride of Urhobo nation. Lagos, Ribway Press c1950.

56p. illus., port. 18cm.
Portrait of author in book.

Social club mu Afrika.

Uganda
M367
P85

Potts, C W K
Social club mu Afrika [Social club in East Africa] Kyakyusibwa F. B. Lubwama. Nairobi, Eagle Press, 1953.

32p. 22½cm.
Written in Luganda.
White author.

1. Africa, East - Clubs. 2. Clubs. I. Title
II. Lubwama, F. B., tr.

M813.5
L96s

So low, so lonely.
Lucas, Curtis
So low, so lonely. New York, Lion Books, Inc. 1952.

158p. 16½cm.

O sobrinho do general.

Brazil
M869.3
Iv7s

Ivo, Lêdo, 1924–
O sobrinho do general. Rio de Janeiro, Editôra Civilização Brasileira [1964]

124p. 18cm. (Novela Brasileira, v.3)

I. Title.

Social conditions.

M301
C83

Covington, Matilda N
A brighter tomorrow; how to live better in every area of human endeavor. New York, Exposition Press [1963]

79p. 21cm.

So you're going to fly.

M623.74
P33s

Peck, James L H.
So you're going to fly, by James L. H. Peck ... with official photographs and diagrams by the author. New York, Dodd, Mead & company, 1941.

xiv, 241 p. front., illus., plates, diagrs. 21cm.

Bibliography: p. 239-241.

1. Aeroplanes—Piloting. 2. Aeronautics, Military. I. Title.

41—51786

Library of Congress TL710.P4

[43f5] 629.1325

Socé, Ousmane, pseud.
see
Diop, Ousmane Socé, 1911–

Social conditions.

M306
N21p

Johnson, Mordecai Wyatt, 1890–
The Negro and his relationships.

(In: National Conference of Social Work. Proceedings, 1937. Chicago, University of Chicago Press, 1937. 23cm. p.56-70)

Social conditions.

M309
P949

Provost, C Antonio, 1910–

The birth of the modern renaissance (and the rise of the U. S. A.) by C. Antonio Provost. Illus. ₍by₎ Art Henkel. ₍1st ed.₎ New York, Pageant Press ₍1965–

v. illus. 21 cm.

Bibliographical footnotes.

1. U. S.—Moral conditions. 2. U. S.—Soc. condit. I. Title.

HN65.P7 309.173 65–29725

Library of Congress ₍2₎

M301
R56t

Social conditions.

Robinson, James Herman.

Tomorrow is today. Philadelphia, Christian Education Press ₍1954₎

127 p. 22 cm.

1. Social conditions. I. Title.

HN18.R57 *301.23 301.153 54–11556 ‡

Library of Congress ₍2₎

Social conditions.- Addresses, essays, lectures.

M973
D541

Diamond, Sigmund, *ed.*

The Nation transformed; the creation of an industrial society. Selected and edited, with introd. and notes by Sigmund Diamond. New York, G. Braziller, 1963.

xiv, 528 p. 24 cm.

Bibliography: p. 524–528.

1. U. S.—Soc. condit.—Addresses, essays, lectures. 2. U. S.—Civilization—Addresses, essays, lectures. I. Title.

HN57.D53 309.173 63–17876

Library of Congress ₍67n4₎

M323
N21a

Social Equality.

National Association for the Advancement of Colored People.

An appeal to the world; A statement on the denial of human rights to minorities in the case of citizens of Negro descent in the United States of America and An appeal to the United Nations for redress. Prepared for the National Association for the Advancement of Colored People, under the editorial supervision of W.E. Burghardt Du Bois. New York, 1947.

94p. tables. 21cm.

A social history of the American Negro.

M310
B73so

Brawley, Benjamin Griffith, 1882–1939.

A social history of the American Negro, being a history of the Negro problem in the United States, including a history and study of the republic of Liberia, by Benjamin Brawley. New York, The Macmillan company, 1921.

xv, 420 p. 22½ cm.

"Select bibliography": p. 390–408.

1. Negroes. 2. Slavery in the U. S. 3. U. S.—Race question. 4. Liberia. I. Title.

Library of Congress E185.61.B82 21–15578

₍a43g1₎

Social life and customs.

M301
H22

Hare, Nathan.

The black Anglo-Saxons. With an introd. by Oliver C. Cox. ₍1st ed. New York₎ Marzani & Munsell ₍1965₎

124 p. 22 cm.

Bibliographical references included in footnotes.

1. Negroes—Soc. life & cust. 2. Class distinction. 3. Assimilation (Sociology) I. Title.

E185.86.H3 301.45196073 65–18681

Library of Congress ₍5₎

M973
R14

Soc. life & cust.

Ramos, Arthur, 1903–1949.

... As culturas negras no novo mundo ... Rio de Janeiro, Civilização brasileira, s/a., 1937.

399, ₍1₎ p. illus. (maps) plates, diagr. 18½ cm. (Bibliotheca de divulgação scientifica, sob a direcção de Arthur Ramos. vol. XII)

1. Negroes in America. 2. Negro race—Soc. life & cust. 3. Negro race—Religion. 4. Folk-lore, Negro. I. Title.

₍*Full name:* Arthur Ramos de Araujo Pereira₎

38–12715

Library of Congress E29.N3R3

₍a44e1₎ 325.26097

Puerto Rico Social life and conditions.
M301
R72

Rosario, Jose Colomban

Problemas sociales; el Negro: Haiti-Estados Unidos-Puerto Rico, por Jose Colomban Rosario y Justina Carrion. San Juan, Negociado de Materiales, Imprenta y Transporte, 1940.

174p. 21cm. (Universidad de Puerto Rico. Boletim, series X, no. 2, December 1939)

Bibliography: p. 161-165.

M973
R47

Social life and customs.

Ringel, Frederick Julius, 1904– ed.

America as Americans see it, edited by Fred J. Ringel; illustrated by over 100 American artists. New York, Harcourt, Brace and co. ₍c1932₎

xviii, 365p. front., illus. (incl. facsim.) plates, ports. 22cm.

First edition.

Partial contents: -Black America, by W.E.B. DuBois; Introduced by Walter White. -Back to Africa by Robert L. Ephraim. -The creative Negro, by James Weldon Johnson; Introduced by Countee Cullen.

Senegal Social medicine.
M610
Sa58

Sankalé, Marc

Médecine sociale au Sénégal, par Marc Sankalé et Pierre Pène. Dakar, Afrique documents, 1960.

104p. illus., map. 24cm. (Cahiers documents, no. 1, March 1960)

Includes bibliography.

Social philosophy for the new Nigeria nation.

Nigeria
M966.9
IL18

Ilogu, Edmund

Social philosophy for the new Nigeria nation. Onitsha, Etudo Limited ₍1962₎

42p. 21½cm.

Social policy.

Ghana
M966.7
G16d
1959

Gardiner, Robert Kweku Atta.

The development of social administration ₍by₎ Robert Kweku Gardiner ₍and₎ Helen O. Judd. 2d ed. London, Oxford University Press, 1959.

208 p. 19 cm.

Includes bibliography.

1. Social policy. 2. Africa, West—Social policy. 3. Gt. Brit.—Social policy. I. Judd, Helen O., joint author. II. Title.

HN18.G29 1959 309.166 60–2188 ‡

Library of Congress ₍61c5₎

Social policy.

Ghana
M966.7
C16d

Gardiner, Robert Kweku Atta.

The development of social administration ₍by₎ Robert Kweku Gardiner ₍and₎ Helen O. Judd. London, Oxford University Press, 1954.

208 p. 19 cm.

1. Social policy. 2. Africa, West—Social policy. 3. Gt. Brit.—Social policy. I. Judd, Helen O., joint author. II. Title.

HN18.G29 56–1903 ‡

Library of Congress ₍8₎

M371.974 Social problems.
Sol3

Desegregation in the public schools.

Consulting editor for the symposium: Kenneth B. Clark. New York, The Society for the Study of Social Problems, 1955.

pp. 197-242.

Issue of Social problems, v.2, no. 4, April 1955.

Partial contents.- Introduction, by Kenneth B. Clark.- Desegregation and social change, by Ira De A. Reid.- The role of the

(Continued on next card)

M371.974 Social problems. Desegregation in the
Sol3 public schools. 1955. (Card 2).

Partial contents - continued.

the NAACP, by Roy Wilkins.- Legal background of the May 17th decision, By Robert L. Carter.- Conclusions, by Kenneth B. Clark.

1. Segregation in education. I. Title.
II. Clark, Kenneth Bancroft, ed.

Social problems.

M814.5
G82

Green, Kirkland W

Fools of the earth; a study of the influence of negative thinking in our time. ₍1st ed.₎ New York, Exposition Press ₍1954₎

138 p. 21 cm.

1. Social problems. I. Title.

HN18.G68 301.15 54–9994 ‡

Library of Congress ₍2₎

M973.9
F46
No.10

Social problems.

Johnson, Charles Spurgeon, 1893–

Fifty years of progress in social development. Pittsburgh, Pittsburgh Courier, 1950.

7p. port. 24cm. (Fifty years of progress)

Social problems in literature.

M810.8
Am3w

American writers' congress, *New York,* **1935.**

American writers' congress, edited by Henry Hart. New York, International publishers ₍°1935₎

viii, 9–192 p. 20cm.

"A congress of American revolutionary writers ... held in New York city on April 26, 27 and 28, 1935."—p. 10.

1. Authors, American — Congresses. 2. American literature — 20th cent.—Hist. & crit. 3. Proletariat. 4. Social problems in literature. I. Hart, Henry, 1903– ed.

35–36744

Library of Congress PS7.A6 1935

——— Copy 2.

Copyright A 88480 ₍36f5₎ 810.6373

Social psychology.

M323
D29c

Davis, Allison, 1902–

Children of bondage; the personality development of Negro youth in the urban South, by Allison Davis and John Dollard, prepared for the American youth commission. Washington, D. C., American council on education, 1940.

xxviii, 299, ₍1₎ p., 1 l. diagrs. 23½cm.

Illustration mounted on cover.

1. Negroes—Moral and social conditions. 2. Personality. 3. Social psychology. I. *Dollard, John, 1900– joint author. II. American council on education. American youth commission. III. Title.

₍*Full name:* William Allison Davis₎

40–13685

Library of Congress E185.86.D38

₍a45r41j²10₎ 325.260975

Social psychology.

M301
F86 ny

Frazier, Edward Franklin, 1894–

Negro youth at the crossways, their personality development in the middle states, by E. Franklin Frazier; prepared for the American youth commission. Washington, D. C., American council on education, 1940.

xxiii, 301, ₍2₎ p. illus. (maps) diagr. 23½ cm.

"This volume ... describes the experiences of Negro boys and girls living in Washington, D. C., and Louisville, Kentucky; these communities were selected as examples of middle-area conditions."—Pref.

1. Negroes—Moral and social conditions. 2. Youth. 3. Personality. 4. Social psychology. 5. Negroes—District of Columbia. 6. Negroes—Louisville, Ky. I. American council on education. American youth commission. II. Title.

40–32764

Library of Congress E185.6.F74

₍42z²7₎ 325.2609753

Social science research council.

M331
L58

Lewis, Edward Erwin, 1900–

The mobility of the Negro; a study in the American labor supply, by Edward E. Lewis ... New York, Columbia university press; London, P. S. King & son, ltd., 1931.

144 p. illus. (maps) 23cm. (*Half-title:* Studies in history, economics and public law, ed. by the Faculty of political science of Columbia university, no. 342)

Published also as thesis (PH. D.) Columbia university.

"The third volume to appear as a result of studies in the field of Negro migration under grants by the Social science research council and the Columbia university Council for research in the social sciences."—Foreword.

"Selected bibliography": p. 134–135.

1. Negroes. 2. Negroes — Employment. 3. Southern states — Econ. condit.—1918– 4. Cotton growing and manufacture—Southern states. I. Social science research council. II. Columbia university. Council for research in the social sciences. III. Title.

Library of Congress H31.C7 no. 342 31–29612

——— Copy 2. E185.8.L47

₍42q2₎ (306.2) 331.6

Social sciences.
M378 D22
Daniel, Walter Green, 1905–
The reading interests and needs of Negro college freshmen regarding social science materials, by Walter Green Daniel ... New York, Teachers college, Columbia university, 1942.
2 p. l., vii–xii p., 1 l., 128 p. incl. tables. 23½cm. (Teachers college, Columbia university. Contributions to education, no. 862)
Bibliography: p. [101]–105. "Titles with authors included in the check list of books relating to social science problems": p. 125–128.
1. Books and reading. 2. Social sciences. 3. Negroes—Education. I. Title.
Library of Congress H62.D28 43—8715
——— Copy 2. LB5.C8 no. 862
[43k5] 307.11753

Socialism.
M816.5 B63
Bohannan, William E.
A Letter to American Negroes. N.Y., Pioneer publishers for the Socialist Workers Party, 1948.
3-15p. 20cm.

Socialism.
M335 W85d
Woodbey, G W
The distribution of wealth, by Rev. G.W. Woodbey... [San Diego, Calif., G.W. Woodbey, 1910.
68p. front. 15cm.

Social sciences–Collections.
M972.9 H83e
Howard university, *Washington, D. C. Graduate school. Division of the social sciences.*
Annual conference.
Washington, D. C., Howard university press, 19
v. 23cm.
Proceedings of the conference.
Issue for 1948 has also distinctive title: The economic future of the Caribbean.
1. Social sciences—Collections. I. Title: The economic future of the Caribbean.
Library of Congress H22.H6 46—46001
[46d2] 330.82

Socialism.
M335 D85
DuBois, William Edward Burghardt, 1868–
Socialism today. [Chicago, Afro-American Heritage Association, 1959]
9p. 18cm.
Portrait on cover.
At head of title: Rejoice not in standing still. A Negro speak of a new world.
Cover title.
1. Socialism. I. Title.

Africa M960 Af78
Socialism in Africa.
Africa's freedom [by] Albert Luthuli [and others] London, Unwin Books [1964]
94p. 18½cm.

M06 Am3 no.2
Social sciences–Miscellanea.
Du Bois, William Edward Burghardt, 1868–
... The conservation of races. By W. E. Burghardt Du Bois. Washington, D. C., The Academy, 1897.
15 p. 23cm. (American negro academy. Occasional papers, no. 2)
1. Social sciences—Miscellanea. 2. U. S.—Race question. 3. Negroes. I. Title.
Library of Congress E184.N3A5 9—24192
——— Copy 2. [a38b1]

Socialism.
M331 J129p
Jackson, Charles.
A practical program to kill jim crow. 2nd ed. enl. New York, Pioneer Publishers for the Socialist Workers Party, 1945.
3-22p. illus. 20cm.

Ghana M335 N65
Socialism in Africa.
Nkrumah, Kwame, Pres. Ghana, 1909–
Consciencism; philosophy and ideology for decolonization and development with particular reference to the African revloution. New York, Monthly Review Press [1965, °1964]
vi, 122p. 23cm.

Haiti M360 H61t
Social service.
Hippolyte, Simone W , 1918–
Travail social; panorama et details. [Port-au-Prince] Imp. Les presses libres, 1951.
141p. port. 20cm.

Trinidad M820 J23in
Socialism.
[James, Cyril Lionel Robert] 1901–
The invading socialist society, by [C.L. R. James] J. R. Johnson, F. Forest, and Ria Stone. New York, Johnson-Forest Tendency, 1947.
63p. 21cm.

Senegal M335 Se5
Socialism in Africa – Addresses, essays, lectures.
Senghor, Léopold Sédar.
On African socialism. Translated and with an introd. by Mercer Cook. New York, Praeger [1964]
xv, 173 p. 21 cm.
Bibliographical references included in "Notes" (p. 167–173)
CONTENTS.—Nationhood: report on the doctrine and program of the Party of African Federation.—The African road to socialism.—The theory and practice of Senegalese socialism.
1. Senegal—Pol. & govt.—Addresses, essays, lectures. 2. Mali—Pol. & govt.—Addresses, essays, lectures. 3. Socialism in Africa—Addresses, essays, lectures. I. Title.
JQ3396.A91S4 1964 64—16419
Library of Congress [64f4]

Social service.
M306 N214f
National Urban League (for Social Service among Negroes)
40th anniversary year book, 1950. [New York, 1951]
128 p. illus. 29 cm.
1. Negroes.
E185.5.N33F67 325.260973 52-69 ‡
Library of Congress [12]

Socialism.
Sénégal M966.3 Se5nt
Senghor, Léopold Sédar, 1906–
Nation et voie Africaine du socialisme. Paris, Présence Africaine, 1961.
138p. 21½cm.

Socialism today.
M335 D85
DuBois, William Edward Burghardt, 1868–
Socialism today. [Chicago, Afro-American Heritage Association, 1959]
9p. 18cm.
Portrait on cover.
At head of title: Rejoice not in standing still. A Negro speak of a new world.
Cover title.
1. Socialism. I. Title.

Social surveys.
M362.7 Sa5
Sanders, Wiley Britton, 1898– ed.
Negro child welfare in North Carolina, a Rosenwald study, directed by Wiley Britton Sanders ... under the joint auspices of the North Carolina State board of charities and public welfare and the School of public welfare, the University of North Carolina. Chapel Hill, Pub. for the North Carolina State board of charities and public welfare by the University of North Carolina press, 1933.
xiv p., 2 l., [3]–326 p. 24cm.
1. Negroes—North Carolina. 2. Negroes—Moral and social conditions. 3. Charities—North Carolina. 4. Children—Charities, protection, etc.—North Carolina. 5. Juvenile delinquency—North Carolina. 6. Social surveys I. North Carolina. State board of charities and public welfare. II. North Carolina. University. School of public welfare. III. Title.
Library of Congress E185.93.N6S27 33—18006
[45t1] 325.2609756

Socialism in Africa.
Nigeria M335 On9
Onuoha, Bede
The elements of African socialism. [London] Andre Deutsch [1965]
139p. 22½cm.
Includes bibliography.
1. Socialism – Africa. 2. Africa – Socialism. I. Title.

Socialist Workers Party.
M816.5 B63
Bohannan, William E.
A Letter to American Negroes. N.Y., Pioneer publishers for the Socialist Workers Party, 1948.
3-15p. 20cm.

Social surveys.
M309.1 Sp3
Spellman, Cecil Lloyd, 1906–
Elm city, a Negro community in action. Tallahassee, Florida A. and M. College, 1947.
75p. tables, maps. 28cm.

Socialism.
Senegal M966.3 Se5nt2
Senghor, Léopold Sédar, 1906–
Nationhood and the African road to socialism. Translated by Mercer Cook. Paris, Presence Africaine [1962]
130p. 21½cm.
Includes bibliography.
1. Africa. 2. Socialism. I. Title. II. Cook, Mercer, tr.

Socialist workers party.
M350 J62
Johnson, J R
Why Negroes should oppose the war, by J. R. Johnson ... [New York, Pub. by Pioneer publishers for the Socialist workers party and the Young people's socialist league (Fourth International) 1939?]
30, [1] p. 21cm.
1. World war, 1939– —Negroes. I. Socialist workers party. II. Young people's socialist league of America. III. Title.
Library of Congress D810.N4J57 44—12148
[2] 940.5403

Socialist Workers Party.

M335.4 Sa8s

Saunders, John.
The struggle for Negro equality; Program of the Socialist Workers Party, by John Saunders and Albert Parker. New York, Pioneer Publishers for the Socialist Workers Party, 1943.

30p. 22cm.

Haiti
M972.94 Solt

La Société Haitienne d'etudes scientifiques.
Travaux du Congres international de philosophie, consacre aux problemes de la connaissance, organised par la société haitienne d'etudes scientifiques et tenu a Port-au-Prince du 24 au 30 Septembre 1944. Sous les auspices du Gouvernement Haitien. Port-au-Prince, Imp. de l'etat, 1947.
447p. 22cm.

1. Haiti. I. Congres International de Philosophie.
II. DuBois, William E. B. -Message,

Société Toussaint - Louverture.

Haiti
M972.94 T64t

Toussaint Louverture, Pierre Dominique, 1746?-1803.
Toussaint Louverture et l'independance de Saint-Dominigue; explication par des documents des traités secrets entre Toussaint-Louverture, les Etats-Unis d'Amérique et l'Angleterre. Port-au-Prince, Société d'Edition et de Librairie, 1946.

145p. 23½cm.
Special number of Le Document, 20 Mai 1946; published under the patronage of the Société Toussaint-Louverture.

Societies.

M06 Am3 no.18, 19

American Negro academy, *Washington, D. C.*
Papers of the American Negro academy ... read at the nineteenth annual meeting of the American Negro academy ... Washington, D. C., December 28th and 29th, 1915. [Washington, 1916]
78 p. 22cm. (Occasional papers, no. 18/19)
CONTENTS.—The sex question and race segregation, by A. H. Grimke.—Message of San Domingo to the African race, by T. G. Steward.—Status of the free Negro prior to 1860, by L. M. Hershaw.—Economic contribution by the Negro to America, by A. A. Schomberg [!]—The status of the free Negro from 1860 to 1870, by William Pickens.—American Negro bibliography of the year, by J. W. Cromwell.
1. Negroes—Societies. 2. Negroes—Bibl. I. Grimke, Archibald Henry, 1849–1930. II. Steward, Theophilus Gould, 1843– III. Hershaw, Lafayette M. IV. Schomburg, Arthur Alfonso, 1874– V. Pickens, William, 1881– VI. Cromwell, John Wesley, 1846–
[r42b2] 16-17783 Revised
Library of Congress E185.5.A51 no. 18/19
——— Copy 2. E185.5.A525

Societies..

M366 B81h

Brown, Sue M (Wilson) "*Mrs.* S. Joe Brown," 1877–
The history of the Order of the eastern star among colored people, by Mrs. S. Joe Brown ... Des Moines, Ia. [The Bystander press] 1925.
3 p. l., [13]–88 p., 1 l. front., plates, ports. 18½cm.

1. Order of the eastern star (Colored) 2. Negroes—Societies.

Library of Congress HS895.E33 1925 25-10755
Copyright A 830384 [2]

Societies.

M304 P19 V.6,no.2

National Afro-American council.
The National Afro-American council, organized 1898. A history of the organization, its objects, synopses of proceedings, constitution and by-laws, plan of organization, annual topics, etc. Comp. by Cyrus Field Adams, secretary ... Washington, D. C., C. F. Adams, 1902.
29, [2] p. 23cm.

1. Negroes—Societies. I. Adams, Cyrus Field, comp.

12-2868
Library of Congress E185.5.N27
[41b1]

Socities.

M368.3 St46

Stuart, Merah Steven, 1878–
An economic detour; a history of insurance in the lives of American Negroes, by M. S. Stuart ... New York, W. Malliet and company, 1940.
xxv, 339 p., 6 l. front., illus. (facsims.) plates, ports. 23½cm.
"Errata" slip inserted.
"First edition."
Bibliography: p. 337-338.

1. Insurance, Life—U. S.—Hist. 2. Negroes—Societies. 3. Negroes—Econ. condit. I. Title.

41-1573
Library of Congress HG8799.S75
[44h2] 368.30973

Societies, Beneficial.

M306 B79c

Brotherly union society.
Constitution and by-laws of the Brotherly Union Society. Instituted April 1823. Philadelphia, William Brown, 1833.
31p. 10½ x 7½cm.

Societies, Literary

M806 P83o

Porter, Dorothy Burnett, 1905-
The organized educational activities of Negro literary societies, 1828-1846. Reprinted from The Journal of Negro education, October, 1936.
555 - 576p. 25cm.

Bahamas
M332 Sm6n

Society.
Smith, James C.
The National providence; essays, by Jas. C. Smith... London, Kegan Paul, Trench, Trubner & Co., 1910.

vi, 1 l. 103p. 21½cm.

Kenya
M967.65 K4?f...

Society, Primitive.

Kenyatta, Jomo.
Facing mount Kenya: the tribal life of Gikuyu, by Jomo Kenyatta, with an introduction by B. Malinowski ... London, Secker and Warburg [1938]
xxv, [1], 339 p. illus. (incl. map) VIII pl. (incl. front. (port.)) 22½cm.
"First published 1938."
"Glossary": p. 319-329.

1. Kikuyu tribe. 2. Ethnology—Africa, East. 3. Society, Primitive. I. Title.

39-8764
Library of Congress DT434.E2K45
[40c2] 572.96765

Society, Primitive.

Kenya
M967.65 K42f4

Kenyatta, Jomo
I skyggen af Mount Kenya [Facing Mount Kenya. Omslaget tegnet af Waldemar Swierzy. Copenhagen] Munksgaard [1964]
256p. 18½cm.
Written in Danish.

1. Kikuyu tribe. 2. Ethnology - Africa, East. 3. Society, Primitive. 4. Africa, East. I. Title.

Society for promoting the emigration of free persons of colour to Hayti.

M972.94 D51c

[Dewey, Loring Daniel] 1791–1867.
Correspondence relative to the emigration to Hayti, of the free people of colour, in the United States. Together with the instructions to the agent sent out by President Boyer. New-York, Printed by M. Day, 1824.
32 p. 22cm.
[Miscellaneous pamphlets, v. 295, no. 4]
Correspondence of Loring D. Dewey and Jean Pierre Boyer, president of Haiti; published by the former.
This proposition to promote the emigration of negroes to Haiti was submitted by Dewey to the American colonization society, but the society rejected it. A new society was organized in June 1824 under the name: Society for promoting the emigration of free persons of colour to Hayti. For reports of the meetings *cf.* p. 28–32.
1. Negroes—Colonization—Haiti. 2. Haiti—Emig. & immig. I. Boyer, Jean Pierre, pres. Haiti, 1776–1850. II. Society for promoting the emigration of free persons of colour to Hayti. III. Title.
[44b1]
Library of Congress AC901.M5 vol. 295 17—5264

M378 B81s

Socio-economic approach to educational problems.
Brown, Ina Corinne, 1896-
Socio-economic approach to educational problems, by Ina Corinne Brown, with an introduction by Fred J. Kelly. Washington, U.S. Govt. Print. Off., 1942.

xii, 166p. maps, tables, diagrs.
(U.S. Office of Education. Miscellaneous no.6)
At head of title: National survey of the higher education of Negroes, v.1.

Sociological survey...

M974.4 D35s

DeBerry, William Nelson 1870-
Sociological survey of the Negro population of Springfield, Mass., edited by William N. DeBerry. Springfield, Mass., The Dunbar community league 1940

15 1 p. tables. 20½cm.

M306 Sol 1913

Sociology - Congresses.
Southern sociological congress. *2d, Atlanta,* 1913.
The human way. Addresses on race problems at the Southern sociological congress, Atlanta, 1913. Edited by James E. McCulloch. Nashville, Southern sociological congress, 1913.
146 p. 24cm.
Also included in "The South mobilizing for social service: addresses delivered at the Southern sociological congress", Nashville, 1913.
Bibliography: p. [144]–146.

1. Negroes. 2. Sociology—Congresses. I. McCulloch, James Edward, 1873– ed. II. Title.

Agr 13-1850
U. S. Dept. of agr. Library for Library of Congress 280So8 E185.61.S72
[a38d1]

Sociology - History.

M301 R75

Roucek, Joseph Slabey, 1902– *ed.*
Contemporary sociology. New York, Philosophical Library [1958]
xii, 1209 p. illus. 24 cm.
Includes bibliographies and bibliographical references.

1. Sociology—Hist.

HM19.R6 301 58—59414
Library of Congress [60q10]

Sociology, Bibical.

M200 O13n

Oliver, C Herbert, 1925–
No flesh shall glory. [Nutley, N. J.] Presbyterian and Reformed Pub. Co., 1959.
96 p. 21 cm.

1. Race. 2. Segregation—Religious aspects. 3. Sociology, Biblical. I. Title.

BT734.O4 261.83 59-14513 ‡
Library of Congress [2]

M200. T42j

Sociology. Biblical.
Thurman, Howard, 1899–
Jesus and the disinherited. New York, Abingdon-Cokesbury Press [1949]
112 p. 20 cm.
"The ... study of which this book is the full development was presented as the Mary L. Smith memorial lectures at Samuel Huston College, Austin, Texas, in April, 1948."

1. Jesus Christ—Teachings. 2. Sociology, Biblical. I. Title.

BS2417.S7T5 232.9 49-8371*
Library of Congress [20]

Sociology, Biblical.

M200 T42r

Thurman, Howard, 1899-
The religion of Jesus and the disinherited.

(In: Johnson, Thomas Herbert, ed. In defense of democracy. New York, Putnam, 1949. 21cm. p.125-135)

Sociology, Christian.

M260 M45g

Mays, Benjamin Elijah, 1895– , comp.
A gospel for the social awakening; selections from the writings of Walter Rauschenbusch, compiled by Benjamin E. Mays, with an introd. by C. Howard Hopkins. New York, Association Press, 1950.
187 p. 20 cm. (A Haddam House book)
Bibliography: p. [6]

1. Sociology, Christian. I. Title.

BR115.S6R38 208.1 51-1462
Library of Congress [10]

Sociology, Rural.

M370
T36s

Thomasson, Maurice Ethan, 1892–
A study of special kinds of education for rural Negroes ₍by₎ Maurice E. Thomasson ... Charlotte, N. C., 1936.
vi, 104 p., 1 l., 23cm.
Thesis (PH. D.)—Columbia university, 1936.
Vita.
"This study was concerned with agencies which offered instruction in fields other than those ordinarily included in the regular public school program ... Researches were conducted ... in the state of Virginia."—p. 2.
Bibliography: p. ₍103₎–104.
1. Negroes—Education. 2. Negroes—Virginia. 3. Sociology, Rural. I. Title: Education for rural Negroes. II. Title: Rural Negroes.
36—21306
Library of Congress LC2802.V8T5 1936
Columbia Univ. Libr. ₍37c2₎ 371.97409755

Sociology, Rural.

M973.
W86 r

Woodson, Carter Godwin, 1875–
The rural Negro, by Carter Godwin Woodson. Washington, D. C., The Association for the study of Negro life and history, inc. ₍©1930₎
xvi p., 1 l., 265 p. illus. (incl. map) 22cm.
"Another by-product of the three-year survey of the social and economic conditions of the Negroes of the United States since the civil war ... undertaken by the Association for the study of Negro life and history in 1926."—Introd.
1. Negroes—Moral and social conditions. 2. Negroes—Employment. 3. Sociology, Rural. 4. Country life—U. S. I. Association for the study of Negro life and history, inc. II. Title.
30—21077
Library of Congress E185.86.W896
₍43u²2₎ 325.26

Jamaica
M972.92
P27

The sociology of slavery.
Patterson, Orlando.
The sociology of slavery: an analysis of the origins, development and structure of Negro slave society in Jamaica. London, MacGibbon & Kee₍1967₎
310 p. 4 plates (incl. 3 maps), tables. 22½ cm. (Studies in society) 63/-
Bibliography: p. 297-301. (B 67-8966)
1. Slavery in Jamaica. I. Title. (Series)
HT1096.P3 301.45'22'097292 67-86315
Library of Congress ₍3₎

M222.11
T14s

A Socratic exposition of Genesis.
Talley, Marshall Alexander.
A Socratic exposition of Genesis; a study of the book of Genesis in the light of modern thought and of New Testament interpretation designed especially for the advancement of the cause of religious education, by Marshall A. Talley ... ₍Indianapolis, ©1935₎
365 p. 19½cm.
1. Bible. O. T. Genesis—Examinations, questions, etc. 2. Bible—Examinations, questions, etc.—O. T. Genesis. I. Title.
35-13797
Library of Congress BS1227.T3
——— Copy 2.
Copyright A 85422 ₍2₎ 222.11

Madagascar
M843
B46s

La soeur inconnue.
Bézoro, Edouard.
La soeur inconnue.
Paris, Editions Eugéne Figuiere ₍c1932₎
184p. 18cm.

Nigeria
M896.2
So2W

Sofola, Samuel Adeniyi.
When a philosopher falls in love. New York, Comet Press Books ₍1956₎
210 p. 21 cm.
A play.
I. Title.
PR6037.O48W5 822.91 56-5954 ‡
Library of Congress ₍3₎

S.Africa
M968
So21a

Soga, John Henderson, 1860–1941.
The Ama-Xosa: life and customs, by John Henderson Soga ... Lovedale, C. P., South Africa, Lovedale press; London, K. Paul, Trench, Trubner & co., ltd. ₍1932₎
xvii p., 3 l., 5-431, ₍1₎ p. front., illus. (plan, map) plates, ports. 24½cm.
1. Kafirs (African people) 2. Bantus. I. Title.
32—35354
Library of Congress DT764.K286
₍a40d1₎ 572.9686

S.Africa
M896
So21s

Soga, John Henderson, 1860-1941
The south-eastern Bantu (Abe-Nguni, Aba-Mbo, Ama-Lala) by J. Henderson Soga. Johannesburg, The Witwatersrand university press, 1930.
xxxi, 490 p., 1 l. front. (port.) map, geneal. tables (part fold.) 22cm. (*Half-title:* "Bantu studies" ... Supplement no. 4)
Errata leaf inserted between p. ₍xxiv₎ and ₍xxv₎
"Editor's introduction" and "A biographical note on the author" signed: R. F. A. H. ₍*i. e.* Reinhold Friedrich Alfred Hoernlé₎
Bibliography: p. ₍xxi₎–xxiii.
1. Bantus. I. Hoernlé, Reinhold Friedrich Alfred, 1880– ed. II. Title.
32-6775
Library of Congress DT764.B286
₍3₎ 572.968

S. Africa
M896
So21in

Soga, John Henderson, 1860-1941, tr.
Inkokeli yomhambi, osuka ekufeni esiya ebomini. Lovedale, South Africa, Lovedale Press, n.d. (1925?).
226 ₍1₎ p.

S. Africa
M968
So21i

Soga, John Henderson, 1860-1941
Inkonzo zamabandla ka-Krestu. Umalatiso wokuqutya kwe-nkonzo, kunye nezimiselo eziya kuba luncedo kubapatiswa be-lizwi lika-Tixo, nakuma-bandla e-nkosi u-Yesu Krestu. Lovedale, South Africa, Lovedale Press, 1934.
104p. 19cm.
"How to conduct a religious service."
1. Africa, South - Religion.

S. Africa
M896
So2u

Soga, John Henderson, 1860-1941, tr.
Uhambo lomhambi. ₍ Part Two. Written by John Bunyan; translated into Xhosa by John Henderson Soga.₎ London, Society for Promoting Christian Knowledge, 1929.
190p. 18½cm.
Bound together with Tiyo Soga's Uhambo lo mhambi. Part One. See card for fuller entry.

S. Africa
M896
So2u

Soga, Tiyo, 1829-1871, tr.
Uhambo lo mhambi, owesuka kweli lizwe, waye esinga kwelo lizayo. Written by John Bunyan. Part One translated into Xhosa by Tiyo Soga. Part Two translated by John Henderson Soga. Lovedale, Lovedale Press, n.d. (1929).
186 ₍1₎; 190p. 18½cm.
Parts I and II bound together as one vol.

Soga, Tiyo, 1829-1871

S. Africa
M896
So2chu

Soga, Tiyo Burnside, 1869-1938, tr.
U-Tiyo Soga; incwadi yobom bake.
₍Written by John A. Chalmers, translated into Xhosa by Tiyo Burnside Soga.₎
Lovedale, Lovedale Institution Press, 1923.
xvi, 158p. port. 18½cm.
Translation of J. A. Chalmer's Life of Tiyo Soga.

S. Africa
M896
So21

Soga, Tiyo Burnside, 1869-1938
Intlalo ka Xosa. Lovedale, South Africa, Lovedale Press, n.d. (1927?).
xi, 250p. 21½cm.
"Customs and beliefs."
1. Africa, South - Social life and customs.

S. Africa
M896
So2chu

Soga, Tiyo Burnside, 1869-1938, tr.
U-Tiyo Soga; incwadi yobom bake.
₍Written by John A. Chalmers, translated into Xhosa by Tiyo Burnside Soga.₎
Lovedale, South Africa, Lovedale Institution Press, 1923.
xvi, 158p. port. 18½cm.
Translation of J.A. Chalmer's Life of Tiyo Soga.
1. Soga, Tiyo, 1829-1871. I. Chalmers, J. A.

Soil.

M630.7
C25h3

Carver, George Washington, 1864-1943.
How to build up and maintain the virgin fertility of our soils. Secon edition..., by George W. Carver...Tuskegee Institute, Alabama, Experiment station, Tuskegee Institute, 1936.
10p. 21½cm.

Le soir; ou, Fleurs haitiennes de sensibilite...

Haiti
M843.91
L13s

Lafontant, Delorme.
... Le soir; ou, Fleurs haïtiennes de sensibilité ... Port-au-Prince, Haïti ₍Imp. du Collège Vertières, 1942.
cover-title, 6 p. l., ₍11₎-346 p. port. 21½cm.
I. Title. ₍*Full name:* Jean Delorme Lafontant₎
44-53543
Library of Congress PQ3949.L2S6
₍2₎ 843.91

Soko risina musoro.

Rhodesia, S.
M496
C44s

Chitepo, H W
Soko risina musoro. Translated and edited with notes by Hazel Carter. London, Oxford University Press, 1958.
61p. 21½cm.

Sokoto, Nigeria (Province) - Biog.

Sudan, French
M966.2
T22

Tedzkiret en-nisian fi akhbar molouk es-Soudan. Traduction française par O. Houdas. Paris, E. Leroux, 1901.
2v.
xiv, 413 p. 29 cm. (Publications de l'École des langues orientales vivantes. 4. sér., v. 20)
Added is a fragment on the history of Sokoto (p. ₍303₎-331) by a certain Hadj Sa'id.
On cover: Documents arabes relatifs à l'histoire du Soudan.
Contents v.1. Texte arabe v.2. Traduction, par O. Houdas
1. Sudan — Biog. 2. Sokoto, Nigeria (Province) — Biog. I. Houdas, Octave Victor, 1840-1916, ed. and tr. II. Title: Documents arabes relatifs à l'histoire du Soudan. (Series: Paris. École des langues orientales vivantes. Publications. 4. sér., v. 20)
PJ7819.S8T4 52-59060
Library of Congress ₍2₎

Sokoto, Nigeria (Province) - History.

Nigeria
M966.9
Ab32

'Abd Allāh ibn Muḥammad, ***Emir of Gwandu,*** **1767 (ca.)–1829.**
Tazyin al-waraqāt, by 'Abdullāh ibn Muḥammad. Edited, with a translation and introductory study of the author's life and times, by M. Hiskett. ₍Ibadan, Nigeria₎ Ibadan University Press, 1963.
144 p. facsims., geneal. table, fold. map. 25 cm.
Bibliographical footnotes.
1. Sokoto, Nigeria (Province)—Hist. I. Hiskett, M., ed. and tr. II. Title.
DT515.9.S6A2 65-4747
Library of Congress ₍1₎

Cameroun
M896.3
P548s

Sola ma chérie.
Philombe, René, 1930-
Sola ma chérie. Yaoundé, Editions Abbia avec la collaboration de CLE, 1966.
124p. 18cm.
I. Title.

Haiti
M972.94
So4b

Solages, F
Face à l'avenir! Conférences dédiées à la jeunesse masculine et féminine de mon pays, aux éducateurs et éducatrices. Port-au-Prince, Haïti, 1948.

166 p. 18 cm.

1. Youth—Religious life. 2. Christian life—Catholic authors. I. Title.

BX2355.S6 248 49-51661*

Library of Congress

Soldiers.

M350
C26

Cashin, Herschel V.
Under fire. With the Tenth U. S. cavalry. Being a brief, comprehensive review of the Negro's participation in the wars of the United States. Especially showing the valor and heroism of the Negro soldiers of the Ninth and Tenth cavalries, and the Twenty-fourth and Twenty-fifth infantries of the regular army; as demonstrated in the decisive campaign around Santiago de Cuba, 1898 ... Thrilling episodes interestingly narrated by officers and men. Famous Indian campaigns and their results. A purely military history of the Negro. With introduction by Major-General Joseph Wheeler ... By Her-

(Continued on next card)

8—23899

[41j1]

Soldiers.

M350
G821

Green, Alfred M
Letters and discussions on the formation of colored regiments, and the duty of the colored people in regard to the great slaveholders' rebellion, in the United States of America. By Alfred M. Green. Philadelphia, Ringwalt-Brown, Steam power printers, 1862.

36p. 21½cm.

Puerto Rico
M863
L63s

... Solar Montoya.

Laguerre, Enrique A.
... Solar Montoya. [San Juan, Isla de Puerto Rico, América [Biblioteca de autores puertorriqueños, 1941]

1 p. l., [5]-351 p., 2 l. 22cm.

A novel.

I. Title.

A 42-3487 Revised

Harvard univ. Library for Library of Congress PQ7439.L28S [r44c2]† 863.6

Soldiers.
Coston, W[illiam] Hilary.

M350
C82

The Spanish-American war volunteer; Ninth United States volunteer infantry roster and muster, biographies, Cuban sketches. Middletown, Pa., The author, 1899.

139 p. illus. 8°.

July 18, 99-7

Library of Congress, no. E725.7.C85. Copyright.

Soldiers.

M350
H27o

Hastie, William Henry, 1904–
On clipped wings; the story of Jim Crow in the Army air corps, by William H. Hastie. [New York, National association for the advancement of colored people, 1943]

27 p. illus. (incl. ports.) 21½cm.

1. U. S. Army—Negro troops. 2. Negroes as soldiers. 3. U. S. Army air forces. I. National association for the advancement of colored people. II. Title.

A 44-3616

Harvard univ. Library for Library of Congress [3]

Africa
M960
J88

Solarin, Tai
A personal view of Nigerian independence. Pp. 231-253.

In: Judd, Peter, ed. African independence. New York, Dell Pub. Co., 1963.

Soldiers.

M815.4
D74m

Douglass, Frederick, 1817-1895.
Men of color, to arms! A call by Frederick Douglass. Rochester, March 2, 1863.

1p. 21½cm.

Soldiers.

M350
M35r

Marshall, Thurgood, 1908-
Report on Korea; The shameful story of the court martials of Negro GIs. New York, NAACP, 1951.

19p. 22cm.

Nigeria
M370
So42

Solarin, Tai.
Towards Nigeria's moral self-government. Ikenne, Tai Solarin, 1959.

95p. 21cm.

1. Nigeria - Education. 2. Education - Nigeria. I. Title.

Soldiers.

M815.4
D74he

Douglass, Frederick, 1817-1895.
The Negro people in a democratic war. Reprinted by the Workers bookshop, New York City.

3p. 22cm.

Soldiers.

M350
N32
1852

Nell, William C.
Services of colored americans, in the wars of 1776 and 1812. By William C. Nell. 2nd ed. Boston, Robert F. Wallcut, 1852.

40p. 30cm.

Nigeria
M370
So42

Solaru, T T
Teacher training in Nigeria, by T. T. Solaru. Edited, and with a final chapter by Ian Espie. Ibadan, Ibadan University. Press, 1964.

109p. maps. 21½cm.
Includes bibliography.

1. Teachers, Training of - Nigeria. 2. Nigeria - Teachers. I. Title. II. Espie, Ian.

Soldiers.

M350
D83

Drinker, Frederick E.
Our war for human rights, being an intensely humanand brilliant account of the World War and why and for what purpose American and the allies are fighting including the horrors and wonders of of modern warfare, the new and strange devices that have come into use, etc... by Fred. E. Drinker... illustrated with 128 genuine pictures.. Washington, D.C., Austin Jenkins co., 1917

xiii, [1], 17-424p. plates. 21½cm.

M350
N32
1851

Soldiers.

Nell, William C.
Services of colored Americans, in the wars of 1776 and 1812. By William C. Nell. Boston, Printed by Prentiss & Sawyer, 1851.

24 p. 23½cm.

1. U. S.—Hist.—Revolution—Negro troops. 2. U. S.—Hist.—War of 1812—Negro troops.

5-23354

Library of Congress E269.N3N4S

Soldiers.

M350
B798

Brown, Earl Louis, 1900–
... The Negro and the war [by] Earl Brown and George R. Leighton ... [New York, Public affairs committee, inc.] 1942.

cover-title, 32 p. diagrs. 21cm. (Public affairs pamphlets, no. 71)

"First edition, August, 1942."
"For further reading": p. 32.

1. Negroes. 2. Negroes—Employment. 3. Negroes as soldiers. I. Leighton, George Ross, 1902– joint author. II. Title.

42-22292

Library of Congress E185.61.B877 [25] 325.260973

Soldiers.

M350
F62

Fleetwood, Christian A.
The Negro as a soldier; written by Christian A. Fleetwood, late sergeant-major 4th U. S. colored troops, for the Negro congress, at the Cotton states and international exposition, Atlanta, Ga., November 11 to November 23, 1895. Published by Prof. Geo. Wm. Cook. Washington, D. C., Howard university print, 1895.

1 p. l., 19 p. 23cm.

1. Negroes. 2. U. S.—History—Civil war—Negro troops. I. Cook, George William, pub. II. Atlanta. Cotton states and international exposition, 1895. III. Title.

A 12—751 x[1]

Stanford univ. Library for Library of Congress E185.68.F59 [a40b1]

Soldiers.

M323
N78t

Reddick, Lawrence Dunbar, 1910-
Letters from a Jim Crow Army.

pp. 371-382.
In: Twice a year, ed. by Dorothy Norman. 1946.

Soldiers.

M815.5
B83
No.7

Bruce, John Edward, 1856-
A defence of the colored soldiers who fought in the war of the rebellion. Their critics answered by ex-union and ex-confederate soldiers, and by John Edward Bruce. "Grit" A Spy at Tom Dixon's Clansman". Yonkers, N.Y.

20p. 21½cm.

Soldiers.

M350
G192

[Garrison, William Lloyd] 1805–1879.
The loyalty and devotion of colored Americans in the revolution and war of 1812. Pub. in Boston, Mass., 1861. New York city, The New York age press, 1918.

24 p. 18cm.

1. U. S.—Hist.—Revolution—Negro troops. 2. U. S.—Hist.—War of 1812—Negro troops. 3. Slavery in the U. S.—Controversial literature—1861. I. Title.

18—22489

Library of Congress E269.N3G242 [36b1]

Soldiers.

M350
T21

Taylor, Susie King, 1848–
Reminiscences of my life in camp with the 33d United States colored troops, late 1st S. C. volunteers, by Susie King Taylor ... Boston, The author, 1902.

xii p., 1 l., 82 p. front., pl., ports. 19½cm.

1. U. S.—Hist.—Civil war—Regimental histories—U. S. inf.—33d. 2. U. S. infantry. 33d regt., 1862–1866. I. Title.

2—30128

Library of Congress E492.94.33dT [a44b1]

Soldiers.

M350 W65 **Wilkes, Laura Eliza,** 1871–
Missing pages in American history, revealing the services of negroes in the early wars in the United States of America, 1641–1815, by Laura E. Wilkes ... [Washington, D. C., Press of R. L. Pendleton, °1919]
91 p. 22cm.
On cover: Armistice edition.
Bibliography: p. 85–87.
1. Negroes as soldiers. 2. U. S.—History, Military. I. Title.
19–10083
Library of Congress E185.63.W68
Copyright A 515580 [3]

Soldiers.

M304 P19 V.6, no.8 Wilkins, J P
History of my brothers in the World War. Also an appendix of valuable information. [lacks imprint]
58p. 19cm.

Soldiers.

M350 W67n **Williams, John Henry.**
A Negro looks at war, by John Henry Williams ... [New York, Workers library publishers, inc., 1940]
31 p. 19cm.
1. Negroes. 2. Negroes as soldiers. I. Title.
44–35049
Library of Congress E185.61.W735
[2] 325.260973

Soldiers.

M350 Yo8m **Young, Charles,** 1864–1922.
Military morale of nations and races, by Charles Young ... Kansas City, Mo., Franklin Hudson publishing co., 1912.
273 p. 22½cm.
Bibliography: p. [7]
1. National characteristics. 2. Ethnopsychology. 3. Soldiers. 4. Morale. I. Title.
14–3326
Library of Congress U21.Y6
[a41b1]

M350 J13 1944 Soldiers–Virginia.
Jackson, Luther Porter
Virginia Negro soldiers and seamen in the Revolutionary war, by Luther Porter Jackson ... Norfolk, Va., Guide Quality press, 1944.
vi, [7]–46p. illus. 23cm.

Soleil cou-coupé.

Martinique M841.91 C33s **Césaire, Aimé.**
Soleil cou-coupé. Paris, K, 1948.
123 p. 23 cm. (Collection Le Quadrangle)
I. Title. (Series)
A 49–2942*
Illinois. Univ. Library for Library of Congress [1]

Soleil de la conscience.

Martinique M844 G49s Glissant, Édouard, 1928–
Soleil de la conscience. Paris, Palaize, 1956.
73p. 22cm.

Le soleil noir point.

Ivory Coast M896.2 N69s Nokan, Charles, 1936–
Le soleil noir point. Préface de Pierre Stibbe. Paris, Présence Africaine [1962]
70p. 21cm.
Portrait of author on back cover.

Le soleil partagé.

Martinique M843.91 Z71s Zobel, Joseph
Le soleil partagé. Paris, Présence Africaine, 1964.
207p. 18cm.
I. Title.

Soleils Caraibes.

Martinique M841.91 L55so Léopold, Emmanuel-Flavia
Soleils Caraibes, poèmes en ce temps de la terre toi qui n'étais que de lumière. Paris, Editions Bellenand, 1953.
158p. 19cm.

South Africa M896.4 W15 Solilo, John
Imbalana Ngo-Ntu.
Pp. 79–84.
Written in Xhosa.
In: Wallis, S. J., comp. and ed. Inkolo namasiko. London, Society for Promoting Christian Knowledge, 1930.

South Africa M896.4 W15 Solilo, John
Intsingiselo Yenkolo Yakwa-Xosa Ku-Yise.
Pp. 7–10.
Written in Xhosa.
In: Wallis, S. J., comp. and ed. Inkolo namasiko. London, Society for Promoting Christian Knowledge, 1930.

The soliloquy of Satan.

M811.5 H38s **Henderson, Elliott Blaine.**
The soliloquy of Satan, and other poems, by Elliott Blaine Henderson ... Springfield, O., The author, 1907.
64 p. front. (port.) 21cm.
1. Title.
7–16931
Library of Congress PS3515.E434S7 1907
Copyright A 175763 [a21c1]

Somali language – Texts.

Somali M496 G13 Galaal, Muuse Haaji Ismaaiil
Hikmad Soomaali. Edited with grammatical introduction and notes by B. W. Andrzejewski. London, Oxford University Press, 1956.
150p. 22cm. (Annotated African texts, 4)
Title in English: Somali wisdom.
Includes bibliography.
1. Somali language – Texts. 2. Tales, Somali. I. Title. II. Andrzejewski, B. W., ed. III. Series.

Somali poetry.

Somalia M896.1 Sy11k Syad, William J F
Khamsine; poèmes. Préface de Léopold S. Senghor. Paris, Présence Africaine [1959]
70p. 20cm.
Text in English or French.

Somalia M967.7 So15 **Somalia.** *Information Services.*
The Somali Peninsula; a new light on imperial motives. [Mogadiscio, 1962]
xiii, 137 p. maps. 26 cm.
Bibliography: p. 131–134.
1. Somaliland—Hist. 2. Somalia—Hist.
DT401.A53 62–58193
Library of Congress [1]

Somalia – History.

Somalia M967.7 So15 **Somalia.** *Information Services.*
The Somali Peninsula; a new light on imperial motives. [Mogadiscio, 1962]
xiii, 137 p. maps. 26 cm.
Bibliography: p. 131–134.
1. Somaliland—Hist. 2. Somalia—Hist.
DT401.A53 62–58193
Library of Congress [1]

Somaliland – History.

Somalia M967.7 So15 **Somalia.** *Information Services.*
The Somali Peninsula; a new light on imperial motives. [Mogadiscio, 1962]
xiii, 137 p. maps. 26 cm.
Bibliography: p. 131–134.
1. Somaliland—Hist. 2. Somalia—Hist.
DT401.A53 62–58193
Library of Congress [1]

Somatology.

M610 C63e13 Cobb, William Montague, 1904–
Education in human biology; an essential for the present and future. Reprinted from the Journal of Negro history, 27:119–155, April 1943.
119–155p. illus. 24cm.

Somatology.

M610 C63p3 Cobb, William Montague, 1904–
Physical anthropology and the Negro in the present crisis. Reprinted from the Journal of the National Medical Association, 34:181–187, Sept., 1942.
181–187p. 28cm.

Somatology.

M610 C63p5 Cobb, William Montague, 1904–
Physical anthropology of the American Negro. Reprinted from the American journal of physical anthropology, 29:114–223, June 1942.
114–223p. tables. 26cm.

Some achievements of the Negro through education.
M370 Guzman, Jessie Parkhurst, 1898-
G98s Some achievements of the Negro through education. Rev. ed. Tuskegee, Alabama, Tuskegee Institute, Dept. of Records and Research, 1950.
34p. 28cm. (Records and research pamphlet, no.1)

Some of my best friends.
M741 Brandon, Brumsic
B734 Some of my best friends. [Westbury, N. Y., 1963]
[12]p. (Chiefly illus.) 21cm.

Somebody please help me.
M813.5 Battles, Jesse Moore, 1935-
B322s Somebody please help me. [New York, Pageant Press [1965]
116 p. 21 cm.
Portrait of author on book jacket.

Some aspects of post-war travel.
M910 Hershaw, Fay McKeene.
H43s Some aspects of post-war travel. Boston, Christopher Pub. House [1950]
81 p. illus. 21 cm.
CONTENTS.—Bermuda in color.—Europe in reconstruction.—Australia.—Some common questions.
1. Voyages and travels. I. Title.
G463.H56 910 50-14358
Library of Congress [8]

Some public health problems...
M610 Nichols, Franklin O
P19 Some public health problems of the Negro.
v.1, no.9 Reprinted from the Journal of social hygiene, vol.8, July 1922.
281-285p.

M89 Somerville, John Alexander, 1882-
So5m Man of color, an autobiography. With a
1951 foreword by P. M. Sherlock. Kingston, Jamaica, Pioneer Press, 1951.
134p. 19cm.
Pocket book edition.

Some aspects of the Negro question in the U. S.
M335.4 Jackson, James Edward, 1914-
J14 Some aspects of the Negro question in the United States. [New York, Communist Party, 1959]
31p. 14cm.
"Reprinted from World Marxist Review, vo. 2, no. 7, July 1959"
Portrait on cover.
1. Communism - U.S. I. Title.

Some simple songs.
M811.4 McGirt, James Ephraim
M17s Some simple songs and a few more ambitious attempts. By James E. McGirt... Philadelphia, George F. Lasher c1901
72p. front. plates. 18cm.

M89 Somerville, John Alexander, 1882-
So5m Man of color, an autobiography. A factual report on the status of the American Negro today. [1st ed.] Los Angeles, L. L. Morrison [1949]
170 p. port. 24 cm. (The Publisher's library, no. 5)
ViHaI
I. Title.
E185.97.S65 325.260973 49-4392*
Library of Congress [25]

Some elements necessary to race development.
M323.1 Moton, Robert Russa, 1867-1940.
M85s Some elements necessary to race development [an address delivered at the Tuskegee Commencement, May 1912] Hampton, Press of the Hampton Normal and Agricultural Institute, 1913.
22p. 13cm.
"Reprinted from the Southern workman for July, 1912."
1. Race question. I. Title.

Some things we saw while abroad.
M910 Lane, James Franklin, 1874-
L24s Some things we saw while abroad; a visit to Europe, the Holy Land and Egypt, by J. F. Lane ... and Mary Edna Lane ... Boston, The Christopher publishing house [°1941]
xv, 17-224 p. plates, ports. 19cm.
1. Europe—Descr. & trav. 2. Palestine—Descr. & trav. 3. Egypt—Descr. & trav. I. Lane, Mrs. Mary Edna (Johnson) 1872- joint author. II. Title.
Library of Congress D975.L24 42-2468
[4] 910.4

Something in common.
M813.5 Hughes, Langston, 1902-
H87so Something in common, and other stories. New York, Hill and Wang [1963]
236 p. 21 cm. (American century series)
I. Title.
Full name: James Langston Hughes.
PZ3.H87313So 63-8189 ‡
Library of Congress [5]

Some essential features of Nkrumaism.
Ghana
M966.7 The Spark.
Sp26 Some essential features of Nkrumaism, by the editors of the Spark. New York, International Publishers [1965, °1964]
127 p. 18 cm. (Little new world paperbacks, LNW-8)
1. Nkrumah, Kwame, Pres. Ghana, 1909- 2. Ghana - Politics. I. Title.
DT510.6.N5S65 1965 320.531 65-24330
Library of Congress [8]

Kenya Some thoughts on native tribunals in Kenya.
M967.62 Oyende, J P
Oy3p Paro mako kuom dohini e Kenya [Some thoughts on native tribunals in Kenya] Nairobi, Eagle Press, 1950.
27p. 18cm. (Paro mag jowadi. Your friends are thinking series)
Written in Luo and English
1. Justice, Administration of - Kenya Colony and Protectorate. 2. Kenya Colony and Protectorate. I. Title. II. Title: Some thoughts on native tribunals in Kenya. III. Series. IV. Series: Your friends are thinking series.

Something to remember; poems.
M811.5 Hammond, Basil Calvin
H18s Something to remember; poems. New York, Exposition Press, 1960.
87p. 20cm.
Portrait of author on book jacket.

Some essentials of race leadership.
Trinidad
M323 Maloney, Arnold Hamilton.
M29s Some essentials of race leadership, by Arnold Hamilton Maloney ... Xenia, O., The Aldine publishing house, 1924.
180, [4] p. 20cm.
1. Negro race. 2. U. S.—Race question. I. Title.
Library of Congress E185.61.M25 24-6120
——— Copy 2.
Copyright A 777566 [2]

Nigeria Some tribal gods of Southern Nigeria.
M290 Egharevba, Jacob Uwadiae, 1893-
Eg39 Some tribal gods of Southern Nigeria. [Benin City, The Author] 1951.
59p. 18cm.
Portrait of author.

M813.5 Sometime tomorrow.
P28s Paulding, James E., 1935-
Sometime tomorrow. New York, Carlton Press [1965]
136p. 21cm.
Portrait of author on book jacket.
I. Title.

Some historical errors of James Ford Rhodes.
M973.8 Lynch, John Roy, 1847-
L99s Some historical errors of James Ford Rhodes, by Major John R. Lynch. Boston, New York, The Cornhill publishing company [°1922]
xx, 115 p. front., ports. 19cm.
1. Rhodes, James Ford, 1848- History of the United States from the compromise of 1850 ... 2. Negroes—Politics and suffrage. I. Title.
Library of Congress E415.7.R479 22-23557
——— Copy 2.
Copyright A 690397 [37d1]

Some Venda folk-tales...
S. Africa
M896.3 Lestrade, G P
L56 Some Venda folk-tales; edited with English translations and notes. Cape Town, The Lovedale Press, 1949.
48p. 25cm.

U.S.
M839 Sommerfelt, Aimee, 1892-
Iv3m Miriam. Translated by Pat Shaw Iversen. London, New York, Abelard-Schuman [1965]
160p. 22cm.
I. Title. II. Iversen, Pat (Shaw), tr.

Søn af de sorte [Native son]

M813.5
W93n45

Wright, Richard
Søn af de sorte [Native son] paa Dansk ved Tom Kristensen. Kobenhavn, Gyldendalske Boghandel, 1942.

298p. 21½cm.

Cuba
M861.6
G94cu

El son entero.

Guillén, Nicolás, 1904-
Cuba libre; tr. from the Spanish by Langston Hughes and Ben Frederic Carruthers; illus. by Gar Gilbert. Los Angeles, Anderson & Ritchie, 1948.

xi, 98p. illus. 28cm.
Limited ed. of 500 copies. Selection from the author's El son entero.

Cuba
M861.6
G94s

El son entero.

Guillén, Nicolas, 1904-
El son entero, suma poetica, 1929-1946, con una carta de D. Miguel de Unamuno. Textos musicales de Eliseo y Emilio Grenet, Alejandro García Corturla y Silvestre Revueltas. Ilustraciones de Carlos Enriquex. Buenos Aires, Editorial Pleamar, 1947.

210p. port. 21cm.

Martinique
M843.91
R39s

Son of Ti-Coyo.

Richer, Clément.
Son of Ti-Coyo; translated from the French by Gerard Hopkins. London, R. Hart-Davis, 1954.

143 p. 21 cm.

"First published in French under the title of Nouvelles aventures de Ti-Coyo et de son requin."

I. Title.

PZ3.R404So 843.91 54-26080 ‡

Library of Congress [1]

Martinique
M843.91
R39s2

Son of Ti-Coyo.

Richer, Clément.
Son of Ti-Coyo. [Translated from the French by Gerard Hopkins. 1st American ed.] New York, Knopf, 1954.

245 p. illus. 21 cm.

I. Title.

PZ3.R404So 2 843.91 54-7200 ‡

Library of Congress [8]

Martinique
M841.91
R66s

Sonate.

Romanette, Irmine
Sonate, poésies, Dessins de Georges Guiraud. Paris, Jouve, 1951, c1950.

190p. port. illus. 19cm.

South Africa
M896
M88

Sondhi, Kuldip, 1924-
Bad Blood.

Pp. 99-107.

In: Mphahlele, Ezekiel, ed. African writing today. Baltimore, Penguin Books, 1967.

M811.5
T84s

The song I sing.

Turner, Adolph John.
The song I sing. New York, Exposition Press [1964]

64p. 20cm.
Portrait of author on book jacket.

Nigeria
M896.1
C45s

Song of a goat.

Clark, John Pepper
Song of a goat. Ibadan, Mbari [1960]

43p. 20½cm.

Nigeria
M896.2
C54

Song of a goat.

Clark, John Pepper, 1935-
Three plays: Song of a goat; The masquerade; The raft. London, Oxford University Press, 1964.

134p. 18½cm.

Uganda
M896.1
P29s

Song of lawino.

p'Bitek Okot, J 0 1931-
Song of lawino. Nairobi, Kenya, East African Publishing House, 1966.

216p. 19cm. (Modern African Library)
Portrait of author on book cover.

I. Title.

M811.5
H55s

A song of magnolia.

Hill, Julious C.
A song of magnolia, by Julious C. Hill ... Boston, Meador publishing company, 1937.

88 p. 20½cm.

I. Title.

37-10980

Library of Congress PS3515.I 4938S 1937
——— Copy 2.
Copyright A 105846 [3] 811.5

South Africa
M896.3
Ab8s

Song of the city.

Abrahams, Peter, 1919-
Song of the city. A novel by Peter Abrahams. London, Published by Dorothy Crisp & co. Ltd. [1943]

179 p. 19 cm.

Niger
M966.26
B664

Songhai.

Boubou Hama, M jt. auth.
~~Boulnois, Jean.~~
L'empire de Gao; histoire, coutumes et magie des Sonrai [par] Jean Boulnois et Boubou Hama. Préf. de Théodore Monod. Paris, Librairie d'Amérique et d'Orient, 1954.

182 p. illus. 19 cm.

1. Songhai. ~~2. Boubou Hama, , joint author.~~ II. Title.

DT551.B6 55-16737 ‡

Library of Congress [60b1]

U.S.
M960
Sk34

Songhai.

Skinner, Elliott Percival, 1924-
~~Chu, Daniel.~~
A glorious age in Africa; the story of three great African empires [by] Daniel Chu and Elliott Skinner. Illustrated by Moneta Barnett. [1st ed.] Garden City, N. Y., Doubleday, 1965.

120 p. col. illus., col. maps. 22 cm. (Zenith books)

I. Chu, Daniel.
1. Africa—History, Juvenile. ~~I. Skinner, Elliott Percival, 1924- joint author.~~ II. Title. 2. Mali. 3. Songhay.

DT23.C5 1965 j960 65-10280

Library of Congress [5]

Cuba
M861.6
G74so
1931

Sóngoro Cosongo.

Guillén, Nicolás, 1904-
...Sóngoro Cosongo; poemas mulatos. La Habana Ucar, Garcia y cia 1931.

57p. 20½cm.

Cuba
M861.6
G94so
1942

Songoro Cosongo y otras poemas.

Guillén, Nicolás, 1904-
Sóngoro Cosongo y otras poemas de Nicolás Guillén; con una carte de don Miguel de Unamuno. [La Habana, La Verónica, 1942]

2 p. l., 9-120 p., 3 l. front. (port.) 17½ cm.

I. Title.

A 42-5576

Harvard Univ. Library for Library of Congress [48d1]

M784
A15

Songs.

Allen, William Francis, 1830-1889, comp.
Slave songs of the United States. New York, A. Simpson & Co., 1867.

115p. illus. 22½cm.

M378H
Ar5h

Songs.

Armstrong, Mary Frances (Morgan) *d.* 1903-
Hampton and its students. By two of its teachers, Mrs. M. F. Armstrong and Helen W. Ludlow. With fifty cabin and plantation songs, arranged by Thomas F. Fenner ... New York, G. P. Putnam's sons, 1874.

255, [1] p. fold, front., illus. 21½cm.

Songs (with music) : p. [171]-255.

1. Hampton, Va. Normal and agricultural institute. 2. Negro songs. I. Ludlow, Helen Wilhelmina, joint author. II. Fenner, Thomas P.

Library of Congress LC2851.H32A7 7-42208
[45k1]

M784
B41

Songs.

Belafonte, Harold, 1927- comp.
Songs Belafonte sings. Illustrated by Charles White. [1st ed.] New York, Duell, Sloan and Pearce [1962]

x, 196 p. illus. 29 cm.

Commentary on each song by Belafonte.
Music editor: Bob Bollard; piano arrangements: Joseph Maxzu.

CONTENTS.—Around the world.—The American Negro.—The West Indies.

1. Folk-songs. 2. Negro songs. 3. Negro spirituals. 4. Music, Popular (Songs, etc.)—West Indies. I. Title.

Full name: Harold George Belafonte.

M1627.B36S6 M62-1000

Library of Congress [5]

M784
B46

Songs.

Berendt, Joachim Ernst, ed.
Spirituals, geistliche lieder der Neger Amerikas. Original texte Melodien und Ubertragungen. Paridam Von Dem Knesebeck. Munchen, Nymphenburger Verlagshandlung, 1955.

87p. illus. 24cm.
White editor.

1. Songs. 2. Spirituals. I. Title.

Songs.
M784 C53
Clark, Edgar Rogie, 1914- , comp.
Negro art songs; album by contemporary composers for voice and piano. New York, Edward B. Marks Music Corp., 1956.
72p. illus. 33cm.

Songs.
M810 H94mu 1935
Hurston, Zora Neale.
Mules and men, by Zora Neale Hurston; with an introduction by Frank Boas ... 10 illustrations by Miguel Covarrubias. Philadelphia, London, Kegan, Paul, Trench, Trubner, 1935.
342, [1] p. front., illus., plates. 22cm.
CONTENTS.—pt. I. Folk tales.—pt. II. Hoodoo.—Appendix. I. Negro songs with music (p. 309-[331]) II. Formulae of hoodoo doctors. III. Paraphernalia of conjure. IV. Prescriptions of root doctors.
1. Folk-lore, Negro. 2. Voodooism. 3. Negroes—Florida. 4. Negroes—Louisiana. 5. Negro songs. I. Title.
35—18525
Library of Congress GR103.H8
[45j2] 398.09759

Songs.
M784 J68
Jolas, Eugene, 1894- tr.
Le Nègre qui chante; chansons traduites et introduction par Eugène Jolas. Paris, Éditions de cahiers libres [1928]
85p. cm.

Songs.
M784 C83
Courlander, Harold, 1908-
Negro folk music, U. S. A. New York, Columbia University Press, 1963.
x, 324p. illus., music. 24cm.
"The music" (melodies with words): p.[221]-287.
Bibliography: [299]-301; Discography: p.[302]-308.

M810 H94mu
Songs.
Hurston, Zora Neale.
Mules and men, by Zora Neale Hurston; with an introduction by Frank Boas ... 10 illustrations by Miguel Covarrubias. Philadelphia, London, J.B. Lippincott company, 1935.
342, 1 p. front, illus., plates. 22cm.
Contents.-pt. I. Folk tales. -pt.II. Hoodoo. -Appendix. I. Negro songs with music (p.309-331) II. Formulae of hoodoo doctors. III. Paraphernalia of conjure. IV. Prescriptions of root doctors.

Songs.
M784 J87
Jubilee songs: as sung by the Jubilee singers... enlarged, compiled by Theodore F. Seward, and George L White, New York, Biglow and Main [c1872]
160 p. 23cm.
Contains Part I and II.

Songs.
M784 D48
Dett, Robert Nathaniel, 1882- *ed.*
Religious folk-songs of the Negro as sung at Hampton institute, edited by R. Nathaniel Dett ... Hampton, Va., Hampton institute press, 1927.
xxvii, 236, [1], ii, xiii p. 24cm.
1. Negro songs. I. Hampton, Va. Normal and agricultural institute. II. Title.
27—10635
Library of Congress M1670.H3 1927
[45m1]

Songs.
M784 J61
Johns, Altona (Trent)
Play songs of the deep south. Illustrated by James A. Porter. Washington, D.C., The Associated Publishers, Inc., [1944]
33p. illus. 27½cm.

Songs.
M784 K38
Kennedy, Robert Emmet, 1877-
Mellows; a chronicle of unknown singers. Decorations by Simmons Persons. New York, Albert and Charles Boni, 1925.
183p. illus. 30cm.

Songs.
MB Em3
Emerson, William Canfield, 1893- *ed.*
Stories and spirituals of the Negro slave, by William C. Emerson, M. D. Boston, R. G. Badger [c1930]
79 p. front., ports. 19½cm.
Includes music.
white author?
1. Negro songs. 2. Negroes—Biog. 3. Slavery in the U. S.—Condition of slaves. I. Title. II. Title: Spirituals of the Negro slave.
30—12872
Library of Congress ML3556.E7
——— Copy 2. E444.E53
[43g1]

Songs.
M784 J63
Johnson, James Weldon, 1871-1938, *ed.*
The book of American Negro spirituals, edited with an introduction of James Weldon Johnson; musical arrangements by J. Rosamond Johnson, additional numbers by Lawrence Brown. New York, The Viking press, 1925.
187 p. 26cm.
1. Negro songs. I. Johnson, John Rosamond, 1873- II. Brown, Lawrence. III. Title. IV. Title: Spirituals.
25—23072
Library of Congress M1670.J67
[45q2] 784.756

Songs.
M784 L23
Landeck, Beatrice.
Echoes of Africa in folk songs of the Americas. Instrumental arrangements by Milton Kaye. English version of foreign lyrics by Margaret Marks. Drawings by Alexander Dobkin. New York, D. McKay Co. [1961]
viii, 184 p. illus. 29 cm.
Includes discussions of the origin of each folk song as well as technics of performance.
Instrumental arrangements consist of accompaniment of the songs by percussion instruments in varying combinations.
Bibliography: p. 182-183. Discography: p. 178-181.
White author.
1. Folk-songs, African—America. 2. Negro songs. 3. Jazz music. 4. Folk-songs, African—America—Discography. I. Kaye, Milton. II. Title.
M1680.L15E3 M 61—1013
Library of Congress [61x15]

Songs.
M784 F53
Fisher, Miles Mark, 1899-
Negro slave songs in the United States. With a foreword by Ray Allen Billington. Ithaca, Cornell University Press for the American Historical Association [1953]
xv, 223 p. 24 cm.
Includes texts of the songs, without the music.
Bibliography: p. 193-213.
1. Negro songs. I. Title.
M1670.F35N4 53—13501
Library of Congress [54w15]

Songs.
M784 J63b
Johnson, James Weldon, 1871-1938, *ed.*
The books of American Negro spirituals, including The book of American Negro spirituals and The second book of Negro spirituals [by] James Weldon Johnson and J. Rosamond Johnson. New York, The Viking press, 1940.
2 v. in 1. 26cm.
A re-issue of the volumes first published separately in 1925 and 1926. Each volume has special t.-p.
Musical arrangements by J. Rosamond Johnson, additional numbers by Lawrence Brown.
1. Negro songs. I. Johnson, John Rosamond, 1873- II. Brown, Lawrence. III. Title. IV. Title: Spirituals.
A 41—546
Cincinnati. Univ. Libr. for Library of Congress M1670.J66 [M1670.J]
[45v3]

Songs.
M784 M35
Marsh, J B T
The story of the Jubilee singers; with their songs. Ed. by J. B. T. Marsh. 7th ed. London, Hodder and Stoughton, 1877.
vi, [2], 248 p. front. (mounted phot.) illus. 17½cm.
1. Jubilee singers. 2. Negro musicians. 3. Negro songs.
6—8204
Library of Congress M1607.F4
[45ol]

Songs.
M784 F52
Fisher, William Arms, 1861- *ed.*
Seventy Negro spirituals, edited by William Arms Fisher ... Boston, Oliver Ditson company; New York, C. H. Ditson & co.; [etc., etc., c1926]
xxxiv, [2], 212 p. ports. 32 x 24½cm. (The musicians library)
Edition for high voice.
Bibliography: p. [xxxiii]-xxxiv.
1. Negro songs. I. Title. II. Title: Spirituals.
26—18007
Library of Congress M1.M9F43H
——— Edition for low voice. M1.M9F43L
Copyright A 950085 [a39q1]

Songs.
M784 J63s
Johnson, James Weldon, 1871-
The second book of negro spirituals, edited with an introduction by James Weldon Johnson; musical arrangements by J. Rosamond Johnson. New York, The Viking press, 1926.
189 p. 26 x 19½cm. $3.50
1. Negro songs. I. Johnson, J. Rosamond, 1873- II. Title: Spirituals.
26-27592
Library of Congress M1670.J672
——— Copy 2.
Copyright E 651256 [8-2]

Songs.
M784 Od8
Odum, Howard Washington, 1884-
The Negro and his songs; a study of typical Negro songs in the south, by Howard W. Odum and Guy B. Johnson. Chapel Hill, University of North Carolina Press; London, Humphrey Milford, Oxford University Press, 1925.
306p. 23cm.

Songs.
M572 F75
Ford, Theodore P.
God wills the Negro; an anthropological and geographical restoration of the lost history of the American Negro people, being in part a theological interpretation of Egyptian and Ethiopian backgrounds. Compiled from ancient and modern sources, with a special chapter of eight Negro spirituals. By Theodore P. Ford, PH. B. Chicago, Ill., The Geographical institute press, 1939.
159 p. incl. front., illus. 28cm.
Includes music.
Bibliographical foot-notes.
1. Negro race. 2. Negro songs. I. Title.
39-2105
Library of Congress GN545.F6
——— Copy 2.
Copyright A 124575 [3] 572.96

Songs.
M784 J63r
Johnson, John Rosamond, 1873- *ed.*
Rolling along in song; a chronological survey of American Negro music, with eighty-seven arrangements of Negro songs, including ring shouts, spirituals, work songs, plantation ballads, chain-gang, jail-house, and minstrel songs, street cries, and blues, edited and arranged by J. Rosamond Johnson. New York, The Viking press, 1937.
224 p. 26cm.
1. Negro songs. I. Title.
37—27426
Library of Congress M1670.J65R6
[40u2] 784.756

Songs.
M784 Od8n
Odum, Howard Washington, 1884-
Negro workaday songs, by Howard W. Odum ... and Guy B. Johnson ... Chapel Hill, The University of North Carolina press; London, H. Milford, Oxford university press, 1926.
3 p. l., [ix]-xii, 2 l., 278 p. illus. (music) diagrs. 23½ cm. (*Half-title:* The University of North Carolina. Social study series)
"Selected bibliography": p. [265]-270.
1. Negro songs. 2. Negro songs—Hist. & crit. I. Johnson, Guy Benton, 1901- joint author. II. Title.
ML3556.O32 26—14118
Library of Congress [54g1]

Ecuador
M863.6
Or8t

Songs.

Ortiz, Adalberto.

... Tierra, son y tambor; cantares negros y mulatos. Prólogo de Joaquín Gallegos Lara y 28 grabados originales de Galo Galecio. México, D. F., Ediciones La Cigarra, 1945.

2 p. l., [7]–81 p., 2 l. illus. 28cm.

Without music.

1. Negroes—Poetry. 2. Negro songs. I. Title.

46-18308

Library of Congress PQ8219.O7T5

[2] 861.6

M784
P63

Songs.

Pike, Gustavus D

The Jubilee singers, and their campaign for twenty thousand dollars. By G. D. Pike ... Boston, Lee and Shepard; New York, Lee, Shepard and Dillingham, 1873.

219 p., 1 l. incl. front. ports. 20½ cm.

Includes a brief account of Fisk university, Nashville.
"Jubilee songs": p. [161]–219.

1. Jubilee singers. 2. Negro musicians. 3. Fisk university, Nashville. 4. Negro songs. I. Title.

6—3203

Library of Congress ML400.P63

[45o1]

Ghana
M784
R54

Songs.

Roberts, J T

A hymn of thanksgiving and other songs. Accra, Accra High School, 1953.

16p. port. 25cm.

M780
Sh66

Songs.

Shirley, Kay, *ed.*

The book of the blues. Annotated by Frank Driggs. Record research by Joy Graeme. Music research by Bob Hartsell. New York, Leeds Music Corp. [1963]

301 p. 32 cm.

Unacc., with guitar chords.
Background notes, list of recordings, and chord diagrams for guitar and tenor banjo, precede each song.

1. Music, Popular (Songs, etc.)—U. S. 2. Folk-songs, American. 3. Negro songs. I. Title.

M1629.S557B6 63-18895/M

Library of Congress [3]

M811.08
T14

Songs.

Talley, Thomas Washington, *comp.*

Negro folk rhymes, wise and otherwise, with a study by Thomas W. Talley ... New York, The Macmillan company, 1922.

xii p., 1 l., 347 p. illus. (incl. music) 19½cm.

1. Negro songs. I. Title.

22—1477

Library of Congress PS595.N3T3

[41t1]

M973
Un3s

Songs.

U. S. *Library of Congress.*

75 years of freedom; commemoration of the 75th anniversary of the proclamation of the 13th amendment to the Constitution of the United States. The Library of Congress. [Washington, U. S. Govt. print. off., 1943]

cover-title, vi, 108 p. col. pl. 26cm.

"The contribution of the American Negro to American culture was the theme of a series of exhibits and concerts in the Library of Congress commencing on December 18th, the 75th anniversary of the proclamation of the Thirteenth amendment, which ended slavery in the United States."—p. v.

1. Negroes. 2. Negro songs. 3. Negro art. 4. Negro literature (American) I. Title.

43-52457

Library of Congress E185.6.U597

[15] 325.260973

M784.4
W58

Songs.

White, Newman Ivey, 1892–1948.

American Negro folk-songs, by Newman I. White ... Cambridge, Harvard university press, 1928.

x p., 2 l., [3]–501 p. 24 cm.

Contains music.
Bibliography: p. [469]–480.

1. Negro songs. I. Title.

ML3556.W4 28—21279

Library of Congress [a55q1]

M813.5
W589

Songs.

Whiting, Helen Adele (Johnson) 1885–

Negro art, music and rhyme, for young folks, by Helen Adele Whiting; illustrations by Lois Mailou Jones. Book II. Washington, D. C., The Associated publishers, inc. [°1938]

[38] p. illus. 23½cm.

Without music.
Book I published under title: Negro folk tales for pupils in the primary grades.

1. Negroes in literature and art. 2. Negro songs. I. Title.

38—17194

Library of Congress PE1119.W55

[45k1] 372.4

M784
W88n

Songs.

Wood, Clement, 1888– *ed.*

... Negro songs, an anthology, edited, with an introduction, by Clement Wood. Girard, Kan., Haldeman-Julius company [°1924]

64 p. 13cm. (Little blue book, no. 626, ed. by E. Haldeman-Julius)

1. Negro songs.

CA 26-62 Unrev'd

Library of Congress PS595.N3W6
———— Copy 2.

Copyright A 816570 [2]

M784
W89a

Songs.

Work, John Wesley, 1901– *ed.*

American Negro songs and spirituals; a comprehensive collection of 230 folk songs, religious and secular, with a foreword by John W. Work. New York, Crown publishers [°1940]

1 p. l., [v]–vii p., 1 l., 259 p. 26cm.

With music.
Bibliography: p. 252–256.

1. Negro songs. I. Title.

A 42-5002

Oberlin college. Library for Library of Congress [M1670.W93A]

[5] 784.756

M784
W89f

Songs.

Work, John Wesley, 1871–1925.

Folk song of the American Negro [by] John Wesley Work ... Nashville, Tenn., Press of Fisk university [°1915]

4 p. l., 5–131 p. illus. (incl. ports.) 23cm.

1. Negro songs. I. Title.

15—22992

Library of Congress ML3556.W78

[a41b1]

M784
C83

Songs - Discography.

Courlander, Harold, 1908–

Negro folk music, U. S. A. New York, Columbia University Press, 1963.

x, 324 p. illus., music. 24 cm.

"The music" (melodies with words) : p. [221]–287.
Bibliography : p. [299]–301 ; Discography : p. [302]–308.

1. Music—Negroes. 2. Negro songs—Hist. & crit. 3. Negro songs—Discography. 4. Negro songs. I. Title.

ML3556.C7 784.756 63—18019/MN

Library of Congress [a63d3]

M784
C83

Songs - History and criticism.

Courlander, Harold, 1908–

Negro folk music, U. S. A. New York, Columbia University Press, 1963.

x, 324 p. illus., music. 24 cm.

"The music" (melodies with words) : p. [221]–287.
Bibliography : p. [299]–301 ; Discography : p. [302]–308.

1. Music—Negroes. 2. Negro songs—Hist. & crit. 3. Negro songs—Discography. 4. Negro songs. I. Title.

ML3556.C7 784.756 63—18019/MN

Library of Congress [a63d3]

M780.9
H22

Songs-Hist. & crit.

Hare, Maud (Cuney) 1874–1936.

Negro musicians and their music, by Maud Cuney-Hare. Washington, D. C., The Associated publishers, inc. [°1936]

xii, 439 p. plates, ports., facsim. 21 cm.

Includes music.
Bibliography : p. 419–423.

1. Negro musicians. 2. Negro songs—Hist. & crit. 3. Music—U. S.—Hist. & crit. 4. Folk-songs, African. 5. Music—Africa.

36—11293

Library of Congress ML3556.H3N4

[37u5] 780.96

M784
K87

Songs - History and criticism.

Krehbiel, Henry Edward, 1854–1923.

Afro-American folksongs; a study in racial and national music, by Henry Edward Krehbiel ... New York and London, G. Schirmer [°1914]

xii, 176 p. 24 cm.

Contains songs with music.

1. Negro songs—Hist. & crit. I. Title.

ML3556.K9 14—1130

Library of Congress [50p½]

M308
L79n2

Songs— Hist. & crit.

Locke, Alain LeRoy, 1886–

... The Negro and his music, by Alain Locke ... Washington, D. C., The Associates in Negro folk education, 1936.

3 p. l., 142 p. 20½ cm. (Bronze booklet no. 2)

"Reading references" at end of each chapter; "Recorded illustrations" at end of most of the chapters.

1. Negro musicians. 2. Negro songs—Hist. & crit. 3. Music—U. S.—Hist. & crit. 4. Jazz music. 5. Phonograph records. I. Title.

37—10637

Library of Congress E185.5.B85 no. 2
———— Copy 2. ML3556.L6N4

[42t2] (325.260973) 784.756

M784
Od8

Songs - History & criticism.

Odum, Howard Washington, 1884–

The Negro and his songs; a study of typical Negro songs in the south, by Howard W. Odum and Guy B. Johnson. Chapel Hill, University of North Carolina Press; London, Humphrey Milford, Oxford University Press, 1925.

306p. 23cm.

M784
Od8n

Songs - History and criticism.

Odum, Howard Washington, 1884–

Negro workaday songs, by Howard W. Odum ... and Guy B. Johnson ... Chapel Hill, The University of North Carolina press; London, H. Milford, Oxford university press, 1926.

3 p. l., [ix]–xii, 2 l., 278 p. illus. (music) diagrs. 23½ cm. (*Half-title:* The University of North Carolina. Social study series)

"Selected bibliography" : p. [265]–270.

1. Negro songs. 2. Negro songs—Hist. & crit. I. Johnson, Guy Benton, 1901– joint author. II. Title.

ML3556.O32 26—14118

Library of Congress [54g½]

Jamaica
M784
M95

Songs - Jamaica.

Murray, Tom, ed. and arr.

Folk songs of Jamaica. London, Oxford University Press [1951]

9p. 25½cm

1. Songs - Jamaica. 2. Folk songs - Jamaica. I. Title.

Trinidad
M780
W671sg

Songs - Trinidad.

Williams, Connie, collector.

12 songs from Trinidad. [Illustrated by Grace West] San Francisco, Panpipes Press, 1958.

15p. illus., port. 18½cm.

S. Africa
M784
M72

Songs, African.

Mohapeloa, J P

Meloli le lithallere tsa Africa. Morija, Basutoland, Morija Sesuto Book Depot, 1947.

68p. 18cm.
Sotho Songs.

1. Songs, African.

Songs, Plantation.
M784
H15
Hallowell, Emily, ed.
Calhoun plantation songs; collected and edited by Emily Hallowell. Boston, C. W. Thompson & Co., 1901.

61p. 27cm.

1. Songs, Plantation. I. Title. II. Title: Plantation songs.

Songs, Religious.
M784
F36r
Fenner, Thomas P
Religious folk songs of the Negro, as sung on the plantations. New ed. Arranged by the musical directors of the Hampton Normal and Agricultural Institute. From the original edition. Hampton, Va., The Institute Press, 1916.

178p. 21½cm.

Songs and music.
M784
H19u
Handy, William Christopher, 1873- 1958ed.
Unsung Americans sung, edited by W. C. Handy. ₍New York? 1944₎
236 p. incl. front., illus. (ports.) 28 cm.
Principally biographical sketches of prominent Negroes, with music written about them. The music is for solo voice or mixed chorus, with piano accompaniment.
Bibliography: p. 235-236.

1. Negroes—Songs and music. I. Title.

M1659.5.N4H 784.8 44—40185
Library of Congress ₍a54f1₎

Songs and tales from the dark continent.
Africa
M784
B92
Burlin, Natalie (Curtis) 1875–1921, *ed.*
Songs and tales from the dark continent, recorded from the singing and the sayings of C. Kamba Simango ... and Madikane Cele ... by Natalie Curtis. New York, Boston, G. Schirmer ₍°1920₎
xxv p., 1 l., 170 p. front., illus., 4 pl., 2 port. 27 cm.
CONTENTS.—Introduction.—C. Kamba Simango.—Simango's letter to the reader.—Proverbs, beliefs and customs, songs and tales of the Ndau tribe, East Africa.—Madikane Čele.—Songs and tales of the Zulin tribe, South Africa.—Simango's farewell to the reader.—Chindau's songs ₍with the music₎ (p. ₍79₎-129)—Zulu songs ₍with the music₎ (p. ₍131₎-149)—Appendix.
1. Folk-songs, African. 2. Folk-lore—Africa. I. Simango, C. Kamba. II. Čele, Madikane Qaṇdeya. III. Title.

ML3760.B98 21—5086
Library of Congress ₍a51q1₎

Songs Belafonte sings.
M784
B41
Belafonte, Harold, 1927- *comp.*
Songs Belafonte sings. Illustrated by Charles White. ₍1st ed.₎ New York, Duell, Sloan and Pearce ₍1962₎
x, 196 p. illus. 29 cm.
Commentary on each song by Belafonte.
Music editor: Bob Bollard; piano arrangements: Joseph Mazzu.
CONTENTS.—Around the world.—The American Negro.—The West Indies.
1. Folk-songs. 2. Negro songs. 3. Negro spirituals. 4. Music, Popular (Songs, etc.)—West Indies. I. Title.
Full name: Harold George Belafonte.

M1627.B86S6 M62-1000
Library of Congress ₍5₎

Songs from Jamaica.
Jamaica
M821.91
M19son
McKay, Claude, 1890-1948.
Songs from Jamaica. London, Augener, Ltd., 1912.
11p. 28½cm.
Words and music.
Six songs.

Songs from the dark.
M811.5
F75s
Ford, Nick Aaron.
Songs from the dark, by Nick Aaron Ford. Boston, Meador publishing company, 1940.
40 p. 20½cm.
Poems.

I. Title.
40-35665
Library of Congress PS3501.F686 1940
——— Copy 2.
Copyright ₍2₎ 811.5

Songs from the wayside.
M811.5
T37so
Thompson, Clara Ann
Songs from the wayside. By Clara Ann Thompson. Rossmoyne, Ohio, Published and sold by the author, 1908.
96p. 17½cm.

Songs from the wilderness.
Ghana
M896.1
P22s
Parkes, Frank Kobina
Songs from the wilderness. London, University of London Press ₍1965₎

64p. 22cm.

I. Title.

...Songs in the night.
M811.5
J15s
Jacobson, Harriet Price
...Songs in the night. New York, the Exposition press c1947
63p. 22½cm.
At head of title: Poems by Harriet Price Jacobson.
Inscribed copy: To the Hon. Arthur B. Spingarn, from the author Harriet Price Jacobson.

Songs of a southerner.
M811.5
M128s
McClellan, George Marion, 1860-1974.
Songs of a southerner, by George Marion McClellan. Boston, Press of Rockwell and Churchill, 1896.

16p. front. 22cm.

Nigeria
M896.1
Ok5s
Songs of Africa.
Okogie, M O
Songs of Africa. Ilfracombe, Arthur H. Stockwell ₍1961₎

47p. port. 18½cm.
Portrait of author in book.

Songs of Caroline.
M811.5
T37s
Thompson, Joseph
Songs of Caroline, by Joseph Thompson. Chicago, Ill., Joseph Thompson 1936
30p. front. 20x11cm.

Songs of creation.
M811.5
C97s
Cuthbert, Marion Vera, 1896-
Songs of creation. New York, Woman's Press ₍1949₎
46 p. 19 cm.

I. Title.
PS3505.U963S6 811.5 49-11890*
Library of Congress ₍2₎

Jamaica
M821.91
M19so
Songs of Jamaica...
McKay, Claude, 18?0-
Songs of Jamaica, by Claude McKay. With an introduction by Walter Jekyll... Kingston, Jamaica, Aston W. Gardner & co., 1912.
140p. front. 18½cm.
Music.

Songs of life.
M811.5
M33s
Margetson, George Reginald.
Songs of life, by George Reginald Margetson. Boston, Sherman, French & company, 1910.
3 p. l., 57 p. 19½cm. $1.00

10-13842
Library of Congress
© June 7, 1910; 2c. June 10, 1910; A 265594; Sherman, French & co., Boston, Mass.

Songs of my people.
M811.5
J624s
Johnson, Charles Bertram.
Songs of my people ₍by₎ Charles Bertram Johnson. Boston, The Cornhill company ₍°1918₎
vi, 55 p., 1 l. 19½cm.

I. Title.
19-5146
Library of Congress PS3501.J55S6 1918
——— Copy 2.
Copyright A 512775 ₍2₎

Songs of the soil.
M811.5
J632s
Johnson, Fenton, 1888-
Songs of the soil, by Fenton Johnson ... New York, F. J. ₍°1916₎
3 p. l., iii, ₍1₎, 39 p. 16½cm. $0.50
Reprinted in part from the Citizen.

I. Title.
16-6071
Library of Congress PS3519.O245S6 1916
Copyright A 427114

Songs of the soul.
M814.5
Sh7s
Shokunbi, Mae (Gleaton)
Songs of the soul, by Mae Gleaton Shokunbi. Philadelphia, Dorrance & company ₍1945₎
viii, 9-76 p. 19cm.
Essays.

I. Title.
45-17723
Library of Congress PS3537.H958S6
₍2₎ 818.5

Songs to a phantom nightingale.
M811.5
M26s
Madgett, Naomi Cornelia Long.
Songs to a phantom nightingale, by Naomi Cornelia Long. New York, Fortuny's publishers, inc. ₍1941₎
80 p. port. 19 cm.
Verse.
"First edition."

I. Title.
PS3525.A318S6 811.5 41-15740 rev
Library of Congress ₍r57c8₎

Sonnendolche; poignards du soleil.
Martinique
M841.91
C33so
Césaire, Aime, 1913-
Sonnendolche; poignards du soleil. Lyrik von den Antillen. Ausgewählt und übertragen von Janheinz Jahn. Heidelberg, Wolfgang Rothe Verlag, 1956.

88p. 24cm.

Haiti M841 V712s

Sonnets au palmiste.

Vilaire, Jean Joseph, 1881-
Sonnets au palmiste. Les Boeufs (poème) Port-au-Prince, Aug. A. Héraux, 1921.

34p. 18½cm.

M811.5 B33

Sonnets for the Ethiopians...

Baxter, Joseph Harvey Lowell.
Sonnets for the Ethiopians and other poems, by J. Harvey L. Baxter. Roanoke, Va., The Magic city press, 1936.

xiv, 113 p. 20cm.

I. Title.

37-189

Library of Congress PS3503.A92966 1936
——— Copy 2.
Copyright A 100982 (2) 811.5

Haiti M841 L13s

Sonnets-Médaillons du dix-neuvième siècle.

Laforest, Edmond
Sonnets-Médaillons du dix-neuvième siècle. Ornés de quatre-vingt-dix portraits authentiques et de douze fleurons originaux. Paris, Lib. Fischbacher, 1909.

LXVIII, 216p. ports. cm. (Collection des poetes Francias de l'etranger)

Ghana M896.2 D36s

Sons and daughters.

De Graft-Johnson, John Coleman, 1919-
Sons and daughters. London, Oxford University Press, 1964.

53p. 18½cm.

MB T14s

The sons of Allen.

Talbert, Horace, 1853-
The sons of Allen, by Rev. Horace Talbert, M. A. Together with a sketch of the rise and progress of Wilberforce university, Wilberforce, Ohio. Xenia, O., The Aldine press, 1906.

3 p. l., v-xiv p., 1 l., 17-286 p. front. (port.) illus. 23cm.

1. Allen, Richard, bp., 1760-1831. 2. Wilberforce university, Wilberforce, O. 3. African Methodist Episcopal church—Clergy. I. Title.

6-15719

Library of Congress BX8443.T3
——— Copy 2.
Copyright A 141603 [a33b1]

Martinique M841.91 R66so

...Sonson de la Martinique.

Romanette, Irmine
...Sonson de la Martinique, roman. Paris, Société Francaise d'Editions littéraires et Techniques, 1932.

248p. 18½cm.
At head of title: Bibliothèque du Hérisson.

M810.9 H55

Soon, one morning.

Hill, Herbert, 1924- ed.
Soon, one morning; new writing by American Negroes, 1940-1962. Selected and edited, with an introd. and biographical notes, by Herbert Hill. [1st ed.] New York, Knopf, 1963.

617 p. 22 cm.

1. Negro literature—U. S. 2. American literature—Negro authors. I. Title.

PS508.N3H5 810.89 62—15567 ‡

Library of Congress [63f5]

M811.5 H55so

A sooner song.

Hill, Julius C
A sooner song, by Julius C. Hill. New York, Empire books [c1935]
63p. 19½cm.

Guiana, French MB9 Eb7s

Sophie, Ulrich.
Le gouverneur général Félix Éboué. Préf. de G. Monnerville. 2. éd. Paris, Larose, 1950. 1949.

91p. port. 26 cm.

1. Éboué, Adolphe Félix Sylvestre, 1884-1944.

[JV1809.E3S] A 53-7869

Harvard Univ. Library for Library of Congress [1]

France M840 D891so

Sophie Printems.

Dumas, Alexandre, 1824-1895.
Sophie Printems, par Alexandre Dumas fils. Bruxelles, Meline, Cans et Cie., 1853.

228p. 15cm.

Nigeria M496 So6

Sorinolu, Ariyo
Gbolohunoro - 200 Tabi Gbedegbeyo [200 sentences or vocabulary] Lagos, Church Missionary Society Bookshop, 1930.

25p. 18½cm.

1. Yoruba reader.

Sororities

see

Greek letter societies

Nigeria M896.3 Ig8s

The sorrows of love.

Iguh, Thomas O
The sorrows of love. Onitsha, Nigeria, A. Onwudiwe and Sons [n.d.]

39p. 21cm.

M323.4 B93a4

Sort protest; de Amerikanske Negeres kamp for ligeberettigelse.

Burns, W Haywood
Sort protest; de Amerikanske Negeres kamp for ligeberettigelse. Glostrup, Det Danske Forlag [1964]

119p. 21cm.
Translation of The voices of Negro protest in America.
Written in Danish.

1. Civil rights. 2. Race question.
I. Title.

M813.5 W93a5

Sort ungdom [Native son]

Wright, Richard, 1908-
Sort ungdom [Native son. Kobenhavn] Gyldendal, 1961.

247p. 21½cm.

Haiti M398 P612

Sortilèges Afro-Haitiens.

Pierre-Louis, Ulysse
Sortilèges Afro-Haitiens (contes et légendes). Préface du Dr. Jean Price-Mars. Port-au-Prince, Imprimerie de l'Etat, 1961.

120p. 18½cm.

Brazil M869.2 M17d

Sortilégio.

Nascimento, Abdias do
Sortilégio.

Pp. 159-197.

In: Nascimento, Abdias do, ed. Dramas para Negroes e prologo para brancos. Rio de Janeiro, Teatro Experimental do Negro, 1961.

I. Title.

Brazil M869.2 N17

Sortilegio (Misterio Negro).

Nascimento, Abdias do, 1914-
Sortilegio (Misterio Negro). Rio, [Teatro Experimental do Negro] 1959.

81p. 22½cm.
"Para National Association for the Advancement of the Colored People, comas homenagens, do autor, Abdias Nascimento, Rio-Setembro—1959."

copy 183.

S. Africa M896.3 M85m

Sotho language.

Motsamai, Edward.
Mehla ea malimo. Morija, Sesuto Book Depot, 1912.

143p. 16cm.
Times of the Cannibals.

S.Africa M896.1 Se7

Sotho language.

Setsoto; Recitations for the elementary schools. Morija, Sesuto Book Depot, 1946.

44p. 15½cm.

Liberia M966.6 B62w

Soudan.

Blyden, Edward Wilmot, 1832-
West Africa before Europe, and other addresses, delivered in England in 1901 and 1903, by Edward Wilmot Blyden ... With an introduction by Casely Hayford ... London, C. M. Phillips, 1905.

4 p. l., iv, 158 p. front. (port.) 19cm.

Includes the author's article, "Islam in the Western Soudan," reprinted from Journal of African society, October, 1902.

1. Africa, West. 2. Negroes—Africa. 3. Mohammedanism.

Library of Congress DT471.B5 6-27329

Le souffle des ancêtres.

Cameroun
M896.3 Nzouankeu, Jacques Mariel, 1938-
N98s Le souffle des ancêtres. Yaounde, Editions Abbia, avec la collaboration de CLE, 1965.

107p. 18cm.
Portrait of author on book cover.
Contents.- Le souffle des ancêtres.- Les dieux de Bangoulap.- Le parole de Mouan Koum.- La dame d'eau.

I. Title.

La Saufriere, St. Vincent-Eruption, 1902.

M972.98 Miller, James Martin, 1859-1939.
M61m The Martinique horror and St. Vincent calamity, containing a full and complete account of the most appalling disaster of modern times ... by J. Martin Miller ... in collaboration with Hon. John Stevens Durham ... Philadelphia, National publishing co. [1902]

8, 17-560 p. 2 front., illus., plates, ports., maps. 23½cm.

Issued also under the title: True story of the Martinique and St. Vincent calamities ... by Prof. John Randolph Whitney.

1. La Soufrière, St. Vincent—Eruption, 1902. 2. Pelée, Mont—Eruption, 1902. 3. St. Vincent. 4. Volcanoes. I. Durham, John Stevens, 1861- joint author. II. Title.

2-17542

Library of Congress F2081.M64 [a44f1]

Soul clap hands and sing.

M813.5 Marshall, Paule, 1929-
M35s Soul clap hands and sing. [1st ed.] New York, Atheneum, 1961.

177 p. 21 cm.
Four short novels.
Portrait of author on book jacket.

I. Title.

PZ4.M369So 61-16515 ‡

Library of Congress [5]

Soul gone home.

M812.5 Hughes, Langston, 1902-
H87s Soul gone home.

(In; One act play magazine, v.1, July 1937. 25cm. p.196-197.)

M252 Soul Magnets
Sp3s Spearman, Henry Kuhns.
Soul magnets; twelve sermons from Testament texts, bt Rev Henry Kuhns Spearman, compiled as a memorail by Miss Elizabeth F. Spearman. [Philadelphia, A.M.E. Book Concern, 1929]

116p. front(port.) 19cm.

Nigeria The Soul of Nigeria.
M966.9 Delano, Isaac O
D37s The soul of Nigeria, by Isaac O. Delano. London, T. Werner Laurie [1937]

251[1]p. front (port) plates. 22cm.

Soul on ice.

M301 Cleaver, Eldridge, 1935-
C58 Soul on ice. With an introd. by Maxwell Geismar. [1st ed.] New York, McGraw-Hill [1967, °1968]

xv, 210 p. 22 cm.
"A Ramparts book."

1. ~~Negroes~~—Psychology. I. Title.

E185.97.C6 301.451'96'073 (B) 67-27277

Library of Congress [10-2]

Soulcraft.

M813.5 Adams, Frankie V
Ad1s Soulcraft; sketches on Negro-white relations designed to encourage friendship, by Frankie V. Adams. Atlanta, Ga., Morris Brown college press, Morris Brown college [1944]

5 p. l., 13-65 p. 22cm.

1. Negroes. I. Title.

45-109

Library of Congress * E185.61.A23 [3] 326.26

The souls of black folk.

M301 DuBois, William Edward Burghardt, 1868-
D853so8 The souls of black folk; essays and sketches. With an introduction by Saunders Redding. Greenwich, Conn., Fawcett Publications, Inc., 1961.

192p. 18cm.

The souls of black folk.

M301 Du Bois, William Edward Burghardt, 1858-
D853so8 The souls of black folk; essays and
1905 sketches. London, Archibald Constable, 1905-

viii, p., 1 l, 264p. 1 l. 22cm.
First English edition.

The souls of black folk

M301 Du Bois, William Edward Burghardt, 1868-
D853so8 The souls of black folk, essays and sketches Chicago, A. C. McClurg & Co., 1903.

viii, 1 l, 264p. 21½cm.

Guinea Soundjata.
M966.24 Niane, Djibril Tamsir.
N51 Soundjata; ou, L'épopée mandingue. Paris, Présence africaine [1960]

154 p. illus. 18 cm.

1. Mali Empire. I. Title. II. Title: L'épopée mandingue.

DT532.2.N5 61-48937 ‡

Library of Congress [1]

Sounds of the struggle.

M323.4 Lincoln, Charles Eric.
L638 Sounds of the struggle; persons and perspectives in civil rights, by C. Eric Lincoln. New York, Morrow, 1967.

252 p. 22 cm.
Includes bibliographical references.

1. ~~Negroes~~—Civil rights—Addresses, essays, lectures. I. Title.

E185.615.L5 323.4'0973 67-29822

Library of Congress [5]

Senegal
M896.1 Sourang, Ibrahima
So84aub Aubades. Préface de Léopold Sédar Senghor, Palais-Miami, Monte-Carlo [Editions Regain, 1964]

42p. 18cm. (Les Cahiers des Poètes de Notre Temps, no. 318)

I. Title. II. Series.

Sénégal
M896.1 Sourang, Ibrahima
So84au Auréoles. Préface de Camille Souyris. Palais Miami, Monte-Carlo [1961]

60p. 18cm. (Cahiers des poètes de notre temps, no. 255)

1. Senegal - Poetry. I. Title. II. Series.

Senegal
M896.1 Sourang, Ibrahima
So84c Chants du crépuscule. Palais-Miami, Monte-Carlo [Editions Regain, 1962]

61p. 18cm. (Les Cahiers des Poètes de Notre Temps, no. 273)

I. Title. II. Series.

La source; poème.

Haiti
M841 Brièrre, Jean Ferdinand, 1909-
B76s La source; poème. Buenos Aires, Collection du Jubilé du Docteur Jean Price Mars, 1956.

38p. 19cm.

Source studies in Southern history, no.1)

MB9 Johnson, William, 1809-1851.
J639 William Johnson's Natchez; the ante-bellum diary of a free Negro. Edited by William Random Hogan and Edwin Adams Davis. [Baton Rouge] Louisiana State University Press [1951]

ix, 812p. illus. facsims. 24cm. (Source studies in Southern history, no.1)

Sous les Bambous.

Haiti
M841 Battier, Alcibiade Fleury, 1841-
B32s Sous les Bambous, poésies par Alcibiade Fleury-Battier ... accompagnées d'un avant-propos de M. Gesner Rafina ... Paris, Imprimerie typographique Kugelmann, 1881.

319 p. 25cm.

"Coup-d'oeil sur le livre des poésies publié par M. A.-F. Battier", signed Edgar La Selve: p. [313]-319.

1. Rafina, Gesner. II. Title.

25-20890

Library of Congress PQ3949.B3S6

Martinique Sous l'oeil fixe du soleir.
M841.91 Desportes, George, 1921-
D46s Sous l'oeile fixe du soleir; poèms masqués. Paris, Debresse-Poésie, 1958.

127p. 19cm.

Sous l'orage (Kany)

Mali
M896.3 Badian, Seyou
B23 Sous l'orage (Kany) Paris, Présence Africaine [c 1963]

153p. 19cm.

Congo, Brazzaville
M967.26
S08 Sousatte, René-Paul.
L'ame Africaine. ‹Brazzaville, Imprimerie du Service de Presse ‹1945›
23p. port. illus. 27cm.
1. Africa. I. Title.

M968
So8r South Africa. Supreme Court.
Appeals ... against invalidation of the separate representation of Voters act, 1951 (Act no. 46 of 1951)
24p. 28cm.
Reprinted from Time's law review, March 23, 1952.
Mimeographed.
(Tracings over)
1. Africa, South. Race question. 2. Harris, Cantel. 3. Franklin, Edgar. 4. Collins, William Daniel. 5. Deane, Edgar Arthur.

The South African way of life...
S. Africa
M968
C135 Calpin, George Harold, 1897- ed.
The South African way of life: values and ideals of a multi-racial society. Edited by G. H. Calpin under the auspices of the South African Institute of International Affairs. New York, Columbia University Press, 1953.
ix, 200 p. plates, tables. 23 cm. (The Way of life series)
Bibliographical footnotes.
1. Africa, South—Soc. condit. 2. Minorities—Africa, South. I. South African Institute of International Affairs. II. Title. (Series)
DT761.C3 1953 968 A 54-8905
Columbia Univ. for Library of Congress Libraries ‹20›†

M323
B81m South.
Browning, Matthew.
My tour through Dixie. Minneapolis, Martin Brown, 1947.
‹9›p. 20cm.

South Africa: the peasants' revolt.
South Africa
M968
M45s Mbeki, Govan Archibald Mvunyelwa, 1910-
South Africa: the peasants' revolt ‹by› Govan Mbeki. Baltimore, Penguin Books ‹1964›
156, ‹3› p. map, port. 18 cm. (Penguin African library, AP9)
Portrait of author on book cover.
1. Africa, South—Native races. 2. Kaffraria—Pol. & govt. 3. Negroes in Africa, South—Segregation. I. Title.
DT846.K2M3 323.1 64-57150
Library of Congress ‹2›

South America.
M378
W52a West Virginia. State college, *Institute. Research council.*
... An adventure in cooperative research; Harry W. Greene, editor; associate editors: Herman G. Canady, Harrison H. Ferrell ‹and others› ... Personnel of Research council: Harry W. Greene, chairman; Hillery C. Thorne, executive secretary ‹and others› ... Institute, W. Va., West Virginia State college ‹1944›
74 p. 23cm. (West Virginia state college bulletin. Ser. 31, no. 1. Feb. 1944)
Cover-title: The Research council at West Virginia State college publishes An adventure in cooperative research.
"Fourth contribution of the Research council."—Introd.
"The second of a series ... in connection with the semi-centennial celebration (1941) of the West Virginia State college."—Introd.
(Continued on next card)
44-42483
‹4›

M304
P19
v.5, no.2 South.
Councill, William Hooper, 1848-
Synopsis of three addresses delivered at the Chautauqua Assembly at Waterloo, Iowa, July 10, 14, 15; at Chautauqua Assembly at Spirit Lake, School of Iowa at Cedar Falls, July 15, 1900. I. Building the South. 2. The children of the South. 3. Negro religion and character: No apology.
‹ n.p. 1900›
18p. 21½cm.

Africa
M968
So8 South Africa behind bars. Johannesburg, South Africa. African National Congress, 1950.
16p. illus. 22cm.
1. South Africa - Race question.

South America.
M378
W52a West Virginia. State college, *Institute. Research council.* ... An adventure in cooperative research ... ‹1944›
(Card 2)
CONTENTS.—The conference in review, by H. C. Thorne.—The theory of educational research, by J. S. Price.—The newer Negro and his education, by F. C. Sumner.—Some suggestions for research in the contribution of the Negro to American life, by John Lovell, jr.—The promotion of biological research, by H. E. Finley.—South America, a new frontier, by V. B. Spratlin.
1. Negroes. 2. Negroes—Education. 3. Negroes in South America. I. Greene, Harry Washington, 1896- ed. II. Title.
44-42483
Library of Congress E185.5.W5
‹4› $25.260973

South.
M975
N31 Du Bois, William Edward Burghardt, 1868-
The Negro in the black belt; Some social sketches. ‹Bulletin of the Labor Dept., no.22, ‹1899›. Pp. 401-417.
In: The Negro in the black belt. Washington, D.C., Dept. of Labor, ‹1897-1902›

South Africa
see also
Africa, South.

Uruguay
M864.6
P41m South America.
Pereda Valdés, Ildefonso, 1899-
... El negro rioplatense, y otros ensayos. Montevideo, C. García & cía, 1937.
187, ‹1› p., 1 l. plates. 17½cm.
CONTENTS.—Contribución al estudio del tema del negro en la literatura castellana hasta fines de la edad de oro.—Contribución al estudio de la música popular brasileña.—Supersticiones africanas del Río de la Plata.—Los pueblos negros del Uruguay y la influencia africana en el habla rioplatense.—Vocabulario de palabras de origen africano en el habla rioplatense.—El diablo mundo y Martín Fierro.—"La mojiganga de la muerte"; una piexa menor poco conocida de Calderón.—Los antiquijotes.—El "no" japonés y la tragedia griega.—Balzac, novelista de una época.—Las ideas ultraconservadoras de Chateaubriand.
1. Negroes in literature and art. 2. Negroes in South America. 3. Literature, Modern—Addresses, essays, lectures. I. Title.
39-10585
Library of Congress PQ8510.P26N4
‹42c1› 864.6

South.
M975
N31 The Negro in the black belt; Some social sketches and other economic and social studies published by the Department of Labor. Washington, D.C. ‹1897-1902›.
1v. (various paging) tables. maps. 23cm.
Eight separately issued Labor Dept. Bulletins.

The South African constitution.
Africa, South
M968
Sp6s Molteno, Donald B , 1908-
The South African constitution.
pp. 193-204.
In: South Africa the road ahead, comp. by Hildegarde Spottiswoode. 1960.

South America—Descr. & trav.
M910
H43m Hershaw, Fay McKeene.
Memories of east South America; an appreciation in story and pictures, by Fay McKeene Hershaw ... Boston, Meador publishing company, 1940.
144 p. incl. front. (map) plates. 20cm.
1. South America—Descr. & trav. I. Title. II. Title: East South America, Memories of.
40-5440
Library of Congress F2223.H42
——— Copy 2.
Copyright A 139001 ‹2› 918

M323
So8 South.
The Southern Negro, 1952; Warning to Ike and the Dixiecrats, a special issue. New York, The Nation, 1952.
243-284p. illus. 29cm.
Special issue of The Nation, September 27, 1952.
Partial contents: -The Negro vote in the South, 1952, by Henry Lee Moon. -How far has southern labor advanced? by George S. Mitchell. -Democrats versus Dixiecrats, by Clarence Mitchell.

South African Institute of International Affairs
S. Africa
M968
C135 Calpin, George Harold, 1897- ed.
The South African way of life: values and ideals of a multi-racial society. Edited by G. H. Calpin under the auspices of the South African Institute of International Affairs. New York, Columbia University Press, 1953.
ix, 200 p. plates, tables. 23 cm. (The Way of life series)
Bibliographical footnotes.
1. Africa, South—Soc. condit. 2. Minorities—Africa, South. I. South African Institute of International Affairs. II. Title. (Series)
DT761.C3 1953 968 A 54-8905
Columbia Univ. for Library of Congress Libraries ‹20›†

The South and the Negro.
M06
J61
no.11 Galloway, Charles Betts, *bp.*, 1849-1909.
... The South and the Negro; an address delivered at the seventh Annual conference for education in the South, Birmingham, Ala., April 26, 1904, by the Rev. Bishop Charles B. Galloway ... New York, The Trustees, 1904.
16 p. 23cm. (Trustees of the John F. Slater fund. Occasional papers. no. 11)
1. Negroes. 2. U. S.—Race question. I. Title.
5-30409
Library of Congress E185.5.J65 no. 11
——— Copy 2. E185.61.G17
‹39e1›

South Africa - Health.
S. Africa
M610
J68im Jolobe, James J R , 1902-
Impilo-ntle; iguqulwe, ngu James J. R. Jolobe, NoE. Thandiwe Makiwane; ku guide to health for adults. Lovedale, Lovedale Press, 1955.
94p. illus. 25cm.

S. Africa
M398
M89 South African legends.
Mukhombo, Aron S
A nkutsulani wa matimu ya batswa; a timhaka ta kale ti khedzelwe. Cleveland, Central Mission Press, 1931.
127p. port. 20½cm.
Tswa legends.

M973.6
C76
1876 South Carolina.
Conference of colored citizens, Columbia, S. C.
An address to the people of the United States, adopted at a conference of colored citizens. held at Columbia, S. C. July 20th and 21st, 1876. Columbia, S. C., Republican printing co., 1876.
13 p. 19cm.

M972
F51

South Carolina.
First anniversary of the proclamation of freedom in South Carolina, held at Beaufort, S.C., January 1, 1864. Beaufort, S.C., Free South Print, 1864.

17p. 21½cm.

M366.1
F87s

South Carolina.
Freemasons. South Carolina. Grand Lodge.
Proceedings. 1st- 1867-
Columbia, S.C., 18 -

v. 22cm. annual
See holdings card for proceedings in library.

M975.7
G65

South Carolina
Gordon, Asa H
Sketches of Negro life and history in South Carolina. Special contributors: Dr. D.H. Sims... Mr. B.E. Mays ... Mr. B.B. Barnwell. Industrial college, Georgia. The author. c1929

xvi, 280p. 22cm.

M975.7
G76m

South Carolina.
Grant, Ulysses S. pres. of U.S.
...Message from the president of the United States, communicating, in answer to a senate resolution of July 20, 1876, information in relation to the slaughter of American citizens at Hamburgh, S.C.
56p. 23cm. (U.S. Congress, 1st sess. Senate. Ex. Doc. no.85)

M973.8
T21

South Carolina.
Taylor, Alrutheus Ambush.
The Negro in South Carolina during the reconstruction by Alrutheus Ambush Taylor, Washington, D.C., The Association for the study of Negro life and history.

iv, 341p. 24cm.

M398.
B75

South Carolina- Folk tales.
Brewer, John Mason, 1896- ed.
Humorous folk tales of the South Carolina Negro... Orangeburg, S.C., South Carolina Negro folklore guild 1945

xxi 64p. illus. 24½cm.

M973
R81r

South Carolina - Politics and government.
DuBois, William Edward Burghardt, 1868-
The black proletariat in South Carolina.

pp. 62-83.

In: Reconstruction in the South, by Edwin Charles Rozwenc. 1952.

S.Africa
M896
So21s

The south-eastern Bantu.
Soga, John Henderson.
The south-eastern Bantu (Abe-Naguni, Aba-Mbo, Ama-Lala) by J. Henderson Soga. Johannesburg, The Witwatersrand university press, 1930.

xxxi, 490 p., 1 l. front. (port.) map, geneal. tables (part fold.) 22cm. (*Half-title:* "Bantu studies" ... Supplement no. 4)

Errata leaf inserted between p. [xxiv] and [xxv]
"Editor's introduction" and "A biographical note on the author" signed: R. F. A. H. [*i. e.* Reinhold Friedrich Alfred Hoernlé]
Bibliography: p. [xxi]-xxiii.

1. Bantus. I. Hoernlé, Reinhold Friedrich Alfred, 1880- ed. II. Title.

32-6775
Library of Congress DT764.B286
[3] 572.968

Kenya
M967.6
M451u

South Nyanza, Kenya - Politics and government.
Mboya, Paul
Utawala na Maendeleo ya local government South Nyanza 1926-1957. (The work and progress of local government in South Nyanza, Kenya: 1926-1957.) Nairobi, The Eagle Press, 1959.

32p. illus. 18½cm.
Text in: Swahili.

1. Kenya - Politics and government. 2. South Nyanza, Kenya - Politics and government.

M813.3
N312

South Carolina-Soc. lif & cust.
Neilson, Peter, 1795-1861.
The life and adventure of Zamba, an African negro king; and his experience of slavery in South Carolina. Written by himself. Corrected and arranged by Peter Neilson. London, Smith, Elder and co., 1847.

xx, 258 p. front. 20½ cm.

Written by Peter Neilson. *cf.* Dict. nat. biog.

1. Slavery in the U. S.—Fiction. 2. South Carolina—Soc. life & cust. I. Title.

7—33168
Library of Congress PZ3.N318L
[a28d1]

M323
R78

South of Freedom.
Rowan, Carl Thomas.
South of freedom. [1st ed.] New York, Knopf, 1952.

270 p. 22 cm.

1. Negroes. 2. U. S.—Race question. I. Title.

E185.61.R86 51—11990 ‡
*301.451 325.260975
Library of Congress [53i⁴7]

M813.5
Sm68s

South street.
Smith, William Gardner, 1926-
South Street. New York, Farrar, Straus and Young [1954]

312 p. 21 cm.

I. Title.

PZ3.S6638So 54-5687 ‡
Library of Congress [7]

M975
M834

The South today, 100 years after Appomattox.
Morris, Willie, *ed.*
The South today, 100 years after Appomattox. [1st ed.] New York, Harper & Row [1965]

ix, 149 p. 22 cm.

Most of these essays, now rev. and extended, originally appeared in a supplement to the April 1965 issue of Harper's magazine.

1. Southern States — Race question. 2. Southern States — Soc. condit. I. Harper's magazine. Supplement. II. Title.

E185.61.M85 301.45196075 65-21004
Library of Congress [5]

M813.5
G76s

South Town.
Graham, Lorenz B
South Town. Chicago, Follett Pub. Co. [1958]

189 p. 23 cm.

I. Title.

PZ4.G74So 58—13128 ‡
Library of Congress [59h7]

U. S.
M968
Am3

Southern Africa in transition.
American Society of African Culture.
Southern Africa in transition. Edited by John A. Davis and James K. Baker. New York, Published for the American Society of African Culture by F. A. Praeger [1966]

xxviii, 427 p. map. 21 cm.

Revisions of papers first presented at the Fourth International Conference of the American Society of African Culture, held at Howard University, Washington, D. C., in the spring of 1963.
Bibliographical footnotes.

1. Africa, Sub-Saharan. 2. Africa, South. I. Davis, John Aubrey, 1912- ed. II. Baker, James K., 1919- ed. III. Howard University, Washington, D. C. IV. Title.

DT733.A7 320.968 65—13968
Library of Congress [67o5]

M641.5
B55s

The southern cookbook;
Bivins, S Thomas.
The southern cookbook; a manual of cooking and list of menus, including recipes used by noted colored cooks and prominent caterers, by S. Thomas Bivins ... Hampton, Va., Press of the Hampton institute, 1912.

239 p. 22½cm. $2.00

1. Cookery, American. I. Title.

12-26875
Library of Congress TX715.B5
Copyright A 328293 [36b1]

M06
J61
no. 12

Southern industrial classes, *Norfolk, Va.*
... Report of the society of the Southern industrial classes, Norfolk, Virginia, to the trustees of the John F. Slater fund and the General education board ... [11th]-
19
Hampton, Va., 19

v. 23cm. (The Trustees of the John F. Slater fund. Occasional papers, no. 12

Report year ends in February.
Short reports are included in the Proceedings of the John F. Slater fund, 1890-1913.

1. ~~Negroes~~—Education. 2. Technical education—Southern states.

7—37620
Library of Congress E185.5.J65 no. 12
[38r19e1]

M323.4
B93f

Southern justice.
Friedman, Leon, *ed.*
Southern justice. With a foreword by Mark DeW. Howe. New York, Pantheon Books [1965]

ix, 306 p. 22 cm.
Bibliographical references included in "Notes" (p. [281]-306)

1. Justice, Administration of—Southern States. 2. Negroes—Legal status, laws, etc. 3. Civil rights—Southern States. I. Title.

323.4 65-14581
Library of Congress [5]

M323
So8

The Southern Negro, 1952; warning to Ike and the Dixiecrats, a special issue. New York, The Nation, 1952.

243-284p. illus. 29cm.
Special issue of The Nation, September 27, 1952.
Partial contents: -The Negro vote in the South, 1952, by Henry Lee Moon. -How far has southern labor advanced? by George S. Mitchell. -Democrats versus Dixiecrats, by Clarence Mitchell.
(Tracings on card 2)

M323
So8

The Southern Negro, 1952. (Card 2)

1. Moore, Harry T. p.267. 2. South. I. a.t. Moon, Henry Lee, 1901- . II. a.t. Mitchell, Clarence M.,1911- . III. a.t. Mitchell, George S.

M027
G47

The southern Negro and the public library.
Gleason, Eliza Valeria (Atkins) 1909-
The southern Negro and the public library; a study of the government and administration of public library service to Negroes in the South, by Eliza Atkins Gleason, with a foreword by Louis R. Wilson. Chicago, Ill., The University of Chicago press [1941]
xvi, 218 p. incl. tables, diagrs. 21 cm. (*Half-title:* The University of Chicago studies in library science)
Issued also in part as thesis (PH. D.) Chicago university, under title: The government and administration of public library service to Negroes in the South.
Bibliography: p. 199-202.
1. Libraries and Negroes. 2. Libraries—Southern states. I. Title.

41—52062
Library of Congress Z711.9.G6
[48r43x2] 027.636

Nigeria
M966.9
An34

Southern Nigeria in transition.
Anene, Joseph C
Southern Nigeria in transition, 1885–1906; theory and practice in a colonial protectorate. Cambridge, Cambridge U. P., 1966.
xii, 360 p. illus., 9 plates (incl. map, ports.) tables. 22½ cm. 45/–
(B 66–5470)
Bibliography: p. 340–346.
1. Nigeria—Hist. I. Title.
DT515.7.A48 966.903 66–70318 rev
Library of Congress ₍r66f5₎

M975
T39

A southern reader.
Thorp, Willard, 1899- ed.
A southern reader. ₍1st ed.₎ New York, Knopf, 1955.
760p. illus. 25cm.

S. Africa
M968
M711

Southern Rhodesia.
Mnyanda, B J
In search of truth; a commentary on certain aspects of Southern Rhodesia's Native Policy. Bombay, Hind Kitabs Ltd., 1954.
173p. port. map 21cm.

M306
Sol
1913

Southern sociological congress. 2d, *Atlanta*, 1913.
The human way. Addresses on race problems at the Southern sociological congress, Atlanta, 1913. Edited by James E. McCulloch. Nashville, Southern sociological congress, 1913.
146 p. 24cm.
Also included in "The South mobilizing for social service: addresses delivered at the Southern sociological congress", Nashville, 1913.
Bibliography: p. ₍144₎–146.
Partial contents: Racial self-respect and racial antagonism, by Charles V. Roman.
1. ~~[illegible]~~ 2. Sociology—Congresses. I. McCulloch, James Edward, 1873- ed. II. Title. III. a.t. Roman.
Agr 13–1850
U. S. Dept. of agr. Library for Library of Congress 280So8 E185.61.S72
₍a33d1₎

M306
Sol
1913

Southern Sociological Congress, 2d, Atlanta, 1913.
The South mobilizing for social service; addresses delivered at the Southern Sociological Congress, Atlanta, Georgia, April 25-29, 1913. Ed. by James E. McCulloch. Nashville, 1913.
702p. 24cm.
Partial contents: Racial self-respect and racial antagonism, by Charles V. Roman.
1. Race problems. I. a.t. Roman. II. McCulloch, James Edward, 1873- ed.

M306
Sol
1919

Southern Sociological Congress. Knoxville. 1919
Distinguished service citizenship. Ed. by J. E. McCulloch. Washington, D. C., Southern Sociological Congress, 1919.
170 p. 23 cm.
Partial contents: Interracial co-operation and the south's new economic conditions, by Monroe Work.
1. Citizenship. 2. Race relations. I. a.t. Work. II. McCulloch, James Edward, 1873- ed.

M306
Sol
1919

Southern Sociological Congress. Houston, 1915.
The New chivalry - health. Edited by James E. McCulloch. Nashville, Southern Sociological Congress, 1915.
555p. 24cm.
Partial contents: The Negro woman and the health problem, by C.V. Roman. City housing of Negroes in relation to health, by J.W. Gilbert. The South and the Health of Negroes, by Monroe N. Work. Recreation as related to the health of Negroes in rural communities, by J.A. Booker;
(continued)

M306
Sol
1919

Southern Sociological Congress. Houston, 1915.
The New chivalry - health. Edited by James E. McCulloch. Nashville, Southern Sociological Congress, 1915. (Card 2)
555p. 24cm.
Health the basis of racial prosperity, by R. R. Wright. Health problems of the Negro church, by L.K. Williams.
1. Health and hygiene. I. a.t. Roman. II. a.t. Gilbert. III. a.t. Work. IV. a.t. Booker. V. a.t. Wright. VI. a.t. Williams.

South
Africa
M496
M11

Southern Sotho-English Dictionary.
Mabille, Adolph, 1836-1894.
Southern Sotho-English Dictionary, by A. Mabille and H. Dieterlen. Reclassified, revised and enlarged by R. A.Paroz. Morija, Basutoland, Morija Sesuto Book Dept., 1950.
xvi, 445p. 21½cm.
White authors.

M323.
C67p

Southern States.
Coleman, Charles C
Patterns of race relations in the South. New York, Exposition Press ₍1949₎
44p. 21cm.

M331
H77t

Southern states.
Hope, John, 1909-
3 southern plants of International Harvester Company, prepared for the NPA Committee of South. Washington, D. C., National Planning Association, 1953.
143 p. tables 23 cm. (National Planning Association. Committee of the South. Report no. 1)

M301
L58b

Southern States.
Lewis, Hylan.
Blackways of Kent. Chapel Hill, University of North Carolina Press, 1955.
xxiv, 337 p. diagrs., tables. 21 cm. (Field studies in the modern culture of the South)
Based on thesis, University of Chicago.
1. Negroes—Southern States. I. Title. (Series)
E185.6.L4 55—62673
*301.451 325.260975
Library of Congress ₍56k10₎

M301
M69

Southern States.
Mitchell, Glenford E *ed.*
The angry black South. Edited by Glenford E. Mitchell and William H. Peace, III. New York, Corinth Books, 1962.
159 p. 21 cm.
Portraits of authors on back of book.
1. Negroes—Southern States. 2. U. S.—Race question. I. Peace, William H., joint ed. II. Title.
E185.61.M67 301.451 61—15876 ‡
Library of Congress ₍62f5₎

M331.1
N21s

Southern States.
National Planning Association. Committee of the South.
Selected studies of Negro employment in the South, prepared for the NPA Committee of the South. Washington, National Planning Association ₍1953-54₎
5v. (x, 483, a-i p.) illus. 23cm.
(Its Report no.6)

M781
R14br

Southern States.
Ramsey, Frederic, 1915–
Been here and gone. New Brunswick, N. J., Rutgers University Press ₍1960₎
177 p. illus. 24 cm.
1. Music—Negroes. 2. Negroes—Southern States. 3. Southern States—Soc. life & cust.—1865- —Illustrations. I. Title.
Full name: Charles Frederic Ramsey.
ML3556.R3 781.775 59—7514
Library of Congress ₍61c20₎

M323
R78g

Southern States.
Rowan, Carl Thomas.
Go South to sorrow. New York, Random House ₍1957₎
246 p. 21 cm.
1. Negroes—Segregation. 2. Negroes—Southern States. I. Title.
E185.61.R855 325.260975 57–5378 ‡
Library of Congress ₍25₎

M973.8
St8

Southern states.
Straker, David Augustus, *d.* 1908.
The new South investigated. By D. Augustus Straker ... Detroit, Mich., Ferguson printing company, 1888.
viii p., 1 l., 11–230 p. front. (port.) 20cm.
1. Southern states. 2. Negroes. I. Title.
1—21330
Library of Congress F215.S89
Copyright 1888: 23618 ₍a30c1₎

M323
W651

Southern states.
Wilkins, Roy, 1901-
Integration crisis in the South; an address delivered at the 14th annual State convention of the NAACP in Charlotte, N. C., October 11th, 1957, and broadcast over radio network facilities of the American Broadcasting Company. New York, National Association for the Advancement of Colored People ₍1957₎
11p. 21½cm.
1. Race relations. 2. Southern states. I. Title.

M630
B87p

₍Southern states—Agriculture₎
Bullock, Benjamin Franklin, 1888–
Practical farming for the South, by B. F. Bullock ... Chapel Hill, The University of North Carolina press, 1944.
xvii, ₍3₎, 3–510 p. illus. 21cm.
"Farm publications": p. 460–486. Bibliography ₍on mulching and sub-surface tillage₎: p. 498.
1. Agriculture—Handbooks, manuals, etc. 2. Agriculture—Southern states. ₍2. Southern states—Agriculture₎ 3. Faulkner, Edward Hubert, 1886- Plowman's folly. I. Title. II. Title: Farming for the South.
Agr 44–211
U. S. Dept. of agr. Library for Library of Congress 31.3B87 S505.B8
₍30₎† 630.2

M301
Se4s

Southern States-Civilization.
Sellers, Charles Grier, *ed.*
The southerner as American. ₍By₎ John Hope Franklin ₍and others₎ Chapel Hill, University of North Carolina Press ₍1960₎
216 p. 24 cm.
Includes bibliography.
1. National characteristics, American. 2. Southern States—Civilization. 3. Southern States—Hist.—Historiography. 4. Southern States—Race question. I. Title.
F209.S44 917.5 60—4104 ‡
Library of Congress ₍61v30₎

M975
T39

Southern States - Civilization.
Thorp, Willard, 1899- ed.
A southern reader. ₍1st ed.₎ New York, Knopf, 1955.
760p. illus. 25cm.

Southern States-Descr. & trav.

M973.5 J95j
Jones, Katharine M 1900- ed.
The plantation South. [1st ed.] Indianapolis, Bobbs-Merrill [1957]
412 p. illus. 22 cm.
Includes bibliography.
White author.

1. Southern States—Descr. & trav. 2. Southern States—Soc. life & cust. 3. Plantation life.

F213.J6 917.5 57—9357 ‡
Library of Congress [a62y^{2}5]

Southern States-Description and travel.

M323 Sa13
Sabourin, Clemonce.
Let the righteous speak! Travel memoirs. [1st ed.] New York, Pageant Press [1957]
89 p. 21 cm.

1. Negroes—Segregation. 2. Southern States—Descr. & trav. I. Title.

E185.61.S25 325.260975 57-8311 ‡
Library of Congress [2]

Southern states-Econ. condit.

M975 D29
Davis, Allison, 1902-
Deep South; a social anthropological study of caste and class, written by Allison Davis, Burleigh B. Gardner and Mary R. Gardner, directed by W. Lloyd Warner. Chicago, Ill., The University of Chicago press [1941]
xv, 558 p. incl. tables, diagrs., forms. 20 cm.

1. Southern states—Soc. condit. 2. Negroes. 3. Southern states—Econ. condit. I. Gardner, Burleigh Bradford, 1904- joint author. II. Gardner, Mary R., joint author. III. Warner, William Lloyd, 1898- ed. IV. Title.
[Full name: William Allison Davis]
41-23645 rev
Library of Congress HN79.A2D3 [r42i7] 309.175

Southern states - Econ. condit.

M378 FB F54b
Fisk University, *Nashville*.
Build the future; addresses marking the inauguration of Charles Spurgeon Johnson. Nashville, Fisk Univ. Press, 1949.
ix, 100 p. 24 cm.
Introd. signed: Edwin R. Embree.
PARTIAL CONTENTS.—Recent economic changes in the South.—The next ten years in education.—Human rights and international relations.

1. Southern states—Econ. condit. 2. Education—Southern states. 3. Civil rights. 4. Johnson, Charles Spurgeon, 1893- I. Embree, Edwin Rogers, 1883- II. Title.

HC107.A13F63 378.9768 49—3360*
Library of Congress [50r49c5]

Southern states—Econ. condit.

M323.! F77
Fortune, Timothy Thomas.
Black and white: land, labor, and politics in the South. By T. Thomas Fortune ... New York, Fords, Howard, & Hulbert, 1884.
iv p., 2 l., [9]-310 p. 17½cm. (*On cover: American questions*)

1. Negroes. 2. U. S.—Race question. 3. Southern states—Econ. condit.
12—2876
Library of Congress E185.61.F74
——— Copy 2.
Copyright 1884: 16803 [38g1]

M301 R27p
Southern states - Econ. condit.
Reid, Ira DeAugustine, 1901-
Poor land and peasantry, by Arthur Raper and Ira DeA. Reid. pp. 15-17, 41-42.

In: North Georgia review; A magazine of the southern regions, winter, 1939-1940.

Southern states-Econ. condit.-1918-

M331 L58
Lewis, Edward Erwin, 1900-
The mobility of the Negro; a study in the American labor supply, by Edward E. Lewis ... New York, Columbia university press; London, P. S. King & son, ltd., 1931.
144 p. illus. (maps) 23cm. (*Half-title: Studies in history, economics and public law, ed. by the Faculty of political science of Columbia university, no. 342*)
Published also as thesis (PH. D.) Columbia university.
"The third volume to appear as a result of studies in the field of Negro migration under grants by the Social science research council and the Columbia university Council for research in the social sciences."—Foreword.
"Selected bibliography": p. 134-135.
1. Negroes. 2. Negroes — Employment. 3. Southern states — Econ. condit.—1918- 4. Cotton growing and manufacture—Southern states. I. Social science research council. II. Columbia university. Council for research in the social sciences. III. Title.
Library of Congress H31.C7 no. 342 31—29612
——— Copy 2. E185.8.L47
[42q2] (306.2) 331.6

M301 R27sh
Southern states - Econ. condit. - 1918-
Reid, Ira DeAugustine, 1901-
Sharecroppers all by Arthur F. Raper and Ira DeA. Reid. Chapel Hill, The University of North Carolina press, 1941.

xp., 21., 3-281p. front. plates. 21½cm.

Southern States - Education.

M370 W65p
Wilkerson, Doxey Alphonso, 1905-
The people versus segregated schools. New York, New Century Publishers, 1955.

15p. 18cm.

M813.5 C79t
Southern States - Fiction.
Cooper, William Arthur, 1895-
Thank God for a song; a novel of Negro church life in the rural south. New York, Exposition Press [1922]

121p. 21cm.

Southern States - Fiction.

M813.5 L139b
LaHon, Vyola Therese
The big lie. New York, Vantage Press [1964]

68p. 20½cm.

Southern States - History - Addresses, essays, lectures.

M973 C886
Crowe, Charles Robert, 1928- ed.
The age of Civil War and Reconstruction, 1830-1900; a book of interpretative essays, edited by Charles Crowe. Homewood, Ill., Dorsey Press, 1966.
x, 479 p. 26 cm. (The Dorsey series in American history)
Includes bibliographies.

1. Southern States—Hist.—Addresses, essays, lectures. 2. U. S.—Hist.—Civil War—Addresses, sermons, etc. 3. Reconstruction—Addresses, essays, lectures. I. Title.

F209.C7 973.08 66-27454
Library of Congress [5]

Southern States-History-Historiography.

M301 Se4s
Sellers, Charles Grier, ed.
The southerner as American. [By] John Hope Franklin [and others] Chapel Hill, University of North Carolina Press [1960]
216 p. 24 cm.
Includes bibliography.

1. National characteristics, American. 2. Southern States—Civilization. 3. Southern States — Hist. — Historiography. 4. Southern States—Race question. I. Title.

F209.S44 917.5 60—4104 ‡
Library of Congress [61r^{2}30]

Southern States-Hist.-1775-1865.

M973 F85m
Franklin, John Hope, 1915-
The militant South, 1800-1861. Cambridge, Belknap Press of Harvard University Press, 1956.
317 p. 22 cm.
Includes bibliography.

1. Southern States—Hist.—1775-1865. 2. Militarism. I. Title.

F213.F75 975 56—10160 ‡
Library of Congress [57x20]

Southern States - History - 1865-1877.

M973.8 R81r
Rozwenc, Edwin Charles, 1915- ed.
Reconstruction in the South. Boston, Heath [1952]
109 p. 24 cm. (Problems in American civilization; readings selected by the Dept. of American Studies, Amherst College)
Bibliography: p. 108-109.
White author.

1. Reconstruction. 2. Southern States—Hist.—1865-1877. I. Title.

E668.R83 973.8 52—1818 ‡
Library of Congress [60g2]

Southern States - Race question.

M323 G12w
Gaines, Gartrell J
Where do we stand? The Negro in the South today. [1st ed.] New York, Vantage Press [1957]
76 p. illus. 21 cm.

1. Southern States—Race question. 2. Negroes. 3. Miscegenation. I. Title.

E185.61.G15 57-7789 ‡
*301.451 325.260975
Library of Congress [30]

Southern States - Race question.

M975 M834
Morris, Willie, ed.
The South today, 100 years after Appomattox. [1st ed.] New York, Harper & Row [1965]
ix, 149 p. 22 cm.
Most of these essays, now rev. and extended, originally appeared in a supplement to the April 1965 issue of Harper's magazine.

1. Southern States — Race question. 2. Southern States — Soc. condit. I. Harper's magazine. Supplement. II. Title.

E185.61.M85 301.45196075 65-21004
Library of Congress [8]

Southern States-Race question.

M301 Se4s
Sellers, Charles Grier, ed.
The southerner as American. [By] John Hope Franklin [and others] Chapel Hill, University of North Carolina Press [1960]
216 p. 24 cm.
Includes bibliography.

1. National characteristics, American. 2. Southern States—Civilization. 3. Southern States — Hist. — Historiography. 4. Southern States—Race question. I. Title.

F209.S44 917.5 60—4104 ‡
Library of Congress [61r^{2}30]

Southern states-Soc. condit.

M975 D29
Davis, Allison, 1902-
Deep South; a social anthropological study of caste and class, written by Allison Davis, Burleigh B. Gardner and Mary R. Gardner, directed by W. Lloyd Warner. Chicago, Ill., The University of Chicago press [1941]
xv, 558 p. incl. tables, diagrs., forms. 20 cm.

1. Southern states—Soc. condit. 2. Negroes. 3. Southern states—Econ. condit. I. Gardner, Burleigh Bradford, 1904- joint author. II. Gardner, Mary R., joint author. III. Warner, William Lloyd, 1898- ed. IV. Title.
[Full name: William Allison Davis]
41-23645 rev
Library of Congress HN79.A2D3 [r42i7] 309.175

Southern States - Social conditions.

M975 M834
Morris, Willie, ed.
The South today, 100 years after Appomattox. [1st ed.] New York, Harper & Row [1965]
ix, 149 p. 22 cm.
Most of these essays, now rev. and extended, originally appeared in a supplement to the April 1965 issue of Harper's magazine.

1. Southern States — Race question. 2. Southern States — Soc. condit. I. Harper's magazine. Supplement. II. Title.

E185.61.M85 301.45196075 65-21004
Library of Congress [8]

M301 R27sh
Southern states - Soc. condit.
Reid, Ira DeAugustine, 1901-
Sharecroppers all by Arthur F. Raper and Ira DeA. Reid. Chapel Hill, The University of North Carolina press, 1941.

xp., 21., 3-281p. front. plates. 21½cm.

Southern states— Soc. life & cust.

M910
B81m

Brown, William Wells, *b.* 1814.
My southern home: or, The South and its people. By Wm. Wells Brown ... ~~3d ed.~~ Boston, A. G. Brown & co., ~~1882.~~ 1880
vii, 253 p. illus. 19½cm.
Portrait.

1. Negroes. 2. Slavery in the U. S. 3. Southern states—Soc. life & cust. I. Title.
2—7807
Library of Congress E185.B88
[37b1-]

Southern States-Soc. life & cust.

M973.5
L95j

Jones, Katharine M 1900– *ed.*
The plantation South. [1st ed.] Indianapolis, Bobbs-Merrill [1957]
412 p. illus. 22 cm.
Includes bibliography.
White author.

1. Southern States—Descr. & trav. 2. Southern States—Soc. life & cust. 3. Plantation life.
F213.J6 917.5 57—9357 ‡
Library of Congress [a62y⅝]

Southern States - Soc.life & cust.-1865-
Illustrations.

M781
R14br

Ramsey, Frederic, 1915–
Been here and gone. New Brunswick, N. J., Rutgers University Press [1960]
177 p. illus. 24 cm.

1. Music — Negroes. 2. Negroes — Southern States. 3. Southern States—Soc. life & cust.—1865— —Illustrations. I. Title.
Full name: Charles Frederic Ramsey.
ML3556.R3 781.775 59—7514
Library of Congress [61c⅞20]

Southern states-Stat.

M301
J63s

Johnson, Charles Spurgeon, 1893–
Statistical atlas of southern counties; listing and analysis of socio-economic indices of 1104 southern counties, by Charles S. Johnson and associates: Lewis W. Jones, Buford H. Junker [and others] ... Chapel Hill, The University of North Carolina press, 1941.
x, 1 l., 355 p. illus. (maps) 26 cm.
"County and state reference lists": p. [290]-355.

1. Southern states—Stat. I. Jones, Lewis Wade, 1910– II. Title.
41-8730
Library of Congress HA218.J6
[8] 317.5

Southern sunbeams.

M811.5
H24s

Harrison, James Minnis, 1873-
Southern sunbeams, a book of poems by James M. Harrison. Richmond, Virginia, The Saint Luke press, 1926.

100p. port. 2[illegible]cm.

M631.114
So8p

Southern tenant farmer's union.
Proceedings... ann al convention 19 .
Memphis, Tenn., Southern tenant farmers' union, 19

v. 23cm.
Library has: 3rd. annual convention proceedings (Jan., 1937)

1. Sharecropping. 2. Farms and-farming.

Southern University, Baton Rouge, La.

MB9
C53c

Cade, John Brother, 1894–
The man christened Josiah Clark; who, as J. S. Clark, became president of a Louisiana State land grant college, by John B. Cade. [1st ed.] New York, American Press [1966]
202 p. 21 cm.
Bibliography: p. 201-202.
Portrait of author on book cover.

1. Clark, Joseph Samuel, 1871-1944. 2. Southern University, Baton Rouge, La. I. Title.
LA2317.C5C3 378.110924 66-17854
Library of Congress [5]

Southern women and racial adjustment...

M06
J61
no. 19

Hammond, *Mrs.* Lily (Hardy) 1859–
Southern women and racial adjustment, by L. H. Hammond. [Lynchburg, Va., J. P. Bell company, inc., printers] 1917.
32 p. 23½cm. (*On cover:* The trustees of the John F. Slater fund. Occasional papers, no. 19)

1. Negroes—Moral and social conditions. I. Title.
17—27879
Library of Congress E185.5.J65 no. 19
[40b1]

The southerner as American.

M301
Se4s

Sellers, Charles Grier, *ed.*
The southerner as American. [By] John Hope Franklin [and others] Chapel Hill, University of North Carolina Press [1960]
216 p. 24 cm.
Includes bibliography.

1. National characteristics, American. 2. Southern States—Civilization. 3. Southern States — Hist. — Historiography. 4. Southern States—Race question. I. Title.
F209.S44 917.5 60—4104 ‡
Library of Congress [61v30]

Trinidad
M820
J23s

Souvarine, Boris.
Stalin; a critical survey of bolshevism, by Boris Souvarine. London, Secker and Warburg [1940]
xiv, 690 p. 22 cm.
Portrait on t.-p.
"Translated by C. L. R. James."
"First published September 1939. Reprinted January 1940."
White author

1. Stalin, Iosif, 1879-1953. 2. Communism—Russia. I. James, Cyril Lionel Robert, 1901– tr.
DK268.S8S62 1940 923.247 40—12536
Library of Congress [a55c½]

... Le souvenir demeure.

Haiti
M841.
B45s

Bernard, Regnor C
... Le souvenir demeure. Préface de mr. Christian Werleigh... [Port-au-Prince, Haiti] Imprimerie "Le Jour," 1940.

cover-title, iv, 5-60p. port. 19½cm.
Poems.

Souvenirs.

Martinique
M972.98
P53s

Philémon, Césaire
Souvenirs. Préface de Thizy. 2e ed.
Paris, Exposition coloniale internationale, 1931.

176p. illus., ports. 22½cm.

Haiti
M972.94
D37s

...Souvenirs d'épopée.
Delienne, Castera
...Souvenirs d'épopée. Port-au-Prince, Haiti, Imp. de l'etat, 1935.
112p. port. (front) illus. 22cm.

Réunion
MB9
V88

Souvenirs d'un marchand de tableaux.
Vollard, Ambroise
Souvenirs d'un marchand de tableaux.
Édition revue et augmentée. Paris, Albin Michel. 1937.
458p. illus. 21cm.

Sousa, João da Cruz e, 1861-1898
see
Cruz e Souza, João da, 1861-1898.

Souza, Ivo de.

West Indies
M325.27
F21

Family Welfare Association, *London.*
The West Indian comes to England; a report prepared for the Trustees of the London Parochial Charities by the Family Welfare Association. Contributors: Douglas Manley, Ivo de Souza, Albert Hyndman, et al. Edited by S. K. Ruck. London, Routledge & K. Paul [1960]
187 p. 23 cm.

1. West Indians in Great Britain. I. Ruck, S. K., ed. II. Title.
DA125.W4F3 325.2729042 60-3053 ‡
Library of Congress [2]

Brazil
M398
S08

Souza Carneiro, A J de.
... Os mitos africanos no Brasil, ciencia do folk-lore; ilustrado com 30 gravuras e as fontes etimologicas de mais de 500 termos afro-brasileiros, ilustrações de Cicero Valladares. São Paulo [etc.] Companhia editora nacional, 1937.
506 p., 1 l. illus. 18½cm. (Biblioteca pedagogica brasileira. Ser. 5.ª: Brasiliana. v. 103)
At head of title: Souza Carneiro.

1. Folk-lore, ~~Negro~~. 2. ~~Negroes in~~ Brazil. I. Title.
38—4942
Library of Congress GR133.B6S6
[45d1] 398.0981

Brazil
M869.1
G58po

Souza Silva, Joaquim Norberto de, 1820-1891.
Gonçalves Diaz, Antonio, 1823-1864.
Poesias de A. Gonçalves Dias. Nova ed., organizada e rev. por J. Norberto de Souza Silva, e precidida de uma notiva sobre o autor e susas obras pelo congeo doutor Fernandes Pinheiro ... Rio de Janeiro, Paris, H. Garnier, 1910.
2 v. front. (port.) 18 cm. (Half title: Brasilia bibliotheca dos melhores autores nacionaes antigos e modernos)

Nigeria
M896.1
So9a

Sowande, J S
Awọn ărofo-orin ti Sọbọ A-ró-bi-odu li ọdun 1930. Ake, Abeokuta, 1931.

47p. 20½cm.
Written in Yoruba.
Translation: A series of poems.
"Alias Sọbọ a-ró-bi-odu"

1. Nigeria-Poetry. I. Title: A ~~series of poems~~.

... Sowing and reaping.

M814.4
W722so

Washington, Booker Taliferro, 1859?-1915.
...Sowing and reaping. New York and Boston, H. M. Caldwell, 1900.

5-29p. 19½cm. (The Character and wisdom series.)

Sowing and reaping and other poems.

M811.5
H86s

Huff, William Henry, 1887-
Sowing and reaping and other poems . Avon, Illinois, Hamlet press, 1950.

77p. 22cm.

Nigeria
[illegible].9
So5o

Sowunmi, Akintunde.
Our land and People. Part III - the west. Lagos, Public Relations Department, n.d.

16p. illus. map 20½cm. (Crownbird Series No. 33)

1. Nigeria.

Nigeria
M896.2
So3d

Soyinka, Wole.
A dance of the forest. London, Ibadan, Oxford University Press, 1963.

89p. 18½ cm.

I. Title.

Nigeria
M896.2
So3f

Soyinka, Wole.
Five plays: A dance of the forests, The lion and the jewel, The swamp dwellers, The trials of Brother Jero ⌊and⌋ The strong breed. London, Oxford University Press, 1964.

276 p. 20 cm. (⌊A Three crowns book⌋)

I. A dance of the forests. II. The lion and the jewel. III. The swamp dwellers. IV. The trials of Brother Jero. V. The strong breed.

PR6069.O9F5 822.914 65-1569
Library of Congress ⌊3⌋

Nigeria
M896.1
So91

Soyinka, Wole.
Idanre, & other poems. London, Methuen, 1967.

88 p. 21 cm. 18/- (B 67-26606)

I. Title.

PR6069.O9 I 8 821 68-77557
Library of Congress ⌊3⌋

Nigeria
M896.3
So96i

Soyinka, Wole
The interpreters. ⌊London⌋ Andre Deutsch ⌊1965⌋

251p. 20cm.

I. Title.

Nigeria
M896.2
So3k

Soyinka, Wole, 1934-
Kongi's Harvest. London, Ibadan ⌊etc.⌋ Oxford U. P., 1967.

⌊5⌋, 90 p. 18½ cm. (Three crowns books) 8/6 (B 67-11141)

I. Title.

PR6069.O9K6 822 67-91651
Library of Congress ⌊3⌋

Nigeria
M896.2
So3L

Soyinka, Wole.
The lion and the jewel. London, Oxford University Press, 1963.

64p. 18cm.

1. African drama. 2. Drama - Africa.
I. Title.

Nigeria
M896.2
So3r

Soyinka, Wole
The road. London, Oxford University Press, 1965.

101p. 18½cm.

1. African drama. I. Title.

Nigeria
M896.2
So3t

Soyinka, Wolè
Three plays. Book design and illustration by Denis Williams. Ibadan, Ibadan University Press, 1963.

118p. 21cm. (Mbari Publications)
Contents: The swamp-dwellers. The trials of Brother Jero. The strong breed.

1. Africa - Drama. I. The swamp dwellers. II. The trials of Brother Jero. III. The strong breed.

Space, time and race or the age of man in America.

Ghana
M573
Ar5s

Armattoe, Raphael Ernest Grail, -1954.
Space, time and race or the age of man in America. An address to Great James St. Women's Guild. ⌊n.p., n.d.⌋

16p. 19cm.

Spain.

M89
K24n

The Negro committee to aid Spain.
A Negro nurse in republican Spain. New York, issued by the Negro committeee to aid Spain... n.d.
14p. port. 18cm.

Spain - Description and travel.

France

Dumas, Alexandre, 1802-1870.
From Paris to Cadiz. Translated and edited by A. E. Murch. London, P. Owen ⌊1958⌋

216 p. illus. 23 cm.

1. Spain—Descr. & trav. I. Title.

DP41.D783 1958 914.6 59-2606 ‡
Library of Congress ⌊2⌋

Spain - Description and travel, - 1951-

M813.5
W93p

Wright, Richard, 1908-
Pagan Spain. ⌊1st ed.⌋ New York, Harper ⌊1957⌋

241 p. 22 cm.

1. Spain—Descr. & trav.—1951- I. Title.
Full name: Richard Nathaniel Wright.

DP43.W7 914.6 56-11091 ‡
Library of Congress ⌊20⌋

Spain - Descr & trav. 1951-

M813.5
W93pa

Wright, Richard, 1908-1960.
Pagan Spain. London, Bodley Head, ⌊c1957⌋

191p. 22cm.

Dominican
Republic
M860.9
H39L

Spanish-American-Civilization.

Henríquez-Ureña, Pedro, 1884-
Literary currents in Hispanic America, by Pedro Henríquez-Ureña. Cambridge, Mass., Harvard university press, 1945.

vi p., 2 l., ⌊3⌋-345 p. 21½ cm. (*Half-title:* The Charles Eliot Norton lectures, 1940-1941)

Bibliographical references included in "Notes" (p. ⌊205⌋-284) Bibliography: p. ⌊285⌋-295.

1. Spanish-American literature—Addresses, essays, lectures. 2. Spanish America—Civilization. I. Title.

A 45—2956

Harvard Univ. Librar,
for Library of Congress ⌊48c⁵⌋

Puerto
Rico
M864
F41

Spanish-American literature-Addresses, essays, lectures.

Ferrer, José.
... Marginalia. Margen del padre Rivera Viera. Puerto Rico ⌊Imprenta Venezuela⌋ 1939.

3 p. l., ⌊9⌋-185 p., 2 l. 19ᶜᵐ.

CONTENTS.—Carmelina Vizcarrondo, la Infancia y Poemas para mi niño. — Vigil: El erial.—Los ídolos del foro, de Carlos Arturo Torres, ensayista colombiano. — Concha Meléndez: Signos de Iberoamérica. — Hostos, ciudadano de América.—Motivos de Carmen Alicia Cadilla.—Acentos y evocaciones: Juan Ramón Jiménez. Maestro. Claridad e iluminación. Cesáreo Rosa-Nieves. Tierra y estrella.

1. Spanish-American literature—Addresses, essays, lectures. I. Title.

Library of Congress PQ7081.F4 40-17011
——— Copy 2. ⌊2⌋ 860.4

Dominican
Republic
M860.9
H39L

Spanish-American literature-Addresses, essays, lectures.

Henríquez-Ureña, Pedro, 1884-
Literary currents in Hispanic America, by Pedro Henríquez-Ureña. Cambridge, Mass., Harvard university press, 1945.

vi p., 2 l., ⌊3⌋-345 p. 21½ cm. (*Half-title:* The Charles Eliot Norton lectures, 1940-1941)

Bibliographical references included in "Notes" (p. ⌊205⌋-284) Bibliography: p. ⌊285⌋-295.

1. Spanish-American literature—Addresses, essays, lectures. 2. Spanish America—Civilization. I. Title.

A 45—2956

Harvard Univ. Librar,
for Library of Congress ⌊48c⁵⌋

Latin
America
M861.08
F56a

Spanish-American poetry-Bio-Bibl.

Fitts, Dudley, 1903- ed.
Anthology of contemporary Latin-American poetry, edited by Dudley Fitts. Norfolk, Conn., New directions ⌊1942⌋

ix, ⌊2⌋, x-xxi, 667p. 23½cm.

Latin
America
M861.08
F56a

Spanish-American poetry-Translations into English.

Fitts, Dudley, 1903- ed.
Anthology of contemporary Latin-American poetry, edited by Dudley Fitts. Norfolk, Conn., New directions ⌊1942⌋

ix, ⌊2⌋, x-xxi, 667p. 23½cm.

Latin
America
M861.08
B21a

Spanish-American poetry (Collections)

Ballagas, Emilio, *ed.*
... Antología de poesía negra hispano americana. Madrid, M. Aguilar, 1935.

3 p. l., ⌊11⌋-182 p., 3 l. illus. 18½ᶜᵐ.

"Indice alfabético de autores y datos sobre los mismos": p. ⌊175⌋-182.

1. Negroes in literature and art. 2. Spanish-American poetry (Collections) I. Title.

Library of Congress PQ7084.B25 36—28887
⌊48c1⌋ 861.0822

Spanish-American poetry (Collections)

Latin
America
M861.08
F56a

Fitts, Dudley, 1903- ed.
Anthology of contemporary Latin-American poetry, edited by Dudley Fitts. Norfolk, Conn., New directions ⌊1942⌋

ix, ⌊2⌋, x-xxi, 667p. 23½cm.

Latin America M808.8 J19
Spanish-American poetry (Collections)
Jahn, Janheinz, comp. and tr.
Rumba macumba; Afrocubanische lyrik. Munchen, Carl Henser Verlag, 1957.
79p 20cm.

Dominican Republic M861.6 B34c
Spanish poetry.
Brazil, Osvaldo
La cruz transparente (Con un mensaje inedito de Alfonso Reyes). Buenos Aires, Editorial Tor, 1939.
124p. 18cm.
The author is from Santo Domingo.

MB9 C82
A spark for my people.
Cotton, Ella Earls.
A spark for my people; the sociological autobiography of a Negro teacher. [1st ed.] New York, Exposition Press [1954]
288 p. 21 cm.
I. Title.
LA2317.C64A3 923.773 54-7034 ‡
Library of Congress [3]

M350 C82
The Spanish-American war volunteer;
Coston, W[illiam] Hilary.
The Spanish-American war volunteer; Middletown, Pa., The author, 1899.
139 p. illus. 8°.

Dominican Republic M861.6 C11
Spanish poetry.
Cabral, Manuel del.
...Trópico negro ... Buenos Aires, Editorial Sopena argentina, s.r. l. [c1941]
154p., 3 l. 20½cm. (Colección "Ayer y hoy")
Poems.
"Primera edición, julio de 1941."

M251 M58
Sparks from the anvil.
Michaux, Lightfoot.
Sparks from the anvil of Elder Michaux, compiled and edited by Pauline Lark. Washington, Happy News Pub. Co., 1950.
ix, 139 p. port. 24 cm.
1. Homiletical illustrations. I. Title.
BV4225.M5 251 50-9492
Library of Congress [3]

Puerto Rico M860 F39
Spanish language - Chrestomathies and readers.
Fernández Junos, Manuel, 1846-1928
Antología Portorriquena; prosa y verso; para lectura escolar. New York, Barnes and Noble, Inc. [1959]
iv, 343p. 18½cm.
White author.

Dominican Republic M861.6 F44c
Spanish poetry.
Fiallo, Fabio, 1865-1942.
...La canción de una vida, poesías; estudio crítico de Rubén Darío, epístola extravagante de Alfonso Camín. Madrid, Editorial "Cristóbal Colón," 1926.
2p. l., [9]-284 p., 1 l. 19½cm.
Imperfect; half-title (?) wanting.

M231 W62
Sparrow, Eugene, 1921-
Why I believe there is a God.
Pp. 88-93.
In: Why I believe there is a God. Chicago, Johnson Pub. Co., 1965.

Dominican Republic M860.9 H39p
Spanish language-Foreign words and phrases-Indian.
Henríquez Ureña, Pedro, 1884-
... Para la historia de los indigenismos ... Buenos Aires [Imprenta de la Universidad de Buenos Aires] 1938.
147 p., 1 l. 22½cm. (Facultad de filosofía y letras de la Universidad de Buenos Aires. Instituto de filología. [Biblioteca de dialectología hispanoamericana, director: Amado Alonso. Anejo III])
"Bibliografía": p. [7]-14.
Contents.—Papa y batata.—El enigma del aje.—Boniato.—Caribe.—Palabras antillanas.
1. Spanish language—Foreign words and phrases—Indian. I. Title.
42-5419
Library of Congress PC4822.H4 [44d1] 462.4

Dominican Republic M863.6 F44cu
Spanish poetry.
Fiallo, Fabio, 1865-1942.
Cuentos frágiles. Madrid, Biblioteca Rubén Darío, 1929.
xvi, 21-210p. 19cm.

M811.4 H23sp
The sparrow's fall...
Harper, Frances Ellen Watkins, b. 1825.
The sparrow's fall... and other poems, by Frances E.W. Harper. [n.p., n.p., n.d.]
22p. port. 16cm.

Puerto Rico M864 T48g
Spanish Language - Grammar.
Timothée, Pedro Carlos, 1864-
Gramatica Castellana para adultos. 2d ed. por Pedro C. Timothée. San Juan, P. R. Cantero, Fernandez & co.
11, iiip. 24cm.
Author is Puerto Rican.

M811.5 H87g
Spanish poetry.
Hughes, Langston, 1902- , tr.
Gypsy ballads, by Federico García Lorca. Translated by Langston Hughes; illus. by John McHee; introduction by Robert H. Glauber. Beloit, Wisconsin, Beloit College, 1951.
40p. 22cm. (Chapbook no.1)
Special issue of the Beloit poetry journal, fall 1951.

M973.9 F46 No.18
Spaulding, Charles Clinton, 1874-1952.
Fifty years of progress in business. Pittsburgh, Pittsburgh Courier, 1950.
7p. port. 24cm. (Fifty years of progress)
1. Business. I. Series.

Portugal M869 D71p
Spanish literature.
Domingues, Mario.
O preto do Charleston (novela) Lisboa, Livraria editora Guimaraes [1932?]
276 p. 18 cm.
1. Spanish literature. I. Title.

Dominican Republic M860.9 H39ci
Spanish poetry (Collections)
Henríquez Ureña, Pedro, 1884- comp.
Cien de las mejores poesías castellanas; selección de Pedro Henríquez Ureña. Buenos Aires, A. Kapelusz & cía., 1929.
289 p., 1 l. 19½cm.
1. Spanish poetry (Collections) I. Title.
30-12731
Library of Congress PQ6176.H4 [3]

M811.5 W152s
Speak nature.
Walker, James Robert
Speak nature. New York, Carlton Press [1965]
122p. 21cm.
I. Title.

MB9 L34m
Spanish literature.
Marín Ocete, Antonio
El negro Juan Latino, ensayo, biográfico y critico. Granada, Libraria, Guevara, 1925.
94p. 27cm.

Ghana M966.7 Sp26
The Spark.
Some essential features of Nkrumaism, by the editors of the Spark. New York, International Publishers [1965, °1964]
127 p. 18 cm. (Little new world paperbacks, LNW-8)
1. Nkrumah, Kwame, Pres. Ghana, 1909- 2. Ghana - Politics. I. Title.
DT510.6.N5S65 1965 320.531 65-24380
Library of Congress [3]

M811.4 D91s
Speakin' o' Christmas...
Dunbar, Paul Laurence, 1872-1906.
Speakin' o' Christmas, and other Christmas and special poems, by Paul Laurence Dunbar; with numerous illustrations. New York, Dodd, Mead and company, 1914.
96 p. front., plates. 18cm $1.00
I. Title.
14-18594
Library of Congress PS1556.S6 1914
Copyright A 387181 [37b1]

M89
Sp3
Spear, Mrs. Chole, 1750?-1815.
Memoir of Mrs. Chloe Spear, a native of Africa, who was enslaved in childhood and died in Boston, Jan. 3, 1815 ... By a lady of Boston ... Boston, J. Loring, 1832.
1 p. l., iii, [9]-108 p. front. 15½cm.

1. Spear, Mrs. Chloe, 1750?-1815. I. A lady of Boston.
14-15962
Library of Congress [31c1] E444.S74

Speech construction.
M808.5
B64s
Bond, Frederick Weldon.
Speech construction, by Frederick W. Bond ... Boston, The Christopher publishing house [°1936]
2 p. l., 7-146 p. 20½cm.
Bibliography: p. 141-146.

1. Speech. 2. Elocution. 3. Oratory. I. Title.
36—10026
Library of Congress PN4121.B53
[37c1] 808.5

M261.8
Sp31
Speers, Wallace Carter, 1896- ed.
Laymen speaking. New York, Association Press, 1947.
207 p. 19 cm.

1. Christian life. 2. Laity.
BV4495.S6 248 47—5820*
Library of Congress [60k½]

M811.5
Sp31w
Spearman, Aurelia L. P. (Childs)
What Christ means to us; a book of religious verse. New York, Carlton Press [1964]
99p. 20½cm.
Portrait of author on book jacket.

1. Poetry. 2. Relgious poetry. I. Title.

Speech on the death of William Lloyd Garrison.
M815.4
D74Sp
Douglass, Frederick, 1817-1895.
Speech on the death of William Lloyd Garrison, at the Garrison memorial meeting in the 15th street Presbyterian church, Monday, June 2, 1879 ... by Frederick Douglass, U. S. marshal of the District of Columbia. [Washington? 1879?]
8 p. 23cm.
Caption title.

1. Garrison, William Lloyd, 1805-1879. I. Title.
11—14857
Library of Congress E449.G2542
[a41b1]

M780
Sp32
Spellman, A B 1935-
Four lives in the bebop business, by A. B. Spellman. New York, Pantheon Books [1966]
xiv, 241 p. 22 cm.
Portrait of author on book jacket.

1. Jazz musicians. 2. Negro musicians. I. Title.
ML394.S74 780.922 66-10410/MN
Library of Congress [8]

M252
Sp3s
Spearman, Henry Kuhns, 1875-1928
Soul magnets; twelve sermons from Testament texts, by Rev. Henry Kuhns Spearman, compiled as a memorial by Mrs. Elizabeth F. Spearman. [Philadelphia, A.M.E. Book Concern, 1929]
116p. front(port.) 19cm.

1. Sermons. I. title

Speeches.
Nigeria
M966.9
Az2re
Azikiwe, Nnamdi, 1904-
Respect for human dignity; an inaugural address delivered by His Excellency Dr. Nnamdi Azikiwe, Governor General and Commander-in-Chief [of the] Federation of Nigeria, 16 November, 1960. [Enugu, Government Printer] 1960.
25p. ports. 25cm.
Biographical data: pp. 19-25.

M309.1
Sp3
Spellman, Cecil Lloyd, 1906-
Elm city, a Negro community in action. Tallahassee, Florida A. and M. College, 1947.
75p. tables, maps. 28cm.
1. Social surveys. I. Title.

M026
S64s
Special collections of Negroana.
Bontemps, Arna Wendell, 1902-
Special collections of Negroana. Reprinted from the Library quarterly. 14:187-206. June 1944.
187-206p. 24cm.

Speeches.
Haiti
M972.94
M31r
Manigat, Leslie
La révolution de 1843; essai d'analyse historique d'une conjoncture de crise. [Port-au-Prince] le Normalien [1959]
31p. 23cm.
Bibliography.

M370
Sp3
Spellman, Cecil Lloyd, 1906-
How to organize and conduct a workshop. Tallahassee, Florida A and M College, 1947.
20 p. 28 cm.
At head of title: Florida Agricultural and Mechanical College bulletin.
Mimeographed.

I. Title. 1. Education-Study and teaching.

Special laughter.
M813.5
W93i
Wright, Richard, 1909-
Introduction.
(In: Nutt, Howard. Special laughter, poems. Prairie City, Illinois, Press of James A. Decker, 1940. pp. ix-xii)

Speeches.
Ghana
M966.7
N65h
Nkrumah, Kwame, 1909-
Hands off Africa. Some famous speeches by Dr. The Rt. Hon. Kwame Nkrumah, P.C., M.P. (First President of the Republic of Ghana); with a tribute to George Padmore written by Tawia Adamafio, General Secretary of C.P. P. Accra, Kwabena Owusu-Akyem [1960]
62p. ports. 21cm.

M89
Sp32
Spellman, Cecil Lloyd, 1906-
Rough steps on my stairway; the life history of a Negro educator. [1st ed.] New York, Exposition Press [1953]
273 p. 21 cm.

1. Teachers—Correspondence, reminiscences, etc. I. Title.
LC2731.S65 923.773 53-5639 ‡
Library of Congress [5]

Special problems of Negro education.
M370
W65s
Wilkerson, Doxey Alphonso, 1905-
Special problems of Negro education, by Doxey A. Wilkerson ... Prepared for the Advisory committee on education. Washington, U. S. Govt. print. off., 1939.
xvi, 171 p. incl. tables. 23cm. ([U. S.] Advisory committee on education. Staff study no. 12)
"Publications of the committee": p. 171.

1. Negroes—Education. I. Title.
39—26926
Library of Congress L111.A93 no. 12
——— Copy 2. LC2801.W5
[43u2] (370.973) 371.9740973

Speeches
M815.3
P97s
Purvis, Robert,
Speeches and letters by Robert Purvis [Published by the request of the "Afro-American League." Correspondence between Robert Purvis and Bayard Taylor. [n.p. 1860?]
23p. front (port) 23½cm.

M378At
At6
Spelman College, Atlanta Ga.
The Atlanta University system; Atlanta University, Morehouse College, Spelman College, The Atlanta University School of Social Work. n.p., 1939.
1 fold. l. 7 columns.
Originally published in the City builder, August 1934.

Speech.
M808.5
B64s
Bond, Frederick Weldon.
Speech construction, by Frederick W. Bond ... Boston, The Christopher publishing house [°1936]
2 p. l., 7-146 p. 20½cm.
Bibliography: p. 141-146.

1. Speech. 2. Elocution. 3. Oratory. I. Title.
36—10026
Library of Congress PN4121.B53
[37c1] 808.5

M815
Sp3d
Speeches delivered at the anti-colonisation meeting in Exeter Hall, London, July 13, 1833, by James Cropper, William Lloyd Garrison, Nathaniel Paul, Daniel O'Connell, Mr. Buckingham, Mr. Hunt, Mr. Abrahams, George Thompson. Boston, Printed by Garrison & Knapp, 1833.
40p. 23½cm.

1. Paul, Nathaniel. Speech, p. 12-16.

M812.5
Sp3f
Spence, Eulalie
Fool's errand, play in one act, by Eulalie Spence... New York, Samuel French, c1927.
26 [6] p. 20cm.
1. Drama I. Title

Jamaica
M823.91 **Spence, Tomas H**
Sp3m
Martin Larwin [by] Tomas H. Spence [and] Eric Heath. [1st ed.] New York, Pageant Press [1954]

187 p. 21 cm.

I. Heath, Eric, joint author. II. Title.

PZ4.S744Mar 54-9325 ‡

Library of Congress [3]

Spiegel, Doris, 1901- illus.
M813.5 **Jackson, Jesse.**
J13
Call me Charley, by Jesse Jackson; illustrations by Doris Spiegel. [New York, Harper & brothers [1945]

5 p. l., 156 p. incl. plates. 21 cm.

"First edition." I-4

I. Spiegel, Doris, 1901- illus. II. Title.

45-9807

Library of Congress PZ7.J1362Cal [47o3]

Spingarn, Arthur Barnett, pp. 70 and 88.
M252 **Imes, William Lloyd, 1889-**
Im2b
The black pastures, an American pilgrimage in two centureis; essays and sermons. [1st ed.] Nashville, Hemphill Press, 1957.

146p. illus. 24cm.

St. Lucia
M610 Spencer, Gerald Arthur, 1902-
Sp3c
Cosmetology in the Negro; a guide to its problems, by Gerald A. Spencer... [New York, The Arlain printing co., 1944]

viii, 9-127p. illus. 19½cm.

1. Skin - Diseases. 2. Health and hygiene. I. Title.

Spiller, Gustav, ed.
M323. Universal races congress. 1st London, 1911.
Sp4p
Papers on inter-racial problems, communicated to the first Universal races congress, held at the University of London, July 26-29, 1911, ed. for the Congress executive, by G. Spiller, Hon. organiser of the Congress, Pub. for the World peace foundation, Ginn and company, Boston, London, P. S. King & son, 1911.

xvi, 485p. 1 l. 25½cm.

Spingarn, Arthur Barnett, 1878- Foreword.
M323 U. S. Supreme Court. Brief for appellants in
Un30
Nos. 1, 2 and 4 and for respondents in No. 10... October Term, 1953.

235p. 23½cm.

St. Lucia
M610 **Spencer, Gerald Arthur, 1902-**
Sp3m
Medical symphony, a study of the contributions of the Negro to medical progress in New York. [New York, °1947]

120 p. ports. 21 cm.

"References": p. 9.

1. Medicine—New York (City) 2. Negro physicians. I. Title.

R292.N7S63 610.97471 48-3224*

Library of Congress [3]

M815.5 Spingarn, Arthur Barnett, 1878-
Sp4a
An address delivered before the fifteenth annual session of the National Association of Teachers in Colored Schools, at Storer College, Harper's Ferry, W.Va., August 1, 1918. Augusta, Ga., National Association of Teachers in Colored Schools, 1918.

8p. 21cm. (National note-book series, no.1)

Reprinted for the U.S. Public Health Service.

1. Veneral diseases.

M811.5 Spingarn, Arthur B - The great Jokesmith
P83
[a poem]
Double blossoms, Helen Keller anthology, compiled by Edna Porter. New York, L. Copeland, 1931.
96p. front. (port.) 20cm.

Africa
M496 Spencer, John Walter, ed.
L57
Leverhulme Conference on Universities and the Language Problems of Tropical Africa, *Ibadan, Nigeria, 1961-1962.*
Language in Africa; papers. Edited by John Spencer. Cambridge [Eng.] University Press, 1963.

vii, 167 p. 23 cm.

English or French.
Bibliographical footnotes.

1. Africa, Sub-Saharan—Languages. 2. Education—Africa, Sub-Saharan. I. Spencer, John Walter, ed. II. Title.

LA1503.7.L46 1961-1962 63-4814

Library of Congress [5]

M811.5 Spingarn, Arthur Barnett, 1878-
J63a2
An appreciation of James Weldon Johnson.

(In: Fisk University. Nashville. James Weldon Johnson. Nashville. 1939. 25cm. 3p.)

M815.5 Spingarn, Joel Elias, 1875-1939.
Sp4r
Racial equality; Address delivered at the twenty-third annual conference of the National Association for the Advancement of Colored People, held at Washington, D.C., May 17, 1932. N.Y., National Association for the Advancement of Colored, 1932.

8p. 23cm.

I. Title.

M813.5 **Spencer, Mary Etta.**
Sp3r
The resentment, by Mary Etta Spencer. [Philadelphia, Printed by A. M. E. book concern, 1921]

4 p. l., [7]-216 p. 20½ cm.

I. Title.

21-20882

Library of Congress PZ3.S7466Re [48c1]

M323 Spingarn, Arthur B
Un33
Statement.

(U.S. Congress. House. Committee on the Judiciary. Anti-lynching. Hearings. Washington, G.P.O., 1920, p.22-27)

M343.3 Spingarn, Joel Elias, 1875-1939.
Sp4s
[Statement at] Hearing before the Committee on the Judiciary, House of Representatives, sixty-fifth Congress, second session on H.R. 11279, to protect citizens against lynching. Washington, Govt. Print., Off., 1918.

14p. 23cm.

At head of title: To protect citizens against lynching.

1. Lynching.

Spero, Sterling D.
M331 **Harris, Abram Lincoln, 1899-**
H24b
The black worker; the Negro and the labor movement, by Sterling D. Spero and Abram L. Harris. New York, Columbia university press, 1931.

x, 509 p., 1 l. 22½ cm.

Issued also as A. L. Harris's thesis (PH. D.) Columbia university. Mr. Harris wrote chapters 2-5, 10, 14-15, 17-19.
"Bibliography of works cited": p. 485-490.

1. Negroes—Employment. 2. Trade-unions—U. S. 3. Labor and laboring classes—U. S. 4. Negroes—Civil rights. 5. U. S.—Race question. I. Harris, Abram Lincoln, 1899- joint author. II. Title. III. Title: The Negro and the labor movement.

31—3610

Library of Congress E185.8.S74 [44p²2] [325.26] 331.6

M815.5 Spingarn, Arthur Barnett, 1878-
Sp4w
The war and veneral diseases among Negroes.

(In: Social hygiene, 4:333-346, July 1918)

1. Veneral diseases.

Spingarn Collection

see

Howard University, Washington, D. C. Founders Library. Moorland Foundation. Arthur B. Spingarn Collection.

Spice of dawns.
M811.5 **Ayers, Vivian.**
Ay2
Spice of dawns; a book of verse. Illus. by Edsel Maurice Cramer. [1st ed.] New York, Exposition Press [1953]

39 p. illus. 21 cm.

I. Title.

PS3501.Y48S58 811.5 53-5142 ‡

Library of Congress [2]

M026 Spingarn, Arthur Barnett, 1878-
H83a
Howard University, Washington, D.C. Founders Library. Moorland Foundation.
The Arthur B. Spingarn collection of Negro authors. Washington, D.C. [1948]

[7]p. facisms. 21cm.

M323 The Spingarn medal, awarded annually for the
Sp46
highest achievement of an American Negro. New York, National Association for the Advancement of Colored People, [1949].

8p. ports. 23cm.

Ghana M966.7 Os22
The spirit and structure of Nkrumah's Convention People's Party.
Osei, Gabriel K
The spirit and structure of Nkrumah's Convention People's Party. [London, G. K. Osei, 1962]
48p. 21½cm.
1. Ghana. 2. Convention People's Party. I. Title.

M784 B62s
Spirituals.
Boatner, Edward
Spirituals triumphant old and new, edited and arranged by Edward Boatner... assisted by Mrs. Willa A. Townsend... Nashville, Tennessee, Sunday school publishing board, c1927.
85p. 22½cm.

M784 H32
Spirituals.
Hayes, Roland, 1887–
My songs; Aframerican religious folk songs arr. and interpreted by Roland Hayes. [1st ed.] Boston, Little, Brown, 1948.
x, 128 p. 20 cm.
"An Atlantic Monthly Press book."
1. Negro spirituals. I. Title.
M1670.H4M9 48–8965*
Library of Congress [58c1]

M815.5 R17s
The spirit of freedom and justice.
Ransome, Reverdy Cassius, 1861–
The spirit of freedom and justice; orations and speeches, by Reverdy C. Ransom. Nashville, Tenn., A.M.E. Sunday School Union, 1926.
175p. portraits, 23cm.

M784 B75
Spirituals.
Breman, Paul, ed.
Spirituals; Noord-Amerikaanse geestelijke volksliederen. Den Haag, Servire [1958]
164p. illus., map. 19½cm.
"To Arthur B. Spingarn, with kindest regards. London, April 27, 1959. Paul Breman."
White editor
1. Spirituals.

M784 J632
Spirituals.
Johnson, Hall, 1888–
The green pastures spirituals, arranged for voice and piano by Hall Johnson. New York, Farrar & Rhinehart, Inc., 1930.
40p. illus. 30cm.

M370 J71s
The Spirit of Piney Woods.
Jones, Laurence Clifton, 1884–
The spirit of Piney Woods, by Laurence C. Jones ... introduction by George Foster Peabody. New York, Chicago [etc.] Fleming H. Revell company [°1931]
2 p. l., 3–93 p. front., plates, ports. 19½cm.
"Addresses delivered on Sunday evenings to the students of Piney Woods country life school."—Foreword.
1. Piney Woods country life school, Braxton, Miss. I. Title.
31–34338
Library of Congress LC2852.B72J63
——— Copy 2.
Copyright A 41914 [30d1] 371.97409762

M784 C35
Spirituals.
Chambers, Herbert Arthur, ed.
The treasury of Negro spirituals; ed. by H. A. Chambers. London, Blandford Press [1953]
125p. cm.
Foreword by Marian Anderson.
"First published in 1953."
White editor.
1. Spirituals. I. Anderson, Marian, 1908– II. Title.

M784 J63
Spirituals.
Johnson, James Weldon, 1871–1938, *ed.*
The book of American Negro spirituals, edited with an introduction of James Weldon Johnson; musical arrangements by J. Rosamond Johnson, additional numbers by Lawrence Brown. New York, The Viking press, 1925.
187 p. 26cm.
1. Negro songs. I. Johnson, John Rosamond, 1873– II. Brown, Lawrence. III. Title. IV. Title: Spirituals.
25–23072
Library of Congress M1670.J67
[45q²2] 784.756

M133.9 Sh12
Spiritualism.
Butcher, Harriet Parke (Shadd)
Beyond communications from the spirit world as received by Harriet Parke Shadd. [n.p., n.p.] 1964.
82p. 19cm.

M740 C86w
Spirituals.
Crite, Allan Rohan, 1910– *illus.*
Were you there when they crucified my Lord; a Negro spiritual in illustrations, by Allan Rohan Crite. Cambridge, Mass., Harvard university press, 1944.
[93] p. illus. 32cm.
Music for the spiritual: p. [13]
1. Jesus Christ—Art. 2. Jesus Christ—Crucifixion. 3. Negro spirituals. I. Title.
A 44–4812
Harvard univ. Library for Library of Congress N8053.C7
[46q4] 741.6385

M784 J63b
Spirituals.
Johnson, James Weldon, 1871–1938, *ed.*
The books of American Negro spirituals, including The book of American Negro spirituals and The second book of Negro spirituals [by] James Weldon Johnson and J. Rosamond Johnson. New York, The Viking press, 1940.
2 v. in 1. 26cm.
A re-issue of the volumes first published separately in 1925 and 1926. Each volume has special t.-p.
Musical arrangements by J. Rosamond Johnson, additional numbers by Lawrence Brown.
1. Negro songs. I. Johnson, John Rosamond, 1873– II. Brown, Lawrence. III. Title. IV. Title: Spirituals.
Cincinnati. Univ. Libr. for Library of Congress M1670.J66 [M1670.J] A 41–546
[45v3]

Sierra Leone M784 B21
Spirituals.
Ballanta-(Taylor), Nicholas George Julius.
Saint Helena Island spirituals; recorded and transcribed at Penn Normal, Industrial and Agricultural School, St. Helena Island, Beaufort County, South Carolina. [New York, G. Schrimer, Inc., 1925]
93p. 26½cm.

M784 D34s
Spirituals.
Deas, E C , arr.
Songs and spirituals of Negro composition; also patriotic songs, songs of colleges and college fraternities and sororities. Chicago, Progressive Book co., 1928.
64p. 22cm.

M784 J68
Spirituals.
Jolas, Eugene, 1894– tr.
Le Nègre qui chante; chansons traduites et introduction par Eugène Jolas. Paris, Éditions de cahiers libres [1928]
85p. cm.

M784 B41
Spirituals.
Belafonte, Harold, 1927– *comp.*
Songs Belafonte sings. Illustrated by Charles White. [1st ed.] New York, Duell, Sloan and Pearce [1962]
x, 196 p. illus. 29 cm.
Commentary on each song by Belafonte.
Music editor: Bob Bollard; piano arrangements: Joseph Mazzu.
CONTENTS.—Around the world.—The American Negro.—The West Indies.
1. Folk-songs. 2. Negro songs. 3. Negro spirituals. 4. Music, Popular (Songs, etc.)—West Indies. I. Title.
Full name: Harold George Belafonte.
M1627.B36S6 M62–1000
Library of Congress [5]

M784 F36c
Spirituals.
Fenner, Thomas P
Cabin and plantation songs as sung by the Hampton students, arranged by Thomas P. Fenner. New York, Putnam's 1880.
255p. 23cm.

M784 R13
Spirituals.
Raim, Walter, *ed.*
The Josh White song book. Biography and song commentaries by Robert Shelton. Illus. by Stu Gross. Chicago, Quadrangle Books [1963]
191 p. illus. 32 cm.
For voice and piano, with chord symbols for guitar.
Discography: p. 190–191.
1. Folk-songs, American. 2. Ballads, American. 3. Negro spirituals. 4. Folk-songs, American—Discography. I. White, Josh. II. Title.
M1629.R16J7 784.4973 63–18475/M
Library of Congress [5]

M784 B46
Spirituals.
Berendt, Joachim Ernst, ed.
Spirituals, geistliche lieder der Neger Amerikas. Original texte Melodien und Ubertragungen. Paridam Von Dem Knesebeck. Munchen, Nymphenburger Verlagshandlung, 1955.
87p. illus. 24cm.
White editor.
1. Songs. 2. Spirituals. I. Title.

M784 F52
Spirituals.
Fisher, William Arms, 1861– *ed.*
Seventy Negro spirituals, edited by William Arms Fisher ... Boston, Oliver Ditson company; New York, C. H. Ditson & co.; [etc., etc., °1926]
xxxiv, [2], 212 p. ports. 32 x 24½cm. (The musicians library)
Edition for high voice.
Bibliography: p. [xxxiii]–xxxiv.
1. Negro songs. I. Title. II. Title: Spirituals.
26–18007
Library of Congress M1.M9F43H
——— Edition for low voice. M1.M9F43L
Copyright A 950085 [a39q1]

M784 Sa5
Spirituals.
Sandilands, Alexander
A hundred and twenty Negro spirituals; selected chiefly with a view to their being used by Africans in Africa. Morija, Basutoland, Morija Sesuto Book Depot, 1951.
158p. 20cm.

Spirituals.

M973 Un3s
U. S. *Library of Congress.*
75 years of freedom; commemoration of the 75th anniversary of the proclamation of the 13th amendment to the Constitution of the United States. The Library of Congress. [Washington, U. S. Govt. print. off., 1943]
cover-title, vi, 108 p. col. pl. 26cm.
"The contribution of the American Negro to American culture was the theme of a series of exhibits and concerts in the Library of Congress commencing on December 18th, the 75th anniversary of the proclamation of the Thirteenth amendment, which ended slavery in the United States."—p. v.
1. Negroes. 2. Negro songs. 3. Negro art. 4. Negro literature (American) I. Title.
Library of Congress E185.6.U597 [15] 43-52457 325.260973

Spirituals.

M784 W58
White, Clarence Cameron, 1880-1960.
Forty Negro spirituals, compiled and arranged for solo voice with pianoforte accompaniment, by Clarence Cameron White. Philadelphia, Theodore Presser Co., 1927.
129p. illus. 31cm.

Spirituals-Hist. & crit.

M200 T42d
Thurman, Howard, 1899–
Deep river; reflections on the religious insight of certain of the Negro spirituals. Illustrated by Elizabeth Orton Jones. [Rev. and enl.] New York, Harper [1955]
98 p. illus. 22 cm.
1. Negro spirituals—Hist. & crit. I. Title.
ML3556.T55 1955 784.756 55-11488 ‡
Library of Congress [30]

Spirituals - Hist. & crit.

M200 T42n
Thurman, Howard, 1899–
The Negro spiritual speaks of life and death. New York, Harper [1947]
55 p. 18 cm. (The Ingersoll lecture, Harvard University, 1947)
1. Negro spirituals—Hist. & crit. I. Title. (Series)
ML3556.T56 784.756 47-12396*
Library of Congress [49n3]

Spirituals - St. Helena Island, Beaufort County South Carolina.

Sierra Leone M784 B21
Ballanta-(Taylor), Nicholas George Julius.
Saint Helena Island spirituals; recorded and transcribed at Penn Normal, Industrial and Agricultural School, St. Helena Island, Beaufort County, South Carolina. [New York, G. Schirmer, Inc., 1925]
93p. 26½cm.

Spirituals, geistliche lieder de Negre Amerikas.

M784 B46
Berendt, Joachim Ernst, ed.
Spirituals, geistliche lieder der Neger Amerikas. Original texte Melodien und Ubertragungen. Paridam Von Dem Knesebeck. Munchen, Nymphenburger Verlagshandlung, 1955.
87p. illus. 24cm.
White editor.
1. Songs. 2. Spirituals. I. Title.

Spirituals of the Negro slave.

MB Em3
Emerson, William Canfield, 1893– *ed.*
Stories and spirituals of the Negro slave, by William C. Emerson, M. D. Boston, R. G. Badger [°1930]
79 p. front., ports. 19½cm.
Includes music.
white author?
1. Negro songs. 2. Negroes—Biog. 3. Slavery in the U. S.—Condition of slaves. I. Title. II. Title: Spirituals of the Negro slave.
Library of Congress ML3556.E57 30-12872
——— Copy 2. E444.E53 [43g1]

M784 B62s
Spirituals triumphant old and new.
Boatner, Edward
Spirituals triumphant old and new. edited and arranged by Edward Boatner... assisted by Mrs. Willa A. Townsend... Nashville, Tennessee, Sunday school publishing board, c1927.
85p. 22½cm.

Kenya M960 M458
Spiro, Herbert J *ed.*
Patterns of African development; five comparisons, edited by Herbert J. Spiro. Englewood Cliffs, N. J., Prentice-Hall [1967]
144 p. 21 cm. (A Spectrum book)
Bibliographical footnotes. White editor.
CONTENTS.—~~Introduction, by H. J. Spiro.—Some reflections on constitutionalism for emergent political orders, by C. J. Friedrich.—Nationalism in a new perspective: the African case, by I. Abu-Lughod.—The challenge of change: Japan and Africa, by C. E. Welch.~~—Borrowed theory and original practice in African politics, by A. A. Mazrui.—~~Repetition or innovation?—By H. J. Spiro.~~
1. Africa—Politics—1960– —Addresses, essays, lectures. I. Title.
DT30.S675 320.9'6 67-14837
Library of Congress [3]

Splendeur.

Haiti M841 L93s
Louis, Janine Tavernier
Splendeur. Port-au-Prince, Imprimerie S. Bissainthe, [n.d.]
[16]p. 21cm.
1. Haitian portry. I. Title.

Splintered darkness.

M811.5 C44
Chisolm William Mason
Splintered darkness. Brooklyn, N.Y., Trilon Press, 1953.
86p. 20cm.

Spokes for the wheel.

M813.5 B774s
Broadus, Robert Deal.
Spokes for the wheel. Muncie, Ind., Kingsman Press [1961]
148 p. 23 cm.
I. Title.
PZ4.B8634Sp 61-59588 ‡
Library of Congress [1]

The sport of the gods.

M813.4 D91s
Dunbar, Paul Laurence, 1872–1906.
The sport of the gods, by Paul Laurence Dunbar ... New York, Dodd, Mead and co., 1902.
3 p. l., 255 p. 19cm.
I. Title.
2–11783
Library of Congress PZ3.D918Sp
Copyright [40b1]

The sport of the Gods.

M813.4 D91s2
Dunbar, Paul Lawrence.
The sport of the Gods. Complete novel by Paul Lawrence Dunbar. Lippincott's magazine, May 1901.
515-594p. 24cm.

MB9 J633
Sports.
Johnson, Jack, 1878–
Jack Johnson in the ring and out, by Jack Johnson ... with introductory articles by "Tad," Ed. W. Smith, Damon Runyon and Mrs. Jack Johnson; special drawings by Edwin William Krauter. Chicago, National sports publishing company, 1927.
4 p. l., 259 p. front., plates, ports. 20 cm.
27-15294
Library of Congress GV1132.J7A18 [2]

Sports.

M796 L95n
Low, Nat
The Negro in sports. San Francisco, The Daily People's World, 19 .
31p. illus. 19cm.

M973.9 F46 No.23
Sports.
Wilson, W Rollo.
Fifty years of progress in the world of sports. Pittsburgh, Pittsburgh Courier, 1950.
7p. illus. port. 24cm. (Fifty years of progress)

Sports.

M796 Y84n
Young, Andrew Sturgeon Nash, 1919–
Negro firsts in sports, by A. S. "Doc" Young. With illus. by Herbert Temple. Chicago, Johnson Pub. Co. [1963]
301 p. illus. 22 cm.
1. Negro athletes. I. Title.
GV697.A1Y6 927.96 63-21535 ‡
Library of Congress [63f10]

Sports—Anecdotes, facetiae, satire, etc.

M796 M45t
Maxwell, Sherman Leander, 1906–
Thrills and spills in sports [by] Jocko Maxwell. New York, Fortuny's [1939]
101 p. 20cm.
"First edition."
1. Sports—Anecdotes, facetiae, satire, etc. I. Title.
40-35013
Library of Congress GV191.M3 [2] 796.0888

Sports-U.S.

M796 H38 1949
Henderson, Edwin Bancroft, 1883–
The Negro in sports. Rev. ed. Washington, Associated Publishers, 1949.
xvi, 507 p. illus., ports. 21 cm.
1. Negro athletes. 2. Sports—U. S. 3. Negroes—Biog. I. Title.
GV161.H4 1949 796.0973 50-6466
Library of Congress [15]

Sports—U.S.

M796 H38
Henderson, Edwin Bancroft, 1883–
The Negro in sports, by Edwin Bancroft Henderson ... Washington, D. C., The Associated publishers, inc. [°1939]
5 p. l., 371 p. illus. (incl. ports.) 21 cm.
1. Negro athletics. 2. Sports—U. S. 3. Negroes—Biog. I. Title.
39-29452
Library of Congress E185.88.H45 [40k5] 796.0973

MB9
Sp72
Sprague, Rosetta Douglass, 1839-
My mother as I recall her. A paper read before Anna Murray Douglass union W.C.T.U., by Rosetta Douglass-Sprague, May 10, 1900. [n.p., n.p.] 1900
11p. port. 22½cm.

1. Douglass, Anna Murray

Ssanyu teribeerera.
Uganda
M896.3
M87s
Mpalanyi, Solomon E K
Ssanyu teribeerera [You can't always be happy] Ebifaananyi byakubibwo. M. E. Gregg. Kampala, Eagle Press, 1961.
32p. 18½cm.
Written in Luganda.

I. Title.

Stalin's blueprint for a Soviet Black Belt in the U.S.A.
M335.4
Sc8st
Schuyler, George Samuel, 1895-
Stalin's blueprint for a Soviet Black Belt in the U.S.A.
pp. 3-9. maps. 23cm.
In: Plain Talk, vol. 9, no. 9, June 1947, pp. 3-9.

MB9
L34s
Spratlin, Valaurez Burwell.
Juan Latino, slave and humanist, by V. B. Spratlin ... New York, Spinner press, inc., 1938.
xiii, 216 p. 24cm.
CONTENTS.—Introduction.—Juan Latino.—"The famous drama of Juan Latino", an adaptation in English from the Spanish of Diego Jiménez de Enciso.—Appendix: Diego Jiménez de Enciso.—Bibliography (p. 212-214)

1. Latino, Juan, 16th cent. I. Ximénes de Enciso, Diego. Comedia famosa de Juan Latino.
Library of Congress PA8540.L615Z8 38—31798
——— Copy 2.
Copyright A 122085 [40d1] 928.7

Uganda
M808.6
Ss24
Ssekawma, J C
Okuwandiika ebbaluwa [Letter writing] Nairobi, Eagle Press, 1960.
108p. 21½cm. (East African Literature Bureau)
Written in Luganda.

1. Letter writing, African. I. Title.

Stances haitienes.
Haiti
M841
V47s
Vaval, Duracine, 1879-
Stances haitienes. Paris, Albert Messein, Editeur, 1912.
175p. 19cm.

Spring in New Hampshire.
Jamaica
M821.91
M19sp
McKay, Claude, 1890-
Spring in New Hampshire and other poems, by Claude McKay. London, Grant Richards, 1920.
40p. 20cm.

M614.8
St12
Stack, Herbert James, 1892-
Careers in safety; choosing a vocation in the field of accident prevention, by Herbert J. Stack ... Charles C. Hawkins ... [and] Walter A. Cutter ... New York and London, Funk and Wagnalls company, 1945.
viii, 152 p. 19½cm. (Kitson careers series, ed. by H. D. Kitson)

1. Accidents—Prevention. I. Hawkins, Charles C., joint author. II. Cutter, Walter Airey, 1902- joint author. III. Title.
45—1287
Library of Congress HV676.A2S64
[46x5] 614.8069

M973
St1
Stanford, Peter Thomas.
The tragedy of the negro in America. A condensed history of the enslavement, sufferings, emancipation, present condition and progress of the negro race in the United States of America, by Rev. P. Thos. Stanford ... Boston, Mass., Authors edition, 1898.
4 p. l., xvi, 230 p. incl. illus., plates, ports. front. 19cm.

I. Title.
Library of Congress E185.S79 12—5317
Copyright 1897: 34173 [36d1]

West Indies
M972.97
L95w
Springer, H W
The West Indies emergent: problems and prospects.
(In: Lowenthal, David. The West Indies Federation. New York, Columbia University Press, 1961. 21cm. p.1-16)
Portrait of author on book jacket.

Tanganyika
M967.8
N89
Stahl, Kathleen Mary, 1918-
Tanganyika: sail in the wilderness. [Foreword by Julius Nyerere] 'S-Gravenhage, Mounton, 1961.
100p. plates. maps. 22cm.
White author.

1. Tanganyika-Description and travel. I. Nyerere, Julius Kambarage, Forward. II. Title.

M811.5
St2
Stanford, Theodore Anthony.
Dark harvest, by theodore Anthony Stanford, with an introduction by Joseph V. Baker. Philadelphia, Pa. [Bureau of Negro affairs] 1936.
ix, 32 [1] p. 23½cm.
Inscribed copy: Theodore Anthony Stanford.

1. Poetry. I. Title.

Springer, Hugh W.
British Guiana
M371.37
F229
Farley, Rawle, 1922-
Discussion and national progress. With a foreword by H. W. Springer. Kingston, Jamaica, W. I., The Pioneer Press [c195-]
60p. 19cm.

1. Discussion. 2. Education of adults. I. Springer, Hugh W. II. Title.

The stake of minorities in national health legislation.
M610
C63st
Cobb, William Montague, 1904-
The stake of minorities in national health legislation. Nashville, Fisk University, Social Science Institute, 1946.
37-41p. 25cm.
Reprinted from A Monthly Summary of Events and Trends in Race Relations.

Stanford University - Hist.
MB9
M23
McDonald, Emanuel B 1884-
Sam McDonald's farm; Stanford reminiscences by Emanuel B. "Sam" McDonald. Stanford, Calif., Stanford University Press, 1954.
422 p. illus. 24 cm.

1. Stanford University—Hist. I. Title.
LD3027.M2 378.794 54-7166 ‡
Library of Congress [5]

Springfield, Mass.
M974.4
D35s
De Berry, William Nelson, 1870-
Sociological survey of the Negro population of Springfield, Mass., edited by William N. DeBerry. Springfield, Mass., The Dunbar community league 1940
15 1 p. tables. 20½cm.

Stalin, Iosif, 1879-
Trinidad
M820
J23s
James, Cyril Lionel Robert, 1901- tr.
Stalin, a critical survey of Bolshevism, by Boris Souvarine. London, Secker and Warburg, 1940.
xiv. 690p. 25cm.

Uganda
M630
St1
Staples, E G
Pwonye me pur [Lectures in elementary agriculture. Translated by Lakana Otim and T. L. Lawrence. Rev. by Tomasi Otim and others] Nairobi, Eagle Press, 1949.
25p. 18½cm.
Written in Acoli.
White author.

1. Agriculture. I. Title. II. Otim, Lakana, tr.

Uganda
M967.61
Sala
Ssali, E M
Abazungu nga bwe tubalaba [Europeans as we see them] Kampala, The Eagle Press, 1952.
28p. 21cm.
Written in Luganda.

1. Uganda.

Stalin, Iosif, 1879-
Trinidad
M820
J23w
James, Cyril Lionel Robert, 1901-
... World revolution, 1917-1936; the rise and fall of the Communist International. London, M. Secker and Warburg, ltd. [1937]
xii, 9-429 p. 22cm.
At head of title: C. L. R. James.
"How much the book owes to the writings of Trotsky, the text can only partially show."—p. xii.

1. Communist International. 2. Communism. 3. Revolutions. 4. World politics. 5. Russia—Pol. & govt.—20th cent. 6. Trotskii, Lev, 1879-1940. 7. Stalin, Iosif, 1879- I. Title.
37—23007
Library of Congress HX11.I 5J25
[45g1] 335.40621

Star by star; poems.
M811.5
M26s
Madgett, Naomi Cornelia (Long)
Star by star; poems, by Naomi Long Madgett. [1st ed.] Detroit, Harlo Press, 1965.
64 p. 23 cm.
Portrait of author on book jacket.

I. Title.
PS3525.A318S7 811.52 65-27463
Library of Congress [3]

A star to steer by.

MB9
M92
Mulzac, Hugh, 1886–
A star to steer by; by Hugh Mulzac, as told to Louis Burnham and Norval Welch. New York, International Publishers [1963]
251 p. illus. 21 cm.

1. Merchant marine—U. S.—Negroes. 2. Merchant marine—U. S.—Officers—Correspondence, reminiscences, etc. I. Burnham, Louis E., 1915 or 16–1960. II. Welch, Norval. III. Title.
E185.63.M8 923.578 63–14260 ‡
Library of Congress [5]

Starkenfirst, roman.

Martinique
M843.9
T17s
Tardon, Raphaël, 1911–
Starkenfirst, roman. Paris, Fasquelle Editeurs, 1947.
201p. 22½cm.
Received Prix des Antilles

M283
C76p
Starkey, Thomas A.
Sermon on church work among the colored people, by Rt. Rev. Thomas A. Starkey.
In: Convocation of Colored Clergy. Proceedings of the first convocation... P. 13-22.

Starr, Frederick, ed.

Liberia
M966.6
An2na
Anderson, Benjamin J K
Narrative of the expedition despatched to Musahdu by the Liberian government under Benjamin J. K. Anderson, sr., esquire in 1874. Ed. by Frederick Starr. Monrovia, College of West Africa Press, 1912.
43p. 23cm.

M973.6
St2c
1849
State convention of the colored citizens of Ohio. Columbus, Ohio.
Minutes and address of the State Convention of colored citizens of Ohio, convened at Columbus, January 10th, 11th, 12th and 13th, 1849. Oberlin, From J. M. Fitch's Power Press, 1849.
28p. 19cm.
1. Congresses and conventions. 2. Ohio.

M973.6
St2c
1850
State convention of the colored citizens of Ohio, Columbus, Ohio.
Minutes of the state convention of the colored citizens of Ohio, convened at Columbus, January 9th, 10th, 11th and 12th, 1850. Columbus, Printed at Ohio Standard Office, by Gale & Cleveland, 1850.
22p. 19cm.
1. Congresses and conventions. 2. Ohio.

M973.6
St2
1848
State convention of coloured citizens, Harrisburg, Pa.
Minutes of the state convention of the coloured citizens of Pennsylvania, convened at Harrisburg, December 13th and 14th, 1848. Philadelphia, Merrihew and Thompson, 1849.
24p. 21cm.
1. Congresses and conventions. 2. Pennsylvania.

M973.6
St2ky
1867
State Convention of Colored Men, Lexington, Ky.
Proceedings of the State Convention of Colored Men, held at Lexington, Kentucky, in the A.M.E. Church, November 26th, 27th, and 28th, 1867. Frankfort, Ky., Frankfort Commonwealth Print, 1867.
13p. 21cm.
1. Congress and conventions.

M973.6
St2al
1851
State Convention of Colored People, Albany, New York.
Proceedings of the state convention of colored people, held at Albany, New York, on the 22d, 23d and 24th of July, 1851. Albany, Charles Van Benthuysen, Printer, 1851.
36p. 19cm.
1. Congresses and conventions.

M973.6
St2h
1865
State equal rights convention, Pennsylvania.
Proceedings of the state equal rights' convention, of tje colored people of Pennsylvania, held in the city of Harrisburg, February 8th, 9th and 10th, 1865, together with a few of the arguments presented suggesting the necessity for holding the convention, and an address to the colored state convention, to the people of Pennsylvania [Philadelphia] Printed for and by order of the convention, 1865.
50p. 21cm.
1. Congresses and conventions. 2. Equal rights league. 3. Pennsylvania.

State laws limiting marriage selection.

M323.3
D27s
Davenport, Charles Benedict, 1866–
... State laws limiting marriage selection examined in the light of eugenics, by Charles B. Davenport ... with two figures and four tables. Cold Spring Harbor [N. Y.] 1913.
66 p. tables (1 fold.) diagrs. (1 fold.) 23cm. (Eugenics record office. Bulletin no. 9)
Bibliography: p. 40.
1. Eugenics. 2. Marriage law—U. S. I. Title.
13–21086
Library of Congress HQ750.A1C5 [33f1]

Statement on foreign policy.

Ghana
M966.7
N65st
Nkrumah, Kwame, 1909–
Statement on foreign policy. In the National Assembly on 3rd September, 1958. Accra, Government Printer, 1958.
6p. 21½cm.

States' laws on race and color...

M323.4
M96s
Murray, Pauli, 1910– ed.
States' laws on race and color, and appendices containing international documents, federal laws and regulations, local ordinances and charts. [Cincinnati, Woman's Division of Christian Service, Board of Missions and Church Extension, Methodist Church] 1950 [i. e. 1951]
x, 746 p. forms. 24 cm.
1. Negroes—Legal status, laws, etc. 2. Race discrimination—U. S. I. Title.
325.260973 51–2354
Library of Congress [51u10]

Ghana
M309.16
B96
States, New.
Busia, Kofi Abrefa.
The challenge of Africa. New York, Praeger [1962]
150 p. 21 cm. (Books that matter)
1. Africa—Soc. condit. 2. States, New. 3. Akans (African people) I. Title.
DT30.B8 1962 309.16 62–21607 ‡
Library of Congress [63i10]

States, New.

Africa
M960
J88
Judd, Peter, ed.
African independence. [New York, Dell Pub. Co., 1963, °1962]
512 p. illus. 17 cm. (A Laurel original, 0088)
Includes bibliography.
White editor.
Partial contents.- African culture trends, by Ezekiel Mphahlele. - A personal view of Nigerian independence, by Tai Solarin. - The legal and
1. Africa, Sub-Saharan—Hist.—Addresses, essays, lectures. 2. States, New. I. Title.
(Continued on next card)
DT352.J8 1963 967 63–550 ‡
Library of Congress [2]

States, New.

Africa
M960
J88
Judd, Peter, ed.
African independence. [New York, Dell Pub. Co., 1963, °1962] (Card 2)
Contents-Continued.
constitutional problems of independence, by H. O. Davies. - Africa and the United Nations, by Alex Quaison-Sackey.

States, New.

St. Lucia
M966
L589
Lewis, William Arthur, 1915–
Politics in West Africa [by] W. Arthur Lewis. Toronto, New York, Oxford University Press, 1965.
90p. map. 19cm (The Whidden lectures, 1965)

States, New.

Ghana
M960
N65
Nkrumah, Kwame, Pres. Ghana, 1909–
Africa must unite. New York, F. A. Praeger [1963]
xvii, 229 p. port., map (on lining papers) 23 cm.
Bibliographical footnotes.
1. Pan-Africanism. 2. Africa—Hist. 3. Ghana—Hist. 4. States, New. I. Title.
DT30.N45 1963 960 63–18462
Library of Congress [64f5]

Statesmen.

Haiti
M972.4
D38t
Delorme, Démesvar.
Les théoriciens au pouvoir. Causeries historiques. Par D. Delorme ... Paris, H. Plon, 1870.
3 p. l., 732 p., 1 l. 23cm.
Contents.—Époque grecque: Périclès, Démosthènes, Solon.—Époque romaine: Cicéron.—Époque française: Avant 89, Mirabeau, Lamartine.
1. History—Addresses, essays, lectures. 2. Statesmen. I. Title. II. Title: Causeries historiques.
25–22817
Library of Congress D7.D4

Statistical atlas of southern counties.

M301
J63s
Johnson, Charles Spurgeon, 1893–
Statistical atlas of southern counties; listing and analysis of socio-economic indices of 1104 southern counties, by Charles S. Johnson and associates: Lewis W. Jones, Buford H. Junker [and others] ... Chapel Hill, The University of North Carolina press, 1941.
x, 1 l., 355 p. illus. (maps) 26 cm.
"County and state reference lists": p. [299]–355.
1. Southern states—Stat. I. Jones, Lewis Wade, 1910– II. Title.
41–8730
Library of Congress HA218.J6 [8] 317.5

Statistics.

M06
J61
no.4
Gannett, Henry, 1846–1914.
... Statistics of the Negroes in the United States, by Henry Gannett ... Baltimore, The Trustees, 1894.
28 p. maps, diagrs. 24½cm. (The trustees of the John F. Slater fund. Occasional papers, no. 4)
1. Negroes. 2. Negroes—Stat. I. Title.
6–31899
Library of Congress E185.5.J65
——— Copy 2. [30d1]

Statistics.

M07 S15 Simpson, George Eaton, 1904–
The Negro in the Philadelphia press ... [by] George Eaton Simpson. Philadelphia, 1936.
xv, 158 p. incl. illus. (map) tables, diagrs. 23cm.
Thesis (PH. D.)—University of Pennsylvania, 1934.
"Planoprinting."
An analysis of Negro material published in the Philadelphia record, Public ledger, Evening bulletin and Philadelphia inquirer during 1908–1932.
Bibliography: p. [153]–156.
1. Negroes. 2. Negroes—Stat. 3. American newspapers—Philadelphia. I. Title.
Library of Congress PN4899.P4S85 1934 37—1807
Univ. of Pennsylvania Libr.
——— Copy 2. [38g5] 071.4811

Statistics of the Negro race, 1927-28.
M370 C12m no.6 U.S., Office of education. Statistical Div.
Statistics of the Negro race, 1927-28. Washington, D.C., G.P.O., 1931.
16p. tables - 23cm. (U.S. Office of education. Pamphlet no. 14, December, 1930)
Editor: David Thompson, Blose.

Zanzibar
M398 St3s4 Steere, Edward, bp. 1828-1882.
Swahili tales (an English translation), by Edward Steere. London, The Sheldon press [1929]
iii, 186p. 19cm.
White author
1. Folklore, Swahili. 2. Tales, African. I. Title.

Statistics.

M323 W67 Williams, Frances Harriet.
The business girl looks at the Negro world, a study course, by Frances Harriet Williams ... New York, The Womans press, 1937.
3 p. l., 55 p. illus. (maps) 21½cm.
1. Negroes—Moral and social conditions. 2. Negroes—Stat. 3. U. S.—Race question. I. Title. 37—4315
Library of Congress E185.61.W73
[42d1] 325.260973

...Statistics of the Negroes in the United States...

M06 J61 no.4 Gannett, Henry, 1846–1914.
... Statistics of the Negroes in the United States, by Henry Gannett ... Baltimore, The Trustees, 1894.
28 p. maps, diagrs. 24½cm. (The trustees of the John F. Slater fund. Occasional papers, no. 4)
1. Negroes. 2. Negroes—Stat. I. Title. 6—31899
Library of Congress E185.5.J65
——— Copy 2. [39d1]

Zanzibar
M398 St3s Steere, Edward, bp. 1828-1882.
Swahili tales, by Edward Steere. A new edition, revised by Alice Werner. London, The Sheldon press, 1929.
185p. 18½cm.
Written in Swahili.
White author.
1. Folklore, Swahili. 2. Tales, African. I. Title. II. Werner, Alice, 1895-1935.

Statistics.

M280 Y33 Year book of Negro churches, with statistics and records of achievements of Negroes in the United States ... 1935/36–
Wilberforce, O., Printed at Wilberforce university [19
v. 22½cm.
Editor: 1935/36– Reverdy C. Ransom.
"Published by authority of the bishops of the A. M. E. church."
1. Negroes. 2. Negroes—Religion. 3. Churches—U. S. 4. Negroes—Stat. I. Ransom, Reverdy Cassius, bp., 1861– ed. II. African Methodist Episcopal church. III. Title: Negro churches, Year book of. 37—22400
Library of Congress E185.7.Y43
[44e1] 325.260973

Africa
M266 St29t Stauffer, Milton Theobald, 1885– ed.
... Thinking with Africa; chapters by a group of nationals interpreting the Christian movement, assembled and edited by Milton Stauffer ... New York, Pub. for the Student volunteer movement for foreign missions by the Missionary education movement of the United States and Canada [°1927]
xviii p., 1 l., 184 p. 19½cm. (Christian voices around the world)
White author.
1. Missions—Africa. 2. Africa—Religion. 3. Africa—Civilization. I. Title. (over) 28—8082
Library of Congress BV3500.S65
[40i1]

Stella.
Haiti
M843.91 B45s Beregeaud, Emeric, 1818-1858.
Stella, par E. Beregeaud. Paris, E. Dentie, Libraire-Editeur, 1859.
viii, 330p. 18½cm.

Statistics, Vital.

M306 At6 no.1 Atlanta University. Conference for the Investigations of City Problems.
Mortality among Negroes in cities; Proceedings of the Conference for the Investigations of City Problems, held at Atlanta University, May 26-27, 1896. Ed. by Thomas N. Chase. Atlanta, Atlanta University Press, 1903.
51p. 22½cm. (Atlanta University publications, no.1)

A
M266 St29t Stauffer, Milton Theobald, 1885– ed.
... Thinking with Africa; chapters by a group of nationals interpreting the Christian movement, assembled and edited by Milton Stauffer ... New York, Pub. for the Student volunteer movement for foreign missions by the Missionary education movement of the United States and Canada [°1927]
xviii p., 1 l., 184 p. 19½cm. (Christian voices around the world)
White author.
1. Missions—Africa. 2. Africa—Religion. 3. Africa—Civilization. I. Title.
(Over) 28—8082
Library of Congress BV3500.S65
[40i1]

M323 St4 Stemons, James Samuel.
As victim to victims; an American Negro laments with Jews, by James Samuel Stemons. New York, Fortuny's [°1941]
268 p. 22½cm.
"First edition."
1. Negroes—Moral and social conditions. 2. Jewish question. 3. Race problems. I. Title. II. Title: An American Negro laments with Jews. 41—9105
Library of Congress E185.61.S8
[42d2] 325.260973

Statistics, Vital.

M304 P19 v.3,no.5 Nathan, Winfred Bertram.
... Health conditions in North Harlem, 1923–1927, by Winfred B. Nathan ... an abstract, by Mary V. Dempsey. New York, National tuberculosis association [°1932]
68 p. incl. maps. 23cm. ([National tuberculosis association] Social research series. no. 2)
The death rates were revised on the basis of the 1930 census population figures. cf. Foreword.
"This study is ... largely a study of negro health."—Introd.
1. Harlem, New York (City)—Sanit. affairs. 2. Negroes—New York (City) 3. Negroes—Mortality. 4. Negroes—Statistics, Vital. 5. New York (City)—Statistics, Vital. 6. Health surveys. I. Dempsey, Mary V., ed. II. Title. 32—21088
Library of Congress RA448.H3N3
[42d1] 614.097471

Barbados
M610 St2n Staupers, Mabel Keaton, 1890–
No time for prejudice; a story of the integration of Negroes in nursing in the United States. New York, Macmillan [1961]
206 p. illus. 22 cm.
1. Negro nurses. I. Title.
RT83.5.S75 610.7306273 61—7432 ‡
Library of Congress [61k10]

M323 St4k Stemons, James Samuel.
The key; a tangible solution of the negro problem, by James Samuel Stemons ... New York, The Neale publishing company, 1916.
156 p. 19cm. $1.00
1. Negroes. 2. U. S.—Race question. I. Title. 17-2334
Library of Congress E185.61.S82
——— Copy 2. [36b1]
Copyright A 455220

Statistics of the education of Negroes.

M370 Un3s U. S. *Office of education. Statistical division.*
... Statistics of the education of Negroes, 1925–1926— Washington, U. S. Govt. print. off., 1928–
v. tables, diagrs. 23cm.
1925–1928, by D. T. Blose; 1929– by D. T. Blose and Ambrose Caliver.
1925–1926, issued as Bureau of education. Bulletin, 1928, no. 19; 1927–1928, as U. S. Office of education. Pamphlet no. 14; 1929–1932—as U. S. Office of education. Bulletin 1935, no. 13; 1938, no. 13
Title varies: 1925–26, Statistics of education of the Negro race.
1927–28, Statistics of the Negro race.
1929–32– Statistics of the education of Negroes.
1. Negroes—Education—[Statistics] I. Blose, David Thompson. II. Caliver, Ambrose, 1894– III. Title.
U. S. Off. of educ. Library LC2801.U61
——— 2d set. L111.A6 E 29—26 (rev. '40)
——— for Library of Congress L111.A6
——— Copy 2. LC2801.A33
[a40r36w2] 371.9740973

The steel makers.
M811.5 H24st Harris, Leon R
The steel makers and other war poems ... by Leon R. Harris. Portsmouth, Ohio T.C. McConnell printery c1918.
15p. 21cm.

M814.5 Ev1s Step of life.
Evans, Phillip.
Subject of life; Step of life; The goodness of a woman. Chicago, The author, 1946.
12p. 17cm.

Statistics of education of the Negro race.
M370 C12m no.5 U.S. Office of education. Statistical Div.
Statistics of education of the Negro race, 1925-1926, by David T. Blose... Washington, D.C., G.P.O. 1928.
42p. tables. 24cm. (U.S. Office of education. Bulletin, 1928, no.19)
Editor: David Thompson Blose

M220 St3b Steele, Algernon Odell, 1900–
The Bible and the human quest. New York, Philosophical Library [°1956]
240 p. 21 cm.
1. Christianity—20th cent. I. Title.
BR121.S82 220.7 57—1204 ‡
Library of Congress [8]

Nigeria
M896.3 St43f Stephen, Felix N
A fool at forty, a very fascinating novel written by a Free Lance Journalist packed with thrills, laughter, humourous and educative. Port Harcourt, Vincent Okeanu [n.d.]
42p. port. 18½cm.
I. Title.

Nigeria
M896.2
St43t

Stephen, Felix N
The trials and death of Lumumba. Onitsha [Nigeria] M.A. Ohaejesi [n.d.]

42p. ports. 20½cm.

1. African drama. 2. Lumumba, Patrice, 1925-1961 - Drama. I. Title.

Nigeria
M896.2
St43tr

Stephen, Felix N
The trials of Lumumba, Jomo Kenyatta and St. Paul. Onitsha, Njoku and Sons Bookshop, n.d.

44p. ports. 21½cm.

1. African drama. I. Title.

Stephen.

M204
St4f

Stephenson, Isaiah H.
First oration on Stephen, the first martyr of the Christian church. ed ed. [n.p. 1898]

8p. 22cm.

M341.1
St41

Stephens, Perry Alexander.
Lasting peace and democracy. [New York, F. Hubner & Co., 1946]

11p. 22cm.

M204
St4f

Stephenson, Isaiah H.
First oration on Stephen, the first martyr of the Christian church. 2d ed. [n.p. 1898]

8p. 22cm.

1. Christianity. 2. Stephen.

Stephenson, Lee, joint author.

M784
W33

Watson, Deek.
The story of the "Ink Spots," by Deek Watson with Lee Stephenson. [1st ed.] New York, Vantage Press [1967]

72 p. 21 cm.

1. Ink Spots. I. Stephenson, Lee, joint author. II. Title.

ML400.W23 784'.0922 67-5817/MN

Library of Congress [3]

Stepping back.

M811.5
B84s

Bryant, Joseph G
Stepping back. Philadelphia, A.M.E. Book Concern, n.d.

16p. ports. 15cm.

1. Poetry. I. Title.

Stepping stones to freedom.

M811.5
R21s

Ragland, James Farley, 1904-
Stepping stones to freedom; poems of pride and purpose. Richmond, Virginia, Quality Printing, c 1960.

30p. port. 23cm.

Haiti
M843.91
St4

Sterlin, Philippe
3 contes. New York, Imp. de l'Etat, 1953.

79p. 18cm.

1. Haitian fiction

M89
Sm1s

Sterling, Dorothy, 1913-
Captain of the Planter; the story of Robert Smalls. Illustrated by Ernest Crichlow. [1st ed.] Garden City, N. Y., Doubleday, 1958.

264 p. illus. 22 cm.

Includes bibliography.

White author.

1. Smalls, Robert, 1839-1915. I. Title. II. Crichlow, Ernest, illustrator.

E185.97.S6S8 923.273 58-5582 ‡

Library of Congress [15]

M973.714
St45

Sterling, Dorothy.
Forever free, the story of the Emancipation Proclamation. Illustrated by Ernest Crichlow. [1st ed.] Garden City, N. Y., Doubleday [1963]

208 p. illus. 22 cm.

Includes bibliography.

White author.

1. Emancipation Proclamation—Juvenile literature. 2. Slavery in the U. S.—Juvenile literature. I. Title.

E453.S83 j 973.7 63-7691 ‡

Library of Congress [5]

M813.5
E14ir

Sterling, Dorothy, 1913- ed.
I have seen war; 25 stories from World War II. New York, Hill and Wang [1960]

278 p. 21 cm.

1. World War, 1939-1945—Anecdotes. I. Title.

D744.S75 940.548 60-14909 ‡

Library of Congress [61k10]

M813.5
St4m

Sterling, Dorothy, 1913-
Mary Jane. Illustrated by Ernest Crichlow. [1st ed.] Garden City, N. Y., Doubleday, 1959.

214 p. illus. 22 cm.

I. Title. II. Crichlow, Ernest, illus.

PZ7.S8376Mar 59-7917 ‡

Library of Congress [59f7]

M817
St45

Sterling, Philip, ed.
Laughing on the outside; the intelligent white reader's guide to Negro tales and humor. Introductory essay by Saunders Redding. Cartoons by Ollie Harrington. New York, Grosset & Dunlap [1965]

254 p. illus. 22 cm.

Bibliography: p. [251]-254.

Includes selections from writings by American Negro authors.

White editor.

1. Negro wit and humor. I. Title. II. Redding, Jay Saunders.

PN6231.N5S7 817.008 65-15349

Library of Congress [5]

M326.
St4

Stevens, Charles Emery, 1815-1893.
Anthony Burns, a history, by Charles Emery Stevens. Boston, J. P. Jewett and company, 1856.

xiv, 15-295 p. 8 pl. (incl. front.) 19cm.

1. Burns, Anthony, 1830?-1862.

Library of Congress E450.B96 14-5642

[a41b1]

Stevens, Edward.

Haiti
M972.94
L49p

Lecorps, Louis Marceau, ed.
... La politique extérieure de Toussaint-Louverture; nos premières relations politiques avec les États-Unis, lettres de Toussaint-Louverture et d'Edward Stevens (1799-1800) Port-au-Prince, Cheraquit, 1935.

1 p. l., ii, [5]-107, vi p., 1 l. port. 22½cm.

At head of title: Ls. Marceau Lecorps.

1. Haiti—For. rel. 2. Haiti—For. rel.—U. S. 3. U. S.—For. rel.—Haiti. I. Toussaint Louverture, Pierre Dominique, 1746?-1803. II. Stevens, Edward.

New York. Public library for Library of Congress A 41-3004

[3]

M306
N21p

Stevens, Myra.
Necessary modifications of child welfare services to meet the needs of dependent Negro children. New York, 1945.

In: National Conference of Social Work. Selected papers at seventy-second annual meeting, 1945. New York, Columbia University, for the Conference, 1945. pp. 305-313.

1. Children - Charities, protection, etc.

M89
St4s

Stevens, Walter James, 1877-
Chip on my shoulder, autobiography of Walter J. Stevens. Boston, Meador publishing company [1946]

315 p. front. (port.) 20½cm.

I. Title.

E185.97.S82A3 325.260973 47-15600

© 12Nov46; author, Roxbury, Mass.; A9041.

Library of Congress [3]

M260
St4h

Stevenson J. W
How to get and keep churches out of debt, and also a lecture on the secret of success in the art of making money. By Rev. J.W. Stevenson. Albany, Weed, Parsons and company, 1886.

xxxi, 283 p. front. 19cm.

1. Churches-Finances.

Uganda
M823
St48

Stevenson, Robert Louis
Ekizinga Ky'Obugagga [Treasure Island] Kyakyusibwa Y. B. Semambo. Kampala, Eagle Press, 1951.

156p. 18cm.

Written in Luganda.

White author.

I. Title. II. Semambo, Yusufu Balirwana, tr.

Kenya
M823
St48t

Stevenson, Robert Louis
Kithamani kya uthwii [Treasure Island. Retold by Haydn Perry] Kitungitwe J. S. Mbiti. Nairobi, Eagle Press, 1955.

45p. 18½cm.

Written in Kamba.

White author.

I. Title. II. Mbiti, John Samuel, 1931- tr.

M326.99B St4 1867
Steward, Austin, *b.* 1794.
Twenty-two years a slave, and forty years a freeman; embracing a correspondence of several years, while president of Wilberforce colony, London, Canada West, by Austin Steward. 4th ed. ~~Rochester, N. Y., Allings & Cory, 1861.~~ Canandaigua, N.Y., The author, 1867.
xii, ⌊13⌋–360 p. front. (port.) 4 pl. 18cm.
4. Slave narratives.
1. Slavery in the U. S.—Virginia. 2. Slavery in the U. S.—New York (State) 3. Wilberforce negro colony, Middlesex Co., Ont. I. Title.
Library of Congress E444.S845 14—17056 ⌊s20f2⌋

M326.99B St4
Steward, Austin, *b.* 1794.
Twenty-two years a slave, and forty years a freeman; embracing a correspondence of several years, while president of Wilberforce colony, London, Canada West, by Austin Steward. Rochester, N. Y., W. Alling, 1857.
xii, ⌊13⌋–360 p. front. (port.) 4 pl. 19cm.
Narrative of slave life in Virginia and in central New York.
1. Slavery in the U. S.—Virginia. 2. Wilberforce negro colony, Middlesex co., Ont. I. Title.
Library of Congress E444.S84 6—34319 ⌊a27d1⌋

M610 P19 v.1 no.1
Steward, Susan Maria Smith, 1845-
Women in medicine; a paper read before the National association of Colored Women's clubs at Wilberforce, Ohio, August 6, 1914, by S. Maria Steward... Wilberforce, Ohio ⌊The author⌋ 1914.
24p. ports. 19½cm.
1. Medicine.

M350 St4r
Steward, Theophilus Gould, 1843–1924
The colored regulars in the United States army, with a sketch of the history of the colored American, and an account of his services in the wars of the country, from the period of the revolutionary war to 1899. Introductory letter from Lieutenant-General Nelson A. Miles ... By Chaplain T. G. Steward ... Philadelphia, A. M. E. book concern, 1904.
344 p. front., ports., maps. 22cm.
1. U. S.—Hist.—War of 1898—Negro troops. ~~2. Negroes.~~
Library of Congress E725.5.N3S8 8–317 Revised ⌊r42b2⌋

MB9 St4f
Steward, Theophilus Gould, 1843-1924
From 1864 to 1914, fifty years in the gospel ministry; twenty-seven years in the pastorate; sixteen years' active service as chaplain in the U.S. army; seven years professor in Wilberforce university; two trips to Europe; a trip in Mexico. In two parts, with appropriate illustrations. Introduction by Rev. Reverdy C. Ransom... By Theophilus Gould Steward... ⌊Philadelphia, Pa., A.M.E. book concern, 1914?⌋
xvii, 19-520p. front., illus. 20½cm.
1. African methodist episcopal church. ~~I. Title.~~

M910 St4
Steward, Theophilus Gould, 1843–1924
The Haitian revolution, 1791 to 1804; or, Side lights on the French revolution, by T. G. Steward ... New York, T. Y. Crowell company ⌊©1914⌋
ix, ⌊3⌋, 292 p. front., pl., ports., map. 19cm.
"List of authorities consulted": p. ⌊x⌋; "Haitian authors of merit with names of their works": p. 273–276.
1. Haiti—Hist.—Revolution, 1791–1804.
Library of Congress F1923.S85 15—292 ⌊42b1⌋

M06 Am3 no.5
Steward, Theophilus Gould, 1843–1924
... How the black St. Domingo legion saved the patriot army in the siege of Savannah, 1779, by T. G. Steward ... Washington, D. C., The Academy, 1899.
15 p. illus. (maps) 23cm. (American negro academy. Occasional papers, no. 5)
1. Savannah—Siege, 1779. 2. U. S.—Hist.—Revolution—Negro troops. 3. France—Army—Infantry—Fontage's legion.
Library of Congress E185.5.A51 no. 5 9–24043 Revised
——— Copy 2. E241.S2S88 ⌊r32e2⌋

Steward, Theophilus Gould, 1843-1924
Message of San Domingo to the African race.

M06 Am3 no. 18, 19
American Negro academy, *Washington, D. C.*
Papers of the American Negro academy ... read at the nineteenth annual meeting of the American Negro academy ... Washington, D. C., December 28th and 29th, 1915. ⌊Washington, 1916⌋
78 p. 22cm. ⌊Occasional papers, no. 18/19⌋
CONTENTS.—The sex question and race segregation, by A. H. Grimke.—Message of San Domingo to the African race, by T. G. Steward.—Status of the free Negro prior to 1860, by L. M. Hershaw.—Economic contribution by the Negro to America, by A. A. Schomberg ⌊!⌋—The status of the free Negro from 1860 to 1870, by William Pickens.—American Negro bibliography of the year, by J. W. Cromwell.
1. Negroes—Societies. 2. Negroes—Bibl. I. Grimke, Archibald Henry, 1849–1930. II. Steward, Theophilus Gould, 1843– III. Hershaw, Lafayette M. IV. Schomburg, Arthur Alfonso, 1874– V. Pickens, William, 1881– VI. Cromwell, John Wesley, 1846–
Library of Congress E185.5.A51 no. 18/19 16–17783 Revised ⌊r42b2⌋
——— Copy 2. E185.5.A525

Steward, Theophilus Gould, 1843-1924, joint author.

M974.9 St4
Steward, William, 1840–
Gouldtown, a very remarkable settlement of ancient date; studies of some sturdy examples of the simple life, together with sketches of early colonial history of Cumberland county and southern New Jersey and some early genealogical records, by William Steward ... and Rev. Theophilus G. Steward ... Philadelphia, Press of J. B. Lippincott company, 1913.
237 p. front., plates, ports. 25cm.
1. Gouldtown, N. J. I. Steward, Theophilus Gould, 1843– joint author.
Library of Congress F144.G6S8 13—15731 ⌊37f1⌋

M974.9 St4
Steward, William, 1840–
Gouldtown, a very remarkable settlement of ancient date; studies of some sturdy examples of the simple life, together with sketches of early colonial history of Cumberland county and southern New Jersey and some early genealogical records, by William Steward ... and Rev. Theophilus G. Steward ... Philadelphia, Press of J. B. Lippincott company, 1913.
237 p. front., plates, ports. 25cm.
1. Gouldtown, N. J. I. Steward, Theophilus Gould, 1843– joint author.
Library of Congress F144.G6S8 13—15731 ⌊37f1⌋

Stewardship, Christian.

M286 R17c
Ransome, William Lee, 1879–
Christian stewardship and Negro Baptists, by W. L. Ransome ... Richmond, Virginia, National ministers' institute, Virginia union university. Richmond, Va., Brown print shop, inc., 1934.
193 p. 20cm.
"A short bibliography": p. 190.
1. Stewardship, Christian. 2. Baptists, Negro. 3. Baptists—Missions. I. National ministers' institute, Virginia. Union university, Richmond. II. Title.
Library of Congress BV772.R25 36–30056
——— Copy 2. ⌊3⌋ 254

M813.5 H87n
Stewart, Donald Ogden, 1894– *ed.*
Fighting words, edited by Donald Ogden Stewart. New York, Harcourt, Brace and company ⌊©1940⌋
5 p. l., 3–168 p. 21cm.
Selected material on various aspects of creative writing, including screen and radio productions, from addresses and discussions at the third congress of the League of American writers held in New York, June 2–5, 1939. Edited by the president of the league.
"First edition."
1. Authorship. I. League of American writers. II. Title.
Library of Congress PN137.S8 40–30022
——— Copy 2.
Copyright ⌊10⌋ 029.6

Stewart, John, 1786-1823.

MB9 St4m
⌊Mitchell, Joseph⌋
The missionary pioneer, or a brief memoir of the life, labours and death of John Stewart (man of colour) founder, under God of the mission among the Wyandott's at Upper Sandusky, Ohio. Published by Joseph Mitchell. New York, Printed by J. C. Totten, 1827.
viii, 96p. 15cm.

Stewart, John.

MB9 St4m
⌊Mitchell, Joseph⌋
The missionary pioneer, or a brief memoir of life, labours, and death of John Stewart, (man of colour) founder, under God of the mission among the Wyandotts at Upper Sandusky, Ohio. Published by Joseph Mitchell. New York, Printed by J.C. Totten, 1827.
viii, 96p. 15cm.
Facsimile reproduction.

Ghana M896.1 St4a
Stewart, MacNeill
Appeal to reason -- to the political leaders of the country this poem is respectfully dedicated --. Accra, 1951.
4p. ports. 18cm.
1. Ghana - Poetry. 2. Poetry - Ghana. I. Danquah, Joseph Boakye, 1895- II. Nkrumah, Kwame, 1909- III. Ollennu,

---

M323 St4n
Stewart, Maxwell Slutz, 1900–
... The Negro in America, by Maxwell S. Stewart. ⌊New York, Public affairs committee, inc., 1944⌋
cover-title, 32 p. 1 illus., diagrs. 21cm. (Public affairs pamphlet, no. 95)
"First edition, August 1944."
"Summary of An American dilemma ... by Gunnar Myrdal."—p. ⌊1⌋
"For further reading": p. 32.
1. Negroes. I. *Myrdal, Gunnar, 1898– An American dilemma. II. Title.
Library of Congress E185.6.M952 44–9455 ⌊35⌋ 325.260973

M910 St4
Stewart, Thomas McCants, 1853–1923
Liberia: the Americo-African republic. Being some impressions of the climate, resources, and people, resulting from personal observations and experiences in West Africa. By T. McCants Stewart ... With an introduction by Dr. G. W. Samson ... New York, E. O. Jenkins' sons, 1886.
107 p. illus. 20½cm.
Inscribed copy: To E. J. Stokes, Esq. With compliments of T. McCants Stewart, May 12th, '86.
1. Liberia. I. Title.
Library of Congress DT625.S85 5–15270 Revised ⌊r30c2⌋

M973.6 N21t 1879
Stowart, William H
The necessity of a National review devoted to the interests of Negro-American. p.52-56. National Conference of Colored Men. Nashville. Proceedings of the National Conference of Colored Men of the United States, held in the State Capitol at Nashville, Tennessee, May 6, 7, 8, and 9, 1879. Washington, D.C., Rufus H. Darby, 1879.
107p. 19cm.

MB9 St5
Still, James, *b.* 1812.
Early recollections and life of Dr. James Still. ⌊Philadelphia⌋ Printed for the author by J. B. Lippincott & co., 1877.
274 p. front. (port.) 19cm.
1. Philadelphia, Pa.
Library of Congress E185.97.S85 14–15943
Copyright 1877; 3478 ⌊37b1⌋

Still, Lavinia.

M326.99B P58k 1941
Pickard, Kate E R
The kidnapped and the ransomed, by Kate E. R. Pickard ... ⌊New York⌋ Negro publication society of America, inc., 1941.
315, ⌊1⌋ p. 22cm. (⌊Negro publication society of America. Publications⌋ Series I, History. No. 1)
"The first edition ... appeared in 1856."—Editor's note.
"Appendix. Seth Conklin ⌊by W. H. Furness⌋": p. 293–315.
1. Still, Peter. 2. Still, Lavinia. 3. Slavery in the U. S.—Kentucky. 4. Slavery in the U. S.—Alabama. 5. Concklin, Seth, 1802–1851. I. Furness, William Henry, 1802–1896. II. Negro publication society of America. III. Title.
Library of Congress E444.S855 43—17335 ⌊45e1⌋ 326.92

Still, Lavinia.

M326.99B P58k
Pickard, Kate E R.
The kidnapped and the ransomed. Being the personal recollections of Peter Still and his wife "Vina," after forty years of slavery. By Mrs. Kate E. R. Pickard. With an introduction, by Rev. Samuel J. May; and an appendix, by William H. Furness, D. D. Syracuse, W. T. Hamilton; New York ⌊etc.⌋ Miller, Orton and Mulligan, 1856.
xxiii (*i. e.* xxi), 25–409 p. 8 pl. (incl. front.) 19 cm.
Pages ix–x omitted in paging.
Added t.-p., engraved.
"Appendix. Seth Concklin ⌊by William H. Furness⌋": p. 377–409.
1. Still, Peter. 2. Still, Lavinia. 3. Slavery in the U. S.—Kentucky. 4. Slavery in the U. S.—Alabama. 5. Concklin, Seth, 1802–1851. I. Furness, William Henry, 1802–1896. II. Title.
Library of Congress E444.S85 14—15958 ⌊48g1⌋

M326.99B
P58k

Still, Peter. 1801-1868.
Pickard, Kate E R.
The kidnapped and the ransomed. Being the personal recollections of Peter Still and his wife "Vina," after forty years of slavery. By Mrs. Kate E. R. Pickard. With an introduction, by Rev. Samuel J. May; and an appendix, by William H. Furness, D. D. Syracuse, W. T. Hamilton; New York, ⌈etc.⌉ Miller, Orton and Mulligan, 1856.
xxiii (*i. e.* xxi), 25–409 p. 8 pl. (incl. front.) 19 cm.
Pages ix–x omitted in paging.
Added t.-p., engraved.
"Appendix. Seth Concklin ⌈by William H. Furness⌉": p. 377–409.
1. Still, Peter. 2. Still, Lavinia. 3. Slavery in the U. S.—Kentucky. 4. Slavery in the U. S.—Alabama. 5. Concklin, Seth, 1802–1851. I. Furness, William Henry, 1802–1896. II. Title.
14—15958
Library of Congress E444.S85
⌈48g1⌉

M326.99B
P58k
1941

Still, Peter, 1801-1868.
Pickard, Kate E R
The kidnapped and the ransomed, by Kate E. R. Pickard ... ⌈New York⌉ Negro publication society of America, inc., 1941.
815, ⌈1⌉ p. 22cm. (⌈Negro publication society of America. Publications⌉ Series I, History. No. 1)
"The first edition ... appeared in 1856."—Editor's note.
"Appendix. Seth Conklin ⌈by W. H. Furness⌉": p. 298-815.
1. Still, Peter. 2. Still, Lavinia. 3. Slavery in the U. S.—Kentucky. 4. Slavery in the U. S.—Alabama. 5. Concklin, Seth, 1802–1851. I. Furness, William Henry, 1802–1896. II. Negro publication society of America. III. Title.
43—17835
Library of Congress E444.S855
⌈45e1⌉ 326.82

M973.6
N21t
1879

Still, William, 1821-1902
Opportunities and capabilities of educated Negroes. p. 56-65.
National Conference of Colored Men. Nashville.
Proceedings of the National Conference of Colored Men of the United States, held in the State Capitol at Nashville, Tennessee, May 6, 7, 8, and 9, 1879. Washington, D.C., Rufus H. Darby, 1879.
107p. 19cm.

M326
St5
1886

Still, William, 1821-1902.
Underground railroad records, with a life of the author, narrating the hardships, hair-breadth escapes, and death struggles of the slaves in their efforts for freedom; together with sketches of some of the eminent friends of freedom, and most liberal aiders and advisers of the road. Illus. with 70 fine engravings... and portraits... rev. ed. Phil., William Still, publisher, 1886.
21, lxiv, 780p. illus. 24cm.
1. Underground railroad. 2. Slavery in the U.S.—Fugitive slaves.

M326
St5

Still, William, 1821-1902.
The underground railroad. A record of facts, authentic narratives, letters & c., narrating the hardships, hairbreadth escapes and death struggles of the slaves in their efforts for freedom, as related by themselves and others, or witnessed by the author; together with sketches of some of the largest stockholders, and most liberal aiders and advisers, of the road. By Williams Still...Philadelphia, Porter E. Coates, 1872.
2p. l., 780p. front. illus., pl. ports. 24cm.
(over)

M780.9
C83

Still, William Grant, 1895-
An Afro-American composer's point of view. Pp. 182-83.
In: Cowell, Henry, ed. American composers on American music. Standford University, Calif. Stanford University Press, 1933.

M973.9
F46
No.19

Still, William Grant, 1895-
Fifty years of progress in music. Pittsburgh, Pittsburgh Courier, 1950.
7p. illus. port. 24cm. (Fifty years of progress)
1. Music. I. Series.

M214.5
W93u

Still, William Grant, 1895-
The Negro and his music in films.
(In: Writers' Congress. University of California at Los Angeles, 1943. Proceedings, Berkeley and Los Angeles, University of California Press, 1944. 23cm. p.(277-79)

M811.5
H87t

Still, William Grant, 1895-
Hughes, Langston, 1902-
Troubled island; An opera in three acts. Libretto. Music by William Grant Still. Libretto by Langston Hughes. Hollywood, Leeds Music Corporation, 1949.
38p. 22cm.

M811.5
El49s

Still waters and other poems.
Elliot, Emily I
Still waters and other poems. Cambridge, The author, 1949.
28p. 19cm.
Portrait attached.

M811.5
C15

Stills, Gordon H
Poems.
(In: Campbell, James E. Temporary reprieve, a collection of original poems. Baltimore, The authors, 1953. pp. 20-46)

MB9
A12m

Stock, Mildred, joint author.
Marshall, Herbert, 1912–
Ira Aldridge, the Negro tragedian, by Herbert Marshall and Mildred Stock. ~~London, Rockliff~~ ⌈1958⌉
355 p. illus. 23 cm. N.Y., Macmillan.
Includes bibliographies.
1. Aldridge, Ira Frederick, d. 1867. I. Stock, Mildred, joint author.
PN2598.A52M3 927.92 59—22897 ‡
Library of Congress ⌈59b15⌉

MB9
A12m2

Stock, Mildred, jt. aut.
Marshall, Herbert, 1912-
Ira Aldridge, the Negro tragedian. By Herbert Marshall and Mildred Stock. London, Rockliff [c1958]
355p. ports. 22cm.
Bibliography: p. 337 - 342
White authors.

M630.7
C25c

Stock and stock breeding.
Carver, George Washington, 1864-1943.
Can live stock be raised profitably in Alabama?..By George W. Carver. Second edition. Tuskegee Institute, Alabama, Tuskegee Institute Press, 1936.
12p. tables. 22cm. (Bulletin no. 41, April 1936)

Nigeria
M966.9
St6o

Stocker, John
Our festival of the arts. Lagos, Public Relations Department, n.d.
19p. illus. 20½cm. (Crownbird Series No. 5)
1. Nigeria - art.

M301
D853r5

Stoddard, Lothrop.
Du Bois, William Edward Burghardt, 1868-
Report of debate conducted by the Chicago forum "Shall the Negro be encouraged to seek cultural equality?" Affirmative: W. E. Burghardt Du Bois...Negative: Lothrop Stoddard ...Chicago, ⌈Chicago forum council, c1929⌉
24p. 19cm.

M252
St67
1924

Stokes, Andrew Jackson, 1859–
Select sermons, by Rev. A. J. Stokes ... ⌈Nashville, Natl. Baptist pub. board, ~~1920~~ c1924
152 p. front. (port.) plates. 20cm.
Revised edition.
I. Title.
Library of Congress 20-8017
——— Copy 2.
Copyright A 566649 ⌈2⌉

M180
J23

Stolen legacy.
James, George G M
Stolen legacy: the Greeks were not the authors of Greek philosophy, but the people of North Africa, commonly called the Egyptians. New York, Philosophical Library ⌈1954⌉
100 p. 22 cm.
1. Philosophy, Ancient—Hist. I. Title.
B171.J3 180 54-4101 ‡
Library of Congress ⌈7⌉

M323.4
St71

Stone, Chuck.
Tell it like it is. New York, Trident Press, 1967 ⌈°1968⌉
211 p. 22 cm.
~~1. Negroes—Civil rights—Addresses, essays, lectures.~~ I. Title.
E185.61.S872 1968 301.451'96'073 68—13435
Library of Congress ⌈68a5⌉

M811.5
St7c

Stone, Leroy Owen,
Continental streamlets (a joint poetical premiere). Poems by Leroy Owen Stone and Percy Edward Johnston. ⌈Washington, D.C., Continental Press, c 1960⌉
7p. 18cm.
1. Poetry. I. Title. II. Percy Edward Johnston, 1930-

South Africa
M896.3
L11s

The stone-country.
La Guma, Alex.
The stone-country. Berlin, Seven Seas Publishers (1967).
189 p. 19 cm. (Seven seas books) DM 2.85
(GDB 68-A1-220)
I. Title. (Series)
PZ4.L178St 68-92036
Library of Congress ⌈1⌉

The stone face.

M813.5 Sm68st

Smith, William Gardner, 1926-
The stone face, a novel. New York, Farrar, Straus [1963]
218 p. 21 cm.

I. Title.

PZ3.S6638St 63-11184

Library of Congress [5]

Stories from the south of Nigeria.

Nigeria M372.8 B813

Brown, Godfrey M
Stories from the south of Nigeria. Illustrated by M. A. Ajayi. London, Allen [c1966]
79p. illus. 18cm. (African social studies for the primary school)

1. Nigeria - Juvenile literature. I. Title.

The story of an African chief.

M896.3 N98

Nyabongo, Akiki K 1905-
The story of an African chief, by Akiki K. Nyabongo; illustrations by Eleanor Maroney; with an introduction by William Lyon Phelps. New York, C. Scribner's sons, 1935.
x p., 2 l., 3-312 p. incl. front., plates. 22cm.

1. Africa, Central—Soc. life & cust. I. Title.

35-7987 Provisional

Library of Congress DT351.N9

—— Copy 2.

Copyright A 83492 [5-5] 916.7

Stores, Retail - Uganda.

Uganda M658 L97

Lumu, Nehemiah Bosa Eryan, 1912-
Oyinza okutunda edduka? [Can you run a shop?] Nairobi, Eagle Press, 1957.
59p. illus.
Written in Luganda.

1. Stores, Retail - Uganda. I. Title.

Stories in verse.

M811.5 H78

Horn, Max T ed.
Stories in verse. New York, Odyssey Press [1943]
430p. 20cm.
Partial contents.- The creation, by James Weldon Johnson.- De Boll Weevil.

1. Poetry. I. Title. II. De Boll Weevil.

The story of Dorothy Stanfield.

M813.5 M58s

Micheaux, Oscar, 1884-
The story of Dorothy Stanfield, based on a great insurance swindle, and a woman! A novel by Oscar Micheaux ... New York, Book supply company, 1946.
416 p. col. front. 22½cm.

I. Title.

46-2507

Library of Congress PZ3.M5808St [5]

M323 St7n

Storey, Moorfield.
The Negro question; An address delivered before the Wisconsin Bar Association, June 27, 1918. New York, NAACP, [1918]
30p. 23cm.
White author ?

1. Race problem. I. Title.

Stories of black folk for little folk.

MB L23s

Landrum, Bessie.
Stories of black folk for little folk, by Bessie Landrum. Atlanta, Ga., A. B. Caldwell publishing co., 1923.
103 p. illus. (ports.) 20½cm.

1. Negroes—Biog. I. Title.

24-2634

Library of Congress E185.96.L25

Copyright A 766907 [2]

The story of George Washington Carver.

M372.4 C35

Chambers, Lucille Arcola
The story of George Washington Carver, scientist. Art by John Neal. New York, C & S Ventures, 1965.
[21]p. illus. 31cm. (Negro pioneers)
"Compliments, of Lucille Arcola Chambers, '67."

I. Title. II. Series.

Storey, Moorfield, 1845-

MB9 St7

Moorfield Storey. Memorial Exercises in Park Street church, Boston, March 19, 1930. Boston, National Association for the Advancement of Colored People [c1930]
vi, 37p. port. (front.) 23cm.

Stories of life.

Kenya M896.3 In7s

Inoti, F M
Stories of life. London, Sheldon Press, 1948.
15p. illus. 15cm. (African home library)

I. Title.

The story of Miqdad & Mayasa.

Kenya M896.1 H119

Hadithi ya Mikidadi na Mayasa.
The story of Miqdad & Mayasa, from the Swahili-Abrabic text of Alice Werner. Medstead, Hampshire, Azania Press, 1932.
90p. illus. 19cm.
Written in Swahili and English.

1. Swahili language - Texts. I. Werner, Alice, 1859-1935, tr. II. Title. III. Title: Miqdad & Mayasa, The story of.

Storey, Moorfield, 1845-

MB9 St7

Wilson, Butler R.
Moorfield Storey and the Negro. In: Moorfield Storey, memorial exercises in Park Street Church, Boston, March 19, 1930. Boston, National Association for the Advancement of Colored People [c1930] p. 49.

Stories of the Benin Empire.

Nigeria M398 S113

Sidahome, Joseph E ,1917-1963.
Stories of the Benin Empire. London, Oxford University Press, 1964.
196p. illus. 21½cm.

Story of Noliswa.

Africa, South M896.3 N24n

Ndawo, Henry Masila
U-Nolishwa. Lovedale, The Lovedale Press, 1939.
126p. port. 18½cm.
Story of Noliswa.
Bound with the author's InXenye YenTsomi Zase Zweni. [Natal, 1920]

MB Em3

Stories and spirituals of the Negro slave...
Emerson, William Canfield, 1893- ed.
Stories and spirituals of the Negro slave, by William C. Emerson, M. D. Boston, R. G. Badger [c1930]
79p. front, ports. 19½cm.
Includes music.
white author?

Stories of the South, old and new.

M813.08 H52s

Hibbard, Clarence Addison, 1887- *ed.*
Stories of the South, old and new, edited by Addison Hibbard, with an introduction, biographical notes, and bibliography by the editor. Chapel Hill, The University of North Carolina press; New York, W. W. Norton & company [c1931]
xvii, 520 p. 22cm.

1. Short stories, American. 2. American literature—Southern states. I. Title.

31—8688

Library of Congress PZ1.H522St [44j2]

The story of Haiti.

M910. M35

Marshall, *Mrs.* Harriet (Gibbs)
The story of Haiti, from the discovery of the island by Christopher Columbus to the present day, by Harriet Gibbs Marshall ... Boston, The Christopher publishing house [c1930]
177 p. front., plates, ports., fold. map. 20½cm.
"List of Haitian music": p. 139-141. "List of Haitian literature": p. 142-147.

1. Haiti—Hist. I. Title.

30—15208

Library of Congress W1011.M36 [42f1] 972.94

Stories from the Caribbean, an anthology.

Jamaica M823.91 Sa3a

Salkey, Andrew, comp.
Stories from the Caribbean, an anthology. Selected and introduced by Andrew Salkey. London, Elek Books [1965]
256p. 21cm.
"For Arthur from Andrew, 5/22/65."

Sierra Leone M966.4 J627

The story of a mission.
Johnson, Thomas Sylvester.
The story of a mission; the Sierra Leone Church, first daughter of C. M. S. With a foreword by the Archbishop of Canterbury. London, S. P. C. K., 1953.
148 p. illus. 23 cm.

1. Church of the Province of West Africa. Dioceses. Sierra Leone—Hist. 2. Church Missionary Society. I. Title.
Full name: Thomas Sylvester Claudius Johnson.

BX5682.S568 53-11016 ‡

Library of Congress [2]

M973 B81a

The story of the American Negro.
Brown, Ina Corinne, 1896-
The story of the American Negro. Decorations by Aaron Douglas. [2d rev. ed.] New York, Friendship Press [1957]
212 p. illus. 20 cm.
Includes bibliography.

1. Negroes. I. Title.

E185.6.B85 1957 57—6581 ‡

*301.451 325.260973

Library of Congress [58q10]

The story of the great war.

M350 B73

Braithwaite, William Stanley Beaumont, 1878–
The story of the great war, by William Stanley Braithwaite; with twelve illustrations in color. New York, Frederick A. Stokes company [°1919]
ix, 371 p. xii col. pl. (incl. front.) 24cm.

1. European war, 1914-1918—Juvenile literature. I. Title.

19—19870

Library of Congress D522.7.B7
——— Copy 2.
Copyright A 561033 [39y1]

The story of the "Ink Spots".

M784 W33

Watson, Deek.
The story of the "Ink Spots," by Deek Watson with Lee Stephenson. [1st ed.] New York, Vantage Press [1967]
72 p. 21 cm.

1. Ink Spots. I. Stephenson, Lee, joint author. II. Title.

ML400.W23 784'.0922 67-5817/MN

Library of Congress [3]

The story of the Negro retold.

M973 W86s 1959

Woodson, Carter Goodwin, 1875-1950.
The story of the Negro retold, by Carter G. Woodson and Charles H. Wesley. 4th ed. rev. and enl. Washington, D.C., The Associated Pub.,Inc., 1959.

472p. illus. 20cm.

The story of the Negro retold.

M973 W86s

Woodson, Carter Godwin, 1875–
The story of the Negro retold, by Carter Godwin Woodson. Washington, D. C., The Associated publishers, inc. [°1935]
viii, 369 p. incl. front., illus. (incl. ports., maps) diagr. 20cm.
"The history of the Negro in the United States."—Pref.
Bibliographies at end of each chapter except chapter XII.

1. Negroes. 2. Slavery in the U. S. I. Title.

36—484

Library of Congress E185.W898
[43t1] 325.260973

Story of the riot.

M974.7 C49

Citizens' protective league, *New York.*
Story of the riot, pub. by the Citizens' protective league. [New York, 1900]
cover-title, 79 p., 1 l. 22½cm.
"Persecution of negroes by roughs and policemen, in the city of New York, August, 1900. Statement and proofs written and compiled by Frank Moss and issued by the Citizens' protective league."

1. New York (City)—Riot, August, 1900. 2. Negroes—New York (City) I. Moss, Frank, 1860– comp. II. Title.

5—42487

Library of Congress F128.9.N3C6
[a29b1]

Stowe, Harriet Elizabeth (Beecher), 1811-1896.

M813.5 H871

Hughes, Langston
Introductory remarks and captions.

(In: Stowe, Harriet Elizabeth (Beecher) Uncle Tom's cabin. New York, Dodd, Mead, [c1952] 22cm.)

Stowe, Mrs. Harriet Elizabeth (Beecher) 1811-1896.

M350 N32c

Nell, William Cooper, 1816-1874.
The colored patriots of the American revolution, with sketches of several distinguished colored persons: to which is added a brief survey of the condition and prospects of colored Americans. By William C. Nell. With an introduction by Harriet Beecher Stowe. Boston, R. F. Wallcut, 1855.
396 p. 2 pl. (incl. front.) fold. facsim. 19½cm.

1. U. S.—Hist.—Revolution—Negro troops. 2. Negroes. I. Stowe, Mrs. Harriet Elizabeth (Beecher) 1811-1896. II. Title.

4—5729

Library of Congress E269.N3N4
[42g1]

Stowe, Lyman Beecher, 1880- joint author.

M814.4 W27s

Scott, Emmett Jay, 1873-
Booker T. Washington, builder of a civilization, by Emmett J. Scott and Lyman Beecher Stowe; illustrated from photographs. Garden City, N.Y., Doubleday, Page & company, 1916.

xx, 331, [1]p. front., plates, ports 24½cm.

M813.4 St7a

[Stowers, Walter H aslip], 1859-
Appointed; an American novel, by Sanda. Detroit, Anderson & Stowers, 1894.

371p. 20cm.
Sanda pseud of Walter H. Stowers and William H. Anderson.

I. Title. II. Anderson, William H., 1858- jt. auth.

M973.8 St8

Straker, David Augustus, 1842-1908
The new South investigated. By D. Augustus Straker ... Detroit, Mich., Ferguson printing company, 1888.
viii p., 1 l., 11-230 p. front. (port.) 20cm.

1. Southern states. 2. Negroes. I. Title.

1—21289

Library of Congress F215.S89
Copyright 1888: 23618 [a30c1]

M910 St8t

Straker, David Augustus, 1842-1908
A trip to the Windward islands; or, Then and now. By D. Augustus Straker ... Detroit, J. H. Stone & co. [°1896]
110 p. front., plates, ports. 22cm.

1. Windward islands—Descr. & trav.

1—27986

Library of Congress F2011.S89
Copyright 1896: 32171 [a31c1]

Strange, A M p.98-106

M378A1 D29p

Davis, Walker Milan, 1908-
Pushing forward; a history of Alcorn A. & M. college and portraits of some of its successful graduates, by W. Milan Davis... Okolona, Miss., The Okolona industrial school, 1938.

x, 124 p. illus, (incl. ports.) 23½cm

Strange sinner.

M813.5 J75

Jordan, Elsie.
Strange sinner. [1st ed.] New York, Pageant Press [1954]
172 p. 21 cm.

I. Title.

PZ4.J818St 54-7603 ‡

Library of Congress [3]

A strange way home.

M813.5 Ea7s

Easterling, Renée.
A strange way home [by] Renée Easterling. [1st ed.] New York, Pageant Press [1952]
136 p. 21 cm.

I. Title.

PZ3.E1315St 52-14506 ‡

Library of Congress [2]

Stranger and alone.

M810 R24s

Redding, Jay Saunders, 1906–
Stranger and alone, a novel. [1st ed.] New York, Harcourt, Brace [1950]
308 p. 21 cm.

I. Title.

PZ3.R246533St 50-5405

Library of Congress [5]

Jamaica M823.91 H35s

Stranger at the gate.

Hearne, John, 1925–
Stranger at the gate. London, Faber and Faber [1956]
304 p. 19 cm.

I. Title.

Full name: John Edgar Caulwell Hearne.

PZ4.H435St 56-36368 ‡

Library of Congress [58b1]

The stranger within our gates...

M323 Im1

Imbert, Dennis I
The stranger within our gates; a South American's impression of America's social problems, by D.I. Imbert. First edition... New Orleans, La., Watson bros. press, 1945.
102p. plate. 15cm.

Streamlets of poetry.

M811.5 P83s

Porter, George W
Streamlets of poetry, by G. W. Porter ... Memphis, Tenn., The author, c1912.
87p. front. 19cm.

The street.

M813.5 P44s 1958

Petry, Ann (Lane), 1911-
The street. London, Harborough Publishing Co., 1958.

203p. 18cm.

The street.

M813.5 P44s 1954

Petry, Ann (Lane), 1911-
The street. New York, New American Library, 1954.

270p. 18cm. (Signet giant, S1123)
Pocket book edition.
"Complete and unabridged."

The street.

M813.5 P44s

Petry, Ann (Lane)
The street. New York, New American Library, 1949.

189p. 18cm. (Signet books)
Pocket book edition.

The street.
M813.5 P44s 1947
Petry, Ann (Lane)
... The street. Boston, Houghton Mifflin company, 1946. London, M. Joseph [1947] 4 p. l., 435, [1] p. 21cm. 312p.
At head of title: Ann Petry.
Illustration on t.-p.
"A Houghton Mifflin literary fellowship novel."
I. Title.
Library of Congress PZ3.P449048t 46-1079 [5]

Strictly on our own.
M610. C63s tr
Cobb, William Montague, 1904-
Strictly on our own. The Oracle, 1947.
12, 13-14p. 28cm.

The strong breed.
Nigeria M896.2 So3f
Soyinka, Wole
Five plays: A dance of the forests, The lion and the jewel, The swamp dwellers, The trials of Brother Jero [and] The strong breed. London, Oxford University Press, 1964.
276p. 20cm. (A Three crowns book)

A street in Bronzeville.
M811.5 B791s
Brooks, Gwendolyn.
A street in Bronzeville, by Gwendolyn Brooks. New York and London, Harper & brothers, 1945.
vi, 57, [1] p. 19½cm.
Poems.
"First edition."
I. Title.
Library of Congress PS3503.R7244S8 45-7550 [46h5] 811.5

Stride toward freedom.
M323 K58s
King, Martin Luther.
Stride toward freedom; the Montgomery story. [1st ed.] New York, Harper [1958]
230 p. illus. 21 cm.
1. Segregation in transportation—Montgomery, Ala. 2. Negroes—Montgomery, Ala. 3. Montgomery, Ala.—Race question. I. Title.
E185.89.T8K5 58-7099 ‡ *301.451 325.2609761
Library of Congress [59d'60]

The strong breed.
Nigeria M896.2 So3t
Soyinka, Wolé
Three plays. Book design and illustration by Dennis Williams. Ibadan, Ibadan University Press, 1963.
118p. 21cm. (Mbari Publications).
Contents: The swamp-dwellers. The trials of Brother Jero. The strong breed.

The strength of Gideon...
M813.4 D91st
Dunbar, Paul Laurence, 1872-1906.
The strength of Gideon, and other stories, by Paul Laurence Dunbar ... with illustrations by E. W. Kemble. New York, Dodd, Mead & company, 1900.
3 p. l., 362 p. front., plates. 18½cm.
Contents.—Strength of Gideon.—Mammy Peggy's pride.—Viney's free papers.—The fruitful sleeping of the Rev. Elisha Edwards.—The ingrate.—The case of 'Ca'line.—The finish of Patsy Barnes.—One man's fortunes.—Jim's probation.—Uncle Simon's Sundays out.—Mr. Cornelius Johnson, office-seeker.—An old-time Christmas.—A mess of pottage.—The trustfulness of Polly.—The tragedy at Three Forks.—The finding of Zach.—Johnsonham, junior.—The faith cure man.—A council of state.—Silas Jackson.
I. Title.
Library of Congress PZ3.D911St 3 0-2516
Copyright 1900 A 9875 [40c1]

Strike a blow and die.
Malawi M968.97 M98
Mwase, George Simeon, ca. 1880-1962.
Strike a blow and die; a narrative of race relations in colonial Africa. Edited and introduced by Robert I. Rotberg. Cambridge, Mass., Harvard University Press, 1967.
xlii, 135 p. map, ports. 22 cm.
Bibliographical footnotes.
1. Chilembwe, John, d. 1915. 2. Malawi—Hist. I. Rotberg, Robert I., ed. II. Title.
DT862.M68 66-21342 968.97'020924 (B)
Library of Congress [5]

M326 St8u
Strother, Horatio T
The Underground railroad in Connecticut. [1st ed.] Middletown, Conn., Wesleyan University Press [1962]
262 p. illus. 22 cm.
1. Underground railroad—Connecticut.
E450.S93 973.7115 62-15122 ‡
Library of Congress [5]

Strength to love.
M252 K58
King, Martin Luther.
Strength to love. [1st ed.] New York, Harper & Row [1963]
146 p. 22 cm.
1. Baptists, Negro—Sermons. 2. Sermons, American. I. Title.
BX6452.K5 252.06 63-12051 ‡
Library of Congress [5]

A string of pearls.
M811.5 P42s
Perkins, Minnie Louise, 1932-
A string of pearls. [Chicago, Ill. c 1945]
16p. port. (on cover) 24cm.

MB9 St8
Stroyer, Jacob, 1849-
My life in the South. By Jacob Stroyer. New and enl. ed. Salem, Salem observer book and job print, 1889.
83 p. 19½ cm.
On verso of t.-p.: Third edition.
"The autobiography of an emancipated slave, born and raised on an extensive plantation in central South Carolina."—Introd.
1. Slavery in the U. S.—South Carolina. I. Title.
Library of Congress E444.S92 14-6299 [48c1]

M306 St85
Strickland, Arvarh E
History of the Chicago Urban League [by] Arvarh E. Strickland. Urbana, University of Illinois Press, 1966.
286 p. 24 cm.
Bibliography: p. [265]-272. Bibliographical footnotes.
Portrait of author on book jacket.
1. Chicago Urban League. 2. Negroes—Chicago. I. Title.
F548.9.N3S76 362.8406277311 66-18826
Library of Congress [5]

Striving to win.
M811.5 M22s
McMorris, Thomas, 1897-
Striving to win. Boston, Christopher Pub. House [1949]
144 p. 20 cm.
Poems.
I. Title.
PS3525.A27755S7 811.5 49-3153*
Library of Congress [2]

The struggle for Negro equality.
M335.4 Sa8s
Saunders, John.
The struggle for Negro equality; Program of the Socialist Workers Party, by John Saunders and Albert Parker. New York, Pioneer Publishers for the Socialist Workers Party, 1943.
30p. 22cm.

M326.99B W24s
Strickland, S.
Negro slavery described by a Negro: being the narrative of Ashton Warner, a native of St. Vincent's. With an appendix containing the testimony of four Christian ministers recently returned from the colonies on the system of slavery as it now exists. By S. Strickland... London, Samuel Maunder, 1831.
144p. 15½cm.
1. Slavery in the U.S. 2. Warner, Ashton. 3. Manumission, Deed of,. 4. Orton, Joseph. 5. Thorpe, John. 6. Trew, J.M. 7. Wright, Wm. 8. Slave narratives.

Stroke of midnight.
M813.5 C78s
Cooper, Alvin Carlos, 1925-
Stroke of midnight. Nashville, Counterpoise, 1949.
xviip. 24cm. (The Counterpoise series, no.2)

The struggle over slavery.
M326 W37
Weaver, Robert Bartow.
The struggle over slavery, by Robert B. Weaver ... Chicago, Ill., The University of Chicago press [°1938]
vii, 83, [1] p. illus. (incl. ports., map, facsim.) 23cm.
"The major portion of this volume consists of descriptions, statements, and explanations taken from source materials."—Pref.
Contents.—Early slavery in America.—Controversies over the extension of slavery.—The secession movement.—The civil war.—Reconstruction in the South.—Bibliography (p. 83-[84])
1. Slavery in the U. S.—Controversial literature. 2. U. S.—Hist.—1849-1877—Sources. I. Title.
Library of Congress E449.W34 38-17444
——— Copy 2.
Copyright A 119120 [5] 326.973

Stricklin, James, illus.
M301 R676
Williamson, Stanford Winfield.
With grief acquainted. Photographs: James Stricklin, Don Sparks [and] Jerry Cogbill. Chicago, Follett Pub. Co. [1964]
127 p. illus., port. 29 cm.
Portrait of author in book
1. Negroes—Moral and social conditions—Pictorial works. I. Stricklin, James, illus. II. Title.
E185.86.W5 301.451 64-21580
Library of Congress [5]

Strong, Edward.
M335.4 C73
The Communist position on the Negro question [by] William Z. Foster, Benjamin J. Davis, jr., Eugene Dennis [and others] ... Introduction by Nat Ross. New York, New century publishers, 1947.
61, [1] p. 22cm.
1. Negroes. 2. Communism—U. S.—1917- I. Foster, William Zebulon, 1881-
E185.61.C752 325.260973 47-24094
Library of Congress [8]

The struggles and trial of Jomo Kenyatta.
Nigeria M396.2 Ig8s
Iguh, Thomas O
The struggles and trial of Jomo Kenyatta. Onitsha, [Nigeria] Appolos & Bros. [n.d.]
56p. illus. port. 20½cm.
1. Kanyatta, Jomo, 1890- - Drama.
I. Title.

Struggles for freedom.

M326.99B Watkins, James, 1823(?)
W32s
Struggles for fre dom; or the life of James Watkins, formerly a slave in Maryland, U.S.; in which is detailed a gr phic account of his extraordinary escape from slavery, notices of the fugitive slave law, the sentiments of American div nes on the subject of slavery, etc. 19th edition... Manchester, Printed for James Watkins, 1860.

x ,11,- 104p. 18½cm.

M39
Sh2s
Stuart, Charles.
A memoir of Grenville Sharp, to which is added Sharp's "Law of retribution," By Charles Stuart. New York, American anti-slavery society, 1836.

156p. front. 19cm.
White author.

1. Sharp, Granville, 1735-1813. 2. Slavery in England. 3. Colonization. 4. Slave trade. 5. Reason, Patrick.

M368.3 **Stuart, Merah Steven,** 1878–
St46
An economic detour; a history of insurance in the lives of American Negroes, by M. S. Stuart ... New York, W. Malliet and company, 1940.

xxv, 339 p., 6 l. front., illus. (facsims.) plates, ports. 23½cm.

"Errata" slip inserted.
"First edition."
Bibliography: p. 337-338.

1. Insurance, Life—U. S.—Hist. 2. Negroes—Societies. 3. Negroes—Econ. condit. I. Title.

41—1578

Library of Congress HG8799.S75
[44h2] 368.30973

M811.08 **Student Nonviolent Coordinating Committee.**
St94
Freedom school poetry. [Compiled by Nancy Cooper] Foreword by Langston Hughes. Atlanta, 1965 [°1966]

47 p. 21 cm.

"Langston Hughes, New York, August 25, 1966."

1. American poetry—Negro authors. 2. Negroes—Civil rights—Poetry. I. Title. II. Hughes, Langston, 1902-

PS591.N4S8 811.00803 65-19797

Library of Congress [3]

Student Volunteer Movement for Kongo, Belgian.
M225 Sheppard, William Henry, 1865-1927.
Sh4e
Experiences of a pioneer missionary on the Congo.

(In: Student Volunteer Movement for Foreign Missions. International Convention, 5th, Nashville, 1906. Students and the modern missionary crusade; addresses... New York, Student Volunteer Movement for Foreign Missions 1906. 24cm. p. 291-296).

Students.

M370 **Scott, John Irving E**
Sc8f
Finding my way. Boston, Meador [1949]

344 p. 21 cm.

Includes "Recommended readings."

1. Students. I. Title.

LB2343.S38 371.8 49-11682*

Library of Congress [15]

South Africa Students, Foreign.
M378.3 Commission on Survey of Foreign Students in
N65 the United States of America.
The foreign student in America; a study, under the auspices of the Friendly Relations Committees of the Young Men's Christian Association. Edited by W. Reginald Wheeler, Henry H. King, and Alexander B. Davidson, with a foreward by Robert E. Speer. New York, Association Press, 1925.

xxxiv, 329p. incl. tables, fold, map. 23½cm.

Students, Foreign - Gt. Brit.

Africa
M323 **Tajfel, Henri,** *ed.*
T139
Disappointed guests; essays by African, Asian, and West Indian students. Edited by Henri Tajfel and John L. Dawson. London, New York, Oxford University Press, 1965.

158, [1] p. 23 cm.

"Issued under the auspices of the Institute of Race Relations."
Bibliography: p. [159]

1. Students, Foreign—Gt. Brit. 2. Gt. Brit.—Race question. 3. Race problems. I. Dawson, John L. M., joint ed. II. Institute of Race Relations. III. Title.

LA637.7.T3 370.196 65-8757

Library of Congress [2]

Studies in African music.

Rhodesia,N.
M780 **Jones, A M**
J71
Studies in African music. London, New York, Oxford University Press, 1959.

2 v. xviii plates (photos.) charts, music. 22, 28 x 32 cm.

Vol. 2 contains music dealt with in text of vol. 1 in full score; principally dance music for voices and percussion.

1. Music, African — Hist. & crit. 2. Music, Primitive. 3. Music, African. I. Title.

ML3760.J63 59—1858

Library of Congress [60j10]

Studies in American literature and history, 1.

M326 **Nichols, Charles Harold.**
N515
Many thousand gone; the ex-slaves' account of their bondage and freedom, by Charles H. Nichols. Leiden, Brill, 1963.

xvi, 229 p. 25 cm. (Studies in American literature and history, 1)

Bibliography: p. [213]-224.

1. Negroes—Biog. 2. Slavery in the U. S.—Conditions of slaves. I. Title. (Series)

E444.N5 64-55501

Library of Congress [2]

Studies in society.

Jamaica
M972.92 Patterson, Orlando.
P27
The sociology of slavery: an analysis of the origins, development and structure of Negro slave society in Jamaica. London, MacGibbon & Kee [1967]

310p. 4 plates (incl. 3 maps), tables. 22 1/2cm. (Studies in society) 63/-
Bibliography: p. 297-301.

1. Slavery in Jamaic. I. Title. (Series)

A study of some Negro-white families in the United States.

M572 **Day, Caroline (Bond)**
D33
A study of some Negro-white families in the United States by Caroline Bond Day with a foreword and notes on the anthropometric data by Earnest A. Hooton. Cambridge, Mass., Peabody museum of Harvard university, 1932.

1 p. l., ix p., 1 l., 126, [1] p. 58 pl. (incl. ports.) 28cm.

1. Ethnology. 2. Negro race. I. Hooton, Earnest Albert, 1887– II. Title.

A 34—1707

Crozer theol. sem. library for Library of Congress [a44d1]

A study of the Sutherland community, Dinwiddie county, Virginia.

M975.5 Roberts, Harry Walter, 1902
R74
A study of the Sutherland community, Dinwiddie County, Virginia. A contribution on behalf of Virginia State College to a cooperative research project of the Conference of Presidents of Negro Land-Grant Colleges and the Tennessee Valley Authority. Petersburg, Virginia State College, 1959.

74p. 23cm. (Virginia State College gazette, v.65, no.3 September 1959)

1. Dinwiddie County, Virginia. 2. Virginia. 3. Sutherland Community, Virginia. I. Title.

The study of the New Testament.

M220 Vass, S[amuel] N 1866-
V44s
The study of the New Testament, by S.N. Vass. Nashville, Tenn., Published by the Sunday School Publishing Board [1932]

197p. 19cm.

M326. **Stutler, Boyd Blynn,** 1889–
St9
Captain John Brown and Harper's Ferry, the story of the raid and the old fire engine house known as John Brown's fort, by Boyd B. Stutler. Harper's Ferry, W. Va., Storer college, 1930.

40 p. illus. (incl. ports., facsims.) 23cm.

Second edition.
White author?

1. Brown, John, 1800-1859. 2. Harper's Ferry, W. Va.—Hist.

30-18184

Library of Congress E451.S932
——— Copy 2.
Copyright A 24990 [3] 973.68

M331 **Styles, Fitzhugh Lee,** 1899–
St99
How to be successful Negro Americans, by Fitzhugh Lee Styles ... A guide to success in life and business for Negroes in America. Boston, The Christopher publishing house [°1941]

xiv, 15-102 p. front. (port.) 19cm.

1. Negroes—Employment. 2. Negroes. I. Title.

41—22996

Library of Congress E185.8.S97
[42d3] 325.260973

M342 **Styles, Fitzhugh Lee,** 1899–
St9
Negroes and the law in the race's battle for liberty, equality and justice under the Constitution of the United States; with causes celebres, by Fitzhugh Lee Styles ... Boston, The Christopher publishing house [°1937]

xi, [1], 13-320 p. front. (port.) 24cm.

The manuscript of the author's address before the National bar association at Baltimore, August 1934, on the battle of the Negro at the bar of justice, is the basis of this book. *cf.* Pref.
Bibliography: p. 320.

1. Negroes — Legal status, laws, etc. 2. Negroes—Biog. 3. Negro lawyers. 4. Law reports, digests, etc.—U. S. I. Title.

37—3583

Library of Congress E185.61.S92
——— Copy 2.
Copyright A 103799 [38g3] 325.260973

M814.5 Subject of life.
Ev1s
Evans, Phillip.
Subject of life; Step of life; The goodness of a woman. Chicago, The author, 1946.

12p. 17cm.

Success.

M131 **Anderson, Garland.**
An2u
Uncommon sense; the law of life in action, by Garland Anderson ... ~~London, L. N. Fowler & co.~~ [New York, The author] [1933]

220 p. 19cm.

1. New thought. 2. Faith-cure. 3. Success. I. Title.

34-488

Library of Congress BF639.A66 1933
——— Copy 2.
Copyright A ad int. 18321 [3] [159.91324] 131.324

Success.

M174 **Pace, Harry Herbert,** 1884–
P11b
Beginning again, by Harry H. Pace. Philadelphia, Dorrance & company, inc. [°1934]

72 p. front. 19½cm.

1. Success. 2. Will. I. Title.

35-734

Library of Congress HF5386.P13
Copyright A 78810 [2] 174

Sudan.

M966.2 Maran, René, 1887-
M32t
Le Tchad de sable et d'or, par René Maran. Documentation de Pierre Deloncle, couverture en couleurs de Charles Fouqueray. Paris, Librairie de la revue francaise [c1931]

159p. 21cm.

Sudan - Biog.

Sudan, French
M966.2
T22

Tedzkiret en-nisian fi akhbar molouk es-Soudan. Traduction française par O. Houdas. Paris, E. Leroux, 1901.

2v. xiv, 418 p. 29 cm. (Publications de l'École des langues orientales vivantes. 4. sér., v. 20)

Added is a fragment on the history of Sokoto (p. ₍303₎-361) by a certain Hadj Sa'id.

On cover: Documents arabes relatifs à l'histoire du Soudan.

Contents - v.1 Texte arabe. v.2. Traduction, par O. Houdas

1. Sudan — Biog. 2. Sokoto, Nigeria (Province) — Biog. I. Houdas, Octave Victor, 1840-1916, ed. and tr. II. Title: Documents arabes relatifs à l'histoire du Soudan. (Series: Paris. École des langues orientales vivantes. Publications. 4. sér., v. 20)

PJ7819.S8T4 52-59060

Library of Congress ₍3₎

Sudan - Hist.

Sudan, Egyptian
M962.4
N56g

Nigumi, Mohammed A

A great trusteeship. London, The Caravel Press ₍1957₎

175 p. illus. 22 cm.

1. Sudan—Hist. 2. British in Sudan. I. Title.

DT108.6.N5 962.4 58-29817 ‡

Library of Congress ₍58c1₎

Sudan - History.

Sudan
M962.4
Y16

Yangu, Alexis Mbali.

The Nile turns red; Azanians chose freedom against Arab bondage. Edited by A. G. Mondini. ₍1st ed. New York₎ Pageant Press ₍°1966₎

xviii, 184 p. map. 21 cm.

Bibliography: p. 182-184.

1. Sudan—Hist. 2. Sudan—Race question. I. Title.

DT108.7.Y3 962.9'04 66-29146

Library of Congress ₍3₎

Sudan - Race question.

Sudan
M962.4
Y16

Yangu, Alexis Mbali.

The Nile turns red; Azanians chose freedom against Arab bondage. Edited by A. G. Mondini. ₍1st ed. New York₎ Pageant Press ₍°1966₎

xviii, 184 p. map. 21 cm.

Bibliography: p. 182-184.

1. Sudan—Hist. 2. Sudan—Race question. I. Title.

DT108.7.Y3 962.9'04 66-29146

Library of Congress ₍3₎

Sudan, Egyptian.

Sudan
Egyptian
MB9
W69i

Wilson, Salim C

I was a slave. (Hatashil Masha Kathish). With twelve half-tone illustrations. London, Stanley Paul and Co., n.d.

256p. ports., illus. 21½cm.

Soudan,
Egyptian
M962.4
Ab1s

Sudan, Egyptian - Hist.

Abbas, Mekki.

The Sudan question; the dispute over the Anglo-Egyptian condominium, 1884-1951. New York, F.A. Praeger ₍1952₎

xix, 201p. maps (1 fold. col.) 23cm. (Colonial and comparative studies)

Bibliography: p. 185-189.

Sudan
Egyptian
M962.4
Sh61

Sudan, Egyptian - Hist.

Shibeika, Mekki.

British policy in the Sudan, 1882-1902. London, New York, Oxford University Press, 1952.

439 p. maps. 23 cm.

Bibliography: p. ₍426₎-430.

1. Sudan, Egyptian—Hist. 2. British in the Sudan. I. Title.

DT108.3.S4 962.4 53-766

Library of Congress ₍2₎

Sudan, Egyptian-Politics and govt.

Nigeria
M966.9
F11s

Fabunmi, L A

The Sudan in Anglo-Egyptian relations; a case study in power politics 1800-1956. London, Longmans, Green and Co., 1960.

466p. 22cm.

Sudan, French.

Mali
M966.2
Ou1e

Ouane, Ibrahima Mamadou, 1908-

L'énigme du Macina. Préface de Maurice Kaouza. Monte-Carlo, Regain, 1952.

187p. 19½cm.

Sudan, French - Folktales.

Mali
M398
Si8

Sissoko, Fily-Dabo

Crayons et protraits. Paris, Imprimerie Union Mulnouse, n.d.

79p. 23cm.

Sudan, French-History.

Mali
M966.2
Ab3d

'Abd al-Raḥmān ibn 'Abd Allāh, *al-Sa'dī*, 1596-ca. 1655.

Documents arabes relatifs à l'histoire du Soudan: Tarikh es-Soudan, par Abderrahman ben Abdallah ben 'Imran ben 'Amir es-Sa'ḍi ... édité par O. Houdaś ... avec la collaboration de Edm. Benoist ... Paris, E. Leroux, 1898-1900.

2 v. 28½cm. (*Half-title:* Publications de l'École des langues orientales vivantes, IVe sér., vol. XII-XIII)

History of Timbuktu and the surrounding region under Moroccan rule during the 16th and 17th centuries.

CONTENTS.—v. 1. Texte arabe.—v. 2. ₍Traduction₎ par O. Houdas.

1. Sudan, French—Hist. 2. Timbuktu—Hist. I. Houdas, Octave Victor, 1840-1916, ed. and tr. II. *Benoist, Edmond, 1871- ed. III. Title. IV. Title: Tarikh es-Soudan.

44-44091

Library of Congress PJ7819.S8A23 ₍3₎

Sudan, French-History.

Mali
M966.2
M31d

Mahmūd Kati ibn al-Hāj al-Mutawakkil Káti 1468-1593.

Documents arabes relatifs à l'histoire du Soudan: Tarikh El-Fettach; ou, chronique du chercheur pour servir a l'histoire des Villes, des Armées et des principaux personages du Tekrour par Mahmoûd ben El 'Hâdj El-Motaouakkel Kâti. tr. Française par O. Houdas et M. Delafosse. Paris, Ernest Leroux, 1913.

2v. 28½cm.

The Sudan in Anglo-Egyptian relations.

Nigeria
M966.9
F11s

Fabunmi, L A

The Sudan in Anglo-Egyptian relations; a case study in power politics 1800-1956. London, Longmans, Green and Co., 1960.

466p. 22cm.

Soudan,
Egyptian
M962.4
Ab1s

The Sudan Question.

Abbas, Mekki.

The Sudan question; the dispute over the Anglo-Egyptian condominium, 1884-1951. New York, F. A. Praeger ₍1952₎

xix, 201 p. maps (1 fold. col.) 23 cm. (Colonial and comparative studies)

Bibliography: p. 185-189.

1. Sudan, Egyptian—Hist. I. Title. (Series)

[DT108.A] A 52-9820

Detroit. Public Library for Library of Congress ₍10₎

Sudanese poetry.

Sudan
M896.1
T28

Tescaroli, Livio, comp.

Poesia Sudanese. ₍Bolonga₎ Editrice Nigrizia, 1961.

119p. illus. 21½cm. (Museum Combonianum, No. 12)

Appendice musicale: p. 87-117.

White compiler.

Suffrage

see

Politics and suffrage

MB9
G19s

Suffrage league of Boston and vicinity. *Garrison centenary committee.*

The celebration of the one hundredth anniversary of the birth of William Lloyd Garrison, by the colored citizens of greater Boston, under the auspices of the Suffrage league of Boston and vicinity, December tenth and eleventh, MCMV, with abridged accounts of celebrations held by certain churches of greater Boston, Sunday evening, December tenth, in response to appeal of the Suffrage league. Reported by Miss Ethel Lewis ... ed. by the secretary of the Suffrage league centenary committee. Boston, The Garrison centenary committee of the Suffrage league of Boston and vicinity, 1906.

3 p. l., 11-75, ₍1₎ p. front. (port.) illus. 24cm.

1. Garrison, William Lloyd, 1805-1879. 2. Boston, Mass. I. Lewis, Ethel.

6-18976

Library of Congress E449.G257

Copyright A 137143 ₍a27d1₎

Haiti
M630
P66p

Sugar cane.

Pierre-Louis, Regnier.

Notes sur la canne à sucre. Port-au-Prince, Barthélemy. ₍1948?₎

20p. 20cm.

Haitian author.

A suggested course of study for county training schools for Negroes in the South.

M06
J61
no. 18

John F. Slater fund.

A suggested course of study for county training schools for negroes in the South. ₍Lynchburg, Va., J. P. Bell company, inc., printers₎ 1917.

79 p. incl. front., illus., plates. plan. 24cm. (*On cover:* The trustees of the John F. Slater fund. Occasional papers, no. 18)

1. Negroes—Education. 2. Teachers, Training of—Southern states. I. Title.

17-30810

Library of Congress E185.5.J65 no. 18

——— Copy 2. ₍a36k1₎

Les suicidés d'une classe.

Haiti
M972.94
Au4

Auguste, Gérard Bonaparte.

Les suicidés d'une classe. Port-au-Prince, Éditions ouvrières, 1957.

xv, 61 p. 21 cm.

1. Labor and laboring classes—Haiti. 2. Haiti—Soc. condit. I. Title.

A 59-3958

Florida. Univ. Library for Library of Congress ₍2₎

Suite pour un visage.

Martinique
M841.91
L55su

Léopold, Emmanuel-Flavia

Suite pour un visage, poème suivi d'une ode. Paris, Éditions des Cahiers Libres, 1926.

23p. 19cm.

Inscribed by author.

Africa
M960
Af83

Sule, Alhaji Maitama, 1927-
Political and economic problems of Africa.

Pp. 83-92.

In: African Conference on Progress through Cooperation. Africa. New York, Dodd, Mead, 1966.

M616
W93e2

Sulfathalidine.
Wright, Louis Tompkins, 1891-1952.
The effect of sulfathalidine on the bleeding and clotting time of the blood and prolongation reduction by the administration of vitamin K, by Louis T. Wright, Frank R. Cole, and Lyndon M. Hill. Reprinted from Surgery, gynecology and obstetrics, 88:201-208, February 1949.

M616
W93s

Sulfathalidine.
Wright, Louis Tompkins, 1891-1952.
Sulfathalidine in low postoperative fistulas of the ileum, by Louis T. Wright, and Frank R. Cole. Reprinted from the American journal of surgery. 75:852-853. June 1948.

Sullivan, May (Miller)

see

Miller, May

Africa
M896
Su5c

Sulzer, Peter, comp.
Christ erscheint am Kongo; Afrikanische Erzählungen und Gedichte gesammelt und Gedichte gesammelt und ubertragen von Peter Sulzer. Heilbronn, Eugen Salzer. [1958,

255p. 20cm.
Biography: p. 248-251.
White compiler.

1. Poetry - Africa. 2. Short stories.
3. Hughes, Langston. I. Title.

Sumner, Charles.
Langston, John Mercer, 1829-1897.
M815
L26

Freedom and citizenship. Selected lectures and addresses of Hon. John Mercer Langston... With an introductory sketch by Rev. J. E. Rankin... Washington, D.C., R. H. Darby, 1883.
286 p. front. (port.) 20cm.

M808.8
P21

The summer fire.
Dodson, Owen Vincent, 1914-
The summer fire.

Pp. 231-245.
(In: The Paris review. Best short stories. New York, Dutton, 1959. 21cm.)

Haiti
M972.94
H24

A summer on the borders of the Caribbean Sea.
Harris, J Dennis.
A summer on the borders of the Caribbean Sea. By J. Dennis Harris. With an introduction by George William Curtis. New York, A. B. Burdick, 1860.
xi, [13]-179 p. 18½cm.

Contents.—Dominican Republic.—Republic of Hayti.—Grand Turk's and Caicos Islands.—British Honduras.—Conclusive summary.—Appendix.

1. Haiti—Descr. & trav. 2. Haiti—Hist. 3. British Honduras. 4. Turks and Caicos Islands. I. Title.

Library of Congress F2171.H29 2—12367
[a42b1]

M323.4
H742

The summer that didn't end.
Holt, Len, 1928-
The summer that didn't end. New York, Morrow, 1965.
351 p. map. 22 cm.

1. Civil rights—Mississippi. 2. ~~Negroes—Civil rights.~~ I. Title.

E185.61.H75 323.4 65-18521
Library of Congress [5]

M323
Su6

Summit Meeting of National Negro Leaders, Washington, D. C., 1958.
Report of proceedings [of] Summit Meeting of Negro Leaders, Washington, D.C., May 12, 13, 1958. Sponsored by National Newspaper Publishers Association. [Washington, National Newspaper Publishers Association] 1958.

137p. illus. 33cm.
Contents.- Speech, by William O. Walker.- Speech, by A. Philip Randolph.- Speech, by Paul H. Cooke.- Address, by Roy Wilkins.-

(Continued on next card)

M323
Su6

Summit Meeting of National Negro Leaders, Washington, D. C., 1958. Report of proceedings. 1958. (Card 2)

Contents - Continued.
Speech by Thurgood Marshall.- How shall we travel the road of freedom together, by F. L. Shuttleworth.
At head of title: Lighting the way to freedom.
Mimeographed.
1. Race relations. 2. Civil rights.
3. Freedom. I. Title. II. National Newspaper Publishers Association.

Sierra Leone
M496
Su6hm

Sumner, A T
A hand-book of the Mende language, by the Rev. A. T. Sumner... Freetown, Government printing office, 1917.
2 p. l., [vii]-xiv, 191 p. 21½cm.

1. Mende language—Grammar.

Library of Congress PL8511.S8 44-17472
[2] 496.4

Sierra Leone
M496
Su6h

Sumner, A. T.
A handbook of the Sherbro language, by Rev. A. T. Sumner. London, The Crown Agents for the colonies, 1921.
xii, 132p. 21½cm.

1. Sherbro language—Grammar ~~2. Sierra Leino-Language~~

Sierra Leone
M496
Su6ht

Sumner, A T
A handbook of the Temne language, by the Rev. A.T. Sumner... Freetown, Sierra Leone West Africa, Government printing office, 1922.
xvi, 157p. 21½cm.

1. Temne language - Grammar.

MB9
Su6

Sumner, Charles, 1811-1874.
A memorial of Charles Sumner ... Boston, 1874.
316 p. front. 22cm.
White author.

I. Elliott, Robert B. Oration. p. 265-287.

MB9
Su6c

Sumner, Charles, 1811-1874.
Cornell, William Mason, 1802-1895, ed.
Charles Sumner; memoir and eulogies. A sketch of his life by the editor, an original article by Bishop Gilbert Haven, and the eulogies pronounced by eminent men. Ed. by William M. Cornell. Boston, J. H. Earle, 1874.

336p. port. plates. 19cm.
Included eulogies by Carl Schurz and G. W. Curtis.

MB9
Su6e

Sumner, Charles, 1811-1874.
Elliott, Robert Browne, 1842-
... Oration of the Hon. Robert B. Elliott, of South Carolina, Delivered in Faneuil Hall, April 14, 1874, under the auspices of the Colored Citizens of Boston. Boston, Published for the Committee of Arrangements, by Charles L. Mitchell, 1874.
[34]p. 23cm.

MB9
Su6e

Sumner, Charles, 1811-1874.
Evangeline, *pseud.*
Oration on Charles Sumner, addressed to colored people ... By Evangeline. Albany, Weed, Parsons & co., printers, 1874.
53 p. 23cm.
Illustrated cover.
Cover-title: Sumner, the friend of humanity. Oration delivered at Washington by Evangeline.
Blank verse.

1. Sumner, Charles, 1811-1874. I. Title.

[33b1] 19-12977
Library of Congress E415.9.S9E9

MB9
Su6g

Sumner, Charles, 1811-1874.
Grimké, Archibald Henry, 1849-1930.
The life of Charles Sumner, the scholar in politics, by Archibald H. Grimke ... New York [etc.] Funk & Wagnalls company, 1892.
viii, [9]-415 p. front. (port.) 19cm. (*On cover: American reformers, ed. by C. Martyn*)

1. Sumner, Charles, 1811-1874.

Library of Congress E176.A52 9—7790
——— Copy 2. E415.9.S9G84
[a39f1]

W. Indies
M523
R14s

Sun.
Ramsay, Obadiah Anderson.
The sun has no heat, by Obadiah Anderson Ramsay. [New York, °1939]
5 p. l., 204 p. chart. 22cm.

1. Cosmology—Curiosa and miscellany. 2. Heat. 3. Sun. I. Title.

Library of Congress QB52.R35 39-33950
——— Copy 2.
Copyright A 134352 [2] 523.0888

M812.5
H87su

The sun do move.
Hughes, Langston, 1902-
The sun do move; A music-play. New York, International Workers Order, 1942.

42p. 36cm.
Mimeographed.

W. Indies
M523
R14s
The sun has no heat.
Ramsay, Obadiah Anderson.
The sun has no heat, by Obadiah Anderson Ramsay. [New York, °1939]
5 p. l., 204 p. chart. 22cm.
1. Cosmology—Curious and miscellany. 2. Heat. 3. Sun. I. Title.
Library of Congress QB52.R35 39-33950
——— Copy 2.
Copyright A 134352 [2] 523.0883

Guinea
M398.2
N51
Sundiata.
Niane, Djibrie Tamsir
Sundiata; an epic of old Mali. Translated by G. D. Pickett. [London] Longmans [1965]
96p. map. 20½cm.
1. Tales, African. I. Title.

M301
D853so6
1954
The suppression of the African slave-trade to the United States of America, 1638-1870.
Du Bois, William Edward Burghardt, 1868-
The suppression of the African slave-trade to the United States of America, 1638-1870. New York, The Social Science Press, 1954.
335p. 22cm.

M915.5
G88
V.1, no.14
Sunday, Billy.
Grimke, Francis James, 1850-1931.
Rev. "Billy" Sunday's Campaign in Washington, D.C., January 6 - March 3, 1918, by Rev. Francis J. Grimke. Washington, 1918
4p. 23cm.

Zanzibar
M398
D64s
Sungura mjanja.
Diva, David Edward
Sungura mjanja [Hare is a rascal] East African tales. Illustrated by Ruth Yudelowitz. Nairobi, Eagle Press, 1953.
29p. illus. 15½cm.
Written in Swahili and English.
1. Africa, East - Folk tales. 2. Tales, African. I. Title. II. Title: Hare is a rascal.

M323.4
B45s
Supreme Court.
Berger, Morroe.
The Supreme Court and group discrimination since 1937. Reprinted Columbia law revise, 49:201-230, February 1949.
201-230p. 26cm.
Inscribed by author: For Arthur B. Spingarn, with my compliments, Morroe Berger.

M268
Sh1s
Sunday-schools.
Shackleford, William H
Sunday school problems, written especially for Sunday school workers, by Wm. H. Shackleford... n.p. A.M.E. Sunday school union n.d.
v. 19½cm.
volume 1 and 2 bound together.

Brazil
M869.3
Am 1p
Suor.
Amado, Jorge, 1912-
O país do carnaval. Cacau. Suor. São Paulo, Livraria Martins Editôra [1944]
317 p. 21 cm. (Obras)
Each pt. previously pub. separately.
I. Title. II. Title: Cacau. III. Title: Suor.
PQ9697.A647P3 1944 869.3 48-13882*
Library of Congress [2]

M323.4
M35s
Supreme Court.
Marshall, Thurgood, 1908-
The supreme court as protector of civil rights; Equal protection of the laws. Reprinted from the Annals of the American Academy of Political and Social Science. Philadelphia, 1951.
101-110p. 24cm.

M220
V44h
Sunday-schools.
Vass, Samuel N 1866-
How to study and teach the Bible, by S. N. Vass ... Teacher training book, National Baptist convention, U. S. A. Nashville, Tenn., Sunday school publishing board [°1922]
2 p. l., 7-633, [1] p. illus., plates, ports., maps, fold. tab. 19½cm.
1. Bible—Study. 2. Sunday-schools. I. Title.
Library of Congress BS600.V3 22-25580
Copyright A 692433 [a33c1]

M301
D853su3
The superior race.
Du Bois, William Edward Burghardt, 1868-
The superior race (an essay) by W.E. Burghardt Du Bois, [n.p., n.p., n.d.]
55-60p. 24½cm.

M304
P19
v.7
no.7
M347.9
W58n
M323
W587ne3
Supreme court.
White, Walter Francis, 1893-
The Negro and the supreme court, by Walter White. Reprinted from Harper's magazine, January, 1931 for the National association for the advancement of colored people, New York.
11p. 24½cm.

M268.76
T66s
Sunday schools - pageants.
Townsend, Willa A arr.
A song in the night time; a Christmas pageant-program for Sunday schools, arranged by Mrs. W.A. Townsend. Nashville, Tenn., Sunday school publishing board n.d.
16p. 23cm.
Music included.

M223.2
P87
A supervised life.
Powell, W H R
A supervised life; or, Impressions from the Twenty-third psalm, by W. H. R. Powell ... [Philadelphia, Press of B. F. Emery company, 1945]
xiii, 145 p. plates. 19cm.
1. Bible. O. T. Psalms xxiii—Sermons. 2. Baptists—Sermons. 3. Sermons, American. I. Title.
45-5226
Library of Congress BS1450 23d.P6
[3] 223.2

M323.4
B45s
The Supreme Court and group discrimination since 1937.
Berger, Morroe.
The Supreme Court and group discrimination since 1937. Reprinted Columbia law revise, 49:201-230, February 1949.
201-230p. 26cm.
Inscribed by author: For Arthur B. Spingarn, with my compliments, Morroe Berger.

M220
Su7c
Sunday-school literature.
National Baptist Convention, U.S.A.
Sunday School Publishing Board. Commentary on the international and improved uniform lessons for 1937. Nashville, The Board, 19
321p. illus. map. 24cm.
Editor: J. T. Brown.

M370
C12su
Supervision of the education of Negroes...
Caliver, Ambrose, 1894-
Supervision of the education of Negroes as a function of state departments of education, by Ambrose Caliver, senior specialist in the education of Negroes ... Federal security agency, Paul V. McNutt, administrator. U. S. Office of education, John W. Studebaker, commissioner. [Washington, U. S. Govt. print. off., 1941]
vi, 45 p. 23cm. (U. S. Office of education. Bulletin 1940, no. 6. Studies of state departments of education. Monograph no. 11)
1. Negroes—Education. 2. Negroes—[U. S.] I. Title.
E 41-105
U. S. Off. of educ. Library for Library of Congress [L111.A6 1940, no. 6]
[10] (370.6173)

Haiti
M843.91
L193
Sur la route de la vie.
Lamothe, Leduc B
Sur la route de la vie; quelques pages de Cudel au coin des amateurs d'art. Préface de Me. J. B. Cinéas. Port-au-Prince, Editions Henri Deschamps, 1960.
112p. 21cm.
Portrait of author in book.

M263
Sc8s
Sunday, The Christian Sabbath.
Scott, Timothy D
Sunday, The Christian Sabbath, a brief discussion of the Sunday question, by the Reverend Timothy D.Scott... Springfield, Ohio, The Whyte printing co. n.d.
137p. front. 20½cm.

M301
D853su6
The suppression of the African slave-trade to the United States of America.
Du Bois, William Edward Burghardt, 1868-
The suppression of the African slave-trade to the United States of America, 1638-1870, by W. E. Burghardt Du Bois ... New York, London, etc.] Longmans, Green, and co., 1896.
xi, 335 p. diagrs. 23 cm. (Half-title: Harvard historical studies, vol. I)
Appendices: A. A chronological conspectus of colonial and state legislation restricting the African slave-trade, 1641-1787.—B. A chronological conspectus of state, national, and international legislation, 1788-1871.—C. Typical cases of vessels engaged in the American slave-trade, 1619-1864.—D. Bibliography (p. [299]-325)
1. Slave-trade—U. S. 2. Slave-trade. I. Title.
2—23269
Library of Congress E441.D81
[39q1] 326.10973

Haiti
M844
B45
Sur les routes qui montent.
Bernard, Regnor C
Sur les routes qui montent. Port-au-Prince, Les Presses Libres, 1954.
67p. 21cm (Collection du cent cinquantenaire)

Haiti
M841
D774
Sur les traces de Caonabo et de Toussaint-Louverture.
Dorismond, Jean Baptiste.
Sur les traces de Caonabo et de Toussaint-Louverture; poèmes caraïbes ₍par₎ Félix Desroussels ₍pseud.₎ Préf. de Jean-Baptiste Dorismond. Port-au-Prince, Impr. de l'État, 1953.
246 p. 21 cm. (Collection du cent-cinquantenaire)
1. Caribbean area—Hist.—Poetry. 2. Poetry of places—Caribbean area. I. Title.
PQ2607.O6473S8 54-32879 ‡
Library of Congress ₍1₎

M617
C24s
Surgery-Cases, clinical reports.
Carter, Sylvester J
Serum amylase findings in chronic alcoholic patients with acute, severe abdominal symptoms. Annals of Surgery, July, 1945.
117-121p. tables. 25cm.

M614
R66su
Survival values diminishing returns and the margin of safety.
Roman, Charles Victor, 1864-1934.
Survival values diminishing returns and the margin of safety. Tuskegee, Tuskegee Institute, 1932.
14p. 23cm.

Haiti
M841.1
R76
Sur les vieux thèmes.
Rouzier, Mona.
Sur les vieux thèmes. Port-au-Prince, N. A. Théodore ₍1958₎
57 p. 18 cm.
Poems.
I. Title.
A 59-2240
Florida. Univ. Library for Library of Congress ₍1₎

Surinam
M988
K83
Surinam.
Kom, A de,
Wij slaven van suriname, door A. De Kom. Amsterdam, Uitgevers-Mij. Contact ₍c1934₎
234p. portrait. 20½cm.

Haiti
M572
B43s
Survivances Africaines en Amérique.
Benjamin, Georges J
Survivances Africaines en Amérique. Série I-Essai d'Antropologie du Télédiol. Paris, Jean D'Halluin, Editeur, 1956.
94p. 19½cm. (Collection Alternance)

Haiti
M841
O88s
...Sur ma flute de bambou.
Orimard, Luc
...Sur ma flute de bambou; poemes... Paris, Les editions de la nef, 1926.
123p. 18½cm.

Nigeria
M896.3
K127s
The surprise packet.
Kamalu, Sigis
The surprise packet. Port Harcourt, V. C. Okeanu ₍n.d.₎
54p. port. 18cm.

Barbados
M823
C55s
The survivors of the crossing.
Clarke, Austin C
The survivors of the crossing. London, Heinemann, 1964.
202p. 19½cm.
Portrait of author on book jacket.
I. Title.

Guinea
M966
N51
Suret-Canale, Jean, jt. auth.
Niane, Djibril Tamsir
Histoire de l'Afrique Occidentale, par Djibril Tamsir Niane et J. Suret-Canale. ₍Paris₎ Présence Africaine ₍1961₎
223p. maps. 24cm.

M323.22
Su7n
Survey associates, inc., New York.
Survey midmonthly.
... The Negro in the cities of the North ... New York, The Charity organization society, °1905.
2 p. l., 96 p. illus., plates. 26cm.
At head of title: Charities publication committee.
Reprint of Charities, October 7, 1905.
1. Negroes. I. Survey associates, inc., New York. II. Title.
6-2281 Revised
Library of Congress E185.9.S96 ₍r45c2₎

Jamaica
M823.91
D37s
Susan Proudleigh.
De Lisser, Herbert George, 1878-
Susan Proudleigh, by Herbert G. de Lisser. London, Methuen & co., ltd. ₍1915₎
309, 21p. 19½cm.

M813.5
An2s
Surgeon in black.
Andrews, Owen M
Surgeon in black. New York, Comet Press Books ₍1956₎
282 p. 21 cm.
I. Title.
PZ4.A554Su 56-12155 ‡
Library of Congress ₍2₎

M323
Su7n
Survey midmonthly
... The Negro in the cities of the North ... New York, The Charity Organization Society, 1905.
96p. illus. tables. 26cm.
Partial contents: -Should Negro business men go south, by Booker T. Washington. -The black vote of Philadelphia, by W.E.B. Du Bois. Social bonds in the black belt: Chicago, by Fannie B. Williams. Negro dependence in Baltimore, by Helen Pendleton.

U.S.
M966.7
An24
Suten dan wani hwe fie.
Anderson, Rosa Claudette.
River, face homeward (Suten dan wani hwe fie); an Afro-American in Ghana. ₍1st ed.₎ New York, Exposition Press ₍1966₎
120, ₍1₎ p. illus., ports. 21 cm.
"References": p. ₍121₎
1. Ghana—Soc. life & cust. I. Title. II. Title: Suten dan wani hwe fie.
DT510.4.A58 916.67 66-8809
Library of Congress ₍3₎

Haiti
M610
P61p
Surgery.
Pierre-Louis, Constant.
Pathologie chirurgicale a l'usage de l'etudiant Haitien. Portau-Prince. Imp. Telhomme, 1948.
386p. illus. 22cm. (Bibliothèque Haitienne)

M323
Su7n
Survey midmonthly
The Negro in the cities of the North ... (card 2)
The Negro today in music, by James W. Johnson. - Social settlement in Washington, by Sarah C. Fernandis. -The Negro Press in America, by L.M. Hershaw. -The Negro in times of industrial unrest, by R.R. Wright.
I. a.t. Washington, B.T. II. a.t. DuBois, W.E.B III. a.t. Wright, R.R. IV. a.t. Hershaw, L.M. V. a.t.Williams VI. a.t. Pendleton, H.B.
F.B.

South Africa
M896.3
S52m
Sutherland, Efua
New life at Kyerefaso.
Pp. 79-86.
In: Rive, Richard, ed. Modern African prose. London, Heinemann Educational Books, 1964.

M016.6
H22p
Surgery--Bibliography.
Harlem Hospital. New York (City)
Partial bibliography of surgical papers by members of the surgical staff of Harlem Hospital, based on material from Harlem Hospital, 1910-1946. New York, Harlem Hospital, 194 .
8p. 28cm.
Mimeographed.

M976.7
W93
Survey of Negroes in Little Rock and North Little Rock...
Writers' program. *Arkansas.*
Survey of Negroes in Little Rock and North Little Rock, compiled by the Writers' program of the Work projects administration in the state of Arkansas. Sponsored by the Urban league of greater Little Rock, Arkansas. ₍Little Rock, °1941₎
4 p. l., 101 p. incl. tables. 28cm.
Bibliography: p. 99-101.
1. Negroes—Little Rock, Ark. 2. Negroes—North Little Rock, Ark. I. Title.
41-4905
Library of Congress F419.L7W85 ₍3₎ 325.2609767

Ghana
M896.1
Su8p
Sutherland, Efua.
Playtime in Africa. Text by Efua Sutherland. Photos. by Willis E. Bell. ₍1st ed.₎ New York, Atheneum, 1962.
56 p. illus. 24 cm.
1. Children in Africa—Juvenile literature. 2. Games. I. Bell, Willis E., illus. II. Title.
PZ9.S9476Pl j916 62-7368 ‡
Library of Congress ₍62k5₎

Ghana
M966.7
Su8
Sutherland, Efua.
The roadmakers. Photos. by William E. Bell. Planned and written by Efua Sutherland. Accra, Ghana Information Services [1961]
unp. (chiefly illus.) 32cm.
1. Ghana-Description and travel. I. Bell, William E. II. Title.

Zanzibar
M896.1
M87
Swahili literature.
Msham, Mwana Kupona (Binti) 1810-1860?
The advice of Mwana Kupona upon the wifely duty, from the Swahili texts, by Alice Werner and William Hichens. Medstead, Hampshire, The Azania press [1934]
95p. illus. 19½cm.

Zanzibar
M398
F25
Bk.1
Swahili sayings from Zanzibar.
Farsi, Shaabar Saleh.
Swahili sayings from Zanzibar. Book 1, Proverbs. Dar es Salaam, East African Literature Bureau, 1962.
52p. 18½cm.
Written in Swahili.
1. Folk-lore - Zanzibar. 2. Swahili proverbs. 3. Zanzibar - Folk-lore. I. Title.

Sutherland Community, Virginia.
M975.5
R74
Roberts, Harry Walter, 1902
A study of the Sutherland community, Dinwiddie County, Virginia. A contribution on behalf of Virginia State College to a cooperative research project of the Conference of Presidents of Negro Land-Grant Colleges and the Tennessee Valley Authority. Petersburg, Virginia State College, 1959.
74p. 23cm. (Virginia State College gazette, v.65, no.3 September 1959)
1. Dinwiddie County, Virginia. 2. Virginia 3. Sutherland Community, Virginia. I. Title.

Swahili literature.
Africa
M896.3
V54
Velten, Carl, 1862- comp.
Swahili prose texts; a selection from the material collected by Carl Velten from 1893 to 1896. Edited and translated by Lyndon Harries. London, Oxford University Press, 1965.
viii, 298 p. 22 cm.
Swahili and English.
The Swahili texts were first published in the compiler's Safari za Wasuaheli and Desturi za Wasuaheli.
1. Swahili literature. I. Harries, Lyndon, ed. and tr. II. Title.
PL8704.A2V4 916.76 65-3830
Library of Congress [2]

Zanzibar
M398
F25
Bk.2
Swahili sayings from Zanzibar.
Farsi, Shaaban Saleh
Swahili sayings from Zanzibar. Book 2 Riddles and superstitions. Dar es Salaam, East African Literature Bureau, 1963.
32p. 18cm.
Written in Swahili.
1. Riddles, African. 2. Folk-lore,- Zanzibar. I. Title.

S. Africa
M896.3
Sw1
Swaartbooi, Victoria N M , 1907-1937
U-Mandisa. Lovedale, Lovedale Press, 1946.
47p. 18cm.
"Mandisa, the bringer of joy."

Zanzibar
M398
Z17
Swahili literature.
Zanzibar tales told by natives of the east coast of Africa; translated from the original Swahili by George W. Bateman, illustrated by Walter Bobbett. Chicago, A. C. McClurg & co., 1901.
8 p. l., [5]-224 p. incl. illus., plates. 19cm.
Added t.-p., illustrated.
Stories about animals.
1. Swahili literature. 2. Folk-lore—Zanzibar. 3. Animals, Legends and stories of. I. Bateman, George W., tr.
1—26205
Library of Congress GR360.Z3Z3
[a42g1]

Zanzibar
M398
St3s
Swahili tales.
Steere, Edward, bp. 1828-1882.
Swahili tales, by Edward Steere. A new edition, revised by Alice Werner. London, The Sheldon press, 1929.
185p. 18½cm.
Written in Swahili.
White author.
1. Folklore, Swahili. 2. Tales, African. I. Title. II. Werner, Alice, 1895-1935.

Tanganyika
M896.3
R54k
Swahili essays.
Robert, Shaaban
Kielezo cha insha [Model essays]
Johannesburg, Witwatersrand University Press, 1957.
111p. 18cm. (Bantu treasury, XIII)
Written in Swahili.
1.Swahili essays. I. Title.

Swahili poetry.
Tanganyika
M967.82
Ab3
Abedi, K Amri
Sheria za kutunga mashairi na diwani ya Amri [The poems of Amri with an essay on Swahili poetry and the rules of versification]
Kampala, The Eagle Press, 1954.
148p. 21½cm.

Zanzibar
M398
St3s4
Swahili tales.
Steere, Edward, bp. 1828-1882.
Swahili tales (an English translation), by Edward Steere. London, The Sheldon press [1929]
iii, 186p. 19cm.
White author
1. Folklore, Swahili. 2. Tales, African. I. Title.

Swahili language - Addresses, essays, lectures.
Tanganyika
M896.4
R54
Robert, Shaaban
Kielezo cha insha [model essays]
Johannesburg, Witwatersrand University Press, 1961.
111p. 18½cm. (The Bantu Treasury, xiii)
"First published 1954".
Written in Swahili.
1. Swahili language - Addresses, essays, lectures. I. Cole, D T ed.

Swahili poetry.
Africa
M896.1
H23
Harries, Lyndon, ed. and tr.
Swahili poetry. Oxford, Clarendon Press, 1962.
xi, 326 p. facsim. 23 cm.
Texts in the Swahili-Arabic script are transliterated and translated into English.
1. Swahili poetry.
PL8704.A2H3 62-6394
Library of Congress [64b1]

M813.5
H66
Swamp Angel.
Hodges, George W
Swamp Angel. New York, New Voices Publishing Company, 1958.
128p. 22cm.
Biography on jacket.

Swahili language - Texts.
Kenya
M896.1
H119
Hadithi ya Mikidadi na Mayasa.
The story of Miqdad & Mayasa, from the Swahili-Abrabic text of Alice Werner. Medstead, Hampshire, Azania Press, 1932.
90p. illus. 19cm.
Written in Swahili and English.
1. Swahili language - Texts. I. Werner, Alice, 1859-1935, tr. II. Title. III. Title: Miqdad & Mayasa, The story of.

Swahili prose texts.
Africa
M896.3
V54
Velten, Carl, 1862- comp.
Swahili prose texts; a selection from the material collected by Carl Velten from 1893 to 1896. Edited and translated by Lyndon Harries. London, Oxford University Press, 1965.
viii, 298 p. 22 cm.
Swahili and English.
The Swahili texts were first published in the compiler's Safari za Wasuaheli and Desturi za Wasuaheli.
1. Swahili literature. I. Harries, Lyndon, ed. and tr. II. Title.
PL8704.A2V4 916.76 65-3830
Library of Congress [2]

Nigeria
M896.2
So3f
The swamp dwellers.
Soyinka, Wole.
Five plays: A dance of the forests, The lion and the jewel, The swamp dwellers, The trials of Brother Jero [and] The strong breed. London, Oxford University Press, 1964.
276p. 20cm. (A Three crowns book)

Tanzania
M396.1
H372
Swahili language - Texts.
Hemedi bin Abdallah bin Said, el Buhriy
Utenzi wa Abdirrahmani na Sufiyani. The History of Abdurrahman and Sufian. by Hemed Abdallah. With translation by Roland Allen and notes by J. W. T. Allen. Dar es Salaam, Eagle Press, 1961.
132p. (Johari za Kiswahili, 2)
Text in Swahili and English.

Zanzibar
M398
F25
Bk.1
Swahili proverbs.
Farsi, Shaabar Saleh.
Swahili sayings from Zanzibar. Book 1, Proverbs. Dar es Salaam, East African Literature Bureau, 1962.
52p. 18½cm.
Written in Swahili.
1. Folk-lore - Zanzibar. 2. Swahili proverbs. 3. Zanzibar - Folk-lore. I. Title.

Nigeria
M896.2
So3t
The swamp dwellers.
Soyinka, Wolé
Three plays. Book design and illustration by Dennis Williams. Ibadan, Ibadan University Press, 1963.
118p. 21cm. (Mbari Publications).
Contents: The swamp-dwellers. The trials of Brother Jero. The strong breed.

Swan, Eugene, joint author.
Haiti M447.9 M13y
McConnell, H Ormonde.
You can learn Creole; a simple introduction to Haitian Creole for English speaking people, by H. Ormonde McConnell ₍and₎ Eugene Swan. Port-au-Prince, Haiti, Impr. de l'État, 1945.
106 p. 24 cm.
Additional text on label mounted on p. ₍89₎
1. Creole dialects—Haiti. I. Swan, Eugene, joint author. II. Title.
PM7854.H3M3 447.9 47-27395*
Library of Congress ₍1₎

Sweet, Ossian.
M343.3 D25a
Darrow, Clarence
Argument of Clarence Darrow in the case of Henry Sweet in the Recorders Court, Detroit, Michigan before the honorable Frank Murphy, April and May, 1926. New York, National Association for the Advancement of Colored People, 1927.
34p. 23cm.
white author.

Swint, Sarah Louise (Johnson) ed.
M811.5 J6282
Johnson, Frank A , 1905-1932
Fireside poems, compiled and edited by Sarah L. Johnson Swint. Rev. memorial ed. New York, Sarah L. Johnson Swint, 1953.
47p. front. (port.) 22cm.
First edition published in 1931.
(in intro. sister says 1932. L. C. card says ₍1931₎ ???

British Guiana MB9 M69
A swarthy boy.
Mittelhölzer, Edgar.
A swarthy boy. London, Putnam ₍1963₎
157p. port. 21½cm.

The sweet flypaper of life.
M813.5 H87sw
Hughes, Langston, 1902- joint author.
The sweet flypaper of life ₍by₎ Roy De Carava and Langston Hughes. ₍New York, Simon and Schuster, 1955₎
98 p. illus. 19 cm.
1. Negroes—New York (City) 2. Harlem, New York (City)—Descr.—Views. I. Hughes, Langston, 1902- joint author. II. Title.
F128.9.N3D4 325.2609747 55—10048 ‡
Library of Congress ₍58k10₎

The Swiss contribution to western civilisation.
Gold Coast M966.7 Ar5sw
Armattoe, Raphael Ernest Grail. -1954.
The Swiss contribution to western civilisation, by Raphael E. G. Armattoe; with a foreword by Professor Julian S. Huxley, F. R. S. Dundalk, W. Tempest, 1944.
91 p. 18½cm.
Errata slip inserted.
1. Switzerland—Civilisation—Hist. I. Title.
45—1070
Library of Congress QD86.A8 ₍46d1₎ 914.94

The sway-backed house.
M813.4 C43u
Chesnut, Charles Waddell, 1858-1932.
The sway-backed house. From the Outlook, November 3, 1900. P. 588-593.

Sweet land of liberty.
M811.5 T36s
Thomas, Charles Cyrus, 1909-
Sweet land of liberty, by Charles Cyrus Thomas ... Dallas, Texas, The Kaleidograph press ₍n.d.₎
8p. 21½cm.

Switzerland.
Ghana MB9 Ar5
Armattoe, Rephael Ernest Grail, 1913-1954.
Personal recollections of the Nobel Laureation Festival. With an appendix listing all the distinguished guests at the Nobel banquet. Londonberry, Lomeshie Research Centre ₍n.d.₎
62p. ports. 25cm.

Swaziland.
M910 J63s
Johnson, Kathryn Magnolia, 1878-
Stealing a nation, a brief story of how Swaziland, a South African kingdom, came under British control without the knowledge or consent of its people, by Kathryn M. Johnson... Chicago, Ill., Pyramid publishing co. c 1939.
50, ₍2₎ p. maps. 17½ cm.

Sweet Potatoes.
M630.7 C25h2
Carver, George Washington, 1864-1943.
How the farmer can save his sweet potatoes and ways of preparing them for the table. (Revised and reprinted) fourth edition. Tuskegee Institute, Alabama, Tuskegee Institute press, 1937.
21p. 23cm. (Bulletin no. 38, November, 1936)

Switzerland - Civilization - History.
Gold Coast M966.7 Ar5sw
Armattoe, Raphael Ernest Grail. -1954.
The Swiss contribution to western civilisation, by Raphael E. G. Armattoe; with a foreword by Professor Julian S. Huxley, F. R. S. Dundalk, W. Tempest, 1944.
91 p. 18½cm.
Errata slip inserted.
1. Switzerland—Civilisation—Hist. I. Title.
45—1070
Library of Congress QD86.A8 ₍46d1₎ 914.94

Sweatt, Heman Marion.
M378 T369s
Thompson, Charles Henry, 1896-
Separate but not equal; The Sweat case. Dallas, Texas State Conference NAACP, 1948.
105-112p. 25cm.
Reprint from Southwest review, Spring 1948.

M811.5 Sw3e
Sweetwine, Charles.
The earth shall conquer you, an epic poem, by Charles Sweetwine. N.Y.C., Charles Sweetwine, ₍c 1945₎
10 unnumb. p. 23cm.
1. Poetry. I. Title.

Switzerland - Description & Travel.
France M914.94 D89
Dumas, Alexandre, 1802-1870.
Travels in Switzerland. Translated by R. W. Plummer and A. Craig Bell. Edited by A. Craig Bell. London, A. Owen ₍1958₎
230 p. illus., port. 20 cm.
Translation and condensation of Impressions de voyage. Suisse.
1. Switzerland—Descr. & trav. I. Title.
DQ23.D823 914.94 60-51296
Library of Congress ₍8₎

M350 Sw3
Sweeney, William Allison, 1851-
History of the American Negro in the great world war, his splendid record in the battle zones of Europe, including a resume of his past services to his country in the wars of the revolution, of 1812, the war of the rebellion, the Indian wars on the frontier, the Spanish-American war, and the late imbroglio with Mexico. By W. Allison Sweeney ... ₍Chicago, Printed by Cuneo-Henneberry company, ©1919₎
xx, 21-307 p. incl. front. plates (part col.) ports. 23cm.
1. European war, 1914-1918—Negroes. 2. Negroes. I. Title: American Negro in the great world war.
19—10990
Library of Congress D639.N4S8 ₍45e1₎

Swift, Job, 1743-1804.
M252 H33s
Haynes, Lemuel, 1753-1833.
₍A sermon₎ delivered at Rutland, (West Parish), October 28th, 1804. Occasioned by the sudden and much lamented death of the late Rev. Job Swift.
pp. ₍23₎-32, in: Job Swift, Discourses on religious subjects...Middlebury, Vermont, Printed by Huntington and Fitch, Nov. 1805.

Somalia M896.1 Sy11k
Syad, William J F
Khamsine; poèmes. Preface de Léopold S. Senghor. Paris, Présence Africaine ₍1959₎
70p. 20cm.
Text in English or French.
1. Poetry - Somali authors. 2. Somali poetry. I. Title. II. Senghor, Léopold Sédar, 1906-

Sweet, Ossian H , 1895-
M343.3 D25a
Darrow, Clarence
Argument of Clarence Darrow in the case of Henry Sweet in the Recorders Court, Detroit, Michigan before the honorable Frank Murphy, April and May, 1926. New York, National Association for the Advancement of Colored People, 1927.
34p. 23cm.
white author.

Swing that music.
M780 Ar5
Armstrong, Louis, 1900-
Swing that music, by Louis Armstrong, with an introduction by Rudy Vallee. Music section edited by Horace Gerlach, with special examples of swing music contributed by Benny Goodman, Tommy Dorsey, Joe Venuti ₍and others₎ ... London, New York ₍etc.₎ Longmans, Green and co., 1936.
xii p., 1 l., 136 p., 11 fold. l. front., ports. 22cm.
Includes a piano score by the author and Horace Gerlach, accompanied by improvisations supplied by ten musicians for their particular instruments (11 fold. l.) A portrait of the musician appears on verso of each improvisation.
"First edition."
1. Jazz music. I. Gerlach, Horace. II. Title.
36—36408
Library of Congress ML3561.A74S8 ₍43j1₎ ₍785₎ 780.973

Sydenham Hospital. New York.
M323.2 L62
Lifting the barriers at Sydenham Hospital. New York, Sydenham Institution.
18p. illus. 23cm.

M813.5 Sy7v
Sydner, W Leon.
Veronica, a novel. [1st ed.] New York, Exposition Press [1956]
207 p. 21 cm.
I. Title.
PZ4.S983Ve 56-8719 ‡
Library of Congress

Haiti M843.91 Sy5
Sylvain, Georges, 1866-1925
... Cric! Crac! Fables de La Fontaine, racontées par un montagnard haïtien, et transcrites en vers créoles par Georges Sylvain. 2. éd. Port-au-Prince (Haïti) En vente chez mme Georges Sylvain, 1929.
2 p. l., 163, [1] p. front. (port.) illus. 17½cm. (Bibliothèque haïtienne)
Autographed presentation copy to Mr. and Mrs. Arthur Spingarn.
I. La Fontaine, Jean de, 1621-1695. Fables. II. Title.
1. Creole verse 2. Haiti
Library of Congress PQ3949.S9C7 42-20688

Sylves.
Madagascar M841 R11v
Rabéarivelo, Jean Joseph, 1901-1937.
Sylves; nobles dedaens, fleurs mêlées, Destinée, Dixains, Sonnets & poèmes d'Iarive. Tananarive, Imprimerie de l'Imerina, 1927.
[102]p. 24cm.

Africa M896.1 Sy25
Sydow, Eckart von, 1885-1942, ed.
Poesia dei popoli primitivi; lirica religiosa, magica e profana. Scelta, introd. e note di Eckart v. Sydow. [Traduzione di Roberto Bazlen. Modena, Guanda, 1951.
197 p. 24 cm. (Collezione Fenice; edizione fuori serie, 15)
Includes selected African poems translated into Italian from African languages.
1. Literature, Primitive. 2. Poetry—Collections. 3. Italian poetry—Translations from foreign literature. I. Title.
4. African poetry.
[PN1347.S] A 52-7577
Illinois. Univ. Library for Library of Congress

Haiti M972.94 Sy58d
Sylvain, Georges, 1866-1925.
Dix annes de lutte pour la liberte 1915-1925. Port-au-Prince, Editions Henri Deschamps, 1957.
2 v. port. 21cm.
1. Haiti - History.

Symphonie en noir majeur poeme.
Haiti M841 F82s
Fouche, Franck
Symphonie en noir majeur poeme; pour Roussan Camille in memoriam. Port-au-Prince, Art Graphique Presse, 1962.
13p. 21½cm.

Haiti M325 Sy5
Sylvain, Benito.
Du sort des indigènes dans les colonies d'exploitation; par Benito Sylvain ... Paris, L. Boyer, 1901.
528 p., 1 l. incl. port. 22½cm.
Autographed presentation copy: A L'illustre tragedienne Sarah Bernhardt respectueux hommage de ma profunde admiration. Benito Sylvain, Paris, 9, Novembre 1901.
1. Native races. 2. Slavery. 3. Colonies.
3-3141
Library of Congress JV305.S9

Haiti M972.94 Sy58l
Sylvain, Georges, 1866-1925.
La lecture recueil de Causeries faites aux conférences post-scolaires du Comité Haitien de l'alliance Française, par Georges Sylvain. Port-au-Prince, Imprimerie de l'Abeille, 1908.
162p. 19½cm.
Autographed presentation copy to Mr. and Mrs. Arthur B. Spingarn.
1. Haiti. I. Comité Haitien de l'Alliance Française.

Africa M960.3 Sy6s
Symposium on Africa, *Wellesley College, 1960.*
Symposium on Africa. Wellesley, Mass., Wellesley College, 1960.
163 p. 28 cm.
1. Africa—Congresses.
DT23.S9 1960 960.3 60-3302
Library of Congress [61c5]

Haiti M972.44 Sy579s
Sylvain, Franck
Sur le vif, notes et impressions pour mon pays. Port-au-Prince, Haiti, Imp. de l'etat, 1946.
30p. 21cm.
1. Haiti.

Haiti M972.94 P19 V.2 no.1,2
Sylvain, Georges, 1866-1925. 1866-1925
Union Patriotique
Bulletin mensuel de l'Union Patriotique publie par le Comité de Port-au-Prince, 1-3. Port-au-Prince, 1920-1921.
v. 21cm.
Georges Sylvain, Administrateur-delegue.

Synthèse de la "jouissance effective" ....
Haiti M972.94 C23s
Carrié, Francois Eugene
Synthèse de la "jouissance effective" des droits de l'homme et des droits du peuple. Port-au-Prince, 1943-1944.
viii, 137, iiip. 21cm. (La Croisade Démocratique)
Mimeographed.

Haiti M972.94 Sy58a
Sylvain, Georges, 1866-1925.
Allocution de Me. Georges Sylvain, administratéur délégue de l'union patriotique, prononcée a Jean Rabel le 19 Août 1923.
4p. 25½cm.
1. Haiti. I. Rabel, Jean.

Haiti M972.94 Sy59m
Sylvain, Jeanne G
Mon Premier livre de geographie cours preparatoire. Haiti, Edition Henri Deschamps, [19]
20p. 17½cm.
1. Haiti-Geography.

Syphilis.
M616.951 H59
Hinton, William Augustus, 1883-
Syphilis and its treatment, by William A. Hinton ... New York, The Macmillan company, 1936.
xvi p., 1 l., 321 p. 22cm. (*Half-title:* Macmillan medical monographs, G. R. Minot ... editorial advisor)
1. Syphilis.
36-13179
Library of Congress RC201.H57 [45d1] 616.951

Haiti M840.9 Au8
1866-1925
Sylvain, Georges, 1866-1925.
Auteurs Hatiens, morceaux choisis, précédes de notices biographiques, par Solon Menos, Dantes Bellegarde, A. Duval, Georges Sylvain; prose. Port-au-Prince, Imp. de F. Smith, 1904.
351p. 19cm. (Oeuvre des écrivains Haitiens)

The sylvan cabin.
M811.5 J699s 1915
Jones, Edward Smyth, 1881-
The sylvan cabin, a centenary ode on the birth of Lincoln, by Edward Smyth Jones; With introduction taken from the N.Y. Times. San Francisco, published by the author, 1915.
9 unnumb. leaves port. (front.) 20½cm.
On cover: Panama-Pacific International Exposition Edition.

Syphilis-Homeopathic treatment.
M615 B73t
Branche, George C
Therapeutic quartan malaria in the treatment of neurosyphilis among Negroes. Reprinted from the Journal of nervous and mental disease, 83:177-190, February 1936.
177-190p. tables, graphs, 23cm.
Inscribed by author: With the writer's compliments, Geo. C. Branche, To Arthur B. Spingarn.
Read at the meeting of the American Psychiatric Association, May 30, 1934.

Haiti M841 Sy9c
Sylvain, Georges, 1866-1925.
...Confidences et mélancolies; poésies par Georges Sylvain (1885-1898). Précédées d'une notice sur la poésie haitienne par l'auteur et d'une préface par Justin Devot. Paris, Atéliers Haitiens, 1901.
140p. 22cm.
1. Haitian poetry. I. Title.

Sylvandire.
France M840 D89sy
Dumas, Alexandre, 1802-1870.
Sylvandire, Bruxelles, Meline, Cans et cie., 1843.
2 vols.

Syphilis-Homeopathic treatment.
M615 B73t2
Branche, George C
Therapeutic quartan malaria in the treatment of neurosyphilis among Negroes, a progress report. Reprinted from American Journal of psychiatry, 96: 967 - 978, January 1940.
967-968p. tables. 24cm.
Inscribed by author: To Arthur B. Spingarn, Geo. C. Branche.
Read at the American Psychiatric Association, Chicago, May 8-12, 1939.

Syria—Descr. & trav.

M910
Se1
Seaton, Daniel P.
The Land of promise; or, The Bible land and its revelation. Illustrated with several engravings of some of the most important places in Palestine and Syria. By D. P. Seaton, D. D., M. D. Philadelphia, Pa., Publishing house of the A. M. E. church, 1895.
ix, 443 p. front. (port.) 16 pl., map. 24½cm.
1. Palestine—Descr. & trav. 2. Syria—Descr. & trav.
Library of Congress DS107.S45 7—14411 [38b1]

S. Africa
M371.97
T11e
Tabata, Isaac B , 1909-
Education for barbarism in South Africa; Bantu (apartheid) education. London, Pall Mall Press, 1960.
100p. 19cm.
1. Negroes in South Africa - Education. I. Title.
LC2808.S7T3 371.97-968 61-24954

Nigeria
M896.3
F13t3
Taiwo ati kehinde; iwe keji.
Fagunwa, Daniel Olorunfemi (b.ca. 1900-)
Taiwo ati kehinde; iwe keji. [Taiwo and Kehinde, Bk. 2] [Lati owo D. O. Fagunwa ati o se iwe L. J. Lewis] 2d ed. Ibadan, Oxford University Press, 1963.
62p. illus. 18cm.
Written in Yoruba.
I. Title.

The system of Dante's Hell.
M813.5
J714s
Jones, LeRoi.
The system of Dante's Hell; [a novel] New York, Grove Press [1965]
154 p. 22 cm.
I. Title.
PZ4.J774Sy 65-23858
Library of Congress [3]

S. Africa
M968
T11
Tabata, Isaac B , 1909-
8 million demand freedom! What about it, Gen. Smuts? New York, Council on African Affairs, 1946.
23p. 20½cm.
1. Africa, South. 2. Smuts, Jan Christiaan, 1870-1951.

Africa
M323
T139
Tajfel, Henri, ed.
Disappointed guests; essays by African, Asian, and West Indian students. Edited by Henri Tajfel and John L. Dawson. London, New York, Oxford University Press, 1965.
158, [1] p. 23 cm.
White editor.
"Issued under the auspices of the Institute of Race Relations."
Bibliography: p. [159]
Partial contents.- Feeling, affection, respect, by Mervyn Morris.- The colour problem at the University: a West Indian's changing
~~1. Students, Foreign—Gt. Brit. 2. Gt. Brit.—Race question. 3. Race problems. I. Dawson, John L. M., joint ed. II. Institute of Race Relations. III. Title.~~
(Continued on next card)
LA637.7.T3 370.196 65-8757
Library of Congress [2]

T.V.A.
See
Tennessee Valley Authority.

M642
H71m
Table etiquette.
Holland, Edwin Clifford
The modern waiter, a formula for correct and perfect dining room service. The waiter's criterion, by E.C. Holland... Columbus, Ohio, Lutheran book concern, 1920.
89p. front, illus. 19½cm.

Africa
M323
T139
Tajfel, Henri, ed. Disappointed guests. 1965. (Card 2)
Partial contents - Continued.
attitudes, by Kenneth Ramchand.- The weary road to whiteness and the hasty retreat into Nationalism, by Elliott Bastein.- The transition from 'Light skinned' to 'coloured', by Patricia Madoo.- Some contexts of blackness, by Sillaty K. Dabo.- The paternal posture, by Chickwenda Nwariaku.- Racialism at the meeting point, by Francis M. Deng.
1. Students, Foreign - Gt. Brit. 2. Gt. Brit. - Race question. 3. Race problems. I. Dawson, John L. M., joint ed. II. Institute of Race Relations. III. Title.

Taanya Ugima-ini.
Kenya
M613.2
H88f3
Humphrey, Norman
Kũiyũria nda tikou gũthodeka mwĩrĩ [Feeding the body is more than filling the stomach. Tr. by J. M. Ruthuku] Nairobi, Eagle Press, 1950.
16p. 22cm. (Taanya Ugima-ini. Aim at healthy living series)
Written in Kikuyu.
White author.
1. Nutrition. I. Title. II. Series. III. Aim at healthy living series. IV. Ruthuku, J. M., tr.

M813.5
A17t
1951
Taffy.
Adams, Alger
Taffy, by Philip B. Kaye, [pseud.] New York, Avon Publishing Co., 1951.
254p. 16cm. (Avon pocket-size books, 377)
"Complete and unabridged."

M812.5
P44
Take a giant step.
Peterson, Louis Stamford, 1922-
Take a giant step, a drama in two acts. New York, French [1954]
110 p. 19 cm.
I. Title.
PS3531.E867T3 812.5 54-31878 ‡
Library of Congress [3]

Kenya
M610
N49
Taanya ũgima-inĩ.
Ngurungu, Sospeter Munuhe, tr.
Muceera na mukundu akundukaga o taguo [V.D. and drunkenness] [Tr. with a new preface by Sospeter Munuhue Ngurungu] Nairobi, Eagle Press, 1950.
16p. 22cm. (Taany ũgima-inĩ. Aim at healthy living series)
Written in Kikuyu)

M813.5
Ad17t
Taffy.
Adams, Alger.
Taffy, a novel by Philip B. Kaye. [pseud.] New York, Crown publishers [c1950]
258p.

Take up your cross.
Cameroun
M896.1
M98t
Mveng, Englebert
Take up your cross. Meditations on the way of the cross. Translated by Douglas Lord. London, Geoffrey Chapman [1963]
[30]p. illus. 20cm.
Translation of Si quelqu'un... chemin de croix.
1. Jesus Christ - Poetry. I. Title.

Taanya Ugimainĩ.
Kenya
M613.2
H88w3
Humphrey, Norman
Ukwenda ng'aragu kana buthi? [Which do you want: starvation or nourishment? Tr. by J. M. Ruthuku] Nairobi, Eagle Press, 1949.
9p. 21½cm. (Taanya Ugimainĩ. Aim at healthy living series)
Written in Kikuyu.
White author.
1. Nutrition. I. Title. II. Series. III. Ruthuku, J. M., tr.

M810
H94n
Taft, Robert Alphonso, 1889-1953.
Hurston, Zora Neale, 1903-
A Negro voter sizes up Taft. Washington, D.C., Taft Committee. [1952]
[12]p. 23cm.
Reprinted from the Saturday evening post, December 18, 1951.

Gold Coast
M966.7
B96r
Takoradi, Gold Coast - Soc. Condit.
Busia, Kofi Abrefa.
Report on a social survey of Sekondi-Takoradi. London, Crown Agents for the Colonies on behalf of the Govt. of the Gold Coast, 1950.
164 p. 2 col. maps (1 fold.) 22 cm.
1. Sekondi, Gold Coast—Soc. condit. 2. Takoradi, Gold Coast—Soc. condit.
HN800.G6S43 309.1667 51—20972
Library of Congress [a52b½]

Congo
Leopoldville
M967.5
K125
Tabalayi; bana betu.
Kalanda, Auguste Mabika, 1932-
Tabalayi; bana betu. [Leopoldville, Imprimerie Concordia, 1963]
93p. 21cm.
Portrait of author on back cover of book.
Written in Luba

Nigeria
M896.3
F13t
Taiwo ati Kehinde.
Fagunwa, D O
Taiwo ati Kehinde. Iwe kerin, lati owo D. O. Fagunwa ati L. J. Lewis. London, Oxford University Press, 1959.
110p. illus. 18½cm.
"First published 1951."
Written in Yoruba.

MB
T14s
Talbert, Horace, 1853-
The sons of Allen, by Rev. Horace Talbert, M. A. Together with a sketch of the rise and progress of Wilberforce university, Wilberforce, Ohio. Xenia, O., The Aldine press, 1906.
8 p. l., v-xiv p., 1 l., 17-286 p. front. (port.) illus. 23cm.
1. Allen, Richard, bp., 1760-1831. 2. Wilberforce university, Wilberforce, O. 3. African Methodist Episcopal church—Clergy. I. Title. 4. Biography.
Library of Congress BX8443.T3 6-15719
——— Copy 2.
Copyright A 141608 [a33b1]

British Guiana
M823.91 Talbot, Dave
T14m The musical bride. New York, Vantage Press, 1962.
249p. 23cm.
Portrait of author on book jacket.
I. Title.

M910 **Talbot, David Abner.**
T14c Contemporary Ethiopia. New York, Philosophical Library [1952]
267 p. 28 cm.
1. Ethiopia. I. Title.
DT378.T3 916.3 52-13211 ‡
Library of Congress [10]

M811.5 A tale of a walled town, and other verses, by B. 8266, —— penitentiary; with an introduction by William Stanley Braithwaite. Philadelphia and London, J. B. Lippincott company, 1921.
T14
120, [1] p. 19½ᶜᵐ.
Inscription written to Mrs. Max Greenbaum by "B.8266 appears on front gly leaf.
I. B. 8266, —— penitentiary. 1. Poetry. 22—714
Library of Congress PS3500.A1T3
—— Copy 2.
Copyright A 654114 [41e1]

The tale of Czar Saltan.
Russia
M891 Pushkin, Aleksandr Sergieevich, 1799-1837.
P97r The Russian wonderland: coq d'or, the tale of the fisherman and the fish, the tale of Czar Saltan. A metrical translation from the Russian of Alexander Poushkin, by Boris Brasol Manning... New York, The Paisley press, 1936.
ix, 62p. 21½cm.

The tale of the fisherman.
Russia
M891 Pushkin, Aleksandr Sergieevich, 1799-1837.
P97r The Russian wonderland: coq d'or, the tale of the fisherman and the fish, the tale of Czar Saltan. A metrical translation from the Russian of Alexander Poushkin, by Boris Brasol Manning... New York The Paisley press, 1936.
ix, 62p. 21½cm.

A tale of three places.
Brit. Guiana
M823.91 Mittelholser, Edgar
M69t A tale of three places. London, Secker and Warburg, 1957.
347p. 20cm.

Tales.
M398 **Dorson, Richard Mercer, 1916-** *ed.*
D73 Negro folktales in Michigan. Cambridge, Harvard University Press, 1956.
245 p. illus. 22 cm.
1. Negro tales. 2. Folk-lore, Negro. 3. Negroes. I. Title.
GR103.D6 398.21 56-6516 ‡
Library of Congress [15]

Tales.
M813.5 **Jones, LeRoi.**
J714t Tales. New York, Grove Press [1967]
132 p. 21 cm.
I. Title.
PZ4.J774Tal 67—27881
Library of Congress [68c2]

Africa Tales, African.
M398 **Arnott, Kathleen.**
Ar66 African myths and legends, retold by Kathleen Arnott. Illustrated by Joan Kiddell-Monroe. [1st American ed.] New York, H. Z. Walck, 1963 [°1962]
211 p. illus. 23 cm. (Oxford myths and legends)
1. Tales, African. 2. Mythology, African. I. Title.
PZ8.1.A73Af 2 398.096 63-7590 ‡
Library of Congress [5]

Africa Tales, African.
M398 **Beier, Ulli,** *ed.*
B396 The origin of life and death: African creation myths. London, Ibadan [etc.] Heinemann, 1966.
x, 65 p. 18½ cm. (African writers series, 23) 5/-
(B 66-17612)
1. Creation. 2. Tales, African. I. Title.
GR355.B4 398.36 66-77882
Library of Congress [3]

Tales, African.
Africa
M398 **Cendrars, Blaise, 1887-** *comp.*
C33b ... The African saga; translated from l'Anthologie nègre by Margery Bianco, with an introduction by Arthur B. Spingarn. New York, Payson & Clarke ltd. [°1927]
378 p. 24½ᶜᵐ.
Maps on lining-papers.
Bibliography: p. 371-378.
1. Tales, African. I. Bianco, Margery (Williams) 1880- tr. II. Title. 27—24330
Library of Congress GR350.C42
[a44l1]

Tales, African.
Senegal
M398 Diop, Birago
D59c Contes choisis; [compiled by] Birago Diop, edited by Joyce A. Hutchinson. Cambridge U. P., 1967.
176p. 21cm.
French text, introduction in English.
The stories in this selection are from Les contes d'Amadou Koumba, 1947, and Les nouveaux contes d'Amadou Koumba, 1958.
Bibliography: p. 4.

Tales, African.
Senegal
M398 Diop, Birago.
D59 Les contes d'Amadou-Koumba. Paris, Fasquelle 1947
189p. port. 19cm. (Ecrits francais d'outre-mer)

Tales, African.
Senegal Diop, Birago, 1906-
M398 Tales of Amadou Koumba; translated [from the French] by Dorothy S. Blair. London, Oxford U. P., 1966.
D59t
xxiii, 134 p. 22½ cm. 16/-
(B 66-11909)
1. Tales, African. I. Amadou-Koumba. II. Title.
GR350.B4813 398.2096 66-74700
Library of Congress [2]

Zanzibar Tales, African.
M398 Diva, David Edward
D64s Sungura mjanja [Hare is a rascal] East African tales. Illustrated by Ruth Yudelowitz. Nairobi, Eagle Press, 1953.
29p. illus. 15½cm.
Written in Swahili and English.
1. Africa, East - Folk tales. 2. Tales, African. I. Title. II. Title: Hare is a rascal.

Tales, African.
Angola
M398 Ennis, Merlin, comp. and tr.
En62 Umbundu; folk tales from Angola. Collected and translated by Merlin Ennis. Comparative analysis by Albert B. Lord. Boston, Beacon Press [1962]
316p. 21cm.

Liberia Tales, African.
M398 Freeman, Edwin O K
F87 More Liberian tales. London, Sheldon Press, 1941.
69p. 18cm.
1. Tales, African. I. Title.

Tales, African.
A
M398 **Frobenius, Leo, 1873-**
F92 ... African genesis. New York, Stackpole sons [°1937]
4 p. l., 13-236 p. illus., plates. 23½ᶜᵐ.
At head of title: Leo Frobenius and Douglas C. Fox.
"The stories in the first and second parts of this book have appeared in the ... Atlantis series of Volksmärchen und volksdichtungen Afrikas by Leo Frobenius, published ... 1921-1924. The stories in the third part of this book have been published in Frobenius' Erythräa, published ... 1931."—Note.
CONTENTS.—The Berbers.—The Sudanese.—Southern Rhodesians.
1. Folk-lore—Africa. 2. Tales, African. I. Fox, Douglas Claughton, 1906- II. Title.
37—35129
Library of Congress GR350.F74
[a42g1] 398.2096

Tales, African.
Africa
M398 **[Frobenius, Leo]** 1873-1938, *ed.*
F92a Atlantis; volksmärchen und volksdichtungen Afrikas ... Muenchen, Veröffentlichungen d. Forschungsinstituts für kulturmorphologie [1921-28]
12 v. illus., plates (part col.) maps (part fold.) plans. 21½ᶜᵐ.
"Herausgegeben von Leo Frobenius."
Each volume has also special t.-p., with imprint: Jena, E. Diederichs.
Vols. 10 and 12 have imprint: Frankfurt M., Veröffentlichungen d. Forschungsinstitutes f. kulturmorphologie.
CONTENTS.—bd. I-III. Volksmärchen der Kabylen.—bd. IV. Märchen aus Kordofan.—bd. V. Dichten und denken im Sudan.—bd. VI. Spielmannsgeschichten der Sahel.—bd. VII. Dämonen des Sudan.—bd. VIII. Erzählungen aus dem West-Sudan.—bd. IX. Volkserzählungen und volksdichtungen aus dem Zentral-Sudan.—bd. X. Die atlantische götterlehre.—bd. XI. Volksdichtungen aus Oberguinea. — bd. XII. Dichtkunst der Kassaiden.
1. Folk-lore—Africa. 2. Tales, African. I. Title.
Library of Congress GR350.F75 22—13973
[41r32e1]

Africa Tales, African.
M398.2 **Fuchs, Peter.**
F95 African Decameron; folk tales from central Africa. Translated from the German by Robert Meister. New York, I. Obolensky [1964, °1963]
208 p. 22 cm.
White editor.
1. Tales, African. I. Title.
GR350.F913 1964 398.2 63-20478
Library of Congress [5]

Africa Tales, African.
M398 Harman, Humphrey.
H22 Tales told near a crocodile; a collection of stories from Nyanza. Illustrated by Grace Huxtable. London, Hutchinson [1962]
151p. 21cm.

Nigeria Tales, African.
M398 Ajibola
It1 **Itayemi, Phebean,** 1927- *comp.*
Folk tales and fables, collected by Phebean Itayemi and P. Gurrey. London, Penguin Books [1953]
122 p. 18 cm. (Penguin West African series, WA 8)

1. Fables, African. 2. Tales, African. I. Gurrey, Percival, joint comp.
Full name: Phebean Ajibola Itayemi.
GR350.I 8 398.2 55-16450 ‡
Library of Congress [3]

Tales, African.
Africa, West
M398.2 Jablow, Alta, comp.
J11 An anthology of West African folklore. Introduction by Paul Goodman. [London] Thames and Hudson [1962, ©1961]
223p. 21cm.
White compiler.

Tales, African.
Uganda
M398 **Kalibala, Ernest Balintuma.**
K12 Wakaima and the clay man, and other African folktales, by E. Balintuma Kalibala and Mary Gould Davis. Illustrated by Avery Johnson. New York, Toronto, Longmans, Green & co. [1946]
6 p. l., 145 p. incl. illus., plates. front. 21cm.
"First edition."

1. Tales, African. I. Davis, Mary Gould, 1882- joint author. II. Johnson, Avery F., 1906- illus. III. Title.
46-3687
Library of Congress PZ8.1.K18Wak
[47u5]

Tales, African.
Africa
M39 Kelsey, Alice Geer.
K29t Tales from Africa, by Alice Geer Kelsey... Cover and decorations by Aaron Douglas. New York, Friendship, c1945.
80p. illus. 23cm.

Nigeria Tales, African.
M966.9 **LeBagola, Bata Kindai Amgoza ibn.**
L78f The folk tales of a savage, by Lobagola; illustrated by Erick Berry. New York, A. A. Knopf, 1930.
7 p. l., 199, [1] p. front., illus. 20½cm.
Illustrated lining-papers.

1. Tales, African. I. Title.
30-21411
Library of Congress GR350.L6
——— Copy 2.
Copyright A 25961 [41j1] 398.21

Tales, African.
Africa, South
M896.3 Ndawo, Henry Masila
N24in Izibongo zenkosi zama-Hlubi nezama-Baca. Natal, The Mariannhill Mission Press, 1928.
39p. 18½cm.
Common folktales - Xhosa, Zulu.
Bound with the author's InXenye YenTsomi Zase Zweni. [Natal, 1920]

Tales, African.
Guinea
M398.2 Niane, Djibrie Tamsir
N51 Sundiata; an epic of old Mali. Translated by G. D. Pickett. [London] Longmans [1965]
96p. map. 20½cm.

1. Tales, African. I. Title.

Tales, African.
Uganda
M967.61 **Nyabongo, Akiki K** 1905-
N98w Winds and lights; African fairy tales, by H. H. Prince Akiki K. Nyabongo; with illustrations by B. Hewitt. New York, N. Y., The Voice of Ethiopia [©1939]
[45] p. illus., port. 24cm.
"Errata" slip mounted on lining-paper.

1. Tales, African. I. Title.
Library of Congress PZ8.1.N98W1 39-17420
——— Copy 2.
Copyright A 131104 [3]

Tales, African.
M740 Porter, James Amos, 1905- illus.
P82 Talking animals, by Wilfrid D. Hambly; illus. by James A. Porter. Washington, D. C., Associated Publishers, 1949.
x, 100p. illus. 28cm.

Zanzibar Tales, African.
M398 Steere, Edward, bp. 1828-1882.
St3s4 Swahili tales (an English translation), by Edward Steere. London, The Sheldon press [1929]
iii, 186p. 19cm.
White author

1. Folklore, Swahili. 2. Tales, African. I. Title.

Tales, African.
Zanzibar
M398 Steere, Edward, bp. 1828-1882.
St3s Swahili tales, by Edward Steere. A new edition, revised by Alice Werner. London, The Sheldon press, 1929.
185p. 18½cm
Written in Swahili.
White author.

Africa Tales, African.
M896 Whiteley, W H. comp.
W58 A selection of African prose. Oxford, Clarendon Press, 1964.
2v. 22cm.
Contents.- v.1. Traditional oral texts.- v.2. Written prose.

M973 Tales, African.
W86am Woodson, Carter Godwin, 1875-
African myths, together with proverbs; a supplementary reader composed of folk tales from various parts of Africa, adapted to the use of children in the public schools, by Carter Godwin Woodson ... Washington, D. C., The Associated publishers, inc. [1928]
xv, 184p. incl. front., illus. 19½cm.

Ghana Tales, Ashanti.
M398 **Appiah, Peggy.**
Ap49 Ananse the spider; tales from an Ashanti village. Pictures by Peggy Wilson. [New York] Pantheon Books [1966]
152 p. illus. 25 cm.
White author.

1. Tales, Ashanti. I. Wilson, Peggy, illus. II. Title.
PZ8.1.A647An 398.24 66-9666
Library of Congress [3]

Tales, Ashanti.
Ghana Prempeh, Albert Kofi
M398 ~~Courlander, Harold, 1908-~~
P91h The hat-shaking dance, and other tales from the Gold Coast, by Harold Courlander, with Albert Kofi Prempeh. Illustrated by Enrico Arno. [1st ed.] New York, Harcourt, Brace [1957]
115 p. illus. 21 cm.

1. Tales, Ashanti. I. Title.
PZ8.1.C8Hat 56-5872 ‡
Library of Congress [57b5]

Tales, Chad.
Chad
M398 Seid, Joseph Brahim
Se4 Au Tchad sous les étoiles. [Paris] Présence Africaine, [1962]
101p. 19cm.

Ethiopia Tales, Ethiopic.
M963 **Courlander, Harold,** 1908-
C83 The fire on the mountain, and other Ethiopian stories, by Harold Courlander and Wolf Leslau. Illustrated by Robert W. Kane. New York, Holt [1950]
141 p. illus., col. plates. 25 cm.

1. Tales, Ethiopic. I. Leslau, Wolf, joint author. II. Title.
GR360.E8C6 398.21 50-7265
Library of Congress [52k3]

Ghana Tales, Ghanaian.
M398 Kyereture, K O. Bonsu
K52 Ashanti heroes. [Illustrated by E. Addo Osafo and Laszlo Acs] Accra, Waterville Publishing House, 1964.
63p. illus., map.

1. Folk-lore - Ghana. 2. Ghana - Folk-lore. 3. Tales, Ghanaian. I. Title.

Tales, Haitian.
Haiti Hyppolite, Michelson Paul
M398 Contes dramatiques Haitiens. Port-au-Prince. Imp. de l'Etat, 1951.
H99c
v. illus., port. 22cm.
At head of title: Bibliotheque de Musee du Peuple Haitien.
Library has: tome I.

Tales, Haitian.
Haiti
M398 Pierre-Louis, Ulysse
P612 Sortilèges, Afri-Haitiens (contes et légendes). Préface du Dr. Jean Price-Mars. Port-au-Prince, Imprimeire de l'Etat, 1961.
120p. 18½cm.

Tales, Hausa.
Nigeria
M398 **Johnston, Hugh Anthony Stephens,** *ed. & tr.*
J64 A selection of Hausa stories; compiled and translated by H. A. S. Johnston. Oxford, Clarendon P., 1966.
l, 241 p. 22½ cm. (Oxford library of African literature) 35/-
(B 66-16882)
Appendix in Hausa.

1. Tales, Hausa. 2. Proverbs, Hausa. I. Title.
PL8234.Z95E5 1966 398.2 66-75454
Library of Congress [3]

Jamaica M398 An1

Tales, Jamaican.

Anancy stories and dialect verse; by Louise Bennett ꜀and others꜆ With an introd. by P. M. Sherlock. ꜀1st ed.꜆ Cover design after a drawing by Stella Shaw. Kingston, Jamaica, Pioneer Press ꜀1950꜆

101 p. 19 cm.

Partial contents: Louise Bennett. Dorothy Clarke. Una Wilson. Claude McKay. Una Marson.

1. Tales, Jamaican. 2. Negro-English dialects—Texts. I. Bennett, Louise.

PZ8.1.A5 51-17383

Library of Congress ꜀3꜆

Kenya M398 M45

Tales, Kamba.

Mbiti, John Samuel, 1931- , ed. and tr.

Akamba stories; ꜀translated and edited by꜆ the Reverend John S. Mbiti. Oxford, Clarendon P., 1966.

x, 240 p. 22½ cm. (Oxford library of African literature) 45/-

(B 67-1173)

Bibliography: p. 41.

1. Tales, Kamba. 2. Kamba tribe. 3. Folklore - Kenya. 4. Tales, Kenya. I. Title.

PL8351.M2 67-72464

Library of Congress ꜀67c2꜆

Kenya M398 M45

Tales, Kenyan.

Mbiti, John Samuel, 1931- , ed. and tr.

Akamba stories; ꜀translated and edited by꜆ the Reverend John S. Mbiti. Oxford, Clarendon P., 1966.

x, 240 p. 22½ cm. (Oxford library of African literature) 45/-

(B 67-1173)

Bibliography: p. 41.

1. Tales, Kamba. 2. Kamba tribe. 3. Folklore - Kenya. 4. Tales, Kenya. I. Title.

PL8351.M2 67-72464

Library of Congress ꜀67c2꜆

Kenya M398 N65

Tales, Kikuyu.

Njururi, Ngumbu, 1930- comp.

Agikuyu folk tales. London, Oxford U. P., 1966.

ix, 109 p. 22½ cm. 18/6

(B 66-11836)

1. Tales, Kikuyu. I. Title.

GR360.K5N55 398.2096762 66-72313

Library of Congress ꜀3꜆

Liberia M398 L55

Tales, Liberian.

The leopard's daughter; a folk tale from Liberia. Translated from the Vai language by Princess Fatima Massaquoi. With illus. by Martha Burnham Humphrey. Boston, Bruce Humphries [1961]

14p. illus. 28cm.

Nigeria M398 Id2n

Tales, Nigerian.

Idewu, Olawale.

Nigerian folk tales as told by Olawale Idewu and Omotayo Adu. Told to and edited by Barbara K. and Warren S. Walker. Text decorations by Margaret Barbour. New Brunswick, N. J., Rutgers University Press ꜀1961꜆

113 p. 22 cm.

1. Tales, Nigerian. I. Adu, Omotayo. II. Walker, Barbara K. III. Walker, Warren S.

GR360.N5 I 3 398.2 61-10268 ‡

Library of Congress ꜀62i5꜆

Nigeria M398 S113

Tales, Nigerian.

Sidahome, Joseph E , 1917-1963.

Stories of the Benin Empire. London, Oxford University Press, 1964.

196p. illus. 21½cm.

U.S. M839 Iv3f

Tales, Norwegian.

Christiansen, Reidar Thorwold, 1886- ed.

Folktales of Norway, edited by Reidar Th. Christiansen. Translated by Pat Shaw Iversen. ꜀London꜆ Routledge & Kegan ꜀1964꜆

284p. 23cm. (Folktales of the world)

Bibliography: p. ꜀263꜆-265.

1. Tales, Norwegian. I. Title. II. Iversen, Esther Patricia (Shaw) tr.

Somali M496 G13

Tales, Somali.

Galaal, Muuse Haaji Ismaaiil

Hikmad Soomaali. Edited with grammatical introduction and notes by B. W. Andrzejewski. London, Oxford University Press, 1956.

150p. 22cm. (Annotated African texts, 4)

Title in English: Somali wisdom.

Includes bibliography.

1. Somali language - Texts. 2. Tales, Somali. I. Title. II. Andrzejewski, B. W., ed. III. Series.

Angola M398 En62

Tales, Umbundu.

Ennis, Merlin, *comp. and tr.*

Umbundu; folk tales from Angola. Collected and translated by Merlin Ennis. Comparative analysis by Albert B. Lord. Boston, Beacon Press ꜀1962꜆

316 p. 21 cm.

1. Tales, Umbundu.

GR360.A5E5 398.2 62-7895 ‡

Library of Congress ꜀5꜆

Tobago M972.98 Ot5L

Tales, West Indian.

Ottley, Carlton Robert, 1914-

Legends, true stories and old sayings from Trinidad and Tobago, collected and told by C. R. Ottley. Port-of-Spain, College Press, 1962.

71p. 20cm.

Jamaica M398 Sh54

Tales, West Indian.

Sherlock, Philip Manderson,

West Indian folk-tales, retold by Philip Sherlock; illustrated by Joan Kiddell-Monroe. London, Oxford U. P., 1966.

(7), 151 p. col. front., illus., col. plates. 23½ cm. (Oxford myths and legends) 17/6

(B 66-687)

1. Tales, West Indian. I. Kiddell-Monroe, Joan, illus. II. Title.

GR120.S5 1966a 398.24 66-70268

Library of Congress ꜀5꜆

Africa M89 K29t

Tales from Africa.

Kelsey, Alice Geer.

Tales from Africa, by Alice Gerr Kelsey... Cover and decorations by Aaron Douglas. New York, Friendship c1945

80p. illus. 23cm.

Senegal M398 D59t

Tales of Amadou Koumba.

Diop, Birago, 1906-

Tales of Amadou Koumba; translated ꜀from the French꜆ by Dorothy S. Blair. London, Oxford U. P., 1966.

xxiii, 184 p. 22½ cm. 16/-

(B 66-11909)

1. Tales, African. I. Amadou-Koumba. II. Title.

GR350.B4813 398.2096 66-74700

Library of Congress ꜀2꜆

M813.5 J632t

Tales of darkest Africa.

Johnson, Fenton, 1888-

Tales of darkest Africa, by Fenton Johnson. Chicago, Ill., The Favorite Magazine ꜀c 1920꜆

34p. 20½cm.

M398 G76t

Tales of Momolu.

Graham, Lorenz B

Tales of Momolu, by Lorenz Graham, illustrated by Letterio Calapai. New York, Reynal & Hitchcock ꜀1946꜆

6 p. l., 3-169 p. incl. illus., plates. 21cm.

1. Children in Africa. I. Title.

PZ9.G74Tal 46-8058

© 18Nov46; author, Corona, N. Y.; A8389.

Library of Congress ꜀5꜆

Jamaica M398 B56

Tales of old Jamaica.

Black, Clinton Vane de Brosse, 1918-

Tales of old Jamaica. Kingston, Pioneer Press ꜀1952꜆

121 p. illus. 19 cm.

1. Jamaica—Hist. I. Title.

F1881.B8 *972.9203 52-31554 ‡

Library of Congress ꜀3꜆

Nigeria M896.3 N97t

Tales out of school.

Nwankwo, Nkem

Tales out of school. Illustrated by Adebayo Ajayi. Lagos, African Universities Press ꜀1963꜆

90p. illus. 20cm. (African Reader's Library, no. 2)

Africa M398 H22

Tales told near a crocodile.

Harman, Humphrey.

Tales told near a crocodile; a collection of stories from Nyanza. Illustrated by Grace Huxtable. London, Hutchinson ꜀1962꜆

151p. 21cm.

M740 P82

Talking animals.

Porter, James Amos, 1905- illus.

Talking animals, by Wilfrid D. Hambly; illus. by James A. Porter. Washington, D. C., Associated Publishers, 1949.

x, 100p. illus. 28cm.

M398 B17t

The talking tree.

Baker, Augusta, *comp.*

The talking tree; fairy tales from 15 lands. Illustrated by Johannes Troyer. ꜀1st ed.꜆ Philadelphia, Lippincott ꜀1955꜆

255 p. illus. 23 cm.

1. Fairy tales. I. Title.

PZ8.B17Tal 55-9507 ‡

Library of Congress ꜀56n5꜆

Talks on citizenship, no. 1.
Tanganyika
M967.82
Om1k
Omari, Dunstan Alfred, 1922- jt. auth.
Kwa nini tuna haja ya serikali? Why do we have government? [By C. W. W. Ryan and D. A. Omari] Dar es Salaam, Eagle Press, 1954.
17p. 18cm. (Mazungumzo juu ya uraia. Talks on citizenship no.1)
Written in Swahili and English.
1. Tanganyika. I. Title. II. Title: Why do we have government? III. Series: Mazungumzo ya uraia, no.1. IV. Series: Talks on citizenship, no. 1. V. Ryan, C. W. W.

Talks on citizenship, no. 2.
Tanganyika
M967.82
Om1m
Omari, Dunstan Alfred, 1922- jt. auth.
Mtu maskini mwenye sh.1,000,000. The poor man with a million shillings. [By C. W. W. Ryan and D. A. Omari] Dar es Salaam, Eagle Press, 1954.
16p. 18cm. (Mazungunmzo ya uraia. Talks on citizenship, no.2)
Writtn in Swahili and English.
1. Money. I. Title. II. Title: The poor man with a million shillings. III. Series: Mazungunmzo ya uraia, no. 2. IV. Talks on citizenship, no. 2. V. Ryan, C. W. W.

Talks on citizanship, no. 3.
Tanganyika
M967.82
Om1ma
Omari, Dunstan Alfred, 1922- jt. auth.
Maendeleo na jasho. Progress & perspiration. [By C. W. W. Ryan and D. A. Omari] Dar es Salaam, Eagle Press, 1954.
19p. 18cm. (Mazungunmzo ya uraia. Talks on citizenship, no. 3)
Written in English and Swahili.
1. Tanganyika. I. Title. II. Title: Progress & perspiration. III. Series: Mazungunmzo ya uraia, no. 3. IV. Series: Talks on citizenship, no. 3. V. Ryan, C. W. W.

Talks on citizenship, no. 4.
Tanganuika
M967.82
Om1t
Omari, Dunstan Alfred, 1922- jt. auth.
Tanganyika, tajiri au maskini? Tanganyika - rich or poor? [By C. W. W. Ryan and and D. A. Omari] Dar es Salaam, 1954.
17p. 18cm. (Mazungumzo ya uraia. Talks on citizanship, no. 4)
Written in Swahili and English.
1. Tanganyika. I. Title. II. Tanganyika - rich or poor? III. Mazungumzo ya uraia, no. 4. IV. Talks on citizenship. no. 4. V. Ryan, C. W. W.

Senegal
M916.63
T145
Tall, Ibra
Un voyage au Senegal. [Tanger, Editions Marocaines et Internationales, 1965.]
[70]p. 15½cm.
1. Senegal - Description and travel. I. Title.

Talladega College. ~~Alabama.~~ Talladega, Ala.
M378Ta
G79
Gray, Arthur D
Inaugural address. The vocation of the church-related college.
(In: The Talladegan, v.70, no.6, May 1953. 30cm. [4]p.)

Talladega college, Talladega, Ala.
M378Ta
C85
Crawford, George Williamson, 1877-
The Talladega manual of vocational guidance (The red book) written and compiled by George W. Crawford ... [Talladega, Ala., Pub. under the auspices and official sponsorship of the Board of trustees of Talladega college [°1937]
x, 146 p. incl. illus. (map) tables, diagrs. 23½cm.
"A bibliography on vocational guidance": p. 141-146.
1. Negroes — Employment. 2. Negroes — Education. 3. Profession, Choice of. 4. Talladega college, Talladega, Ala. I. Title.
37-5167
Library of Congress E185.8.C86
——— Copy 2.
Copyright A 106261 [38d3] [371.425] 326.260973

M378Ta
T14r
Talladega College, Talladega, Alabama. President
Report ...
Talladega, Alabama,
v. illus. 22cm. annual.
Title varies.
See holdings card for issues in library.

Talladega College, Talladega, Ala. Savery Library.
M323
H73n
Holmes, Dwight Oliver Wendell, 1877-
The Negro chooses democracy. Reprinted from the Journal of Negro education. [8:620-633]. October, 1939.
Dedicatory address, The Savery Library, Talladega College, April 16, 1939.

The Talladega manual of vocational guidance.
M378Ta
C85
Crawford, George Williamson, 1877-
The Talladega manual of vocational guidance (The red book) written and compiled by George W. Crawford ... [Talladega, Ala., Pub. under the auspices and official sponsorship of the Board of trustees of Talladega college [°1937]
x, 146 p. incl. illus. (map) tables, diagrs. 23½cm.
"A bibliography on vocational guidance": p. 141-146.
1. Negroes — Employment. 2. Negroes — Education. 3. Profession, Choice of. 4. Talladega college, Talladega, Ala. I. Title.
37-5167
Library of Congress E185.8.C86
——— Copy 2.
Copyright A 106261 [38d3] [371.425] 326.260973

M222.11
T14s
Talley, Marshall Alexander, 1877-
A Socratic exposition of Genesis; a study of the book of Genesis in the light of modern thought and of New Testament interpretation designed especially for the advancement of the cause of religious education, by Marshall A. Talley ... [Indianapolis, °1935]
365 p. 19½cm.
1. Bible. O. T. Genesis—Examinations, questions, etc. 2. Bible—Examinations, questions, etc.—O. T. Genesis. I. Title.
35-13797
Library of Congress BS1227.T3
——— Copy 2.
Copyright A 85422 [2] 222.11

Talley, Marshall Alexander, 1877- joint author.
M286
Ad1n
Adams, C C
Negro Baptists and foreign missions; C. C. Adams and Marshall A. Talley, authors. Philadelphia, Pa., The Foreign mission board of the National Baptist convention, U. S. A., inc. [°1944]
84 p. 18½cm.
1. Baptists, Negro—Missions. 2. National Baptist convention of the United States of America—Missions. I. Talley, Marshall Alexander, 1877- joint author. II. National Baptist convention of the United States of America. Foreign mission board. III. Title.
45-15372
Library of Congress BV2521.A85
[3] 266.61

M811.08
T14
Talley, Thomas Washington, 1868-1952, comp.
Negro folk rhymes, wise and otherwise, with a study by Thomas W. Talley ... New York, The Macmillan company, 1922.
xii p., 1 l., 347 p. illus. (incl. music) 19½cm.
1. ~~Negro~~ songs. I. Title.
22—1477
Library of Congress PS595.N3T3
[41t1]

Talmud Selections.
M296
R91
Russell, Charles L ed. and tr.
Light from the Talmud ... by Charles L. Russell. New York, Bloch Publishing Co., 1942.
iv, 200p. incl. tab. 20cm.
Hebrew and English on opposite pages.

Tam-Tam schwarz.
Senegal
M986.1
Se5t
Senghor, Léopold Sédar, 1906-
Tam-Tam schwarz; gesänge vom Senegal. Ausgewählt und übertragen von Janheinz Jahn. Heidelberg, Wolfgang Rothe, 1955.
63p. 24cm.
Biography: p. 60-62

U. S.
M968
Am3
Tambo, Oliver, 1917-
Passive resistance in South Africa.
Pp. 217-224.
In: American Society of African Culture. Southern Africa in transition. New York, Praeger, 1966.

Tambourines to glory.
M813.5
H87tr
Hughes, Langston
Trommeln zur Selighkeit; roman. Germany, Verlegt Bei Kindler, 1959.
268p. 19cm.
Title: Tambourines to glory.
"To Arthur Spingarn, this German translation of 'Tambourines to Glory' - Sincerely, Langston Hughes. New York, April 25, 1960."
1. Title.

Tambourines to glory, a novel.
M813.5
H87t
Hughes, Langston, 1902-
Tambourines to glory, a novel. New York, J. Day Co. [1958]
188 p. 21 cm.
I. Title. *Full name: James Langston Hughes.*
PZ3.H87313Tam 58-13324 ‡
Library of Congress [7]

Tanganyika.
Tanganyika
M967.82
Am7p
Amri, Daudi
Polisi na raia [The police and the public] Kampala, The Eagle Press, 1951.
32p. illus. 18½cm.
Written in Swahili and English.
1. Tanganyika.

Tanganyika.
M338.9
G92s
Kiano, J G
Kenya, Uganda, and Tanganyika.
Pp. 49-53.
In: Science and the new nations, edited by Ruth Gruber. 1961.

Tanganyika.
Tanganyika
M967.82
K83u
Kombo, S M
Ustaarabu na maendeleo ya Mwafrika [The civilisation and development of the African] Nairobi, The Eagle Press, 1950.
60p. 18cm.
Written in Swahili.
1. Tanganyika.

Tanganyika.
Tanganyika
M967.82 Mnyampala, Mathias E
M71h Historia, milia, na desturi za Wagogo wa Tanganyika [History and customs of the Wagogo of Tanganyika] Kampala, The Eagle Press, 1954.

116p. 15cm. (Custom and tradition in East Africa series)

Written Swahili.

Tanganyika.
Tanganyika
M967.82 Mzirai, Robert R
M99 Maandishi ya barua zetu. Kimetungwa na. Kampala, The Eagle Press, 1957.

107p. 18½cm.
Written in Swahili.
English translation: The writing of letters.

Tanganyika.
Tanganyika
M967.82 Omari, Dunstan Alfred, 1922- jt. auth.
Om1k Kwa nini tuna haja ya serikali? Why do we have government? [By C. W. W. Ryan and D. A. Omari] Dar es Salaam, Eagle Press, 1954.

17p. 18cm. (Mazungumzo juu ya uraia. Talks on citizenship no.1)
Written in Swahili and English.

1. Tanganyika. I. Title. II. Title: Why do we have government? III. Series: Mazungumzo ya uraia, no.1. IV. Series: Talks on citizenship, no. 1. V. Ryan, C. W. W.

Tanyanyika.
Tanganyika
M967.82 Omari, Dunstan Alfred, 1922- jt. auth.
Om1ma Maendeleo na jasho. Progress & perspiration. [By C. W. W. Ryan and D. A. Omari] Dar es Salaam, Eagle Press, 1954.

19p. 18cm. (Mazungunmzo ya uraia. Talks on citizenship, no. 3)
Written in English and Swahili.

1. Tanganyika. I. Title. II. Title: Progress & perspiration. III. Series: Mazungunmzo ya uraia, no. 3. IV. Series: Talks on citizenship, no. 3. V. Ryan, C. W. W.

Tanganyika.
Tanganuika
M967.82 Omari, Dunstan Alfred, 1922- jt. auth.
Om1t Tanganyika, tajiri au maskini? Tanganyika - rich or poor? [By C. W. W. Ryan and D. A. Omari] Dar es Salaam, 1954.

17p. 18cm. (Mazungumzo ya uraia. Talks on citizenship, no. 4)
Written in Swahili and English.

1. Tanganyika. I. Title. II. Tanganyika - rich or poor? III. Mazungumzo ya uraia, no. 4. IV. Talks on citizenship. no. 4. V. Ryan, C. W. W.

Tanganyika.
Tanganyika
M967.82 Kiwa, R L
R52h Hadithi za rafiki saba; Hadithi tamu za zamani. [Tales told by seven friends] Nairobi, The Eagle Press, 1951.

45p. illus. 21½cm.
Written in Swahili.

Tanganyika.
Tanganyika
M967.82 Robert, Shaaban
R54r Kusadikika. Nchi Iloyo Angani. London, Thomas Nelson and sons, ltd. 1951.

57p. illus. 18½cm.

Tanganyika.
Tanganyika
M967.82 Thonya, Lucius Mbasha
T38 Siusa hapo kale [Wisdom of the past] methali katika hadithi, Kingoni kimefasiriwa kwa kiswahili. Dar es Salaam, Eagle Press, 1960.

95p. illus. 21½cm.

1. Tanganyika. 2. Angoni. I. Title.

Tanganyika Tanganyika - Description and travel.
M967.8 Stahl, Kathleen, Mary, 1918-
M89 Tanganyika: sail in the wilderness. [Forward by Julius Nyerere] 'S-Gravenhage, Mounton, 1961.

100p. plates. maps. 22cm.
White author.

1. Tanganyika-Description and travel. I. Nyerere, Julius Kambarage, Forward. II. Title.

Tanganyika - Folktales.
Tanganyika
M967.82 Kayombo, Innocent K
K18s Stories of our Tanganyika forefathers. Illus. by K.M. Kadege. London, Sheldon Press, 1952.

29p. illus. 18cm.

Tanganyika. - History.
Tanganyika
M967.82 Lemenye, Justin
L54m Maisha ya sameni ole kivasis yaani Justin Lemenye [The life of Justin Lemenye] Kampala, The Eagle Press, 1953.

71p. port. illus. 18½cm.

Written in Swahili.

Tanganyika - History.
Tanganyika
M967.82 Ntiro, S J
N88d Desturi za Wachagga [Customs and traditions of the Chagga people of Tanganyika] Nairobi, The Eagle Press, 1953.

50p. illus. 22½cm.
Written in Swahili.

Tanganyika - Short stories.
Tanganyika
M967.82 Ulenge, Yussuf
U12 Nguzo ya maji; na hadithi nyingine; [The pillar of water, and other stories.] Nairobi, The Eagle Press, 1951.

22p. illus. 19cm.

Tanganyika Tanganyika: sail in the wilderness.
M967.8 Stahl, Katheleen Mary, 1918-
N89 Tanganyika: sail in the wilderness. [Forward by Julius Nyerere] 'S-Gravenhage, Mounton, 1961.

100p. plates. maps. 22cm.
White author.

1. Tanganyika-Description and travel. I. Nyerere, Julius Kambarage, Forward. II. Title.

Tanganyika - rich or poor?
Tanganuika
M967.82 Omari, Dunstan Alfred, 1922- jt. auth.
Om1t Tanganyika, tajiri au maskini? Tanganyika - rich or poor? [By C. W. W. Ryan and D. A. Omari] Dar es Salaam, 1954.

17p. 18cm. (Mazungumzo ya uraia. Talks on citizenship, no. 4)
Written in Swahili and English.

1. Tanganyika. I. Title. II. Tanganyika - rich or poor? III. Mazungumzo ya uraia, no. 4. IV. Talks on citizenship. no. 4. V. Ryan, C. W. W.

Tanganyika, tajiri au maskini?
Tanganuika
M967.82 Omari, Dunstan Alfred, 1922- jt. auth.
Om1t Tanganyika, tajiri au maskini? Tanganyika - rich or poor? [By C. W. W. Ryan and D. A. Omari] Dar es Salaam, 1954.

17p. 18cm. (Mazungumzo ya uraia. Talks on citizenship, no. 4)
Written in Swahili and English.

1. Tanganyika. I. Title. II. Tanganyika - rich or poor? III. Mazungumzo ya uraia, no. 4. IV. Talks on citizenship. no. 4. V. Ryan, C. W. W.

Tango (Dance)
Argentina
M982 Rossi, Vicente.
R73 ... Cosas de negros; los oríjenes del tango y otros aportes al folklore rioplatense. Rectificaciones históricas. Rio de la Plata [Córdoba, Imprenta argentina] 1926.

436 p., 2 l., 7 p. illus. (music) 26cm.

1. Negroes in Argentine republic. 2. Negroes in Uruguay. 3. Folklore, Negro. 4. Negroes—Dancing. 5. Tango (Dance) I. Title.

27—25000

Library of Congress F3021.N3R8
[a45d1]

M287.8 Tanner, Benjamin Tucker, *bp.*, 1835–1923.
T15 An apology for African Methodism, by Benj. T. Tanner. Baltimore, 1867.

xxiii, [13]–468 p. 20cm.

1. African Methodist Episcopal church. I. Title.

22—15342

Library of Congress BX8443.T4
[a38b1]

M204 Tanner, Benjamin Tucker, 1835-1923.
T15c The color of Solomon - What? "My beloved is white and ruddy." A monograph. By Bishop Benjamin Tucker Tanner ... Introduction by William S. Scarborough... Philadelphia, A.M.E. book concern, 1895.

xiii, 14-93p. front., plates. 19½cm.

1. Ethonology. I. Title.

M287.8 Tanner, Benjamin Tucker, 1835-1923
T15ou An outline of our history and government for African Methodist churchmen, ministerial and lay, in catechetical form. Two parts with appendix, by B.T. Tanner... Introduction by B.F. Lee. [n.p., n.p., c 1884]
206p. illus. 20cm.
1. African Methodist Episcopal church.

M973.6 Tanner, Benjamin Tucker, bp. 1835-1923.
N21t The theory and practice of American Christianity, p. 70-79.
1879 National Conference of Colored Men. Nashville.
Proceedings of the National Conference of Colored Men of the United States, held in the State Capitol at Nashville, Tennessee, May 6, 7, 8, and 9, 1879. Washington, D.C., Rufus H. Darby, 1879.

107p. 19cm.

M331
T15

Tanneyhill, Anna Elizabeth,
From school to job: guidance for minority youth. [1st ed. New York, Public Affairs Committee, 1953]
28 p. illus. 19 cm. (Public affairs pamphlet, no. 200)

1. Negroes—Employment. I. Title.
E185.8.T32 331.98 53-4285 ‡
Library of Congress [20]

Tante-Bella.
Cameroons, Fr.
M896.3
Ow5tb

Owono, Joseph
Tante-Bella; roman d'aujourd'hui et de demain. Yaounde, Librairie au Messager, 1959.
293p. 20cm.
Portrait of author on front of book.

Martinique
M843.9
T17b

Tardon, Raphaël, 1911-
Bleu des Iles, recits Martiniquais, Fasquelle Editeurs, 1946.
209p. 19cm.

1. Martinican fiction. 2. Martinique-Fiction.
I. Title.

West Indies
M808.8
H839

Tardon, Raphaël, 1911-
Calderon's revolt. Translated by Patrick Bowles.
Pp. 214-221
In: Howes, Barbara, ed. From the Green Antilles. New York, Macmillan, 1966.

Martinique
M843.9
T17c

Tardon, Raphaël, 1911-
La Caldeira, roman. Paris, Fasquelle Editeurs, 1949.
264p. 23cm.

1. Martinican fiction. 2. Martinique - Fiction.
I. Title.

Martinique
M843.9
T17c

Tardon, Raphaël, 1911-
Christ au Poing, roman. Paris, Fasquelle [1950]
267 p. 21 cm.

1. Martinican fiction
I. Title.
PQ2639.A734C48 843.91 A 51-4993
Illinois. Univ. Library for Library of Congress [1]

Martinique
M893.9
T17co

Tardon, Raphaël, 1911-
Le corbat de Schoelcher. Paris, Fasquelle Editeurs, 1948.
127p. 19cm.

1. Schoelcher, Victor, 1804-1893. I. Title.

Martinique
M323
T17n

Tardon, Raphaël, 1911-
Noirs et blancs; une solution: l'apartheid? Paris, Denoël, 1961.
171p. 18½cm.

1. Africa, South - Race relations.
2. Apartheid. I. Title.

Martinique
M843.9
T17s

Tardon, Raphaël, 1911-
Starkenfirst, roman. Paris, Fasquelle Editeurs, 1947.
201p. 22½cm.
Received Prix des Antilles

1. Martinican fiction. 2. Slavery - Fiction.
I. Title.

Haiti
MB9
T64t

Tardon, Raphael, 1911-
Toussaint Louverture. Le Napoleon noir. Paris, Bellenand, 1951.
254p. 19cm.

1. French literature--Martiniquan author.
2. Toussaint Louverte, Pierre Dominique, 1746?-1803.

M323
N21

Target for 1963, goals of the fight for freedom.
National Association for the Advancement of Colored People.
Target for 1963, goals of the fight for freedom. New York, 1954.
15 p. cm.

Tarikh El-Fettach.
Mali
M966.2
M31d

Mahmūd Kati ibn al-Hāj al-Mutawakkil Kāti 1468-1593.
Documents arabes relatifs à l'histoire du Soudan: Tarikh El-Fettach; ou chronique du chercheur pour servie a l'histoire des Villes, des Armées et des principaux personages du Tekrour par Mahmoûd ben El 'Hadj El-Mataouakkel Kâti. tr. Française par O. Houdas et M. Delafosse, Paris, Ernest Leroux, 1913.
2v. 28½cm.

Tarikh es-Soudan.
Mali
M966.2
Ab3d

'Abd al-Raḥmān ibn 'Abd Allāh, *al-Sa'dī*, 1596-ca. 1655.
Documents arabes relatifs à l'histoire du Soudan: Tarikh es-Soudan, par Abderrahman ben Abdallah ben 'Imran ben 'Amir es-Sa'di ... édité par O. Houdas ... avec la collaboration de Edm. Benoist ... Paris, E. Leroux, 1898-1900.
2 v. 28½ᶜᵐ. (*Half-title:* Publications de l'École des langues orientales vivantes, ivᵉ sér., vol. XII-XIII)
History of Timbuktu and the surrounding region under Moroccan rule during the 16th and 17th centuries.
CONTENTS.—v. 1. Texte arabe.—v. 2. [Traduction] par O. Houdas.
1. Sudan, French—Hist. 2. Timbuktu—Hist. I. Houdas, Octave Victor, 1840-1916, ed. and tr. II. *Benoist, Edmond, 1871- ed. III. Title. IV. Title: Tarikh es-Soudan.
44-44091
Library of Congress PJ7819.S8A23 [3]

MB9
D82t

Tarry, Ellen, 1906-
Katharine Drexel, friend of the neglected. Illustrated by Donald Bolognese. New York, Farrar, Straus & Cudahy [1958]
190 p. illus. 22 cm. (Vision books, 32)

1. Drexel, Katharine, 1858-1955.
BX4705.D755T3 922.273 58-5456 ‡
Library of Congress [7]

MB9
M37t

Tarry, Ellen, 1906-
Martin de Porres, saint of the New World. Illustrated by James Fox. London, Burns and Oates; New York, Vision Books [1963]
178 p. illus. 22 cm. (Vision books, 57)

1. Martin de Porres, Saint, 1579-1639. 2. Saints.
BX4700.M397T3 1963 j 92 63-9924 ‡
Library of Congress [5]

M813.5
T17m2

Tarry, Ellen, 1906-
My dog Rinty, by Ellen Tarry and Marie Hall Ets, illustrated by Alexander and Alexandra Alland. New York, The Viking press, 1946. [1964]
[48] p. incl. front., illus. 24½ x 19½ cm.
"First published May 1946."

1. Dogs—Legends and stories. I. Ets, Marie Hall, 1895- joint author. II. Title.
PZ10.3.T1386My 46-4736
Library of Congress [50h1]

M813.5
T17m

Tarry, Ellen, 1906-
My dog Rinty, by Ellen Tarry and Marie Hall Ets, illustrated by Alexander and Alexandra Alland. New York, The Viking press, 1946.
[48] p. incl. front., illus. 24½ x 19½ᶜᵐ.
"First published May 1946."

2. Children's stories
1. Dogs—Legends and stories. I. Ets, Marie Hall, joint author. II. Title.
Library of Congress PZ10.3.T1386My 46-4736
[47m5]

M813.5
T17h

Tarry, Ellen, 1906-
Hezekiah Horton, by Ellen Tarry; pictures by Oliver Harrington. New York, The Viking press, 1942.
89 p. illus. (part col.) 24ᶜᵐ.
"First published August 1942."

1. Children's stories
I. Title. II. Harrington, Oliver illus.
42-18466
Library of Congress PZ7.T18He
[43e2]

M813.5
T17

Tarry, Ellen, 1906-
Janie Belle, by Ellen Tarry, illustrated by Myrtle Sheldon. New York, Garden City publishing co., inc., °1940.
[30] p. illus. 26½ x 20ᶜᵐ.
Illustrated title on two leaves.

1. Children's stories
I. *Sheldon, Myrtle, 1893- illus. II. Title.
40-32086
Library of Congress PZ7.T18Jan
——— Copy 2.
Copyright [5]

M813.5
T17r

Tarry, Ellen, 1906-
The runaway elephant. Pictures by Oliver Harrington. New York, Viking Press, 1950.
87 p. col. illus. 25 cm.

1. Children's stories
I. Harrington, Oliver, illus. II. Title.
PZ10.3.T1386Ru 50-8883
Library of Congress [3]

MB9
T17

Tarry, Ellen, 1906-
The third door; the autobiography of an American Negro woman. New York, D. McKay Co. [1955]
304 p. 21 cm.

I. Title.
E185.97.T27A3 920.5 55-14466 ‡
Library of Congress [56p5]

MB9
J64t
Tarry, Ellen, 1906-
Young Jim; the early years of James Weldon Johnson. New York, Dodd, Mead [1967]
xii, 230 p. facsims., ports. 22 cm.

1. Johnson, James Weldon, 1871-1938—Juvenile literature. I. Title.

PS3519.O2625Z89 67-22194
Library of Congress [5]

Taxation - Haiti.

Haiti
M354
J16g
Jacques, Jean F.
Guide pratique de l'enregistrement facilitant la perception des droits du fisc et le tarif des timbres à l'usage des inspecteurs-receveurs et des contrôleurs de l'enregistrement, des notaires, arpenteurs, greffliers, huissiers et des parties contractantes. Port-au-Prince, Imp. de l'Etat, 1948.
22p. 23½cm.

M231
W62
Taylor, Gardner Calvin, 1918-
Why I believe there is a God.

Pp. 102-107.

In: Why I believe there is a God. Chicago, Johnson Pub. Co., 1965.

M813.5
T178f
Tarter, Charles Lewis, 1907-
Family of destiny. [1st ed.] New York, Pageant Press [1954]
277 p. 21 cm.

I. Title.

PZ4.T194Fam 54-12344 ‡
Library of Congress [2]

M973.8
T21
Taylor, Alrutheus Ambush, 1893-1954
The Negro in South Carolina during the reconstruction by Alrutheus Taylor, Wash., D.C., The Association for the study of Negro life and history c1924
iv, 341p. 24cm.

1. South Carolina. 2. Reconstruction - South Carolina.

M811.5
T21
Taylor, Gloria Lee, 1916-
Dreams for sale. Poems. [1st ed.] New York, Exposition Press [1953]
64 p. 21 cm.

I. Title.

PS3539.A895D7 811.5 53-12049 ‡
Library of Congress [2]

M335.4
R54f
Taruc, Luis, 1913-
Born of the people. With a foreword by Paul Robeson. New York, International Publishers [1953]
286 p. illus. 21 cm.

1. Hukbong Mapagpalaya ng Bayan (Philippine Islands) I. Title.

DS686.2.T3A3 991.4 53-10412 ‡
Library of Congress [5]

M973.8
T21ne
Taylor, Alrutheus Ambush, 1893-1954
The Negro in Tennessee, 1865-1880, by Alrutheus Ambush Taylor ... Washington, D. C., The Associated publishers, inc., 1941.
5 p. l., 306 p. 23½cm.
Bibliography: p. 267-278. Bibliographical notes: p. 275-300.

1. Negroes—Tennessee. I. Title. 41-5247
Library of Congress E185.93.T3T3
[43h1] 325.2609768

MB
T21o
Taylor, Harold William, 1903-
One tenth of a nation, by Harold W. Taylor. Corona, L. I., N. Y., Progressive book shop, °1946.
31 p. 15 x 11½cm.
Contributions made by the Negro people in building a democratic America. cf. Foreword.
Bibliography: p. 31. "Books to read": p. 31.

1. Negroes. 2. Negroes—Biog. I. Title.

E185.6.T3 325.260973 47-15548
Library of Congress [3]

A taste for blood.
M813.5
W52t
West, John B
A taste for blood. New York, The New American Library, 1960.
144p. 18cm. (Signet Book)
Portrait of author on book cover.

M973.8
T21n
Taylor, Alrutheus Ambush, 1893-1954
The Negro in the reconstruction of Virginia, by Alrutheus Ambush Taylor ... Washington, D. C., The Association for the study of Negro life and history [°1926]
iv, 300 p. 24½cm.
Bibliography: p. 287-292.

1. Negroes—Virginia. 2. Reconstruction—Virginia. I. Association for the study of Negro life and history, inc. II. Title.
27-5705
Library of Congress E185.93.V8T3
[43g1]

Nigeria
M966.9
C88g
Taylor, J C
Crowther, Samuel Adjai, 1806-1891.
The gospel on the banks of the Niger. Journals and notices of the native missionaries accompanying the Niger expedition of 1857-1859. By the Rev. John Christopher Taylor. London, Church Missionary House, 1859.
x, 451p. map. 20cm.

M341.6
T18
Tate, Merze, 1905-
The disarmament illusion; the movement for a limitation of armaments to 1907, by Merze Tate ... New York, The Macmillan company, 1942.
xiv, 398 p. 22cm.
Half-title: Bureau of international research, Harvard university and Radcliffe college.
"First printing."
Bibliography: p. [363]-378.

1. Disarmament. I. Bureau of international research of Harvard university and Radcliffe college.
42-17792
Library of Congress JX1974.T3
[20] 341.6

M323
T21c
Taylor, Cæsar Andrew Augustus P.
The conflict and commingling of the races; a plea not for the heathens by a heathen to them that are not heathens. By Cæsar A. A. P. Taylor. New York, Broadway publishing company, 1913.
3 p. l., xv, 119 p. 20cm.

1. U. S.—Race question. ~~2. Negroes.~~ I. Title.
13-10926
Library of Congress E185.61.C22
Copyright A 347353 [a37b1]

M780
T21t
Taylor, J Hillary
Taylor's music questionnaire. 250 questions and answers upon many phases of the art for the music lover, student, amateur and musician, by J. Hillary Taylor. Washington, D.C., The author c1936
28p. 21cm.
1. Music.

M325.3
T18t
Tate, Merze, 1905- ed.
Trust and non-self-governing territories; Papers and proceedings of the tenth annual conference of the Division of the Social Sciences, The Graduate School, Howard University, April 8th and 9th, 1947, ed. by Merze Tate. Washington, D. C., Howard University, Graduate School, 1948.
128p. 23cm. (Howard University. Studies in Social sciences, v.6, no.1)

1. Trusteeship. I. Howard University, Wash. D.C. Division of Social Sciences. II. Series.

MB9
T19
Taylor, Douglas
World of a pullman porter. New York, [n.d.]
48p. illus., ports. 21cm.
Portrait of author in book and on front cover.

I. Title.

Taylor, Julius H., ed.
M500
M36n
Maryland. Morgan State College, *Baltimore.*
The Negro in science, by the Calloway Hall editorial committee: Julius H. Taylor, editor [and others. Baltimore] Morgan State College Press [1955]
viii, 192 p. illus. 26 cm.
Includes bibliographies.

1. Science—Addresses, essays, lectures. 2. Negro scientists. I. Taylor, Julius H., ed. II. Title.

Q171.M312 504 55-63107
Library of Congress [56e2]

M341.6
T18u
Tate, Merze, 1905-
The United States and armaments. Cambridge, Harvard Univ. Press, 1948.
xii, 312 p. 24 cm.
"Much of the material of Part I ... is in [the author's] The disarmament illusion."
"Short titles used in footnotes": p. [275]-278. "Selective bibliography": p. 278-286.

1. Disarmament. 2. U. S.—Defenses. I. Title.

JX1974.T32 341.6 48-5607*
Library of Congress [48q7]

Trinidad
M972.98
T212
Taylor, Edward
The mayor's report for the Mayoral terms 1960-1961 and 1961-1962. Port-of-Spain, P.N.M. Pub. Co., Ltd., 1962.
12p. illus. 28½cm.
Portrait of author.

1. Trinidad.

M245
T21c
Taylor, Marshall W
A collection of revival hymns and plantation melodies, by Marshall W. Taylor... Musical composition by Miss Josephine Robinson. Copied by Miss Amelia C. and Hettie C. Taylor. Cincinnati: Marshall W. Taylor. and W.C. Echols, 1883.
276p. front. 16½cm.
1. Hymns. I. Robinson, Josephine

MB9
T21f
Taylor, Marshall W 1878–
The fastest bicycle rider in the world, the story of a colored boy's indomitable courage and success against great odds; an autobiography by Marshall W. "Major" Taylor. Worcester, Mass., Wormley publishing company [°1928]
6 p. l., 431 p. front. (port.) illus. 23½cm.
1. Cycling. I. Title.
Library of Congress GV1051.T2A3 29–29836
——— Copy 2.
Copyright A 9600 [3]

M350
T21
Taylor, Susie King, 1848–
Reminiscences of my life in camp with the 33d United States colored troops, late 1st S. C. volunteers, by Susie King Taylor ... Boston, The author, 1902.
xii p., 1 l., 82 p. front., pl., ports. 19½cm.
1. U. S.—Hist.—Civil war—Regimental histories—U. S. inf.—33d. 2. U. S. infantry. 33d regt., 1862–1866. I. Title. 3. Soldiers.
Library of Congress E492.94.33dT 2–30128
[a44b1]

Congo
Brazzaville
M896.1
T2v
Tchicaya U'Tamsi, Gerald Felix
Le ventre. Paris, Présence Africaine [1964]
135p. 20cm.
I. Title.

M540
T21f
Taylor, Moddie Daniel, 1912–
First principles of chemistry. Illus. by Wilma Riley. Princeton, N. J., Van Nostrand [1960]
688 p. illus. 24 cm.
Includes bibliography.
1. Chemistry. 2. Chemistry, Physical and theoretical.
QD31.T28 540 60–9036 ‡
Library of Congress [25]

A
M398
T21a
Taylor, W E , compiler.
African aphorisms or saws from Swahili-land. Collected, translated and annotated by W. E. Taylor. With a preface by W. Salter Price. London, The Sheldon Press, 1924.
182p. 16cm.

M811.5
R62t
Teach me to live.
Roe, Helene
Teach me to live; a selection of prose poems. [n.p.] 1963
19p. illus. 23cm.
Portrait of author in book.
I. Title.

M343.3
G65
Taylor, Recy.
Gordon, Eugene, 1890–
Equal justice under law, by Earl Conrad and Eugene Gordon; foreword by Henrietta Buckmaster, cover by Bert Adams. New York, Committee for Equal Justice for Mrs. Recy Taylor, n.d.
15p. port. 23cm.

Nigeria
M966.9
Ab32
Tazyīn al-waraqāt, by 'Abdullāh ibn Muhammad.
'Abd Allāh ibn Muḥammad, *Emir of Gwandu*, 1767 (ca.)–1829.
Tazyīn al-waraqāt, by 'Abdullāh ibn Muḥammad. Edited, with a translation and introductory study of the author's life and times, by M. Hiskett. [Ibadan, Nigeria] Ibadan University Press, 1963.
144 p. facsims., geneal. table, fold. map. 25 cm.
Bibliographical footnotes.
1. Sokoto, Nigeria (Province)—Hist. I. Hiskett, M., ed. and tr. II. Title.
DT515.9.S6A2 65–4747
Library of Congress [1]

M811.5
W25t
The teacher and other poems.
Warren, Samuel Enders, 1903–
The teacher and other poems. Houston, Texas, privately printed, 1953.
23p. 22cm.

M304
P19
v.6
no.5
Taylor, Robert W.
Harriet Tubman, the heroine in ebony. By Robert W. Taylor, with introduction by Booker T. Washington. Boston, Mass., George H. Ellis, printer, 1901.
16p. port. 19½cm.
1. Tubman, Harriet (Ross).

Martinique
M843.9
M32t
Le Tchad de sable et d'or.
Maran, René, 1887–
Le Tchad de sable et d'or, Documentation de Pierre Deloncle, couverture en couleurs de Charles Fouqueray. Paris, Librairie de la revue française [c1931]
159p. 21cm.

Nigeria
M370
So42
Teacher training in Nigeria.
Solaru, T T
Teacher training in Nigeria, by T. T. Solaru. Edited, and with a final chapter by Ian Espie. Ibadan, Ibadan University Press, 1964.
109p. maps. 21½cm.
Includes bibliography.

Jamaica
M823.91
T21b
Taylor, Stanley Arthur Goodwin, 1894–
Buccaneer Bay. Kingston, Jamaica, Pioneer Press [1952]
243 p. 19 cm.
I. Title.
PZ4.T246Bu 53–26148 ‡
Library of Congress [3]

Congo,
Brazzaville
M896.1
T2f4
Tchicaya U'Tamsi, Gerald Felix
Brush fire. [Translated by Langodare Akanji. Ibadan, Mbari Publications [1964]
[65]p. illus. 23½cm.
Translation of Feu de Brausse.
1. African poetry. I. Title.
II. Mbari Publications.

M370.
C54
Teacher-training programs for Negroes.
Clark, Felton Grandison, 1903–
The control of state-supported teacher-training programs for Negroes, by Felton G. Clark ... New York city, Teachers college, Columbia university, 1934.
vi, 118 p. fold. diagr. 23½cm. (Teachers college, Columbia university. Contributions to education, no. 605)
Issued also as thesis (PH. D.) Columbia university.
Bibliography: p. 104–107.
1. Teachers, Training of—U. S. 2. Negroes—Education. I. Title. II. Title: Teacher-training programs for Negroes.
Library of Congress LC2731.C55 1934 a 34–25345
——— Copy 2. LB5.C8 no. 605
Copyright A 72895 [a35t5] 370.7373

Jamaica
M823.91
T21c
Taylor, Stanley Arthur Goodwin, 1894–
The capture of Jamaica, a historical novel. Kingston, Jamaica, Pioneer Press, 1951.
164p. 19cm.
1. Jamaica - Hist. - Fiction. I. Title.

Congo,
Brazzaville
M896.1
T2f
Tchicaya U'Tamsi, Gerald Felix
Feu de brousse; poém parléen 17 vivions. Paris [Caractères, 1957]
85p. 20cm.
1. African poetry. I. Title.

M304
P19
v.7
no.19
Teachers.
The National notebook, vol. 1, no.1, Augusta, Ga., National association of teachers in colored schools, Ja 1919.
18p. 25½cm.
Editor: Silas X. Floyd.

Jamaica
M823.91
T21p
Taylor, Stanley Arthur Goodwin, 1894–
Pages from our past. Kingston, Jamaica, Pioneer Press [1954]
183 p. 19 cm.
1. Jamaica—Hist.—Fiction. I. Title.
PZ4.T246Pag 55–43679 ‡
Library of Congress [1]

South Africa
M896
M88
Tchicaya U'Tamsi, Gerald Felix
Presence.
Pp. 123–124.
In: Mphahlele, Ezekiel, ed. African writing today. Baltimore, Penguin Books, 1967.

MB9
C55
Teachers - Correspondence, reminiscences, etc.
Clark, Septima (Poinsette) 1898–
Echo in my soul, by Septima Poinsette Clark with LeGette Blythe. Foreword by Harry Golden. [1st ed.] New York, Dutton, 1962.
243 p. illus. 21 cm.
An autobiography.
1. Negro teachers—Correspondence, reminiscences, etc. I. Blythe, LeGette, 1900– II. Title.
E185.97.C59A3 923.773 62–14718 ‡
Library of Congress [10]

Teachers - Correspondence, reminiscences, etc.

M89
M846

Morton, Lena Beatrice.
My first sixty years: passion for wisdom. New York, Philosophical Library [1965]
175 p. port. 22 cm.

1. Negro teachers—Correspondence, reminiscences, etc. I. Title.

LC2731.M6 923.773 65-11951

Library of Congress [5]

Teachers-Correspondence, reminiscences, etc.

M89
Sp32

Spellman, Cecil Lloyd, 1906-
Rough steps on my stairway; the life history of a Negro educator. [1st ed.] New York, Exposition Press [1953]
273 p. 21 cm.

1. Negro teachers—Correspondence, reminiscences, etc. I. Title.

LC2731.S65 923.773 53-5639 ‡

Library of Congress [5]

Teachers - Salaries, pensions, etc.

M323
N21

National association for the advancement of colored people.
Teachers' salaries in black and white, a pamphlet for teachers and their friends, prepared by the National association for the advancement of colored people ... New York, N. Y. [1942]
15 p. illus. (ports.) 23cm.
"Reprinted February, 1942."

1. Teachers—U. S.—Salaries, pensions, etc. 2. Negroes—Education. I. Title.

Library of Congress LB2843.N4N35 43-8223
[3] 371.161

Teachers—Salaries, pensions, etc.

M370
T37p

Thompson, Charles Henry, 1896-
Progress in the elimination of discrimination in white and Negro teacher's salaries, [editorial] Reprinted from the Journal of Negro education. 9:1-4, January 1940.

Teachers—Tennessee.

M370.
G66

Gore, George William, 1901-
In-service professional improvement of Negro public school teachers in Tennessee, by George W. Gore, jr. ... New York, Teachers college, Columbia university, 1940.
xi p., 1 l., 142 p. incl. illus., tables. 23½cm. (Teachers college, Columbia university. Contributions to education, no. 786)
Issued also as thesis (PH. D.) Columbia university.
Bibliography: p. 123-130.

1. Negroes—Education. 2. Teachers, Training of—Tennessee. 3. Education — Tennessee. 4. Teachers — Tennessee. I. Title. II. Title: Negro public school teachers in Tennessee.

Library of Congress LC2802.T2G6 1940 a 40-30014
——— Copy 2. LB5.C8 no. 786
Copyright A 139131 [41k10] 371.97409768

Teachers, Interchange of.

M910
Ad17

Adams, Effie Kaye.
Experiences of a Fulbright teacher. Boston, Christopher Pub. House [1956]
215 p. 21 cm.

1. Pakistan—Descr. & trav. 2. Voyages and travels—1950- 3. Teachers, Interchange of. I. Title.

DS379.A6 *915.47 56-2860 ‡

Library of Congress [57g5]

Teachers, Training of

M370
C12m
no.3

Caliver, Ambrose, 1894-
...Education of Negro teachers, by Ambrose Caliver. Washington, D.C., U.S. government printing office, 1933.
123p. 24cm. (National survey of the education of teachers, bulletin 1933, no.10) Volume 4.
1. Teacher training. I. Title

Teachers, Training of.

M378.
G83a

Greene, Harry Washington, 1896-
... An adventure in experimental co-operative teaching; a general account of recent work in progressive education conducted jointly by members of the Department of education of the Ohio state university and the West Virginia state college, by Harry W. Greene ... Institute, W. Va., 1938.
vi, [7]-36 p. 22½cm. (West Virginia state college bulletin ... November, 1938. ser. 25, no. 6 ... Contribution no. 9 of the Dept. of education)
Bibliography: p. 32-36.

1. Teachers, Training of. 2. Education—Experimental methods. I. Ohio state university, Columbus. College of education. II. West Virginia state college, Institute. III. Title.

A 40-1473

Teachers college library, for Library of Congress Columbia univ. [2]

Teacher, Training of -Louisiana.

M370.
M11

McAllister, Jane Ellen, 1899-
The training of Negro teachers in Louisiana, by Jane Ellen McAllister ... New York city, Teachers college, Columbia university, 1929.
vi, 95 p. 23½cm. (Teachers college, Columbia university. Contributions to education; no. 364)
Published also as thesis (PH. D.) Columbia university.
Bibliography: p. 95.

1. Teachers, Training of—Louisiana. 2. Negroes—Education. 3. Negroes—Louisiana. I. Title. II. Title: Negro teachers in Louisiana, The training of.

Library of Congress LC2802.L8M3 1929 a 30-11081
——— Copy 2. LB5.C8 no. 364
Copyright A 21710 [41m1] 370.7

Nigeria
M370
So42

Teachers, Training of - Nigeria.
Solaru, T T
Teacher training in Nigeria, by T. T. Solaru. Edited, and with a final chapter by Ian Espie. Ibadan, Ibadan University Press, 1964.
109p. maps. 21½cm.
Includes bibliography.

Teachers, Training of -Southern states.

M06
J61
no. 18

[John F. Slater fund]
A suggested course of study for county training schools for negroes in the South. [Lynchburg, Va., J. P. Bell company, inc., printers] 1917.
70 p. incl. front., illus., plates. plan. 24cm. (*On cover:* The trustees of the John F. Slater fund. Occasional papers, no. 18)

1. Negroes—Education. 2. Teachers, Training of—Southern states. I. Title.

17-30810

Library of Congress E185.5.J65 no. 18
——— Copy 2. [a38g1]

Teachers, Training of— Tennessee.

M370.
G66

Gore, George William, 1901-
In-service professional improvement of Negro public school teachers in Tennessee, by George W. Gore, jr. ... New York, Teachers college, Columbia university, 1940.
xi p., 1 l., 142 p. incl. illus., tables. 23½cm. (Teachers college, Columbia university. Contributions to education, no. 786)
Issued also as thesis (PH. D.) Columbia university.
Bibliography: p. 123-130.

1. Negroes—Education. 2. Teachers, Training of—Tennessee. 3. Education — Tennessee. 4. Teachers — Tennessee. I. Title. II. Title: Negro public school teachers in Tennessee.

Library of Congress LC2802.T2G6 1940 a 40-30014
——— Copy 2. LB5.C8 no. 786
Copyright A 139131 [41k10] 371.97409768

Teachers, Training of—U.S.

M370
C12e

Caliver, Ambrose, 1894-
Education of teachers for improving majority-minority relationships. Course offerings for teachers to learn about racial and national minority groups. By Ambrose Caliver ... Federal security agency. Paul V. McNutt, administrator. U. S. Office of education, John W. Studebaker, commissioner. Washington, U. S. Govt. print. off., 1944.
iv, 64 p. incl. illus., tables. 23cm. (U. S. Office of education. Bulletin 1944, no. 2)
"Selected references and sources of information": p. 60-64.

1. U. S.—Race question. 2. Minorities. 3. Teachers, Training of—U. S. 4. Universities and colleges—Curricula. I. Title.

E 45—7

U. S. Off. of educ. Library for Library of Congress L111.A6 1944, no. 2
——— Copy 2. E184.A1C3
[46k3]† (370.6173) 325.73

Teachers, Training of — U.S.

M370.
C54

Clark, Felton Grandison, 1903-
The control of state-supported teacher-training programs for Negroes, by Felton G. Clark ... New York city, Teachers college, Columbia university, 1934.
vi, 118 p. fold. diagr. 23½cm. (Teachers college, Columbia university. Contributions to education, no. 605)
Issued also as thesis (PH. D.) Columbia university.
Bibliography: p. 104-107.

1. Teachers, Training of—U. S. 2. Negroes—Education. I. Title. II. Title: Teacher-training programs for Negroes.

Library of Congress LC2731.C55 1934 a 34-25345
——— Copy 2. LB5.C8 no. 605
Copyright A 72895 [a35t5] 370.7878

Teachers, Training of-"U. S.

M370
C71

Colson, Edna Meade, 1888-
An analysis of the specific references to Negroes in selected curricula for the education of teachers, by Edna Meade Colson ... New York, Teachers college, Columbia university, 1940.
x p., 1 l., 178 p. incl. tables. 23½cm. (Teachers college, Columbia university. Contributions to education, no. 822)
Issued also as thesis (PH. D.) Columbia university.
Bibliography: p. 163-178.

Education.
1. Negroes. 2. Teachers, Training of—U. S. I. Title.

41-3012

Library of Congress E185.6.C7 1940
——— Copy 2. LB5.C8 no. 822
[43r41m2] 375.825260973

Teachers College studies in education.

M378
N66n

Noble, Jeanne L
The Negro woman's college education. New York, Teachers College, Columbia University, 1956.
x, 163p. form, 39 tables. 22cm. (TC studies in education)
Bibliography: p. 145-150.

Teachers' salaries in black and white,...

M323
N21

National association for the advancement of colored people.
Teachers' salaries in black and white, a pamphlet for teachers and their friends, prepared by the National association for the advancement of colored people ... New York, N. Y. [1942]
15 p. illus. (ports.) 23cm.
"Reprinted February, 1942."

1. Teachers—U. S.—Salaries, pensions, etc. 2. Negroes—Education. I. Title.

Library of Congress LB2843.N4N35 43-8223
[3] 371.161

Teaching.

MB9
C79r

Coppin, Fanny Jackson, 1837-1913.
Reminiscences of school life, and hints on teaching, by Fanny Jackson Coppin. Introduction by William C. Bolivar. [Philadelphia, Pa., A.M.E. Book Concern, 1913]
191p. port (front.) 20½cm.
Introduction by William C. Bolivar.

Teaching.

M370
J71

Jones, Gilbert Haven, 1881-
Education in theory and practice, by Gilbert H. Jones ... Boston, R. G. Badger [1919]
396 p. 20½cm. (*Lettered on cover:* Library of educational methods)
"Reference reading" at end of chapters.
Bibliography: p. 389-392.

1. Education. 2. Teaching. I. Title.

19-11720

Library of Congress LB1025.J67
Copyright A 530083 [s24d2]

Teaching techniques for cerebral palsied children.

M371.91
P419

Perkins, Fannie Lee (LaGrone)
Teaching techniques for cerebral palsied children, by Fannie Lee L. Perkins. [1st ed.] New York, Vantage Press [1964, °1963]
117 p. 21 cm.
Bibliography: p. 58-60.

1. Cerebral palsied children—Education. I. Title.
2. Handicapped children-Education.

LC4580.P4 371.91 64-4181

Library of Congress [5]

Teage, Hilary.

M326.5
Ar5

[Armistead, Wilson] 1819?-1868.
Calumny refuted by facts from Liberia; with extracts from the inaugural address of the coloured President Roberts; an eloquent speech of Hilary Teage, a coloured senator; and extracts from a discourse by H. H. Garnett, a fugitive slave, on the past and present condition, and destiny of the coloured race. Presented to the Boston Anti-slavery bazaar, U. S., by the author of "A tribute for the negro". London, C. Gilpin; New York, W. Harned, Anti-slavery office; [etc., etc.] 1848.
46 p. 18cm.
1. Liberia. 2. Negroes — Colonization—Africa. I. Roberts, Joseph Jenkins, pres. of Liberia, 1809-1876. II. Teage, Hilary. III. Garnett, H. H. IV. Title.

[33b1] 24-3758

Library of Congress DT632.A5

M813.5
T22c
Teague, Robert L , 1929?-
The climate of Candor; a novel of the 1970's. New York, Pageant Press, 1961.
198p. 21cm.
Brief biographical sketch of author on back of book jacket.
I. Title.

S. Africa
M39
Ab8
Tell freedom.
Abrahams, Peter, 1919-
Tell freedom. London, Faber and Faber [1954]
311 p. 21 cm.
Autobiographical.
I. Title.
Full name: Peter Henry Abrahams.
PR6001.B62T4 1954a 54-31865 ‡
Library of Congress [4]

Haiti
M944
G93t
Témoignages.
Guéry, Fortuna (Augustin)
Témoignages. Port-au-Prince, H. Deschamps, 1950.
108p. 20cm.

M150
T22
Teague, Wilbur A
Decline in American democracy. New York, Vantage Press [1963]
98p. 20½cm.
Portrait of author on book jacket.
1. Philosophy. I. Title.

S. Africa
M39
Ab8
amer. ed.
Tell freedom.
Abrahams, Peter, 1919-
Tell freedom; memories of Africa. [1st American ed.] New York, Knopf, 1954.
370 p. 22 cm.
I. Title.
Full name: Peter Henry Abrahams.
PR6001.B62T4 928.2 54-5266 ‡
Library of Congress [20]

Senegal
M966.3
T24p
Tempels, Placide, Father.
La philosophie bantoue. Traduit du néerlandais par A. Rubbens. [Paris] Éditions africaines, 1949]
125 p. illus. 25 cm. (Collection Présence africaine)
Introduction by Alioune Diop.
Bantu philosophy. I. Diop, Alioune - Introduction.
GN657.B2T414 572.968 50-63936
Library of Congress [4]

Brazil
M869.3
M18t
Teatro.
Machado de Assis, Joaquim Maria, 1839-1908.
... Teatro. Colyido por Mario de Alencar. Rio de Janeiro, Paris, Garneir, [n.d.]
369p. 1 l., 19cm.

M323.4
St71
Tell it like it is.
Stone, Chuck.
Tell it like it is. New York, Trident Press, 1967 [1968]
211 p. 22 cm.
1. Negroes—Civil rights—Addresses, essays, lectures. I. Title.
E185.61.S872 1968 301.451'96'073 68-15435
Library of Congress [68n5]

M614
R66d
Temperance.
Roman, Charles Victor, 1864-1934.
The dethronement of a king. Reprinted from the Journal of the National Medical Association, April-June, 1913.
12p. 19cm.

M338.9
G92s
Technical assistance.
International Conference on Science in the Advancement of New States, Rehovot, Israel, 1960.
Science and the new nations, proceedings. Edited by Ruth Gruber. New York, Basic Books [1961]
xv, 314 p. illus., ports. 24 cm.
Sponsored by the Weizmann Institute of Science.
1. Underdeveloped areas. 2. Technical assistance. 3. Science—Social aspects. I. Gruber, Ruth, 1911- ed. II. Title.
HC60.I 545 1960 338.9 61-11992
Library of Congress [15]

Zambia
M392
M11
Tell me, Josephine.
Maango, David
"Tell me, Josephine." [By David Maango, Barbara Hall and Kay Sifuniso] Edited by Barbara Hall. [Foreword by Kenneth D. Kaunda] New York, Simon and Schuster, 1964.
142p. 21cm.
Selections from the Tell me, Josephine column started in February, 1960, by the Central African mail, a weekly paper in Northern Rhodesia.
(Over)

M811.5
T24
Temple, George Hannibal
The epic of Columbus' bell and other poems. Reading, Pa., Press of the Reading Eagle, 1900.
80p. front. (port.) 18cm.
I. Title.

M06
J61
no. 12
Technical education - Southern states.
Southern industrial classes, Norfolk, Va.
... Report of the society of the Southern industrial classes, Norfolk, Virginia, to the trustees of the John F. Slater fund and the General education board ... [11th]-
19
Hampton, Va., 19
v. 23cm. (The Trustees of the John F. Slater fund. Occasional papers, no. 12)
Report year ends in February.
Short reports are included in the Proceedings of the John F. Slater fund, 1899-1913.
1. Negroes—Education. 2. Technical education—Southern states.
Library of Congress E185.5.J65 no. 12 7-37620
[38r19e1]

M810
H94te
Tell my horse.
Hurston, Zora Neale.
Tell my horse, by Zora Neale Hurston. Philadelphia, New York [etc.] J. B. Lippincott company [1938]
301 p. front., plates, ports. 22cm.
Illustrated lining-papers.
"Songs of worship to voodoo gods" (words and music): p. 279-301.
1. Jamaica—Soc. life & cust. 2. Haiti—Soc. life & cust. 3. Haiti—Pol. & govt.—1844- 4. Voodooism. 5. Negroes in Haiti. I. Title.
38-27984
Library of Congress F1886.H87
[44i2] 917.292

Northern Rhodesia
M968.94
K16
Temple, Merfyn F
Kaunda, Kenneth, 1924-
Black government; a discussion between Colin Morris and Kenneth Kaunda. Lusaka, Northern Rhodesia, United Society for Christian Literature, 1960.
116p. ports. 22cm.
Biographies included.

Sudan, French
M966.2
T22
Tedzkiret en-nisian fi akhbar molouk es-Soudan. Traduction française par O. Houdas. Paris, E. Leroux, 1901.
xiv, 415 p. 29 cm. (Publications de l'École des langues orientales vivantes. 4. sér., v. 20)
Added is a fragment on the history of Sokoto (p. [309]-321) by a certain Hadj Sa'îd.
On cover: Documents arabes relatifs à l'histoire du Soudan.
Contents - v. 1. Texte arabe. v. 2. Traduction, par Houdas.
1. Sudan—Hist. 2. Sokoto, Nigeria (Province)—Hist. 3. Houdas, Octave Victor, 1840-1916, ed. and tr. II. Title: Documents arabes relatifs à l'histoire du Soudan. (Series: Paris. École des langues orientales vivantes. Publications. 4. sér., v. 20)
PJ7819.S8T4 52-59060
Library of Congress [1]

Sierra Leone
M496
Su6ht
Temne language - Grammar.
Sumner, A T
A handbook of the Temne language, by the Rev. A. T. Sumner... Freetown, Sierra Leone West Africa, Government printing office, 1922.
xvi, 157p. 21½cm.

M811.5
C15t
Temporary reprieve.
Campbell, James E
Temporary reprieve; a collection of original poems, by James E. Campbell and Gordon H. Stills. With an interpretation by Bernard R. Byrd. Baltimore, Morgan State College, 1953.
46p. 21½cm.

M813.5
B19an4
Tejn, Michael, tr.
Baldwin, James
Mod en anden himmel [Another country] [Copenhagen] Steen Hasselbalchs Forlag, 1963.
447p. 22cm.
Portrait of author on book cover.
"Oversat fra engelskaf Michael Tejn"

Madagascar
M969
R11t
Témoignage malgache et colonialisme.
Rabemananjara, Jacques, 1913-
Témoignage malgache et colonialisme. Paris, Présence africaine [1956]
46 p. 19 cm. (Collection "Le Colonialisme," 2)
First ed. published in 1946 under title: Un Malgache vous parle.
1. Madagascar—Pol. & govt. I. Title.
JQ3453 1956.R3 57-30796 ‡
Library of Congress [8]

Africa
M39
P41t
Ten Africans.
Perham, Margery Freda, 1896- ed.
Ten Africans, edited by Margery Perham. London, Faber and Faber limited [1936]
356 p. front., plates, ports., fold. map. 23cm.
Contents.—Introduction, by Margery Perham.—The story of Bwembya of the Bemba tribe, northern Rhodesia, recorded by Audrey I. Richards.—The story of Udo Akpabio of the Anang tribe, southern Nigeria, recorded by W. Groves.—The story of Ndansi Kumalo of the Matabele tribe, southern Rhodesia, recorded by J. W. Posselt and Margery Perham.—The story of Rashid Bin Hassani of the Bisa tribe, northern Rhodesia, recorded by W. F. Baldock.—The story of Nosente, the mother of compassion of the Xhosa tribe, South Africa, recorded by
(Continued on next card)
36-24346
[8]

Africa Ten Africans.

MB9 P41t
Perham, Margery Freda, 1896- *ed.* **Ten Africans ... ₍1936₎ (Card 2)**

CONTENTS—Continued.

Monica Hunter.—The story of Amini Bin Saidi of the Yao tribe of Nyasaland, recorded by D. W. Malcolm.—The story of Parmenas Mockerie of the Kikuyu tribe, Kenya, written by himself.—The story of Martin Kayamba Mdumi, M. B. E., of the Bondei tribe, written by himself.—The story of Gilbert Coka, of the Zulu tribe of Natal, South Africa, written by himself.—The story of Kofoworola Aina Moore, of the Yoruba tribe, Nigeria, written by herself.

1. Africa—Biog. 2. Bantus. I. Title.

36-24346

Library of Congress DT18.P38 1936

Copyright A ad int. 21866 ₍3₎ 920.06

"Ten con ten."

Puerto Rico
M864 C23t
Carrion, Madura Tomás
"Ten con ten." Impresiones de un Viaje á la América de Norte. Puerto Rico, "La Republica Española," 1906.

4-200p. 17cm.
Presentation copy inscribed by author, 1906.

M01 T25
Tennessee. *Dept. of education. Division of school libraries.*
The Negro; a selected list for school libraries of books by or about the Negro in Africa and America, compiled by the Division of school libraries. Revised and reprinted through courtesy of the Julius Rosenwald fund. Nashville, Tenn., State department of education, 1941.

48 p. illus. 23cm.

Classified and annotated, with author and title index.
"A list of bibliographies consulted": p. 10-11.

1. ~~Negroes~~—Bibliography I. Title.

41-9406

Library of Congress Z1361.N39T3 1941
₍44f2₎ 016.325260973

Tennessee.

M366.1 F87t5
Freemasons. Tennessee. Grand Lodge.
Proceedings. 1st- 1870-
Nashville, 18 -

v. 22½cm. annual
See holdings card for proceedings in library.

Tennessee.

M286 F95
Fuller, Thomas Oscar, 1867-
History of the Negro Baptists of Tennessee, by T. O. Fuller ... ₍Memphis, Tenn., Haskins print, °1936₎

346 p. front., plates, ports. 18½cm.

1. Baptists, Negro—Tennessee. 2. Negroes—Tennessee. I. Title: Negro Baptists of Tennessee.

36-16378

Library of Congress BX6444.T4F8
₍44c1₎ 286.1768

Tennessee.

MB9 F95t
Fuller, Thomas Oscar, 1867-
Twenty years in public life, 1890-1910, North Carolina-Tennessee, by Thomas O. Fuller. Nashville, Tenn., National Baptist publishing board, 1910.

279, ₍1₎ p. illus., ports. 20 cm.

1. Negroes—North Carolina. 2. North Carolina—Pol. & govt.—1865- 3. Negroes—Tennessee. I. Title.

E185.97.F9 10-18964 rev

Library of Congress ₍r47b1₎

Tennessee.

M610 B44
Joint health education committee, *Nashville.*
Rural Negro health; a report on a five-year experiment in health education in Tennessee, by Michael J. Bent, M. D., and Ellen F. Greene, M. A., for the Joint health education committee. Nashville, Tenn., Julius Rosenwald fund, 1937.

85 p. diagrs. 23cm.

"General references": p. 79-83.

1. Negroes—Tennessee. 2. Hygiene—Study and teaching. 3. Hygiene, Public—Tennessee. I. Bent, Michael James, 1885- II. Greene, Ellen F. III. Title.

38-21257

Library of Congress RA420.J73
₍41m2₎ 613.07

Tennessee.

M973.8 T21ne
Taylor, Alrutheus Ambush.
The Negro in Tennessee, 1865-1880, by Alrutheus Ambush Taylor ... Washington, D. C., The Associated publishers, inc., 1941.

5 p. l., 306 p. 23½cm.
Bibliography: p. 267-273. Bibliographical notes: p. 275-300.

1. Negroes—Tennessee. I. Title.

41-5247

Library of Congress E185.93.T3T3
₍43h1₎ 325.2609768

Tennessee Centennial, p. 31-44.

M973 H13s
Haley, James T. comp.
Sparkling gems of race knowledge worth reading. A compendium of valuable information and wise suggestions that will inspire noble effort at the hands of every race-loving man, woman, and child... Comp. and arranged by James T. Haley...Nashville, Tenn., J. T. Haley & company, 1897.

200p. incl. front., illus., ports. 20½cm.

Tennessee Colored Agricultural and Mechanical Association.

M815.4 D74ad2
Douglass, Frederick, 1817-1895.
Address delivered by Hon. Frederick Douglass, at the third annual fair of the Tennessee colored agricultural and mechanical association on Thursday, September 18, 1873 at Nashville, Tenn. Washington, New national era, 1873.

19p. 22cm.

M976.8 D29r
Tennessee Valley Authority.
Davis, John P
Report of the chief social and economic problems of Negroes in the TVA: A survey prepared for the National Association for the Advancement of Colored People. New York, 1935.

41p. tables. 28cm.
Mimeographed.

Tensions and destiny.

M248 E15
Ellison, John Malcus, 1892-
Tensions and destiny. Richmond, John Knox Press, 1953.

185 p. 21 cm.

1. Christian life. I. Title.

BV4501.E5875 248 53-8461 ‡

Library of Congress ₍8₎

M616 W93e5
Teropterin.
Wright, Louis Tompkins, 1891-1952.
An evaluation of teropterin therapy in metastatic neoplasms, by Solomon Weintraub, Isidore Arons, Louis T. Wright, and others. Reprinted from New York State journal of medicine, 51:2159-2162, September 15, 1951.

M616 W93u
Teropterin.
Wright, Louis Tompkins, 1891-1952.
Use of teropterin in neoplastic disease; a preliminary clinical report, by S. P. Lehv, L. T. Wright, S. Weintraub, and I. Arons. Reprinted from the Transaction of the New York Academy of Sciences, 10:75-81, January 1948.

75-81p. tables, graphs, illus. 25cm.
Inscribed: To Arthur from Louis.

Terre d'Enchantements.

Haiti M843.91 L135t
Lagazy, Madeleine, 1911-
Terre d'enchantements, roman. Port-au-Prince, Haiti, Imprimerie de l'etat ₍1951₎

285 p. illus. 24 cm.

I. Title.

PQ2623.A27285T4 52-27962 ‡

Library of Congress ₍1₎

Terras do sem fim.

Brazil M869.3 Am1t
Amado, Jorge, 1912-
Terras do sem fim. 8 ed. Capa de Clóvis Graciano. São Paulo, Livraria Martins Editôra, 1957.

296p. 22cm. (Obras v. 8)

La terre inquiète.

Martinique M841.91 G49t
Glissant, Édouard, 1928-
La terre inquiète. ₍poems₎ Frontispice de Wifredo Lam. Paris, Éditions du Drago, 1955.

67p. 20cm.

Haiti M841 D73t
La terre qui s'ouvre.
Dorismond, Jacques.
La terre qui s'ouvre. Préface de Antonio Vieux; dessin par l'auteur. Port-au-Prince, L'Etat, 1950.

39p. port. 21cm. (Collection Haitiana)

MB9 T27
Terrell, Mary (Church) 1863- 1954
A colored woman in a white world, by Mary Church Terrell. Washington, D. C., Ransdell inc. ₍°1940₎

7 p. l., 436, ₍1₎ p. front. (port.) 23½cm.
Autobiography.

I. Title.

₍Full name: Mary Eliza (Church) Terrell₎

40-34942

Library of Congress E185.97.T47
₍a44h2₎ 920.7

M814.5 W89
Terrell, Mary (Church), 1863- 1954
Solving the colored woman's problem.

(In: World Fellowship of Faiths. International Congress. 1st, Chicago and New York, 1933-1934. Addresses...New York, Liveright Publishing Corporation ₍1935₎ cm. p. 304-316.)

Terrell, Mary (Church) 1863-1954 - Juvenile literature.
Quarles, Benjamin, jt. auth.

MB Qu26
~~Sterling, Dorothy, 1913-~~
Lift every voice; the lives of Booker T. Washington, W. E. B. Du Bois, Mary Church Terrell, and James Weldon Johnson ₍by₎ Dorothy Sterling and Benjamin Quarles. Illustrated by Ernest Crichlow. ₍1st ed.₎ Garden City, N. Y., Doubleday, 1965.

116 p. illus., ports. 22 cm. (Zenith books)

1. Washington, Booker Taliaferro, 1859-1915—Juvenile literature. 2. Du Bois, William Edward Burghardt, 1868-1963—Juvenile literature. 3. Terrell, Mary (Church) 1863-1954—Juvenile literature. 4. Johnson, James Weldon, 1871-1938—Juvenile literature. I. Quarles, Benjamin, joint author. II. Title.

E185.96.S77 920.073 65-17237

Library of Congress ₍5₎

Terrell, Mary Church, 1863-1954.
MB9 T27s Shepperd, Gladys Byram
Mary Church Terrell respectable person. Baltimore, Human Relations Press, 1959.

125p. port. 23½cm.

Guadeloupe. La terreur noire a la Guadeloupe.
M972.97 B341 Bazile, Corneille
...La terreur noire a la Guadeloupe. Pointe-a-Pitre, Imprimerie Information ₍1925₎

144p. port. 20½cm.

Terrisse, André, joint author.
Coast
M448 D125 Dadié, Bernard B
Les belles histoires de Kacou Ananzè l'araignée ₍par₎ Bernard Dadié ₍et₎ André Terrisse. Imagé par Alain Grée. Livre de lecture courante. Cours élémentaire des écoles africaines. Paris, F. Nathan ₍1963?₎

191 p. col. illus. 22 cm.

"Une partie importante des textes ... adaptée d'après un volume paru aux éditions Présence africaine sous le titre 'Le pagne noir' par Bernard Dadié."

1. French language—Text-books for foreigners—African. I. Terrisse, André, joint author. II. Title.

PC2129.A5D3 65-58061

Library of Congress ₍1₎

M343.3 H23t2 Terror in Tennessee.
Harrington, Oliver W
Terror in Tennessee. New York, National Association for the Advancement of Colored People. Legal Defense and Education Fund, 1946.

10p. illus. 21cm.

M343.3 H23t Terror in Tennessee.
Harrington, Oliver W
Terror in Tennessee; The truth about the Columbia outrages. New York, Committee of 100, ₍1946?₎

10p. illus. 21cm.
Reprint of pamphlet issued by NAACP.

M343.3 H23t4 Terror in Tennessee.
Harrington, Oliver W.
Terror in Tennessee. The truth about the Columbia outrages. New York, Nat'l Comm. for Justice in Columbia, Tennessee. ₍1946?₎

8p. 25cm.

Congo Leopoldville Tervuren. Musée Royal de l'Afrique Centrale. Archives d'ethnographie, no. 4.
M967.5 Iy9 Iyandza-Lopoloko, Joseph, 1927-
Bobongó; danse renommée des Ekonda du Lac Léopold II, une institution parascolaire. Tervuren, Belgique, Musee Royal de l'Afrique Centrale, 1961.

169p. illus. map. 26½cm. (Tervuren. Musée Royal de l'Afrique Centrale. Archives d'ethnographie, no. 4)

1. Congo. 2. Congo - Native races. I. Title. II. Series.

Sudan
M896.1 T28 Tescaroli, Livio, comp.
Poesia Sudanese. ₍Bolonga₎ Editrice Nigrizia, 1961.

119p. illus. 21½cm. (Museum Combonianum, No.12)
Appendice musicale: p. 87-117.
White compiler.

1. Sudanese poetry. I. Title.

O tesouro do vale aprazivel; romance.
M813.5 Y46t Yerby, Frank, 1916-
O tesouro do vale aprazivel; romance. (The treasure of Pleasant Valley). Tradução de Bernice Xavier. Rio de Janeiro, Livraria José Olympio Editôra, 1959.

214p. 23½cm.

Le testament de M. de Chauvelin.
France M840 D89te Dumas, Alexandre, 1802-1870.
Le testament de M. de Chauvelin, par Alexandre Dumas. Le Havre, Chez les Mêri Tiero Doorman, 1850.

212p. 15cm.
At head of title: Les mille et un fantomes.

... Testament of youth.
M811.5 F45t Fields, Maurice C 1915-1938.
... Testament of youth. New York, Pegasus publishing company ₍°1940₎

32 p. 20cm.

Poems.
"First edition."

I. Title.

41-6400

Library of Congress PS3511.I 8T4 1940 ₍2₎ 811.5

Testing whether that nation.
M323.4 Am3t American Civil Liberties Union.
Testing whether that nation. 41st annual report, 1960-1961. New York, American Civil Liberties Union, 1961.

80p. 23cm.

Gold Coast
M966.7 T29a Tete-Ansá, Winfred, 1889-
Africa at work, by W. Tete-Ansá ₍n.p., n.p., c1930₎

95p. port. plates. 23cm.

1. Africa, West-Econ. condit. 2. Africa, West-Indus. 3. Gold Coast. I. Title.

Ghana
M896.3 T29s Tetteh-Lartey, A. C. V. B
The school days of Shango Salomon. Cambridge, University Press, 1965.

78p. illus. 18cm.

I. Title.

Dahomey
M966.8 T29 Tevoedjre, Albert, 1929-
L'Afrique révoltée. Préf. d'Alioune Diop. Paris, Présence africaine ₍1958₎

157 p. illus., ports. 20 cm. (Tribune de la jeunesse, 1)

Errata leaf inserted.
Portrait of author.

1. Nationalism—Africa. 2. France—Colonies—Africa. I. Title.

DT33.T4 59-30412

Library of Congress ₍8₎

Dahomey
M960 T29 Tevoedjre, Albert, 1929-
Contribution à une synthèse sur le problème de la formation des cadres africaine en vue de la croissance économique. Préface d'Alfred Savoy. Paris, Diloutremer, ₍1965₎

152p. 27cm.
Thesis (Ph.D.) Université de Fribourg.

1. Africa - Economic development.

Texas.
M324 B75n Brewer, John Mason, 1896-
Negro legislators of Texas and their descendants; a history of the Negro in Texas politics from reconstruction to disfranchisement, by J. Mason Brewer ... with an introduction by Herbert P. Gambrell ... Dallas, Tex., Mathis publishing co. ₍°1935₎

x, 134 p. ports. (1 fold.) map. 20cm.

1. Negroes—Texas. 2. Negroes—Politics and suffrage. 3. Texas—Pol. & govt.—1865- 4. Negroes—Biog. I. Title. II. Title: Negro in Texas politics.

35-17051

Library of Congress E185.93.T4B7
—— —— Copy 2.
Copyright A 86409 ₍36d3₎ 325.2609764

Texas.
M370. D29 Davis, William Riley, 1886-
The development and present status of Negro education in east Texas, by William R. Davis ... New York city, Teachers college, Columbia university, 1934.

viii, 150 p. illus. (maps) diagrs. 23½cm. (Teachers college, Columbia university. Contributions to education, no. 626)

Issued also as thesis (PH. D.) Columbia university.
Bibliography: p. 139-150.

1. Negroes—Education. 2. Negroes—Texas. I. Title: Negro education in east Texas.

35-8311

Library of Congress LC2802.T4D3 1934 a
—— —— Copy 2. LB5.C8 no. 626
Copyright A 77765 ₍12₎ 371.97409764

Texas
M301 D853wh Dubois, William Edward Burghardt, 1868-
What the Negro has done for the United States and Texas. Washington, U. S. Govt. print. off., 1936.

folder (10 p.) 20½cm.

Texas.
M813.5 G759 Graham, Katheryn Campbell.
Under the cottonwood; a saga of Negro life in which the history, traditions and folklore of the Negro of the last century are vividly portrayed. By Katheryn Campbell Graham. New York, W. Malliet and company, 1941.

262 p. 23½cm.

"First edition."

1. Negroes—Texas. I. Title.

42-22316 Revised

Library of Congress E185.93.T4G7 ₍r43d3₎ 325.2609764

M976.4 H14p Texas.
Hall, Charles Edward, 1868-1952
Progross of the Negro in Texas. Washington, D. C., Dept. of Commerce, Bureau of the Census.

7p. tables cm.

M89 H81h

Texas.
Hamilton, Jeff.
"My master," the inside story of Sam Houston and his times, by his former slave Jeff Hamilton as told to Lenoir Hunt, with a foreword by Franklin Williams, Dallas Texas., Manfred, Van Nort & Co., c1940.

141p. illus. 23cm.

M378Te J63

Texas.
Johnson, Ozie Harold.
Price of freedom. ₍Houston? Tex.₎ ©1954.

117 p. 24 cm.

1. Texas Southern University. School of Law. 2. Negroes—Texas. 3. Discrimination in education. 4. Law—Study and teaching—Texas. I. Title.

371.974 54-31912 ‡

Library of Congress ₍1₎

M606 T36

Texas.
Thomas, Jesse O 1883–
Negro participation in the Texas centennial exposition, by Jesse O. Thomas. Boston, The Christopher publishing house ₍©1938₎

154 p. front. (port. group) plates. 20cm.

1. Negroes—Texas. 2. Dallas. Texas centennial central exposition, 1936. I. Title.

38-30208

Library of Congress E185.93.T4T5

₍42d1₎ 325.260973

M976.4 Ya1n

Texas.
Yancy, J W
The Negro blue - book of Washington county, Texas, by J. W. Yancy... Brenham, Texas, Brenham banner press, 1936
viii, 138p. illus. 23cm.

M976.4 W67

Texas - Cattle.
Williams, Jerome Aredell
The tin box; a story of Texas cattle and oil. New York, Vantage Press, 1958.

275p. 21cm.

M287.8 K19h

Texas-Churches.

Kealing, Hightower T
History of African Methodism in Texas, by H. T. Kealing. Waco. Texas, C. F. Blanks, 1885.
288p. plates. 19½cm.

M304 P19 v.3,no.8

Texas-Education.

Conference on education for Negroes in Texas.
... Proceedings of the 1st– annual Conference on education for Negroes in Texas ... ₍Prairie View, Tex., 1930–

v. 23 cm.

1930-31 issued as a Prairie View standard, Prairie View state college, Prairie View, Tex. (Texas, State normal and industrial college, Prairie View)
1932– issued as Bulletin, Prairie View state normal and industrial college. v. 24, no. 1; v. 25, no. 1; v. 26, no. 1

(Continued on next card)
E 30—404 (rev '35)

₍40r35f2₎

West Indies M823.91 F38p

Texas - Fiction.
Ferguson, Ira Lunan
Ocee McRae, Texas; a novel of passion, petroleum and politics in the Pecos River Valley. New York, Exposition Press ₍1962₎

182p. 22cm.

M976.4 W67

Texas - Oil.
Williams, Jerome Aredell
The tin box; a story of Texas cattle and oil. New York, Vantage Press, 1958.

275p. 21cm.

M324 B75n

Texas - Politics and government - 1865–
Brewer, John Mason, 1896–
Negro legislators of Texas and their descendants; a history of the Negro in Texas politics from reconstruction to disfranchisement, by J. Mason Brewer ... with an introduction by Herbert P. Gambrell ... Dallas, Tex., Mathis publishing co. ₍©1935₎

x, 134 p. ports. (1 fold.) map. 20cm.

1. Negroes—Texas. 2. Negroes—Politics and suffrage. 3. Texas—Pol. & govt.—1865– 4. Negroes—Biog. I. Title. II. Title: Negro in Texas politics.

35-17051

Library of Congress E185.93.T4B7

——— Copy 2.

Copyright A 86409 ₍36d3₎ 323.2609764

M89 C91h

Texas - Politics and government - 1865-
Hare, *Mrs.* Maud (Cuney) 1874–1936.
Norris Wright Cuney; a tribune of the black people, by his daughter, Maud Cuney Hare; with an introduction by James S. Clarkson ... New York, The Crisis publishing company, 1913.

xv p., 1 l., 230 p. pl., 2 port. (incl. front.) 19½cm.

Cuney was a prominent Republican politician in Texas.

1. Cuney, Norris Wright, 1846-1899. 2. Texas—Pol. & govt.—1865–

14—11337

Library of Congress E185.97.H27

Copyright A 371957 ₍a38b1₎

M378Tex W85

Texas. Agricultural and Mechanical College, Prairie View.
Woolfolk, George Ruble.
Prairie View, a study in public conscience, 1878-1946. ₍1st ed.₎ New York, Pageant Press ₍1962₎

404 p. illus. 21 cm.

1. Texas. Agricultural and Mechanical College, Prairie View.

LC2851.T424 378.764249 61-18006 ‡

Library of Congress ₍10₎

M378Te J63

Texas Southern University. School of Law.
Johnson, Ozie Harold.
Price of freedom. ₍Houston? Tex.₎ ©1954.

117 p. 24 cm.

1. Texas Southern University. School of Law. 2. Negroes—Texas. 3. Discrimination in education. 4. Law—Study and teaching—Texas. I. Title.

371.974 54-31912 ‡

Library of Congress ₍1₎

M323 N21

Text-books.
National Association for the Advancement of Colored People.
Anti-Negro propaganda in school textbooks, with a foreword by Walter White. New York, 1939.

18p. 21cm.
Partial list of books to be examined: p.17-18.

M371.32 S1.52

Textbooks - History.
Sloan, Irving
The Negro in modern American history textbooks: a study of the Negro in selected junior and senior high history textbooks as of September, 1966. ₍Chicago₎ American Federation of Teachers ₍1966₎

47p. 20cm.
White author?

M370. C22

Textbooks-U.S.
Carpenter, Marie Elizabeth.
The treatment of the Negro in American history school textbooks; a comparison of changing textbook content, 1826 to 1939, with developing scholarship in the history of the Negro in the United States ₍by₎ Marie Elizabeth Carpenter. Published with the approval of Professor Erling M. Hunt, sponsor. ₍Menasha, Wis., George Banta publishing company, ©1941₎

4 p. l., 137 p. 23½cm.

Bibliography: p. ₍130₎-137. Bibliographical foot-notes.

1. Negroes. 2. U. S.—Hist.—Historiography. 3. Text-books—U. S. I. Title.

41—8011

Library of Congress E185.C3

₍41d2₎ 323.260973

U. S. M959.3 L837

Thailand, the war that is, the war that will be.
Lomax, Louis Emanuel, 1922–
Thailand; the war that is, the war that will be ₍by₎ Louis E. Lomax. New York, Random House ₍1967₎

xiii, 175 p. map. 22 cm.
Portrait of author on book jacket.

1. Guerrillas—Thailand. 2. Communism—Thailand. I. Title.

DS586.L6 959.3'04 67—25075

Library of Congress ₍68a5₎

Martinique M841.91 T32ch

Thaly, Daniel Desiré Alin, 1879-
Chansons de mer et d'outre mer. Paris, Editions de la Phalange, 1911.

108p. 19½cm.

1. Martinican poetry. I. Title.

Martinique M841.91 T32c

Thaly, Daniel Desiré Alin, 1879-
Chants de l'Atlantique suivis de sous le ciel des Antilles. Paris, La Muse Française. Garnier Editeur, 1928.

128p. port. 19½cm.

1. Martinican poetry. I. Title.

Martinique M841.91 T32cl

Thaly, Daniel Desiré Alin, 1879-
La clarté du Sud; poèmes. Toulouse, Société Proviciale d'Edition, 1905.

107p. 18½cm.
Inscribed presentation copy

1. Martinican poetry. I. Title.

Martinique M972.98 D87m

Thaly, Daniel Desiré Alin, 1879-
De flacon de rhum.

(In: Dufougere, William. Madinina ... Paris, Berger-Levrault, 1929. p. 221-222)

Martinique
M972.98 Thaly, Daniel Desiré Alin, 1879-
D87m D'Ile Lointaine.

(In: Dufourgere, William. Madinina ... Paris, Berger-Levrault, 1929. p. 219-220)

Martinique
M841.91 Thaly, Daniel Desiré Alin, 1879-
T32n Nostalgies françaises (1908-1913). Paris, Editions de là Phalange, 1913.

134p. 19cm.
"Hommage de l'auteur a Monsieur le Prince de Bauffremont. Daniel Thaly, Roseau 14 Mon 1916.

I. Title.

Martinique
M841.91 Thaly, Daniel Desiré Alin, 1879-
T32p Paysages inviolés.

(In: Le Beffroi, 74:17-22, Janvier 1908)

1. Martinican poetry. I. Title.

French Guiana
M841.08 Thaly, Daniel Desiré Alin, 1879-
D18 Damas, Leon G ed., 1912-
Poètes d'expression française ₍d'Afrique Noire, Madagascar, Réunion, Guadeloupe, Martinique, Indochine, Guyane₎ 1900-1945. Paris, Éditions du Seuil ₍1947₎

322 p. (Latitudes françaises, 1)
Collection "Pierres vives."

1. French poetry—20th cent. I. Title. (Series. Series: Collection "Pierres vives")

A 49-3183*

Illinois. Univ. Library for Library of Congress ₍1₎

Martinique Thaly, Daniel Desiré Alin, 1879-
M972.98 Thomarel, André
T36p Parfums et saveurs des Antilles. Préface de Daniel Thaly, illustré par Ardachès Baldjian. ₍Paris, Ch. Ebener, 1934₎
42p. plates. 32cm.

Thank God for a song.
M813.5 Cooper, William Arthur, 1895-
C79t Thank God for a song; a novel of Negro church life in the rural south. New York, Exposition Press, ₍1962₎

121p. 21cm.

I. Title.

Thanksgiving day addresses.
Grimke, Francis James, 1850-
M815.5 Excerpts from a thanksgiving sermon by Francis J.
G88 Grimke ... Delivered November 26, 1914, and Two let-
v.1, ters addressed to Hon. Woodrow Wilson ... ₍Washing-
no.13 ton, Printed by R. L. Pendleton, 1914₎
8 p. 22½ᶜᵐ.

1. U. S.—Race question. 2. Thanksgiving day addresses.

Library of Congress E185.61.G8754 18-4034
——— Copy 2.

Thanksgiving sermons.
M815.2 Jones, Absalom, 1746-1818.
J71t A Thanksgiving sermon, preached January 1, 1808, in St. Thomas's or the African Episcopal Church, Philadelphia: an account of the abolition of the African slave trade, on that day by the congress of the United States.. Philadelphia, Printed for the use of the congregation, Fry and Kammerer, printers, 1808.

22 ₍2₎p. 21½cm.

Nigeria
M966.9 Thanni, Ade.
T32o Our coronation visitors. Lagos, Public Relations Department, n.d.

32p. illus. 20½cm. (Crownbird Series No. 35 (Special)

1. Nigeria.

That big broozer.
M813.5 Graham, Benzell.
G761t That big broozer. Illustrated by Paul Galdone. New York, Morrow, 1959.
80 p. illus. 22 cm.

I. Title.

PZ10.3.G728Th 59-5126 ‡

Library of Congress ₍60f5₎

That which concerneth me.
M811.5 Baxter, Joseph Harvey Lowell.
B33t That which concerneth me; sonnets and other poems, by J. Harvey L. Baxter. Roanoke, Va., The Magic city press, 1934.
viii, 87 p. 20ᶜᵐ.

I. Title. 1. Poetry.

Library of Congress PS3503.A929T5 1934 34-35084
——— Copy 2.
Copyright A 75642 ₍2₎ 811.5

Theal, George McCall, 1837-1919.
S. Africa
M398 Bleek, Wilhelm Heinrich Immanuel, 1827-1875, *comp.*
B61b Specimens of Bushman folklore, collected by the late W. H. I. Bleek, PH. D., and L. C. Lloyd; ed. by the latter; with an introduction by George McCall Theal ... Translation into English; illustrations; and appendix. London, G. Allen & company, ltd., 1911.
xl, 468 p. plates (part col.) ports. (2 col., incl. front.) 22½ᶜᵐ.
"The original Bushman text ... is printed side by side with the English translation."

1. Folk-lore—Africa, South. 2. Bushmen. I. Lloyd, Lucy C., ed. II. Theal, George McCall, 1837-1919. III. Title: Bushmen folklore.

11—20041

Library of Congress GR360.B9B4 ₍48e1₎

Haiti
M843.91 Théard, Gaston.
T34c Contes Haitiens. Port-au-Prince, Editions Campagnie Lithographique d'Haiti, 1949.

114p. 17cm.

1. Haitian fiction. I. title

Haiti
M843.91 Theard, Gaston
T343 Le jacot de Madame Cicéron; contes et récits. Port-au-Prince, Haiti ₍Imp. Telhome₎ 1944.

102p. port. 18½cm.

1. Haitian fiction. I. Title.

M973.9 Theater.
F46 Lewis, Theophilus.
No.11 Fifty years of progress in the theatre. Pittsburgh, Pittsburgh Courier, 1950.

7p. illus. 24cm. (Fifty years of progress)

Theater.
M792 Mitchell, Loften.
M694 Black drama; the story of the American Negro in the theatre. ₍1st ed.₎ New York, Hawthorn Books ₍1967₎
248 p. illus., ports. 24 cm.

1. Negroes—in literature. 2. Theater—U. S. 3. Negroes—Moral and social conditions. I. Title.

PS338.N4M5 792'.0973 66-22313

Library of Congress ₍5₎

Theater -Drama.
M812.5 Hughes, Langston, 1902-
H87c Calvacade of the Negro theatre, by Langston Hughes and Arna Bontemps, for the American Negro Exposition, Chicago, Illinois, July 4th - September 4th. New York, Maxim Lieber, 1940.

12p. 28cm.
Typewritten.

Theater - Production and direction.
Kenya
M896.2 MacPherson, Margaret
M c4 Let's make a play. With the acted version of Kintu; a play by E. C. N. Kironde. Kampala, Eagle Press, 1960.

vii, 44p. 21½cm.
White author.

1. Theater - Production and direction.
2. Drama. I. Title. II. Kironde, E. C. N. Kintu.

Theater-U.S. - Hist.
M792 Fletcher, Tom, 1873-1954.
F63 100 years of the Negro in show business; the Tom Fletcher story. 1st ed. New York, Burdge ₍1954₎
337 p. illus. 23 cm.

1. Negro minstrels. 2. Theater—U. S.—Hist. I. Title.

ML3561.N4F5 927.8 55-1843 ‡

Library of Congress ₍2₎

Theater-Haiti.
Haiti
M972.94 Fouchard, Jean, 1912-
F82a Artistes et répertoire des scènes de Saint-Domingue. Port-au-Prince, Impr. de l'État, 1955.
271 p. 21 cm.
Includes bibliographical references.

1. Theater—Haiti. 2. Music—Haiti. I. Title.

PN2416.F58 56-58737

Library of Congress ₍2₎

Theater-Haiti.
Haiti
M972.94 Fouchard, Jean, 1912-
F82t Le théâtre a Saint-Domingue. Port-au-Prince, Impr. de l'État, 1955.
353 p. illus. 21 cm.

1. Theater—Haiti. I. Title.

PN2416.F6 56-28710 ‡

Library of Congress ₍2₎

Theatre - New York (City)

M974.7
C55

Mitchell, Loften
The Negro Theatre and the Harlem community.

Pp. 146-156.

In: Clarke, John Henrik, ed. Harlem, a community in transition, New York, Citadel Press, 1965.

Theater - U.S. - Yearbooks.

M812.5
B46

The Best plays. 1894/99- , 1958-1959.
New York [etc.] Dodd, Mead [etc.]
v. illus. 21 cm.
Title varies: 1947/48-1949/50, The Burns Mantle best plays and the year book of the drama in America.—1950/51-1951/52, The Best plays and the year book of the drama in America.—1952/53, The Burns Mantle yearbook. The Best plays.
Other slight variations in title.
Added t. p., 1953/54- The Burns Mantle yearbook.
Editors: 1894/99, G. P. Sherwood, J. Chapman.—1899/1900-1946/47, B. Mantle (with G. P. Sherwood, 1899/1900-1909/10)—1947/48-1951/52, J. Chapman.—1952/53- L. Kronenberger.
INDEXES:
1899/1909-1949/50. 1 v.
1. Drama—20th cent. 2. Theater—U. S.—Yearbooks. 3. Drama—Bibl. I. Mantle, Robert Burns, 1873-1948, ed. II. Chapman, John Arthur, 1900- ed. III. Sherwood, Garrison P., ed. IV. Kronenberger, Louis, 1904- ed.
PN6112.B45 812.5082 20—21432*
Library of Congress [62r56t44 15]

Le théâtre a Saint-Domingue.

Haiti
M972.94
F82t

Fouchard, Jean, 1912-
Le théâtre a Saint-Domingue. Port-au-Prince, Impr. de l'État, 1955.
353 p. illus. 21 cm.

1. Theater—Haiti. I. Title.
PN2416.F6 56-28710 ‡
Library of Congress [4]

Le théatre Négro-Africain et ses fonctions sociales.

Senegal
M792
T68t

Traoré, Bakary
Le théatre Négro-Africain et ses fonctions sociales. Paris, Présence Africaine, 1958.

159p. 22½cm.
Bibliographie: p. 151-153.

Their eyes were watching God.

M810.
H94th

Hurston, Zora Neale.
Their eyes were watching God; a novel, by Zora Neale Hurston. Philadelphia, London, J. B. Lippincott company [c1937]
286 p. 21cm.

I. Title.
37—18658
Library of Congress PZ3.H9457Th
[41g1]

Haiti
M841.
T34m

Thélemaque, Louis Edm.
Miscellanees. Poems, avec une préface de J. B. Cineas. Haiti [Imprimerie du Seminaire Adventiste, 1949

136p. 19cm.

1. Haitian poetry.

Africa
M266
St29t

Thema, Richard Victor Selope, 1886-1955 and Jones, J. D. Rheinallt.
Our changing life and thought in South Africa.

Pp. 36-64.

In: Stauffer, Milton Theobald, ed. Thinking with Africa; chapters by a group of nationals interpreting the Christian Movement.
(cont. on next card)

Africa
M266
St29t

Thema, Richard Victor Selope, 1886-1955 and Jones, J. D. Rheinallt. Our changing life... (card 2)

New York, Published for the Student Volunteer Movement for Foreign Missionary Education Movement of the United States and Canada, 1927.

South Africa
M896
M88

Themba, Can, 1923-
The Urchin

Pp. 274-283

In: Mphahlele, Ezekiel, ed. African writing today. Baltimore, Penguin Books, 1967.

Thémistocle-Épaminondas Labasterre.

Haiti
M843.91
M33t

Marcelin, Frédéric, 1848-1917.
... Thémistocle-Épaminondas Labasterre; petit récit haïtien. Paris, P. Ollendorff, 1901.
3 p. l., 323 p. 16cm.

I. Title.
25-30466 Revised
Library of Congress PQ3949.M3T5
[r44b2]

Martinique Théo le Paladin Martiniquais.

M843.91
Z69t

Zizine, Pierre
Théo le Paladin Martiniquais; récit. Paris, Les Editions du Scorpion c1959.

190p. 19cm. (Collection Alternance).

Theological seminaries.

M207
D22

Daniel, William Andrew, 1895-
The education of Negro ministers, by W. A. Daniel; based upon a survey of theological schools for Negroes in the United States made by Robert L. Kelly and W. A. Daniel. New York, George H. Doran company [c1925]
vii p., 2 l., 13-187 p. 19½cm.
"The Institute of social and religious research ... is responsible for this publication."

1. Theological seminaries. 2. Theology—Study and teaching. 3. Negroes—Education. I. Institute of social and religious research. II. Title. III. Title: Negro ministers, The education of.
25—15962
Library of Congress BV4080.D8
[39p2]

M207
D22n

Theological Seminaries.
Daniel, William Andrew, 1895-
Negro theological seminary survey, abstract.

(IN: Chicago. University of. Abstracts of theses submitted... August 1924-June 1925. Chicago, 1927. 23 cm. pp. 233-237)

Theology— Collected works—20th cent.

M208.1
G88

Grimké, Francis James, 1850-1937.
The works of Francis J. Grimké, edited by Carter G. Woodson ... Washington, D. C., The Associated publishers, inc. [1942]
4 v. 23½cm.
CONTENTS.—I. Addresses mainly personal and racial.—II. Special sermons.—III. Stray thoughts and meditations.—IV. Letters.

1. Presbyterian church — Collected works. 2. Theology — Collected works—20th cent. 3. U. S.—Race question. I. Woodson, Carter Godwin, 1875- ed.
42—18902
Library of Congress BX8915.G73
[43d2] 208.1

Theology-Study and teaching.

M207
D22

Daniel, William Andrew, 1895-
The education of Negro ministers, by W. A. Daniel; based upon a survey of theological schools for Negroes in the United States made by Robert L. Kelly and W. A. Daniel. New York, George H. Doran company [c1925]
vii p., 2 l., 13-187 p. 19½cm.
"The Institute of social and religious research ... is responsible for this publication."

1. Theological seminaries. 2. Theology—Study and teaching. 3. Negroes—Education. I. Institute of social and religious research. II. Title. III. Title: Negro ministers, The education of.
25—15962
Library of Congress BV4080.D8
[39p2]

Theology, Doctrinal.

M230.41
M48

Melanchthon, Philipp, 1497-1560.
The Loci communes of Philip Melanchthon, with a critical introduction by the translator, Charles Leander Hill ... and a special introduction by Dean E. E. Flack ... Boston, Meador publishing company [c1944]
274 p. 20½cm.
Bibliographical foot-notes. "Bibliographia Melanchthoniana": p. 268-274.

1. Theology, Doctrinal. 2. Lutheran church—Doctrinal and controversial works. I. Hill, Charles Leander, tr. II. Title.
45—1360
Library of Congress BR336.L62
[46g2] 230.41

Theology, Postoral.

M251
R56a

Robinson, James Herman.
Adventurous preaching. [1st ed.] Great Neck, N. Y., Channel Press [1956]
186 p. 21 cm. (The Lyman Beecher lectures at Yale, 1955)

1. Preaching. 2. Theology, Pastoral. I. Title.
BV4211.2.R6 251 56-13819 ‡
Library of Congress [7]

Les théoriciens au pouvoir.

Haiti
M972.4
D 38t

Delorme, Démesvar.
Les théoriciens au pouvoir. Causeries historiques. Par D. Delorme ... Paris, H. Plon, 1870.
3 p. l., 732 p., 1 l. 23cm.
CONTENTS.—Époque grecque: Périclès, Démosthènes, Solon.—Époque romaine: Cicéron.—Époque française: Avant 89, Mirabeau, Lamartine.

1. History—Addresses, essays, lectures. 2. Statesmen. I. Title. II. Title: Causeries historiques.
25-22817
Library of Congress D7.D4

The theory and practice of Creole grammar.

M447.9
T36t

Thomas, J J.
The theory and practice of Creole grammar. By J. J. Thomas ... Port-of-Spain, The Chronicle publishing office, 1869.
viii, 134 p., 1 l. 21cm.

1. Creole dialects. 2. Creole dialects—Trinidad. I. Title.
3—28762
Library of Congress PM7851.T5
[a39d1]

Trinidad
M440
T36t2

Theory and practice of Creole grammar.

Thomas, J J.
The theory and practice of Creole grammar. By J. J. Thomas ... Port-of-Spain, The Chronicle publishing office, 1869.
viii, 134 p., 1 l. 21cm.

Trinidad - Creole dialects
1. Creole dialects. Grammar 2. ~~Creole dialects—Trinidad~~ I. Title.
3—28762
Library of Congress PM7851.T5
[a39d1]

The theory of economic growth.

St. Lucia
M330
L58t

Lewis, William Arthur, 1915-
The theory of economic growth. London, Allen & Unwin [1955]
453 p. 23 cm.

1. Industry. I. Title.
HD21.L43 330.1 55-43952 ‡
Library of Congress [61b2]

Therapeutics.
M616
W93e
Wright, Louis Tompkins, 1891-1952
The effect of formo-cibazol alone and in combination with chloretracycline on the bacterial flora of the colon of man, by Milton Marmell, James C. DiLorenzo, Louis T. Wright, and William I. Metzger. Antibiotics & chemotherapy, 1953.

1129-1134p. illus. tables 26cm.
Reprinted from Antibiotics and chemotherapy, November 1953.

Therapeutics.
M616
W928f
Wright, Jane Cooke
Further observations on the use of triethylene melamine in neoplastic diseases, by Jane C. Wright, Aaron Prigot, Louis T. Wright and Isidore Aarons. Chicago, American Medical Association, 1952.

18p. illus. tables 26cm.
Reprinted with additions from the A.M.E. archives of internal medicine, March 1952.

Therapeutics.
M616
W928i
Wright, Jane Cooke
In vivo and in vitro effects on chemotherapeutic agents on human neoplastic diseases; A preliminary report on the comparison of the effects of chemotherapeutic agents on humna tumors in tissue culture and the effects of each such agent in the patient from whom the tissue for culture was taken, by Jane C. Wright, Jewel I. Plummer, Rosette Spoerri Coidan and Louis T. Wright. New York, Harlem Hospital bulletin, 1953.

58-63p. 23cm.
Reprinted from the Harlem Hospital bulletin, September 1953.

M616
W93t
Therapeutics.
Wright, Louis Tompkins, 1891-1952
The treatment of acute gonorrhea in male patients with an aureomycin-triple sulfonamide combination, by Louis T. Wright and William I. Metzger. St. Louis, American Journal of Syphilis, Gonorrhea, and Venereal Diseases, 1953.

7p. tables 26cm.
Reprinted from the American Journal of Syphilis, Gonorrhea, and Venereal Diseases, May 1953

Therapeutics.
M616
W93v
Wright, Louis Tompkins, 1891-1952
A vehicle for the tropical use of certain therapeutic agents, by Aaron Prigot, Louis T. Wright, and Eugene T. Quash, Reprinted from Antibiotics and chemotherapy, 1953.

418-420p. illus. 25cm.
Reprinted from the Antibiotics and chemotherapy, April 1953.

There is a song.
M811.5
J546t
Jewell, Aander
There is a song. New York, Pageant Press [1967]

31p. 21cm.

I. Title.

There is confusion.
M813.5
F27t
Fauset, Jessie Redmon.
There is confusion, by Jessie Redmon Fauset ... New York, Boni and Liveright, 1924.
297 p. 20cm.

1. Title.
Library of Congress PZ3.F276Th 24—7817
——— Copy 2.
Copyright A 777815 [35e1]

There is something within.
M815.5
M82t
Morrison, Elizabeth (Jenkins)
There is something within; a series of talks given before religious, educational and parents' groups, by E. J. Morrison, assisted by Mr. and Mrs. H. Holliday. Detroit, Harlo Press, 1964.

126p. 20½cm.
Picture of author on book jacket.

I. Title.

There was once a slave.
M813.5
G76t
Graham, Shirley.
... There was once a slave ... The heroic story of Frederick Douglass. New York, J. Messner, inc. [1947]
ix, 310 p. 22cm.
"Received the Julian Messner award for the best book combating intolerance in America."
Bibliography: p. 309-310.

1. Douglass, Frederick, 1817?-1895. I. Title.
[Full name: Lola Shirley (Graham) McCanns]
E449.D758 923.673 47—2086
Library of Congress [47u14]

These black bodies and this sunburnt face.
M811.5
R52
Rivers, Conrad Kent, 1933–
These black bodies and this sunburnt face. Cleveland, Free Lance Press, 1962.
28 p. 22 cm.
Poems.

I. Title.
PS3535.I 895B5 62–21042 ‡
Library of Congress [5]

These low grounds.
M813.5
T86t
Turpin, Waters Edward, 1910–
These low grounds, by Waters Edward Turpin. New York, London, Harper & brothers, 1937.
4 p. l., 344 p. 21cm.
"First edition."

I. Title. 37–19647
Library of Congress PZ3.T867Th
——— Copy 2.
Copyright A 106681 [5]

These my people.
Jamaica
M823.91
T37t
Thompson, Claude.
These my people, by Claude Thompson. Kingston, Jamaica, The Herald ltd., printers [194–?]
4 p. l., 78 p. 21½cm.

I. Title. A 45-830
New York. Public library for Library of Congress [2]

These rights they seek.
M323.4
C55
Clarke, Jacquelyne (Johnson)
These rights they seek; a comparison of goals and techniques of local civil rights organizations. Washington, Public Affairs Press [1962]
85 p. 24 cm.
Includes bibliography.

1. Negroes—Alabama. 2. Negroes—Civil rights. I. Title.
E185.93.A3C55 323.41 61–15690 ‡
Library of Congress [10]

Thesis-writing.
M378 Ho
H83m
Howard university, Washington, D. C.
The Graduate School.

A manual of research and thesis-writing for graduate students. Washington, D. C., Howard university, The graduate school, 1941.
80p. 21cm.

They came in chains.
M810
R24th
Redding, Jay Saunders, 1906–
They came in chains; Americans from Africa. [1st ed.]

320p. 22cm. (The Peoples of America series)
Bibliography: p. 304-308.

They crashed the color line!
MB
N21t
National urban league.
They crashed the color line! ...New York City, Department of industrial relations, National urban league [c1937]

31p. illus. 23cm. (On cover: The color line series, no. 5.)

They knew Lincoln.
MB9
L63was
Washington, John E.
They knew Lincoln, by John E. Washington, with an introduction by Carl Sandburg ... New York, E. P. Dutton & co., inc., 1942.
8 p. l., 11-244, [21] p. front., plates, ports., facsims. 22½cm.
"Personal narrative of a Negro boy and man who sought all that could be possibly known about Abraham Lincoln from Negroes having impressions on facts he considered worth record."—Introd.
"First edition."

1. Lincoln, Abraham, pres. U. S., 1809-1865. 2. Negroes—District of Columbia. I. Title.
42-8268
Library of Congress E457.15.W32
[30] 923.173

They loved him; a dialogue thesis written in diary form...
M286
B87
Bullock, Samuel Howard.
They loved him; a dialogue thesis written in diary form, setting forth the dramatic story of the Pleasant Hill Baptist Church. [Roxbury? Mass., 1951]
244 p. 21 cm.
Includes the author's thesis, Staley College of Spoken Word, "Radio preaching today": p. 148-190.

1. Boston. Pleasant Hill Baptist Church. I. Title.
BX6445.B6P55 286.1744 51-30703
Library of Congress [1]

They sang through the crisis.
M248
E15t
Ellison, John Malcus, 1889–
They sang through the crisis; dealing with life's most critical issues. Chicago, Judson Press [1961]
159 p. 22 cm.
Includes bibliography.
Portrait of author on book jacket.

1. Christian life. I. Title.
BV4501.2.E4 248.42 61–14615 ‡
Library of Congress [3]

... They seek a city.
M973
B64t
Bontemps, Arna Wendell, 1902–
... They seek a city. Garden City, New York, Doubleday, Doran and company, inc., 1945.
xvii p., 1 l., 266 p. 21½cm.
At head of title: Arna Bontemps and Jack Conroy.
"First edition."
"A selected list of references and sources": p. 253-258.

1. Negroes—Hist. 2. Negroes—Biog. 3. Migration, Internal—U. S. I. Conroy, Jack, 1899– joint author. II. Title.
45—35114
Library of Congress E185.6.B75
[47g²5] 325.260973

They showed the way.
MB
R65
Rollins, Charlemae Hill.
They showed the way; forty American Negro leaders. New York, Crowell [1964]
165 p. 21 cm.

1. Negroes—Biog. I. Title.
E185.96.R6 920.073 64—20692
Library of Congress [65k9]

They speak of dawns.
M811.5 LaGrone, Oliver
L13t They speak of dawns; a duo-poem; written for the Centennial year of the Emancipation Proclamation: 1863, in 1863. «Narrating: The Journeys of two modern contemporary travelers: the astronaut, the freedom rider» Brinkley Printers, 1963.

1 v. illus. 20½cm.

Things fall apart.
Nigeria
M896.3 Achebe, Chinua
Ac4 Things fall apart. London, Heinemann, 1958.

185p. 19cm.

I. Title.

Thirikari ya handu o handŭ Kenya.
Kenya
M967.62 La Fontaine, Sidney Hubert, 1887-
L18 Thirikari ya handu o handŭ Kenya; [Local government in Kenya] ihumo o na ũkũria wayo, rĩandĩkĩtwo nĩ S. H. La Fontaine magĩteithanagia wĩra wa rĩo na J. H. Mower. [Translated into Kikuyu by Mathayo Njeroge] Nairobi, Eagle Press, 1955.

63p. 21½cm.
Written in Kikuyu.

1. Local government - Kenya Colony and Protectorate. I. Title. II. Mower, J. H. III. Njerage, Mathayo, tr.

They who preach.
M251 Ellison, John Malcus, 1892-
E15t They who preach. Nashville, Broadman Press [1956]
180 p. 21 cm.

1. Preaching. I. Title.

BV4211.2.E4 251 56-13821 ‡
Library of Congress [5]

... Thinking with Africa.
M266 Stauffer, Milton Theobald, 1885- ed.
St29t ... Thinking with Africa; chapters by a group of nationals interpreting the Christian movement, assembled and edited by Milton Stauffer ... New York, Pub. for the Student volunteer movement for foreign missions by the Missionary education movement of the United States and Canada [°1927]
xviii p., 1 l., 184 p. 19½cm. (Christian voices around the world)

1. Missions—Africa. 2. Africa—Religion. 3. Africa—Civilization. I. Title.

28—8082
Library of Congress BV3500.S65 [40i1]

Thirkield, W.P. - Present weaknesses of the ministry.
M323 Negro Christian student conference. *Atlanta*, 1914.
N69 The new voice in race adjustments; addresses and reports presented at the Negro Christian student conference, Atlanta, Georgia, May 14-18, 1914. A. M. Trawick, editor ... Pub. by order of the executive committee of the conference. New York city, Student volunteer movement [1914]
1 p. l., [v]-vi p., 1 l., 230 p. 23½cm.
"Best books on the Negro in America and Africa": p. 221-224.

1. Negroes—Congresses. 2. U. S.—Race question. I. Trawick, Arcadius McSwain, 1869- ed. II. Title.

A 15-837
Springfield. Public library for Library of Congress E185.5.N88 [a35f1]

Senegal
M960 Thiam, Doudou.
T346 The foreign policy of African States: ideological bases, present realities, future prospects. Pref. by Roger Decottignies. [Translation with revisions by the author] New York, Praeger [1965]
xv, 134 p. 23 cm.
Bibliographical footnotes.

1. Africa—Politics—1960- 2. Pan-Africanism. I. Title.

DT31.T513 327.6 65-21845
Library of Congress [5]

The third door.
M9 Tarry, Ellen, 1906-
T17 The third door; the autobiography of an American Negro woman. New York, D. McKay Co. [1955]
304 p. 21 cm.

I. Title.

E185.97.T37A3 920.5 55—14466 ‡
Library of Congress [56p5]

Thirteen Americans.
MB9 Tobias, Channing H , 1882-
T55 [Autobiographies]

(In: Thirteen Americans: their spiritual autobiographies, ed. by Louis Finkelstein. New York, Institute of Religious and Social Studies; distributed by Harper [1953]. 21cm. pp.177-199)

Senegal
M966.3 Thiam, Doudou
T346 La portée de la citoyenneté française dans les territoires d'outremer. These pour le doctorat en droit ... Paris, Société d'Éditions Africaines, 1953.

180p. 25cm.

1. France - colonies

The third generation.
M813.5 Himes, Chester B 1909-
H57t The third generation. [1st ed.] Cleveland, World Pub. Co. [1954]
350 p. 21 cm.

I. Title.

PZ3.H57Th 53—13947 ‡
Library of Congress [54d3]

Thirty years a slave.
M326.99B Hughes, Louis, 1832-
H87 Thirty years a slave. From bondage to freedom. The institution of slavery as seen on the plantation and in the home of the planter. Autobiography of Louis Hughes. Milwaukee, South Side printing company, 1897.

210p. front. (port) plans (facsims) 21½cm.

Senegal
MB9 Thiam, Medoune Diarra
B219t Cheickh Ahmadou Bamba: fondateur du Mouridisme (1850-1927). [Conakry, Imprimerie Nationale, 1964]

32p. illus., ports. 27cm.
Portrait of author in book.

1. Bamba, Cheickh Ahmadou; 1850-1927. 2. Mouridisme.

Third ward.
M813.5 Lucas, Curtis
L96t Third ward, Newark. New York, Lion Books,
1952 Inc., 1952.

160p. 16cm. (Lion books 80)
Pocket book edition.

Thirty years of freedom.
M812.5 Tillman, Katherine D
T46t Thirty years of freedom; a drama in four acts, by Katherine D. Tillman. [n.p., n.p., n.d.]
32p. 17cm.

Madagascar
M969.1 Thierry, Solange
T34m Madagascar. [Madagascar, 196?]

189p. illus. 18cm.

1. Madagascar-History.

Third ward, Newark.
M813.5 Lucas, Curtis.
L96t ... Third ward, Newark. Chicago, New York, Ziff-Davis publishing company [1946]
3 p. l., 238 p. 21cm.

I. Title.
PZ3.L9614Th 46-8619
© 30Nov46; author, Newark, N. J.; A8896.

Library of Congress [4]

M323 Thirty years of lynching in the U.S.
N21 National association for the advancement of colored people.
Thirty years of lynching in the United States, 1889-1918. New York, The National association for the advancement of colored people, 1919.
105 p. incl. maps, tables, diagrs. 23cm.

1. Lynch law. I. Title.

20—13596
Library of Congress HV6457.N3 [37d1]

Things fall apart.
Nigeria
M896.3 Achebe, Chinua.
Ac4t Things fall apart. New York, McDowell, Obolensky
1959 [1959]
215 p. 22 cm.

I. Title.
Full name: Albert Chinua Achebe.

PZ4.A17Th 813.5 59-7114 rev ‡
Library of Congress [r59c2]

The third woman;
M896.2 Danquah, Joseph Boakye.
D23t The third woman; a play in five acts, by J. B. Danquah. London and Redhill, United society for Christian literature [1943]
151, [1] p. 18cm.
"First published 1943."

I. United society for Christian literature, London. II. Title.

A 45-1224
New York. Public library for Library of Congress PR6007.A516T5
[3]† 822.91

This America is also my country.
M910 Tomas, Rosai J 1926-
T59 This America is also my country. New York, Pageant Press [1965]

131p. 21cm.
Portrait of author on book jacket.

1. Voyages and travels. I. Title.

This bird must fly.
M323
R54b
Robertson, Julius Winfield.
This bird must fly, by Julius Winfield Robertson. Washington, D. C., Unity press and pamphlet service [°1944]
118 p. 22cm.
1. Negroes. I. Title.
Library of Congress E185.61.R67 45-14887
[2] 325.260973

This is Liberia.
M910
D29t
Davis, Stanley A
This is Liberia; a brief history of this land of contradictions, with biographies of its founders and builders. New York, William-Frederick Press, 1953.
151 p. 23 cm.
1. Liberia—Descr. & trav. I. Title.
DT626.D3 966.6 52-12928 ‡
Library of Congress [3]

Haiti
M842
T35
Thoby, Armand, 1841-1899.
Jacques Bonhomme d'Haiti, en sept tableaux. Port-au-Prince, Imprimerie Dme F. Smith, 1901.
xx, 148p. 21cm.
1. Haitian drama. I. Title.

M811.5
B815e
This generation.
Brown, Sterling Allen, 1901-
Eight poems.
Contents: Transfer. -Old Lem. -Conjured. Colloquy. -Bitter fruit of the tree. -Slim in hell. Break of day. Glory, glory.
(In: Anderson, George Kumler, ed. This generation; a selection of British and American literature ... New York, Scott, Foresman, 1939. 25½cm. p. 762-768).

This is my country too.
M301
W673
Williams, John Alfred, 1925-
This is my country too [by] John A. Williams. [New York] New American Library [1965]
xix, 169 p. 21 cm. (An NAL-World book)
1. U. S.—Race question. 2. U. S.—Desc. & trav.—1960- I. Title.
E185.61.W734 301.451 65-17842
Library of Congress [5]

Thoby, Perceval
M972.94
P19
V.2,no.8
Union Nationaliste
Dépossessions, "Le lati-fundia Américain" contre "La petite propriété d'Haiti." port-au-Prince, Imp. de "La Presse".
39p. 24cm.

M170
T34
This I believe: 2; The personal philosophies of one hundred thoughtful men and women in all walks of life - twenty of whom are immortals in the history of ideas, eighty of whom are our contemporaries of today. Written for Edward R. Murrow. Edited by Raymond Swing. New York, Simon and Schuster, 1954.
233p. 20cm.
Partial contents: Ralph J. Bunche. Hubert T. Delany. Walter White.
I. Bunche, Ralph J II. Delany, Hubert T III. White, Walter IV. Murrow, Edward R
1. Conduct of life.

South Africa
M896.3
Ab8t
This island now.
Abrahams, Peter
This island now. London, Faber & Faber [1966]
255p. 21cm.

Haiti
M843.91
T35b
Thoby-Marcelin, Philippe, 1904-
The beast of the Haitian hills, by Philippe Thoby-Marcelin and Pierre Marcelin, translated from the French, La bête du Museau, by Peter C. Rhodes. New York, Toronto, Rinehart & company, inc. [1946]
5 p. l., 3-210 p. 19½cm.
I. Marcelin, Pierre, 1908- joint author. II. Rhodes, Peter C., tr. III. Title. 1. Haitian fiction
[Full name: Émile Philippe Thoby-Marcelin]
PZ3.T35Be 843.91 46-8130
© 7Nov46; 2c 12Oct46; publisher, New York; A8804.
Library of Congress [5]

M170
B881
This I believe (Radio Program)
This I believe. Writers for Edward R. Murrow. London, Hamilton, 1952-1953.
2v. 21cm.
Statements originally prepared for presentation on the radio program, "This I believe."
Contents.- [1] The living philosophies of one hundred thoughtful men and women in all walks of life, edited by E. P. Morgan.-
(Continued on next card)

This morning, this evening, so soon.
M813.5
B19t
The Best American short stories ... and the Yearbook of the American short story ... 1915- Boston, Houghton Mifflin company [1916]-
v. 19½-21cm.
Title varies: 1915-41, The Best short stories. 1942- The Best American short stories.
Editors: 1915-41, E.J.O'Brien.-1942- Martha Foley. Imprint varies: 1915-25, Boston, Small, Maynard & company.-1926-32, New York, Dodd, Mead and company.-1933- Boston, Houghton Mifflin company.
White author.

Haiti
M843.91
T35c
Thoby-Marcelin, Philippe, 1904-
Canapé-Vert, by Philippe Thoby-Marcelin and Pierre Marcelin; translated by Edward Larocque Tinker. New York, Toronto, Farrar & Rinehart inc. [1944]
xxvii, 225 p. col. front. 21cm.
Illustrated lining-papers.
"Prize winning novel, second Latin American contest."
I. *Marcelin, Pierre, 1908- joint author. II. Tinker, Edward Larocque, 1881- tr. III. Title. 1. Haitian fiction
[Full name: Émile Philippe Thoby-Marcelin]
44-1710
Library of Congress PZ3.T35Can
[46t5]

M170
B881
This I believe (Radio Program) This I believe, 1952-1953. (Card 2)
(Contents. - Continued)
2. The personal philosophies of one hundred thoughtful men and women in all walks of life, twenty of whom are immortals in the history of ideas, eighty of whom are our contemporaries of today, edited by R. Swing.
1. Conduct of life. I. Title. II. Bunche, Ralph. [This I believe]

This race of mine.
M811.5
W154t
Walker, William
This race of mine, by William Walker... Chicago, Ill., Wm. Walker, c 1938.
29p. port. 21½cm.

Haiti
M843.91
T35ca
Thoby-Marcelin, Philippe, 1904-
... Canapé-vert ... New York, N. Y., Éditions de la Maison française, inc., °1944.
2 p. l., [7]-255 p. 19cm.
At head of title: Philippe Thoby-Marcelin et Pierre Marcelin.
"Prix du roman haïtien, deuxième concours latino-américain."
I. *Marcelin, Pierre, 1908- joint author. II. Title.
1. Haitian fiction [Full name: Émile Philippe Thoby-Marcelin]
44-8279
Library of Congress PQ3949.T45C3
[3] 843.91

This I believe.
M170
B881
This I believe (Radio Program)
This I believe. Writers for Edward R. Murrow. London, Hamilton, 1952-1953.
2v. 21cm.
Statements originally prepared for presentation on the radio program, "This I believe."
Contents.- [1] The living philosophies of one hundred thoughtful men and women in all walks of life, edited by E. P. Morgan.-
(Continued on next card)

This thing called religion.
M248
T75
Tross, Joseph Samuel Nathaniel.
This thing called religion, by J. S. Nathaniel Tross ... Charlotte, N. C., 1934.
xviii, 21-132 p., 1 l. 19cm.
"A brief bibliography": p. 129-132.
I. Title.
Library of Congress BR125.T76 34-33849
Copyright A 75083 [2] 248

Haiti
M843.91
T35p2
Thoby-Marcelin, Phillippe, 1904-
Marcelin, Pierre, 1908-
Le crayon de Dieu, roman [par] Pierre Marcelin [et] Philippe Thoby-Marcelin. Paris, La Table ronde [1952]
254 p. 19 cm.
Marcelin, Pierre, 1908- joint author. II. Title.
Full name: Léonce Perceval Pierre Marcelin.
A 52-10337
Illinois. Univ. Library for Library of Congress [1]

This I believe.
M170
B881
This I believe (Radio Program) This I believe, 1952-1953. (Card 2)
(Contents. - Continued)
2. The personal philosophies of one hundred thoughtful men and women in all walks of life, twenty of whom are immortals in the history of ideas, eighty of whom are our contemporaries of today, edited by R. Swing.
1. Conduct of life. I. Title. II. Bunche, Ralph. [This I believe]

This world is hard.
Nigeria
M896.3
OL3w
Olisah, Sunday Okenwa, 1936-
This world is hard. Onitsha, Nigeria, The Author [n.d.]
20p. 18cm.

Haiti
M700
T35
Thoby-Marcelin, Philippe, 1904-
Haiti, by Philippe Thoby-Marcelin. [English translation by Eva Thoby-Marcelin] Washington, D.C., Pan American Union, 1959.
59p. illus., 18cm. (Art in Latin America today)
Bibliography: p. 58-59.
1. Art - Haiti. I. Title.

Haiti
M843.91
T35pa
Thoby-Marcelin, Philippe, 1904-
Panorama de l'art haïtien. Port-au-Prince, Impr. de l'État, 1956.
75 p. 20 cm.

1. Art—Haiti—Hist. I. Title.

A 57-5914

Florida. Univ. Library for Library of Congress

Guadeloupe
M843.91 Thomarel, André.
T36
Nuits tropicales. Avant-propos de René Marna. Paris, Les Editions du Scorpion, 1960.
159p. 19cm. (Collection Alternance.)

1. Martinique - Fiction. I. Title. II. Maran, Rene, 1887-

S. Africa
M398
T36b
Thomas, E W
Bushman stories. Cape Town, Oxford University, 1950.
75p. 19cm.
Author white

1. Africa, South - Folktales. I. Title.

Haiti
M843.91 Thoby-Marcelin, Philippe, 1904-
T35p
The pencil of God, by Philippe Thoby-Marcelin and Pierre Marcelin; translated by Leonard Thomas, with an introd. by Edmund Wilson. Boston, Houghton Mifflin, 1951.
xvii, 204 p. 22 cm.

I. Marcelin, Pierre, 1908- joint author. II. Title.
1. Haitian fiction Full name: Émile Philippe Thoby-Marcelin.

PZ3.T35Pe 843.91 50-5883

Library of Congress

Martinique
M972.98 Thomarel, André
T36p
Parfums et saveurs des Antilles. Préface de Daniel Thaly, illustré par Ardachés Baldjian. [Paris, Ch. Ebener, 1934]
42p. plates. 32cm.
This edition is printed on Japanese paper.

1. Martinique. I. Baldjian, Ardaches, illus. II. Thaly, Daniel Desire Alin, 1879- III. Title.

M285
T36t
Thomas, Edgar Garfield, 1880-
The first African Baptist church of North America, by Rev. Edgar Garfield Thomas ... Savannah, Ga. [1925]
144 p. front., illus. 19cm.

1. Savannah. First African Baptist church. I. Title.

26-4814

Library of Congress BX6480.S45F53 [a45c1]

West Indies
M808.8
H839
Thoby-Marcelin, Philippe, 1904-
The submarine. Translated by Eva Thoby-Marcelin.
Pp. 195-201.
In: Howes, Barbara, ed. From the green Antilles. New York, Macmillan, 1966.

Martinique
M972.98
T36r
Thomarel, André
...Regrets et tendresses. Préface de Robert Chauvelot, 1936.
76p. 19cm.
At head of title: Sous le ciel des Antilles.

1. Martinique. I. Title.

M323
T59b
Thomas, Issac Lemuel,
The birth of a nation, a hyperbole versus a Negro's plea for fair play, by Issac L. Thomas. Philadelphia, Wm. H. Watson, 1916.
64p. 22½cm.

1. Race relations. I. Title.

M975
N31
Thom, William Taylor.
The Negroes of Litwalton, Virginia: A social study of the Oyster Negro. [Bulletin of the Labor Dept., no.37, 1901. pp. 1115-1170.
In: The Negro in the black belt... Washington, D.C., Dept. of Labor, [1897-1902]

1. Litwalton, Virginia. 2. Virginia.
I. Title. I.t - Negro in the black belt.

St. Kitts
M972.97
T36m
Thomas, Alexander, 1909-
Many a night's journey. New York, Comet Press Books, 1957.
143 p. 21 cm. (A Reflection book)
Autobiographical.

I. Title.

CT275.T536A3 818.5 57-8119 ‡

Library of Congress [4]

Trinidad
M398
T36
1890
Thomas, J J.
Froudacity; West Indian fables by James Anthony Froude, explained by J. J. Thomas... Philadelphia, Gebbie and company, 1890.
261p. 19½cm.

West Indies - Folk-lore
1. ~~[struck out]~~ I. Title.

M975 Thom, William Taylor.
N31
The Negroes of Sandy Spring, Maryland: A social study. Bulletin of the Labor Dept., no.32. 1901. pp. 43-102.
In: The Negro in the black belt... Washington, D.C., Dept. of Labor, [1897-1902]

1. Sandy Spring, Maryland. 2. Maryland.
I. Title. II. T.- Negro in the black belt.

M811.5
T36b
Thomas, Charles Cyrus, 1909-
A black lark caroling, by Charles Cyrus Thomas. Dallas, Tex., The Kaleidograph press [c1936]
xii p., 2 l., 17-73 p. 20cm.
Poems.

I. Title. 1. Poetry. 37-4734

Library of Congress PS3539.H565B6 1936
——— Copy 2.
Copyright A 104348 [2] 811.5

Trinidad
M398
T36
1889
Thomas, J J.
Froudacity; West Indian fables by James Anthony Froude, explained by J. J. Thomas ... London, T. F. Unwin, 1889.
261 p. 12°.

West Indies - Folk-lore
1. ~~[struck out]~~ I. Title.

Library of Congress 1-11139

M975
N31
Thom, William Taylor.
The Negroes of Sandy Spring Maryland: A social tudy. Bulletin of the Labor Dept., no. 32. 1901 pp. 43-102.
In: The Negro in the black belt... Washington, D.C., Dept. of Labor, [1897-1902]

M811.5
T36s
Thomas, Charles Cyrus, 1909-
Sweet land of liberty, by Charles Cyrus Thomas ... Dallas, Texas, The Kaleidograph press [n.d.]
8p. 21½cm.

1. Poetry. I. Title.

Trinidad
M440
T36t
Thomas, J J.
The theory and practice of Creole grammar. By J. J. Thomas ... Port-of-Spain, The Chronicle publishing office, 1869.
viii, 134 p., 1 l. 21cm.
"Errata" at end of book.

1. Creole dialects. 2. ~~Creole dialects—Trinidad.~~ Trinidad - Creole dialects Grammar I. Title.

Library of Congress PM7851.T5 3-28762 [a30d1]

Martinique
M972.98
T36c
Thomarel, André
Contes & paysages de la Martinique. [Wood-cuts by P. A. Bailly.] Fort-de-France, Imprimerie Antillaise, 1930.
160p. illus. 24cm.

1. Martinique--Description and travel.
2. Martinique--Fiction. I. Bailly, P.A., illus.

M811.5
T36y
Thomas, Charles Cyrus, 1909-
Young bough blossoming. Hollywood, Calif. 1954.
33p. 24cm.
Inscribed by author.

1. title

Trinidad
M440
T36t2
Thomas, J J.
The theory and practice of Creole grammar. By J. J. Thomas ... Port-of-Spain, The Chronicle publishing office, 1869.
viii, 134 p., 1 l. 21cm.
Much later reprint.
Introduction included, 188 .

Trinidad - Creole dialects
1. Creole dialects. 2. ~~[struck out]~~ Grammar I. Title.

Library of Congress PM7851.T5 3-28762 [a30d1]

M306
N21p

Thomas, Jesse O.
The effect of changing economic conditions upon the living standards of Negroes. In: National Conference of Social Work. Pp. 455-466, 1928.

MB9
T36

Thomas, Jesse O 1885–
My story in black and white; the autobiography of Jesse O. Thomas. Foreword by Whitney M. Young, Jr. [1st ed.] New York, Exposition Press [1967]
300 p. 21 cm. (An Exposition-banner book)

I. Title.

E185.97.T49A3 973.9'0924 (B) 67-24271

Library of Congress [5]

M606
T36

Thomas, Jesse O 1885–
Negro participation in the Texas centennial exposition, by Jesse O. Thomas. Boston, The Christopher publishing house [©1938]
154 p. front. (port. group) plates. 20cm.

1. ~~Negroes~~—Texas. 2. Dallas. Texas centennial central exposition, 1936. I. Title.

Library of Congress E185.93.T4T5 38-30208
[42d1] 325.260973

M306
N21p

Thomas, Julius A
The economic situation of national minorities.

pp. 88-95
In: National Conference of Social Work. Proceedings, 1947.

MB9
T366

Thomas, Piri, 1928–
Down these mean streets. [1st ed.] New York, Knopf, 1967.
xiii, 333 p. 22 cm.
Autobiographical.
Portrait of author on book jacket.

1. Puerto Ricans in New York (City)—Personal narratives. I. Title. 2. Harlem, New York (City)

F128.9.P8T5 301.451'67'97471 66-19402

Library of Congress [5]

Thomas, Ruby L jt auth.

MB
C42

Cherry, Gwendolyn S
Portraits in color; the lives of colorful Negro women, by Gwendolyn Cherry, Ruby Thomas, and Pauline Willis. [1st ed.] New York, Pageant Press [1962]

224p. illus. 21cm.

Liberia
M966.6
T36

Thomas, W H
History of Liberia (revised and illustrated) Brewerville, Liberia, Lott Carey Mission press [c1935]

[iv] 61 p. plates. 20½ cm.

1. Liberia.

M813.5
T361

Thomas, Will, 1905–
Love knows no barriers (God is for white folks). Rev. ed. New York, New American Library, 1950.

207p. 18cm. (Signet books)
At head of cover title: Original title: God is for white folks.
Pocket book edition.

I. Title. II. God is for white folks.

M813.5
T36s

Thomas, Will, 1905–
The seeking. New York, A. A. Wyn [1953]
290 p. 22 cm.
Autobiographical.

1. ~~Negroes~~. I. Title.

E185.97.T52A3 52-6928 ‡

Library of Congress *301.451 325.2609743
[53b10]

M973
T36

Thomas, William Hannibal, 1843–
The American Negro; what he was, what he is, and what he may become; a critical and practical discussion, by William Hannibal Thomas. New York, The Macmillan company; London, Macmillan & co., ltd., 1901.
xxvi p., 1 l., 440 p. 21cm.

1. ~~Negroes~~. I. Title.

1—29974

Library of Congress E185.T46
[41g1]

M304
P19
v.5
no. 3

Thomas, William Hannibal, 1843-
Walker, Charles Thomas, 1858-
Reply to William Hannibal Thomas. An address by Rev. C. T. Walker... lacks imprint.

31p. port. 23cm.

M370
T36s

Thomasson, Maurice Ethan, 1892–
A study of special kinds of education for rural Negroes [by] Maurice E. Thomasson ... Charlotte, N. C., 1936.
vi, 104 p., 1 l., 23cm.
Thesis (PH. D.)—Columbia university, 1936.
Vita.
"This study was concerned with agencies which offered instruction in fields other than those ordinarily included in the regular public school program ... Researches were conducted ... in the state of Virginia."—p. 2.
Bibliography: p. [103]–104.

1. ~~Negroes~~—Education. 2. ~~Negroes~~—Virginia. 3. Sociology, Rural. I. Title: Education for rural Negroes. II. Title: Rural Negroes.

Library of Congress LC2802.V8T5 1936 36—21306
Columbia Univ. Libr. [37c2] 371.97409755

M811.5
T371e

Thompson, Aaron Belford.
Echoes of spring. By Aaron Belford Thompson ... Rossmoyne, O., The author, 1901. 1904.
2 p. l., 76, [2] p. port. 17½cm.

I. Title. 1. Poetry.

1-22913

Library of Congress PS3539.H63E4 1901
Copyright A 9503 [a19b1]

M811.5
T371h

Thompson, Aaron Belford.
Harvest of thoughts. By Aaron Belford Thompson ... With an introduction by James Whitcomb Riley. Illustrated by G. T. Haywood. Indianapolis, Ind., The author, ©1907.
3 p. l., 110 p. plates, port., facsim. 18cm.

I. Title. 1. Poetry. 7-22263 Revised

Library of Congress PS3539.H63H3 1907
[r42b2] 811.5

M811.5
T371h

Thompson, Aaron Belford.
Morning songs. By Aaron Belford Thompson. Rossmoyne, O., The author, 1899.
82 p., 1 l. port. 18cm.

I. Title. 1. Poetry.

6-77 Revised

Library of Congress PS3539.H63M6 1899
Copyright 1899: 70950

M306
Am35

Thompson, Charles Henry, 1896-
The educational achievements of Negro children.

(In: American Academy of Political and Social Science, Philadelphia. The American Negro. Philadelphia, 1928. 24cm. p. 193-208.

M973.9
F46
No.20

Thompson, Charles Henry, 1896-
Fifty years of progress in higher education. Pittsburgh, Pittsburgh Courier, 1950.

7p. port. 24cm. (Fifty years of progress)

1. Education, Higher. I. Series.

M370
T37p

Thompson, Charles Henry, 1896-
Progress in the elimination of discrimination in white and Negro teacher's salaries, [editorial] Reprinted from the Journal of Negro education. 9:1-4, January 1940.

1. Teachers--Salaries, pensions, etc.

M378
T369s

Thompson, Charles Henry, 1896-
Separate but not equal; The Sweat case. Dallas, Texas State Conference NAACP, 1948.

105-112p. 25cm.
Reprint from Southwest review, Spring 1948.

1. Sweatt, Heman Marion. 2. Education - Southern states.

Thompson, Charles Henry, 1896-
Symposium: the new south and higher education; discussion, pp. 62-67.

M371.974
T87n

Tuskegee Institute.
The new south and higher education: what are the implications for higher education of the changing socio-economic conditions of the south? A symposium and ceremonies held in connection with the inauguration of Lutther Hilton Foster, fourth president of Tuskegee Institute [October 31 and November 1, 1953. Tuskegee, Ala.] Dept. of Records and Research, Tuskegee Institute, 1954

x, 145p. map. 24cm.

M811.5
T37g

Thompson, Clara Ann.
A garland of poems, by Clara Ann Thompson ... Boston, The Christopher publishing house [©1926]
96 p. 20½cm.

I. Title. 1. Poetry.

26-15258

Library of Congress PS3539.H645G3 1926
Copyright A 901617 [2]

M811.5
T37so
Thompson, Clara Ann
Songs from the wayside. By Clara Ann Thompson. Rossmoyne, Ohio, Published and sold by the author, 1908.
96p. 17½cm.
1. Poetry. I. Title

M811.5
T372w
Thompson, Clara Ann.
What means this beating of the sheep? Poem by Clara Ann Thompson. ⌈Rossmoyne, Ohio, Box 17, 1921⌉
⌈8⌉ p. 17cm.
1. Poetry

Jamaica
M823.91
Sa3a
Thompson, Claude
The house of many doors.
Pp. 203-210.
In: Salkey, Andrew, comp. Stories from the Caribbean. London, Elek Books, 1965.

Jamaica
M820
H38
Thompson, Claude
Spring planting.
Pp. 51-60.
In: Hendriks, A. L., ed. The independence anthology of Jamaican literature. Kingston, Arts Celebration Committee, Ministry of Development and Welfare, 1962.

Jamaica
M823.91
Sa3a
Thompson, Claude
The stragglers.
Pp. 200-202.
In: Salkey, Andrew, comp. Stories from the Caribbean. London, Elek Books, 1965.

Jamaica
M823.91
T37t
Thompson, Claude.
These my people, by Claude Thompson. Kingston, Jamaica, The Herald ltd., printers ⌈194-?⌉
4 p. l., 78 p. 21½cm.
I. Title. 1. Jamaican fiction
A 46-630
New York. Public library for Library of Congress ⌈2⌉

M323.1
T372
Thompson, Daniel Calbert.
The Negro leadership class. Englewood Cliffs, N. J., Prentice-Hall ⌈1963⌉
174 p. 21 cm. (A Spectrum book)
Includes bibliography.
1. Negroes—New Orleans—Case studies. 2. Community leadership—Case studies. 3. Negroes—Civil rights. I. Title.
4. Leadership.
F379.N5T45 301.155 63-8286 ‡
Library of Congress ⌈5⌉

M323
T37
Thompson, Edgar Tristram, 1900- *ed.*
Race relations and the race problem, a definition and an analysis. Edgar T. Thompson, editor; contributors: Robert E. Park, Edward B. Reuter, S. J. Holmes ⌈and others⌉ ... Durham, N. C., Duke university press, 1939.
xv, 338 p. incl. illus. (maps) tables, diagrs. 23½cm. (*Half-title:* Duke university publications)
"A Duke university centennial publication."
CONTENTS.—Introduction, by E. T. Thompson.—The nature of race relations, by R. E. Park.—Competition and the racial division of labor, by E. B. Reuter.—The trend of the racial balance of births and deaths, by S. J. Holmes.—Racial competition for the land, by R. B. Vance.—Patterns of race conflict, by G. B. Johnson.—The Negro as a contrast conception,
(Continued on next card)
39—21842
⌈451²3⌉

M323
T37
Thompson, Edgar Tristram, 1900- *ed.* Race relations and the race problem ... 1939. (Card 2)
CONTENTS—Continued.
by L. C. Copeland.—The plantation: the physical basis of traditional race relations, by E. T. Thompson.—A comparative study of American caste, by W. L. Warner and Allison Davis.—Race mixture and the mulatto, by E. V. Stonequist.—Race relations and social change, by C. S. Johnson.—A bibliography of race relations (p. ⌈305⌉-328)
4. Davis, Allison. A comparative study of American caste. p. 219-46.
5. Johnson, Charles S. Race relations and social change. p. 271-305
1. U. S.—Race question. 2. Negroes. 3. Race problems. I. Title.
39—21842
Library of Congress E184.A1T5
⌈451²3⌉ 325.260973

M910
T37
Thompson, Era Bell.
Africa, land of my fathers. ⌈1st ed.⌉ Garden City, N. Y., Doubleday, 1954.
281 p. illus. 22 cm.
1. Africa—Native races. 2. Africa—Descr. & trav. I. Title.
DT15.T48 916 54-10091 ‡
Library of Congress ⌈25⌉

M910
T37af
Thompson, Era Bell
Afrika land meiner väter. ⌈Africa, land of my fathers⌉ Freiburg, Verlagsanstalt Hermann Klemm, 1954.
250p. 20cm.
1. Africa. I. Title.

MB9
T37a
Thompson, Era Bell.
... American daughter. Chicago, The University of Chicago press ⌈1946⌉
x, 300, ⌈1⌉ p. 19½cm.
Autobiography.
I. Title.
A 46—10
Chicago. Univ. Library for Library of Congress E185.97.T58
⌈46z7⌉† 920.7

MB9
T37a
Lond. ed.
Thompson, Era Bell.
American daughter, by Era Bell Thompson. London, Victor Gollancz Ltd., 1946.
214p. 19cm.
I. Title.

M301
Eb74
Thompson, Era Bell
Some of my best friends are White
Pp. 153-158
In: Ebony. The white problem in America. Chicago, Johnson Pub. Co., 1966.

Thompson, George, 1804-1878.

M815.4
D74co
Douglass, Frederick, 1817-1895.
The Constitution of the United States: is it pro-slavery or anti-slavery? By Frederick Douglass. A speech delivered in Glasgow, March 26, 1860, in reply to an attack made upon his view by Mr. George Thompson. ⌈Halifax, T. and W. Birtwhistle, printers, 1860?⌉
16 p. 18½cm.
Caption title.
From the Glasgow daily mail.
1. U. S. Constitution. 2. Slavery in the U. S. 3. Thompson, George, 1804-1878.
A 17-1156
Title from Harvard Univ. Printed by L. C.

Thompson, George, 1804-1878, ed.

M326.99B
G76
Grandy, Moses, *b.* 1786?
Narrative of the life of Moses Grandy; late a slave in the United States of America ... 1st American from the last London ed. ... Boston, O. Johnson, 1844.
iv, ⌈5⌉-45 p., 1 l. 16½cm.
Introduction signed: George Thompson.
1. Slavery in the U. S.—North Carolina. I. Thompson, George, 1804-1878, ed.
⌈35b1⌉ 11-6095
Library of Congress E444.G75

Thompson, Henry C., p. 23-28.

M326.5
G19
Garrison, William Lloyd, 1805-1879.
Thoughts on African colonization: or, An impartial exhibition of the doctrines, principles and purposes of the American colonization society. Together with the resolutions, addresses and remonstrances of the free people of color... By Wm. Lloyd Garrison. Boston, Printed and pub. by Garrison and Knapp, 1832.
iv, 160, 76 p. 23cm.

M326.99B
T37
Thompson, John, 1812-
The life of John Thompson, a fugitive slave; containing his history of 25 years in bondage, and his providential escape. Written by himself. Worcester, John Thompson, 1856.
143p. 18½cm.
1. Thompson, John, 1812- 2. Slave narrative.

Thompson, John, 1812-

M326.99B
T37
Thompson, John, 1812-
The life of John Thompson, a fugitive slave; containing his history of 25 years in bondage, and his providential escape. Written by himself. Worcester, John Thompson, 1856.
143p. 18½cm.

M815.4
D73at
Thompson, John W.
An authentic history of the Douglass monument; biographical facts and incidents in the life of Frederick Douglass ... By J. W. Thompson ... Rochester, N. Y., Rochester herald press, 1903.
204 p., 1 l. 4 pl., 12 port. (incl. front.) 22cm.
1. Douglass, Frederick, 1817-1895. 2. Rochester, N. Y. Douglass monument.
3—15416
Library of Congress E449.D78
⌈44b1⌉

M811.5
T37s
Thompson, Joseph
Songs of Caroline, by Joseph Thompson. Chicago, Ill., Joseph Thompson 1936
30 p. front. 20x11cm.
Inscribed copy: Sincerely, Joseph Thompson.
1. Poetry. I. Title.

M331.88 T371 Thompson, Louise.
The IWO and the Negro people; A message and an appeal from Louise Thompson and Samuel Patterson. New York, International Workers Order, n.d.
[12]p. illus. ports. 15x11cm.
1. International Workers Order. 2. Trade unions. I. Patterson, Samuel C.

M331.88 T371 1943 Thompson, Louise.
The IWO and the Negro people; A message & an appeal from Louise Thompson and Samuel C. Patterson. New York, International Workers Order, 1943.
22p. illus. ports. 15x23cm.
1. International Workers Order. 2. Trade unions. I. Patterson, Samuel C.

M811.5 T375a Thompson, Minnie E. Coleman.
Amateur efforts of Minnie E. Coleman Thompson. n.p. n.d.
29p. 22cm.
Mimeographed.
1. Poetry.

M811.5 T37et Thompson, Priscilla Jane.
Ethiope lays. By Priscilla Jane Thompson. Rossmoyne, O., The authoress, 1900.
4 p. l., 95 p. port. 17½ cm.
I. Title.
0-2850 rev
Library of Congress PS3539.H68E7 1900 [r19b1]

M811.5 T37g Thompson, Priscilla Jane.
Gleanings of quiet hours. By Priscilla Jane Thompson ... Rossmoyne, O., The author, °1907.
3 p. l., 100 p. front. (port.) 17½ cm.
I. Title. 1. Poetry.
8—6633
Library of Congress PS3539.H68G5 1907 [a48b1]

Sierra Leone M966.4 T373 Thompson, T J
The jubilee and centenary volume of Fourah Bay College, Freetown, Sierra Leone, by T.J. Thompson. Sierra Leone, The Elsiemay Printing Works, 1930.
173, vi, i-xxiv p. portraits, illus. 24½cm.
1. Fourah Bay College, Freetown, Sierra Leone. 2. Africa, West - Education. 3. Sierra Leone-Education.

Africa M966.4 T37p Thompson, T J
The people's appeal for an intermediate court of appeal and an efficient system for the administration of justice in the colony and protectorate of Sierra Leone, by T.J. Thompson... London The Caxton press, 1911.
34p. 21cm. (The people's series)
1. Sierra Leone- Politics and government.

M794.1 T37c Thompson, Theophelus A , 1855-
Chess problems, by Theophelus A. Thompson. Dubuque, Iowa, [Printed by John J. Brownson] 1873.
63p. illus. 20cm.
1. Chess.

MB T38p Thoms, Adah B.
Pathfinders, a history of the progress of colored graduate nurses, compiled by Adah B. Thoms ... with biographies of many prominent nurses ... [New York, Printed at Kay printing house, inc., °1929]
xvi, 240 p. front., 1 illus., plates, ports. 23½cm.
1. Nurses and nursing. 2. Negroes—Biog. Biography 3. Women, Negro. Bio. 4. Nurses and nursing—Study and teaching. I. Title.
[Full name: Adah B. Glassell Thoms]
29—19412
Library of Congress RT71.T45 [41g1]

Tanganyika M967.82 T38 Thonya, Lucius Mbasha
Siasa hapo kale [Wisdom of the past] methali katika hadithi, Kingoni kimefasiriwa kwa kiswahili. Dar es Salaam, Eagle Press, 1960.
95p. illus. 21½cm.
Written in Swahili.
1. Tanganyika. 2. Angoni. I. Title.

Thorez, Maurice.
Martinique M843 C331e Césaire, Aimé, 1913-
Letter to Maurice Thorez. Paris, Presence Africaine [c1957]
16p. 18cm.

Thorez, Maurice.
Martinique M843 C331 Césaire, Aimé, 1913-
Lettre a Maurice Thorez. 2ed. Paris, Présence Africaine, 1956.
16p. 18cm.

Thorne, Jack, pseud. See Fulton, David B.

MB9 T39f Thornhill, C J
From hobo to cannibal king. With sixteen pages of illustrations in half-tone. London, Stanley Paul & Co., 1928.
285p. illus. 23cm.

M811.5 T39b Thornton, George Bennett, 1881-
Best poems, containing all the poetical works of George B. Thornton. 2d ed. Wilberforce, Ohio [1949]
86 p. port. 22 cm.
PS3539.H833 1949 811.5 50-1402
Library of Congress [2]

M811.5 T39b Thornton, George Bennett, 1881-
Best poems of George B. Thornton ... [Orangeburg, S. C., G. B. Thornton, 1937.
cover-title, 28 p. illus. (port.) 21½cm.
Blank page for "Autographs" (p. 28)
"Biographical sketch": p. [1]
1. Poetry
38-31017
Library of Congress PS3601.T5B4 1937 [3] 811.5

M811.5 T39g Thornton, George Bennett, 1881-
Great poems. First edition. Wilberforce, Ohio, George B. Thornton c1945 ix, 41p. front. 22cm.
1. Poetry.

M811.5 T39s Thornton, George Bennett , 1881-
Selections from Thornton with notes; a collection of classical poetry... 1st ed. Wilberforce, Ohio. The Author, 1954.
60p. 21cm.
1. Poetry

M323 T39 Thornton, M W 1878-
The white Negro; or, A series of lectures on the race problem. By Rev. M. W. Thornton ... Burlington, Ia., C. Lutz printing and publishing co., 1894.
99 p. front. (port.) 19½cm.
1. XXXXX 2. XXXX—Race question.
12—5302
Library of Congress E185.5.T51
Copyright 1894: 8396 [a38b1]

M975 T39 Thorp, Willard, 1899- ed.
A southern reader. [1st ed.] New York, Knopf, 1955.
760 p. illus. 25 cm.
Contains selections from writings of Solomon Thorp, Frederick Douglass, William Johnson, Sterling Brown, Booker T. Washington, W. E. B. Dubois, J. Saunders Redding, Carl Thomas Rowan, and Booker T. Washington.
white editor
1. Southern States—Civilization. 2. American literature—Southern States. I. Title.
Full name: William Willard Thorp.
F209.T48 917.5 53—9473 ‡
Library of Congress [61q2]

M301 T39d Thorpe, Earl Endris,
The desertion of man; a critique of philosophy of history. Baton Rouge, La., Ortlieb Press [1958]
181 p. 22 cm.
1. History—Philosophy. I. Title.
D16.8.T46 901 58-40977 ‡
Library of Congress [1]

M301
T39m
Thorpe, Earl Endris,
The mind of the Negro; an intellectual history of Afro-Americans. Baton Rouge, La., Printed by Ortlieb Press [1961]
562 p. 24 cm.
Includes bibliography.

1. Negroes—Intellectual life. 2. Negroes—Psychology.
I. Title.
E185.82.T5 325.2670973 61—16125 ‡
Library of Congress [62k5]

Thoughts from the mind.
M153
S14t
Simmons, James W
Thoughts from the mind. New York, Exposition Press, 1962.
94p. 23cm.
Portrait of author on book jacket.
"An Exposition-Banner book."

Three adventurous men.
M813.5
W46t
Wells, Moses Peter
Three adventurous men. New York, Carlton Press, 1963.
55p. 20cm. (A Geneva book)
Portrait of author on book jacket.

M301
T39n
Thorpe, Earl Endris,
Negro historians in the United States. Baton Rouge, La., Fraternal Press [1958]
188 p. 22 cm.
Includes bibliography.

1. Negroes—Hist—Historiography. 2. Historians, Negro.
I. Title.
E175.T5 *301.451 325.260973 58—2987 ‡
Library of Congress [61k5]

Thoughts in verse.
M811.4
R79t
Rowe, George Clinton, 1853-1903.
Thoughts in verse. A volume of poems, by George Clinton Rowe ... Charleston, S. C., Kahrs, Stolze & Welch, printers, 1887.
118 p. port. 18½cm.

I. Title.
29-30627
Library of Congress PS2735.R55T5
Copyright 1887: 13869

M323
T41
Three articles on the Negro problem.
Should the color line go? by Hon. Robert Watson Winston; The Negro's greatest enemy, by Marcus Garvey; The Negro Exodus from the South, by Eric D. Waldron. [New York, Universal Negro Improvement Association, 1924]
M304
P19
V.5,
no.15
29p. 22cm.
I. Winston, Robert W. - Should the color line go? II. Garvey, Marcus- The Negro's greatest enemy. III. Waldron, Eric D. The Negro exodus from the South. 1. Race problem

---

M326.99B
J24s
Thorpe, John.
Strickland, S.
Negro slavery described by a Negro: being the narrative of Ashton Warner, a native of St. Vincent's. With an appendix containing the testimony of four Christian ministers recently returned from the colonies on the system of slavery as it now exists. By S. Strickland... London, Samuel Maunder, 1831.
144p. 15½cm.

Thoughts of a postman.
M811.5
R51t
Ritch, Manly.
Thoughts of a postman, by Manly Ritch. 3d ed. Boston, The Christopher publishing house [1926]
ix, 101 p. front. (port.) 21cm.
Poems.

I. Title.
26-14061
Library of Congress PS3535.I 84T5 1926
Copyright A 901278 [2]

---

3 brave men tell how freedom comes to an old South City, Nashville, Tenn.
M323
J132
Jackson, James Edward
3 brave men tell how freedom comes to an old South City, Nashville, Tenn. [New York, Publisher's New Press, 1963]
27p. 22½cm

1. Race relations. 2. Nashville, Tenn.
I. Title.

Thou shalt not kill.
Guyana
M364
M342
Marks, I Alexander
Thou shalt not kill. New York, Carolton Press [1967]
125p. 21cm.
Portrait of author on book jacket.

1. Crime. I. Title.

Thoughts of idle hours.
M811.5
W64t
Wilds, *Mrs.* Myra Viola.
Thoughts of idle hours, by Myra Viola Wilds ... illustrations by Lorenzo Harris ... Nashville, Tenn., National Baptist publishing board, 1915.
81 p. front. (port.) illus. 16cm. $0.65

I. Title.
15-19093
Library of Congress PS3545.I 358T5 1915
Copyright A 410560

The three day Negro.
M973
S15t
Simons, R. E
The three day Negro, yesterday, today, tomorrow, by R.E. Simons.
n.p., n.p.n n.d.
25p. 15cm.

M811.5
P81t
Thoughtless thinks by a thinkless thought-er..
Popel, Esther, 1896-
Thoughtless thinks by a thinkless thought-er.. Dedicated to my mother and my six best friends, by Esther A. B. Popel. Lacks imprint.
16p. port. 16cm.
Inscribed on title page: "A first venture to raise money for college expenses! It netted $100! Esther Popel.

Nigeria
M966.9
Aw6t
Thoughts on Nigerian constitution.
Awolowo, Obafemi, 1909-
Thoughts on Nigerian constitution. Ibadan, London, Oxford U. P., 1966.
xii, 196 p. front. (map), tables. 21½ cm. 10/6
(B 67-10848)

1. Nigeria—Pol. & govt. I. Title.
JQ3083 1966.A9 342.669'03 67-90818
Library of Congress [3]

Three Finger Jack's treasure.
Jamaica
M823.91
Sh54t
Sherlock, Philip Manderson.
Three Finger Jack's treasure. Illustrated by William Reeves. London, New York, Macmillan, 1961 [i. e. 1962]
176 p. illus. 21 cm.

I. Title.
PZ7.S5452Th 2 62-612 ‡
Library of Congress [5]

Gold Coast
M966.7
C89t
1791
Thoughts and sentiments on the evil of slavery.
Cugoano, Ottobah.
Thoughts and sentiments on the evil of slavery; or the nature of servitude as admitted by the law of God, compared to the modern slavery of the Africans in the West Indies; in an answer to the advocates for slavery and oppression. Addressed to the sons of Africa, by a native. London: Printed for, and sold by the author, no.12. Queen Street, Grosvenor Square. 1791.
[6] - 46 [3]p. 23½cm.

A thousand years of West African history.
Nigeria
M966
Aj18
Ajayi, Jacob F Ade, *ed.*
A thousand years of West African history: a handbook for teachers and students by J. F. Ade Ajayi and Ian Espie; with a foreword by K. O. Dike. Ibadan, London, Ibadan U. P.; Nelson, 1965.
xi, 543 p. maps, diagr. 22½ cm. 25/-
(B 66-3530)
Bibliography: p. [496]-505.

1. Africa, West—Hist. I. Espie, Ian, joint ed. II. Title.
DT471.A4 966 66-71412
Library of Congress [5]

Three generations...
MB9
C16
[Cansler, Charles W] 1871-
Three generations; the story of a colored family of eastern Tennessee. [Kingsport, Tenn.] Priv. print. [Kingsport press, inc.] 1939.
viii, 173 p. port. 21cm.
Foreword signed: C. W. C. [i. e. Charles W. Cansler]

1. Negroes. 2. Cansler family. I. Title.
39—22425
Library of Congress E185.97.C256
——— Copy 2.
Copyright A 132050 [40r3] 325.260973

Thoughts for today upon the past, present...
M973
Em1t
Embry, James Crawford, 1834-1897.
Thoughts for today upon the past, present and future of the colored Americans in six chapters, by Rev. J. C. Embry... Fort Scott, Kansas, Pioneer book and job publishing house, 1878.
66p. 14½cm.

M814.4
W272in
Thrasher, Max Bennett, 1860-1903.
Washington, Booker Taliaferro, 1859?-1915
Introduction.
(In: Thrasher, Max Bennet. Tuskegee; its story and its work. Boston, Small, Maynard & company, 1900. 19cm. p.xv-xvi)

Three immortals.
British Guiana
M820
C14t
Cameron, Norman Eustace.
Three immortals; a collection of three plays. Georgetown, B. G., Printed at F. A. Persick, 1953.
189 p. illus., music. 22 cm.
CONTENTS.—Adoniya.—Sabaco.—Ebedmelech.

I. Title.
A 61-82
Florida. Univ. Library for Library of Congress [5]

M301
T413

Three Negro classics: Up from slavery. The souls of black folk. The autobiography of an ex-colored man. With an introd. by John Hope Franklin. [New York, Avon Books, 1965]

xxv, 511 p. 19 cm. (Avon library, W102)

Includes music.

1. Negroes. 2. Tuskegee Institute. I. Washington, Booker Taliaferro, 1856-1915. Up from slavery. II. DuBois, William Edward Burghardt, 1868-1963. The souls of the black folk. III. Johnson, James Weldon, 1871-1938. The autobiography of an ex-colored man. IV. Franklin, John Hope. Introduction.

E185.97.W278 301.451 65-3044

Library of Congress [5]

M646.7
P83

Three Negro pioneers in beauty culture.

Porter, Gladys L

Three Negro pioneers in beauty culture, by Gladys L. Porter. [1st ed.] New York, Vantage Press [1966]

48 p. ports. 21 cm.

Bibliography: p. 48.

1. Beauty operators. I. Title.

TT955.A1P6 646.720922 65-28002

Library of Congress [2]

M811.5
AM8t

Three shades of blue.

Anthony, James K

Three shades of blue. [1st ed.] New York, Vantage Press [1956]

63 p. 21 cm.

Poems.

I. Title.

PS3501.N725T5 811.5 56-5823 ‡

Library of Congress [2]

M331
H77t

3 southern plants of International Harvester Company.

Hope, John, 1909-

3 southern plants of International Harvester Company, prepared for the NPA Committee of South. Washington, D. C., National Planning Association, 1953.

143 p. tables 23 cm. (National Planning Association. Committee of the South. Report no. 1)

M210
B81t
1852

Three years in Europe.

Brown, William Wells, b. 1815.

Three years in Europe: or, Places I have seen and people I have met. By W. Wells Brown, a fugitive slave. With a memoir of the author, by William Farmer, esq. London, C. Gilpin; [etc., etc.] 1852.

[iii]-xxxii, 312 p. front. (port.) 16½cm.

An enlarged edition appeared in 1855 under title: The American fugitive in Europe.

1. Gt. Brit.—Descr. & trav. I. Farmer, William, 1802- II. Title.

Library of Congress DA625.B88 8-6127

[a34b1]

M378
M541

Three years in Mississippi.

Meredith, James Howard, 1933-

Three years in Mississippi [by] James Meredith. Bloomington, Indiana University Press [1966]

328 p. 24 cm.

Autobiographical.

1. Mississippi. University—Hist. I. Title.

LD3412.9.M4A3 378.762 66-12731

Library of Congress [5]

Nigeria
M896.2
L125

Three Yoruba plays.

Ladipo, Duro

Three Yoruba plays: Ọba Koso, Ọba Mọrọ [and] Ọba Waja. English adaptations by Ulli Beier. Ibadan, Mbari Publications [1964]

75p. 21½cm.

Contents.- Ọba Koso [The king does not hang.- Ọba Mọrọ [The ghost catcher.- Ọba Waja [The king is dead]

1. African drama. I. Beier, Ulli, tr. II. Title. III. Mbari Plubications.

M977.4
T41

A thrilling narrative from the lips of the sufferers of the late Detroit riot, March 6, 1863, with the hair breadth escapes of men, women and children, and destruction of colored men's property, not less than $15,000. Detroit, Mich. Published by the author. 1863. Hattiesburg, Miss., The Book farm, 1945.

cover-title, 1 p. l., 24 p. 21½cm. (Heartman's historical series no. 72)

"One hundred and thirty-six copies reprinted from the copy in the Charles F. Heartman collection of material relating to Negro culture." "Lithoprinted."

1. Detroit—Riot, 1863. 2. Negroes—Detroit. Roto

45-9856

Library of Congress F574.D4T5

[4] 977.434

M796
M45t

Thrills and spills in sports.

Maxwell, Sherman Leander, 1906-

Thrills and spills in sports [by] Jocko Maxwell. New York, Fortuny's [1939]

101 p. 20cm.

"First edition."

1. Sports—Anecdotes, facetiae, satire, etc. I. Title.

40-85013

Library of Congress GV191.M3

[2] 796.0988

Africa, South
M968
Sp6s

Through coloured glasses.

Ross, Richard Ernest van der. 1921-

Through coloured glasses.

pp. 237-248.

In: South Africa the road ahead, comp. by Hildegarde Spottiswoode. 1960.

M811.5
D29t

Through sepia eyes.

Davis, Frank Marshall

Through sepia eyes, by Frank Marshall Davis. Decorations by William Fleming. Chicago, Black cat press, 1938.

10p. illus. 24½cm.

British Guiana
M823.91

Thunder returning.

Mittelholzer, Edgar, 1909-

Thunder returning; a novel in the Leitmotiv manner. London, Secker and Warburg, 1961.

240p. 20½cm.

M811.5
B64t

"Thunderbolts"

Borders, William Holmes, 1905-

"Thunderbolts" [by] William Holmes Borders. [Atlanta, Morris Brown college press, c1942]

50p. illus. 23½cm.

Poems.

M200
T42c

Thurman, Howard, 1900-

The creative encounter; an interpretation of religion and the social witness. [1st ed.] New York, Harper [1954]

153 p. 20 cm.

"The substance ... in essentially the present form, was given as the Merrick lectures at Ohio Wesleyan University in March, 1954."

1. Experience (Religion) 2. Religion. I. Title.

BR110.T48 248 54-11664 ‡

Library of Congress [25]

M200
T42d

Thurman, Howard, 1900-

Deep is the hunger; meditations for apostles of sensitiveness. [1st ed.] New York, Harper [1951]

x, 212 p. 22 cm.

An expansion of the author's Meditations for apostles of sensitiveness, published in 1948.

1. Devotional literature. I. Title. II. Title: Meditations for apostles of sensitiveness.

BV4832.T558 242 51-9391

Library of Congress [51h7]

M200
T42d

Thurman, Howard, 1900-

Deep river; reflections on the religious insight of certain of the Negro spirituals. Illustrated by Elizabeth Orton Jones. [Rev. and enl.] New York, Harper [1955]

93 p. illus. 22 cm.

1. Negro spirituals—Hist. & crit. I. Title.

ML3556.T55 1955 784.756 55-11483 ‡

Library of Congress [30]

M200
T42di

Thurman, Howard, 1900-

Disciplines of the spirit. [1st ed.] New York, Harper & Row [1963]

127 p. 22 cm.

1. Devotional literature. I. Title.

BV4832.2.T527 242 63-17716

Library of Congress [7-1]

M371.974
T87n

Thurman, Howard, 1900-

The dream of order in the mind of God, pp. 87-91.

Tuskegee Institute.

The new south and higher education: what are the implications for higher education of the changing socio-economic conditions of the south? A symposium and ceremonies held in connection with the inauguration of Luther Hilton Foster, fourth president of Tuskegee Institute [October 31 and November 1, 1953. Tuskegee, Ala.] Dept. of Records and Research, Tuskegee Institute, 1954.

x, 145p. map. 24cm.

M200
T42f

Thurman, Howard, 1900-

Footprints of a dream; the story of the Church for the Fellowship of All Peoples. New York, Harper [1959]

157 p. illus. 20 cm.

1. San Francisco. Church for the Fellowship of All Peoples. I. Title.

BX9999.S3C5 289.9 59-11412 ‡

Library of Congress [20]

M200
T42g

Thurman, Howard, 1900-

God and the race question.

(In: Together. New York, Abingdon-Cokesbury Press, 1945. 19cm. p. 113-120)

1. Christianity - Adresses, essays, lectures. I. Title.

M200
T42gr

Thurman, Howard, 1900-

The growing edge. [1st ed. New York] Harper [1956]

181 p. 22 cm.

1. Baptists—Sermons. 2. Sermons, American. I. Title.

BX6333.T5G7 252.06 56-12058 ‡

Library of Congress [10]

M200
T421
Thurman, Howard, 1900-
The inward journey. [1st ed.] New York, Harper [1961]
155 p. 22 cm.

1. Devotional literature. I. Title.
BV4832.2.T53 242 61-12833 ‡
Library of Congress [10]

M200
T42j
Thurman, Howard, 1900-
Jesus and the disinherited. New York, Abingdon-Cokesbury Press [1949]
112 p. 20 cm.
"The ... study of which this book is the full development was presented as the Mary L. Smith memorial lectures at Samuel Huston College, Austin, Texas, in April, 1948."

1. Jesus Christ—Teachings. 2. Sociology, Biblical. I. Title.
BS2417.S7T5 232.9 49-8371*
Library of Congress [20]

M301
T426
Thurman, Howard, 1900-
The luminous darkness; a personal interpretation of the anatomy of segregation and the ground of hope. [1st ed.] New York, Harper & Row [1965]
xi, 113 p. 20 cm.

1. Negroes—Segregation. 2. Church and race problems. I. Title.
E185.61.T47 301.45196073 65-20445
Library of Congress [5]

M200
T42m
Thurman, Howard, 1900-
Meditations of the heart. [1st ed.] New York, Harper [1953]
216 p. 22 cm.

1. Devotional literature. I. Title.
BV4832.T57 242 53-10980 ‡
Library of Congress [10]

M200
T42a
Thurman, Howard, 1900-
The Negro spiritual speaks of life and death. New York, Harper [1947]
56 p. 18 cm. (The Ingersoll lecture, Harvard University, 1947)

1. Negro spirituals—Hist. & crit. I. Title. II. Series.
ML3556.T56 784.756 47-12396*
© Harper & Bros.; 12Nov47; A18748.
Library of Congress [5]

M200
T42r
Thurman, Howard, 1900-
The religion of Jesus and the disinherited.
(In: Johnson, Thomas Herbert, ed. In defense of democracy. New York, Putnam, 1949. 21cm. p.125-135).

I. Title. 1. Sociology, Biblical
2. Jesus Christ - Teachings
II. Johnson, Thomas Herbert, ed. In defense of democracy. III. In defense of democracy.

M231
W62
Thurman, Howard, 1900-
Why I believe there is a God.
Pp. 116-120.
In: Why I believe there is a God. Chicago, Johnson Pub. Co., 1965.

Thurman, Howard, 1900- . Introduction.
M231
W62
Why I believe there is a God; sixteen essays by Negro clergymen. With an introd. by Howard Thurman. Chicago, Johnson Pub. Co., 1965.
xiii, 120 p. 22 cm.

1. God—Proof—Addresses, essays, lectures. I. Title: Negro clergymen, sixteen essays by.
BT102.W5 231.082 65-17082
Library of Congress [5]

Thurman, Howard, 1900- , pp. 159-184.
M8
H38f
Henderson, Dorothy (McLaughlin) 1900-
Biographical sketches of six humanitarians whose lives have been for the greater glory. Symbol designs by Douglas C. Henderson. [1st ed.] New York, Exposition Press [1958]
188 p. illus. 21 cm.

1. Biography. I. Title: For the greater glory.
CT105.H45 920.02 58-4777 ‡
Library of Congress [2]

M979.4
T42
Thurman, Sue Bailey.
Pioneers of Negro origin in California. San Francisco, Acme Publishing Company, 1949.
70 p. 21 cm.

1. California. I. Title.

Thurman, Sue Bailey, ed.
M641.5
N21
National Council of Negro Women.
The historical cookbook of the American Negro. Published under the auspices of the Council's Archives and Museum Dept. Compiled and edited by Sue Bailey Thurman, chairman. [Washington] Corporate Press, °1958.
144 p. illus. 22 cm.

1. Cookery, Negro. 2. Cookery, American. I. Thurman, Sue Bailey, ed. II. Title.
TX715.N326 59-24514 ‡
Library of Congress [1]

M813.5
T42b
Thurman, Wallace, 1902-1934
The blacker the berry; a novel of negro life, by Wallace Thurman. New York, The Macaulay company, 1929.
6 p. l., 9-262 p. 19½cm.

I. Title.
29-8978
Library of Congress PZ3.T4258Bl
[43d1]

M813.5
T421
Thurman, Wallace, 1902-1934
Infants of the spring, by Wallace Thurman ... New York, The Macaulay company [°1932]
284 p. 19½cm.

I. Title.
Library of Congress PZ3.T4258 In 32-765
——— Copy 2.
Copyright A 46754 [3]

M813.5
T42in
Thurman, Wallace, 1902-1934
The interne, by Wallace Thurman ... and A. L. Furman. New York, The Macaulay company [°1932]
252 p. 19½cm.

I. Furman, Abraham L., joint author. II. Title.
Library of Congress PZ3.T4258 Int 32-11559
——— Copy 2.
Copyright A 49820 [3]

M974.8
T926s
Thurman, Wallace, 1902-1934.
Negro life in New York's Harlem, a lively picture of a popular and interesting section by Wallace Thurman. Girard Kansas, Haldeman-Julius publication °1928
64p. 13cm. (Little blue book no. 494, edited by E. Haldeman-Julius)
1. Harlem, New York (City).

175111

Thursday's child.
M89
K65
Kitt, Eartha.
Thursday's child. [1st ed.] New York, Duell, Sloan and Pearce [1956]
250 p. illus. 21 cm.
Autobiographical.

1. Musicians—Correspondence, reminiscences, etc. I. Title.
ML420.K5A3 927.8 56-9590 ‡
Library of Congress [15]

Martinique Ti-Coyo and his shark.
M843.91
R39t
Richer, Clément.
Ti-Coyo and his shark: an immoral fable. [Translated from the French by Gerard Hopkins. 1st American ed.] New York, Knopf, 1951.
235 p. illus. 21 cm.

I. Title.
PZ3.R404Ti 51-11057
Library of Congress [53g2]

Martinique
...Ti-coyo et son requin.
M843.91
R39t2
Richer, Clément.
... Ti-coyo et son requin. Paris, Plon [1941]
2 p. l., 248 p., 1 l. 18½cm.

I. Title.
45-34517
Library of Congress PQ2635.I 32T5
[2] 843.91

Ti-Coyo und sein hai (Ti-Coyo et son requin.)
Martinique
M843.91
R39t3
Richer, Clément, 1915-
Ti-Coyo und sein hai(Ti-Coyo et son requin.) Darmstadt und Genf, Holle, 1953.
231p. 19cm.

Tibati, Cameroun.
Cameroun
M967.11
M725
Mohamadou, Eldridge
L'histoire de Tibati, chefferie Foulbe du Cameroun. Yaounde, Editions Abbia avec la collaboration de CLE, 1965.
72p. 18cm. illus., maps.

1. Fulahs. 2. Tibati, Cameroun. I. Title.

Africa
M896
T43
Tibble, Anne (Northgrave) ed.
African-English literature; a short survey and anthology of prose and poetry up to 1965. Edited by Anne Tibble. [New York] October House [1965]
304 p. 23 cm.
Bibliography: p. 292-302.
White editor.

1. English literature—Africa. I. Title.
PR9799.T5 1965 820.8096 65-22929
Library of Congress [5]

Gold Coast
M966.7 Tidsley, Alfred.
T45r The remarkable work achieved by Rev. Dr. Mark C. Rayford, in promotion of the spiritual and material welfare of the natives of West Africa, and proposed developments; with a foreword by Rev. Thos. Nightingale and appreciations from the President of the United States of America, the King of England, the President of France. London, Morgan & Scott, 1926.

36, [2] p. port. illus. fascms. 22cm.
(Tracings over)

The tie that binds...
M813.5 Dreer, Herman, 1889–
D81t The tie that binds; a novel of a youth who seeks to understand life. Boston, Meador Pub. Co. [1958]

374 p. 21 cm.

I. Title.

PZ3.D813Ti 58-8270 ‡

Library of Congress [2]

Upper Volta
M398 Tiendrebeogo, Yamba, 1907–
T443 Contes du larhallé; suivis d'un recueil de proverbes et de devises du pays mossi. Rédigés et présentés par Robert Pageard. Ouagadougou, Chez l'auteur, 1963.

215 p. 21 cm.

1. Upper Volta - Folk-lore. 2. Folk-lore - Upper Volta. I. Title.

Upper Volta
M966.68 Tiendrebéogo, Yamba, 1907–
T44 Histoire et coutumes royales des Mossi de Ouagadougou; rédaction et annotations de Robert Pageard. Ouagadougou, Chez le Larhallé Naba, 1964.

208p. ports. 20cm.

1. Ivory Coast - Social life and customs. 2. Ivory Coast - History. 3. Ouagadougou, Ivory Coast. I. Title.

Ecuador Tierra, son y tambor.
M863.6 Ortiz, Adalberto.
Or8t ... Tierra, son y tambor; cantares negros y mulatos. Prólogo de Joaquín Gallegos Lara y 28 grabados originales de Galo Galecio. México, D. F., Ediciones La Cigarra, 1945.

2 p. l., [7]–81 p., 2 l. illus. 28cm.

Without music.

1. Negroes—Poetry. 2. Negro songs. I. Title.

46-18308

Library of Congress PQ8219.O7T5
[2] 861.6

M331.833 Tillman, James Albert, 1926–
T466 Not by prayer alone; a report on the Greater Minneapolis Interfaith Fair Housing Program [by] James A. Tillman, Jr. Philadelphia, United Church Press [1964]

223 p. 23 cm.

1. Greater Minneapolis Interfaith Fair Housing Program. 2. Discrimination in housing—Minneapolis. 3. Negroes—Housing. 4. Church and race problems. I. Title. 5. Minneapolis.

E185.89.H6T5 301.451 64-19721

Library of Congress [5]

M812.5 Tillman, Katherine Davis
T46t Thirty years of freedom; a drama in four acts, by Katherine D. Tillman. [n.p., n.p., n.d.]
32p. 17cm.

1. Drama. I. Title.

M326.99B Tilmon, Levin, 1807–1863.
T46t A brief miscellaneous narrative of the more early part of the life of L. Tilmon, pastor of a colored Methodist Congregational church in the city of New York. Written by himself. Jersey City, W. W. & L. A. Pratt, printers, 1853.

1 p. l., 97 p. 17cm.

Verso of p. 89 unnumbered and blank.

1. Slavery in the U. S. I. Title.
2. Slave narratives.

37-12163

Library of Congress BX8473.T5A3
[2] 922.773

Timbuctoo.
Haiti Durand, Oswald, 1840–1906.
M844. René Caillié et Tombouctou. Paris, Tours
D93r Maison Mame c1938.

128p. illus. 21cm.

Timberlake, Clarence L.
M89 Dawson, Osceola Aleese.
T48d The Timberlake story. [Carbondale, Ill., Dunaway-Sinclair, 1959.

165 p. illus. 21 cm.

Portrait of author on book jacket.

1. Timberlake, Clarence L.

E185.97.T55D3 923.773 60-18528 ‡

Library of Congress [5]

La timbrologie Haitienne, 1881–1954.
Haiti Montès, Léon
M383 La timbrologie Haitienne, 1881–1954. Port-au-
M76 Prince. Henri Deschamps, 1954.

1v. 205p. illus. 21cm.

Timbuktu-History.
Mali
M966.2 'Abd al-Raḥmān ibn 'Abd Allāh, *al-Sa'dī*, 1596–*ca.* 1655.
Ab3d Documents arabes relatifs à l'histoire du Soudan: Tarikh es-Soudan, par Abderrahman ben Abdallah ben 'Imran ben 'Amir es-Sa'ḍi ... édité par O. Houdaś ... avec la collaboration de Edm. Benoist ... Paris, E. Leroux, 1898–1900.

2 v. 28½cm. (*Half-title:* Publications de l'École des langues orientales vivantes, IVe sér., vol. XII–XIII)

History of Timbuktu and the surrounding region under Moroccan rule during the 16th and 17th centuries.

CONTENTS.—v. 1. Texte arabe.—v. 2. [Traduction] par O. Houdas.

1. Sudan, French—Hist. 2. Timbuktu—Hist. I. Houdas, Octave Victor, 1840–1916, ed. and tr. II. *Benoist, Edmond, 1871– ed. III. Title. IV. Title: Tarikh es-Soudan.

44-44001

Library of Congress PJ7819.S8A23
[8]

Mali Timbuktu- History.
M966.2 Mahmūd Kati ibn al-Hāj al-Mutawakkil Kāti
M31d 1468–1593.
Documents arabes relatifs à l'histoire du Soudan: Tarikh El-Fettach; ou, chronique du chercheur pour servir a l'histoire des Villes, des Armées et des principaux personages du Tekrour par Mahoûd ben El 'Hâdj El-Motaouakkel Kâti. tr. Française par O. Houdas et M. Delafosse. Paris, Ernest Leroux, 1913.
2v. 28½cm.

Timeless issues.
M252 Wynn, Daniel Webster, 1919–
W98 Timeless issues [by] Daniel W. Wynn. New York, Philosophical Library [1957]

x, 144 p. 22 cm.

1. Methodist Church—Sermons. 2. Sermons, American. I. Title.

BX8472.W9 252.07 66-20219

Library of Congress [5]

M407 Timmons, Eleanor Lewis
T48 Teaching English. New York, Vantage Press, [1958]

96p. 20cm.

Picture and biographical sketch of the author on the book jacket.

1. English language - study and teaching.
2. Literature - study and teaching.

Puerto Rico
M864. Timotheo, Pedro Carlos, 1864–
T48 El consultor, folleto de amena literatura, con informacion utilisima para padres, maestros y estudiantes, relacion de professonale y altos funcionarios, comerciantes de San Juan, etc. Compilado por Pedro C. Timothee. San Juan, P. R., 1929.

112p. 19cm.

1. Puerto Rico - Directory.

Puerto Rico
M864 Timothée, Pedro Carlos, 1864–
T48c Cuentos populares por Pedro C. Timothée. 2d. ed. San Juan, Puerto Rico, 1923.

223p. 20cm.

1. Puerto Rican fiction.

Puerto Rico
M864 Timothée, Pedro Carlos, 1864–
T48g Gramatica Castellana para adultos. 2d. ed. por Pedro C. Timothée. San Juan, P. R. Cantero, Fernandez & co.

11, iiip. 24cm.
Author is Puerto Rican.

1. Spanish language - grammar.

Sierra Leone
M39 Timothy, Bankole
N65t Kwame Nkrumah, his rise to power. London, George Allen & Unwin, Ltd. 1955.

198p. portraits. 21cm.

1. Gold Coast. 2. Nkrumah, Kwame, 1909–

M252 Tindley, Charles Albert, 1856–1933
T49b A book of sermons, by Rev. Charles Albert Tindley ... with introductory remarks by Rt. Rev. J.S. Caldwell... A brief sketch of the writer's life, in his own words to Dr. S.W. Thomas... Philadelphia, Pa., Edward T. Duncan [n.d.]

151p. front. 20½cm.

1. Sermons.

M252 Tindley, Charles Albert, 1856–1933.
T49b Book of sermons, by Rev. Chas. A. Tindley,
1932 with an introduction, by Bishop J.S. Caldwell. Philadelphia, Published by Charles A. Tindley, 1932.

viii, 153p. front (port.) 19½cm.

1. Sermons.

M3
T49e

Tinker, Edward Larocque, 1881-
Les écrits de langue française en Louisiane au XIXe siècle; essais biographiques at bibliographiques par Edward Larocque Tinker ... Paris, H. Champion, 1932 [i. e. 1933]

2 p. l., 502 p. incl. plates, facsims. 25½cm. (*Added t.-p.:* Bibliothèque de la Revue de littérature comparée ... t. 85)

Authors, including Negroes, arranged alphabetically, with biographical and critical sketches written to show the characteristic French spirit which has left an impress in Louisiana, followed by the author's works including English titles of those writing in both languages. The location of a copy of the work is given, if known.

white author.

(Continued on next card)

33—21149

[45h1]

Tinker, Edward Larocque, 1881- Les écrits de langue française en Louisiane ... 1932 [i. e. 1933] (Card 2)

While information about the periodical literature is scattered under the names of the founders or editors, the author's "Bibliography of the French newspapers and periodicals of Louisiana," published in the American antiquarian society's Proceedings for Oct. 1932 and separately by the Society in 1933, serves in the nature of a supplement for that part of the French publications of Louisiana.

1. American literature—Louisiana—Bio-bibl. 2. American literature (French) — Louisiana — Bio-bibl. 3. French literature—American authors—Bibl. 4. Creoles. 5. Louisiana—Civilization. I. Title.

33—21149

Library of Congress Z1289.T59

[45h1] [016.84] 016.81

M447.9
T49g

Tinker, Edward Larocque, 1881-
Gombo, the Creole dialect of Louisiana, with a bibliography, by Edward Larocque Tinker.

(*In* American antiquarian society, Worcester, Mass. Proceedings. Worcester, Mass., 1935. 25cm. n. s., v. 45, p. 101-142)

"A bibliography of the writings in and about the Creole dialect of Louisiana": p. 129-142.

1. Creole dialects — Louisiana. 2. French language—Dialects—Louisiana. I. Title.

A 38-848

Newberry library for Library of Congress [E172.A35 n. s., vol. 45]

[38c2] (978.062) 447.9

Haiti
M843.91
T35c

Tinker, Edward Larocque, 1881- tr.

Thoby-Marcelin, Philippe, 1904-
Canapé-Vert, by Philippe Thoby-Marcelin and Pierre Marcelin; translated by Edward Larocque Tinker. New York, Toronto, Farrar & Rinehart inc. [1944]

xxvii, 225 p. col. front. 21cm.

Illustrated lining-papers.
"Prize winning novel, second Latin American contest."

I. *Marcelin, Pierre, 1908- joint author. II. Tinker, Edward Larocque, 1881- tr. III. Title.

[*Full name:* Émile Philippe Thoby-Marcelin]

44—1710

Library of Congress PZ3.T35Can

[46t5]

A tinkling in the twilight.

British Guiana
M823.91
M69ti

Mittelholzer, Edgar, 1909-
A tinkling in the twilight; a novel. London, Secker & Warburg, 1959.

269p. 19½cm.

Tinsley, Tomi Carolyn, jt. author.

M811.5
H24t

Harris, Helen C.
Triad. Poems by Helen C. Harris, Lucia Mae Pitts [and] Tomi Carolyn Tinsley. Privately published, December, 1945.

95p. 21cm.

Tinsley, Tomi Carolyn jt. author.

M811.5
H24t

Harris, Helen C
Triad. Poems by Helen C. Harris, Lucia Mae Pitts [and] Tomi Carolyn Tinsley. Privately published, December, 1945.
95p. 21cm.

Haiti
M520
T491

Tippenhauer, Louis Gentil, 1867-
Die insel Haiti. Von L. Gentil Tippenhauer ... Mit 30 holzschnitten, 29 abbildungen in lichtdruck und 6 geologischen tafeln in farbendruck. Leipzig, F. A. Brockhaus, 1893.

xviii, 693, [1] p. illus., plates. 32½cm.

"Bibliographie": p. [672]-693.

1. Haiti.

6—29524

Library of Congress F1901.T59

[42d1]

Haiti
M520
T49p

Tippenhauer, Louis Gentil, 1867-
Le précalcul astronomique du comportement de notre vitalite importante consequence de la decouverte de la loi du temps. n. p., n.d.

4p. 23cm.
At head of title: Communication importante.

Haiti
M520
T49pr

Tippenhauer, Louis Gentil, 1867-
La préconnaissance du futur; interview relative a la decouverte de la loi du temps. Port-au-Prince, Fondation Internationale de Meterologie de Port-au-Prince, 1950.

32p. illus. 23cm.
Interview de Pierre Moraviah Morpeau avec ...Docteur Louis Gentil Tippenhauer.

I. Title. 1. Morpeau, Pierre Moravia.

La tireuse de cartes.

M812.3
Se4n
no.3

Séjour, Victor, 1816-1874.
La tireuse de cartes; drame en cinq actes et un prologue, en prose, par Victor Séjour. 2. éd. Paris, Michel Lévy frères, 1860.

2 p. l., iii, 131 p. 19½cm.

I. Title.

34-19717

Library of Congress PQ1222.Z76 no. 1

(842.80623) 842.89

Guadeloupe
M841
T51b

Tirolien, Guy
Balles d'or; poemes. [Paris, Présence Africaine, 1960]

91p. 16½cm.

1. Poetry - Guadeloupe. I. Title.

M616
P73

Tissues - Culture.

Plummer, Jewel I.
Triethylene melamine in vitro studies; I. Mitotic a;terations produced in chick fibroblast tissue cultures, by Jewel I. Plummer, Louis T. Wright, Grace Antikajian, and Solomon Weintraub. Cancer Research, Inc., 1952.

796-800p. tables graphs 27cm.
Reprinted from Cancer Research, November 1952.

Les Titans de 1804.

Haiti
M972.94
G25p

Gayot, Gerard G
Presente les Titans de 1804. Condense. Preface du professeur Lucien P. Balmir. [Montreal, 1955]

143p. port. 21cm.

Titien Vecelli.

France
M840
D89mic

Dumas, Alexandre, 1824-1895
Michel-ange suivi de Titien Vecelli. Bruxelles et Leipzig, Meline, Cans, et compagnie, 1844.

278p. 15½cm.

Titine grosbonda.

Guadeloupe
M843.91
C35t

Chambertrand, Gilbert de.
Titine grosbonda. Paris, Fasquelle Editeurs [1947]

250p. front (port.) 18cm.

Tituba - Juvenile fiction.

M813.5
P44t

Petry, Ann (Lane) 1911-
Tituba of Salem Village, by Ann Petry. New York, Crowell [1964]

254 p. 21 cm.

Portrait of author on book cover.

1. Tituba—Juvenile fiction. 2. Witchcraft—Salem, Mass.—Juvenile literature. I. Title.

PZ7.P4473Ti 64-20691

Library of Congress [7-1]

Tituba of Salem Village.

M813.5
P44t

Petry, Ann (Lane) 1911-
Tituba of Salem Village, by Ann Petry. New York, Crowell [1964]

254 p. 21 cm.

Portrait of author on book cover.

1. Tituba—Juvenile fiction. 2. Witchcraft—Salem, Mass.—Juvenile literature. I. Title.

PZ7.P4473Ti 64-20691

Library of Congress [7-1]

Tivi (African people)

Nigeria
M966.9
Ak5a

Akiga.
Akiga's story; the Tiv tribe as seen by one of its members; translated and annotated by Rupert East ... London, New York [etc.] Pub. for the International institute of African languages & cultures by the Oxford university press, 1939.

xv, 436 p. front., plates, ports. 22cm.

Map on lining-papers.
"The extracts which have been translated and reproduced in this book form only about a half of the original manuscript."—p. 7.

1. Tivi (African people) 2. Ethnology—Nigeria. I. *East, Rupert, ed. and tr. II. International institute of African languages and cultures. III. Title.

40-8326

Library of Congress DT515.A7

[3] 572.96697

To be equal.

M323.4
Y87

Young, Whitney M
To be equal [by] Whitney M. Young, Jr. [1st ed.] New York, McGraw-Hill [1964]

254 p. 22 cm.

1. Negroes—Civil rights. 2. Negroes—Moral and social conditions. I. Title.

E185.61.Y73 323.41 64-23179

Library of Congress [7-1]

To flower.

M811.5
D23t

Danner, Margaret
To flower; poems. Hemphill Press, 1963.

30p. 23cm.
"For Arthur B. Spingarn - March 17, 1964 - Margaret Danner."

I. Title.

To get my name in the Kingdom Book.
M811.5 McGehee, Maud
Mc17t To get my name in the Kingdom book. Atlanta, Franklin Printing Co., 1962.

42p. 22½cm.

I. Title.

To make a poet black.
M810. Redding, Jay Saunders.
R24to To make a poet black ₍by₎ J. Saunders Redding. Chapel Hill, The University of North Carolina press, 1939.

x p., 2 l., ₍3₎–142 p. 22cm.
"Factual material and critical opinion on American Negro literature."—Pref.
Bibliography: p. ₍131₎–136.

1. Negro literature—Hist. & crit. I. Title.

39—27275

Library of Congress PS153.N5R4
——— Copy 2.
Copyright A 127898 ₍41k3₎ 810.9

811.5 To no special land.
R33 Reynolds, Evelyn Crawford.
To no special land; a book of poems, by Eve Lynn ₍pseud.₎ With a foreword by Mary McLeod Bethune. ₍1st ed.₎ New York, Exposition Press ₍1953₎

64 p. 21 cm.

I. Title.

PS3535.E945T6 811.5 53–7871 ‡

Library of Congress ₍3₎

To secure these rights.
M323 U. S. *President's Committee on Civil Rights.*
Un3t To secure these rights, the report of the President's Committee on Civil Rights. Washington, U. S. Govt. Print. Off., 1947.

xii, 178 p. illus., maps. 25 cm.
Charles E. Wilson, chairman.

1. Civil rights—U. S. I. Wilson, Charles Erwin, 1890– II. Title.
JC599.U5A32 1947 323.4 47—46486*

Library of Congress ₍48x15₎

To Sir, with love.
Brit. Guiana
M823.91 Braithwaite, E R
B73t1 To Sir, with love. London, The Bodley Head, 1959.

188p. 19½cm.

To Sir, with love.
Brit. Guiana
M823.91 Braithwaite, E R
B73t To Sir, with love. Englewood, Cliffs, N. J., Prentice-Hall, Inc., 1959.

216p. 20½cm.
Portrait of author on book jacket.

To stem this tide.
M301 Johnson, Charles Spurgeon, 1893–
J63t To stem this tide, a survey of racial tension areas in the United States ₍by₎ Charles S. Johnson and associates. Boston and Chicago, The Pilgrim press, 1943.

x, 142 p. 20cm.
"The Julius Rosenwald fund of Chicago sponsored this study ... ₍which was₎ made by the Institute of social studies at Fisk university ... under the direction of Dr. Charles S. Johnson."—Pref.
Bibliographical foot-notes.

1. Negroes. 2. U. S.—Race question. I. Fisk university, Nashville. Social science institute. II. Title.

44—247

Library of Congress E185.61.J685
₍46d²7₎ 325.260973

Toad-song.
M811.5 Hunt, Evelyn Tooley
H89t Toad-song; a collection of Haiku and other small poems. ₍New York, Apple Press, 1966₎

48p. 18cm.
Autographed.

I. Title.

Toads for supper.
Nigeria
M896.3 Ike, Vincent Chukwuemeka
Ik3t Toads for supper. London, Harvill Press ₍1965₎

192p. 20cm.
Portrait of author on book jacket.

M810 A toast to love and death.
B73t Brawley, Benjamin Griffith, 1882–1939.
A toast to love and death, by Benjamin Griffith Brawley. ₍eight lines of verse₎ ₍Atlanta₎ Atlanta Baptist College Print, 1902.

29p. 17cm.

Tobago, Island of.
Tobago
M972.98 Ottley, Carlton Robert, 1914–
Ot5to Tobago legends and West Indian lore. ₍Trinidad, 1950₎

137p. illus. 19cm.

Tobago, Island of.
Tobago
M972.98 Ottley, Carlton Robert, 1914–
Ot5tr Trindad; land of the calypso, steelband, humming bird, pitch lake, and the Cardura. Tobago, Robinson Crusoe's Isle. Port-of-Spain, Trinidad, 1954.

36p. illus. 21½cm.

MB9 Tobias, Channing H eggie , 1882–1961
T55 Autobiography.
(In: Thirteen Americans: their spiritual autobiographies, ed. by Louis Finkelstein. New York, Institute of Religious and Social Studies; distributed by Harper ₍1953₎. 21cm. pp.177–199)

I. Finkelstein, Louis, 1895– ed.
II. title - Thirteen American.

M355.2 Tobias, Channing H eggie , 1882–1961
H18f The importance of national unity.

(In: Hampton Institute. Conference on the participation of the Negro in national defense. Findings and principal addresses. Hampton, Va. 28cm. p. 52–55)

Tobias, Channing Heggie, 1882–1961
M378. New York (City) Mayor's Committee on Unity.
N42r Report on inequality of opportunity in higher education. New York, 1946.

19p. 26cm.

M323 Tobias, Channing H eggie , 1882–1961
T55w World implications of race. New York, Foreign Missions Conference of North America, 1944.

11–15p. 23cm.
Bound with Redfield, Robert. Race and human nature: an anthropologists view.
At head of title: Challenge of race.

1. Race question.

M06 Tobias, Channing H eggie , 1882–1961
Am35 The Work of the Young Men's and Young Women's Christian Associations with Negro youth.

(In: American Academy of Political and Social Science, Philadelphia. The American Negro. Philadelphia, 1928. 24cm. p. 283–286.

Tobias, Channing Heggie, 1882–1961
M323 U. S. *President's Committee on Civil Rights.*
Un3t To secure these rights, the report of the President's Committee on Civil Rights. Washington, U. S. Govt. Print. Off., 1947.

xii, 178 p. illus., maps. 25 cm.
Charles E. Wilson, chairman.

1. Civil rights—U. S. I. Wilson, Charles Erwin, 1890– II. Title.
JC599.U5A32 1947 323.4 47—46486*

Library of Congress ₍48x15₎

M267.3 Tobias, Channing Heggie, 1882–1961
Yo8b Young Men's Christian Associations. International Convention. Centennial.
Between two centuries: report of the Centennial International Y.M.C.A. Convention. New York, Association Press, 1951.

209p. ports. illus. 23cm.
Partial contents: Conditions of world peace and world unity, by Ralph Bunche.-Living is a Christian calling, by Benjamin Mays.

Tobias, Channing Heggie, 1882–1961
On securing strong and able students for the ministry.
M323 Negro Christian student conference. *Atlanta*, 1914.
T69 The new voice in race adjustments; addresses and reports presented at the Negro Christian student conference, Atlanta, Georgia, May 14–18, 1914. A. M. Trawick, editor ... Pub. by order of the executive committee of the conference. New York city, Student volunteer movement ₍1914₎

1 p. l., ₍v₎–vi p., 1 l., 230 p. 23½cm.
"Best books on the Negro in America and Africa": p. 221–224.

1. Negroes—Congresses. 2. U. S.—Race question. I. Trawick, Arcadius McSwain, 1869– ed. II. Title.

A 15–837

Springfield. Public library for Library of Congress E185.5.N38
₍a35f1₎

Tobias, Channing Heggie, 1882–1961.
On the work of the International Committee, YMCA.
M323 Negro Christian student conference. *Atlanta*, 1914.
T69 The new voice in race adjustments; addresses and reports presented at the Negro Christian student conference, Atlanta, Georgia, May 14–18, 1914. A. M. Trawick, editor ... Pub. by order of the executive committee of the conference. New York city, Student volunteer movement ₍1914₎

1 p. l., ₍v₎–vi p., 1 l., 230 p. 23½cm.
"Best books on the Negro in America and Africa": p. 221–224.

1. Negroes—Congresses. 2. U. S.—Race question. I. Trawick, Arcadius McSwain, 1869– ed. II. Title.

A 15–837

Springfield. Public library for Library of Congress E185.5.N38
₍a35f1₎

M841.8 Toby-Marcelin, Philippe, 1904-
T35 Canape-Vert by Philippe Thoby-Marcelin and Pierre Marcelin; translated by Edward Larocque Tinker. New York; Toronto, Farrar & Rinehart inc. (1944)

xxvii, 225 p. col. front. 21cm.

159212

Togoland Togoland.
M966.81 Equaggo, (Mrs.) Rose Y ,comp.
Eq2 First justice - then peace in connection with the Ewe and Togoland unification problem. ꜀Accra, West African Graphic Co., 1952꜆

36p. illus. map 20cm.

Toleration.

M323 Institutate for religious and social studies.
In8u Jewish theological seminary of America.
... Unity and difference in American life, a series of addresses and discussions, edited by R. M. MacIver. New York, and London, Pub. by Institute for religious & social studies, distributed by Harper & brothers 1947

5p. l., 3-168p. 21cm. (Religion and civilization series.)

MB9 Todd, Thomas Wingate.
T56c Cobb, William Montague, 1904-
Thomas Wingate Todd, an appreciation. Reprinted from the American journal of physical anthropology, 25:1-3, April-June 1939.

3p. 25cm.

Gold Coast Togoland-Civilization.
M966.7 Armattoe, Raphael Ernest Grail, -1954.
Ar5g The golden age of West African civilization, by Dr. R.E.G. Armattoe ... With an introduction by Prof. Dr. E. Schroedinger ... ꜀Londonderry?꜆ Pub. for the Lomeshie research centre by "The Londonderry sentinel," 1946.

98 (i.e. 116) p. incl. front. (port.) plates. 25½ cm.

M811.5 Tolson, Melvin Beaunorus, 1900-1966
T58h Harlem gallery, by M. B. Tolson. With an introd. by Karl Shapiro. New York, Twayne ꜀1965-

v. 21 cm.

Poetry.

CONTENTS.—book I. The curator.
Portrait of author on book jacket.

1. Negroes — New York (City) — Poetry. 2. Harlem, New York (City) — Descr. — Poetry. 3. Poetry of places — Harlem, New York (City) I. Title.

PS3539.O334H3 811.52 64-25063

Library of Congress ꜀5꜆

Todd, Walter E.
M811.5 Fireside musings ~~(poems)~~ second editions by Walter E. Todd. Washington, D. C., Murray brothers, 1908./1909
T56f 52 p., 1 l. port. 18cm.

8-20855

Library of Congress (Copyright 1908 A 209240)

Togoland (French)
Togoland (Fr)
M843 Ananou, David
An14 Le fils du fetiche; roman. Paris, Nouvelles Editions Latines, 1955.

198p. 18½cm.

1. Togoland (French)

M811.5 Tolson, Melvin Beaunorus, 1900-1966
T58l Libretto for the Republic of Liberia. New York, Twayne Publishers ꜀1953꜆
unpaged. 22 cm.

1. Liberia—Hist.—Poetry. I. Title.

PS3539.O334L5 811.5 53-13482 ‡

Library of Congress ꜀7꜆

M811.5 Todd, Walter E.
T56a A little sunshine, by Walter E. Todd. Washington, D. C., Murray bros. printing co. ꜀1917꜆
61 p., 1 l. front. (port.) 16cm. $0.50
Poems.
꜀First edition꜆

I. Title. 1. Poetry.
Library of Congress PS3601.T7L5 1917 17-30029
——— Copy 2.
Copyright A 477525

Togoland, West Africa.
Africa
MB9 Kuku, Aaron, 1860-1929.
K951 The life of Aaron Kuku of Eweland born 1860-died 1929, told by himself. Translated and abridged from the German version of Rev. P. Wiegrabe, and published by kind permission of the Verlag der Norddeutschen Mission, Bremen. London, The Sheldon Press, 1931.

24p. 18cm. (Little books for Africa)

M810.9 Tolson, Melvin Beaunorus, 1900-1966
H55am A poet's odyssey.

Pp. 181-195.

In: Hill, Herbert, ed. Anger and beyond. New York, Harper & Row, 1966.

M811.5 Todd, Walter E.
T56b A little sunshine, by Walter E. Todd. ꜀n.p., n.p., n.d.꜆

61p. front. (port.) 15cm.
Poems.

1. Poetry. I. Title.

The toiler's life.

M811.5 Harleston, Edward Nathaniel, 1869-
H22 The toiler's life; poems, by Edward Nathaniel Harleston; with an introduction by L. S. Crandall. Philadelphia, The Jenson press, 1907.
xv, 238 p. front. (port.) 19½cm.
Introduction (biographical) by L. S. Crandall.

I. Title. 7—32835

Library of Congress PS3515.A6T8
Copyright A 182881 ꜀a30b1꜆

M811.5 Tolson, Melvin Beaunorus, 1900-1966
T58 Rendezvous with America, by Melvin B. Tolson. New York, Dodd, Mead & company, 1944.
xii, 121 p. 19cm.
Poems.

I. Title. 1. Poetry.
Library of Congress PS3539.O334R4 44—7183
꜀45h3꜆ 811.5

M811.5 Todd, Walter E
T56p. Parson Johnson's lecture, by Walter E. Todd. Washington, D.C., Murray bros., 1906.
45p. front. 19cm.

1. Poetry
I. Title

Toleration.

M323 Council against intolerance in America.
C831 An American answer to intolerance. Teacher's manual no. 1, junior and senior high schools. Experimental form, 1939. New York city, Council against intolerance in America, 1939.
130 p., 1 l. 23 cm.
"Prepared by Frank Walser, with the assistance of Annette Smith and Violet Edwards."
"Bibliography of plays suitable for high school production": p. 117-118.
Bibliography: p. 119-130.
1. Propaganda. 2. Prejudices and antipathies. 3. Toleration. I. ~~Walser, Frank, tr. Smith, Annette, tr. Edwards, Violet.~~ IV. Title. V. Title: Intolerance. 1. Race relations. II. White, Walter, 1893-1955. A 40—2271
New York Univ. Wash. Sq. Library HM263.C7 for Library of Congress HM263.C6 ꜀a50m1꜆ 301.1523

M01 Tolson, Ruth M ,comp.
T58ht Hampton Institute press publications; a bibliography. Hampton, Virginia, Hampton Institute, 1959.

6p. 28cm.
Mimeographed.

1. Bibliographies. 2. Hampton Institute - Hampton, Virginia.- Bibliographies. I. Title.

Togoland.
Togoland
M966.81 Chapman, D A
C36h The human geography of Eweland (Anlo district). Paris, Librairie d'Amerique et d'Orient, 1950.

꜀79꜆ - 101p. maps. 27cm.
At head of title: Premiere Conference International des Africanistes de l'Ouest. tome 1.

Toleration.
M301 Frazer, Charles Rivers, 1879-
F84 White man, black man. ꜀1st ed.꜆ New York, Exposition Press ꜀1965꜆
60 p. 21 cm.

1. ~~U.S.~~—Race question. ~~2. Negroes.~~ 3. Toleration. I. Title.

E185.61.F826 301.45196073 65—8471

Library of Congress ꜀5꜆

Venezuela
M869.1 Tomás, Benito Luciano.
T59h Harlemitta dreams, by Benito Luciano Tomás. New York, 1934.
95 p. ~~illus. (port.) 20 cm.~~

I. Title. 1. Poetry.
Library of Congress PS3539.O34H3 1934 34-31635
——— Copy 2.
Copyright A 76089 ꜀3꜆ 811.5

M910
T59
Tomas, Rossi J 1926-
This America is also my country. New York, Pageant Press [1965]
131p. 21cm.
Portrait of author on book jacket.
1. Voyages and travels. I. Title.

Tomatoes.
M630.7
C25h6
Carver, George Washington, 1864-1943.
How to grow the tomato and 115 ways to prepare it for the table. Second edition..., by George W. Carver... Tuskegee Institute, Alabama, Experimental Station, Tuskegee Normal and Industrial Institute, 1936.
36p. 22½cm. (Bulletin no.35, April 1918)

M811.5
T59v
Tomlin, J Henri
Varied verses, a book of poems, by J. Henri Tomlin. Tampa, Fla., The author, c 1937
92p. 16½cm.
1. Poetry. I. Title.

Tomorrow is today.
M301
R56t
Robinson, James Herman.
Tomorrow is today. Philadelphia, Christian Education Press [1954]
127 p. 22 cm.
1. Social conditions. I. Title.
HN18.R57 *301.23 301.153 54-11556 ‡
Library of Congress [2]

Tomorrow was yesterday.
M812.5
B817t
Brown, James Nelson, 1933-
Tomorrow was yesterday; a play in nine scenes. New York, Exposition Press [1966]
57p. 21cm.
Portrait of author on book jacket.

Tomorrow's church in today's world...
M261
L61t
Licorish, David Nathaniel, 1904-
Tomorrow's church in today's world; a study of the twentieth-century challenge to religion. [1st ed.] New York, Exposition Press [1956]
172 p. 21 cm.
1. Church and social problems. 2. Church. I. Title.
HN31.L55 *261.8 55-9408 ‡
Library of Congress [2]

M811.5
T61y
Toney, Ieda Mai.
The young scholar, & other poems; with a critical introd. by Charles Leander Hill. Boston, Meador Pub. Co. [1951]
82 p. port. 21 cm.
I. Title. 1. Poetry
PS3539.O42Y6 811.5 51-5072
Library of Congress [2]

M817.08
B46a
Toomer, Jean, 1894-1967
Blood-burning moon.
(In: The Best American Short stories...1923. Boston, Houghton Mifflin, 1923. 21cm. p. 385-393.)

M810.8
Am29
Toomer, Jean, 1894-1967
Blue meridian [poem].
(In: The American caravan. 1936. New York, The Macaulay company, 1936. 22cm. pp. 633-653).

M813.5
T61
Toomer, Jean, 1894-1967
Cane [by] Jean Toomer; with a foreword by Waldo Frank ... New York, Boni and Liveright [c1923]
xi, [1] p., 2 l., 239 p. 19½ cm.
First edition.
I. Title.
23-12749
Library of Congress PZ3.T6184Ca
[a36c1]

M813.6
T61
Toomer, Jean, 1894-1967
Cane [by] Jean Toomer; with a foreword by Waldo Frank ... New York, Boni and Liveright [c1923]
xi, [1] p., 2 l., 239 p. 19½ cm.
First edition
I. Title.
23-12749
Library of Congress PZ3.T6184Ca
[a36c1]

M811.5
T61e
Toomer, Jean, 1894-1967
Essentials, by Jean Toomer. Definitions and aphorisms. Private ed. Chicago [The Lakeside press] 1931.
4 p. l., lxiv p. 18½cm.
"This edition is limited to one thousand numbered copies." This copy is ~~not numbered~~. 404.
1. Aphorisms. I. Title. 1. Poetry.
32-14189
Library of Congress PN6271.T65
——— Copy 2.
Copyright A 52188 [2] 818.5

M811.08
F825
Toomer, Jean, 1894-1967
[Poems]
(In: Four Negro poets: ... New York, Simon & Schuster, n.d. 21½cm. p. 12-14).

M323
T61
Toomer, Jean, 1894-1967
Race problems and modern society.
(In: Problems of civilization ... New York, D. Van Nostrand company, 1929. 18 cm. p. 67-114)
1. Race problems. I. Problems of civilization.

M810.8
Am29
Toomer, Jean, 1894-1967
Winter on earth.
(In: The American caravan. 1928. New York, The Macaulay company, 1928. 24cm. pp. 694-715).

M810.8
Am29
Toomer, Jean, 1894-1967
York beach.
(In: The American caravan. 1929. New York, The Macaulay company, 1929. 21cm. pp. 12-83).

Toomer, Jean, 1894-1967. Winter on earth. pp. 694-715
M810.8
Am3
1928
The Second American caravan, a yearbook of American literature... New York, The Macaulay company [1928]
v. 21½cm. ([v.3]: 21cm)
Editors: 1927, Van Wyck Brooks, Alfred Kreymborg, Lewis Mumford and Paul Rosenfeld. - 1928 - Alfred Kreymborg, Lewis Mumford and Paul Rosenfeld
Title varies: 1927, The American caravan, 1928 - The Second American caravan. 1929, The New American caravan. 1931, The American caravan, IV. 1936, The New caravan.
(over)

Ghana
M966
B63
Topics in West African history.
Boahen, Adu
Topics in West African history [by] A Adu Boahen. London, Longmans, 1966.
viii, 174p. map. 20cm. (Forum series)
Bibliography: p. 156-158.
1. Africa, West - History. I. Title.

MB
T629
Toppin, Edgar Allan, 1928- joint author.
~~Dobler, Lavinia G~~
Pioneers and patriots: the lives of six Negroes of the Revolutionary era [by] Lavinia Dobler and Edgar A. Toppin. Illustrated by Colleen Browning. [1st ed.] Garden City, N.Y., Doubleday, 1965.
118 p. illus., facsims., ports. 22 cm. (Zenith books)
1. ~~Negroes~~—Biog.—Juvenile literature. ~~I. Toppin, Edgar Allan, 1928- joint author.~~ II. Title.
E185.96.D6 j 920 65-17241
Library of Congress [5]

Torias; contes et proverbes créoles.
Haiti
M398
H75t
Hon, Addin.
Torias; contes et proverbes créoles. Port-au-Prince, Impr. du Collége Vertiéres, 1945.
50p. 20cm.
Errata leaf inserted.

The tornado in my mouth; poems.
M811.5
B55t
Black, Austin, 1928-
The tornado in my mouth; poems. [1st ed.] New York, Exposition Press [1966]
80 p. 22 cm.
I. Title.
PS3552.L28T6 811.54 66-8653
Library of Congress [3]

Zambia
XXXXXXX
M398.
T63
Torrend, J.
Specimens of Bantu folk-lore from northern Rhodesia; texts (collected with the help of the phonograph) and English translations by J. Torrend ... London, K. Paul, Trench, Trubner & co., ltd.; New York, E. P. Dutton & co., 1921.
iv, 187 p. illus. (map, music) 22½ cm.
1. Folk-lore, Bantu. 2. Folk-songs, African.
21—10554
Library of Congress [a33d1]

A touch of Midas.
Brit. Guiana
M823.91 Carew, Jan. Rynveld, 1923-
C18t
A touch of Midas. New York, Coward-McCann [1958]
288 p. 21 cm.
I. Title.
PZ4.C269To 58-10380 ‡
Library of Congress [5]

Touré, Sékou, Pres. Guinea, 1922-
Africa's destiny, pp. 35-47.
Africa
M960.3
D87a
Duffy, James, 1923- ed.
Africa speaks. Edited by James Duffy and Robert A. Manners. Princeton, N. J., Van Nostrand [1961]
223p. 23cm.

Puerto Rico
M861.
T63
Torres Rivera, Enrique, *ed.*
Parnaso portorriqueño, antología esmeramamente seleccionada de los mejores poetas de Puerto Rico por Enrique Torres Rivera. Barcelona, Maucci [1920]
351 p. 18½ cm.
1. Puerto Rican poetry (Collections) I. Title.
41-21059 Revised
Library of Congress PQ7434.T6
[r42c2] 861.0822

M811.5
B977t
Touch stone.
Butler, Anna Land
Touch stone. Wilmington, Delaware Poetry Center, 1961.
29p. 23cm.
1. Poetry. I. Title.

Guinea, Fr.
M966.52
T64a
Touré, Sékou, Pres. Guinea, 1922-
L'action politique du parti démocratique de Guinée. Paris, Présence Africaine, 1959.
249p. 21½cm.
Portrait of author on book.
1. Guinea, French - Politics and government.

Tôt ou tard.
Congo
(Democratic Republic)
M967.5
K13t
Kanza, Thomas R
Tôt ou tard ... (Ata ndele ...) Bruxelles, Le Livre africain [1959?]
87 p. 19 cm.
1. Nationalism—Congo, Belgian. 2. Congo, Belgian—Native races. I. Title.
DT644.K3 60-31883 ‡
Library of Congress [5]

Senegal
M966.3
B12
Toucouleurs.
Ba, Oumar
Notes sur la democratie en pays Toucouleur. [Dakar, Imprimerie A. Diop, n.d.]
52p. 22cm.
1. Toucouleurs. 2. Senegal - Native races. I. Title.

Guinea
M966.52
T64ac
Touré, Sékou, *Pres. Guinea*, 1922-
L'action politique du Parti démocratique de Guinée pour l'émancipation africaine. [Conakry, Impr. nationale, 1959-
v. illus. 24 cm.
Library has vol. 2 only.
1. Nationalism—Guinea, French. 2. Parti démocratique de Guinée. I. Title.
DT543.T6 60-22321 rev ‡
Library of Congress [r62b1]

Tote see.
Brazil
M869.3
Am1to
Amado, Jorge, 1912-
Tote see. Hamburg, Rowohlt Verlag, 1959.
220p. 18cm.

Toucouleurs.
Senegal
M966.3
D59
Diop, Abdoulaye Bara
Société Toucouleur et migration (enquete sur l'immigration Toucouleur à Dakar. [Dakar, Institut Francais d'Afrique Noire, 1965]
232p. illus, maps. (Initiations et études, no. XVIII)
Includes bibliography.

Africa
M960
F76
Touré, Sékou, Pres. Guinea, 1922-
Africa's future and the world.
Pp. 314-326.
In: Foreign Affairs (New York). Africa. New York, Praeger, 1964.

M261.8
T64
Tottress, Richard E
Heaven's entrance requirements for the races. [Rev. ed.] New York, Comet Press Books, 1957.
50 p. 21 cm. (A Reflection book)
1. U. S.—Race question. I. Title. 2. Christianity.
BR115.R3T6 1957 *261.8 57-8115 ‡
Library of Congress [5]

Tounka, nouvelle.
Senegal
M896.3
Sa1t
Sadji, Abdoulaye, 1910-
Tounka, nouvelle. Paris, Présence Africaine [1965]
90p. 17½cm.
I. Title.

Guinea, Fr.
M966.52
T64c
Touré, Sékou, Pres. Guinea, 1922-
Congrès général de l'U.G.T.A.N. (Union Générale des Travilleurs de l'Afrique Noire). Conakry 15-18 Janiver 1959. Rapport d'Orientation et de Doctrine présenté par Sékou Touré. Paris, Présence Africaine, 1959.
75p. 20cm.
1. Africa. I. Union Générale des Travailleurs de l'Afrique Noire.

A touch of innocence.
MB9
D92to
Dunham, Katherine.
A touch of innocence. [1st ed.] ~~New York, Harcourt, Brace [1959]~~ London, Cassell, 1960.
312 p. 22 cm.
Autobiographical.
Portrait of author on book jacket.
I. Title.
GV1785.D82A3 927.933 59—10256 ‡
Library of Congress [60x15]

La tour de Nesle, par Alexandre Dumas, père;
France
M840.
D89ta
Dumas, Alexandre, 1802-1870.
La tour de Nesle, par Alexandre Dumas, père; edited with introduction, notes and vocabulary by T. A. Daley ... Williamsport, Pa., The Bayard press [°1935]
v, 100 p. 21 cm.
A drama originally written by Fréderic Gaillardet was rewritten by Dumas and first published in 1832 as the work of "MM. Gaillardet et * * *". In 1839 it was reprinted giving both authors' names.
1. Marguerite de Bourgogne, queen consort of Louis x, 1290-1315—Drama. I. *Gaillardet, Fréderic, 1808-1882, joint author. II. Daley, Tatham Ambersley, ed. III. Title.
35-13054
Library of Congress PQ2227.T6 1935
——— Copy 2.
Copyright A 90530 [5] 842.77

Guinea, Fr.
M966.52
T64g
Touré, Sékou, Pres. Guinea, 1922-
Guinée; prélude à l'indépendance. Introduction by Jacques Rabemananjara. Paris, Presence Africaine, 1958.
175p. 24cm.
Portrait of author on book.
1. Guinea, French - Politics and government. I. Title.

A touch of innocence.
MB9
D92t
Dunham, Katherine.
A touch of innocence. [1st ed.] New York, Harcourt, Brace [1959]
312 p. 22 cm.
Autobiographical.
I. Title.
GV1785.D82A3 927.933 59—10256 ‡
Library of Congress [59k10]

Cameroun
M967.11
R629
Le tour du Cameroun en 59 jours.
Rifoe, Simon, 1943-
Le tour du Cameroun en 59 jours. Yaounde, Editions CLE, 1965.
58p. illus., map. 18cm.
Portrait of author on book jacket.
1. Cameroun - Description and travel. I. Title.

Guinea, Fr.
M966.52
T64e
Touré, Sékou, Pres. Guinea, 1922-
Expérience Guinéenne et unité Africaine. Preface, by Aimé Cesaire. Paris, Présence Africaine, 1959.
436p. 22½cm.
Portrait of author on book
1. Guinea, French. I. Cesaire, Aimé.

Guinea
M966.52 Touré, Sékou, Pres. Guinea, 1922-
T64in The international policy of the democratic party of Guinea. [n.p., Orientale de Publicité, n.d.]

241p. port. 24cm.
Cover title.
Collection of speeches, extracts of reports and speeches and remarks made by the author.

1. Guinea - Politics and government.
I. Title.

Haiti Toussaint Louverture, François Dominique, 1743-
M972.94 1803.
Scit Scharon, Faine.
Toussaint Louverture et la Révolution de St-Domingue. Port-au-Prince, Impr. de l'État [1957-
v. 24 cm.
Includes bibliography.
Library has: v. 2

1. Haiti—Hist.—Revolution, 1791-1804. 2. Toussaint Louverture, François Dominique, 1743-1803. 3. Haiti—Hist.—To 1791.

F1923.S35 60-43228 ‡
Library of Congress [2]

Toussaint Louverture, Pierre Dominique, 1746?-1803.
Haiti
MB9 Brutus, Timoléon C
T64b Rançon du génie; ou, La leçon de Toussaint Louverture, par Timoléon C. Brutus ... Port-au-Prince, Haïti, N. A. Théodore, 1945-
v. plates, port. 22½cm. (On cover: Collection "Pro patria")
"Bibliographie des ouvrages lus ou consultés pour écrire Rançon du génie."—v. 1, p. [i]-iii (1st group)

1. Toussaint Louverture, Pierre Dominique, 1746?-1803. I. Title.
46-20686
Library of Congress F1923.T785
[2] 923.27294

M813.4 Tourgée, Albion Winegar, 1838-1905.
T64f A fool's errand. Edited by John Hope Franklin. Cambridge, Belknap Press of Harvard University Press, 1961.
1961 404 p. 22 cm. (The John Harvard library)

1. Reconstruction—Fiction. 2. Ku-Klux Klan. I. Title.

PZ3.T64Fo 7 61-13744 ‡
Library of Congress [62f5]

Haiti
MB9 Toussaint l'ouverture: A biography and auto-
T64 biography. Boston, James Redpath, 1863.

x [11] - 372p. front. map. 19½cm.

I. Toussaint L'ouverture, Pierre Dominique, 1746? - 1803.
1. Haiti.
2. Christophe, Henri, King of Haiti, 1767-1820.

Toussaint - Louverture Bierre Dominique,
Martinique 1746?-1803.
MB9 Césaire, Aimé, 1913-
T64tc Toussaint Louverture; la révolution française et le proelème colonial.
Paris, Le Club Française du Livre, 1960.

288p. illus. 21cm.

Tourist trade development board of Jamaica, Kingston, Jamaica.
Jamaica Olley, Philip Peter, ed.
M972.92 Guide to Jamaica, compiled and edited by Philip P. Olley ...
O14g for the Tourist trade development board, Kingston, Jamaica, B. W. I. [Glasgow, Printed by R. Maclehose and co., ltd., The University press] 1937.
347 p. incl. front., illus., plates. maps (part fold.) 17½cm.
"First published 1937."

1. Jamaica—Descr. & trav.—Guide-books. I. Tourist trade development board of Jamaica, Kingston, Jamaica.
38—7270
Library of Congress F1869.O55
[38d3] 917.292

Toussaint Louverture, Pierre D.
Haiti
M972.94 [Morpeau, Moravia] ed.
M82d Documents inedits pour l'histoire. Correspondance concernant l'emprisonnement et la mort de Toussaint Louverture. Procès-verbal de l'autopsie de son cadavre au Fort de Jouv (Jura) France et rapport des médecin et chirurg en memoire du commissaire Julien Raymond sur la colonie de Saint-Domingue au premier consul Bonaparte publiés par M. Morpeau. Port-au-Prince, Imprimerie et Librairie der Sacre Coeur, 1920.
16p. 23cm.

Toussaint Louverture, Pierre Dominque.
Haiti 1746?-1803
M342 Ducasse, Vendenesse Estepha, 1872-
D85f Fort de joux, ou les derniers moments de Toussaint Louverture, drame historique en un acte. Port-au-Prince, Editions - Veteran [n.d.]

36p. illus. 17½cm.

1. Toussaint Louverture, Pierre Dominique, 1746?-1803. I. Title.

Congo Les touristes Congolais visitent.
Leopoldville
M914 Dimbamba, S
D59 Les touristes Congolais visitent la Belgique et l'exposition universelle de Bruxelles. [Leopoldville, Imprimerie le-Courrier d'Afrique, 1958]

29p. illus. 21cm. (Temps Nouveaux)

Haiti Toussaint Louverture, Pierre Dominique, 1746?-1803
MB9 Toussaint Louverture a travers sa correspond-
T64a ence, (1794-1798). Haiti, 1953.

480p. 20cm.
On cover: Tri-cinquantenaire de la Republique d'Haiti, 1804-1954.

1. Haiti - Hist. - To 1791
I. Gerard, M Laurent

Toussaint Louverture, Pierre Dominque,
Haiti 1746-1803.
M972.94 Edouard, Emmanuel
Ed6p ...Le panthéon haïtien, par Emmanuel-Edouard. Précédé d'une lettre a LL. MM. l'empereur du Brésil et le roi d'Espagne... Paris, Auguste Ghio, Editeur [1885]
76p. 19cm.

Toussaint, A. jt. auth.
Mauritius
M015.698 Adolphe, H
Ad72 Bibliography of Mauritius (1502-1954), covering the printed record, manuscripts, archivalia and carographic manterial, by A. Toussaint and H. Adolphe. Port Louis, Esclapon Ltd., 1956.

884p. 23cm.

Haiti
M972.94 Toussaint Louverture, Pierre Dominique, 1746?-1803.
T64t Toussaint Louverture et l'independance de Saint-Domingue; explication par des documents des Traités secrets entre Toussaint-Louverture, les Etats-Unis d'Amérique et l'Angleterre. Port-au-Prince, Société d'Edition et de Librairie, 1946.

145p. 23½cm.
Special number of Le Document, 20 Mai 1946; published under the patronage of the Société Toussaint-Louverture.
1. Haiti - Hist. - Revolution, 1791-
2. Haiti - For. Rel. - U.S. 3. Haiti - For. Rel.- Gt. Brit. 4. U.S. For rel.- Haiti. (over)

Toussaint Louverture, Pierre Dominique, 1746?-1803.
M812.5 Hill, Leslie Pinckney, 1880-
H55 Toussaint L'Ouverture, a dramatic history, by Leslie Pinckney Hill. Boston, The Christopher publishing house [°1928]
137, [1] p. front. (port.) 20½cm.

1. Toussaint Louverture, Pierre Dominique, 1746?-1803.
28—10695
Library of Congress PS3515.I 495T6 1928
[48d1]

La Toussaint des énigmes.
Algeria
M896.1 Aba, Noureddine
Ab12t La Toussaint des énigmes. Paris, Présence Africaine, 1963.

95p. 19½cm.
Portrait of author on book cover.

1. African poetry. I. Title

Toussaint Louverture, Pierre Dominique, 1746?-1803.
Haiti
MB9 Alexis, Stephen.
T64a3 Black liberator; the life of Toussaint Louverture. Tr. from the French by William Stirling. London, E. Benn. 1949.

227p. illus. ports. map. (on lining papers) 22cm.
An abridgment of Toussaint Louverture, libérataur d'Haiti.

Toussaint Louverture, François Dominique,
Trinidad 1743-1803.
M820 James, Cyril Lionel Robert, 1901-
J23b2 The Black Jacobins; Toussaint L'Ouverture and the San Domingo Revolution. 2d ed., rev. New York, Vintage Books [1963]
xi, 426 p. map. 19 cm.
"V242."
Bibliography: p. [379]-389.

1. Toussaint Louverture, François Dominique, 1743-1803. 2. Haiti—Hist.—Revolution, 1791-1804. I. Title.

F1923.T85 1963 972.9403 63-15043
Library of Congress [5]

Haiti
M972.94 Toussaint-Louverture, François-Dominique,
M35s
pp. 11-41

In Jean Price Mars' Silhouettes de Nègres et de Négrophiles. 1959.

Haiti Toussaint Louverture, Pierre Dominique,
MB9 1746?-1803.
T64a2 Alexis, Stéphen.
Black liberator; the life of Toussaint Louverture. Tr. from the French by William Stirling. New York, Macmillan Co., 1949.
227 p. illus., ports., map (on lining-papers) 22 cm.
An abridged translation of the author's Toussaint Louverture, libérateur d'Haïti.

1. Toussaint Louverture, Pierre Dominique, 1746?-1803. I. Title.

F1923.T683 923.27294 49—9931*
Library of Congress [50q5]

Toussaint Louverture, Pierre Dominique,
Trinidad 1746?-1803
M820 James, Cyril Lionel Robert, 1901-
J23b The black Jacobins; Toussaint Louverture and the San Domingo revolution [by] C. L. R. James. New York, The Dial press [1938]
xvi, 328 p. front., plates, ports., fold. map. 22cm.
Printed in Great Britain.
Bibliography: p. 317-322.

1. Toussaint Louverture, Pierre Dominique, 1746?-1803. 2. Haiti—Hist.—Revolution, 1791-1804. I. Title.
39-8293
Library of Congress F1923.T85
[8] 972.94

Toussaint Louverture, Pierre Dominique,
Trinidad 1746?-1803
M820
J23j
James, Cyril Lionel Robert, 1901-
Les Jacobins noirs; Toussaint Louverture et la revolution de Saint-Domingue par P.I.R. (i.e. C.L.R.) James. Tr. de l'anglais par Pierre Naville. Paris Gallimard 1949.
xix, 362p. map. 23cm. (La Suite des temps, 22)

Toussaint Louverture, Pierre Dominique, 1746?-1803.
Haiti
MB9
T64nt
Nemours, Alfred, 1883-
... Toussaint Louverture fonde à Saint-Domingue la liberté et l'égalite, avec des documents inédits. Port-au-Prince, Haïti, Imp. du Collège Vertières, 1945.
104 p. group port. 23cm.
At head of title: Général Nemours.
"Bibliographie": p. 97-102.
1. Toussaint Louverture, Pierre Dominique, 1746?-1803. 2. Haiti—Hist.—Revolution, 1791-1804.
F1923.T89072 923.27294 A 46-6000
New York. Public library for Library of Congress ₍2₎†

Toussaint Louverture, Pierre Dominique, 1746?-1803.
Haiti
MB9
T64
Toussaint l'ouverture: A biography and autobiography. Boston, James Redpath, 1863.
X ₍11₎ - 372p. front. map. 19½cm.

Toussaint Louverture, Pierre Dominique,
Trinidad 1746?-1803
M820
J23t
James, Cyril Lionel Robert, 1901-
Toussaint Louverture (Act II, Scene I)
(In: Life and letters to-day, 14:7-18, Spring 1936)

Toussaint Louverture, Pierre Dominque, 1746-1803
Haiti
MB9
T64nh
Nemours, Alfred, 1883-
... Histoire de la famille et de la descendance de Toussaint-Louverture. Avec des documents inédits et les portraits des descendants de Toussaint-Louverture jusqu'à nos jours. Port-au-Prince, Haiti, Imprimerie de l'État, 1941.
4 p. l., vii-viii, 308 p. front., pl., ports. 23cm.
At head of title: Général Nemours.
Bibliography: p. 290-302.
1. Toussaint Louverture, Pierre Dominique, 1746?-1803. 2. Louverture family. I. Title.
A 41-1743
Harvard univ. Library for Library of Congress F1923.T8907
₍48c1₎ 923.27294

Martinique
M842.91
G49m
Toussaint Louverture, Pierre Dominique, 1746?-1803-Drama.
Glissant, Edouard, 1928-
Monsieur Toussaint; théâtre. Paris, Éditions du Seuil, 1961.
237p. 18½cm.

Haiti
MB9
T641
Toussaint Louverture, Pierre Dominique, 1746?-1803.
Laurent, Gérard M
Coup d'œil sur la politique de Toussaint-Louverture. ₍Port-au-Prince, H. Deschamps, cover 1949₎
xix, 350, ₍4₎ p. illus. 20 cm.
"Bibliographie": p. ₍351₎-₍352₎
1. Toussaint Louverture, Pierre Dominique, 1746?-1803. 2. Haiti—Hist.—Revolution, 1791-1804.
F1923.T858 923.27294 50-19137
Library of Congress ₍1₎

Toussaint Louverture, Pierre Dominque, 1746?-1803.
Haiti
M972.94
M34his
Nemours, Alfred, 1883-
Histoire de la captivité et de la mort de Toussaint Louverture. Notre pèlerinage au Fort de Joux, avec les documents inedits. Paris, Editions Berger-Levrault, 1929.
315 ₍2₎ p. 22cm.
At head of title: Général Nemours.

M813.5
B64d
Toussaint Louverture, Pierre Dominique, 1746-1803—Fiction.
Bontemps, Arna Wendell, 1902-
Drums at dusk; a novel by Arna Bontemps. New York, The Macmillan company, 1939.
8 p. l., 226 p. illus. 21cm.
"First printing."
1. Haiti—Hist.—Revolution, 1791-1804—Fiction. 2. Toussaint Louverture, Pierre Dominique, 1746-1803—Fiction. I. Title.
39-10640 Revised
Library of Congress PZ3.B64376Dr
₍r41l3₎

Toussaint Louverture, Pierre Dominique, 1746?-1803.
Haiti
M972.94
L49p
Lecorps, Louis Marceau, ed.
... La politique extérieure de Toussaint-Louverture; nos premières relations politiques avec les États-Unis, lettres de Toussaint-Louverture et d'Edward Stevens (1799-1800) Port-au-Prince, Cheraquit, 1935.
1 p. l., ii, ₍3₎-107, vi p., 1 l. port. 22½cm.
At head of title: La. Marceau Lecorps.
1. Haiti—For. rel. 2. Haiti—For. rel.—U. S. 3. U. S.—For. rel.—Haiti. I. Toussaint Louverture, Pierre Dominique, 1746?-1803. II. Stevens, Edward.
A 41-3004
New York. Public library for Library of Congress ₍2₎

Toussaint Louverture, Pierre Cominique, 1746?-1803.
Haiti
MB9
T64p
Pauléus Sannon, H.
Histoire de Toussaint-Louverture, par H. Pauléus Sannon ... Port-au-Prince (Haiti) Impr. A. A. Héraux, 1920-
v. port. 24cm.
1. Toussaint Louverture, Pierre Dominique, 1746?-1803. 2. Haiti—Hist.—Revolution, 1791-1804.
20-22229
Library of Congress F1923.T898
₍44b1₎

Martinique
MB9
T64tc
Toussaint Louverture.
Césaire, Aimé, 1913-
Toussaint Louverture; la révolution française et le proelème colonial. Paris, Le Club Française du Livre, 1960.
288p. illus. 21cm.

Haiti
M972.94
M821i
Toussaint Louverture, Pierre Dominique, 1746-1803.
Morpeau ₍Moravia₎
Instruction pour tous. Conference sur Toussaint Louverture, prononcée en 1921 au théatre cinématographique aux Gonaives et a Parisiana au Port-au-Prince, par M. Morpeau. Port-au-Prince, Imp. V. Pierre-Noel ₍1922₎
42p. 25cm.

Toussaint-Louverture, Pierre Dominique, 1746?-1803.
Haiti
MB9
T64re
Saint-Rémy, Joseph.
Vie de Toussaint-L'Ouverture. Par Saint-Remy. Paris, Moquet, 1850.
xi, 408 p. front. (port.) 22½cm.
1. Toussaint-Louverture, Pierre Dominique, 1746?-1803. 2. Haiti—Hist.—Revolution, 1791-1804.
14-3387
Library of Congress F1923.T9
₍35b1₎

Tout pour plaire.
M813.5
H57to
Himes, Chester B , 1909-
Tout pour plaire. (The big gold dream). Traduit de l'américain par Yves Malartic. London, Librairie, 1959.
250p. 18cm.
Portrait of author on back of book jacket.

Haiti
MB9
T64m
Toussaint Louverture, Pierre Dominque, 1746-1802
Mossell, Charles W
Toussaint L'Ouverture, the hero of Saint Domingo, soldier statesman, martyr; or, Hayti's struggle, triumph, independence, and achievements. By Rev. C. W. Mossell ... Lockport, N. Y., Ward & Cobb, 1896.
2 p. l., ₍vii₎-xxx, ₍31₎-485, x p. front., illus., plates, ports., fold. map. 23 cm.
The work includes (p. ₍31₎-319) without acknowledgment, a translation of Thomas Prosper Gragnon-Lacoste's Toussaint Louverture. Paris, 1877.
1. Toussaint Louverture, Pierre Dominique, 1746-1803. 2. Haiti—Hist.—Revolution, 1791-1804. 3. Haiti—Hist.—1804- I. Gragnon-Lacoste, Thomas Prosper, b. 1820.
1-6703
Library of Congress F1923.T80
₍33e1₎

Toussaint Louverture, Pierre Dominique, 1746?-1803.
Haiti
MB9
L93s
Scharon, Faine
Toussaint Louverture et la révolution de St.-Domingue. Port-au-Prince, Imprimerie de l'Etat, 1957.
217p.

Senegal
M966.3
Se5pr
Touze, R L
Bignona en Casamance. Préface de Léopold Sédar Senghor. Dakar, Editions Sepa ₍1963₎
214p. illus., maps. 18cm.
White author.
1. Senegal - Description and travel. I. Title. II. Senghor, Léopold Sédar, 1906- Preface.

Toussaint Louverture, Pierre Dominique, 1746-1803.
Haiti
M972.94
N34hi
Nemours, Alfred, 1883-
... Histoire des relations internationales de Toussaint Louverture. Avec des documents inédits. Port-au-Prince, Haïti, Impr. du Collège Vertières, 1945.
208 p. incl. port. 22½ cm.
At head of title: Général Nemours.
"Liste des ouvrages du général Nemours": p. ₍7₎-₍9₎ "Bibliographie": p. 202-206.
1. Toussaint Louverture, Pierre Dominique, 1746?-1803. 2. Haiti—For. rel. I. Title.
A 45-4110
Harvard Univ. Library for Library of Congress ₍48c1₎

Haiti
MB9
T64t
Toussaint Louverto, Pierre Dominique, 1746?-1803.
Tardon, Raphael, 1911-
Toussaint Louverture. Le Napoleon noir. Paris, Bellenand, 1951.
254p. 19cm.

Panama
M986.2
W52t
Toward a better understanding.
Westerman, George W
Toward a better understanding. Preface by Gil Blas Tejeira. 2nd ed. ₍Panama₎ 1946.
20 p. 22 cm.
English and Spanish text, separately pated; added t.p. in Spanish.
Inscribed by author: Sincere regards, G. W. Westerman.
____ ______cop. 2. Inscribed by author: To Walter White with compliments. G. W. Westerman.

Toward interracial fellowship.
M323.2 Federal Council of the Churches of Christ in
F31t America. Dept. of Race Relations.
Toward interracial fellowship. New York, 1939.
7p. 22cm. (Interracial publications, no.42)
18th annual report.

Toward job adjustment...
Granger, Lester Blackwell, 1896–
M331 Toward job adjustment, with specific reference to the vocational problems of racial, religious and cultural minority
G76t groups, by Lester B. Granger ... Louis H. Sobel ... ₍and₎ William H. H. Wilkinson ... Prepared under the direction of Committee on minority groups, Section on employment and vocational guidance, Welfare council of New York city. ₍New York₎ Welfare council of New York city ₍°1941₎
78 p., 1 l. illus. 21½cm.
Bibliography: 76–78.
1. Interviewing. 2. Employment agencies. 3. Minorities. I. Sobel, Louis Harry, joint author. II. Wilkinson, William H. H. III. Welfare council of New York city. Section on employment and vocational guidance. IV. Title.
Library of Congress HD5861.G65 41-16628
₍10₎ 331.11511

Towards a Pax Africana.
Kenya Mazrui, Ali Al'Amin.
M960 Towards a Pax Africana; a study of ideology and ambi-
M458t tion ₍by₎ Ali A. Mazrui. ₍Chicago₎ University of Chicago Press ₍1967₎
xi, 287 p. 23 cm. (The Nature of human society series)
Bibliographical references included in "Notes" (p. 243-277)
1. Nationalism—Africa. I. Title. 2. Africa-Nationalism.
DT30.M35 1967a 320.9'6 67-12232
Library of Congress ₍7₎

Towards Nigeria's moral self-government.
Nigeria
M370 Solarin, Tai,
So42 Towards Nigeria's moral self-government. Ikenne, Tai Solarin, 1959.
95p. 21cm.

Jamaica Towards the stars.
M821.91 Marson, Una. M , 1905–
M35t Towards the stars; poems by Una Marson, with a foreword by L. A. G. Strong. Bickley, Kent, University of London press ltd. ₍1945₎
63 p. 16½cm.
"First printed February 1945."
I. Title.
Library of Congress PR6025.A695T6 45-6860
₍3₎ 821.91

The towers of Toron.
M813.5 Delany, Samuel R
D37t The towers of Toron. New York, Ace Books ₍1964₎
140p. 16cm.

Town life today.
Ghana
M966.7 Busia, Kofi Abrefa, 1913–
W83p Town life today.
pp. 236-242.
In: Pageant of Ghana, by Freda Wolfson. 1958.

Town on trial.
M813.5 Hooks, Nathaniel, 1926–
H76t Town on trial, a novel of racial violence in a southern town. ₍1st ed.₎ New York, Exposition Press ₍1959₎
165 p. 21 cm.
I. Title.
PZ4.H788To 59-3594 ‡
Library of Congress ₍2₎

Townsend, Henry.
Nigeria
M966.9 Crowther, Samuel Adjai, 1806-1891.
C88s Slave trade-African squadron. Letters from the Rev. Samuel Crowther ... and the Rev. Henry Townsend ... London, John Mortimer, 1850.
15p. 22cm.

M287.8 Townsend, Vince M 1869–
T66 Fifty-four years of African Methodism; reflections of a presiding elder on the law and doctrine of the African Methodist Episcopal Church. ₍1st ed.₎ New York, Exposition Press ₍1953₎
158 p. 21 cm.
1. African Methodist Episcopal Church—Government. 2. African Methodist Episcopal Church—Doctrinal and controversial works. I. Title.
BX8447.T68 287.8 53-11271 ‡
Library of Congress ₍3₎

M812.5 Townsend, Willa A
T66b Because he lives, a drama of the resurrection, in three parts... by Mrs. Willa A. Townsend... Nashville, Tenn., Sunday school publishing board of the National Baptist convention, c1924.
30 ₍2₎p. 19cm.
Music.
1.Drama. I.Title.

M812.5 Townsend, Willa A
T66b Because he lives, a drama of the resurrection, in three parts... by Mrs. Willa A. Townsend... Nashville, Tenn., Sunday school publishing board of the National Baptist convention, c1924.
30 ₍2₎p. 19cm.
Music.
1.Drama. I.Title.

M268.76 Townsend, Willa A arr.
T66s A song in the night time; a Christmas pageant-program for Sunday schools, arranged by Mrs. W.A. Townsend. Nashville, Tenn., Sunday school publishing board ₍n.d.₎
16p. 23cm.
Music included.
1. Pageants - Sunday school
2. Sunday schools - pageants.

Africa,
South
M780 Tracey, Hugh
T671e Lalela Zulu; 100 Zulu lyrics. With illustrations by Eric Byrd. Foreword by A. W. Hoernle. Johannesburg, Published by African Music Society, 1948.
121p. illus. 25cm.
White author.
1. Zulu-Music. 2. Music-Zulu. I. Title.

Track thirteen.
M813.5 Graham, Shirley
G760 Track thirteen.
(In: Welch, Constance, ed. Yale radio plays; ... Boston, Mass., Expression company, c1940. 21cm. p.131-63.)

Trade unions.
M331 Alston, Christopher C.
A17h Henry Ford and the Negro people. Wash., D. C. National Negro Congress and the Michigan Negro Congress, 1940.
22p. 19cm.

M331.88 Trade unions.
B53 The Birth of a union; what the press of the nation has to say about the new red cap; Excerpts from news stories, feature articles and editorials of leading American newspapers since 1938. Edited by Ernest Calloway. Chicago, United Transport Service Employees of American, Educational Department, 1940.
26p. 28cm.

M331.88 Trade unions.
C76c Congress of Industrial Organizations.
The CIO and the Negro worker together for victory. Washington, D.C.k Congress of Industrial Organizations, 194 .

M331 Trade unions.
C76c Congress of Industrial Organizations.
The C.I.O. and the Negro worker. Washington, Congress of Industrial Organizations, ₍193 ₎
7p. 10x23cm.

Trade unions.
M306 Hill, Timothy Arnold, 1888-
N21p Social significance to minority groups of recent labor developments.
(In: National Conference of Social Work. Proceedings, 1937. Chicago, University of Chicago Press, 1937. 23cm. p. 399-408)

Trade Unions.
M323. National Association for the Advancement of
N21 Colored People.
The Negro and the labor union with especial reference to the action of the American Federation of Labor in conference at Atlantic City, June, 1919. New York, 1919.
₍3₎ p. 24cm.

M331.88
N21n
Trade unions.
National Maritime Union.
The N.M.U. fights jim crow. New York, 1943.

13p. illus. 23cm.

Trinidad
M330
P13v
Trade Unions.
Padmore, George, 1903- ed.
The voice of coloured labour; Speeches and reports of colonial delegates to the world trade union conference, 1945. Manchester, Panaf Service [1945]

55p. 22cm.

M331.88
T371
Trade unions.
Thompson, Louise.
The IWO and the Negro people; A message and an appeal from Louise Thompson and Samuel Patterson. New York, International Workers Order, n.d.

[12]p. illus. ports. 15x11cm.

M331.88
T371
1943
Trade unions.
Thompson, Louise.
The IWO and the Negro people; A message & an appeal from Louise Thompson and Samuel C. Patterson. New York, International Workers Order, 1943.

22p. illus. ports. 15x23cm.

South Africa
M331.88
L56
Trade-unions - Africa, South.
Letsoaba, J
The fight for trade union rights in South Africa. [London, Union of Democratic Control Publications, n.d.]

13p. 21½cm.

1. Trade-unions - Africa, South.
2. Africa, South - Labor and laboring classes. I. Title.

M331
F85
Trade-unions—New York (City)
Franklin, Charles Lionel, 1910–
The Negro labor unionist of New York; problems and conditions among Negroes in the labor unions in Manhattan with special reference to the N. R. A. and post-N. R. A. situations, by Charles Lionel Franklin ... New York, 1936.
2 p. l., 7–417 p. 22½ᶜᵐ.
Thesis (PH. D.)—Columbia university, 1936.
Vita.
Published also as Studies in history, economics and public law, ed. by the Faculty of political science of Columbia university, no. 420.
Bibliography: p. 398–402.
1. Negroes—New York (City) 2. Negroes—Employment. 3. Trade-unions—New York (City) 4. Labor and laboring classes—New York (City) I. Title. II. Title: Negroes in the labor unions in Manhattan.

36—34118

Library of Congress E185.8.F732
Columbia Univ. Libr. [39d1] 331.88007471

M331
C31
Trade-unions— U.S.
Cayton, Horace R.
Black workers and the new unions, by Horace R. Cayton and George S. Mitchell. Chapel Hill, The University of North Carolina press, 1939.
xviii, 473 p. 23½ᶜᵐ.
"Three industries have been chosen for examination: iron and steel, meat packing, and railroad car shops."—Introd.
Bibliography: p. [458]–467.

1. Negroes—Employment. 2. Trade-unions—U. S. 3. Labor and laboring classes—U. S. I. Mitchell, George Sinclair, 1902- joint author. II. Title.

39–27580

Library of Congress E185.8.C39
[6] 331.6

M331
H24b
Trade-unions— U.S.
Harris, Abram Lincoln, 1899-
The black worker; the Negro and the labor movement, by Sterling D. Spero and Abram L. Harris. New York, Columbia university press, 1931.
x, 509 p., 1 l. 22½ cm.
Issued also as A. L. Harris's thesis (PH. D.) Columbia university.
Mr. Harris wrote chapters 2-5, 10, 14-15, 17-19.
"Bibliography of works cited": p. 485-496.

1. Negroes—Employment. 2. Trade-unions—U. S. 3. Labor and laboring classes—U. S. 4. Negroes—Civil rights. 5. U. S.—Race question. I. Harris, Abram Lincoln, 1899- joint author. II. Title. III. Title: The Negro and the labor movement.

31—3610

Library of Congress E185.8.S74
[44p^{1}2] [325.26] 331.6

M331
N21
Trade-unions-U.S.
National urban league (for social service among Negroes)
Negro membership in American labor unions, by the Department of research and investigations of the National urban league, Ira De A. Reid, director. New York, N. Y. [The Alexander press, 1930]
175 p. 23½ᶜᵐ.

1. Negroes—Employment. 2. Trade-unions—U. S. I. Title.

30—29407

Library of Congress E185.8.N31
[44r39l1] [331.8808] 325.26

St. Lucia
M330
L582
Trade-unions—West Indies, British.
Lewis, William Arthur, 1915–
Labour in the West Indies; the birth of a workers' movement, by W. Arthur Lewis; with a preface by A. Creech Jones, M. P. London, V. Gollancz ltd. and the Fabian society, 1939.
44 p. 21½ᶜᵐ. (*On cover:* Fabian society. Research series, no. 44)

1. Labor and laboring classes—West Indies, British. 2. Trade-unions—West Indies, British. I. Title.

41-9878

Library of Congress HX11.N42 no. 44
[2] (355.1062) 331.8809729

Virgin Islands
M811.5
C86t
Trade winds.
Creque, Cyril Felix William, 1899-
Trade winds. Newport, R. I., Franklin Print. House, 1934.

110p. 22½cm.

Peru
M985
P18t
... Tradiciones peruanas escogidas.
Palma, Ricardo, 1833–1919.
... Tradiciones peruanas escogidas (edición crítica) Prólogo, selección y notas de Luis Alberto Sánchez. Santiago de Chile, Ediciones Ercilla, 1940.
3 p. l., [9]–215, [3] p. 18ᶜᵐ. (*Half-title:* Biblioteca Amauta (Serie América) [V. 1])
"Noticia bibliográfica": p. 14–16.

1. Legends—Peru. 2. Peru—Hist. I. Sánchez, Luis Alberto, 1900- ed. II. Title.
[*Full name:* Manuel Ricardo Palma]

41—9583

Library of Congress F3400.P1732
[44e1] 985

Africa
M960
R245
Tradition et modernisme en Afrique noire.
Recontres internationales, Bouaké, Ivory Coast, 1962.
Tradition et modernisme en Afrique noire. Paris, Editions du Seuil [1965]
317p. 21cm.
"Organisées par le Centre cultural du Monastère bénedictin de Bouaké (Cote d'Ivoire)
Partial contents.- Les traditions africaines, gages de progrès, by Amadou Hampaté Ba.-

---

Guyana
M801
H249
Tradition, the writer and society.
Harris, Theodore Wilson.
Tradition, the writer and society: critical essays; with an appendix by C. L. R. James. London, Port of Spain, New Beacon, 1967.
75 p. 18½ cm. 8/-

(B 67-16502)

1. Literature and society—Addresses, essays, lectures. I. Title.

PR6058.A692T7 801 67-101761

Library of Congress [3]

British Guiana
M823.09
H24
Tradition and the West Indian novel.
Harris, Wilson
Tradition and the west Indian novel; a lecture delivered to the London West Indian Students' Union on Friday, 15th May, 1966. With an introduction by C. R. R. James. [London, London West Indian Students' Union, 1965]
17p. 21cm.

1. West Indian fiction - History and criticism. I. Title. II. James, C L R Introduction.

Haiti
M133
R44
La tradition voudoo et le voudoo haïtien.
Rigaud, Milo, 1904–
La tradition voudoo et le voudoo haïtien: son temple, ses mystères, sa magie. Photos. de Odette Mennesson-Rigaud. Paris, Niclaus, 1953.
433 p. illus., port., map. 28 cm.

1. Voodooism. 2. Folk-lore—Haiti. I. Title.

BL2490.R53 133.4 53—33161

Library of Congress [54c1]

Martinique
M842.91
C33t
La tragédie du roi Christophe.
Césaire, Aimé. 1913-
La tragédie du roi Christophe. Paris, Présence Africaine, 1963.

161p. 18cm.
Portrait of author on back cover.

1. Drama - Martinique. I. Title.

Haiti
M327.7
D46
Tragédies Américaines.
Desinor, Yvan M
Tragédies Américaines. Port-au-Prince, Imprimerie de l'Etat, 1962.

171p. 21cm.

1. Pan Americanism. I. Title.

M813.5
P68t
Tragedies of life.
Pitts, Gertrude.
Tragedies of life; takes place in the United States, by Gertrude Pitts ... Newark, N. J., ©1939.
62 p. 18ᶜᵐ.

I. Title.

39-25324

Library of Congress PZ3.P689Tr
—— —— Copy 2.
Copyright A 133698 [2]

M811.09
M84
Tragedy.
Morton, Lena Beatrice.
Negro poetry in America, by Lena Beatrice Morton. Boston, Mass., The Stratford company, 1925.
4 p. l., 71 p. illus. (music) 16ᶜᵐ.
"The tragedy": p. 67–71.
Bibliography: p. 66; "References used": p. 71.

1. Negro poetry (American)—Hist. & crit. 2. Tragedy. I. Title.

25—15782

Library of Congress PS310.N4M6
—— —— Copy 2.
Copyright A 861050 [41g1]

Nigeria
M020.7
Uz7
The tragedy of Prince Hamlet.
Uzodinma, Eddy C C
The tragedy of Prince Hamlet. Questions and answers; running analysis and critical essay; Macbeth and Hamlet contrasted. [Onitsha, Nigeria, Etudo, 1963]

83p. 21cm.

M973 St1

The tragedy of the Negro in America.

Stanford, Peter Thomas.

The tragedy of the negro in America. A condensed history of the enslavement, sufferings, emancipation, present condition and progress of the negro race in the United States of America, by Rev. P. Thos. Stanford ... Boston, Mass., Authors edition, 1898.

4 p. l., xvi, 230 p. incl. illus., plates, ports. front. 19cm.

1. Negroes.

Library of Congress E185.S79 12—5317

Copyright 1897: 34173 [a56d1]

M808.4 Sc8t

Tragic, The.

Scott, Nathan A *ed.*

The tragic vision and the Christian faith. New York, Association Press [1957]

346 p. 21 cm. (A Haddam House book)

Includes bibliography.

1. Religion in literature. 2. Tragic, The. 3. Christianity—Philosophy. I. Title.

PN49.S34 801 57—11604 ‡

Library of Congress [58x10]

M808.4 Sc8t

The tragic vision and the Christian faith.

Scott, Nathan A *ed.*

The tragic vision and the Christian faith. New York, Association Press [1957]

346 p. 21 cm. (A Haddam House book)

Includes bibliography.

1. Religion in literature. 2. Tragic, The. 3. Christianity—Philosophy. I. Title.

PN49.S34 801 57—11604 ‡

Library of Congress [58x10]

M973 R56d

Train ride to Arkansas.

Johnson, Mordecai Wyatt, 1890-

Train ride to Arkansas.

pp. 233-235.

In: The day I was proudest to be an American, by Donald B. Robinson. 1958.

M370 M11

The training of Negro teachers in Louisiana.

McAllister, Jane Ellen, 1899–

The training of Negro teachers in Louisiana, by Jane Ellen McAllister ... New York city, Teachers college, Columbia university, 1929.

vi, 95 p. 23½cm. (Teachers college, Columbia university. Contributions to education; no. 364)

Published also as thesis (PH. D.) Columbia university. Bibliography: p. 95.

1. Teachers, Training of—Louisiana. 2. Negroes—Education. 3. Negroes—Louisiana. I. Title. II. Title: Negro teachers in Louisiana, The training of.

Library of Congress LC2802.L8M3 1929 a 30—11031

——— Copy 2. LB5.C8 no. 364

Copyright A 21710 [41m1] 370.7

M811.5 H55t

A traipsin' heart.

Hill, Mildred Martin.

A traipsin' heart, by Mildred Martin Hill. New York, W. Malliet and co., 1942.

4p. l., 7-61p. 23½cm.

Poems.

M170 K67t

Traits of character illustrated in Bible light.

Kletzing, Henry F 1850–

Traits of character illustrated in Bible light. Together with short sketches of marked and marred manhood and womanhood, by H. F. Kletzing ... and E. L. Kletzing ... Naperville, Ill., Kletzing brothers, 1898.

1 p. l., vii, 8-371 p. incl. front., illus., ports. 20½cm.

1. Characters and characteristics. 2. Biography. I. Kletzing, Elmer L., joint author. II. Title.

Library of Congress BF831.K64 10—32088

Copyright 1898: 21453 [41d1]

M621 T85t

Transistors.

Turner, Rufus P

Transistors: theory and practice. New York, Gernsback Publications [1954]

144 p. illus. 22 cm. (Gernsback library, no. 51)

1. Transistors.

TK7872.T73T8 *621.34 621.38 54—10401 ‡

Library of Congress [54e5]

M811.5 W65t

Transitory.

Wilkinson, Henry Bertram, 1889-

Transitory, a poem by Henry B. Wilkinson. Dedicated to a peaceful world. Boston privately printed for the author by the Popular Poetry Publishers, [c1941]

20p. 16cm.

autographed copy

M331.88 B53

Transport workers.

The Birth of a union; what the press of the nation has to say about the new red cap; Excerpts from news stories, feature articles and editorials of leading American newspapers since 1938. Edited by Ernest Calloway. Chicago, United Transport Service Employees of America, Educational Department, 1940.

26p. 28cm.

M323.4 J56

Transportation--Segregation.

Jim crow cars abolished; According to the decision of the United States Supreme Court... Chicago, The Hansberry Foundation. [194].

10p. 22cm.

M323 R92

Transportation - Segregation.

Rustin, Bayard

We challenged Jim Crow! A report on the journey of reconciliation April 9-23, 1947, by George Houser and Bayard Rustin. New York, Fellowship of Reconciliation; Congress of Racial Equality, 1947.

15p. 22cm.

Senegal M966.3 T688

Traoré, Bakary.

Forces politiques en Afrique noire, par Bakari Traoré, Mamadou Lô et Jean-Louis Alibert ... Paris, Presses universitaires de France, 1966.

viii, 312 p. 24 cm. (Travaux et recherches de la Faculté de droit et des sciences économiques de Paris. Série "Afrique," no 2) 20 F. (F 66-12565)

Includes bibliographies.

1. Political parties—Senegal. 2. Africa, Sub-Saharan—Politics. I. Title. (Series: Paris. Université. Faculté de droit et des sciences économiques. Série "Afrique," no 2) II. Lo, Mamadou. III. Alibert, Jean-Louis.

JQ3396.A979T7 329.9'668 67-74794

Library of Congress [2]

Senegal M792 T68t

Traoré, Bakary

Le théâtre Négro-Africain et ses fonctions sociales. Paris, Présence Africaine, 1958.

159p. 22½cm.

Bibliographie: p. 151-153.

1. Africa - Theatre. I. Title.

Senegal M610 T68

Traore, Dominique

Comment le noir se soigne-t-il? Ou médecine et magie Africaines. Paris, Présence Africaine, [1965]

643p. 21½cm.

1. Medicine - Africa. 2. Africa - Social life and customs. I. Title.

Guinea M966.52 T68

Traore, Mamadou, 1916-

Connaissance de la République de Guinée. [n.p.] Ministère de l'Information et du Tourisme de la République de Guinée [1960]

56p. 23½cm.

At head of title: Mamadou Traore Rayautra.

1. Guinea. I. Title.

Guinea M960 T68

Traore, Mamadou, 1916-

Considerations sur la loi-cadre dans les territoires d'outre-mer par Ray Autra [pseud] Porto-Novo, Dahomey, Union Démocratique Dahomeene [n.d.]

30p. 21cm.

1. France - Colonies - Africa. 2. Africa - Politics and government. I. Title.

Guinea M896.1 T68v

Traore, Mamadou, 1916-

Vers la liberté; poemes, [par] Ray Autra [pseud.] Pekin, Librairie du Nouveau Monde, 1961.

61p. 21½cm.

1. African poetry. I. Title.

Traumatism

See

Wounds and injuries under names of organs and regions of body, e.g. Chest--Wounds and injuries.

Haiti M360 H61t

Travail social.

Hippolyte, Simone W , 1918-

Travail social; panorama et details. [Port-au-Prince] Imp. Les presses libres, 1951.

141p. port. 20cm.

Brazil M869.1 C27e

Travassos, Renato.

Castro Alves, Antonio de, 1847-1871.

... Espumas fluctuantes. Nova ed. Prefacio de Renato Travassos. Rio [de Janeiro] Editora Guanabara, Waissman, Reis & cia. ltda., 1932.

210, [2] p. 19cm.

At head of title: Castro Alves. Poems.

I. Travassos, Renato. II. Title.

Library of Congress PQ9697.C35E8 1932 33-10462

[2] 869.1

Travel.
M39 D72c
Dorr, David F
A colored man round the world. By a quadroon. [Ohio] Printed for the author, 1858.
192p. front. 20½cm.

Travel.
France M840 D89q
Dumas, Alexandre, 1802-1879.
Quinze jours au sinai. Bruxelles, Meline, Cans et Cie., 1839.
2 vols. in 1 16cm.

Travel.
France M840 D89ve
Dumas, Alexandre, 1802-1870
Le veloce, ou; Tanger, Alger et Tunis. Bruxelles, Meline, Cans et cie., 1849.
3 vols in 2. 16cm.

Travel.
M910 T69
Travelguide. New York, Travelguide, Inc., 1955.
126p. illus. 23cm.

Travel books.
M973 P93
Price, Willard.
The negro around the world, by Willard Price ... pictorial maps by George Annand. New York, George H. Doran company [°1925]
75 p. incl. front., maps. 19½cm.
1. Negro race. I. Title.
25—9188
Library of Congress HT1581.P7 [s25d3]

Travel in Switzerland.
France M914.94 D89
Dumas, Alexandre, 1802–1870.
Travels in Switzerland. Translated by R. W. Plummer and A. Craig Bell. Edited by A. Craig Bell. London, A. Owen [1958]
230 p. illus., port. 20 cm.
Translation and condensation of Impressions de voyage. Suisse.
1. Switzerland—Descr. & trav. I. Title.
DQ23.D823 914.94 60-51296
Library of Congress [8]

Mali M496 T69c
Travélé, Moussa
Le catéchisme des noirs; électeurs du Sénégal et des colonies, par Moussa - Mangoumbel, [pseud.] Bordeaux, Imprimerie Générale D'Émile Crugy, 1899.
80p. 18½cm.
I. Title.

Mali M496 T69pe
Travélé, Moussa.
Petit dictionnaire Français-Bambara et Bambara-Français, par Moussa Travélé. Paris, Librarie Paul Geuthner, 1913.
281p. 18cm.
1. Bambara language - Dictionnaries.

Mali M496 T69p
Travélé, Mossa.
Petit manuel Français-Bambara, par Moussa Travele. 2e edition revue et augmentée. Paris, Librairie orientaliste Paul Geuthner, 1923.
89p. 19cm.
1. Bambara language-Grammar.

Mali M398 T69p
Travélé, Moussa.
Proverbs et contes Bambara accompagnés d' une traduction française et précédés d'un abrégéde droit coutumier Bambara et Malinke, par Moussa Travélé. Paris, Librairie Orientaliste Paul Geuthner, 1923.
240p. 22cm.
1. Bambara folktales.

M910 T69
Travelguide. New York, Travelguide, Inc., 1955.
126p. illus. 23cm.

The traveller of the East.
Basutoland M896.3 M72t
Mofolo, Thomas, 1875?-
The traveller of the East, by Thomas Mofolo. London, Society for Promoting Christian knowledge, n.d.
125p. 18cm.

Trawick, Arcadius McSwain, 1869- ed.
M323 T69
Negro Christian student conference. *Atlanta*, 1914.
The new voice in race adjustments; addresses and reports presented at the Negro Christian student conference, Atlanta, Georgia, May 14–18, 1914. A. M. Trawick, editor ... Pub. by order of the executive committee of the conference. New York city, Student volunteer movement [1914]
1 p. l., [v]–vi p., 1 l., 230 p. 23½cm.
"Best books on the Negro in America and Africa": p. 221–224.
1. Negroes—Congresses. 2. U. S.—Race question. I. Trawick, Arcadius McSwain, 1869- ed. II. Title.
A 15–837
Springfield. Public library for Library of Congress E185.5.N38 [a35f1]

The treasure of Pleasant Valley.
M813.5 Y46t
Yerby, Frank, 1916–
The treasure of Pleasant Valley. New York, Dial Press, 1955.
348 p. 21 cm.
I. Title.
Full name: Frank Garvin Yerby.
PZ3.Y415Tr 55–9940 ‡
Library of Congress [15]

The treasure of Pleasant Valley.
M813.5 Y46t
Yerby, Frank, 1916-
O tesouro do vale aprazivel; romance. (The treasure of Pleasant Valley). Tradução de Bernice Xavier. Rio de Janeiro, Livraria José Olympio Editôra, 1959.
214p. 23½cm.

A treasury of East African literature.
Kenya M398 G26
Gecaga, Bethuel Mareka
Gwata ndaĩ, ndaĩ na ng'ano. [Riddles and stories, a miscellany. Illustrated by W. S. Agutu] Nairobi, Eagle Press, 1950.
39p. illus. 18½cm. (Mabuku ma kuiga muthithu wa maundu maitu. [A treasury of East African literature])
Written in Kikuyu.
1. Riddles, African. 2. Folk-lore - Kenya. I. Title. II. Series: A treasury of East African literature. III. Agutu, W. S., illus.

A treasury of East African Literature.
Zanzibar M896.3 Om1h
Omar, C A Shariff
Hadithi ya hazina binti Sultani. [The tale of Hazina, the Sultan's daughter] Nairobi, Eagle Press, 1951.
33p. illus. 21½cm. (A Treasury of East African Literature)
Written in Swahili.
I. Title. II. Series.

Treasury of East African literature.
Zanzibar M896.3 Om1k
Omar, C A Shariff
Kisa cha hasan-Li-Basir. [The adventures of Hasan-Li-Basir] Nairobi, Eagle Press, 1951.
30p. illus. 21cm. (Treasury of East African literature)
Written in Swahili.
I. Title. II. Series.

Treasury of East African stories.
Kenya M896.3 M29s
Malo, S
Sigend Luo ma duogo chuny [Merry stories] Ogor gi W. S. Agutu. Nairobi, Eagle Press, 1951.
42p. illus. 21½cm. (Treasury of East African stories)
Written in Luo.
1. Short stories - Kenya. I. Title. II. Agutu, W. S., illus. III. Series.

A treasury of the blues.
M784 H19tr
Handy, William Christopher, 1873– *ed.*
A treasury of the blues; complete words and music of 67 great songs from Memphis blues to the present day. With an historical and critical text by Abbe Niles. With pictures by Miguel Covarrubias. [New York?] C. Boni; distributed by Simon and Schuster [1949]
258 p. illus. 29 cm.
First ed. published in 1926 under title: Blues, an anthology.
"A selective bibliography": p. 254–255.
1. Music, Popular (Songs, etc.)—U. S. I. Niles, Abbe, 1894– II. Title.
M1630.18.H26B5 1949 784 49—50282*
Library of Congress [56f²2]

The treasury of Negro spirituals.
M784 C35
Chambers, Herbert Arthur, ed.
The treasury of Negro spirituals; ed. by H. A. Chambers. London, Blandford Press [1953]
125p. cm.
Foreword by Marian Anderson.
"First published in 1953."
White editor.
1. Spirituals. I. Anderson, Marian, 1908- II. Title.

Treat it gentle.

MB9
B37
Béchet, Sidney.
Treat it gentle. London, Cassell [1960]
vii, 245 p. illus., ports. 23 cm.
Imprint stamped on t. p.: New York, Hill & Wang.
"A catalogue of the recordings of Sidney Béchet, compiled by David Mylne": p. 221-240.

1. Béchet, Sidney. I. Title.
ML419.B23A3 927.8 60-4214
Library of Congress [3]

Trees-Haiti.

Haiti
M972.94
B94
Burr-Reynaud, Frédéric, 1884-
... Visages d'arbres et de fruits haïtiens. Port-au-Prince, Haïti [Impr. du Collège Vertières] 1940.
6 p. l., 9-218 p. front. (port.) 20½cm.
Errata leaf mounted on p. [3] of cover.

1. Trees—Haiti. 2. Fruit. I. Title.
44-38584
Library of Congress PQ3949.B8V5
[3] 581.97294

M371.974
T87n
Trent, William Johnson, 1873-
Salutation to the new president for th United Negro College Fund, p. 120.
Tuskegee Institute.
The new south and higher education: what are the implications for higher education of the changing socio-economic conditions of the south? A symposium and ceremonies held in connection with the inauguration of Luther Hilton Foster, fourth president of Tuskegee Institute [October 31 and November 1, 1953. Tuskegee, Ala.] Dept. of Records and Research, Tuskegee Institute, 1954.
x, 145p. map. 24cm.

Treat it gentle.

MB9
B37a
Béchet, Sidney.
Treat it gentle. ~~London, Cassell [1960]~~ New York, Hill and Wang [1960]
vii, 245 p. illus., ports. 23 cm.
~~Imprint stamped on t. p.: New York, Hill & Wang.~~
"A catalogue of the recordings of Sidney Béchet, compiled by David Mylne": p. 221-240.

1. Béchet, Sidney. I. Title.
ML419.B23A3 927.8 60-4214
Library of Congress [3]

Trees along the highway.

M811.5
P93
Pritchard, Gloria Clinton.
Trees along the highway. New York, Comet Press Books [1953]
26 p. 23 cm.
Poems.

I. Title.
PS3531.R67T7 811.5 54-1228 rev
Library of Congress [r54c3]

M343.3
D34s
Trenton, New Jersey.
Dean, Elwood.
The story of the Trenton six. New York, New Century, 1949.
23p. 19cm.

The treatment of rheumatism...

M610
P19
v.1, no.5
Jackson, Algernon Brashear, 1878-
The treatment of rheumatism by injection of magnesium sulphate, by Algernon Brashear Jackson... Reprinted from "The Practitioner for January, 1912.
3p. 24½cm.
Bound in: Medical pamphlets.

France
M841
So3t
Le trembleur.
Ségalas, Anaïs (Menard) 1814-1895.
Le trembleur, comedie en deux actes, mêlée de couplets, par mme Anaïs Ségalas, représentée, pour la première fois, à Paris, sur le Second Theatre.-Français le 8 septembre 1849.
14 p. 23½ cm.

M323.
N212
Trenton, New Jersey.
National Association for the Advancement of Colored People. Legal Defense and Educational Fund.
The fantastic case of the Trenton six. New York, 1951.
5p. 22cm.

The treatment of the Negro in American history school textbooks.

M371.32
C22
Carpenter, Marie Elizabeth.
The treatment of the Negro in American history school textbooks; a comparison of changing textbook content, 1826 to 1939, with developing scholarship in the history of the Negro in the United States [by] Marie Elizabeth Carpenter. Published with the approval of Professor Erling M. Hunt, sponsor. [Menasha, Wis., George Banta publishing company, °1941]
4 p. l., 137 p. 23½cm.
Bibliography: p. [130]-137. Bibliographical foot-notes.

1. Negroes. 2. U. S.—Hist.—Historiography. 3. Text-books—U. S. I. Title.
41—8011
Library of Congress E185.C2
[41d2] 325.260973

Nigeria
M966.9
T72h
Tremearne, Arthur John Newmann, 1877-1915.
Hausa superstitions and customs; an introduction to the folklore and the folk, by Major A. J. N. Tremearne ... with forty-one illustrations, over two hundred figures in the text, and a map. London, J. Bale, sons & Danielsson, ltd., 1913.
xv, 548 p. illus., plates, fold. map. 23½cm.

1. Hausas. 2. Folk-lore, Hausa.
13—15578
Library of Congress GN653.T7
[44f1]

M343.3
D34s
Trenton six.
Dean, Elwood.
The story of the Trenton six. New York, New Century, 1949.
23p. 19cm.

The treatment of tuberculosis...

M610
P19
V.1
no.4
Jackson, Algernon Brashear, 1878-
The treatment of tuberculosis, encouraging results with calcium cacodylate and calcium iodide. By Algernon Brashear Jackson... Reprinted from the New York medical journal for May 24, 1913.
10p. 20½cm.

The trend of the races.

M323.2
H33t
Haynes, George Edmund, 1880-
The trend of the races [by] George Edmund Haynes ... with an introduction by James H. Dillard. New York, Council of women for home missions and Missionary education movement of the United States and Canada [°1922]
xvi p., 1 l., 205 p. front., plates. 19½cm.
"A select reading list": p. 201-205.

1. Negroes. 2. U. S.—Race question. I. Title.
22—15670
Library of Congress E185.61.H48
[38d1]

M323.
N212
Trenton six.
National Association for the Advancement of Colored People. Legal Defense and Educational Fund.
The fantastic case of the Trenton six. New York, 1951.
5p. 22cm.

Bahamas
M821
C89
Tree, Iris
In Nassau, [poem].
(In: Culmer, Jack, comp. A book of Bahamian verse. 2d ed. London, J. Culmer, 1948. 23cm. p. 41.)

M371.974
T87n
Trenholm, Harper Council, 1900-
Salutation to the new president for the American Teachers Association, p. 119.
Tuskegee Institute.
The new south and higher education: what are the implications for higher education of the changing socio-economic conditions of the south? A symposium and ceremonies held in connection with the inauguration of Luther Hilton Foster, fourth president of Tuskegee Institute [October 31 and November 1, 1953. Tuskegee, Ala.] Dept. of Records and Research, Tuskegee Institute, 1954.
x, 145p. map. 24cm.

M326.99B
W24s
Trow, J.M.
Strickland, S.
Negro slavery described by a Negro: being the narrative of Ashton Warner, a native of St. Vincent's. With an appendix containing the testimony of four Christian ministers recently returned from the colonies on the system of slavery as it now exists. By S. Strickland... London, Samuel Maunder, 1831.
144p. 15½cm.

Egypt
M896.2
H13t
The tree climber.
ad-Hakim, Tewfik
The tree climber; a play in two acts. Translated from the Arabic by Denys Johnson-Davies. London, Oxford University Press, 1966.
87p. 19cm.

I. Title.

M811.5
T72m
Trent, Hattie Covington
My memory gems. North Carolina, Livingstone College, 1948.
87p. ports. 22cm.
Autographed.

1. Poetry. I. Title.

Puerto Rico
M863
L13t
El 30 de febrero.
Laguerre, Enrique A
... El 30 de febrero (vida de un hombre interino) San Juan de Puerto Rico, Biblioteca de autores puertorriqueños, 1943.
338 p., 2 l. 20½cm.
A novel.

I. Title.
A 43-3168
Harvard univ. Library for Library of Congress PQ7439.L3T7
[3]† 863.6

The trey of sevens.

M350. Hornsby, Henry Haywood, 1923-
H78t The trey of sevens. Dallas, Mathis, Van Nort [1946]
xvii, 126 p. illus., ports. 20 cm.
"Based on activities of Battery 'C' of the 777th Field Artillery Battalion in the Ninth Army sector."—p. xii.
Map on lining-papers.

1. World War, 1939-1945—Personal narratives, American. 2. U. S. Army. 777th Field Artillery Battalion. 3. World War, 1939-1945—Campaigns—Western. I. Title.

D769.34 777th.H6 940.542 47—27938*
Library of Congress [50c1]

The trial of Obafemi Awolowo.

Nigeria
M966.9 Jakande, L K
J21 The trial of Obafemi Awolowo, by L. K. Jakande. London, Secker & Warburg; Lagos, John West Publications, 1966.
xiv, 354 p. front. (port.) 7 plates (incl. facsims., ports.) 22½ cm. 42/- (B 66-24229)

1. Awolowo, Obafemi, 1909- 2. Nigeria—Pol. & govt. I. Title.

343.31 67-71081
Library of Congress [3]

MB9 A tribute of respect, commemorative of the
B81tr worth and sacrifice of John Brown of Ossawatomie; it being a full report of the speeches made and the resolutions adopted by the citizens of Cleveland at a meeting held in the Melodeon on the evening of the day on which John Brown was sacrificed by the Commonwealth of Virginia: together with a sermon, commemorative of the sad event... Cleveland, Published for the benefit of the widows and families of the Revo-

---

Triad.

M811.5 Harris, Helen C.
H24t Triad. Poems by Helen C. Harris, Lucia Mae Pitts [and] Tomi Carolyn Tinsley. Privately published, December, 1945.
95p. 21cm.

The trials and death of lumumba.

Nigeria
M896.2 Stephen, Felix N
St43t The trials and death of Lumumba. Onitsha [Nigeria] M.A. Ohaejesi [n.d.]
42p. ports. 20½cm.

Card 2

MB9 lutionists of Harper's Ferry, 1859.
B81tr 62p. 21½cm.

1. Brown, John. I. Langston, C H., p. 16-23.

The trial and the fire.

M813.5 Ramsey, LeRoy L.
R149 The trial and the fire. New York, Exposition Press [1967]
160p. 21cm.
Portrait of author on book cover.

I. Title.

Nigeria The trials of Brother Jero.
M896.2 Soyinka, Wole
So3f Five plays: A dance of the forests, The lion and the jewel, The swamp dwellers, The trials of Brother Jero [and] The strong breed. London, Oxford University Press, 1964.
276p. 20cm. (A Three crowns book)

Tricks.

M133 Black Herman's easy pocket tricks which
B56 you can do. All new tricks... [New York, Martin Publishing Co., n.d.]
160p. illus. 22½cm.

Trial by fire and 25 other full length sermons.

M252 Borders, William Holmes, 1905-
B64t Trial by fire and 25 other full length sermons. Atlanta, Georgia, Author, 195?
127p. port. 23cm.

Nigeria The trials of Brother Jero.
M896.2 Soyinka, Wolè
So3t Three plays. Book design and illustration by Dennis Williams. Ibadan, Ibadan University Press, 1963.
118p. 21cm. (Mbari Publications).
Contents: The swamp-dwellers. The trials of Brother Jero. The strong breed.

Trigo, Felipe, 1864-1916.

M808.3 Watkins, Alma Taylor.
W32 Eroticism in the novels of Felipe [sic] Trigo. New York, Bookman Associates [1954]
162 p. 23 cm.
Includes bibliography.

1. Trigo, Felipe, 1864-1916. I. Title.

PQ6637.R5Z9 863.6 54-8091 ‡
Library of Congress [1]

The trial of Chief Awolowo.

Nigeria
M896.2 Mbah, A N
M45t The trial of Chief Awolowo and twenty others; a drama. Onitsha, Appolos Brothers Press, 1963.
40p. 21cm.

Nigeria The trials of Lumumba, Jomo Kenyatta and St. Paul.
M896.2 Stephen, Felix N
St43tr The trials of Lumumba, Jomo Kenyatta and St. Paul. Onitsha, Njoku and Sons Bookshop, n.d.
44p. ports. 21½cm.

Trinidad.

Trinidad
M972.98 Achong, Tito Princilliano.
Ac4m ... The Mayor's annual report. A review of the activities of the Port-of-Spain City council, with discourses on social problems affecting the Trinidad community, for the municipal year 1942-43, by his worship the Mayor Alderman Tito Pachong. Boston, Meador Publishing Co., [1944]
343p.

The trial of Hitler.

Nigeria
M896.2 Oleyede, S P
OL2 The trial of Hitler; a play. Aba [Nigeria] International, n.d.
12p. 15cm.

The Triangle's end.

M813.5 Jones, William H 1910-
J73 The triangle's end, a novelette. [1st ed.] New York, Exposition Press [1954]
79 p. 21 cm.

I. Title.

PZ4.J8Tr 54-5750 ‡
Library of Congress [2]

Trinidad.

Trinidad
M796.358 James, Cyril Lionel Robert.
J23 Beyong a boundary. London, Hutchinson 1963.
255p. 21½cm.

The Trial of Jomo Kenyatta.

Kenya
M967.65 Slater, Montagu
S11t The Trial of Jomo Kenyatta. London, Secker & Warburg, 1955.
255p. 21cm.
White Author

1. Kenya - Politics and government. I. Kenyatta, Jomo. II. Title.

A tribute for the Negro.

M973 Armistead, Wilson, 1819?-1868.
Ar5t A tribute for the Negro; being a vindication of the moral, intellectual, and religious capabilities of the coloured portion of mankind; with particular reference to the African race. Illustrated by numerous biographical sketches, facts, anecdotes, etc. ... By Wilson Armistead. Manchester, W. Irwin; American agent, W. Harned, New York; [etc., etc.] 1848.
xxxv, 564 p. front., plates, ports., facsims. 23½cm.
Title and text within ornamental borders.

1. Negro race. I. Title.

12—30165
Library of Congress HT1581.A6
——— Copy 2. [41e1]

Trinidad.

Trinidad
M972.98 Mendes, Alex. L
M52m The marine fishes of Trinidad [by] Alex. L. Mendes. Trinidad, B. W. I., Trinidad publishing co., ltd., 1940.
28p. 21½cm.
Inscribed copy: To Captain A. A. Cepriani, with the compliments of the author, Alex. L. Mendes, 31 July 1940.

Trinidad
Tobago
M972.98
Ot5a
Ottley, Carlton Robert, 1914-
An account of the life in Spanish Trinidad (from 1498-1787) with a chronological table of events and sundry appendices. Trinidad, Printed by the college press, 1955.
135p. illus. 21cm.

Trinidad.
Tobago
M972.98
Ot5tr
Ottley, Carlton Robert, 1914-
Trinidad; land of the calypso, steelband, humming bird, pitch lake, and the Cascura. Tobago, Robinson Crusoe's Isle. Port-of-Spain, Trinidad, 1954.
36p. illus. 21½cm.

Trinidad.
M326.5
P33r
Peck, Nathaniel.
Report of Messrs. Peck and Price, who were appointed at a meeting of the free colored people of Baltimore, held on the 25th November, 1839, delegates to visit British Guiana and the Island of Trinidad; and other information, showing the advantages to be derived by immigrating to those colonies.
32p. 23½cm.

Trinidad.
Martinique
M972.98
P53a
Philip, John Baptist.
An address to the Right Hon. Earl Bathurst. His Majesty's Principal of State for the Colonies, relative to the claims which the coloured population of Trinidad have to the same civil and political privileges with their white fellow-subjects. By a free mulatto of the Island. London, Printed in the year 1824.
298p. 20cm.

Trinidad
Trinidad
M972.98
T212
Taylor, Edward
The mayor's report for the Mayoral terms 1960-1961 and 1961-1962. Port-of-Spain, P.N.M. Pub. Co., Ltd., 1962
12p. illus. 28½cm.
Portrait of author.

Trinidad.
Trinidad
M972.9
W67c
Williams, Eric, ed.
Caribbean historical review. Port-of-Spain, Trinidad Pub. Co., 1951.
152p. 21½cm. (Historical Society of Trinidad and Tobago ... No. 2. Dec. 1951)
Partial contents.- The caribbean bookshelf: the sugar economy of the Caribbean, by Eric Williams.

Trinidad.
Trinidad
M972.98
W67f
Williams, Erice Eustace, 1911-
Federation; two public lectures. [Port-of-Spain, Printed for the People's National Movement by the College Press, 1956]
60p. 21½cm.

Trinidad
Trinidad
M972.98
W67m
Williams, Eric Eustace, 1911-
Massa day done; a masterpiece of political and sociological analysis. Address delivered on Wednesday, March 27, 1961. Port-of-Spain, PNM Pub. Co., 1961.
19p. 21cm.
Portrait of author on front cover.

Trinidad - Creole dialects.
Trinidad
M440
T36t
Thomas, J J.
The theory and practice of Creole grammar. By J. J. Thomas ... Port-of-Spain, The Chronicle publishing office, 1869.
viii, 134 p., 1 l. 21cm.
1. Creole dialects. 2. Creole dialects—Trinidad. I. Title.
Library of Congress PM7851.T5 8—28762 [a30d1]

Trinidad - Creole dialects.
Trinidad
M440
T36t2
Thomas, J J.
The theory and practice of Creole grammar. By J. J. Thomas ... Port-of-Spain, The Chronicle publishing office, 1869.
viii, 134 p., 1 l. 21cm.
Much later reprint.
Introduction included, 188 .
1. Creole dialects. 2. Creole dialects—Trinidad. I. Title.
Library of Congress PM7851.T5 8—28762 [a30d1]

Trinidad - Description and travel.
Trinidad
M917.298
R14
Rampersad, Felix Alban
Trinidad, gem of the Caribbean. Port-of-Spain, Quick-Service Printing Co., n.d.
128p. illus. 21cm.

Trinidad - Economic condition.
Trinidad
M972.98
R39
Richardson, E C
Onward Trinidad; the solution to our economic and social problems. [Port-of-Spain, Enterprise Electric Printery, n.d.]
25p. 22½cm.
1. Trinidad - Economic condition.
2. Trinidad - Social conditions. I. Title.

Trinidad - Economic conditions.
Trinidad
M972.98
R56
Robinson, Arthur N R
Budget speech, 1965. Friday, 15th January, 1965. [Trinidad, Government Printery] 1965.
40p. 23cm.
1. Trinidad - Economic conditions.
2. Budget - Trinidad.

Trinidad - poetry.
Trinidad
M821
C88p
Cruickshank, Alfred M
Poems in all moods, by Alfred M. Cruickshank ... Port of Spain, Trinidad, Belle Eau Road, 1937.
viii, [10] - 203p. 19½cm.

Trinidad - Poetry.
Trinidad
M821
D24c
Darlington, Levi A
Calliope, by Levi A. Darlington. Trinidad, Cosmopolitan Printing Works, 1938.
124p. 19½cm.

Trinidad - Political parties.
Trinidad
M329
W67ap
Williams, Eric Eustace, 1911-
The approach of independence; an address to the fourth annual convention of the People's National Movement. [Port-of-Spain, P.N.M. Publishing, Co., 1960]
23p. 21cm.

Trinidad - Political parties.
Trinidad
M329
W67o
Williams, Eric Eustace, 1911-
Our fourth anniversary, the last lap; political leader's address on September 24, 1960, at the University of Woodford Square, marking the fourth year of P. N. M.'s first term of office. [Port-of-Spain, P.N.M. Publishing Co., 1960]
15p. 21cm.
Portrait on cover.

Trinidad - Political parties.
Trinidad
M329
W67p
Williams. Eric Eustace, 1911-
Perspectives for our party; address delivered to the third annual convention of the People's National Movement on October 17, 1958. [Port-of-Spain, P.N.M. Publishing Co., 1958]
20p. 22cm.

Trinidad - Social conditions.
Tinidad
M972.98
R39
Richardson, E C
Onward Trinidad; the solution to our economic and social problems. [Port-of-Spain, Enterprise Electric Printery, n.d.]
25p. 22½cm.

Trinidad - Songs.
Trinidad
M780
W671sg
Williams, Connie, collector.
12 songs from Trinidad. [Illustrated by Grace West] San Francisco, Panpipes Press, 1958.
15p. illus., port. 18½cm.

Trinidad, gem of the Caribbean.
Trinidad
M917.298
R14
Rampersad, Felix Alban
Trinidad, gem of the Caribbean. Port-of-Spain, Quick-Service Printing Co., n.d.
128p. illus. 21cm.

Trinidad and Tobago

Tobago
M352.2
Ot5

Ottley, Carlton Robert
A historical account of the Trinidad and Tobago police force from the earliest times. Trinidad, The Author, 1964.

152p. illus., port. 18½cm.

Trinidad and Tobago.

Tobago
M972.98
Ot5L

Ottley, Carlton Robert, 1914-
Legends, true stories and old sayings from Trinidad and Tobago, collected and told by C. R. Ottley. Port-of-Spain, College Press, 1962.

71p. 20cm.

Trinidad and Tobago.

Trinidad
M972.9
T737

Trinidad and Tobago. Central Statistical Office.
Research papers, no.1-
Port of Sapin, 1963-

v. 23cm.

Contents.- Employment in Trinidad and Tobago, by Jack Harewood.- Growth and structural change in the economy of Trinidad and Tobago 1951-1961., by Frank Rampersad.
1. Trinidad and Tobago. 2. Employment - Trinidad and Tobago.

Trinidad
M972.98
W67s

Trinidad and Tobago.
Williams, Eric Eustace, 1911-
Speech on independence at the special convention January 27-28, 1962. Port-of-Spain, PNM Pub. Co., 1962.

51p. port. 21cm.

Trinidad
M330
R56

Trinidad and Tobago - Economic policy.
Robinson, Arthur N R
Economic development in Trinidad and Tobago; a lecture. [Port-of-Spain, P. N. M. Pub. Co., n.d.]

15p. 21cm.
Portrait of author on front cover.

1. Trinidad and Tobago - Economic policy. I. Title.

Trinidad and Tobago - History.

Trinidad
M972.98
W67h

Williams, Eric Eustace, 1911-
History of the people of Trinidad and Tobago. Port-of-Spain, Trinidad, Printed by PNM Pub. Co., 1962.
viii, 294 p. maps (on p. [2]-[3] of cover) 21 cm.
Bibliography: p. [285]-288.
Autographed.

1. Trinidad and Tobago—Hist. I. Title.

F2119.W5 64-778 rev

Library of Congress [r64b1]

Trinidad
M972.9
T737

Trinidad and Tobago. Central Statistical Office.
Research papers, no.1-
Port of Sapin, 1963-

v. 23cm.

Contents.- Employment in Trinidad and Tobago, by Jack Harewood.- Growth and structural change in the economy of Trinidad and Tobago 1951-1961., by Frank Rampersad.
1. Trinidad and Tobago. 2. Employment - Trinidad and Tobago.

Trinity college, Hartford, Conn.

MB9
W67

Proctor, Charles Hayden, 1848?-1890.
The life of James Williams, better known as Professor Jim, for half a century janitor of Trinity college. By C. H. Proctor ... Hartford, Case, Lockwood and Brainard, printers, 1873.
79 p. front. (port.) 17½ cm.

1. Williams, James, b. 1790? 2. Trinity college, Hartford, Conn.

13—33803

Library of Congress E185.97.W72 [48b1]

Trisection of angle.

Sherrod, Fletcher.
Geometry; the trisection of the angle and theorems and corollaries leading to it. Revised, 1933. Fletcher Sherrod, author and publisher. New Orleans, La., °1932-1933.
[14] p. diagrs. 21½cm.

1. Trisection of angle. I. Title.

CA 33-572 Unrev'd

Library of Congress QA468.S45 1933
Copyright AA 122420 513.9

Brazil
M869.3
L62t
1915

Triste fim de polycarpo quaresma.
Lima Barreto, Afonso Henrique de, 1881-1922
Triste fim de polycarpo quaresma. Rio de Janeiro, Revista dos Tribunaes, 1915.

352p. 19cm.

Tritriva.

Madagascar
M842.91
R11ag

Rabemananjara, Jacques, 1913-
Agapes des dieux: Tritriva; tragédie malgache. Paris, Présence Africaine [1962]

265p. 19cm.

Haiti
M972.94
H86t

The triumph of fascism.
Hudicourt, Max Lelio
The triumph of fascism; or, the Haitian-American mutual responsibilities in the Haitian affairs. New York, Comite de Lutte pour une Haiti Democratique, [1945].

16p. port. 29cm.

The triumphs of Ephraim.

M817.4
M17t

McGirt, James Ephraim.
The triumphs of Ephraim by James E. McGirt. Philadelphia [The McGirt Publishing Co.] 1907.

131p. front. (port.) illus. 20cm.

Haiti
M972.94
F82tr

Trois discours.
Fouchard, Jean, 1912-
Trois discours; avant-propos de Leon Leleau. Port-au-Prince, Imprimerie de l'Etat, 1962.

76p. 19cm.

Haiti
M842
Sa3t

Trois noms, trois marques, trois papas;
Salnave, Théophile.
Trois noms, trois marques, trois papas; mélodrame en Créole. Imp. Duchemin, [1951]

32p. 20cm.

Trois prètendants; un mari;

Cameroons
M896.2
Oy6t

Oyono, Guillaume
Trois prétendants; un mari; pièce en quatre actes et un intermède. Yaoundé [Cameroun] Editions CLE, 1964.
126p. 18cm.
Portrait of author on book cover.

1. African drama. I. Title.

Tropic death.

M813.5
W16t

Walrond, Eric.
Tropic death, by Eric Walrond. New York, Boni & Liveright, 1926.
282, [1] p. 19½cm.
Contents.—Drought.—Panama gold.—The yellow one.—The wharf rats.—The palm porch.—Subjection.—The beach pin.—The white snake.—The vampire bat.—Tropic death.

I. Title. 26—18164

Library of Congress PZ3.W166Tr
——— Copy 2.
Copyright A 949614 [30d1]

Les tropicales poemes.

Haiti
M841
J38

Jeremie, Mea de
Les tropicales poemes. Port-au-Prince, Imprimerie Rasoir, 1960.

17p. 22cm. (Collection Louverture)

1. Haitian poetry. I. Title.

Dominican Republic
M861.6
C11

Trópico negro ...
Cabral, Manuel del.
... Trópico negro ... Buenos Aires, Editorial Sopena argentina, s. r. l. [°1941]
154 p., 3 l. 20½cm. (Colección "Ayer y hoy")
Poems.
"Primera edición, julio de 1941."

I. Title.

A 43-5095

Harvard univ. Library for Library of Congress [2]

Tropics— Diseases and hygiene.

Sierra Leone
M966.4
H78p

Horton, James Africanus Beale.
Physical and medical climate and meteorology of the west coast of Africa with valuable hints to Europeans for the preservation of health in the tropics. By James Africanus B. Horton ... London, J. Churchill & sons, 1867.
xix, 321 p. 23½cm.

1. Africa, West—Climate. 2. Medical geography—Africa, West. 3. Tropics—Diseases and hygiene.

Library of Congress RA943.H82 7—39467
[a27d1]

M248
T75

Tross, Joseph Samuel Nathaniel.
This thing called religion, by J. S. Nathaniel Tross ... Charlotte, N. C., 1934.
xviii, 21-132 p., 1 l. 19cm.
"A brief bibliography": p. 129-132.

I. Title.

34-33849

Library of Congress BR125.T76
Copyright A 75063 [2] 248

Trotskii, Lev, 1879-1940.

Trinidad
M320
J23w

James, Cyril Lionel Robert, 1901–
... World revolution, 1917–1936; the rise and fall of the Communist International. London, M. Secker and Warburg, ltd. [1937]
xii, 9–429 p. 22cm.
At head of title: C. L. R. James.
"How much the book owes to the writings of Trotsky, the text can only partially show."—p. xii.
1. Communist International. 2. Communism. 3. Revolutions. 4. World politics. 5. Russia—Pol. & govt.—20th cent. 6. Trotskii, Lev, 1879–1940. 7. Stalin, Iosif, 1879– I. Title.
Library of Congress HX11.I 5J25 37—25067
[45g1] 335.40621

Haiti
MB9
D38t

Trouillot, Ernst
Demesvar Delorme; le journaliste - le diplomate. Port-au-Prince, Imprimerie N. A. Theodore, 1958.
160p. ports. 23½cm.
1. Delorme, Demesvar, 1831-1901. 2. Haiti-Politics and government.

S. Africa
M968
T76m

True, Patrick.
Marena a Batho. London, Thomas Nelson and sons, ltd., 1944.
125p. 18cm.
1. Africa, South - History.

M784
T75

Trotter, James Monroe, 1844-1912
Music and some highly musical people: containing brief chapters on I. A description of music. II. The music of nature. III. A glance at the history of music. IV. The power, beauty, and uses of music. Following which are given sketches of the lives of remarkable musicians of the colored race. With portraits, and an appendix containing copies of music composed by colored men. By James M. Trotter ... Boston, Lee and Shepard; New York, C. T. Dillingham, 1878.
353 p., 1 l., 152 p. incl. pl. front., ports. 19½cm.
Music: Appendix, p. 4–152.
1. Negro musicians.
Library of Congress ML60.T85 5—38550
[41c1]

Haiti
M972.94
T75c

Trouillot, Hencock
La condition des Negres domestiques a Saint-Domingue. Port-au-Prince, Haiti, 1955.
30p. 23cm.
1. Saint Domingue. 2. Haiti-history.

Nigeria
M896.3
Ak5t

True confession of a girl.
Akinsuroju, Olurundayomi, 1925-
True confession of a girl. Lagos, Nigeria, Udo-Na-Meche Bookshop, 1961.
43p. 20cm.

M323
Un33

Trotter, William.
Statement.
(U.S. Congress. House. Committee on the Judiciary. Anti-lynching. Hearings. Washington, G.P.O., 1920. p.27-31)

Haiti
MB9
B41t

Trouillot, Henock
M. Dantès Bellegarde un ecrivain d'autrefois Port-au-Prince, Imprimerie N.A. Theodore, 1957.
131p. 24cm. (Collection "Haitiana")
1. Bellegarde, Dantès, 1877- 2. Haiti.

The true criteria.

M811.5
Ea7

Warrick, Calvin Horatio.
The true criteria and other poems, by C. Horatio Warrick. Kansas City, Mo., The Sojourner press, 1924.
120 p. port. 20½cm.
I. Title.
Library of Congress PS3545.A763T7 1924 24-22094 Revised
[r41c2]

Nigeria
M896.3
K122

Trouble for the "Tornadoes".
Kaine, E O
Trouble for the "Tornadoes". Lagos, Western Region Literature Committee, 1953.
32p. 19cm.
I. Title.

Haiti
M840.9
T75

Trouillot, Henock
Les origines sociales de la litterature Haitienne. Port-au-Prince, Imprimerie N. A. Theodore, 1962.
376p. 23½cm.
Special number, Revue de la societe Haitienne d'histoire de geographie et de geologie. January-July, 1962, v. 32, no. 109.
1. Haitian literature. 2. Literature - Haiti. I. Title.

M813.5
L58

A true fairy tale.
Lewis, Alethia (Lightner)
A true fairy tale; illustrated by Gloria Bultman. Boston, Christopher Pub. House [1952]
107 p. illus. 21 cm.
1. Carver, George Washington, 1864?–1943—Fiction. I. Title.
PZ7.L5846Tr 52-8235 ‡
Library of Congress [3]

Nigeria Trouble in form six.
M896.3
Ek8t

Ekwensi, Cyprian Odiatu Duaka, 1921–
Trouble in Form Six; drawings by Prue Theobalds. Cambridge, Cambridge U. P., 1966.
78 p. illus. 18½ cm. 3/6 (B 66-4075)
1. Readers—1950– I. Title.
PE1121.E55 428.64 66-10246
Library of Congress [5]

Haiti
M972.94
T75p

Trouillot, Henock
La pensee de docteur Jean Price-Mars. Port-au-Prince, 1956.
101p. port. 23cm. (Numero special - Revue de la Societe Haitienne d'Histoire de Geographie et de Geologie. Vol. 29, No. 102, Juillet-Octobre 1956)
1. Mars, Jean Price, 1876-

M323
C88t

True freedom for Negro and white labor.
Crosswaith, Frank R
True freedom for Negro and white labor. by Frank R. Crosswaith and Alfred Baker Lewis; with introduction by Norman Thomas. New York, Negro Labor News Service, 1926.
59p. tables. 18cm.

M301
R93

The trouble with being a mama.
Rutland, Eva.
The trouble with being a mama. New York, Abingdon Press [1964]
143 p. 21 cm.
Autobiographical.
1. Segregation. ~~1. Negroes.~~ 2. Children—Management. I. Title.
E185.625.R8 301.451 64-21136
Library of Congress [4-1]

MB
T75

Troup, Cornelius V
Distinguished Negro Georgians. Dallas, Royal Pub. Co. [1962]
208 p. 21 cm.
Includes bibliography.
"To Dr. Arthur Spingarn, a great humanitarian, with the compliments of the author, C.V.Troup."
~~1. Negroes—Georgia.~~ 2. Georgia—Biog. I. Title.
E185.93.G4T7 920.0758 62-52066 ‡
Library of Congress [5]

True historical facts about Africa.

U.S.
M960
K83

Kollock, Shadie.
True historical facts about Africa, by Shadie Kollock [and] Phillip Alegbe. New York, Carlton Press, 1961.
52 p. illus. 21 cm. (A Reflection book)
1. Africa—Hist.—Outlines, syllabi, etc. I. Alegbe, Phillip, joint author. II. Title.
DT22.K6 960 62-311 ‡
Library of Congress [5]

Troubled island.

M811.5
H87t

Hughes, Langston, 1902-
Troubled island; An opera in three acts. Libretto. Music by William Grant Still. Libretto by Langston Hughes. Hollywood, Leeds Music Corporation, 1949.
38p. 22cm.

Uganda
M613.2
T75

Trowell, H C
Mmere ki gye tusaanira okulya? [What food should we eat?] kya H. C Trowell ne R. G. Ladin. Kyakyusibwa John W. S. Kasirye ne Aloni Lubwama. Nairobi, Eagle Press, 1951.
23p. illus. 18½cm. (Asika Obulamu Series) Written in Luganda.
1. Nutrition. I. Title. II. Kasirye, John W. S., tr. III. Lubwama, Aloni, jt. tr. IV. Series.

Sierra Leone
M896.3
N54t

The truly married woman.
Nicol, Abioseh Davidson, 1929-
The truly married woman and other stories. Illustrated by J. H. Vandi. London, Oxford University Press, 1965.
120p. 18½cm.
I. Title.

Trumbull Park.
M813.5
B81t
Brown, Frank London.
Trumbull Park, a novel. Chicago, Regnery [1959]
432 p. 21 cm.
I. Title.
PZ4.B8774Tr 813.54 59—8460 ‡
Library of Congress [59f5]

Truth, Sojourner, d. 1883.
M326.99B
T77g
1875
[Gilbert, Olive]
Narrative of Sojourner Truth; a bonds-woman of olden time, emancipated by the New York Legislature in the early part of the present century; with a history of her labors and correspondence drawn from her "Book of life." Boston, For the author, 1875.
xi, [1]-324p. front. (port.) illus. 20cm.
Narrative of Sojourner Truth, by Olive Gilbert. Book of life, by Frances W. Titus.
1. Truth, Sojourner, d. 1883. I. Titus, Frances W. II. Title.
29—25244
Library of Congress E185.97.T875
[a35b1]

The truth that makes men free.
M813.5
W21t
Ward, Thomas Playfair, 1895-
The truth that makes men free; a novel. [1st ed.] New York, Pageant Press [1955]
154 p. 21 cm.
I. Title.
PZ4.W266Tr 55-11983 ‡
Library of Congress

M811.5
J41t
Trumpet, Welborn Victor
Jenkins, Welborn Victor
Trumpet in the new moon and other poems, by Welborn Victor Jenkins. Foreword by E.H. Webster. Boston, The Peabody Press, 1934.
62p. 19cm.

Truth, Sojourner, d. 1883.
M326.99B
T77g
1850
[Gilbert, Olive]
Narrative of Sojourner Truth, a northern slave, emancipated from bodily servitude by the state of New York, in 1828. With a portrait ... Boston, Printed for the author, 1850.
xi, [1], [13]-144 p. incl. front. (port.) $18\frac{1}{2}$cm.
1. Truth, Sojourner, d. 1883. I. Title. 11—27426
Library of Congress E185.97.T87
[a37d1]

Basutoland Tseleng ea Bophelo.
M896
M71t2
Mocoancoeng, Jacob G
Tseleng ea Bophelo, le lithothokiso tse ncha [The path of life, a drama and new poems. 2d ed.] Johannesburg, Witwatersrand University Press, 1955.
52p. 19cm. (The Bantu treasury x, ed. by C. M. Doke)
Written in Sotho.

The trumpet sounds.
MB9
H358
Hedgeman, Anna (Arnold)
The trumpet sounds; a memoir of Negro leadership. [1st ed.] New York, Holt, Rinehart and Winston [1964]
202 p. 22 cm.
Portrait of author on book jacket.
1. Negroes—Civil rights. 2. Negroes—Moral and social conditions. I. Title.
E185.97.H44 323.4 64-21938
Library of Congress [7-1]

The truth about interracial marriage.
M323.3
G174
Gardner, LeRoy.
The truth about interracial marriage. [St. Paul? 1965]
ii, 143 p. 23 cm.
1. Miscegenation. 2. Negroes. I. Title.
HQ1031.G3 301.422 65-26932
Library of Congress [3]

Tseleng ea bophelo le lithothokiso tse nchla.
Basutoland
M896
M71
Mocoancoeng, Jac G
Tseleng ea bophelo le lithothokiso tse nchla [The path of life and new poems. 2nd ed.] Johannesburg, Witwatersrand University Press, 1955.
52p. $18\frac{1}{2}$cm. (The Bantu treasury, X)
Written in Sotho.
I. Title.

M325.3
T18t
Trusteeship.
Tate, Merze, ed.
Trust and non-self-governing territories; Papers and proceedings of the tenth annual conference of the Division of the Social Sciences, The Graduate School, Howard University, April 8th and 9th, 1947, ed. by Merze Tate. Washington, D. C., Howard University, Graduate School, 1948.
128p. 23cm. (Howard University. Studies in Social sciences, v.6, no.1)

The Truth about the West African Land Question.
Gold Coast
M966.7
H33t
Hayford, Casely Archie, 1898-
The truth about the West African land question, by Casely Hayford...London, C.M. Phillips, 1913.
304, 8p. 22cm.

Tshadda river.
M966.96
C88j
Crowther, Samuel Adjai, 1806-1891.
Journal of an expedition up the Niger and Tshadda rivers, undertaken by Macgregor Laird Esq. in connection with the British government in 1854. By the Rev. Samuel Crowther. With map and appendix. London, Church missionary house, 1855.
xxiii, maps. $20\frac{1}{2}$cm.

Trusts, Industrial.
Cuba
M338.8
L13t
Lafargue, Paul, 1842-1911.
Les trusts américains; leur action—économique—sociale—politique; par Paul Lafargue ... Paris, V. Giard & E. Brière, 1903.
vi, [7]-146 p., 1 l. 19cm.
1. Trusts, Industrial.
4-6974
Library of Congress

Truth is beauty.
M811.5
F94t
Fulger, Willie E
Truth is beauty. [1st ed.] New York, Vantage Press [c1963]
68p. 21cm.
Poems.

Tshaka.
S. Africa
M896.1
D24a
Darlow, D J
African heroes - Ntsikana, Tshaka, Khama, Moshoeshoe. Poems, by D.J. Darlow. [Lovedale, Lovedale Press [n.d.]
75p. illus. $21\frac{1}{2}$cm.
1. African poetry. 2. Ntsikana. 3. Tshaka. 4. Khama, 5. Moshoeshoe.

Truth.
M177.3
C16t
Cannon, Noal Calwell W
Truth. Instruction. to youth. Seek ye after knowledge. Written by Rev. N. C.W. Cannon. Reprinted by James Nelson. Rochester, C. S. Mc Connell & co., 1843.
24p. $20\frac{1}{2}$cm.

"Truth is stranger than fiction."
M326.99B
H39t
1879
Henson, Josiah
"Truth is stranger than fiction." An autobiography of the Rev. Josiah Henson (Mrs. Harriet Beecher Stowe's "Uncle Tom"), from 1789-1879. With a preface by Mrs. Harriet Beecher Stowe, introductory notes by Wendell Phillips and John G. Whittier, and an appendix on the exodus, by Bishop Gilbert Haven. Boston, B. B. Russell & company, 1879.
xxiv, 336p. front. (port.) plates. 19cm.

Tshaka.
M896.1
D24a
Darlow, D J
African heroes - Ntsikana, Tshaka, Khama, Moshoeshoe. Poems, by D.J. Darlow. [Lovedale S.A.] Lovedale press [n.d.]
75p. illus. $21\frac{1}{2}$cm.

Truth, Sojourner, d. 1883.
MB9
T77f
Fauset, Arthur Huff, 1899-
Sojourner Truth, God's faithful pilgrim [by] Arthur Huff Fauset ... Chapel Hill, The University of North Carolina press [c1938]
viii p., 2 l., 187 p. front. (port.) 21cm. (Half-title: The Chapel Hill series of Negro biographies, edited by Benjamin Brawley)
"Selected bibliography": p. 181-182.
1. Truth, Sojourner, d. 1883.
Library of Congress E185.97.T85 38—27497
—— Copy 2.
Copyright A 118614 [39g5] 922

Truth, stranger than fiction.
M326.99B
H39f
Henson, Josiah, 1789-1883.
Father Henson's story of his own life. Introd. by Walter Fisher. New York, Corinth Books [1962]
212p. illus. 19cm. (The American experience Series, AE18)

Tshaka.
S. Africa
M896
D851
Dube, John Langalibalele. -1946.
Insila ka Tshaka. [Mariannhill] Icindezelwe Ngokwesitatu, 1933.
80p. front(port.) $18\frac{1}{2}$cm.

Tshaka.

M896.3 D851
Dube, John Langalebalele.
Insila ka Tshaka. Mariannhill, Mission press, 1933.

80p. front (port.) 18½cm.

Intimate attendants of Tshaka in Zulu.

S. Africa M896 D85j
Tshaka.
Dube, John Langalebalele, -1946.
Jeqe, the Bodyservant of King Tshaka (Insila ka Tshaka), by John Dube. Translated from the Zulu by Professor J. Boxwell. Lovedale, The Lovedale Press, 1951.

84p. 23cm.

S. Africa M896.1 T78i
Tshaka, R M
Iintsika zentlambo ye-tyhume. Lovedale press, 1953.

95p. 18½cm.
Title: Pillars of the Tyhume Valley.
Xhosa poems

1. Xhosa poety.

South Africa M896.4 W15
Tshefu, Izaac
Ubukumkani Bamandulo Kwa-Xosa

Pp. 1-6.
Written in Xhosa.

In: Wallis, S. J., comp. and ed. Inkolo namasiko. London, Society for Promoting Christian Knowledge, 1930.

Tshekedi Khama of Bechuanaland.

Bechuanaland MB9 K52g
Gabatshwane, S M
Tshekedi Khama of Bechuanaland; great statesman and politician. Foreword by Margery Perham. London, Oxford University Press, 1961.

69p. illus., port. 18½cm.

1. Khama, Tshekedi, 1905-
2. Bechuanaland. I. Title.

Nigeria M896.2 Ig8ts
Tshombe of Katanga.
Iguh, Thomas O
Tshombe of Katanga; a drama. «Onitsha, Nigeria, A. Onwudiwe & Sons, n.d.»

54p. ports. 21cm.

S. Africa M896.3 T78u
Tsotsi, Liziwe L
U-Ntabaziya-duma. Lovedale, Lovedale Press, 1952.

89p. 18cm.
A novel in the new Xhosa orthography.

S. Africa M398 M89
Tswa language.
Mukhombo, Aron S
A nkutsulani wa matimu ya batswa; a timhaka ta kale ti khedzelwe. Cleveland, Central Mission Press, 1931.

127p. port. 20½cm.
Tswa legends.

Tswana (Bantu tribe) - Kings and rulers.

South Africa M896.1 Sch16
Schapera, Isaac, 1905- *ed. and tr.*
Praise-poems of Tswana chiefs. Translated and edited with an introd. and notes, by I. Schapera. Oxford, Clarendon Press, 1965.

vi, 255 p. geneal. tables, map. 23 cm. (Oxford library of African literature)

Bibliography: p. ₍246₎-247.

1. Sechuana poetry. 2. Tswana (Bantu tribe)—Kings and rulers. I. Title.

PL8651.7.S3 896.3 65-8539

Library of Congress ₍2₎

Tswana language.

A M896.2 Sh1
Shakespeare, William.
Dintshontsho tsa bo-Juliuse Kesare, ke William Shakespeare. Di fetoletswe mo puong ya Setswana ke Solomon Tshekiso Plaatje; di siamisitswe e bile di rulagantswe ke G. P. Lestrade. Johannesburg, University of Witwatersrand, press, 1942.

75p. 17½cm.

Tswana literature.

A M370 K52t
Kgasi, Micah.
Thuto ke eng. Lovedale, Lovedale press, 1945.

44p. 18cm.

What is education?

M616 B641
Tuberculosis.
Bontemps, Arna Wendell, 1902-
The low-down on tuberculosis. National Tuberculosis Association, 1941.

7p. illus. 23cm.

Tuberculosis.

M616 C81u
Cordice, John Walter Vincent
Use of pyrazinamide (aldinamide) in the treatment of tuberculous lymphadenopathy and draining sinuses, a preliminary report, by John W.V. Cordice, Lyndon M. Hill, and Louis T. Wright. Journal of the National Medical Association, 1953.

87-98p. illus. tables 27cm.
Reprinted from Journal of the National Medical Association, March 1953.

M610 P19 v.1, no.3
Tuberculosis.
Jackson, Algernon Brashear, 1878-
Artificial hyperaemia and its therapeutic application (after Bier), by Algernon Brashear Jackson... Reprinted from the New York medical journal for October 17, 1908.
11p. 20½cm.

Tuberculosis.

M610 P19 V.1 No.4
Jackson, Algernon Brashear, 1878-
The treatment of tuberculosis, encouraging results with calcium cacodylate and calcium iodide. By Algernon Brashear Jackson... Reprinted from the New York medical journal for May 24, 1913.

10p. 20½cm.

Tuberculosis-Philadelphia.

M304 P19 v.1 no.15
Mossell, Sadie Tanner.
... A study of the negro tuberculosis problem in Philadelphia, by Sadie T. Mossell ... Philadelphia, Henry Phipps institute, 1923.

v, 7-29, ₍3₎ p. illus. (maps) diagr. 26cm.

At head of title: University of Pennsylvania.
"This study was made under the auspices of the Whittier centre and the Henry Phipps institute; it was revised by the Philadelphia health council and Tuberculosis committee."

1. Tuberculosis—Philadelphia. 2. Negroes—Philadelphia. I. Pennsylvania. University. Henry Phipps institute.

Library of Congress RC313.A57M6 25—20530

₍a28c1₎

Tubman, Harriet (Ross)

MB9 T79s
Bradford, Sarah Elizabeth (Hopkins) "*Mrs. J. M. Bradford*," b. 1818.
Scenes in the life of Harriet Tubman. By Sarah H. Bradford. Auburn ₍N. Y.₎ W. J. Moses, printer, 1869.

2 p. l., 132 p. front. (port.) 18½cm.

1. Tubman, Harriet (Ross) I. Title.

7-31857

Library of Congress E444.T89

₍35g1₎

MB9 T79p
Tubman, Harriet (Ross), 1815?-1913.
Petry, Ann (Lane), 1911-
The girl called Moses; the story of Harriet Tubman. London, Methuen & Co., 1960.

205p. 19½cm.

Tubman, Harriet (Ross) 1815?-1913.

M813.5 P44h
Petry, Ann (Lane) 1911-
Harriet Tubman, conductor on the Underground Railroad. New York, Crowell ₍1955₎

247 p. 21 cm.

1. Tubman, Harriet (Ross) 1815?-1913—Fiction.

PZ3.P44904Har 55—9215 ‡

Library of Congress ₍56a7₎

Tubman, Harriet(Ross).

M304 P19 v.5, no.5
Taylor, Robert W.
Harriet Tubman, the heroine in ebony. By Robert W. Taylor, with introduction by Booker T. Washington. Boston, Mass., George H. Ellis, printer, 1901.
16p. port. 19½cm.

Liberia M966.6 T79p
Tubman, William V S *Pres. Liberia*, 1895-
President Tubman of Liberia speaks; edited by E. Reginald Townsend. London, Consolidated Publications Co. ₍1959₎

201 p. illus. 25 cm.
Portrait of author on book jacket.

1. Liberia.

DT624.T8 923.1666 60-34031 ‡

Library of Congress ₍1₎

Tubman, William V.S., Pres. of Liberia, 1895.
Liberia
M966.6 Liberian Information Service.
T79p The plot that failed; the story of the attempted assisination of President Tubman. Monrovia, Liberian Information Service ⌈1959⌉
68p. ports. 21cm.
Autographed: "This was stolen from my house John B. Falconer by Arthur Spingarn."

M796
T83 Tunnell, Emlen.
Footsteps of a Giant, by Emlen Tunnell with Bill Gleason. ⌈1st ed.⌉ Garden City, N. Y., Doubleday, 1966.
288 p. 22 cm.
1. Football.
I. Gleason, William. II. Title.
GV939.T8A3 796.332640924 65-10776
Library of Congress ⌈5⌉

MB9
T94 Turner, Bridges Alfred, 1908-
From a plow to a doctorate so what? Hampton, Virginia, Hampton Institute, 1945.
89p. port. illus. 22½cm.
I. title

Tubman, William V. S., 1895-
M966.6 Knight, J. Emery.
K741 Liberia's eighteenth president. ⌈Monrovia, Liberia, 1946⌉
64p. port. 25cm.

Puerto Rico
Tuntún de pasa y grifería.
M861. Palés Matos, Luis.
P17 ... Tuntún de pasa y grifería; poemas afroantillanos. San Juan de Puerto Rico, Biblioteca de autores puertorriqueños, 1937.
133 p., 2 l. 17cm.
I. Title.
39-12503
Library of Congress PQ7439.P24T8
⌈2⌉ 861.6

Turner, Geneva Calcier, joint author.
MB Derricotte, Elise Palmer.
D44w Word pictures of the great, by Elise Palmer Derricotte ... Geneva Calcier Turner ... ⌈and⌉ Jessie Hailstalk Roy ... illustrated by Lois Mailou Jones. Washington, D. C., The Associated publishers inc. ⌈1941⌉
xiii, 280 p. incl. front., illus. 21½cm.
Illustrated lining-papers in color.
"Books to read" at end of each section.
1. Negroes—Biog. I. Turner, Geneva Calcier, joint author. II. Roy, Jessie Hailstalk, joint author. III. Title.
41-13255
Library of Congress E185.96.D4
⌈a44g2⌉ [325.260973] 920.073

Tulip mania. 17th cent.-Fiction.
France Dumas, Alexandre, 1802-1870.
M840 La tulipe noire. Bruxelles, Meline,
D89tu Cans et cie., 1850.
2 vols in one. 15cm.

Tũrĩrĩa kĩ?
Kenya
M613.2 Culwick, G M
C89w Tũrĩrĩa kĩ? ⌈What shall we eat?⌉Tr. by D. Wahome Ndabi⌉ Nairobi, Eagle Press, 1950.
24p. illus. 21½cm. (Taanya Ũgima-ini. Aim at healthy living series)
Written in Kikuyu.
White author.
1. Nutrition. I. Title. II. Ndabi, D. Wahome, tr.

U.S.
M960 Turner, Henry McNeal (1834-1915)
C76a The American Negro and the fatherland.
Pp. 195-198.
In: Congress on Africa, Atlanta, 1895. Africa and the American Negro, Atlanta, Gamma Theological Seminary, 1896.
McNeil
1833-1915

La tulipe noire.
France Dumas, Alexandre, 1802-1870.
M840 La tulipe noire. Bruxelles, Meline, Cans et
D89tu cie., 1850.
2 vols in one. 15cm.

Turks and Caicos Islands.
Haiti
M972.94 Harris, J Dennis.
H24 A summer on the borders of the Caribbean Sea. By J. Dennis Harris. With an introduction by George William Curtis. New York, A. B. Burdick, 1860.
xi, ⌈13⌉-179 p. 18½cm.
CONTENTS.—Dominican Republic.—Republic of Hayti.—Grand Turk's and Caicos Islands. — British Honduras.—Conclusive summary. —Appendix.
1. Haiti—Descr. & trav. 2. Haiti—Hist. 3. British Honduras. 4. Turks and Caicos Islands. I. Title.
2—12387
Library of Congress F2171.H29
⌈a42b1⌉

M262 Turner, Henry McNeal, 1834-1915.
T85g The genius and theory of Methodist policy, or the machinery of Methodism. Practically illustrated through a series of questions and answers, by Bishop H.M. Turner...Philadelphia, A.M.E. Church ⌈1885⌉
xii, 342p.
1. Methodism. I. Title.

Tulsa, Oklahoma
M976.6
P24e Parrish, Mary E Jones
Events of the Tulsa disaster, by Mrs. Mary E. Jones Parrish. ⌈n.p., n.p., n.d.⌉
112p. plates. 22cm.
Cover title.

Turn to the dark.
Basutoland
M896.3 Mopeli-Paulus, Attwell Sidwell, 1913-
M79t Turn to the dark, by A. S. Mopeli-Paulus & Miriam Basner. London, Cape ⌈1956⌉
287 p. 21 cm.
I. Basner, Miriam, 1920- joint author. II. Title.
PZ4.M828Tu 57-27405 ‡
Library of Congress ⌈5⌉

Turner, Henry Mc Neal, 1834-1915.
MB9 Pontan, M. M.
T85p Life and times of Henry M. Turner... by M. M. Pontan... Atlanta, Ga., A.B. Caldwell Pub. Co., 1917.
⌈24⌉ - 173p. front. (port.) 20cm.

Tunde in trouble.
Nigeria
M896.3 Tong, Raymond
T61t Tunde in trouble, by Raymond Tong and Ernest Edyang. Illustrated by Zelide Teague. London, Cassell, 1958.
80p. 18½cm.
1. Nigeria - short stories. I. Title.

M811.5 Turner, Adolph John.
T84s The song I sing. New York, Exposition Press ⌈1964⌉
64p. 20cm.
Portrait of author on book jacket.
1. Poetry. I. Title.

Turner, Henry McNeal, 1834-1915.
MB Simmons, William J 1849-
S14 Men of mark: eminent, progressive and rising. By Rev. William J. Simmons ... With an introductory sketch of the author by Rev. Henry M. Turner ... Cleveland, O., G. M. Rewell & co., 1887.
1138 p. front., ports. 23½ cm.
1. Negroes—Biog. I. Turner, Henry McNeal, 1834-1915.
6—5585
Library of Congress E185.96.S45
⌈a36d1⌉

Tuneful tales.
M811.5 Wiggins, Bernice Love, 1897-
W63t Tuneful tales, by Bernice Love Wiggins. El Paso, Tex., 1925.
174 p. 20cm.
In verse.
I. Title.
26-1848
Library of Congress PS3545.I 246T8 1925
Copyright A 875896 ⌈2⌉

M813.5 Turner, Allen Pelzer, 1889-
T85o Oaks of Eden, a novel. New York, Exposition Press ⌈1951⌉
135 p. 23 cm.
I. Title.
PZ4.T745Oak 51-11875
Library of Congress ⌈5⌉

M323 Turner, Henry McNeal, 1834-1915.
T85 Speech on the eligibility of colored members to seats in the Georgia legislature, delivered before that body September 3rd, 1868. ⌈Augusta, Ga., E. H. Pughe Printer, 1868⌉
16p. 21½cm.
An extract.
1. Civil rights.

Turner, Henry McNeil, 1834-1915.
M39 T85q
Quarto - centennial of H.M. Turner as bishop in the A.M.E. church, celebrated in St. Paul A.M.E. church, Saint Louis, Missouri. Nashville, Tenn., A.M.E. Sunday School union, 1905.
147p. 19cm.

M981 T84s
Turner, Lorenzo Dow, 1895-
Some contacts of Brazilian ex-slaves with Nigeria, West Africa. Reprinted from the Journal of Negro history, 27:55-67, January 1942.
Address delivered November 1941 at meeting of Association for Study of Negro Life and History.
Inscribed: To Mr. Arthur B. Spingarn, with the cordial regards of Lorenzo D. Turner, Nashville, Tenn. Jan. 14, 1945.
1. Brazil--African customs.

M910 T85u
Turner, Walter Lee
Under the skin in Africa; a complete outline of the history of the Republic of Liberia. Hot Springs, Arkansas, Connelly Printing Co., 1928.
152p. port. 18½cm.
1. Liberia - History.

M301 D122
Turner, John Briscoe, 1922-
Who has the revolution or thoughts on the second reconstruction, by John B. Turner and Whitney M. Young.
Pp. 678-693.
In: Daedalus. The Negro American. Boston, Houghton Mifflin, 1966.
I. Young, Whitney Moore, 1921- jt. auth.

Turner, Lorenzo Dow, 1895- , joint editor
M810.8 C88
Cromwell, Otelia ed.
Readings from negro authors, for schools and colleges, with a bibliography of negro literature, by Otelia Cromwell ... Lorenzo Dow Turner ... Eva B. Dykes ... New York, Harcourt, Brace and company [°1931]
xii, 388 p. 21cm.
"A bibliography of negro literature": p. 371-388; contains "Collateral reading."
1. Negro literature (American) 2. Negro literature (American)—Bibl. 3. American literature—Negro authors. I. Turner, Lorenzo Dow, joint ed. II. Dykes, Eva Beatrice, joint ed. III. Title.
31-31497
Library of Congress PS508.N3C7
[a45m1] 810.8

M910 T85m
Turner, Zatella R.
My wonderful year, by Zatella R. Turner. Boston, The Christopher publishing house [°1939]
xi, 13-117 p. front. 19½cm.
1. England—Descr. & trav. 2. Europe—Descr. & trav.—1919- I. Title.
39-31520
Library of Congress D921.T87
——— Copy 2.
Copyright A 134074 [2] 914

M427. T85a
Turner, Lorenzo Dow, 1895-
Africanisms in the Gullah dialect. [Chicago] Univ. of Chicago Press [1949]
xi, 317 p. maps, diagr. 24 cm.
Bibliography: p. 293-299.
1. Negro-English dialects. 2. Gullah dialect I. Title.
PM7875.G8T8 427.9 49-10175*
Library of Congress [8]

M812.5 T85e
Turner, Lucy M.
The exodus, a Negro drama in three acts with three songs, by Lucy M. Turner. East St. Louis, Ill., Lucy M. Turner [c 1931.]
25p. 25cm.
1. Drama. I. Title.

Haiti
M972.94 T86e
Turnier, Alain
Les États-Unis et le marché Haïtien. Washington, 1955.
354p. 20½cm.
1. Haiti.

M810.9 T85
Turner, Lorenzo Dow, 1895-
Anti-slavery sentiment in American literature prior to 1865, by Lorenzo Dow Turner ... Washington, D. C., The Association for the study of Negro life and history, inc. [°1929]
viii, 188 p. 24cm.
"This study ... in 1926, was ... submitted to ... the University of Chicago in candidacy for the degree of doctor of philosophy."—Pref.
Bibliography: p. 158-182.
1. Slavery in the U. S.—Controversial literature. 2. American literature—Hist. & crit. 3. Slavery in the U. S.—Bibl. I. Title.
30-7026
Library of Congress PS310.S6T8
——— Copy 2.
Copyright A 19871 [40j1]

M811.5 T85
Turner, Lucy Mae.
'Bout cullud folkses; poems by Lucy Mae Turner. New York, H. Harrison [1938]
64 p. 22cm.
I. Title. 1. Poetry.
38-31464
Library of Congress PS3501.T8B6 1938
——— Copy 2.
Copyright A 120807 [3] 811.5

Turning point in freedom road.
M335.4 L62
Lightfoot, Claude
Turning point in freedom road; the fight to end jim crow now. New York, New Century Publishers, 1962.
32p. 18½cm.
1. Communism. 2. Race problems. I. Title.

Turner, Lorenzo Dow, 1895- The impact of Western education on the African's way of life.
M960 H12a
Haines, Charles Grove, 1906- ed. p. 147-65.
Africa today. Baltimore, Johns Hopkins Press [°1955]
xvi, 510 p. illus., maps. 24 cm.
Based on the proceedings of the conference on contemporary Africa which the Johns Hopkins University School of Advanced International Studies sponsored in Washington in August 1954.
Bibliographical footnotes.
1. Africa. I. Title.
DT5.H25 960 55—6220
Library of Congress [56x15]

MB9 T857
Turner, Robert Emanuel, 1875-
Memories of a retired Pullman porter. [1st ed.] New York, Exposition Press [1954]
191 p. illus. 21 cm.
1. Porters—Correspondence, reminiscences, etc. I. Title.
Full name: Robert Emanuel Hammond Turner.
HD8039.R37T8 923.873 54-10978 ‡
Library of Congress [2]

MB9 T86u
Turpeau, David Dewitt
Up from the can-brakes, an autiobiography, by David Dewitt Turpeau, Sr. [Cincinnati, 1942]
43p. 20cm.
1. Cincinnati, Ohio. I. Title.

M306 H431
Turner, Lorenzo Dow, 1895-
Linguistic research and African survivals.
(In: Herskovits, M. J. The interdisciplinary aspects of Negro studies. Bulletin of the American Council of Learned Societies, no. 32, September 1941. pp. 68-78.)

M621 T85
Turner, Rufus P
Basic electronic test instruments: their operation and use. New York, Technical Division, Rinehart Books [1953]
254 p. illus. 24 cm.
1. Electronic apparatus and appliances. I. Title. II. Title: Electronic test.
TK7870.T87 *621.34 621.38 53-5782 ‡
Library of Congress [58n10]

M813.5 T86o
Turpin, Waters Edward, 1910-1968
... O Canaan! A novel. New York, Doubleday, Doran & company, inc., 1939.
5 p. l., 3-311 p. 20½cm.
At head of title: Waters E. Turpin.
"First edition."
I. Title.
39-27606
Library of Congress PZ3.T8670
[44k1]

M427. T85m
Turner, Lorenzo Dow, 1895-
...Notes on the sounds and vocabulary of Gullah. Reprinted... from Publication of the American Dialect Society, no.3, May 1945.
13-28p. 22½cm.
Inscribed copy: To Dr. Arthur B. Spingarn, with the cordial regards of Lorenzo D. Turner, December 9, 1945.
1. Gullah - Dialect. I. Title

M621 T85t
Turner, Rufus P
Transistors: theory and practice. New York, Gernsback Publications [1954]
144 p. illus. 22 cm. (Gernsback library, no. 51)
1. Transistors.
TK7872.T73T8 *621.34 621.38 54-10401 ‡
Library of Congress [54e5]

M813.5 T86r
Turpin, Waters Edward, 1910-1968
The rootless. [1st ed.] New York, Vantage Press [1957]
340 p. 21 cm.
I. Title.
PZ3.T867Ro 56-12795 ‡
Library of Congress [2]

M813.5
T86t
Turpin, Waters Edward, 1910-1968
These low grounds, by Waters Edward Turpin. New York, London, Harper & brothers, 1937.
4 p. l., 344 p. 21cm.
"First edition."
1. Title. 37-19647
M813.5 T86
Library of Congress PZ3.T867Th
——— Copy 2.
Copyright A 106681 [5]

MB9
M85h
Tuskegee Institute.
Hughes, William Hardin, 1881- ed.
Robert Russa Moton of Hampton and Tuskegee, edited by William Hardin Hughes [and] Frederick D. Patterson. Chapel Hill, University of North Carolina Press [1956]
238 p. illus. 24 cm.
"Volume of tributes to the life of Dr. Robert Russa Moton."
1. Moton, Robert Russa, 1867-1940. 2. Tuskegee Institute. 3. Hampton Institute, Hampton, Va. I. Patterson, Frederick Douglas, 1901- joint ed.
E185.97.M92H8 923.773 56-14299 ‡
Library of Congress [57f7]

MB9
C154
Tuskegee Normal and Industrial Institute
Campbell, Thomas Monroe, 1883-
The school comes to the farmer; the autobiography of T. M. Campbell, with foreword by Jackson Davis. Illus. with photographs. New York, Longmans, Green, 1947.
7-64p. illus. 18½cm.

M808
F75
Turpin, Waters Edward, 1910-1968, joint author
Ford, Nick Aaron.
Basic skills for better writing; a guide and practice book for those who intend to master the essentials of good English, by Nick Aaron Ford and Waters E. Turpin. New York, Putnam [1959]
192 p. 28 cm.
1. English language—Rhetoric. 2. English grammar—1870- I. Turpin, Waters Edward, 1910- joint author. II. Title.
PE1408.F52 808 59-10041 ‡
Library of Congress [10]

M301
T413
Tuskegee Institute.
Three Negro classics: Up from slavery. The souls of black folk. The autobiography of an ex-colored man. With an introd. by John Hope Franklin. [New York, Avon Books, 1965]
xxv, 511 p. 19 cm. (Avon library, W102)
Includes music.
1. Negroes. 2. Tuskegee Institute. I. Washington, Booker Taliaferro, 1856-1915. Up from slavery. II. DuBois, William Edward Burghardt, 1868-1963. The souls of the black folk. III. Johnson, James Weldon, 1871-1938. The autobiography of an ex-colored man.
E185.97.W278 301.451 65-3044
Library of Congress [5]

M814.4
W272i
Tuskegee Normal and Industrial Institute.
Washington, Booker Taliaferro, 1859?-1915
Introduction.
(In: Thrasher, Max Bennet. Tuskegee, its story and its work. Boston, Small, Maynard & company, 1900. 19cm. p.xv-xvi)

M808
F75
1962
Turpin, Waters Edward, 1910-1968 jt. auth.
Ford, Nick Aaron.
Basic skills for better writing. Form B: a guide and practice book for those who intend to master the essentials of good English, by Nick Aaron Ford and Waters E. Turpin. New York, Putnam [1962]
192 p. 28 cm.
1. English language—Rhetoric. 2. English language—Grammar—1870- I. Turpin, Waters Edward, 1910- joint author. II. Title.
PE1408.F52 1962 428 62-13803 ‡
Library of Congress [5]

M814.4
W27au4
1963
Tuskegee Institute.
Washington, Booker Taliaferro, 1859?-1915.
Up from slavery, an autobiography. Garden City, N. Y., Doubleday, 1963.
243 p. illus. 22 cm.
1. Tuskegee Institute. I. Title.
E185.97.W3163 923.773 63-3987 ‡
Library of Congress [5]

M814.4
W27as
Tuskegee normal and industrial institute.
Washington, Booker Taliaferro, 1859?-1915.
The story of my life and work, Booker T. Washington ... with an introduction by Dr. J. L. M. Curry ... illustrated ... by Frank Beard. Toronto, Ont., Naperville, Ill. [etc.] J. L. Nichols & co. [°1900]
423 p. incl. illus., plates, ports. front. 21cm.
Plates and portraits printed on both sides.
1. Tuskegee normal and industrial institute. 0-3304
Library of Congress E185.97.W29 [44j1]

M350
F85
The Tuskegee airmen; the story of the Negro in the U. S. Air Force.
Francis, Charles E
The Tuskegee airmen; the story of the Negro in the U. S. Air Force. Boston, Bruce Humphries [1956, °1955]
225 p. illus. 22 cm.
1. World War, 1939-1945—Negroes. 2. Negroes in aeronautics. 3. U. S. Army Air Forces. I. Title.
D810.N4F76 940.541273 53-11824 ‡
Library of Congress [57d5]

M378Tu
W578
Tuskegee Institute, Tuskegee, Ala.
Whiting, Helen Adele (Johnson) 1885-
Booker T. Washington's contribution to education. Charlotte, N. C., Mimeograph Press, Kluttz Mail Advertising Service [n.d.]
160p. port. diagr. 27cm.
Mimeographed.

M814.4
W272t
Tuskegee, Ala. Normal and industrial institute.
Washington, Booker Taliaferre, 1859?-1915, ed.
Tuskegee & its people: their ideals and achievements, ed. by Booker T. Washington. New York, D. Appleton and company, 1905.
xvi, 354 p. front., plates, ports. 21cm.

M814.4
W272t
Tuskegee & its people.
Washington, Booker Taliaferro, 1859?-1915, ed.
Tuskegee & its people: their ideals and achievements, ed. by Booker T. Washington. New York, D. Appleton and company, 1905.
xiv, 354 p. front., plates, ports. 21cm.
The volume here presented has been edited by Mr. Emmett J. Scott, executive secretary of the Tuskegee institute. The task of editing which the principal had expected to perform has been so well done that it has only been necessary to review the manuscript after its preparation for the publishers, and to forego the strict editorial revisioning planned. cf. General introduction.
CONTENTS.—I. The school and its purposes.—II. Autobiographies by graduates of the school.
1. Tuskegee, Ala. Normal and industrial institute. I. Scott, Emmett Jay, 1873- ed. II. Title. 5-17294
Library of Congress LC2851.T82W2 [44j1]

M630.7
G25
Tuskegee Institute. Dept. of Records and Research. Records and research pamphlet no. 3.
Guzman, Jessie Parkhurst, 1898-
George Washington Carver, a classified bibliography. [Tuskegee Institute, Ala.] Dept. of Records and Research, Tuskegee Institute 1953 [i. e. 1954]
26, [1] p. 27 cm. (Records and research pamphlet no. 3)
Cover title.
"Parts I, II, and III also printed in the Bulletin of bibliography, beginning with the August-December [i. e. May-August] 1953 issue."
Erratum slip mounted on p. [27]
1. Carver, George Washington, 1864?-1943—Bibl. (Series: Tuskegee Institute. Dept. of Records and Research. Records and research pamphlet no. 3)
Z8150.7.G8 012 54-23533
Library of Congress [1]

M814.4
W27au2
Tuskegee Normal and Industrial Institute.
Washington, Booker Taliferro, 1859?-1915.
Up from slavery, an autobiography. New York, Pocket Books Inc., 1940.
236p. 16½cm.

M371.974
T87n
Tuskegee Institute.
The new South and higher education: what are the implications for higher education of the changing socio-economic conditions of the South? A symposium and ceremonies held in connection with the inauguration of Luther Hilton Foster, fourth president of Tuskegee Institute [October 31 and November 1, 1953. Tuskegee, Ala.] Dept. of Records and Research, Tuskegee Institute, 1954.
x, 145 p. map. 24 cm.
(Continued on next card) 54-12394
[5615]

M06
J61
no.8
Tuskegee Negro conferences.
Johnson, John Quincy,
...Report of the fifth Tuskegee Negro conference, 1896, by John Quincy Johnson... Baltimore, The Trustees, 1896.
27p. 24cm.

M814.4
W27au2
1902
Tuskegee normal and industrial institute.
Washington, Booker Taliaferro, 1859?-1915.
Up from slavery; an autobiography, by Booker T. Washington. London, Grant Richards, 1902.
ix, 330 p. front. (port.) 20½cm.
Originally published in the Outlook. cf. Pref.
1. Tuskegee normal and industrial institute. I. Title. 1-31242
Library of Congress E185.97.W3
——— Copy 2. [45g²2]

M371.974
T87n
Tuskegee Institute. The new South and higher education ... 1954. (Card 2)
PARTIAL CONTENTS.—Population distribution and composition in the new South, by D. J. Bogue.—The reorganization of the Southern economy, by B. U. Ratchford.—The extension of citizenship, by G. S. Mitchell.—Changes in values and attitudes, their implications for higher education, by I. D. Reid.—The dream of order in the mind of God, by H. Thurman.—The role of education in our times, by J. D. Russell.—Inaugural statement, by L. H. Foster.
1. Universities and colleges—Southern States. 2. Negroes—Education—Southern States. I. Title.
LA228.T8 371.974 54-12394
Library of Congress [5615]

M370.
C15
Tuskegee normal and industrial institute.
Campbell, Thomas Monroe, 1883-
The Movable school goes to the Negro farmer, by Thomas Monroe Campbell ... Tuskegee Institute, Ala., Tuskegee institute press [°1936.
xiv, 170 p. front., plates, ports. 23½cm.
CONTENTS.—pt. I. Semi-autobiography.—pt. II. The school on wheels.
1. Agricultural education—Alabama. 2. Negroes—Education. 3. Negroes—Alabama. 4. Tuskegee normal and industrial institute. 5. U. S. Extension service. I. Title.
36-7891
Library of Congress LC2802.A2C3
[44m1] 371.97409761

M814.4
W27au
1902
Tuskegee normal and industrial institute.
Washington, Booker Taliaferro, 1859?-1915.
Up from slavery; an autobiography, by Booker T. Washington. New York, Doubleday, Page & co., 1902.
ix, 330 p. front. (port.) 20½cm.
Originally published in the Outlook. cf. Pref.
1. Tuskegee normal and industrial institute. I. Title. 1-31242
Library of Congress E185.97.W3
——— Copy 2. [45g²2]

Tuskegee normal and industrial institute.

M814.4 W27au 1901
Washington, Booker Taliaferro, 1859?–1915.
Up from slavery; an autobiography, by Booker T. Washington. New York, Doubleday, Page & co., 1901.
ix, 330 p. front. (port.) 20½cm.
Originally published in the Outlook. cf. Pref.

1. Tuskegee normal and industrial institute. I. Title.
Library of Congress E185.97.W3 1—31242
——— Copy 2.
[45g²2]

M814.4 W27au
Tuskegee normal and industrial institute.
Washington, Booker Taliaferro, 1859?–1915.
Working with the hands; being a sequel to "Up from slavery," covering the author's experiences in industrial training at Tuskegee, by Booker T. Washington; illustrated from photographs by Frances Benjamin Johnston. New York, Doubleday, Page & company, 1904.
x, 246 p. front. (port.) 31 pl. 20½ cm.
Subscription edition with a special introduction not in the trade edition.

1. Tuskegee normal and industrial institute. I. Title.
E185.97.W32 4—12107
Library of Congress [56o½]

Tuskegee normal and industrial institute.

M814.4 W27 aw
Washington, Booker, Taliaferro, 1859?–1915.
Working with the hands; being a sequel to "Up from slavery," covering the author's experiences in industrial training at Tuskegee, by Booker T. Washington; illustrated from photographs by Frances Benjamin Johnston. New York, Doubleday, Page & company, 1904.
x, 246 p. front. (port.) 31 pl. 20½cm.

1. Tuskegee normal and industrial institute. I. Title.
4—12107
Library of Congress E185.97.W32
[42p1]

Tuskegee normal and industrial institute.

M378Tu W58
Whiting, Joseph Livingston, 1877–
Shop and class at Tuskegee; a definitive story of the Tuskegee correlation technique, 1910–1930, by J. L. Whiting. Boston, Chapman & Grimes [°1941]
114 p. front., plates, map, tables, diagrs. 21cm.

1. Tuskegee normal and industrial institute. I. Title.
42-4090
Library of Congress LC2851.T82W5
[4] 378.761

M630 J71c
Tuskegee Normal and Industrial Institute. Rural Life Council.
Jones, Lewis Wade, 1910-
The changing status of the Negro in southern agriculture; Proceedings of Tuskegee Rural Life Conference, June 18, 19, 20, 1950, ed. by Lewis W. Jones. Tuskegee Institute, Alabama, The Rural Life Council, 1950.
325p. 23cm. (Rural life information series)

M251 J63t
Tuskegee talks.
Johnson, Henry Theodore, 1857-
Tuskegee talks. Ministerial training and qualification, by H.T. Johnson... Philadelphia, Press of international printing co. c1902
viii, 49p. front. 23cm.

Congo Leopoldville M325 M89
La tutelle internationale et le problème des unions administratives.
Mulenzi, Janvier.
La tutelle internationale et le problème des unions administratives. Préf. de Guy Malengreau. Louvain, Nauwelaerts, 1955.
228 p. 21 cm.
Includes bibliography.

1. International trusteeships. I. Title.
JX4021.M9 57—26550 ‡
Library of Congress [5]

Nigeria M896.3 T88aj
Tutuola, Amos.
Ajaiyi and his inherited poverty. London, Faber, 1967.
5–235 p. 20½ cm. 25/- (B 67-25588)

I. Title.
PZ4.T968Aj 67–114493
Library of Congress [3]

Nigeria M896.3 T88b
Tutuola, Amos, 1902-
The brave African huntress. Illustrated by Ben Enwonwu. London, Faber and Faber [1958]
150p. 20cm.

I. Title. II. Enwonwu, Ben, illus.

Nigeria M896.3 T88br
Tutuola, Amos, *1920 -*
The brave African huntress. New York, Grove Press [°1958]
150 p. illus. 21 cm.

I. Title.
PZ7.T885Br 2 58–8977 ‡
Library of Congress [5]

Nigeria M896.3 T88f
Tutuola, Amos
Feather woman of the jungle. London, Faber and Faber, 1962.
132p. 21cm.

1. Nigeria - Fiction. I. Title.

Nigeria M896.3 T88p
Tutuola, Amos, *1920-*
L'Ivrogne dans la Brousse [The palm-wine drinkard and his dead palm-wine tapster in the deads' town] Traduit de l'Anglais par Raymond Queneau. Roman. Paris, Gallimard, 1953.
197p. 19cm.

I. Title.

Nigeria M896.3 T88m
Tutuola, Amos, *1920-*
My life in the Bush of Ghosts; with a foreword by Geoffrey Parrinder. London, Faber and Faber [1954]
174 p. 21 cm.

I. Title.
PZ4.T968My 54–21629 ‡
Library of Congress [3]

Nigeria M896.3 T88m Amer. ed.
Tutuola, Amos.
My life in the Bush of Ghosts. With a foreword by Geoffrey Parrinder. New York, Grove Press [1954]
174 p. 21 cm.

I. Title.
[PZ4] 54–12101 ‡
Printed for U. S. Q. B. R. by Library of Congress [5]

Nigeria M896.3 T88p
Tutuola, Amos.
The palm-wine drinkard and his dead palm-wine tapster in the Dead's Town. New York, Grove Press [1953]
130 p. 21 cm.

I. Title.
PZ4.T968Pal 2 53–8397 ‡
Library of Congress [3]

Nigeria M896.3 T88p
Tutuola, Amos.
The palm-wine drinkard and his dead palm-wine tapster in the Deads' Town. London, Faber and Faber [1952]
125 p. 21 cm.

I. Title. 1. Nigeria - Fiction.
PZ4.T968Pal 52–43382 ‡
Library of Congress [53b1]

Nigeria M896.3 T88s
Tutola, Amos.
Simbi and the satyr of the dark jungle. London, Faber and Faber, 1955.
136p. 20½cm.

1. Nigeria - fiction. I. Title.

M811.4 W59t 1890
Twasinta's Seminoles.
Whitman, Albery Allson, 1851-1901.
Twasinta's Seminoles; or Rape of Florida. By Albery A. Whitman. Third ed. carefully rev. St. Louis, Nixon-Jones printing co., 1890.
96p. incl. front. (port.) 26cm.

Twasinta's Seminoles.

M811.4 W59t
Whitman, Albery A 1851–
Twasinta's Seminoles; or, Rape of Florida. By Albery A. Whitman. Rev. ed. St. Louis, Nixon-Jones printing co., 1885.
97 p. incl. front. (port.) 19½cm.

1. Seminole Indians—Poetry. I. Title.
31—28855
Library of Congress PS3187.W3T8
Copyright 1885: 19359 [37b1]

U.S. M839 Iv3t
The twelve dancing princesses and other fairy tales.
David, Alfred, comp.
The twelve dancing princesses and other fairy tales; a new selection with an introd. by Alfred and Mary Elizabeth David. New York, New American Library 1964.
319p. 18cm.
"A Signet book."
Partial contents.- The tinderbox; The swineherd; The princess on the pea; The ugly duckling; The nightingale and The little mermaid by Hans Christian Andersen; Translated by Pat Shaw Iversen.

M813.5 W93t
12 million black voices.
Wright, Richard, 1909–
12 million black voices; a folk history of the Negro in the United States; text by Richard Wright, photo-direction by Edwin Rosskam. New York, The Viking press, 1941.
152 p. illus. 26cm.
"First published in October 1941."

1. Negroes—Moral and social conditions. I. *Rosskam, Edwin, 1903– II. Title.
[Full name: Richard Nathaniel Wright]
41—25589
Library of Congress E185.6.W9
[45n2] 325.260973

12 Nigger-songs.

Congo, Leopoldville
M896.1
K127
Kalombo, Vidye
12 Nigger-songs. Naar het Kiluba van Vidye Kalombo. Op sonnetten getrokken door Gaston Burssens. Antwerpen, De Sikkel, 1945.
20p. 18cm.
Van dit boek werden gedruk 120 exx. op Van Gelder, genummerd van 1 tot 120. Dit is nummer 77.
Written in Flemish.
I. Burssens, Gaston, 1896- tr. II. Title.

Twenty - eight years a slave;

MB9
J63t
Johnson, Thomas L.
Twenty - eight years a slave; or the story of my life in three continents, by Thomas L. Johnson... Bourne mouth, W. mate and sons, limited, 1909.
xvi, 266 p. front., plates. 19cm.

Twenty-two years a slave.

M326.99B
St4
1867
Steward, Austin, *b.* 1794.
Twenty-two years a slave, and forty years a freeman; embracing a correspondence of several years, while president of Wilberforce colony, London, Canada West, by Austin Steward. 4th ed. ~~Rochester, N. Y., Allings & Cory, 1861.~~ Canandaigua, N.Y. The Author, 1867.
xii, [13]-360 p. front. (port.) 4 pl. 18cm.
1. Slavery in the U. S.—Virginia. 2. Slavery in the U. S.—New York (State) 3. Wilberforce negro colony, Middlesex Co., Ont. I. Title.
Library of Congress E444.S845 14—17056
[a20f2]

---

12 songs from Trinidad.

Trinidad
M780
W671sg
Williams, Connie, collector.
12 songs from Trinidad. [Illustrated by Grace West] San Francisco, Panpipes Press, 1958.
15p. illus., port. 18½cm.

Twenty-five.

M811.5
R55
Robinson, Golia W
Twenty-five; a collection of poems and lyrics. New York, William-Frederick Press, 1953.
22 p. 22 cm. (The William-Frederick poets, 98)
I. Title.
PS3535.O25645T9 811.5 53-8208 ‡
Library of Congress [2]

Twenty-two years a slave, and forty years a freeman.

M326.99B
St4
Steward, Austin, *b.* 1794.
Twenty-two years a slave, and forty years a freeman; embracing a correspondence of several years, while president of Wilberforce colony, London, Canada West, by Austin Steward. Rochester, N. Y., W. Alling, 1857.
xii, [13]-360 p. front. (port.) 4 pl. 19cm.
Narrative of slave life in Virginia and in central New York.
1. Slavery in the U. S.—Virginia. 2. Wilberforce negro colony, Middlesex co., Ont. I. Title.
Library of Congress E444.S84 6—34319
[a27d1]

---

12 Spanish American poets.

Cuba
M861.6
G94
Guillen, Nicolas, 1904-
[Poems].
(In: 12 Spanish American poets, an anthology, ed. by H.R. Hays... New Have, Yale University Press, 1943. 21cm. pp. 218-237)

Twenty-five years history of the grand fountain.

M366.5
B94
Burrell, William Patrick, 1865-
Twenty-five years history of the grand fountain of the united order of true reformers, 1881-1905. Illustrated. By W. P. Burrell and D. E. Johnson, Sr. Richmond, Va., 1909.
513p. front. ports. 22cm.

Twenty years in public life.

MB9
F95t
Fuller, Thomas Oscar, 1867-
Twenty years in public life, 1890-1910, North Carolina-Tennessee, by Thomas O. Fuller. Nashville, Tenn., National Baptist publishing board, 1910.
279, [1] p. illus., ports. 20 cm.
1. Negroes—North Carolina. 2. North Carolina—Pol. & govt.—1865- 3. Negroes—Tennessee. I. Title.
E185.97.F9 10-18964 rev
Library of Congress [r47b1]

W. Indies
M821.08
T91
Twelve West-Indian poems for children.
British Guiana, for private circulation of Govt. Training College for Teachers class of 1952.
15 p. 15 cm.
Contents: Walter McA. Lawrence. Leo (Egbert Martin). F.E. Brassington. A.F. Seymour. J. Hamilton Holder. Reginald Henry. J. W. Harper-Smith. George Campbell. Archie Lindo. Una Marson. Frank Collymore.
1. West Indian poetry.

Twenty-five years in the Black belt.

MB9
Ed4t
Edwards, William James, 1869-
Twenty-five years in the Black belt, by William J. Edwards ... Boston, The Cornhill company [°1918]
xvii p., 1 l., 143, [1] p. front. (port.) plates (incl. ports.) 19½ cm.
Autobiographical narrative and history of the Snow Hill normal and industrial institute, Snow Hill, Ala.
1. Snow Hill normal and industrial institute, Snow Hill, Ala. I. Title.
E185.82.E25 19—5302
Library of Congress [54e1]

Twenty years of court decisions.

M371.974
G93
Guzman, Jessie Parkhurst, 1898-
Twenty years of court decisions affecting higher education in the South, 1938-1958. Tuskegee, Alabama, Tuskegee Institute, Department of Records and Research, 1960.
36p. 23cm.
1. Segregation in education - Cases - Digests. I. Title.

M326.99B
An19t
Twelvetrees, Harper, 1823-1881, *ed.*
The story of the life of John Anderson, the fugitive slave. Ed. by Harper Twelvetrees, M. A., chairman of the John Anderson committee. London, W. Tweedie, 1863.
xv, 182 p. front. (port.) 19½cm.
1. Anderson, John, b. 1831? I. Allen, W C. 2. Slave narratives
Library of Congress E450.A54 15-13278

Twenty-five years in the Black belt...

MB9
Ed4t
Edwards, William James, 1869-
Twenty-five years in the Black belt, by William J. Edwards ... Boston, The Cornhill company [°1918]
xvii p., 1 l., 143, [1] p. front. (port.) plates (incl. ports.) 19½cm.
Autobiographical narrative and history of the Snow Hill normal and industrial institute, Snow Hill, Ala.
1. Snow Hill normal and industrial institute, Snow Hill, Ala. I. Title.
Library of Congress E185.82.E25 19—5302
[44d1]

Twi Grammar.

Ghana
M966.7
Ak7
Akrofi, C A
Twi Kasa Mmara; a Twi grammar in Twi. With a foreword by Prof. D. Westermann. London, Longmans, Green and Co., 1958.
110p. 18½cm.

Twentieth century Jamaica.

Jamaica
M823.91
D37t
De Lisser, Herbert George, 1878-
Twentieth century Jamaica, by H. G. De Lisser ... Kingston, Jamaica, The Jamaica times limited, 1913.
3 p. l., [5]-208 p. 7 pl., 2 port. (incl. front.) 20cm.
1. Jamaica—Descr. & trav. 2. Jamaica—Soc. life & cust. I. Title.
15-24481 Revised
Library of Congress F1871.D35
[r44b2]

Malagasy
M841
K11tw
24 poems.
Rabearivelo, Jean-Joseph.
24 poems. [Translated by Gerald Moore and Ulli Beier] Designed and illustrated by M. E. Betts. Ibadan, Mbari Publications, 1962.
[40]p. illus. 21-1/2cm.
I. Title. II. Mbari Publications.

Twice a year.

M323
N78t
Norman, Dorothy, ed.
Twice a year. A book of literature, the arts and civil liberties. New York, Twice A Year Press, 1946.
513p. 23cm.
Double Number - Fourteen - Fifteen
Fall - Winter - 1946-1947.
Richard Wright, Association editor.

Twentieth century Negro literature;

M973
C89t
Culp, Daniel Wallace, *ed.*
Twentieth century Negro literature; or, A cyclopedia of thought on the vital topics relating to the American Negro, by one hundred of America's greatest Negroes; ed. and arranged by D. W. Culp ... Naperville, Ill., Toronto, Can. [etc.] J. L. Nichols & co. [1902]
472 p. front., port. 24½ cm.
Portraits have text on verso.
1. Negroes--Education. I. Title.
2—10128
Library of Congress M185.5.C97
[a40g1]

Twenty-one Negro spirituals p. 98-106.

M810
F31
Federal writers' project.
American stuff; an anthology of prose & verse by members of the Federal writers' project, with sixteen prints by the Federal art project. New York, The Viking press, 1937,
xvii, [1], 301 p. plates. 22cm.

Twilight and the tortoise.

Nigeria
M896.3
Ak52
Akinsemoyin, Kunle
Twilight and the tortoise. Illustrated by Stephen Erhabor. Lagos, African Universities Press, 1963.
80p. 20cm. (African reader's library, 3)

M811.5
T92
Twilight dreams; the poetry of Homer Preston Johnson, John Robert Jackson [and] Robert Milum Baker. New York, Exposition Press [1950]

63p. 23cm.

1. American poetry - 20th cent. I. Johnson, Homer Preston, 1929- II. Jackson, John Robert. III. Baker, Robert Milum, 1929-

---

Two ways and other stories.

M813.5
H55
Hill, Roy L ,1925-
Two ways and other stories. State College, Pennsylvania, Commercial Printing Company, 1959.

43p. 23½cm.
Inscribed.

MB9
B22t
Tyson, *Mrs.* Martha (Ellicott) 1795-1873.
Banneker, the Afric-American astronomer. From the posthumous papers of Martha E. Tyson. Ed. by her daughter ... Philadelphia, Friends' book association, 1884.

vii, 9-72 p. incl. facsim. 17½cm.
Introduction signed: "A. T. K." [*i. e.* Anne T. Kirk]

1. Banneker, Benjamin, 1731-1806. I. Kirk, Anne T., ed.
4-18065
Library of Congress QB36.B22T9
[a41d1]

Sierra Leone
M896.3
N54tw
Two African tales.
Nicol, Abioseh Davidson, 1929-
Two African tales: The leopard hunt, and The devil at Yolahun Bridge. Illustrated by Hassan Bangurah. Cambridge [Eng.] University Press, 1965.
76 p. illus. 21 cm.

I. Title. II. Title: The leopard hunt. III. Title: The devil at Yolahun Bridge.
PZ7.N559Tw 65-19166
Library of Congress [3]

M813.5
D27t
Two weeks to find a killer.
Davis, Charles
Two weeks to find a killer. New York, Carlton Press [1966]

77p. 21cm.
Portrait of author on book jacket.

S. Africa
M896
N23u
U-Meweewe.
Ndawo, Henry Masila
U-Meweewe. Lovedale, Lovedale Press, 1951.

162p. port. 18½cm.

Two and one.

M813.5
M26tw
Madden, Will Anthony
Two and one; two short stories and a play. New York, Exposition Press, 1961.

50p. 21cm.
Portrait of author on back of book jacket.

M252
P38t
A two years' absence.
Pennington, James William Charles, 1812-1871
A two years' absence, or a farewell sermon, preached in the Fifth Congregational Church, by J.W.C. Pennington. Nov. 2d., 1845. Hartford, Published by H. T. Wells, 1845.

31p. 22½cm.

UN and peace-making.
M815.5
B88u
Bunche, Ralph Johnson, 1904-
UN and peace-making. n.p., [1950]

15p. 28cm.
Address delivered in Denver, May 11, 1950.
Mimeographed.

350
M920.9
H92
Two colored women with the American expeditionary forces.
Hunton, *Mrs.* Addie D (Waites)
Two colored women with the American expeditionary forces, by Addie W. Hunton and Kathryn M. Johnson ... Brooklyn, N. Y., Brooklyn eagle press [°1920]
256 p. front., 1 illus., plates, ports. 19cm.

1. European war, 1914-1918—Negroes. 2. European war, 1914-1918—War work—Y. M. C. A. 3. European war, 1914-1918—Personal narratives. I. Johnson, Kathryn Magnolia, 1878- II. Title.
21-287
Library of Congress D639.N4H8
[43g1]

A
M398
M89
Twsa language.
Mukhombo, Aron S
A nkutsulani wa matimu ya batswa: a timhaka ta kale ti khedzelwe. Celveland, Central Mission press, 1931.

127p. port. 20½cm.

Twsa legends.

U-Nolishwa.
Africa, South
M896.3
N24in
Ndawo, Henry Masila
U-Nolishwa. Lovedale, The Lovedale Press, 1939.

126p. port. 18½cm.
Story of Noliswa.
Bound with the author's InXenye YenTsomi Zase Zweni. «Natal, 1920»

M378
G83t
... Two decades of research and creative writings at West Virginia state college.
Greene, Harry Washington, 1896-
... Two decades of research and creative writings at West Virginia state college, compiled by Harry W. Greene ... Institute, W. Va., West Virginia state college [1939]
iv p., 1 l., [7]-24 p. 23cm. (West Virginia state college bulletin. Ser. 26, no. 4. Aug.-Nov. 1939)
Contribution no. 2 of the Research council at West Virginia state college.
Publications of West Virginia state college.
Z5055.U5W46
(Continued on next card)
E 40-5 rev
[r46c2]

S. Africa
M784
T95
Tyamzashe, Ben J P , 1890-
Five S. S. C. part songs for Native schools, by B. J. P. Tyamzashe. Lovedale, South Africa, Lovedale Press, 1943.

16p. 18½cm.

1. Africa - Music.

U-nomsa (a novel)
Africa, South
M896.3
S16n
Sinxo, Guybon B.
U-nomsa (a novel). «Lovedale. Lovedale Press «1922»

84p. 18cm.

Two distinct religions.

M210
M76t
Montgomery, Leroy Jeremiah
Two distinct religions, Christianity and the religion of Jesus Christ, by Leroy Jeremiah Montgomery... Houston, Texas, Informer publishing company n.d.

69p. 17½cm.

M268
T97
Tyms, James Daniel, 1905-
The rise of religious education among Negro Baptists; a historical case study, by James D. Tyms. [1st ed.] New York, Exposition Press [1966, °1965]
xiv, 408 p. 21 cm. (An Exposition-university book)
Bibliography: p. [397]-403.

1. Baptists, Negro—Education. I. Title. 2. Religious education.
BX6450.T93 268.86133 66-1120
Library of Congress [3]

M815.4
D739u
U. S. Grant and the colored people.
[Douglass, Frederick] 1817-1895.
U. S. Grant and the colored people. His wise, just, practical, and effective friendship thoroughly vindicated by incontestable facts in his record from 1862 to 1872. Words of truth and soberness! He who runs may read and understand!! Be not deceived, only truth can endure!!! [Washington, 1872]
8 p. 24cm.
Caption title.
Signed: Frederick Douglass.

1. Grant, Ulysses Simpson, pres. U. S., 1822-1885. 2. Negroes—Politics and suffrage. 3. Campaign literature, 1872—Republican. I. Title.
12-6966
Library of Congress E185.2.D73
[32b1]

M811.5
Od5t
Two Gun Bill
Oden, Thomas Hildred.
Two Gun Bill [by] Benny Burleigh [pseud.] New York, Comet Press Books [1957]
44 p. 21 cm.
Poems.

I. Title.
PS3529.D45T85 811.5 57-7019 ‡
Library of Congress [2]

M973.2
T97
Tyndall, John William, 1877-
The origin of the black man, by John W. Tyndall ... St. Louis, Mich., Metropolitan correspondence Bible college [°1927]
8 p. l., 114, [1] p. 19cm.

Second edition revised and enlarged.

1. Negro race. I. Title.
27-15666
Library of Congress HT1589.T8
[2]

Uganda
M967.61
Ad45
Uganda.
Adimola, A B
Lobo Acoli [A geographical survey of Acoli district] Kampala, East African Literature Bureau, 1956.

37p. illus., maps. 21½cm.
Written in Acoli.

Uganda
Uganda
M967.61
An9
Anywar, Reuben Stephen
Acoli ki ker megi. Nairobi, The Eagle Press, 1954.
223p. 18cm.

Uganda.
Uganda
M967.61
M8p
Mubiru, Wilson
Paspalum [The value of Paspalum grass] Nairobi, The Eagle Press, n.d.
18p. illus. 20½cm.
Written in Luganda.

Uganda.
Uganda
M967.61
N87m
Nsimbi, Michael B
Muddu awulira. ("The obedient servant...") Michael B. Wamala. Nairobi, The Eagle Press, 1959.
82p. 21½cm.
Text in: Luganda.
1. Uganda

Uganda.
Uganda
M967.61
B17b
Bakaluba, E
Buganda n'ensimbi zaayo: [Buganda and its systems of currency.] Kampala, The Eagle Press, 1951.
20p. 18½cm.

Uganda
Uganda
M967.61
M890
Pt. I.
Mulira, Enoch E K
Olugero lwa Kintu [Story of the first king of Buganda] Part I. Nairobi, The Eagle Press, 1951.
31p. illus. 20cm.
Written in Luganda.

Uganda.
Uganda
M967.61
N87w
Nsimbi, Michael B
Waggumbulizi. Eyawandiika; Omugaso gw' Okugunjulwa, Siwa Muto Lugero, Olulimi Oluganda, Muddu Awulira. Kampala, Uganda Bookshop, 1952.
111p. illus. 18½cm.
I. Title. 1. Uganda

Nyasaland Uganda.
M967.61
H34
Head, M E
Ensi mwe tuli n'abanti Nga bwe bagyeyambisa [The land and how men use it] Ebifaananyi bya J. Rubadiri. Nairobi, Eagle Press, 1953.
8 p. illus. 18 cm.
Written in Luganda.
White author.
1. Uganda. I. Rubadiri, J., tr. I. Title.

Uganda.
Uganda
M967.61
M890
Pt.II
Mulira, Enoch E K
Olugero lwa Kintu [Story of Kintu the first king of Buganda: Pt. II] Nairobi, The Eagle Press, 1951.
30p. illus. 20cm.
Written in Luganda.

Uganda.
Uganda
M967.61
N88ek
Ntungqweisko, Yemima K
Ekirooto ky'omufuzi era ekimuli sekisumuluzó [The ruler's dream and the key flower] Nairobi, The Eagle Press, 1949. African home library No. 37.
14p. 18cm.
Written in Luganda.
1. Uganda.

Uganda.
Uganda
M967.61
K11e
Kagwa, Apolo, 1864?-1927.
Ekitabo kye mpisa za Baganda (the customs of Baganda in the Luganda language) kyawandikibwa, Sir Apolo Kagwa... Kampala, Uganda printing and publishing co., 1918.
XV, 319p. port. (front.) 19½cm.

Uganda.
Uganda
M967.61
M91t
Mulira, E M K
Troubled Uganda. London, Fabian Publications and Victor Gollancz [1950]
44p. 18cm. (Colonial controversy series, no.6)

Uganda.
Uganda
M967.61
N88e
Ntungwerisho, Yemima K
Ensulo era n'ekitole ky'ebbumba [The source and a handful of clay] Nairobi, The Eagle Press, 1949.
10p. 18½cm.
(African home library, No. 63)
Written in Luganda.
1. Uganda.

Uganda.
M338.9
G92s
Kiano, J G
Kenya, Uganda, and Tanganyika.
Pp. 49-53.
In: Science and the new nations, edited by Ruth Gruber. 1961.

Uganda.
Uganda
M967.61
M89L
Mukwaya, A B
Land tenure in Buganda; present day tendencies. Nairobi, The Eagle Press, 1953.
79p. tables graphs 21cm.

Uganda.
Uganda
M967.61
Sa1a
Ssali, E M
Abazungu nga bwe tubalaba [Europeans as we see them] Kampala, The Eagle Press, 1952.
28p. 21cm.
Written in Luganda.
1. Uganda.

Uganda.
Uganda
M967.61
K62e
Kintu, Quintin Y
Ettaka n'ebika mu Busoga [Busoga land tenure by D. W. Roberston and Quintin Y. Nairobi, The Eagle Press, 1955.
90p. map 18cm.
Written in Luganda (Custom and tradition in East Africa series)
1. Uganda.

Uganda
Uganda
M967.61
N87o
Nsimbi, M B
Olulimi Oluganda [Correct Luganda] Nairobi, The Eagle Press, 1955.
52p. 21½cm.

Uganda - Agriculture.
Uganda
M630
M37u
Masefield, G. B
Omulimi w'omu Uganda [The Uganda farmer] Kyakyusibwa E. Bulera. Nairobi, Eagle Press, 1951.
186p. illus. 18cm.
Written in Luganda.
1. Agriculture - Uganda. 2. Uganda - Agriculture. I. Title. II. Bulewa, E., tr.

Uganda.
Uganda
M967.61
M8e
Mubiru, Wilson
Ebyafa e Ssaayi [The story of Ssaayi] Nairobi, The Eagle Press, 1952.
9p. illus. 18cm.
Written in Luganda.

Uganda.
Uganda
M967.61
N87a
Nsimbi, Michael B
Amannya amaganda n'ennono zaago. Kampala, East African Literature Bureau, 1956.
323p. illus., maps. 21½cm.

Uganda - Athletics.
Uganda
M967.61
K14o
Kakoza, Polycarp K
Omupira[Football] Nairobi, The Eagle Press, 1953.
74p. illus. 21cm.
Written in Luganda.

Uganda - Cookery.

Uganda
M967.61
K81c

Koeune, Esther
Cooking for the family in East Africa. Nairobi, The Eagle Press, 1953.

91p. illus. 18cm.

1. Uganda - Cookery. I. Title.

Uganda - Economic conditions.

Uganda
M967.61
O12ki

Olinga, Enoch O
Kimonyia oni akwap. (The Country is crying out for us; a discussion of economic, social and health problems) Nairobi, The Eagle Press, 1959.

28p. illus. 21½cm.
Text in: Teso

1. Uganda - Social conditions. 2. Uganda - Economic conditions. 3. Uganda-Health.

Uganda - Education.

Uganda
M370
Ad44

Adimola, A B
The development of primary education in Acholi. Kampala, East African Literature Bureau, 1962.

79p. 32cm.
Mimeographed.

1. Education - Uganda. 2. Uganda - Education. I. Title.

Uganda - Education.

Uganda
M967.61
M91v

Mulira, Enoch M K
The vernacular in African education. London, Longmans, Green and Co., [1951]

55p. 18½cm.

Uganda-Folklore.

Uganda
M967.61
K11en

Kagwa, Apolo, 1867-1927.
Engero za Baganda (Uganda folklore stories) ezaku'nganyizibwa Sir Apolo Kagwa... London, The Sheldon press, 1927.

viii, 120p. front. 18cm.

Uganda - Folklore.

Uganda
M896.3
Se3s

Segganyi, Edward A K
Ssebato bafuma. (Short stories and folklore). [By] Edward A. K. Segganyi, Erasmus K. Kizito ne Jechoada K. S. Mukalazi. ... Nairobi, The Eagle Press, 1959.

164p. illus. 18½cm.
Text in: Luganda.

Uganda - Folktales.

Uganda
M967.61
N51e

Nganwa, Kesi K
Emi twarize ya wakami [Traditional stories of the Ankole people of Uganda] Nairobi, The Eagle Press, 1951.

35p. 21cm.

Uganda - Health.

Uganda
M967.61
K81te

Koeune, Esther
The teaching of health-training in the Junior school; Book One: Class I to III. Illustrations by Susan Grave Morris. Nairobi, The Eagle Press, 1953.

106p. illus. 18cm.

1. Uganda - Health.

Uganda - Health.

Uganda
M967.61
K81t

Koeune, Esther
The Teaching of health-training in the Junior school; Book Two-Class IV. Illustrations by Susan Grave Morris and Ruth Yudelowitz. Nairobi, The Eagle Press, 1953.

75p. illus. 18cm.

1. Uganda - Health.

Uganda - health.

Uganda
M967.61
O12k

Olinga, Enoch
Kidar Aijarakon [Look after you life.] Kampala, The Eagle Press [1952]

48p. 18cm.

Uganda - History

Uganda
M967.61
G79

Gray, John Milner
Ebyafaayo ebitonotono ku Uganda [Short history of Uganda] Kyakyusibwa Vencent Lule. Kampala, East African Literature Bureau, 1956.

25p. 21½cm.
Written in Luganda.
White author.

1. Uganda - History. I. Lule, Vencent, tr. II. Title.

Uganda-History.

Uganda
M967.61
K11ek

Kagwa, Sir Apolo, 1864?-1927.
Ekitabo kya basekabaka bebuganda, Nabebunyoro, Nakekoki, Nabetoro Nabenkole. London, Luzac & co., 1912.

340p. 18cm.

History of the Kings of Buganda, Bunyoro, Koki, Toro and Ankole in the Luganda Language.

Uganda - history.

Uganda
M967
K151

Katiti, C B
Ishe - katabazi. Nairobi, The Eagle Press, 1947.
40p. illus. 21cm.
"Traditional stories of the Ankole people of Uganda."

1. Uganda - history. 2. Banyankole.

Uganda - history.

Uganda
M967.61
K15o

Katyanku, Lucy Olive and Bulera, Semu Obwomezi bw'omulama Duhaga II: Life of Dunhaga II, The Mukama of Bunyoro. Nairobi, The Eagle Press, 1950.

71p. port. illus. 21½cm. (A treasury of East African history)
Written in Runyoro.

Uganda - History.

Uganda
M967.61
Ok2t

Okech, Lacito
Tekwaro ki ker lobo acholi [History and chieftainship records of the land of the Acholi people of Uganda] Nairobi, The Eagle Press, 1953.

90p. 21cm.

Uganda - Hygiene.

Uganda
M967.61
M46

Medical Headquarters, Entebee, Uganda.
The laws that protect your health; a book of village hygiene with special reference to Uganda. Nairobi, East African Literature Bureau, 1956.

56p. illus. diagrs. 24½cm.

Uganda - medicine.

Uganda
M967.61
Se5g

Sembeguya, F G
Genda olabe omuisawo [Go and see the doctor] Nairobi, East African Literature Bureau, 1956.

42p. 21cm.
Written in Luganda.

Uganda - Native races.

Uganda
M967.61
Ob5

Oboth-Ofumbi, Arphaxed Charles K, 1932-
Padhola [History and customs of the Jo Pahdola] Nairobi, Eagle Press, 1960.

84p. 21½cm.
Written in Luo (Ludoma)

1. Jopadhola. 2. Uganda - Native races. I. Title.

Uganda - Politics and government.

Uganda
M967.61
K12c

Kale, John K ,ed.
Colonialism is incompatible with peace.

31p. 21½cm.

1. Uganda - Politics and government. I. Title.

Uganda - Politics and government.

Uganda
M967.61
K12U

Kale, John K ,ed.
Uganda: colonial regime versus national aspirations. Cairo Mondiale Press, 195?

32p. 21½cm.

1. Uganda - Politics and government. I. Title.

Uganda - Proverbs.

Uganda
M398
Ea67

East African Literature Bureau
Engero ezimu [Proverbs. Illustrated by L. N. Sekaboga] Kampala, Eagle Press, 1951.
11p. illus. 18cm. (Eagle improve your reading series, no. I)
Written in Luganda.

1. African. 2. Uganda - Proverbs. I. Title. II. Series. III. Sekaboga, L. N., illus.

Uganda - Proverbs.
Uganda
M398 Kagoro, E D
K119 Ezimu ha nfumo z'abatooro hali Nyinanyowe, N'abagenzi Bange [Batooro proverbs] Kampala. Eagle Press, 1956.
iv, 15p. 21cm.
Written in Nyora-Tooro.
1. Proverbs, African. 2. Uganda - Proverbs. I. Title.

Uganda - Proverbs.
Uganda
M398 Onen, S F
On2a Agda yil ku wade; lem'abola ku titi. (Alur proverbs and riddles.) Nairobi, The Eagle Press, 1959.
26p. 18cm.
Text in: Lwo (Alur)
1. Uganda - Proverbs. 2. Uganda - Riddles.

Uganda - Riddles.
Uganda
M398 Onen, S F
On2a Agda yil ku wade; lem'abola ku titi. (Alur proverbs and riddles.) Nairobi, The Eagle Press, 1959.
26p. 18cm.
Text in: Lwo (Alur)
1. Uganda - Proverbs. 2. Uganda - Riddles.

Uganda - short stories.
Uganda
M896.3 Segganyi, Edward A K
Se3s Ssebato bafuma. (Short stories and folklore).
S [By] Edward A. K. Segganyi, Erasmus K. Kizito ne Jechoada K. S. Mukalazi. ... Nairobi, The Eagle Press, 1959.
164p. illus. 18½cm.
Text in: Luganda.

Uganda - Social conditions.
Uganda
M967.61 Olinga, Enoch O
O12ki Kimonyia oni akwap. (The Country is crying out for us; a discussion of economic, social and health problems) Nairobi, The Eagle Press, 1959.
28p. illus. 21½cm.
Text in: Teso.
1. Uganda - Social conditions. 2. Uganda - Economic conditions. 3. Uganda-Health.

Uganda - Soc. life & cust.
Africa, South
M968 Jabavu, Noni.
J111d2 Drawn in color: African contrasts. New York, St. Martin's Press [1962, °1960]
208 p. 22 cm.
"A personal account of ... [the autnor's] experiences and impressions of the differences between East and South Africa in their contact with westernisation."
1. Africa, South—Soc. life & cust. 2. Uganda—Soc. life & cust. I. Title.
DT761.J25 1962 916.8 62-8319 ‡
Library of Congress [10]

Uganda - Soc. life & cust.
Africa, South
M968 Jabavu, Noni.
J11d Drawn in colour: African contrasts. London, Murray [1960]
xii, 208 p. fold. map. 23 cm.
"A personal account of ... [the author's] experiences and impressions of the differences between East and South Africa in their contact with westernisation."
Portrait of author on book jacket.
1. Africa, South—Soc. life & cust. 2. Uganda—Soc. life & cust. I. Title.
DT761.J25 916.8 60—2618
Library of Congress [60e5]

Uganda
M657 Uganda. Department of Commerce.
Ug1 Kutumia hesabu; kitabu cha kuwasaidia, Waafrika katika biashara. Using accounts, a handbook to assist Africans in trade. Kampala, Eagle Press, 1956.
39p. illus. 25cm.
Written in English and Swahili.
1. Africa - Business. 2. Accounting. 3. Business - Africa. 4. Bookkeeping. I. Title.

Uganda Folklore.
Uganda
M967.61 Kagwa, Sir Apolo, 1864?-1927.
K11t The tales of Sir Apolo, Uganda folklore and proverb. With an introduction by the translator the Rev. Canon F. Rowling. Illustrated by Savile Lumley. London, The Religious Tract Society n.d.
95p. port. 18½cm.
1. Uganda Folklore. 2. Africa-Folklore.

Uganda literature
Uganda
M967.61 Nganwa, Kesi K.
N51a Abakozire eby'okutangaza. Omuri. Ankole. Nairobi, Published for the Ankole literature committee by The Eagle Press, 1949.
36p. illus. 21cm.

Uganda: colonial regime versus national aspirations.
Uganda
M967.61 Kale, John K ,ed.
K12U Uganda: colonial regime versus national aspirations. Cairo Mondiale Press, 195?
32p. 21½cm.
1. Uganda - Politics and government. I. Title.

M646.7 Uggams, Leslie.
Ug4 The Leslie Uggams beauty book, by Leslie Uggams with Marie Fenton. Englewood Cliffs, N. J., Prentice-Hall [1966]
178 p. illus., ports. 26 cm.
1. Beauty, Personal. I. Fenton, Marie, joint author. II. Title.
RA778.U3 646.72 66—24987
Library of Congress [67d7]

Ugubudele Namazimuzimu.
South Africa
M896.2 Ndebele, Nimrod N T
N24u2 Ugubudele Namazimuzimu [Gubudele and the Cannibals] (umdlalo osenzo-sinye esinemiboniso emihlanu). [Reprinted in the new orthography] Johannesburg, Witwatersrand University Press, 1959.
62p. 18cm. (Bantu treasury, edited by D. T. Cole, VI)
1. Drama - Zulu. 2. Zulu - Drama. I. Title. II. Title: Gubudele and the Cannibals. III. Series

---

Uhambo Luka Gqoboka.
Africa, South
M896.3 Ndawo, Henry Masila
N24in Uhambo Luka Gqoboka. Lovedale, Lovedale Institution Press, 193?
93p. 18½cm.
Gqoboka's travels.
Bound with the author's InXenye YenTsomi Zase Zweni. «Natal, 1920»

Uhuru na umoja.
Tanganyika
M960 Nyerere, Julius Kambarage, *Pres. Tanzania*, 1922-
N98 Freedom and unity: Uhuru na umoja; a selection from writings and speeches, 1952-65 [by] Julius K. Nyerere. London, Nairobi [etc.] Oxford U. P., 1967.
xiii, 366 p. front., 8 plates (incl. ports.) 22½ cm. 45/-
(B 67-8232)
1. Africa—Politics—Addresses, essays, lectures. I. Title. II. Title: Uhuru na umoja.
DT446.N9A5 320.9'6 67-77497
Library of Congress [3]

Uhuru wa watumwa.
Kenya
M967.6 Mbotela, James Juma
M45u Uhuru wa watumwa [The slaves who were brought to Freetown] Nairobi, Eagle Press, 1951.
102p. illus. 18cm.
Written in Swahili.
English ed. has title: The freeing of the slaves in East Africa.
1. Africa, British East - History. 2. Slavery in Africa. I. Title.

Ujiongezee maarifa.
Zanzibar
M001 Diva, David Edward
D64 Ujiongezee maarifa [Increase your knowledge, Bk. I-VIII. [Dar es Salaam] Eagle Press [1950]
8v. illus. 17½cm.
I. Title.

Ukawamba.
Malawi
M896.3 Nkomba, Lester L
N65u Ukawamba. Edited by Guy Atkins. Cape Town; London, Oxford University Press, 1953.
134p. 18½cm. (Annotated African Texts - II: Cewa)

Ukufa kukashaka.
South Africa
M896.3 Zondi, Elliot
Z76u Ukufa kukashaka. [The death of Chaka] Johannesburg, Witwatersrand University Press, 1960.
45p. 18½cm. (The Bantu Treasury, xiv)
Written in Zulu.
I. Title. II. Series.

Ukwenda ng'aragu kana buthi?
Kenya
M613.2 Humphrey, Norman
H88w3 Ukwenda ng'aragu kana buthi? [Which do you want: starvation or nourishment? Tr. by J. M. Ruthuku] Nairobi, Eagle Press, 1949.
9p. 21½cm. (Taanya Ūgimaini. Aim at healthy living series)
Written in Kikuyu.
White author.
1. Nutrition. I. Title. II. Series. III. Ruthuku, J. M., tr.

Tanganyika
M967.82 Ulenge, Yussuf
U12 Nguzo ya maji; na hadithi nyingine; [The pillar of water, and other stories.] Nairobi, The Eagle Press, 1951.
22p. illus. 19cm.
Written in Swahili
1. Tanganyika - short stories.

...The ultimate criminal.

M06
Am3
no. 17

Grimké, Archibald Henry, 1849–
... The ultimate criminal. Annual address [by] Archibald H. Grimke ... Washington, D. C., The Academy, 1915.
14 p. 22cm. (The American negro academy. Occasional papers, no. 17)

1. Negroes—Crime. I. Title

Library of Congress E185.5.A51 no. 17 15-10359
——— Copy 2. E185.65.G85

Umvuzo wesoono.

S. Africa
M896.3
D64u

Dlova, E S M
Umvuzo wesoono. Lovedale, The Lovedale Press, 1954.

172p. 18½cm.

The uncalled.

M813.4
D91u3

Dunbar, Paul Laurence, 1872–1906.
The uncalled; a novel, by Paul Laurence Dunbar ... New York, Dodd, Mead and company, 1898.
3 p. l., 255 p. 18½cm.

I. Title.

Library of Congress PZ3.D911U8 98-1206 Revised
——— Copy 2.
Copyright 1898: 55550 [r30d2]

Uma lira dos vinte anos poesia.

Brazil
M869.1
Iv7u

Ivo, Lêdo
Uma lira dos vinte anos poesia. Rio de Janeira, Livraria São José, [1962]

197p.

I. Title.

Umyezo.

South Africa
M896
J68u2

Jolobe, James J R
Umyezo. [Xhosa poems] Amazwi okugabula izigcawu enziwe ngu Dr. W. G. Bennie. [Reprinted in new orthography] Johannesburg, Witwatersrand Press, 1957.

87p. 18cm. (The Bantu treasury, ed. by D. T. Cole, II)

1. Xhosa Poetry. 2. Poetry, African.
I. Title. II. Series.

The uncalled.

M813.4
D91u

Dunbar, Paul Laurence, 1872–1906.
The uncalled; a novel, by Paul Laurence Dunbar ... New York, Dodd, Mead and company, 1898.
3 p. l., 255 p. 18½cm.

I. Title.

Library of Congress PZ3.D911U8 98—1206
[42r30f1]

M39
D34u

Umbala.
Dean, Harry.
Umbala, the adventures of a Negro sea-captain in Africa and the seven seas in his attempts to found an Ethiopian empire; an autobiographical narrative by Captain Harry Dean, written with the assistance of Sterling North. London, George G. Harrap & co., ltd. [1929]

Umyezo.

M896.
J68u

Jolobe, James J R
Umyezo [by] James J. R. Jolobe, B.A. Amazwi okugabula izigcawu enziwe ngu W. G. Bennie. Johannesburg, The University of the Witwatersrand press, 1944.

vii, 71, [1]p. 18cm.

Uncle Paul.

British Guiana
M823.91
M69u

Mittelhölzer, Edgar
Uncle Paul. London, McDonald [1963]

222p. 20cm.

Umbundu; folk tales from Angola.

Angola
M398
En62

Ennis, Merlin, comp. and tr.
Umbundu; folk tales from Angola. Collected and translated by Merlin Ennis. Comparative analysis by Albert B. Lord. Boston, Beacon Press [1962]

316p. 21cm.

Umzali wolahleko.

S. Africa
M896.3
S16u

Sinxo, Guybon B
Umzali wolahleko (a novel). Lovedale, Lovedale Press, 1944.

64p. 18½cm.

Uncle Tom's Cabin.

M813.5
H87i

Hughes, Langston
Introductory remarks and captions.

(In: Stowe, Harriet Elizabeth (Beecher) Uncle Tom's cabin. New York, Dodd, Mead, [1952] 22cm.)

Umbuso ka Shaka.

South Africa
M896.3
N87

Ntuli, F L
Umbuso ka Shaka. [Translated] from Nada the lily [R. Haggard] Mariannhill, Natal, Mariannhill Mission Press [1933]

350p. 18½cm.
Written in Zulu.

1. Zululand - History - Fiction.
I. Haggard, Sir Henry Rider, 1856-1925. Nada the lily. II. Title.

Un Africain.

Algeria
M965
Af8m

Manuel de politique Musulmane.
Paris, Brossard, 1925.

189p. 19cm.

Uncle Tom's children.

M813.5
W93u2

Wright, Richard, 1909–
I figli dello Zio Tom. Einaudi, 1949.

318p. cm.

Umfundisi wase-mtuqwasi (i-novel).

Africa, South
M896.3
S16n

Sinxo, Guybon B.
Umfundisi wase-mtuqwasi (i-novel). «Lovedale» Lovedale Institution Press, «1927»

89p. 18½cm.

France
M848
Sa8m

Un du Normandie-Niémen.

Sauvage, Roger, 1917–
Un du Normandie-Niémen. Préf. du colonel Pouyade. [Givors] A. Martel [1950]
316 p. illus., ports. 21 cm.
"Il a été tiré ... 500 exemplaires sur Alfa Mousse des Papeteries Navarre numérotés 1 à 450 et H-C1 à H-C1. 131."

1. France combattante. Forces aériennes françaises libres. Régiment Normandie-Niémen. 2. World War, 1939–1945—Aerial operations, French. 3. World War, 1939–1945—Personal narratives, French. I. Title.

D788.S39 940.544944 51-17012
Library of Congress [1]

Uncle Tom's Children.

M813.5
W93u
1947

Wright, Richard, 1909–
Uncle Tom's children. New York, Penguin Books, 1947.

185p. 18cm.
Pocket book edition.

Umulimo wa nkoko.

[Zambia]
M896.3
C46u

Chitupa, Rodwell Pardon
Umulimo wa nkoko. Lusaka, Publications Bureau [1962]

[15]p. 18½cm.
Written in Bemba.

I. Title.

The uncalled.

M813.4
D91u2

Dunbar, Paul Lawrence, 1872-1906.
The uncalled. Lippincott's magazine, May 1898.

579-669p. 25cm.

Uncle Tom's children.

M813.5
W93un

Wright, Richard, 1908-1960.
Uncle Tom's children. 1st ed. New York, Penguin Books [1947]

185p. 18cm. (Penguin Books)
Pocket book edition.
"Complete and unabridged."

Uncle Tom's children.

M813.5 W93u **Wright, Richard, 1909–**
Uncle Tom's children, five long stories by Richard Wright. New York and London, Harper & brothers [1938]
xxx, 384 p. 21cm.
CONTENTS. — The ethics of living Jim Crow; an autobiographical sketch.—I. Big boy leaves home.—II. Down by the riverside.—III. Long black song.—IV. Fire and cloud.—V. Bright and morning star.
I. Title.
[Full name: Richard Nathaniel Wright]
Library of Congress PZ3.W935Un 2 40–29877 [2]

Underdeveloped areas.

M338.9 C83 **Cox, Oliver Cromwell, 1901–**
Capitalism and American leadership. New York, Philosophical Library [1962]
xx, 328 p. 23 cm.
Bibliography: p. 311–322.
1. Capitalism. 2. U. S.—Economic policy. 3. Underdeveloped areas. I. Title.
HB501.C78 338.9173 61–10606
Library of Congress [10]

M811.5 Un2b **Underhill, Irvin W** 1868–
The brown madonna and other poems, by Irvin W. Underhill, Sr. Philadelphia, Pa. [c1929]
95p. 18cm.
1. Poetry
I. Title

Uncommon sense.

M131 An2u **Anderson, Garland.**
Uncommon sense; the law of life in action, by Garland Anderson ... ~~London, L. N. Fowler & co.~~ [1933] [New York, The author]
220 p. 19cm.
1. New thought. 2. Faith-cure. 3. Success. I. Title.
Library of Congress BF639.A68 1933 34–488
——— Copy 2.
Copyright A ad int. 18321 [3] [159.91324] 131.324

Underdeveloped areas.

M338.9 G92a **International Conference on Science in the Advancement of New States, *Rehovot, Israel, 1960.***
Science and the new nations, proceedings. Edited by Ruth Gruber. New York, Basic Books [1961]
xv, 314 p. illus., ports. 24 cm.
Sponsored by the Weizmann Institute of Science.
1. Underdeveloped areas. 2. Technical assistance. 3. Science—Social aspects. I. Gruber, Ruth, 1911– ed. II. Title.
HC60.I 545 1960 338.9 61–11992
Library of Congress [15]

M811.5 Un2 **Underhill, Irvin W** 1868–
Daddy's love, and other poems, by Irvin W. Underhill ... Philadelphia, Pa. [A. M. E. book concern, printers, 1916]
87 p. 19cm. $0.60
I. Title. 1. Poetry.
Library of Congress PS3541.N4D3 1916 17–548
Copyright A 453468

Under fire.

M350 C26 **Cashin, Herschel V.**
Under fire. With the Tenth U. S. cavalry. Being a brief, comprehensive review of the Negro's participation in the wars of the United States. Especially showing the valor and heroism of the Negro soldiers of the Ninth and Tenth cavalries, and the Twenty-fourth and Twenty-fifth infantries of the regular army; as demonstrated in the decisive campaign around Santiago de Cuba, 1898 ... Thrilling episodes interestingly narrated by officers and men. Famous Indian campaigns and their results. A purely military history of the Negro. With introduction by Major-General Joseph Wheeler ... By Her-
(Continued on next card)
[41j1] 8–23892

Underground railroad.

M326.99B L82 **Loguen, Jermain Wesley, 1814–1872.**
The Rev. J. W. Loguen, as a slave and as a freeman. A narrative of real life. Syracuse, N. Y., J. G. K. Truair & co., printers, 1859.
x, [11]–454 p. front. (port.) 18cm.
Written in the third person, but apparently the work of Loguen. Two letters at end of volume are dated 1860.
"Testimony of Rev. E. P. Rogers," including a poem "Loguen's position": p. 445–450.
1. Slavery in the U. S.—Fugitive slaves. 2. Slavery in the U. S.—Anti-slavery movements. 3. Underground railroad. I. Rogers, Elymas Payson, d. 1861.
Library of Congress E444.L83 14–15518 [43r42d1]

Understanding minority groups.

M323 G44u **Gittler, Joseph Bertram, 1912– ed.**
Understanding minority groups. Contributors: John Collier [and others] New York, Wiley [1956]
xii, 139 p. illus. 24 cm.
Includes bibliographical references.
1. Minorities—~~U. S.~~ I. Collier, John, 1884– II. Title.
E184.A1G5 325.73 56–11777
Library of Congress [57f15]

Under the cottonwood.

M813.5 G759 **Graham, Katheryn Campbell.**
Under the cottonwood; a saga of Negro life in which the history, traditions and folklore of the Negro of the last century are vividly portrayed. By Katheryn Campbell Graham. New York, W. Malliet and company, 1941.
262 p. 23½cm.
"First edition."
1. Negroes—Texas. I. Title.
42–22816 Revised
Library of Congress E185.93.T4G7 [r43d3] 325.2609764

Underground railroad.

M326. M69 1860 **Mitchell, William M.**
The underground railroad from slavery to freedom. By the Rev. W. M. Mitchell ... 2d ed. London, W. Tweedie; [etc., etc.] 1860.
ix, [10]–191 p. front. (port.) 16½cm.
1. Underground railroad. 2. Slavery in the U. S.—Fugitive slaves. 3. Negroes—Ontario.
10–34489
Library of Congress E450.M68 [a36b1]

Understanding the Negro protest.

M323.4 H34 **Heacock, Roland T**
Understanding the Negro protest, by Roland T. Heacock. [1st ed.] New York, Pageant Press [1965]
188 p. 21 cm.
Portrait of author on book jacket.
1. Negroes—Civil rights. I. Title.
E185.61.H45 323.4 65–17618
Library of Congress [5]

Under the sun.

Jamaica M823.91 D37u De Lisser, Herbert George, 1878–
Under the sun: a Jamaica comedu, by Herbert G. de Lisser. London, Ernest Benn Limited [1937]
269p. 18½cm.

M326 St5 1886

Underground railroad.
Still, William, 1821-1902.
Underground railroad records, with a life of the author, narrating the hardships, hairbreadth escapes, and death struggles of the slaves in their efforts for freedom; together with sketches of some of the eminent friends of freedom, and most liberal aiders and advisers of the road. Illus. with 70 fine engravings... and portraits... rev. ed. Phil., William Still, publisher. 1886.
21, lxiv, 780p. illus. 24cm.

Undertakers and undertaking.

M393 P61e Pierce, Samuel Henry, 1913-
Excerpts from a mortician's workshop. Atlanta, Georgia, Board of Directors of the Georgia Funeral Directors and Embalmers Assoc., 1958.
144p. illus. 21½cm.

Underdeveloped areas.

M909.82 C76a **Conference on Tensions in Development, *Oxford University, 1961.***
Restless nations; a study of world tensions and development. Foreword by Lester B. Pearson. ~~New York, Dodd, Mead, 1962.~~ London, Allen and Unwin [1962]
217 p. 22 cm.
Sponsored by the Council on World Tensions.
1. Underdeveloped areas. 2. Economic assistance. 3. World politics—1955– I. Council on World Tensions. II. Title.
HC60.C63 1961 338.91 62–16328 ‡
Library of Congress [64r7]

M326 St5

Underground railroad.
Still, William, 1821-1902.
The underground railroad. A record of facts, authentic narratives, letters & c., narrating the hardships, hairbreadth escapes and death struggles of the slaves in their efforts for freedom, as related by themselves and others, or witnessed by the author; together with sketches of some of the largest stockholders, and most liberal aiders and advisers of the road. By William Still...Philadelphia, Porter E. Coates, 1872.
2p. 1., 780p. front. illus., pl. ports. 24cm.

Haiti M841 Un2p **Underwood, Edna (Worthley) 1873– tr.**
The poets of Haiti, 1782–1934, translated by Edna Worthley Underwood; woodcuts by Pétion Savain, glossary by Charles F. Pressoir. Portland, Me., The Mosher press, 1934.
xiii, 159 p., 1 l. incl. illus., pl. 19cm.
Includes biographical matter.
1. Haitian poetry (French)—Translations into English. 2. English poetry—Translations from Haitian (French) I. Title.
Library of Congress PQ3946.Z5E5 1934 34–22300 [a42e1] 841.0822

Underdeveloped areas.

M909.82 C76 **Conference on Tensions in Development, *Oxford University, 1961.***
Restless nations; a study of world tensions and development. Foreword by Lester B. Pearson. New York, Dodd, Mead, 1962.
217 p. 22 cm.
Sponsored by the Council on World Tensions.
1. Underdeveloped areas. 2. Economic assistance. 3. World politics—1955– I. Council on World Tensions. II. Title.
HC60.C63 1961 338.91 62–16328 ‡
Library of Congress [64r7]

Underground railroad - Connecticut.

M326 St8u **Strother, Horatio T**
The Underground railroad in Connecticut. [1st ed.] Middletown, Conn., Wesleyan University Press [1962]
262 p. illus. 22 cm.
1. Underground railroad—Connecticut.
E450.S93 973.7115 62–15122 ‡
Library of Congress [5]

... Une etape de l'evolution haitienne.

Haiti M972.94 M35e **Mars, Price.**
... Une étape de l'évolution haïtienne. Port-au-Prince, Haïti, Impr. "La Presse" [1929?]
viii, [9]–208 p. 24½cm. (Bibliothèque haïtienne)
CONTENTS. — L'intelligence haïtienne, études de socio-psychologie.—Les croyances, le sentiment et le phénomène religieux chez les nègres de St.-Domingue; conférence prononcée à la Société d'histoire et de géographie en 1926.—Magic island, par W. B. Seabrook ...—La Noël des humbles.—Les opinions à propos de "Black Haiti", une biographie de la fille aînée de l'Afrique, par Blair Niles.
1. Haiti—Soc. condit. 2. Haiti—Intellectual life. 3. National characteristics, Haitian. 4. Negroes in Haiti. I. Title.
30–15008
Library of Congress F1921.M36 [2]

Une femme chante.

Haiti
M841.
W63f

Wiener, Jacqueline.
Une femme chante. Duexieme edition. Port-au-Prince, L'Etat, ⌊1951?⌋

59p. port. 21cm.

I. Title. 1. Haitian poetry.

France
M840
D89fi

Une fille du regent.
Dumas, Alexandre, 1802-1870.
Une fille du regent. Bruxelles et Leipzig, Meline, Cans et Compagnie, 1844.

3v. 18cm.

Cameroun
M896.3
Oy4v

Une vie de Boy.
Oyono, Ferdinand.
Une vie de Boy; roman. Paris, Rene Julliard, 1956.

183p. 19cm.

M331
H76b

Unemployed-U.S.
Hoover, Isaac James.
Banishing the ghost of unemployment, by Isaac James Hoover. Boston, Meador publishing company, 1934.

2 p. l., 7-105 p. 19½cm.
"The fallacies of the 'new deal' exposed."—Publisher's announcement.

1. Unemployed—U. S. 2. U. S.—Economic policy. 3. National industrial recovery act, 1933. I. Title.

Library of Congress HD5724.H6 34-39702
———— Copy 2.
Copyright A 78288 ⌊5⌋ 331.137973

M331
M93s

Unemployment.
Murchison, John Prescott
⌊Statement at⌋ Hearings before the Committee on Labor, House of Representatives, seventy-second Congress, first session on Relief of distress due to unemployment. Wash., D.C., Govt. Print. Off., 1932.

45-51p. 23cm.
At head of title: Relief of distress due to unemployment. Detached copy.

M304
P19
V.7
no.32

Unemployment.
National urban league.
Unemployment status of Negroes; a compilation of facts and figures respecting unemployment among Negroes in one hundred and six cities. New York, National urban league, 1931.

56p. 26cm.

M813.5
G87u

Unfettered.
Griggs, Sutton Elbert, 1872-
Unfettered, a novel by Sutton E. Griggs. Nashville, The Orion publishing co., 1902.

276p. 22cm.

M323.4
J135

Unholy shadows and freedom's holy light.
Jackson, Joseph Harrison, 1900-
Unholy shadows and freedom's holy light, by J. H. Jackson. Nashville, Townsend Press ⌊1967⌋

xii, 270 p. group ports. 22 cm.
Bibliography: p. 264-266.

1. ~~Negroes~~—Civil rights. I. Title.

E185.61.J15 301.451'96'073 67-29805
Library of Congress ⌊5⌋

M813.5
W52

An unimportant man.
West, Dorothy
An unimportant man.

pp. 124-53 19cm.
In: Copy, 1929; stories, plays, poems and essays. New York, D. Appleton and Company, 1939.

M973.8
Ow2u

Union League of America.
Owens, Susie Lee.
Union League of America; Political activities in Tennessee, the Carolinas, and Virginia, 1865-1870, an abridgement. New York, New York University, 1947.

23p. 23cm.

M972.94
P19
V.2,no.8

Union Nationaliste
Depossessions, "Le lati-fundia Américain" contre "La petite propriété d'Haiti." port-au-Prince, Imp. de "La Presse"

39p. 24cm.

1. Haiti. I. Thoby, Perceval.

Haiti
M972.94
P19
V.2
no.1,2

Union Patriotique
Bulletin mensuel de l'Union Patriotique publie par le Comité de Port-au-Prince, 1-3. Port-au-Prince, 1920-1921.
v. 21cm.
Georges Sylvain, Administrateur-delgue.
See holdings card for issues in library.

1. Haiti - Periodicals. I. Sylvain, Georges.

Haiti
M972.94
P19

Union Patriotique
Bulletin mensuel

Volume	Year	Month	Volume	Year	Month
2					
no.1	1920	Dec.			
no.2&3	1921	Jan.-Feb.			

Haiti
M972.94
P19
V.2,no.5

Union Patriotique
Le procès pour les élections législatives du 10 janvier 1924... Port-au-Prince, Imp. Edmond Chevet, 1923.

45p. 23cm.
At head of title: Union Patriotique, Comité de Port-au-Prince.

1. Haiti-Pol. & govt. - 1844.

Haiti
M972.94
P19
V.2,no.4

Union Patriotique.
Séance publique tenue au Théatre Parisiana, le 16 Février 1925, la mission Hudicourt à Washington,et à Lima ... Port-au-Prince, Imp. V. Pierre-Noel, 1925.

24p. 19½cm.
At head of title: Union patriotique. Comité Central de Port-au-Prince.

1. Hudicourt, Pierre Lelio. 2. Haiti - For. rel. - U.S.

M323.
J632a

Union patriotique haitienne.
Johnson, James Weldon, 1871-
L'autonomie d'Haïti, par James Weldon Johnson. Qurtre ⌊!⌋ articles reproduits de la revue "The Nation", comprenant le compte-rendu d'une enquête effectuée pour le compte de l'Association nationale pour l'avancement des gens de couleur, et traduits en français par les soins de l'Union patriotique haïtienne. New York, Association nationale pour l'avancement des gens de couleur; Port-au-Prince, Comité central de l'Union patriotique, 1921.
35 p. 21½cm.
1. Haiti—For. rel.—U. S. 2. U. S.—For. rel.—Haiti. 3. Haiti—Pol. & govt.—1844- I. The Nation, New York. II. National association for the advancement of colored people. III. Union patriotique haïtienne. IV. Title. *Translation* *of* Self-determining Haiti.
22-24487
Library of Congress F1926.J83
⌊2⌋ [827.T294] 972.94

Sénégal
M966.3
D62u

L'unité culturelle de l'Afrique noire;
Diop, Cheikh Anta
L'unité culturelle de l'Afrique noire; domaines du patriarcat et du matriarcat dans l'antiquité classique. Paris, Présence Africaine, 1959.

203p. 22½cm.

Haiti
M972.94
M35u

L'Unité politique de l'ile d'Haiti s'est-elle opérée en 1822...
Mars, Jean Price, 1876-
L'Unité politique de l'ile d'Haiti s'est-elle opérée en 1822 par la violence ou par le libre ralliement des Dominicains à la République d'Haiti?

(In: Revue de la Société à Histoire et de Géographie d'Haiti. Port-au-Prince, Haiti, 1937. 24cm. v.8, Octobre 1937. p.1-27)

M910
Un3

United aid for Ethiopia.
Ethiopia. ⌊New York city, United aid for Ethiopia. 1936⌋
26p. 19cm.

1. Ethiopia

Tanzania
M341.13
B478

United Nations.
Barros, Romeo Julius.
African States and the United Nations versus apartheid; the efforts of the African States to affect South Africa's apartheid policy through the United Nations. New York, Carlton Press ⌊1967⌋

132 p. 21 cm. (A Hearthstone book)
Includes legislation.
Bibliography: p. 111-125.

1. Africa, South—Native races. 2. United Nations—Africa, South. I. United Nations. II. Title.

DT763.B37 341.13'9'68 68-427
Library of Congress ⌊5⌋

M815.5
B88u

United Nations.
Bunche, Ralph Johnson, 1904-
UN and peace-making. n.p., ⌊1950⌋

15p. 28cm.
Address delivered in Denver, May 11, 1950.
Mimeographed.

M301
D853ne3
United Nations.
Du Bois, William Edward Burghardt, 1868-
The Negro and imperialism. NAACP radio broadcast, Station WEVD, November 15, 1944.

9unnumb. p. 35cm.
Mimeographed.

M301
F86r
United Nations Educational Scientific and Cultural Organization.
Frazier, Edward Franklin, 1894-
The race question, drafted by Ernest Beaglehold, Juan Comas, L.A. Costa Pinto Franklin Frazier, and others. UN2300, 195 .

9p. 21cm. (Publication 791)
At head of title: UNESCO and its programme.

Nigeria
M966.9
D37a
United society for Christian literature, London.
Delano, Isaac O
An African looks at marriage, by Isaac O. Delano...London and Redhill, United society for Christian literature [1944]

47p. 18cm. (African's own library no.5)

Ghana
M341.139
L85
United Nations.
Longdon, J E
Mr. Amoa learns about Uno, by J. E. Longdon and Ella Griffin. Cover design by R. Ohene Akyeampong. Accra, Bureau of Ghana Languages, 1959.

9p. 22cm.

M323
N213p
... United Nations on behalf of 13 million oppressed Negro citizens of U.S.A.
[National Negro Congress]
A petition... to the United Nations on behalf of 13 million oppressed Negro citizens of the United States of America. New York, 1946.

15p. 23cm.
Contains also: The oppression of the American Negro: the facts, by Herbert Aptheker: p. 8-14.

Nigeria
M966.9
D37n
United Society for Christian literature, London.
Delano, Isaac O
Notes and comments from Nigeria, by Isaac O. Delano...London, The United Society for Christian literature [1944]

64p. 18½cm. (Africa's own library no.8)

M341.1
P31
United Nations.
Peace on earth by Trygve Lie and others.
Introduction by Robert E. Sherwood. New York, Hermitage House, 1949.

251p. 22cm.

M973.8
P38u
The united Negro: His problems and his progress.
Penn, Irvine Garland, 1867- ed.
The united negro: his problems and his progress, containing the addresses and proceedings the Negro young people's Christian and educational congress, held August 6-11, 1902; introduction by Bishop W. J. Gaines ... edited by Prof. I. Garland Penn ... Prof. J. W. E. Bowen ... Atlanta, Ga., D. E. Luther publishing co., 1902.

xxx, 600 p. illus., plates, ports. 21cm.

1. Negroes—Moral and social conditions. 2. Negroes—Religion. I. Bowen, John Wesley Edward, 1855- joint ed. II. Title.

3—1895

Library of Congress E185.5.P41
[a45e1]

Nigeria
MB9
R17
United society for Christian literature, London
Delano, Isaac O
The singing minister of Nigeria; the life of the Rev. Canon J. J. Ransome-Kuti, by Isaac O. Delano ... London, United society for Christian literature [1942]

63, [1] p. 18½cm. (Half-title: Africa's own library, no. 2)

1. Ransome-Kuti, Josaiah Jesse, 1855-1930. 2. Missions — Nigeria. I. United society for Christian literature, London. II. Title.

44-35618

Library of Congress BV3625.N6R3
[3]
922

Panama
M986.2
W52n
United Nations.
Westerman, George W
Non-self-governing territories and the United Nations. Panama, 1958.

33p. 22½cm.
Spanish text: 36p.

M366.5
B94
United order of true reformers.
Burrell, William Patrick, 1865-
Twenty-five years history of the grand fountain of the united order of true reformers, 1881-1905. Illustrated. By W. P. Burrell and D. E. Johnson, Sr. Richmond, Va., 1909.

513p. front. ports. 22cm.

Gold Coast
M896.2
F44f
United society for Christian literature, London.
Fiawoo, F Kwasi.
The fifth landing stage, a play in five acts, by F. Kwasi Fiawoo ... A free translation from the Ewe original. London and Redhill, United society for Christian literature [1943]

87, [1] p. 18cm.
"First published 1943."

I. United society for Christian literature, London. II. Title.

45-8281

Library of Congress PL8164.Z95E5 1943
[3]
896.4

Haiti
M972.94
N34
United Nations. Charter.
Nemours, Alfred, 1883-
... La charte des Nations unies; étude comparative de la charte avec: les propositions de Dumbarton Oaks, le covenant de la Société des nations, les conventions de la Haye, les propositions et doctrines inter américaines. Port-au-Prince, Haïti, H. Deschamps, 1945.

xv, 17-188 p., 1 l. 20½cm.
At head of title: Général Nemours.
"Liste des ouvrages du général Nemours": p. viii-x.

1. United nations. Charter.

JX1976.N36 341.1 46-22436

Library of Congress [2]

MB9
817d
United order of true reformers.
Davis, Daniel Webster, 1862-
The life and public services of Rev. Wm. Washington Browne, founder of the Grand fountain u. o. of true reformers ... written by D. Webster Davis ... with an introduction by Rt. Rev. Benjamin F. Lee ... [Richmond, Va.] Mrs. M. A. Browne-Smith [1910]

x, 11-192 p. front., plates, ports. 22½cm. $1.00

1. Browne, William Washington, 1849-1897.

10-26175

Library of Congress

© Sept. 10, 1910; 2c. Nov. 7, 1910; A 275211; Mary A. Browne-Smith, Richmond, Va.

Sierra Leone
M966.4
G68
United society for Christian literature, London.
Gorvie, Max.
Our people of the Sierra Leone protectorate, by Max Gorvie. London and Redhill, United society for Christian literature [1944]

64, [1] p. 18½cm. (Half-title: Africa's own library, no. 6)
"First published 1944."

1. Ethnology—Sierra Leone. I. United society for Christian literature, London. II. Title.

A 46-333

New York. Public library for Library of Congress [3]

Tanzania
M341.13
B478
United Nations - Africa, South.
Barros, Romeo Julius.
African States and the United Nations versus apartheid; the efforts of the African States to affect South Africa's apartheid policy through the United Nations. New York, Carlton Press [1967]

182 p. 21 cm. (A Hearthstone book)
Includes legislation.
Bibliography: p. 111-125.

1. Africa, South—Native races. 2. United Nations—Africa, South. I. United Nations. II. Title.

DT763.B37 341.13'9'68 68-427

Library of Congress [5]

M331.1
H77e
United Packinghouse Workers of America.
Hope, John, 1909-
Equality of opportunity; a union approach to fair employment. With an introd. by Hubert Humphrey. Washington, Public Affairs Press [1956]

xii, 142 p. diagrs. 24 cm.
Includes bibliographical references.

1. Discrimination in employment—U. S. 2. United Packinghouse Workers of America. I. Title.

HD4903.5.U58H6 331.11 56—6587

Library of Congress [56g5]

Rhodesia, N.
M968.94
M18L
United society for Christian literature, Lond.
Mackintosh, Catharine Winkworth.
Lewanika, paramount chief of the Barotse and allied tribes, 1875-1916, by C. W. Mackintosh. London and Redhill, United society for Christian literature [1942]

63, [1] p. 18½cm. (Half-title: Africa's own library, no. 4)
"First published 1942."

1. Lewanika, king of Barotseland, d. 1916. 2. Missions—Barotseland. I. United society for Christian literature, London.

44-35596

Library of Congress DT964.B3M18
[2]
968.951

Sénégal
M966.3
Se5afr
United Nations - Senegal.
Senghor, Léopold Sédar, 1906-
L'Afrique a l'O.N.U., XVIe session. [Paris] Présence Africaine, 1961.

55p. 18cm.
French and English.

1. United Nations - Senegal. 2. Senegal. I. Title.

Gold Coast
M966.7
D23t
United society for Christian literature, London.
Danquah, Joseph Boakye, 1895-
The third woman; a play in five acts, by J. B. Danquah. London and Redhill, United society for Christian literature [1943]

151, [1] p. 18cm.
"First published 1943."

I. United society for Christian literature, London. II. Title.

A 45-1224

New York. Public library for Library of Congress PR6007.A516T5
[3]
822.91

M356
Evln
U. S. Army.
Evans, James Carmichael, 1900-
The Negro in the army, policy and practice; A summary prepared for the Secretary of the Army, by James C. Evans. Wash. D.C., Dept. of the Army, 1948.

Irregularly paged. 32cm.
Mimeographed.

U. S. Army.

M323 N78t Reddick, Lawrence Dunbar, 1910-
Letters from a Jim Crow Army.

pp. 371-382.
In: Twice a year, ed. by Dorothy Norman. 1946.

U.S. Army - Courts-martial and courts of inquiry

see

Courts-martial an' courts of inquiry.

U. S. Army—Negro troops.

M350 H27o **Hastie, William Henry, 1904–**
On clipped wings; the story of Jim Crow in the Army air corps, by William H. Hastie. [New York, National association for the advancement of colored people, 1943]

27 p. illus. (incl. ports.) 21½cm.

1. U. S. Army—Negro troops. 2. Negroes as soldiers. 3. U. S. Army air forces. I. National association for the advancement of colored people. II. Title.

A 44-3616

Harvard univ. Library for Library of Congress [3]

U.S. Army-Recruiting, enlistment, etc.- Civil War.

MB9 Ay2f **Ayers, James T 1805–1865.**
The diary of James T. Ayers, Civil War recruiter; ed., with an introd., by John Franklin. Springfield, Printed by authority of the State of Illinois, 1947.

xxv, 138 p. illus., port., facsims. 24 cm. (Occasional publications of the Illinois State Historical Society)

On cover: Publication no. 50.

1. U. S.—Hist.—Civil War—Personal narratives. 2. U. S.—Hist.—Civil War—Negro troops. 3. U. S. Army—Recruiting, enlistment, etc.—Civil War. I. Franklin, John Hope, 1915– ed. II. Title. (Series: Illinois State Historical Society. Occasional publications. Series: Illinois State Historical Society. Publicaton no. 50)

F536.I 34 no. 50 — Copy 3. 973.781 E601.A9 48—45066*

Library of Congress [a59f²2]

U. S. Army. 33d Infantry (Colored)

M350 H53a **Higginson, Thomas Wentworth, 1823–1911.**
Army life in a black regiment. With notes and a biographical introd. by John Hope Franklin. Foreword by E. Franklin Frazier. Boston, Beacon Press [1962]

300 p. 21 cm.

1. U. S.—Hist.—Civil War—Regimental histories—U. S.—33d Infantry (Colored) 2. U. S. Army. 33d Infantry (Colored) 3. U. S.—Hist.—Civil War—Personal narratives. I. Title.

E492.94 33d.H5 1962 973.7415 62-9217 ‡

Library of Congress [5]

U. S. Army. 761st tank battalion.

[?]C An2c **Anderson, Trezzvant W**
Come out fighting; the epic tale of the 761st tank battalion, 1942–1945, by Trezzvant W. Anderson. [Salzburg, Printed by Salzburger druckerei und verlag, 1945]

xv, 135 p. illus. (incl. ports., maps) fold. tab. 30cm.

1. World war, 1939–1945—Regimental histories—U. S.—761st tank battalion. 2. World war, 1939–1945—Negroes. 3. U. S. Army. 761st tank battalion. 4. World war, 1939–1945—Campaigns—Western. I. Title.

A 46-3127

Harvard univ. Library for Library of Congress D769.306 761st.A6 [5]† 940.542

U.S. Army. 777th Field Artillery Battalion.

M350 H78t **Hornsby, Henry Haywood, 1923–**
The trey of sevens. Dallas, Mathis, Van Nort [1946]

xvii, 126 p. illus., ports. 20 cm.

"Based on activities of Battery 'C' of the 777th Field Artillery Battalion in the Ninth Army sector."—p. xii.
Map on lining-papers.

1. World War, 1939–1945—Personal narratives, American. 2. U. S. Army. 777th Field Artillery Battalion. 3. World War, 1939–1945—Campaigns—Western. I. Title.

D769.34 777th.H6 940.542 47—27938*

Library of Congress [50c½]

U. S. Army Air Forces.

M350 F85 **Francis, Charles E**
The Tuskegee airmen; the story of the Negro in the U. S. Air Force. Boston, Bruce Humphries [1956, ©1955]

225 p. illus. 22 cm.

1. World War, 1939–1945—~~Negroes~~. 2. Negroes in aeronautics. 3. U. S. Army Air Forces. I. Title.

D810.N4F76 940.541273 53—11824 ‡

Library of Congress [57d5]

U. S. Army air forces.

M350 H27o **Hastie, William Henry, 1904–**
On clipped wings; the story of Jim Crow in the Army air corps, by William H. Hastie. [New York, National association for the advancement of colored people, 1943]

27 p. illus. (incl. ports.) 21½cm.

1. U. S. Army—Negro troops. 2. Negroes as soldiers. 3. U. S. Army air forces. I. National association for the advancement of colored people. II. Title.

A 44-3616

Harvard univ. Library for Library of Congress [3]

U.S. artillery, 12th colored regiment, 1863-1865.

MB9 M349m Marrs, Elijah P. 1840
Life and history of the Rev. Elijah P. Marrs... Louisville, Ky., The Bradley & Gilbert company, 1885.

146p. 1 l. front. (port.) 19½cm.

M331.833 Un3b U.S. Attorney General
Brief for the United States as amicus curiae in the Supreme Court of the United States [in the cases] of Shelly v. Fitzgerald on writ of certiorari to the Supreme Court of the State of Missouri; McGhee v. Sipes on writ of certiorari to the Supreme Court of the State of Michigan; Hurd v. Hodge on writ of certiorari to the United States Court of Appeals for the District of Columbia, Wash., D.C., Govt. Print. Off., 1941.

123p. 23cm.

Tracings on back.

U.S. Bureau of refugees, freedmen and abandoned lands.

MB(D37r Whipper, Frances E Rollin
Life and public services of Martin R. Delany, subassistant commissioner, Bureau relief of refugees, freedmen, and of abandoned lands, and late major 104th U.S. colored troops. Boston, Lee and Shepard, 1868.

367p. 20cm.

M312 Un3cr **U. S.** *Bureau of the census.*
... Negro population 1790–1915. Washington, Govt. print. off., 1918.

844 p. incl. maps, tables, diagrs. 30cm.

At head of title: Department of commerce. Bureau of the census. Sam. L. Rogers, director.
"Prepared by Dr. John Cummings in the Division of revision and results, under the general supervision of Dr. Joseph A. Hill."—"Letter of transmittal," p. 13.

1. Census

1. ~~Negroes~~ Population I. Cummings, John, 1868–1936. II. Hill, Joseph Adna, 1860– III. Title.

18—26864

Library of Congress HA205.A33 [42t2]

M312 Un3n 1935 **U. S.** *Bureau of the Census.*
... Negroes in the United States, 1920–32. Prepared under the supervision of Z. R. Pettet, chief statistician for agriculture, by Charles E. Hall, specialist in Negro statistics. Washington, U. S. Govt. print. off., 1935.

xvi, 845 p. incl. maps, tables, diagrs. 30cm.

At head of title: U. S. Department of commerce. Daniel C. Roper, secretary. Bureau of the census. William Lane Austin, director.
"This report supplements the volume, "Negro population in the United States, 1790–1915," published by the Bureau of the census in 1918."—p. iii.

1. Census 2. Population.

1. Negroes. I. Pettet, Zellmer Roswell, 1880– II. Hall, Charles Edward, 1868–

35—26735

Library of Congress HA205.A33 1920-32 [45w1] 325.260973

M312 Un3n 1915 **U. S.** *Bureau of the census.*
... Negroes in the United States. Washington, Govt. print. off., 1915.

207 p. incl. illus. (maps) tables. diagrs. 31cm. (*Its* Bulletin 129)

At head of title: Dept. of commerce. Bureau of the census. Wm. J. Harris, director.
To be followed by a more complete and comprehensive report on the same subject. *cf.* Letter of transmittal.
"Prepared in the Division of revisions and results under the general supervision of Dr. Joseph A. Hill, expert special agent. The statistical tables were planned and arranged by ... Charles E. Hall, William Jennifer, and Robert A. Pelham."—Letter of transmittal, p. 5.

1. ~~Negroes~~ Census. 2. Population I. ~~Hill, Joseph Adna, 1860–1938.~~ I. Hall, Charles E. II. Jennifer, William III. Pelham, Robert A. 15-26207 Revised 2

Library of Congress — 2d set. HA201.1900.A12 no. 129 E185.6.U585 [r43d2]

M312 Un3n **U. S.** *Bureau of the census.*
... Negroes in the United States. Washington, Govt. print. off., 1904.

333 p. incl. charts, diagrs. double front. 29 x 22½cm. (Bulletin 8)

At head of title: Department of commerce and labor. Bureau of the census. S. N. D. North, director.
The tables were prepared under the supervision of W. C. Hunt, chief statistician and W. F. Willcox, special agent of the Census bureau; the section on the Negro farmer was prepared by W. E. B. Du Bois. *cf.* p. 9.

1. Census 2. Population

1. ~~Negroes.~~ I. ~~Hunt, William Chamberlin, 1856–1929.~~ ~~II. Willcox, Walter Francis, 1861–~~ III. Du Bois, William Edward Burghardt, 1868–

9—5910

Library of Congress — Copy 2. HA201 1900.A12 no. 8 E185.6.U58 [45d1]

U. S. cavalry. 10th regt. 1866-

M350 C26 **Cashin, Herschel V.**
Under fire. With the Tenth U. S. cavalry. Being a brief, comprehensive review of the Negro's participation in the wars of the United States. Especially showing the valor and heroism of the Negro soldiers of the Ninth and Tenth cavalries, and the Twenty-fourth and Twenty-fifth infantries of the regular army; as demonstrated in the decisive campaign around Santiago de Cuba, 1898 ... Thrilling episodes interestingly narrated by officers and men. Famous Indian campaigns and their results. A purely military history of the Negro. With introduction by Major-General Joseph Wheeler ... By Her-

(Continued on next card)

8—23892

[41j1]

M323.4 Un3r **U. S.** *Commission on Civil Rights.*
Report. 1959–
[Washington, U. S. Govt. Print. Off.]

v. diagrs. 24 cm.

1. Civil rights—U. S. I. Johnson, George M.

JC599.U45A3 323.40973 59—62177

Library of Congress [60f10]

Haiti

M972.94 Un3r **U. S.** *Commission on education in Haiti.*
... Report of the United States Commission on education in Haiti. October 1, 1930. Washington, U. S. Govt. print. off., 1931.

vii, 74, [2] p. incl. map, tables. 24½cm. ([Publication, no. 166] Latin American series, no. 5)

R. R. Moton, chairman.

Haiti - Education

1. [struck out] I. Moton, Robert Russa, 1867– II. [struck out] ... no. 5. IV. Title.

31-26635

Library of Congress — Copy 2. LA491.U6 1930 F1401.U65 no. 5 [33f3] 379.7294

U.S. Committee on Fair Employment Practice (1943-1946)

M331.1 N21f **National Community Relations Advisory Council.**
FEPC reference manual prepared by the Committee on Employment Discrimination of the National Community Relations Advisory Council. 1948 ed. New York [1948]

70 p. 22 cm.

Bibliography: p. 69–70.

1. Discrimination in employment—U. S. 2. U. S. Committee on Fair Employment Practice (1943–1946) I. Title.

HD4903.N25 331.11 48-4697*

Library of Congress [2]

U. S. Congress.

M973 M69q **Mitchell, George Washington, 1865–**
The question before Congress, a consideration of the debates and final action by Congress upon various phases of the race question in the United States, by Geo. W. Mitchell. Philadelphia, Pa., The A. M. E. book concern [©1918]

247 p. 23½cm.

1. Slavery in the U. S. 2. Negroes. 3. U. S.—Race question. I. Title.

18—21546

Library of Congress E441.M68 [33g1]

M B9
C25u

U.S. Congress. House. Committee on public lands.
U. S. *Congress. Senate. Committee on public lands and surveys.*
George Washington Carver national monument, Missouri. Joint hearing before the Committee on public lands and surveys, United States Senate, and the Committee on public lands, House of representatives, Seventy-eighth Congress, first session, on S. 37, S. 312, and H. R. 647, bills to provide for the establishment of the George Washington Carver national monument. February 5, 1943 ... Washington, U. S. Govt. print. off., 1943.
iii, 63 p. 23^{cm}.
Joseph C. O'Mahoney, presiding.
1. George Washington Carver national monument. I. U. S. Congress. House. Committee on public lands.
45-14743
Library of Congress SB482.M8A53 1943
[3] 917.7873

U.S. Congress. Senate. Committee on Public Lands and Surveys. George Washington Carver national monument ... (card 2)

Contains statements by John P. Davis. Dr. G. Lake Imes. Dr. Mordecai Johnson. C.A. Franklin. Mary McLeod Bethune. Leslie Perry.

MB9
C25u

U. S. *Congress. Senate. Committee on public lands and surveys.*
George Washington Carver national monument, Missouri. Joint hearing before the Committee on public lands and surveys, United States Senate, and the Committee on public lands, House of representatives, Seventy-eighth Congress, first session, on S. 37, S. 312, and H. R. 647, bills to provide for the establishment of the George Washington Carver national monument. February 5, 1943 ... Washington, U. S. Govt. print. off., 1943.
iii, 63 p. 23^{cm}.
Joseph C. O'Mahoney, presiding.
1. George Washington Carver national monument. I. U. S. Congress. House. Committee on public lands.
45-14743
Library of Congress SB482.M8A53 1943
[3] 917.7873

M323
Un33

U.S. Congress. House. Committee on the Judiciary.
Anti-lynching; Hearings before the Committee on the Judiciary, House of Representatives, sixty-sixth Congress, second session on H. R. 259, 4123, and 11873. Washington, Govt. Print. Off., 1920.

1. Lynch law. I. a.t. Spingarn, Arthur B. II. a.t. Trotter, William. III. a.t. Johnson, James Weldon. IV. a.t. Grimke, Archibald Henry. V. a.t. Cook, George William.

M343.3
Un3c

U. S. *Congress. Senate. Committee on the judiciary.*
Crime of lynching. Hearings before a subcommittee of the Committee on the judiciary, United States Senate, Seventy-sixth Congress, third session, on H. R. 801, an act to assure to persons within the jurisdiction of every state due process of law and equal protection of the laws, and to prevent the crime of lynching. February 6, 7, March 5, 12, and 13, 1940 ... Washington, U. S. Govt. print. off., 1940.
iii, 204 p. incl. tables. 23^{cm}.
Printed for the use of the Committee on the judiciary.
Frederick Van Nuys, chairman of subcommittee.
1. Lynch law. I. Title.
40-8628
Library of Congress HV6457.A5 1940
——— Copy 2. [41c2] 343.2

Ghana
M966.7
B96

U. S. *Congress. Senate. Committee on the Judiciary.*
Is U. S. money aiding another Communist state? Hearing before the Subcommittee to Investigate the Administration of the Internal Security Act and Other Internal Security Laws of the Committee on the Judiciary, United States Senate, Eighty-seventh Congress, second session. Testimony of K. A. Busia, December 3, 1962. Washington, U. S. Govt. Print. Off., 1963.
iii, 165 p. illus., ports. 24 cm.
1. Economic assistance, American—Ghana. 2. Communism—Ghana. I. Busia, Kofi Abrefa. II. Title. 3. Ghana
HC517.G6U5 63-61892
Library of Congress [64c2]

M814.4
W27u

U.S. Congress. Senate Committee on Banking and Currency.
Hearing on H.R. 6528; An act to authorize the coinage of 50 cent pieces to commemorate the life and perpetuate the ideals and teachings of Booker T. Washington, July 23, 1945.
16p. 23cm.
At head of title: Booker T. Washington Commemorative Coin.

1. Washington, Booker Taliaferro, 1859?-1915.

U.S . Constitution.

M815.4
D74co

Douglass, Frederick, 1817-1895.
The Constitution of the United States: is it pro-slavery or anti-slavery? By Frederick Douglass. A speech delivered in Glasgow, March 26, 1860, in reply to an attack made upon his view by Mr. George Thompson. [Halifax, T. and W. Birtwhistle, printers, 1860?]
16 p. 18½^{cm}.
Caption title.
From the Glasgow daily mail.

1. U. S. Constitution. 2. Slavery in the U. S. 3. Thompson, George, 1804-1878.
A 17-1156
Title from Harvard Univ. Printed by L. C.

U. S. Constitution. 13th amendment.

M342.73
B79d

[The Brotherhood of liberty]
Justice and jurisprudence: an inquiry concerning the constitutional limitations of the Thirteenth, Fourteenth, and Fifteenth amendments ... Philadelphia, J. B. Lippincott company, 1889.
1 p. l., xxxix, 578 p. 22½^{cm}.
Preface signed: The Brotherhood of liberty.

1. U. S. Constitution. 13th amendment. 2. U. S. Constitution. 14th amendment. 3. U. S. Constitution. 15th amendment. 4. Negroes—U. S. I. Title.
9-21553
Library of Congress JK169.13th 1889
[a41c1]

U. S. Constitution. 14th amendment.

M342.73
B79d

[The Brotherhood of liberty]
Justice and jurisprudence: an inquiry concerning the constitutional limitations of the Thirteenth, Fourteenth, and Fifteenth amendments ... Philadelphia, J. B. Lippincott company, 1889.
1 p. l., xxxix, 578 p. 22½^{cm}.
Preface signed: The Brotherhood of liberty.

1. U. S. Constitution. 13th amendment. 2. U. S. Constitution. 14th amendment. 3. U. S. Constitution. 15th amendment. 4. Negroes—U. S. I. Title.
9-21553
Library of Congress JK169.13th 1889
[a41c1]

U.S. Constitution, 14th Amendment.

M331.833
M66r

Ming, William R , 1911-
Racial restrictions and the fourteenth amendment: The restrictive covenant cases. Reprinted from the University of Chicago law review, 16:203-238, Winter 1949.
203-238p; 24cm.

U. S. Constitution. 15th amendment.

M342.73
B79d

[The Brotherhood of liberty]
Justice and jurisprudence: an inquiry concerning the constitutional limitations of the Thirteenth, Fourteenth, and Fifteenth amendments ... Philadelphia, J. B. Lippincott company, 1889.
1 p. l., xxxix, 578 p. 22½^{cm}.
Preface signed: The Brotherhood of liberty.

1. U. S. Constitution. 13th amendment. 2. U. S. Constitution. 14th amendment. 3. U. S. Constitution. 15th amendment. 4. Negroes—U. S. I. Title.
9-21553
Library of Congress JK169.13th 1889
[a41c1]

M325
Un3n

U.S. Department of labor. Division of Negro economics.
The Negro at work during the world war and during reconstruction. Statistics, problems and policies relating to the greater inclusion of Negro wage earners in American industry and agriculture... Washington, Government printing office, 1921.
144p. diagrs., tables. 22½cm.
Bound with: Negro migration in 1916-17, by U.S. Department of labor.
over

M325
Un3n

U.S. Department of labor. Division of Negro economics.
Negro migration in 1916-17. Reports by R. H. Leavell, T. R. Snavely, T. J. Woofter, Jr., W. T. B. Williams and Francis D. Tyson, with an introduction by J. H. Dillard. Washington, Government printing office, 1919.
158p. tables. 23cm.
1. Migration. 2. Labor and laboring classes. I. Haynes, George Edmund, 1880- II. Title.

U.S. Dept. of labor. Division of Negro economics.

M331.
Un3

U. S. *Women's bureau.*
... Negro women in industry. Washington, Govt. print. off., 1922.
v, 65, [1] p. front. 23^{cm}. (Bulletin no. 20)
At head of title: U. S. Department of labor. James J. Davis, secretary. Women's bureau. Mary Anderson, director.
"This investigation was made by Miss Emma L. Shields ... in conjunction with the Division of Negro economics in the Department of labor."—Letter of transmittal.
1. Negroes—Employment. 2. Woman—Employment—U. S. 3. Women, Negro. I. U. S. Dept. of labor. Division of Negro economics. II. Shields, Emma L. III. Title.
L 22-164
U. S. Dept. of labor. Libr. for Library of Congress HD6008.A35 no. 20
[a41n1]

M347.9
Un34

U. S. District Court. Virginia (Eastern District) Richmond Division.
National Association for the Advancement of Colored People, a corporation, N.A.A.C.P. Legal Defense and Educational Fund, Incorporated, a corporation, plaintiffs, against Kenneth C. Patty...defendants. Civil actions nos. 2435 and 2436. [n.p.] NAACP Legal Defense and Educational Fund [n.d.]
64p. 27cm.
"A reprint of the decision."
1. National Association for the Advancement of Colored People.

U.S. Extension service.

M379.173
C15

Campbell, Thomas Monroe, 1883-
The Movable school goes to the Negro farmer, by Thomas Monroe Campbell ... Tuskegee Institute, Ala., Tuskegee institute press [°1936].
xiv, 170 p. front., plates, ports. 23½^{cm}.
CONTENTS.—pt. I. Semi-autobiography.—pt. II. The school on wheels.

1. Agricultural education—Alabama. 2. Negroes—Education. 3. Negroes—Alabama. 4. Tuskegee normal and industrial institute. 5. U. S. Extension service. I. Title.
36-7891
Library of Congress LC2802.A2C3
[44m1] 371.97409761

U.S. Hist.-Civil War-Personal narratives.

M350
H53

Higginston, Thomas Wentworth, 1823-1911.
Army life in a black regiment. Boston, Fields, Osgood, & Co., 1870.

296p. 18cm.

U.S. infantry-33d colored regt., 1862-1866.

M350
H53

Higginson, Thomas Wentworth, 1823-1911.
Army life in a black regiment. Boston, Fields, Osgood, & Co., 1870.

296p. 18cm.

U. S. infantry. 33d regt., 1862-1866.

M350
T21

Taylor, Susie King, 1848-
Reminiscences of my life in camp with the 33d United States colored troops, late 1st S. C. volunteers, by Susie King Taylor ... Boston, The author, 1902.
xii p., 1 l., 82 p. front., pl., ports. 19½^{cm}.

1. U. S.—Hist.—Civil war—Regimental histories—U. S. inf.—33d. 2. U. S. infantry. 33d regt., 1862-1866. I. Title.
2-30128
Library of Congress E492.94.33dT
[a44b1]

U.S. Infantry. 33d regt., 1862-1866

M350
T21

Taylor, Susie King, 1848-
Reminiscences of my life in camp with the 33d United States colored troops, late 1st S. C. volunteers, by Susie King Taylor ... Boston, The author, 1902.
xii, 82p. front., pl., ports. 19½cm.

M973 Un3s
U. S. *Library of Congress.*
75 years of freedom; commemoration of the 75th anniversary of the proclamation of the 13th amendment to the Constitution of the United States. The Library of Congress. [Washington, U. S. Govt. print. off., 1943]
cover-title, vi, 108 p. col. pl. 26cm.
"The contribution of the American Negro to American culture was the theme of a series of exhibits and concerts in the Library of Congress commencing on December 18th, the 75th anniversary of the proclamation of the Thirteenth amendment, which ended slavery in the United States."—p. v.
1. Negroes. 2. Negro songs. 3. Negro art. 4. Negro literature (collections) I. Title.
Library of Congress E185.6.U597 43-52457 [15] 325.260973

U.S. Military academy. West Point.
M89 F64
Flipper, Henry Ossian, 1856–
The colored cadet at West Point. Autobiography of Lieut. Henry Ossian Flipper, U. S. A., first graduate of color from the U. S. Military academy. New York, H. Lee & co., 1878.
4 p. l., [7]-322 p. 2 port. (incl. front.) 19cm.
1. U. S. Military academy, West Point.
15—21526
Library of Congress U410.P1F6
Copyright 1879: 29 [39d1]

U. S. National Archives.
M026 L58
Lewinson, Paul, 1900–
A guide to documents in the National Archives: for Negro studies, compiled by Paul Lewinson for the Committee on Negro Studies of the American Council of Learned Societies. Washington, 1947.
x, 28 p. 24 cm. (American Council of Learned Societies Devoted to Humanistic Studies. Committee on Negro Studies. Publications, no. 1)
1. Negroes—Bibl. I. U. S. National Archives. (Series)
A 50-2611
Columbia Univ. for Library of Congress Libraries [3]

M359 H24
U. S. Navy.
Harris, Paul N. 1914–
Base company 16. New York, Vantage Press [1963]
201p. 20½cm.

M323 N21
U. S. Navy.
National Association for the Advancement of Colored People.
Our democratic navy... New York, 1941.
[4]p. 22cm.

M323 N212
U. S. Navy.
National Association for the Advancement of Colored People. Legal Defense and Educational Fund.
Mutiny? The real story of how the Navy branded 50 fear-shocked sailors as mutineers. New York, 1945.
16p. 21cm.

U.S. Navy Dept.
M359 N331 1948
Nelson, Dennis Denmark, 1907–
The integration of the Negro into the United States Navy, 1776–1947, with a brief historical introduction. [Washington, 1948]
1 v. (various pagings) illus., ports. 27 cm.
Cover title.
"A monograph from the thesis by the same title submitted to the Department of Sociology, Howard University, in partial fulfillment of the requirements for the degree of master of arts."
Seal of Navy Department, United States of America, on cover.
"Navexos-P-526."
Bibliography: p. 209-212.
1. U. S. Navy—Negroes. 2. Negroes as seamen. I. U. S. Navy Dept. II. Title.
E185.63.N4 1948 325.260973 48—46195*
Library of Congress [48c2]

M331 Un3u
U. S. *Office of adviser on Negro affairs.*
The urban Negro worker in the United States, 1925–1936 ... Sponsored by the United States Department of the interior. Administered by the Office of the adviser on Negro affairs ... Washington, U. S. Govt. print. off., 1938–
v. tables, diagrs., forms. 29cm.
Vol. 1 has subtitle: An analysis of the training, types, and conditions of employment and the earnings of 200,000 skilled and white-collar Negro workers.
Vol. 2 has subtitle: Male Negro skilled workers in the United States, 1930–1936. Library has vol. 2.
1. Negroes—Employment. 2. Negroes—Econ. condit. I. Title.
II. Weaver, Robert Clifton, 1907– 38-26495
Library of Congress E185.8.U535
——— Copy 2. [10] 331.6

M331 W37
U.S. Office of Adviser on Negro Affairs.
Weaver, Robert Clifton, 1907–
Male Negro skilled workers in the United States, 1930–1936, by Robert C. Weaver, Administrator of survey, Ira DeA. Reid ... Preston Valien ... Charles S. Johnson ... Sponsored by United States Department of the Interior ... Washington, D. C. Govt. Print. Off., 1939.
vi, 87p. tables, graphs 29cm.

M378 B81s
U.S. Office of Education.
National Survey of the higher education of Negroes.
Brown, Ina Corinne, 1896–
Socio-economic approach to educational problems, by Ina Corinne Brown, with an introduction by Fred J. Kelly. Washington, U.S. Govt. Print. Off., 1942.
xii, 166p. maps, tables, diagrs.
(U.S. Office of Education. Miscellaneous no.6)
At head of title: National survey of the higher education of Negroes, v.1.

M370 C12n
U.S. Office of Education.
National survey of the higher education of Negroes. v.4
Caliver, Ambrose, 1894–
National survey of the higher education of Negroes, a summary. Washington, U.S. Govt. Print. Off., 1943.
50p. 29cm. (U.S. Office of Education. Miscellaneous, no.6)
At head of title: National survey of the higher education of Negroes, v.4)

U.S. Office of education. Project in vocational education and guidance of Negroes.
M370. C12v
Caliver, Ambrose, 1894–
... Vocational education and guidance of Negroes; report of a survey conducted by the Office of education, by Ambrose Caliver, senior specialist in the education of Negroes ... United States Department of the interior. Harold L. Ickes, secretary. Office of education, J. W. Studebaker, commissioner. Washington, U. S. Govt. print. off., 1938.
x, 137 p. incl. tables, diagrs. 23cm. (U. S. Office of education. Bulletin, 1937, no. 38)
At head of title: Project in vocational education and guidance of Negroes.
On p. [2] of cover: National survey of vocational education and guidance of Negroes.
(Continued on next card)
E 39-3 †
[a46d²3]†

M370 Un3s
U. S. *Office of education. Statistical division.*
... Statistics of the education of Negroes, 1925–1926— Washington, U. S. Govt. print. off., 1928–
v. tables, diagrs. 23cm.
1925–1928, by D. T. Blose; 1929– by D. T. Blose and Ambrose Caliver.
1925–1926, issued as Bureau of education. Bulletin, 1928, no. 19; 1927–1928, as U. S. Office of education. Pamphlet no. 14; 1929–1932— as U. S. Office of education. Bulletin 1935, no. 13; 1938, no. 13
Title varies: 1925–26, Statistics of education of the Negro race.
1927–28, Statistics of the Negro race.
1929–32, Statistics of the education of Negroes.
1. Negroes—Education—[Statistics] I. Blose, David Thompson. II. Caliver, Ambrose, 1894– III. Title.
U. S. Off. of educ. Library LC2801.U61
——— 2d set. L111.A6 E 29—26 (rev. '40)
for Library of Congress L111.A6
——— Copy 2. LC2801.A83
[a40r36w2] 371.9740973

M370 Un3s
U.S. Office of Education. Statistical Division
Statistics of the education of Negroes, 1925–26–

Volume	Year	Month	Volume	Year	Month
	1925-26 -	M370 C12m no.5			
	1927-28 -	" no.6			
	1929-30				
	1931-32				
	1933-34				
	1935-36				

M370 C12m no.5
U.S. Office of education. Statistical Div.
Statistics of education of the Negro race, 1925-1926, by David T. Blose... Washington, D.C., G.P.O. 1928.
42p. tables. 24cm. (U.S. Office of education. Bulletin, 1928, no.19)
Editor: David Thompson Blose
1. Education - Statistics
I. Title

M370 C12m no.6
U.S., Office of education. Statistical Div.
Statistics of the Negro race, 1927-28. Washington, D.C., G.P.O., 1931.
16p. tables - 23cm. (U.S. Office of education. Pamphlet no.14, December, 1930)
Editor: David Thompson, Blose.
1. Education - Statistics
I. Title

Nigeria M309.22 Ob3
U. S. Peace Corps.
Obi, Enuenwemba.
Peace-corpsism. [1st ed.] New York, Pageant Press [1962]
78 p. 20 cm.
Portrait of author on book jacket.
1. U. S. Peace Corps. I. Title.
HC60.5.O2 309.2206173 62-20947 ‡
Library of Congress [5]

M309.2 Sm55
U.S. Peace Corps-Ghana.
Smith, Ed, 1937–
Where to, black man? Chicago, Quadrangle Books, 1967.
221 p. 22 cm.
1. U. S. Peace Corps—Ghana. I. Title.
HC60.5.S6 309.2'235'667 67-21640 rev
Library of Congress [r68f3]

M323 Un3t
U. S. *President's Committee on Civil Rights.*
To secure these rights, the report of the President's Committee on Civil Rights. Washington, U. S. Govt. Print. Off., 1947.
xii, 178 p. illus., maps. 25 cm.
Charles E. Wilson, chairman.
autographed copy Tobias Channing T
1. Civil rights—U. S. I. Wilson, Charles Erwin, 1890– II. Title.
JC599.U5A32 1947 323.4 47—46486*
Library of Congress [48x15]

U.S. Senate.
M973 L82s
Logan, Rayford Whittingham, 1897–
The Senate and the Versailles mandate system, by Rayford W. Logan ... Washington, D. C., The Minorities publishers, 1945.
vi p., 1 l., 112 p. 22½cm.
Bibliography: p. 105-106.
1. U. S. Senate. 2. Mandates. I. Title.
45—8821
Library of Congress JX4021.L6 [46g2] 321.027

M323 Un30
U.S. Supreme Court.
Brief for appellants in Nos. 1, 2 and 4 and for respondents in No. 10 on reargument. No. 1-Oliver Brown, et al., Appellants, vs. Board of Education of Topeka, et al., Appellees. No. 2-Harry Briggs, Jr., et al., Appellants vs. R. W. Elliott, et al., Appellees. No. 4-Dorothy E. Davis, et al., Appellants, vs. County School Board of Prince Edwards County, Appellees. No. 10-Francis B. Gebhart, et al., Petitioners, vs. Ethel Louise Belton, et al., Respondents. Appeals from the United States District Court for the District of Kansas, the Eastern District of South Carolina
(continued on next card)

M323
Un30
U. S. Supreme Court. Brief for appellants in Nos. 1, 2 and 4 and for respondents in No. 10... (Card 2)

and the Eastern District of Virginia, and on Petition for a Writ of Certiorari to the Supreme Court of Delaware, respectively. In the Supreme Court of the United States, October Term, 1953.

235p. 23½cm.

1. Segregation in education. 2. NAACP - School segregation brief. I. Spingarn, Arthur Barnett, 1878- Foreword.

U.S. Supreme Court.
M973.
W86fo
Woodson, Carter Godwin, 1875- ed.
Fifty years of Negro citizenship as qualified by the United States supreme court, by C.G.Woodson. Reprinted from the Journal of Negro history, 6: January 1921.
53p. 25cm.
Bound with: Free Negro owners of slaves in the United States, by C.G. Woodson.

U. S. - Armed Forces - Negroes.
M350
J634
Johnson, Jesse J., 1914-
Ebony brass; an autobiography of Negro frustration amid aspiration, by Jesse J. Johnson, New York, William-Frederick Press, 1967.
141 p. 23 cm.

1. U. S.—Armed Forces—Negroes. I. Title.

U53.J6A3 355.3'39'0924 67-14249
Library of Congress

M323
Un301
U. S. Supreme Court.
Brief for appellants in nos. 1, 2 and 3 and for respondents in no. 5 on further reargument. No. 1-Oliver Brown, et al., appellants, vs. Board of Education of Topeka, et al., appelles. No. 2-Harry Briggs, Jr., et al., appellants, vs. R. W. Elliott, et al., appelles. No.3-Dorothy E. Davis, et al., appellants, vs. County School Board of Prince Edward County, Virginia, et al., appelles. No.5-Francis B. Gebhart, et al., petitioners, vs. Ethel Louise Belton, et al., respondents. Appelas from the United States (continued on next card)

M331
Un3
U. S. *Women's bureau.*
... Negro women in industry. Washington, Govt. print. off., 1922.
v, 65, [1] p. front. 23cm. (Bulletin no. 20)
At head of title: U. S. Department of labor. James J. Davis, secretary. Women's bureau. Mary Anderson, director.
"This investigation was made by Miss Emma L. Shields ... in conjunction with the Division of Negro economics in the Department of labor."—Letter of transmittal.

1. Negroes—Employment. 2. Woman—Employment—U. S. 3. Woman, Negro. I. U. S. Dept. of labor. Division of Negro economics. II. Shields, Emma L. III. Title.
L 22—164
U. S. Dept. of labor. Libr. for Library of Congress HD6098.A35 no. 20
[a41n1]

U.S. - Civilization.
Nigeria
M973
C54
Clark, John Pepper, 1935-
America, their America. [London] Deutsch [1964]
221p. 22½cm.
Portrait of author on book jacket.

M323
UN301
U.S. Supreme Court. Brief for appellants in Nos. 1, 2 and 3 and for respondents in no. 5 ... (Card 2)
District Courts for the District of Kansas, the Eastern District of South Carolina and the Eastern District of Virginia and on petition for a Writ of Certiorari to the Supreme Court of Delaware, respectively. In the Supreme Court of the United States, October Term, 1954.
31p. 23cm.
1. Segregation in education.

U. S. Work projects administration.
M01
H83
Howard university, *Washington, D. C. Founders library. Moorland foundation.*
A catalogue of books in the Moorland foundation, compiled by workers on projects 271 and 328 of the Works progress administration, Margaret R. Hunton and Ethel Williams, supervisors, Dorothy B. Porter, director. Washington, D. C., Howard university, 1939.
2 p. l., ii numb. l., 94, 106, 159, 23, 88, 19 p. 27½ x 21½cm.
Each part preceded by leaf with half-title not included in paging (6 leaves)
Mimeographed.
1. Negroes—Bibl. 2. Negro literature—Bibl. I. *Porter, Dorothy (Burnett) 1905- II. Hunton, Margaret R. III. Williams, Ethel. IV. U. S. Work projects administration.
39-14329 Revised
Library of Congress Z1361.N39H8
[r44f2] 016.325260973

U. S. - Civilization.
Ivory Coast
M973
D12p
Dadie, Bernard B , 1916-
Patron de New York. Paris, Présence Africaine, 1964.
308p. 18½cm.
1. U. S. - Civilization. 2. U. S. - Social life and customs. I. Title.

M323
Un3h
U.S. Supreme Court.
Reply brief for appellants on reargument. No.2 - Harry Briggs, Jr., et al., appellants, vs. R.W.Elliott, et.al., appelles. No.4 - Dorothy E. Davis, et al., appellants, vs. County School Board of Prince Edward County, appelles. Appeal from the United States District Court for the Eastern District of South Carolina and the Eastern District of Virginia. In the Supreme Court of the United States, October Term, 1953.
40p. 23cm.
1. Segregation in education.

United States - Defenses.
M355.2
H18f
Hampton Institute. Hampton Va. Conference on the Participation of the Negro in National Defense.
Findings and principal addresses. Hampton, Va., 1940.
61p. 28cm.
Addresses at inauguration of Dr. Malcolm S. Mac Lean.

U.S.-Civilization-Addresses, essays, lectures.
M973
R56d
Robinson, Donald B 1913- ed.
The day I was proudest to be an American. [1st ed.] Garden City, N. Y., Doubleday, 1958.
288 p. 22 cm.

1. U. S.—Civilization—Addresses, essays, lectures. 2. U. S.—Hist.—Anecdotes. I. Title.
E169.1.R722 917.3 58-10037 ‡
Library of Congress [30]

M323
N212
U. S. Supreme Court.
National Association for the Advancement of Colored People. Legal Defense and Educational Fund.
Segregation in public schools; brief for reargument in the Supreme Court of the United States, October term, 1953.
xxxii, 235 p. 24 cm.

Haiti
M844
L96t
United States--Description and travel.
Lubin, J Dieudonné.
Travaux de recherches et de documentation aux Etats-Unis et impressions de voyage. Port-au-Prince, L'Etat, 1951.
69p. port. 17cm.

U.S. - Civilization - Addresses, essays, lectures.
M323
M45
Smith, Huston, ed.
The search for America. Edited by Huston Smith, with Richard T. Heffron and Eleanor Wieman Smith. [Englewood Cliffs, N. J.] Prentice-Hall [1959]
176 p. 21 cm. (Spectrum paperbacks, S-9)
"Based on the National educational television series [The search for America]"

1. U. S.—Civilization—Addresses, essays, lectures. 2. U. S.—Relations (general) with foreign countries. I. Title.
E169.1.S62 917.3 59-15720 ‡
Library of Congress [30]

M323.4
Un3n
U.S. Supreme Court
Petition for Writ of Certiorari to the Supreme Court of Alabama. National Association for the Advancement of Colored People, a corporation, petitioner, v. State of Alabama, ex rel. John Patterson, Attorney General. In the Supreme Court of the United States, October Term, 1956.
22p. 23cm.
1. National Association for the Advancement of Colored People.

United States-For. rel. - Haiti.
M972.94
P19
V.2,no.9
Holly, Alonzo Potter Burgess, 1865-
Our future relations with Haiti. Philadelphia, American Academy of Political and Social Science, 1931.
5p. 23cm.
Reprinted from Elements of an American foreign policy, vol. 156 of The Annals of the American Academy of Political and Social Science, July 1931.

U.S. - Civilization - Addresses, essays, lectures.
M323.4
W65d
Wrage, Ernest J ed.
Contemporary forum; American speeches on twentieth-century issues, edited by Ernest J. Wrage [and] Barnet Baskerville. New York, Harper [1962]
376 p. 25 cm.

1. American orations. 2. U. S.—Civilization—Addresses, essays, lectures. 3. U. S.—Pol. & govt.—20th cent.—Addresses, essays, lectures. I. Baskerville, Barnet, joint ed. II. Title.
PS668.W7 815.5082 62-10074 ‡
Library of Congress [10]

M342.73
M615
U.S. Supreme Court.
Miller, Loren.
The petitioners; the story of the Supreme Court of the United States and the Negro. New York, Pantheon Books [1966]
xv, 461 p. 22 cm.
Bibliographical references included in "Notes" (p. [433]-455)

1. U. S. Supreme Court. 2. Negroes—Legal status, laws, etc. I. Title.
342.73 65-14382
Library of Congress [5]

United States - Guide books.
M310.
H11h
Hackley, Edwin H.
Hackley & Harrison's hotel and apartment guide for colored travelers, board, rooms, garage accomodations, etc. in 300 cities in the United States and Canada, 1930/ Philadelphia, Pa., Hackley & Harrison publishing company, 1930.
48p. 23½cm.

U.S. - Defenses.
M341.6
T18u
Tate, Merze.
The United States and armaments. Cambridge, Harvard Univ. Press, 1948.
xii, 312 p. 24 cm.
"Much of the material of Part I ... is in [the author's] The disarmament illusion."
"Short titles used in footnotes": p. [275]-278. "Selective bibliography": p. 278-286.

1. Disarmament. 2. U. S.—Defenses. I. Title.
JX1974.T32 341.6 48-5607*
Library of Congress [48q7]

U.S.-Descr. & trav.

Guadeloupe
M910
C17s

Capitaine, Alexandre, 1894–
La situation économique et sociale des États-Unis à la fin du XVIIIe siècle (d'après les voyageurs français) par Alexandre Capitaine ... Paris, Les Presses universitaires de France, 1926.
xx, 162 p., 1 l. 25½cm.

1. U. S.—Descr. & trav. 2. U. S.—Soc. condit. 3. U. S.—Econ. condit. I. Title.

26—18783

Library of Congress E164.C28 [42c1]

M99
M48
1851

U.S. - Descr. & trav.
Melbourn, Julius, b. 1790.
Life and opinions of Julius Melbourn; with sketches of the lives and characters of Thomas Jefferson, John Quincy Adams, John Randolph, and several other eminent American statesmen. Ed. by a late member of Congress. Syracuse, Hall, 1851.

xii, 258p. (port.) 20cm.

U.S.-Descr. & trav.

MB9
M48

Melbourn, Julius, b. 1790.
Life and opinions of Julius Melbourn; with sketches of the lives and characters of Thomas Jefferson, John Quincy Adams, John Randolph, and several other eminent American statesmen. Ed. by a late member of Congress. Syracuse, Hall & Dickson; [etc., etc.] 1847.
239 p. front. (port.) 20cm.

1. Slavery in the U. S.—North Carolina. 2. U. S.—Descr. & trav. 3. U. S.—Pol. & govt.—1815–1861. I. Hammond, Jabez Delano, 1778–1855, ed.

12—30047

Library of Congress E338.M51 [45c1]

U. S. - Description and travel - 1960-

M301
W673

Williams, John Alfred, 1925–
This is my country too [by] John A. Williams. [New York] New American Library [1965]
xix, 169 p. 21 cm. (An NAL-World book)

1. U. S.—Race question. 2. U. S.—Desc. & trav.—1960– I. Title.

E185.61.W734 301.451 65–17842

Library of Congress [5]

U. S. - Economic conditions.

Guadeloupe
M910
C17s

Capitaine, Alexandre, 1894–
La situation économique et sociale des États-Unis à la fin du XVIIIe siècle (d'après les voyageurs français) par Alexandre Capitaine ... Paris, Les Presses universitaires de France, 1926.
xx, 162 p., 1 l. 25½cm.

1. U. S.—Descr. & trav. 2. U. S.—Soc. condit. 3. U. S.—Econ. condit. I. Title.

26—18783

Library of Congress E164.C28 [42c1]

U. S. - Economic policy.

M331
H76b

Hoover, Isaac James.
Banishing the ghost of unemployment, by Isaac James Hoover. Boston, Meador publishing company, 1934.
2 p. l., 7–105 p. 19½cm.
"The fallacies of the 'new deal' exposed."—Publisher's announcement.

1. Unemployed—U. S. 2. U. S.—Economic policy. 3. National industrial recovery act, 1933. I. Title.

34–39702

Library of Congress HD5724.H6
——— Copy 2.
Copyright A 78288 [5] 331.137973

U. S. - Emigration and immigration.

M301
R27n4

Reid, Ira De Augustine, 1901–
The Negro immigrant, his background, characteristics and social adjustment, 1899–1937, by Ira De A. Reid ... New York, Columbia university press; London, P. S. King & son, ltd., 1939.
261 p. incl. tables. 23cm. (*Half-title:* Studies in history, economics and public law, ed. by the Faculty of political science of Columbia university. no. 449)
Issued also as thesis (PH. D.) Columbia university.
Bibliography: p. 253–258.

1. Negroes. 2. U. S.—Race question. 3. U. S.—Emig. & immig. I. Title.

39–19999

Library of Congress H31.C7 no. 449
——— Copy 2. JV6895.N4R4 1939 a
Copyright A 126486 [40k5] (308.2) 325.260973

U.S. - Foreign relations.

M327
W73

Winston, Henry, 1911-
New Colonialism U.S. style. [New York, New Outlook Publishers, 1965]
30p. port. 18½cm.

1. U.S. - Foreign relations. I. Title.

U. S. - Foreign relations - Haiti.

M972.94
B18

Balch, Emily Greene, 1867– ed.
Occupied Haiti; being the report of a committee of six disinterested Americans representing organizations exclusively American, who, having personally studied conditions in Haiti in 1926, favor the restoration of the independence of the Negro republic, edited by Emily Greene Balch. New York, The Writers publishing company, inc., 1927.
viii p., 1 l., 186 p. 19½cm.

1. Haiti—Pol. & govt.—1844– 2. Haiti—For. rel.—U. S. 3. U. S.—For. rel.—Haiti. I. Title.

27—16258

Library of Congress F1926.B17 [47q1]

U. S. - Foreign relations - Haiti.

Haiti
M972.94
B38c

Beauvoir, Vilfort.
Le contrôle financier du gouvernement des États-Unis d'Amérique sur la république d'Haïti, par Vilfort Beauvoir ... préface de m. Marc Réglade ... Paris, Recueil Sirey, 1930.
1 p. l., [v]–xi, 268 p., 1 l. 25½cm.
"Bibliographie": p. [251]–263.

1. Finance—Haiti. 2. Haiti—For. rel.—U. S. 3. U. S.—For. rel.—Haiti. I. Title.

31–8143

Library of Congress HJ858.B4 [37c1] 336.7294

U. S. - Foreign relations - Haiti.

Haiti
M972.94
B41o

Bellegarde, Dantès, 1877–
... L'occupation américaine d'Haïti, ses conséquences morales et économiques. Port-au-Prince, Chéraquit, 1929.
3 p. l., 44 p. 24cm.

1. Haiti—Hist.—1844– 2. U. S.—For rel.—Haiti. 3. Haiti—For. rel.—U. S. I. Title.

[*Full name:* Louis Dantès Bellegarde]

32—21642

Library of Congress F1926.B42 [45c1] 972.94

U. S. - Foreign relations - Haiti.

Haiti
M972.94
B41re

Bellegarde, Dantès, 1877–
... La résistance haïtienne (l'occupation américaine d'Haïti); récit d'histoire contemporaine. Montréal, Éditions Beauchemin, 1937.
2 p. l., [9]–175 p., 2 l. incl. front. (map) plates. 20½cm.
Bibliographical foot-notes.

1. Haiti—Hist.—1844– 2. U. S.—For. rel.—Haiti. 3. Haiti—For. rel.—U. S. I. Title.

[*Full name:* Louis Dantès Bellegarde]

A C 38—1300

New York. Public library for Library of Congress F1926.B44 [a43c1]

U. S. - Foreign relations - Haiti.

Haiti
MB9
D25d

Danache, B
Le président Dartiguenave et les Américains. Port-au-Prince, Impr. de l'État, 1950.
164 p. illus., port. 22 cm.

1. Dartiguenave, Sudre, Pres. Haiti. 2. Haiti—Hist.—1844– 3. Haiti—For. rel.—U. S. 4. U. S.—For. rel.—Haiti.

F1926.D28D3 923.17294 51–2664

Library of Congress [2]

U. S. - Foreign relations - Haiti.

Haiti
M972.94
F51r

Firmin, Anténor, 1850–1911.
M. Roosevelt, président des États-Unis et la République d'Haïti, par A. Firmin ... New York, Hamilton bank note engraving and printing company; Paris, F. Pichon et Durand-Auzias, 1905.
x, 501, [1] p. front. (port.) 19cm.

1. Haiti—For. rel.—U. S. 2. U. S.—For. rel.—Haiti. 3. Haiti—Pol. & govt.—1844– 4. Roosevelt, Theodore, pres. U. S., 1858–1919.

6—26

Library of Congress F1921.F52 [43f1]

U. S. - Foreign relations - Haiti.

Haiti
M972.94
H86p

Hudicourt, Pierre Lelio
Pour notre libération économique et financière. [Port-au-Prince, Édition du Parti socialiste populaire, 1946]
25 p. 21 cm.

1. Haiti—Economic policy. 2. Finance—Haiti. 3. Haiti—For. rel.—U. S. 4. U. S.—For. rel.—Haiti. I. Title.

A 48-6316*

Harvard Univ. Library for Library of Congress [1]

U. S. - Foreign relations - Haiti.

M323
J632a

Johnson, James Weldon, 1871–
L'autonomie d'Haïti, par James Weldon Johnson. Quatre [!] articles reproduits de la revue "The Nation", comprenant le compte-rendu d'une enquête effectuée pour le compte de l'Association nationale pour l'avancement des gens de couleur, et traduits en français par les soins de l'Union patriotique haïtienne. New York, Association nationale pour l'avancement des gens de couleur; Port-au-Prince, Comité central de l'Union patriotique, 1921.
35 p. 21½cm.

1. Haiti—For. rel.—U. S. 2. U. S.—For. rel.—Haiti. 3. Haiti—Pol. & govt.—1844– I. The Nation, New York. II. National association for the advancement of colored people. III. Union patriotique haïtienne. IV. Title. *Translation of* Self-determining Haiti.

32–24487

Library of Congress F1926.J63 [2] [327.7294] 972.94

U. S. - Foreign relations - Haiti.

M323
J632s

Johnson, James Weldon, 1871–1938.
Self-determining Haiti, by James Weldon Johnson. Four articles reprinted from the Nation embodying a report of an investigation made for the National association for the advancement of colored people, together with official documents ... [New York, The Nation, °1920]
48 p. 23cm.

M323
J632e
no.3

1. Haiti—For. rel.—U. S. 2. U. S.—For. rel.—Haiti. 3. Haiti—Pol. & govt. I. The Nation, New York. II. National association for the advancement of colored people. III. Title.

A 21—1238

Stanford univ. Library for Library of Congress [a41d1]

U. S. - Foreign relations - Haiti.

Haiti
M972.94
L49p

Lecorps, Louis Marceau, ed.
... La politique extérieure de Toussaint-Louverture; nos premières relations politiques avec les États-Unis, lettres de Toussaint-Louverture et d'Edward Stevens (1799–1800) Port-au-Prince, Cheraquit, 1935.
1 p. l., ii, [3]–107, vi p., 1 l. port. 22½cm.
At head of title: La. Marceau Lecorps.

1. Haiti—For. rel. 2. Haiti—For. rel.—U. S. 3. U. S.—For. rel.—Haiti. I. Toussaint Louverture, Pierre Dominique, 1746?–1803. II. Stevens, Edward.

A 41–3004

New York. Public library for Library of Congress [2]

U. S. - Foreign relations - Haiti.

M973
L82d

Logan, Rayford Whittingham.
The diplomatic relations of the United States with Haiti, 1776–1891, by Rayford W. Logan. Chapel Hill, The University of North Carolina press, 1941.
xi p., 2 l., 516 p. 24cm.
Bibliography: p. [459]–496. Bibliographical foot-notes.

1. U. S.—For. rel.—Haiti. 2. Haiti—For. rel.—U. S. I. Title.

41–6260

Library of Congress E183.8.H2L6 [42k4] 327.73097294

U. S. - Foreign relations - Haiti.

Haiti
M972.94
T64t

Toussaint Louverture, Pierre Dominique, 1746?-1803.
Toussaint Louverture et l'independance de Saint-Dominigue; explication par des documents des Traités secrets entre Toussaint-Louverture, les Etats-Unid d'Amérique et l'Angleterre. Port-au-Prince, Société d'Edition et de Librairie, 1946.
145p. 23½cm.
Special number of Le Document, 20 Mai 1946; published under the patronage of the Société Toussaint-Louverture.

U.S.-History.

M973
Ep7e
1943

Eppse, Merl R
An elementary history of America, including the contributions of the Negro race, by Merl R. Eppse ... and A. P. Foster ... Nashville, Tenn., National publication company, 1943.
xi, 350 p. front., illus. (incl. maps, ports.) 20½cm.
"Revised and enlarged."
Bibliography: p. 348–350.

1. Negroes. 2. U. S.—Hist. 3. Slavery in the U. S.—Hist. I. Foster, Austin Powers, 1859– joint author.

43–15927

Library of Congress E185.E684 1943 [3] 325.260973

U.S.— Hist.

M973 Ep7e

Eppse, Merl R.
An elementary history of America, including the contributions of the Negro race, by Merl R. Eppse ... and A. P. Foster ... Chicago, Nashville [etc.] National educational publishing co., inc., 1939.
xi, 312 p. front., illus. (incl. ports.) 20½cm.
Includes bibliographies.
1. Negroes. 2. U. S.—Hist. 3. Slavery in the U. S.—Hist. I. Foster, Austin Powers, 1859– joint author. II. Title.
39—1901
Library of Congress E185.E684
[44n2] 325.260973

U.S. - History.

M973 F85L

Franklin, John Hope, 1915– jt. auth.
Land of the free; a history of the United States, by John W. Caughey, John Hope Franklin [and] Ernest R. May. Educational advisers: Richard M. Clowes, [and] Alfred T. Clark, Jr. Pasadena, Calif., Designed and produced by the W. Ritchie Press for Franklin Publications, 1965.
xi, 658 p. illus. (part col.) maps, ports. 27 cm.
Includes bibliographical references.
1. U. S.—Hist. ~~I. Franklin, John Hope, 1915– joint author.~~ II. May, Ernest R., joint author. III. Title.
E178.1.C36 973 65–27033
Library of Congress [5]

U.S. - History.

M973 H55f

Hill, Arthur C 1918–
From yesterday thru tomorrow, by Arthur C. Hill and J. W. Miller. New York, Vantage Press [1951]
142 p. 23 cm.
1. Negroes. 2. Slavery in the U. S. I. Miller, Jesse W., 1920– joint author. II. Title.
E185.6.H5 325.260973 51–2475
Library of Congress [10]

U.S. - History.

M973 R24n

Reddick, Lawrence Dunbar, 1910–
The Negro in the building of America. New York, National Committee for the Participation of Negroes in the American Common World's Fair of 1920 in New York, 1940.
4-7p. 23cm.
In: Souvenir program of Negro week on the American Common, World's Fair of 1940 in New York.

U.S.-History-Anecdotes.

M973 R56d

Robinson, Donald B 1913– *ed.*
The day I was proudest to be an American. [1st ed.] Garden City, N. Y., Doubleday, 1958.
238 p. 22 cm.
1. U. S. — Civilization — Addresses, essays, lectures. 2. U. S. — Hist.—Anecdotes. I. Title.
E169.1.R722 917.3 58–10037 ‡
Library of Congress [30]

U.S.-Hist.-Historiography.

M370. C22

Carpenter, Marie Elizabeth.
The treatment of the Negro in American history school textbooks; a comparison of changing textbook content, 1826 to 1939, with developing scholarship in the history of the Negro in the United States [by] Marie Elizabeth Carpenter. Published with the approval of Professor Erling M. Hunt, sponsor. [Menasha, Wis., George Banta publishing company, °1941]
4 p. l., 137 p. 23cm.
Bibliography: p. [130]–137. Bibliographical foot-notes.
1. Negroes. 2. U. S.—Hist.—Historiography. 3. Text-books—U. S. I. Title.
41—8011
Library of Congress E185.C2
[41d2] 325.260973

U.S. - History - Personal narrative.

M89 R57

Robinson, W H , 1848–
From log cabin to the pulpit; or fifteen years in slavery by W. H. Robinson. [Eau Claire, Wis., James H. Tifft, 1913.
200p. illus. 19½cm.

U. S.-Hist.-Revolution.

Bahamas M972.96 B46e

Bethell, Arnold Talbot.
The early settlers of the Bahama islands, with a brief account of the American revolution. Most of the historical facts contained in this book are taken from the archives of the colony. By A. Talbot Bethell ... Nassau, N. P., Bahamas. Holt, Eng., Printed by Rounce & Wortley [~~1937~~] 1926
166 p. front. 22cm.
"Second edition."
Errata slip inserted.
1. Bahamas—Hist. 2. Bahamas—Biog. 3. U. S.—Hist.—Revolution. I. Title.
31–13972
Library of Congress F1656.B562
[3] 972.96

U. S.—Hist.—Revolution.

M350 N32 1852

Nell, William C.
Services of colored americans, in the wars of 1776 and 1812. By William C. Nell. 2nd ed. Boston, Robert F. Wallcut, 1852.
40p. 30cm.

U. S.—Hist.—Revolution.

M350 N32 1851

Nell, William C.
Services of colored Americans, in the wars of 1776 and 1812. By William C. Nell. Boston, Printed by Prentiss & Sawyer, 1851.
24 p. 23½cm.
1. U. S.—Hist.—Revolution—Negro troops. 2. U. S.—Hist.—War of 1812—Negro troops.
5–23354
Library of Congress E269.N3N48

U.S. - Hist. --Revolution.

Haiti M972.94 N34ha

Nemours, Alfred, 1883–
Haiti et la Guerre de l'Indépendance Américaine. Port-au-Prince, Henri Deschamps, 1952.

U.S.-History-Revolution.

M973 Qu2n

Quarles, Benjamin.
The Negro in the American Revolution. Chapel Hill, Published for the Institute of Early American History and Culture, Williamsburg, Va., by University of North Carolina Press [1961]
xiii, 231 p. front. 24 cm.
Bibliography: p. [201]–223.
1. U. S.—Hist.—Revolution—Negroes. I. Institute of Early American History and Culture, Williamsburg, Va. II. Title.
Full name: Benjamin Arthur Quarles.
E269.N3Q3 973.315967 61—66795
Library of Congress [62k10]

U.S. - Hist. - Revolution - Fiction.

M813.5 Y46be

Yerby, Frank, 1916–
Bride of liberty. [1st ed.] Garden City, N. Y., Doubleday, 1954.
219 p. illus. 22 cm. (Cavalcade books)
1. U. S.—Hist.—Revolution—Fiction. I. Title.
Full name: Frank Garvin Yerby.
PZ7.Y48Br 54–7595 ‡
Library of Congress [10]

U.S.-Hist.-Revolution-Negro troops.

M350 G191

[Garrison, William Lloyd, 1805–1879.
The loyalty and devotion of colored Americans in the revolution and war of 1812. Pub. in Boston, Mass., 1861. New York city, The New York age press, 1918.
24 p. 18cm.
1. U. S.—Hist.—Revolution—Negro troops. 2. U. S.—Hist.—War of 1812—Negro troops. 3. Slavery in the U. S.—Controversial literature—1861. I. Title.
18—22489
Library of Congress E269.N3G242
[36b1]

U.S.-History-Revolution-Negro troops.

M350 G19L 1861

Garrison, William Lloyd.
The loyalty and devotion of colored Americans in the Revolution and War of 1812. Boston, R. F. Wallcut, 1861.
24p. 18cm.

U.S.—Hist.—Revolution— Negro troops.

M973. M45

Mazyck, Walter H.
George Washington and the Negro, by Walter H. Mazyck ... Washington, D. C., The associated publishers, inc. [°1932]
vii p., 1 l., 180 p. 19½cm.
1. Washington, George, pres. U. S.—Associates and employees. 2. Slavery in the U. S.—Virginia. 3. U. S.—Hist.—Revolution—Negro troops. I. Title.
32—4101
Library of Congress E312.17.M38
——— Copy 2.
Copyright A 47409 [38j2] 923.173

U.S.—Hist.—Revolution— Negro troops.

M350 N32c

Nell, William Cooper, 1816–1874.
The colored patriots of the American revolution, with sketches of several distinguished colored persons: to which is added a brief survey of the condition and prospects of colored Americans. By William C. Nell. With an introduction by Harriet Beecher Stowe. Boston, R. F. Wallcut, 1855.
396 p. 2 pl. (incl. front.) fold. facsim. 19½cm.
1. U. S.—Hist.—Revolution—Negro troops. 2. Negroes. I. Stowe, Mrs. Harriet Elizabeth (Beecher) 1811–1896. II. Title.
4—5729
Library of Congress E269.N3N4
[42g1]

U. S.-Hist.-Revolution-Negro troops.

M06 Am3 no.5

Steward, Theophilus Gould, 1843–
... How the black St. Domingo legion saved the patriot army in the siege of Savannah, 1779, by T. G. Steward ... Washington, D. C., The Academy, 1899.
15 p. illus. (maps) 23cm. (American negro academy. Occasional papers, no. 5)
1. Savannah—Siege, 1779. 2. U. S.—Hist.—Revolution—Negro troops. 3. France—Army—Infantry—Fontage's legion.
9–24043 Revised
Library of Congress E185.5.A51 no. 5
——— Copy 2. E241.S2638
[r32e2]

U.S.— Hist.—Revolution— Negro troops.

M350 W67h

Williams, George Washington, 1849–1891.
A history of the Negro troops in the war of the rebellion, 1861–1865, preceded by a review of the military services of Negroes in ancient and modern times, by George W. Williams ... New York, Harper & brothers, 1888.
2 p. l., [ix]–xvi, 353 p. front. (port.) 1 illus., pl. 20½cm.
1. U. S.—Hist.—Civil war—Negro troops. 2. U. S.—Hist.—Revolution—Negro troops. I. Title.
2—17113
Library of Congress E540.N3W7
[42d1]

U.S.-Hist.-Revolution Negro troops.

M350 W86

Wilson, Joseph Thomas, 1836–1891.
The black phalanx; a history of the Negro soldiers of the United States in the wars of 1775–1812, 1861–'65. By Joseph T. Wilson ... Hartford, Conn., American publishing company, 1888.
9 p. l., 21–528 p. incl. front., illus., plates, ports. 22½cm.
Bibliography: p. 517.
CONTENTS.—pt. I. The wars for independence.—pt. II. The war between the states.—pt. III. Miscellany.
1. U. S.—Hist.—Civil war—Negro troops. 2. U. S.—Hist.—Revolution—Negro troops. 3. U. S.—Hist.—War of 1812—Negro troops. I. Title.
2—17127
Library of Congress E185.63.W8
[45k1]

U. S.—Hist.—War of 1812.

M350 N33 1852

Nell, William C.
Services of colored americans, in the wars of 1776 and 1812. By William C. Nell. 2nd ed. Boston, Robert F. Wallcut, 1852.
40p. 30cm.

U. S.—Hist.—War of 1812.

M350 N32 1851 **Nell, William C.**
Services of colored Americans, in the wars of 1776 and 1812. By William C. Nell. Boston, Printed by Prentiss & Sawyer, 1851.
24 p. 23½cm.
1. U. S.—Hist.—Revolution—Negro troops. 2. U. S.—Hist.—War of 1812—Negro troops.
5-23354
Library of Congress E269.N3N43

U.S. - History - Civil War - Addresses, sermons, etc.

M973 C886 **Crowe, Charles Robert,** 1928- ed.
The age of Civil War and Reconstruction, 1830-1900; a book of interpretative essays, edited by Charles Crowe. Homewood, Ill., Dorsey Press, 1966.
x, 479 p. 26 cm. (The Dorsey series in American history)
Includes bibliographies.
1. Southern States—Hist.—Addresses, essays, lectures. 2. U. S.—Hist.—Civil War—Addresses, sermons, etc. 3. Reconstruction—Addresses, essays, lectures. I. Title.
F209.C7 973.08 66-27454
Library of Congress [5]

U.S.-Hist.-Civil war-Negro troops.

M810 B81n **Brown, William Wells,** b. 1815.
The negro in the American rebellion, his heroism and his fidelity, by William Wells Brown ... Boston, Lee & Shepard, 1867.
xvi, 380 p. 19cm.
1. U. S.—Hist.—Civil war—Negro troops. I. Title.
3-5868
Library of Congress E540.N3B8 [37g1]

M350 G19R U.S.-Hist.-War of 1812-Negro troops.

Garrison, William Lloyd, 1805-1879.
The loyalty and devotion of colored Americans in the revolution and war of 1812. Pub. in Boston, Mass., 1861. New York city, The New York age press, 1918.
24 p. 18cm.
1. U. S.—Hist.—Revolution—Negro troops. 2. U. S.—Hist.—War of 1812—Negro troops. 3. Slavery in the U. S.—Controversial literature—1861. I. Title.
18-22489
Library of Congress E269.N3G242 [36b1]

U.S.-Hist.-Civil War-Campaigns and battles

M350 C55b Clark, Peter H
The black brigade of Cincinnati; being a report of its labors and a muster-roll of its members; together with various orders, speeches, etc., relating to it. By Peter H. Clark. Cincinnati, Printed by J. B. Boyd, 1864.
30p. 22½cm.

U.S. - Hist - Civil War - Negro troops.

M815.4 D74a Douglass, Frederick, 1817-1895.
Addresses of the Hon. W.D. Kelley, Miss Anna E. Dickinson, and Mr. Frederick Douglass at a mass meeting...Philadelphia, July 6, 1863, for the promotion of colored enlistments. [Philadelphia, 1863].
7p. 22cm.

U.S.-History-War of 1812-Negro troops.

M350 G19R 1861 Garrison, William Lloyd.
The loyalty and devotion of colored Americans in the Revolution and War of 1812. Boston, R. F. Wallcut, 1861.
24p. 18cm.

U.S.-History - Civil war - Enlistments.

M815.4 D74m **Douglass, Frederick, 1817-1895.**
Men of color, to arms! A call by Frederick Douglass.
Rochester, March 2, 1863.
1p. 21½cm.

U.S.— History—Civil war—Negro troops.

M350 F62 **Fleetwood, Christian A.**
The Negro as a soldier; written by Christian A. Fleetwood, late sergeant-major 4th U. S. colored troops, for the Negro congress, at the Cotton states and international exposition, Atlanta, Ga., November 11 to November 23, 1895. Published by Prof. Geo. Wm. Cook. Washington, D. C., Howard university print, 1895.
1 p. l., 19 p. 23cm.
1. Negroes. 2. U. S.—History—Civil war—Negro troops. I. Cook, George William, pub. II. Atlanta. Cotton states and international exposition, 1895. III. Title.
A 12—751 r1
Stanford univ. Library for Library of Congress E185.63.F59 [a40b1]

U.S.-Hist.-War of 1812-Negro troops.

M350 W86 **Wilson, Joseph Thomas,** 1836-1891.
The black phalanx; a history of the Negro soldiers of the United States in the wars of 1775-1812, 1861-'65. By Joseph T. Wilson ... Hartford, Conn., American publishing company, 1888.
9 p. l., 21-528 p. incl. front., illus., plates, ports. 22½cm.
Bibliography: p. 517.
CONTENTS.—pt. I. The wars for independence.—pt. II. The war between the states.—pt. III. Miscellany.
1. U. S.—Hist.—Civil war—Negro troops. 2. U. S.—Hist.—Revolution—Negro troops. 3. U. S.—Hist.—War of 1812—Negro troops. I. Title.
2—17127
Library of Congress E185.63.W8 [45k1]

U.S.- History - Civil war - Enlistments.

M815.4 D74ne Douglass, Frederick, 1817-1895.
The Negro people in a democratic war.
Reprinted by the Workers bookshop, New York City.
3p. 22cm.

U. S. - Hist. - Civil War - Negro troops.

M973.7 W516 **Wesley, Charles Harris,** 1891-
Ohio Negroes in the Civil War. [Columbus] Ohio State University Press for the Ohio Historical Society [1962]
46 p. 24 cm. (Publications of the Ohio Civil War Centennial Commission, no. 6)
Includes bibliography.
1. U. S.—Hist.—Civil War—Negro troops. 2. Negroes—Ohio. I. Title.
E525.O337 no. 6 62-63753 ‡
Library of Congress [5]

U.S.—Hist.—1849-1877—Sources.

M326 W37 **Weaver, Robert Bartow.**
The struggle over slavery, by Robert B. Weaver ... Chicago, Ill., The University of Chicago press [°1938]
vii, 83, [1] p. illus. (incl. ports., map, facsim.) 23cm.
"The major portion of this volume consists of descriptions, statements, and explanations taken from source materials."—Pref.
CONTENTS.—Early slavery in America.—Controversies over the extension of slavery.—The secession movement.—The civil war.—Reconstruction in the South.—Bibliography (p. 83-[84])
1. Slavery in the U. S.—Controversial literature. 2. U. S.—Hist.—1849-1877—Sources. I. Title.
38-17444
Library of Congress E449.W34
——— Copy 2.
Copyright A 119120 [5] 326.973

U.S.-History-Civil war-Enlistment.

M815.4 D74a **Douglass, Frederick, 1817-1895.**
Negroes and the national war front. An address by Frederick Douglass, with a foreword, by James.W. Ford. New York, Workers library, 1942.
15p. 13cm.

U.S.— Hist.—Civil war—Negro troops.

M89 D37r Whipper, Frances E. Rollin.
Life and public services of Martin R. Delany, subassistant commissioner, Bureau relief of refugees, freedmen, and of abandoned lands, and late major 104th U. S. colored troops. By Frank A. Rollin ... Boston, Lee and Shepard, 1868.
367 p. 20cm.
1. Delany, Martin Robison, 1812-1885. 2. U. S.—Hist.—Civil war—Negro troops. 3. U. S. Bureau of refugees, freedmen and abandoned lands.
7—21560
Library of Congress E185.97.D33 [48e1]

U. S. - Hist. - Civil war.

M973 A12 **Alexander, William T.**
History of the colored race in America. Containing also their ancient and modern life in Africa ... the origin and development of slavery ... the civil war ... Prepared and arranged by Wm. T. Alexander ... Kansas City, Mo., Palmetto publishing co., 1887.
2 p. l., 600 p. front. (port. group) plates, ports. 24cm.
1. Negroes. 2. Slavery in the U. S.—Hist. 3. U. S.—Hist.—Civil war.
4—11144
Library of Congress E185.A4 [a37e1]

U.S.-History-Civil War-Fiction.

M813.5 Y46c **Yerby, Frank,** 1916-
Captain Rebel. New York, Dial Press [1956]
343 p. 21 cm.
1. U. S.—Hist.—Civil War—Fiction. I. Title.
Full name: Frank Garvin Yerby.
PZ3.Y415Cap 56-11248 ‡
Library of Congress [15]

U.S.—Hist.—Civil war— Negro troops.

M350 W67h **Williams, George Washington,** 1849-1891.
A history of the Negro troops in the war of the rebellion, 1861-1865, preceded by a review of the military services of Negroes in ancient and modern times, by George W. Williams ... New York, Harper & brothers, 1888.
2 p. l., [ix]-xvi, 353 p. front. (port.) 1 illus., pl. 20½cm.
1. U. S.—Hist.—Civil war—Negro troops. 2. U. S.—Hist.—Revolution—Negro troops. I. Title.
2—17113
Library of Congress E540.N3W7 [42d1]

M973 Q25 U.S.-Hist.-Civil War.

Quarles, Benjamin.
The Negro in the Civil War. [1st ed.] Boston, Little, Brown [1953]
xvi, 379 p. illus. 21 cm.
Bibliography: p. [349]-360.
1. U. S.—Hist.—Civil War—Negroes. I. Title.
E540.N3Q3 973.715 53—7309
Library of Congress [54x10]

U.S.-Hist.-Civil War-Negro troops.

M89 Ay2f **Ayers, James T** 1805-1865.
The diary of James T. Ayers, Civil War recruiter; ed., with an introd., by John Franklin. Springfield, Printed by authority of the State of Illinois, 1947.
xxv, 138 p. illus., port., facsims. 24 cm. (Occasional publications of the Illinois State Historical Society)
On cover: Publication no. 50.
1. U. S.—Hist.—Civil War—Personal narratives. 2. U. S.—Hist.—Civil War—Negro troops. 3. U. S. Army—Recruiting, enlistment, etc.—Civil War. I. Franklin, John Hope, 1915- ed. II. Title. (Series: Illinois State Historical Society. Occasional publications. Series: Illinois State Historical Society. Publicaton no. 50)
F536.I 34 no. 50 973.781 48—45066*
——— Copy 3. E601.A9
Library of Congress [a50f*2]

U.S.-Hist.-Civil war-Negro troops.

M350 W86 **Wilson, Joseph Thomas,** 1836-1891.
The black phalanx; a history of the Negro soldiers of the United States in the wars of 1775-1812, 1861-'65. By Joseph T. Wilson ... Hartford, Conn., American publishing company, 1888.
9 p. l., 21-528 p. incl. front., illus., plates, ports. 22½cm.
Bibliography: p. 517.
CONTENTS.—pt. I. The wars for independence.—pt. II. The war between the states.—pt. III. Miscellany.
1. U. S.—Hist.—Civil war—Negro troops. 2. U. S.—Hist.—Revolution—Negro troops. 3. U. S.—Hist.—War of 1812—Negro troops. I. Title.
2—17127
Library of Congress E185.63.W8 [45k1]

U. S. - History - Civil War - Negroes - Juvenile literature.

M973 R24w

Reddick, Lawrence Dunbar, 1910- jt. auth.

Worth fighting for; a history of the Negro in the United States during the Civil War and Reconstruction ₍by₎ Agnes McCarthy and Lawrence Reddick. Illustrated by Colleen Browning. ₍1st ed.₎ Garden City, N. Y., Doubleday, 1965.

118 p. col. illus., ports. 22 cm. (Zenith books)

1. Negroes—History, Juvenile. 2. U. S.—Hist.—Civil War—Negroes—Juvenile literature. I. Reddick, Lawrence Dunbar, 1910- joint author. II. Title.

E185.2.M23 973.715 65-10281

Library of Congress ₍5₎

U.S.-Hist.-Civil War-Personal narratives.

MB9 Ay2f

Ayers, James T 1805-1865.

The diary of James T. Ayers, Civil War recruiter; ed., with an introd., by John Franklin. Springfield, Printed by authority of the State of Illinois, 1947.

xxv, 138 p. illus., port., facsims. 24 cm. (Occasional publications of the Illinois State Historical Society)

On cover: Publication no. 50.

1. U. S.—Hist.—Civil War—Personal narratives. 2. U. S.—Hist.—Civil War—Negro troops. 3. U. S. Army—Recruiting, enlistment, etc.—Civil War. I. Franklin, John Hope, 1915- ed. II. Title. (Series: Illinois State Historical Society. Occasional publications. Series: Illinois State Historical Society. Publicaton no. 50)

F536.I 34 no. 50 973.781 48-45066*

——— Copy 3. E601.A9

Library of Congress ₍a59f2₎

U. S. - Hist. - Civil War - Personal narratives.

M350 H53a

Higginson, Thomas Wentworth, 1823-1911.

Army life in a black regiment. With notes and a biographical introd. by John Hope Franklin. Foreword by E. Franklin Frazier. Boston, Beacon Press ₍1962₎

300 p. 21 cm.

1. U. S.—Hist.—Civil War—Regimental histories—U. S.—33d Infantry (Colored) 2. U. S. Army. 33d Infantry (Colored) 3. U. S.—Hist.—Civil War—Personal narratives. I. Title.

E492.94 33d.H5 1962 973.7415 62-9217 ‡

Library of Congress ₍5₎

MB9 M349m

U.S. - Hist. - Civil War - Personal narratives.

Marrs, Elijah P. 1840-

Life and history of the Rev. Elijah P. Marrs... Louisville, Ky., The Bradley & Gilbert company, 1885.

146p. 1 l. front (port.) 19½cm.

U.S.-Hist.-Civil War-Regimental histories-U.S. in infantry-33d.

M350 H53

Higginston, Thomas Wentworth, 1823-1911.

Army life in a black regiment. Boston, Fields, Osgood, & Co., 1870.

296p. 18cm.

U. S.-Hist.-Civil war-Regimental histories-U.S. inf.-33d.

M350 T21

Taylor, Susie King, 1848-

Reminiscences of my life in camp with the 33d United States colored troops, late 1st S. C. volunteers, by Susie King Taylor ... Boston, The author, 1902.

xii p., 1 l., 82 p. front., pl., ports. 19½cm.

1. U. S.—Hist.—Civil war—Regimental histories—U. S. inf.—33d. 2. U. S. infantry. 33d regt., 1862-1866. I. Title.

2—30123

Library of Congress E492.94.33dT ₍a44b1₎

U. S. - Hist. - Civil War - Regimental histories - U. S. - 33d Infantry (Colored)

M350 H53a

Higginson, Thomas Wentworth, 1823-1911.

Army life in a black regiment. With notes and a biographical introd. by John Hope Franklin. Foreword by E. Franklin Frazier. Boston, Beacon Press ₍1962₎

300p. 21cm.

U.S. - History - 1865-1898

M973.8 Ow2u

Owens, Susie Lee

Union League of America; Political activities in Tennessee, the Carolinas, and Virginia, 1865-1870, an abridgement. New York, New York University, 1947.

23p. 23cm.

U. S.—Hist.—War of 1898.

M350 J63

Johnson, Edward Augustus, 1860-

History of Negro soldiers in the Spanish-American war, and other items of interest. By Edward A. Johnson ... Raleigh, Capital printing co., 1899.

147 p. front., plates, ports. 22cm.

1. U. S.—Hist.—War of 1898. 2. U. S.—Hist.—War of 1898—Negro troops.

99—4743

Library of Congress E725.5.N3J6

——— Copy 2.

Copyright 1899: 31418 ₍a40r29b1₎

U. S.-Hist.-War of 1898- Negro troops

M350 C26

Cashin, Herschel V.

Under fire. With the Tenth U. S. cavalry. Being a brief, comprehensive review of the Negro's participation in the wars of the United States. Especially showing the valor and heroism of the Negro soldiers of the Ninth and Tenth cavalries, and the Twenty-fourth and Twenty-fifth infantries of the regular army; as demonstrated in the decisive campaign around Santiago de Cuba, 1898 ... Thrilling episodes interestingly narrated by officers and men. Famous Indian campaigns and their results. A purely military history of the Negro. With introduction by Major-General Joseph Wheeler ... By Her-

(Continued on next card)

8—23892

₍41j1₎

U. S.—Hist.—War of 1898—Negro troops.

M350 J63

Johnson, Edward Augustus, 1860-

History of Negro soldiers in the Spanish-American war, and other items of interest. By Edward A. Johnson ... Raleigh, Capital printing co., 1899.

147 p. front., plates, ports. 22cm.

1. U. S.—Hist.—War of 1898. 2. U. S.—Hist.—War of 1898—Negro troops.

99—4743

Library of Congress E725.5.N3J6

——— Copy 2.

Copyright 1899: 31418 ₍a40r29b1₎

U.S.—Hist.—War of 1898—Negro troops.

M973 N42

A new Negro for a new century; an accurate and up-to-date record of the upward struggles of the Negro race. The Spanish-American war, causes of it; vivid descriptions of fierce battles; superb heroism and daring deeds of the Negro soldier ... Education, industrial schools, colleges, universities and their relationship to the race problem, by Prof. Booker T. Washington. Reconstruction and industrial advancement by N. B. Wood ... The colored woman and her part in race regeneration ... by ... Fannie Barrier Williams ... Chicago, Ill., American publishing house ₍1900₎

428 p. front., illus. (ports) 20cm.

(Continued on next card)

0—5252

₍44g1₎

U.S.—Hist.—War of 1898—Negro troops.

M350 St4r

Steward, Theophilus Gould, 1843-

The colored regulars in the United States army, with a sketch of the history of the colored American, and an account of his services in the wars of the country, from the period of the revolutionary war to 1899. Introductory letter from Lieutenant-General Nelson A. Miles ... By Chaplain T. G. Steward ... Philadelphia, A. M. E. book concern, 1904.

344 p. front., ports., maps. 22cm.

1. U. S.—Hist.—War of 1898—Negro troops. 2. Negroes.

8-317 Revised

Library of Congress E725.5.N3S8 ₍r42b2₎

U. S. - Hist. - War of 1898- Regimental histories- U. S. cav. - 10th.

M350 C26

Cashin, Herschel V.

Under fire. With the Tenth U. S. cavalry. Being a brief, comprehensive review of the Negro's participation in the wars of the United States. Especially showing the valor and heroism of the Negro soldiers of the Ninth and Tenth cavalries, and the Twenty-fourth and Twenty-fifth infantries of the regular army; as demonstrated in the decisive campaign around Santiago de Cuba, 1898 ... Thrilling episodes interestingly narrated by officers and men. Famous Indian campaigns and their results. A purely military history of the Negro. With introduction by Major-General Joseph Wheeler ... By Her-

(Continued on next card)

8—23892

₍41j1₎

U. S.-History, Military.

M350 W65

Wilkes, Laura Eliza, 1871-

Missing pages in American history, revealing the services of negroes in the early wars in the United States of America, 1641-1815, by Laura E. Wilkes ... ₍Washington, D. C., Press of R. L. Pendleton, °1919₎

91 p. 22cm.

On cover: Armistice edition.
Bibliography: p. 85-87.

1. Negroes as soldiers. 2. U. S.—History, Military. I. Title.

19-10083

Library of Congress E185.63.W68

Copyright A 515580 ₍3₎

U. S. - Politics and government.

M06 Am3 no.6

Love, John L.

The disfranchisement of the negro, by John L. Love ... Washington, D. C., The Academy, 1899.

27 p. 23cm. (American negro academy. Occasional papers, no. 6)

1. U. S.—Pol. & govt. 2. Negroes—U. S.

9—21947

Library of Congress E184.N3A5

——— Copy 2. JK1924.L89

₍35b1₎

U. S.-Pol. & govt.-Handbooks, manuals, etc.

M973 N51s

Nichols, James Lawrence, d. 1895.

Safe citizenship; or, Issues of the day ... and a complete dictionary of civil government. By J. L. Nichols ... 2d ed. Naperville, Ill., Toronto, Ont., J. L. Nichols & co., 1896.

1 p. l., 7-591 p. incl. illus., port. front. 18cm.

1. U. S.—Pol. & govt.—Handbooks, manuals, etc.

3-4376 Revised

Library of Congress JK246.N5 1896

Copyright 1896: 33454 ₍r30d2₎

MB9 M48 1851

U.S. - Pol. & govt. - 1815-1861.

Melbourn, Julius, b. 1790.

Life and opinions of Julius Melbourn; with sketches of the lives and characters of Thomas Jefferson, John Quincy Adams, John Randolph, and several other eminent American statesmen. Ed. by a late member of Congress. Syracuse, Hall 1851.

xii, 258p. (port.) 20cm.

U.S.-Pol. & govt.-1815-1861.

MB9 M48

Melbourn, Julius, b. 1790.

Life and opinions of Julius Melbourn; with sketches of the lives and characters of Thomas Jefferson, John Quincy Adams, John Randolph, and several other eminent American statesmen. Ed. by a late member of Congress. Syracuse, Hall & Dickson; etc., etc.₎ 1847.

239 p. front. (port.) 20cm.

1. Slavery in the U. S.—North Carolina. 2. U. S.—Descr. & trav. 3. U. S.—Pol. & govt.—1815-1861. I. Hammond, Jabez Delano, 1778-1855, ed.

12—30047

Library of Congress E338.M51

₍45c1₎

U.S.—Pol. & govt.—1865-1877.

M301 D853b8

Du Bois, William Edward Burghardt, 1868-

Black reconstruction; an essay toward a history of the part which black folk played in the attempt to reconstruct democracy in America, 1860-1880, by W. E. Burghardt Du Bois ... New York, Harcourt, Brace and company ₍°1935₎

6 p. l., 3-746 p. 22cm.

"First edition."
Bibliography: p. 731-737.

1. Reconstruction. 2. Negroes. 3. Negroes—Politics and suffrage. 4. Negroes—Employment. 5. U. S.—Pol. & govt.—1865-1877. I. Title.

35—8545

Library of Congress E668.D83

₍45g2₎ 325.260973

U.S.-Pol. & govt.-1865-1898.

M815 L26

Langston, John Mercer, 1829-1897.

Freedom and citizenship. Selected lectures and addresses of Hon. John Mercer Langston ... With an introductory sketch by Rev. J. E. Rankin ... Washington, D. C., R. H. Darby, 1883.

286 p. front. (port.) 20cm.

1. Negroes. 2. U. S.—Pol. & govt.—1865-1898. I. Rankin, Jeremiah Eames, 1828-1904. II. Title.

15—10680

Library of Congress E185.6.L28

Copyright 1883: 19154 ₍40b1₎

U. S. - Pol. & govt. - 1953-1961.
M973.92 M83
Morrow, Everett Frederic, 1909–
Black man in the White House; a diary of the Eisenhower years by the administrative officer for special projects, the White House, 1955-1961. New York, Coward-McCann [1963]
308 p. 22 cm.
1. U. S.—Pol. & govt.—1953-1961. 2. Negroes—Civil rights. 3. Presidents—U. S.—Staff. 4. Eisenhower, Dwight David, Pres. U. S., 1890– I. Title.
E835.M58 323.40973 63—13310 ‡
Library of Congress [64f14]

U.S. - Relations (general) with foreign countries.
M323 M45
Smith, Huston, ed.
The search for America. Edited by Huston Smith, with Richard T. Heffron and Eleanor Wieman Smith. [Englewood Cliffs, N. J., Prentice-Hall [1959]
176 p. 21 cm. (Spectrum paperbacks, S-9)
"Based on the National educational television series (The search for America)"
1. U. S.—Civilization—Addresses, essays, lectures. 2. U. S.—Relations (general) with foreign countries. I. Title.
E169.1.S62 917.3 59—15720 ‡
Library of Congress [20]

The United States and Africa.
M973 Am3
American Assembly.
The United States and Africa; background papers prepared for the use of participants and the Final report of the Thirteenth American Assembly, Arden House, Harriman Campus of Columbia University, Harriman, New York, May 1-4, 1958. Final ed. [New York] 1958.
xiv, 252 p. illus., maps. 23 cm.
1. U. S.—Relations (general) with Africa. 2. Africa—Relations (general) with the U. S. I. Title.
DT38.A65 1958 960 58—10601
Library of Congress [59r*20]

M329.6 B79
U.S. - Pol. & govt. - 20th cent.
Brooke, Edward William, 1919–
The challenge of change; crisis in our two-party system, by Edward W. Brooke. [1st ed.] Boston, Little, Brown [1966]
xviii, 269 p. 22 cm.
Bibliography: p. 267-269.
1. U. S.—Pol. & govt.—20th cent. 2. Republican Party—Hist. 3. U. S.—Social policy. I. Title.
E743.B77 329.6 66—16557
Library of Congress [5]

U. S. - Relations (general) with Latin America.
M973.8 F854
Hyman, Harold Melvin, 1924– , ed.
New frontiers of the American Reconstruction, edited by Harold M. Hyman. Urbana, University of Illinois Press, 1966.
x, 156p. 24cm.
Papers presented at a conference held at the University of Illinois in April 1965.
Includes bibliographical footnotes.
White editor.
Partial contents.- Reconstruction and the Negro, by John Hope Franklin.

The United States and armaments.
M341.6 T18u
Tate, Merze.
The United States and armaments. Cambridge, Harvard Univ. Press, 1948.
xii, 312 p. 24 cm.
"Much of the material of Part I ... is in [the author's] The disarmament illusion."
"Short titles used in footnotes": p. [275]-278. "Selective bibliography": p. 278-286.
1. Disarmament. 2. U. S.—Defenses. I. Title.
JX1974.T32 341.6 48—5607*
Library of Congress [48q7]

M323.4 W65d
U.S. - Politics and government - 20th century - Addresses, essays, lectures.
Wrage, Ernest J ed.
Contemporary forum; American speeches on twentieth-century issues, edited by Ernest J. Wrage [and] Barnet Baskerville. New York, Harper [1962]
376 p. 25 cm.
1. American orations. 2. U. S.—Civilization—Addresses, essays, lectures. 3. U. S.—Pol. & govt.—20th cent.—Addresses, essays, lectures. I. Baskerville, Barnet, joint ed. II. Title.
PS668.W7 815.5082 62—10074 ‡
Library of Congress [10]

U. S. - Social conditions.
Guadeloupe M910 C17s
Capitaine, Alexandre, 1894–
La situation économique et sociale des États-Unis à la fin du XVIIIe siècle (d'après les voyageurs français) par Alexandre Capitaine ... Paris, Les Presses universitaires de France, 1926.
xx, 162 p., 1 l. 25½cm.
1. U. S.—Descr. & trav. 2. U. S.—Soc. condit. 3. U. S.—Econ. condit. I. Title.
26—18783
Library of Congress E164.C28 [42c1]

The United States of West Africa and Realpolitik.
Nigeria M966.9 O19
Olugboji, Dayo
The United States of West Africa and realpolitik. Lagos, Nigeria Press, 1959.
44p. 22cm.

U.S. M960 D82
U.S. - Relations (general) with Africa.
American Assembly.
The United States and Africa. Edited by Walter Goldschmidt. Rev. ed. New York, F. A. Praeger [1963]
xvi, 298 p. maps (1 fold.) diagrs., tables. 22 cm.
Originally prepared as background reading for participants in the American Assembly, 1958.
1. U. S.—Relations (general) with Africa. 2. Africa—Relations (general) with the U. S. I. Goldschmidt, Walter Rocha, 1913– ed. II. Title.
DT38.A65 1963 309.16 63—20154
Library of Congress [64a7]

U. S. - Social conditions.
M323 Im1
Imbert, Dennis I
The stranger within our gates; a South American's impression of America's social problems, by D. I. Imbert. First edition... New Orleans, La., Watson bros. press, 1945.
102p. plate. 15cm.

M615.4 P272
United States Pharmacopoeia.
Patrick, Thomas William, 1872–
A little fun with the U.S.P. (8th revision) before it leaves us. Boston, n.d.
[5] p. 18cm.

U.S.-Relations (general) with Africa.
M973 Am3
American Assembly.
The United States and Africa; background papers prepared for the use of participants and the Final report of the Thirteenth American Assembly, Arden House, Harriman Campus of Columbia University, Harriman, New York, May 1-4, 1958. Final ed. [New York] 1958.
xiv, 252 p. illus., maps. 23 cm.
1. U. S.—Relations (general) with Africa. 2. Africa—Relations (general) with the U. S. I. Title.
DT38.A65 1958 960 58—10601
Library of Congress [59r*20]

M329.6 B79
U. S. - Social policy.
Brooke, Edward William, 1919–
The challenge of change; crisis in our two-party system, by Edward W. Brooke. [1st ed.] Boston, Little, Brown [1966]
xviii, 269 p. 22 cm.
Bibliography: p. 267-269.
1. U. S.—Pol. & govt.—20th cent. 2. Republican Party—Hist. 3. U. S.—Social policy. I. Title.
E743.B77 329.6 66—16557
Library of Congress [5]

M331.88 B53
United Transport Service Employees of America.
The Birth of a union; what the press of the nation has to say about the new red cap; Excerpts from news stories, feature articles and editorials of leading American newspapers since 1938. Edited by Ernest Calloway. Chicago, United Transport Service Employees of America, Educational Department, 1940.
26p. 28cm.

U. S.-Relations (general) with Africa.
M323.4 F229
Farmer, James, 1920–
Freedom, when? With an introd. by Jacob Cohen. New York, Random House [1966, °1965]
xxiv, 197 p. 22 cm.
1. Negroes—Civil rights. 2. Congress of Racial Equality. 3. U. S.—Relations (general) with Africa. 4. Africa—Relations (general) with the U. S. I. Title.
E185.61.F19 323.4 65—18104
Library of Congress [5]

United society for Christian literature, London.
Sierra Leone M966.4 G68
Gorvie, Max.
Our people of the Sierra Leone protectorate, by Max Gorvie. London and Redhill, United society for Christian literature [1955]
64, [1] p. 18½cm.

... Unity and difference in American life ...
M323 In8a
Institute for religious and social studies, *Jewish theological seminary of America.*
... Unity and difference in American life, a series of addresses and discussions, edited by R. M. MacIver. New York and London, Pub. by Institute for religious & social studies, distributed by Harper & brothers [1947]
5 p. l., 3-168 p. 21 cm. (Religion and civilization series)
CONTENTS.—The common ground: Three paths to the common good, by Louis Finkelstein. The rise of an American culture, by Allan Nevins. What common ground has America won? By L. K. Frank.—The dividing issues: The racial issue, by E. F. Frazier. The ethnic issue, by Vilhjalmur Stefansson. The economic issue, by Eli Ginzberg.
(Continued on next card)
47—2731
[49k7]

U.S. - Relations (general) with Canada.
M973.8 F854
Hyman, Harold Melvin, 1924– , ed.
New frontiers of the American Reconstruction, edited by Harold M. Hyman. Urbana, University of Illinois Press, 1966.
x, 156p. 24cm.
Papers presented at a conference held at the University of Illinois in April 1965.
Includes bibliographical footnotes.
White editor.
Partial contents.- Reconstruction and the Negro, by John Hope Franklin.

The United States and Africa.
U.S. M960 D82
American Assembly.
The United States and Africa. Edited by Walter Goldschmidt. Rev. ed. New York, F. A. Praeger [1963]
xvi, 298 p. maps (1 fold.) diagrs., tables. 22 cm.
Originally prepared as background reading for participants in the American Assembly, 1958.
1. U. S.—Relations (general) with Africa. 2. Africa—Relations (general) with the U. S. I. Goldschmidt, Walter Rocha, 1913– ed. II. Title.
DT38.A65 1963 309.16 63—20154
Library of Congress [64a7]

M341.1 Un3p
Universal Negro Improvement Association.
Petition of the Universal Negro Improvement Association and African Communities League, representing the interest of the four hundred million Negroes Indiginies of Africa, the British subjects in the West Indies, South and Central America, and the citizens, and other Negro inhabitants of the United States of America and those of Asia and Europe, to the League of Nations. [New York, The Association, [1922]
7 leaves 28cm.
1. Race problems. I. Garvey, Marcus. I. Title.

Universal Negro Improvement Association.

Jamaica
M323
G19

Garvey, Marcus, 1887-1940.
Aims and objects of movement for solution of Negro problem outlined... by Marcus Garvey. [New York, Press of the Universal Negro Improvement Association, 1924]

[11] 21cm.

Universal Negro Improvement Association.

Jamaica
M323 .
G19

Garvey, Marcus, 1887-1940.
An appeal to the soul of white America. The solution to the problem of competition between two opposite races. Negro leader appeals to the conscience of white race to save his own. [New York, Press of the Universal Negro Improvement Association, 1924]
[7] 21cm.

Universal Negro Improvement Association.

M304
P19
V.5, no.15

Garvey, Marcus, 1887-1940.
The Negro's greatest enemy. In: Three articles on the Negro problem. (Published in Current History Magazine, Sept. 1923) p. 11-22.

Universal Negro improvement association.

Jamaica
M89
G199

Garvey, Marcus, 1887-1940.
Philosophy and opinions of Marcus Garvey, edited by Amy Jacques-Garvey ... 1st ed. New York city, The Universal publishing house, 1923-25
2 v. front., port. 21½ᶜᵐ.
Inscribed: With the compliments of A. Jacques Garvey.

I. Garvey, Mrs. Amy Jacques, ed.

23—9826

Library of Congress HT1581.G8
[a43d1]

M323.
Sp4p

Universal races congress. 1st, London, 1911.
Papers on inter-racial problems, communicated to the first Universal races congress, held at the University of London, July 26-29, 1911, ed., for the Congress executive, by G. Spiller, Hon. organiser of the Congress. Pub. for the World peace foundation, Ginn and company, Boston. London, P. S. King & son, 1911.

xvi, 485p., 1 l. 25½cm.
1. Race problems. I. Spiller, Gustav, ed.-
II. Inter-racial problems, Papers on.

Universal salvation.

M252
H33u
1805

Haynes, Lemuel, 1753-1833.
[Universal salvation, a very ancient doctrine: With some account of the life and character of its author. A sermon, delivered at Rutland, West-Parish, in the year 1805. by Lemuel Haynes, A.M. Rutland, Printed by William Fay, January, 1806.

vi, 18p. 17½cm.

For other editions of this title see author entry.

Universalism: faith in mankind.

M191
M363

Martin, Clarence.
Universalism: faith in mankind. [1st ed.] New York, Vantage Press [1964]
88 p. illus. 21 cm.

1. Humanism. I. Title.

B945.M383U5 191 64-22777
Library of Congress [5]

The universe of universes.

M113
W64

Wilhite, William Hugh.
The universe of universes, by William Hugh Wilhite. St. Louis, Mo., Keymer Printing company, 1923.

117 [10]p. 19½cm.

M370
C12n

Universities and colleges.
Caliver, Ambrose, 1894-
National survey of the higher education of Negroes, a summary. Washington, U.S. Govt. Print. Off., 1943.

50p. 29cm. (U.S. Office of Education. Miscellaneous, no.6)
At head of title: National survey of the higher education of Negroes, v.4.

Universities and colleges— . .

M378
D29

Davis, John Warren, 1888–
... Problems in the collegiate education of Negroes, by President John W. Davis ... Institute, W. Va., 1937.
56 p. 23ᶜᵐ. (West Virginia state college bulletin, June 1937. Ser. 24, no. 4)
Contribution no. 8 of the Department of education.
Publications of West Virginia State college.

1. Negroes—Education. 2. Universities and colleges—U. S. I. Title. II. Title: Collegiate education of Negroes.

E 37-208 Revised

U. S. Off. of educ. Library for Library of Congress LC2781.D85
[r44d2]† 378.73

Universities and colleges.

M304
P19
v.3,
no.12

Davis, John Warren, 1888–
... Land-grant colleges for Negroes, by President John W. Davis, West Virginia state college ... Institute, W. Va. [1934]
73 p. incl. tables, diagr. 23ᶜᵐ. (West Virginia state college. Dept. of education. Contribution no. 6)
At head of title: West Virginia state college bulletin ... April, 1934. Series 21, no. 5. Publications of West Virginia state college.
First published in abridged form in the Journal of Negro education. July, 1933. *cf.* foot-note, p. [3]
Bibliography: p. [69]–73.
1. Agricultural colleges—U. S. 2. Negroes—Education. 3. Universities and colleges—U. S. I. Title.

A 35–750

Title from Rochester Univ. LC2801.D26 1934
Printed by L. C.
[3]

Universities and colleges

M378
F92

From servitude to service; being the Old South lectures on the history and work of southern institutions for the education of the Negro. Boston, American Unitarian Association, 1905.

3p. l., v -x, 232p. 20cm.
Partial contents: -Howard University, by K. Miller. -Tuskegee Institute, by R.C. Bruce. Hampton Institute, by H. B. Frissell. Atlanta University, by W.E.B. Du Bois.

Universities and colleges— . .

M378
H73

Holmes, Dwight Oliver Wendell, 1877–
The evolution of the Negro college, by Dwight Oliver Wendell Holmes ... New York city, Teachers college, Columbia university, 1934.
xi, 221 p. 23½ᶜᵐ. (Teachers cllege, Columbia university. Contributions to education, no. 609)
Issued also as thesis (PH. D.) Columbia university.
Bibliography: p. 211–221.

1. Negroes—Education. 2. Universities and colleges—U. S. I. Title. II. Title: The Negro college.

34—33609

Library of Congress LC2801.H57 1934 a
——— Copy 2. LB5.C8 no. 609
Copyright A 75062 [40o2] [378.73] 371.9740973

Universities and colleges. . .

M301
J63ne2

Johnson, Charles Spurgeon, 1893–
The Negro college graduate, by Charles S. Johnson ... Chapel Hill, The University of North Carolina press, 1938.
xvii, 399 p. incl. tables, diagrs. maps (part fold.) 23½ᶜᵐ.
Bibliography: p. 378-384.

1. Negroes—Education. 2. Negroes—Moral and social conditions. 3. Universities and colleges—U. S. I. Title.

38—9887

Library of Congress LC2781.J6
——— Copy 2.
Copyright A 116318 [40w5] 371.9740973

Universities and colleges.

M378F
N49

Neyland, Leedell W
The history of Florida Agricultural and Mechanical University [by] Leedell W. Neyland [and] John W. Riley. Gainesville, University of Florida Press, 1963.
xi, 303 p. illus., ports. 24 cm.
Bibliography: p. 281-282.

1. Florida. Agricultural and Mechanical University, Tallahassee. I. Riley, John W., joint author.

LC2851.F63N4 630.711 63-17301
Library of Congress [5]

Universities and colleges. . .

M378
ScSn

Scott, John Irving E
Negro students & their colleges. Boston, Meador Pub. Co. [1949]
179 p. 21 cm.

1. Negroes—Education. 2. Universities and colleges—U. S.—Direct. I. Title.

L901.S48 378.73 49-6113*
Library of Congress [15]

Universities and colleges. . .
U. S. *Office of education.*

M378
Un3na

National survey of the higher education of Negroes ... Federal security agency, Paul V. McNutt, administrator. U. S. Office of education, John W. Studebaker, commissioner. Washington, U. S. Govt. print. off., 1942–43.
4 v. maps, tables, diagrs. 29 x 23 cm. (*Its* Misc[ellaneous] no. 6)
CONTENTS.—[I] Socio-economic approach to educational problems, by Ina C. Brown, with an introduction by F. J. Kelly.—[II] General studies of colleges for Negroes.—[III] Intensive study of selected colleges for Negroes, by L. E. Blauch and M. D. Jenkins. IV. A summary, by Ambrose Caliver.

(Continued on next card)
E 42–362 rev
[r45v7]†

Universities and colleges - Curricula.

M370
C12e

Caliver, Ambrose, 1894–
Education of teachers for improving majority-minority relationships. Course offerings for teachers to learn about racial and national minority groups. By Ambrose Caliver ... Federal security agency. Paul V. McNutt, administrator. U. S. Office of education, John W. Studebaker, commissioner. Washington, U. S. Govt. print. off., 1944.
iv, 64 p. incl. illus., tables. 23ᶜᵐ. (U. S. Office of education. Bulletin 1944 no. 2)
"Selected references and sources of information": p. 60-64.
1. U. S.—Race question. 2. Minorities. 3. Teachers, Training of—U. S. 4. Universities and colleges—Curricula. I. Title.

E 45—7

U. S. Off. of educ. Library for Library of Congress L111.A6 1944, no. 2
——— Copy 2. E184.A1C3
[46k3]† (370.6173) 325.73

Universities and colleges - Curricula.

M378
C16p

Canady, Herman George, 1901–
... Psychology in Negro institutions, by Herman G. Canady ... Institute, W. Va., West Virginia state college [1939]
24 p. tables. 23ᶜᵐ. (West Virginia state college bulletin. Series 26, no. 3. June, 1939)
"Contribution no. 1 of the Research council at West Virginia state college—curricula studies."

1. Psychology—[Study and] teaching. 2. Universities and colleges—U. S.—Curricula. 3. Negroes—Education. I. Title. II. Title: Negro institutions.

E 39-308

U. S. Off. of educ. Library for Library of Congress LC2801.C4
[4]

Universities and colleges - Curricula.

M378
W15c

Wallace, William James Lord, 1908–
... Chemistry in Negro colleges, by William J. L. Wallace ... [Institute, W. Va., 1940]
34 p. tables. 22½ᶜᵐ. (West Virginia state college bulletin ... Ser. no. 2. Apr. 1940)
Contribution no. 3 of the Research council, West Virginia state college.
Publications of West Virginia state college.

1. Chemistry—[Study and] teaching—[Universities and colleges] 2. Universities and colleges—U. S.—Curricula. 3. Negroes—Education. I. Title. II. Title: Negro colleges.

E 40-853 Revised

U. S. Off. of educ. Library for Library of Congress QD40.W26
[r44c2]† 540.71173

Universities and colleges— Graduate work.

M378
F81f

Foster, Laurence, 1903–
The functions of a graduate school in a democratic society [by] Laurence Foster. New York, N. Y., Huxley house, 1936.
ix, 168 p. tables (1 fold.) 23½ᶜᵐ.

1. Universities and colleges—Graduate work. I. Title: A graduate school.

36—9428

Library of Congress LB2371.F6
——— Copy 2.
Copyright A 98736 [39g1] 378.1553

Universities and colleges—Religion.

M378
M21r
McKinney, Richard Ishmael, 1906–
Religion in higher education among Negroes, by Richard I. McKinney ... New Haven, Yale university press; London, H. Milford, Oxford university press, 1945.
xvi, 165, [1] p. incl. tables. 23½cm. (*Half-title:* Yale studies in religious education, XVIII)
"The complete results of this study were presented as a dissertation ... for the degree of doctor of philosophy in Yale university [1942]"—p. xii.
Bibliography: p. [149]–161.
1. Negroes — Education. 2. Negroes — Religion. 3. Universities and colleges—Religion. I. Title.
A 45—4633
Yale univ. Library for Library of Congress BV1610.M33 [4617]†

Universities and colleges - Africa.

Africa
M370
C83
Cowan, Laing Gray, *ed.*
Education and nation-building in Africa. Edited by L. Gray Cowan, James O'Connell [and] David G. Scanlon. New York, F. A. Praeger [1965]
x, 403 p. 21 cm.
Bibliography: p. 397–403.
1. Education—Africa—Addresses, essays, lectures. 2. Nationalism—Africa—Addresses, essays, lectures. I. O'Connell, James, 1925– joint ed. II. Scanlon, David G., joint ed. III. Title.
LA1501.C6 1965 370.96 65–12198
Library of Congress [5]

Universities and colleges - Nigeria.

Nigeria
M370
Ik3
Ikejiani, Okechukwu, ed.
Nigeria education. Edited and introduced by Okechukwu Ikejiani with a foreword by Nnamdi Azikiwe. Ikeja, Nigeria, Longmans of Nigeria, 1964.
xix, 234p. 22cm.

Universities and colleges—South Carolina.

M378
M22
McMillan, Lewis Kennedy.
Negro higher education in the State of South Carolina. [Orangeburg? S. C., 1953, °1952]
xii, 296 p. facsims. 24 cm.
1. Negroes—Education—South Carolina. 2. Universities and colleges—South Carolina. I. Title.
LC2802.S6M25 378.757 53—2401
Library of Congress [54c2]

Universities and colleges—Southern States.

M371.974
T87n
Tuskegee Institute.
The new South and higher education: what are the implications for higher education of the changing socio-economic conditions of the South? A symposium and ceremonies held in connection with the inauguration of Luther Hilton Foster, fourth president of Tuskegee Institute [October 31 and November 1, 1953. Tuskegee, Ala.] Dept. of Records and Research, Tuskegee Institute, 1954.
x, 145 p. map. 24 cm.
~~(Continued on next card)~~
54—12394
[5615]

Universities and colleges- Southern states.

M06
J61
no. 21
Williams, William Taylor Burwell, 1866–1941.
Report on negro universities and colleges, by W. T. B. Williams ... [Baltimore?] 1922.
28 p. incl. tables. 23cm. (*On cover:* The Trustees of the John F. Slater fund. Occasional papers, no. 21)
1. Negroes—Education. 2. Universities and colleges—Southern states. I. Title.
23—7445
Library of Congress E185.5.J65 no. 21
——— Copy 2. E185.82.W72
[a44f1]

M06
J61
no. 24
University commission on southern race questions.
Five letters of the University commission on southern race questions. [Charlottesville, Va.] 1927.
22 p. 23cm. (*On cover:* The Trustees of the John F. Slate fund. Occasional papers no. 24)
The first four letters appeared in 1916–19 under title: Four open letters from the University commission on race questions to the college men of the South.
CONTENTS. — Lynching. — Education.—Migration.—A new reconstruction.—Interracial cooperation.—Introductory address (Knoxville, Tenn., 1919)—Southern educators appeal for enforcement of law.
1. U. S.—Race question.
28—28327
Library of Congress E185.5.J65 no. 24
——— Copy 2. E185.61.U588
[89d1]

M06
J61
no. 24
University commission on southern race questions.
Five letters of the University commission on southern race questions. [Charlottesville, Va.] 1927.
22 p. 23cm. (*On cover:* The Trustees of the John F. Slate fund. Occasional papers no. 24)
The first four letters appeared in 1916–19 under title: Four open letters from the University commission on race questions to the college men of the South.
CONTENTS. — Lynching. — Education.—Migration.—A new reconstruction.—Interracial cooperation.—Introductory address (Knoxville, Tenn., 1919)—Southern educators appeal for enforcement of law.
1. U. S.—Race question.
28—28327
Library of Congress E185.5.J65 no. 24
——— Copy 2. E185.61.U588
[89d1]

University documents.

M378
P83p
Porter, Dorothy Burnett, 1905–
The preservation of university documents; with special reference to Negro colleges and universities. Washington, D.C., 1942.
"Reprinted from the Journal of Negro Education, October, 1942, p. 527–528."
527–528p. 25cm.

Unkhoswe waanyanja.

Malawi
M968.97
K29
Kalekebu, Bennett E
Unkhoswe waanyanja. [Dialogues on guardianship] Edited by Guy Atkins. Cape Town: London. Oxford University Press, 1952.
124p. 18½cm. (Annotated African Texts. Mananja, I)
Written in Nyanja.
1. Nyanja (African people) 2. Nyasaland. I. Title.

Unmasked.

M974.8
M78
Moore, Martha Edith (Bannister) 1910–
Unmasked; the story of my life on both sides of the race barrier, by Martha B. Moore. [1st ed.] New York, Exposition Press [1964]
106 p. 21 cm.
1. Discrimination—Pittsburgh. 2. Pittsburgh. I. Title.
E185.97.M8A3 301.451 64–4395
Library of Congress [5]

M614
R66u
The unsatisfied valence.
Roman, Charles Victor, 1864–
The unsatisfied valence. Reprinted from Journal of the National Medical Association, v.9, no.4.

Unsichtbar (Invisible man).

M813.5
El412
Ellison, Ralph,
Unsichtbar (Invisible man). Berlin, S. Fischer, 1954.
589p. 20½cm.

Unsung American sung.

M784
H19u
Handy, William Christopher, 1873–1958. *ed.*
Unsung Americans sung, edited by W. C. Handy. [New York? 1944]
236 p. incl. front., illus. (ports.) 28 cm.
Principally biographical sketches of prominent Negroes, with music written about them. The music is for solo voice or mixed chorus, with piano accompaniment.
Bibliography: p. 235–236.
1. Negroes—Songs and music. I. Title.
M1659.5.N4H 784.8 44—40185
Library of Congress [a54f1]

Unsung heroes.

MB
H33
Haynes, Elizabeth (Ross)
Unsung heroes, by Elizabeth Ross Haynes. New York, Du-Bois and Dill, 1921.
279 p. illus. (incl. ports.) 20½cm.
CONTENTS.—Frederick Douglass.—Paul Laurence Dunbar.—Booker T. Washington.—Harriet Tubman.—Alexander S. Pushkin.—Blanche Kelso Bruce.—Samuel Coleridge-Taylor.—Benjamin Banneker.—Phillis Wheatley—Toussaint L'Ouverture—Josiah Henson.—Sojourner Truth.—Crispus Attucks.—Alexandre Dumas.—Paul Cuffé.—Alexander Crummell.—John Mercer Langston.
1. Negroes—Biog. I. Title.
22—5452
Library of Congress E185.96.H4 [44g1]

Untangled.

M811.5
J13u
Jackson, Aurilda.
Untangled. [1st ed.] New York, Vantage Press [1956]
40 p. 21 cm.
Poems.
I. Title.
PS3519.A29U6 811.5 56–5496 ‡
Library of Congress [2]

Unto my heart.

M811.5
Ep7
Epperson, Aloise (Barbour)
Unto my heart, and other poems. Boston, Christopher Pub. House [1953]
201 p. 21 cm.
I. Title.
PS3509.P67U55 811.5 53–6801 ‡
Library of Congress [2]

Unwritten history.

M287.8
C79
Coppin, Levi Jenkins, *bp.*, 1848–
Unwritten history, by Bishop L. J. Coppin ... Philadelphia, Pa., A. M. E. book concern [°1919]
375 p. front., ports. 20cm.
I. Title.
Library of Congress BX8495.C6A3 20–9308
[2]

M813.5
El4u
Uomo invisibile.
Ellison, Ralph
Uomo invisibile [Invisible man] Traduzione di Carlo Fruettero e Luciano Gallino. Torino Giulio Einaudi Editore, 1956.
545p. 22½cm.
"For Arthur Spingarn, Sincerely Ralph Ellison."
Italian text.

Up! up! the ladder.

M370
W58u
Whiting, Helen Adele.
Up! up! the ladder. Atlanta, the author, 1948.
32p. illus, 23cm.

Up from slavery.

M814.4
W27au5
Washington, Booker Taliaferro, 1859?–1915.
Tokoloho bokhobeng; or Up from slavery phetolelo sesothong ke Herbert H. Lekhethoa. Morija, Basutoland, Morija Sesuto Book Depot, 1947.
146p. 18½cm.
Translated into Sesuto.

Up from slavery.

M814.4 W27au4 1963 Washington, Booker Taliaferro, 1859?-1915.
Up from slavery, an autobiography. Garden City, N. Y., Doubleday, 1963.
243 p. illus. 22 cm.

1. Tuskegee Institute. I. Title.

E185.97.W3163 923.773 63-3987 ‡
Library of Congress [5]

Up from slavery.

M814.4 W27au2 1940 Washington, Booker Taliaferro, 1859?-1915.
Up from slavery, an autobiography. New York, Pocket Books Inc., 1940.
236p. 16½cm.

Up from slavery.

M814.4 W27au2 Washington, Booker Taliaferro, 1859?-1915.
Up from slavery; an autobiography, by Booker T. Washington. London, Grant Richards, 1902.
ix, 330 p. front. (port.) 20½cm.
Originally published in the Outlook. cf. Pref.

1. Tuskegee normal and industrial institute. I. Title. 1—31242
Library of Congress E185.97.W3
——— Copy 2. [45g²2]

Up from slavery.

M814.4 W27au 1902 Washington, Booker Taliaferro, 1859?-1915.
Up from slavery; an autobiography, by Booker T. Washington. New York, Doubleday, Page & co., 1902.
ix, 330 p. front. (port.) 20½cm.
Originally published in the Outlook. cf. Pref.

1. Tuskegee normal and industrial institute. I. Title. 1—31242
Library of Congress E185.97.W3
——— Copy 2. [45g²2]

Up from slavery.

M814.4 W27au 1901 Washington, Booker Taliaferro, 1859?-1915.
Up from slavery; an autobiography, by Booker T. Washington. New York, Doubleday, Page & co., 1901.
ix, 330 p. front. (port.) 20½cm.
Originally published in the Outlook. cf. Pref.

1. Tuskegee normal and industrial institute. I. Title. 1—31242
Library of Congress E185.97.W3
——— Copy 2. [45g²2]

Up from the cane-brakes.

MB9 T86u Turpeau, David Dewitt
Up from the cane-brakes, an autobiography, by David Dewitt Turpeau, [Sr. Cincinnati, 1942]
43p. 20cm.

The upbuilding of a race.

M252 V59u Vernon, William Tecumseh, 1871-
The upbuilding of a race; or, The rise of a great people, a compilation of sermons, addresses and writings on education, the race question and public affairs. By William Tecumseh Vernon ... Introduction by Rev. H. T. Johnson ... Quindaro, Kan., Industrial students printers, 1904.
4 p. l., 7-153 p. port. 21cm.

1. Negroes. I. Title. 5-17896
Library of Congress E185.5.V54 [a35b1]

Upper classes - Nigeria.

M910 Sm9n Smythe, Hugh H
The new Nigerian elite [by] Hugh H. Smythe and Mabel M. Smythe. Stanford, Calif., Stanford University Press, 1960.
ix, 196 p. map. 24 cm.
Bibliographical references included in "Notes" (p. [175]-191)

1. Upper classes—Nigeria. 2. Nigeria—Soc. condit. I. Smythe, Mabel M., joint author. II. Title.

HN800.N5S56 301.4409669 60—13870
Library of Congress [61f10]

Upper Volta

M966.25 D59e Upper Volta.
Dim Delobsom, A A.
... L'empire du mogho-naba; coutumes des Mossi de la Haute-Volta. Préface de Robert Randau. Paris, Les éditions Domat-Montchrestien, 1932.
3 p. l., vii, 303 p. front., plates, ports., map. 25½cm. (Institut de droit comparé. Études de sociologie et d'ethnologie juridiques ... XI)
Cover dated 1933.

1. Mossi (African people) 2. Customary law—Upper Volta. 3. Ethnology—Upper Volta. I. Title.
33-18717
Library of Congress [3]

Upper Volta Upper Volta - Folk-lore.
M398 T443 Tiendrebeogo, Yamba, 1907-
Contes du larhallé; suivis d'un recueil de Proverbes et de devises du pays mossi. Rédigés et présentés par Robert Pageard. Ouagadougou, Chez l'auteur, 1963.
215 p. 21 cm.

1. Upper Volta - Folk-lore. 2. Folk-lore - Upper Volta. I. Title.

The upward path.

M810.8 P93 Pritchard, Myron Thomas, 1853- comp.
The upward path; a reader for colored children with an introduction by Robert R. Moton ... comp. by Myron T. Pritchard ... and Mary White Ovington ... New York, Harcourt, Brace and Howe [°1920]
xi, [1], 255 p. incl. front., illus. 19½cm.

1. Readers and speakers—1870- I. Ovington, Mary White, 1865- joint comp. II. Title. III. Title: Colored children, Reader for.
Library of Congress PE1126.N3P8 20—16616
Copyright A 597468 [41o1]

The urban complex.

M301.36 W37 Weaver, Robert Clifton, 1907-
The urban complex; human values in urban life [by] Robert C. Weaver. [1st ed.] Garden City, N. Y., Doubleday, 1964.
xii, 297 p. 22 cm.
Bibliographical footnotes.

1. Urbanization—U. S. 2. Urban renewal—U. S. 3. Metropolitan areas—U. S. 4. Cities and towns—Growth. I. Title.

HT123.W38 301.360973 64-15800
Library of Congress [5]

Urban misery in an American City.

M323 N78t Wright, Richard, 1909-1960.
Urban misery in an American City; juvenile delinquency in Harlem.
pp. 339-346.
In: Twice a year, ed. by Dorothy Norman. 1946.

The urban Negro in the South.

M301 C24 Carter, Wilmoth Annette, 1916-
The urban Negro in the South. [1st ed.] New York, Vantage Press [1962]
272 p. illus. 22 cm.
Includes bibliography.

1. Negroes—Raleigh, N. C. 2. Negroes as businessmen. I. Title.

F264.R1C3 301.451 62-4678 ‡
Library of Congress [5]

M301 R27u The urban Negro worker in the United States, 1925-1936.
Reid, Ira De Augustine, 1901-
The urban Negro worker in the United States, 1925-1936; An analysis of the training types, and conditions of employment and the earnings of 200,000 skilled and white-collar Negro workers. Volume I, statistics by regions, by Ira De A. Reid, Preston Valien, and Charles S. Johnson... Washington, D. C., Govt. Print. Off. 1938.
127p. tables. cm.

M331 W37 The Urban Negro worker in the United States.
Weaver, Robert Clifton, 1907-
Male Negro skilled workers in the United States, 1930-1936, by Robert C. Weaver, Administrator of survey, Ira DeA. Reid ... Preston Valien ... Charles S. Johnson ... Sponsored by United States Department of the Interior .... Washington, D.C. Govt. Print. Off., 1939.
vi, 87p. tables graphs 29cm.

Urban renewal.

M301.36 W379 Weaver, Robert Clifton, 1907-
Dilemmas of urban America [by] Robert C. Weaver. Cambridge, Mass., Harvard University Press, 1965.
ix, 138p. 21cm. (The Godkin lectures at Harvard University, 1965)

Urban renewal.

M301.36 W37 Weaver, Robert Clifton, 1907-
The urban complex; human values in urban life [by] Robert C. Weaver. [1st ed.] Garden City, N. Y., Doubleday, 1964.
xii, 297 p. 22 cm.
Bibliographical footnotes.

1. Urbanization—U. S. 2. Urban renewal—U. S. 3. Metropolitan areas—U. S. 4. Cities and towns—Growth. I. Title.

HT123.W38 301.360973 64-15800
Library of Congress [5]

Urbanization.

M301.36 W37 Weaver, Robert Clifton, 1907-
The urban complex; human values in urban life [by] Robert C. Weaver. [1st ed.] Garden City, N. Y., Doubleday, 1964.
xii, 297 p. 22 cm.
Bibliographical footnotes.

1. Urbanization—U. S. 2. Urban renewal—U. S. 3. Metropolitan areas—U. S. 4. Cities and towns—Growth. I. Title.

HT123.W38 301.360973 64-15800
Library of Congress [5]

Urhobo
see

Sobo (African people)

Colombia
MB9 Ob2u Uribe, Juan De D.
Candelario Obeso, por Juan de D. Uribe y Antonio J. Restrepo. Bogota, Imprenta de Vapor de Zalamea Hermanes, 1886.
28p. 17cm.

1. Obeso, Candelario, 1849-1884. 2. Colombia, literature in. I. Restrepo, Antonio Jose, jt. auth.

M616
W93s
Urinary organs.
Wright, Louis Tompkins, 1891-1952.
Subcutaneous injuries of the urinary tract, by Frank R. DelUca, Louis T. Wright, Lyndon M. Hill, Norman F. Laskey, and Aaron Prigot. New York, The Harlem Hospital Bulletin, 1953.
64-73p. tables 23cm.
Reprinted from The Harlem Hospital Bulletin, September 1953.

Cuba
M972.91
Ur7p
Urrutia, Gustavo E.
Puntos de vista del nuevo Negro. Conferencia del arquitecto Gustavo E. Urrutia, inaugural del ciclo de conferencias de caracter social científico y educacional, ofrecido por el instituto en su centro de estudios, pronunciada el dia de Julio de 1937.
40p. 17½cm.
1. Cuba.

Chad
M967.43
V23
Ursu, enfant de la brousse.
Valamu, Buna
Ursu, enfant de la brousse, récit. Préface du R.P. Ravier. Illustrations de Pierre Joubert. Paris, Éditions Alsatia ₑ1961ₒ
247p. illus., map. 20cm.
1. Chad - Social life and customs.
I. Title.

Uruguay
M864.6
P41m
Uruguay.
Pereda Valdés, Ildefonso, 1899–
... El negro rioplatense, y otros ensayos. Montevideo, C. García & cía, 1937.
137, ₍1₎ p., 1 l. plates. 17½cm.
CONTENTS.—Contribución al estudio del tema del negro en la literatura castellana hasta fines de la edad de oro.—Contribución al estudio de la música popular brasileña.—Supersticiones africanas del Río de la Plata.—Los pueblos negros del Uruguay y la influencia africana en el habla rioplatense.—Vocabulario de palabras de origen africano en el habla rioplatense.—El diablo mundo y Martín Fierro.—"La mojiganga de la muerte"; una pieza menor poco conocida de Calderón.—Los antiquijotes.—El "no" japonés y la tragedia griega.—Balzac, novelista de una época.—Las ideas ultraconservadoras de Chateaubriand.
1. Negroes in literature and art. 2. Negroes in South America. 3. Literature, Modern—Addresses, essays, lectures. I. Title.
39—10565
Library of Congress PQ8519.P26N4
₍42c1₎ 864.6

Argentina
M982
R73
Uruguay.
Rossi, Vicente.
... Cosas de negros; los orígenes del tango y otros aportes al folklore rioplatense. Rectificaciones históricas. Río de la Plata ₍Córdoba, Imprenta argentina₎ 1926.
436 p., 2 l., 7 p. illus. (music) 26cm.
1. Negroes in Argentine republic. 2. Negroes in Uruguay. 3. Folklore, Negro. 4. Negroes—Dancing. 5. Tango (Dance) I. Title.
27—25000
Library of Congress F3021.N3R8
₍a45d1₎

Brazil
M869.1
G142u
O Uruguay precedido de um estudo critico por Francisco Pacheco.
Gama, José Basilio da, 1740-1795
O Uruguay precedido de um es udo critico por Francisco Pacheco. Rio de Janeiro, Livraria Classica de Alves & comp., 1893.
78p. port. (front.) 16cm.

Tanganyika
M896.3
M99u
Usia wa baba na hadithi nyingine.
Mwonge, Elias G L
Usia wa baba na hadithi nyingine ₍Father's last will and other Heke stories₎ Dar es Salaam, East African Literature Bureau, 1962.
14p. illus. 18cm. (Hadith za Tanganyika, Kitabu cha Tano)
Written in Swahili.
I. Title. II. Series.

Usuman, Sheku
See
Fodio, Othman Dan.

U'Tamsi, Gerald-Félix Tchicaya
see
Tchicaya U'Tamsi, Gerald-Félix

Tanzania
M896.1
H372
Utenzi wa Abdirrahmani na Sufiyani.
Hemedi bin Abdallah bin Said, el Buhriy
Utenzi wa Abdirrahmani na Sufiyani. The History of Abdurrahman and Sufian. by Hemed Abdallah. With translation by Roland Allen and notes by J. W. T. Allen. Dar es Salaam, Eagle Press, 1961.
132p. (Johari za Kiswahili, 2)
Text in Swahili and English.

Zanzibar
M896.2
C47
Utenzi wa vita vya Uhud.
Chum, Haji, comp.
Utenzi wa vita vya Uhud. The epic of the battle of Uhud. Collected and compiled by Haji Chum. Edited, with a translation and notes, by H. E. Lambert. Dar es Sallam, East African Literature Bureau, 1962.
97p. 21-1/2cm. (Johari za kiswahili, 3)
Written in English and Swahili.
White compiler.
I. Title. II. Title: The epic of the battle of Uhud. III. Series.

Tanzania
M896.1
H372u
Utenzi wa vita Vya wadachi Kutamalaki mrima 1307 A. H.
Hemedi bin Abdallah bin Said, el Buhriy.
Utenzi wa vita Vya wadachi Kutamalaki mrima 1307 A. H.; the German conquest of the Swahili Coast, 1891 A. D. by Hemedi bin Abdallah bin said bin Abdallah bin Masudi el Buhriy. 2d ed. Translation and notes by J. W. T. Allen. Nairobi, Eagle Press, 1960.
84p. 22cm. (Johari Za Kiswahili)
Text in Swahili and English.
~~(Continued on next card)~~

MB9
H74
Utica normal and industrial institute, Utica Institute, Miss.
Holtzclaw, William Henry, 1870?–
The black man's burden, by William H. Holtzclaw ... with an introduction by Booker T. Washington ... illustrated by portraits and views. New York, The Neale publishing company, 1915.
232 p. front., plates, ports. 21cm.
Autobiography, with a history of the Utica normal and industrial institute for the training of colored young men and young women, Utica Institute, Mississippi.
1. Utica normal and industrial institute, Utica Institute, Miss. I. Title.
15—16220
Library of Congress E185.97.H75
——— Copy 2.
Copyright A 406878 ₍40h1₎

Zambia
M896.3
C43u
Uwakalema Takaleka.
Chibamba, Abraham R
Uwakalema Takaleka ₍A leopard cannot change its spots₎ (Joni Bowa na Janet Phiri). Lusaka, A. J. Levin in association with the Publications Bureau of Northern Rhodesia and Nyasaland, 1962.
59p. 18cm.
Written in Bemba.
I. Title.

Nigeria
M966.9
Uw1
Uwanaka, Charles U.
Awolowo and Akintola in political storm. Yaba, Published by the author and printed by John Okwesa and Company. ₑ1964ₒ
119p. port., 20½cm.
1. Nigeria - Politics. I. Title. 2. Awolowo, Obafemi, 1909- 3. Akintola, S L.

Nigeria
M966.9
Uz7n
Uzo, T M
The Nigerian political evolution, by T. M. Uzo... Lagos, C. M.S. Bookshops, ₑ1950ₒ.
80 p. map. 22 cm.
1. Nigeria-Pol. & govt.

Nigeria
M820.7
Uz7m
Uzodinma, Eddy C C
Shakespeare: Macbeth. Questions and answers with summaries and critical appreciation. Onitsha, Nigeria, Etudo ₑ1962ₒ
68p. 20½cm.
1. Shakespeare, William - Study.
I. Title.

Nigeria
M820.7
Uz7
Uzodinma, Eddy C C
The tragedy of Prince Hamlet. Questions and answers; running analysis and critical essay; Macbeth and Hamlet contrasted. ₑOnitsha, Nigeria, Etudo, 1963ₒ
85p. 21cm.
1. Shakespeare, William - Study.
I. Title.

Nigeria
M896.3
Uz7L
Uzoh, John E
Love shall never end. Onitsha ₑNigeria. Njoku and Sons Bookshop ₑn.d.ₒ
48p. 21½cm.
I. Title.

Martinique
M841.91
L55v
Le vagabond.
Léopold, Emmanuel-Flavia
Le vagabond, poème. Carcassonne, Gabelle, 1931.
5p. 26cm.
Il a été tiré de ce poème: 10 exemplaires sur Japon numerotés de I à X, 10 exemplaires sur Holland numérotés de 11 à 20, et 500 exemplaires sur papier Bibliophile.
Inscribed by author.

Senegal
M966.3
D62n
Valaf.
Diop, Cheikh Anta
Nations Nègres et culture. Paris, Éditions Africaines, 1955.
390p. illus. plates 25cm.

Chad
M967.43
V23

Valamu, Buna
Ursu, enfant de la brousse, récit. Préface du R.P. Ravier. Illustrations de Pierre Joubert. Paris, Éditions Alsatia ₍c1961₎
247p. illus., map. 20cm.
1. Chad - Social life and customs. I. Title.

Puerto Rico
M864
Sch6

Valdes, Gabriel de la Concepcion, 1809-1844.
Schomburg, Arthur Alfonso, 1874-1938.
Placido; an epoch in Cuba's struggle for liberty. Reprinted from The New Century. Norfolk, Va., Dec. 25, 1909.
Inscribed: "To A.B. Spingarn Esq. Many thanks for 'Darkwaters'.

M301
R27u

Valien, Preston, 1914-
Reid, Ira De Augustine, 1901-
The urban Negro worker in the United States, 1925-1936; An analysis of the training t pes, and conditions of employment and the earnings of 200,000 skilled and white-collar Negro workers, by Ira De A. Reid, Preston Valien, and Charles S. Johnson ... Washington, D.C., Govt. Print. Off., 1938.
127p. tables 31cm.
Cover title: The Urban Negro worker in the United States, 1925-1936, Volume I.

M811.08
L29c
1845

Valcour, B
Lanusse, Armand, 1812-1867, comp.
Les Cenelles, choix de poesies indigenes ... Nouvelle Orleans, Imprime par H. Lauve et compagnie, 1845.
214p. 16½cm.

M301
R27n5

Valentine, William Robert, 1879-
Reid, Ira DeAugustine, 1901-
The Negro in New Jersey; report of a survey by the Interracial committee of the New Jersey Conference of Social Work in cooperation with the state Department of Institutions and Agencies. ₍Ira DeA. Reid, director₎ ₍Newark₎ 1932.
116p. incl. front. (map) diagrs. 28cm.

Haiti
M840.09
V24p

Valmy-Baysse, Jean, 1874-
... La poésie française chez les noirs d'Haïti; conférence faite le 4 juin 1903 ... sous les auspices de la Nouvelle revue moderne. Paris, Nouvelle revue moderne ₍1903?₎
46 p., 1 l. 22½ cm.
At head of title: J. Valmy-Baysse.
With this is bound: Lespès, P. Haïti devant la France. Port-au-Prince, 1801.
1. Haitian poetry (French) 2. ~~French poetry—Haitian authors.~~ I. Title.
Library of Congress PQ3942.V3 25—24084
₍a48b½₎

Cuba
M861.5
V23

Valdes, Gabriel de la Concepcion, 1809-1844.
Poesias de Placido (Gabriel de la Concepcion Valdes) Nueva ed. Paris, Mexico, Libreria de la Vdo de Ch. Bouret, 1904.
352p. 17½cm.
1. Cuban poetry.

Trinidad
M39
V23

Valerio, Eusebio Atanasio.
Sieges and fortunes of a Trinidadian in search of a doctor's diploma. Philadelphia, Dewey and Eakins, 1909.
10-48 p. port. 21 cm.
1. Valerio, Eusebio Atanasio.

Bahamas
M332.
Sm61

Value.
Smith, James Carmichael, 1852-
Inter-temporary values; or, The distribution of the produce in time. By James C. Smith ... London, K. Paul, Trench, Trübner, & co., ltd., 1906.
2 p. l., 136 p. incl. tables. charts (1 fold.) 22ᶜᵐ.
Appendixes: A. Coinage act, 1870.—B. ₍Miscellaneous charts₎—C. Wholesale and retail prices.—D. The double monetary unit.—E. Inter-temporary value.
1. Money. 2. Value.
A 10-1897
Title from National Monetary Commission. Printed by L. C.

Cuba
MB
C12p

Valdes, Gabriel de la concepcion, 1809-1844.
Calcagno, Francisco, 1827-1903.
Poetas de color, por Francisco Calcagno. Plácido, Manzano, Rodriguez, Echemendía, Silveira, Medina. Habana, Imp. militar de la v. de Soler y compañia, 1878.
1 p. l., ₍5₎-54 p. 23½ᶜᵐ.
1. Poets, Cuban. 2. Negro authors. I. Title.
22-9233
₍84b1₎
Library of Congress PQ7380.C3

Trinidad
M39
V23

Valerio, Eusebio Atanasio.
Valerio, Eusebio Atanasio.
Sieges and fortunes of a Trinidadian in search of a doctor's diploma. Philadelphia, Dewey and Eakins, 1909.
10-48 p. port. 21 cm.

Bahamas
M332
Sm6m

Value.
Smith, James Carmichael, 1852-
Money and profit-sharing; or, The double standard money system, by Jas. C. Smith ... London, K. Paul, Trench, Trübner & co., lᵈ, 1908.
xix, 232 p. incl. tables. fold. tab., fold. diagr. 22ᶜᵐ.
1. Money. 2. Profit-sharing. 3. Currency question—Gt. Brit. 4. Value. I. Title. II. Title: Double standard money system.
9—3071
Library of Congress HG221.S62

Cuba
M972.91
C57m

Valdes, Gabriel de la Concepcion, 1809-1844.
Clavijo Tisseur, Arturo, 1886-
Mis palabras en publico, panegiricos y conferencias. Santiago de Cuba, "Editorial Ros," 1941.
156 ₍3₎p. 19½cm.

M371.974
V23

Valien, Bonita Harrison,
The St. Louis story: a study of desegregation. New York, Anti-Defamation League of B'nai B'rith, 1956.
72p. 23cm.
1. Segregation in education. 2. St. Louis - Segregation in education.

M026
V26c

Van Jackson, Wallace.
The Countee Cullen Memorial Collection at Atlanta University. Reprint from the Crisis, May 1947.
2p. 28cm.
1. Libraries--Special collection. ~~2. Countee Cullen Memorial Collection.~~
2. Atlanta. University. Trevor Arnett Library. Negro Collection. Countee Cullen Collection.

Cuba
M861.5
V23g

Valdes, Gabriel de la Concepcion, 1809-1844.
García Garófalo y Mesa, Manuel, 1887-
... Plácido, poeta y mártir. México, Ediciones Botas, 1938.
205 p., 2 l. 19ᶜᵐ.
At head of title: M. García Garófalo Mesa.
"Plácido, poeta y mártir; Plácido, dichter und martyrer, por Durama de Ochoa ₍seudónimo de₎ Eduardo Machado Gómes. Hannover—1865. Traducido del francés": p. ₍270₎-295.
1. Valdés, Gabriel de la Concepción, 1809-1844. I. Machado y Gómes, Eduardo, 1836-1877. Plácido, dichter und martyrer. II. Title.
39—8206
Library of Congress PQ7389.V3Z59
₍44c1₎ 861.59

M301
M39

Valien, Preston, 1914-
The Montgomery bus protest as a social movement.
Pp. 112-127.
In: Masuoka, Jitsuichi, ed. Race relations. Chapel Hill, University of North Carolina Press, 1961

M813.5
V34am

Van Peebles, Melvin, 1932-
Un Américan en enfer, roman. Traduit de l'American par Paule-Eugénie Truffert. Paris, Editions Denoël ₍1965₎
259p. 20½cm.
I. Title.

M326
G87a
1853

Valdes, Gabriel de la Concepcion, 1809-1844.
Griffiths, Julia ed.
Autographs for freedom. Boston, J.P. Jewett and co.; Cleveland, O., Jewett, Proctor, and Worthington; etc., 1853.
viii, 263p. incl. front. 2pl. 19½cm.
A collection of signed articles, poems, etc., by men and women prominent in the anti-slavery movement. Most of the signatures are in facsimile.
(For other editions of this title, see entries under editor's name)

M301
M39

Valien, Preston, 1914- ..., joint editor
Masuoka, Jitsuichi, 1903- ed.
Race relations: problems and theory; essays in honor of Robert E. Park. Edited by Jitsuichi Masuoka and Preston Valien. Chapel Hill, University of North Carolina Press ₍1961₎
x, 290 p. 24 cm.
Bibliographical footnotes.
1. Race problems — Addresses, essays, lectures. 2. ~~U. S.~~ — Race question—Addresses, essays, lectures. 3. Park, Robert Emory, 1868-1942. I. Valien, Preston, joint ed. II. Title.
HT1521.M29 301.451 61—66070
Library of Congress ₍62q5₎

M813.5
V34o

Van Peebles, Melvin, 1932-
Un ours pour le F. B. I. Traduit de l'american par Paule Truffert. Paris, Buchet/Chastel ₍1964₎
190p. 19½cm.
I. Title.

M811.5 J63a2
Van Vechten, Carl, 1880-
My friend: James Weldon Johnson.

(In: Fisk University. Nashville. James Weldon Johnson. Nashville. 1939. 25cm. [3]p.)

Brazil M869.3 M18se
Varias historias.
Machado de Assis, Joaquim Maria, 1839-1908.
The attendant's confession. The fortune teller. Life. [Selections from Varias historias]

(In: Goldberg, Isaac, ed. Brazilian tales. Boston, The Four Seas company, 1921. 19cm. pp. 43-104.)

M811.5 P91v
"Various Moods"
Prentice, Bessie Elizabeth
"Various Moods" with Marie. Los Angeles, n.p., c 1940
26p. port. 16½cm.
Autographed copy: "Marie Prentice. D.E.S. no. 37 Victory chapter."

M813.5 V37
Van Vechten, Carl, 1880-
Nigger heaven, by Carl Van Vechten. New York, London, A. A. Knopf, 1926.
5 p. l., 3-286 p., 1 l. 19½cm.
Autographed note on front fly leaf from Van Vechten to A.B.S. concerning the poems of Langston Hughes included in this book. Autographed presentation copy from Hughes to A.B.S. (To Arthur Spingarn, Sincerely, Langston)
I. Title.
Library of Congress PZ3.V368Ni [3] 26-15403

Haiti M841. R1v
Les variations tropicales et Les mandragores.
Roy, Herard C L.
... Les variations tropicales et Les mandragores. Port-au-Prince, Haiti, Imprimerie de l'état [193-?]
101 p. 19½cm.
Poems.
I. Title. II. Title: Les mandragores.
Library of Congress PQ3949.R75V3 [2] 841.91 42-11373

Mexico M860.4 L55
Vasconcelos, Jose, 18th cent.
León, Nicolás, 1859-
El negrito poeta mexicano y sus populares versos. Contribucion para el folk-lore nacional, por el Dr. N. Leon ... Mexico, Imprenta del Museo nacional, 1912.
234 p. front. 18½cm.
1. Vasconcelos, José, 18th cent.
Library of Congress PQ7297.L4N3 ——— Copy 2. [a28c1] 13-17185

MB9 V37s
Van Vechten, Carl, 1880-
Schuyler, George Samuel, 1895-
The Van Vechten revolution. Reprinted from Phylon, fourth quarter, 1950.

8p. 23cm.

MB W56v
Varick family (Richard Varick)
Wheeler, Benjamin Franklin, 1854-
The Varick family, by Rev. B. F. Wheeler, D. D., with many family portraits. [Mobile? Ala., °1907]
3 p. l., 5-58 p., 1 l. front., ports., geneal. tab. 16cm.
Descendants of James Varick, founder of the African Methodist Episcopal Zion church.
1. Varick family (Richard Varick) 2. Varick, James, 1750-1827?
Library of Congress CS71.V3 1907 7-21721
Copyright A 179450

M326 G87a 1854
Vashon, George Boyer, ca1820-1878.
Vincent Oge. [poem]

(In: Griffiths, Julia ed. Autographs for freedom. Auburn, Alden, Beardsley. 1854. 19½cm. Pp. 44-60).

M811.5 V27c
Vance, Hart
Cui bono? Dallas, Texas, The author, 1919

12p. 18½cm.

1. Poetry. I. Title.

MB W56v
Varick, James, 1750-1827.
Wheeler, Benjamin Franklin, 1854-
The Varick family, by Rev. B. F. Wheeler, D. D., with many family portraits. [Mobile? Ala., °1907]
3 p. l., 5-58 p., 1 l. front., ports., geneal. tab. 16cm.
Descendants of James Varick, founder of the African Methodist Episcopal Zion church.
1. Varick family (Richard Varick) 2. Varick, James, 1750-1827?
Library of Congress CS71.V3 1907 7-21721
Copyright A 179450

M220 V44h
Vass, Samuel Nathaniel, 1866-1938
How to study and teach the Bible, by S. N. Vass ... Teacher training book, National Baptist convention, U. S. A. Nashville, Tenn., Sunday school publishing board [°1922]
2 p. l., 7-633, [1] p. illus., plates, ports., maps, fold. tab. 19½cm.
1. Bible—Study. 2. Sunday-schools. I. Title.
Library of Congress BS600.V3 22-25580
Copyright A 692433 [a33c1]

M301. J63c
Vance, Rupert Bayless, ed.
Johnson, Charles Spurgeon, 1893-
The collapse of cotton tenancy. Summary of Field studies & statistical surveys, 1933-35, by Charles S. Johnson, Edwin R. Embree [and] W. W. Alexander. Chapel Hill, The University of North Carolina press, 1935.
ix p., 1 l., 81 p. 21 cm.
"Detailed investigations have been carried out by corps of students, under the direction of Dr. Rupert B. Vance and his colleagues of the University of North Carolina Institute for research in social science, and of Professor Charles S. Johnson and his associates in the Department of social science of Fisk university ... The present brief summary ... is issued for general readers."—Note.
"Selected bibliography": p. 79-81.
(Continued on next card)
[44h5] 35-25767

M813.5 B94v
Varied harvest.
Loveman, Amy, ed.
Varied harvest; a miscellany of writing by Barnard College women, edited by Amy Loveman, Frederica Barach, and Marjorie M. Mayer. New York, Putnam [1953]
304 p. 22 cm.
1. American literature (Selections: Extracts, etc.) 2. Barnard College, New York—Alumnae. I. Title.
PS508.W7L6 810.82 53—12900 ‡
Library of Congress [15]

M220 V44p
Vass, S[amuel] N athaniel, 1866-1938
Principles and methods of religious education, Nashville, Tenn. Sunday School Publishing Board, c1932.

378, 2p. illus. 20cm.

1. Religious education.

Liberia M896.3 V28c
Vanderpuije, Nii Akrampahene, 1925-
The counterfeit corpse. New York, Comet Press Books [°1956]
138 p. 21 cm.

Portrait of author on book jacket.
I. Title.
PZ4.V239Co 56-12338 ‡
Library of Congress [2]

M811.5 T59v
Varied verses.
Tomlin, J Henri
Varied verses, a book of poems, by J Henri Tomlin. Tampa. Fla., The author, c1937
92p. 16½cm.

M220 V44s
Vass, S[amuel] N athaniel , 1866-1938
The study of the New Testament, by S.N. Vass. Nashville, Tenn., Published by the Sunday School Publishing Board c1932].

197p. 19cm.

Bible N.T.
1. ~~XXXXXXXXXXX~~ 2~~XXXXXX~~ I.Title.

M811.5 V28r
Vandyne, William Johnson
Revels of fancy, by William Johnson Vandyne [two lines of verse] Boston A.F. Grant, publishers, 1891.
50p. 17½cm.
1. Poetry
I. Title

M8115 P91va
"Various moods"
Prentice, Bessie Elizabeth
"Various moods" with Marie. Volume II. Los Angeles, Burris, printer, c1944.
27p. 16cm.
cover title.

M220 V44st
Vass, S[amuel] Nathaniel, 1866-1938
The study of the Old Testament, by S.N. Vass. The Vass Leadership training series. Nashville, Tenn., Published by the Sunday School Publishing Board c1932].

228p. 19cm.

Bible O.T.
1. ~~XXXXXXXXXXXXXXXXXX~~

Vassall, William F

The origin of Christianity; a brief study of the world's early beliefs and their influence on the early Christian church, including an examination of the lost books of the Bible. [1st ed.] New York, Exposition Press [1952]

183 p. 21 cm.

1. Religions — Hist. 2. Christianity — Origin. 3. Bible. N. T. Apocryphal books—Criticism, interpretation, etc. I. Title.

BL80.V27 290 52-10685 ‡

Library of Congress [3]

Haiti
M972.94
V44e

Vastey, Pompée Valentin, *baron* de, *d.* 1820?

An essay on the causes of the revolution and civil wars of Hayti, being a sequel to the political remarks upon certain French publications and journals concerning Hayti. By the Baron de Vastey ... Tr. from the French by W. H. M. B. Exeter [Eng.] Printed at the Western luminary office, 1823.

2 p. l., ix, 249, [1], cxviii p. 21½cm.

1. Haiti—Hist.—Revolution, 1791-1804. 2. Haiti—Hist.—1804-1844. I. B., W. H. M., tr.

Library of Congress F1921.V34 10—8112

[44e1]

Haiti
M972.94
V44p

Vastey, Pompée Valentin, baron de, d.1820?

Political remarks on some French works and newspapers, concerning Haiti, by the Baron de Vastey... at Sans Couci, from the King's printing office, 1817, the 14th of Independence. Translated exclusively for the Pamphletier. London, 1818.

[165] - 239p. 21½cm.

1. Haiti. I. Title.

Haiti
M972.94
V44r

Vastey, Pompée Valentin, baron de, c.1820?

Reflexions on the blacks and whites. Remarks upon a letter addressed by M. Mazeres, a French ex-colonist, to J. C. L. Sismonde de Sismondi, containing observations on the blacks and whites, the civilization of Africa, the kingdom of Hayti, &c. Translated from the French of the Baron DeVastey by W.H.M.B. London, Sold by J. Hatchard, 190 Piccadilly, and may be had of the Booksellers in general [1817]

83p. 17cm.

1. Haiti. 2.Africa. I. Sismonde de Sismondi, J.C.L. II. Mazeres, M

Guadeloupe
M972.97
V46g

Vauchelet, Emile, 1830-1913.

La Guadeloupe ses enfants célèbres (Leonard, Lethière, Bernard, Poirie St. Aurèle), par Vauchelet. Paris, Augustin Challamel, 1894.

130p. 18cm.

1. West Indian literature. 2. Creole dialects, literature. 3. Leonard, Nicolas Germain, 1744-1793. 4. Bernard, Jean 1774-1844.

M813.5
V46

Vaught, Estella V

Vengeance is mine. New York, Comet Press, 1959.

62p. 21cm.

Portrait of author on book jacket.

I. Title.

Haiti
M840.9
V47h

Vaval, Duraciné, 1879-

Histoire de la littérature haïtienne; ou, "L'âme noire", par Duraciné Vaval ... Port-au-Prince (Haiti) Imprimerie Aug A. Héraux, 1933.

8 p. l., [5]-506 p. port. 22cm.

1. Haitian literature (French)—Hist. & crit. 2. French literature—Haitian authors. I. Title: "L'âme noire".

36-19861

Library of Congress PQ3948.H3V3

[2] 840.9

Haiti
M840.9
V44l

Vaval, Duraciné, 1879-

... La litterature Haitienne; essais critiques ... Paris, Bibliotheque Internationale d'Edition, E. Sansot,& Cie, 1911.

330p. front. 19½cm.

1. Haitian literature. I. Title.

Haiti
M841
V47s

Vaval, Duraciné, 1879-

Stances haitienes. Paris, Albert Messein, Editeur, 1912.

175p. 19cm.

1. Haitian poetry. I. Title.

Latin America
M861.08
F56a

Vaval, Duraciné, 1879- 1879-

Pp. 460-461. In -

Fitts, Dudley, 1903- ed.

Anthology of contemporary Latin-American poetry, edited by Dudley Fitts. Norfolk, Conn., New directions [1942]

ix, [2], x-xxi, 667 p. 23½ cm.

Added t.-p.: Antología de la poesía americana contemporánea.

English and original text (Spanish, Portuguese or French) on opposite pages.

"Biographical and bibliographical notes, by H. R. Hays": p. 581-641.

1. Spanish-American poetry (Collections) 2. Spanish-American poetry—Translations into English. 3. English poetry—Translations from Spanish. 4. Spanish-American poetry—Bio-bibl. I. Hays, Hoffman Reynolds. II. Title.

PQ7084.F5 861.6082 43—485

Library of Congress [54r43k^{4}7]

Vei (Negro tribe)

M910
E15

Ellis, George Washington, 1875-1919.

Negro culture in West Africa; a social study of the Negro group of Vai-speaking people, with its own invented alphabet and written language shown in two charts and six engravings of Vai script, twenty-six illustrations of their arts and life, fifty folklore stories, one hundred and fourteen proverbs, and one map, by George W. Ellis ... Introduction by Frederick Starr ... New York, The Neale publishing company, 1914.

290 p. front., plates, map. 20½cm.

1. Vei (Negro tribe) 2. Folk-lore, Vei. 3. Vei language. I. Title.

Library of Congress DT630.5.V2E6 15—1680

[42i1]

Vei language.

M910
E15

Ellis, George Washington, 1875-1919.

Negro culture in West Africa; a social study of the Negro group of Vai-speaking people, with its own invented alphabet and written language shown in two charts and six engravings of Vai script, twenty-six illustrations of their arts and life, fifty folklore stories, one hundred and fourteen proverbs, and one map, by George W. Ellis ... Introduction by Frederick Starr ... New York, The Neale publishing company, 1914.

290 p. front., plates, map. 20½cm.

1. Vei (Negro tribe) 2. Folk-lore, Vei. 3. Vei language. I. Title.

Library of Congress DT630.5.V2E6 15—1680

[42i1]

La veillée; poèmes.

Haiti
M841
An88v

Antoine, Yves.

La veillée; poèmes. [Port-au-Prince, 1964?]

62 p. port. 21 cm.

Portrait of author in book.

I. Title.

PQ3949.2.A5V4 65-46746

Library of Congress [1]

French Guiana
M841
D18v

Veillées noires.

Damas, Léon G 1912-

Veillées noires. [2. éd.] Paris, Éditions Stock, 1943.

220 p. 19 cm.

Short stories.

I. Title.

PQ2607.A425V4 843.91 A 51-100

New York. Public Libr. for Library of Congress [1]†

Brazil
MB9
M18v

Vellinho, Moysés

Machado de Assis; histórias mal contadas e outros assuntos. Rio de Janeiro, Libraria São José, 1960.

106p. 19cm.

1. Machado de Assis, Joaquim Maria, 1837-1908. I. Title.

Africa
M896.3
V54

Velten, Carl, 1862- comp.

Swahili prose texts; a selection from the material collected by Carl Velten from 1893 to 1896. Edited and translated by Lyndon Harries. London, Oxford University Press, 1965.

viii, 298 p. 22 cm.

Swahili and English.

The Swahili texts were first published in the compiler's Safari za Wasuaheli and Desturi za Wasuaheli.

~~1. Swahili literature. I. Harries, Lyndon, ed. and tr. II. Title.~~

(Continued on next card)

PL8704.A2V4 916.76 65-3830

Library of Congress [2]

Africa
M896.3
V54

Velten, Carl, 1862- comp. Swahili prose texts. 1965. (Card 2)

Partial contents.- Safari Yangu ya Bara Afrika, ya Seleman bin Mwenye Chande.- Safari Yangu ya Urusi na ya Siberia, ya Salim bin Abakari.- My journey up-country in Africa, by Selemani bin Mwenye Chande.- My journey to Russia and Siberia, by Salim bin Abakari.

White author.

1. Swahili literature. I. Harries, Lyndon, ed. and tr. II. Title.

Venda - Folk-tales.

S. Africa
M896.3
L56

Lestrade, G P

Some Venda folk-tales; edited with English translations and notes. Cape Town, The Lovedale Press, 1949.

48p. 25cm.

M326.99B
V55n

[Veney, Bethany]

The Narrative of Bethany Veney, a slave woman. With introduction by Rev. Bishop Mallalieu, and commendatory notices from Rev. V. A. Cooper and Rev. Erastus Spaulding. Worcester, Mass., 1889.

46p. front. (port.) 19½cm.

1. Slave narrative. 2. Slavery in the U.S.

Venereal diseases.

Kenya
M610
N49

Ngurungu, Sospeter Munuhe, tr.

Muceera na mukundu akundukaga o taguo [V.D. and drunkenness] [Tr. with a new preface by Sospeter Munuhue Ngurungu] Nairobi, Eagle Press, 1950.

16p. 22cm. (Taanya ũgima-inĩ. Aim at healthy living series)

Written in Kikuyu.

Venereal diseases.

M815.5
Sp4a

Spingarn, Arthur Barnett, 1878-

An address delivered before the fifteenth annual session of the National Association of Teachers in Colored Schools, at Storer College, Harper's Ferry, W.Va., August 1, 1918. August, Ga., National Association of Teachers in Colored Schools, 1918.

8p. 21cm. (National note-book series, no.1)

Reprinted for the U.S. Public Health Service

Venereal diseases.
M815.5 Spingarn, Arthur Barnett, 1878-
Sp4w The war and veneral diseases among Negroes.
(In: Social hygiene, 4:333-346, July 1918.)

Verbe noir.
Africa
M960 Achille, Louis T
Ac6a Verbe noir.
Pp. 31-44.
In: Aspects de la culture noire. 1958.

M252 **Vernon, William Tecumseh, 1871-1944**
V59u The upbuilding of a race; or, The rise of a great people, a compilation of sermons, addresses and writings on education, the race question and public affairs. By William Tecumseh Vernon ... Introduction by Rev. H. T. Johnson ... Quindaro, Kan., Industrial students printers, 1904.
4 p. l., 7-158 p. port. 21cm.
1. Negroes. I. Title.
5-17896
Library of Congress E185.5.V54
[a35b1]

Venereal diseases.
M815.5 Spingarn, Arthur Barnett, 1878-
Sp4w The war and veneral diseases among Negroes. New York, American Social Hygiene Association, 1918.
333-346p. 26cm.
Reprinted from Social Hygiene, 4:333-346, July 1918.

French Guiana
M398 **Verderosa, Constantin.**
V58 Les chaines du passé; légende en Guyane. Paris, L. Soulanges [1961]
46 p. 20 cm.
I. Title.
Illinois. Univ. Library for Library of Congress [1] A 61-4743

Veronica, a novel.
M813.5 **Sydnor, W Leon.**
Sy7v Veronica, a novel. [1st ed.] New York, Exposition Press [1956]
207 p. 21 cm.
I. Title.
PZ4.S982Ve 56-8719 ‡
Library of Congress [2]

La vengeance de la terre.
Haiti
M843.91 Cineas, Jean Baptiste
C49v ... La vengeance de la terre. Roman paysan. Port-au-Prince, Haiti, Imprimerie du College Vertieres [1933]
162p. 21cm.

The vernacular in African education.
Uganda
M967.61 Mulira, Enoch M K
M91v The vernacular in African education. London, Longmans, Green and Co., [1951]
55p. 18½cm.

Veronica my daughter.
Nigeria
M896.2 Ogali, Ogali Agu, 1931-
Oglv Veronica my daughter; a drama. Aba [Nigeria] Okeudo and Sons Press [n.d.]
40p. port. 20½cm.
Portrait of author in book.

La vengeance de Mama.
Haiti
M843.91 **Marcelin, Frédéric, 1848-1917.**
M33v ... La vengeance de Mama, roman haïtien. Paris, P. Ollendorff, 1902.
2 p. l., 276 p. 16cm.
I. Title.
25-20471
Library of Congress PQ3949.M3V4
[a44b1]

Vernacular literature.
Ghana
M496.3 Baeta, C G
B14h Hints to authors of vernacular books. London, The Sheldon Press, n.d.
24p. 16cm.
(Published with the approval of the Education Department of the Gold Coast)

Guinea Vers la liberté.
M896.1 Traore, Mamadou, 1916-
T68v Vers la liberté; poemes, [par] Ray Autra [pseud.] Pekin, Librairie du Nouveau Monde, 1961.
61p. 21½cm.
1. African poetry. I. Title.

Vengeance is mine.
M813.5 Vaught, Estella V
V46 Vengeance is mine. New York, Comet Press, 1959.
62p. 21cm.

Haiti
M843.91 **Verne, Marc.**
V59 ... Marie Villarceaux, un roman d'amour ... [Port-au-Prince] Haïti, H. Deschamps [1945]
xxii p., 1 l., 25-255 p. 20½cm. (*On cover:* Collection haïtienne)
I. Title. 1. Haitian fiction
PQ3949.V4M3 A 47-1717
New York. Public library for Library of Congress [2]†

... Vers les cimes.
Haiti
M841. Daniel, Neptune.
D22v ... Vers les cimes. [Port-au-Prince, Haiti, Imprimé à la Societé Biblique, 1946]
52p. 21cm.

The vengeance of the gods...
M323 Pickens, William, 1881-1954.
P58v The vengeance of the gods, and three other stories of real American color line life, by William Pickens ... introduction by Bishop John Hurst ... Philadelphia, Pa., The A. M. E. book concern [°1922]
125 p. 20cm.
CONTENTS.—The vengeance of the gods.—The superior race.—Passing the buck.—Tit for tat.
I. Title.
Library of Congress PZ3.P5853Ve 22-15210
——— Copy 2.
Copyright A 674947 [3]

Haiti Vernet, E Louis
M610 Le médecin Haitien discrédité par les siens,
V59 essai de combat contre une oeuvre injuste, néfaste et antipatriotique. Une réhabilitation nécessaire, à l'approche de la grande fête commémorative du 150 ème anniversaire de l'indépendance du peuple haitien. Port-au-Prince, Les Presses Libres, n.d.
40p. 21cm.
"Petite contribution aux travaux de reparations (materielles et morales) entrepris par notre gouvernement en vu des prochaines Solennites du ler Janvier 1954."
1. Haiti - medicine.

Vers une théodicée bantoue.
Congo (Léopoldville)
M200 Lufuluabo, Francois-Marie
L96 Vers une théodicée bantoue. Mechliniae, Imprimi potest, 1961.
50p. 22½cm.

Le ventre.
Congo
Brazzaville
M896.1 Tchicaya U'Tamsi, Gerald Felix
T2v Le ventre. Paris, Présence Africaine [1964]
135p. 20cm.
I. Title.

Haiti
M972.94 **Vernet, E Louis.**
V590 ... Les oubliés de chez nous, question hygiéno-sociale, par E. Louis Vernet ... [Port-au-Prince] Imprimerie A. P. Barthélemy [1945?]
6 p. l., [12]-48 p., 1 l. 20½cm. (Bibliothèque haïtienne)
1. Leprosy—Haiti. I. Title.
RC154.55.H3V4 614.546 Med 47-1314 rev
Library of Congress [r47c2]

Verse along the way.
M910 **Hershaw, Fay McKeene.**
H43v Verse along the way. [1st ed.] New York, Exposition Press [1954]
48 p. 21 cm.
I. Title.
PZ8.3.H436Ve 54-11911 ‡
Library of Congress [2]

Verse fragments.
M811.5
N51v
Nichols, James Emanuel
Verse fragments. New York, Vantage Press, 1958.
77p. 21cm.

Verses from a humble cottage.
M811.5
R43v
Ridout, Daniel Lyman.
Verses from a humble cottage, by Daniel Lyman Ridout. [Hampton, Va., Hampton institute press, 1924]
28 p. 19cm.
I. Title.
Library of Congress PS3535.I 4365V4 1924 24-18782
Copyright A 802879 [2]

Vesey, Denmark, d. 1822.
M06
Am3
no.7
Grimké, Archibald Henry, 1849-1930.
... Right on the scaffold, or, The martyrs of 1822. By Mr. Archibald H. Grimke ... Washington, D. C., The Academy, 1901.
24 p. 23cm. (American negro academy. Occasional papers, no. 7)
1. Charleston, S. C.—Slave insurrection, 1822. 2. Vesey, Denmark, d. 1822.
Library of Congress E184.N3A5 9—23294
——— Copy 2. F279.C4G9
[a35b1]

Vesey, Paul, pseud.
M811.5
A15e
Allen, Samuel W
Elfenbeinzahne; ivory tusks, gedichte eines Afroamerikaners, Von Paul Vesey. Heidelberg, Wolfgang Rothe, c1956.
47p. 24cm.

M355.11
B63o
Veterans.
Bolte, Charles G
Our Negro veterans, by Charles G. Bolte and Louis Harris. N.Y., Public Affairs Committee, 1947.
31p. graphs. 21cm.
For further reading: p.31.

Veterans.
M362.11
C63s
Cobb, William Montague, 1904-
Statement of W. Montague Cobb, representing the National Medical Committee of the National Association for the Advancement of Colored People, in opposition to S. 1414; A bill to provide for the establishment of a veterans hospital for Negro veterans at the birthplace of Booker T. Washington in Franklin County, Va., 1948.
5p. 28cm.
Mimeographed.

M355.11
M31i
Veterans.
Manhattan Medical Society.
Identical care and treatment by the federal government; An open letter to the American Legion from The Manhattan Medical Society. New York, The Society, 1932.
3-10p. 23cm.

Veterans.
M323
N21
[National Association for the Advancement of Colored People]
Veterans' handbook. New York, NAACP, n.d.
24p. 18cm.

Veterans - Employment - U.S.
M331
H86
Hudson, Roy.
Post-war jobs for veterans, negroes, women, by Roy Hudson. New York, Workers library publishers, 1944.
24 p. illus. 19cm.
1. Veterans—Employment—U. S. 2. Negroes—Employment. 3. Woman—Employment—U. S. I. Title.
A 45-2552
Harvard univ. Library for Library of Congress HD5724.H83 331.137
[3]†

Vi kan ikke vente
M323.4
K58a4
King, Martin Luther
Vi kan ikke vente [Why we can't wait] Oversat af Sophus H. Johansen. København Jespersen of Pios Forlag, 1965.
151p. 21½cm.
Written in Danish.

Viard, Ducis, ed.
Haiti
M972.94
N22h
Nau, Émile, *baron*, 1812-1860.
Histoire des caciques d'Haïti; par le baron Émile Nau. 2. éd. publiée avec l'autorisation des héritiers de l'auteur par Ducis Viard. Paris, G. Guérin et c[ie], 1894.
viii, 365 p. incl. port. plates, port., fold. map. 23cm.
"Notice biographique, Émile Nau": p. [vii]-viii.
Appendice: Géographie primitive d'Haïti; De la langue et de la littérature des aborigènes d'Haïti.—Flore indienne d'Haïti par Eugène Nau.
1. Haiti—Hist.—To 1791. 2. Botany—Haiti. 3. Indians of the West Indies—Haiti. I. Viard, Ducis, ed. II. Nau, Eugène. III. Title.
2—12695
Library of Congress F1911.N28
[37e1]

Viaud, Leonce.
Haiti
M133
Aulc
Aubourg, Michel.
Ceremony of petro rite (voodoo cult), by Michel Aubourg and Leonce Viaud. Port-au-Prince, Imp. Commerce, n.d.
8p. 17½cm.

Vibraciones, producciones poeticas.
Cuba
M861.6
R85v
Ruiz Suarez, Bernardo
Vibraciones, producciones poeticas. Habana, casa Editoria: Gutierrez y compania, [n.d.]
145p. port. 17cm.

Vibrations of my heartstrings.
M811.5
Sa9v
Savage, Eudora V
Vibrations of my heartstrings, by Eudora V. Savage. New York, The Exposition press [1944]
4 p. l., 11-94 p. 19½cm. [Poets of America. Series four]
I. Title.
44—41841
Library of Congress PS3537.A9267V5 811.5
[46c1]

Vice - Chicago.
M364
Sm42
Smith, Joseph.
Sin corner and Joe Smith; a story of vice and corruption in Chicago. Forewords by Alderman Leon M. Depres and Jack Mabley. New York, Exposition Press [1963]
119p. 21cm.

The victims.
M813.5
L513v
Lee, James F 1928-
The victims. [1st ed.] New York, Vantage Press [1959]
190 p. 21 cm.
1. Juvenile delinquency. I. Title.
PZ4.L478Vi 59-65075 ‡
Library of Congress [2]

Victims of our fear.
M808.81
M83
Morris, Tina, ed.
Victims of our fear. [Blackburn, Eng.] Screeches Publication. n.d.
[36]p. 25½cm.
Mimeographed.
White editor.

Victor, Jean Baptiste Thomas, 1823-1856.
See also
Cochinat, Victor.

Haiti
M972.94
V66v
Victor, René.
... Vues sociologiques. Port-au-Prince, Haiti, Impr. de l'État [1940]
254 p. 19cm.
Haiti - Education
1. Haiti—Civilization. 2. ~~Education—Haiti.~~ 3. Haiti—Intellectual life. I. Title.
41-20876
Library of Congress F1926.V65 917.294
[2]

Haiti
M972.94
V66v
Victor, René.
... Vues sociologiques. Port-au-Prince, Haiti, Impr. de l'État [1940]
254 p. 19cm.
1. Haiti—Civilization. 2. Education—Haiti. 3. Haiti—Intellectual life. I. Title.
41-20876
Library of Congress F1926.V65 917.294
[2]

Haiti
M398
V66v
Victor, René, *of Port-au-Prince?*
Les voix de nos rues. [Port-au-Prince, 1949]
98 p. 16 x 24 cm.
"Édition du bi-centenaire de la fondation de Port-au-Prince."
Unaccompanied melodies: p. 61-98.
Haitian folksongs Haitian folklore
1. ~~Folk-songs, Haitian.~~ 2. Cries. 3. ~~Peddlers and peddling.~~ I. Title.
M1681.H2V5 49-53968*
Library of Congress [4]

Victor.

M910
B53v

Roach, Thomas E

Victor, by Thomas E. Roach ... Boston, Meador publishing company [1943]

143 p. 20½cm.

"A story of the life and mission of the author."—Pref.

I. Title.

Library of Congress BR1725.R6A3 43-6662
[2] 922

La vie contemporaine.

Haiti
M972.94
P44v

Phareaux, Lallier C

La vie contemporaine. Port-au-Prince, Impr. de l'État, 1953.

630 p. illus. 21 cm. (Collection du Tricinquantenaire de l'Indépendance d'Haïti)

1. Haiti—Civilization. I. Title.

F1915.P5 54-34975 ‡
Library of Congress [1]

... Viejo, roman.

Haiti
M843.91
C27v

Casseus, Maurice A.

... Viejo, roman. [Port-au-Prince, Haïti; Éditions "La Presse" [1935]

2 p. l., [vii]-x, 158 p., 1 l. 21cm.

At head of title: Maurice Casseus.

I. Title.

Library of Congress PQ3949.C3V5 42-11548
[2]

The Victor Olaiya story.

Nigeria
M780
D28

Davies, Hezekiah Olufela, 1943-

The Victor Olaiya story; a biography of Nigeria's evil genous of highly life, Victor Abimbola Olaiya. [Ikeja, Nigeria, Sankey Printing Works, n.d.]

52p. illus. 18cm.
Cover title.

Haiti
M847.91
M56v

Vie d'exil.

Messac, Achille

Vie d'exil. Roman. Haiti, Port-au-Prince, 1955.

245p. 16cm.

... Viento y espuma...

Puerto Rico
M861
P17v

Palés Matos, Vicente, 1903-

... Viento y espuma, cuentos y poemas ... Mayagüez, P. R., Editorial Puerto Rico, 1945.

2 p. l., 7-252 p., 1 l. 20cm. (*Half-title:* Obras completas, vol. I)

Biblioteca Autores antillanos.
"Printed in Argentine."

I. Title.

PQ7439.P243V5 868.6 A F 47-3609
Northwestern univ. Libr. for Library of Congress [3]†

Victory.

M811.08
B73v

Braithwaite, William Stanley Beaumont, 1878- *comp.*

Victory! celebrated by thirty-eight American poets, brought together by William Stanley Braithwaite, with an introduction by Theodore Roosevelt. Boston, Small, Maynard & company [°1919]

viii, 84 p. 24cm.

1. European war, 1914-1918—Poetry. I. Title.

19-26576
Library of Congress D526.2.B66
[43q1]

Vie de Frédéric, esclave Americain.

M815.4
D73av

Douglass, Frederick, 1817-1895.

Vie de Frédéric, esclave Americain, exrite par Lui-même. Traduite de L'anglais par S.K. Parkes. Paris, Pagnerre, éditeur, 1848.

196p. 18cm.

Haiti
M841
V67c

Vieux, Isnard

La chanson du desert. Haiti, Imp. Ebcn-ozer, n.d.

56 p. 24 cm. (Collection Chants d'espoirs)

I. Title. 1. Haitian poetry.

Victory over myself.

MB9
P26

Patterson, Floyd.

Victory over myself. With Milton Gross. [New York] B. Geis Associates; distributed by Random House [1962]

244p. illus. 22cm.

La vie en blues.

MB9
W29v

Waters, Ethel, 1900-

La vie en blues (His eye is on the sparrow), by Ethel Waters et Charles Samuels. Roman traduit de l'anglais par Georges Belmont. Préface de Hugues Panassié. Paris, Robert Laffont, [1952]

381p. port. 19cm.

Le vieux piquet...

Haiti
M972.94
J26v

Janvier, Louis Joseph, 1855-

Le vieux piquet; scène de la vie haïtienne. Paris, Imp. A. Parent, A. Davy Succ., 1884.

36p. 16cm. (Bibliothèque démocratique Haïtienne)

Brazil
M869.3
L62v

...Vida e morte de M. J. Gonzaga de Sá...

Lima Barreto, Afonso Henrique de, 1881-1922.

...Vida e morte de M. J. Gonzaga de Sá... S. Paulo, Editora Brasiliense, 1956.

At head of title: Lima Barreto.
Novel
316p. port. 21cm.

Vie et aventures de John Davys.

France
M840
D89vi

Dumas, Alexandre, 1802-1870.

Vie et aventures de John Davys. Bruxelles, Meline, Cans et cie., 1840.

2 v. 15cm.

... Le vieux Port-au-Prince...

Haiti
M972.94
L16v

Lamaute, Emmanuel.

... Le vieux Port-au-Prince (une tranche de la vie haïtienne) suivi de quelques faits et dates ... Port-au-Prince, Haïti, Imprimerie de la Compagnie lithographique d'Haïti, 1939.

4 p. l., 7-256 p. front., plates (incl. music) ports. (part fold.) 22½cm.

"Errata": slip inserted.

1. Port-au-Prince, Haiti—Descr. 2. Port-au-Prince, Haiti—Soc. life & cust. 3. Port-au-Prince, Haiti—Hist.—Chronology. I. Title.

41-31912
Library of Congress F1929.P8L3
[2] 917.294

Dahomey
M960
V66

Viderot, Toussaint

A la recherche de la personnalité Négro-Africaine; Tu Gagneras ton pain à la sueuer de ton front. Monte-Carol, Éditions Regain [1960]

216p. illus. 21½cm.

1. Africa - Civilization. 2. Africa - Social Conditions. I. Title.

La vie intérieure, poèmes.

Martinique
M847.9
M32v

Maran, René, 1887-

...La vie intérieure, poèmes, (1909-1912) Paris, Edition du Beffroi, 1912.

163p. 19cm.

The view from here.

M070.432
J13

Jackson, James Edward, 1914-

The view from here. New York, Publishers New Press, [1963]

210p. 20½cm.
Portrait of author on book cover.

1. Editorials. I. The Worker. II. Title.

Dahomey
M896.2
V66p

Viderot, Toussaint.

Pour toi, nègre mon frère ... "Un homme comme les autres." [Par] Toussaint Viderot "Mensah." Monte Carlo, Éditions Regain [1960]

154 p. 19 cm.

A play.

I. Title.

A 61-4375
Illinois. Univ. Library for Library of Congress [1]

Vie et mort de Sylvia.

Brit. Guiana
M823.91
M69v

Mittelholzer, Edgar, 1909-

Vie et mort de Sylvia (The life and death of Sylvia); roman, traduit de l'anglais par Jacques et Jean Tournier. Paris, Librairie Plon, [1956]

339p. 20cm. (Feux Croises, ames et terres etrangeres)

A view from the hill.

West Indies
M823.91
F77v

Forster, Christine

A view from the hill. New York, Vantage Press [1964]

100p. 21cm.

The views and meditations of John Brown.

M811.5
W67v

Williams, Edward W.
The views and meditations of John Brown. By Edward W. Williams ... [Washington, 1893?]
16 p. 24cm.
In verse.

1. Brown, John, 1800-1859. 2. Harpers Ferry, W. Va.—John Brown raid, 1859. I. Title.
8—33640
Library of Congress E451.W72
——— Copy 2. [a40b1]

Haiti
M841
V71a

Vilaire, Etzer, 1872-1953.
...Années tendres. Le flibustier. Page d'amour, 1888-1897. Paris, Librarie Fischbacher, 1907.
XLII, 256p. port. 19½cm.
At head of title: Collection des pôetes Français de l'etranger.

1. Haitian poetry. I. Title.

Haiti
M841
V71po

Vilaire, Etzer, 1872- 1953.
... Poèmes de la mort, 1898-1905. Paris, Fischbacher, 1907.
2 p. l., xxxiv, 306 p. incl. front. (port.) 18cm. (Collection des poètes français de l'étranger ...)

I. Title. 1. Haitian poetry.
25-24082
Library of Congress PQ3949.V53P6

Haiti
M841
V71p

Vilaire, Etzer, 1872- 1953.
... Poésies complètes ... Éd. définitive. Paris, A. Messein, 1914-19.
3 v. 19cm.
CONTENTS.—t. 1. Années tendres.—t. 2. Poèmes de la mort.—t. 3. Nouveaux poèmes.

1. Haitian poetry. I. Title.
41-34576
Library of Congress PQ3949.V53 1914
[2] 841.91

Haiti
M841
V712a

Vilaire, Jean Joseph, 1881-
...Aube. Sonnets Indiens. Poesies avec une preface d'Etzer Vilaire. Paris, Librairie de Progres Vulgarisateur..., 1914.
x, 126p. 18cm.

1. Haitian poetry. I. Title.

Haiti
M843.91
V71e

Vilaire, Jean Joseph, 1881-
... Entre maîtres et esclaves; contes ... Port-au-Prince, Haiti [Imp. Telhomme] 1943.
3 p. l., 11-180 p. 21cm.
CONTENTS.—Le dernier boucan.—Avec elles.—Le retour en Afrique.—La noël de l'esclave.—Un double crime.—Après la nuit.—Ballio.—L'amour et la gloire.—La mère et la fille.—La dernière maîtresse.

I. Title. 1. Haitian fiction
44-53640
Library of Congress PQ3949.V55E5
[2] 843.91

1881-

Haiti
M841
V712p

Vilaire, Jean Joseph, 1881-
Paysages et Paysans au crepuscule du coeur. Poesies. Paris, Albert Messein, editeur. 1930.
96p. 19cm.

1. Haitian literature. I. title

Haiti
M841
V712pe

Vilaire, Jean-Joseph, 1881-
Pensées et réflexions. Port-au-Prince, Imp. de l'Etat, 1949.
182p. 15cm.

I. Title. 1. Haitian poetry

Haiti
M841
V712s

Vilaire, Jean Joseph, 1881-
Sonnets au palmiste. Les Boeufs(poème) Port-au-Prince, Aug.A. Héraux,1921.
34p. 18½cm.

1. Haitian poetry. I. Title.

S. Africa
M968
V71

Vilakazi, Absolom Lawrence, 1914-
Zulu transformations: a study of the dynamics of social change. Pietermaritzburg, South Africa, University of Natal Press, 1962.
x, 168p. maps, diagrs. 25cm.
"Originally presented as a PhD. Thesis to the University of Natal."
Bibliography: p. 163-165.
(over)

S. Africa
M896
V71a

Vilakazi, Benedict Wallet Bambatha, 1906-1947
Amal'ezulu. Johannesburg, South Africa, The University of the Witwatersrand Press, 1945.
46p. 18cm.
Poems in Zulu.

1. Zulu poetry.

S. Africa
M896
V71i3

Vilakazi, Benedict Wallet Bambatha, 1906-1947
Inkondlo kaZulu. With an Introduction by Innes B. Gumede. Fourth and new edition. Johannesburg, South Africa, Witwatersrand University Press, 1955.
63p. illus. 18cm. (Bantu Treasury #1, edited by C. M. Doke.)
Written in Zulu.

1. Poetry - Zulu. 2. Zulu - Poetry.
I. Title.

S. Africa
M896
V71nj

Vilakazi, Benedict Wallet Bambatha, 1906-1947
Nje-nempela. Mariannhill, South Africa, Mariannhill Mission Press, 1944.
218p. front. 19cm.

S. Africa
M896
V71n

Vilakazi, Benedict Wallet Bambatha, 1906-1947
Noma nini. Marianhill, South Africa, Mariannhill Mission Press, n.d. (1935).
184p. front. illus. 19cm.

1. Zulu language - Texts. I. Title.

S. Africa
M896
V71n

Vilakazi, Benedict Wallet Bambatha, 1906-1947
Zulu-English dictionary, compiled by C. M. Doke and B. W. Vilakazi. Johannesburg, Witwatersrand University Press, 1948.
xxvi, 903p. 26cm.
"The preparation of this dictionary was carried out under the auspices of the Bantu Studies Dept. of the Univ. of the Witwatersrand and the Native Education Dept., Natal."
1. Zulu lang.—Dictionaries - English.
2. Doke, Clement Martyn, 1893- jt. author

... Vilbrun Guillaume-Sam ce Méconnu.

Haiti
MB9
G94m

Mars, Jean Price, 1876-
... Vilbrun Guillaume-Sam ce Méconnu. Port-au-Prince, 1961.
175p. illus., port. 21½cm.

Haiti
M972.94
P19
V.1,no.6

Villard, Suirad
Conseils a mon pays, tolérer pour améliorer. Port-au-Prince, Imp. de l'Abeille, 1908.
36p. 19cm.

1. Haiti-Pol.& govt. - 1844-

Ville cruelle.

Cameroons
M896.3
B55v

Biyidi, Alexandre, 1932-
Ville cruelle by Eza Boto [pseud.] Paris, Editions Africaines [1955]
219p. 18½cm.

Haiti
M972.94
V74e

Vincent, Sténio, *pres. Haiti*, 1874-
... Efforts et résultats. Port-au-Prince, Haiti, Imprimerie de l'état [1938]
3 p. l., [9]-298 p., 3 l. 22cm.

1. Haiti—Pol. & govt.—1844- 2. Haiti—Soc. condit. I. Title.
30—11651
Library of Congress F1926.V76
[41c1] 972.94

Haiti
M972.94
V74

Vincent, Sténio, *pres. Haiti*, 1874-
... En posant les jalons ... Port-au-Prince, Haiti, Imprimerie de l'état, 1939.
4 v. 21½cm.
A collection of articles and addresses.
CONTENTS.—t. 1. Introduction.—t. 2. 1930-1933.—t. 3. 1934-1936.—t. 4. 1937-1939.

1. Haiti—Pol. & govt.—1844- 2. Haiti—Hist.—1844-
3. Haiti—Econ. condit. 4. Haiti—Economic policy. I. Title.
40—14254
Library of Congress F1926.V77
[42c1] 972.94

Haiti
M972.94
R44s

Vincent, Sténio, Pres. Haiti, 1874-

Rigaud, Milo, 1904-
Sténio Vincent révélé par la justice et par l'opinion publique. Port-au-Prince, H. Deschamps [1957]
97 p. illus. 27 cm.

1. Vincent, Sténio, Pres. Haiti, 1874-
A 58-2090
Florida. Univ. Library for Library of Congress [1]

M343.3
Am3v

Violence in Peekskill.
American Civil Liberties Union.
Violence in Peekskill; A report of the violations of civil liberties at two Paul Robeson concerts near Peekskill, N.Y., August 27th and September 4th, 1949. New York, ⌜1949?⌝

51p. illus. 20cm.
Original report issued in multigraphed form December, 1949.

Brazil
M869.3
Am1v

The violent land.
Amado, Jorge, 1912-
The violent land, b Jorge Amado, translated from the Portuguese (Terras do sem fim) by Samuel Putnam. New York, A. A. Knopf, 1945.

6 p. l., 335, ⌜1⌝ p. 19 cm.

"First American edition."

Virgin Islands
M641
J726

Virgin Islands.
Jones, Trandailer
Impressions of nutrition habits in the Virgin Islands. ⌜Saint Thomas, V. I.⌝ Nutrition Division, Virgin Islands Department of Health ⌜1952⌝

54p. illus. 23cm.

1. Nutrition. 2. Virgin Islands. I. Title.

Virgin Is.
M972.97
J29vi

Virgin Islands - Descr. & trav.
Jarvis, Jose Antonio, 1901-
Virgin Islands picture book, by J. Antonio Jarvis and Rufus Martin. Philadelphia, Dorrance ⌜1948⌝

118 p. illus., ports., map (on lining-papers) 24 cm.

1. Virgin Islands—Descr. & trav. I. Martin, Rufus, joint author.

F2136.J39 917.297 48-5234*

Library of Congress ⌜10⌝

Virgin Island
M822.81
J29k

Virgin Island - Drama - Slaves.
Jarvis, Jose Antonio, 1901-
The King's mandate; the story of the liberation of the Negro slaves of the Virgin Islands in 1848. Dramatized in three acts. Charlotte Amalie, Academy Limited Editions, 196?

53p. illus. 21½cm.

Virgin Is.
M811.5
G42v

Virgin Islands - Folk-lore.
Gimenez, J P , comp.
Virgin islands folklore and other poems, compiled and arranged by J. P. Gimenez. New York, Frank Harding (agent), c1933.

100, ⌜2⌝ p. 27½cm.

Virgin Is.
MB9
P67J

Virgin islands—Painters.
Jarvis, Jose Antonio, 1901-
Camille Pissarro (painter from the Virgin islands) by J. Antonio Jarvis. Charlotte Amalie, V. I., The Art league of St. Thomas ⌜1947⌝

31 p. incl. port. 20 x 15½cm.
Bibliography: p. 31.

1. *Pissarro, Camille, 1830-1903.

ND553.P55J3 927.5 47-24605

Library of Congress ⌜2⌝

Virgin Is.
M972.97
J29v

The Virgin islands and their people.
Jarvis, Jose Antonio, 1901-
The Virgin islands and their people, by J. Antonio Jarvis ... Philadelphia, Dorrance & company ⌜1944⌝

vii p., 2 l., 13-178 p. incl. front., map. plates. 19½cm.

1. Virgin islands of the United States—Descr. & trav. 2. Virgin islands of the United States—Soc. life & cust. 3. Virgin islands of the United States—Pol. & govt. I. Title.

44-7897

Library of Congress F2136.J37
⌜45n5⌝ 917.297

Virgin Is.
M811.5
G42v

Virgin islands folklore and other poems.
Gimenez, J P , comp.
Virgin islands folklore and other poems, compiled and arranged by J. P. Gimenez. New York, Frank Harding (agent), c 1933.

100, ⌜2⌝ p. 27½cm.

Virgin Is.
M972.97
J29v

Virgin islands of the United States-Descr.& trav.
Jarvis, Jose Antonio, 1901-
The Virgin islands and their people, by J. Antonio Jarvis ... Philadelphia, Dorrance & company ⌜1944⌝

vii p., 2 l., 13-178 p. incl. front., map. plates. 19½cm.

1. Virgin islands of the United States—Descr. & trav. 2. Virgin islands of the United States—Soc. life & cust. 3. Virgin islands of the United States—Pol. & govt. I. Title.

44-7897

Library of Congress F2136.J37
⌜45n5⌝ 917.297

Virgin Islands
M972.97
H556

Virgin Islands of the United States - History.
Hill, Valdemar A
A golden jubilee; Virgin Islanders on the go under the American flag, by Valdemar A. Hill, Sr. New York, Carlton Press ⌜1967⌝

174 p. 21 cm. (A Hearthstone book)
Bibliography: p. 172-174.

1. Virgin Islands of the United States—Hist. I. Title.

F2136.H57 972.97'22 68-2236

Library of Congress ⌜3⌝

Virgin Is.
M972.97
J29

Virgin islands of the United States-Hist.
Jarvis, Jose Antonio, 1901-
Brief history of the Virgin islands, by J. Antonio Jarvis ... St. Thomas, V. I., The Art shop ⌜1938⌝

258 p. front., illus. (map) plates, ports. 20cm.
Bibliography: p. 257-258.

1. Virgin islands of the United States—Hist.

38-23723

Library of Congress F2136.J36
———— Copy 2.
Copyright A 119936 ⌜5⌝ 972.97

Virgin Is.
M972.97
J29v

Virgin islands of the United States - Politics and government.
Jarvis, Jose Antonio, 1901-
The Virgin islands and their people, by J. Antonio Jarvis ... Philadelphia, Dorrance & company ⌜1944⌝

vii p., 2 l., 13-178 p. incl. front., map. plates. 19½cm.

1. Virgin islands of the United States—Descr. & trav. 2. Virgin islands of the United States—Soc. life & cust. 3. Virgin islands of the United States—Pol. & govt. I. Title.

44-7897

Library of Congress F2136.J37
⌜45n5⌝ 917.297

Virgin Is.
M972.97
J29v

Virgin islands of the United States - Social life and customs.
Jarvis, Jose Antonio, 1901-
The Virgin islands and their people, by J. Antonio Jarvis ... Philadelphia, Dorrance & company ⌜1944⌝

vii p., 2 l., 13-178 p. incl. front., map. plates. 19½cm.

1. Virgin islands of the United States—Descr. & trav. 2. Virgin islands of the United States—Soc. life & cust. 3. Virgin islands of the United States—Pol. & govt. I. Title.

44-7897

Library of Congress F2136.J37
⌜45n5⌝ 917.297

M326.99B
Ad1n

Virginia.
Adams, John Quincy, b. 1845.
Narrative of the life of John Quincy Adams, when in slavery, and now as a freeman. Harrisburg, Pa., Sieg, printer, 1872.

64 p. 11½cm.
Account of the author's experiences as a slave in Virginia before 1862.

1. Slavery in the U. S.—Virginia.

14-5640

Library of Congress E444.A2
⌜a41b1⌝

M975
N31

Virginia
Du Bois, William Edward Burghardt, 1898-
The Negroes of Farmville, Virginia: A social study. ⌜bulletin of the Labor Dept., no.14, 1898⌝ pp. 1-38.

In: The Negro in the black belt... Washington, D.C., Dept. of Labor, ⌜1897-1902⌝

M366.1
F87v

Virginia.
Freemasons. Virginia. Grand Lodge.
Minutes. 1st- 1875-
Petersburg, 18 -

v. 22cm annual.
Place of publication varies.
See holdings card for proceedings in library.

M975.5
J135

Virginia.
Jackson, Luther Porter, 1892-
... Free Negro labor and property holding in Virginia, 1830-1860, by Luther Porter Jackson ... New York, London, D. Appleton-Century company, incorporated ⌜1942⌝

xix, 8-270 p. incl. tables. 23cm.
At head of title: The American historical association.
Bibliography: p. 230-238.

1. Negroes—Virginia. 2. Freedmen in Virginia. 3. Negroes—Econ. condit. 4. Negroes—Employment. I. American historical association. II. Title.

42-25804

Library of Congress E185.93.V8J18
⌜45x5⌝ 325.2609755

M370.
J13

Virginia.
Jackson, Luther Porter, 1892-
A history of the Virginia state teachers association, by Luther P. Jackson... Norfolk, Virginia, The Guide publishing co., inc., 1937.

112p. plates. 23cm.

M266
J63

Virginia.
Johnson, James H
The pine tree mission. By James H.A. Johnson... Baltimore, J. Lanahan, 1893.
114p. port. plates. 18cm.

M975.5
M36n

Virginia.
Martin, Robert E
Negro disfranchisement in Virginia. Washington, D.C., Howard University, 1938.

49-188p. (Howard University studies in the social sciences. v.1, no.1)
Mimeographed.
Bound with Africa and the rise of capitalism by Wilson E. Williams.

Virginia.

M89
J31

Randolph, Edwin Archer, 1854–

The life of Rev. John Jasper, pastor of Sixth Mt. Zion Baptist church, Richmond, Va.; from his birth to the present time, with his theory on the rotation of the sun. By E. A. Randolph, LL. B. Richmond, Va., R. T. Hill & co., 1884.

xii, 167 p. front. (port.) 19½ᶜᵐ.

1. Jasper, John, 1812–1901. 2. Negroes—Virginia.

12–10713

Library of Congress E185.97.J39
Copyright 1884: 7138 [a26c1]

Virginia.

M975.5
R74

Roberts, Harry Walter, 1902

A study of the Sutherland community, Dinwiddie County, Virginia. A contribution on behalf of Virginia State College to a cooperative research project of the Conference of Presidents of Negro Land-Grant Colleges and the Tennessee Valley Authority. Petersburg, Virginia State College, 1959.

74p. 23cm. (Virginia State College gazette, v.65, no.3 September 1959)

1. Dinwiddie County, Virginia. 2. Virginia 3. Sutherland Community, Virginia. I. Title.

Virginia.

M973.8
T21n

Taylor, Alrutheus Ambush.

The Negro in the reconstruction of Virginia, by Alrutheus Ambush Taylor ... Washington, D. C., The Association for the study of Negro life and history [°1926]

iv, 300 p. 24½ᶜᵐ.

Bibliography: p. 287–292.

1. Negroes—Virginia. 2. Reconstruction—Virginia. I. Association for the study of Negro life and history, inc. II. Title.

27–5705

Library of Congress E185.93.V8T3
[43g1]

Virginia.

M975
N31

Thom, William Taylor.

The Negroes of Litwalton, Virginia: A social study of the Oyster Negro. [Bulletin of the Labor Dept., no.37, 1901. pp. 1115-1170.

In: The Negro in the black belt... Washington, D.C., Dept. of Labor, [1897-1902]

Virginia.

M370.
T36s

Thomasson, Maurice Ethan, 1892–

A study of special kinds of education for rural Negroes [by] Maurice E. Thomasson ... Charlotte, N. C., 1936.

vi, 104 p., 1 l., 23ᶜᵐ.

Thesis (PH. D.)—Columbia university, 1936.

Vita.

"This study was concerned with agencies which offered instruction in fields other than those ordinarily included in the regular public school program ... Researches were conducted ... in the state of Virginia."—p. 2.

Bibliography: p. [103]–104.

1. Negroes—Education. 2. Negroes—Virginia. 3. Sociology, Rural. I. Title: Education for rural Negroes. II. Title: Rural Negroes.

36–21306

Library of Congress LC2802.V8T5 1936
Columbia Univ. Libr. [37c2] 371.97409755

Virginia.

M975.5
W93

Writers' program. *Virginia.*

The Negro in Virginia, compiled by workers of the Writers' program of the Work projects administration in the state of Virginia ... Sponsored by the Hampton institute. New York, Hastings house, 1940.

xii, 380 p. plates, ports. 21ᶜᵐ.

Map on lining-papers.

Bibliography: p. 353–367.

1. Negroes—Virginia. I. Title.

40–12192

Library of Congress E185.93.V8W7
——— Copy 2.
Copyright [4] 325.2609755

Virginia-Politics and government.

M975.5
J13n

Jackson, Luther Porter

Negro office-holders in Virginia, 1865-1895, by Luther Porter Jackson ... Norfolk, Va., Guide quality press, 1945.

88p. illus. 23cm.

Virginia-Politics and suffrage.

M324
Eq2s

Equal suffrage. Address from the colored citizens of Norfolk, Va., to the people of the United States. Also an account of the agitation among the colored people of Virginia for equal rights. With an appendix concerning the rights of colored witnesses before the state courts. New Bedford, Mass., E. Anthony & sons, printers, 1865.

cover-title, 26 p. 22ᶜᵐ.

1. Negroes—Virginia—Politics and suffrage.

9–32794†

[30d1]

Library of Congress JK1929.V6E6

Virginia-Revolutionary war-Soldiers.

M350
J13
1944

Jackson, Luther Porter

Virginia Negro soldiers and seamen in the Revolutionary war, by Luther Porter Jackson... Norfolk, Va., Guide Quality press, 1944.

vi, [7]-46p. illus. 23cm.

Virginia - Rural conditions.

M975.5
EL59

Ellison, John Malcus, 1889- jt. auth.

Negro life in rural Virginia, 1865-1934, by William Edward Garnett and John Malcus Ellison. [Blacksburg, Va., Virginia Polytechnic Institute, 1934]

35p. illus., maps. 23cm. (Virginia Polytechnic Institute Bulletin 295)

1. Virginia - Rural conditions. 2. Rural conditions. I. Garnett, William Edward. II. Title.

Virginia. University. Library. Tracey W. McGregor Library.

MB9
J35

Jefferson, Isaac, *b.* 1775.

Memoirs of a Monticello slave, as dictated to Charles Campbell in the 1840's by Isaac, one of Thomas Jefferson's slaves. Edited by Rayford W. Logan. Charlottesville, Published by the University of Virginia Press for the Tracy W. McGregor Library, 1951.

45 p. port. 24 cm.

"Appeared simultaneously in the autumn 1951 William and Mary quarterly."

"Bibliographical note": p. 37–38.

1. Jefferson, Thomas, Pres. U. S., 1743–1826. 2. Monticello, Va. I. Campbell, Charles, 1807–1876. II. Virginia. University. Library. Tracy W. McGregor Library. III. Title.

E444.J4 923.173 51—13833

Library of Congress [52m5]

Virginia Negro soldiers and seamen in the Revolutionary war.

M350
J13
1944

Jackson, Luther Porter

Virginia Negro soldiers and seamen in the Revolutionary war, by Luther Porter Jackson ... Norfolk, Va., Guide Quality press, 1944.

vi, [7]-46p. illus. 23cm.

M01
H91a

Virginia State College, Petersburg.

Hunter, John McNeil, 1901- , ed.

Abstracts of masters theses... at the Virginia State College for Negroes and abstracts of research completed by members of the Virginia State College for Negroes faculty; Edited by John M. Hunter and William R. Simms. Petersburg, Virginia State College, 1941.

95p. 23cm.

Graduate research number of the Virginia State College Gazette, 47:1-95, March 1941.

M370.
J13

Virginia state teachers association.

Jackson, Luther Porter, 1892-

A history of the Virginia state teachers association, by Luther P. Jackson... Norfolk Virginia, The Guide publishing co., inc., 1937.

112p. plates. 23cm.

Virginia union university, Richmond.

M378V
V81

Fisher, Miles Mark, *ed.*

Virginia union university and some of her achievements, edited by Miles Mark Fisher ... Twenty-fifth anniversary, 1899–1924. [Richmond, Brown print shop, inc., °1924]

110 p., 1 l. incl. front., illus., ports. 28ᶜᵐ.

Bibliography: p. 110.

1. Virginia union university, Richmond.

25–6407

Library of Congress LC2851.V72F5
——— Copy 2.
Copyright A 799198 [2]

Virginia University Library. Tracy W. McGregor Library.

MB9
J35
1951

Jefferson, Isaac, b. 1775.

Memoirs of a Monticello slave, as dicated to Charles Campbell in the 1840's by Isaac, one of Thomas Jefferson's slaves. Charlottesville, Published by the University of Virginia Press for the Tracy W. McGregor Library, 1951

86p. port. 24cm.

Jamaica
M821.91
V81w

Virtue, Vivian L., 1911-

Wings of the morning. Poems by Vivian L. Virtue. Kingston, Jamaica, The New Dawn Press, 1938.

xiv, 86p. 18cm.

~~1. Poetry—Jamaica~~ 2. Jamaican poetry. I. Title.

Martinique
M841.9
M32vi

Le visage calme, stances.

Maran, René.

... Le visage calme, stances. ~~7.6d.~~... Paris, Aux éditions du Monde nouveau, 1922.

3 p. l., [3]–86, [1] p., 1 l. 19½ᶜᵐ.

"L'edition originale."

"... quatre cent cinquante exemplaire sur papier Alfa satine, ... no. 219)

I. Title.

23–6702

Library of Congress PQ2625.A74V5 1922
Copyright A—Foreign 21496
[2]

Haiti
M972.94
B94

...Visages d'arbres et de fruits haitiens.

Burr-Reynaud, Frédéric, 1884–

... Visages d'arbres et de fruits haïtiens. Port-au-Prince, Haïti [Impr. du Collège Vertières, 1940.

6 p. l., 9–218 p. front. (port.) 20½ᶜᵐ.

Errata leaf mounted on p. [2] of cover.

1. Trees—Haiti. 2. Fruit. I. Title.

44–53584

Library of Congress PQ3949.B8V5
[3] 581.97294

Haiti
M841
L56

Visages familiers.

Lescouflair, Georges

Visages familiers. Paris, Éditions d'Artrey, n.d.

103p. 19cm.

Bahamas
M821.8
B71v

The vision, and other poems.

Boyd, John.

The vision, and other poems, in blank verse, by John Boyd, a man of colour. Pub. for the author's benefit, and prefaced by some preliminary observations, by C. R. Nesbitt... Exeter, Printed by R. J. Trewman; London, Longman and co., 1834.

xix, 23, [1] p. 19cm.

A vision of life, and other poems.
M811.4
J13v
Jackson, A J
A vision of life, and other poems. By A. J. Jackson. Hillsborough, O., Printed at the Highland news office, 1869.
52p. 20cm.

Visions of the dusk.
M811.5
J632v
Johnson, Fenton, 1888–
Visions of the dusk, by Fenton Johnson ... New York, F. J. ⌜1915⌝
4 p. l., (1), 71 p. front. (port.) 16½cm. $1.00
Poems.

I. Title.

Library of Congress PS3519.O245V5 1915 15-11885
Copyright A 406052

Visits of state - U. S.
MB9
F46m
Fields, Alonzo.
My 21 years in the White House. New York, Coward-McCann ⌜1961⌝
223 p. 22 cm.
Portrait of author on book jacket.

1. Washington, D. C. White House. 2. Washington, D. C.—Soc. life & cust. 3. Presidents—U. S.—Biog. 4. Presidents—U. S.—Wives. 5. Visits of state—U. S. I. Title.

F204.W5F5 923.173 61—15068 ‡
Library of Congress ⌜62b5⌝

A visual history of Ghana.
Ghana
M966.7
M41
Mate, C M O
A visual history of Ghana; illustrated by Ann and Donald Goring. London, Evans Brothers, 1959.
64p. illus. 24½cm.

Tanganyika
M398.6
M47
Vitendawili.
Meena, E K
Vitendawili ⌜Riddles⌝ Kutoka makabila mbalilbali ya Tanganyika, kimetungwa na E. K. Meena, G. V. Mmari na H. H. Sangiwa. London, Oxford University Press, 1960.
27p. illus. 18½cm.
Written in Swahili.

1. Riddles, African. I. Mmari, G. V., jt. auth. II. Sangiwa, H. H., jt. auth. III. Title.

The vixens.
M813.5
Y46v
Yerby, Frank, 1916–
The vixens, a novel by Frank Yerby. New York, The Dial press, 1947.
347 p. 21 cm.

1. Reconstruction—Fiction. I. Title.
PZ3.Y415Vi 47—3065
© 23Apr47; Frank Yerby, Valley Stream, L. I.; A12200.

Library of Congress ⌜48k5⌝

Vocational and civic guidance for the Negro youth.
M370.
Ev2c
Everett, Faye Philip, *ed.*
The colored situation; a book of vocational and civic guidance for the Negro youth, by Faye Philip Everett ... Boston, Meador publishing company, 1936.
312 p. illus. (ports.) 20½cm.
On cover: The colored situation ⌜by⌝ Faye P. Everett & others. "Articles and books written by Dr. A. B. Jackson": p. 242-243.

1. Negroes—Employment. 2. Profession, Choice of. 3. Negroes—Moral and social conditions. I. Title. II. Title: Vocational and civic guidance for the Negro youth.

36—9272
Library of Congress E185.8.E94 ⌜4212⌝ [371.425] 325.260973

Vocational education.
M06
J61
no.22
Brawley, Benjamin Griffith, 1882–
Early effort for industrial education, by Benjamin Brawley ... ⌜Charlottesville? Va.⌝ 1923.
15 p. 23cm. (*On cover:* The Trustees of the John F. Slater fund. Occasional papers, no. 22)

1. Negroes—Education. 2. Vocational education. 23—16211
Library of Congress E185.5.J65 no. 22 ⌜35d1⌝

Vocational education..
M370.
C12v
Caliver, Ambrose, 1894–
... Vocational education and guidance of Negroes; report of a survey conducted by the Office of education, by Ambrose Caliver, senior specialist in the education of Negroes ... United States Department of the interior. Harold L. Ickes, secretary. Office of education, J. W. Studebaker, commissioner. Washington, U. S. Govt. print. off., 1938.
x, 137 p. incl. tables, diagrs. 23cm. (U. S. Office of education. Bulletin, 1937, no. 38)
At head of title: Project in vocational education and guidance of Negroes.
On p. ⌜2⌝ of cover: National survey of vocational education and guidance of Negroes.
(Continued on next card)
E 39-3 †
⌜a46d3⌝†

M306
M21p
Vocational education.
McDougald, Elise Johnson
The School and its relation to the vocational life of the Negro.
(In: National Conference of Social Work. Proceedings, 1923. Chicago University of Chicago, 1923. 22cm. p. 415-418)

Vocational education.
M360.71
Sa7v
Sargent, Harvey Owen, 1876?–1936.
... Vocational education in agriculture for negroes; recommendations for the establishment of agricultural schools and programs for Negroes. May, 1926. Issued by the Federal board for vocational education, Washington, D. C. Washington, Govt. print. off., 1926.
ix, 92 p. incl. tables, diagrs. 23cm. (U. S. Federal board for vocational education. Bulletin no. 111. Agricultural series no. 28)
"Prepared ... by H. O. Sargent."—p. ix.
1. Agricultural education. 2. Negroes⌜—Vocational⌝ education. I. Title.
E 26-235 rev
U. S. Off. of educ. Library for Library of Congress LC1045.A28 no. 111 LC1045.A25 no. 111 ⌜r36f2⌝

...Vocational education and guidance of Negroes... 1938.
M370.
C12v
Caliver, Ambrose, 1894–
... Vocational education and guidance of Negroes; report of a survey conducted by the Office of education, by Ambrose Caliver, senior specialist in the education of Negroes ... United States Department of the interior. Harold L. Ickes, secretary. Office of education, J. W. Studebaker, commissioner. Washington, U. S. Govt. print. off., 1938.
x, 137 p. incl. tables, diagrs. 23cm. (U. S. Office of education. Bulletin, 1937, no. 38)
At head of title: Project in vocational education and guidance of Negroes.
On p. ⌜2⌝ of cover: National survey of vocational education and guidance of Negroes.
(Continued on next card)
E 39-3 †
⌜a46d3⌝†

...Vocational education in agriculture for negroes;
M360.71
Sa7v
Sargent, Harvey Owen, 1876?–1936.
... Vocational education in agriculture for negroes; recommendations for the establishment of agricultural schools and programs for Negroes. May, 1926. Issued by the Federal board for vocational education, Washington, D. C. Washington, Govt. print. off., 1926.
ix, 92 p. incl. tables, diagrs. 23cm. (U. S. Federal board for vocational education. Bulletin no. 111. Agricultural series no. 28)
"Prepared ... by H. O. Sargent."—p. ix.
1. Agricultural education. 2. Negroes⌜—Vocational⌝ education. I. Title.
E 26-235 rev
U. S. Off. of educ. Library for Library of Congress LC1045.A28 no. 111 LC1045.A25 no. 111 ⌜r36f2⌝

Vocational guidance.
M136.77
B87f
Bullock, Ralph W.
Fundamental needs of Negro boys and young men, by Ralph W. Bullock, ⌜New York, 1933⌝
34p. 17½cm.

Vocational guidance.
M304
P19
v.7
No.30
Hill, T Arnold.
The problem of self in vocational adjustment. by T. Arnold Hill. Reprinted from Opportunity, April 1932.
1p. 29cm.

Vocational guidance.
M304
P19
v.7
no.25
National urban league
After the depression - What? Statement of the purposes and plans of the third vocational opportunity campaign to improve the status of Negro workers. New York City, National urban league 1932
4p. 28cm.

Vocational guidance.
M304
P19
v.7
no.5
National ruban league
The right vocation; program helps for high schools and colleges participating in the vocational opportunity campaign, April 17-24, 1932. New York, National urban league 1932.
4p. 24½cm.

M304
P19
v.7, no.26
Vocational guidance.
National urban league
Vocational mindedness, a statement of the purpose and plans of the vocational opportunity campaign to improve the status of Negro workers. New York, National urban league ⌜1931⌝
4p. 28cm.

M370
N213m
Vocational guidance.
National Urban League. Dept. of Industrial Relations.
My vocation, with special reference to the problems faced by Negro youth. New York, nd
16p. 19cm.

Vocational guidance - Bibliography.
M304
P19
v.7
no. 28
National urban league.
Vocational guidance: bibliography. New York, National urban league, 1932.
9p. 28cm.
Mimeographed.

Nigeria
M896.3
Ok1v
The voice.
Okara, Gabriel
The voice, a novel. ⌜London⌝ A. Deutsch ⌜1964⌝
157p. 19cm.
Portrait of author on book jacket.

A voice from bleeding Africa...

Liberia
M966.6
B62r
Blyden, Edward Wilmot, 1832-1912.
A voice from bleeding Africa, on behalf of her exiled children, by Edward W. Blyden. Liberia, G. Killian, printer 1856.

33p. 20cm.

A voice from Harper's Ferry.

M326.
An2
Anderson, Osborne Perry, 1830-1872.
A voice from Harper's Ferry. A narrative of events at Harper's Ferry; with incidents prior and subsequent to its capture by Captain Brown and his men. By Osborne P. Anderson, one of the number. Boston, Printed for the author, 1861.

72 p. 19ᶜᵐ.

1. Brown, John, 1800-1859. 2. Harpers Ferry, W. Va.—John Brown raid, 1859. I. Title.

5—34829

Library of Congress E451.A55
——— Copy 2. [40g1]

A voice from the South.

M323.41
C78
[Cooper, Anna Julia (Haywood)] 1859–
A voice from the South. By a black woman of the South. Xenia, O., The Aldine printing house, 1892.

3 p. l., iii p., 1 l., [9]–304 p. front. (port.) 18ᶜᵐ.

CONTENTS.—Womanhood a vital element in the regeneration and progress of a race.—The higher education of woman.—"Woman vs. the Indian."—The status of woman in America.—Has America a race problem; if so, how can it best be solved?—The Negro as presented in American literature.—What are we worth?—The gain from a belief.

1. Negroes. 2. U. S.—Race question. 3. Women in the U. S. I. A black woman of the South. II. Title.

12—2877

Library of Congress E185.6.C77
[a43r37g1]

The voice in the wilderness.

M370.
H24v
Harris, Marquis LaFayette, 1907–
The voice in the wilderness, by M. LaFayette Harris ... Boston, The Christopher publishing house [°1941]

xi, 13-149 p. 19ᶜᵐ.

1. Education—Philosophy. 2. Education, Higher. 3. Negroes—Education. I. Title.

41—9851

Library of Congress LC2801.H3
[45e1] 370.1

The voice of coloured labour.

Trinidad
M330
P13v
Padmore, George, 1903- ed.
The voice of coloured labour; Speeches and reports of colonial delegates to the world trade union conference, 1945. Manchester, Panaf Service [1945]

55p. 22cm.

The voice of God.

M252
C36
Chappelle, E. E.
The voice of God. New York, Carlton Press [1963]
119p. 20½cm.

Voice of Humanity.

M811.5
P429v
Perry, John Sinclair.
Voice of humanity; song of the New World. Boston, Christopher Pub. House [1952]

46 p. 21 cm.

I. Title.

PS3531.E69V6 811.5 52-26306 ‡

Library of Congress [1]

The voice of Mizraim.

M811.5
P16v
Paisley, John Walter.
The voice of Mizraim, by John Walter Paisley. New York and Washington, The Neale publishing company, 1907.

122 p. 19ᶜᵐ.

Poems.

I. Title.

7-38904

Library of Congress PS3531.A29V6 1907
Copyright A 190329 [a36b1] 811.5

M071
V87
Voice of the fugitive, v.1-2, Jan. 1851-Dec. 1852. Sandwich, Canada West, 1851-52.

2v. 49cm. semi-weekly.
H. Bibb, editor.
52 no. in 2v. lacks: v.2, no.6,7,8.

1. Newspapers. 2. Slaves, Fugitive.

M071
V87
Voice of the fugitive. Sandwich, Canada West.

Volume	Year	Month	Volume	Year	Month
v.1-	1851	Jan-Dec.			
v.2	1852	Jan-Dec. Lacks nos. 6,7,8.			

The voice of the Negro, 1919.

M323
K45
Kerlin, Robert Thomas, 1866–
The voice of the Negro, 1919, by Robert T. Kerlin ... New York, E. P. Dutton & company [°1920]

xii p., 1 l., 188 p. front. (ports.) 19½ cm.

"A compilation from the colored press of America for the four months immediately succeeding the Washington riot. It is designed to show the Negro's reaction to that and like events following, and to the world war and the discussion of the treaty."—Pref.

1. Negroes. 2. U. S.—Race question. I. Title.

20—13609

Library of Congress E185.61.K4
[45e1]

Virgin Is. Voice of the Virgin Islands.
M811.5
G42vo
Gimenez, Joseph Patrick.
Voice of the Virgin Islands. Philadelphia, Dorrance [1952]

50 p. 20 cm. (Contemporary poets of Dorrance, 440)

I. Title.

PS3513.I 7V6 811.5 53-5901 ‡

Library of Congress [2]

Ghana
M896.8
V87v
Voices of Ghana; literary contributions to the Ghana broadcasting system 1955-57. Accra, Government Printer, 1958.

266p. 21½cm.

1. Literature - Africa. 2. African Anthology.

Voices of Ghana.

M808.8
N42
v.15
New world writing. 1st-
Apr. 1952-
[New York, New American Library.
v. 18 cm. (N. A. L. Mentor books)

1. Literature, Modern—20th cent. 2. American literature—20th cent.

PN6014.N457 808.8 52—1806

Library of Congress [54j5]

The voices of Negro protest in America.

M323.4
B93
Burns, W Haywood.
The voices of Negro protest in America. With a foreword by John Hope Franklin. London, New York, Oxford University Press, 1963.

88 p. 19 cm.

"Issued under the auspices of the Institute of Race Relations, London."
Bibliography: p. [86]-88.

1. Negroes—Civil rights. 2. U. S.—Race question. I. Title.

E185.61.B96 323.40973 63-6378

Library of Congress [5]

Jamaica
M821.91
M97v
Voices of spring.
Musson, Flora Elaine
Voices of spring. Port-au-Spain, B.W.I., Guardian Commercial Printery, 1943.

39p. port. 23cm.

Jamaica
H823.91
H35v
Voices under the window.
Hearne, John, 1925–
Voices under the window. London, Faber and Faber [1955]

168 p. 20 cm.

I. Title.

Full name: John Edgar Caulwell Hearne.

PZ4.H435Vo 55-58526 ‡

Library of Congress [2]

Voix d'Afrique... échos du monde.

Senegal
M808.8
D67
Diboti, Max Ekoka, ed.
Voix d'Afrique ... échos du monde; livre de lecture, cours moyen classes terminales [par] M. Diboti Ekoka [et] Richard Dogbeh. Illustrations de Tanguy de Rémur. Paris, Librairie Istra [1965]

255p. illus. 21½cm.

1. Readers and speakers - Text-books - Africa. 2. French language - Readers and speakers - Africa. I. Dogveh, Richard, jt. ed. II. Title.

Voix dans le soir.

Haiti
M841
P54v
Philoctete, Raymond
Voix dans le soir; poèmes. Port-au-Prince, Edition "La Semeuse," 1945.

20p. 21cm.

Les voix de nos rues.

Haiti
M398
V66v
Victor, René, *of Port-au-Prince?*
Les voix de nos rues. [Port-au-Prince, 1949]

98 p. 16 x 24 cm.

"Édition du bi-centenaire de la fondation de Port-au-Prince."
Unaccompanied melodies: p. 61-98.

1. Folk-songs, Haitian. 2. Cries. 3. Peddlers and peddling. I. Title.

M1681.H2V5 49-53968*

Library of Congress [4]

Voix du centenaire, poèmes héroiques.

Haiti
M972.94
P19
V.1,no.9
Chevry, Arsène
Voix du centenaire, poèmes héroiques. Port-au-Prince, Imp. de l'Abeille, 1904.

49p. 19cm.

M808.81 Vojáka, Knihovna, comp.
V85 Černošska poesie; světová antologie. Praha, Naše Vojsko, 1958.

371p. illus. 21cm.
Biographies: pp. 361-371.
Czech translations.
White author.

1. Poetry - Anthologies.

Haiti Voodooism.
M972.94 [Holly, Arthur C]
H72du Les daimons du culte voudo par l'ésotériste haïtian Her-Ra-Ma-El (Dr. Arthur Holly). Port-au-Prince, Haiti, 1919.

xi, 522p. 23cm.

Voodooism.
Haiti Mars, Jean Price-, 1876–
M398. ... Ainsi parla l'oncle...; essais d'ethnographie. [Port-
M35 au-Prince, Imprimerie de Compiègne, 1928.

8 p. l., iv, 243 p. illus. (incl. map, facsims., music) 25cm. (Bibliothèque haïtienne)

"Errata": 2 p. inserted.
"Bibliographie": p. [237]-239.

1. Folk-lore—Haiti. 2. Ethnology—Haiti. 3. Haiti—Soc. life & cust. 4. Voodooism. 5. Ethnology—Africa. I. Title.

33—13308

Library of Congress GR121.H3M3
[47d1] 398.097294

Martinique Volancoes.
M972.98 Miller, James Martin, 1859–1939.
M61m The Martinique horror and St. Vincent calamity, containing a full and complete account of the most appalling disaster of modern times ... by J. Martin Miller ... in collaboration with Hon. John Stevens Durham ... Philadelphia, National publishing co. [1902]

8, 17-560 p. 2 front., illus., plates, ports., maps. 23½cm.

Issued also under the title: True story of the Martinique and St. Vincent calamities ... by Prof. John Randolph Whitney.

1. La Soufrière, St. Vincent—Eruption, 1902. 2. Pelée, Mont—Eruption, 1902. 3. St. Vincent. 4. Volcanoes. I. Durham, John Stevens, 1861– joint author. II. Title.

2-17542

Library of Congress F2081.M64
[a44f1]

Haiti Voodooism.
M972.94 Holley, Arthur
H72d Les daimons du culte voudo, par l'estériste Haitien Her-Ra-Ma-El (Dr. Arthur Holly). Port-au-Prince, Haiti, Imp. Edmond Chenet, 1918.

xi, 523p. 23cm.

Voodooism.
Haiti
M972.94 Mars, Louis
M352c ...La crise de possession dans le voudou, essais de psychiatrie comparee [by] Louis Mars... Port-au-Prince, Haiti, Imprimerie de l'Etat, 1946.

XV, 103p. 20cm. (Bibliotheque de l'Institut d'Ethnologie de Port-au-Prince).

Réunion Vollard, Ambroise
M89 Souvenirs d'un marchand de tableaux.
V88 Édition revue et augmentée. Paris, Albin Michel, 1937.

458p. illus. 21cm.

I. title

Voodooism
Haiti
M972.94 Holley, Arthur
H72d Les daimons du culte voudo, par l'esotériste Haitien Her-Ra-Ma-El (Dr. Arthur Holly). Port-au-Prince, Haiti, Imp. Edmond Chenet, 1918

xi, 523p. 23cm.

Haiti Voodooism.
M133 Rigaud, Milo, 1904–
R44 La tradition voudoo et le voudoo haïtien: son temple, ses mystères, sa magie. Photos. de Odette Mennesson-Rigaud. Paris, Niclaus, 1953.

433 p. illus., port., map. 23 cm.

1. Voodooism. 2. Folk-lore—Haiti. I. Title.

BL2490.R53 133.4 53—33161

Library of Congress [54c1]

Les volontaires de 1814.

M812:3 Séjour, Victor, 1816-1874.
Se4 Les volontaires de 1814; drame en cinq,
no.3 actes et quatorze tableaux. Paris, Michel Lévy Frères, 1862.

130p. 19cm.

Voodooism.

M810 Hurston, Zora Neale.
H94mu Mules and men, by Zora Neale Hurston; with an introduc-
1936 tion by Frank Boas ... 10 illustrations by Miguel Covarrubias. Philadelphia, London, Kegan, Paul, Trench, Trubner, 1936.

342, [1] p. front., illus., plates. 22cm.

Contents.—pt. I. Folk tales.—pt. II. Hoodoo.—Appendix. I. Negro songs with music (p. 309-[331]) II. Formulae of hoodoo doctors. III. Paraphernalia of conjure. IV. Prescriptions of root doctors.

1. Folk-lore, Negro. 2. Voodooism. 3. Negroes—Florida. 4. Negroes—Louisiana. 5. Negro songs. I. Title.

35—18525

Library of Congress GR103.H8
[45f2] 398.09759

Voorhees, Lillian Welch, ed.

M811.08 The Brown thrush, anthology of verse by Negro students ...
B81 Bryn Athyn, Pa., Claremont, Calif., Lawson-Roberts publishing company [°1932–

v. illus. 23cm.

Vol. 1, edited by Lillian W. Voorhees, Robert W. O'Brien; v. 2, edited by Helen M. O'Brien, Lillian W. Voorhees, Hugh M. Gloster.
Vol. 2, published Memphis, Tenn., The Malcolm-Roberts publishing co.

1. College verse. 2. Negro poetry (American) I. Voorhees, Lillian Welch, ed. II. O'Brien, Robert Welch, ed. III. O'Brien, Helen M., ed. IV. Gloster, Hugh Morris, ed.

32—18258

Library of Congress PS591.N4B67
——— Copy 2.
Copyright A 52920 [37r36e1] 811.50822

Voltaique.
Senegal
M896.3 Ousane, Sembene.
Ou8v Voltaique; nouvelles. [Paris] Présence Africaine [1962]

204p. 20cm.

Voodooism.

M810 Hurston, Zora Neale.
H94mu Mules and men, by Zora Neale Hurston; with an introduction by Frank Boas ... 10 illustrations by Miguel Covarrubias. Philadelphia, London, J. B. Lippincott company, 1935.

342, [1] p. front., illus., plates. 22cm.

Contents.—pt. I. Folk tales.—pt. II. Hoodoo.—Appendix. I. Negro songs with music (p. 309-[331]) II. Formulae of hoodoo doctors. III. Paraphernalia of conjure. IV. Prescriptions of root doctors.

1. Folk-lore, Negro. 2. Voodooism. 3. Negroes—Florida. 4. Negroes—Louisiana. 5. Negro songs. I. Title.

35—18525

Library of Congress GR103.H8
[45f2] 398.09759

M812.5 Voteur, Ferdinand.
V94m My unfinished portrait; drama in three acts and seven scenes. Boston, Bruce Humphries [°1951]

78 p. 24 cm.

I. Title.

PS3543.O98M9 812.5 52-14695 ‡

Library of Congress [3]

Voodoism.
Haiti
M133 Aubourg, Michel.
Aulc Ceremony of petro rite (voodoo cult), by Michel Aubourg and Leonce Viaud. Port-au-Prince, Imp. Commerce, n.d.

8p. 17½cm.

Voodooism.

M810 Hurston, Zora Neale.
H94te Tell my horse, by Zora Neale Hurston. Philadelphia, New York [etc.] J. B. Lippincott company [°1938]

301 p. front., plates, ports. 22cm.

Illustrated lining-papers.
"Songs of worship to voodoo gods" (words and music) : p. 279-301.

1. Jamaica—Soc. life & cust. 2. Haiti—Soc. life & cust. 3. Haiti—Pol. & govt.—1844– 4. Voodooism. 5. Negroes in Haiti. I. Title.

38—27034

Library of Congress F1886.H87
[44f2] 917.292

Voteur, Ferdinand.
M812.5 A right angle triangle. The prince and the singer. By
V94r Ferdinand Voteur. [New York, Ardsley publishing company, °1938]

4 p. l., 11-213 p. 20½cm.

Plays.

I. Title. II. Title: The prince and the singer.

39-11806

Library of Congress PS3543.O98R5 1938
——— Copy 2.
Copyright D pub. 62936 [2] 812.5

Haiti Voodooism.
M972.94 Denis, Lorimer
D95e ...Evolution stadiale du vodou by Lorimer Denis and Francois Duvalier. Port-au-Prince, Haiti, Imprimerie de l'etat, 1944.

28p. 23cm.

Voodoism.
Haiti
M133 Marcelin, Milo.
M33m Mythologie vodou (rite rada) I; préface de F. Morisseau Leory; illustration de Hector Hyppolite. Port-au-Prince, Les Éditions Haitiennes, 1949.

139p. illus. 23½cm.

Voting.

M324 Clayton, Edward Taylor, 1921–
C579 The Negro politician, his success and failure [by] Edward T. Clayton. With and introd. by Martin Luther King, Jr. Chicago, Johnson Pub. Co., 1964.

xiv, 213p. 22cm.

Voting.
M324 Ross, Hilliard Franklin
R73e The election of 1936, by Hilliard Franklin Ross. New York, N.Y. The author 1936.
36p. 22cm.

Liberia Voyages and travels.
M966.6 Blyden, Edward Wilmot, 1832-1912.
B62f From West Africa to Palestine. By Edward W. Blyden, M.A. Freetown, Sierra Leone, T.J. Sawyer; [etc., etc.] 1873.
viii, [9]-201p. front. 22cm.

Voyages and travels.
M910 Tomas, Ros. i J 1926-
T59 This America is also my country. New York, Pageant Press [1965]
131p. 21cm.
Portrait of author on book jacket.
1. Voyages and travels. I. Title.

Voting
see also
Politics and suffrage

Voyages and travels.
MB9 Dean, Harry, 1864-
D34 p The Pedro Gorino; the adventures of a Negro sea-captain in Africa and on the seven seas in his attempts to found an Ethiopian empire; an autobiographical narrative by Captain Harry Dean, with the assistance of Sterling North. Boston and New York, Houghton Mifflin company, 1929.
xvi, 262 p. illus. 22½cm.
1. Seafaring life. 2. Voyages and travels. 3. Africa, South. I. North, Sterling, 1906- II. Title.
29-6322
Library of Congress G530.D4
[a44u1]

Voyages and travels.-1950-
M910 Adams, Effie Kaye.
Ad17 Experiences of a Fulbright teacher. Boston, Christopher Pub. House [1956]
215 p. 21 cm.
1. Pakistan—Descr. & trav. 2. Voyages and travels—1950- 3. Teachers, Interchange of. I. Title.
DS379.A6 *915.47 56—2860 ‡
Library of Congress [57g5]

Voting restrictions in the 13 southern states.
M324 Committee of Editors and Writers of the South.
C73v Voting restrictions in the 13 southern states. Atlanta, the Committee, 1944.
[12]p. illus. graphs. 23cm.

Voyages and travels.
MB9 Harrison, Juanita.
H24m My great, wide, beautiful world, by Juanita Harrison; arranged and prefaced by Mildred Morris. New York, The Macmillan company, 1936.
xii p., 1 l., 318 p. 20½cm.
"Condensed version first appeared in the 1935 autumn numbers of the Atlantic monthly."—Pref.
1. Voyages and travels. I. Morris, Mildred, ed. II. Title.
Library of Congress G463.H33 36—27252
[43i2] 910.4

Voyages and travels- 1951 -
MB9 Schuyler, Philippa Duke.
Sc8a Adventures in black and white. Foreword by Deems Taylor. [1st ed.] New York, R. Speller [1960]
302 p. illus. 22 cm.
An account of the author's travels in sixty countries.
1. Voyages and travel—1951- I. Title.
ML417.S42A3 927.8 60-9609 ‡
Library of Congress [10]

Haiti Vouillon, Francis.
M972.94 Etheart, Liautaud, 1826-1888.
Et3v La verite A. M. Vouillon. Port-au-Prince, Imp. R. Etheart, 1884.
120p. 22cm.

Voyages and travels.
M910 Hershaw, Fay McKeene.
H43s Some aspects of post-war travel. Boston, Christopher Pub. House [1950]
81 p. illus. 21 cm.
CONTENTS.—Bermuda in color.—Europe in reconstruction.—Australia.—Some common questions.
1. Voyages and travels. I. Title.
G463.H56 910 50-14358
Library of Congress [3]

Voyages around the world.
M910 Hershaw, Fay McKeene.
H43 a Around the world with Hershaw and Collins, by Fay McKeene Hershaw and Flaurience Sengstacke Collins. Boston, Meador publishing company, 1938.
151 p. incl. front., illus. 20½cm.
1. Voyages around the world. I. Collins, Mrs. Flaurience Sengstacke, joint author. II. Title.
Library of Congress G440.H53 38-7307
——— Copy 2.
Copyright A 115275 [3] 910.4

Haiti Vox Nigri.
M841 Roker, Samuel J
R74 Vox Nigri. Port-au-Prince, Editions Panorama, 1963.
31p. 22cm.
"To Mr. Roy Wilkins who deeply loves his race and the Negroes all over the world. Cordially from the author, Port-au-Prince, June 27, 1963."
1. Haitian poetry. I. Title.

Voyages and travels.
Haiti
M910 Lescouflair, Georges, 1882-
L56m Mon vieux carnet; voyages--pensees--considerations--journal 1927. Montreal, Beauchemin, 1958.
178p. 16½cm.

Voyages around the world.
M910 Paynter, John H.
P29 Joining the navy; or, Abroad with Uncle Sam. By Jno. H. Paynter ... Hartford, Conn., American publishing company, 1895.
298 p. front., plates, ports. 20½cm.
1. Voyages around the world.
[29c1] 5-38244†
Library of Congress G440.P34

Senegal Un voyage au Senegal.
M916.63 Tall, Ibra
T145 Un voyage au Senegal. [Tanger, Editions Marocaines et Internationales, 1965.]
[70]p. 15cm.

Voyages and travels.
Congo, Leopoldville
M910 Malula, Jos
M29 Congo-Belgique. [Bruxelles, Ultramure, 1953]
46p. illus. port. 21½cm.
Portrait of author in book.

M813.5 Vroman, Mary Elizabeth.
V96e Esther, a novel. New York, Bantam Books [1963]
154 p. 18 cm.
"J2590."
I. Title.
PZ4.V984Es 63-14175
Library of Congress [2]

Voyages and travels.
Blyden, Edward Wilmot, 1832-1912.
M915.69 From West Africa to Palestine. By Edward W. Bly-
B62 den, M. A. Freetown, Sierra Leone, T. J. Sawyer; [etc., etc.] 1873.
viii, [9]-201 p. front. 22cm.
Printed in Great Britain.
1. Palestine—Descr. & trav. 2. Voyages and travels. I. Title.
15-1109
Library of Congress G490.B7

Voyages and travels.
MB9 Smith, Amanda (Berry) 1837-1915.
Sm5 An autobiography; the story of the Lord's dealings with Mrs. Amanda Smith, the colored evangelist; containing an account of her life work of faith, and her travels in America, England, Ireland, Scotland, India and Africa, as an independent missionary. With an introduction by Bishop Thoburn ... Chicago, Meyer & brother, 1893.
xvi, 17-506 p. front., plates, ports. 20½cm.
1. Evangelistic work. 2. Voyages and travels.
14-18153
Library of Congress BV3785.S56A3 1893
[34b1]

M371.85 Vroman, Mary Elizabeth.
V966 Shaped to its purpose: Delta Sigma Theta—the first fifty years. New York, Random House [1965]
x, 213 p. 22 cm.
1. Delta Sigma Theta. I. Title.
LJ145.D58V7 371.856 64-8777
Library of Congress [3]

...Vues sociologiques.
M972.94 V66v
Victor, René.
... Vues sociologiques. Port-au-Prince, Haiti, Impr. de l'État [1940]
254 p. 19cm.

1. Haiti—Civilization. 2. Education—Haiti. 3. Haiti—Intellectual life. I. Title.

41-20876
Library of Congress F1926.V65
[2] 917.294

Wait till next year; the life story of Jackie Robinson.
M B9 R56w
Rowan, Carl Thomas.
Wait till next year; the life story of Jackie Robinson, by Carl T. Rowan with Jackie Robinson. New York, Random House [1960]
339 p. illus. 24 cm.
Portrait of author on book jacket.

1. Robinson, John Roosevelt, 1919- I. Title.

GV865.R6R64 927.96357 60-5566 ‡
Library of Congress [61f15]

Africa
M896.1 W137
Wake, Clive, ed.
An anthology of African and Malagasy poetry in French. London, Oxford University Press, 1965.
179p. 18½cm.
White editor.

1. African poetry. 2. Malagasy poetry. I. Title.

Africa
M960 Am3
Wachuku, Jaja A.
The relation of Amsac and the American Negro to Africa and Pan-Africanism.
Pp. 361-376.
In: American Society of African Culture. Pan-Africanism reconsidered. Berkeley, University of California Press, 1962.

Waiters.
M641 C15h
Campbell, Tunis G
Hotel keepers, head waiters, and housekeepers' guide. Boston, Print. by Coolidge and Wiley, 1848.
192 p. illus. 12 cm.

1. Waiters. 2. Cookery, American. I. Title.

TX925.C3 47-28726*
Library of Congress [1]

Wake, Clive, jt. comp.
Senegal
M896 Se5p
Senghor, Léopold Sédar, 1906-
Prose and poetry. Selected and translated by John Reed and Clive Wake. London, Oxford University Press, 1965.
181p. 18½cm.
Includes bibliography.

1. African literature. I. Title. II. Reed, John, comp. III. Wake, Clive, jt. comp.

Senegal
M330 W11
Wade, Abdoulaye
Économie de l'ouest Africain (Zone Franc); unité et croissance. [Préface de Henri Bartoli] Paris, Présence Africaine, 1959.
371p. diagrs., tables. 21½cm

1. Africa, West - Economic conditions. I. Title.

Waiters.
M642 H71m
Holland, Edwin Clifford
The modern waiter, a formula for correct and perfect dining room service. The waiter's criterion, by E.C. Holland... Columbus, Ohio, Lutheran book concern, 1920.
89p. front, illus. 19½cm.

Barbados
M796.358 W14
Walcott, Clyde
Island cricketers. London, Hodder and Stoughton, [1958]
188p. port. illus. 19½cm.

1. Cricket.

Wages-New York (City)
M323.2 H33n
Haynes, George Edmund, 1880-
The Negro at work in New York city; a study in economic progress, by George Edmund Haynes ... New York, 1912.
2 p. l., 7-150 p. incl. tables, diagrs. 25cm.
Thesis (PH. D.)—Columbia university, 1912.
Vita.
Published also as Studies in history, economics and public law, ed. by the Faculty of political science of Columbia university, vol. XLIX, no. 3, whole no. 124.
"Select bibliography": p. 154-156.

1. Negroes—New York (City) 2. Labor and laboring classes—New York (City) 3. Wages—New York (City) I. Title.

12-28454
Library of Congress E185.93.N56H41
Columbia Univ. Libr. 326.073
[45b1]

The waiters.
M813.5 F539 1954
Fisher, William
The waiters. New York, New American Library, 1954.
223p. 18cm. (Signet books, 1907)
Pocket book edition.
"Complete and unabridged."

Kenya
M967.62 W139
Wako, Daniel M
Akabaluyia bemumbo [Customs of the Western Abaluyia people of the Nyanza Province, Kenya] [Illus. by Oren Libuko] Kampala, Eagle Press, 1954.
64p. map. illus. 21cm. (Custom and tradition in East Africa)
Written in Luyia.

1. Kenya - Native races. I. Title. II. Series.

Senegal
M966.3 D63
Wages - Senegal.
Diouf, Coumba N'Doffène
La question des salaires au Sénégal, 1965; notes et commentaires mis en ordre et présentés par Coumba N'Doffène Diouf, Georges Vermot-Gauchy et Charles Francis Brun. [Dakar] Librairie Clairafrique [1966]
82p. illus. 24cm. (Dossiers Africains, no. 2)

The waiters.
M813.5 F539
Fisher, William, 1909-
The waiters. [1st ed.] Cleveland, World Pub. Co. [1953]
295 p. 21 cm.

I. Title.

PZ4.F537Wai 52-13237 ‡
Library of Congress [3]

St. Lucia
M821.91 W14c
Walcott, Derek, 1930-
The castaway and other poems. London, Jonathan Cape [1965]
62p. 22½cm.

I. Title.

Waggumbulizi.
Uganda
M967.61 N87w
Nsimbi, Michael B
Waggumbulizi. Eyawandiika; Omugaso gw' Okugunjulwa, Siwa Muto Lugero, Olulimi Oluganda, Muddu Awulira. Kampala, Uganda Bookshop, 1952.
111p. illus. 18½cm.

I. Title. 1. Uganda

Guyana
M823.91 H24wa
The waiting room.
Harris, Theodore Wilson
The waiting room. London, Faber, 1967.
80 p. 19 cm. 18/-
(B 67-9763)

I. Title.

PZ4.H318Wai 68-77319
Library of Congress [3]

St. Lucia
M821.91 W14i
Walcott, Derek, 1930-
In a green night, poems 1948-1960. London, Jonathan Cape [1962]
79p. 21cm.

1. Poetry - St. Lucia. 2. St. Lucia - Poetry. I. Title.

Wagoner, Isabella

See

Truth, Sojourner

Wakaima and the clay man...
Uganda
M398 K12
Kalibala, Ernest Balintuma.
Wakaima and the clay man, and other African folktales, by E. Balintuma Kalibala and Mary Gould Davis. Illustrated by Avery Johnson. New York, Toronto, Longmans, Green & co. [1946]
6 p. l., 145 p. incl. illus., plates. front. 21cm.
"First edition."

1. Tales, African. I. Davis, Mary Gould, 1882- joint author. II. Johnson, Avery F., 1906- illus. III. Title.

46-3687
Library of Congress PZ8.1.K13Wak
[47u5]

St. Lucia
M822.91 W142i
Walcott, Derek, 1900-
Ione; a play with music. [Mona, Jamaica] Extra-mural Dept., University College of the West Indies [1957?]
55 p. 22 cm. (Caribbean plays, no. 8)

I. Title. (Series)

A 57-6627
Florida. Univ. Library for Library of Congress [1]

Trinidad
M822.91 Walcott, Derek, 1900-
H55 Malcauchon or the six in the rain.

Pp. 149-174.

In: Hill, Erroll G., ed. Caribbean plays, v.2. Mona, Jamaica, Mona, University of the West Indies, 1965.

St. Lucia
M822.91 Walcott, Derek, 1900-
W14s The sea at dauphin. [Jamaica] Extra-Mural Dept., University College of the West Indies, 1958.

23p. 21cm. (Caribbean plays no. 4)

I. Title.

St. Lucia
M821.91 Walcott, Derek, 1900-
W14s Selected poems. New York, Farrar, Straus [1964]

x, 85 p. 22 cm.

Portrait of author on book jacket.

I. Title.

PR6045.A26A17 1964 821.914 64-17912

Library of Congress [5]

M811.4 Walden, Islay, 1849-1884.
W14 Walden's miscellaneous poems, which the author desires to dedicate to the cause of education and humanity. 2d ed. Washington, published by the author, 1873.

96p. 15cm.

1. Poetry. I. Howard University, Washington, D. C.

Waldo, Samuel Putnam, 1780- 1826.

MB 9
H33m
Haynes, Lemuel, 1753-1833.

Mystery developed; or, Russell Colvin, (supposed to be murdered,) in full life: and Stephen and Jesse Boorn, (his convicted murderers,) rescued from ignominious death by wonderful discoveries. Containing, I. A narrative of the whole transaction, by Rev. Lemuel Haynes, A. M. II. Rev. Mr. Haynes' sermon, upon the developement of the mystery. III. A succinct account of the indictment, trial and conviction of Stephen and Jesse Boorn. 2d ed. Hartford: Published by William S. Marsh, R. Storrs.... printer. 1820.

48 p. 22½cm.

(Continued on next card)

[35d1] 2-6202

Waldron, Eric D. The Negro Exodus from the South.

M323
T41
Three articles on the Negro problem. Should the color line go? by Hon. Robert Watson Winston; The Negro's greatest enemy, by Marcus Garvey; The Negro Exodus from the South, by Eric D. Waldron. New York, Universal Negro Improvement Association, 1924.

29p. 22cm.

M304 Waldrond, Eric D.
P19 The Negro exodus from the South; In:
V.5, no.15 Three articles on the Negro problem. (Published in current history magazine, Sept. 1923) p. 23-29.

M323
T41

1. Migration

a.e.t.

M306 Waldron, John Milton, 1863-
N212 The problem's solution.

(In: National Negro Conference. Proceedings. New York, [1909] p. 159-166.)

A walk in the night.

Africa, South
M896.3 La Guma, Alex.
L11 A walk in the night. Ibadan, Nigeria, Mbari Publications [n.d.]

90p. 21½ cm.

I. Title.

South Africa A walk in the night and other stories.
M896.3 La Guma, Alex.
L11w A walk in the night, and other stories. London, Heinemann, 1967.

[8], 136 p. 20½ cm. 18/- (B 67-12615)

I. Title.

PZ4.L178Wal 4 67-112215

Library of Congress [2]

Walker, Barbara K.

Nigeria
M398
Id2n
Idewu, Olawale.

Nigerian folk tales as told by Olawale Idewu and Omotayo Adu. Told to and edited by Barbara K. and Warren S. Walker. Text decorations by Margaret Barbour. New Brunswick, N. J., Rutgers University Press [1961]

113 p. 22 cm.

1. Tales, Nigerian. I. Adu, Omotayo. II. Walker, Barbara K. III. Walker, Warren S.

GR360.N5 I 3 398.2 61-10268 ‡

Library of Congress [62l5]

M814.4 Walker, Charles Thomas, 1858- 1921
W15f ...Forty years of freedom. The American Negro: his hindrances and progress. Philadelphia, Christian banner print, 1903.

32p. 15cm.

At head of title: Address by Rev. C.T. Walker...

I. Title

M304 Walker, Charles Thomas, 1858-1921
P19 The Negro Problem. Its scriptural
v.3, no.1 solution, by Rev. Charles T. Walker, delivered at Tabernacle Baptist Church, Augusta Georgia, Sunday, June 4, 1893. Augusta, Ga., Chronicle Job Printing Co., 1893.

16p. 23cm.

1. Sermons.

M304 Walker, C[harles] T[homas] 1858-1921
P19 Reply to William Hannibal Thomas.
v.5, no.3 An address by Rev. C.T. Walker... [lacks imprint]

31p. port. 23cm.

1. Thomas, William Hannibal, 1843-

Walker, Charles Thomas, 1858-1921 - The church as a medium for race expression

M323
T69
Negro Christian student conference. *Atlanta*, 1914.

The new voice in race adjustments; addresses and reports presented at the Negro Christian student conference, Atlanta, Georgia, May 14-18, 1914. A. M. Trawick, editor ... Pub. by order of the executive committee of the conference. New York city, Student volunteer movement [1914]

1 p. l., [v]-vi p., 1 l., 230 p. 23½cm.

"Best books on the Negro in America and Africa": p. 221-224.

1. Negroes—Congresses. 2. U. S.—Race question. I. Trawick, Arcadius McSwain, 1869- ed. II. Title.

A 15-837

Springfield. Public library for Library of Congress E185.5.N38

[a35f1]

Walker, Charles Thomas, 1858-1921 - How we may improve our colored churches in the country

M323
T69
Negro Christian student conference. *Atlanta*, 1914.

The new voice in race adjustments; addresses and reports presented at the Negro Christian student conference, Atlanta, Georgia, May 14-18, 1914. A. M. Trawick, editor ... Pub. by order of the executive committee of the conference. New York city, Student volunteer movement [1914]

1 p. l., [v]-vi p., 1 l., 230 p. 23½cm.

"Best books on the Negro in America and Africa": p. 221-224.

1. Negroes—Congresses. 2. U. S.—Race question. I. Trawick, Arcadius McSwain, 1869- ed. II. Title.

A 15-837

Springfield. Public library for Library of Congress E185.5.N38

[a35f1]

Walker, Charles Thomas, 1858-1921

MB9
W15
Floyd, Silas Xavier, 1869-

Life of Charles T. Walker, D. D., ("The black Spurgeon".) pastor Mt. Olivet Baptist church, New York city. By Silas Xavier Floyd, A. M. With an introduction by Robert Stuart MacArthur, D. D. Nashville, Tenn., National Baptist publishing board, 1902.

193 p. illus. (incl. ports.) 19½cm.

1. Walker, Charles Thomas, 1858-

22-6806

Library of Congress BX6455.W3F5

[40c1]

M813.5 Walker, Claudius Roland.
W147L The legacy of a bet. New York, Carlton Press, 1962.

149p. 20cm. (A Geneva book)

Portrait of author on book jacket.

I. Title.

M813.5 Walker, Claudius Roland
W147s Sabih. New York, Carlton Press [1965]

147p. 21cm.

Portrait of author on book cover.

I. Title.

M813.5 Walker, Constance Warrick
W15d Dee-Dee and the monkeys; a little girl's adventure. New York, Exposition Press, 1959.

27p. illus. 21cm.

Portrait of author on book jacket.

I. Title.

Ethiopia
M963 Walker, Craven Howell, 1878-
W15a The Abyssinian at home, by C.H. Walker. London, The Sheldon Press, 1933.

xii, 220p. 19cm.

White author.

"This book is a translation of Amharic notes, which are the statements of natives..."

I. Title. 1. Ethiopia - Social life & Cust.

M326
W15
1829
Walker, David, 1785-1830.
Walker's appeal, in four articles, together with a preamble to the colored citizens of the world, but in particular, and very expressly to those of the United States of America. Written in Boston, in the state of Massachusetts, Sept. 28, 1829. Boston, Published by David Walker, 1829.
76p. 22cm.
First edition.
Bound with Walker's appeal... 2d ed., 1830.

M326
W15
1829
Walker, David, 1785-1830.
Walker's appeal, ... Boston, 1829. (card 2)
Association copy: William Lloyd Garrison. Autographed by Francis Jackson Garrison. 125 Highland St., Roxbury 1888.
For other editions of this title, see entries under author's name.
1. Slavery in the U.S. - Controversial literature - 1830.

M326
W15
1829
Walker, David, 1785-1830.
Walker's appeal, in four articles, together with a preamble, to the colored citizens of the world, but in particular, and very expressly to those of the United States of America. Written in Boston, in the state of Massachusetts, Sept. 28, 1829. 2d ed. with corrections, & c. by David Walker, 1830.
9-96p. 22cm.
Includes: An address to the slaves of the United States, by Henry Highland Garnet, p. ₍89₎-96.
Bound with Walker's appeal... 1st ed. 1829.

M326
W15
1830
2d. ed.
Walker, David, 1785-1830.
Walker's appeal, in four articles, together with a preamble, to the colored citizens of the world, but in particular, and very expressly to those of the United States of America. Written in Boston, in the state of Massachusetts, Sept. 28, 1829. 2d ed. with corrections, & c. Boston; Published by David Walker, 1830.
80p. 21½cm.

M326
W15
1830
3rd ed.
Walker, David, 1785-1830.
Walker's appeal, in four articles; together with a preamble, to the coloured citizens of the world, but in particular, and very expressly, to those of the United States of America, written in Boston, State of Massachusetts, September 28, 1829. 3rd and last ed. with additional notes, corrections & c. Boston: Revised and published by David Walker, 1830.
88p. 22cm.

Walker, David, 1785-1830. Walker's appeals, in four articles; together with a preamble, to the coloured citizens of the world.
M326
W15
1965
Aptheker, Herbert, 1915-
One continual cry; David Walker's Appeal to the colored citizens of the world, 1829-1830, its setting & its meaning, together with the full text of the third, and last, edition of the Appeal. New York, Published for A. I. M. S. by Humanities Press ₍1965₎
150 p. 22 cm.
Bibliography: p. 149-150.
1. Slavery in the U. S.—Controversial literature—1830. I. Walker, David, 1785-1830. Walker's appeal, in four articles; together with a preamble, to the coloured citizens of the world. II. Title.
E446.W2A6 301.4522 65-16708
Library of Congress ₍8₎

M285
W15
Walker, James Garfield
Presbyterianism and the Negro, by Rev. James Garfield Walker... Greensboro, N.C. ₍n.p., n.d.₎
92p. front. 23cm.
~~1. Presbyterians.~~ I Title
2. Churches.
1. Presbyterian Church in the U.S.A.

M811.5
W152b
Walker, James Robert.
Be firm my hope. New York, Comet Press Books ₍1955₎
114 p. 23 cm.
Poems.
I. Title.
PS3545.A486B4 811.5 55-8496 ‡
Library of Congress ₍2₎

M811.5
W152me
Walker, James Robert.
Menus of love. New York, Carlton Press, 1963.
130p. 20cm. (A Lyceum book)
Portrait of author on book jacket.
1. Poetry. I. Title.

M811.5
W152m
Walker, James Robert.
Musings of childhood. New York, Comet Press Books, 1960.
115p. 21cm.
Portrait of author on book jacket.
1. Poetry. I. Title.

M811.5
W152s
Walker, James Robert
Speak nature. New York, Carlton Press ₍1965₎
122p. 21cm.
I. Title.

Walker, Joseph E p. 89-92
M378A1
D29p
Davis, Walker Milan, 1908-
Pushing; forward; a history of Alcorn A. & M. college and portraits of some of its successful graduates, by W. Milan Davis... Okolona, Miss., The Okolona industrial shhool, 1938.
x, 124 p. illus, (incl. ports.) 23½cm

Walker, Maggie Lena.
MB 9
W15d
₍Dabney, Wendell Phillips₎ 1865-
Maggie L. Walker and the I. O. of Saint Luke; the woman and her work. Cincinnati, O., The Dabney publishing co. ₍1927₎
137 p. front., plates, ports. 19½cm.
1. Walker, Maggie Lena. 2. Independent order of Saint Luke.
44-50462
Library of Congress E185.97.W13D3
₍2₎

M811.5
W153
Walker, Margaret, 1915-
For my people, by Margaret Walker, with a foreword by Stephen Vincent Benét. New Haven, Yale university press, 1942.
58 p. 24½cm. (*Half-title:* The Yale series of younger poets, ed. by S. V. Benét. ₍41₎)
Poems.
"Portrait on jacket"
I. Title. 1. Poetry.
A 42-4985
Yale univ. Library for Library of Congress PS3545.A517F6
₍45q4₎† 811.5

M813.5
W153j
Walker, Margaret, 1915-
Jubilee. Boston, Houghton Mifflin, 1966.
xiii, 497 p. map (on lining papers) 22 cm.
Portrait of author on book jacket.
I. Title.
PZ4.W1814Ju 66-11916
Library of Congress ₍66c25₎

MB9
W15h
Walker, Thomas Calhoun, 1862-1953.
The honey-pod tree; the life story of Thomas Calhoun Walker. New York, J. Day Co. ₍1958₎
320 p. illus. 21 cm.
I. Title.
E185.97.W133A3 923.473 58-10117 ‡
Library of Congress ₍58f5₎

M323
T69
Walker, Thomas Calhoun, 1862-1953.
How we may improve our colored churches in the country.
(In: Negro Christian Student Conference. Atlanta, 1914. The new voice in race adjustments; addresses and reports ... New York, Student Volunteer Movement, 1914. 23½cm. p. 139-145).

M910
W15h
Walker, Thomas Hamilton Beb, 1873-
History of Liberia, by Thomas H. B. Walker ... Boston, The Cornhill publishing company ₍1921₎
xx p., 1 l., 175 p. incl. front. plates, ports. 18½cm.
1. Liberia—Hist.
22-1383
Library of Congress DT631.W3
——— Copy 2.
Copyright A 654227 ₍41d1₎

M813.5
W15j
Walker, Thomas Hamilton Beb 1873-
J. Johnson; or, "The unknown man"; an answer to Mr. Thos. Dixon's "Sins of the fathers." By Thos. H. B. Walker ... De Land, Fla., The E. O. Painter printing co. ₍1915₎
3 p. l., 192 p. front., plates. 19cm. $1.00
1. Dixon, Thomas, 1864- The sins of the father. II. Title.
15-16777
Library of Congress PZ3.W1482J
Copyright A 411057

M910
W15p
Walker, Thomas Hamilton Bob 1873-
The presidents of Liberia. A biographical sketch for students. Containing biographies of the presidents and some of the leaders in the making of the republic. With portraits, by Thos. H. B. Walker ... Jacksonville, Fla. ₍Mintz printing co.₎ 1915.
4 p. l., 11-96, ₍7₎ p. incl. plates, ports. 19½cm. $1.25
1. Liberia—Presidents. I. Title.
15-8010
Library of Congress DT636.A3W3
——— Copy 2.
Copyright A 398286

Walker, Warren S.
Nigeria
M398
Id2n
Idewu, Olawale.
Nigerian folk tales as told by Olawale Idewu and Omotayo Adu. Told to and edited by Barbara K. and Warren S. Walker. Text decorations by Margaret Barbour. New Brunswick, N. J., Rutgers University Press ₍1961₎
113 p. 22 cm.
1. Tales, Nigerian. I. Adu, Omotayo. II. Walker, Barbara K. III. Walker, Warren S.
GR360.N5 I 3 398.2 61-10268 ‡
Library of Congress ₍62i5₎

M811.5
W154e

Walker, William
Poem book no.8 of everyday life poetry, by William Walker... Chicago, Ill., Wm. Walker, c1942.

16p. port. 22cm.

1. Poetry.

M811.5
W154ed

Walker, William
Poem book number ten by W.M. Walker... Chicago. Ill., The author, c1943.

20p. front. 21cm.

1. Poetry.

M811.5
W154t

Walker, William
This race of mine, by William Walker... Chicago, Ill., Wm. Walker, c 1938.

28p. port. 21½cm.

1. Poetry. I. Title

M811.5
W154a

Walker, William
Walker's no.2 all occasion poem book, every day life poetry, by William Walker... Chicago, William Walker [c1944]
206p. front. 19½cm..

1. Poetry

M811.5
W154el

Walker, William
Walker's book no.9 of everyday life poetry [by] Wm. Walker. Chicago. Ill., Wm. Walker, c1943.

16p. port. 21½cm.

1. Poetry.

M815.5
W154c

Walker, William.
Walker's complete book of welcome address and response for all occasion... Chicago, Ill., The author, c 1944.
31p. port. 21cm.

1. Orations.

M323
Su6

Walker, William O
Speech.

Pp. 17-25.

In: Summit Meeting of National Negro Leaders, Washington, D.C. Report. Washington, National Newspaper Publishers Association, 1958.

Wallace, Daniel Webster, 1860-1939.

MB9
W15b

Branch, Hettye (Wallace)
The story of "80 John," a biography of one of the most respected Negro ranchmen in the Old West. [1st ed.] New York, Greenwich Book Publishers [1960]

59 p. 22 cm.

1. Wallace, Daniel Webster, 1860-1939. 2. Cattle trade—Mitchell Co., Tex. 3. Ranch life.

F392.M6B7 60-11709 ‡

Library of Congress [5]

Jamaica
M821.91
W15r

Wallace, George B.
Random reveries, by George B. Wallace. With an introduction by Hon. B. H. Easter.. Jamaica n.p. 1944.

95p. 20½cm.

1. Jamaica Poetry. I. Title.

M812.5
W15

Wallace, Richetta G (Randolph)
Mount Olivet yesterday and today, a panorama in five acts. n.p. 1953.

28p. 25cm.
"Presented May 1953 ... in celebration of Mount Olivet's Seventy-fifth Anniversary. Inscribed by author.

1. Mount Olivet Baptist Church - Drama

M378
W15c

Wallace, William James Lord, 1908–
... Chemistry in Negro colleges, by William J. L. Wallace ... [Institute, W. Va., 1940]
34 p. tables. 22½cm. (West Virginia state college bulletin ... Ser. no. 2. Apr. 1940)

Contribution no. 3 of the Research council, West Virginia state college. Publications of West Virginia state college.

1. Chemistry — [Study and] teaching—[Universities and colleges] 2. Universities and colleges — U. S. — Curricula. 3. Negroes — Education. I. Title. II. Title: Negro colleges.

E 40-353 Revised

U. S. Off. of educ. Library for Library of Congress QD40.W26 [r44c2]† 540.71173

Waller, Emily Mary, tr.

France
M840
D89a2

Dumas, Alexandre, 1802-1870.
My memoirs, by Alexandre Dumas, tr. by E. M. Waller, with an introduction by Andrew Lang ... With a frontispiece. New York, The Macmillan company, 1907-09.

6 v. fronts. (v. 3-4, 6: ports.) 20cm.

Printed in Great Britain.
"The translator has, in the main, followed the edition published at Brussels in 1852-56, in the preface to which the publishers state that they have printed from 'le manuscrit autographe' of the author."

I. Waller, Emily Mary, tr. II. Lang, Andrew, 1844-1912.

8-3121

Library of Congress PQ2230.A8W3 [45h1]

South Africa
M896.4
W15

Wallis, S J comp. and ed.
Inkolo namasiko A-Bantu [Bantu beliefs and customs] Prize essays in Xosa. Edited and prepared for press by S. J. Wallis. London, Society for Promoting Christian Knowledge [1930]

92p. 19cm.
"Essays...written by Natives of South Africa in open competition for prize offered by S.P.C.K.

(Continued on next card)

South Africa
M896.4
W15

Wallis, S J comp and ed.
Inkolo namasiko A-Bantu [1930] (Card 2)

Contents.- Ubukumkani Bamandulo Kwa-Xosa [by] Isaac Tshefu.- Intsingiselo Yenkolo Yakwa-Xosa Ku-Yise [by] John Solilo.- Ukuzibon-akalisa Kuka-Moya Oyingcwele Nomesebenzi Wake Eku-Lungiseleni Abantu I-Vangeli [by] E. F. Daniel.- Ukucinga Kwabantsundu Ngentlalo Yompefumlo Emva Kokufa [by] A. D. Nyoka.- Ukudlelana Kobu-Kristu Namasiko Olwaluko Lwabantu Abantsundu [by] James A. Calata.-

(Continued on next card)

South Africa
M896.4
W15

Wallis, S J comp. and ed.
Inkolo namasiko A-Bantu [1930] (Card 3)

Contents - Continued.
Ukufana Kobu-Kristu Namasiko Olwendo Lwesintu [by] Victor Harold Lokwe.- Ubugqira Kwa-Ntu [by] Sol Makeba.- Imbalana Ngo-Ntu [by] John Solilo.½ Ukukubekisa Kobu-Gqwira Entla-Lweni Yobu-Kristu [by] Elda Blanche Ntsonkota.

Walls, Mary E., joint author.

M973
C67

Coleman, Joseph E
Another chosen people—American Negroes, by Joseph E. Coleman and Mary E. Walls. Philadelphia, 1961 [°1962]
118 p. 23 cm.
Includes bibliography.

1. Negroes—Hist. I. Walls, Mary E., joint author. II. Title.

E185.C65 1962 63-41131 ‡

Library of Congress [2]

MB9
P93

Walls, William Jacob, bp., 1885–
Joseph Charles Price, educator and race leader, by William Jacob Walls. Boston, The Christopher publishing house [1943]
xx p., 1 l., 23-568 p. plates, ports. 20½cm.
Bibliography: p. 537-549.

1. Price, Joseph Charles, 1854-1893.

43-7960

Library of Congress E185.97.P9W3 [45f1] 923.773

M231
W62

Walls, William Jacob, 1885–
Why I believe there is a God.

Pp. 42-48.

In: Why I believe there is a God. Chicago, Johnson Pub. Co., 1965.

The walls of Jericho.

M813.5
F53w

Fisher, Rudolph, 1897–
The walls of Jericho, by Rudolph Fisher ... New York & London, A. A. Knopf, 1928.
5 p. l., 3-307, [1] p. 19½cm.

I. Title.

28-13899

Library of Congress PZ3.F5367Wa [41e1]

M811.08
W166

Walrond, Eric, 1898– comp.
Black and unknown bards; a collection of Negro poetry, selected by Eric Walrond and Rosey Pool. Kent [England] The Hand & Flower Press [1958]
43p. 21cm.

1. Poetry. I. Pool, Rosey, jt. comp. II. Title.

M810.8
Am29

Walrond, Eric, 1898–
City love.

(In: The American caravan, 1927. New York, The Macaulay company, 1927. 24cm. pp. 485-493).

M812.5 Walrond, Eric, 1898-
B29e Introduction.

(In: Basshe, Emanuel Jo. Earth, a play in seven scenes. N.Y., The Macaulay company, c1927. p. vii-xiii.)

M813.5 **Walrond, Eric, 1898-**
W16t Tropic death, by Eric Walrond. New York, Boni & Liveright, 1926.

282, [1] p. 19½cm.

CONTENTS.—Drought.—Panama gold.—The yellow one.—The wharf rats.—The palm porch.—Subjection.—The beach pin.—The white snake.—The vampire bat.—Tropic death.

I. Title. 26—18164

Library of Congress PZ3.W166Tr
——— Copy 2.
Copyright A 940614 [89d1]

M813.5 Walrond, Eric, 1898-
W16w The wharf rats.
Pp. 237-250.

In: Copy, 1927. New York, D. Appleton, 1927.

I. Title

M811.3 **Walser, Richard Gaither, 1908-**
H78a The black poet; being the remarkable story (partly told my [sic] himself) of George Moses Horton, a North Carolina slave, by Richard Walser. Drawings by Claude Howell. New York, Philosophical Library [1966]

vii, 120 p. illus. 22 cm.
White author.
Includes poems of George Horton.

1. Horton, George Moses, 1798?-ca. 1880. I. Title.

PS1999.H478Z9 66-18817

Library of Congress [8]

M306 Walters, Alexander, 1858-1917.
N212 Civil and political status of the Negro.

(In: National Negro Conference. Proceedings. New York, [1909] p. 167-173)

M39 Walters, Alexander, 1858-1917.
W17 My life and work, by Alexander Walters ... New York, Fleming H. Revell company [c1917]
272p. front. 21cm.

1. Afro-American Council. 2. A.M.E. Zion Church.

M329.3 Walters, Alexander, 1858 - 1917-
W17r Reasons why the Negro should vote the Democratic ticket in this campaign. By Alexander Walters... [n.p., n.p., n.d.]
16 [1] p. illus. 19cm.
1. Democratic party.

M910 Walton, Lester Aglar, 1882-1965
W17r Remarks of the Hon. Lester A. Walton... at cornerstone laying of the American Legation, Monrovia, Liberia, December 24, 1939. Monrovia, Liberia, The Lone Star Publishing co.

3p. 15cm.

M910 Walton, Lester Aglar, 1882-1965
W17e Education; Commencement address delivered to the members of the graduating class of Liberia College, Monrovia, November 30, 1938. Monrovia, Liberia, Weekly Mirror, [1938].

8p. 22cm.

1. Liberia--Education.

M813.5 **Wamble, Thelma.**
W18 All in the family. [1st ed.] New York, New Voices Pub. Co. [1953]
190 p. 23 cm.

I. Title.

PZ4.W243A1 53-23305 ‡

Library of Congress [3]

Wand of noble wood.
Nigeria
M896.3 Nzekwu, Onuora, 1928-
N98w Wand of noble wood. London, Hutchinson, 1961.

208p. 19cm.

Wannenburgh, Alf, 1936-
Africa, South
M896.3 Rive, Richard, 1931- ed.
R52 Quartet; new voices from South Africa: Alex La Guma, James Matthews, Alf Wannenburgh, Richard Rive. New York, Crown Publishers [1963]
223p. 22cm.

Short stories.

War
M172.1 Darton, Andrew W
D25c ... Citizenship in wartime. New York, Fortuny's c1940 .

47p. front. (port.) 18½cm.
First edition.

M355.2 War.
J73L Jones, Claudia.
Lift every voice for victory. New York, New Age, 1942.

14p. illus. 19cm.

The war and the Negro people.
M304 **Ford, James W 1893-**
P19 The war and the Negro people, by James W. Ford ... [New
v.2 no.4 York, Workers library publishers, 1942.
15 p. 19cm.

M335.4
F75w

1. World war, 1939- —Negroes. I. Title.
45-13492

Library of Congress D810.N4F73
[2] 940.5403

War correspondents.
M350 Afro-American Company, Baltimore, Md.
Af8t This is our war. Selected stories of six war correspondents who were sent overseas, by the Afro-American newspapers. Baltimore, Philadelphia, Richmond and Newark. Original drawings by Francis Yancey. Baltimore, The Afro-American Co., 1945.

216p. illus. 17½cm.

War in Africa;
M304 **Ford, James W 1893-**
P19 War in Africa; Italian fascism prepares to enslave Ethiopia,
V.1,no.11 by James W. Ford and Harry Gannes ... [New York, Workers library publishers, 1935]
M335.4 31, [1] p. illus. (map) 19cm.
F75wi

1. Italo-Ethiopian war, 1935-1936. I. Gannes, Harry, joint author. II. Title.

Library of Congress DT387.8.F6 44-11577
[2]

War in heaven, and other poems.
M811.5 **Love, Melvin.**
L94w War in heaven, and other poems. [1st ed.] New York, Exposition Press [1954]
64 p. 21 cm.

I. Title.

PS3523.O825W3 811.5 54-8969 ‡

Library of Congress [2]

M811.5 War poems.
P44w Peters, Ada Tress
War poems, by Peters sisters, [n.p., n. p., 1919]

83p. photo, 18½ cm.

War poems of the United nations.
M811.08 **Davidman, Joy, ed.**
D28w ... War poems of the United nations; three hundred poems, one hundred and fifty poets from twenty countries. Sponsored by the League of American writers. Edited by Joy Davidman. New York, Dial press, 1943.

ix, 395 p. 21cm.

At head of title: The songs and battle cries of a world at war.

1. World war, 1939- —Poetry. 2. English poetry—20th cent. 3. American poetry—20th cent. 4. English poetry—Translations from foreign literature. I. Title.
43-18223

Library of Congress D745.2.D3
[40] 940.5491

M39 Ward, Matthew
W199 Indignant heart. New York, New Books, 1952.

184 p. 18 cm.
Pocketbook edition.

I. Title. 1. Labor and laboring classes-Bio.

M89 W21
Ward, Samuel Ringgold, 1817-1967
Autobiography of a fugitive Negro: his anti-slavery labours in the United States, Canada, & England. By Samuel Ringgold Ward ... London, J. Snow, 1855.
xii, 412 p. front. (port.) 18½ cm.
1. Slavery in the U. S.—Anti-slavery movements.
Library of Congress E449.W27 13—22943
[48b1]

M813.5 W23a
Waring, Robert Lewis, 1863-
As we see it, by Robert L. Waring. Washington, D. C., Press of C. F. Sudwarth, 1910.
233 p. front. 23cm.
I. Title.
Library of Congress PZ3.W2237A 10—5053
Copyright A 256768 [a36b1]

Ghana M896.1 D36g
Warren, Yaw.
Dei-Anang, Michael Francis, 1909-
Ghana glory; poems on Ghana and Ghanaian life [by] Michael Dei-Anang & Yaw Warren. Foreword by Kwame Nkrumah. [London] Nelson [1965]
69p. illus.
"The poems on pages 1 to 32 are by Michael Dei-Anang".
I. Warren, Yaw. II. Title.

M813.5 W21r
Ward, Thomas Playfair, 1895-
The right to live. [1st ed.] New York, Pageant Press [1953]
249 p. 21 cm.
I. Title.
PZ7.W216Ri 53-10072 ‡
Library of Congress [2]

M326.99B W24s
Warner, Ashton.
Strickland, S.
Negro slavery described by a Negro: being the narrative of Ashton Warner, a native of St. Vincent's. With an appendix containing the testimony of four Christian ministers recently returned from the colonies on the system of slavery as it now exists. By S. Strickland ... London, Samuel Maunder, 1831.
144p. 15½cm.

M811.5 W25t
Warrick, Calvin Horatio.
The true criteria and other poems, by C. Horatio Warrick. Kansas City, Mo., The Sojourner press, 1924.
120 p. port. 20½cm.
I. Title. 1. Poetry.
Library of Congress PS3545.A758T7 1924 24-22084 Revised
[r41c2]

M813.5 W21t
Ward, Thomas Playfair, 1895-
The truth that makes men free; a novel. [1st ed.] New York, Pageant Press [1955]
154 p. 21 cm.
I. Title.
PZ4.W256Tr 55-11983 ‡
Library of Congress [2]

M326.5 Am3r
Warner, Daniel Bashiel, pres. of Liberia.
Address.
(In: American Colonization Society. Memorial of the semi-centennial anniversary ... January 15, 1867. With documents concerning Liberia. Washington, The Society, 1867. 24cm. p. 37-57).

M350 M14w
The war's greatest scandal.
MacDonald, Dwight
The war's greatest scandal; The story of jim crow in uniform, by Dwight Macdonald, research by Nancy Macdonald. New York, March on Washington Movement, [1943]
15p. illus. 23cm.

M784
Ware, Charles Pickard, 1840-1921, jt. comp.
Allen, William Francis, 1830-1889, comp.
Slave songs of the United States. New York, A. Simpson & Co., 1867.
115p. illus. 22½cm.

M326.5 Am3r
Warner, Daniel Bashiel, pres. of Liberia.
Annual message.
(In: American Colonization Society. Memorial of the semi-centennial anniversary ... January 15, 1867. With documents concerning Liberia. Washington, The Society, 1867. 24cm. p. 162-76).

M06 J61 no. 7
Washington, Booker Taliaferro, 1856-1915.
Address at opening of Atlanta exposition.
Bacon, Alice Mabel, 1858-1918.
... The negro and the Atlanta exposition, by Miss Alice M. Bacon ... Baltimore, The Trustees, 1896.
28 p. 24½cm. (The trustees of the John F. Slater fund. Occasional papers, no. 7)
Address by Booker T. Washington, at opening of Atlanta exposition, September 18, 1895, p. 12-16.
1. Negroes. 2. Atlanta. Cotton states and international exposition, 1895. I. Washington, Booker Taliaferro, 1859?-1915. II. Title.
Library of Congress E185.5.J65 no. 7 8—18186
——— Copy 2. [35c1]

MB9 W23j
Warfield, Bernis.
Johnson, Lois Phelps.
I'm gonna fly; the biography of Bernis Warfield. [1st ed.] Saint Paul, Macalester Park Pub. Co. [1959]
176 p. 21 cm.
1. Warfield, Bernis. I. Title.
BX6455.W34J6 922.673 60-19260 ‡
Library of Congress [1]

M813.5 W24m
Warner, Samuel Jonathan, 1896-
Madam President-elect; a novel. [1st ed.] New York, Exposition Press [1956]
249 p. 21 cm.
I. Title.
PZ4.W284Mad 56-8728 ‡
Library of Congress [2]

M814.4 W272a
Washington, Booker Taliaferro, 1856-1915.
An address by Booker T. Washington... delivered on the occasion of the unveiling of the Shaw Monument, Boston, Mass., May 31, 1897.
"Cover title. 10p. 9x16cm.
"From The Boston evening transcript of June 1."
1. Shaw, Robert Gould, 1837-1863.

M323.22 Su7n
Waring, James H N Some causes of criminality, p.45-49.
Survey midmonthly.
...The Negro in the cities of the North... New York, The Charity organization society, c1905.
2 p. l., 96 p. illus., plates. 26cm.

Ghana MB9 W25
Warren, Guy
I have a story to tell ... Accra, Guinea Press, ltd., 1962.
203p. illus. 21cm.
Portrait of author.
1. Jazz music. I. Title.

M323 T69
Washington, Booker Taliaferro, 1856-1915 - The basis of race progress in the South.
Negro Christian student conference. *Atlanta*, 1914.
The new voice in race adjustments; addresses and reports presented at the Negro Christian student conference, Atlanta, Georgia, May 14-18, 1914. A. M. Trawick, editor ... Pub. by order of the executive committee of the conference. New York city, Student volunteer movement [1914]
1 p. l., [v]-vi p., 1 l., 230 p. 23½cm.
"Best books on the Negro in America and Africa": p. 221-224.
1. Negroes—Congresses. 2. U. S.—Race question. I. Trawick, Arcadius McSwain, 1869- ed. II. Title.
Springfield. Public library for Library of Congress E185.5.N58 A 15-837
[a35f1]

M304 P19 v.4, no.12
Waring, James H N
Work of the Colored law and order league, Baltimore, Md., by James H. N. Waring. Cheyney, Pa., Committee of twelve for the advancement of the interests of the Negro race [1908?]
29 p. illus. (maps) diagrs. 22½cm.
1. Colored law and order league, Baltimore. 2. ~~Negroes~~—Baltimore. I. Committee of twelve for the advancement of the interests of the Negro race, Cheyney, Pa.
Stanford univ. Library for Library of Congress F189.B1W28 A 11-2097 Revised
[r43b2]†

M811.5 W25t
Warren, Samuel Enders, 1903-
The teacher and other poems. Houston, Texas, privately printed, 1953.
23p. 22cm.
Autographed: "To Mr. Arthur B. Spingarn for the Spingarn collection."
1. Poetry. I. Title.

M814.4 W272bi
Washington, Booker Taliaferro, 1856-1915.
[Bishop Potter and the Negro, address]
(In: New York. People's Institute. Memorial to Henry Codman Potter by the People's Institute, Cooper Union,... December twentieth, MCMVIII. New York, [Cheltenham Press] 1909. 21cm. pp. 60-67)
1. Potter, Henry Codman, bp., 1834-1908
I. New York. People's Institute

M814.4 W272b
Washington, Booker Taliaferro, 1856-1915.
Black-belt diamonds; gems from the speeches, addresses, and talks to students of Booker T. Washington ... selected and arranged by Victoria Earle Matthews; introduction by T. Thomas Fortune. New York, Fortune and Scott, 1898.
xii, 115 p. front. (port.) 18cm.
1. Quotations. I. Matthews, Victoria Earle. II. Title.
Library of Congress E185.6.W3 98-582 Revised
Copyright 1898: 40043 [r32c2]

M973.8 Am3
Washington, Booker Taliaferro, 1856-1915.
Industrial education and the public schools.
(In: American Academy of Political and Social Science. The Negro's progress in fifty years ... Philadelphia, 1913. 25cm. p. 219-232.)

M814.4 W272n2
Washington, Booker Taliaferro, 1856-1915.
The Negro in the South, his economic progress in relation to his moral and religious development; being the William Levi Bull lectures for the year 1907, by Booker T. Washington ... and W. E. Burghardt Du Bois ... Philadelphia, G. W. Jacobs & company [1907]
222 p. 19½cm.
CONTENTS.—I. The economic development of the Negro race in slavery, by B. T. Washington.—II. The economic development of the Negro race since its emancipation, by B. T. Washington.—III. The economic revolution in the South, by W. E. B. Du Bois.—IV. Religion in the South, by W. E. B. Du Bois.—Notes to chapters III and IV (Bibliography: p. 220-222)
1. Negroes. I. Du Bois, William Edward Burghardt, 1868- II. Title. (over)
Library of Congress E185.6.W316 7-21310
[45i1]

M814.4 W272c
Washington, Booker Taliaferro, 1856-1915.
Character building; being addresses delivered on Sunday evenings to the students of Tuskegee institute by Booker T. Washington. New York, Doubleday, Page & company, 1902. 1903.
7 p. l., 3-291 p. front. 20½cm.
1. Character. 2. Negroes—Education. I. Title.
Library of Congress BJ1581.W15 2-17836
[41i1]

M323 N31
Washington, Booker Taliaferro, 1856.-1915, ed.
Industrial education for the Negro p. 7-30.
The Negro problem; a series of articles by representative American Negroes of today; contributions by Booker T. Washington ... W. E. Burghardt Du Bois, Paul Laurence Dunbar, Charles W. Chesnutt, and others. New York, J. Pott & company, 1903.
234 p. front., ports. 19cm.
CONTENTS.—Washington, B. T. Industrial education for the Negro.—Du Bois, W. E. B. The talented tenth.—Chesnutt, C. W. The disfranchisement of the Negro.—Smith, W. H. The Negro and the law.—Kealing, H. T. The characteristics of the Negro people.—Dunbar, P. L. Representative American Negroes.—Fortune, T. T. The Negro's place in American life at the present day.
1. Negroes. I. Washington, Booker Taliaferro, 1859?-1915, ed.
Library of Congress E185.5.N39 3-23404
[41j1]

M814.4 W272p
Washington, Booker Taliaferro, 1856-1915.
Putting the most into life, by Booker T. Washington ... New York, T. Y. Crowell & co. [1906]
4 p. l., 35, [1] p. front. (port.) 19½cm.
"The chapters in this little book were originally part of a series of Sunday evening talks given by the principal to the students of the Tuskegee normal and industrial institute."
1. Negroes. I. Title.
Library of Congress E185.6.W318 6-36165
Copyright [a39g1]

M814.4 W272d
Washington, Booker Taliaferro, 1856-1915.
Daily resolves, by Booker T. Washington. London, Ernest Nister, 1896.
17p. illus. 14½cm.
I. Title.

M814.4 W272in
Washington, Booker Taliaferro, 1856-1915
Introduction.
(In: Thrasher, Max Bennet. Tuskegee; its story and its work. Boston, Small, Maynard & company, 1900. 19cm. p.xv-xvi)
I. Thrasher, Max Bennett, 1860-1903
1. Tuskegee Normal and Industrial Institute

M814.4 W272q
Washington, Booker Taliaferro, 1856-1915.
Quotations of Booker T. Washington, compiled by E. Davidson Washington ... [Tuskegee, Ala., Tuskegee institute press, 1938]
37, [1] p. illus., port. 22½cm.
I. Washington, Ernest Davidson, comp.
Library of Congress E185.6.W3185 38-10576
——— Copy 2.
Copyright A 119867 [39c2] 825.260073

M814.4 W272e
Washington, Booker Taliaferro, 1856-1915.
... Education of the negro, by Booker T. Washington ... [Albany, N. Y., J. B. Lyon company, 1900]
44 p. 24½cm. (Monographs on education in the United States, ed. by N. M. Butler. 18)
At head of title: Department of education for the United States commission to the Paris exposition of 1900.
"This monograph is contributed to the United States educational exhibit by the state of New York."
1. Negroes—Education.
Library of Congress LB5.B89 no. 18 5—1982
[a32e1]

M814.4 W272i
Washington, Booker Taliaferro, 1856-1915.
Is the Negro having a fair chance? By Booker T. Washington. Tuskegee, Alabama, Tuskegee Institute Press, 1912.
39p. 19½cm.
Reprinted from The Century Magazine.

M306 N21c
Washington, Booker, Taliaferro, 1856-1915
The rural Negro and the South.
(In: National Conference of Charities and Correction. Proceedings ... forty-first annual session, May 8-15, 1914. Fort Wayne, Indiana, Fort Wayne Printing Co., 1914. 21cm. p. 121-127.)

M815.4 D737w
Washington, Booker Taliaferro, 1856-1915.
... Frederick Douglass, by Booker T. Washington ... Philadelphia and London, G. W. Jacobs & company [1907]
14 p., 1 l., [15]-365 p. front. (port.) 19½cm. (*Half-title:* American crisis biographies, ed. by E. P. Oberholtzer ...)
Series title also at head of t.-p.
Bibliography: p. [353]
1. Douglass, Frederick, 1817-1895.
Library of Congress E449.D8 7—8512
——— Copy 2.
Copyright A 155150 [a26j2]

M814.4 W272m
Washington, Booker Taliaferro, 1856-1915.
The man farthest down; a record of observation and study in Europe, by Booker T. Washington, with the collaboration of Robert E. Park. Garden City, New York, Doubleday, Page & company, 1912.
4 p. l., 3-390 p., 1 l. fold. map. 20½cm.
1. Labor and laboring classes—Europe. 2. Poor—Europe. I. Park, Robert E., joint author. II. Title.
Library of Congress HD4851.W3 12—23003
——— Copy 2.
Copyright A 320538 [a39k1]

M814.4 W272e
Washington, Booker Taliaferro, 1856-1915.
Selected speeches of Booker T. Washington ... edited by E. Davidson Washington. Garden City, N. Y., Doubleday, Doran & company, inc., 1932.
xvi p., 1 l., 283 p. front. (port.) 20cm.
"First edition."
1. Negroes. I. Washington, Ernest Davidson, ed.
Library of Congress E185.6.W319 32—18704
[47g1] 825.26

M814.4 W272f
Washington, Booker Taliaferro, 1856-1915.
The future of the American negro [by] Booker T. Washington. Boston, Small, Maynard & company, 1902.
4 p. l., vii-x, 3-244 p. front. (port.) 19cm.
1. Negroes. I. Title.
Library of Congress E185.6.W313 0—2908
——— Copy 2.
Copyright 1900 A 10092 825 [a25m2] Ism

M814.4 W27am
Washington, Booker Taliaferro, 1856-1915.
My larger education; being chapters from my experience, by Booker T. Washington ... illustrated from photographs. Garden City, New York, Doubleday, Page & company, 1911.
viii, 313 p. front., plates, ports. 20½cm.
1. Negroes. I. Title.
Library of Congress E185.97.W28 11—29623
[36j1]

M323 Su7n
Washington, Booker Taliaferro, 1856-1915.
Should Negro business men go south.
(In: Survey midmonthly. The Negro in the cities of the North. New York, The Charity Organization Society, 1905. 26cm. p.17-19).

M814.4 W272f
Washington, Booker Taliaferro, 1856-1915.
The future of the American negro [by] Booker T. Washington. Boston, Small, Maynard & company, 1899.
4 p. l., vii-x, 3-244 p. front. (port.) 19cm.
1. Negroes. I. Title.
Library of Congress E185.6.W313 0—2908
——— Copy 2.
Copyright 1900 A 10092 825 [a25m2] Ism

M814.4 W272n
Washington, Booker Taliaferro, 1856-1915.
The Negro in business, by Booker T. Washington ... Boston, Chicago, Hertel, Jenkins & co. [c1907]
1 p. l., 379 p. 18 pl. (incl. front., ports.) 20½ cm.
Plates printed on both sides.
1. Negroes—Employment. I. Title.
Library of Congress E185.8.W31 7—37616
[41g1]

M814.4 W722so
Washington, Booker Taliferro, 1856-1915.
...Sowing and reaping. New York and Boston, H. M. Caldwell, 1900.
5-29p. 19½cm. (The Character and wisdom series).
1. Conduct of life. 2. Education.
I. Title.

M814.4 W27as
Washington, Booker Taliaferro, 1856-1915.
The story of my life and work, Booker T. Washington ... with an introduction by Dr. J. L. M. Curry ... illustrated ... by Frank Beard. Toronto, Ont., Naperville, Ill. [etc.] J. L. Nichols & co. [1900]
423 p. incl. illus., plates, ports. front. 21cm.
Plates and portraits printed on both sides.
1. Tuskegee normal and industrial institute.
0—3304
Library of Congress E185.97.W29 [44j1]

M814.4 W27au2 1902
Washington, Booker Taliaferro, 1856-1915.
Up from slavery; an autobiography, by Booker T. Washington. London, Grant Richards, 1902.
ix, 330 p. front. (port.) 20½cm.
Originally published in the Outlook. cf. Pref.
1. Tuskegee normal and industrial institute. I. Title.
1—31242
Library of Congress E185.97.W3 — Copy 2. [45g*2]

M814.4 W27bo
Washington, Booker Taliaferro, 1856--1915.
Boone, Theodore Sylvester, 1896-
The philosophy of Booker T. Washington, the apostle of progress, the pioneer of the new deal, by Theodore S. Boone ... with introduction by L. K. Williams. [Fort Worth, Tex., Manney printing co., 1939]
xix, 311 p. pl., port. 20cm.
Bibliography: p. vii-xi.
1. Washington, Booker Taliaferro, 1859?-1915. I. Title.
39-17748
Library of Congress E185.97.W14 — Copy 2.
Copyright A 130418 [3] 923.773

M814.4 W272st
Washington, Booker Taliaferro, 1856-1915.
The story of the Negro, the rise of the race from slavery, by Booker T. Washington ... New York, Doubleday, Page & company, 1909.
2 v. front. (port.) 21 cm.
~~1. Negroes.~~
9—29958
Library of Congress E185.W316 [43h1]

M814.4 W27au 1902
Washington, Booker Taliaferro, 1856-1915.
Up from slavery; an autobiography, by Booker T. Washington. New York, Doubleday, Page & co., 1902
ix, 330 p. front. (port.) 20½cm.
Originally published in the Outlook. cf. Pref.
1. Tuskegee normal and industrial institute. I. Title.
1—31242
Library of Congress E185.97.W3 — Copy 2. [45g*2]

M811.5 C59r
Washington, Booker Taliaferro, 1856-1915
Clem, Charles Douglass, 1875-
Booker T. Washington [a poem]
Broadside 16½ x 27½cm.

M814.4 W272st2
Washington, Booker Taliaferro, 1856-1915.
The story of the Negro, the rise of the race from slavery, by Booker T. Washington ... London, T. Fisher Unwin, 1909.
2 v. front. (port.) 21 cm.
1. Negroes.
E185.W316 9—29958
Library of Congress [58i1]

M808.81 R228 Autumn 1960
Washington, Booker Taliaferro 1856-1915
Up from slavery. [Condensed version]
Pp. 261-318.
In: Reader's digest. Reader's digest condensed books. Pleasantville, N. Y., Reader's Digest Association, 1960.

M814.4 W272d
Washington, Booker Taliaferro, 1856-1915.
Drinker, Frederick E.
Booker T. Washington, the master mind of a child of slavery; an appealing life story rivaling in its picturesque simplicity and power those recounted about the lives of Washington and Lincoln. A biographical tale destined to live in history and furnish an inspiration for present and future generations; a human interest story depicting the life achievements of a great leader of a rising race ... By Frederick E. Drinker, editor and author. Splendidly illustrated with photographic pictures. Memorial ed. [Philadelphia, Printed by National publishing co., 1915]
(Continued on next card)
16—2034
[a38b1]

M814.4 W27au5
Washington, Booker Taliaferro, 1856 -1915.
Tokoloho bokhobeng: or Up from slavery phetolelo sesothong ke Herbert H. Lekhethoa. Morija, Basutoland, Morija Sesuto Book Depot, 1947.
146p. 18½cm.
Translated into Sesoto
I. Title - (Up from slavery)
II. Tr. - Lekhethoa, Herbert H.

M814.4 W27au4 1963
Washington, Booker Taliaferro, 1856-1915.
Up from slavery, an autobiography. Garden City, N. Y., Doubleday, 1963.
243 p. illus. 22 cm.
1. Tuskegee Institute. I. Title.
E185.97.W3163 923.773 63-3987 ‡
Library of Congress [5]

M301 D853s38 1905
Washington, Booker Taliaferro, 1856-1915
Du Bois, William Edward Burghardt, 1868-
The souls of black folk; essays and sketches London, Archibald Constable, 1905-
viii, p., 1 l, 264p. 1 l. 22cm.
First English edition.

M814.4 W272t
Washington, Booker Taliaferro, 1856-1915, ed.
Tuskegee & its people: their ideals and achievements, ed. by Booker T. Washington. New York, D. Appleton and company, 1905.
xiv, 354 p. front., plates, ports. 21cm.
The volume here presented has been edited by Mr. Emmett J. Scott, executive secretary of the Tuskegee institute. The task of editing which the principal had expected to perform has been so well done that it has only been necessary to review the manuscript after its preparation for the publishers, and to forego the strict editorial revisioning planned. cf. General introduction.
CONTENTS.—I. The school and its purposes.—II. Autobiographies by graduates of the school.
1. Tuskegee, Ala. Normal and industrial institute. I. Scott, Emmett Jay, 1873- ed. II. Title.
5—17294
Library of Congress LC2851.T82W2 [44j1]

M301 T413
Washington, Booker Taliaferro, 1856-1915.
Up from slavery.
Three Negro classics: Up from slavery. The souls of black folk. The autobiography of an ex-colored man. With an introd. by John Hope Franklin. [New York, Avon Books, 1965]
xxv, 511p. 19cm. (Avon library, W102)
1. Negroes. 2. Tuskegee Institute. I. Washington, Booker Taliaferro, 1856-1915. Up from slavery. II. DuBois, William Edward Burghardt, 1863-1963. The souls of the black folk. III. Johnson, James Weldon, 1871-1938. The autobiography of an ex- colored man.

M301 D853s08
Washington, Booker Taliaferro, 1856-1915
Du Bois, William Edward Burghardt, 1868-
The souls of black folk, essays and sketches Chicago, A. C. McClurg & Co., 1903.
viii, 1 l, 264p. 21½cm.

M814.4 W27au? 1940
Washington, Booker Taliferro, 1856 -1915.
Up from slavery, an autobiography. New York, Pocket Books Inc., 1940.
236p. 16½cm.
I. Title. 1. Tuskegee Normal and Industrial Institute.

M814.4 W27aw
Washington, Booker, Taliaferro, 1856-1915.
Working with the hands; being a sequel to "Up from slavery," covering the author's experiences in industrial training at Tuskegee, by Booker T. Washington; illustrated from photographs by Frances Benjamin Johnston. New York, Doubleday, Page & company, 1904.
x, 246 p. front. (port.) 31 pl. 20½cm.
1. Tuskegee normal and industrial institute. I. Title.
4—12107
Library of Congress E185.97.W32 [42p1]

M814.4 W27f
Washington, Booker Taliaferro, 1856-1915.
[Fauset, Arthur Huff]
... Booker T. Washington ... Philadelphia, Ethiopian publishing company, 1924.
63 p. incl. front., illus., ports. 17cm. (Ethiopian classic series)
By Arthur H. Fauset and Tanner G. Duckrey.
1. Washington, Booker Taliaferro, 1859-1915. I. Duckrey, Tanner Grant, joint author. II. Title.
CA 24-637 Unrev'd
Library of Congress E185.97.W22 — Copy 2.
Copyright A 779980

M814.4 W27au 1901
Washington, Booker Taliaferro, 1856-1915.
Up from slavery; an autobiography, by Booker T. Washington. New York, Doubleday, Page & co., 1901.
ix, 330 p. front. (port.) 20½cm.
Originally published in the Outlook. cf. Pref.
1. Tuskegee normal and industrial institute. I. Title.
1—31242
Library of Congress E185.97.W3 — Copy 2. [45g*2]

M814.4 W27au
Washington, Booker Taliaferro, 1856-1915.
Working with the hands; being a sequel to "Up from slavery," covering the author's experiences in industrial training at Tuskegee, by Booker T. Washington; illustrated from photographs by Frances Benjamin Johnston. New York, Doubleday, Page & company, 1904.
x, 246 p. front. (port.) 31 pl. 20½ cm.
Subscription edition with a special introduction not in the trade edition.
1. Tuskegee normal and industrial institute. I. Title.
E185.97.W32 4—12107
Library of Congress [56o1]

M814.4 W27fr
Washington, Booker Taliaferro, 1856 -1915.
Frazier, Edward Franklin, 1894-
The Booker T. Washington papers.
(In: The Library of Congress quarterly journal of current acquisitions. v.2, no.2, February 1945, p.23-31)

Washington, Booker Taliaferro, 1856-1915.
M813.5 G76b
Graham, Shirley.
Booker T. Washington, educator of hand, head, and heart. Front. and jacket by Donald W. Lambo. New York, Messner [1955]
192 p. illus. 22 cm.
1. Washington, Booker Taliaferro, 1859?-1915.
Full name: Lola Shirley (Graham) McCanns.
E185.97.W226 923.773 55—9855 ‡
Library of Congress [56h7]

Washington, Booker Taliaferro, 1856-1915.
M814.4 W27s
Scott, Emmett Jay, 1873-
Booker T. Washington, builder of a civilization, by Emmett J. Scott and Lyman Beecher Stowe; illustrated from photographs. Garden City, N.Y., Doubleday, Page & company, 1916.
xx, 331, [1]p. front., plates, ports. 24½cm.

Washington, Ernest Davidson, ed.
M814.4 W272o
Washington, Booker Taliaferro, 1859?-1915.
Selected speeches of Booker T. Washington ... edited by E. Davidson Washington. Garden City, N. Y., Doubleday, Doran & company, inc., 1932.
xvi p., 1 l., 283 p. front. (port.) 20cm.
"First edition."
1. Negroes. I. Washington, Ernest Davidson, ed.
32—18704
Library of Congress E185.6.W319
[47g1] 325.26

Washington, Booker Taliaferro, 1856-1915.
MB9 W26h
Hawkins, Hugh, ed.
Booker T. Washington and his critics; the problem of Negro leadership. Boston, Heath [1962]
113 p. 24 cm. (Problems in American civilization)
Includes bibliography.
Contains selections from the writings of Booker T. Washington, Rayford W. Logan, W. E. B. DuBois, Kelly Miller and H. M. Bondd
1. Washington, Booker Taliaferro, 1859?-1915. 2. Negroes—Segregation.
E185.97.W235 923.773 62-4235 ‡
Library of Congress [10]

Washington, Booker Taliaferro, 1856 -1915.
M814.4 W27u
U.S. Congress. Senate Committee on Banking and Currency.
Hearing on H.R. 6528; An act to authorize the coinage of 50 cent pieces to commemorate the life and perpetuate the ideals and teachings of Booker T. Washington, July 23, 1945. Washington, G.P.O., 1946.
16p. 23cm.
At head of title: Booker T. Washington Commemorative Coin.

M709.6 W27
Washington, Forrester Blanchard, 1887-
Contemporary artists of Africa. New York, Division of Social Research and Experimentation, Harmon Foundation [1960]
iii p., 82 l. 28 cm.
Cover title.
Bibliographical references included in "Acknowledgments" (p. iii)
1. Artists, African. 2. Art—Africa. I. Title.
3. Art schools.
N7380.W3 709.6 60-2950
Library of Congress [5]

Washington, Booker Taliaferro, 1856-1915.
M814.4 W27j
Jackson, Walter Clinton, 1879-
A boy's life of Booker T. Washington, by W.C. Jackson ... New York, The Macmillan company, 1923.
xi, 147p. incl. front., illus. 19cm.

Washington, Booker Taliaferro, 1856-1915.
M378Tu W578
Whiting, Helen Adele (Johnson) 1885-
Booker T. Washington's contribution to education. Charlotte, N. C., Mimeograph Press, Kluttz Mail Advertising Service [n.d.]
160p. port. diagr. 27cm.
Mimeographed.

M306 N21p
Washington, Forrester Blanchard, 1887-
The effect of changed economic conditions upon the living standards of Negroes.
(In: National Conference of Social Work. Proceedings, 1928. p. 466-78).

Haiti M844 L96t
Washington, Booker Taliaferro, 1856-1915.
Lubin, J Dieudonné.
Travaux de recherches et de documentation aux Etats-Unis et impressions de voyage. Port-au-Prince, L'Etat, 1951.
69p. port. 17cm.

Washington, Booker Taliaferro, 1856-1915 - Juvenile literature.
MB Qu26
Quarles, Benjamin, jt. auth.
~~Sterling, Dorothy, 1913-~~
Lift every voice; the lives of Booker T. Washington, W. E. B. Du Bois, Mary Church Terrell, and James Weldon Johnson [by] Dorothy Sterling and Benjamin Quarles. Illustrated by Ernest Crichlow. [1st ed.] Garden City, N. Y., Doubleday, 1965.
116 p. illus., ports. 22 cm. (Zenith books)
1. Washington, Booker Taliaferro, 1859-1915—Juvenile literature. 2. Du Bois, William Edward Burghardt, 1868-1963—Juvenile literature. 3. Terrell, Mary (Church) 1863-1954—Juvenile literature. 4. Johnson, James Weldon, 1871-1938—Juvenile literature. I. Quarles, Benjamin, joint author. II. Title.
E185.96.S77 920.073 65-17287
Library of Congress [5]

M306 N21p
Washington, Forrester Blanchard, 1887-
The Negro and relief, In: National Conference of social work. Pp. 178-194, 1934.

Washington, Booker Taliaferro, 1856-1915.
M06 J61 no. 17
... Memorial addresses in honor of Dr. Booker T. Washington. Lynchburg, Va., J. P. Bell company, inc., printers, 1916.
cover-title, 31 p. 23cm. (The trustees of the John F. Slater fund. Occasional papers no. 17)
"A memorial meeting in honor of Dr. Booker T. Washington was held in Carnegie hall, New York city ... February 11, 1916. The meeting was held under the auspices of Hampton institute, Tuskegee institute, and the National league on urban conditions."—Note, p. [2]
1. Washington, Booker Taliaferro, 1859?-1915.
16—17488
Library of Congress E185.5.J65 no. 17
——— Copy 2. E185.97.W25
[a39b1]

Washington, Chester L.
MB9 L93m
Louis, Joe, 1914-
My life story, by Joe Louis ... New York, Duell, Sloan and Pearce [1947]
188, [2] p. plates, ports. 22cm.
"An Eagle book."
"Written with the editorial aid of Chester L. Washington and Haskell Cohen."
"First edition."
Contains J. Louis' autograph
1. Washington, Chester L. II. Cohen, Haskell.
GV1132.L6A3 927.9683 47-30240
© 19Mar47; author, New York; A11564.
Library of Congress [25]

M06 Am35
Washington, Forrester Blanchard, 1887-
Recreational facilities for the Negro.
(In: American Academy of Political and Social Science, Philadelphia. The American Negro. Philadelphia, 1928. 24cm. p. 272-282.

Washington, Booker Taliaferro, 1856-1915
M323 M690
Mitchell, Arthur W , 1883-
Overcoming difficulties under adverse conditions, address...in the House of Representatives, Thursday, April 6, 1939. Washington, Govt. Print. Off. 1939.
15p. 23cm.
Founder's Day address delivered at Tuskegee Institute, Alabama, April 2, 1939.

M813.5 W276y
Washington, Doris V
Yulan; a novel. New York, Carlton Press, 1964.
100p. 20cm.
Portrait of author on book jacket.
I. Title.

Washington, George, pres. U.S.— Associates and employees.
M973. M45
Mazyck, Walter H.
George Washington and the Negro, by Walter H. Mazyck ... Washington, D. C., The associated publishers, inc. [c1932]
vii p., 1 l., 180 p. 19½cm.
1. Washington, George, pres. U. S.—Associates and employees. 2. Slavery in the U. S.—Virginia. 3. U. S.—Hist.—Revolution—Negro troops. I. Title.
32—4101
Library of Congress E312.17.M38
——— Copy 2.
Copyright A 47400 [33j2] 923.173

Washington, Booker Taliaferro, 1856—1915.
M973 N42
A new Negro for a new century; an accurate and up-to-date record of the upward struggles of the Negro race. The Spanish-American war, causes of it; vivid descriptions of fierce battles; superb heroism and daring deeds of the Negro soldier ... Education, industrial schools, colleges, universities and their relationship to the race problem, by Prof. Booker T. Washington. Reconstruction and industrial advancement by N. B. Wood ... The colored woman and her part in race regeneration ... by ... Fannie Barrier Williams ... Chicago, Ill., American publishing house [1900]
428 p. front., illus. (ports) 20cm.
(Continued on next card)
0—5252
[44g1]

Washington, Ernest Davidson, comp.
M814.4 W272q
Washington, Booker Taliaferro, 1859?-1915.
Quotations of Booker T. Washington, compiled by E. Davidson Washington ... [Tuskegee, Ala., Tuskegee institute press, 1938]
87, [1] p. illus., port. 22½cm.
1. Washington, Ernest Davidson, comp.
38—19576
Library of Congress E185.6.W3185
——— Copy 2.
Copyright A 119867 [39c2] 325.260973

Washington, George, pres. U.S.—Fiction.
M813.1 H55
Hill, John H.
Princess Malah, by John H. Hill. Washington, D. C., The associated publishers, inc. [c1933]
vii p., 1 l., 330 p. 21cm.
1. Washington, George, pres. U. S.—Fiction. 2. Washington, Mrs. Martha (Dandridge) Custis, 1731-1801—Fiction. 3. Slavery in the U. S.—Virginia—Fiction. I. Title.
33—3600
Library of Congress PZ3.H5521Pr
——— Copy 2.
Copyright A 60229 [a33e1]

MB9
L63was
Washington, John Edwin,
They knew Lincoln, by John E. Washington, with an introduction by Carl Sandburg ... New York, E. P. Dutton & co., inc., 1942.
3 p. l., 11-244, [2] p. front., plates, ports., facsims. 22½ᶜᵐ.
"Personal narrative of a Negro boy and man who sought all that could be possibly known about Abraham Lincoln from Negroes having impressions on facts he considered worth record."—Introd.
"First edition."
1. Lincoln, Abraham, pres. U. S., 1809-1865. 2. Negroes—District of Columbia. I. Title. II. Keckley, Elizabeth. Companion and confidente of Mrs. Lincoln. p42-2825.
Library of Congress E457.15.W32
[80] 923.173

M277
W27
Washington, Joseph R
Black religion; the Negro and Christianity in the United States [by] Joseph R. Washington, Jr. Boston, Beacon Press [1964]
ix, 308 p. 22 cm.
Bibliographical references included in "Notes" (p. 298-308)
1. ~~Negroes~~—Religion. I. Title. II. Title: The Negro and Christianity in the United States. 2. Church history.
BR563.N4W3 277.3 64-13529
Library of Congress [8]

Washington, Mrs. Martha (Dandridge) Curtis, 1731-1801—Fiction.
M813.1
H55
Hill, John H.
Princess Malah, by John H. Hill. Washington, D. C., The associated publishers, inc. [c1933]
vii p., 1 l., 330 p. 21ᶜᵐ.
1. Washington, George, pres. U. S.—Fiction. 2. Washington, Mrs. Martha (Dandridge) Custis, 1731-1801—Fiction. 3. Slavery in the U. S.—Virginia—Fiction. I. Title.
33-3000
Library of Congress PZ3.H5521Pr
——— Copy 2.
Copyright A 60229 [a33e1]

MB9
W27m
Washington, Vivian Edwards, 1914-
Mount Ascutney. New York, Comet Press Books, 1958.
66p. 20½cm.
Picture and biographical sketch of the author on the book jacket.
1. Washington, Vivian Edwards, 1914-
I. Title.

Washington, Vivian Edwards, 1914-
MB9
W27m
Washington, Vivian Edwards, 1914-
Mount Ascutney. New York, Comet Press Books, 1958.
66p. 20½cm.
Picture and biographical sketch of the author on the book jacket.

Washington, D.C.
MB9
Ar6
Coleman, Lucretia H. Newman
Poor Ben: a story of real life...
Nashville, Tenn., A.M.E. Sunday school union, 1890.
220p. port. (front.) illus. 19cm.

Washington, D. C.
M973.6
C76w
1870
Colored National Labor Convention, Washington, D. C.
Proceedings of the Colored National labor convention held in Washington, D. C., on December 6th, 7th, 8th, 9th and 10th, 1869. Washington, D. C., Printed at the office of the New Era, 1870.
46p. 19cm.

Washington, D.C.
M331
G46
Glazier, Harlan E.
No Negro need apply; A brief glance at the employment situation in the District of Columbia as related to colored citizens, by Harlan E. Glazier, sponsored by the Inter-Racial Committee of the District of Columbia. Washington, The Committee, n.d.
8p. graphs. 23cm.

Washington, D.C.
M343.3
K63w
Kirksey, Thomas.
Who stopped the race riots in Washington; real causes and effects of race clashes in the District of Columbia, by T. Kirksey... J. Henry Hewlett... Washington, D.C., Murray bros., n.d.
12p. 23½cm.

Washington, D. C.
M973.6
N21w
National convention of colored men, Washington, D. C.
Proceedings of the national convention of the colored men of America, held in Washington, D. C. on January 13, 14, 15 and 16, 1869. Washington, D. C., Great Republic book and newspaper printing establishment, 1869.
42, xv p. 21cm.

Washington, D.C.
M323.22
Su7n
Survey midmonthly.
... The Negro in the cities of the North ... New York, The Charity organization society, [c1905.
2 p. l., 96 p. illus., plates. 26ᶜᵐ.
At head of title: Charities publication committee.
Reprint of Charities, October 7, 1905.
1. Negroes. I. Survey associates, inc., New York. II. Title.
6-2281 Revised
Library of Congress E185.9.S96
[r45c2]

Washington, D. C.
M658.7
W27
Washington Afro-American.
The Washington Afro-American report on characteristics of the Washington Negro market. its product buying and brand preferences in 1945, compiled by the Washington Afro-American, from a survey conducted by the Research company of America. Washington, D.C. c1945.
92p. illus., diagrs. 28x22cm.

Washington, D. C.-Amusements.
M975.3
J71
Jones, William Henry. 1896-
Recreation and amusement among Negroes in Washington, D. C.; a sociological analysis of the Negro in an urban environment, by William H. Jones ... Washington, D. C., Howard university press, 1927.
4 p. l., xi-xv, 17-216 p. plates (1 fold.) map, diagr. 21½ cm. (*Half-title:* Howard university studies in urban sociology)
Bibliography: p. 203-207.
1. Negroes—District of Columbia. 2. Washington, D. C.—Amusements. 3. Negroes—Moral and social conditions. I. Title.
27-24235
Library of Congress E185.93.D6J7
[3]

Washington, D.C.-Churches.
M206
H36
Helping Hand Club.
The history of the Helping Hand Club of the Nineteenth Street Baptist Church. Washington, D.C. The Associated Publishers, 1948.
86p. port. 19½cm.

Washington, D.C.-Descr.-Guide-books.
M975.3
F31
Federal writers' project.
Washington, city and capital. Federal writers' project, Works progress administration ... Washington, 1937. Washington, D. C., U. S. Govt. print. off. [1937]
xxvi, 1140, [1] p. incl. front., illus., port., plans. maps (part fold.; part in pocket) 24 cm. (American guide series)
Maps on lining-papers.
Bibliography: p. 1094-1100.
1. Washington, D. C.—Descr.—Guide-books. 2. Washington, D. C.—Hist. 3. Washington, D. C.—Intellectual life. 4. Washington, D. C.—Suburbs. I. Title.
37-26377
Library of Congress F199.F38
[48f2] 917.53

Washington, D.C. - Soc. life & cust.
MB9
F46m
Fields, Alonzo.
My 21 years in the White House. New York, Coward-McCann [1961]
223 p. 22 cm.
Portrait of author on book jacket.
1. Washington, D. C. White House. 2. Washington, D. C.—Soc. life & cust. 3. Presidents—U. S.—Biog. 4. Presidents—U. S.—Wives. 5. Visits of state—U. S. I. Title.
F204.W5F5 923.173 61-15068 ‡
Library of Congress [62b5]

Washington, D.C.-Hist.
M975.3
F31
Federal writers' project.
Washington, city and capital. Federal writers' project, Works progress administration ... Washington, 1937. Washington, D. C., U. S. Govt. print. off. [1937]
xxvi, 1140, [1] p. incl. front., illus., port., plans. maps (part fold.; part in pocket) 24 cm. (American guide series)
Maps on lining-papers.
Bibliography: p. 1094-1100.
1. Washington, D. C.—Descr.—Guide-books. 2. Washington, D. C.—Hist. 3. Washington, D. C.—Intellectual life. 4. Washington, D. C.—Suburbs. I. Title.
37-26377
Library of Congress F199.F38
[48f2] 917.53

M371.974
K77d
Washington, D.C. - Public Schools.
Knox, Ellis O
Democracy and the District of Columbia public schools; a study of recently integrated public schools. Washington, Judd & Detweiler, 1957.
viii, 131 p. tables. 24 cm.
Bibliography: p. 123-128.
1. Washington, D. C.—Public schools. 2. Segregation in education. I. Title.
LA255.K6 371.974 57-2405
Library of Congress [2]

Washington county, Texas.
M976.4
Yaln
Yancy, J W
The Negro blue - book of Washington county, Texas, by J. W. Yancy... Brenham, Texas, Brenham banner press, 1936
viii, 138p. illus. 23cm.

Washington, D.C. Dunbar High School.
M373
D912h
Hundley, Mary (Gibson)
The Dunbar story, 1870-1955. With an introd. by Robert C. Weaver. [1st ed.] New York, Vantage Press [1965]
179 p. [4] plates. 21 cm.
"Alma mater. Words by Dr. A. J. Cooper. Music by Miss M. L. Europe": (close score, for chorus SATB) : p. [4]
Includes bibliographies.
1. Washington, D. C. Dunbar High School. I. Title.
LD7501.W3D8 373.753 65-5375
Library of Congress [3]

Washington, D. C. Frederick Douglass memorial home.
M015.4
D739z
Historical records survey. *District of Columbia.*
Calendar of the writings of Frederick Douglass in the Frederick Douglass memorial home, Anacostia, D. C. Prepared by District of Columbia Historical records survey, Division of professional and service projects, Work projects administration. Sponsored by the Board of commissioners of the District of Columbia. Washington, D. C., District of Columbia Historical records survey, 1940.
7 p. l., 93 numb. l. 27½ᶜᵐ.
Reproduced from type-written copy.
"Publications of District of Columbia Historical records survey": leaves 92-93.
1. Douglass, Frederick, 1817-1895—Bibl. 2. Negroes—Bibl. 3. Slavery in the U. S.—Bibl. I. Washington, D. C. Frederick Douglass memorial home. II. Title.
41-52933
Library of Congress Z8616.D7H57
[8] 012

Washington, D.C. Lincoln status (Lincoln park)

M815.4 D74o

Douglass, Frederick, 1817–1895.

Oration by Frederick Douglass, delivered on the occasion of the unveiling of the freedmen's monument in memory of Abraham Lincoln, in Lincoln park, Washington, D. C., April 14th, 1876. With an appendix. ~~Washington, D. C., Gibson brothers, printers, 1876.~~ N.Y., Fred. Douglass historical-cultural league 1940

cover-title, 21 p. 23ᶜᵐ. 17 cm. 34

1. Lincoln, Abraham, pres. U. S.—Addresses, sermons, etc. 2. Washington, D. C. Lincoln statue (Lincoln park)

Library of Congress E457.8.D73 12—6733 [28d1]

Washington, D.C. Lincoln statue (Lincoln park)

M815.4 D74or

Douglass, Frederick, 1817–1895.

Oration by Frederick Douglass, delivered on the occasion of the unveiling of the freedmen's monument in memory of Abraham Lincoln, in Lincoln park, Washington, D. C., April 14th, 1876. With an appendix. Washington, D. C., Gibson brothers, printers, 1876.

cover-title, 21 p. 23ᶜᵐ.

1. Lincoln, Abraham, pres. U. S.—Addresses, sermons, etc. 2. Washington, D. C. Lincoln statue (Lincoln park)

Library of Congress E457.8.D73 12—6733 [28d1]

Washington, D. C. Summit Meeting of National Negro Leaders, 1958.

see

Summit Meeting of National Negro Leaders, Washington, D. C., 1958.

Washington, D.C. White House.

MB9 F46m

Fields, Alonzo.

My 21 years in the White House. New York, Coward-McCann [1961]

223 p. 22 cm.

Portrait of author on book jacket.

1. Washington, D. C. White House. 2. Washington, D. C.—Soc. life & cust. 3. Presidents—U. S.—Biog. 4. Presidents—U. S.—Wives. 5. Visits of state—U. S. I. Title.

F204.W5F5 923.173 61—15068 ‡

Library of Congress [62b5]

Washington, D.C. White House.

MB9 P23m

Parks, Lillian (Rogers)

My thirty years backstairs at the White House [by] Lillian Rogers Parks in collaboration with Frances Spatz Leighton. New York, Fleet Pub. Corp. [1961]

346 p. 21 cm.

Portrait of author on book jacket.

1. Presidents—U. S.—Biog. 2. Presidents—U. S.—Wives. 3. Washington, D. C. White House. I. Title.

E176.1.P37 923.173 61—7626 ‡

Library of Congress [61t30]

Washington, D.C. Bethel Literary and Historical Association

see

Bethel Literary and Historical Association

M658.7 W27

Washington Afro-American.

The Washington Afro-American report on characteristics of the Washington Negro market...its product buying and brand preferences in 1945, compiled by the Washington Afro-American, from a survey conducted by the Research company of America. Washington, D.C. c1945.

92p. illus., diagrs. 28x22cm.

1. Market surveys-Washington, D.C.
2. Washington, D.C. I. Research company of America, N.Y. II. Hayden(Harry) company, N.Y. III. Title.

The Washington Afro-American report on characteristics of the Washington Negro market...

M658.7 W27

Washington Afro-American.

The Washington Afro-American report on characteristics of the Washington Negro market...its product buying and brand preferences in 1945, compiled by the Washington Afro-American, from a survey conducted by the Research company of America. Washington, D.C. c1945.

92p. illus., diagrs. 28x22cm.

M323. W279

Washington conference on the race problem in the United States, *Washington, D. C.*, 1903.

How to solve the race problem. The proceedings of the Washington conference on the race problem in the United States under the auspices of the National sociological society, held at the Lincoln temple Congregational church; at the Nineteenth street Baptist church and at the Metropolitan A. M. E. church, Washington, D. C., November 9, 10, 11, and 12, 1903. Addresses, resolutions and debates by eminent men of both races and in every walk of life. Washington, D. C., Beresford, printer, 1904.

1 p. l., 286 p. front., illus. (port.) 23½ᶜᵐ.

Edited by Jesse Lawson. [45p1]

~~1. Negroes. 2.~~ Race question. I. Lawson, Jesse, ed. II. National sociological society.

Library of Congress E185.5.W32 4—14581

Washington, city and capital.

M975.3 F31

Federal writers' project.

Washington, city and capital. Federal writers' project, Works progress administration ... Washington, 1937. Washington, D. C., U. S. Govt. print. off. [1937]

xxvi, 1140, [1] p. incl. front., illus., port., plans. maps (part fold.; part in pocket) 24 cm. (American guide series)

Maps on lining-papers.
Bibliography: p. 1094–1100.

1. Washington, D. C.—Descr.—Guide-books. 2. Washington, D. C.—Hist. 3. Washington, D. C.—Intellectual life. 4. Washington, D. C.—Suburbs. I. Title.

Library of Congress F199.F38 37—26377 [48i²2] 917.53

Washington federation of churches. Interracial committee.

M331.833 J71

Jones, William Henry, 1896–

The housing of negroes in Washington, D. C.; a study in human ecology, by William Henry Jones ... Washington, D. C., Howard university press, 1929.

191 p. incl. front. (port.) plates, maps, diagrs., form. 22ᶜᵐ.

"An investigation made under the auspices of the Interracial committee of the Washington federation of churches."
Bibliography: p. [157]–158.

1. Negroes—District of Columbia. 2. Negroes—Moral and social conditions. 3. Housing—Washington, D. C. I. Washington federation of churches. Interracial committee. II. Title.

Library of Congress E185.93.D6J6 29—22528 [41i1]

M323 W281

Wassom, R Conkling

A larger manhood for the Negro ... by R. Conkling Wassom. Kansas City, Mo., Franklin Hudson publishing co., 1914.

80 [1]p. 17½cm.

I. Title.

Africa M896 W28

Westberg, Per, comp.

Afrika berättar. Malö-Lund, Bo Cavefors Bokförlag, 1961.

438p. 21½cm.
Includes bibliography.
White compiler.

1. African literature - Translations into the Swedish. I. Title.

Wasted travail.

M813.5 R72

Rosebrough, Sadie Mae

Wasted travail. New York, Vantage Press, Inc., 1951.

90p. 21½cm.

The watchword is forward!

M812.5 C15w

Campbell, Dick

The watchword is forward! A playlet, by Dick Campbell. Written for the Madison Square Garden mass meeting of the march on Washington movement. New York, city, Juen 16th, 1942.

23p. 21cm.

Inscribed copy: "To Arthur Spingarn from Dick Campbell."

M813.5 W31c

Waterman, Charles Elmer, 1858–

Carib queens, by Charles E. Waterman. Boston, The Chapple publishing company, ltd., 1932.

viii, 198 p. 18½ᶜᵐ.

CONTENTS.—Defilee.—Marie-Louise.—The Creole empress.

1. Haiti—Hist.—Fiction. 2. Joséphine, empress consort of Napoleon I, 1763–1814—Fiction. I. Title.

Library of Congress PZ3.W31Car 32-33294

——— Copy 2.

Copyright A 58062 [3]

M794 B56s

Waters, Archie, 1918– , jt. author.

Black, Clyde, 1912–

The secrets of Spanish pool checkers, also known as pool checkers or Polish minor checkers, by Clyde "Kingrow" Black and Archie "Checkerboard" Waters. New York [1948–

v. illus. 23 cm.

1. Checkers. I. Waters, Archie, 1918– joint author. II. Title.

GV1463.B57 794.2 48-19338*

Library of Congress [1]

MB9 W29h

Waters, Ethel, 1900–

His eye is on the sparrow; an autobiography by Ethel Waters with Charles Samuels. [1st ed.] Garden City, N. Y., Doubleday, 1951.

278 p. illus. 22 cm.

ViHaI

1. Musicians—~~Correspondence, reminiscences, etc.~~ 2. Jazz music. I. Title.

ML420.W24A3 927.8 51-9726

Library of Congress [25]

MB9 W29v

Waters, Ethel, 1900–

La vie en blues (His eye is on the sparrow), by Ethel Waters et Charles Samuels. Roman. Traduit de l'anglais par Georges Belmont. Préface de Hugues Panassié. Paris, Robert Laffont, [1952]

381p. port. 19cm.

I. Title.

M808.3 W32

Watkins, Alma Taylor.

Eroticism in the novels of Filipe [sic] Trigo. New York, Bookman Associates [1954]

162 p. 23 cm.

Includes bibliography.

1. Trigo, Felipe, 1864–1916. I. Title.

PQ6637.R5Z9 863.6 54-8091 ‡

Library of Congress [3]

M326.99B W32s

Watkins, James, 1823(?)

Struggles for freedom; or the life of James Watkins, formerly a slave in Maryland, U.S.; in which is detailed a graphic account of his extraordinary escape from slavery, notices of the fugitive slave law, the sentiments of American divines on the subject of slavery, etc. 19th edition... Manchester, Printed for James Watkins, 1860.

x [1], -104p. 18½cm.

1. Slave narratives. 2. Slavery in the U.S. I. Title.

M301 J63e5 Watkins, Mark Hanna, 1903-
The West African "bush" school.

(In: Johnson, Charles S. ed. Education and the cultural process ... The American journal of sociology, May 1943. Pp. 38-47)

M326 G87a 1854 Watkins, William James
The work goes bravely on.

(In: Griffiths, Julia ed. Autographs for freedom. Auburn, Alden, Beardsley, 1854. 19½cm. Pp. 156-57).

Watu wa Africa ya mashariki.
Kenya M896.2 K96n Kuria, Henry
Nakupenda, lakini ... [I love you, but ...] Nairobi, Eagle Press, 1957.
42p. 22cm. (Watu wa Africa ya mashariki)
Written in Swahili.

I. Title. II. Series

M265.1 W32h Watkins, S D
Human and divine baptism, by Rev. S.D. Watkins [Charlotte, N.C., A.M.E. Zion publication house, 1927]
34p. front. 20cm.

1. Baptism I. Title

Watkins, William James
M973.6 N21cl 1854 National emigration convention, Cleveland, Ohio.
Arguments, pro and con, on the call for a national emigration convention, to be held in Cleveland, Ohio, August, 1854, by Frederick Douglass, W. J. Watkins, J. M. Whitfield. With a short appendix of the statistics of Canada, West Indies, Central and South America. Published by M. T. Newsome. Detroit, George E. Pomeroy & co., 1854.
34p. 19cm.

Mo1 W36 Waxman, Julia.
Race relations, a selected list of readings on racial and cultural minorities in the United States, with special emphasis on Negroes, by Julia Waxman. Chicago, Ill., Julius Rosenwald fund, 1945.
47 p. 22½cm.
Classified and annotated.

1. ~~Negroes~~—Bibl. 2. ~~U.S.~~—Race question—Bibl. 3. Minorities—~~U.S.~~—Bibl. I. Julius Rosenwald fund. II. Title.
45-7918
Library of Congress Z1361.N39W3
[20] 016.3251

M810.8 W32 Watkins, Sylvestre Cornelius, 1911- , editor.
Anthology of American Negro literature, edited by Sylvestre C. Watkins, with an introduction by John T. Frederick. New York, The Modern library [1944]
xvii, 481 p. 18½ cm. (*Half-title:* The modern library of the world's best books)
"Bibliographical notes": p. [457]-481.

1. ~~Negro~~ literature (American) 2. ~~American literature—Negro authors.~~ I. Title.
44-6528
Library of Congress PS508.N3W3
[48b2] 810.82

M784 W33 Watson, Deek.
The story of the "Ink Spots," by Deek Watson with Lee Stephenson. [1st ed.] New York, Vantage Press [1967]
72 p. 21 cm.

1. Ink Spots. I. Stephenson, Lee, joint author. II. Title.
3. Musicians.
ML400.W23 784'.0922 67-5817/MN
Library of Congress [8]

Way down south.
M792 M97w Muse, Clarence
Way down south, by Clarence Muse and David Arlen. Wood cuts by Blanding Sloan. Hollywood, Calif., David Graham Fischer Publisher, 1932.

145p. illus. 26½cm.

M394.1 W32p Watkins, Sylvestre Cornelius, 1911- *comp.*
The pleasures of smoking as expressed by those poets, wits and tellers of tales who have drawn their inspiration from the fragrant weed. New York, H. Schuman [1948]
xii, 203 p. illus. 25 cm.

1. Smoking. I. Title.
GT3020.W37 394.1 48-9635*
Library of Congress [5]

M326.99B W33 Watson, Henry
Narrative of Henry Watson, a fugitive slave. Written by himself. Boston, Published by Bela Marsh, 1848.
48p. 18½cm.

1. Slavery in the U. S.
2. Slave narratives.

The way of worship in everyday life.
M240 Im2w Imes, William Lloyd, 1889-
The way of worship in everyday life; a course of studies in devotion. [Winona Lake, Indiana, Light and Life Press, 1947]

48p. 15½cm.
Inscribed by author: With best wishes to a great bibliophile Mr. Arthur B. Spingarn October 1947.

M03 W32 Watkins, Sylvestre Cornelius, 1911-
The pocket book of Negro facts. Chicago, Bookmark Press [1946]
24 p. 21 cm.
Cover title.
"Books by and about Negroes": p. 21-22.

1. ~~Negroes~~ History. 2. ~~Negroes—Biog.~~ Biography I. Title.
E185.6.W34 325.260973 47-308 rev*
Library of Congress [r49i8]

M811.5 W33 Watson, Nana.
Reap the harvest. New York, William-Frederick Press, 1952.
31 p. 22 cm. (The William-Frederick poets: 95)

I. Title.
PS3545.A8728R4 811.5 52-11783 ‡
Library of Congress [3]

M287.8 W36c Wayman, Alexander Walker, bp. 1821-1895.
Cyclopaedia of African Methodism, by Alexander W. Wayman ... Baltimore, Methodist Episcopal Book Depository, 1882.
viii, 190p. 19½cm.

1. African Methodist Episcopal Church.
~~2. Churches.~~

M813.5 W32m Watkins, Violette Peaches.
My dream world of poetry; poems of imagination, reality, and dreams. [1st ed.] New York, Exposition Press [1955]
128 p. 21 cm.

I. Title.
PS3545.A8284M9 811.5 55-11196 ‡
Library of Congress [2]

M813.5 W337c Watson, Roberta Bruce
Closed doors. New York, Exposition Press [1967]
95p. 21cm.
Portrait of author on book jacket.

I. Title.

MB9 Sh8w Wayman, Alexander Walker, bp. 1821-1895.
The life of Rev. James Alexander Shorter, one of the bishops of the African M. E. church, by Alexander W. Wayman. With an introduction by Rev. James H. A. Johnson... Baltimore, J. Lanahan, 1890.
50p., front. 19½cm
Presentation copy.
Inscribed copy: Rev. Doctor Bowen, with compliments of the author.
1. African Methodist Episcopal Church.
2. Shorter, James Alexander, 1817-1887.

M326 G87a 1854 Watkins, William James
The evils of colonization.

(In: Griffiths, Julia ed. Autographs for freedom. Auburn, Alden, Beardsley, 1854. 19½cm. Pp. 198-200).

Watts, Isaac, 1674-1748.
MB9 W34d Davis, Arthur Paul, 1904-
Isaac Watts, his life and works, by Arthur Paul Davis ... [New York, 1943]
xi, 307 p. 21cm.
Thesis (PH. D.)—Columbia university, 1942.
"First edition."
Published also without thesis note.
Vita.
"Bibliography I. Works of Isaac Watts": p. 271-281. "Bibliography II. General": p. 282-295.

1. Watts, Isaac, 1674-1748. A 43-1740
Columbia univ. Libraries for Library of Congress BX5207.W8D3 1943 a
[44c1]† [922.2] 922.342

M287.6 W36m Wayman, Alexander Walker, bp. 1821-1895.
Manual, or guide book for the administration of the discipline of the African M.E. church. By Alex. W. Wayman ... Philadelphia, A. M. E. Book Rooms, 1886.
84p. 17½cm.

1. African Methodist Episcopal Church.

M287.8
W36m
Wayman, Alexander Walker, *bp.*, 1821-1895.
My recollections of African M. E. ministers, or, Forty years' experience in the African Methodist Episcopal church. By Rev. A. W. Wayman ... With an introduction by Rev. B. T. Tanner, D. D. Philadelphia, A. M. E. book rooms, 1881.
xxi, 250 p. front. (port.) 20cm.
I. Title. II. Title: Forty years' experience in the African Methodist Episcopal church.
1. African Methodist Episcopal Church 37-12169
Library of Congress BX8478.W35A4
Copyright 1881: 761 [2] 922.773

Wayne Co., Mich. - Pol. & govt.
MB9
P36m
Mallas, Aris A
Forty years in politics; the story of Ben Pelham, by Aris A. Mallas, Jr., Rea McCain [and] Margaret K. Hedden. Detroit, Wayne State University Press, 1957.
92 p. illus. 24 cm.
1. Pelham, Benjamin B., 1862-1948. 2. Finance, Public—Wayne Co., Mich. 3. Wayne Co., Mich.—Pol. & govt. I. Title.
F572.W4P4 923.573 57—10562 ‡
Library of Congress [59f5]

The ways of white folks.
M813.5
H87w
Hughes, Langston, 1902-
The ways of white folks [by] Langston Hughes. New York, A. A. Knopf, 1934.
7 p. l., 3-248 p., 1 l. 19½cm.
Short stories.
"First edition."
I. Title. 34—27175
Library of Congress PZ3.H87318Way
[44h1]

Weaver, Robert Clifton, 1907-
M331.833
Am3h
American council on race relations.
Hemmed in A B C's of race restrictive housing covenants. [Chicago, Ill., American council on race relations, 1945]
14p. illus. 23cm.

We can't run away from here.
M813.5
Sc2w
Screen, Robert Martin
We can't run away from here. New York, Vantage Press, 1958.
55p. 21cm.

We challenged Jim Crow!
M323
R92
Rustin, Bayard
We challenged Jim Crow! A report on the journey of reconciliation April 9-23, 1947, by George Houser and Bayard Rustin. New York, Fellowship of Reconciliation; Congress of Racial Equality, 1947.
15p. 22cm.

We charge genocide.
M343.3
C49w
Civil Rights Congress.
We charge genocide; The historic petition to the United Nations for relief from a crime of the United States government against the Negro people. New York, Civil Rights Congress, 1951.
239p. 24cm.

We fished all night.
M813.5
M85w
1953
Motley, Williard, 1912-
We fished all night. New York, New American Library, 1953.
598p. 18cm. (Signet books)
Pocket book edition.

We fished all night.
M813.5
M85w
Motley, Willard, 1912-
We fished all night. New York, Appleton-Century-Crofts [1951]
560 p. 22 cm.
I. Title.
PZ3.M8573We 51-14180 ‡
Library of Congress [7]

We have tomorrow.
MB
B64w
Bontemps, Arna Wendell, 1902-
We have tomorrow, by Arna Bontemps, illustrated with photographs by Marian Palfi. Boston, Houghton Mifflin company, 1945.
vi p., 2 l., 131 p. front., ports. 20cm.
CONTENTS.—The Campbell kid: E. Simms Campbell.—A girl who liked hats: Mildred E. Blount.—Strangers and friends: Horace E. Clayton.—Beatrice's secret: Beatrice Johnson Trammell.—Fiddler's progress: Dean Dixon.—He was fired: Sylvestre C. Watkins.—The judge's boy: Douglas Watson. — Sailor's dream: Emmett M. May. — Her own idea: Hazel Scott.—They called him a ham: Algernon P. Henry.—Star's return: James E. Lu Valle.—Wings on his shoulders: Benjamin Davis, jr.
1. Negroes—Biog. I. Title. 45—8344
Library of Congress E185.96.B6
[47h²5] 325.260973

We hold these truths.
M813.5
H87a
Hughes, Langston, 1902-
Anti-Semitism and Negroes.
(In: League of American Writers. "We hold these truths..." New York, The League of American Writers, 1939. 20cm. p.58-59)

We lift our voices...
M811.5
C83w
Cowdery, Mae V
We lift our voices and other poems, by Mae V. Cowdery. With a frontispiece for the title poem, by Allan Freelon and an introduction by William Stanley Braithwaite. Philadelphia, Alpress, 1936.
68p. front. 21cm.
This is no. 291 of 350 numbered copies.

We sing America.
M973
C97
Cuthbert, Marion Vera, 1896-
We sing America, by Marion Cuthbert; illustrations by Louise E. Jefferson. New York, Friendship press [©1936]
viii p., 1 l., 117 p. illus. 20cm.
Includes songs with music.
1. Negroes. I. Title. 36-28988 rev
Library of Congress E185.6.C975
[r43k2] 325.260973

We who would die...
M811.5
D63
Dismond, Henry Binga, 1891-
We who would die, and other poems, including Haitian vignettes, by Binga Dismond; illustrations by E. Simms Campbell. New York, W. Malliet and company, 1943.
[68] p. illus. 23½cm.
I. Title. 43-3078
Library of Congress PS3507.I 74W4
[3] 811.5

Wealth.
M335
W85d
Woodbey, G W
The distribution of walth, by Rev. G.W. Woodbey... [San Diego, Calif., G.W. Woodbey] 1910.
68p. front. 15cm.

The Weary blues.
M811.5
H87c
Hughes, Langston, 1902-
Cernoch si zpiva blues. Praha, Statni Nakladatelstvi Krasne Literatury, 1957.
157p. illus. 20cm.
Translation of: The Weary blues.
"Especially for Arthur Spingarn, Sincerely, Langston Hughes, New York February 20, 1958."
I. Title: The Weary Blues.

The weary blues.
M811.5
H87wh
Hughes, Langston, 1902-
The weary blues. [Japanese translation] n.p., 1958.
71p. 16cm.
In Japanese.

The weary blues.
M811.5
H87w
Hughes, Langston, 1902-
The weary blues, by Langston Hughes; with an introduction by Carl Van Vechten. New York, A. A. Knopf, 1926.
109 p. 19½cm.
Poems.
I. Title. 26—4730
Library of Congress PS3515.U274W4 1926
[39k1]

A weary stranger without a home.
M784
R56w
Robinson, A B
A weary stranger without a home. Asheville, North Carolina, The author, [1941].
[2]p. 24cm. (Trumpets of Gabriel, Jubilee anthems, no.2)

The Weather family.
Brit. Guiana
M823.91
M69we
Mittelholzer, Edgar, 1909-
The Weather family; a novel. London, Secker & Warburg, 1958.
339p. 23cm.

Brit. Guiana
The Weather in Middenshot.
M823.91
M69w
Mittelhölzer, Edgar.
The weather in Middenshot, a novel. [1st American ed.] New York, J. Day Co. [1953, ©1952]
280 p. 20 cm.
I. Title.
PZ3.M6977We 2 53-1289 ‡
Library of Congress [3]

M343.3
W371
Weatherford, Willis Duke, 1875
Lynching, removing its causes; Address delivered before the Southern Sociological Congress, New Orleans, La., April 14, 1916. Southern Sociological Congress, 1916.

18p. 16cm.

1. Lynching.

M331
W37
Weaver, Robert Clifton, 1907-
Male Negro skilled workers in the United States, 1930-1936, by Robert C. Weaver, Administrator of survey, Ira DeA. Reid ... Preston Valien ... Charles S. Johnson ... Sponsored by United States Department of the Interior .... Washington, D.C. Govt. Print. Off., 1939.

vi, 87p. tables graphs 29cm.
At head of title: The Urban Negro worker in the United States, 1925-1936, volume II.

M323
R72
Weaver, Robert Clifton, 1907-
Negro labor since 1929.

(In: Rose, Arnold, ed. Race prejudice and discrimination;... New York, Knopf, 1951. 22cm. pp. 117-131)

M323
W37
Weatherford, Willis Duke, 1875-
Race relations; adjustment of whites and Negroes in the United States, by Willis D. Weatherford ... and Charles S. Johnson ... Boston, New York ₍etc.₎ D. C. Heath and company ₍°1934₎

x, 590 p. 22½ cm. (On cover: Social relations series)
Bibliography: p. 558-576.

~~1. Negroes.~~ 2. U. S.—Race question. 3. ~~Negroes~~—Moral and social conditions. 4. Slavery in the U. S. I. Johnson, Charles Spurgeon, 1893- joint author. II. Title.

34—36788

Library of Congress E185.W42
₍40h³₂₎ 325.260973

M331
W37
Weaver, Robert Clifton, 1907-
Male Negro skilled workers ... (card 2)

Vol. 1 of above work has title: An analysis of the training, types, and conditions of employment and the earnings of 200,000 skilled and white-collar Negro workers.

1. Employment. 2. Economic conditions. I. Title. II. The Urban Negro worker in the United States. III. U.S. Office of Adviser on Negro Affairs.

M323
W379
Weaver, Robert Clifton, 1907-
Summary of conference and plans for future. ₍Conference on Research in Race Relations, University of Chicago, July 26-30, 1952₎
Reprinted from Inventory of research in racial and cultural relations, v. 5, no.2-3, Winter-spring, 1953.

204-213p. 24cm.

1. Race relations.

M326
W37
Weaver, Robert Bartow.
The struggle over slavery, by Robert B. Weaver ... Chicago, Ill., The University of Chicago press ₍°1938₎

vii, 83, ₍1₎ p. illus. (incl. ports., map, facsim.) 23cm.
"The major portion of this volume consists of descriptions, statements, and explanations taken from source materials."—Pref.
Contents.—Early slavery in America.—Controversies over the extension of slavery.—The secession movement.—The civil war.—Reconstruction in the South.—Bibliography (p. 83-₍84₎)

1. Slavery in the U. S.—Controversial literature. 2. U. S.—Hist.—1849-1877—Sources. I. Title.

38-17444

Library of Congress E449.W34
——— Copy 2.
Copyright A 119120 ₍5₎ 326.973

M810.8
M77p
Weaver, Robert Clifton, 1907-
The Negro comes of age in industry.

(In: Moon, Bucklin, ed. Primer for white folks. Garden City, N.Y. Doubleday, Doran, 1945. 21½cm. pp. 439-450).

M301.36
W37
Weaver, Robert Clifton, 1907-
The urban complex; human values in urban life ₍by₎ Robert C. Weaver. ₍1st ed.₎ Garden City, N. Y., Doubleday, 1964.

xii, 297 p. 22 cm.
Bibliographical footnotes.

1. Urbanization—~~U. S.~~ 2. Urban renewal—~~U. S.~~ 3. Metropolitan areas—~~U. S.~~ 4. Cities and towns—Growth. I. Title.

HT123.W38 301.360973 64-15800
Library of Congress ₍5₎

M973
R72
Weaver, Robert Clifton, 1907-
The changing structure of the American city and the Negro.

Pp. 135-146.

In: Rose, Arnold Marshall, ed. Assuring freedom to the free. Detroit, Wayne State University, 1964.

M331
W37ne
Weaver, Robert Clifton, 1907-
The Negro comes of age in industry. Washington, D.C., National CIO Committee to Abolish Racial Discrimination, 1943.

54-59p. 25½cm.
Reprinted from the Atlantic Monthly, September 1943.

1. Employment 2. Labor and laboring class.

Weaver, Robert Clifton, 1907-
M323
C43
Chicago. Mayor. Conference on Race Relations. February 1944.
Proceedings ... Chicago, The Committee, 1944.

64p. 28cm.

M323
Am3m
Weaver, Robert Clifton, 1907-
Defense industries and the Negro.

(In: American Academy of Political and Social Science. Minority peoples in a nation at war. Philadelphia, 1942. p. 60-66).

M331.833
W37n
Weaver, Robert Clifton, 1907-
The Negro ghetto. New York, Harcourt, Brace & co., 1948.

xviii, 404p. 21cm.

1. Housing. I. Title.

M813.5
W38s
Webb, Charles Lewis.
Sasebo diary. New York, Vantage Press ₍1964₎
129p. 20½cm.

Portrait of author on book jacket.

I. Title. 1. Korean War, 1950-1951-Fiction.

M301.36
W379
Weaver, Robert Clifton, 1907-
Dilemmas of urban America ₍by₎ Robert C. Weaver. Cambridge, Mass., Harvard University Press, 1965.

ix, 138 p. 21 cm. (The Godkin lectures at Harvard University, 1965)
"Based on the Godkin lectures ... delivered at Harvard University."
Bibliographical references included in "Notes" (p. ₍121₎-131)

1. Urban renewal—U. S. I. Title. (Series: Godkin lectures, Harvard University, 1965)

HT175.U6W4 65-22056
Library of Congress ₍5₎

M331.833
W37n3
Weaver, Robert Clifton, 1907-
The Negro in a program of public housing. Reprinted from Opportunity, July 1938.

6p. illus. 28cm.

1. Housing. I. Title.

M813.3
W38g
Webb, Frank J
The Garies and their friends. By Frank J. Webb. With an introductory preface by Mrs. Harriet B. Stowe. London, G. Routledge & co., 1857.
vi, 2, 392p. 19½cm.
First edition.

I. Title.

M973.9
F46
No.21
Weaver, Robert Clifton, 1907-
Fifty years of progress in housing. Pittsburgh, Pittsburgh Courier, 1950.

7p. port. 24cm. (Fifty years of progress)

1. Housing. I. Series.

M331
W37n
Weaver, Robert Clifton, 1907-
Negro labor, a national problem ₍by₎ Robert C. Weaver. New York, Harcourt, Brace and company ₍1946₎

xiv, 329 p. 21cm.
"First printing."
"Selected bibliography": p. 317-321.

1. Negroes—Employment. I. Title.
2. Labor and laboring classes. 46-25023

Library of Congress E185.8.W38
₍35₎ 331.96

M350
W38m
Webb, Percy R , 1917-
Memoranda of a soldier. New York, Vantage Press, 1961.

61p. 20cm.
Portrait of author on back of book jacket.

1. U.S.-World War II, 1941-1945.
I. Title.

M07
W41
Wedlock, Lunabelle.
... The reaction of Negro publications and organizations to German anti-Semitism, by Lunabelle Wedlock, M. A. Washington, D. C., The Graduate school, Howard university, 1942.
4 p. l., [7]-208 p. 23½ cm. (The Howard university studies in the social sciences, vol. III, no. 2)

1. Negroes. 2. Jewish question. 3. Jews in Germany. I. Title.
Library of Congress H31.H66 vol. 3, no. 2 [48f1] (308.2) 325.260973 43—431

'Weh down souf...
M811.4
D29
Davis, Daniel Webster, 1862-
'Weh down souf, and other poems [by] Daniel Webster Davis. Illustrations [by] William L. Sheppard ... Cleveland, The Helman-Taylor company, 1897.
vi, 7-136 p. front., 3 pl. 18½cm.
Appendix: Introduction to the author's first volume of poems [Idle moments] by John H. Smythe.
Glossary.

I. Title.
Library of Congress PS1514.D56 [32b1] 24-11131
Copyright 1897: 67169

M396
W46g
1951
Wellington, Joseph, 1888-
The glory of womanhood, a discourse delivered before the Empire State Federation of Women's Clubs, the Shiloh Benevolent Society of Staten Island, the Book-lovers Club of New York, inc. [and] the Young Women's Elite Society of New York. Foreword by Nannie C. Burden. New York, Exposition Press [1951]
40 p. 21 cm.

1. Woman. I. Title.
HQ1233.W37 1951 396 51-4238
Library of Congress [2]

Weed.
M813.5
C783w
Cooper, Clarence L
Weed, a novel. Evanston, Ill., Regency Books [1961]
159p. 18cm.

Dominican Republic
M796.357
AL73
Weiskopf, Herm, joint author.
Alou, Felipe, 1935-
Felipe Alou: my life and baseball, by Felipe Alou with Herm Weiskopf. Waco, Tex., Word Books [1967]
154 p. illus., ports. 23 cm.

I. Weiskopf, Herm, joint author. II. Title: My life and baseball.
GV865.A38A3 796.3576'4'0924 67-18977
Library of Congress [5]

M396
W46g
Wellington, Joseph, 1888-
The glory of womanhood. Empire state federation of woman's clubs address, by Joseph Wellington...
New York, Alliance press c1932
45p 18 cm.

1. Women I Title

Weeds and other poems.
M811.5
C85
Crawford, Isaac
Weeds and other poems. Brooklyn, N.Y., The Author, 1952.
61p. 19cm.

...Der Weisse Neger ein leben zwischen...
M813.5
J63w
Johnson, James Weldon
...Der Weisse Neger ein leben zwischen den rassen mit einem begleitwort . von Frederick Delius. Frankfurt A. M., Frankfurter Societats-Druckerei, 1928.
208p. 23cm.
Inscribed copy: Dear Arthur: I hope to get you to read this to me some day, so that I may be sure what it's about. Jim.

M06
Am35
Wells, J L
Lockawanna steel mill, illus.
(In: American Academy of Political and Social Science. The American Negro. Philadelphia, 1928. 24cm. frontispiece)

Congo (Leopoldville)
M967.5
W41c
Weeks, John H.
Congo life and folklore; part I, life on the Congo as described by a brass rod; part II, thirty-three native stories as told round the evening fires, by the Rev. John H. Weeks ... London, The Religious tract society, 1911.
xxii p., 1 l., 468 p. front., illus., plates, port. 21½cm.

1. Congo. 2. Ethnology—Congo. 3. Folk-lore—Congo. I. Title.
Library of Congress DT650.W4 [n41d1] 12—782

Welborne, Anthony W., 1840- p. 202-03.
M286
W61h
Whitted, J A
A history of the Negro Baptists of North Carolina, by Rev. J.A. Whitted... Raleigh, Presses of Edwards and Broughton printing co., 1908.
212p. front. plates - 22½cm.

M323
W46f
Wells, Moses Peter
Faults of the world. New York, Carlton Press, 1962.
150p. 23cm.
"A Reflection book."
Portrait of author on book jacket.

1. Race relations. I. Title.

M338.9
G92s
Weeks, Rocheforte L
Liberia.
Pp. 38-44.
In: Science and the new nations, edited by Ruth Gruber. 1961.

1. Liberia. I. Title.

Welch, Norval.
M89
M92
Mulzac, Hugh, 1886-
A star to steer by; by Hugh Mulzac, as told to Louis Burnham and Norval Welch. New York, International Publishers [1963]
251 p. illus. 21 cm.

1. Merchant marine—U. S.—Negroes. 2. Merchant marine—U. S.—Officers—Correspondence, reminiscences, etc. I. Burnham, Louis E., 1915 or 16-1960. II. Welch, Norval. III. Title.
E185.63.M8 923.573 63-14260 ‡
Library of Congress [5]

M813.5
W46t
Wells, Moses Peter
Three adventurous men. New York, Carlton Press, 1963.
55p. 20cm. (A Geneva book)
Portrait of author on book jacket.

1. Short stories. I. Title.

Kenya
M896.3
N49w
Weep not, child.
Ngugi, James, 1938-
Weep not, child. London, Heinemann, 1964.
153p. 18½cm.

Welfare council of New York city. Section on employment and vocational guidance.
M331
G76t
Granger, Lester Blackwell, 1896-
Toward job adjustment, with specific reference to the vocational problems of racial, religious and cultural minority groups, by Lester B. Granger ... Louis H. Sobel ... [and] William H. H. Wilkinson ... Prepared under the direction of Committee on minority groups, Section on employment and vocational guidance, Welfare council of New York city. [New York] Welfare council of New York city [°1941]
78 p., 1 l. illus. 21½cm.
Bibliography: 76-78.
1. Interviewing. 2. Employment agencies. 3. Minorities. I. Sobel, Louis Harry, joint author. II. Wilkinson, William H. H. III. Welfare council of New York city. Section on employment and vocational guidance. IV. Title.
Library of Congress HD5861.G65 [10] 331.11511 41-16628

M813.5
W46w
Wells, Moses Peter.
Working for progress. New York, Carlton Press, 1963.
32p. 20cm. (A Geneva book)
Portrait of author on book jacket.

I. Title.

M811.1
H18
Wegelin, Oscar, 1876-
Jupiter Hammon, American Negro poet; selections from his writings and a bibliography, by Oscar Wegelin; with five facsimiles. New York, Ninety-nine copies printed for C. F. Heartman, 1915.
51 p. incl. front. facsims. (1 fold.) 24cm. (*On verso of half-title: Heartman's historical series, no. 13*)
"No. 77 of 91 copies printed on Alexandra Japan paper."

1. Hammon, Jupiter, b. ca. 1720.
Library of Congress PS767.H15Z8 [42c1] 16—730

En welke is onze zonde.
Brit. Guiana
M823.91
M69wel
Mittelholzer, Edgar, 1909-
En welke is onze zonde; roman. Amsterdam, EM. Querido's Uigeversmij, 1953.
295p. 21cm.
Title: Shadows move among them.
Dutch edition.

M572
W46a
Wells, Robert Gilbert, 1865-
Anthropology applied to the American white man and Negro, by Robert Gilbert Wells. Buxton, Iowa, Wells & company [1905]
239 [2] p. front., plates. 19cm.

1. Anthropology

MB9
W48
Wendell, Bruce.
The future of the pianoforte; A plea for its continued maintenance as the corner stone of musical culture in the home. Antiqua, 1936.

(In: Bruce Wendell; Introductory memoir... Antiqua, n.p., 1936. pp.22-25.)

Zanzibar
M398
St3s
Werner, Alice, 1895-1935.
Steere, Edward, bp. 1828-1882.
Swahili tales, by Edward Steere. A new edition, revised by Alice Werner. London, The Sheldon press, 1929.

185p. 18½cm.
Written in Swahili.
White author.

1. Folklore, Swahili. 2. Tales, African. I. Title. II. Werner, Alice, 1895-1935.

M378
W51
1948
Wesley, Charles Harris, 1891-
The history of Alpha Phi Alpha; A development in Negro college life. Washington, D.C., Foundation publishers, 1948.

463p. illus. 22cm.

1. Alpha Phi Alpha.

MB9
W48
Wendell, Bruce.
Bruce Wendell; Introductory memoir with biographical notes, by [Aethiops] Antiqua, n.p., 1936.

26p. port. 17cm.

M896.3
St3s
Werner, Alice.
Steere, Edward.
Swahili tales, by Edward Steere. A new revised edition. Revised by Alice Werner. London, The Sheldon press, 1929.

185p. 18½cm.

M378
W51
Wesley, Charles Harris, 1891-
The history of Alpha phi alpha; a development in Negro college life, by Charles H. Wesley ... Washington, D. C., The Foundation publishers, Howard university [1935, 1929.
1x 296 p. illus. (incl. ports.) fold. pl. 22½cm.
"Second edition, revised and enlarged."
"National Alpha phi alpha hymn" (words and music): p. [311]-[319]

1. Alpha phi alpha. 2. Negroes. I. Title: Negro college life.

Library of Congress LJ121.A55W4 1935 36-3087
——— Copy 2.
Copyright A 90328 [3] 371.855

Nigeria
M896.1
G25y
Wenger, Susanne.
Gbadamosi, Bakare, comp.
Yoruba poetry, collected and translated by Bakare Gbadamosi and Ulli Beier. Eight Silkscreen prints and ten vignettes by Susanne Wenger. Ibadan, Nigeria Printing and Publishing Co., 1959.
68p. illus. 26½cm.
A special publication of "Black Orpheus"

M973
W51c
Wesley, Charles Harris, 1891-
The changing African historical tradition. Reprint from the Journal of Human Relations, Volume VIII, Numbers 3 and 4.

21p. 23cm.
Bibliography: 352-354.

1. Africa - History. I. Title.

M366.5
W51h
Wesley, Charles Harris, 1891-
History of the Improved Benevolent and Protective Order of Elks of the World, 1898-1954. Washington, Association for the Study of Negro Life and History [1955]
508 p. illus. 23 cm.

1. Elks of the World, Improved Benevolent and Protective Order of.

HS2259.E53W4 *366.5 55-13609 ‡
Library of Congress [a56c2]

M740
C86w
Were you there...
Crite, Allan Rohan, 1910- illus.
Were you there when they crucified my Lord; a Negro spiritual in illustrations, by Allan Rohan Crite. Cambridge, Mass., Harvard university press, 1944.
[93] p. illus. 32cm.
Music for the spiritual: p. [13]

1. Jesus Christ—Art. 2. Jesus Christ—Crucifixion. 3. Negro spirituals. I. Title.

Harvard univ. Library for Library of Congress N8053.C7 A 44-4812
[46q4] 741.6385

M973.8
W51
Wesley, Charles Harris, 1891
The collapse of the confederacy, by Charles H. Wesley. Published under the direction of The Department of history, Howard University, Washington, D. C.
373-422p. 26cm.
In: Howard university record, 16: May 1922.

1. Confederate States of America-History. I. Title

M366.1
W51h
Wesley, Charles Harris, 1891-
The history of the Prince Hall Grand Lodge of Free and Accepted Masons of the State of Ohio, 1849-1960; an epoch in American fraternalism. Wilberforce, Ohio, Central State College Press [1961]
457 p. illus. 24 cm.

1. Freemasons. Ohio. Grand Lodge (Negro)
2 Hall, Prince
HS887.O3W4 366.109771 61-30649 ‡
Library of Congress [3]

Kenya
M896.1
H119
Werner, Alice, 1859-1935, tr.
Hadithi ya Mikidadi na Mayasa.
The story of Miqdad & Mayasa, from the Swahili-Arabic text of Alice Werner. Medstead, Hampshire, Azania Press, 1932.
90p. illus. 19cm.
Written in Swahili and English.
1. Swahili language - Texts. I. Werner, Alice, 1859-1935, tr. II. Title. III. Title: Miqdad & Mayasa, The story of.

M973.8
W51
Wesley, Charles Harris, 1891-
The collapse of the confederacy, by Charles H. Wesley ... Washington, D. C., The Associated publishers, inc., 1937.
xiii, 225 p. 18½cm.
"A complete revision and expansion of an essay ... first published as a brief account in one of the Howard university studies in history."—Pref.
Bibliography: p. 195-211.

1. Confederate States of America—Hist. I. Title.

38-2881
Library of Congress E487.W56
[43p2] 973.716

M973
W51n
Wesley, Charles Harris, 1891-
Neglected history; essays in Negro history by a college president: Charles H. Wesley. Wilberforce, Ohio, Central State College Press, 1965.
200 p. 23 cm.
Bibliographical references included in "Historical notes" p. 186-187)

1. Negroes—Hist.—Addresses, essays, lectures. I. Title.

E185.W46 973.0917496 65-5958
Library of Congress [3]

Jamaica
M398
J38
Werner, Alice, 1859-1935.
Jekyll, Walter, comp. and ed.
Jamaican song and story: Annancy stories, digging sings, ring tunes, and dancing tunes, collected and edited by Walter Jekyll: with an introduction by Alice Werner, and appendices on traces of African melody in Jamaica by C. S. Myers, and on English airs and motifs in Jamaica, by Lucy E. Broadwood ... London, Pub. for the Folk-lore society by D. Nutt, 1907.
xxxviii p., 1 l., 288 p. illus. (music) 22½cm. (Added t.-p.: ... Publications of the Folk-lore society, LV)

I. Werner, Alice, 1859-1935. II. Myers, C. S. III. Broadwood, Lucy Etheldred, d. 1929.

7-23639
Library of Congress GR121.J2J4
[44h1]

M370
W51ed
Wesley, Charles Harris, 1891-
Education for citizenship in a democracy. [Washington, D.C.,] 1941.
"Reprinted from the Journal of Negro Education, January 1941, p. 68-78."
68-78p. 25cm.

1.Education. I.Title.

M323.
W51
Wesley, Charles Harris, 1891- ed.
... The Negro in the Americas, edited by Charles H. Wesley ... Washington, D. C., The Graduate school, Howard university [1940]
3 p. l., 86 p. 23½cm. (Public lectures of the Division of the social sciences of the Graduate school, Howard university. vol. 1)
CONTENTS.—The Negro in the British West Indies, by Eric Williams.—Notes on the Negro in the French West Indies, by L. T. Achille.—The Negro in Spanish America, by R. W. Logan.—The Negro in Brazil, by Richard Pattee.—The Haitian nation, by Dantes Bellegarde.—Race, migration and citizenship, by Ira De A. Reid.—The Negro in the United States and Canada, by C. H. Wesley.
1. Negroes in America. I. Title. 1. West Indies. 2. Brazil. 3. Haiti.
Library of Congress H31.H65 vol. 1 40-34239
——— Copy 2. 129.N8W5
[44f1] (306.2) 325.26007

Zanzibar
M896.1
K57
Werner, Alice, 1895-1935.
Kusham, Kwana Kupona (Binti) 1810-1860?
The advice of Mwana Kupona upon the wifely duty, from the Swahili texts, by Alice Werner and William Hichens. Medstead, Hampshire, The Azania press [1934]
95p. illus. 19½cm.

1. African poetry. 2. Swahili literature. I. Werner, Alice, 1895-1935. II. Hichens, William.

M973
W51f
Wesley, Charles Harris, 1891- Foreword.
Year.
Year's pictorial history of the American Negro. [Maplewood, N. J., C. S. Hammond, 1965]
144 p. illus., facsims., ports. 30 cm.
Bibliography: p. 142.

1. Negroes—Hist. 2. Negroes—Civil rights. I. Title.

E185.Y4 301.451 65-18139
Library of Congress [42-1]

M326.
W51n
Wesley, Charles Harris, 1891-
The Negro in the organization of abolition. Reprinted from Phylon, 2:223-235. Third quarter 1941.

223-235p. 25cm.
Paper read at the meeting of the American Historical Association, 1940.

1. Abolitionists 2. Slavery in the U.S.-Anti-slavery societies I. title

M331
W51
Wesley, Charles Harris, 1891–
Negro labor in the United States, 1850–1925; a study in American economic history, by Charles H. Wesley ... New York, Vanguard press, 1927.
xiii, 343 p. illus. (map) $18\frac{1}{2}$cm.
Bibliography: p. 321–330.

1. Negroes—Employment. I. Title.
27–7288
Library of Congress HD6305.C7W4
[44h1]

M973.8
W51n
Wesley, Charles Harris, 1891–
The Negroes of New York in the emancipation movement. Reprinted from the Journal of Negro history, 24:65–103, January 1939.
65–103p. $24\frac{1}{2}$cm.

1. Slavery in the U.S. – Emancipation
2. ~~Emancipation~~ 3. Abolitionists
I. title

M973.7
W516
Wesley, Charles Harris, 1891–
Ohio Negroes in the Civil War. [Columbus, Ohio State University Press for the Ohio Historical Society [1962]
46 p. 24 cm. (Publications of the Ohio Civil War Centennial Commission, no. 6)
Includes bibliography.

1. U. S.—Hist.—Civil War—Negro troops. 2. Negroes—Ohio. I. Title.
E525.O337 no. 6 62–63753 ‡
Library of Congress [5]

MB9
A17w
Wesley, Charles Harris, 1891–
Richard Allen, apostle of freedom, by Charles H. Wesley ... Washington, D. C., The Associated publishers, inc. [©1935]
xi p., 2 l., 300 p. front. (port.) 20cm.
Bibliography: p. 277–285.

1. Allen, Richard, bp., 1760–1831. 2. African Methodist Episcopal church.
36–272
Library of Congress BX8449.A6W4
[40g1] 922.773

Wesley, Charles Harris, 1891– jt. author.
M973
W86s
1959
Woodson, Carter Goodwin, 1875–1950.
The story of the Negro retold, by Carter G. Woodson and Charles H. Wesley. 4th ed. rev. and enl. Washington, D.C., The Associated Pub.,Inc., 1959.
472p. illus. 20cm.

M973
W51t
Wesley, Charles Harris, 1891–
The treatment of the Negro in the teaching of United States history. Reprinted from Social Education, 7:295–300, November 1943.
295–300p. 27cm.

1. History– Study and teaching

M811.5
W517d
Wess, Deborah Fuller
Drippings from a poet's pen. [Washington Bell Print, 1949]
37p. 23cm.
Autographed.

I. Title.

M813.5
W521
West, Dorothy.
The living is easy. Boston, Houghton, Mifflin Co., 1948.
347 p. 22 cm.

I. Title.
PZ3.W5174Li 48–6871*
Library of Congress [4]

M813.5
W52
West, Dorothy
An unimportant man.
pp. 124–53 19cm.
In: Copy, 1929; stories, plays, poems and essays. New York, D. Appleton and Company, 1939.

I. Title.

M813.5
W52b
West, John B
Bullets are my business. New York, The New American Library, 1960.
128p. 18cm. (Signet Book)

I. Title.

M813.5
W52c
West, John B
Cobra venom. New York, The New American Library, 1960.
126p. 18cm. (Signet Book)

I. Title.

M813.5
W52d
West, John B.
Death on the rocks. [New York] New American Library [1961]
128p. 18cm.
"A Signet book."

1. Title.

M813.5
W52e
West, John B
An eye for an eye. New York, The New American Library, 1959.
144p. 18cm. (A Signet Book)

I. Title.

M813.5
W52t
West, John B
A taste for blood. New York, The New American Library, 1960.
144p. 18cm. (Signet Book)
Portrait of author on book cover.

I. Title.

M813.5
W53c
West, William, 1933–
Cornered. New York, Carlton Press, 1964.
134p. 20½cm.
Portrait of author on book jacket.

I. Title.

Sierra Leone West Africa in history.
M966
C768a
Conton, William Farquhar, 1925–
West Africa in history, [by] W. F. Conton. Revised new ed. London, Allen & Unwin, 1966–
v. maps, table. $21\frac{1}{2}$ cm. v. 2: 9/6 (v. 2: B 66–13706)
CONTENTS.—
v. 2. Since 1800.

1. Africa, West—Hist. I. Title.
DT471.C65 966 66–74863
Library of Congress [2]

Sierra Leone
M966
C768
West Africa in history.
Conton, William Farquhar, 1925–
West Africa in history. London, Allen & Unwin, [1961–63]
2 v. illus., port., maps. 22 cm.
CONTENTS.—v. 1. Before the Europeans.—v. 2. Sovereignty lost and regained.

1. Africa, West—Hist. I. Title.
DT471.C64 62–5214 rev ‡
Library of Congress [r64c2]

West Africa on the March.
M966.7
Ag9w
Agyeman, Nana Yaw Twum Dush.
West Africa on the march, an intimate survey of problems and potentialities. New York, William-Frederick Press, 1952.
73 p. 22 cm.

1. Africa, West. I. Title.
DT494.A6 966 52–9947 ‡
Library of Congress [2]

West Africa vignettes.
M910
F28w2
Fax, Elton C
West Africa vignettes. [Translations by Jacques Leger. 2d ed. New York] American Society of African Culture [1963]
92 p. illus., ports., map. 26 cm.
French and English.

1. National characteristics, West African. 2. Africa, West—Biog.—Portraits. I. Title.
DT494.F3 1963 916.6 63–11211
Library of Congress [3]

West Africa vignetts.
M910
F28w
Fax, Elton C
West Africa vignettes. [New York] American Society of African Culture [1960]
62 p. illus. 26 cm.

1. National characteristics, West African. 2. Africa, West—Biog.—Portraits. I. Title.
DT494.F3 916.6 60–11410 ‡
Library of Congress [3]

West African Affairs, No. 5.
Gold Coast
M966.7
J73
Jones-Quartey, K. A. B.
Problems of the press. London, The Bureau of Current Affairs, n.d.
15p. $22\frac{1}{2}$cm. (West African Affairs, no.5)

West African Folk-tales.
Gold Coast
M966.7 Barker, William Henry, 1882-
B24w West African folk-tales, collected and arranged by W.H. Barker...and Cecilia Sinclair. London, George G. Harrap & Co., 1917.

184p. front., plates. 19cm.
Printed in Great Britain.

The West African intellectual community.
Africa, West
M370 **International Seminar on Inter-university Co-operation in**
In8 West Africa, *Freetown, Sierra Leone, 1961.*
The West African intellectual community; papers and discussions. ₍Ibadan, Nigeria₎ Published for the Congress for Cultural Freedom by Ibadan University Press, 1962.

356 p. 22 cm.

Held under the joint auspices of Fourah Bay College and the Congress for Cultural Freedom, 11-16 December 1961.

1. Education—Africa, West—Congresses. I. Freetown, Sierra Leone. Fourah Bay College. II. Congress for Cultural Freedom. III. Title.

LA1503.I 5 1961 63-6250

Library of Congress ₍2₎

Ghana West African Soviet Union.
M966 Awoonor-Renner, Bankole
Aw96 West African Soviet Union. London, Wans Press, 1946.

31p. 18½cm.

West India Emancipation.
M252 Pennington, James William Charles, 1812-1871.
P38a An address delivered at Newark, N.J. at the first anniversary of West India Emancipation. August 1, 1839. By J.W.C. Pennington. Newark, N.J., Aaron Guest Printer, 1839.

12p. 20cm.

West Indian cricket.
British Guiana
M796 Nicole, Christopher, 1930-
N54 West Indian cricket; the story of cricket in the West Indies with complete records. London, Phoenix Sports Books ₍1957₎

256p. ports. 22cm.

West Indian drama.
Trinidad
M822.91 Hill, Errol G ed.
H55 Caribbean plays, vol. 2. With an introduction by C. L. R. James. [Mona, Jamaica] Extra-Mural Dept., University of the West Indies, 1965.

174p. 21cm.

West Indian fiction.
Guadeloupe
M843.9 Baghio'o, Jean Louis
B14i Issandre le mulatre. Preface de Katherine Dunham. Paris, Fasquelle Éditeurs, 1949.

v. 174p. front (port.) 19cm.

West Indian fiction.
Guadeloupe
M843.91 Blancan, André.
B59j Scènes de la vie créole; Jacques Danglemont, par André Blancan. Paris, Martory & c^ie, 1917.

4p. l., 408p. 18½cm. fr. 3.50

West Indian fiction.
Guadeloupe
M843.91 Chambertrand, Gilbert de.
C35t Titine grosbonda. Paris, Fasquelle Editeurs ₍1947₎

250p. front (port.) 18cm.

West Indian fiction.
Martinique
M843.91 Sainville, Léonard.
Sa2d Dominique, nègre esclave. Paris, Fasquelle, 1951.

327p. 19cm.

West Indian fiction - History and criticism.
British Guiana
M823.09 Harris, Wilson
H24 Tradition and the West Indian novel; a lecture delivered to the London West Indian Students' Union on Friday, 15th May, 1966. With an introduction by C. R. R. James. ₍London, London West Indian Students' Union, 1965₎

17p. 21cm.

1. West Indian fiction - History and criticism. I. Title. II. James, C L R Introduction.

Jamaica West Indian folk-tales.
M398 **Sherlock, Philip Manderson,** 1902
Sh54 West Indian folk-tales, retold by Philip Sherlock; illustrated by Joan Kiddell-Monroe. London, Oxford U. P., 1966.

₍7₎, 151 p. col. front., illus., col. plates. 22½ cm. (Oxford myths and legends) 17/6 (B 66-637)

1. Tales, West Indian. I. Kiddell-Monroe, Joan, illus. II. Title.

GR120.S5 1966a 398.24 66-70268

Library of Congress ₍5₎

The West Indian in Britain.
Jamaica
M972.92 Manley, Douglas
M31 The West Indian in Britain, by Clarence Senior and Douglas Manley. Edited by Norman MacKenzie. London, Fabian Colonial Bureau, 1956.

29p. 21½cm.

West Indian literature.
Guadeloupe
M848 Baudot, Paul, 1801-1870.
B32o ...Oeuvres créoles; poésies, fables, théatre, contes. Basse-Terre, Guadeloupe, Imprimerie du governement, 1923.

vii, 165p. 19cm.

West Indian literature.
Guadeloupe
M972.97 Lara, H Adolphe.
L319c Contributionde la Guadeloupe a la pensée francaise, 1635-1935. Preface de Léon Hennique. Paris, Editions Jean Crès, 1936.

301p. portraits. 22cm.

West Indian literature.
Guadeloupe
M972.97 Lara, Oruno
L321 La litterature Antillaise. Aux pays bleus. Notes de litterature et d'art etudes et critiques. La litterature Antillaise et le regionalisme chez les creoles ... Paris, Librairie "Le progres Vulgarisateur Fernand Drubay, 1913.

xiv. 206p. port. 18cm.

West Indian literature.
Guadeloupe
M972.97 Lara, Oruno.
L32s Sous le ciel bleu de la Guadeloupe ... Paris, Librairie Fischbacker, 1912.

174p. port. 18cm.

West Indian literature.
Jamaica
M823.91 Salkey, Andrew, comp.
Sa3a Stories from the Caribbean, an anthology. Selected and introduced by Andrew Salkey. London, Elek Books ₍1965₎

256p. 21cm.
"For Arthur from Andrew, 5/22/65."

West Indian literature.
Guadeloupe
M972.97 Vauchelet, Emile, 1830-1913.
V46g La Guadeloupe ses enfants célèbres (Leonard Lethière, Bernard, Poirie St. Auréle), par Vauchelet. Paris, Augustin Challamel, 1894.

130p. 18cm.

West Indies West Indian narrative.
M823 **Ramchand, Kenneth,** *comp.*
R144 West Indian narrative: an introductory anthology. London, Nelson, 1966.

xii, 226 p. illus. (ports.) 19½ cm. 12/6 (B 66-9738)

Includes excerpts from English novelists dealing with the West Indies.
Col. maps on endpapers.

1. English fiction (Collections) 2. West Indies in literature. I. Title.

PZ1.R138We 66-74111

Library of Congress ₍5₎

West Indian poetry.
Virgin Is.
M811.5 Anduze, Aubrey
An29r Reminiscence. St. Thomas, Virgin Islands, The Art Shop, 1940.

89p. 22½cm.

West Indian poetry.

Africa M808.81 B75 Brent, P L ed.
Young Commonwealth poets '65. London, Heinemann in assocation with Cardiff Commonwealth Arts Festival [1965]

216p. 22½cm.
White editor.

1. Poetry - Collection. 2. African poetry. 3. West Indian poetry. I. Title.

West Indian poetry.

Trinidad M821 C88p Cruickshank, Alfred M.
Poems in all moods, by Alfred M. Cruickshank ... Port-of-Spain, Trinidad, Belle Eau Road, 1937.

viii, [10] - 203p. 19½cm.

West Indian poetry.

Trinidad M821 D24c Darlington, Levi A.
Calliope, by Levi A. Darlington. Trinidad, Cosmopolitan Printing Works, 1938.

124p. 19½cm.

West Indian poetry.

Virgin Is. M811.5 G42v Gimenez, J P , comp.
Virgin Islands folklore and other poems, compiled and arranged by J. P. Gimenez. New York, Frank Harding (agent), c1933.

100, [2] p. 27½cm.

West Indian poetry.

Virgin Is. M811.5 H286 Hatchette, Wilfred Irvin
Youth's flight, a collection of poems. St. Thomas, Virgin Island, Art Shop Press, 1938.

30p. 20½cm.

West Indian poetry.

Virgin Is. M811.5 J29b Jarvis, Jose Antonio, 1901-
Bluebeards last wife. Charlotte Amalie, V. I. Jarvis Art Gallery, 1951.

25p. 21cm.
Inscribed by author.

West Indian poetry.

Virgin Is. M811.5 J29f Jarvis, Jose Antonio, 1901-
Fruits in passing, poems. St. Thomas, Virgin Islands, The Art Shop [c1932]

99p. illus. 17cm.
Autographed.

West Indian Poetry.

Trinidad M821.91 L17p Lambert, Calvin Stollmeyer, 1913?-
Poems of a West-Indian. London, "Poetry of to-day", 1938.

35p. 20cm.

Trinidad M821.91 L17s West Indian Poetry.

Lambert, Calvin Stollmeyer, 1913?-
Selected poems of a West-Indian, by Calvin S. Lambert. London, The Fortune press [1940]

57, [1] p. 19½cm.

A 41-624

Harvard univ. Library for Library of Congress [3]

W. Indies M821.08 T91 West Indian poetry.
Twelve West-Indina poems for children. British Guiana, for private circulation of Govt. Training College for Teachers class of 1952.

15 p. 15 cm.
Contents: Walter McA. Lawrence. Leo (Egbert Martin). F.E. Brassington. A.F. Seymour. J. Hamilton Holder. Reginald Henry. J.W. Harper-Smith. George Campbell. Archie Lindo. Una Marson. Frank Collymore.

West Indian poetry - Collections.

West Indies M821.08 K98 Kyk-over-al anthology of West Indian poetry.
Revised by A. J. Seymour. Georgetown, British Guiana, 1957.

99p. 23cm. (Kykoveral 22)

West Indian stories.

Jamaica M823.91 Sa3w Salkey, Andrew, 1928- , ed.
West Indian stories. London, Faber and Faber, 1960.

224p. 20cm.

West Indian story.

Jamaica M972.9 Sh54w Sherlock, Philip Manderson
West Indian story. London, Longmans, 1960.

vii, 134p. illus. 19cm.
Map of theWest Indies and British Caribbean Federation Territories on lining papers.

1. West Indies - History. I. Title.

Barbados M972.9 H85 West Indians - History.
Hoyos, F A
The rise of West Indian democracy; the life and times of Sir Grantley Adams. [n.p.] Advocate Press, 196?.

228, x p. ports. 21cm.

1. Adams, Sir Grantley Herbert, 1898- 2. West Indians - History. I. Title.

West Indians in Great Britain.

West Indies M325.27 F21 **Family Welfare Association, *London*.**
The West Indian comes to England; a report prepared for the Trustees of the London Parochial Charities by the Family Welfare Association. Contributors: Douglas Manley, Ivo de Souza, Albert Hyndman, et al. Edited by S. K. Ruck. London, Routledge & K. Paul [1960]

187 p. 23 cm.

1. West Indians in Great Britain. I. Ruck, S. K., ed. II. Title.

DA125.W4F3 325.2729042 60-3053 ‡

Library of Congress [2]

Barbados M942 M45 West Indians in Great Britain.
Maxwell, Neville George Anthony.
The power of Negro action, by Neville Maxwell. [London] N. G. A. Maxwell [1966]

1-59 p. 22 cm. 3/-
Bibliography: p. 57-58. (B 66-5406)

1. West Indians in Great Britain. 2. Negroes in Great Britain. 3. Gt. Brit.—Race question. I. Title.

DA125.W4M3 301.45196042 66-70698

Library of Congress [5]

Jamaica M972.92 G191m West Indies.
Garvey, Amy Jacques
Memorandum correlative of Africa, West Indies and the Americas, sent to the representatives of the United Nations... by Mrs. Amy Jacques Garvey. Jamaica, n.d.

65p. 21cm.

West Indies.

M813.5 H87fbw **Hughes, Langston, 1902-**
The first book of the West Indies. Pictures by Robert Bruce. New York, F. Watts [1956]

62 p. illus. 23 cm. ([First books, 70)

1. West Indies. I. Title.
Full name: James Langston Hughes.

F1608.H8 917.29 55-11846 ‡

Library of Congress [20]

West Indies.

Haiti M972.9 M819d Morisseau-Leroy, Felix, 1912-
...Le destin des Caraïbes. El destino del Caribe. Port-au-Prince, Haiti [Imprimerie Telhomme] 1941.

1p. l., [1], 6-107, [1]p. 21cm.
French and Spanish on opposite pages, numbered in duplicate.

West Indies.

M323.2 W5k **Wesley, Charles Harris, 1891-** *ed.*
... The Negro in the Americas, edited by Charles H. Wesley ... Washington, D. C., The Graduate school, Howard university [1940]

3 p. l., 86 p. 23½cm. (Public lectures of the Division of the social sciences of the Graduate school, Howard university. vol. 1)

CONTENTS.—The Negro in the British West Indies, by Eric Williams.—Notes on the Negro in the French West Indies, by L. T. Achille.—The Negro in Spanish America, by R. W. Logan.—The Negro in Brazil, by Richard Pattee.—The Haitian nation, by Dantes Bellegarde.—Race, migration and citizenship, by Ira De A. Reid.—The Negro in the United States and Canada, by C. H. Wesley.

1. Negroes in America. I. Title.

40-34259

Library of Congress H31.H65 vol. 1
——— Copy 2. E29.N3W5

[44f1] (308.2) 325.26007

Trinidad M972.9 W67c West Indies.
Williams, Eric, ed.
Caribbean historical review. Port-of-Spain, Trinidad Pub. Co., 1951.

152p. 21½cm. (Historical Society of Trinidad and Tobago ... No. 2. Dec. 1951)
Partial contents.- The caribbean bookshelf: the sugar economy of the Caribbean, by Eric Williams.

1. Trinidad. 2. Caribbean area. 3. West Indies. I. Title.

West Indies.

Trinidad
M300
W67n
Williams, Eric, 1911-
... The Negro in the Caribbean, by Eric Williams ... Washington, D. C., The Associates in Negro folk education, 1942.
4 p. l., 119 p. incl. tab. 22cm. (Bronze booklet no. 8)
"Reference notes": p. 110-114. "Select bibliography": p. 115-117.
1. Negroes in the West Indies. I. Title.
42-16832
Library of Congress E185.5.B85 no. 8
——— Copy 2. F1623.W48
[45j2] (825.200078) 825.2000729

West Indies-Biography.

Puerto Rico
M264
Sch6s
Schomburg, Arthur Alfonso, 1874-1938
Some interesting facts [program notes].
(In: Business and Professional Men's Forum Inc. Program of second annual entertainment and dance. New York, 1936. 27cm.)

West Indies - Civilization.

Trinidad
M323
M29af
Maloney, Arnold Hamilton, 1888-
After England—we; nationhood for Caribbea. Boston, Meador Pub. Co. [1949]
183 p. map. 21 cm.
1. West Indies—Pol. & govt. 2. West Indies—Econ. condit.—1918- 3. West Indies—Civilization. I. Title.
F1608.M28 972.9 49-5870*
Library of Congress [3]

West Indies—Commerce.

Jamaica
M972.92
H55p
Hill, Richard, 1795-1872.
The Picaroons; or, one hundred and fifty years ago: being a history of commerce and navigation in the West Indian seas. By the Honorable Richard Hill...communicated to the Port Royal reading society. Dublin, John Falconer, 1869.
80p.

West Indies - Communism.

Martinique
M343
C331e
Césaire, Aimé, 1913-
Letter to Maurice Thorez. Paris, Presence Africaine [c1957]
16p. 18cm.

West Indies - Descr. & trav.

M910
D92p
Dunham, Katharine
[Preface]
(In: Leaf, Earl. Isles of rhythm. New York, A. S. Barnes, [1948]. 24cm. p.vii-ix)

West Indies - Description and travel.

MB9
P93m
Prince, *Mrs.* Nancy (Gardener) *b.* 1799.
A narrative of the life and travels of Mrs. Nancy Prince. Boston, The author, 1850.
87, [1] p. 16cm.
1. Russia—Soc. life & cust. 2. West Indies—Descr. & trav.
[29b1] 20-18619
Library of Congress CT275.P848A3

West Indies - Description and travel - 1951-

Martinique
M972
F66
Florentiny, Édouard.
Les Antilles toutes nues. Paris, L. Soulanges, 1966.
159 p. 19 cm. 10 F. (F 66-8067)
Illustrated cover.
1. West Indies—Soc. condit. 2. West Indies—Descr. & trav.—1951- I. Title.
F1612.F55 66-73468
Library of Congress [5]

West Indies - Description and travel - Poetry.

Cuba
M861.6
G94w
Guillén, Nicolás, 1904-
... West Indies ltd.; poemas. La Habana, Cuba [Imp. Ucar, García y cía.] 1934.
4 p. l., 5-48 p. 19½ x 15½cm.
1. Poetry of places—West Indies. 2. West Indies—Descr. & trav.—Poetry. I. Title.
44-37199
Library of Congress PQ7389.G84W4
[3]

West Indies - Economic conditions.

M301
F86e
Frazier, Edward Franklin, 1894- ed.
The economic future of the Caribbean. Editors, E. Franklin Frazier and Eric Williams. Washington, Howard University Press, 1944.
94p. 23cm. (Howard University. Division of Social Sciences. Conference 7th)

West Indies - Economic conditions.

W.Indies
M972.9
B41
Latin American economic institute.
... Economic problems of the Caribbean area; speeches, addresses and abstracts of papers, delivered at the public conference held in New York city jointly with the Women's international league for peace and freedom on May 1, 1943, by Dantes Bellegarde, Lawrence Berenson [and others] ... New York, 1943.
cover-title. 60 p. 23cm. (*Its* Pamphlet series, no. 7)
1. West Indies—Econ. condit. I. Women's international league for peace and freedom. II. Title.
44-47231.
Library of Congress HC161.L26 no. 7
[45d2] (330.82) 330.9729

West Indies - Economic conditions - 1918-

Trinidad
M323
M29af
Maloney, Arnold Hamilton, 1888-
After England—we; nationhood for Caribbea. Boston, Meador Pub. Co. [1949]
183 p. map. 21 cm.
1. West Indies—Pol. & govt. 2. West Indies—Econ. condit.—1918- 3. West Indies—Civilization. I. Title.
F1608.M28 972.9 49-5870*
Library of Congress [3]

West Indies-Emigration and Immigration.

Jamaica
M972.92
M31
Manley, Douglas
The West Indian in Britain, by Clarence Senior and Douglas Manley. Edited by Norman MacKenzie. London, Fabian Colonial Bureau, 1956.
29p. 21½cm.

West Indies - Federation.

Trinidad
M820
J231
James Cyril Lionel Robert, 1901-
Lecture on federation (West Indies and British Guiana). Delivered June 1958 at Queen's College. Demerara, Argosy Co., Ltd., 1958.
25p. 21cm.
1. West Indies - Federation. 2. British Guiana - Federation.

West Indies-Folklore.

Tobago
M972.98
Ot5to
Ottley, Carlton Robert, 1914-
Tobago legends and West Indian lore. [Trinidad, 1950]
137p. illus. 19cm.

West Indies - Folk-lore.

Trinidad
M398
T36
1890
Thomas, J J.
Froudacity; West Indian fables by James Anthony Froude, explained by J. J. Thomas ... Philadelphia, Gebbie and company, 1890.
261p. 19½cm.

West Indies - Folk-lore.

Trinidad
M398
T36
1889
Thomas, J J.
Froudacity; West Indian fables by James Anthony Froude, explained by J. J. Thomas ... London, T. F. Unwin, 1889.
261 p. 12°.
Library of Congress 1-11139

West Indies - History.

Jamaica
MB9
Ol4
Olivier, Sydney Haldane Olivier, baron, 1859-1943.
Letters and selected writings, edited with a memoir by Margaret Olivier. With some impressions by Bernard Shaw. London, Allen & Unwin, 1948.
252p. plates, ports. 22cm.

West Indies West Indies - History.

M972.9
P24s
Parry, John Horace.
A short history of the West Indies, by J. H. Parry and P. M. Sherlock. London, Macmillan; New York, St. Martin's Press, 1956.
316 p. illus. 23 cm.
Includes bibliography.
1. West Indies—Hist. I. Sherlock, Philip Manderson, joint author.
F1621.P33 972.9 56-58641 ‡
Library of Congress [57k10]

West Indies - History.

Jamaica
M972.9
Sh54w
Sherlock, Philip Manderson
West Indian story. London, Longmans, 1960.
vii, 134p. illus. 19cm.
Map of the West Indies and British Caribbean Federation Territories on lining papers.
1. West Indies - History. I. Title.

West Indies - History.

Jamaica
M972.9
Sh54we
Sherlock, Philip Manderson.
West Indies [by] Philip Sherlock. London, Thames & Hudson [1966]
215 p. illus. (incl. ports.) 3 maps, facsims, table. 21½ cm. (New nations and peoples) 35/-
(B 66-22385)
Bibliography: p. 194-198.
1. West Indies—Hist. I. Title.
F1621.S5 972.9 66-66325
Library of Congress [2]

West Indies - History - Sources.
Trinidad
M972.9
W67b
Williams, Eric Eustace, 1911-
British historians and the West Indies. Port-of-Spain, P.N.M. Pub. Co., Ltd., 1964.
187p. 21cm.
Includes bibliography.
Portrait of author on back cover.

Trinidad
M323
M29af
West Indies - Politics and government.
Maloney, Arnold Hamilton, 1888-
After England—we; nationhood for Caribbea. Boston, Meador Pub. Co. [1949]
183 p. map. 21 cm.
1. West Indies—Pol. & govt. 2. West Indies—Econ. condit.—1918- 3. West Indies—Civilization. I. Title.
F1608.M28 972.9 49-5870*
Library of Congress [3]

Jamaica
M972.9
Sh54we
West Indies.
Sherlock, Philip Manderson.
West Indies [by] Philip Sherlock. London, Thames & Hudson [1966]
215 p. illus. (incl. ports.) 8 maps, facsims., table. 21½ cm. (New nations and peoples) 35/-
(B 66-22385)
Bibliography: p. 194-196.
1. West Indies—Hist. I. Title.
F1621.S5 972.9 66-66325
Library of Congress [2]

Trinidad
M972.9
W67d
West Indies - History - Sources.
Williams, Eric Eustace, 1911-
Documents of West Indian history, Port-of-Spain, PNM Pub. Co., 1963-
v. 21cm.
Contents: V. 1 From the Spanish discovery to the British conquest of Jamaica, 1492-1955.
Autographed.
Portrait of the author on back cover.

Trinidad
M972.9
W67p
West Indies - Politics and government.
Williams, Eric Eustace, 1911-
Perspectives for the West Indies [speech delivered at San Fernando on Monday, May 30th, 1960. Port-of-Spain, P.N.M. Pub. Co., 1960]
12p. 21cm.
1. West Indies - Politics and government. I. Title

Trinidad
M917.29
C246
The West Indies; islands in the sun.
Carley, Wilfred.
The West Indies; islands in the sun. [Camden, N. J.] Nelson [1967]
224 p. illus., map. 22 cm. (World neighbors)
Bibliography: p. 218.
1. West Indies. Juvenile literature. I. Title.
F1608.3.C35 917.29'03'5 67-13917
Library of Congress [3]

Trinidad
M917.29
C246
West Indies - Juvenile literature.
Carley, Wilfred.
The West Indies; islands in the sun. [Camden, N. J.] Nelson [1967]
224 p. illus., map. 22 cm. (World neighbors)
Bibliography: p. 218.
1. West Indies. Juvenile literature. I. Title.
F1608.3.C35 917.29'03'5 67-13917
Library of Congress [3]

Jamaica
M823.91
Sa3w
West Indies - Short stories.
Salkey, Andrew, 1928- , ed.
West Indian stories. London, Faber and Faber, 1960.
224p. 20cm.

Barbados
M823
L18p
West Indies, British.
Lamming, George, 1927-
The pleasures of exile. London, M. Joseph [1960]
232 p. 23 cm.
1. Colonies. 2. West Indies, British. I. Title.
PR6023.A518P5 828.91 60-51766 ‡
Library of Congress [2]

Jamaica
M972.92
H55p
West Indies—Navigation.
Hill, Richard, 1795-1872.
The Picaroons; or, one hundred and fifty years ago: being a history of commerce and navigation in the West Indian seas. By the Honorable Richard Hill...communicated to the Port Royal reading society. Dublin, John Falconer, 1869.
30p.

West Indies
M325.27
F21
West Indies - Social conditions.
Family Welfare Association, *London.*
The West Indian comes to England; a report prepared for the Trustees of the London Parochial Charities by the Family Welfare Association. Contributors: Douglas Manley, Ivo de Souza, Albert Hyndman, et al. Edited by S. K. Ruck. London, Routledge & K. Paul [1960]
187 p. 23 cm.
1. West Indians in Great Britain. I. Ruck, S. K., ed. II. Title.
DA125.W4F3 325.2729042 60-3053 ‡
Library of Congress [2]

Windward Is.
M330
L58L
West Indies, British.
Lewis, William Arthur, 1915-
Labour in the West Indies; the birth of a workers' movement, by W. Arthur Lewis; with a preface by A. Creech Jones, M. P. London, V. Gollancz ltd. and the Fabian society, 1939.
44 p. 21½cm. (*On cover:* Fabian society. Research series, no. 44)
1. Labor and laboring classes—West Indies, British. 2. Trade-unions—West Indies, British. I. Title.
41-6678
Library of Congress HX11.N42 no. 44
[2] (355.1062) 331.6800729

Trinidad
M972.98
W67r
West Indies - Political conventions.
Williams, Eric Eustace, 1911-
Responsibilities of the party member by Dr. Eric Williams, premier of Trinidad and Tobago; full text of the political leader's address to the fifth annual convention on Friday, September (1960). [Port-of-Spain, P.N.M., 1960]
16p. 21cm.

Martinique
M972
F66
West Indies - Social conditions.
Florentiny, Édouard.
Les Antilles toutes nues. Paris, L. Soulanges, 1966.
159 p. 19 cm. 10 F.
(F 66-6987)
Illustrated cover.
1. West Indies—Soc. condit. 2. West Indies—Descr. & trav.—1951- I. Title.
F1612.F55 66-73468
Library of Congress [5]

Jamaica
M972.9
Sh54
West Indies, British.
Sherlock, Philip Manderson.
Caribbean citizen. London, New York, Longmans, Green [1957]
158 p. illus. 19 cm.
1. West Indies, British. I. Title.
A 58-4133 ‡
Wisconsin. Univ. Libr. for Library of Congress [2]

Trinidad
M972.98
W67r
West Indies - Political parties.
Williams, Eric Eustace, 1911-
Responsibilities of the party member by Dr. Eric Williams, premier of Trinidad and Tobago; full text of the political leader's address to the fifth annual convention on Friday, September (1960). [Port-of-Spain, P.N.M., 1960]
16p. 21cm.

Nigeria
M966.9
El4f
West Indies (Federation).
Elias, Taslim Olawale
Federation vs. confederation and the Nigerian Federation. Trinidad, Office of the Premier of Trinidad and Tobago, 1960.
50p. 24½cm.

Trinidad
M300
W67e
West Indies, British - Education.
Williams, Eric Eustace, 1911-
Education in the British West Indies. Foreword by John Dewey. Port-of-Spain, Printed by Guardian Commercial Printery, [1950]
xix, 167p. 22cm.
At head of title: The Teachers' Economic and Cultural Association, ltd.

Trinidad
M972.9
J23
West Indies - Politics.
James, C L R , 1901-
Party politics in the West Indies. San Juan, Vedic Enterprises, n.d.
175p. 22cm.
Portrait of author on back cover.

West Indies
M972.97
L95w
West Indies (Federation)
Lowenthal, David.
The West Indies Federation; pespectives on a new nation. New York, Columbia University Press, 1961.
142 p. illus. 21 cm. (American Geographical Society. Research series, no. 23)
Includes bibliography.
1. West Indies (Federation)
F2131.L8 972.97 61-7176 ‡
Library of Congress [61k10]

Trinidad
M972.9
W67
West Indies, British - History.
Williams, Eric Eustace, 1911- , ed.
The British West Indies at Westminster. Part I: 1789-1823. Extracts from the debates in parliament. Port-of-Spain, Historical Society of Trinidad and Tobago, 1954.
136p. 21cm.

Nigeria
M966.9
EL4f
West Indies, British - Politics and government.
Elias, Taslim Olawale
Federation vs. confederation and the Nigerian Federation. Trinidad, Office of the Premier of Trinidad and Tobago, 1960.
50p. 24½cm.

M370
W52b
West Virginia. *State dept. of education.*
Biennial report.
Charleston ,etc., 18
v. illus. (incl. plans) plates, ports., maps, tables, diagrs. 23cm.
Report year irregular.
Title, : Annual report of the general superintendent of public schools.
1890/92 includes "History of education in West Virginia. By B. S. Morgan and J. F. Cork."
Library has: 1928
1. Education—West Virginia. 2. West Virginia - Education
6-7382 Revised
Library of Congress L214.B2
r45e2
379.754

M370
G61m
West Virginia. School for the colored deaf and blind, Institute.
Goodlett, Carlton Benjamin.
... The mental abilities of twenty-nine deaf and partially deaf Negro children, by Carlton B. Goodlett and Vivian R. Greene (with a foreword by Harry W. Greene) ... Charleston, W. Va., Jarrett printing company, 1940.
23 p. incl. illus., tables, diagr. 23cm. (West Virginia state college bulletin ... Ser. no. 4. June, 1940)
"Contribution no. 1 of the Departments of psychology and education, West Virginia state college, in cooperation with the West Virginia school for the colored deaf and blind, Institute, West Virginia."
"Publications of West Virginia state college."
Bibliographical foot-notes.
1. Mental tests. 2. Negroes—Education. 3. Deaf—Education and institutions. 3. Deaf and dumb—West Virginia. I. Greene, Vivian R., joint author. II. West Virginia. School for the colored deaf and blind, Institute. III. Title.
U. S. Off. of educ. Library for Library of Congress
BF432.N5G6
a44c1
E 40-403
371.912

Trinidad
M820
J23c
West Indies, British-Pol. & govt.
James, Cyril Lionel Robert, 1901-
The case for West-Indian self government by C. L. R. James. London, L. and Virginia Woolf at the Hogarth press, 1933.
32 p. 18½cm. (On cover: Day to day pamphlets, no. 16)
1. West Indies, British—Pol. & govt. I. Title.
34-34780
Library of Congress F2131.J26
3
972.97

M975.4
H55n
West Virginia.
Hill, Tyler Edward, 1883-
The Negro in West Virginia; Report of T. Edward Hill, director, Bureau of Negro Welfare and Statistics of the state of West Virginia to governor Ephraim F. Morgan. Charleston, W. Va. 1922.
102, iiip. 23cm.

M378
W52a
West Virginia. State college, *Institute. Research council.*
... An adventure in cooperative research; Harry W. Greene, editor; associate editors: Herman G. Canady, Harrison H. Ferrell and others ... Personnel of Research council: Harry W. Greene, chairman; Hillery C. Thorne, executive secretary and others ... Institute, W. Va., West Virginia State college 1944
74 p. 23cm. (West Virginia state college bulletin. Ser. 31, no. 1. Feb. 1944)
Cover-title: The Research council at West Virginia State college publishes An adventure in cooperative research.
"Fourth contribution of the Research council."—Introd.
"The second of a series ... in connection with the semi-centennial celebration (1941) of the West Virginia State college."—Introd.
(Continued on next card)
44-42483
4

Guadeloupe
M325
C16a
West Indies, French.
Candace, Gratien, 1873-
Les Antilles dans la prosperite des ports francais depuis trois siecles.
(In: Denis, Serge, ed. Nos Antilles... Orleans, G. Luzeray; Paris, Maison du Livre Francais, 1935. 25½cm. p.65-79)

M975.4
P84n
West Virginia.
Posey, Thomas Edward, 1901-
The Negro citizen of West Virginia, by Thomas E. Posey ... Institute, W. Va., Press of West Virginia state college 1934
1 p. l., 5-119 p. plates, ports., diagrs. 24cm.
Bibliography: p. 110-112.
1. Negroes—West Virginia. I. Title.
37-27796
Library of Congress E185.93.W5P6
2
325.2609754

M378
W52a
West Virginia. State college, *Institute. Research council.* ... An adventure in cooperative research ... 1944
(Card 2)
CONTENTS.—The conference in review, by H. C. Thorne.—The theory of educational research, by J. S. Price.—The newer Negro and his education, by F. C. Sumner.—Some suggestions for research in the contribution of the Negro to American life, by John Lovell, jr.—The promotion of biological research, by H. E. Finley.—South America, a new frontier, by V. B. Spratlin.
1. Research. ~~1. Negroes.~~ 2. ~~Negroes~~—Education. 3. ~~Negroes in~~ South America. I. Greene, Harry Washington, 1896- ed. II. Title.
44-42483
Library of Congress E185.5.W5
4
325.260973

West Indies
M823
R144
West Indies in literature.
Ramchand, Kenneth, *comp.*
West Indian narrative: an introductory anthology. London, Nelson, 1966.
xii, 226 p. illus. (ports.) 19½ cm. 12/6
(B 66-9738)
Includes excerpts from English novelists dealing with the West Indies.
Col. maps on endpapers.
1. English fiction (Collections) 2. West Indies in literature. I. Title.
PZ1.R188We
66-74111
Library of Congress
5

M975.4
W52
West Virginia.
West Virginia. Bureau of Negro Welfare and Statistics.
Report.
Charleston, 1922-
v. 23½cm. Biennial.
1925 report has title: The Negro in West Virginia.
Report year edns June 30.
See holdings card for issues incollection.

M378
G83t
West Virginia. State college, Institute—Bibl.
Greene, Harry Washington, 1896-
... Two decades of research and creative writings at West Virginia state college, compiled by Harry W. Greene ... Institute, W. Va., West Virginia state college 1939
iv p., 1 l., 7-24 p. 23cm. (West Virginia state college bulletin. Ser. 26, no. 4. Aug.-Nov. 1939)
Contribution no. 2 of the Research council at West Virginia state college.
Publications of West Virginia state college.
Z5055.U5W45
(Continued on next card)
E 40-3 rev
r46e2

Cuba
M861.6
G94w
...West Indies ltd.; poemas.
Guillén, Nicolás, 1904-
... West Indies ltd.; poemas. La Habana, Cuba Imp. Ucar, García y cía. 1934.
4 p. l., 5-48 p. 19½ x 15½cm.
1. Poetry of places—West Indies. 2. West Indies—Descr. & trav.—Poetry. I. Title.
44-37199
Library of Congress PQ7389.G84W4
2

M975.4
W52
West Virginia.
West Virginia, Bureau of Negro welfare and statistics
Report
Charleston, 1922
v. 23½cm.
Report year ends June 30.

M975.4
W87w
West Virginia and its struggle for statehood.
Woodward, Isaiah Alfonso, 1913-
West Virginia and its struggle for statehood, 1861-1863. Baltimore, Wolk Pub. Co., 1954
44 p. illus., ports., map. 22 cm.
Bibliography: p. 39-42.
1. West Virginia—Pol. & govt. I. Title.
E536.W65 975.4 54-37068
Library of Congress
1

M975.4
W52
West Virginia. Bureau of Negro Welfare and Statistics.
Report.
Charleston. 1922-
v. 23½cm. Biennial.
1925 report had title: The Negro in West Virginia.
Report year ends June 30.
See holdings card for issues in collection.
1. West Virginia.
I. Hill, Tyler Edward.

M370
W52b
West Virginia - Education.
West Virginia. *State dept. of education.*
Biennial report.
Charleston ,etc., 18
v. illus. (incl. plans) plates, ports., maps, tables, diagrs. 23cm.
Report year irregular.
Title, : Annual report of the general superintendent of public schools.
1890/92 includes "History of education in West Virginia. By B. S. Morgan and J. F. Cork."
1. Education—West Virginia.
6-7382 Revised
Library of Congress L214.B2
r45e2
379.754

M378
G83a
West Virginia state college, Institute.
Greene, Harry Washington, 1896-
... An adventure in experimental co-operative teaching; a general account of recent work in progressive education conducted jointly by members of the Department of education of the Ohio state university and the West Virginia state college, by Harry W. Greene ... Institute, W. Va., 1938.
vi, 7-86 p. 22½cm. (West Virginia state college bulletin ... November, 1938. ser. 25, no. 6 ... Contribution no. 9 of the Dept. of education)
Bibliography: p. 82-86.
1. Teachers, Training of. 2. Education—Experimental methods. I. Ohio state university, Columbus. College of education. II. West Virginia state college, Institute. III. Title.
A 40-1473
Teachers college library, for Library of Congress
Columbia univ.
2

M975.4
W52
West Virginia. Bureau of Negro Welfare and Statistics. Report. (biennial)

Volume	Year	Month	Volume	Year	Month
	1925-26				
	1933-34				
	1937-38				
	1939-40				

M975.4
W87w
West Virginia - Pol. & govt.
Woodward, Isaiah Alfonso, 1913-
West Virginia and its struggle for statehood, 1861-1863. Baltimore, Wolk Pub. Co., 1954
44 p. illus., ports., map. 22 cm.
Bibliography: p. 39-42.
1. West Virginia—Pol. & govt. I. Title.
E536.W65 975.4 54-37068
Library of Congress
1

MB9
W52
Westberry, Ransom William, 1871-
Wilson, John R.
Life and speeches of Ransom W. Westberry, by Prof. John R. Wilson... Atlanta, Ga., A.B. Caldwell publishing company, 1921.
130p. , illus. 23cm.

U. S.
M968
Am3
Westerfield, Samuel Z 1919-
The economic future of Central Africa.

Pp. 138-144.

In: American Society of African Culture. Southern Africa in transition. New York, Praeger, 1966.

Panama
M986.2
W52n
Westerman, George W
Non-self-governing territories and the United Nations. Panama, 1958.

33p. 22½cm.
Spanish text: 36p.
"Best wishes, G. W. Westerman."

1. United Nations. 2. Non-self-governing territories. I. Title.

Panama
M986.2
W52u
Westerman, George W
Urban housing in Panama and some of its problems. Panama, Imprenta de la Academia, 1955.

43p. tables 23½cm.

1. Panama - Housing. 2. Housing - Panama.

Panama
M986.2
W52b
Westerman, George W
Blocking them at the canal (Failure of the red attempt to control local workers in the vital Panama Canal area). Panama, Imprenta de la Academia, 1952.

67p. 23cm.

I. Title 1. Canal zone
2. Communism - Canal zone

Panama
M986.2
W52pi
Westerman, George W
Pioneers in Canal Zone education. [Canal Zone], La Boca and Silver City Occupational High Schools, 1949.

21p. illus. 24cm.

1. Canal Zone. - Education.

Africa
M89
W52a
Westermann, Diedrich, 1875-
Autobiographies d'Africains. Onze autobiographies d'indigènes originaires de diverses régions de l'Afrique et représentant des métiers et des degrés de culture différents. Traduction française de L. Homburger. Paris, Payot, 1943.
328p. map. 22½cm.

1. Africa - Biographies. 2. Biography. 3. Mqhayi, Samuel Edward Kroune, 1875-
4. Akiga, Benjamin, 1908-

Panama
M89
M52w
Westerman, George W
Carlos Antonio Mendoza father of Panama's Independence Act in commemoration of the Centennial of his birth, October 31, 1856. Panama, Published by the Bellas Artes Department and also publications from the Educational Department Panama, 19??
83p. illus., port. 21½cm.
Bound with: Carlos Antonio Mendoza padre del acta de independencia de Panama. 83p.

1. Mendoza, Carlos Antonio, 1856-
2. Panama-History.

Panama
M986.2
W52pl
Westerman, George W comp.
A plea for higher education of Negroes on the canal zone, arranged by George W. Westerman. [El Panama-America, 1942]

34p. 22cm.
"Seven addresses presented under the sponsorship of the Canal Zone ColoredTeachers Association."

I. Canal Zone Colored Teachers Association.

M323.4
W52
Westin, Alan F ed.
Freedom now! The civil-rights struggle in America. Edited by Alan F. Westin. New York, Basic Books [1964]

xv, 346p. 22cm.

Bibliography: p. [239]-341.
White editor.
Partial contents.- Letter from Birmingham jail, by Martin Luther King.- Freedom now - but, what then, by Loren Miller.- Black Muslims and civil rights, by Malcom X.- The March on
(Continued on next card)

Panama
M986.2
W52f
Westerman, George W
Fifty years (1903-1953) of treaty negotiations between the United States and Republic of Panama. Panama, Imprenta de la Academia, 1953?

26p. 21cm.
Spanish text - 26p.

1. Panama.

Panama
M986.2
W52so
Westerman, George W
Sore spots in United States-Panama Relations Address given at International House, Chicago, by George W. Westerman, associate editor, "The Panama Tribune," and delegate to the Inter-American Press Association's 8th Annual Meeting on October 16, 1952 under sponsorship of the Labor-Education Division of Roosevelt College. N.Y., The Isthmian Civic Society, 1952.

9p. 21cm.
Spanish text 10p.

1. Panama.

M323.4
W52
Westin, Alan F ed.
Freedom now! [1964]
(Card 2)

Washington movement during World War II, by A. Philip Randolph.- Jobs for Negroes - the unfinished revolution, by A. Philip Randolph.- Humiliation stalks them, by Roy Wilkins.- Negroes and the police in Los Angeles by Loren Miller.- The sit-in comes to Atlanta, by C. Eric Lincoln.- A debate over "compensation" prorams, by Whitney M. Young and Kyle
(Continued on next card)

Panama
M986.2
W5213
Westerman, George W ed.
In memoriam; The tribute of a sorrowing group on the passing of the late Franklin Delano Roosevelt. Panama, Isthmian Negro Youth Congress, 1945.

16p. 22cm.
Inscription: To A.B. Spingarn, President NAACP from ?

1. Roosevelt, Franklin Delano, Pres. of U.S. 1882-1945.

Panama
M986.2
W52sc
Westerman, George W
School segregation on the Panama Canal Zone.

Pp. 276-87 22½cm.
Reprinted from Phylon, The Atlanta University Review of Race and Culture, Third Quarter, 1954.

1. Panama Canal - Segregation in education.

M323.4
W52
Westin, Alan F ed.
Freedom now! [1964]
(Card 3)

Haselden.- Middle-class Negroes and the Negro masses by Whitney M. Young.

1. Civil rights - Addresses, essays, lectures. 2. Civil rights - Bibliography.
I. Title.

Panama
M986.2
W521
Westerman, George W
Introduction.

(In: An exhibit on the races of mankind, prepared by Linda Samuels. Panama, Isthmian Negro Youth Congress, 1946. 21 cm. pp.)

Inscribed by Linda R. Samuels: Very truly yours.

1. Anthropoly. I. Samuels, Linda R.

Panama
M986.2
W52s
Westerman, George W
A Study of socio-economic conflicts on the Panama Canal Zone. Panama City, Liga Civica Nacional.

26, 29p. 22cm.

1. Panama Canal Zone. 2 Panama I. Title.
I. t-Estudio de los conflictos socio-economicos en la Zona del Canal.

The Wharf Rate.

M813.5
W16w
Walrond, Eric, 1898 -
The wharf rate.
pp. 237-250.

In: Copy, 1927. New York, D. Appleton, 1927.

I. Title

Panama
M986.2
W52m
Westerman, George W
A minority group in Panama; Some aspects of West Indian life. 3rd ed. Panama, National Civic League, 1950.

32 p. 21 cm.
English and Spanish text, separately paged; added t.p. in Spanish.
Inscribed by author: Sincere regards, G.W. Westerman.

1. Panama. I. Title. II. t.-Un grupo minoritario en Panama

Panama
M986.2
W52t
Westerman, George W
Toward a better understanding. Preface by Gil Blas Tejeira. 2nd ed. [Panama] 1946.

20 p. 22 cm.
English and Spanish text, separately paged; added t.p. in Spanish.
Inscribed by author: Sincere regards, G.W. Westerman.
______ cop. 2. Inscribed by author: To Walter White with compliments, G. W. Westerman
1. Panama. I. Title. II. t.-Hacia una major compresion.

"What became of race prejudice?"

M323
Et3w
Etheridge, Frank Oscar
"What became of race prejudice?" By Frank Oscar Etheridge. New York, William-Frederick press, 1943.
23p. 13½cm.

What caused the Detroit riot?
M323. White, Walter Francis, 1893-
W587w What caused the Detroit riot? An analysis by Walter and Thurgood Marshall. New York, NAACP, 1943.
37p. 22½cm.

What it means to be a communist.
M335.4 Winston, Henry.
W73w What it means to be a communist. New York, New Century, 1951.
15p. port. 19cm.

What ye sow.
M812.5 Huntley, Elizabeth (Maddox)
H91w What ye sow. [1st ed.] New York, Comet Press Books [1955]
97 p. 22 cm.
A play.
I. Title.
PS3515.U683W5 812.5 55-8499 ‡
Library of Congress [5]

What Christ means to us.
M811.5 Spearman, Aurelia L. P. (Childs)
Sp31w What Christ means to us; a book of religious verse. New York, Carlton Press [1964]
99p. 20½cm.

What manner of man.
MB9 Bennett, Lerone.
K58b What manner of man; a biography of Martin Luther King, Jr., by Lerone Bennett, Jr. With an introd. by Benjamin E. Mays. Chicago, Johnson Pub. Co., 1964.
227 p. illus., ports. 25 cm.
1. King, Martin Luther. I. Title.
E185.97.K5B4 922.673 64-66315
Library of Congress [5]

What's happening?
M817.5 Gregory, Dick.
G86w What's happening? Photos. by Jerry Yulsman. [1st ed.] New York, Dutton, 1965.
126 p. illus. 28 cm.
1. Negro wit and humor. 2. Negroes—Civil rights—Humor, caricatures, etc. I. Title.
PN6231.N5G68 817.54 65-19973
Library of Congress [5]

What do the people of Africa want?
M910 Robeson, Eslanda (Goode)
R54w What do the people of Africa want? By Mrs. Paul Robeson. N.Y., Council on African affairs, 1945.
23p. illus. map. 20cm.

What the Negro has done for the United States and Texas.
M301 Dubois, William Edward Burghardt, 1868-
D853wh What the Negro has done for the United States and Texas, by W. E. B. DuBois. [Washington, U. S. Govt. print. off., 1936]
folder (10 p.) 20½cm.
1. Negroes. I. Title. 36-26594
Library of Congress E185.6.D82
——— Copy 2. [5] 325.260973

What's happening in school integration?
M370 Fleming, Harold C
F62 What's happening in school integration? By Harold C. Fleming and John Constable. [1st ed. New York, Public Affairs Committee, 1956]
20 p. illus. 19 cm. (Public affairs pamphlet no. 244)
1. Discrimination in education. I. Constable, John, joint author. II. Title.
LB3062.F49 371.974 57-666 ‡
Library of Congress [25]

M220.8 What if the shoe were on the other foot?
H72 Holley, Joseph Winthrop, 1874-
What if the shoe were on the other foot? Slavery in reverse. New York, William-Frederick Press, 1953.
30 p. 22 cm.
1. Negroes. I. Title.
E185.61.H72 *301.451 325.26 53-10281 ‡
Library of Congress [5]

What the Negro thinks.
M323.1 Moton, Robert Russa, 1867-1940.
M85 What the Negro thinks, by Robert Russa Moton. Garden City, N. Y., Doubleday, Doran and company, inc., 1929.
vii p., 2 l., 267 p. 21½cm.
"First edition."
1. Negroes. 2. U. S.—Race question. I. Title.
29—9727
Library of Congress E185.61.M934
[45y1]

What's wrong with lottery?
M174.6 Bernard, Ruth Thompson.
B45 What's wrong with lottery? By Ruth Thompson Bernard. Boston, Meador publishing company [1943]
122 p. 20cm.
1. Gambling. 2. Lotteries. I. Title.
43-18105
Library of Congress HV6713.B47
[5] 174.6

M301 What is civilization? By Maurice Maeterlinck, Dhan Gopal
D853a9 Mukerji, and others, with an introduction by Hendrik Van Loon. New York, Duffield & company, 1926.
6 p. l., 216, [1] p. front., illus. 21½cm.
A majority of these articles first appeared in the Forum. *cf.* Publisher's note.
CONTENTS.—The answer of India, by D. G. Mukerji.—The answer of Africa, by W. E. B. DuBois.—The answer of the middle ages, by R. A. Cram.—The age of Pericles, by P. Shorey.—The answer of China, by C.-F. Liu.—Ancient Egypt, by M. Maeterlinck.—The answer of ancient America, by H. Spinden.—Women and modern civilization, by R. Traquair.—America's democracy of bad manners, by Elizabeth R. Pennell.
1. Civilization. I. ~~Maeterlinck, Maurice, 1862-~~ II. Mukerji, ~~Dhan Gopal, 1890-1936.~~ III. DuBois, W. E. B., 1868- The answer of Africa p. 43-57.
26—11844
Library of Congress CB5.W5
[43q1]

What the Negro wants.
M973 Logan, Rayford Whittingham, 1897- *ed.*
L82 w What the Negro wants, edited by Rayford W. Logan ... Chapel Hill, The University of North Carolina press [1944]
xxiii p., 1 l., 352 p. 23cm.
"Who's who": p. 345-352.
1. Negroes. I. Title.
44—47086
Library of Congress E185.61.L65
[46u²14] 325.260973

M973 Wheadon, Augusta Austin.
W56 The Negro from 1863 to 1963. [1st ed.] New York, Vantage Press [1964, °1963]
91 p. 21 cm.
Bibliography: p. 91.
Portrait of author on book jacket.
History.
1. ~~Negroes.~~ 2. ~~Negroes—Biog.~~ I. Title.
E185.6.W55 325.2670973 64-3233
Library of Congress [5]

Uganda What is freedom.
M323 Lucas, Eric, ed.
B31 What is freedom. London, Oxford University Press, 1963.
136p. 18cm.

What shall the harvest be?
M252 Bowen, John Wesley Edward, 1855-
B67w What shall the harvest be? A national sermon; or, A series of plain talks to the colored people of America, on their problems, by the Rev. J. W. E. Bowen, Ph. D., in the Asbury Methodist Episcopal church. Washington, D.C., Press of the Stafford printing co., 1892.
87p. front. (port) 22½cm.

M811.1
W56e Wheatley, Phillis, afterwards Phillis Peters,
1770 1753?-1784.
An elegiac poem, on the death of the celebrated divine and eminent servant of Jesus Christ, the Reverend and learned George Whitefield, chaplain to the Right Honourable the Countess of Huntingdon, &c. &c. who made his exit from this transitory state, to dwell in the celestial realms of bliss, on Lord's-day, 30th September, 1770, when he was siez'd with a fit of the asthma, at Newbury-Port, near Boston, New England. In which is a condolatory address

---

What is the unpardonable sin?
M233.2 Clarke, Andral Wellington, 1896-
C55w What is the unpardonable sin? By A. Wellington Clarke, TH. B. Boston, Mass., Meador publishing company [°1929]
64 p. 19½cm.
1. Sin. I. Title.
30-5798
Library of Congress BT721.C6
Copyright A 17468 [2]

What we saw in England.
Tanganyika
M967.82 Kayamba, H Martin Th , 1891-1940.
K18t Tulivyoona na tulivyofanya ingereza. London, The Sheldon Press, 1932.
132p. illus. port. 19cm.
Written in Swahili.
Translation: What we saw in England.
I. Title: What we saw in England.

M811.1
W56e Wheatley, Phillis, afterwards Phillis Peters,
1770 1753?-1784. An elegiac poem ...
(card 2)
to his truly noble benefactress the worthy and pious Lady Huntingdon; and the orphan-children in Georgia, who, with many thousands are left, by the death of this great man, to lament the loss of a father, friend, and benefactor. By Phillis, a servant girl, of 17 years of age, belonging to Mr. J. Wheatley, of Boston:--She has been but 9 years in this country from Africa.

M811.1 W56e 1770 Wheatley, Phillis, afterwards Phillis Peters, 1753?-1784.
An elegiac poem ... (card 3)

Boston: Printed and sold by Ezekiel Russell, in Queen-street, and John Boyles, in Marlboro'-street [1770]

8 p. 19½cm.
Added to.-p., illus.

1. Whitefield, George, 1714-1770. 2. Poetry.

M811.1 W56m 1834 Wheatley, Phillis, *afterwards* Phillis Peters, 1753?-1784.
Memoir and poems of Phillis Wheatley, a native African and a slave. Dedicated to the friends of the Africans ... Boston, G. W. Light, 1834.
viii, [9]-108 p. front. (port.) 17½cm.
Memoir (p. [9]-29) by Margaretta Matilda Odell.

I. Odell, Margaretta Matilda. 30-20914

Library of Congress PS866.W5 1834 [42b1]

M811.1 W56po 1886 Wheatley, Phillis, afterwards Phillis Peters, 1753?-1784
Poems on various subjects, religious and moral. By Phillis Wheatley, negro servant to Mr. John Wheatley, of Boston, in New England. With memoirs, by W. H. Jackson. Cleveland, Ohio, The Rewell publishing co. [c1886]

149p. front. (port.) 17½cm.
Includes sketches of Phillis Wheatley, Benjamin Banneker, Thomas Fuller and James Durham (p.117-149)

Broadside M811.1 W56e 1770 Wheatley, Phillis, afterwards Phillis Peters, 1753?-1784.
An elegiac poem, on the death of that celebrated divine, and eminent servant of Jesus Christ, the late Reverend, and pious George Whitefield, Chaplain to the Right Honourable the Countess of Huntingdon, &c. &c. who made his exit from this transitory state, to dwell in the celestial realms of bliss, on Lord's-day, 30th of September, 1770, when he was seiz'd with a fit of asthma, at Newbury-Port, near Boston, in New England.

M811.1 W56m 1835 Wheatley, Phillis, afterwards Phillis Peters, 1753?-1784.
Memoir and poems of Phillis Wheatley, a native African and a slave. Dedicated to the friends of the Africans. Second edition. Boston, Light & Horton, 1835.

viii, [9] 110p. front. (port.) 17½cm.
Memoir (p. [9]-29) by Margaretta Matilda Odell.

M811.1 W56po 1816 Wheatley, Phillis, afterwards Phillis Peters, 1753?-1784.
Poems on various subjects, religious and moral. By Phillis Wheatley, Negro servant to Mr. John Wheatley, of Boston, on New-England. London, printed. Reprinted in New-England, 1816.
120 p. 17cm.

1. Poetry.

Broadside M811.1 W56e 1770 Wheatley, Phillis ...
An elegiac poem. (card 2)

In which is a condolatory address to his truly benefactress the worthy, and pious Lady Huntingdon, and the orphan-children in Georgia; who, with many thousands, are left, by the death of this great man, to lament the loss of a father, friend, and benefactor. By Phillis, a servant girl, of 17 years of age, belonging to Mr. J. Wheatley, of Boston: -and has been but 9 years in this country from Africa.

M811.1 W56m 1838 Wheatley, Phillis, afterwards Phillis Peters, 1753?-1784.
Memoir and poems of Phillis Wheatley, a native African and a slave. Also, poems by a slave...Third edition. Boston, Published by Isaac Knapp, 1838.

155p. 16½cm.
Contains poems by George Moses Horton, p. 125 -155.

1. Poetry. I. Horton, George Moses.

M811.1 W56po 1802 Wheatley, Phillis, afterwards Phillis Peters, 1753?-1784.
Poems on various subjects, religious and moral. By Phillis Wheatley, Negro servant to Mr. John Wheatley of Boston, in New England. Dedicated to the Countess of Huntingdon. Walpole, N. H. Printed for Thomas & Thomas, by David Newhall, 1802.

86p. 15cm.
1. Poetry.

Broadside M811.1 W56e 1770 Wheatley, Phillis ...
An elegiac poem. (card 3)

Boston, Sold by Ezekiel Russell, in Queen-Street, and John Boyles, in Marlboro Street. 1770.

Broadside. 40½ x 33cm.
Framed.

1. Whitefield, George, 1714-1770.
2. Poetry.

M811.1 W56o Wheatley, Phillis, afterwards Phillis Peters, 1753?-1784.
An Ode on the birthday of Pompey Stockbridge. [n.p. n.d.]
Broadside. 10.5 x 915 cm.
This ode was probably written by Phillis Wheatley. The subject is Negro.

1. Poetry.

M811.1 W56po 1793 Wheatley, Phillis, *afterwards* Phillis Peters, 1753?-1784.
Poems on various subjects, religious and moral. By Phillis Wheatley, negro servant to Mr. John Wheatley, of Boston, in New-England. Albany: Re-printed, from the London edition, by Barber & Southwick, for Thomas Spencer, book-seller, Market-street, 1793.
viii, 9-89, [3] p. 15½ cm.
Signatures: [A]-L⁴, M².

30-20912

Library of Congress PS866.W5 1793 [48b1]

M811.1 W56e 1771 Wheatley, Phillis, afterwards Phillis Peters, 1753?-1784.
An elegiac poem on the death of that celebrated Divine and eminent servant of Jesus Christ, the Reverend and learned Mr. George Whitefield...p. 29 -31. In: Ebenezer Pemberton, Heaven the residence of saints. A sermon occasioned by the sudden and much lamented death of the Rev. George Whitefield... Boston, Printed: London, reprinted, for E. and C. Dilly in the Poultry; and sold at the chapel in Tottenham-Court Road, and at the Tabernacle near Moorfields, 1771.
31p. 20cm.
1. Poetry

M811.1 W56po 1915 Wheatley, Phillis, *afterwards* Phillis Peters, 1753?-1784.
... Poems and letters; first collected edition, ed. by Chas. Fred. Heartman; with an appreciation by Arthur A. Schomburg. New York, C. F. Heartman [1915]
111 p. incl. front. (port.) 24½cm. (*Verso of half-title: Heartman's historical series, no. 8*)
At head of title: Phillis Wheatley (Phillis Peters)
~~No. [illegible]~~
No. 4 of nine copies printed on Japan vellum paper.
I. Heartman, Charles Frederick, 1883- II. Schomburg, Arthur Alfonso, 1874- 1. Poetry

15-22732

Library of Congress PS866.W5 1915 [36b1]

M811.1 W56po 1787 Wheatley, Phillis, *afterwards* Phillis Peters, 1753?-1784.
Poems on various subjects, religious and moral. By Phillis Wheatley, negro servant to Mr. John Wheatley, of Boston, in New-England. Philadelphia: Printed by Joseph James, in Chesnut-street, 1787.
55, [1] p. 16½cm.
~~[illegible]~~

1 Poetry

26-374

Library of Congress PS866.W5 1787 [2]

M811.1 W56el 1784 Wheatley, Phillis, afterwards Phillis Peters, 1753?-1784.
An elegy, sacred to the memory of that great divine, the Reverend and learned Dr. Samuel Cooker, who departed this life December 29, 1783, aetatis 59. By Phillis Peters. Boston, Printed and sold by E. Russell, in Essex-Street, near Liberty Pole, MDCC,LXXIV.

8p. 18cm.

1. Poetry. 2. Cooper, Samuel, d.1783.

M811.1 W56poe 1930 Wheatley, Phillis, *afterwards* Phillis Peters, 1753?-1784.
The poems of Phillis Wheatley, edited with introduction and notes by Charlotte Ruth Wright. Philadelphia, Pa., The Wrights, 1930.
xii p., 1 l., 15-104 p. front. (port.) 19cm.
"A few books with contents relating to Phillis Wheatley": p. 99-100.

1. Wright, Charlotte Ruth, ed. 30-29133

Library of Congress PS866.W5 1930
——— Copy 2.
Copyright A 30148 [2] 811.1

M811.1 W56po 1786 Wheatley, Phillis, *afterwards* Phillis Peters, 1753?-1784.
Poems on various subjects, religious and moral. By Phillis Wheatley, negro servant to Mr. John Wheatley, of Boston, in New-England. London: Printed. Philadelphia: Re-printed, and sold by Joseph Crukshank, in Market-street, between Second and Third-streets. 1786.
vi, [2], [9]-66, [2] p. 15½cm.

Manuscript notes on last two pages.

26-376

Library of Congress PS866.W5 1786 [2]

M811.1 W56L 1916 Wheatley, Phillis, afterwards Phillis Peters, 1753?-1784.
Life and works of Phillis Wheatley, containing her complete poetical works, numerous letters, and a complete biography of the famous poet of a century and a half ago, by G. Herbert Renfro. Also a sketch of the life of Mr. Renfro by Leila Amos Pendleton. Washington, D.C. 1916

112p. portrait, 19cm.
1. Renfro, Gloster Herbert, 1867-1894.
2. Poetry. I. Pendleton, Leila Amos.

M811.1 W56poem 1773 Wheatley, Phillis, afterwards Phillis Peters, 1753? - 1784.
Poems on comic, serious, and moral subjects. By Phillis Wheatley, Negro-servant to Mr. John Wheatley of Boston in New England. The second edition, corrected. London, J. French, bookseller [1773]
124p. front. 18cm.
A unique edition of the first edition-"Poems on various subjects, religious and moral, by Phillis Wheatley, with variant title page.

M811.1 W56po 1773 Wheatley, Phillis, *afterwards* Phillis Peters, 1753?-1784.
Poems on various subjects, religious and moral. By Phillis Wheatley, Negro servant to Mr. John Wheatley, of Boston, in New England. London: Printed for A. Bell, bookseller, Aldgate; and sold by Messrs. Cox and Berry, King-street, Boston. MDCCLXXIII.
v, [1] p., 1 l., [9]-124, [3] p. front. (port.) 17½cm.
Signatures: [A]-Q⁴.

1 Poetry

30-20911

Library of Congress PS866.W5 1773
——— Copy 2. [39b1]

Wheatley, Phillis, afterwards Phillis Peters, 1753-1784.
M39.5 Eq51 Equiano, Olaudah. c. 1745
The interesting narrative of the life of Olaudah Equiano, or Gustavus Vassa, the African. Written by himself ... To which are added, Poems on various subjects, by Phillis Wheatly, Negro servant to Mr. John Wheatly of Boston in New England. Halifax, Printed at the office of J. Nicholoson & co., 1814
514, [2] p. front. (port.) 17½ cm.
I. Wheatley, Phillis, afterwards Phillis Peters, 1753-1784.
Library of Congress HT869.E6A3 1813 5—41226 [a48d1]

Wheeler, Benjamin Franklin, 1854-1919, *comp.*
M811.08 V56 Cullings from Zion's poets, by B. F. Wheeler, D. D. [Mobile? Ala., °1907]
384 p. front., ports. 20cm.
1. Religious poetry, American. 2. Negro poetry (American) I. Title.
Library of Congress PS595.R4W5 8—20853
Copyright A 178145 [a37b1] 811.0822

When peoples meet...
M300 L79w Locke, Alain Le Roy, 1886- ed.
When peoples meet; a study in race and culture contacts, edited by Alain Locke ... and Bernhard J. Stern ... New York, Committee on workshops, Progressive education association [°1942]
xii, 756 p. 24½ cm. (*Half-title:* Progressive education association publications. Committee on workshops)
1. Acculturation. 2. Minorities. 3. Race problems. I. Stern, Bernhard Joseph, 1894- joint ed. II. Title.
Library of Congress CB5.L6 42—326 [45g²5] 901

Wheatley, Phillis, afterwards Phillis Peters, 1753-1784.
M39 Eq51 1814 Poems on various subjects.
Equiano, Olaudah, b. 1745.
The interesting narrative of the life of Olaudah Equiano, or Gustavus Vass, the African, written by himself ... To which are added, Poems on various subjects, by Phillis Wheatly, Negro servant to Mr. John Wheatly at the office of J. Nicholoson & Co., 1814.
514 2 p. front. (port.) 17½cm.

M8 W56v Wheeler, Benjamin Franklin, 1854- 1919
The Varick family, by Rev. B. F. Wheeler, D. D., with many family portraits. [Mobile? Ala., °1907]
3 p. l., 5-58 p., 1 l. front., ports., geneal. tab. 16cm.
Descendants of James Varick, founder of the African Methodist Episcopal Zion church.
1. Varick family (Richard Varick) 2. Varick, James, 1750-1827?
Library of Congress CS71.V3 1907 7-21721
Copyright A 179450

When the melon is ripe.
M39 G76w Grant, Daniel T 1914-
When the melon is ripe; the autobiography of a Georgia Negro high school principal and minister. [1st ed.] New York, Exposition Press [1955]
174 p. 21 cm.
1. U. S.—Race question. I. Title.
E185.97.G7A3 325.260973 55-12465 ‡
Library of Congress [3]

M811.1 W56s 1915 oversize Wheatley, Phillis, afterwards Phillis Peters, 1753?-1784.
Six broadsides relating to Phillis Wheatley (Phillis Peters) with portrait and facsimile of her handwriting. New York, printed for Chas. Fred Heartman, 1915.
8 leaves, facsims. front. (port.) 38cm.

South Africa M378.3 N65 Wheeler, W. Reginald, ed.
Commission on Survey of Foreign Students in the United States of America.
The foreign student in America; a study, under the auspices of the Friendly Relations Committees of the Young Men's Christian Association. Edited by W. Reginald Wheeler, Henry H. King, and Alexander B. Davidson, with a foreward by Robert E. Speer. New York, Association Press, 1925.
xxxiv, 329p. incl. tables, fold, map. 23½cm.

When the word is given.
M297 L83 Lomax, Louis E 1922-
When the word is given; a report on Elijah Muhammad, Malcolm X, and the Black Muslim world. [1st ed.] Cleveland, World Pub. Co. [1963]
223 p. illus., ports. 21 cm.
"Suggested additional reading": p. 213-214.
1. Black Muslims. I. Title.
BP222.L6 290 63—21624
Library of Congress [64f3]

Wheatley, Phillis, afterwards, Phillis Peters, 1753?-1784.
M811.1 W56h 1915 Heartman, Charles Frederick, 1883-
Phillis Wheatley (Phillis Peters); a critical attempt and a bibliography of her writings by Chas. Fred. Heartman. New York, The author, 1915.
44 [3] p. front. (port.)

Nigeria M896.2 So2W When a philospher falls in love.
Sofola, Samuel Adeniyi.
When a philosopher falls in love. New York, Comet Press Books [1956]
210 p. 21 cm.
A play.
I. Title.
PR6037.O48W5 822.91 56-5954 ‡
Library of Congress [2]

"When thou prayest"
M248 M38wt Massey, James Earl.
"When thou prayest"; an interpretation of Christian prayer according to the teachings of Jesus. Anderson, Ind., Warner Press [1960]
64 p. 19 cm.
1. Prayer. I. Title.
BV215.M37 248.32 60-11403 ‡
Library of Congress [2]

Wheatley, Phillis, afterwards Phillis Peters, 1753?-1784 - Bibliography.
Puerto Rico M864 Sch6b Schomburg, Arthur Alfonso, 1874-
A bibliographical checklist of American Negro poetry, comp. by Arthur A. Schomburg. New York, C. F. Heartman, 1916.
57 p. 25cm. (*Added t.-p.:* Bibliographica americana; a series of monographs ed. by Charles F. Heartman. vol. II)
Printed on one side of leaf only.
"Bibliography of the poetical works of Phillis Wheatley (copyrighted by Charles F. Heartman) (reprinted from Heartman's 'Phillis Wheatley (Phillis Peters)')": p. 47-57.
1. Negro poetry (American)—Bibl. 2. Wheatley, Phillis, afterwards Phillis Peters, 1753?-1784—Bibl. I. Heartman, Charles Frederick, 1883-
Library of Congress Z1231.P7S3 17—7194 [a40b1]

When Africa awakes.
M973 H237w Harrison, Hubert H.
When Africa awakes; the "inside story" of the stirrings and strivings of the new negro in the western world, by Hubert H. Harrison ... New York city, The Porro press, 1920.
146 p. illus. (port.) 18½cm.
1. Negroes. 2. U. S.—Race question. I. Title.
Library of Congress E185.61.H31 22-4902 [2]

Whence waters flow.
M811.5 M55w Merritt, Alice Haden, 1905-
Whence waters flow; poems for all ages from Old Virginia. Richmond, Dietz Press [1948]
69 p. illus. 26 cm.
I. Title.
PS3525.E677W5 811.5 49-10264*
Library of Congress [4]

Wheatley, Phillis, afterwards Phillis Peters, 1753?-1784 - Fiction.
M813.5 G76s Graham, Shirley.
The story of Phillis Wheatley; illus. by Robert Burns. New York, J. Messner [1949]
176 p. illus., port. 22 cm.
"Sources": p. 172.
1. Wheatley, Phillis, afterward Phillis Peters, 1753?-1784—Fiction.
Full name: Lola Shirley (Graham) McCanns.
PZ7.G757St 49—10767*
Library of Congress [50c5]

When Malindy sings.
M811. D91w Dunbar, Paul Laurence, 1872-1906.
When Malindy sings [poems] by Paul Laurence Dunbar; illustrated with photographs by the Hampton institute camera club; decorations by Margaret Armstrong. New York, Dodd, Mead and co., 1903.
3 p. l., 9-144 p. incl. front., illus. 22cm.
Blue ornamental borders.
I. Title.
Library of Congress PS1556.W4 1903 3—27952 [45b1]

Where do we go from here.
M323.4 K58w King, Martin Luther, 1929-1968.
Where do we go from here: Chaos or community? [1st ed.] New York, Harper & Row [1967]
209 p. 22 cm.
Bibliographical references included in "Notes" (p. 203-204)
1. Negroes—Hist.—1964- 2. Negroes—Civil rights. I. Title. II. Title: Chaos or community.
E185.615.K5 301.451'96'073 67—17072
Library of Congress [67z7]

The wheel that made wishes come true.
M813.5 W98w Wynbush, Octavia B.
The wheel that made wishes come true, by Octavia B. Wynbush; illustrations by George Greene. Philadelphia, Dorrance and company [°1941]
59 p. front., illus. 19½cm.
I. Title.
Library of Congress PZ8.W98Wh 41-14761 [4]

When people behave like sputniks (as I saw them).
M252 H91w Huntley, Thomas Elliott
When people behave like sputniks (as I saw them). New York, Vantage Press, 1960.
112p. 20½cm.

M323 G12w Where do we stand? The Negro in the South today.
Gaines, Gartrell J
Where do we stand? The Negro in the South today. [1st ed.] New York, Vantage Press [1957]
76 p. illus. 21 cm.
1. Southern States—Race question. 2. Negroes. 3. Miscegenation. I. Title.
E185.61.G15 57-7789 ‡
*301.451 325.260975
Library of Congress [20]

Trinidad M823.91 H41w

Where the hummingbird flies.
Hercules, Frank.
Where the hummingbird flies. [1st ed.] New York, Harcourt, Brace [1961]
212p. 21cm.
Portrait of author on book jacket.

M813.5 B946

Whip me, whop me pudding and other stories.
Burroughs, Margaret (Taylor)
Whip me, whop me pudding and other stories of Riley Rabbit and his fabulous friends. [Introduction by Charlemae Rollins. Chicago, Proga Press, 1966.
59p. illus. 21cm.
"To Mr. Arthur B. Spingarn, in appreciation, Margaret T. Burroughs, 3/30/67".
I. Title.

M811.5 W58p

White, Charles Frederick, 1876-
Plea of the negro soldier, and a hundred other poems, by Corporal Charles Fred. White ... Easthampton, Mass., Press of Enterprise printing company [°1908]
170, [2] p. front. (port.) 19cm.
1. Title. 1. Poetry.
Library of Congress PS3174.W58 8—18064
Copyright A 203554 [a31d1]

M309.2 Sm55

Where to, black man?
Smith, Ed, 1937-
Where to, black man? Chicago, Quadrangle Books, 1967.
221 p. 22 cm.
1. U. S. Peace Corps—Ghana. I. Title.
HC60.5.S6 309.2'235'667 67-21640 rev
Library of Congress [r68f3]

MB9 D37r

Whipper, Frances E. Rollin.
~~Rollin, Frank A.~~
Life and public services of Martin R. Delany, subassistant commissioner, Bureau relief of refugees, freedmen, and of abandoned lands, and late major 104th U. S. colored troops. By Frank A. Rollin ... Boston, Lee and Shepard, 1868.
367 p. 20cm.
1. Delany, Martin Robison, 1812-1885. 2. U. S.—Hist.—Civil war—Negro troops. 3. U. S. Bureau of refugees, freedmen and abandoned lands.
Library of Congress E185.97.D33 7—21560
[43e1]

MB W58

White, Charles Frederick, 1876-
Who's who in Philadelphia; a collection of thirty biographical sketches of Philadelphia colored people ... together with cuts and information of some of their leading institutions and organizations, by Charles Fred. White ... with an introduction by R. R. Wright, jr., PH. D., and containing additional articles by C. J. Perry, B. F. Lee, jr., R. R. Wright, jr., and Charles Fred. White ... Philadelphia, The A. M. E. book concern [°1912]
206 p., 1 l. incl. illus., plates. 24 cm.
1. Negroes—Philadelphia. I. Title.
Library of Congress F158.9.N3W5 12—14969
[48b½]

Kenya M170 G12

Where we are now.
Gakwa, Silvanus Njendu
Harĩa tũrĩ rĩu. Where we are now. Nairobi, Eagle Press, 1949.
[25p. 18½cm. (Merciria ma arata anyu. Your friends are thinking series)
Written in English and Kikuyu.
1. Ethics. I. Title. II. Series. III. Series: Your friends are thinking series. IV. Title: Where we are now.

M815.2 W64w

Whipper, William, 1805-1885
An address delivered in Wesley church in the evening of June 12 before the Colored Reading Society of Philadelphia, for mental improvement. By William Whipper. Philadelphia, Printed by John Young [c1828]
22p. 20½cm.
I. Colored Reading Society. 1. Addresses.

M784 W58

White, Clarence Cameron, 1880-1960.
Forty Negro spirituals, compiled and arranged for solo voice with pianoforte accompaniment, by Clarence Cameron White. Philadelphia, Theodore Presser Co., 1927.
129p. illus. 31cm.
1. Spirituals.

St. Lucia M966 L589

The Whidden lectures, 1965.
Lewis, William Arthur, 1915-
Politics in West Africa [by] W. Arthur Lewis. Toronto, New York, Oxford University Press, 1965.
90 p. map. 19 cm. (The Whidden lectures, 1965)
1. Africa, West—Politics. 2. States, New. I. Title. (Series)
DT471.L57 320.966 65—8469
Library of Congress [66e2]

MB9 W64w

Whipper, William, 1805-1885
Eulogy on William Wilberforce, esq., delivered at the request of the people of colour of the city of Philadelphia ... on the sixth day of December, 1833. By William Whipper. Philadelphia, Printed by W. P. Gibbons [1833?]
iv, [5]-35 p. 21½cm.
1. Wilberforce, William, 1759-1833.
Library of Congress HT1029.W5W4 11-34676
[a34b1]

MB9 W58b

White, George.
A brief account of the life, experience, travels, and gospel labours of George White, an African; written by himself and revised by a friend ... New York, John C. Totten, 1810.
60p. 17cm.
1. Biography.

Trinidad M823.91 L94w

While gods are falling.
Lovelace, Earl, 1935-
While gods are falling. Chicago, H. Regnery Co., 1966.
254 p. 21 cm.
I. Title.
PZ4.L889Wh 66-17746
Library of Congress [3]

M813.5 K22w

Whistle for Willie.
Keats, Ezra Jack.
Whistle for Willie. New York, Viking Press [1964]
33 p. col. illus. 21 x 24 cm.
I. Title.
PZ7.K2253Wh 64-13595
Library of Congress [14-1]

M323 W58d

White, George Henry, 1852-1918.
Defense of the Negro race—charges answered ... Speech of Hon. George H. White, of North Carolina, in the House of representatives, January 29, 1901. Washington [Govt. print. off.] 1901.
14 p. 24cm.
1. Negroes—Politics and suffrage.
Library of Congress E185.6.W58 12—11525
[a41b1]

French Guiana MB9 W57

Whily-Tell, A E
Je suis un civilisé. Paris, Société d'Impressions de Lancry, 1953.
253p. port. 24½cm.
"To Mr. Arthur B. Spingarn, with my best regards, A. E. Whily-Tell."
Portrait of author in book.
1. Whily-Tell, A. E. 2. Baker, Josephine, 1906- 3. Folies Bergére. I. Title.

M811.5 W58s

Whitaker, Christine D
The singing teakettle; poems for children. [1st ed.] New York, Exposition Press [1956]
40 p. 21 cm.
I. Title.
PZ8.3.W58 55-11838 ‡
Library of Congress [2]

M784 J87

White, George L. comp.
Jubilee songs: as sung by the Jubilee singers... enlarged, compiled by Theodore F. Seward, and George L. White. New York, Biglow and Main [c1872]
160p. 23cm.
Contains Part I and II.

French Guiana MB9 W57

Whily-Tell, A E
Whily-Tell, A E
Je suis un civilisé. Paris, Société d'Impressions de Lancry, 1953.
253p. port. 24½cm.
"To Mr. Arthur B. Spingarn, with my best regards, A. E. Whily-Tell."
Portrait of author in book.
1. Whily-Tell, A. E. 2. Baker, Josephine, 1906- 3. Folies Bergére. I. Title.

M616 W58

Whitaker, James C
Magnamycin - a new antibiotic, by James C. Whitaker, Aaron Prigot, Milton Marmell and E. Gates Morgan. St. Louis, American Journal of Syphilis, Gonorrhea, and Venereal Diseases, 1953.
3-7p. illus. 25cm.
Reprinted from the September 1953 issue of the American Journal of Syphilis, Gonorrhea, and Venereal Diseases.
1. Antibiotics.

MB9 C79r

White, Jacob C.
Coppin, Fanny Jackson, 1837-1913.
Reminiscences of school life, and hints on teaching, by Fanny Jackson Coppin. Introduction by William C. Bolivar. [Philadelphia, Pa., A.M.E. Book Concern, 1913]
191p. port (front.) 20½cm.
Introduction by William C. Bolivar.

White, Josh.
M784 R13 Raim, Walter, *ed.*
The Josh White song book. Biography and song commentaries by Robert Shelton. Illus. by Stu Gross. Chicago, Quadrangle Books ⌐1963⌐
191 p. illus. 32 cm.
For voice and piano, with chord symbols for guitar.
Discography: p. 190-191.
1. Folk-songs, American. 2. Ballads, American. 3. Negro spirituals. 4. Folk-songs, American—Discography. I. White, Josh. II. Title.
M1629.R16J7 784.4973 63-18475/M
Library of Congress ⌐5⌐

MB W58g White, Laureen, 1908–
Giants lived in those days. ⌐1st ed.⌐ New York, Pageant Press ⌐1959⌐
188 p. 21 cm.
1. Abolitionists. 2. Slavery in the U. S.—Anti-slavery movements. I. Title.
E449.W58 923.673 59-1450 ‡
Library of Congress ⌐2⌐

M784.4 W58 White, Newman Ivey, 1892-1948.
American Negro folk-songs, by Newman I. White ... Cambridge, Harvard university press, 1928.
x p., 2 l., ⌐3⌐-501 p. 24 cm.
Contains music.
Bibliography: p. ⌐469⌐-480.
White author.
1. Negro songs. I. Title.
ML3556.W4 28-21279
Library of Congress ⌐a55q1⌐

M811.08 W58 White, Newman Ivey, 1892– *ed.*
An anthology of verse by American Negroes, edited with a critical introduction, biographical sketches of the authors, and bibliographical notes by Newman Ivey White ... and Walter Clinton Jackson ... with an introduction by James Hardy Dillard ... Durham, N. C., Trinity college press, 1924.
2 p. l., iii-xi, 250 p. 20½cm. (*Half-title:* Trinity college publications)
"Bibliographical and critical notes": p. 214-237.
White editor.
1. Negro poetry (American) I. Jackson, Walter Clinton, 1879– joint ed. II. Title.
24-8398
Library of Congress PS591.N4W5 ⌐42k1⌐

M214.5 W73u White, Walter Francis, 1893-1955
Address.
(In: Writers' Congress. University of California at Los Angeles, 1943. Proceedings, Berkeley and Los Angeles, University of California Press, 1944. 23cm. p.14-18.)

M323 W587ad White, Walter Francis, 1893-1955
Address at the tenth Constitutional Convention of the Congress of Industrial Organizations, November 25, 1948, Portland, Oregon.
(In: Congress of Industrial Organizations. Proceedings of the tenth Constitutional convention, November 25, 1948. 23cm. p.20-25)

M170 T34 White, Walter Francis, 1893-1955
All or nothing.
(In: This I believe; 2; The personal philosophies of one hundred thoughtful men and women ... New York, Simon and Schuster, 1954. 20cm. pp. 154-155)

M323 W587a White, Walter Francis, 1893-1955
...The American Negro and his problems, a comprehensive picture of a serious and pressing situation... Girard, Kansas, Haldeman-Julius publications ⌐1927⌐
64p. 12cm. (Little blue book no. 788, edited by E. Haldeman-Julius)
1. Race problems

M973.9 F46 No.22 White, Walter Francis, 1893-1955
Civil rights; Fifty years of fighting. Pittsburgh, Pittsburgh Courier, 1950.
10p. port. 24cm. (Fifty years of progress)
1. Civil rights. I. Series.

M06 Am35 White, Walter Francis, 1893- 1955
The color line in Europe.
(In: American Academy of Political and Social Science, Philadelphia. The American Negro. Philadelphia, 1928. 24cm. p. 331-336.

M304 P19 v.7 no.8 White, Walter Francis, 1893-1955
The color line in Europe. Reprinted from the Annals of the American academy of political and social science, November, 1928.
6p. 23½cm.
1. Europe - Race relations.
2. Race relations - Europe.
I. Title

MB On2 White, Walter Francis, 1893- 1955
The cry of the mob, autobiography.
(In: On our way. New York, Holiday House, 1952. 22cm. p. 362-372).

M304 P19 v.7 no. 1 White, Walter Francis, 1893-1955.
Election by terror in Florida, by Walter F. White. Reprinted from the New Republic of January 12, 1921. N.Y.C., National association for the advancement of the colored people, 1921
11p. 20¼cm.
M323 W587el
1. Elections - Florida. 2. Politics.

M323 W587et White, Walter Francis, 1893-1955.
L'étincelle (The fire in the flint) traduit de l'anglais par Marguerite Humbert-Zeller ... Paris, Plon [1928]
2p. l., 263p. 19cm.
At head of title: Walter F. White.
Inscribed copy: For Arthur Spingarn- Another burden for his Negroana shelves - with warmest regards, Walter White, New York City, 6 December 1928.
I. Humbert-Zeller, Marguerite, tr. II. Title. III. Title: Fire in the flint.

M323 W587f12 White, Walter Francis, 1893-1955
⌐The fire in the flint⌐ by Walter White. ⌐Translated into the Japanese by Yonezo Hiramara. 2d ed. ⌐Tokio, Bonjinsha⌐
322 ⌐1⌐ p. 22cm.
Inscribed copy: "For Arthur B. Spingarn, ever cordially, Walter White. Has "new Japanese title, the equivalent of'lynching'" A.B.S.
I. Fire in the Flint.

M323. W587f12 1935 White, Walter Francis, 1893—1955
The fire in the flint, by Walter F. White ⌐translated by Yonezo Hiramara. Tokio, Bonjin-Sha⌐ 1935.
322p. 22cm.
Forword quotes Sinclair Lewis and Zona Gale.
Inscribed copy: For Arthur B. Spingarn. Cordially, Walter White, 1935.
I. Hiramara, Yonezo, tr. II. Title: The fire in the [fli]nt (Japanese)

M323. W587fi 1925 White, Walter Francis, 1893- 1955
The fire in the flint ⌐by⌐ Walter F. White. London, Williams and Norgate, Ltd., 1925.
⌐289⌐ p. 20cm.
"Inscribed copy. For Arthur B. Spingarn. This copy of the first (and only) English edition. Ever cordially, Walter White
I. Title

M323. W587fi 1924 White, Walter Francis, 1893-1955
The fire in the flint ⌐by⌐ Walter F. White. New York, A. A. Knopf, 1924.
300 p. 20cm.
Inscribed copy: "To Arthur Spingarn - My best friend, and I might add, my severest critic ! Ever sincerely, Walter. New York City 19 August 1924
I. Title.
24-21400
Library of Congress PZ3.W5857Fi ⌐37r30h1⌐

M323 W587f1 White, Walter Francis, 1893-1955
... Flight. New York, A. A. Knopf, 1926.
300 p., 1 l. 19½cm.
At head of title: Walter White.
Inscribed copy: "For Arthur B. Spingarn with the warm regard of his friend, Walter White.
I. Title.
26-9564
Library of Congress PZ3.W5857Fl ⌐44r32f1⌐

M323 F587h White, Walter Francis, 1893-1955.
How far the promised land? New York, Viking Press, 1955.
244 p. 22 cm.
1. U. S.—Race question. 2. Negroes. I. Title.
E185.61.W6 325.260973 55-9638 ‡
Library of Congress ⌐56v³15⌐

M973 R47 White, Walter Francis, 1893-1955, Introduction.
Du Bois, William Edward Burghardt, 1868-
Black America; Introduction by Walter White.
(In: Ringel, Frederick J. ed. America as Americans see it. New York, Harcourt, Brace, ⌐c1932⌐ 22cm. p. 139-155).

M323.
W587i
White, Walter Francis, 1893-1955
It's our country, too; The Negro demands the right to be allowed to fight for it. Reprinted from The Saturday Evening Post, December 14, 1940.
8p. 23cm.
I. Title.

M323
L14
White, Walter Francis, 1893-1955
The Negro problem in America.
(In: Laidler, Harry W. The role of the races in our future civilization. New York. League for Industrial Democracy, 1942. 23cm. p. 36-39).

White, Walter Francis, 1893-1955
M323
C831
Council against intolerance in America.
An American answer to intolerance. Teacher's manual no. 1, junior and senior high schools. Experimental form, 1939. New York city, Council against intolerance in America, 1939.
130 p., 1 l. 28 cm.
"Prepared by Frank Walser, with the assistance of Annette Smith and Violet Edwards."
"Bibliography of plays suitable for high school production": p. 117-118.
Bibliography: p. 119-130.
1. Propaganda. 2. Antipathies and prejudices. 3. Toleration. I. Walser, Frank. II. Smith, Annette. III. Edwards, Violet. IV. Title. V. Title: Intolerance.
A 40—2271
New York Univ. Wash. Sq. Library HM263.C7
for Library of Congress HM263.C6
[a40k1] 301.1523

M323
W586am
1949
White, Walter, Francis, 1893-1955
A man called White. The autobiography of Walter White. London, Victor Gollancz Ltd., 1949.
vii, 382p. front. (port) 21½cm.
I. Title.

M323
W587ne
White, Walter Francis, 1893-1955
The Negro's contribution to American culture, the sudden flowering of a genius-laden artistic movement, by Walter White. Girard Kansas, Haldeman - Julius publications c1928
64p. 12½cm. (Little blue book no. 1306, edited by E. Haldeman - Julius)
1. Literature 2. Culture I. Title

M740
D74
White, Walter Francis, 1893-1955.
Douglas, Aaron, illus.
Black magic, by Hamish Miles. Illus. by Aaron Douglas. New York, Viking Press, 1929.
vi, 218 p. 22 cm.
A group of stories on the modern Negro.
Walter White assisted the author.

M323
W586am
White, Walter Francis, 1893-1955
A man called White, the autobiography of Walter White. New York, Viking Press, 1948.
viii, 382. 22cm.
Inscribed: For Arthur and Marian.
Affectionately Walter White.
I. Title

M814.5
W93u
White, Walter Francis, 1893-1955
Resolution on international cultural cooperation.
(In: Writers' Congress. University of California at Los Angeles, 1943. Proceedings, Berkeley and Los Angeles, University of California Press, 1944. 23cm. p. 277-279.)

M323
N21
White, Walter Francis, 1893-1955
National Association for the Advancement of Colored People.
Anti-Negro propaganda in school textbooks, with a foreword by Walter White. New York, 1939.
18p. 21cm.
Partial list of books to be examined: p.17-18.

M323
W587m
White, Walter Francis, 1893-1955
Massacring whites in Arkansas. The Nation, December 6, [19]
2p. 31cm.
1. Riots--Arkansas. 2. Phillips County. Arkansas.

M323
W587ri
White, Walter Francis, 1893-1955
... A rising wind. Garden City, New York. Doubleday, Doran and company, inc., 1945.
155p. 19½cm.
At head of title: Walter White.
"First edition."
1. World war, 1939-1945--Negroes. I. Title.

White, Walter Francis, 1893-1955
M323
N21
National association for the advancement of colored people.
The lynchings of May, 1918 in Brooks and Lowndes counties, Georgia. An investigation made and published by the National association for the advancement of colored people. New York city, September, 1918.
6p. 24cm.

M323.
W587n
1928
White, Walter. Francis, 1893-1955
Negeren, fortælling fra sydstatene. Med forord av nini roll anker. Oversatt av E.R.H. og N.R.A. Oslo, H. Aschehoug & co., 1928.
145p. 19½cm.
Translation into the Norwegian of Fire in the Flint.
1. Anker, Nini Roll, tr. II. Fire in the Flint.

M323.
W587ro
White, Walter Francis, 1893-1955
Rope & faggot; a biography of Judge Lynch, by Walter White. New York & London, A. A. Knopf, 1929.
xiii p., 2 l., [3]-272, iv p., 1 l. incl. tables. front. 21½cm.
Bibliography: p. 269-272.
Inscribed copy: For Arthur B. Spingarn with the affectionate regard of Walter White.
1. Lynch law. 2. Negroes. 3. U. S.—Race question. I. Title. II. Title: A biography of Judge Lynch.
29—10015
Library of Congress HV6457.W45
[44e1]

M335.4
P42w
White chauvinism and the struggle for peace.
Perry, Pettis.
White chauvinism and the struggle for peace. N.Y., New Century, 1952.
5-22p. 20cm.

M323
W587ne2
M304
P19
v.7
no.9
White, Walter Francis, 1893-1955
The Negro and the Communists, by Walter White. Reprinted from Harper's magazine, December, 1931 for the National association for the advancement of colored people.
13p. 24cm.
1. Communism.

M323.
W587w
White, Walter Francis, 1893-1955
What caused the Detroit riot? An analysis by Walter White and Thurgood Marshall. New York, NAACP, 1943.
37p. 22½cm.
1. Riots - Detroit. 2. Detroit - Riots, 1943.- I. Marshall, Thurgood, jt. author. II. Title.

... The white face.
Trinidad
M823.91
Of4w
Offord, Carl Ruthven.
... The white face. New York, R. M. McBride & company [1943]
317 p. 21cm.
"First edition."
I. Title.
43-8249
Library of Congress PZ3.O825Wh
[4]

M304
P19
v.7
no.7
M323
W587ne3
M347.9
W58n
White, Walter Francis, 1893-1955
The Negro and the supreme court, by Walter White. Reprinted from Harper's magazine, January, 1931 for the National association for the advancement of colored people, New York.
11p. 24½cm.
1. Supreme Court 2. Laws and legislation

M323
Am3m
White, Walter Francis, 1893-1955. What the Negro thinks of the army.
American academy of political and social science, Philadelphia.
... Minority peoples in a nation at war, edited by J. P. Shalloo ... and Donald Young ... Philadelphia, 1942.
viii, 276 p. 23½cm. (Its Annals, v. 223, September 1942)
CONTENTS.—The need for national solidarity.—The Negro and the war.—Minorities of alien origin.—The treatment of minorities in a democracy.
1. U. S.—Foreign population. 2. Negroes. 3. World war, 1939- — U. S. I. Shalloo, Jeremiah Patrick, 1898- ed. II. Young, Donald Ramsey, 1898- joint ed. III. Title.
42-36334
Library of Congress H1.A4 vol. 223
——— Copy 2. E184.A1A53
[45] (306.273) 323.173

White Fathers.
Tanganyika
M967.82
R84w
Kittler, Glenn D
The White Fathers. Introd. by Bishop Laurian Rugambwa. [1st ed.] New York, Harper [1957]
299 p. illus. 22 cm.
1. White Fathers.
BV2300.W5K5 [266.2] 276 57-6134 ‡
Library of Congress [20]

White horse in Harlem.
M813.5 R56w
Robinson, John Terry
White horse in Harlem. New York, Pageant Press [1965]

159p. 21cm.

I. Title.

M977.4 G87w
White hypocrisy and black lethargy.
Grisby, Snow F
White hypocrisy and black lethargy. Detroit, The author, 1937.

58p. 23cm.
Autographed.

White man, black man.
M301 F84
Frazer, Charles Rivers, 1879-
White man, black man. [1st ed.] New York, Exposition Press [1965]
69 p. 21 cm.

1. U. S.—Race question. 2. Negroes. 3. Toleration. I. Title.

E185.61.F826 301.45196073 65—8471

Library of Congress [66d4]

White man, listen!
M813.5 W93ec
Wright, Richard, 1909-
Ecoute, homme blanc (White man, listen!) Traduit de l'Américan par Dominique Guillet. Paris, Calmann-Lévy, Editeurs, 1959.

225p. 19cm.

1. Race relations. I. Title. II. Title: White man, listen!

White man, listen!
M813.5 W93es
Wright, Richard, 1909-
'Escucha, hombre blanco! (White man, listen!) Traducción de Floreal Mazía. Buenos Aires, Editorial Sudamericana, 1959.

178p. 20½cm.

1. Race relations. I. Title. II. Title: 'Escucha, hombre blanco!

White man, listen!
M813.5 W93w
Wright, Richard, 1908-
White man, listen! [1st ed.] Garden City, N. Y., Doubleday, 1957.
190 p. 22 cm.

1. Negro race. I. Title.

Full name: Richard Nathaniel Wright.

HT1581.W7 *301.451 325.26 57—9702 ‡

Library of Congress [58x15]

M323 C91w
The white man's duty.
Cunard, Nancy, 1896-
The white man's duty, by Nancy Cunard and George Padmore... 2nd edition. Manchester, Panaf service, ltd., 1945.

51p. 21½cm.

M813.5 Ot8
White marble lady.
Ottley, Roi, 1906-
White marble lady. New York, Farrar, Straus and Giroux [1965]
278 p. 22 cm.

I. Title.

PZ4.O894Wh 65-13727

Library of Congress [8]

White mother.
MB9 L51s 1958
Sams, Jessie (Bennett)
White mother. [1st ed.] London, Michael Joseph, 1958.

224p. 21cm.
Autobiographical.

White mother.
MB9 L51s
Sams, Jessie (Bennett)
White mother. [1st ed.] New York, McGraw-Hill [1957]
241 p. 21 cm.
Autobiographical.

1. Lee, Rossie. I. Title.

CT275.L344S3 920.7 57-12911 ‡

Library of Congress [25]

White papers for white Americans.
M301 H43w
Hernton, Calvin C
White papers for white Americans [by] Calvin C. Hernton. [1st ed.] Garden City, N. Y., Doubleday, 1966.
185 p. 22 cm.
Portrait of author on book jacket.

1. U. S.—Race question. 2. Negroes—Psychology. I. Title.

E185.61.H53 301.45196073 66-12244

Library of Congress [5]

The white peril.
M270 M85w
Moses, W H
The white peril, by W. H. Moses... [Philadelphia, Pa., Lisle - Carey press, 1919]
xxxii, 260p. 19cm.

M323.2 W58r
White Plains, New York, Human Relations Center.
Report to the White Plains schools, 1948. White Plains, N.Y., 1948.

25p. 28cm.
Mimeographed.

1. Race relations.

M323.22 W58r
White Plains. New York. Human Relations Center.
Report to the White Plains schools, July 1, 1948. White Plains, New York, 1948.

25p. 28cm.
Mimeographed.

1. ~~Interracial~~ Race relations.

M323.2 W65p
White Plains, New York. Human Relations Center
Wilkins, Marjorie V
Pioneer in human relations. Reprinted from New York State education, February 1949.

4p. 25cm.

The white problem in America.
M301 Eb74
Ebony.
The white problem in America, by the editors of Ebony. Chicago, Johnson Pub. Co., 1966.
v, 181 p. 22 cm.
"First published as a special issue of Ebony magazine, August, 1965."

1. U. S.—Race question. 2. Negroes—Civil rights. I. Title.

E185.615.E2 323.40973 66-24419

Library of Congress [5]

A white song and a black one.
M811.5 C82w
Cotter, Joseph Seamon, 1861-
A white song and a black one, by Joseph S. Cotter. Louisville, Ky., The Bradley & Gilbert co., 1909.
64 p. incl. front. (port.) 18cm.

I. Title.

Library of Congress PS1449.C4W5 9—22188

Copyright A 244598 [a38b1]

The white witch of Rosehall.
Jamaica M823.91 D37w
De Lisser, Herbert George, 1878-
The white witch of Rosehall, by Herbert G. de Lisser. London, Ernest Benn Limited, 1929.

286p. 19cm.

M811.5 N98w
Whitecaps.
Nyabongo, Virginia Lee (Simmons)
Whitecaps [by] Virginia Simmons. [Yellow Springs, O., The Antioch press, 1942]

79p. illus. 21cm.

Broadside M811.1 W56e 1770
Whitefield, George, 1714-1770.
Wheatley, Phillis, afterwards Phillis Peters, 1753?-1784.
An elegiac poem, on the death of that celebrated divine, and eminent servant of Jesus Christ, the late Reverend, and pious George Whitefield, Chaplain to the Right Honourable the Countess of Huntingdon, &c. &c. who made his exit from this transitory state, to dwell in the celestial realms of bliss, on Lord's-day, 30th of September, 1770, when he was seiz'd with a fit of asthma, at Newbury-Port, near Boston, in New England.

Broadside M811.1 W56e 1770
Whitefield, George, 1714-1770.
Wheatley, Phillis ...
An elegiac poem. (card 2)

In which is a condolatory address to his truly benefactress the worthy, and pious Lady Huntingdon, and the orphan-children in Georgia; who, with many thousands, are left, by the death of this great man, to lament the loss of a father, friend, and benefactor. By Phillis, a servant girl, of 17 years of age, belonging to Mr. J. Wheatley, of Boston: -and has been but 9 years in this country from Africa.

Broadside
M811.1
W56e
1770

Whitefield, George, 1714-1770.
Wheatley, Phillis ...
An elegiac poem. (card 3)

Boston, Sold by Ezekiel Russell, in Queen-Street, and John Boyles, in Marlboro Street. 1770.

Broadside. 40½ x 33cm.
Framed.

M811.1
W56e
1770

Whitefield, George, 1714-1770.
Wheatley, Phillis, afterwards Phillis Peters, 1753?-1784.
An elegiac poem, on the death of the celebrated divine and eminent servant of Jesus Christ, the Reverend and learned George Whitefield, chaplain to the Right Honourable the Countess of Huntingdon, &c. &c. who made his exit from this transitory state, to dwell in the celestial realms of bliss, on Lord's-day, 30th September, 1770, when he was seiz'd with a fit of the asthma, at Newbury-Port, near Boston, New England. In which is a condolatory address

---

M811.1
W56e
1770

Whitefield, George, 1714-1770.
Wheatley, Phillis, afterwards Phillis Peters, 1753?-1784.
An elegiac poem ... (card 2)

to his truly noble benefactress the worthy and pious Lady Huntingdon; and the orphan-children in Georgia, who, with many thousands are left, by the death of this great man, to lament the loss of a father, friend, and benefactor. By Phillis, a servant girl, of 17 years of age, belonging to Mr. J. Wheatley, of Boston;--She has been but 9 years in this country from Africa.

M811.1
W56e
1770

Whitefield, George, 1714-1770.
Wheatley, Phillis, afterwards Phillis Peters, 1753?-1784.
An elegiac poem ... (card 3)

Boston: Printed and sold by Ezekiel Russell, in Queen-street, and John Boyles, in Marlboro'-street [1770]

8 p. 19½cm.
Added t.-p., illus.

Africa
M896
W58

Whiteley, W H. comp.
A selection of African prose. Oxford, Clarendon Press, 1964.

2v. 22cm.
Contents.- v.1. Traditional oral texts.- v.2. Written prose.
White compiler.

1. African literature. 2. Tales, African. 3. Literature-Africa. I. Title.

M811.4
W58a

Whitfield, James M.
America and other poems. By J. M. Whitfield. Buffalo, J. S. Leavitt, 1853.
2 p. l., [vii]-viii, [9]-85 p. 15½cm.

I. Title. 1. Poetry.

Library of Congress PS3180.W65 31-28848
——— Copy 2.

M326
G87a
1853

Whitfield, James M
How long? [poem]

(In: Griffiths, Julia ed. Autographs for freedom. Boston, Jewett, 1853. 19½cm. Pp. 46-54).

M973.6
N21cl
1854

Whitfield, James M ,
National emigration convention, Cleveland, Ohio
Arguments, pro and con, on the call for a national emigration convention, to be held in Cleveland, Ohio, August, 1854, by Frederick Douglass, W. J. Watkins, & J. M. Whitfield. With a short appendix of the statistics of Canada, West Indies, Central and South America. Published by M. T. Newsome. Detroit, George E. Pomeroy & co., 1854.
34p. 19cm.

M811.5
W58a

Whiting, Helen Adele Johnson, 1885-1959
Along the road (verse for children) by Helen Adele Whiting. [Atlanta, Ga., Superior printing company, 1938]

19p. illus. 19cm.

1. Poetry— Children. I. Title.

M378Tu
W578

Whiting, Helen Adele (Johnson) 1885-1959
Booker T. Washington's contribution to education. Charlotte, N. C., Mimeograph Press, Kluttz Mail Advertising Service [n.d.]

160p. port. diagr. 27cm.
Mimeographed.

1. Washington, Booker Taliaferro, 1859-1915. 2. Education. 3. Tuskegee Institute, Tuskegee.

M370
W58c

Whiting, Helen Adele (Johnson) 1885-1959
Climbing the economic ladder. [Atlanta, 1948]
100 p. illus. 23 cm.
Cover title.
"Selected references for understanding and improving Southern life": p. 99-100.

1. ~~Negroes~~—Econ. condit. 2. ~~Negroes~~—Moral and social conditions. 3. ~~Negroes~~—Education. I. Title.

E185.8.W48 325.260975 49-601*
Library of Congress [7]

Whiting, Helen Adele Johnson, 1885-1959, jt. author.

M813.5
C16

Cannon, Elizabeth Perry.
Country life stories, some rural community helpers, by Elizabeth Perry Cannon ... & Helen Adele Whiting ... introduction by Mabel Carney ... illustrated by Vernon Winslow ... New York, E. P. Dutton & co., inc., 1938.
xiii, [2], 17-95 p. incl. col. front., illus. (part col.) 19½cm.
"This book is intended to serve as a social studies reader for pupils on the elementary level in small rural schools."—Foreword.
"First edition."

1. Readers and speakers—1870- I. Whiting, Helen Adele, joint author. II. Title.
38-9190
Library of Congress PE1127.F4C3
[3] [323.354] 372.4

M370
W58f

Whiting, Helen Adele (Johnson) 1885-1959
For human welfare, being notes from records of some phases of the Georgia program of Negro rural elementary schools and communities, 1935-1943, by Helen Adele Whiting. [Atlanta, Morris Brown college press, 1946]
63 p. incl. illus., forms. 28cm.
Errata slip inserted.

1. ~~Negroes~~—Education. 2. Project method in teaching. 3. Education—Georgia. I. Title.
46-7025
Library of Congress LC2802.G4W47
[5] 371.974

M813.5
W589

Whiting, Helen Adele (Johnson) 1885-1959
Negro art, music and rhyme, for young folks, by Helen Adele Whiting; illustrations by Lois Mailou Jones. Book II. Washington, D. C., The Associated publishers, inc. [°1938]
[38] p. illus. 23½cm.
Without music.
Book I published under title: Negro folk tales for pupils in the primary grades.

1. ~~Negroes in~~ literature and art. 2. ~~Negro~~ songs. I. Title.
38—17194
Library of Congress PE1119.W55
[45k1] 372.4

M813.5
W589n

Whiting, Helen Adele (Johnson) 1885-1959
Negro folk tales, for pupils in the primary grades, by Helen Adele Whiting; illustrations by Lois Mailou Jones. Book I. Washington, D. C., The Associated publishers, inc. [°1938]
[28] p. illus. 23½ cm.
Book II published under title: Negro art, music and rhyme, for young folks.

1. Folk-lore, Negro. I. Title. II. Jones, Lois Mailou illus. 38—17132
Library of Congress PE1119.W54
[a45d1] 372.4

M370.
W58pl

Whiting, Helen Adele Johnson, 1885-1959
Planning together and following through, being ways of cooperating for inservice growth of Jeanes supervising teachers of Georgia Negro elementary schools. [n.p., n.p., c 1945]
46p. 23cm.
1. Education 2. Jeanes fund - Teachers.
I. Title

M370
W58 pr

Whiting, *Mrs.* Helen Adele (Johnson) 1885-1959
Primary education. 2d ed. By Helen Adele Whiting. Boston, The Christopher publishing house [°1927]
148 p. illus. 20½cm.
Contains references.

1. Education of children. I. Title.
27-18410 Revised
Library of Congress LB1511.W5 1927
Copyright A 996915 [r39c2]

M370.
W58u

Whiting, Helen Adele.Johnson, 1885-1959
Up! up! the ladder. Atlanta, the author, 1948.

32p. illus. 23cm.

1. Economic conditions. I. Title.

M378Tu
W58

Whiting, Joseph Livingston, 1877-
Shop and class at Tuskegee; a definitive story of the Tuskegee correlation technique, 1910-1930, by J. L. Whiting. Boston, Chapman & Grimes [°1941]
114 p. front., plates, map, tables, diagrs. 21cm.

1. Tuskegee normal and industrial institute. I. Title.
42-4090
Library of Congress LC2851.T82W5
[4] 378.761

M811.4
W591

Whitman, Albery Allson, 1851-1901.
An idyl of the South, by Albery A. Whitman: an epic poem in two parts. New York, The Metaphysical publishing company, 1901.
5 p. l., [7]-126 p. 19½cm.

I. Title.
1-31988 Revised
Library of Congress PS3187.W2 I 3
[r42c2]

M811.4
W59l

Whitman, Albery Allson, 1851-1901.
Leelah misled; a poem. By A. A. Whitman. Elizabeth-town [Ky.] , Richard Larue, printer, 1873.

39p. 14cm.

1. Poetry. I. Title.

M811.4 W59n
Whitman, Albery Allson, 1851-1901.
Not a man, and yet a man: by A. A. Whitman. Springfield, O., Republic printing company, 1877.
254 p. front. (port.) 19½cm.
Poems.
1. Slavery in the U. S.—Poetry. I. Title. 1. Poetry.
31-28854 Revised
Library of Congress PS3187.W2N6
[r42b2]

M811.4 W59r
Whitman, Albery Allson, 1851-1901.
The rape of Florida, by Albery A. Whitman. St. Louis, Nixon - Jones Printing Co. 1884.
95p. front. 19cm.
1. Poetry.
I. Title.

M811.4 W59t 1890
Whitman, Albery Allson, 1851-1901.
Twasinta's Seminoles; or Rape of Florida. By Albery A. Whitman. Third ed. carefully rev. St. Louis, Nixon-Jones printing co., 1890.
96p. incl. front. (port.) 26cm.
1. Seminole Indians - Poetry. 2. Poetry.
I. Title.

M811.4 W59t
Whitman, Albery Allson, 1851-1901
Twasinta's Seminoles; or, Rape of Florida. By Albery A. Whitman. Rev. ed. St. Louis, Nixon-Jones printing co., 1885.
97 p. incl. front. (port.) 19½cm.
1. Seminole Indians—Poetry. I. Title.
2. Poetry.
31-28855
Library of Congress PS3187.W2T8
Copyright 1885: 10359 [37b1]

M811.5 W61
Whitney, Salem Tutt, 1879-1934
Mellow musings, by Salem Tutt Whitney, with an introduction by Thomas L. G. Oxley... Boston, Mass., The Colored poetic league of the world, 1926.
XXV, 126p. plates. 19cm.
1. Poetry. I. Title.

M286 W61h
Whitted, J A
A history of the Negro Baptists of North Carolina, by Rev. J.A. Whitted,.. Raleigh, Presses of Edwards and Broughton printing co., 1908.
212p. front, plates - 22½cm.
1. Baptists - North Carolina
2. Cowen, Harry, 1810 -1904 p. 199-200
3. Parker, Thomas, 1830- p. 200 - 01
4. Williams, Arnold B., 1804 - 1886 p. 201-02.
5. Welborne, Anthony W., 1840- p.202-03.

M242 W58c
Whittier, A Gerald
Christian meditations. New York, Carlton Press, 1961.
178p. 23cm.
Portrait of author on book jacket.
1. Religion. 2. Devotional literature.
I. Title.

Whittier, John Greenleaf, 1807-1892.
M326.99B W67n 1838
Williams, James, b. 1805.
Narrative of James Williams. An American slave; who was for several years a driver on a cotton plantation in Alabama ... New-York, The American anti-slavery society, 1838.
xxiii, [25]-108 p. front. (port.) 15cm.
Written by J. G. Whittier from the verbal narrative of Williams. cf. G. R. Carpenter, John Greenleaf Whittier, 1903, p. 165.
1. Slavery in the U. S.—Alabama. I. Whittier, John Greenleaf, 1807-1892. II. American anti-slavery society, New York. III. Title.
17-5248
Library of Congress E444.W748
[30c1]

Africa M398.9 W61
Whitting, Charles Edward Jewel, comp.
Hausa and Fulani proverbs. Lagos, Government Printer, 1940.
192p. 26cm.
Hausa and English.
White compiler.
1. Proverbs, Hausa. 2. Proverbs, Fulah.
I. Title.

Who killed the Congo?
M910 Sc8
Schuyler, Philippa Duke.
Who killed the Congo? New York, Devin-Adair Co., 1962.
310 p. illus. 21 cm.
1. Congo (Leopoldville) I. Title.
DT652.S3 967.5 62-13468 ‡
Library of Congress [10]

Who stopped the race riots in Washington;
M34.3 K63w
Kirksey, Thomas
Who stopped the race riots in Washington; real causes and effects of race clashes in the District of Columbia, by T. Kirksey... J. Henry Hewlett... Washington, D.C., Murray bros., n.d.
12p. 32½cm.

The whole armour.
British Guiana M823.91 H24w
Harris, Wilson
The whole armour. London, Faber and Faber, 1962.
128p. 19cm.

Who's who among the colored Baptists of the United States.
MB B13
Bacote, Samuel William, ed.
Who's who among the colored Baptists of the United States... Ed. by Samuel William Bacote... Kansas City, Mo., Franklin Hudson Publishing Co., 1913-
v. front. ports. 20½cm.

MB W62w
Who's who in colored America; a biographical dictionary of notable living persons of Negro descent in America ... v. 1- 1927-
New York, N. Y., Who's who in colored America corp. [c1927-
v. ports. 28cm.
Editor: 1927- J. J. Boris.
1. ~~Negroes—Biog.~~ Biography I. Boris, Joseph J., 1888- ed.
27-8470
Library of Congress E185.96.W54
[45x2]

MB P41w
Who's who in colored Louisiana, 1930; A. E. Perkins ... editor. Baton Rouge, La., Douglas loan co., inc. [1930]
158, [1] p. illus., plates (1 fold.) ports., facsim. 21cm.
1. Negroes—Louisiana. 2. ~~Negroes—Biog.~~ Biography 3. ~~Louisiana—Biog.~~ I. Perkins, Archie Ebenezer, 1879- ed.
33-19208
Library of Congress E185.93.L6W5
[a44b1] 325.26

Who's who in Philadelphia.
MB W58
White, Charles Frederick.
Who's who in Philadelphia; a collection of thirty biographical sketches of Philadelphia colored people ... together with cuts and information of some of their leading institutions and organizations, by Charles Fred. White ... with an introduction by R. R. Wright, jr., PH. D., and containing additional articles by C. J. Perry, B. F. Lee, jr., R. R. Wright, jr., and Charles Fred. White ... Philadelphia, The A. M. E. book concern [c1912]
206 p., 1 l. incl. illus., plates. 24 cm.
1. Negroes—Philadelphia. I. Title.
12-14969
Library of Congress F158.9.N3W5
[48b1]

Who's who in the American Negro press.
M07 H55w
Hill, Roy L
Who's who in the American Negro press. Dallas, Royal Pub. Co. [1960]
80 p. 21 cm.
Bibliography: p. 70.
1. Negro press. 2. Negroes—Biog. I. Title.
PN4888.N4H5 071.3 60-4017
Library of Congress [61d3]

MB W62
Who's who of the colored race; a general biographical dictionary of men and women of African descent ... Chicago, 1915-
v. illus. 20cm.
Vol. 1 edited by Frank Lincoln Mather.
Vol. 1: Memento edition, half-century anniversary of Negro freedom in U. S.
1. Negroes—Biog. I. Mather, Frank Lincoln, ed.
15-25373
Library of Congress E185.96.W6
[a25g1]

Why do we have government?
Tanganyika M967.82 Om1k
Omari, Dunstan Alfred, 1922- jt. auth.
Kwa nini tuna haja ya serikali? Why do we have government? [By C. W. W. Ryan and D. A. Omari] Dar es Salaam, Eagle Press, 1954.
17p. 18cm. (Mazungumzo juu ya uraia. Talks on citizenship no.1)
Written in Swahili and English.
1. Tanganyika. I. Title. II. Title: Why do we have government? III. Series: Mazungumzo ya uraia, no.1. IV. Series: Talks on citizenship, no. 1. V. Ryan, C. W. W.

Why harlots hate married men and love bachelors.
Nigeria M896.3 M74w
Moneyhard, C N Onuoha
Why harlots hate married men and love bachelors. Port Harcourt, Fenu Press [n.d]
32p. illus., ports. 20½cm.
Portrait of author in book.
Cover title.

Why I am a communist.
M335.4 D29w
Davis, Benjamin Jefferson, 1903-
Why I am a communist. New York, New Century, 1947.
23p. port. (cover) 18½cm.
Reprint of article in Phylon, June 1947.

M231
W62
Why I believe there is a God; sixteen essays by Negro clergymen. With an introd. by Howard Thurman. Chicago, Johnson Pub. Co., 1965.
xiii, 120 p. 22 cm.
Contents.- Why I believe there is a God, by B. E Mays.- Why I believe there is a God, by J. H. Evans.- Why I believe there is a God, by J. H. Robinson.- Why I believe there is a God, by G. W. Baber.- Why I believe there is a God,
~~1. God—Proof—Addresses, essays, lectures. I. Title: Negro clergymen, sixteen essays by.~~
BT102.W5 231.082 65-17082
Library of Congress [5]

M301
D852g
Why was Du Bois fired?
Graham, Shirley, 1904-
Why was Du Bois fired?
(In: Masses & mainstream, 1:15-27, November 1948)

Haiti
M841
W634p
Wiener, Wanda Ducoste
Pétal par pétale. [Paris, Maitre-Imprimeur, 1962.
29p. 4 plates. 24cm. (Collection "L'ile heureuse.")
"... Toute ma cordialite a Arthur Spingarn, Wanda Ducaster Wiener, New York, 1962".
I. Title.

M231
W62
Why I believe there is a God. 1965. (Card 2)
Contents continued.
by J. H. Howard.- Why I believe there is a God, by E. P. Murchison.- Why I believe there is a God, by W. J. Walls.- Why I believe there is a God, by W. J. Faulkner.- Why I believe there is a God, by Hubert Singleton.- Why I believe there is a God, by J. G. Lavalais.- Why I believe there is a God, by H. V. Richardson.- Why I believe there is a God, by W. H. Borders.- Why I believe there is a God, by
(Continued on next card)

Why we can't wait.
M323.4
K58
King, Martin Luther.
Why we can't wait. [1st ed.] New York, Harper & Row [1964]
xii, 178 p. illus., ports. 22 cm.
1. ~~Negroes~~—Civil rights. I. Title.
E185.61.K54 301.451 64-19514
Library of Congress [64f7]

The wife of his youth.
M813.4
C42w
Chesnutt, Charles Waddell, 1858-1932.
The wife of his youth, and other stories of the color line; by Charles W. Chesnutt. With illustrations by Clyde O. De Land. Boston and New York, Houghton, Mifflin and company, 1899.
3 p. l., 323, [1] p. front., plates. 20cm.
Contents.—The wife of his youth.—Her Virginia mammy.—The sheriff's children.—A matter of principle.—Cicely's dream.—The passing of Grandison.—Uncle Wellington's wives.—The bouquet.—The web of circumstance.
I. Title.
6—113
Library of Congress PZ3.C4253W [a42g1]

M231
W62
Why I believe there is a God. 1965. (Card 3)
Contents continued.
E. F. Jackson.- Why I believe there is a God, by G. C. Taylor.- Why I believe there is a God, by W. E. Fauntroy.- Why I believe there is a God, by Howard Thurman.
1. God - Proof - Addresses, essays, lectures. I. Title: Negro Clergymen, sixteen essays by. II. Thurman, Howard. Introduction.

Wia wa mũndũ mũka e mũsyĩ.
Kenya
M396
G19w
Garrioch, L H
Wia wa mũndũ mũka e mũsyĩ [The work of women in the home. Tr. by T. N. Malinda] Nairobi, Eagle Press, 1950.
16p. 18cm.
Written in Kamba.
Cover title.
White author.
1. Home labor - Kenya. I. Title.

The wig, a mirror image.
M813.5
W92w
Wright, Charles Stevenson, 1932-
The wig, a mirror image [by] Charles Wright. New York, Farrar, Straus and Giroux [1966]
179 p. 21 cm.
Portrait of author on book jacket.
I. Title.
PZ4.W9477Wi 66-11706
Library of Congress [5]

Why I sit-in.
M323
P84wy
Posey, Barbara Ann
Why I sit-in; the girl who started a nationwide civil-rights movement tells how and why she sits and waits. New York, NAACP, 1960.
4p. port. 22cm.
Reprinted from Datebook magazine.

West Indies
M823
C23
Wickham, John
Breaking point.
(In: Caribbean anthology of short stories,... Kingston, Jamaica, Pioneer Press 1953. 19cm. pp. 79-86.)

M811.5
W63t
Wiggins, Bernice Love, 1897-
Tuneful tales, by Bernice Love Wiggins. El Paso, Tex., 1925.
174 p. 20cm.
In verse.
Inscribed copy: To Arthur B. Spingarn. Sincerely, Bernice Love Wiggins. 819 Jefferson Blvd., Los Angeles, Calif.
I. Title. 1. Poetry. 7-2-1928.
26-1848
Library of Congress PS3545.I 246T8 1925
Copyright A 875896 [2]

Ghana
M843
Of6
Why kibi ritual murder?
Ofori, David
Why kibi ritual murder? An inside story of a sensational so-called "ritual murder" case. [Accra, Heal Press, 1954]
36p. illus., ports. 21cm.
Portrait of author on t.p.

M813.5
W633g
Wideman, John Edgar.
A glance away. [1st ed.] New York, Harcourt, Brace & World [1967]
186 p. 21 cm.
I. Title.
PZ4.W638Gl 67-19103
Library of Congress [5]

Wilberforce, William, 1759-1833.
M89
W64h
Hughes, Benjamin F
Eulogium on the life and character of William Wilberforce, delivered and published at the request of the people of color of the city of New York, twenty-second of October, 1833, by Benjamin F. Hughes, (a man of color) New York, Printed at the office of the Emancipator, 1833.
16p. 22cm.

M350
J62
Why Negroes should oppose the war.
Johnson, J R
Why Negroes should oppose the war, by J. R. Johnson ... [New York, Pub. by Pioneer publishers for the Socialist workers party and the Young people's socialist league (Fourth International) 1939?]
30, [1] p. 21cm.
1. World war, 1939- —Negroes. I. Socialist workers party. II. Young people's socialist league of America. III. Title.
44-12148
Library of Congress D810.N4J57 [2] 940.5408

M811.5
C61w
The widening light.
Clifford, Carrie Williams,
The widening light, by Carrie Williams Clifford. Boston, Walter Reid Co., [c1922]
ix, 65p. 23cm.

Wilberforce, William, 1759-1833.
M89
W64w
Whipper, William.
Eulogy on William Wilberforce, esq., delivered at the request of the people of colour of the city of Philadelphia ... on the sixth day of December, 1833. By William Whipper, Philadelphia, Printed by W. P. Gibbons [1833?]
iv, [5]-35 p. 21½cm.
1. Wilberforce, William, 1759-1833.
11-34676
Library of Congress HT1029.W5W4 [a34b1]

... Why race riots?
M323.
B81w
Brown, Earl Louis, 1900-
... Why race riots? Lessons from Detroit, by Earl Brown ... [New York, Public affairs committee, inc., 1944.
cover-title, 31, [1] p. illus., diagrs. 21cm. (Public affairs pamphlets, no. 87)
"First edition, January, 1944."
"For further reading": p. 31.
1. Detroit—Riot, 1943. 2. Negroes—Detroit. 3. U. S.—Race question. I. Title.
44—5826
Library of Congress F574.D4B58 [46q5] 977.434

Haiti
M841
W63f
Wiener, Jacqueline
Une femme chante. Duexieme edition. Port-au-Prince, L'Etat [1951?]
59p. port. 21cm.
I. Title. 1. Haitian poetry.

Wilberforce Negro colony, Middlesex Co., Ont.
M326.99B
St4
1867
Steward, Austin, b. 1794.
Twenty-two years a slave, and forty years a freeman; embracing a correspondence of several years, while president of Wilberforce colony, London, Canada West, by Austin Steward. 4th ed. ~~Rochester, N. Y., Allings & Cory, 1861.~~ Canadigua, N. Y., The Author, 1867.
xii, [13]-360 p. front. (port.) 4 pl. 18cm.
1. Slavery in the U. S.—Virginia. 2. Slavery in the U. S.—New York (State) 3. Wilberforce negro colony, Middlesex Co., Ont. I. Title.
14—17056
Library of Congress E444.S845 [a20f2]

Willerforce Negro colony, Middlesex co., Ont.

M326.99B St4
Steward, Austin, b. 1794.
Twenty-two years a slave, and forty years a freeman; embracing a correspondence of several years, while president of Wilberforce colony, London, Canada West, by Austin Steward. Rochester, N. Y., W. Alling, 1857.
xii, [13]-360 p. front. (port.) 4 pl. 19cm.
Narrative of slave life in Virginia and in central New York.
1. Slavery in the U. S.—Virginia. 2. Wilberforce negro colony, Middlesex co., Ont. I. Title.
Library of Congress E444.S84 6—34319 [a27d1]

Wilberforce University, Wilberforce, Ohio.

MB9 Sm5d
Smith, David.
Biography of Rev. David Smith, of the A.M.E. Church, being a complete history, embracing over sixty years labor in the advancement of the Redeemer's kingdom on earth, Including "the history of the origin and development of Wilberforce University". Xenia, O., Printed at the Xenia Gazette Office, 1881.
vii, [1l] - 135p. front.

South Africa M896.3 Ab8w 1950
Wild conquest.
Abrahams, Peter, 1919–
Wild conquest. [1st ed.] New York, Harper [1950]
309 p. 21 cm.
I. Title.
Full name: Peter Henry Abrahams.
PZ3.A1576Wi 50-7364
Library of Congress [5]

Wilberforce philanthropic association, New York.

M326 S11o
Sidney, Joseph.
An oration, commemorative of the abolition of the slave trade in the United States; delivered before the Wilberforce philanthropic association, in the city of New-York, on the second of January, 1809. By Joseph Sidney. New-York, Printed for the author, J. Seymour, printer, 1809.
20 p. 20cm.
1. Slavery in the U. S.—Controversial literature—1809. 2. Slave-trade—U. S. I. Wilberforce philanthropic association, New York.
10-32480
Library of Congress E446.S56

Wilberforce university, Wilberforce, Ohio.

MB T14s
Talbert, Horace, 1853–
The sons of Allen, by Rev. Horace Talbert, M. A. Together with a sketch of the rise and progress of Wilberforce university, Wilberforce, Ohio. Xenia, O., The Aldine press, 1906.
3 p. l., v-xiv p., 1 l., 17-286 p. front. (port.) illus. 23cm.
1. Allen, Richard, bp., 1760-1831. 2. Wilberforce university, Wilberforce, O. 3. African Methodist Episcopal church—Clergy. I. Title.
6-15719
Library of Congress BX8443.T3
——— Copy 2.
Copyright A 141603 [a33b1]

Wilder Weg.

S.Africa M896.3 Ab8wi
Abrahams, Peter, 1919-
Wilder Weg; ein roman (Wild conquest.) Zürich, Im Verlag der Archo, 1952.
332p. 19cm.

Wilberforce University, Wilberforce, Ohio.

MB B80p
Brown, Hallie Quinn, ed.
Pen pictures of pioneers of Wilberforce, compiled and edited by Hallie Q. Brown ... illustrated from photographs from widely different sources. [Xenia, O., The Aldine publishing company, °1937]
96 p. illus. (incl. ports.) 20½cm.
1. Wilberforce university, Wilberforce, O. I. Title.
37-13020
Library of Congress LC2851.W61B7
——— Copy 2.
Copyright A 107185 [3] 378.771

Wilberforce University, Wilberforce, Ohio.
see also
Central State College. Wilberforce, Ohio.

M813.5 B439w
A wilderness of vines.
Bennett, George Harold, 1930–
A wilderness of vines [by] Hal Bennett. [1st ed.] Garden City, N. Y., Doubleday, 1966.
345 p. 22 cm.
I. Title.
PZ4.B4696Wi 66-17441
Library of Congress [5]

M977.1 J66h
Wilberforce university, Wilberforce, Ohio.
Joiner, William A
A half century of freedom of the Negro in Ohio, compiled and arranged by W. A. Joiner.. Xenia. O., Press of Smith Adv. Co., 1915?
134p. illus. 22½cm.

Wilbur, Marguerite Knowlton (Eyer) tr.

France M843 D89j
Dumas, Alexandre, 1802-1870.
The journal of Madame Giovanni, by Alexandre Dumas, translated from the French edition (1856) by Marguerite E. Wilbur, with a foreword by Frank W. Reed. New York, Liveright publishing corporation [1944]
xxxi p., 1 l., 404 p. 22½ cm.
Has been attributed to Vicomtesse de Saint Mars. *cf.* Bibliothèque nationale, Catalogue général, and Quérard, J. M., Les supercheries littéraires dévoilées.
French edition, 1856, has title: Taïti-Marquises-Californie; journal de madame Giovanni, rédigé et publié par Alexandre Dumas.
I. Saint Mars, Gabrielle Anne Cisterne de Courtiras, vicomtesse de, 1804-1872, supposed author. II. Wilbur, Marguerite Knowlton (Eyer) tr. III. Title.
PZ3.D89Jo 843.76 44—1899
Library of Congress [59q1]

M811.5 W64t
Wilds, Mrs. Myra Viola.
Thoughts of idle hours, by Myra Viola Wilds ... illustrations by Lorenzo Harris ... Nashville, Tenn., National Baptist publishing board, 1915.
81 p. front. (port.) illus. 16cm. $0.65
Autographed copy: Myra Viola Wilds
I. Title.
15-19093
Library of Congress PS3545.I358T5 1915
Copyright A 410560

Wilberforce university, Wilberforce, Ohio.

M378w M17
McGinnis, Frederick Alphonso.
A history and an interpretation of Wilberforce university, by Frederick A. McGinnis ... Wilberforce, O. [Blanchester, O., Printed at the Brown publishing co.] 1941.
xii, 215 p. incl. tab. front., plates, ports. 23½cm.
Bibliography: p. 203-208.
1. Wilberforce university, Wilberforce, O.
41-9156
Library of Congress LC2851.W62M2 [3] 378.771

Wilbur, Marguerite Knowlton (Eyer) tr.

France M840 B89jo
Dumas, Alexandre, 1802-1870.
The journal of Madame Giovanni, by Alexandre Dumas, translated from the French edition (1856) by Marguerite E. Wilbur. London, Hammond, Hammond & co. ltd [°1944]
305 p. 22½cm.
Has been attributed to Vicomtesse de Saint Mars. *cf.* Bibl. nat. Cat. gén., and Quérard, J. M. Les supercheries littéraires dévoilées.
French edition, 1856, has title: Taïti-Marquises-Californie; journal de madame Giovanni, rédigé et publié par Alexandre Dumas.
I. Saint Mars, Gabrielle Anne Cisterne de Courtiras, vicomtesse de, 1804-1872, supposed author. II. Wilbur, Marguerite Knowlton (Eyer) tr. III. Title.
45-6399
Library of Congress PZ3.D89Jo 2 [3] 843.76

M811.5 W65bh
Wilentz, Elias, ed.
The beat scene. Photos. by Fred McDarrah. Edited and with an introd. by Elias Wilentz. New York, Corinth Books, Distributed by The Citadel Press, 1960.
185 p. illus. 21 cm.
Verse and prose.
1. American literature—20th cent. 2. Bohemianism. I. Title.
PS536.W47 810.91 60-10628 ‡
Library of Congress [10]

Wilberforce University, Wilberforce, Ohio.

M287.8 P29r
Payne, Daniel Alexander, 1811-1893.
Response of Bishop Payne to Rev. R.C. Ransom. [n.p., n.p., n.d.]
4unnumb. p. 24cm.
Response to an article written by Reverdy C. Ransom and published in the Christian Recorder, Sept. 1890.

The wild coast.

British Guiana M823.91 C18w
Carew, Jan Ryveld, 1923-
The wild coast. London, Secker & Warburg, 1958.
256p. 23cm.
Picture and biographical sketch of the author on the book jacket.

M113 W64
Wilhite, William Hugh.
The universe of universes, by William Hugh Wilhite. St. Louis, Mo., Keymer Printing company, 1923.
117 [10]p. 19½cm.
1.Metaphysics. I.Title.

Wilberforce University, Wilberforce, Onio.

M378W R17s
Ransom, Reverdy Cassius, bp., 1861-
School days at Wilberforce, by Reverdy C. Ransom. [Springfield, Ohio, The New Era Co., 1892].
66p. front., port. 20½cm.

Wild conquest.

South Africa M896.3 Ab8w 1951
Abrahams, Peter, 1919-
Wild conquest. London, Faber and Faber, 1951.
382p. 19cm.

M370 W65f
Wilkerson, Doxey Alphonso, 1905–
Federal aid to education; to perpetuate or diminish existing educational inequalities? By Doxey A. Wilkerson. Issued April, 1937. Chicago, American federation of teachers [1937]
12 p. incl. tables. 21½cm.
1. Education and state—U. S. 2. Education—~~U. S.~~—Finance. 3. Public schools—U. S.—Finance. ~~4. Negroes—Education—Finance.~~ I. Title.
E 40-448
U. S. Off. of educ. Library for Library of Congress LB2825.W66 [2]

M304 P19 v.2, no.10 M335.4 W65n

Wilkerson, Doxey Alphonso, 1905–
... The Negro people and the Communists. [New York] Workers library publishers, inc., 1944.
23 p. 18cm.
At head of title: Doxey A. Wilkerson.
Portrait on title-page.
1. Negroes. 2. Communism—U. S. I. Title.
Harvard univ. Library for Library of Congress E185.61.W67 [45c1] A 44—2215

M350 W65

Wilkes, Laura Eliza, 1871–
Missing pages in American history, revealing the services of negroes in the early wars in the United States of America, 1641–1815, by Laura E. Wilkes ... [Washington, D. C., Press of R. L. Pendleton, °1919]
91 p. 22cm.
On cover: Armistice edition.
Bibliography: p. 85–87.
1. Negroes as soldiers. 2. U. S.—History, Military. I. Title.
Library of Congress E185.63.W68 19-10083
Copyright A 515580 [3]

M323.4 W65d

Wilkins, Roy, 1901–
Deep south crisis.
Pp. 344–351.
In: Wrage, E. J., ed. Contemporary forum. New York, Harper, 1962.

M370 W65p

Wilkerson, Doxey Alphonso, 1905–
The people versus segregated schools. New York, New Century Publishers, 1955.
15p. 18cm.
1. Segregation in education. 2. Southern States - Education.

MB9 D74wi

Wilkes, Laura Eliza, 1871–
The story of Frederick Douglass, with quotations and extracts, by Laura E. Wilkes... Washington, D.C., R.L. Pendleton, Printer, 1909.
46p. front. 15½cm.
Copyrighted November 1899.
1. Douglass, Frederick, 1817–1895.

M323.4 G58

Wilkins, Roy, 1901–
Emancipation and militant leadership.
Pp. 25–46.
In: Goldwin, Robert A.,ed. 100 years of emancipation. Chicago, Rand McNally, 1964.

M370 W65s

Wilkerson, Doxey Alphonso, 1905–
Special problems of Negro education, by Doxey A. Wilkerson ... Prepared for the Advisory committee on education. Washington, U. S. Govt. print. off., 1939.
xvi, 171 p. incl. tables. 23cm. ([U. S.] Advisory committee on education. Staff study no. 12)
"Publications of the committee": p. 171.
1. Negroes—Education. I. Title.
Library of Congress L111.A98 no. 12 39—26926
——— Copy 2. LC2801.W5
[43u2] (370.973) 371.9740973

Wilkins, Helen J., joint author.

M267.5 M41i

Bell, Juliet Ober, 1895–
Interracial practices in community Y. W. C. A.'s; a study under the auspices of the Commission to gather interracial experience, as requested by the sixteenth National convention of the Y. W. C. A.'s of the U. S. A., conducted by Juliet O. Bell, PH. D., and Helen J. Wilkins. New York, N. Y., National board, Y. W. C. A., 1944.
3 p. l., 116 p. 21½cm.
"Recommendations related to interracial practices in community Y. W. C. A.'s to be submitted for action to the seventeenth National convention" (8 p.) inserted.
1. U. S.—Race question. 2. Negroes. 3. Young women's Christian associations. I. Wilkins, Helen J., joint author. II. Young women's Christian associations. U. S. National board. Commission to gather interracial experience. III. Title.
Library of Congress E185.61.B4 44-7133
[4] 267.43265

M323 W65e

Wilkins, Roy, 1901–
The enemies of mankind.
Pp. 14–19.
In: Freedom House, New York. Vital speeches. New York, Freedom House, 1963.

M335.4 W65

Wilkerson, Doxey Alphonso, 1905–
Why Negroes are joining the communist party. New York, The communist party, 1946.
15p. 19cm.
1. Communism - U.S.

M304 P19 V.6, no.8

Wilkins, J P.
History of my brothers in the World War –, Also an appendix of valuable information. [lacks imprint]
58p. 19cm.
1. World War I. 2. Soldiers.

M323 N214w

Wilkins, Roy, 1901–
40 years of the NAACP, keynote address at 40th annual conference, National Association for the Advancement of Colored People, Los Angeles, California, July 12, 1949. New York, NAACP, 1949.
16p. 21x10cm.
1. National Association for the Advancement of Colored People

---

Wilkerson, Doxey Alphonso, 1905–

M371.974 W65

National Association of Intergroup Relations Officials. Commission on School Integration.
Public school segregation and integration in the North; analysis and proposals of the [NAIRO] Commission on School Integration [prepared by Doxey A. Wilkerson] Washington, 1963.
vi, 104p. tables. 22cm.
Special issue of the Journal of Intergroup Relations.
Bibliography: p. 87–104.
(Continued on next card)

M323.2 W65p

Wilkins, Marjorie V
Pioneer in human relations. Reprinted from New York State education, February 1949.
4p. 25cm.
1. Race relations. 2. White Plains, New York. Human Relations Center.

M323.4 W52

Wilkins, Roy, 1901–
Humiliation stalks them.
pp. 158–161.
In: Westin, Alan F. Freedom now. New York, Basic Books, 1964.

Wilkerson, Doxey Alphonso, 1905–

M370 Sm51e

Smith, Payson, 1873–
Education in the forty-eight states, by Payson Smith, Frank W. Wright and associates ... Prepared for the Advisory committee on education. Washington, U. S. Govt. print. off., 1939.
xv, 199 p. incl. tables. 23cm. ([U. S.] Advisory committee on education. Staff study no. 1)
Bibliographical foot-notes. "Publications of the committee": p. 199.
1. Education—U. S. I. Wright, Frank Watson, 1880– joint author. II. Title.
Library of Congress L111.A98 no. 1 39—26774
——— Copy 2. LA210.S58
[42x3] (370.973) 370.973

M323 Su6

Wilkins, Roy, 1901–
Address.
Pp. 61–65.
In: Summit Meeting of National Negro Leaders, Washington, D.C. Report. Washington, National Newspaper Publishers Association, 1958.

M323 W65i

Wilkins, Roy, 1901–
Integration crisis in the South; an address delivered at the 14th annual State convention of the NAACP in Charlotte, N. C., October 11th, 1957, and broadcast over radio network facilities of the American Broadcasting Company. New York, National Association for the Advancement of Colored People [1957]
11p. 21½cm.
1. Race relations. 2. Southern states. I. Title.

MB9 W65h

Wilkerson, James.
Wilkerson's history of his travels and labors, in the United States, as a missionary, in particular, that of the Union seminary, located in Franklin Co., Ohio, since he purchased his liberty in New Orleans, La., &c. Columbus, O., 1861.
43 p. 22½cm.
Library of Congress E185.97.W68 13-26819

M323 W65c

Wilkins, Roy, 1901–
The conspiracy to deny equality; an address delivered at the 46th annual NAACP convention in Atlantic City, N. J., June 25, 1955. New York, National Association for the Advancement of Colored People [1955]
15p. 21½cm
1. Civil rights. I. Title.

M323 W65k

Wilkins, Roy, 1901–
Keynote address, NAACP 54th annual National Convention, Morrison Hotel, Chicago, Ill., July 1, 1963.
[6]p. 28cm.
I. Title.

M323
W65m
Wilkins, Roy, 1901-
The meaning of the sit-ins. New York, National Association for the Advancement of Colored People, 1960]
11p. 23cm.
1. Sit-in demonstrations. 2. Civil rights. I. Title.

M07
W65
Wilkins, Roy, 1901-
The Negro press hits back. Toronto, Reprinted from the Magazine digest, April 1943,
3-7p. 19cm.
1. Newspapers. 2. Press. I. Title.

M323
W65n
Wilkins, Roy, 1901-
The Negro wants full equality. New York, Committee of 100 [1945]
14p. 23cm.
Reprinted from What the Negro wants, ed. by Rayford Logan 1944.
1. Equality. I. Title.

M371.974
Sol3
Wilkins, Roy, 1901-
The role of the NAACP.
Pp. 201-203
Negro author.
In: Social problems. Desegregation in the public schools. New York, Society for the Study of Social Problems, 1955.

M323
W65se
Wilkins, Roy, 1901-
Segregation, the top executive officer of the National Association for the Advancement of Colored People and the author of Weep no more, my lady discuss the pros and cons of that Supreme Court decision. Edited by W. E. Debman. Raleigh, W. E. Debnam, 1955.
43p 19½cm.
1. Civil rights. I. Debman, W. E., ed.

M323
D22
Wilkins, Roy, 1901-
What the Negro American wants: an interview.
Pp. 26-44.
In: Bradford, Daniel, ed. Black, white and gray. New York, Sheed and Ward, 1964.

M811.5
W65d
Wilkinson, Henry Bertram, 1889–
Desert sands, a volume of verse touching various topics, by Henry B. Wilkinson ... London, A. H. Stockwell, ltd. [1933]
108 p., 2 l. 18½cm.
I. Title. 1. Poetry.
A 40-3142
No. Carolina. Univ. Libr. for Library of Congress PS3545.D
[2]

M811.5
W65i
Wilkinson, Henry Bertram, 1889–
Idle hours, by Henry B. Wilkinson. New York, F. H. Hitchcock [°1927]
5 p. l., 86 p. 19½cm.
Poems.
"Only two hundred and fifty copies of this book have been printed and the type distributed."
I. Title. 1. Poetry.
28-5706
Library of Congress PS3545.I 396 I 4 1927
Copyright A 1013904 [3]

M811.5
W65s
Wilkinson, Henry Bertram, 1889–
Shady-rest, by Henry B. Wilkinson ... New York, F. H. Hitchcock [°1928]
5 p. l., 69 p. 19½cm.
Poems.
"Only two hundred and fifty copies of this book have been printed and the type distributed."
I. Title. 1. Poetry.
28-21570
Library of Congress PS3545.I 39385 1928
Copyright A 1054264 [2]

M811.5
W65t
Wilkinson, Henry Bertram, 1889-
Transitory, a poem by Henry B. Wilkinson. Dedicated to a peaceful world. Boston, privately printed for the author by the Popular Poetry Publishers, [c1941]
20p. 16cm.
autographed copy
1. Poetry
I. Title

M616
W93pe
Wilkinson, Robert Shaw, 1899- .
Wright, Louis Tompkins, 1891-1952.
Penetrating stab wounds of the abdomen and stab wounds of the abdominal wall; A review of 184 consecutive cases, by Louis T. Wright, Robert S. Wilkinson and Joseph L. Gaster. Reprinted from Surgery, 6:241-260, August 1959.

M331
G76t
Wilkinson, William H.H.
Granger, Lester Blackwell, 1896–
Toward job adjustment, with specific reference to the vocational problems of racial, religious and cultural minority groups, by Lester B. Granger ... Louis H. Sobel ... [and] William H. H. Wilkinson ... Prepared under the direction of Committee on minority groups, Section on employment and vocational guidance, Welfare council of New York city. [New York] Welfare council of New York city [°1941]
78 p., 1 l. illus. 21½cm.
Bibliography: 76–78.
1. Interviewing. 2. Employment agencies. 3. Minorities. I. Sobel, Louis Harry, joint author. II. Wilkinson, William H. H. III. Welfare council of New York city. Section on employment and vocational guidance. IV. Title.
41-16628
Library of Congress HD5861.G65
[10] 331.11511

Will.
M174
P11b
Pace, Harry Herbert, 1884–
Beginning again, by Harry H. Pace. Philadelphia, Dorrance & company, inc. [°1934]
72 p. front. 19½cm.
1. Success. 2. Will. I. Title.
35-784
Library of Congress HF5386.P18
Copyright A 78810 [2] 174

William Johnson's Natchez.
M89
J639
Johnson, William, 1809-1851.
William Johnson's Natchez; the ante-bellum diary of a free Negro. Edited by William Ransom Hogan and Edwin Adams Davis. [Baton Rouge] Louisiana State University Press [1951]
ix, 812 p. illus., facsims. 24 cm. (Source studies in Southern history, no. 1)
1. Natchez, Miss.—Soc. life & cust. I. Title. (Series)
E185.97.J697A3 325.2609762 51—3480
Library of Congress [52k5]

Williams, Arnold B., 1804-1886 p. 201-02.
M286
W61h
Whitted, J A
A history of the Negro Baptists of North Carolina, by Rev. J.A. Whitted... Raleigh, Presses of Edwards and Broughton printing co., 1908.
212p. front. plates - 22½cm.

M301
R75
Williams, Chancellor, 1902-
Africa.
pp. 1085-1094
In: J.S. Roučeks Contemporary sociology. 1958.
I. Faculty contribution.

M323
W67a
Williams, Chancellor, 1902-
And if I were white, a reply to the if I were a Negro series by prominent white writers. By Chancellor Williams. Washington, D.C., Shaw Publishing Co. [c1946]
63p. front (port.) 19½cm.
1. Race relations.

M813.5
W67h
Williams, Chancellor, 1902–
Have you been to the river? A novel. [1st ed.] New York, Exposition Press [1952]
258 p. 21 cm.
I. Title.
PZ3.W67143Hav 52-10988 ‡
Library of Congress [2]

M813.5
W67
Williams, Chancellor, 1902–
The raven, by Chancellor Williams. Philadelphia, Dorrance and company [1943]
2 p. l., iii-iv p., 1 l., 7-562 p. 23½ cm.
A novel.
1. Poe, Edgar Allan, 1809-1849—Fiction. I. Title.
43-17566
Library of Congress PZ3.W67143Rav
[5]

M910
W67r
Williams, Chancellor, 1902–
The rebirth of African civilization. Washington, Public Affairs Press [1961]
328 p. 24 cm.
Includes bibliography.
1. Africa, Sub-Saharan—Civilization. I. Title. II. Faculty contributions.
DT352.W5 916.7 61-11689 ‡
Library of Congress [5]

M350
W67
Williams, Charles Halston, 1886–
Sidelights on Negro soldiers, by Charles H. Williams ... with an introduction by Benjamin Brawley. Boston, B. J. Brimmer company, 1923.
248 p. 22cm.
"First edition." June 1923.
Special edition... of one hundred and twenty-five copies, of which this is number 1.
Autographed copy.
1. European war, 1914-1918—Negroes. I. Title.
24—2170
Library of Congress D639.N4W5
——— Copy 2.
Copyright A 760790 [30e1]

Trinidad
M780 W671sg
Williams, Connie, collector.
12 songs from Trinidad. [Illustrated by Grace West] San Francisco, Panpipes Press, 1958.

15p. illus., port. 18½cm.

1. Trinidad - Songs. 2. Songs - Trinidad. I. Title.

M973 W67f
Williams, Daniel Barclay, 1861–
Freedom and progress, and other choice addresses on practical, scientific, educational, philosophic, historic and religious subjects, by Professor Daniel B. Williams ... with an introductory sketch of the author, by John Mitchell, jr. ... Petersburg, Va., D. B. Williams, 1890.
150 p. front. (port.) 18½cm.

~~1. Negroes.~~ I. Title.

Library of Congress E185.5.W72 15–23538
Copyright 1890: 844

Jamaica
M823.91 Sa3a
Williams, Denis
A long long pause.

Pp. 218-222.

In: Salkey, Andrew, comp. Stories from the Caribbean. London, Elek Books, 1965.

British Guiana
M823.91 W67o
Williams, Denis, 1923-
Other leopards. [London, New Authors Limited, 1963]

221p. 21½ cm.

Portrait of author on book jacket.

1. Title.

M811.5 W67v
Williams, Edward W.
The views and meditations of John Brown. By Edward W. Williams ... [Washington, 1893?]
16 p. 24cm.
In verse.

1. Brown, John, 1800–1859. 2. Harpers Ferry, W. Va.—John Brown raid, 1859. I. Title.

Library of Congress E451.W72 8–33640
——— Copy 2. [a40b1]

Williams, Egbert Austin, 1875-1922.

MB9 W671r
Rowland, Mabel, *ed.*
Bert Williams, son of laughter; a symposium of tribute to the man and to his work, by his friends and associates, with a preface by David Belasco; edited by Mabel Rowland. New York city, The English crafters [©1923]
xvii p., 1 l., 218 p. front., plates, ports., facsim. 19½ cm.

1. Williams, Egbert Austin, 1875–1922.

Library of Congress PN2287.W46R6 23–8629 [8]

Trinidad
M329 W67ap
Williams, Eric Eustace, 1911-
The approach of independence; an address to the fourth annual convention of the People's National Movement. [Port-of-Spain, P.N.M. Publishing Co., 1960]

23p. 21cm.

1. People's National Party. 2. Trinidad - Political parties. 3. Political parties - Trinidad. I. Title.

Trinidad
M972.9 W67b
Williams, Eric Eustace, 1911-
British historians and the West Indies. Port-of-Spain, P.N.M. Pub.,Co., Ltd., 1964.

187p. 21cm.
Includes bibliography.
Portrait of author on back cover.

1. West Indies - History - Sources. I. Title.

W. Indies
M972.9 B41
Williams, Eric Eustace, 1911-
British possessions.

(In: Latin American Economic Institute. Economic problems of the Caribbean area; ... New York, 1943. 23cm. p. 20-23).

Trinidad
M972.9 W67
Williams, Eric Eustace, 1911- , ed.
The British West Indies at Westminster. Part I: 1789-1823. Extracts from the debates in parliament. Port-of-Spain, Historical Society of Trinidad and Tobago, 1954.

136p. 21cm.

1. West Indies, British - History.

Trinidad
M300. W67c
Williams, Eric Eustace, 1911-
Capitalism & slavery [by] Eric Williams. Chapel Hill, The University of North Carolina press [1944]
ix, 285 p. 22½cm.
Bibliographical references included in "Notes" (p. 213–261) Bibliography: p. 262–270.
"Based on a doctoral dissertation, 'The economic aspect of the abolition of the British West Indian slave trade and slavery,' submitted to the Faculty of modern history of Oxford university in September, 1938."—p. 262.

1. Gt. Brit.—Indus.—Hist. 2. Slave trade—Gt. Brit. I. Title.

Library of Congress HC254.5.W5 44–47876 [80] 330.942

Eustace, 1911–

Trinidad
M972.9 W67c
Williams, Eric. Eustace, 1911- ed.
Caribbean historical review. Port-of-Spain, Trinidad Pub. Co., 1951.

152p. 21½cm. (Historical Society of Trinidad and Tobago ... No. 2. Dec. 1951)
Partial contents.- The caribbean bookshelf: the sugar economy of the Caribbean, by Eric Williams.

1. Trinidad. 2. Caribbean area. 3. West Indies. I. Title.

Trinidad
M972.9 W67d
Williams, Eric Eustace, 1911-
Documents of West Indian history, Port-of Spain, PNM Pub. Co., 1963-

v. 21cm.
Contents: V. 1. From the Spanish discovery to the British conquest of Jamaica, 1492-1955.
Autographed.
Portrait of the author on back cover.

1. West Indies - History - Sources. 2. Jamaica - History. I. Title.

Trinidad
M972.98 W67f
Williams, Eric Eustace, 1911-
Federation; two public lectures. [Port-of-Spain, Printed for the People's National Movement by the College Press, 1956]

60p. 21½cm.

1. Trinidad. I. Title.

Trinidad
M300. W67e
Williams, Eric Eustace, 1911–
Education in the British West Indies. Foreword by John Dewey. Port-of-Spain, Printed by Guardian Commercial Printery [1950]
xix, 167 p. 22 cm.
At head of title: The Teachers' Economic and Cultural Association, ltd.
Label mounted on cover: Distributors in U. S. A., University Place Book Store, New York.
Bibliography: p. 153–158.

1. Education—West Indies, British. I. Title.

LA481.W5 370.9729 51—12986
Library of Congress [52c1]

Trinidad
MB9 G15w
Williams, Eric Eustace, 1911-
Gandhi; a broadcast by Eric Williams on the 90th anniversary of the birth of Mahatma Gandhi. Port-of-Spain, P. N. M. Publishing Co., [n.d.]

4p. 21cm.

1. Gandhi, Mohandas Karamchand, 1869-1948. ~~I. Title.~~

Trinidad
M972.98 W67h
Williams, Eric Eustace, 1911–
History of the people of Trinidad and Tobago. Port-of-Spain, Trinidad, Printed by PNM Pub. Co., 1962.
viii, 294 p. maps (on p. [2]–[3] of cover) 21 cm.
Bibliography: p. [285]–288.
Autographed.

1. Trinidad and Tobago—Hist. I. Title.

F2119.W5 64–773 rev
Library of Congress [r64b1]

Trinidad
M972.98 W67m
Williams, Eric Eustace, 1911-
Massa day done; a masterpiece of political and sociological analysis. Address delivered on Wednesday, March 27, 1961. Port-of-Spain, PNM Pub. Co., 1961.

19p. 21cm.
Portrait of author on front cover.

1. Trinidad. I. Title.

Trinidad
M300. W67n
Williams, Eric Eustace, 1911-
... The Negro in the Caribbean, by Eric Williams ... Washington, D. C., The Associates in Negro folk education, 1942.
4 p. l., 119 p. incl. tab. 22cm. (Bronze booklet no. 8)
"Reference notes": p. 110–114. "Select bibliography": p. 115–117.

1. ~~Negroes in the~~ West Indies. I. Title.

Library of Congress E185.5.B85 no. 8 42—16832
——— Copy 2. F1623.W48
[45j2] (325.260973) 325.2609729

Trinidad
M329 W67o
Williams, Eric Eustace, 1911-
Our fourth anniversary, the last lap; political leader's address on September 24, 1960, at the University of Woodford Square, marking the fourth year of P.N.M.'s first term of office. [Port-of-Spain, P.N.M. Publishing Co., 1960]
15p. 21cm.
Portrait on cover.
1. People's National Movement. 2. Trinidad - Political parties. 3. Political parties.- Trinidad. I. Title.

Trinidad
M329 W67p
Williams, Eric Eustace, 1911-
Perspectives for our party; address delivered to the third annual convention of the People's National Movement on October 17, 1958. [Port-of-Spain, P.N.M. Publishing Co., 1958]
20p. 22cm.

1. People's National Movement. 2. Trinidad - Political parties. 3. Political parties - Trinidad. I. Title.

M306
M451
Williams, Eric Eustace, 1911-
[Problems of economic research] Added comment respecting the West Indies.

(In: Herskovits, M. J. The interdisciplinary aspects of Negro studies. Bulletin of the American Council of Learned Societies, no. 32, September 1941. pp. 58-64.)

Trinidad
M972.98
W67r
Williams, Eric Eustace, 1911-
Responsibilities of the party member by Dr. Eric Williams, premier of Trinidad and Tobago; full text of the political leader's address to the fifth annual convention on Friday, September (1960). [Port-of-Spain, P.N.M., 1960]

16p. 21cm.

continued on next card.

Trinidad
M972.98
W67r
Williams, Eric Eustace, 1911-
Responsibilities of the party member... [Port-of-Spain, P.N.M., 1960] (Card 2.)

1. Political parties - West Indies. 2. West Indies - Political parties. 3. Political conventions - West Indies. 4. West Indies - Political conventions. I. Title.

Trinidad
M972.98
W67s
Williams, Eric Eustace, 1911-
Speech on independence at the special convention January 27-28, 1962. Port-of-Spain, PNM Pub. Co., 1962.

51p. port. 21cm.

1. Trinidad and Tobago.

Trinidad
M972.98
W67y
Williams, Eric Eustace, 1911- , comp.
Yearbook of Caribbean research 1948. Survey of research and investigation in Caribbean Commission territories. Compiled by Research Branch, Central Secretariat Caribbean Commission Port-of-Spain, Trinidad, Caribbean Commission 1949.

v. 23cm.

1. Caribbean-Yearbooks. 2. Yearbooks-Caribbean.

Williams, Eric Eustace, 1911- ed.
M301
F86e
Frazier, Edward Franklin, 1894- ed.
The economic future of the Caribbean. Editors, E. Franklin Frazier and Eric Williams. Washington, Howard University Press, 1944.

94p. 23cm. (Howard University. Division of Social Sciences. Conference 7th)

Williams, Eric Eustace, 1911-
Jamaica
M39
J67j
James, Cyril Lionel Robert, 1901-
A convention appraisal, Dr. Eric Williams of Trinidad and Tobago; a biographical sketch. [Port-of-Spain P.N.M. Publishing Co., 1960]
16p. 22cm.
Portrait on cover.
Autographed.

1. Williams, Eric Eustace, 1911-
I. Title.

MB
W67
Williams, Ethel Naomi (Langley) 1909-
Biographical directory of Negro ministers, by Ethel L. Williams. New York, Scarecrow Press, 1965.

xi, 421 p. 22 cm.

Bibliography: p. 407-412.

1. Negro clergy—U. S.—Biog.—Dictionaries. I. Title.

BR563.N4W5 262.140922 (B) 65-13562

Library of Congress [2-1]

Williams, Ethel Naomi Langley, 1909-
M01
H83
Howard university, *Washington, D. C. Founders library. Moorland foundation.*
A catalogue of books in the Moorland foundation, compiled by workers on projects 271 and 328 of the Works progress administration, Margaret R. Hunton and Ethel Williams, supervisors, Dorothy B. Porter, director. Washington, D. C., Howard university, 1939.
2 p. l., ii numb. l., 94, 166, 159, 28, 33, 19 p. 27½ x 21½cm.
Each part preceded by leaf with half-title not included in paging (6 leaves)
Mimeographed.
1. Negroes—Bibl. 2. Negro literature—Bibl. I. *Porter, Dorothy (Burnett) 1905- II. Hunton, Margaret R. III. Williams, Ethel. IV. U. S. Work projects administration.
39-14329 Revised
Library of Congress Z1361.N39H8
[r44f2] 016.32526097З

M323
Su7n
Williams, Fannie Barrier,
Social bonds in the black belt. Chicago.

(In: Survey midmonthly. The Negro in the cities of the North. New York. The Charity Organization Society, 1905. 26cm. p. 4-44).

Williams, Fannie Barrier.

M973
N42
A new Negro for a new century; an accurate and up-to-date record of the upward struggles of the Negro race. The Spanish-American war, causes of it; vivid descriptions of fierce battles; superb heroism and daring deeds of the Negro soldier ... Education, industrial schools, colleges, universities and their relationship to the race problem, by Prof. Booker T. Washington. Reconstruction and industrial advancement by N. B. Wood ... The colored woman and her part in race regeneration ... by ... Fannie Barrier Williams ... Chicago, Ill., American publishing house [1900]

428 p. front., illus. (ports) 20cm.

(Continued on next card)

0—5252

[44g1]

M248
W67
Williams, Florence B
The guiding light. Baltimore, National Baptist Training Union Board Publisher, 1962.

94p. 21½cm.

1. Christian life. 2. Religion in poetry. I. Title.

M610
P19
v.1, no.13
Williams, Florence Chapman
Health work among Negroes in North Carolina, by Mrs. F.C. Williams... Reprinted by the North Carolina tuberculosis association, Sanatorium, N.C. from the Southern Workman for September 1920.
8p., illus. 25cm.
1. Health - North Carolina.

M610
P19
v.1
13. Williams, Florence Chapman.
Health work among Negroes in North Carolina.
14. Pennsylvania. Dept. of welfare.
Directory of Pennsylvania institutions caring for the sick and the aged.
15. Mossell, Sadie T. A study of the Negro tuberculosis problem in Philadelphia.

M323
W67
Williams, Frances Harriet.
The business girl looks at the Negro world, a study course, by Frances Harriet Williams ... New York, The Womans press, 1937.

3 p. l., 55 p. illus. (maps) 21½cm.

1. Negroes—Moral and social conditions. 2. Negroes—Stat. 3. U. S.—Race question. I. Title.

37—4315

Library of Congress E185.61.W73

[42d1] 325.260973

M370
W67p
Williams, Frances Harriet.
Pudge grows up; Series of meetings for high school girls, by Frances Williams and Wenonah Logan. New York, Womans press, 1936.

28p. 28cm.

1. Girls- Societies and clubs.
I. Logan, Wenonah Bond. II. Title.

Williams, Francis. To the most upright and valiant man, George Haldane, Esq., governor of the Island of Jamaica...v.2, p.481-482.
M972.92
L85h
[Long, Edward] 1734-1813.
The history of Jamaica; or, General survey of the antient and modern state of that island ... London, T. Lowndes, 1774.
3v. fold. fronts. 28x22cm.

Williams, Francis, v.2, p.475-485.
M972.92
L85h
[Long, Edward] 1734-1813.
The history of Jamaica; or, General survey of the antient and modern state of that island... London, T. Lowndes, 1774.
3v. fold. fronts. 28x22cm.

Williams, Francis.
Martinique
M972.98
P53a
Philip, John Baptist, -1829.
An address to the Right Hon. Earl Bathurst, His Majesty's Principal of State for the Colonies, relative to the claims which the coloured population of Trinidad have to the same civil and political privileges with their white fellow-subjects. By a free mulatto of the Island. London, Printed in the year 1824.

298p. 20cm.

M324
W67a
Williams, Franklin Hall, 1917-
An American principle realized. Reprinted from The Pacific spectator, v.6, no.4, Autumn 1952.
[7]p. 23cm.

1. Politics and suffrage
2. Grandfather clause

Africa
M960
P26
Williams, Frederick Rotimi Alade.
Ministers, civil servants, and the public. Pp. 126-130.

In: Passin, Herbert, ed. Africa; the dynamics of change. Ibadan, Ibadan University Press, 1963.

Africa
M808.83
B396

Williams, Gaston Bart
The bed-sitter.

Pp. 36-45.

In: Black Orpheus. Black Orpheus; an anthology of African and Afro-American prose. New York, McGraw-Hill, 1965.

Ghana
M896.1
W672r

Williams, George Awoonor, 1935-
Rediscovery and other poems. Ibadan, Mbari Publications [1964]

36p. 20cm.

I. Title.

M973
W67

Williams, George Washington, 1849–1891.
History of the Negro race in America from 1619 to 1880. Negroes as slaves, as soldiers, and as citizens; together with a preliminary consideration of the unity of the human family, an historical sketch of Africa, and an account of the Negro governments of Sierra Leone and Liberia. By George W. Williams ... Popular ed. ... New York & London, G. P. Putnam's sons [c1882]

2 v. in 1. front. (port.) 24cm.
Vol. 2 has half-title only.

1. Negroes. 2. Sierra Leone. 3. Liberia.

20—4240

Library of Congress E185.W69
[43d1]

M350
W67h

Williams, George Washington, 1849–1891.
A history of the Negro troops in the war of the rebellion, 1861–1865, preceded by a review of the military services of Negroes in ancient and modern times, by George W. Williams ... New York, Harper & brothers, 1888.

2 p. l., [ix]–xvi, 353 p. front. (port.) 1 illus., pl. 20½cm.

1. U. S.—Hist.—Civil war—Negro troops. 2. U. S.—Hist.—Revolution—Negro troops. I. Title.

2—17113

Library of Congress E540.N3W7
[42d1]

Williams, Henry Llewellyn, jr., tr.

France
M840
D89Lo

Dumas, Alexandre, 1802–1870.
Louise de La Vallière; or, The love of Bragellone [!] A continuation of "The three musketeers", "Twenty years after", and "Bragelonne, the son of Athos". By Alex. Dumas. New rev. translation by H. Llewellyn Williams. New York, The F. M. Lupton publishing company [c1892]

459 p. 19cm. (*On cover:* The elite series. no. 9)
Written in collaboration with Auguste Maquet.
A translation of the middle portion of the Vicomte de Bragelonne.
Sequel: The man in the iron mask.
1. La Vallière, Louise Françoise de La Baume Le Blanc, duchesse de, 1644–1710—Fiction. 2. France—Hist.—Louis XIV, 1643–1715—Fiction. 3. Man in the iron mask—Fiction. I. Maquet, Auguste, 1813–1888, joint author. II. Williams, Henry Llewellyn, jr., tr. III. Title.

6—43023

Library of Congress (⊕) (PZ3.D89Lo 2)
Copyright 1892: 5323 [a37g1]

M811.5
W67

Williams, Henry Roger, 1869–
Heart throbs—poems of race inspiration—written by H. Roger Williams ... Mobile, Ala., Gulf city printing co., inc., 1923.

80 p. incl. port. 21cm.

I. Title. 1. Poetry.

23-6889

Library of Congress PS3545.I 5282H4 1923
——— Copy 2.
Copyright A 698788 [2]

Williams, Henry Roger, 1869- ed.

M034
P19
V.5,no.9

Mobile Emancipation Association, Mobile, Ala.
Programme fifty-sixty anniversary, January 1, 1919; together with the names of all officers of the association, the members of the executive committee, also a complete report of the retiring general chairman, Dr. H. Roger Williams. Lacks imprint.

12p. 23cm.

M153
W672

Williams, Herbert L 1917-
Adventure into thought. New York, Exposition Press [1964]

69p. 21cm.

1. Philosophy. I. Title.

M326.99B
W68

Williams, James
Narrative of the cruel treatment of James Williams, a Negro apprentice in Jamaica, from 1st August, 1834, till the purchase of his freedom in 1837, by Joseph Sturge, of Birmingham, by whom he was brought to England. Glasgow: Printed by Aird and Russell, 1837.

20p. 21cm.

1. Slave narratives. 2. Slavery in the West Indies.

M326.99B
W67na

Williams, James
A narrative of events, since the first of August, 1834. An apprenticed labourer in Jamaica. London, Printed by John Haddon, 1834.

23p. 17½cm.

1. Slavery, in Jamaica. 2. Williams, James, b. 1805.

Williams, James

M326.99B
W67na

Williams, James
A narrative of events, since the first of August, 1834. An apprenticed labourer in Jamaica. London, Printed by John Haddon, 1834.

23p. 17½cm.

Williams, James, b. 1790?

MB9
W67

Proctor, Charles Hayden, 1848?–1890.
The life of James Williams, better known as Professor Jim, for half a century janitor of Trinity college. By C. H. Proctor ... Hartford, Case, Lockwood and Brainard, printers, 1873.

79 p. front. (port.) 17½ cm.

1. Williams, James, b. 1790? 2. Trinity college, Hartford, Conn.

13—33803

Library of Congress E185.97.W72
[48b½]

M326.99B
W67n
1838

Williams, James, b. 1805.
Narrative of James Williams. An American slave; who was for several years a driver on a cotton plantation in Alabama ... New-York, The American anti-slavery society, 1838.

xxiii, [25]–108 p. front. (port.) 15cm.

Written by J. G. Whittier from the verbal narrative of Williams. *cf.* G. R. Carpenter, John Greenleaf Whittier, 1903, p. 165.

1. Slavery in the U. S.—Alabama. I. Whittier, John Greenleaf, 1807–1892. II. American anti-slavery society, New York. III. Title.

17—5248

Library of Congress E444.W748
[39c1]

M326.99B
W67n

Williams, James, b. 1805
Narrative of James Williams, an American slave. In anti-slavery examiner no.6
1838
8p. 30cm
1. Slavery in the U.S. - Alabama.
I. American anti-slavery society, New York.
II. Title. 2. Slave narratives.

MB9
W67k

Williams, James H 1864–1927.
Blow the man down! A Yankee seaman's adventures under sail; an autobiographical narrative based upon the writings of James H. Williams as arranged and edited by Warren F. Kuehl. [1st ed.] New York, Dutton, 1959.

255 p. illus. 22 cm.

1. Merchant seamen—U. S. I. Kuehl, Warren F., 1924– ed. II. Title.

HD8039.S42U74 923.873 59—5821 ‡

Library of Congress [59q15]

Jamaica
M823.91
Sa3w

Williams, Jan,
Arise, my love.

pp. 148-155

In Andrew Salkey's West Indian Stories. 1960.

M976.4
W67

Williams, Jerome Aredell
The tin box; a story of Texas cattle and oil. New York, Vantage Press, 1958.

275p. 21cm.

1. Texas - Oil. 2. Texas - Cattle. 3. Cattle - Texas. 4. Oil - Texas.

M974.7
C55

Williams, Jim
The need for a Harlem.

Pp. 157-166.

In: Clarke, John Henrik, ed. Harlem, a community in transition. New York, Citadel Press, 1965.

M910
W67

Williams, John Alfred, 1925–
Africa: her history, lands and people, told with pictures. [1st ed.] New York, Cooper Square Publishers, 1962.

128 p. illus., ports., maps. 28 cm.

1. Africa—Hist.—Pictorial works.

DT21.W5 960 62-19529

Library of Congress [5]

M813.08
W67

Williams, John Alfred, 1925- ed.
The angry black [stories and articles by James Baldwin and others] New York, Lancer Books [1962]

160p. 18cm. (Lancer original, 172-625)
Partial contents.- Theatre: the Negro in and out, by James Baldwin.- Mother dear and daddy, by Junius Edwards.- The death of Clifton, by Ralph Ellison.- Name in print, by Langston Hughes.- Son in the afternoon, by John A.

(Continued on next card)

M813.08
W67

Williams, John Alfred, 1925- ed. The angry black [stories and articles by James Baldwin and others] 1933. (Card 2)

Contents - Continued.
Williams.- The plea, by Richard Wright.

1. Short stories-Race relations. I. Title.

M813.5 W672a Williams, John Alfred, 1925-
The angry ones. New York, Ace Books, inc., 1960.

192p. 16½cm.

1. Title.

M974.7 C55 Williams, John Alfred, 1925-
Harlem nightclub.

Pp. 167-179.

In: Clarke, John Henrik, ed. Harlem, a community in transition. New York, Citadel Press, 1965.

M813.5 W68m **Williams, John Alfred, 1925-**
The man who cried I am; a novel, by John A. Williams. [1st ed.] Boston, Little, Brown [1967]
408 p. 22 cm.

I. Title.

PZ4.W72624Man 67—18103
Library of Congress [68f5]

M813.5 W672n **Williams, John Alfred, 1925-**
Night song. New York, Farrar, Straus and Cudahy [1961]
219 p. 21 cm.
Portrait of author on book jacket.

I. Title.

PZ4.W72624Ni 61-16740 ‡
Library of Congress [5]

M813.5 W68s **Williams, John Alfred, 1925-**
Sissie. New York, Farrar, Straus and Cudahy [1963]
277 p. 22 cm.

I. Title.

PZ4.W72624Si 63-8551 ‡
Library of Congress [5]

M813.08 W67 Williams, John Alfred, 1925-
Son in the afternoon.
Pp. 134-141.

In: Williams, John Alfred, ed. The angry blacks. New York. Lancer Books, 1962.

M301 W673 **Williams, John Alfred, 1925-**
This is my country too [by] John A. Williams. [New York] New American Library [1965]
xix, 169 p. 21 cm. (An NAL-World book)
Portrait of author on book cover.

1. ~~U. S.~~—Race question. 2. U. S.—Desc. & trav.—1960- I. Title.

E185.61.W734 301.451 65-17842
Library of Congress [5]

Nigeria M960 Ob82 Williams, John Alfred, 1925- joint author
Obukar, Charles.
The modern African, by Charles Obukar and John Williams. London, Macdonald & Evans, 1965.
x, 149 p. illus., ports. 23 cm.

1. Africa, Sub-Saharan—Soc. condit. ~~I. Freyberg, Fritz Karl, 1944- joint author.~~ II. Title.

HN797.O2 66-34229
Library of Congress [1]

M350 W67n **Williams, John Henry.**
A Negro looks at war, by John Henry Williams ... [New York, Workers library publishers, inc., 1940]
31 p. 19cm.

1. Negroes. 2. Negroes as soldiers. I. Title.

44-35949
Library of Congress E185.61.W735 [2] 325.260973

M39 EL56w Williams, John R
The duke of note, Ellington life story. [Los Angeles, Duke Ellington Life Story Foundation, n.d.]

23p. 21½cm.

1. Ellington, Duke. I. Title.

M306 Sol 1919 Williams, Lacy Kirk.
Health problems of the Negro church.

(In: Southern Sociological Congress. Houston 1915. The New chivalry - health. Nashville, Southern Sociological Congress, 1915. 24cm. pp. 427-436)

M811.5 W6731 **Williams, Louis Albion.**
In memory of George Washington Carver (a funeral sermon) by Louis Albion Williams; frontispiece by Fred Carlo. Cleveland, O., The American weave magazine [1944]
15 p. illus. (port.) 20½cm.
In verse.
Inscribed copy: Jan.21, 1945. Best wishes to Mr. Roy Wilkins. Sincerely, Louis Albion Williams. To Arthur B. Spingarn. From Roy Wilkins. Ja. 29-45 1. Carver, George Washington, 1864?-1943. 2. Poetry.

44-30848
Library of Congress S417.C3W5 [2] 811.5

MB9 W67m Williams, Maria P
My work and public sentiment, by Maria P. Williams ... Kansas City, Mo. Burton publishing co. [c1916]
272p. front. plates. 20cm.

1. Women. I. Title.

M728.6 W67n **Williams, Paul R** 1894-
New homes for today, by Paul R. Williams, A. I. A. Hollywood [Calif.] Murray & Gee, incorporated, 1946.
95 p. illus. (incl. plans) 27½ x 21½cm.
On cover: Remodeling interiors; duplexes, ranch houses.

1. Architecture, Domestic—Designs and plans. 2. House decoration. I. Title.

46—3841
Library of Congress NA7127.W612 [47z7] 728.6084

M728.6 W67s **Williams, Paul R** 1894-
The small home of tomorrow, by Paul R. Williams, A. I. A. Hollywood, Murray & Gee, incorporated, 1945.
2 p. l., 7-95 p. illus. (incl. port., plans) 28 x 21½ cm.

1. Architecture, Domestic—Designs and plans. I. Title.

45—6335
Library of Congress NA7127.W614 [47f5] 728.6

M325 W67d Williams, Peter, 1780?-1840
A discourse delivered in St. Philip's church, for the benefit of the coloured community of Wilberforce, in Upper Canada, on the Fourth of July, 1830. By Rev. Peter Williams, New York, Printed by G. F. Bunce, 1830.

16p. 19cm.

1. Colonization. 2. Canada.

MB9 C89w 1818 Williams, Peter, 1780?-1840.
A discourse, delivered on the death of Capt. Paul Cuffe, before the New-York African institution, in the African Methodist Episcopal Zion Church, October 21, 1817, By Peter Williams, jun.-a man of colour. Published by request of some members of that institution, New-York printed, York: Reprinted for W. Alexander... 1818.
vi, 30p. 20½cm.

1. Cuffe, Paul, 1759-1818.

MB9 C89w 1817 **Williams, Peter, 1780?-1840.**
A discourse, delivered on the death of Capt. Paul Cuffe, before the New-York African institution, in the African Methodist Episcopal Zion church, October 21, 1817. By Peter Williams, jun. Pub. by request of some of the members of the African institution. New-York. B. Young and co. print., no. 86 Nassau-street. 1817.
16 p. 22cm.
[Miscellaneous pamphlets, v. 876, no. 15]

1. Cuffee, Paul, 1759-1818.

19-10109
Library of Congress AC901.M5 vol. 876 [2]

M815.2 W67o **Williams, Peter, 1780?-1840.**
An oration on the abolition of the slave trade; delivered in the African church, in the city of New-York, January 1, 1808 ... By Peter Williams, jun., a descendant of Africa. New-York: Printed by Samuel Wood. no. 362 Pearl-street. 1808.
26, [2] p. 22cm.
~~[Markoe pamphlets, v. 33, no. 14]~~

1. Slave-trade—U. S. I. Sipkins Henry - introductory added.

19—10108
Library of Congress AC901.M2 vol. 33 [31b1]

M815.2 W670 **Williams, Peter, 1780?-1840.**
An oration on the abolition of the slave trade; delivered in the African church, in the city of New-York, January 1, 1808 ... By Peter Williams, jun., a descendant of Africa. New-York: Printed by Samuel Wood. no. 362 Pearl-street. 1808.
26, [2] p. 22cm.
[Markoe pamphlets, v. 33, no. 14]

1. Slave-trade—U. S.

19—10108
Library of Congress AC901.M2 vol. 33 [31b1]

M813.5 W684p Williams, Richard L.
Parson Wiggins' son.
New York, Carlton Press [c1964]

117p. 21cm. (A Geneva book)
Portrait of author on book jacket.

I. Title.

M301
G623
Williams, Robert Franklin, 1925-
Can Negroes afford to be pacifists?

Pp. 270-277.

In: Goodman, Paul, 1911- ed. Seeds of liberation. New York, G. Braziller, 1965.

M323.1
W67
Williams, Robert Franklin, 1925-
Negroes with guns. Edited by Marc Schleifer. New York, Marzani & Munsell [°1962]
128 p. illus. 21 cm.

1. Negroes—Monroe, N. C. 2. Civil rights—Monroe, N. C. I. Title.

F264.M75W5 323.1 63-1716 ‡
Library of Congress [1]

MB9
W66bw
Williams, Rose Berthenia Clay, 1910-
Black and white orange; an autobiography. New York, Vantage Press, 1961.

135p. 20cm.
Portrait of author on back of book jacket.

1. Williams, Rose Berthenia Clay, 1910-
I. Title.

Williams, Rose Berthenia Clay, 1910-

MB9
W66bw
Williams, Rose Berthenia Clay, 1910-
Black and white orange; an autobiography. New York, Vantage Press, 1961.

135p. 20cm.
Portrait of author on back of book jacket.

Williams, Sally, American slave.

M326.99B
Au5
Aunt Sally; or, The cross the way to freedom. A narrative of the slave-life and purchase of the mother of Rev. Isaac Williams, of Detroit, Michigan ... Cincinnati, American reform tract and book society, 1862.
vii, 9-216 p. front. (port.) illus., port. group. 15½cm.
Slave life in North Carolina and Alabama.

1. Williams, Sally, American slave. 2. Slavery in the U. S.—North Carolina. 3. Slavery in the U. S.—Alabama. I. American reform tract and book society, Cincinnati, pub.
15—23529
Library of Congress E444.W79
[a37b1]

Williams, Tennessee, 1911-

MB9
W674j
Jackson, Esther Merle.
The broken world of Tennessee Williams. Madison, University of Wisconsin Press, 1965.
xxiii, 179 p. illus., port. 23 cm.
Works of Tennessee Williams: p. 161-168.
Bibliography: p. 165-169.

1. Williams, Tennessee, 1911- I. Title.

PS3545.I 5365Z7 812.54 64-8489
Library of Congress [5]

M364
W67p
Williams, Thomas C
The people v. Diaz and DeJesus, brief v. [To the honorable members of the legislature] A series of miscarriages of justice... culminating in the railroading of two Puerto Rican youths to the chair. New York, 1946.

71p. 22cm.

1. Law reports, digests, etc.

M06
J61
no. 15
Williams, William Taylor Burwell, 1866-1941
Duplication of schools for Negro youth, by W. T. B. Williams. [Lynchburg, Va., J. P. Bell company, incorporated, printers] 1914.
22 p. illus. (map) 23½cm. (*On cover: The trustees of the John F. Slater fund. Occasional papers, no. 15*)

1. Negroes—Education.
15—10337
Library of Congress E185.5.J65 no. 15
[38b1]

M06
J61
no.21
Williams, William Taylor Burwell, 1866-1941.
Report on negro universities and colleges, by W. T. B. Williams ... [Baltimore?] 1922.
28 p. incl. tables. 23cm. (*On cover: The Trustees of the John F. Slater fund. Occasional papers, no. 21*)

1. Negroes—Education. 2. Universities and colleges—Southern states. I. Title.
23—7445
Library of Congress E185.5.J65 no. 21
——— Copy 2. E185.82.W72
[a44f1]

M975.5
W56n
Williams, Wilson E
Africa and the rise of capitalism. Washington, D.C., Howard University, 1938.

1-48p. (Howard University. Studies in the social sciences, v.1, no.1)
Mimeographed.
Bound with Negro disfranchisement in Virginia, by Robert Martin.

1. Africa--Economic conditions. I. Title. II. Series.

M366.1
W67n
Williamson, Harry Albro, 1875-
The Negro in Masonic literature, compiled by Harry A. Williamson... [New York, Prince Hall Masonic publishing co., c 1922]

30p. 21½cm.

1. Free masons. I. Title.

M304
P19
v.6, no.2
Williamson, Harry Albro, 1875-
Negroes and freemasonry. [lacks imprint, 1920]
24p. 18cm.

1.Masonry. 2.Freemasons.

M366.1
Am3
Williamson, Harry Albro, 1875-
Negroes and freemasonry [part 2] The American freemason. 7:153-196, February 1916.

1. Secret societies. 2. Freemasons.
I. Title.

M366.1
Am3
Williamson, Harry Albro, 1875-
Negroes and freemasonry [part1] The American freemason. 7:104-111, January 1916.

1. Secret societies. 2. Freemasons.
I. Title.

M366.1
W67p
1946
Williamson, Harry Albro, 1875-
The Prince Hall primer. rev. ed. New York. The author, 1946.

59p. 19½cm.

1. Freemasons - Handbooks, manuals, etc.
I. Title.

M366.1
W67p
1925
Williamson, Harry Albro, 1875-
The Prince Hall primer, a historical quiz. New York, Prince Hall Masonic Publishing co., 1925.

24p. 18½cm. (Midget Library no.1)

1. Free masons - Handbooks, manuals, etc.
I. Title.

M364
W674
Williamson, Henry, *pseud.*
Hustler! [By] Henry Williamson. Edited by R. Lincoln Keiser. With a commentary by Paul Bohannan. [1st ed.] Garden City, N. Y., Doubleday, 1965.
xi, 222 p. 22 cm.
Autobiographical.

1. Prisoners—Personal narratives. I. Keiser, R. Lincoln, 1937- ed. II. Title.

HV6248.W49A3 364.15 65-10686
Library of Congress [5]

Jamaica
M821.91
W67p
Williamson, Solomon Jeffrey, 1878-1941.
Poetical works; ed. by H. F. Williamson. Boston, B. Humphries [1948, °1947]
247 p. illus., port. 21 cm.

PR6045.I 562 1948 821.91 49-3532* ‡
Library of Congress [3]

M301
R676
Williamson, Stanford Winfield.
With grief acquainted. Photographs: James Stricklin, Don Sparks [and] Jerry Cogbill. Chicago, Follett Pub. Co. [1964]
127 p. illus., port. 29 cm.
Portrait of author in book.

1. Negroes—Moral and social conditions—Pictorial works. I. Stricklin, James, illus. II. Title.

E185.86.W5 301.451 64-21580
Library of Congress [5]

Willie Mae.

MB9
W89K
Kytle, Elizabeth Larisey.
Willie Mae. [1st ed.] New York, Knopf, 1958.
243 p. 21 cm.

1. Workman, Willie Mae (Cartwright) 2. Negroes—Georgia. I. Title.
E185.97.W62K9 325.2609758 58—7560 ‡
Library of Congress [58x20]

Willis, Pauline S jt. auth.

MB
C42
Cherry, Gwendolyn.
Portraits in color; the lives of colorful Negro women, by Gwendolyn Cherry, Ruby Thomas, and Pauline Willis. [1st ed.] New York, Pageant Press [1962]

224p. illus. 21cm.

M306 W67a
Willkie Memorial Building. Seven Organizations.
Annual report at the birthday anniversary dinner in memory of Wendell L. Willkie. New York, Willkie Memorial of Freedom, 1947.
20p. 23cm.
Contents: Freedom House; - Public education Association; - World Student Service Fund; - National Association for the Advancement of Colored People; - Citizens' Housing Council of New York, Common Council of New York, Common Council for American Unity; - Anti-Defamation League and Metropolitan Council of B'nai B'rith.
I. National Association for the Advancement of Colored People.

M370 W69e
Wilson, Charles H 1905–
Education for Negroes in Mississippi since 1910, by Charles H. Wilson, sr. ... Boston, Meador publishing company [1947]
641 p. illus. (incl. ports.) 20½cm.
Bibliography: p. 595-607.
1. Negroes—Mississippi. 2. Negroes—Education. 3. Education—Mississippi. I. Title.
LC2802.M7W5 371.974 47-3639
© 16Apr47; Edward K. Meador, Boston; A12739.
Library of Congress [5]

M350 W69
Wilson, Joseph Thomas, 1836-1891.
The black phalanx; a history of the Negro soldiers of the United States in the wars of 1775-1812, 1861-'65. By Joseph T. Wilson ... Hartford, Conn., American publishing company, ~~1888~~ 1897
9 p. l., 21-528 p. incl. front., illus., plates, ports. 22½cm.
Bibliography: p. 517.
Contents.—pt. I. The wars for independence.—pt. II. The war between the states.—pt. III. Miscellany.
1. U. S.—Hist.—Civil war—Negro troops. 2. U. S.—Hist.—Revolution—Negro troops. 3. U. S.—Hist.—War of 1812—Negro troops. I. Title.
2—17127
Library of Congress E185.63.W8 [45k1]

M796 W68
Wills, Maury, 1932–
It pays to steal [by] Maury Wills, as told to Steve Gardner. Englewood Cliffs, N. J., Prentice-Hall [1963]
186 p. illus. 22 cm.
1. Baseball. I. Gardner, Steve. II. Title.
GV865.W55A3 796.357 63—14721 ‡
Library of Congress [64f7]

MB9 R24g
Wilson, Charles H 1905–
God! Make me a man! A biographical sketch of Dr. Sidney Dillion Redmond. Boston, Meador Pub. Co. [1950]
61 p. port. 21 cm.
1. Redmond, Sidney Dillion, 1871-1948. I. Title.
E185.97.R4W5 920 50-7842
Library of Congress [5]

MB9 W52
Wilson, John R
Life and speeches of Ransom W. Westberry, by Prof. John R. Wilson... Atlanta, Ga., A.B. Cadwell publishing company, 1921.
130p. illus. 23cm.
1. Westberry, Ransom William, 1871–
2. Orations.

Brit. Guiana M827.91 W68
Wills, S E
50 local limericks, or 50 laughs by S.E. Wills. Georgetown, British Guiana, 1920.
12p. 21cm.
1. Limericks. 2. Humor. I. British Guiana.

M326.99B N81 1853
Wilson, David, 1818-1887, ed.
Northup, Solomon, b. 1808.
... Twelve years a slave. Narrative of Solomon Northup, a citizen of New-York, kidnapped in Washington city in 1841, and rescued in 1853, from a cotton plantation near the Red river, in Louisiana. Auburn, Derby and Miller; Buffalo, Derby, Orton and Mulligan; [etc., etc.] 1853.
xvi, [17]-336 p. front., pl. 19½cm.
At head of title: Tenth thousand.
Preface signed: David Wilson.
1. Plantation life. 2. Slavery in the U. S.—Louisiana. I. Wilson, David, 1818-1887, ed.
10—34503
Library of Congress E444.N87 [30h1]

M813.5 W69sk
Wilson, Pat
The sign of Kelos. New York, Carlton Press, 1961.
36p. 21cm.
Portrait of author on back of book jacket.
I. Title.

MB9 St7
Wilson, Butler R.
Moorfield Storey and the Negro. In: Moorfield Storey, memorial exercises in Park Street Church, Boston, March 19, 1930. Boston, National Association for the Advancement of Colored People [c1930] p. 49.
1. Storey, Moorfield, 1845–

MB9 W69L
Wilson, Eddie.
Lawrence, Versie Lee.
Deep south showman. New York, Carlton Press, 1962.
33p. 20½cm.

Ghana M398 Ap49
Wilson, Peggy, illustrator.
Appiah, Peggy.
Ananse the spider; tales from an Ashanti village. Pictures by Peggy Wilson. [New York] Pantheon Books [1966]
152 p. illus. 25 cm.
1. Tales, Ashanti. I. Wilson, Peggy, illus. II. Title.
PZ8.1.A647An 398.24 66-9666
Library of Congress [3]

Jamaica M372.92 W69m
Wilson, C A
Men with backbone and other pleas for progress, by Rev. C.A. Wilson. Second edition. Kingston, Jamaica, The Educational supply company, 1913.
98 3 p. plates. 19cm.
1. Jamaica - Biography. I. Title.

MB9 W69
Wilson, H E
Our Nig; or, sketches from the life of a free black in a two story white house, north. Showing that slavery's shadows fall even there.. By "Our Nig." Boston, Geo. C. Rand, 1859.
140p. 21cm.
1. Slavery in the U. S. I. Title.

Sudan, Egyptian MB9 W69i
Wilson, Salim C
I was a slave. (Hatashil Masha Kathish). With twelve half-tone illustrations. London, Stanley Paul and Co., n.d.
256p. ports., illus. 21½cm.
1. Sudan, Egyptian. 2. Dinka (African Tribe). I. Title.

M813.5 W688h
Wilson, Carl Thomas David.
The half caste, by Carl T. D. Wilson. Ilfracombe [Eng.] A. H. Stockwell [1964]
207 p. 19 cm.
Portrait of author on book jacket.
I. Title. 1. London - Fiction.
PZ4.W7457Hal 65-71410
Library of Congress [1]

M355.2 W69c
Wilson, J Finley, 1881-1952
The colored Elks and national defense; Improved Benevolent and Protective Order of Elks of the World, 1941.
15p. cover port. 24cm.
Foreword by Elizabeth Gordon.
1. Elks of the World, Improved Benevolent and Protective Order.

Jamaica M398 An1
Wilson, Una
Anancy stories.
(In: Anancy stories and dialect verse.... 1st ed. Kingston, Jamaica, Pioneer Press, [1950]. 19cm. pp. 86-89)

M366.3 W69o
Wilson, Charles B.
The official manual and history of the Grand United Order of Odd Fellows in America... prepared by Charles B. Wilson. Philadelphia, George F. Lasher, 1894.
357p. port. 20½cm.

M326 H87
Wilson, J. Finley, 1881-1952, jt. editor
Hueston, William C, 1880- , ed.
The John Brown reader, edited, with foreword by William C. Hueston and J. Finley Wilson. Designed by Edward H. Lawson, Sr. Washington, D.C., Murray Brothers, For the I.B.P.O. Elks of the World, 1949.
96p. illus. 22½cm.

Jamaica M398 W69
Wilson, Una
Anancy stories, retold by Una Wilson. Kingston, Jamaica Times (Press) Ltd. 1947.
83 p. 19cm.
1. Jamaican folk-lore.
I. Title.

M973.9
F46
No.23
Wilson, W Rollo.
Fifty years of progress in the world of sports. Pittsburgh, Pittsburgh Courier, 1950.

7p. illus. port. 24cm. (Fifty years of progress)

1. Sports. I. Series.

Nigeria
M896.3
Eg19w
Wind versus polygamy...
Egbuna, Obi B
Wind versus polygamy; where "wind" is the "wind of change" and polygamy the "change of eves". London, Faber and Faber [1964]

128p. 19cm.

M812.5
M61
Wings over dark waters.
Miller, Clifford L
Wings over dark waters, a poetic drama. [1st ed.] New York, Great Concord Publishers [1954]
270 p. illus. 21 cm.

I. Title.
PS3525.I 5223W5 812.5 54-8457 ‡
Library of Congress [2]

M252
W69
Wilson, William Green
From son-lit skies. New York, Carlton Press, 1964.

58p. 21cm.
Portrait of author on book jacket.

1. Sermons, American. I. Title.

A
M398
N98
Winds and lights;
Nyabongo, Akiki K 1905–
Winds and lights; African fairy tales, by H. H. Prince Akiki K. Nyabongo; with illustrations by B. Hewitt. New York, N. Y., The Voice of Ethiopia [°1939]
[45] p. illus., port. 24cm.
"Errata" slip mounted on lining-paper.

1. Tales, African. I. Title.
Library of Congress PZ8.1.N86Wi 39-17420
——— Copy 2.
Copyright A 131104 [3]

M811.5
W731
Winston, Bessie Brent.
Life's red sea and other poems. Washington, Review and Herald publishing association, 1950.

32p. 14cm.

I. Title. 1. Poetry.

M811.5
W69r
Wilson, William Green, 1867–
Rhymes & sketches from the cabin fireside, by William Green Wilson. [Selma, Ala., Lloyd printing company, °1931]
2 p. l., 62, [2] p. 21½cm.

I. Title. 1. Poetry.
Library of Congress PS3545.I 643R5 1931 CA 31-1104 Unrev'd
——— Copy 2.
Copyright A 45073 811.5

Kenya
M173
W73
Windstedt, R O
Mũtũũrĩre na mwĩcirĩrie mwega [Right living and right thinking] Ritauritwo ni J. P. Mathenge na A. H. Kanyuru. Nairobi, Eagle Press, 1954.
89p. 18cm.
Written in Kikuyu.
White author.

1. Ethics. I. Title. II. Mathenge, J. P., tr. III. Kanyuru, A. H., jt. tr.

M323
W73
Winston, Henry M. ,1911–
Introduction.
Pp. 3-5.

In: Winston, Henry M. Negro freedom. New York, New Currents Publishers, 1964.

M326
G87a
1854
Wilson, William J
A leaf from my scrapbook.

(In: Griffiths, Julia ed. Autographs for freedom. Auburn, Alden, Beardsley, 1854. 19½cm. Pp. 165-73).

M910
St8t
Windward islands–Descr. & trav.
Straker, David Augustus, *d.* 1908.
A trip to the Windward islands; or, Then and now. By D. Augustus Straker ... Detroit, J. H. Stone & co. [°1896]
110 p. front., plates, ports. 22cm.

1. Windward islands—Descr. & trav.
Library of Congress F2011.S89 1-27986
Copyright 1896: 52171 [a31c1]

M304
P19
v.1
no.10
Winston, Henry M 1911–
Life begins with freedom. New York, New Age Publishers, 1937.

5-39p. 19cm.

1. Communism.

M364
W71r
Wiltwyck School for Boys. Esopus, New York.
[Report] [Esopus, New York, 194]

[143p. illus. 23cm.

1. Juvenile detention homes.

M811.5
B815w
Wine of Youth.
Brown, Robert Harvey.
Wine of youth. New York, Exposition Press [1949]
46 p. 23 cm.
Poems.

I. Title.
PS3503.R82842W5 811.5 49-11978*
Library of Congress [2]

M335.4
W73n
Winston, Henry M. , 1911–
Negro-white unity. New York, New Outlook Publishers, 1967.

31p. 20cm.

1. Race relations. 2. Communism.
I. Title.

U. S.
M968
Am3
Wina, Arthur Nutulli Lubinda
Theories of multiracialism: problems of political equality.

Pp. 317-323.

In: American Society of African Culture. Southern Africa in transition. New York, Praeger, 1966.

M811.5
H55w
The wings of oppression.
Hill, Leslie Pinckney, 1880–
The wings of oppression, by Leslie Pinckney Hill. Boston, The Stratford co., 1921.
5 p. l., 124 p. 19½cm.
Poems.

I. Title. 1. Poetry.
Library of Congress PS3515.I 495W5 1921 21-15040
[42c1]

M323
W73
Winston, Henry M , 1911–
Old jim crow has got to go. New York, New Age Publishers, 1941.

15p. 19cm.

I. Communist Party of the United States.
1. Jim Crow. 2. Segregation.

250019

M813.5
M58w
The wind from nowhere...
Micheaux, Oscar, 1884-1951.
The wind from nowhere... By Oscar Micheaux. New York, Book Supply Co., 1944.

385p. illus. 21½cm.

Jamaica
M821.91
V81w
Wings of the morning.
Virtue, Vivian L., 1911–
Wings of the morning. Poem by Vivian L. Virtue. Kingston, Jamaica, The New Dawn Press, 1938.

xiv, 86p. 18cm.

M323
W73n
Winston, Henry M. , 1911–
Negro freedom, a goal for all Americans, by Henry M. Winston [and others. New York, New Currents Publishers, 1964.

56p. 18½cm.
Contents.- Introduction, by Henry M. Winston.- Negro freedom is in the interest of every American, by Gus Hall.- Building a Negro and white alliance for progress, by Claude Lightfoot.- The battle for America, by William L. Patterson.
(Continued on next card)

M323
W73n
Winston, Henry M. , 1911-
Negro freedom, a goal for all Americans. New York, New Currents Publishers, 1964.
(Card 2)

1. Civil rights. 2. Race relations. I. Title.

M327
W73
Winston, Henry M , 1911-
New Colonialism U.S. style. [New York, New Outlook Publishers, 1965]
30p. port. 18½cm.

1. U.S. - Foreign relations. I. Title.

M335.4
W73w
Winston, Henry M , 1911-
What it means to be a communist. New York, New Century, 1951.
15p. port. 19cm.

1. Communism. I. Title.

M304
P19
v.5, no.15
Winston, Robert Watson.
Should the color line go. In: Three articles on the Negro Problem (Published in Current History Magazine, Sept. 1923) p. 1-10.
White author.

M323
T41

1. Miscegenation

A winter piece.
M811.1
H18w
Hammon, Jupiter, b. ca. 1720.
A winter piece: being a serious exhortation, with a call to the unconverted; and a short contemplation on the death of Jesus Christ. Written by Jupiter Hammon, A Negro man belonging to Mr. John Lloyd, of Queen's Village, on Long Island, now in Hartford. Published by the author with the assistance of his friends. Hartford: Printed for the author, MDCCLXXXII.
24p. 18cm.
Contains: A poem for children with thoughts on death, p.23-24.

M06
J61
no.16
Winton, George Beverly, 1861-
Sketch of Bishop Atticus G. Haygood, by Rev. G. B. Winton, D. D. [Lynchburg, Va., J. P. Bell company, inc., printers] 1915.
24 p. 23 cm. (On cover: The trustees of the John F. Slater fund. Occasional papers, no. 16)
"Adapted from the Journal of the General conference of the Methodist Episcopal church, South, for the year 1898."
Brief extracts from Dr. Haygood's speeches and writings: p. 8-28.

1. Haygood, Atticus Greene, bp., 1839-1896.
15—18900
Library of Congress E185.5.J65 no. 16
[48b½]

Wisdom in Ethiopia.
M910
R45
Riley, Willard D
Wisdom in Ethiopia. [1st ed.] New York, Vantage Press [1959]
66 p. 22 cm.

1. Negroes—Religion. I. Title.
BR563.N4R54 241 59-3659 ‡
Library of Congress [2]

Wisdom's call.
M323
G87w
Griggs, Sutton Elbert, 1872-
Wisdom's call, by Sutton E. Griggs ... Nashville, Tenn., The Orion publishing co., 1911.
2 p. l., vii-viii p., 1 l., 11-193 p. 19 cm.

1. U. S.—Race question. I. Title.
11—30416
Library of Congress E185.61.G85
[48g½]

Wise, James.
M342
R15
Randolph, Asa Philip, 1889-
Chart and compass.
(In: Wise, James W. Our Bill of rights: what it means to me,...1941. New York, Bill of Rights Sesqui-centennial Committee, 1941. pp. 112-113)

M248
W75
Wise, Namon.
The Namon Wise story. New York, Carlton Press [1964]
38p. 21cm. (A Reflection book)
Autobiographical.
Portrait of author on book jacket.

1. Christian life. I. Title.

The wise fool.
M811.5
K58
King, Bert Roscoe, 1887-
The wise fool. New York Exposition Press, 1959.
79p. 20½cm.

M973
W75
Wish, Harvey, 1909- *ed.*
The Negro since emancipation. Englewood Cliffs, N. J., Prentice-Hall [1964]
vi, 184 p. 21 cm. (A Spectrum book)
Bibliography: p. 183-184.
White editor.
An anthology of excerpts from the writings of 15 Negro leaders.

1. ~~Negroes~~—Hist.—Addresses, essays, lectures. 2. ~~U.S.~~—Race question—Addresses, essays, lectures. I. Title. 3. Biography.
E185.61.W79 301.451 64-23550
Library of Congress [5]

M252
W75e
Wisher, Daniel W , 1853-
Echoes from the gospel trumpet; three sermons and a paper, by Daniel W. Wisher ... New York, E. Scott Co., c1896
109p. port. (front.) 17½cm.

1. Sermons. I. Title.

Wit and humor.
M817.5
C22
Carpenter, Ben
Simple Simon; a portfolio. Los Angeles, Calif., Carpto Publishing Co., 1962.
61p. 24cm.

Wit and humor.
M817
C24
Carter, Randall Albert, *bp.*, 1867-
Canned laughter, by Randall Albert Carter ... Cincinnati, O., Printed for the author [by] the Caxton press [1923]
212 p. 20cm.

1. American wit and humor. 2. Negro wit and humor. I. Title.
23-14386
Library of Congress PN6161.C375
——— Copy 2.
Copyright A 759366 [2]

Wit and humor.
M817
C81
Corrothers, James David, 1869-
The Black cat club; Negro humor & folk-lore, by James D. Corrothers; illustrated by J. K. Bryans. New York [etc.] Funk & Wagnalls co., 1902.
v, 7-264 p. front., illus. 19cm.

1. Negro wit and humor. I. Title.
2—7102
Library of Congress PN6161.C662
[38e1]

Wit and humor.
M817.5
G86w
Gregory, Dick.
What's happening? Photos. by Jerry Yulsman. [1st ed.] New York, Dutton, 1965.
125 p. illus. 23 cm.

1. Negro wit and humor. 2. Negroes—Civil rights—Humor, caricatures, etc. I. Title.
PN6231.N5G68 817.54 65-19973
Library of Congress [5]

Wit and humor.
M817.5
H874
Hughes, Langston, 1902- *ed.*
The book of Negro humor. New York, Dodd, Mead [1966]
265 p. 22 cm.

1. Negro wit and humor. I. Title.
PN6231.N5H8 817.008 65-24461
Library of Congress [5]

Wit and humor.
M323
P58am
Pickens, William, 1881- 1954.
American Æsop; Negro and other humor, by William Pickens ... Boston, The Jordan & More press, 1926.
xx, 183 p. front. 20 cm.

1. Wit and humor. 2. Negro wit and humor. I. Title.
26—12677
Library of Congress PN6161.P58
[48d½]

M817
St45
Wit and humor.
Sterling, Philip, *ed.*
Laughing on the outside; the intelligent white reader's guide to Negro tales and humor. Introductory essay by Saunders Redding. Cartoons by Ollie Harrington. New York, Grosset & Dunlap [1965]
254 p. illus. 22 cm.
Bibliography: p. [251]-254.

1. Negro wit and humor. I. Title.
PN6231.N5S7 817.008 65-15349
Library of Congress [5]

Wit and humor, Pictoral.
Guadeloupe
M741
C35
Chambertrand, Gilbert de
Choses et gens de mon patelin. Paris, Éditions Louis Soulanges, 1961.
28p. illus. 22cm.

Wit and humor, Pictorial.
M813.5 H23b
Harrington, Oliver.
Bootsie and others; a selection of cartoons by Ollie Harrington. Introd. by Langston Hughes. New York, Dodd, Mead [1958]
unpaged. illus. 26 cm.
1. Negro wit and humor, Pictorial. I. Title.
NC1429.H333A43 741.5973 58-13095 ‡
Library of Congress [5]

M323. W77
Withers, Zachary.
Our inheritance, by Z. Withers ... Oakland, Cal., Tribune publishing co. print, 1909.
104 p. front. (port.) 18½cm.
"This essay ... argues for the rights of my [the negro] people before an unbiased and just American public."
Inscribed copy: With kindest regards, Z Withers, Elmhurst, Calif. Baker Ave. Box 323.
1. Negroes. I. Title.
Library of Congress E185.6.W82 9-17565
Copyright A 242779 [34b1]

Ghana M966.7 W83p
Wolfson, Freda.
Pageant of Ghana. London, Oxford University Press, 1958.
266 p. illus. 28 cm. (West African history series)
1. Ghana—Hist. I. Title.
DT510.W6 966.7 58-3099 ‡
Library of Congress [50h5]

Guadeloupe M741 P36
Wit and humor, Pictorial.
Pélage, *1
La Guadeloupe vye [gravures et dessins humoristiques de Al Pélage. Préface de E. Isaac. Basse-Terre, Guadelope, Imprimerie Officiele, n.d.]
22 leaves 23cm.
Cover title.

M811.5 W77b
Witherspoon, James William, 1893-
A breath of the muse, a volume of poetic browsings containing several prose writings, by J. William Witherspoon. Illustrated, Columbia, S.C., Hampton publishing company, 1927.
132p. plates. 20cm.
1. Poetry. I. Title.

Woman-Employment.
M304 P19 v.1, no.3
Gordon, Eugene, 1890-
The position of Negro women, by Eugene Gordon and Cyril Briggs ... [New York, Workers library publishers, 1935]
15, [1] p. 15½cm.
Caption title: Negro women workers in the U. S. A.
Illustration on t.-p.
1. Women, Negro. 2. Woman—Employment. I. Briggs, Cyril V., 1888- joint author. II. Title. III. Title: Negro women workers in the U. S. A.
Library of Congress E185.8.G67 45-48360
[2]

The wit and wisdom of the Haytians.
M972.94 B48w
Bigelow, John, 1817-1911, comp.
The wit and wisdom of the Haytians. By John Bigelow. New York, Scribner & Armstrong, 1877.
1 p. l., 112 p. 21½cm.
1. Proverbs, Haitian. I. Title.
Library of Congress PN6519.H3B6 13-33675

Nigeria M966.9 Or1w
Without bitterness.
Orizu, Akweke Abyssinia Nwafor, 1920-
Without bitterness; western nations in post-war Africa, by A. A. Nwafor Orizu. New York, N. Y., Creative age press, inc. [1944]
xiv, 395 p. 21cm.
1. Africa—Civilization. 2. Africa—Native races. 3. Nigeria—Soc. condit. 4. Reconstruction (1939-)—Africa. I. Title.
Library of Congress DT14.07 44-7985
[46q²7] 960

Woman-Employment-U. S.
M396.5 B81n
Brown, Mrs. Jean (Collier)
... The Negro woman worker, by Jean Collier Brown ... Washington, U. S. Govt. print. off., 1938.
v, 17 p. pl. 23cm. (Bulletin of the [U. S.] Women's bureau, no. 165)
At head of title: United States Department of labor. Frances Perkins, secretary. Women's bureau. Mary Anderson, director.
"Selected references on Negro women workers": p. 16-17.
1. Women, Negro. 2. Woman—Employment—U. S. I. Title.
U. S. Dept. of labor Libr. for Library of Congress HD6093.A3 no. 165 HD6093.A35 no. 165 L 39-7
——— Copy 2. [a40f3] (331.406173)

Witchcraft-Salem, Mass.-Jevenile literature.
M813.5 P44t
Petry, Ann (Lane) 1911-
Tituba of Salem Village, by Ann Petry. New York, Crowell [1964]
254 p. 21 cm.
Portrait of author on book cover.
1. Tituba—Juvenile fiction. 2. Witchcraft—Salem, Mass.—Juvenile literature. I. Title.
PZ7.P4473Ti 64-20691
Library of Congress [7-1]

France M840 D89tu
Witt, Johan de, 1625-1672-Fiction.
Dumas, Alexandre, 1802-1870.
La tulipe noire. Bruxelles, Meline, Cans et cie., 1850.
2 vols in one. 15cm.

Woman—Employment—U. S.
M331 H86
Hudson, Roy.
Post-war jobs for veterans, negroes, women, by Roy Hudson. New York, Workers library publishers, 1944.
24 p. illus. 19cm.
1. Veterans—Employment—U. S. 2. Negroes—Employment. 3. Woman—Employment—U. S. I. Title.
Harvard univ. Library for Library of Congress HD5724.H83 A 45-2552
[3]† 331.137

With a Carib eye.
Brit. Guiana M823.91 W69wi
Mittelhölzer, Edgar.
With a Carib eye. London, Secker & Warburg, 1958.
192 p. illus. 21 cm.
1. Caribbean area—Descr. & trav. I. Title.
Full name: Edgar Austin Mittelhölzer.
F2171.M55 917.29 58-44418 ‡
Library of Congress [1]

The wolf and the lamb.
M323. D11
Dabney, Wendell Phillips, 1865-
The wolf and the lamb, by Wendell P. Dabney. Cincinnati, O., The author, c 1913.
Cover-title. 15p. illus. 23cm.

A Woman called Fancy.
M813.5 Y46w
Yerby, Frank, 1916-
A woman called Fancy. New York, Dial Press, 1951.
340 p. 21 cm.
I. Title.
Full name: Frank Garvin Yerby.
PZ3.Y415Wo 51-3370
Library of Congress [10]

With Christ in the mount...
Barbados M252 B69
Boyce, Edward H
With Christ in the mount; mountain experiences in the life of Christ. [Sermons] New York, Exposition Press [1951]
128 p. 23 cm.
1. Sermons, American. I. Title.
BV4253.B64 252 51-5040
Library of Congress [2]

Wolf Kitty.
M813.5 B41w
Bellinger, Claudia
Wolf Kitty. Washington, Vantage Press, 1958.
173p. 21½cm.

A woman called Fancy.
M813.5 Y46w 1953
Yerby, Frank, 1916-
A woman called Fancy. New York, Pocket Books, Inc., 1953.
324p. 16cm. (Cardinal edition C 102)
Pocket book edition.

With grief acquainted.
M301 R676
Williamson, Stanford Winfield.
With grief acquainted. Photographs: James Stricklin, Don Sparks [and] Jerry Cogbill. Chicago, Follett Pub. Co. [1964]
127 p. illus., port. 29 cm.
Portrait of author in book.
1. Negroes—Moral and social conditions—Pictorial works. I. Stricklin, James, illus. II. Title.
E185.86.W5 301.451 64-21580
Library of Congress [5]

"Wolf snout"...
M610 C63w
Cobb, William Montague, 1904-
"Wolf snout" and other anomalies in monovular twins: a case report. Reprinted from the Freedmen's hospital bulletin, 1:27-32, September 1934.
6p. illus. 28cm.

A woman in her prime.
Ghana M896.3 K83w
Konadu, Samuel Asare, 1932-
A woman in her prime [by] S. A. Konadu. London, Heinemann, 1967.
[5], 108 p. 19 cm. 18/-
(B 67-6524)
I. Title.
PZ4.K818Wo 67-91691
Library of Congress [3]

Woman's American Baptist home mission society.
MB
B74
Brawley, Benjamin Griffith, 1882–
Women of achievement; written for the Fireside schools, under the auspices of the Women's American Baptist home mission society, by Benjamin Brawley ... [Chicago, Woman's American Baptist home mission society, °1919]
92 p., 1 l. ports. 18cm.
CONTENTS.—Introduction: The Negro woman in American life.—Harriet Tubman.—Nora Gordan.—Meta Warrick Fuller.—Mary McLeod Bethune.—Mary Church Terrell.
1. Negroes—Biog. 2. Woman—Biog. 3. Women, Negro. I. Woman's American Baptist home mission society. II. Title.
19—4709
Library of Congress E185.96.B82
[42f1]

Woman's missionary society guide.
M266
B43w
Bennett, Ambrose
Woman's missionary society guide, arranged and edited by Ambrose Bennett. Nashville, Tenn., National Baptist convention [n.d.]
99p. 19½cm.

Women.
M396.5
B81n
Brown, Mrs. Jean (Collier)
... The Negro woman worker, by Jean Collier Brown ... Washington, U. S. Govt. print. off., 1938.
v, 17 p. pl. 23cm. (Bulletin of the [U. S.] Women's bureau, no. 165)
At head of title: United States Department of labor. Frances Perkins, secretary. Women's bureau. Mary Anderson, director.
"Selected references on Negro women workers": p. 16–17.
1. Women, Negro. 2. Woman—Employment—U. S. I. Title.
L 39—7
U. S. Dept. of labor Libr. for Library of Congress HD6008.A3 no. 165 HD6008.A35 no. 165
——— Copy 2. [a40f3] (331.406173)

Women.
M393
C83b
Crummell, Alexander, 1819–1898.
The black woman of the South. Her neglects and her needs. By Alex. Crummell ... [Washington, B. S. Adams, printer, 1883]
16 p. 23½cm.
Caption title.
"Address delivered before the Freedman's aid society of the Methodist Episcopal church at Ocean Grove, 13th August, 1883."
1. Women, Negro. I. Title.
19–3282
[37b1]
Library of Congress E185.86.C95

Women.
M370
C89
Cuthbert, Marion Vera, 1896–
Education and marginality; a study of the Negro woman college graduate, by Marion Vera Cuthbert ... New York city, 1942.
xviii, 167 p. incl. tables. 24cm.
Thesis (PH. D.)—Columbia university, 1942.
Vita.
Bibliography: p. 161–166.
1. Women, Negro. 2. Education of women—U. S. 3. Negroes—Education. 4. Negroes—Moral and social conditions. I. Title.
A 42—5888
Columbia univ. Libraries for Library of Congress LC2781.C8
[44e2]† 376.873

Women.
M367
D27t
Davis, Elizabeth Lindsey
The story of the Illinois Federation of Colored Women's Clubs, 1900-1922.
137p. ports. 22cm.

Women.
M396
F95p
[Fulton, David Bryant], 1863–
... A plea for social justice for the negro woman ... Issued by the Negro society for historical research, Yonkers, N. Y. [New York, Lincoln press ass'n., 1912.
cover-title, 11 p. 17½cm. (Negro society for historical research. Occasional paper no. 2)
Signed: Jack Thorne [pseud.]
1. Women, Negro. I. Title.
30–28450
Library of Congress E185.5.N4 no. 2
[2] 325.26

Women.
M304
P19
v.1, no.3
Gordon, Eugene, 1890–
The position of Negro women, by Eugene Gordon and Cyril Briggs ... [New York, Workers library publishers, 1935]
15, [1] p. 15½cm.
Caption title: Negro women workers in the U. S. A.
Illustration on t.-p.
1. Women, Negro. 2. Woman—Employment. I. Briggs, Cyril V., 1888– joint author. II. Title. III. Title: Negro women workers in the U. S. A.
45–48360
Library of Congress E185.8.G67
[2]

Women.
M973
H13s
Haley, James T *comp.*
Sparkling gems of race knowledge worth reading. A compendium of valuable information and wise suggestions that will inspire noble effort at the hands of every race-loving man, woman, and child ... Comp. and arranged by James T. Haley ... Nashville, Tenn., J. T. Haley & company, 1897.
200 p. incl. front., illus., ports. 20½cm.
1. Negroes.
12-4235
Library of Congress E185.5.H16
Copyright 1897: 38849 [37b1]

Women.
M396
Io8s
Iota Phi Lambda Sorority.
Survey on white collar occupations of Negro women... [1947] the Sorority, 1948.
11p. graphs. 23cm.

Women.
M396
J71e
Jones, Claudia.
An end to the neglect of the problems of the Negro woman. New York, National Women's Commission, 1949.
19p. 19cm.
Reprinted from Political Affairs (June 1949)

Women.
M396
J71w
Jones, Claudia
Women in the struggle for peace and security. New York, National Women's Commission, Communist Party, 1950.
16 p. 20cm.
Reprinted from Political Affairs, March 1950.

Women.
M658
K25n
Keene, Josephine Bond,
National directory of Negro business and professional women. Philadelphia, the author, 1942.
[19]p. illus. 21cm.

Women.
M973.9
F46
No.13
McKenzie, Marjorie.
Fifty years of progress for Negro women. Pittsburgh, Pittsburgh Courier, 1950.
11p. illus. 24cm. (Fifty years of progress)

Women.
M378
N66n
Noble, Jeanne L.
The Negro woman's college education. New York, Teachers College, Columbia University, 1956.
x, 163 p. form, 39 tables. 22 cm. (TC studies in education)
Bibliography: p. 145–150.
1. Women, Negro. 2. Education of women—U. S. I. Title. (Series: Teachers College studies in education)
LC1605.N6 378.73 56–8941
Library of Congress [10]

Women.
M304
P19
v.3, no.9
Powell, W H R
The Negro and the bread line. The danger of his remaining. Some things he should do to get out, and Is Negro womanhood equal to its task of constructive leadership in these days of distressing unemployment.
[Philadelphia, James Printing Co. 1931]
[22]p. 22cm.

M614
R66n4
Women.
Roman, Charles Victor, 1864-1934.
The Negro woman and the health problem. Reprinted from the Journal of the National Medical Association, 7:182-191, July-Sept. 1915.

Women.
M610
P19
V.1
no.1
Steward, S Maria, 1845.
Women in medicine; a paper read before the National association of colored women's clubs at Wilberforce, Ohio, August 6, 1914, by S. Maria Steward.. Wilberforce, Ohio The author 1914
24p. ports. 19½cm.

Women.
M396
W46g
1951
Wellington, Joseph, 1888–
The glory of womanhood, a discourse delivered before the Empire State Federation of Women's Clubs, the Shiloh Benevolent Society of Staten Island, the Book-lovers Club of New York, inc. [and] the Young Women's Elite Society of New York. Foreword by Nannie C. Burden. New York, Exposition Press [1951]
40 p. 21 cm.
1. Woman. I. Title.
HQ1233.W37 1951 396 51–4288
Library of Congress [2]

Women
M396
W46g
Wellinton, Joseph
The glory of womanhood. Empire state federation of woman's clubs address, by Joseph Wellington...
New York, Alliance press c1932
45p 18 cm.

Women
M89
W67m
Williams, Maria P
My work and public sentiment, by Maria P. Williams ... Kansas City, Mo., Burton Publishing Co., c1916
272p. front. plates. 20cm.

Women - Biographies.

MB
B74

Brawley, Benjamin Griffith, 1882–
Women of achievement; written for the Fireside schools, under the auspices of the Women's American Baptist home mission society, by Benjamin Brawley ... ₍Chicago, Woman's American Baptist home mission society, °1919₎
92 p., 1 l. ports. 18cm.
CONTENTS.—Introduction: The Negro woman in American life.—Harriet Tubman.—Nora Gordan.—Meta Warrick Fuller.—Mary McLeod Bethune.—Mary Church Terrell.
1. Negroes—Biog. 2. Woman—Biog. 3. Women, Negro. I. Woman's American Baptist home mission society. II. Title.
19—4709
Library of Congress E185.96.B82
₍42f1₎

Women - Biographies.

MB
B80h

Brown, Hallie Quinn, *comp.*
Homespun heroines and other women of distinction, compiled and edited by Hallie Q. Brown ... foreword by Mrs. Josephine Turpin Washington ... ₍Xenia, O., The Aldine publishing company, °1926₎
viii, 248, ₍2₎ p. front., ports. 23½cm.
1. Negroes—Biog. 2. Woman—Biog. 3. Women, Negro. I. Title.
26—18256
Library of Congress E185.96.B84
——— Copy 2.
Copyright A 950521 ₍38d2₎

Women - Biographies

MB
D22

Daniel, Sadie Iola
Women builders. Washington, D.C., The Associated Publishers, Inc., 1931.
xviii p., 1l, 187p. plates, ports. 19½cm.
Contents. -Lucy Craft Laney. -Maggie Lena Walker. -Janie Porter Barrett. -Mary McLeod Bethune. -Nannie Helen Burroughs. -Charlotte Hawkins Brown. -Jane Edna Hunter.

Women - Biographies

MB
T38p

Thoms, Adah B.
Pathfinders, a history of the progress of colored graduate nurses, compiled by Adah B. Thoms ... with biographies of many prominent nurses ... ₍New York, Printed at Kay printing house, inc., °1929₎
xvi, 240 p. front., 1 illus., plates, ports. 23½cm.
1. Nurses and nursing. 2. Negroes—Biog. 3. Women, Negro. 4. Nurses and nursing—Study and teaching. I. Title.
₍*Full name:* Adah B. Glassell Thoms₎
29—19412
Library of Congress RT71.T45
₍41g1₎

Women-Employment

M304
P19
v.3, no.4

₍Mc Dougald, Gertrude E.₎
A n w day for the colored woman worker. A study of the colored women in industry in New York City... Investigators Miss Jessie Clark and Mrs. Gertrude E. Mc Dougald. New York, Chas. P. Young, Co. 1919.
39p. illus. 22½cm.

Women - Employment

M331.
Wn3

U. S. *Women's bureau.*
... Negro women in industry. Washington, Govt. print. off., 1922.
v, 65, ₍1₎ p. front. 23cm. (Bulletin no. 20)
At head of title: U. S. Department of labor. James J. Davis, secretary. Women's bureau. Mary Anderson, director.
"This investigation was made by Miss Emma L. Shields ... in conjunction with the Division of Negro economics in the Department of labor."—Letter of transmittal.
1. Negroes—Employment. 2. Woman—Employment—U. S. 3. Women, Negro. I. U. S. Dept. of labor. Division of Negro economics. II. Shields, Emma L. III. Title.
L 22—164
U. S. Dept. of labor. Libr. for Library of Congress HD6093.A85 no. 20
₍a41n1₎

Women - Health and hygiene.

Cuba
M613
L32s

Lara Mena, María Julia de.
Salud y belleza; divulgaciones científicas sobre anatomía, fisiología, patología, higiene y estética de la mujer, por la dra. María Julia de Lara ... Con un juicio crítico del profesor dr. W. H. Hoffmann ... Con 260 ilustraciones. La Habana, Cuba, Casa editora "La Propagandista," s. a., 1940.
xxxv, 663 p. illus. (incl. ports., facsim.) col. pl., tables, diagrs. 24cm.
"Bibliografía" at end of chapter 7.
1. Woman—Health and hygiene. I. Title.
A 41-189 rev
Harvard univ. Library for Library of Congress ₍r46c2₎

Women - Juvenile literature.

MB
C42

Cherry, Gwendolyn S
Portraits in color; the lives of colorful Negro women, by Gwendolyn Cherry, Ruby Thomas, and Pauline Willis. ₍1st ed.₎ New York, Pageant Press ₍1962₎
224 p. illus. 21 cm.
Includes bibliography.
1. Negroes—Biog.—Juvenile literature. 2. Women, Negro—Juvenile literature. I. Title.
E185.96.C45 j 920 61-18864 ‡
Library of Congress ₍10₎

Women—Legal status, laws, etc.

Cuba
M972.91
G98m

Gutiérrez, José Margarito, 1855–
La mujer, defensa de sus derechos e ilustración; ensayo literario por José Margarito Gutiérrez. 2. ed. Habana, Imprenta de Rambla, Bouza y ca., 1929.
2 p. l., ₍3₎–66 p. 23cm.
1. Woman—Social and moral questions. 2. Woman—Legal status, laws, etc. I. Title.
30-29572
Library of Congress HQ1227.G9 1929
₍2₎ 396.2

Women— Social and moral questions.

Cuba
M972.91
G98m

Gutiérrez, José Margarito, 1855–
La mujer, defensa de sus derechos e ilustración; ensayo literario por José Margarito Gutiérrez. 2. ed. Habana, Imprenta de Rambla, Bouza y ca., 1929.
2 p. l., ₍3₎–66 p. 23cm.
1. Woman—Social and moral questions. 2. Woman—Legal status, laws, etc. I. Title.
30-29572
Library of Congress HQ1227.G9 1929
₍2₎ 396.2

Leopoldville,
Congo, Women-Belgian Congo.

M967.5
B63p

Bolamba, Antoine Roger.
...Les problemes de l'evolution de la femme noire. Preface de M. Robert Godding. Elisabethville, Editions de l'Essor du Congo, 1949.
167 p. 19½ cm.
Belgian Congo author.

Congo, Women, African.
Leopoldville

M396
M28

Makonga, Bonaventure
La mere Africaine. Bruxelles, Editions Remarques Congolaises, 1964.
113p. ports. 19cm. (Collection Etudes Congolaises, no. 11)
Portrait of author in book.
1. Women in the Congo. 2. Women, African. I. Title.

Women builders.

MB
D22

Daniel, Sadie Iola.
Women builders, by Sadie Iola Daniel. Washington, D. C., The Associated publishers, inc. ₍°1931₎
xviii p., 1 l., 187 p. plates, ports. 19½cm.
CONTENTS.—Lucy Craft Laney.—Maggie Lena Walker.—Janie Porter Barrett.—Mary McLeod Bethune.—Nannie Helen Burroughs.—Charlotte Hawkins Brown.—Jane Edna Hunter.
1. Negroes—Biog. 2. Woman—Biog. 3. Woman, Negro. 4. Negroes—education. I. Title.
32—3462
Library of Congress E185.96.D23
₍43x2₎ [325.26] 923.773

Women in Haiti-Biog.

Haiti
M396
L62

Ligue féminine d'action sociale (*Haiti*)
Femmes haïtiennes. ₍Port-au-Prince, H. Deschamps, 1953?₎
263 p. 21 cm. (Collection du tricinquantenaire de l'indépendance d'Haïti)
1. Women in Haiti—Biog. I. Title.
F1914.L55 54-27866
Library of Congress ₍1₎

Women in medicine.

M610
P19
V.1
no.1

Steward, S Maria, 1845-
Women in medicine; a paper read before the National association of colored women's clubs at Wilberforce, Ohio, August 6, 1914, by S. Maria Steward... Wilberforce, Ohio The author 1914
24p. ports. 19½cm.

Women in Nigeria.

Nigeria
M966.9
B11

Baba *of Karo,* 1890 (*ca.*)–1951.
Baba of Karo, a woman of the Muslim Hausa. ₍Autobiography recorded₎ by M. F. Smith. With an introd. and notes by M. G. Smith; pref. by Daryll Forde. London, Faber and Faber ₍1954₎
299 p. illus. 23 cm.
1. Hausas. 2. Women in Nigeria. I. Smith, Mary Felice, 1924–
DT515.B115 1954 54–4526 ‡
Library of Congress ₍56c2₎

Nigeria
M200
C46

Women in Nigeria.
Okunsanya, I O S.
The place of women in the new Nigeria. Pp. 21-22.
In: Christian Council of Nigeria. Building for tomorrow. Lagos, 1960.

Congo, Women in the Congo.
Leopoldville

M396
M28

Makonga, Bonaventure
La mere Africaine. Bruxelles, Editions Remarques Congolaises, 1964.
113p. ports. 19cm. (Collection Etudes Congolaises, no. 11)
Portrait of author in book.
1. Women in the Congo. 2. Women, African. I. Title.

Women in the struggle for peace and security.

M396
J71w

Jones, Claudia
Women in the struggle for peace and security. New York, National Women's Commission, Communist Party, 1950.
16 p. 20cm.
Reprinted from Political Affairs, March 1950.

Women in the U.S.

M323.
C78

₍Cooper, Anna Julia (Haywood)₎ 1859–
A voice from the South. By a black woman of the South. Xenia, O., The Aldine printing house, 1892.
3 p. l., iii p., 1 l., ₍9₎–304 p. front. (port.) 18cm.
CONTENTS.—Womanhood a vital element in the regeneration and progress of a race.—The higher education of woman.—"Woman vs. the Indian."—The status of woman in America.—Has America a race problem; if so, how can it best be solved?—The Negro as presented in American literature.—What are we worth?—The gain from a belief.
1. ~~Negroes.~~ 2. U. S.—Race question. 3. Women in the U. S. I. A black woman of the South. II. Title.
12—2877
Library of Congress E185.6.C77
₍a43r37g1₎

Women in the U. S.

M06
J61
no.9

Hobson, *Mrs.* Elizabeth Christophers (Kimball) 1831-1912.
... A report concerning the colored women of the South, by Mrs. E. C. Hobson and Mrs. C. E. Hopkins. Baltimore, The Trustees ₍J. Murphy & co., printers₎ 1896.
15 p. 24cm. (Trustees of the John F. Slater fund. Occasional papers, no. 9)
1. Negroes. 2. Women in the U. S. I. Hopkins, Mrs. Charlotte Everett (Wise) joint author.
6—10234
Library of Congress E185.5.J65 no. 9
——— Copy 2. E185.86.H68
₍a35d1₎

M396 C26
Women in the U. S. - Addresses,essays,lectures
Cassara, Beverly Benner, ed.
American women: the changing image. Contributors: Ethel J. Alpenfels ⌈and others⌉ Boston, Beacon Press ⌈1962⌉
141 p. 21 cm.
Includes bibliography.
Partial contents.- Women in education, by Vivian C. Mason.
1. Women in the U. S.—Addresses, essays, lectures. I. Title.
HQ1419.C3 301.4242 62-13636 ‡
Library of Congress ⌈5⌉

MB B74
Women of achievement.
Brawley, Benjamin Griffith, 1882–
Women of achievement; written for the Fireside schools, under the auspices of the Women's American Baptist home mission society, by Benjamin Brawley ... ⌈Chicago, Woman's American Baptist home mission society, °1919⌉
92 p., 1 l. ports. 18ᶜᵐ.
CONTENTS.—Introduction: The Negro woman in American life.—Harriet Tubman.—Nora Gordan.—Meta Warrick Fuller.—Mary McLeod Bethune.—Mary Church Terrell.
1. Negroes—Biog. 2. Woman—Biog. 3. Women, Negro. I. Woman's American Baptist home mission society. II. Title.
19—4709
Library of Congress E185.96.B82
⌈42f1⌉

West Indies M972.9 B41
Women's international league for peace and freedom.
Latin American economic institute.
... Economic problems of the Caribbean area; speeches, addresses and abstracts of papers, delivered at the public conference held in New York city jointly with the Women's international league for peace and freedom on May 1, 1943, by Dantes Bellegarde, Lawrence Berenson ⌈and others⌉ ... New York, 1943.
cover-title, 60 p. 23ᶜᵐ. (*Its* Pamphlet series, no. 7)
1. West Indies—Econ. condit. I. Women's international league for peace and freedom. II. Title.
44—47231.
Library of Congress HC161.L26 no. 7
⌈45d2⌉ (330.82) 330.9729

M264 B54
The wonder of prayer.
Bishop, Shelton Hale.
The wonder of prayer. Greenwich, Conn., Seabury Press, 1959.
95 p. 20 cm.
1. Prayer. I. Title.
BV210.2.B57 264.1 59-5700 ‡
Library of Congress ⌈5⌉

Jamaica MB9 Se2s
Wonderful adventures of Mrs. Seacole in many lands.
Seacole, Mary.
Wonderful adventures of Mrs. Seacole in many lands. Edited by W. J. S. With an introductory preface by W. H. Russell ... London, J. Blackwood, 1857.
xii, 200 p. double front. 17ᶜᵐ.
Largely devoted to an account of the author's experiences as a sutler during the Crimean war.
1. Crimean war, 1853-1856—Personal narratives. I. S., W. J., ed. II. Title.
A 25-224
H. E. Huntington library for Library of Congress

M910 H81
Wonderful Ethiopians of the ancient Cushite...
Houston, Drusilla Dunjee. -1941.
Wonderful Ethiopians of the ancient Cushite empire, by Drusilla Dunjee Houston ... Oklahoma City, Okla., The Universal publishing company, 1926–
v. illus. 20½ᶜᵐ.
Inscribed: "For the Spingarn Library, the author.
1. Cushites. 2. Negro race. 3. Civilization, Ancient. I. Title. II. Title: Cushite empire.
27—5026
Library of Congress GN545.H6
——— Copy 2.
Copyright A 907452 ⌈30d1⌉

M813.5 W85n
Wooby, Philip
Nude to the meaning of tomorrow. New York, Exposition Press, 1959.
285p. 21cm.
Portrait of author on book jacket.
I. Title.

M784 W85n
Wood, Clement, 1888– ed.
... Negro songs, an anthology, edited, with an introduction, by Clement Wood. Girard, Kan., Haldeman-Julius company ⌈°1924⌉
64 p. 13ᶜᵐ. (Little blue book, no. 626, ed. by E. Haldeman-Julius)
Inscribed copy: For Arthur B. Spingarn, with the sincere wishes of his friend, Clement Wood.
1. Negro songs.
Library of Congress PS595.N3W6 CA 26-62 Unrev'd
——— Copy 2.
Copyright A 816570 ⌈2⌉

M813.5 W849
Wood, Lillian E.
"Let my people go". Philadelphia, Pa., A.M.E. book concern, n.d.
132p. 22cm.
I. Title.

M813.5 W85h
Wood, Odella Phelps.
High ground, a novel by Odella Phelps Wood. New York, The Exposition press ⌈1946⌉ [c1945]
8 p. l., 200 p. 19½ᶜᵐ.
I. Title.
PZ3.W85225Hi 47-18972
Library of Congress ⌈8⌉

M811.5 W85
Wood, Odella Phelps.
Recaptured echoes, by Odella Phelps Wood. New York, The Exposition press ⌈1944⌉
64 p. 19½ᶜᵐ. ⌈Poets of America. Series four⌉
I. Title. 1. Poetry.
45-166
Library of Congress * PS3545.O484R4
⌈8⌉ 811.5

M335 W85d
Woodbey, G W
The distribution of wealth, by Rev. G.W. Woodbey... [San Diego, Calif., G.W. Woodbey] 1910.
68p. front. 15cm.
1. Socialism
2. Wealth
I. Title

M395 W86
Woods, E M.
The negro in etiquette: a novelty. St. Louis, Buxton & Skinner, 1899.
1 p. l., 163 p. port. 12°.
Mar. 1, 1900-166
I. Title.
Library of Congress, no. Copyright.

M813.5 W86
Woods, William B 1935–
Lancaster triple thousand; a novel of suspense. ⌈1st ed.⌉ New York, Exposition Press ⌈1956⌉
77 p. 21 cm.
Portrait of author on jacket.
I. Title.
PZ4.W898Lan 56-7473 ‡
Library of Congress ⌈8⌉

M973 W86 ah
Woodson, Carter Godwin, 1875–1950
The African background outlined; or, Handbook for the study of the Negro, by Carter G. Woodson. Washington, D. C., The Association for the study of Negro life and history, inc. ⌈°1936⌉
viii, 478 p. illus. (maps) 22½ᶜᵐ.
Includes bibliographies.
1. Africa—Hist. 2. Negroes in Africa. 3. Africa—Civilization. 4. Negro race. 5. Negroes. I. Association for the study of Negro life and history, inc. II. Title. III. Title: Handbook for the study of the Negro.
36—8432
Library of Congress DT8.W65
⌈44z1⌉ [325.26] 960

M973 W86ah
Woodson, Carter Godwin, 1875– 1950
African heroes and heroines, by Carter Godwin Woodson. Washington, D. C., The Associated publishers, inc. ⌈°1939⌉
6 p. l., 249 p. illus. 20½ cm.
Bibliography: p. 227-240.
1. Africa—Hist. 2. Africa—Biog. I. Title.
39—17702
Library of Congress DT21.W6
⌈43h2⌉ 960

M973 W86 a
Woodson, Carter Godwin, 1875– 1950
African myths, together with proverbs; a supplementary reader composed of folk tales from various parts of Africa, adapted to the use of children in the public schools, by Carter Godwin Woodson ... Washington, D. C., The Associated publishers, inc. ⌈°1928⌉
xv, 184 p. incl. front., illus. 19½ᶜᵐ.
1. Tales, African. 2. Readers and speakers—1870– I. Title.
29—1210
Library of Congress PE1127.G4W7
⌈44o2⌉

M973 W86 c
Woodson, Carter Godwin, 1875– 1950
A century of Negro migration, by Carter G. Woodson ... Washington, D. C., The Association for the study of Negro life and history, 1918.
vii, 221 p. maps, diagrs. 20½ᶜᵐ.
Bibliography: p. 193-211.
1. Negroes. I. Title. II. Title: Negro migration.
18—17856
Library of Congress E185.9.M89
⌈47q1⌉

M973. W86 e
Woodson, Carter Godwin, 1875–1950
The education of the Negro prior to 1861; a history of the education of the colored people of the United States from the beginning of slavery to the civil war, by C. G. Woodson ... New York and London, G. P. Putnam's sons, 1915.
v, 454 p. 20½ᶜᵐ.
Bibliography: p. 390-434.
1. Negroes—Education. I. Title.
15—11678
Library of Congress LC2741.W7
⌈45o1⌉

M973. W86fo
Woodson, Carter Godwin, 1875-1950 ed.
Fifty years of Negro citizenship as qualified by the United States supreme court, by C.G. Woodson. Reprinted from the Journal of Negro history, 6: January 1921.
53p. 25cm.
Bound with: Free Negro owners of slaves in the United States, by C.G.Woodson.
1. U.S. Supreme Court. I. Title
2. Citizenship
3. Laws and legislation

M973. W86fr
Woodson, Carter Godwin, 1875–1950
Free negro heads of families in the United States in 1830, together with a brief treatment of the free negro, by Carter G. Woodson ... Washington, D. C., The Association for the study of negro life and history, inc. ⌈°1925⌉
lviii, 296 p. 25½ᶜᵐ.
"Second of a series of documentary studies of the free negro provided for by a grant ... from the Laura Spelman Rockefeller memorial in 1921."—Foreword.
Bibliographical foot-notes.
1. Negroes—Direct. 2. Negroes. I. Laura Spelman Rockefeller memorial, New York. II. Association for the study of negro life and history, inc. III. Title.
25—27636
Library of Congress E185.W887
⌈45n1⌉

M973 W86fo

Woodson, Carter Godwin, 1875–1950 *ed.*
Free Negro owners of slaves in the United States in 1830, together with Absentee ownership of slaves in the United States in 1830, compiled under the direction of, and edited by Carter G. Woodson ... Washington, D. C., The Association for the study of Negro life and history ₍°1924₎
viii, 78 p. 25ᶜᵐ.
This statistical report was made possible by an appropriation obtained from the Laura Spelman Rockefeller memorial. *cf.* Foreword.
1. Slavery in the U. S. 2. Negroes—Directory. I. Association for the study of Negro life and history, inc. II. Laura Spelman Rockefeller memorial, New York. III. Title. IV. Title: Absentee ownership of slaves in the United States in 1830. 3. Free Negroes
Library of Congress E185.W8873 25—28062
₍44n1₎

M973 W86ne

Woodson, Carter Godwin, 1875–1950
Negro makers of history, by Carter G. Woodson ... Washington, D. C., The Associated publishers, inc. ₍°1928₎
2 p. l., iii–vi, 362 p. illus. (incl. ports., facsims.) double map. 20 cm.
"An adaptation of ₍the author's₎ The Negro in our history to the capacity of children in the elementary schools."—Pref.
History.
1. Negroes. 2. Slavery in the U. S. I. Title.
Library of Congress E185.W895 29—458
₍43j1₎

Woodson, Carter Godwin, 1875–1950

M331 A87

Association for the study of Negro life and history, inc.
The Negro as a business man, by J. H. Harmon, jr., Arnett G. Lindsay, and Carter G. Woodson. Washington, D. C., The Association for the study of Negro life and history, inc. ₍°1929₎
v, 111 p. 25 cm.
CONTENTS.—The Negro as a local business man.—The Negro in banking.—Insurance business among Negroes.
1. Negroes—Employment. I. Harmon, John Henry, jr. II. Lindsay, Arnett Grant. III. Woodson, Carter Godwin, 1875– IV. Title.
Library of Congress E185.8.A84 30—21076
₍48j1₎ 325.26

M973 W86h

Woodson, Carter Godwin, 1875–1950
The history of the Negro church, by Carter G. Woodson ... Washington, D. C., The Associated publishers ₍°1921₎
x, 330 p. front., plates, ports. 20½ᶜᵐ.
1. Negroes—Religion. I. Title. II. Title: Negro church, The history of the.
Library of Congress BR563.N4W6 22—685
₍44q1₎

M973 W86 no

Woodson, Carter Godwin, 1875–1950*ed.*
Negro orators and their orations, by Carter G. Woodson ... Washington, D. C., The Associated publishers, inc. ₍°1925₎
xi p., 1 l., 711 p. 22½ᶜᵐ.
1. Orations. I. Title.
Library of Congress PS663.N4W6 25—20434
₍45h1₎

Woodson, Carter Godwin, 1875–1950

M331 G82n

Greene, Lorenzo Johnston, 1899–
The Negro wage earner, by Lorenzo J. Greene and Carter G. Woodson. Washington, D. C., The Association for the study of Negro life and history, inc. ₍°1930₎
xiii p., 1 l., 388 p. incl. tables, diagrs. 22½ᶜᵐ.
Bibliography: p. ₍369₎–380.
1. Negroes — Employment. 2. Negroes — Moral and social conditions. I. Woodson, Carter Godwin, 1875– II. Association for the study of Negro life and history, inc. III. Title.
Library of Congress E185.8.G79 31—493
₍44r37z1₎ 325.26

M973. W86m

Woodson, Carter Godwin, 1875–1950 *ed.*
The mind of the Negro as reflected in letters written during the crisis, 1800–1860, edited by Carter G. Woodson ... Washington, D. C., The Association for the study of Negro life and history, inc. ₍°1926₎
5 p. l., v–xxxii, 672 p. 24ᶜᵐ.
1. Negroes. 2. Negroes—Moral and social conditions. 3. Slavery in the U. S.—Emancipation. I. Association for the study of Negro life and history, inc. II. Title.
Library of Congress E185.W8877 26—14304
₍45m1₎

M973 W86n

Woodson, Carter Godwin, 1875– 1950
The Negro professional man and the community, with special emphasis on the physician and the lawyer, by Carter Godwin Woodson. Washington, D. C., The Association for the study of Negro life and history, inc. ₍°1934₎
1 p. l., v–xviii, 365 p. diagr. 23½ᶜᵐ.
"₍This study forms₎ a part of the effort of the Association for the study of Negro life and history to portray the social and economic conditions obtaining among Negroes in the United States since the civil war."—Foreword.
1. Negroes—Employment. 2. Negroes—Moral and social conditions. 3. Negro physicians. 4. Negro lawyers. I. Association for the study of Negro life and history, inc. II. Title.
Library of Congress E185.82.W88 34—10066
₍34f5₎ 325.260973

Woodson, Carter Goodwin, 1875–1950ed.

M208.1 G88

Grimké, Francis James, 1850–1937.
The works of Francis J. Grimké, edited by Carter G. Woodson ... Washington, D. C., The Associated publishers, inc. ₍1942₎
4 v. 23½ᶜᵐ.
CONTENTS.—I. Addresses mainly personal and racial.—II. Special sermons.—III. Stray thoughts and meditations.—IV. Letters.
1. Presbyterian church — Collected works. 2. Theology — Collected works—20th cent. 3. U. S.—Race question. I. Woodson, Carter Godwin, 1875– ed.
Library of Congress BX8915.G78 42—18902
₍43d2₎ 208.1

M973 W86m

Woodson, Carter Godwin, 1875–1950
The mis-education of the Negro, by Carter Godwin Woodson. Washington, D. C., The Associated publishers, inc. ₍°1933₎
xiv p., 1 l., 207 p. 19 cm.
1. Negroes—Education. 2. Negroes—Moral and social conditions. 3. Negroes—Employment. I. Title.
Library of Congress E185.82.W88 33—3606
₍45i1₎ 371.974

M973 W86 r

Woodson, Carter Godwin, 1875– 1950
The rural Negro, by Carter Godwin Woodson. Washington, D. C., The Association for the study of Negro life and history, inc. ₍°1930₎
xvi p., 1 l., 265 p. illus. (incl. map) 22ᶜᵐ.
"Another by-product of the three-year survey of the social and economic conditions of the Negroes of the United States since the civil war ... undertaken by the Association for the study of Negro life and history in 1926."—Introd.
1. Negroes—Moral and social conditions. 2. Negroes—Employment. 3. Sociology, Rural. 4. Country life—U. S. I. Association for the study of Negro life and history, inc. II. Title.
Library of Congress E185.86.W896 30—21077
₍43u2₎ 325.26

M975.4 W87w

Woodward, Isaiah Alfonso, 1913–
West Virginia and its struggle for statehood, 1861–1863. ₍Baltimore, Wolk Pub. Co., 1954₎
44 p. illus., ports., map. 22 cm.
Bibliography: p. 39–42.
1. West Virginia—Pol. & govt. I. Title.
E536.W65 975.4 54–37068
Library of Congress ₍1₎

M973 W86n

₍Woodson, Carter Goodwin, 1875–1950₎
The Negro a factor in the history of the world; Remarks of Hon. Arthur W. Mitchell of Illinois in the House of Representatives. Washington, Govt. Print. Off., 1940.
3–8p. 23cm.
Letter from Dr. Woodson read by Representative Mitchell.
I. Mitchell, Arthur W., 1883–

M973 W86s 1959

Woodson, Carter Godwin, 1875–1950.
The story of the Negro retold, by Carter G. Woodson and Charles H. Wesley. 4th ed. rev. and enl. Washington, D.C., The Associated Pub.,Inc., 1959.
472p. illus. 20cm.
1. Slavery in the U.S. I. Wesley, Charles Harris, 1891– , jt. author. II. Title.

M323 W879

Woofter, Thomas Jackson, 1893– *ed.*
Negro problems in cities; a study made under the direction of T. J. Woofter, jr. Garden City, N. Y., Doubleday, Doran & company, inc. ₍°1928₎
xiii p., 2 l., 17–284 p. illus. (maps) diagrs., form. 19½ᶜᵐ.
"The Institute of social and religious research ... is responsible for this publication."
CONTENTS.—pt. 1. Neighborhoods, by T. J. Woofter, jr.—pt. 2. Housing, by Madge Headley.—pt. 3. Schools, by W. A. Daniel.—pt. 4. Recreation, by H. J. McGuinn.
1. Negroes—Moral and social conditions. I. Headley, Madge. II. Daniel, William Andrew, 1895– III. McGuinn, Henry J. IV. Institute of social and religious research. V. Title.
Library of Congress E185.86.W91 28—8612
——— Copy 2.
Copyright A 1069386 ₍40x2₎

M973 W86 1928

Woodson, Carter Godwin, 1875– 1950
The Negro in our history, by Carter G. Woodson.. fifth edition (further revised and enlarged). Washington, D.C., The Associated publishers, inc. ₍c1928₎
xxx, 628p. front. illus. 21½cm.
1. Slavery in the U.S. 2. History
I. Title

M973 W86s

Woodson, Carter Godwin, 1875–1950
The story of the Negro retold, by Carter Godwin Woodson. Washington, D. C., The Associated publishers, inc. ₍°1935₎
viii, 369 p. incl. front., illus. (incl. ports., maps) diagr. 20ᶜᵐ.
"The history of the Negro in the United States."—Pref.
Bibliographies at end of each chapter except chapter XII.
History
1. Negroes. 2. Slavery in the U. S. I. Title.
Library of Congress E185.W896 36—434
₍45t1₎ 325.260973

M378Tex W85

Woolfolk, George Ruble.
Prairie View, a study in public conscience, 1878–1946. ₍1st ed.₎ New York, Pageant Press ₍1962₎
404 p. illus. 21 cm.
Portrait of author on book jacket.
1. Texas. Agricultural and Mechanical College, Prairie View. 2. Education, Higher – Texas.
LC2851.T424 378.764249 61–18006 ‡
Library of Congress ₍10₎

M973 W86

Woodson, Carter Godwin, 1875– 1950
The Negro in our history, by Carter G. Woodson ... Washington, D. C., The Associated publishers, inc. ₍°1922₎
xv, 393 p. incl. front., illus. 20ᶜᵐ.
1. History 2. Slavery in the U. S. I. Title.
Library of Congress E185.W89 22—14504
₍a35p2₎

M304 P19 v.4, no.21

Woodson, Carter Godwin, 1875–1950
Ten years of collecting and publishing the records of the Negro. Washington D.C. The association for the study of Negro life and History. 1925.
Reprinted from the Journal of Negro history, v.x. no.4, Oct. 1925; p. 398–606.

A word from Africa.

Tanganyika
M967.82 R84w

Kittler, Glenn D
The White Fathers. Introd. by Bishop Laurian Rugambwa. ₍1st ed.₎ New York, Harper ₍1957₎
299 p. illus. 22 cm.
1. White Fathers.
BV2300.W5K5 ₍266.2₎ 276 57–6134 ‡
Library of Congress ₍20₎

The Word on the Brazos.

M398 B75w

Brewer, John Mason, 1896–
The Word on the Brazos; Negro preacher tales from the Brazos bottoms of Texas. Foreword by J. Frank Dobie; illus. by Ralph White, Jr. Austin, University of Texas Press, 1953.
109 p. illus. 24 cm.
First edition.
Autographed by authors.

1. Folk-lore, Negro. 2. Folk-lore—Brazos Valley. 3. ~~Negroes~~—Religion. I. Title.

GR103.B7 398.21 53—10834 ‡
Library of Congress [54k5]

Word pictures of the great.

MB D44w

Derricotte, Elise Palmer.
Word pictures of the great, by Elise Palmer Derricotte ... Geneva Calcier Turner ... [and] Jessie Hailstalk Roy ... illustrated by Lois Mailou Jones. Washington, D. C., The Associated publishers inc. [°1941]
xiii, 280 p. incl. front., illus. 21½ cm.
Illustrated lining-papers in color.
"Books to read" at end of each section.

1. Negroes—Biog. I. Turner, Geneva Calcier, joint author. II. Roy, Jessie Hailstalk, joint author. III. Title.

41—13255
Library of Congress E185.96.D4
[a44g2] [825.260973] 920.073

M784 W88f

Work, Frederick Jerome, 1880– ed.
Folk songs of the American Negro. Edited by Frederick J. Work ... Introduction by John W. Work, Jr. ... Nashville, Tenn. National B.Y.P. U. Board, n.d.
94p. 2 p. 23½cm.
Music.
Cover title: Folk songs, plantation and jubilee melodies ...

1. Folk songs. I. Work, John Wesley, 1901–
II. Title.

M784 W88f 1907

Work, Frederick Jerome, 1880– ed.
Folk songs of the American Negro, no.1, edited by Frederick J. Work. Introduction by John W. Work. Nashville, tenn., Work bros. & Hart Co., 1907.
48p. 20½cm.

1. Folk songs.
I. Title. II. Work, John Wesley, 1901–

M784 W89f

Work, John Wesley, 1871–1925.
Folk song of the American Negro [by] John Wesley Work ... Nashville, Tenn., Press of Fisk university [°1915]
4 p. l., 5–131 p. illus. (incl. ports.) 23 cm.

1. Negro songs. I. Title.

15—22992
Library of Congress ML3556.W78
[a41b1]

M784 W89a

Work, John Wesley, 1901– *ed.*
American Negro songs and spirituals; a comprehensive collection of 230 folk songs, religious and secular, with a foreword by John W. Work. New York, Crown publishers [°1940]
1 p. l., [v]–vii p., 1 l., 259 p. 26 cm.
With music.
Bibliography: p. 252–256.

1. ~~Negro songs~~. I. Title.

A 42–5002
Oberlin college. Library for Library of Congress [M1670.W89A]
[5] 784.756

M784 W88f

Work, John Wesley, 1901–
Work, Frederick Jerome, ed.
Folk songs of the American Negro. Edited by Frederick J. Work ... Introduction by John W. Work, Jr. ... Nashville, Tenn. National B.Y.P.U. Board, n.d.
94p. 2 p. 23½cm.
Music.
Cover title: Folk songs, plantation and jubilee melodies ...

M784 W88f 1907

Work, John Wesley, 1901–
Work, Frederick Jerome, ed.
Folk songs of the American Negro, no.1, edited by Frederick J. Work. Introduction by John W. Work. Nashville, Tenn., Work bros. & Hart Co., 1907.
48p. 20½cm.

M01 W89

Work, Monroe Nathan, 1866–1945 *comp.*
A bibliography of the Negro in Africa and America, compiled by Monroe N. Work ... New York, The H. W. Wilson company, 1928.
xxi, [1] p., 1 l., 698 p. 26½ cm.
Classified, with author index.
"List of periodicals from which references for the bibliography were taken": p. [661]–674.
"A bibliography of bibliographies on Africa": pt. I, p. [242]–247.
"A bibliography of bibliographies on the Negro in the United States": pt. II, p. [630]–636.

(Continued on next card)
28—17150
[42w2]

M01 W89

Work, Monroe Nathan, 1866–1945 *comp.* A bibliography of the Negro in Africa and America ... 1928. (Card 2)
"A bibliography of bibliographies on the West Indies": pt. II, p. [665]–658.
"A bibliography of bibliographies on Latin America": pt. II, p. [650]–660.

1. Negroes—Bibl. 2. Negroes in Africa—Bibl. 3. Negroes in America—Bibl. I. Title: The Negro in Africa and America, A bibliography of.

28—17150
Library of Congress Z1361.N39W8
[42w2]

M306 Sol 1919

Work, Monroe Nathan, 1866–1945.
Interracial co-operation and the south's new economic conditions.
(In: Southern Sociological Congress. Knoxville, 1919. "Distinguished service citizenship." Washington, D.C., Southern Sociological Congress 1919. 23 cm. p. 122–29).

M973.8 Am3

Work, Monroe Nathan, 1866–1945.
Negro criminality in the south.
(In: American Academy of Political and Social Science. The Negro's progress in fifty years ... Philadelphia, 1913. 25cm. p. 74–80.)

M06 Am35

Work, Monroe Nathan, 1866–1945.
The Negro in business and the professions.
(In: American Academy of Political and Social Science, Philadelphia. The American Negro. Philadelphia, 1928. 24cm. p. 138–144.

Work, Monroe Nathan, 1866– 1945 ed.

M310 N31

Negro year book, an annual encyclopedia of the Negro ...
1912–
Tuskegee Institute, Ala., Negro year book publishing co., °1912–
v. illus. (incl. maps) diagrs. 19½–24 cm.
No editions were published for 1920/21, 1923/24, 1927/28–1929/30.
Editor: 1912: M. N. Work.
Publishers: 1912, Negro year book co.—1914/15– Negro year book publishing co.
Title varies slightly.

1. Negroes—Year-books. I. Work, Monroe Nathan, 1866– ed.

12—14974
Library of Congress E185.5.N41
[43t2]

M323 W89p

Work, Monroe Nathan, 1866–1945.
Problems of adjustment of race and class in the South. Reprinted from Social forces, 16:108–117, October 1937.

1. Race problems. I. Title.

M306 Sol 1919

Work, Monroe Nathan, 1866–1945
The south and the health of Negroes.
(In: Southern Sociological Congress. Houston 1915. The New chivalry - health. Nashville, Southern Sociological Congress, 1915. 24cm. pp. 412–421)

The work of the Afro-American woman.

MB M85

Mossell, (Mrs.) N F
The work of the Afro-American woman, by Mrs. N.F. Mossell. Philadelphia, Geo. S. Ferguson company, 1894.
178p. frton. 17½cm.

The Worker.

M070.432 J13

Jackson, James Edward, 1914–
The view from here. New York, Publishers New Press, [1963]
210p. 20½cm.
Portrait of author on book cover.

1. Editorials. I. The Worker.
II. Title.

Workers battle automation.

M331 D41

Denby, Charles
Workers battle automation. [Detroit, News and Letters, 1960]
62p. illus. 17cm.

1. Labor and laboring classes. 2. Automation. I. Title

Working for Progress.

M813.5 W46w

Wells, Moses Peter.
Working for progress. New York, Carlton Press, 1963.
32p. 20cm. (A Geneva book)

Working with the hands...

M814.4 W27au

Washington, Booker Taliaferro, 1859?–1915.
Working with the hands; being a sequel to "Up from slavery," covering the author's experiences in industrial training at Tuskegee, by Booker T. Washington; illustrated from photographs by Frances Benjamin Johnston. New York, Doubleday, Page & company, 1904.
x, 246 p. front. (port.) 31 pl. 20½ cm.
Subscription edition with a special introduction not in the trade edition.

1. Tuskegee normal and industrial institute. I. Title.

E185.97.W32 4—12107
Library of Congress [56c4]

Workman, Willie Mae (Cartwright)

MB9 W89K **Kytle, Elizabeth Larisey.**
Willie Mae. [1st ed.] New York, Knopf, 1958.
243 p. 21 cm.

1. Workman, Willie Mae (Cartwright) 2. ~~Negroes—Georgia.~~ I. Title.

E185.97.W62K9 325.2609758 58—7560 ‡
Library of Congress [58x20]

A world of peoples.

Ghana M301 G166 **Gardiner, Robert Kweku Atta.** 1914–
A world of peoples [by] Robert Gardiner. London, British Broadcasting Corporation, 1966.
93 p. 22 cm. (The Reith lectures, 1965) 15/- (B 66-7753)
Includes bibliographies.
Portrait of author on book jacket.

1. Race problems. 2. Prejudices and antipathies. I. British Broadcasting Corporation. II. Title. (Series)

HT1521.G3 1966 301.45 66—71229
Library of Congress [67f5]

... world revolution, 1917-1936.

Trinidad M320 J23w **James, Cyril Lionel Robert,** 1901–
... World revolution, 1917–1936; the rise and fall of the Communist International. London, M. Secker and Warburg, ltd. [1937]
xii, 9–429 p. 22cm.
At head of title: C. L. R. James.
"How much the book owes to the writings of Trotsky, the text can only partially show."—p. xii.

1. Communist International. 2. Communism. 3. Revolutions. 4. World politics. 5. Russia—Pol. & govt.—20th cent. 6. Trotskiĭ, Lev, 1879–1940. 7. Stalin, Iosif, 1879– I. Title.

37—23067
Library of Congress HX11.I 5J25 [45g1] 335.40621

M811.08 W89a **Works Progress Administration. New Jersey.**
An Anthology of Negro poetry by Negroes and others, arranged by Beatrice F. Wormley, and Charles Carter, Under the supervision of Benjamin F. Seldon [Newark, N.J. n.d.]

135p. 28cm.
Mimeographed.

1. Poetry - anthologies.

World politics.

Trinidad M320 J23w **James, Cyril Lionel Robert,** 1901–
... World revolution, 1917–1936; the rise and fall of the Communist International. London, M. Secker and Warburg, ltd. [1937]
xii, 9–429 p. 22cm.
At head of title: C. L. R. James.
"How much the book owes to the writings of Trotsky, the text can only partially show."—p. xii.

1. Communist International. 2. Communism. 3. Revolutions. 4. World politics. 5. Russia—Pol. & govt.—20th cent. 6. Trotskiĭ, Lev, 1879–1940. 7. Stalin, Iosif, 1879– I. Title.

37—23067
Library of Congress HX11.I 5J25 [45g1] 335.40621

World Trade Union Conference, 1945-

Trinidad M330 P13v **Padmore, George, 1903- ed.**
The voice of coloured labour; speeches and reports of colonial delegates to the world trade union conference, 1945. Manchester, Panaf Service [1945]

55p. 22cm.

The world and Africa.

M301 D853wo2 **Du Bois, William Edward Burghardt,** 1868–1963.
The world and Africa; an inquiry into the part which Africa has played in world history. An enl. ed., with new writings on Africa, 1955–1961. New York, International Publishers [1965]
xii, 352 p. illus., maps. 21 cm.
Bibliographical footnotes.

1. Africa—Hist. I. Title.

DT21.D8 1965 960 65–16392
Library of Congress [3]

World politics - 1945 -

Haiti M327 B43c **Benjamin, Georges J**
Contribution à l'histoire diplomatique et contemporaine. Port-au-Prince, Impr. de l'État [1951]
314 p. port. 20 cm.
Includes texts of treaties and official correspondence, part in translation.
Bibliography: p. [311]–314.

1. Haiti—For. rel. 2. Haiti—For. rel.—Dominican Republic. 3. Dominican Republic—For. rel.—Haiti. 4. World politics—1945–

F1926.B46 327.7294 51–5708
Library of Congress [2]

A world view of the American Negro.

M323 N78t **Wright, Richard, 1909-1960.**
A world view of the American Negro.

pp. 346-348.
A letter.
In: Twice a year, ed. by Dorothy Norman. 1946.

The world and Africa.

M301 D853wo **Du Bois, William Edward Burghardt,** 1868–
The world and Africa; an inquiry into the part which Africa has played in world history, by W. E. Burghardt Du Bois. New York, The Viking press, 1947.
xii, 276 p. illus. (incl. maps) 21 cm.
Bibliographical references included in the foreword.

1. Africa—Hist. I. Title.

RT21.D8 960 47—30075
Library of Congress [49c5]

World politics - 1955-

M909.82 C76a **Conference on Tensions in Development,** *Oxford University, 1961.*
Restless nations; a study of world tensions and development. Foreword by Lester B. Pearson. ~~New York, Dodd, Mead, 1962.~~ London, Allen and Unwin [1962]
217 p. 22 cm.
Sponsored by the Council on World Tensions.

1. Underdeveloped areas. 2. Economic assistance. 3. World politics—1955– I. Council on World Tensions. II. Title.

HC60.C63 1961 338.91 62—16328 ‡
Library of Congress [64v7]

World War I

see

European war, 1914-1918

M814.5 W89 **World fellowship of faiths.** *International congress. 1st, Chicago and New York,* 1933–1934.
World fellowship; addresses and messages by leading spokesmen of all faiths, races and countries, edited by Charles Frederick Weller ... New York, Liveright publishing corporation [°1935]
xviii, 986 p. 22 cm.
"This book ... condenses and co-ordinates the 242 addresses delivered by 199 spokesmen ... in the 83 meetings held ... by the first International congress of the World fellowship of faiths."—p. v.

1. Religions—Congresses. 2. Religions—Addresses, essays, lectures. I. Weller, Charles Frederick, 1870– ed.

36—2382
Library of Congress BL21.W6 1933–1934 [48k1] 290.631

World politics - 1955-

M909.82 C76 **Conference on Tensions in Development,** *Oxford University, 1961.*
Restless nations; a study of world tensions and development. Foreword by Lester B. Pearson. New York, Dodd, Mead, 1962.
217 p. 22 cm.
Sponsored by the Council on World Tensions.

1. Underdeveloped areas. 2. Economic assistance. 3. World politics—1955– I. Council on World Tensions. II. Title.

HC60.C63 1961 338.91 62—16328 ‡
Library of Congress [64v7]

World war, 1939-1945.

M350 An2c **Anderson, Trezzvant W**
Come out fighting; the epic tale of the 761st tank battalion, 1942–1945, by Trezzvant W. Anderson. [Salzburg, Printed by Salzburger druckerei und verlag, 1945]
xv, 135 p. illus. (incl. ports., maps) fold. tab. 30cm.

1. World war, 1939–1945—Regimental histories—U. S.—761st tank battalion. 2. World war, 1939–1945—Negroes. 3. U. S. Army. 761st tank battalion. 4. World war, 1939–1945—Campaigns—Western. I. Title.

Harvard univ. Library for Library of Congress D769.306 761st.A6 [5]† A 46–3127 940.542

M814.5 W89 World Fellowship of Faiths. International Congress 1st, Chicago and New York, 1933-1934. World fellowship; addresses... (card 2)

Partial contents: -Solving the colored woman's problem. -The Negro, the hope or despair of Christianity, by Reverdy C. Ransom. -Overcoming racial and religious prejudices, R.R. Wright, Jr. -Interracial co-operation and good will.

World politics - 1945 - Addresses, essays, lectures.

M301 G623 **Goodman, Paul,** 1911– *ed.*
Seeds of liberation. New York, G. Braziller [1965]
xviii, 551 p. 22 cm.

1. World politics—1945– —Addresses, essays, lectures. 2. Civilization, Modern—1950– —Addresses, essays, lectures. I. Title.

D839.3.G56 081 65–12888
Library of Congress [20]

World war, 1939-1945.

M323 Am3m **American academy of political and social science,** *Philadelphia.*
... Minority peoples in a nation at war, edited by J. P. Shalloo ... and Donald Young ... Philadelphia, 1942.
viii, 276 p. 25½cm. (*Its* Annals, v. 223, September 1942)
CONTENTS.—The need for national solidarity.—The Negro and the war.—Minorities of alien origin.—The treatment of minorities in a democracy.

1. U. S.—Foreign population. 2. Negroes. 3. World war, 1939– — U. S. I. Shalloo, Jeremiah Patrick, 1896– ed. II. Young, Donald Ramsey, 1898– joint ed. III. Title.

Library of Congress H1.A4 vol. 223 42-36334
——— Copy 2. E184.A1A53
[45] (306.273) 323.173

MB9 T19 World of a pullman porter.
Taylor, Douglas
World of a pullman porter. New York, [n.d.]

48p. illus., ports. 21cm.
Portrait of author in book and on front cover.

World problems of the Negro people.

M304 P19 v.1 no.2 **Ford, James W**
World problems of the Negro people. (a reputation of George Padmore) New York, issued by the Harlem section of the communist party [n.d.]

24p. 15cm. (Series on Negro problems)

World War, 1939-1945

M910 B58 **Blake, Alfred Egbert,** 1906–
Convoy to India, by Al Ethelred Blakeley [pseud.] Brooklyn, Trilon Press, 1953.
214 p. 22 cm.

1. World War, 1939–1945—Negroes. 2. India—Descr. & trav. I. Title.

D810.N4B5 940.5403 53–20847 ‡
Library of Congress [1]

World war, 1939-1945.

M304 p19 v.2 no.3 Ford, James W 1893-
The Negro people and the new world situation, by James W. Ford. ₍New York, Workers library publishers, inc., 1941₎
15 p. 19ᶜᵐ.
"James W. Ford ₍biographical sketch₎": p. ₍2₎
M335.4 F75n2
1. World war, 1939- —Negroes. I. Title.
42-15016
Library of Congress D810.N4F7
₍2₎ 940.5403

World war, 1939-1945.

M304 P19 v.2 no.4 Ford, James W 1893-
The war and the Negro people, by James W. Ford ... ₍New York, Workers library publishers, 1942.
15 p. 19ᶜᵐ.
1. World war, 1939- —Negroes. I. Title.
45-13492
Library of Congress D810.N4F73
₍2₎ 940.5403

M335.4 F75w World war, 1939-1945.
Ford, James W , 1893-
The war and the Negro people. New York, Workers Library, 1942.
15p. 19cm.

World War, 1939-1945.

M350 F85 Francis, Charles E
The Tuskegee airmen; the story of the Negro in the U. S. Air Force. Boston, Bruce Humphries ₍1956, °1955₎
225 p. illus. 22 cm.
1. World War, 1939-1945—Negroes. 2. Negroes—in aeronautics. 3. U. S. Army Air Forces. I. Title.
D810.N4F76 940.541273 53—11824 ‡
Library of Congress ₍57d5₎

World war, 1939-1945—

M350. F98 Furr, Arthur, 1895-
Democracy's Negroes, by Arthur Furr ... A book of facts concerning the activities of Negroes in world war II. Boston, Mass., The House of Edinboro ₍1947₎
315 p. incl. front., plates, ports. 20½ᶜᵐ.
1. World war, 1939-1945—Negroes. I. Title.
D810.N4F85 940.5403 47-1670
© 1Feb47; The House of Edinboro, publishers; A10469.
Library of Congress ₍5₎

World War, 1939-1945.

M350 H242 Harris, Elbert Leroy
Let the ammunition roll: The story of a Negro GI. N.Y. Exposition press, 1948.
30p. 22cm.

World war, 1939-1945

M350. J62 Johnson, J R
Why Negroes should oppose the war, by J. R. Johnson ... ₍New York, Pub. by Pioneer publishers for the Socialist workers party and the Young people's socialist league (Fourth International) 1939?₎
30, ₍1₎ p. 21ᶜᵐ.
1. World war, 1939- —Negroes. I. Socialist workers party. II. Young people's socialist league of America. III. Title.
44-12148
Library of Congress D810.N4J57
₍2₎ 940.5403

World war, 1939-1945.

M323 J71j Jones, Claudia.
Jim-Crow in uniform, by Claudia Jones ... ₍New York, New age publishers, 1940₎
23, ₍1₎ p. 18½ᶜᵐ.
1. World war, 1939- —Negroes. I. Title.
44-34122
Library of Congress D810.N4J6
₍2₎ 325.260973

World War, 1939-1945.

M350 M14w MacDonald, Dwright
The war's greatest scandal: The story of jim crow in uniform, by Dwight Macdonald, research by Nancy Macdonald. New York, March on Washington Movement, [1943]
15p. illus. 23cm.

M350 Ow2n World war, 1939-1945.
Owen, Chandler.
Negroes and the war. Washington, D. C., Office of War Information, 194 .
6p. illus. 34cm.

World War, 1939-1945.

M350 S13n Silvera, John D.
The Negro in World War II, by John D. Silvera. Baton Rouge, La. Military press of Louisiana, 1946.
140 unnumbered p. illus. 27cm.

World war, 1939-1945—

M323. W587ri White, Walter Francis, 1893-
... A rising wind. Garden City, New York, Doubleday, Doran and company, inc., 1945.
155 p. 19½ᶜᵐ.
At head of title: Walter White.
"First edition."
1. World war, 1939-1945—Negroes. I. Title.
45—9285
Library of Congress D810.N4W48
₍47i7₎ 940.5403

World War, 1939-1945.

M910 Y4a Yergan, Max. 1894-
Africa in the war. New York, Council on African Affairs.
8p. 20cm.
M304 P19 V.2, no.7

France M848 Sa8m World war, 1939-1945—Aerial operations, French.
Sauvage, Roger, 1917-
Un du Normandie-Niémen. Préf. du colonel Pouyade. ₍Givors₎ A. Martel ₍1950₎
316 p. illus., ports. 21 cm.
"Il a été tiré ... 500 exemplaires sur Alfa Mousse des Papeteries Navarre numérotés 1 à 450 et H-C₁ à H-C₅. 131."
1. France combattante. Forces aériennes françaises libres. Régiment Normandie-Niémen. 2. World War, 1939-1945—Aerial operations, French. 3. World War, 1939-1945—Personal narratives, French. I. Title.
D788.S39 940.544944 51-17012
Library of Congress ₍1₎

World War, 1939-1945-Anecdotes.

M813.5 E14ir Sterling, Dorothy, 1913- ed.
I have seen war; 25 stories from World War II. New York, Hill and Wang ₍1960₎
273 p. 21 cm.
1. World War, 1939-1945—Anecdotes. I. Title.
D744.S75 940.548 60—14909 ‡
Library of Congress ₍61k10₎

World war, 1939-1945-Campaigns-Western.

M350 An2c Anderson, Trezzvant W
Come out fighting; the epic tale of the 761st tank battalion, 1942-1945, by Trezzvant W. Anderson. ₍Salzburg, Printed by Salzburger druckerei und verlag, 1945₎
xv, 135 p. illus. (incl. ports., maps) fold. tab. 30ᶜᵐ.
1. World war, 1939-1945—Regimental histories—U. S.—761st tank battalion. 2. World war, 1939-1945—Negroes. 3. U. S. Army. 761st tank battalion. 4. World war, 1939-1945—Campaigns—Western. I. Title.
A 46-3127
Harvard univ. Library for Library of Congress D769.306 761st.A6
₍5₎† 940.542

World War, 1939-1945 - Campaigns - Western.

M350. H78t Hornsby, Henry Haywood, 1923-
The trey of sevens. Dallas, Mathis, Van Nort ₍1946₎
xvii, 126 p. illus., ports. 20 cm.
"Based on activities of Battery 'C' of the 777th Field Artillery Battalion in the Ninth Army sector."—p. xii.
Map on lining-papers.
1. World War, 1939-1945—Personal narratives, American. 2. U. S. Army. 777th Field Artillery Battalion. 3. World War, 1939-1945—Campaigns—Western. I. Title.
D769.34 777th.H6 940.542 47—27938*
Library of Congress ₍50c₁₎

World war, 1939-1945 - Fiction.

M813.5 K55an Killens, John Oliver, 1916-
And then we heard the thunder. ₍1st ed.₎ New York, Knopf, 1963 ₍°1962₎
485 p. 22 cm.
1. World War, 1939-1945—Fiction. I. Title.
PZ4.K48An 2 62-15560 ‡
Library of Congress ₍5₎

World war, 1939-1945-Peace.

M910 C73 Committee on Africa, the war, and peace aims.
The Atlantic charter and Africa from an American standpoint; a study by the Committee on Africa, the war, and peace aims. The application of the "eight points" of the charter to the problems of Africa, and especially those related to the welfare of the African people living south of the Sahara, with related material on African conditions and needs. New York city, 1942.
xi, 164 p. fold. map. 23ᶜᵐ.
"Selected African bibliography": p. 144-150.
D754.A3C6 1942
(Continued on next card)
42-18394 Revised
₍46c7₎

World war, 1939-1945—Peace.

M301 D853c7 Du Bois, William Edward Burghardt, 1868-
Color and democracy: colonies and peace, by W. E. B. Du Bois ... New York, Harcourt, Brace and company ₍1945₎
5 p. l., 3-143 p. illus. (map, music) 19½ᶜᵐ.
"First edition."
1. World war, 1939-1945—Peace. 2. Colonies. I. Title.
45—35105
Library of Congress D816.D8
₍46r10₎ 940.531

World War, 1939-1945- Personal narratives, American.

M350. H78t Hornsby, Henry Haywood, 1923-
The trey of sevens. Dallas, Mathis, Van Nort ₍1946₎
xvii, 126 p. illus., ports. 20 cm.
"Based on activities of Battery 'C' of the 777th Field Artillery Battalion in the Ninth Army sector."—p. xii.
Map on lining-papers.
1. World War, 1939-1945—Personal narratives, American. 2. U. S. Army. 777th Field Artillery Battalion. 3. World War, 1939-1945—Campaigns—Western. I. Title.
D769.34 777th.H6 940.542 47—27938*
Library of Congress ₍50c₁₎

France
M948
Sa8m

World war, 1939-1945--Personal narratives, French.

Sauvage, Roger, 1917–
Un du Normandie-Niémen. Préf. du colonel Pouyade. ₍Givors₎ A. Martel ₍1950₎
316 p. illus., ports. 21 cm.
"Il a été tiré ... 500 exemplaires sur Alfa Mousse des Papeteries Navarre numérotés 1 à 450 et H-C1 à H-C2. 181."

1. France combattante. Forces aériennes françaises libres. Régiment Normandie-Niémen. 2. World War, 1939–1945—Aerial operations, French. 3. World War, 1939–1945—Personal narratives, French. I. Title.

D788.S39 940.544944 51–17012
Library of Congress ₍1₎

Haiti
M341
B94ce

World war, 1939-1945 -Poetry.

Burr-Reynaud, Frédéric, 1884–
... C'est la guerre... Poèmes. Port-au-Prince, Haïti, Impr. du Collège Vertières ₍194–₎
54 p. 17cm.

1. World war, 1939– —Poetry. I. Title.

44–53605
Library of Congress PQ3949.B8C2
₍2₎ 841.91

M811.5
C46c

World War, 1939-1945 - Poetry.

Christian, Marcus Bruce, 1900–
The common peoples' manifesto of World War II. New Orleans, Les Cenelles Society of Arts & Letters, 1948.
28 p. illus. 24 cm.
"Number 50 of an edition of 105 copies."
CONTENTS.—Proem: Men on horseback.—The common peoples' manifesto, a poem written in five parts.—Apologia: The ballad of rebellious men.

1. World War, 1939–1945—Poetry. I. Title.

PS3505.H87C6 811.5 49–16147*
Library of Congress ₍1₎

M811.08
D28w

World war, 1939-1945-Poetry.

Davidman, Joy, *ed.*
... War poems of the United nations; three hundred poems, one hundred and fifty poets from twenty countries. Sponsored by the League of American writers. Edited by Joy Davidman. New York, Dial press, 1943.
ix, 395 p. 21 cm.
At head of title: The songs and battle cries of a world at war.

1. World war, 1939–1945—Poetry. 2. English poetry—20th cent. 3. American poetry—20th cent. 4. English poetry—Translations from foreign literature. I. Title.

43–18223
Library of Congress D745.2.D3
₍a50w²2₎ 940.5491

M350
An2c

World war, 1939-1945 - Regimental histories - U. S. - 761st tank battalion.

Anderson, Trezzvant W
Come out fighting; the epic tale of the 761st tank battalion, 1942–1945, by Trezzvant W. Anderson. ₍Salzburg, Printed by Salzburger druckerei und verlag₎ 1945₎
xv, 135 p. illus. (incl. ports., maps) fold. tab. 30cm.

1. World war, 1939–1945—Regimental histories—U. S.—761st tank battalion. 2. World war, 1939–1945—Negroes. 3. U. S. Army. 761st tank battalion. 4. World war, 1939–1945—Campaigns—Western. I. Title.

A 46–3127
Harvard univ. Library
for Library of Congress D769.306 761st.A6
₍5₎† 940.542

M910
C73

World war, 1939-1945-Africa.

Committee on Africa, the war, and peace aims.
The Atlantic charter and Africa from an American standpoint; a study by the Committee on Africa, the war, and peace aims. The application of the "eight points" of the charter to the problems of Africa, and especially those related to the welfare of the African people living south of the Sahara, with related material on African conditions and needs. New York city, 1942.
xi, 164 p. fold. map. 23cm.
"Selected African bibliography": p. 144–150.

D754.A34C6 1942
(Continued on next card)
₍46c²7₎ 42–18394 Revised

M350
Af8t

World, War, 1939-1945.

Afro-American Company, Baltimore, Md.
This is our war. Selected stories of six war correspondents who were sent overseas, by the Afro-American newspapers. Baltimore, Philadelphia, Richmond and Newark. Original drawings by Francis Yancey. Baltimore, The Afro-American Co., 1945.

216p. illus. 17½cm.

M350
W38m

World War, 1941-1945.

Webb, Percy R , 1917–
Memoranda of a soldier. New York, Vantage Press, 1961.

61p. 20cm.

M973
R63w

World's great men of color...

Rogers, Joel Augustus, 1880–
World's great men of color ... By J. A. Rogers ... New York, N. Y., J. A. Rogers ₍1946–47₎
2 v. illus. (incl. ports.) 23½cm.
On cover: 3000 B. C. to 1946 A. D.
Paged continuously.
"First edition."
Includes bibliographies.

1. Negro race—Biog. I. Title.

DT18.R59 325.26 46–8140 rev
Library of Congress ₍r47h2₎

M973
R63 w3
1935

World's greatest men and women of African descent.

Rogers, Joel Augustus, 1880–
World's greatest men and women of African descent. Small ed. By J. A. Rogers ... New York city, J. A. Rogers, ©1935.
71 p. illus. (incl. ports.) 23cm.
"Limited edition."

1. Negroes—Biog. I. Title.

CA 35–182 Unrev'd
Library of Congress DT18.R6 1935
₍48b1₎ 325.26

M973
R63w5

World's greatest men of African descent.

Rogers, Joel Augustus, 1880–
World's greatest men of African descent... by J.A. Rogers... N. Y. C., J.A. Rogers, 1931.

iv, 79p. illus. 23cm.

M301
D853w

Worlds of color.

Du Bois, William Edward Burghardt, 1868–
Worlds of color. New York, Mainstream Publishers, 1961.
349 p. 22 cm. (*His* The black flame, a trilogy, book 3)
Portrait of author on book jacket.

1. Negroes. I. Title.

PZ3.D8525Wo 61–3560 ‡
Library of Congress ₍5₎

M796
W89

Worrell, Frank, 1924–
Cricket punch. London, S. Paul; ₍stamped: distributed by Sportshelf, New Rochelle, N. Y., 1959₎
143 p. illus. 22 cm.
Portrait of author on book jacket.

1. Cricket. *Full name:* Frank Maclinne Mortimer Worrell.

GV915.W66A3 796.358 59–4048 ‡
Library of Congress ₍2₎

M398
B75wo

Worser days and better times.

Brewer, John Mason, 1896–
Worser days and better times; the folklore of the North Carolina Negro, by J. Mason Brewer. With pref. & notes by Warren E. Roberts. Drawings by R. L. Toben. Chicago, Quadrangle Books ₍1965₎
192 p. illus. 22 cm.
Bibliography: p. 17–18.

1. Folk-lore, Negro. 2. Folk-lore—North Carolina. I. Title.

GR103.B72 398.0917496 65–18245
Library of Congress ₍66d2₎

M572
A15w

The worshiping tribe.

Allyn, Henry.
The worshiping tribe, by Henry Allyn. Los Angeles, Calif., Midland press ₍©1940₎
2 p. l., 133 p. 19½cm.

1. Ethnology. I. Title.

42–32788
Library of Congress GN335.A55
₍2₎ 572

M973
R24w

Worth fighting for.

Reddick, Lawrence Dunbar, 1910– jt. auth.
Worth fighting for; a history of the Negro in the United States during the Civil War and Reconstruction ₍by₎ Agnes McCarthy and Lawrence Reddick. Illustrated by Colleen Browning. ₍1st ed.₎ Garden City, N. Y., Doubleday, 1965.
118 p. col. illus., ports. 22 cm. (Zenith books)

1. Negroes—History, Juvenile. 2. U. S.—Hist.—Civil War—Negroes—Juvenile literature. ~~I. Reddick, Lawrence Dunbar, 1910– joint author.~~ II. Title.

E185.2.M23 973.715 65–10261
Library of Congress ₍5₎

M811.5
W89s

Wortham, Anne, 1941–
Silence. New York, Pageant Press ₍1965₎

51p. 21cm.
Poems and essays.

I. Title.

M973
L614n

Worthy, William.

Liberation Committee for Africa.
Nationalism, colonialism and the United States one minute to twelve; a forum. First anniversary celebration, June 2, 1961. ₍New York₎ Photo-Offset Process, 1961.

39p. 23cm.

Ghana
M966.7
Ed82

Would you be a Ghana hero?

Edu, John E
Would you be a Ghana hero? Kumasi, J. E. Edu ₍1959₎

30p. ports. 21cm.

British Guiana
M823.91
M69wo

The wounded and the worried.

Mittelholzer, Edgar.
The wounded and the worried. London, Putnam, ©1962.

223p. 21cm.

I. Title.

M616.
W93u3

Wounds.

Wright, Louis Tompkins, 1891-1952.
The use of alkyl-dimethyl-benzyl- ammonium chloride in injury, by Louis T. Wright, and Robert S. Wilkinson. Reprinted from the American journal of surgery, 44:626-630, June 1939.

Inscribed: To my friend Arthur from Louis.

M616
W93pe
Wounds--Treatment.
Wright, Louis Tompkins, 1891-1952.
Penetrating stab wounds of the abdomen and stab wounds of the abdominal wall; A review of 184 consecutive cases, by Louis T. Wright, Robert S. Wilkinson and Joseph L. Gaster.
Reprinted from Surgery, 6:241-260, August 1939.

M323.4
W65d
Wrage, Ernest J ed.
Contemporary forum; American speeches on twentieth-century issues, edited by Ernest J. Wrage [and] Barnet Baskerville. New York, Harper [1962]
376 p. 25 cm.
"To Arthur B. Spingarn in appreciation of his long service to freedom and particularly for his wisdom on many a trying occasion. Affectionately, Roy Wilkins, May, 1966."
~~1. American orations. 2. U. S.—Civilization—Addresses, essays, lectures. 3. U. S.—Pol. & govt.—20th cent.—Addresses, essays, lectures. I. Baskerville, Barnet, joint ed. II. Title.~~
(Continued on next card)
PS668.W7 815.5082 62-10074 ‡
Library of Congress [10]

M323.4
W65d
Wrage, Ernest J ed. Contemporary forum; American speeches on twentieth-century issues. [1962] (Card 2)
Partial contents.- Deep south crisis, by Roy Wilkins.
1. American orations. 2. U.S - Civilization - Addresses, essays, lectures. 3. U.S. - Pol. & govt. - 20th cent. - Addresses, essays, lectures. I. Baskerville, Barnet, joint ed. II. Title.

S. Africa
M896.3
Ab8Wr
A wreath for Udomo.
Abrahams, Peter, 1919-
A wreath for Udomo. [1st American ed.] New York, Knopf, 1956.
356 p. 22 cm.
I. Title.
Full name: Peter Henry Abrahams.
PZ3.A1576Wr 56-5768 ‡
Library of Congress [5715]

S. Africa
M896.3
Ab8wr2
A wreath for Udomo.
Abrahams, Peter, 1919-
A wreath for Udomo. London, Faber and Faber [1956]
309 p. 20 cm.
I. Title.
Full name: Peter Henry Abrahams.
PZ3.A1576Wr 2 56-32194 ‡
Library of Congress [8]

Martinique
M965
F21d4
The wretched of the earth.
Fanon, Frantz, 1925-1961.
The wretched of the earth. Pref. by Jean-Paul Sartre. Translated from the French by Constance Farrington. [Harmondsworth, Eng.] Penguin Books [1967]
255p. 18cm.
Translation of Les deamnés de la terre.
1. France—Colonies—Africa. 2. Algeria—Hist.—1945- 3. Offenses against the person. I. Title.
DT33.F313 301.24 65-14196
Library of Congress [67f3]

Martinique
M965
F21d3
The wretched of the earth.
Fanon, Frantz, 1925-1961.
The wretched of the earth. Pref. by Jean-Paul Sartre. Translated from the French by Constance Farrington. New York, Grove Press [1965, °1963]
255 p. 21 cm.
Translation of Les damnes de la terre.
1. France—Colonies—Africa. 2. Algeria—Hist.—1945- 3. Offenses against the person. I. Title.
DT33.F313 301.24 65-14196
Library of Congress [5]

Senegal
M796.81
Se5
Wrestling.
Sène, Moustapha
La Lutte Sénégalaise [n.p., 1966]
18p. ports. 21cm.
"Comité de participation du Sénégal au premier festival mondial des arts Nègres."
Portrait of author on t.p.
1. Wrestling. I. Title.

M811.5
W931c
Wright, Beatrice.
Color scheme; selected poems. [1st ed.] New York, Pageant Press [1957]
59 p. 21 cm.
I. Title.
PS3545.R16C6 811.5 57-9944 ‡
Library of Congress [2]

M811.5
W93b
Wright, Bruce McMarion, 1917-
From the shaken tower, poems by Bruce McM. Wright. Cardiff [England] William Lewis (printers) 1944.
38p. 18½cm.
1. Poetry.

M813.5
W92m
Wright, Charles Stevenson, 1932-
The messenger. New York, Farrar, Straus [1963]
217 p. 22 cm.
I. Title.
PZ4.W9477Me 63-11709 ‡
Library of Congress [5]

M813.5
W92w
Wright, Charles Stevenson, 1932-
The wig, a mirror image [by] Charles Wright. New York, Farrar, Straus and Giroux [1966]
179 p. 21 cm.
Portrait of author on book jacket.
I. Title.
PZ4.W9477Wi 66-11706
Library of Congress [5]

M910
W93b
Wright, Charlotte (Crogman)
Beneath the Southern Cross; the story of an American bishop's wife in South Africa. [1st ed.] New York, Exposition Press [1955]
184 p. 21 cm.
1. Missions—Africa, South. 2. African Methodist Episcopal Church—Missions. I. Title.
BV3555.W7 [266.78] 276.8 55-11138 ‡
Library of Congress [2]

M811.1
W56poe
Wright, Charlotte Ruth, ed.
Wheatley, Phillis, *afterwards* Phillis Peters, 1753?-1784.
The poems of Phillis Wheatley, edited with introduction and notes by Charlotte Ruth Wright. Philadelphia, Pa., The Wrights, 1930.
xii p., 1 l., 15-104 p. front. (port.) 19cm.
"A few books with contents relating to Phillis Wheatley": p. 99-100.
I. Wright, Charlotte Ruth, ed.
Library of Congress PS866.W5 1930 30-29183
——— Copy 2.
Copyright A 30148 [2] 811.1

M811.5
W671
Wright, Ethel Williams.
Of men and trees; poems. [1st ed.] New York, Exposition Press [1954]
64 p. 21 cm.
I. Title.
PS3545.R34O5 811.5 54-9542 ‡
Library of Congress [2]

M616
W928c
Wright, Jane Cooke
The effect of a folic acid antagonist A-methopterin, on the level of the circulating eosinophils in humans, by Jane C. Wright with technical assistance of Inga Hjelt. Blood, the Journal of Hematology, 1952.
743-748p. 26cm.
Reprinted from Blood, the Journal of Hematology July, 1952.

M616
W928f
Wright, Jane Cooke
Further observations on the use of triethylene melamine in neoplastic diseases, by Jane C. Wright, Aaron Prigot, Louis T. Wright and Isidore Aarons. Chicago, American Medical Association, 1952.
18p. illus. tables 26cm.
Reprinted with additions from the A.M.E. archives of internal medicine, March 1952.
1. Therapeutics. I. Wright, Louis Tompkins, 1891-1952, jt. author.

M616
W928i
Wright, Jane Cooke
In vivo and in vitro effects on chemotherapeutic agents on human neoplastic diseases; A preliminary report on the comparison of the effects of chemotherapeutic agents on human tumors in tissue culture and the effects of each such agent in the patient from whom the tissue for culture was taken, by Jane C. Wright, Jewel I. Plummer, Rosette Spoerri Coidan and Louis T. Wright. New York, Harlem Hospetal bulletin, 1953.
58-63p. 23cm.
Reprinted from the Harlem Hospital bulletin September 1953.
1. Therapeutics. I. Plummer, Jewel I. II. Wright, Louis Tompkins, 1891-1952.

M616
W93
Wright, Louis Tompkins, 1891-1952
Address.
(In: The Louis T. Wright Library of Harlem Hospital. Journal of the National Meidcal Association, July 1952. p. 306-309)

M616
W93a
Wright, Louis Tompkins, 1891-1952.
Anorectogenital lymphogranuloma venereum and granuloma inguinale treated with aureomycin, by Aaron Prigot, Louis T. Wright, Myra A. Logan and others. Reprinted from the New York State journal of medicine, 40:1911-1917, August 15, 1949.
1. Aureomycin. 2. Lymphogranuloma venereum. 3. Medical research.

M616
W93al
Wright, Louis Tompkins, 1891-1952
Antibacterial action of oral aureomycin on the contents of the colon of man, by William I. Metzger, Louis T. Wright, Robert F. Morton. Antibiotics and chemotherapy, 1952.
91-102p. 25cm.
Reprinted from Antibiotics and chemotherapy, v. 2, February 1952.
1. Antibiotics.

M616
W93a2

Wright, Louis Tompkins, 1891-1952.
Aureomycin, a new antibiotic with virucidal properties; A preliminary report on successful treatment in twenty-five cases of lymphogranuloma venereum, by Louis T. Wright, Murray Sanders, and Myra A. Logan. Chicago, American Medical Association, 1948.

12p. tables. 22cm.
Reprinted, with additions, from the Journal of the American Medical Association, 138:408-412, October 9, 1948.

1. Aureomycin. 2. Lymphogranuloma venereum 3. Medical research.

M616
W93a4

Wright, Louis Tompkins, 1891-1952.
Aureomycin as an adjunct in the treatment of major burns, by Louis T. Wright, Joseph A. Tamerin, William I. Metzer, and Arthur L. Garnes. Reprinted from Surgery, 29:763-771, May 1951.

11p. illus. 26cm.

1. Aureomycin. 2. Burns and scalds. 3. Medical research.

Wright, Louis Tompkins, 1891-1952.

M616
H55

Hill, Lyndon M
Aureomycin as an adjunct to excisional surgery in the treatment of cervical tuberculosis lymphadenitis, by Lyndon M. Hill, John W.V. Cordice and Louis T. Wright. Journal of the National Medical Association, 1952.

440-445p. tables 27cm.
Reprinted from the Journal of the National Medical Association, November 1952.

M616
W93au3

Wright, Louis Tompkins, 1891-1952.
Aureomycin hydrochloride in actinomycosis, Louis T. Wright, and Harry J. Lowen. Chicago, American Medical Association, 1950.

5p. illus. 22cm.
Reprinted from the Journal of the American Medical Association, 144:21-22, September 2, 1950.

1. Actinomycosis. 2. Medical research. 3. Aureomycin.

M616
W93au4

Wright, Louis Tompkins, 1891-1952.
Aureomycin in the treatment of cervical tuberculous lymphadenopathy, report of twenty-five cases, by John W. V. Cordice, Lyndon M. Hill and Louis T. Wright. Reprinted from the Harlem hospital bulletin, 3:162-176, March 1951.

1. Aureomycin. 2. Medical research.

M616
W93au5

Wright, Louis Tompkins, 1891-1952
Aureomycin in urinary tract infections, by William I. Metzger, Louis T. Wright, Frank R. De Luca, and others. The Journal of Urology, 1952.

374-388p. 25cm.
Reprinted from the Journal of Urology, v. 67, March 1952.

1. Antibiotics.

M616
W93c

Wright, Louis Tompkins, 1891-1952.
Congenital arteriovenous aneurysm of right upper extremity, by Louis T. Wright, and Arthur C. Logan. Reprinted from the American journal of surgery, new series, 48:658-663, June 1940.

1. Blood vessels. 2. Aneurism. 3. Medical research.

Wright, Louis Tompkins, 1891-1952, joint author.

M616
C81u

Cordice, John Walter Vincent
Use of pyrazinamide (aldinamide) in the treatment of tuberculous lymphadenopathy and draining sinuses, a preliminary report, by John W.V. Cordice, Lyndon M. Hill, and Louis T. Wright. Journal of the National Medical Association, 1953.

87-98p. illus. tables 27cm.
Reprinted from Journal of the National Medical Association, March 1953.

M616
W93d

Wright, Louis Tompkins, 1891-1952.
Deaths from dicumarol, by Louis T. Wright and Milton Rothman. Chicago, American Medical Association, 1951.

6p. graphs. 26cm.
Reprinted with additions from the A.M.A. Archives of surgery, 62:23-28, January 1951.

1. Dicumarol. 2. Medical research.

M610
P19
v.1
no.12

Wright, Louis Tompkins, 1891-1952
Diagnosis and treatment of fractured skulls by Louis T. Wright, Jesse J. Greene and David H. Smith... Reprinted from the Archives of surgery, vol. 27, November 1933.
19p. 25½cm.
1. Fractures 2. Medicine
I. Title
II. Greene, Jesse J.

M616
W93e

Wright, Louis Tompkins, 1891-1952
Effect of esters of parahydroxybenzoic acid on Candida and yeast-like fungo, by William I. Metzger, Louis T. Wright, and James C. Dilorenzo American Medical Association, 1954.

18p. 21cm.
Reprinted from the Journal of the American Medical Association, May??, 1954.

1. Antibiotics.

M616
W93e

Wright, Louis Tompkins, 1891-1952
The effect of formo-cibazol alone and in combination with chlortetracycline on the bacterial flora of the colon of man, by Milton Marmell, James C. DiLorenzo, Louis T. Wright, and William I. Metzger. Antiobiotics & chemotherapy, 1953.

1129-1134p. illus. tables 26cm.
Reprinted from Antibiotics and chemotherapy, November 1953.

1. Antiseptic medication. 2. Therapeutics

M616
W93e2

Wright, Louis Tompkins, 1891-1952.
The effect of sulfathalidine on the bleeding and clotting time of the blood and prolongation reduction by the administration of vitamin K, by Louis T. Wright, Frank R. Cole, and Lyndon M. Hill. Reprinted from Surgery, gynecology and obstetrics, 88:201-208, February 1949.

1. Blood--Coagulation. 2. Sulfathalidine. 3. Medical research.

M616
W93e3

Wright, Louis Tompkins, 1891-1952
An evaluation of abdominal paracentesis as a diagnostic aid in subcutaneous injuries of the peritoneal cavity, by Aaron Prigot, Louis T. Wright and Peter J. Marchisello; New York, The Harlem Hospital Bulletin, 1953.

21-24p. tables 23cm.
Reprinted from the Harlem Hospital Bulletin, June 1953.
1. Abdomen.

M616
W93e5

Wright, Louis Tompkins, 1891-1952.
An evaluation of teropterin therapy in metastatic neoplasms, by Solomon Weintraub, Isidore Arons, Louis T. Wright, and others. Reprinted from New York State journal of medicine, 51:2159-2162, September 15, 1951.

1. Cancer. 2. Teropterin. 3. Medical research.

Wright, Louis Tompkins, 1891-1952, jt.author

M616
W928f

Wright, Jane Cooke
Further observations of the use of triethylene melamine in neoplastic diseases, by Jane C. Wright, Aaron Prigot, Louis T. Wright and Isidore Aarons. Chicago, American Medical Association, 1952.

18p. illus. tables 26cm.
Reprinted with additions from the A.M.E. archives of internal medicine, March 1952.

M616
W93g

Wright, Louis Tompkins, 1891-1952.
Gunshot wounds of the abdomen, by Robert S. Wilkinson, Lyndon M. Hill and Louis T. Wright. Reprinted from Surgery, 19:415-429, March 1946.

15p. tables. 26cm.
Inscribed: To Arthur from Louis.

1. Abdomen--Wounds and injuries. 2. Gunshot wounds. 3. Medical research.

M616
W93h

Wright, Louis Tompkins, 1891-1952
Head injuries by Louis T. Wright.

(In: Scudder, Charles L. Treatment of fractures. Philadelphia, W.B. Saunders, 1938. 25½cm. pp. 417-459).

Reprint of chapter xxii.

1. Head - wounds and injuries.
2. Medical research.

M616
W63i

Wright, Louis Tompkins, 1891-1952.
Incidence of asymptomatic lymphogranuloma venereum in a municipal hospital, by Louis T. Wright, Gerald A. Spencer, and Abraham Oppenheim. Reprinted from American journal of syphillis, gonorrhea, and venereal diseases, 31:282-288, May 1947.

1. Lymphogranuloma venereum. 2. Medical research.

Wright, Louis Tompkins, 1891-1952

M616
W93

The Louis T. Wright Library of Harlem Hospital. Journal of the National Medical Association, 1952.

296-309p.
Reprinted from Journal of the National Medical Association, vol. 44, July 1952.

M616
W93l

Wright, Louis Tompkins, 1891-1952.
Lymphogranulomatous strictures of the rectum; a resume of four hundred and seventy-six cases, by Louis T. Wright, W. Adrian Freeman and Joel V. Bolden. Reprinted from the Archives of Surgery, 53:499-544, November 1946.

Inscribed: To Arthur from Louis.

1. Lymphogranuloma venereum. 2. Medical research.

M616
W93n

Wright, Louis Tompkins, 1891-1952
A new aureomycin dressing, rationale and use in the treatment of surface wounds, by Joseph A. Tamerin, William I. Metzger, and Louis T. Wright. New York, American Journal of Surgery, 1953.

325-330p. 25cm.
Reprinted from the American Journal of Surger September 1953.

1. Antibiotics.

M616
W93py

Wright, Louis Tompkins, 1891-1952.
Pyoderma gangrenosum in chronic non-specific ulcerative colitis treated with aureomycin, by Louis T. Wright, and Selig Strax. Reprinted from the Harlem Hospital bulletin, 1:99-112, December 1948.

1. Aureomycin. 2. Skin-Homeopathic treatment. 3. Medical research.

M616
W93s

Wright, Louis Tompkins, 1891-1952.
Streptokinase-streptodornase in the local treatment of burns, by Frances E. Stein, Louis T. Wright, and Aaron Prigot. New York, The Harlem Hospital bulletin, 1953.

134-146p. 23cm.
Reprinted from the Harlem Hospital bulletin, March 1953.

1. Burns and scalds.

M616
W93ob

Wright, Louis Tompkins, 1891-1952.
Oblique subcervical (reverse intertrochanteric) fractures of the femur. American Orthopaedic Association, 1947.

4p. illus. 26cm.
Reprinted from the Journal of bone and joint surgery 29:707-710, July 1947.

1. Bones. 2. Medical research.

M616
W93r4

Wright, Louis Tompkins, 1891-1952.
Recent advances in antibiotic therapy, by Selig Strax and Louis T. Wright. Reprinted New York State journal of medicine, 49:1797-1801, August 1, 1949.

1. Aureomycin. 2. Antibiotics. 3. Medical research.

M616
W93s

Wright, Louis Tompkins, 1891-1952
Subcutaneous injuries of the urinary tract, by Frank R. DeLuca, Louis T. Wright, Lyndon M. Hill, Norman F. Laskey, and Aaron Prigot. New York, The Harlem Hospital Bulletin, 1953.

64-73p. tables 23cm.
Reprinted from The Harlem Hospital Bulletin, September 1953.

1. Urinary organs. I. Hill, Lyndon M jt. author.

M616
W93op

Wright, Louis Tompkins, 1891-1952.
Operative reduction and fixation by means of a specially devised blade plate for the treatment of supracondylar and T fractures of the lower end of the femur and T fractures of the upper end of the tibia, preliminary report. Reprinted from the Harlem Hospital bulletin, 1:17-24, June 1948.

1. Bones. 2. Medical research.

M616
W93r6

Wright, Louis Tompkins, 1891-1952.
Rectal strictures due to lymphogranuloma venereum, with especial reference to Pauchet's excision operation, by Louis T. Wright, Benjamin N. Berg, Joel V. Bolden and W. Adrian Freeman. Reprinted from Surgery, Gynecology and Obstetrics, 82:449-462, April 1946.

Inscribed: To Arthur from Louis, May 10, 1946.

1. Lymphogranuloma venereum. 2. Medical research.

M616.
W93s

Wright, Louis Tompkins, 1891-1952.
Sulfathalidine in low postoperative fistulas of the ileum, by Louis T. Wright, and Frank R. Cole. Reprinted from the American journal of surgery. 75:852-853, June 1948.

1. Sulfathalidine. 2. Intestines. 3. Medical research.

M616
W93os

Wright, Louis Tompkins, 1891-1952.
Osseous changes associated with lymphogranuloma venereum, by Louis T. Wright, and Myra Logan. Reprinted from the Archives of surgery, 39:108-121, July 1939.

1. Lymphogranuloma venereum. 2. Medical research.

M616
W93r7

Wright, Louis Tompkins, 1891-1952
The role of antibiotics in surgery. New York, The Harlem Hospital Bulletin, 1952.

37-48p. 23cm.
Reprinted from The Harlem Hospital Bulletin, v.5, no.2.

1. Antibiotics.

M616
W93t3

Wright, Louis Tompkins, 1891-1952.
Traumatic rupture of the intestines without penetrating wounds, by Louis T. Wright, Aaron Prigot, and Frances E. Stein. Reprinted from the Harlem Hospital bulletin, 1:116-139, December 1948.

1. Intestines. 2. Medical research.

M616
W93pe

Wright, Louis Tompkins, 1891-1952.
Penetrating stab wounds of the abdomen and stab wounds of the abdominal wall; A review of 184 consecutive cases, by Louis T. Wright, Robert S. Wilkinson and Joseph L. Gaster. Reprinted from Surgery, 6:241-260, August 1939.

1. Wounds--Treatment. 2. Abdomen--Wounds. I. Wilkinson, Robert Shaw, 1899- . II. Gaster, Joseph L.

M616
W93r

Wright, Louis Tompkins, 1891-1952
Rupture of hollow and solid viscera in the newborn, an analysis of twenty-five cases, by Frances E. Stein and Louis T. Wright. New York, The Harlem Hospital Bulletin, 1953.

32-57p. 23cm.
Reprinted from the Harlem Hospital Bulletin, September 1953.

1. Hernia.

M616
W93t2

Wright, Louis Tompkins, 1891-1952.
Traumatic rupture of the liver without penetrating wounds, a study of thirty-two cases. Chicago, American Medical Association, 1947.

20p. tables. 27cm.
Reprinted from the Archives of surgery, 54:613-632, June 1947.

1. Liver. 2. Medical research.

M616
W93pr

Wright, Louis Tompkins, 1891-1952
The practical aspects and the differentiation between lymphogranuloma venereum and cancer. New York, The Harlem Hospital Bulletin, 1953.

74-77p. 23cm.
Reprinted from the Harlem Hospital Bulletin, September 1953.

1. Cancer.

M616
W93s

Wright, Louis Tompkins, 1891-1952.
Sensitivities of freshly-isolated microorganisms to seven antibiotics with special emphasis on carbomycin and erythromycin preliminary report by Boris A. Shidlovsky, Milton Marmell, Aaron Prigot and Louis T. Wright. New York, Medical Encyclopedia, Inc., 1954.

548-559p. tables 26cm.
Reprinted from Antibiotics annual, 1953-1954.

1. Antibiotics.

M616
W93t

Wright, Louis Tompkins, 1891-1952
Traumatic subcutaneous rupture of abdominal viscera, by Aaron Prigot and Louis T. Wright. New York, The Harlem Hospital Bulletin, 1953.

104-111p. tables 23cm.
Reprinted from The Harlem Hospital Bulletin, December 1952.

1. Hernia.

M616
W93pr

Wright, Louis Tompkins, 1891-1952.
Prevention of postoperative adhesions in rabbits with streptococcal metabolites, Louis T. Wright, David H. Smith, Milton Rothman and others. Society for Experimental Biology and Medicine, 1950.

[3]p. illus. 25cm.
Reprinted from Proceedings of the Society.

1. Adhesion. 2. Medical research.

M616
W93s

Wright, Louis Tompkins, 1891-1952
Some experiences with pilonidal cysts. New York, The Harlem Hospital Bulletin, 1952.

18-26p. illus. 23cm.
Reprinted from the Harlem Hospital Bulletin, June 1952.

1. Cysts.

M616
W93t

Wright, Louis Tompkins, 1891-1952
The treatment of acute gonorrhea in male patients with an aureomycin-triple sulfonamide combination, by Louis T. Wright and William I. Metzger. St. Louis, American Journal of Syphilis, Gonorrhea, and Venereal Diseases, 1953.

7p. tables 26cm.
Reprinted from the American Journal of Syphilis, Gonorrhea, and Venereal Diseases, May 1953.

1. Therapeutics

M616
W93t5
Wright, Louis Tompkins, 1891-1952.
Treatment of acute peritonitis with aureomycin, by Louis T. Wright, William I. Metzger, and Edward B. Shapero. Reprinted from the American journal of surgery, 78:15-22, July 1949.

1. Aureomycin. 2. Peritonitis. 3. Medical research.

M616
W93t7
Wright, Louis Tompkins, 1891-1952.
The treatment of lymphogranuloma venereum and granuloma inguinale in humans with aureomycin, by L. T. Wright, M. Sanders, M. A. Logan, and others. Reprinted from the Annals of the New York Academy of Sciences, 51:318-330, November 30, 1948.

1. Aureomycin. 2. Lymphogranuloma venereum. 3. Medical research.

M616
W93t8
Wright, Louis Tompkins, 1891-1952.
Treatment of non-specific ulcerative colitis with aureomycin, by Louis T. Wright, Selig Strax, and Jerome A. Marks. Reprinted from the Annals of western medicine and surgery, November 1950.

1. Intestines. 2. Aureomycin. 3. Medical research.

M616
W93t
Wright, Louis Tompkins, 1891-1952
The treatment of soft tissue infections with an aureomycin-triple sulfonamide combination, by James C. DiLorenzo, Louis T. Wright, and William I. Metzger. New York, Medical Society of the State of New York, 1954.

1631-1633p. tables 25cm.
Reprinted from the New York Journal of Medicine, June 1, 1954.

1. Antibiotic

M616
W93u3
Wright, Louis Tompkins, 1891-1952.
The use of alkyl-dimethyl-benzyl-ammonium chloride in injury, by Louis T. Wright, and Robert S. Wilkinson. Reprinted from the American journal of surgery, 44:626-630, June 1939.

Inscribed: To my friend Arthur from Louis.

1. Wounds. 2. Medical research.

M616
W93u5
Wright, Louis Tompkins, 1891-1952.
Use of teropterin in neoplastic disease; a preliminary clinical report, by S. P. Lehv, L. T. Wright, S. Weintraub, and I. Arons. Reprinted from the Transaction of the New York Academy of Sciences, 10:75-81, January 1948.

75-81p. tables, graphs, illus. 25cm.
Inscribed: To Arthur from Louis.

1. Teropterin. 2. Cancer. 3. Medical research.

M616
W93v
Wright, Louis Tompkins, 1891-1952
A vehicle for the tropical use of certain therapeutic agents, by Aaron Prigot, Louis T. Wright, and Eugene T. Quash. Reprinted from Antibiotics and chemotherapy, 1953.

418-420p. illus. 25cm.
Reprinted from the Antibiotics and chemotherapy, April 1953.

1. Therapeutics. I. Quash, Eugene T. jt. aurhor.

Wright, Louis Tompkins, 1891-1952.
M616
W93
Cobb, William Montague, 1904-
Louis Tompkins Wright, 1891-1952. Journal of the National Medical Association, 1953.

130-148p. illus. 27cm.
"Scientific publications by Dr. Wright and associates": pp.146-148.
Reprinted from the Journal of the National Medical Association, March 1953.

Wright, Louis Tompkins, 1891-1952.
M616
P73
Plummer, Jewel I.
Triethylene melamine in vitro studies; I. Mitotic alterations produced in chick fibroblast tissue cultures, by Jewel I. Plummer, Louis T. Wright, Grace Antikajian, and Solomon Weintraub. Cancer Research, Inc., 1952.

796-800p. tables graphs 27cm.
Reprinted from Cancer Research, November 1952.

Wright, Louis Tompkins, 1891-1952.
M616
W9281
Wright, Jane Cooke
In vivo and in vitro effects on chemotherapeutic agents on human neoplastic diseases; A preliminary report on the comparison of the effects of chemotherapeutic agents on human tumors in tissue culture and the effects of each such agent in the patient from whom the tissue for culture was taken, by Jane C. Wright, Jewel I. Plummer, Rosette Spoerri Coidan and Louis T. Wright. New York, Harlem Hospital bulletin, 1953.

58-63p. 23cm.
Reprinted from the Harlem Hospital bulleti September 1953.

M370
W92
Wright, *Mrs.* Marion Manola (Thompson) 1904-1962.
The education of Negroes in New Jersey ₍by₎ Marion M. Thompson Wright ... New York, Teachers college, Columbia university, 1941.

ix p., 1 l., 227 p. 23½cm. (Teachers college, Columbia university. Contributions to education, no. 815)

Issued also as thesis (PH. D.) Columbia university.
Bibliography: p. 212-227.

1. Negroes—Education. 2. Negroes—New Jersey. I. Title.

41-19695 Revised
Library of Congress LC2802.N5W7 1941
₍r42i3₎ 371.97409749

M974.9
W93n
Wright, Marion Manola (Thompson), 1904-1962.
New Jersey laws and the Negro. Washington D.C., The Association for the Study of Negro Life and History, 1943.

45p. 24cm.
Reprinted from the Journal of Negro History. 28, no.2. April, 1943.
Inscribed by author: To Arthur B. Spingarn, Marion Thompson Wright, May 1943.

1. Laws and legislation 2. New Jersey
I. title

MSS
W93
Wright, Nathan.
Black power~~, and urban unrest; creative possibilities. ₍1st ed.₎~~ New York, Hawthorn Books ₍1967₎
~~200 p. 22 cm.~~ 185 leaves. 28cm.
~~Bibliographical references included in "Notes" (p. 195)~~
"Uncorrected proofs."

1. ~~Negroes~~—Civil rights. 2. ~~U. S.~~—Race question. 3. ~~Negroes~~—Psychology. I. Title.

E185.615.W7 323.4'0973 67-15556
Library of Congress ₍7₎

M323.4
W934
Wright, Nathan.
Black power and urban unrest; creative possibilities. ₍1st ed.₎ New York, Hawthorn Books ₍1967₎
200 p. 22 cm.
Bibliographical references included in "Notes" (p. 195)

1. Negroes—Civil rights. 2. U. S.—Race question. 3. Negroes—Psychology. I. Title.

E185.615.W7 323.4'0973 67—15556
Library of Congress ₍68t10₎

M265.3
W93
Wright, Nathan.
One bread, one body. Foreword by James A. Pike. Greenwich, Conn., Seabury Press, 1962.
148 p. 22 cm.
Includes bibliographies.

1. Lord's Supper—Anglican Communion. I. Title.

BX5949.C5W73 265.3 62-9618 ‡
Library of Congress ₍5₎

M309.1
W934
Wright, Nathan.
Ready to riot. ₍1st ed.₎ New York, Holt, Rinehart and Winston ₍1968₎
148 p. illus., maps. 22 cm.
Bibliographical footnotes.

1. Newark, N. J.—Soc. condit. 2. Negroes—Newark, N. J. I. Title.

HN80.N685W74 309.1'749'32 68-12218
Library of Congress ₍15-2₎

M252
W93r
Wright, Nathan.
The riddle of life, and other sermons. Boston, Bruce Humphries ₍1952₎
98 p. 24 cm.

1. Protestant Episcopal Church in the U. S. A.—Sermons. 2. Sermons, American. I. Title.

BX5937.W7R5 252.03 52-14342 ‡
Library of Congress ₍3₎

M813.08
Sch81
Wright, Richard, 1908-1960
Almos a man.

Pp. 107-118.

In: Schulman, L. M., ed. Come out the wilderness. New York, Popular Library, 1965.

Ghana
M966.7
W83p
Wright, Richard, 1908-1960
American angles.

pp. 252-253.
In: Pageant of Ghana, by Freda Wolfson. 1958.

I. Title.

M810.8
Am29
Wright, Richard, 1908-1960
Big boy leaves home.

(In: The American caravan, 1936. New York, The Macaulay company, 1936. 22cm. pp. 124-158).

M813.5
W93a
Wright, Richard, 1908-1960
Black boy, a record of childhood and youth by Richard Wright. New York and London, Harper & brothers ₍1945₎
5 p. l., 3-228 p., 1 l. 21cm.
"First edition."
Portrait on jacket.

I. Title.
₍Full name: Richard Nathaniel Wright₎
Library of Congress PS3545.R815Z5 45—2254
₍47b7₎ 928.1

M813.5
W93ab2
Wright, Richard, 1908-1960.
Black boy; a record of childhood and youth by Richard Wright. [London] Victor Gollancz, [1947]

296p. 18cm. (Readers Union)

I. Title.

M813.5
W93ab
Wright, Richard, 1908-1960.
Black boy; a record of childhood and youth by Richard Wright. [New York] New American Library [1945]

207p. 18cm. (Signet Books)
Pocket book edition
"Complete and unabridged."

I. Title.

M813.5
W93bl
Wright, Richard, 1908-1960
Black power; a record of reactions in a land of pathos. [1st ed.] New York, Harper [1954]

358 p. illus. 22 cm.

1. Gold Coast—Descr. & trav. 2. Gold Coast—Soc. condit. I. Title.
Full name: Richard Nathaniel Wright.

DT511.W7 916.67 54—10082 ‡
Library of Congress [55f15]

M813.5
W93bL2
Wright, Richard, 1908- 1960
Black power; a record of reactions in a land of pathos. [1st ed.] ~~New York, Harper [1954]~~ London, D. Dobson [1954]

358 p. illus. 22 cm.

1. Gold Coast—Descr. & trav. 2. Gold Coast—Soc. condit. I. Title.
Full name: Richard Nathaniel Wright.

DT511.W7 916.67 54-10082 rev ‡
Library of Congress [r56b²14]

M813.5
W93b
Wright, Richard, 1908-1960
Bright and morning star by Richard Wright. New York, International publishers [c1938]

48p. 20cm.

I. Title.

M813.08
C554
Wright, Richard, 1908-1960.
Bright and morning star
Pp. 75-108

In: Clarke, John Henrik, ed. American Negro short stories. New York, Hill and Wang, 1966.

U.S.
M960
W93c
Wright, Richard, 1908-1960
The color curtain; a report on the Bandung Conference. Foreword by Gunnar Myrdal. [1st ed.] Cleveland, World Pub. Co. [°1956]

221 p. 22 cm.

1. Asian-African Conference, Bandung, Java, 1955. I. Title.
Full name: Richard Nathaniel Wright.

DS35.A8 1955d 950 56-5734 ‡
Library of Congress [30]

U. S.
M960
W93c3
Wright, Richard, 1908- 1960
The colour curtain, a report on the Bandung conferences. Foreword by Gunnar Myrdal. London, Dobson [1956]

187p. illus., ports. 21cm.

1. Asian-African conference, Bandung, Java, 1955. I. Title.

M813.5
W93in
Wright, Richard, 1908-1960
De la inocencia a la pesadilla. (Savage holiday). Traduccion de Leon Mirlas. Buenos Aires, Editorial Sudamericana, 1956.

252p. 18½cm.

I. Title. II. Title: Savage holiday.

M813.5
W93L2
Wright, Richard, 1908-1960.
Den lange drøm [The long dream] pa Dansk ved Kurt Kreutzfeld. [København] Gyldendal, 1959.

330p. 23cm.

Written in Danish.

1. Title. II. Title: The long dream.

M813.5
W93d
Wright, Richard, 1908-1960
Le dieu de mascarde (savage holiday); roman. Traduit de l'américan par Jane Fillion. Paris, Les Éditions Mondiales [1955]

269p. 21cm.

I. Title.

M810.8
C884
1945
Wright, Richard, 1908-1960
Early days in Chicago.

(In: Cross section ... A collection of new American writing, 1945. New York, L. B. Fischer, 1945. p. 306-342).

M813.5
W93ec
Wright, Richard, 1908-1960
Écoute, homme blanc (White man, listen!) Traduit de l'Américan par Dominique Guillet. Paris, Calmann-Levy, Éditeurs, 1959.

225p. 19cm.

1. Race relations. I. Title. II. Title: White man, listen!

M813.5
W93ei
Wright, Richard, 1908-1960
Eight men. [1st ed.] Cleveland, World Pub. Co. [1961]

250 p. 21 cm.
Short stories.
Portrait of author on book jacket.

I. Title.
Full name: Richard Nathaniel Wright.

PZ3.W9352Ei 61—5636 ‡
Library of Congress [61k10]

M813.5
W93ei2
Wright, Richard, 1908-1960
Eight men. New York, Avon Book Division, [1961]

191p.
Short stories.

I. Title.

M813.5
W93e
Wright, Richard, 1908-1960
Un enfant du pays (Native son) Roman tr. de l'américain par Hélène Bokanowski et Marcel Duhamel. Paris, A. Michel [1947]

488 p. 21 cm.

I. Title.
Full name: Richard Nathaniel Wright.

PS3545.R815N252 48-14096*‡
© Éditions Albin Michel; 10Jun47; AF4948.

Library of Congress [1]

M813.5
W93en
Wright, Richard, 1908-1960
Les enfants de l'Oncle Tom (Uncle Tom's children) Tr. de l'américain par Marcel Duhamel. Paris, A. Michel [1947, °1946]

250 p. 19 cm.

I. Title.
Full name: Richard Nathaniel Wright.

PS3545.R815U53 48-14180*‡
© Albin Michel; 15Sep47; AF4967.

Library of Congress [1]

M813.5
W93enl
Wright, Richard, 1908-1960.
Les enfants de l'oncle Tom (Uncle Tom's children). Traduit de l'américain par Marcel Duhamel suivi de Là-bas, près de la Rivière traduit par Boris Vian. [Paris, Albin Michel, °1946]

241p. 17cm. (Le livre de poche)
Pocket book edition.

I. Title. II. Là-bas, près de la Rivière.

M813.5
W93enl
Wright, Richard, 1908-1960.
Les enfants de l'oncle Tom (Uncle Tom's children). Traduit de l'américain par Marcel Duhamel suivi de Là-bas, près de la Rivière traduit par Boris Vian. [Paris] Albin Michel [c1946]

241p. 17cm. (Le livre de poche)
Pocket book edition.

I. Title. II. Là-bas, près de la Rivière.

M813.5
W93es
Wright, Richard, 1908-1960
¡Escucha, hombre blanco! (White man, listen!) Traducción de Floreal Mazía. Buenos Aires, Editorial Sudamericana, 1959.

178p. 20½cm.

1. Race relations. I. Title. II. Title: ¡Escucha, hombre blanco!

M813.5
W929e
Wright, Richard, 1908-1960
[Essay on communism].

(In: The God that failed ... New York, Harper, [1950, c1949] 22cm. pp. 115-162)

1. Communism
I. Title--The God that failed.

M810.8
M77p Wright, Richard, 1908-1960
The ethics of living Jim Crow.

(In: Moon, Bucklin, ed. Primer for white folks. Garden City, N. Y. Doubleday, Doran, 1945. 21½cm. pp. 252-262).

M810.8
F31 Wright, Richard, 1908-1960
The ethics of living Jim Crow.

(In: Federal Writers' Project. American stuff; an anthology of prose & verse... New York, The Viking press, 1937. pp. 39-52.)

M813.5
W93ex Wright, Richard, 1908-1960
El extraño. (The outsider). Traducción de León Mirlas. Buenos Aires, Editorial Sudamericana, 1954.

615p. 18½cm.

I. Title. II. Title: The Outsider.

M813.5
W93i2 Wright, Richard, 1908-1960
I figli dello Zio Tom. Einaudi, 1949.

318p. cm.
Titolo originale: Uncle Tom's children.

I. Title. II. Uncle Tom's children.

M813.5
W93f Wright, Richard, 1908-1960
Fire and cloud [drama].

(In: Kozlenko, William, ed. American scenes. N.Y., John Day, 1941. 21cm. p.51-71.)

1. Drama. I. Title.

M813.5
W93fi Wright, Richard, 1908-1960.
Fishbelly (The long dream). Traduit de l'Americain par Helene Bokanowski. Paris, Julliard [1960]

459p. port. 21cm. (Les lettres nouvelles, 3)

I. Title.

Wright, Richard, 1908-1960.
Foreword, pp. vii-xii.

M784
O13b Oliver, Paul.
Blues fell this morning; the meaning of the blues. With a foreword by Richard Wright. London, Cassell and Co., Ltd., 1960.

355p. 21½cm.

M813.5
W93f Wright, Richard, 1908-1960
[Foreword to - Letters from the Tombs].

(In: Schappes, Morris Urman. Letters from the Tombs, ed. by Louis Lerman... New York, Schappes Defense Committee, [1941]. p.v-vi)

M813.5
W93Law3 Wright, Richard, 1908-1960.
Glad dag i Chicago [Lawd today. Omslag] Gyldendals Tranebøger, 1965.

243p. 18½cm.
Written in Danish.

I. Title.

M813.5
W93he Wright, Richard, 1908-1960
Heidnisches Spanien [Pagan Spain] Hamburg, Classen Verlag, 1958.

332p. 22½cm.

I. Title.

M813.5
W93h Wright, Richard, 1908-1960
How "Bigger" was born; the story of Native son, one of the most significant novels of our time, and how it came to be written [by] Richard Wright. [New York] Harper & brothers [°1940]

2 p. l., 39 p. 20½cm.
"First edition." K-P

1. Wright, Richard, 1908- Native son. I. Title.
[Full name: Richard Nathaniel Wright]

Library of Congress PS3545.R815N35 40-35061
——— Copy 2.
Copyright [4] 813.5

M813.5
W931 Wright, Richard, 1908-1960.
Introduction.

(In: Nutt, Howard. Special laughter, poems. Prairie City, Illinois, Press of James A. Decker, 1940. pp. ix-xii)

M813.5
W93k Wright, Richard, 1908-1960.
De kleurbarriere; een verslag van de Conferentie van Bandung. s'Gravenhage, Uitgeverij W. van Hoeve, 1957.

204p. ports. 21cm.
Title: The color curtain.

I. Title.

M813.5
W93 la Wright, Richard, 1908-1960.
De lange droom; roman. Leiden, A. W. Sijthoff, 1959.

380p. 19½cm.
Title: The long dream.

M813.5
W93Law2 Wright, Richard, 1908-1960.
Lawd today. [London] Anthony Blond [1965]

219p. 21cm.

I. Title.

PZ3.W9352Law 63—11769 ‡
Library of Congress [67f5]

M813.5
W93Law Wright, Richard, 1908-1960.
Lawd today. New York, Walker [1963]

189 p. 22 cm.

I. Title. Full name: Richard Nathaniel Wright.

PZ3.W9352Law 63-11769 ‡
Library of Congress [5]

M813.5
W931 Wright, Richard, ~~1908~~ 1909-
The long dream, a novel. [1st ed.] Garden City, N. Y., Doubleday, 1958.

384 p. 22 cm.

I. Title. Full name: Richard Nathaniel Wright.

PZ3.W9352Lo 58—12059 ‡
Library of Congress [58f10]

M810.8
C884
1944 Wright, Richard, 1909-
The man who lived underground, novelette.

(In: Cross section ... A collection of new American writing, 1944. New York, L. B. Fischer, 1944. p. 58-102).

M813.5
W93a2 Wright, Richard, 1909-
Mi vida de Negro, de la miñez y la juventud, tr. de Clara Diament. Buenos Aires, Editorial Sudamericana. [1946].

391p. 19cm.
Spanish translation of Black boy.

I. Title.

M813.5
W93n6 Wright, Richard, 1908-1960
Native son. New York, New American Library, 1950.

413p. 18cm. (Signet books)

Pocket book edition.

I. Title.

M813.5
W93n7 Wright, Richard, 1908-1960
Native son (the biography of a young American) a play in ten scenes by Paul Green and Richard Wright, from the novel by Richard Wright. A Mercury production by Orson Welles, presented by Orson Welles and John Houseman. New York and London, Harper & brothers [°1941]

ix p., 1 l., 148 p. front. 21cm. Pictures on jacket.
Includes songs with music.
"First edition."

I. °Green, Paul, 1894- joint author. II. Title.
[Full name: Richard Nathaniel Wright]

Library of Congress PS3545.R815N25 41-6481
[12] 812.5

M813.5 W93n4 Wright, Richard, 1908-1960
Native son, by Richard Wright ... New York and London, Harper & brothers, 1940.
xi, 359 p. 21 cm.
"First edition." A-P

I. Title.

Library of Congress PZ3.W9352Nat ₍45o1₎ 40—4862

M813.5 W93o 1954 Wright, Richard, 1908-1960
The outsider. New York, New American Library, 1954.
384p. 18cm. (Signet giant. S1114)
Pocket book edition.
"Complete and unabridged."

I. Title

M323 N78t Wright, Richard, 1908-1960.
Psychiatry goes to Harlem.
pp. 348-354.
In: Twice a year, ed. by Dorothy Norman, 1946.

1. Harlem, New York

M813.5 W93n9 Wright, Richard, 1908-1960
Native son. New York, Grosset & Dunlap Publishers, 1940.
359p. 19½cm.

I. Title.

M813.5 W93ou Wright, Richard, 1908-1960.
The outsider. ₍New York₎ New American Library ₍c1953₎
384p. 18cm. (Signet Books)
Pocket book edition
"Complete and unabridged."

I. Title.

M813.5 Wright, Richard, 1908-1960. Preface.
Himes, Chester B , 1909-
La croisade de Lee Gordon (Lonely Crusade): roman. Preface de Richard Wright. Traduit de l'Americain par Yves Malartic. ₍Paris₎ Corrêa ₍c1952₎
384p. 19cm. (La chemin de la vie)

M813.5 W93n3 Wright, Richard, 1908-1960.
Native son. London, Victor Gollancz, 1940.
459p. 20cm.

I. Title.

M813.5 W93o Wright, Richard, 1908-1960
The outsider. ₍1st ed.₎ New York, Harper ₍1953₎
405 p. 22 cm.

I. Title. *Full name:* Richard Nathaniel Wright.

PZ3.W9352Ou 53-5383 ‡
Library of Congress ₍10₎

M813.5 W93p Wright, Richard, 1908-1960
Puissance noire. Traduit de l'Américain par Roger Giroux. Paris, Corrêa, Buchet-Chastel, 1955.
400p. 19cm.
Translation of "Black Power."

1. Gold Coast.

M813.5 W93n5 Wright, Richard, 1908-1960
Native son. New York, Grosset & Dunlap, 1940.
359p. 21cm.

I. Title.

M813.5 W93p Wright, Richard, 1908-1960
Pagan Spain. ₍1st ed.₎ New York, Harper ₍1957₎
241 p. 22 cm.

1. Spain—Descr. & trav.—1951- I. Title.
Full name: Richard Nathaniel Wright.
DP43.W7 914.6 56-11091 ‡
Library of Congress ₍20₎

M813.5 W93a2 Wright, Richard, 1908-1960
Ragazzo Negro. Einaudi, 1952.
359p. 19cm.
"Titolo originale: Black boy.
I. Title. I. t.- Black boy.

M813.5 W93n2 Wright, Richard, 1908-1960
Native son. New York, Harper, 1939.
134 (i.e. 268)p. 30cm.
Inscription: Kind wishes. Paul Robeson.
Galley proof.

I. Title.

M813.5 W93pa Wright, Richard, 1908-1960.
Pagan Spain. London, Bodley Head, ₍c1957₎
191p. 22cm.

1. Spain - Descr & trav. 1951- I. Title.

M813.5 W93s Wright, Richard, 1908-1960.
Sangre Negra (Native son). Traducción de Pedro Lecuona. Buenos Aires, Editorial Sudamericana, 1959.
567p. 18½cm.

I. Title. II. Title: Native son.

M813.5 W93ne Wright, Richard, 1908-1960
El Negrito. (The Black boy). Madrid, Afrodisio Aguado, S. A., 1957
345p. 19cm.
Portrait of author on book jacket.

I. Title. II. Title: El Negrito.

M813.5 W93n8 Wright, Richard, 1908-1960
Paura, romanzo. III edizione. Roma, Bompiani, 1951.
582p. 20cm.
Titolo originale: Native son.
I. Title. II. t.Paura.

M813.5 W93s Wright, Richard, 1908-1960
... Sangre negra ("Native son") Traducción de Pedro Lecuona. Buenos Aires, Editorial sudamericana ₍1941₎
4 p. l., 11-566, ₍1₎ p., 2 l. 18ᶜᵐ. (*On cover:* Colección Horizonte)

I. Lecuona, Pedro, tr. II. Title.
₍*Full name:* Richard Nathaniel Wright₎
42-18505
Library of Congress PS3545.R815N253 ₍3₎

M813.5 W93u4 Wright, Richard, 1908-1960
Onkel Toms børn ₍Uncle Tom's children₎ Pa dansk ven Kurt Kreutzfeld. ₍København₎ Gyldendal, 1957.
245p. 21cm.
Written in Danish.

I. Title.

M813.08 W67 Wright, Richard, 1908-1960
The plea.
Pp. 142 -160.

In: Williams, John Alfred, ed. The angry blacks. New York. Lancer Books, 1962.

M813.5 W93sa Wright, Richard, 1908-1960
Savage holiday. New York, Avon Publications 1954.
220p. 18cm. (Avon red & gold edition T-86)
Pocket book edition.
"Complete and unabridged."

I. Title

M813.5
W93a

Wright, Richard, 1908-1960
Schwarz unter weiss fern von Afrika. (12 million black voices). Frankfurt am Main, Europaische verlagsanstalt GMBH., 1948.

unnumb. leaves, illus. 23½cm.

M813.5
W93n45

Wright, Richard, 1908-1960
Søn af de sorte [Native son] paa Dansk ved Tom Kristensen. Kobenhavn, Gyldendalske Boghandel, 1942.

298p. 21½cm.

I. Title.

M813.5
W93n8

Wright, Richard, 1908-1960
Son av sitt land. Stockholm. Bonniers Folkbibliotek, 1952.

416p. 18cm.
Swedish translation of - Native Son

M813.5
W93a5

Wright, Richard, 1908-1960
Sort ungdom [Native son. Kobenhavn] Gyldendal, 1961.

247p. 21½cm.

I. Title.

M813.5
W93a3

Wright, Richard, 1908-1960
Sort ungdom. Paa Dansk ved Tom Kristensen. Kǿ benhavn, Glydendalske Boghandel Nordisk verlag, 1947.

275p. 20cm.
Danish translation of Black Boy.

M813.5
W93ol

Wright, Richard, 1908-1960
... Le transfuge (The outsider) Traduit de l'Americain par Guy de Montlaur. Roman. Paris, Gallimard, 1955.

488p. 21cm.

French translation of-The outsider.

M813.5
W93t

Wright, Richard, 1908-1960
12 million black voices; a folk history of the Negro in the United States; text by Richard Wright, photo-direction by Edwin Rosskam. New York, The Viking press, 1941.

152 p. illus. 26cm.

"First published in October 1941."

1. ~~Negroes~~—Moral and social conditions. I. *Rosskam, Edwin, 1903- II. Title.

[Full name: Richard Nathaniel Wright]

41—25589

Library of Congress E185.6.W9
[45n2] 325.260073

M813.5
W93un

Wright, Richard, 1908-1960.
Uncle Tom's children. 1st ed. New York, Penguin Books [1947]

185p. 18cm. (Penguin Books)
Pocket book edition.
"Complete and unabridged."

I. Title.

M813.5
W93u
1947

Wright, Richard, 1908-1960
Uncle Tom's children. New York, Penguin Books, 1947.

185p. 18cm.
Pocket book edition.

I. Title.

M813.5
W93u

Wright, Richard, 1908-1960
Uncle Tom's children, five long stories by Richard Wright. New York and London, Harper & brothers [c1938]

xxx, 384 p. 21cm.

CONTENTS.—The ethics of living Jim Crow; an autobiographical sketch.—I. Big boy leaves home.—II. Down by the riverside.—III. Long black song.—IV. Fire and cloud.—V. Bright and morning star.

First edition of new edition.

I. Title.

[Full name: Richard Nathaniel Wright]

40-29877

Library of Congress PZ3.W935Ua 2
[2]

M323
N78t

Wright, Richard, 1908-1960.
Urban misery in an American City; juvenile delinquency in Harlem.

pp. 339-346.
In: Twice a year, ed. by Dorothy Norman. 1946.

1. Juvenile delinquency-Harlem, N.Y. 2. Harlem, N.Y.-Juvenile delinquency. 3. New York (City)-Juvenile delinquency. I. Title.

M813.5
W93w

Wright, Richard, 1908-1960
White man, listen! [1st ed.] Garden City, N. Y., Doubleday, 1957.

190 p. 22 cm.

1. Negro race. I. Title.

Full name: Richard Nathaniel Wright.

HT1581.W7 *301.451 325.26 57—9702 ‡

Library of Congress [58x15]

M323
N78t

Wright, Richard, 1908-1960.
A world view of the American Negro.

pp. 346-348.
A letter.
In: Twice a year, ed. by Dorothy Norman. 1946.

I. Title.

M813.5
W93z

Wright, Richard, 1908-1960.
Zoon van Amerika. Vertaald door Mevr. Mr. A. W. Ebbinge - Van Nes. Den Haag, Zuid-Hollandsche Uitgevers Maatschappij [n.d.]

383p. 23cm.

I. Title.

M813.5
W93z

Wright, Richard, 1908-1960.
Zwarte Kracht. Terugblik op een verblijf Aan De Goudkust. Leiden, A. S. Sijthoff's Uitgeversmij N. V., 1956.

310p. 23cm.
Title: Black power.

Wright, Richard, 1908-1960

M813.5
E14r

The Antioch review.
The Antioch review anthology; essays, fiction, poetry, and reviews from the Antioch review. Edited by Paul Bixler. [1st ed.] Cleveland, World Pub. Co. [1953]

470p. 22cm.

Wright, Richard, 1908-1960
Native son.

M813.5
W93h

Wright, Richard, 1909-
How "Bigger" was born; the story of Native son, one of the most significant novels of our time, and how it came to be written [by] Richard Wright. [New York] Harper & brothers [c1940]

2 p. l., 39 p. 20½cm.

"First edition."

1. Wright, Richard, 1909- Native son. I. Title.

[Full name: Richard Nathaniel Wright]

40-35061

Library of Congress PS3545.R815N35
——— Copy 2.
Copyright [4] 813.5

M370.
W93n

Wright, Richard Robert, 1855-1947
A brief historical sketch of negro education in Georgia, by Richard R. Wright ... Savannah, Ga., Robinson printing house, 1894.

58 p. 22½cm.

1. ~~Negroes~~—Education.—Georgia 2. ~~Negroes~~—Georgia.—Education

E 9-1666

Library, U. S. Office of Education LC2802.G4W9
——— Copy 2.
Library of Congress LC2802.G4W7
[a34b1]

M287.8
W93

Wright, Richard Robert, 1878-1967 *ed.*
... Centennial encyclopedia of the African Methodist Episcopal church, containing principally the biographies of the men and women, both ministers and laymen, whose labors during a hundred years, helped make the A. M. E. church what it is; also short historical sketches of annual conferences, educational institutions, general departments, missionary societies of the A. M. E. church, and general information about African Methodism and the Christian church in general; being a literary contribution to the celebration of the one hundredth anniversary of the formation of the African Methodist Episcopal church

(Continued on next card) 17-734

M287.8
W93

Wright, Richard Robert, 1878-1967 *ed.* ... Centennial encyclopedia of the African Methodist Episcopal church ... (Card 2)

denomination by Richard Allen and others, at Philadelphia, Penna., in 1816, by Richard R. Wright, jr. ... editor-in-chief, assisted by John R. Hawkins ... associate editor; introduction by Bishop L. J. Coppin ... [v. 1]- Philadelphia, Pa. [Printed by Book concern of the A. M. E. church, c1916]-

v. illus. (incl. ports.) 30½cm.

At head of title: 1816, 1916.

I. Hawkins, John Russell, 1862- joint ed. II. Title.
1. African Methodist Episcopal Church. Biography

Library of Congress
——— 2d set.
Copyright A 455003

MB9
W938

Wright, Richard Robert, 1878-1967
87 years behind the black curtain; an autobiography, by Richard R. Wright, Jr. Philadelphia, Rare Book Co., 1965.

351 p. 24 cm.

1. African Methodist Episcopal Church—Clergy—Correspondence, reminiscences, etc. 2. Negro clergy—Correspondence, reminiscences, etc. I. Title.

BX8449.W7A3 287.83 (B) 66-8242

Library of Congress [3]

M306
Sol
1919
Wright, Richard Robert, 1878-1967
Health the basis of racial prosperity.

(In: Southern Sociological Congress. Houston 1915. The New chivalry - health. Nashville, Southern Sociological Congress, 1915. 24cm. pp. 437-446)

M974.8
W93n
Wright, Richard Robert, 1878-1967
The Negro in Pennsylvania; a study in economic history ... By Richard R. Wright, jr. ⌊Philadelphia, A. M. E. book concern, printers, 1912⌋

250 p. 23½cm.

Thesis (PH. D.)—University of Pennsylvania, 1911.
Bibliography: p. 233-250.

1. Negroes—Pennsylvania.

12—21986

Library of Congress E185.93.P41W9
⌊42b1⌋

M323
Su7n
Wright, Richard Robert, 1878-1967
The Negro in times of industrial unrest.

(In: Survey midmonthly. The Negro in the cities of the North. New York, The Charity Organization Society, 1905. 26cm. p.69-72).

S.P.

M973.8
Am3
Wright, Richard Robert, 1878-1967
The Negro in unskilled labor.

(In: American Academy of Political and Social Science. The Negro's progress in fifty years ... Philadelphia, 1913. 25cm. p. 19-27.)

M323
W93n
Wright, Richard Robert, 1878-1967
The negro problem; being extracts from two lectures on "The sociological point of view in the study of race problems," and "The negro problem; what it is not and what it is," by R. R. Wright, jr. ⌊Philadelphia, Printed by the A. M. E. book concern, °1911⌋

47 p. 18cm. $0.25

1. Negroes. 2. U. S.—Race question. I. Title.

12-1050

Library of Congress E185.61.W95
Copyright A 305268

M975
N31
Wright, Richard Robert Jr., 1878-1967
The Negroes of Xenia, Ohio: a social study. ⌊Bulletin of the Labor Dept., no.48, 1903⌋ pp. 1007-1044.

In: The Negro in the black belt... Washington, D.C., Dept. of Labor, ⌊1897-1902⌋

1. Xenia, Ohio. 2. Ohio.

M214.5
W89
Wright, Richard Robert, 1878-1967
Overcoming racial and religious prejudices.

(In: World Fellowship of Faiths. International Congress. 1st, Chicago and New York, 1933-1934. Addresses... New York, Liveright Publishing Corporation ⌊1935⌋ cm. p. 319-322.)

Wright, Richard Robert. What does the Negro want in our democracy? p. 539-545 1919.

M306
N21p
National conference of social work.
Proceedings ... Selected papers ⌊of the⌋ ... annual meeting. 1st-
1874- Library has: 1919, 1924
New York ⌊etc.⌋ 1874-19

v. ports., tables (part fold.) diagrs. 22-24 cm.
Issued under earlier names of the conference as follows: 1874, Conference of boards of public charities; 1875-79, Conference of charities; 1880-81, Conference of charities and corrections; 1882-1916, National conference of charities and correction (varies slightly)
Title varies slightly.
Vol. for 1874 (originally published in the Journal of social science, no. 6) was issued without title by the American social science association; reprinted in 1885 under title Proceedings of the first Conference of charities and correction.

(Continued on next card)
8-35377 rev 2
⌊r46p°20⌋

Wright, Richard Robert, 1855-1947

M815.5
L54r
Lemon, Harriet Beecher Stowe Wright, comp.
Radio speeches of Major R. R. Wright, Sr. compiled by his daughter, Harriet Beecher Stowe Lemon. Philadelphia, Pa., The Farmer Press, 1949

189p. 18½cm.

Wright, Richard Robert, 1878-1967

MB
W58
White, Charles Frederick.
Who's who in Philadelphia; a collection of thirty biographical sketches of Philadelphia colored people ... together with cuts and information of some of their leading institutions and organizations, by Charles Fred. White ... with an introduction by R. R. Wright, jr., PH. D., and containing additional articles by C. J. Perry, B. F. Lee, jr., R. R. Wright, jr., and Charles Fred. White ... Philadelphia, The A. M. E. book concern ⌊°1912⌋

206 p., 1 l. incl. illus., plates. 24 cm.

1. Negroes—Philadelphia. I. Title.

12—14969

Library of Congress F158.9.N3W5
⌊48b1⌋

Wright, Richard Robert, 1855-1947.

MB9
W937h
Haynes, Elizabeth (Ross)
The black boy of Atlanta. Boston, House of Edinboro ⌊1952⌋

237 p. illus. 21 cm.

1. Wright, Richard Robert, 1855-1947. I. Title.

E185.97.W87H3 923.273 52-7005 ‡

Library of Congress ⌊5⌋

M323
W94
Wright, Rutherford R.
What the Negro needs; A post-war plan to integrate the Negro's activities and build toward full social and economical security,

27p. port. 30cm.
White author.

M811.5
W938
Wright, Sarah E
Give me a child, by Sarah E Wright and Lucy Smith. Philadelphia, Kraft Publishing Company, 1955.

40p. illus. 27cm.
"To Arthur B. Spingarn with respect and admiration and very best wishes. Lucy Smith, Dec. 28, 1955."
"To Arthur Spingarn, my best wishes and gratitude for your interest. Sarah E.Wright, 12/28/55"

I. Smith, Lucy, jt. auth. II. Title.

M301
Ah5n
Wright, Stephen Junious, 1910-
The new Negro in the South.

(In: Ahmann, Mathew H ed. The new Negro. Notre Dame, Ind., Fides Publishers ⌊1961⌋ 21cm. pp. 1-22)

Wright, Stephen Junious, 1910-

M301
Ah5n
Ahmann, Mathew H *ed.*
The new Negro. Contributors: Stephen J. Wright ⌊and others⌋ In the symposium: James Baldwin ⌊and others⌋ Notre Dame, Ind., Fides Publishers ⌊1961⌋

xii, 145 p. 21 cm.

Includes papers presented at the 1st convention of the National Catholic Conference for Interracial Justice, held in Detroit in 1961.

1. Negroes—Addresses, essays, lectures. I. Wright, Stephen J. II. National Catholic Conference for Interracial Justice. 1st convention, Detroit, 1961. III. Title.

E185.6.A26 301.451 61—17712

Library of Congress ⌊62f5⌋

M974.7
W93a
Wright, Theodore Sedgewick, 1797-1847
An address to the three thousand colored citizens of New York who are the owners of one hundred and twenty thousand acres of land in the state of New York, given to them by Gerrit Smith... September 1, 1846. New York, n.p. 1846.

20p. 23cm.

1. New York. I. Ray, Charles B. II. Smith, J. McCune.

Wright, Theodore Sedgewick, 1797-1847 joint auth.

M325.3
C81c
Cornish, Samuel E *d. 1859?*
The colonization scheme considered, in its rejection by the colored people—in its tendency to uphold caste—in its unfitness for Christianizing and civilizing the aborigines of Africa, and for putting a stop to the African slave trade: in a letter to the Hon. Theodore Frelinghuysen and the Hon. Benjamin F. Butler; by Samuel E. Cornish and Theodore S. Wright ... Newark ⌊N. J.⌋ Printed by A. Guest, 1840.

26 p. 20½cm.

1. Negroes—Colonization—Africa. I. Wright, Theodore S., d. 1849? joint author.

11-8707

Library of Congress E448.C81

M326.99B
W24s
Wright, W.
Strickland, S.
Negro slavery described by a Negro: being the narrative of Ashton Warner, a native of St. Vincent's. With an appendix containing the testimony of four Christian ministers recently returned from the colonies on the system of slavery as it now exists. By S. Strickland... London, Samuel Maunder, 1831.

144p. 15½cm.

M323.
W93m
The Writers' Board.
The myth that threatens America. New York, The Board,

3-35p. 21cm.

1. Prejudice. I. Title.

Writers' Conference on the Northwest, Portland, Or., 1946.

M979
C44
Chittick, Victor Lovitt Oakes, 1882- *ed.*
Northwest harvest, a regional stocktaking. Contributions by Peter H. Odegard ⌊and others⌋ New York, Macmillan Co., 1948.

xvi, 226 p. 22 cm.

"The printed record of the Writers' Conference on the Northwest, held in Portland, Oregon, October 31, November 1 and 2, 1946, under the joint sponsorship of the Library Association of Portland and Reed College."

1. Northwest, Pacific. 2. Alaska. I. Odegard, Peter H., 1901- II. Writers' Conference on the Northwest, Portland, Or., 1946. III. Title.

F852.C57 979.50082 48—5145*

Library of Congress ⌊40u10⌋

M814.5
W93u
Writers' congress, *University of California at Los Angeles,* 1943.
Writers' congress; the proceedings of the conference held in October 1943 under the sponsorship of the Hollywood writers' mobilization and the University of California. Published in coöperation with the Writers' congress continuations committee of the Hollywood writers' mobilization. Berkeley and Los Angeles, University of California press, 1944.

xx, 663 p. incl. front. (facsim.) 23cm.

1. Authors. 2. ~~World war, 1939- —Addresses, sermons, etc.~~ 2. Radio I. Hollywood writers' mobilization. ~~II. California. University. University at Los Angeles.~~ 3. Minorities 4. Motion picture

A 44-3435

California. Univ. Libr. for Library of Congress ⌊12⌋

M976.7
W93
Writers' program. *Arkansas.*
Survey of Negroes in Little Rock and North Little Rock, compiled by the Writers' program of the Work projects administration in the state of Arkansas. Sponsored by the Urban league of greater Little Rock, Arkansas. ₍Little Rock, °1941₎
4 p. l., 101 p. incl. tables. 23ᶜᵐ.
Bibliography: p. 99–101.
1. Negroes—Little Rock, Ark. 2. Negroes—North Little Rock, Ark. I. Title.
Library of Congress F419.L7W85 41-4905 ₍3₎ 325.2609767

M973
W93c
Writer's program. Illinois.
Cavalcade of the American Negro, compiled by the workers of the Writer's programs of the work projects administration in the state of Illinois; frontispiece by Adrian Troy of the Illinois Art project. Chicago, Diamond jubilee exposition authority, 1940.
95p. incl. front. 23cm.
1. Chicago, American Negro Exposition, 1940. 2. Art. 3. Literature. 4. Drama. 5. Journalism. I. Title.

M978.2
W93n
Writers' program. *Nebraska.*
The Negroes of Nebraska, written and compiled by workers of the Writers' program, Work projects administration in the state of Nebraska. Sponsored by the Omaha urban league community center. Drawings by Paul Gibson. Lincoln, Neb., Woodruff printing company, 1940.
48 p. illus. 21½ᶜᵐ.
1. Negroes—Nebraska. I. Title.
Library of Congress E185.93.N5W7 40—13925 ₍42d1₎ 325.2609782

M975.5
W93
Writers' program. *Virginia.*
The Negro in Virginia, compiled by workers of the Writers' program of the Work projects administration in the state of Virginia ... Sponsored by the Hampton institute. New York, Hastings house, 1940.
xii, 380 p. plates, ports. 21ᶜᵐ.
Map on lining-papers.
Bibliography: p. 353–367.
1. Negroes—Virginia. I. Title.
Library of Congress E185.93.V8W7 40-12192
——— Copy 2.
Copyright ₍4₎ 325.2609755

M01
H18
Writers' program. Virginia.
Hampton, Va. Normal and agricultural institute. *Collis P. Huntington library.*
A classified catalogue of the Negro collection in the Collis P. Huntington library, Hampton institute. Compiled by workers of the Writers' program of the Works projects administration in the state of Virginia. Sponsored by Hampton institute. ₍n. p.₎ 1940.
5 p. l., 255, ₍85₎ p. 27½ᶜᵐ.
Reproduced from type-written copy.
1. Negroes—Bibl.—Catalogs. 2. Negroes in Africa—Bibl. I. Writers' program. Virginia. II. Title.
Library of Congress Z1361.N39H3 40-28842
——— Copy 2. ₍3₎ 016.325260978

Writers' War Board,
See
Writers' Board.

M029.6
M95c
Writing.
Murphy, Beatrice M
Catching the editor's eye; a manual for writers. Rev. Washington, D.C., Author 1962.
10p. 21½cm.

M070
Sh26
Writing for the weeklies.
Shaw, O'Wendell.
Writing for the weeklies: how to earn sparetime money as a weekly newspaper correspondent. Columbus, Ohio, Russwurm Press, °1962.
28 p. 23 cm.
1. Journalism—Authorship. 2. Negro press. I. Title.
PN147.S47 61-18806 ‡
Library of Congress ₍2₎

Africa
M896
B75
Writing in French from Senegal to Cameroon.
Brench, Anthony Cecil, *comp.*
Writing in French from Senegal to Cameroon ₍by₎ A. C. Brench. London, Oxford U. P., 1967.
₍6₎, 153 p. 18½ cm. (A Three crowns book) 10/6
(B 67-18147)
French text, introduction and notes in English.
Bibliography: p. 142–153.
1. French literature—African authors. I. Title.
PQ3985.B7 848 67-108366
Library of Congress ₍3₎

Kenya
M967.62
B65p
Wwang'ombe, Peter.
Bostock, P G
The peoples of Kenya; the Taita. London, MacMillan and Co. Ltd., 1950.
42p. illus. map. 18½cm.

MB9
St4m
Wyandott Mission.
₍Mitchell, Joseph₎
The missionary pioneer, or a brief memoir of the life, labours, and death of John Stewart(man of colour) founder, under God of the mission among the Wyandotts at Upper Sandusky, Ohio. Published by Joseph Mitchell. New York, Printed by J.C. Totten, 1827.
viii, 96p. 15cm.

MB9
J136
Wylie, Evan McLeod, 1916-
Jackson, Mahalia, 1911-
Movin' on up. With Evan McLeod Wylie. ₍1st ed.₎ New York, Hawthorn Books ₍1966₎
212, ₍7₎ p. illus., ports. 24 cm.
Discography: p. ₍215₎, ₍218₎–₍219₎
1. Musicians—Correspondence, reminiscences, etc. I. Wylie, Evan McLeod, 1916– II. Title.
ML420.J17A3 784.0924 66-22315/MN
Library of Congress ₍5₎

M813.5
W98w
Wynbush, Octavia B.
The wheel that made wishes come true, by Octavia B. Wynbush; illustrations by George Greene. Philadelphia, Dorrance and company ₍°1941₎
59 p. front., illus. 19½ᶜᵐ.
I. Title.
Library of Congress PZ8.W988Wh 41-14761 ₍4₎

M323
W98c
Wynn, Daniel Webster, 1919-
The chaplin speaks. Boston, Bruce Humphries, Inc., 1956.
50p. 21½cm.
I. Title.

M171.1
W98
Wynn, Daniel Webster, 1919–
Moral behavior and the Christian ideal; an explanation of Christian ethics for the layman in our time. ₍1st ed.₎ New York, American Press ₍°1961₎
123 p. 22 cm.
Portrait of author on book jacket.
1. Christian ethics. I. Title.
BJ1261.W9 171.1 61-9470 ‡
Library of Congress ₍5₎

M323
W98n
Wynn, Daniel Webster, 1919–
The NAACP versus Negro revolutionary protest; a comparative study of the effectiveness of each movement. ₍1st ed.₎ New York, Exposition Press ₍1955₎
115 p. 21 cm. (Exposition—University book)
Bibliography: p. ₍108₎–110.
~~1. Negroes~~—Civil rights. 2. National Association for the Advancement of Colored People. 3. Communism—U. S.—1917– I. Title.
E185.61.W98 325.260973 54—13180
Library of Congress ₍56h5₎

M252
W98
Wynn, Daniel Webster, 1919–
Timeless issues ₍by₎ Daniel W. Wynn. New York, Philosophical Library ₍1967₎
x, 144 p. 22 cm.
1. Methodist Church—Sermons. 2. Sermons, American. I. Title.
BX8472.W9 252.07 66-20219
Library of Congress ₍5₎

Jamaica
M823.91
W99h
Wynter, Sylvia.
The hills of Hebron, a Jamaican novel. New York, Simon and Schuster, 1962.
315 p. 22 cm.
I. Title.
PZ4.W9895Hi 62-14285 ‡
Library of Congress ₍5₎

Jamaica
M823.91
W99h2
Wynter, Sylvia.
The hills of Hebron, a Jamaican novel. ~~New York, Simon and Schuster, 1962.~~ London, Jonathan Cape [1962] ~~315 p. 22 cm.~~ 283p. 20cm.
I. Title.
PZ4.W9895Hi 62-14285 ‡
Library of Congress ₍5₎

M811.5
C541a
Xavier university, New Orleans.
Clark, Peter Wellington, *ed.*
Arrows of gold; an anthology of Catholic verse from "America's first Catholic college for colored youth," edited by Peter Wellington Clark. New Orleans, La., Xavier university press, 1941.
x, 85, ₍1₎ p. pl. 21ᶜᵐ.
1. Negro poetry (American) 2. College verse—Xavier university, New Orleans. 3. American literature—Catholic authors. 4. American literature—Southern states. I. Xavier university, New Orleans. II. Title.
Library of Congress PS591.N4C5 41—10132 ₍41c2₎ 811.50822

M975
M31
Xenia, Ohio.
Wright, Richard Robert, Jr., 1878-
The Negroes of Xenia, Ohio: A social study ₍Bulletin of the Labor Dept., no. 48, 1903₎ pp. 1007-1044.
In: The Negro in the black belt... Washington, D.C., Dept. of Labor, ₍1897-1902₎

S.Africa
M296
J68a

Xhosa essays.

Jolobe, James J R , 1902-
Amavo ₍by₎ James J.R. Jolobe ₍Introduction by₎ R.T. Bokwe. Johannesburg, University of Witwatersrand Press, 1945.

72p. 18½cm.

Africa, South
M896.3
N24in

Xhosa language.

Ndawo, Henry Masila
Uhambo Luka Gqoboka. Lovedale, Lovedale Institution Press, 193?

93p. 18½cm.
Oqoboka's travels.
Bound with the author's InXenye YenTsomi Zase Zweni. ‹Natal, 1920›

South Africa
M896
J68u2

Xhosa Poetry.

Jolobe, James J R
Umyezo. ₍Xhosa poems₎ Amazwi okugabula izigcawu enziwe ngu Dr. W. G. Bennie. ₍Reprinted in new orthography₎ Johannesburg, Witwatersrand Press, 1957.

87p. 18cm. (The Bantu treasury, ed. by D. T. Cole, II)

1. Xhosa Poetry. 2. Poetry, African. I. Title. II. Series.

S. Africa
M496
M31

Xhosa grammar.

Manyase, L T
Indlela yokubalwa kwamagama esi-Xhosa ngolobalo olutsha. Lovedale, Lovedale Press, 1952.

20p. 18cm.

Africa, South
M896.3
N24in

Xhosa language.

Ndawo, Henry Masila
U-Nolishwa. Lovedale, The Lovedale Press, 1939.

126p. port. 18½cm.
Story of Noliswa.
Bound with the author's InXenye YenTsomi Zase Zweni. ‹Natal, 1920›

S. Africa
M896.1
M31a

Xhosa poetry.

Mama, G Soya
Amaqunube (imiHobe yesiXhosa), ngu G. Soya Mama no A. Z. T. Mbebe. London, Oxford University Press, 1950.

61p. 19cm.

S.Africa
M896
J68x

Xhosa grammatical terminology.

Jolobe, James J R 1902-
Xhosa grammatical terminology (amazwi emigaqo yentetho yesixhosa) by J. R. Arosi and J. J. R. Jolbe. Lovedale, The Lovedale Press, 1951.

20p. 18cm.

S. Africa
M572
N24u

Xhosa language.

Ndawo, Henry Masila.
UNomathamsanqa noSigebenga-i Gazi liYintSikelelo noXolelaniso-imbali engokuwa Kuka-Ntu nokusindiswa Kwakhe. Lovedale, Lovedale press, 1943.

48p. 18½cm.
"Nomathamsanqa and Sigebenga: a story of the fall and rise of the Ntu. In Xhosa.

S. Africa
M896
M87in

Xhosa poetry.

Mqhayi, Samuel Edward Krune, 1875-
I-nzuzo... ₍by₎ S.E.K. Mqhayi ₍with an introduction by₎ Rev. R. Godfrey. Johannesburg. The University of Witwatersrand press, 1942.

viii, 96 p. port. 17 cm.

South Africa
M89
M99

Xhosa Language.

Mzimba, Livingstone Ntibane.
Ibali lobomi nomsebenzi womfi umfundisi Pambani Jeremiah Mzimba. Libalwe ngunyana wake U-Livingstone Ntibane Mzimba. Lovedale, Lovedale Institution Press, 1923.

93p. port. illus. 21cm.
Work of Rev. P. J. Mzimba.

S. Africa
M896.2
Ou51

Xhosa language.

Ouless, E U.
Iziganeko zom-Kristu-uhambo lo mbambi-senziwe undlalo, ngu E.U. Ouless. Lovedale, Lovedale Institution press, 1928.

35p. 18½cm.

S. Africa
M896
M871

Xhosa poetry.

Mqhayi, Samuel Edward Krune, 1875-
...Imihobe nemibongo, yokufundwa ezikolweni. Yenziwe. London, The Sheldon press ₍1927₎

viii, 116 p. 16½ cm.
At head of title: xosa poetry for schools.

Africa, South
M896.3
N24in

Xhosa language.

Ndawo, Henry Masila
InXenye YenTsomi Zase Zweni. Natal, Mariannhill Mission Press, 1920.

73p. illus. 18½cm.
Common folktales - Xhosa, Zulu.

S.Africa
M896
So21in

Xhosa language.

Soga, John Henderson
Inkokele yomhambi osuka ekufeni esiya ebomini; iguqulwe. Lovedale, Lovedale Institution Press, 1925.

227p. 18½cm.
Traveler's guide from life to death, tr. by J. H. Soga.

South Africa
M896
M87in2

Xhosa Poetry.

Mqhayi, Samuel Edward Krune, 1875-
Inzuzo ₍Reward₎ Amazwi okugabula izigcawu enziwe ngu Rev. R. Godfrey. ₍Reprinted in new orthography₎ Johannesburg, Witwatersrand University Press, 1957.
96p. 18cm. (Bantu treasury, edited by D. T. Cole, VII)
Written in Zhosa.

1. Poetry - Xhosa. 2. Xhosa Poetry. I. Title.

Africa, South
M896.3
N24in

Xhosa language.

Ndawo, Henry Masila
Izibongo zenkosi zama-Hlubi nezama-Baca. Natal, The Mariannhill Mission Press, 1928.

39p. 18½cm.
Common folktales - Xhosa, Zulu.
Bound with the author's InXenye YenTsomi Zase Zweni. ‹Natal, 1920›

M968
Z62

Xhosa language.

Zibi, Shadrack F.
U-kayakulu: umhlaba otengwa e Rustenburg... Lamanqaku alencwadana aqokelelwe ngu D.D.T. Jabavu. Lovedale, Lovedale institution press₍1930₎

38p. 18½cm.
In Xhosa. Facts concerning land which has been released at Rustenburg for purchase by Africans.

S. Africa
M896.1
N49i

Xhosa Poetry.

Ngani, Alfred Z
Intlaba-mkhosi (izibongo zesiXhosa). Lovedale, The Lovedale Press, 1952.

60p. 18½cm.

S. Africa
M572
N241

Xhosa language.

Ndawo, Henry Masila.
Iziduko zama-Hlubi. Lovedale, Lovedale press, 1939.

39p. 18½cm.
Family names of the Hlubi tribe in Xhosa.

1. Ethnology. 2. Xhosa language.

S. Africa
M968
J11im

Xhosa people.

Jabavu, Davidson Don Tengo, 1885-
Imbumba yamaNyama. Lovedale, Lovedale Press, 1952.

v, 105 p. 19 cm.

S. Africa
M896.1
T781

Xhosa poetry.

Tshaka, R M
Iintsika zentlambo ye-tyhume. Lovedale press, 1953.

95p. 18½cm.

Xhosa poetry.
S. Africa
M896.1 Yali-Manisi, D L P
Y12 Izibongo zeenkosi zama-Xhosa; zabuy' iindlezan' entlazaneni. Lovedale, The Lovedale Press, 1952.

141p. 18½cm.

1. Xhosa poetry.

Ximenez de Encise, Diego. Comedia famosa de Juan Latino.
MB9
L34s Spratlin, Valaurez Burwell
Juan Latino, slave and humanist. New York, Spinner Press, Inc., 1938.

xii, 216p. 24cm.
Contents. -Introduction. -Juan Latino. -"The famous drama of Juan Latino", an adaptation in English from the Spanish of Diego Jimenez de Enciso.

Xosa

see

Xhosa

S. Africa
M968 Xuma, Alfred Bitini, 1890-1962
Xu8 Reconstituting the Union of South Africa; or a more rational union policy. Address delivered before a public meeting of the Bantu Studies Club of the University of the Witwatersrand, May 30th 1932. Lovedale, South Africa, Lovedale Press, 1932.

23p. 21½cm.

1. South Africa.

Nigeria Yaba roundabout murder.
M896.3 Ekwensi, Cyprian
Ek87y Yaba roundabout murder. Lagos, Tortoise Series Books [1962]

54p. illus. 21cm.
Nigerian author.

(Yale Judaica Series, v.6)
Ethiopia
M296 Leslau, Wolf
L566 Falasha anthology, translated from Ethiopic sources with an introduction by Wolf Leslau. New Haven, Yale University Press, 1951.

222p. illus. 21½cm. (Yale Judaica Series, v.6)
Includes bibliography.
White author.

1. Judaism - Collections. 2. Falashas. 3. Ethiopic literature - Translations into English. I. Title. II. Series.

Yale University. James Weldon Johnson Memorial Collection.
MO26 Bontemps, Arna Wendell, 1902-
B64j The James Weldon Johnson Memorial Collection of Negro Arts and Letters. Yale University Library Gazette, 18:18-26, October 1943.

18-26p. port. 26cm.

S. Africa
M896.1 Yali-Manisi, D L P
Y12 Izibongo zeenkosi zama-Xhosa; zabuy' iindlezan' entlazaneni. Lovedale, The Lovedale Press, 1952.

141p. 18½cm.

1. Xhosa poetry.

MB9 Yancey, Asa H , 1881-
Y151 Interpositionulification; what the Negro may expect. New York, Comet Press Books, 1959.

134p. 20cm.
Portrait of author on book jacket.

I. Title.

MB9 Yancey, Asa H , 1881-
Y1512 Interpositionulification or what the Negro may expect. Rev. ed. New York, Carlton Press [©1959]

136p. illus. 22cm.
Autobiographical.
Portrait of author on book jacket.

I. Title.

M811.5 Yancey, Bessie (Woodson) 1882-
Y15 Echoes from the hills; a book of poems, by Bessie Woodson Yancey. Washington, D. C., The Associated publishers, inc. [©1939]

vi, 62 p. 19½cm.

I. Title. 1. Poetry.

Library of Congress PS3547.A353 1939 40—530
[a45c1] 811.5

Liberia
M966.6 Yancey, Ernest Jerome.
Y15r The recent Liberian crisis and its causes; an address delivered at Buffalo, New York, August 12 and 14, 1934 under auspices of the Buffalo Liberian research society, by Ernest Jerome Yancey [n.p., n.p., c 1934]

12p. 23½cm.

1. Liberia.

Liberia
M966.6 Yancey, Ernest Jerome.
Y15h Historical lights of Liberia's yesterday and today, by Ernest Jerome Yancy, A. B. [Xenia, O., The Aldine publishing company, ©1934]

xi, [1] p., 1 l., 15-323 p. incl. illus., port. 20cm.
"First edition."
Bibliography: p. xi.
Music: p. 293-302.

1. Liberia—Hist. 2. Liberia—Pol. & govt. I. Title.

Library of Congress DT631.Y3 35—608
——— Copy 2.
Copyright A 79022 [36d2] 966.6

Liberia
M966.6 Yancy, Ernest Jerome
Y15re The Republic of Liberia. London, George Allen & Unwin, 1959.

144p. port. illus. 18½cm.

1. Liberia - Politics and government.
I. Title.

M976.4 Yancy, J W
Yaln The Negro blue - book of Washington county, Texas, by J. W. Yancy... [Brenham, Texas, Brenham banner press, 1936]
viii, 138p. illus. 23cm.
Inscribed copy: "The Crisis, compliments of J. W. Yancy."
1. Washington county, Texas.
2. Texas
3. Biography. I. Title

Sudan Yangu, Alexis Mbali.
M962.4 The Nile turns red; Azanians chose freedom against Arab bondage. Edited by A. G. Mondini. [1st ed. New York] Pageant Press [©1966]
Y16
xviii, 184 p. map. 21 cm.
Bibliography: p. 182-184.

Portrait of author on book jacket.

1. Sudan—Hist. 2. Sudan—Race question. I. Title.
II. Mondini, A G ed.
DT108.7.Y3 962.9'04 66-29146

Library of Congress [3]

Yao language - Grammar.
Malawi
M496.3 Abdallah, Yohanna B
Ab32 Chikala cha wayao, uwalembile nde Yohanna B. Abdallah. Soni uwalundenye nde Meredith Sanderson. Zomba, Nyasaland, Government Printing Office, 1919.

60, 60p. 21½cm.
Yao and English; added t.p. in English.
1. Yao language - Grammar. I. Title.
II. Sanderson, Meredith, tr.

The yardarm of Murphey's kite.
M811.5 Mason, Mason Jordan
M38y The yardarm of Murphey's kite. Ranches of Taos, New Mexico, Motive Press, 1956.

58p. illus. 24½cm.

Yayá Garcia.
Brazil
M869.3 Machado de Assis, Joaquim Maria, 1839-1908.
M18y ... Yayá Garcia, por Machado de Assis. Nova ed. Rio de Janeiro, Paris, Garnier ~~[1920]~~ 1919

2 p. l., 320 p. 19cm. (Collecção dos autores celebres da litteratura brasileira)

I. Title.

Library of Congress PQ9697.M18Y3 1925 31-29253
869.3

"Ye shall not surely die."

M252 Haynes, Lemuel, 1753-1833.
H33y "Ye shall not surely die." A short sermon, by Rev. Lemuel Haynes. Published by the American Tract Society, no.451

4p. 17½cm.

M973 Year.
W51f Year's pictorial history of the American Negro. [Maplewood, N. J., C. S. Hammond, 1965]

144 p. illus., facsims., ports. 20 cm.
Bibliography: p. 142.

1. Negroes—Hist. 2. Negroes—Civil rights. I. Title.
II. Wesley, Charles Harris, 1891- Foreword.
E185.Y4 301.451 65-18139

Library of Congress [42-1]

M280
Y33
Year book of Negro churches, with statistics and records of achievements of Negroes in the United States ... 1935/36–
Wilberforce, O., Printed at Wilberforce university [19
v. 22½cm.
Editor: 1935/36– Reverdy C. Ransom.
"Published by authority of the bishops of the A. M. E. church."
1. Negroes. 2. Negroes—Religion. 3. Churches—U. S. 4. Negroes—Stat. I. Ransom, Reverdy Cassius, bp., 1861– ed. II. African Methodist Episcopal church. III. Title: Negro churches, Year book of.
37—22400
Library of Congress E185.7.Y43
[44e1] 325.260973

Year - books - Sierra Leone.
Sierra Leone
M966.4
Sily
Sierra Leone Year Book, 1960,
[Sierra Leone] Daily Mail [1960],
v. ports. 18cm.

Nigeria
M896.1
Y391
Yemitan, E Oladipupo (1923–)
Ijala, aré ode [Poem singing, the hunter's play] Ibadan, Oxford University Press, 1963.
85p. illus. 18½cm.
Written in Yoruba.
I. Title.

Jamaica
M821.08
Ye3
Year book of the Jamaica poetry league, 1939–
Kingston, Jamaica, The New Dawn Press, 1939–
v. 21cm.
Compiled by Archie Lindo.
See holdings card for issues in library.
1. Jamaican poetry. I. Lindo, Archie.

The year in San Fernando.
Trinidad
M823.91
An86y
Anthony, Michael
The year in San Fernando. [London]
Andre Deutsch [1965]
190p. 20cm.

Gold Coast
M966.7
Ye3a
Yen, Kwesi.
The Achievements of Dr. Kwame Nkrumah.
Accra, The Heal Press, 1954.
19p. port. 18cm.
1. Nkrumah, Kwame, 1910–

Jamaica
M821.08
Ye3
Year book of the Jamaica poetry league.

Volume	Year	Month	Volume	Year	Month
	1939				
	1940				
	1941				
	1942				

Yearbook of American poetry.
M811.08
B73
Braithwaite, William Stanley Beaumont, 1878– ed.
Anthology of magazine verse for 1913–29 and yearbook of American poetry, edited by William Stanley Braithwaite. New York, G. Sully and company, inc. [1913]–29.
17 v. 22 cm.
1926: Sesqui-centennial edition.
Imprint varies: 1913–14, Cambridge, Mass., Issued by W. S. B.—1915, New York, Gomme & Marshall.—1916, New York, L. J. Gomme.—1917–22, Boston, Small, Maynard & company.—1923–27, Boston, B. J. Brimmer company.—1928, New York, H. Vinal, ltd.—1929, New York, G. Sulley and company, inc.
1. American poetry—20th cent. I. Title. II. Title: Magazine verse. III. Title: Yearbook of American poetry.
15—26325
Library of Congress PS614.B7
[47r36m1]

Gold Coast
M966.7
Ye3s
Yen, Kwesi.
The street boys on the march to freedom.
Accra, The Quality Press [1954]
23p. 17½cm.
1. Gold Coast-Pol. and Govt. 2. Gold Coast-Biography. 3. Nkrumah, Kwame, 1910–

Year-books.
M310
M96
The Negro handbook ... 1942–
New York, N. Y., W. Malliet and company, 1942–
v. tables. 24 cm.
Editor: 1942– Florence Murray.
"Books and periodicals, a list of books by and about Negroes": 1942, p. 194–200.
1. Negroes—Year-books. I. Murray, Florence, ed.
42—22818
Library of Congress E185.5.N382
[45k*7] 325.260973

Yearbook of the American short story.
M813.08
B46a
The Best American short stories ... and the Yearbook of the American short story ... 1915–
Boston, Houghton Mifflin company [1916]
v. 19½–21 cm.
Title varies: 1915–41, The Best short stories.
1942– The Best American short stories.
Editors: 1915–41, E. J. O'Brien.—1942– Martha Foley.
Imprint varies: 1915–25, Boston, Small, Maynard & company.—1926–32, New York, Dodd, Mead and company.—1933– Boston, Houghton Mifflin company.
1. Short stories, American. 2. Short stories—Bibl. I. O'Brien, Edward Joseph Harrington, 1890–1941, ed. II. Foley, Martha, ed. III. Yearbook of the American short story.
16—11387
Library of Congress PZ1.B446235
[49r43u²30] 813.0822

M813.5
Y46be
Yerby, Frank, 1916–
Benton's Row. New York, Dial Press, 1954.
346 p. 21 cm.
I. Title.
Full name: Frank Garvin Yerby.
PZ3.Y415Be 54–10533 ‡
Library of Congress [10]

Year-books.
M310
N31
Negro year book, an annual encyclopedia of the Negro ... 1912–
Tuskegee Institute, Ala., Negro year book publishing co., °1912–
v. illus. (incl. maps) diagrs. 19½–24cm.
No editions were published for 1920/21, 1923/24, 1927/28–1929/30.
Editor: 1912: M. N. Work.
Publishers: 1913, Negro year book co.—1914/15– Negro year book publishing co.
Title varies slightly.
1. Negroes—Year-books. I. Work, Monroe Nathan, 1866– ed.
12—14974
Library of Congress E185.5.N41
[43t2]

Year's pictorial history of the American Negro.
M973
W51f
Year.
Year's pictorial history of the American Negro. [Maplewood, N. J., C. S. Hammond, 1965]
144 p. illus., facsims., ports. 20 cm.
Bibliography: p. 142.
1. Negroes—Hist. 2. Negroes—Civil rights. I. Title.
E185.Y4 301.451 65–18139
Library of Congress [42-1]

M813.5
Y46bo
Yerby, Frank, 1916–
Bride of liberty. [1st ed.] Garden City, N. Y., Doubleday, 1954.
219 p. illus. 22 cm. (Cavalcade books)
1. U. S.—Hist.—Revolution—Fiction. I. Title.
Full name: Frank Garvin Yerby.
PZ7.Y48Br 54–7595 ‡
Library of Congress [10]

Year - books - Caribbean.
Trinidad
M972.98
W67y
Williams, Eric Eustace, 1911– , comp.
Yearbook of Caribbean research 1948.
Survey of research and investigation in Caribbean Commission territories. Compiled by Research Branch, Central Secretariat Caribbean Commission Port-of-Spain, Trinidad, Caribbean Commission 1949.
v. 23cm.

M811.5
Y361
Yeiser, Idabelle, -1954
Lyric and legend. [Poems] Boston, Christopher Pub. House [1947]
77 p. 21 cm.
I. Title. 1 Poetry
PS3547.E4L8 811.5 47–8097*
© Idabelle Yeiser, Philadelphia; 7Oct47; A17678.
Library of Congress [1]

M813.5
Y46c
Yerby, Frank, 1916–
Captain Rebel. New York, Dial Press [1956]
343 p. 21 cm.
1. U. S.—Hist.—Civil War—Fiction. I. Title.
Full name: Frank Garvin Yerby.
PZ3.Y415Cap 56–11248 ‡
Library of Congress [15]

Year - books - National Urban League.
M306
N21a
National Urban League.
... And the pursuit of happiness. 40th anniversary year book. New York, National Urban League, 1950.
128p. ports. illus. 28½cm.

Yellow fever-Philadelphia, 1793.
M974.8
J71n
[Jones, Absalom]
A narrative of the proceedings of the black people, during the late awful calamity in Philadelphia, in the year 1793: and a refutation of some censures, thrown upon them in some late publications. By A. J. and R. A. Philadelphia: Printed for the authors, by William W. Woodward, at Franklin's head, no. 41, Chesnut-street. 1794.
28 p. 18½cm.
"To Matthew Clarkson, esq. mayor of the city of Philadelphia [with reply]": p. 21–23. "An address to those who keep slaves, and approve the practice": p. 23–26. "To the people of colour": p. 26–27. "A short address to the friends of him who hath no helper" [signed Absalom Jones, Richard Allen, followed by five stanzas of verse]: p. 27–28.
(Continued on next card)
2–13737
[a38b1]

M813.5
Y46d
1953
Yerby, Frank, 1916–
The devil's laughter. ~~New York, Dial Press~~ 1953. London, The Book Club,
~~376p.~~ 21 cm.
300p.
I. Title.
Full name: Frank Garvin Yerby.
PZ3.Y415De 53–9319 ‡
Library of Congress [12]

M813.5 Y46d2
Yerby, Frank, 1916-
The devil's laughter. London, William Heinemann, 1953.
378p. 19½cm.
I. Title.

M813.5 Y46d
Yerby, Frank, 1916-
The devil's laughter. New York, Dial Press, 1953.
376 p. 21 cm.
First edition.
I. Title.
Full name: Frank Garvin Yerby.
PZ3.Y415De 53-9819 ‡
Library of Congress [12]

M813.5 Y46di
Yerby, Frank, 1916-
Les diablesses (The vixens). Traduit de l'anglais par M. N. Repond et R. Villemin. Paris, Marguerat, 1949.
348p. 19cm.
I. Title.

M813.5 Y46fa
Yerby, Frank, 1916-
Fairoaks, a novel. New York, Dial Press [1957]
405 p. 21 cm.
First edition.
I. Title.
Full name: Frank Garvin Yerby.
PZ3.Y415Fai 57-11707 ‡
Library of Congress [58h10]

M813.5 Y46fa
Yerby, Frank, 1916-
De familie fox (The foxes of Harrow). L. J. Veen's Uitgeversmaatschappij [1946?]
401p. 24cm.
I. Title.

M813.5 Y46fl
Yerby, Frank, 1916-
Floodtide. N. Y., Dial Press, 1950.
342 p. 22 cm.
I. Title.
Full name: Frank Garvin Yerby.
PZ3.Y415Fl 50-9227
Library of Congress [10]

M813.5 Y46fl 1952
Yerby, Frank, 1916-
Floodtide. London, The Book Club, 1952.
276p.
I. Title.
Full name: Frank Garvin Yerby.

M813.5 Y46fl 1953
Yerby, Frank, 1916-
Floodtide. New York, Pocket Books, Inc., 1953.
358p. 16cm.
Pocket book edition.
I. Title.

M813.5 Y42f2
Yerby, Frank, 1916-
The Foxes of Harrow. ~~Garden City, N. Y., Sun Dial Press [1947, c1946]~~ London, The Book Club [1949]
~~xiii, 408 p. 21 cm.~~ 340 p. 18 cm.
I. Title.
PZ3.Y415Fo 2 47-5613
Library of Congress [7]

M813.5 Y46f 1949
Yerby, Frank, 1916
The Foxes of Harrow. New York, Pocket Books, Inc., 1949.
372p. 16cm.
Pocket book edition.
I. Title

M813.5 Y46f
Yerby, Frank, 1916-
The foxes of Harrow [by] Frank Yerby. New York, The Dial press, 1946.
viii p., 1 l., 534 p. 20½cm.
I. Title.
46-25030
Library of Congress PZ3.Y415Fo [47k5]

M813.5 Y46ga
Yerby, Frank, 1916-
The Garfield honor. New York, The Dial Press, 1961.
347p. 20½cm.
I. Title.

M813.5 Y46gr
Yerby, Frank, 1916-
Gillian. New York, Dial Press, 1960.
346 p. 21 cm.
I. Title.
Full name: Frank Garvin Yerby.
PZ3.Y415Gi 60-14688 ‡
Library of Congress [7]

M813.5 Y46go
Yerby, Frank, 1916-
Goat song; a novel of ancient Greece. New York, Dial Press, 1967.
498 p. 24 cm.
1. Greece—Hist.—Fiction. I. Title.
PZ3.Y415Gm 67-16540
Library of Congress [5]

M813.5 Y46g2
Yerby, Frank, 1916-
The Golden Hawk. A Cardinal edition. New York, Pocket Books, Inc., 1948.
354p. 16cm.
I. Title.

M813.5 Y46g
Yerby, Frank, 1916-
The Golden hawk. New York, The Dial press, 1948.
346p. 20cm.
1. Title. 1. Fiction.

M813.5 Y46g2
Yerby, Frank, 1916-
The golden hawk. New York, Pocket books, 1948.
354p. 16cm.
Pocket book edition.
I. Title.

M813.5 Y46g3
Yerby, Frank, 1916-
Gouden havik; een liefde aan de Caraibische Zee. Geautoriseerde vertaling van Martin Denijs. Den Haag, Zuid-Hollansche Uitgevers Maatschappij [n. d.]
299p. 23cm.
Title: The golden hawk.
Dutch edition.
I. Title.

M813.5 Y46gri
Yerby, Frank, 1916-
Griffin's Way, a novel. New York, Dial Press, 1962.
345 p. 22 cm.
I. Title.
Full name: Frank Garvin Yerby.
PZ3.Y415Gr 62-18845 ‡
Library of Congress [5]

M813.5 Y46t4
Yerby, Frank, 1916-
Guld og Kaerlighed [The treasure of pleasant valley. Overstat af Michael Tejn] København, Nyt Nordisk Forlag, Arnold Busck, 1957.
229p. 22cm.
I. Title.

M813.5 Y46h
Yerby, Frank, 1916-
Health card. Pp. 42-51.
In: O. Henry memorial award prize stories of 1944. ed. by Herschel Brickell. New York, Doubleday, 1944.
I. Title.

M813.08 C554 Yerby, Frank, 1916-
The homecoming
Pp. 147-156

In: Clarke, John Henrik, ed. American Negro short stories. New York, Hill and Wang, 1966.

M813.5 Y46s 1954 Yerby, Frank, 1916-
The Saracen blade. New York, Pocket Books, inc., 1954.

418p. 16cm.
Cardinal edition.

I. Title.

M813.5 Y46w Yerby, Frank, 1916-
A woman called Fancy. New York, Dial Press, 1951.
340 p. 21 cm.

I. Title.
Full name: Frank Garvin Yerby.
PZ3.Y415Wo 51-8370
Library of Congress [10]

M813.5 Y46j Yerby, Frank, 1916-
Jarrett's Jade, a novel. New York, Dial Press, 1959.
342 p. 21 cm.

I. Title.
Full name: Frank Garvin Yerby.
PZ3.Y415Jar 59-15486 ‡
Library of Congress [20]

M813.5 Y46s Yerby, Frank, 1916-
The Saracen blade, a novel. New York, Dial Press, 1952.
406 p. 21 cm.

I. Title.
Full name: Frank Garvin Yerby.
PZ3.Y415Sar 52-5616 ‡
Library of Congress [12]

M813.5 Y46w Yerby, Frank, 1916-
A woman called Fancy. New York, Pocket Books, Inc., 1953.

324p. 16cm. (Cardinal edition C 102)
Pocket book edition.

I. title

M813.5 Y46k Yerby, Frank, 1916-
Katoen bloeit onder de galden. Een verhaal van liefde, haat en hartstocht in Louisiana. Geautoriseerde vertaling van M. L. Ohl. Den Haag, Ad. M. C. Stok, 1954.

304p. 23cm.
Title: Benton's row.
Dutch edition

M813.5 Y46se Yerby, Frank, 1916-
The serpent and the staff. New York, Dial Press, 1958.
377 p. 21 cm.

I. Title.
Full name: Frank Garvin Yerby.
PZ3.Y415Se 58-12778 ‡
Library of Congress [12]

Yerby, Frank Garvin, 1916-

see

Yerby, Frank, 1916-

M813.5 Y46od Yerby, Frank, 1916-
An odor of sanctity; a novel of medieval Moorish Spain. New York, Dial Press [1965]
vi, 563 p. 24 cm.

I. Title.
PZ3.Y415Od 65-23964
Library of Congress [5]

M813.5 Y46t Yerby, Frank, 1916-
O tesouro do vale aprazivel; romance. (The treasure of Pleasant Valley). Traducão de Bernice Xavier. Rio de Janeiro, Livraria José Olympio Editôra, 1959.

214p. 23½cm.

I. Title. II. Title: The treasure of Pleasant Valley.

M910 C759 Yergan, Max, 1892-
Africa - new perspectives, main address of the conference.

(In: Council on African Affairs. Conference on Africa - New Perspectives. Proceedings. New York, 1944. 21cm. p.10-12)

M813.5 Y46o Yerby, Frank, 1916-
The old gods laugh, a modern romance. New York, Dial Press, 1964.
408 p. 22 cm.

I. Title.
PZ3.Y415Ol 64-15225
Library of Congress [5]

M813.5 Y46t Yerby, Frank, 1916-
The treasure of Pleasant Valley. New York, Dial Press, 1955.
348 p. 21 cm.

I. Title.
Full name: Frank Garvin Yerby.
PZ3.Y415Tr 55-9940 ‡
Library of Congress [15]

M910 Y4a3 Yergan, Max, 1892-
Africa, the west and Christianity [by] Max Yergan. For distribution to the general committee of The World Student Christian Federation, Mysore, India, December 5-16, 1928.

50p. 23cm.

1. Africa I. title

M813.5 Y46pi Yerby, Frank, 1916-
Pietro chevalier d'amour (The Saracen Blade); roman. Traduit de l'anglais par Michèle Laurent. Paris, Editions Denoel [1954]

411p. 21½cm.

I. Title.

M813.5 Y46vs Yerby, Frank, 1916-
The Vixens. New York, Pocket Books, Inc. 1950.

340p. 16cm.
Pocket book edition.

M910 Y4a3 Yergan, Max, 1892-
Africa, the west and Christianity [by] Max Yergan. For distribution to the general committee of The World Student Christian Federation, Myrose, India, December 5-16, 1928.

50p. 23cm.

Spingarn

M813.5 Y46p Yerby, Frank, 1916-
Pride's castle. New York, Pocket Books, Inc., 1952.

382p. 16cm. (Cardinal edition C 21)
Pocket book edition.

I. title

M813.5 Y46v Yerby, Frank, 1916-
The vixens, a novel by Frank Yerby. New York, The Dial press, 1947.

347p. 21cm.

1. Reconstruction - Fiction. I. Title.

M910 Y4a Yergan, Max, 1892-
Africa in the war. New York, Council on African Affairs.

8p. 20cm.

M304 P19 V.2, no.7
I. title 1. World War, 1939-1945.

M323 Y4d
Yergan, Max, 1892-
Democracy and the Negro people today. Washington, D.C., National Negro Congress, 194 .
3-15p. 19cm.
1. Race problems. I. Title.

M304 P19 v.2, no.8
Yergan, Max, 1892-
Democracy and the Negro people today. Washington, D.C., National Negro Congress, [1940].
3-14p. port. (cover) 15cm.
1. National Negro Congress.

M910 Y4g
Yergan, Max, 1892-
Gold and poverty in South Africa; a study of economic organization and standards of living, by Max Yergan ... The Hague, New York, International industrial relations institute, with the co-operation of the International committee on African affairs, 1938.
24 p. 24½cm. [International industrial relations institute. Social economic series]
1. Africa, South—Econ. condit.—1918- 2. Africa, South—Native races. I. Title.
Library of Congress HD5091.S7Y45 39-15318
[3] 330.968

MB9 B799n
Yergan, Max, 1892-
The Negro and justice; A plea for Earl Browder, by Max Yergan and Paul Robeson. New York, Citizens' Committee to Free Earl Browder, 1941.
11p. illus. 19cm.
1. Browder, Earl. I. Robeson, Paul, 1898- II. Title.

M960 H12a
Yergan, Max, 1892- The communist threat in Africa, p. 262-280.
Haines, Charles Grove, 1906- ed.
Africa today. Baltimore, Johns Hopkins Press [1955]
xvi, 510 p. illus., maps. 24 cm.
Based on the proceedings of the conference on contemporary Africa which the Johns Hopkins University School of Advanced International Studies sponsored in Washington in August 1954.
Bibliographical footnotes.
1. Africa. I. Title.
DT5.H25 960 55—6220
Library of Congress [56x15]

M266 St29t
Yergan, Max, 1892- Youth's challenge to Youth, p.157-84.
Stauffer, Milton Theobald, 1885- ed.
... Thinking with Africa; chapters by a group of nationals interpreting the Christian movement, assembled and edited by Milton Stauffer ... New York, Pub. for the Student volunteer movement for foreign missions by the Missionary education movement of the United States and Canada [1927]
xviii p., 1 l., 184p. 19½cm. (Christian voices around the world)

Africa M398 J114
Yes and no.
Jablow, Alta.
Yes and no; the intimate folklore of Africa. Introd. by Paul Goodman. New York, Horizon Press [1961]
223 p. 22 cm.
"Dilemma tales, proverbs, stories of love, and adult riddles."
1. Folk-lore—Africa, West. I. Title.
GR350.J3 398.0966 61-8508 ‡
Library of Congress [15]

Yes I can.
MB9 D287
Davis, Sammy, 1925-
Yes I can; [the story of Sammy Davis, Jr., by Sammy Davis, Jr., and Jane and Burt Boyar. New York, Farrar, Straus & Giroux, 1965]
612 p. ports. 22 cm.
I. Boyar, Jane, joint author. II. Boyar, Burt, joint author. III. Title.
PN2287.D322A3 792.70924 (B) 64-11456
Library of Congress [3]

Nigeria M331 Y48
Yesufu, Tijani M
An introduction to industrial relations in Nigeria. [London] Published for the Nigerian Institute of Social and Economic Research by the Oxford University Press, 1962.
ix, 190 p. tables. 23 cm.
"Based upon a thesis ... University of London."
Bibliographical footnotes.
1. Industrial relations—Nigeria.
HD8791.N5Y4 331.109669 63-189
Library of Congress [3]

Yo viajo por un mundo encantado.
M811.5 H87y
Hughes, Langston, 1902-
Yo viajo por un mundo encantado. (I Wonder as I Wander). Buenos Aires, Compañia General Fabril Editora, 1959.
417p. 19½cm.
Portrait of author on book jacket.
"This book dedicated to ... Sincerely, Langston Hughes, Feb. 25, 1960."
I. Title. II. Title: I Wonder as I Wander.

Nigeria M896.3 Aj74
Yomi in Paris.
Ajose, Audrey.
Yomi in Paris; with drawings by Mick Pilcher. Cambridge, Cambridge U. P., 1966.
87 p. illus. 18½ cm. 4/- (B 66-12458)
1. English language—Text-books for foreigners. 2. Readers—1950- I. Title.
PE1128.A43 428.644 66-73973
Library of Congress [3]

Nigeria M896.3 Aj74y
Yomi's adventure.
Ajose, Audrey
Yomi's adventure. With drawings by Mick Pilcher. Cambridge, University Press, 1964.
90p. illus. 18½cm.

Yondo, Elolongue Epanya
see
Epanya Yondo, Elolongue

Jamaica M966.9 C15p
Yoruba. - Description and travel.
Campbell, Robert
A pilgrimage to my motherland. An account of a journey among the Egbas and Yorubas of Central Africa, in 1859-60. By Robert Campbell ... of the Niger Valley exploring party ... New-York, T. Hamilton; Philadelphia, The author, 1861.
145p. front. (port) double map. 19cm.

Jamaica M966.9 C15p2
Yoruba - Description and travel.
Campbell, Robert
A pilgrimage to my motherland; or, Reminiscences of a sojourn among the Egbas and Yorubas of Central Africa, in 1859-60. By Robert Campbell. With an introduction by Sir Culling E. Eardley. London, William John Johnson, 1861.
116p. front. 19cm. illus.

M910 D37o
Yoruba-Descr. & trav.
Delany, Martin Robison, 1812-1885
Official report of the Niger Valley exploring party. By M. R. Delany, chief commissioner to Africa. New York, T. Hamilton; [etc., etc.] 1861.
4 p. l., [5]-75 p. 22½cm.
1. Liberia—Descr. & trav. 2. Yoruba—Descr. & trav. 3. Negroes—Colonization—Africa. I. Delany, Martin Robison, 1812-1885. II. Title.
5-15242
Library of Congress DT513.N68
——— Copy 2.

Nigeria M496 D37ag
Yoruba - Grammar.
Delano, Isaac O
Agbékà Ọrọ Yoruba; appropriate words and expressions in Yoruba. London, Oxford University Press, 1960.
160p. 18½cm.

Nigeria M496 D37at
Yoruba - Grammar.
Delano, Isaac O
Atúmò ede Yoruba (a short Yoruba grammar and dictionary). London, Oxford University Press, 1958.
209p. maps. 19cm.

Nigeria M966.9 J63h
Yoruba—Hist.
Johnson, Samuel, d. 1901.
The history of the Yorubas from the earliest times to the beginning of the British protectorate, by the Rev. Samuel Johnson ... Ed. by Dr. O. Johnson ... London, G. Routledge & sons, ltd., 1921.
lv, 684 p. front. (port.) fold. map. 22cm.
1. Yoruba—Hist. I. Johnson, Obadiah, ed.
22-9406
Library of Congress DT513.J6
[2]

Nigeria M896.1 G25y
Yoruba - Poetry.
Gbadamosi, Bakare, comp.
Yoruba poetry, collected and translated by Bakare Gbadamosi and Ulli Beier. Eight silkscreen prints and ten vignettes by Susanne Wenger. Ibadan, Nigeria Printing and Publishing Co., 1959.
68p. illus. 26½cm.
A special publication of "Black Orpheus"

Nigeria M398 L14p
Yoruba - Proverbs.
Lakeru, J A ,comp.
Awọn owe ilẹ wa. Abeokuta, E.N.A. Press, 1916.
32p. 18½cm.
Translation: The proverbs of our land (Yoruba proverbs)

Yoruba - Songs.
Nigeria M784 R17a
Ransome-Kuti, Josaiah Jesse, 1855-1930.
Awọn orin mimọ ni ede ati Ohùn Ilẹ Wa. Yoruba sacred songs. Lagos, C.M.S. Bookshop, 1925.
Pp. 556-617 18½cm.
Translation: A series of sacred songs in the language and the tone of our land.

Yoruba language.
Nigeria M966.9 C88g 1852
Crowther, Samuel Adjai, 1860-1891.
A grammar and vocabulary of the Yoruba language, compiled by the Rev. Samuel Crowther, together with introductory remarks by O.E. Vidal. London, Seeley, 1852.
v., 291p. 22cm.

Nigeria M496 D37c
Yoruba language - Grammar.
Delano, Isaac O
Conversation in Yoruba and English, London, Heinemann Educational Books [1963].
81p. 18cm.

Nigeria M966.9 Aj51
Yoruba, History of.
Ajisafe, Ajayi Kọlawọle
Iwe itan Abeokuta. Bungay, Suffolk. Printed for the authors by Richard Clay & Sons, 1924.
192p. portraits. 18½cm.

Nigeria M966.9 C88j 1854
Yoruba language.
Crowther, Samuel Adjai, 1806-1891.
Journal of an expedition up the Niger and Tshadda rivers, undertaken by Macgregor Laird Esq. in connection with the British government in 1854. By the Rev. Samuel Crowther. With map and appendix. London, Church Missionary house, 1855.
xxxi, 233p. maps. 20½cm.

Nigeria M496.5 L331
Yoruba language - Grammar.
Laṣebikan, Ebenezer Latunde.
Learning Yoruba. London, Oxford University Press, 1958.
81 p. 19 cm.
1. Yoruba language—Grammar.
PL8821.L3 496.5 61-21789 ‡
Library of Congress [2]

Nigeria M496 Ak5y
Yoruba African language simplified.
Akinwunmi, Muniru Akanbi, 1922-
Yoruba (African) language simplified. Brooklyn, N. Y., Akinwunmi Enterprises, Merchandising Agency, 1960.
48p. port. 23½cm. (a library of African cultures)
Portrait of author on back of book.

Yoruba language.
Nigeria M966.9 C88v 1843
Crowther, Samuel Adjai, 1806-1891.
Vocabulary of the Yoruba language. Part I.- English and Yoruba. Part II.-Yoruba and English. To which are prefixed the grammatical elements of the Yoruba language. By Samuel Crowther... London. Printed for the Church Missionary society, 1843.
vii, 196p. 20cm.

Nigeria M496 L33
Yoruba language - Grammar.
Laṣebikan, Ebenezer Latunde
Ojúlówó Yoruba. Iwe kini: awon ilu nlá nlá ilẹ Yoruba. London, Oxford University Press [1961]
84p. illus. 18½cm..
"First published 1954."

Nigeria M641.5 M35k
Yoruba cookery.
Mars, J A , compiler.
Kudeti book of Yoruba cookery. Lagos, The Church Missionary Society's Bookshop, 1936.
39p. 20cm.

Nigeria M496 D37at
Yoruba language.
Delano, Isaac O
Atúmọ̀ ede Yoruba (a short Yoruba grammar and dictionary). London, Oxford University Press, 1958.
209p. maps. 19cm.

Nigeria M496 L45
Yoruba language - Grammar.
Layeni, Olasiji
Yoruba course for secondary schools, Book I. Lagos, Pacific Printers [1962]
131p. 21cm.

Yoruba course for secondary schools.
Nigeria M496 L45
Layeni, Olasiji
Yoruba course for secondary schools, Book I. Lagos, Pacific Printers [1962]
131p. 21cm.

Nigeria M966.9 K96e
Yoruba Language.
Kuye, J G
English principia, or grammar Gẹsi for primary schools and private tuition, containing copious exercises for translation, with vocabularies, by J.G. Kuye. Fifth edition. Lagos, published by the author, 1925.
xii, 13-15p. 19cm.

Nigeria M372.4 Od8 Bk. 2
Yoruba language - Grammar.
Odujinrin, J S A
ABD asiko; apa kejo. [Ebute-Metta, Nigeria Service Printers. 1963.
55p. illus. 18cm.
Written in Yoruba.

Nigeria M966.9 Oj5
Yoruba culture.
Ojo, G J Afolabi.
Yoruba culture: a geographical analysis [by] G. J. Afolabi Ojo; foreword by S. O. Biobaku. Ife, University; London, University of London P. [1967]
308 p. front., 20 plates, maps, plans, tables. 22½ cm. 30/- (B 67-1219)
Revision of author's thesis, National University of Ireland. Bibliography: p. [279]-290.
1. Yoruba. I. Title. II. Biobaku, S O
DT513.O36 1967 916.69 67-78331
Library of Congress [2]

Nigeria M896.2 Od8ag
Yoruba language - Drama.
Odunjo, J F
Agbàlọwọmeri bàlẹ jọntolo; itàn eré aládun. Enti ti o ya àwòran rẹ ni J. K. Oye. London, Longmans, Green and Co., 1958.
76p. illus.
Written in Yoruba.

Nigeria M372.4 Od8 Bk.3
Yoruba language - Grammar.
Odujinrin, J S A
Iwe kika; asiko. Part III. Lagos, Olufunmiso Printing Works, 1961.
124p. illus. 18½cm.
Written in Yoruba.

Nigeria M896.1 Aj5g
Yoruba language.
Ajisafe, Ajayi Kilawole.
O rúnmìlà, nipa A. K. Ajisafe. (A ko Gbodo da a Jo Laigbase.) Bungay, Suffolk, Printed for the author by Richard Clay & Sons, Ltd., 1923.
16 p. 18 cm.
Bound with: Ajisafe, A. K. Gbadebo Alake ... 1922.

Nigeria M496 B115
Yoruba language - Grammar.
Babalọla, Adeboye
Iwé èdè Yorùbá [Yoruba course for secondary schools] Fun awọn akẹkọ ni Ile-Iwe Giga; apa kini. [Ikeja, Nigeria] Longmans, [1963]
139p. illus. 18½cm.
Written in Yoruba.

Nigeria M896.1 At47 Bk. 1
Yoruba language - Poetry.
Atilade, Emmanuel Adekunle, 1911-
Iwe ikilọ fun awọn ọdọ; Apa I. Lagos, New Nigeria Press [n.d.]
36p. 18cm.
Written in Yoruba.

Nigeria M896.1 At47 Bk. 3
Yoruba language - Poetry.
Atilade, Emmanuel Adekunle, 1911-
Iwe ikilọ fun awọn ọdọ; Apa III. Lagos, New Nigeria Press ‹n.d.›
32p. 18cm.
Written in Yoruba.

Nigeria M896.1 At47 Bk. 4
Yoruba language - Poetry.
Atilade, Emmanuel Adekunle, 1911-
Iwe ikilọ fun awọn ọdọ; apa 4. Lagos, New Nigeria Press ‹n.d.›
30p. 18cm.
Written in Yoruba.

Nigeria M896.1 At47 Bk. 5
Yoruba language - Poetry.
Atilade, Emmanuel Adekunle, 1911-
Iwe ikilọ fun awọn ọdọ; Apa 5. Lagos, New Nigeria Press ‹n.d.›
29p. 18cm.
Written in Yoruba.

Nigeria M896.1 At47 Bk. 6
Yoruba language - Poetry.
Atilade, Emmanuel Adekunle, 1911-
Iwe ikilọ fun awọn ọdọ; Apa 6. Lagos, New Nigeria Press ‹n.d.›
27p. 18cm.
Written in Yoruba.

Nigeria M372.4 At47 Bk. I
Yoruba language - Readers and speakers.
Atilade, Emmanuel Adekunle, 1911-
Akoka Yoruba, Apa I. ‹Lagos, Ife Olu Printing Works ‹n.d.›
32p. illus. 18cm.

Nigeria M372.4 Od8 Bk. 1
Yoruba language-Readers and speakers.
Odujinrin, J S A
ABD asiko; apa kin-ni. Lagos, Olufunmiso Printing Works, 1963?
56p. illus. 18cm.

Nigeria M372.4 Od8 Bk. 2
Yoruba language - Readers and speakers.
Odujinrin, J S A
ABD asiko; apa kejo. ‹Ebute-Metta, Nigeria Service Printers› 1963.
55p. illus. 18cm.
Written in Yoruba.

Nigeria M372.4 Od83iw Bk.6
Yoruba language -Readers and speakers.
Ọdunjọ, J Folahan
Iwe-kẹfà alawiye. Eni ti o ya àwòrán rẹ̀ ni Cyril Deakins. London, Longmans, 1961.
128p. illus. 18½cm.
Translated title: Yoruba Alawiye readers, 6.
Written in Yoruba.

Nigeria M372.4 Od83iw Bk. 2
Yoruba language - Readers and speakers.
Odunjo, J Folahan
Iwe-keji Alawiye, fun awọn ọmọde; ati awọn agbà ti o nkọ iwe Yoruba ni kikà. London, Longmans, Green and Co., 1949.
64p. illus. 18½cm.
Translated title: Yoruba Alawiye readers, 2.
Written in Yoruba.

Nigeria M372.4 Od83i
Yoruba language - Readers and speakers.
Odunjo, J Folahan
Iwe-kini Alawiye; fun alakòbẹ̀rẹ̀ ẹ̀kọ́ Yoruba l'omode ati l'agbà. Eni ti o ya àwòran rẹ̀ ni Tayo Aiyegbusi. Ikeja ‹Nigeria› Longmans of Nigeria, 1963.
62p. illus. 18½cm.
Translated title: Alawiye primer and reader.
Written in Yoruba.

Nigeria M372.4 Od83iw Bk. 3
Yoruba language - Readers and speakers.
Ọdunjọ, J Folahan
Iwe-kẹta alawiye. ‹ 2nd ed. London› Longmans ‹1960›
97p. illus. 18½cm.
Translated title: Yoruba Alawiye reader, 3.
Written in Yoruba.

Nigeria M372.4 At47 Bk. 3
Yoruba language - Texts.
Atilade, Emmanuel Adekunle, 1911-
Akoka Yoruba, Apa keta. Lagos, New Nigeria Press ‹1962›
96p. illus. 21cm.
Written in Yoruba.

Nigeria M966.9 B11or
Yoruba marriage.
Babamuboni, I E
Oro ife toto; si awon ti o no ju obinrin kan lo. Lagos, Tanimola Printing & Book-Binding Works, 1926.
15p. 18cm.

Nigeria M728 Oj5
Yoruba palaces.
Ojo, G J Afolabi.
Yoruba palaces: a study of Afins of Yorubaland ‹by› G. J. Afolabi Ojo. London, University of London P. ‹1967›
112 p. plates, maps, plans, tables. 21 cm. 12/6
(B 67-2079)
Bibliography: p. 106.
1. Palaces—Yoruba. I. Title.
NA1597.Y6O38 728.8'2 67-75209
Library of Congress ‹2›

Nigeria M966.9 Aj51
Yoruba people.
Ajisafẹ, Ajayi Kọlawọle.
The laws and customs of the Yoruba people, by A.K. Ajisafẹ. London, George Routledge & Sons, Ltd., 1924.
97p. front. 17½cm.

Nigeria M896.1 B112
Yoruba poetry.
Babalọla, S A
The content and form of Yoruba ijala. Oxford, Clarendon P., 1966.
xiv, 395 p. 22½ cm. (Oxford library of African literature) 70/-
(B 67-1175)
Based on thesis, University of London.
Bibliography: p. ‹394›-395.
1. Folk-songs, Yoruba—Hist. & crit. I. Title. II. Title: Ijala.
PL8823.5.B3 67-72415
Library of Congress ‹2›

Africa M896 B36
Yoruba poetry.
Babalola, Adeboye.
Ijala; the traditional poetry of Yoruba hunters.
Pp. 12-22.
In: Beier, Ulli, comp., Introduction to African literature. London, Longmans, 1967.

Nigeria M496 K96a
Yoruba Primer.
Kuyẹ, J G
ABD alaworan. (ABD Yoruba pictorial primer with pictures). Sixth edition. n.p., 1929.
25p. illus. 17cm.

Nigeria M496 K96iw
Yoruba primer.
Kuyẹ, J G
Iwe alaworan keji. (Second Yoruba reader with pictures). Third edition. n.p., 1922.
64p. illus. 17cm.

Nigeria M496 K96i
Yoruba primer.
Kuyẹ, J G
Iwe alaworan kini. (First Yoruba reader with pictures). Second edition. n.p., 1923.
53p. illus. 17cm.

Nigeria M496 K96p
Yoruba primer.
Kuyẹ, J G
Primer gẹsi. Fifth edition. Rev. and enl. Lagos, The Church Missionary Society Bookshop, 1930.
55p. 18½cm.

Yoruba reader.

Nigeria
M496
So6

Sorinolu, Ariyo
Gbolohunoro - 200 Tabi Gbedegbeyo ⌈200 sentences or vocabulary⌉ Lagos, Church Missionary Society Bookshop, 1930.

25p. 18½cm.

Nigeria
M784
K58

Yoruba sacred music from Ekiti.
King, Anthony.
Yoruba sacred music from Ekiti. ⌈Nigeria⌉ Ibadan University Press, 1961.

ix, 45, xlix p. illus., music. 22 cm.
Music: xlix p. at end.

1. Music, African. 2. Music, Primitive. 3. Yorubas—Music. 4. Percussion music—Hist. & crit. I. Title.

ML3760.K47 62-759

Library of Congress ⌈1⌉

A
M784
Aw6

Yoruba songs.

⌈Ransome-Kuti, Josiah Jessie, 1855-1930⌉
Awọn orin momọ ni ed ati ohùn ile wa. Yoruba sacred songs. Lagos, C.M.S. Bookshop, 1925.

556-617p. 18½cm.

Nigeria
M966.9
Aj1ly

Yoruba warfare in the nineteenth century.
Ajayi, J F Ade.
Yoruba warfare in the nineteenth century, by J. F. Ade Ajayi and Robert Smith. Cambridge ⌈Eng.⌉ University Press, 1964.

x, 160 p. maps, plans, plate. 23 cm.
Bibliography: p. 148-151. Bibliographical footnotes.

1. Yorubas. 2. Nigeria—Hist. I. Smith, Robert Sydney. II. Title.

DT513.A48 966.9 64-21522

Library of Congress ⌈5⌉

Nigeria
M966.9
Aj1ly

Yorubas.
Ajayi, J F Ade.
Yoruba warfare in the nineteenth century, by J. F. Ade Ajayi and Robert Smith. Cambridge ⌈Eng.⌉ University Press, 1964.

x, 160 p. maps, plans, plate. 23 cm.
Bibliography: p. 148-151. Bibliographical footnotes.

1. Yorubas. 2. Nigeria—Hist. I. Smith, Robert Sydney. II. Title.

DT513.A48 966.9 64-21522

Library of Congress ⌈5⌉

Nigeria
M966.9
M782

Yorubas.
Moore, E A Ajisafe
The laws and customs of the Yoruba people. Abeokuta, Nigeria, M. A. Ola Fola Bookshops ⌈n.d.⌉

85p. 18cm.

1. Nigeria - Native races. 2. Yorubas. I. Title.

Nigeria
M966.9
Oj5

Yorubas.
Ojo, G J Afolabi.
Yoruba culture: a geographical analysis ⌈by⌉ G. J. Afolabi Ojo; foreword by S. O. Biobaku. Ife, University; London, University of London P. ⌈1967⌉

303 p. front., 20 plates, maps, plans, tables. 22½ cm. 30/-
(B 67-1219)
Revision of author's thesis, National University of Ireland.
Bibliography: p. ⌈279⌉-290.

1. Yorubas. I. Title. II. Biobaku, S O.

DT513.O36 1967 916.69 67-78331

Library of Congress ⌈5⌉

Nigeria
M966.9
L621

Yorubas - Folklore.
Lijadu, E M
Ifa: imole rè ti ise ipilè ìsin ni ile Yoruba, ⌈Sayings of the Yoruba⌉ nipa E.M. Lijadu. Exeter, printed by James Townsend & Sons, 1923.

72p. front. (port.) 21½cm.
In Yoruba.

Nigeria
M966.9
Og9s

Yorubas - Folklore.
Ogumefu, M I
The staff of Oranyan and other Yoruba tales, by M. I. Ogumefu. London, The Sheldon Press, ⌈1930⌉

iv, 5-32p. illus. 18½cm.

Nigeria
M966.9
Og9t

Yorubas - Folklore.
Ogumefu, M I
Tales of tortoise, Yoruba tales, by M. I. Ogumefu. London, The Sheldon Press ⌈n.d.⌉

v. 7-32p. illus. 18½cm.

Nigeria
M966.9
Og9y

Yorubas - Folklore.
Ogumefu, M I
Yoruba legends. London, The Sheldon Press ⌈1929⌉

87p. 17½cm.

Nigeria
M784
K58

Yorubas - Music.
King, Anthony.
Yoruba sacred music from Ekiti. ⌈Nigeria⌉ Ibadan University Press, 1961.

ix, 45, xlix p. illus., music. 22 cm.
Music: xlix p. at end.

1. Music, African. 2. Music, Primitive. 3. Yorubas—Music. 4. Percussion music—Hist. & crit. I. Title.

ML3760.K47 62-759

Library of Congress ⌈1⌉

Nigeria
M784
Og9y

Yorubas - Music.
Ogumefu, Ebun.
Yoruba melodies, adapted by Ebun Ogumefu. London, Society for promoting Christian knowledge ⌈1929⌉

16 p. 18½ cm.

Nigeria
M784
P54

Yorubas-Music.
Phillips, Ekundayo
Yoruba music (African); fusion of speech and music. Johannesburg, African Music Society, 1953.

58p. diagrs. 24½cm.

Nigeria
M966.9
At8a

Yorubas - Religion.
Atundaolu, H.
Awon enia inu bibeli, nipa H.Atundaolu... Lagos ⌈n.p.⌉ 1906.

vii, 208p. 18½cm.
Personalities in the Bible
In Yoruba.

Nigeria
M966.9
B11o

Yorubas - Religion.
Babamuboni, I E
Ojo Oluwa (Sunday) lati owo Mr. I.E. Babamuboni. Lagos, Tanimola printing and bookbinding works, 1927.

12p. 18½cm.
In Yoruba.

Nigeria
M290
Id5

Yorubas - Religion.
Idowu, E Bolaji.
Olódùmarè; God in Yoruba belief. ⌈London⌉ Longmans ⌈1962⌉

222 p. illus. 23 cm.

1. Yorubas—Religion. I. Title. II. Title: God in Yoruba belief.

BL2480.Y6I3 62-52364 ‡

Library of Congress ⌈2⌉

Nigeria
M966.9
J71i

Yorubas - Religion.
Jones, Melville, bp.
Isin Kristi ati Isin Momodu, ⌈Christianity and Mohammedanism⌉ lati owo Bisopu Melville Jones. Lagos, printed and published by the C.M.S. Press, 1920.

62p. 19cm.
In Yoruba.

Nigeria
M966.9
L96

Yorubas - Religion.
Lucas, J Olumide
The religion of the Yorubas; being an account of the religious beliefs and practices of the Yoruba peoples of Southern Nigeria, especially in relation to the religion of ancient Egypt. Lagos, C.M.S. Bookshop, 1948.

420p. illus. 21½cm.

Nigeria
M966.9
Og9a

Yorubas - Religion.
Ogunbiye, Thomas A J.
Awọn Serafu ⌈by⌉ Thos. A. J. Ogunbiye. Lagos, C.M.S. press, 1926.

14p. 18½cm.
In Yoruba.

Nigeria
M966.9
L621

Yorubas - Religious life.
Lijadu, E M
IFA: imọlẹ rẹ̀ ti iṣe ipilẹ̀ ìsin ni ilẹ Yoruba. Exeter, James Townsend & Sons, 1923.

72p. Portrait, 21½cm.
Translation: A Yoruba god: its foundation of worship in Yoruba land.

M811.5
H87p
Yoseloff, Thomas, 1913– *ed.*
Seven poets in search of an answer: Maxwell Bodenheim, Joy Davidman, Langston Hughes, Aaron Kramer, Alfred Kreymborg, Martha Millet, Norman Rosten. A poetic symposium edited by Thomas Yoseloff, with an introductory note by Shaemas O'Sheel. New York, B. Ackerman, incorporated [1944]
8 p. l., 15-118 p. illus. (ports.) 24cm.
1. American poetry—20th cent. I. Bodenheim, Maxwell, 1893- II. Davidman, Joy. III. *Hughes, Langston, 1902- IV. Kramer, Aaron. V. Kreymborg, Alfred, 1883- VI. Millet, Martha. VII. Rosten, Norman. VIII. Title.
Library of Congress PS614.Y58 44-4241
[10] 811.5082

Guinea
M896.1
Yo83
Youla, Nabi
Moussa, enfant de Guinée; Aux enfants de Guinée et a leurs petits amis de tous les pays. Regensburg, Josef Habbel [1964]
[68]p. illus. 30cm.
Text in French and Dutch.
I. Title.

M350
Yo8m
Young, Charles, 1864–1922.
Military morale of nations and races, by Charles Young ... Kansas City, Mo., Franklin Hudson publishing co., 1912.
273 p. 22½cm.
Bibliography: p. [7]
1. National characteristics. 2. Ethnopsychology. 3. Soldiers. 4. Morale. I. Title.
Library of Congress U21.Y6 14–8826
[a41b1]

Nigeria
M618.2
Ad35
You and your baby.
Adeniyi-Jones. O., jt auth.
You and your baby [by] W. R. F. Collis [and] O. Adeniyi-Jones. Lagos, African Universities Press [1961]
94p. 18½cm. illus.

Youmba.
Martinique
M843.9
M32ba
1938
Maran, René, 1887–
... Batouala; véritable roman nègre. Éd. définitive. Paris, A. Michel [1938]
3 p. l., [9]-250 p., 2 l. 19cm.
CONTENTS.—Batouala.—Youmba, la mangouste.
I. Title. II. Title: Youmba, la mangouste.
Library of Congress PQ2625.A74B29 1938 38-23341
Copyright A—Foreign 39301
[2]

M06
Am35
Young, Donald Ramsey, 1898– ed.
American academy of political and social science, *Philadelphia.*
The American Negro ... Editor in charge of this volume: Donald Young ... Philadelphia, The American academy of political and social science, 1928.
viii, 359 p. front., illus. (maps) diagrs. 24cm. (*Its* Annals. vol. CXXXX [no. 229] November, 1928)
Contains bibliographies.
CONTENTS.—Foreword.—Race relations.—The Negro as an element in the population of the United States.—The legal status of the Negro.—The economic achievement of the Negro. — The mental ability and achievement of the Negro.—Organizations for social betterment.—Race relations in other lands.
1. Negroes. 2. Negro race. 3. U. S.—Race question. 4. Race problems. I. Young, Donald Ramsey, 1898– ed. II. Title.
Library of Congress H1.A4 vol. CXXXX 28—29716
———— Copy 2. E185.6.A38
[41k2]

Nigeria
M333
Ek34
You and your landlord and you and the law of libel and slander.
Ekineh, Aliyi.
You and your landlord and you and the law of libel and slander. Lagos, Megida Printers and Publishers [1961]
50p. 22½cm. (Megida legal guide series, no. 1)

Youmba, la mangouste.
Martinique
M843.9
M32y
Maran, René, 1887–
Youmba, la mangouste.
(In: Les Oeuvres libres, v. 159. Paris, Fayard, 1934. 19cm. p.[5]-48)

M813.5
Y84
Young, James L
Helen Duval; a French romance, by James L. Young (Colored) San Francisco, The Bancroft Company, 1891.
202p. 19cm.
I. Title.

You can learn Creole;
Haiti
M447.9
M31y
McConnell, H Ormonde.
You can learn Creole; a simple introduction to Haitian Creole for English speaking people, by H. Ormonde McConnell [and] Eugene Swan. Port-au-Prince, Haïti, Impr. de l'État, 1945.
108 p. 24 cm.
Additional text on label mounted on p. [89]
1. Creole dialects—Haiti. I. Swan, Eugene, joint author. II. Title.
PM7854.H3M3 447.9 47-27395*
Library of Congress [1]

M796
Y84g
Young, Andrew Sturgeon Nash, 1919–
Great Negro baseball stars, and how they made the major leagues. New York, A. S. Barnes [1953]
248 p. illus. 21 cm.
1. Baseball—Biog. 2. Negro athletes. I. Title.
GV865.Y6A3 796.357 52-12609 ‡
Library of Congress [15]

M231.74
Yo8s
Young, Lucinda Smith.
The seven seals. "A sinner's dream", "conversion," "Daniel in the lion's den," "meditation," "distance of falling," vision of the judgement," vision of after the judgement," By Madame Lucinda Smith-Young. Philadelphia, Pa., J. Gordon Baugh, 1903.
199p. front. plates. 18½cm.
1. Revelations. 2. Dreams. I. Title.

You can't build a chimney from the top.
MB9
H72y
Holley, Joseph Winthrop, 1874–
You can't build a chimney from the top; the South through the life of a Negro educator. New York, William-Frederick Press, 1948.
226p. illus. ports. 23cm.

M796
Y84g
Young, Andrew Sturgeon Nash, 1919–
Great Negro baseball stars, and how they made the major leagues. New York, A. S. Barnes [1953]
248 p. illus. 21 cm.
Paper binding
1. Baseball—Biog. 2. Negro athletes. I. Title.
GV865.Y6A3 796.357 52-12609 ‡
Library of Congress [15]

M973
Y86
Young, Margaret (Buchner)
The first book of American Negroes, by Margaret B. Young. New York, F. Watts [1966]
86 p. illus., ports. 23 cm.
~~1. Negroes—Juvenile literature.~~ I. Title.
1. History - Juvenile literature.
E185.Y6 j917.3 66-31407
Library of Congress [5]

M813.5
B64y
You can't pet a possum.
Bontemps, Arna Wendell, 1902–
You can't pet a possum, by Arna Bontemps; with illustrations by Ilse Bischoff. New York, W. Morrow and company, 1934.
4 p. l., 120 p. illus., col. plates. 20½cm.
I. Title.
34–32567 Revised
Library of Congress PZ7.B6443Yo
[r44e2]

M796
Y84n
Young, Andrew Sturgeon Nash, 1919–
Negro firsts in sports, by A. S. "Doc" Young. With illus. by Herbert Temple. Chicago, Johnson Pub. Co. [1963]
301 p. illus. 22 cm.
1. Negro athletes. I. Title.
GV697.A1Y6 927.96 62—21535 ‡
Library of Congress [63f10]

M649.1
Y86
Young, Margaret Buchner,
How to bring up your child without prejudice, by Margaret B. Young. [1st ed. New York, Public Affairs Committee, 1965]
20 p. col. illus. 18 cm. (Public affairs pamphlet no. 373)
Cover title.
Bibliography: p. 20.
"Illustrations by Ernest Crichlow."
1. Prejudices and antipathies (Child psychology) I. Title.
2. Child study. II. Crichlow, Ernest, illus.
BF723.P75Y6 65–5635
Library of Congress [10]

You in your small corner.
Jamaica
M822.91
R24y
Reckford, Barry
You in your small corner; a play. London [s.p.], n.d.
[56] leaves. 22cm.
"To Arthur Spingarn with great respect & affection. Barry Reckford."
Mimeographed.

MB9
L69y
Young, Andrew Sturgeon Nash, 1919–
Sonny Liston, the champ nobody wanted, by A. S. "Doc" Young. Chicago, Johnson Pub. Co. [1963]
224 p. illus. 21 cm.
1. Liston, Sonny. 2. Boxing.
GV1132.L5Y6 927.9683 63–15659 ‡
Library of Congress [5]

M977.8
Yo8y
Young, Nathan Benjamin, 1862-1933
Your St. Louis and Mine."
St. Louis, N.B. Young [1937]
80p. illus. 25½cm.
1. St. Louis, Mo.
I. Title

M814.5
Yo8p

Young, Plummer Bernard, 1884-
A plea for understanding, editorials reprinted from the Norfolk Journal and guide. Norfolk, Va. Guide Publishing co., 1935.

2 fold, l., 6 columns. 25cm.
Contents: -Our educational dilemma and proposed court action as a remedy; -Let us understand each other.

1. Education--Virginia. I. Title.

Africa
M896.3
Yo8a

Young, T Cullen, ed.
African new writing; short stories by African authors. London, Lutterworth Press [1947]

126 p. 19 cm.

1. Short stories. I. Title.

PZ1.Y85Af 48-13317*

Library of Congress [1]

Young, T. Cullen, tr.

Malawi
M968.97
N87m

Ntara, Samuel Yosia, 1904 *or* 5-
Man of Africa, by Samuel Yosia Ntara; translated and arranged from the original Nyanja by T. Cullen Young. Foreword by Professor Julian Huxley ... London, The Religious tract society [1934]

180, [1] p. front., plates. 19cm.

"Prize-winning biography under authority of the International institute of African languages and cultures ... 1933."—p. [2]

1. Ethnology—Nyasaland. I. Young, T. Cullen, tr. II. Religious tract society, London. III. International institute of African languages and cultures.

35-6977

Library of Congress DT864.N8

[5] 572.96897

M973
R72

Young, Whitney Moore, 1921-
Civil rights action and the Urban League.
Pp. 210-219.

In: Rose Arnald Marshall, ed. Assuring freedom to the free. Detroit, Wayne State University, 1964.

M323.4
W52

Young, Whitney Moore, 1921-
A debate over "compensation" programs, by Whitney M. Young, Jr., and Kyle Haselden.

pp. 279-289.

In: Westin, Alan F. Freedom now. New York, Basic Books, 1964.

M301
Eb74

Young, Whitney Moore, 1921-
The high cost of discrimination
Pp. 21-30

In: Ebony. The white problem in America. Chicago, Johnson Pub. Co., 1966.

M331
G43

Young, Whitney Moore, 1921-
Jobs and people.

Pp. 25-37.

In: Ginzberg, Eli, ed. The Negro challenge to the business community. New York, McGraw-Hill, 1964.

Young, Whitney Moore, 1921-
Middle-class Negroes and the Negro masses.
pp. 315-319.

M323.4
W52

Westin, Alan F ed.
Freedom now! The civil-rights struggle in America. Edited by Alan F. Westin. New York, Basic Books [1964]

xv, 346 p. 22 cm.

Bibliography: p. [329]-341.

1. Negroes — Civil rights — Addresses, essays, lectures. 2. Civil rights—U. S.—Addresses, essays, lectures. I. Title.

E185.61.W54 301.451 64-17401

Library of Congress [5]

M323
Y87

Young, Whitney Moore, 1921-
Preface.

(In Halsey, Margaret. Color blind. New York, McGraw-Hill, 1965. p. ix-xiv)

M323.4
Y87

Young, Whitney Moore, 1921-
To be equal [by] Whitney M. Young, Jr. [1st ed.] New York, McGraw-Hill [1964]

254 p. 22 cm.

1. Negroes—Civil rights. 2. Negroes—Moral and social conditions. I. Title.

E185.61.Y73 323.41 64-23179

Library of Congress [7-1]

M975
M834

Young, Whitney Moore, 1921-
A vanishing era.

Pp. 100-101.

In: Morris, Willie, ed. The South today. New York, Harper & Row [1965]

Young, Whitney Moore, 1921- joint author.

M301
D122

Turner, John Briscoe, 1922-
Who has the revolution or thoughts on the second reconstruction, by John B. Turner and Whitney M. Young.

Pp. 678-693.

In: Daedalus. The Negro American. Boston, Houghton Mifflin, 1966.

Young bough blossoming.

M811.5
T36y

Thomas, Charles Cyrus, 1909-
Young bough blossoming. Hollywood, Calif. 1954.

33p. 24cm.
Inscribed by author.

Africa
M808.81
B75

Young Commonwealth poets '65.
Brent, P L ed.
Young Commonwealth poets '65. London, Heinemann in assocation with Cardiff Commonwealth Arts Festival [1965]

216p. 22½cm.
White editor.

1. Poetry - Collection. 2. African poetry. 3. West Indian poetry. I. Title.

A young hunter.

M285
Sh4y

Sheppard, William Henry, 1865-1927.
A young hunter, a true story of Central Africa. By Rev. W.H. Sheppard... [Louisville, Ky., The author, n.d.]

7p. illus. 17½cm.

Young Jim; the early years of James Weldon Johnson.

MB9
J64t

Tarry, Ellen, 1906-
Young Jim; the early years of James Weldon Johnson. New York, Dodd, Mead [1967]

xii, 230 p. facsims., ports. 22 cm.

1. Johnson, James Weldon, 1871-1938—Juvenile literature. I. Title.

PS3519.O2625Z89 67-22194

Library of Congress [3]

Young men.

M815.4
M43y

Matthews, William E.
'Young manhood: it's relations to a worthy future.' Address delivered before the literary societies of Wilberforce university, commencement week, June 15th, 1880, by William E. Matthews ... [Washington? D. C., 1880]

cover-title, 1 p. l., 15 p. 20½cm.

1. Young men. 15-17286

Library of Congress BJ1671.M6

Young men's Christian associations.

MB9
H91h

Hunton, Addie D. (Waite)
William Alphaeus Hunton; a pioneer prophet of young men, by Addie W. Hunton. New York, Association press, 1938.

xii, 176 p. 21cm.

1. Hunton, William Alphaeus, 1863-1916. 2. Young men's Christian associations.

39-10087

Library of Congress BV1085.H8H8

[a45d1] 922

Young men's Christian association.

M267.3
Y87m

Young men's Christian associations. *Association of secretaries.*
Men working; the Y. M. C. A. program and the present needs of youth; being an account of the work of the Young men's Christian association as portrayed in the proceedings of the forty-sixth conference of the Association of secretaries at Silver bay on lake George, New York, June 8-13, 1936 ... New York, Association press [°1936]
178 p. 23½cm.
Edited by L. K. Hall.
"A selected bibliography": p. 171-178.
1. Young men's Christian associations. 2. Youth. I. Hall, Lawrence Kingsley, 1886- ed. II. Title.

A 37-093

Pittsburgh. Univ. Libr.
for Library of Congress [42c1]

Young men's Christian associations (Colored)

M267.3
Ar7

Arthur, George Robert, 1879-
Life on the Negro frontier; a study of the objectives and the success of the activities promoted in the Young men's Christian associations operating in "Rosenwald" buildings [by] George R. Arthur. New York, Association press, 1934.

viii, 259 p. plates, maps. 19½cm.

1. Young men's Christian associations (Colored) 2. Rosenwald, Julius, 1862-1932. 3. Julius Rosenwald fund. 4. Negroes—Moral and social conditions. I. Title.

35-27187

Library of Congress BV1190.A7

—— —— Copy 2.

Copyright A 84475 [5-5] 267.3650973

Young Men's Christian Associations. Association of Secretaries.

M267.3
Ar7

Arthur, George Robert, 1879-
Area project of the Wabash Avenue Department.

(In: Young Men's Christian Associations. Association of Secretaries. Men working; the Y.M.C.A. program... New York, Association, Press, c1936. 24cm. p. 57-59).

M267.3 Yo8b
Young Men's Christian Associations. International Convention. Centennial.
Between two centuries: report of the Centennial International Y.M.C.A. Convention. New York, Association Press, 1951.
209p. ports. illus. 23cm.
Partial contents: Conditions of world peace and world unity, by Ralph Bunche.–Living is a Christian calling, by Benjamin Mays.
I. Title. II. Tobias, Channing.

M973 P942
The young Negro in America, 1960-1980.
Proctor, Samuel Dewitt, 1921-
The young Negro in America, 1960-1980, by Samuel D. Proctor. New York, Association Press [1966]
160 p. 21 cm.
Bibliographical references included in "Notes by chapters" (p. 159-160)
1. Negroes—Civil rights. 2. Negroes—Hist. I. Title.
E185.61.P76 301.45196073 66-15750
Library of Congress [5]

M350 J62
Young people's socialist league of America.
Johnson, J R
Why Negroes should oppose the war, by J. R. Johnson ... [New York, Pub. by Pioneer publishers for the Socialist workers party and the Young people's socialist league (Fourth International) 1939?]
30, [1] p. 21cm.
1. World war, 1939- —Negroes. I. Socialist workers party. II. Young people's socialist league of America. III. Title.
44-12148
Library of Congress D810.N4J57 [2] 940.5403

M811.5 T61y
The young scholar.
Toney, Ieda Mai.
The young scholar, & other poems; with a critical introd. by Charles Leander Hill. Boston, Meador Pub. Co. [1951]
82 p. port. 21 cm.
I. Title.
PS3539.O42Y6 811.5 51-5072
Library of Congress [2]

M396 H11c
Young women.
Hackley, E Azalia.
The colored girl beautiful, by E. Azalia Hackley ... Kansas City, Mo., Burton publishing company [1916]
8 p. l., 9-208 p. 20 cm.
"This volume has been compiled from talks given to girls in colored boarding schools."—Foreword.
1. Young women. 2. Conduct of life. I. Title.
18—20407
Library of Congress BJ1681.H3 [a48b1]

M267.5 B41i
Young women's christian associations.
Bell, Juliet Ober, 1895-
Interracial practices in community Y. W. C. A.'s; a study under the auspices of the Commission to gather interracial experience, as requested by the sixteenth National convention of the Y. W. C. A.'s of the U. S. A., conducted by Juliet O. Bell, PH. D., and Helen J. Wilkins. New York, N. Y., National board, Y. W. C. A., 1944.
8 p. l., 116 p. 21½cm.
"Recommendations related to interracial practices in community Y. W. C. A.'s to be submitted for action to the seventeenth National convention" (8 p.) inserted.
1. U. S.—Race question. 2. Negroes. 3. Young women's Christian associations. I. Wilkins, Helen J., joint author. II. Young women's Christian associations. U. S. National board. Commission to gather interracial experience. III. Title.
44-7133
Library of Congress E185.61.B4 [4] 267.43265

M267.5 B41i
Young women's Christian associations. U. S. National board. Commission to gather interracial experience.
Bell, Juliet Ober, 1895-
Interracial practices in community Y. W. C. A.'s; a study under the auspices of the Commission to gather interracial experience, as requested by the sixteenth National convention of the Y. W. C. A.'s of the U. S. A., conducted by Juliet O. Bell, PH. D., and Helen J. Wilkins. New York, N. Y., National board, Y. W. C. A., 1944.
8 p. l., 116 p. 21½cm.
"Recommendations related to interracial practices in community Y. W. C. A.'s to be submitted for action to the seventeenth National convention" (8 p.) inserted.
1. U. S.—Race question. 2. Negroes. 3. Young women's Christian associations. I. Wilkins, Helen J., joint author. II. Young women's Christian associations. U. S. National board. Commission to gather interracial experience. III. Title.
44-7133
Library of Congress E185.61.B4 [4] 267.43265

M813.5 K55y 1956
Youngblood.
Killens, John O
Youngblood. London, The Bodley Head, 1956.
566p. 20cm.

M813.5 K55y
Youngblood.
Killens, John O
Youngblood. New York, Pocket Books, Inc., 1955.
519p. 16cm.

M813.5 K55
Youngblood.
Killens, John O
Youngblood. New York, Dial Press, 1954.
566 p. 21 cm.
I. Title.
PZ4.K48Yo 54-7128 ‡
Library of Congress [8]

M323.2 F31y
Your community and its unity.
Federal Council of the Churches of Christ in America. Dept. of Race Relations.
Your community and its unity; How you can help improve race relations. New York, the Council, 1944.
31p. illus. 18cm. (Interracial publication, no.34

Kenya M170 G12
Your friends are thinking series.
Gakwa, Silvanus Njendu
Haria tūrī rīu. Where we are now. Nairobi, Eagle Press, 1949.
[25p. 18½cm. (Merciria ma arata anyu. Your friends are thinking series)
Written in English and Kikuyu.
1. Ethics. I. Title. II. Series. III. Series: Your friends are thinking series. IV. Title: Where we are now.

Kenya M967.6 K23
Your friends are thinking series.
Kebaso, John K 1911-
Jinsi Afrika mashariki inavyowiwa deni kubwa na utawala wa dola ya kiingereza. East Africa owes much to British rule. Nairobi, Eagle Press, 1953.
[47]p. 18½cm. (Mawazo ya wenzenu. Your friends are thinking series)
Written in Swahili and English.
1. Africa, British East - Politics and government. I. Title. II. Title: East Africa owes much to British rule. III. Series. IV. Series: Your friends are thinking series.

Kenya M967.62 Oy3
Your friends are thinking series.
Oyende, J P
Chifu hodari wa kiafrika. The ideal African chief. Nairobi, Eagle Press, 1951.
14p. 18cm. (Mawazo ya wenzenu. Your friends are thinking series)
Written Swahili and English.
1. Leadership. 2. Africa - Native races. I. Title. II. Title: The ideal African chief. III. Series. IV. Series: Your friends are thinking series.

Kenya M967.62 Oy3p
Your friends are thinking series.
Oyende, J P
Paro mako kuom dohini e Kenya [Some thoughts on native tribunals in Kenya] Nairobi, Eagle Press, 1950.
27p. 18cm. (Paro mag jowadi. Your friends are thinking series)
Written in Luo and English
1. Justice, Administration of - Kenya Colony and Protectorate. 2. Kenya Colony and Protectorate. I. Title. II. Title: Some thoughts on native tribunals in Kenya. III. Series. IV. Series: Your friends are thinking series.

Kenya M376 R112
Your friends are thinking series.
Rabuku, Martin A
Puonjrwok mar nyako [A girl's education] Nairobi, Eagle Press, 1950.
23p. 18cm. (Paro mag jowadu. Your friends are thinking series)
Written in Luo and English.
1. Education of women. I. Title. II. Title: A girl's education. III. Series.

M973 R63y
Your history from the beginning of time to the present.
Rogers, Joel Augustus, 1880-
Your history from the beginning of time to the present, by J.A. Rogers. Pittsburgh, Pa., Pittsburgh Courier, 1940.
96 unnumb. p. illus. 30cm.

M813.5 G76y
Your most humble servant.
Graham, Shirley.
Your most humble servant. New York, Messner [1949]
. 235 p. 22 cm.
"Notes on sources": p. 227-235.
1. Banneker, Benjamin, 1731-1806. I. Title.
Full name: Lola Shirley (Graham) McCanns.
QB36.B22G7 925.2 49—11346*
Library of Congress [50z7]

M810 B73y
Your Negro neighbor.
Brawley, Benjamin Griffith, 1882-
Your Negro neighbor, by Benjamin Brawley ... New York, The Macmillan company, 1918.
3 p. l., 100 p. front. (port.) 17cm.
1. Negroes. I. Title.
18—12720
Library of Congress E185.5.B82 [41b1]

M610 C63y
Your nose won't tell.
Cobb, William Montague, 1904-
Your nose won't tell. Reprinted from the Crisis, 45:332, 336, October 1938.
one leaf, 3 columns. 30cm.

M977.8 Yo8y
Your St. Louis and Mine.
Young, N B editor.
Your St. Louis and Mine.
St. Louis, N.B. Young [1937]
80p. illus. 25½cm.

You're not alone.
[illegible]304 Gordon, Eugene, 1890-
[illegible] You're not alone. New York, International Workers Order, 1940.
v.2, no.9
59p. illus. 15cm.

Youth.
M324 Armattoe, Raphael Ernest Grail.
Ar5p The pttern youth: an interim report. Reprinted from Nature, vol. 152, Aug 21, 1943. p. 217.

Youth.
M267.3 Arthur, George Robert, 1879-
Ar7 Area project of the Wabash Avenue Department.
(In: Young Men's Christian Assoications. Association of Secretaries. Men working; the Y.M.C.A. program... New York, Association Press, ©1936. 24cm. p. 57-59)

Haiti
M972.94 Youth.
C73f Comhaire-Sylvain, Suzanne
Food and leisure among the African youth of Leopoldville (Belgian Congo). Cape Town, University of Cape Town, 1950.
124p. 33cm. (Communications from the School of African studies, new series, no. 25)

Youth.
M301 Frazier, Edward Franklin, 1894-
F86 ny Negro youth at the crossways, their personality development in the middle states, by E. Franklin Frazier; prepared for the American youth commission. Washington, D. C., American council on education, 1940.
xxiii, 301, [2] p. illus. (maps) diagr. 23½ cm.
"This volume ... describes the experiences of Negro boys and girls living in Washington, D. C., and Louisville, Kentucky; these communities were selected as examples of middle-area conditions."—Pref.
1. Negroes—Moral and social conditions. 2. Youth. 3. Personality. 4. Social psychology. 5. Negroes—District of Columbia. 6. Negroes—Louisville, Ky. I. American council on education. American youth commission. II. Title.
Library of Congress E185.6.F74 40—32764
[42r7] 325.2609753

Youth.
M323 National association for the advancement of colored people.
N21 Resources in Negro youth. New York city, National association for the advancement of colored people, 1940.
18p. 20cm.

Youth.
M975.8 National Youth Administration. Georgia.
N21n Negro youth in Georgia study their problems: Based on the first state Negro youth conference ..., by William H. Shell and Gabriel S. Alexander. [Atlanta, 1940]
85p. 28cm. (Bulletin, no.3)
Mimeographed.

Youth-Religious life.
Haiti
M972.94 Solages, F
So4b Face à l'avenir! Conférences dédiées à la jeunesse masculine et féminine de mon pays, aux éducateurs et éducatrices. Port-au-Prince, Haïti, 1948.
166 p. 18 cm.
1. Youth—Religious life. 2. Christian life—Catholic authors. I. Title.
BX2355.S6 248 49-51661*
Library of Congress [1]

Youth - Harlem, New York (City).
M362.7 Harlem Youth Opportunities Unlimited, *New York.*
H226 Youth in the ghetto; a study of the consequences of powerlessness and a blueprint for change. [1st ed.] New York, 1964.
xxi, 614 p. illus., maps, tables. 28 cm.
Bibliographical footnotes.
1. Harlem, New York (City)—Soc. condit. 2. Youth—Harlem, New York (City) 3. ~~Negroes~~—New York (City) I. Title.
HN80.N5H3 64-16399
Library of Congress [5]

Youth in the ghetto.
M362.7 Harlem Youth Opportunities Unlimited, *New York.*
H226 Youth in the ghetto; a study of the consequences of powerlessness and a blueprint for change. [1st ed.] New York, 1964.
xxi, 614 p. illus., maps, tables. 28 cm.
Bibliographical footnotes.
1. Harlem, New York (City)—Soc. condit. 2. Youth—Harlem, New York (City) 3. ~~Negroes~~—New York (City) I. Title.
HN80.N5H3 64-16399
Library of Congress [5]

M813.5 Youth of color.
T368y Thomason, Caroline Wasson.
Youth of color, a novel. New York, Exposition Press [1951]
208 p. 23 cm.

Youth's flight, a collection of poems.
Virgin Is.
M811.5 Hatchette, Wilfred Irvin
H28y Youth's flight, a collection of poems. St. Thomas, Virgin Island, Art Shop Press, 1938.
30p. 20½cm.

M811.08 Yoseloff, Thomas, 1913- *ed.*
Yo8 Seven poets in search of an answer: Maxwell Bodenheim, Joy Davidman, Langston Hughes, Aaron Kramer, Alfred Kreymborg, Martha Millet, Norman Rosten. A poetic symposium edited by Thomas Yoseloff, with an introductory note by Shaemas O'Sheel. New York, B. Ackerman, incorporated [1944]
8 p. l., 15-118 p. illus. (ports.) 24cm.
1. American poetry—20th cent. I. Bodenheim, Maxwell, 1893- II. Davidman, Joy. III. *Hughes, Langston, 1902- IV. Kramer, Aaron. V. Kreymborg, Alfred, 1883- VI. Millet, Martha. VII. Rosten, Norman. VIII. Title.
Library of Congress PS614.Y58 44-4241
[10] 811.5082

Yulan; a novel.
M813.5 Washington, Doris V
W276y Yulan; a novel. New York, Carlton Press, 1964.
100p. 20cm.
Portrait of author on book jacket.
I. Title.

Zalka Peetruza and other poems.
M811.5 Dandridge, Raymond Garfield.
D19z Zalka Peetruza and other poems, by Raymond Garfield Dandridge. Cincinnati, The McDonald Press, 1928.
xiii, 107p. port. 24cm.
autographed presentation copy.

Zamal.
France
M841 Albany, Jean.
Al3z Zamal. Paris, Éditions Bellenand [1951]
64 p. 20 cm.
Poems.
I. Title.
PQ2601.L311Z3 A 52-2789
Illinois. Univ. Library for Library of Congress [2]†

Zamba, an African Negro King.
M813.3 Neilson, Peter, 1795-1861.
N312 The life and adventure of Zamba, an African Negro king; and his experience of slavery in South Carolina. Written by himself. Corrected and arranged by Peter Neilson. London, Smith, Elder and co., 1950.
xx, 258p. front. 20½cm.
Written by Peter Neilson. cf. Dict. nat. biog

Zambia - History.
Zambia
M968.94 Kaunda, Kenneth David, Pres. Zambia, 1924-
K16k Kenneth Kaunda of Zambia; selections from his writings, edited by Thomas Patrick Melady. New York, Issued for the Africa Service Institute of New York by Praeger [1964]
254p. 22cm.

Zambia shall be free.
Rhodesia, Northern
MB9 ~~Kaunda, Kenneth D~~ 1924-
K16a Zambia shall be free; an autobiography. New York, Praeger [1963, °1962]
202 p. illus. 19 cm. (Books that matter)
1. Rhodesia, Northern—Pol. & govt. I. Title.
DT963.K3 968.94 63-8622 ‡
Library of Congress [5]

Zambia shall be free.
Northern Rhodesia
MB9 Kaunda, Kenneth D 1924- London,
K16 Zambia shall be free; an autobiography. ~~New York, Praeger [1963, °1962]~~ Heinemann, 1962.
202 p. illus. 19 cm. (Books that matter)
1. Rhodesia, Northern—Pol. & govt. I. Title.
DT963.K3 968.94 63-8622 ‡
Library of Congress [5]

Kenya
M967.62 Zani, Z M S
Z1m Mashairi yangu [my poems] Kampala, The Eagle Press, 1953.
279p. 18½cm.
1. Kenya-poetry.

Zanzibar. Zanzibar
M967.8 Om1
Omar, C A Shariff
Kisiwa cha Pemba; historia na masimulizi [History and traditions of the Island of Pemba] Nairobi, Eagle Press, 1951.
21p. illus., port., maps. 21cm.
Written in Swahili.
1. Pemba. - History. 2. Pemba. - Social life and customs. 3. Zanzibar. I. Title.

Zanzibar - Fiction
Zanzibar
M896.3 F25k
Farsy, Muhammad Saleh, 1925-
Kurwa na doto [Kurwa and Doto] maelezo ya makazi katika kijiji cha Unguja yaani Zanzibar. Dar es Salaam, Eagle Press, 1960.
62p. 18½cm.
Written in Swahili.
1. Zanzibar - Fiction. I. Title.

Zanzibar - Social life and customs.
Zanzibar
M392 F26
Farsy, Muhammad Saleh, 1925-
Ada za harusi, katika unguja [Marriage customs in Zanzibar] Dar es Salaam, East African Literature Bureau, 1956.
51p. illus. 18cm. (Desturi na masimulizi ya Afrika ya mashariku)
Written in Swahili.
1. Marriage - Zanzibar. 2. Zanzibar - Social life and customs. I. Title.

Zanzibar
M398 Z17
Zanzibar tales told by natives of the east coast of Africa; translated from the original Swahili by George W. Bateman, illustrated by Walter Bobbett. Chicago, A. C. McClurg & co., 1901.
3 p. l., [5]-224 p. incl. illus., plates. 19cm.
Added t.-p., illustrated.
Stories about animals.
1. Swahili literature. 2. Folk-lore—Zanzibar. 3. Animals, Legends and stories of. I. Bateman, George W., tr.
Library of Congress GR360.Z3Z3 1—26205
[a42g1]

Colombia
M869.3 Z17d
Zapata Olivella, Manuel
Detrás del rostro, novela. Madrid, Aguilar [1963]
159p.
I. Title.

Zeitlin, Ida, tr.
France
M843 C67r
Colette, Sidonie Gabrielle, 1873-
... The ripening; translated from the French by Ida Zeitlin. New York, Farrar & Rinehart, incorporated [°1932]
3 p. l., 3-244 p. 20cm.
At head of title: Colette.
I. Zeitlin, Ida, tr. II. Title. *Translation of Le blé en herbe.*
Library of Congress PZ3.C6796R1 32-21436 Revised
——— Copy 2.
Copyright A 53725 [r36d2] 843.91

Zelenzné město. (Iron city).
M813.5 B799z
Brown, Lloyd Louis, 1913-
Zelenzné město. (Iron city). Praha, Statni Nakladatelstvi, 1953.
251p. 20cm.

M811.08 Z44T
Zenkevitch, Ivan Kushkeen Michael, ed.
Poets of America. XX century, an anthology. Moscow, Literary Art State Publishing House, 1939.
288p. 22cm.
Text in Russian.
1. (Poetry-Collections) II. Hughes, Langston, 1902- III. Brown, Sterling Allen, 1901- IV. Cullen, Countee, 1903-1946.

South Africa
M968 Z62
Zibi, Shadrack F 1879-1954
U-kayakulu: umhlaba otengwa e Rustenburg... Lamanqaku alencwadana aqokelelwe ngu D.D.T. Jabavu. Lovedale, Lovedale institution press [1930]
38p. 18½cm.
In Xhosa. Facts concerning land which has been released at Rustenburg for purchase by Africans.
1. Xhosa language. I. Jabavu, Davidson Don Tengo, 1885- 2. Africa - land tenure.

South Africa
M968 Z62
Zibi, Shadrack F 1879-1954.
U-kayakulu: umhlaba otengwa e Rustenburg... Lamanqaku alencwadana aqokelelwe ngu D.D.T. Jabavu. Lovedale, Lovedale Institution Press [1930]
38p. 18½cm.
In Xhosa. Facts concerning land which has been released at Rustenburg for purchase by Africans.

Zik.
Nigeria
M966.9 Az2z
Azikiwe, Nnamdi, 1904-
Zik; a selection from the speeches of Nnamdi Azikiwe. Cambridge, University Press, 1961.
344p. port. 22cm.
Portrait of author on book jacket.

Zik of new Africa.
Nigeria
M89 Az3ik
Ikeotuonye, Vincent C
Zik of new Africa. London, P. R. Macmillan Ltd., 1961.
262p. 23cm.
Portrait of biographee on front of book.

Nigeria
M966.9 Az2zi
Zik on African unity.
Azikiwe, Benjamin Nnamdi, 1904-
Zik on African unity; opening address to the heads of African and Malagasy States Conference in Lagos, 25th Jan. 1962 & Respect for human dignity; inaugural address delivered on 16th November 1960. Lagos, Udo-Na-Meche Stores, 1962.
21p. 22½cm.
Cover title.

M323 Z65
Zilton, A W
The negative forces vs. the positive qualities. n.p., n.p., 1942.
40p. illus. (ports) 23cm.
Cover title.
1. Race relations. I. Title.

M910 C77s
Zimeo.
Cook, Mercer, 1903- ed.
Saint Lambert's Zimeo. Edited with foreword, notes and vocabulary by Mercer Cook and Guichard Parris. Atlanta, Atlanta University, 1936.
28 p. 28 cm. (The Atlanta University french series)

Zinunula omunaku.
Uganda
M896.3 K17z
Kawere, Edward K N
Zinunula omunaku [They buy a poor man] Nairobi, Eagle Press, 1954.
109p. 21cm.
Written in Luganda.
I. Title.

Zipporah, the maid of Midian.
M813.5 B78z
Brockett, Joshua Arthur.
Zipporah, the maid of Midian, by Joshua A. Brockett ... [Zion, Ill., Zion printing and publishing house, °1926]
257, [3] p. front. (port.) 23½cm.
Blank pages for "Memoranda" ([3] at end)
I. Title.
Library of Congress PZ3.B7834Zi 26-24558
——— Copy 2.
Copyright A 958415 [2]

Africa
M896 C771
Zirimu, Elvania Namukwaya, 1938-
Keeping up with the Mukasas.
Pp. 141-151.
In: Cook, David ed. Origin East Africa. London, Heinemann Educational Books, 1965.

Martinique
M843.91 Z69t
Zizine, Pierre
Théo le Paladin Martiniquais; récit. Paris, Les Editions du Scorpion °1959.
190p. 19cm. (Collection Alternance).
1. Martinique - Fiction. I. Title.

Martinique
M843.9 Z71
Zobel, Joseph, 1915-
Diab' - là; roman antillais. Préface de Georges Pillement. Paris, Nouvelles Editions Latines [1946]
174p. 18½cm.
1. Martinique - fiction. 2. Martinican fiction. I. Title.

Martinique
M843.91 Z71e
Zobel, Joseph, 1915-
La fête à Paris, roman. Paris, La Table ronde [1953]
258 p. 19 cm.
Biography of author and portrait pasted in.
I. Title.
A 53-6642
Illinois. Univ. Library for Library of Congress [1]

South Africa
M896 Zobel, Joseph, 1915-
M88 Flowers! Lovely Flowers!

Pp. 164-172.

In: Mphahlele, Ezekiel, ed. African writing today. Baltimore, Penguin Books, 1967.

West Indies
M808.8 Zobel, Joseph, 1915-
H839 The gift. Translated by Merloyd Lawrence.

Pp. 205-213.

In: Howes, Barbara, ed. From the Green Antilles. New York, Macmillan, 1966.

Martinique
M843.91 Zobel, Joseph, 1915-
Z71r La rue Cases-Nègres. [Roman. Paris, Les Quatre Jeudis [1955]

240 p. 21 cm.

I. Title.

Illinois. Univ. Library for Library of Congress A 56-8135 [1]

Martinique
M843.91 Zobel, Joseph, 1915-
Z71s Le soleil partagé. Paris, Présence Africaine, 1964.

207p. 18cm.

I. Title.

South Africa
M896.3 Zondi, Elliot
Z76u Ukufa kukashaka. [The death of Chaka] Johannesburg, Witwatersrand University Press, 1960.

45p. 18½cm. (The Bantu Treasury, xiv)
Written in Zulu.

I. Title. II. Series.

Zoology.

Kenya
M574 Kago, Fred K
K119 Citũmbe cia ngai [God's creatures. London, Macmillan, 1959.

48p. illus. 18cm.
"Published in association with the East African Literature Bureau."
Written in Kikuyu.

1. Natural history. 2. Zoology. I. Title.

Zoon van Amerika.

M813.5 Wright, Richard, 1909-1960.
W93z Zoon van Amerika. Vertaald door Mevr. Mr. A. W. Ebbinge - Van Nes. Den Haag, Zuid-Hollandsche Uitgevers Maatschappij [n.d.]

383p. 23cm.

MB9 Zuber, Osburn.
C25z Negro scientist shows 'way out' for Southern farmers; a story of George Washington Carver of Tuskegee, by Osburn Zuber.
21p. port. 22½cm.
This article appeared in the Montgomery Advertiser, December 22, 1929.

1. Carver, George Washington, 1864-1943.

Zulu - Drama.

South Africa
M896.2 Ndebele, Nimrod N T
N24u2 Ugubudele Namazimuzimu [Gubudele and the Cannibals] (umdlalo osenzo-sinye esinemiboniso emihlanu). [Reprinted in the new orthography] Johannesburg, Witwatersrand University Press, 1959.

62p. 18cm. (Bantu treasury, edited by D. T. Cole, VI)

1. Drama - Zulu. 2. Zulu - Drama. I. Title. II. Title: Gubudele and the Cannibals. III. Series

---

Zulu - Grammar.

S.Africa
M496.3 Nyembezi, C L Sibusio
N981 Learn Zulu. Pietermaritzburg, Shuter and Shooter, 1957.

151p. 18½cm.

Zulu-Music.

Africa, South
M780 Tracey, Hugh
T671e Lalela Zulu; 100 Zulu lyrics. With illustrations by Eric Byrd. Foreword by A. W. Hoernle. Johannesburg, Published by African Music Society, 1948.

121p. illus. 25cm.

Zulu - Poetry.

South Africa
M896 Vilakazi, Benedict Wallet, 1906-1947.
V71i3 Inkondlo Kazulu [Zulu poems] Namazwi ebika alotshwe ngu Dr. Innes B. Gumede. [4th ed.] Johannesburg, Witwatersrand University Press, 1955.

63p. illus. 18cm. (Bantu treasury, edited by C. M. Doke, I)

1. Poetry - Zulu. 2. Zulu - Poetry. I. Title.

Zulu language-Dictionaries-English.

S.Africa
M896 Vilakazi, Benedict Wallet, 1906-1947
V71z Zulu-English dictionary, comp. by C.M. Doke and B.W. Vilakazi. Johannesburg, Witwatersrand Univ. Press, 1948.

xxvi, 903p. 26cm.

Zulu language - Texts.

S. Africa
M896 Vilakazi, Benedict Wallet, 1906-1947.
V71i Inkondlo kazulu. [by] B. Wallet Vilakazi, Namazwi ebika alotshwe ngu Dr. Innes B. Gumede. Johannesburg, The University of the Witwatersrand press, 1935.

xiii, 100p., 1 L. incl. front. 18cm.

Zulu language - Texts.

S.Africa
M896 Vilakazi, Benedict Wallet, d. 1947.
V71n Noma nini. Mariannhill, Natal, Yacindezelwa Emshinini Was'emhalthuzane [prof. 1939]

184p. illus. 19cm.

Zulu literature - History and criticism.

South Africa
M896 Nyembezi, Cyril Lincoln Sibusiso, 1919-
N98r A review of Zulu literature. University lecture delivered in the University of Natal, Pietermaritzburg, 7th June, 1961. Pietermaritzburg, University of Natal Press, 1961.

10p. 21½cm.

1. Zulu literature - History and criticism.

Zulu music.

Natal
M968.4 Mseleku, William J
M87z Zulu solfa music, by William J. Mseleku. Durban, Natal, The Orient Music saloon, 1936.

31p. port. 24½cm.

Zulu poetry.

S.Africa
M896 Vilakazi, Benedict Wallet, 1906-1947.
V71a Amal'ezulu [by] B. Wallet Vilakazi. Johannesburg. The University of Witwatersrand Press, 1945.

46p. 18cm.
Poems. in Zulu.

Zulu proverbs.

S. Africa
M398.9 Nyembezi, C L Sibusiso
N98 Zulu proverbs. Johannesburg, Witwatersrand University press, 1954.

238p. 22½cm.

Zulu transformations...

Africa, South
M968 Vilakazi, Absolom.
V71 Zulu transformations: a study of the dynamics of social change. Pietermaritzburg, University of Natal Press, 1962.

x, 168 p. maps, diagrs. 25 cm.

"Originally presented as a Ph. D. thesis to the University of Natal."
Bibliography: p. 163-165.

1. Zulus. 2. Social change—Case studies. I. Title.
3. Africa, South - Social life and customs.
DT878.Z9V5 63-36287

Library of Congress [1]

Zululand - History - Fiction.

South Africa
M896.3 Ntuli, F L
N87 Umbuso ka Shaka. [Translated] from Nada the lily [R. Haggard] Mariannhill, Natal, Mariannhill Mission Press [1933]

350p. 18½cm.
Written in Zulu.

1. Zululand - History - Fiction. I. Haggard, Sir Henry Rider, 1856-1925. Nada the lily. II. Title.

South Africa
M968
M98

Zululand - Social life and customs.

Mutwa, Vusamazulu Credo
Indaba, my children. Johannesburg, Blue Crane Books [1965]

562p. illus., ports. 25cm.

1. Zulus. 2. Zululand - Social life and customs. 3. Africa, South - Native races. I. Title.

South Africa
M968
M98

Zulus.

Mutwa, Vusamazulu Credo
Indaba, my children. Johannesburg, Blue Crane Books [1965]

562p. illus., ports. 25cm.

1. Zulus. 2. Zululand - Social life and customs. 3. Africa, South - Native races. I. Title.

Zulus.

Africa, South
M968
V71

Vilakazi, Absolom.
Zulu transformations: a study of the dynamics of social change. Pietermaritzburg, University of Natal Press, 1962.

x, 168 p. maps, diagrs. 25 cm.

"Originally presented as a Ph. D. thesis to the University of Natal."
Bibliography: p. 163-165.

1. Zulus. 2. Social change—Case studies. I. Title.
3. Africa, South - Social life and customs.
DT878.Z9V5 63-36287

Library of Congress [1]

S. Africa
M968
Z85u

Zungu, Andreas Z.
Ukuthuthuka Kwesizwe esinsundu (Development of the Bantu people) Pietermartizburg, Shuter & Shooter, [1936]

79p. illus. 18cm.

1. Bantus. 2. Africa, South.

Nigeria
M966.9
M31z

Zuwan turawa nijeriya ta arewa.
Mani, Abdulmalik
Zuwan turawa nijeriya ta arewa. [Local history of Nigeria] Zaria, Norla; London, Longmans, Green and Co., 1957.

218p. 18½cm.
Written in Hausa.

Music Catalog

MUSIC CATALOG

*NEGRO COMPOSERS

Abbott, Francis H comp.

Eight Negro songs (from Bedford Co., Va.). Collected by Francis H. Abbott; edited by Alfred J. Swan. New York, Enoch & sons ₍1923₎
47 p. fol.

Score: medium solo voice with piano accompaniment. Negro dialect.

Explanatory comments and notes on dialect are given for each song.

(continued on next card)

Abbott, Francis H comp. Eight Negro songs... ₍1923₎ (Card 2)

Contents: 1. Who gon bring you chickens? -2. Muh reguluh dram. -3. Ole ark movin'. -4. Squirl he tote a bushy tail. -5. Bookuh red. -6. De bad man's ball. -7. Dat lonesome road. -8. Vanderbilt's daughter.

BHC CPL NYPLS
BPL NYPL42 YJWJ

---

*Accooe, William J

Baby, I'se done throwed you down. ₍Popular song₎. Words Cole and Johnson...;music by Willis Accooe. New York, Howley, Haviland & co.,₍c1899₎.
5 p. fol.

Score: medium solo voice ₍key of G₎ with piano accompaniment. Negro dialect.

"Words by Bob Cole"- caption title.

LC ABSpl

---

*Accooe, William J

...Cause I'se in society now. ₍Popular song₎ Words by Hen. Wise; music by Will Accooe. New York, Howley, Haviland & Dresser ₍1901₎
4 p. fol.
Illus. cover (col.)

Score: medium solo voice ₍key of F₎ with piano accompaniment.

ABSpl
HMC
LC

---

*Accooe, William J

...Love has claimed its own... ₍Popular song₎ Words by S. B. Cassin; music by Will Accooe. New York; Shapiro, Bernstein & Von Tilzer. ₍c1901₎.
5 p. fol.

Score: high solo voice ₍Key of Bb₎ with piano accompaniment. English words

"Featured by Harry Fairleigh in Geo. Lederer's production, The Casino Girl"—at end of title.

LC
ABS pl

---

*Accooe, William J

My Samoan beauty. ₍Popular song.₎ Words by Arthur Trevelyan; music by Will Accooe. Chicago, Bernstein & Von Tilzer. ₍c1901.₎
5 p. fol.

Score: medium solo voice ₍key of F₎ with piano accompaniment. English words.

LC
ABS pl

---

*Accooe, William J

... The phrenologist coon. ₍Popular song₎. Words by *Ernest Hogan; music by Will Accooe. New York, Jos. W. Stern & co. ₍c1901₎. Publ. pl. no. 3256 .
6 p. fol.

Score: medium solo voice ₍key of Eb₎ with piano accompaniment. Negro dialect.

LC
ABSpl

Accooe, William J
The stars are still shining for you

---

*Adams, Alton A.

The governer's own. March ₍ for band ₎ By Alton A. Adams. New York: Carl Fischer Co., ₍c1921₎ Publ. pl. no. 22252.
25 parts. 8°.

Parts: full band.

ABS pl

---

*Adams, Alton A.

Virgin Islands. March for band. By Alton A. Adams. Boston: Walter Jacobs. Publ. pl. no. 4134.
20 parts. 8°

Parts: full band.

ABSpl

---

*Adams, Wellington Alexander, 1879-

...Hymn of freedom (Let freedom's music ring.) Hymn. Words and music by Wellington Adams. New York, Edward B. Marks music co. ₍c1928₎ Publ. pl. no. 9505.
5 p. 8°.
Bound in black spiral notebook no. 4.
Score: SATB with piano accompaniment. English words.

At head of title: "First prize Rodman Wanamaker prize composition."

ABSpl

---

*Adams, Wellington Alexander .

The newborn king. Chorus. By Wellington Adams. New York: Lorenz Publishing Co. ₍c1933₎.
5p. 8° (No. 4055)

Score: SATB with piano accompaniment. English words.

ABSpl

---

*Adams, Wellington Alexander .

Shine, oh, shine. (In "Spiritual" style) ₍Chorus.₎ Words and music by Wellington Adams. New York: Lorenz Pub. Co., ₍c1933₎ Publ. pl. no. L -XL- 69
5p. fol

Score: SATB with piano accompaniment. English words.

ABSpl

---

*Adams, Wellington Alexander, 1879-

Six of the twelve Negro spirituals, arranged for solo voice by *William Grant Still...edited by Wellington Adams. Vol.1. New York, Handy brother music co.,inc.₍c1937₎
61p. fol.

Score: solo voice with piano accompaniment. Negro dialect.
Preface by Mr. Adams.

ABSpl
HMC
LC ZWpl

---

*Aldridge, Amanda Ira, 1866-

Blue days of June. Song. Words by Fred. E. Weatherly; music by Montague Ring pseud. New York, Chappell and co., ltd., c1915. Publ. pl. no. 26041.
4 p. fol.

Score: low solo voice ₍key of C₎ with piano accompaniment. English words.

ABSpl

---

*Aldridge, Amanda Ira, 1866-

The bride. Song. Words by P. J. O'Reilly; music by Montague Ring pseud. New York, Chappell and co., ltd., c1910. Publ. pl. no. 24483.
5 p. fol.

Score: high solo voice ₍ key of F ₎ with piano accompaniment. English words.

ABSpl LC

Aldridge, Amanda Ira, 1866-

An Eastern lullaby. (Camel-bells).
(In Aldridge, Amanda Ira, Two songs of the desert... New York, c1923, p. 2-5.)

Score: low solo voice key of F minor

ABSpl LC

---

*Aldridge, Amanda Ira, 1866-

Evening.
(In Aldridge, Amanda Ira, Through the day. London, c1910, p. 10-13.)

Score: medium solo voice key of Ab

ABSpl HMC LC ZWpl

---

*Aldridge, Amanda Ira, 1866-

...June in Kentucky. One of Two little southern songs. Words by Fred. G. Bowles; music by Montague Ring pseud. London, Chappell and co., ltd. c1912. Publ. pl. no. 25206.
3 p. fol.

Score:

ABSpl LC

---

*Aldridge, Amanda Ira, 1866-

...Kentucky love song. ₍One of₎ Two little southern songs. Words by Fred. G. Bowles; music by Montague Ring pseud. London, Chappell and co., ltd. c1912. Publ. pl. no. 25206.
5 p. fol.

Score: medium solo voice ₍key of Ab₎ with piano accompaniment. English words.

ABSpl LC

*Aldridge, Amanda Ira, 1866-

Little rose in my hair. Song. Words by Eileen Price-Evans; music by Montague Ring [pseud.] ...London, Chappell and co., ltd., [c1917] Publ. pl. no. 26611.
5 p. fol.

Score: medium solo voice [key of E^b] with piano accompaniment. English words.

ABSpl LC

---

*Aldridge, Amanda Ira, 1866-

Mirette. Serenade [for piano] By Montague Ring pseud. London, Walsh, Holmes and co., ltd., [c1934] Publ. pl. no. W.H.&Co.ltd.1862.
6 p. fol.

Score: piano solo.

ABSpl

Aldridge, Amanda Ira, 1866-
Montague Ring [pseud.]

A noontide song

---

*Aldridge, Amanda Ira, 1866-

Morning.
(In Aldridge, Amanda Ira, Through the day. London, c1910, p. 2-5.)

Score: medium solo voice key of E^b

ABSpl HMC LC ZWpl

---

*Aldridge, Amanda Ira, 1866-

Noon.
(In Aldridge, Amanda Ira, Through the day. London, c1910, p. 6-9.)

Score: medium solo voice key of E^b

ABSpl HMC LC ZWpl

---

*Aldridge, Amanda Ira, 1866-

...Three African dances. Music by Montague Ring [pseud.] London, Chappell and co., ltd. c1913 Publ. pl. no. 25490.
8 p. and 12 parts. fol. (Chappell's orchestral selections no. 109.)

Score: piano-conductor and 12 parts.

ABSpl ZWpl

---

*Aldridge, Amanda Ira, 1866-

'Tis morning. Song. Words by *Paul Laurence Dunbar; music by Montague Ring pseud. New York, G. Ricordi and co. [c1925] Publ. pl. no. E. & Co. 1455.
6 p. fol.

Score: high solo voice [key of E^b] with piano accompaniment. English words.

ABSpl

---

*Aldridge, Amanda Ira, 1866-

Through the day. Three songs... The words by P. J. O'Reilly; the music by Montague Ring [pseud.] ...London, Boosey and co. c1910. Publ. pl. no. H.6461.
13 p. fol.

Score: medium solo voice with piano accompaniment. English words.

Contents: 1. Morning. 2. Noon. 3. Evening.

ABSpl HMC LC
ZWpl

---

*Aldridge, Amanda Ira, 1866-

...Two little southern songs. Words by Fred. G. Bowles; music by Montague Ring pseud. London, Chappell and co., ltd. c1912. Publ. pl. no. 25206.
2 v. fol.

Score: low solo voice with piano accompaniment. English words.

Contents: Kentucky love song. June in Kentucky.

ABSpl LC

---

*Aldridge, Amanda Ira, 1866-

Two songs of the desert... Words by Fred. G. Bowles; music by Montague Ring pseud. New York, G. Ricordi and co. [c1923] Publ. pl. no. E & Co. 1333.
7 p. fol.

Score: low solo voice with piano accompaniment. English words.

Contents: An Eastern lullaby. (Camel-bells) A warrior's love song.

ABSpl LC

---

*Aldridge, Amanda Ira, 1866-

A warrior's love song.
(In Aldridge, Amanda Ira, Two songs of the desert... New York, c1923, p. 6-7.)

Score: low solo voice key of C minor

ABSpl LC

---

*Allen, Thomas S.

...Good-bye Mister Greenback. [Popular Song] Words and music by Thomas S. Allen. Boston: Walter Jacobs pub. [c1906] Publ. pl. no. 1266.
5p. fol

Score: medium solo voice with piano accompaniment. Negro dialect.

ABSpl

---

*Allen, Thomas S.

Oh gee—oh me, never-no-more. [Popular Song] Words and music by Thomas S. Allen. Boston: Daly music pub. [c1909.]
5p. fol

Score: medium solo voice with piano accompaniment English words.

ABSpl

Allen, William Francis, 1830-1889 comp.

Slave songs of the United States. By William Francis Allen, Charles Pickard Ware and, Lucy McKim Garrison. New York, P. Smith, 1929.
115 p. 23 cm.

"Copyright 1867. Reprinted 1929".

Includes: unaccompanied melodies and Negro dialect for 137 songs.

CPL ChPL HMC HPSpl YJWJ

Alter, Louis

Ma kinda love. [Popular song] Lyric by Jo' Trent; music by Louis Alter. New York, Robbins music corp. [c1929] Publ. pl. no. S H 521.
5 p. fol.

Score: medium solo voice with piano accompaniment. English words.

ABSpl

---

*Anderson, Alfred
Thompson, DeKoven

When tomorrow comes. Popular song ; words by Russel Smith; music by *DeKoven Thompson and Alfred Anderson. Chicago, Will Rossiter, c1912.
5 p. fol.

Score: medium solo voice with piano accompaniment [key of B^b] English words.

ABSpl LC

---

*Andrews, Ismay

Tradition. Words and music by Ismay Andrews; arranged by *Hall Johnson. Dance interpreted by Emilia Caesar. New York, *Handy bros. music co., inc. [c1935]
7 p. fol.

Score: low solo voice [key of E^b] with piano accompaniment.

Dedicated to Hall Johnson.

ABSpl
HMC
YJWJ *Hope*

Arbelo, Fernando

...Big chief De Sota (Fox-trot song). Words by *Andy Razaf; music by Fernando Arbelo. NY: Joe Davis, inc. [c1936] Publ. pl. no. 3639.
5p. fol.

Score: medium solo voice with piano accompaniment. English words.

ABSpl

---

*Armstrong, Daniel Louis, 1900-

Honeymooning in Manhattan. [Popular song] By Horace Gerlach and Louis Armstrong. New York, Chappell & co. [c1937] Publ. pl. no. C-742.
5 p. fol.

Score: medium solo voice with piano accompaniment. English words.

ABSpl

---

*Armstrong, Daniel Louis, 1900-

If we never meet again. [Popular song] By Horace Gerlach and Louis Armstrong. New York, Southern music publ. co., inc. [c1936]
5 p. fol.

Score: medium solo voice with piano accompaniment. English words.

ABSpl

---

*Armstrong, Daniel Louis, 1900-

I've got a heart full of rhythm. [Popular song] Words and music by Louis Armstrong. New York, Schuster and Miller inc. [c1938]
5 p. fol.

Score: medium solo voice with piano accompaniment. English words.

ABSpl

*Armstrong, Daniel Louis, 1900-

Louis Armstrong's original tunes. Swing solo folio with trumpet solos. New York, *Clarence Williams music pub. co., inc. ⌊c1938⌋
20 p. fol.

Score: medium solo voice with piano accompaniment; and trumpet solo parts. English words.

Contents: 1. When you leave me alone to pine. -2. Satchel mouth swing. 3. West end blues. -4. Where were you last night? -5. Tomorrow night. -6. High society. -7. Everybody loves my baby. -8. Oh, sand me!
ABSpl

---

*Armstrong, Daniel Louis, 1900-

Ol' man Mose. ⌊Popular song⌋ By Louis Armstrong and Zilner Trenton Randolph. New York, Santly bros.-Joy, inc., ⌊c1936⌋
5 p. fol.

Score: medium solo voice with piano accompaniment. English words.

ABSpl

Austin, Lovie
Bleeding Hearted Blues

Baily, Phoebe M
Stay Free America

---

*Baker, George A.

...Always be doing. ⌊Popular song. Words by George Carlisle; Music by George Baker.⌋ New York: M. Witmark & sons, ⌊c1906⌋. Publ. pl. no. 7643
5p. fol

Score: medium solo voice ⌊Key of G⌋ with piano accompaniment. English words.
T.P. has portraits of Messrs. Carlisle and Baker.

ABSpl
LC

---

*Baker, George A.

...My answer's No. ⌊Popular song. Words by George Carlisle; Music by George Baker.⌋ New York, M. Witmark & sons. ⌊c1906.⌋ Publ. pl. no. 7596.
5p. fol

Score: medium solo voice ⌊Key of G⌋ with piano accompaniment. English words.

ABSpl
LC

---

*Baker, George A.

...My Queen Diann. ⌊Popular Song. Words by George Carlisle; Music by George Baker.⌋ New York: M. Witmark & Sons. ⌊c1906.⌋ Publ. pl. no. 7594.
5p. fol

Score: medium solo voice ⌊Key of C⌋ with piano accompaniment. English words.

ABSpl
LC

---

*Baker, George A

Zelda. ⌊Popular song⌋ Words by *George Carlisle; music by George Baker. New York: M. Witmark & Sons. ⌊c1906⌋ Publ. pl. no. M.W.& Sons. 7601.
5p. fol

Score: medium solo voice with piano accompaniment. English words.

ABSpl

---

*Ballanta-Taylor, Nicholas George Julius arr.

Saint Helena Island spirituals. Recorded and transcribed at Penn normal, industrial and agricultural school, St. Helena Island, Beaufort County, South Carolina. By Nicholas George Julius Ballanta(Taylor) of Freetown, Sierra Leone, West Africa. New York, G. Schirmer, inc., c1925.
93 p. 27 1/2 cm.

Close score: SATB, mostly; a few are unaccompanied melodies. Negro dialect.

(continued on next card)

---

*Ballanta-Taylor, Nicholas George Julius arr.
Saint Helena Island... c1925. (Card 2)

A collection of 115 spirituals from St. Helena.

CPL HMC ICN LC NYPL42 NYPLS YJWJ

---

*Ballanta-Taylor, Nicholas George Julius, 1894-

...Redimentes opportunitatem. The Accra High School Song. Words by J. T. Roberts; music by N. G. J. Ballanta.
1 leaf. 8°.

Close Score: SATB. English words.

ABSpl

---

*Barbour, J. Berni

Doan' let Satan git yo' (on de judgment day) Negro spiritual. Lyric and music by J. Berni Barbour. New York: Edward B. Marks music co. ⌊c1927⌋ Publ. pl. no. 9459.
9p. fol.

Score: Soprano solo with piano accompaniment and optional bass solo obligato. Negro dialect.

ZWpl
ABSpl

---

*Barbour, J Berni

...Done laid down all ma' burden (Laid down dis heavy load). Negro spiritual. Lyric and music by J. Berni Barbour. New York: Edward B. Marks music co., ⌊c1927⌋ Publ. pl. no. 9465
5p. fol.

Score: medium solo voice ⌊Key of F⌋ with piano accompaniment. Negro dialect.
Dedicated to Dr. *Nathaniel Dett.
"Series of different Negro spirituals introducing musical arrangements with new ideas in basses and harmonies "at head of title.
ABSpl
ZWpl

---

*Barbour, J Berni

I'm ready to go. (Negro spiritual) Lyric and music by J. Berni Barbour. New York: Edward B. Marks music co., ⌊c1927⌋ Publ. pl. no. 9460.
5p. fol.

Score: medium solo voice ⌊Key of A♭⌋ with piano accompaniment. Negro dialect.

ZWpl
ABSpl

---

*Barbour, J Berni

...In a de mornin'. (Negro spiritual) Introducing musical arrangements with new ideas in basses and harmonies; lyric and music by J. Berni Barbour. New York, Edward B. Marks music co. ⌊c1927⌋ Publ. pl. no. 9467.
7 p. fol.

Score: high voice ⌊key of F⌋; coda with 4 part women's chorus as accompaniment to solo voice. Piano accompaniment. Negro dialect.

Dedicated to *Prof. J. Wes Mundy, choirmaster, Chicago, Ill.
ABSpl NYPLS YJWpl

---

*Barbour, J. Berni.

...Nicodemus (Yo' mus' be born agin). Original spiritual from Plantation suite; Lyric and music by J. Berni Barbour. New York: Edward B. Marks music co. ⌊c1927.⌋ Publ. pl. no. 9457.
3p. fol.

Score: medium solo voice ⌊Key of F⌋ with piano accompaniment. Negro dialect.
Dedicated to *Thomas Waller, organist.

ABSpl
ZWpl

---

*Barbour, J. Berni

The Sphinx. (Egyptian intermezzo) ⌊Song⌋ Words and music by J. Berni Barbour. New York: *Pace & Handy Music Co., inc. ⌊c1920.⌋
5p. fol.

Score: medium solo voice with piano accompaniment. English words.

ABSpl

Barés, Basile
La Capricieuse

Barés, Basile
Creole Music

Barés, Basile
Delphine

Barés, Basile
Mamie Waltz

Barés, Basile
Minuit Valse de Salon

Benjamin, Bennie
Each Time That I Puff on My Cigarette

Benjamin, Bennie
Oh! What It Seemed to Be

Barés, Basile
Regina

Benjamin, Bennie
I Burned a Match

Benjamin, Bennie
Pianissimo

Barés, Basile
La Seduisante

Benjamin, Bennie
I Can't Get Up the Nerve

Benjamin, Bennie
Rumors are Flying

Barés, Basile
Varietés du Carnaval

Benjamin, Bennie
I Don't See Me in Yours Eyes Anymore

Benjamin, Bennie
Strictly Instrumental

Barés, Basile
The Wedding - Heel and Toe

Benjamin, Bennie
I Don't Want to Set the World on Fire

Benjamin, Bennie
Surrender

Benjamin, Bennie
Ashes in the Tray

Benjamin, Bennie
I Want to Thank Your Folks

Benjamin, Bennie
The Storm's All Over

Benjamin, Bennie
Cancel the Flowers

Benjamin, Bennie
Melody Time

Benjamin, Bennie
When the Lights Go on Again

*Berry, Leon, 1909-1944.

Christopher Columbus. (A rhythm cocktail) Words by *Andy Razaf; music by Leon Berry. NY: Joe Davis Inc. [c1936] Publ. pl. no. 3622.
5p. fol.

Score: medium solo voice with piano accompaniment. English words.

ABSpl

---

*Berry, Leon, 1909-1944.

Uptown rhapsody. (Duck soup) [for piano] By Teddy Hill & Leon Berry. NY: Exclusive publications, inc. [c1936]
3p. fol.

Score: piano solo

ABSpl

---

*Berry, Leon, 1909-1944.

...William Tell. (Novelty fox-trot song). Words by *Andy Razaf; music by Leon Berry. NY: Joe Davis, inc. [c1936] Publ. pl. no. 3660.
5p. fol.

Score: medium solo voice with piano accompaniment. English words.

ABSpl

Bethune, Thomas, 1849-1908.

Battle of Manassas. [By] Blind Tom. Cleveland, S. Brainard's sons pub. c1884. Publ. pl. no. 4907.
11 p. fol.

Score: piano solo.

Highly ornamented title page in colors.

ABSpl
LC

Bethune, Thomas, 1849-1908.

Virginia polka. By Tom. The blind Negro boy pianist only 10 years old. New York, Horace Waters, c1860.
4 p. fol.

Score: piano solo.
Caption title.

Cover title page has a full length portrait of composer at age of 10.
ABSpl
ZWpl

---

*Bishop, Walter

Ain't gonna swing no more. [Popular song] By Walter Bishop, *Willie (The Lion) Smith, and Basil G. Adlam. New York, Mills music inc., [c1938]
5 p. fol.

Score: medium solo voice piano accompaniment. English words.

ABSpl

Bishop, Walter

Williams, Clarence
...The Brown Bomber, the kid from Alabam'. [Popular] song Words and music by Dan Dougherty, Walter Bishop, and *Clarence Williams. New York, *Clarence Williams music pub. co. [c1935]
3 p. fol.

Score: medium solo voice key of F with piano accompaniment. English words.

Caption title: "Look out for the Brown Bomber, the kid from Alabam'".

Portrait of "Joe Louis" on cover.
ABSpl
LC

---

*Bishop, Walter.

The Duke of Harlem. [Rhythm trot song. By Walter Bishop. New York: Edward B. Marks music co., [c1930]
Publ. pl. no. 9668.
5p. fol.

Score: medium solo voice with piano accompaniment. English words.

ABSpl

---

* Bishop, Walter
*Smith, Willie (The Lion)
Feelin' low. [Popluar song] By Mitchell Parish, *Willie (The Lion) Smith and Walter Bishop. New York, Mills music inc., [c1938]
5 p. fol.

Score: medium solo voice with piano accompaniment. English words.

ABSpl

---

*Bishop, Walter

The man from Scotland Yard. [Popular song] Words and music by Will Gregory and Walter Bishop. New York: Modern music publ. co., [c1934]
5p. fol.

Score: medium solo voice with piano accompaniment. English words.

ABSpl

---

*Bishop, Walter

Monkeys is the swaziest people! [Popular song] By Lew Lehr; Walter Bishop and Basil G. Adlam. New York: Mills music inc., [c1938]
5p. fol.

Score: medium solo voice with piano accompaniment. English words.

ABSpl

---

*Bishop, Walter

The old stamping ground. (a swing lament) By Walter Bishop, Willie Smith and E. P. La Freniere. New York: Roy music co., [c1938]
5 p. fol

Score: medium solo voice with piano accompaniment. English words

ABSpl

---

*Bivins, Nathan

... Deed I'm done with you. [Popular song] Words and music by Nathan Bivins. New York, M. Witmark & sons. [c1900] Publ. pl. no. 2260.
6 p. fol.

Score: medium solo voice [key of B♭] with piano accompaniment. English words.

ABSpl
LC

Bivins, Nathan
I Ain't Seen No Messenger Boy

---

*Bivins, Nathan
I want some one to care for me (or, Rosy Lee) [Popular song.] By Nathan Bivins... New York, Willis Woodward & co., [c1901.]
5 p. fol.

Score: medium solo voice with piano accompaniment. English words.

ABSpl
LC

---

*Bivins, Nathan

I'se a picking my company now. [Popular song.] Words and music by Nathan Bivins. New York, T. B. Harms & co. [c 1899.]
4 p. fol.

Score: medium solo voice with piano accompaniment. Negro dialect.
Reprinted as the Musical Supplement to the New York Sunday Press, Nov. 11, 1900.

ABSpl

---

*Bivins, Nathan

She certainly looks good to me. [Popular song.] Words and music by Nathan Bivins... New York, Howley, Haviland & Dresser, [c1903.]
5 p. fol.

Score: medium solo voice [key of C] with piano accompaniment. Negro dialect.

LC
ABSpl

Bivins, Nathan

Tell me baby do, or, Whose lil' babe is you. [Popular song] Words and music by Nathan Bivins...New York, Dave Fitzgibbon, Butler & co. [c1901]
5 p. fol.

Score: medium solo voice [key of B♭] with piano accompaniment. Negro dialect.

ABSpl

---

*Bivins, Nathan

You can't fool me no more. [Popular song.] By Nathan Bivins. New York, Shapiro, Bernstein & Von Tilzer. [c1900.]
5 p. fol.

Score: medium solo voice [key of B♭] with piano accompaniment. Negro dialect.

ABSpl
LC

---

*Bivins, Nathan

You can't join this show. [Popular song.] Words and music by Nathan Bivins. New York, Howley, Haviland & Dresser, [c1902]
5 p. fol.

Score: medium solo voice [key of G] with piano accompaniment. English words.

ABSpl
LC

---

*Bivins, Nathan

You were never introduced to me ... [Popular song] Words and music by Nathan Bivins... New York, Howley, Haviland & Dresser, [c1902.]
6 p. fol.

Score: medium solo voice [key of B♭] with piano accompaniment. Negro dialect.
"Sung with tremendous success by Anna Driver, with Tide of Life Co."

LC
ABSpl

*Blake, J Hubert, 1887-
*McPherson, Richard Cecil
Ain't we got love. [Popular song] By *Cecil Mack pseud. *J. Milton Reddie & Eubie Blake... New York Mills music inc. [c1937.]
5p. fol.

Score: medium solo voice with piano accompaniment. English words.
Caption title.
"From the musical production, 'Swing it'." - Cover title page.

ABSpl

---

*Blake, J Hubert, 1887-
*Europe, James Reese
All of no man's land is ours. [Popular song] [By Lieut. *Jim Europe, Lieut. *Noble Sissle and Eubie Blake] New York, M. Witmark & sons [c1919] Publ. pl. no. 16003.
3 p. fol.

Score: medium solo voice [key of F] with piano accompaniment. English words.

aBSpl

---

*Blake, J Hubert, 1887-
*Sissle, Noble
Baby buntin'. [Popular song] Lyric and music by *Noble Sisle and Eubie Blake. New York: M. Witmark & Sons, [c1923] Publ. pl. no. M. W. & Sons 16779
5p. fol.

Score: medium solo voice with piano accompaniment. English words.

From the musical comedy, "Elsie".
Caption title

ABSpl

---

*Blake, J Hubert, 1887-

Baby mine. [Popular song] Words by *Andy Razaf; music by Eubie Blake. New York: Shapiro, Bernstein & co., inc. [c1930]
5p. fol.

Score: medium solo voice with piano accompaniment. English words.

From Lew Leslie's "Blackbirds of 1930"
Caption title.

ABSpl

---

*Blake, J Hubert, 1887-
*Sissle, Noble
Baltimore buzz. Novelty for trot song. Lyric and music by *Noble Sisle and Eubie Blake. New York: M. Witmark & sons [c1921] Publ. pl. no. M.W.&Sons 16461.
5p. fol.

Score: medium solo voice with piano accompaniment. English words.

From the musical comedy. "Shuffle Along."
Caption title.

ABSpl

---

*Blake, J Hubert, 1887-
*Sissle, Noble
Bandana days... [Popular song] Lyrics and music by *Noble Sissle and Eubie Blake. New York; M. Witmark & Sons [c1921] Publ. pl. no. M.W. & Sons 16451.
5 p. fol.

Score: medium solo voice with piano accompaniment. English words.
From the musical comedy, "Shuffle Along".
Caption title.
ABSpl

---

*Blake, J Hubert, 1887-
*McPherson, Richard Cecil
By the sweat of your brow. [Popular song] By *Cecil Mack pseud J. Milton Reddie & Eubie Blake. New York: Mills music inc., [c1937]
5p. fol.

Score: medium solo voice with piano accompaniment. English words.

From the musical production, "Swing it".
Caption title.

ABSpl

---

*Blake, J Hubert, 1887-
*Sissle, Noble
Daddy, won't you please come home. Fox trot song. Lyric and music by *Noble Sissle and Eubie Blake. New York: M. Witmark and Sons, [c1921] Publ. pl. no. M.W. & Sons 16454.
5 p. fol.

Score: medium solo voice with piano accompaniment. English words.
From the musical comedy, "Shuffle along."
Caption title.
ABSpl

---

*Blake, J Hubert, 1887-
*Sissle, Noble
Dixie moon. [Popular song] Lyrics and music by *Noble Sissle and Eubie Blake... New York: Harms Inc. [c1924] Publ. pl. no. 7024.
7 p. fol.

Score: medium solo voice with piano accompaniment. English words.
From the musical comedy, "The chocolate dandies."
Caption title.

ABSpl

---

*Blake, J Hubert, 1887-
*Sissle, Noble
Everybody's struttin' now. [Popular song] Lyric and music by *Noble Sissle and Eubie Blake. New York: M. Witmark & Sons, [c1923] Publ. pl. no. 16782.
5 p. fol.

Score: medium solo voice with piano accompaniment. English words.
From the musical comedy, "Elsie."
Caption title.
ABSpl

---

*Blake, J Hubert, 1887-
*Sissle, Noble
Everything reminds me of you... [Popular song] Lyrics and music by *Noble Sissle and Eubie Blake. New York: M. Witmark & Sons., [c 1921] Publ. pl. no. M. W. & Sons 16419.
5 p. fol.

Score: medium solo voice with piano accompaniment. English words.
From the musical comedy, "Shuffle along."
Caption title.

ABSpl

Blake, J Hubert
Goodnight Angeline

Blake, J Hubert, 1887-
*McPherson, Richard Cecil
Green and blue. [Popular song] By *Cecil Mack, J. Milton Reddie and Eubie Blake... New York: Mills Music Inc. [c1937]

5 p. fol.

Score: medium solo voice with piano accompaniment. English words.
Caption title.
From the musical production, "Swing it."
ABSpl

---

*Blake, J Hubert, 1887-

Green pastures. [Popular song] Words by Will Morrissey; music by Eubie Blake. New York: Shapiro, Bernstein & co. [c1930]
5p. fol.

Score: medium solo voice with piano accompaniment. English words.

ABSpl

---

*Blake, J Hubert, 1887-
*Sissle, Noble
Gypsy blues... [Popular song] Lyrics and music by Noble Sissle and Eubie Blake. New York: M. Witmark & Sons, [c1921] Publ. pl. no. M.W. & Sons 16420.
5 p. fol.

Score: medium solo voice with piano accompaniment. English words.

From the musical comedy, "Shuffle along".
Caption title.

ABSpl

---

*Blake, J Hubert, 1887-
*Sissle, Noble
I like to walk with a pal like you. Fox trot song. Lyric and music by *Noble Sissle and Eubie Blake. New York: M. Witmark & Sons [c1922] Publ. pl. no. 8119.
5 p. fol.

Score: medium solo voice with piano accompaniment. English words.
From the musical comedy, "Elsie".
Caption title.
ABSpl

---

*Blake, J Hubert, 1887-
*Sissle, Noble
If you've never been vamped by a brown skin, you've never been vamped at all... [Popular song] Words and music by *Noble Sissle and Eubie Blake. New York: M. Witmark & Sons, [c1921] Publ. pl. no. 16487.
5 p. fol.

Score: medium solo voice with piano accompaniment. English words.
From the musical comedy, "Shuffle along."
Caption title.
ABSpl

---

*Blake, J Hubert, 1887-
*Sissle, Noble
I'm craving for that kind of love. [Popular song] Lyric and music by *Noble Sissle and Eubie Blake. New York: M. Witmark & Sons [c1921] Publ. pl. no. M. W. & Sons 16453.
5 p. fol.

Score: medium solo voice with piano accompaniment. English words.
From the musical comedy, "Shuffle along."
Caption title.

ABSpl

---

*Blake, J Hubert, 1887-

I'm just simply full of jazz. [Popular song] Words by *Noble Sissle; music by Eubie Blake. New York: M. Witmark & sons. [c1921] Publ. pl. no. M.W. & sons 16064.
5p. fol.

Score: medium solo voice with piano accompaniment. English words.

From the musical comedy, "Shuffle along".
Caption title.

ABSpl

---

*Blake, J Hubert, 1887-
*Sissle, Noble
I'm just wild about Harry. One step song. Lyric and music by *Noble Sissle and Eubie Blake. New York: M. Witmark & Sons [c1921] Publ. pl. no. 16482.
5 p. fol.

Score: medium solo voice with piano accompaniment. English words.
From the musical comedy, "Shuffle along."
Caption title.

ABSpl

---

*Blake, J Hubert, 1887-
*Sissle, Noble
In honeysuckle time, when Emaline said she'd be mine. Novelty fox trot song. Words and music by *Noble Sissle and Eubie Blake. [c1921] Publ. pl. no. M. W. & Sons 16481.
5 p. fol.

Score: medium solo voice with piano accompaniment. English words.
From the musical comedy, "Shuffle along."
Caption title.
ABSpl

*Blake, J Hubert, 1887-

It ain't being done no more. [Popular song] Lyric by George Sherzer; music by Gene Irwin and Eubie Blake. New York: Handy Brothers Music Co. Inc., [c1935]

5 p. fol.

Score: medium solo voice with piano accompaniment. English words.

ABSpl

Blake, J Hubert, 1887-
Sissle, Noble

Jassamine Lane. [Popular song] Lyrics and music by Noble Sissle and Eubie Blake. New York: Harms inc. [c1924] Publ. pl. no. 7018.

7p. fol.

Score: medium solo voice with piano accompaniment. English words.
Caption title.
From the musical comedy, "Bamville."

ABSpl

---

*Blake, J Hubert, 1887-

Jingle step. [Popular song] Lyric by *Noble Sissle; music by Eubie Blake. New York: M. Witmark & Sons, [c1922] Publ. pl. no. M. W. & Sons 16742.
5 p. fol.

Score: medium solo voice with piano accompaniment. English words.
From the musical comedy, "Elsie."
Caption title.
ABSpl

---

*Blake, J Hubert, 1887-
*Sissle, Noble
Kentucky Sue. [Popular song]...Lyric and music by *Noble Sissle and Eubie Blake. New York: M. Witmark & Sons, [c1921] Publ. pl. no. M. W. & Sons 16356.
5 p. fol.

Score: medium solo voice with piano accompaniment. English words.
From the musical comedy, "Shuffle along."
Caption title.
ABSpl

---

*Blake, J Hubert, 1887-
*Sissle, Noble
Lady of the moon. [Popular song] By *Noble Sissle and Eubie Blake... London: Keith Prowse & Co. Ltd. [c1925] Publ. pl. no. K.P. 2996.
4 p. fol.

Score: medium solo voice with piano accompaniment. English words.
From the musical revue, "Still dancing!"
Caption title.

ABSpl

---

*Blake, J Hubert, 1887-
*Sissle, Noble
Low down blues. Fox trot song. Words and music by *Noble Sissle and Eubie Blake. New York: M. Witmark & Sons. [c1921] Publ. pl. no. M. W. & Sons 16450.
5 p. fol.

Score: medium solo voice with piano accompaniment. English words.
From the musical comedy, "Shuffle along."
Caption title.
ABSpl

---

*Blake, J Hubert, 1887-
*Sissle, Noble
Love will find a way. [Popular song] Words and music by *Noble Sissle and Eubie Blake. New York: M. Witmark & Sons, [c1921] Publ. pl. no. M. W. & Sons 16418.
5 p. fol.

Score: medium solo voice with piano accompaniment. English words.
From the musical comedy, "Shuffle along."
Caption title.
ABSpl

---

*Blake, J Hubert, 1887-

Loving you the way I do... [Popular song] Lyric by Jack Scholl and Will Morrissey; music by Eubie Blake. New York: Shapiro, Bernstein & co. [c1930]
5p. fol.

Score: medium solo voice with piano accompaniment. English words.

From the musical show, "Hot Rhythm".
Caption title

ABSpl
OCPpl

---

*Blake, J Hubert, 1887-

Mammy's lit'l choc'late cullud chile. Song. Lyric by *Noble Sissle; music by Eubie Blake. New York: M. Witmark & Sons. [c1919] Publ. pl. no. M. W. & Sons 16031.
6 p. fol.

Score: medium solo voice [key of F] Negro dialect.

ABSpl
LC

---

*Blake, J Hubert, 1887-
*Sissle, Noble
Manda. [Popular song] Lyrics and music by *Noble Sissle and [Eubie] Blake... New York: Harms, Inc. [c1924] Publ. pl. no. 7019.
5 p. fol.

Score: medium solo voice with piano accompaniment. English words.
Caption title.
From the musical comedy, "The chocolate dandies."

ABSpl

---

*Blake, J Hubert, 1887-

Memories of you. [Popular song] Lyric by *Andy Razaf; music by Eubie Blake. New York: Shapiro, Bernstein & Co. inc. [c1930.]
5 p. fol.

Score: medium solo voice with piano accompaniment. English words.
"From Lew Leslie's Blackbirds of 1930"--cover title page.
Caption title.
ABSpl
YJWJ

---

*Blake, J Hubert, 1887-
*Sissle, Noble
My crinoline girl. Fox trot song. Lyric and music by *Noble Sissle and Eubie Blake. New York: M. Witmark & Sons, [c1923] Publ. pl. no. M. W. & Sons 16781.
5 p. fol.

Score: medium solo voice with piano accompaniment. English words.
From the musical comedy, "Elsie."
Caption title.

ABSpl

---

*Blake, J Hubert, 1887-

My handy man ain't handy no more... [Popular song] Lyric by *Andy Razaf; music by Eubie Blake. New York: Shapiro, Bernstein & Co. Inc. [c1930]
5 p. fol.

Score: medium solo voice with piano accompaniment. English words.
"Introduced by *Ethel Waters in Lew Leslie's Blackbirds of 1930"--at end of title.
Caption title.
ABSpl

---

*Blake, J Hubert, 1887-

Oriental blues.. [Popular song] Lyrics and music by *Noble Sissle and Eubie Blake. New York: M. Witmark & Sons, [c1921] Publ. pl. no. M. W. & Sons 16335.
5 p. fol.

Score: medium solo voice with piano accompaniment. English words.
From the musical comedy, "Shuffle along."
Caption title.
ABSpl

---

*Blake, J Hubert, 1887-

Pickaninny shoes. [Popular song] Lyric by Noble Sissle; music by Eubie Blake. New York: M. Witmark & sons. [c1920] Publ. pl. no. M. W. & sons 16223
4p. fol.

Score: medium solo voice with piano accompaniment Negro dialect.

ABSpl

---

*Blake, J Hubert, 1887-
*Sissle, Noble
A regular guy. [Popular song] Lyric and music by *Noble Sissle and Eubie Blake. New York: M. Witmark & Sons, [c1922] Publ. pl. no. M. W. & Sons 16591.
5 p. fol.

Score: medium solo voice with piano accompaniment. English words.
From the musical comedy, "Elsie."
Caption title.
ABSpl

---

*Blake, J Hubert, 1887-

Roll, Jordan. (A new spiritual) Lyric by Andy Razaf; music by Eubie Blake. New York: Shapiro, Bernstein & Co. Inc. [c1930]
5 p. fol.

Score: medium solo voice with piano accompaniment. English words.

ABSpl

---

*Blake, J Hubert, 1887-

Sand flowers. [Popular song] Lyric by *Noble Sissle; music by Eubie Blake. New York: M. Witmark & Sons, [c1922] Publ. pl. no. M. W. & Sons 16743.
5 p. fol.

Score: medium solo voice with piano accompaniment. English words.
From the musical comedy, "Elsie."
Caption title.
ABSpl

---

*Blake, J Hubert, 1887-
*Sissle, Noble
Shuffle along. One step song. Words and music by *Noble Sissle and Eubie Blake. New York: M. Witmark & Sons, [c1921] Publ. pl. no. M. W. & Sons 16452.
5 p. fol.

Score: medium solo voice with piano accompaniment. English words.
From the musical comedy, "Shuffle along."
Caption title.
ABSpl

---

*Blake, J Hubert, 1887-
*Sissle, Noble
Shuffle along. Selection a medley of tunes from the musical comedy, "Shuffle along" for piano. By *Noble Sissle and Eubie Blake; arranged by Geo. J. Trinkaus. New York: M. Witmark & Sons [c1921] Publ. pl. no. M. W. & Sons 16507.
11 p. fol.

Score: piano solo

ABSpl

---

*Blake, J Hubert, 1887-
*Sissle, Noble
Sing me to sleep, dear mammy. [Popular song] Words and music by *Noble Sissle and Eubie Blake. New York: M. Witmark & Sons [c1921] Publ. pl. no. M. W. & Sons 16484
5 p. fol.

Score: medium solo voice with piano accompaniment. English words.
From the musical comedy, "Shuffle along."
Caption title.

ABSpl

*Blake, J Hubert, 1887-

The slave of love. [Popular song] Words by *Noble Sissle; music by Eubie Blake. New York: Harms, inc., c1924 Publ. pl. no. 7100.
5 p. fol.

Score: medium solo voice with piano accompaniment. English words.
From the musical comedy, "The chocolate dandies."
Caption title.
ABSpl

*Blake, J Hubert, 1887-

That lindy hop. [Popular song] Lyric by *Andy Razaf; music by Eubie Blake. New York: Shapiro, Bernstein & co., inc. [c1930]
5 p. fol.

Score: medium solo voice with piano accompaniment. English words.

ABSpl
YJWJ

*Blake, J Hubert, 1887-
*Sissle, Noble
There's a million little cupids in the sky. [Popular song] Lyrics and music by *Noble Sissle and Eubie Blake. New York: Harms inc., [c1924] Publ. pl. no. 7017.
5 p. fol.

Score: medium solo voice with piano accompaniment. English words.
Caption title.
From the musical comedy, "In Bamville."
ABSpl

*Blake, J Hubert, 1887-

Truckin' on down. (Harlem's latest dance craze) [Popular song] Words by *Arthur Porter; music by Eubie Blake. New York: *Handy Brothers Music Co., inc., [c1935]
5 p. fol.

Score: medium solo voice with piano accompaniment. English words.

ABSpl
HMC
LC
ZWpl

*Blake, J Hubert, 1887-
*Sissle, Noble
Two hearts in tune. [Popular song] Lyric and music by *Noble Sissle and Eubie Blake. New York: M. Witmark & Sons, [c1922] Publ. pl. no. M. W. & Sons 16592.
5 p. fol.

Score: medium solo voice with piano accompaniment. English words.
From the musical comedy, "Elsie."
Caption title.
ABSpl

*Blake, J Hubert, 1887-

Vision girl. Oriental fox-trot song... [Popular song] Lyric by *Noble Sissle; music by Eubie Blake. New York: M. Witmark & Sons, [c1920] Publ. pl. no. M. W. & Sons 16227.
5 p. fol.

Score: medium solo voice with piano accompaniment. English words.
"Sung by Helen Bolton in "The Midnight Rounders' featuring Eddie Cantor."—at end of title.
ABSpl

*Blake, J Hubert, 1887-
*Sissle, Noble
Why? [Popular song] Written and composed by *Noble Sissle and Eubie Blake. London: Keith Prowse & Co. Ltd. [c1925] Publ. pl. no. K.P.2984.
5 p. fol.

Score: medium solo voice with piano accompaniment. English words.
"I would like to know"—at head of title

ABSpl

*Blake, J Hubert, 1887-
*Sissle, Noble
With you. Fox trot ballad. Lyric and music by *Noble Sissle and Eubie Blake. New York: M. Witmark & Sons, [c1922] Publ. pl. no. M. W. & Sons 16593.
5 p. fol.

Score: medium solo voice with piano accompaniment. English words.
From the musical comedy, "Elsie."
Caption title.

ABSpl

*Blake, J Hubert, 1887-
*Sissle, Noble
You were meant for me. [Popular song] Written and composed by *Noble Sissle and Eubie Blake. New York: Harms inc., [c1924] Publ. pl. no. 6966.
5 p. fol.

Score: medium solo voice with piano accompaniment. English words.
Introduced in "Andre Charlot's Revue of 1924."

ABSpl

*Blake, J Hubert, 1887-

You're lucky to me. [Popular song] Lyric by Andy Razaf; music by Eubie Blake. New York: Shapiro, Bernstein & Co., [c1930]
5p. fol.

Score: medium solo voice with piano accompaniment. English words.

"Introduced by *Ethel Waters in Lew Leslie's Blackbirds of 1930" — at end of title.
Caption title

ABSpl
YJWJ

*Bland, James Allen, 1856-1911.

... Carry me back to old Virginny. Song and chorus. Words and music by James A. Bland... Boston, John F. Perry & co. [c1878] Publ. pl. no. 1,403.
5 p., front., illus., plates, fol.

Score: verse, medium solo voice [key of A♭]; chorus, SATB, with piano accompaniment. Negro dialect.

ABSpl
HMC

*Bland, James Allen, 1856-1911.

...Carry me back to old Virginny. [Song; [Words and music] by James A. Bland. Boston, Oliver Ditson co. [c1906] Publ. pl. no. 4-94-64116.
5 p. fol.

Score: medium voice [key of A♭] with chorus arranged for SATB. Negro dialect.
(Also available for small orchestra and piano, full orchestra and piano, piano solo, duet for S & T (with violin obligato))

"Sung with great success by Alma Gluck."
(continued on next card)

*Bland, James Allen, 1856-1911. ...Carry me back to old Virginny... [c1906] (Card 2)

In YJWJ is a recording by Alma Gluck. She is a former celebrated soprano of Metropolitan Opera House.

ABSpl
NYPLS
YJWJ

*Bland, James Allen, 1856-1911.

...De angels am a coming. [Minstrel song] Words and music by Jas. A. Bland. New York, Hitchcock's music store, c1880.
5 p. fol.

Score: verse for medium solo voice [key of G]; chorus, SATB with piano accompaniment. Negro dialect.

"James A. Bland's ... great Ethiopian songs." — Head of title.

ABSpl
LC

*Bland, James Allen, 1856-1911.

...De golden wedding. [Minstrel song. Words and music] by James A. Bland, of Sprague's Georgia minstrels... [Arranged by J. H. W.] Boston, John F. Perry & co. [c1880] Publ. pl. no. 1,623.
5 p. fol.

Score: verse for medium solo voice [key of F]; chorus, SATB with piano accompaniment. Negro dialect.

ABSpl
LC

*Bland, James Allen, 1856-1911.

In the evening by the moonlight. [Song; [Words and music] by James Bland; [arranged by Bernice Manoloff] Chicago, Calumet music co. [c1937]
[4] p. fol.

Score: medium voice "with ukulele chords, guitar chords and special Hawaiian guitar chords." Negro dialect.

ABSpl
NYPLS

*Bland, James Allen, 1856-1911.

...In the morning by the bright light... A famous end song. Words and music by James A. Bland. Boston, John F. Perry & co., c1879. Publ. pl. no. 1510.
5 p. fol.
Illus. cover title.

Score: verse for medium solo voice; chorus, SATB. Negro dialect.

ABSpl
LC
HMC

*Bland, James Allen, 1856-1911.

...Listen to the silver trumpet's sounding. Great character song and chorus by Jas. A. Bland... Boston, White, Smith & co., c1880. Publ. pl. no. 3981.
5 p. fol.

Score: medium solo voice [key of B♭] with piano accompaniment. Negro dialect.

ABSpl
LC

*Bland, James Allen, 1856-1911.

...Oh! dem golden slippers. [Song and chorus] Words and music by James A. Bland, of Sprague's Georgia minstrels; [arranged by F. Louis] Boston, John F. Perry & co., c1879.
5 p. fol.

Score: verse for medium solo voice [key of G]; chorus, SATB with piano accompaniment. Negro dialect.

~~LC~~
ABS

*Bland, James Allen, 1856-1911.

...Oh dem golden slippers. [Minstrel] Song. Words and music by James A. Bland; arranged by Harold Potter. New York, Mills music inc. [c1923]
3 p. fol. (Edition Supreme)

Score: medium solo voice [key of E♭] with piano accompaniment. Negro dialect.

ABSpl

*Bland, James Allen, 1856-1911.

Old fashioned homestead. Song and chorus. Words and music by James Bland. Boston, Oliver Ditson co., c1883. Publ. pl. no. 50044.
5 p. fol.

Score: verse, medium solo voice [key of G] with piano accompaniment; chorus, SATB. English words.

ABSpl
LC

*Bland, James Allen, 1856-1911.
...Rose Pachoula. ⌊Song;⌋ Words by Mannie Friend; music by Jas. A. Bland. New York, Mrs. Pauline Lieder publ., c1881. Publ. pl. no. Mrs. P. L. 108.
5 p. fol.
Score: high solo voice ⌊key of C;⌋ with piano accompaniment. English words.
ABSpl
LC

*Bland, James Allen, 1856-1911.
..."Tapioca." A genuine Negro plantation song and chorus. Written and composed by James A. Bland... Baltimore, Md., Otto Sutro & co., c1891.
5 p. fol.
Score: medium solo voice ⌊key of D;⌋ with piano accompaniment. Negro dialect.
ABSpl
LC

Bland, James
Uncle Joe, or the cabin by the stream.

*Bland, James Allen, 1856-1911.
...You could have been true. Song and chorus. Words by Mannie Friend; music by James A. Bland; arranged by Ned Straight. New York, Hitchcock's music store, c1881.
5 p. fol.
Score: verse, high solo voice ⌊key of B♭,⌋ with piano accompaniment; chorus, SATB. English words.
ABSpl

*Boatner, Edward H 1898- arr.
I want Jesus o walk with me. Negro spiritual. ⌊Arranged⌋ by Edward Boatner. New York, Galaxy music corp. ⌊c1939⌋ Publ. pl. no. G. M. 1008.
5 p. fol.
Score: medium solo voice with piano accompaniment. English words.
ABSpl

*Boatner, Edward H , 1898- arr.
...O Lord, I done done. Negro spiritual. Arranged by Edward Boatner. Boston, Oliver Ditson co. ⌊c1925⌋ Publ. pl. no. 75373.
5 p. fol.
Score: medium solo voice with piano accompaniment. Negro dialect.
ABSpl

*Boatner, Edward H , 1898- arr.
Oh, what a beautiful city! Traditional Negro spiritual; arranged for voice and piano by Edward Boatner. New York, G. Schirmer, inc. ⌊c1940⌋ Publ. pl. no 38855.
5 p. fol.
Score: medium solo voice ⌊key of G⌋ with piano accompaniment. Negro dialect.
ZWpl
ABSpl

*Boatner, Edward H , 1898- arr.
On ma journey...Negro spiritual. Arranged by Edward Boatner. New York, G. Ricordi & co., inc. ⌊c1928⌋ Publ. pl. no. N. Y. 711.
9 p. fol.
Score: low solo voice with piano accompaniment. Negro dialect.
ABSpl

*Boatner, Edward H , 1898- arr.
Trampin'. Negro spiritual. Music by Edward H. Boatner. New York, Galaxy music corp. ⌊c1931⌋
6 p. fol.
Score: low solo voice with piano accompaniment. Negro dialect.
ABSpl
LC

*Boatner, Edward H , 1898- arr.
...Wade in de water. Negro spiritual. Arranged by Edward Boatner. Boston, Oliver Ditson co., ⌊c1925⌋ Publ. pl. no. 75322.
5 p. fol.
Score: medium solo voice ⌊key of E♭ minor⌋ with piano accompaniment. Negro dialect.
ABSpl

*Bonds, Margaret
The Negro speaks of rivers. ⌊Song.⌋ Words by *Langston Hughes; music by Margaret Bonds.... New York, *Handy brothers music co., inc. ⌊c1942⌋
7 p. fol.
Score: medium solo voice ⌊key of D⌋ with piano accompaniment. English words.
ABSpl
HMC
ZWpl
HPSpl

*Bowman, Elmer S
*Smith, Christopher
All in down and out (Sorry I ain't got it, you could get it, if I had it). ⌊Popular song;⌋ Words by *R. C. McPherson (Cecil Mack); music by* ⌊Chris;⌋ Smith, ⌊Billy B.;⌋ Johnson and Elmer Bowman. New York, Gotham-Attucks music co. ⌊c1906;⌋
5 p. fol.
Score: medium solo voice ⌊key of B♭;⌋ with piano accompaniment. English words.
ABSpl

*Bowman, Elmer S
*Smith, Christopher
Clorindy. An Ethiopian serenade. By Smith and Bowman. New York, Howley, Haviland and Dresser. ⌊c1903⌋
5 p. fol.
Score: medium solo voice ⌊key of F⌋ with piano accompaniment. Negro dialect.
ABSpl

*Bowman, Elmer S
*Smith, Christopher
In the jungle I'm a queen. ⌊Popular song;⌋ Words and music by *Smith and Bowman. New York, Shapiro, Bernstein & co., ⌊c1903⌋
4p. fol.
Score: medium solo voice ⌊key of A♭⌋ with piano accompaniment. English words.
ABSpl
LC

*Bowman, Elmer S
*Smith, Christopher
Mister Moon, kindly come out and shine. ⌊Minstrel song⌋ By *Smith and Elmer Bowman. Boston, Walter Jacobs, ⌊c1903⌋ Publ. pl. no. 792.
5p. fol.
Score: medium solo voice ⌊key of A♭⌋ with piano accompaniment. Negro dialect.
ABSpl

*Brown, Harry
*Smith, Christopher
...No, no, positively no. ⌊Popular song.⌋ Words and music by *Chris Smith and Harry Brown. New York, Herbert H. Taylor, inc. ⌊c1907⌋
5p. fol.
Score: medium solo voice ⌊key of F⌋ with piano accompaniment. English words.
ABSpl

*Bowman, Elmer S
*Smith, Christopher
...That sneaky snakey rag (The snake). ⌊Popular song.⌋ Words and music by *Chris Smith and Elmer Bowman. New York, Haviland pub. co. ⌊c1912;⌋
5 p. fol.
Score: medium solo voice ⌊key of G;⌋ with piano accompaniment. English words.
ABSpl

*Bowman, Elmer S
*Smith, Christopher
Your face looks familiar to me. ⌊Popular song;⌋ Words and music by* ⌊Chris;⌋ Smith and ⌊Elmer;⌋ Bowman. Boston, G. W. Setchell ⌊c1902;⌋
5 p. fol.
Score: medium solo voice ⌊key of A♭;⌋ with piano accompaniment. English words.
ABSpl

*Bowman, Theodore
...Coon's day in May. Coon song. Words by *Chris Smith; music by Theo. Bowman. New York, F. A. Mills. ⌊c1898⌋
5 p. fol.
Score: low solo voice ⌊key of E♭⌋ with piano accompaniment. Negro dialect.
ABSpl

*Boyd, Wyneberry
Make a joyful noise unto God. Anthem. Words and music by Wyneberry Boyd. New York, *Handy bros. music co., inc. ⌊c1938;⌋
13 p. 8vo.
Score: SATB with bass, baritone and tenor soli. Piano accompaniment. English words.
Bound in black spiral notebook no. 4.
ABSpl HPSpl

*Bradford, Perry
Black bottom dance. ⌊Popular song;⌋ By Gus Horsley and Perry Bradford. New York, Perry Bradford music co. ⌊c1926⌋
5 p. fol.
Score: medium solo voice with piano accompaniment. English words.
ABSpl

*Bradford, Perry

...Crazy blues. [Popular song] By Perry Bradford. New York, Clarence Williams music pub. co., inc. [c1920] Publ. pl. no. 949.
5 p. fol.

Score: medium solo voice [key of B^b] with piano accompaniment. English words.

ABSpl
LC

*Bradford, Perry

Dixieland echoes. A collection of five descriptive Negro songs composed and edited by Perry Bradford and *James P. Johnson... New York, *Perry Bradford, inc. [c1928]
29 p. fol.

Score: solo voice with piano accompaniment. Negro dialect.

Contents: -1. Echoes of ole Dixie land. -2. Honey.

*Bradford, Perry

Double-crossin' papa (You can't double cross me) [Popular song] By Perry Bradford. New York, *Perry Bradford music co. [c1924]
5p. fol.

Score: medium solo voice with piano accompaniment. English words.

ABSpl

*Bradford, Perry

Echoes of ole Dixie land. [Song] Composed and edited by Perry Bradford and *James P. Johnson... New York, *Perry Bradford, inc. [c1928]
(In Bradford, Perry, Dixieland echoes. New York, 1928, p. 3-8.)

Score: high solo voice [key of D^b] with piano accompaniment. Negro dialect.

"We picture a log cabin scene in Alabama, with fathers, mothers, sons and daughters after their evening meal at sundown" - Foreword.
ABSpl NYPL42 NYPLS LC

*Bradford, Perry

Ev'rybody mess aroun'. [Popular song and dance] By Perry Bradford. New York, Perry Bradford music pub. co. [c1926]
5 p. fol.

Score: medium solo voice with piano accompaniment. English words.

ABSpl

*Bradford, Perry

Frankie. [Popular song] Words by Marion Dickerson; music by Perry Bradford. New York, *Perry Bradford music co., inc. [c1921]
5 p. fol.

Score: medium solo voice with piano accompaniment. English words.

ABSpl

*Bradford, Perry

Honey. [Song] Composed and edited by Perry Bradford and *James P. Johnson... New York, *Perry Bradford, inc. [c1928]
(In Bradford, Perry, Dixieland echoes. New York, 1928, p. 8-11.)

Score: high solo voice [key of B^b] with piano accompaniment. Negro dialect.

"A crooning Negro lullaby, with love for its theme." - Foreword.
ABSpl LC
NYPL42
NYPLS

*Bradford, Perry

I don't let no one man worry me. [Popular song] By Perry Bradford. New York, *Perry Bradford music pub. co. [c1923]
5p. fol.

Score: medium solo voice with piano accompaniment. English words.

ABSpl
LC

*Bradford, Perry

Liza Jane'sweddin'. [Song] By Perry Bradford... New York, *Perry Bradford, inc. [c1928]
(In Bradford, Perry, Dixieland echoes, New York, 1928, p. 25-29.)

Score: medium solo voice [key of F] with piano accompaniment. Negro dialect.

"A terpsichorean jazz classic, with words that describe the happenings at a Negro wedding." -Foreword
ABSpl LC
NYPL42
NYPLS

*Bradford, Perry

Mississippi river flood. Descriptive. [Song] Composed and edited by Perry Bradford and *James P. Johnson... New York, *Perry Bradford, inc. [c1928]
(In Bradford, Perry, Dixieland echoes. New York, 1928, p. 12-19.)

Score: high solo voice [key of C] with piano accompaniment. Negro dialect.

"A Negro musical poem, of the Mississippi river flood, with style descriptive." - Foreword.
ABSpl LC
NYPL42 NYPLS

*Bradford, Perry

Scratchin' the gravel...A dancing song. By Jack Yellen, Charlie Pierce and Perry Bradford. New York, Chas. K. Harris pub. [c1917]
3 p. fol.

Score: medium solo voice with piano accompaniment. English words.

ABSpl

*Bradford, Perry

We'll meet again. Waltz ballad. By Perry Bradford. New York, Perry Bradford music pub. co. [c1927]
5 p. fol.

Score: medium solo voice with piano accompaniment. English words.

From the musical comedy, "Black bottom".

ABSpl

*Bradford, Perry

Wicked blues. [Popular song] Words and music by Perry Bradford. New York, Perry Bradford music pub. co. [c1922]
5 p. fol.

Score: medium solo voice with piano accompaniment. English words.

ABSpl

• Bradford, Perry

You can't keep a good man down. [Popular song] By Perry Bradford...New York, Perry Bradford music pub. co. [c1920]
5 p. fol.

Score: medium solo voice with piano accompaniment. English words.

ABSpl

Braga, Francisco
Album (4 compositions)

Braga, Francisco
Valse Romantique

Branen, Jeff T
If I could See As Far Ahead as I Can See Behind

*Brooks, Shelton

All night long. [Popular song] Words and music by Shelton Brooks... Chicago, Will Rossiter [c1912]
6 p. fol.

Score: medium solo voice [key of E^b] with piano accompaniment. English words.

ABSpl
NYPLS- In folio, "Five songs by Shelton Brooks."

*Brooks, Shelton

The cosey rag. By Shelton Brooks... Chicago, Will Rossiter [c1911]
5 p. fol.

Score: low solo voice [key of B^b] with piano accompaniment. English words.

ABSpl

*Brooks, Shelton

The darktown strutters' ball (I'll be down to get you in a taxi, honey). [Popular song] Words and music by Shelton Brooks... New York, Feist, inc. [c1917]
3 p. fol.

Score: low solo voice [key of C] with piano accompaniment. English words.

LC
NYPLS-(In folio, "Five songs by Shelton Brooks")
ABSpl
NBEL-(Full orchestra, arr. by Jimmy Dale; full band, arr. Harry L. Alford; orchestral accom. arr. by F. H. Klickmann)

*Brooks, Shelton

Don't leave your little blackbird blue. [Popular song] By *Joe Jordan, *Porter Grainger, and Shelton Brooks. New York, Harms, inc. [c1930] Publ. pl. no. 8578.
5 p. fol.

Score: medium solo voice [key of C] with piano accompaniment. English words.

Introduced in "Brown Buddies", featuring *Bill Robinson & Adelaide Hall.
ABSpl

*Brooks, Shelton

...Ev'ry day. Or, I want you every day. [Popular song] Words by W. R. Williams; music by Shelton Brooks. Chicago, Will Rossiter [c1918]
3 p. fol.

Score: high solo voice [key of E^{b}] with piano accompaniment. English words.

3 copies

ABSpl

---

*Brooks, Shelton

If anybody here wants a real kind mama (Here's your opportunity). [Popular song] By Shelton Brooks. New York, Blues music pub. co. [c1923]
5 p. fol.

Score: medium solo voice [key of B^{b}] with piano accompaniment. English words.

Sung by Ethel Ridley on Columbia record No. 3941.

ABSpl

---

*Brooks, Shelton

If I were a bee and you were a red, red rose. [Popular song] Words and music by Shelton Brooks. New York, Maurice Abraham music co. [c1915]
5p. fol.

Score: medium solo voice with piano accompaniment. English words.

ABSpl
LC

---

*Brooks, Shelton

I'm sorry for the day I laid my eyes on you. [Popular song] By Shelton Brooks. New York, Strand music pub. co. [c1915]
5 p. fol.

Score: low solo voice [key of B^{b}] with piano accompaniment. English words.

ABSpl

---

*Brooks, Shelton

Jean. [Popular song] Words by Ernie Erdman and Benny Davis; music by Shelton Brooks. New York, Waterson & Snyder co. [c1919] Publ. pl. no. 1012.
5 p. fol.

Score: medium solo voice [key of G] with piano accompaniment. English words.

ABSpl
NYPLS - In folio, "Five songs by Shelton Brooks."

---

*Brooks, Shelton

Kentucky rose. [Popular song] By Shelton Brooks... New York, Strand music pub. co. [c1915]
5 p. fol.

Score: low solo voice [key of B^{b}] with piano accompaniment. English words.

ABSpl

---

*Brooks, Shelton

Since you turned me down. [Popular song] By Shelton Brooks. New York, Strand music pub. co. [c1915]
5 p. fol.

Score: low solo voice [key of B flat] with piano accompaniment. English words.

ABSpl

---

*Brooks, Shelton

...Some of these days. [Popular song] Words and music by Shelton Brooks... Chicago, Will Rossiter [c1910]
6 p. fol.

Score: medium solo voice [key of G] with piano accompaniment. English words. Chorus also arranged for male or mixed quartet.

NBCL - (arr. for dance orchestra by Paul Sterrett.)
NYPLS - (In folio, "Five songs by Shelton Brooks")
ABSpl

---

*Brooks, Shelton

Swing that thing. [Popular song] Words and music by Shelton Brooks... New York, *Handy bros. music co. [c1934]
5 p. fol.

Score: medium solo voice [key of B^{b}] with piano accompaniment. English words.

ABSpl
LC

---

*Brooks, Shelton

Tell me why you want to go to Paree (You can get the same sweet loving here at home). [Popular song] By Shelton Brooks. New York, McCarthy & Fisher (inc.) [c1919]
3 p. fol.

Score: medium solo voice [key of B^{b}] with piano accompaniment. English words.

ABSpl

---

*Brooks, Shelton

There'll come a time (when you'll feel lonely.) [Popular song] Words and music by Shelton Brooks... Chicago, Harold Rossiter music co. [c1911]
5 p. fol.

Score: medium solo voice [key of B^{b}] with piano accompaniment. English words.

ABSpl

---

*Brooks, Shelton

...Walkin' the dog. [Popular song] Words and music by Shelton Brooks. Chicago, Will Rossiter [c1916]
3 p. fol.

Score: medium solo voice [key of B^{b}] with piano accompaniment. English words.

ABSpl

---

*Brooks, Shelton

Why do you make me love you - then break my heart? [Popular song] Words and music by Shelton Brooks. Chicago, Will Rossiter [c1917]
3 p. fol.

Score: medium solo voice [key of B^{b}] with piano accompaniment. English words.

ABSpl

---

*Brooks, Shelton

You ain't talking to me. [Popular song] Words by Mat Marshall. Music by Shelton Brooks. Chicago, Will Rossiter, [c1909]
5 p. fol.

Score: medium solo voice [key of G] with piano accompaniment. English words.

ABSpl

---

*Brown, Charlotte Hawkins, 1883-

...Saved. [Sacred song.] ...Words and music by Charlotte Hawkins Brown. Sedalia, N. C., Charlotte Hawkins Brown publisher. [c1927.]
5 p. fol.

Score: medium solo voice with piano accompaniment. English words.
Also includes an arrangement for SATB.

ABSpl

Brown, Lawrence
Great Gittin' Up Mornin'

Brown, Lawrence
Hammer Song

Brown, Lawrence
I Got a Robe

Brown, Lawrence
I'm Goin' to Tell God all my Troubles

Brown, Lawrence
No More

---

*Brown, Lawrence

...Ev'ry time I feel de spirit. (In Brown, Lawrence. Spirituals. London, 1923, p. 16-19.)

Score: low solo voice with piano accompaniment. Negro dialect.

ABSpl CBSL LC NYPLS YJWJ ZWpl

*Brown, Lawrence

...I know de Lord's laid his hands on me. (In Brown, Lawrence. Spirituals. London, 1923, p. 9-12.)

Score: low solo voice with piano accompaniment. Negro dialect.

ABSpl CBSL LC NYPLS YJWJ ZWpl

---

*Brown, Lawrence

...Nobody knows de trouble I've seen. (In Brown, Lawrence. Spirituals. London, 1923, p. 3-5.)

Score: low solo voice with piano accompaniment. Negro dialect.

ABSpl CBSL LC NYPLS YJWJ ZWpl

Brown, Lawrence
Poor Wayfarin' Stranger

---

*Brown, Lawrence

...Sometimes I feel like a motherless child. (In Brown, Lawrence. Spirituals. London, 1923, p. 6-9.)

Score: low solo voice with piano accompaniment. Negro dialect.

ABSpl CBSL LC NYPLS YJWJ ZWpl

---

*Brown, Lawrence

Spirituals. Five Negro songs; arranged by Lawrence Brown. London, Schott and co. [c1923] Publ. pl. no. 4145.
19 p. fol.

Score: low solo voice with piano accompaniment. Negro dialect.

Contents: 1. Nobody knows de trouble I've seen. 2. Sometimes I feel like a motherless child. 3. I know de Lord's laid his hands on me. 4. Swing low, sweet chariot. 5. Ev'ry time I feel de spirit.

ABSpl CBSL LC NYPLS YJWJ ZWpl

---

*Brown, Lawrence

Steal away. Negro folk song; arranged by Laurence Brown. Boston, Winthrop Rogers, ltd. [c1922] Publ. pl. no. 4095.
6 p. fol.

Score: low voice [key of F] with piano accompaniment. Negro dialect.

ABSpl
NYPLS
YJWJ
LC

---

*Brown, Lawrence

...Swing low, sweet chariot. (In Brown, Lawrence. Spirituals. London, 1923, p. 13-15.)

Score: low solo voice with piano accompaniment. Negro dialect.

ABSpl CBSL LC NYPLS YJWJ ZWpl

Browne, Samuel Rodney
Blue Grotto

MSS
Typed letter attached.

---

*Bryan, Frederick M

Allies triumphant march. For piano Composed by Fred'k M. Bryan. New York, *Pace and Handy music co., inc. [c1919]
3 p. fol.

Score: piano solo.

ABSpl

---

*Bryan, Frederick M

Mauvolyene waltz. [For piano] By Frederick M. Bryan. New York, Pace and Handy music co., inc. [c1918]
3 p. fol.

Score: piano solo.

ABSpl

---

*Brymn, James Timothy

After tea (save a waltz for me). [Popular song] By Tim Brymn, *Chris Smith and *Clarence Williams. New York, *Clarence Williams music pub. co. [c1925]
5 p. fol.

Score: medium solo voice [key of C] with piano accompaniment. English words.

ABSpl

---

*Brymn, James Timothy

Build a nest for Birdie. [Popular song] Words by *R. C. McPherson (Cecil Mack)... music by Jas. T. Brymn... New York, Gotham-Attucks [c1906]
5 p. fol.

Score: medium solo voice [key of A^b] with piano accompaniment. English words.

ABSpl
LC

---

*Bryan, James T.

...Come after breakfast (Bring 'long your lunch and leave 'fore supper time.) [Popular song] By James T. Brymn, * Chris Smith and James *Burris. New York, Jos. W. Stern & co. [c1909] Publ. pl. no. 6435.
5p. fol.

Score: medium solo voice [key of B^b] with piano accompaniment. Negro dialect.

ABSpl

---

*Brymn, James Timothy

Consolation lane. [Popular song] By Brymn, *Smith and *Burris. New York, Jos. W. Stern & co. c1909 Publ. pl. no. 6436.
(In Ten choice Negro folksongs for voice and pianoforte. New York, [n.d.] p. 28-30.)

Score: medium solo voice [key of E^b] with piano accompaniment. English words.
Caption title.

ABSpl
BHC

---

*Brymn, James Timothy

...The darktown grenadiers. (March song) Words by *Billy Johnson. music by James T. Brymn. New York, Hamilton S. Gordon, c1905. Publ. pl. no. 11433.
5 p. fol.

Score: medium solo voice [key of F] with piano accompaniment. English words.

Excerpt from the musical comedy, "The smart set."

ABSpl
LC

---

*Brymn, James Timothy

Don't tell it to me. [Popular song] Words by *R. C. McPherson; music by Jas. T. Brymn. New York, Shapiro, Bernstein & co. [c1902]
5 p. fol.

Score: medium solo voice [key of G] with piano accompaniment. English words.

ABSpl
LC

---

*Brymn, James Timothy

...Down in sunny Alabama (Angeline). A coon love song. Words by James Burrell; music by James T. Brymn. New York, Richard A. Saalfield, c1901.
4 p. fol.

Score: medium solo voice [key of G] with piano accompaniment. English words.

"Musical supplement to the New York Sunday press, Sunday, Feb. 17, 1901." - Head of title.

ABSpl
LC

---

*Brymn, James Timothy

Ghost of the blues. [Popular song] By Tim Brymn and Sidney Bechet. New York, *Clarence Williams music pub. co. [c1924]
5 p. fol.

Score: medium solo voice [key of G] with piano accompaniment. English words.
Excerpt from the musical comedy, "Dinah."

ABSpl

---

*Brymn, James Timothy

Good night Lucinda. [Popular song] Words by *R. C. McPherson; music by Jas. T. Brymn. New York, Shapiro, Bernstein & co. [c1902]
5 p. fol.

Score: medium solo voice [key of G] with piano accompaniment. Negro dialect.

Introduced by John C. Slavin in Klaw & Erlanger's production of Mark Twain's "Huckleberry Finn."

ABSpl

---

*Brymn, James Timothy

...I'm going to steal away. [Popular song] Words and music by James T. Brymn. New York, Hamilton S. Gordon, c1905. Publ. pl. no. 11437.
5 p. fol.

Score: medium solo voice [key of E^b] with piano accompaniment. English words.

ABSpl
LC

---

*Brymn, James Timothy

I take things easy. [Popular song] Words and music by *[R. C.] McPherson and Brymn. New York, Shapiro, Bernstein & co. [c1903]
5 p. fol.

Score: medium solo voice with piano accompaniment. English words.

"Professional copy."

ABSpl
LC

*Brymn, James Timothy

Josephine, my Jo. [Popular song] Words by *R. C. McPherson; music by Jas. T. Brymn. New York, Shapiro, Bernstein & co. [c1901]
5 p. fol.

Score: medium solo voice [key of B^b] with piano accompaniment. English words.

ABSpl

*Brymn, James Timothy

Kickapoo dance. The latest Parisian sensation. It has entirely supplanted the fad of last season, the cakewalk. [Popular song for piano] Composed by Jas. T. Brymn. New York, Jos. W. Stern & co. [c1904] Publ. pl. no. 3987.
5 p. fol.

Score: piano solo.

ABSpl
LC

Brymn, James T

Old handerchief head.

Brymn, James T.

Patiently I Wait for Thee Love

Brymn, James T

Porto Rico

*Brymn, James Timothy

La rumba (El danson sociadal) Tango Argentine. [Popular song for piano] By J. Tim Brymn... New York, Jos. W. Stern & co. [c1913] Publ. pl. no. 7431.
5 p. fol.

Score: piano solo.

LC
ABSpl
CCPpl
NYPLS

*Brymn, James Timothy

Lindy, what you're gwine to do? [Popular song] Words by Frank Montgomery; music by J. T. Brymn. New York, Hamilton S. Gordon [c1905] Publ. pl. no. 11432.
5 p. fol.

Score: medium solo voice [key of G] with piano accompaniment. Negro dialect.

"As sung with great success by *Ernest Hogan, the unbleached American" - Title page.

ABSpl
LC

*Brymn, James Timothy

...Morning, noon and night (Serenade). [Popular song] Words by *Billy Johnson; music by James T. Brymn. New York, Hamilton S. Gordon, c1905. Publ. pl. no. 11439.
5 p. fol.

Score: medium solo voice [key of G] with piano accompaniment. English words.

ABSpl
LC

*Brymn, James Timothy

My little Zulu babe. [Popular song] Words by W. S. Estren; music by Jas. T. Brymn. New York, Windsor music co. [c1900]
5 p. fol.

Score: medium solo voice [key of F] with piano accompaniment. English words.

"Originally introduced and featured by the Real Coons, Williams and Walker." - Head of title. (On title page is also a photograph inset of *Williams and *Walker in costume for this song.)

ABSpl

*Brymn, James Timothy

My Louise. [Popular song] Words by W. S. Estren; music by Jas. T. Brymn. New York, F. S. Mills music pub. [c1900]
5 p. fol.

Score: medium solo voice [key of E^b] with piano accompaniment. English words.

ABSpl

*Brymn, James Timothy

...O-San. (Japanese song) [Popular song] Words by *Billy Johnson; music by James T. Brymn. New York, Hamilton S. Gordon, c1905. Publ. pl. no. 11441.
5 p. fol.

Score: medium solo voice [key of A^b] with piano accompaniment. English words.

ABSpl
LC

*Brymn, James Timothy

...Please let me sleep. [Popular song] Words by *R. C. McPherson; music by James T. Brymn. New York, Harry von Tilzer music pub. co. [c1902]
5 p. fol.

Score: low solo voice [key of B^b] with piano accompaniment. English words.

ABSpl
LC

*Brymn, James Timothy

...Powhatanna (Indian song). [Popular song] Words by *Billy Johnson; music by James T. Brymn. New York, Hamilton S. Gordon, c1905. Publ. pl. no. 11440.
5 p. fol.

Score: medium solo voice [key of F] with piano accompaniment. English words.

ABSpl
LC

*Brymn, James Timothy

Remember. A song. Words by James Burrell; music by James T. Brymn. New York, Leo. Feist pub. [c1902]
5 p. fol.

Score: high solo voice [key of B^b] with piano accompaniment. English words.

ABSpl
LC

*Brymn, James Timothy

Rowena. A characteristic Indian love song. Words and music by James. T. Brymn... New York, American music pub. co. [c1904]
5 p. fol.

Score: medium solo voice [key of G] with piano accompaniment. English words.

LC
ABSpl

*Brymn, James Timothy

Send the rent and you needn't come home. [Popular song] Words by *R. C. McPherson; music by James T. Brymn. New York, T. B. Harms & co. [c1903]
6 p. fol.

Score: high solo voice [key of G] with piano accompaniment. English words.
Caption title

ABSpl
LC

*Brymn, James Timothy

Shout, sister, shout! [Popular song] By *Clarence Williams, Tim Brymn and *Alexander Hill. New York, *Clarence Williams music pub. co. [c1930]
5 p. fol.

Score: medium solo voice [key of A^b] with piano accompaniment. English words.

Featured by the Boswell sisters in a Brunswick recording and as a N. B. C. feature.

ABSpl

*Brymn, James Timothy

Stop! Rest a while... [Popular song] By L. Wolfe Gilbert and Tim Brymn. New York, L. Wolfe Gilbert [c1921]
5 p. fol.

Score: medium solo voice [key of E^b] with piano accompaniment. English words.
Excerpt from the musical revue, "Put and Take".

ABSpl

*Brymn, James Timothy

Those tantalizing eyes (Oh Lize, those eyes, those eyes.) [Popular song] Words by *R. C. McPherson; music by Jas. T. Brymn. New York, Shapiro, Bernstein & co. [c1902]
5 p. fol.

Score: medium solo voice [key of G] with piano accompaniment. English words.

ABSpl
LC

*Brymn, James Timothy

Toot-toot! Dixie bound in the mornin'. [Popular song] By *Chris Smith and J. Tim Brymn... New York, *Handy bros. music co., inc. [c1903]
5 p. fol.

Score: medium solo voice with piano accompaniment. English words.

ABSpl

*Brymn, James Timothy

"Travel on." (Coon song) Words by *Billy Johnson; music by James T. Brymn. New York, Hamilton S. Gordon, c1905. Publ. pl. no. 11442.
5 p. fol.

Score: medium solo voice [key of A^b] with piano accompaniment. English words.

From the musical comedy, "The Smart Set."

ABSpl
LC

*Brymn, James Timothy

...Waiting for love again. Song. Words by W. S. Estren; music by James T. Brymn. New York, Richard A. Saalfield publ. ꜀c1901꜁
4 p. fol.

Score: medium solo voice with piano accompaniment. English words.

ABSpl
LC

---

*Burleigh, Henry Thacker, 1866- arr.

꜀An ante-bellum sermon. Song. Tune: Joshua fit de battl' ob Jerico. Words by *Paul Laurence Dunbar; arranged by H. T. Burleigh꜁
(In Burleigh, H. T., "Plantation melodies, old and new. p. 16-18)

Score: medium solo voice ꜀key of G꜁ with piano accompaniment. Negro dialect.

ABSpl NYPLS
HMC YJWJ
LC Zwpl
NYPL42

---

*Burleigh, Henry Thacker, 1866-

꜀"De black-bird an' de crow." Tune: We will go er-pickin' up cohn. Words by R. E. Phillips; arranged by H. T. Burleigh꜁
(In Burleigh, H. T., "Plantation melodies, old and new." p. 10,11)

Score: medium solo voice ꜀key of A^b꜁ with piano accompaniment. Negro dialect.

ABSpl NYPLS
HMC YJWJ
LC ZWpl
NYPL42

---

*Burleigh, Henry Thacker, 1866-

Achievement. Song. The poem by Frances Bacon Paine; music by H. T. Burleigh. New York, William Maxwell music co. ꜀c1905꜁ Publ. pl. no. 766.
3 p. fol.

Score: low solo voice ꜀key of A^b꜁ with piano accompaniment. English words.

LC
ABSpl

---

*Burleigh, Henry Thacker, 1866-

And as the gulls soar. Song. Poem by Frances Bacon Paine; music by H. T. Burleigh. New York, William Maxwell music co. ꜀c1905꜁ Publ. pl. no. 786.
3 p. fol.

Score: low solo voice ꜀key of F꜁ with piano accompaniment. English words.
Bound in Vol. 1.

ABSpl
LC

---

*Burleigh, Henry Thacker, 1866- arr.

De blin' man stood on de road an' cried. ꜀Negro spiritual for solo voice꜁ Text from St. Mark 10:46, 52; arranged by H. T. Burleigh. New York, G. Ricordi & co., inc. ꜀c1928꜁ Publ. pl. no. NY743.
6 p. fol.

Score: low solo voice ꜀key of D^b꜁ with piano accompaniment. Negro dialect.
Bound in Vol. 3.

ABSpl

---

*Burleigh, Henry Thacker, 1866-

Adoration. Song. Words by Dora Lawrence Houston; music by H. T. Burleigh. New York, G. Ricordi & co. ꜀c1921꜁ Publ. pl. no. NY115.
5 p. fol.

Score: high solo voice ꜀key of F꜁ with piano accompaniment. English words.
Bound in Vol. 1.

LC
ABSpl

---

*Burleigh, Henry Thacker, 1866-

Apart. Song. Words by Frances Bacon Paine; music by H. T. Burleigh. New York, William Maxwell music co. ꜀c1905꜁ Publ.pl. no. 765.
3 p. fol.

Score: low solo voice ꜀key of B^b꜁ with piano accompaniment.

ABSpl
LC

---

*Burleigh, Henry Thacker, 1866-

...Bring her again to me. ꜀Song꜁
(In Burleigh, Henry Thacker. Two poems by W. E. Henley. p. 1-3)

Score: high solo voice ꜀key of F꜁ with piano accompaniment. English words.

ABSpl
LC

---

*Burleigh, Henry Thacker, 1866-

Ahmed's song of farewell.
(In Burleigh, H. T. Saracen songs. New York, c1914, p. 18-21.)

Score: high solo voice ꜀key of B꜁ with piano accompaniment. English words.
Caption title.

ABSpl
HPSpl
HMC
NYPLS

---

*Burleigh, Henry Thacker, 1866- arr.

...Balm in Gilead. ꜀Negro spiritual for solo voice꜁ Text from Jeremiah 8:22; arranged by H. T. Burleigh. New York, G. Ricordi & co., inc. ꜀c1919꜁ Publ. pl. no. 116578.
6 p. fol.

Score: low solo voice ꜀key of G꜁ with piano accompaniment. Negro dialect.
Bound in Vol. 3.

ABSpl
LC
ZWpl

---

*Burleigh, Henry Thacker, 1866- arr.

By an' by. ꜀Negro spiritual for solo voice꜁ Arranged by H. T. Burleigh. New York, G. Ricordi & co., inc. ꜀c1917꜁ Publ. pl. no. 116408.
5 p. fol.

Score: high solo voice ꜀key of A^b꜁ with piano accompaniment. Negro dialect.
Bound in Vol. 3.

ABSpl
ZWpl

---

*Burleigh, Henry Thacker, 1866- arr.

...Ain't goin' to study war no mo'. ꜀Negro spiritual for solo voices꜁ Arranged by H. T. Burleigh. New York, G. Ricordi & co. ꜀c1922꜁ Publ. pl. no. NY268.
6 p. fol.

Score: high solo voice ꜀key of B^b꜁ with piano accompaniment. Negro dialect.
Bound in Voll 3.

ABSpl
BPL
ZWpl

---

*Burleigh, Henry Thacker, 1866-

Before meeting. Song. Words by Arthur Symons; music by H. T. Burleigh. New York, G. Ricordi & co., inc., c1921. Publ. pl. no. NY64.
7 p. fol.

Score: high solo voice ꜀key of G^b꜁ with piano accompaniment. English words.
Bound in Vol. 1.

ABSpl
LC

---

*Burleigh, Henry Thacker, 1866-

...By the pool at the third Rosses. Song. Words by Arthur Symons...music by H. T. Burleigh... New York, G. Ricordi & co., c1916. Publ. pl. no. 116255.
6 p. fol.

Score: high solo voice ꜀key of D^b꜁ with piano accompaniment. English words.
Bound in Vol. 1.
Dedicated to John McCormack.

LC
ABSpl
HPSpl

---

*Burleigh, Henry Thacker, 1866-

Almona (song of Hassan)
(In Burleigh, H. T. Saracen songs. New York, 1914, p. 3-5.)

Score: high solo voice ꜀key of A꜁ with piano accompaniment. English words.
Caption title.

ABSpl
HPSpl
HMC
NYPLS

---

*Burleigh, Henry Thacker, 1866-
Behold that Star

---

*Burleigh, Henry Thacker, 1866-

Carry me back to the pine wood. Song. Words anon.; music by H. T. Burleigh. New York, William Maxwell music co. ꜀c1909꜁ Publ. pl. no. 1164.
3 p. fol.

Score: low solo voice ꜀key of G꜁ with piano accompaniment. English words.
Bound in Vol. 1.

ABSpl
LC

---

*Burleigh, Henry Thacker, 1866-

Among the fuchsias. ꜀Song꜁
(In Burleigh, H. T. Five songs of Laurence Hope. New York, 1915, p. 12-15.)

Score: high solo voice ꜀key of $F^{\#}$꜁ with piano accompaniment. English words.
Caption title.

ABSpl NYPLS
HPSpl NYPL42
HMC LC
ZWpl

---

*Burleigh, Henry Thacker, 1866-

...A birthday song. ꜀Song. From꜁ Three songs for baritone or mezzo-soprano with piano accompaniment by H. T. Burleigh; ꜀words by Christina Rossetti꜁ New York, G. Schirmer ꜀c1898꜁ Publ. pl. no. 14093.
5 p. fol.

Score: medium solo voice ꜀key of A꜁ with piano accompaniment. English words.

ABSpl
HMC
LC
NYPLS

---

*Burleigh, Henry Thacker, 1866-

Come with me. Song. Words by Lura Kelsey Clendening; music by H. T. Burleigh. New York, G. Ricordi & co., inc. ꜀c1921꜁ Publ. pl. no. NY62.
7 p. fol.

Score: high solo voice ꜀key of F꜁ with piano accompaniment. English words.
Bound in Vol. 1.

ABSpl
LC

*Burleigh, Henry Thacker, 1866-

A corn song. Song. Words by *Paul Laurence Dunbar; music by H. T. Burleigh. New York, G. Ricordi & co. ₍c1920₎ Publ. pl. no. 19.
11 p. fol.

Score: high solo voice ₍key of G^{b}₎ with piano accompaniment. Negro dialect.
Bound in Vol. 3.

ABS
LC

---

*Burleigh, Henry Thacker, 1866- arr.

...Don't yo' dream of turnin' back... Negro folk song (not spiritual) ₍for solo voice₎ Music by H. T. Burleigh. New York, G. Ricordi & co., inc. ₍c1921₎ Publ. pl. no. NY156.
5 p. fol.

Score: low solo voice ₍key of F₎ with piano accompaniment. Negro dialect.
Bound in Vol. 3.

LC
ZWpl
ABSpl

---

*Burleigh, Henry Thacker, 1866-

Elysium. Song. The words by *James Weldon Johnson; music by H. T. Burleigh. New York, G. Ricordi & co., inc. ₍C1914₎ Publ. pl. no. 116048.
6 p. fol.

Score: high solo voice ₍key of E^{b}₎ with piano accompaniment. English words.
Bound in Vol. 1.

LC
ABS

---

*Burleigh, Henry Thacker, 1866- arr.

...Couldn't hear nobody pray. ₍Negro spiritual for solo voice₎ Arranged by H. T. Burleigh. New York, G. Ricordi & co., inc. ₍c1922₎ Publ. pl. no. NY240.
6 p. fol.

Score: low solo voice ₍key of D^{b}₎ with piano accompaniment. Negro dialect.
Bound in Vol. 3.

ABSpl
ZWpl

---

*Burleigh, Henry Thacker, 1866- arr.

...Don't you weep when I'm gone. ₍Negro spiritual for solo voice₎ Text from Jeremiah 22:10; arranged by H. T. Burleigh. New York, G. Ricordi & co., inc. ₍c1919₎ Publ. pl. no. 116600.
6 p. fol.

Score: medium solo voice ₍key of G^{b}₎ with piano accompaniment. Negro dialect.
Bound in Vol. 3.

LC
BPL
ABSpl

---

*Burleigh, Henry Thacker, 1866-

...Ethiopia saluting the colors. Song. The poem by Walt Whitman; music by H. T. Burleigh. New York, G. Ricordi & co., inc., c1916. Publ. pl. no. 116339.
10 p. fol.

Score: low solo voice ₍key of C^{m}₎ with piano accompaniment. English words.
Bound in Vol. 1.

#PSpl ABS
LC

Burleigh, Henry Thacker, 1866-
De Creation - Scandalize My Name.

---

*Burleigh, Henry Thacker, 1866- arr.

...The dove and the lily (Swedish folk song). Arranged by H. T. Burleigh. New York, G. Ricordi & co., c1917. Publ. pl. no. 116415.
7 p. fol.

Score: high solo voice ₍key of G₎ with piano accompaniment. English words.
Bound in Vol. 1.
At head of title: "Sung by Mr. Charles Harrison."

ABS
LC
BuGL

Burleigh, Henry Thacker, 1866-
Ethiopia's Paean of Exaltation.

---

*Burleigh, Henry Thacker, 1866- arr.

Dar's a meetin' here tonight. ₍Negro spiritual for solo voice₎ Arranged by H. T. Burleigh. Boston, Oliver Ditson co. ₍c1926₎ Publ. pl. no. ML-3329.
5 p. fol.

Score: high solo voice ₍key of E^{b}₎ with piano accompaniment. Negro dialect.
Caption title.
Bound in Vol. 3.

ZWpl
ABSpl

---

*Burleigh, Henry Thacker, 1866-

Down by the sea. Song...Words by George O'Connell; music by H. T. Burleigh. New York, G. Ricordi & co., inc. ₍c1919₎ Publ. pl. no. 116539.
6 p. fol.

Score: low solo voice ₍key of E^{b}₎ with piano accompaniment. English words.
Bound in Vol. 1.

LC
ABSpl

---

*Burleigh, Henry Thacker, 1866- arr.

...Ev'ry time I feel de spirit. ₍Negro spiritual arranged for solo voice by₎ H. T. Burleigh. New York, G. Ricordi & co. ₍c1925₎ Publ. pl. no. 462.
7 p. fol.

Score: high solo voice ₍key of F₎ with piano accompaniment. Negro dialect.
Bound in Vol. 3.

ABSpl
BPL
LC
NYPLS
ZWpl

---

*Burleigh, Henry Thacker, 1866- arr.

...Deep river. Song. Old Negro melody. Arranged by H. T. Burleigh... New York, G. Ricordi & co., c1917. Publ. pl. no. 116059.
5 p. fol.

Score: high solo voice ₍key of F₎ with piano accompaniment. English words.

ABSpl
LC
ZWpl

---

*Burleigh, Henry Thacker, 1866-

The dream love. A song. Words by Alexander Groves; music by H. T. Burleigh. New York, G. Ricordi & co. ₍c1923₎ Publ. pl. no. 363.
5 p. fol.

Score: high solo voice ₍key of A^{b}₎ with piano accompaniment. English words.
BOUND in Vol. 1.

ABS
BuGL
LC

---

*Burleigh, Henry Thacker, 1866-

Exile. Song. Words by Inez Maree Richardson; music by H. T. Burleigh. New York, G. Ricordi & co. ₍c1922₎ Publ. pl. no. 320.
5 p. fol.

Score: low solo voice ₍key of A minor₎ with piano accompaniment. English words.
Bound in Vol. 1.

ABSpl
LC

Burleigh, Henry Thacker, 1866-
Didn't My Lord Deliver Daniel

---

*Burleigh, Henry Thacker, 1866-

Dreams tell me truly. Song. Words by Frederic G. Bowles; music by H. T. Burleigh. New York, G. Ricordi & co., c1917. Publ. pl. no. 116424.
6 p. fol.

Score: high solo voice ₍key of G₎ with piano accompaniment. English words.
Bound in Vol. 1.

LC
ABSpl

Burleigh, Henry Thacker, 1866-
Ezekiel Saw de Wheel

---

*Burleigh, Henry Thacker, 1866- arr.

Don't be weary traveler. ₍Negro spiritual for solo voice₎ Arranged by H. T. Burleigh. New York, G. Ricordi & co., inc. ₍c1928₎ Publ. pl. no. NY744.
5 p. fol.

Score: low solo voice ₍key of D₎ with piano accompaniment. Negro dialect.
Bound in Vol. 3.

ABSpl

---

*Burleigh, Henry Thacker, 1866- arr.

...Dry bones. ₍Negro spiritual. Text from Ezekiel 37₎ arranged by₎ H. T. Burleigh. New York, G. Ricordi & co. ₍c1930₎
8 p. fol.

Score: medium solo voice ₍key of G minor₎ with piano accompaniment.
Bound in Vol. 3.
"To "Paul Robeson." - Head of title.

ABSpl
BuGL

Burleigh, Henry Thacker, 1866-
A Fatuous Tragedy

•Burleigh, Henry Thacker, 1866-

[Five songs of Laurence Hope [pseud.] Set to music by H. T. Burleigh. New York, G. Ricordi & co., c1915. Publ. pl. nos. 114196-and 116283.
20 p. fol.

Score: medium solo voice with piano accompaniment. English words.
Bound in Vol. 1.
Contents: 1. Worth while. -2. The jungle flower. -3. Kashmiri song. -4. Among the fuchsias. -5. Till I wake.
Prefatory note by H. E. Krehbiel.
ABSpl HPSpl LC NYPLS ZWpl

•Burleigh, Henry Thacker, 1866- arr.

...De gospel train, or ("Git on bo'd lit'l' children") [Negro spiritual for solo voice; Arranged by H. T. Burleigh. New York, G. Ricordi & co., inc. [c1921] Publ. pl. no. NY81.
6 p. fol.

Score: high solo voice [key of B^b] with piano accompaniment. Negro dialect.
Bound in Vol. 3.

LC
ABSpl
ZWpl

•Burleigh, Henry Thacker, 1866-

He sent me you. Song. Words by Frederick H. Martens; music by H. T. Burleigh. New York, G. Ricordi & co., c1915. Publ. pl. no. 116132.
5 p. fol.

Score: high solo voice [key of A^b] with piano accompaniment. English words.
Bound in Vol. 1.

LC
ABSpl

•Burleigh, Henry Thacker, 1866-

Folk song (I love my Jean). Song. Poem by Robert Burns; music by H. T. Burleigh. New York, William Maxwell music co. [c1904] Publ. pl. no. 586.
4 p. fol.

Score: low solo voice [key of E^b] with piano accompaniment. Scotch dialect.
Bound in Vol. 1.

ABSpl
LC

•Burleigh, Henry Thacker, 1866-

The grey wolf. Scena. Words by Arthur Symons; music by H. T. Burleigh. New York, G. Ricordi & co., inc., c1915. Publ. pl. no. 116222.
11 p. fol.

Score: high solo voice [key of D^b] with piano accompaniment. English words.
Bound in Vol. 1.

ABSpl
BuGL
HPSpl - autographed to M... [illegible]aughter by composer.
LC

•Burleigh, Henry Thacker, 1866- arr.

Hear de lambs a-cryin'. [Negro spiritual. Anthem; Text from John 21:15-17; arranged by H. T. Burleigh. New York, G. Ricordi & co., inc. [c1927] Publ. pl. no. NY658.
13 p. fol.

Score: SATB with alto or baritone solo and with piano reduction for rehearsal only. Negro dialect.
Bound in Vol. 3.

ABSpl

•Burleigh, Henry Thacker, 1866-

Fragments. Song... Words by •Jessie Fauset; music by H. T. Burleigh. New York, G. Ricordi & co. [c1919] Publ. pl. no. 116597.
3 p. fol.

Score: low solo voice [key of E^b] with piano accompaniment. English words.
Bound in Vol. 1.

LC ABS

Burleigh, Henry Thacker, 1866-
Hail to the King.

•Burleigh, Henry Thacker, 1866-

Hearts. Song. Words by C. M. Wilmerding; music by H. T. Burleigh. New York, G. Ricordi & co., c1915. Publ. pl. no. 116242.
5 p. fol.

Score: high solo voice [key of D] with piano accompaniment. English words.
Bound in Vol. 1.

LC
ABSpl

•Burleigh, Henry Thacker, 1866- arr.

Give me Jesus. [Negro spiritual for solo voice; Arranged ... by H. T. Burleigh. New York, G. Ricordi & co., inc. [c1926] Publ. pl. no. NY594.
5 p. fol.

Score: low solo voice [key of C] with piano accompaniment. Negro dialect.
Bound in Vol. 3.

ABSpl

Burleigh, Henry Thacker, 1866-
De Ha'nt

•Burleigh, Henry Thacker, 1866- arr.

... Heav'n, heav'n. [Negro spiritual. Arranged] by H. T. Burleigh. New York, G. Ricordi & co. [c1921] Publ. pl. no. NY78.
6 p. fol.

Score: low solo voice [key of A^b] with piano accompaniment. Negro dialect.
Bound in Vol. 3.

ABSpl
ZWpl

•Burleigh, Henry Thacker, 1866-

...The glory of the day was in her face. [Song from "Passionale" a set of four songs for tenor. Music] by H. T. Burleigh; lyrics by •James Weldon Johnson... New York, G. Ricordi & co., inc. [c1915] Publ. pl. no. 116175.
6 p. fol.

Score: high solo voice [key of E^b] with piano accompaniment. English words.

ABSpl NYPLS
HMC YJWJ
LC

•Burleigh, Henry Thacker, 1866- arr.

Hard trials. [Negro spiritual for solo voice; Text from Matthew 8:20; 14:21; arranged by H. T. Burleigh. New York, G. Ricordi & co., inc. [c1919] Publ. pl. no. 116582.
7 p. fol.

Score: medium solo voice [key of E^b] with piano accompaniment. Negro dialect.
Bound in Vol. 3.

LC
BPL
ABSpl
ZWpl

•Burleigh, Henry Thacker, 1866-

Heigh-ho! Song. The words by James E. Campbell; the music by H. T. Burleigh... New York, William Maxwell music co. [c1904] Publ. pl. no. 603.
7 p. fol.

Score: low solo voice [key of B^b] with piano accompaniment. English words.
Bound in Vol. 1.

LC ABS

•Burleigh, Henry Thacker, 1866- arr.

...Go down Moses. Let my people go! [Negro spiritual. Text from Exodus VIII; arranged by H. T. Burleigh] New York, G. Ricordi & co. [c1917] Publ. pl. no. 116427.
6 p. fol.

Score: high solo voice [key of B^m] with piano accompaniment. Negro dialect.
Bound in Vol. 3.

ABS
LC
ZWpl

•Burleigh, Henry Thacker, 1866-

Have you been to Lons. Song. Words by Gordon Johnstone; music by H. T. Burleigh... New York, G. Ricordi & co. [c1920] Publ. pl. no. 116490.
7 p. fol.

Score: high solo voice [key of F] with piano accompaniment. English words.

Bound in Vol. 1.

ABSpl
LC

•Burleigh, Henry Thacker, 1866-

...Her eyes twin pools. [Song. From "Passionale," a set of four songs for tenor. Music] by H. T. Burleigh; lyrics by •James Weldon Johnson... New York, G. Ricordi & co. [c1915] Publ. pl. no. 116172.
5 p. fol.

Score: low solo voice [key of E^b] with piano accompaniment. English words.

ABSpl YJWJ
HMC
LC

•Burleigh, Henry Thacker, 1866- arr.

...Go tell it on de mountains! (Christmas song of the plantation) [Negro spiritual for solo voice, Arranged by] H. T. Burleigh. New York, G. Ricordi & co., inc. [c1927] Publ. pl. no. NY696.
7 p. fol.

Score: medium solo voice [key of G] with piano accompaniment. Negro dialect.
Caption title.
Bound in Vol. 3.

ABSpl LC
ZWpl BPL

•Burleigh, Henry Thacker, 1866-

He met her in the meadow. Song. [No author given;] music by H. T. Burleigh. New York, G. Ricordi & co. [c1921] Publ. pl. no. 220.
5 p. fol.

Score: high solo voice [key of A^b] with piano accompaniment. English words.
Bound in Vol. 1.

ABSpl

•Burleigh, Henry Thacker, 1866- arr.

He's jus' de same today. [Negro spiritual for solo voice; From Calhoun, Lowndes co., Alabama. Text from Exodus 14:22 and I Samuel 17:49; arranged by H. T. Burleigh. New York, G. Ricordi & co., inc. [c1919] Publ. pl. no. 116581.
7 p. fol.

Score: high solo voice [key of B^b] with piano accompaniment. Negro dialect.
Bound in Vol. 3.
ABSpl
BPL

*Burleigh, Henry Thacker, 1866-

His helmet's blaze. Almona's song of Youssouf to Hassan.
(In Burleigh, H. T. Saracen songs. New York, 1914, p. 8,9.)

Score: high solo voice ⌊key of A^m⌋ with piano accompaniment. English words.
Caption title.

ABSpl
HPSpl
HMC
NYPLS

---

*Burleigh, Henry Thacker, 1866- arr.

...I got a home in-a dat rock. ⌊Negro spiritual for solo voice⌋ Arranged by H. T. Burleigh. New York, G. Ricordi & co., inc. ⌊c1926⌋ Publ. pl. no. NY543.
7 p. fol.

Score: low solo voice ⌊key of F⌋ with piano accompaniment. Negro dialect.
Bound in Vol. 3.

BPL
LC
ABSpl

---

*Burleigh, Henry Thacker, 1866-

I want to die while you love me. ⌊Song⌋ Words by *Georgia Douglas Johnson; music by H. T. Burleigh. New York, G. Ricordi & co. ⌊c1919⌋ Publ. pl. no. 116599.
6 p. fol.

Score: low solo voice ⌊key of D⌋ with piano accompaniment. English words.
Bound in Vol. 1.

ABSpl
HMC
LC
NYPLS

---

*Burleigh, Henry Thacker, 1866-

His word is love. Sacred song. Words by Fred. G. Bowles; music by H. T. Burleigh. New York, G. Ricordi & co., c1914. Publ. pl. no. 116075.
7 p. fol.

Score: high solo voice ⌊key of A^b⌋ with piano accompaniment. English words.

ABSpl
LC

---

*Burleigh, Henry Thacker, 1866-

I hear his footsteps, music sweet. Almona's song of delight.
(In Burleigh, H. T. Saracen songs. New York, 1914, p. 10-12.)

Score: high solo voice ⌊key of E^m⌋ with piano accompaniment. English words.
Caption title.

ABSpl
HPSpl
HMC NYPLS

---

*Burleigh, Henry Thacker, 1866-

If life be a dream. Song. Words by Frank L. Stanton; music by H. T. Burleigh. New York, William Maxwell music co. ⌊c1904⌋ Publ. pl. no. 673.
6 p. fol.

Score: low solo voice ⌊key of D⌋ with piano accompaniment. English words.
Bound in Vol. 1.

ABSpl
LC
ZWpl

Burleigh, Henry Thacker, 1866-
Ho, Ro, My Nut Brown Maiden

Burleigh, Henry Thacker, 1866-
I Hope My Mother Will Be There

---

*Burleigh, Henry Thacker, 1866-

...If you but knew. ⌊Song. From⌋ Three songs for baritone or mezzo-soprano with piano accompaniment by H. T. Burleigh; ⌊words from "The martian" translated from the French⌋ New York, G. Schirmer ⌊c1898⌋ Publ. pl. no. 14094.
5 p. fol.

Score: medium solo voice ⌊key of E⌋ with piano accompaniment. English words.

ABSpl
HMC
NYPLS
ZWpl

---

*Burleigh, Henry Thacker, 1866- arr.

Hold on (Keep your hand on the plow). Negro spiritual. Arranged by H. T. Burleigh. New York, G. Ricordi & co., inc. ⌊c1938⌋ Publ. pl. no. 1113.
13 p. 8°.

Score: SATB with medium solo obligato throughout and with piano reduction for rehearsal only. Negro dialect.

ABSpl

---

*Burleigh, Henry Thacker, 1866- arr.

I know de Lord's laid his hands on me. ⌊Negro spiritual⌋ arranged by H.T.Burleigh. New York, G Ricordi & co. c1924. Publ. pl. no. NY 495.
7 p. fol.

Score: High solo voice ⌊key of F⌋ with piano accompaniment. Negro dialect.
Bound in Vol. 3.

BPL
LC
ABSpl
ZWpl

---

*Burleigh, Henry Thacker, 1866-

I'll be dar to meet yo'. ⌊Song. From⌋ Two plantation songs. ⌊Words by Beverly Garrison;⌋ music by H. T. Burleigh. New York, William Maxwell music co. ⌊c1905⌋ Publ. pl. no. 882-7a.
6 p. fol.

Score: high solo voice ⌊key of F⌋ with piano accompaniment. Negro dialect.

ABSpl
LC

---

*Burleigh, Henry Thacker, 1866-

The hour glass. Song. The poem by Alexander Groves; music by H. T. Burleigh... New York, G. Ricordi & co. ⌊c1914⌋ Publ. pl. no. 114136.
5 p. fol.

Score: medium solo voice ⌊key of B^b⌋ with piano accompaniment. English words.
"With incidental use of a theme from the liturgy of the Dresden church."
Bound in Vol. 1.

ABSpl
NYPLS

---

*Burleigh, Henry Thacker, 1866-

I remember all. Song. Words by Arthur Symons; music by H. T. Burleigh. New York, G. Ricordi & co. ⌊c1919⌋ Publ. pl. no. 116601.
6 p. fol.

Score: low solo voice ⌊key of A^b⌋ with piano accompaniment. English words.
Bound in Vol. 1.

LC
ABSpl

---

*Burleigh, Henry Thacker, 1866-

In summer. Song. Words by Josephine Nichols; music by H. T. Burleigh. New York, G. Ricordi & co., c1917. Publ. pl. no. 116419.
5 p. fol.

Score: high solo voice ⌊key of G minor⌋ with piano accompaniment. English words.
Bound in Vol. 1.

ABSpl

---

*Burleigh, Henry Thacker, 1866- arr.

⌊I doan' want fu' t' stay hyeah no longah.⌋ Tune: "Danville chariot." Words by R. E. Phillips; arranged by H. T. Burleigh.
(In Burleigh, H. T., "Plantation melodies, old and new." p. 3-5)

Score: medium solo voice ⌊key of E^b⌋ with piano accompaniment. Negro dialect.

ABSpl NYPLS
HMC YJWJ
LC ZWpl
NYPL42

---

*Burleigh, Henry Thacker, 1866- arr.

I stood on de ribber of Jerdon. ⌊Negro spiritual for solo voice⌋ Arranged by H. T. Burleigh. New York, G. Ricordi & co., inc. ⌊c1918⌋ Publ. pl. no. 116506.
6 p. fol.

Score: low solo voice ⌊key of F⌋ with piano accompaniment. Negro dialect.

ABSpl
LC
ZWpl

---

*Burleigh, Henry Thacker, 1866-

In the great somewhere. Song... Words by Harold Robe; music by H. T. Burleigh. New York, G. Ricordi & co. ⌊c1919⌋ Publ. pl. no. 116559.
7 p. fol.

Score: low solo voice ⌊key of E^b⌋ with piano accompaniment. English words.
Bound in Vol. 1.
"Sung by John McCormack at all his engagements." - Title page.

ABSpl
LC

---

*Burleigh, Henry Thacker, 1866- arr.

I don't feel no-ways tired, or ("I am seekin' for a city"). ⌊Negro spiritual for solo voice⌋ Text from Hebrews 11:14, 16; arranged by H. T. Burleigh. New York, G. Ricordi & co., inc. ⌊c1917⌋ Publ. pl. no. 116410.
6 p. fol.

Score: medium solo voice ⌊key of C⌋ with piano accompaniment. Negro dialect.
Bound in Vol. 3.

BPL
LC
ABSpl
ZWpl

---

*Burleigh, Henry Thacker, 1866- arr.

...I want to be ready. Walk in Jerusalem jus' like John. ⌊Negro spiritual arranged by H. T. Burleigh; text from Rev. 21:16 and Acts 2⌋ New York, G. Ricordi & co. ⌊c1917⌋ Publ. pl. no. 116409.
5 p. fol.

Score: medium solo voice ⌊key of E^b⌋ with piano accompaniment. Negro dialect.
Bound in Vol. 3.

ABSpl
BPL
LC
ZWpl

---

*Burleigh, Henry Thacker, 1866-

In the wood of Finvara. Song. Words by Arthur Symons; music by H. T. Burleigh. New York, G. Ricordi & co., inc. ⌊c1917⌋ Publ. pl. no. 116002.
5 p. fol.

Score: low solo voice ⌊key of D^b⌋ with piano accompaniment. English words.
Bound in Vol. 1.

LC
ABSpl
HPSpl - autographed to [illegible] by HTB.

*Burleigh, Henry Thacker, 1866-

It was nothing but a rose. Song. Words anon.; music by H. T. Burleigh. New York, William Maxwell music co. [c1910; Publ. pl. no. 1237.
5 p. fol.

Score: low solo voice [key of B^b, with piano accompaniment. English words.
Bound in Vol. 1.

ABSpl

*Burleigh, Henry Thacker, 1866-

Just my love and I (boat song). Song. Words by *Louise Alston Burleigh; music by H. T. Burleigh. New York, William Maxwell music co. [c1904; Publ. pl. no. 596.
6 p. fol.

Score: high solo voice [key of F; with piano accompaniment. English words.
Bound in Vol. 1.

ABSpl
LC
HPSpl

*Burleigh, Henry Thacker, 1866- arr.

...Little David, play on your harp. [Negro spiritual for solo voice; Arranged by H. T. Burleigh. New York, G. Ricordi & co., inc. [c1921; Publ. pl. no. NY145.
6 p. fol.

Score: high solo voice [key of A^b, with piano accompaniment. Negro dialect.
Bound in Vol. 4.

NYPL42
BPL
ABSpl ZWpl
LC

*Burleigh, Henry Thacker, 1866- arr.

I've been in de storm so long. [Negro spiritual for solo voice; Arranged by H. T. Burleigh. New York, G. Ricordi & co., inc. [c1927; Publ. pl. no. NY695.
7 p. fol.

Score: low solo voice [key of B^b, with piano accompaniment. Negro dialect.
Bound in Vol. 3.

BPL
LC
ABSpl

*Burleigh, Henry Thacker, 1866-

Kashmiri song.
(In Burleigh, H. T. Five songs of Laurence Hope. New York, 1915, p. 8-11.)

Score: high solo voice [key of B^m] with piano accompaniment. English words.
Caption title.
ABSpl NYPLS
HPSpl NYPL42
HMC LC
ZWpl

*Burleigh, Henry Thacker, 1866- arr.

Little child of Mary. From the Negro spiritual "De new-born baby." Words and music adapted and arranged by H. T. Burleigh... New York, G. Ricordi & co., inc. [c1932; Publ. pl. no. NY889.
5 p. fol.

Score: high solo voice [key of G^m, with piano accompaniment. English words.

ABSpl
LC

*Burleigh, Henry Thacker, 1866-
Just because. 1914. 12244.
In the key of D.

Bound in Vol. 1.

ABS

*Burleigh, Henry Thacker, 1866-

...Just you. Song. Words by Madge Marie Miller; music by H. T. Burleigh. New York, G. Ricordi & co., c1915. Publ. pl. no. 116130.
5 p. fol.

Score: high solo voice [key of A^b, with piano accompaniment. English words.
Bound in Vol. 1.

HPSpl
LC
ABSpl

*Burleigh, Henry Thacker, 1866-

...The little house of dreams. Song. Words by Arthur Wallace Peach; music by H. T. Burleigh. New York, G. Ricordi & co. [c1922; Publ. pl. no. 340.
5 p. fol.

Score: high solo voice [key of A^b, with piano accompaniment.
Bound in Vol. 1.
At head of title: Sung by Mr. John McCormack.

ABSpl
BuGL
LC

*Burleigh, Henry Thacker, 1866-

...Jean. Song. The words by Frank L. Stanton; the music by H. T. Burleigh... New York, William Maxwell music co. [c1903; Publ. pl. no. 542.
6 p. fol.

Score: medium solo voice [key of D^b, with piano accompaniment. English words.
Bound in Vol. 1.

ABS
LC

*Burleigh, Henry Thacker, 1866-

Keep a good grip on de hoe! [Song. From] Two plantation songs. [Words by Howard Weeden; music by H. T. Burleigh. New York, William Maxwell music co. [c1905; Publ. pl. no. 882-7b.
5 p. fol.

Score: medium solo voice [key of A; with piano accompaniment. Negro dialect.

ABSpl
LC

*Burleigh, Henry Thacker, 1866-

Little mother of mine. [Song; Words by Walter H. Brown; music by H. T. Burleigh. New York, G. Ricordi & co., inc., c1917. Publ. pl. no. 116438.
7 p. fol.

Score: medium solo voice [key of E^b, with piano accompaniment. English words.
Bound in Vol. 1.

LC ABS

*Burleigh, Henry Thacker, 1866- arr.

John's gone down on de island. [Negro spiritual for solo voice. Text from Revelations 1;; arranged... by H. T. Burleigh. New York, G. Ricordi & co., inc. [c1917; Publ. pl. no. 116444.
6 p. fol.

Score: high solo voice [key of A^b, with piano accompaniment. Negro dialect.
Bound in Vol. 3.
ABSpl
BPL
LC

*Burleigh, Henry Thacker, 1866- arr.

...Let us cheer the weary traveler. [Negro spiritual for solo voice; Arranged by H. T. Burleigh. New York, G. Ricordi & co., inc. [c1919; Publ. pl. no. 116577.
6 p. fol.

Score: high solo voice [key of D^b, with piano accompaniment. Negro dialect.
Bound in Vol. 4.
ABSpl
BPL
LC
ZWpl

*Burleigh, Henry Thacker, 1866- arr.

...Lonesome valley. [Negro spiritual for solo voice; Arranged by H. T. Burleigh. New York, G. Ricordi & co., inc. [c1926; Publ. pl. no. NY596.
5 p. fol.

Score: medium solo voice [key of E minor; with piano accompaniment. Negro dialect.
Bound in Vol. 4.
"Go down in de lonesome valley." - Caption title.

ABSpl
ZWpl

*Burleigh, Henry Thacker, 1866-

The jungle flower. [Song]
(In Burleigh, H. T. Five songs of Laurence Hope. New York, 1915, p. 4-7.)

Score: high solo voice [key of A^b] with piano accompaniment. English words.
Caption title.
ABSpl NYPLS
HPSpl NYPL42
HMC LC
ZWpl

*Burleigh, Henry Thacker, 1866-

...Life. [Song. From] Three songs for baritone or mezzo-soprano with piano accompaniment by H. T. Burleigh; [words by John Boyle O'Reilly; New York, G. Schirmer [c1898; Publ. pl. no. 14095.
3 p. fol.

Score: medium solo voice [key of C; with piano accompaniment. English words.

ABSpl
LC

*Burleigh, Henry Thacker, 1866-

Love found the way. A song. Words by Jesse Winne; music by H. T. Burleigh. New York, G. Ricordi & co. [c1922; Publ. pl. no. NY310.
7 p. fol.

Score: low solo voice [key of C; with piano accompaniment. English words.
Bound in Vol. 2.

ABSpl

Burleigh, Henry Thacker, 1866-
Just a Wearin' For You.

*Burleigh, Henry Thacker, 1866-

Listen to yo' gyarder angel. Song. Words by Robert Underwood Johnson; music by H. T. Burleigh. New York, G. Ricordi & co., inc. [c1920; Publ. pl. no. NY14.
6 p. fol.

Score: medium solo voice [key of A^b; with piano accompaniment. Negro dialect.

LC
ABSpl

*Burleigh, Henry Thacker, 1866-

Love found the way. A song. Words by Jesse Winne; music by H. T. Burleigh. New York, G. Ricordi & co. [c1922; Publ. pl. no. NY309.
7 p. fol.

Score: high solo voice [key of E^b, with piano accompaniment.
Bound in Vol. 2.

ABSpl
BuGL

*Burleigh, Henry Thacker, 1866- arr.

Love watches (an Irish fragment). Song. Words and melody by George F. O'Connell; arranged by H. T. Burleigh. New York, G. Ricordi & co. [c1920, Publ. pl. no. NY15.
6 p. fol.

Score: high solo voice [key of B^{b}, with piano accompaniment. English words.
Bound in Vol. 2.

ABSpl

---

*Burleigh, Henry Thacker, 1866-

Lovely dark and lonely one. [Song, poem by *Langston Hughes; music by H. T. Burleigh... New York, G. Ricordi and co., inc., [c1935, Publ. pl. no. 1014.
3 p. fol.

Score: Medium solo voice [key of C, with piano accompaniment. English words.
Bound in Vol. 1.
Poem is from the book "The Dream Keeper," Langston Hughes.

ABSpl HMC HPS (Autographed to HPS by Mr. Burleigh)
YJWJ ZWpl LC

---

*Burleigh, Henry Thacker, 1866-

Love's dawning. A song. Poem by *Louise Alston Burleigh; music by H. T. Burleigh. New York, William Maxwell music co. [c1906, Publ. pl. no. 883.
5 p. fol.

Score: low solo voice [key of F, with piano accompaniment. English words.
Bound in Vol. 2.

ABSpl
LC

---

*Burleigh, Henry Thacker, 1866-

Love's garden. Song. The poem by M. Heuchling; the music by H. T. Burleigh... New York, William Maxwell music co. [c1902, Publ. pl. no. 527.
6 p. fol.

Score: high solo voice [key of A^{b}, with piano accompaniment. English words.
Bound in Vol. 2.

ABSpl
LC

---

*Burleigh, Henry Thacker, 1866-

Love's likeness. [A song, Poem by Madge Marie Miller; music by H. T. Burleigh... New York, G. Ricordi & co. [c1927, Publ. pl. no. 694.
5 p. fol.

Score: medium solo voice [key of C, with piano accompaniment. English words.
Bound in Vol. 2.

ABSpl
BuGL
LC

---

*Burleigh, Henry Thacker, 1866-

Love's pleading. Song. Poem by Leontine Stanfield; music by H. T. Burleigh... New York, William Maxwell music co. [c1904, Publ. pl. no. 585.
6 p. fol.

Score: medium solo voice [key of E, with piano accompaniment. English words.
Bound in Vol. 2.

ABSpl
BuGL
LC ZWpl

---

*Burleigh, Henry Thacker, 1866- arr.

["Ma Lawd's a-writin' down time." Tune: He sees all you do, an' hyeahs all you see [sic, Words by R. E. Phillips; arranged by H. T. Burleigh,
(In Burleigh, H. T., "Plantation melodies, old and new." p. 6,7)

Score: medium solo voice [key of F, with piano accompaniment. Negro dialect.

ABSpl YJWJ
HMC ZWpl
NYPL42
NYPLS

---

*Burleigh, Henry Thacker, 1866-

Malay boat song. Song. Words by Laurence Hope; music by H. T. Burleigh. New York, William Maxwell music co. [c1906, Publ. pl. no. 861.
6 p. fol.

Score: high solo voice [key of D, with piano accompaniment. English words.
Bound in Vol. 2.

ABSpl
LC

---

*Burleigh, Henry Thacker, 1866-

...Mammy's li'l' baby. Cradle song. Poem by *Louise Alston Burleigh; music by H. T. Burleigh... New York, William Maxwell music co. [c1903, Publ. pl. no. 569.
4 p. fol.

Score: high solo voice [key of F, with piano accompaniment. English words.
Bound in Vol. 2.
"Specially composed for and sung by Mme. Schumann-Heink." - Head of title.

ABSpl ZWpl
LC

---

*Burleigh, Henry Thacker, 1866-

The man in white. Song. Words anon.; music by H. T. Burleigh. New York, G. Ricordi & co. [c1917, Publ. pl. no. NY248.
5 p. fol.

Score: medium solo voice [key of G, with piano accompaniment. English words.
Bound in Vol. 2.
A song for children.

ABSpl

---

*Burleigh, Henry Thacker, 1866-

Memory. Song. Words by Arthur Symons; music by H. T. Burleigh. New York, G. Ricordi & co., c1915. Publ. pl. no. 116218.
5 p. fol.

Score: medium solo voice [key of D, with piano accompaniment. English words.
Bound in Vol. 2.

LC
ABSpl

---

*Burleigh, Henry Thacker, 1866- arr.

My Lord, what a mornin'. [Negro spiritual for solo voice, Text from Revelations 6:10; arranged by H. T. Burleigh. New York, G. Ricordi & co., inc. [c1918, Publ. pl. no. 116493.
6 p. fol.

Score: high solo voice [key of F, with piano accompaniment. Negro dialect.
Bound in Vol. 4.

ABSpl
BPL
LC
ZWpl

---

*Burleigh, Henry Thacker, 1866-

[My Merlindy Brown. Negro serenade. Words by James Edwin Campbell; music by H. T. Burleigh,
(In Burleigh, H. T., "Plantation melodies, old and new." p. 12, 13)

Score: medium solo voice [key of F, with piano accompaniment. Negro dialect.

ABSpl NYPLS
HMC YJWJ
LC ZWpl
NYPL42

---

*Burleigh, Henry Thacker, 1866- arr.

My way's cloudy. [Negro spiritual for solo voice, Arranged by H. T. Burleigh. New York, G. Ricordi & co., inc. [c1917, Publ. pl. no. 116445.
6 p. fol.

Score: medium solo voice [key of D^{b}, with piano accompaniment. Negro dialect.
Bound in Vol. 4.

LC
ABSpl
BPL

---

*Burleigh, Henry Thacker, 1866-

Myrra (I know of two bright eyes). Song. [No author given, music by H. T. Burleigh. New York, William Maxwell music co. [c1909, Publ. pl. no. 1177.
5 p. fol.

Score: high solo voice [key of A^{b}, with piano accompaniment. English words.
Bound in Vol. 2.

ABSpl
LC

---

*Burleigh, Henry Thacker, 1866-

[Negro lullaby. Song. Words by James Edwin Campbell; music by H. T. Burleigh,
(In Burleigh, H. T., "Plantation melodies, old and new." p. 14, 15)

Score: medium solo voice [key of F, with piano accompaniment. Negro dialect.

ABSpl YJWJ
HMC ZWpl
LC
NYPL42
NYPLS

---

*Burleigh, Henry Thacker, 1866- Negro minstral melodies. New York, 1909. (card #2)

Contents: 1. Angel Gabriel. -2. Angels, meet me at the crossroads. -3. Balm of Gilead. -4. Come where my love lies dreaming. -5. Darling Nellie Gray. -6. Dearest Mae. -7. De camptown races (or "Gwine to run all night!")-8. Jim along Josie. -9. Kingdom coming. -10. Massa's in de col', col' ground. -11. My old Kentucky home. -12. Nelliewas a lady. -13. Nelly Bly. -14. Oh! Dem golden slippers! -15. Oh! Susanna. -16. Old black Joe. -17. Old cabin home. -18. Old folks at home. 19- Shine on. -20. Tom-Big-Bee river. -21. Wake Nicodemus. ABSpl HMC LC NYPLS ZWpl

---

*Burleigh, Henry Thacker, 1866- arr.

...Nobody knows de trouble I've seen. [Negro spiritual for solo voice, Arranged by H. T. Burleigh. New York, G. Ricordi & co., inc. [c1917, Publ. pl. no. 116436.
6 p. fol.

Score: high solo voice [key of A^{b}, with piano accompaniment. Negro dialect.
Bound in Vol. 4.

BPL
LC
ABSpl
ZWpl

---

*Burleigh, Henry Thacker, 1866-

Now sleeps the crimson petal. Song. The words by [Alfred, Tennyson; music by H. T. Burleigh. New York, William Maxwell music co. [c1908, Publ. pl. no. 1075.
5 p. fol.

Score: low solo voice [key of B^{b}, with piano accompaniment. English words.

ABSpl
LC

---

*Burleigh, Henry Thacker, 1866-

O love of a day. Song. Poem by Randolph Hartley; music by H. T. Burleigh. New York, William Maxwell music co. [c1905, Publ. pl. no. 752.
6 p. fol.

Score: high solo voice [key of G, with piano accompaniment. English words.
Bound in Vol. 2.

ABSpl
LC

---

*Burleigh, Henry Thacker, 1866- arr.

O Lord have mercy on me. Negro spiritual. Arranged by H. T. Burleigh. New York, G. Ricordi & co. [c1935, Publ. pl. no. N. Y. 987.
5 p. 8°.

Score: SATB with piano reduction for rehearsal only. Negro dialect.

ABSpl

*Burleigh, Henry Thacker, 1866-

O, night of dream and wonder. Almona's song. (In Burleigh, H. T. Saracen songs. New York, 1914, p. 6,7.)

Score: high solo voice ₍key of B^b minor₎ with piano accompaniment. English words.

Caption title.

ABSpl
HPSpl
HMC
NYPLS

*Burleigh, Henry Thacker, 1866- arr.

Oh Peter go ring dem bells. ₍Negro spiritual for solo voice; Text from Revelations 8:10; arranged by H. T. Burleigh. New York, G. Ricordi & co., inc. ₍c1918₎ Publ. pl. no. 116494.
5 p. fol.

Score: low solo voice ₍key of F₎ with piano accompaniment. Negro dialect.
Bound in Vol. 4.

ABSpl
LC

*Burleigh, Henry Thacker, 1866
Plantation melodies... c1901 (card 2)

2. Ma Lawd's a-writin' down time.-3. When de Debble comes 'round. -4. De black-bird and de crow. -5. My Merlinda Brown. -6. A Negro serenade. -7. Negro lullaby. -8. An antebellum sermon.

ABSPL NYPLS CPL
HMC YJWJ ZWpl
NYPL42 LC

*Burleigh, Henry Thacker, 1866-

O perfect love. Wedding song. The words by D. F. Blomfield; ₍the₎ music by H. T. Burleigh. Philadelphia, Theodore Presser co. ₍c1904₎ Publ. pl. no. 12268.
7 p. fol.

Score: high solo voice ₍key of A^b₎ with piano accompaniment.
Bound in Vol. 2.

ABSpl
BuGL
ZWpl

*Burleigh, Henry Thacker, 1866- arr.

...Oh! Rock me, Julie. ₍Song. From Afro-American folksongs by H. E. Krehbiel; arranged by H. T. Burleigh.₎ New York, G. Ricordi & co. ₍c1921₎ Publ. pl. no. NY152.
3 p. fol.

Score: high solo voice ₍key of C₎ with piano accompaniment. English words.
Bound in Vol. 4.

"Words and melody received by Mr. Krehbiel from Mr. George W. Cable." — Footnote, p. 2.
"The melody is based on the 'whole tone' scale."

LC ABS

*Burleigh, Henry Thacker, 1866-

The prayer I make for you. Song. Words by Harold Robe; music by H. T. Burleigh. New York, G. Ricordi & co. ₍c1921₎ Publ. pl. no. NY117.
7 p. fol.

Score: high solo voice ₍key of B^b₎ with piano accompaniment. English words.
Bound in Vol. 2.

LC
ABSpl

*Burleigh, Henry Thacker, 1866- arr.

...O rocks, don't fall on me. ₍Negro spiritual for solo voice; Arranged by H. T. Burleigh. New York, G. Ricordi & co., inc. ₍c1922₎ Publ. pl. no. NY270.
7 p. fol.

Score: high solo voice ₍key of F₎ with piano accompaniment. Negro dialect.
Bound in Vol. 4.

BPL
LC
ABSpl

*Burleigh, Henry Thacker, 1866- arr.

...Oh, wasn' dat a wide ribber? ₍Negro spiritual for solo voice; Arranged by H. T. Burleigh. New York, G. Ricordi & co., inc. ₍c1924₎ Publ. pl. no. NY439.
7 p. fol.

Score: medium solo voice ₍key of E^b₎ with piano accompaniment. Negro dialect.
Bound in Vol. 4.

BPL
LC
ABSpl
ZWpl

*Burleigh, Henry Thacker, 1866-

The prayer. Song. Words by Arthur Symons... Music by H. T. Burleigh. New York, G. Ricordi & co., c1915. Publ. pl. no. 116217.
5 p. fol.

Score: high solo voice ₍key of A^b₎ with piano accompaniment. English words.

ABSpl
ZWpl
LC

Burleigh, Henry Thacker, 1866-
O Southland

*Burleigh, Henry Thacker, 1866-

On Inishmaan. Isles of Aran. Song. Words by Arthur Symons; music by H. T. Burleigh. New York, G. Ricordi & co., inc. ₍c1917₎ Publ. pl. no. 116425.
5 p. fol.

Score: low solo voice ₍key of E^b₎ with piano accompaniment. English words.
Bound in Vol. 2.

ABSpl
LC

*Burleigh, Henry Thacker, 1866-

Promis' lan' (a hallelujah song). Words by Mrs. N. J. Corey; music by H. T. Burleigh. New York, G. Ricordi & co., inc. ₍c1917₎ Publ. pl. no. 116394.
7 p. fol.

Score: high solo voice ₍key of F₎ with piano accompaniment. Negro dialect.
Bound in Vol. 4.

LC ABS

*Burleigh, Henry Thacker, 1866-

O why art thou not near me (serenade). Song. Words anon.; music by H. T. Burleigh... New York, William Maxwell music co. ₍c1904₎ Publ. pl. no. 690.
6 p. fol.

Score: high solo voice ₍key of G₎ with piano accompaniment. English words.
Bound in Vol. 2.

ABSpl
LC

*Burleigh, Henry Thacker, 1866-

One day. Song. Words by Mary Blackwell Sterling; music by H. T. Burleigh. New York, William Maxwell music co. ₍c1904₎ Publ. pl. no. 597.
5 p. fol.

Score: medium solo voice ₍key of F₎ with piano accompaniment. English words.
Bound in Vol. 2.

ABSpl
LC

*Burleigh, Henry Thacker, 1866-

...Request. Song. Words by Laurence Hope; music by H. T. Burleigh. New York, William Maxwell music co. ₍c1905₎ Publ. pl. no. 814.
5 p. fol.

Score: low solo voice ₍key of E^b₎ with piano accompaniment. English words.

ABSpl
LC

*Burleigh, Henry Thacker, 1866- arr.

Oh didn't it rain. ₍Negro spiritual for solo voice; Text from Genesis 7:4; arranged by H. T. Burleigh. New York, G. Ricordi & co., inc. ₍c1919₎ Publ. pl. no. 116528.
6 p. fol.

Score: high solo voice ₍key of B^b₎ with piano accompaniment. Negro dialect.
Bound in Vol. 4.

BPL
ABSpl
ZWpl

*Burleigh, Henry Thacker, 1866-

One year (1914-1915). Song. Poem by Margaret M. Harlan; music by H. T. Burleigh... New York, G. Ricordi & co., c1916. Publ. pl. no. 116258.
5 p. fol.

Score: high solo voice ₍key of C₎ with piano accompaniment.
Bound in Vol. 2.

ABSpl
LC

Burleigh, Henry Thacker, 1866-
Ride on, King Jesus.

*Burleigh, Henry Thacker, 1866-

Oh, my love. Song. Words by Harriet Gaylord; music by H. T. Burleigh... New York, G. Ricordi and co. ₍c1919₎ Publ. pl. no. 116591.
6 p. fol. (square)

Score: high voice only ₍key of E^b₎ with piano accompaniment. English words.

ABS
NYPLS
ZWpl

*Burleigh, Henry Thacker, 1866

Plantation melodies, old and new. Words by R. E. Phillips; J. E. Campbell; *Paul Lawrence Dunbar; music composed, or transcribed and adapted by H. T. Burleigh, NY, G. Schirmer, c1901, Publ. pl. no. 15445.
18 p. fol.

Score: medium solo voice with piano accompianiment. Negro dialect.
Bound in Vol. 4.

Contents: 1.- I doan' want fu' t' stay hyeah no longah.-2

ABS (continued on next card)

*Burleigh, Henry Thacker, 1866-

...Ring, my bawnjer, ring. ₍Song. From, "Two plantation songs for medium voice." Words by James E. Campbell; ₍music by₎ H. T. Burleigh. New York, G. Schirmer, inc. ₍c1902₎ Publ. pl. no. 16014.
3 p. fol.

Score: low solo voice ₍key of B^b₎ with piano accompaniment. Negro dialect.

ABSpl
LC

*Burleigh, Henry Thacker, 1866- arr.

Run to Jesus. ₍Negro spiritual for solo voice₎ Arranged by H. T. Burleigh. Boston, Oliver Ditson co. ₍c1926₎ Publ. pl. no. ML-3308.
3 p. fol.

Score: low solo voice ₍key of C minor₎ with piano accompaniment. Negro dialect.
Bound in Vol. 4.

ABS This song was given to the Jubilee singers by Hon. Frederick Douglass, at Wa[shi]ngton, D. C., with the (continued on next card)

*Burleigh, Henry Thacker, 1866- Run to Jesus. ₍c1926₎ (Card 2)

interesting statement, that it first suggested to him the thought of escaping from slavery." - Footnote, p.2.
Bound in Vol. 4.

ABSpl

*Burleigh, Henry Thacker, 1866-

The sailor's wife. Song. Words by Mary Stewart Cutting; music by H. T. Burleigh. New York, G. Ricordi & co., c1917. Publ. pl. no. 116416.
7 p. fol.

Score: low solo voice ₍key of A^b₎ with piano accompaniment. English words.
Bound in Vol. 2.

ABSpl
LC

*Burleigh, Henry Thacker, 1866-

Saracen songs. Lyrics by Fred. G. Bowles; set to music by H. T. Burleigh. New York, G. Ricordi & co. c1914. Publ. pl. no. 114182.
21 p. fol.
[Bound in Vol. 2]

Score: high solo voice with piano accompaniment. English words.

Contents: 1. Aloma. -2. O, night of dream and wonder. -3. His helmet['s] blaze. -4. I hear his footsteps, music sweet. -5. Thou art weary. -6. This (continued on next card)

*Burleigh, Henry Thacker, 1866- Saracen songs. 1914. (card # 2)

is Nirvana. -7. Ahmed's song of farewell.

ABSpl
HPSpl
HMC
NYPLS

*Burleigh, Henry Thacker, 1866-

Savior divine. ₍Sacred song₎ Words by R. Palmer; music by H. T. Burleigh. New York, William Maxwell music co. ₍c1907₎ Publ. pl. no. 1030.
7 p. fol.

Score: medium solo voice ₍key of A^b₎ with piano accompaniment. English words.

ABSpl

*Burleigh, Henry Thacker, 1866- arr.

...Scandalize' my name...Negro folk song (not spiritual) ₍for solo voice. From Calhoun, Lowndes County, Alabama. Arranged by H. T. Burleigh₎ New York, G. Ricordi & co., inc. ₍c1921₎ Publ. pl. no. NY154.
3 p. fol.

Score: medium solo voice ₍key of A^b₎ with piano accompaniment. Negro dialect.

LC
YJWI
ABSpl

*Burleigh, Henry Thacker, 1866-

Since Molly went away. Song. Words by Frank L. Stanton; music by H. T. Burleigh. New York, William Maxwell music co. ₍c1907₎ Publ. pl. no. 976.
6 p. fol.

Score: low solo voice ₍key of C₎ with piano accompaniment. English words.
Bound in Vol. 2.

ABSpl
LC

*Burleigh, Henry Thacker, 1866-
Sinner please doan le t dis harves' pass. 1917. 116406.

Bound in Vol. 4.

ABS

*Burleigh, Henry Thacker, 1866- arr.

...Sinner, please don't let this harves' pass. ₍Negro spiritual for solo voice. Arranged by H. T. Burleigh₎ New York, G. Ricordi & co., inc. ₍c1917₎ Publ. pl. no. 116406.
5 p. fol.

Score: medium solo voice ₍key of E minor₎ with piano accompaniment. Negro dialect.
2 cop.

LC BPL
ABSpl ZWpl

*Burleigh, Henry Thacker, 1866-

Sleep, li'l chile, go sleep! A Negro lullaby. Words by George V. Hobart; music by H. T. Burleigh. Chicago, Harry von Tilzer co. ₍c1902₎
5 p. fol.

Score: low solo voice ₍key of G₎ with piano accompaniment. Negro dialect.

ABSpl

*Burleigh, Henry Thacker, 1866-

The soldier. Song. The words by Rupert Brooke...the music by H. T. Burleigh. New York, G. Ricordi & co., c1916. Publ. pl. no. 116316.
8 p. fol.

Score: medium solo voice ₍key of E^b minor₎ with piano accompaniment. English words.
Bound in Vol. 2.

ABSpl

*Burleigh, Henry Thacker, 1866- arr.

Sometimes I feel like a motherless child. ₍Negro spiritual for solo voice. Arranged by H. T. Burleigh₎ New York, G. Ricordi & co., inc. ₍c1918₎ Publ. pl. no. 116497.
6 p. fol.

Score: medium solo voice ₍key of F^m₎ with piano accompaniment. Negro dialect.
Bound in Vol. 4.

ABSpl
LC
ZWpl

*Burleigh, Henry Thacker, 1866-

...Somewhere. Song... Words by James Whedon; music by H. T. Burleigh. New York, William Maxwell music co. ₍c1907₎ Publ. pl. no. 978.
5 p. fol.

Score: high solo voice ₍key of D₎ with piano accompaniment. English words.

ABSpl
LC

*Burleigh, Henry Thacker, 1866-

...Southern lullaby. For mixed voices. ₍Words by George V. Hobart; music by₎ H. T. Burleigh. New York, G. Ricordi & co. ₍c1920₎ Publ. pl. no. NY22.
8 p. 8°.

Score: SATB with S solo and with piano reduction for rehearsal only. Negro dialect.

LC
ABSpl

*Burleigh, Henry Thacker, 1866-
Southland sketches for violin and piano. (Andante). 1916. 116310.

Bound in Vol. 2.

ABS

*Burleigh, Henry Thacker, 1866-

...The spring my dear is no longer spring. ₍Song₎ (In Burleigh, Henry Thacker. Two poems by W. E. Henley. p. 4-6)

Score: high solo voice ₍key of A^b₎ with piano accompaniment. English words.

ABSpl
LC

*Burleigh, Henry Thacker, 1866- arr.

...Stan' still Jordan. ₍Negro spiritual for solo voice. Arranged by H. T. Burleigh₎ New York, G. Ricordi & co., inc. ₍c1926₎ Publ. pl. no. NY598.
7 p. fol.

Score: high solo voice ₍key of G^m₎ with piano accompaniment. Negro dialect.
Bound in Vol. 4.

ABSpl
BPL
LC

*Burleigh, Henry Thacker, 1866- arr.

...Steal away. ₍Negro spiritual for solo voice₎ Arranged by H. T. Burleigh. New York, G. Ricordi & co., inc. ₍c1921₎ Publ. pl. no. NY157.
6 p. fol.

Score: low solo voice ₍key of F₎ with piano accompaniment. Negro dialect.
Bound in Vol. 4.

ABSpl
ZWpl

*Burleigh, Henry Thacker, 1866- arr.

Swing low, sweet chariot. ₍Negro spiritual for solo voice₎ Text from II Kings 2:11; arranged by H. T. Burleigh. New York, G. Ricordi & co., inc. ₍c1917₎ Publ. pl. no. 116451.
6 p. fol.

Score: high solo voice ₍key of A^b₎ with piano accompaniment. Negro dialect.
Bound in Vol. 4.

ABSpl
BPL
LC
ZWpl

*Burleigh, Henry Thacker, 1866-

...Tarry with me, o my savior! Sacred song. Poem by C. L. Smith; music by H. T. Burleigh. New York, William Maxwell music co. ₍c1911₎ publ. pl. no. 1283.
7 p. fol.

Score: low solo voice ₍key of D^b₎ with piano accompaniment. English words.

ABSpl

*Burleigh, Henry Thacker, 1866-

Tell me once more. Song... Words by Fred. G. Bowles; music by H. T. Burleigh. New York, G. Ricordi & co. [c1920] Publ. pl. no. 116618.
7 p. fol.

Score: low solo voice [key of F] with piano accompaniment. English words.
Bound in Vol. 2.

ABSpl zWpl
LC

*Burleigh, Henry Thacker, 1866-

Tide. Song. The poem by Frances Bacon Paine; the music by H. T. Burleigh. New York, William Maxwell music co. [c1905] Publ. pl. no. 768.
5 p. fol.

Score: low solo voice [key of D^b] with piano accompaniment. English words.
Bound in Vol. 2.

ABSpl
LC

*Burleigh, Henry Thacker, 1866-

...Under a blazing star. Song. Words by Mildred Seitz; music by H. T. Burleigh. New York, G. Ricordi & co. [c1918] Publ. pl. no. 116508.
6 p. fol.

Score: low solo voice [key of B minor] with piano accompaniment. English words.
Bound in Vol. 2.

At head of title: "Sung by John McCormack."

LC
ABSpl zWpl

*Burleigh, Henry Thacker, 1866-

This is Nirvana. Yussouf's song to Almona. (In Burleigh, H. T. Saracen songs. New York, 1914, p. 15-17.)

Score: high solo voice [key of E^b] with piano accompaniment. English words.
Caption title.

ABSpl
HPSpl
HMC
NYPLS

*Burleigh, Henry Thacker, 1866-

Till I wake. [Song]
(In Burleigh, H. T. Five songs of Laurence Hope. New York, 1915, p. 16-20.)

Score: high solo voice [key of D^m] with piano accompaniment. English words.
Caption title.

ABSpl NYPLS
HPSpl NYPL42
HMC LC
ZWpl

*Burleigh, Henry Thacker, 1866-

The victor. Song. Words by George O'Connell; music by H. T. Burleigh. New York, G. Ricordi & co., inc., c1919. Publ. pl. no. 116550.
7 p. fol.

Score: high solo voice [key of F] with piano accompaniment. English words.
Bound in Vol. 2.

ABSpl
LC

*Burleigh, Henry Thacker, 1866-

Thou art weary. Almona's song to Yussouf. (In Burleigh, H. T. Saracen songs. New York, 1914, p. 13,14.)

Score: high solo voice [key of G^b] with piano accompaniment. English words.
Caption title.

ABSpl
HPSpl
HMC NYPLS

*Burleigh, Henry Thacker, 1866-

...Till I wake. Song. Words by Laurence Hope... Music by H. T. Burleigh. New York, G. Ricordi & co., c1926. Publ. pl. no. 116283.
7 p. fol.

Score: high solo voice [key of F] with piano accompaniment. English words.

At head of title: "Sung by Mr. John McCormack."

NYPLS
ABSpl
HPSpl
LC

*Burleigh, Henry Thacker, 1866- arr.

Wade in de water. [Negro spiritual for solo voice] Arranged by H. T. Burleigh. New York, G. Ricordi & co., inc. [c1925] Publ. pl. no. NY497.
7 p. fol.

Score: high solo voice [key of F minor] with piano accompaniment. Negro dialect.
Bound in Vol. 4.

LC zWpl
ABSpl BPL

*Burleigh, Henry Thacker, 1866-

...Three shadows. Song. The poem by Dante Gabriel Rossetti; the music by H. T. Burleigh. New York, G. Ricordi & co., inc., c1916. Publ. pl. no. 116327.
7 p. fol.

Score: high solo voice [key of E^b] with piano accompaniment. English words.
Bound in Vol. 2.

ABSpl
LC
ZWpl

*Burleigh, Henry Thacker, 1866- arr.

'Tis me, O Lord, [or] Standin' in de need of pray'r). [Negro spiritual for solo voice. Arranged by H. T. Burleigh] New York, G. Ricordi & co., inc. [c1918] Publ. pl. no. 116524.
5 p. fol.

Score: medium solo voice [key of A^b] with piano accompaniment. Negro dialect.
Bound in Vol. 4.

BPL
LC
ABSpl

*Burleigh, Henry Thacker, 1866-

Waiting. Song. Poem by Martha Gilbert Dickinson; music by H. T. Burleigh. New York, William Maxwell music co. [c1904] Publ. pl. no. 703.
6 p. fol.

Score: high solo voice [key of F] with piano accompaniment. English words.
Bound in Vol. 2.

ABSpl BPL
LC

*Burleigh, Henry Thacker, 1866-

...Three songs for baritone or mezzo-soprano with piano accompaniment by H. T. Burleigh... New York, G. Schirmer [c1898] Publ. pl. nos. 14093-5.
3 v. fol.

Score: medium solo voice [various keys] with piano accompaniment. English words.
Bound in Vol. 2.

Contents: 1. A birthday song. -2. If you but knew. -3. Life. (missing)

ABSpl
LC

*Burleigh, Henry Thacker, 1866-

The trees have grown so. Song. Words by John Hanlon; music by H. T. Burleigh. New York, G. Ricordi & co. [c1923] Publ. pl. no. NY358.
5 p. fol.

Score: high solo voice [key of F] with piano accompaniment. English words.
Bound in Vol. 2.

ABSpl
ZWpl
LC

*Burleigh, Henry Thacker, 1866- arr.

Walk together children. Negro spiritual. Arranged by H. T. Burleigh. New York, G. Ricordi & co., inc. [c1938] Publ. pl.no. N. Y. 1118.
5 p. 8°.

Score: SSA with piano reduction for rehearsal only. Negro dialect.

ABSpl

*Burleigh, Henry Thacker, 1866-

Through love's eternity. Song. Poem by C. C. Stoddard; music by H. T. Burleigh. New York, William Maxwell music co. [c1906] Publ. pl. no. 904.
5 p. fol.

Score: low solo voice [key of F] with piano accompaniment. English words.

ABSpl
LC

*Burleigh, Henry Thacker, 1866-

...Two poems by W. E. Henley (a) Bring her again to me; (b) The spring my dear is no longer spring. Set to music by H. T. Burleigh... New York, G. Ricordi & co., c1914. Publ. pl. no. 116062, 3.
6 p. fol.

Score: high solo voice with piano accompaniment. English words. (missing)
Bound in Vol. 2.

ABSpl
HPSpl
LC

*Burleigh, Henry Thacker, 1866-

The way o' the world. Song. Poem by Frank L. Stanton; music by H. T. Burleigh. New York, William Maxwell music co. [c1904] Publ. pl. no. 701.
6 p. fol.

Score: high solo voice [key of E^b] with piano accompaniment. English words.
Bound in Vol. 2.

LC
ABSpl

*Burleigh, Henry Thacker, 1866-

Thy heart. Song for mezzo-soprano or baritone. Words (from the Sanskrit) by A. V. Williams Jackson; music by H. T. Burleigh. New York, G. Schirmer, c1902. Publ. pl. no. 15893.
3 p. fol.

Score: medium solo voice [key of B] with piano accompaniment. English words.
Bound in Vol. 2.

ABSpl
HMC
LC

*Burleigh, Henry Thacker, 1866-

Two words. Song. Words by Edward Oxenford; music by H. T. Burleigh. New York, William Maxwell music co. [c1908] Publ. pl. no. 1155.
7 p. fol.

Score: low solo voice [key of F] with piano accompaniment. English words.

ABSpl zWpl
LC

*Burleigh, Henry Thacker, 1866- arr.

Weepin' Mary. [Negro spiritual for solo voice] Text from John 20:11; arranged by H. T. Burleigh. New York, G. Ricordi & co., inc. [c1917] Publ. pl. no. 116428.
3 p. fol.

Score: high solo voice [key of F^m] with piano accompaniment. Negro dialect.
Bound in Vol. 4.

ABSpl
BPL
LC
NYPL42 zWpl

*Burleigh, Henry Thacker 1866-

Were I a star. Song. Words by A. Musgrove Robarts; music by H. T. Burleigh. New York, G. Ricordi & co. [c1919] Publ. pl. no. 116547.
5 p. fol.

Score: high solo voice, key of A♭, with piano accompaniment. English words.
Bound in Vol. 2.

ABS
ZWpl
LC

---

*Burleigh, Henry Thacker, 1866- arr.

Were you there? [Negro spiritual for solo voice] Arranged by H. T. Burleigh. New York, G. Ricordi & co., inc. [c1924] Publ. pl. no. NY446.
6 p. fol.

Score: medium solo voice [key of F] with piano accompaniment. Negro dialect.
Bound in Vol. 4.

ABSpl
ZWpl

---

*Burleigh, Henry Thacker, 1866- arr.

["When de debble comes 'round." Tune: You shall have er new hidin'-place dat day. Words by R. E. Phillips; arranged by H. T. Burleigh]
(In Burleigh, H. T., "Plantation melodies, old and new." p. 8-9)

Score: Medium solo voice [key of F] with piano accompaniment. Negro dialect.

ABSpl NYPLS
HMC YJWJ
LC ZWpl
NYPL42

---

*Burleigh, Henry Thacker, 1866- arr.

Who is dat yondah? [Negro spiritual for solo voice] From the collection of *Eva A. Jessye. Arranged by H. T. Burleigh. New York, G. Ricordi & co., inc. [c1930]
6 p. fol.

Score: low solo voice [key of D minor] with piano accompaniment. Negro dialect.
Bound in Vol. 4.

ABSpl

---

*Burleigh, Henry Thacker, 1866-

Worth while. [Song]
(In Burleigh, H. T. Five songs of Laurence Hope. New York, 1915, p. 1-3.)

Score: high solo voice [key of D] with piano accompaniment. English words.
Caption title.

ABSpl NYPLS
HPSpl NYPL42
HMC LC
ZWpl

---

*Burleigh, Henry Thacker, 1866-

You ask me if I love you. Song. Words by Lillian Bennett Thompson; music by H. T. Burleigh. New York, William Maxwell music co. [c1907] Publ. pl. no. 1011.
7 p. fol.

Score: low solo voice [key of F] with piano accompaniment. English words.
Bound in Vol. 2.

ABSpl
LC

---

*Burleigh, Henry Thacker, 1866- arr.

You'll git dar in de mornin'. [Song] From "Two plantation songs for medium voice." Words by F. L. Stanton; [music by] H. T. Burleigh. New York, G. Schirmer, inc. [c1902] Publ. pl. no. 15894.
3 p. fol.

Score: medium solo voice with piano accompaniment. Negro dialect.

ABSpl

---

*Burleigh, Henry Thacker, 1866- arr.

You may bury me in de eas'. [Negro spiritual for solo voice] Text from I Corinthians 15:52; arranged by H. T. Burleigh. New York, G. Ricordi & co., inc. [c1917] Publ. pl. no. 116449.
6 p. fol.

Score: high solo voice [key of F^m] with piano accompaniment. Negro dialect.
Bound in Vol. 4.

ABSpl
BPL
LC
ZWpl

---

*Burleigh, Henry Thacker, 1866- arr.

You goin' to reap jus' what you sow. Negro spiritual. [Arranged by] H. T. Burleigh. New York, G. Ricordi & co., inc. [c1938] Publ. pl. no. 1134.
9 p. 8°.

Score: SATB with piano reduction for rehearsal only. Negro dialect.

ABSpl

---

*Burleigh, Henry Thacker, 1866-

The young warrior (Il giovane guerriero) Song. Words by *J. Weldon Johnson; Italian text by Edoardo Petri; music by H. T. Burleigh... New York, G. Ricordi & co. [c1915] Publ. pl. no. 116235.
7 p. fol.

Score: low solo voice [key of F] with piano accompaniment. English and Italian words.

ABSpl ZWpl
HMC
LC
YJWJ

---

*Burleigh, Henry Thacker, 1866-

The young warrior. (Il giovane guerriero) Song. The words by *J. Weldon Johnson; the Italian text by Edoardo Petri; the music by H. T. Burleigh... New York, G. Ricordi & co. [c1915] Publ. pl. no. 116236.
7 p. fol.

Score: high solo voice [key of A^b] with piano accompaniment. English words.
Bound in Vol. 2.

LC
ZWpl - Laid in is the vocal part with Italian words.
ABS

---

*Burleigh, Henry Thacker, 1866-

... Your eyes so deep. [Song. From "Passionale" a set of four songs for tenor. Music] by H. T. Burleigh; lyrics by *James Weldon Johnson... New York, G. Ricordi & co., inc. [c1915] Publ. pl. no. 116174.
7 p. fol.

Score: medium solo voice [key of B^b] with piano accompaniment. English words.

ABSpl
NYPLS
YJWJ
LC

---

*Burleigh, Henry Thacker, 1866-

...Your lips are wine. [Song. From "Passionale" a set of four songs for tenor. Music] by H. T. Burleigh; lyrics by *James Weldon Johnson. New York, G. Ricordi & co., inc. [c1915] Publ. pl. no. 116173.
6 p. fol.

Score: medium solo voice [key of B^b] with piano accompaniment. English words.

ABSpl YJWJ
LC
NYPLS

---

*Burleigh, Henry Thacker, 1866-

Yours alone. Song. Words by Edward Oxenford; music by H. T. Burleigh. New York, William Maxwell music co. [c1909] Publ. pl. no. 1195.
7 p. fol.

Score: high solo voice [key of A] with piano accompaniment. English words.
Bound in Vol. 2.

ABSpl

Burlin, Natalie Curtis, comp. and ed.

...Negro folk songs. Recorded by Natalie Curtis Burlin... New York, G. Schirmer, 1918, 19.
4 v. in 3, 25½ cm. (Hampton series nos. 6716, 6726, 6756, 6766)

Score: TTBB, with piano accompaniment. Negro dialect.

Contents: Vol. I, Spirituals: -1. O ride on, Jesus. -2. Go down, Moses. -3. Couldn't hear

(continued on next card)

Burlin, Natalie Curtis, comp. and ed. Negro folk songs... 1918, 19. (Card 2)

nobody pray. -4. Good news, chariots comin'.
Vol. II. Spirituals. -1. Tis me, O Lord. -2. Listen to de lambs. -3. O ev'ry time I feel de spirit. -4. Gods a gwine ter move all de troubles away.
VOL. III. Work and Play songs. -1. Cott'n-pickin' song. -2. Cott'n-dance song. -3. Cott'n packin' song. -4. Corn-shuckin' song.
Vol. IV. Work and Play songs. -1. Peanut-pickin' song. -2. Hammerin' song. -3. Lullaby. -4. Chickahanka. -5. Hyah, rattler. -6. Old rags, bottles, rags. -7. 'Liza-Jane.

BPL NYPLS YJWJ
LC NYPL42 HMC

Burns, Jeanne
Got a Need for You.

---

*Burris, James

*Brymn, James T.
...Come after breakfast (Bring 'long your lunch and leave 'fore supper time.) [Popular song. By James T. *Brymn, Chris *Smith and James Burris. New York, Jos. W. Stern & co. [c1909] Publ. pl. no. 6435.
5p. fol.

Score: medium solo voice [key of B^b] with piano accompaniment. Negro dialect.

ABSpl

---

*Burris, James

Consolation land. [Popular song. By Brymn, Smith and Burris. New York, Jos. W. Stern & co. [c1909] Publ. pl. no. 6436.
(In Ten choice Negro folksongs for voice and pianoforte. New York, [n.d.] p. 28-30.)

Score: medium solo voice [key of E^b] with piano accompaniment. English words.
Caption title.

ABSpl
BHO

---

*Butler, Frank S

Blossoms. [For orchestra] By Frank S. Butler. New York, Emil Ascher. [c1927.]
17 pts. 3 p. 8 vo.

Score: piano-conductor; and parts.

ABSpl

---

*Calhoun, W Arthur

...Down in the valley awaiting for my Jesus, [arranged by] W. Arthur Calhoun. New York, *Handy bros. music co., inc. [c1936]
5 p. 8°.

Score: SATB with piano accompaniment. English words.
Bound in black spiral notebook no. 4.
An adaptation of excerpts from two Negro spirituals: "Steal away"; and "A little talk with Jesus makes it right."

ABS

(continued on next card)

*Calhoun, W Arthur ...Down in the valley awaiting for my Jesus... [c1936] (Card 2)

"...Dedicated to my dear friend and former pupil, Mr. Roland Hayes."

Bound in black spiral notebook no. 4.

ABSpl
NYPLS

---

*Calloway, Cabell, 1908-

Boog-it. [Popular song] Words and music by Cab Calloway, Buck Ram and Jack Palmer. New York, Regent music corp. c1940 [ ]

5 p. fol.

Score: medium solo voice [key of F] with piano accompaniment. English words.

ABSpl

---

*Calloway, Cabell, 1908-

Do I care? No! No! [Popular song] By Cab Calloway, Dan Shapiro, Jerry Seelen and Lester Lee... New York, Edward B. Marks music corp. c1940 [ ] Publ. pl. no. 11,112.

5 p. fol.

Score: medium solo voice with piano accompaniment. English words.

ABSpl

---

*Calloway, Cabell, 1908-

Hep-hep! The jumpin' jive. [Popular song] By Cab Calloway, Frank Froeba and Jack Palmer. New York, Edward B. Marks music corp. c1939 [ ] Publ. pl. no. 11036.

5 p. fol.

Score: medium solo voice with piano accompaniment. English words.

ABSpl

Calloway, Cabell
The Jive's Been Here and Gone

---

*Calloway, Cabell, 1908-

Lavender languor. [Popular song] Music by Cab Calloway; lyrics by Corinne Gould. New York, Lus bros. music publ. [c1935]

5 p. fol.

Score: medium solo voice with piano accompaniment. English words.

ABSpl

---

*Calloway, Cabell, 1908-

Minnie, the moocher (The Ho de ho [popular] song). Words and music by Cab Calloway and Irving Mills. New York, Gotham music service, inc. [c1931]

5 p. fol.

Score: medium solo voice with piano and ukulele accompaniment.

ABSpl
YJMJ

Calloway, Cabell
Ogeechee River Lullaby

---

*Calloway, Cabell, 1908-

The scat song. [Popular song] Words by Mitchell Parish; music by Frank Perkins and Cab Calloway. New York, Mills music publishers [c1932]

5 p. fol.

Score: medium solo voice with piano accompaniment. English words.

ABSpl

Calloway, Cabell
That Man's Here Again

Carle, William J.

"I shall trust the Lord." [Sacred song] Words by George A. Opharrow; music by Wm. J. Carle. c1919. [no publisher given]

1 leaf fol.

Score: SATB. English words.

This leaf is in an elaborate folder on which is printed the picture of the author of the text.

ABSpl

Carmichael, Hoagy

Sing it way down low. [Popular song] By Hoagy Carmichael and Jo Trent. New York, Southern music publ. co., inc. [1932]

3 p. fol.

Score: medium solo voice with piano accompaniment.

ABSpl

---

*Carter, Bennett Lester, 1907-

Blues in my heart. [Popular song] Words and music by King Carter and Irving Mills. New York, Gotham music service, inc. [c1931]

5 p. fol.

Score: medium solo voice with piano accompaniment. English words.

ABSpl

---

*Carter, Bennett Lester, 1907-

Blue interlude. [Popular song] Words and music by Benny Carter, Manny Kurtz and Irving Mills. New York, Exclusive publications, inc. [c1935]

3 p. fol.

Score: medium solo voice with piano accompaniment. English words.

ABSpl

Caturla, Alejandro Garcia
Bito Manué

Caturla, Alejandro Garcia
Dos Danzas Cubanas

Charles, L
Delia Gone, One More Roun' Delia Gone

Charlton, Melville
Poème Érotique

Chase, Newell

I want it sweet like you. [Popular song] Lyric by Jo. Trent; music by Newell Chase... New York, Words and music publ. inc., [c1937]

5p. fol.

Score: medium solo voice with piano accompaniment. English words.

"From the RKO picture, 'Rarris in the spring'" — at end of title.

ABSpl

Chevalier de Saint-Georges (Le), 1745-1799.

Les caquets. Rondo en staccato. Pour violon et piano. Par Chevalier de St. Georges; harmonise et orchestre par Marius Casadesus. Paris: Editions Max Eschig. [c1938] Publ. pl. no. M. E. 5587.

12 p. fol.

Score: violin and piano; and violin part.

ABSpl

---

*Clark, H. Qualli

Ev'rything is going up. [Popular song.] Lyric by Bilby Curtis; music by H. Qualli Clark. New York, *Pace & Handy music co., inc. [c1920]

3 p. fol.

Score: medium solo voice with piano accompaniment. English words.

ABSpl

Clark, H Qualli
Make That Trombone Laugh

*Clark, H Qualli

Pee Gee's blues. Words by *Alex Rogers; music by H. Qualli Clark. NY: *Pace and Handy music co., inc., [c1919]
5p. fol.

Score: medium solo voice [key of G] with piano accompaniment. English words.

"Dedicated to P. G. Lowery of Barnum and Bailey's circus."

ZNpl
ABSpl

*Clarke, Edgar Rogie

There's a man goin' roun'. Negro spiritual for mixed voices. Arranged by Edgar Rogie Clarke. New York, *Handy Brothers music co., inc. [c1940.]
7 p. 8 vo.

Score: SATB with soprano solo throughout, and with piano accompaniment. Negro dialect.

ABSpl

*Cochran, Arthur Myron, 1878-

A communion service based on Negro spirituals By A. Myron Cochran. Manuscript. [n.d.]
14 p. 8 vo.

Score: SATB. English words.

"A setting of the office of the Communion Service of the Protestant Episcopal Church based upon some of the best of the Negro spirituals. By A. Myron Cochran, Rector of

(continued on next card)

*Cochran, Arthur Myron, 1878- (Card 2)

A communion service...

the Church of the Holy Trinity, Nashville, Tennessee, one time Curate and organize of the chapel of St. Simon the Cyrenian, Philadelphia, Pa., and Rector of St. Ambrose Church, Raleigh, N. C. and Director of Music at St. Augustine's College, Raleigh, N. C." -- cover title page.

ABSpl

*Cole, Robert Allen, 1868 - 1911.

Ada, my sweet potater! [Popular song] Words by Chas. A. Hunter; music by Bob Cole and *James Reese Europe. New York, Jos. W. Stern & co. [c1908]
Publ. pl. no. 6115.
5 p. fol.

Score: medium solo voice [key of B flat] with piano accompaniment. Negro dialect.

ABSpl
LC

*Cole, [Robert Allen], 1868-1911
The black four hundred's ball. March song and chorus. Words by *Billy Johnson; music by Bob Cole. New York, Howley, Haviland & co., [c1896].
5 p. fol.

Score: medium solo voice with piano accompaniment. English words.

ABSpl
LC

*Cole, Robert Allen, 1868 - 1911.

Christening of a little black coon. [Popular song] Words by *Billy Johnson; music by Bob Cole. New York, Howley, Haviland & co. [c1897]
5 p. fol.

Score: medium solo voice [key of B flat] with piano accompaniment. English words.

ABSpl

*Cole, Robert Allen, 1868-1911.

The Conjure man. [Popular song] Words by *J. W. Johnson; music by Bob Cole. New York, Jos. W. Stern and co. [c1905] Publ. pl. no. 4668.
5p. fol.

Score: medium solo voice [key of F] with piano accompaniment. Negro dialect.

Cover title page states: "By Cole and Johnson Bros."

ABSpl
LC

*Cole, Robert Allen, 1868-1911.

The coontown regiment. March song. [Popular song] Words and music by Bob Cole and *Billy Johnson. New York: Howley, Haviland & Co. [c1898]

5p. fol.

Score: medium solo voice with piano accompaniment. English words.

ABSpl

*Cole, Robert Allen, 1868 - 1911.

Darkies' delights. (Introducing: "Carve dat possum.") [Popular song] Words by *J. W. Johnson; music by Bob Cole. New York, Jos. W. Stern & co. [c1903] Publ. pl. no. 3937.
(In Ten choice Negro folksongs for voice and pianoforte. New York, [n.d.] p. 31-32.)

Score: medium solo voice [key of F] with piano accompaniment. Negro dialect.
Caption title.

ABSpl
BHC

*Cole, Robert Allen, 1868 - 1911.

Father's got a job. [Popular song] Words by Bob Cole and *J. W. Johnson; music by Bob Cole. New York, Jos. W. Stern & co. [c1906] Publ. pl. no. 4943.
5 p. fol.

Score: medium solo voice [key of G] with piano accompaniment. English words.

ABSpl

*Cole, Robert Allen, 1868 - 1911.

"Gimme de leavin's." [Popular song] Words by *J. W. Johnson; music by Bob Cole. New York, Jos. W. Stern & co. [c1904] Publ. pl. no. 4205.
5 p. fol.

Score: medium solo voice [key of G] with piano accompaniment. Negro dialect.

Excerpt from the musical show, "Alabama blossom".

ABSpl

*Cole, Robert Allen, 1868 - 1911.

...He handed me a lemon. [Popular song] Words and music by Bob Cole. New York, Jos. W. Stern & co. [c1906] Publ. pl. no. 5164.
5 p. fol.

Score: medium solo voice [key of G] with piano accompaniment. English words.

ABSpl

Cole, Robert Allen
I'm thinkin' bout you honey, all the time

*Cole, Robert Allen, 1868-1911.

The katy-did, the cricket and the frog. [Popular music] Words by *J. W. Johnson; music by Bob Cole... New York, Jos. W. Stern and co. [c1903] Publ. pl. no. 3512.
5p. fol.

Score: medium solo voice [key of A^b] with piano accompaniment. English words.

"Introduced by Marie Cahill in 'Nancy Brown'" - at end of title.

ABSpl
LC

*Cole, Robert Allen
*Johnson, John Rosamond, 1873-

Lazy moon. [Popular song] Words by *Bob Cole; music by Rosamond Johnson. New York, Jos. W. Stern & co. [c1903] Publ. pl. no. 3708.
(In Ten choice Negro folksongs for voice and pianoforte. New York, [n.d.] p. 15-17.)

Score: medium solo voice [key of G] with piano accompaniment. English words.
Caption title.

ABSpl
BHC

*Cole, Robert Allen, 1868 - 1911.

"Leave it to Bill!" [Popular song] Words and music by Bob Cole. New York, Jos. W. Stern & co. [c1904] Publ. pl. no. 4181.
5 p. fol.

Score: medium solo voice [key of E flat] with piano accompaniment. Negro dialect.

LC
ABSpl

*Cole, Robert Allen, 1868 - 1911.

Louisiana Lize. [Popular song] Composed by Bob Cole; words and music edited by *J. W. and Rosamond Johnson. New York, Jos. W. Stern & co. [c1899] Publ. pl. no. 1053.
5 p. fol.

Score: low solo voice [key of F] with piano accompaniment. Negro dialect.

ABSpl

*Cole, Robert Allen, 1868-1911.
The luckiest coon in town. [Popular song] By *Billy Johnson and Bob Cole. New York: Howley, Haviland & Co., [c1899].
5 p. fol.

Score: medium solo voice [key of G] with piano accompaniment. Negro dialect.

ABSpl
LC

*Cole, Robert Allen, 1868-1911.

...The maid of Timbuctoo. [Popular song. Words by *J. W. Johnson; music by Bob Cole] New York, Jos. W. Stern and co. [c1903] Publ. pl. no. 3767.
5p. fol.

Score: mediumsolo voice [key of G] with piano accompaniment. English words.

"Introduced by Miss Lillian Russell at Weber and Field's Broadway music hall in 'Whoop dee-doo'" - title page.

LC
HHC
ABSpl

Cole, Robert Allen and Johnson
Magdline my southern queen

*Cole, Robert Allen
*Johnson, John Rosamond, 1873-

Moonlight on the Mississippi. [Popular song] Words by *Bob Cole; music by Rosamond Johnson. New York, Jos. W. Stern & co. [c1903] Publ. pl. no. 3681.
(In Ten choice Negro folksongs for voice and pianoforte. New York, [n.d.] p. 25-27.)

Score: medium solo voice [key of G] with piano accompaniment. English words.
Caption title.

ABSpl
BHC

*Cole, Robert Allen, 1868-1911.

A prepossessing little maid. [Popular song.] Lyric by *J. W. Johnson; music by Bob Cole. New York, Jos. W. Stern and co. [c1904] Publ. pl. no. 3971.
4p. fol.

Score: medium solo voice [Key of B^b] with piano accompaniment. English words.
Caption title.

LC
ABSpl

Cole, Robert Allen
The Maiden with the Dreamy Eyes. Arr. by Frank Saddler.

*Cole, Robert Allen
*Johnson, John Rosamond, 1873-

"Mudder knows." [Popular song] Lyrics by *Bob Cole; music by Rosamond Johnson. New York, Jos. W. Stern & co. [c1903] Publ. pl. no. 7974.
(In Ten choice Negro folksongs for voice and pianoforte. New York, [n.d.] p. 8-10.)

Score: medium solo voice key of F with piano accompaniment. Negro dialect.
Caption title.

ABSpl
BHC

*Cole, Robert Allen, 1868-1911.
...Roaming round the town. [Popular song. Lyric by *J. W. Johnson; music by Bob Cole.] New York, Jos. W. Stern & co. [c1905] Publ. pl. no. 4349.
6 p. fol.

Score: medium solo voice [key of A flat] with piano accompaniment. English words.

LC
ABSpl

*Cole, Robert Allen, 1868-1911.

The maiden with the dreamy eyes. [Popular song] Words by *J. W. Johnson; music by Bob Cole. New York, Jos. W. Stern and co. [c1901] Publ. pl. no. 3284.
5p. fol.

Score: medium solo voice [key of B^b] with piano accompaniment. English words.

Cover title page states: "By J. W. Johnson, Bob Cole and Rosamond Johnson."

Sung by Anna Held in "The Little Duchess".

ABSpl.

*Cole, Robert Allen, 1868-1911.

My Lu-Lu San. [Popular song. A Japanese love song] Words by *J. W. Johnson; music by Bob Cole. New York, Jos. W. Stern and co. [c1905] Publ. pl. no. 4402.
5p. fol.

Score: medium solo voice [key of G] with piano accompaniment. English words.

"As sung in 'Mr. Hamlet of Denmark,' 17th annual production of 'The Mask and Wig Club.'" -title page.

LC
ABSpl

*Cole, Robert Allen, 1868 - 1911.

Sambo and Dinah. [Popular song] Lyrics by Bob Cole and *James W. Johnson; music by Bob Cole. New York, Jos. W. Stern & co. [c1904] Publ. pl. no. 4301.
7 p. fol.

Score: medium solo voice [key of G] with piano accompaniment. Negro dialect.
Excerpt from the musical show, "Humpty dumpty".
ABSpl
HMC

*Cole, Robert Allen, 1868 - 1911.

"M'aimez vous?" (Do you love me?) [Popular song] Words and music by Robert Allen Cole. New York, Jos. W. Stern & co., [c1910] Publ. pl. no. 6687.
5 p. fol.

Score: medium solo voice [key of G] with piano accompaniment. English words.
Caption title.
"By Cole and Johnson." -Cover title page.

ABSpl

*Cole, Robert Allen, 1868-1911.

My one and only". [Popular song] Lyrics by *J. W. Johnson; music by Bob Cole. New York, Jos. W. Stern and co. [c1906] Publ. pl. no. 4990.
5p. fol.

Score: low solo voice [key of B^b] with piano accompaniment. English words.

Cover title page states: "Latest song successes of Cole and Johnson Bros."

ABSpl

*Cole, Robert Allen, 1868-1911.

"Save it for me." [Popular song] Words by *Jas. W. Johnson; music by Bob Cole. New York, Jos. W. Stern and co. [c1903] Publ. pl. no. 3748.
5p. fol.

Score: medium solo voice [key of G] with piano accompaniment. English words.

LC
ABSpl

*Cole, Robert Allen, 1868-1911.

"Man, man, man." [Popular song] Lyric by *James W. Johnson; music by Bob Cole. New York, Jos. W. Stern and co. [c1904] Publ. pl. no. 4314.
6p. fol.

Score: medium solo voice [key of A^b] with piano accompaniment. English words.

Cover title page states: "By Cole and Johnson Bros."

ABSpl

*Cole, Robert Allen, 1868-1911.

No coons allowed! [Popular song] Words by *Billy Johnson; music by Bob Cole. New York, Howley, Haviland and co. [c1897]
5p. fol.

Score: medium solo voice [key of E^b] with piano accompaniment. Negro dialect.

Excerpt from the musical comedy "A Trip to Coontown."

ABSpl
LC

*Cole, Robert Allen
*Johnson, John Rosamond, 1873-

Sugar babe. [Popular song] Lyric by *Bob Cole; music by J. Rosamond Johnson. New York, Jos. W. Stern & co. [c1907] Publ. pl. no. 5836.
(In Ten choice Negro folksongs for voice and pianoforte. New York, [n.d.] p. 5-7.)

Score: medium solo voice [key of E^b] with piano accompaniment. Negro dialect.
Caption title.

ABSpl
BHC

*Cole, Robert Allen, 1868 - 1911.

Mexico. [Popular song] Lyrics by Bob Cole and *James W. Johnson; music by Bob Cole. New York, Jos. W. Stern & co. [c1904] Publ. pl. no. 4304.
7 p. fol.

Score: high solo voice [key of B flat] with piano accompaniment. English words.
Excerpt from the musical show, "Humpty dumpty".
ABSpl

*Cole, Robert Allen
*Johnson, John Rosamond, 1873-

Nobody's lookin' at the owl and the moon. [Popular song] Words by *J. W. Johnson and *Bob Cole; music by Rosamond Johnson. New York, Jos. W. Stern & co., c1901. Publ. pl. no. 3258.
(In Ten choice Negro folksongs for voice and pianoforte. New York, [n.d.] p. 2-4.)

Score: medium solo voice [key of F] with piano accompaniment. Negro dialect.
Caption title.
ABSpl
BHC

*Cole, Robert Allen, 1868 - 1911.

Under the bamboo tree. [Popular song] By Bob Cole. New York, Jos. W. Stern & co. [c1902] Publ. pl. no. 3384.
5 p. fol.

Score: medium solo voice [key of E flat] with piano accompaniment. English words.

"By Cole and Johnson bros." - Cover title page.
2 copies
ABSpl

*Cole, Robert Allen, 1868-1911.

Mr. Coon you're alright in your place. [Popular song] By Bob Cole and *Billy Johnson,,, New York, Howley, Haviland & co. [c1899]
5 p. fol.

Score: medium solo voice [key of E^b] with piano accompaniment. Negro dialect.

ABSpl

*Cole, Robert Allen, 1868-1911.

On the road to Monterey. [Popular song] Words and music by Bob Cole. New York, Jos. W. Stern and co. [c1908] Publ. pl. no. 6148.
6p. fol.

Score: medium solo voice with piano accompaniment. English words.

From the musical show "Red Moon."

LC
ABSpl

*Cole, Robert Allen, 1868-1911
The wedding of the Chinee and the coon. [Popular song] Words by *Billy Johnson; music by Bob Cole; [arranged by Theo. F. Morse.] New York: Howley, Haviland and Co. [c1897]
5 p. fol.

Score: low solo voice [key of E flat] with piano accompaniment. Negro dialect.

ABSpl
LC

*Cole, Robert Allen, 1868-1911.

"Won't your mama let you come out and play?" [Popular song] Lyrics by *J. W. Johnson; music by Bob Cole. New York, Jos. W. Stern and co. [c1906] Publ. pl. no. 4991. 6p. fol.

Score: medium solo voice [key of B♭] with piano accompaniment. English words.

"Written especially for the 18th production of The Mask and Wig Club, University of Pennsylvania."- cover title page.

LC
ABSpl

---

*Coleridge-Taylor, Samuel, 1875-1912.

Andalla. (In Coleridge-Taylor, Samuel. Moorish tone-pictures for pianoforte. Opus 19, no. 1. London, 1897. p. 1-6)

Score: piano solo.

ABSpl
LC

---

*Coleridge-Taylor, Samuel, 1875-1912.

Beside the ungathered rice he lay. (In Coleridge-Taylor, Samuel. ...Three choral ballads. London, c1904. p. 1-21)

Score: piano-vocal (SATB). English words.

ABSpl
LC

---

*Cole, Robert Allen, 1868-1911.

Zel-Zel. An Arabian love song. Lyric by *J. W. Johnson; music by Bob Cole. New York, Jos. W. Stern and co. [1905] Publ. pl. no. 4340. 5p. fol.

Score: medium solo voice [key of A♭] with piano accompaniment. English words. Caption title.

LC
ABSpl

---

*Coleridge-Taylor, Samuel, 1875-1912.

As the moon's soft splendour. [To a lady singing to her accompaniment on the guitar] Song. The poem by [P. B.] Shelley; the music composed by S. Coleridge-Taylor. Opus 37, no. 5... London, Novello & co., ltd., c1899. Publ. pl. no. 10866. 5 p. fol.

Bound V. I.

Score: low solo voice [key of B] with piano accompaniment. English words.

ABSpl
LC

---

*Coleridge-Taylor, Samuel, 1875-1912.

Big lady moon. [One of] "Five fairy ballads" ... The words by Kathleen Easmon; the music by S. Coleridge-Taylor. London, Boosey & co. [c1909] Publ. pl. no. H.6428. 5 p. fol.

Score: high solo voice [key of D♭] with piano accompaniment. Negro dialect.

ABSpl
LC
ZWpl
HMC

---

*Coleridge-Taylor, Samuel, 1875-1912.

An African love song. (In Coleridge-Taylor, Samuel. African romances. Opus 17, no. 1. London, 1897. p. 1-5)

Bound V. I.

Score: medium solo voice with piano accompaniment. English words.

ABSpl
LC
NYPL42

---

*Coleridge-Taylor, Samuel, 1875-1912.

...The atonement. [A sacred cantata. Words by Alice Parsons; music] by S. Coleridge-Taylor. [Opus 53] London, Novello & co. [c1903] Publ. pl. no. 11726. 4 v. 8°. (Novello's separate chorus parts)

Parts: S, C, T, B. English words.

LC ABS

Coleridge-Taylor, Samuel, 1875-1912
Big Lady Moon. Song from five Fairy ballads.

Bound V. I.

---

*Coleridge-Taylor, Samuel, 1875-1912.

African romances. Song cycle. Words by *Paul Laurence Dunbar. Music by S. Coleridge-Taylor. Opus 17. London, Augener & co., ltd. [c1897] Publ. pl. no. 11114. 21 p. fol. (Augener's edition no. 8817)

Bound V. I.

Score: medium solo voice with piano accompaniment. English words.

Contents: 1. An African love song. -2. A prayer. -3. A starry night. -4. Dawn. -5. Ballad. -6. Over the hills. -7. How shall I woo thee?

ABSpl LC NYPL42

---

*Coleridge-Taylor, Samuel, 1875-1912.

Ballad. (In Coleridge-Taylor, Samuel. African romances. Opus 17, no. 5. London, 1897. p. 13-16)

Bound V. I.

Score: medium solo voice with piano accompaniment. English words.

ABSpl
LC
NYPL42

Coleridge-Taylor, Samuel
A Birthday

---

*Coleridge-Taylor, Samuel, 1875-1912.

...African suite for the pianoforte. By S. Coleridge-Taylor. Opus 35... London, Augener & co., ltd. [c1898] Publ. pl. no. 11368. 4 v. fol. (Augener's edition no. 6103)

Bound V. I.

Score: piano solos.

Contents: 1. Introduction. -2. A Negro love-song. -3. Valse. -4. Dance negre.

ABSpl
LC
ZWpl

---

*Coleridge-Taylor, Samuel, 1875-1912.

...Ballade in A minor for full orchestra. Composed by S. Coleridge-Taylor. Opus 33. Arrangement for pianoforte solo by the composer... London, Novello & co., ltd., c1898. Publ. pl. no. 10675. 20 p. fol.

Score: piano solo; originally for full orchestra.

"Composed for the Gloucester musical festival, 1898." - Head of title.

LC

---

*Coleridge-Taylor, Samuel, 1875-1912.

A blood-red ring hung round the moon. Song. The poem by Barry Dane; the music composed by S. Coleridge-Taylor. (Opus 37, no. 3) London, Novello & co., ltd., c1899. Publ. pl. no. 10857. 5 p. fol.

Bound V. I.

Score: low solo voice [key of G^m] with piano accompaniment. English words.

ABSpl
LC
ZWpl
HMC

---

*Coleridge-Taylor, Samuel, 1875-1912.

Ah, sweet, thou little knowest!. Song. Words by Thomas Hood; music by S. Coleridge-Taylor. London, G. Ricordi & co. [c1904] Publ. pl. no. 109582. 6 p. fol.

Bound V. I.

Score: high solo voice [key of A] with piano accompaniment. English words.

ABSpl
LC

---

*Coleridge-Taylor, Samuel, 1875-1912.

Beat, beat, drums! [Song. No. 6 of] Six American lyrics. [Words by Walt Whitman; music] composed by S. Coleridge-Taylor. [Opus 45, no. 6]... London, Novello & co., ltd. [c1903] Publ. pl. no. 11562. 7 p. fol.

Bound V. I.

Score: low solo voice with piano accompaniment. English words.

Orchestral accompaniment may be had from publisher.

ABSpl
LC

---

*Coleridge-Taylor, Samuel, 1875-1912.

A blood-red ring hung round the moon. Song. Poem by Barry Dane; music by S. Coleridge-Taylor. Opus 37, no. 3. London, Novello & co., ltd. [c1920] Publ. pl. no. 14690. 5 p. fol.

Bound V. I.

Score: medium solo voice [key of C^m] with piano accompaniment. English words.

LC

Coleridge-Taylor, Samuel
Alone with mother

(In five fairy ballads)

---

*Coleridge-Taylor, Samuel, 1875-1912.

Beauty and song. [Song. One of] "Three song poems"... Words by Thomas Moore; music by S. Coleridge-Taylor. [Opus 50, no. 3]... New York, Boosey & co., c1905. Publ. pl. no. E & S 3237. 6 p. fol.

Bound V. I.

Score: low solo voice with piano accompaniment. English words.

ABSpl

---

*Coleridge-Taylor, Samuel, 1875-1912.

...Breeze scene. [Opus 44 (47), no. 2] From "Incidental music to Herod." By S. Coleridge-Taylor ...London, Augener & co., c1901. Publ. pl. no. 11986. p. 5-8. fol.

Score: piano solo. Originally scored for full orchestra.

LC

*Coleridge-Taylor, Samuel, 1875-1912.

The bridal day. (I hear the flutes) [Song. Words by] Annie Andros Hawley; [music by] S. Coleridge-Taylor. New York, Arthur P. Schmidt co. [c1918] Publ. pl. no. A.P.S. 11883.
5 p. fol.
Bound V. I.
Score: medium solo voice [key of E^b] with piano accompaniment. English words.

ABSpl
LC

*Coleridge-Taylor, Samuel, 1875-1912.

Canoe song. [Song] The words by Isabella Crawford; the music composed by S. Coleridge-Taylor. (Opus 37, no. 2)... London, Novello & co., ltd., c1899. Publ. pl. no. 10840.
5 p. fol.
Bound V. I.
Score: low solo voice [key of D^b] with piano accompaniment.

ABSpl
LC

*Coleridge-Taylor, Samuel, 1875-1912.

In dark fens of the dismal swamp.
(In Coleridge-Taylor, Samuel. Two choral ballads. 2nd set. Opus 54. London, 1905. p. 13-31)

Score: SSAATTBB with piano accompaniment. English words.

Full score and orchestral parts may be obtained on hire from the publishers.

ABSpl LC
HMC

*Coleridge-Taylor, Samuel, 1875-1912.

[Cameo. No. 1 in F] By S. Coleridge-Taylor. Opus 56, no. 1... London, Augener & co., c1904. Publ. pl. no. 12705.
p. 1-7. fol.
Bound V. I.
Score: piano solo.

ABS
LC

*Coleridge-Taylor, Samuel, 1875-1912.

Comfort. [Song. Words by] Elizabeth Barrett Browning; [music by] S. Coleridge-Taylor. Opus 42, no. 4. London, Novello & co., ltd., c1900. Publ. pl. no. 11085.
p. 16-19. fol.
Bound v. IV
Score: low solo voice [key of F] with piano accompaniment.
Caption title.

From "The Soul's expression," a song cycle.

LC

*Coleridge-Taylor, Samuel, 1875-1912.

...Dance. [Opus 47, no. 3] From "Incidental music to Herod." By S. Coleridge-Taylor... London, Augener & co., c1901. Publ. pl. no. 11986.
p. 9-13. fol.

Score: piano solo. Originally scored for full orchestra.

LC

*Coleridge-Taylor, Samuel, 1875-1912.

[Cameo. No. 2 in D] By S. Coleridge-Taylor. Opus 56, no. 2... London, Augener & co., c1904. Publ. pl. no. 12705.
p. 8-13. fol.
Bound V. I.
Score: piano solo.

ABS
LC

*Coleridge-Taylor, Samuel, 1875-1912.

...Concerto in G minor for violin and orchestra. Composed by S. Coleridge-Taylor. Opus 80. (Post-humous) London, Metzler & co., ltd., c1912. Publ. pl. no. M & co. 221.
65 p. fol.

Score: violin and piano; and violin part originally scored for violin and orchestra.

Contents: 3 movements.

ABSpl

*Coleridge-Taylor, Samuel, 1875-1912.

...Danse negre. [From] African suite for the pianoforte by S. Coleridge-Taylor. Opus 35, no. 4. London, Augener & co., ltd. [c1898] Publ. pl. no. 11267.
9 p. fol.
Bound V. I.
Score: piano solo.

ABSpl
LC

*Coleridge-Taylor, Samuel, 1875-1912.

[Cameo. No. 3 in G] By S. Coleridge-Taylor. Opus 56, no. 3... London, Augener & co., c1904. Publ. pl. no. 12705.
p. 14-17. fol.
Bound V. I.
Score: piano solo.

ABS
LC

Coleridge-Taylor, Samuel
A corn song. [1 sharp]

Bound V. I.

ABS

*Coleridge-Taylor, Samuel, 1875-1912.

The dark eye has left us. [Song. No. 4 of] Six American lyrics. Words by Whittier; music; composed by S. Coleridge-Taylor. [Opus 45, no. 4]... London, Novello & co., ltd. [c1903] Publ. pl. no. 11560.
6 p. fol.
Bound V. I.
Score: low solo voice with piano accompaniment. English words.

ABSpl
LC

*Coleridge-Taylor, Samuel, 1875-1912.

Cameo.
(In Coleridge-Taylor, Samuel. Melodies for piano. Selected, arranged and revised by Alex Roloff... London. p. 10-15)

Score: piano solo, simplified version; originally a piano solo in the suite, "Cameos," no. 3.

ABSpl
LC

Coleridge-Taylor, Samuel
A corn song. [4 sharps]

Bound V. I.

ABS

*Coleridge-Taylor, Samuel, 1875-1912.

Dawn.
(In Coleridge-Taylor, Samuel. African romances. Opus 17, no. 4. London, 1897. p. 12)

Score: medium solo voice with piano accompaniment. English words.

ABSpl
LC
NYPL42

*Coleridge-Taylor, Samuel, 1875-1912.

...Cameos. [Three pieces for piano] by S. Coleridge-Taylor. Opus 56, nos. 1, 2, 3... London, Augener & co., c1904. Publ. pl. no. 12705.
3 v. fol. (Augener's edition no. 6099)
Bound V. I.
Scores: piano solos.

Contents: no. 1 in F; no. 2 in D; no. 3 in G.

ABS
LC

*Coleridge-Taylor, Samuel, 1875-1912.

A dance.
(In Coleridge-Taylor, Samuel. Hiawathan sketches for violin and piano. Opus 16, no. 3. London, 1897. p. 13-17)

Score: violin and piano; and violin part.
Bound v. II

ABS
LC

*Coleridge-Taylor, Samuel, 1875-1912.

...The death of Minnehaha. A cantata for soprano and baritone solo, chorus, and orchestra. The words written by H. W. Longfellow; the music composed by S. Coleridge-Taylor. (Opus 30, no. 2)... London, Novello & co., ltd., c1899. Publ. pl. no. 8299.
51 p. 8°.

Score: piano-vocal. English words. Originally with orchestral accompaniment.

First performance: North Staffordshire musical festival, Hanley, Oct. 26, 1899.

"Scenes from the Song of Hiawatha, no. 2."-Head of title. ABSpl LC NYPLS

*Coleridge-Taylor, Samuel, 1875-1912.

Candle lightin' time. [Song] Words by *Paul Laurence Dunbar; music by S. Coleridge-Taylor. Cincinnati, The John Church co. [c1911] Publ. pl. no. 16499.
7 p. fol.
Bound V. I.
Score: low voice [key of E^m] Negro dialect.

ABSpl
LC
NYPLS

*Coleridge-Taylor, Samuel, 1875-1912.

...Danse negre from the "African suite." By S. Coleridge-taylor. Opus 35, no. 4. London, Augener & co. [c1901] Publ. pl. no. 11368.
9 p. fol. (Augener's edition no. 6100)

Score: piano solo.
(Also arranged for orchestra and violin and piano.)

ABSpl
ZWpl

Coleridge-Taylor, Samuel
Deep River

*Coleridge-Taylor, Samuel, 1875-1912.

...Demande et repose. From the "Petite suite de concert" for violin and piano by S. Coleridge-Taylor. Opus 77, no. 2. New York, G. Schirmer ₍c1911₎ Publ. pl. no. 27136.
7 p. fol.

Score: piano and violin and violin part; originally scored for full orchestra.

ABSpl

Coleridge-Taylor, Samuel
Drake's Drum

---

*Coleridge-Taylor, Samuel, 1875-1912.

...Dreaming forever. ₍Song. One of₎ "Three song poems" ... Words by Thomas Moore; music by S. Coleridge-Taylor. ₍Opus 50, no. 1₎ ... New York, Boosey & co. ₍c1905₎ Publ. pl. no. 3233.
7 p. fol.

Score: low solo voice ₍key of D₎ with piano accompaniment. English words.

ABSpl

---

*Coleridge-Taylor, Samuel, 1875-1912.

Earth fades! Heaven breaks on me. Words by ₍Robert₎ Browning.
(In Coleridge-Taylor, Samuel. In memoriam. Three rhapsodies for low voice and pianoforte. Opus 24, no. 1. London, ₍n.d.₎ p. 1-3)

Score: low solo voice with piano accompaniment. English words.

ABSpl

Coleridge-Taylor, Samuel
The Easter Moon

---

*Coleridge-Taylor, Samuel, 1875-1912.

...Ethiopia saluting the colours. Concert march for orchestra by S. Coleridge-Taylor. Opus 51... London, Augener & co. ₍c1902₎ Publ. pl. no. 12307.
13 p. fol. (Augener's edition no. 6106a)

Score: piano solo. Originally scored for full orchestra.
"Pianoforte solo by the composer."

ABSpl
LC

---

*Coleridge-Taylor, Samuel, 1875-1912.

An explanation. Song with pianoforte accompaniment. By S. Coleridge-Taylor. Boston, Arthur P. Schmidt ₍c1914₎ Publ. pl. no. 10304.
5 p. fol.

Score: medium voice ₍key of B^b₎. English words. (Also arranged for high voice ₍key of D₎)

ABSpl
LC
NYPLS
ZWpl

---

*Coleridge-Taylor, Samuel, 1875-1912.

...Fairy roses. ₍One of₎ "Five fairy ballads"... The words by Kathleen Easmon; music by S. Coleridge-Taylor. London, Boosey & co. ₍c1909₎ Publ. pl. no. 6428.
7 p. fol.

Score: medium solo voice ₍key of A₎ with piano accompaniment. English words.

ABSpl
LC
ZWpl

---

*Coleridge-Taylor, Samuel, 1875-1912.

Five fairy ballads... ₍Song suite₎ The words by Kathleen Easmon; the music by S. Coleridge-Taylor. London, Boosey & co. ₍c1909₎ Publ. pl. no. H. 6828.
5 v. fol.

Score: solo voice with piano accompaniment. English words or Negro dialect.

Contents: 1. Sweet baby butterfly. -2. Alone with mother. -3. Big lady moon. -4. The stars. -5. Fairy roses.
ABSpl LC ZWpl

---

*Coleridge-Taylor, Samuel, 1875-1912.

...Four African dances for violin with pianoforte accompaniment. By S. Coleridge-Taylor. Opus 58 ₍nos. 1-4₎ ... London, Augener & co., c1904. Publ. pl. no. 12837.
4 v. fol.
Bound v. I.
Score: violin and piano; and violin part.

Contents: No. 1 in G minor; No. 2 in F major; No. 3 in A major; No. 4 in D minor.

LC ZWpl ABS

---

*Coleridge-Taylor, Samuel, 1875-1912.

Four characteristic waltzes. Composed by S. Coleridge-Taylor. (Opus 22) Arranged for the pianoforte by the composer. London, Novello, Ewer & co., c1898. Publ. pl. no. 10560.
19 p. fol.

Score: piano solos.

ABSpl
LC

Coleridge-Taylor, Samuel
Four Novelletten (no.1)

Coleridge-Taylor, Samuel
Four Novelletten (no.4)

---

*Coleridge-Taylor, Samuel, 1875-1912.

From the east.
(In Coleridge-Taylor, Samuel. Melodies for piano. Selected, arranged and revised by Alex Roloff... London. p. 6,7)

Score: piano solo; originally a part-song (SSC), "We strew these opiate flowers." Also published as solo entitled, "The oasis." (See cards)

ABSpl
LC

---

*Coleridge-Taylor, Samuel, 1875-1912.

...Eleanore. Song. The poem by Eric Mackay; the music composed by S. Coleridge-Taylor. (Opus 37, no. 6) ... London, Novello & co., ltd. ₍c1921₎ Publ. pl. no. 14785.
4 p. fol.
Bound V. II
Score: medium solo voice ₍key of C₎ with piano accompaniment. English words.

Orchestral arrangement available from publisher.

ABSpl
LC

---

*Coleridge-Taylor, Samuel, 1875-1912.

...Eleanore. Song. The poem by Eric Mackay; the music composed by S. Coleridge-Taylor. (Opus 37, no. 6)... London, Novello & co., ltd., c1899. Publ. pl. no. 10867.
4 p. fol.
Bound v. II
Score: high solo voice ₍key of D₎ with piano accompaniment. English words.

Orchestral arrangement available from publisher.
ABS
LC

---

*Coleridge-Taylor, Samuel, 1875-1912.

Erstwhile they ride, the forest maiden acknowledges her love.
(In Coleridge-Taylor, Samuel. Forest scenes. Characteristic pieces for pianoforte. Opus 55. London, 1907. p. 14-19.)

Score: piano solo.

ABSpl
LC

Coleridge-Taylor, Samuel
Fairy roses song from five fairy ballads.

Bound V. II

ABS

Coleridge-Taylor, Samuel

Five and twenty sailermen.

Bound v. II.

ABS

---

*Coleridge-Taylor, Samuel, 1875-1912.

...Forest scenes. Characteristic pieces for pianoforte by S. Coleridge-Taylor. Opus 66... London, Augener, ltd. ₍c1907₎ Publ. pl. no. 13552.
25 p. fol. (Augener's edition, no. 6097)
Bound v. II.
Score: piano solos.

Contents: 1. The lone forest maiden (p. 1-4). -2. The phantom lover arrives (p. 5-8). -3. The phantom tells his tale of longing (p. 9-13). -4. Erstwhile they ride the forest maiden acknowledges her love (p. 14-19). -5. Now proudly they journey together towards the grea[illegible]t city (p. 20-25).
ABSpl LC

---

*Coleridge-Taylor, Samuel, 1875-1912.

Four characteristic waltzes. Composed by S. Coleridge-Taylor. (Opus 22, nos. 1-4); arranged for violin and pianoforte by the composer... London, Novello, Ewer & co., c1898. Publ. pl. no. 10566.
21 p. fol.
Bound v. II
Score: violin and piano; and violin part. Originally for full orchestra.

This earlier edition titles the waltzes by number only.

ABS
LC

*Coleridge-Taylor, Samuel, 1875-1912.

...Four characteristic waltzes. Composed by S. Coleridge-Taylor (Opus 22, nos. 1-4); arranged for violin and pianoforte by the composer... London, Novello & co., ltd., c1903. Publ. pl. no. 10566.
4 v. fol.
Bound v. II
Scores: violin and piano; and violin parts. Originally for full orchestra.

Contents: 1. Valse Bohemienne. -2. Valse rustique. -3. Valse de la Reine. -4. Valse Mauresque.

This is the same music as the earlier edition with the addition of titles for each waltz.

ABSpl LC

---

*Coleridge-Taylor, Samuel, 1875-1912.

Grief. ‹Song. Words by› Elizabeth Barrett Browning; ‹music by› S. Coleridge-Taylor. Opus 42, no. 3. London, Novello & co., ltd., c1900. Publ. pl. no. 11085.
p. 11-15. fol.
Bound v. IV
Score: low solo voice with piano accompaniment.
Caption title.

From "The Soul's expression," a song cycle.

LC

---

*Coleridge-Taylor, Samuel, 1875-1912.

If I could love thee. Song. The poem by *Louise Alston Burleigh; the music by S. Coleridge-Taylor... New York, William Maxwell music co. ‹c1905› Publ. pl. no. 731.
6 p. fol.
Bound v. III
Score: low solo voice ‹key of F› with piano accompaniment. English words.

ABSpl

---

*Coleridge-Taylor, Samuel, 1875-1912.

Genevieve. Song. The poem by Samuel Taylor Coleridge; the music by S. Coleridge-Taylor... New York, William Maxwell music co. ‹c1905› Publ. pl. no. 736.
9 p. fol.
Bound v. II
Score: high solo voice ‹key of F› with piano accompaniment. English words.

ABSpl
LC

Coleridge-Taylor, Samuel

The guest. Song with pianoforte accompaniment.

9p.

Bound v. II

ABS

---

*Coleridge-Taylor, Samuel, 1875-1912.

If thou art sleeping maiden (Portuguese). Words by Longfellow.
(In Coleridhe-Taylor, S. Southern love songs. Opus 12, no. 4. London, 1896. p. 11-13.)

Score: high solo voice ‹key of F› with piano accompaniment. English words.

Also arranged for piano solo entitled, "Serenade." (See card)

ABSpl
LC

---

*Coleridge-Taylor, Samuel, 1875-1912.

...The gift-rose. ‹Song. Words by› Dr. Frederic Petersen; ‹music by› S. Coleridge-Taylor. Boston, Oliver Ditson co. ‹c1907› Publ. pl. no. 5-37-66582.
5 p. fol.

Score: high solo voice ‹key of D› with piano accompaniment.

ABSpl
BuGL
RMC
LC
ZWpl

---

*Coleridge-Taylor, Samuel, 1875-1912.

...Hiawathan sketches for violin and pianoforte. By S. Coleridge-Taylor. Opus 16... London, Augener, ltd. ‹c1897› Publ. pl. no. 11074.
17 p. fol. (Augener's edition no. 7356)

Score: violin and piano; and violin part.

Contents: 1. A tale. -2. A song. -3. A dance.
Bound v. II

ABSpl
LC

---

*Coleridge-Taylor, Samuel, 1875-1912.

In memoriam. Three rhapsodies for low voice and pianoforte, composed by S. Coleridge-Taylor. Opus 24. London, Augener & co. ‹n.d.› Publ. pl. no. 11278.
9 p. fol.

Score: low solo voice with piano accompaniment. English words.

Contents: 1. Earth fades! Heaven breaks on me. -2. Substitution. -3. Weep not, beloved friends.

ABSpl
ZWpl

---

*Coleridge-Taylor, Samuel, 1875-1912.

A gipsy dance.
(In Coleridge-Taylor, Samuel. Gipsy movements for violin with pianoforte accompaniment. Opus 20, no. 3. London, 1897. p. 9-16)

Score: violin and piano; and violin part.
Bound v. II

ABSpl
LC

Coleridge-Taylor, Samuel

Hiawatha's wedding feast. Op. 30, No. 1. pub. no. 14389.
38p.

Bound v. III

ABS

---

*Coleridge-Taylor, Samuel, 1875-1912.

In the Sierras.
(In Coleridge-Taylor, Samuel. Melodies for piano. Selected, arranged and revised by Alex Roloff... London. p. 23)

Score: piano solo; originally a part-song (SATB) entitled "Dead in the Sierras." Opus 67, no. 2.

ABSpl
LC

---

*Coleridge-Taylor, Samuel, 1875-1912.

A gipsy song.
(In Coleridge-Taylor, Samuel. Gipsy movements for violin with pianoforte accompaniment. Opus 20, no. 2. London, 1897. p. 1-8)

Score: violin and piano; and violin part.
Bound v. II

ABSpl
LC

---

*Coleridge-Taylor, Samuel, 1875-1912.

Her love. ‹Song. No. 3 of› Six American lyrics. ‹Words by Ella Wheeler Wilcox; music› composed by S. Coleridge-Taylor. ‹Opus 45, no. 3›... London, Novello & co., ltd. ‹c1903› Publ. pl. no. 11559.
9 p. fol.
Bound v. II
Score: low solo voice ‹key of F› with piano accompaniment. English words.

ABSpl
LC

---

*Coleridge-Taylor, Samuel, 1875-1912.

...Incidental music to "Herod." Suite for orchestra by S. Coleridge-Taylor. Opus 47, no. 1-4. Transcribed for the pianoforte by the composer... London, Augener & co. ‹c1901› Publ. pl. no. 11986.
17 p. fol. (Augener's edition no. 6105)

Score: piano solo. Originally scored for full orchestra.

Contents: 1. Processional. -2. Breeze scene. -3. Dance. -4. Finale.

ABSpl

---

*Coleridge-Taylor, Samuel, 1875-1912.

...Gipsy suite. (Violin and pianoforte) ‹By› S. Coleridge-Taylor. Opus 20 ‹nos. 1-4› London, Augener & co. ‹c1904› Publ. pl. no. 12680.
28 p. fol. (Augener's edition no. 11340)
Bound v. II
Score: violin and piano; and violin part in pocket on back cover.

Contents: No. 1 Lament and tambourine. No. 4 Waltz.

ABSpl
LC

---

*Coleridge-Taylor, Samuel, 1875-1912.

How shall I woo thee?
(In Coleridge-Taylor, Samuel. African romances. London, 1897. p. 19-21)
Bound V. I.
Score: medium solo voice with piano accompaniment. English words.
Also published separately.

ABSpl
LC
NYPL42
ZWpl

Coleridge-Taylor, Samuel
Intermezzo

---

*Coleridge-Taylor, Samuel, 1875-1912.

The Gitanos, a cantata-operetta for female voices ...Words by Edward Oxenford; music by S. Coleridge-Taylor. Opus 26. London, Augener & co. ‹1898?› Publ. pl. no. 11247.
40 p. 8°. (Augener's edition no. 9088)

Score: S, 2 Mz, and 2 C soli, SSA chorus with piano accompaniment. English words.
Bound v. II

ABSpl

---

*Coleridge-Taylor, Samuel, 1875-1912.

Idyll.
(In Coleridge-Taylor, Samuel. Melodies for piano. Selected, arranged and revised by Alex Roloff... London. p. 2-5)

Score: piano solo; originally a part-song (SSC), "How they so softly rest." Also published as solo with other words entitled, "Our idyll." (See cards)

ABSpl
LC

---

*Coleridge-Taylor, Samuel, 1875-1912.

...Introduction. ‹From› African suite for the pianoforte by S. Coleridge-Taylor. Opus 35, no. 1. London, Augener & co., ltd. ‹c1898› Publ. pl. no. 11368.
5 p. fol.

Score: piano solo.

ABSpl
LC

*Coleridge-Taylor, Samuel, 1875-1912.

The island of gardens. From "Songs of sun and shade." The poem by Marguerite Radclyffe-Hall; the music by S. Coleridge-Taylor. New York, Boosey & co. ©1911. Publ. pl. no. 1135.
5 p. fol.
Bound v. III
Score: low solo voice (key of C) with piano accompaniment. English words.

ABSpl
HMC

*Coleridge-Taylor, Samuel, 1875-1912.

Life and death. Song with pianoforte accompaniment. By S. Coleridge-Taylor. New York, Arthur P. Schmidt co. ©1914. Publ. pl. no. 14770.
5 p. fol.
Bound v. III
Score: medium solo voice (key of B♭) with piano accompaniment.

ABSpl

*Coleridge-Taylor, Samuel, 1875-1912.

Love's passing. Song. The poem by *Louise Alston Burleigh; the music by S. Coleridge-Taylor. New York, William Maxwell music co. ©1905. Publ. pl. no. 737.
7 p. fol.
Bound v. III
Score: low solo voice (key of F) with piano accompaniment. English words.

ABSpl

Coleridge-Taylor, Samuel

Keep those eyes. MSS.

Bound v. III

ABS

*Coleridge-Taylor, Samuel, 1875-1912.

The links of love. Song. Verse by Greville E. Matheson; music by S. Coleridge-Taylor... New York, John Church co. ©1910. Publ. pl. no. 16426.
7 p. fol.
Bound v. III
Score: low solo voice (key of Em) with piano accompaniment. English words.

ABSpl
HMC

Coleridge-Taylor, Samuel

Low-breathing winds. pub. no. 10299

Bound v. III

ABS

Coleridge-Taylor, Samuel
Keep those eyes. Duet for soprano and tenor. 1903.

8p.

Bound v. III

*Coleridge-Taylor, Samuel, 1875-1912.

The lone forest maiden.
(In Coleridge-Taylor, Samuel. Forest scenes. Characteristic pieces for pianoforte. Opus 55. London, 1907. p. 1-4.)

Score: piano solo.

ABSpl
LC

Coleridge-Taylor, Samuel

Low-breathing winds. pub. no. 14639.

ABS

*Coleridge-Taylor, Samuel, 1875-1912.

...A king there lived in Thule. Song. The words from the German, by Stephen Phillips and J. Comyns Carr; the music by S. Coleridge-Taylor. (Opus 70) London, Boosey & co., ©1908. Publ.pl. no. 6021.
7 p. fol.
Bound v. III
Score: high solo voice with piano accompaniment. English words.

From the Incidental music to "Faust."

ABSpl
LC

*Coleridge-Taylor, Samuel, 1875-1912.

Loud he sang the psalm of David.
(In Coleridge-Taylor, Samuel. ...Three choral ballads. London, ©1904. p. 36-51)

Score: piano-vocal (SATB). English words.

ABSpl
LC

*Coleridge-Taylor, Samuel, 1875-1912.

Lucy (words by Wordsworth).
(In Coleridge-Taylor, Samuel. Three songs. Opus 29, no. 1. London (n.d.) p. 1-4)

Score: high solo voice with piano accompaniment. English words.

ABSpl

*Coleridge-Taylor, Samuel, 1875-1912.

Kubla Khan. A rhapsody for solo, chorus and orchestra. Words by (Samuel Taylor) Coleridge; music by S. Coleridge-Taylor. (Opus 61) London, Houghton & co. ©1905. Publ. pl. no. H & co. 559.
50 p. 8°.

Score: contralto solo and SATB with piano accompaniment. English words.

First performance: Queen's Hall, 1906, by the Handel's Society.

ABSpl
LC

*Coleridge-Taylor, Samuel, 1875-1912.

...Love is like the roses. (Song. Words by Robert Buchanan; music by) S. Coleridge-Taylor. New York, Arthur P. Schmidt co. ©1918. Publ. pl. no. A. P. S. 12347.
5 p. fol.

Score: low solo voice with piano accompaniment. English words.

ABSpl
LC

*Coleridge-Taylor, Samuel, 1875-1912.

Mary (words by Wordsworth.)
(In Coleridge-Taylor, Samuel. Three songs. Opus 29, no. 2. London. (n.d.) p. 5-8)

Score: high solo voice with piano accompaniment. English words.

ABSpl

*Coleridge-Taylor, Samuel, 1875-1912.

Lament and tambourine.
(In Coleridge-Taylor, Samuel. Gipsy suite for violin and pianoforte. Opus 20, no. 1. London, 1904. p. 1-14)

Score: violin and piano; and violin part in pocket on back cover.

ABSpl
LC

Coleridge-Taylor, Samuel
A Lovely Little Dream

*Coleridge-Taylor, Samuel, 1875-1912.

...Melodies for piano (by) S. Coleridge-Taylor... Selected, arranged and revised by Alex Roloff... London, Augener, ltd. (various copyright dates, 1896-1915) Publ. pl. nos. 14906, 14834.
25 p. fol. (Album series no. 28)

Score: piano solos.

This compilation was made after composer's death of excerpts from larger piano works, transcriptions of choral and other vocal numbers, etc.

(continued on next card)

Coleridge-Taylor, Samuel
Lament for Pianoforte

Coleridge-Taylor, Samuel
Love's Mirrow

*Coleridge-Taylor, Samuel, 1875-1912. ...Melodies for piano. London, (1896-1915) (Card 2)

Contents: 1. Idyll. -2. From the east. -3. Serenade. -4. Cameo. -5. Minguillo. -6. Zarifa. -7. In the Sierras. -8. Reflection.

ABSpl

*Coleridge-Taylor, Samuel, 1875-1912.

Minguillo.
(In Coleridge-Taylor, Samuel. Melodies for piano. Selected, arranged and revised by Alex Roloff... London. p. 16-18)

Score: piano solo; originally a song from the song cycle, "Southern love songs."

ABSpl
LC

Coleridge-Taylor, Samuel
My Lady

---

*Coleridge-Taylor, Samuel, 1875-1912.

O thou, mine other, stronger part. ⌈Song. No. 1 of⌉ six American lyrics. ⌈Words by Ella Wheeler Wilcox; music⌉ composed by S. Coleridge-Taylor. ⌈Opus 45, no. 1⌉... London, Novello & co., ltd. ⌈c1903⌉ Publ. pl. no. 11557.
5 p. fol.

Score: low solo voice ⌈key of E⌉ with piano accompaniment. English words.

ABSpl
LC

---

*Coleridge-Taylor, Samuel, 1875-1912.

Minguillo (ancient Spanish). Words by Lockhart.
(In Coleridge-Taylor, Samuel. Southern love songs. Opus 12, no. 3. London, 1896. p. 10,11)

Score: high solo voice ⌈key of A^b⌉ with piano accompaniment. English words.

Also arranged for piano solo. (See card)

ABSpl
LC

---

*Coleridge-Taylor, Samuel, 1875-1912.

My love (a Spanish ditty). Words by Longfellow.
(In Coleridge-Taylor, Samuel. Southern love songs. Opus 12, no. 1. London, 1896. p. 1-5)

Score: high solo voice ⌈key of A⌉ with piano accompaniment. English words.

Orchestral arrangement available from publisher.

ABSpl
LC

---

*Coleridge-Taylor, Samuel, 1875-1912.

Oh! my lonely, lonely, lonely pillow (stanzas to a Hindoo air). Words by Byron.
(In Coleridge-Taylor, Samuel. Southern love songs. Opus 12, no. 5. London, 1896. p. 14-15)

Score: high solo voice ⌈key of C⌉ with piano accompaniment. English words.

ABSpl
LC

---

*Coleridge-Taylor, Samuel, 1875-1912.

...Minnehaha. ⌈Piano⌉ Suite from the Hiawatha ballet music... By S. Coleridge-Taylor. ⌈Opus 82, no. 2⌉ London, Hawkes & son ⌈c1925⌉ Publ. pl. no. H.&S.6313.
31 p. fol.

Score: piano solos; originally scored for full orchestra.
"This suite has been selected from music written by Coleridge-Taylor for his great Hiawatha ballet. It contains numbers not already published in Hiawatha ballet suite, and has been arranged and orchestrated by Percy E. Fletcher." - End of Caption title.

(continued on next card)

---

*Coleridge-Taylor, Samuel, 1875-1912.

...A Negro love-song for violin and pianoforte. By S. Coleridge-Taylor. ⌈Opus 35, no. 2⌉ London, Augener & co., c1898. Publ. pl. no. 11395.
9 p. fol. (Augener's edition no. 7359B)

Score: violin and piano; and violin part.

ABSpl
LC
ZWpl

---

*Coleridge-Taylor, Samuel, 1875-1912.

Oh, roses for the flush of youth. ⌈One of⌉ Six sorrow songs for contralto voice... Words by Christina G. Rossetti; music by S. Coleridge-Taylor. Opus 57, no. 3. London, Augener & co., c1904. Publ. pl. no. 12715.
5 p. fol.

Score: low solo voice with piano accompaniment.

ABSpl
LC

Coleridge-Taylor, Samuel
O Mistress Mine

---

*Coleridge-Taylor, Samuel, 1875-1912.

...A Negro love-song. ⌈From⌉ the African suite for the pianoforte by S. Coleridge-Taylor. Opus 35, no. 2. London, Augener & co., ltd. ⌈c1898⌉ Publ. pl. no. 11368.
7 p. fol.

Score: piano solo.

ABSpl
LC

---

*Coleridge-Taylor, Samuel, 1875-1912.

Oh what comes over the sea. ⌈One of⌉ Six sorrow songs for contralto voice... Words by Christina G. Rossetti; music by S. Coleridge-Taylor. Opus 57, no. 1. London, Augener & co., c1904. Publ. pl. no. 12715.
3 p. fol.

Score: low solo voice ⌈key of D^m⌉ with piano accompaniment.

ABSpl
LC

---

*Coleridge-Taylor, Samuel, 1875-1912.

...Moorish dance for pianoforte. By S. Coleridge-Taylor. Opus 55. London, Augener & co., c1904. Publ. pl. no. 12682.
17 p. fol. (Augener's edition no. 6107)

Score: piano solo.

ABSpl
LC

---

*Coleridge-Taylor, Samuel, 1875-1912.

Now proudly they journey together towards the great city.
(In Coleridge-Taylor, Samuel. Forest scenes. Characteristic pieces for pianoforte. Opus 55. London, 1907. p. 20-25.)

Score: piano solo.

ABSpl
LC

Coleridge-Taylor, Samuel

Onaway! awake, beloved! Pub. no. 10723

Bound v. III

ABS

---

*Coleridge-Taylor, Samuel, 1875-1912.

...Moorish tone-pictures for the pianoforte (2) By S. Coleridge-Taylor. Opus 19, no. 1... London, Augener's ltd. ⌈c1897⌉ Publ. pl. no. 11145.
12 p. fol. (Augener's edition no. 6101)

Score: piano solos.

Contents: Andalla. -Zarifa.

ABSpl
LC

---

*Coleridge-Taylor, Samuel, 1875-1912.

O praise me not. ⌈Song. No. 2 of⌉ Six American lyrics. ⌈Words by Ella Wheeler Wilcox; music⌉ composed by S. Coleridge-Taylor. ⌈Opus 45, no. 2⌉... London, Novello & co., ltd. ⌈c1903⌉ Publ. pl. no. 11558.
5 p. fol.

Score: low solo voice ⌈key of G⌉ with piano accompaniment. English words.

ABSpl
LC
ZWpl

---

*Coleridge-Taylor, Samuel, 1875-1912.

Once only. Rhapsody for voice and piano. ⌈Words by⌉ Robert Louis Stevenson ⌈from⌉ "Youth and love"; ⌈music by⌉ S. Coleridge-Taylor. Boston, Oliver Ditson co. ⌈c1906⌉ Publ. pl. no. 5-19-65712.
7 p. fol.

Score: medium solo voice ⌈key of D⌉ with piano accompaniment. English words.
Caption title.

ABSpl
ZWpl
LC
HMC

Coleridge-Taylor, Samuel
My Algonoquin

---

*Coleridge-Taylor, Samuel, 1875-1912.

O ship that sailest slowly on. ⌈Song. No. 5 of⌉ Six American lyrics. ⌈Words by Ella Wheeler Wilcox; music⌉ composed by S. Coleridge-Taylor. ⌈Opus 45, no. 5⌉ ... London, Novello & co., ltd. ⌈c1903⌉ Publ. pl. no. 11561.
6 p. fol.

Score: low solo voice ⌈key of A⌉ with piano accompaniment. English words.

ABSpl
LC

---

*Coleridge-Taylor, Samuel, 1875-1912.

Othello. Orchestral suite... Composed by S. Coleridge-Taylor... London, Metzler & co., ltd., c1912. Publ. pl. no. M & co. (1909) ltd. 206.
20 p. fol.

Score: piano solos; originally scored for full orchestra.

Contents: 1. Dance. -2. Children's intermezzo. -3. Funeral march. -4. The willow song. -5. Military march.

ABSpl
LC

*Coleridge-Taylor, Samuel, 1875-1912.

Othello. Suite... By Samuel Coleridge-Taylor. London, J. B. Cramer & co., ldt. c1912. Publ. pl. no. M & co. (1909) ltd. 206.
20 p. fol.

Score: piano solos; originally scored for full orchestra.

Contents: 1. Dance. -2. Children's intermezzo. -3. Funeral march. -4. The willow song. -5. Military march.
ZWpl

Coleridge-Taylor, Samuel
Prelude

*Coleridge-Taylor, Samuel, 1875-1912.

She dwells by great Kenhawa's side.
(In Coleridge-Taylor, Samuel. ...Three choral ballads. London, c1904. p. 22-35)

Score: piano-vocal (SATB). English words.

ABSpl
LC

*Coleridge-Taylor, Samuel, 1875-1912.

Over the hills.
(In Coleridge-Taylor, Samuel. African romances. Opus 17, no. 6. London, 1897. p. 17, 18)

Score: medium solo voice with piano accompaniment. English words.
Also published separately.

ABSpl
LC
NYPL42

Coleridge-Taylor, Samuel
Question and Answer

Coleridge-Taylor, Samuel

She rested by the broken brook. pub..no.72722

Bound v. III

ABS

Coleridge-Taylor, Samuel
Papillon

*Coleridge-Taylor, Samuel, 1875-1912.

"The quadroon girl."
(In Coleridge-Taylor, Samuel. Two choral ballads. 2nd set. Opus 54, nos. 4 and 5. London, c1905. p. 1-12)

Score: SSA with baritone solo and piano accompaniment. English words.

ABSpl
HMC
LC

*Coleridge-Taylor, Samuel, 1875-1912.

She sat and sang alway. ₍One of₎ Six sorrow songs for contralto voice... Words by Christina G. Rossetti; music by S. Coleridge-Taylor. Opus 57, no. 4. London, Augener & co., c1904. Publ. pl. no. 12715.
4 p. fol.

Score: low solo voice with piano accompaniment.

ABSpl
LC

*Coleridge-Taylor, Samuel, 1875-1912.

Petite suite de concert for pianoforte by S. Coleridge-Taylor. ₍Opus 77, nos. 1-4₎... London, Hawkes & son, c1916. Publ. pl. no. H. & S. 5440.
23 p. fol.

Score: piano solos.

Contents: 1. La caprice de nannette. -2. Demande et reponse. -3. Un sonnet d'amour. -4. La tarantelle fretillante.

ABSpl
LC

*Coleridge-Taylor, Samuel, 1875-1912.

Reflection.
(In Coleridge-Taylor, Samuel. Melodies for piano. Selected, arranged and revised by Alex Roloff... London. p. 24, 25)

Score: piano solo; originally no. 2 of "Six sorrow songs" entitled "When I am dead my dearest," and for violin and piano as "Regret." (See cards)

ABSpl
LC

*Coleridge-Taylor, Samuel, 1875-1912.

Six American lyrics. Composed by S. Coleridge-Taylor. ₍Opus 45, nos. 1-6. Lyrics by various authors₎ London, Novello & co., ltd. ₍c1903₎ Publ. pl. nos. 11557-11562.
6 v. fol.

Score: low solo voice with piano accompaniment. English words.

Contents: 1. O thou, mine other, stronger part. -2. O praise me not. -3. Her love. -4. The dark eye has left us. -5. O ship that sailest slowly on. -6. Beat, beat, drums!
ABSpl LC

*Coleridge-Taylor, Samuel, 1875-1912.

The phantom lover arrives.
(In Coleridge-Taylor, Samuel. Forest scenes. Characteristic pieces for pianoforte. Opus 55. London, 1907. p. 5-8.)

Score: piano solo.

ABSpl
LC

*Coleridge-Taylor, Samuel, 1875-1912.

Scenes de ballet. ₍Four piano solos by₎ S. Coleridge-Taylor. ₍Opus 64, no. 1-4₎ London, Augener ltd. ₍c1906₎ Publ. pl. no. 13355.
27 p. fol. (Augener's edition no. 6098)

Score: piano solos.

Contents: No. 1 in C; No. 2 in A; No. 3 in A^{b}; No. 4 in B^{b}.

ABSpl
LC

Coleridge-Taylor, Samuel

Six sorrow songs.

23p, pub. no. 12715 Augener's ed. No.8870A

Bound v. IV

ABS

*Coleridge-Taylor, Samuel, 1875-1912.

The phantom tells his tale of longing.
(In Coleridge-Taylor, Samuel. Forest scenes. Characteristic pieces for pianoforte. Opus 55. London, 1907. p. 9-13.)

Score: piano solo.

ABSpl
LC

*Coleridge-Taylor, Samuel, 1875-1912.

...Scenes from an imaginary ballet for the pianoforte. By S. Coleridge-Taylor. Opus 74, no. 1. London, Winthrop Rogers, ltd. ₍c1911₎ Publ. pl. no. 2764.
17 p. fol.

Score: piano solos.

ABSpl

*Coleridge-Taylor, Samuel, 1875-1912.

...Six sorrow songs for contralto voice... Words by Christina G. Rossetti; music by S. Coleridge-Taylor. Opus 57... London, Augener & co., c1904. Publ. pl. no. 12715.
23 p. fol. (Augener's edition no. 8870)

Score: low solo voice with piano accompaniment.

Contents: 1. Oh what comes over the sea. -2. When I am dead, my dearest. -3. Oh, roses for the flush of youth. -4. She sat and sang alway. -5. Unmindful of the roses. -6. Too late for love.
ABSpl LC

*Coleridge-Taylor, Samuel, 1875-1912.

A Prayer.
(In Coleridge-Taylor, Samuel. African romances. Opus 17, no. 2. London, 1897. p. 6-8)

Score: medium solo voice with piano accompaniment. English words.

ABSpl
LC
NYPL42

*Coleridge-Taylor, Samuel, 1875-1912.

Serenade.
(In Coleridge-Taylor, Samuel. Melodies for piano. Selected, arranged and revised by Alex Roloff... London, p. 8,9)

Score: piano solo; originally a song entitled "If thou art sleeping, maiden" from the song cycle, "Southern love songs."

ABSpl
LC

*Coleridge-Taylor, Samuel, 1875-1912.

Sleep, sleep, O king. Minstrel's song from "Herod." The words by Stephen Phillips; the music by S. Coleridge-Taylor. New York, Boosey & co., c1900. Publ. pl. no. E & S 2781.
7 p. fol.

Score: high solo voice ₍key of C₎ with piano accompaniment. English words.

ABSpl
LC

*Coleridge-Taylor, Avril

Sleeping and waking. ₍Song₎ Music by Avril Coleridge-Taylor; poem by Norman Notley. New York, Galaxy music corp. ₍c1939₎ Publ. pl. no. G.M.1017. 3 p. fol.

Score: medium solo voice ₍key of E^b₎ with piano accompaniment. English words.

ABSpl
ZWpl

*Coleridge-Taylor, Samuel, 1875-1912.

...The soul's expression (four sonnets) by Elizabeth Barrett Browning... Set to music by S. Coleridge-Taylor. Opus 42, nos. 1-4; London, Novello & co., ltd., c1900. Publ. pl. no. 11085. 19 p. fol.
Bound v. IV

Score: solo voice with piano accompaniment.

First performance: Hereford musical festival, Sept. 13, 1900.

Contents: 1. The soul's expression. -2. Tears. -3. Grief. -4. Comfort.
ABSpl

Coleridge-Taylor, Samuel
Suite De Pièces (1-4)

*Coleridge-Taylor, Samuel, 1875-1912.

...Sometimes I feel like a motherless child. An American Negro melody. Song. Transcribed by S. Coleridge-Taylor. (Opus 59, no. 1-(22); arranged by *William Arms Fisher. Opus 19, no. 2. Boston, Oliver Ditson co. ₍c1917₎ Publ. pl. no. 5-150-72070. 7 p. fol.
Bound v. III

Score: medium solo voice ₍key of E^m₎ with piano accompaniment. English words.

ABSpl
LC
ZWpl

*Coleridge-Taylor, Samuel, 1875-1912.

The soul's expression. ₍Song. Words by₎ Elizabeth Barrett Browning; ₍music by₎ S. Coleridge-Taylor. Opus 42, no. 1. London, Novello & co., ltd., c1900. Publ. pl. no. 11085. p. 1-5. fol.
Bound v. IV

Score: medium solo voice with piano accompaniment. Caption title.

From "The soul's expression," a song cycle.

LC

*Coleridge-Taylor, Samuel, 1875-1912.

Suite from the Hiawatha ballet music... By S. Coleridge-Taylor. Opus 82, no. 1... London, Hawkes & son, c1919. Publ. pl. no. H. & S. 5706. 25 p. fol.

Score: piano solos; originally scored for full orchestra.
This album has been adapted from the original score, and arranged for piano solo by Percy Fletcher.

Contents: 1. The wooing. -2. The marriage feast. -3. A. Bird scene. -3. B. Conjurer's dance. -4. Departure. -5. The reunion.
ABSpl ZWpl

*Coleridge-Taylor, Samuel, 1875-1912.

A song.
(In Coleridge-Taylor, Samuel. Hiawathan sketches for violin and piano. Opus 16, no. 2. London, 1897. p. 8-12)

Score: violin and piano; and violin part.
Bound v. II

ABS
LC

*Coleridge-Taylor, Samuel, 1875-1912.

...Southern love songs. ₍A song cycle₎ set to music by S. Coleridge-Taylor. Opus 12... London, Augener & co. ₍c1896₎ Publ. pl. no. 10976. 15 p. fol. (Augener's edition no. 8819)
Bound v. IV
Score: high solo voice with piano accompaniment. English words.

Contents: 1. My love (a Spanish ditty). -2. Tears (a lament). -3. Minguillo (ancient Spanish). -4. If thou art sleeping maiden (Portuguese). -5. Oh! my lonely, lonely, lonely pillow (stanzas to a Hindoo air).
ABSpl LC ZWpl

Coleridge-Taylor, Samuel

Suite from the Hiawatha ballet music. Nos. 1-5.

25p. pub. no. 5706
Bound v. II

ABS

Coleridge-Taylor, Samuel
Song of the Nubian girl. pub. no. 13002

Bound v. III

ABS

*Coleridge-Taylor, Samuel, 1875-1912.

Spring had come. ₍Song. Kam der lenz mit seinem glanze₎ From scenes from the "Song of Hiawatha." The words written by H. W. Longfellow; the music by S. Coleridge-Taylor. (Opus 30, no. 4)... London, Novello & co., ltd., c1900. Publ. pl. no. 11151. 6 p. fol.
Bound v. IV
Score: high solo voice ₍key of D₎ with piano accompaniment. English and German words. Originally with orchestral accompaniment.
ABSpl ZWpl
LC

*Coleridge-Taylor, Samuel, 1875-1912.

Suite from the incidental music to St. Agnes' eve for pianoforte by S. Coleridge-Taylor. London, Hawkes & son, c1922. Publ. pl. no. H. & S. 6009. 10 p. fol.
Bound v. IV
Score: piano solos; originally scored for full orchestra.

Contents: 1. That ancient beadsman heard the prelude soft. -2. Her maiden eyes divine. -3. Porphyro, "now tell me where is Madeline."

ABSpl
HMC

*Coleridge-Taylor, Samuel, 1875-1912.

"Songs of sun and shade." Song cycle. Poems by Marguerite Radclyffe-Hall; music by S. Coleridge-Taylor. London, Boosey & co., c1911. Publ. pl. no. H. 8222. 18 p. fol.
Bound v. III
Score: low solo voice with piano accompaniment. English words.

Contents: 1. You lay so still in the sunshine. -2. Thou hast bewitched me, beloved. -3. The rainbow-child. -4. Thou art risen, my beloved. -5. This is the island of gardens.
ABSpl

*Coleridge- Taylor, Samuel, 1875-1912.

A starry night.
(In Coleridge-Taylor, Samuel. African romances. Opus 17, no. 3. London, 1897. p. 8-11)
Bound v. I
Score: medium solo voice with piano accompaniment. English words.

ABSpl
LC
NYPl42

*Coleridge-Taylor, Samuel, 1875-1912.

A summer idyll. Song. The words by Hilda Hammond-Spencer; the music by S. Coleridge-Taylor... London, Boosey & co. ₍c1906₎ Publ. pl. no. E.S. 3551. 7 p. fol.
Bound v. IV
Score: high solo voice ₍key of G₎ with piano accompaniment. English words.

ABSpl
LC

*Coleridge-Taylor, Samuel, 1875-1912.

...Songs with pianoforte accompaniment. ₍By₎ S. Coleridge-Taylor. New York, The Arthur P. Schmidt co. v. fol.

Scores: solo voice with piano accompaniment. English words.

Contents: 1. Life and death. -2. An explanation. -3. Low-breathing winds. -4. Tell, O tell me. -5. The guest. -6. My lady. -7. Love's mirror. -8. My pretty fisher maiden. -9. Thy sapphire eyes. -10. The bridal day.
ABSpl - has nos. 1, 2, 4, 6, 7, 10. LC

*Coleridge-Taylor, Samuel, 1875-1912.

...The stars. ₍One of₎ "Five fairy ballads"... The words by Kathleen Easmon; the music by S. Coleridge-Taylor. London, Boosey & co. ₍c1909₎ Publ. pl. no. H.6428. 7 p. fol.

Score: low solo voice ₍key of E^b₎ with piano accompaniment. Negro dialect.

LC
ABS

*Coleridge-Taylor, Samuel, 1875-1912.

...Sweet baby butterfly. ₍One of₎ "Five fairy ballads"... The words by Kathleen Easmon; the music by S. Coleridge-Taylor. London, Boosey & co. ₍c1909₎ Publ. pl. no. 6428. 5 p. fol.

Score: low solo voice ₍key of F₎ with piano accompaniment. English words.

ABSpl
LC
ZWpl
HMC

*Coleridge-Taylor, Samuel, 1875-1912.

Sons of the sea. Song. The words by Sarojini Naidu; the music by S. Coleridge-Taylor... London, Novello & co., ltd., c1910. Publ. pl. no. 13182. 9 p. fol.

Score: medium solo voice ₍key of F^m₎ with piano accompaniment. English words.

ABSpl
LC

*Coleridge-Taylor, Samuel, 1875-1912.

Substitution. Words by Elizabeth Barrett Browning.
(In Coleridge-Taylor, Samuel. In memoriam. Three rhapsodies for low voice and pianoforte. Opus 24, no. 2. London, ₍n.d.₎ p. 4-7)

Score: low solo voice with piano accompaniment. English words.

ABSpl

Coleridge-Taylor, Samuel

Sweet baby butterfly. Song from five fairy ballads.
5p. pub. no. 6427
Bound v. IV

ABS

*Coleridge-Taylor, Samuel, 1875-1912.

Sweet evenings come and go, love. Song. The words by George Eliot; the music by S. Coleridge-Taylor. Opus 37, no. 4. London, Novello & co., ltd., c1899. Publ. pl. no. 10838.
4 p. fol.
Bound v. IV

Score: high solo voice ‹key of B♭› with piano accompaniment. English words.

ABSpl
LC

---

*Coleridge-Taylor, Samuel, 1875-1912.

Three dream dances. ‹Piano solos› By S. Coleridge-Taylor. ‹Opus 74, no. 2›... London, Ascherberg, Hopwood & Crew, ltd. ‹c1911› Publ. pl. no. A.H. & C. ltd. 5368a.
18 p. fol.

Score: piano solos. Originally scored for full orchestra.

Contents: No. 1 in D; No. 2 in F; No. 3 in G.

ABSpl zwpl
LC

---

*Coleridge-Taylor, Samuel, 1875-1912. Two choral ballads by Longfellow... London ‹c1905› (Card 2)

"Full score and orchestra part may be obtained on hire by arrangement with publisher."

ABSpl
HMC
LC

---

*Coleridge-Taylor, Samuel, 1875-1912.

A tale.
(In Coleridge-Taylor, Samuel. Hiawathan sketches for violin and piano. Opus 16, no. 1. London, 1897. p. 1-7)

Score: violin and piano; and violin part.
Bound v. II

ABS
LC

---

*Coleridge-Taylor, Samuel, 1875-1912.

...Three-fours. Valse suite. ‹By› S. Coleridge-Taylor. Opus 71. ‹London› Augener ltd. ‹c1909› Publ. pl. no. 13895.
25 p. fol. (Augener's edition no. 6073)
Bound v. IV
Score: piano solos.

Contents: No. 1 in A minor; No. 2 in A♭; No. 3 in G minor; No. 4 in D; No. 5 in E♭; No. 6 in C minor.

ABSpl
LC
zwpl

---

*Coleridge-Taylor, Samuel, 1875-1912.

...Two gipsy movements for violin with pianoforte accompaniment by S. Coleridge-Taylor. ‹Opus 20, no. 2 and 3› ... London, Augener & co., c1897. Publ. pl. no. 11163.
16 p. fol. (Augener's edition no. 7357)

Score: violin and piano; and violin part.

Contents: No. 2, A gipsy song. No. 3, A gipsy dance.

ABSpl
LC

---

*Coleridge-Taylor, Samuel, 1875-1912.

Tears (a lament). ‹No author given›
(In Coleridge-Taylor, Samuel. Southern love songs. Opus 12, no. 2. London, 1896. p. 6-9)

Score: high solo voice ‹key of D♭› with piano accompaniment. English words.

ABSpl
LC

Coleridge-Taylor, Samuel
Three Humoresques

---

*Coleridge-Taylor, Samuel, 1875-1912.

Unmindful of the roses. ‹One of› Six sorrow songs for contralto voice... Words by Christina G. Rossetti; music by S. Coleridge-Taylor. Opus 57, no. 5. London, Augener & co., c1904. Publ. pl. no. 12715.
4 p. fol.

Score: low solo voice ‹key of D› with piano accompaniment.

ABSpl
LC

---

*Coleridge-Taylor, Samuel, 1875-1912.

Tears. ‹Song. Words by› Elizabeth Barrett Browning; ‹music by› S. Coleridge-Taylor. Opus 42, no. 2. London, Novello & co., ltd., c1900. Publ. pl. no. 11085.
p. 6-10. fol.
Bound v. IV
Score: medium solo voice with piano accompaniment. Caption title.

From "The Soul's expression," a song cycle.

LC

---

*Coleridge-Taylor, Samuel, 1875-1912.

Three songs. Songs. Composed by S. Coleridge-Taylor. Opus 29, nos. 1-3. London, Augener & co., ‹n.d.› Publ. pl. no. 11295.
13 p. fol.
Bound v. IV
Score: high solo voice with piano accompaniment. English words.

Contents: 1. Lucy. -2. Mary. -3. Jessy.

ABSpl

---

*Coleridge-Taylor, Samuel, 1875-1912.

Valse Bohemienne. No. 1 of Four characteristic waltzes. Composed by S. Coleridge-Taylor. (Opus 22, no. 1); arranged for violin and pianoforte by the composer. London, Novello & co., ltd., c1903. Publ. pl. no. 10566.
p. 1-4. fol.

Score: piano and violin; and violin part.

ABSpl
LC

Coleridge-Taylor, Samuel
Tell, O Tell Me

Coleridge-Taylor, Samuel

Thou art riden, my beloved.
4p. pub. no. 842
Bound v. IV

ABS

---

*Coleridge-Taylor, Samuel, 1875-1912.

Valse de la Reine. No. 3 of Four characteristic waltzes. Composed by S. Coleridge-Taylor. (Opus 22, no. 3); arranged for violin and pianoforte by the composer. London, Novello & co., ltd., c1903.
p. 10-15. fol.

Score: piano and violin; and violin part.

ABSpl
LC

---

*Coleridge-Taylor, Samuel, 1875-1912.

...Three choral ballads by Longfellow ‹1st set;› set to music as 4-part songs (SATB) by S. Coleridge-Taylor. Opus 54... London, Breitkopf & Hartel ‹c1904› Publ. pl. no. L.65.
51 p. 8°.
Bound v. IV
Score: piano-vocal (SATB). English words.

Contents: 1. Beside the ungathered rice he lay. -2. She dwells by great Kenhawa's side. -3. Loud he sang the psalm of David.
(continued on next card)

---

*Coleridge-Taylor, Samuel, 1875-1912.

Too late for love. ‹One of› Six sorrow songs for contralto voice... Words by Christina G. Rossetti; music by S. Coleridge-Taylor. Opus 57, no. 6. London, Augener & co., c1904. Publ. pl. no. 12715.
7 p. fol.

Score: low solo voice with piano accompaniment.

Orchestral arrangement available from publisher.

ABSpl
LC

---

*Coleridge-Taylor, Samuel, 1875-1912.

...Valse. ‹From› African suite for the pianoforte by S. Coleridge-Taylor. Opus 35, no. 3. London, Augener & co., ltd. ‹c1898› Publ. pl. no. 11368.
8 p. fol.
Bound v. I
Score: piano solo.

ABSpl
LC

---

*Coleridge-Taylor, Samuel, 1875-1912. ...Three choral ballads by Longfellow... London, c1904. (Card 2)

"Full score and orchestral parts may be obtained on hire by arrangement with the publishers." - Title page.

ABSpl
LC

---

*Coleridge-Taylor, Samuel, 1875-1912.

Two choral ballads by Longfellow ‹2nd set› with accompaniment of orchestra or pianoforte by S. Coleridge-Taylor. Opus 54, no. 4 and 5. London, Breitkopf & Hartel ‹c1905› Publ. pl. no. L.75.
31 p. 8°.
Bound v. IV
Score: piano-vocal score (SSA and SSAATTBB). English words.

Contents: 1. The quadroon girl (p. 1-12). -2. In dark fens of the dismal swamp (p. 13-31)
(continued on next card)

---

*Coleridge-Taylor, Samuel, 1875-1912.

Valse Mauresque. No. 4 of Four characteristic waltzes. Composed by S. Coleridge-Taylor. (Opus 22, no. 4); arranged for violin and pianoforte by the composer. London, Novello and co., ltd., c1903.
p. 16-21. fol.

Score: piano and violin; and violin part.

ABSpl
LC

*Coleridge-Taylor, Samuel, 1875-1912.

Valse rustique. No. 2 of Four characteristic waltzes. Composed by S. Coleridge-Taylor. (Opus 22, no. 2); arranged for violin and pianoforte by the composer. London, Novello & co., ltd., c1903. p. 5-9. fol.

Score: piano and violin; and violin part.

ABSpl
LC

*Coleridge-Taylor, Samuel, 1875-1912.

Twenty-four Negro melodies. Transcribed for the piano by S. Coleridge-Taylor. Opus 59, no. 1. With a preface by Booker T. Washington... Boston, Oliver Ditson company [c1905] Publ. pl. nos. 865-888.
127 p. fol. (The musician's library)

Score: piano solos.

Also published separately.

(continued on next card)

Coleridge-Taylor, Samuel

Violin concerto in G minor.
18p.

Bound V. I.

ABS

*Coleridge-Taylor, Samuel, 1875-1912.

Viking song. [Song.] Words by David McKee Wright; music by S. Coleridge-Taylor. Boston, Oliver Ditson co. [c1914] Publ. pl. no. 5-146-71907.
7 p. fol.
Bound v. IV
Score: low solo voice [key of E♭] with piano accompaniment. English words. Originally arranged as part-song for SC.

ABSpl
BuGL
ZWpl

*Coleridge-Taylor, Samuel, 1875-1912. Twenty-four Negro melodies... Boston, c1905. (Card 2)

Contents: 4 songs from Southeast Africa: 1. At the dawn of day (Loko ku ti ga). -2. The stones are very hard (Maribye ma nonoha mgopfu). -3. Take nabandji (Thata nabandji). -4. They will not lend me a child (A ba boleki mwana!). 2 Songs from South Africa: 5. Song of conquest (Ringendje). -6. Warrior's song. 1 song from West Africa: -7. Aloba. 1 song from West Indies: -8. The bamboula (African dance). 16 songs from America: -9. The angels changed my name. -10. Deep river. -11. Didn't my Lord deliver Daniel? -12. Don't be weary, traveler.

(continued on next card)

*Coleridge-Taylor, Samuel, 1875-1912.

When I am dead, my dearest. [One of] Six sorrow songs for contralto voice... Words by Christina G. Rossetti; music by S. Coleridge-Taylor. Opus 57, no. 2. London, Augener & co., c1904. Publ. pl. no. 12715.
5 p. fol.

Score: low solo voice [key of F] with piano accompaniment.

Arranged as a piano solo entitled "Reflection"; and for violin and piano, "Regret." (See cards)
ABSpl LC

*Coleridge-Taylor, Samuel, 1875-1912.

Waltz.
(In Coleridge-Taylor, Samuel. Gipsy suite for violin and pianoforte. Opus 20, no. 4. London, 1904. p. 15-28)

Score: violin and piano; and violin part in pocket on back cover.

ABSpl
LC

*Coleridge-Taylor, Samuel, 1875-1912. Twenty-four Negro melodies... Boston, c1905. (Card 3)

-13. Going up. -14. I'm troubled in mind. -15. I was way down a-yonder (Dum-a-lum). -16. Let us cheer the weary traveler. -17. Many thousand gone. -18. My Lord delivered, Daniel. -19. Oh, he raise a poor Lazarus. -20. Pilgrim's song. -21. Run, Mary, run. -22. Sometimes I feel like a motherless child. -23. Steal away. -24. Wade in the water.

ABSpl NYPL42
BPL NYPL58
HMC NYPLS
LC ZWpl

(continued on next card)

*Coleridge-Taylor, Samuel, 1875-1912.

Who calls? Song. From "Endymion's dream." The words by C. R. B. Barrett; the music by S. Coleridge-Taylor... London, Novello & co., ltd. [c1913] Publ. pl. no. 13908.
12 p. fol.
Bound v. IV
Score: high solo voice [key of B♭] with piano accompaniment. English words.
This is another version of "Who calls?" the tenor scena from "Endymion's dream" and is published separately.
ABSpl
LC

*Coleridge-Taylor, Samuel, 1875-1912.

Weep not, beloved friends. Words by Chiabrera.
(In Coleridge-Taylor, Samuel. In memoriam. Three rhapsodies for low voice and pianoforte. Opus 24, no. 3. London, [n.d.] p. 8,9)

Score: low solo voice with piano accompaniment. English words.

ABSpl

*Coleridge-Taylor, Samuel, 1875-1912. Twenty-four Negro melodies... Boston, c1905. (Card 4)

The songs from Africa are developments of airs from Henri Alexandre Junod and Henry Edward Krehbiel. (See cards)

Nos. 4, 11, 15, 18 and 22 are arranged as trios for violin, violoncello, and piano; nos. 4, 5, 7, 12 and 14 for orchestra; no. 10 for violin and piano.

*Coleridge-Taylor, Samuel, 1875-1912.

You'll love me yet! Song. The poem written by Robert Browning; the music composed by S. Coleridge-Taylor. (Opus 37, no. 1) ... London, Novello & co., ltd., c1899. Publ. pl. no. 10818a.
4 p. fol.
Bound v. IV
Score: low solo voice [key of G^m] with piano accompaniment. English words.

ABSpl
LC

*Coleridge-Taylor, Samuel, 1875-1912.

...The willow song. Words from Shakespeare's "Othello." Music by S. Coleridge-Taylor. Opus 79. London, Metzler & co. [c1912] Publ. pl. no. M & co. (1909) ltd. 190.
5 p. fol.

Score: low solo voice [key of G^m] with piano accompaniment. English words.

ABSpl
LC

*Coleridge-Taylor, Samuel, 1875-1912.

...Until. [Song. Words by] Frank Dempster Sherman. [Music by] S. Coleridge-Taylor. Boston, Oliver Ditson co. [c1908] Publ. pl. no. 5-40-66759.
5 p. fol.

Score: medium solo voice with piano accompaniment. English words.
Caption title.

ABSpl
LC
ZWpl

*Coleridge-Taylor, Samuel, 1875-1912.

Zarifa.
(In Coleridge-Taylor, Samuel. Melodies for piano. Selected, arranged and revised by Alex Roloff. London. p. 19-22)

Score: piano solo, simplified version. Originally a piano solo in a suite entitled, "Moorish tone pictures," no. 2.

ABSpl
LC

*Coleridge-Taylor, Avril

...Wyndore. (Windover) For choir and orchestra. By Avril Coleridge-Taylor. London, J. & W. Chester ltd. [c1936]
9 p. 8°.

Score: piano-vocal (SATB) score with piano accompaniment. To be sung throughout on the syllable "ah." Originally scored for "wordless chorus and orchestra."

Performance time: 7 minutes.

(continued on next card)

*Coleridge-Taylor, Samuel, 1875-1912.

...Valse-caprice for violin et piano par S. Coleridge-Taylor. Opus 23. London, Augener & co. [c1898] Publ. pl. no. 11223.
13 p. fol. (Augener's edition no. 7358)

Score: violin and piano; and violin part.

Bowing and fingering marks by William Henley.

ABSpl
LC

*Coleridge-Taylor, Samuel, 1875-1912.

Zarifa.
(In Coleridge-Taylor, Samuel. Moorish tone-pictures for pianoforte. Opus 19, no. 1. London, 1897. p. 7-12)

Score: piano solo.

ABSpl
LC

*Coleridge-Taylor, Avril ...Wyndore. (Windover) London [c1936] (Card 2)

"To all my mutual friends who have helped me by their encouragement, especially Albert Coates, Roger Quilter, Fritz Hart, John Fry and Eldridge Newman, I dedicate this work with affection and gratitude." - Head of title.

Orchestral score available on hire from the publisher.

ABSpl

*Coleridge-Taylor, Samuel, 1875-1912.

The violet bank. Song. The poem by Darling; the music by S. Coleridge-Taylor. New York, The William Maxwell co. [c1905] Publ. pl. no. 788.
7 p. fol.

Score: high solo voice [key of C] with piano accompaniment. English words.

ABSpl
LC

*Cook, B Consuelo

... The lost summer. Song. Words by Fenton Johnson; music by B. Consuelo Cook. Chicago, Clayton F. Summy Co., [c1915.] Publ. pl. no. C.F.S. Co. 1658.
6 p. fol.

Score: medium solo voice with piano accompaniment. English words.
"Dedicated to and sung by Mme Ernestine Schumann-Heink" -- at head of title.

ABSpl

*Cook, Will Marion, 1869- 1944.

Any old place in Yankee land is good enough for me. [Popular song] Words by *Alex Rogers; music by Will Marion Cook and *Chris Smith. New York, Gotham-Attucks music co. [c1908]
5 p. fol.

Score: medium solo voice with piano accompaniment. English words.
Caption title.
In bound vol.
Excerpt from the Negro musical comedy "Bandana land." ABS
LC

*Cook, Will Marion, 1869-1944.

Darktown is out tonight. [Song] Words and music by Will Marion [pseud.] New York, M. Witmark & sons [c1898] Publ. pl. no. 1835.
7 p. fol.

Score: medium solo voice [key of B♭] with piano accompaniment. Negro dialect.
Caption title.
In bound vol.
Excerpt from the Negro musical show, "Clorindy."

ABSpl
LC

*Cook, Will Marion, 1869-1944.

Gems from "Clorindy" or "The origin of the cake-walk." A Negro musical farce. Libretto by *Paul Laurence Dunbar; music by Will Marion [pseud.] ... New York, M. Witmark & sons [c1898] Various publ. pl. nos.
7 v. fol.

Score: medium solo voice with piano accompaniment. Negro dialect.
In bound vol. (continued on next card)
ABS

*Cook, Will Marion, 1869- 1944.

As the sunflower turns to the sun. [Song] Words by Richard Grant; music by Will Marion Cook. New York, Gotham music co. [c1904]
5 p. fol.

Score: medium solo voice [key of A♭] with piano accompaniment. English words.
Caption title.
In Bound Vol.

ABSpl
LC

*Cook, Will Marion, 1869- 1944.

Dinah. [Popular song] Lyric by *Alex Rogers; music by Will Marion Cook. New York, Gotham-Attucks music co. [c1907]
5 p. fol.

Score: medium solo voice with piano accompaniment. Negro dialect.
Caption title.
In bound vol.
Excerpt from the Negro musical comedy, "Bandana land." ABS

LC

*Cook, Will Marion, 1869-1944. Gems from "Clorindy" ... [c1898] (Card 2)

Contents: 1. Darktown is out tonight. -2. Love in a cottage is best. -3. Dance Creole. -4. Who dat say chicken in dis crowd. -5. Hottest coon in Dixie. -6. Jump back. -7. Clorindy two step (introducing "Hottest coon in Dixie" and "Darktown is out tonight.")

In bound vol.

ABSpl

*Cook, Will Marion, 1869-1944.

Bon bon buddy (The chocolate drop) [Popular song] Lyric by *Alex Rogers; music by Will Marion Cook. New York, Gotham-Attucks music co. [c1907]
5 p. fol.

Score: medium solo voice with piano accompaniment. Negro dialect.
Caption title.

Excerpt from the Negro musical comedy, "Bandana land."
ABSpl. YJWJ
LC

*Cook, Will Marion, 1869-1944.

...Down de lover's lane. (Plantation croon) Words by *Paul Laurence Dunbar. [From "Two Negro songs." Music by Will Marion Cook. New York, G. Schirmer, inc. [c1902] Publ. pl. no. 23719.
5 p. fol.

Score: medium solo voice with piano accompaniment. Negro dialect.
In bound vol.

ABSpl

*Cook, Will Mercer

Georgia Lee and me. [Popular song.] By Billy De. Beck, Mercer Cook and J. Russel Robinson. New York, De Sylva, Brown and Henderson, Inc. [c1932.]
3 p. fol.

Score: medium solo voice with piano accompaniment. English words.

ABSpl

*Cook, Will Marion, 1869-1944.

...Brown-skin baby mine. Words by Will Marion Cook and *Cecil Mack. [From] "Two Negro songs." Music by Will Marion Cook. New York, G. Schirmer, inc. [c1902] Publ. pl. no. 23820.
5 p. fol.

Score: medium solo voice with piano accompaniment. Negro dialect.
In bound vol.
Copyrighted in 1902 as "The little gipsy maid." Changed to Negro dialect in this edition. (See card)
ABSpl LC

*Cook, Will Marion, 1869- 1944.

Evah dahkey is a king. [Song] Words by E. P. Moran and *Paul Laurence Dunbar; music by John H. [sic] Cook.
(Music supplement of the New York American and Journal, Sunday, Oct. 26, 1902. p. 5-8. fol)

Score: medium solo voice with piano accompaniment.
In bound vol.
"As sung by *Williams and *Walker in *Dunbar and Cook's operetta, "In Dahomey." Published by permission of Harry von Tilzer music pub. co. owners of the copyright."
HPSpl ABS

*Cook, Will Marion, 1869-1944.

Good evenin'. [Song.] Words by *Paul Laurence Dunbar; music by Will Marion Cook. New York, Harry von Tilzer [c1902]
5 p. fol.

Score: medium solo voice with piano accompaniment.
Caption title.
In bound vol.

ABSpl
LC

*Cook, Will Marion, 1869-1944.

Clorindy two step (introducing "Hottest coon in Dixie" and "Darktown is out tonight.") From "Gems from 'Clorindy' or 'The origin of the cake-walk'." A Negro musical farce. Libretto by *Paul Laurence Dunbar; music by Will Marion [pseud.] New York, M. Witmark & sons [c1898] Publ. pl. no. 1371.
7 p. fol.

Score: piano solo.
In bound vol.

ABSpl

*Cook, Will Marion, 1869-1944.

...Exhortation (a Negro sermon). Words by *Alex Rogers. One of "Three Negro songs" by Will Marion Cook. New York, G. Schirmer, inc. [c1912] Publ. pl. no. 23763.
5 p. fol.

Score: low solo voice [key of A minor] with piano accompaniment. Negro dialect.
In bound vol.

ABSpl
ZWpl

*Cook, Will Marion, 1869- 1944.

Hottest coon in Dixie. [Song] Words by *Paul Laurence Dunbar; music by Will Marion [pseud.] New York, M. Witmark & sons [c1898]
5 p. fol.

Score: medium solo voice [key of G] with piano accompaniment. English words.
Caption title.
In bound vol.
Excerpt from the Negro musical show, "Clorindy."
ABSpl
LC

*Cook, Will Marion, 1869- 1944.

Creole Dance. [From] "Gems from 'Clorindy' or 'The origin of the cake-walk'." A Negro musical farce. Libretto by *Paul Laurence Dunbar; music by Will Marion [pseud.] New York, M. Witmark & sons [c1898] Publ. pl. no. 1850.
7 p. fol.

Score: piano solo.
In bound volume.

ABSpl

*Cook, Will Marion, 1869-1944.

An explanation. Characteristic Negro verses by *James Weldon Johnson; music by Will Marion Cook. New York, G. Schirmer [c1914] Publ. pl. no. 24889.
7 p. fol.

Score: high solo voice [key of C] with piano accompaniment. Negro dialect.
In bound vol.

ABSpl
ZWpl
HMC

*Cook, Will Marion, 1869-1944.

I'm coming Virginia. [Popular song] Words by Will Marion Cook; music by *Donald Heywood. New York, Robbins music corp. [c1927]
5 p. fol.

Score: medium solo voice [key of F] with piano accompaniment. English words.
In bound vol.

ABSpl

*Cook, Will Marion, 1869-1944 .

Darktown barbecue (Darktown was out at dat barbecue). [Song] Words and music by Will Marion Cook. New York, The York music co. [1904]
5 p. fol.

Score: medium solo voice with piano accompaniment. Negro dialect.
In bound vol.

ABSpl

*Cook, Will Marion, 1869-1944.

Gal o mine (Caroline). [Popular song] Lyric by *Cecil Mack; melody by Will Marion Cook. New York, Art music, inc. [c1918]
6 p. fol.

Score: medium solo voice [key of G] with piano accompaniment. English words.
In bound vol.

ABSpl

*Cook, Will Marion, 1869-1944.

In bandana land. [Popular song] Lyric by "Mord." Allen; music by Will Marion Cook. New York, Gotham-Attucks music co. [c1907]
5 p. fol.

Score: medium solo voice [key of G] with piano accompaniment. Negro dialect.
Caption title.

Excerpt from the Negro musical comedy, "Bandana land."
ABSpl
LC

*Cook, Will Marion, 1869-1944.

In de evenin'. [Popular song] Words by *Alex Rogers; music by Will Marion Cook. New York, Harry von Tilzer music pub. co. [c1910]
5 p. fol.

Score: medium solo voice [key of D] with piano accompaniment. Negro dialect.
In bound vol.

ABSpl

---

*Cook, Will Marion, 1869-1944.

It's allus de same in Dixie. Popular song; Words by Harry B. Smith; music by Will Marion Cook. New York, Gotham music co., inc. [c1904]
5 p. fol.

Score: medium solo voice [key of B^b] with piano accompaniment. Negro dialect.
Caption title.
In bound vol.

ABSpl
LC

---

*Cook, Will Marion, 1869-1944.

Julep song. "The good old mint julip for me." [Song] Words by Richard Grant; music by Will Marion Cook. [n.i.] c1904 by John H. Cook pub. co.
5 p. fol.

Score: low solo voice [key of B^b] with piano accompaniment. English words.
Caption title.
In bound vol.

LC
ABS

---

*Cook, Will Marion, 1869-1944.

Jump back. Negro love song. Words by *Paul Laurence Dunbar; music by Will Marion [pseud.] New York, M. Witmark & sons [c1898]
5 p. fol.

Score: medium solo voice [key of C] with piano accompaniment. Negro dialect.
Caption title.

Excerpt from the Negro musical show, "Clorindy."

ABSpl
LC

Cook, Will Marion
Just the Same

---

*Cook, Will Marion, 1869-1944.

...The little gypsy maid. [Song] Words by Harry B. Smith and *Cecil Mack. [pseud.]; music by Will Marion Cook. New York, Harry von Tilzer music co., c1902.
5 p. fol.

Score: medium solo voice [key of G] with piano accompaniment. English words.
Caption title.
In bound vol.

LC
ABS

---

*Cook, Will Marion, 1869-1944.

Love me with a tiger love... [Popular song] from "The deacon and the lady." Words by Addison Burkhardt; music by Will Marion Cook. New York, Harry von Tilzer music pub. co. [c1910]
5 p. fol.

Score: medium solo voice [key of G] with piano accompaniment. English words.
In bound vol.

ABSpl

---

*Cook, Will Marion, 1869-1944.
Lovie Joe. 1910.

In bound vol.

ABS

---

*Cook, Will Marion, 1869-1944.

...Mammy. Song. Words by *Lester A. Walton; music by Will Marion Cook. New York, Art music, inc. [c1916]
5 p. fol.

Score: medium solo voice [key of C] with piano accompaniment. Negro dialect.
In bound vol.

ABSpl

---

*Cook, Will Marion, 1869-1944.

Mammy's 'lasses candy chile. [Popular song] Words by *Cecil Mack; music by Will Marion Cook. New York, Shapiro music pub. [c1909]
5 p. 27 cm.

Score: medium solo voice [key of F] with piano accompaniment. Negro dialect.
In bound vol.

ABSpl
HMC

---

*Cook, Will Marion, 1869-1944.
Mandy Lou. 1905.

In bound vol.

ABS

---

*Cook, Will Marion, 1869-1944.

Molly Green. [Popular song] Words by *Cecil Mack [pseud.] music by Will Marion Cook. New York, Harry von Tilzer [c1902]
5 p. fol.

Score: medium solo voice [key of D] with piano accompaniment. English words.
Excerpt from the musical comedy, "In Dahomey."

LC
ABSpl

---

*Cook, Will Marion, 1869-1944.

My lady. [Song] Words by *Paul Laurence Dunbar, refrain by W. M. C.; music by Will Marion Cook. New York, G. Schirmer [c1914] Publ. pl. no. 24961
7 p. fol.

Score: high solo voice [key of G] with piano accompaniment. Negro dialect.

Dedicated "To the lady with the brown hair, red lips, black eyes and tender heart."
In bound vol.

BPL
ABSpl
LC

---

*Cook, Will Marion, 1869-1944.

My lady frog. [Song] Words and music by Will Marion Cook and *Will Accoe. New York, Harry von Tilzer music pub. co., 1902.
4 p. fol.

Score: medium solo voice [key of A^b] with piano accompaniment. English words.
Caption title.
In bound vol.

ABS
LC

---

*Cook, Will Marion, 1869-1944.

My lady's lips am like de honey. [Popular song] Words by *James Weldon Johnson; music by Will Marion Cook. New York, G. Schirmer [c1915] Publ. pl. no. 25558.
5 p. fol.

Score: medium solo voice [key of G] with piano accompaniment. Negro dialect.
In bound vol.

YJWJ
ABSpl

---

*Cook, Will Marion, 1869- 1944.

My little Irish canary (Mary Ann). [Popular song] Words by Andrew B. Sterling; music by Will Marion Cook. New York, Howley, Dresser & co. [c1904]
5 p. fol.

Score: medium solo voice [key of D] with piano accompaniment. English words.
Caption title.
In bound vol.

LC
ABSpl

---

*Cook, Will Marion, 1869-1944.

On Emancipation day. [Popular song] Words by *Paul Laurence Dunbar; music by Will Marion Cook. New York, Harry von Tilzer music pub. co. [c1902]
4 p. fol.

Score: medium solo voice with piano accompaniment. Negro dialect.
In bound vol.

ABS
LC HMC

---

*Cook, Will Marion, 1869-1944.

...The Pensacola mooch. [Popular song] By *Ford T. Dabney and Will Marion Cook. New York, Harry von Tilzer music publ co. [c1910]
5 p. fol.

Score: medium solo voice [key of G] with piano accompaniment. English words.
In bound vol.

ABSpl

---

*Cook, Will Marion, 1869-1944.

...Rain song. [Words by *Alex. Rogers; music] by Will Marion Cook... New York, G. Schirmer, [c1912] Publ. pl. no. 23595.
7 p. fol.

Score: high voice [key of E^b] with piano accompaniment. Negro dialect.
In bound vol.

ABS
HMC
NYPLS
LC

---

*Cook, Will Marion, 1869-1944.

Red, red rose. [Popular song] Words by *Alex Rogers; music by Will Marion Cook. New York, Gotham-Attucks music co. [c1908]
5 p. fol.

Score: medium solo voice [key of B^b] with piano accompaniment. English words.
Caption title.
In bound vol.

Excerpt from the Negro musical comedy, "Bandana land."

ABS
LC

---

*Cook, Will Marion, 1869-1944.

Returned; "Empty and so silent now the old cabin stands." [Song] Words by *Paul Laurence Dunbar; music by Will Marion Cook. Chicago, Harry von Tilzer,
4 p. fol.

Score: medium solo voice with piano accompaniment. English words.
In bound vol

YJWJ ABS
LC

*Cook, Will Marion, 1869- 1944.

Selections from "The Southerners" a musical romance Libretto and lyrics by Richard Grant and *Will Mercer; music by Will Marion Cook. New York, York music co. [c1904]
25 p. fol.

Score: medium solo voice with piano accompaniment.

Contents: -1. Julep song ("The good old mint julep for me.") -2. As the sunflower turns to the sun.

(continued on next card)

---

*Cook, Will Marion, 1869- 1944.

There's a place in the old vacant chair... Popular song. Words and music by Will Marion Cook. New York, Gotham music pub. co. [c1905]
5 p. fol.

Score: medium solo voice [key of G] with piano accompaniment. English words.

"To my mother." - At end of title.
In bound vol.

ABSpl

---

*Cook, Will Marion, 1869-1944.

Whoop 'er up! (with a whoop, la! la!) [Popular song] Words by Andrew B. Sterling; music by Will Marion Cook. New York, Harry von Tilzer music pub. co. [c1910]
5 p. fol.

Score: medium solo voice [key of E^b] with piano accompaniment. English words.
In bound vol.

"Sung with great success by Marie Cahill in Daniel V. Arthur's musical comedy production, "Judy forgot." - Cover title page.

ABSpl

---

*Cook, Will Marion, 1869-1944. Selections from "The Southerner" ... [c1904] (Card 2)

-3. Mandy Lou. -4. Where the lotus blossoms grow. -5. Darktown barbecue. -6. Allus the same in Dixie. -7. Lotus blossoms (characterisque) -8. Daisy Deane. -9. Dandy Dan. -10. Slumber song ("Sweet dreams, dear one, of thee") -11. Good evenin'.

ABSpl

---

*Cook, Will Marion, 1869-1944.

Three Negro songs. By Will Marion Cook. New York, G. Schirmer, inc. [c1912]
3 v. fol.

Scores: solo voice with piano accompaniment. Negro dialect.

ABSpl
ZWpl

---

*Cook, Will Marion. 1869-1944.

...Wid de moon, moon, moon. Negro love song. Words by William Moore; music by Will Marion Cook. Chicago, Will Marion Cook pub. (2700 State St.) [c1907]
6 p. fol.

Score: high solo voice [key of F] with piano accompaniment. Negro dialect.
In bound vol.

LC
ABSpl

---

*Cook, Will Marion, 1869-1944.

She's dancing Sue. [Song] Words by Charles S. Sager; music by Will Marion Cook and *Will Accoe. New York, Harry von Tilzer music pub. co., c1902.
5 p. fol.

Score: medium solo voice [key of G] with piano accompaniment. English words.
Caption title.
In bound vol.

LC
ABS

---

*Cook, Will Marion, 1869- 1944.

Three Negro songs by Will Marion Cook. New York, G. Schirmer, inc. [c1912] Publ. pl. no. 23763.
15 p. fol.

Score: solo voice with piano accompaniment. Negro dialect.

Contents: 1. Swing along. -2. Exhortation (a Negro sermon). -3. Rain song.

ABSpl

---

*Cooke, Charles L. 1891-1958.

Always in my dreams. [Popular song.] Lyric by Kack Yellen; music by Charles L. Cooke and Abe Olman. New York, Forster Music publ. inc., [c1921.]
5 p. fol.

Score: medium solo voice with piano accompaniment. English words.

ABSpl

---

*Cook, Will Marion, 1869-1944.

...Springtime. [Springtime is a comin'] Words by Phil. H. Armstrong; music by Will Marion Cook. New York, G. Schirmer [c1914] Publ. pl. no. 24933.
5 p. fol.

Score: high solo voice [key of A] with piano accompaniment. Negro dialect.
In bound vol.

ABSpl
HMC
LC

---

*Cook, Will Marion, 1869-1944.

...Troubled in mind. Negro spiritual arranged and adapted... [by] Will Marion Cook... words by *Mercer Cook. New York, G. Schirmer, inc. [c1929] Publ. pl. no. 34831.
5 p. fol.

Score: low solo voice [key of C^m] with piano accompaniment. Negro dialect.
In bound vol.

ABSpl
HMC
ZWpl

---

*Cooke, Charles L. 1891-1958.

Blame it on the blues. A weary blue [for piano] by Char. L. Cooke. New York, Jerome H. Remick & Co. [c1914]
5 p. fol.

Score: piano solo.

ABSpl

---

*Cook, Will Mercer

Stop the sun, stop the moon (My man's gone). [Popular song] By Harty Cook, J. Russel Robinson and Mercer Cook. New York, DeSylva, Brown & Henderson, inc. [c1932]
5 p. fol.

Score: medium solo voice with piano accompaniment. English words.

ABSpl

Cook, Will Marion
Until Then

---

*Cooke, Charles L 1891-1958.

Daisy days. [Popular song] Lyric by Gus Kahn; music by Walter Blaufuss and Chas. L. Cooke. New York, Jerome H. Remick & co. [c1921] Publ. pl. no. 2185.
5 p. fol.

Score: medium solo voice [key of A^b] with piano accompaniment. English words.

ABSpl

---

*Cook, Will Marion, 1869-1944.
Sweetie, Dear. 1906.

In bound vol.

ABS

---

*Cook, Will Marion, 1869-1944.

What would you be a-doing. From "The wild rose." [Popular song] Words by W. S. Estren and Eugene Parke; music by Will Marion Cook. New York, Harry von Tilzer music pub. co. [c1902]
5 p. fol.

Score: medium solo voice [key of E^b] with piano accompaniment. English words.

ABSpl
LC

---

*Cooke, Charles L 1891-1958.

Do you ever dream of me? [Popular song] By Dave Goldye and Chas. L. Cooke. Chicago, Ted Browne music co., inc. [c1925]
5 p. fol.

Score: medium solo voice [key of G] with piano accompaniment. English words.

ABSpl

---

*Cook, Will Marion, 1869-1944.

...Swing along. [Song] Words and music by Will Marion Cook... New York, G. Schirmer, inc. [c1912] Publ. pl. no. 23600.
7 p. fol.

Score: medium voice [key of E^b] with piano accompaniment. Negro dialect.
In bound vol.

ABSpl
HMC
LC

---

*Cook, Will Marion, 1869- 1944.

Who dat say chicken in dis crowd. [Song] Words by *Paul Laurence Dunbar; music by Will Marion [pseud.] New York, M. Witmark & sons [c1898] Publ. pl. no. 1320.
5 p. fol.

Score: medium solo voice [key of G] with piano accompaniment. Negro dialect.
Caption title.
In bound vol.

Excerpt from the Negro musical show, "Clorindy."

ABSpl
LC

---

*Cooke, Charles L 1891-1958.

The girl of the golden west. [Popular] song. Lyrics by Haven Gillespie; music by Egbert Van Alstyne and Charles L. Cooke... New York, Jerome H. Remick & co. [c1923] Publ. pl. no. 361.
5 p. fol.

Score: medium solo voice [key of G] with piano accompaniment. English words.

ABSpl

*Cooke, Charles L 1891-1958.

Goodbye pretty butterflies. ₍Popular song₎ Lyric by Jack Yellen; music by Chas. L. Cooke and Abe Olman. Chicago, Forster music pub., inc. ₍c1921₎
5 p. fol.

Score: medium solo voice ₍key of C₎ with piano accompaniment.

ABSpl

*Cooke, Charles L 1891-1958.

Lucy. A jazz waltz ₍for piano₎ By Egbert Van Alstyne; compiled and arranged by Chas. L. Cooke. New York, Jerome H. Remick & co. ₍c1919₎ Publ. pl. no. 763.
5 p. fol.

Score: piano solo.

ABSpl

*Cooke, Charles L, 1891-1958

On the Banda isles in the Banda sea. Oh me! Oh my! Oh me! ₍Popular song₎ By *Alonzo Govern and Chas. L. Cooke. New York, Handy Brothers music co., inc. ₍c1938₎
5 p. fol.

Score: medium solo voice with piano accompaniment. English words.

ABSpl

*Cooke, Charles L 1891-1958. arr.

Songs from Michael Todd's "Hot Mikado", the new musical hit based on the Gilbert and Sullivan classic Modern rhythm adaptations by Charles L. Cooke. New York, Robbins Music Corp. ₍c1939₎
28 p. fol.

Score: medium solo voice with piano accompaniment. English words.
Contents: A wond'ring minstrel, I.
"I", the living "I"
I've got 'em on the list
Let the punishment fit the crime
The flowers that bloom in the spring

ABSpl

*Cooke, Charles L 1891-1958, arr. ...

Songs from Michael Todd's "Hot Mikado" ... New York, Robbins Music Corp. ₍c1939₎ (card 2)

Contents: Three little maids from school are we
Tit-willow

ABSpl

*Cooke, Charles L 1891-1958.

Such is life. Rag fox trot ₍for piano₎. By Chas. L. Cooke. New York, Jerome H. Remick & co. ₍c1915.₎ Publ. pl. no. 167.
5 p. fol. (Popular edition)

Score: piano solo.

ABSpl

*Creamer, Henry S 1879-

After you've gone. ₍Popular song₎ By ₍Henry Creamer₎ and ₍*Turner₎ Layton. New York, Triangle music pub. co. ₍c1929₎
5p. fol.

Score: medium solo voice with piano accompaniment. English words.

ABSpl
LC

*Creamer, Henry S 1879-

...Come along. I'm through with worryin.' "Featured in Ziegfeld Follies, 1922." ₍Popular song₎ By ₍Henry₎ Creamer and ₍Turner₎ Layton. New York, Irving Berlin, inc. ₍c1922₎
7p. fol. (operatic edition)

Score: medium solo voice with piano accompaniment. English words. With ad lib. S A chorus arrangement to accompany solo voice in verse.

ABSpl
LC

*Creamer, Henry S 1879-

The cute little wifflin' dance. ₍Popular song₎ By Henry Creamer and *J. Turner Layton. New York, Broadway music corp. ₍c1917₎
3p. fol.

Score: medium solo voice with piano accompaniment. English words.

LC
ABSpl

*Creamer, Henry S 1879-

Everybody's crazy (bout thedoggone blues but I'm happy... ₍Popular song₎ By ₍Henry₎ Creamer and ₍Turner₎ Layton. New York, Broadway music corp. ₍c1918₎
3p. fol.

Score: medium solo voice with piano accompaniment. English words.

"The instantaneous hit, sung by *Bert Williams in the Ziegfeld Follies, 1917-18." - at end of title.

ABSpl

*Creamer, Henry S 1879-

Goodbye Alexander. Good-bye honey-boy. ₍Popular song₎ By ₍Henry₎ Creamer and *Turner Layton. New York, Broadway music corp. ₍c1918₎
3p. fol.

Score: medium solo voice with piano accompaniment. English words.

A war song.

ABSpl

*Creamer, Henry S 1879-

I can't let 'em suffer (for the want of love.)

₍Popular song₎ By ₍Henry₎ Creamer and Turner Layton. New York, Broadway music corp. ₍c1918₎
3p. fol.

Score: medium solo voice with piano accompaniment. English words.

ABSpl

*Creamer, Henry S 1879-

I need lovin'. ₍Popular₎ song. By Henry Creamer and *Jimmy Johnson. New York, Jerome H. Remick & co. ₍c1926₎ Publ. pl. no. 274.
5 p. fol.

Score: medium solo voice ₍key of G₎ with piano accompaniment. English words.

ABSpl
YJWJ

*Creamer, Henry S 1879-

I'll sing you a song about dear old Dixie land. Novelty song... By ₍Henry₎ Creamer and ₍*Turner₎ Layton. New York, M. Witmark and sons, ₍c1919₎ publ. pl. no. M. W. and sons 16042.
5p. fol.

Score: medium solo voice with piano accompaniment. English words.

LC
ABSpl

Creamer, Henry S
I'm waiting for you Liza Jane

*Creamer, Henry S , 1879-

Its always the fault of the man. ₍Popular song₎ By Henry S. Creamer and *Turner Layton. New York, Charles K. Harris, publ. ₍c19..₎
5p. fol.

Score: medium solo voice with piano accompaniment. English words.
Caption title

Excerpt from the musical comedy, "Three showers."

LC
ABSpl

*Creamer, Henry S , 1879-

Look what you've done. ₍Popular song₎ By Henry Creamer and ₍Turner₎ Layton. New York, Broadway music corp., ₍c1918₎
5p. fol.

Score: medium solo voice with piano accompaniment. English words.

ABSpl

*Creamer, Henry S , 1879-

Meet me when the stars am shining. ₍Popular song₎ By ₍Henry₎ Creamer and ₍Turner₎ Layton. New York, Broadway music corp. ₍c1919₎
3p. fol.

Score: medium solo voice with piano accompaniment. Negro dialect.

ABSpl

*Creamer, Henry S , 1879

Oh! Lawdy. (Something's done got between Ebaneezer and me) ₍Popular song₎ By ₍*Henry₎ Creamer and ₍Turner₎ Layton. New York, Broadway music corp. ₍c1919₎
3p. fol.

Score: medium solo voice with piano accompaniment. English words.

LC
ABSpl

*Creamer, Henry S , 1879-

One and two and three and four rock-a-bye. ₍Popular song.₎ By ₍Henry₎ Creamer and ₍Turner₎ Layton. New York, Broadway music corp. ₍c1919₎
3p. fol.

Score: medium solo voice with piano accompaniment. English words.

LC
ABSpl

*Creamer, Henry S 1879-

Show me how. ₍Popular song₎ By *Henry Creamer and *Turner Layton. New York, Charles K. Harris publisher. ₍c1920₎
5p. fol.

Score: medium solo voice with piano accompaniment. English words.

ABSpl

*Creamer, Henry S 1879-

Somebody love me. Fox-trot ballad. By Henry Creamer and *Turner Layton...New York, Charles K. Harris publisher. [c1922]
5p. fol.

Score: medium solo voice with piano accompaniment. English words.

ABSpl

---

*Creamer, Henry S 1879-

Sweet Emalina, my gal. [Popular song] Words and music by Henry Creamer and [Turner] Layton. New York, Broadway music corp. [c1917]
3p. fol.

Score: medium solo voice with piano accompaniment. English words.

ABSpl
HMC

---

*Creamer, Henry S 1879-

Sweet 'n pretty. [Popular song.] By Henry Creamer and *Turner Layton. New York, Broadway music corp. [c1918]
5p. fol.

Score: medium solo voice with piano accompaniment. English words.

ABS
ABSpl

---

*Creamer, Henry S 1879-

That's it. Fox trot [for piano] By Henry Creamer and *Turner Layton. New York, Artmusic, inc. [c1917]
6p. fol.

Score: piano solo

LC
ABSpl

---

*Creamer, Henry

There's a rainbow in the sky. [Popular song] Words and music by *Henry Creamer and Turner Layton. New York: Waterson, Berlin & Snyder co. [c1922] Publ. pl. no. 1257.
5 p. fol.

Score: medium solo voice with piano accompaniment. English words.

ABSpl

---

*Creamer, Henry S 1879-

'Way down yonder in New Orleans [Popular song] ... Lyrics by *Henry Creamer; music by Turner Layton. New York: Shapiro, Bernstein & co. [c1922]
5 p. fol.

Score: medium solo voice with piano accompaniment. English words.

"Creole Producing Co. presents 'Strut Miss Lizzie' with Creamer and Layton and all star Creole cast at the Times Square Theater, New York." at end of title.

ABSpl

Creamer, Henry S

Whoa, Tillie, take your time

Creamer, Henry S

With the coming of tomorrow

---

*Crowdus, Reuben Ernest, 1865-1909.

...All coons look alike to me. [Minstrel song] Words and music by Ernest Hogan [pseud.] New York, M. Witmark & sons [c1906]
6 p. fol.

Score: medium solo voice [key of F] with piano accompaniment. Negro dialect.

"May Irwin's new coon song hits... sung by her in the successful comedy, 'Courted into court'." - Title page.

ABSpl

---

*Crowdus, Reuben Ernest, 1865-1909.

...De congregation will please keep their seats (Kase dis bird am mine) [Minstrel song] by Ernest Hogan [pseud.] New York, M. Witmark & sons [c1900] Publ. pl. no. 2287.
6 p. fol.

Score: low solo voice [key of F] with piano accompaniment. Negro dialect.

LC
ABSpl

---

*Crowdus, Reuben Ernest, 1865-1909.

...Contribution box. [Minstrel song] Words by *Henry S. Creamer; music by *Will H. Vodery and Ernest Hogan [pseud.] New York, M. Witmark & sons [c1907] Publ. pl. no. M.W. & sons 8090.
5 p. fol.

Score: high solo voice [key of F] with piano accompaniment. English words.

Excerpt from "The Oyster man," musical comedy.

ABSpl
LC

---

*Crowdus, Reuben Ernest, 1865-1909.

He may get over it, but he'll never look the same. [Popular song] By Hogan [pseud.] Steely and Coe. New York, Jos. W. Stern & co. [c1903] Publ. pl. no. 3689.
6 p. fol.

Score: low solo voice [key of F] with piano accompaniment. English words.

ABSpl
LC

---

*Crowdus, Reuben Ernest, 1865-1909.

...He used to be a friend of mine. [Minstrel song] Words by Wm. Murray; music by Ernest Hogan [pseud.] New York, Sol Bloom [c1902]
5 p. fol.

Score: medium solo voice [key of F] with piano accompaniment. Negro dialect.

ABSpl
LC

---

*Crowdus, Reuben Ernest, 1865-1909.

Is everybody happy? [Popular song] Words by Frank Williams; music by Ernest Hogan [pseud.] and *Tom Lemonier. Chicago, Chas. K. Harris, [c1905]
6 p. fol.

Score: medium solo voice [key of G] with piano accompaniment. Negro dialect.

"...From the musical production 'Rufus Rastus'." - Title page.

ABSpl
LC NBCL (with full orchestra accompaniment

---

*Crowdus, Reuben Ernest, 1865-1909.

La Pas Ma La. [Minstrel song] Words and music by Ernest Hogan [pseud.] Kansas City, Mo., J. R. Bell [c1895]
5 p. fol.

Score: medium solo voice [key of C] with piano accompaniment. Negro dialect.

ABSpl
LC

---

*Crowdus, Reuben Ernest, 1865-1909.

Mina. [Popular song] Words by *Henry S. Creamer; music by *Will H. Vodery and *Ernest Hogan [psued.] New York, M. Witmark & sons [c1907] Publ. pl. no. M.W. & sons 8097.
5 p. fol.

Score: low solo voice [key of F] with piano accompaniment. English words.

From "The Oyster man," musical comedy.

ABSpl

---

*Crowdus, Reuben Ernest, 1865-1909.

The missionary man. [Minstrel song] Words by Steve Cassin; music by Ernest Hogan [pseud.] New York, Jos. W. Stern & co. [c1902] Publ. pl. no. 3465.
6 p. fol.

Score: medium solo voice [key of F] with piano accompaniment. Negro dialect.

"Words and music by Ernest Hogan introduced by Gus Hill's Smart Set Co in 'Enchantment'."

(continued on next card)

---

*Crowdus, Reuben Ernest, 1865-1909. The missionary man... New York [c1902] (Card 2)

Portrait inset of *Mattie Wilkes, "The phenomenal soprano."

ABSpl
LC

---

*Crowdus, Reuben Ernest, 1865-1909.

...My little jungle queen. A Congo love song. Words by Jas. O'Dea; written and composed by Ernest Hogan [pseud.] and Theo. H. Northrup. New York, Jos. W. Stern & co. [c1900] Publ. pl. no. 3072.
5 p. fol.

Score: medium solo voice [key of F] with piano accompaniment. Negro dialect.

ABSpl
LC

---

*Crowdus, Reuben Ernest, 1865-1909.

My sweet Moana. [Popular song] Words by *Billy McClain; music by Ernest Hogan [pseud.] New York, Jos. W. Stern & co. [c1902] Publ. pl. no. 3404.
5 p. fol.

Score: medium solo voice [key of B♭] with piano accompaniment. English words.

"Introduced by The Smart Set Co in 'Enchantment'." - Title page.

ABSpl

---

*Crowdus, Reuben Ernest, 1865-1909.

"Obadiah" (You took de'vantage of me). [Popular song] By Ernest Hogan [pseud.] and *James Reese Europe. New York, The Gotham music pub. co. [c1905]
5 p. fol.

Score: medium solo voice [key of G] with piano accompaniment. Negro dialect.

ABSpl

*Crowdus, Reuben Ernest, 1865-1909.

...R-A-Z-O-R, dat am a black man's friend. [Minstrel song] Words by Billy Clark; music by Ernest Hogan [pseud.] New York, Helf and Hager co. [c1904]
5 p. fol.

Score: medium solo voice [key of G] with piano accompaniment. Negro dialect.

"In time of peace, prepare for war." - Head of title.

ABSpl
LC

---

*Crowdus, Reuben Ernest, 1865-1909.

Roll on, Mr. Moon. [Minstrel song] By Ernest Hogan [pseud.] New York, Jos. W. Stern & co. [c1902] Publ. pl. no. 3406.
5 p. fol.

Score: medium solo voice [key of D] with piano accompaniment. English words.

"By *Billy McClain and Ernest Hogan" as produced in The Smart Set in "Enchantment." - Cover title-page.

ABSpl
LC

---

*Crowdus, Reuben Ernest, 1865-1909.

'Taint no disgrace to run when you're skeered. [Popular song] Words by James Burris; music by Ernest Hogan peeud. and *Chris. Smith. New York, Whitney-Warner pub. co. [c1903]
6 p. fol.

Score: medium solo voice [key of A^b] with piano accompaniment. English words.

ABSpl

---

*Crowdus, Reuben Ernest, 1865-1909.

...Wink, wink, wink, Mr. Owl. [Minstrel song] Lyrics by Jas. O'Dea; written and composed by Ernest Hogan [pseud.] and Teho. H. Northrup. New York, Jos. W. Stern & co. [c1900] Publ. pl. no. 3103.
5 p. fol.

Score: medium solo voice [key of E^b] with piano accompaniment. English words.

"Introduced at the New York Theatre with special scenery and electrical effects by the popular female baritone Emma Carus." - Head of title.

ABSpl LC

---

*Dabney, Ford T 1883-

Anoma. Characteristic rag. By Ford Dabney. New York, Jerome H. Remick and co. [c1910]
5 p. fol.

Score: piano solo.

ABSpl LC

---

*Dabney, Ford T 1883-

Call me dear. [Song] Words by *Henry S. Creamer; music by Ford T. Dabney. New York, Francis, Day & Hunter, c1908. Publ. pl. no. F. D. & H. 401.
5 p. fol.

Score: low solo voice [key of B^b] with piano accompaniment. English words.

ABSpl

---

*Dabney, Ford T 1883-
Europe, James Reese
Castle innovation tango. (Argentine tango). [For piano] By *James Reese Europe and Ford T. Dabney. New York, Jos. W. Stern & co. [1914] Publ. pl. no. 7766.
5 p. fol.

Score: piano solo.

ABSpl

---

*Dabney, Ford T 1883-
Europe, James Reese
Castle lame duck waltz. [For piano] By *James Reese Europe and Ford T. Dabney. New York, Jos. W. Stern & co. [c1914] Publ. pl. no. 7785.
5 p. fol.

Score: piano solo.

ABSpl

---

*Dabney, Ford T 1883-
Europe, Reese
Castles' half and half. [For piano] By *James Reese Europe and Ford T. Dabney. New York, Jos. W. Stern & co. [1914] Publ. pl. no. 7764.
5 p. fol.

Score: piano solo.

ABSpl

---

*Dabney, Ford T 1883-

The Georgia grind. [For piano] By Ford T. Dabney. New York, Jos. W. Stern & co. [c1915] Publ. pl. no. 7963.
5 p. fol.

Score: piano solo.

ABSpl

---

*Dabney, Ford T 1883-

Jungle rose. Fox-trot song. Lyric by *"Jo' Trent; music by Ford Dabney. New York, Leo Feist, inc. [c1927] Publ. pl. no. 5987.
5 p. fol.

Score: high solo voice [key of B^b] with piano accompaniment. English words.

ABSpl

Dabney, Ford T
The Last Waltz

---

*Dabney, Ford T 1883-

Oh! You angel (Rag) [for piano] ... by Ford T Dabney. New York, Shapiro music publisher. [c1911]
5 p. fol.

Score: piano solo

Composer given as Fred Dabney on page 2. (Pages 3 & 4 missing)

ABSpl

---

*Dabney, Ford T 1883-

Oh! you devil. Rag. Composed by Ford T. Dabney. New York, Shapiro music pub. [c1909]
5 p. fol.

Score: piano solo.

"As intorduced by Aida Overton Walker, America's foremost colored comedienne" — at end of title. (Cover title page has photograph of Aida Overton Walker in costume.)

ABSpl LC

---

*Dabney, Ford T 1883-

Porto Rico. Rag-intermezzo [for piano] Composed by Ford T. Dabney. New York, Shapiro music pub. [c1910]
5 p. fol.

Score: piano solo.

ABSpl

---

*Dabney, Ford T 1883-

S-H-I-N-E. [Popular song] Words by *Cecil Mack, pseud. and Lew Brown; music by Ford Dabney. New York, Shapiro, Bernstein and co., [c1924]
3 p. fol.

Score: medium solo voice [key of E^b] with piano accompaniment. English words.

ABSpl
LC

---

*Dabney, Ford T 1883-

That minor strain. [Popular song] Words by *Cecil Mack; music by Ford Dabney. New York, Gotham-Attucks music co. [c1910]
5 p. fol.

Score: medium solo voice [key of G] with piano accompaniment. English words.

Sung by *Bert Williams in Ziegfeld's "Follies of 1910."

ABSpl

---

*Dabney, Wendell Phillips, 1886-

Baby chile. Song. Words and music by W. P. Dabney... Cincinnati, O., Dabney publ. co. [c1924]
3 p. fol.

Score: low solo voice [key of G] with piano accompaniment. English words.

ABSpl

---

*Dabney, Wendell Phillips, 1886-

God our Father. A prayer [Song] Words and music by Wendell P. Dabney... Cincinnati, O., Dabney music co. [c1904]
3 p. fol.

Score: verse, medium solo voice with piano accompaniment; chorus, SATB. English words.

ABSpl - Inscribed to Mr. Spingarn by the composer as of 1/8/39.

---

*Dabney, Wendell Phillips, 1886-

If you must be caught. [Popular song] Words and music by Wendell Phillips Dabney... Cincinnati, O., Dabney pub. co. [c1920]
3 p. fol.

Score: medium solo voice [key of E^b] with piano accompaniment. English words.

Arranged by Artie Matthews.

ABSpl

---

*Dabney, Wendell Phillips, 1886-

...Lonely tonight. [Song] Poem by W. P. D.; music by W. P. Dabney. Cincinnati, O., Geo. Jaberg music co. [c1894]
5 p. fol.

Score: high solo voice [key of G] with piano accompaniment. English words.

ABSpl
LC
NYPLS

*Dabney, Wendell Phillips, 1886-

...March overture for the piano-forte. By W. P. Dabney. Richmond, Va., Walter D. Moses & co., c1889.
5 p. fol.

Score: piano solo.

ABSpl
NYPLS

---

*Dabney, Wendell Phillips, 1886-

My old sweetheart. Song. Words and music by W. P. Dabney. Cincinnati, O., Dabney publishing co. [c1921]
3 p. fol.

Score: high solo voice [key of G] with piano accompaniment. English words.

ABSpl
NYPLS.

---

*Dabney, Wendell Phillips, 1886-

... That old leathern trunk. A ballad for middle voice. Words and music by W. P. Dabney. Richmond, Va., Walter D. Moses & co., c1893.
5 p. fol.

Score: high solo voice [key of A^b] with piano accompaniment. English words.

ABSpl
LC
NYPLS

---

*Dabney, Wendell Phillips, 1886-

...You will miss the colored soldiers... [Song] Words and music by W. P. Dabney. Cincinnati, O., Dabney pub. co. [c1907]
5 p. fol.

Score: medium solo voice [key of F] with piano accompaniment. English words.

ABSpl
LC

Dacre, Harry

I can't think ob nothin' else but you. (Luli Lu) Words and music by Harry Dacre. New York, Jos. W. Stern & co. [c1896] Publ. pl. no. 587.
(In Ten choice Negro folksongs for voice and pianoforte. New York, [n.d.] p. 18-20.)

Score: medium solo voice [key of G] with piano accompaniment. Negro dialect.

ABSpl
BHC

---

*Davis, Blevins

"How do I love thee" Sonnet XLIII of poem by Elizabeth Barrett Browning; musical setting by Blevins Davis. New York, *Handy Brothers Music Co., Inc. [c1936]
5 p. fol.

Score: medium solo voice with piano accompaniment. English words.

ABSpl

---

*Davis, Gussie Lord, 1863-1899.

...Baby's laughing in her sleep. [Song] Words and music by Gussie L. Davis... New York, George Propheter, jr. publisher [c1886]
5 p. fol.

Score: verse, medium solo voice with piano accompaniment; chorus, SATB. English words.

ABSpl

---

*Davis, Gussie Lord, 1863-1899.

Beyond pardon - beyond recall. Song with waltz refrain. Written and composed by Gussie L. Davis... New York, W. B. Gray & co. [c1894]
5 p. fol.

Score: medium solo voice [key of B^b] with piano accompaniment. English words.

ABSpl

---

*Davis, Gussie Lord, 1863-1899.

Clime up de ladder to de clouds. Ethiopian song composed by Gussie L. Davis. New York, Hitchcock and McCargo publ. co., l'td. [c1891]
5 p. fol.

Score: high solo voice [key of A^b] with piano accompaniment. Negro dialect.

ABSpl
LC

Davis, Gussie Lord

Dance Picaninnies, Dance

---

*Davis, Gussie Lord, 1863-1899.

Dig away, Dempsey, dig away. [Song] Words and music by Gussie L. Davis. New York, Howley, Haviland & co. [c1898]
5 p. fol.

Score: high solo voice [key of E^b] with piano accompaniment. English words.

ABSpl
LC

---

*Davis, Gussie Lord, 1863-1899.

..."Down in poverty row." [Popular song] Words by Gussie L. Davis; music by Arthur Trevelyan. New York, Jos. W. Stern & co. [c1896]
5 p. fol.

Score: medium solo voice [key of G] with piano accompaniment. English words.

ABSpl

---

*Davis, Gussie Lord, 1863-1899.

...Every day at the station. Descriptive song and chorus. By Gussie L. Davis. New York, Carleton Cavanagh & co. [c1897]
5 p. fol.

Score: high solo voice [key of E^b] with piano accompaniment. English words.

ABSpl

---

*Davis, Gussie Lord, 1863-1899.

...Fair Virginia from Virginia. Song and chorus. By Raymond A. Browne and Gussie L. Davis... New York, Howley, Haviland & co. [c1899]
5 p. fol.

Score: medium solo voice [key of A^b] with piano accompaniment. English words.

ABSpl

---

*Davis, Gussie Lord, 1863-1899.

...The fatal wedding... [Descriptive waltz song] Words by Wm. H. Windom; music by Gussie L. Davis. New York, Spaulding & Gray [c1893]
5 p. fol.

Score: medium solo voice [key of G] with piano accompaniment. English words.

ABSpl

---

*Davis, Gussie Lord, 1863-1899.

...The girl I love, loves me. [Popular song] Words and music by Gussie L. Davis. Chicago, Will Rossiter, c1896.
5 p. fol.

Score: medium solo voice [key of G] with piano accompaniment. English words.

ABSpl

---

*Davis, Gussie Lord, 1863-1899.

Have pity judge, she's my mother. Song and chorus. Composed by Gussie L. Davis. New York, Hamilton S. Gordon, c1898. Publ. pl. no. 11152.
5 p. fol.

Score: medium solo voice [key of A^b] with piano accompaniment. English words.

ABSpl

---

*Davis, Gussie Lord, 1863-1899.

..."He carved his mother's name upon the tree." [Song] Words by Henry V. Neal; music by Gussie L. Davis. New York, Feist & Frankenthaler [c1899]
5 p. fol.

Score: medium solo voice [key of B^b] with piano accompaniment. English words.

ABSpl

---

*Davis, Gussie Lord, 1863-1899.

Hold out dat light! Comic [minstrel] song and chorus by Gussie L. Davis. Brooklyn, N. Y., Chas. W. Held, c1891. Publ. pl. no. 146.
5 p. fol.

Score: high solo voice [key of F] with piano accompaniment. Negro dialect.

ABSpl
LC

---

*Davis, Gussie Lord, 1863-1899.

Hold your temper Casey! Comic song and chorus. By Gussie L. Davis... New York, Spaulding & Gray [c1894]
5 p. fol.

Score: medium solo voice [key of F] with piano accompaniment. English words.

ABSpl
LC

---

*Davis, Gussie Lord, 1863-1899.

In the baggage coach ahead. Song and refrain. Words and music by Gussie L. Davis. New York, Edward B. Marks music co. [c1932] Publ. pl. no. 9317.
5 p. fol.

Score: medium solo voice [key of A^b] with piano accompaniment. English words.

ABSpl

*Davis, Gussie Lord, 1863-1899. In the baggage coach ahead... [c1896] (Card 2)

mandolins, guitar and piano; mandolin solo; mandolin and guitar; two mandolins and guitar; orchestra accompaniment to song; waltz orchestra, 10 parts and piano and 14 parts and piano.

ABSpl

*Davis, Gussie Lord, 1863-1899.

Mine alone. Song with waltz refrain. Words and music by Gussie L. Davis... New York, W. B. Gray & co. [c1895]
5 p. fol.

Score: high solo voice [key of G] with piano accompaniment. English words.

ABSpl
LC

*Davis, Gussie Lord, 1863-1899.

...There's always a home for you. Song and chorus. Words and music by Gussie L. Davis... New York, W. B. Gray & co. [c1899]
6 p. fol.

Score: medium solo voice [key of G] with piano accompaniment. English words.

ABSpl

*Davis, Gussie Lord, 1863-1899.

It's a good thing, push it along! Topical song and chorus. Words and music by Gussie L. Davis. New York, Spaulding & Gray [c1894]
5 p. fol.

Score: high solo voice [key of E^b] with piano accompaniment. English words.

ABSpl

*Davis, Gussie Lord, 1863-1899.

My Creole Sue. [Popular song] Words and music by Gussie L. Davis. New York, Hamilton S. Gordon, c1898. Publ. pl. no. 11153.
5 p. fol.

Score: verse, medium solo voice with piano accompaniment; chorus SATB. English words.

ABSpl

*Davis, Gussie Lord, 1863-1899.

Trusting only you. [Song] By Gussie L. Davis. New York, Howley, Haviland & co. [c1896]
5 p. fol.

Score: medium solo voice [key of E^b] with piano accompaniment. English words.

ABSpl

*Davis, Gussie Lord, 1863-1899.

...Just a sorter hangin' roun'. Song and chorus. Words by Nita A. Pierson; music by Gussie L. Davis... New York, Howley, Haviland & co. [c1898]
5 p. fol.

Score: medium solo voice [key of E^b] with piano accompaniment. Negro dialect.

"Music for April." - Head of title.

ABSpl
LC

*Davis, Gussie Lord, 1863-1899.

The mystery of the village. Descriptive song and refrain. Words and music by Gussie L. Davis... New York, New York music co. [c1894]
5 p. fol.

Score: high solo voice [key of F] with piano accompaniment. English words.

ABSpl

*Davis, Gussie Lord, 1863-1899.

..."T'was a sad trip coming back." [Song] Words and music by Gussie L. Davis... New York, Spaulding & Gray [c1895]
5 p. fol.

Score: medium solo voice [key of A^b] with piano accompaniment. English words.

ABSpl

*Davis, Gussie Lord, 1863-1899.

The last kiss grandma gave me. Song and chorus. Words by Edgar Seldon; music by Gussie L. Davis. London, C. Sheard & co. Copyrighted, no date given.
6 p. fol.

Score: medium solo voice [key of G] with piano accompaniment. English words.

ABSpl

*Davis, Gussie Lord, 1863-1899.

Only a Bowery boy. (A true picture of Bowery life) [Song] Words by Chas. B. Ward; music by Gussie L. Davis... New York, New York music co., c1894.
5 p. fol.

Score: high solo voice [key of E^b] with piano accompaniment. English words.

ABSpl

*Davis, Gussie Lord, 1863-1899.

...We sat beneath the maple on the hill. Song and chorus. By Gussie L. Davis... Cincinnati, O., F. W. Helmick, c1880.
5 p. fol.

Score: verse, low solo voice with piano accompaniment; chorus, SATB. English words.

ABSpl
LC

*Davis, Gussie Lord, 1863-1899.

The light-house by the sea. [Song] Words and music by Gussie L. Davis; arranged for guitar by Will Foden. Cincinnati, O., J. C. Groene & co., c1887.
6 p. fol.

Score: verse, medium solo voice; chorus, SATB, with guitar accompaniment. English words.

ABSpl

*Davis, Gussie Lord, 1863-1899.

...The pastor's resignation. Descriptive song by Gussie L. Davis... New York, W. B. Gray & co. [c1895]
5 p. fol.

Score: medium solo voice [key of E^b] with piano accompaniment. English words.

ABSpl

*Davis, Gussie Lord, 1863-1899.

...When the mighty ship begins to roll. Negro song and chorus. Music and words by Gussie L. Davis... New York, W. B. Gray & co. [c1898]
6 p. fol.

Score: medium solo voice [key of D] with piano accompaniment. English words.

ABSpl

*Davis, Gussie Lord, 1863-1899.

...Mamma, does you love your honey? [Minstrel song and chorus. Words by Henry Wise; music; by Gussie L. Davis. New York, Spaulding & Gray [c1894]
5 p. fol.

Score: medium solo voice [key of E] with piano accompaniment. Negro dialect.

ABSpl
LC

*Davis, Gussie Lord, 1863-1899.

Picture 84. Descriptive song and refrain. Words by Chas. B. Ward; music by Gussie L. Davis. New York, T. B. Harms & co. [c1894]
5 p. fol.

Score: medium solo voice [key of B^b] with piano accompaniment. English words.

ABSpl

*Davis, Gussie Lord, 1863-1899.

...Won't you take me back to Dixie. [Minstrel song] Written by Gussie L. Davis; words and music revised by Edw. B. Marks and Geo. Rosey. New York, Jos. W. Stern & co. [c1899]
5 p. fol.

Score: low solo voice [key of F] with piano accompaniment. English words.

ABSpl

*Davis, Gussie Lord, 1863-1899.

...The midway in the moon. [Song and chorus] Words and music by Gussie L. Davis... New York, Spaulding & Gray [c1895]
5 p. fol.

Score: medium solo voice [key of G] with piano accompaniment. English words.

ABSpl
LC

*Davis, Gussie Lord, 1863-1899.

Sing again that sweet refrain. Or, Far from the old folks at home. [Song] Words and music by Gussie L. Davis... New York, W. B. Gray & co. [c1894]
6 p. fol.

Score: medium solo voice [key of E^b] with piano accompaniment. English words.

Also arranged for mandolin and piano; mandolin solo; mandolin and guitar; male quartette; banjo solo; zither; and guitar with voice.

ABSpl

*Dawson, William Levi, 1899-

Ain' - a that good news. Negro spiritual; arranged by William L. Dawson. Tuskegee Institute, Ala., Music press [c1937]
8 p. 8 vo. (Tuskegee choir series, no. 104.)

Score: TTBB, with piano reduction, for rehearsal only. Negro dialect.

ABSpl HMC LC

*Dawson, William Levi, 1899-

...Forever thine. Song. Words and music by William L. Dawson. Tuskegee Institute. Alabama, William L. Dawson pub. [c1920]
5 p. fol.

Score: medium solo voice with piano accompaniment [key of A♭] English words.

ABSpl

---

*Dawson, William Levi, 1899-

Go to sleep. Lullaby. Words by *Vernon N. Ray; music by William L. Dawson. Chicago, H. T. FitzSimons pub. [c1926] Publ. pl. no. 1006.
5 p. 8° (Aeolian series of choral music)

Score: SATB, with piano reduction for rehearsal only. English words.

ABSpl

---

*Dawson, William Levi, 1899-

I couldn't hear nobody pray. Negro spiritual; arranged by William L. Dawson. Chicago, H. T. FitzSimons pub. [c1926] Publ. pl. no. 2008.
7 p. 8° (Aeolian series of choral music)

Score: SATB, and soprano solo, with piano accompaniment for rehearsal only. Negro dialect.

ABSpl

---

*Dawson, William Levi, 1899-

...Jesus walked this lonesome valley. Negro spiritual. From the singing of my cousin, Mrs. *Blanche Dawson-Roney, Tuskegee Institute, Ala.; arranged by William L. Dawson. Chicago, Gamble hinged music co. [c1927] Publ. pl. no. 818.
5 p. fol.

Score: low solo tenor with piano accompaniment. [key of E♭] Negro dialect.
Caption title.

ABSpl LC ZWpl

---

*Dawson, William Levi, 1899-

King Jesus is a-listening. Negro folk-song; arranged by William L. Dawson. Chicago, H. T. FitzSimons pub. [c1925] Publ. pl. no. 2004.
7 p. 8° (Aeolian series of choral music)

Score: SATB, with piano reduction for rehearsal only. Negro dialect.

ABSpl

---

*Dawson, William Levi, 1899-

The mongrel Yank ("A Yankee is a mixture of many races"). Poem by Allen Quade; music by William L. Dawson, Opus 6. Chicago, Gamble hinged music co. [c1930] Publ. pl. no. 939.
14 p. 8°. (Gamble's collection of secular part songs for men's voices).

Score: TTBB with piano accompaniment. English words.

ABSpl

---

*Dawson, William Levi, 1899-

...My Lord what a mourning. Negro spiritual. Text from St. Matthew 24: 29; music arranged by William L. Dawson. Chicago, H. T. FitzSimons pub. [c1927]
5 p. fol.

Score: low solo voice [key of D] with piano accompaniment. English words.

Dedicated to Miss *Marian Anderson.

ABSpl

---

*Dawson, William Levi, 1899-

Oh, what a beautiful city. [Negro spiritual for mixed chorus] Edited and arranged by William L. Dawson. Tuskegee Institute, Ala., Music press [c1934]
11 p. 8° (Tuskegee choir series, no. 100.)

Score: SATB, with piano reduction for rehearsal only. Negro dialect.

ABSpl LC HMC ZWpl

---

*Dawson, William Levi, 1899-

...Out in the fields. Song. Poem by Elizabeth Barrett Browning; music by William L. Dawson. Chicago, Gamble hinged music co. [c1929] Publ. pl. no. 874.
5 p. fol.

Score: medium solo voice with piano accompaniment [key of C] English words.

ABSpl

---

*Dawson, William Levi, 1899-

Soon - a will be done. Negro spiritual; arranged by William L. Dawson. Tuskegee Institute, Ala., Music press [c1934]
10 p. 8 vo. (Tuskegee choir series, no. 102.)

Score: SATB, with piano reduction, for rehearsal only. Negro dialect.
Caption title

ABSpl HMC LC

---

*Dawson, William Levi, 1899-

...Talk about a child that do love Jesus. Negro spiritual. From the author's collection; arranged by William L. Dawson. Chicago, H. T. FitzSimons pub. [c1927] Publ. pl. no. 2015.
5 p. 8° (Aeolian series of choral music)

Score: SATTBB, with soprano solo and piano accompaniment for rehearsal only.

ZWpl
ABS

---

*Dawson, William Levi, 1899-

...Talk about a child that do love Jesus. Negro spiritual. From the author's collection. Arranged by William L. Dawson. Chicago, H. T. FitzSimons pub. [c1927]
5 p. fol.

Score: low solo voice with piano accompaniment [key of E minor] Negro dialect.

ABSpl

---

*Dawson, William L.

...You got to reap just what you sow. Negro spiritual; arranged by William L. Dawson. Chicago, Gamble hinged music co. [c1928] Publ. pl. no. 839.
5 p. fol.

Score: low solo voice with piano accompaniment [key of E♭] Negro dialect.

Dedicated to Paul Robeson.

ABSpl

Deas, Lawrence

...All I wants is ma chickens. [Popular song] Words and music by Deas & Wilson; arranged by W. H. Tyers. New York, Jos. W. Stern & co., [c1898]
6p. fol.

Score: medium solo voice with piano accompaniment Negro dialect.

Excerpt from the musical show, "A trip to coontown"

ABSpl

---

*Delaney, Tom

The jazz-me blues. [Popular song] By Tom Delaney. New York, Palmetto Music Publ. Co., [c1921.]
5 p. fol.

Score: medium solo voice with piano accompaniment. English words.

ABSpl

---

*Delaney, Tom

You may go, but you'll come back some day. [Popular song.] Words and music by Tom Delaney. New York, Triangle Music Publ. Co., [c1925.]
5 p. fol.

Score: medium solo voice with piano accompaniment. English words.

ABSpl

Denniker, Paul

Farewell. Ballad. Lyric by Andy Razaf; melody by Paul Denniker. NY: Joe Davis, inc. [c1933]
3p. fol.

Score: median solo voice with piano accompaniment. English words.

ABSpl

Denniker, Paul
Hawaiian love-bird

Denniker, Paul
The language of love

See
Andy Razaf

Denniker, Paul

Natiesha (Bright eyes). An Indian love song. The poem by *Andrea Razaf; the melody by Paul Denniker. NY: Forrest S. Chilton. [c1926]
5p. fol.

Score: median solo voice [key of E♭] with piano accompaniment. English words.

ABSpl

Denniker, Paul

Perhaps... [Popular song] Words by *Andy Razaf; music by Paul Denniker. New York, Triangle music co. [c1929]
5 p. fol.

Score: medium voice [key of G] with piano and ukulele or banjulele banjo accompaniment.

ABSpl
NYPLS

Denniker, Paul

S'posin'. Ballad fox-trot. Words by Andy Razaf; music by Paul Denniker. NY: Triangle music publ co. ⌈c1929⌉
5p. fol.

Score: medium solo voice with piano accompaniment. English words.

ABSpl

Denniker, Paul

... Won'tcha? A musical question. ⌈Popular song.⌉ Words by Andy Razaf; music by Paul Denniker. NY: Joe Davis, inc. ⌈c1929⌉
5p. fol.

Score: medium solo voice with piano accompaniment. English words.

ABSpl

Denniker, Paul

The world's greatest sweetheart is you. ⌈Popular⌉ song. Words by Andy Razaf; music by Paul Denniker. NY: Triangle music pub. co., inc. ⌈c1929⌉
5p. fol.

Score: medium solo voice with piano accompaniment. English words.

ABSpl

Denniker, Paul

(You'll always be) welcome. Waltz ballad. Words by Andy Razaf; music by Paul Denniker. NY: Joe Davis, inc. ⌈c1929⌉
5p. fol.

Score: medium solo voice with piano accompaniment. English words.

ABSpl

---

*Dett, Robert Nathaniel, 1882-1943.

America the beautiful. O beautiful for spacious skies. ⌈Hymn⌉ Words by Katherine Lee Bates; music by R. Nathaniel Dett. New York, J. Fischer & bro. ⌈c1918⌉ Publ. pl. no. J. F. & B. 4582.
1 p. 8 vo.

Close score: SATB. Familiar English text.
Bound in black spiral notebook. no.1.

ABS
HMC

---

*Dett, Robert Nathaniel, 1882-1943 arr.

... As by the streams of Babylon. For solo voice (preferably soprano) with accompaniment of four-part chorus of mixed voices, a cappella. ⌈Music by⌉ Thomas Campian, First book of ayres (1613); arr. by R. Nathaniel Dett. ⌈New York⌉ G. Schirmer (inc.) c1933. Publ. pl. no. 36047.
4 p. 8vo. (G. S. octavo choruses no. 7713)

Score: high solo voice (preferably soprano) with SATB accompaniment and piano reduction for rehearsal only. English words.

ABSpl ZWpl
LC

---

*Dett, Robert Nathaniel, 1882-1943.

As children walk ye in God's love. ⌈Anthem⌉ (Based on a traditional Negro melody.) ⌈Music by⌉ R. Nathaniel Dett. New York, G. Schirmer, inc., ⌈c1930.⌉ Publ. pl. no. 34911.
9 p. 8 vo. (G. S. octabo choruses no. 7398)

Score: TTBB with tenor solo and with piano reduction for rehearsal only. English words.
Bound in black spiral notebook. no.1.

ABSpl
LC

---

*Dett, Robert Nathaniel, 1882-1943.

...As his own soul. Piano solo. ⌈One of⌉ eight Bible vignettes for the piano. By R. Nathaniel Dett... New York, Mill music inc. ⌈c1942⌉
5 p. fol.

Score: piano solo.

ABSpl
ZWpl

---

*Dett, Robert Nathaniel, 1882-1943.

Ave Maria (Guide me and lead me) ...⌈Anthem⌉ English text by Frederick H. Martens; music by R. Nathaniel Dett. New York, G. Schirmer, inc., ⌈c1930⌉. Publ. pl. no. 34905.
7 p. 8 vo. (G. S. octavo choruses no. 7395)

Score: SATB with baritone solo and piano reduction for rehearsal only. English and Latin words.
Bound in black spiral notebook. no.1.

ABSpl

---

*Dett, Robert Nathaniel, 1882-1943.

Barcarolle. Morning. (In Dett, R. Nathaniel, In the bottoms. The characteristic suite for the piano. Chicago, 1913, p. 14-23.)

Score: piano solo.
Caption title
Bound in vol.

LC
Zwpl
ABSpl

---

*Dett, Robert Nathaniel, 1882-1943.

...Barcarolle of tears. Piano solo. ⌈One of⌉ eight Bible vignettes for the piano. By R. Nathaniel Dett. New York, Mills music inc. ⌈c1943⌉
6 p. fol.

Score: piano solo.

ABSpl
ZWpl

---

*Dett, Robert Nathaniel, 1882-1943.

Beyond the dream; piano solo from the romantic suite, "Enchantment" by R. Nathaniel Dett. New York, John Church co. ⌈c1922⌉ Publ. pl.no. 18543.
9 p. fol.

Score: piano solo.
In bound vol.

ABSpl
LC
ZWpl

---

*Dett, Robert Nathaniel, 1882-1943.

The chariot jubilee. Motet. For tenor solo and chorus of mixed voices, accompaniment of organ (piano) or orchestra. By R. Nathaniel Dett. New York ⌈etc.⌉ The John Church co. ⌈c1919⌉ Publ. pl. no. 18124.
31 p. 8°.

Score: tenor solo with SSAATTBB and organ or piano accompaniment. English words.
Orchestra accompaniment available.

ABSpl
LC

(continued on next card)

---

*Dett, Robert Nathaniel, 1882-1943. The chariot jubilee... New York ⌈c1919⌉ (Card 2)

Written "for the Syracuse Festival chorus, performed by them and the Cleveland Symphony orchestra, with Lambert Murphy soloist, in Keith's theatre, Syracuse, May 4, 1921." According to Mr. Dett this "marks the first attempt to develop the spiritual into an oratorio form." - Interview Dett, Washington, D. C., 7/23/43

---

*Dett, Robert Nathaniel, 1882-1943, arr.

Cotton needs pickin'. A worksong arranged by R. Nathaniel Dett.
(In Williams, Charles H., Cotton needs pickin'. Norfolk, Va., 1928.)

Score: piano solo.

Illustrations of the dance steps for this piece are by *Hampton Institute students.

ABSpl NYPLS

---

*Dett, Robert Nathaniel, 1882-

Dance. Juba. (In Dett, R. Nathaniel, In the bottoms. The characteristic suite for the piano. New York, 1913, p. 24-28.)

Score: piano solo.
Caption title
Bound in vol.

LC
Zwpl
ABSpl

---

*Dett, Robert Nathaniel, 1882-1943.

Dance of desire; piano solo from the romantic suite, "Enchantment" by R. Nathaniel Dett. New York, John Church co. ⌈c1922⌉ Publ. pl. no. 30630.
11 p. fol.

Score: piano solo.
Bound in vol.

ABSpl
LC
ZWpl

---

*Dett, Robert Nathaniel, 1882-1943.

...Desert interlude. Piano solo. ⌈One of⌉ eight vignettes for the piano. By R. Nathaniel Dett... New York, Mills music co inc. ⌈c1942⌉
4 p. fol.

Score: piano solo.

ABSpl
ZWpl

---

*Dett, Robert Nathaniel, 1882-1943.

Don't you weep no more, Mary. ⌈Anthem. Based on a Negro melody in the collection of R. N. D. Music by R. Nathaniel Dett.⌉ New York, G. Schirmer, inc. ⌈c1930⌉ Publ. pl. no. 34906.
8 p. 8 vo.

Score: SATB with piano reduction for rehearsal only. English words.
Bound in black spiral notebook. no.1.

ABSpl
LC

---

*Dett, Robert Nathaniel, 1882-1943. arr.

...Drink to me only with thine eyes. ⌈Chorus. Words by⌉ Ben Johnson. ⌈Music arranged by⌉ R. Nathaniel Dett. New York, F. Fischer & bro., c1933. Publ. pl. no. J. F. & B. 6700.
12 p. 8°. (Fischer edition no. 6700)

Score: SAATBB with piano reduction for rehearsal only. English words.
Bound in black spiral notebook. no.1.
A brilliant arrangement of the familiar tune.

ABSpl LC
HMC ZWpl

---

*Dett, Robert Nathaniel, 1882-1943.

...Enchantment. A romantic suite for the piano on an original program... ⌈By⌉ R. Nathaniel Dett. Cincinnati, ⌈etc.⌉ The John Church co. ⌈c1922⌉ Publ. pl. nos. 18540-18543.
4 v. fol.

Scores: piano solos.
Bound in vol.

Contents: 1. Incantation. -2. Song of the shrine. -3. Dance of desire. -4. Beyond the dream.

ABSpl
LC - second set of nos. I & II autograph dedication
ZWpl to Mrs. Frederic Coolidge on titlepage.

*Dett, Robert Nathaniel, 1882-1943.

...Father Abraham. Piano solo. ₍One of₎ eight Bible vignettes for the piano. By R. Nathaniel Dett... New York, Mills music inc. ₍c1941₎
8 p. fol.

Score: piano solo.

ABSpl
ZWpl

---

*Dett, Robert Nathaniel, 1882-

Honey. Humoresque (In Dett, R. Nathaniel, In the bottoms. The characteristic suite for the piano. New York, 1913, p. 12, 13.)

Score: piano solo.
Caption title.
Bound in vol.

LC
Zwpl
ABSpl

---

*Dett, Robert Nathaniel, 1882-1943, arr.

I'm so glad trouble don't last alway. Negro spiritual from the collection of R. N. D.; ₍arranged by₎ R. Nathaniel Dett. New York, John Church ₍c1919₎ Publ. pl. no. 18150.
5 p. fol.

Score: medium solo voice ₍key of F₎ with piano accompaniment. English words.
Bound in vol.
Caption title.

ABSpl
LC
ZWpl

---

*Dett, Robert Nathaniel, 1882-1943. arr.

...Follow me. ₍A Negro spiritual from the collection of Mrs. Catherine Fields-Gay ₍arranged by₎ R. Nathaniel Dett. New York, John Church co. ₍c1919₎ Publ. pl. no. 18209.
8 p. fol.

Score: medium solo voice ₍key of A^b₎ with piano accompaniment. English words.
Bound in vol.

ABSpl
LC
ZWpl

---

*Dett, Robert Nathaniel, 1882-1943.

Hymn to Parnassus. Song. ₍Verse 1, anonymous, verse 2 by the composer; music by₎ R. Nathaniel Dett. New York, Mills music inc. ₍c1942₎
5 p. fol.

Score: medium solo voice ₍key of C₎ with piano accompaniment. English words.

ABSpl
ZWpl

---

*Dett, Robert Nathaniel, 1882-1943.

...In the bottoms. Characteristic suite for the piano by R. Nathaniel Dett... Chicago, Clayton F. Summy co. ₍c1913₎ Publ. pl. no. C.F.S. co. 1465.
28 p. fol. (Summy edition no. 61)

Score: piano solos.
Bound in vol.
Contents: 1. Prelude, p. 1-8. -2. His song, p. 9-11. -3. Honey, p. 12,13. -4. Barcarolle, p. 14-23. -5. Dance juba, p. 24-28.

ZWpl LC ABSpl

---

*Dett, Robert Nathaniel, 1882-1943.

...Go not far from me, O God. ₍Anthem. Based on two traditional Negro melodies in the collection of R. N. D.₎ ₍Words and music by₎ R. Nathaniel Dett. New York, J. Fischer & bro. ₍c1933₎ Publ. pl. no. J. F. & B. 6698.
11 p. 8 vo. (Cantate domino no. 6698)

Score: SATB with baritone solo and with piano reduction for rehearsal only. English words.
Bound in black spiral notebook. no.1.

ABSpl
HMC
LC
ZWpl

---

*Dett, Robert Nathaniel, 1882-1943.

...I am the true vine. Piano solo. ₍One of₎ eight Bible vignettes for the piano. By R. Nathaniel Dett... New York, Mills music inc. ₍c1943₎
5 p. fol.

Score: piano solo.

ABSpl
ZWpl

Dett, Robert Nathaniel, 1882-1943.

Incantation; piano solo from the romantic suite, "Enchantment" by R. Nathaniel Dett. New York, John Church co. ₍c1922₎ Publ. pl. no. 30618.
9 p. fol.

Score: piano solo.
Bound in vol.

LABSpl
ZWpl

---

*Dett, Robert Nathaniel, 1882-1943.

Go on, brother. Negro spiritual. Setting by R. Nathaniel Dett; featured with success by Miss Dorothy Maynor. New York, Mills music inc. ₍c1942₎
3 p. fol.

Score: medium solo voice ₍key of F^m₎ with piano accompaniment. English words.

ZWpl
ABS

---

*Dett, Robert Nathaniel, 1882-1943.

...I'll never turn back no more. ₍Athem. Theme traditional after the singing of Mr. Dola Miller. Additional texts from "Church hymns and tunes." Music by₎ R. Nathaniel Dett. New York, J. Fischer & bro. ₍c1917₎ Publ. pl. no. J. F. & B. 4435.
8 p. 8 vo.
Bound in black spiral notebook. no.1.
Score: SATB with soprano obligato and with piano reduction for rehearsal only. English words.

ABSpl
LC
ZWpl

---

*Dett, Robert Nathaniel, 1882-1943.

Iorana. Tahitian maiden's love song. Words by J. Henry Quine; music by R. Nathaniel Dett. Chicago, Clayton F. Summy co. ₍c1935₎ Publ. pl. no. C.F.S. 3019.
7 p. fol.

Score: medium solo voice ₍key of G B₎ with piano accompaniment. English words.

LC
ZWpl
A.BS

---

*Dett, Robert Nathaniel, 1882-1943.

Go on, mule! An army camp folk song, developed by *J. Fletcher Bryant and R. Nathaniel Dett. New York, J. Fischer & bro. ₍c1918₎ Publ. pl. no. J. F. & B. 4578.
5 p. fol.

Score: medium solo voice with piano accompaniment. Negro dialect.
Bound in vol.

ABSpl

---

*Dett, Robert Nathaniel, 1882-1943. arr.

I'm a-trav'ling to the grave. Negro spiritual. ₍Arranged₎ by R. Nathaniel Dett. New York, Mills music inc. ₍c1943₎
5 p. fol.

Score: high solo voice ₍key of G₎ with piano accompaniment. Negro dialect.

ZWpl
ABS

Dett, Robert Nathaniel, 1882-1943
Lead gently, Lord, and slow

---

*Dett, Robert Nathaniel, 1882-1943.

God understands. ₍Song₎ Verse by Katrina Trask; music by R. Nathaniel Dett... Cincinnati, The John Church co. ₍c1926₎ Publ. pl. no. 19061.
5 p. fol.

Score: medium solo voice ₍key of G₎ with piano accompaniment. English words.
Bound in vol.

ABSpl
LC
ZWpl

---

*Dett, Robert Nathaniel, 1882-1943.

I'm a goin' to see my friedns again. A Negro folk song derivative. From the singing of *Rev. J. Fletcher Bryant; arranged by R. Nathaniel Dett. New York, John Chruch co. ₍c1924₎ Publ. pl. no. 18764.
5 p. fol.

Score: high solo voice with piano accompaniment. Negro dialect.
Bound in vol.

ABSpl
ZWpl

---

*Dett, Robert Nathaniel, 1882-1943. arr.

...Listen to the lambs. A religious characteristic in the form of an anthem. ₍By₎ R. Nathaniel Dett. Arranged for 3 part chorus by Grace Helen Nash. New York, G. Schirmer inc. ₍c1914 and 1929₎ Publ. pl. no. 34372.
8 p. 8°. (Schirmer secular choruses for mixed voices, no. 7337)
Bound in black spiral notebook. no.1.
Score: 3 part chorus of mixed voices (SAB) with piano reduction "for rehearsal only." English words.

ABSpl

---

*Dett, Robert Nathaniel, 1882-

His song. (In Dett, R. Nathaniel, In the bottoms. The characteristic suite for the piano. New York 1913. p. 9-11)

Score: piano solo.
Caption title
Bound in vol.

LC
Zwpl
ABSpl

---

*Dett, Robert Nathaniel, 1882-1943.

...I'm goin' to thank God. Negro spiritual. Accompaniment by R. Nathaniel Dett. New York, J. Fischer & bro. ₍c1940₎ Publ. pl. no. J. F. & B. 7696.
4 p. fol.

Score: high solo voice ₍key of B^b₎ with piano accompaniment. Negro dialect.

At head of title: "Dedicated to Miss Dorothy Maynor for whom it was especially written and set."

ABSpl
LC
ZWpl

---

*Dett, Robert Nathaniel, 1882-1943.

Madrigal divine. Piano solo. ₍One of₎ eight Bible vignettes for the piano. By R. Nathaniel Dett... New York, Mills music inc. ₍c1943₎
5 p. fol.

Score: piano solo.

ABSpl
ZWpl

*Dett, Robert Nathaniel, 1882-1943.

...Magic moon of molten gold. [Song; The verse by Frederick H. Martens; music by; R. Nathaniel Dett. New York, John Church co. [c1919; Publ. pl. no. 18211.

17 p. fol.

Bound in vol.

Score: high solo voice with piano accompaniment. English words.

ABSpl
LC
ZWpl

---

*Dett, Robert Nathaniel, 1882-1943.

...A man goin' roun' takin' names. A Negro folk song derivative, from the singing of Captain *Walter R. Brown of Hampton Institute; [arranged by] R. Nathaniel Dett. New York, John Church co. [c1924] Publ. pl. no. 18765.

5 p. fol.

Bound in vol.

Score: low solo voice with piano accompaniment. English words.

Caption title.

ABSpl
LC
ZWpl

---

*Dett, Robert Nathaniel, 1882-1943.

...Martha complained. Piano solo. [One of; eight Bible vignettes for the piano. By R. Nathaniel Dett... New York, Mills music inc. [c1942]

7 p. fol.

Score: piano solo.

ABSpl
ZWpl

---

*Dett, Robert Nathaniel, 1882-1943.

My day. [Song; Verse by Daniel S. Twohig; music by R. Nathaniel Dett. New York, John Church co. [c1929; Publ. pl. no. 19311.

5 p. fol.

Bound in vol.

Score: medium solo voice [key of G; with piano accompaniment. English words.

ABSpl
LC
ZWpl

---

*Dett, Robert Nathaniel, 1882-1943.

Nepenthe and the muse; a composition for the piano by R. Nathaniel Dett. New York, John Church co. [c1922; Publ. pl. no. 18544.

6 p. fol.

Score: piano solo.

Bound in vol.

ABSpl
LC

---

*Dett, Robert Nathaniel, 1882-1943. arr.

Now we take this feeble body. Negro funeral hymn. [Arranged; by R. Nathaniel Dett. New York, Mills music inc. [c1943]

5 p. fol.

Score: high solo voice [key of A^b; with piano accompaniment. English words.

ZWpl
ABS

---

*Dett, Robert Nathaniel, 1882-1943.

...O Holy Lord... [Anthem; Text from "The story of the jubilee singers." [Music by; R. Nathaniel Dett. New York, G. Schirmer inc. [c1916; Publ. pl. no. 27011.

8 p. 8°. (G. S. octavo choruses no. 6579)

Score: SSAATTBB with piano reduction "for rehearsal only." English words.

Bound in black spiral notebook. no.1.

ABSpl
NYPLS

---

*Dett, Robert Nathaniel, 1882-1943.

O Lord, the hard-won miles. Sacred song for voice and piano. Words by *Paul Laurence Dunbar; music by R. Nathaniel Dett. New York, G. Schirmer, inc. [c1934] Publ. pl. no. 36033.

5 p. fol.

Score: low solo voice [key of E^b] with piano accompaniment. English words.

Bound in vol.

HMC
ZWpl

---

*Dett, Robert Nathaniel, 1882-1943. arr.

Oh, the land I am bound for. Negro folk-song derivative. [Arranged by; R. Nathaniel Dett. New York, John Church co. [c1923; Publ. pl. no. 18658.

5 p. fol.

Score: low solo voice with piano accompaniment. English words.

Bound in vol.

ABSpl
LC
ZWpl

---

*Dett, Robert Nathaniel, 1882-1943.

Open yo' eyes. Song. Text from "The album of a heart"; music [and words; by R. Nathaniel Dett. Philadelphia, Theodore Presser co. [c1923; Publ. pl. no. 19031.

7 p. fol.

Score: high solo voice [key of C; with piano accompaniment. Negro dialect.

Bound in vol.

ABSpl
LC

---

*Dett, Robert Nathaniel, 1882-1943.

...The ordering of Moses. Biblical folk scene for soli, chorus and orchestra. Text based on scripture and folk lore; compiled and set to music by R. Nathaniel Dett. New York, J. Fischer & bro. [c1937; Publ. pl. no. J.F. & B. 7230.

123 p. 27 cm. (Fischer edition no. 7230)

Score: SATB with STA and 2 Bs. soloists. English words.

Performed at Musical festival at Cincinnati, May 7, 1937 under direction of Eugene Goossens.

ABSpl HMC LC YJWJ ZWpl

---

*Dett, Robert Nathaniel, 1882-1943.

...Other sheep. Piano solo. [One of; eight Bible vignettes for the piano. By R. Nathaniel Dett... New York, Mills music inc. [1943]

14 p. fol.

Score: piano solo.

ZWpl
ABSpl

Dett, Robert Nathaniel, 1882-1943

The place where the rainbow ends

---

*Dett, Robert Nathaniel, 1882-1943. arr.

...Poor me. Negro folk song derivative. Melody from Work brothers' "Folk songs of the American Negro;" [arranged by] R. Nathaniel Dett. NewYork, John Church co. [c1923] Publ. pl. no. 18656.

5 p. fol.

Score: medium solo voice with piano accompaniment. English words.

Bound in vol.

Dedicated "to *Miss Marian Anderson."

ABSpl
ZWpl

---

*Dett, Robert Nathaniel, 1882-

Prelude. Night <In Dett, R. Nathaniel, In the bottoms. The characteristic suite for the piano. New York, 1913. p. 4-8]

Score: piano solo.

Caption title

Bound in vol.

LC
ZWpl
ABSpl

---

*Dett, Robert Nathaniel, 1882-1943.

...Ride on, Jesus. Negro spiritual. Accompaniment by R. Nathaniel Dett. New York, J. Fischer & bro. [c1940] Publ. pl. no. J. F. & B. 7695.

4 p. fol.

Score: high solo voice [key of E^b] with piano accompaniment. Negro dialect.

"Setting requested and made especially for Miss Dorothy Manor" - at head of title.

ABSpl
LC
ZWpl

---

*Dett, Robert Nathaniel, 1882-1943. arr.

Rise up shepherd and follow. Christmas spiritual set for anthem with solo and accompaniment by R. Nathaniel Dett... New York, F. Fischer & bro. [c1936; Publ. pl. no. J.F. & B. 7218.

7 p. 8°.

Bound in black spiral notebook. no.1.

Score: SATB with solo (any voice) with piano accompaniment. English words.

ABSpl
LC
ZWpl

---

*Dett, Robert Nathaniel, 1882-1943.

Sit down, servant, sit down. Negro folk-scene for low or medium voice and piano by R. Nathaniel Dett. New York, G. Schirmer, inc. [c1932] Publ. pl. no. 35805.

7 p. fol.

Bound in vol.

Score: low voice [key of F] with piano accompaniment. Negro dialect.

HMC
LC
ZWpl

---

*Dett, Robert Nathaniel, 1882-1943.

Somebody's knocking at your door. Negro spiritual. [By] R. Nathaniel Dett. New York, John Church co. [c1919; Publ. pl. no. 18210.

9 p. fol.

Bound in vol.

Score: medium solo voice with piano accompaniment. English words.

ABSpl
ZWpl

---

*Dett, Robert Nathaniel, 1882-1943.

Song of the shrine; piano solo from the romantic suite, "Enchantment" by R. Nathaniel Dett. New York, John Church co. [c1922; Publ. pl. no. 18541.

5 p. fol.

Score: piano solo.

Bound in vol.

ABSpl
LC
ZWpl

---

*Dett, Robert Nathaniel, 1882-1943.

The soul of America, defend! Song. [Words and music; by R. Nathaniel Dett. New York, Mills music inc. [c1942]

3 p. fol.

Score: medium solo voice [key of E^b, with piano accompaniment. English words.

ZWpl
ABS

*Dett, Robert Nathaniel, 1882-1943.

A thousand years ago or more. Song. Words by Frederick H. Martens; music by R. Nathaniel Dett. New York, John Church co. ₍c1919₎ Publ. pl. no. 18212.
9 p. fol.

Score: high solo voice with piano accompaniment. English words.
Bound in vol.

ABSpl
LC

*Dett, Robert Nathaniel, 1882-1943.

...The voice of the sea. Song. Words from "The album of a heart"; music ₍and words₎ by R. Nathaniel Dett. New York, John Church co. ₍c1924₎ Publ. pl. no. 18819.
5 p. fol.
Bound in vol.

Score: low solo voice with piano accompaniment. English words.

ABSpl
LC

*Dett, Robert Nathaniel, 1882-1943.

...Wasn't that a mighty day?...₍Anthem. Traditional melody from the collection of R. N. D. arranged by R. Nathaniel Dett.₎ New York, G. Schirmer, inc. ₍c1933₎ Publ. pl. no. 36402.
9 p. 8 vo. (G. S. octavo choruses no. 7712)
Bound in black spiral notebook. no.1.
Score: SATBB, with baritone and alto soli ad lib. Piano reduction for rehearsal only. English words.

"This number can be performed by a solo quartet by omitting the first 8 measures." - note p. 2.

ABSpl
LC
NBCL

*Dett, Robert Nathaniel, 1882-1943.

...Weeping Mary. ₍Anthem. Afro-American folk song. Arranged by₎ R. Nathaniel Dett. New York, J. Fischer & bro. ₍c1918₎ Publ. pl. no. J. F. & B. 4434.
8 p. 8 vo.
Bound in black spiral notebook. no.1.

Score: SATB with soprano solo and with piano reduction for rehearsal only. English words.

ABSpl
LC
ZWpl

*Dett, Robert Nathaniel, 1882-1943.

...Were thou the moon. Song. Text from "The album of a heart"; music ₍and words₎ by R. Nathaniel Dett. New York, John Church co. ₍c1924₎ Publ. pl. no. 18818.
5 p. fol.
Bound in vol.
Score: low solo voice ₍key of F₎ with piano accompaniment. English words.

ABSpl
LC
ZWpl

*Dett, Robert Nathaniel, 1882-1943.

What kind of shoes you going to wear? Negro spiritual. ₍Arranged₎ by R. Nathaniel Dett. New York, Mills music inc. ₍c1943₎
5 p. fol.

Score: medium solo voice ₍key of A^b₎ with piano accompaniment. Negro dialect.

ZWpl
ABS

*Dett, Robert Nathaniel, 1882-1943.

The winding road. Song. Words by Tertius van Dyke; music by R. Nathaniel Dett. Philadelphia, Theodore Presser co. ₍c1923₎ Publ. pl. no. 19030.
7 p. fol.

Score: low solo voice ₍key of E^b₎ with piano accompaniment. English words.
Bound in vol.

ABSpl
LC
ZWpl

*Dett, Robert Nathaniel, 1882-1943.

...Zion hallelujah. Negro folk song derivative. Song from the collection of R. N. D. as sung by "Miss Baytop; ₍arranged by₎ R. Nathaniel Dett. New York, John Church co. ₍c1923₎ Publ. pl. no. 18657.
5 p. fol.

Score: medium solo voice with piano accompaniment. English words.
Bound in vol.

ABSpl
LC
ZWpl

*Diton, Carl Rossini, 1886- arr.

...An' he never spoke a mumbelin' word; for 6 part chorus of mixed voices, arranged by C. R. Diton. New York, G. Schirmer, inc. ₍c1921₎ Publ. pl. no. 29797.
4 p. 8vo. (G. S. secular choruses no. 6885)

Score: 6 part (SSATBB) mixed chorus a cappella with reduced piano part for rehearsal. Negro dialect.
Bound in black spiral notebook no. 2.

ABSpl
HMC
BPL

*Diton, Carl Rossini, 1886- arr.

...At the beautiful gate. Negro spiritual; anthem. Arranged by C. R. Diton. New York, G. Schirmer, inc. ₍c1921₎ Publ. pl. no. 29796.
4 p. 8vo. (G. S. secular choruses no. 6883)

Score: 5 part chorus of mixed voices (SSATB) with piano reduction for rehearsal only. English words.
Bound in black spiral notebook no. 2.

ABSpl
BPL

*Diton, Carl Rossini, 1886- arr.

A collection of six Negro partsongs. Arranged by C. R. Diton. New York, G. Schirmer, inc. c1915-21 Publ. pl. nos. 29796-98; 29791,2; 29736.
6 v. 8vo. (Schirmer's standard secular choruses, nos. 6882-85; 6100, 6099.)

Bound in black spiral notebook no. 2.
Scores: SATB, with piano reduction for rehearsal only. Negro dialect.
ABS

Contents: 1. Roll, Jordan roll. -2. At the (continued on next card)

*Diton, Carl Rossini, 1886- arr. A collection of six Negro part songs. 1915-21. (card 2)

beautiful gate. -3. Poor mourner's got a-home at last. -4. An' He never spoke a mumberlin' word. -5. Little David, play on your harp. -6. Deep river.

Bound in black spiral notebook no. 2.

ABSpl
BPL

*Diton, Carl Rossini, 1886- arr.

Deep river. Negro spiritual; anthem. Arranged by Carl R. Diton. New York, G. Schirmer, inc. ₍c1915₎ Publ. pl. no. 25491.
4 p. 8vo. (G. S. Secular choruses no. 6099)

Score: 5 part chorus of mixed voices (SSATB) with piano reduction for rehearsal only. English words.
Bound in black spiral notebook no. 2.

ABSpl
BPL

*Diton, Carl Rossini, 1886- arr.

Ev'ry time I feel the spirit. Negro spiritual; anthem. Arranged by Carl R. Diton. New York, G. Schirmer, inc. ₍c1915₎ Publ. pl. no. 25493.
4 p. 8vo.

Score: 5 part chorus of mixed voices (SSATB) with piano reduction for rehearsal only. English words.
Bound in black spiral notebook no. 2.

ABSpl

*Diton, Carl Rossini, 1886- arr.

Little David, play on your harp. Negro spiritual; anthem. Arranged by Carl R. Diton. New York, G. Schirmer, inc. ₍c1915₎ Publ. pl. no. 25492.
5 p. 8vo (G. S. octavo choruses no. 6100)

Score: 5 part chorus of mixed voices (SSATB) with piano reduction for rehearsal only. English words.
Bound in black spiral notebook no. 2.

ABSpl
BPL

*Diton, Carl Rossini, 1886- arr.

Pilgrim's song. For 5 part chorus of mixed voices by Carl R. Diton. New York, G. Schirmer, inc. ₍c1915₎ Publ. pl. no. 25011.
3 p. 8vo. (G. S. choruses, no. 5957)

Score: SSATB, a cappella; with piano reduction for rehearsal only. Negro dialect.
Bound in black spiral notebook no. 2.
HMC
NYPL42
ABSpl

*Diton, Carl Rossini, 1886- arr.

...Poor mourner's got a-home at last. Negro spiritual. Anthem. Arranged by C. R. Diton. New York, G. Schirmer, inc. ₍c1921₎ Publ. pl. no. 29736.
5 p. 8vo. (G. S. octavo choruses no. 6884)

Score: 8 part chorus of mixed voices (SSAATTBB) with piano reduction for rehearsal only. English words.
Bound in black spiral notebook no. 2.

ABSpl

*Diton, Carl Rossini, 1886- arr.

Roll, Jordan, roll. Negro spiritual; anthem. Arranged by C. R. Diton. New York, G. Schirmer, inc. ₍c1921₎ Publ. pl. no. 29798.
5 p. 8vo. (G. S. octavo choruses no. 6882)

Score: 4 part chorus of mixed voices (SATB) with piano reduction for rehearsal only. English words.
Bound in black spiral notebook no. 2.

ABSpl
BPL

*Diton, Carl Rossini, 1886- arr.

Swing low, sweet chariot. Negro spiritual, harmonized by Carl Diton, arranged by Elliot Schenck. Philadelphia, Theodore Presser ₍c1920₎ Publ. pl. no. 15698.
6 p. 8vo.

Score: 4 part chorus of mixed voices (SATB) with piano accompaniment. Negro dialect.
Bound in black spiral notebook no. 2.

ABSpl

Dixon, Will H
Ardente ivresse

Dixon, Will H
Brazilian dreams

Dixon, Will H
Dance of the bugs

Dixon, Will H
Delicioso

*Dixon, Will H.

Go 'long, mule, go 'long... Chorus Words by Alfred Andersen; music by Will H. Dixon. New York, G. Schirmer, inc. c1915. Publ pl. no. 25795.

8 p. 8vo (G. S. 8vo choruses #6153)

Score: TTBB with piano accompaniment. Negro dialect.

NBCL
ABSpl

Dixon, Will H
September eve - a trot

Dorsey, James Elmo
Go tell it on the mountain

*Dorsey, Thomas A , 1899-

All alone. Gospel song By *G. T. Byrd; arranged by Thomas A. Dorsey. Chicago, Thomas A. Dorsey, publ.
1 leaf. 8vo.

Score: medium solo voice with piano accompaniment. English words.

ABSpl
ZWpl

*Dorsey, Thomas A , 1899-

Gospel medley of He that believeth, Let's go down to Jordan, Holy Ghost get'n us ready for that great day. A special arrangement for choir and chorus. Arranged by Thomas A. Dorsey. Chicago, Thomas A. Dorsey publ. c1933
3 p. 8vo.

Score: medium solo voice with piano accompaniment. English words.

ABSpl
Zwpl

*Dorsey, Thomas A , 1899-

How about you? America's greatest revival song. Gospel song Words and music by Thomas A. Dorsey. Chicago, Thomas A. Dorsey publ. c1930
1 leaf. 8vo.

Score: medium solo voice with piano accompaniment. English words.

ABSpl

*Dorsey, Thomas A , 1899-

I don't know why I have to cry sometime. Gospel song By Thomas A. Dorsey. Chicago, Thomas A. Dorsey publ. c1942
1 leaf. 8vo.

Score: medium solo voice with piano accompaniment. English words.

ABSpl
Zwpl

*Dorsey, Thomas A , 1899-

If I don't get there. Gospel song By Thomas A. Dorsey. Chicago, Thomas A. Dorsey, publ.
1 leaf. 8vo.

Score: medium solo voice with piano accompaniment. English words.

ABSpl
Zwpl

Dorsey, Thomas A
I'm going to walk right in and make myself at home.

*Dorsey, Thomas A , 1899-

I'm in your care. Gospel song By Bessie Mitchell arranged by Thomas A. Dorsey. Chicago, Thomas A. Dorsey, publ.
1 leaf. 8vo.

Score: medium solo voice with piano accompaniment. English words.

ABSpl
Zwpl

*Dorsey, Thomas A , 1899-

It just suits me. Old time spiritual. Gospel song Arranged by Thomas A. Dorsey, Chicago, Thomas A. Dorsey publ.
1 leaf. 8vo.

Score: medium solo voice with piano accompaniment. English words.

ABSpl
Zwpl

*Dorsey, Thomas A , 1899-

I want to go there. Gospel song Words and music by Thomas A. Dorsey. Chicago, Thomas A. Dorsey publ. c1942
1 leaf.

Close score: SATB. English words.

ABSpl
Zwpl

*Dorsey, Thomas A , 1899-

Let us go back to God. Gospel song Words and music by Thomas. A. Dorsey. Chicago, Thomas A. Dorsey publ. c1942
1 leaf. 8vo.

Score: medium solo voice with piano accompaniment. English words.

ABSpl
ZWpl

*Dorsey, Thomas A , 1899-

A little talk with Jesus. Gospel solo. Poem set to music by Thomas A. Dorsey. Chicago, Thomas A. Dorsey publ.
1 leaf. 8vo.

Score: medium solo voice with piano accompaniment. English words.

ABSpl
ZWpl

*Dorsey, Thomas A , 1899-

The Lord knows just what I need. Gospel song By Thomas A. Dorsey. Chicago, Thomas A. Dorsey publ. c1942
1 leaf. 8vo.

Score: medium solo voice with piano accompaniment. English words.

ABSpl
Zwpl

*Dorsey, Thomas A , 1899-

My desire. Gospel song Words and music by Thomas A. Dorsey. Chicago, Thomas A. Dorsey publ. c1937
4 p. fol.

Score: medium solo voice with piano accompaniment. English words. With arrangement on p. 4 which is suitable for SA or SATB.

ABSpl
ZWpl

*Dorsey, Thomas A , 1899-

Shake my mother's hand for me. Gospel song By Thomas A. Dorsey. Chicago, Thomas A. Dorsey publ. c1932
1 leaf. 8vo.

Score: verse for medium solo voice with piano accompaniment; chorus for SATB. English words.

ABSpl
ZWpl

*Dorsey, Thomas A , 1899-

Some day I'm goin' to see my Jesus. Gospel song By Thomas A. Dorsey. Chicago, Thomas A. Dorsey publ. c1941
3 p. 8vo.

Score: verse for medium solo voice; chorus, SATB with medium solo obligato. English words.

ABSpl
ZWpl

*Dorsey, Thomas A , 1899-

Take my hand, precious Lord. Gospel song Words and arrangement by Thomas A. Dorsey. Chicago, Thomas A. Dorsey publ.
1 leaf. 8vo.

Score: medium solo voice with piano accompaniment. English words.

ABSpl
ZWpl

*Dorsey, Thomas A , 1899-

There's a God some-where. [Gospel song] By Thomas A. Dorsey. Chicago, Thomas A. Dorsey publ. [c1942]
1 leaf. 8vo.

Close score: SATB. English words.

ABSpl
ZWpl

---

*Dorsey, Thomas A , 1899-

Thy kingdom come. [Gospel song] By Thomas A. Dorsey. Chicago, Thomas A. Dorsey publ. [c1943]
1 leaf. 8vo.

Close score: SATB. English words.

ABSpl
ZWpl

---

*Dorsey, Thomas A , 1899-

...Walking up the King's highway. [Gospel song] Arranged and verses by Mary Gardner and Thomas A. Dorsey. Chicago, Thomas A. Dorsey publ. [c1940]
1 leaf. 8vo.

Close score: SATB with soprano obligato. English words.

ABSpl
ZWpl

---

*Dorsey, Thomas A , 1899-

What the world need is Jesus most of all. [Gospel song] By Thomas A. Dorsey. Chicago, Thomas A. Dorsey publ. [c1942]
1 leaf. 8vo.

Close score: SATB. English words.

ABSpl
ZWpl

---

*Dorsey, Thomas A , 1899-

When I've done my best. [Gospel song] By Thomas A. Dorsey. Chicago, Thomas A. Dorsey publ. [c1931]
1 leaf. 8vo.

Score: medium solo voice with piano accompaniment. English words.

ABSpl
ZWpl

---

*Dowell, Edgar

Harlem(Harlem's heaven to me). [Popular song] Words by *Arthur Porter; *music by Edgar Dowell, New York, *Handy Brothers Music Co., Inc. [c1934]
5 p. fol.

Score: medium solo voice with piano accompaniment. English words.

ABSpl

Durante, Jimmy

Daddy, your mama is lonesome for you. Blues fox-trot song. Words by Chris Smith and Bob Schafer ; music by Jimmy Durante. New York, Edward B. Marks music co. [c1921]
5p. fol.

Score: medium solo voice [key of C] with piano accompaniment. Negro dialect.

ABSpl

Durante, Jimmy
I've got my habits on

Edmonds, Shepard N
Dat's just what "expotentisious" means

---

*Edmonds, Shepard N..

... 'Deed I do. March and two-step [for piano] By Shepard N. Edmonds. New York, Windsor music co. [c1904]
5 p. fol.

Score: piano solo.

Arranged by E. Rosales.

ABSpl

---

*Edmonds, Shepard N.

Ding-a-ling, ding. Or, Ma baby don't treat me right! [Popular song] Words and music by Shepard N. Edmonds. New York, Jos. W. Stern & co. [c1902] Publ. pl. no. 3322.
5 p. fol.

Score: low solo voice [key of F] with piano accompaniment. Negro dialect.

ABSpl
LC

---

*Edmonds, Shephard N.

I ain't goin' back to Baltime' no mo'. Coon song by Shephard Edmonds...New York, Jerome Remick & co., [c1906]

5p.. fol.

Score: medium solo voice [key of E♭] with piano accompaniment. Negro dialect.

ABSpl
LC

---

*Edmonds, Shephard N

I'm crazy about it. [Popular song.] Words and music by Shephard N.Edmonds...New York, Shephard N. Edmonds music publ. co., [c1905.]

5p.. fol.

Score: medium solo voice [Key of F] with piano accompaniment.. Negro dialect.
Caption title.

LC
ABSpl

Edmonds, Shepard N
I'm gon' to live anyhow till I die

---

*Edmonds, Shephard N.

"The Kissing trust." or "Since Malinda Hinda's in the syndicate. [Popular song] Words and music by Shephard N. Edmonds. New York; Charles B. Ward. [c1901.]

5p. fol.

Score: medium solo voice [Key of A♭] with piano accompaniment. English words.

ABSpl

---

*Edmonds, Shepard N

She's my Irene. [Popular song] Words and music by Shepard N. Edmonds. New York, T. B. Harms [c1899]
4 p. fol.

Score: medium solo voice [key of G] with piano accompaniment. English words.

ABSpl

---

*Edmonds, Shepard N

Summertime is the time for me. [Popular song] Words and music by Sheppard [sic] Edmonds. New York, F. A. Mills [c1910]
5 p. fol.

Score: medium solo voice [key of C] with piano accompaniment. English words.

ABSpl

---

*Edmonds, Shepard N

You can't fool all the people all the time. [Popular song] Written by Shepard N. Edmonds... New York, Jos. W. Stern & co. [c1903] Publ. pl. no. 3548.
6 p. fol.

Score: medium solo voice [key of F] with piano accompaniment. Negro dialect.
Caption title.

ABSpl
LC

Elie, Justin
Doll's parade

Elie, Justin
The echo (Isma-o)

Elie, Justin
Haytian legend

Elie, Justin
Homesickness (Nostalgie)

Elie, Justin
Tropical dance

Ellington, ₛDukeₛ Edward Kennedy
Blue feeling

Elie, Justin
Indian dance and ritual

*Elkins, William C arr.

"Dere's a man goin' 'round takin' names." Arrangement of a Negro spiritual by William C. Elkins. New York, *Handy bros., inc. ₍c1933₎
5 p. 8°.

Score: 5 part chorus for male voices (TTTBB) with piano accompaniment. Negro dialect.
Bound in black spiral notebook no. 4.

ABSpl

Ellington, ₛDukeₛ Edward Kennedy
Blue reverie

Elie, Justin
Kiskaya

*Elkins, William C arr.

Time ain't long. Negro spiritual. Arranged by William C. Elkins. New York, *Handy bros. music co., inc. ₍c1933₎
5 p. 8°.

Score: 5 part male chorus (TTTBB) unaccompanied.
Bound in black spiral notebook no. 4.

ABSpl

Ellington, ₛDukeₛ Edward Kennedy
Boy meets horn

Elie, Justin
Nocturne

*Ellington, Edward Kennedy, 1899-

Alabamy home. ₍Popular song₎ Words and music by Dave Ringle and Duke Ellington. New York, Exclusive publications, inc., ₍c1937₎
5p. fol.

Score: medium solo voice ₍key of G₎ with piano accompaniment. English words.

ABSpl
LC

Ellington, ₛDukeₛ Edward Kennedy
Caravan

Elie, Justin
Prayer at eventide

Ellington, ₛDukeₛ Edward Kennedy
Battle of Swing

*Ellington, Edward Kennedy, 1899-

Choo-choo (I gotta hurry home). ₍Popular song₎ By Dave Ringle, Duke Ellington and Bob Schafer. New York, Broadway music corp., ₍c1924₎
5p. fol.

Score: medium solo voice ₍key of F₎ with piano accompaniment. English words.

ABSpl

Elie, Justin
Queen of the night

Ellington, ₛDukeₛ Edward Kennedy
Bird of paradise

Ellington, ₛDukeₛ Edward Kennedy
The Creole love call

Elie, Justin
Rumba

*Ellington, Edward Kennedy, 1899-

Black butterfly. By Duke Ellington. New York, Exclusive publications, inc., ₍c1937₎
3p. fol.

Score: piano solo.

ABSpl
LC

Ellington, ₛDukeₛ Edward Kennedy
Do nothin' till you hear from me

Ellington, «Duke» Edward Kennedy
Don't get around much anymore

Ellington, «Duke» Edward Kennedy
I'm just a lucky so-and so

---

*Ellington, Edward Kennedy, 1899-

...La de doody doo. ⌊Popular song⌋ By Duke Ellington, Edward J. Lambert, and Stephen Richards. New York, Exclusive publications inc., ⌊c1938⌋
5p. fol.

Score: medium solo voice ⌊key of C⌋ with piano accompaniment. English words.

ABSpl

Ellington, «Duke» Edward Kennedy
Don't you know I care

---

*Ellington, Edward Kennedy, 1899-

I'm so in love with you. ⌊Popular song⌋ Words and music by Irving Mills and Duke Ellington...New York, Mills music, inc., ⌊c1930⌋
5p. fol.

Score: medium solo voice ⌊key of C⌋ with piano accompaniment. English words.

ABSpl
LC

---

*Ellington, Edward Kennedy, 1899-

Mood indigo. By Duke Ellington, Irving Mills and Albany ⌊?⌋ Bigard. New York, Gotham music service, inc., ⌊c1931⌋
5p. fol.

Score: piano solo.

ABSpl
LC

Ellington, «Duke» Edward Kennedy
Dusk on the desert

---

*Ellington, Edward Kennedy, 1899-

In a sentimental mood. ⌊Popular song⌋ Music by Duke Ellington; lyrics by Irving Mills and Manny Kurtz. New York, Exclusive pub. inc., ⌊c1935⌋
5p. fol.

Score: medium solo voice ⌊key of F⌋ with piano accompaniment. English words.

ABSpl

---

*Ellington, Edward Kennedy, 1899-

Prelude to a kiss. ⌊Popular song⌋ Lyric by Irving Gordon and Irving Mills; music by Duke Ellington. New York, Exclusive publications, inc., ⌊c1938⌋
5p. fol.

Score: medium solo voice with piano accompaniment. English words.

Professional copy.

ABSpl

Ellington, «Duke» Edward Kennedy
I didn't know about you

---

*Ellington, Edward Kennedy, 1899-

It don't mean a thing (if it ain't got that swing). ⌊Popular song⌋ Words by Irving Mills; music by Duke Ellington. New York, Gotham music service, ⌊c1932⌋
3p. fol.

Score: medium solo voice ⌊key of B^b⌋ with piano accompaniment. English words.

ABSpl
LC

---

*Ellington, Edward Kennedy, 1899-

Pyramid. ⌊Popular song⌋ Words by Irving Gordon and Irving Mills; music by Duke Ellington and *Juan Tizol. New York, Exclusive publications inc., ⌊c1938⌋
5p. fol.

Score: medium solo voice ⌊key of A^b⌋ with piano accompaniment. English words.

ABSpl

---

*Ellington, Edward Kennedy, 1899-

I let a song go out of my heart. ⌊Popular song⌋ Words by Irving Mills, Henry Nemo and John Redmond; music by Duke Ellington. New York, Mills music inc., ⌊c1938⌋
5p. fol. 2 copies

Score: medium solo voice with piano accompaniment. English words.

ABSpl

---

*Ellington, Edward Kennedy, 1899-

...Jig Walk (Charleston) ⌊Popular song⌋ Lyric by *"Jo" Trent; melody by Duke Ellington. New York, Robbins-Engle inc., ⌊c1925⌋ Publ. pl. no. SH 232.
5p. fol.

Score: medium solovvoice ⌊key of E^b⌋ with piano accompaniment. English words.

"The sensational hit of the production, 'Chocolate kiddies'...as introduced in America by Ben Bernie and his orchestra." -- title page.

ABSpl

---

*Ellington, Edward Kennedy, 1899-

Rockin' in rhythm. By Duke Ellington, Irving Mills and *Harry Carney. New York, Gotham music service, inc., ⌊c1931⌋
5p. fol.

Score: piano solo.

LC
ABSpl

---

*Ellington, Edward Kennedy, 1899-

If you were in my place (What would you do?) ⌊Popular song⌋ Words by Irving Mills and Henry Nemo; music by Duke Ellington. New York, Mills Music inc., ⌊c1938⌋
5p. fol.

Score: medium solo voice ⌊key of F⌋ with piano accompaniment. English words.

ABSpl

Ellington, «Duke» Edward Kennedy
Jump for joy

---

*Ellington, Edward Kennedy, 1899-

Scattin' at the kit kat. ⌊Popular song⌋ Lyric by Irving Mills; music by Duke Ellington. New York, Exclusive pub. inc., c1937.
5p. fol.

Score: medium solo voice ⌊key of A^b⌋ with piano accompaniment. English words.

ABSpl

Ellington, «Duke» Edward Kennedy
I'm beginning to see the light

Ellington, «Duke» Edward Kennedy
Just a-sittin' and a-rockin'

---

*Ellington, Edward Kennedy, 1899-

Solitude. ⌊Popular song⌋ Music by Duke Ellington; words by Eddie De Lange and Irving Mills. New York, Milsons music publishing corp., ⌊c1934⌋
3p. fol.

Score: medium solo voice ⌊key of E^b⌋ with piano accompaniment. English words.

"Featured by Little Jack Little and his orchestra."

ABSpl
LC

*Ellington, Edward Kennedy, 1899-

...Streamlined piano solos. By Duke Ellington (Edward Kennedy Ellington). New York, Mills music inc., [vod & v publ. pl. nos.]
31p. fol.

Score: piano solos.

Contents: 1. Blues I love to sing (p. 29-31) By Duke Ellington and Bub Miley (c1927) Gotham music service inc.

(continued on next card)

*Ellington, Edward Kennedy, 1899- Card #2

...Streamlined piano solos. New York.

2. Blue bubbles. (p. 26-28) By Duke Ellington. (Gotham music service inc., [c1928])
3. Birmingham break-down. By Duke Ellington. (p. 17-19) (Gotham music service, inc., [c1927])
4. Cincinnati daddy. By Duke Ellington. (p. 12-13) (Gotham music service inc., [c1930])
5. East St. Louis Toodle-O. (p. 14-16) By Duke Ellington. (Gotham music service inc., [c1927])

(continued on next card)

*Ellington, Edward Kennedy, 1899- Card #3

...Streamlined piano solos. New York.

6. Jazz lips. (p. 10) By Duke Ellington. (Gotham music service inc., [c1930])
7. Jubilee stomp. (p. 23-25) By Duke Ellington. (Gotham music service inc., [c1928])
8. The Mooch (p. 7-9) By Duke Ellington and Irving Mills. (Gotham music service inc., [c1928])
9. Sophisticated lady (Also published as a song) By Duke Ellington; piano score by James Matte. (p. 4-6) (Gotham music service inc., [c1933])

(continued on next card)

*Ellington, Edward Kennedy Card #4

...Streamlined piano solos. New York.

10. Take it easy. By Duke Ellington. (p. 20-21) (Gotham music service inc., [c1928])

ABSpl

Ellington, [Duke] Edward Kennedy
Swanee river rhapsody

*Ellington, Edward Kennedy, 1899-

Yearning for love. [Popular song] Music by Duke Ellington; lyric by Mitchell Parish and Irving Mills. New York, Exclusive publications, inc. [c1936]
5p. fol.

Score: medium solo voice with piano accompaniment. English words.

ABSpl

*Ellington, Edward Kennedy, 1899

You gave me the gate (And I'm swingin'). [Popular song] Words by Irving Gordon, J. B. McNeely and Jimmy Farmer; music by Duke Ellington. New York, Exclusive publications, inc., [c1938]
3p. fol.

Score: medium solo voice [Key of C] with piano accompaniment. English words.

ABSpl

Engel, S Clarance
Let me change your name Miss Mandy

*Evanti, Lillian

The mighty rapture. [Song] Edwin Markham's poem, "Victory in defeat"; music by Lillian Evanti. New York, Handy brothers music co., inc. [c1943]
5 p. fol.
Score: medium solo voice with piano accompaniment. English words.

ABSpl ZWpl

Evanti, Lillian
My little prayer. [Song] Poem by Mrs. Bruce Evans; music by Lillian Evanti. New York, Handy brothers music co., inc. [c1943]

3 p. fol
Score: medium solo voice with piano accompaniment. English words.

ABSpl ZWpl

*Europe, James Reese, 1881-1919.
Cole, Bob
Ada, my sweet potater! [Popular song] Words by Chas. A. Hunter; music by *Bob Cole and James Reese Europe. New York, Jos. W. Stern & co. [c1908] Publ. pl. no. 6115.
5 p. fol.

Score: medium solo voice [key of B flat] with piano accompaniment. Negro dialect.
Excerpt from "The red moon".

ABSpl
LC

*Europe, James Reese, 1881-1919.

All of no man's land is ours. [Popular song] [By Lieut. Jim Europe, Lieut. *Noble Sissle and *Eubie Blake] New York, M. Witmark & sons [c1919] Publ. pl. no. 16003.
3 p. fol.

Score: medium solo voice [key of F] with piano accompaniment. English words.
Caption title.

ABSpl
LC

*Europe, James Reese, 1881-1919.
*Smith, Christopher
Ballin' the jack. Fox trot [for piano] By *Chris. Smith and James Reese Europe. New York, Jos. W. Stern & co. [c1914] Publ. pl. no. 7823.
5 p. fol.

Score: piano solo.

ABSpl
LC

*Europe, James Reese, 1881-1919.

Blue eyed Sue. [Popular song] Words and music by Jas. R. Europe. New York, Sol Bloom [c1904]
5 p. fol.

Score: medium solo voice [key of G] with piano accompaniment. English words.
Caption title.

ABSpl
LC

*Europe, James Reese, 1881-1919.

Castles' half and half. [For piano] By James Reese Europe and *Ford T. Dabney. New York, Jos. W. Stern & co. [1914] Publ. pl. no. 7754.
5 p. fol.

Score: piano solo.

ABSpl
LC

*Europe, James Reese, 1881-1919.

Castle house rag. Trot and one step. By James Reese Europe. New York, Jas. W. Stern and co., [c1914] Publ. pl. no. 7737.
5 p. fol.

Score: piano solo.
Caption title

"Introduced by Mr. and Mrs. Vernon Castle" — title page.

ABSpl

*Europe, James Reese, 1881-1919.

Castles in Europe. The innovation trot [for piano] By James Reese Europe. New York, Jos. W. Stern & co. [c1914] Publ. pl. no. 7733.
3 p. fol.

Score: piano solo.

ABSpl
LC

*Europe, James Reese, 1881-1919.

Castle innovation tango. (Argentine tango). [For piano] By *James Reese Europe and *Ford T. Dabney. New York, Jos. W. Stern & co. [1914] Publ. pl. no. 7766.
5 p. fol.

Score: piano solo.

ABSpl

*Europe, James Reese, 1881-1919.

Castle lame duck waltz. [For piano] By James Reese Europe and *Ford T. Dabney. New York, Jos. W. Stern & co. [c1914] Publ. pl. no. 7785.
5 p. fol.

Score: piano solo.

ABSpl

Europe, James Reese
Castle perfect trot

*Europe, James Reese, 1881-1919.

Congratulations... Castle lame duck waltz. [For piano] By James Reese Europe; arranged by J. Louis von der Mehden, jr. New York, G. Ricordi & co. [c1914] Publ. pl. no. 116058.
6 p. fol.

Score: piano solo.

ABSpl - This copy is a different arrangement of the original score under the title "Castle Lame Duck Waltz" (see card)

*Europe, James Reese, 1881-1919.

The coon band parade. For piano By James R. Europe. New York, Sol. Bloom ⌊c1905⌋
5 p. fol.

Score: piano solo.

ABSpl LC

---

*Europe, James Reese, 1881-1919.

Good night Angeline. ⌈Popular song⌉ ⌈By Lieut. James Reese Europe, Lieut. *Noble Sissle and *Eubie Blake⌉ New York, M. Witmark & sons ⌈c1919⌉
Publ. pl. no. 15988.
3 p. fol. 2 copies

Score: medium solo voice ⌈key of G⌉ with piano accompaniment. English words.
Caption title.

ABSpl LC

---

*Europe, James Reese, 1881-1919.

I ain't had no lovin' in a long time. ⌈Popular song⌉ Words by *Bob Cole; music by James Reese Europe. New York, Jos. W. Stern & co. ⌈c1908⌉
Publ. pl. no. 6103.
6 p. fol.

Score: medium solo voice ⌈key of F⌉ with piano accompaniment. Negro dialect.

ABSpl

---

*Europe, James Reese, 1881-1919.

I've got the finest man. ⌈Popular song⌉ Words by *Henry S. Creamer; music by James Reese Europe. New York, Waterson, Berlin & Snyder co. ⌈c1912⌉
5 p. fol.

Score: medium solo voice ⌈key of B^b⌉ with piano accompaniment. English words.

ABSpl

Europe, James Reese
Mirandy

---

*Europe, James Reese, 1881-1919.

My heart goes thumping and bumping for you. ⌈Popular song⌉ Words and music by Jas. R. Europe. New York, Sol Bloom ⌈c1904⌉
5 p. fol.

Score: medium solo voice ⌈key of F⌉ with piano accompaniment. English words.

ABSpl LC

---

*Europe, James Reese, 1881-1919.

"Obadiah" (You took de'vantage of me). ⌈Popular song⌉ By *Ernest Hogan and James Reese Europe. New York, The Gotham music pub. co. ⌈c1905⌉
5 p. fol.

Score: medium solo voice ⌈key of G⌉ with piano accompaniment. Negro dialect.

ABSpl LC

---

*Europe, James Reese, 1881-1919.

On patrol in no man's land. ⌈Popular song⌉ ⌈By Lieut. James Reese Europe, Lieut. *Noble Sissle and *Eubie Blake⌉ New York, M. Witmark & sons ⌈c1919⌉
3 p. fol.

Score: medium solo voice ⌈key of E^b⌉ with piano accompaniment. English words.
Caption title.

ABSpl LC

---

*Europe, James Reese, 1881-1919.

On the gay Luneta. ⌈Popular song⌉ Lyric by *Bob Cole; music by James Reese Europe. New York, Jos. W. Stern & co. ⌈c1906⌉ Publ. pl. no. 5156.
5 p. fol.

Score: high solo voice ⌈key of E flat⌉ with piano accompaniment. English words.
Excerpt from "The shoo-fly regiment" by Cole and Johnson.

ABSpl LC Filed under Johnson, J. R.

---

*Europe, James Reese, 1881-1919.

Pliney come out in the moonlight. Popular song Words by *Bob Cole; music by James Reese Europe. New York, Jerome H. Remick & co. ⌊c1910⌋
5 p. fol.

Score: medium solo voice ⌊key of G⌋ with piano accompaniment. English words.
Caption title.

Excerpt from the musical show, "Red moon".

ABSpl

---

*Europe, James Reese, 1881-1919.

Someone is waiting down in Tennessee. ⌈Popular song⌉ Words by *Cecil Mack; music by James Reese Europe. New York, Waterson, Berlin & Snyder co. ⌈c1913⌉
5 p. fol.

Score: low solo voice ⌈key of B^b⌉ with piano accompaniment. English words.

ABSpl LC

---

*Europe, James Reese, 1881-1919.

Valse Marguerite (Hesitation)... ⌈For piano⌉ Composed by James Reese Europe. New York, Jos. W. Stern & co. ⌈c1914⌉ Publ. pl. no. 7769.
5 p. fol.

Score: piano solo.

ABSpl

---

*Europe, James Reese, 1881-1919.

Zolo. Jungle song. ⌊Popular song.⌋ By *John Larkins and James R. Europe. Boston, G. W. Setchell publisher ⌊c1904⌋
5 p. fol.

Score: medium solo voice with piano accompaniment ⌊key of A^b.⌋ English words.

ABSpl LC

Evanti, Lillian
Himno Pan-Americano

---

*Evanti, Lillian

The mighty rapture. ⌊Song⌋ Edwin Markham's poem, "Victory in defeat"; music by Lillian Evanti. New York, Handy brothers music co., inc. ⌊c1943⌋
5 p. fol.

Score: medium solo voice with piano accompaniment. English words.

ABSpl ZWpl

Evanti, Lillian

My little prayer. ⌊Song⌋ Poem by Mrs. Bruce Evans; music by Lillian Evanti. New York, Handy brothers music co., inc. ⌊c1943⌋

3 p. fol

Score: medium solo voice with piano accompaniment. English words.

ABSpl ZWpl

Evanti, Lillian
Speak to him thou

Evanti, Lillian
Twenty-third psalm

---

*Farrell, William H.

After tonight (You won't forget me). ⌈Popular song⌉ Words and music by William H. Farrell. New York, Haviland pub. co. ⌈c1917⌉
5 p. fol.

Score: medium solo voice ⌈key of F⌉ with piano accompaniment. English words.

ABSpl

---

*Farrell, William H.

Hoochy-coochy eyes. ⌈Popular song⌉ Words and music by William H. Farrell and Arthur W. Lange. New York, Millbrook music pub. co. ⌈c1909⌉
5 p. fol.

Score: high solo voice ⌈key of G⌉ with piano accompaniment. English words.

ABSpl

---

*Farrell, William H.

I'm going mad over you. ⌈Popular song⌉ Words by Charles G. Kane- music by William H. Farrell. New York, Gotham-Attucks music co. ⌈c1909⌉
5 p. fol.

Score: medium solo voice ⌈key of G⌉ with piano accompaniment. English words.

ABSpl

Farrell, William H
Lucy

*Farrell, William H

Mama's blues (Papa's blues). [Popular song] By *Jas. P. Johnson and William H. Farrell. New York, Haviland pub. co. [c1917]
5 p. fol.

Score: medium solo voice [key of B^b] with piano accompaniment. English words.

ABSpl

*Farrell, William H

My little jungle maid. [Popular song] Words by *Henry S. Creamer and Charles A. Parker; music by William H. Farrell. New York, Gotham-Attucks music co. [c1910]
5 p. fol.

Score: medium solo voice [key of C] with piano accompaniment. English words.

ABSpl

*Farrell, William H

Not tonight. [Popular song] Words by *Cecil Mack; music by William H. Farrell. New York, Waterson, Berlin & Snyder co. [c1913]
5 p. fol.

Score: medium solo voice [key of C] with piano accompaniment. English words.

ABSpl

*Farrell, William H

Stop it. [Popular song] By *Jas. P. Johnson and Wm. H. Farrell. New York, Haviland pub. co. [c1917]
3 p. fol.

Score: high solo voice [key of E^b] with piano accompaniment. English words.

ABSpl

*Farrell, William F.

When I get back from over there. [Popular song] Words and music by DeWitt H. Morse and William H. Farrell. New York, Haviland pub. co. [c1918]
3 p. fol.

Score: medium solo voice [key of G] with piano accompaniment. English words.

ABSpl

*Farrell, William F.

Who will be with you when I go away? Or (When I'm far away from you.) [Popular song] Words and music by Wm. H. Farrell. New York, Haviland pub. co. [c1913]
5 p. fol.

Score: high solo voice [key of C] with piano accompaniment. English words.

ABSpl

Fisher, William Arms, 1861-

Seventy Negro spirituals; edited by William Arms Fisher ... Boston, Oliver Ditson co. [c1926]
212 p., port., fol. (The musicians library)

Score: high solo voice with piano accompaniment. Negro dialect.

Includes: Introduction (p. [vii] - xix)
Tabulated analysis of scales and metre of 5 books of spirituals (574 songs) (p. [xx])
Biographical notes (p. [xxi] - xxiii) include Burleigh, Bootner and J. . Johnson.
(continued on next card)

Fisher, William Arms, 1861- Seventy Negro spirituals... [c1926] (Card 2)

Photographs of contributors including above named.
Notes on songs (p. [xxv] - xxxi.)
Bibliography, annotated (p. [xxxiii] - xxxiv) listed chronologically 1856-1925.

Also published in New York by Chas. H. Ditson and Co., and in Chicago by Lyon and Healy, inc.

xwpl
NYPL42
NYPLS
LC

Fitzgerald, Ella
A-tisket a-tasket

Fitzgerald, Ella
Chew-chew-chew chew your bubble gum

Fitzgerald, Ella
I found my yellow basket

*Fitzgerald, Ella, ca.1918-

Spinnin' the web. [Popular song] Words by *J. C. Johnson; music by *Chick Webb and Ella Fitzgerald. New York, Famous music corp. [c1938]
5 p. fol.

Score: medium solo voice with piano accompaniment. English words.

ABSpl

Flatow, Leon.

Oh say! Can I see you tonight. [Popular] Song. Words by *Henry Creamer and Joe Schuster; music by Leon Flatow. New York: Jerome H. Remick & Co. [c1926] Publ. pl. no. 988.
5p. fol

Score: medium solo voice with piano accompaniment. English words.

ABSpl
NYPLS

*Ford, Frank W.

...America's victory; sweet liberty. Song...Words by Bessie V. Johnson; music by Frank W. Ford. Burlington, Iowa: Progressive Music Publ.Co., [c1918.]
3p. fol.

Score: medium solo voice with piano accompaniment. English words.

ABSpl

*Foresythe, Reginald, 1907-

Bit. A novelty for piano. By Reginald Foresythe. New York, Robbins music corp. [c1934] Publ. pl. no. 1266.
5 p. fol.

Score: piano solo.

ABSpl
LC

*Foresythe, Reginald, 1907-

The greener the grass. A novelty for piano. By Reginald Foresythe. New York, Robbins music corp. [c1934] Publ. pl. no. SH 1282.
3 p. fol.

Score: piano solo.

ABSpl

*Foresythe, Reginald, 1907-

He's a son of the south. Novelty song Words by *Andy Razaf and Joe Davis; music by Reginald Foresythe. New York, Joe Davis, inc. [c1933] Publ. pl. no. 1105.
3 p. fol.

Score: medium solo voice [key of E^b] with piano accompaniment. English words.

ABSpl
LC

*Foresythe, Reginald, 1907-

Mississippi basin. Fox-trot song. Words by *Andy Razaf; music by Reginald Foresythe. New York, Joe Davis inc. [c1933] Publ. pl. no. 1117.
3 p. fol.

Score: low solo voice [key of F] with piano accompaniment. English words.

ABSpl
LC

*Foresythe, Reginald, 1907-

Serenade for a wealthy widow. A novelty for piano by Reginald Foresythe. New York, Robbins music corp. [c1934] Publ. pl. no. S. H. 1203.
6 p. fol.

Score: piano solo with lyrics ad. lib.

Lyric by Dorothy Fields and Jimmy McHugh.

ABSpl
LC

*Fowler, Lemuel

He may be your man, but he comes to see me sometimes. [Popular song.] By Lemuel Fowler. Chicago: Ted Browne music co., [c1922.]

5 p. fol.

Score: medium solo voice with piano accompaniment. English words.

ABSpl

*Fowler, LeMuel

Wondrin' why I'm lonesome (and if you're lonesome too). ⌜Popular song⌝ By Lem Fowler. NY: *W. C. Handy ⌜c1928⌝
5p. fol.

Score: medium solo voice ⌜key of E♭⌝ with piano accompaniment. English words.

A BSpl
ZWpl

Franklin, Dave

Buzz, Mirandy. ⌜Popular song⌝ Lyrics by *Henry Creamer; music by Dave Franklin. New York: Shapiro, Bernstein & Co. ⌜c1922⌝
5 p. fol.

Score: medium solo voice with piano accompaniment. English words.
Caption title.
From the musical comedy, "Strut Miss Lizzie."

ABSpl

---

*Freeman, Henry Lawrence, 1875-

If thou didst love. Song. Words and music by H. Lawrence Freeman. New York, Handy brothers music co., inc. ⌜c1935⌝
6 p. fol.

Score: high solo voice ⌜key of G♭⌝ with piano accompaniment. English words.

ZWpl
ABSpl
HMC

---

*Freeman, Henry Lawrence, 1875-

Voodoo. ⌜An opera⌝ Act III. Lyrics and music by H. Lawrence Freeman. Photostat of manuscript.
32 p. fol.

Score: SATB and 2 solo voices with piano accompaniment. English words.

ABSpl

---

*Freeman, Henry Lawrence, 1875-

Whither? Song. Words and music by H. Lawrence Freeman. New York, Handy bros. music co., inc. ⌜c1935⌝
4 p. fol.

Score: high solo voice ⌜key of G⌝ with piano accompaniment. English words.

HMC
ABSpl
ZWpl

---

*Freeman, Henry Lawrence, 1875-

Zulu King. (Witch-hunt). A symphonic poem by H. Lawrence Freeman. Photostat of manuscript.
49 p. fol.

Score: piano-vocal score. English words.

ABSpl

---

*Furth, Seymour

As you and I. ⌜Popular song⌝ Words by Billy Johnson; music by Seymour Furth. New York, T. B. Harms & co., ⌜c1902⌝
5p. fol.

Score: low solo voice ⌜key of B♭⌝ with piano accompaniment. English words.

ABSpl

---

*Furth, Seymour

My Leonora Lee. ⌜Popular Song⌝ Words by Billy Johnson; music by Seymour Furth. New York, T. B. Harms & co., ⌜c1902⌝
5p. fol.

Score: medium solo voice ⌜key of B♭⌝ with piano accompaniment. English words.

ABSpl

Garcia, José Mauricio Nunes
Andante

Garcia, José Mauricio Nunes
Fugato

Gibbs, A Harrington

Runnin' wild. An ebony jazz tune. Words by Joe Grey and Leo Wood; music by A. Harrington Gibbs. New York, Leo. Feist, inc., ⌜c1922⌝ Publ. pl. no. 5156.
5 p. fol.

Score: medium solo voice with piano accompaniment. English words.

ABSpl
NBCL - (arr. for small orchestra by Sam Danks)

---

*Gomes, Antonio Carlos, 1836-1896.

A mocidade academica. Hymno. Musica de A. Carlos Gomes; poesia do. Dr. Bitencourt Sampaio. Rio de Janeiro: Sampaio A raujo & Cia. Publ. pl. no. 2759.
5 p. fol.

Score: high solo voice with piano accompaniment. Portuguese words.

ABSpl

---

*Gomes, Antonio Carlos, 1836-1896.

Addio. Romance para meio soprano ou baritono. Musica de A. Carlos Gomes. S. Paulo, Graphic Mangione. Publ. pl. no. 2650
5 p. fol.

Score: medium solo voice with piano accompaniment. Italian words.
Bound in vol. 2.

ABSpl

---

*Gomes, Antonio Carlos, 1836-1896.

...Ah! contemplar m'e dato in te l'aurora. Duetto Odalea e Condor. From Act III of the lyric opera, "Condor". Poesia de Mario Canti; musica de Carlos Gomes. Milao: Arthur Demarchi.
10 p. fol.

Score: S & T duet with piano accompaniment. Portuguese words.

Edicao especial para o Brazil.

ABSpl

---

*Gomes, Antonio Carlos, 1836-1896.

Analia ingrata! Romance. Canto. Musica de A. Carlos Gomes. Rio de Janeiro: Sampaio A raujo & Cia.
5 p. fol.

Score: high solo voice with piano accompaniment. Portugese words.
Bound in vol. 2.

ABSpl

---

*Gomes, Antonio Carlos, 1836-1896.

As Bahianas. Modinha. Os anjo bahianos nos fazem morrer, modinha, por Carlos Gomes. Rio de Janeiro: Arthur Napoleao & Ca. Publ. pl. no. 1352.
5 p. fol.

Score: high solo voice with piano accompaniment. Portugese words.
Bound in vol. 2.

ABSpl

---

*Gomes, Antonio Carlos, 1836-1896.
Atto quarto. Aria. 98122.

Bound in vol. 2.

ABS

---

*Gomes, Antonio Carlos, 1836-1896.
Atto quarto; romanza. 98124.

Bound in vol. 2.

ABS

---

*Gomes, Antonio Carlos, 1836-1896.
Atto terzo. Aria. 98120.

Bound in vol. 2.

ABS

---

*Gomes, Antonio Carlos, 1836-1896.

...Avea sultana altera. Serenata Adin. From Act III of the lyric opera, "Condor". Poesia de Mario Canti; musica de Carlos Gomes. Milao: Arthur Demarchi.
3 p. fol.

Score: Soprano solo with piano accompaniment. Portuguese words.

Edicao especial para o Brazil.

ABSpl

---

*Gomes, Antonio Carlos, 1836-1896.

Ballata Adin. Nel regno de le rose una sorgente. Aria from the lyric opera "Condor". Poesia de Mario Canti; musica de Carlos Gomes. Milao: Arthur Demarchi.
7 p. fol.
Bound in vol. 1
Score: high solo voice with piano accompaniment. Portuguese words.

Edicao especial para o Brazil.

ABSpl

*Gomes, Antonio Carlos, 1836-1896.

... Ballabili ed inno della regina. ⌐for four hands⌐. From the lyric opera, "Maria Tudo" di Emilia Prago; musica di Carlos Gomes; reduzione di Nicolo Celega para pianoforte a 4 mani. Milano: Edizioni Ricordi. Publ. pl. no. 46997.
41 p. fol.

Score: piano duet for 4 hands.

ABSpl

*Gomes, Antonio Carlos, 1836-1896.

...Febbre fatal, sogno crudel d'ebra follia! Frase Odiea. ⌐From Act III of the lyric opera, "Condor"⌐ Posesia de Mario Canti; musica de Carlos Gomes. Milano: Arthur Demarchi.
4 p. fol.

Score: high solo voice with piano accompaniment. Portuguese words.

Edicao especial para o Brazil.

ABSpl

*Gomes, Antonio Carlos, 1836-1896.

Hymno triumphal. Para grande orchestra e banda. Por A. Carlos Gomes; reducoao para piano a 2 maos. Rio de Janiero: Narciso, Arthur Napoleao & Migeuz. Publ. pl. no. 2164.
5 p. fol.
Bound in vol. 2.
Score: piano solo.

"Expressamente escripta para e grande festival do terceiro centenario de Luiz de Connoes, e executada em 10 de Junho de 1880 no Imperial Theatre D Pedro 2°, do Rio de Janeirol." — cover title page.

"A camoes" — at head of title.

ABSpl

*Gomes, Antonio Carlos, 1836-1896.

...C'era una voita un principle. Ballata. ⌐From the opera, "Il Guarany".⌐ Di A.C.Gomes. Milano: G. Ricordi & C. Pub. pl. no. 54337.
16 p. fol.

Score: soprano solo with piano accompaniment. Italian words.

ABSpl

*Gomes, Antonio Carlos, 1836-1896.

Forma sublime, eterea. Romanza. ⌐De la opera, "Salvator Rosa".⌐ Di A.C.Gomes. Milano: G. Ricordi & C. Publ. pl. no. 109957.
8 p. fol.

Score: Tenor solo with piano accompaniment.

ABSpl

*Gomes, Antonio Carlos, 1836-1896.

Il Guarany; opera-ballo in quattro atti, libretto di Antonio Scalvini, musica di A. Carlos Gomes. Prima rappresentazione, Milano, Teatro alla Scala, 19 marzo 1870. Opera completa per canto e piano-forte...Milano: G. Ricordi & C. ⌐ca 1892⌐ Publ. pl. no. 53426.
447 p. front. (port.) fol.
Bound in vol.
Score: piano-vocal. Italian words.

ABSpl
NYPL42

*Gomes, Antonio Carlos, 1836-1896.

Conselhos. (Cancao popula Brazileira) Poesia do Dr. Velho Experiente; musica de A. Carlos Gomes. Rio de Janeiro: Sampaio Araujo & Cia. Publ. pl. no. 3885.
6 p. fol.

Score: high solo voice with piano accompaniment. Portuguese words.
Bound in vol. 2.

ABSpl

*Gomes, Antonio Carlos, 1836-1896.
Fosca melodramma in quattro atti...Scena e duetto. 7703.

Bound in vol. 1.

ABS

*Gomes, Antionio Carlos, 1836-1896

Il Guarany. Opera-ballo in quattro atti. Musica di A. C. Gomes. Riduzione per pianoforte a quattro mani di Nicolo Celega. Milano: G. Ricordi & C. Publ. pl. nos. 92398-408-409; 923399-408-409, 92404.
4 v. in 1. fol.
Score: piano solos
Bound in vol. 1.
Contents: 1. Introduzione, Ballebile e Azione Mimica.
2. Passo selvaggio.
3. Passo delle freccie
4. Gran marcia-baccanale Indiano.

ABSpl

*Gomes, Antonio Carlos, 1836-1896.

...Di sposo...di padre...le gioie serene. Aria. ⌐De la opera,⌐ "Salvator Rosa". Di A.C.Gomes. Milano: G. Ricordi & C. Publ. pl. no. 110083.
5 p. fol.

Score: Ba solo with piano accompaniment. Italian words.

ABSpl

*Gomes, Antonio Carlos, 1836-1896.

...Fosca. Symphonia para piano a duas maos. De Carlos Gomes; Transcripcao de Souza Lima. Sao Paulo: Edicoes Ricordi. Publ. pl. no. B.A.7172.
11 p. fol.

Score: piano solo.
Bound in vol. 1.

ABSpl

*Gomes, Antonio Carlos, 1836-1896.

Io ti vidi. Canzone. Parole di M. Marcello; musica de A. Carlos Gomes. Rio de Janeiro: Sampairo Araujo & Cia. Publ. pl. no. 1355.
4 p. fol.

Score: high solo voice with piano accompaniment. Italian words.
Bound in vol. 2.

ABSpl

*Gomes, Antonio Carlos, 1836-1896.

Dolce rimprovero. Romance. Musica de A. Carlos Gomes; poesia de Emilio Ducati. Rio de Janeiro: Sampaio Araujo and Cia. Publ. pl. no. ~~2446~~. 2646.
4 p. fol.

Score: medium solo voice with piano accompaniment. Italian words.
Bound in vol. 2.

ABSpl

*Gomes, Antonio Carlos, 1836-1896.

...Gentile di cuore. Polacca. ⌐From the opera, "Il Guarany".⌐ Di A.C. Gomes. Publ. pl. no. 54336.
7 p. fol.

Score: soprano solo with piano accompaniment. Italian words.

ABSpl

*Gomes, Antonio Carlos, 1836-1896

Mamma dice...Arietta. Parole di G. E. Ducati; musica di A. Carlos Gomes. Rio de Janeiro: F. de Sampaio. Publ. pl. no. 3555.
7 p. fol.

Score: medium solo voice with piano accompaniment Italian words.
Bound in vol. 2.

ABSpl

*Gomes, Antonio Carlos, 1836-1896.

...Fantasia briliante. Para piano. ⌐Transcription⌐ by J. Famagaili. ⌐From the opera, "Fosca" of Carlos Gomes. Rio de Janeiro: Arthur Napoleao & Cia. Publ. pl. no. 2199.
11 p. fol.

Score: piano solo.

ABSpl

*Gomes, Antonio Carlos, 1836-1896.
Gran Marcia - baccanale indiano. 92401.

Bound in vol. 1.

ABS

*Gomes, Antonio Carlos, 1836-1896

Marcha nupcial. ⌐Para piano⌐ Por Carlos Gomes. Rio de Janeiro: Sampaio Araujo & Cia. Publ; pl. no. 3664
9 p. fol.

Score: piano solo
Bound in vol. 2.

ABSpl

*Gomes, Antonio Carlos, 1836-1896.
Passo Selvaggio. 92399-408-09.

Bound in vol. 1.

ABS

*Gomes, Antonio Carlos, 1836-1896.

Grande valsa de bravura... ⌐para piano⌐ por A. Carlos Gomes. ⌐No publisher or date given.⌐
13 p. fol. (Obl)

Score: piano solo
Bound in vol. 2.

ABSpl

*Gomes, Antonio Carlos, 1836-1896.

Masaniello. ⌐Aria de la opera, "Salvator Rosa"⌐ Dramma lirico di Antonio Ghislanzoni; musica di A. Carlos Gomes; reduzioni por canto e pianoforte di N. Celega. Milano: G. Ricordi & C, Publ. pl. no. 44000.
10 p. fol.

Score: Ba solo with piano and 2 choruses (SATB & TB) as accompaniment. Italian words.
Bound in vol. 2.

"Rappresentato per la prima volta al Teatro Carlo Felice, a Genova, il 21 marza 1874." — cover title page.

ABSpl

*Gomes, Antonio Carlos, 1836-1896.

...Mia piccirella, deh! Vieni allo mare. Canzonetta. [From the opera, "Salvator Rosa."] Di A. C. Gomes Milano: G. Ricordi & C. Publ. pl. no. 109831.
8 p. fol.

Score: Soprano solo with piano accompaniment. Italian words.

Dramma di Antonio Ghislanzoni.

ABSpl

---

*Gomes, Antonio Carlos, 1836-1896.

Monologo de Odalea. From the lyric opera, "Condor". Poesia de Mario Canti; musica de Carlos Gomes. Rio de Janeiro: Sampaio Araujo & Cia. Publ. pl. no. 6919.
5 p. fol.

Score: soprano solo with piano accompaniment. Portuguese words.

ABSpl

---

*Gomes, Antonio Carlos, 1836-1896.

Monologo di Zuleida. From the lyric opera, "Condor". Poesia de Mario Canti; musica de Carlos Gomes. Rio de Janiero: Sampaio Araujo & Cia. Publ. pl. no. 6920.
7 p. fol.

Score: S solo; with piano accompaniment. Portuguese words.

ABSpl

---

*Gomes, Antonio Carlos, 1836-1896.

Notturno - Preludio. From Act III of the lyric opera, "Candor". Del Carlos Gomes. Milao: Arthur Demarchi. Publ. pl. no. A 2046 D.
3 p. fol.

Score: piano solo.

Edicao especial para o Brazil.
Bound in vol. 1.

ABSpl

---

*Gomes, Antonio Carlos, 1836-1896.

Overture to the opera, "Il Guarany". By A. Carlos Gomes; arranged by Ross Jungnickel for orchestra. New York: G. Schirmer, Inc., [c] 1912 Publ. pl. no. 22869.
11 p. fol. (Miscellany, no. 83)

Score: piano-conductor and 14 parts including violin obligato.

ABSpl

---

*Gomes, Antonio Carlos, 1836-1896.
Passo delle freccie. 92400-408-09.

Bound in vol. 1.

ABS

---

*Gomes, Antonio Carlos, 1836-1896.

...Per me solo! Bozzetto per voce di baritono. Parole di E. Ducati; musica di Carlos Gomes. Milano: Arturo Demarchi.
5 p. fol.

Score: medium solo voice with piano accompaniment. Italian words.
Bound in vol. 2.
ABSpl

---

*Gomes, Antonio Carlos, 1836-1896.

...Perche di meste lagrime. Duetto. [From the opera, "Il Guarany".] Di A. C. Gomes. Milano: G. Ricordi & C. Publ. pl. no. 110178.
8 p. fol.

Score: S & T duet with piano accompaniment. Italian words.

ABSpl

---

*Gomes, Antonio Carlos, 1836-1896.

...Povera Bambola! Canto. Parole e musica di Carlos Gomes...Milano: Arturo Demarchi.
5 p. fol.

Score: medium solo voice with piano accompaniment. Italian words.
Bound in vol. 2.

ABSpl

---

*Gomes, Antonio Carlos, 1836-1896.

...Preludio. Para piano a duas maos. [From the lyrical opera, "Maria Tudor" by Carlos Gomes.] Transcripcao de Souza Lima. Sao Paulo: Edicoes Ricordi. Publ. pl. no. B. A. 7170.
7 p. fol.
In vol. 2.
Score: piano solo.

ABSpl

---

*Gomes, Antonio Carlos, 1836-1896.

...Quale orribile peccato. Aria. [From the opera, "Fosca".] De Carlos Gomes. S. Paulo: Edicoes Ricordi. Publ. pl. no. B. A. 7177.
10 p. fol.

Score: soprano solo with piano accompaniment. Portuguese words.

ABSpl

---

*Gomes, Antonio Carlos, 1836-1896.

...Quando nascesti tu. Tomanza - Americo. Aria de "Lo Schiavo", dramma lirico in quattro atti di Rodolfo Paravicini; musica di A. Carlos Gomes. Milano: G. Ricordi & C. Publ. pl. no. 98118.
5 p. fol.

Score: T solo with piano accompaniment. Italian words.

ABSpl

---

*Gomes, Antonio Carlos, 1836-1896.

Quartetto. [From Act III of the lyric opera, "Condor".] Poesia de Mario Canti; musica de Carlos Gomes. Milao: Arthur Demarchi.
21 p. fol.

Score: S MzT & B quartet with piano accompaniment. Portuguese words.

Edicao especial para o Brazil.
Bound in vol. 1.

ABSpl

---

*Gomes, Antonio Carlos, 1836-1896.

...Quem sabe? [Tao longe de mim distante] — Modinha. Poesia do Dr. F. L. Bittencourt Sampaio; musica de A. Carlos Gomes. Rio de Janeiro: Sampaio Araujo & Cia. Publ. pl. no. 2276.
3 p. fol.

Score: high solo voice with piano accompaniment. Portuguese words.
Bound in vol. 2.

ABSpl

---

*Gomes, Antonio Carlos, 1836-1896.

...Romanza di Fabiani. [Aria from the opera, "Maria Tudor".] De Carlos Gomes. S. Paulo: Edicoes Ricordi. Publ. pl. no. B. A. 7176.
7 p. fol.

Score: T solo with piano accompaniment. Italian words.

ABSpl

---

*Gomes, Antonio Carlos, 1836-1896.

Romanza di Giovanna. [Aria from the opera, "Maria Tudor".] De Carlos Gomes. S. Paulo: Edicoes Ricordi. Publ. pl. no. B. A. 7175.
7 p. fol.

Score: soprano solo with piano accompaniment. Italian words.

ABSpl

---

*Gomes, Antonio Carlos, 1836-1896.

...Scena e duetto — Maria e Fabiani. From "Maria Tudor", dramma lirico in quattro atti, di Emilio Prago; musica di Carlos Gomes...Riduzione per canto e pianoforte di Nicolo Celega...Milano: Edizioni Ricordi. Publ. pl. no. 46403.
14 p. fol.

Score: S & T duet with piano accompaniment. Italian words.
Bound in Vol. 2.

(continued on next card)
ABS

---

*Gomes, Antonio Carlos, 1836-1896. ...Scena e duetto...Milano. (Card 2)

"Rappresentato per la prima volta al Teatro alla Scala in Milano, il 27 Marzo 1879." — cover title page.

Bound in vol. 2.

ABSpl

---

*Gomes, Antonio Carlos, 1836-1896.

Sento una forza indomita. Duetto. [From the opera-ballet, "Il Guarany"] by A. Carlos Gomes. Riduzione per canto con accompto di pianoforte di Nicolo Celega. Milano: G. Ricordi & C. Publ. pl. no. 88528.
15 p. fol.

Score: soprano and tenor duet with piano accompaniment. Italian words.

ABSpl

---

*Gomes, Antonio Carlos, 1836-1896.

...Sento una forza indomita. Duetto. [From the opera, "Il Guarany".] Di A. C. Gomes. Milano: G. Ricordi & C. Publ. pl. no. 110177.
9 p. fol.

Score: S & T duet with piano accompaniment. Italian words.

ABSpl

---

*Gomes, Antonio Carlos, 1836-1896.

...Sulle rive di Chiaja. Scena e duetto, Isabella e Salvatore. [From the opera, "Salvator Rosa"] Di A. C. Gomes. Milano: G. Ricordi & C. Publ. pl. no. 110179.
19 p. fol.

Score: S & T duet with piano accompaniment. Italian words.

ABSpl

*Gomes, Antonio Carlos, 1836-1896.

...Vagando la notte — por l'arida piaggia. Duetto Zuleida e Condor. ₍From the lyric opera "Condor". Poesia de Mario Canti; musica de Carlos Gomes. Milao: Arthur Demarchi.
10 p. fol.

Score: Mz & T duet with piano accompaniment. Portuguese words.

Edicao especial para o Brazil.

ABSpl

*Gomes, Antonio Carlos, 1836-1896.

...Volate, colate. Romanza. ₍De la opera, "Salvator Rosa"₎ Di A. C. Gomes. Milano: G. Ricordi & C. Publ. pl. no. 109832.
6 p. fol.

Score: S solo with piano accompaniment. Italian words.

ABSpl

*Grainger, Porter

...Aunt Jemima (I'm coming home). ₍Popular song₎ By Porter Grainger, Freddie Johnson and Nat Reed. New York, Equitable music corp. ₍c1925₎
7 p. fol.

Score: medium solo voice with piano accompaniment. English words.

ABSpl

Grainger, Porter
By an old southern river

*Grainger, Porter
*Williams, Clarence
I'm gettin' my bonus in love. ₍Song₎ By *Clarence Williams and Porter Grainger. New York, *Clarence Williams music pub. co., inc. ₍c1931₎
4 p. fol.

Score: medium solo voice with piano accompaniment. English words.

ABSpl

*Grainger, Porter

Laughin' cryin' blues. The novel laughin-crying song. By Porter Grainger and Bob Ricketts. New York, Zipf music publ. co. ₍c1923₎
5 p. fol.

Score: medium solo voice with piano accompaniment. English words.

ABSpl

*Grainger, Porter

Mistreatin' daddy. ₍Popular song₎ By Porter Grainger and Bob Ricketts. New York, Rainbow music corp., ₍c1923₎
5 p. fol.

Score: medium solo voice with piano accompaniment. English words.

ABSpl

*Grainger, Porter

Taint nobody's biz-ness if I do. ₍Popular song₎... By Porter Grainger and Everett Robbins. New York, *Clarence Williams music pub. co., inc. ₍c1922₎
5 p. fol. 2 copies

Score: medium solo voice with piano accompaniment. English words.

ABSpl

*Grainger, Porter

'Tain't nobody's biz-ness if I do. ₍Popular song₎ Words and music by Porter Grainger, Graham Prince and *Clarence Williams. New York, *Clarence Williams music pub. co., inc. ₍c1936₎
3 p. fol.

Score: medium solo voice ₍key of B^{b}₎ with piano accompaniment. English words.

LC
ABSpl

Gumble, Albert
You better stop messin' around.

*Hall, Purnell Fleetwood

Christian travelers' triumphant praise. Anthem. Words and music by Purnell Fleetwood Hall. New York, *Handy bros. music co., inc. ₍c1939₎
7 p. 8°.

Score: 4 part chorus with sporano obligato and piano accompaniment. English words.
Bound in black spiral notebook no. 4.

ABSpl

*Hall, Purnell Fleetwood

I will lift up mine eyes. ₍Vocal duett... By Purnell Fleetwood Hall. New York, Handy brothers music co., inc. ₍c1939₎
9 p. fol.

Score: soprano and tenor duet with piano accompaniment. English words.

ABSpl

*Hall, Purnell Fleetwood

Let us all bow together. Negro spiritual arranged by Purnell Fleetwood Hall. New York, *Handy bros. music co., inc. ₍c1939₎
9 p. 8°.

Score: 4 part chorus (SATB) with soprano or tenor solo and piano accompaniment. English words.
Bound in black spiral notebook no. 4.

ABSpl

Hallowell, Emily comp.

Calhoun plantation songs. Collected and edited by Emily Hallowell. Boston: C. W. Thompson & co. ₍c1901₎
61 p. 8 vo.

Score: SATB for most; unaccompanied melody for several. Negro dialect.

54 Negro spirituals

Contents: 1. Amazing grace. -2. Am I born to die? -3. Band ob music. -4. Calvary. -5.

(continued on next card)

Hallowell, Emily comp. Calhoun plantation songs. ₍c1901₎ (Card 2)

De blin' man. -6. Done foun' my los'sheep. -7. Dum-a-lum. -8. End o'dat morning. -9. Fo' de Lord. -10. Go Mary an' toll de bell. -11. Good Lord, shall I be de one? -12. Gwine to shout all over God's heavn. -13. Hammering judgment. -14. Hear Gabriel blow in dat morn. -15. He's jus' de same today. -16. Hold out yo' light. -17. Holy is my God. -18. I done been home. -19. I done done. -20. I know my Jesus loves me. -21. I'll meet you way up

(continued on next card)

Hallowell, Emily comp. Calhoun plantation songs. ₍c1901₎ (Card 3)

yonder. -22. In de army. -23. Jacob's ladder long an' tall. -24. Jesus lock' de lion' jaw. -25. John de Bunyan. -26. Keep a-inching along. -27. Kind Savior. -28. Listed in de field o' battle. -29. My soul wants something dat's new. -30. O dat sun gwine down. -31. O Lord write my name. -32. O who dat coming over yonder. -33. Praying in de lan'. -34. Redeem', redeem'. -35. Roll de ol' chariot along. -36. Serving my God. -37. Sister Hannah. -38. Singing on de ol'

(continued on next card)

Hallowell, Emily comp. Calhoun plantation songs. ₍c1901₎ (Card 4)

church groun'. -39. Sitting down side ob my Jesus. -40. Somebody knocking at yo' do'. -41. Sorry to tell. -42. So sad. -43. Takes a little bit ob man to rock Dan. -44. Tall angel at de bar. -45. Tell it. -46. Thank God I'm in de field. -47. Until I reach-a my home. -48. Way up on de mountain. -49. We are climbing Jacob's ladder. -50. What you gwine to do when yo' lamp burn' down? -51. Wheel in de middle ob a wheel. -52. Where shall I be when de firs' trumpet soun'. -53. Wrastlin Jacob. -54. You got a right.

LC HMC ZWpl

Handman, Lou
Send back my honeyman.

Handy, Elizabeth

Stay. A torch ballad. Words by *Andy Razaf; music by Elizabeth Handy. New York: *Handy Bro. Music Co., inc. ₍c1936₎
5 p. fol.

Score: medium solo voice with piano accompaniment. English words.

A BSpl

Handy, Lucile Marie
Deep River blues.

Handy, William Christopher, 1873-

Aunt Hagar's blues. New revised edition ... ₍Song₎ By Wm. C. Handy ... New York, Richmond-Robbins, Inc. ₍c1921₎
5 p. fol.

Score: medium solo voice with piano accompaniment. Negro dialect.

"Adaptation from W.C. Handy's original selection, 'Aunt Hagar's Children'." —at end of caption title.

HPSpl ZWpl
ABSpl LC

Handy, William Christopher
Atlanta Blues

Handy, William Christopher
Aunt Hargar's childrens' blues

---

*Handy, William Christopher, 1873-

The basement blues (Low-downer than any low-down blues). Words and music by W. C. Handy. New York, *Handy gouge music pub. [c1924]
5 p. fol.

Score: medium solo voice key of C with piano accompaniment. Negro dialect.

ABSpl
BHC

Handy, William Christopher
Beale Street Blues.

1927 Pace & Handy Music Co.

---

*Handy, William Christopher, 1873-

Beale street blues. Words and music by W. C. Handy. New York, *Handy bros. music co. [c1917]
5 p. fol.

Score: medium solo voice [key of B^b] with piano accompaniment. Negro dialect.

ABSpl
BHC

Handy, William Christopher
Beale Street Serenade

Handy, William Christopher
Black Patti

---

*Handy, William Christopher, 1873-

Blues; an anthology. Edited by W. C. Handy; with an introduction by Abbe Niles; illustrations by Miguel Covarrubias. New York, Albert & Charles Boni [c1926]
180 p., front., illus. (incl. music) plates, fol.

Music: p. 49-180.

Score: solo voice with piano accompaniment for all but three. Negro dialect.

(continued on next card)

---

*Handy, William Christopher, 1873- Blues; an anthology ... [c1926] (Card 2)

These songs are classified under three headings: 1. The folk-song basis. -2. Blue-black. -3. The white viewpoint.

Contents: 1. Train's a comin'. -2. Cheer the weary traveller. -3. Somebody's wrong about dis Bible. -4. Joe Jacobs. -5. Goin' to see my Sarah. -6. Juba. -7. Sail away ladies. -8. Come on Eph! -9. A typical stomp. -10. Careless love. -11. Ever after on. -12. Vesta and Matties. -13. Got no more home. -14. Friendless blues. -15.

(continued on next card)

---

*Handy, William Christopher, 1873- Blues; an anthology ... [c1926] (Card 3)

Joga blues. -16. St. Louis blues. -17. Loveless love. -18. Joe Turner blues. -19. Snakey blues. -20. Goin' down that long, long lonesome road. -21. Florida blues. -22. Hesitating blues. -23. Aunt Hagar's children. -24. Stingaree blues. -25. West Texas blues. -26. Deep river blued. -27. Hooking car blues. -28. Blind man blues. -29. Banjo blues. -30. The blues I've got. -31. Rockpile blues. -32. Mississippi Delta blues. -33. Mountain top blues. -34. Kansas city blues.

(continued on next card)

---

*Handy, William Christopher, 1873- Blues; an anthology ... [c1926] (Card 4)

-35. Long gone blues. -36. John Henry blues. -37. Atlanta blues. -38. Chicago gouge. -39. Gouge of Armour Avenue. -40. Dallas blues. -41. You'll think of e. -42. Blue gummed blues. -43. Harlem blues. -44. Homesickness blues. -45. Left all alone again blues. -46. You don't know the half of it Dearie blues. -47. Concerto in F. -48. Krazy Kat. -49. Rhapsody in blue.

ABSPL HMC NYPL42 NYPLS ZWpl
BHC LC YJWJ

---

*Handy, William Christopher, 1873-

...Careless love. (Folk melody) By W. C. Handy. New York, *Handy brothers music co. inc. [c1935]
5 p. fol.

Score: high solo voice [key of A^b] with piano accompaniment. English words.
Caption title.

7 extra verses by Martha E. Koenig and *Spencer Williams on p. 5.

ABSpl

---

*Handy, William Christopher, 1873-

Chantez les bas. Sing 'em low. [Creole blues] words and music by W.C. Handy. New York, *W.C. Handy, Music Publisher, [c1931]
5 p. fol.

Score: low solo voice [key of E^b] with piano accompaniment. Negro dialect.

ABSpl
LC

---

*Handy, William Christopher, 1873-

Darktown reveilee (adaptation from W. C. Handy's famous "Bugle blues.") Lyric by Walter Kirsch; melody by *Chris Smith and W. C. Handy. New York, Robbins music corp. [c1923]
5 p. fol.

Score: medium solo voice [key of F] with piano accompaniment. Negro dialect.

ABSpl
BHC
LC

Handy, William Christopher
Finis (4 copies)

---

*Handy, William Christopher, 1873-

... Friendless blues. Song words by *Mercedes Gilbert; music by W.C. Handy. New York, Handy Bros. Music Co., Inc. [c1926]
5 p. fol.

Score: medium solo voice [key of E^b] with piano accompaniment. English words.

ABSpl
HPSpl

---

*Handy, William Christopher, 1873-

Go and get the enemy blues. [Song] Words by Langston Hughes; music by W. C. Handy and *Clarence Jones. New York, *Handy bros. music co., inc. [c1942]
5 p. fol.

Score: medium solo voice with piano accompaniment. English words.

Also arranged for dance orchestra.

ABSpl
LHpl
ZWpl [HPSpl]

---

*Handy, William Christopher, 1873- arr.

Go down, Moses (Let my people go) a Negro spiritual arranged by W. C. Handy; adapted for organ by W. C. Simon. New York, *Handy bros. music co., inc. [c1930]
7 p. 8 vo.

Score: organ solo.

ABSpl
YJWJ

---

*Handy, William Christopher, 1873-

The good Lord sent me you. Song. By Elsie Francis, Stella Francis, and W.C. Handy. New York, *Handy bros. music co., inc. [c1936]
4 p. fol.

Score: low solo voice [key of D minor] with piano accompaniment. English words.

ABSpl
LC

---

*Handy, William Christopher, 1873

Harlem blues. Song. By W.C. Handy ... New York, published by W.C. Handy [c1922]
8 p. fol.

Score: low solo voice [key of C] with piano accompaniment. Negro dialect.

"Foreword" by George W. Harris.

ZWpl ABSpl
ABSpl LC
YJWJ

---

*Handy, William Christopher, 1873-

The hesitating blues. By W. C. Handy. New York, *Pace & Handy music co. [c1915]
5 p. fol.

Score: medium solo voice with piano accompaniment. English words.

ABSpl
YJWJ
[HPSpl]

*Handy, William Christopher, 1873-

Hist de window Noah. Negro spiritual. Arranged for mixed voices by William C. Handy. New York, William C. Handy, Publisher. [c1933]
7 p. 8vo.

Score: SATB with piano accompaniment. Negro dialect.

ABSpl
HMC

---

*Handy, William Christopher, 1873- arr.

Nobody knows the trouble I see. [Negro spiritual] [Arranged by W. C. Handy] New York, *Handy bros. music co. [c1936]
5 p. fol.

Score: medium solo voice [key of C minor] with piano accompaniment. Negro dialect.

ABSpl
BHC
HPSpl

---

*Handy, William Christopher, 1873-

Saint Louis blues. Words and music by W. C. Handy. New York, Handy bros. music co., inc. [c1914]
5 p. fol.

Score: medium solo voice [key of G] with piano accompaniment. Negro dialect.
Caption title

"First introduced and popularized by Ted Lewis, pioneer in blues and jazz," — at end of title.

BHC ABSpl
ZWpl HMC YJWJ HPSpl WORL

---

*Handy, William Christopher, 1873-

The hooking cow blues. (A Texas jazz song.) Words and music by Douglass Williams; jazz and blues music by W.C. Handy. New York, Pace & Handy Music Co. [c1917]
3 p. fol.

Score: medium solo voice with piano. English words.

ABSpl

Handy, William Christopher
Oh, didn't he ramble

Handy, William Christopher
Shine like a morning star

---

*Handy, William Christopher, 1873- arr.

I'll never turn back no more. [Negro spiritual. Arranged by W. C. Handy] New York, *Handy bros. music co. [c1935]
3 p. fol.

Score: high solo voice [key of A minor] with piano accompaniment. Negro dialect.

ABSpl
BHC
ZWpl
HPSpl

---

*Handy, William Christopher, 1873-

Ole Miss blues. Lyric revised by Walter Hirsch; [music] by W. C. Handy. New York, Robbins music corp. [c1923]
5 p. fol.

Score: medium solo voice [key of G] with piano accompaniment. Negro dialect.

ABSpl
BHC
LC HPSpl

---

*Handy, William Christopher, 1873-

Somebody's wrong about dis Bible. [Chorus] By W.C. Handy; stanzas by Arthur J. Neale. New York, W.C. Handy Music Publisher. [c1930]
3 p. 8vo.

Score: SATB. Negro dialect.

ZWpl
HMC
ABSpl

Handy, William Christopher
The Jogo Blues

---

*Handy, William Christopher, 1873-

Opportunity. [Song] Poem by Walter Malone; music by W.C. Handy. New York, W.C. Handy Music, publisher. [c1934]
5 p. fol.

Score: medium solo voice [key of F] English words.

ABSpl

---

*Handy, William Christopher, 1873-

Sounding brass and tinkling cymbals. [Song] Dedicated to jazz orchestra conductors by the grandfather of jazz, W. C. Handy. New York, *W. C. Handy music pub. [c1929]
4 p. fol.

Score: medium solo voice [key of F] with piano accompaniment. English words.

ABSpl
YJWJ
ZWpl

---

*Handy, William Christopher, 1873- arr.

Long gone. [Song] Words by *Chris Smith; music by W. C. Handy. [New York, *Pace & Handy music co., inc. c1920]
5 p. fol.

Score: medium solo voice with piano accompaniment. Negro dialect.

ABSpl
YJWJ

Handy, William Christopher
Pasadena

---

*Handy, William Christopher, 1873-

Sundown blues (Hurry sundown and let tomorrow come). [Words and music] by W. C. Handy. New York, *Handy bros. music co. [c1923]
5 p. fol.

Score: medium solo voice [key of E^b] with piano accompaniment. Negro dialect.

Caption title.

ABSpl
BHC
LC HPSpl

---

*Handy, William Christopher, 1873

... Loveless Love. A blues novelty song by W.C. Handy. New York, Handy Bros. Music Co., [c1929]

7 p. fol.

Score: medium solo voice with piano accompaniment. English words.

ABSpl

Handy, William Christopher
Remembered

---

*Handy, William Christopher, 1873-

... The temple of music. [Chorus] A tribute to Robert T. (Bob) Motts. By W. C. Handy and *Joe Jordan. New York, Handy Bros. Music Co., Inc. [c1940]
4 p. 8vo.

Score: SATB. English words.

"Unsung Americans --sung. (Negro history in song --edited by W.C. Handy)" --at head of title.

ABSpl

---

*Handy, William Christopher, 1873-

Memphis Blues. [Song] By W.C. Handy. New York, Joe Morris Music Co., [c1913]
5 p. fol.

Score: medium solo voice with piano accompaniment. English words.

"Featured by Mae West in the Paramount production 'Belle of the Nineties'" -- at end of title.

ABSpl

---

*Handy, William Christopher, 1873- , arr.

The rough rocky road. (I'm most done travelling.) Negro spiritual. Arranged by W.C. Handy. New York, *Handy Bros. Music Co., Inc. [c1921]
5 p. fol.

Score: low solo voice [key of E^b] with piano accompaniment. Negro dialect.

ABSpl

---

*Handy, William Christopher, 1873- ed.

Ten songs from unsung Americans--sung (Negro history in song). Edited by W. C. Handy. For voice with piano accompaniment... New York, Handy bros. music co., inc [c1943]
10 v. 8 vo.

Scores: solo voice with piano accompaniment. English words.

Contents: 1*Booker Taliaferro Washington.

(cont. on next card)

*Handy, William Christopher, 1873- ed. (Card 2)

Ten songs from unsung Americans--sung...

Contents...

2. *Frederick Douglas. 3. Private *Robert Harold Brooks. 4. *Dorie Miller. 5. The Curator (* 6. *Richard Allen. 7. *Ira Aldridge. 8. *George Washington Carver. 9. Lincoln's Gettysburg Address. 10. A soldier's prayer.

ZWPL
HMC

---

*Handy, William Christopher, 1873-

W.C.Handy's famous blues for the Hawaiian guitar, including "Saint Louis blues". Arrangements by John Martell, NY, *Handy Bros. Music Co. inc., [c 1938]
47 p. fol.

Part: guitar solo. Also the notes and diagram system is given for the player who does not wish to read the music part.

(continued on next card)

---

*Hare, Maud Cuney

Six Creole folk-songs. With original Creole and translated English text. By Maud Cuney Hare... New York, Carl Fischer. [c1921] Publ. pl. no. 21859.
24 p. fol.

Score: medium solo voice with piano accompaniment. French patois and English words.

Contents: 1. Aurore Pradere (A love song). -2. Carde piti mulet la (Musieu Bainjo). -3. Belle Layotte (A love song). -4. Quand Mo-te jeune (Bal fini). -5. Aine, de, trois, Caroline (Song of longing). -6. Dialogue d'Amour. (Song of Mockery).

LC
ABSpl

---

*Handy, William Christopher, 1873- arr.

'Tis the old ship of Zion. [Negro spiritual] [Arranged by W. C. Handy] New York, *Handy bros. music co. [c1935]
4 p. 8 vo.

Score: SATB; with piano accompaniment. Negro dialect.

ABSpl
BHC

---

*Handy, William Christopher, 1873
W.C.Handy's famous blues...NY c 1938 (Card 2)

Contents: 1. Saint Louis blues,- 2. John Henry blues,- 3. Way down south where the blues began.

ABSpl

Hawthorne, Alice
Listen to the mocking bird
See Richard Milburn

---

*Handy, William Christopher, 1873- arr.

Train's a comin'. Negro spiritual. (In Handy, W. C. Blues; an anthology. New York, 1926, p. 49)

Score: medium solo voice with piano accompaniment. Negro dialect.

ABSPL	HMC	NYPL42	YJWJ
BHC	LC	NYPLS	ZWpl

---

*Handy, William Christopher, 1873-

Wall Street blues. [Song] Words by Margaret Gregory and W. C. Handy. New York, *W. C. Handy music pub. [c1929]
6 p. fol.

Score: medium solo voice with piano accompaniment. English words.

The author acknowledges extra stanzas contributed by *Spencer Williams, E. Abbe Niles and Arthur J. Neale.

ABSpl
YJWJ HPSpl

---

*Hayes, Roland W 1887-

A fragrant flower. Song... [Words and music] By R. W. Hayes. Boston, C. W. Thompson and co. [c1916] Publ. pl. no. T. & co. 1904.
5 p. fol.

Score: high solo voice [key of D^b] with piano accompaniment. English words.

ZWpl-Mss. copy of song.
ABSpl
LC

---

*Handy, William Christopher, 1873-

Vesuvius; (There's a red glow in the sky above Vesuvius) a timely plea for universal peace. [Song] Poem by *Andy Razaf; title and music by William C. Handy. New York, *Handy bros. music co., inc. [c1935]
5 p. fol.

Score: medium solo voice [key of C] with piano accompaniment. English words.

ABSpl
YJWJ
ZWpl
HPSpl

---

*Handy, William Christopher, 1873-

Way down south where the blues began. By W. C. Handy. New York, *Handy bros. music co., inc. [c1932]
5 p. fol.

Score: medium solo voice [key of G] with piano accompaniment. English words.

HPSpl
ABSpl
LC
YJWJ
ZWpl

---

*Hayes, Roland W 1887-

Sit down. Negro spiritual. Arranged by Roland Hayes. New York, G. Ricordi and co. [c1923] Publ. pl. no. N.Y. 365.
7 p. fol.

Score: low solo voice with piano accompaniment. Negro dialect.

ABSpl
LC

---

*Handy, William Christopher, 1873-

W. C. Handy's collection of Negro spirituals for mixed voices, male voices; also vocal solos with piano accompaniment [arranged by W. C. Handy]... New York, *Handy bros. music co., inc. [c1938]
116 p. 8 vo.

Score: TTBB for 8; SATB for 21; medium solo voice for 3. All with piano accompaniment. Negro dialect.

(continued on next card)

---

*Handy, William Christopher, 1873-

"When the black man has a nation of his own." [Male quartet.] Words by *J. M. Miller; music by W. C. Handy. Arranged by *William C. Elkins. New York, *Handy bros. music co., inc. [c1933]
5 p. 8 vo.
Bound in black spiral notebook no. 4.
Score: TTBB; with piano accompaniment. English words.

ABSpl

---

*Hebron, J Harvey

Good-night. Song with violin obligato. Poem by *Paul Lawrence [sic] Dunbar; music by J. Harvey Hebron Philadelphia, M. D. Swisher pub. [c1913]
5 p. fol.

Score: medium solo voice with piano accompaniment and violin obligato (ad lib.) English words.

ABSpl

---

*Handy, William Christopher, 1873- W. C. Handy's collection of Negro spirituals... [c1938] (Card 2)

Contents: 1. Nobody knows the trouble I see. -2. I'll never turn back no more. -3. The rough rocky road (I'm most done travellin') -4. Room enough. -5. I've just come from the fountain. -6. My Lord's writing all the time. -7. Been a listening. -8... You better mind. -9. Get right, church, get right. -10. ...See the sign of the judgment. -11. Children, you'll be called on. -12. I want to be ready.

(continued on next card)

Handy, William Christopher
Yellow dog blues

---

*Hebron, J Harvey

Longing. Song. Poem by *Paul Laurence Dunbar; music by J. Harvey Hebron. Philadelphia, M. D. Swisher pub. [c1915]
5 p. fol.

Score: medium solo voice with piano accompaniment. English words.

ABSpl

---

*Handy, William Christopher, 1873- W. C. Handy's collection of Negro spirituals... [c1938] (Card 3)

-13. The gospel train. -14. The rocks and the mountains. -15. Sunday morning band. -16. I'll be there in the morning. -17. I'm drinking from a fountain (that never runs day). -18. Stand on the rodk a little longer. -19. We'll go on and serve the Lord. -20. Turn back Pharaoh's army, hallelu.

Hanley, James F

Any way the wind blows. [Popular song] By *Henry Creamer and James F. Hanley. New York: Shapiro, Bernstein & co. [c1924]
5 p. fol.

Score: medium solo voice with piano accompaniment. English words.

ABSpl

---

*Hemmenway, James

The Philadelphia Hop waltz... [For piano] By J. Hemmenway. Philadelphia, George Willig. [No date given]
3 p. fol.

Score: piano solo.

"As performed by Hemmenway's band, Washington Hall, and dedicated to the Ladies of Philadelphia..." — at end of title.

ABSpl

*Henderson, James Fletcher, 1898-

It's wearin' me down. ⌊Popular song⌋ Words by J. C. Johnson; music by Fletcher Henderson. New York, Harms inc. ⌊c1932⌋ Publ. pl. no. 8845.
5 p. fol.

Score: medium solo voice with piano accompaniment. English words.

ABSpl

---

*Henderson, Fletcher

Whoopee! ⌊Popular song⌋ By William Morice, Geo. J. Bennett and Fletcher Henderson. New York, Mimic music publ. co. ⌊c1927⌋
5 p. fol.

Score: medium solo voice with piano accompaniment. English words.

ABSpl

---

*Henry, S R

The colored major. Characteristic march and two-step ⌊for piano⌋ By S. R. Henry. New York, The Lyceum publ. co., ⌊c1900⌋
5 p. fol.

Score: piano solo.

ABSpl

Heyman, Edward
Heart of Mine

---

*Heywood, Donald

Back in circulation. ⌊Popular song⌋ Words and music by Donald Heywood. New York, Mills music pub. ⌊c1938⌋
5 p. fol.

Score: medium solo voice ⌊key of F⌋ with piano accompaniment. English words.
Excerpt from musical show, "Black rhythm"

ABSpl

---

*Heywood, Donald

Brown sugar. ⌊Popular song⌋ Words and music by Donald Heywood. New York, Remick music corp. ⌊c1932⌋ Publ. pl. no. 2317.
5 p. fol.

Score: medium solo voice ⌊key of C⌋ with piano accompaniment. English words.

Excerpt from "The black berries of 1932"

ABSpl

---

*Heywood, Donald

Charleston ball. ⌊Popular song⌋ Lyrics and music by Donald Heywood. New York, Edward B. Marks music co. ⌊c1925⌋ Publ. pl. no. 9349.
5 p. fol.

Score: medium solo voice ⌊key of C⌋ with piano accompaniment. Negro dialect.

ABSpl

---

*Heywood, Donald

Clorinda. ⌊Popular song⌋ Words and music by Donald Heywood. New York, Robbins music corp. c1927 Publ. pl. no. SH372.
5p. fol.

Score: medium solo voice ⌊key of E^b⌋ with piano accompaniment. English words.
Caption title.

Sung by *Ethel Waters in the musical show, "Africana".
LC
ABSpl

---

*Heywood, Donald

First thing in the morning. ⌊Popular song⌋ Words and music by Donald Heywood. New York, Remick music corp. ⌊c1932⌋ Publ. pl. no. 2318.
5 p. fol.

Score: medium solo voice ⌊key of C⌋ with piano accompaniment. English words.

ABSpl

---

*Heywood, Donald

Home beyond the river. ⌊Popular song⌋ Words and music by Donald Heywood. New York G. Schirmer (inc.) ⌊c1932⌋ Publ. pl. no. 35912.
5 p. fol.

Score: medium solo voice ⌊key of E^b⌋ with piano accompaniment. Negro dialect.

ABSpl

---

*Heywood, Donald

...I'm coming Virginia. ⌊Popular song⌋ Words by *Will Marion Cook; music by Donald Heywood. New York, Robbins music corp. ⌊c1927⌋ Publ. pl. no. SH324.
5 p. fol.

Score: medium solo voice ⌊key of F⌋ with piano accompaniment. English words.

YJWJ
ABSpl

---

*Heywood, Donald

Laz'rus. ⌊Song⌋ From Donald Heywood's "Blow, Gabriel blow," a Negro folk drama presented by The Negro art theatre. Story, lyrics and music by Donald Heywood; staged by Edgar J. Ulmer; additional lyrics by Hal Hode. New York, *Handy bros. music co., inc. ⌊c1935⌋
10 p. fol.

Score: high solo voice ⌊key of E^b⌋ with piano accompaniment. Negro dialect.

ABSpl

Heywood, Donald
The penalty of love

---

*Heywood, Donald

Smile. ⌊Popular song⌋ Words and music by Donald Heywood. New York, Robbins music corp. ⌊c1927⌋ Publ. pl. no. SH373.
5p. fol.

Score: medium solo voice ⌊key of A^b⌋ with piano accompaniment. English words.
Caption title.

Sung by *Ethel Waters in the musical show, "Africana".
ABSpl
LC

Hill, Alexander
Armful o' sweetness

Hill, Alexander
Draggin' my heart around

---

*Hill, Alexander, 1907-1937.

I would do anything for you. ⌊Popular song⌋ By Alexander Hill, Bob Williams and *Claude Hopkins. New York, Mayfair music corp. ⌊c1932⌋
5 p. fol.

Score: medium solo voice ⌊key of E^b⌋ with piano accompaniment. English words.

ABSpl
LC

---

*Hill, Alexander, 1907-1937.

Keep a song in your soul. ⌊Popular song⌋ Words and music by *Thomas Waller and Alexander Hill. New York: Joe Davis inc., ⌊c1930⌋ Publ. pl. no. 1034.
5p. fol.

Score: medium solo voice with piano accompaniment. English words.

ABSpl

Hill, Alexander
Let's have a jubilee

---

*Hill, Alexander, 1907-1937.
*Waller, Thomas "Fats"

Little Brown Betty. ⌊Popular song⌋ Words and music by Alex Hill and *Fats Waller. New York: Red Star music co. ⌊c1931⌋
5p. fol.

Score: medium solo voice ⌊key of B^b⌋ with piano accompaniment. English words.

ABSpl
LC

Hill, Alexander
Long about midnight

Hill, Alexander
Passing time with me

*Hill, Alexander, 1907-1937.

Shout, sister, shout! ⌐Popular song¬ By *Clarence Williams, *Tim Brymn and Alexander Hill. New York, *Clarence Williams music pub. co. ⌐c1930¬
5 p. fol.

Score: medium solo voice ⌐key of A♭¬ with piano accompaniment. English words.

ABSpl

Hill, Alexander
A song (how the first song was born)

Hill, Alexander
Take this little rose

Hill, Alexander
There must have been a devil in the moon.

*Hill, JohnLeubrie ,1873-1916.

At the ball, that's all. ⌐Popular song¬ Words and music by J. Leubrie Hill. New York, Jerome H. Remick & co. ⌐c1913¬
5 p. fol.

Score: medium solo voice ⌐key of D¬ with piano accompaniment. English words.

ABSpl
LC

*Hill, John Leubrie, 1873-1916.

Boo-loo beau. (I love him with a love that never dies.) ⌐Popular song¬ Words by Eddie Leonard; music by J. Leubrie Hill. New York, Jos. W. Stern and co. ⌐c1910¬ Publ. pl. no. 6708.
5p. fol.

Score: medium solo voice ⌐key of F¬ with piano accompaniment. English words.

LC
ABSpl

Hill, John Leubrie
Daffy-down-dilly

*Hill, John Leubrie, 1873-1916.

...Dear old Dixie. ⌐Popular song¬ Words and music by J. Leubrie Hill. New York, Jerome H. Remick and co. ⌐c1913¬
6p. fol.

Score: medium solo voice ⌐key of F¬ with piano accompaniment. English words.

"From the Darktown Follies in a three act musical comedy entitled 'My friend from Kentucky'; book, lyrics, music and staging by J. Leubrie Hill."

Cover title page has photograph inset of composer.

ABSpl

*Hill, John Leubrie, 1873-1916.

Every little motion. ⌐Popular song¬ Words and music by J. Leubrie Hill...New York, Jerome H. Remick and co. ⌐c1914¬
5p. fol.

Score: medium solo voice with piano accompaniment English words.

"From Ziegfeld Follies, 1914" -- cover title.

ABSpl

*Hill, John Leubrie, 1873-1916.

I know your face but I can't call your name. ⌐Popular song¬ by John L. Hill and Adolph Henderson. New York, Jos. W. Stern and co. ⌐c1902¬ Publ. pl. no. 3385.
5p. fol.

Score: medium solo voice ⌐key of G¬ with piano accompaniment. English words.

"Sung with great success by *George H. Walker" -- title page.

ABSpl

*Hill, John Leubrie, 1873-1916.

Molasses candy song. ⌐Popular song¬ Words by Eddie Leonard; music by J. Leubrie Hill. New York, Jos. W. Stern and co. ⌐c1910¬ Publ. pl. no. 6658.
5p. fol.

Score: low solo voice ⌐key of G¬ with piano accompaniment. English words.

ABSpl

*Hill, John Leubrie, 1873-1916.

My trombone man. ⌐Popular song¬ Lyrics by Harold Atteridge; music by J. Leubrie Hill. New York, G. Schirmer, ⌐c1915¬ Publ. pl. no. 25847.
P. 34-40 (detached from the score) fol.

Score: medium solo voice ⌐key of G¬ with piano accompaniment. English words.

"As sung in the Winter Garden Company's Annual production, 'The Passing Show of 1915'" -- title page.

ABSpl

*Hill, John Leubrie, 1873-1916.

Rock me in the cradle of love. ⌐Popular song¬ Words and music by J. Leubrie Hill. New York, Jerome Remick and co. ⌐c1914¬
6p. fol.

Score: medium solo voice ⌐key of F¬ with piano accompaniment. English words.

Excerpt from the musical comedy, "My friend from Kentucky".

ABSpl
LC

*Hill, John Leubrie, 1873-1916.

Rosey Posey. ⌐Popular song¬ Lyrics by Harold Atteridge; music by J. Leubrie Hill. New York, G. Schirmer ⌐c1915¬ Publ. pl. no. 25848.
5p. fol.

Score: medium solo voice ⌐key of G¬ with piano accompaniment. English words.

"As sung in the Winter Garden Company's production 'A World of Pleasure'" -- title page.

ABSpl

*Hill, John Leubrie, 1873-1916.

Syncopation. ⌐Popular song¬ Words and music by J. Leubrie Hill. New York, G. Schirmer ⌐c1915¬ Publ. pl. no. 26201.
5p. fol.

Score: high solo voice ⌐key of G¬ with piano accompaniment. English words.

"As sung in the Winter Garden Company's production, 'A World of Pleasure'" -- title page.

LC
ABSpl

*Hillman, Charles

Preparedness blues. ⌐For piano¬ By Chas. Hillman. New York, Pace and Handy music co. ⌐c1917¬
3 p. fol.

Score: piano solo.

ABSpl

Hillman, Roc
I bought a wooden whistle

*Hines, Earl

You can depend on me. ⌐Popular song¬ Words and music by Charles Carpenter, Louis Dunlap and Earl Hines. New York, Southern music pub. co., inc. ⌐c1932¬
5 p. fol.

Score: medium solo voice with piano accompaniment. English words.

ABSpl

Hines, Earl
Thinkin' of you

Hogan, Ernest, pseud. (William Fields Crowdus)
All Coons look alike to me

Hogan, Ernest, pseud. (William Fields)
Crowdus
Contribution box-Mina.

Hogan, Ernest, pseud. (William Fields)
Crowdus
De congregation will please keep their seats

Hogan, Ernest, pseud. (William Fields)
He may get over it, but... Crowdus

Hogan, Ernest, pseud. (William Fields)
Crowdus
He used to be a friend of mine

Hogan, Ernest, pseud. (William Fields)
Is everybody happy Crowdus

Hogan, Ernest, pseud. (William Fields)
La pasmala Crowdus

Hogan, Ernest, pseud. (William Field)
The missionary man Crowdus

Hogan, Ernest, pseud. (William Fields)
My little jungle queen Crowdus

Hogan, Ernest, pseud. (William Fields)
My sweet Moana Crowdus

Hogan, Ernest, pseud. (William Fields)
Crowdus
Razor dat am a black man's friend

Hogan, Ernest, pseud. (William Fields)
Roll on Mr. Moon Crowdus

Hogan, Ernest, pseud. (William Fields)
Wink, Wink, Wink Mr. Owl. Crowdus

*Holland, Justin Minor, 1819- arr.

Her bright smile haunts me still. [Song] Words by J. E. Carpenter; music by W. T. Wrighton; arranged for guitar and voice by Justin Holland. Cleveland, Brainard and co. c1858. Publ. pl. no. 358.
5 p. fol.

Score: medium solo voice with guitar accompaniment. English words.

ABSpl

*Holland, Justin Minor, 1819- arr.

...Spanish fandango. For the guitar. By Justin Holland. Cleveland, S. Brainard & co. [c1856]
5 p. fol.

Part: guitar solo.

ABSpl
LC

Holland, Justin
Hunting rondo

Hoover, Joe

Rhythm king. [Popular song] Words by Jo' Trent; music by Joe Hoover. New York, Waterson Berlin & Snyder co. [c1928] Publ. pl. no. 1863.

5p. fol.

Score: medium solo voice with piano accompaniment. English words.

"Featured by Ben Bernie" -- title cover.

ABSpl

*Hopkins, Claude, ca. 1900-

Crazy fingers.
(In Hopkins, Claude. Original piano solos. New York, 1937, p. 14-16.)

Score: piano solo.

ABSpl
LC

*Hopkins, Claude, ca 1900-

Cryin' my heart out for you. [Popular song] Lyric by *J. C. Johnson; music by Claude Hopkins. New York, Southern music pub. co. inc. [c1936]
5 p. fol.

Score: medium solo voice [key of B♭] with piano accompaniment. English words.

ABSpl
LC

*Hopkins, Claude, ca 1900-

Deep dawn. Torch ballad. Lyric by *J. C. Johnson; music by Claude Hopkins. New York, *Handy bros. music co. inc. [c1936]
5 p. fol.

Score: medium solo voice [key of G] with piano accompaniment. English words.

ABSpl
LC
ZWpl

*Hopkins, Claude, ca. 1900-

Grotesque.
(In Hopkins, Claude. Original piano solos. New York, 1937, p. 8-10)

Score: piano solo.

ABSpl
LC

*Hopkins, Claude, ca. 1900-

Hopkins' scream.
(In Hopkins, Claude. Original piano solos. New York, 1937, p. 4-7.)

Score: piano solo.

ABSpl
LC

*Hopkins, Claude, ca 1900-
Hill, Alexander
I would do anything for you. Popular song By *Alexander Hill, Bob Williams and Claude Hopkins. New York, Mayfair music corp. c1932
5 p. fol.

Score: medium solo voice key of E^b with piano accompaniment. English words.

ABSpl
LC

---

*Hopkins, Claude, ca. 1900-

Original piano solos. Five original modern novelty piano solos composed and arranged by Claude Hopkins. New York, JoeDavis, inc., c1937 Publ. pl. nos. 3726-3730.
18 p. fol.

Contents: 1. Hopkins' scream. -2. Grotesque. -3. Sand fiddler. -4. Crazy fingers. -5. Retrospection.

ABSpl
LC

---

*Hopkins, Claude, ca. 1900-

Retrospection.
(In Hopkins, Claude. Original piano solos. New York, 1937, p. 17-18.)

Score: piano solo.

ABSpl
LC

---

*Hopkins, Claude, ca. 1900-

(Sand fiddler.
In Hopkins, Claude. Original piano solos. New York, 1937, p. 11-13.)

Score: piano solo.

ABSpl
LC

---

*Hopkins, Claude, ca. 1900-

Thru' with love affairs. Popular song Lyric by J. C. Johnson; music by Claude Hopkins. New York, Stasny-Lang, inc. c1936
5 p. fol. 2 copies

Score: medium solo voice with piano accompaniment. English words.

ABSpl

---

*Hopkins, Claude, ca. 1900-

What can I do to convince you? (I love you? Popular song Words and music by Frede Liscombe and Claude Hopkins. New York, Goebel and Liscombe music publ. c1933
5 p. fol. 2 copies

Score: medium solo voice with piano accompaniment. English words.

On page 2 is a novelty piano solo arrangement of the same by Claude Hopkins.

ABSpl

---

*Huffman, Ethel Brown

Singable songs for tiny tots; rote songs for primary grades. Set to music by Ethel Brown Huffman. St. Louis, Shattinger c1935
25 p. $25\frac{1}{2}$ cm.

Score: unison voices with piano accompaniment. English words.
Contains 27 songs, and instructions for dramatizing each.

NYPLS - gift of A. A. Schomburg
ABSpl

---

*Hughes, Langston
*Price, Florence Bond
Songs to the dark virgin. Song. Words by Langston Hughes; music by *Florence B. Price. New York, G. Schirmer, inc. c1941 Publ. pl. no. 39462O.
5 p. fol.

Score: medium solo voice key of G with piano accompaniment. English words.

This song is in the repertory of *Marian Anderson.
ABSpl
YJWJ - inscribed to Carl Van Vechten by Langston Hughes.
ZWpl

Ingham, Nelson

Talkin' to myself. [Popular song] [Words and music] by Nelson Ingham and Chas. Smith. New York, Joe Morris music co. [c1928]

5p fol.

Score: medium solo voice [key of E^b] with piano and ukulele accompaniment. English words.

ABSpl

---

*Jackson, Eugene Aldama arr.

Don't be weary, traveller. Negro spiritual arranged by E. Aldama Jackson. New York, H. W. Gray co. c1919, Publ. pl. no. M. S. 158.
6 p. 8°. (Modern series no. 158)

Score: SATB with alto solo and piano accompaniment. English words.
Bound in black spiral notebook no. 4.

ABSpl

---

*Jackson, Eugene Aldama arr.

Go down Moses. Negro spiritual arranged by E. Aldama Jackson. New York, H. W. Gray co. c1919; Publ. pl. no. M.S. 157.
7 p. 8°. (Modern series no. 157)

Score: SATB with soprano solo and piano accompaniment. English words.
Bound in black spiral notebook no. 4.

ABSpl
LC

Card I
*Jackson, Marylou India

Negro spirituals and hymns. Arranged for women's choruses and quartettes. By Marylou I. Jackson... New York, J. Fischer & bro., 1935.
59 p. 8 vo.

Scores: SSAA with piano reduction for rehearsal only for 25 songs.
Contents: 1. We are climbing Jacob's ladder (spiritual of aspiration) 2. My Lord! What a mornin' (A judgement day spiritual) 3. Dere's no

---

Card II
*Jackson, Marylou India

hidin' place. (Judgment day spiritual) 4. Steal away. (A communion with God). 5. Hallelujah (Baptismal spiritual) 6. Scandalize my name. (Folk song) 7. Let us break bread together. (Communion spiritual) 8. Done foun' my los' sheep. (Revival spiritual). 9. Cert'nly Lawd. (Confession spiritual) 10. Go tell it on the mountain. (A Christmas spiritual) 11. Go down Moses (Deliverance spiritual) 12. A witness (A Bibleistic and confession spiritual) 13. Joshua fit de battle of Jericho. (Bibleistic spiritual). 14. Gwinter sing all along de way.

Card III
*Jackson, Marylou India

Negro spirituals and hymns...
(A war spiritual). 15. Lord, I want to be a Christian (A prayer; spiritual of aspiration). 16. Shine on me. (Gospel hymn) 17. Trampin' (A spiritual of determination) 18. You better min'. (A warning spiritual). 19. Let us cheer the weary traveler. (A spiritual of hope, faith, and inspiration). 20. Ain't goin' a study war no more. (A peace spiritual) 21. Good news (A death spiritual) 22. Crucifixion (Bibleistic spiritual) 23. I can't stay away (Bibleistic spiritual) 24. Is there anybody here? (A confession spiritual)
LC HMC ZWpl
NYPLS ABSpl

---

*Jessye, Eva A

My spirituals, edited & arranged,. By Eva A. Jessye; Illustrated by Millar of the Roland company; New York: Robbins - Engil, inc. c1927, publ. pl. no. B.F. 39.
81 p. fol.

Score: solo voice with piano accompaniment. Negro dialect.

Contents: 1. Who is dat yondah? -2. Spirit O' the Lord done fell on me. -3. An' I

(continued on next card)

---

*Jessye, Eva A My spirituals, edited & arranged, (Card 2)

cry. -4. Bles' my soul an' gone. -5. I been buked an' I been scorned. -6. Stan' steady. -7. Ain't got long to stay heah. -8. March down to Jerdon. -9. John saw de holy numbah. -10. I'm a po' lil' orphan. -11. When Moses smote de water. -12. So I can write my name. -13. I can't stay away. -14. Tall angel at the bar. -15. Got a home at las'. -16. I'se might tired.

ABSpl HMC NYPL42 YJWJ
CPL LC NYPLS ZWpl

---

*Jessye, Eva A

Ain't got long to stay heah. Negro spiritual.
[In Jessye, Eva A. My spirituals. New York, 1927, 34,35.]

Score: medium solo voice with piano accompaniment. Negro dialect.

ABSpl HMC NYPL42 YJWJ
CPL LC NYPLS ZWpl

---

*Jessye, Eva A

An' I cry. Negro spiritual.
[In Jessye, Eva A. My spirituals. New York, 1927, p 16,17.]

Score: medium solo voice with piano accompaniment. Negro dialect.

ABSpl HMC NYPL42 YJWJ
CPL LC NYPLS ZWpl

---

*Jessye, Eva A

Bles' my soul an' gone. Negro spiritual.
[In Jessye, Eva A. My spirituals. New York, 1927, p 20.]

Score: medium solo voice with piano accompaniment. Negro dialect.

ABSpl HMC NYPL42 YJWJ
CPL LC NYPLS ZWpl

---

*Jessye, Eva A

Got a home at las'. Negro spiritual.
[In Jessye, Eva A. My spirituals. New York, 1927, p 74,75.]

Score: medium solo voice with piano accompaniment. Negro dialect.

ABSpl HMC NYPL42 YJWJ
CPL LC NYPLS ZWpl

---

*Jessye, Eva A

I been buked an' I been scorned. Negro spiritual.
[In Jessye, Eva A. My spirituals. New York, 1927, p 24,25]

Score: medium solo voice with piano accompaniment. Negro dialect.

ABSpl HMC NYPL42 YJWJ
CPL LC NYPLS ZWpl

*Jessye, Eva A

I can't stay away. Negro spiritual. [In Jessye, Eva A. My spirituals. New York, 1927, p 65,67.]

Score: medium solo voice with piano accompaniment. Negro dialect.

ABSpl HMC NYPL42 YJWJ
CPL LC NYPLS ZWpl

*Jessye, Eva A

Stan' steady. Negro spiritual. [In Jessye, Eva A. My spirituals. New York, 1927, p 30,31.]

Score: medium solo voice with piano accompaniment. Negro dialect.

ABSpl HMC NYPL42 YJWJ
CPL LC NYPLS ZWpl

*Johns, Albert
Boardwalk parade. 1903. 5531.

In bound vol.

ABS

*Jessye, Eva A

I'm a po' lil' orphan. Negro spiritual. [In Jessye, Eva A. My spirituals. New York, 1927, p 50,51.]

Score: medium solo voice with piano accompaniment. Negro dialect.

ABSpl HMC NYPL42 YJWJ
CPL LC NYPLS ZWpl

*Jessye, Eva A

Tall angel at the bar. Negro spiritual. [In Jessye, Eva A. My spirituals. New York, 1927, p 70.]

Score: medium solo voice with piano accompaniment. Negro dialect.

ABSpl HMC NYPL42 YJWJ
CPL LC NYPLS ZWpl

*Johns, Albert
Clementine and I. 1903.

In bound vol.

ABS

*Jessye, Eva A

I'se mighty tired. Negro spiritual. [In Jessye, Eva A. My spirituals. New York, 1927, p 80,81.]

Score: medium solo voice with piano accompaniment. Negro dialect.

ABSpl HMC NYPL42 YJWJ
CPL LC NYPLS ZWpl

*Jessye, Eva A

When Moses smote de water. Negro spiritual. [In Jessye, Eva A. My spirituals. New York, 1927, p 54,55.]

Score: medium solo voice with piano accompaniment. Negro dialect.

ABSpl HMC NYPL42 YJWJ
CPL LC NYPLS ZWpl

*Johns, Albert
Dance Rybenesque. 1902.

In bound vol.

ABS

*Jessye, Eva A

John saw de holy numbah. Negro spiritual. [In Jessye, Eva A. My spirituals. New York, 1927, p 44,45.]

Score: medium solo voice with piano accompaniment. Negro dialect.

ABSpl HMC NYPL42 YJWJ
CPL LC NYPLS ZWpl

*Jessye, Eva A

Who is dat yonday? Negro spiritual. [In Jessye, Eva A. My spirituals. New York 1927, p 6,7.]

Score: medium solo voice with piano accompaniment. Negro dialect.

ABSpl HMC NYPL42 YJWJ
CPL LC NYPLS ZWpl

*Johns, Albert

The darling of my dreams. Song. Words by Chas. Noel Douglas; music by Al. Johns. New York, M. Witmark & sons ₍c1903₎ Publ. pl. no. 5532.
5 p. fol.

Score: medium solo voice ₍key of E^b₎ with piano accompaniment. English words.

ABSpl
LC

*Jessye, Eva A

March down to Jerdon. Negro spiritual. [In Jessye, Eva A. My spirituals. New York, 1927, p 40,41.]

Score: medium solo voice with piano accompaniment. Negro dialect.

ABSpl HMC NYPL42 YJWJ
CPL LC NYPLS ZWpl

*Johns, Albert

...Ain't that lovin'. ₍Popular song₎ Words by Elmer Bowman; music by *Al. Johns. New York, F. A. Mills ₍c1901₎
4 p. fol.

Score: medium solo voice ₍key of F₎ with piano accompaniment. Negro dialect.
In bound vol.

ABSpl

*Johns, Albert

Dorothy. Song... Words by Harrison Armstrong; music by Al Johns. New York, Howley, Haviland & co. ₍c1900₎
5 p. fol.

Score: low solo voice ₍key of E^b₎ with piano accompaniment. English words.

ABSpl
LC

*Jessye, Eva A

So I can write my name. Negro spiritual. [In Jessye, Eva A. My spirituals. New York, 1927, p 60,61.]

Score: medium solo voice with piano accompaniment. Negro dialect.

ABSpl HMC NYPL42 YJWJ
CPL LC NYPLS ZWpl

*Johns, Albert

Araby. Characteristic intermezzo ₍for piano₎ By Al. Johns. New York, M. Witmark & sons. ₍c1903₎ Publ. pl. no. 6005.
6p. fol.

Score: piano solo.

ABSpl
LC

*Johns, Albert
Ethiopia; an African intermezzo. 1903. 5224.

In bound vol.

ABS

*Jessye, Eva A

Spirit O' the Lord done fell on me. Negro spiritual. [In Jessye, Eva A. My spirituals. New York, 1927, p 10,11.]

Score: medium solo voice with piano accompanimemt. Negro dialect.

ABSpl HMC NYPL42 YJWJ
CPL LC NYPLS ZWpl

*Johns, Albert
At a garden party. 1902.

In bound vol.

ABS

*Johns, Albert

Fellowcraft. March and two-step ₍for piano₎ by Al. Johns. New York, F. A. Mills ₍c1901₎
4 p. fol.

Score: piano solo.

ABSpl

*Johns, Albert

Go way back and sit down. [Popular song] Words by Elmer Bowman; music by *Al Johns. New York, F. A. Mills [c1901]
5 p. fol.
In bound vol.
Score: medium solo voice [key of d] with piano accompaniment. Negro dialect.

ABSpl

*Johns, Albert

I've got company and you can't come in. Song and chorus Words by *Elmer Bowman; music by Al. Johns. New York, Howley, Haviland & Dresser, [c1902]
6p. fol.
Score: medium solo voice [key of F] with piano accompaniment. Negro dialect.
Caption title.

LC
ABSpl

*Johns, Albert
Sometime, someday, somewhere. 1903.

In bound vol.

ABS

*Johns, Albert

...Honey lamb. Song. Poem by *Henry Troy; music by Albert Johns... New York, The Penn music co. [c1914]
5 p. fol.
Score: high solo voice [key of F] with piano accompaniment. Negro dialect.

ABSpl
LC

*Johns, Albert

My lady love. [Popular song] Words by *Elmer Bowman; music by Al. Johns. New York, F. A. Mills [c1900]
3 p. fol.
Score: low solo voice [key of B♭] with piano accompaniment. English words.

ABSpl
NYPLS
LC

Johns, Albert
The sound of my sweethearts name

*Johns, Albert

I can't get no money from home. [Popular song] Words by Elmer Bowman; music by *Al. Johns. New York, F. A. Mills [c1901]
4 p. fol.
In bound vol.
Score: low solo voice [key of F] with piano accompaniment. Negro dialect.

ABSpl

*Johns, Albert

The matinee girls' parade. Popular song Words by Vincent P. Bryan; music by Al. Johns. New York, F. A. Mills, [c1901]
4p. fol.
In bound vol.
Score: medium solo voice [key of B♭] with piano accompaniment. English words.
Caption title.

ABS
LC

*John, Albert
Take a little walk. 1904. 6051.

In bound vol.

ABS

*Johns, Albert

I thought I heard somebody calling me. (Gin and Jim sounded so much the same) [Popular song] Words and music by Al Johns. New York, F. A. Mills music pub. [c1898]
4 p. fol.
Score: medium solo voice [key of C] with piano accompaniment.

ABSpl
LC

*Johns, Albert
The Mississippi Bubble/ characteristic march and two-step. 1902.

In bound vol.

ABS

*Johns, Albert
Toba; a dream of the Holy land. 1902.

In bound vol.

ABS

*Johns, Albert
Ianthia; march. 1902.

In bound vol.

ABS

*Johns, Albert
On Broadway in Dahomey Bye and Bye. 1902.

In bound vol.

ABS

*Johns, Albert

We can't always have the one that we love. [Popular song] Words by Ben F. Barnett; music by Al. Johns. New York, Howley, Haviland & Dresser [c1902]
5 p. fol.
Score: medium solo voice [key of B♭] with piano accompaniment. English words.

ABSpl
LC

*Johns, Albert
If I but thought you cared for me. 1902.

In bound vol.

ABS

*Johns, Albert
Pretty Sal. 1901.

In bound vol.

ABS

Johnson, F Hall
City called heaven

*Johns, Albert
In Dahomey; characteristic march and cake walk. 1902.

In bound vol.

ABS

*Johns, Albert.
Sallie! 1904. 6210.

In bound vol.

ABS

*Johnson, F Hall, 1888-

His name so sweet. Negro spiritual; arranged by Hall Johnson. New York, Carl Fischer, inc. [c1934] Publ. pl. no. 26646.
7 p. fol. (Sheet music edition v. 1222)
Score: high solo voice [key of G] with piano accompaniment. Negro dialect.
Caption title

ABSpl LC ZWpl

*Johnson, F Hall, 1888-

Honor! Honor! Negro spiritual; arranged by Hall Johnson. New York, Carl Fischer, inc. ⌊c1934⌋ Publ. pl. no. 26644.
7 p. fol. (Sheet music edition, v.1220.)

Score: medium solo voice ⌊key of B♭⌋ with piano accompaniment. Negro dialect.
Caption title

ZWpl LC ABSpl

*Johnson, F Hall, 1888- arr.

The green pastures spirituals. Arranged for voice and piano by Hall Johnson. New York, Farrar and Rinehart, inc., c1930.
40 p. fol.

Score: solo voice with piano accompaniment. Negro dialect.

Contents: 1. Oh, rise an' shine. 2. When de saints come marchin' in. 3. Cert'n'y, Lord. 4. My God is so high. 5. Hallelujah!
(continued on next card)

*Johnson, F Hall, 1888- (Card 2)

Contents...
6. In bright mansions above. 7. Doncher let nobody turn you roun'. 8. Run, sinner, run! 9. You better min'! 10. Dere's no hidin' place down here. 11. Some o' these days. 12. I want to be ready. 13. De ol' ark's a-moverin'. 14. Witness. 15. My Lord's a-writin' all de time. 16. Go down, Moses. 17. Oh, Mary, doncher weep. 18. Lord, I don't feel noways tired. 19. Joshua fit de battle of Jerico. 20. I can't stay away. 21. Hail! De King of Babylon! 22. Death's go'n' ter lay his col', icy hands on me. 23. De blin' man stood on de road an' cried. (continued on next card)

*Johnson, F Hall, 1888- (Card 3)

Contents...

24. Hallelujah! King Jesus.

CPL
NYPL3
NYPL42
YJWJ
LC
ZWpl
HMC

*Johnson, F Hall, 1888-

Jesus, lay your head in de winder... Negro spiritual selected and arranged by Hall Johnson... New York, Robbins music corp. ⌊c1930⌋ Publ. pl. no. S.H. 541.
5 p. fol.

Score: medium solo voice ⌊key of A minor⌋ with piano accompaniment. Negro dialect.

ABSpl LC ZWpl

Johnson, F Hall
On the dusty road

*Johnson, F Hall, 1888-

'Steal away. Negro spiritual; arranged by Hall Johnson. New York, Carl Fischer, inc. ⌊c1934⌋ Publ. pl. no. 26645.
5 p. fol. (Sheet music edition v.1221.)

Score: medium solo voice ⌊key of G⌋ with piano accompaniment. Negro dialect.
Caption title

ABSpl LC ZWpl

*Johnson, F Hall, 1888- arr.
*Andrews, Ismay

Tradition. Words and music by *Ismay Andrews; arranged by Hall Johnson. Dance interpreted by Emilia Caesar. New York, *Handy bros. music co., inc. ⌊c1935⌋
7 p. fol.

Score: low solo voice ⌊key of E♭⌋ with piano accompaniment.

Dedicated to Hall Johnson.
ABSpl
HMC
YJWJ

Johnson, F Hall
Way up in heaven

*Johnson, Haven

My last affair. ⌊Popular song⌋ Words and music by Haven Johnson. New York, Chappell and co., inc., ⌊c1936⌋ Publ. pl. no. C-623.
5 p. fol.

Score: medium solo voice with piano accompaniment. English words.

ABSpl

*Johnson, James C

Believe it, beloved. ⌊Popular song⌋ music by J. C. Johnson; lyric by George Whiting and Nat Schwartz. New York, Broadway music corp. ⌊c1934⌋
5 p. fol.

Score: medium solo voice with piano accompaniment. English words.

ABSpl

*Johnson, James C

Dancin' 'way your sin. ⌊Popular song⌋ Words and music by J. C. Johnson. New York, Harms, inc. ⌊c1930⌋ Publ. pl. no. 8588.
5 p. fol.

Score: medium solo voice with piano accompaniment. Negro dialect.

ABSpl

*Johnson, James C

Dip your brush in the sunshine (and keep on painting away) ⌊Popular song⌋ Words by *Andy Razaf; music by J. C. Johnson. New York, Joe Davis, inc. ⌊c1931⌋ Publ. pl. no. 1054.
5 p. fol.

Score: medium solo voice with piano accompaniment. English words.

ABSpl

*Johnson, James C

Don't let your love go wrong. ⌊Popular song⌋ Lyrics by George Whiting and Nat Schwartz; music by J. C. Johnson. New York, Broadway music corp. ⌊c1934⌋
5 p. fol.

Score: medium solo voice with piano and ukulele accompaniment.

YJWJ
ABSpl

Johnson, James C
Dusky stevedore

*Johnson, James C

Empty arms. ⌊Popular song⌋ By J. C. Johnson and Lew Rosser. New York, Johnson-Rosenberg music publ. ⌊c1927⌋
3 p. fol.

Score: medium solo voice with piano accompaniment.

ABSpl

*Johnson, James C

...Futurustic. Novelty song. By *Andy Razaf and J. C. Johnson... New York, Triangle music publ. co., inc. ⌊c1928⌋
5 p. fol.

Score: medium solo voice with piano accompaniment. English words.

ABSpl

Johnson, James C
Guess who's in town

*Johnson, James C

I see you everywhere (and still you're far away). ⌊Popular song⌋ Lyric by George Whiting and Nat Schwartz; music by J. C. Johnson. New York, Keit-Engel, inc. ⌊c1932⌋
3 p. fol.

Score: medium solo voice with piano accompaniment. English words.

ABSpl

*Johnson, James C

Louisiana. ⌊Popular song⌋ Words by *Andy Razaf and Bob Schafer; music by J. C. Johnson. New York, Al Piantadosi music publ. ⌊c1928⌋
5 p. fol.

Score: medium solo voice with piano accompaniment. Negro dialect.

ABSpl

*Johnson, James C

Love and kisses. ⌊Popular song⌋ Words by George Whiting and Nat Schwartz; music by J. C. Johnson. New York, Broadway music corp. ⌊c1935⌋
5 p. fol.

Score: medium solo voice with piano accompaniment. English words.

ABSpl

Johnson, James C
Love I'm Calling

*Johnson, James C

Three kisses. ₍Popular song.₎ Words by George Whiting and Bob Schafer; music by J. C. Johnson. New York, Sterling songs, inc. ₍c1932₎
3 p. fol.

Score: medium solo voice with piano and ukulele accompaniment.

YJWJ
aBSpl

*Johnson, James Price, 1897-

Aintcha got music. ₍Choral arrangement₎ Lyric by *Andy Razaf; music by James P. Johnson; choral arrangement by *W. C. Handy. New York, *Handy bros. music co., inc. ₍c1932₎
15 p. 8°.

Score: SSAATTBB; with piano accompaniment. English words.

YJWJ
ABSpl

Johnson, James C
My love will never grow old

*Johnson, James C
Trav'lin' all along. ₍Popular song₎ Words and music by J. C. Johnson. New York, Harms, inc. ₍c1930₎ Publ. pl. no. S-336.
5 p. fol.

Score: medium solo voice with piano accompaniment. English words.

ABSpl

*Johnson, James Price, 1897-

...Carolina shout. Negro classic. (Syncopated piano solo) by James P. Johnson. New York, *Clarence Williams music pub. ₍c1926₎
7 p. fol.

Score: piano solo.

ABSpl
LC

Johnson, James C
Remember who you're promised to

*Johnson, James C

Two seats in the balcony. ₍Popular song₎ Words by Nat Schwartz; music by J. C. Johnson. San Francisco, Sherman, Clay and co. ₍c1935₎
5 p. fol.

Score: medium solo voice with piano accompaniment. English words.

ABSpl

Johnson, James Price
Charleston

*Johnson, James C

Rhythm and romance. ₍Popular song₎ Words by George Whiting and Nat Schwartz; music by J. C. Johnson. New York, Broadway music corp. ₍c1935₎
5 p. fol.

Score: medium solo voice with piano accompaniment. English words.

ABSpl

*Johnson, James C

When? Paul Whiteman's greatest success. ₍Popular song₎ Words by *Andy Razaf and Bob Schafer; music by J. C. Johnson. New York, Irving Berlin, inc. ₍c1928₎
5 p. fol.

Score: medium solo voice with piano accompaniment. English words.

ABSpl

*Johnson, James Price, 1897-

"Cotton pickin'." (Jubilee song) Composed and edited by *Perry Bradford and James P. Johnson... New York, *Perry Bradford, inc. ₍c1928₎
(In Johnson, James P., "Dixieland echoes". New York, 1928, p. 20-24.)

Score: high solo voice ₍key of B^b₎ with piano accompaniment. Negro dialect.

"A descriptive gem, telling how the Negroes celebrate the event by singing, dancing, banjo
(continued on next card)

*Johnson, James Price, 1897-"Cotton pickin'."... ₍c1928₎ (Card 2)

playing and giving thanks to the Lord for their good crops." - Foreword.

ABSpl
NYPL42
NYPLS

Johnson, James C
Right about face

*Johnson, James C

Without a shadow of a doubt. ₍Popular song.₎ Words by George Whiting and Nat Schwartz; music by J. C. Johnson. New York, Broadway music corp. ₍c1936₎
5 p. fol.

Score: medium solo voice with piano and guitar, ukulele or banjo accompaniment. English words.

YJWJ
aBSpl

*Johnson, James C

Somebody loses — Somebody wins. ₍Popular song₎ Words by George Whiting and Nat Schwartz; music by J. C. Johnson. New York, Santly bros., inc. ₍c 1932₎
5 p. fol.

Score: medium solo voice with piano accompaniment. English words.

ABSpl

*Johnson, James C

You stayed away too long. ₍Popular song₎ Lyric by George Whiting and Nat Schwartz; music by J. C. Johnson. New York, Broadway music corp. ₍c1935₎
5 p. fol.

Score: medium solo voice with piano accompaniment. English words.

ABSpl

*Johnson, James Price, 1897-

Dixieland echoes. A collection of five descriptive Negro songs composed and edited by *Perry Bradford and James P. Johnson... New York, *Perry Bradford, inc. ₍c1928₎
29 p. fol.

Score: solo voice with piano accompaniment. Negro dialect.

Contents: -1. Echoes of ole Dixie land. -2. Honey. -3. Mississippi river flood. Descriptive.
(continued on next card)

*Johnson, James C

Take your tomorrow (and give me today). ₍Popular song₎ Words by *Andy Razaf; music by J. C. Johnson. New York, Triangle music publ. ₍c1928₎
5 p. fol.

Score: medium solo voice with piano accompaniment. English words.

ABSpl

*Johnson, James Price, 1897-

Alabama stomp. ₍Popular song₎ Lyric by *Henry Creamer; melody by Jimmy Johnson. New York, Robbins-Engle inc. ₍c1926₎ Publ. pl. no. SH317.
5 p. fol. 2 copies

Score: medium solo voice ₍key of E^b₎ with piano accompaniment. English words.

"...as features in Earl Carroll's 'Vanities,' 5th edition." -Title page.

ABSpl

*Johnson, James Price, Dixieland echoes... ₍c1928₎ (Card 2)

-4. "Cotton pickin'." (Jubilee song). -5. Liza Jane's weddin'.

ABSpl
NYPL42
NYPLS - inscribed to Arthur Schomburg by both composers.

•Johnson, James Price, 1897-

Don't cry baby (A sobbing serenade). ₍Song₎ Lryics by Stella Unger and Saul Bernie; music by Jimmy Johnson. New York, Saul Bernie inc. ₍c1929₎ 4 p. fol.

Score: medium solo voice ₍key of E^b₎ with piano accompaniment. English words.

ABSpl

•Johnson, James Price, 1897-

I need you. ₍Popular song₎ Lyric by •Perry Bradford; music by Jimmy Johnson. New York, M. Witmark & sons ₍c1929₎ Publ. pl. no. 8684. 5 p. fol.

Score: medium solo voice ₍key of B^b₎ with piano accompaniment. English words.
Caption title.

From "the modern musical novelty success, 'Messin' around'." - Title page.

ABSpl

•Johnson, James Price, Echoes of ole Dixie land... ₍c1928₎ (Card 2)

"We picture a log cabin scene in Alabama, with fathers, mothers, sons and daughters after their evening meal at sundown." - Foreword.

•Johnson, James Price, 1897-

Ebony Dreams (Novelty piano solos) By James P. Johnson. New York, •Perry Bradford, inc. ₍c1928₎ 6 p. fol.

Score: piano solo.

ABSpl

•Johnson, James Price, 1897-

Ivy. (Cling to me). Words by •Alex Rogers; music by Isham Jones and Jimmy Johnson. New York, Irving Berlin, inc. ₍c1922₎ 5 p. fol.

Score: medium solo voice ₍key of G₎ with piano accompaniment. English words.

ABSpl

•Johnson, James Price, 1897-

...Mister deep blue sea. ₍Popular song₎ Words and music by Gene Austin and Jimmy Johnson. New York, Famous music corp. ₍c1936₎ 5 p. fol.

Score: low solo voice ₍key of C₎ with piano accompaniment. English words.
Caption title.

"Featured by May West in the Paramount picture, 'Klondike Annie'." - Title page.

ABSpl

•Johnson, James Price, 1897-

Echoes of ole Dixie land. ₍Song₎ Composed and edited by •Perry Bradford and James P. Johnson... New York, •Perry Bradford, inc. ₍c1928₎ (In Johnson, James P., "Dixieland echoes." New York, 1928, p. 3-8.)

Score: high solo voice ₍key of D^b₎ with piano accompaniment. Negro dialect.

ABSpl (continued on next card)
NYPl42
NYPLS - inscribed to Arthur Schomburg by both composers.

•Johnson, James Price, 1897-

I was so weak, love was so strong. ₍Popular song₎ Lyric by •Andy Razaf; music by James P. Johnson. New York, •Handy bros. music co. ₍c1932₎ 5 p. fol.

Score: medium solo voice ₍key of E^b₎ with piano accompaniment. English words.
Caption title.

From "Harlem hotcha," Connie's Inn new revue. Featured by Don Redman and his Connie's Inn orchestra.

ABSpl LC YJWJ

•Johnson, James Price, 1897-

My headache (There goes my headache). ₍Popular song₎ Lyric by •Andy Razaf; music by James P. Johnson. New York, •Handy bros. music co., inc. ₍c1932₎ 5 p. fol.

Score: medium solo voice ₍key of E^b₎ with piano accompaniment. English words.
Caption title.

From the musical revue, "Harlem hotcha."

ABSpl YJWJ
LC

•Johnson, James Price, 1897-

Give me the sunshine. ₍Popular song₎ Words by Con Conrad and •Henry Creamer; music by Jimmy Johnson. New York, Harms, inc. ₍c1928₎ Publ. pl. no. 8146. 5 p. fol. 2 copies

Score: medium solo voice with piano accompaniment. English words.
Caption title.

From the musical comedy, "Keep shufflin'."

ABSpl
LC

•Johnson, James Price, 1897-

Jungle nymphs. Novellette; ₍for piano₎ By James P. Johnson. New York, Jack Mills, inc. ₍c1924₎ 6 p. fol.

Score: piano solo.

ABSpl

Johnson, James Price
Old fashioned love

•Johnson, James Price, 1897-

I don't love nobody but you. ₍Popular song₎ Lyric by •Perry Bradford; music by Jimmy Johnson. New York, M. Witmark & sons ₍c1929₎ Publ. pl. no. 8683. 5 p. fol.

Score: low solo voice ₍key of B^b₎ with piano accompaniment. English words.
Caption title.

From "Messin' around" a modern musical novelty.

ABSpl

•Johnson, James Price, 1897-

Love bug. ₍Popular song₎ Words and music by •Cecil Mack ₍pseud.₎ and Jimmy Johnson. New York, Harms inc. ₍c1923₎ Publ. pl. no. 6873. 5 p. fol.

Score: low solo voice ₍key of F₎ with piano accompaniment. English words.
Caption title.

From Miller and Lyles' "Runnin' wild."

ABSpl
LC

•Johnson, James Price, 1897-

Open your heart. ₍Popular song₎ Words and music by •Cecil Mack and Jimmy Johnson. New York, Harms, inc. ₍c1923₎ Publ. pl. no. 6866. 5 p. fol.

Score: medium solo voice ₍key of B^b₎ with piano accompaniment. English words.
Caption title.

Excerpt from title Miller and Lyles', "Runnin' wild" musical show.

ABSpl

•Johnson, James Price, 1897-

If I could be with you (one hour tonight). Song. By •Henry Creamer and Jimmy Johnson. New York, Jerome H. Remick & co. ₍c1925₎ Publ. pl. no. 232. 5 p. fol.

Score: medium solo voice ₍key of E^b₎ with piano accompaniment. English words.

ABSpl

•Johnson, James Price, 1897-

Mama's blues (Papa's blues). ₍Popular song₎ By Jas. P. Johnson and •William H. Farrell. New York, Haviland pub. co. ₍c1917₎ 5 p. fol.

Score: medium solo voice ₍key of B^b₎ with piano accompaniment. English words.

ABSpl

•Johnson, James Price, 1897-

A porter's love song to a chambermaid. (Novelty ballad) Words by •Andy Razaf; music by Jimmy Johnson. New York, Joe Davis inc. ₍c1932₎ 3 p. fol.

Score: medium solo voice ₍key of F₎ with piano accompaniment. English words.

ABSpl

•Johnson, James Price, 1897-

I need lovin'. ₍Popular₎ song. By •Henry Creamer and Jimmy Johnson. New York, Jerome H. Remick & co. ₍c1926₎ Publ. pl. no. 274. 5 p. fol.

Score: medium solo voice ₍key of G₎ with piano accompaniment. English words.

ABSpl
YJWJ

•Johnson, James Price, 1897-

Mississippi river flood. Descriptive. ₍Song₎ Composed and edited by •Perry Bradford and James P. Johnson... New York, •Perry Bradford, inc. ₍c1928₎ (In Johnson, James P., "Dixieland echoes." New York, 1928, p. 12-19.)

Score: high solo voice ₍key of C₎ with piano accompaniment. Negro dialect.

"A Negro musical poem, of the Mississippi river flood, with style descrintive." - Foreword.

ABSpl
NYPl42
NYPLS

•Johnson, James Price, 1897-

She's the hottest gal in Tennessee. ₍Popular song₎ Words by •Henry Creamer; music by Jimmy Johnson... New York, Shapiro and Bernstein & co. ₍c1926₎ 5 p. fol.

Score: medium solo voice ₍key of B^b₎ with piano accompaniment. English words.
Caption title.

"As featured in the Christie talking play, 'The Lady Fare' ... a Paramount picture." - Title page.

ABSpl

*Johnson, James Price, 1897-

'Sippi. [Popular song] Words by Con Conrad and *Henry Creamer; music by Jimmy Johnson. New York, Harms inc. [c1928] Publ. pl. no. 8147.
6 p. fol.

Score: medium solo voice [key of E♭] with piano accompaniment. Negro dialect.
Caption title.

From Miller and Lyles' "Keep shufflin."

ABSpl
LC

---

*Johnson, James Price, 1897-

Skiddle-de skow. [Popular song] Lyric by *Perry Bradford; music by Jimmy Johnson. New York, M. Witmark & sons [c1929] Publ. pl. no. 8685.
5 p. fol.

Score: medium solo voice [key of A♭] with piano accompaniment. English words.
Caption title.

From the musical comedy, "Messin' Around."

ABSpl

---

*Johnson, James Price, 1897-

Sorry that I strayed away from you. [Popular song] Lyric by *Perry Bradford; music by Jimmy Johnson. New York, M. Witmark & sons [c1929] Publ. pl. no. 8686.
5 p. fol.

Score: medium solo voice [key of A♭] with piano accompaniment. English words.
Caption title.

From the musical comedy, "Messin' around."

ABSpl

---

*Johnson, James Price, 1897-

The Spanish in my eyes. [Popular song] By Enric Madriguera and Jimmy (J.P.) Johnson. New York, F. B. Haviland pub. co. [c1934]
5 p. fol.

Score: high solo voice [key of E♭] with piano accompaniment. English words.

ABSpl

---

*Johnson, James Price, 1897-

Stop it. [Popular song] By Jas. P. Johnson and *Wm. H. Farrell. New York, Haviland pub. co. [c1917]
3 p. fol.

Score: high solo voice [key of E♭] with piano accompaniment. English words.

ABSpl

---

*Johnson, James Price, 1897-

Stop that dog. [Popular song] Lyric by *Andy Razaf; music by James P. Johnson. New York, *Handy bros. music co., inc. [c1932]
5 p. fol.

Score: medium solo voice [key of A♭] with piano accompaniment. English words.
Caption title.

From the musical revue, "Harlem hotcha."

ABSpl
LC
YJWJ

Johnson, James Price
There goes my headache

---

*Johnson, James Price, 1897-

When I can't be with you. [Popular song] By *Andy Razaf and Jimmy (J.P.) Johnson... New York, Southern music pub. co., inc. [c1931]
5 p. fol.

Score: medium solo voice [key of E♭] with piano accompaniment. English words.

ABSpl

---

*Johnson, James Price, 1897-

Yamekraw. A Negro-rhapsody [for piano] by James P. Johnson. New York, *Perry Bradford, inc. [c1927]
26 p. fol.

Score: piano solo.

"A genuine Negro treatise on spiritual, syncopated and 'blue' melodies... expressing the religious fervor and happy moods of the natives of Yamekraw, a Negro settlement situated on the outskirts of Savannah, Ga." - From the Publisher's foreword.

ABSpl - Inscribed by the composer to Mr. Spingarn, 1/30/36. NYPL42 NYPLS

---

*Johnson, James Price, 1897-

Yes, I love you, honey. [Popular song] Words by *Jo' Trent; music by Jimmy Johnson. New York, Harms, inc. [c1931] Publ. pl. no. 8772.
5 p. fol.

Score: medium solo voice [key of A♭] with piano accompaniment. English words.
Caption title.

"Featured in 'Sugar Hill' with Miller and Lyle..."

ABSpl

Johnson, James Price
You for me, me for you from now on

Johnson, James Price
Your love I crave

---

*Johnson, James Price, 1897-

Your love is all that I crave. [Popular song] Lyric by A. Dubin and *Perry Bradford; music by Jimmy Johnson. New York, M. Witmark & sons [C1929] Publ. pl. no. 8757.
5 p. fol.

Score: medium solo voice [key of G] with piano accompaniment. English words.
Caption title.

"Song hit from Warner Bros. 'Show of Shows'." - Title page.

ABSpl

---

*Johnson, James Price, 1897-

Yours all yours. [Popular song] Lyric by *Andy Razaf; music by James P. Johnson. New York, *Handy bros. music co., inc. [c1932]
5 p. fol.

Score: medium solo voice [key of E♭] with piano accompaniment. English words.
Caption title.

From the musical revue, "Harlem Hotcha."

ABSpl
LC
YJWJ

---

*Johnson, John Rosamond, 1873-

...Album of Negro spirituals. Newly adapted and arranged by J. Rosamond Johnson... New York, Edward B. Marks music corp. [c1940] Publ. pl. nos. 11191-11215, 11225.
56 p. fol. (Radio city edition)

Score: medium solo voice with piano accompaniment. Negro dialect.

Contents: De band o'Gideon. -Deep river. -Didn't my Lord deliver Daniel? -Ev'ry time I feel de spirit. -Ezekiel saw de wheel. -Gimme dat old time religion. -Git on bo'd little child'en.
(continued on next card)

---

*Johnson, John Rosamond, 1873- ...Album of Negro spirituals... New York [c1940] (Card 2)

-Go down Moses. -Goin' to shout all over God's heab'n. -I been in de storm, so long. -I couldn't hear nobody pray. -I'm a-rollin'. -Joshua fit the battle o'Jerico. -Lis'en to de lam's. -Lit'le David play on yo' harp. -Nobody knows de trouble I see. -Now let me fly. -O, rocks don't fall on me. -Peter, go ring-a dem bells. -Peter on de sea, sea, sea, sea. -Roll Jordan roll. -Sometimes I feel like a motherless child. -Standin' in the need of prayer. -Steal away to Jesus. -Swing low sweet chariot. -Were you there when they crucified my Lord?

ABSpl LC ZWpl

---

*Johnson, John Rosamond, 1873-

...The animals' convention. [Popular song] Words by *J. W. Johnson; music by Rosamond Johnson. New York, Jos. W. Stern & co. [c1902] Publ. pl. no. 3441.
6 p. fol.

Score: medium solo voice [key of G] with piano accompaniment. Negro dialect.

"Written by Cole and Johnson Bros." - Cover title.

(continued on next card)

---

*Johnson, John Rosamond
The awakening.

---

*Johnson, John Rosamond, 1873-

Dry bones. Descriptive characteristic shout song for mixed voices, by J. Rosamond Johnson. New York, *Handy bros. music co., inc. [c1938]
7 p. 8vo.

Score: Mixed chorus (SATB) with piano accompaniment. Negro dialect.
Bound in black spiral notebook no. 3.

ABS
HMC
ZWpl
YJWJ

---

*Johnson, John Rosamond, 1873-

...Go chain de lion down. (Negro spiritual) [Arranged] for mixed voices by J. Rosamond Johnson. New York, *Handy brothers music co., inc. [c1935]
5 p. 8°.

Score: SATB with piano accompaniment. Negro dialect.
Bound in black spiral notebook no. 3.

ABS
HMC
LC
ZWpl

---

*Johnson, John Rosamond, 1873- arr.

...Go down Moses. (Negro spiritual) [Arranged] for mixed voices by J. Rosamond Johnson. New York, *Handy bros. music co., inc. [c1938]
9 p. 8°.

Score: SAATTBB with piano accompaniment. Negro dialect.
Bound in black spiral notebook no. 3.

ABS
HMC
ZWpl

*Johnson, John Rosamond, 1873-

Big Indian chief. ₍Popular song₎ Words by *Bob Cole; music by Rosamond Johnson. New York, Jos. W. Stern & co. ₍c1904₎ Publ. pl. no. 3974.
5 p. fol.

Score: medium solo voice with piano accompaniment.

"Written by Cole and Johnson bros." - Cover title.

ABSpl
YJWJ
LC

*Johnson, John Rosamond, 1873-

Congo love song. ₍Popular song₎ Words by *J₍ames₎ W₍eldon₎ Johnson; music by J₍ohn₎ Rosamond Johnson. New York, Jos. W. Stern and co., ₍c1903₎ Publ. pl. no. 3510.
5 p. fol.

Score: medium solo voice ₍key of G₎ with piano accompaniment. English words.
Cover title-page states: "By Cole & Johnson Bros"

ABSpl
YJWJ
LC

*Johnson, John Rosamond, 1873- ..."Dis aint no time for an argument." ... New York, ₍c1906₎ (Card 2)

"Written especially for and introduced by the Jest and Song Club, Schenectady, N. Y. at the Sixth Annual Performance." - Head of title.

ABSpl
LC

*Johnson, John Rosamond, 1873-

Big Indian chief. Two step ₍for piano₎ By *Bob Cole and *Johnson Bros. ₍James Weldon and J. Rosamond Johnson₎ New York, Jos. W. Stern & co. ₍c1904₎ Publ. pl. no. 4010.
6 p. fol.

Score: piano solo.

ABSpl

*Johnson, John Rosamond, 1873-

..."De chain gang" (Musical episode) based on work songs of the southland for male voices with descriptive continuity and light effects ... ₍by₎ J. Rosamond Johnson. ... New York, *Handy bros. music co. ₍c1938₎
32 p. fol.

Score: TTBB chorus with 3 soli, piano accompaniment. Negro dialect.

From the book "Rolling along in song." (Viking press)

LC
ABSpl
HPSpl
ZWpl

*Johnson, John Rosamond, 1873- arr.

Do don't touch-a my garment. Negro spiritual. Arranged by J. Rosamond Johnson. ₍London, J. Curwen, inc., c1926₎
6 p. fol. (Curwen edition)

Score: low solo voice ₍key of G₎ with piano accompaniment. Negro dialect.

ABSpl
NBCL

*Johnson, John Rosamond, 1873-

"The big red shawl." Popular song. Words by *Bob Cole; music by J. Rosamond Johnson. New York, Jos. W. Stern & co. ₍c1908₎ Publ. pl. no. 6101.
4 p. fol.

Score: medium solo voice with piano accompaniment.

ABSpl
YJWJ

*Johnson, John Rosamond, 1873- arr.

De lam' done been down here an' died. Adaptation from an old Negro spiritual by J. Rosamond Johnson. (In Johnson, J. Rosamond, "Sixteen new Negro spirituals." p. 18)

Score: medium solo voice ₍key of A^b₎ with piano accompaniment. Negro dialect.

ABSpl
BHC
HMC
LC
ZWpl

*Johnson, John Rosamond, 1873-

"Don't butt in." ₍Minstrel song₎ Words by *Bob Cole and *J. W. Johnson; music by Rosamond Johnson. New York, Jos. W. Stern & co. ₍c1901₎ Publ. pl. no. 3239.
6 p. fol.

Score: medium solo voice ₍key of E^b₎ with piano accompaniment. Negro dialect.

ABSpl
LC

*Johnson, John Rosamond, 1873-

"The bleeding moon." ₍Popular song₎ Words by *Bob Cole; music by J. Rosamond Johnson. New York, Jos. W. Stern & co. ₍c1908₎ Publ. pl. no. 6170.
5 p. fol.

Score: high solo voice ₍key of F₎ with piano accompaniment. English words.

Excerpt from the operetta, "The Red Moon."

ABSpl
CCPpl
LC

*Johnson, John Rosamond, 1873-

...De little pickaninny's gone to sleep. ₍Song₎ Words by *J. W. Johnson; music by J. Rosamond Johnson. Boston, Oliver Ditson co. ₍c1910₎ Publ. pl. no. 5-64-67973.
7 p. fol.

Score: medium solo voice ₍key of F₎ with piano accompaniment. Negro dialect.

ABSpl

*Johnson, John Rosamond, 1873-

Ev'ry woman's eyes. ₍Popular song₎ Lyric by *James Weldon Johnson; music by J. Rosamond Johnson. New York, Jos. W. Stern & co. ₍c1912₎ Publ. pl. no. 7201.
5 p. fol.

Score: medium solo voice ₍key of B^b₎ with piano accompaniment. English words.

ABSpl
LC

*Johnson, John Rosamond, 1873-

Champagne Charlie. Song successes introduced by Peter F. Dailey in the new successful comedy "Champagne Charlie" by Augustus Thomas... ₍By₎ *Cole and Johnson. New York, Jos. W. Stern &co., c1901.
4 v. fol.

Scores; Medium solo voice with piano accompaniment. English words or Negro dialect.

(continued on next card)

*Johnson, John Rosamond, 1873-

"Dem lovin' words sound mighty good to me." ₍Popular song₎ Lyric by *J. W. Johnson; music by Rosamond Johnson. New York, Jos. W. Stern & co. ₍c1905₎ Publ. pl. no. 4652.
5 p. fol.

Score: medium solo voice ₍key of F₎ with piano accompaniment. Negro dialect.

"By Cole and Johnson." - Cover title.

ABSpl
LC

*Johnson, John Rosamond, 1873-

"Excuse me Mister Moon." ₍Popular song₎ Words by *James W. Johnson; music by J. Rosamond Johnson. New York, Jos. W. Stern & co. ₍c1912₎ Publ. pl. no. 7058.
5 p. fol.

Score: medium solo voice ₍key of F₎ with piano accompaniment. English words.

Sung by Alice Lloyd in "Little Miss Fix-it."

ABSpl

*Johnson, John Rosamond, 1873- Champagne Charlie ... New York, c1901. (Card 2)

Contents: 1. "I don't want to be no actor man." Music by *Bob Cole. -2. "Gin" Music by *J. Rosamond Johnson. -3. "My castle on the Nile." - Music by *J. Rosamond Johnson. -4. "Nobody's lookin' but de owl an' de moon." - Music by *J. Rosamond Johnson.

ABSpl - has above excerpts.
LC " " "

*Johnson, John Rosamond, 1873- arr.

₍Dere's a meetin' here tonight. Negro spiritual by J. Rosamond Johnson.₎ (In Johnson, J. Rosamond, "Sixteen new Negro spirituals." p. 17)

Score: medium solo voice ₍key of D₎ with piano accompaniment. Negro dialect.

ABSpl
BHC
HMC
LC
ZWpl

*Johnson, John Rosamond, 1873-

Floating down the Nile. ₍Popular song₎ Lyric by *Jas. W. Johnson; music by J. Rosamond Johnson. New York, Jos. W. Stern & co. ₍c1906₎ Publ. pl. no. 5136.
6 p. fol.

Score: medium solo voice ₍key of D₎ with piano accompaniment. Negro dialect.

From "The Shoo-fly Regiment." by Cole & Johnson.

ABSpl
LC

Johnson, John Rosamond
Come out Dinah on the Green

*Johnson, John Rosamond, 1873-

... "Dis aint no time for an argument." ₍Minstrel song₎ Words by *James W. Johnson; music by Rosamond Johnson. New York, Jos. W. Stern & co. ₍c1906₎ Publ. pl. no. 4899.
5 p. fol.

Score: low solo voice ₍key of G₎ with piano accompaniment. Negro dialect.

"By Cole and Johnson." - Cover title.

(continued on next page)

*Johnson, John Rosamond, 1873-

...For thee! ₍Song. Words by J. A. Middleton; music by₎ J. Rosamond Johnson. Boston, Oliver Ditson co. ₍c1910₎ Publ. pl. no. 5-63-67959.
5 p. fol.

Score: high solo voice ₍key of D₎ with piano accompaniment. English words.

ABSpl

•Johnson, John Rosamond, 1873-

"The flowers of Dixie land." ₍Popular song₎ Words by Edgar Smith; music by Rosamond Johnson. New York, Jos. W. Stern & co. ₍c1903₎ Publ. pl. no. 3768.
5 p. fol.

Score: high solo voice ₍key of A^b₎ with piano accompaniment. English words.

"Words by Edgar Smith, music by Cole and Johnson Bros." - Cover title page.
"Introduced by Miss Lillian Russell in 'Whoop-dee-doo'."
ABSpl LC

•Johnson, John Rosamond, 1873-

If you'll be my Eve (I'll build an Eden for you) ₍Popular song₎ ₍Words by •James W. Johnson; music by J. Rosamond Johnson.₎ New York, Jos. W. Stern & co. ₍c1912₎ Publ. pl. no. 7059.
5 p. fol.

Score: low solo voice ₍key of C₎ with piano accompaniment. English words.

"Alice Lloyd's song success in the sparkling musical play, 'Little Miss Fix-it'." - End of title.
ABSpl LC

•Johnson, John Rosamond, 1873- arr.

₍I wish I had died in Egypt lan'. Negro spiritual by J. Rosamond Johnson.₎
(In Johnson, J. Rosamond, ₍Sixteen new Negro spirituals." p. 13)

Score: medium solo voice ₍key of F₎ with piano accompaniment. Negro dialect.

ABSpl
BHC
HMC
LC
ZWpl

•Johnson, John Rosamond, 1873-

Gin. ₍Minstrel song₎ Words by •Bob Cole and •J. W. Johnson; music by Rosamond Johnson. New York, Howley, Haviland & Dresser, ₍c1901₎
5 p. fol.

Score: medium solo voice ₍key of F₎ with piano accompaniment. Negro dialect.

"As sung by Peter F. Dailey in new successful comedy... 'Champagne Charlie!"
ABSpl
LC

•Johnson, John Rosamond, 1873-

...I told my love to the roses. ₍Song. Poem by J. A. Middleton; music by₎ J. Rosamond Johnson. New York, G. Schirmer ₍c1916₎ Publ. pl. no. 26631.
5 p. fol.

Score: low solo voice ₍key of F₎ with piano accompaniment. English words.

ABSpl

•Johnson, John Rosamond, 1873- arr.

...Joshua fit de battle o' Jerico. (Negro spiritual) ₍arranged₎ for mixed voices by J. Rosamond Johnson. New York, •Handy bros. music co., inc. ₍c1936₎
9 p. 8°.
Bound in black spiral notebook no. 3.
Score: SSAATB with piano accompaniment. Negro dialect.
ABS
HMC
LC
NYPLS
ZWpl

•Johnson, John Rosamond, 1873- arr.

₍Goin' to see my mother. (Some o' dese mornin's). Negro spiritual by J. Rosamond Johnson.₎
(In Johnson, J. Rosamond, "Sixteen new Negro spirituals." p. 22, 23)

Score: medium solo voice ₍key of G₎ with piano accompaniment. Negro dialect.

ABSpl
BHC
HMC
LC
ZWpl

•Johnson, John Rosamond, 1873-

I'll keep a warm spot in my heart for you. ₍Popular song₎ Lyric by •J. W. Johnson; music by J. Rosamond Johnson. New York, Jos. W. Stern & co. ₍c1906₎ Publ. pl. no. 4942.
5 p. fol. 2 copies

Score: medium solo voice ₍key of C₎ with piano accompaniment. English words.

ABSpl
HMC

•Johnson, John Rosamond, 1873-

Lazy moon. ₍Popular song₎ Words by •Bob Cole; music by Rosamond Johnson. New York, Jos. W. Stern & co. ₍c1903₎ Publ. pl. no. 3708.
5 p. fol.

Score: medium solo voice ₍key of G₎ with piano accompaniment. English words.

"Famous song successes of Cole and Johnson bros." - Cover title page.
ABSpl
LC

•Johnson, John Rosamond, 1873-
•Williams, Egbert Austin
The harbor of lost dreams. ₍Popular song₎ Words by •Alex Rogers; music by •Bert A. Williams; arranged by J. Rosamond Johnson. Chicago, Will Rossiter pub. ₍c1909₎
5 p. fol.

Score: medium solo voice with piano accompaniment. English words.
Caption title.

Excerpt from musical comedy, "Mr. Lode of Koal."
ABSpl
LC

•Johnson, John Rosamond, 1873-
•Cole, Robert Allen
I'm thinkin' 'bout you honey, all the time. ₍Popular song₎ By •₍Bob₎ Cole and ₍J. Rosamond₎ Johnson. New York, M. Witmark & sons ₍c1901₎ Publ. pl. no. 3600.
5 p. fol.

Score: medium solo voice ₍key of G₎ with piano accompaniment. Negro dialect.

ABSpl
LC

•Johnson, John Rosamond, 1873-

₍Leanin' on de Lord. Negro spiritual by J. Rosamond Johnson.₎
(In Johnson, J. Rosamond, "Sixteen new Negro spirituals." p. 16)

Score: medium solo voice ₍key of D₎ with piano accompaniment. Negro dialect.

ABSpl
BHC
HMC
LC
ZWpl

•Johnson, John Rosamond, 1873-

"Hello Ma Lulu!" ₍Popular song₎ Lyrics by •J. W. Johnson; music by Rosamond Johnson. New York, Jos. W. Stern & co. ₍c1905₎ Publ. pl. no. 4332.
5 p. fol.

Score: medium solo voice ₍key of G₎ with piano accompaniment. Negro dialect.

"Written by Cole and Johnson bros." - Cover title.

ABSpl
LC

•Johnson, John Rosamond, 1873-

₍I'm troubled, Lord. Negro spiritual by J. Rosamond Johnson.₎
(In Johnson, J. Rosamond, "Sixteen new Negro spirituals." p. 10)

Score: low solo voice ₍key of A^b₎ with piano accompaniment. Negro dialect.

ABSpl
BHC
HMC
LC
ZWpl

•Johnson, John Rosamond, 1873-

Life is a game of checkers. ₍Popular song₎ Words by •Bob Cole and Chas. Hunter; music by J. Rosamond Johnson. New York, Jos. W. Stern & co. ₍c1908₎ Publ. pl. no. 6192.
6 p. fol.

Score: medium solo voice ₍key of E^b₎ with piano accompaniment. English words.

Excerpt from "The red moon."

ABSpl
LC

•Johnson, John Rosamond, 1873- arr.

... I ain't goin' study war no more. (Negro peace jubilee song) ₍Arranged₎ for mixed voices by J. Rosamond Johnson. New York, •Handy brothers music co., inc. ₍c1938₎
7 p. 8°.

Score: SATB with piano accompaniment. Negro dialect.
Bound in black spiral notebook no. 3.
ABS
HMC
ZWpl

•Johnson, John Rosamond, 1873- arr.

₍I'm walkin' on borrow'd lan'. Negro spiritual by J. Rosamond Johnson.₎
(In Johnson, J. Rosamond, "Sixteen new Negro spirituals." p. 8)

Score: medium solo voice ₍key of A^b₎ with piano accompaniment. Negro dialect.

ABSpl ZWpl
BHC
HMC
LC

•Johnson, John Rosamond, 1873-

...Lift every voice and sing. Hymn. Words by •James W. Johnson; music by J. Rosamond Johnson. New York, Edward B. Marks music co. ₍c1921₎ Publ. pl. no. 8979.
5 p. fol.

Score: high solo voice ₍key of B^b₎ with piano accompaniment. English words.

"National Negro hymn." - Head of title.
LC
ABSpl NYPLS
HMC YJWJ

•Johnson, John Rosamond, 1873-

..."I cant think of nothin' in the wide, wide world but you." ₍Popular song₎ Lyric by •Bob Cole; music by •J. Rosamond Johnson. New York, Jos. W. Stern & co. ₍c1907₎ Publ. pl. no. 5878.
5 p. fol. 2 copies

Score: medium solo voice ₍key of E^b₎ with piano accompaniment. English words.

"The hit of "The Shoo-fly regiment." - Head of title.

ABSpl LC

•Johnson, J₍ohn₎ Rosamond, 1873-

"I've lost my teddy bear." ₍Popular song₎ Lyric by Bob Cole; music by Bob Cole and Rosamond Johnson. New York, Jos. W. Stern and co., ₍c1908₎ Publ. pl. no. 6079.
4 p. fol.

Score: Medium solo voice ₍key of B^b₎ with piano accompaniment. English words.
Excerpt from the operetta, "The Red Moon".

ABSpl
YJWJ

•Johnson, John Rosamond, 1873-

Li'l gal. ₍Song₎ Words by •Paul Laurence Dunbar; music by J. Rosamond Johnson. New York, Jos. W. Stern & co. ₍c1917₎ Publ. pl. no. 8248.
7 p. fol.

Score: low solo voice ₍key of C₎ with piano accompaniment. Negro dialect.

ABSpl
HMC
YJWJ

*Johnson, John Rosamond, 1873-

"Lit'l gal." [Song; Words by *Paul Laurence Dunbar; music by Rosamond Johnson. New York, Jos. W. Stern & co. [c1902, Publ. pl. no. 3397.

(In Ten choice Negro folksongs for voice and pianoforte. New York, n.d. p. 21-24.)

Score: medium solo voice key of C with piano accompaniment. Negro dialect.

Caption title.

ABSpl
BHC

*Johnson, John Rosamond, 1873-

Mississippi River (Keep on croonin') [Popular song; Lyric by Frank Abbot; music by J. Rosamond Johnson. New York, Edward B. Marks music corp. [c1932, Publ. pl. no. 9930.
5 p. fol.

Score: low solo voice [key of E^b] with piano accompaniment. Negro dialect.

ABSpl

*Johnson, John Rosamond, 1873-

...Nobody's lookin' but de owl and de moon. [Popular song, Words by *J. W. Johnson and *Bob Cole; music by Rosamond Johnson. New York, Jos. W. Stern & co. [c1901, Publ. pl. no. 3258.
5 p. fol.

Score: medium solo voice with piano accompaniment. Negro dialect.

"A stirring American song." -- at head of title.

ABSpl
YJWJ
LC

*Johnson John Rosamond, 1873-
*Cole, Robert Allen

Louisiana Lize. [Popular song; Composed by *Bob Cole; words and music edited by *J. W. and Rosamond Johnson. New York, Jos. W. Stern & co. [c1899; Publ. pl. no. 1053.
5 p. fol.

Score: low solo voice [key of F] with piano accompaniment. Negro dialect.

ABSpl

*Johnson, John Rosamond, 1873-

Moonlight on the Mississippi. [Popular song; Words by *Bob Cole; music by Rosamond Johnson. New York, Jos. W. Stern & co. [c1903; Publ. pl. no. 3681.
5 p. fol.

Score: medium solo voice [key of G] with piano accompaniment. English words.

ABSpl
LC

*Johnson, John Rosamond, 1873-

...No use in askin' 'cause you know the reason why. [Popular song. Words by *J. W. Johnson; music by Rosamond Johnson.] New York, Jos. W. Stern & co. [c1901; Publ. pl. no. 3241.
6 p. fol.

Score: high solo voice [key of G] with piano accompaniment. Negro dialect.

LC
ABSpl

*Johnson, John Rosamond, 1873-

...Lovely daughter of Allah (An Arabian episode) [Popular song; Lyric by *James Weldon Johnson; music by J. Rosamond Johnson. New York, Jos. W. Stern & co. [c1912; Publ. pl. no. 7187.
5 p. fol.

Score: low solo voice [key of F] with piano accompaniment. English words.

ABSpl

*Johnson, John Rosamond, 1873-

...Morning, noon and night. [Song. Words by *James Weldon Johnson; music by] J. Rosamond Johnson. New York, G. Schirmer [c1916; Publ. pl. no. 26650.
5 p. fol.

Score: low solo voice [key of E^b] with piano accompaniment. English words.

ABSpl

*Johnson, John Rosamond, 1873-

O, come let us sing. [Popular song. Chorus; Words by Noble Sissle; music by J. Rosamond Johnson... New York, *Handy brothers music co., inc. [c1934;
6 p. 8°.

Score: SATB with piano accompaniment. English words.

Bound in black spiral notebook no. 3.

"Chicago World's Fair edition choral arrangement as sung in the pageant, 'O, sing a new song.'" - End of title.

ABS
LC ZWpl

*Johnson, John Rosamond, 1873-

...Ma Mississippi belle. [Popular song; Words by *J. W. Johnson and *Bob Cole; music by Rosamond Johnson. New York, Jos. W. Stern & co. [c1900; Publ. pl. no. 3063.
5 p. fol.

Score: medium solo voice [key of F] with piano accompaniment. Negro dialect.

"Sung in her new play, 'The Belle of Bridgeport' by ... May Irwin." - Head of title.

ABSpl
LC

*Johnson, John Rosamond, 1873- arr.

[Move, members, move Dan-u-el. Negro spiritual by J. Rosamond Johnson.]

(In Johnson, J. Rosamond, "Sixteen new Negro spirituals." p. 19)

Score: high solo voice [key of F] with piano accompaniment. Negro dialect.

ABSpl
BHC
HMC
LC
ZWpl

*Johnson, John Rosamond, 1873- arr.

[O gimme de wings, for to move along. Negro spiritual by J. Rosamond Johnson.]

(In Johnson, J. Rosamond, "Sixteen new Negro spirituals." p. 11)

Score: medium solo voice [key of F] with piano accompaniment. Negro dialect.

ABSpl
BHC
HMC
LC
ZWpl

*Johnson, John Rosamond, 1873-

...Mandy, won't you letmebe your beau? [Popular song. Words by *Bob Cole; music by Rosamond Johnson.] New York, Jos. W. Stern & co. [c1902; Publ. pl. no. 3319.
5 p. fol.

Score: medium solo voice [key of G] with piano accompaniment. English words.

"By J. W. Johnson, Bob Cole and Rosamond Johnson." - Cover title page.

ABSpl
LC

*Johnson, John Rosamond, 1873-

"Mudder knows." [Popular song; Words by *Bob Cole; music by Rosamond Johnson. New York, Jos. W. Stern & co. [c1903; Publ. pl. no. 3757.
5 p. fol.

Score: medium solo voice [key of F] with piano accompaniment. Negro dialect.

"By... Cole and Johnson Bros." - Cover title page.

ABSpl
LC

*Johnson, John Rosamond, 1873- arr.

[O, holy Lord! Negro spiritual by J. Rosamond Johnson.]

(In Johnson, J. Rosamond, "Sixteen new Negro spirituals." p. 12)

Score: medium solo voice [key of G] with piano accompaniment. Negro dialect.

ABSpl
BHC
HMC
LC
ZWpl

*Johnson, John Rosamond, 1873-

Mem'ries of violets. Song The words by Estelle Pugsley Hart; the music by J. Rosamond Johnson... New York, G. Ricordi & co., c1914. Publ. pl. no. 114300.
6 p. fol.

Score: high solo voice [key of D] with piano accompaniment. English words.

ABSpl YJWJ
LC ZWpl

*Johnson, John Rosamond, 1873-

... "My castle on the Nile." [Popular song] Words by *J. W. Johnson and *Bob Cole; music by J. Rosamond Johnson. New York, Jos. W. Stern & co. [c1901; Publ. pl. no. 3264.
4 p. fol.

Score: medium solo voice [key of G] with piano accompaniment. Negro dialect.

ABSpl
NYPLS
YJWJ
LC

*Johnson, John Rosamond, 1973- arr.

...O, wasn't that a wide river. (Negro spiritual) [Arranged] for mixed voices by J. Rosamond Johnson. New York, *Handy bros. music co., inc. [c1935;
5 p. 8°.

Score: SATB with piano accompaniment. Negro dialect.

ABS Bound in black spiral notebook no. 3.
HMC
LC
ZWpl

*Johnson, John Rosamond, 1873-

...The merango (El merengue) Characteristic Cuban dance. [By] Rosamond Johnson... New York, Jos. W. Stern & co. [c1915] Publ. pl. no. 4504.
7 p. fol.

Score: piano solo.

ABSpl
LC
YJWJ

*Johnson, John Rosamond, 1873- arr.

[My good Lord done been here (Bless my soul an' gone). Negro spiritual by J. Rosamond Johnson.]

(In Johnson, J. Rosamond, "Sixteen new Negro spirituals." p. 20, 21)

Score: medium solo voice [key of F] with piano accompaniment. Negro dialect.

ABSpl
BHC
HMC
LC
ZWpl

*Johnson, John Rosamond, 1873-

The old flag never touched the ground. (Patriotic march song) Words by *J. W. Johnson and *Bob Cole; music by Rosamond Johnson. New York, Edward B. Marks music co., c1901. Publ. pl. no. 3238.
5 p. fol.

Score: medium solo voice [key of A^b] with piano accompaniment. English words.

ABSpl

*Johnson, John Rosamond, 1873-

[On Lalawana's shore. (Fay Templeton's South Sea Island love song) Popular song. Words by *J. W. Johnson; music by Rosamond Johnson.] New York, Jos. W. Stern & co. [c1904] Publ. pl. no. 4162.
5 p. fol.

Score: low solo voice [key of G] with piano accompaniment. English words.

ABSpl
LC

Johnson, John Rosamond
The Saint Vitus Rag

---

*Johnson, John Rosamond, 1873- ed.

Sixteen new Negro spirituals, arranged and adapted by J. Rosamond Johnson. New York, *Handy bros. music co. [c1929]
23 p. fol.

Score: medium solo voice with piano accompaniment. Negro dialect.

Contents: 1. Wake up, Jacob, day is a breakin'. -2. Tell Jesus I done done, all I can -3. I'm walkin' on borrow'd lan'. -4. Where

(continued on next card)

---

*Johnson, John Rosamond, 1873-

"The pathway of love" ... [Popular song] Lyric by *Bob Cole; music by J. Rosamond Johnson. New York, Jos. W. Stern & co. [c1908] Publ. pl. no. 6116.
6 p. fol.

Score: high solo voice [key of E^b] with piano accompaniment. English words.

Excerpt from "The red moon."

"Sung by *Abbie Mitchell." - End of title.

ABSpl LC
CCPpl

---

*Johnson, John Rosamond, 1873- arr.

...Same train. (Negro spiritual) [Arranged] for mixed voices by J. Rosamond Johnson. New York, *Handy bros. music co., inc. [c1935]
6 p. 8°.

Score: SATB with piano accompaniment. Negro dialect.
ABS Bound in black spiral notebook no. 3.
HMC
LC
ZWpl

---

*Johnson, John Rosamond, 1873- ed. Sixteen new Negro spirituals....c1929. (Card 2)

shall I go? -5. I'm troubled Lord. -6. O gimme de wings, for to move along. -7. O, holy Lord! -8. I wish I had died in Egypt lan'. -9. Tell John don't call de roll (Sinner man so hard to believe). -10. You got to die. -11. Leanin' on de Lord. -12. Dere's a meetin' here tonight. -13. De lam' done been down here an' died. -14 Move, members, move Dan-u-el. -15. My good Lord done been here (Bless my soul an' gone). -16. Goin' to see my mother (Some o' dese mornin's.

ABSpl BUC HMC LC NYPL42 NYPLS
HPSpl YJWJ ZWpl

---

*Johnson, John Rosamond, 1873-

Phoebe Brown. [Popular song] Words by Bob Cole; music by J. Rosamond Johnson. New York, Jerome H. Remick & co. [c1909] Publ. pl. no. 2786.
5 p. fol.

Score: medium solo voice [key of F] with piano accompaniment. English words.
Caption title.

Excerpt from the musical production, "The red moon."

ABSpl

---

*Johnson, John Rosamond, 1873-

Selections from "Humpty Dumpty." By [*Bob] Cole and Johnson bros. [James Weldon and J. Rosamond;] arranged for piano by Andor Pinter. New York, Jos. W. Stern & co. [c1905] Publ. pl. no. 4426.
11 p. fol.

Score: piano solo.

Includes melodies of: 1. Peter Piper. -2. Any old tree. -3. Mexico. -4. When the harvest moon is shining on the river. -5. Sambo and Dinah. -6. The banana man. -7. In sweet loveland. -8. On Lalawana's shore. -9. Lindy. ABSpl

---

Johnson, John Rosamond
A song of the heart for 4 voices.

---

*Johnson, John Rosamond, 1873-

...The pretty little squaw, from Utah. [Popular song. Words by *Bob Cole; music by Rosamond Johnson.] New York, Jos. W. Stern & co. [c1904] Publ. pl. no. 4171.
5 p. fol.

Score: medium solo voice [key of G] with piano accompaniment. English words.

ABSpl
LC

Johnson, John Rosamond
Shoo-fly regiment

(3 compositions)

---

*Johnson, John Rosamond, 1873-

Song of the heart. [Song] The words by Margaret Graham; the music by J. Rosamond Johnson... New York, G. Ricordi & co., c1918. Publ. pl. no. 116373.
7 p. fol.

Score: medium solo voice [key of D^b] with piano accompaniment. English words.
ABSpl
HPSpl - Autographed by composer to HPS, July 24, 1942.
LC NYPL42 ZWpl

---

*Johnson, John Rosamond, 1873-

"The pussy and the bow-bow." [Popular song] Lyric by *James W. Johnson; music by Rosamond Johnson. New York, Jos. W. Stern & co. [c1904] Publ. pl. no. 4300.
6 p. fol.

Score: medium solo voice [key of G] with piano accompaniment. English words.

"By Cole and Johnson Bros." - Cover title page.

Excerpt from "Humpty Dumpty."
ABSpl

Johnson, John Rosamond
The Shoo-fly Regiment

(5 compositions)

---

*Johnson, John Rosamond, 1873- arr.

...Steal away to Jesus. (Negro spiritual) [Arranged] for mixed voices by J. Rosamond Johnson. New York, *Handy bros. music co., inc. [c1937]
7 p. 8°.
Bound in black spiral notebook no. 3.
Score: SSAATBB with soprano or tenor solo and piano accompaniment. Negro dialect.
ABS
HMC
LC
ZWpl

---

*Johnson, John Rosamond, 1873-

Roll them cotton bales. [Popular song] Words by *James W. Johnson; music by J. Rosamond Johnson. New York, Jos. W. Stern & co. [c1914] Publ. pl. no. 7741.
5 p. fol.

Score: low solo voice with piano accompaniment.

ABSpl
YJWJ

Johnson, John Rosamond
Since you went away.

---

*Johnson, John Rosamond, 1873-

Sugar Babe. [Popular song] Words by *Bob Cole; music by J. Rosamond Johnson. New York, Jos. W. Stern & co. [c1907] Publ. pl. no. 5836.
5 p. fol.

Score: medium solo voice [key of E^b] with piano accompaniment. Negro dialect.

Excerpt from "The Shoo-fly Regiment."

ABSpl
LC

---

*Johnson, John Rosamond, 1873-

Run, brudder rabbit, run! [Popular song] Lyric by *Jas. W. Johnson; music by J. Rosamond Johnson. New York, Jos. W. Stern & co. [c1906] Publ. pl. no. 5138.
(In Ten choice Negro folksongs for voice and pianoforte. New York, [n.d.] p. 11-14.)

Score: medium solo voice [key of F] with piano accompaniment. Negro dialect.
Caption title.
ABSpl
BHC

---

*Johnson, John Rosamond, 1873-

Singin' wid a sword in ma han'. Negro spiritual. Arranged by J. Rosamond Johnson. [London, J. Curwen & sons, ltd., c1925]
6 p. fol. (Curwen edition)

Score: low solo voice [key of F] with piano accompaniment. Negro dialect.

"Melody by courtesy of *Miss H. B. Lee, Palmer Memorial Institute, Sedalia, N. C." - End of title.

ABSpl

Johnson, John Rosamond
Sweetness, I love you best of all

*Johnson, John Rosamond, 1873-

Sweetness, -I love you the best of all. ⌈Popular song⌉ Words and music by J. Rosamond Johnson. New York, Jos. W. Stern & co. ⌈c1910⌉ Publ. pl. no. 6654.
5 p. fol.

Score: medium solo voice ⌈key of G⌉ with piano accompaniment. English words.

"Introduced by Cole and Johnson's Sambo Girls with Edgar Connor." - End of title.

ABSpl

*Johnson, John Rosamond, 1873-

"There's a very pretty moon tonight." ⌈Popular song⌉ Words by *J. W. Johnson; music by Rosamond Johnson. New York, Jos. W. Stern & co. ⌈c1903⌉ Publ. pl. no. 3921.
5 p. fol.

Score: medium solo voice ⌈key of F⌉ with piano accompaniment. English words.

"By Cole and Johnson Bros... as sung in Klaw & Erlanger's production of The Drury Lane Extravaganza, 'Mother Goose'." - Cover title-page.

ABSpl LC

*Johnson, John Rosamond, 1873-

...Walk together, children. A triumphant Negro march song, arranged by J. Rosamond Johnson. Boston, Oliver Ditson co. ⌈c1917⌉ Publ. pl. no. 72213.
5 p. fol.

Score: high solo voice ⌈key of F⌉ with piano accompaniment.

ABSpl
LC
YJWJ

*Johnson, John Rosamond, 1873- arr.

...The tale of a pig. (Mock ballad). Composed by Frederick V. Bowers; arranged by J. Rosamond Johnson. New York, Edward B. Marks music corp. ⌈c1935⌉ Publ. pl. no. 10,278.
5 p. fol.

Score: medium solo voice ⌈key of E^b⌉ with piano accompaniment, with chorus arranged for TTBB. English words.

ABSpl

*Johnson, John Rosamond, 1873-

..."There's always something wrong." ⌈Popular song⌉ Words by *Bob Cole; music by Rosamond Johnson. New York, Jos. W. Stern & co. ⌈c1917⌉ Publ. pl. no. 5639.
5 p. fol.

Score: medium solo voice ⌈key of G⌉ with piano accompaniment. Negro dialect.

⌈Sung with tremendous success by Cole and Johnson in their new play, 'The Shoo-fly Regiment'."- Head of title.

ABSpl LC

*Johnson, John Rosamond, 1873-

...W'en de colo'ed ban' comes ma'chin' down de street... ⌈Popular song⌉ Words by *Paul Laurence Dunbar; music by Rosamond Johnson. New York, Howley, Haviland & Dresser ⌈c1903⌉
6 p. fol.

Score: high solo voice ⌈key of D⌉ with piano accompaniment. Negro dialect.

"As sung in Klaw & Erlanger's colossal 'Mr. Blue Beard'; greatest musical spectacular entertainment in the world. From the theatre Royal, Drury Lane, London." - End of title.

ABSpl LC

*Johnson, John Rosamond, 1873-

...Tango dreams. The new Maurice Brazilian tango ⌈for piano⌉ Composed by J. Rosamond Johnson. New York, Jos. W. Stern & co. ⌈c1914⌉ Publ. pl. no. 7746.
5 p. fol.

Score: piano solo with a chorus for high solo voice with piano accompaniment. English words (ad lib)

ABSpl

*Johnson, John Rosamond, 1873-

Three questions. A ballad. ⌈Poem by *James Weldon Johnson; music by⌉ J. Rosamond Johnson. New York, Harold Flammer, inc. ⌈c1917⌉ Publ. pl. no. 157C.
5 p. fol.

Score: high solo voice ⌈key of D⌉ with piano accompaniment. English words.

ABSpl
LC

*Johnson, John Rosamond, 1873-

"When the moon comes peeping o'er the hill." ⌈Popular song⌉ Words by *Bob Cole; music by Rosamond Johnson. New York, Jos. W. Stern & co. ⌈c1902⌉ Publ. pl. no. 3431.
5 p. fol.

Score: high solo voice ⌈key of F⌉ with piano accompaniment. English words.

"By ... Cole and Johnson Bros." - Cover title-page.
"As sung by Irene Bentley in the comedy opera success, 'A girl from Dixie'." - End of title.

ABSpl LC

*Johnson, John Rosamond, 1873-

...Tell me, dusky maiden. ⌈(A travesty) Minstrel song⌉ Words by *J. W. Johnson and *Bob Cole; music by Rosamond Johnson. New York, Howley, Haviland & Dresser ⌈c1901⌉
7 p. fol.

Score: duet for high and medium voices ⌈key of E^b⌉ with piano accompaniment. Includes some Negro dialect.

(continued on next card)

*Johnson, John Rosamond, 1873-

...Two eyes. ⌈Popular song⌉ Words by *J. W. Johnson; music by Rosamond Johnson. New York, Jos. W. Stern & co. ⌈c1903⌉ Publ. pl. no. 3536.
5 p. fol.

Score: low solo voice ⌈key of C⌉ with piano accompaniment. English words.

"Famous song successes, Cole and Johnson Bros." - Cover title-page.
"Introduced by Marie Cahill in 'Nancy Brown'."- Head of title.

ABSpl LC

*Johnson, John Rosamond, 1873- arr.

⌈Where shall I go? To ease my trembalin' mind. Negro spiritual by J. Rosamond Johnson⌉
(In, Johnson, J. Rosamond, "Sixteen new Negro spirituals." p. 9)

Score: medium solo voice ⌈key of A^b⌉ with piano accompaniment. Negro dialect.

ABSpl
BHC
HMC
LC
ZWpl

*Johnson, John Rosamond, 1873- ...Tell me, dusky maiden... New York, ⌈c1901⌉ (Card 2)

Makes use of the melodies of "When you ain't got no money," "All coons look alike to me," and "Just because I made dem goo goo eyes."

Excerpt from the musical show, "The sleeping beauty and the beast."

ABSpl
LC
YJWJ

*Johnson, John Rosamond, 1873-

Treat me like a baby doll. ⌈Popular song⌉ Lyric by *J. W. Johnson; music by J. Rosamond Johnson. New York, Jos. W. Stern & co. ⌈c1914⌉ Publ. pl. no. 7743.
5 p. fol.

Score: medium solo voice ⌈key of G⌉ with piano accompaniment. English words.

ABSpl

*Johnson, John Rosamond, 1873-
Who built de Ark? 1938.

Bound in black spiral notebook no. 3.

ABS

*Johnson, John Rosamond, 1873- arr.

⌈Tell Jesus I done done, all I can. Negro spiritual by J. Rosamond Johnson.⌉
(In Johnson, J. Rosamond, ⌈Sixteen new Negro spirituals." p. 7)

Score: low solo voice ⌈key of F⌉ with piano accompaniment. Negro dialect.

ABSpl
BHC
HMC
LC
ZWpl

*Johnson, John Rosamond, 1873- comp.

Utica jubilee singers spirituals. Taken down by J. Rosamond Johnson; with introduction by C. W. Hyne. New York: Oliver Ditson co ⌈c1930⌉. Publ pl no. 76619-149.
149 p. fronts., illus., 27 1/2 cm.

Score: TTBB with piano accompaniment. Negro dialect.

Contents: 38 songs.

BPL HMC CPL NYPL42 NYPLS

*Johnson, John Rosamond, 1873-

Who do you love? ⌈Popular song⌉ Lyric by *Bob Cole; music by J. Rosamond Johnson. New York, Jos. W. Stern & co. ⌈c1906⌉ Publ. pl. no. 5151.
6 p. fol.

Score: medium solo voice ⌈key of B^b⌉ with piano accompaniment. English words.

Excerpt from "The Shoo-fly Regiment."

ABSpl
LC

*Johnson, John Rosamond, 1873- arr.

⌈Tell John, don't call de roll. (Sinner man so hard to believe). Negro spiritual by J. Rosamond Johnson⌉
(In Johnson, J. Rosamond, "Sixteen new Negro spirituals." p. 14)

Score: medium solo voice ⌈key of F⌉ with piano accompaniment. Negro dialect.

ABSpl ZWpl
BHC
HMC
LC

*Johnson, John Rosamond, 1873- arr.

⌈Wake up, Jacob, day is a breakin'. Adaptation from an old Negro spiritual by J. Rosamond Johnson⌉
(In Johnson, J. Rosamond, "Sixteen new Negro spirituals. p. 6)

Score: low solo voice ⌈key of G⌉ with piano accompaniment. Negro dialect.

ABSpl
BHC
HMC
LC
ZWpl

*Johnson, John Rosamond, 1873-

...Why don't the band play? ⌈Popular song⌉ Words by *Bob Cole and *J. W. Johnson; music by Rosamond Johnson. New York, Jos. W. Stern & co. ⌈c1900⌉ Publ. pl. no. 3065.
6 p. fol.

Score: medium solo voice ⌈key of A^b⌉ with piano accompaniment. English words.

ABSpl
LC

*Johnson, John Rosamond, 1873- arr.

[You got to die. Negro spiritual by J. Rosamond Johnson.]
(In Johnson, J. Rosamond, "Sixteen new Negro spirituals." p. 15)

Score: low solo voice [key of F] with piano accompaniment. Negro dialect.

ABSpl
BHC
HMC
LC
ZNpl

---

*Johnson, William B

From Egypt to the Zululand. [Popular song] Words and music by Billy Johnson. New York, Hamilton S. Gordon publisher, [c1905] Publ. pl. no.11420.
5p. fol.

Score: medium solo voice [key of G] with piano accompaniment. English words.

LC
ABSpl

Johnson, William B
Since Mandy Green's got opera on her brain

---

*Johnson, Lukie

Has anybody seen my Corinne? [Popular song] Words by Roger Graham; music by Lukie Johnson. New York, Jos. W. Stern & co. [c1918] Publ. pl. no. 8684.
3 p. fol.

Score: medium solo voice with piano accompaniment. English words.

ABSpl

---

*Johnson, William B
*Smith, Christopher
Good-bye, I'll see you some more. [Popular song] By*Chris. Smith and Billy B. Johnson... Brooklyn, New York, Hirsekorn and Selig c1905
5 p. fol.

Score: medium solo voice key of F with piano accompaniment. Negro dialect.

Pictures of Billy B. Johnson,*Estelle Johnson, and *Chris Smith on title page.

ABSpl

Johnson, William B
That great big yaller Coon from Baltimore

---

*Johnson, William B
*Smith, Christopher
All in down and out (Sorry I ain't got it, you could get it, if I had it). [Popular song] Words by *R. C. McPherson (Cecil Mack); music by *Chris, Smith, [Billy B.] Johnson and *Elmer Bowman. New York, Gotham-Attucks music co. [c1906]
5 p. fol.

Score: medium solo voice [key of B^b] with piano accompaniment. English words.

LC
ABSpl

---

*Johnson, William B

I am going back to my old Georgia home. [Popular song] By Billy Johnson. New York, T. B. Harms & co., [c1901]
5p. fol.

Score: medium solo voice [key of G] with piano accompaniment. English words.

ABSpl
LC

---

*Johnson, William B

...Sweeter dan a sugar cane. Darket love song and refrain...Words and music by Billy Johnson. New York, M. Witmark & sons. [c1903] Publ. pl. no. 5220.
5p. fol.

Score: medium solo voice [key of B^b] with piano accompaniment. Negro dialect.

LC
ABSpl

Johnson, William B
Angel face

---

*Johnson, William B

"I belong to the government now." [Popular song] Words and jusic by Billy Johnson. New York, Harry Von Tilzer music pub. co. [c1903]
5p. fol.

Score: low solo voice [key of F] with piano accompaniment. Negro dialect.

ABSpl

---

*Johnson, William B

Sweethearts one, two and three. [Popular song] Words and music by Billy Johnson. New York, Frank K. Root & co., [c1909]
5p. fol.

Score: low solo voice [key of G] with piano accompaniment. English words.

ABSpl

---

*Johnson, William B
*Smith, Christopher
Business is business with me. [Popular song] Words by Billy B. Johnson; music by *Chris Smith. Boston, G. W. Setchell, pub. [c1907]
5 p. fol.

Score: medium solo voice [key of A^b] with piano accompaniment. English words.

ABSpl

Johnson, William B
I'm keeping my love lamp burning for you

---

*Johnson, William B

Swing me honey, swing me. [Popular song] Lyric by J. Will Callahan and Billy Johnson; music by Billy Johnson. New York, Frank K. Root & co., [c1914]
5p. fol.

Score: medium solo voice [key of F] with piano accompaniment. Negro dialect.

ABSpl

---

*Johnson, William B

The doctor calls me somnambulist coon. [Popular song] Words and music by Billy Johnson. New York, M. Witmark & sons [c1902] Publ. pl. no. 4735.
4p. fol.

Score: medium solo voice [key of B^b] with piano accompaniment. Negro dialect.

LC
ABSpl

---

*Johnson, William B
*Cole, Robert Allen
The luckiest coon in town. [Popular song] By Billy Johnson and *Bob Cole. New York, Howley, Haviland & co., [c1899]
5p. fol.

Score: medium solo voice [key of G] with piano accompaniment. Negro dialect.

ABSpl

---

*Jones, Clarence M

Am I a butterfly? (To whom you say good-bye) [Popular song] Lyric by Walter Hirsch; music by Clarence M. Jones. New York, Frank K. Root and co. [c1918]
3 p. fol.

Score: medium solo voice with piano accompaniment. English words.

ABSpl

---

*Johnson, William B

Down on the Amazon. [Popular song] By Billy Johnson. New York, The Dowling Sutton music pub. co., [c1903]
5p. fol.

Score: low solo voice [key of B^b] with piano accompaniment. English words.

LC
ABSpl

---

*Johnson, William B
*Cole, Robert Allen
Mr. Coon you're alright in your place. [Popular song] By *Bob Cole and Billy Johnson... New York, Howley, Haviland & co. [c1899]
5 p. fol.

Score: medium solo voice [key of E^b] with piano accompaniment. Negro dialect.

ABSpl

---

*Jones, Clarence M

Black bottom's got 'em (and won't behave)...[Popular song] Lyric by Will H. Hendrickson; music by Clarence M. Jones and Glenn M. Coleman. Chicago, Glenn M. Coleman and co. music publ. [c1927]
5 p. fol.

Score: medium solo voice with piano accompaniment. English words.

ABSpl

*Jones, Clarence M

...Daddy long legs. Hesitation waltz for piano By Clarence M. Jones. New York, Frank K. Root and co. [c1914]
5 p. fol.

Score: piano solo.

ABSpl

*Jones, Irving.
Fare thee well, that means good-bye. Words by Irving Jones and music by Maxwell Silver. 1905.

In bound vol.

ABS

*Jones, Irving

My money never gives out. [Popular song] Words and music by Irving Jones. New York, Feist and Frankenthaler [c1900]
5p. fol.

Score: medium solo voice [key of B^b] with piano accompaniment. Negro dialect.
Caption title.

LC
ABSpl

*Jones, Clarence M

How'd you like to go a-honeymooning? [Popular song] Lyric by Arthur J. Lamb; music by Clarence M. Jones. New York, Frank K. Root and co. [c1916]
5 p. fol.

Score: medium solo voice with piano accompaniment. English words.

ABSpl

*Jones, Irving.
Get your money's worth. 1897.

In bound vol.

ABS

*Jones, Irving

...Possumala dance. Or, My honey. [Popular song] Words and music by Irving Jones. New York, Willis, Woodward & co. , c1894.
7p. fol.

Score: medium solo voice [key of F] with piano accompaniment. English words.

LC
ABSpl

*Jones, Clarence M

My keepsake is a heartache (My dream of love is o'er) [Popular song] Lyric by Arthur J. Lamb; music by Clarence Jones. New York, Frank K. Root and co. [c1915]
5 p. fol.

Score: medium solo voice with piano accompaniment. English words.

ABSpl

*Jones, Irving.
Give me back dem clothes. 1899.

In bound vol.

ABS

*Jones, Irving.
Take your clothes and go. 1897.

In bound vol.

ABS

*Jones, Clarence M

One wonderful night (you told me you loved me). [Popular song.] Words by E. Clinton Keithley and Joe Lyons; music by Clarence M. Jones. New York, Frank K. Root and co. [c1914]
5 p. fol.

Score: medium solo voice with piano accompaniment. English words.

ABSpl

*Jones, Irving
Home aint nothing like this. 1902.

In bound vol.

ABS

*Jones, Irving

..."There ain't no use to keep on hanging around." [Popular song] Words and music by Irving Jones. New York, Feist and Frankenthaler [c1899]
4p. fol.

Score: medium solo voice with piano accompaniment. Negro dialect.

"Composed expressly for the New York Sunday World. Part III. The Sunday World's Album of Ten New Original Songs" -- at head of title.
Arr. by *William H. Tyers.
ABSpl

*Jones, Clarence M

Sweet cookie mine. [Popular song] Lyric by Jack Frost; music by Clarence M. Jones. New York, Frank K. Root and co., [c1917]
3 p. fol.

Score: medium solo voice with piano accompaniment. English words.

ABSpl

*Jones, Irving

...I don't allow no coon to hurt my feelin's. [Popular song] Words and music by Irving Jones of Jones, Grant & Jones. New York, Jos. W. Stern & co. [c1898]
5p. fol.
In bound vol.
Score: high solo voice [key of E^b] with piano accompaniment. Negro dialect.

Portraits of Irving Jones, Burt Grant and Sadie Jones on title page.
ABS

(continued on next card)

*Jones, Irving
Mills, Kerry
"Under the chicken tree." [Popular song] Words by Irving Jones; music by Kerry Mills. New York, F. A. Mills, [c1908]
6p. fol.

Score: medium solo voice with piano accompaniment. English words.

ABSpl

*Jones, Clarence M

...Thanks for the lobster (Merci du homard). One or two-step or tango [for piano] By Clarence Jones. New York, Frank K. Root and co. [c1914]
5 p. fol.

Score: piano solo.

ABSpl

*Jones, Irving.
I'm lending money to the government now. 1900.

In bound vol.

ABS

*Jones, Irving.
You don't handle nuff money for me. 1898.

In bound vol.

ABS

*Jones, Irving

"The Blackville Derby ball." [Popular song] Words and music by I. Irving Jones; arranged by Joseph Clander. Milwaukee, Wis., Chas. K. Harris, [c1897]
5p. fol.

Score: medium solo voice [key of G] with piano accompaniment. English words.
Caption title.

ABSpl
LC

Jones, Irving
I'm livin' easy

ABSpl
no cd. made

*Jones, Irving.
You don't need nothin' for your nerves. Words by Irving Jones and music by Maxwell Silver. 1905.

In bound vol.

ABS

*Jones, Laurence C

Sweet memories of Dixie. ⌊By Laurence C. Jones⌋ Piney Woods, Miss., Laurence C. Jones publisher ⌊c1924⌋
3 p. fol.

Score: medium solo voice with piano accompaniment. English words.

ABSpl

---

*Joplin, Scott, -1917.

Euphonic sounds. A syncopated novelty ⌊for piano⌋ By Scott Joplin... New York, Seminary music co. ⌊c1909⌋
5 p. fol.

Score: piano solo.

Photograph of composer on title page.

ABSpl
LC

---

*Joplin, Scott, -1917.

Ragtime dance. A stop-time two step. By Scott Joplin. St. Louis, Stark music co. ⌊c1906⌋
5 p. fol.

Score: piano solo.
Caption title.

ABSpl
LC

Jones, Stephen

'Twas a kiss in the moonlight. ⌊Popular song⌋ Words by Con Conrad and Henry Creamer; music by Stephen Jones. New York: Harms, inc. ⌊c1928⌋ Publ. pl. no. 8148.
5 p. fol.

Score: medium solo voice with piano accompaniment. English words.
From the musical comedy, "Keep shufflin'".

ABSpl

---

*Joplin, Scott, -1917.

Heliotrope bouquet. A slow drag two step. By Scott Joplin and Louis Chauvin. St Louis, Stark music pub. co. ⌊c1907⌋ Publ. pl. no. 121.
5 p. fol.

Score: piano solo.

ABSpl

---

*Joplin, Scott, -1917.

...Rose leaf rag. A ragtime two step. By Scott Joplin... Boston, Daly music publisher ⌊c1907⌋
5 p. fol.

Score: piano solo.

ABSpl
LC

---

*Joplin, Scott, -1917.

...The cascades. A rag. The masterpiece of Scott Joplin. St. Louis, John Stark & sons ⌊c1904⌋
5 p. fol.

Score: piano solo.

ABSpl
LC

---

*Joplin, Scott, -1917.

Maple leaf rag. By ... Scott Joplin... St. Louis, Stark music co. ⌊c1899⌋ Publ. pl. no. 1-3.
5 p. fol.

Score: piano solo.

ABSpl

---

*Joplin, Scott, -1917. arr.

...Sensation. A rag by Joseph F. Lamb; arranged by Scott Joplin. St. Louis, Stark music co. ⌊c1908⌋ Publ. pl. no. 134.
5 p. fol.

Score: piano solo.

ABSpl

---

*Joplin, Scott, -1917.

...The chrysanthemum. An Afro-American intermezzo. By Scott Joplin. St. Louis, John Stark & son ⌊c1904⌋
5 p. fol.

Score: piano solo.

ABSpl
LC

---

*Joplin, Scott, -1917.

Original rags. Picked by Scott Joplin; arranged by Charles N. Daniels. New York, Jerome H. Remick & co. ⌊c1899⌋
5 p. fol.

Score: piano solo.

ABSpl

---

*Joplin, Scott, -1917.

Stoptime rag. By Scott Joplin... New York, Jos. W. Stern & co. ⌊c1910⌋ Publ. pl. no. 6490.
5 p. fol.

Score: piano solo.

ABSpl

---

*Joplin, Scott, -1917.

Country club. Ragtime two step. By Scott Joplin. New York, Seminary music co. ⌊c1909⌋
6 p. fol.

Score: piano solo.

ABSpl
NYPLS

---

*Joplin, Scott, -1917.

...Paragon rag. By...Scott Joplin... New York, Seminary music co. ⌊c1909⌋
7 p. fol.

Score: piano solo.

ABSpl
LC

---

*Joplin, Scott, -1917.

"Sugar cane." A ragtime two step. By Scott Joplin. New York, Seminary music co. ⌊c1908⌋
6 p. fol.

Score: piano solo.

ABSpl

---

*Joplin, Scott, -1917.

The easy winners. A ragtime two step. By Scott Joplin. St. Louis, Mo., John Stark & son ⌊c1901⌋
5 p. fol.

Score: piano solo.

ABSpl

Joplin, Scott
Pineapple rag

ABSpl
no cd. made

---

*Joplin, Scott, -1917.

...Sunflower slow drag. A ragtime two-step. By Scott Joplin and Scott Hayden... St. Louis, John Stark and sons, c1901.
5 p. fol.

Score: piano solo.

ABSpl
LC

---

*Joplin, Scott, -1917.

Elite syncopations. ⌊By⌋ Scott Joplin. St. Louis, John Stark & son ⌊c1902⌋ Publ. pl. no. 6-4.
5 p. fol.

Score: piano solo.

ABSpl
LC

---

*Joplin, Scott, -1917.

Pleasant moments. Ragtime waltz by Scott Joplin ... New York, Seminary music co. ⌊c1909⌋
6 p. fol.

Score: piano solo.

ABSpl

---

*Joplin, Scott, -1917.

Treemonisha. Opera in three acts. Words and music by Scott Joplin... New York, Scott Joplin publ. ⌊c1911⌋
230 p. fol.

Score: piano-vocal. English words and Negro dialect.

Cast of characters includes: 3 sopranos, 3 tenors, 1 baritone, 4 basses, and SATB chorus.

ABSpl LC NYPLS
FMC - autographed by Mrs. Joplin, donor of score.

•Joplin, Scott, -1917.

Wall street "rag." [For piano] By Scott Joplin. New York, Seminary music co. [c1909]
3 p. fol.

Score: piano solo.

ABSpl

Jordan, Joe
Do you dig Jim

•Jordan, Joe

Happiness. Ballad. Words and music by Fred Fischer and Joe Jordan. New York, Chas. K. Harris pub. [c1918]
3 p. fol.

Score: medium solo voice with piano accompaniment. English words.

ABSpl

•Jordan, Joe

Lovie Joe. [Popular song] Words by •Will Marion Cook; music by Joe Jordan. New York, Harry von Tilzer [c1910]
5 p. fol.

Score: medium solo voice with piano accompaniment. English words.
Caption title.

ABSpl

•Jordan, Joe

Oh, say wouldn't it be a dream. [Popular song] Words by Earl C. Jones; music by Joe Jordan. Chicago, Chas. K. Harris [c1905]
5 p. fol. 2 copies

Score: low solo voice [key of E^b] with piano accompaniment. English words.

"...from the musical production, 'Rufus Rastus' " featuring •Ernest Hoga.

ABSpl
LC

Jordan, Joe
So lonesome

• Jordan, Joe

Take your time. [Popular song] Words by Harrison Stewart; music by Joe Jordan. New York, Gotham-Attucks music co. [c1907]
5 p. fol.

Score: medium solo voice with piano accompaniment.

Extra verses by Tom Brown.

YJWJ
ABSpl

•Jordan, Joe

The tango. Two-step. [For piano] By Joe Jordan. Chicago, Will Rossiter [c1913]
5 p. fol.

Score: piano solo.

ABSpl
LC

Josefovits, Teri
When the river Don runs dry

See
Razafkeriefo, Paul Andrea

ABSpl
no cd. made

Joy, Len

The verdict is --Life (with you). [Popular song] Words by Andy Razaf; music by Len Joy. NY: Joe Davis inc. [c1930]
5p. fol.

Score: medium solo voice with piano accompaniment. English words.

ABSpl

Jubilee songs, as sung by Slaytons jubilee singers. Chicago: Thayer and Jackson stationery co., [c18--]
16 p. 8°

Score: SATB. Negro dialect.

Group portrait on cover.
Contents: 1. Dar's a jubilee. 2. Swing low, sweet chariot. 3. Roll, Jordan, roll. 4. When de rocks ode mountains. 5. De gospel train. 6. Steal away. 7. A few more years. 8. Put on

---

Jubilee songs... (Card 2)

your golden sword. 9. What kind of shoes are you going to wear? 10. Was you there? 11. King Immanuel. 12. Prepare me, Lord. 13. The Lord's prayer. 14. Peter, go ring dem bells. 15. Joshua at Jerico. 16. Halleluyah.

LC
HUL

Kennedy, R obert Emmet, 1877- Card 1

Mellows. A chronicle of unknown singers by R. Emmet Kennedy; decorations by Simmons Persons. New York: Albert & Charles Boni c1925
183 p. fol. illus.

Score: solo voice with piano accompaniment for 27 songs; 21 unaccompanied melodies. Negro dialect.
Contents: The harmonized songs are: 1. Rock Mount Sinai. 2. Dry bones. 3. God down, death. 4. I'm goin' home on a cloud. 5. Who's goin' to

---

Kennedy, Robert Emmet, 1877- Card 2

Mellows...

close my dyin' eyes? 6. Po' lil Jesus. 8. Trouble was hard. 9. I got a home in the rock. 10. O Lord, how long? 11. Lonesome valley. 12. Blind man stood on the road and cried. 13. I fold up my arms and I wonder. 14. If you can't come, send one angel down. 15. I got two wings. 16. He never said a mumblin' word. 17. Dat suits me. 18. O Mary, what you weepin' about? 19. My soul

---

Kennedy, Robert Emmet, 1877- Card 3

Mellows...

wants to go home to glory. 20. I'm a soldier of de cross. 21. Toll de bell, angel, I jus' got over. 22. Heaven. 23. Li'l David, play on yo' harp. 24. De ole mule. 25. My baby in a Guinea-blue gown. 26. Grumbellin' people. 27. Honey baby.
"Negro work songs, street cries and spirituals" --label on back
Includes character sketches of his singers.

HMC
HPSpl

Knox, Herbert F
Dance a'la mandarin

ABSpl
no cd. made

Kortlander, Max
I'm a good gal (but I'm a thousand miles from home!) [Popular song] Words by Spencer Williams; music by Max Kortlander...New York, Leo Feist inc. [c1924]
Publ. pl. no. 5509
5 p. fol.

Score: medium solo voice with piano accompaniment. English words.

ABSpl

---

*Layton, John Turner
•Creamer, Henry
After you've gone. [Popular song] By [•Henry] Creamer and [Turner] Layton. New York, Triangle music pub. co. [c1929]
5p. fol.

Score: medium solo voice with piano accompaniment. English words.

ABSpl
LC

---

*Layton, John Turner
•Creamer, Henry
...Come along. I'm through with worryin.' "Featured in Ziegfeld Follies, 1922." [Popular song] By •[Henry] Creamer and [Turner] Layton. New York, Irving Berlin, inc. [c1922]
7p. fol. (operatic edition)

Score: medium solo voice with piano accompaniment. English words. With ad lib. S A chorus arrangement to accompany solo voice in verse.

ABSpl
LC

---

*Layton, John Turner

Cool river. Song.
(In Layton, Turner. Creole love songs. A song cycle. New York, 1923, p. 3-7.)

Score: high solo voice [key of E^b] with piano accompaniment. English words.

ABSpl
LC
NYPLS
ZWpl

---

*Layton, John Turner

Creole love songs. A song cycle. Poems by Gordon Johnstone; music by Turner Layton. New York, Composers' music corp. [c1923] Publ. pl. no. 801.
19 p. fol.

Score: high solo voice with piano accompaniment. English words.

Contents: 1. Cool river. -2. Tenderness. -3. I took my mother's heart. -4. Hunger.

LC
ZWpl
ABSpl
NYPL 42

*Layton, John Turner
*Creamer, Henry
The cute little wifflin' dance. [Popular song] By Henry Creamer and J. Turner Layton. New York, Broadway music corp. [c1917]
3p. fol.

Score: medium solo voice with piano accompaniment. English words.

LC
ABSpl

*Layton, John Turner
*Creamer, Henry
I can't let 'em suffer (for the want of love). [Popular song] By [Henry] Creamer and [Turner] Layton. New York, Broadway music corp. [c1918]
3p. fol.

Score: medium solo voice with piano accompaniment. English words.

ABSpl

*Layton, John Turner
*Creamer, Henry
Its always the fault of the men. [Popular song] By *Henry S. Creamer and Turner Layton. New York, Charles K. Harris, publ. [c1920]
5p. fol.

Score: medium solo voice with piano accompaniment. English words.
Caption title

Excerpt from the musical comedy, "Three showers."

LC
ABSpl

*Layton, John Turner

Dear old southland. [Popular song] Lyric by *Henry Creamer; music by Turner Layton. New York, Jack Mills, inc. [c1921]
5p. fol.

Score: low solo voice [key of F] with piano accompaniment. Negro dialect.

LC
ABSpl
HMC
NBCL (arr. for full time orchestra by J. Dale)

*Layton, John Turner

I took my mother's heart. Song.
(In Layton, Turner. Creole love songs. A song cycle. New York, 1923, p. 12-15.)

Score: high solo voice [key of A] with piano accompaniment. English words.

LC
ZWpl
ABSpl
NYPL 42

*Layton, John Turner

The little gray road of love. [Song] Words by Gordon Johnstone; music by Turner Layton. New York, Harms Inc. [c1922] Publ. pl. no. 6421.
5p. fol.

Score: medium solo voice with piano accompaniment. English words.

ABSpl

*Layton, John Turner

Easy goin' man. [Popular] song...Lyric and music by Darl MacBoyle and Turner Layton. New York, Jerome H. Remick and co. [c1924]
5p. fol.

Score: medium solo voice with piano accompaniment. English words.
Caption title:

Excerpt from the musical comedy, "Runnin' wild."

LC
ABSpl

*Layton, John Turner
*Creamer, Henry
If, and But

*Layton, John Turner
*Creamer, Henry
Look what you've done. [Popular song] By Henry Creamer and [Turner] Layton. New York, Broadway music corp., [c1918]
3p. fol.

Score: medium solo voice with piano accompaniment. English words.

ABSpl

*Layton, John Turner
*Creamer, Henry
Everybody's crazy (bout the doggone blues but I'm happy... [Popular song] By [Henry] Creamer and [Turner] Layton. New York, Broadway music corp. [c1918]
3p. fol.

Score: medium solo voice with piano accompaniment. English words.

"The instantaneous hit, sung by *Bert Williams in the Ziegfeld Follies, 1917-18." - at end of title.

ABSpl

*Layton, John Turner

If you'll come back. [Popular] song. By Sam Ehrlich and Turner Layton. New York, Jerome H Remick and co., [c1924]
5p. fol.

Score: medium solo voice with piano accompaniment. English words.

ABSpl

*Layton, John Turner
*Creamer, Henry
Love me sweetheart mine

*Layton, John Turner
*Creamer, Henry
Goodbye Alexander. Good-bye honey-boy. [Popular song] By *[Henry] Creamer and [Turner] Layton. New York Broadway music corp. [c1918]
3p. fol.

Score: medium solo voice with piano accompaniment. English words.

A war song.

ABSpl

*Layton, John Turner
*Creamer, Henry
I'll sing you a song about dear old Dixie land. Novelty song...By [Henry] Creamer and [Turner] Layton. New York, M. Witmark and sons, [c1919] publ. pl. no. M.W. and sons 16042.
5p. fol.

Score: medium solo voice with piano accompaniment. English words.

LC
ABSpl

*Layton, John Turner
*Creamer, Henry
Meet me when the stars am shining. [Popular song] By [Henry] Creamer and [Turner] Layton. New York, Broadway music corp. [c1919]
3p. fol.

Score: medium solo voice with piano accompaniment. Negro dialect.

ABSpl

Layton, John Turner
*Creamer, Henry
How wonderful You are

*Layton, John Turner
*Creamer, Henry
I'm waiting for you

Layton, Turner
The night the stars and you

ABSpl

*Layton, John Turner

Hunger. Song.
(In Layton, Turner. Creole love songs. A song cycle. New York, 1923, p. 16-19.)

Score: high solo voice [key of C^m] with piano accompaniment. English words.

LC
ABSpl
NYPLS
ZWpl

*Layton, John Turner
*Creamer, Henry
It must be love

*Layton, Turner
*Creamer, Henry
Oh! Lawdy. (Something's done got between Ebenezer and me) [Popular song] By [Henry] Creamer and [Turner] Layton. New York, Broadway music corp. [c1919]
3p. fol.

Score: medium solo voice with piano accompaniment. English words.

LC
ABSpl

*Layton, John Turner
*Creamer, Henry
The old love is the true love

*Layton, John Turner
*Creamer, Henry
Sweet Emaline, my gal. [Popular song] Words and music by *Henry Creamer and [Turner] Layton. New York, Broadway music corp. [c1917]
3p. fol.

Score: medium solo voice with piano accompaniment. English words.

ABSpl
HMC

*Layton, John Turner
*Creamer, Henry
Who, Tillie, take your time

*Layton, John Turner
*Creamer, Henry
One and two and three and four rock-a-bye. [Popular song.] By *Henry Creamer and [Turner] Layton. New York, Broadway music corp. [c1919]
3p. fol.

Score: medium solo voice with piano accompaniment. English words.

LC
ABSpl

*Layton, John Turner
Creamer, Henry
Sweet 'n pretty. [Popular song.] By *Henry Creamer and Turner Layton. New York, Broadway music corp. [c1918]
5p. fol.

Score: medium solo voice with piano accompaniment. English words.

ABS
ABSpl

*Layton, John Turner
*Creamer, Henry
With the coming of tomorrow. Song. Lyric and music by *Henry Creamer and Turner Layton. New York: Jerome H. Remick & co. [c1921] Publ. pl. no. 2167.
5 p. fol.

Score: medium solo voice with piano accompaniment. English words.

ABSpl

*Layton, John Turner
*Creamer, Henry
One of the boys

*Layton, John Turner

Tenderness. Song.
(In Layton, Turner. Creole love songs. A song cycle. New York, 1923, p. 8-11.)

Score: high solo voice [key of F] with piano accompaniment. English words.

ABSpl
LC
NYPLS
ZWpl

Lemonier, Tom
The coon with the panama

*Layton, John Turner
*Creamer, Henry
Open your heart

*Layton, John Turner

Thank God the drums are silent. Song. Words by Gordon Johnstone; music by Turner Layton. New York, Harms, inc. [c1922] publ. pl. no. 6420.
5p. fol.

Score: medium solo voice with piano accompaniment. English words.

ABSpl

*Lemonier, Thomas

Dear old moonlight. [Popular song] Words by *Henry S. Creamer; music by Tom Lemonier. New York, Gotham-Attucks music co., [c1909]
5p. fol.

Score: medium solo voice [key of A^b] with piano accompaniment. English words.

ABSpl

*Layton, John Turner
*Creamer, Henry
Show me how. [Popular song] By *Henry Creamer and Turner Layton. New York, Charles K. Harris publisher. [c1920]
5p. fol.

Score: medium solo voice with piano accompaniment. English words.

ABSpl

*Layton, John Turner
*Creamer, Henry
That's it. Fox trot [for piano] By *Henry Creamer and [Turner] Layton. New York, Art music, inc. [c1917]
6p. fol.

Score: piano solo

LC
ABSpl

*Lemonier, Thomas

Fazie. [Popular song] Words by Frank Montgomery; music by Tom Lemonier. New York, Hamilton S. Gordon pub. [c1905] Publ. pl. no. 11419.
5p. fol.

Score: medium solo voice [key of G] with piano accompaniment. English words.

ABSpl

*Layton, John Turner
*Creamer, Henry
Somebody loves me. Fox-trot ballad. By *Henry Creamer and Turner Layton...New York, Charles K. Harris publisher. [c1922]
5p. fol.

Score: medium solo voice with piano accompaniment. English words.

ABSpl

*Layton, John Turner
Creamer, Henry
There's a rainbow in the sky. [Popular song] Words and music by *Henry Creamer and Turner Layton. New York: Waterson, Berlin & Snyder co. [c1922] Publ. pl. no. 1267.
5 p. fol.

Score: medium solo voice with piano accompaniment. English words.

ABSpl

*Lemonier, Thomas

...I'll be your dewdrop Rosey. Popular song and refrain. Words by Richard H. Gerard; music by Tom Lemonier. New York, Witmark & sons, [c1904] Publ. pl. no. 6810.
5p. fol.

Score: medium solo voice [key of B^b] with piano accompaniment. English words.

"Sung with great success by Joseph Hart and Carrie DeMar in 'Foxy Grandpa'" -- title page.

ABSpl
LC

*Layton, John Turner
Creamer, Henry
Strut, Miss Lizzie. [Popular song] By *Henry Creamer and Turner Layton. New York, Jack Mills, inc. [c1921]
5p. fol.

Score: medium solo voice [key of B^b] with piano accompaniment. English words.

ABSpl

*Layton, John Turner
*Creamer, Henry
'Way down yonder in New Orleans [Popular song] ... Lyrics by *Henry Creamer; music by Turner Layton. New York: Shapiro, Bernstein & co. [c1922]
5 p. fol.

Score: medium solo voice with piano accompaniment. English words.

"Creole Producing Co. presents 'Strut Miss Lizzie' with Creamer and Layton and all star Creole cast at the Times Square Theater, New York." at end of title.

ABSpl
IJMJ

Lemonier, Tom
In my old home

*Lemonier, Thomas

Just one word of consolation. [Popular song] Words by Frank B. Williams; music by Tom Lemonier. New York, Vogel music co., inc., [c1933]
5p. fol.

Score: medium solo voice [key of A^b] with piano accompaniment. English words.

ABSpl

---

*Lemonier, Thomas

...The leader of the ball...[Minstrel song] Words by *R. C. McPherson; music by Tom Lemonier. New York, Jos. W. Stern & co. [c1901] Publ. pl. no. 3267.
5p. fol.

Score: medium solo voice [key of C] with piano accompaniment. Negro dialect.

Excerpt from *Williams &*Walker's musical play, "The sons of Ham".

ABSpl

---

*Lemonier, Thomas

Love me all the time. [Popular song] Words and music by Tom Lemonier. New York, *Nathan Bivins music pub. [c1906]
5p. fol.

Score: medium solo voice [key of A^b] with piano accompaniment. English words.

ABSpl
LC

---

*Lemonier, Thomas

Lovie dear. [Popular song] Words by Fred Bonny; music by Tom Lemonier. New York, Rogers bros. music pub. co. [c1911]
5p. fol.

Score: medium solo voice [key of B^b] with piano accompaniment. English words.

ABSpl

---

*Lemonier, Thomas

...My dear Luzon. [Popular song] Words by J. A. Shipp music by Tom Lemonier. New York, F. A. Mills, [c1904]
6p. fol.

Score: medium solo voice [key of G] with piano accompaniment. English words.

"Featured...by *Williams and Walker in the musical comedy, 'In Dahomey'" -- at head of title.

ABSpl

---

*Lemonier, Thomas

Remember (and be careful ev'ry day) Chorus Lyric by *Lew Payton; music by Tom Lemonier. New York, *Pace and Handy music co. inc. [c1919]
7p. 8°

Score: TTBB with piano accompaniment. English words.
Bound in black spiral notebook no. 4.

ABSpl

---

*Lemonier, Thomas

Remember (and be careful ev'ry day). [Popular song] Lyric by *Lew Payton; music by Tom Lemonier. New York, Pace & Handy music co. [c1919]
3p. fol.

Score: medium solo voice [key of B^b] with piano accompaniment. English words.

ABSpl

---

*Lemonier, Thomas

...When the grand army's out on parade. Popular song Words by Frank B. Williams; music by Tom Lemonier. New York, Nathan Bivins music pub. co. [c1905]
5p. fol.

Score: medium solo voice [key of C] with piano accompaniment. English words.

"Respectfully dedicated to the Grand Army of the Republic." -- at head of title.

ABSpl

---

*Lillard, James A.
*Talbert, Wen
Hip hip hooray for Roosevelt. [Campaign song] Words by P. K. Masson; music by *Wen Talbert and Jas. Lillard. Forest Hills, L. I., Masson publisher, c1932
5 p. fol.

Score: medium solo voice with piano accompaniment. English words.

ABSpl

Linet, Hank

Hank's songs of the sunny South for the ukulele. By Hank Linet. New York, Robbins-Engel pub. [c1925] Publ. pl. no. B. F. 12-16.
15 p. fol.

Score: melody and words with ukulele diagrams of chords.

ABSpl

Link, Harry

Gone. [Popular song] Lyrics by *Andy Razaf and *Thomas Waller; music by Harry Link. NY: Santly Bros. Inc., [c1930]
5p. fol.

Score: medium solo voice with piano accompaniment. English words.

ABSpl

Lomax, John Avery, 1872-

American ballads and folk songs; collected and compiled by John A. Lomax... and Alan Lomax. New York, The Macmillan co., 1934.
612 p. 24 cm.

Unaccompanied melodies for many; words only for many more. Negro songs distributed throughout the book; especially under such headings as: Songs from Southern chain gangs; Negro bad men; The blues; Creole Negroes, reels; and, Negro spirituals.
Foreword by George Lyman Kittredge of Harvard university.

HMC
NYPLS
LC

---

*Lucas, Ann Lawrence
Smalls, Alonzo
Claribel. Waltz song. Poem by Ann Lawrence-Lucas; music by Alonzo P. Smalls. [c1922] No publisher given
5 p. fol.

Score: medium solo voice [key of E^b] with piano accompaniment. English words.

ABSpl

Lunceford, James Melvin, 1902-
Buz-Buz-Buz will you be my honey

---

*Lunceford, James Melvin, 1902-

Honey, keep your mind on me. [Popular song] Words and music by Allan Roberts, Porter Roberts and Jimmy Lunceford. New York, Words and music, inc. [c1937]
5 p. fol.

Score: medium solo voice with piano accompaniment. English words.

ABSpl

---

*Lunceford, James Melvin, 1902-

If I had rhythm in my nurseryrhymes. [Popular song] Music by Jimmy Lunceford and Saul I. Chaplin; words by Sammy Cahn and Don Raye. New York, Select music pub. inc., [c1935]
5 p. fol. 2 copies

Score: medium solo voice [key of F] with piano accompaniment. English words.

ABSpl
LC

Lunceford, James Melvin, 1902-
Rhythm is our business

Mack, Cecil See

McPherson, Richard Cecil

---

*Maddox, Yolande arr.

Were you there? Negro spiritual arranged by Yolande Maddox. New York, *Handy bros. music co., inc. [c1936]
5 p. 8vo.

Score: SATB with mezzo soprano solo and piano accompaniment.
Bound in black spiral notebook no. 4.

NYPLS
ABSpl

---

*Maddox, Yolande arr.

When you come out the wilderness. Negro spiritual. Arranged by Yolande Maddox. New York, *Handy bros. music co., inc. [c1936]
7 p. 8vo.

Score: 4 part chorus for mixed voices (SATB) with soprano solo. English words.
Bound in black spiral notebook no. 4.

NYPLS
ABSpl

McCanns, Shirley Graham
I promise

ABSpl
no cd. made

McDaniels, Gough D

... Freedman's song. ⌐Chorus⌐ Poem from "Afro-American competition by Gough D. McDaniels; music by Franz C. Bornschein. New York, J. Fischer and bro. ⌐c1936⌐ Publ. pl. no. J. F. & B. 7085.
16 p. 8vo.

Score: SATB with piano accompaniment.

Time of performance: 8 minutes.

ABSpl

McNeil, J Charles
Pretty little baby

ABSpl
no cd. made

---

*McPherson, R ichard Cecil, ca. 1883-1944.

Ain't we got love. ⌐Popular song⌐ By Cecil Mack pseud *J. Milton Reddie & *Eubie Blake...New York: Mills music inc. ⌐c1937⌐
5p. fol.

Score: medium solo voice with piano accompaniment. English words.
Caption title.
"From the musical production, 'Swing it.'" - Cover title page.

ABSpl

---

*McPherson, Richard Cecil, ca. 1883-1944.

Brand-new ⌐Popular song⌐ By Cecil Mack pseud. and *Chris. Smith. New York, Ted Snyder co. ⌐c1912⌐
5 p. fol.

Score: medium solo voice ⌐key of G⌐ with piano accompaniment. English words.
Caption title.

ABSpl

---

*McPherson, Richard Cecil, ca. 1883-1944.

By the sweat of your brow. ⌐Popular song⌐ By *Cecil Mack pseud *J. Milton Reddie & *Eubie Blake. New York: Mills music inc., ⌐c1937⌐
5p. fol.

Score: medium solo voice with piano accompaniment. English words.

From the musical production, "Swing it".
Caption title.

ABSpl

---

*McPherson, Richard Cecil, ca. 1883-1944.

Green and blue. ⌐Popular song⌐ By *Cecil Mack, J. Milton Reddie and Eubie Blake... New York: Mills Music Inc. ⌐c1937⌐
5 p. fol.

Score: medium solo voice with piano accompaniment. English words.
Caption title.
From the musical production, "Swing it."

ABSpl

---

*McPherson, Richard Cecil, ca. 1883-1944.

If I were a flower in the garden of love. ⌐Popular song⌐ Words and music by Cecil Mack ⌐pseud⌐ and Chris Smith. New York, Maurice Richmond music co. c1916
5p. fol.

Score: medium solo voice ⌐key of C⌐ with piano accompaniment. English words.

ABSpl

~~Smith, Christopher~~
*McPherson, Richard Cecil

Scaddle - de - mooch. ⌐Popular song⌐ Words and music by *Cecil Mack and Chris Smith. New York, Jos. W. Stern & co. ⌐c1915⌐ Publ. pl. no. 8010.
5 p. fol.

Score: medium solo voice ⌐key of G⌐ with piano accompaniment. English words.

ABSpl

---

*Margetson, Edward

Break forth into joy. A festival anthem. ⌐Text from⌐ Isaiah 52:9; 55:1,6,12; ⌐Music by⌐ Edward Margetson. New York, J. Fischer & bro. ⌐c1936⌐ Publ. pl. no. J.F. & B. 7196.
16 p. 8°.

Score: SATB with organ accompaniment. English words.

ABSpl
ZWpl

---

*Margetson, Edward

By the waters of Babylon. Anthem. Adapted from Psalm 137; ⌐music by⌐ Edward Margetson. New York, G. Schirmer, inc. ⌐c1932⌐ Publ. pl. no. 35895.
12 p. 8°.

Score: SATB with piano reduction for rehearsal only. English words.

ABSpl
ZWpl

---

*Margetson, Edward

...A Christmas roundelay. A Christmas carol for mixed voices. By Edward Margetson. New York, H. W. Gray co. ⌐c1931⌐
6 p. 8°.

Score: SATB with piano reduction for rehearsal only. English words.

ABSpl

---

*Margetson, Edward

Dark'ning night the land doth cover. Evening anthem for mixed voices with soprano solo. ⌐Words from an⌐ Old Greek translation; ⌐music by⌐ Edward Margetson. New York, Galaxy music corp. ⌐c1937⌐ Publ. pl. no. G.M. 745.
11 p. 8°.

Score: SATB with soprano solo and piano reduction for rehearsal only. English words.

ABSpl
LC

---

*Margetson, Edward

...Far from my heavenly home. Motet for mixed voices. Words by Rev. H. F. Lyte; ⌐music by⌐ Edward Margetson. New York, J. Fischer & bro. ⌐c1932⌐ Publ. pl. no. J.F. & B. 6607.
8 p. 8°.

Score: SSAATTBB with piano reduction for rehearsal only. English words.

ABSpl
HMC
ZWpl

---

*Margetson, Edward

He stooped to bless. Short anthem for mixed voices. Words anonymous; ⌐music by⌐ Edward Margetson. New York, J. Fischer & bro. ⌐c1936⌐ Publ. pl. no. J.F. & B. 7198.
4 p. 8°.

Score: SATB with soprano solo with piano reduction for rehearsal only. English words.

ABSpl
ZWpl

---

*Margetson, Edward

...Lord, what am I. Anthem for mixed chorus with soprano and tenor solo... ⌐Words by⌐ Lope de Vega (1562-1635); translated by H. W. Longfellow; set to music by Edward Margetson. New York, The H. W. Gray co., c1936.
7 p. 8°. (No. 1374)

Score: SATB, with soprano and tenor solo with piano reduction for rehearsal only. English words.
Caption title.

ABSpl
LC

---

*Margetson, Edward

Now sleeps the crimson petal. A madrigal. Words by Lord Tennyson; music by Edward Margetson. New York, J. Fischer & bro. ⌐c1931⌐ Publ. pl. no. J.F. & B. 6504.
5 p. 8°.

Score: SATB with piano reduction for rehearsal only. English words.

ABSpl
HMC
ZWpl

---

*Margetson, Edward

O come, let us sing. ⌐Anthem. Text from⌐ Psalm 95; ⌐music by⌐ Edward Margetson. New York, J. Fischer & bro., c1935. Publ. pl. no. J.F. & B. 6971.
16 p. 8°.

Score: SATB with Ba solo and with piano reduction for rehearsal only. English words.
Caption title.

ABSpl ZWpl
HMC
LC

---

*Margetson, Edward

O mistress mind. A madrigal. Words by ⌐William⌐ Shakespeare; ⌐music by⌐ Edward Margetson. New York, J. Fischer & bro. ⌐c1931⌐ Publ. pl. no. J.F. & B. 6505.
5 p. 8°.

Score: SATB with piano reduction for rehearsal only. English words.

ABSpl
HMC
ZWpl

---

*Margetson, Edward

O my deir hert, young Jesus sweit. A Christmas carol. ⌐Words⌐ anonymous; ⌐music by⌐ Edward Margetson. New York, J. Fischer & bro. ⌐c1931⌐ Publ. pl. no. J.F. & B. 6555.
4 p. 8°.

Score: SSA with piano reduction for rehearsal only. Old English words.

ABSpl
HMC
ZWpl

---

*Margetson, Edward

O taste and see. Anthem. ⌐Words from⌐ Psalm 34: 8-11; ⌐music by⌐ Edward Margetson. New York, J. Fischer & bro. ⌐c1936⌐ Publ. pl. no. 7197.
11 p. 8°.

Score: SATB with piano reduction for rehearsal only. English words.

ABSpl
ZWpl

---

*Margetson, Edward

...Search me, O Lord. Anthem. ⌐Words from⌐ Psalm 139:23, 24; 140:1-4, 8, 10; ⌐music by⌐ Edward Margetson. New York, J. Fischer & bro. ⌐c1935⌐ Publ. pl. no. J. F. & B. 6969.
16 p. 8°.

Score: SATB with piano reduction for rehearsal only. English words.

ABSpl
HMC
ZWpl

*Margetson, Edward

...Sing we a joyous measure. Christmas Carol-anthem for mixed chorus. Words compiled by E. M.; [music by] Edward Margetson. New York, H. W. Gray co. [c1936]
8 p. 8°.

Score: SATB with piano reduction for rehearsal only. English words.

ABSpl

---

*Margetson, Edward

Softly now the light of day. Anthem. [Words by] Bishop George W. Doane; [music by] Edward Margetson. New York, J. Fischer & bro. [c1935] Publ. pl. no. J.F. & B. 6972.
10 p. 8°.

Score: SSAATTBB with piano reduction for rehearsal only. English words.

ABSpl
HMC
ZWpl

---

*Margetson, Edward

Weep you no more [sad fountains] A madrigal for SATB. Words anonymous; [music by] Edward Margetson. New York, J. Fischer & bro. [c1932] Publ. pl. no. J. F. & B. 6606.
4 p. 8°.

Score: SATB with piano reduction for rehearsal only. English words.

ABSpl
HMC
ZWpl

The Mark Stern "Ragtime" song folio, No. 2. Fifteen late popular ragtime successes by *Williams and *Walker, Heelan and Helf, Ed. Rogers, *Bowman and *Johns, *Irving Jones, *Hogan and Northrup, Monroe H. Rosenfeld, *Bob Cole, Deas and Wilson. New York, Jos. W. Stern & co. [c1897-1902]
55 p. fol.

Score: medium solo voice with piano accompaniment. English words or Negro dialect.

(continued on next card)

The Mark Stern "Ragtime" song Folio No. 2...
New York, [c1897-1902] (Card 2)

Contents: 1. What de watermelon grow. -2. All I wants is ma chickens. -3. The missionary man. -4. The oriental coon. -5. Look here Mr. Yaller man. -6. I've got chicken on the brain. -7. The emblem of an independent coon. -8. Dat certain party. -9. When Zacharias leads the band. -10. I got de headache now. -11. I've got money locked up in a vault. -12. Nigger, nigger, never die. -13. He's up against the real thing now. -14. Wink, wink, wink, Mr. Owl. -15. When Cindy sings a rag-time song.

ABSpl

Card I

Marks, Edward Bennet, 1865-

They all sang. From Tony Pastor to Rudy Vallee. As told to Abbott J. Liebling by Edward B. Marks. New York: The Viking Press c1934
321 p. 26½cm.
Illus. (port. and music)
Chapter beginning p. 87 especially discusses the Negroes of minstrel and early vaudeville days. Frequent references to Negroes will be found throughout the book.
Lists "1545 songs outstanding in my memory" (p. 223-269); list includes many by Negroes.

Card II

Marks, Edward Bennet, 1865-

They all sang...

Contains rare photographs of *Williams and *Walker, *James Weldon Johnson, *J. Rosamond Johnson, and *Bob Cole.

ZWpl
NYPLS--Presentation copy of Harry T. Burleigh
YJWJ
LC
HMC

---

*Moore, Ruth

The kitchenette across the hall. [Popular song] Words and music by Ruth Moore. New York, *Handy Brother music co., inc. [c1935.]
4 p. fol.

Score: low solo voice with piano accompaniment. English words.

ABSpl

---

*Milady, Samuel Lucas, 1848-1916.

Careful man (his great motto song). By G. Grosse. [One of] "The world-renowned Sam Lucas' songs..." Boston, White, Smith & co., n. d. Publ. pl. no. 4055.
5 p. fol.

Score: verses for medium solo voice with piano accompaniment; chorus (SATB)

LC
ABSpl

Milady, Samuel Lucas, 1848-1916

Careful man. pub. no. 4055

Bound v. Songs Lucas

ABS

---

*Milady, Samuel Lucas, 1848-1916.

Carve dat possum... Original [minstrel] song and chorus by the author of words and music, Sam Lucas... Boston, John F. Perry & co., c1875. Publ. pl. no. 675.
3 p. fol.

Score: verse medium solo voice [key of Am] with piano accompaniment, chorus (SATB) Negro dialect.

"Arranged by Hubert Hersey."

LC
ABSpl
BHC
HMC

---

*Milady, Samuel Lucas, 1848-1916.

Children, I'm gwine to shine. By Sam Lucas. [One of] "The world-renowned Sam Lucas' songs..." Boston, White, Smith & co., n. d. Publ. pl. no. 4399.
5 p. fol.

Score: verses medium solo voice with piano accompaniment; chorus (SATB)

ABSpl

---

*Milady, Samuel Lucas, 1848-1916.

Children, I'm gwine to shine. [Song & chorus. Written expressly for Williams and Sully by Sam Lucas] Boston, White, Smith & co. [c1881] Publ. pl. no. 4399.
5 p. fol.
Bound v. Songs Lucas.
Score: verse for medium solo voice; chorus, SATB. Negro dialect.

Titlepage has portrait of the composer.

ABS
LC

---

*Milady, Samuel Lucas, 1848-1916.

Daffney do you love me? Words by Sam Lucas; music by Henry Hart. [One of] "The world-renowned Sam Lucas' songs..." Boston, White, Smith & co., c1875. Publ. pl. no. 2172.
5 p. fol.

Score: verses medium solo voice [key of D] with piano accompaniment; chorus (SATB). Negro dialect.

LC
ABSpl

---

*Milady, Samuel Lucas, 1848-1916.

...De coon dat had de razor. Song and chorus. Words by Professor William F. Quown; music by Sam Lucas. Boston, White, Smith & co. [c1885] Publ. pl. no. 6063.
5 p. fol.

Score: medium solo voice with piano accompaniment. Negro dialect.

ABSpl
LC

---

*Milady, Samuel Lucas, 1848-1916.

De coon's salvation army. [Popular song] Words and music by Sam Lucas. Boston, Oliver Ditson & co., n.d. Publ. pl. no. 31.
5 p. fol.

Score: low solo voice [key of E^b] with piano accompaniment. Negro dialect.

ABSpl

---

*Milady, Samuel Lucas, 1848-1916.

...De day I was sot free! Words and music by Sam Lucas. [One of] "The world-renowned Sam Lucas' songs..." Boston, White, Smith & co., n.d.
5 p. fol.

Score: verses medium solo voice [key of G] with piano accompaniment; chorus (SATB). Negro dialect.

ABSpl

---

*Milady, Samuel Lucas, 1848-1916.

...De day I was sot free. [Song and dance. Words and music by Sam Lucas] Boston, White, Smith & co. [c1878] Publ. pl. no. 3326.
5 p. fol.
Bound v. Songs Lucas
Score: verse for low solo voice; chorus, SATB. Negro dialect.

"Sam Lucas' great songs." - Head of title.

Titlepage has portrait of composer.

LC
ABS

---

*Milady, Samuel Lucas, 1848-1916.

De old ship ob Zion. [One of] "Two favorite songs." Written and sung by Sam Lucas. Boston, W. A. Evans & bro. [c1881]
5 p. fol.

Score: verses medium solo voice [key of C] with piano accompaniment; chorus (SATB). Negro dialect.

ABSpl

---

*Milady, Samuel Lucas, 1848-1916.

Dem silver slippers. Words and music by Sam Lucas. [One of] "The world-renowned Sam Lucas' songs..." Boston, White, Smith & co. [c1879] Publ. pl. no. 3723.
5 p. fol.

Score: verses medium solo voice [key of E^b] with piano accompaniment; chorus (SATB). Negro dialect.

LC
ABSpl

---

*Milady, Samuel Lucas, 1848-1916.

Dis darkey's growing old. Words and music by Sam Lucas. [One of] "The world-renowned Sam Lucas' songs..." Boston, White, Smith & co. [c1881] Publ. pl. no. 4422.
5 p. fol.

Score: verses medium solo voice [key of G] with piano accompaniment; chorus (SATB). Negro dialect.

LC
ABSpl

*Milady, Samuel Lucas, 1848-1916.

...Gentle Mary of the lea. Words and music by Sam Lucas. [One of] "The world-renowned Sam Lucas' songs..." Boston, White, Smith & co. [c1882] Publ. pl. no. 4887.
5 p. fol.

Score: verses medium solo voice [key of F] with piano accompaniment; chorus (SATB). English words.

ABSpl

*Milady, Samuel Lucas, 1848-1916.

...Jeremiah Brown. "That Brown." "That Brown." Song and chorus. [Words and music] by Sam Lucas. Boston, White, Smith & co. [c1882] Publ. pl. no. 4875.
5 p. fol.

Score: verse for medium solo voice; chorus, SATB with piano accompaniment. English words.

ABSpl
LC

*Milady, Samuel Lucas, 1848-1916.

Rasper's birthday party. Song and chorus. Words and music by Sam Lucas. Boston, Oliver Ditson [c1886] Publ. pl. no. 123.
5 p. fol.

Score: medium solo voice with piano accompaniment. Negro dialect.

ABSpl

*Milady, Samuel Lucas, 1848-1916.

Get up with the lark. Words and music by Sam Lucas. [One of] "The world-renowned Sam Lucas' songs..." Boston, White, Smith & co. [c1882] Publ. pl. no. 4793.
5 p. fol.

Score: verses medium solo voice [key of B^b] with piano accompaniment; chorus (SATB). English words.

LC
ABSpl

*Milady, Samuel Lucas, 1848-1916.

The jolly dude. Song. [Written and composed] by Sam Lucas. Boston, White, Smith & co. [c1883] Publ. pl. no. 5099.
5 p. fol.

Score: medium solo voice [key of F] with piano accompaniment. English words.

LC
ABSpl

*Milady, Samuel Lucas, 1848-1916.

...Rasper's birthday party. [Song & chorus. Words and music by Sam Lucas] Boston, Chas. D. Blake & co. [c1886] Publ. pl. no. 123-3 C.D.B. & co.
5 p. fol.
Bound v. Songs Lucas
Score: medium solo voice and unison chorus with piano accompaniment. Negro dialect.
ABS

LC

*Milady, Samuel Lucas, 1848-1916.

Goodbye, Annie darling. Song. Words and music by Sam Lucas. Boston, White, Smith & co. [c1886] Publ. pl. no. 6215.
5 p. fol.

Score: verses medium solo voice [key of G] with piano accompaniment; chorus (SATB). English words.

ABSpl

*Milady, Samuel Lucas, 1848-1916.

...Meet me at de sunrise in de morning. Song [by] Sam Lucas. [One of] "The world-renowned Sam Lucas' songs..." Boston, White, Smith & co. [c1881] Publ. pl. no. 4456.
5 p. fol.

Score: verses medium solo voice [key of G] with piano accompaniment; chorus (SATB). Negro dialect.

ABSpl

*Milady, Samuel Lucas, 1848-1916.

Ring dem heavenly bells. [Song] Written and composed by Sam Lucas. Boston, Russell bros. [c1883]
5 p. fol.

Score: medium solo voice [key of D] with piano accompaniment. Negro dialect.

LC
ABSpl

*Milady, Samuel Lucas, 1848-1916.

...Grandfather's old arm chair. [Song and chorus. Words by George Russell Jackson; music] by Sam Lucas. [One of] "The world-renowned Sam Lucas' songs..." Boston, White, Smith & co. [c1877] Publ. pl. no. 2922.
5 p. fol.
Bound v. Songs Lucas
Score: verses medium solo voice [key of D] with piano accompaniment; chorus (SATB). English words.

ABSpl

*Milady, Samuel Lucas, 1848-1916.

...Mother's calling baby home. Song and chorus. [Words by George Russell Jackson; music by Sam Lucas] From "The world-renowned Sam Lucas' songs..." Boston, White, Smith & co. [c1881] Publ. pl. no. 4163.
5 p. fol.

Score: verses medium solo voice [key of A^b] with piano accompaniment; chorus (SATB). English words.

ABSpl

*Milady, Samuel Lucas, 1848-1916.

Sam Lucas' great sensational and motto songs. Words and music by Sam Lucas. Boston, Oliver Ditson & co., c1884.
7 v. fol.

Score: verse, medium solo voice with piano accompaniment; chorus, SATB. Negro dialect.

Contents: -1. De coon's salvation army. -2. My thoughts are of thee... -3. Dat coon in number 4. -4. Dear mother waits for me. -5. The level headed mare. -6. Dar's a lock [illegible] on de chicken coop door. -7. Rasper's birthday party.
ABSpl

*Milady, Samuel Lucas, 1848-1916.

...Hannah, boil dat cabbage down. Song and chorus by Sam Lucas. Boston, White, Smith & co. [c1878] Publ. pl. no. 2892.
5 p. fol.

Score: verses medium solo voice [key of G] with piano accompaniment; chorus (SATB). Negro dialect.

LC
ABSpl

*Milady, Samuel Lucas, 1848-1916.

My thoughts are of thee... [Popular song] Words and music by Sam Lucas. Boston Oliver Ditson [c1884] Publ. pl. no. 43.
5 p. fol.

Score: medium solo voice [key of d] with piano accompaniment. English words.

ABSpl

*Milady, Samuel Lucas, 1848-1916.

Shivering and shaking out in the cold. Song and chorus by Sam Lucas of Callender's original Georgia minstrels. New York, White-Smith music pub. co. [c1878] Publ. pl. no. 2174.
5 p. fol.

Score: verse, medium solo voice [key of E^b] with piano accompaniment; 4 part mixed chorus (SATB). Negro dialect.

ABSpl
LC

*Milady, Samuel Lucas, 1848-1916.

I'm thinking of the golden past. Song and chorus by Sam Lucas. New York, White-Smith music pub. co. [C1892] Publ. pl. no. 8699.
5 p. fol.

Score: verses medium solo voice [key of F] with piano accompaniment; chorus (SATB). English words.

ABSpl

*Milady, Samuel Lucas, 1848-1916.

... Oh, I'll meet you dar. Song and chorus. Words and music by Sam Lucas. [One of] "The world-renowned Sam Lucas' songs..." Boston, White, Smith & co. [c1880] Publ. pl. no. 3942.
5 p. fol.

Score: verses medium solo voice [key of A] with piano accompaniment; chorus (SATB). Negro dialect.

LC
ABSpl

*Milady, Samuel Lucas, 1848-1916.

...Starlight on the sea. Waltz song. Words and music by Sam Lucas. Boston, White, Smith & co. [c1882] Publ. pl. no. 4891.
7 p. fol.

Score: high solo voice [key of B] with piano accompaniment. English words.

ABSpl

*Milady, Samuel Lucas, 1848-1916.

I'se gwine in de valley. Plantation song and chorus. By Sam Lucas. Boston, White, Smith & co. [c1879] Publ. pl. no. 2842.
5 p. fol.

Score: verse for medium solo voice; chorus, SATB. Negro dialect.

ABSpl
LC

*Milady, Samuel Lucas, 1848-1916.

...Put on the long white robe. [Song & chorus. Words and music by Sam Lucas.] Boston, White, Smith & co., c1879. Publ. pl. no. 3739.
5 p. fol.

Score: verse for medium solo voice; chorus, SATB with piano accompaniment. Negro dialect.

"To Jas. Bland." - Head of caption title.

"Sam Lucas' 3 great songs." - Head of title.

LC
ABSpl

*Milady, Samuel Lucas, 1848-1916.

... Strolling in the park in the moonlight. [Comic song. Words by George Russell; music by] Sam Lucas. New York, W. A. Evans & bro. pub. [c1882]
5 p. fol.

Score: medium solo voice [key of G] with piano accompaniment. English words.

LC
ABSpl

*Milady, Samuel Lucas, 1848-1916.

...Susan Brown's wedding. Jubilee song and chorus by Sam Lucas. Boston, White, Smith & co., c1884. Publ. pl. no. 5606.
5 p. fol.

Score: verses medium solo voice [key of G] with piano accompaniment; chorus (SATB). Negro dialect.

LC
ABSpl

*Milady, Samuel Lucas, 1848-1916.

Talk about your Moses (camp meeting hymn). Words and music by Sam Lucas. From "The world-renowned Sam Lucas' songs..." Boston, White, Smith & co. [c1880] Publ. pl. no. 3968.
5 p. fol.

Score: medium solo voice with piano accompaniment.

ABSpl
YJWS

*Milady, Samuel Lucas, 1848-1916.

That's what the little bird whispered to me. Motto song. Words and music by Sam Lucas. Boston, White, Smith & co. [c1885] Publ. pl. no. 5764.
5 p. fol.

Score: medium solo voice [key of G] with piano accompaniment. English words.

LC
ABSpl

*Milady, Samuel Lucas, 1848-1916.

Things that make a man feel like a fool. [Song.] Words and music by Sam Lucas. Boston, White, Smith & co. [c1885] Publ. pl. no. 6094.
5 p. fol.

Score: medium solo voice [key of G] with piano accompaniment. English words.

LC
ABSpl

*Milady, Samuel Lucas, 1848-1916.

We ought to be thankful for that. A comic song by Sam Lucas. New York, White-Smith music pub. co. [c1892] Publ. pl. no. 8698.
5 p. fol.

Score: verses medium solo voice [key of A] with piano accompaniment; chorus (SATB). Negro dialect.

LC
ABSpl

*Milady, Samuel Lucas, 1848-1916.

...White kid slippers. [Minstrel song] Words by Geo. Russell Jackson; music by Sam Lucas. Boston, W. A. Evans & bro. [c1883]
5 p. fol.

Score: medium solo voice [key of A^b] with piano accompaniment. Negro dialect.

"Companion song to 'Golden slippers'." - Head of title.

ABSpl
LC

*Milady, Samuel Lucas, 1848-1916.

The world-renowned Sam Lucas' songs, as sung by him with great success. Boston, White, Smith & co. [various copyright dates]
25 v. fol.

Score: verses for medium solo voice; chorus, SATB with piano accompaniment.

Contents: 1. Careful man (His great motto song). -2. Children, I'm gwine to shine. -3. Daffney do you love me? -4. De day I was sot free!

(continued on next card)

*Milady, Samuel Lucas, 1848-1916. The world-renowned Sam Lucas' songs... Boston, (Card 2)

-5. Dem silver slippers. -6. Dis darkey's growing old. -7. ...Gentle Mary of the lea. -8. Get up with the lark. -9. Grandfather's old arm chair. -10. I'se gwine in de valley. -11. ...Meet me at de sunrise in de morning. -12. Mother's calling baby home. -13. Oh, I'll meet you dar. -14. Put on my long white robe. -15. You know the sort of fellow I mean (motto song). -16. Talk about your Moses (camp meeting hymn). -17. Don't you hear the baby crying. -18. Every day will be Sunday bye and bye. -19. Hannah, boil dat cabbage down.

(continued on next card)

*Milady, Samuel Lucas, 1848-1916. The world-renowned Sam Lucas' songs... Boston, (Card 3)

-20. On the banks by the river side. -21. Shivering and shaking out in the cold. -22. When we meet in the sweet bye and bye. -23. What kind of shoes are you gwine to wear. -24. I'm Grant, & I've travelled around the world. -25. Down by de sunrise.

LC

*Milady, Samuel Lucas, 1848-1916.

...You know the sort of fellow I mean. [Motto song. By Sam Lucas] Boston, White, Smith & co. [c1881] Publ. pl. no. 4476.
5 p. fol.

Score: medium solo voice [key of A] with piano accompaniment. English words.

ABSpl
LC

Milburn, Richard
... Listen to the mocking bird. 1900.

*Milburn, Richard

...Listen to the Mocking bird. [Song] Melody by Richard Milburn; written and arranged by Alice Hawthorne [Pseud] Philadelphia: Winner and Shuster, [c1855.]

Score: medium solo voice with piano accompaniment. English words. Chorus also arranged for SATB with piano accompaniment.

"Sentimental Ethiopian ballad -- at head of title.

ABSpl
NYPES

Miller, Bob

Strut long papa. [Popular song] Words by Trebor Rellim; music by Bob Miller; arranged by John L. Herman. New York, Edward B. Marks music co., [c1923.] Publ. pl. no. 9135.
5 p. fol.

Score: medium solo voice with piano accompaniment. English words.

ABSpl

Mills, Kerry
Under the chicken tree

ABSpl
no cd. made

*Moore, Phil

...Shoo-shoo baby. [Popular song] By Phil Moore. Featured by The Andrew sisters in the Universal picture "Three cheers for the boys." New York, Leeds music corp. [c1943]
3 p. fol.

Score: low solo voice [key of F] with piano accompaniment. English words.

ABSpl
ZWpl

*Morgan, William Astor arr.

Four and twenty elders. Negro spiritual arranged by Jean Stor [pseud.] New York, *Handy bros. music co., inc. [c1937]
11 p. 8°.

Score: 4 part choral for mixed voices (SATB) with piano accompaniment. English words.
Bound in black spiral notebook no. 4.

ABSpl
ZWpl

*Morgan, William Astor, arr.

Going to hold out to the end. Negro spiritual arranged by Jean Stor [pseud.] New York, *Handy bros. music co., inc. [c1936]
10 p. 8°.

Score: 4 part choral for mixed voices (SATB) with piano accompaniment. English words.
Bound in black spiral notebook no. 4.

ABSpl
ZWpl

*Morgan, William Astor, arr.

Hold the wind. Negro spiritual arranged by Jean Stor [pseud.] New York, *Handy bros. music co., inc. [c1933]
10 p. 8°.

Score: 4 part chorus for mixed voices with bass solo. Piano accompaniment. English words.
Bound in black spiral notebook no. 4.

ABSpl
ZWpl

*Morgan, William Astor, 1890- arr.

I want Jesus to walk with me. Negro spiritual. Arranged for solo voice by Jean Stor pseud. New York, Handy bros. music co., inc. [c1935]
5 p. fol.

Score: low solo voice with piano accompaniment. English words.

ABSpl ZWpl

*Morgan, William Astor, arr.

...My way is cloudy. Negro spiritual arranged by Jean Stor [pseud.] New York, *Handy bros. music co., inc. [c1933]
6 p. 8°.

Score: SATB with baritone solo. Piano accompaniment. English words.
Bound in black spiral notebook no. 4.

ABSpl
ZWpl

*Morgan, William Astor, arr.

Pale horse and rider. Negro spiritual based on the text from Revelations 6:8. Arranged by Jean Stor [pseud.] New York, *Handy bros. music co., inc. [c1936]
11 p. 8°.

Score: choral for mixed voices (SATB) with mezzo soprano and tenor soli and piano accompaniment.
Bound in black spiral notebook no. 4.

ABSpl
ZWpl

*Morgan, William Astor, arr.

...Sit down. Negro spiritual choral arrangement by Jean Stor. New York, *Handy bros. music co., inc. c1933;
11 p. 8°.

Score: SATB with soprano solo with piano accompaniment. Negro dialect.
Bound in black spiral notebook no. 4.
Dedicated to the *Jean Stor symphony choir.

ABSpl
ZWpl

*Morgan, William Astor, arr.

This is a sin trying world. A Negro spiritual march arranged by Jean Stor. New York, *Handy bros. music co., inc. c1936;
11 p. 8°.

Score: SATB with soprano solo. Piano accompaniment. English words.
Bound in black spiral notebook no. 4.

ABSpl
ZWpl

*Morice, William

That's why my heart cries out for you. Popular song. Words and music by William Morice. New York, Mimic Music publ. co. c1927
5 p. fol.

Score: medium solo voice with piano accompaniment. English words.

ABSpl

Muse, Clarence
Alley-way of my dreams

*Morton, Ferdinand Joseph, 1885-1941.

Billy goat stomp. Orchestration by Fred (Jelly Roll) Morton; arranged by *Tiny Parham. Chicago, Melrose bros. music co. c1927
3 p. and 12 parts. 8vo.

Score: piano-conductor score; and parts for dance orchestra.

ABSpl

*Morton, Ferdinand Joseph, 1885-1941.

Black bottom stomp. By "Jelly Roll" Morton; arranged by Elmer Schoebel. Chicago, Melrose bros. music co. c1926
2 p. and 12 parts. 8vo.

Score: piano-conductor score; and parts for dance orchestra.

ABSpl

*Morton, Ferdinand Joseph, 1885-1941.

...Chicago Breakdown. Special jazz arrangement for orchestra By "Jelly Roll" Morton...A rranged by Elmer Schoebel, Chicago Melrose Bros . Music Co. c 1925
2 p. and 12 parts. 8vo

Score: piano conductor score and parts for jazz orchestra.

ABSpl

*Morton, Ferdinand Joseph, 1885-1941

...Grandpa's spells. Special jazz arrangement for orchestra By "Jelly Roll" Morton. .., arranged by Elmer Schoebel, Chicago, Melrose Bros. Music Co. c1925
2 p. and 12 parts. 8vo

Score: piano conductor; and parts for jazz orchestra.

ABSpl

*Morton, Ferdinand Joseph, 1885-1941

King Porter Stomp. F or piano by Ferdinand Morton. Chicago: Melrose Bros. c1925
6 p. fol.

Score: piano solo

ABSpl

*Morton, Ferdinand Joseph, 1885-1941.

..London blues. Orchestration. By Ferd "Jelly Roll" Morton...; arranged by F. Alexander. Chicago, Melrose bros. music co. c1923
2 p. and 12 parts. 8vo.

Score: piano-conductor; and parts for jazz orchestra.

ABSpl

*Morton, Ferdinand Joseph, 1885-1941.

..Midnight Mamma. Special jazz arrangement for orchestra By "Jelly Roll" Morton; arranged by Elmer Schoenbel. Chicago, Melrose bros. music co. c1925
2 p. and 12 parts. 8vo.

Score: piano-conductor; and parts for jazz orchestra.

ABSpl

Muse, Clarence
Lazy rain

*Muse, Clarence

When it's sleepy time down south. Popular song. Words and music by *Leon and *Otis Rene and Clarence Muse. New York, Mills Music inc. c1931.
5 p. fol.

Score: medium solo voice with piano accompaniment. English words.

ABSpl
YJWJ

*Nickerson, Camille Lucie arr.

...You don' know when. Negro spiritualistic song of death. Arranged by Camille Nickerson. New York, *Handy brothers music co., inc. c1939
5 p. fol.

Score: medium solo voice with piano accompaniment. Negro dialect.

ABSpl

Niles, John Jacob, 1892-

Singing soldiers. Illustrated by Margaret Thorniley Williamson. New York, Scribner, 1927.
171 p. 22½ cm.

Score: many unison; about half with piano accompaniment. Negro dialect.
Includes words and music for 29 songs.

The songs of the Negro soldier in World War I as recorded and arranged with piano accompaniment

(continued on next card)

Niles, John Jacob, 1892- Singing soldiers... 1927. (Card 2)

by author: -1. Going home song. -2. Whale song. -3. Don't close does gates. -4. Crap-shootin' Charley. -5. Diggin'. -6. I'm a warrior. -7. Oh, I don't want to go. -8. Lordy, turn your face. -9. Goodbye, Tennessee. -10. He's a burden-bearer. -11. I don't want any more France. -12. For I'se weary. -13. Ole ark. -14. Gimmie song. -15. Scratch. -16. "Soldier man blues." -17. Deep sea blues. -18. Chicken butcher. -19. Jackass song. -20. We wish the same to

(continued on next card)

Niles, John Jacob, 1892 Singing soldiers... 1927. (Card 3)

you. -21. Grave-diggers. -22. Ghost song. -23. Jail house. -24. Roll, Jordan, roll. -25. Long gone. -26. Pray for forgiveness. -27. Clean clothes song. -28. Destroyer song. -29. Georgia.

HMC
BPL
NYPLS

Odum, Howard Washington, 1884-

Negro workaday songs, by Howard W. Odum... and Guy B. Johnson... Chapel Hill, University of North Carolina press; London, H. Milford, Oxford university press c1926;
278 p., illus. (music) diagr., 23½ cm. (Univ. of N. C. social study series)
Unaccompanied melodies for 14 songs; words for 248 songs. Negro dialect.
Selected bibliography: p. 265-70.

YJWJ
BHC
HMC
NYPLA2
NYPLS
LC

*Oliver, Joseph, 1885-1938.

Chime blues. For orchestra By Joseph (King) Oliver...Chicago, Melrose bros. music co. c1923
2 p. and 10 parts. 8vo.

Score: piano-conductor; and parts for dance orchestra.

ABSpl

*Oliver, Joseph, 1885-1938.

West End blues. Popular song Words by *Clarence Williams; music by *Joe Oliver. New York, *Clarence Williams music pub. co., c1928
5 p. fol.

Score: medium solo voice with piano accompaniment. English words.

ABSpl

The old cabin home. Song; Author unknown;

(In *Burleigh, H. T. Negro minstrel melodies... c1909, p. 30,31.)

Score: medium solo voicewith piano accompaniment. Negro dialect.

ABSpl
BHC
HMC
ZWpl

Opharrow, George A
Carle, William J
I Shall Trust the Lord

---

*Overstreet, W. Benton

Jazbo Johnson's syncopating band. [Popular song] Words and music by W. Benton Overstreet. New York, Handy bros. music co., inc. [c1921]
5 p. fol.

Score: high solo voice with piano accompaniment. Negro dialect.

ABSpl

---

*Overstreet, W Benton

Play it a long time papa (Blues). By W. Benton Overstreet. New York, Clarence Williams music pub. co., inc. [c1923]
5 p. fol.

Score: medium solo voice with piano accompaniment. English words.

ABSpl

Packay, Peter
I want a little change

Palmer, Jack

Treat me like a baby. [Popular song] Lyric by Andy Razaf; music by Jack Palmer. NY: Meyer Cushman, inc. [c1931]
5p. fol.

Score: medium solo voice with piano accompaniment. English words.

ABSpl

---

*Parker, Kaye arr.

Hold on. Negro spiritual arranged by Kaye Parker. New York, *Handy bros. music co., inc. [c1934]
13 p. 8vo.

Score: 7 part chorus for mixed voices (SSATBBB) with piano accompaniment. Negro dialect.
Bound in black spiral notebook no. 4.

ABSpl
ZWpl

---

*Parker, Kaye

Night again. [Popular song] Lyric by Ted Koehler; music by Kaye Parker. New York, Lawrence music publishers, inc. c1932
3 p. fol.

Score: medium solo voice with piano accompaniment. English words.

ABSpl

---

*Parker, Kaye, arr.

Wade in the water. Negro spiritual arranged by Kaye Parker. New York, *Handy bros. music co., inc. [c1935]
7 p. 8vo.

Score: 7 part chorus for mixed voices (SSATBBB) with piano accompaniment. Negro dialect.
Bound in black spiral notebook no. 4.

ABSpl
ZWpl

Parrish, Lydia (Austin) comp.

Slave songs of the Georgia Sea Islands. By Lydia Parrish; music transcribed by Creighton Churchill and Robert MacGimsey; introduction by Olin Downes. New York, Creative press, inc., 1942 [c1942]
256 p., front., plates, ports., map, 28½ cm.

Unaccompanied melodies for 60 songs. Negro dialect.

"A selected bibliography": p. 253-256.
NYPL42 HMC
NYPLS LC
YJWJ

Card II
Parrish, Lydia (Austin) comp.

Slave songs of the Georgia Sea Islands...

Contents: 60 songs.
A selected bibliography: p. 253-256.
Contents: I. African survivals. 1. Calling the wind. 2. Rockah mh moomba. 3. I wok om a mona. 4. Fallewell shisha Maley. 5. Byum by-e. 6. Afro-american shout songs. 7. Ha'k'e angels. 8. Until I die. 9. Where was Peter. 10. Plumb de line. 11. Down to de mire. 12. Eli ah can't

---

Card III
Parrish, Lydia (Austin comp.

Slave songs of the Georgia Sea Islands...

stan'. 13. Moonlight-starlight. 14. Knee-bone. 15. Blow Gabriel. 16. Good-bye everybody. II. Ring-play, dance & fiddle songs. 17. Emma you my darlin'. 18. Go roun' the border Susie. 19. Sangaree. 20. It's cold frosty mornin'. 21. Throw me anywhere. 22. Gimme him. 23. Way down in the ole Peedee. 24. Johnny come a long time. 25. I jing-a-ling. III. Religious songs. 26.

Card IV
Parrish, Lydia (Austin) comp.

Norah, hist the windah. 27. Believer I know. 28. That suits me. 29. Wasn' that a wonder. 30. I heard the angels singin'. 31. Can't hide sinner. 32. John, John. 33. When I rise cryin' holy. 34. No hidin' place. 35. Livin' humble. 36. Swing low sweet chariot. 37. Zion. 38. My God is a rock in a weary land. 39. Wade in nuh watuh children. 40. Sabbath has no end. 41. In that old field. 42. Jesus gon tuh make up my dyin' bed. 43. O de robe. 44. Ride on conquering King. 45. Aye Lord, time is drawin' nigh. 46. Nummer me on. 47. In

---

Card V
Parrish, Lydia (Austin) comp.

Slave songs of the Georgia Sea Islands... some lonesome graveyard. IV. Work songs. 48. Call me hangin' Johnny. 49. Knock a man down. 50. Sand Anna. 51. Pay me my money down. 52. Debt I owe. 53. Ragged Leevy. 54. Goodbye My Riley O. 55. Ole tar river. 56. Shilo Brown. 57. Anniebelle. 58. Do remember. 59. Peas an' the rice. 60. Oh when I come to die. 61. Five fingers in the boll.
HMC BPL
LC BHC
NYPLS
NYPL42
YJWJ

---

*Payton, David

I'm dying with the worried blues. [Popular song] Words by W. E. Browning; music by Dave Payton, Jr. New York, *Pace and Handy music co., inc. [c1919]
5 p. fol.

Score: medium solo voice with piano accompaniment. English words.

ABSpl

---

*Payton, Lew

All the wrongs you've done to me (They're bound to come back to you.)...By Lew Payton, *Chris Smith and Edgar Dowell. New York, Clarence Williams music co, inc. [c1924]
5p. fol.

Score: low solo voice [key of G] with piano accompaniment. English words.

"As featured by Lew Payton and Johnny Hudgins in The Chocolate Dandies" -- at end of title.

ABSpl

---

*Perrin, Sidney L

...Arabela Jones, will you accept my hand. The plea of a love-sick darkey, cleverly worded and set to music by *Hillman and Perrin... New York, W. B. Gray and co., [c1897]
6 p. fol.

Score: medium solo voice with piano accompaniment [key of F] English words.

"Featured by the 'white but cullud ladies', The Nichols Sisters, dur- ing their trip around the world." — title page.

ABSpl LC

---

*Perrin, Sidney L

I wants to be some kind of a show girl too. [Popular song] Words and music by Sidney L. Perrin... New York, M. Witmark and sons, [c1903] Publ. pl. no. 5513.
5 p. fol.

Score: medium solo voice with piano accompaniment. [key of G] Negro dialect.

"Sung by Clara Bloodgood in Charles Frohman's production... 'The girl with the green eyes'" - title page.

ABSpl LC

---

*Perrin, Sidney L

In gayest darktown. The latest and best characteristic composition. By Sidney Perrin... New York, W. B. Gray and co., [c1899]
6 p. fol.

Score: piano solo.

ABSpl LC

---

*Perrin, Sidney L

...Just to please you, Sue. Coon love song and refrain. Popular song Words and music by Sidney L. Perrin. New York, M. Witmark and sons, [c1902] Publ. pl. no. 4922.
5 p. fol.

Score: medium solo voice with piano accompaniment [key of G] Negro dialect.

ABSpl LC

---

*Perrin, Sidney L

Lina, ma lady. A serenade. [Song] Words by Carroll Fleming; music by Sidney L. Perrin. New York, Rogers bros. music pub. co., [c1900]
5 p. fol.

Score: medium solo voice with piano accompaniment [key of D] Negro dialect.

"As sung in John J. McNally's latest comedy, 'The Rogers Bros. in Central Park'" - title page.

ABSpl LC

---

*Perrin, Sidney L

Mammy's little pumpkin colored coons. Plantation slumber song. Written and composed by *Hillman and Perrin... New York, M. Witmark and sons, [c1897]
6 p. fol.

Score: medium solo voice with piano accompaniment [key of B♭] Negro dialect.

"Introduced with great success by Julius P. Witmark in Rich and Harris' new production, 'The Good Mr. Best'" — at end of title.

ABSpl LC NYPLS

*Perrin, Sidney L

My Afro-Mexican queen. ⌐Popular song⌐ Words and music by Sidney L. Perrin. New York, M. Witmark and sons, ⌐c1903⌐ Publ. pl. no. 5489.
5 p. fol.

Score: medium solo voice with piano accompaniment. ⌐key of C⌐ Negro dialect.

ABSpl LC

---

*Perrin, Sidney L

My Dinah. ⌐Popular song⌐ Words and music by Sidney L. Perrin... New York, Hugo V. Schlam. ⌐c1900⌐ Publ. pl. no. 693.
5 p. fol.

Score: medium solo voice with piano accompaniment ⌐key of G⌐ English words.

"As sung with great success by *Johnson and *Dean" whose pictures are on the cover.

ABSpl LC

---

*Perrin, Sidney L

My Dixie queen (Coontown loyalty). ⌐Popular song⌐ Words and music by Sidney L. Perrin. New York, M. Witmark and sons, ⌐c1901⌐ Publ. pl. no. 4531.
6 p. fol.

Score: medium solo voice with piano accompaniment ⌐key of C⌐ Negro dialect.

"As sung by Anna Laughlin in Geo. W. Lederer's production, 'The New Yorkers'" — title page.

ABSpl LC

---

*Perrin, Sidney L

Pickaninny Mine, come hide away. ⌐Popular song⌐ Words by Hen. Wise; music by Sid. Perrin. New York, T. B. Harms and co. ⌐c1899⌐
6 p. fol.

Score: medium solo voice with piano accompaniment. ⌐key of B^b⌐ Negro dialect.

ABSpl LC

---

*Perrin, Sidney L

The rareback's ball. ⌐Popular song⌐ By Sidney L. Perrin. New York, Raymond music pub. co., ⌐c1901⌐
5 p. fol.

Score: medium solo voice with piano accompaniment ⌐key of E^b⌐ Negro dialect.

ABSpl

---

*Perrin, Sidney L

Show your invitation (Or, you can't come in.) Popular song By *Al. Brown and Sidney Perrin... New York, M. Witmark and sons, ⌐c1901⌐ Publ. pl. no. 3602.
5 p. fol.

Score: medium solo voice with piano accompaniment ⌐key of G⌐ Negro dialect.

ABSpl LC

Peyton, Eddie
Hey, stop kissing my sister

---

*Phillips, William King

The Florida blues. ⌐for piano⌐ By Wm. King Phillips. New York, Pace and Handy ⌐c1916⌐
5 p. fol.

Score: piano solo.

ABSpl

Pinckney, Lloyd
My cookie and me

---

*Pinkard, Maceo

Adorable Dora. ⌐Popular song⌐ By Archie Gottler, Sidney Clare and Maceo Pinkard. NY: Waterson, Berlin & Snyder co. ⌐c1928⌐ Publ. pl. no. 1862.
5p. fol.

Score: medium solo voice with piano accompaniment. English words.

ABSpl

---

*Pinkard, Maceo

Another mule kitched in you stall. ⌐Popular song⌐ Words by Wm. Tracey; music by Maceo Pinkard. NY: Shapiro, Bernstein & co. ⌐c1921⌐
5p. fol.

Score: medium solo voice with piano accompaniment. English words.

ABSpl

---

*Pinkard, Maceo

At twilight. ⌐Popular song⌐ Lyric by Wm. Tracey; music by Maceo Pinkard. NY: Gene Austin, inc. ⌐c1929⌐
5p. fol.

Score: medium solo voice ⌐key of E^b⌐ with piano accompaniment. English words.

ABSpl
E

---

*Pinkard, Maceo

'Bammy (The land that gave me mammy) ⌐Popular song⌐ Words by William Tracey; music by Maceo Pinkard. NY: Goodman & Rose, inc. ⌐c1922⌐
5p. fol.

Score: medium solo voice with piano accompaniment English words.

ABSpl

---

*Pinkard, Maceo

...Barefoot boy. Song. Words by Will J. Hart; music by Maceo Pinkard. NY: Jos. W. Stern & co. ⌐c1918⌐ Pulb. pl. no. 8672.
5p. fol.

Score: medium solo voice with piano accompaniment. Englsih words. Refrain also arranged for TTBB.

ABSpl

---

*Pinkard, Maceo

Come on, baby! ⌐Popular song⌐ Words and music by Maceo Pinkard, Archie Gottler and Sidney Clare. New York, Ager, Yellow and Bornstein, inc. ⌐c1928⌐
5 p. fol.

Score: medium solo voice with piano and ukulele accompaniment.

YJWJ
ABSpl

---

*Pinkard, Maceo

Congratulations. Ballad fox-trot. By Maceo Pinkard, Coleman Goetz and Green and Stept. NY: Green and Stapt inc. ⌐c1929⌐
5p. fol.

Score: medium solo voice with piano accompaniment. English words.

ABSpl

---

*Pinkard, Maceo

Dawning. ⌐Popular song⌐ Words and music by Abner Silver and Maceo Pinkard. New York, Irving Berlin, inc. ⌐c1927⌐
5 p. fol.

Score: medium solo voice with piano and ukulele accompaniment.
Ukulele arrangement by May Singhi Breen.

YJWJ
ABSpl

---

*Pinkard, Maceo

Desdemona (That personal friend of mine). ⌐Popular song⌐ Words and music by Maceo Pinkard. NY: Jerome H. Remick and co. ⌐c1925⌐
5p. fol.

Score: medium solo voice with piano accompaniment. English words.

ABSpl

---

*Pinkard, Maceo

Dixie is Dixie once more. Dancing Mose is back in civy clothes. ⌐Popular song⌐ Words by Wm Tracey; music by Maceo Pinkard. NY: Shapiro, Bernstein and co. ⌐c1919⌐
3p. fol.

Score: medium solo voice with piano accompaniment. Negro dialect.

ABSpl

---

*Pinkard, Maceo

Does my sweetie do - and how. ⌐Popular song⌐ By Sidney Holden, Alex Belledna and Maceo Pinkard. NY: Shapiro, Bernstein and co., ⌐c1925⌐
5p. fol.

Score: medium solo voice ⌐key of G⌐ with piano accompaniment. English words.

ABSpl
LC

---

*Pinkard, Maceo

Don't be like that. ⌐Song⌐ By Archie Gottler, Charles Tobias and Maceo Pinkard. New York, Shapiro Bernstein and co. ⌐c1928⌐
5p. fol.

Score: medium solo voice with piano and ukulele accompaniment.
Ukulele arrangement by A. J. Franchini.

YJWJ
ABSpl

*Pinkard, Maceo

Don't cry little girl, don't cry. ⌐Popular song¬ Words and music by Maceo Pinkard. New York, Shapiro, Bernstein and co. ⌐c1918¬
3p. fol.

Score: medium solo voice with piano accompaniment. English words.

ABSpl

---

*Pinkard, Maceo

I love to see the evenin' sun go down (so I can be with you) ⌐Popular song¬ Words and music by Maceo Pinkard and Jack Palmer. New York, Harms, inc. ⌐c1932, Publ. pl. no. 8802.
5 p. fol.

Score: medium solo voice with piano and ukulele banjo or guitar accompaniment.

YJWJ
ABSpl

---

*Pinkard, Maceo

I'm satisfied (Beside that sweetie o'mine). ⌐Popular song¬ Lyric by Jack Yellen; music by Maceo Pinkard. New York, Ager, Yellen and Bornstein inc., ⌐c1924¬
5p. fol.

Score: medium solo voice with piano accompaniment. English words.

ABSpl

---

*Pinkard Maceo

Gingham girl. (Fox-trot-ballad) Words by Darl Mc Boyle; music by Maceo Pinkard....New York, *Maceo Pinkard music publisher ⌐c1920¬
5p. fol.

Score: medium solo voice with piano accompaniment. English words.

ABSpl

---

*Pinkard, Maceo

I wonder. ⌐Popular song¬ By Abner Silver, Maceo Pinkard and Benny Davis. New York, Irving Berlin, inc. ⌐c1928¬
5p. fol.

Score: medium solo voice with piano accompaniment. English words.

ABSpl

---

*Pinkard Maceo

I'm so sorry. Ballad-fox-trot By Maceo Pinkard and Murray Rich. New York, *Pinkard inc. music pub. ⌐c1931¬
5p. fol.

Score: medium solo voice with piano accompaniment. English words.

ABSpl

---

*Pinkard, Maceo

Give and take. ⌐Popular song¬ Words by Dave Dreyer; music by Maceo Pinkard and Joseph Cherniovsky. New York, Irving Berlin, inc. ⌐c1928¬
5p. fol.

Score: medium solo voice with piano accompaniment. Entlish words.

Theme song of the musical production, "Give and take" featuring Jean Hersholt, George Sidney and George Lewis. -- Cover title page.

ABSpl

---

*Pinkard, Maceo

I wonder what's become of Joe? ⌐Popular song¬ By Roy Tuek and Maceo Pinkard. New York, Shapiro, Bernstein and co. ⌐c1926¬
5p. fol.

Score: medium solo voice with piano accompaniment. English words.

ABSpl

Pinkard, Maceo
Is that religion

---

*Pinkard, Maceo

Harlem's poppin' ⌐Popular song¬ Words by Wm. Tracey; music by Maceo Pinkard. New York, *Pinkard publications, ⌐c1940¬
5p. fol.

Score: medium solo voice ⌐key of G¬ with piano accompaniment. Negro dialect.

ABSpl
LC

---

*Pinkard, Maceo

I'll be a friend with pleasure. ⌐Popular song¬ By Maceo Pinkard. New York, Mills music inc. ⌐c1930¬
5p. fol.

Score: medium solo voice ⌐key of G¬ with piano accompaniment. English words.

ABSpl
LC

---

*Pinkard, Maceo

Jazz babies' ball. (Song-Jazz dance) Words by Charles Bayha; music by Maceo Pinkard. New York, Shapiro, Bernstein and co, ⌐c1920¬
5p. fol.

Score: medium solo voice with piano accompaniment. English words.

ABSpl

---

*Pinkard, Maceo

Here come the show boat. ⌐Popular song¬ Words by Billy Rose ; music by Maceo Pinkard. New York, Shapiro, Bernstein & co. ⌐c1927¬
5 p. fol.

Score: medium solo voice with piano and ukulele accompaniment.

HMC
YJWJ
ABSpl

---

*Pinkard, Maceo

I'm a real kind mama, lookin' for a lovin' man. ⌐Popular song¬ Words by Roger Graham; music by Maceo Pinkard. New York, Frank K. Root and co. ⌐c1917¬
3p. fol.

Score: medium solo voice with piano accompaniment. English words.

AB Spl

---

*Pinkard, Maceo

Jo-Anne. ⌐Popular song¬ By Abner Silver, Maceo Pinkard and Joe Ward. New York, Shapiro, Bernstein and co. ⌐c1928¬
5p. fol.

Score: medium solo voice with piano accompaniment. English words.

ABSpl

---

*Pinkard, Maceo

"He's had no lovin' for a long long time." ⌐Popular song¬ Words by Wm. Tracey; music by Maceo Pinkard. New York, Broadway music corp. ⌐c1919¬
3p. fol.

Score: medium solo voice with piano accompaniment. English words.

ABSpl

Pinkard, Maceo
I'm always stuttering

---

*Pinkard, Maceo

Just leave it to me. ⌐Popular song¬ Words by Wm Tracey; music by Maceo Pinkard. New York, Shapiro, Bernstein and co ⌐c1919¬
3p. fol.

Score: medium solo voice with piano accompaniment. English words.

ABSpl

---

*Pinkard, Maceo

How'd ya like to meet me in the moonlight? ⌐Popular song¬ Words by Gene Austin and Sam Coslow; music by Maceo Pinkard. New York, Bibo Bloedon and Lang music pub. ⌐c1926¬
5p. fol.

Score: medium solo voice with piano accompaniment. English words.

ABSpl

Pinkard, Maceo
I'm feeling delivilish

---

*Pinkard, Maceo

Lila. Popular song Words and music by Maceo Pinkard, Archie Gottler and Charles Tobias. New York, De Sylva, Brown & Henderson, inc. ⌐c1928¬
3 p. fol.

Score: low solo voice with piano and ukulele accompaniment.

YJWJ
ABSpl

*Pinkard, Maceo

"Liza". ⌈Popular song.⌉ Words by Nat Vincent; music by Maceo Pinkard. New York, Harms inc. ⌈c1922⌉ Publ. pl. no. 6648
5p. fol.

Score: medium solo voice with piano accompaniment. English words.

ABSpl

*Pinkard, Maceo

Someone's stolen my sweet sweet baby. ⌈Popular⌉ Song Lyric by Lew Brown and Sidney Clare; music by Maceo Pinkard. New York, Jerome H Remick and co. ⌈c1926⌉
5p. fol.

Score: medium solo voice with piano accompaniment. English words.

ABSpl

*Pinkard, Maceo

Those draftin' blues. ⌈Popular song⌉ Words and music by Maceo Pinkard. New York, Jos. W. Stern and co. ⌈c1918⌉
3p. fol.

Score: medium solo voice with piano accompaniment. English words.

ABSpl

*Pinkard, Maceo

Mammy o' mine. ⌈Popular song⌉ Words by W⌈illiam⌉ Tracey; music by Maceo Pinkard. New York, Shapiro, Bernstein & co. ⌈c1919⌉
3 p. fol.

Score: medium voice ⌈key of G⌉ with piano accompaniment. Negro dialect.

NYPLS
YJWJ
ABSpl

*Pinkard, Maceo

Sugar (that sugar baby o' mine). ⌈Popular song⌉ Words by Sidney Mitchell and Edna Alexander; music by Maceo Pinkard. New York, *W. C. Handy music pub., c1927.

Score: medium solo voice with piano and ukulele accompaniment.

Professional copy.

YJWJ
ABSpl

*Pinkard, Maceo

Wait'll it's moonlight. ⌈Popular song⌉ Lyric by Frank Bannister; music by Maceo Pinkard. New York, Broadway music corp. ⌈c1925⌉
5p. fol.

Score: medium solo voice with piano accompaniment. Englisht words.

ABSpl

*Pinkard, Maceo

Okay, baby. ⌈Popular song⌉ Words by William Tracey; music by Maceo Pinkard. New York, Mills music inc. ⌈c1930⌉
5p. fol.

Score: medium solo voice ⌈key of B^b⌉ with piano accompaniment. English words.

ABSpl
LC

*Pinkard, Maceo

Sweet man. Fox trot song with a Charleston rhythm. Words by Roy Turk; music by Maceo Pinkard. New York: Leo. Feist inc. ⌈c1925⌉ Publ. pl. no. 5630.
5p. fol.

Score: medium solo voice with piano accompaniment. English words.

ABSpl

Pinkard, Maceo
The Whole world knows I love you

*Pinkard, Maceo

Our cottage isn't for sale any more. ⌈Popular song⌉ Lyric by William Tracey; music by Maceo Pinkard, New York, Mills music inc. ⌈c1930⌉
5p. fol.

Score: medium solo voice ⌈key of C⌉ with piano accompaniment. English words.

LC
ABSpl

*Pinkard, Maceo

Tail spin (You're flying high -- but you'll do a tail spin fo me). Eyrics and music by Maceo Pinkard. New York, Gene Austin, inc. ⌈c1930⌉
5p. fol.

Score: medium solo voice with piano accompaniment. English words. On back of cover is a special instrumental chorus: arranged for piano, violin, saxophone, guitar, and ukulele as accompaniment for voices.
"From the all- sepia musicle production, 'Change your luck'" -- at end of title.

ABSpl

*Pinkard, Maceo

Who'll love you while I'm gone. ⌈Popular song⌉ Words and music by Maceo Pinkard. NY: Shapiro, Bernstein and co. ⌈c1918⌉
3p. fol.

Score: medium solo voice with piano accompaniment. English words.

ABSpl

*Pinkard, Maceo

Pile of logs and stone (called home). ⌈Popular song⌉ Words and music by Maceo Pinkard. New York, *Clarence Williams music pub. ⌈c1925⌉
5p. fol.

Score: medium solo voice with piano accompaniment. English words.

ABSpl

*Pinkard, Maceo

Them there eyes. ⌈Popular song⌉ Words and music by Maceo Pinkard, William Tracey and Doris Tauber. New York, Irving Berlin, inc. ⌈c1930⌉
5 p. fol.

Score: low solo voice with piano and ukulele accompaniment.
Ukulele arrangement by May Singhi Breen.

YJWJ
ABSpl

Pinkard, Maceo
Will "ya" huh?

*Pinkard, Maceo

Planning. ⌈Popular song⌉ By Maceo Pinkard. New York, Harms inc. c1922 Publ. pl. no. 6649
5p. fol.

Score: medium solo voice with piano accompaniment. English words.

ABSpl

*Pinkard, Maceo

There must be somebody else. ⌈Popular song⌉ By Archie Gottler, Sidney Clare and Maceo Pinkard. New York, Irving Berlin, inc. ⌈c1927⌉
5p. fol.

Score: medium solo voice with piano accompaniment. English words.

ABSpl

Pinkard, Maceo
You look like an angel (but there's devil in you)

Pinkard, Maceo
Sincerely yours

*Pinkard, Maceo

This is the day for Aunt Jemima! ! Aunt Jemima's Jubilee. ⌈Popular song⌉ Words by William Tracey; music by Maceo Pinkard. New York, Fred Fisher, inc. ⌈c1921⌉
5p. fol.

Score: medium solo voice with piano accompaniment. English words.

ABSpl

*Pinkard, Maceo

You'll be sorry but you'll be sorry too late. ⌈Popular song⌉ Words by William Tracey; music by Maceo Pinkard. New York, Shapiro, Bernstein and co. ⌈c1919⌉
3p. fol.

Score: medium solo voice with piano accompaniment. English words.

ABSpl

Piron, Armand J
High society

Lyrics by Clarence Williams

---

*Piron, Armand J

I wish I could shimmy like my sister Kate. ⌐Popular song¬ Words and music by A. J. Piron. New York, *Clarence Williams music pub. co., inc. ⌐c1922¬
5 p. fol.

Score: medium solo voice with piano accompaniment. English words.

ABSpl

Piron, Armand J
New Orleans wiggle.

---

*Piron, Armand J
Williams, Clarence
You can have it. I don't want it. ⌐Popular song¬ By May Hill, *Clarence Williams and Armand J. Piron. New York. Frank K. Root and co. ⌐c1917¬
3 p. fol.

Score: medium solo voice with piano accompaniment. English words.

ABSpl

Pollack, Lew

Vamping Sal. The Sheba of Georgia. Fox trot song. Lyrics by *Henry Creamer; music by Lew Pollack. New York, M. Witmark and sons, ⌐c1923¬ Publ. pl. no. M.W.&Sons 16792.
5 p. fol.

Score: medium solo voice with piano accompaniment. English words.

ABSpl

Pohl, Frédéric
Trois psalmodies nègres
(4 copies)

Pollack, Lew
I'm feeling blue for Mammy Lou

See

Henry Creamer

---

*Porter, Dick

...Ten fingers and a Porter. ⌐Popular song¬ Words and music by Dick Porter. San Francisco, Sherman, Clay and co. ⌐c1936¬
5 p. fol.

Score: medium solo voice with piano accompaniment. English words.

Dick Porter's theme song.

ABSpl

---

*Price, Florence Bond

Anticipation (La anticipacion) One of 5 easy compositions for piano by Florence B. Price. Chicago, McKinley music co. ⌐c1928¬ Publ. pl. no. 2241.
5 p. fol. (World-famous McKinley edition of standard teaching music)
Score: piano solo.

This composition is #1 in a series of five pieces for grade 2: A study in phrasing.

ABSpl

Price, Florence Bond
At the cotton gin

---

*Price, Florence Bond

The butterfly. Piano solo, by Florence B. Price. New York, Carl Fischer ⌐c1936¬ Publ. pl. no. 27643.
5 p. fol. (Sheet music edition P 2100)

Score: piano solo. (Grade 3)

ABSpl

---

*Price, Florence Bond

Doll waltz (Vals de la muneca). One of 5 easy compositions for piano by Florence B. Price. Chicago, McKinley music co. ⌐c1928¬ Publ. pl. no. 2242.
3 p. fol. (World-famous edition of standard teaching music)
Score: piano solo.

This composition is #2 in a series of five pieces for grade 2: a study in rests.

ABSpl

---

*Price, Florence Bond Easy compositions for piano... c1928. (Card 2)

Contents: valsante). -5. The waterfall (La cascada).

ABSpl

---

*Price, Florence Bond

The engine (La maquine de vapor). One of 5 easy compositions for piano by Florence B. Price. Chicago, McKinley music co. ⌐c1928¬ Publ. pl. no. 2243.
3 p. fol. (World-famous McKinley edition of standard teaching music.)
Score: piano solo.

This composition is #3 in a series of 5 pieces for grade 2: a study in staccato and short phrases.

ABSpl

---

*Price, Florence Bond

The gnat and the bee. Piano solo by Florence Price. New York, Carl Fischer ⌐c1936¬ Publ. pl. no. 27642.
5 p. fol. (Sheet music edition P 2098)

Score: piano solo.

Grade III

ABSpl
ZWpl

Price, Florence Bond
Levee dance

Price, Florence Bond
Mellow twilight

---

*Price, Florence Bond

The moon bridge. Song...Words by Mary Rolefson Gamble; music by Florence B. Price. Chicago, Gamble Hinged music co. ⌐c1930¬ Publ. pl. no. 937.
6 p. fol.

Score: high solo voice ⌐key of F¬ with piano accompaniment. English words.

ABSpl
ZWpl
HMC
LC

---

*Price, Florence Bond

My soul's been anchored in the Lord...Spiritual arranged by Florence Price. Chicago, Gamble Hinged music co. ⌐c1937¬ Publ. pl. no. 1292.

Score: medium solo voice ⌐key of A minor¬ with piano accompaniment. Negro dialect.

"As sung by *Marion Anderson (Victor record #1799)" -- at end of title.

ZWpl
HMC
ABSpl

---

*Price, Florence Bond

Nobody knows the trouble I've seen. Spiritual. Arranged for piano by Florence B. Price. Philadelphia, Theodore Presser co. ⌐c1938¬ Publ. pl. no. 26701.
3 p. fol.

Score: piano solo.

ABSpl
ZWpl
HMC
ChPL

---

*Price, Florence Bond

The rose. Piano solo by Florence Price. New York, Carl Fischer, ⌐c1936¬ Publ. pl. no. 27638.
5 p. fol. (Sheet music edition P 2091).

Score: piano solo.

Grade II.

ABSpl
ZWpl

*Price, Florence Bond

A Sachem's pipe. Piano solo by Florence Price. New York, Carl Fischer ⌞c1935⌟ Publ. pl. no. 27275. 5 p. fol. (Sheet music edition P. 2060).

Score: piano solo.

Grade III.

ABSpl
ZWpl

*Price, Florence Bond

Songs to the dark virgin. Song. Words by *Langston Hughes; music by Florence B. Price. New York, G. Schirmer, inc. ⌞c1941⌟ Publ. pl. no. 39462C. 5 p. fol.

Score: medium solo voice ⌞key of C⌟ with piano accompaniment. English words.

This song is in the repertory of *Marian Anderson.

ABSpl
YJWJ-inscribed to Carl Van Vechten by Langston Hughes.
ZWpl

*Price, Florence Bond

Tecumseh. Piano solo by Florence Price...New York, Carl Fischer, inc. ⌞c1935⌟ Publ. pl. no. 27277. 5 p. fol. (Sheet music edition P. 2062).

Score: piano solo.

Grade III.

ABSpl
HMC
ZWpl

*Price, Florence Bond

Three little Negro dances for piano. By Florence B. Price. Philadelphia, Theodore Presser co. ⌞c1933⌟ Publ. pl. nos. 26030-32. 3 v. fol.

Scores: piano solos.

Grade III½.

Contents: 1. Hoe cake. -2. Rabbit foot. -3. Tickling toes.

LC
ABSpl
ZWpl
HMC

*Price, Florence Bond

"Three sketches for little pianists" by Florence B. Price. Philadelphia, Theodore Presser co. ⌞c1937⌟ Publ. pl. nos. 26510-12. 3 v. fol.

Scores: piano solos.

A series of teaching pieces for grade I.

Contents: 1. Bright eyes. -2. Cabin song. -3. A morning sunbeam.

LC
ZWpl
ABSpl

*Price, Florence Bond

The waterfall (La cascada). ⌞One of 5⌟ easy compositions for piano. By Florence B. Price. Chicago, McKinley music co. c1928 Publ. pl. no. 2245. 3 p.fol. (World-famous McKinley edition of standard teaching music).

Score: piano solo.

This composition is #5 in a series of 5 pieces for grade 2: a study in arpeggio forms.

ABSpl

*Price, Florence Bond

The waltzing fairy (El duende valsante). ⌞One of 5⌟ easy compositions for piano by Florence B. Price. Chicago, McKinley music co. ⌞c1928⌟ Publ. pl. no. 2244. 5 p. fol. (World-famous McKinley edition of standard teaching music)

Score: piano solo.

This composition is #4 in a series of 5 pieces for grade 2: a study in legato staccato and phrasing.

ABSpl

*Price, Florence Bond

...The Zephyr (El Cefiro). Mexican folk-song... Transcribed for piano by Florence B. Price. Chicago, McKinley music co., ⌞c1928⌟ Publ. pl. no. 2279. (World-famous McKinley edition of standard teaching music). 5 p. fol.

Score: piano solo (Grade 3).

Grade III.

"A study in phrasing and pedaling"--at head of title.

ABSpl

Prince, Charles A

Not lately. Character song. Words by E. Deacey; music by Chas. A. Prince. New York, Triangle music pub. co. ⌞c1922⌟ 5 p. fol.

Score: medium solo voice with piano accompaniment. English words.

"The last song featured and sung for the Columbia records by the late *Bert Williams." - Cover title page.

ABSpl

Razafkeriefo, Paul Andrea, 1895-
Cryin' mood

*Razafkeriefo, Paul Andrea, 1895-

Every time I pick a sweetie. ⌞Popular song⌟ By *Phil Worde, *Allie Moore and Andrea Razaf. NY: *Handy bros. music co., inc. ⌞c1927⌟ 5p. fol.

Score: medium solo voice ⌞key of F⌟ with piano accompaniment. English words.

ZWpl
ABSpl

*Razafkeriefo, Paul Andrea, 1895-

Link, Harry
Gone. ⌞Popular song.⌟ By Harry Link, Andy Razaf and *Thomas Waller. New York: Santly bros. inc. ⌞c1930⌟ 5p. fol.

Score: medium solo voice ⌞key of E^b⌟ with piano accompaniment. English words.

ABSpl
LC

*Razafkeriefo, Paul Andrea, 1895-

Hands off! Thats my gal. ⌞Popular song⌟ Words and music by Andy Razaf and Paul Denniker. NY: Elliot-Chilton & co., inc. ⌞c1926⌟ 5p. fol.

Score: medium solo voice with piano accompaniment. English words.

ABSpl

*Razafkeriefo, Paul Andrea, 1895-

If it ain't love. ⌞Popular song⌟ Words and music by Andy Razaf, *Donald Redmon and *Thomas Waller. NY: Davis, Coots & Engel, inc. ⌞c1932⌟ 5 p. fol.

Score: medium solo voice with piano accompaniment. English words.

ABSpl

*Razafkeriefo, Paul Andrea, 1895-

Imagine. ⌞Popular⌟ song. Words and music by Will Osborne, Andy Razaf, and Paul Denniker. NY: Joe Davis, inc. ⌞c1930⌟ . 5p. fol. 2 copies

Score: medium solo voice with piano accompaniment. English words.

ABSpl

*Razafkeriefo, Paul Andrea, 1895-

It's you who taught it to me. (Novelty song) Words and music by John Harley, Joe Davis and Andy Razaf. New York, Georgia music corp. ⌞c1939⌟ 3 p. fol.

Score: medium solo voice ⌞key of F⌟ with piano accompaniment. English words.

ABSpl

Razafkeriefo, Paul Anirea, 1895-
A lover's lullaby

*Razafkeriefo, Paul Andrea, 1895-

...Make believe ball room. (Fox-trot song) Words and music by Andy Razaf and Paul Denniker. NY: Joe Davis, inc. ⌞c1936⌟ Publ. pl. no. 3655. 3p. fol.

Score: medium solo voice with piano accompaniment. English words.

ABSpl

*Razfkeriefo, Paul Andrea, 1895-

The milkman's matinee. (Novelty song) Words and music by Paul Denniker, Joe Davis and Andy Razaf. NY: Joe Davis, inc. ⌞c1936⌟ Publ. pl. no. 3667. 3p. fol.

Score: medium solo voice with piano accompaniment. English words.

ABSpl

*Razfkeriefo, Paul Andrea, 1895-

My Joe Louis of love. ⌞Popular song⌟ Words and music by Andy Razaf and Paul Denniker. NY: Handy brothers music co. inc. ⌞c1935⌟ 5p. fol.

Score: medium solo voice with piano accompaniment. English words.

ABSpl

*Razfkeriefo, Paul Andrea, 1895-

Nero. (A "burning" rhythm song). Words and music by Andy Razaf, Paul Denniker and Joe Davis. NY: Joe Davis, inc. ⌞c1937⌟ Publ. pl. no. 3710. 5p. fol.

Score: medium solo voice with piano accompaniment. English words.

ABSpl

*Razafkeriefo, Paul Andrea, 1895-

On rainy days. [Popular song] By Andy Razaf and *Thomas (Fats) Waller. New York; Mills music, inc. [c1938] 5p. fol.

Score: medium solo voice with piano accompaniment. English words.

ABSpl

Razfkeriefo, Paul Andrea, 1895-

On revival day. (A rhythmic spiritual). Words and music by Andy Razaf. NY: Joe Davis, inc., [c1930] Publ. pl. no. 1008. 5p. fol.

Score: medium solo voice with piano accompaniment. English words.

ABSpl

Razafkeriefo, Paul Andrea, 1895-
Peach tree St.

Razafkeriefo, Paul Andrea
Patty cake, patty cake

Razafkeriefo, Paul Andrea, 1895-
Rhythm lullaby

---

*Razfkeriefo, Paul Andrea, 1895-

She belongs to me. Novelty fox-trot. Words and music by Howard Johnson, Andy Razaf, and Paul Denniker, NY: Triangle music publ co., inc. [c1926] 5p. fol.

Score: medium solo voice with piano accompaniment. English words.

ABSpl

---

*Razkeriefo, Paul Andrea, 1895-

That rhythm parade. [Popular song] By Andy Razaf, *Russell Wooding and Paul Denniker. NY: Mills music, inc., [c;935] 3p. fol.

Score: medium solo voice with piano accompaniment. English words.

Excerpt from Connie's "Hot Chocolates of 1935"

ABSpl

---

*Razafkeriefo, Paul Andrea, 1895-

Throw out your chest (Keep up your chin). [Popular song] By Joe Davis, Andy Razaf, and Bob Emmerich. NY: Joe Davis, inc. [c1934] Publ. pl. no. 2012. 3p. fol.

Score: medium solo voice with piano accompaniment. English words.

ABSpl

---

*Razafkeriefo, Paul Andrea, 1895-

Unsophisticated Sue. [Popular song] By Nat Simon, Harold Reymond and Andy Razaf. NY: Superior music, inc. [c1934] 3p. fol.

Score: medium solo voice with piano accompaniment. English words.

ABSpl

---

*Razafkeriefo, Paul Andrea, 1895-

Willow tree. (A musical misery) [Popular song] By Andy Razaf and *Thomas Waller. New York: Harms, inc., [c1928] Publ. pl. no. 8-188. 5p. fol.

Score: medium solo voice with piano accompaniment. English words.
Caption title.
Excerpt from the musical show, "Keep Shufflin'."

LC
ABSpl

---

*Reddie, J Milton.
*McPherson, Richard Cecil

Ain't we got love. [Popular song] By *Cecil Mack pseud J. Milton Reddie and*Eubie Blake...New York Mills music inc. [c1937] 5p. fol.

Score: medium solo voice with piano accompaniment. English words.
Caption title.
"From the musical production, 'Swing it'." - Cover title page.

ABSpl

---

*Reddie, J Milton
*McPherson, Richard Cecil

By the sweat of your brow. [Popular song] By *Cecil Mack, pseud J. Milton Reddie &*Eubie Blake. New York: Mills music inc., [c1937] 5p. fol.

Score: medium solo voice with piano accompaniment. English words.

From the musical production, "Swing it".
Caption title.

ABSpl

---

*Reddie, J Milton
*McPherson, Richard Cecil

Green and blue. [Popular song]: By *Cecil Mack, J. Milton Reddie and Eubie Blake... New York: Mills Music Inc. [c1937] 5 p. fol.

Score: medium solo voice with piano accompaniment. English words.
Caption title.
From the musical production, "Swing it."

ABSpl

---

*Reddie, J Milton

Took mah babe away. A Negro lamentation. Lyric and music by J. Milton Reddie. New York, Handy bros. music co., inc. [c1935] 3 p. fol.

Score: medium solo voice [key of E minor] with piano accompaniment. English words.

ABSpl HMC ZWpl

---

*Redman, Donald, 1900-

Chant of the weed. [For piano] By Donald Redman. New York, Gotham music service, inc. [c1932] 3 p. fol.

Score: piano solo.

ABSpl

Redman, Donald
Cherry

---

*Redman, Donald, 1900-

Honey, how I long for you. [Popular song] By *Jo Trent? Edgar Dowell, and Don Redman. New York, Broadway music corp., [c1931] 5 p. fol.

Score: medium solo voice [key of E^b] with piano accompaniment. English words.

ABSpl
LC

---

*Redman, Donald, 1900-

How can I hi-de-hi when I feel so low-de-low! [Popular song] By *Mercer Cook, Don Redman and J. Russell Robinson. New York, DeSylva, Brown and Henderson, inc. [c1932] 3 p. fol.

Score: medium solo voice with piano accompaniment. English words.

ABSpl

---

*Redman, Donald

How'm I doin'? [Popular song] Words and music by Lem Fowler and Don Redman. New York, Mills music, inc. [c1932] 3 p. fol.

Score: medium solo voice [key of B^b] with piano accompaniment. English words.

ABSpl
LC

Redman, Donald
I heard

---

*Redmon, Donald, 1900-

If it ain't love. [Popular song] Words and music by Andy Razaf, *Donald Redmon and *Thomas Waller. NY: Davis, Coots & Engel, inc. [c1932] 5p. fol.

Score: medium solo voice with piano accompaniment. English words.

ABSpl

*Redman, Donald, 1900-
*Razafkeriefo, Paul Andrea
If it ain't love. [Popular song] Words and music by *Andy Razaf, Donald Redman and *Thomas Waller. New York: Radio music co. [c1932.]
5p. fol.

Score: medium solo voice with piano accompaniment. English words.

ABSpl

---

*Redman, Donald, 1900-

My dreams. Ballad. Words by *Mercer cook; music by Don Redman. New York, *Sandy bros. music co., inc. [c1936]
5 p. fol.

Score: medium solo voice [key of E^b] with piano accompaniment. English words.
Caption title.

LC
ABSpl
ZWpl

---

*Redman, Donald, 1900-

Too bad. [Popular song] Words by Tom Gindhart; music by Don Redman and Herman Stein. Chicago, Forster music publ. inc. [c1936]
4 p. fol.

Score: medium solo voice [key of F] with piano accompaniment. English words.

ABSpl
LC

---

*Reed, Nat

Happy. [Popular song] Words by Bob Joffe; music by Nat Reed. New York, Harms, inc., [c1930] Publ. pl. no. 8580.
5 p. fol.

Score: medium solo voice with piano accompaniment. English words.

ABSpl

---

*Reed, Nat

Missouri. [Popular song] By Nat Reed. New York, Harms, inc., [c1930] Publ. pl. no. 8577.
5 p. fol.

Score: medium solo voice with piano accompaniment. English words.

ABSpl

Rich, Max

My bluebird was caught in the rain. [Popular song] Words by *Henry Creamer; music by Max Rich. New York, Irving Berlin, inc. [c1930]
5 p. fol.

Score: medium solo voice with piano and ukulele accompaniment.

YJWJ
ABSpl

---

*Roberts, C Luckeyth, ca. 1893-

Doggone whippoorwill. [Popular song] Lyrics by *Alex Rogers; music by C. Luckeyth Roberts. New York, Shapiro, Bernstein & co., [c1923]
5p. fol.

Score: medium solo voice [key of C] with piano accompaniment. English words.

Excerpt from the musical show, "Go-go".

ABSpl
NYPLS

---

*Roberts, C Luckeyth, ca. 1893-

Go-go bug. [Popular song] Lyrics by *Alex Rogers; music by C. Luckeyth Roberts. New, Shapiro, Bernstein & co., [c1923]
5p. fol.

Score: medium solo voice [key of G] with piano accompaniment. English words.

Excerpt from the musical show, "Go-go".

ABSpl

---

*Roberts, C Luckeyth, ca. 1893-

I wonder if you can be happy without me. [Popular song] Words by Louise Bascom Barrat; music by Luckey Roberts. Chicago, The Braun organization music pub. [c1936]
5 p. fol.

Score: medium solo voice [key of C] with piano accompaniment. English words.

ABSpl

---

*Roberts, C Luckeyth, ca. 1893-

Isabel. [Popular song] Lyrics by *Alex Rogers; music by C. Luckeyth Roberts. New York, Shapiro, Bernstein & co., [c1923]
5p. fol.

Score: medium solo voice [key of F] with piano accompaniment. English words.

Excerpt from the musical show, "Go-go".

ABSpl

---

*Roberts, C Luckeyth, ca. 1893-

The junk man rag...Novel one step for piano... Written by C. Luckeyth Roberts ("Luckey"); New York, Jos. W. Stern & co., [c1913] Publ. pl. no. 7446.
5p. fol.

Score: piano solo.
Caption title.

ABSpl
LC

Roberts, C Luckeyth, ca. 1893-

Massachusetts

ABSpl

---

*Roberts, C Luckeyth, ca. 1893-

Mo'lasses. [Popular song] Lyric by *Alex Rogers; music by C. Luckeyth Roberts. New York, Shapiro, Bernstein & co., inc. [c1923]
5p. fol.

Score: medium solo voice [key of G] with piano accompaniment. Negro dialect.

Excerpt from the musical show, "Go-go".

ABSpl
NYPLS

Roberts, C Luckeyth, ca. 1893-

Moonlight cocktail

ABSpl.

---

*Roberts, C Luckeyth, ca. 1893-

Music box rag. Fox trot. By C. Luckeyth Roberts. New York, Jos. W. Stern & co., [c1914] Publ. pl. no. 7863.
5p. fol.

Score: piano solo.

Also published for orchestra.

ABSpl

---

*Roberts, C Luckeyth, ca. 1893-

Railroad blues. [Popular song] Lyric by Haven Gillespie and Howard Washington; music by C. Luckeyth Roberts. Chicago Van Alstyne & Curtis, [c1920]
5p. fol.

Score: medium solo voice [key of G] with piano accompaniment. English words.

"Published for song or foxtrot" -- title page.

ABSpl

---

*Roberts, C Luckeyth, ca. 1893-

...The robin and the red, red rose. [Popular song] Words by *Alex Rogers; music by C. Luckeyth Roberts. New York, T. B. Harms and Francis, Day and Hunter. [c1915] Publ. pl. no. 5246.
5 p. fol.

Score: medium solo voice [key of E^b] with piano accompaniment. English words.

"Nora Bayles' successful song creation" -- at head of title.

ABSpl

Roberts, C Luckeyth, ca. 1893-

Rock-a-bye baby blues

ABSpl.

---

*Roberts, C Luckeyth, ca. 1893-

...Rockaway. (The swaying rag song rage). Words by Howard Johnson and *Alex Rogers; music by C. Luckeyth Roberts. New York, Leo Feist inc., [c1917] Publ. pl. no. 3636.
3p. fol.

Score: medium solo voice [key of F] with piano accompaniment. English words.

"Sung by Sophie Tucker" whose picture is on cover.

ABSpl

---

*Roberts, C Luckeyth, ca. 1893-

Rosetime and you. [Popular song] Lyrics by *Alex Rogers; music by C. Luckeyth Roberts. New York, Shapiro, Bernstein & co., [c1923]
5p. fol.

Score: medium solo voice [key of F] with piano accompaniment. English words.

Excerpt from the musical show, "Go-go".

ABSpl
LC

---

*Roberts, C Luckeyth, ca. 1893-

Struttin' the blues away. [Popular song] Lyrics by *Alex Rogers; music by C. Luckeyth Roberts. New York, Shapiro, Bernstein & co., [c1923]
5p. fol.

Score: medium solo voice [key of C] with piano accompaniment. English words.

Excerpt from the musical show, "Go-go".

NYPLS
ABSpl

Roberts, C Luckeyth, ca. 1893-

The tremolo trot.

ABSpl.

---

*Roberts, C Luckeyth, ca. 1893-

Uno. ⌊Popular song⌋ Lyrics by *Alex Rogers; music by C. Luckeyth Roberts. New York, Shapiro, Bernstein & co., ⌊c1923⌋
5p. fol.

Score: medium solo voice ⌊key of E♭⌋ with piano accompaniment. English words.

Excerpt from the musical show, "Go-go".

NYPLS
ABSpl

---

*Roberts, C Luckeyth, ca. 1893-

When you dance with a wonderful girl. ⌊Popular song⌋ Words by *Alex Rogers; music by C. Luckeyth Roberts. New York, Shapiro, Bernstein & co., ⌊c1923⌋
5p. fol.

Score: medium solo voice ⌊key of F⌋ with piano accompaniment. English words.

Excerpt from the musical show, "Go-go".

ABSpl
NYPLS

Robinson, Avery arr.

...Hail the crown. ⌊Spiritual⌋ Arranged by Avery Robinson. Boston, Oliver Ditson co. ⌊c1924⌋ Publ. pl. no. 74976.
5 p. fol.

Score: high solo voice with piano accompaniment. Negro dialect.

Tune from Miss Mildred J. Hill's collection of Negro sacred songs.

At head of title: "A[rr]anged for and sung by *Roland Hayes."
NYPL58 ZWpl ABSpl

---

*Robinson, A B

Lord, I'm convinced that Thy Word is true... ⌊Gospel song⌋ Words and music by Elder A. B. Robinson. ⌊No publisher given⌋ ⌊c1943.⌋
4 p. fol.

Score: SAT, with piano accompaniment; English words. Also arranged on page 4 for SATB, hymn style.

ABSpl

---

*Robinson, A B

Yes, I'll be true. ⌊Gospel song⌋ Words and music by Elder A. B. Robinson. ⌊No publisher given⌋ c1943.
1 leaf. 8°

Score: SATB. English words.

ABSpl

Robinson, J. Russel

Funny little you. ⌊Popular song⌋ Lyric by Andy Razaf; music by J. Russel Robinson. NY: M Witmark and sons ⌊c1930⌋ Publ. pl. no. M. W. and sons 17670.
5p. fol.

Score: medium solo voice with piano accompaniment. English words.

ABSpl

Robinson, J Russel

Hello, sweetheart, hello! ⌊Popular song⌋ Words by *Noble Sissle; music by J. Russel Robinson. New York: DeSylva, Brown & Henderson, Inc. ⌊c1932⌋
5 p. fol. 2 copies

Score: medium solo voice with piano accompaniment. English words.

ABSpl

Robinson, J Russel

Hold up your hands (in the name of the law of love). ⌊Popular song⌋ Words by *Mercer Cook and Thos. Blandford; music by J. Russel Robinson. New York, Marlo music corp. ⌊c1932⌋
3 p. fol.

Score: medium solo voice with piano and ukulele accompaniment.

Introduced by Kate Smith.

ABSpl
YJWJ
HMC

Robinson, J Russel

Is I in love? I is. ⌊Popular song⌋ Words by *Mercer Cook; music by J. Russel Robinson. New York, De Sylva Brown & Henderson, Inc. ⌊c1932⌋
3 p. fol.

Score: medium solo voice with piano accompaniment. Negro dialect.

ABSpl
YJWJ

Robinson, J. Russell
Ringtail Blues

Robinson, J Russel

Roamin' for romance. ⌊Popular song⌋ Words by *Mercer Cook; music by J. Russel Robinson. New York, De Sylva, Brown & Henderson, inc. ⌊c1932⌋
5 p. 8°.

Score: medium solo voice with piano and ukulele accompaniment.

ABSpl
YJWJ

Robinson, J Russel

Yeah man. ⌊Popular song⌋ Words by Noble Sissle; music by J. Russel Robinson. New York: DeSylva, Brown and Henderson, Inc. ⌊c1932⌋
3 p. fol.

Score: medium solo voice with piano accompaniment. English words.

ABSpl

---

*Robinson, Bill, 1878-

Is ev'rything copesetic? ⌊Popular song⌋ By Bill Robinson, Connie Bemis & Lew Porter. New York, Mills music publishers. ⌊c1936⌋
5 p. fol.

Score: medium solo voice with piano accompaniment. English words.

ABSpl

---

*Rogers, Alexander

...I'm a Jonah man. ⌊Popular song⌋ Words and music by *Alex Rogers. New York, M. Witmark & sons, ⌊c1903⌋ Publ. pl. no. 5163.
6p. fol.

Score: medium solo voice ⌊key of F⌋ with piano accompaniment. Negro dialect.

"Williams and Walker's crowning success...sung in every performance of their latest musical-production, 'In Dahomey'" --at head of title.

Four extra verses and choruses on p. 6.

ABSpl
LC

---

*Rogers, Alexander

...Never! ⌊Popular song⌋ Words and music by Alex. Rogers. New York, The Attucks music pub. co. ⌊c1904⌋
5p. fol.

Score: medium solo voice ⌊key of D⌋ with piano accompaniment. English words.

"A darktown determination"-- at head of title.

ABSpl
LC

---

*Rogers, Alexander

Save your money, John... ⌊Popular song⌋ Words and music by Les Copeland and Alex Rogers. New York, Triangle music pub. co. ⌊c1909⌋
5p. fol. 2 copies

Score: medium solo voice with piano accompaniment. English words.

"Introduced by the eminent comedian: Bert A. Williams in Ziegfeld's Follies" -- at end of title.

ABSpl

---

*Rogers, Alexander

...Why Adam sinned. ⌊Popular song⌋ Words and music by Alex Rogers...New York, The Attucks music co. c1904
5p. fol.

Score: medium solo voice ⌊key of G⌋ with piano accompaniment. Negro dialect.

ABSpl
LC

Roldan, Amadeo
The "diablito" dances

Roldan, Amadeo
Negro baby's lullaby

---

*Rose, Dave

Keep on loving me. ⌊Popular song⌋ Words by Billy Johnson, late of Cole and Johnson; music by Dave Rose ...New York, Willis Woodward & co., ⌊c1906⌋ Publ. pl. no. 1578.
5p. fol.

Score: low solo voice ⌊key of B♭⌋ with piano accompaniment. English words.

ABSpl

Ruben, Louis A.

The night, the wind, and me. [Popular song] Words by *Andy Razaf; music by Louis A. Ruben. NY: Louis A. Ruben publisher. [c1935]
5p. fol.

Score: mediam solo voice with piano accompaniment. English words.

ABSpl

Rubin, Ada

The meetin's called to order. (A modern rhythmic spiritual) Words by Andy Razaf and Joe Davis; music by Ada Rubin. NY: Joe Davis, inc. [c1936] Publ. pl. no. 3623.
5p. fol.

Score: medium solo voice with piano accompaniment. English words.

ABSpl

Russ, Elmo
Cross

Lyric by Langston Hughes

---

*Ryder, Noah Francis arr.

...An' I cry. Negro spiritual [arranged by] Noah F. Ryder. New York, *Handy bros. music co., inc. [c1939]
8 p. 8vo.

Score: 4 part chorus for mixed voices (SATB) with soprano solo and piano accompaniment.
Bound in black spiral notebook no. 2.

ABSpl

---

*Ryder, Noah Francis arr.

...Balm in Gilead. Negro spiritual arranged by Noah F. Ryder. New York, *Handy bros. music co. [c1938]
5 p. 8vo.

Score: 4 part chorus for mixed voices (SATB) with piano accompaniment. English words.
Bound in black spiral notebook no. 2.

ABSpl

---

*Ryder, Noah Francis arr.

...By and by. Negro spiritual arranged by Noah F. Ryder. New York, *Handy bros. music co., inc. [c1938]
5 p. 8vo.

Score: 4 part chorus for mixed voices (SATB) with soprano solo. Negro dialect.
Bound in black spiral notebook no. 2.

ABSpl

---

*Ryder, Noah Francis arr.

...Done paid my vow. Arranged by Noah F. Ryder. New York, *Handy bros. music co., inc. [c1938]
9 p. 8vo.

Score: 4 part chorus for mixed voices (SATB) with piano solo. English words.
Bound in black spiral notebook no. 2.

ABSpl

---

*Ryder, Noah Francis arr.

... Don't be weary traveler. Negro spiritual arranged by Noah F. Ryder. New York, *Handy bros. music co., inc. [c1939]
6 p. 8vo.

Score: 8 part chorus for mixed voices (SSAATTBB) with alto solo and piano accompaniment. English words.
Bound in black spiral notebook no. 2.

ABSpl

---

*Ryder, Noah Francis arr.

Gonna journey away. Anthem. Words and music by Noah F. Ryder. New York, *Handy bros. music co., inc. [c1939]
8 p. 8vo.

Score: part for SATB, part for SABaTB with contralto solo. Negro dialect.
Bound in black spiral notebook no. 2.

ABSpl

---

*Ryder, Noah Francis arr.

Great day. Negro spiritual arranged by Noah F. Ryder. New York, *Handy bros. music co., inc. [c1938]
5 p. 8vo.

Score: 4 part chorus for mixed voices (SATB) and piano accompaniment. English words.
Bound in black spiral notebook no. 2.

ABSpl

---

*Ryder, Noah Francis arr.

Gwine up. Negro spiritual arranged by Noah F. Ryder. New York, *Handy bros. music co., inc. [c1935]
4 p. 8vo.

Score: 4 part chorus for mixed voices (SATB) with baritone solo and piano accompaniment. Negro dialect.
Bound in black spiral notebook no. 2.

ABSpl

---

*Ryder, Noah Francis arr.

...Hear the lambs a crying. Negro spiritual arranged by Noah F. Ryder. New York, *Handy bros. music co. [c1938]
5 p. 8vo.

Score: 4 part chorus for mixed voices (SATB) with piano accompaniment. English words.
Bound in black spiral notebook no. 2.

ABSpl

---

*Ryder, Noah Francis arr.

I got a mother in the heaven. Negro spiritual arranged by Noah F. Ryder. New York, *Handy bros. music co., inc. [c1938]
5 p. 8vo.

Score: 4 part chorus for mixed voices (SATB) with piano accompaniment. English words.
Bound in black spiral notebook no. 2.

ABSpl

---

*Ryder, Noah Francis arr.

I heard the preaching of the elders. Negro spiritual. Anthem. Arranged by Noah F. Ryder. New York, *Handy bros. music co., inc. [c1938]
7 p. 8vo.

Score: 4 part chorus for mixed voices (SATB) with soprano solo, with piano accompaniment. English words.
Bound in black spiral notebook no. 2.

ABSpl

---

*Ryder, Noah Francis arr.

I will never betray my Lord. Arranged by Noah F. Ryder. New York, *Handy bros. music co., inc. [c1935]
5 p. 8vo.

Score: 4 part chorus for mixed voices (SATB) with piano accompaniment. English words.
Bound in black spiral notebook no. 2.

ABSpl

---

*Ryder, Noah Francis arr.

In bright mansions above. Negro spiritual; anthem. [Arranged by] Noah F. Ryder. New York, *Handy bros. music co., inc. [c1939]
6 p. 8vo.

Score: 4 part chorus for mixed voices (SATB) with piano accompaniment. English words.
Bound in black spiral notebook no. 2.

ABSpl

---

*Ryder, Noah Francis arr.

Lord, I want to be a Christian. Traditional spiritual arranged by Noah F. Ryder. New York, *Handy bros. music co., inc. [c1938]
6 p. 8vo.

Score: 4 part chorus for mixed voices (SATB) with piano accompaniment. English words.
Bound in black spiral notebook no. 2.

ABSpl

---

*Ryder, Noah Francis arr.

My Lord is so high. Traditional Negro spiritual arranged by Noah F. Ryder. New York, *Handy bros. music co., inc. [c1939]
8 p. 8vo.

Score: 4 part chorus for mixed voices (SATB) with soprano and tenor soli and piano accompaniment. English words.
Bound in black spiral notebook no. 2.

ABSpl

---

*Ryder, Noah Francis arr.

No more auction block. Negro spiritual [arranged by] Noah F. Ryder. New York, *Handy bros. music co., inc.
4 p. 8vo.

Score: 4 part chorus for mixed voices (SATB) with soprano solo. English words.
Bound in black spiral notebook no. 2.

ABSpl

---

*Ryder, Noah Francis arr.

...Nobody knows de trouble I see. Traditional Negro spiritual arranged by Noah F. Ryder. New York, *Handy bros. music co. [c1938]
5 p. 8vo.

Score: 4 part chorus for mixed voices (SATB) with piano accompaniment. English words.
Bound in black spiral notebook no. 2.

ABSpl

---

*Ryder, Noah Francis arr.

O lem'me shine. Negro spiritual arranged by Noah F. Ryder. New York, *Handy bros. music co., inc. [c1935]
5 p. 8vo.

Score: 4 part chorus with mixed voices (SATB) with baritone solo. Negro dialect.
Bound in black spiral notebook no. 2.

ABSpl

*Ryder, Noah Francis arr.

Run to Jesus. A Negro spiritual arranged by Noah F. Ryder. New York, *Handy bros. music. co., inc. [c1936]
7 p. 8vo.

Score: 4 part chorus for mixed voices (SATB) with baritone solo. English words.
Bound in black spiral notebook no. 2.

ABSpl

*Ryder, Noah Francis arr.

Sunrise. Anthem. Words and music by Noah F. Ryder. New York *Handy bros. music co., inc. [c1939]
8 p. 8vo.

Score: 4 part chorus for mixed voices (SATB) with piano accompaniment.
Bound in black spiral notebook no. 2.

ABSpl

Saint-Georges, Chevalier de

See

Chevalier de Saint-Georges

Sam will oblige - song by Sam and his sister

See
Edwin S. Brill

Sampson, Edgar
Dark rapture

Sampson, Edgar
Don't be that way

*Sampson, Edgar

If dreams come true. [For piano] By Edgar Sampson. New York, Milsons music publishing corp., [c1934]
3 p. fol.

Score: piano solo.

ABSpl

*Sampson, Edgar arr.
Stone, Gregory
"Let's dance." Benny Goodman's theme song. Lyric by Fanny May Baldridge; music by Gregory Stone and Josef Bonime; new arrangement by Edgar Sampson. New York, Edward B. Marks music corp. [c1935] Publ. pl. no. 10979.
5 p. fol.

Score: medium solo voice [key of C] with piano accompaniment. English words.

ABSpl

Sampson, Edgar
Stomping at the Savoy

*Sawyer, Jacob J

My Lord is writin' down time. [Song] Composed by Jacob J. Sawyer. New York, National music co., c1883.
3 p. fol.

Score: high solo voice with piano accompaniment. Negro dialect.

ABSpl

Sawyer, Jacob J
Oleander Blossom's birthday party

Schuyler, Philippa
Five little pieces

Schuyler, Philippa
Three little pieces

Scott, Hazel
A rainy night in G

Scott, Tom
The creation

Shipp, J A
Fare Thee, on ma' way, jes' gone

Simon, Nat
I never slept a wink last night

words by Andy Razaf

*Sissle, Noble Lee, 1889-
*Europe, James Reese
All of no man's land is ours. [Popular song] [By Lieut. *Jim Europe, Lieut. Noble Sissle and *Eubie Blake] New York, M. Witmark & sons [c1919] Publ. pl. no. 16003.
3 p. fol.

Score: medium solo voice [key of F] with piano accompaniment. English words.

ABSpl

*Sissle, Noble Lee, 1889-

Baby buntin'. [Popular song] Lyric and music by Noble Sissle and *Eubie Blake. New York: M. Witmark & Sons, [c1923] Publ. pl. no. M. W. & Sons 16779.
5p. fol.

Score: medium solo voice with piano accompaniment. English words.

From the musical comedy, "Elsie".
Caption title.

ABSpl

*Sissle, Noble Lee, 1889-

Baltimore buzz. Novelty fox trot song. Lyric and music by Noble Sissle and Eubie Blake. New York: M. Witmark & sons [c1921] Publ. pl. no. M.W. & sons 16461.
5p. fol.

Score: medium solo voice with piano accompaniment. English words.

From the musical comedy, "Shuffle Along."
Caption title.

ABSpl

*Sissle, Noble

Bandana days... Popular song Lyrics and music by *Noble Sissle and Eubie Blake. New York: M. Witmark & Sons c1921 Publ. pl. no. M.W. & Sons 16451.
5 p. fol.

Score: medium solo voice with piano accompaniment. English words.
From the musical comedy, "Shuffle Along."
Caption title.
ABSpl

Sissle, Noble

Daddy, won't you please come home. Fox trot song. Lyric and music by *Noble Sissle and Eubie Blake. New York: M. Witmark and Sons. c1921 Publ. pl. no. M.W. & Sons 16454.
5 p. fol.

Score: medium solo voice with piano accompaniment. English words.
From the musical comedy. "Shuffle along."
Caption title.
ABSpl

*Sissle, Noble

I like to walk with a pal like you. Fox trot song. Lyric and music by *Noble Sissle and Eubie Blake. New York: M. Witmark & Sons.⌊c1922⌋Publ. pl. no. 8119.
5 p. fol.

Score: medium solo voice with piano accompaniment. English words.
From the musical comedy, "Elsie."
Caption title.
ABSpl

*Sissle, Noble
*Blake, J Hubert
Oriental blues... ⌊Popular song⌋ Lyrics and music by *Noble Sissle and Eubie Blake. New York: M. Witmark & Sons,⌊c1921⌋ Publ. pl. no. M. W. & Sons 16335.
5 p. fol.

Score: medium solo voice with piano accompaniment. English words.
From the musical comedy, "Shuffle along."
Caption title.
ABSpl

Sissle, Noble

Dixie moon. ⌊Popular song⌋ Lyrics and music by *Noble Sissle and Eubie Blake... New York: Harms Inc. ⌊c1924⌋ Publ. pl. no. 7024.
7 p. fol.

Score: medium solo voice with piano accompaniment. English words.
From the musical comedy, "The chocolate dandies."
Caption title.
ABSpl

Sissle, Noble
I'm craving for that kind of love.

*Sissle, Noble

Why? Popular song Written and composed by *Noble Sissle and Eubie Blake. London: Keith Prowse & Co. Ltd. c1925 Publ. pl. no. K.P.2984.
5 p. fol.

Score: medium solo voice with piano accompaniment. English words.
"I would like to know"--at head of title.
ABSpl

*Sissle, Noble

Everybody's sturttin' now. ⌊Popular song⌋ Lyric and music by *Noble Sissle and Eubie Blake. New York: M. Witmark & Sons,⌊c1923⌋ Publ. pl. no. 16782.
5 p. fol.

Score: medium solo voice with piano accompaniment. English words.
From the musical comedy, "Elsie."
Caption title.
ABSpl

Sissle, Noble
I'm just wild about Harry. Fox trot.

*Sissle, Noble

Kentucky Sue. ⌊Popular song⌋...Lyric and music by *Noble Sissle and Eubie Blake. New York: M. Witmark & Sons. ⌊c1921⌋ Publ. pl. no. M. W. & Sons 16356.
5 p. fol.

Score: medium solo voice with piano accompaniment. English words.
From the musical comedy, "Shuffle along."
Caption title.
ABSpl

*Sissle, Noble

Everything reminds me of you... ⌊Popular song⌋ Lyrics and music by *Noble Sissle and Eubie Blake. New York: M. Witmark & Sons. ⌊c 1921⌋ Publ. pl. no. M. W. & Sons 16419.
5 p. fol.

Score: medium solo voice with piano accompaniment. English words.
From the musical comedy, "Shuffle along."
Caption title.
ABSpl

*Sissle, Noble

I'm just wild about Harry. One step song. Lyric and music by *Noble Sissle and Eubie Blake. New York: M. Witmark & Sons ⌊c1921⌋ Publ. pl. no. 16482.
5 p. fol.

Score: medium solo voice with piano accompaniment. English words.
From the musical comedy, "Shuffle along."
Caption title.
ABSpl

*Sissle, Noble

Lady of the moon. ⌊Popular song⌋ By *Noble Sissle and Eubie Blake... London: Keith Prowse & Co. Ltd. ⌊c1925⌋ Publ. pl. no. K.P. 2996.
4 p. fol.

Score: medium solo voice with piano accompaniment. English words.
From the musical revue, "Still dancing!"
Caption title.
ABSpl

*Sissle, Noble Lee, 1889-
*Europe, James Reese
Good night Angeline. ⌊Popular song⌋ ⌊By Lieut. *James Reese Europe, Lieut. Noble Sissle and *Eubie Blake⌋ New York, M. Witmark & sons ⌊c1919⌋ Publ. pl. no. 15988.
5 p. fol.

Score: medium solo voice ⌊key of G⌋ with piano accompaniment. English words.

ABSpl

*Sissle, Noble

In honeysuckle time, when Emaline said she'd be mine. Novelty fox trot song. Words and music by *Noble Sissle and Eubie Blake. ⌊c1921⌋ Publ. pl. no. M. W. & Sons 16481.
5 p. fol.

Score: medium solo voice with piano accompaniment. English words.
From the musical comedy, "Shuffle along"
Caption title.
ABSpl

*Sissle, Noble

Love will find a way. ⌊Popular song⌋ Words and music by *Noble Sissle and Eubie Blake. New York: M. Witmark & Sons, ⌊c1921⌋ Publ. pl. no. M. W. & Sons 16418.
5 p. fol.

Score: medium solo voice with piano accompaniment. English words.
From the musical comedy, "Shuffle along."
Caption title.
ABSpl

Sissle, Noble Lee, 1889-

Gypsy blues... ⌊Popular song⌋ Lyrics and music by *Noble Sissle and Eubie Blake. New York: M. Witmark & Sons, ⌊c1921⌋ Publ. pl. no. M.W. & Sons 16420.
5 p. fol.

Score: medium solo voice with piano accompaniment. English words.
From the musical comedy, "Shuffle along."
Caption title.
ABSpl

Sissle, Noble

Jassamine Lane. [Popular song] Lyrics and music by Noble Sissle and Eubie Blake. New York; Harms inc. [c1924] Publ. pl. no. 7018.
7p. fol.
Score: medium solo voice with piano accompaniment. English words.
Caption title.
From the musical comedy, "In Bamville."
ABSpl

*Sissle, Noble

Low down blues. Fox trot song. Words and music by *Noble Sissle and Eubie Blake. New York: M. Witmark & Sons. ⌊c1921⌋ Publ. pl. no. M. W. & Sons 16450.
5 p. fol.

Score: medium solo voice with piano accompaniment. English words.
From the musical comedy, "Shuffle along."
Caption title.
ABSpl

*Sissle, Noble

If you've never been vamped by a brown skin, you've never been vamped at all... ⌊Popular song⌋ Words and music by *Noble Sissle and Eubie Blake. New York: M. Witmark & Sons,⌊c1921⌋ Publ. pl. no. 16487.
5 p. fol.

Score: medium solo voice with piano accompaniment. English words.
From the musical comedy, "Shuffle along."
Caption title.
ABSpl

*Sissle, Noble
*Blake, J Hubert, 1887-

Jingle step. Novelty fox trot song. Lyric by *Noble Sissle; music by Eubie Blake. New York: M. Witmark & Sons, ⌊c1922⌋ Publ. pl. no. M. W. & Sons 16742.
5 p. fol.

Score: medium solo voice with piano accompaniment. English words.
From the musical comedy, "Elsie."
Caption title.
ABSpl

*Sissle, Noble

Manda. ⌊Popular song⌋ Lyrics and music by *Noble Sissle and Eubie Blake... New York: Harms, Inc.⌊c1924⌋ Publ. pl. no. 7019.
5 p. fol.

Score: medium solo voice with piano accompaniment. English words.
Caption title.
From the musical comedy, "The chocolate dandies."
ABSpl

*Sissle, Noble

My crinoline girl. Fox trot song. Lyric and music by *Noble Sissle and Eubie Blake. New York: M. Witmark & Sons, ⌐c1923¬ Publ. pl. no. M. W. & Sons 16781.
5 p. fol.

Score: medium solo voice with piano accompaniment. English words.
From the musical comedy, "Elsie."
Caption title.
ABSpl

*Sissle, Noble

With you. Fox trot ballad. Lyric and music by *Noble Sissle and Eubie Blake... New York: M. Witmark & Sons, ⌐c1922¬ Publ. pl. no. M. W. & Sons 16593.
5 p. fol.

Score: medium solo voice with piano accompaniment. English words.
From the musical comedy, "Elsie."
Caption title.
ABSpl

*Smith, Christopher
Affection. 1905. 2002.

Bound in vol.

ABS

*Sissle, Noble

A regular guy. ⌐Popular song¬ Lyric and music by *Noble Sissle and Eubie Blake. New York: M. Witmark & Sons, ⌐c1922¬ Publ. pl. no. M. W. & Sons 16591.
5 p. fol.

Score: medium solo voice with piano accompaniment. English words.
From the musical comedy, "Elsie."
Caption title.
ABSpl

*Sissle, Noble

You were meant for me. ⌐Popular song¬ Written and composed by *Noble Sissle and Eubie Blake. New York: Harms inc., ⌐c1924¬ Publ. pl. no. 6966.
5 p. fol.

Score: medium solo voice with piano accompaniment. English words.
Introduced in "Andre Charlot's Revue of 1924."

ABSpl

*Smith, Christopher
After All That I've Been to You! 1912.

Bound in vol.

ABS

*Sissle, Noble

Shuffle along. One step song. Words and music by *Noble Sissle and Eubie Blake. New York: M. Witmark & Sons, ⌐c1921¬ Publ. pl. no. M. W. & Sons 16452.
5 p. fol.

Score: medium solo voice with piano accompaniment. English words.
From the musical comedy, "Shuffle along."
Caption title.

ABSpl

Smalls, Alonzo P
Claribel

Poem by Ann Lawrence Lucas

*Smith, Christopher
After tea (save a waltz for me). 1925.

Bound in vol.

ABS

*Sissle, Noble

Shuffle along. Selection a medley of tunes from the musical comedy. "Shuffle along" for piano. By *Noble Sissle and Eubie Blake; arranged by Geo. J. Trinkaus. New York: M. Witmark & Sons ⌐c1921¬ Publ. pl. no. M. W. & Sons 16507.
11 p. fol.

Score: piano solo

ABSpl

*Smith, Bessie, ca 1897-1937.

Jail house blues. ⌐Popular song¬ By Bessie Smith and *Clarence Williams...New York, *Clarence Williams music pub. co., inc. ⌐c1924¬
5 p. fol.

Score: medium solo voice with piano accompaniment. Negro dialect.

ABSpl

*Smith, Christopher

All in down and out (Sorry I ain't got it, you could get it, if I had it). ⌐Popular song¬ Words by *R. C. McPherson (Cecil Mack); music by ⌐Chris¬ Smith and ⌐Billy B.¬ Johnson and *Elmer Bowman. New York, Gotham-Attucks music co. ⌐c1906¬
5 p. fol.

Score: medium solo voice ⌐key of B^b¬ with piano accompaniment. English words.

ABSpl

*Sissle, Noble

Sing me to sleep, dear mammy. ⌐Popular song¬ Words and music by *Noble Sissle and Eubie Blake. New York: M. Witmark & Sons ⌐c1921¬ Publ. pl. no. M. W. & Sons 16484
5 p. fol.

Score: medium solo voice with piano accompaniment. English words.
From the musical comedy, "Shuffle along."
Caption title.

ABSpl

*Smith, Charles
Ingham, Nelson
Talkin' to Myself

*Smith, Christopher
All the little lovin' that I had for you is gone, gone, gone. 1913. 7617.

Bound in vol.

ABS

*Sissle, Noble

There's a million little cupids in the sky. ⌐Popular song¬ Lyrics and music by *Noble Sissle and Eubie Blake. New York: Harms inc., ⌐c1924¬ Publ. pl. no. 7017.
5 p. fol.

Score: medium solo voice with piano accompaniment. English words.
Caption title.
From the musical comedy, "In Bamville."

ABSpl

*Smith, Christopher
McPherson, Richard Cecil
...Abraham Lincoln Jones, or (The christening). Words and music by *Cecil Mack and Chris Smith. New York, Gotham-Attucks music co. ⌐c1909¬
5 p. fol.

Score: medium solo voice ⌐key of B^b¬ with piano accompaniment. Negro dialect.

A Bert Williams song.

ABSpl

*Smith, Christopher
*Payton, Lew
All the wrongs you've done to me (They're bound to come back to you.)...By *Lew Payton, Chris Smith and Edgar Dowell. New York, Clarence Williams music co., inc. ⌐c1924¬
5p. fol.

Score: low solo voice ⌐key of G¬ with piano accompaniment. English words.

"As featured by Lew Payton and Johnny Hudgins in The Chocolate Dandies" — at end of title.

ABSpl

*Sissle, Noble

Two hearts in tune. ⌐Popular song¬ Lyric and music by *Noble Sissle and Eubie Blake. New York: M. Witmark & Sons, ⌐c1922¬ Publ. pl. no. M. W. & Sons 16592.
5 p. fol.

Score: medium solo voice with piano accompaniment. English words.
From the musical comedy, "Elsie."
Caption title.

ABSpl

Smith, Christopher
Ain't my sugar sweet

*Smith, Christopher
Ballin' the Jack. 1913. 7616.

Bound in vol.

ABS

*Smith, Christopher

Ballin' the jack. Fox trot [for piano] By Chris. Smith and *Jame Reese Europe. New York, Jos. W. Stern & co. [c1914] Publ. pl. no. 7823.
5 p. fol.

Score: piano solo.

ABSpl

*Smith, Christopher
Does you love me as you used to, Miss Jane? 1904.

Bound in vol.

ABS

*Smith, Christopher

Forget me. Song Lyric by *James Burris; music by Christopher Smith. New York, Jos. W. Stern & co. [c1915] Publ. pl.no. 7962.
5p. fol.

Score: medium solo voice [key of B^b] with piano accompaniment. English words.

ABSpl

Smith, Christopher
Boom, tum, ta-ra-ra zing boom

*Smith, Christopher
Don't believe all you hear, honey. 1901.

In bound vol.

ABS

*Smith, Christopher

...Gee! But ain't America a grand old place. [Popular song] Words and music by Chris Smith...New York, Jos. W. Stern & co. [c1909] Publ. pl.no. 6439.
5p. fol.

Score: medium solo voice [key of B^b] with piano accompaniment. English words.

ABSpl

*Smith, Christopher
*McPherson, Richard Cecil
Brand-new! [Popular song] *By Cecil Mack pseud. and Chris. Smith. New York, Ted Snyder co. [c1912]
5 p. fol.

Score: medium solo voice [key of G] with piano accompaniment. English words.
Caption title.

ABSpl

*Smith, Christopher
*McPherson, Richard Cecil
Down among the sugar cane. [Popular song] Words by Avery & Hart; music by *Cecil Mack and Chris Smith. New York, Gotham-Attucks music co. [c1908]
4 p. fol.

Score: medium solo voice with piano accompaniment.

"As sung by Bert Williams."

YJWJ
ABSpl

*Smith, Christopher
Gimme hush money. 1905.

In bound vol.

ABS

*Smith, Christopher

Business is business with me. [Popular song] Words by Billy B. Johnson; music by Chris Smith. Boston, G. W. Setchell, pub. [c1907]
5 p. fol.

Score: medium solo voice [key of A^b] with piano accompaniment. English words.

ABSpl

*Smith, Christopher
Down in Honky Tonky Town. 1916.

In bound vol.

ABS

*Smith, Christopher

Good-bye, I'll see you some more. [Popular song] By Chris. Smith and *Billy B. Johnson..Brooklyn, New York, Hirsekorn and Selig [c1905]
5 p. fol.

Score: medium solo voice [key of F] with piano accompaniment. Negro dialect.

Pictures of *Billy B. Johnson, *Estelle Johnson, and Chris Smith on title page.

ABSpl

*Smith, Christopher

Clorindy. An Ethiopian serenade. By Smith and Bowman. New York, Howley, Haviland and Dresser. [c1903]
5 p. fol.

Score: medium solo voice [key of F] with piano accompaniment. Negro dialect.

ABSpl

*Smith, Christopher

Fifteen cents. [Popular song] Words and music by Chris Smith. New York, Haviland pub. co.[c1903]
5 p. fol.

Score: medium solo voice [key of B^b] with piano accompaniment. English words.

ABSpl

*Smith, Christopher
Good morning Carrie! 1901.

In bound vol.

ABS

*Smith, Christopher
*Brymn, James T.
...Come after breakfast (Bring 'long your lunch and leave 'fore supper time.) [Popular song] By James T. *Brymn, Chris Smith and James *Burris. New York, Jos. W. Stern & co. [c1909] Publ. pl.no. 6435.
5p. fol.

Score: medium solo voice [key of B^b] with piano accompaniment. Negro dialect.

ABSpl

*Smith, Christopher

...Fifty-fifty. [Popular song] Lyric by *Jim Burris; music by Chris Smith. New York, Jos. W. Stern & co. [c1914] Publ. pl. no. 7683.
5p. fol.

Score: medium solo voice [key of F] with piano accompaniment. English words.

ABSpl

*Smith, Christopher

...He's a cousin of mine. [Popular song.] Lyric by *Cecil Mack...; music by Chris Smith and Silvia Hein... New York, Gotham-Attucks music co. [c1906]
5 p. fol.

Score: medium solo voice [key of B^b] with piano accompaniment. English words.

"Featured in Daniel V. Arthur's production of "Marrying Mary"." - at end of title
"Mary Cahill's song success" at head of title

ABSpl
Lc

*Smith, Christopher
Dinner bells. 1904. 4206.

Bound in vol.

ABS

*Smith, Christopher

Fishing [Song] Words and music by Chris Smith... Chicago, Thompson & co.
5p. fol.

Score: medium solo voice [key of B^b] with piano accompaniment. English words.

ABSpl

*Smith, Christopher
Honky Tonky. One step. 1916.

In bound vol.

ABS

*Smith, Christopher

I have shed my last tears for you. [Popular song] Words by N. H. Jefferson; music by Chris Smith. New York, Jos. W. Stern. [c1914] Publ. pl. no. 7791.
5p. fol.

Score: medium solo voice [key of G] with piano accompaniment. English words.

ABSpl

---

*Smith, Christopher

If we were alone. [Popular song] Words and music by Chris Smith. Boston, Daly music pub. [c1912]
5p. fol.

Score: medium solo voice [key of B^b] with piano accompaniment. English words. Chorus also arr. for male quartet (TTBB).

ABSpl

---

*Smith, Christopher

In the jungle I'm a queen. [Popular song] Words and music by Smith and *Bowman. New York, Shapiro, Bernstein & co., [c1903]
4p. fol.

Score: medium solo voice [key of A^b] with piano accompaniment. English words.

ABSpl
LC

---

*Smith, Christopher
I want a little lovin', sometimes. 1912.

In bound vol.

ABS

---

*Smith, Christopher

I'm glad you're goin', goodbye. [Popular song] Words and music by Chris Smith. New York, F. B. Haviland pub. co. [c1912]
5 p. fol.

Score: medium solo voice [key of G] with piano accompaniment. English words.

ABSpl

---

*Smith, Christopher

In watermelon time. [Popular song] Words by *James Burris; music by Christopher Smith. New York, M. Witmark & sons, [c1909] Publ. pl. no. 8875.
5p. fol.

Score: low solo voice [key of A^b] with piano accompaniment. Negro dialect.

ABSpl

Smith, Christopher
I want to know where Tosti went

---

*Smith, Christopher

I'm going back to Broadway. [Popular song] Words by Ferd E. Mierisch; music by Chris Smith. New York, F. B. Haviland pub. co. inc., [c1913]
5p. fol.

Score: medium solo voice [key of G] with piano accompaniment. English words.

ABSpl

---

*Smith, Christopher

It takes a good man to do that. [Popular song] Words and music by Jack Elliott Bayha and Chris Smith. New York, Stark and Cowan inc. [c1921]
5p. fol.

Score: medium solo voice [key of G] with piano accompaniment. English words.

ABSpl

Smith, Christopher
I wants to pick a bone with you

---

*Smith, Christopher

I'm haunted by that Swanee river song. [Popular song] Words by Henry Troy; music by Chris Smith and Joseph Carlton. New York, Rainbow music corp. [c1924]
5 p. fol.

Score: medium solo voice [key of F] with piano accompaniment. English words.

ABSpl

---

*Smith, Christopher
It's a pretty thing. 1916.

In bound vol.

ABS

---

*Smith, Christopher
If I ever get back to Cincinnati. 1906.

In bound vol.

ABS

Smith, Christopher
I'm with you just call on me

---

*Smith, Christopher

It's hard to love somebody (who's loving somebody else). [Popular song] Lyric by *Cecil Mack [pseud.] music by Chris Smith. New York, Gotham-Attucks music co. [c1907]
5 p. fol.

Score: medium solo voice [key of G] with piano accompaniment. English words.

"Introduced by *Aida Overton Walker in *Williams' and Walker's latest success 'Bandanna land'."

ABSpl

---

*Smith, Christopher

...If he comes in, I'm going out. [Popular song] Lyric by *Cecil Mack [pseud.] music by Chris Smith. New York, Gotham-Attucks music co. [c1910]
5 p. fol.

Score: medium solo voice [key of G] with piano accompaniment. English words.

At head of title: "Sung with great success by Stella Mayhew in 'The barnyard Romeo'."

ABSpl

Smith, Christopher
In a year from now

---

*Smith, Christopher

Jazbo Johnson's hokum band. Fox trot by Chris Smith. [From] "Perfection dance folio no. 2 for piano.." New York, Jos. W. Stern & co. [c1917] Publ. pl. no. 8559.
2 p. fol.

Score: piano solo.

ABSpl

---

*Smith, Christopher
*McPherson, Richard Cecil
If I were a flower in the garden of love. [Popular song] Words and music by *Cecil Mack [pseud.] and Chris Smith. New York, Maurice Richmond music co. [c1916]
5p. fol.

Score: medium solo voice [key of C] with piano accompaniment. English words.

ABSpl

---

*Smith, Christopher

In a year from now. [Popular song] Words by Ferd E. Mierisch; music by Chris Smith. New York, F. B. Haviland pub. co. [c1913]
5p. fol.

Score: medium solo voice [key of G] with piano accompaniment. English words.

ABSpl

---

*Smith, Christopher
The Jungle ball. 1914. 7840.

In bound vol.

ABS

*Smith, Christopher

...Just an old friend of the family. [Popular song] Words by *R. C. McPherson (Cecil Mack); music by Chris Smith. New York, Gotham-Attucks music co. [c1907]
5 p. fol.

Score: medium solo voice [key of G] with piano accompaniment. English words.

ABSpl

*Smith, Christopher

Mister Moon, kindly come out and shine. [Minstrel song] By Smith and Elmer *Bowman. Boston, Walter Jacobs, [c1903] Publ. pl. no. 792.
5p. fol.

Score: medium solo voice [key of A^b] with piano accompaniment. Negro dialect.

ABSpl

Smith, Christopher
Oi yoi yoi yoi

*Smith, Christopher

...Keep it up (Keep it up all the time). Fox trot. Words and music by Chris. Smith. New York, Maurice Richmond music co. [c1914]
5 p. fol.

Score: medium solo voice [key of B^b] with piano accompaniment. English words.

ABSpl

*Smith, Christopher

My last dollar. [Popular song] Words by Charles Bayha; music by Chris Smith. New York, Shapiro, Bernstein & co. [c1921]
5 p. fol.

Score: medium solo voice [key of F] with piano accompaniment. Negro dialect.

Introduced by Bert Williams.

ABSpl

Smith, Christopher Card # 1
Perfection dance folio # 2 for piano

*Smith, Christopher
Lily of France. 1914.

In bound vol.

ABS

*Smith, Christopher
My Sweet Savannah Lize. 1903. 11388.

In bound vol.

ABS

*Smith, Christopher Card #2

Perfection dance folio #2 for piano, containing song hits of the season. New York, [c1917]

3. In the sweet bye and bye. Fox trot by Chris Smith. (p. 14-15)
4. It takes a long tall brown skin gal (to make a preacher lay his Bible down) by Chris Smith (p. 7-9)

ABSpl

*Smith, Christopher

... 'Long in pumpkin-pickin' time. [Popular song] Words by *Cecil Mack; music by Chris Smith. New York, Gotham-Attucks music co. [c1908]
5 p. fol.

Score: medium solo voice [key of F] with piano accompaniment. Negro dialect.

ABSpl

*Smith, Christopher
Never let the same bee sting twice. 1916.

In bound vol.

ABS

Smith, Christopher
Piping rock

*Smith, Christopher

Love is a grand old thing so gimme little bit of lovin'. [Popular song] Words by *Elmer Bowman and Jack Drisland; music by Chris Smith. New York, F. B. Haviland pub. co. [c1912]
5p. fol.

Score: medium solo voice [key of B^b] with piano accompaniment. English words.

ABSpl

*Smith, Christopher

...No, no, positively no. [Popular song] Words and music by *Chris Smith and *Harry Brown. New York, Herbert H. Taylor, inc. [c1907]
5p. fol.

Score: medium solo voice [key of F] with piano accompaniment. English words.

ABSpl

Smith, Christopher
Please don't love anybody else but me

*Smith, Christopher
*Brooks, Shelton
Mighty day. [Popular song] By Chris Smith and *Shelton Brooks. New York, *Perry Bradford, inc. [c1921]
5 p. fol.

Score: medium solo voice [key of C] with piano accompaniment. English words.

ABSpl

*Smith, Christopher
Nobody has more trouble than me. 1905. 4588.

In bound vol.

ABS

*Smith, Christopher

Shame on you! [Popular song] Words and music by Chris Smith and John Larkins. New York, Jos. W. Stern & co. [c1904] Publ. pl. no. 4178.
5 p. fol.

Score: medium solo voice [key of B^b] with piano accompaniment. Negro dialect.

ABSpl
NBCL - arranged for full orchestra by Walter C. Schel

*Smith, Christopher
The missing link. 1922.

In bound vol.

ABS

*Smith, Christopher

...Oh! so sweet. [Popular song] Words by Joe McCarthy and Joe Goodwin; music by Chris Smith. New York, Leo Feist, inc. [c1912] Publ. pl. no. 2965.
5p. fol.

Score: medium solo voice [key of E^b] with piano accompaniment. English words.

ABSpl

*Smith, Christopher

Slip on your gingham gown. [Popular song] Words by *James Burris; music by Chris Smith. New York, M. Witmark & sons. [c1909] Publ. pl. no. 8718.
5 p. fol.

Score: medium solo voice [key of A^b] with piano accompaniment. English words.

ABSpl
LC

*Smith, Christopher
Sweetie don't. 1905. 4347.

In bound vol.

ABS

*Smith, Christopher

There's a time and place for everything. Coon song. Words by *Al Brown; music by Chris Smith. New York-Detroit, Jerome H. Remick & co. [c1906]
5p. fol.

Score: medium solo voice [key of G] with piano accompaniment. English words.

ABSpl
LC

*Smith, Christopher
Yo' wasting time. 1904.

In bound vol.

ABS

*Smith, Christopher
Taint de kind o'grub I've been gettin' down home. 1905. 4339.

In bound vol.

ABS

*Smith, Christopher

Trans-mag-ni-fi-can-bam-dam-u-al-i-ty. [Popular song] Words by *James Burris; music by Chris Smith. Detroit, Jerome H. Rémick & co. [c1909]
5p. fol.

Score: high solo voice [key of E^b] with piano accompaniment. Negro dialect.

LC
NBCL] (orches. parts in mss. arr. by W. C. Schad.)
ABSpl

*Smith, Christopher

You'll never need a doctor no more. [Popular song] Words and music; by Chris Smith. New York, Skidmore music co, inc. [c1921]
3 p. fol.

Score: medium solo voice [key of G] with piano accompaniment. Negro dialect.

"Introduced by Bert Williams in his 1921 riot, 'Broadway brevities'." - Cover title page.

ABSpl

*Smith, Christopher
*Hogan, Ernest
'Taint no disgrace to run when you're skeered. [Popular song] Words by James Burris; music by *Ernest Hogan pseud. and Chris. Smith. New York, Whitney-Warner pub. co. [c1903]
6 p. fol.

Score: medium solo voice [key of A^b] with piano accompaniment. English words.

ABSpl

*Smith, Christopher

The undertaker man. [Popular song] Words and music by Chris Smith. Chicago, Harold Rossiter music co. [c1911]
5 p. fol.

Score: medium solo voice [key of B^b] with piano accompaniment. English words.

ABSpl

*Smith, Christopher

You're in the right church but the wrong pew. [Popular song] Words by *Cecil Mack; music by Chris Smith. New York, Gotham-Attucks music co. [c1908]
5 p. fol.

Score: medium solo voice with piano accompaniment.

"As sung by Bert Williams."

YJWJ
ABSpl

*Smith, Christopher

...That puzzlin' rag. [Popular song. Words and music] by *Elmer Bowman and Chris Smith. New York, Haviland pub. co. [c1912]
5 p. fol.

Score: medium solo voice [key of G] with piano accompaniment. English words.

ABSpl

*Smith, Christopher

When everything seems to go wrong. [Popular song] Words by Ferd. E. Mierisch; music by Chris Smith. New York, Haviland pub. co. [c1913]
5 p. fol.

Score: medium solo voice [key of G] with piano accompaniment. English words.

ABSpl

*Smith, Christopher

Your face looks familiar to me. [Popular song] Words and music by [Chris] Smith and *[Elmer] Bowman. Boston, G. W. Setchell. [c1902]
5 p. fol.

Score: medium solo voice [key of A^b] with piano accompaniment. English words.

ABSpl

*Smith, Christopher

...That sneaky snakey rag (The snake). [Popular song] Words and music by Chris Smith and *Elmer Bowman. New York, Haviland pub. co. [c1912]
5 p. fol.

Score: medium solo voice [key of G] with piano accompaniment. English words.

ABSpl

*Smith, Christopher
When I want a little loving. 1913. 7537.

In bound vol.

ABS

*Smith, N Clark, 1877-1933.

Banana walk (St. Helena island melodies). [In Smith, N. Clark-, Negro folk suite. Chicago, c1925, p. 7-11]

Score: piano solo.

ABSpl
LC

*Smith, Christopher

...That's where friendship ends. [Popular song.] Words by *R. C. McPherson; music by Chris Smith... New York, Gotham-Attucks music co. [c1907]
5 p. fol.

Score: medium solo voice [key of F] with piano accompaniment. English words.

LC
ABSpl

*Smith, Christopher
Why! Hello, Bill, Who's Yo' Friend? 1904.

In bound vol.

ABS

*Smith, N. Clark- 1877 - 1933. arr.

...Come out the wilderness. Bahama folk song. [Anthem.] Arranged by N. Clark-Smith. Chicago, Lyon & Healy, [c1923]
3 p. 8°.

Score: SATB with piano accompaniment. Negro dialect.

ABSpl
LC

*Smith, Christopher
There's a big cry baby in the moon. 1909. 2668.

In bound vol.

ABS

*Smith, Christopher
Yo' eyes are open, but yo' sound asleep. 1907.

In bound vol.

ABS

*Smith, N Clark, 1877-1933. arr.

...Couldn't hear, nobody pray. [From Negro choral symphony for tenor [or contralto] solo, male chorus and orchestra. By N. Clark-Smith.. Chicago, Lyon & Healy, [c1821]
8p. 8°. (Century of Progress edition)

Score: TTBB with tenor or contralto solo and piano accompaniment. Negro dialect.

At head of title: "Echo melody from Negro choral symphony".

ABSpl

*Smith, N Clark- 1877 - 1933, arr.

...The crucifixion. An Easter-tide melody, 1913. Anthem for mixed voices. By N. Clark-Smith. Chicago, Lyon & Healy, c1922, 4 p. fol.

Score: SATB with piano accompaniment. Negro dialect.

ABSpl
LC

---

*Smith, N Clark, 1877-1933.

Pine apple lament (Martinique melody). [In Smith; Negro folk suite. Chicago, c1925. p. 5-7]

Score: piano solo.

ABSpl
LC

---

*Smith, N Clark, 1877-1933. arr.

...That muttering thunder. The storm cloud. (A primitive African melody). By N. Clark-Smith. Chicago, Lyon & Healy publishers, c1924.
3p. fol.

Score: medium solo voice [key of A^{b}] with piano accompaniment. Negro dialect.

ABSpl

---

*Smith, N Clark- 1877 - 1933, arr.

...Lord, I wish I could. Bahama folk song. Anthem. Arranged by N. Clark-Smith. Chicago, Lyon & Healy, c1923,
3 p. 8°.

Score: SATB with piano accompaniment. Negro dialect.

Caption title.

ABSpl
LC

---

*Smith, N Clark, 1877-1933.

Prayer. [From] "Negro choral symphony. (Heart of emancipation). [Chorus] Poem by *Kelly Miller; music by N. Clark-Smith. Chicago, Lyon & Healy, c1917]
8p. 8°.

Score: SATB and soprano solo [key of E^{b}] with piano accompaniment. English words.

ZWpl
ABSpl

---

*Smith, Russell

Let not your heart be troubled. (From XIV chapter of St. John) Negro spiritual. Music by Russell Smith. New York, W. C. Handy music publisher c1928]
5 p. fol.

Score: medium solo voice with piano accompaniment. English words.

ABSpl

---

*Smith, N Clark

Negro choral symphony. By N. Clark Smith, Chicago, Lyon and Healy, various copyright dates. (Century Progress edition).
5 v. 8°

Score: choruses for mixed, male and women's voices; soli (vocal and piano) piano accompaniment. Orchestra accompaniment available from Lyon and Healy on hire.

(continued on next page)

---

*Smith, N Clark, 1877-1933. arr.

...Prelude (Congo melody). [From] the Negro choral symphony. Piano soloo chorus and orchestra. By N. Clark-Smith...Chicago, Lyon & Healy, c1933]
8p. 8°. (Century of Progress edition)

Score: piano solo with TTBB and optional soli. Negro dialect.

Wanamaker prize award, 1930.

ABSpl

---

*Smith, Willie, 1897-
*Bishop, Walter

Ain't gonna swing no more. [Popular song] By *Walter Bishop, Willie (the Lion) Smith, and Basil G. Adlam. New York, Mills music inc., c1938]
5 p. fol.

Score: medium solo voice with piano accompaniment. English words.

ABSpl

---

*Smith, N Clark ....Negro choral symphony, Chicago. (Card two)

Contents: Part 1. Prelude (Congo melody), -2. Couldn't hear nobody pray (Echo melody), -3. Prayer, -4. Spiritual jubilee, -5. The prima donna song.

ABpl

---

*Smith, N Clark, 1877-1933.

The prima donna song. [From] "Negro choral symphony". Part V - Finale. Chorus. By N. Clark-Smith. Chicago, Lyon & Healy, c1933] Publ. pl. no. 35475.
12p. 8°. (Century of Progress edition)

Score: SA, TTBB (ad. lib.), soprano solo [key of B^{b}] with piano accompaniment. English words.

ABSpl

---

*Smith, Willie

Curfew time in Harlem. (Novelty song). Words and music by Willie (The Lion) Smith and Neil Laurence. New York, Joe Davis, inc., c1938] Publ. pl. no. 3838.
3 p. fol.

Score: medium solo voice with piano accompaniment. English words.

ABSpl

---

*Smith, N Clark, 1877-1933.

...Negro folk suite... By N. Clark-Smith, (Bac. Mus.) (Chicago Musical College)...Chicago, Lyon & Healy, inc. c1925]
11p. fol.

Score: piano solos.

There are editorial notes by the composer preceding each piece; also an explanatory note inside title page by Ruth Louise Allan of the American Conservatory of Music, Chicago.

(see next card)

---

*Smith, N Clark, 1877-1933. arr.

...Spiritual jubilee. [From] "Negro choral symphony". Part IV (Alabamy). By N. Clark-Smith. Chicago, Lyon & Healy, c1933]
8p. 8°. (Century of Progress edition)

Score: SATB with soprano and tenor soli [key of E^{b}] with piano accompaniment. Negro dialect.

ABSpl

---

*Smith, Willie, 1897 -

Feelin' low. [Popular song] By Mitchell Parish, Willie (The Lion) Smith and *Walter Bishop. New York, Mills music inc., c1936]
5 p. fol.

Score: medium solo voice with piano accompaniment. English words.

ABSpl

---

*Smith, N Clark, 1877-1933. Card #2

...Negro folk suite... Chicago. c1925

Contents: 1. Orange dance (British Guinea). 2. Pine apple lament (Martinique melody). 3. Banana walk (St. Helena Island melody).

Also arranged for violin and piano; violin, cello, and piano; and full orchestra.

ABSpl
LC

---

*Smith, N Clark- 1877 - 1933, arr.

...Steal away to Jesus (Folk-song anthem) By N. Clark-Smith. Chicago, Lyon & Healy, c1916,
7 p. 8°.

Score: SSAATTBB with piano accompaniment. Negro dialect.

ZWpl
ABSpl

---

*Smith, Willie, 1897 -

Modern piano solos. By Willie Smith. New York, Leo Feist, inc., c1939] Publ pl nos. 6940, 7038, 7039, 7041, 7042, 7044.
25 p. fol

Score: piano solos

Contents: 1. Morning air. -2. Passionette. -3. Finger buster. -4. Tango a la caprice. -5. Rippling waters

(continued on next card)

---

*Smith, N Clark, 1877-1933.

The orange dance. [In Smith, N. Clark-, Negro folk suite. Chicago. c1925. p. 3-5]

Score: piano solo.

ABSpl
LC

---

*Smith, N Clark- 1877 - 1933, arr.

Swing low, sweet chariot (Folk-song anthem) By N Clark-Smith. Chicago, Lyon & Healy, c1921.
9 p. 8°.

Score: SATB with optional alto, tenor and baritone soli, with piano accompaniment. Negro dialect.

Wanamaker prize song, 1931.

ABSpl
ZWpl

---

*Smith, Willie, 1897 - (Card 2)

Modern piano solos.

-6. No local stops. -7. Concentratin'

*Smith, Willie, 1897 -
*Bishop, Walter
The old stamping ground. (a swing lament) By *Walter Bishop, Willie Smith and E. P. La Freniere: Roy music co., ⌞c1938⌟
5 p. fol

Score: medium solo voice with piano accompaniment. English words.

ABSpl

---

*Smith, Willie, 1897 -

Piano marmalade. (Novelty piano solo.) By Willie (The Lion) Smith. New York, Mills music, inc., ⌞c1937⌟

5 p. fol

Score: piano solo

ABSpl
LC

---

*Stewart, Hilbert Earl -1943. arr.

Love song. Song. The words by *Paul Lawrence Dunbar; the music by Hilbert Earl Stewart. Chicago, Gamble Hinged music co. ⌞c1918⌟ Publ. pl. no. 547.
5 p. fol.

Score: medium solo voice with piano accompaniment English words.

ABSpl HSpl ZWpl

---

*Stewart, Hilbert Earl -1943 arr.

...O brothers, you'll be called on. Negro spiritual. Arranged by Hilbert Earl Stewart. Boston, Oliver Ditson co. ⌞c1926⌟ Publ. pl. no. 75517.
5 p. fol.

Score: medium solo voice ⌞key of C⌟ with piano accompaniment. English words.

ABSpl LC ZWpl

---

*Still, William Grant, 1895-

All God's chilun got shoes. ⌞Song. Arranged for solo voice by William Grant Still⌟
(In William Grant Still, "Six of the twelve Negro spirituals arranged for solo..." New York, ⌞c1937⌟ p. 21-27a)

Score: medium solo voice ⌞key of G⌟ with piano accompaniment. Negro dialect.

LC
ABSpl
ZWpl

---

*Still, William Grant, 1895-

A bit of wit.
(In Still, William Grant. Seven traceries. For piano. New York, c1940. p. 22-24)

Score: piano solo.

ABSpl
LC
NYPL42
ZWpl

---

*Still, William Grant, 1895-

...The breath of a rose. ⌞Song. One of⌟ Two poems set to music by William Grant Still... ⌞Poem by *Langston Hughes.⌟ New York, G. Schirmer, inc. ⌞c1928⌟ Publ. pl. no. 33804.
5 p. fol.

Score: high or medium solo voice ⌞key of G^bm⌟ with piano accompaniment. English words.

ABSpl
LC
NYPL42
ZWpl

---

*Still, William Grant, 1895-

Brown baby (Southern blues). ⌞Song⌟ Lyric by *Paul Henry ⌞pseud.⌟; music by Willie M. Grant ⌞pseud.⌟ New York, Edward B. Marks music co. ⌞c1923⌟ Publ. pl. no. 9111.
5 p. fol. (genuine struttin'-blues series by natural born writers of "blues.")

Score: medium solo voice ⌞key of C⌟ with piano accompaniment. English words.

ABSpl
LC

---

*Still, William Grant, 1895-

Cloud cradles.
(In Still, William Grant. Seven traceries. For piano. New York, c1940. p. 1-4)

Score: piano solo.

ABSpl
LC
NYPL42
ZWpl

---

*Still, William Grant, 1895-

Dark horsemen.
(In Still, William Grant. ...Three visions. For piano solo... New York, c1936. p. 1-3)

Score: piano solo.

ABSpl
HMC
LC
NYPL42
ZWpl

---

*Still, William Grant, 1895-

A deserted plantation. By William Grant Still... New York, Robbins music corp. ⌞c1936⌟
13 p. fol.

Score: piano solos; originally an orchestral suite.

A musical picture of the meditations of Uncle Josh, an old colored man who was the sole occupant of a dying plantation, and who delights in basking in its past glory.

Contents: A. Spiritual. -B. Young missy. -C. Dance. ABSpl LC ZWpl

---

*Still, William Grant, 1895-

...Dance.
(In Still, William Grant. A deserted plantation. New York, c1936. p. 10-13)

Score: piano solo.

ABSpl
LC
ZWpl

---

*Still, William Grant, 1895-

Great camp meeting. ⌞Song. Arranged for solo voice by William Grant Still⌟
(In William Grant Still, "Six of the twelve Negro spirituals arranged for solo..." New York, ⌞c1937⌟ p. 55-61)

Score: medium solo voice ⌞key of F⌟ with piano accompaniment. Negro dialect.

LC
ABSpl
ZWpl

---

*Still, William Grant, 1895-

Gwinter sing all along de way. ⌞Song. Arranged for solo voice by William Grant Still⌟
(In William Grant Still, "Six of the twelve Negro spirituals arranged for solo..." New York, ⌞c1937⌟ p. 11-19)

Score: medium solo voice ⌞key of F⌟ with piano accompaniment. Negro dialect.

LC
ABSpl
ZWpl

Still, William Grant

Here's one

---

*Still, William Grant, 1895-

...In memoriam: The colored soldiers who died for democracy. ⌞For orchestra⌟ By William Grant Still. Phila., Delkas music pub. co. ⌞c1943⌟
16 p. 8°.

Score: full orchestra in miniature.

Score and parts available on rental from publisher.

ABSpl
HPSpl
ZWpl

---

*Still, William Grant, 1895-

Keep me f'om sinkin' down. ⌞Song. Arranged for solo voice by William Grant Still⌟
(In William Grant Still, "Six of the twelve Negro spirituals arranged for solo..." New York, ⌞c1937⌟ p. 39-45)

Score: low solo voice ⌞key of D⌟ with piano accompaniment. Negro dialect.

LC
ABSpl
ZWpl

---

*Still, William Grant, 1895-

Lawd ah wants to be a Christian. ⌞Song. Arranged for solo voice by William Grant Still⌟
(In William Grant Still, "Six of the twelve Negro spirituals arranged for solo..." New York, ⌞c1937⌟ p. 47-53)

Score: high solo voice ⌞key of G^b⌟ with piano accompaniment. Negro dialect.

LC
ABSpl
ZWpl

---

*Still, William Grant, 1895-

Lenox Ave. Choreographic street scenes. Scenario by Verna Arvey; music by William Grant Still... New York, J. Fischer and bro. ⌞c1938⌟ Publ. pl. no. J.F. & B. 0379.
41 p. fol.

Score: piano-vocal (SSATBB) for two choral episodes. Negro dialect.

Performance time: approximately 25 minutes.

(continued on next card)

---

*Still, William Grant, 1895- Lenox Ave...
New York, c1938. (Card 2)

Explanatory text in English. Illustrated title-page. "Choreography by Norma Gould."

Originally commissioned by C. B. S. First presented over National hookup on 5/23/37, with Howard Barlow conducting. Later transformed into a ballet first performed by Dance theatre group of L. A. on 5/1/38 with choreography by Norma Gould and with Charles Teske dancing role of "The man from down south."

(continued on next card)

---

*Still, William Grant, 1895- Lenox Ave...
New York, c1938. (Card 3)

A series of 10 orchestral episodes and finale, built on scenes the composer has witnessed in Harlem.

ABSpl
HMC
LC
NYPL42
ZWpl

*Still, William Grant, 1895-

Lis'en to de lam's. [Song. Arranged for solo voice by William Grant Still]
(In William Grant Still, "Six of the twelve Negro spirituals arranged for solo..." New York, [c1937] p. 29-37)

Score: high solo voice [key of G] with piano accompaniment. Negro dialect.

LC
ABSpl
ZWpl

*Still, William Grant, 1895-

Radiant pinnacle.
(In Still, William Grant. ...Three visions. For piano solo... New York, c1936. p. 8-12)

Score: piano solo.

ABSpl
HMC
LC
NYPL42
ZWpl

*Still, William Grant, 1895- Six of the twelve Negro spirituals... [c1937] (Card 3)

"Literary treatments" consists of 6 poems and 6 "stories depicting Negro life at the time these spirituals were inspired." A poem and story introduces each song.

LC
ABSpl
ZWpl
HMC

*Still, William Grant, 1895-

Memphis man (A love-sick blues). [Popular song] Words by *Paul Henry [pseud.]; music by Willy M. Grant [pseud.] New York, Edward B. Marks music co. [c1923] Publ. pl. no. 9103.
5 p. fol. (genuine struttin'-blues series by natural born writers of "blues.")

Score: medium solo voice [key of E^b] with piano accompaniment. English words.

ABSpl
LC

*Still, William Grant, 1895-

Rising tide. [Song] Commissioned for the theme exhibit by the New York World's Fair, 1939, inc. Lyrics by Albert Stillman; music by William Grant Still. New York, J. Fischer & bro. [c1939] Publ. pl. no. J.F. & B. 7525.
5 p. fol.

Score: medium solo voice [key of A^b] with piano accompaniment. English words.
Orchestral arrangement available on rental from publisher.

ABSpl LC
HMC ZWpl

*Still, William Grant, 1895-

...Spiritual.
(In Still, William Grant. A deserted plantation. New York, c1936. p. 2-5)

Score: piano solo.

ABSpl
LC
ZWpl

*Still, William Grant, 1895-

Muted laughter.
(In Still, William Grant. Seven traceries. For piano. New York, c1940. p. 8-10)

Score: piano solo.

ABSpl
LC
NYPL42
ZWpl

*Still, William Grant, 1895-

Rising tide. Commissioned for the theme exhibit by the New York World's Fair, 1939, inc. Lyrics by Albert Stillman; music by William Grant Still... New York, J. Fischer & bro. [c1939] Publ. pl. no. J. F. & B. 7526.
3 p. 20 pts. fol.

Score: piano-conductor, and parts. Vocal part optional.

LC
ABSpl
ZWpl
HMC

*Still, William Grant, 1895-

Summerland.
(In Still, William Grant. ...Three visions. For piano solo... New York, c1936. p. 4-7)

Score: piano solo.

ABSpl
HMC
LC
NYPL42
ZWpl

*Still, William Grant, 1895-

Mystic pool.
(In Still, William Grant. Seven traceries. For piano. New York, c1940. p. 5-7)

Score: piano solo.

ABSpl
LC
NYPL42
ZWpl

*Still, William Grant, 1895-

...Scherzo from Afro-American symphony, by William Grant Still... New York, J. Fischer & bro. [c1938] Publ. pl. no. J.F. & B. 0366.
7 p. fol. (Fischer edition)

Score: piano-conductor score; and parts.

"Reduced instrumentation from the original for symphony orchestra."

Performance time: 4 minutes.

ABSpl LC
HMC ZWpl

*Still, William Grant, 1895-

...Three visions. For piano solo... [By] William Grant Still. New York, J. Fischer & bro. [c1936] Publ. pl. no. J.F. & B. 7119.
12 p. fol. (Fischer edition no. 7119)

Score: piano solos.

Contents: 1. Dark horsemen. -2. Summerland. -3. Radiant pinnacle.

No. 2 is published also for small orchestra, arranged by composer.

ABSpl HMC LC NYPL42 ZWpl

*Still, William Grant, 1895-

Out of the silence.
(In Still, William Grant. Seven traceries. For piano. New York, c1940. p. 11-14)

Score: piano solo.

ABSpl
LC
NYPL42
ZWpl

*Still, William Grant, 1895-

Seven traceries. For piano. By William Grant Still. New York, J. Fischer & bro. [c1940] Publ. pl. no. 7632.
24 p. fol. (Fischer edition)

Score: piano solos.

Contents: 1. Cloud cradles. -2. Mystic pool. -3. Muted laughter. -4. Out of the silence. -5. Woven silver. -6. Wailing dawn. -7. A bit of wit.

Introduction by Verna Arvey.

ABSpl LC NYPL42 ZWpl

*Still, William Grant, 1895-

Wailing dawn.
(In Still, William Grant. Seven traceries. For piano. New York, c1940. p. 18-21)

Score: piano solo.

ABSpl
LC
NYPL42
ZWpl

*Still, William Grant, 1895-

Plain chant for America. For baritone voice with orchestral accompaniment. Poem by Katherine Garrison Chapin; music by William Grant Still... New York, J. Fischer & bro. [c1941] Publ. pl. no. J.F. & B. 7800.
14 p. fol. (Fischer edition no. 7800)

Score: Ba solo with piano accompaniment. English words. Originally for voice and orchestra.
Orchestral parts obtainable from publisher for larg or small orchestra.

Dedicated to the President of the United States and Mrs. Franklin Delano Roosevelt.

ABSpl HMC LC NYPL42 YJWJ ZWpl

*Still, William Grant, 1895-

Six of the twelve Negro spirituals arranged for solo voice by William Grant Still; *Ruby Berkley Goodwin, author of the "Literary treatments"; illustrations by Albert Barbelle; edited by *Wellington Adams. Vol. I. New York, *Handy bros. music co., inc. [c1937]
61 p. illus., fol.
Cover title: Twelve Negro spirituals.

Score: solo voice with piano accompaniment. Negro dialect.

(continued on next card)

*Still, William Grant, 1895-

Woven silver.
(In Still, William Grant. Seven traceries. For piano. New York, c1940. p. 15-17)

Score: piano solo.

ABSpl
LC
NYPL42
ZWpl

*Still, William Grant, 1895-

Quit dat fool'nish (to Shep, my mischievous dog) By William Grant Still. New York, J. Fischer & bro. [c1938] Publ. pl. no. J.F. & B. 7460.
5 p. fol.

Score: piano solo.

ABSpl
HMC
LC
ZWpl

*Still, William Grant, 1895- Six of the twelve Negro spirituals... [c1937] (Card 2)

Contents: -1. Gwinter sing all along de way. -2. All God's chillun got shoes. -3. Lis'en to de lam's. -4. Keep me f'om sinkin' down. -5. Lawd ah wants to be a Christian. -6. Great camp meeting.

Biographical sketch of William Grant Still by Verna Arvey; preface by Wellington Adams, p. [5]

(continued on next card)

*Still, William Grant, 1895-

...Young missy.
(In Still, William Grant. A deserted plantation. New York, c1936. p. 6-9)

Score: piano solo.

ABSpl
LC
ZWpl

*Still, William Grant, 1895-

Winter's approach. ⌊Song. One of⌋ Two poems set to music by William Grant Still... ⌊Poem by *Paul Laurence Dunbar.⌋ New York, G. Schirmer, inc. ⌊c1928⌋ Publ. pl. no. 33805.
5 p. fol.

Score: high solo voice ⌊key of A^b⌋ Negro dialect.

ABSpl
LC
ZWpl

Stockhausen, Linda
Jamaica folk songs Part I.

---

*Stone, Fred S

The belle of the Philippines. March, two-step characteristic for piano By Fred S. Stone. New York, The Whitney-Warner pub. co. ⌊c1903⌋
6 p. fol.

Score: piano solo.

ABSpl

Stone, Fred S
The bos'n rag

Stone, Fred S
Ma ragtime baby

Stone, Fred S
Silks and rags

Stone, Gregory
"Lets Dance" arranged by Edgae Sampson

---

*Stone, Walter

...The burden, Lord, Thou gavest me. ⌊Sacred song⌋ lyric by Bessie V. Johnson; music by Walter Stone. Burlington, Iowa, Bessie V. Johnson Pub. n.d.
3 p. fol.

Score: medium solo voice ⌊key of B^b⌋ with piano accompaniment. English words.

"Professional copy" -- at head of title.

ABSpl

---

*Stone, Walter

To mother. ⌊Song⌋ Lyric by Bessie V. Johnson; music by Walter Stone. Photostat copy of manuscript. ⌊n.d.⌋
2 p. fol.

Score: medium solo voice ⌊key of D⌋ with piano accompaniment. English words.

ABSpl

---

*Stor, Jean (pseud.) Morgan, William Astor.

Bound in black spiral notebook no. 4.

ABS

Stor, Jean
I want Jesus to walk with me

Straight, Charley
I never had the blues until I left old Dixie-land. ⌊Popular song⌋ Words by Spencer Williams; music by Charley Straight. New York, *Pace and Handy music co., inc. ⌊c1919⌋
3 p. fol.

Score: medium solo voice with piano accompaniment. English words.

ABSpl

Sunshine, Marion
One side of me

Swanson, Howard
Cahoots

Swanson, Howard
A death song

Swanson, Howard
Ghosts in love

Swanson, Howard
In time of silver rain

Swanson, Howard
I will lie down in autumn

Swanson, Howard
Joy

Swanson, Howard
The junk man

Swanson, Howard
The Negro speaks of rivers

Swanson, Howard
Night song

Swanson, Howard
Nocturne

Swanson, Howard
Pierrot

Swanson, Howard
Saw a grave upon a hill

Swanson, Howard
Still life

Swanson, Howard
To be or not to be

Swanson, Howard
The valley

Sweatman, Wilber C
Old folks rag

*Sweatman, Wilber

That's got 'em. Rag ⌐for piano⌐ By Wilber Sweatman. New York, Triangle music pub. co., ⌐c1919⌐
3 p. fo 2 copies

Score: piano solo

ABSpl

*Talbert, Wendell arr.

Deep river. Negro spiritual. Arranged for mixed voices by Wen Talbert. New York, *Handy bros. music co., inc. ⌐c1934⌐
7 p. 8 vo.
Bound in black spiral notebook no. 4.
Score: SSAATTBB with piano accompaniment English words.

ABSpl HMC
NYPIS ZWpl

*Talbert, Wendell Phillips arr.

Drinking of the vine. Negro spiritual as sung by Southernaires quartette, arranged by "Wen" Talbert. New York, *Handy bros. music co., inc. ⌐c1939⌐
5 p. 8°.
Bound in black spiral notebook no. 4.
Score: 4 parts for male voices (TTBB) with piano accompaniment. English words.

ABSpl

*Talbert, Wendell

Hip hip hooray for Roosevelt. Campaign song Words by P. K. Masson; music by Wen Talbert and *Jas. Lillard. Forest Hills, L. I., Masson publisher, ⌐c1932⌐
5 p. fol.

Score: medium solo voice with piano accompaniment. English words.

ABSpl

Talbert, Wendell
Maybe I'm gettin' old blues

*Talbert, Wendell Phillips arr.

Show me the way to go. Negro spiritual as sung by the Southernaires quartette, arranged by "Wen" Talbert. New York, *Handy bros. music co., inc. ⌐c1939⌐
5 p. 8°.

Score: 4 parts for male voices (TTBB) with piano accompaniment. English words.
Bound in black spiral notebook no. 4.

ABSpl

Taylor, Roumel William
I'm so glad he's mine

Ten choice Negro folksongs for voice and pianoforte. New York, Globe music co., ⌐n.d.⌐ Publ. pl. nos. 3258, 5836, 7974, 5138, 3708, 587, 3307, 3681, 6436, 3937.
32 p. fol.

Score: medium solo voice with piano accompaniment. Negro dialect for 7; English words for 3.

Contents: -1. Nobody's lookin' but the owl and the moon. -2. Sugar babe. -3. "Mudder knows." -4. Run brudder Rabbit, run! -5. Lazy moon. -6. I can't think ob nothin' else but you. (Luli Lu). -7. "Lit'l Gal."

(continued on next card)

Ten choice Negro folksongs...⌐n.d.⌐ (Card 2)

-8. Moonlight on the Mississippi. -9. Consolation land. -10. Darkies' delight.

ABSpl
BHC

*Tharpe, Rosetta comp.

Eighteen original Negro spirituals. By Sister Rosetta Tharpe. New York, Mills music publishers, c1938
32 p. fol.

Score: medium solo voice with piano accompaniment for 18 songs. Negro dialect.
"Spirituals with an original and appealing religious quality set down exactly as sung by Sister Tharpe since infancy in Negro churches all over the country"— Cover title page.
ABSpl

*Thomas, A Jack

...Lord, I ain't got long to stay. A motet from the symphonic poem: "Etude en noir" by A. Jack Thomas. New York, *Handy bros. music co., inc. ⌐c1939⌐
16 p. 8°.

Score: 8 part chorus for mixed voices (SSAATTBB) with tenor solo and piano accompaniment. English words.
Bound in black spiral notebook no. 4.

HMC
ABSpl
ZWpl

*Thomas, Carlette C

Benediction. Anthem. Words by F. B. Whitney; music by Carlette C. Thomas. New York, Galaxy music corp. ⌐c1932⌐ Publ. pl. no. G. M. 573.
6 p. 8 vo.

Score: 5 part chorus for mixed voices (SSATB) with piano reduction for rehearsal only. English words.
Bound in black spiral notebook no. 4.

ABSpl

*Thomas, Millard G

He burns me up! And he knocks me cold! ⌐Popular song⌐ Words by Bob Joffe; music by Millard G. Thomas. New York, *Handy brothers music co., inc. ⌐c1929⌐
5 p. fol.

Score: medium solo voice with piano accompaniment. English words.

ABSpl

*Thomas, Millard G

On a mountain trail. ⌊Popular song⌋ Lyric by Oliver King; music by Millard G. Thomas. New York, King music publishing co. ⌊c1934⌋
5 p. fol.

Score: medium solo voice with piano accompaniment. English words.

ABSpl

---

*Thomas, Millard G

There's a castle in Spain. ⌊Popular song⌋ Lyric by Gus Schilling; music by Millard Thomas. New York, King music publishing co., ⌊c1934⌋
5 p. fol.

Score: medium solo voice with piano accompaniment. English words.

ABSpl

---

*Thomas, Millard G

Waltz time is dream time (when you'r in love.) ⌊Popular song.⌋ Lyric by Gus Schilling; music by Millard G. Thomas. New York, King music publishing co., ⌊c1934⌋
5 p. fol.

Score: medium solo voice with piano accompaniment. English words.

ABSpl

---

*Thompson, James DeKoven, 1878-1934.

...Dear Lord, remember me. Sacred song; composed by James DeKoven Thompson. Chicago, Lyon & Healy, ⌊c1897⌋
5 p. fol.

Score: medium solo voice with piano accompaniment ⌊key of E♭⌋ English words.

Cover title page has photograph of composer who at that time was the organist of the St. Thomas Church in Chicago.

ABSpl LC ZWpl

---

*Thompson, James DeKoven, 1878-1934.

Goodnight sweetheart. ⌊Ballad⌋ lyric by *Alfred Anderson; music by DeKoven Thompson. Chicago, Will Rossiter, c1911.
5 p. fol.

Score: medium solo voice with piano accompaniment⌊key of Eb⌋ English words.

ABSpl LC

---

*Thompson, James DeKoven, 1878-1934.

...The home beyond. Sacred song. By DeKoven Thompson. Chicago, Lyon and Healy, ⌊c1915⌋
5 p. fol.

Score: medium solo voice with piano accompaniment⌊key of B♭⌋ English words.

"To my friend Mr. George H. Webster" — at head of title.

ABSpl LC

---

*Thompson, James DeKoven, 1878-1934.

If I forget. ⌊Song⌋ Words by *Alfred Anderson; music by DeKoven Thompson. Chicago, Harold Rossiter music co., ⌊c1911⌋
5 p. fol.

Score: low solo voice with piano accompaniment ⌊key of C⌋ English words.

"As featured by Mmd Schumann-Heink" — title page.

ABSpl LC

---

*Thompson, James DeKoven, 1878-1934.

I love you dear. ⌊Song⌋ lyrics by G. Franklin Proctor and *Alfred Anderson; music by DeKoven Thompson. New York, Whitney Warner pub. co. ⌊c1915⌋ Publ. pl. no. 29.
5 p. fol.

Score: high solo voice with piano accompaniment⌊key of B♭⌋ English words.

ABSpl LC

---

*Thompson, James DeKoven, 1878-1934.

June will come again. A song of hope...; words by W. H. Hendrickson; music by DeKoven Thompson. New York, G. Schirmer, inc. ⌊c1924⌋ Publ. pl. no. 32674.
5 p. fol.

Score: high solo voice with piano accompaniment. English words.

ABSpl

---

*Thompson, James DeKoven, 1878-1934.

Love comes but once. Song...;lyric by *Alfred Anderson; music by DeKoven Thompson. New York, Jerome H. Remick and co. ⌊c1916⌋ Publ. pl. no. 304.
5 p. fol. (Library edition)

Score: medium solo voice with piano accompaniment⌊key of C⌋ English words.

ABSpl LC

---

*Thompson, James DeKoven, 1878-1934.

...Mandy, w'en you comin' back. Song...; lyric by *Alfred Anderson; music by DeKoven Thompson. New York, Jerome H. Remick and co., c1916 Publ. pl. no. 302.
5 p. fol. (Library edition)

Score: medium solo voice with piano accompaniment ⌊key of F⌋ Negro dialect.

ABSpl

---

*Thompson, James DeKoven, 1878-1934.

When I think of home and you. Ballad. Lyric by *Alfred Anderson; melody by DeKoven Thompson. Chicago, Will Rossiter, c1910.
5 p. fol.

Score: v medium solo voice with piano accompaniment; chorus also arranged for male quartet (TTBB) or mixed (SATB) ⌊key of A♭⌋ English words.

ABSpl

---

*Thompson, James DeKoven, 1878-1934.

When tomorrow comes. Popular song ; words by Russel Smith; music by DeKoven Thompson and *Alfred Anderson. Chicago, Will Rossiter, c1912.
5 p. fol.

Score: medium solo voice with piano accompaniment ⌊key of B♭⌋ English words.

ABSpl LC

---

*Thompson, James DeKoven, 1878-1934.

Your heart. Ballad. Lyric by Benjamin Blood; melody by DeKoven Thompson... Chicago, Harold Rossiter music co., ⌊c1913⌋
4 p. fol.

Score: medium solo voice with piano accompaniment ⌊key of F⌋ English words.

"As featured by Viola Victoria" — title page.

ABSpl

Tindley, C A
Some day

---

*Tizol, Juan, 1900-
*Ellington, Edward Kennedy

Pyramid. ⌊Popular song⌋ Words by Irving Gordon and Irving Mills; music by *Duke Ellington and Juan Tizol. New York, Exclusive publications inc., ⌊c1938⌋
5p. fol.

Score: medium solo voice ⌊key of A♭⌋ with piano accompaniment. English words.

ABSpl

---

*Trent, Joe

'Cause I feel low-down. ⌊Popular song⌋ Words by Jo' Trent; music by Peter DeRose. New York, Irvin Berlin, inc. ⌊c1928⌋
5 p. fol.

Score: medium solo voice with piano accompaniment. English words.

ABSpl

---

*Trent, Joe

Dixie dawn. A Southern fox-trot song. Words by Joe Trent; music by Peter DeRose. New York, Leo. Feist, inc. ⌊c1928⌋ Publ. pl. no. 6073.
5 p. fol.

Score: medium solo voice with piano accompaniment. English words.

ABSpl

Trent, Joe
De Rose, Peter
Easy goin'

Trent, Joe
De Rose, Peter
Either you do or you don't

Trent, Joe
De Rose, Peter
Georgia pines

Trent, Joe
Here you come with love

*Trent, Joe

Muddy water (A Mississippi moan). ⌐Popular song⌐ Words by "Jo" Trent; music by Peter De Rose and Harry Richman. New York, Broadway music corp. ⌐c1926⌐
5 p. fol.

Score: medium solo voice with piano accompaniment. Negro dialect.

ABSpl

Troy, Henry
Who broke the lock off the hen house door

*Trent, Joe

I don't know nobody, and nobody knows me... ⌐Popular song.⌐ Words and music by "Jo" Trent and Will Donaldson. New York, Fred Fisher, inc. ⌐c1924⌐
5 p. fol.

Score: medium solo voice with piano accompaniment. English words.

Featured by *Miller and Lyles in the musical comedy "Running Wild" -- cover title.

LC
ABSpl

Trent, Joe
Alter, Louis
My kinda love (2 copies)

Lyric by Jo Trent

*Turner, Lucy Mae

Set God's heaven on fire. Negro spiritual. Words and music by Lucy M. Turner. East St. Louis, Ill., Lucy M. Turner publisher ⌐c1931⌐
5 p. fol.

Score: SATB, with piano accompaniment. English words.

ABSpl

*Trent, Joe

I just roll along having my ups and downs. ⌐Popular song⌐ By Jo' Trent and Peter DeRose. New York, Irving Berlin inc. ⌐c1927⌐
5 p. fol.

Score: medium solo voice with piano accompaniment. English words.

ABSpl

Trent, Joe
De Rose, Peter
No one but you knows how to love

*Turpin, Tom

...Bowery Buck. Ragtime two step. Arranged by D. S. De Lisle; composed by Tom Turpin. St. Louis, Mo., Rob't De Yong & co. ⌐c1899⌐
5 p. fol.

Score: piano solo.

"Published also for orchestra."

LC
ABSpl

Trent, Joe
Chase, Newell
I want it sweet like you

Lyrics by Jo Trent

*Trent, Joe

Pinin' for dat freedom day. ⌐A spiritual song⌐ Words and music by Jo' Trent. New York, Harms, inc., ⌐c1930⌐ Publ. pl. no. C.H. 8035.
6 p. fol. 2 copies

Score: medium solo voice ⌐key of F⌐ with piano accompaniment. Negro dialect.

ABSpl
NBCL-string quintet (oboe, horn, viba ad.lib.) harmonium and piano accompaniment arr. by T. Jarecki.

*Turpin, Tom

The St. Louis rag. ⌐For orchestra⌐ By Tom Turpin; arranged by Lee Orean Smith. New York, Emil A. Scher, inc. ⌐c1903⌐
2 p. 10 pts. 8°.

Score: piano-conductor; and parts for dance orchestra.

ABSpl

*Trent, Joe

Lazy weather. A slow easy goin' fox-trot. By Jo' Trent and Peter DeRose. New York, Leo. Feist, inc. ⌐c1927⌐ Publ. pl. no. 5970.
5 p. fol.

Score: medium solo voice with piano accompaniment. English words.

ABSpl

Trent, Joe
Carmichael, Hoagy
Sing it way down low

Twenty songs of Harlem. Introducing favorite songs of Ethel Waters, Bert Williams, Bill (Bojangles) Robinson, Duke Ellington, Cab Calloway, Louis Armstrong, Thomas (Fats) Waller... New York, Shapiro, Bernstein and co., inc. ⌐c1938⌐
63 p. fol.

Score: solo voice with piano accompaniment. English words or Negro dialect.

(continued on next card)

*Trent, Joe

Linda. ⌐Popular song⌐ Words by Charlie Tobias and Jo' Trent; music by Peter DeRose. New York, Joe Morris music co., ⌐c1931⌐
5 p. fol.

Score: medium solo voice with piano accompaniment. English words.

ABSpl

Trent, Joe
Robison, Willard
Wake up, chill'un wake up

Twenty songs of Harlem... (Card 2)

Contents: 1. Memories of you. 2. I want a little girl. 3. Somebody else, not me. 4. The moon shines on the moonshine. 5. Royal garden blues. 6. Bessie couldn't help it. 7. Don't cry, little girl, don't cry. 8. You're lucky to me. 9. Loving you the way I do. 10. Headin' for Harlem. 11. Lawd, you made the night too long. 12. Princess Nicotine. 13. The man from the South. 14. Cinderella Brown. 15. Just a crazy song. 16. I ain't gonna give nobody none of this jelly roll.

ABSpl

Trent, Joe
De Rose, Peter
Lazy weather

*Trent, Joe

Yes she do, no she don't. (I'm satisfied with my girl) ⌐Popular song⌐ Words by Jo' Trent; music by Peter De Rose. New York, Broadway music corp., ⌐c1927⌐
5 p. fol.

Score: medium solo voice with piano accompaniment. English words.

ABSpl

Tyers, William H
Deas, Lawrence
All I want is ma chickens

Tyers, William H
Aunt Mandy's wedding march

---

*Tyers, William H 1870-

Dance of the Philippines. Characteristic. By Wm. H. Tyers. New York, F. A. Mills, ⌞c1898⌟
6p. fol.

Score: piano solo.

ABSpl

Tyers, William H
Forest and stream

---

*Tyers, William H 1870-

Love's menu. (Menu d' amour). Intermezzo. By Wm. H. Tyers. New York, M. Witmark & sons. ⌞c1906⌟ Publ. pl. no. M. W. & sons 7497.
7p. fol.

Score: piano solo.

ABSpl
LC

---

*Tyers, William H 1870-

Maori. A Samoan song. Adapted from the instrumental number. "Maori, a Samoan dance. Words by*Henry S. Creamer; music by Wm. H. Tyers...New York, Waterson Berlin & Snyder co., ⌞c1909⌟
5p. fol.

Score: low solo voice ⌞key of C⌟ with piano accompaniment. English words.

ABSpl

---

*Tyers, William H 1870-

La Mariposa (The butterfly.) Dance characteristic. By Wm. H. Tyers. New York, Jos. W. Stern & co., ⌞c1899⌟
5p. fol.

Score: piano solo.

ABSpl

---

*Tyers, William H 1870-

Scene de ballet. Polka mazurka (Yorke) By Wm. H. Tyers. New York, F. A. Mills, c1898.
6p. fol.

Score: piano solo.

ABSpl

Tyers, William H
Summer moon

---

*Tyers, William H 1870-

Trocha. The official tango. By Wm. H. Tyers. New York, F. A. Mills, ⌞c1913⌟
5p. fol.

Score: piano solo.

ABSpl

---

*Tyler, Jesse Gerald

Good-night. ⌞Song.⌟ Words by *Paul Laurence Dunbar; ⌞music by⌟ Gerald Tyler. New York, G. Ricordi, inc. ⌞c1921⌟ Publ. pl. no. 30266.
5p. fol.

Score: medium solo voice ⌞key of G⌟ with piano accompaniment. English words.
Caption title.

To Roland Hayes.

LC
ABSpl
HMC

---

*Tyler, Jesse Gerald

...Ships that pass in the night. ⌞Song.⌟ Words by *Paul Laurence Dunbar; music by Gerald Tyler. New York, G. Schirmer, inc. ⌞c1921⌟ Publ. pl. no. 30265.
5p. fol.

Score: medium solo voice with piano accompaniment. English words.
Caption title.

HMC
ABSpl
LC

---

*Tyler, Jesse Gerald

Syrian lullaby. ⌞Song. Words by⌟ Alice Cunningham music by Gerald Tyler. New York, G. Schirmer, inc. ⌞c1921⌟ Publ. pl. no. 30264.
3p. fol.

Score: medium solo voice ⌞key of G⌟ with piano accompaniment. English words.
Caption Title

LC
HMC
ABSpl

---

*Tyler, Jesse Gerald

Three songs for low or medium voice with piano accompaniment. By Gerald Tyler...New York, G. Schirmer, inc. ⌞c1921⌟ Publ. pl. nos. 30264-66.
3v. fol.

Scores: solo voice with piano accompaniment. English words.

Contents: 1. Ships that pass in the night. 2. Syrian lullaby. 3. Good-night.

ABSpl
LC
HMC

---

*Vaughan, James J

Manyanna. ⌞Popular song⌟ Lyrics by S. Tutt Whitney and J. Homer Tutt; music by Jas. J. Vaughan. New York, Jos. W. Stern & co., ⌞c1915⌟ Publ. pl. no. 8038.
5 p. fol.

Score: medium solo voice with piano accompaniment. English words.

In the musical comedy, "George Washington Bullion Abroad."
ABSpl

---

*Vaughan, James J

Me an' da minstrel ban'. ⌞Popular song⌟ Words by *Alex Rogers; music by James Vaughan. New York, Attucks music publ. co. ⌞c1904⌟
5 p. fol.

Score: medium solo voice with piano accompaniment. Negro dialect.

ABSpl

---

*Vodery, William Henry Bennett, 1885-

All for you. Song. Words by Harold Robe; music by W. H. Vodery... New York, G. Ricordi and co. ⌞c1920⌟ Publ. pl. no. N.Y.33.
6 p. fol.

Score: high solo voice with piano accompaniment ⌞key of C⌟ English words.

ABSpl LC

Vodery, Will Henry Bennett
But where

Vodery, Will Henry Bennett
Carolina fox trot

Vodery, Will Henry Bennett
Cruel and brutal

---

*Vodery, Will Henry Bennett, 1885-
*Williams, Egbert Austin
The darktown poker club. ⌞Popular song⌟ Words by Jean Havez; music by *Bert Williams and Will H. Vodery. New York, Jerome H. Remick & co. ⌞c1914⌟
5 p. fol.

Score: medium solo voice with piano accompaniment. English words.

ABSpl
NBCL - arranged for full orchestra by Bial, Mackie, and Gerstle.

---

*Vodery, William Henry Bennett, 1885-

O, let us sing (a new song.) Popular song ... Lyrics by *Noble Sissle; music by Will H. Vodery... New York, Handy bros. music co., inc. ⌞c1934⌟
3 p. fol.

Score: medium solo voice with piano accompaniment. English words.

"As sung in the Chicago World's Fair Pageant, 'O, sing a new song', by Noble Sissle and Onah L. Spencer, presenting the works of the

(continued on next card)

*Vodery, William Henry Bennett, 1885- (Card 2)

O, let us sing...

following composers: *Harry T. Burleigh, *Will Marion Cook, *Harry Lawrence Freeman, *William C. Handy, *J. Rosamond Johnson, *Major N. Clark Smith, *William Grant Still, and *Will H. Vodery." — at end of title.

ABSpl LC ZWpl

Von Tilzer, Albert

Teasing. Popular song Words by *Cecil Mack pseud music by Albert von Tilzer. New York, The York music co. [c1904]

5 p. fol.

Score: medium solo voice with piano accompaniment. English words.

ABSpl

---

*Walker, George W 1873-1911.
*Williams, Egbert Austin

...I don't like no cheap man. [Popular song] Words and music by *[Egbert Austin] Williams and Walker; arranged by *W. H. Tyers. New York, Jos. W. Stern & co. [c1897]

5 p. fol.

Score: medium solo voice [key of E] with piano accompaniment. Negro dialect.

ABSpl
FMC
LC

---

*Walker, George W 1873-1911.
*Williams, Egbert Austin

If you love your baby make goo goo eyes. Or, "The game of goo-goo eyes." [Popular song] Words and music by *[Egbert Austin] Williams and Walker. New York, Hurtig & Seamon pub. [c1900]

5 p. fol.

Score: medium solo voice with piano accompaniment. English words.

ABSpl

---

*Walker, George W 1873-1911.
*Williams, Egbert Austin

...Look out dar down below. [Popular song] Words and music by *[Egbert Austin] Williams and Walker. New York, W. B. Gray & co. [c1897]

5 p. fol.

Score: medium solo voice with piano accompaniment. Negro dialect.

ABSpl
LC

---

*Walker, George W 1873-1911.
*Williams, Egbert Austin

...The medicine man. [Popular song] Words and music by *[Egbert Austin] Williams and Walker. New York, Jos. W. Stern & co. [c1899] Publ. pl. no. 1097.

5 p. fol.

Score: low solo voice [key of F] with piano accompaniment. Negro dialect.

ABSpl
LC

---

*Walker, George W 1873-1911.
*Williams, Egbert Austin

...Snap shot Sal. [Popular song] Written and composed by *[EGbert Austin] Williams and Walker. [Published as a] Supplement to the New York World Sunday, October 1, 1899. [c1899]

4 p. fol.

Score: medium solo voice with piano accompaniment. Negro dialect.

"Composed expressly for the New York Sunday World." Head of title.

ABSpl

---

*Walker, George W 1873-1911.
*Williams, Egbert Austin

...When it's all goin' out and nothin' comin' in... [Popular song] Words and music by *[Egbert Austin] Williams and Walker; words revised by *James W. Johnson. New York, Jos. W. Stern & co. [c1902] Publ. pl. no. 3346.

6 p. fol.

Score: medium solo voice with piano accompaniment. Negro dialect.

"New song hits introduced by Williams and Walker's own big co." - Head of title.

ABSpl LC

---

*Walker, George W 1873-1911.
*Williams, Egbert Austin

..."When Miss Maria Johnson marries me." [Popular song] Words and music by *[Egbert Austin] Williams and Walker... New York, Spaulding & Gray pub. [c1896]

5 p. fol.

Score: medium solo voice with piano accompaniment. Negro dialect.

ABSpl
LC

---

*Walker, George W 1873-1911.
*Williams, Egbert Austin

...Why don't you get a lady of your own. [Popular song] By *[Egbert Austin] Williams and Walker. New York, Jos. W. Stern & co. [c1898] Publ. pl. no. 610.

6 p. fol.

Score: medium solo voice [key of C] with piano accompaniment. Negro dialect.

Title page has portraits of the composers.

ABSpl
LC

Walker, Marshall
Who calls you sweet mama now?

---

*Waller, Thomas, 1904-1944.

Ain't-cha glad, [Popular song] Words by *Andy Razaf; music by Thomas Waller. New York: Keit-Engel, inc. [c1933]

3p. fol.

Score: medium solo voice [key of G] with piano accompaniment. English words.

LC
ABSpl

---

*Waller, Thomas, 1904-1944.

Ain't misbehavin' (I'm saving my love for you). [Popular song] Words by *Andy Razaf; music by Thomas Waller and Harry Brooks. New York: Mills Music Inc. [c1929]

5p. fol.

Score: medium solo voice [key of E^b] with piano accompaniment. English words.

WOEL
ABSpl
NYPLS
YJWJ

Waller, Thomas "Fats"
All that meat and no potatoes

---

*Waller, Thomas, 1904-1944.

...Alligator crawl. (Novelty fox-trot) [Popular song] Words by *Andy Razaf and Joe Davis; Music by Thomas "Fats" Waller. New York; Joes Davis, Inc., [c1937] Publ. pl. no. 3750.

5p. fol.

Score: medium solo voice [key of C] with piano accompaniment. English words.

ABSpl
LC

Waller, Thomas "Fats"
Angeline

Waller, Thomas "Fats"
Anita

---

*Waller, Thomas, 1904-1944.

Blue, turning grey over you. [Popular song] Words by *Andy Razaf; music by Thomas Waller. New York: Triangle music publ. Co. [c1930]

5p. fol.

Score: medium solo voice [key of C] with piano accompaniment. English words.

ABSpl
LC

Waller, Thomas "Fats"
Buddie

---

*Waller, Thomas, 1904-1944.
*Williams, Spencer

Charleston hound... [Popular song] Words by *Spencer Williams and Eddie Rector; music by *Clarence Williams and Thomas "Fat" Waller...New York, Clarence Williams music pub. co., inc. [c1926]

5 p. fol.

Score: medium solo voice with piano accompaniment. Negro dialect.

ABSpl

Waller, Thomas "Fats"
Choo choo

*Waller, Thomas, 1904-1944.

Concentratin' (on you) [Popular song] Words by *Andy Razaf; music by Thomas Waller. New York: Santly bros. inc. [c1931.]
5p. fol.

Score: medium solo voice [key of E♭] with piano accompaniment. English words.

YJWJ
ABSpl
LC

*Waller, Thomas, 1904-1944.

Honeysuckle Rose. [Popular song] Lyric by *Andy Razaf; music by Thomas Waller. New York: Santly bros. inc. [c1929]
5p. fol.

Score: medium solo voice with piano accompaniment. English words.

ABSpl

Waller, Thomas "Fats"
Inside this heart of mine

*Waller, Thomas, 1904-1944.

Dixie Cinderella. [Popular song] Lyric by *Andy Razaf; music by Thomas Waller and Harry Brooks. New York: Mills music, inc. [c1929.]
5p. fol.

Score: medium solo voice with piano accompaniment. English words.

ABSpl

*Waller, Thomas, 1904-1944.
*Williams, Clarence Augustus

I can see you all over the place. [Popular song] By *Clarence Williams and Thomas "Fats" Waller. New York: *Clarence Williams music pub. co., inc. [c1926] Publ. pl. no. 1143.
3p. fol.

Score: medium solo voice [key of F] with piano accompaniment. English words.

LC
ABSpl

*Waller, Thomas, 1904-1944.
Link, Harry

I've got a feeling I'm falling. [Popular song] By Billy Rose, Harry Link and Thomas Waller. New York: Santly bros., inc. [c1929.]
5p. fol.

Score: medium solo voice with piano accompaniment. English words.

ABSpl

Waller, Thomas "Fats"
Doin' what I please

*Waller, Thomas, 1904-1944.

I didn't dream it was love. [Popular song] Words and music by Elliot Grennard, Thomas Waller and Con Conrad. New York, Harms inc. [c1932] Publ. pl. no. C 8831.
5 p. fol.

Score: medium solo voice [key of G] with piano accompaniment. English words.

ABSpl

*Waller, Thomas, 1904-1944.

Keep a song in your soul. [Popular song.] Words and music by Thomas Waller and *Alexander Hill. New York: Joe Davis inc., [c1930] Publ. pl. no. 1034.
5p. fol.

Score: medium solo voice with piano accompaniment. English words.

ABSpl

*Waller, Thomas, 1904-1944.
*Razafkeriefo, Paul Andrea

Gone. [Popular song] By Harry Link, *Andy Razaf and Thomas Waller. New York: Santly bros. inc. [c1930]
5p. fol.

Score medium solo voice [key of E♭] with piano accompaniment. English words.

ABSpl
LC

*Waller, Thomas, 1904-1944.
*Razafkeriefo, Paul Andrea

If it ain't love. [Popular song] Words and music by *Andy Razaf. *Donald Redman and Thomas Waller. New York, Radio music co., inc. [c1932]
5 p. fol.

Score: medium solo voice with piano accompaniment. English words.

ABSpl

*Waller, Thomas, 1904-1944.

Keepin' out of mischief now. [Popular song] Words by *Andy Razaf ; music by Thomas Waller. New York: Con Conrad music pub. [c1932] Publ. pl. no. C8785.
5p. fol.

Score: medium solo voice [key of C] with piano accompaniment. English words.

LC
ABSpl

Waller, Thomas "Fats"
Got myself another jockey now

*Waller, Thomas, 1904-1944.
*Williams, Clarence

If you like me (like I like you) [Popular song] By *Clarence Williams, Thomas (Fats) Waller and *Spencer Williams, New York: *Clarence Williams music pub. co., inc. [c1929.]
5p. fol.

Score: medium solo voice with piano accompaniment English words.

ABSpl

*Waller, Thomas, 1904-1944.
*Hill, Alexander

Little Brown Betty. [Popular song] Words and music by *Alex Hill and Fats Waller. New York: Red Star music co. [c1931.]
5p. fol.

Score: medium solo voice [key of B♭] with piano accompaniment. English words.

ABSpl
LC

*Waller, Thomas, 1904-1944.

Gotta be, gonna be mine. [Popular song] Words by *Andy Razaf; music by Thomas Waller. New York: Lawrence music publisher, inc. [c1932]
3p. fol.

Score: medium solo voice [key of E♭] with piano accompaniment. English words.

ABSpl
LC

*Waller, Thomas, 1904-1944.

I'm crazy 'bout my baby (and my baby's crazy 'bout me). Novelty song. Words by *Alexander Hill; music by Thomas Waller. New York: Joe Davis, inc., [c1931] Publ. pl. no. 1040.

Score: medium solo voice [key of E♭] with piano accompaniment. English words.

LC
ABSpl
YJWJ

Waller, Thomas "Fats"
Lonesome me (2 copies)

*Waller, Thomas, 1904-1944.

Heart of stone. [Popular song] Lyric by Alexander Hill; music by Thomas Waller. New York: Walter Donaldson music publishers. [c1931] Publ. pl. no. 110.
5. fol.

Score: medium solo voice [key of E♭] with piano accompaniment. English words.

LC
ABSpl

*Waller, Thomas, 1904-1944.

I'm more than satisfied. [Popular song] Lyric by Ray Klagas; melody by Thomas Waller. New York: Robbins music corp. [c1927] Publ. pl. no. S H 387.
5p. fol.

Score: medium solo voice with piano accompaniment. English words.

ABSpl
YJWJ

*Waller, Thomas, 1904-1944.

Meditation. (Piano solo) By "Fats" Waller. New York: Triangle music pub. co., inc. [c1927]
6p. fol.

Score: piano solo.

ABSpl

*Waller, Thomas, 1904-1944.

Moonlight mood. [Popular song] Lyric by *J.C. Johnson; music by Thomas "Fats" Waller. New York: Mills music inc., [c1938]
5p. fol.

Score: medium solo voice with piano accompaniment. English words.

ABSpl

*Waller, Thomas, 1904-1944.

The panic is on. [Popular song: Words and music by George and Bert Clarke, Winston Tharp and "Fats" Waller. New York: Irving Berlin, inc. [c1938]
5p. fol.

Score: medium solo voice with piano accompaniment. English words.

ABSpl

Waller, Thomas "Fats"
Sittin' up waiting for you

Waller, Thomas "Fats"
Moppin' and boppin'

*Waller, Thomas, 1904-1944.

Prisoner of love. Ballad. Lyric by *Andy Razaf; melody composed by Thomas Waller. New York: Joe Davis, inc. [c1930] Pub. pl. no. 1020.
5p. fol.

Score: medium solo voice [key of C] with piano accompaniment. English words.

ABSpl

*Waller, Thomas, 1904-1944.

Strange as it seems. [Popular song.] Words by *Andy Razaf; music by Thomas Waller. New York: Lawrence music publishers, inc., [c1932]
3p. fol.

Score: medium solo voice [key of E^b] with piano accompaniment. English words.

ABSpl
LC

*Waller, Thomas, 1904-1944.

My fate is in your hands. [Popular song] Lyric by *Andy Razaf; music by Thomas Waller. New York: Santly bros. inc. [c1929]
5p. fol.

Score: medium solo voice [key of F] with piano accompaniment. English words.

ABSpl
LC

*Waller, Thomas, 1904-1944.

Rhythm man. [Popular song] Lyric by *Andy Razaf; music by Thomas Waller and Harry Brooks. New York: Mills music inc. c1929.
5p. fol.

Score: medium solo voice with piano accompaniment. English words.

ABSpl

*Waller, Thomas, 1904-1944.

Sugar Rose. [Popular song.] Words by Phil Ponce; music by "Fats" Waller. New York: Chappell & Co., inc. [c1936] Publ. pl. no. C-574.
5p. fol.

Score: medium solo voice [key of C] with piano accompaniment. English words.

ABSpl
[illegible]

*Waller, Thomas, 1904-1944.

My heart's at ease. [Popular song] Words by Joe Young; music by Thomas Waller. New York: Irving Berlin, inc. [c1932]
5p. fol.

Score: medium solo voice [key of C] with piano accompaniment. English words.

ABSpl
LC

*Waller, Thomas, 1904-1944.

Rollin' down the river. [Popular song] Lyric by R. Stanley Adams; music by Thomas Waller. New York: Santly bros., inc. [c1930]
5p. fol.

Score: medium solo voice with piano accompaniment. English words.

ABSpl
YWJ

*Waller, Thomas, 1904-1944.

Sweet Savannah Sue. [Popular song] Lyric by *Andy Razaf; music by Thomas Waller and Harry Brooks. New York: Mills music, inc., [c1929]
5p. fol.

Score: medium solo voice with piano accompaniment. English words.

ABSpl
ABS

Waller, Thomas "Fats"
Off time

*Waller, Thomas, 1904-1944.

Say it with your feet. [Popular song] Lyric by *Andy Razaf; music by Thomas Waller and Harry Brooks. New York: Mills music inc., [c1929]
5p. fol.

Score: medium solo voice with piano accompaniment. English words.

ABSpl

*Waller, Thomas, 1904-1944.

Swingin' the operas. Contained in this folio are excerpts from the original versions of the operas plus a Fats Waller piano conception of each as played by him in personal appearances and broadcasts all over the country. By Fats Waller. New York: Mills music inc., [c1939]
31p. fol.

Score: piano solos
Contents: Ah! so pure. (From "Martha")
(continued on next card)

*Waller, Thomas, 1904-1944.
*Razafkeriefo, Paul Andrea
On rainy days. [Popular song] By *Andy Razaf and Thomas (Fats) Waller. New York: Mills music, inc. [c1938]
5p. fol.

Score: medium solo voice with piano accompaniment. English words.

ABSpl

*Waller, Thomas, 1904-1944.
*Williams, Clarence Augustus
Senorita Mine. [Popular song. Lyric by *Spencer Williams and Eddie Rector; music by *Clarence Williams and Thomas (Fats) Waller] New York: *Clarence Williams music pub. co., Inc., [c1926]
5p. fol.

Score: medium solo voice with piano accompaniment. English words.

ABSpl

*Waller, Thomas, 1904-1944. -2-

Swingin' the operas, 1939.
Then you'll remember me. (From "The Bohemian girl")
Sextet. (From Lucia di Lammermoor")
My heart at thy sweet voice (From "Samson and Delilah")
Intermezzo (From "Cavalleria Rusticana")
Serenade. (From "Les Millions D'Arlequin")
Ah! I have sighed to rest me. (From "Il Trovatore")
Vesti la giubba. (From "Pagliacci")
(continued on next card)

*Waller, Thomas, 1904-1944.

...Original piano conceptions. A unique folio containing the original versions of songdom's foremost popular classics plus Fats Waller's modern conceptions. By "Fats Waller". New York: Mills music, inc. [n.d.]
31 p. fol.

Score: piano solos.

Contents: Dinah. -Ain't misbehavin'.-Margie.-Girl of my Dreams.-Who's sorry now.-Between the devil and the deep blue sea.-For me and my gal.-Just a girl that men forget.-Mary Lou.-Sweet Mam[illegible]-

ABSpl
LC

*Waller, Thomas, 1904-1944.

Sheltered by the stars, cradled by the moon, covered by the night. [Popular song] Words by Joe Young; music by Thomas Waller. New York: Irving Berlin, inc [c1932.]
5p. fol.

Score: medium solo voice [key of C] with piano accompaniment. English words.

ABSpl
LC

*Waller, Thomas, 1904-1944 -3-

Swingin' the operas, 1939...
Over the summer sea. (From " Rigoletto")
Waltz. (From "Faust")

ZWpl
ABSpl

*Waller, Thomas, 1904-1944.

...Swingtime in Scotland. [A collection of swingtime arrangements of Scotch ballads for the piano, by] "Fats" Waller. New York: Mills music, inc. [c1938]
24p. fol.

Score: medium solo voice with piano accompaniment. for 10 Scotch ballads in original form. English words. Each is followed by composers in swingtime conception for piano.

Contents: 1. Loch Lomond. 2. Annie Laurie.
(Continued on next card)

-2-
*Waller, Thomas, 1904-1944.
...Swingtime in Scotland, 1938...

3. The Campbells are comin'.
4. Comin' thro' the Rye.
5. Auld lang syne.
6. Robin Adair.
7. O my love is like a red, red rose.
8. Charlie is my darling.
9. Bonnie Mary of Argyle.
10. The blue bells of Scotland.

ABSpl

*Waller, Thomas, 1904-1944.

Take it from me-I'm takin' to you. [Popular song] Lyric by R. Stanley Adams; music by Thomas Waller. New York: Santly bros. inc., [c1931.]
5p. fol.

Score: medium solo voice [key of G] with piano accompaniment. English words.

ABSpl
LC
YJWJ

*Waller, Thomas, 1904-1944.

Tall timber. [Popular song] Words by *Andy Razaf; music by Thomas Waller. New York: Miller music inc. [c1933] Publ. pl. no. 184.
5p. fol.

Score: medium solo voice [key of G] with piano accompaniment. English words.

ABSpl
LC

Waller, Thomas "Fats"
That rhythm man

Waller, Thomas "Fats"
There's a man in my life

*Waller, Thomas, 1904-1944.

What did I do to be so black and blue. [Popular song] Lyrics by *Andy Razaf; music by Thomas Waller and Harry Brooks. New York: Mills music inc. [c1929]
5p. fol.

Score: medium solo voice with piano accompaniment. English words.

ABSpl

*Waller, Thomas, 1904-1944.

When Gabriel blows his horn. [Popular song] Words by *Andy Razaf; music by Thomas Waller. New York: Nattrass-Schenck, inc., [c1932.]
3p. fol.

Score: medium solo voice with piano accompaniment English words.

ABSpl

*Waller, Thomas, 1904-1944.
*Razafkeriefo, Paul Andrea
Willow tree. (A musical misery) [Popular song] By *Andy Razaf and Thomas Waller. New York: Harms, inc., [c1928] Publ. pl. no. S-188.

Score: medium solo voice with piano accompaniment. English words.
Caption title.
Excerpt from the musical show, "Keep Shufflin'."

LC
ABSpl

Waller, Thomas "Fats"
Zonky

Warren, Harry

Clementine. (From New Orleans) Popular song Words by *Henry Creamer; music by Harry Warren. New York, Shapiro, Bernstein & co. [c1927]
5 p. fol.

Score: medium solo voice with piano accompaniment. English words.

ABSpl

*Webb, Harry

The clearing house blues. Popular song By Sadie Honesty and Harry Webb. New York, *Harry Webb music pub. co. [c1924]
5 p. fol.

Score: medium solo voice with piano accompaniment. English words.

ABSpl

Weldon, Frank

My pathway of love. (Fox trot song) Words by Andy Razaf; music by Frank Weldon and Anthony Trini. NY: Joe Davis, inc., [c1930] Publ. pl. no. 1009.
5p. fol.

Score: medium solo voice with piano accompaniment. English words.

ABSpl

Weldon, Frank

(You are mine) till the end of the waltz. (Waltz song) Lyric by Andy Razaf; music by Frank Weldon. NY: Joe Davis, inc. [c1931] Publ. pl. no. 1058.
5p. fol.

Score: medium solo voice with piano accompaniment. English words.

ABSpl

* White, Clarence Cameron, 1880-

Bandanna sketches (From Negro spirituals.) By Clarence Cameron White, Op. 12; violin and piano... New York, Carl Fischer, inc. [c1918] Publ. pl. nos. 21176-9.
4 v. fol.
Bound
Scores: violin and piano; and violin parts.

Contents: 1. Chant (Nobody knows de trouble I've seen.) 2. Lament (I'm troubled in mind.)
(Continued on next card)

* White, Clarence Cameron, 1880- (Card 2)

Bandanna sketches...
Contents...
3. Slave song (Many thousand gone.) 4. Negro dance (Sometimes I feel like a motherless child.)

ABSpl LC ZWpl

* White, Clarence Cameron, 1880-

...Bear the burden. Negro spiritual; arranged for voice and piano by Clarence Cameron White... New York, Carl Fischer [c1921] Publ. pl. no. 21945.
5 p. fol. (Sheet music edition V724)
Bound v.
Score: medium solo voice [key of E^b] with piano accompaniment. Negro dialect.

From "Cabin memories."

ABSpl LC ZWpl

* White, Clarence Cameron, 1880-

Cabin song. (From the cotton fields.) For violin and piano By Clarence Cameron White, Op. 18, no. 1; free arrangement for piano solo by Arthur Friedheim. New York, Carl Fischer, inc. [c1927] Publ. pl. no. 24162.
5 p. fol. (Sheet music edition P1582)
Bound v.
Score: piano solo; originally for violin and piano.
Caption title

ABSpl LC ZWpl

* White, Clarence Cameron, 1880-

Camp song (Water boy.) Traditional Negro melody freely transcribed for violin and piano by Clarence Cameron White, Op. 26, no. 1. New York, Carl Fischer, inc. [c1927] Publ. pl. no. 24107.
5 p. fol. (Sheet music ed. B. 2060)
Bound v.
Score: Violin and piano; and violin part.
Caption title.

ABSpl LC

* White, Clarence Cameron, 1880-

...Caprice. By Clarence Cameron White, Op. 17, no. 2. New York, Carl Fischer [c1922] Publ. pl. no. 22435.
5 p. fol.
Bound v.
Score: violin and piano; and violin part.

ABSpl LC

* White, Clarence Cameron, 1880-

Chant (Nobody knows de trouble I've seen.) [From "Bandanna sketches"... by Clarence Cameron White for violin and piano. New York, Carl Fischer [c1918] Publ. pl. no. 21176.
5 p. fol.
Bound v.
Score: violin and piano; and violin part.

ABSpl LC ZWpl

White, Clarence Cameron, 1880-

Compositions by Clarence Cameron White for the pianoforte, Op. 16... Boston, C. W. Thompson and co. [c1919] Publ. pl. nos. 2381, 2402, 2515. 3 v. fol.

Scores: piano solos.

Contents: 1. Improvisation. 2. Kashmiru (oriental sketch.) 3. Dance caprice.

ABSpl - has nos. 1 and 2.
LC

White, Clarence Cameron, 1880- arr.

...I want Jesus to walk with me. Negro spiritual. [Arranged by] Clarence Cameron White. New York, Carl Fischer, inc. [c1940; Publ. pl. no. 28986. 5p. fol. (Sheet music ed. V1485)

Score: medium solo voice with piano accompaniment. English words.

"Dedicated to Miss Marian Anderson."

ABSpl

White, Clarence Cameron, 1880-

Pilgrim song. Based on the Negro spiritual ("Somebody's knocking at your door") [Arranged by] Clarence Cameron White. New York, Carl Fischer, inc. [c1936] Publ. pl. no. 27471. 7 p. fol.

Bound v.
Score: violin and piano; and violin part. Caption title

ABSpl LC ZWpl

White, Clarence Cameron, 1880-

...Compositions for violin and piano. By Clarence Cameron White, New York, Carl Fischer, inc. [c1922] Publ pl nos. 22434-7. 4 v. fol.

Bound v.
Scores: violin and piano; and violin parts.

Contents: 1. Twilight. 2. Caprice 3. Serenade. 4. Valse coquette.

ABSpl LC

White, Clarence Cameron, 1880- arr.

...I'm goin' home. Negro spiritual; arranged for voice and piano by Clarence Cameron White... New York, Carl Fischer, inc. [c1921] Publ Publ. pl. no. 21946. 5 p. fol.

Bound v.
Score: medium solo voice [key of E] with piano accompaniment. Negro dialect.

From "Cabin memories."

ABSpl LC ZWpl

White, Clarence Cameron, 1880-

Plantation song. Based on the Negro spiritual ("Swing low, sweet chariot") [Arranged by] Clarence Cameron White, Op. 27, no. 3 New York, Carl Fischer, inc. [c1936] Publ. pl. no. 27470. 7 p. fol. (Sheet music edition B2347)

Bound v.
Score: Violin and piano; and violin part. Caption title

ABSpl LC ZWpl

White, Clarence Cameron, 1880-

... Concert paraphrases of traditional Negro melodies for violin and piano. By Clarence Cameron White, Op. 27, nos. 1-4. New York, Carl Fischer, inc. [c1927, 1936] Publ. pl. nos. 24107, 24108, 27470, 27471. 4 v. fol.

Bound v.
Scores: violin and piano; and violin parts.

Contents: 1. Camp song (water boy.) 2. Levee dance (go down, Moses. 3. Plantation song (swing low, sweet chariot.)

(continued on next card)

White, Clarence Cameron, 1880-

...Improvisation. [By] Clarence Cameron White, [Op. 16, no. 1] Boston, C. W. Thompson and co. [c1919] Publ. pl. no. T and co. 2381. 7 p. fol.

Score: piano solo.

ABSpl LC

White, Clarence Cameron
Poor little Jesus

White, Clarence Cameron, 1880- (Card 2)

Contents...

4. Pilgrim song (somebody's knocking at your door.)

ABSpl LC

White, Clarence Cameron, 1880-

Lament (I'm troubled in mind.) [From] "Bandanna sketches"... by Clarence Cameron White for violin and piano. New York, Carl Fischer [c1918] Publ. pl. no. 21177. 5 p. fol.

Bound v.
Score: violin and piano; and violin part.

ABSpl LC ZWpl

White, Clarence Cameron, 1880-

Reflets. For the pianoforte. By Clarence Cameron White, Op. 24, no. 1 Philadelphia, Theodore Presser co. [c1925] Publ. pl. no. 22928. 3 p. fol.

Bound v.
Score: piano solo.

ABSpl LC

White, Clarence Cameron, 1880- arr.

... Down by de ribber side. Negro spiritual: Arranged for voice and piano by Clarence Cameron White. New York, Carl Fischer, inc. [c1921] Publ. pl. no. 21947. 5 p. fol.

Bound v.
Score: medium solo voice [key of F] with piano accompaniment. Negro dialect.

From "Cabin memories."

ABSpl LC ZWpl

White, Clarence Cameron, 1880-

Levee dance. Based on the Negro spiritual ("Go down Moses") [Arranged by] Clarence Cameron White, Op. 26, no. 2. New York, Carl Fischer, inc. [c1927] Publ. pl. no. 24108. 9 p. fol.

Bound v.
Score: violin and piano; and violin part. Caption title

ABSpl LC ZWpl

White, Clarence Cameron, 1880-

...Scotch Idyl. [By] Clarence Cameron White, Op. 26. New York, Carl Fischer, inc. [c1925] Publ. pl. no. 23411. 8 p. fol. (Sheet music edition B1891)

Bound v.
Score: violin and piano; and violin part.

ABSpl LC

White, Clarence Cameron, 1880-

...From the cotton fields. For violin with pianoforte accompaniment. By Clarence Cameron White, Op. 18; freely arranged for piano solo by Arthur Friedheim. New York, Carl Fischer, inc. [c1927] Publ. pl. nos. 24162-4. 3 v. fol.

Bound v.
Scores: piano solos.

Contents: 1. Cabin song. 2. On the Bayou. 3. Spiritual.

ABSpl LC ZWpl

White, Clarence Cameron, 1880-

Negro dance (sometimes I feel like a motherless child.) [From] "Bandanna sketches."... by Clarence Cameron White for violin and piano. New York, Carl Fischer [c1918] Publ. pl. no. 21179. 7 p. fol.

Bound v.
Score: violin and piano; and violin part.

ABSpl LC ZWpl

White, Clarence Cameron, 1880-

Sérénade. [By] Clarence Cameron White, Op. 17, no. 3. New York, Carl Fischer [c1922] Publ. pl. no. 22436. 5 p. fol.

Bound v.
Score: violin and piano; and violin part.

ABSpl LC

White, Clarence Cameron, 1880-

Hush, mah honey. Cradle song...Words by Helen Boardman Knox; music by Clarence Cameron White. Boston, C. W. Thompson & co. [c1920; Publ. pl. no. T & co. 2601. 5 p. fol.

Bound v.
Score: low solo voice [key of G] with piano accompaniment. Negro dialect.

ABSpl
LC

White, Clarence Cameron, 1880-

On the Bayou. (From the cotton fields.) For violin and piano By Clarence Cameron White, Op. 18, no. 2; free arrangement for piano solo by Arthur Friedheim. New York, Carl Fischer, inc. [c1927] Publ. pl. no. 24163. 5 p. fol. (Sheet music edition P1583)

Bound v.
Score: piano solo; originally for violin and piano. Caption title

ABSpl LC ZWpl

White, Clarence Cameron, 1880-

Slave song (many thousand gone.) [From] "Bandanna sketches."... by Clarence Cameron White for violin and piano. New York, Carl Fischer [c1918] Publ. pl. no. 21178. 5 p. fol.

Bound v.
Score: violin and piano; and violin part.

ABSpl LC ZWpl

* White, Clarence Cameron, 1880-

Spiritual. (From the cotton fields.) By Clarence Cameron White, Op. 18, no. 3. New York, Carl Fischer, inc. [c1920] Publ. pl. no. 21808.
5 p. fol. (Sheet music edition B1201.)

Bound v.
Score: Violin and piano; and violin part.
Caption title
Based on the spiritual: "Poor mourner's got a home at last!"

ABSpl LC ZWpl

* White, Clarence Cameron, 1880-

Tambour. (Haitian meringue). By Clarence Cameron White for piano. New York, Carl Fischer, inc. [c1930] Publ. pl. no. 25819.
7 p. fol.
Bound v.
Score: piano solo.

ABSpl LC

* White, Clarence Cameron, 1880- arr.

Traditional Negro spirituals. Twenty concert and community choruses for mixed voices (a cappella). Arranged by Clarence Cameron White. New York, Carl Fischer, inc. [c1940] Publ. pl. no. 28854.
23 p. 8°

Score: SATB. Negro dialect.

Contents: 1. Can I ride? 2. Cert'nly Lord! 3. Down by the river-side.

(continued on next card)

* White, Clarence Cameron, 1880- (Card 2)

Contents...
4. Every time I feel the spirit. 5. Get on board, little children. 6. Hear the good news! 7. I got a robe. 8. I heard of a city called heaven. 9. In that great gettin' up mornin'. 10. I want Jesus to walk with me. 11. Look away. 12. Lonesome valley. 13. Lord, hear me prayin'. 14. Old time religion. 15. Ride on Jesus. 16. Steal away. 17. Trouble will bring you down. 18. Walk together children. 19. We are climbing Jacob's ladder. 20. Were you there?

ZWpl

* White, Clarence Cameron, 1880-

...Triumphal march. By Clarence Cameron White, Op. 30. Philadelphia, Theodore Presser co. c1927 Publ. pl. no. 23547.
5 p. fol.
Bound v.
Score: piano solo.

ABSpl LC

* White, Clarence Cameron, 1880-

...Twilight. [By Clarence Cameron White, Op. 17, no. 1. New York, Carl Fischer [c1922] Publ. pl. no. 22434.
5 p. fol.
Bound v.
Score: Violin and piano; and violin part.

ABSpl LC

* White, Clarence Cameron, 1880-

Valse coquette. [By] Clarence Cameron White, Op. 17, no. 4. New York, Carl Fischer [c1922] Publ. pl. no. 22437.
5 p. fol.
Bound v.
Score: violin and piano; and violin part.

ABSpl LC

*White, Clarence Cameron, 1880-

The violinist's daily dozen. Twelve special studies for the development of correct finger action in violin playing, by Clarence Cameron White. Chicago, Gamble hinged music co. [c1924] Publ. pl. no. 697.
6 p. fol.

Score: exercises (unaccompanied) for violin.

ABSpl
LC

*White, Joseph, 1830-1890.

Jeunesse. Habanera. Pour deux ou quatre violons (ad libit)... Par Joseph White, Op. 29... Paris, Rene Gilles [c1897] Publ. pl. no. U.T.W. 352.
5 p. fol.

Score: violin and piano; and parts for 2 or 4 violins (ad lib.)

ABSpl LC NYPLS
ZWpl

*White, Joseph, 1830-1890.

...La Jota Aragonesa. Caprice. Pour le violon avec accompagnement de piano. [Par] Joseph White, Op. 5. Paris, Choudens [n.d.] Publ. pl. no. G.G. 1596.
12 p. fol.

Score: violin and piano; and violin part.

Dedication: "A sa Majeste Catholique Isabelle II, Reine d'Espagne." — at head of title.

ABSpl

*White, Joseph, 1830-1890.

Romance sans paroles. 2me. Pour le violon avec accompagnement de piano. Par Joseph White, Op. 8. New York, Edward Schuberth and co. [n.d.] Publ. pl. no. 716.
6 p. fol.

Score: violin and piano; with violin part.

ABSpl

*White, Joseph, 1830-1890.

...Six etudes pour violon. Par Joseph White, Op. 13. Paris, Lemoine et fils, editeurs. [ca.1868] Publ. pl. no. S.2936.
21 p. fol.

Score: violin part only.

ABSpl

*White, Joseph, 1830-1890.

...Styrienne. Morceau de concert. Pour le violon avec accompt. de piano. Par Joseph White, Op. 11... London, Schott et co. [n.d.] Publ. pl. no. E. C. 4460.
13 p. fol. 2 copies

Score: violin and piano; and violin part.

Dedication: "A mon ami, Aime Gros, 2nd edition"— at head of title.

ABSpl

*White, Joseph, 1830-1890.

...Troisieme. Romance sans paroles. Pour violon and piano. Par Joseph White, Op. 18. Paris, Heugel and Cie,[n.d.] Publ. pl. no. H et Cie 9656.
5 p. fol. 2 copies

Score: violin and piano; and violin part.

ABSpl

White, Joseph
Valse Caprice. Violon avec accomp. de piano. Op. 23

*White, Joseph, 1830-1890.

...Violinesque. Pour violon... Par J. White, Op. 32. Paris, Ulysse T. du Wast, editeur, [n.d.] Publ. pl. no. U.T.W. 377.
15 p. fol.

Score: violin and piano; and violin part.

ABSpl

*White, Joseph, 1830-1890.

...Zamacueca. Danse Chilienne. Pour violon avec accompt. de piano. Par Joseph White, Op. 30. Paris, Rene Gilles, c1897. Publ. pl. no. U.T.W. 354.
7 p. fol.

Score: violin and piano; an violin part.

ABSpl

White, Newman Ivey

American Negro folk-songs. By Newman I. White... Cambridge, Harvard University press [c1928]
501 p. 24½cm.

Includes music: text only for "more than 800 songs"; unaccompanied melody for 15 "specimen tunes" (p. 406-412)
Bibliography (p. 469 --480)
This volume is a good discussion on origin and development of Negro songs, with an excellent bibliography.
LC HMC
NYPLS
BHS

*Whitman, Alberta

Think of me little Daddy. [Popular song] By Bert Whitman. New York, "Pace and Handy music co., inc. [c1919]
3 p. fol.

Score: medium solo voice with piano accompaniment. English words.

ABSpl

Willet, Chappie
Let my people go, now.

Lyrics by Langston Hughes

*Williams, Charles H

Charleston. Characteristic Negro dance. (In Williams, Charles H., Cotton needs pickin'. Norfolk, Va. 1928.)

Score: piano solo.

Illustrations of the dance steps for this piece are by *Hampton Institute students.

ABSpl
NYPLS

*Williams, Charles H

"Cotton needs pickin'." Characteristic Negro folk dances. ⌐Norfolk, Va., The Guide publishing co., c1928¬ 24 p. fol.

Score: 7 piano solos.

Contents: Cotton needs pickin'. -2. Plantation days. -3. Charleston. -4. Going up the mountain. -5. Granddaddy is dead. -6. Go in and out the window. -7. Peep squirrel.

ABSpl NYPLS

*Williams, Clarence Agustus, 1893-

Baby, won't you please come home. ⌐Popular song¬ Words and music by Clarence Williams and Chas. Warfield. New York, *Clarence Williams music pub. co., inc. ⌐c1930¬ 5 p. fol.

Score: medium solo voice with piano accompaniment. English words.

ABSpl

*Williams, Clarence Agustus, 1893-
*Williams, Spencer

I ain't gonna give nobody none o' this jelly roll. Jazz song. By *Spencer Williams and Clarence Williams...New York, Shapiro Bernstein & co. ⌐c1919¬ 3 p. fol.

Score: medium solo voice with piano accompaniment. English words.

ABSpl

*Williams, Charles H

Cotton needs pickin'. A work song arranged by *R. Nathaniel Dett.
(In Williams, Charles H., Cotton needs pickin'. Norfolk, Va. 1928.)

Score: piano solo.

Illustrations of the dance steps for this piece are by *Hampton Institute students.

ABSpl
NYPLS

Williams, Clarence
Beer garden blues

*Williams, Clarence, 1893-

I can see you all over the place. ⌐Popular song¬ By Clarence Williams and *Thomas "Fats" Waller. New York: Clarence Williams music pub. co., inc. c1926 Publ. pl. no. 1143.
3p. fol.

Score: medium solo voice ⌐key of F¬ with piano accompaniment. English words.

LC
ABSpl

*Williams, Charles H

Go in and out the window. A singing game. Characteristic Negro dance.
(In Williams, Charles H., Cotton needs pickin'. Norfolk, Va. 1928.)

Score: piano solo.

The dance steps for this piece are illustrated by *Hampton Institute students.

ABSpl
NYPLS

*Williams, Clarence Agustus, 1893-

...The Brown Bomber, the kid from Alabam'. ⌐Popular song¬ Words and music by Dan Dougherty, *Walter Bishop and Clarence Williams. New York, *Clarence Williams music pub. co., ⌐c1935¬
3 p. fol.

Score: medium solo voice ⌐key of F¬ with piano accompaniment. English words.

Caption title: "Look out for the Brown Bomber, the kid from Alabam'".

(continued on next card)

Williams, Clarence
I can't think of anything but you

*Williams, Charles H

Going up the mountain. A singing game. Characteristic Negro dance.
(In Williams, Charles H., Cotton needs pickin'. Norfolk, Va. 1928.)

Score: piano solo.

The dance steps for this piece are illustrated by *Hampton Institute students.

ABSpl
NYPLS

*Williams, Clarence Agustus, 1893- ...The Brown Bomber, the kid from Alabam'...New York, c1935 (Card 2)

Portrait of "Joe Louis" on cover.

ABSpl
LC

*Williams, Clarence Agustus, 1893-

I like to go back in the evening (to that old sweetheart of mine). ⌐Popular song¬ Words by Richard W. Pascoe; music by H. O'Reilly Clint and Clarence Williams. New York, *Clarence Williams music pub. co. inc. ⌐c1933¬
5 p. fol.

Score: medium solo voice with piano accompaniment. English words.

ABSpl

*Williams, Charles H

Peep squirrel Children's game song and dance.
(In Williams, Charles H., Cotton needs pickin'. Norfolk, Va. 1928.)

Score: piano solo.

The dance steps for this piece are illustrated by *Hampton Institute students.

ABSpl
NYPLS

*Williams, Clarence Agustus, 1893-

Charleston hound... ⌐Popular song¬ Words by *Spencer Williams and Eddie Rector; music by *Clarence Williams and *Thomas "Fat" Waller... New York, *Clarence Williams music pub. co., inc. ⌐c1926¬
5 p. fol. 2 copies

Score: medium solo voice with piano accompaniment. Negro dialect.

ABSpl

*Williams, Clarence, 1893-

If you like me (like I like you). ⌐Popular song¬ By Clarence Williams, *Thomas (Fats) Waller and *Spencer Williams. New York: *Clarence Williams music pub. co., inc. ⌐c1929¬
5p. fol.

Score: medium solo voice with piano accompaniment English words.

ABSpl

*Williams, Charles H

Plantation days. Characteristic Negro dance.
(In Williams, Charles H., Cotton needs pickin'. Norfolk, Va. 1928.)

Score: piano solo.

Illustrations of the dance steps for this piece are by *Hampton Institute students.

ABSpl
NYPLS

Williams, Clarence
Dispossessin' me

*Williams, Clarence Agustus, 1893-

I'm gettin' my bonus in love. ⌐Song¬ By Clarence Williams and *Porter Grainger. New York, *Clarence Williams music pub. co., inc. ⌐c1931¬
4 p. fol.

Score: medium solo voice with piano accompaniment. English words.

ABSpl

Williams, Clarence
After tonight

*Williams, Clarence Agustus, 1893-

Gulf coast blues. ⌐Popular song¬ By Clarence Williams. New York, *Clarence Williams music pub. co. inc. ⌐c1923¬
5 p. fol.

Score: medium solo voice with piano accompaniment. English words.

ABSpl

*Williams, Clarence Agustus, 1893-

I'm falling for you. ⌐Popular song¬ Words and music by Joe Trafalgar Hubert and Clarence Williams. New York, *Clarence Williams music pub. co., inc. ⌐c1938¬
5 p. fol.

Score: medium solo voice with piano accompaniment. English words.

ABSpl

Williams, Clarence
I'm going back to bottomland

---

*Williams, Clarence

Shout, sister, shout! [Popular song] By Clarence Williams, *Tim Brymn and Alexander Hill. New York, *Clarence Williams music pub. co. [c1930]
5 p. fol.

Score: medium solo voice [key of A^b] with piano accompaniment. English words.

Featured by the Boswell sisters in a Brunswick recording and as a N. B. C. feature.

ABSpl

---

*Williams, Clarence Agustus, 1893-

You don't know my mind blues. [Song] Words by Virginia Liston and Sam Gray; music by Clarence Williams. New York, *Clarence Williams music pub. co., inc. [c1924]
5 p. fol.

Score: medium solo voice with piano accompaniment. English words.

ABSpl

Williams, Clarence
I'm going to take my bimbo...

---

*Williams, Clarence Agustus, 1893-

Springtime on parade. [Popular song] By Fred Feibel, Geo. Dunbar and Clarence Williams. New York, *Clarence Williams music pub. co., inc. [c1933]
4 p. fol.

Score: medium solo voice [key of G] with piano accompaniment. English words.

ABSpl
LC

---

*Williams, Clarence Agustus, 1893-

...You're some pretty doll. [Popular song] Words and music by Clarence Williams...New York, Shapiro, Bernstein & co., [c1917]
3 p. fol.

Score: medium solo voice with piano accompaniment. English words.

ABSpl

---

*Williams, Clarence Agustus, 1893-
*Smith, Bessie

Jail house blues. [Popular song] By *Bessie Smith and Clarence Williams...New York, *Clarence Williams music pub. co., inc. [c1924]
5 p. fol.

Score: medium solo voice with piano accompaniment. Negro dialect.

ABSpl

Williams, Clarence
Steamboat days

---

*Williams, Egbert Austin, 1875-1922.

Believe me. [Popular song] Words by *Alex Rogers; music by Bert A. Williams. Chicago, Will Rossiter, c1909.
5 p. fol.

Score: low solo voice [key of D] with piano accompaniment. Negro dialect.
Caption title.

Excerpt from musical comedy, "Mr. Lode of Koal."

ABSpl
LC

Williams, Clarence
More than that

---

*Williams, Clarence Agustus, 1893-

Sugar blues. [Popular song] Words by Lucy Fletcher; music by Clarence Williams...New York, *Clarence Williams music pub. co., inc. [c1923]
5 p. fol.

Score: low solo voice with piano accompaniment. English words.

ABSpl
WOrL - arranged for dance orchestra.

---

*Williams, Egbert Austin, 1875-1922.

Borrow from me. [Popular song] Words by Jean Ravez; music by Bert Williams. New York, Jerome H. Remick & co. [c1912]
5 p. fol.

Score: medium solo voice with piano accompaniment. English words.

Song hit of the Ziegfeld Follies.

ABSpl
LC

---

*Williams, Clarence Agustus, 1893-
*Williams, Spencer

Papa-de-da-da. (A New Orleans stomp) [Popular song] By Clarence Todd, *Spencer Williams and Clarence Williams. New York, *Clarence Williams music pub. co., inc. [c1930]
5 p. fol.

Score: medium solo voice with piano accompaniment. English words.

"Featured by the *Berry Brothers in Lew Leslie's 'Blackbirds of 1930'"-- cover-title page.

ABSpl

---

*Williams, Clarence Agustus, 1893-
*Grainger, Porter

'Tain't nobody's biz-ness if I do. [Popular song] Words and music by *Porter Grainger, Graham Prince and Clarence Williams. New York, *Clarence Williams music pub. co., inc. [c1936]
3 p. fol.

Score: medium solo voice [key of B^b] with piano accompaniment. English words.

LC
ABSpl

---

*Williams, Clarence, 1893-

Senorita Mine. [Popular song.] Lyric by *Spencer Williams and Eddie Rector; music by Clarence Williams and Thomas (Fats) Waller. New York: *Clarence Williams music pub. co., Inc., [c1926]
5p. fol.

Score: medium solo voice with piano accompaniment. English words.

ABSpl

---

*Williams, Clarence
*Williams, Spencer

Yama yama blues. [Popular song] By Spencer Williams and *Clarence Williams. New York, Shapiro, Bernstein and co., [c1919]
3 p. fol.

Score: medium solo voice with piano accompaniment. English words.

ABSpl
ZWpl

---

*Williams, Egbert Austin, 1875-1922.

...Chicken. As long as it's got feathers I'm its fren'. Amen. [Popular song] Words by *Henry S. Creamer; music by Bert Williams. New York, Gotham-Attucks music co. [c1910]
5 p. fol.

Score: medium solo voice with piano accompaniment. English words.

ABSpl

---

*Williams, Egbert Austin, 1875-1922.

Constantly... [Popular song] Words by *Harry B. Smith and [*James] Burris; music by Bert Williams. New York, Jerome H. Remick & co. [c1910]
5 p. fol.

Score: medium solo voice with piano accompaniment. Negro dialect.

Sung in the "Follies of 1910" by Bert Williams.

ABSpl
LC

Williams, Clarence
The shim sham shimmy dance

---

*Williams, Clarence Agustus, 1893-

You can have it, I don't want it. [Popular song] By May Hill, Clarence Williams and *Armand J. Piron. New York, Frank K. Root and co. [c1917]
3 p. fol.

Score: medium solo voice with piano accompaniment. English words.

ABSpl

---

*Williams, Egbert Austin, 1875-1922.

The darktown poker club. [Popular song] Words by Jean Havez; music by Bert Williams and *Will H. Vodery. New York, Jerome H. Remick & co. [c1914]
5 p. fol.

Score: medium solo voice with piano accompaniment. English words.

ABSpl
NBCL - arranged for full orchestra by Bial, Mackie, and Gerstle.

*Williams, Egbert Austin, 1875-1922.

Dat's harmony. ₍Popular song₎ Words by Grant Clarke; music by Bert Williams. New York, Jerome H. Remick & co. ₍c1911₎
5 p. fol.

Score: medium solo voice with piano accompaniment. Negro dialect.

Sung by Bert Williams in the "Follies of 1911."

ABSpl

*Williams, Egbert Austin, 1875-1922.

I'm cured. ₍Popular₎ song. Lyric by Jean C. Havez; music by Bert Williams. New York, Jerome H. Remick & co. ₍c1904₎
6 p. fol.

Score: medium solo voice with piano accompaniment. English words.

Sung by Bert Williams in the Ziegfeld Follies, 1914.

ABSpl
LC

*Williams, Egbert Austin, 1875-1922.

Miss Georgia. ₍Popular song₎ ... Words by *Alex Rogers; music by Bert A. Williams. New York, The Attucks music pub. co. ₍c1905₎
5 p. fol.

Score: medium solo voice with piano accompaniment. Negro dialect.

ABSpl

*Williams, Egbert Austin, 1875-1922.

Fas', fas' world. ₍Popular song₎ Words by *Alex Rogers; music by Bert A. Williams. New York, Gotham-Attucks music co. ₍c1907₎
5 p. fol.

Score: medium solo voice with piano accompaniment. Negro dialect.
Caption title.

Excerpt from the Negro musical comedy, "Bandana land."
ABSpl
LC

*Williams, Egbert Austin, 1875-1922.

The island of by and by... ₍Popular song₎ Words by *Alex Rogers; music by Bert A. Williams. New York, Gotham-Attucks music co. ₍c1906₎
5 p. fol. 2 copies

Score: medium solo voice ₍key of E^b₎ with piano accompaniment. English words.

Excerpt from the musical show, "Abyssinia."

ABSpl
LC

*Williams, Egbert Austin, 1875-1922.

Nobody. ₍Popular song₎ ...Words by *Alex Rogers; music by Bert A. Williams. New York, The Attucks music pub. co. ₍c1905₎
5 p. fol.

Score: medium solo voice with piano accompaniment. English words.

7 extra verses on p. 5.

ABSpl YJWJ
HMC
LC

*Williams, Egbert Austin, 1875-1922.

...The fortune telling man. ₍Popular song₎ Words and music by Williams and *₍George W.₎ Walker. New York, Jos. W. Stern & co. ₍c1901₎ Publ. pl. no. 3142.
5 p. fol.

Score: medium solo voice ₍key of E^b₎ with piano accompaniment. Negro dialect.

LC
NBCL - Arranged for small orchestra by Walter C. Schad.
ABSpl

*Williams, Egbert Austin, 1875-1922.

It ain't no use to sing dem songs to me. ₍Popular song₎ Words and music by Williams and *₍George W.₎ Walker. New York, Jos. W. Stern & co. ₍c1902₎ Publ. pl. no. 3430.
5 p. fol.

Score: medium solo voice with piano accompaniment. Negro dialect.

ABSpl
LC

*Williams, Egbert Austin, 1875-1922.

...No coon can come too black for me. ₍Popular song₎ By ₍ ₎ Smart and Williams. New York, Howley, Haviland & co. ₍c1898₎
6 p. fol.

Score: medium solo voice with piano accompaniment. Negro dialect.

ABSpl

*Williams, Egbert Austin, 1875-1922.

The harbor of lost dreams. ₍Popular song₎ Words by *Alex Rogers; music by Bert A. Williams; arranged by *J. Rosamond Johnson. Chicago, Will Rossiter pub. ₍c1909₎
5 p. fol.

Score: medium solo voice with piano accompaniment. English words.
Caption title.

Excerpt from musical comedy, "Mr. Lode of Koal."
ABSpl
LC

Williams, Egbert Austin
The jolly jungle boys

Williams, Egbert Austin
Rastus Johnson USA

*Williams, Egbert Austin, 1875-1922.

...I don't like no cheap man. ₍Popular song₎ Words and music by Williams and *₍George W.₎ Walker; arranged by *W. H. Tyers. New York, Jos. W. Stern & co. ₍c1897₎
5 p. fol.

Score: medium solo voice ₍key of E₎ with piano accompaniment. Negro dialect.

ABSpl
HMC
LC

*Williams, Egbert Austin, 1875-1922.

Let it alone. ₍Popular song₎ Words by *Alex Rogers; music by Bert A. Williams. New York, Gotham-Attucks music co. ₍c1906₎
5 p. fol.

Score: medium solo voice with piano accompaniment. Negro dialect.

Six extra verses and choruses on page ₍2₎

ABSpl
HMC
LC
YJWJ

*Williams, Egbert Austin, 1875-1922.

...Snap shot Sal. ₍Popular song₎ Written and composed by Williams and *₍George W.₎ Walker. ₍Published as a₎ Supplement to the New York World Sunday, October 1, 1899. ₍c1899₎
4 p. fol.

Score: medium solo voice with piano accompaniment. Negro dialect.

"Composed expressly for the New York Sunday World." -Head of title.

ABSpl

*Williams, Egbert Austin, 1875-1922.

I'd rather have nothin' all of the time, than somethin' for a little while. ₍Popular song₎ Words by John B. Lowitz; music by Bert A. Williams. New York, Gotham-Attucks music co. ₍c1908₎
5 p. fol.

Score: medium solo voice with piano accompaniment. English words.

Excerpt from the musical show, "Bandana land."

ABSpl
LC

*Williams, Egbert Austin, 1875-1922.

...Look out dar down below. ₍Popular song₎ Words and music by Williams and *₍George W.₎ Walker. New York, W. B. Gray & co. ₍c1897₎
5 p. fol.

Score: medium solo voice with piano accompaniment. Negro dialect.

ABSpl
LC

*Williams, Egbert Austin, 1875-1922. arr.

...Somebody lied. ₍Popular song₎ ...By Jeff T. Branen and Evans Lloyd; adapted by Bert A. Williams. Chicago, Will Rossiter music publisher, c1907.
6 p. fol.

Score: medium solo voice with piano accompaniment. English words.

Extra verses by Jeff T. Branen on p. 6.

ABSpl

*Williams, Egbert Austin, 1875-1922.

If you love your baby make goo goo eyes. Or, "The game of goo-goo eyes." ₍Popular song₎ Words and music by Williams and *₍George W.₎ Walker. New York, Hurtig & Seamon pub. ₍c1900₎
5 p. fol.

Score: medium solo voice with piano accompaniment. English words.

ABSpl

*Williams, Egbert Austin, 1875-1922.

...The medicine man. ₍Popular song₎ Words and music by Williams and *₍George W.₎ Walker. New York, Jos. W. Stern & co. ₍c1899₎ Publ. pl. no. 1097.
5 p. fol.

Score: low solo voice ₍key of F₎ with piano accompaniment. Negro dialect.

ABSpl
LC

*Williams, Egbert Austin, 1875-1922.

Tale of the monkey maid. Or, (Die trying) ₍Popular song₎ Words by *Alex Rogers; music by Bert A. Williams. New York, Gotham-Attucks music co. (inc.) ₍c1906₎
6 p. fol.

Score: medium solo voice with piano accompaniment. English words.

ABSpl

*Williams, Egbert Austin, 1875-1922.

That's a plenty. [Popular song] Words by *Henry S. Creamer; music by Bert A. Williams. Chicago, Will Rossiter pub., c1909.
5 p. fol.

Score: medium solo voice with piano accompaniment. English words.

"Mister, mister, oh listen like a friend." - Head of title.

ABSpl

---

*Williams, Egbert Austin, 1875-1922

A trip to coon town. [Popular song] Words by *Bob Cole and *Billy Johnson; music by Bert Williams... New York, Howley, Haviland co. [c1897]
5 p. fol.

Score: medium solo voice [key of F] with piano accompaniment. English words.

ABSpl
HMC
LC

---

*Williams, Egbert Austin, 1875-1922.

The vampire. [Popular song] Lyric by Earl Jones and Gene Buck; music by Bert A. Williams... New York, Jerome H. Remick & co. [c1914]
5 p. fol.

Score: medium solo voice with piano accompaniment. English words.

Sung by Bert Williams in the Ziegfeld Follies, 1914.

ABSpl

---

*Williams, Egbert Austin, 1875-1922.

...When it's all goin' out and nothin' comin' in... [Popular song] Words and music by Williams and *[George W.] Walker; words revised by *James W. Johnson. New York, Jos. W. Stern & co. [c1902] Publ. pl. no. 3346.
6 p. fol.

Score: medium solo voice with piano accompaniment. Negro dialect.

"New song hits introduced by Williams and Walker's own big co." - Head of title.

ABSpl LC

---

*Williams, Egbert Austin, 1875-1922.

..."When Miss Maria Johnson marries me." [Popular song] Words and music by Williams and *[George W.] Walker... New York, Spaulding & Gray pub. [c1896]
5 p. fol.

Score: medium solo voice with piano accompaniment. Negro dialect.

ABSpl
LC

Williams, Egbert Austin
When the moon shines

Williams, Egbert Austin
Where my forefathers died

---

*Williams, Egbert Austin, 1875-1922.

...Why don't you get a lady of your own. [Popular song] By Williams and *[George W.] Walker. New York, Jos. W. Stern & co. [c1898] Publ. pl. no. 610.
6 p. fol.

Score: medium solo voice [key of C] with piano accompaniment. Negro dialect.

Title page has portraits of the composers.

ABSpl
LC

---

*Williams, Egbert Austin, 1875-1922.

You're gwine to get somethin' what you dont expect... [Popular song] Words by Vincent Bryan; music by Bert Williams. New York, Leo Feist [c1910] Publ. pl. no. 2584.
5 p. fol.

Score: medium solo voice with piano accompaniment. Negro dialect.
Caption title.

Sung by Bert Williams in the "Ziegfeld Follies of 1910."

ABSpl
LC

---

*Williams, Egbert Austin, 1875-1922.

Williams and Walker's album of gems; from their original musical farce comedy, "The policy players." [Various composers] New York, Hurtig & Seamon pub. [c1899]
17 p. fol.

Score: 3 songs for solo voice, with piano accompaniment; 7 songs, melody only; 3 songs, words only. English words or Negro dialect.

Contents: 1. Whose gwine to get the money. By Williams and Walker.

(continued on next card)

---

*Williams, Egbert Austin, 1875-1922. Williams and Walker's album of gems... New York, Hurtig & Seamon pub. [c1899] (Card 2)

-2. Dream interpreter. By Williams and Walker. -3. I cert'n'ly was a very busy man. By Bennett & Northrup. -4. Gwine to catch a gig today. By Williams and Walker. -5. Ghost of a coon. By Williams and Walker. -6. The colored band. By Williams and Walker. -7. The Broadway coon. By Williams and Walker. -8. Honolulu belles. By Williams and Walker. -9. The man in the moon might tell. By J. A. Shipp. -10. The medicine man. By Williams and Walker.

(continued on next card)

---

*Williams, Egbert Austin, 1875-1922. Williams and Walker's album of gems... New York, Hurtig & Seamon pub. [c1899] (Card 3)

-11. Gladys. By Theo. H. Northrup. -12. Take me as I am. Words by Joe Hurtig; music by Andy Lewis. -13. Policy players. By Williams and Walker.

ABSpl

---

*Williams, La Salle J arr.

O Satan! your kingdom must come down. Negro spiritual arranged by La Salle J. Williams. New York, *Handy bros. music co., inc. [c1938]
9 p. 8°.

Score: SATB with baritone solo and piano accompaniment. English words.

Bound in black spiral notebook no. 4.

HMC
ZWpl
ABSpl

---

*Williams, Spencer

Ain't got no worry (As long as you're my baby). Words and music by Spencer Williams. New York, Mills music, inc. [c1930]
5 p. fol.

Score: medium solo voice with piano accompaniment. English words.

ABSpl

---

*Williams, Spencer

Black man (be on yo' way)... By Spencer Williams. New York, *Spencer Williams music co., inc. c1923
5 p. fol.

Score: medium solo voice with piano accompaniment. Negro dialect.

ABSpl

---

*Williams, Spencer

The blues singer (from Alabam) [Popular song] By Agnes Castleton and Spencer Williams. New York, *Handy bros. music co. inc., [c1929]
5 p. fol.

Score: medium solo voice [key of E^b] with piano accompaniment. English words.

ABSpl
ZWpl

---

*Williams, Spencer

Driftin' tide. [Popular song] By Pat Castleton and Spencer Williams. New York, Mills music, inc., [c1934]
3 p. fol.

Score: medium solo voice with piano accompaniment. English words.

ABSpl

---

*Williams, Spencer

Everybody love my baby—but my baby don't love nobody but me. [Popular song] Words and music by Spencer Williams and Jack Palmer. New York, *Clarence Williams music pub. co., inc. [c1924]
5 p. fol.

Score: medium solo voice with piano accompaniment. English words.

LC
ABSpl

Williams, Spencer
Farewell to Storyville.

---

*Williams, Spencer

...Give me just a little bit of your love. [Popular song] Words and music by Jack Palmer and Spencer Williams. New York, *Handy bros. music co., inc. [c1925]
5 p. fol.

Score: low solo voice [key of C] with piano accompaniment. English words.

ABSpl
ZWpl

---

*Williams, Spencer

Got to cool my doggies now. Peppy dance song. By Bob Schafer, Babe Thompson and Spencer Williams. New York, *Clarence Williams music pub. co., Inc. [c1922]
5 p. fol.

Score: medium solo voice with piano accompaniment. English words.

ABSpl

•Williams, Spencer

Great camp meetin' ground (a modern rhythmic spirtual,) Words and music by Spencer Williams and Joe Davis. New York, Joe Davis, inc. ⌐c1938.¬
3 p. fol.

Score: Medium solo voice with piano accompaniment. Negro dialect.

ABSpl

Williams, Spencer
Kortlander, Max.
I'm a good gal.

*Williams, Spencer

Moan, you moaners. (A rhythmic spirtual) Words and music by Spencer Williams. New York, Joe Davis Inc., ⌐c1931¬ Publ. pl. no. 1044.
5 p. fol.

Score: medium solo voice⌐key of C¬with piano accompaniment. Negro dialect.

ABSpl
LC

*Williams, Spencer

Hot Eskimo. ⌐Popular song¬by Fay Meisel, Spencer Williams and Bob Schaefer. New York, Denton and Haskin music co., ⌐c1925¬
6 p. fol.

Score: medium solo voice with piano accompaniment. English words.

ABSpl

Williams, Spencer
It took a wild, wild woman

Williams, Spencer
My home in Oklahoma

*Williams, Spencer

I ain't gonna give nobody none o' this jelly roll. Jazz song. By *Spencer Williams and*Clarence Williams...New York, Shapiro Bernstein & co.⌐c1919¬
3 p. fol.

Score: medium solo voice with piano accompaniment. English words.

ABSpl

*Williams, Spencer

I've found a new baby. ⌐Popular song¬ By Jack Palmer and Spencer Williams. New York, *Clarence Williams music pub. co., inc. ⌐c1926¬
5 p. fol.

Score: medium solo voice with piano accompaniment. English words.

ABSpl

Williams, Spencer
My June love

*Williams, Spencer

I ain't got nobody much (and nobody cares for me)... ⌐Popular song¬ Lyric by Roger Graham; music by Spencer Williams. New York, Frank K. Root & co. ⌐c1916¬
5 p. fol.

Score: medium solo voice with piano accompaniment. Negro dialect.

ABSpl

William, Spencer
Jungle Blues

Williams, Spencer
Neglected blues

*Williams, Spencer

...I want a good man (and I want him bad). ⌐Popular Song.¬ By Herb Magidson, Michael Cleary and Spencer Williams...New York, Triangle music publ. co., inc. ⌐c1928¬
5 p. fol.

Score: medium solo voice with piano accompaniment. English words.

ABSpl

*Williams, Spencer

...Just a crazy song. (Hi-hi-hi). ⌐Popular song¬ By Chick Smith and Spencer Williams. New York, Shapiro Bernstein and co., ⌐c1931¬
5 p. fol.

Score: medium solo voice with piano accompaniment. English words.

LC
ABSpl

*Williams, Spencer

Papa-de-da-da. (A New Orleans stomp) ⌐Popular song¬ By Clarence Todd, Spencer Williams and *Clarence Williams. New York, *Clarence Williams music pub. co., inc. ⌐c1930¬
5 p. fol.

Score: medium solo voice with piano accompaniment. English words.

"Featured by the *Berry Brothers in Lew Leslie's 'Blackbirds of 1930'"--cover-title page.

ABSpl

*Williams, Spencer

If I had my way 'bout my sweetie. ⌐Popular song¬ By Jack Palmer and Spencer Williams...New York, Harry D. Squires inc. ⌐c1925¬
5 p. fol.

Score: medium solo voice with piano accompaniment. English words.

ABSpl

Williams, Spencer
Just one more day

*Williams, Spencer

Paradise blues. Oh pretty papa! Oh pretty papa! ⌐Popular song¬ Lyric by Walter Hirsch; music by Spencer Williams. New York, McKinley music co. ⌐c1916.¬
5 p. fol.

Score: medium solo voice ⌐key of E^b¬ with piano accompaniment. English words.

ABSpl
LC

*Williams, Spencer
*Williams, Clarence Augustus

If you like me (like I like you). ⌐Popular song¬ By *Clarence Williams, *Thomas (Fats) Waller and Spencer Williams. New York: *Clarence Williams music pub. co., inc. ⌐c1929¬
5p. fol.

Score: medium solo voice with piano accompaniment. English words.

ABSpl

*Williams, Spencer

May I bring you flowers, Mademoiselle? ⌐Popular song¬ Poem by Jack Scholl and Bradford Browne; melody by Spencer Williams and Al. Piantadosi. New York, Al Piantadosi music publisher ⌐c1929¬
5 p. fol.

Score: medium solo voice with piano accompaniment. English words.

ABSpl

*Williams, Spencer

Parting. Waltz ballad. By Johnnie Tucker, Bob Schafer and Spencer Williams. New York, Joe Mittenthal, inc. ⌐c1922¬
5 p. fol.

Score: low solo voice with piano accompaniment. English words.

ABSpl

*Williams, Spencer
*Robinson, J Robinson
Ringtail blues. ⌐Popular song⌐ (A vocal adaptation of the famous instrumental). By J. Russell Robinson and Spencer Williams. New York, *Pace and Handy music co. inc., ⌐c1918⌐
3 p. fol.
Score: medium solo voice with piano accompaniment. English words.
ABSpl

Williams, Spencer
Straight, Charley
I never had the blues until I left old Dixie-land.

*Williams, Spencer
...Wednesday night waltz. ⌐Popular⌐Song by Spencer Williams. New York, Triangle music publ. co., inc., ⌐c1928⌐
5 p. fol.
Score: medium solo voice with piano accompaniment. English words.
ABSpl

Williams, Spencer
Sandman Blues

*Williams, Spencer
Struttin' at the strutter's ball. ⌐Popular song⌐ Words and music by Spencer Williams. New York, Leo Feist inc. ⌐c1922⌐ Publ. pl. no. 5069.
5 p. fol.
Score: medium solo voice ⌐key of E^b⌐ with piano accompaniment. Negro dialect.
ABSpl

*Williams, Spencer
Wonder. Fox-trot ballad. Lyric by *Andy Razaf... Music by Spencer Williams and Cliff Burwell. New York, Joe Davis inc. ⌐c1930⌐ Publ. pl. no. 1015.
3 p. fol.
Score: medium solo voice ⌐key of F⌐ with piano accompaniment. English words.
ABSpl
LC

Williams, Spencer
Santa Claus is Bringing you home for Christmas

*Williams, Spencer
Talkin' 'bout home. (Fox-trot song). By Spencer Williams and Agnes Castleton... New York, Triangle music pub. co. ⌐c1928⌐
5 p. fol.
Score: medium solo voice with piano accompaniment. English words.
ABSpl

*Williams, Clarence
Yama yama blues. ⌐Popular song⌐ by *Spencer Williams and Clarence Williams. New York, Shapiro, Bernstein and co., ⌐c1919⌐
3 p. fol.
Score: medium solo voice with piano accompaniment. English words.
ABSpl
ZWpl

*Williams, Spencer
Shim-me-sham-wabble. ⌐Popular⌐Song by Spencer Williams. New York, Jos. W. Stern & co. ⌐c1917⌐ Publ. pl. no. 8340.
3 p. fol.
Score: medium solo voice with piano accompaniment. English words.
ABSpl

*Williams, Spencer
...That makes me give in. ⌐Popular song⌐ Words and music by Spencer Williams. New York, Triangle music pub. co. ⌐c1930⌐
5 p. fol.
Score: medium solo voice with piano accompaniment. English words.
Words for 4 extra choruses printed preceding the music on p. 2.
ABSpl
LC

*Wilson, Clarence Hayden
They have led my Lord away. Negro spiritual. Arranged by Clarence Hayden Wilson. New York, Handy brothers music co., inc ⌐c1939⌐
5 p. fol.
Score: medium solo voice with piano accompaniment. English words.
ABSpl

*Williams, Spencer
Snake hips. A jungle jazz. Words and music by Spencer Williams. New York, Leo Feist inc., ⌐c1923⌐ Publ. pl. no. 5202.
5 p. fol.
Score: medium solo voice with piano accompaniment. English words.
ABSpl

*Williams, Spencer
Tired o' the blues... (Mournful Mamma's wail) ⌐Popular song⌐ By Spencer Williams. New York, *Spencer Williams music co. inc. ⌐c1923⌐
5 p. fol.
Score: medium solo voice with piano accompaniment. English words.
ABSpl

Woodworth, Julian
When you press your lips to mine. (Fox-trot ballad) Words by Andy Razaf; music by Julian Woodworth...NY: Joe Davis, inc., ⌐c1930⌐ Publ. pl. no. 1016.
5p. fol. 2 copies
Score: medium solo voice with piano accompaniment. English words.
ABSpl

*Williams, Spencer
Solitude. A weird inspiration. ⌐For piano⌐ By Spencer Williams. New York, Triangle music pub. co. ⌐c1928⌐
7 p. fol.
Score: piano solo.
ABSpl

*Williams, Spencer
Tishomingo blues. ⌐Popular song⌐ Words and music by Spencer Williams. New York, Jos. W. Stern and co. ⌐c1917⌐ Publ. pl. no. 8509.
3 p. fol.
Score: medium solo voice with piano accompaniment. English words.
ABSpl

*Work, John Wesley, 1901-
...For the beauty of the earth. Hymn-anthem. Words by Folliott S. Pierpong; music by John W. Work. New York, Fischer and bro. ⌐c1936⌐ Publ. pl. no. J. F. & B. 6851.
8 p. 8vo.
Score: SATB with S and Ba soli. Organ accompaniment. English words.
Bound in black spiral notebook no. 2.
ZWpl
HMC
ABSpl

*Williams, Spencer
Steppin' on the puppy's tail. ⌐Popular song⌐ Words and music by Spencer Williams. New York, Frank K. Root & co. ⌐c1917⌐
3 p. fol.
Score: medium solo voice with piano accompaniment. English words.
ABSpl

*Williams, Spencer
Treatin' me low-down. ⌐Popular song⌐ Words by Jack Scholl; music by Spencer Williams. New York, Al Piantadosi music pub. co., ⌐c1929⌐
5 p. fol.
Score: medium solo voice with piano accompaniment. English words.
ABSpl

*Work, John Wesley, 1901- arr.
Going home to live with God. Adapted from a Negro spiritual by John W. Work. New York, J. Fischer and bro. ⌐c1936⌐ Publ. pl. no. J. F. & B. 6836.
8 p. 8°.
Score: TTBB with tenor solo, and piano reduction for rehearsal only. English words.
Bound in black spiral notebook no. 2.
HMC
ABSpl
ZWpl

*Work, John Wesley, 1901

...How beautiful upon the mountains. Motet. Text from Isaiah 52:7-8; music by John W. Work. New York, Galaxy music corp. [c1934] Publ. pl. no. G. M. 633.
11 p. 8°.

Score: SATB with piano reduction for rehearsal only. English words.
Bound in black spiral notebook no. 2.

ABSpl

*Work, John Wesley, 1901- arr.

...Po' ol' Laz'rus, Negro spiritual. Anthem. Arranged by John W. Work. New York, J. Fischer and bro. [c1931] Publ. pl. no. J. F. & B. 6513.
11 p. 8°.

Score: TTBB with piano reduction for rehearsal only. Negro dialect.
Bound in black spiral notebook no. 2.

HMC
ZWpl
ABSpl

*Work, John Wesley, 1901- arr.

...Stand the storm. Adapted from the Negro spiritual by John W. Work. New York, J. Fischer and bro. [c1931] Publ. pl. no. J. F. & B. 6514.
13 p. 8°.

Score: TTBB with tenor solo and piano reduction for rehearsal only. English words.
Bound in black spiral notebook no. 2.

HMC
ABSpl
ZWpl

*Work, John Wesley, 1901- arr.

Wasn't that a mighty day. Adapted from a Negro spiritual by John W. Work. New York, J. Fischer and bro. [c1934] Publ. pl. no. J. F. & B. 6835.
7 p. fol.

Score: SATB with tenor solo and piano reduction for rehearsal only. English words.
Bound in black spiral notebook no. 2.

HM C
ZWpl
ABSpl